The New College
GERMAN & ENGLISH
Dictionary

The New College
GERMAN & ENGLISH
Dictionary

JOHN C. TRAUPMAN, Ph.D.
St. Joseph's University, Philadelphia

Dedicated to serving

AMSCO

our nation's youth

AMSCO SCHOOL PUBLICATIONS, INC.
315 HUDSON STREET / NEW YORK, N.Y. 10013

The front cover shows Katz Castle overlooking the Rhine, photo courtesy of the German National Tourist Office; the back cover shows the Rathaus and St. Peter's Cathedral, Bremen, photo courtesy of the German Information Center.

THE NEW COLLEGE GERMAN & ENGLISH DICTIONARY

ISBN 0-87720-584-1

Published by Amsco School Publications, Inc., by arrangement with the copyright owners.

Printed in the United States of America

1 2 3 4 5 6 7 8 9

Contents

JOHN C. TRAUPMAN received his B.A. in German and in Latin at Moravian College and his M.A. and Ph.D. in Classics at Princeton University. He is Chairman of the Department of Classical Languages at St. Joseph's University (Philadelphia). He served as president of the Philadelphia Classical Society, of the Pennsylvania Classical Association, and of the Classical and Modern Language League. He has published widely in learned journals and is the author of *The New College Latin & English Dictionary* and an associate editor of *The Scribner-Bantam English Dictionary*.

EDWIN B. WILLIAMS (1891-1975), under whose editorship *The New College German & English Dictionary* was prepared, was Chairman of the Department of Romance Languages, Dean of the Graduate School, and Provost of the University of Pennsylvania. Among his many works on the Spanish, Portuguese, and French languages are *The Williams Spanish and English Dictionary* and *The New College Spanish & English Dictionary*. He created and coordinated the New College series of original dictionaries—French, German, Italian, Latin, and Spanish.

HOW TO USE THIS DICTIONARY

HINWEISE FÜR DEN BENUTZER

All entry words are treated in a fixed order according to the parts of speech and the functions of verbs. On the German-English side: past participle, adjective, adverb, pronoun, preposition, conjunction, interjection, transitive verb, reflexive verb, reciprocal verb, intransitive verb, impersonal verb, auxiliary verb, substantive; on the English-German side: adjective, substantive, pronoun, adverb, preposition, conjunction, transitive verb, intransitive verb, auxiliary verb, impersonal verb, interjection.

Alle Stichwörter werden in einheitlicher Reihenfolge gemäß der Wortart und der Verbfunktion behandelt. Im deutsch-englischen Teil: Partizip Perfekt, Adjektiv, Adverb, Pronomen, Präposition, Konjunktion, Interjektion, transitives Verb, reflexives Verb, reziprokes Verb, intransitives Verb, unpersönliches Verb, Hilfsverb, Substantiv; im englisch-deutschen Teil: Adjektiv, Substantiv, Pronomen, Adverb, Präposition, Konjunktion, transitives Verb, intransitives Verb, Hilfsverb, unpersönliches Verb, Interjektion.

The order of meanings within an entry is as follows: first, the more general meanings; second, the meanings with usage labels; third, the meanings with subject labels in alphabetical order; fourth, illustrative phrases in alphabetical order.

Die verschiedenen Bedeutungen sind innerhalb eines Stichwortartikels in folgender Anordnung gegeben: zuerst die allgemeinen Bedeutungen; dann die Bedeutungen mit Bezeichnung der Sprachgebrauchsebene; dann die Bedeutungen mit Bezeichnung des Sachgebietes, in alphabetischer Reihenfolge; zuletzt die Anwendungsbeispiele, in alphabetischer Reihenfolge.

Subject and usage labels (printed in roman and in parentheses) refer to the preceding entry word or illustrative phrase in the source language (printed in boldface), e.g.,

Die Bezeichnungen der Sprachgebrauchsebene und des Sachgebiets (in Antiqua und in Klammern) beziehen sich auf das vorangehende Stichwort oder Anwendungsbeispiel in der Ausgangssprache (halbfett gedruckt), z.B.

mund′tot *adj*—**j–n m. machen** (fig) silence s.o.
Pinke [′pɪŋkə] *f* (–;) (coll) dough

Words in parentheses and in roman coming after a meaning serve to clarify that meaning, e.g.,

Kursiv gedruckte Wörter in Klammern, die nach einer Bedeutung stehen, sollen diese Bedeutung illustrieren, z.B.

überschau′en *tr* look over, survey; overlook (*a scene*)

Words in parenthese and in roman type coming after or before a meaning are optional additions to the word in the target language, e.g.,	In Antiqua gedruckte Wörter in Klammern, die nach oder vor einer Bedeutung stehen, sind wahlfreie Erweiterungen des Wortes der Zielsprache, z.B.

Tanne ['tanə] *f* (–;–n) fir (tree)
Pap'rikaschote *f* (green) pepper

Meaning discriminations are given in the source language and are in italics, e.g.,	Bedeutungsdifferenzierungen sind in der Ausgangssprache angegeben und kursiv gedruckt, z.B.

überrei'zen *tr* overexcite; (*Augen, Nerven*) strain
earn [ʌrn] *tr* (*money*) verdienen; (*interest*) einbringen

Since vocabulary entries are not determined on the basis of etymology, homographs are listed as a single entry.	Da die Etymologie bei der Anführung der Stichwörter unberücksichtigt bleibt, sind gleichgeschriebene Wörter als ein und dasselbe Stichwort verzeichnet.

The entry word is represented within the entry by its initial letter followed by a period (if the entry word contains more than three letters), provided the form is identical. The same applies to a word that follows the parallels. The entry word is not abbreviated within the entry when associated with suspension points, e.g.,	Innerhalb eines Stichwortartikels wird das Stichwort (wenn es mehr als drei Buchstaben enthält) durch seinen Anfangsbuchstaben und einen Punkt angegeben, vorausgesetzt, daß die betreffende Form mit dem Stichwort identisch ist. Das Gleiche gilt für ein Wort, das nach den Vertikalstrichen steht. Wenn ein Stichwort innerhalb eines Stichwortartikels in Verbindung mit Auslassungspunkten angegeben ist, wird es nicht abgekürzt, z.B.

weder ... noch

Parallels are used (a) to separate parts of speech, (b) to separate transitive, reflexive, reciprocal, intransitive, impersonal, and auxiliary verbs, (c) to separate verbs taking HABEN from those taking SEIN, (d) to indicate a change in pronunciation of the entry word, depending on the meaning, e.g.,	Es ist der Zweck der Vertikalstriche, (a) Wortarten voneinander zu trennen, (b) transitive, reflexive, reziproke, intransitive, unpersönliche Verben und Hilfsverben zu trennen, (c) Verben mit dem Hilfsverb HABEN von Verben mit dem Hilfsverb SEIN zu trennen, (d) verschiedene Aussprachen des Stichwortes je nach Bedeutung anzuzeigen, z.B.

bow [baʊ] *s* Verbeugung *f;* (naut) Bug *m* . . .
 ‖ [bo] *s* (*weapon*) Bogen *m;* . . .

(e) to show change from a strong verb to a weak verb and vice versa, (f) to show a change in the case governed by	(e) den Wechsel von einem starken zu einem schwachen Verb und umgekehrt anzuzeigen, (f) den Wechsel in einem

a preposition where the entry word is a preposition, (g) to show a shift of accent, e.g.,

von einer Präposition regierten Fall anzuzeigen, wo das Stichwort selbst eine Präposition ist, (g) unterschiedliche Stellungen des Akzents anzuzeigen, z.B.

ü′bergießen *tr* . . . ‖ **übergie′ßen** *tr* . . .

The centered period in the English word on the German-English side marks the point at which the following letters are dropped before irregular plural endings are added. The centered period in the entry word on the English-German side marks the point at which the following letters are dropped before irregular plural endings are added to nouns and inflections are added to verbs. The centered period in the phonetic spelling indicates diaeresis, e.g.,

Der auf Mitte stehende Punkt im Stichwort des deutsch-englischen Teils zeigt die Stelle an, wo die nachfolgenden Buchstaben abzutrennen sind, bevor unregelmäßige Pluralendungen angefügt werden können. Der auf Mitte stehende Punkt im Stichwort des englisch-deutschen Teils zeigt die Stelle an, wo die nachfolgenden Buchstaben abzutrennen sind, bevor unregelmäßige Pluralendungen an Hauptwörter and Flexionen an Verben angefügt werden können. Der auf Mitte stehende Punkt in der Lautschrift zeigt Diärese an, z.B.

befähigt [bə′fe·ɪçt]

On the German-English and the English-German side, in the case of a transitive verb, the meaning discrimination in parentheses before the target word is always the object of the verb. On the German-English side, in the case of an intransitive verb, the meaning discrimination in parentheses before the target word is always the subject of the verb. On the English-German side, the suggested subject of a verb is prefaced by the words "said of".

Im deutsch-englischen und im englisch-deutschen Teil ist die bei transitiven Verben in Klammern vor dem Wort in der Zielsprache angegebene Bedeutungsdifferenzierung immer das Objekt des Verbs. Im deutsch-englischen Teil ist bei intransitiven Verben die vor dem Wort in der Zielsprache angegebene Bedeutungsdifferenzierung immer das Subjekt des Verbs. Im englisch-deutschen Teil stehen vor dem beabsichtigten Subjekt eines Verbs die Worte "said of."

Inflections are generally not shown for compound entry words, since the inflections have been shown where the components are entry words. However, when the last component of a compound noun on the German-English side has various inflections depending on meaning, the inflection is shown for the compound, e.g.,

Bei zusammengesetzten Stichwörtern ist die Flexion im Allgemeinen nicht angegeben, da sie unter den als Stichwörter angeführten Teilen des Kompositums angegeben ist. Falls jedoch der letzte Teil eines deutschen Kompositums je nach der Bedeutung verschieden flektiert wird, ist die Flexion für das Kompositum angegeben, z.B.

Ton′band *n* (–[e]s;⁼er) . . .

German verbs are regarded as reflexive regardless of whether the reflexive pronoun is the direct or indirect object of the verb.

Deutsche Verben gelten als reflexiv ohne Rücksicht darauf, ob das Reflexivpronomen das direkte oder indirekte Objekt des Verbs ist.

On the English-German side, when the pronunciation of an entry word is not given, stress in the entry word is shown as follows: a high-set primary stress mark ′ follows the syllable that receives the primary stress, and a high-set secondary stress mark ′ follows the syllable that receives the secondary stress. When the pronunciation of an entry word *is* provided [given in brackets], a high-set primary stress mark ˈ *precedes* the syllable that receives the primary stress, and a *low*-set secondary stress mark ˌ *precedes* the syllable that receives the secondary stress.

On the German-English side, when the pronunciation of an entry word is not given, a high-set primary stress mark ′ follows the syllable of the entry word that receives the primary stress. When the pronunciation of the entry *is* provided [given in brackets], a high-set primary stress mark ˈ *precedes* the syllable that receives the primary stress. (Because opinions on the system of secondary stress in German differ widely, secondary stress marks are not employed in this Dictionary.)

Wo die Aussprache des Stichwortes im englisch-deutschen Teil nicht angegeben ist, wird die Betonung des Stichwortes folgendermaßen angedeutet: Das stärkere, obere graphische Zeichen ′ steht nach der Silbe mit dem Haupttonakzent, und das schwächere, obere Zeichen ′ steht nach der Silbe mit dem Nebentonakzent. Wo hingegen die Aussprache des Stichwortes im englisch-deutschen Teil [in eckigen Klammern] angegeben ist, steht das stärkere, obere Zeichen ˈ *vor* der Silbe mit dem Haupttonakzent und das schwächere, *untere* Zeichen ˌ *vor* der Silbe mit dem Nebentonakzent.

Wo die Aussprache das Stichwortes im deutsch-englischen Teil nicht angegeben ist, steht das starke Zeichen ′ nach der Stichwortsilbe mit dem Haupttonakzent. Wo hingegen die Aussprache des Stichwortes im deutschenglischen Teil [in eckigen Klammern] angegeben ist, steht das starke Zeichen ˈ *vor* der Silbe mit dem Haupttonakzent. (Wegen der widersprüchlichen Theorien, die die Frage des Nebentonakzents im Deutschen umgeben, wendet dieses Wörterbuch keine Nebentonakzente für die deutschen Wörter an.)

Proper nouns and general abbreviations are listed in their alphabetical position in the main body of the Dictionary.

Eigennamen und allgemeine Abkürzungen sind in den beiden Hauptteilen des Wörterbuches in alphabetischer Reihenfolge angegeben.

This Dictionary contains approximately 75,000 "entries." As entries are counted (a) nonindented boldface headwords and (b) elements that could have been set nonindented as separate headwords, too, but that for reasons of style and typography are grouped under the nonindented headwords, namely, separate parts of speech and boldface idioms and phrases.

Dieses Wörterbuch enthält ungefähr 75.000 "Stichwörter." Die folgenden Elemente gelten als Stichwörter: (a) die nicht eingerückten fettgedruckten Wörter am Anfang eines Stichwortartikels und (b) Elemente, die man auf dieselbe Weise hatte drucken können, die aber aus Stil– und Typographiegründen eingerückt wurden, nämlich die unterschiedlichen Wortarten und die fettgedruckten Redewendungen.

I wish to express my appreciation to the many persons on whose help I relied in researching and compiling this Dictionary. I am particularly indebted to Edwin B. Williams, Walter D. Glanze, Donald Reis, Rudolf Pillwein, and Helmut Kreitz.

J. C. T.

PART ONE

German-English

A

A, a [ɑ] *invar n* A, a; (mus) A; **das A und O** the beginning and the end; (*das Wichtigste*) the most important thing

Aal [ɑl] *m* (-[e]s;-e) eel; (nav) torpedo

aal'glatt' *adj* (fig) sly as a fox

Aas [ɑs] *n* (-es;-e) carrion; (sl) louse

ab [ap] *adv* off; away; down; on, e.g., **von heute ab** from today on; (theat) **exit, exeunt**, e.g., **Hamlet ab** exit Hamlet; **ab und zu** now and then || *prep* (*dat*) from, e.g., **ab Frankfurt** from Frankfurt; minus, e.g., **ab Skonto** minus discount

ab'ändern *tr* alter; (*völlig*) change; (*mildern*) modify; (parl) amend

Ab'änderung *f* (-;-en) alteration; change; modification; (parl) amendment

Ab'änderungsantrag *m* (parl) (proposed) amendment

ab'arbeiten *tr* work off || *ref* work hard

Ab'art *f* variety, type

ab'arten *intr* (SEIN) deviate from type

Ab'bau *m* (-[e]s;) demolition; reduction; cutback; layoff; (chem) decomposition; (min) exploitation

ab'bauen *tr* demolish; (*Maschinen, Fabriken*) dismantle; (*Steuern, Preise, Truppen*) reduce; (*Zelt*) take down; (*Lager*) break; (*Angestellte*) lay off; (chem) decompose; (min) work, exploit

ab'beißen §53 *tr* bite·off || *intr* take a bite

ab'bekommen §99 *tr* (*seinen Teil*) get; (*Schmutz*) get out; (*Deckel*) get off; **du wirst was a.!** you're going to get it!

ab'berufen §122 *tr* (dipl) recall

ab'bestellen *tr* cancel

ab'betteln *tr*—**die ganze Straße a.** beg up and down the street; **j-m etw a.** chisel s.th. from s.o.

ab'biegen §57 *tr* bend, twist off; (*Gefahr*) avert; (*Plan*) thwart; **das Gespräch a.** change the subject || *intr* (SEIN) branch off; (fig) get off the track; **in e-e Seitenstraße a.** turn down a side street; **nach links a.** turn left; **von e-r Straße a.** turn off a road

Ab'bild *n* picture, image

ab'bilden *tr* represent

Ab'bildung *f* (-;-en) illustration, figure

ab'binden §59 *tr* untie; (*Kalb*) wean; (*Arm*) apply a tourniquet to; (surg) tie off || *intr* (*Zement*) set

Ab'bitte *f* apology; **A. tun wegen** apologize for

ab'bitten §60 *tr* apologize for || *intr* apologize

ab'blasen §61 *tr* blow off; (fig) call off || *intr* (mil) sound the retreat

ab'blättern *intr* (SEIN) shed leaves; (*Farben, Haut*) flake, peel

ab'blenden *tr* dim; (cin) fade out; (phot) stop down || *intr* (aut) dim the lights; (nav) darken ship; (phot) stop down the lens

Ab'blendlicht *n* (aut) low-beam lights

ab'blitzen *intr* (SEIN) be unsuccessful; **j-n a. lassen** snub s.o.

ab'blühen *intr* stop blooming || *intr* (SEIN) fade

ab'böschen *tr* slope; (*Mauer*) batter

ab'brausen *tr* hose down || *ref* shower off || *intr* (SEIN) (coll) roar off

ab'brechen §64 *tr* break off; (*Belagerung*) raise; (*Gebäude*) demolish; (*Zelt*) take down; (sport) call; **das Lager a.** break camp || *intr* (SEIN) (& fig) break off

ab'bremsen *tr* slow down; (*Streik*) prevent; (*Motoren*) (aer) rev || *intr* put on the brakes; (aer) fishtail

ab'brennen §97 *tr* burn off; (*Feuerwerk*) set off; (*Geschütz*) fire; (chem) distil out; (metal) refine; (naut) bream; **ich bin vollkommen abgebrannt** (coll) I'm dead broke || *intr* (SEIN) burn down

ab'bringen §65 *tr* (*Fleck*) remove; (*gestrandetes Schiff*) refloat; **davon a. zu** (*inf*) dissuade from (*ger*); **vom rechten Weg a.** lead astray; **vom Thema a.** throw off; **von der Spur a.** throw off the scent; **von e-r Gewohnheit a.** break of the habit

ab'bröckeln *intr* crumble; (*Farbe*) peel (off); (*Preis, Aktie*) go slowly down; (*Mitglieder*) fall off

Ab'bruch *m* (*e-s Zweiges, der Beziehungen*) breaking off; (*e-s Gebäudes*) demolition; (*Schaden*) damage; **A. des Spiels** (sport) calling of the game; **A. tun** (*dat*) harm, spoil; **auf A. verkaufen** sell at demolition value; (*Maschinen*) sell for junk

ab'brühen *tr* (culin) scald

ab'brummen *tr* (*Strafe*) (coll) serve, do || *intr* (SEIN) (coll) clear out

ab'buchen *tr* (*abschreiben*) write off; (acct) debit

ab'bürsten *tr* brush off

ab'büßen *tr* atone for; **e-e Strafe a.** serve time; **er hat es schwer a. müssen** (coll) he had to pay for it dearly

Abc [ɑbe'tse] *n* (-;-) ABC's

Abc'-Schütze *m* (-n;-n) pupil

ab'danken *tr* dismiss; (*pensionieren*)

3

retire || *intr* resign; (*Herrscher*) abdicate; (mil) get a discharge
ab'decken *tr* uncover; (*Tisch*) clear; (*Bett*) turn down; (*Vieh*) skin; (*e-e Schuld*) pay back; (mil) camouflage; (phot) mask
ab'dichten *tr* seal (off); (*Loch*) plug up; (*mit weichem Material*) pack; (naut) caulk
ab'dienen *tr* (*Schuld*) work off; (mil) serve (*one's term*)
ab'drehen *tr* twist off; (*Gas, Licht, Wasser*) turn off || *intr* turn away
ab'dreschen §67 *tr* thrash
Ab'druck *m* (-s;-e) reprint; offprint; copy; (*Abguß*) casting; (phot, typ) proof || *m* (-s;-̈e) impression, imprint
ab'drucken *tr* print
ab'drücken *tr* (*abformen*) mold; (*Gewehr*) fire; (*Pfeil*) shoot; (*umarmen*) hug; **den Hahn a.** pull the trigger || *ref* leave an impression || *intr* pull the trigger
ab'duschen *ref* shower off
Abend ['abənt] *m* (-s;-e) evening; **am A.** in the evening; **bunter A.** social; (telv) variety show; **des Abends** in the evening(s); **zu A.** essen eat dinner
A'bendblatt *n* evening paper
A'bendbrot *n* supper, dinner
A'benddämmerung *f* twilight, dusk
A'bendessen *n* supper, dinner
abendfüllend ['abəntfʏlənt] *adj* full-length (*movie*)
A'bendgesellschaft *f* party (*in the evening*)
A'bendland *n* West, Occident
abendländisch ['abəntlɛndɪʃ] *adj* occidental
a'bendlich *adj* evening || *adv* evenings
A'bendmahl *n* supper; **das Heilige A.** Holy Communion
abends ['abənts] *adv* in the evening
Abenteuer ['abəntɔɪ·ər] *s* (-s;-) adventure; **galantes A.** (love) affair
a'benteuerlich *adj* adventurous; (*Unternehmen*) risky
aber ['abər] *adv* yet, however; (before adjectives and adverbs) really, indeed; **a. und abermals** over and over again; **hundert und a. hundert** hundreds and hundreds of || *conj* but || *interj*—aber, aber! now, now! || **Aber** *n* (-s;-s) but; **hier gibt es kein A.!** no ifs and buts
A'berglaube *m* superstition
abergläubisch ['abərglɔɪbɪʃ] *adj* superstitious
ab'erkennen §97 *tr*—**j-m etw a.** deny s.o. s.th.; (jur) dispossess s.o. of s.th.
Ab'erkennung *f* (-;-en) denial; (jur) dispossession
abermalig ['abərmalɪç] *adj* repeated
abermals ['abərmals] *adv* once more
ab'ernten *tr* reap, harvest
ab'fahren §71 *tr* cart away; (*Strecke*) cover; (*Straße*) wear out; (*Reifen*) wear down || *intr* (SEIN) depart; drive off
Ab'fahrt *f* departure
Ab'fall *m* (*der Blätter*) falling; (*Bö-*

schung) steep slope; (*von e-m Glauben*) falling away; (*von e-r Partei*) defection; (*Sinken*) drop, decrease; **Abfälle** garbage, trash; chips, shavings
ab'fallen §72 *intr* (SEIN) fall off; (*von e-r Partei*) defect; (*vom Glauben*) fall away; (*abnehmen*) decrease, fail; (*Kunden*) stay away; (sport) fall behind; **a. gegen** compare badly with; **es wird etw für dich a.** there'll be s.th. in it for you; **körperlich a.** lose weight; **steil a.** drop away
abfällig ['apfelɪç] *adj* disparaging
Ab'fallprodukt *n* by-product
ab'fangen §73 *tr* catch; (*Angriff*) foil; (*Brief*) intercept; (aer) pull out of a dive; (*U-Boot*) (nav) trim; (sport) catch (up with); **j-m die Kunden a.** steal s.o.'s customers
ab'färben *intr* (*Farben*) run; (*Stoff*) fade; **a. auf** (*acc*) stain; (fig) rub off on
ab'fassen *tr* compose, draft; (*erwischen*) catch
Ab'fassung *f* (-;-en) wording; composition
ab'faulen *intr* (SEIN) rot away
ab'fegen *tr* sweep off, whisk off
abfertigen ['apfertɪgən] *tr* get ready for sending off; (*Gepäck*) check; (*Zollgüter*) clear; (*Kunden*) wait on; (*abweisen*) snub; (*verwaltungsmäßig*) (adm) process;
Ab'fertigung *f* (-;-en) dispatch; snub; zollamtliche A. clearance
ab'feuern *tr* fire; (rok) launch
ab'finden §59 *tr* (*Gläubiger*) satisfy; (*Partner*) buy off; (*entschädigen*) (für) compensate (for) || *ref*—**sich a. lassen** settle for a lump-sum payment; **sich a. mit** put up with; come to terms with
Ab'findung *f* (-;-en) satisfaction; lump-sum settlement
Ab'findungsvertrag *m* lump-sum settlement
abflachen ['apflaxən] *tr* level; (*abschrägen*) bevel || *ref* flatten out
abflauen ['apflau·ən] *intr* (SEIN) slack off; (*Interesse*) flag; (*Preis*) go down; (st. exch.) ease off
ab'fliegen §57 *intr* (SEIN) take off
ab'fließen §76 *intr* (SEIN) flow off, drain off
Ab'flug *m* takeoff, departure
Ab'fluß *m* discharge; drain, gutter, gully; **See ohne A.** lake without outlet
Ab'flußrinne *f* drainage ditch
Ab'flußrohr *n* drainpipe; soil pipe; (*vom Dach*) downspout
ab'fordern *tr*—**j-m etw a.** demand s.th. from s.o.
ab'fragen *tr*—**j-n etw a.** question s.o. about s.th.; quiz s.o. on s.th.
ab'fressen §70 *tr* eat up; crop, chew off; (*Metall*) corrode
ab'frieren §77 *intr* (SEIN) be nipped by the frost; **abgefroren** frostbitten
Abfuhr ['apfur] *f* (-;-en) removal; (*Abweisung*) (coll) cold shoulder, snub

ab'führen *tr* lead away; *(festnehmen)* arrest; (fencing) defeat ‖ *intr* cause the bowels to move

Abführmittel [ˈapfʏrmɪtəl] *n* laxative

ab'füllen *tr (Wein, Bier)* bottle

Ab'gabe *f (Auslieferung)* delivery; *(Verkauf)* sale; *(Steuer)* tax; *(Zoll)* duty; *(der Wahlstimme)* casting; *(e–s Urteils)* pronouncing; *(e–r Meinung)* expressing; (fb) pass; **Abgaben** taxes, fees

ab'gabenfrei *adj* tax-free, duty-free

abgabenpflichtig [ˈapgabənpflɪçtɪç] *adj* taxable, subject to duty

Ab'gang *m* departure; *(von e–m Amt)* retirement; *(von der Schule)* dropping out; graduation; *(Verlust)* loss; *(Abnahme)* decrease; (gym) finish; (pathol) discharge; (pathol) miscarriage; (theat) exit; **guten A. haben** sell well

abgängig [ˈapgɛŋɪç] *adj* lost, missing; (com) marketable

Ab'gangsprüfung *f* final examination

Ab'gangspunkt *m* point of departure

Ab'gas *n* (aut) exhaust; (indust) waste gas

ab'geben §80 *tr (Paß)* hand over; *(Gepäck)* check; *(abliefern)* deliver; *(Schulheft)* hand in; *(Urteil)* pass; *(Meinung)* express; *(Gutachten)* give; *(Amt)* lay down; *(gute Ernte)* yield; *(Schuß)* fire; *(Wahlstimme)* cast; *(Waren)* sell, let go; *(sich eignen als)* act as, serve as; **be cut out to be**; (elec) deliver; (fb) pass; (phys) give off; **e–e Offerte a.** (jur) make an offer; **e–n Narren a.** play the fool; **er würde e–n guten Vater a.** he would make a good father; **j–m eins a.** (coll) let s.o. have it; **j–m von etw a.** share s.th. with s.o. ‖ *ref*—**sich a.** mit bother with; associate with; spend time on

abgebrannt [ˈapgəbrant] *adj* (coll) broke

abgebrüht [ˈapgəbryt] *adj* (fig) hardened

abgedroschen [ˈapgədrɔʃən] *adj* trite, hackneyed; *(Witz)* stale

abgefeimt [ˈapgəfaɪmt] *adj* cunning; out-and-out

abgegriffen [ˈapgəgrɪfən] *adj* well-thumbed

abgehackt [ˈapgəhakt] *adj* jerky

abgehärmt [ˈapgəhɛrmt] *adj* careworn, drawn

ab'gehen §82 *intr* (SEIN) leave, depart; *(Brief)* go off; *(Knopf)* come off; *(Schuß)* go off; *(Farbe)* fade; *(Seitenweg)* branch off; *(vom Gesprächsgegenstand)* digress, go off; *(vom rechten Wege)* stray; *(aus e–m Amt)* resign, retire; *(von der Bühne)* retire; *(von der Schule)* drop out; graduate; (com) sell; (theat) exit; **bei Barzahlung gehen fünf Prozent ab** you get a five-percent reduction for paying cash; **davon kann ich nicht a.** I must insist on it; **er geht mir sehr ab** I miss him a lot; **nicht a. von** stick to; **reißend a.** sell like hotcakes; ‖ *ref*—**sich** [dat] **nichts a.**

lassen deny oneself nothing ‖ *impers* —**es geht ihm nichts ab** he lacks for nothing; **es gehen mir zehn Dollar ab** I am ten dollars short; **es ist alles glatt abgegangen** everything went well

ab'gehend *adj (Post, Beamte)* outgoing; *(Zug)* departing

abgekämpft [ˈapgəkɛmpft] *adj* exhausted

abgekartet [ˈapgəkartət] *adj (Spiel)* fixed; **abgekartete Sache** put-up job

abgeklappert [ˈapgəklapərt] *adj* hackneyed

abgeklärt [ˈapgəklɛrt] *adj* mellow, wise

abgelebt [ˈapgəlept] *adj* decrepit

abgelegen [ˈapgəlegən] *adj* out-of-the-way, outlying

ab'gelten §83 *tr* meet, satisfy

abgemacht [ˈapgəmaxt] *adj* settled ‖ *interj* agreed!

abgemagert [ˈapgəmagərt] *adj* emaciated

abgemessen [ˈapgəmɛsən] *adj* measured; *(genau)* exact; *(Rede)* deliberate; *(Person)* stiff, formal

abgeneigt [ˈapgənaɪkt] *adj* reluctant; *(dat)* averse to; **ich bin durchaus nicht a.** (coll) I don't mind if I do

Ab'geneigtheit *f* (–;) aversion

abgenutzt [ˈapgənʊtst] *adj* worn out

Abgeordnete [ˈapgəʔɔrdnətə] §5 *mf* delegate; (pol) representative; deputy *(member of the Bundestag)*; (Brit) Member of Parliament

Ab'geordnetenhaus *n* House of Representatives; (Brit) House of Commons

abgerissen [ˈapgərɪsən] *adj* torn; *(zerlumpt)* ragged; *(ohne Zusammenhang)* incoherent, disconnected

Abgesandte [ˈapgəzantə] §5 *mf* envoy

abgeschieden [ˈapgəʃidən] *adj* secluded; *(verstorben)* deceased, late

Ab'geschiedenheit *f* (–;) seclusion

abgeschliffen [ˈapgəʃlɪfən] *adj* polished

abgeschlossen [ˈapgəʃlɔsən] *adj* isolated; *(Leben)* secluded; *(Ausbildung)* completed

abgeschmackt [ˈapgəʃmakt] *adj* tactless, tasteless; (fig) insipid

abgesehen [ˈapgəzeˑən] *adj*—**a. davon, daß** not to mention that; **a. von** aside from, except for

abgespannt [ˈapgəʃpant] *adj* tired out

abgestanden [ˈapgəʃtandən] *adj* stale

abgestorben [ˈapgəʃtɔrbən] *adj (Pflanze, Gewebe)* dead; *(Glied)* numb

abgestumpft [ˈapgəʃtumpft] *adj* blunt; *(Kegel)* truncated; (fig) dull; *(gegen)* indifferent (to)

abgetakelt [ˈapgətakəlt] *adj (Person)* seedy; *(Schiff)* unrigged

abgetan [ˈapgətan] *adj* settled

abgetragen [ˈapgətragən] *adj* threadbare

abgetreten [ˈapgətretən] *adj* worn-down

ab'gewinnen §52 *tr* win; **e–r Sache Geschmack a.** acquire a taste for s.th.; **e–r Sache Vergnügen a.** derive pleas-

ure from s.th.; **j–m e–n Vorteil a.**
gain an advantage over s.o.
abgewirtschaftet [ˈapgəvɪrtʃaftət] *adj*
run-down
ab'gewöhnen *tr*—**ich kann es mir nicht
a.** I can't get it out of my system;
j–m etw a. break s.o. of s.th.
abgezehrt [ˈapgətsert] *adj* emaciated
ab'gießen §76 *tr* pour off; (*Statue*)
cast; (chem) decant; (culin) strain
off
Ab'glanz *m* reflection
ab'gleiten §86 *intr* (SEIN) slip off; (**an**
dat) glance off (*s.th.*); (aer, aut)
skid; (st. exch.) decline
Ab'gott *m* idol
Abgötterei [apgœtəˈraɪ] *f* (–;–en) idolatry; **A. treiben** worship idols; **mit
j–m A. treiben** idolize s.o.
abgöttisch [ˈapgœtɪʃ] *adj* idolatrous ‖
adv—**a. lieben** idolize
Ab'gottschlange *f* boa constrictor
ab'graben §87 *tr* (*Bach*) divert; (*Feld*)
drain; (*Hügel*) level
ab'grämen *ref* eat one's heart out
ab'grasen *tr* (*Wiese*) graze on; (fig)
scour, search
ab'greifen §88 *tr* wear out (*by constant handling*); (*Buch*) thumb
ab'grenzen *tr* mark off, demarcate; delimit; (fig) differentiate
Ab'grund *m* abyss; precipice
abgründig [ˈapgryndɪç] *adj* precipitous; (fig) deep, unfathomable
ab'gucken *tr* (coll) copy, crib; (coll)
pick up a habit from ‖ *intr* (coll)
copy, crib
Ab'guß *m* (sculp) cast; **A. in Gips**
plaster cast
ab'hacken *tr* chop off; (*Baum*) chop
down
ab'haken *tr* unhook, undo; (*in e–r
Liste*) check off; (telp) take off (*the
receiver*)
ab'halftern *tr* unharness; (fig) sack
ab'halten §90 *tr* hold off; (*Vorlesung*)
give; (*Regen*) keep out; (*Versammlung, Parade*) hold; (**von**) keep
(from)
Ab'haltung *f* (–;–en) hindrance; (*e–r
Versammlung*) holding; (*e–s Festes*)
celebration
ab'handeln *tr* (*Thema*) treat; (*erörtern*) discuss; **er läßt sich nichts a.**
he won't come down (*in price*); **etw
vom Preise a.** get s.th. off the price
(*by bargaining*)
abhanden [apˈhandən] *adv*—**a. kommen** get lost; **a. sein** be missing
Ab'handlung *f* (–;–en) essay; (*Vortrag
in e–m gelehrten Verein*) paper;
(*Doktorarbeit*) thesis, dissertation;
(*mündlich*) discourse, discussion
Ab'hang *m* slope
ab'hängen *tr* (*vom Haken*) take off;
(*e–n Verfolger*) shake off; (rr) uncouple ‖ *intr* (telp) hang up; **a. von**
depend on; be subject to (*s.o.'s approval*)
abhängig [ˈaphɛŋɪç] *adj* (*Stellung*) subordinate; (*Satz*) dependent; (*Rede*)
indirect; (*Kasus*) oblique; (**von**) dependent (on), contingent (upon)

Ab'hängigkeit *f* (–;–en) dependence;
(gram) subordination; **gegenseitige
A.** interdependence
ab'härmen *ref* pine away; **sich a. wegen** (or **über** *acc*) fret about
ab'härten *tr* harden; (gegen) inure (to)
‖ *ref* (gegen) become hardened (to)
ab'hauen §93 *tr* cut off; chop off ‖
§109 *intr* (SEIN) (coll) scram, get lost
ab'häuten *tr* skin, flay
ab'heben §94 *tr* lift off; (*Rahm*) skim;
(*Geld*) withdraw; (*Dividende*) collect; (*Haut*) (surg) strip off ‖ *ref* become airborne; (**von**) contrast (with)
Ab'hebung *f* (–;–en) lifting; (*vom
Bankkonto*) withdrawal; (cards) cutting
Ab'hebungsformular *n* withdrawal slip
ab'heften *tr* (*Briefe*) file; (sew) tack
ab'heilen *intr* (HABEN & SEIN) heal up
ab'helfen §96 *intr* (dat) (e–m *Unrecht*)
redress; (*e–r Schwierigkeit*) remove;
(*e–m Mangel*) relieve; **dem ist nicht
abzuhelfen** that can't be helped
ab'hetzen *tr* drive hard, work to death;
(hunt) hunt down ‖ *ref* rush; tire
oneself out
Ab'hilfe *f* remedy, redress; **A. schaffen** take remedial measures; **A.
schaffen für** remedy, redress
ab'hobeln *tr* plane (down)
abhold [ˈaphɔlt] *adj* (*dat*) ill-disposed
(towards), averse (to)
Abholdienst [ˈapholdinst] *m* pickup
service
ab'holen *tr* fetch, call for, pick up
ab'holzen *tr* clear (of trees), deforest
Abhörapparat [ˈaphøraparat] *m* (mil,
nav) listening device
ab'horchen *tr* overhear; (med) sound;
(rad, telp) monitor
ab'hören *tr* overhear, eavesdrop on;
(*Studenten*) quiz; (*Schallplatte, Tonband*) listen to; (mil) intercept;
(telp) monitor
Ab'hörgerät *n* bugging device
Ab'hörraum *m* (rad, telv) control
room
Ab'irrung *f* (–;–en) deviation; (opt)
aberration
Abitur [abɪˈtur] *n* (–s;–e) final examination (*at end of junior college*);
das A. bestehen graduate
Abiturient –in [abɪturɪˈɛnt(ɪn)] §7 *mf*
graduate (*of a junior college*)
Abitur'zeugnis *n* diploma (*from senior
high school or junior college*)
ab'jagen *tr* drive hard; **j–m etw a.** recover s.th. from s.o. ‖ *ref* run one's
head off
abkanzeln [ˈapkantsəln] *tr* (coll) give
(*s.o.*) a good talking to
ab'kauen *tr* chew off ‖ *ref*—**sich** [*dat*]
die Nägel a. bite one's nails
ab'kaufen *tr*—**j–m etw a.** buy s.th.
from s.o.
Abkehr [ˈapker] *f* (–;) turning away;
estrangement; (*Verzicht*) renunciation
ab'kehren *tr* turn away, avert; (*mit
dem Besen*) sweep off ‖ *ref* turn
away; become estranged
ab'klappern *tr* (coll) scour, search

ab'klatschen *tr* imitate slavishly; make an exact copy of; (*beim Tanzen*) cut in on; (typ) pull (*a proof*)
ab'klingen §142 *intr* (SEIN) (*Farbe*) fade; (*Töne*) die away; (*Schmerz*) ease off
ab'klopfen *tr* beat off, knock off; (*Teppich*) beat; (med) tap, percuss || *intr* stop the music (*with the rap of the baton*)
ab'knabbern *tr* (coll) nibble off
ab'knallen *tr* fire off; (sl) bump off
ab'knicken *tr* snap off || *intr* (SEIN) snap off
ab'knipsen *tr* pinch off, snip off; (*Film*) use up
ab'knöpfen *tr* unbutton; **j-m Geld a.** squeeze money out of s.o.
ab'knutschen *tr* (coll) pet
ab'kochen *tr* boil; (*Obst*) stew; (*Milch*) scald || *intr* cook out
ab'kommandieren *tr* detach, detail
ab'kommen §99 *intr* (SEIN) (**von**) get away (from); (*Mode*) go out of style; (naut) become afloat (again); **auf zwei Tage a.** get away for two days; **gut** (or **schlecht**) **a.** (sport) get off to a good (or bad) start; **hoch** (or **tief**) **a.** aim too high (or low); **vom Kurs a.** go off course; **vom Boden a.** become airborne; **vom Thema a.** get off the subject; **vom Wege a.** lose one's way, stray; **von der Wahrheit a.** deviate from the truth; **von e-r Ansicht a.** change one's views || **Abkommen** *n* (-s;-) (com, pol) agreement; (jur) settlement
abkömmlich ['apkœmlıç] *adj*—**a. sein** be able to get away
Abkömmling ['apkœmlıŋ] *m* (-s;-e) descendant, scion
ab'koppeln *tr* uncouple
ab'kratzen *tr* scratch off; (*Schuhe*) scuff up || *intr* (*sterben*) (sl) croak; (*abhauen*) (sl) beat it; **kratz ab!** drop dead!
ab'kriegen *tr* (coll) get off or out
ab'kühlen *tr, ref & intr* cool off
Abkunft ['apkunft] *f* (-;) lineage
ab'kürzen *tr* shorten; (*Inhalt*) abridge; (*Wort*) abbreviate; (math) reduce
Ab'kürzung *f* (-;-en) shortening; abridgement; abbreviation; (*kürzerer Weg*) shortcut
ab'küssen *tr* smother with kisses
ab'laden §103 *tr* unload; (*Schutt*) dump
Ab'ladeplatz *m* dump; (mil) unloading point
Ab'lage *f* (*für Kleider*) cloakroom; (*Lagerhaus*) depot, warehouse; (*abgelegte Akten*) files; (mil) dump
ab'lagern *tr* (*Wein, usw.*) age; (geol) deposit || *ref* (geol) be deposited || *intr*—**a. lassen** age, season
Ab'laß *m* (-lasses;-lässe) outlet, drain; (com) deduction; (eccl) indulgence
ab'lassen §104 *tr* leave off; (*Bier*) tap; (*Dampf*) let off; (*Teich, Faß*) drain; (*Waren*) sell; **etw vom Preise a.** knock s.th. off the price; **j-m etw billig a.** (com) let s.o. have s.th. cheaply || *intr* desist, stop; **a. von** let go of, give up

Ablativ ['ablatif] *m* (-s;-e) ablative
Ab'lauf *m* overflow; (*e-r Frist, e-s Vertrags*) expiration; (*der Ereignisse*) course; (sport) start
ab'laufen §105 *tr* (*Strecke*) run; (*Stadt*) scour; (*Schuhe*) wear out; **j-m den Rang a.** get the better of s.o.; **outrun s.o.** || *intr* (SEIN) run away; (*Zeit*) expire; (*ausfallen*) turn out; (com) fall due; (sport) start
Ab'laut *m* ablaut
Ab'leben *n* demise, decease
ab'lecken *tr* lick (off)
ab'legen *tr* (*Last, Waffen*) lay down; (*ausziehen*) take off; (*Schwert*) lay aside; (*die alte Haut*) slough; (*Karten*) discard; (*Akten, Dokumente*) file; (*Briefe*) sort; (*Namen*) drop, stop using; (*Sorgen, Kummer*) put away; (*Prüfung, Gelübde, Eid*) take; (*Predigt*) deliver; (*Gewohnheit*) give up; (*Rechenschaft*) render, give; **Bekenntnis a.** make a confession; **die Maske a.** (fig) throw off all disguise; **die Trauer a.** come out of mourning; **ein volles Geständnis a.** come clean; **Probe a.** furnish proof; **seine Fehler a.** mend one's ways; **Zeugnis a.** (für or gegen) testify (for or against) || *intr* take off one's coat or hat and coat); **bitte, legen Sie ab!** please take your things off
Ab'leger *m* (-s;-) (bot) shoot; (com) subsidiary; (hort) slip, cutting
ab'lehnen *tr* refuse, turn down; (*Antrag*) reject; (*Zeugen*) challenge; (*Erbschaft*) renounce; **durch Abstimmung a.** vote down
ab'lehnend *adj* negative
Ab'lehnung *f* (-;-en) refusal
ab'leiern *tr* recite mechanically
ab'leisten *tr* (*Eid*) take; **den Militärdienst a.** (mil) serve one's time
ab'leiten *tr* lead away; (*Herkunft*) trace back; (*Fluß, Blitz*) divert; (*Wasser*) drain off; (*Wärme*) conduct; (chem) derive; (elec) shunt; (gram, math) derive; **abgeleitetes Wort** derivative || *ref* (aus, von) be derived (from)
Ab'leitung *f* (-;-en) (*e-s Flusses*) diversion; (*des Wassers*) drainage; (elec, phys) conduction; (gram, math) derivation; (phys) convection
ab'lenken *tr* turn away, divert; (*Gefahr, Verdacht*) ward off; (fencing) parry; (opt, phys) deflect
Ab'lenkung *f* (-;-en) diversion; distraction; (opt) refraction
ab'lernen *tr*—**j-m etw a.** learn s.th. from s.o.
ab'lesen §107 *tr* read off; (*Zähler*) read; (*Obst*) pick; **es j-m vom Gesicht a., daß** tell by looking at s.o. that
ab'leugnen *tr* deny, disown; (*Glauben*) renounce
Ab'leugnung *f* (-;-en) denial, disavowal
ab'liefern *tr* deliver, hand over, surrender
Ab'lieferung *f* (-;-en) delivery; (*der Schußwaffen*) surrender

ab'liegen §108 *intr* (*Wein*) mature; (*Obst*) ripen ‖ *intr* (SEIN) be remote
ab'löschen *tr* extinguish; (*Stahl*) temper; (*Tinte*) blot; (*Kalk*) slake
ab'lösen *tr* loosen, detach; (*Posten*) relieve; (*Schuld*) discharge; (*Pfand*) redeem; (*Haut*) peel off ‖ *ref* (bei) take turns (at)
Ab'lösung *f* (-;-en) loosening; relief; discharge
ab'machen *tr* undo, untie; (*erledigen*) settle, arrange; (*Vertrag*) conclude; (*Rechnung*) close
Ab'machung *f* (-;-en) settlement
abmagern ['apmɑgərn] *intr* (SEIN) grow thin, thin down
Ab'magerung *f* (-;) emaciation
ab'mähen *tr* mow
ab'malen *tr* portray; (fig) depict
Ab'marsch *m* departure
ab'marschieren *intr* (SEIN) march off
Ab'mattung *f* (-;) fatigue
ab'melden *tr* (*Besuch*) (coll) call off; der ist bei mir abgemeldet (coll) I've had it with him; **j-n bei der Polizei a.** give notice to the police that s.o. is leaving town ‖ *ref* (mil) report off duty
ab'messen §70 *tr* measure (off); (*Worte*) weigh; (*Land*) survey
ab'montieren *tr* dismantle; (*Geschütz*) disassemble; (*Reifen*) take off ‖ *ref* (aer) (coll) disintegrate in the air
ab'mühen *ref* exert oneself, slave
ab'murksen *tr* (sl) do in
ab'nagen *tr* gnaw (off); (*Knochen*) pick
Ab'nahme *f* (-;-n) (*Verminderung*) (an dat) reduction (in), drop (in); (*des Gewichts*) loss; (*des Mondes*) waning; (*des Tages*) shortening; (*e-s Eides*) administering; (*e-r Rechnung*) auditing; (*indust*) final inspection; (surg) amputation; **A. der Geschäfte** decline in business; **A. e-r Parade** reviewing of the troops; **bk. finden** be sold; **in A. geraten** decline, wane
ab'nehmen §116 *tr* take off, remove; (*Wäsche*) take down; (*Schnurrbart*) shave off; (*wegnehmen*) take away; (*Hörer*) lift, unhook; (*Strom*) use; (*Obst*) pick; (*Eid*) administer; (*Waren*) purchase; (*Rechnung*) audit; (*prüfen*) inspect and pass; (*Verband*) remove; (phot) take; (surg) amputate; **aus Berichten a.** gather from reports; **das kann ich dir nicht a.** I can't accept what you are saying; **die Parade a.** inspect the troops; **j-m die Arbeit a.** take the work off s.o.'s shoulders; **j-m die Beichte a.** hear s.o.'s confession; **j-m die Maske a.** unmask s.o., expose s.o.; **j-m die Verantwortung a.** relieve s.o. of responsibility; **j-m ein Versprechen a.** make s.o. make a promise; **j-m zuviel a.** charge s.o. too much ‖ *intr* diminish; (*Preise*) drop; (*Wasser*) recede; (*Kräfte*) fail; (*Mond*) be on the wane; **an Dicke a.** taper; **an Gewicht a.** lose weight; **an Kräften a.** lose strength ‖ **Abnehmen**

n (-s;) decrease; **im A. sein** be on the decrease
Ab'nehmer **-in** §6 *mf* buyer, consumer; (*Kunde*) customer; (*Hehler*) fence
Ab'neigung *f* (-;-en) (gegen, vor dat) aversion (to, for), dislike (of)
abnorm [ap'nɔrm] *adj* abnormal
Abnormität [apnɔrmɪ'tet] *f* (-;-en) abnormity, monstrosity
ab'nötigen *tr* (dat) extort (from)
ab'nutzen, ab'nützen *tr* wear out ‖ *ref* wear out, become worn out
Ab'nutzung *f* (-;-en) wear and tear; (*Abrieb*) abrasion; (mil) attrition
Ab'öl *n* (-s;-e) used oil
Abonnement [abɔn(ə)'mɑ̃] *n* (-s;-s) (auf acc) subscription (to)
Abonnements'karte *f* commutation ticket
Abonnent **-in** [abɔ'nɛnt(ɪn)] §7 *mf* subscriber
abonnieren [abɔ'nirən] *tr* subscribe to; **abonniert sein auf** (acc) have a subscription to ‖ *intr* (auf acc) subscribe (to)
ab'ordnen *tr* delegate, deputize
Ab'ordnung *f* (-;-en) delegation
Abort [a'bɔrt] *m* (-s;-e) toilet ‖ [a'bɔrt] *m* (-s;-e) abortion
ab'passen *tr* measure, fit; (*abwarten*) watch for; (*auflauern*) waylay
ab'pfeifen §88 *tr* (sport) stop
ab'pflücken *tr* pluck (off)
ab'placken, ab'plagen *ref* work oneself to death, slave
ab'platzen *intr* (SEIN) come loose
Abprall ['apral] *m* rebound; (*Geschoß*) richochet
ab'prallen *intr* (SEIN) rebound; ricochet
ab'pressen *tr* extort
ab'putzen *tr* clean (off); (*polieren*) polish; (*Mauer*) roughcast, plaster
ab'raten §63 *intr*—**j-m von etw a.** advise s.o. against s.th.
Ab'raum *m* (-es;) rubble; (min) overburden
ab'räumen *tr* clear away; (*Tisch*) clear off ‖ *ref* (coll) calm down
ab'reagieren *tr* (*Spannung, Erregung*) work off ‖ *ref* (coll) calm down
ab'rechnen *tr* subtract; (*Spesen*) account for; (com) deduct ‖ *intr* settle accounts
Ab'rechnung *f* (-;-en) (*von Konten*) settlement; (*Abzug*) deduction; **A. halten** balance accounts
Ab'rede *f* agreement, arrangement; **in A. stellen** deny
ab'reden *intr*—**j-m von etw a.** dissuade s.o. from s.th.
ab'reiben *tr* rub off; (*Körper*) rub down
Ab'reise *f* departure
ab'reisen *intr* (SEIN) (**nach**) depart (for)
ab'reißen §53 *tr* tear off; (*Haus*) tear down; (*Kleid*) wear out ‖ *intr* (SEIN) tear off
ab'richten *tr* (*Tier*) train; (*Pferd*) break in; (*Brett*) dress
Ab'richter **-in** §6 *mf* trainer
ab'riegeln *tr* (*Tür*) bolt; (mil) seal off

ab'ringen §142 *tr*—**j-m etw a.** wrest s.th. from s.o.
ab'rinnen §121 *intr* (SEIN) run off, run down
Ab'riß *m* summary, outline; (*Skizze*) sketch
ab'rollen *tr* & *ref* unroll, unwind (| *intr* (SEIN) unroll, unwind
ab'rücken *tr* push away, move back || *intr* (SEIN) clear out; (fig) dissociate oneself; (mil) march off
Ab'ruf *m* recall; **auf A.** on call
ab'rufen §122 *tr* call away; (*Zug*) call out, announce
ab'runden *tr* round off
ab'rupfen *tr* pluck (off)
ab'rüsten *tr* & *intr* disarm
Ab'rüstung *f* (–;) disarmament
ab'rutschen *intr* (SEIN) slip (off)
absacken ['apzakən] *intr* (SEIN) sink; (*Flugzeug*) pancake
Ab'sage *f* cancellation; (*Ablehnung*) refusal
ab'sagen *tr* cancel || *intr* decline; (*dat*) renounce, repudiate
ab'sägen *tr* saw off
ab'sahnen *tr* (& fig) skim (off)
Ab'satz *m* stop, pause, break; (*Zeileneinrückung*) indentation; (*Abschnitt*) paragraph; (*des Schuhes*) heel; (*der Treppen*) landing; (*Vertrieb*) market, sale(s); **ohne A.** without a break
ab'satzfähig *adj* marketable
Ab'satzgebiet *n* territory (*of a salesman*)
Ab'satzmarkt *m* (com) outlet
Ab'satzstockung *f* slump in sales
ab'saugen *tr* suck off; (*Teppich*) vacuum
Ab'saugventilator *m* exhaust fan
ab'schaben *tr* scrape off
ab'schaffen *tr* abolish, do away with; (*Mißbrauch*) redress; (*Diener*) dismiss
ab'schälen *tr* peel
ab'schalten *tr* switch off
ab'schätzen *tr* (*Wert*) estimate; (*für die Steuer*) assess, appraise
abschätzig ['apʃetsɪç] *adj* disparaging
Ab'schaum *m* (–[e]s;) (& fig) scum
ab'scheiden §112 *tr* part, sever; (physiol) excrete; (physiol) secrete || *intr* (SEIN) pass away, pass on
Ab'scheu *m* (–[e]s;) (**vor** *dat,* **gegen**) abhorrence (of), disgust (at)
ab'scheuern *tr* scrub off, scour; (*Haut*) scrape; (*abnutzen*) wear out
abscheu'lich *adj* atrocious
ab'schicken *tr* send away; (*Post*) mail
ab'schieben §130 *tr* shove off; deport
Abschied ['apʃit] *m* (–[e]s;–e) (*Weggang*) departure; (*Entlassung*) dismissal; (mil) discharge; **A. nehmen von** take leave of; (*e–m Amt*) resign, retire from
Ab'schiedsfeier *f* farewell party
Ab'schiedsrede *f* valediction
Ab'schiedsschmaus *m* farewell dinner
ab'schießen §76 *tr* (*Gewehr*) fire, shoot; (*Flugzeug*) shoot down; (*Panzer*) knock out; (rok) launch; **j–n a.** bring about s.o.'s downfall
ab'schinden §167 *tr* skin || *ref* slave

ab'schirmen *tr* screen (off); (**gegen**) guard (against)
ab'schlachten *tr* butcher; (fig) massacre
Ab'schlag *m* discount; (golf) tee shot; **auf A.** in part payment, on account
ab'schlagen §132 *tr* knock off; (*Baum*) fell; (*Angriff*) repel; (*Bitte*) refuse; **das Wasser a.** pass water || *intr* (golf) tee off
abschlägig ['apʃlegɪç] *adj* negative; **a. bescheiden** turn down
Ab'schlagszahlung *f* installment
ab'schleifen §88 *tr* grind off; (fig) refine, polish || *ref* become refined
ab'schleppen *tr* drag away, tow away
Ab'schleppwagen *m* tow truck
ab'schleudern *tr* fling off, catapult
ab'schließen §76 *tr* lock (up); (*Straße*) close off; (*Rechnung*) close, settle; (*Bücher*) balance; (*Vertrag*) conclude; (*Rede*) wind up; (*Wette*) wager || *ref* seclude oneself, shut oneself off || *intr* conclude
ab'schließend *adj* definitive; (*Worte*) concluding || *adv* definitively; (*schließlich*) in conclusion
Ab'schluß *m* completion; (*e–s Vertrags*) conclusion; (*Geschäft*) transaction, deal; (*Verkauf*) sale; (*Rechnungs-, Konto-, Buch-*) closing; (mach) seal
ab'schmeicheln *tr*—**j-m etw a.** coax s.th. out of s.o.
ab'schmelzen §133 *tr* (*Erz*) smelt; (*Schnee*) melt || *intr* (SEIN) melt
ab'schmieren *tr* copy carelessly; (coll) beat up; (aut) lubricate || *intr* (SEIN) (aer) (coll) crash
ab'schnallen *tr* unbuckle, unstrap
ab'schnappen *intr* (SEIN) (coll) stop dead; (coll) die
ab'schneiden §106 *tr* cut (off); (*Hecke*) trim; **den Weg. a.** take a shortcut; **j-m das Wort a.** cut s.o. short; **j-m die Ehre a.** steal s.o.'s good name || *intr*—**gut a.** do well
Ab'schnitt *m* cut, cutting; (*Teilstück*) part, section; (*im Scheckbuch*) stub; (*Kapitel*) section, paragraph; (math) segment; (mil) sector
ab'schnüren *tr* untie; (surg) ligature; **j-m den Atem a.** choke s.o.
ab'schöpfen *tr* skim off
ab'schrägen *tr* & *ref* slant, slope
ab'schrauben *tr* unscrew
ab'schrecken §134 *tr* scare off; (*abbringen*) deter
ab'schreiben §62 *tr* copy; (*Schularbeit*) crib; (*uneinbringliche Forderung*) write off; (*Literaturwerk*) plagiarize; (*Wert*) depreciate || *intr* send a refusal
Ab'schreiber **–in** §6 *mf* plagiarist
Ab'schreibung *f* (–;–en) write-off
ab'schreiten §86 *tr* pace off; (mil) review; **die Front a.** review the troops
Ab'schrift *f* copy, transcript; (com, jur) duplicate
ab'schriftlich *adj* & *adv* in duplicate
ab'schuften *ref* work oneself to death
ab'schürfen *ref*—**sich** [*dat*] **die Haut a.** skin oneself

Ab'schürfung ƒ (-;-en) abrasion
Ab'schuß *m* (*e-r Waffe*) firing; (*e-r Rakete*) launching; (*e-s Panzers*) knocking out; (*e-s Flugzeugs*) downing, kill; (hunt) kill
abschüssig ['apʃʏsɪç] *adj* sloping; (*steil*) steep
Ab'schußrampe ƒ launch pad
ab'schütteln *tr* shake off
ab'schwächen *tr* weaken; (*vermindern*) diminish, reduce; (*Farben*) tone down ‖ *ref* (*Preis*) decline
ab'schweifen *intr* (SEIN) stray, digress
Ab'schweifung ƒ (-;-en) digression
ab'schwellen §119 *intr* (SEIN) go down; (*Lärm, Gesang*) die down
ab'schwenken *intr* (SEIN) swerve
ab'schwören *intr* (*dat*) (*dem Glauben*) deny; (*dem Trunk*) swear off
ab'segeln *intr* (SEIN) set sail
absehbar ['apzebɑr] *adj* foreseeable
ab'sehen §138 *tr* foresee; **es abgesehen haben auf** (*acc*) be out to get ‖ *intr*—a. **von** disregard; refrain from
ab'seifen *tr* soap down
abseits ['apzaɪts] *adv* aside; (sport) offside ‖ *prep* (*genit*) off
ab'senden §140 *tr* send (off), dispatch; (*Post*) mail; (*befördern*) forward
Ab'sender –in §6 *mf* sender, dispatcher
Ab'sendung ƒ (-;-en) sending, dispatching; mailing, shipping
ab'sengen *tr* singe off
Absentismus [apzɛn'tɪsmʊs] *m* (-;) absenteeism
ab'setzen *tr* (*Betrag*) deduct; (*Last*) set down; (*entwöhnen*) wean; (*Beamten*) remove; (*König*) depose; (*Fallschirmtruppen, Passagiere*) drop; (com) sell; (typ) set up ‖ *ref* settle, set; (mil) disengage ‖ *intr* stop, pause
Absetzung ƒ (-;-en) dismissal
Ab'sicht ƒ intention, purpose; **in der A.** with the intention; **mit A.** on purpose; **ohne A.** unintentionally
ab'sichtlich *adj* intentional ‖ *adv* on purpose, intentionally
ab'sitzen §144 *tr* (*Strafzeit*) serve, do ‖ *intr* (SEIN) (*vom Pferde*) dismount; **a. lassen** (chem) let settle
absolut [apzo'lut] *adj*
absolvieren [apzɔl'virən] *tr* absolve; (*Studien*) finish; (*Hochschule*) graduate from; (*Prüfung*) pass
abson'derlich *adj* peculiar, strange
ab'sondern *tr* separate, segregate; (*Kranken*) isolate; (physiol) secrete ‖ *ref* keep aloof
absorbieren [apzɔr'birən] *tr* absorb
ab'speisen *tr* feed; **j-n mit schönen Worten a.** put s.o. off with polite words
abspenstig ['apʃpɛnstɪç] *adj*—a. **machen** lure away; **j-m a. werden** desert s.o.
ab'sperren *tr* shut off, block off; (*Tür*) lock; (*Strom*) cut off; (*Gas*) turn off
ab'spielen *tr* play through to the end; (*Schallplatte, Tonband*) play; (*Tonbandaufnahme*) play back ‖ *ref* take place
ab'sprechen §64 *tr* dispute, deny; (*ab-*

machen) arrange; **j-m das Recht a. zu** (*inf*) dispute s.o.'s right to (*inf*)
ab'sprechend *adj* (*Urteil*) unfavorable; (*Kritik*) adverse; (*tadelnd*) disparaging
ab'springen §142 *intr* (SEIN) jump down, jump off; (*Ball*) rebound; (*Glasur*) chip; (*abschweifen*) digress; (aer) bail out, jump; **a. von** quit, desert
Ab'sprung *m* jump; (*ins Wasser*) dive; (*des Balles*) rebound
ab'spulen *tr* unwind, unreel
ab'spülen *tr* rinse (off)
ab'stammen *intr* (SEIN) (**von**) be descended (from); (**von**) be derived (from)
Abstammung ƒ (-;-en) descent, extraction; (gram) derivation
Ab'stand *m* distance; (*räumlich und zeitlich*) interval; **A. nehmen von** refrain from; **A. zahlen** pay compensation
abstatten ['apʃtatən] *tr* (*Besuch*) pay; (*Bericht*) file; (*Dank*) give, return
ab'stauben *tr* dust off; (sl) swipe
ab'stechen §64 *tr* (*töten*) stab; (*Rasen*) cut; (*Hochofen*) tap; (*Karten*) trump ‖ *intr*—**gegen** (or **von**) **etwa a.** contrast with s.th.
Ab'stecher *m* (-s;-) side trip; (*Umweg*) detour; (fig) digression
ab'stecken *tr* (*Haar*) unpin, let down; (*Kleid*) pin, fit; (surv) mark off
ab'stehen §146 *intr* (*entfernt sein*) (**von**) be, stand away (from); (*Ohren, usw.*) stick out ‖ *intr* (HABEN & SEIN) (**von**) refrain (from)
ab'steigen §148 *intr* (SEIN) get down, descend; **in e-m Gasthof a.** stay at a hotel
ab'stellen *tr* (*Last*) put down; (*Radio, Gas, usw.*) turn off; (*Motor*) switch off; (*Auto*) park; (*Mißstand*) redress; (mil) detach, assign; **a. auf** (*acc*) gear to
Ab'stellraum *m* storage room
ab'stempeln *tr* stamp
ab'sterben §149 *intr* (SEIN) die off; (*Pflanzen*) wither; (*Glieder*) get numb
Abstieg ['apʃtik] *m* (-[e]s;) descent
ab'stimmen *tr* tune; (com) balance; **a. auf** (*acc*) (fig) atune (to) ‖ *intr* (*über acc*) vote (on)
Abstinenzler –in [apstɪ'nɛntslər(ɪn)] §6 *mf* teetotaler
ab'stoppen *tr* stop; (sport) clock
ab'stoßen §150 *tr* push off; (*Waren*) get rid of, sell; (*Schulden*) pay off; (*Geweih*) shed; (fig) disgust, sicken; (phys) repel ‖ *ref*—**sich** [*dat*] **die Hörner a.** (fig) sow one's wild oats ‖ *intr* (SEIN) shove off
ab'stoßend *adj* repulsive
abstrakt [ap'strakt] *adj* abstract
ab'streichen *tr* (*abwischen*) wipe off; (*Rasiermesser*) strop; (*abhaken*) check off; (bact) swab; (com) deduct
ab'streifen *tr* (*Handschuh, usw.*) take off; (*Haut*) slough off; (*Gewohnheit*) break ‖ *intr* (SEIN) deviate, stray
ab'streiten §86 *tr* contest, dispute

Ab'strich m (beim Schreiben) downstroke; (Abzug) cut; (bact) swab
ab'stufen tr (Gelände) terrace; (Farben) shade off
abstumpfen ['apstumpfən] tr blunt
Ab'sturz m fall; (Abhang) precipice; (aer) crash
abstürzen intr (SEIN) fall down; (aer) crash
ab'suchen tr (Gebiet) scour, comb
Ab·szeß [ap'stsɛs] m (-szesses; -szesse) abscess
Abt [apt] m (-[e]s;-̈e) abbot
ab'takeln tr unrig; (coll) sack, fire
ab'tasten tr probe; (rad) scan
Abtei [ap'taɪ] f (-;-en) abbey
Ab'teil m compartment
ab'teilen tr divide, partition
Ab'teilung f (-;-en) department, division; (im Krankenhaus) ward; (arti) battery; (mil) detachment, unit
Ab'teilungsleiter -in §6 mf department head, section head
Ab'teilungszeichen n hyphen
Äbtissin [ɛp'tɪsɪn] f (-;-nen) abbess
ab'tönen tr tone down, shade off
ab'töten tr (Bakterien) kill; (das Fleisch) mortify
Abtrag ['aptrɑk] m (-[e]s;-̈e)—j-m A. leisten compensate s.o.; j-m A. tun hurt s.o.
ab'tragen §132 tr carry away; (Gebäude) raze; (Kleid) wear out; (Schuld) pay
abträglich ['aptreklɪç] adj detrimental
ab'treiben §62 tr drive away; (Leibesfrucht) abort || intr (SEIN) drift away; **vom Kurs a.** drift off course
Ab'treibung f (-;-en) abortion
ab'trennen tr separate, detach; (Glied) sever; (Genähtes) unstitch
ab'treten §152 tr wear out (by walking); (aufgeben) cede, turn over || intr (SEIN) retire, resign; (theat) exit
Ab'treter m (-s;-) doormat
Ab'tretung f (-;-en) (von Grundeigentum) transfer; (pol) cession
ab'trocknen tr dry || intr (SEIN) dry
ab'tropfen intr (SEIN) trickle, drip
ab'trudeln intr (SEIN) go into a tailspin; (coll) toddle off, saunter off
abtrünnig ['aptrʏnɪç] adj unfaithful; (eccl) apostate; **a. werden** defect
Ab'trünnigkeit f (-;) desertion, defection; (eccl) apostasy
ab'tun §154 tr (ablegen) take off; (beiseite schieben) get rid of; (töten) kill; (erledigen) settle; **a. als** dismiss as; **kurz a.** make short work of; **mit e-m Achselzucken a.** shrug off
ab'urteilen tr pass final judgment on
ab'verlangen tr—j-m etw a. demand s.th. of s.o.
ab'wägen §156 tr weigh
ab'wälzen tr roll away; (Schuld) shift
ab'wandeln tr (Thema) vary; (Hauptwort) (gram) decline; (Zeitwort) (gram) conjugate
ab'wandern intr (SEIN) wander off; (Bevölkerung) migrate; (Arbeitskräfte) drift away
Ab'wanderung f (-;-en) exodus, migration

Ab'wandlung f (-;-en) variation; (e-s Hauptwortes) declension; (e-s Zeitwortes) conjugation
ab'warten tr wait for; (Anweisung) await; **das bleibt abzuwarten!** that remains to be seen! **s-e Zeit a.** bide one's time || intr wait and see
abwärts ['apvɛrts] adv down, downwards; **mit ihm geht es a.** (coll) he's going downhill
ab'waschen §158 tr wash (off)
ab'wechseln tr & intr alternate
ab'wechselnd adj alternate
Ab'wechs(e)lung f (-;-en) variation; (Mannigfaltigkeit) variety; (Zerstreuung) diversion, entertainment
Ab'weg m wrong way; **auf Abwege führen** mislead; **auf Abwege geraten** go wrong
Ab'wehr f (-;-en) defense; (e-s Stoßes, usw.) warding off; (mil) counter-espionage service
ab'wehren tr ward off, avert
ab'weichen §85 intr (SEIN) deviate, diverge; (verschieden sein) differ
Ab'weichung f (-;-en) deviation; difference; (math) divergence
ab'weiden tr graze on
ab'weisen §118 tr refuse, turn down; (Angriff) repel; (Berufung) deny
ab'weisend adj (gegen) unfriendly (to)
Ab'weisung f (-;-en) refusal; (jur) denial; (mil) repulse
ab'wenden tr turn away, turn aside; (Augen) avert; (Aufmerksamkeit) divert; (Krieg, Gefahr) prevent || §140 & 120 ref (von) turn away (from)
ab'werfen §160 tr throw off; (Bomben) drop; (Blätter, Geweih) shed; (Gewinn) bring in, yield; (Zinsen) bear; (Karten) discard; (Joch) shake off
ab'werten tr devaluate
Ab'wertung f (-;-en) devaluation
abwesend ['apvezənt] adj absent, missing; (fig) absent-minded
Ab'wesenheit f (-;) absence; (fig) absent-mindedness
ab'wickeln tr unwind, unroll; (Geschäfte) transact; (Schulden) settle; (Aktiengesellschaft) liquidate || ref unwind; (fig) develop **sich gut a.** (com) turn out well
ab'wiegen §57 tr weigh
ab'wischen tr wipe off, wipe clean
Abwurf ['apvurf] m drop(ping); (Bomben) release; (Ertrag) yield
ab'würgen tr wring the neck of; (aut) stall
ab'zahlen tr pay off
ab'zählen tr count off
Ab'zahlung f (-;-en) payment in installments; (Rate) installment; **auf A.** on terms
Ab'zahlungsgeschäft n deferred-payment system
ab'zapfen tr (Bier) tap; (Blut) draw
Ab'zehrung f emaciation; consumption
Ab'zeichen n distinguishing mark, badge; (mil) decoration
ab'zeichnen tr copy, draw, sketch;

(*Dokument*) initial || *ref* become apparent; (**gegen**) stand out (against)
Ab'ziehbild *n* decal
ab'ziehen §163 *tr* pull off; (*Kunden*) lure away; (*Reifen*) take off; (*Bett*) strip; (*vom Preise*) deduct, knock off; (*vervielfältigen*) run off; (*Abziehbild*) transfer; (*Schlüssel vom Loch*) take out; (*Rasiermesser*) strop; (*Wein*) draw; (*Truppen*) withdraw; (*Aufmerksamkeit*) divert; (arith) deduct; (phot) print; (typ) pull || *intr* (SEIN) depart; (*abmarschieren*) march off; (*Rauch*) disperse
Ab'zug *m* (*e–r Summe*) deduction; (*Rabatt*) rebate, allowance; (*Skonto*) discount; (*am Gewehr*) trigger; (*Weggang*) departure; (*für Wasser*) outlet; (*für Rauch*) escape; (mil) withdrawal; (phot) print; (typ) proof sheet
abzüglich ['aptsyklɪç] *prep* (*genit* or *acc*) less, minus
Ab'zugsbogen *m* proof sheet
Ab'zugspapier *n* duplicating paper; (phot) printing paper
Ab'zugsrohr *n* drainpipe
ab'zweigen *tr* divert || *intr* (SEIN) branch off
ach [ax] *interj* oh!; ah!; **ach so!** oh, I see!; **ach was!** nonsense!; **ach wo!** of course not!
Achse ['aksə] *f* (–;–n) axis; (*am Wagen*) axle; (mach) shaft; **auf der A.** on the move; **per A.** by truck; **by rail**
Achsel ['aksəl] *f* (–;–n) shoulder; **auf die leichte A. nehmen** make light of; **mit den Achseln zucken** shrug one's shoulders; **über die Achseln ansehen** look down on
Ach'selbein *n* shoulder blade
Ach'selgrube *f*, **Ach'selhöhle** *f* armpit
Ach'selträger –in §6 *mf* opportunist
acht [axt] *adj* eight; **alle a. Tage** once a week; **in a. Tagen** within a week; **über a. Tage** a week from today || **Acht** *f* (–;–en) eight || *f* (–;) (*Bann*) outlawry; (*Obacht*) care, attention; **in die A. erklären** outlaw; (fig) ostracize; **sich in a. nehmen vor** (*dat*) watch out for
achtbar ['axtbar] *adj* respectable
achte ['axtə] §9 *adj* & *pron* eight
achteckig ['axtekɪç] *adj* octagonal
Achtel ['axtəl] *n* (–s;–) eighth (*part*)
achten ['axtən] *tr* (*beachten*) respect; (*schätzen*) esteem; (*erachten*) consider || *intr—a.* **auf** (*acc*) pay attention to; **a. darauf, daß** see to it that
ächten ['eçtən] *tr* outlaw, proscribe; (*gesellschaftlich*) ostracize
ach'tenswert *adj* respectable
achter(n) ['axtər(n)] *adv* aft, astern
acht'geben §80 *intr* (**auf** *acc*) pay attention (*to*); **gib acht!** watch out!
acht'los *adj* careless
Acht'losigkeit *f* (–;) carelessness
acht'sam *adj* ['axtzam] cautious; (**auf** *acc*) attentive (to); (**auf** *acc*) careful (of)
Acht'samkeit *f* (–;) carefulness

achttägig ['axttegɪç] *adj* eight-day; eight-day old; one-week
Ach'tung *f* (–;) attention; (**vor** *dat*) respect (for); **A.!** watch out!; (mil) attention!
ach'tungsvoll *adj* respectful; (*als Briefschluß*) Yours truly
acht'zehn *adj* & *pron* eighteen || **Achtzehn** *f* (–;–en) eighteen
acht'zehnte §9 *adj* & *pron* eighteenth
achtzig ['axtsɪç] *adj* eighty
achtziger ['axtsɪgər] *invar adj* of the eighties; **die a. Jahre** the eighties || **Achtziger** –in §6 *mf* octogenarian
achtzigste ['axtsɪçstə] §9 *adj* eightieth
ächzen ['eçtsən] *intr* groan, moan
Acker ['akər] *m* (–s;⸚) soil, (arable) land, field; (*Maß*) acre
Ackerbau (Ak'kerbau) *m* farming
ackerbautreibend ['akərbautraɪbənt] *adj* agricultural
Ackerbestellung (Ak'kerbestellung) *f* cultivation, tilling
Ackerland (Ak'kerland) *n* arable land
ackern ['akərn] *tr* & *intr* plow
addieren [a'dirən] *tr* & *intr* add
Addiermaschine [a'dirmaʃinə] *f* adding machine
Addition [adɪ'tsjon] *f* (–;–en) addition
ade [a'de] *interj* farewell!; bye-bye!
Adel ['adəl] *m* (–s;) nobility, noble birth; (*edle Gesinnung*) noble-mindedness
ad(e)lig ['ɑd(ə)lɪç] *adj* noble, titled; nobleman's || **Ad(e)lige** §5 *m* nobleman || §5 *f* noblewoman
A'delsstand *m* nobility
Ader ['ɑdər] *f* (–;–n) vein
adieu [a'djø] *interj* adieu!
Adjektiv ['atjɛktif] *n* (–s;–e) adjective
Adjutant –in [atju'tant(ɪn)] §7 *mf* adjutant; (*e–s Generals*) aide(-de-camp)
Adler ['ɑdlər] *m* (–s;–) eagle
Ad'lernase *f* aquiline nose
Admiral [atmɪ'rɑl] *m* (–[e]s;–e) admiral
Admiralität [atmɪralɪ'tet] *f* (–;) admiralty
adoptieren [adɔp'tirən] *tr* adopt
Adoption [adɔp'tsjon] *f* (–;–en) adoption
Adoptiv- [adɔp'tif] *comb. fm.* adoptive
Adressat –in [adrɛ'sɑt(ɪn)] §7 *mf* addressee; (*e–r Warensendung*) consignee
Adresse [a'drɛsə] *f* (–;–n) address; **an die falsche A. kommen** (fig) bark up the wrong tree; **per A.** care of
adressieren [adra'sirən] *tr* address; (*Waren*) consign
adrett [a'drɛt] *adj* smart, neat
Advent [at'vɛnt] *m* (–s;–e) Advent
Adverb [at'vɛrp] *n* (–[e]s;–ien [-ɪ·ən]) adverb
Advokat –in [atvo'kɑt(ɪn)] §7 *mf* lawyer
Affäre [a'ferə] *f* (–;–n) affair
Affe ['afə] *m* (–n;–n) ape, monkey; **e–n Affen haben** (sl) be drunk
Affekt [a'fɛkt] *m* (–[e]s;–e) emotion; (*Leidenschaft*) passion
affektiert [afɛk'tirt] *adj* affected

Affektiert'heit *f* (-;-en) affectation
äffen ['ɛfən] *tr* ape, mimic
Af'fenliebe *f* doting
Af'fenpossen *pl* monkeyshines
Af'fenschande *f* crying shame
Af'fentheater *n* farce, joke
affig ['afɪç] *adj* affected; *(geckenhaft)* foppish
Äffin ['ɛfɪn] *f* (-;-nen) female ape, female monkey
Afrika ['afrɪka] *n* (-s;) Africa
afrikanisch [afrɪ'kanɪʃ] *adj* African
After ['aftər] *m* (-s;-) anus
AG, A.G., A.-G. *abbr* (Aktiengesellschaft) stock company
ägäisch [ɛ'gɛ·ɪʃ] *adj* Aegean
Agende [a'gɛndə] *f* (-;-n) memo pad
Agent -in [a'gɛnt(ɪn)] §7 *mf* agent, representative; *(Geheim-)* secret agent
Agentur [agɛn'tur] *f* (-;-en) agency
aggressiv [agrɛ'sif] *adj* aggressive
Ägide [ɛ'gidə] *f* (-;-n) aegis
Agio ['aʒɪ·o] *n* (-s;-s) premium
Agitation [agɪta'tsjon] *f* (-;-en) agitation, rabble-rousing
Agi·tator [agɪ'tatər] *m* (-s;-tatoren) [ta'torən] (& mach) agitator
agitatorisch [agɪta'torɪʃ] *adj* inflammatory
agitieren [agɪ'tirən] *intr* agitate
Agraffe [a'grafə] *f* (-;-n) clasp
agrarisch [a'grarɪʃ] *adj* agrarian
Ägypten [ɛ'gʏptən] *n* (-s;) Egypt
Ägypter -in [ɛ'gʏptər(ɪn)] §6 *mf* Egyptian
ägyptisch [ɛ'gʏptɪʃ] *adj* Egyptian
ah [a] *interj* ah!
Ahle ['alə] *f* (-;-n) awl, punch
Ahn [an] *m* (-(e)s & -en;-en) ancestor
ahnden ['andən] *tr* (*strafen*) punish; *(rächen)* avenge
Ahn'dung *f* (-;) revenge
ähneln ['ɛnəln] *intr* (*dat*) resemble
ahnen ['anən] *tr* have a premonition of, suspect; *(erfassen)* divine
Ah'nentafel *f* family tree
ähnlich ['ɛnlɪç] *adj* alike; *(dat)* similar (to), analogous (to): **das sieht ihm ä.** that's just like him; **j–m ä sehen** look like s.o.
Ähn'lichkeit *f* (-;-en) *(mit)* resemblance (to)
Ah'nung ['anʊŋ] *f* (-;-en) *(Vorgefühl)* presentiment, hunch; *(böse)* misgiving; *(Argwohn)* suspicion; **keine A. haben** have no idea
ah'nungslos *adj* unsuspecting
ah'nungsvoll *adj* full of misgivings
Ahorn ['ahɔrn] *m* (-[e]s;-e) maple
Ähre ['ɛrə] *f* (-;-n) *(Korn)* ear; *(e–r Blume)* spike; **Ähren lesen** glean
Ais ['a·ɪs] *n* (-;-) (mus) A sharp
Akade·mie [akadə'mi] *f* (-;-mien) ['mi·ən]) academy; university
Akademiker -in [aka'demɪkər(ɪn)] §6 *mf* university graduate
akademisch [aka'demɪʃ] *adj* academic; university
Akazie [a'katsjə] *f* (-;-n) acacia
akklimatisieren [aklɪmatɪ'zirən] *tr* acclimate || *ref* become acclimated
Akkord [a'kɔrt] *m* (-[e]s;-e) chord;

(Vereinbarung) accord; (com) settlement; **im A. arbeiten** do piecework
Akkord'arbeit *f* piecework
Akkordeon [a'kɔrdɛ·ɔn] *n* (-s;-s) accordion
akkreditieren [akrɛdɪ'tirən] *tr* accredit; open an account for
Akkreditiv [akrɛdɪ'tif] *n* (-[e]s;-e) *(Beglaubigungsschreiben)* credentials; (com) letter of credit
Akkumula·tor [akʊmu'latər] *m* (-s; -toren** ['torən]) storage battery
akkurat [akʊ'rat] *adj* accurate
Akkusativ ['akuzatif] *m* (-[e]s;-e) accusative (case)
Akrobat [akro'bat] §7 *m* acrobat
Akrobatik [akro'batɪk] *f* (-;) acrobatics
Akrobatin [akro'batɪn] §7 *f* acrobat
Akt [akt] *m* (-[e]s;-e) act, action; (paint) nude; (theat) act
Akte ['aktə] *f* (-;-n) document; record, file; (jur) instrument; **zu den Akten legen** file; (fig) shelve
Ak'tendeckel *m* file folder
Ak'tenklammer *f* paper clip
Ak'tenmappe *f* brief case, portfolio
ak'tenmäßig *adj* documentary
Ak'tenschrank *m* file cabinet
Ak'tentasche *f* brief case
Ak'tenzeichen *n* file number
Aktie ['aktsjə] *f* (-;-n) stock
Ak'tienbesitzer -in §6 *mf* stockholder
Ak'tienbörse *f* stock exchange
Ak'tiengesellschaft *f* corporation
Ak'tieninhaber -in §6 *mf* stockholder
Ak'tienmakler -in §6 *mf* stockbroker
Ak'tienmarkt *m* stock market
Ak'tienschein *m* stock certificate
Aktion [ak'tsjon] *f* (-;-en) action; *(Unternehmung)* campaign, drive; *(polizeiliche)* raid; (mil) operation; **Aktionen** activity
Aktionär -in [aktsjɔ'ner(ɪn)] §8 *mf* stockholder
aktiv [ak'tif] *adj* active; *(Bilanz)* favorable; (chem) activated; (gram) active; **a. werden** become a member *(of a student club)* || **Aktiv** *n* (-s;) (gram) active voice
Aktiva [ak'tiva] *pl* assets; **A. und Passiva** assets and liabilities
Aktiv'posten *m* asset
aktuell [aktu'el] *adj* current, topical || **Aktuelle** *pl* (journ) newsbriefs
Akustik [a'kʊstɪk] *f* (-;) acoustics
akustisch [a'kʊstɪʃ] *adj* acoustic(al)
akut [a'kut] *adj* acute
Akzent [ak'tsɛnt] *m* (-[e]s;-e) accent (mark); *(Nachdruck)* emphasis; (phonet) stress
akzentuieren [aktsɛntu'irən] *tr* accent; (fig) stress, accentuate
akzeptieren [aktsɛp'tirən] *tr* accept
Alabaster [ala'bastər] *m* (-s;) alabaster
Alarm [a'larm] *m* (-[e]s;-e) alarm; **A. blasen** (or **schlagen**) (mil & fig) sound the alarm; **blinder A.** false alarm
Alarm'anlage *f* alarm system; warning system *(in civil defense)*
alarm'bereit *adj* on the alert

Alarm'bereitschaft *f* (state of) readiness; **in A.** on the alert
alarmieren [alar'mirən] *tr* alert; alarm
Alaun [a'laun] *m* (-s;-e) alum
Álaun'stift *m* steptic pencil
Albanien [al'banjən] *n* (-s;) Albania
albanisch [al'banıʃ] *adj* Albanian
albern ['albərn] *adj* silly
Al·bum ['albʊm] *n* (-s;-ben [bən]) album
Alchimist [alçı'mıst] §7 *m* alchemist
Alge ['algə] *f* (-;-n) alga; seaweed
Algebra ['algebra] *f* (-;) algebra
algebraisch [alge'bra·ıʃ] *adj* algebraic
Algerien [al'gerjən] *n* (-s;) Algeria
algerisch [al'gerıʃ] *adj* Algerian
Algier ['alʒir] *n* (-s;) Algiers
Alibi ['alibı] *n* (-s;-s) alibi
Alimente [alı'mentə] *pl* child support
alimentieren [alımen'tirən] *tr* pay alimony to; (*Kind*) support
Alkohol ['alkɔhol] *m* (-s;-e) alcohol
al'koholfrei *adj* non-alcoholic
Alkoholiker –in [alkɔ'holıkər(ın)] §6 *mf* alcoholic
alkoholisch [alkɔ'holıʃ] *adj* alcoholic
all [al] *adj* all; (*jeder*) every; (*jeder beliebige*) any; **alle beide** both (of them); **alles Gute!** take care!; (*im Brief*) best wishes; **alle zehn Minuten** every ten minutes; **alle zwei Tage** every other day; **auf alle Fälle** in any case || *indef pron* each, each one; everyone, everything; all; **aller und jeder** each and every one; **in allem** all told; **vor allem** above all, first of all
alle ['alə] *adv* all gone; **a. machen** finish off; **a. sein** be all gone; **a. werden** run low
Allee [a'le] *f* (-;-n) (tree-lined) avenue; (tree-lined) walk
Allego·rie [alegɔ'ri] *f* (-;-rien ['ri·ən]) allegory
allegorisch [ale'gorıʃ] *adj* allegoric(al)
allein [a'laın] *adj* alone || *adv* alone; only; however; no fewer than, no less than; **schon a.** der Gedanke mere thought
Allein'berechtigung *f* exclusive right
Allein'flug *m* solo flight
Allein'handel *m* monopoly
Allein'herrschaft *f* autocracy
Allein'herrscher –in §6 *mf* autocrat
allei'nig *adj* (*ausschließlich*) sole, exclusive; (*einzig*) only
allein'stehend *adj* alone in the world; (*unverheiratet*) single; (*Gebäude*) detached
Allein'verkauf *m*, **Allein'vertrieb** *m* franchise
al'lemal *adv* every time; **ein für a.** once and for all
al'lenfalls *adv* if need be; (*vielleicht*) possibly; (*höchstens*) at most
allenthalben ['alənt'halbən] *adv* everywhere
al'lerart *invar adj* all kinds of
al'lerbe'ste §9 *adj* very best; **aufs a.** in the best possible manner
al'lerdings' *adv* (*gewiß*) certainly (*strong affirmative answer*); (*zugestehend*) admittedly, I must admit

al'lerer'ste §9 *adj* very first, first ... of all
Aller·gie [aler'gi] (-;-gien ['gi·ən]) allergy
allergisch [a'lergıʃ] *adj* allergic
al'lerhand' *invar adj* all kinds of; (*viel*) a lot of || *indef pron* —das ist a.! that's great!; das ist doch a.! the nerve!
Allerhei'ligen *invar n* All Saints' Day
allerlei ['alər'lai] *invar adj* all kinds of || **Allerlei** *n* (-s;-s) hotchpotch; (*mus*) medley
al'lerlet'zte §9 *adj* very last, last of all; latest
allerliebste ['alər'lipstə] §9 *adj* dearest ... of all; (*Kind*) sweet
al'lermei'ste §9 *adj* most; **am allermeisten** most of all; chiefly
al'lernäch'ste §9 *adj* very next
al'lerneu'este §9 *adj* latest, newest
Allersee'len *invar n* All Souls' Day
allesamt [alə'zamt] *adv* all together
al'lezeit *adv* always
Allge'genwart *f* omnipresence
all'gemein *adj* general, universal
All'gemeinheit *f* universality; (*Öffentlichkeit*) public
Allheil'mittel *n* cure-all
Allianz [alı'ants] *f* (-;-en) alliance
alliieren [alı'irən] *ref*—**sich a. mit** ally oneself with
alliiert [alı'irt] *adj* allied || **Alliierte** §5 *mf* ally
alljähr'lich *adj* annual, yearly
All'macht *f* omnipotence
allmäch'tig *adj* omnipotent, almighty
allmählich [al'melıç] *adj* gradual
allnächt'lich *adj* nightly
allseitig ['alzaitıç] *adj* all-round || *adv* from all sides, on all sides
All'tag *m* daily routine
alltäg'lich *adj* daily; (*fig*) everyday
all'tags *adv* daily; (*wochentags*) weekdays
All'tags– *comb.fm.* everyday; (*fig*) commonplace
All'tagsmensch *m* common man
All'tagswort *n* (-[e]s;-"er) household word
allwissend [al'vısənt] *adj* omniscient
allwö'chentlich *adj* & *adv* weekly
allzu– *comb.fm.* all too
all'zumal *adv* one and all, all together
all'zusammen *adv* all together
Alm [alm] *f* (-;-en) Alpine meadow
Almanach ['almanax] *m* (-[e]s;-e) almanac
Almosen ['almozen] *n* (-s;-) alms
Alp [alp] *m* (-[e]s;-e) elf, goblin; (*Alptraum*) nightmare
Alp'druck *m* (-[e]s;), **Alp'drücken** *n* (-s;) nightmare
Alpen ['alpən] *pl* Alps
Alphabet [alfa'bet] *n* (-[e]s;-e) alphabet
alphabetisch [alfa'betıʃ] *adj* alphabetical
alpin [al'pin] *adj* alpine
als [als] *adv* as, like || *conj* than; when, as; but, except; **als ob** as if
alsbald' *adv* presently, immediately
alsdann' *adv* then, thereupon

also ['alzo] *adv* so, thus; therefore, consequently; **na a.!** well then!

alt [alt] *adj* (älter ['ɛltər], älteste ['ɛltəstə] §9) *adj* old; (*bejahrt*) aged; (*gebraucht*) second-hand; (*abgestanden*) stale; (*antik*) antique; (*Sprache*) ancient ‖ **Alt** *m* (-[e]s;-e) contralto ‖ **Alte** §5 *m* (coll) old man; **die Alten** the ancients; **mein Alter** (coll) my husband ‖ **Alte** §5 *f* (coll) old woman; **meine Alte** (coll) my wife

Altan [al'tɑn] *m* (-[e]s;-e), **Altane** [al'tɑnə] *f* (-;-n) balcony, gallery

Altar [al'tɑr] *m* (-[e]s;-̈e) altar

alt'bewährt *adj* long-standing

Alt'eisen *n* scrap iron

Alt'eisenhändler *m* junk dealer

Alter ['altər] *n* (-s;-) age; (*Greisen-*) old age; (*Zeit-*) epoch; (*Dienst-*) seniority; **er ist in meinem A.** he is my age; **im A. von** at the age of; **mittleren Alters** middle-aged

altern ['altərn] *intr* (SEIN) age

Alternative [altɛrna'tivə] *f* (-;-n) alternative

Al'tersgrenze *f* age limit; (*für Beamte*) retirement age

Al'tersheim *n* home for the aged

Al'tersrente *f* old-age pension

al'tersschwach *adj* decrepit; senile

Al'tersschwäche *f* (feebleness of) old age

Al'tersversorgungskasse *f* old-age pension fund

Altertum ['altərtum] *n* (-s;) antiquity

altertümlich ['altərtymlıç] *adj* ancient; (*Möbel*) antique; (*veraltet*) archaic

Al'tertumsforscher -in §6 *mf* archaeologist; (*Antiquar*) antiquarian

Al'tertumskunde *f*, **Al'tertumswissenschaft** *f* study of antiquity; classical studies

althergebracht ['alt'hergəbraxt] *adj* long-standing, traditional

alther/kömmlich *adj* ancient, traditional

Altist [al'tıst] §7 *m* alto (*singer*)

Altistin [al'tıstın] §7 *f* contralto (*female singer*)

alt'klug *adj* precocious

ältlich ['ɛltlıç] *adj* elderly

Alt'meister *m* past master; (sport) champion

alt'modisch *adj* old-fashioned

Alt'stadt *f* old (part of the) city

Alt'stadtsanierung *f* urban renewal

Alt'stimme *f* alto; contralto (*female voice*)

altväterlich ['altfetərlıç], **altväterisch** ['altfetərıʃ] *adj* old-fashioned; old-time

Alt'warenhändler -in §6 *mf* second-hand dealer

Altweibersommer [alt'vaıbərzɔmər] *m* Indian summer; (*Spinnweb*) gossamer

Aluminium [alu'minjum] *n* (-s;) aluminum

am [am] *contr* **an dem**

amalgamieren [amalga'mirən] *tr* amalgamate

Amateur [ama'tør] *m* (-s;-e) amateur

Amazone [ama'tsonə] *f* (-;-n) Amazon

Am·boß ['ambɔs] *m* (-bosses;-bosse) anvil

ambulant [ambu'lant] *adj* ambulatory ‖ *adv*—a. **Behandelte** out-patient

Ambulanz [ambu'lants] *f* (-;-en) outpatient clinic; (*Krankenwagen*) ambulance

Ameise ['amaızə] *f* (-;-n) ant

Amerika [a'merıka] *n* (-s;) America

Amerikaner -in [amerı'kanər(ın)] §6 *mf* American

amerikanisch [amerı'kanıʃ] *adj* American

Ami ['ami] *m* (-s;-s) (sl) Yank ‖ *f* (-;-s) American cigarette

Amme ['amə] *f* (-;-n) nurse, wet-nurse

Amnes·tie [amnes'ti] *f* (-;-tien) ['ti·ən]) amnesty

amnestieren [amnes'tirən] *tr* pardon

A·mor ['amɔr] (-s;-moren ['morən]) (myth) Cupid

Amortisation [amɔtıza'tsjon] *f* (-;-en) amortization

Amortisations'kasse *f* sinking fund

amortisieren [amɔrtı'zirən] *tr* amortize

Ampel ['ampəl] *f* (-;-n) hanging lamp; (*Verkehrs-*) traffic light

Ampere [am'per] *n* (-s;-) ampere

Amphibie [am'fibjə] *f* (-;-n) amphibian

Amphi'bienpanzerwagen *m* amphibious tank

Amphitheater [am'fite·atər] *n* (-s;-) amphitheater

Ampulle [am'pulə] *f* (-;-n) phial

Amputation [amputa'tsjon] *f* (-;-en) amputation

amputieren [ampu'tirən] *tr* amputate

Amputierte [ampu'tirtə] §5 *mf* amputee

Amsel ['amzəl] *f* (-;-n) blackbird

Amt [amt] *n* (-[e]s;-̈er) office; (*Pflicht*) duty, function; (dipl) post; (eccl) divine service; (telp) exchange

amtieren [am'tirən] *intr* be in office, hold office; (eccl) officiate

amt'lich *adj* official

Amts– *comb.fm.* official, of (an) office

Amts'antritt *m* inauguration

Amts'befugnis *f* competence

Amts'bereich *m* jurisdiction

Amts'bewerber -in §6 *mf* office seeker

Amts'bezirk *m* jurisdiction

Amts'blatt *n* official bulletin

Amts'eid *m* oath of office

Amts'enthebung *f* dismissal

Amts'führung *f* administration

amts'gemäß *adj* official ‖ *adv* officially

Amts'gericht *n* district court

Amts'gerichtsrat *m* (official rank of) district-court judge

Amts'geschäfte *pl* official duties

Amts'gewalt *f* (official) authority

Amts'handlung *f* official act

Amts'niederlegung *f* resignation

Amts'schimmel *m* bureaucracy; (coll) red tape

Amts'siegel *n* seal of office

Amts'sprache *f* official language; (coll) officialese, gobbledygook
Amts'tracht *f* robes
Amts'träger **–in** §6 *m/* officeholder
Amts'verletzung *f* misconduct in office
Amts'weg *m*—**auf dem Amtswege** through official channels
Amts'zeichen *n* (telp) dial tone
Amulett [amu'lɛt] *n* (-[e]s;-e) amulet
amüsant [amy'zant] *adj* amusing
amüsieren [amy'zirən] *tr* amuse, entertain || *ref* amuse oneself; (*sich gut unterhalten*) enjoy oneself
an [an] *adv* on; onward || *prep* (*dat*) at, against, on, upon, by, to; (*Grad, Maß*) in; **an sich** per se; **an und für sich** properly speaking; **es ist an dir zu** (*inf*) it's up to you to (*inf*) || *prep* (*acc*) at, on, upon, against, to
analog [ana'lok] *adj* analogous
Analo·gie [analɔ'gi] *f* (-;-gien ['gi·ən]) analogy
Analphabet **–in** [analfa'bet(ın) §7 *m/* illiterate
Analphabetentum [analfa'betəntum] *n* (-s;), **Analphabetismus** [analfabe'tısmus] *m* (-;) illiteracy
analphabetisch [analfa'betıʃ] *adj* illiterate
Analyse [ana'lyzə] *f* (-;-n) analysis; (gram) parsing; **durch A.** analytically
analysieren [analy'zirən] *tr* analyze; (gram) parse
Analy·sis [a'nalyzıs] *f* (-;-sen [ana-'lyzən]) (math) analysis
Analytiker **–in** [ana'lytıkər(ın)] §6 *m/* analyst
analytisch [ana'lytıʃ] *adj* analytic(al)
Anämie [anɛ'mi] *f* (-;) anemia
anämisch [an'emıʃ] *adj* anemic
Ananas ['ananas] *f* (-;-se) pineapple
Anarchie [anar'çi] *f* (-;) anarchy
anästhesieren [anɛstɛ'zirən] *tr* anesthetize
Anästheti·kum [anɛs'tetıkum] *n* (-s; -ka [ka]) anesthetic
an'atmen *tr* breathe on
Anato·mie [anatɔ'mi] *f* (-;-mien ['mi·ən)] anatomy
anatomisch [ana'tomıʃ] *adj* anatomical
an'backen §50 *tr* bake gently || *intr* (HABEN & SEIN) cake on
an'bahnen *tr* pave the way for
anbandeln ['anbandəln] *intr*—**a. mit** flirt with
An'bau *m* (-[e]s;) cultivation || *m* (-[e]s;-bauten) annex, new wing
an'bauen *tr* cultivate; (*Gebäudeteil*) add on
An'baufläche *f* (arable) acreage
An'baumöbel *pl* sectional furniture
An'beginn *m* outset
an'behalten §90 *tr* keep (*garment*) on
anbei [an'baɪ] *adv* enclosed (herewith)
an'beißen §53 *tr* bite into, take the first bite of || *intr* nibble at the bait; (fig) bite
an'belangen *tr*—**was mich anbelangt** as far as I am concerned, as for me
an'bellen *tr* bark at
anberaumen ['anbəraumən] *tr* schedule
an'beten *tr* (& fig) worship

An'betracht *m*—**in A.** (*genit*) in consideration of, in view of
an'betteln *tr* bum, chisel
An'betung *f* (-;) worship
an'betungswürdig *adj* adorable
an'bieten §58 *tr* offer || *ref* offer one's services
an'binden §59 *tr* tie (up) || *intr*—**mit j-m a.** pick a quarrel with s.o.
an'blasen §61 *tr* blow at, blow on
An'blick *m* look, view, sight
an'blicken *tr* look at; (*besehen*) view; (*mustern*) eye
an'blinzeln *tr* wink at
an'brechen §64 *tr* (*Vorräte*) break into; (*Flasche, Kiste*) open || *intr* (SEIN) (*Tag*) dawn; (*Nacht*) come on
an'brennen §97 *tr* light || *intr* (SEIN) catch fire; (*Speise*) burn
an'bringen §65 *tr* bring, fetch; (*befestigen*) (**an** *acc*) attach (to): (*Bitte*) make; (*Klage*) lodge; (*Geld*) invest; (*Tochter*) marry off; (*Waren*) sell, get rid of; (*Bemerkung*) insert; (*Licht, Lampe*) install; (*Geld*) (coll) blow
An'bruch *m* break; **bei A. der Nacht** at nightfall; **bei A. des Tages** at daybreak
an'brüllen *tr* roar at
Andacht ['andaxt] *f* (-;-en) devotion; (*Gottesdienst*) devotions
andächtig ['andɛçtıç] *adj* devout
an'dauern *intr* continue, last; (*hartnäckig sein*) persist
An'denken *n* (-s;-) remembrance; souvenir; **zum A. an** (*acc*) in remembrance of
andere ['andərə] §9 *adj & pron* other; (*folgend*) next; **ein anderer** another; another one; **kein anderer** no one else
ändern ['ɛndərn] *tr* change; (*Wortlaut*) modify || *ref* change
andernfalls ['andərn'fals] *adv* (or) else
anders ['andərs] *adj* else; (**als**) different (from); **a. werden** change || *adv* otherwise differently
an'dersartig *adj* of a different kind
anderseits ['andər'zaıts] *adv* on the other hand
an'derswo' *adv* somewhere else
anderthalb ['andərt'halp] *invar adj* one and a half
Än'derung *f* (-;-n) change, variation; modification
Än'derungsantrag *m* amendment
anderwärts ['andər'verts] *adv* elsewhere
anderweitig ['andər'vaıtıç] *adj* other, further || *adv* otherwise; elsewhere
an'deuten *tr* indicate, suggest; (*anspielen*) hint at, allude to; (*zu verstehen geben*) imply, intimate
an'deutungsweise *adv* by way of suggestion
an'dichten *tr*—**j-m etw a.** impute s.th. to s.o.
An'drang *m* rush; crowd; heavy traffic; (*von Arbeit*) pressure
an'drehen *tr* turn on; **j-m etw a.** palm s.th. off on s.o.

an'drohen *tr—j-m etw a.* threaten s.o. with s.th.
an'drücken *tr—etw a.* an *(acc)* press s.th. against
an'eignen *ref—sich [dat]* **a.** appropriate; *(Gewohnheit)* acquire; *(Meinungen)* adopt; *(Sprache)* master; *(widerrechtlich)* appropriate, usurp
aneinan'der *adv* together
aneinan'dergeraten §63 *intr* (SEIN) come to blows
Anekdote [anɛk'doːtə] *f* (-;-n) anecdote
an'ekeln *tr* disgust, nauseate
an'empfehlen §147 *tr* recommend
An'erbieten *n* (-s;-) offer, proposal
an'erkennbar *adj* recognizable
an'erkennen §97 *tr* (als) recognize (as); (als) acknowledge (as); *(Schuld)* admit; *(billigen)* approve; *(lobend)* appreciate; *(Anspruch)* allow; **nicht a.** repudiate, disown; (sport) disallow
An'erkennung *f* (-;-en) acknowledgement; recognition; appreciation; admission; **lobende A.** honorable mention
anfachen ['anfaxən] *tr* *(Feuer)* fan; *(Gefühle)* inflame; *(Haß)* stir up
an'fahren §71 *tr* *(herbeibringen)* carry, convey; *(anstoßen)* run into; (fig) snap at; (naut) run afoul of || *intr* (SEIN) drive up; *(losfahren)* start off
An'fall *m* attack
an'fallen §72 *tr* attack, assail || *intr* (SEIN) accumulate, accrue
anfällig ['anfɛlɪç] *adj* (für) susceptible (to)
An'fang *m* beginning, start; **von A. an** from the very beginning
an'fangen §73 *tr & intr* begin, start
Anfänger -in ['anfɛŋər(ɪn)] §6 *mf* beginner; *(Neuling)* novice
anfänglich ['anfɛŋlɪç] *adj* initial
an'fangs *adv* at the start, initially
An'fangsbuchstabe *m* initial (letter)
An'fangsgründe *pl* rudiments, elements
an'fassen *tr* take hold of; *(behandeln)* handle, touch || *intr* lend a hand
an'faulen *intr* (SEIN) begin to rot
anfechtbar ['anfɛçtbar] *adj* debatable, questionable; (jur) contestable
an'fechten §74 *tr* *(Richtigkeit)* contest; *(beunruhigen)* trouble; (jur) challenge
An'fechtung *f* (-;-en) (eccl) temptation; (jur) challenge
an'fertigen *tr* make, manufacture
an'feuchten *tr* moisten, wet
an'feuern *tr* inflame; (sport) cheer
an'flehen *tr* implore
an'fliegen §57 *tr* (aer) approach
An'flug *m* *(Anzeichen)* suggestion, trace; *(oberflächliche Kenntnis)* smattering; *(dünner Überzug)* film; **A. von Bart** down; **leichter A. von** slight case of
an'fordern *tr* call for, demand; (mil) requisition
an'fragen *intr* (**über** *acc,* **wegen, nach**) ask (about *s.th.*); (**bei**) inquire (of *s.o.*)
an'fressen §70 *tr* gnaw; *(Metall)* corrode

anfreunden ['anfrɔɪndən] *ref* (**mit**) make friends (with)
an'frieren §77 *intr* (SEIN) begin to freeze; **a. an** *(acc)* freeze onto
an'fügen *tr* (an *acc*) join (to)
an'fühlen *tr & ref* feel
Anfuhr ['anfur] *f* (-;-en) delivery
an'führen *tr* lead; *(Worte)* quote; *(Grund)* adduce; *(täuschen)* take in, fool; (mil) lead, command
An'führer -in §6 *mf* leader; (mil) commander; (pol) boss
An'führung *f* quotation
An'führungszeichen *n* quotation mark
an'füllen *tr & ref* fill up
An'gabe *f* *(Erklärung)* statement; *(beim Zollamt)* declaration; (coll) showing off; **Angaben** data; directions; **nähere Angaben machen** give particulars; **wer hat die A.?** whose serve is it?
an'geben §80 *tr* *(mitteilen)* state; *(bestimmen)* appoint; *(anzeigen)* inform against; *(vorgeben)* pretend; *(Preis)* quote || *intr* (coll) show off; (cards) deal first; (tennis) serve
An'geber -in §6 *mf* informer; *(Prahler)* show-off
angeblich ['angeplɪç] *adj* alleged
an'geboren *adj* innate, natural
An'gebot *n* offer; *(bei Auktionen)* bid; **A. und Nachfrage** supply and demand
angebracht ['angəbraxt] *adj* advisable; **es für a. halten zu** *(inf)* see fit to *(inf);* **gut a.** appropriate; **schlecht a.** ill-timed
angegossen ['angəgɔsən] *adj—wie a. sitzen** fit like a glove
angeheiratet ['angəhaɪratət] *adj* related by marriage
angeheitert ['angəhaɪtərt] *adj* tipsy
an'gehen §82 *tr* charge, attack; *(Problem)* tackle; **das geht dich gar nichts an** that's none of your business; **j-n um etw a.** approach s.o. for s.th. || *intr* (SEIN) begin; *(zulässig sein)* be allowable; *(leidlich sein)* be tolerable; **das geht nicht an** that won't do
an'gehend *adj* future, prospective
an'gehören *intr* (dat) be a member (of)
Angehörige ['angəhøːrɪgə] §5 *mf* member; **nächste Angehörigen** next of kin; **seine Angehörigen** his relatives
Angeklagte ['angəklaːktə] §5 *mf* defendant; *(wenn verhaftet)* suspect
Angel ['aŋəl] *f* (-;-n) fishing tackle; *(e-r Tür)* hinge; **aus den Angeln heben** (& fig) unhinge
an'gelangen *intr* (SEIN) (**an** *dat,* **bei**) arrive (at)
an'gelegen *adj—sich [dat]* **etw a. sein lassen** make s.th. one's business
An'gelegenheit *f* (-;-en) affair, business
angelehnt ['angəlent] *adj* ajar
An'gelgerät *n* fishing tackle
An'gelhaken *m* fish(ing) hook
angeln ['aŋəln] *intr* (**nach**) fish (for)
An'gelpunkt *m* pivot, central point
An'gelrute *f* fishing rod

angelsächsisch ['aŋəlzɛksɪʃ] adj Anglo-Saxon
An'gelschnur f fishing line
angemessen ['angəmɛsən] adj suitable (ausreichend) adequate; (annehmbar) reasonable; (Benehmen) proper; (dat) in keeping (with); für a. halten think fit
angenehm ['angənem] adj pleasant; sehr a! pleased to meet you!
angeregt ['angərekt] adj lively
angeschlagen ['angəʃlɑgən] adj chipped; (Boxer) groggy; (mil) hard-hit
angesehen ['angəze-ən] adj respected; (ausgezeichnet) distinguished
An'gesicht n countenance, face; von A. by sight
an'gesichts prep (genit) in the presence of; (fig) in view of
angestammt ['angəʃtamt] adj hereditary
Angestellte ['angəʃtɛltə] §5 mf employee; die Angestellten the staff
angetan ['angətɑn] (mit) clad (in); a. sein von have a liking for; ganz danach a. zu (inf) very likely to (inf)
angetrunken ['angətruŋkən] adj tipsy
angewandt ['angəvant] adj applied
angewiesen ['angəvizən] adj—a. sein auf (acc) have to rely on
an'gewöhnen tr—j—m etw a. accustom s.o. to s.th.
An'gewohnheit f (-;-en) habit
an'gleichen §85 tr adapt, adjust
Angler –in ['aŋlər(ɪn)] §6 mf fisher
an'gliedern tr link, attach; (Gesellschaft) affiliate
an'greifen §88 tr (anfassen) handle; (Vorräte) draw on, dip into; (Körper) affect; (mil) attack
an'greifend adj aggressive, offensive
An'greifer –in §6 mf aggressor
an'grenzen intr (an acc) be adjacent (to), border (on)
An'griff m attack
An'griffskrieg m war of aggression
an'griffslustig adj aggressive
Angst [aŋst] f (-;=e) fear, anxiety
ängstigen ['ɛŋstɪgən] tr alarm || ref (vor) be afraid (of); (um) be alarmed (about)
ängstlich ['ɛŋstlɪç] adj uneasy, jittery; (besorgt) anxious; (sorgfältig) scrupulous; (schüchtern) timid
Angst'zustände pl jitters
an'haben §89 tr have on; j–m etw a. have s.th. on. s.o.; j–m etw a. können be able to harm s.o.
an'haften intr (dat) stick (to)
an'haken tr check off; (an acc) hook (onto)
an'halten §90 tr stop; (Atem, Ton) hold; || intr stop; (andauern) continue, last
an'haltend adj continuous
An'halter m—per A. fahren hitch-hike
An'haltspunkt m clue, lead
An'hang m (-[e]s;=e) appendix; (Gefolgschaft) following; (jur) codicil
an'hängen §92 & §109 tr (Hörer) hang up; (hinzufügen) add on; j–m e–e Krankheit a. infect s.o. with a disease; j–m e–n Prozeß a. bring suit

against s.o.; j–m etw a. pin s.th. on s.o. || §92 intr (an dat) adhere (to)
An'hänger –in §6 mf follower || m (Schmuck) pendant; (aut) trailer
anhänglich ['anhɛŋlɪç] adj (an acc) attached (to), devoted (to)
Anhängsel ['anhɛŋzəl] m (-s;-) appendage, adjunct
an'hauchen tr breathe on
an'häufen tr & ref pile up
An'häufung f (-;-en) accumulation
an'heben §94 tr lift (up); (Lied) strike up; (aut) jack up
an'heften tr fasten; (annähen) stitch
an'heilen tr & intr heal up
anheim'fallen §72 intr (SEIN) (dat) devolve (upon)
anheim'stellen tr (dat) leave (to)
An'höhe f rise, hill
an'hören tr listen to, hear || ref —sich gut a. sound good
Anilin [anɪ'lin] n (-s;) aniline
Animier'dame f B-girl
animieren [anɪ'mirən] tr encourage
Anis [a'nis] m (-es;-e) anise
an'kämpfen intr (gegen) struggle (against)
An'kauf m purchase
an'kaufen tr purchase
Anker ['aŋkər] m (-s;-) anchor; (elec) armature; vor A. gehen drop anchor
ankern ['aŋkərn] intr anchor
an'ketten tr (an acc) chain (to)
An'klage f accusation, charge; (jur) indictment; A. erheben prefer charges; die A. vertreten be counsel for the prosecution; unter A. stellen indict
an'klagen tr (wegen) accuse (of), charge (with), indict (for)
An'kläger –in §6 mf accuser; (jur) prosecutor
An'klageschrift f (bill of) indictment
an'klammern tr (an acc) clip (to) || ref (an acc) cling (to)
An'klang m (an acc) reminiscence (of), trace (of); A. finden be well received, catch on
an'kleben tr (an acc) paste (on), stick (on) || intr (HABEN & SEIN) stick
an'kleiden tr & ref dress
an'klingeln tr ring, call up || intr—bei j–m a. ring s.o.'s doorbell
an'klopfen intr (an acc) knock (on)
an'knipsen tr switch on
an'knüpfen tr tie, attach; (Gespräch) start || intr (an acc) link up (with)
an'kommen §99 intr (SEIN) (in dat) arrive (at); (bei) be well received (by); (bei) get a job (with); es darauf a. lassen take one's chances; es kommt ganz darauf an, ob it (all) depends on whether
Ankömmling ['ankœmlɪŋ] m (-s;-e) newcomer, arrival
an'kündigen tr announce, proclaim; j–m etw a. notify s.o. of s.th.
An'kündigung f (-;-en) announcement
Ankunft ['ankunft] f (-;=e) arrival
an'kurbeln tr crank up; die Wirtschaft a. prime the economy
an'lachen tr laugh at
An'lage f (Anordnung) plan, layout;

(*Bau*) construction; (*Errichtung*) installation; (*Fabrik*) plant, works; (*Garten*) park, grounds; (*Fähigkeit*) ability, aptitude (*im Brief*) enclosure; in der A. enclosed
An'lagekapital *n* invested capital; permanent assets
an'langen *tr*—was mich anlangt as far as I'm concerned ‖ *intr* (SEIN) arrive
An·laß ['anlas] *m* (-lasses;-lässe) occasion; (*Grund*) reason, motive; A. geben zu give rise to; ohne allen A. without any reason
an'lassen §104 *tr* (*Kleid*) keep on; (*Motor*) start (up); (*Wasser*) turn on; (*Pumpe*) prime; (*Stahl*) temper; j-n hart a. rebuke s.o. sharply ‖ *ref* sich gut a. shape up
Anlasser ['anlasər] *m* (-s;-) starter
anläßlich ['anleslɪç] *prep* (*genit*) on the occasion of
An'lauf *m* run, start
an'laufen §105 *tr* run at; (*Hafen*) put into ‖ *intr* (SEIN) (*Motor*) start up; (*Brille*) fog up; (*Metall*) tarnish; (*anwachsen*) accumulate; (*Schulden*) mount up; (*Film*) start, come on; angelaufen kommen come running up; ins Rollen a. (fig) get rolling; rot a. blush
an'legen *tr* (an *acc*) put (on), lay (on); (*Garten; Geld*) lay out; (*Kapital*) invest; (*Leitung*) install; (*Verband*) apply; (*Kolonie*) found ‖ *ref*—sich a. mit have a run-in with ‖ *intr* put ashore; moor
An'legeplatz *m* pier
an'lehnen *tr* (an *acc*) lean (against); (*Tür*) leave ajar ‖ *ref* (an *acc*) lean (against); (fig) be based (on), rely (on)
Anleihe ['anlaɪ-ə] *f* (-;-n) loan
an'leiten *tr* (zu) guide (to); a. in (*dat*) instruct in
An'leitung *f* (-;-en) guidance; (*Lehre*) instruction
an'lernen *tr* train, break in
an'liegen §108 *intr* (*passen*) fit; (an *dat*) lie near, be adjacent (to); eng a. fit tight; j-m a. pester s.o. ‖ **Anliegen** *n* (-s;-) request; ein A. an j-n haben have a request to make of s.o.
an'liegend *adj* adjacent; (*Kleid*) tight-fitting; (*im Brief*) enclosed
an'locken *tr* lure (on)
an'machen *tr* (*Licht*) switch on; (*Feuer*) light; (*zubereiten*) prepare; (an *acc*) attach (to)
an'malen *tr* paint
an'marschieren *intr* (SEIN) approach
anmaßen ['anmasən] *ref*—sich [*dat*] etw a. usurp s.th.; sich [*dat*] a., etw zu sein pretend to be s.th.
an'maßend *adj* arrogant
An'meldeformular *n* registration form
an'melden *tr* announce; report; (*Anspruch, Berufung*) file; (*Konkurs*) declare; (*Patent*) apply for; (*educ*) register; (sport) enter ‖ *ref* (bei) make an appointment (with); (zu) enroll (in); (mil) report in
an'merken *tr* note down; j-m etw a. notice s.th. in s.o.

an'messen §70 *tr*—j-m etw a. measure s.o. for s.th.
An'mut *f* (-;) charm, attractiveness
an'mutig *adj* charming
an'nageln *tr* (an *acc*) nail (to)
an'nähen *tr* (an *acc*) sew on (to)
annähernd ['annɛ·ərnt] *adj* approximate
An'näherung *f* (-;-en) approach
An'näherungsversuch *m* (romantic) pass; attempt at reconciliation
an'näherungsweise *adv* approximately
An'nahme *f* (-;-n) acceptance; (*Vermutung*) assumption
annehmbar ['annembar] *adj* acceptable
an'nehmen §116 *tr* accept, take; (*vermuten*) assume, suppose, guess; (*Glauben*) embrace; (*Gewohnheit*) acquire; (*Gesetz*) pass; (*Kind*) adopt; (*Arbeiter*) hire; (*Farbe, Gestalt*) take on; (*Titel*) assume; etw als erwiesen a. take s.th. for granted ‖ *ref* (*genit*) take care of
annektieren [anɛk'tirən] *tr* annex
Annexion [anɛ'ksjon] *f* (-;-en) annexation
Annonce [a'nõsə] *f* (-;-n) advertisement
annoncieren [anõ'sirən] *tr* advertise
anöden [a'nødən] *tr* bore to death
anonym [ano'nym] *adj* anonymous
an'ordnen *tr* arrange; (*befehlen*) order
an'packen *tr* grab hold of, seize; (*Problem*) tackle
an'passen *tr* fit; (*Worte*) adapt; ‖ *ref* (dat or an *acc*) adapt oneself (to)
an'passungsfähig *adj* adaptable
an'pflanzen *tr* plant, cultivate
an'pflaumen *tr* (coll) kid
anpöbeln ['anpøbəln] *tr* mob
an'pochen *tr* (an *acc*) knock (on)
An'prall *m* impact; (*e-s Angriffs*) brunt
an'prallen *intr* (SEIN) (gegen, an *acc*) collide (with), run (into)
an'preisen *tr* praise; j-m etw a. recommend s.th. to s.o.
An'probe *f* fitting, trying on
an'probieren *tr* try on
an'pumpen *tr*—j-n a. um hit s.o. for
an'quatschen *tr* talk the ears off
an'raten §63 *tr* advise, recommend
an'rechnen *tr* charge; hoch a. appreciate; j-m etw a. charge s.o. for s.th.
An'recht *n* (auf *acc*) right (to)
An'rede *f* address
an'reden *tr* address, speak to
an'regen *tr* stimulate; suggest
An'reiz *m* incentive
an'reizen *tr* stimulate; spur on
an'rennen §97 *intr* (SEIN) (gegen) run (into); angerannt kommen come running
an'richten *tr* (*Schaden*) cause, do; (culin) prepare
anrüchig ['anrʏçɪç] *adj* disreputable
an'rücken *intr* (SEIN) approach
An'ruf *m* (telephone) call
an'rufen §122 *tr* call; (*Gott*) invoke; (*Schiff*) hail; (jur) appeal to; (mil) challenge; (telp) call up
an'rühren *tr* touch; (*Thema*) touch on; (*mischen*) stir
An'sage *f* announcement

an'sagen *tr* announce; (*Trumpf*) declare
An'sager –in §6 *mf* announcer
an'sammeln *tr* gather; (*anhäufen*) amass; (*Truppen*) concentrate || *ref* gather; (*Zinsen*) accumulate
ansässig ['anzɛsıç] *adj* residing; **a. werden** (or **sich a. machen**) settle || **Ansässige** §5 *mf* resident
An'satz *m* start; (*Mundstück*) mouthpiece; (*Spur*) trace; (*in e-r Rechnung*) charge; (*Schätzung*) estimate; (*geol*) deposit; (*mach*) attachment; (*math*) statement
an'saugen §125 *tr* suck in; (*Pumpe*) prime
an'schaffen *tr* procure; (*kaufen*) get, purchase; **Kinder a.** (coll) have kids
an'schalten *tr* switch on
an'schauen *tr* look at
an'schaulich *adj* graphic
An'schauung *f* outlook, opinion; (*Vorstellung*) perception; (*Auffassung*) conception; (*Erkenntnis*) intuition; (*Betrachtung*) contemplation
An'schauungsbild *n* mental image
An'schauungsmaterial *n* visual aids
An'schein *m* appearance
an'scheinend *adj* apparent, seeming
an'scheinlich *adv* apparently
an'schicken *ref* get ready
an'schieben §130 *tr* give (*s.th.*) a push
anschirren ['anʃırən] *tr* harness
An'schlag *m* (an *acc*, gegen) striking (against); (*Anprall*) impact; (*Attentat*) attempt; (*Bekanntmachung*) notice; (*e-r Uhr*) stroke; (*e-r Taste*) hitting; (*Berechnung*) calculation; (*e-s Gewehrs*) firing position; (*Komplott*) plot; (*mach*) stop (*for arresting motion*); (*mus*) touch; (*tennis*) serve; **A. spielen** play tag
An'schlagbrett *n* bulletin board
an'schlagen §132 *tr* (an *acc*) fasten (to); (*Plakat*) post; (*Gewehr*) level; (*Tasse, usw.*) chip; (*Taste*) hit; (*einschätzen*) estimate; (*Gegner*) (box) have in trouble; **e-n anderen Ton a.** (fig) change one's tune || *ref* bump oneself || *intr* (*Wellen*) (an *acc*) beat against); (*Hund*) let out a bark; (*Arznei*) work
An'schlagzettel *m* notice; poster
an'schließen §76 *tr* padlock; (*anketten*) chain; (*verbinden*) connect; (*anfügen*) join; (*com*) affiliate; (*elec*) plug in || *ref* (*dat*, **an** *acc*) join, side with || *intr* (*Kleid*) be tight
an'schließend *adj* (**an** *acc*) subsequent (to); adjacent (to) || *adv* next, then
An'schluß *m* connection; (*pol*) annexation, union; **sie sucht A.** (coll) she is looking for a man
An'schlußbahn *f* (rr) branch line
An'schlußdose *f* (elec) receptacle
An'schlußschnur *f* (elec) cord
An'schlußzug *m* connection, connecting train
an'schmachten *tr* make eyes at
an'schmiegen *ref* (an *acc*) nestle up (to); (*Kleid*) (an *acc*) cling (to)
anschmiegsam ['anʃmikzɑm] *adj* accommodating; cuddly

an'schmieren *tr* smear; (coll) bamboozle
an'schnallen *tr* buckle || *ref* fasten one's seat belt
an'schnauzen *tr* snap at, bawl out
an'schneiden §106 *tr* cut into; (*Thema*) take up
An'schnitt *m* first cut
an'schrauben *tr* (an *acc*) screw on (to)
an'schreiben §62 *tr* write down; (*Spielstand*) mark; (*dat*) charge (to): (com) write to; **etw a. lassen** buy s.th. on credit
An'schreiber –in §6 *mf* scorekeeper
An'schreibetafel *f* scoreboard
an'schreien §135 *tr* yell at
An'schrift *f* address
An'schriftenmaschine *f* addressograph
anschuldigen ['anʃuldıgən] *tr* accuse
an'schwärzen *tr* blacken, disparage
an'schwellen *tr* cause to swell; (*Unkosten, usw.*) swell || §119 *intr* (SEIN) swell up, puff up; increase
an'schwemmen *tr* wash (*s.th.*) ashore; (geol) deposit
an'sehen §138 *tr* look at; (fig) regard || **Ansehen** *n* (–s;–) appearance; (*Achtung*) reputation; (*Geltung*) prestige, authority; **von A.** by sight; of high repute
ansehnlich ['anzenlıç] *adj* good-looking; (*beträchtlich*) considerable; (*eindrucksvoll*) imposing
An'sehung *f* (–;) **—in A.** (*genit*) in consideration of
anseilen ['anzaılən] *tr* rope together
an'setzen *tr* (an *acc*) put (on), apply (to): (*zum Kochen*) put on; (*Frist, Preis*) set; (*abschätzen*) rate; (*berechnen*) charge; (*Knospen*) put forth || *intr* begin; (*fett werden*) get fat
An'sicht *f* view; (*Meinung*) opinion; **zur A.** on approval
an'sichtig *adj*—**a. werden** (*genit*) catch sight of
An'sichtspostkarte *f* picture postcard
An'sichtssache *f* matter of opinion
An'sichtsseite *f* frontal view, façade
An'sichtssendung *f* article(s) sent on approval
ansiedeln *tr* & *ref* settle
An'siedler –in §6 *mf* settler
An'siedlung *f* (–;–en) settlement
An'sinnen *n* (–s;–) unreasonable demand
an'spannen *tr* stretch; (*Pferd*) hitch up; (fig) exert, strain
An'spannung *f* (–;–en) exertion, strain
an'speien §135 *tr* spit on
an'spielen *tr* (cards) lead with || *intr* (auf *acc*) allude (to); (mus) start playing; (sport) kick off, serve, break
An'spielung *f* (–;–en) allusion, hint
an'spitzen *tr* sharpen (*to a point*)
An'sporn *m* spur, stimulus
an'spornen *tr* spur
An'sprache *f* (an *acc*) address (to); **e-e A. halten** deliver an address
an'sprechen §64 *tr* speak to, address; (*Ziel, Punkt*) make out; **a. als** regard as; **j–n a. um** ask s.o. for || *intr* (*dat*) appeal to, interest; (auf *acc*) respond (to)

an'sprechend *adj* appealing
an'springen §142 *tr* leap at ‖ *intr* (SEIN) (*Motor*) start (up); **angesprungen kommen** come skipping along
an'spritzen *tr* sprinkle, squirt
An'spruch *m* claim; **A. haben auf** (*acc*) be entitled to; **A. machen** (or **erheben**) **auf** (*acc*), **in A. nehmen** demand, require, claim; **große Ansprüche stellen** ask too much
an'spruchslos *adj* unpretentious
an'spruchsvoll *adj* pretentious; (*wählerisch*) choosey, hard to please
an'spucken *tr* spit on
an'spülen *tr* wash ashore; (geol) deposit
an'stacheln *tr* goad on
Anstalt ['anʃtalt] *f* (-;-en) institution, establishment; **Anstalten treffen zu** make preparations for
An'stand *m* (*Schicklichkeit*) decency; (*Bedenken*) hesitation; (*Einwendung*) objection; (hunt) blind
anständig ['anʃtendɪç] *adj* decent
An'standsbesuch *m* formal call
An'standsdame *f* chaperone
An'standsgefühl *n* tact
an'standshalber *adv* out of politeness, out of human decency
an'standslos *adv* without fuss
an'starren *tr* stare at, gaze at
anstatt [an'ʃtat] *prep* (genit) instead of
an'stauen *tr* dam up ‖ *ref* pile up
an'staunen *tr* gaze at (*in astonishment*)
an'stecken *tr* stick on; (*Ring*) put on; (*anzünden*) set on fire; (*Zigarette, Feuer*) light; (pathol) infect ‖ *ref* become infected
an'steckend *adj* infectious; (*durch Berührung*) contagious
An'steckung *f* (-;-en) infection; (*durch Berührung*) contagion
an'stehen §146 *intr* (**nach**) line up (for): (*zögern*) hesitate; **j-m gut a.** fit s.o. well, become s.o.
an'steigen §148 *intr* (SEIN) rise, ascend; (*zunehmen*) increase, mount up
an'stellen *tr* (**an** *acc*) place (against); (*beschäftigen*) hire; (*Versuch, usw.*) (*Vergleich*) draw; (*Heizung, Radio*) turn on ‖ *ref* (**nach**) line up (for); **sich a., als ob** act as if; **stell dich nicht so dumm an!** don't play dumb!
anstellig ['anʃtelɪç] *adj* skillful
An'stellung *f* (-;-en) hiring; job
an'steuern *tr* steer for
Anstieg ['anʃtik] *m* (-[e]s;-e) rise; (*e-s Weges*) grade
an'stieren *tr* stare at, glower at
an'stiften *tr* instigate
An'stifter **-in** §6 *mf* instigator
an'stimmen *tr* (*Lied*) strike up; (*Geheul*) let out
An'stoß *m* impact; (*Antrieb*) impulse; (*Ärgernis*) offense; (sport) kickoff; **den A. geben zu** start
an'stoßen §150 *tr* bump against; (*Ball*) kick off; (*Wagen*) give a push; (*mit dem Ellbogen*) nudge, poke ‖ *intr* clink glasses; **a. an** (*acc*) adjoin; **bei j-m a.** shock s.o.; **mit den Gläsern a.** clink glasses; **mit der Zunge a.** lisp ‖

intr (SEIN)—**mit dem Kopf a. an** (*acc*) bump one's head against
an'stoßend *adj* adjoining
anstößig ['anʃtøsɪç] *adj* shocking
an'strahlen *tr* beam on; (fig) beam at; (*mit Scheinwerfern*) floodlight
an'streben *tr* strive for
an'streichen §85 *tr* paint; (*Fehler*) underline; (*anhaken*) check off
An'streicher *m* house painter
an'streifen *tr* brush against, graze
an'strengen *tr* exert; (*Geist*) tax; **e-n Prozeß a.** file suit ‖ *intr* be a strain
an'strengend *adj* strenuous, trying
An'strengung *f* (-;-en) exertion, effort
An'strich *m* (*Farbe*) paint; (*Überzug*) coat (*of paint*); (fig) tinge
An'sturm *m* assault, charge
antarktisch [ant'arktɪʃ] *adj* antarctic
an'tasten *tr* touch, finger
An'teil *m* share, portion; (*Quote*) quota; (st. exch.) share; **A. nehmen an** (*dat*) take part in; (fig) sympathize with
an'teilmäßig *adj* proportional
An'teilnahme *f* (-;) (**an** *dat*) participation (in); (*Mitleid*) sympathy
Antenne [an'tɛnə] *f* (-;-n) antenna, aerial; (ent) antenna, feeler
Antibioti·kum [antɪbɪ'otɪkʊm] *n* (-s; -ka [ka]) antibiotic
antik [an'tik] *adj* ancient; classical ‖
Antike *f* (-;-n) (classical) antiquity; (*Kunstwerk*) antique
Anti'kenhändler **-in** §6 *mf* antique dealer
Antilope [antɪ'lopə] *f* (-;-n) antelope
Antipa·thie [antɪpa'ti] *f* (-;-thien ['ti·ən]) antipathy
an'tippen *tr & intr* tap
Antiqua [an'tikva] *f* (-;) roman (type)
Antiquar **-in** [antɪ'kvar(ɪn)] §8 *mf* antique dealer; second-hand bookdealer
Antiquariat [antɪkva'rjat] *n* (-[e]s;-e) second-hand bookstore
antiquarisch [antɪ'kvarɪʃ] *adj* secondhand
Antiquität [antɪkvɪ'tet] *f* (-;-en) antique
Antlitz ['antlɪts] *m* (-es;-e) (Bib, poet) countenance
Antrag ['antrak] *m* (-[e]s;ːe) (*Angebot*) offer; (*Vorschlag*) proposal; (*Gesuch*) application; (pol) motion
an'tragen §132 *tr* offer; (*vorschlagen*) propose ‖ *intr*—**a. auf** (*acc*) make a motion for; propose, suggest
An'tragsformular *n* application form
Antragsteller **-in** ['antrakʃtelər(-ɪn)] §6 *mf* applicant; (parl) mover
an'treffen §151 *tr* meet; find at home
an'treiben §62 *tr* drive on, urge on; (*Schiff*) propel; (*anreizen*) egg on ‖ *intr* (SEIN) wash ashore
an'treten §152 *tr* (*Amt, Erbschaft*) enter (upon); (*Reise*) set out on; (*Motorrad*) start up ‖ *intr* (SEIN) take one's place; (mil) fall in; (sport) enter
An'trieb *m* (-s;-e) (*Beweggrund*) motive; (*Anreiz*) incentive; (mech) drive, impetus; **aus eigenem A. on**

one's own initiative; **neuen A. verleihen** (*dat*) give fresh impetus to
An'tritt *m* (-[e]s;-e) beginning, start;
(*e-s Amtes*) entrance upon
an'tun §154 *tr* (*Kleid*) put on; **j-m**
etw a. do s.th. to s.o.
Antwort ['antvɔrt] *f* (-;-en) answer
antworten ['antvɔrtən] *intr* (auf *acc*)
reply (to), answer; **j-m a.** answer s.o.
an'vertrauen *tr* entrust; (*mitteilen*)
tell, confide
an'verwandt *adj* related ‖ **Anver-
wandte** §5 *mf* relative
an'wachsen §155 *intr* (SEIN) begin to
grow; grow together; (*Wurzel schlagen*) take root; (*zunehmen*) increase
Anwalt ['anvalt] *m* (-[e]s;-̈e) attorney
An'waltschaft *f* legal profession, bar
an'wandeln *tr*—mich wandelte die Lust
an zu (*inf*) I got a yen to (*inf*); was
wandelte dich an? what got into
you?
An'wandlung *f* (-;-en) impulse, sudden feeling; (*von Zorn*) fit
An'wärter -in §6 *mf* candidate; (mil)
cadet, officer candidate
Anwartschaft ['anvartʃaft] *f* (-;) expectancy; (*Aussicht*) prospect
an'wehen *tr* blow on ‖ *intr* (SEIN)
drift
an'weisen §118 *tr* (*beauftragen*) instruct; (*zuteilen*) assign; (*Geld*) remit
An'weisung *f* (-;-en) instruction; assignment; (fin) money order
anwendbar ['anvɛntbɑr] *adj* (auf *acc*)
applicable (to); (**für, zu**) that can be
used (for)
an'wenden §140 *tr* (auf *acc*) apply
(to); (**für, zu**) use (for)
An'wendung *f* (-;-en) application;
use
an'werben §149 *tr* recruit
an'werfen §160 *tr* (*Motor*) start up
An'wesen *n* estate, property; presence
anwesend ['anvezənt] *adj* present ‖
Anwesende §5 *mf* person present;
verehrte Anwesende! ladies and
gentlemen!
An'wesenheit *f* (-;) presence
an'wurzeln *ref & intr* (SEIN) take root;
wie angewurzelt rooted to the spot
An'zahl *f* (-;) number, quantity
an'zahlen *tr* pay down ‖ *intr* make a
down payment
an'zapfen *tr* tap
An'zeichen *n* indication, sign; (*Vorbe-
deutung*) omen; (pathol) symptom
Anzeige ['antsaɪgə] *f* (-;-n) (*Ankündigung*) announcement, notice; (*Reklame*) ad; (med) advice; **kleine
Anzeigen** classified ads
an'zeigen *tr* announce; notify; (*Symp-
tome, Fieber*) show, indicate; (*bei
der Polizei*) report, inform against;
(*inserieren*) advertise
An'zeigenvermittlung *f* advertising
agency
an'zetteln *tr* (*Verschwörung*) hatch
an'ziehen §163 *tr* pull; (& fig) attract;
(*Kleid*) put on; (*e-e Person*) dress;
(*Riemen, Schraube*) tighten; (*Bremse*)
apply; (*Beispiele, Quellen*) quote ‖

intr pull, start pulling; (*Preis*) go up;
(chess) go first
An'ziehung *f* (-;-en) attraction; (*Zitat*)
quotation
An'ziehungskraft *f* appeal; (& phys)
attraction; (astr) gravitation
An'zug *m* suit; (mil) uniform; **in A.
sein** (*Armee*) be approaching;
(*Sturm*) be gathering; (*Gefahr*) be
imminent
anzüglich ['antsylɪç] *adj* offensive; **a.
werden** become personal
an'zünden *tr* set on fire; (*Feuer*) light
an'zweifeln *tr* doubt, question
apart [a'part] *adj* charming; (coll)
cute
Apathie [apa'ti] *f* (-;) apathy
apathisch [a'pɑtɪʃ] *adj* apathetic
Apfel ['apfəl] *m* (-s;-̈) apple
Ap'felkompott *n* stewed apples
Ap'felmus *n* applesauce
Ap'felsaft *m* apple juice
Apfelsine [apfəl'zinə] *f* (-;-n) orange
Ap'feltorte *f* apple tart; **gedeckte A.**
apple pie
Ap'felwein *m* cider
Apostel [a'pɔstəl] *m* (-s;-) apostle
Apostroph [apo'strof] *m* (-[e]s;-e)
apostrophe
Apotheke [apo'tekə] *f* (-;-n) phar-
macy
Apotheker -in [apo'tekər(ɪn)] §6 *mf*
druggist
Apothe'kerwaren *pl* drugs
Apparat [apa'rɑt] *m* (-[e]s;-e) ap-
paratus, device; (phot) camera; (rad,
telv) set; (telp) telephone; **am A.!**
speaking
Appell [a'pɛl] *m* (-[e]s;-e) appeal;
(mil) roll call; (mil) inspection
appellieren [apɛ'lirən] *intr* (& jur)
(an *acc*) appeal (to)
Appetit [apɛ'tit] *m* (-[e]s;-e) appetite
Appetit'brötchen *n* canapé
appetit'lich *adj* appetizing; (*Mädchen*)
attractive
applaudieren [aplau'dirən] *tr & intr*
applaud
Applaus [a'plaus] *m* (-es;-e) applause
Appretur [aprɛ'tur] *f* (-;-en) (tex)
finish
Aprikose [aprɪ'kozə] *f* (-;-n) apricot
April [a'prɪl] *m* (-[s];-e) April
Aquarell [akva'rɛl] *n* (-[e]s;-e) water-
color; watercolor painting
Aqua·rium [a'kvɑrjum] *n* (-s;-rien
[rɪ·ən]) aquarium
Äqua·tor [ɛ'kvɑtər] *m* (-s;-toren
['torən]) equator
Ära ['ɛra] *f* (-;Ären ['ɛrən]) era
Araber -in ['arabər(ɪn)] §6 *mf* Arab
Arabien [a'rabjən] *n* (-s;) Arabia
arabisch [a'rabɪʃ] *adj* Arabian; (*Zif-
fer*) Arabic
Arbeit ['arbaɪt] *f* (-;-en) work
arbeiten ['arbaɪtən] *tr & intr* work
Arbeiter ['arbaɪtər] *m* (-s;-) worker;
A. und Unternehmer *pl* labor and
management
Ar'beiterausstand *m* walkout, strike
Ar'beitergewerkschaft *f* labor union
Arbeiterin ['arbaɪtərɪn] *f* (-;-nen)
working woman, working girl

Ar'beiterschaft f (-;) working class
Arbeitertum ['arbaɪtərtum] n (-s;) working class, workers
Ar'beitgeber -in §6 m/ employer
Ar'beitnehmer -in §6 m/ employee
arbeitsam ['arbaɪtzɑm] adj industrious
Ar'beitsanzug m overalls; (mil) fatigue clothes, fatigues
Ar'beitseinkommen n earned income
Ar'beitseinstellung f work stoppage
ar'beitsfähig adj fit for work
Ar'beitsgang m process; operation (single step of a process)
Ar'beitsgemeinschaft f team; (educ) workshop
Ar'beitsgerät n equipment, tools
Ar'beitskommando n (mil) work detail
Ar'beitskraft f labor force; **Arbeitskräfte** personnel
Ar'beitslager n work camp
Ar'beitsleistung f (work) quota; (e-r Maschine, Fabrik) output
Ar'beitslohn m wages, pay
ar'beitslos adj unemployed
Ar'beitslosenunterstützung f unemployment compensation
Ar'beitslosigkeit f unemployment
Ar'beitsmarkt m labor market
Ar'beitsminister m secretary of labor
Ar'beitsministerium n department of labor
Ar'beitsnachweis m, **Ar'beitsnachweisstelle** f employment agency
Ar'beitsniederlegung f walkout, strike
ar'beitsparend adj labor-saving
Ar'beitspause f break, rest period
Arbeitspferd n (& fig) workhorse
Ar'beitsplatz m job, place of employment
Ar'beitsrecht n labor law
ar'beitsscheu adj work-shy, lazy
Ar'beitsschicht f shift
Ar'beitsstätte f place of employment; workshop; yard
Ar'beitsstelle f job, position
Ar'beitstag m workday
Ar'beitsvermittlung f employment agency
Ar'beitsversäumnis n absenteeism
Ar'beitszeug n tools
Ar'beitszimmer n study; workroom
archaisch [ar'çɑ·ɪʃ] adj archaic
Archäologe [arçɛ·ɔ'logə] m (-n;-n) archaeologist
Archäologie [arçɛ·ɔlɔ'gi] f (-;) archaeology
Archäologin [arçɛ·ɔ'logɪn] f (-;-nen) archaeologist
archäologisch [arçɛ·ɔ'logɪʃ] adj archaeological
Architekt -in [arçɪ'tɛkt(ɪn)] §7 m/ architect
Architektur [arçɪtɛk'tur] f (-;-en) architecture
Ar·chiv [ar'çif] n (-[e]s;-chive ['çivə]) archives; (für Zeitungen) morgue
Areal [are'ɑl] n (-s;-e) area
Are·na [a'rena] f (-;-nen [nən]) arena
arg [ark] adj (ärger ['ɛrgər]; ärgste ['ɛrkstə] §9) bad, evil, wicked; (coll) awful; (schlimm) grave; (Raucher)

heavy || **Arg** n (-s;) malice, cunning || **Arge** §5 m Evil One || §5 n evil
Argentinien [argɛn'tinjən] n (-s;) Argentina
Argentinier -in [argɛn'tinjər(ɪn)] §6 m/ Argentinean
Ärger ['ɛrgər] m (-s;) irritation; mit j-m Ä. haben have trouble with s.o.
är'gerlich adj (auf acc or über acc) annoyed (at); irritating, annoying
ärgern ['ɛrgərn] tr annoy || ref (über acc) be annoyed (at)
Ärgernis ['ɛrgərnɪs] n (-ses;-se) scandal, offense; (Mißstand) nuisance
Arg'list f craft, cunning
arg'listig adj crafty, cunning
arg'los adj guileless; (nichtsahnend) unsuspecting
Argwohn ['arkvon] m (-s;) suspicion
argwöhnen ['arkvønən] tr suspect
argwöhnisch ['arkvønɪʃ] adj suspicious
Arie ['arjə] f (-;-n) aria
Arier -in ['arjər(ɪn)] §6 Aryan
arisch ['arɪʃ] adj Aryan
Aristokrat [arɪstə'krat] m (-en;-en) aristocrat
Aristokra·tie [arɪstəkra'ti] f (-;-tien ['ti·ən]) aristocracy
Aristokratin [arɪstə'kratɪn] f (-;-nen) aristocrat
Arithmetik [arɪt'metɪk] f (-;) arithmetic
Arktis ['arktɪs] f (-;) Arctic
arktisch ['arktɪʃ] adj arctic
arm [arm] adj (ärmer ['ɛrmər], ärmste ['ɛrmstə] §9 (an dat) poor in) || **Arm** m (-[e]s;-e) arm; (e-s Flusses) branch
Armatur [arma'tur] f (-;-en) armature; **Armaturen** fittings, mountings
Armatu'renbrett n instrument panel; (aut) dashboard
Arm'band n (-[e]s;-̈er) bracelet; watchband; (Armabzeichen) brassard
Arm'banduhr f wrist watch
Arm'binde f brassard; (med) sling
Ar·mee [ar'me] f (-;-meen ['me·ən]) army
Ärmel ['ɛrməl] m (-s;-) sleeve
Är'melaufschlag m cuff
Är'melkanal m English Channel
är'mellos adj sleeveless
Armen- [armən] comb.fm. for the poor
Ar'menhaus n poorhouse
Armenien [ar'menjən] n (-s;) Armenia
armenisch [ar'menɪʃ] adj Armenian
Ar'menpflege f public assistance
Ar'menunterstützung f public assistance, welfare
Ar'menviertel n slums
Armesün'dermiene f hangdog look
Arm'lehne f arm, armrest
Arm'leuchter m candelabrum
ärmlich ['ɛrmlɪç] adj poor, humble
arm'selig adj poor, wretched; (kläglich) paltry
Armut ['armut] f (-;) poverty
Arm'zeichen n semaphore
Aro·ma [a'roma] n (-s;-men [mən], -mata [mata]) aroma
aromatisch [arɔ'matɪʃ] adj aromatic
Arrest [a'rɛst] m (-[e]s;-e) arrest;

(*in der Schule*) detention; (jur) impounding, seizure
Arsch [arʃ] *m* (-es;–e) (sl) ass
Arsch'backe *f* (sl) buttock
Arsch'kriecher *m* (sl) brown-noser
Arsch'lecker *m* (sl) brown-noser
Arsen [ar'zen] *n* (-s;) arsenic
Arsenal [arzɛ'nɑl] (-s;–e) arsenal
Art [art] *f* (-;–en) sort, kind; nature; (*Rasse*) race, breed; species; (*Weise*) manner; (*Verfahren*) procedure; (*Muster*) model; **das ist keine Art!** that's no way to behave!
art'eigen *adj* true to type
arten ['artən] *intr* (SEIN)—a. nach take after
Arterie [ar'terjə] *f* (-;–n) artery
artig ['artıç] *adj* (*brav*) good, well-behaved; (*höflich*) polite
Artikel [ar'tikəl] (-s;–) (com, gram, journ) article
Artillerie [artılə'ri] *f* (-;) artillery
Artillerie'aufklärer *m* artillery spotter
Artischocke [artı'ʃɔkə] *f* (-;–n) artichoke
Artist –in [ar'tıst(ın)] §7 *mf* artist; (*beim Zirkus*) performer
Arznei [arts'naı] *f* (-;–en) medicine, medication, drug
Arznei'kraut *n* herb, medicinal plant
Arznei'kunde *f,* **Arznei'kunst** *f* pharmaceutics; pharmacology
Arznei'mittel *n* medication
Arzt [artst] *m* (-[e]s;–e) doctor
Ärztin ['ɛrtstın] *f* (-;–nen) doctor
ärztlich ['ɛrtstlıç] *adj* medical
As [as] *n* (Asses; Asse) ace ‖ *n* (-;-) (mus) A flat
Asbest [as'bɛst] *m* (-[e]s;–e) asbestos
asch'bleich *adj* ashen, pale
Asche ['aʃə] *f* (-;–n) ash(es), cinders
Aschen– *comb.fm.* ash; cinder; funerary
A'schenbahn *f* cinder track
A'schenbecher *m* ashtray
Aschenbrödel ['aʃənbrød̦əl] *n* (-s;–) Cinderella; drudge
Aschermittwoch [aʃər'mıtvɔx] *m* (-s; –e) Ash Wednesday
asch'fahl *adj* ashen, pale
äsen ['ezen] *intr* graze, feed
asiatisch [azı'atıʃ] *adj* Asiatic
Asien ['azjən] *n* (-s;) Asia
Asket [as'ket] *m* (-en;–en) ascetic
asketisch [as'ketıʃ] *adj* ascetic
Asphalt [as'falt] *m* (-[e]s;) asphalt
asphaltieren [asfal'tirən] *tr* asphalt
Asphalt'pappe *f* tar paper
aß [as] *pret* of **essen**
Assistent –in [asıs'tent(ın)] §7 *mf* assistant
Assistenz [asıs'tɛnts] *f* (-;–en) assistance
Assistenz'arzt *m,* **Assistenz'ärztin** *f* intern
Ast [ast] *m* (-es;–e) bough, branch; (*im Holz*) knot, knob
ästhetisch [ɛs'tetıʃ] *adj* esthetic(al)
Asthma ['astma] *n* (-s;) asthma
ast'rein *adj* free of knots; **nicht ganz a.** (coll) not quite kosher
Astrologe [astro'logə] *m* (-n;–n) astrologer

Astrologie [astrolo'gi] *f* (-;) astrology
Astronaut [astro'naut] *m* (-en;–en) astronaut
Astronom [astro'nom] *m* (-en;–en) astronomer
Astronomie [astrono'mi] (-;) astronomy
astronomisch [astro'nomıʃ] *adj* astronomic(al)
Astrophysik [astrofY'zik] *f* (-;) astrophysics
Asyl [a'zyl] *n* (-[e]s;–e) asylum, sanctuary; (*Obdach*) shelter; **ohne A.** homeless
Atelier [atɛ'lje] *n* (-s;–s) studio
Atem ['atəm] *m* (-s;) breath
A'tembeklemmung *f* shortness of breath
A'temholen *n* (-s;) respiration
a'temlos *adj* breathless
A'temnot *f* breathing difficulty
A'tempause *f* breathing spell
a'temraubend *adj* breath-taking
A'temzug *m* breath
Atheismus [ate'ısmʊs] *m* (-;) atheism
Atheist –in [ate'ıst(ın)] §7 *mf* atheist
Äther ['etər] *m* (-s;) ether
Athlet [at'let] *m* (-en;–en) athlete
Athletik [at'letık] *f* (-;) athletics
Athletin [at'letın] *f* (-;–nen) athlete
athletisch [at'letıʃ] *adj* athletic
Atlantik [at'lantık] *m* (-s;) Atlantic
At·las ['atlas] *m* (-';) (myth) Atlas ‖ *m* (-lasses; –lanten ['lantən] & –lasse) atlas ‖ *m* (- & –lasses;–lasse) satin
atmen ['atmən] *tr & intr* breathe
Atmosphäre [atmo'sfɛrə] *f* (-;–n) (& fig) atmosphere
atmosphärisch [atmo'sfɛrıʃ] *adj* atmospheric; **atmosphärische Störungen** (rad) static
At'mung *f* (-;) breathing
Atom [a'tom] *n* (-s;–e) atom
Atom– *comb. fm.* atom, atomic
Atom'abfall *m* fallout; atomic waste
atomar [ato'mar] *adj* atomic
Atom'bau *m* atomic structure
atom'betrieben *adj* atomic-powered
Atom'bombe *f* atomic bomb
Atom'bombenversuch *m* atomic test
Atom'-Epoche *f* atomic age
Atom'kern *m* atomic nucleus
Atom'müll *m* atomic waste
Atom'regen *m* fallout
Atom'schutt *m* atomic waste
ätsch [etʃ] *interj* (to express gloating) serves you right!, good for you!
Attentat [aten'tat] *n* (-s;–e) attempt (*on s.o.'s life*); assassination
Attentäter –in [aten'tetər(ın)] §6 *mf* assailant, would-be assassin; assassin
Attest [a'tɛst] *n* (-es;–e) certificate
attestieren [atɛs'tirən] *tr* attest (to)
Attrappe [a'trapə] *f* (-;–n) dummy
Attribut [atrı'but] *n* (-[e]s;–e) attribute; (gram) attributive
atzen ['atsən] *tr* feed
ätzen ['ɛtsən] *tr* corrode; (med) cauterize (typ) etch
ät'zend *adj* corrosive; caustic
Au [au] *f* (-;–en) (poet) mead, meadow

au *interj* ow!, ouch!; oh!

Aubergine [ɔbɛr'ʒin(ə)] *f* (-;-n) eggplant

auch [aux] *adv* also, too; *(selbst)* even

Audienz [au'djɛnts] *f* (-;-en) audience; (jur) hearing

auf [auf] *adv* up; **auf und ab** up and down;**von Kind auf** from childhood on ‖ *prep (dat)* on, upon; **auf der ganzen Welt** in the whole world; **auf der Universität** at the university ‖ *prep (acc)* on; up; to; **auf den Bahnhof gehen** go to the station; **auf deutsch** in German; **drei aufs Dutzend** three to a dozen; **es geht auf vier Uhr zu** it's going on four; **Monat auf Monat** verging month after month passed ‖ *interj* get up! ‖ **Auf** *n*—**das Auf und Nieder** the ups and downs

auf'arbeiten *tr (Rückstände)* catch up on; *(verbrauchen)* use up; *(erneuern)* renovate; (mach) recondition ‖ *ref* work one's way up

auf'atmen *intr* breathe a sigh of relief

aufbahren ['aufbarən] *tr* lay out

Auf'bau *m* (-[e]s;) construction; structure; organization; *(Anlage)* arrangement, setup; (chem) synthesis ‖ *m* (-[e]s;-ten) structure; (aer) framework; (aut) body; (naut) superstructure

auf'bauen *tr* erect; *(Organization)* establish; (chem) synthesize; (mach) assemble ‖ *ref*—**er baute sich vor mir auf** he planted himself in front of me; **sich** [*dat*] **e-e Existenz a.** make a life for oneself

auf'bäumen *ref* rear; (fig) rebel

auf'bauschen *tr* puff up; (fig) exaggerate

auf'begehren *intr* flare up; **(gegen)** protest (against), rebel (against)

auf'behalten §90 *tr* keep on; keep open

auf'bekommen §99 *tr (Tür)* get open; *(Knoten)* loosen; *(Hausaufgabe)* be assigned

auf'bereiten *tr* prepare, process

auf'bessern *tr (Gehalt)* improve, raise

auf'bewahren *tr* keep, store; **das Gepäck a. lassen** check one's baggage

auf'bieten §58 *tr* summon; *(Brautpaar)* announce the banns of; (mil) call up

auf'binden §58 *tr* tie up; *(lösen)* untie; **j-m etw a.** put s.th. over on s.o.

auf'blähen *tr* inflate, distend

auf'blasen §61 *tr* inflate ‖ *ref* get puffed up

auf'bleiben §62 *intr* (SEIN) *(Tür)* stay open; *(wachen)* stay up

auf'blenden *intr* turn on the high beam

auf'blicken *intr* glance up

auf'blitzen *intr* (HABEN & SEIN) flash

auf'blühen *intr* (SEIN) begin to bloom

auf'bocken *tr* (aut) jack up

auf'brauchen *tr* use up

auf'brausen *intr* (HABEN & SEIN) bubble, seethe; *(Wind)* roar; (fig) flare up

auf'brausend *adj* effervescent; irascible

auf'brechen §64 *tr* break up; break open; (hunt) eviscerate ‖ *intr* (SEIN)

burst open; *(fortgehen)* **(nach)** set out (for)

auf'bringen §65 *tr* bring up; *(Geld, Truppen)* raise; *(Schiff)* capture; *(Kraft)* gather; *(Mut)* get up; *(erzürnen)* infuriate

Auf'bruch *m* departure

auf'brühen *tr* bring to a boil

auf'bügeln *tr* iron, press; refresh *(one's knowledge of s.th.)*

aufbürden ['aufbʏrdən] *tr*—**j-m etw a.** saddle s.o. with s.th.

auf'decken *tr* uncover; *(Bett)* turn down; *(Tischtuch)* spread

auf'drängen *tr* force open; **j-m etw a.** force s.th. on s.o.

auf'drehen *tr* turn up; *(Uhr)* wind; *(Hahn)* turn on; *(Schraube)* unscrew; *(Strick)* untwist ‖ *intr (Wagen)* increase speed; (coll) step on it, get a move on

auf'dringlich *adj* pushy; *(Farben)* gaudy

Auf'druck *m* print, imprint

auf'drücken *tr* impress, imprint, affix; *(öffnen)* squeeze open

aufeinan'der *adv* one after the other

Aufeinan'derfolge *f* succession; series

aufeinan'derfolgen *intr* (SEIN) follow one another

aufeinan'derfolgend *adj* successive

Aufenthalt ['aufenthalt] *m* (-[e]s;-e) holdup, delay; **ohne A.** nonstop

Auf'enthaltsgenehmigung *f* residence permit

Auf'enthaltsort *m (Wohnsitz)* residence; *(Verbleib)* whereabouts

Auf'enthaltsraum *m* lounge

auf'erlegen *tr* impose ‖ *ref*—**sich** [*dat*] **die Pflicht a. zu** *(inf)* make it one's duty to *(inf)*; **sich** [*dat*] **Zwang a.** müssen have to restrain oneself

auf'erstehen §146 *intr* (SEIN) rise (from the dead)

Auf'erstehung *f* (-;) resurrection

auf'erwecken *tr* raise from the dead

auf'erziehen §163 *tr* bring up, raise

auf'essen §70 *tr* eat up

auf'fädeln *tr (Perlen)* string

auf'fahren §71 *tr (Fahrzeuge)* park; *(Geschütze)* bring up; *(Wein, Speisen)* serve up ‖ *intr* (SEIN) rise, mount; *(im Auto)* pull up; *(in Erregung)* jump (up); (arti) move into position; **a. auf** *(acc)* run into

Auf'fahrt *f* ascent; *(Zufahrt)* driveway

auf'fallen §72 *intr* (SEIN) be conspicuous; **j-m a.** strike s.o.

auf'fallend, auf'fällig *adj* striking; noticeable; *(Farben)* loud, gaudy

auf'fangen §73 *tr (Ball, Worte)* catch; *(Briefe, Nachrichten)* intercept

auf'fassen *tr* comprehend; *(deuten)* interpret; *(Perlen)* string

Auf'fassung *f* (-;-en) understanding; interpretation; *(Meinung)* view

auf'finden §59 *tr* find *(after searching)*

auf'fliegen §57 *intr* (SEIN) fly up; *(Tür)* fly open; *(scheitern)* fail; **a. lassen** break up *(e.g., a gang)*

auf'fordern *tr* call upon, ask

Auf'forderung *f* (-;-en) invitation; (jur) summons

auf'frischen *tr* freshen up, touch up
auf'führen *tr* (*Bau*) erect; (*Schauspiel*) present; (*eintragen*) enter; (*Zeugen*) produce; (*anführen*) cite; (*mit*) post; **einzeln a.** itemize || *ref* behave, act
Auf'führung *f* (-;-en) erection; performance; entry; specification; behavior
auf'füllen *tr* fill up
Auf'gabe *f* task, job; (*e-s Briefes*) mailing; (*des Gepäcks*) checking; (*e-r Bestellung*) placing; (*e-s Amtes, e-s Geschäfts*) giving up; (*educ*) homework; (*jur*) waiver; (*math*) problem; (*mil*) assignment
auf'gabeln *tr* (& coll) pick up
Auf'gang *m* ascent; (*Treppe*) stairs; (*astr*) rising
auf'geben §80 *tr* give up; (*Amt*) resign; (*Post*) mail; (*Gepäck*) check in; (*Anzeige*) place; (*Preis*) quote; (*Arbeit*) assign; (*Telegramm*) send
auf'geblasen *adj* (fig) uppity
Auf'gebot *n* public notice; (eccl) banns; (mil) call-up
auf'gebracht *adj* angry, irate
auf'gedonnert *adj* (coll) dolled up
auf'gehen §82 *intr* (SEIN) rise; (*Tür*) open; (*Pflanzen*) come up; (arith) go into; **genau a.** come out exactly
auf'geklärt *adj* enlightened
auf'geknöpft *adj* (coll) chatty
auf'gekratzt *adj* (coll) chipper
Auf'geld *n* surcharge; premium
auf'gelegt *adj* (zu) disposed (to)
auf'geräumt *adj* (fig) good-humored
auf'geschlossen *adj* open-minded; (für) receptive (to)
auf'geschmissen *adj* (coll) stuck
auf'gestaut *adj* pent-up
auf'geweckt *adj* smart, bright
auf'geworfen *adj* (*Lippen*) pouting; (*Nase*) turned-up
auf'gießen §76 *tr* (auf *acc*) pour (on); (*Tee, Kaffee*) make, brew
auf'graben §87 *tr* dig up
auf'greifen §88 *tr* pick up; (*Dieb*) catch; (fig) take up
auf'haben §98 *tr* (*Hut*) have on; (*Tür, Mund*) have open; (*Aufgabe*) have to do
auf'hacken *tr* hoe up
auf'haken *tr* unhook
auf'halten §90 *tr* hold up; (*Tür*) hold open; (anhalten) stop, delay || *ref* stay; (wohnen) live; **sich über etw a.** find fault with s.th.
Auf'hängeleine *f* clothesline
auf'hängen §92 *tr* hang up; **j-m etw a.** push s.th. on s.o.; (*Wertloses*) palm s.th. off on s.o.
auf'häufen *tr* & *ref* pile up
auf'heben §94 *tr* lift up, pick up; (bewahren) preserve; (ungültig machen) cancel; (*Gesetz*) repeal; (ausgleichen) cancel out, offset; (*Strafe, Belagerung*) lift; **gut aufgehoben sein** be in good hands
auf'heitern *tr* cheer up || *ref* cheer up; (*Gesicht*) brighten; (*Wetter*) clear up
auf'hellen *ref* & *intr* brighten
auf'hetzen *tr* incite, egg on

auf'holen *tr* hoist; (*Verspätung*) make up for || *intr* catch up
auf'horchen *intr* prick up one's ears
auf'hören *intr* stop, quit
auf'jauchzen *intr* shout for joy
auf'kaufen *tr* buy up; (*Markt*) corner
auf'klären *tr* clear up; enlighten; (mil) reconnoitre || *ref* clear up; (*Gesicht*) light up, brighten
Auf'klärer *m* (-s;-) (aer) reconnaissance plane; (mil) scout
Auf'klärung *f* (-;-en) explanation; enlightenment; (mil) reconnaissance
Auf'klärungsbuch *n* sex-education book
Auf'klärungsspähtrupp *m* reconnaissance patrol
auf'kleben *tr* (auf *acc*) paste (onto)
auf'klinken *tr* unlatch
auf'knacken *tr* crack open
auf'knöpfen *tr* unbutton
auf'knüpfen *tr* (lösen) untie; (hängen) (coll) string up
auf'kochen *tr* & *intr* boil
auf'kommen §99 *intr* (SEIN) come up, rise; (*Gedanke*) occur; (*Mode*) come into fashion; (*Schiff*) appear on the horizon; **a. für** answer for; (*Kosten*) defray; **a. gegen** stand up against, cope with; **a. von** recover from ||
Aufkommen *n* (-s;) rise; recovery
auf'krempeln *tr* roll up
auf'kreuzen *intr* (coll) show up
auf'kriegen *tr* see **aufbekommen**
auf'lachen *intr* burst out laughing
auf'laden §103 *tr* load up; (*Batterie*) charge || *ref*—**sich** [*dat*] **etw a.** saddle oneself with s.th.
Auf'lage *f* edition, printing; (*e-r Zeitung*) circulation; (*Steuer*) tax; (*Stütze*) rest, support
auf'lassen §104 *tr* leave open; (*Fabrik, Bergwerk*) abandon
auf'lauern *intr* (*dat*) lie in wait (for)
Auf'lauf *m* gathering, crowd; (*Tumult*) riot; (com) accumulation; (culin) soufflé
auf'laufen §105 *intr* (SEIN) rise; (anwachsen) accrue; (*Schiff*) get stranded; (*Panzer*) get stuck
auf'leben *intr* (SEIN) revive
auf'lecken *tr* lick up
auf'legen *tr* (auf *acc*) put (on); (*Steuer*) impose; (*Hörer*) hang up; (*Buch*) publish; (*Karten*) lay on the table; (*Liste*) make available for inspection; (*Anleihe*) float; (*Faß Bier*) put on || *intr* (telp) hang up
auf'lehnen *tr* (auf *acc*) lean (on) || *ref* (auf *acc*) lean (on); (gegen) rebel (against)
Auf'lehnung *f* (-;-en) rebellion; resistance
auf'lesen §107 *tr* pick up, gather
auf'liegen §108 *intr* (auf *dat*) lie (on); (zur Ansicht) be displayed
auf'lockern *tr* loosen; (*Eintönigkeit, Vortrag*) break (up)
auf'lösbar *adj* soluble; solvable
auf'lösen *tr* untie; (öffnen) loosen; (entwirren) disentangle; (*Versammlung*) break up; (*Heer*) disband; (*Ehe*) dissolve; (*Verbindung*) sever; (*Firma*) liquidate; (*Rätsel*) solve;

(*zerlegen*) break down; dissolve; (*entziffern*) decode; **ganz aufgelöst** all out of breath
Auf′lösung *f* (-;-en) solution; disentanglement; (*e-r Versammlung, Ehe*) breakup; (*Zerfall*) disintegration; (*von Beziehungen*) severance; (com) liquidation
auf′machen *tr* open (up); (*Geschäft*) open; (*Dampf*) get up; (coll) do up (*e.g., big, tastefully*) ‖ *ref* (*Wind*) rise; (**nach**) set out (for)
Auf′machung *f* (-;-en) layout, format; (*Kleidung*) outfit
Auf′marsch *m* parade; (mil) concentration; (*zum Gefecht*) (mil) deployment
auf′marschieren *intr* (SEIN) parade; (*strategisch*) assemble; (*taktisch*) deploy
auf′merken *tr* (**auf** *acc*) pay attention (to)
aufmerksam [′aʊfmɛrkzɑm] *adj* (**auf** *acc*) attentive (to)
Auf′merksamkeit *f* (-;) attention
auf′möbeln *tr* (coll) dress up; (*anherrschen*) (sl) chew out; (*aufmuntern*) (coll) pep up ‖ *ref* (coll) doll up
auf′muntern *tr* cheer up
Auf′nahme *f* (-;-n) taking up; (*Empfang*) reception (*Zulassung*) admission; (*von Beziehungen*) establishment; (*Inventur*) stock-taking; (electron) recording; (phot) photograph
Auf′nahmeapparat *m* camera; recorder
Auf′nahmegerät *n* camera; recorder
Auf′nahmeprüfung *f* entrance exam
auf′nehmen §116 *tr* take up; (*erfassen*) grasp; (*Diktat*) take down; (*Gast*) receive; (*Inventar*) take; (*Geld*) borrow; (*Anleihe*) float; (*Spur*) pick up; (*Beziehungen*) establish; (*eintragen*) enter; (*durch*) *Tonband, Schallplatte* record; (geog) map out; (phot) take
auf′opfern *tr* offer up, sacrifice
auf′päpeln *tr* spoon-feed
auf′passen *intr* pay attention; look out; **paß auf!** watch out!
auf′pflanzen *tr* set up; (*Seitengewehr*) fix
auf′platzen *intr* (SEIN) burst (open)
auf′polieren *tr* polish up
auf′prägen *tr* (**auf** *acc*) (& fig) impress (on)
auf′prallen *intr* (**auf** *acc*) crash (into)
auf′pumpen *tr* pump up
auf′putschen *tr* incite; (coll) pep up
auf′putzen *tr* dress up; clean up ‖ *ref* dress up
auf′raffen *tr* pick up ‖ *ref* stand up; (fig) pull oneself together
auf′ragen *intr* tower, stand high
auf′räumen *tr* (*Zimmer*) straighten up; (*wegräumen*) clear away ‖ *intra*—**a. mit** do away with, get rid of
Auf′räumungsarbeiten *pl* clearance
auf′rechnen *tr* add up; (acct) balance
auf′recht *adj* upright, erect
auf′rechterhalten §90 *tr* maintain
auf′regen *tr* excite, stir up; (*unruhig machen*) disturb, upset
Auf′regung *f* (-;-en) excitement

auf′reiben §62 *tr* rub off; (*wundreiben*) rub sore; (*vertilgen*) destroy; (*Heer*) grind up; (*Kräfte*) sap; (*Nerven*) fray ‖ *ref* worry onself to death
auf′reibend *adj* wearing, exhausting
auf′reihen *tr* string, thread
auf′reißen §53 *tr* tear open; (*Straße*) tear up; (*Tür*) fling open; (*Augen*) open wide; (*zeichnen*) sketch ‖ *intr* (SEIN) split open, crack
auf′reizen *tr* provoke, incite; (*stark erregen*) excite
auf′reizend *adj* provoking, annoying; (*Rede*) inflammatory; (*Anblick*) sexy
auf′richten *tr* erect, set up; (*trösten*) comfort ‖ *ref* sit up
auf′richtig *adj* upright, sincere
Auf′richtigkeit *f* sincerity
auf′riegeln *tr* unbolt
Auf′riß *m* front view
auf′rollen *tr* roll up; (*entfalten*) unroll
auf′rücken *intr* (SEIN) advance; (**zu**) be promoted (to)
Auf′ruf *m* (*Aufschrei*) outcry; (*Aufforderung*) call; (mil) call-up
auf′rufen §122 *tr* call on; (*appellieren an*) appeal to; (*Banknoten*) call in
Auf′ruhr *m* uproar; (*Tumult*) riot
auf′rühren *tr* stir up
aufrührerisch [′aʊfryrərɪʃ] *adj* inflammatory, rebellious; (mil) mutinous
auf′runden *tr* round out
auf′rüsten *tr* & *intr* arm; rearm
Auf′rüstung *f* (-;-en) rearmament
auf′rütteln *tr* wake up (*by shaking*)
auf′sagen *tr* recite; (*ein Ende machen mit*) terminate
auf′sammeln *tr* gather up
aufsässig [′aʊfzɛsɪç] *adj* hostile; (*widerspenstig*) rebellious
Auf′satz *m* superstructure; (*auf dem Tische*) centerpiece; (*Schularbeit*) essay, composition; (*in der Zeitung*) article; (golf) tee; (mil) gun sight
auf′saugen §125 *tr* suck up; absorb
auf′schauen *intr* look up
auf′scheuchen *tr* scare up
auf′scheuern *tr* scrape
auf′schichten *tr* stack (up), pile (up)
auf′schieben §130 *tr* push up; (*Tür*) push open; (*verschieben*) postpone
auf′schießen §76 *intr* (SEIN) shoot up
Auf′schlag *m* (**auf** *acc*) striking (upon), impact (on); (*an Kleidung*) cuff, lapel; (*Steuer-*) surtax; (*Preis-*) price hike; (tennis) service, serve
auf′schlagen §132 *tr* (*öffnen*) open; (*Ei*) crack; (*Karte, Ärmel*) turn up; (*Zelt*) pitch; (*Wohnung*) take up; (*Preis*) raise; (*Knie, usw.*) bruise; (*Ball*) serve ‖ *intr* (SEIN) (*Tür*) fly open; (*Flugzeug*) crash; (*Ball*) bounce; (tennis) serve
auf′schließen §76 *tr* unlock, open ‖ *ref* (*dat*) pour out one's heart (to) ‖ *intr* (mil) close ranks
auf′schlitzen *tr* slit open
Auf′schluß *m* information; (chem) decomposition
auf′schlußreich *adj* informative
auf′schnallen *tr* buckle; unbuckle
auf′schnappen *tr* snap up; (*Nachricht*) pick up

Auf'schneidemaschine *f* meat slicer
auf'schneiden §106 *tr* cut open; (*Fleisch*) slice ‖ *intr* (coll) talk big
Auf'schneider *m* boaster
Auf'schnitt *m*—**kalter A.** cold cuts
auf'schnüren *tr* untie, undo
auf'schrauben *tr* unscrew; (**auf** *acc*) screw (on)
auf'schrecken §134 *tr* startle; (*Wild*) scare up ‖ *intr* (SEIN) be startled
Auf'schrei *m* scream, yell; (fig) outcry
auf'schreiben §62 *tr* write down
auf'schreien §135 *intr* scream, yell
Auf'schrift *f* inscription; (*Anschrift*) address; (*e–r Flasche*) label
Auf'schub *m* deferment, postponement; (*Verzögerung*) delay; (jur) stay
auf'schürfen *tr* scrape; (*Bein*) skin
auf'schwellen §119 *intr* (SEIN) swell up; (*Fluß*) rise
auf'schwemmen *tr* bloat
auf'schwingen §142 *ref* (& fig) soar; **sich a., etw zu tun** bring oneself to do s.th.
Auf'schwung *m* (& fig) upswing
auf'sehen §138 *intr* look up ‖ **Aufsehen** *n* (–s;) sensation, stir
auf'sehenerregend *adj* sensational
Auf'seher –**in** §6 *mf* supervisor; (*im Museum*) guard; (*im Geschäft*) floorwalker
auf'sein §139 *intr* (SEIN) be up; (*Tür*) be open
auf'setzen *tr* put on; (*aufrichten*) set up; (*schriftlich*) compose, draft ‖ *ref* sit up ‖ *intr* (aer) touch down; (rok) splash down
Auf'sicht *f* inspection, supervision
Auf'sichtsbeamte *m*, **Auf'sichtsbeamtin** *f* inspector, supervisor
Auf'sichtsbehörde *f* control board
Auf'sichtsdame *f* floorwalker
Auf'sichtsherr *m* floorwalker
Auf'sichtsrat *m* board of trustees; (*Mitglied*) trustee
auf'sitzen §144 *intr* (SEIN) sit up; (auf *dat*) sit (on), rest (on); **j–m a.** be taken in by s.o.; **j–n a. lassen** stand s.o. up
auf'spannen *tr* stretch, spread; (*Regenschirm*) open
auf'sparen *tr* save (up)
auf'speichern *tr* store (up)
auf'sperren *tr* unlock; (*Augen, Tür*) open wide
auf'spielen *tr* strike up ‖ *ref* (mit) show off (with) ‖ *intr* play dance music
auf'spießen *tr* spear, pierce
auf'sprengen *tr* force open; (*mit Sprengstoff*) blow up
auf'springen §142 *intr* (SEIN) jump up; (*Tür*) fly open; (*Ball*) bounce; (*Haut*) chap, crack
auf'spritzen *tr* (*Farbe*) spray up ‖ (sl) shoot up ‖ *intr* (SEIN) squirt up
auf'sprudeln *intr* (SEIN) bubble (up)
auf'spulen *tr* wind up
auf'spüren *tr* track down, ferret out
auf'stacheln *tr* goad; (fig) stir up
auf'stampfen *intr*—**mit dem Fuß a.** stamp one's foot
Auf'stand *m* insurrection, uprising

aufständisch ['aufʃtendɪʃ] *adj* insurgent ‖ **Aufständischen** *pl* insurgents
auf'stapeln *tr* stack up, pile up
auf'stechen §64 *tr* puncture; (surg) lance
auf'stecken *tr* (*Flagge*) plant; (*Haar*) pin up; (coll) give up; **j–m ein Licht a.** enlighten s.o.
auf'stehen §146 *intr* (HABEN) stand open ‖ *intr* (SEIN) stand up, get up; (gegen) revolt (against)
auf'steigen §148 *intr* (SEIN) climb; (*Reiter*) mount; (*Rauch*) rise; (*Gewitter*) come up; (*Tränen*) well up; **a. auf** (*acc*) get on
auf'stellen *tr* set up, put up; (*Beispiel*) set; (*Behauptung*) make; (*Wachposten*) post; (*Bauten*) erect; (*Leiter*) raise (*Waren*) display; (*Maschine*) assemble; (*als Kandidaten*) nominate; (*Regel, Problem*) state; (*Lehre*) propound; (*Rekord*) set; (*Liste*) make out; (*Rechnung*) draw up, make out; (*Stühle*) arrange; (*Falle*) set; (*Bedingungen, Grundsätze*) lay down; (*Beweis*) furnish ‖ *ref* station oneself
Auf'stellung *f* (–;–en) erection; assertion; list, schedule; (mil) formation; (pol) nomination; (sport) lineup
auf'stemmen *tr* pry open ‖ *ref* prop oneself up
Auf'stieg *m* climb; (*Steigung*) slope; (fig) advancement
auf'stöbern *tr* ferret out; (fig) unearth
auf'stoßen §150 *tr* push open ‖ *ref*—**sich** [*dat*] **das Knie a.** skin one's knee ‖ *intr* (HABEN) (sl) belch ‖ *intr* (HABEN & SEIN) bump, touch; (*Schiff*) touch bottom ‖ *intr* (SEIN)—**j–m a.** strike s.o., cross s.o.'s mind
auf'streichen §85 *tr* (*Butter*) spread
auf'streuen *tr* (auf *acc*) sprinkle (on)
Auf'strich *m* upstroke; (*auf Brot*) spread
auf'stützen *tr* prop up
auf'suchen *tr* search for; (*nachschlagen*) look up; (*Ort*) visit; (*aufsammeln*) pick up; (*Arzt*) go to see
Auf'takt *m* upbeat; (fig) prelude
auf'tauchen *intr* (SEIN) turn up, appear; (*Frage*) crop up; (*U-Boot*) surface; (*Gerücht*) arise
auf'tauen *tr* & *intr* (SEIN) thaw
auf'teilen *tr* divide up
Auftrag ['auftrak] *m* (–[e]s;–e) (*Anweisung*) orders, instructions; (*Bestellung*) order, commission; (*Sendung*) mission; **in A. von** on behalf of
auf'tragen §132 *tr* instruct, order; (*Speise*) serve; (*Farben, Butter*) put on; (*Kleidungsstück*) wear out; (surv) plot; **j–m etw a.** impose s.th. on s.o. ‖ *intr*—**dick** (or **stark**) **a.** (sl) put it on thick
Auf'traggeber –**in** §6 *mf* employer; (*Besteller*) client, customer
Auf'tragsformular *n* order blank
auf'tragsgemäß, auf'trag(s)mäßig *adv* as ordered, according to instructions
auf'treffen §151 *intr* (SEIN) strike
Auf'treffpunkt *m* point of impact
auf'treiben §62 *tr* (*Staub; Geld*) raise;

(*Wild*) flush; (*aufblähen*) distend; (*Teig*) cause to rise

auf'trennen *tr* rip, undo, unstitch

auf'treten §152 *tr* (*Tür*) kick open ‖ *intr* (SEIN) step, tread; (*erscheinen*) appear; (*handeln*) act, behave; (*eintreten*) occur, crop up; (*pathol*) break out; (*theat*) enter ‖ **Auftreten** *n* (-s;) appearance; occurrence; behavior; **sicheres A.** poise

Auf'trieb *m* drive; buoyancy; (aer & fig) lift; (agr) cattle drive; **j-m A. geben** encourage s.o.

Auf'tritt *m* (*Streit*) scene, row; (theat) entrance (*of an actor*); (theat) scene

auf'trumpfen *intr* play a higher trump; **gegen j-n a.** go to s.o. better

auf'tun §154 *tr* & *ref* open

auf'türmen *tr* & *intr* pile up

auf'wachen *intr* (SEIN) awaken, wake up

auf'wachsen §155 *intr* (SEIN) grow up

auf'wallen *intr* (SEIN) boil, seethe; (fig) surge, rise up

Auf'wallung *f* (-;-en) (fig) outburst

Aufwand ['aufvant] *m* (-[e]s;-e) (an *dat*) expenditure (of); (*Prunk*) show

auf'wärmen *tr* warm up; (fig) drag up

Auf'wartefrau *f* cleaning woman

auf'warten *intr* (*dat*) wait on; **a. mit** oblige with, offer

Auf'wärter –in §6 *mf* attendant ‖ *f* cleaning woman

aufwärts ['aufvɛrts] *adv* upward(s)

Auf'wärtshaken *m* (box) uppercut

Auf'wartung *f* (-;) attendance; (*bei Tisch*) service; (*Besuch*) call; **j-m seine A. machen** pay one's respects to s.o.

Aufwasch ['aufvaʃ] *m* (-es;) washing; dirty dishes

auf'waschen §158 *tr* & *intr* wash up

auf'wecken *tr* wake (up)

auf'weichen *tr* soften; soak ‖ *intr* (SEIN) become soft; become sodden

auf'weisen §118 *tr* produce, show

auf'wenden §140 *tr* spend, expend; **Mühe a.** take pains

auf'werfen §160 *tr* throw up; (*Tür*) fling open; (*Graben*) dig; (*Frage*) raise ‖ *ref*—**sich a. zu** set oneself up as

auf'wickeln *tr* wind up; (*Haar*) curl; (*loswickeln*) unwind

aufwiegeln ['aufvigəln] *tr* instigate

Aufwiegler –in ['aufviglər(ɪn)] §6 *mf* instigator

aufwieglerisch ['aufviglərɪʃ] *adj* inflammatory

Auf'wind *m* updraft

auf'winden §59 *tr* wind up; (*Anker*) weigh ‖ *ref* coil up

auf'wirbeln *tr* (*Staub*) raise; **viel Staub a.** (coll) make quite a stir

auf'wischen *tr* wipe up

auf'wühlen *tr* dig up; (*Wasser*) churn up; (fig) stir up

auf'zählen *tr* enumerate, itemize

auf'zäumen *tr* bridle

auf'zehren *tr* consume

auf'zeichnen *tr* make a sketch of; (*notieren*) write down, record

aufzeigen *tr* point out

auf'ziehen §163 *tr* pull up; (*öffnen*) pull open; (*Uhr*) wind; (*Saite*) put on; (*Perlen*) string; (*Kind*) bring up; (*Tier*) breed; (*Pflanzen*) grow; (*Flagge, Segel*) hoist (*Anker*) weigh; (*Veranstaltung*) arrange, organize; (coll) kid ‖ *intr* (SEIN) approach, pull up

Auf'zucht *f* breeding, raising

Auf'zug *m* elevator; (*e-r Uhr*) winder; (*Aufmarsch*) parade , procession; (gym) chin-up; (theat) act

auf'zwingen §142 *tr*—**j-m etw a.** force s.th. on s.o.; **j-m seinen Willen a.** impose one's will on s.o.

Augapfel ['aukpfəl] *m* eyeball; (fig) apple of the eye

Auge ['augə] *n* (-s;-n) eye; (*auf Würfeln*) dot; (hort) bud; (typ) face

äugeln ['ɔigəln] *intr.*—**ä. mit** wink at

Augen– [augən] *comb.fm.* eye, of the eye(s), in the eye(s); visual; (anat) ocular, optic(al)

Au'genblick *m* moment, instant

au'genblicklich *adj* momentary; (*sofortig*) immediate, instantaneous

Au'genblicksmensch *m* hedonist; impulsive person

Au'genbraue *f* eyebrow

Au'genbrauenstift *m* eyebrow pencil

au'genfällig *adj* conspicuous, obvious

Au'genhöhle *f* eye socket

Au'genlicht *n* eyesight

Au'genlid *n* eyelid

Au'genmaß *n* sense of proportion; **ein gutes A. haben** have a keen eye; **nach dem A.** by eye

Au'genmerk *n* attention

Au'gennerv *m* optic nerve

Au'genschein *m* inspection; (*Anschein*) appearances; **in A. nehmen** inspect

au'genscheinlich *adj* obvious

Au'genstern *n* pupil; iris

Au'gentäuschung *f* optical illusion

Au'gentrost *m* sight for sore eyes

Au'genwasser *n* eyewash

Au'genweide *f* sight for sore eyes

Au'genwimper *f* eyelash

Au'genwinkel *m* corner of the eye

Au'genzeuge *m*, **Au'genzeugin** *f* eyewitness

–äugig [ɔigɪç] *comb.fm.* –eyed

August [au'gust] *m* (-[e]s & -;-e) August

Auktion [auk'tsjon] *f* (-;-en) auction

Auktio·nator [auktsjo'nator] *m* (-s; –natoren [na'torən]) auctioneeer

auktionieren [auktsjo'nirən] *tr* auction off, put up for auction

Au·la ['aula] *f* (-;-s & –len [lən]) auditorium

aus [aus] *adv* out; **von ... aus** from, e.g., **vom Fenster aus** from the window ‖ *prep* (*dat*) out of, from; **because of**

aus'arbeiten *tr* elaborate; finish ‖ *ref* work out, take physical exercise

Aus'arbeitung *f* (-;-en) elaboration; (*schriftlich*) composition; (*körperlich*) workout; (tech) finish

aus'arten *intr* (SEIN) get out of hand; (in *acc*) degenerate (into)

aus'atmen *tr* exhale

aus'baden tr (coll) take the rap for
aus'baggern tr dredge
Aus'bau m (-[e]s;) completion; expansion, development
aus'bauen tr complete; (erweitern) expand, develop
aus'bedingen tr stipulate
aus'bessern tr repair; (Kleid) mend; (Bild) retouch
aus'beulen tr take the dents out of
Aus'beute f (Ertrag) output; (Gewinn) profit, gain
ausbeuten ['ausbɔɪtən] tr exploit
aus'biegen §57 tr bend out || intr (SEIN) curve; (dat, **vor** dat) make way (for)
aus'bilden tr develop; (lehren) train, educate; (mil) drill || ref train
Aus'bilder m (mil) drill instructor
aus'bitten §60 ref—sich [dat] **etw a.** ask for s.th.; insist on s.th.
aus'bleiben §62 intr (SEIN) stay out; stay away; be missing
aus'bleichen §85 tr & intr (SEIN) bleach; fade
aus'blenden tr (cin, rad) fade-out
Aus'blick m (**auf** acc) view (of); (fig) outlook
aus'bohren tr bore (out), drill (out)
aus'borgen ref—sich [dat] **etw a. von** borrow s.th. from
aus'brechen §64 tr break off || intr (SEIN) (aus) break out (of)
aus'breiten tr & ref spread; extend
aus'brennen §97 tr burn out, gut; (Sonne) parch; (med) cauterize || intr (SEIN) burn out; (Haus) be gutted
Aus'bruch m outbreak; (e-s Vulkans) eruption; (e-s Gefangenen) break-out; (des Gelächters) outburst
aus'brüten tr incubate; hatch
Ausbuchtung ['ausbuxtuŋ] f (-;-en) bulge
ausbuddeln ['ausbudəln] tr (coll) dig out
aus'bügeln tr iron out
Aus'bund m (**von**) very embodiment (of)
ausbürgern ['ausbγrgərn] tr expatriate
aus'bürsten tr brush out
Aus'dauer f perseverance
aus'dauern intr persevere, persist
aus'dauernd adj persevering; (bot) perennial
aus'dehnen tr & ref stretch, expand; (Organ) dilate
aus'denken §66 tr think out; think up; nicht auszudenken inconceivable
aus'deuten tr interpret, explain
aus'dienen intr serve one's time
aus'dorren intr (SEIN) dry up; wither
aus'dörren tr dry up, parch
aus'drehen tr turn out; turn off
Aus'druck m expression
aus'drücken tr squeeze out; (fig) express
ausdrücklich ['ausdryklɪç] adj express, explicit
aus'druckslos adj expressionless
aus'drucksvoll adj expressive
Aus'drucksweise f way of speaking
aus'dünsten tr exhale, give off || intr evaporate; (schwitzen) sweat

auseinan'der adv apart; separately
auseinan'derfallen §72 intr (SEIN) fall apart
auseinan'dergehen §82 intr (SEIN) part; (Versammlung) break up; (Meinungen) differ; (Wege) branch off; (auseinanderfallen) come apart
auseinan'derhalten §90 tr keep apart
auseinan'derlaufen §105 intr (SEIN) (Menge) disperse; (Wege) diverge
auseinan'dernehmen §116 tr take apart
auseinan'dersetzen tr explain || ref—sich mit etw a. come to grips with s.th.; sich mit j-m a. have it out with s.o.; (gütlich) come to an understanding with s.o.
Auseinan'dersetzung f explanation; (Erörterung) discussion, controversy; (Übereinkommen) arrangement
aus'erkoren adj chosen; predestined
aus'erlesen adj choice || §107 tr choose, select
aus'ersehen §138 tr destine
aus'erwählen tr pick out, choose
aus'fahren §71 tr (Straße, Gleis) wear out; (aer) let down; **den Motor a.** (coll) open it up; **die Kurve a.** not cut the corner || intr (SEIN) drive out; (naut) put to sea; (rr) pull out
Aus'fahrt f departure; exit; (Spazierfahrt) ride, drive; (Torweg) gateway
Aus'fall m falling out; (Ergebnis) result; (Verlust) loss; (fencing) lunge; (mach) breakdown; (mil) sally
aus'fallen §72 intr (SEIN) fall out; (nicht stattfinden) fail to take place; (ausgelassen werden) be omitted; (versagen) go out of commission; (Ergebnis) turn out; (mil) sortie
aus'fallend adj aggressive, insulting
aus'fechten §74 tr (Kampf) fight; (Streit) settle (by fighting)
aus'fegen tr sweep (out)
aus'fertigen tr finish; (Paß) issue; (Scheck) write out; (Schriftstück) draw up, draft; **doppelt a.** draw up in duplicate
aus'findig adj—a. machen find out; (aufspüren) trace
aus'fliegen §57 intr (SEIN) fly out; (wegfliegen) fly away; (von Hause wegziehen) leave home; go on a trip
aus'fließen §76 intr (SEIN) flow out
Aus'flucht f evasion; Ausflüchte machen dodge, beat around the bush
aus'fluchten tr align
Aus'flug m trip, outing
Ausflügler ['ausflyglər] m (-s;-) tourist, vacationer
Aus'fluß m outflow; (Eiter) discharge; (Ergebnis) outcome; (Mündung) outlet
aus'folgen tr hand over
aus'forschen tr investigate; sound out
aus'fragen tr interrogate, quiz
aus'fressen §70 tr empty (by eating); (chem) corrode; (geol) erode; **was hast du denn ausgefressen?** (coll) what were you up to?
Ausfuhr ['ausfur] f (-;-en) export
Aus'fuhrabgabe f export duty
ausführbar ['ausfyrbar] adj feasible

aus'führen *tr* carry out; export, ship; (*Auftrag*) fill; (*darlegen*) explain
Aus'fuhrhändler –in §6 *mf* exporter
ausführlich ['ausfyrlıç] *adj* detailed ‖ *adv* in detail, in full
Aus'führung *f* (–;–en) carrying out, performance; (*Qualität*) workmanship; (*Darlegung*) explanation; (*e–s Gesetzes, Befehls*) implementation; (*Fertigstellung*) completion; (*e–s Verbrechens*) perpetrations; (*typ*) type, model; copy
Aus'fuhrwaren *pl* exports
aus'füllen *tr* fill out; (*Zeit*) occupy; (*Lücke; Stellung*) fill
Aus'gabe *f* (*Verteilung*) distribution; (*von Geldern*) expenditure; (*von Briefen*) delivery; (*e–s Buches*) edition; (*von Aktien*) issue
Aus'gang *m* exit; (*Auslaß*) outlet; (*Ergebnis*) result; (*Ende*) close, end; (aer) gate
Aus'gangspunkt *m* starting point
Aus'gangssprache *f* source language
aus'geben §80 *tr* give out, distribute; (*Aktien; Befehl*) issue; (*Geld*) spend; (*Briefe*) deliver; (*Karten*) deal ‖ *ref*—sich a. für pass oneself off as
ausgebeult ['ausgəbɔɪlt] *adj* baggy
Aus'geburt *f* figment
aus'gedehnt *adj* extensive
aus'gedient *adj* retired; (educ) emeritus
aus'gefallen *adj* (fig) eccentric, odd
aus'gefeilt *adj* (fig) flawless
aus'geglichen *adj* (*Person*) well-balanced; (*Styl*) balanced
aus'gehen §82 *intr* (SEIN) go out; (*Vorräte, Geld, Geduld*) run out; (*Haar*) fall out; (*Farbe*) fade; **a. auf** (*acc*) aim at, be bent on; **a. von** proceed from; **die Sache ging von ihm aus** it was his idea; **frei a.** get off scot-free; **gut a.** turn out well; **leer a.** come away empty-handed; **wenn wir davon a., daß** going on the assumption that
Aus'gehverbot *n* curfew
aus'gekocht *adj* (*Lügner*) out-and-out; (*Verbrecher*) hardened
aus'gelassen *adj* boisterous
aus'geleiert *adj* trite; worn-out; (*Gewinde*) stripped
aus'gemacht *adj* settled; downright
ausgenommen *prep* (*acc*) except; **niemand a.** bar none
aus'gepicht *adj* inveterate
aus'gerechnet *adv* just, of all …; **a. Sie!** you of all people!
aus'geschlossen *adj* out of the question, impossible
Ausgesiedelte ['ausgəzidəltə] §5 *mf* evacuee, displaced person
aus'gestalten *tr* make arrangements for
aus'gesucht *adj* choice
aus'gezeichnet *adj* excellent
ausgiebig ['ausgibıç] *adj* abundant; (*ergiebig*) productive
aus'gießen §76 *tr* pour out, pour away
Aus'gleich *m* (–s;–e) (*Ersatz*) compensation; (*Vergleich*) compromise; (acct) settlement; (tennis) deuce
aus'gleichen §85 *tr* level, smooth out; (*Konten*) balance; (*Verlust*) compensate for ‖ *ref* cancel one another out

Ausgleichs– *comb.fm.* balancing, compensating
Aus'gleichung *f* (–;–en) equalization; settlement; compensation
aus'gleiten §86 *intr* (SEIN) slip
aus'graben §87 *tr* dig out, dig up; (*Leiche*) exhume; (archeol) excavate
aus'greifen §88 *intr* reach out; **weit ausgreifend** far-reaching
Ausguck ['ausguk] *m* (–s;–e) lookout
aus'gucken *intr* (nach) be on the lookout (for)
Aus'guß *m* sink; (*Tülle*) spout, nozzle
aus'haken *tr* unhook
aus'halten §90 *tr* endure, stand ‖ *intr* persevere, stick it out
aus'handeln *tr* get by bargaining
aushändigen ['aushendɪgən] *tr* hand over, surrender
Aus'hang *m* notice, shingle
Aus'hängeschild *n* (–[e]s;–er) sign board, shingle; (fig) front, cover
aus'harren *intr* hold out, last
aus'hauchen *tr* breathe out, exhale
aus'heben §94 *tr* lift out; (*Tür*) lift off its hinges; (*Truppen*) recruit
aushecken ['aushɛkən] *tr* (fig) hatch
aus'heilen *tr* heal completely ‖ *intr* (SEIN) heal up
aus'helfen §96 *intr* (dat) help out
Aus'hilfe *f* (temporary) help; (temporary) helper; makeshift
Aushilfs– *comb.fm.* temporary, emergency
Aus'hilfsarbeit *f* part-time work
Aus'hilfslehrer –in §6 *mf* substitute teacher
aus'hilfsweise *adv* temporarily
aus'höhlen *tr* hollow out
aus'holen *tr* (*ausfragen*) sound out ‖ *intr* (*beim Schwimmen*) stroke; **mit dem Arm a.** raise the arm (*before striking*); **weit a.** start from the beginning
aus'horchen *tr* sound out, pump
aus'hülsen *tr* (*Bohnen, usw.*) shell
aus'hungern *tr* starve (out)
aus'husten *tr* cough up
aus'kehlen *tr* groove
Aus'kehlung *f* (–;–en) groove
aus'kehren *tr* sweep (out)
aus'kennen §97 *ref* know one's way; (*in e–m Fach*) be well versed
Aus'klang *m* end, close
aus'klappen *tr* pull out (*a fold-away bed*)
aus'kleiden *tr* line, panel; (*ausziehen*) undress ‖ *ref* undress
aus'klopfen *tr* beat the dust out of
ausklügeln ['ausklygəln] *tr* figure out (*ingeniously*)
aus'kneifen §88 *intr* (SEIN) beat it
aus'knipsen *tr* (coll) switch off
ausknobeln ['ausknobəln] *tr* figure out
aus'kochen *tr* boil out; boil clean
aus'kommen §99 *intr* (SEIN) come out, get out; (*ausreichen*) manage ‖ **Auskommen** *n* (–s;) livelihood
auskömmlich ['auskœmlıç] *adj* adequate
aus'kosten *tr* relish
aus'kramen ['auskramən] *tr* (*aus Schubladen*) drag out; (fig) show off

aus'kratzen *tr* scratch out; (surg) curette

aus'kriechen §102 *intr* (SEIN) be hatched

aus'kugeln *ref*—*sich* [*dat*] **den Arm a.** dislocate the shoulder

aus'kundschaften *tr* explore; (mil) scout

Auskunft ['auskʊnft] *f* (–;ⁿe) information, piece of information

Auskunftei [aʊskʊnf'taɪ] *f* (–;–en) private detective agency

Aus'kunftschalter *m* information desk

aus'kuppeln *tr* uncouple; (*die Kupplung*) release ‖ *intr* disengage the clutch

aus'lachen *tr* laugh at ‖ *ref* have a good laugh

aus'laden §103 *tr* unload; (*Gast*) put off ‖ *intr* project, jut out ‖ **Ausladen** *n* (–s;) unloading; projection

Aus'lage *f* (*von Geld*) outlay; (*Unkosten*) expenses; (*von Waren*) display; (*Schaufenster*) display window

Aus'land *n* foreign country, foreign countries; **im A. leben** live abroad; **ins A. gehen** go abroad

Ausländer –in ['aʊslɛndər(ɪn)] §6 *mf* foreigner, alien

aus'ländisch *adj* foreign, alien

Auslands– comb.fm. foreign

Aus·laß ['aʊslas] *m* (–lasses;–lässe) outlet

aus'lassen §104 *tr* let out; (*weglassen*) omit; (*Wut*) (**an** *dat*) vent (on) ‖ *ref* express one's opinion

Aus'lassung *f* omission; (*Bemerkung*) remark

Aus'lassungszeichen *n* (gram) apostrophe; (typ) caret

Aus'lauf *m* sailing; room to run

aus'laufen §105 *intr* (SEIN) run out; (*Schiff*) put out to sea; (*Farbe*) run; **a. in** (*acc*) end in; (*Straße*) run into

Aus'läufer *m* (geol)) spur; (hort) runner

aus'leben *tr* live out ‖ *ref* make the most of one's life ‖ *intr* die

aus'lecken *tr* lick clean

aus'leeren *tr* empty ‖ *ref* have a bowel movement

aus'legen *tr* lay out; (*Waren*) display; (*erklären*) construe; (*Geld*) advance; (*Fußboden*) cover (*with carpeting*); (*Minen*) lay; (*Schlinge*) set; **falsch a.** misconstrue, misinterpret

Aus'leger –in §6 *mf* interpreter ‖ *m* outrigger; (*e–s Krans*) boom

aus'leihen §81 *tr* lend (out) ‖ *ref*—**sich** [*dat*] **etw a.** borrow s.th.

aus'lernen *intr* finish one's apprenticeship; **man lernt nie aus** one never stops learning

Aus'lese *f* pick, choice

aus'lesen §107 *tr* pick out; (*Buch*) finish reading

aus'liefern *tr* deliver, turn over; (*verteilen*) distribute; (*Verbrecher*) extradite; **j–m ausgeliefert sein** be at s.o.'s mercy

aus'liegen §108 *intr* (SEIN) be on display

aus'löffeln *tr* spoon out; **etw a. zu ha**ben have to face the consequences of s.th.

aus'löschen *tr* (*Feuer*) extinguish; (*Licht*) put out; (*Schreiben*) erase

aus'losen *tr* draw lots for

aus'lösen *tr* loosen, release; (*Gefangen*) ransom; (*Pfand*) redeem

Aus'löser *m* (–s;–) release

aus'loten *tr* (naut & fig) plumb

aus'lüften *tr* air, ventilate

aus'machen *tr* (*Feuer*) put out; (*sichten*) make out; (*betragen*) amount to; (*Fleck*) remove; (*Licht*) turn out; (*bilden*) constitute; (*vereinbaren*) agree upon; **es macht nichts aus** it doesn't matter

aus'malen *tr* paint ‖ *ref*—*sich* [*dat*] **etw a.** picture s.th.

aus'marschieren *intr* (SEIN) march out

Aus'maß *n* measurement; dimensions; **in großem A.** on a large scale; (fig) to a great extent

ausmergeln ['aʊsmɛrgərln] *tr* exhaust

ausmerzen ['aʊsmɛrtsən] *tr* reject; (*ausrotten*) eradicate

aus'messen §70 *tr* measure; survey

aus'misten *tr* (*Stall*) clean; (fig) clean up

aus'mustern *tr* discard; (mil) discharge

Aus'nahme *f* (–;–n) exception

Aus'nahmezustand *m* state of emergency

aus'nahmslos *adj* & *adv* without exception

aus'nahmsweise *adv* by way of exception

aus'nehmen §116 *tr* take out; (*Fisch, Huhn*) clean; (*ausschließen*) exclude; (sl) clean out (of money) ‖ *ref*—**sich gut a.** look good

aus'nutzen, aus'nützen *tr* utilize; (*Gelegenheit*) take advantage of

aus'packen *tr* unpack; (*Geheimnis*) disclose ‖ *intr* (coll) unburden oneself, open up

aus'pfeifen §88 *tr* hiss (off the stage)

aus'plappern *tr* blurt out, blab out

aus'plaudern *tr* blab out

aus'plündern *tr* ransack; (coll) clean out (of money)

aus'polstern *tr* stuff, pad

aus'posaunen *tr* (coll) broadcast

aus'probieren *tr* try out, test

Aus'puff *m* (–[e]s;–e) exhaust

Aus'puffleitung *f* (aut) manifold

Aus'puffrohr *n* exhaust pipe

Aus'pufftopf *m* (aut) muffler

aus'pumpen *tr* pump out; **ausgepumpt** (coll) exhausted

aus'putzen *tr* (*reinigen*) clean out; (*schmücken*) adorn ‖ *ref* dress up

aus'quartieren *tr* put out (*of s.o.'s room*)

aus'radieren *tr* erase

aus'rangieren *tr* (coll) scrap

aus'rauben *tr* rob, ransack

aus'räumen *tr* (*Schrank*) clear out; (*Möbel*) remove; (med) clean out

aus'rechnen *tr* figure out

aus'recken *tr* stretch ‖ *ref*—*sich* [*dat*] **den Hals a.** crane one's neck

Aus'rede *f* evasion, excuse

aus'reden *tr*—**j–m etw a.** talk s.o. out

of s.th. || *ref* make excuses || *intr* finish speaking
aus′reiben §62 *tr* rub out; (mach) ream
aus′reichen *tr* suffice, be enough
aus′reichend *adj* sufficient
Aus′reise *f* departure; way out
aus′reißen §53 *tr* tear out || *ref—er reißt sich* [*dat*] **dabei kein Bein aus** he's not exactly killing himself || *intr* (SEIN) run away
Aus′reißer *m* runaway
aus′renken *tr* dislocate
aus′richten *tr* straighten; (*in e–e Linie bringen*) align; (*vollbringen*) accomplish; (*Botschaft, Gruß*) convey
aus′roden *tr* root out; (*Wald*) clear
aus′rollen *tr* roll out || *intr* (SEIN) (aer) taxi to a standstill
ausrotten [′ausrɔtən] *tr* root out; (*Volk, Tierrasse*) exterminate; (*Übel*) eradicate
aus′rücken *tr* (*Kupplung*) disengage || *intr* (SEIN) march off; run away
Aus′ruf *m* outcry; (*öffentlich*) proclamation; (gram) interjection
aus′rufen §122 *tr* call out; exclaim; **a. als** (or **zum**) proclaim
Aus′rufungszeichen *n* exclamation point
aus′ruhen *ref* & *intr* rest
aus′rupfen *tr* pluck
aus′rüsten *tr* equip, fit out; arm
aus′rutschen *intr* (SEIN) slip (out)
Aus′saat *f* sowing; (& fig) seed(s)
aus′säen *tr* sow; (fig) disseminate
Aus′sage *f* statement; (gram) predicate; (jur) affidavit
aus′sagen *tr* state || *intr* give evidence, make a statement
Aus′sagesatz *m* declarative sentence
Aus′sageweise *f* (gram) mood
Aus′satz *m* leprosy
Aussätzige [′auszetsɪgə] §5 *mf* leper
aus′saugen §125 *tr* suck dry; (fig) bleed white
Aus′sauger –in §6 *mf* (coll) bloodsucker
aus′schalten *tr* (*Licht, Radio, Fernseher*) turn off; (fig) shut out
Aus′schalter *m* circuit breaker
Aus′schank *m* sale of alcoholic drinks; (*Kneipe*) bar, taproom
aus′scharren *tr* dig up
Aus′schau *f—A.* **halten nach** be on the lookout for
aus′schauen *intr—a.* **nach** look out for; look like; **gut schaust du aus!** what a mess you are!
aus′scheiden §112 *tr* eliminate; (physiol) excrete, secrete || *intr* (SEIN) retire, resign; (sport) drop out; **das scheidet aus!** that's out!
Aus′scheidung *f* (–;–en) elimination; retirement; (physiol) excretion, secretion
Aus′scheidungskampf *m* elimination bout
aus′schelten §83 *tr* scold, berate
aus′schenken *tr* pour (*drinks*)
aus′scheren *intr* (aus) veer away (from)
aus′schiffen *tr* disembark; (*Ladung*) unload || *ref* disembark
aus′schimpfen *tr* scold, take to task

aus′schirren *tr* unharness
aus′schlachten *tr* cut up; (*Flugzeuge, usw.*) cannibalize; (*ausnutzen*) make the most of
aus′schlafen §131 *tr* sleep off || *ref* & *intr* get enough sleep
Aus′schlag *m* rash; (*e–s Zeigers*) deflection; **den A. geben** turn the scales
aus′schlagen §132 *tr* knock out; (*Feuer*) beat out; (*Metall*) hammer out; (*Innenraum*) line; (*Angebot*) refuse || *intr* bud; sprout; (*Pferd*) kick; (*Pendel*) swing; (*Zeiger*) move || *intr* (SEIN) turn out
aus′schlaggebend *adj* decisive
aus′schließen §76 *tr* lock out; (*von der Schule*) expel; (*ausscheiden*) exclude; (sport) disqualify
aus′schließlich *adj* exclusive, sole || *adv* exclusively, only || *prep* (*genit*) exclusive of
aus′schlürfen *tr* sip
aus′schmieren *tr* grease; (mit) smear (with); (fig) pull a fast one on; (mas) point
aus′schmücken *tr* adorn, decorate; (*Geschichte*) embellish
aus′schnaufen *intr* get one's wind
aus′schneiden §106 *tr* cut out; **tief ausgeschnitten** low-cut, low-necked
Aus′schnitt *m* cut; (*Zeitungs–*) clipping; (*Kleid–*) neckline; (*literarisch*) extract; (geom) sector
aus′schreiben §62 *tr* write out (in full); finish writing; (*ankündigen*) announce; (*Formular*) fill out; (*Rezept*) make out
aus′schreiten §86 *tr* pace off || *intr* (SEIN) walk briskly
Aus′schreitung *f* (–;–en) excess
Aus′schuß *m* waste, scrap; (*Komitee*) committee
Aus′schußware *f* (indust) reject
aus′schütten *tr* pour out, spill; (*Dividende*) pay || *ref—sich vor Lachen a.* split one's sides laughing
aus′schwärmen *intr* (SEIN) swarm out; (*Truppen*) deploy
aus′schwatzen *tr* blab out, blurt out
aus′schweifend *adj* (*Phantasie*) wild; (*liederlich*) wild, dissolute
Aus′schweifung *f* (–;–en) excess; curve; digression
aus′schwemmen *tr* rinse out; wash out
aus′schwenken *tr* rinse
aus′schwitzen *tr* sweat out; exude
aus′sehen §138 *intr* look; **nach j–m a.** look out for s.o.; **nach Regen a.** look like rain; **wie sieht er aus?** what does he look like? || **Aussehen** *n* (–s;) look(s); appearance(s)
außen [′ausən] *adv* outside; **nach a.** out(wards)
außen-, Außen- *comb.fm.* external; outer; exterior; outdoor; foreign
Au′ßenaufnahme *f* (phot) outdoor shot
Au′ßenbahn *f* (sport) outside lane
aus′senden §140 *tr* send out
Au′ßenfläche *f* outer surface
Au′ßenminister *m* Secretary of State; (Brit) Foreign Secretary
Au′ßenpolitik *f* foreign policy
Au′ßenseite *f* outside

Außenseiter ['aʊsənzaɪtər] *m* (-s;-) dark horse, long shot; (*Einzelgänger*) loner; (*Nichtfachmann*) layman
Außenstände ['aʊsənʃtendə] *pl* accounts receivable
Au'ßenstelle *f* branch office
außer ['aʊsər] *prep* (*genit*)—a. **Landes** abroad || *prep* (*dat*) outside, out of; except, but; besides, in addition to; a. **Hause** not at home; a. **sich sein** be beside oneself
au'ßeramtlich *adj* unofficial, private
außerdem ['aʊsərdem] *adv* also, besides; moreover, furthermore
au'ßerdienstlich *adj* unofficial, private; (mil) off duty
äußere ['ɔɪsərə] §9 *adj* outer, exterior, external || **Äußere** §5 *n* exterior
au'ßerehelich *adj* extra-marital; (*Kind*) illegitimate
au'ßergewöhnlich *adj* extraordinary
außerhalb ['aʊsərhalp] *prep* (*genit*) outside, out of
äußerlich ['ɔɪsərlɪç] *adj* external, outward; (*oberflächlich*) superficial
Äu'ßerlichkeit *f* superficiality; (*Formalität*) formality; **Äußerlichkeiten** externals; formalities
äußern ['ɔɪsərn] *tr* express || *ref* (über *acc*) express one's views (about); (in *dat*) be manifested (in)
au'ßerordentlich *adj* extraordinary; **außerordentlicher Professor** associate professor
äußerst ['ɔɪsərst] *adj* outermost; (fig) extreme, utmost || *adv* extremely, highly || **Äußerste** §5 *n* extremity, extreme(s); **aufs Ä.** to the utmost; **bis zum Äußersten** to extremes; to the bitter end
außerstande ['aʊsərʃandə] *adj* unable
Äu'ßerung *f* (-;-en) (*Ausdruck*) expression; (*Bemerkung*) remark
aus'setzen *tr* set out, put out; (*an der Küste*) maroon; (*Kind; dem Wetter*) expose; (*Boot*) lower; (*Wachen*) post; (*Belohnung*) hold out, promise; (*Tätigkeit*) discontinue; **auszusetzen haben** an (*dat*) find fault with || *intr* stop, halt
Aus'sicht *f* (auf *acc*) view (of); (fig) (auf *acc*) hope (of); **in A. nehmen** consider, plan
aus'sichtslos *adj* hopeless
Aus'sichtspunkt *m* vantage point
aus'sichtsreich *adj* promising
Aus'sichtsturm *m* lookout tower
aussichtsvoll *adj* promising
aus'sieben *tr* sift out; (fig) screen
aus'siedeln *tr* evacuate by force
Aus'siedlung *f* (-;-en) forced evacuation
aus'sinnen §121 *tr* think up, devise
aussöhnen ['aʊszønən] *tr* reconcile
aus'sondern *tr* (*trennen*) separate; (*auswählen*) single out; (*physiol*) excrete
aus'spähen *tr* spy out || *intr* (nach) keep a lookout (for), reconnoiter
aus'spannen *tr* stretch; extend; (*Zugtiere*) unhitch || *intr* relax
Aus'spannung *f* (-;) relaxation
aus'speien §135 *tr* spit out
aus'sperren *tr* lock out, shut out

aus'spielen *tr* (*Karten*) lead with; (*Preis*) play for || *intr* lead off
aus'spionieren *tr* spy out
Aus'sprache *f* pronunciation; (*Erörterung*) discussion, talk
aus'sprechen §64 *tr* pronounce; (*deutlich*) articulate; (*ausdrücken*) express || *ref* (über *acc*) speak one's mind (about); (für; gegen) declare oneself (for; against); **sich mit j-m über etw** a. talk s.th. over with s.o. || *intr* finish speaking
Aus'spruch *m* statement
aus'spülen *tr* rinse
aus'spüren *tr* trace (down)
aus'staffieren *tr* fit out, furnish
aus'stampfen *tr* stamp out
Aus'stand *m* walkout
aus'ständig *adj* on strike, striking; (fin) in arrears, outstanding
ausstatten ['aʊsʃtatən] *tr* furnish, equip; (*Tochter*) give a dowry to
Aus'stattung *f* (-;-en) furnishings; equipment; trousseau
aus'stechen §64 *tr* cut out; (*Auge*) poke out; (fig) outdo
aus'stehen §146 *tr* endure, stand || *intr* still be expected, be overdue
aus'steigen §148 *intr* (SEIN) get out, get off
aus'stellen *tr* exhibit; (*Wache*) post; (*Quittung, Scheck*) make out; (*Paß*) issue
Aus'stellung *f* (-;-en) exhibit; issuance; criticism
Aus'stelungsdatum *n* date of issue
aus'sterben §149 *intr* (SEIN) die out
Aus'steuer *f* hope chest, dowry
aus'stopfen *tr* stuff, pad
Aus'stoß *m* (indust) output
aus'stoßen §150 *tr* knock out; (*vertreiben*) eject; (*Seufzer, Schrei, Fluch*) utter; (*Torpedo*) launch; (math) eliminate; (phonet) elide; (phys) emit
Aus'stoßrohr *n* torpedo tube
Aus'stoßung *f* (-;-en) ejection; utterance; (gram) elision
Aus'stoßzahlen *pl* (indust) production figures
aus'strahlen *tr* & *intr* radiate
aus'strecken *tr* & *ref* stretch out
aus'streichen §85 *tr* cross out; (*glätten*) smooth out; (*Bratpfanne*) grease
aus'streuen *tr* strew, scatter, spread
aus'strömen *tr* & *intr* (SEIN) pour out
aus'studieren *tr* study thoroughly
aus'suchen *tr* pick out
Aus'tausch *m* exchange
aus'tauschbar *adj* exchangeable; interchangeable
aus'tauschen *tr* exchange; interchange
Aus'tauschstoff *m* substitute
Aus'tauschstück *n* spare part
aus'teilen *tr* distribute, deal out
Auster ['aʊstər] *f* (-;-n) oyster
aus'tilgen *tr* exterminate, wipe out
aus'toben *tr* give vent to || *ref* (*Person*) let one's hair down; (*Kinder*) raise a rumpus; (*Gewitter*) stop raging
aus'tollen *ref* make a racket
Austrag ['aʊstrak] *m* (-[e]s;)—**bis zum A. der Sache** until the matter is decided; **zum A. bringen** bring to a

head; (jur) settle; **zum A. kommen** come up for a decision

aus'tragen §132 *tr* carry out; (*Briefe*) deliver; (*Kleider*) wear out; (*Meisterschaft*) decide; (*Klatschereien*) spread; (acct) cancel

Aus'träger *m* deliveryman

Australien [aʊs'traljən] *n* (-s;) Australia

Australier –**in** [aʊs'traljər(ɪn)] §6 *mf* Australian

aus'treiben §62 *tr* drive out; exorcise

aus'treten §152 *tr* (*Feuer*) tread out; (*Schuhe, Treppen*) wear out || *intr* (SEIN) step out; (*Blut*) come out; (coll) go to the bathroom; **a. aus** leave (*school, a company, club*)

aus'trinken §143 *tr* drink up, drain

Aus'tritt *m* withdrawal

aus'trocknen *tr* & *intr* (SEIN) dry up

aus'tüfteln *tr* puzzle out

aus'üben *tr* (*Aufsicht, Macht*) exercise; (*Beruf*) practice; (*Pflicht*) carry out; (*Einfluß, Druck*) exert; (*Verbrechen*) commit; **ausübende Gewalt** executive power

Aus'verkauf *m* clearance sale

aus'verkaufen *tr* sell out; close out

aus'wachsen §155 *tr* outgrow

Aus'wahl *f* choice, selection

aus'wählen *tr* select, pick out

Aus'wanderer –**in** §6 *mf* emigrant

aus'wandern *intr* (SEIN) emigrate

auswärtig ['aʊsvertɪç] *adj* out-of-town; (*ausländisch*) foreign

auswärts ['aʊsverts] *adv* outward(s); out, away from home; (*außer der Stadt*) out of town; (*im Ausland*) abroad

Aus'wärtsspiel *n* away game

aus'wechselbar *adj* interchangeable

aus'wechseln *tr* exchange, interchange; (*ersetzen*) replace

Aus'weg *m* way out; escape

Ausweich– *comb.fm.* evasive; alternate; substitute; emergency; reserve

aus'weichen §85 *intr* (SEIN) (*dat*) make way (for), get out of the way (of); (*dat*) evade; **a. auf** (*acc*) switch to

aus'weichend *adj* evasive

Aus'weichklausel *f* escape clause

Aus'weichlager *n* emergency store

Aus'weichstelle *f* passing zone

Aus'weichstraße *f* bypass

Aus'weichziel *n* secondary target

aus'weinen *ref* have a good cry || *intr* stop crying

Ausweis ['aʊsvaɪs] *m* (-s;-e) identification (card); (com) statement

aus'weisen §118 *tr* expel; (*aus Besitz*) evict; (*verbannen*) banish, deport; (*zeigen*) show || *ref* prove one's identity

Aus'weispapiere *pl* identification papers

Aus'weisung *f* (-;-en) expulsion; eviction; deportation

aus'weiten *tr* & *ref* widen, expand

auswendig ['aʊsvendɪç] *adj* outer || *adv* outside; outwardly; by heart

aus'werfen §160 *tr* throw out; (*Graben*) dig; (*Summe*) allocate; (*Lava*) eject; (*Blut, Schleim*) spit up; (angl) cast

aus'werten *tr* evaluate; (*ausnützen*) utilize; (*Statistik*) interpret

aus'wickeln *tr* unwrap

aus'wiegen §57 *tr* weigh out

aus'wirken *tr* knead || *ref* take effect; **sich a. auf** (*acc*) affect; **sich** [*dat*] **etw bei j–m a.** obtain s.th. from s.o.

Aus'wirkung *f* (-;-en) effect

aus'wischen *tr* wipe out; wipe clean; **j–m eins a.** play a dirty joke on s.o.

aus'wittern *tr* season || *intr* weather

aus'wringen §142 *tr* wring out

Aus'wuchs *m* outgrowth; (pathol) tumor

Aus'wurf *m* throwing out; (fig) scum; (mach) ejection

aus'zacken *tr* indent; (*wellenförmig*) scallop

aus'zahlen *tr* pay out; pay off || *ref*— **es zahlt sich nicht aus** it doesn't pay

aus'zählen *tr* count out

aus'zanken *tr* scold

aus'zehren *tr* consume, waste

Aus'zehrung *f* (-;) consumption

aus'zeichnen *tr* mark, tag; (*ehren*) honor; (fig) distinguish

Aus'zeichnung *f* (-;-en) labeling; decoration, honor; distinction

aus'ziehen §163 *tr* pull out; (*Kleid*) take off; (*Stelle*) excerpt; (*Zeichnung*) ink in; (chem) extract || *ref* undress || *intr* (SEIN) set out; (*aus e–r Wohnung*) move out

aus'zischen *tr* hiss off the stage

Aus'zug *m* departure; moving; excerpt; (*Abriß*) summary; (Bib) Exodus; (chem) extract; (com) statement

aus'zugsweise *adv* in summary form

aus'zupfen *tr* pluck out

authentisch [aʊ'tentɪʃ] *adj* authentic

Auto ['aʊto] *n* (-s;-s) auto(mobile)

Au'tobahn *f* superhighway

Au'tobus *m* bus

Autodidakt [aʊtodɪ'dakt] *m* (-en;-en) self-educated person

Au'todroschke *f* taxi

Au'tofahrer –**in** §6 *mf* motorist

Au'tofahrschule *f* driving school

Au'tofahrt *f* car ride, drive

Au'tofalle *f* speed trap

Autogramm [aʊto'gram] *n* (-[e]s;-e) autograph

Autogramm'jäger –**in** §6 *mf* autograph hound

Au'tokino *n* drive-in movie

Au'tokolonne *f* motorcade

Autokrat [aʊto'krat] *m* (-en;-en) autocrat

autokratisch [aʊto'kratɪʃ] *adj* autocratic

Automat [aʊto'mat] *m* (-en;-en) vending machine; (*Musik–*) jukebox; (*Spiel–*) slot machine

Automa'tenrestaurant *n* automat

automatisch [aʊto'matɪʃ] *adj* automatic

Automobil [aʊtomo'bil] *n* (-[e]s;-e) automobile

autonom [aʊto'nom] *adj* autonomous

Autonomie [aʊtono'mi] *f* (-;) autonomy

Au·tor ['aʊtor] *m* (-s;-toren ['torən]) author

Autoreparatur'werkstatt ƒ auto repair shop, garage
Autorin [auˈtorɪn] ƒ (-;-nen) authoress
autorisieren [autɔrɪˈzirən] tr authorize
autoritär [autɔrɪˈter] adj authoritarian
Autorität [autɔrɪˈtet] ƒ (-;-en) authority
Au'toschlosser m automobile mechanic
Au'toschuppen m carport

Au'tounfall m automobile accident
avancieren [avãˈsirən] intr (SEIN) advance; (zu) be promoted (to)
avisieren [avɪˈzirən] tr advise, notify
Axt [akst] ƒ (-;ːe) ax
Azalee [atsaˈleːə] ƒ (-;-n) azalea
Azetat [atseˈtɑt] n (-[e]s;-e) acetate
Azeton [atseˈton] n (-s;) acetone
Azetylen [atsetyˈlen] n (-s;) acetylene
azurn [aˈtsurn] adj azure, sky-blue

B

B, b [be] invar n B, b; (mus) B flat
babbeln ['babəln] intr babble
Baby ['bebi] n (-s;-s) baby
Babysitter ['bebɪzɪtər] m (-s;-) babysitter
Bach [bax] m (-[e]s;ːe) brook, creek
Backe ['bakə] ƒ (-;-n) cheek; jaw (of a vise); (mach) die
backen ['bakən] §50 (& pret **backte**) tr bake; (in der Pfanne) fry || (pret **backte**; pp **gebacken**) intr bake || §109 intr (HABEN & SEIN) cake; stick
Backenbart (Bak'kenbart) m side whiskers
Backenstreich (Bak'kenstreich) m slap
Backenzahn (Bak'kenzahn) m molar; kleiner (or vorderer) B. bicuspid
Bäcker ['bɛkər] m (-s;-) baker
Bäckerei [bɛkəˈraɪ] ƒ (-;-en) bakery
Back'fett n shortening
Back'fisch m fried fish; (fig) teenager
Back'fischalter n teens (of girls)
Back'form ƒ cake pan
Back'hähnchen n fried chicken
Back'hendel n (Aust) fried chicken
Back'huhn n fried chicken
Back'obst n dried fruit
Back'ofen m baking oven
Back'pfeife ƒ slap in the face, smack
Back'pflaume ƒ prune
Back'pulver n baking powder
Back'stein m brick
Back'trog m kneading trough
Back'waren pl baked goods
Back'werk n pastries
Bad [bɑt] n (-[e]s;ːer) bath; bathroom; (Badeort) spa
Ba'deanstalt ƒ public baths; public pool
Ba'deanzug m swim suit
Ba'dehaube ƒ bathing cap
Ba'dehose ƒ bathing trunks
Ba'dekappe ƒ bathing cap
Ba'demantel m bathrobe
baden ['badən] tr & ref bathe || intr take a bath; **b. gehen** go swimming
Ba'deort m bathing resort; spa
Ba'destrand m bathing beach
Ba'detuch n bath towel
Ba'dewanne ƒ bathtub
Badende ['badəndə] §5 mƒ bather
Ba'dewärter –n §6 mƒ lifeguard; bathhouse attendant
Ba'dezimmer n bathroom
baff [baf] adj dumbfounded

Bagage [baˈgaʒə] ƒ (-;) (fig) rabble; (mil) baggage
Bagatelle [bagaˈtɛlə] ƒ (-;-n) trifle
Bagatel'lesache ƒ petty offense
bagatellisieren [bagatɛlɪˈzirən] tr minimize, make light of
Bagger ['bagər] m (-s;-) dredge
baggern ['bagərn] tr & intr dredge
bähen ['be·ən] intr bleat
Bahn [bɑn] ƒ (-;-en) way, path; (aer) runway; (astr) orbit; (aut) lane; (rr) railroad; (sport) course, track; (Eis-) (sport) rink; **auf die schiefe B. geraten** go astray; **B. brechen** (dat) pave the way (for); **mit der B. fahren** travel by train
bahn'brechend adj pioneering, epoch-making
Bahn'brecher –in §6 mƒ pioneer
Bahn'damm m railroad embankment
bahnen ['banən] tr—e–n Weg. b. clear a path, open up a path
Bahn'fahrt ƒ train trip
bahn'frei adj free on board, f.o.b.
Bahn'hof m railroad station
Bahn'hofshalle ƒ concourse
Bahn'hofsvorsteher m stationmaster
Bahn'linie ƒ railroad line
Bahn'schranke ƒ (rr) barrier
Bahn'steig m (rr) platform
Bahn'strecke ƒ (rr) line, track
Bahn'übergang m railroad crossing
Bahn'wärter m (rr) signalman
Bahre ['barə] ƒ (-;-n) stretcher; bier
Bahr'tuch n pall
Bai [baɪ] ƒ (-;-en) bay
Baiser [bɛˈze] m & n (-s;-s) meringue cookie
Baisse ['besə] ƒ (-;-n) (com) slump
Bais'sestimmung ƒ downward trend
Baissier [bɛsˈje] m (-s;-s) (st.exch.) bear
Bajonett [bajoˈnet] n (-s;-e) bayonet
Bake ['bakə] ƒ (-;-n) beacon
Bakterie [bakˈterjə] ƒ (-;-n) bacterium
Bakte'rienforscher –in §6 mƒ bacteriologist
Bakte'rienkunde ƒ bacteriology
Balance [baˈlãsə] ƒ (-;-n) balance
balancieren [balãˈsirən] tr & intr balance
bald [balt] adv (eher ['e·ər]; **eheste** ['e·əstə] §9 soon; (beinahe) nearly
baldig ['baldɪç] adj speedy; (Antwort) early

baldigst ['baldɪgst] *adv* very soon; at the earliest possible moment
Balg [balk] *m* (-[e]s;ːe) skin, pelt; (*Hülse*) shell, husk; **Bälge** bellows; **j-m den B. abziehen** fleece s.o. ‖ *m & n* (-[e]s;ːer) (coll) brat
balgen ['balgən] *ref* roll around, romp; (*raufen*) scuffle ‖ **Balgen** *m* (-s;-) (phot) bellows
Balgerei [balgə'raɪ] *f* (-;-en) scuffle
Balken ['balkən] *m* (-s;-) beam, rafter
Bal'kenwerk *n* framework
Balkon [bal'kon] *m* (-s;-e) balcony
Ball [bal] *m* (-[e]s;ːe) ball; (*Tanz*) ball
Ballade [ba'ladə] *f* (-;-n) ballad
Ballast ['balast] *m* (-[e]s;-e) ballast; (fig) drag; (coll) padding
ballen ['balən] *tr*—**die Faust b.** clench one's fist ‖ *ref* form a cluster ‖ **Ballen** *m* (-s;-) (anat) ball; (com) bale; (pathol) bunion
ballern ['balərn] *intr* (coll) bang away
Ballett [ba'let] *n* (-[e]s;-e) ballet
Ballistik [ba'lɪstɪk] *f* (-;) ballistics
Ballon [ba'lon] *m* (-s;-s) balloon
Ball'saal *m* ballroom
Ball'schläger *m* (sport) bat
Ball'spiel *n* ball game
Bal'lung *f* (-;-en) (mil) massing (of troops)
Balsam ['balzam] *m* (-s;-e) balm, balsam; (fig) balm
balsamieren [balza'mirən] *tr* embalm
balzen ['baltsən] *intr* perform a mating dance
Bambus ['bambus] *m* (-;- & -ses;-se) bamboo
Bam'busrohr *n* bamboo, bamboo cane
banal [ba'nal] *adj* banal
Banane [ba'nanə] *f* (-;-n) banana
Banause [ba'nauzə] *f* (-n;-n) philistine
banausisch [ba'nauzɪʃ] *adj* narrow-minded
Band [bant] *m* (-[e]s;ːe) volume; (*Einband*) binding ‖ *n* (-[e]s;-e) bond, tie; **Bande** chains, shackles ‖ *n* [-[e]s;ːer) (*e-s Hutes, usw.*) band; (*Bindfaden*) string; (*zum Schmuck*) ribbon; tape; (anat) ligament; (electron) recording tape; (rad) band; **am laufenden B.** continuously
Bandage [ban'daʒə] *f* (-;-n) bandage
bandagieren [banda'ʒirən] *tr* bandage
Bande ['bandə] *f* (-;-n) band, gang, crew; (billiards) cushion
Ban'denkrieg *m* guerilla war(fare)
Ban'denmitglied *n* gangster; (mil) guerilla
Ban'denunwesen *n* gangsterism; partisan activities
bändigen ['bendɪgən] *tr* tame; (fig) subdue, overcome, master
Bandit [ban'dit] *m* (-en;-en) bandit
Band'maß *n* tape measure
Band'säge *f* band saw
Band'scheibe *f* (anat) disk
Band'scheibenquetschung *f* slipped disk
Band'wurm *m* tapeworm
bang(e) [baŋ(ə)] *adj* scared, anxious; (*Gefühl*) disquieting; **j-m b. machen** scare s.o. ‖ **Bange** *f* (-;) fear

Bangigkeit ['baŋɪçkaɪt] *f* (-;) fear
Bank [baŋk] *f* (-;ːe) bench; pew; (geol) layer, bed ‖ *f* (-;-en) bank
Bank'anweisung *f* check
Bank'ausweis *m* bank statement
Bank'einlage *f* bank deposit
Bankett [baŋ'ket] *n* (-s;-e) banquet
bank'fähig *adj* negotiable
Bank'guthaben *n* bank balance
Bank'halter **-in** §6 *mf* banker (*in games*)
Bankier [baŋk'je] *m* (-s;-s) banker
Bank'konto *n* bank account
bank'mäßig *adj* by check
bankrott [baŋk'rɔt] *adj* bankrupt ‖ *m* (-[e]s;-e) bankruptcy
Bank'verkehr *m* banking (*activity*)
Bank'wesen *n* banking
Bann [ban] *m* (-[e]s;-e) ban; (Zauber) spell; (eccl) excommunication
bannen ['banən] *tr* banish; (*Geister*) exorcize; (eccl) excommunicate
Banner ['banər] *n* (-s;-) banner; standard
Ban'nerträger *m* standard-bearer
Bann'fluch *m* anathema
Bann'kreis *m* spell; **in j-s B. geraten** come under s.o.'s spell
Bann'meile *f* (fig) city limits
Bann'ware *f* contraband
bar [bar] *adj* bare; (*rein*) pure, sheer; (fin) cash ‖ *adv* cash ‖ *prep* (*genit*) devoid of, lacking ‖ **Bar** *f* (-;-s) bar, taproom
Bär [ber] *m* (-en;-en) bear; (astr) Dipper; **j-m e-n B. aufbinden** tell s.o. a fish story
Bar- *comb.fm.* cash
Baracke [ba'rakə] *f* (-;-n) barrack; (wooden) hut
Barbar -in [bar'bar(ɪn)] §7 *mf* barbarian
Barbarei [barba'raɪ] *f* (-;-en) barbarism; (*Grausamkeit*) barbarity
barbarisch [bar'barɪʃ] *adj* barbarous; barbaric, primitive
bärbeißig ['berbaɪsɪç] *adj* surly
Bar'bestand *m* cash on hand
Bar'betrag *m* amount in cash
Barbier [bar'bir] *m* (-s;-e) barber
barbieren [bar'biran] *tr* shave; (fig) fleece
Barett [ba'ret] *n* (-[e]s;-e) beret
barfuß ['barfus] *adv* barefoot
barfüßig ['barfysɪç] *adj* barefooted
barg [bark] *pret* of **bergen**
Bar'geld *n* cash
barhäuptig ['barhɔɪptɪç] *adj* bareheaded
Bar'hocker *m* bar stool
Bariton ['barɪtɔn] *m* (-s;-e) baritone
Barkasse [bar'kasə] *f* (-;-n) launch
Bärme ['bermə] *f* (-;) yeast, leaven
barmherzig [barm'hertsɪç] *adj* merciful
Bar'mittel *pl* cash
barock [ba'rɔk] *adj* baroque ‖ **Barock** *m & n* (-s;) baroque; baroque period
Barometer [barɔ'metər] *n* (-s;-) barometer
Baron [ba'ron] *m* (-s;-e) baron
Baronin [ba'ronɪn] *f* (-;-nen) baroness

Barre ['barə] *f* (-;-n) bar
Barren ['barən] *m* (-s;-) bar; ingot; (gym) parallel bars
Barriere [bar'jerə] *f* (-;-n) barrier
barsch [barʃ] *adj* gruff, rude ‖ **Barsch** *m* (-es;-e) (ichth) perch
Barschaft ['barʃaft] *f* (-;) cash
barst [barst] *pret* of **bersten**
Bart [bart] *m* (-[e]s;⸚) beard; (*e-r Katze*) whiskers; (*e-s Fisches*) barb; **der B. ist ab!** the jig is up!; **sich** [*dat*] **e-n B. wachsen lassen** grow a beard
bärtig ['bertɪç] *adj* bearded
bart'los *adj* beardless
Bar'verlust *m* straight loss
Basalt [ba'zalt] *m* (-[e]s;-e) basalt
Basar [ba'zar] *m* (-s;-e) bazaar
Ba·sis ['bazɪs] *f* (-;-sen [zən]) basis; (archit, math, mil) base
Baß [bas] *m* (Basses;Bässe) (mus) bass
Baß'geige *f* bass viol, contrabass
Bassin [ba'sɛ̃] *n* (-s;-s) reservoir; swimming pool; (naut) dock, basin
Baß'schlüssel *m* bass clef
Baß'stimme *f* bass (voice), basso
basta ['basta] *interj*—**und damit b.!** and that's that!
Bastard ['bastart] *m* (-[e]s;-e) bastard; (bot) hybrid
Bastei [bas'taɪ] *f* (-;-en) bastion
basteln ['bastəln] *intr* tinker
Bast'ler **-in** §6 *mf* hobbyist
bat [bat] *pret* of **bitten**
Bataillon [batal'jon] *n* (-s;-e) battalion
Batte·rie [batə'ri] *f* (-;-rien ['ri·ən] battery
Bau [bau] *m* (-[e]s;) erection, construction, building; (*Bauart*) structure, design; (*Körper-*) build; **er ist beim Bau** he is in the building trade; **er ist vom Bau** (coll) he's in the racket; **im Bau** under construction ‖ *m* (-[e]s;-ten) building; **auf dem Bau** at the construction site ‖ *m* (-[e]s;-e) burrow, hole; (min) mine **–bau** *m comb.fm.* –construction, –building; –culture; –mining
Bau'abnahme *f* building inspection
Bau'arbeiter *m* construction worker
Bau'art *f* build; structure; type, model
Bauch [baux] *m* (-[e]s;⸚e) belly, stomach; (*Leib*) bowels; (coll) potbelly
Bauch– *comb.fm.* abdominal
bauchig ['bauxɪç] *adj* bulging; convex
Bauch'klatscher *m* belly flop
Bauch'laden *m* vendor's tray
Bauch'landung *f* belly-landing
Bauch'redner **-in** §6 *mf* ventriloquist
Bauch'speicheldrüse *f* pancreas
Bauch'weh *n* stomach ache, bellyache
bauen ['bau·ən] *tr* build; erect; make, manufacture; (*ackern*) till; (*anbauen*) grow ‖ *intr* build; (**an** *dat*) work (at); (**auf** *acc*) depend (on), trust
Bauer ['bau·ər] *m* (-s & -n;-n) farmer; (cards) jack; (chess) pawn ‖ *m* (-s;-) builder ‖ *m & n* (-s;-) birdcage
Bäuerchen ['bɔɪ·ərçən] *n* (-s;-) small farmer; (baby's) burp

Bäuerin ['bɔɪ·ərɪn] *f* (-;-nen) farmer's wife
bäuerisch ['bɔɪ·ərɪʃ] *adj* boorish
Bau'erlaubnis *f* building permit
bäuerlich ['bɔɪ·ərlɪç] *adj* rural
Bau'ernbursche *m* country lad
Bau'erndirne *f* country girl
Bauernfänger ['bau·ərnfɛŋər] *m* (-s;-) confidence man
Bau'erngut *n*, **Bau'ernhof** *m* farm
Bau'fach *n* architecture
bau'fällig *adj* dilapidated
Bau'genehmigung *f* building permit
Bau'gerüst *n* scaffold(ing)
Bau'gewerbe *n* building trade
Bau'gewerkschule *f* school of architecture and civil engineering
Bau'grundstück *n* building site
Bau'holz *n* lumber
Bau'kasten *m* building set
Bau'kunst *f* architecture
bau'lich *adj* architectural; structural; **in gutem baulichen Zustand** in good repair
Baum [baum] *m* (-[e]s;⸚e) tree; (mach) shaft, axle; (naut) boom
Bau'meister *m* building contractor, builder; architect
baumeln ['baumaln] *intr* dangle
bäumen ['bɔɪmən] *ref* rear
Baum'garten *m* orchard
Baum'grenze *f* timber line
Baum'krone *f* treetop
Baum'schere *f* pruning shears
Baum'schule *f* nursery (*of saplings*)
Baum'stamm *m* tree trunk
baum'stark' *adj* strong as an ox
Bau'muster *n* model (number)
Baum'wolle *f* cotton
Baum'wollkapsel *f* cotton boll
Baum'wollsamt *m* velveteen
Bau'plan *m* ground plan
Bau'platz *m* building lot
Bau'rat *m* (-[e]s;⸚e) building inspector
Bausch [bauʃ] *m* (-[e]s;⸚e) pad, wad; (*e-s Segels*) bulge, belly; **in B. und Bogen** wholesale
bauschen ['bauʃən] *tr, ref & intr* bulge, swell
bauschig ['bauʃɪç] *adj* puffy; baggy
Bau'schule *f* school of architecture and civil engineering
Bau'sparkasse *f* building and loan association
Bau'stahl *m* structural steel
Bau'stein *m* building stone; brick
Bau'stelle *f* building site; road construction
Bau'stoff *m* building material
Bau'techniker *m* construction engineer
Bau'unternehmer *m* contractor
Bau'unternehmung *f* building firm, building contractors
Bau'werk *n* building, edifice
Bau'wesen *n* building industry
Bau'zaun *m* hoarding
Bau'zeichnung *f* blueprint
Bayer **-in** ['baɪ·ər(ɪn)] §6 *mf* Bavarian
bayerisch ['baɪ·ərɪʃ] *adj* Bavarian
Bayern ['baɪ·ərn] *n* (-s;) Bavaria
Bazillenträger [ba'tsɪləntregər] *m* germ carrier

Bazil·lus [ba'tsɪlʊs] *m* (-;-len [lən]) bacillus

be- [bə] *insep pref*

beabsichtigen [bə'apzɪçtɪgən] *tr* intend; (mit) mean (by)

beach'ten *tr* pay attention to; (*merken*) note, notice; (*befolgen*) observe; (*berücksichtigen*) consider

beach'tenswert *adj* noteworthy

Beach'tung *f* (-;) attention; notice; observance; consideration

Beamte [bə'amtə] *m* (-n;-n) official

Beam'tenherrschaft *f* bureaucracy

Beam'tenlaufbahn *f* civil service career

Beamtentum [bə'amtəntum] *n* (-[e]s;) officialdom, bureaucracy

Beamtin [bə'amtɪn] *f* (-;-nen) official

beäng'stigen *tr* make anxious, alarm

beanspruchen [bə'an/prʊxən] *tr* claim; (*Zeit, Raum*) require; **zu stark beansprucht werden** be worked too hard

beanstanden [bə'an/tandən] *tr* object to, find fault with; (*Waren*) reject; (*Wahl*) contest; (*Recht*) challenge

Bean'standung *f* (-;-en) objection; complaint

bean'tragen *tr* propose; (**bei**) apply for (to)

beant'worten *tr* answer

Beant'wortung *f* (-;-en) answer

bear'beiten *tr* work; (*Land*) cultivate; (*Buch, Text*) revise; (*Wörterbuch*) compile; (*für die Bühne*) adapt; (*ein Manuskript*) prepare; (*Thema; Kunden*) work on; (*Person*) try to influence; (chem) treat; (*Auftrag*) (com) handle; (*Fall*) (jur) handle; (metal) machine, tool; (mus) arrange

bearg'wöhnen *tr* be suspicious of

beaufsichtigen [bə'aʊfzɪçtɪgən] *tr* supervise; (*Arbeiten*) superintend; (*Kinder*) look after; (educ) proctor; **streng b.** keep a sharp eye on

beauf'tragen *tr* commission, appoint; (mit) entrust (with)

Beauftragte [bə'aʊftraktə] §5 *mf* representative; (com) agent

bebau'en *tr* cultivate; (*Gelände*) build up

beben ['bebən] *intr* (**vor**) tremble (with), shake (with); (*Erde*) quake

bebrillt [bə'brɪlt] *adj* bespectacled

Becher ['beçər] *m* (-s;-) cup, mug

bechern ['beçərn] *intr* (coll) booze

Becken ['bɛkən] *n* (-s;-) basin, bowl; (anat) pelvis; (mus) cymbal

bedacht [bə'daxt] *adj* (**auf** *acc*) intent (on); **auf alles b.** sein think of everything; **darauf b.** sein **zu** (*inf*) be anxious to (*inf*) || **Bedacht** *m*—**B. nehmen auf** (*acc*) take into consideration; **mit B.** deliberately; with caution

bedächtig [bə'dɛçtɪç], **bedachtsam** [bə'daxtzam] *adj* cautious, deliberate

bedan'ken *ref*—**ich würde mich bestens b., wenn** (iron) I would be most indignant if; **sich b. bei j—m für** thank s.o. for

Bedarf [bə'darf] *m* (-[e]s;) demand; requirement; (**an** *dat*) need (of); **bei B.** if required; **den B. decken** meet the demand; **nach B.** as required;

seinen B. decken an (*dat*) get one's supply of

Bedarfs'artikel *pl* needs, supplies

Bedarfs'fall *m*—**im B.** in case of need

Bedarfs'güter *pl* consumer goods

Bedarfs'haltestelle *f* optional bus or trolley stop

Bedarfs'träger *m* consumer

bedauerlich [bə'daʊ·ərlɪç] *adj* regrettable

bedau'erlicherweise *adv* unfortunately

bedauern [bə'daʊ·ərn] *tr* pity, feel sorry for; regret, deplore || **Bedauern** *n* (-s;) (**über** *acc*) regret (over); (*Mitleid*) (mit) pity (for)

bedau'ernswert *adj* pitiful, pitiable

bedecken (bedek'ken) *tr* cover; **bedeckt** overcast

Bedeckung (Bedek'kung) *f* (-;-en) cover; escort; (mil) escort; (nav) convoy

beden'ken §66 *tr* consider; (*beachten*) bear in mind; (*im Testament*) provide for || *ref* deliberate, think a matter over; **sich e-s anderen b.** change one's mind || **Bedenken** *n* (-s;-) (*Erwägung*) consideration, reflection; (*Einwand*) objection; (*Zweifel*) doubt, scruple

bedenk'lich *adj* (*ernst*) serious, critical; (*gefährlich*) risky; (*heikel*) ticklish; (*Charakter*) questionable

bedeu'ten *tr* mean; **das hat nichts zu b.** that doesn't matter; **j—m b., daß** make it clear to s.o. that

bedeu'tend *adj* important; (*beträchtlich*) considerable

bedeutsam [bə'dɔɪtzam] *adj* significant; (*Blick*) meaningful

Bedeu'tung *f* (-;-en) meaning; (*Wichtigkeit*) importance

bedeu'tungsvoll *adj* significant

bedie'nen *tr* wait on, serve; (*Maschine*) operate || *ref* (*genit*) make use of; **bedienen Sie sich** help yourself || *intr* wait on people; (cards) follow suit

Bedie'nung *f* (-;) service; servants; waitresses

Bedienungs- *comb.fm.* control

Bedie'nungsanweisung *f* instructions

Bedie'nungsmannshaft *f* gun crew

bedingen [bə'dɪŋən] *tr* condition, stipulate; (*in sich schließen*) imply; **bedingt** conditioned, conditional

bedin'gungsweise *adv* conditionally

bedrän'gen *tr* press hard; (*beunruhigen*) pester; **bedrängte Lage** state of distress; **bedrängte Verhältnisse** financial difficulties

Bedrängnis [bə'drɛnnɪs] *f* (-;-se) distress; **in ärgster B.** in dire straits

bedro'hen *tr* threaten, menace

bedroh'lich *adj* threatening

bedrucken (bedruk'ken) *tr* print on; (*Stoff*) print

bedrücken (bedrük'ken) *tr* oppress

bedür'fen §69 *intr* (*genit*) require

Bedürfnis [bə'dʏrfnɪs] *n* (-ses;-se) need, requirement; (*Wunsch*) desire; **Bedürfnisse** necessities; **das dringende B. haben zu** (*inf*) have the urge to (*inf*)

Bedürf'nisanstalt *f* comfort station
bedürf'nislos *adj* having few needs
bedürftig [bə'dyrftıç] *adj* needy; **b.
sein** (*genit*) be in need of
Beefsteak ['bifstek] *n* (-s;-s) steak;
Deutsches B. hamburger
beehren [bə'erən] *tr* honor ‖ *ref—*
sich b. zu (*inf*) have the honor of
(*ger*)
beei'len *ref* hurry (up)
beein'drucken *tr* impress
beeinflussen [bə'aınflusən] *tr* influence
Beein'flussung *f* (-;) (*genit*) influence
(on), effect (on); (pol) lobbying
beeinträchtigen [bə'aıntrɛçtıgən] *tr*
(*Ruf*) damage; (*Wert*) detract from;
(*Rechte*) encroach upon; (*Aussichten*) hurt, spoil
been'den, been'digen *tr* end, conclude;
(*Arbeit*) complete
beengen [bə'ɛŋən] *tr* confine, cramp;
sich beengt fühlen feel cramped;
(fig) feel restricted
beer'ben *tr—j—n b.* inherit s.o.'s estate
beerdigen [bə'erdıgən] *tr* bury, inter
Beer'digung *f* (-;-en) burial
Beere ['berə] *f* (-;-n) berry
Beet [bet] *n* (-[e]s;-e) (agr) bed
befähigen [bə'fe·ıgən] *tr* enable,
qualify
befähigt [bə'fe·ıçt] *adj* able, capable
Befä'higung *f* (-;-en) qualification;
(*Fähigkeit*) ability
befahl [bə'fal] *pret* of **befehlen**
befahrbar [bə'farbar] *adj* (*Weg*) passable; (*Wasser*) navigable
befah'ren §71 *tr* travel; (*Meer*) sail;
(*Fluß*) navigate; (*Küste*) sail along;
(*Schacht*) go down into
befal'len §72 *tr* strike, attack; infest
befan'gen *adj* embarrassed; (*schüchtern*) shy; (*voreingenommen*) prejudiced; (*parteiisch*) partial
befas'sen *tr* touch, handle ‖ *ref—sich
b.* **mit** concern oneself with
befehden [bəfedən] *tr* make war on
Befehl [bə'fel] *m* (-s;-e) order, command; **auf B.** (*genit*) by order of
befeh'len §51 *tr* order, command; **was
b. Sie?** what is your pleasure?
befehligen [bə'felıgən] *tr* command,
be in command of
Befehls'form *f* imperative mood
Befehlshaber [bə'felshabər] *m* (-s;-)
(mil) commanding officer; (nav)
commander in chief; **oberster B.**
supreme commander
befehlshaberisch [bə'felshabərıʃ] *adj*
imperious
Befehls'stelle *f* command post
befe'stigen *tr* (**an** *dat*) fasten (to), attach (to); (mil) fortify
Befe'stigung *f* (-;-en) fortification
befeuchten [bə'fɔıçtən] *tr* moisten, wet
befeu'ern *tr* (aer, naut) mark with
lights; (mil) fire on, shoot at
befin'den §59 *tr* deem ‖ *ref* be, feel ‖
Befinden *n* (-s;) judgment, view;
(state of) health; **je nach B.** according to taste
befindlich [bə'fıntlıç] *adj* present, to

be found; **all die im Hafen befind-
lichen Schiffe** the ships (present) in
the harbor; **b. sein** happen to be
beflecken (beflek'ken) *tr* stain, taint
beflissen [bə'flısən] *adj* (*genit*) keen
(on), interested (in) ‖ **Beflissene** §5
mf (*genit*) student (of)
befohlen [bə'folən] *pp* of **befehlen**
befol'gen *tr* obey, comply with
Befol'gung *f* (-;) observance
beför'dern *tr* ship; (*spedieren*) forward; (*im Rang*) promote; (*fördern*)
further
Beför'derungsmittel *n* means of transportation
befra'gen *tr* question, interrogate;
poll; (*um Rat*) consult
befrakt [bə'frakt] *adj* in tails
befrei'en *tr* free; liberate; (*vom Militärdienst*) exempt; (*von e-r Aufgabe*)
excuse; (*von Sorgen, e-r Last*) relieve
Befrei'ung *f* (-;-en) freeing; liberation;
exemption; rescue
befremden [bə'frɛmdən] *tr* surprise,
astonish; strike as odd ‖ **Befremden**
n (-s;) surprise, astonishment
befreunden [bə'frɔındən] *ref—sich
mit etw b.** reconcile oneself to s.th.;
sich mit j—m b. make friends with
s.o.
befrieden [bə'fridən] *tr* pacify
befriedigen [bə'fridıgən] *tr* satisfy
befrie'digend *adj* satisfactory
befristen [bə'frıstən] *tr* set a time
limit on
Befri'stung *f* (-;-en) time limit
befruchten [bə'fruxtən] *tr* (*Land*)
make fertile; (*schwängern*) impregnate; (*Ei*) fertilize; **künstlich b.** in-
seminate; (bot) pollinate
befugt [bə'fukt] *adj* authorized
befüh'len *tr* feel, touch
Befund' *m* (-[e]s;-e) findings, facts
befürch'ten *tr* fear, be afraid of
Befürch'tung *f* (-;-en) apprehension
befürworten [bə'fyrvortən] *tr* support;
(*anraten*) recommend
begabt [bə'gapt] *adj* gifted, talented
Bega'bung *f* (-;-en) aptitude; (natural)
gift, talent
Bega'bungsprüfung *f* intelligence test
begann [bə'gan] *pret* of **beginnen**
begatten [bə'gatən] *tr* mate with ‖
ref copulate, mate
bege'ben §80 *tr* (*Anleihen*) float, place;
(*Wertpapiere*) sell ‖ *ref* go; occur;
es begab sich (Bib) it came to pass;
sich an die Arbeit b. set to work;
sich auf die Flucht b. take to flight;
sich auf die Reise b. set out on a
trip; **sich b.** (*genit*) renounce; **sich
in Gefahr b.** expose oneself to danger
Bege'benheit *f* (-;-en) event, incident
begegnen [bə'gɛgnən] *intr* (SEIN) (*dat*)
meet, come upon; (*Schwierigkeiten,
Feind*) encounter; (*Gefahr*) face
bege'hen §82 *tr* walk on; walk along;
(*Verbrechen, Irrtum*) commit; (*Fest*)
celebrate
Begehr [bə'ger] *m & n* (-s;) desire; request; (econ) demand
begehren [bə'gerən] *tr* wish for; crave;

(Bib) covet; **etw von j-m b.** ask s.o.
for s.th. || *intr* (**nach**) yearn (for)
begeh′renswert *adj* desirable
begehr′lich *adj* covetous
begehrt [bə'gert] *adj* in demand
begeistert [bə'gaɪstərt] *adj* enthusiastic
Begei′sterung *f* (-;) enthusiasm
Begier [bə'gir] *f* (-;) var of **Begierde**
Begierde [bə'girdə] *f* (-;-n) desire;
(fleshly) appetite; eagerness; craving
begierig [bə'giriç] *adj* eager; (*Augen*)
hungry; (**nach, auf** *acc*) desirous
(of); **b. zu** (*inf*) eager to (*inf*)
begie′ßen §76 *tr* water; (culin) baste;
das wollen wir b. we want to celebrate it (*by drinking*)
Beginn [bə'gɪn] *m* (-[e]s;) beginning; (*Ursprung*) origin
beginnen [bə'gɪnən] §52 *tr* & *intr*
begin
beglaubigen [bə'glaubɪgən] *tr* certify,
authenticate; (*Gesandten*) accredit
Beglau′bigung *f* (-;) authentication;
accreditation
Beglau′bigungsschreiben *n* (dipl) credentials
beglei′chen §85 *tr* balance; (*Rechnung*)
pay in full; (*Streit*) settle
begleiten [bə'glaɪtən] *tr* accompany;
escort; see (*e.g., off, home*); **hinaus
b.** see to the door
Beglei′ter –in §6 *mf* companion
Begleit′erscheinung *f* concomitant
Begleit′musik *f* background music
Begleit′schreiben *s* covering letter
Beglei′tung *f* (-;-en) company; escort;
(*Gefolge*) retinue; (mus) accompaniment
beglück′wünschen *tr* (**zu**) congratulate
(on)
Beglück′wünschung *f* (-;-en) congratulation
begnadet [bə'gnɑdət] *adj* highly gifted
begnadigen [bə'gnɑdɪgən] *tr* pardon;
(pol) grant amnesty to
Begna′digung *f* (-;-en) pardon; amnesty
begnügen [bə'gnygən] *ref* (**mit**) content oneself (with), be satisfied (with)
begonnen [bə'gɔnən] *pp* of **beginnen**
begra′ben §87 *tr* bury
Begräbnis [bə'grepnis] *n* (-ses;-se)
burial; funeral
Begräb′nisfeier *f* funeral
Begräb′nisstätte *f* burial place
begradigen [bə'grɑdɪgən] *tr* straighten;
(tech) align
begrei′fen §88 *tr* touch, handle; (*verstehen*) grasp; (*enthalten*) comprise
begreif′lich *adj* understandable
begreif′licherweise *adv* understandably
begren′zen *tr* bound; limit, restrict
Begren′zung *f* (-;-en) limitation
Begriff [bə'grɪf] *m* (-[e]s;-e) idea,
notion; (*Ausdruck*) term; (philos)
concept; **im B. sein zu** (*inf*) be on
the point of (*ger*)
begriffen [bə'grɪfən] *adj*—**b. sein in**
(*dat*) be in the process of
begrün′den *tr* found, establish; (*Behauptung*) substantiate, prove
Begrün′der –in §6 *mf* founder

Begrün′dung *f* (-;-en) establishment;
proof; (*Grund*) ground, reason
begrüßen *tr* greet; welcome
begünstigen [bə'gynstɪgən] *tr* favor;
(*fördern*) promote, support; (jur)
aid and abet
Begün′stiger *m* (-s;-) accessory after
the fact
Begünstigte [bə'gynstɪçtə] §5 *mf* (ins)
beneficiary
Begün′stigung *f* (-;-en) promotion,
encouragement; support, backing;
(jur) aiding and abetting
begut′achten *tr* give an expert opinion
on; **b. lassen** obtain expert opinion on
begütert [bə'gytərt] *adj* well-to-do
begütigen [bə'gytɪgən] *tr* appease
behaart [bə'hɑrt] *adj* hairy
behäbig [bə'hebɪç] *adj* comfort-loving;
(*beleibt*) portly
behaftet [bə'haftət] *adj* afflicted
behagen [bə'hɑgən] *intr* (*dat*) please,
suit || **Behagen** *n* (-s;) pleasure
behaglich [bə'hɑklɪç] *adj* pleasant;
(*traulich*) snug, cozy
behal′ten §90 *tr* keep, retain; **Recht b.**
turn out to be right
Behälter [bə'heltər] *m* (-s;-) container;
box; (*für Öl, usw.*) tank
behan′deln *tr* treat; deal with; handle
behän′gen §92 *tr* hang; deck out
beharren [bə'harən] *intr* remain (unchanged); (**in** *dat*) persevere (in);
(**auf** *dat*) persist (in), stick (to)
beharrlich [bə'harlɪç] *adj* steadfast
behau′en §93 *tr* hew
behaupten [bə'hauptən] *tr* declare, assert; (*festhalten*) maintain, retain;
allege || *ref* stand one's ground;
(*Preise*) remain steady
behausen [bə'hauzən] *tr* lodge, house
Behau′sung *f* (-;-en) dwelling
behe′ben §94 *tr* (*Schwierigkeiten*) remove; (*Zweifel*) dispel; (*Schaden*)
repair; (*Lage*) remedy; (*Geld*) withdraw; (*Schmerzen*) eliminate
beheimatet [bə'haɪmatət] *adj*—**b. sein
in** (*dat*) reside in; come from
Behelf [bə'helf] *m* (-[e]s;-e) expedient; makeshift
behel′fen §96 *ref* (**mit**) make do (with)
Behelfs– *comb.fm.* temporary
behelfs′mäßig *adj* temporary, makeshift
behelligen [bə'helɪgən] *tr* bother
Behel′ligung *f* (-;-en) bother, trouble
behende [bə'hendə] *adj* agile, quick;
(*gewandt*) handy; (*geistig*) smart
beherbergen [bə'herbergən] *tr* take in,
put up (*as guest*)
beherr′schen *tr* (*Land*) rule; (*Sprache*)
master; (*Gefühle*) control; (*überragen*) tower over; **den Luftraum b.**
(mil) have air supremacy
Beherr′scher –in §6 *mf* ruler || *m*
master || *f* mistress
beherzigen [bə'hertsɪgən] *tr* take to
heart, remember
beherzt [bə'hertst] *adj* courageous
behe′xen *tr* bewitch; (fig) captivate
behilflich [bə'hɪlflɪç] *adj* helpful
behin′dern *tr* hinder; hamper; block
behor′chen *tr* overhear

Behörde [bə'hørdə] *f* (-;-n) authority, board; *die Behörden* the authorities
behördlich [bə'hørtlıç] *adj* official
behü'ten *tr* (**vor** *dat*) protect (against); **Gott behüte!** God forbid!
behutsam [bə'hutzɑm] *adj* wary
bei [baɪ] *prep* (*dat*) (*Ort*) by, beside, at, with, in; (*in Anschriften*) in care of, c/o; (*Zeit, Umstände*) at, by, during, on; (*Zustände, Eigenschaften*) at, while, in; **bei mir haben** have on me; **bei meiner Ehre** upon my honor; **bei Schiller** in the works of Schiller; **bei uns** at our house; **bei weitem** by far
bei'behalten §90 *tr* retain, keep
Bei'blatt *n* supplement
bei'bringen §65 *tr* obtain, procure; (*Beweise, Zeugen*) produce; (*Arznei, Gift*) administer; (*Wunde, Niederlage, Schlag, Verluste*) inflict; **j-m die Nachricht schonend b.** break the news gently to s.o.; **j-m etw b.** teach s.o. s.th., make s.th. clear to s.o.
Beichte ['baɪçtə] *f* (-;-n) confession
beichten ['baɪçtən] *tr* (eccl) confess
Beicht'kind *n* (eccl) penitent
Beicht'stuhl *m* (eccl) confessional
beide ['baɪdə] *adj* both; two ‖ *pron* both; two; **keiner von beiden** neither of them
beiderlei ['baɪdər'laɪ] *invar adj* both kinds of
beiderseitig ['baɪdər'zaɪtıç] *adj* bilateral; (*gemeinsam*) mutual
beiderseits ['baɪdər'zaɪts] *adv* on both sides; mutually, reciprocally ‖ *prep* (*genit*) on both sides of
beieinan'der *adv* together; **gut b. sein** (coll) be in good shape
Bei'fahrer –**in** §6 *mf* relief driver; passenger (*next to the driver*)
Bei'fall *m* approval; applause
bei'fällig *adj* approving; (*Bericht*) favorable ‖ *adv* approvingly
Bei'fallklatschen *n* clapping, applause
Bei'fallsgeschrei *n* loud cheering
Bei'fallsruf *m* cheer
Bei'film *m* (cin) second feature
bei'folgend *adj* enclosed
bei'fügen *tr* add; (*e-m Brief*) enclose
bei'fügend *adj* (gram) attributive
Bei'fügung *f* (-;-en) addition; enclosure; (gram) attributive
Bei'gabe *f* extra; funerary gift
bei'geben §80 *tr* add; assign ‖ *intr* give in; **klein b.** knuckle under
Bei'geschmack *m* taste, flavor; tinge
Bei'hilfe *f* aid; (*Stipendium*) grant; (*Unterstützung*) subsidy; allowance; (jur) aiding and abetting
bei'kommen § 99 *intr* (SEIN) (*dat*) get the better of; (*dat*) reach; (*e-r Schwierigkeit*) overcome
Beil [baɪl] *n* (-[e]s;-e) hatchet
Bei'lage *f* (*im Brief*) enclosure; (*e-r Zeitung*) supplement; **Fleisch mit B.** meat and vegetables
beiläufig ['baɪlɔɪfıç] *adj* incidental; casual ‖ *adv* by the way, incidentally; **b.** erwähnen mention in passing
bei'legen *tr* add; (*Titel*) confer; (*Wichtigkeit*) attach; (*Streit*) settle; **etw**

e-m Brief b. enclose s.th. in a letter ‖ *intr* heave to
Bei'leid *n* (-s;) condolence(s)
bei'liegen §108 *intr*—**e-m Brief b.** be enclosed in a letter; **j-m b.** lie with s.o
beim *abbr* **bei dem**
bei'messen §70 *tr* attribute, impute
bei'mischen *tr* mix in
Bein [baɪn] *n* (-[e]s;-e) leg; (*Knochen*) bone; (fig) foot; **j-m ein B. stellen** trip s.o.
beinahe ['baɪnɑ·ə], [baɪ'nɑ·e] *adv* almost, nearly
Bei'name *m* appellation; (*Spitzname*) nickname
Bein'bruch *m* fracture, broken leg
Bein'schiene *f* (surg) splint; (sport) shin guard
Bein'schützer *m* (sport) shin guard
Bein'stellen *n* (sport) tripping
bei'ordnen *tr* assign, appoint (*s.o.*) as assistant; (*dat*) place (*s.th.*) on a level (with)
beipflichten ['baɪpflıçtən] *intr* (*dat*) agree with (*s.o.*), agree to (*s.th.*)
Bei'programm *n* (cin) second feature
Bei'rat *m* (-s;-̈e) adviser, counselor; (*Körperschaft*) advisory board
beir'ren *tr* mislead
beisammen [baɪ'zamən] *adv* together
Beisam'mensein *n* (-s;) being together; gathering, reunion; **geselliges B.** social; informal reception
Bei'satz *m* addition; (*bei Legierung*) alloy; (gram) appositive
Bei'schlaf *m* sexual intercourse
bei'schließen §76 *tr* enclose
Bei'schluß *m*—**unter B. von allen Dokumenten** with all documents attached
bei'schreiben §62 *tr* write in the margin; add as a postscript
Bei'schrift *f* postscript
Bei'sein *n* (-s;) presence
beisei'te *adv* aside; **b. schaffen** remove; (coll) do (*s.o.*) in
bei'setzen *tr* bury, inter
Bei'sitzer *m* associate judge
Bei'spiel *n* example; **zum B.** for example
bei'spielhaft *adj* exemplary
bei'spiellos *adj* unparalleled
bei'spielsweise *adv* by way of example
bei'springen §142 *intr* (*dat*) come to the aid of
beißen ['baɪsən] §53 *tr* & *intr* bite
bei'ßend *adj* biting; stinging, pungent, acrid; sarcastic; (*Reue*) bitter
Beiß'korb *m* muzzle
Beiß'zahn *m* (anat) incisor
Beiß'zange *f* pincers, nippers
Bei'stand *m* aid, support; (*Person*) assistant
bei'stehen §146 *intr* (*dat*) stand by, back, support
Bei'steuer *f* contribution
bei'steuern *tr* contribute
bei'stimmen *intr* (*dat*) agree with
Bei'stimmung *f* (-;) approval
Bei'strich *m* comma
Beitrag ['baɪtrɑk] *m* (-[e]s;-̈e) contribution; (*e-s Mitglieds*) dues

bei'tragen §132 *tr & intr* contribute
bei'treiben §62 *tr* collect; (*Abgaben*)
exact; (mil) commandeer, requisition
bei'treten §152 *intr* (SEIN) (*dat*) join;
(*j–s Meinung*) concur in
Bei'tritt *m* joining; concurrence
Bei'wagen *m* (aut) sidecar
Bei'werk *n* (-[e]s;) accessories
bei'wohnen *intr* (*dat*) attend; (*e–m
Ereignis*) be witness to; (*j–m*) have
intercourse with (s.o.)
Bei'wort *n* (-[e]s;ᵘer) epithet; (gram)
adjective
Beize ['baɪtsə] *f* (-;-n) corrosive;
(wood) stain; (*Falken–*) falconry;
(culin) marinade
beizeiten [baɪ'tsaɪtən] *adv* on time;
(*frühzeitig*) early
beizen ['baɪtsən] *tr* (*ätzen*) corrode;
(*Holz*) stain; (*Wunde*) cauterize;
(hunt) go hawking
bejahen [bə'jɑ·ən] *tr* say 'yes' to
beja'hend *adj* affirmative
bejahrt [bə'jɑrt] *adj* aged
bekämp'fen *tr* fight, oppose
bekannt [bə'kant] *adj* known; familiar;
(*berühmt*) well-known || **Bekannte**
§5 *mf* acquaintance
Bekannt'gabe *f* announcement
bekannt'geben §80 *tr* announce
bekannt'lich *adv* as is well known
bekannt'machen *tr* announce; (*Gesetz*)
promulgate
Bekannt'machung *f* (-;-en) publication, announcement; (*Plakat*) poster
Bekannt'schaft *f* (-;) acquaintance;
(coll) acquaintances
bekeh'ren *tr* convert || *ref* (zu) become
a convert (to)
Bekehrte [bə'kertə] §5 *mf* convert
beken'nen §97 *tr* (*Sünde*) confess; (*zugestehen*) admit; **Farbe b.** follow
suit; (fig) put one's cards on the
table || *ref*—**sich schuldig b.** plead
guilty; **sich zu e–r Religion b.** profess a religion; **sich zu e–r Tat b.**
own up to a deed; **sich zu j–m b.**
stand by s.o., believe in s.o.
Bekennt'nis *n* (eccl) confession; (*Konfession*) denomination
bekla'gen *tr* deplore; (*Tod*) mourn ||
ref (über *acc*) complain (about), find
fault (with)
bekla'genswert *adj* deplorable
Beklagte [bə'klɑktə] §5 *mf* defendant
beklat'schen *tr* applaud
bekle'ben *tr* paste; (*mit Etiketten*)
label; **e–e Mauer mit Plakaten b.**
paste posters on a wall
beklei'den *tr* clothe, dress; (*Mauer*)
face, cover; (*Amt*) hold
beklem'men *tr* stifle, oppress
Beklem'mung *f* (-;-en) worry, anxiety;
Beklemmungen claustrophobia
beklommen [bə'kləmən] *adj* uneasy
bekom'men §99 *tr* get; obtain; receive;
(*Schnupfen*) catch; (*Risse*) develop
|| *intr* (*dat*) do good; **j–m schlecht b.**
do s.o. harm; **wohl bekomm's!** to
your health!
bekömmlich [bə'kœmlɪç] *adj* digestible; (*gesund*) healthful; (*zuträglich*)
wholesome

beköstigen [bə'kœstɪgən] *tr* board,
feed || *ref*—**sich selbst b.** do one's
own cooking
bekräf'tigen *tr* (*Vorschlag*) support;
(*bestätigen*) substantiate; **mit e–m
Eid b.** seal with an oath
bekrän'zen *tr* wreath, crown
bekreu'zen, bekreu'zigen *ref* cross
oneself, make the sign of the cross
bekrie'gen *tr* make war on
bekrit'teln *tr* criticize, pick at
bekrit'zeln *tr* scribble on, doodle on
beküm'mern *tr* worry, trouble || *ref*
(um) concern onself (with), bother
(about)
beküm'mert *adj* (über *acc*) worried
(about)
bekunden [bə'kundən] *tr* manifest,
show; (*öffentlich*) state publicly
bela'den §103 *tr* load; (fig) burden
Belag [bə'lɑk] *m* (-[e]s;ᵘ) covering;
coat(ing); flooring; layer; surface
bela'gern *tr* besiege, beleaguer
Bela'gerung *f* (-;-en) siege
Belang [bə'laŋ] *m* (-[e]s;e) importance, consequence; **Belange** interests
belan'gen *tr* (jur) sue; **was mich be-
langt** as far as I am concerned
belang'los *adj* unimportant
bela'sten *tr* load (down); (*Grundstück*) encumber; (fig) burden; (acct)
charge; (jur) incriminate
belästigen [bə'lestɪgən] *tr* annoy,
bother; (*mit Fragen*) pester; (*unabsichtlich*) inconvenience
Bela'stung *f* (-;-en) load; encumbrance; (fig) burden; (acct) debit;
die Zeiten größter B. the peak hours
Bela'stungsprobe *f* (fig) acid test
Bela'stungszeuge *m* witness for the
prosecution
belau'fen §105 *ref*—**sich b. auf** (*acc*)
amount to, come to
belau'schen *tr* overhear
bele'ben *tr* animate; (*Getränk*) spike;
wieder b. revive
belebt [bə'lept] *adj* animated, lively
Bele'bungsmittel *n* stimulant
Beleg [bə'lek] *m* (-s;-e) (*Beweisstück*)
evidence; (*Unterlage*) voucher; (*Beispiel*) example; (jur) exhibit
bele'gen *tr* cover; (*Platz*) take, occupy;
(*bemannen*) man; (*beweisen*) verify;
(*Vorlesung*) register for; **ein Brötchen mit Schinken b.** make a ham
sandwich; **mit Beispielen b.** exemplify; **mit Fliesen b.** tile; **mit Steuern
b.** tax; **mit Teppichen b.** carpet ||
ref become coated
Beleg'schaft *f* (-;-en) crew; personnel;
shift
Beleg'schein *m* voucher; receipt
Beleg'stelle *f* reference
belegt [bə'lekt] *adj* (*Platz*) reserved;
(*Zunge*) coated; (*Stimme*) husky;
(telp) busy; **belegtes Brot** sandwich
beleh'ren *tr* instruct || *ref*—**sich b.
lassen** listen to reason
beleh'rend *adj* instructive
Beleh'rung *f* (-;-en) instruction;
(*Lehre*) lesson; (*Rat*) advice; **zu
Ihrer B.** for your information

beleibt [bə'laɪpt] *adj* stout
beleidigen [bə'laɪdɪgən] *tr* offend
belei'digend *adj* offensive
bele'sen *adj* well-read
beleuch'ten *tr* light (up), illuminate; (fig) throw light on
Beleuch'ter *m* (aer) pathfinder; (theat) juicer
Beleuch'tung *f* (-;-en) lighting, illumination; (fig) elucidation
Beleuch'tungskörper *m* lighting fixture
Belgien ['bɛlgjən] *n* (-s;) Belgium
Belgier –in ['bɛlgjər(ɪn)] §6 *mf* Belgian
belgisch ['bɛlgɪʃ] *adj* Belgian
belichten [bə'lɪçtən] *tr* (phot) expose
Belich'tung *f* (-;-en) exposure
belie'ben *intr* please || *impers* (*dat*)— wenn es Ihnen beliebt if you please || **Belieben** *n* (-s;) liking; **es steht in Ihrem B.** it's up to you; **nach B.** as you like
beliebig [bə'libɪç] *adj* any (you please) || *adv* as ... as you please
beliebt [bə'lipt] *adj* favorite; (**bei**) popular (with)
Beliebt'heit *f* (-;) popularity
belie'fern *tr* supply, furnish
bellen ['bɛlən] *intr* bark
belob(ig)en [bə'lob(ɪg)ən] *tr* praise; commend; (mil) cite
beloh'nen *tr* reward
belü'gen §111 *tr* lie to, deceive
belustigen [bə'lʊstɪgən] *tr* amuse
bemächtigen [bə'mɛçtɪgən] *intr* (*genit*) seize, get hold of; (mil) seize
bemä'keln *tr* criticize, carp at
bema'len *tr* paint; decorate
bemängeln [bə'mɛŋəln] *tr* criticize
bemannen [bə'manən] *tr* man
Beman'nung *f* (-;-en) (nav) crew
bemänteln [bə'mɛntəln] *tr* gloss over; (*Fehler, Fehltritt*) cover up
bemerk'bar *adj* perceptible
bemer'ken *tr* notice; (*äußern*) remark
bemer'kenswert *adj* remarkable
Bemer'kung *f* (-;-en) note; remark
bemes'sen §70 *tr* measure; proportion
bemit'leiden *tr* pity, feel sorry for
bemittelt [bə'mɪtəlt] *adj* well-to-do
bemogeln [bə'mogəln] *tr* cheat
bemü'hen *tr* trouble, bother; **bemüht sein zu** (*inf*) take pains to (*inf*) || *ref* bother, exert oneself; **sich für j–n b.** intervene for s.o.; **sich um etw b.** make an effort to obtain s.th.; **sich um j–n b.** attend to s.o.; **sich zu j–m b.** go to s.o.
Bemü'hung *f* (-;-en) bother; effort
bemüßigt [bə'mysɪçt] *adj*—**sich b. fühlen zu** (*inf*) feel obliged to (*inf*)
bemu'stern *tr*—**ein Angebot b.** (com) send samples of an offer
bemuttern [bə'mʊtərn] *tr* mother
benachbart [bə'naxbart] *adj* neighboring; (*Fachgebiet*) related, allied
benachrichtigen [bə'naxrɪçtɪgən] *tr* notify; put on notice
Benach'richtigung *f* (-;-en) notification; notice
benachteiligen [bə'naxtaɪlɪgən] *tr*

place at a disadvantage, handicap; discriminate against
benebelt [bə'nebəlt] *adj* covered in mist; (fig) groggy
benedeien [bene'daɪ•ən] *tr* bless
beneh'men §116 *tr*—**j–m etw b.** take s.th. away from s.o. || *ref* behave || **Benehmen** *n* (-s;) behavior
beneiden [bə'naɪdən] *tr*—**j–n um etw b.** begrudge s.o. s.th.
benei'denswert *adj* enviable
benen'nen §97 *tr* name, term
Bengel ['bɛŋəl] *m* (-s;–) rascal
benommen [bə'nɔmən] *adj* dazed
benö'tigen *tr* need
benutz'bar *adj* usable
benut'zen, benüt'zen *tr* use, make use of
Benut'zerkarte *f* library card
Benzin [bɛnt'sin] *n* (-s;-e) gasoline
Benzin'behälter *m* gas tank
beobachten [bə'obaxtən] *tr* observe; (*polizeilich*) keep under surveillance; (med) keep under observation
Beob'achtung *f* (-;-en) observation; (*e–s Gesetzes*) observance
beor'dern *tr* order (to go to a place)
bepacken [bepak'ken] *tr* load (down)
bepflan'zen *tr* plant
bequem [bə'kvem] *adj* comfortable; cozy; (*Stellung*) soft; (*Raten, Lösung*) easy; (*faul*) lazy; **b. zur Hand haben** have handy
berappen [bə'rapən] *tr* (coll) shell out
bera'ten §63 *tr* (über *acc*) advise (on); discuss || *ref & intr* (über *acc*) confer (about), deliberate (on)
bera'tend *adj* advisory, consulting
beratschlagen [bə'ratʃlagən] *intr* (über *acc*) consult (on); **mit j–m b.** consult s.o., confer with s.o.
berat'schlagend *adj* advisory
Bera'tung *f* (-;-en) advice; (jur, med) consultation; **in B. sein** be under consideration
Bera'tungsstelle *f* counseling center
berau'ben *tr* (*genit*) rob (of); (*genit*) dispossess (of); (*genit*) deprive (of); (*genit*) bereave (of)
berech'nen *tr* calculate, figure out; (*schätzen*) estimate; (com) charge
berech'nend *adj* calculating
Berech'nung *f* (-;-en) calculation
berechtigen [bə'rɛçtɪgən] *tr* authorize; justify, warrant; (zu) entitle (to)
Berech'tigung *f* (-;-en) right, authorization; justification; (zu) title (to)
bereden [bə'redən] *tr* talk over, discuss; **j–n zu etw b.** talk s.o. into s.th. || *ref*—**sich mit j–m über etw b.** confer with s.o. on s.th.
beredsam [bə'retzam] *adj* eloquent
beredt [bə'ret] *adj* eloquent
Bereich *m & n* (-[e]s;-e) region; range; (fig) field, sphere; **es fällt nicht in meinen B.** it's not within my province
bereichern [bə'raɪçərn] *tr* enrich
berei'fen *tr* cover with frost; (aut) put tires on
berei'nigen *tr* (*Streit, Konto*) setttle; (*Mißverständnis*) clear up
berei'sen *tr* tour

bereit [bə'raɪt] *adj* ready
bereiten [bə'raɪtən] *tr* prepare; (*Kaffee*) make; (*Freude*) give
Bereit'schaft *f* (-;) readiness; team, squad; (mil) alert
bereit'stellen *tr* make available
Berei'tung *f* (-;-en) preparation; (*Herstellung*) manufacture
bereit'willig *adj* ready, willing
bereu'en *tr* rue, regret
Berg [berk] *m* (-[e]s;-e) mountain; (*Hügel*) hill; **über alle Berge sein** be off and away; **zu Berge stehen** stand on end
bergab' *adv* downhill, down the mountain
bergauf' *adv* uphill; up the mountain
Berg'bahn *f* mountain railroad
Berg'bau *m* (-[e]s;) mining
Berg'bewohner **-in** §6 *mf* mountaineer
bergen ['bergən] §54 *tr* rescue; (*enthalten*) hold; (*Gefahr*) involve; (*Segel*) take in; (naut) salvage; (poet) conceal; (rok) recover || *ref*—**in sich b.** involve
bergig ['bergɪç] *adj* mountainous
Berg'kessel *m* gorge
Berg'kette *f* mountain range
Berg'kluft *f* ravine, gully
Berg'kristall *m* rock crystal, quartz
Berg'land *n* hill country
Berg'mann *m* (-[e]s;-leute) miner
Berg'predigt *f* Sermon on the Mount
Berg'recht *n* mining law
Berg'rücken *m* ridge
Berg'rutsch *m* landslide
Berg'schlucht *f* gorge, ravine
Berg'spitze *f* mountain peak
Berg'steiger **-in** §6 *mf* mountain climber
Berg'steigerei *f* mountain climbing
Berg'sturz *m* landslide
Ber'gung *f* (-;-en) rescue; (naut) salvage; (rok) recovery
Ber'gungsarbeiten *pl* salvage operations
Ber'gungsschiff *n* salvage vessel; (rok) recovery ship
Berg'wacht *f* mountain rescue service
Berg'werk *n* mine
Berg'wesen *n* mining
Bericht [bə'rɪçt] *m* (-[e]s;-e) report
berichten [bə'rɪçtən] *tr & intr* report
Berichterstatter **-in** [bə'rɪçtərʃtatər (ɪn)] §6 *mf* reporter; correspondent; (rad) commentator
Bericht'erstattung *f* (-;) reporting
berichtigen [bə'rɪçtɪgən] *tr* rectify; (*Text*) emend; (*Schuld*) pay off
berie'chen §102 *tr* sniff at; (fig) size up || *recip* (coll) sound each other out
Berlin [ber'lin] *n* (-s;) Berlin
Bernstein ['bernʃtaɪn] *m* amber
bersten ['berstən] §55 *intr* (SEIN) (**vor** *dat*) burst (with)
berüchtigt [bə'rʏçtɪçt] *adj* notorious
berücken (berük'ken) *tr* captivate
berücksichtigen [bə'rʏkzɪçtɪgən] *tr* (*erwägen*) consider; (*in Betracht ziehen*) make allowance for
Berück'sichtigung *f* (-;-en) consideration

Beruf' *m* (-[e]s;-e) vocation; profession; (*Gewerbe*) trade; (*Tätigkeit*) occupation; (*Laufbahn*) career
beru'fen *adj* called; authorized || §122 *tr* call; (*ernennen*) appoint; (*Geister*) conjure up || *ref*—**sich auf ein Gesetz b.** quote a law (*in support*); **sich auf j-n b.** use s.o.'s name as a reference
beruf'lich *adj* professional; vocational
Berufs– *comb.fm.* professional; vocational
Berufs'diplomat *m* career diplomat
Berufs'genossenschaft *f* professional association; trade association
Berufs'heer *n* regular army
Berufs'schule *f* vocational school
Berufs'sportler **-in** §6 *mf* professional
berufs'tätig *adj* working
Beru'fung *f* (-;-en) call; vocation; appointment; (jur) appeal; **B. einlegen** (jur) appeal; **unter B. auf** (*acc*) referring to
Beru'fungsgericht *n* appellate court
beru'hen *intr* (**auf** *dat*) be based (on); (**auf** *dat*) be due (to); **e-e Sache auf sich b.** lassen let a matter rest
beruhigen [bə'ru·ɪgən] *tr* calm; appease
beru'higend *adj* soothing; reassuring
Beru'higung *f* (-;) calming; appeasement, pacification; reassurance; (*der Lage*) stabilization; **zu meiner großen B.** much to my relief
Beru'higungsmittel *n* sedative
berühmt [bə'rymt] *adj* (**wegen**) famous (for)
Berühmt'heit *f* (-;-en) renown; (*berühmte Persönlichkeit*) celebrity
berüh'ren *tr* touch; (*erwähnen*) touch on; (*wirken auf*) affect; (*Zug*) pass through || *ref* come in contact, meet
Berüh'rung *f* (-;-en) touch; contact
besä'en *tr* sow; (*bestreuen*) strew; **mit Sternen besät** star-spangled
besa'gen *tr* say; (*bedeuten*) mean
besagt [bə'zakt] *adj* aforesaid
besänftigen [bə'zenftɪgən] *tr* calm; appease || *ref* calm down
Besatz' *m* trimming
Besat'zung *f* (-;-en) garrison; occupation; army of occupation; (aer, nav) crew
Besat'zungsarmee *f* army of occupation
Besat'zungsbehörde *f* military government
besau'fen §124 *ref* (coll) get drunk
beschä'digen *tr* damage || *ref* injure oneself
beschaf'fen *adj*—**ich bin eben so b.** that's the way I am; **übel b. sein** be in bad shape || *tr* get, procure; (*Geld*) raise
Beschaf'fenheit *f* (-;-en) quality, property; (*Zustand*) state; (*Art*) nature; (*Anlage*) design
Beschaf'fung *f* (-;-en) procuring; (*Erwerb*) acquisition
beschäftigen [bə'ʃeftɪgən] *tr* occupy; keep busy; (*anstellen*) employ; **beschäftigt sein bei** work for (*a company*); **beschäftigt sein mit** be busy with

beschä'men *tr* shame, make ashamed; beschämt sein be ashamed
Beschau' *f* inspection
beschau'en *tr* look at; inspect
beschau'lich *adj* contemplative
Bescheid [bə'ʃaɪt] *m* (-[e]s;-e) answer; (*Anweisung*) instructions, directions; (*Auskunft*) information; (jur) decision; B. hinterlassen bei leave word with; B. wissen be well-informed; j-m B. geben (or sagen) give s.o. information or directions
beschei'den *adj* modest; (*Preise*) moderate; (*Auswahl*) limited; (*einfach*) simple, plain ‖ §112 *tr* inform; (*beordern*) order, direct; (*vorladen*) summon; (*zuteilen*) allot; abschlägig b. turn down; es ist mir beschieden it fell to my lot ‖ *ref* be satisfied
Beschei'denheit *f* (-;) modesty
bescheinigen [bə'ʃaɪnɪgən] *tr* (*Empfang*) acknowledge; (*bezeugen*) certify
Beschei'nigung *f* (-;-en) acknowledgement; certification; (*Schein*) certificate; (*im Brief*) to whom it may concern
beschei'ßen §53 *tr* (sl) cheat
beschen'ken *tr*—j-n b. mit present s.o. with
bescheren [bə'ʃerən] *tr* give gifts to
Besche'rung *f* (-;-en) distribution of gifts (*especially at Christmas*); e-e schöne B. (coll) a nice mess
beschicken (beschik'ken) *tr* (*mit Waren*) supply; (*Messe*) exhibit at, send exhibits to; (*Kongreß*) send delegates to; (*Hochofen*) feed, charge
beschie'ßen §76 *tr* shoot up; (mil, phys) bombard
beschimp'fen *tr* insult, call (*s.o.*) names
beschir'men *tr* shield, protect
beschla'fen *tr* (e–e Frau) sleep with; (e–e Sache) sleep on
Beschlag' *m* (-s;̈e) hardware; (*Huf-*) horse shoes; (*auf Fensterscheiben*) steam, vapor; (*Überzug*) thin coating; in B. nehmen confiscate; (*Schiff*) seize; (*Gehalt*) attach
beschla'gen *adj*—b. in (*dat*) well-versed in ‖ §132 *tr* cover, coat; (*Metallverzierungen*) fit, mount; (*Pferd*) shoe ‖ *ref & intr* steam up; (*Mauer*) sweat; (*Metall*) oxidize
beschlagnahmen [bə'ʃlaknɑmən] *tr* confiscate; (*Schuldnervermögen*) attach; (mil) requisition; (naut) seize
beschlei'chen §85 *tr* stalk, creep up on
beschleunigen [bə'ʃlɔɪnɪgən] *tr* accelerate, speed up
Beschleu'niger *m* (-s;-) accelerator
beschlie'ßen §76 *tr* end, wind up; (*sich entschließen*) decide
Beschluß' *m* conclusion; decision; resolution; (jur) order; unter B. under lock and key; zum B. in conclusion
beschluß'fähig *adj*—b. sein have a quorum; beschlußfähige Anzahl quorum
beschmie'ren *tr* smear, coat; grease
beschmut'zen *tr* soil, dirty

beschnei'den §106 *tr* clip, trim; (fig) curtail; (surg) circumcise
beschneit [bə'ʃnaɪt] *adj* snow-covered
beschönigen [bə'ʃønɪgən] *tr* (*Fehler*) whitewash, cover up, gloss over
beschrän'ken *tr* limit
beschränkt' *adj* limited; (*Verhältnisse*) straitened; (*geistig*) dense
beschrei'ben §62 *tr* describe; use up (*in writing*)
Beschrei'bung *f* (-;-en) description
beschrei'ten §86 *tr* walk on; den Rechtsweg b. take legal action
beschriften [bə'ʃrɪftən] *tr* inscribe; (*Kisten*) mark; (*mit Etikett*) label
Beschrif'tung *f* (-;-en) inscription; lettering; (*erläuternde*) caption
beschuldigen [bə'ʃʊldɪgən] *tr* (*genit*) accuse (of), charge (with)
beschummeln [bə'ʃuməln] *tr* (coll) (um) cheat (out of)
Beschuß' *m* test firing
beschüt'zen *tr* protect, defend
beschwat'zen *tr* gossip about; j–n dazu b. zu (*inf*) talk s.o. into (*ger*)
Beschwerde [bə'ʃverdə] *f* (-;-n) trouble; (*Klage, Krankheit*) complaint
beschweren [bə'ʃverən] *tr* burden ‖ *ref* (über *acc*) complain (about)
beschwer'lich *adj* troublesome
beschwichtigen [bə'ʃvɪçtɪgən] *tr* appease; (*Hunger*) satisfy; (*Gewissen*) soothe
beschwin'deln *tr* (um) swindle (out of)
beschwingt [bə'ʃvɪŋt] *adj* lively
beschwipst [bə'ʃvɪpst] *adj* tipsy, high
beschwö'ren *tr* swear to; (*Geister*) conjure up; (*bitten*) implore, entreat
Beschwö'rungsformel *f* incantation
beseelen [bə'zelən] *tr* inspire, animate
beseelt' *adj* animated; (*von Hoffnungen*) filled; (*Spiel*) inspired
bese'hen §138 *tr* look at; inspect
beseitigen [bə'zaɪtɪgən] *tr* eliminate, remove, clear away; (*Übel, Fehler*) redress; (*Schwierigkeit*) overcome; (*töten*) do away with; (pol) purge
Besen ['bezən] *m* (-s;-) broom
Be'senstiel *m* broomstick
besessen [bə'zesən] *adj* (von) obsessed (by); (*vom Teufel*) possessed
Beses'senheit *f* (-;-en) obsession; (*vom Teufel*) possession
beset'zen *tr* occupy; (*mit Juwelen*) set off; (*Amt, Rolle*) fill; (*Hut*) trim
besetzt' *adj* (*Platz, Abort*) occupied; (*Stelle*) filled; (*Kleid*) trimmed, set off; (telp) busy
Besetzt'zeichen *n* (telp) busy signal
Beset'zung *f* (-;-en) decoration; (e–r Stelle) filling; (mil) occupation; (theat) cast
besichtigen [bə'zɪçtɪgən] *tr* view; tour; inspect; (mil) inspect, review
Besich'tigung *f* (-;-en) sightseeing; inspection; (mil) inspection, review
besie'deln *tr* colonize; populate
besie'geln *tr* seal
besie'gen *tr* defeat; (*Widerstand*) overcome; (*Gefühle*) master
besin'nen §121 *ref* consider; (auf *acc*) think (of); sich anders b. change

one's mind; **sich e–s Besseren b.** think better of it
besinn'lich *adj* reflective
Besin'nung *f* (–;) consciousness; reflection; **j–n zur B. bringen** bring s.o. to his senses
besin'nungslos *adj* unconscious; (*unüberlegt*) senseless
Besitz' *m* (–es;–e) possession; **in B. nehmen** take possession of
bestiz'anzeigend *adj* possessive
besit'zen §144 *tr* own, possess
Besit'zer –in §6 *mf* possessor, owner
Besitz'ergreifung *f* (–;–en) occupancy; seizure
Besitz'stand *m* ownership; (fin) assets
Besitztum [bə'zɪtstum] *n* (–s;⸚er) possession
Besit'zung *f* (–;–en) possession, property; (*Landgut*) estate
besoffen [bə'zɔfən] *adj* (coll) soused
besohlen [bə'zolən] *tr* sole
besolden [bə'zɔldən] *tr* pay
Besol'dung *f* (–;–en) pay, salary
beson'dere §9 *adj* particular, special
Beson'derheit *f* (–;–en) peculiarity; (com) specialty
beson'ders *adv* especially; separately
besonnen [bə'zɔnən] *adj* prudent; (*bedacht*) considerate; level-headed
besor'gen *tr* take care of; (*beschaffen*) procure, get; (*befürchten*) fear
Besorgnis [bə'zɔrknɪs] *f* (–;–se) concern; (*Furcht*) fear
besorg'niserregend *adj* alarming
besorgt [bə'zɔrkt] *adj* (um) worried (about), anxious (for)
Besor'gung *f* (–;–en) care; procurement; (*Auftrag*) errand; **Besorgungen machen** run errands
bespre'chen §64 *tr* discuss; (*Buch*) review; **e–e Schallplatte b.** make a recording ‖ *ref* confer
Bespre'cher –in §6 *mf* reviewer, critic
bespren'gen *tr* sprinkle
besprit'zen *tr* splash; spray
besser ['bɛsər] *adj & adv* better
bessern ['bɛsərn] *tr* better, improve ‖ *ref* improve
Bes'serung *f* (–;–en) improvement; **baldige B.** speedy recovery
Bes'serungsanstalt *f* reform school
Bestand' *m* (–[e]s;⸚e) existence; (*Vorrat*) stock, inventory; (*Kassen–*) cash on hand; (*Baum–*) stand; **B. an** (*dat*) number of; **B. an kampffähigen Truppen** effective strength; **B. haben, von B. sein** have endurance, be lasting
bestän'dig *adj* constant, steady
Bestands'aufnahme *f* inventory
Bestand'teil *m* component; ingredient
bestär'ken *tr* strengthen, fortify
bestätigen [bə'ʃtetɪgən] *tr* confirm; (*Zeugnis*) corroborate; (*Empfang*) acknowledge; (*Vertrag*) ratify ‖ *ref* prove true, come true
bestatten [bə'ʃtatən] *tr* bury, inter
Bestat'tungsinstitut *n* funeral home
bestau'ben, bestäuben (bə'ʃtɔɪbən) *tr* cover with dust; sprinkle; (bot) pollinate
beste ['bɛstə] §9 *adj* best; **am besten**

best (of all); **auf dem besten Weg sein zu** be well on the way to; **aufs b. in the best way; der erste b.** anybody
beste'chen §64 *tr* bribe; (fig) impress
beste'chend *adj* fascinating, charming
bestech'lich *adj* open to bribery
Beste'chung *f* (–;) bribery
Beste'chungsgeld *n* bribe
Besteck [bə'ʃtɛk] *n* (–[e]s;–e) kit; (*Tisch–*) single service; (aer, naut) reckoning, position; (med) set of instruments
bestecken (bestek'ken) *tr* stick; (culin) garnish
beste'hen §146 *tr* undergo; (*Prüfung*) pass ‖ *intr* exist, be; (gegen) hold one's own (against); (*in e–r Prüfung*) pass; **b. auf** (*dat*) insist on; **b. aus** consist of; **b. in** (*dat*) consist in
beste'hend *adj* existing, extant; present
besteh'len §147 *tr* (um) rob (of)
bestei'gen §148 *tr* climb; (*Schiff*) board; (*Pferd*) mount; (*Thron*) ascend
Bestell'buch *n* order book
bestel'len *tr* order; (*Zimmer*) reserve; (*Zeitung*) subscribe to; (*ernennen*) appoint; (*Briefe*) deliver; (*Feld*) till; (*kommen lassen*) send for
Bestell'zettel *m* order slip
be'stenfalls *adv* at best
besteu'ern *tr* tax
bestialisch [bɛst'jɑlɪʃ] *adj* beastly
Bestie ['bɛstjə] *f* (–;–n) beast
bestim'men *tr* determine; (*Zeit, Preis*) set; (*ernennen*) appoint; (*Begriff*) define; (gram) modify; (math) find; **j–n b. zu** (or **für**) destine s.o. for; talk s.o. into ‖ *intr* decree; **b. in** (*dat*) have a say in; **b. über** (*acc*) dispose of
bestimmt' *adj* determined; definite; particular ‖ *adv* definitely
Bestim'mung *f* (–;–en) determination; (*e–r Zeit, e–s Preises*) setting; destination; mission, goal; (*e–s Begriffs*) definition; (*Schicksal*) fate; (*Vorschrift*) regulation; (*e–s Vertrags*) provision; (gram) modifier; **mit B. nach** (naut) heading for; **seiner B. übergeben** dedicate, open
bestra'fen *tr* punish
bestrah'len *tr* irradiate; (med) give radiation treatment to
bestre'ben *ref* strive, endeavor ‖ **Bestreben** *n* (–s;) tendency
Bestre'bung *f* (–;–en) effort
bestrei'chen §85 *tr* spread; (*mit Feuer*) rake; **mit Butter b.** butter
bestrei'ken *tr* strike
bestrei'ten §86 *tr* contest; fight; (*Ausgaben*) defray; (*Recht*) challenge; (*leugnen*) deny; **e–e Unterhaltung allein b.** do all the talking
bestreu'en *tr* (mit) strew (with)
bestricken (bestrik'ken) *tr* (fig) charm
bestücken [bə'ʃtykən] *tr* arm, equip
bestür'men *tr* storm; (fig) bombard
Bestür'mung *f* (–;–en) storming
bestür'zen *tr* dismay
Besuch [bə'zux] *m* (–[e]s;–e) visit; (*Besucher*) visitor(s), company;

(genit) visit (to); **auf B. gehen** pay a visit

besu'chen *tr* visit; *(Gasthaus, usw.)* frequent; *(Schule, Versammlung)* attend; *(Kino)* go to

Besu'cher –in §6 *mf* visitor, caller

Besuchs'zeit *f* visiting hours

besudeln *tr* soil, stain

betagt [bə'takt] *adj* advanced in years

beta'sten *tr* finger, touch, handle

betätigen [bə'tetɪgən] *tr* set in operation; *(Maschine)* operate; *(Bremse)* apply ‖ *ref*—**sich nützlich b.** make oneself useful; **sich politisch b.** be active in politics

betäuben [bə'tɔɪbən] *tr* deafen; stun; *(Schmerz)* deaden; *(durch Rauschgift)* drug, dope; *(med)* anesthetize

Betäu'bungsmittel *n* drug; painkiller; *(med)* anesthetic

Bete ['betə] *f* (–;–n) beet

beteiligen [bə'taɪlɪgən] *tr* **(an** *dat*, **bei)** give *(s.o.)* a share (in) ‖ *ref* **(an** *dat)* participate (in)

Betei'ligung *f* (–;–en) participation; *(Teilhaberschaft)* partnership; *(Teilnehmerzahl)* attendance

beten ['betən] *tr & intr* pray

beteuern [bə'tɔɪ·ərn] *tr* affirm

betiteln [bə'titəln] *tr* entitle

Beton [be'ton] *m* (–s;) concrete

betonen [bə'tonən] *tr* (Silbe) stress, accent; *(nachdrücklich)* emphasize

betonieren [betə'nirən] *tr* cement

Betonmisch'maschine *f* cement mixer

betören [bə'tørən] *tr* infatuate

Betracht' *m* (–[e]s;) consideration; **außer B. lassen** rule out; **es kommt nicht in B.** it is out of the question; **in B. ziehen** take into account, consider

betrachten [bə'traxtən] *tr* look at; consider

beträchtlich [bə'trɛçtlɪç] *adj* considerable

Betrach'tung *f* (–;–en) observation; consideration; meditation; **Betrachtungen anstellen über** *(acc)* reflect on

Betrag [bə'trak] *m* (–[e]s;–̈e) amount; **über den B. von** in the amount of

betra'gen §132 *tr* amount to ‖ *ref* behave ‖ **Betragen** *n* (–s;) behavior

betrau'en *tr* entrust

betrau'ern *tr* mourn for

Betreff [bə'tref] *m* (–[e]s;) *(am Briefanfang)* re; **in B.** *(genit)* in regard to

betref'fen §151 *tr* befall; *(berühren)* affect, hit; *(angehen)* concern; **betrifft** *(acc)* re; **was das betrifft** as far that is concerned; **was mich betrifft** I for one

betreffs [bə'trefs] *prep (genit)* concerning

betrei'ben §62 *tr* carry on; *(leiten)* manage; *(Beruf)* practice; *(Studien)* pursue; *(Maschine)* operate

betre'ten *adj* embarrassed ‖ §152 *tr* step on; set foot on or in; *(Raum)* enter; *(unbefugt)* trespass on

betreuen [bə'trɔɪ·ən] *tr* look after

Betrieb [bə'trip] *m* (–s;–e) operation,

running; *(Unternehmen)* business; *(Anlage)* plant; *(Werkstatt)* workshop; (fig) rush, bustle; **aus dem B. ziehen** take out of service; **außer B.** out of order; **großer B.** hustle and bustle; **in vollem B.** in full swing

betriebsam [bə'tripzam] *adj* enterprising, active

Betrieb'samkeit *f* (–;) hustle

betriebs'fähig *adj* in working order

betriebs'fertig *adj* ready for use

Betriebs'ingenieur *m* production engineer

Betriebs'kosten *pl* operating costs

Betriebs'leiter *m* superintendent

Betriebs'material *n* (rr) rolling stock

Betriebs'prüfer –in §6 *mf* auditor

Betriebs'ruhe *f*—**heute B.** (public sign) closed today

Betriebs'stoff *m* fuel

Betriebs'störung *f* breakdown

Betriebs'wirtschaft *f* industrial management

betrin'ken §143 *ref* get drunk

betroffen [bə'trɔfən] *adj* shocked, stunned; *(heimgesucht)* afflicted

betrü'ben *tr* sadden, distress

betrüb'lich *adj* sad, distressing

betrübt [bə'trypt] *adj* sad, sorrowful

Betrug [bə'truk] *m* (–[e]s;) fraud, swindle; **frommer B.** white lie

betrü'gen §111 *tr* cheat, swindle

Betrügerei [bətrygə'raɪ] *f* (–;–en) deceit, cheating

betrü'gerisch *adj* deceitful; fraudulent

betrunken [bə'trʊnkən] *adj* drunk

Bett [bɛt] *n* (–[e]s;–en) bed

Bett'decke *f* bedspread

Bettelei [bɛtə'laɪ] *f* (–;) begging

betteln ['bɛtəln] *intr* **(um)** beg (for)

betten ['bɛtən] *tr* put to bed ‖ *ref* **make onself a bed; bed down**

Bett'genosse *m* bedfellow

Bett'gestell *n* bedstead

Bett'himmel *m* canopy *(over a bed)*

bettlägerig ['bɛtlegərɪç] *adj* bedridden

Bett'laken *n* bed sheet

Bettler –in ['bɛtlər(ɪn)] §6 *mf* beggar

Bett'stelle *f* bedstead

Bettuch (Bett'tuch) *n* sheet

Bet'tung *f* (–;) bedding; (mil) emplacement; (rr) bed

Bett'vorleger *m* bedside rug

Bett'wäsche *f* bed linen

Bett'zeug *n* bedding

betupfen [bə'tʊpfən] *tr* dab (at); (surg) swab

beugen ['bɔɪgən] *tr* bend; (fig) humble; (gram) inflect ‖ *ref* bend; bow

Beu'gung *f* (–;–en) bending; bowing; (gram) inflection

Beule ['bɔɪlə] *f* (–;–n) lump; *(Geschwür)* boil; *(kleiner Blechschaden)* dent

beunruhigen [bə'ʊnru·ɪgən] *tr* make uneasy, worry, disturb

Beun'ruhigung *f* (–;–en) anxiety, uneasiness; disturbance

beurkunden [bə'urkʊndən] *tr* authenticate

beurlauben [bə'urlaubən] *tr* grant leave of absence to; *(vom Amt)* suspend; (mil) furlough; **sich b. lassen**

ask for time off ‖ *ref* (**bei**) take one's leave (of)
beur'teilen *tr* evaluate; (**nach**) judge (by); **falsch b.** misjudge
Beute ['bɔɪtə] *f* (–;) booty, loot; **zur B. fallen** (*dat*) fall prey to
Beutel ['bɔɪtəl] *m* (–s;–) bag, pouch; purse; (billiards) pocket
beu'telig *adj* baggy
Beu'tezug *m* raid
bevölkern [be'fœlkərn] *tr* populate
Bevöl'kerung *f* (–;–en) population
bevollmächtigen [be'fɔlmɛçtɪgən] *tr* authorize; (jur) give (*s.o.*) power of attorney
Bevoll'mächtigte §5 *mf* authorized agent; proxy; (pol) plenipotentiary
bevor [bə'for] *conj* before; **bevor . . . nicht** until
bevormunden [be'formʊndən] *tr* treat in a patronizing manner
bevor'raten *tr* stock; stockpile
bevorrechtet [bə'forrɛçtət] *adj* privileged
bevor'stehen §146 *intr* be imminent, be on hand; **bevorstehend** forthcoming; **j–m b.** be in store for s.o.
bevorzugen [bə'fortsugən] *tr* prefer
bevor'zugt *adj* preferential; high-priority; privileged; favorite
bewa'chen *tr* guard, watch over
bewach'sen §155 *tr* overgrow, cover
Bewa'chung *f* (–;–en) guard, custody
bewaff'nen *tr* arm
Bewaff'nung *f* (–;) armament, arms
Bewahr'anstalt *f* detention home
bewah'ren *tr* keep, preserve; (**vor** *dat*) save (from), protect (against)
bewäh'ren *tr* prove ‖ *ref* prove one's worth; **sich nicht b.** prove a failure
Bewah'rer –**in** §6 *mf* keeper
bewahrheiten [bə'varhaɪtən] *tr* verify ‖ *ref* come true
bewährt [bə'vert] *adj* tried, trustworthy
Bewah'rung *f* (–;) preservation
Bewäh'rung *f* (–;–en) testing, trial; (jur) probation
Bewäh'rungsfrist *f* (jur) probation; **j–m B. zubilligen** put s.o. on probation
Bewäh'rungsprobe *f* test
bewaldet [bə'valdət] *adj* woody
bewältigen [bə'vɛltɪgən] *tr* (*Hindernis*) overcome; (*Lehrstoff*) master
bewandert [bə'vandərt] *adj* experienced
Bewandtnis [bə'vantnɪs] *f* (–;) circumstances, situation
bewäs'sern *tr* water, irrigate
bewegen [bə'vegən] *tr* move, stir ‖ *ref* move, stir; (*von der Stelle*) budge; (*Temperatur*) vary; (*exerzieren*) take exercise; (astr) revolve ‖ §56 *tr* prompt, induce
Beweg'grund *m* motive; incentive
beweg'lich *adj* movable; (*behend*) agile; (*Geist*) versatile; (*Zunge*) glib
Beweg'lichkeit *f* (–;) mobility; agility; versatility
bewegt [bə'vekt] *adj* agitated; (*ergreifend*) stirring; (*Stimme*) trembling; (*Unterhaltung*) lively; (*Leben*) eventful; (*unruhig*) turbulent
Bewe'gung *f* (–;–en) movement; mo-

tion; move; (*Gebärde*) gesture; (fig) emotion; **in B. setzen** set in motion
Bewe'gungsfreiheit *f* room to move; (fig) leeway, freedom of action
bewe'gungslos *adj* motionless
beweh'ren *tr* arm; (*Beton*) reinforce
beweihräuchern [bə'vaɪrɔɪçərn] *tr* (fig) flatter; (eccl) incense
bewei'nen *tr* mourn, shed tears over
Beweis [bə'vaɪs] *m* (–es;–e) (**für**) proof (of), evidence (of)
beweisen [be'vaɪzən] §118 *tr* prove, demonstrate; (*bestätigen*) substantiate
Beweis'führung *f* argumentation
Beweis'grund *m* argument
Beweis'kraft *f* cogency, force
beweis'kräftig *adj* convincing
Beweis'last *f* burden of proof
Beweis'stück *n* exhibit
bewen'den *intr*—**es dabei b. lassen** leave it at that ‖ **Bewenden** *n*—**damit hat es sein B.** there the matter rests
bewer'ben §149 *ref*—**sich b. um** apply for; (*kandidieren*) run for; (*Vertrag*) bid for; (*Preis*) compete for; (*Frau*) court
Bewer'ber –**in** §6 *mf* applicant; candidate; bidder; competitor ‖ *m* suitor
Bewer'bungsformular *n* application form
Bewer'bungsschreiben *n* written application
bewer'fen §160 *tr* pelt; (*Mauer*) plaster
bewerkstelligen [bə'verkʃtɛlɪgən] *tr* manage, bring off
bewer'ten *tr* (**auf** *acc*) value (at), appraise (at); **b. mit fünf Punkten** give five points (e.g., *a performance*); **zu hoch b.** overrate
Bewer'tung *f* (–;–en) valuation
bewilligen [bə'vɪlɪgən] *tr* approve, grant
Bewil'ligung *f* (–;–en) approval; permit
bewillkommnen [bə'vɪlkɔmnən] *tr* welcome
bewir'ken *tr* cause, occasion, effect
bewir'ten *tr* entertain
bewirt'schaften *tr* (*Acker*) cultivate; (*Betrieb*) manage; (*Mangelware*) ration
Bewir'tung *f* (–;) hospitality
bewitzeln [bə'vɪtsəln] *tr* poke fun at
bewog [bə'vok] *pret* of **bewegen**
bewogen [bə'vogən] *pp* of **bewegen**
bewoh'nen *tr* inhabit, occupy
Bewoh'ner –**in** §6 *mf* (*e–s Landes*) inhabitant; (*e–s Hauses*) occupant
bewölken [bə'vœlkən] *tr* cloud ‖ *ref* cloud over, get cloudy
bewölkt' *adj* cloudy, overcast
Bewöl'kung *f* (–;) clouds
bewun'dern *tr* admire
bewun'dernswert, **bewun'dernswürdig** *adj* admirable
bewußt [bə'vʊst] *adj* conscious; **die bewußte Sache** the matter in question
bewußt'los *adj* unconscious
Bewußt'sein *n* consciousness; **bei B. sein** be conscious
Bewußt'seinsspaltung *f* schizophrenia
bezah'len *tr* pay; (*Gekauftes*) pay for

Bezah'lung f (-;-en) payment; (*Lohn*) pay

bezäh'men tr tame; (fig) control

bezau'bern tr bewitch; (fig) fascinate

bezeich'nen tr (*zeichnen*) mark; (*bedeuten*) signify; (*benennen*) designate; (*kennzeichnen*) characterize; (*zeigen*) point out

bezeich'nend adj characteristic

Bezeich'nung f (-;-en) marking, mark; (*Name*) name; (*Ausdruck*) term

bezei'gen tr show, manifest, express

bezeu'gen tr attest; (jur) testify to

bezichtigen [bə'tsɪçtɪgən] tr accuse

bezieh'bar adj (*Ware*) obtainable; (*Wohnung*) ready for occupancy; (auf acc) referable (to)

bezie'hen §163 tr (*Polstermöbel*) cover; (*Wohnung*) move into; (*Universität*) go to; (*geliefert bekommen*) get; (*Gehalt*) draw; (auf acc) relate (to), refer (to); **das Bett frisch b.** change the bed linens; **die Stellung b.** (mil) occupy the position; **die Wache b.** (mil) go on guard duty ‖ ref become overcast; **sich auf j-n b.** use s.o.'s name as a reference

Bezie'hung f (-;-en) relation, connection, respect; **in B. auf** (acc) in respect to; **in guten Beziehungen stehen zu** be on good terms with

bezie'hungslos adj unrelated; irrelevant

Bezie'hungssatz m relative clause

bezie'hungsweise adv respectively

Bezie'hungswort n [-[e]s; ̈-er) (gram) antecedent

beziffern [bə'tsɪfərn] tr (auf acc) estimate (at) ‖ ref—sich b. auf (acc) amount to, number

Bezirk [bə'tsɪrk] m (-s;-e) district, ward, precinct; (*Bereich*) sphere

Bezug' m (-[e]s; ̈-e) cover, case; (von *Waren*) purchase; (von *Zeitungen*) subscription; (*Auftrag*) order; **Bezüge** earnings; **B. nehmen auf** (acc) refer to; **in B. auf** (acc) in reference to

bezüglich [bə'tsyklɪç] adj (auf acc) relative (to); **bezügliches Fürwort** relative pronoun ‖ prep (genit) concerning, as to, with regard to

Bezugnahme [bə'tsuknamə] f—unter B. auf (acc) with reference to

Bezugs'anweisung f delivery order

bezugs'berechtigt adj entitled to receive ‖ **Bezugsberechtigte** §5 mf (ins) beneficiary

bezwecken [bə'tsvɛkən] tr aim at, have in mind; (mit) intend (by)

bezwei'feln tr doubt, question

bezwin'gen §142 tr conquer; (fig) control, master

Bibel ['bibəl] f (-;-n) Bible

Bi'belforscher –in §6 mf Jehovah's Witness

Biber ['bibər] m (-s;-) beaver

Bibliothek [bɪblɪ·ɔ'tek] f (-;-en) library

Bibliothekar –in [bɪblɪ·ɔte'kar(ɪn)] §8 mf librarian

biblisch ['biblɪʃ] adj biblical

bieder ['bidər] adj honest; (*leichtgläubig*) gullible

Bie'dermann m (-[e]s; ̈-er) honest man

biegen ['bigən] §57 tr bend; (gram) inflect ‖ ref—sich vor Lachen b. double up with laughter ‖ intr (SEIN) bend; **um die Ecke b.** go around the corner

biegsam ['bikzam] adj flexible

Bie'gung f (-;-en) bend, bending; (gram) inflection

Biene ['binə] f (-;-n) bee

Bie'nenfleiß m—mit B. arbeiten work like a bee

Bie'nenhaus n beehive

Bie'nenkorb m beehive

Bie'nenstich m bee sting; (culin) almond pastry

Bie'nenstock m beehive

Bie'nenzucht f beekeeping

Bier [bir] n (-[e]s;-e) beer

bie'ten ['bitən] §58 tr offer; **b. auf** (acc) bid for ‖ ref present itself; **das läßt er sich nicht b.** he won't stand for it

Bigamie [bɪga'mi] f (-;) bigamy

bigott [bɪ'gɔt] adj bigoted

Bigotterie [bɪgɔtə'ri] f (-;) bigotry

Bilanz [bɪ'lants] f (acct) balance; (acct) balance sheet

Bilanz'abteilung f auditing department

bilanzieren [bɪlan'tsirən] intr balance

Bild [bɪlt] n (-es; ̈-er) picture; image; (*Bildnis*) portrait; (in e-m *Buch*) illustration; (*Vorstellung*) idea; (rhet) metaphor, figure of speech; **im Bilde sein** be in the know

Bild'band m (-[e]s; ̈-e) picture book ‖ n (-[e]s; ̈-er) (telv) video tape

Bild'bandgerät n video tape recorder

Bild'betrachter m slide viewer

Bildchen ['bɪltçən] n (-s;-) small picture; (cin) frame

Bild'einstellung f (-;-en) focusing

bilden ['bɪldən] tr form, fashion, create; (*entwerfen*) design; (*gründen*) establish; (*Geist*) educate, develop; (*Gruppe*) constitute ‖ ref form, be produced; develop; educate oneself

bil'dend adj instructive; **bildende Künste** fine arts, plastic arts

bil'derreich adj (*Buch*) richly illustrated; (*Sprache*) picturesque, ornate

Bil'derschrift f picture writing

Bil'dersprache f imagery

Bil'derstürmer m iconoclast

Bild'frequenz f camera speed

Bild'funk m television

bild'haft adj pictorial; graphic

Bildhauer ['bɪlthau·ər] m (-s;-) sculptor

Bildhauerei ['bɪlthau·əraɪ] f (-;) sculpture

Bildhauerin ['bɪlthau·ərɪn] f (-;-nen) sculptress

bild'hübsch adj pretty as a picture

Bild'karte f photographic map; (cards) face card

bild'lich adj pictorial; figurative

Bildner –in ['bɪldnər(ɪn)] §6 mf sculptor ‖ m (fig) molder ‖ f sculptress

Bildnis ['bɪltnɪs] n (-ses;-se) portrait

Bild'röhre f picture tube, TV tube

bildsam ['bɪltzam] adj plastic; (fig) pliant

Bild'säule f statue
Bild'schirm m television screen
bild'schön adj very beautiful
Bild'schriftzeichen n hieroglyph
Bild'seite f head, obverse
Bild'signal n video signal
Bild'stock m wayside shrine
Bild'streifen m filmstrip; (journ) comic strip
Bild'sucher m (phot) viewfinder
Bild'teppich m tapestry
Bild'ton'kamera f sound-film camera
Bil'dung f (-;-en) formation; shape; education, culture
Bil'dungsanstalt f educational institution
Bild'werfer m projector
Bild'werk n sculpture; imagery
Billard ['bɪljart] n (-s;) billiards
Bil'lardkugel f billiard ball
Bil'lardloch n pocket
Bil'lardstab, Bil'lardstock m cue
Billett [bɪl'jet] m (-s;-e) ticket
Billett'ausgabe f, **Billett'schalter** m ticket office; (theat) box office
billig ['bɪlɪç] adj cheap; (Preis) low; (Ausrede, Trost) poor
billigen ['bɪlɪgən] tr approve
Bil'ligung f (-;) approval
Billion [bɪl'jon] f (-;-en) trillion; (Brit) billion
bimbam ['bɪm'bam] interj ding-dong || **Bimbam** m—heiliger **B.!** holy smokes!
bimmeln ['bɪməln] intr (coll) jingle; (telp) ring
Bimsstein ['bɪmsʃtaɪn] m (-s;-e) pumice stone
Binde ['bɪndə] f (-;-n) band; (Krawatte) tie; (Armschlinge) sling; (für Frauen) sanitary napkin; (med) bandage
Bin'deglied n link; (fig) bond, tie
binden ['bɪndən] §59 tr bind, tie
Bin'destrich m hyphen; **mit B. schreiben** hyphenate
Bin'dewort n (-[e]s;ᵉer) conjunction
Bind'faden m string, twine; **es regnet Bindfäden** it's raining cats and dogs
Bin'dung f (-;-en) binding; tie, bond; obligation; (mus) ligature
binnen ['bɪnən] prep (genit & dat) within; **b. kurzem** before long
Binnen- comb.fm. inner; internal; inland; domestic, home
Bin'nengewässer n inland water
Bin'nenhandel m domestic trade
Bin'nenland n inland; interior; **im B.** inland
Binse ['bɪnzə] f (-;-n) rush, reed; **in die Binsen gehen** (coll) go to pot
Bin'senwahrheit f truism
Biochemie [bɪ·oçe'mi] f (-;) biochemistry
Biogra·phie [bɪ·ogra'fi] (-;-phien ['fi·ən] biography
biographisch [bɪ·ə'grafɪʃ] adj biographic(al)
Biologie [bɪ·olo'gi] f (-;) biology
biologisch [bɪ·ə'logɪʃ] adj biological
Biophysik [bɪ·ofʏ'zik] f (-;) biophysics
Birke ['bɪrkə] f (-;-n) birch
Birma ['bɪrma] n (-s;) Burma

Birne ['bɪrnə] f (-;-n) pear; (elec) bulb; (Kopf) (sl) bean
bis [bɪs] prep (acc) (zeitlich) till, until; (örtlich) up to, to; **bis an** (acc) up to; **bis auf** (acc) except for; **bis nach** as far as || conj until, till
Bisamratte ['bizamratə] f (-;-n) muskrat
Bischof ['bɪʃəf] m (-;ᵉe) bishop
bischöflich ['bɪʃøflɪç] adj episcopal
Bi'schofsamt n episcopate
Bi'schofsmütze f miter
Bi'schofssitz m episcopal see
Bi'schofsstab m crosier
bisher [bɪs'her] adv till now
bisherig [bɪs'herɪç] adj former, previous; (Präsident) outgoing
Biskuit [bɪs'kvit] m & n (-[e]s;-e) biscuit
bislang' adv till now
biß [bɪs] pret of **beißen** || **Biß** m (Bisses; Bisse) bite; sting
bißchen ['bɪsçən] n (also used as invar adj & adv) bit, little bit
Bissen ['bɪsən] m (-s;-) bit, morsel
bissig ['bɪsɪç] adj biting, snappish
Bistum ['bɪstum] n (-s;ᵉer) bishopric
bisweilen [bɪs'vaɪlən] adv sometimes
Bitte ['bɪtə] f (-;-n) request; **e-e B.** einlegen bei intercede with
bitten ['bɪtən] §60 tr ask || intr b. für intercede for; **b. um** ask for; **wie bitte?** I beg your pardon? || interj **bitte!** please!; you are welcome!
bitter ['bɪtər] adj bitter
bit'terböse adj (coll) furious
Bit'terkeit f (-;) bitterness
bit'terlich adv bitterly; deeply
Bit'tersalz n Epsom salts
Bittgang ['bɪtgaŋ] m (-[e]s;ᵉe) (eccl) procession
Bittsteller ['bɪtʃtelər] m (-s;-) petitioner, suppliant
Biwak ['bivak] n (-s;-s) bivouac
biwakieren [biva'kirən] intr bivouac
bizarr [bi'tsar] adj bizarre
blähen ['ble·ən] tr inflate, distend || ref swell || intr cause gas
blaken ['blakən] intr smolder
Blamage [bla'maʒə] f (-;-n) disgrace
blamieren [bla'mirən] tr embarrass || ref make a fool of oneself
blank [blaŋk] adj bright; (Schuh) shiny; (bloß) bare; (Schwert) drawn; (sl) broke; **blanke Waffe** side arms; **b. ziehen** draw one's sword
Blankett [blaŋ'ket] n (-s;-e) blank
blanko ['blaŋko] adv—**b. lassen** leave blank; **b. verkaufen** sell short
Blan'koscheck m blank check
Blan'kovollmacht f blanket authority
Blank'vers m blank verse
Bläschen ['blesçən] n (-s;-) small blister; small bubble
Blase ['blazə] f (-;-n) blister; bubble; (coll) gang; (anat) bladder; **Blasen werfen** (Farbe) blister; **Blasen ziehen** (Haut) blister
Bla'sebalg m pair of bellows
blasen ['blazən] tr blow; (Instrument) play || intr blow
Bla'senleiden n bladder trouble
Bläser ['blezər] m (-s;-) blower

blasiert [bla'zirt] *adj* blasé
blasig ['blɑzɪç] *adj* blistery; bubbly
Blas'instrument *n* wind instrument
Blasphe·mie [blasfɛ'mi] *f* (-;-mien [-'mi·ən]) blasphemy
blasphemieren [blasfɛ'mirən] *intr* blaspheme
Blas'rohr *n* blowpipe; peashooter
blaß [blas] *adj* pale; **keine blasse Ahnung** not the foggiest notion
Blässe ['blɛsə] *f* (-;) paleness, pallor
Blatt [blat] *n* (-s;ᵘer) leaf; (*Papier-*) sheet; (*Gras-*) blade
Blatter ['blatər] *f* (-;-n) pustule; **die Blattern** smallpox
blätterig ['blɛtərɪç] *adj* leafy; scaly
blättern ['blɛtərn] *intr*—**in e-m Buch b.** page through a book
Blat'ternarbe *f* pockmark
Blät'terwerk *n* foliage
Blatt'gold *n* gold leaf, gold foil
Blatt'laus *f* aphid
Blatt'pflanze *f* house plant
blättrig ['blɛtrɪç] *adj var* of **blätterig**
Blatt'zinn *n* tin foil
blau [blau] *adj* (& *fig*) blue; (*coll*) drunk; **blaues Auge** black eye; **keinen blauen Dunst haben** (*coll*) not have the foggiest notion; **mit e-m blauen Auge davonkommen** (*coll*) get off easy ‖ **Blau** *n* (-s;-s) blue; blueness
blau'äugig *adj* blue-eyed
Blau'beere *f* blueberry
Bläue ['blɔɪ·ə] *f* (-;) blue; blueness
bläuen ['blɔɪ·ən] *tr* dye blue
bläulich ['blɔɪlɪç] *adj* bluish
blau'machen *intr* (*coll*) take off from work
Blech [blɛç] *n* (-[e]s;-e) sheet metal; (*sl*) baloney; (*mus*) brass
Blech'büchse *f* tin can
blechen ['blɛçən] *tr* (*coll*) pay out ‖ *intr* (*coll*) cough up the dough
Blech'instrument *n* brass instrument
blecken ['blɛkən] *tr*—**die Zähnen b.** bare one's teeth
Blei [blaɪ] *n* (-[e]s;) lead
Bleibe ['blaɪbə] *f* (-;-n) place to stay
bleiben ['blaɪbən] §62 *intr* (SEIN) remain, stay; **am Leben b.** survive; **bei etw b.** stick to s.th.; **dabei bleibt es!** that's final!; **für sich b.** keep to oneself; **sich** [*dat*] **gleich b.** never change; **und wo bleibe ich?** (*coll*) and where do I come in?
blei'bend *adj* lasting, permanent
bleich [blaɪç] *adj* pale ‖ **Bleiche** *f* (-;) bleaching; paleness
blei'chen *tr* bleach; make pale ‖ *intr* (SEIN) bleach; (*verblassen*) fade
Bleich'gesicht *n* paleface
Bleich'mittel *n* bleach
bleiern ['blaɪ·ərn] *adj* leaden
Blei'soldat *m* tin soldier
Blei'stift *m* pencil
Bleistiftspitzer ['blaɪʃtɪftʃpɪtsər] *m* (-s;-) pencil sharpener
Blende ['blɛndə] *f* (-;-n) window blind; shutter; (*phot*) diaphragm
blen'den *tr* blind; (*bezaubern*) dazzle
blen'dend *adj* fabulous
Blen'der *m* (-s;-) (*coll*) fourflusher

Blendling ['blɛntlɪŋ] *m* (-s;-e) (*Mischling*) mongrel; (*bot*) hybrid
Blick [blɪk] *m* (-[e]s;-e) glance, look; (*auf acc*) view (of)
blicken (blik'ken) *intr* (**auf acc, nach**) glance (at), look (at); **sich b. lassen** show one's face
Blick'fang *m* (*coll*) eye catcher
blieb [blip] *pret* of **bleiben**
blies [blis] *pret* of **blasen**
blind [blɪnt] *adj* (**für, gegen**) blind (to); (*Spiegel*) clouded; (*trübe*) dull; (*Alarm*) false; (*Patrone*) blank; **blinder Passagier** stowaway
Blind'band *m* (-[e]s;ᵘe) (*typ*) dummy
Blind'boden *m* subfloor
Blind'darm *m* appendix
Blind'darmentzündung *f* appendicitis
Blind'darmoperation *f* appendectomy
Blin'denheim *n* home for the blind
Blin'denhund *m* Seeing-Eye dog
Blin'denschrift *f* braille
Blind'flug *m* blind flying
Blind'gänger *m* (*mil*) dud
Blind'landung *f* instrument landing
blindlings ['blɪntlɪŋs] *adv* blindly
Blind'schreiben *n* touch typing
blinken ['blɪŋkən] *intr* blink, twinkle; (*Sonne*) shine; (*mil*) signal
Blin'ker *m*, **Blink'licht** *n* (*aut*) blinker
blinzeln ['blɪntsəln] *intr* blink, wink
Blitz [blɪts] *m* (-es;-e) lightning; (*fig* & *phot*) flash
Blitz'ableiter *m* lightning rod
blitz'blank' *adj* shining; spick and span
Blitz'krieg *m* blitzkrieg
Blitz'licht *n* (*phot*) flash
Blitz'lichtaufnahme *f* (*phot*) flash shot
Blitz'lichtbirne *f* (*phot*) flash bulb
Blitz'lichtgerät *n* flash gun
Blitz'lichtröhre *f* (*phot*) electronic flash, flash tube
Blitz'schlag *m* stroke of lightning
blitz'schnell' *adj* quick as lightning
Blitz'strahl *m* flash of lightning
Block [blɔk] *m* (-s;ᵘe) block, log; (*Stück Seife*) cake; (*von Schokolade*) bar; (*von Löschpapier*) pad; (*geol*) boulder; (*metal*) ingot; (*pol*) bloc
Blockade [blɔ'kɑdə] *f* (-;-n) blockade
Blocka'debrecher *m* blockade runner
blocken (blok'ken) *tr* (*sport*) block
Block'haus *n* log cabin
blockieren [blɔ'kirən] *tr* block up; (*mil*) blockade
Block'kalender *m* tear-off calendar
Block'schrift *f* block letters
blöd(e) ['blød(ə)] *adj* stupid, idiotic; feeble-minded; (*schüchtern*) shy
Blöd'heit *f* (-;) stupidity, idiocy
Blö'digkeit *f* (-;) shyness
Blöd'sinn *m* idiocy; nonsense
blöd'sinnig *adj* idiotic ‖ *adv* idiotically; (*sehr*) (*coll*) awfully
blöken ['bløkən] *intr* bleat; (*Kuh*) moo
blond [blɔnt] *adj* blond, fair ‖ **Blonde** §5 *m* blond ‖ *f* blonde
blondieren [blɔn'dirən] *tr* bleach
Blondine [blɔn'dinə] *f* (-;-n) blonde
bloß [blos] *adj* bare; (*nichts als*) mere ‖ *adv* only; barely
Blöße ['bløsə] *f* bareness; nakedness; (*fig*) weak point

bloß'legen *tr* lay bare
bloß'stellen *tr* expose
blühen ['bly·ən] *intr* blossom, bloom; (*Backen*) be rosy; (fig) flourish
Blume ['blumə] *f* (-;-n) flower; (*des Weins*) bouquet; (*des Biers*) head
Blu'menbeet *n* flower bed
Blu'menblatt *n* petal
Blu'mengewinde *n* garland, festoon
Blu'menhändler –in §6 *mf* florist
Blu'menkelch *m* calyx
Blu'menkohl *m* cauliflower
Blu'menstaub *m* pollen
Blu'mentopf *m* flowerpot
Bluse ['bluzə] *f* (-;-n) blouse
Blut [blut] *n* (-[e]s;) blood; **bis aufs B.** almost to death; **B. lecken** taste blood; **heißes B.** hot temper
Blut'andrang *m* (pathol) congestion
blut'arm *adj* anemic
Blut'armut *f* anemia
Blut'bahn *f* bloodstream
Blut'bild *n* blood count
blut'dürstig *adj* bloodthirsty
Blüte ['blytə] *f* (-;-n) blossom, flower, bloom; (fig) prime
Blut'egel *m* leech
bluten ['blutən] *intr* bleed
Blü'tenblatt *n* petal
Blü'tenstaub *m* pollen
Blu'terguß *m* bruise
Blu'terkrankheit *f* hemophilia
Blü'tezeit *f* blooming period; (fig) heyday
Blut'farbstoff *m* hemoglobin
Blut'gerinnsel *n* blood clot
Blut'hund *m* bloodhound
blutig ['blutɪç] *adj* bloody
blut'jung' *adj* very young, green
Blut'körperchen *n* corpuscle
Blut'kreislauf *m* blood circulation
blut'leer, blut'los *adj* bloodless
Blut'pfropfen *m* blood clot
Blut'probe *f* blood test
Blut'rache *f* blood feud
Blut'rausch *m* mania to kill
blutrünstig ['blutrʏnstɪç] *adj* gory
Blut'sauger *m* bloodsucker, leech
Blut'schande *f* incest
blutschänderisch ['blutʃɛndərɪʃ] *adj* incestuous
Blut'spender –in §6 *mf* blood donor
blut'stillend *adj* coagulant
Blut'sturz *m* hemorrhage
Bluts'verwandte §5 *mf* blood relation
Blut'übertragung *f* blood transfusion
blut'unterlaufen *adj* bloodshot
Blut'vergießen *n* (-s;) bloodshed
blut'voll *adj* lively, vivid
Blut'wasser *n* lymph
Blut'zeuge *m*, **Blut'zeugin** *f* martyr
Bö [bø] *f* (-;-en) gust, squall
Bob [bɔb] *m* (-s;-s) bobsled
Bock [bɔk] *m* (-[e]s; ⁼e) buck; ram; he-goat; (*Kutsch-*) driver's seat; (tech) horse; **B. springen** play leapfrog; **e–n B. schießen** pull a boner
bockbeinig ['bɔkbaɪnɪç] *adj* stubborn
bocken ['bɔkən] *intr* buck; (*sich aufbäumen*) rear; (*ausschlagen*) kick; (*brunsten*) be in heat; (aut) hesitate
bockig ['bɔkɪç] *adj* thickheaded
Bock'sprung *m* caper; leapfrog

Boden ['bodən] *m* (-s;⁼) (*Erd-*) ground, soil; (*Meeres-*) bottom; (*Fuß-*) floor; (*Dach-*) attic; (*Trocken-*) loft; **B. fassen** get a firm footing; **zu B. drücken** crush
Bo'denertrag *m* (agr) yield
Bo'denfenster *n* dormer window
Bo'denfläche *f* floor space; (agr) acreage
Bo'denfliese *f* floor tile
Bodenfräse ['bodənfrezə] *f* (-;-n) Rotortiller
Bo'denhaftung *f* roadability
Bo'denkammer *f* attic
bo'denlos *adj* bottomless; (fig) unmitigated
Bo'denmannschaft *f* (aer) ground crew
Bo'denreform *f* agrarian reform
Bo'densatz *m* grounds, sediment
Bodenschätze ['bodənʃɛtsə] *pl* mineral resources
Bo'densee *m* (-s;) Lake Constance
bo'denständig *adj* native, indigenous
bog [bok] *pret* of biegen
Bogen ['bogən] *m* (-s;⁼) bow; (*Kurve*) curve; (*Papier-*) sheet; (*beim Schilaufen*) turn; (*beim Eislaufen*) circle; (archit) arch; (math) arc; **den B. raushaben** have the hang of it; **den B. überspannen** (fig) go too far; **e–n großen B. um j–n machen** give s.o. wide berth
Bo'genfenster *n* bow window
bo'genförmig *adj* arched
Bo'gengang *m* arcade; archway
Bo'genschießen *n* (-s;) archery
Bo'genschütze *m* archer
Bo'gensehne *f* bowstring
Bohle ['bolə] *f* (-;-n) plank
Böhme ['bømə] *m* (-n;-n) Bohemian
Böhmen ['bømən] *n* (-s;) Bohemia
Bohne ['bonə] *f* (-;-n) bean; **blaue Bohnen** bullets; **grüne Bohnen** string beans
Boh'nermasse *f* polish; floor polish
bohnern ['bonərn] *tr* wax, polish
Boh'nerwachs *n* floor wax
Bohr– [bor] *comb.fm.* drill, drilling, bore, boring
bohren ['borən] *tr* drill, bore
Bohrer *m* (-s;-) drill; (ent) borer
Bohr'insel *f* offshore drilling platform
Bohr'presse *f* drill press
Bohr'turm *m* derrick
böig ['bø·ɪç] *adj* gusty; (aer) bumpy
Boje ['bojə] *f* (-;-n) buoy
Böller ['bœlər] *m* (-s;-) mortar
böllern ['bœlərn] *intr* fire a mortar
Bollwerk ['bɔlvɛrk] *n* (-s;-e) bulwark
Bolzen ['bɔltsən] *m* (-s;-) bolt; dowel
Bombardement [bɔmbardə'mɑ̃] *n* (-s; -s) bombardment
bombardieren [bɔmbar'dirən] *tr* bombard
Bombe ['bɔmbə] *f* (-;-n) bomb, bombshell; (coll) smash hit
Bomben– *comb.fm.* bomb, bombing, huge
Bom'benabwurf *m* bombing; **gezielter B.** precision bombing
Bom'benerfolg *m* (theat) smash hit
bom'benfest *adj* bombproof
Bom'benflugzeug *n* bomber

Bom'bengeschäft n (coll) gold mine
Bom'benpunktzielwurf m precision bombing
Bom'benreihenwurf m stick bombing
Bom'bensache f (coll) humdinger
Bom'benschacht m bomb bay
Bom'benschütze m bombardier
Bom'bentrichter m bomb crater
Bom'benzielanflug m bombing run
Bom'benzielgerät n bombsight
Bon [bõ] m (-s;-s) sales slip; (*Gutschein*) credit note
Bonbon [bõ'bõ] m & n (-s;-s) piece of candy; **Bonbons** candy
Bonbonniere [bõbɔnɪ'erə] f (-;-n) box of candy
Bonze ['bɔntsə] m (-;-n) (coll) big shot, bigwig; (pol) boss
Boot [bot] n (-[e]s;-e) boat
Boots'mann m (-es;-leute) boatswain; (nav) petty officer
Bord [bɔrt] m (-es;e) edge; bookshelf; (naut) board, side; **an B.** aboard, on board; **von B. gehen** leave the ship
Bordell [bɔr'dɛl] n (-s;-e) brothel
Bord'karte f boarding pass
Bord'schütze m aerial gunner
Bord'schwelle f curb
Bord'stein m curb
Bord'waffen pl (aer, mil) armament
Bord'wand f ship's side
Borg [bɔrk] m (-s;) borrowing; **auf B.** on credit; on loan
borgen ['bɔrgən] tr (**von, bei**) borrow (from); loan out, lend
Borke ['bɔrkə] f (-;-n) bark
Born [bɔrn] m (-es; -e) (poet) fountain
borniert [bɔr'nirt] adj narrow-minded
Borsäure ['bɔrzɔɪrə] f (-;) boric acid
Börse ['bœrzə] f (-;-n) purse; stock exchange
Bör'senkurs m market price; quotation
Bör'senmakler -in §6 mf stockbroker
Bör'senmarkt m stockmarket
Bör'sennotierung f (st.exch.) quotation
Bör'senpapiere pl stocks, shares, securities
Borste ['bɔrstə] f (-;-n) bristle
borstig ['bɔrstɪç] adj birstly; (fig) crusty
Borte ['bɔrtə] f (-;-n) trim; braid; (*Saum*) hem
bös [bøs] var of **böse**
bös'artig adj nasty; (*Tier*) vicious; (pathol) malignant
Böschung ['bœʃʊŋ] f (-;-en) slope; (*e-s Flusses*) bank; (rr) embankment
böse ['bøzə] adj bad, evil, nasty; angry || **Böse** §5 mf wicked person || m devil || n evil; harm
Bösewicht ['bøzəvɪçt] m (-s;-e) villain
boshaft ['boshaft] adj malicious; wicked; (*tückisch*) spiteful
bossieren [bɔ'sirən] tr emboss
bös'willig adj malicious, willful
bot [bot] pret of **bieten**
Botanik [bɔ'tɑnɪk] f (-;) botany
Botaniker -in §6 mf botanist
botanisch [bɔ'tɑnɪʃ] adj botanic(al)
Bote ['botə] m (-n;-n) messenger
Bo'tengang m errand
Botin ['botɪn] f (-;-nen) messenger

Bot'schaft f (-;-en) message, news; (*Amt*) embassy; (*Auftrag*) mission
Botschafter -in ['bot/aftər(ɪn)] §6 ambassador
Bottich ['bɔtɪç] m (-s;-e) tub; vat
Bouillon (bʊl'jõ] f (-;-s) bouillon
Bowle ['bolə] f (-;-n) punch
boxen ['bɔksən] tr & intr box
Bo'xer m (-s;-) boxer
Box'kampf m boxing match
Boykott [bɔɪ'kɔt] m (-s;-e) boycott
boykottieren [bɔɪkɔ'tirən] tr boycott
brach [brɑx] pret of **brechen** || adj fallow
brachte ['braxtə] pret of **bringen**
brackig ['brakɪç] adj brackish
Branche ['brɑ̃ʃə] f (-;-n) line of business; (com) branch
Brand [brant] m (-[e]s;ːe) burning; fire; (coll) thirst; (agr) blight; (pathol) gangrene **in B. geraten** catch fire; **in B. setzen** (or **stecken**) set on fire
Brand'blase f blister
Brand'bombe f incendiary bomb
Brand'brief m urgent letter
Brand'direktor m fire chief
branden ['brandən] intr surge, break
Brand'fackel f firebrand
brandig ['brandɪç] adj (agr) blighted; (pathol) gangrenous
Brand'mal n brand; (fig) moral stigma
brand'marken tr stigmatize
Brand'mauer f fire wall
brandschatzen ['brant/atsən] tr sack
Brand'stifter -in §6 mf arsonist
Bran'dung f (-;) breakers
Bran'dungswelle f breaker
Brand'wunde f burn
Brand'zeichen n brand
brannte ['brantə] pret of **brennen**
Branntwein ['brantvaɪn] m brandy
Brasilien [bra'ziljən] n (-s;) Brazil
Bratapfel ['brɑtapfəl] m baked apple
braten ['brɑtən] §63 tr & intr roast; (*im Ofen*) bake; (*auf dem Rost*) broil, grill; (*in der Pfanne*) fry || **Braten** m (-s;-) roast
Bra'tensoße f gravy
Brat'fisch m fried fish
Brat'huhn n broiler
Brat'kartoffeln pl fried potatoes
Brat'pfanne f frying pan, skillet
Bratsche ['brat/ə] f (-;-n) viola
Bräu [brɔɪ] m & n (-[e]s;) brew
Brauch [braʊx] m (-[e]s;ːe) custom
brauchbar ['braʊxbɑr] adj useful
brauchen ['braʊxən] tr need; (*Zeit*) take; (*gebrauchen*) use
Brauchtum ['braʊxtum] n (-s;) tradition
Braue ['braʊ·ə] f (-;-n) eyebrow
brauen ['braʊ·ən] tr brew
Brau'er m (-s;-) brewer
Brauerei [braʊ·ə'raɪ] f (-;-en), **Brau'haus** n brewery
braun [braʊn] adj brown; (*Pferd*) bay
Bräune ['brɔɪnə] f (-;) brown; sun tan; (pathol) diphtheria
bräunen ['brɔɪnən] tr tan; (culin) brown || ref & intr tan
bräunlich ['brɔɪnlɪç] adj brownish
Braus [braʊs] m (-es;) noise; revelry

Brause ['brauzə] ƒ (-;-n) soda, soft drink; (Duschbad) shower; (an Gießkannen) nozzle
Brau'sebad n shower
Brau'sekopf m hothead
Brau'selimonade ƒ soda, soft drink
brau'sen tr spray, water || intr bubble; (toben) roar || intr (SEIN) rush
Braut [braut] ƒ (-;⁻e) fiancée; bride
Braut'ausstattung ƒ trousseau
Braut'führer m usher
Bräutigam ['brɔitɪgam] m (-s;-e) fiancé; bridegroom
Braut'jungfer ƒ (-;-n) bridesmaid; **erste B.** maid of honor
Braut'kleid n bridal gown
Braut'leute pl engaged couple
bräutlich ['brɔitlɪç] adj bridal; nuptial
Braut'schatz m dowry
Braut'werber –in §6 mƒ matchmaker
Braut'werbung ƒ courting
Braut'zeit ƒ period of engagement
Braut'zeuge m best man
brav [braf] adj well-mannered, good, honest
Brav'heit ƒ good behavior
Bravour [bra'vur] ƒ (-;) bravado
Brech'eisen n crowbar, jimmy
brechen ['breçən] §64 tr break; (Papier) fold; (Steine) quarry; (Blumen) pick; (coll) vomit; (opt) refract; **die Ehe b.** commit adultery || ref break; (opt) be refracted || intr (SEIN) break; (coll) vomit
Brech'reiz m nausea
Brech'stange ƒ crowbar
Bre'chung ƒ (-;-en) (opt) refraction
Brei [brai] m (-s;-e) paste; pap, gruel; **zu B. schlagen** beat to a pulp
breit [brait] adj broad, wide
breitbeinig ['braitbainiç] adv with legs outspread
breit'drücken tr flatten (out)
Brei'te ƒ (-;-n) width; latitude
Brei'tengrad m degree of latitude
breit'machen ref take up (too much) room; (fig) throw one's weight around
breit'schlagen §132 tr (coll) persuade
breitschulterig ['braitʃultəriç] adj broad-shouldered
breitspurig ['braitʃpuriç] adj (coll) pompous; (rr) broad-gauge
breit'treten §152 tr belabor
Breit'wand ƒ (cin) wide screen
Bremsbelag ['bremsbəlak] m brake lining
Bremse ['bremzə] ƒ (-;-n) brake; (ent) horsefly
bremsen ['bremzən] tr brake; (fig) curb; (atom phys) slow down || intr brake
Brem'ser m (-s;-) brakeman
Brems'flüssigkeit ƒ brake fluid
Brems'fußhebel m brake pedal
Brems'klotz m wheel chock
Bremsleuchte ['bremslɔiçtə] ƒ, **Brems'licht** n (aut) brake light
Brems'rakete ƒ (rok) retrorocket
Brems'schuh m brake shoe
brems'sicher adj skidproof
Brems'spur ƒ skid mark
Brems'wagen m (rr) caboose

Brems'weg m braking distance
Brennapparat ['brenaparat] m still
brennbar ['brenbar] adj inflammable, combustible
brennen §97 tr burn; (Branntwein) distil; (Kaffee) roast; (Haar) curl; (Ziegel) fire || intr burn; smart
Bren'ner m (-s;-) burner; distiller
Brennerei [brenə'rai] ƒ (-;-en) distillery
Brenn'holz n firewood
Brenn'material n fuel
Brenn'ofen m kiln
Brenn'punkt m focus; **im B. stehen** be the focal point
Brenn'schere ƒ curler
Brenn'schluß m (rok) burnout
Brenn'spiegel m concave mirror
Brenn'stoff m fuel
brenzlig ['brentslɪç] adj (Geruch) burnt; (Situation) precarious
Bresche ['breʃə] ƒ (-;-n) breach; **e-e B. schlagen** make a breach
Brett [bret] n (-[e]s;-er) board; plank; (für Bücher, Geschirr) shelf; **Bretter** (coll) skis; (theat) stage; **Schwarzes B.** bulletin board
Bret'terbude ƒ shack
Bret'terverschlag m wooden partition
Brett'säge ƒ ripsaw
Brezel ['bretsəl] ƒ (-;-n) pretzel
Brief [brif] m (-[e]s;-e) letter; **Briefe wechseln** correspond
Brief'ausgabe ƒ mail delivery
Briefbeschwerer ['brifbəʃverər] m (-s;-) paperweight
Brief'bestellung ƒ mail delivery
Brief'beutel m mail bag
Brief'bogen m piece of notepaper
Brief'bote m mailman, postman
Briefchen ['brifçən] n (-s;-) note; **B. Streichhölzer** book of matches
Brief'einwurf m slot in a mailbox; letterdrop; mailbox
Brief'fach n pigeonhole; post-office box
Brief'freund –in §8 mƒ pen pal
Brief'hülle ƒ envelope
Brief'kasten m mailbox
Brief'klammer ƒ paper clip
Brief'kopf m letterhead
Brief'kurs m (st.exch.) selling price
brief'lich adj written; **brieflicher Verkehr** correspondence || adv by letter
Brief'mappe ƒ folder
Brief'marke ƒ postage stamp
Brief'markenautomat m stamp machine
Brief'ordner m ring binder
Brief'papier n stationery; note paper
Brief'porto n postage
Brief'post ƒ first-class mail
Brief'schaften pl correspondence
Brief'stempel m postmark
Brief'tasche ƒ billfold, wallet
Brief'taube ƒ carrier pigeon
Brief'träger m mailman, postman
Brief'umschlag m envelope
Brief'verkehr m correspondence
Brief'waage ƒ postage scales
Brief'wahl ƒ absentee ballot
Brief'wechsel m correspondence
briet [brit] pret of **braten**

Brigade [brɪˈgɑdə] *f* (-;-n) brigade
Briga'degeneral *m* brigadier general; (Brit) brigadier
Brikett [brɪˈkɛt] *n* (-[e]s;-s) briquette
brillant [brɪlˈjant] *adj* brilliant ‖ **Brillant** *m* (-en;-en) precious stone (esp. diamond)
Brille [ˈbrɪlə] *f* (-;-n) eyeglasses; (*für Pferde*) blinkers; (*Toilettenring*) toilet seat; **B. mit doppeltem Brennpunkt** bifocals
Bril'lenbügel *m* sidepiece (*of glasses*)
Bril'lenfassung *f* eyeglass frame
Bril'lenschlange *f* cobra
bringen [ˈbrɪŋən] §65 *tr* bring, take; **an sich b.** acquire; **es mit sich b.**, **daß** bring it about that; **es zu etw b.** achieve s.th.; **etw hinter sich b.** get s.th. over and done with; **etw über sich** (or **übers Herz**) **b.** be able to bear s.th.; **j-n auf etw b.** put s.o. on to s.th.; **j-n außer sich b.** enrage s.o.; **j-n dazu b. zu** (*inf*) get s.o. to (*inf*); **j-m um etw b.** deprive s.o. of s.th.; **j-n zum Lachen b.** make s.o. laugh; **unter die Leute b.** circulate
brisant [brɪˈzant] *adj* high-explosive
Brise [ˈbrizə] *f* (-;-n) breeze
Britannien [brɪˈtanjən] *n* (-s;) Britain
Brite [ˈbrɪtə] *m* (-n;-n) Briton, Britisher; **die Briten** the British
Britin [ˈbrɪtɪn] *f* (-;-nen) Briton, British woman
britisch [ˈbrɪtɪʃ] *adj* British
Broché [brɔˈʃe] *n* (-s;) broché; brocaded fabric
Bröckchen [ˈbrœkçən] *n* (-s;-) bit; morsel, crumb; fragment
bröck(e)lig [ˈbrœk(ə)lɪç] *adj* crumbly
bröckeln [ˈbrœkəln] *tr & intr* crumble
brocken [ˈbrɔkən] *tr*—**Brot in die Suppe b.** break bread into the soup ‖ **Brocken** *m* (-s;-) piece, bit; lump; **Brocken** *pl* scraps, bits and pieces; **harter B.** (coll) tough job
brockenweise [brɔkˈkenweise] *adv* bit by bit
brodeln [ˈbrodəln] *intr* bubble, simmer
Brokat [brɔˈkɑt] *m* (-s;-e) brocade
Brombeere [ˈbrɔmberə] *f* (-;-n) blackberry
Bromid [brɔˈmit] *n* (-[e]s;-e) bromide
Bronchitis [brɔnˈçitɪs] *f* (-;) bronchitis
Bronze [ˈbrɔ̃sə] *f* (-;-n) bronze
Brosche [ˈbrɔʃə] *f* (-;-n) brooch
broschieren [brɔˈʃirən] *tr* stitch; brocade; **broschiert** with stapled binding
Broschüre [brɔˈʃyrə] *f* (-;-n) brochure
Brösel [ˈbrøzəl] *m* (-s;-) crumb
Brot [brot] *n* (-[e]s;-e) bread; loaf; **geröstetes B.** toast
Brot'aufstrich *m* spread
Brötchen [ˈbrøtçən] *n* (-s;-) roll
Brot'erwerb *m* livelihood, living
Brot'geber *m*, **Brot'herr** *m* employer
Brot'kasten *m* breadbox
brot'los *adj* unemployed; unprofitable
Brot'neid *m* professional jealousy
Brot'röster *m* (-s;-) toaster
Brot'schnitte *f* slice of bread
Brot'studium *n* bread-and-butter courses
Brot'zeit *f* breakfast

Bruch [brux] *m* (-[e]s;ˑˑe) breaking; break, crack; breakage; (aer) crash; (geol) fault; (math) fraction; (min) quarry; (pathol) hernia; (surg) fracture; **B. machen** crash-land; **in die Brüche gehen** go to pot; **zu B. gehen** break ‖ [brux] *m & n* (-s;ˑˑe) bog
Bruch'band *n* (-s;ˑˑer) (surg) truss
Bruch'bude *f* shanty
brüchig [ˈbrүçɪç] *adj* fragile, brittle
Bruch'landung *f* crash landing
Bruch'rechnung *f* fractions
Bruch'stück *n* fragment, chip; **Bruchstücke** (fig) scraps, snatches
bruch'stückhaft *adj* fragmentary
Bruch'teil *m* fraction; **im B. e-r Sekunde** in a split second
Bruch'zahl *f* fractional number
Brücke [ˈbrүkə] *f* (-;-n) bridge; (*Teppich*) small (narrow) rug; (gym) backbend
Brückenkopf (Brük'kenkopf) *m* bridgehead
Brückenpfeiler (Brük'kenpfeiler) *m* pier of a bridge
Brückenwaage (Brük'kenwaage) *f* platform scale
Brückenzoll (Brük'kenzoll) *m* bridge toll
Bruder [ˈbrudər] *m* (-sˑˑ) brother; (*Genosse*) companion; (eccl) lay brother
brüderlich [ˈbrydərlɪç] *adj* brotherly
Brüderschaft [ˈbrydərʃaft] *f* (-;-en) brotherhood; fraternity
Brühe [ˈbry·ə] *f* (-;-n) broth; (*Fleisch-*) gravy; **in der B. stecken** be in a jam
brühen [ˈbry·ən] *tr* boil; scald
brüh'heiß' *adj* piping hot
Brüh'kartoffeln *pl* potatoes boiled in broth
Brüh'würfel *m* bouillon cube
brüllen [ˈbrylən] *tr & intr* roar, bellow; (*Sturm*) howl; (*Ochse*) low; **b. vor Lachen** roar with laughter
Brummbär [ˈbrumber] *m* (-en;-en) grouch
brummen [ˈbrumən] *tr* mumble; grumble; growl ‖ *intr* mumble; grumble; growl; (*summen*) buzz, hum; (*Orgel*) boom; (*im Gefängnis*) do time, do a stretch
brummig [ˈbrumɪç] *adj* grouchy
brünett [brүˈnɛt] *adj* brunet(te) ‖ **Brünette** §5 brunette
Brunft [brunft] *f* (-;) rut
Brunft'zeit *f* rutting season
Brunnen [ˈbrunən] *m* (-s;-) well; (*Spring-*) spring
Brunnenkresse [ˈbrunənkresə] *f* (-;-n) watercress
Brunst [brunst] *f* (-;) rut, heat; (fig) ardor, passion
brunsten [ˈbrunstən] *intr* be in heat
brünstig [ˈbrүnstɪç] *adj* in heat; (fig) passionate
brüsk [brusk] *adj* brusque
brüskieren [brusˈkirən] *tr* snub
Brust [brust] *f* (-;ˑˑ) breast, chest
Brust'bein *n* breastbone, sternum
Brust'bild *n* portrait; (sculp) bust
brüsten [ˈbrүstən] *ref* show off

Brust′fellentzündung *f* pleurisy
Brust′kasten *m*, **Brust′korb** *m* thorax
Brust′schwimmen *n* breast stroke
Brust′stück *n* (culin) brisket
Brust′ton *m* —**im B. der Überzeugung** with utter conviction
Brust′umfang *m* chest measurement; (*bei Frauen*) bust measurement
Brü′stung *f* (-;-en) balustrade
Brust′warze *f* nipple
Brust′wehr *f* breastwork
Brut [brut] *f* (-;-en) brood; (pej) scum
brutal [brʊ′tɑl] *adj* brutal
Brut′apparat *m*, **Brut′ofen** *m* incubator
brüten [′brytən] *tr* hatch; (fig) plan ‖ *intr* incubate; **b. auf** (*dat*) (fig) sit on; **b. über** (*dat*) brood over; pore over
brutto [′brʊto] *adj* (com) gross
Brut′tosozialprodukt *n* gross national product
Bube [′bubə] *m* (-n;-n) boy; (*Schurke*) rascal; (cards) jack
Bu′benstreich *m*, **Bu′benstück** *n* prank; dirty trick
bübisch [′bybɪʃ] *adj* rascally
Buch [bux] *n* (-[e]s;-̈er) book; (cards) straight
Buch′besprechung *f* book review
Buchbinderei [′buxbɪndəraɪ] *f* (-;-en) bookbindery; (*Gewerbe*) bookbinding
Buch′binderleinwand *f* buckram
Buch′deckel *m* book cover
Buch′drama *n* closet drama
Buch′druck *m* printing, typography
Buch′drucker *m* printer
Buch′druckerei *f* print shop; (*Gewerbe*) printing
Buche [′buxə] *f* (-;-n) beech
Buchecker [′buxɛkər] *f* (-;-n) beechnut
buchen [′buxən] *tr* book, reserve; (com) enter
Bücher– [byçər] *comb.fm.* book
Bü′cherabschluß *m* balancing of books
Bücherausgabe *f* circulation desk
Bü′cherbrett *n* bookshelf
Bücherei [byçə′raɪ] *f* (-;-en) library
Bü′cherfreund *m* bibliophile
Bü′chergestell *n* bookrack, bookcase
Bü′cherregal *n* bookshelf; bookcase
Bü′cherrevision *f* audit
Bü′cherrevisor *m* auditor; accountant
Bü′cherschrank *m* bookcase
Bü′cherstütze *f* book end
Buch′führung *f* bookkeeping, accounting
Buch′halter –in §6 *mf* bookkeeper
Buch′haltung *f* bookkeeping; accounting department
Buch′händler –in §6 *mf* book dealer
Buch′handlung *f* bookstore
Büchlein [′byçlaɪn] *n* (-s;-) booklet
Buch′macher *m* bookmaker
Buch′prüfer –in §6 *mf* auditor
Buchsbaum [′buksbaum] *m* boxwood
Buchse [′buksə] *f* (-;-n) (mach) bushing
Büchse [′byksə] *f* (-;-n) box, case; (*Dose*) can; (*Gewhr*) rifle
Büch′senfleisch *n* canned meat

Büch′senöffner *m* can opener
Buchstabe [′buxʃtabə] *m* (-n;-n) letter
buchstabieren [buxʃta′birən] *tr & intr* spell
buchstäblich [′buxʃtepliç] *adj* literal
Bucht [buxt] *f* (-;-en) bay
Buch′umschlag *m* book jacket
Bu′chung *f* (-;-en) booking; (acct) entry
Buckel [′bukəl] *m* (-s;-) hump; (coll) back; **B. haben** be hunchback; **e–n B. machen** arch its back
buck(e)lig [′buk(ə)lɪç] *adj* hunchbacked ‖ **Buck(e)lige** §5 *mf* hunchback
bücken [′bykən] *tr & ref* bow (down)
Bückling [′byklɪŋ] *m* (-s;-e) bow
Bude [′budə] *f* (-;-n) booth, stall; (coll) shanty; (coll) hole in the wall
Budget [by′dʒe] *n* (-s;-s) budget
Büfett [by′fe], [by′fet] *n* (-s;-s) buffet, sideboard; counter; (*Schanktisch*) bar; **kaltes B.** cold buffet
Büffel [′byfəl] *m* (-s;-) buffalo
Büffelei [byfə′laɪ] *f* (-;-en) cramming
büffeln [′byfəln] *intr* (für) cram (for)
Bug [buk] *m* (-[e]s;-e) (aer) nose; (naut) bow; (zool) shoulder, withers
Bügel [′bygəl] *m* (-s;-) handle; (*Kleider–*) coat hanger; (*Steig–*) stirrup; (*e–r Säge*) frame
Bü′gelbrett *n* ironing board
Bü′geleisen *n* iron, flatiron
Bü′gelfalte *f* crease
bü′gelfrei *adj* drip-dry
bügeln [′bygəln] *tr* iron, press
Bü′gelsäge *f* hacksaw
bugsieren [buk′sirən] *tr* tow
Buhldirne [′buldɪrnə] *f* (-;-n) bawd
buhlen [′bulən] *intr* have an affair; **um j–s Gunst b.** curry favor with s.o.
Bühne [′bynə] *f* (-;-n) stage; platform
Büh′nenanweisung *f* stage direction
Büh′nenaussprache *f* standard pronunciation
Büh′nenausstattung *f*, **Büh′nenbild** *n* set
Büh′nenbildner –in §6 *mf* stage designer
Büh′nendeutsch *n* standard German
Büh′nendichter –in §6 *mf* playwright
Büh′nendichtung *f* drama, play
Büh′nenkünstler *m* actor
Büh′nenkünstlerin *f* actress
Büh′nenleiter –in §6 *mf* stage manager
Büh′nenstück *n* play, stage play
buk [buk] *pret* of **backen**
Bukarest [′bukarest] *n* (-s;) Bucharest
Bulette [bu′letə] *f* (-;-n) meatball
Bulgarien [bul′garjən] *n* (-s;) Bulgaria
Bullauge [′bulaugə] *n* (-s;-en) porthole
Bulldogge [′buldɔgə] *f* (-;-n) bulldog
Bulle [′bulə] *m* (-n;-n) bull; brawny fellow; (sl) cop ‖ *f* (-;-n) (eccl) bull
bullern [′bulərn] *intr* bubble, boil; (*Feuer*) roar; (*Sturm*) rage
Bummel [′buməl] *m* (-s) stroll
Bummelei [bumə′laɪ] *f* (-;-en) dawdling; loafing; sloppiness
bummelig [′buməlɪç] *adj* slow; sloppy
bummeln [′buməln] *intr* loaf; dawdle; (*Autos*) crawl ‖ *intr* (SEIN) stroll

Bum′melstreik *m* slowdown
Bum′melzug *m* (coll) slow train, local
Bummler [′bumlər] *m* (-s;-) loafer, bum; slowpoke; gadabout
Bums [bums] *m* (-es;-e) thud, thump, bang ‖ *interj* boom!; bang!
bumsen [′bumsən] *intr* thud, thump, bump; (sl) have intercourse
Bums′lokal *n* (coll) dive, joint
Bund [bunt] *m* (-[e]s;⸗) union, federation; (*Schlüssel-*) ring; (*Rand an Hose*) waistband; (*Ehe*) bond; (mach) flange; (mus) fret; (pol) federal government; **im Bunde mit** with the cooperation of ‖ *n* (-[e]s;- & -e) bunch, bundle
Bündel [′byndəl] *n* (-s;-) bunch, bundle; (phys) beam
Bundes– *comb.fm.* federal
Bun′desgenosse *m* ally, confederate
Bun′desgerichtshof *m* federal supreme court
Bun′deslade *f* ark of the covenant
bun′desstaatlich *adj* state; federal
Bun′destag *m* lower house
bündig [′byndıç] *adj* binding; (*überzeugend*) convincing; (*treffend*) succint; **b. liegen** be flush
Bündnis [′byntnıs] *n* (-ses;-se) agreement, pact, alliance
Bunker [′buŋkər] *m* (-;-) bin; (agr) silo; (aer) air-raid shelter; (mil) bunker; (nav) submarine pen
bunt [bunt] *adj* colored; (*mehrfarbig*) multicolored; (*gefleckt*) dappled; (*gemischt*) varied, motley; (*Farbe*) bright, gay; (*Wiese*) gay with flowers; **bunter Abend** variety show; **buntes Durcheinander** complete muddle
Bunt′metall *n* nonferrous metal
Bunt′stift *m* colored pencil, crayon
Bürde [′byrdə] *f* (-;-n) burden
Burg [burk] *f* (-;-en) fortress, stronghold; citadel; castle
Bürge [′byrgə] *m* (-;-n) bondsman, guarantor, surety; **B. sein für** (or **als B. haften für**) stand surety for (*s.o.*); vouch for (*s.th.*)
bürgen [′byrgən] *intr*—**b. für** put up bail for (*s.o.*); vouch for (*s.th.*)
Bürger –in [′byrgər(ın)] §6 *mf* citizen; member of the middle class; commoner
Bür′gerkrieg *m* civil war
bür′gerlich *adj* civic; civil; middle-class; (*nicht überfeinert*) plain
Bür′germeister *m* mayor
Bür′gerrecht *n* civil rights
Bür′gerschaft *f* (-;) citizens

Bür′gersteig *m* sidewalk
Bürgschaft [′byrkʃaft] *f* (-;-en) security, guarantee; (jur) bail; **gegen B. freilassen** release on bail
Büro [by′ro] *n* (-s;-s) office
Büro′angestellte §5 *mf* clerk
Büro′bedarf *m* office supplies
Büro′klammer *f* paper clip
Büro′kraft *f* office worker; **Bürokräfte** office personnel
Bürokrat [byro′krat] *m* (-en;-en) bureaucrat
Bürokra·tie [byrokra′ti] *f* (-;-tien [′ti·ən]) bureaucracy; (fig) red tape
bürokratisch [byro′kratıʃ] *adj* bureaucratic
Bursch(e [′burʃ(ə)] *m* (-[e]n;-[e]n) boy, fellow; (mil) orderly; **ein übler B.** a bad egg
burschikos [burʃı′kos] *adj* tomboyish; devil-may-care
Bürste [′byrstə] *f* (-;-n) brush; (coll) crewcut
bürsten [′byrstən] *tr* brush
Bürzel [′byrtsəl] *m* (-s;-) rump (*of bird*)
Bus [bus] *m* (-ses;-se) bus
Busch [buʃ] *m* (-es;⸗e) bush; forest
Büschel [′byʃəl] *m* & *n* clump, bunch, cluster; (*Haar-*) tuft; (elec) brush
Busch′holz *n* brushwood
buschig [′buʃıç] *adj* bushy; shaggy
Busch′klepper *m* bushwacker
Busch′messer *n* machete
Busch′werk *n* bushes, brush
Busen [′buzən] *m* (-s;-) bosom, breast; (*Bucht*) bay, gulf; (fig) bosom
Bussard [′busart] *m* (-s;-e) buzzard
Buße [′busə] *f* (-n;-n) penance; (*Sühne*) atonement; (*Strafgeld*) fine
büßen [′bysən] *tr* atone for, pay for
Büßer –in [′bysər(ın)] §6 *mf* penitent
Busserl [′busərl] *n* (-s;-n) kiss
buß′fertig *adj* repentant
Bussole [bu′solə] *f* (-;-n) compass
Büste [′bystə] *f* (-;-n) bust
Bü′stenhalter *m* brassière, bra
Bütte [′bytə] *f* (-;-n) tub; vat
Butter [′butər] *f* (-;) butter
But′terbrot *n* bread and butter
But′terdose *f* butter dish
But′termilch *f* buttermilk
buttern [′butərn] butter ‖ *intr* make butter
byzantinisch [bytsan′tinıʃ] *adj* Byzantine
Byzanz [by′tsants] *n* (-′;) Byzantium
bzw. *abbr* (**beziehungsweise**) respectively

C

C, c [tze] *invar n* C, c;(meteor) centigrade; (mus) C
Café [ka′fe] *n* (-s;-s) café; coffee shop
Camping [′kempıŋ] *n* (-s;-s) camping
Canaille [ka′naljə] *f* (-;-n) scoundrel
Cäsar [′tsezar] *m* (-s;) Caesar
Cellist –in [tʃɛ′lıst(ın)] §7 *mf* cellist

Cello [′tʃɛlo] *n* (-s;-s) cello
Cellophan [tsɛlo′fan] *n* (-s;) cellophane
Celsius [′tsɛlzjus] centigrade
Cembalo [′tʃɛmbalo] *n* (-s;-s) harpsichord
Ces [tsɛs] *n* (-;-) (mus) C flat

Champagner [ʃamˈpanjər] *m* (-s;-) champagne
Champignon [ˈʃampɪnjõ] *m* (-s;-s) mushroom
Chance [ˈʃansə] *f* (-;-n) chance
Chaos [ˈkaɔs] *n* (-;) chaos
chaotisch [kaˈɔtɪʃ] *adj* chaotic
Charak·ter [kaˈraktər] *m* (-s;-tere [ˈterə]) character; (mil) honorary rank
Charak′terbild *n* character sketch
Charak′tereigenschaft *f* trait
charak′terfest *adj* of a strong character
charakterisieren [karaktɛrɪˈzirən] *tr* characterize
Charakteristik [karaktɛˈrɪstɪk] *f* (-; -en) characterization
Charakteristi·kum [karaktɛˈrɪstɪkum] *n* [-s;-ka [ka]) characteristic
charakteristisch [karaktɛˈrɪstɪʃ] *adj* (für) characteristic (of)
charak′terlich *adj* of character ‖ *adv* in character
charak′terlos *adj* wishy-washy
Charak′terzug *m* characteristic, trait
Charge [ˈʃarʒə] *f* (-;-n) (metal) charge; (mil) rank; **Chargen** (mil) non-coms
charmant [ʃarˈmant] *adj* charming
Charme [ʃarm] *m* (-s;) charm, grace
Chas·sis [ʃaˈsi] *n* (-sis [ˈsi[s]]; -sis [ˈsis]) chassis
Chaus·see [ʃɔˈse] *f* (-;-seen [ˈse·ən]) highway
Chef [ʃɛf] *m* (-s;-s) chief, head; (com) boss; (culin) chef; **C. des Generalstabs** chief of staff; **C. des Heeresjustizwesens** judge advocate general
Chemie [çeˈmi] *f* (-;) chemistry; **technische C.** chemical engineering
Chemie′faser *f* synthetic fiber
Chemikalien [çemɪˈkaljən] *pl* chemicals
Chemiker –in [ˈçemɪkər(ɪn)] §6′ *mf* chemist; student of chemistry
chemisch [ˈçemɪʃ] *adj* chemical; **chemische Reinigung** dry cleaning
Chemotechniker –in [çemɔˈtɛçnɪkər- (ɪn)] §6 *mf* chemical engineer
Chiffre [ˈʃifər] *f* (-;-n) cipher; code; (in Anzeigen) box number
Chif′freschrift *f* code
chiffrieren [ʃiˈfrirən] *tr* code
China [ˈçina] *n* (-s;) China
Chinese [çiˈnezə] *m* (-n;-n;), **Chinesin** [çiˈnezɪn] *f* (-;-nen) Chinese
chinesisch [çiˈnezɪʃ] *adj* Chinese
Chinin [çiˈnin] *n* (-s;) quinine
Chirurg [çiˈrurg] *m* (-en;-en) surgeon
Chirurgie [çirurˈgi] *f* (-;) surgery
chirurgisch [çiˈrurgɪʃ] *adj* surgical
Chlor [klor] *n* (-s;) chlorine
chloren [ˈklorən] *tr* chlorinate
Chlorid [kloˈrit] *n* (-[e]s;-e) chloride
Chloroform [klɔrɔˈfɔrm] *n* (-s;) chloroform

chloroformieren [klɔrɔfɔrˈmirən] *tr* chloroform
Cholera [ˈkolera] *f* (-;) cholera
cholerisch [kɔˈlerɪʃ] *adj* choleric
Chor [kor] *m* (-s;ⁿe) choir; chorus
Choral [kɔˈral] *m* (-s;ⁿe) Gregorian chant; (Prot) hymn
Chor′altar *m* high altar
Chor′anlage *f* (archit) choir
Chor′bühne *f* choir loft
Choreograph –in [kɔrɛ·ɔˈgraf(ɪn)] §7 *mf* choreographer
Chor′hemd *n* surplice
Chor′stuhl *m* choir stall
Christ [krɪst] *m* (-s;) Christ ‖ *m* (-en; -en) Christian
Christ′abend *m* Christmas Eve
Christ′baum *m* Christmas tree
Chri′stenheit *f* (-;) Christendom
Christentum [ˈkrɪstəntum] *n* (-s;) Christianity
Christin [ˈkrɪstɪn] *f* (-;-nen) Christian
Christ′kind *m* Christ child
christ′lich *adj* Christian
Christ′nacht *f* Holy Night
Chri·stus [ˈkrɪstus] *m* (-sti [sti];) Christ; **nach Christi Geburt A.D.**; **vor Christus B.C.**
Chri′stusbild *n* crucifix; picture of Christ
Chrom [krom] *n* (-s;) chromium, chrome
chromatisch [krɔˈmatɪʃ] *adj* chromatic
Chromosom [krɔmɔˈzom] *n* (-s;-en) chromosome
Chronik [ˈkronɪk] *f* (-;-en) chronicle
chronisch [ˈkronɪʃ] *adj* chronic
Chronist –in [krɔˈnɪst(ɪn)] §7 *mf* chronicler
Chronolo·gie [krɔnɔlɔˈgi] *f* (-;-gien [ˈgi·ən]) chronology
chronologisch [krɔnɔˈlogɪʃ] *adj* chronological
circa [ˈtsɪrka] *adv* approximately
Cis [tsɪs] *n* (-;-) (mus) C sharp
Clique [ˈklɪkə] *f* (-;-n) clique
Cocktail [ˈkɔktel] *m* (-s;-s) cocktail
Conferencier [kõferãˈsje] *m* (-s;-s) master of ceremony
Couch [kautʃ] *f* (-;-es) couch
Countdown [ˈkauntdaun] *m* (-s;-s) (rok) countdown
Couplet [kuˈple] *n* (-s;-s) song (in a musical)
Coupon [kuˈpõ] *m* (-s;-s) coupon
Courage [kuˈraʒə] *f* (-;) courage
Courtage [kurˈtaʒə] *f* (-;-n) brokerage
Cousin [kuˈzẽ] *m* (-s;-s) cousin
Cousine [kuˈzinə] *f* (-;-n) cousin
Cowboy [ˈkaubɔɪ] *m* (-s;-s) cowboy
creme [krem] *adj* cream-colored ‖ **Creme** [ˈkrem(ə)] *f* (-;) cream; custard
Crew [kru] *f* (-;) crew; (nav) cadets (of the same year)
Cut [kœt] *m* (-s;-s) cutaway

D

D, d [de] *invar n* D, d; (mus) D
da [da] *adv* there; then; in that case,
   da und da at such and such a place;
   wieder da back again ‖ *conj* since,
   because; when
dabei [da'baɪ] *adv* nearby; besides,
   moreover; at that; at the same time;
   (*trotzdem*) yet; **d.** bleiben stick to
   one's point; **d. sein** be present, take
   part; **d. sein zu** (*inf*) be on the point
   of (*ger*); **es ist nichts d.** there's nothing to it
da capo [da'kapo] *interj* encore!
Dach [dax] *n* (–[e]s;ːer) roof; (fig)
   shelter; **unter D. und Fach** under
   cover
Dach′boden *m* attic
Dach′decker *m* roofer
Dach′fenster *n* dormer window; sky-
   light
Dach′first *m* ridge of a roof
Dach′geschoß *n* top floor
Dach′gesellschaft *f* holding company
Dach′kammer *f* attic room
Dach′luke *f* skylight
Dach′organisation *f* parent company
Dach′pappe *f* roofing paper
Dach′pfanne *f* roof tile
Dach′rinne *f* rain gutter; eaves
Dach′röhre *f* downspout
Dachs [daks] *m* (–es;–e) badger; **ein
   frecher D.** a young whippersnapper
Dachs′hund *m* dachshund
Dach′sparren *m* rafter
Dach′stube *f* attic, garret
Dach′stuhl *m* roof framework
dachte ['daxtə] *pret* of **denken**
Dach′traufe *f* rain gutter
Dach′werk *n* roof
Dach′ziegel *m* roof tile
dadurch [da'durç] *adv* through it;
   thereby; by this means; **dadurch, daß**
   by (*ger*)
dafür [da'fyr] *adv* for it or them; in
   its place; that's why; therefore
Dafür′halten *n*—**nach meinem D.** in
   my opinion
dagegen [da'gegən] *adv* against it or
   them; in exchange for it or them; in
   comparison; on the other hand; **etw
   d. haben** have an objection; **ich bin
   d.** I'm against it
daheim [da'haɪm] *adv* at home
daher [da'her] *adv* from there; therefore; (bei Verben der Bewegung)
   along ‖ ['daher] *adv* that's why
dahin [da'hɪn] *adv* there, to that place;
   (*vergangen*) gone; (bei Verben der
   Bewegung) along; **bis d.** that far, up
   to there; until then; **es steht mir
   bis d.** I'm fed up with it
da′hinauf *adv* up there
da′hinaus *adv* out there
dahin′geben §80 *tr* give away; give up
dahin′gehen §82 *intr* (SEIN) walk along;
   pass; (*sterben*) pass away; **dahinge-
   hend, daß** to the effect that
dahingestellt [da'hɪngəʃtɛlt] *adj*—**d.**

   sein lassen, ob leave the question
   open whether
dahin′leben *intr* exist from day to day
dahin′raffen *tr* carry off
dahin′scheiden §112 *intr* (SEIN) pass on
dahin′schwinden *intr* (SEIN) dwindle
   away; fade away; pine away
dahin′stehen §146 *impers*—**es steht dahin** it is uncertain
dahin′ten *adv* back there
dahin′ter *adv* behind it or them
dahinterher′ *adv*—**d. sein, daß** be insistent that
dahin′terkommen §99 *intr* (SEIN) find
   out about it; get behind the truth
   of it
dahin′tersetzen *tr* put (*s.o.*) to work
   on it
dahin′welken §113 *intr* (SEIN) fade
   away
dahin′ziehen §163 *intr* (SEIN) move
   along
Dakapo [da'kapo] *n* (–s;–s) encore
da′lassen §104 *tr* leave behind
dalli ['dalɪ] *interj*—**mach d.!** step on
   it!
damalig ['damalɪç] *adj* of that time
damals ['damals] *adv* then, at that
   time
Damast [da'mast] *m* (–es;–e) damask
Dame ['damə] *f* (–;–n) lady; (*beim
   Tanz*) partner; (cards, chess) queen;
   (checkers) king; **e–e D. machen**
   crown a checker; **meine D.!** madam!;
   meine Damen und Herrn! ladies and
   gentlemen!
Da′mebrett *n* checkerboard
Da′menbinde *f* sanitary napkin
Da′mendoppelspiel *n* (tennis) women's
   doubles
Da′meneinzelspiel *n* (tennis) women's
   singles
Da′mengesellschaft *f* hen party
da′menhaft *adj* ladylike
Da′menhemd *n* chemise
Da′menschneider –in §6 *mf* dressmaker
Da′menwäsche *f* lingerie
Da′mespiel *n* checkers
damisch ['damɪʃ] *adj* dopey
damit [da'mɪt] *adv* with it or them;
   by it; thereby; **d. hat's noch Zeit**
   that can wait; **es ist nichts d.** it is
   useless ‖ *conj* in order that, to
dämlich ['demlɪç] *adj* dopey
Damm [dam] *m* (–[e]s;ːe) dam; dike;
   embankment; causeway; breakwater;
   pier; (fig) barrier; (anat) perineum;
   auf dem D. sein feel up to it; **wieder
   auf dem D. sein** be on one's feet
   again
Dämmer ['demər] *m* (–s;) (poet) twilight
dammerig ['demərɪç] *adj* dusky, dim
Däm′merlicht *n* dusk, twilight
dämmern ['demərn] *intr* dawn, grow
   light; (*am Abend*) grow dark, become twilight

Däm'merung *f* (-;-en) (*Morgenrot*) dawn; (*am Abend*) dusk, twilight

Dämmplatte ['dɛmplatəl *f* acoustical tile

Dämmstoff ['dɛm/tɔf] *m* insulation

Damm'weg *m* causeway

Dämon ['demɔn] *m* (-s; Dämonen [de'monən] demon

dämonisch [de'moniʃ] *adj* demoniacal

Dampf [dampf] *m* (-[e]s;̈e) steam; vapor; (*Angst*) (coll) fear; (*Hunger*) (coll) hunger; (vet) broken wind; **D. dahinter machen** (coll) step on it

dampfen ['dampfən] *intr* steam || *intr* (SEIN) steam along, steam away

dämpfen ['dɛmpfən] *tr* (*dünsten*) steam; (*Lärm*) muffle; (*Farben, Gefühle, Lichter*) subdue; (*Stoß*) absorb; (*Begeisterung*) dampen; **mit gedämpfter Stimme** under one's breath

Dampfer ['dampfər] *m* (-s;-) steamer

Dämpfer ['dɛmpfər] *m* (-s;-) (culin) steamer, boiler; (mach) baffle; (mus) mute; (*beim Klavier*) (mus) damper; **e-n D. aufsetzen** (*dat*) put a damper on

Dampf'heizung *f* steam heat

Dampf'kessel *m* steam boiler, boiler

Dampf'maschine *f* steam engine

Dampf'schiffahrtslinie *f* steamship line

Dämp'fungsfläche *f* (aer) stabilizer

Dampf'walze *f* steam roller

Damspiel ['dam/pil] *n* var of **Damespiel**

danach [da'nɑx] *adv* after it or them; accordingly; according to it or them; afterwards; **d. fragen** ask about it; **d. streben** strive for it; **d. sieht er auch aus** that's just what he looks like

Däne ['denə] *m* (-n;-n) Dane

daneben [da'nebən] *adv* next to it or them || *adv* in addition

dane'bengehen §82 *intr* (SEIN) go amiss

dane'benhauen *intr* miss; (fig) be wrong

Dänemark ['denəmark] *n* (-s;) Denmark

dang [daŋ] *pret* of **dingen**

daniederliegen [da'nidərligən] §108 *intr* (fig) be down; **d. an** (*dat*) be laid up with

Dänin ['denɪn] *f* (-;-nen) Dane

dänisch ['denɪʃ] *adj* Danish

dank [daŋk] *prep* (*dat*) thanks to || **Dank** *m* (-[e]s;) thanks; gratitude; **Gott sei D.!** thank God!, thank heaven!

dankbar ['daŋkbər] *adj* thankful; (*lohnend*) rewarding, profitable

Dank'barkeit *f* (-;) gratitude

danken ['daŋkən] *intr* (*dat*) thank; **danke!** thanks!; (*bei Ablehnung*) no, thanks!; **danke schön!** thank you!; **nichts zu d.!** you are welcome!

dan'kenswert *adj* meritorious; rewarding

dank'sagen *intr* return thanks

Danksagung ['daŋkzɑguŋ] *f* (-;) thanksgiving

Dank'sagungstag *m* Thanksgiving Day

Dank'schreiben *n* letter of thanks

dann [dan] *adv* then; **d. und wann** now and then

dannen ['danən] *adv*—**von d. away**

daran [da'ran] *adv* on, at, by, in, onto it or them; **das ist alles d.!** that's great!; **er ist gut d.** he's well off; **er tut gut d. zu** (*inf*) he does well to (*inf*); **es ist nichts d.** there's nothing to it; **ich will wissen, wie ich d. bin** I want to know where I stand; **jetzt bin ich d.** it's my turn; **nahe d. sein zu** (*inf*) be on the point of (*ger*); **was liegt d.?** what does it matter?

daran'gehen §82 *intr* (SEIN) go about it; **d. gehen zu** (*inf*) proceed to (*inf*)

daran'setzen *tr*—**alles d. zu** (*inf*) do one's level best to (*inf*)

darauf [da'rauf] *adv* on it or them; after that; **d. kommt es an** that's what matters; **gerade d. zu** straight towards; **gleich d.** immediately afterwards; **ich lasse es d. ankommen** I'll risk it

daraufhin [darauf'hɪn] *adv* thereupon

daraus [da'raus] *adv* of it, from it; from that; from them; hence; **d. wird nichts!** nothing doing!; **es wird nichts d.** nothing will come of it

darben ['darbən] *intr* live in poverty

darbieten ['darbitən] §58 *tr* present

Dar'bietung *f* (-;-en) presentation; (theat) performance

dar'bringen §65 *tr* present, offer

Dardanellen [darda'nɛlən] *pl* Dardanelles

darein [da'rain] *adv* into it or them

darein'reden *intr* interrupt; **er redet mir in alles d.** he interferes in all that I do

darin [da'rɪn] *adv* in it or them

dar'legen *tr* explain; state

Dar'legung *f* (-;-en) explanation

Darleh(e)n ['darle(ə)n] *n* (-s;-) loan

Dar'leh(e)nskasse *f* loan association

Darm [darm] *m* (-[e]s;̈e) intestine, gut; (*Wursthaut*) skin

Darm- *comb.fm.* intestinal

Darm'entzündung *f* enteritis

Darm'fäule *f* dysentery

dar'stellen *tr* describe; show, depict, portray; represent; mean; plot, chart; (indust) produce; (theat) play the part of

Dar'steller -in §6 *mf* performer

Dar'stellung *f* (-;-en) representation; portrayal; account, version; (indust) production; (theat) performance

dar'tun §154 *tr* prove; demonstrate

darüber [da'rybər] *adv* over it or them; (*querüber*) across it; (*betreffs*) about that; **d. hinaus** beyond it; moreover; **ich bin d. hinweg** I've gotten over it

darum [da'rum] *adv* around it or them; (*deshalb*) therefore; **er weiß d.** he's aware of it; **es ist mir nur d. zu tun, daß** all I ask is that

darunter [da'runtər] *adv* below it or them; among them; (*weniger*) less; **d. leiden** suffer from it; **zehn Jahre und d.** ten years and under

das [das] §1 *def art* the || §1 *dem adj* & *dem pron* this, that; **das und das**

such and such ‖ §11 *rel pron* which, that, who

da'sein §139 *intr* (SEIN) be there; be present; exist; **es ist schon alles mal dagewesen** there's nothing new under the sun; **noch nie dagewesen** unprecedented ‖ **Dasein** *n* (-s;) being, existence, life

Da'seinsberechtigung *f* raison d'être

daselbst [da'zɛlpst] *adv* just there; ibidem; **wohnhaft d.** address as above

dasjenige ['dasjenɪɡə] §4,3 *dem adj* that ‖ *dem pron* the one

daß [das] *conj* that; **daß du nicht vergißt!** be sure not to forget!; **daß er doch käme!** I wish he'd come; **es sei denn, daß** unless

dasselbe [das'zɛlbə] §4,3 *dem adj & dem pron* the same

da'stehen §146 *intr* stand there; **einzig d.** be unrivaled; **gut d.** be well-off; **wie stehe ich nun da!** how foolish I look now!

Daten ['dɑtən] *pl* data

Da'tenverarbeitung *f* data processing

datieren [da'tirən] *tr & intr* date

Dativ ['dɑtif] *m* (-s;-e) dative (case)

dato ['dɑto] *adv*—**bis d.** to date

Dattel ['datəl] *f* (-;-n) (bot) date

Da·tum ['dɑtum] *n* (-s;-ten [tən]) date; **Daten** data, facts; **heutigen Datums** of today; **neueren Datums** of recent date; **welches D. haben wir heute?** what's today's date?

Daube ['daubə] *f* (-;-n) (barrel) stave

Dauer ['dau·ər] *f* (-;) length, duration; permanence; **auf die D.** in the long run; **für die D. von** for a period of; **von D.** sein last, endure

Dau'erauftrag *m* standing order

Dau'erbelastung *f* constant load

Dau'erertrag *m* constant yield

Dau'erfeuer *n* (mil) automatic fire

Dau'erflug *m* endurance flight

Dau'ergeschwindigkeit *f* cruising speed

dau'erhaft *adj* lasting, durable; *(Farbe)* fast

Dau'erkarte *f* season ticket; (rr) commutation ticket

Dau'erlauf *m* (long-distance) jogging

dauern ['dau·ərn] *tr*—**er dauert mich** I feel sorry for him ‖ *intr* last, continue; **die Fahrt dauert fünf Stunden** the trip takes five hours; **es wird nicht lange d., dann** it won't be long before; **lange d.** take a long time

Dau'erplisseé *n* permanent pleat

Dau'erprobe *f* endurance test

Dau'erschmierung *f* self-lubrication

Dau'erstellung *f* permanent job

Dau'erton *m* (telp) dial tone

Dau'erversuch *m* endurance test

Dau'erwelle *f* permanent wave

Dau'erwirkung *f* lasting effect

Dau'erwurst *f* hard salami

Dau'erzustand *m* permanent condition; **zum D. werden** get to be a regular thing

Daumen ['daumən] *m* (-s;-) thumb; **D. halten!** keep your fingers crossed!; **die D. drehen** twiddle one's thumbs; **über den D. peilen** (or **schätzen**) give a rough estimate of

Dau'menabdruck *m* thumb print

Dau'menindex *m* thumb index

Daune ['daunə] *f* (-;-n) downy feather; **Daunen** down

Dau'nenbett *n* feather bed

Davit ['dɛvɪt] *m* (-s;-s) (naut) davit

davon [da'fɔn] *adv* of it or them; from it or them; about it or them; away

davon'kommen §99 *intr* (SEIN) escape

davon'laufen §105 *intr* (SEIN) run away; ‖ **Davonlaufen** *n*—**es ist zum D.** (coll) it's enough to drive you insane

davon'machen *ref* take off, go away

davon'tragen §132 *tr* carry off; win

davor [da'for] *adv* in front of it or them; of it or them; from it or them

dawider [da'vidər] *adv* against it

dazu [da'tsu] *adv* thereto; to it or them; in addition to that; for that purpose; about it or them; with it or them

dazu'gehörig *adj* belonging to it; proper, appropriate

da'zumal *adv* at that time

dazu'tun §154 *tr* add ‖ **Dazutun** *n*—**ohne sein D.** without any effort on his part

dazwischen [da'tsvɪʃən] *adv* in between; among them

dazwi'schenfahren §71 *intr* (SEIN) jump in to intervene

dazwi'schenfunken *intr* (coll) butt in

dazwi'schenkommen §99 *intr* (SEIN) intervene

Dazwischenkunft [da'tsvɪʃənkunft] *f* (-;) intervention

dazwi'schentreten §152 *intr* (SEIN) intervene

Debatte [dɛ'batə] *f* (-;-n) debate, discussion; **zur D. stehen** be under discussion; **zur D. stellen** open to discussion

debattieren [dɛba'tirən] *tr & intr* debate, discuss

Debet ['debet] *n* (-s;) debit; **im D. stehen** be on the debit side

Debüt [de'by] *n* (-s;-s) debut

Debütantin [debY'tantɪn] *f* (-;-nen) debutante

debütieren [debY'tierən] *intr* make one's debut

Dechant [dɛ'çant] *m* (-en;-en) (educ; R.C.) dean

dechiffrieren [dɛʃɪf'rirən] *tr* decipher

Deck [dek] *n* (-s;-s) deck

Deck'anstrich *m* final coat

Deck'bett *n* feather bed

Deck'blatt *n* overlay

Decke ['dɛkə] *f* (-;-n) cover, covering; *(Bett-)* blanket; *(Tisch-)* tablecloth; *⟨Zimmer-⟩* ceiling; *(Schicht)* layer; **mit j-m unter e-r D. stecken** be in cahoots with s.o.; **sich nach der D. strecken** make the best of it

Deckel ['dɛkəl] *m* (-s;-) lid, cap; *(Buch-)* cover; **j-m eins auf den D. geben** (coll) chew s.o. out

decken ['dɛkən] *tr* cover; *(Tisch)* set; **das Tor d.** guard the goal ‖ *ref* coincide ‖ *intr* cover

Deckenbeleuchtung (**Dek'kenbeleuchtung**) *f* (-;) ceiling lighting

Deckenlicht (Dek'kenlicht) *n* ceiling light; skylight; (aut) dome light

Deck'farbe *f* one-coat paint

Deck'konto *n* secret account

Deck'mantel *m* pretext, pretense

Deck'name *m* pseudonym; alias; (mil) code name, cover name

Deck'offizier *m* (nav) warrant officer

Deck'plane *f* awning; tarpaulin

Deckung (Dek'kung) *f* (-;-en) covering; protection; roofing; (box) defense; (com) security, surety; collateral

deckungsgleich (dek'kungsgleich) *adj* congruent

defekt [de'fɛkt] *adj* defective || **Defekt** *m* (-[e]s;-e) defect

defensiv [defɛn'zif] *adj* defensive || **Defensive** [defɛn'zivə] *f* (-;-n) defensive

definieren [defɪ'nirən] *tr* define

definitiv [defɪnɪ'tif] *adj* (endgültig) definitive; (bestimmt) definite

Defizit ['defɪtsɪt] *n* (-s;-e) deficit

Degen ['degən] *m* (-s;-) sword; (poet) warrior; (typ) compositor

degradieren [degra'dirən] *tr* demote

Degradie'rung *f* (-;-en) demotion

dehnbar ['denbar] *adj* elastic; (Metall) ductile; (fig) vague, loose

dehnen ['denən] *tr* stretch; extend; expand; (Worte) drawl out; (Vokal) lengthen; (mus) sustain || *ref* stretch out; expand

Deh'nung *f* (-;-en) extension; expansion; dilation; (ling) lengthening

Deich [daɪç] *m* (-[e]s;-e) dike; (Damm) bank, embankment

Deichsel ['daɪksəl] *f* (-;-n) pole

deichseln ['daɪksəln] *tr* (coll) manage

dein [daɪn] §2 poss adj your, thy

deinerseits ['daɪnər'zaɪts] *adv* on your part

deinesgleichen ['daɪnəs'glaɪçən] *invar pron* your own kin, your equals, the likes of you

deinethalben ['daɪnət'halbən], **deinetwegen** ['daɪnət'vegən], **deinetwillen** ['daɪnət'vɪlən] *adv* for your sake; because of you, on your account

deinige ['daɪnɪgə] *poss pron* yours

Dekan [de'kan] *m* (-s;-e) dean

deklamieren [dekla'mirən] *tr & intr* declaim; recite

Deklination [deklɪna'tsjon] *f* (-;-en) declension

deklinieren [deklɪ'nirən] *tr* decline

dekolletiert [dekɔle'tirt] *adj* lownecked; (Dame) bare-necked

Dekorateur [dekɔra'tør] *m* (-s;-e) decorator, interior decorator

Dekoration [dekɔra'tsjon] *f* (-;-en) decoration; (theat) scenery

dekorieren [dekɔ'rirən] *tr* decorate

Dekret [de'kret] *n* (-[e]s;-e) decree

delikat [delɪ'kat] *adj* delicate; (lecker) delicious

Delikt [de'lɪkt] *n* (-[e]s;-e) offense

Delle ['delə] *f* (-;-n) dent; dip

Delphin [del'fin] *m* (-s;-e) dolphin

Delta ['delta] *n* (-s;-s) delta

dem [dem] §1 def art, dem adj & dem pron || §11 rel pron

Demagoge [dema'gogə] *m* (-n;-n) demagogue

Dementi [de'mɛnti] *n* (-s;-s) official denial

dementieren [demɛn'tirən] *tr* deny (officially)

dem'entsprechend *adj* corresponding || *adv* correspondingly, accordingly

dem'gegenüber *adv* in contrast

dem'gemäß *adv* accordingly

dem'nach *adv* therefore; accordingly

dem'nächst *adv* soon, before long; (theat) (public sign) coming soon

demobilisieren [demɔbɪlɪ'zirən] *tr & intr* demobilize

Demokrat [demo'krat] *m* (-en;-en) democrat

Demokra·tie [demɔkra'ti] *f* (-;-tien ['ti·ən]) democracy

Demokratin [demo'kratɪn] *f* (-;-nen) democrat

demokratisch [demo'kratɪʃ] *adj* democratic

demolieren [demo'lirən] *tr* demolish

Demonstrant –in [demɔn'strant(ɪn)] §7 *mf* demonstrator

demonstrieren [demɔn'strirən] *tr & intr* demonstrate

Demontage [demɔn'taʒə] *f* (-;) dismantling

demontieren [demɔn'tirən] *tr* dismantle

demselben [dem'zɛlbən] §4,3 dem adj & dem pron

Demut ['demut] *f* (-;) humility

demütig ['demytɪç] *adj* humble

demütigen ['demytɪgən] *tr* humble; (beschämen) humiliate

De'mütigung *f* (-;-en) humiliation

de'mutsvoll *adj* submissive

dem'zufolge *adv* accordingly

den [den] §1 def art, dem adj & dem pron || §11 rel pron whom

denen ['denən] §11 rel pron to whom

Denkarbeit ['deŋkarbaɪt] *f* (-;) brainwork

Denkart ['deŋkart] *f* var of **Denkungsart**

Denkaufgabe ['deŋkaufgabə] *f* brain twister, problem

denkbar ['deŋkbar] *adj* conceivable; (vorstellbar) imaginable

denken ['deŋkən] §66 *tr* think, consider; was d. Sie zu tun? what do you intend to do? || *ref*—bei sich (or für sich) d. think to oneself; denke dir e–e Zahl think of a number; d. Sie sich in ihre Lage imagine yourself in her place; sich [dat] etw d. imagine s.th.; was denkst du dir eigentlich? what do you think you're doing? || *intr* think; das gibt mir zu d. that set me thinking; d. an (acc) think about

denk'faul *adj* mentally lazy

Denk'fehler *m* fallacy, false reasoning

Denk'mal *n* (-s;-e & ⁼er) monument

Denk'schrift *f* (pol) memorandum

Denkungsart ['deŋkuŋsart] *f* way of thinking, mentality

Denk'weise *f* way of thinking, mentality

denk'würdig *adj* memorable

Denk'zettel *m*—j–m e–n D. geben teach.o. a lesson

denn [dɛn] *adv* then; **es sei denn, daß** unless || *conj* for

dennoch ['dɛnɔx] *adv* nevertheless, all the same, (but) still

Dentist –in [dɛn'tɪst(ɪn)] §7 *mf* dentist

Denunziant –in [dɛnʊn'tsjant(ɪn)] §7 *mf* informer

denunzieren [dɛnʊn'tsirən] *tr* denounce

Depesche [dɛ'pɛʃə] *f* (–;–n) dispatch

De·ponens [dɛ'ponɛns] *n* (–;–ponenzien** [pɔ'nɛntsjən]) (gram) deponent

deponieren [dɛpo'nirən] *tr* (com) deposit

deportieren [dɛpɔr'tirən] *tr* deport

Depot [dɛ'po] *n* (–s;–s) depot; warehouse; storage; safe; safe deposit

Depp [dɛp] *m* (–s;–e) (coll) dope

Depression [dɛprɛ'sjon] *f* (–;–en) depression

der [der] §1 *def art* the || §1 *dem adj & dem pron* this, that; **der und der** such and such, so and so || §11 *rel pron* who, which, that; (to) whom

der'art *adv* so, in such a way; (coll) that

der'artig *adj* such, of that kind

derb [dɛrp] *adj* coarse; tough; rude

Derb'heit *f* (–;–en) coarseness; toughness; crude joke

dereinst' *adv* some day

deren ['derən] §11 *rel pron* whose

derenthalben ['derənt'halbən], **derentwegen** ['derənt'vegən], **derentwillen** ['derənt'vɪlən] *adv* for her sake, for their sake

dergestalt ['dergə'ʃtalt] *adv* so

dergleichen ['der'glaɪçən] *invar dem adj* such; similar; of that kind || *invar dem pron* such a thing; **und d.** and the like; **und d. mehr** and so on

derjenige ['derjenɪgə] §4,3 *dem adj* that || *dem pron* the one; he

dermaßen [der'masən] *adv* so, in such a way

derselbe [der'zɛlbə] §4,3 *dem adj & dem pron* the same

derweilen ['der'vaɪlən] *adv* meanwhile

derzeit ['der'tsaɪt] *adv* at present

derzeitig ['der'tsaɪtɪç] *adj* present; then, of that time

des [dɛs] *n* (–;–) (mus) D flat

Desaster [dɛ'zastər] *n* (–s;–) disaster

Deserteur [dɛzɛr'tør] *m* (–s;–e) deserter

desertieren [dɛzɛr'tirən] *intr* (SEIN) desert

desgleichen ['des'glaɪçən] *invar dem pron* such a thing || *invar rel pron* the likes of which || *adv* likewise

deshalb ['dɛshalp] *adv* therefore

Desinfektion [dɛsɪnfɛk'tsjon] *f* (–;–en) disinfection

Desinfektions'mittel *n* disinfectant

desinfizieren [dɛsɪnfi'tsirən] *tr* disinfect

Despot [dɛs'pot] *m* (–en;–en) despot

despotisch [dɛs'potɪʃ] *adj* despotic

Dessin [dɛ'sɛ̃] *n* (–s;–s) design

destillieren [dɛstɪ'lirən] *tr* distill

desto ['dɛsto] *adv* the; **d. besser** the better, all the better

deswegen ['dɛs'vegən] *adv* therefore

Detail [dɛ'taɪ(l)] *n* (–s;–s) detail; (com) retail

Detail'geschäft *n* retail store

Detail'händler –in §6 *mf* retail dealer

detaillieren [dɛta'jirən] *tr* relate in detail; specify; itemize

Detek·tiv [dɛtɛk'tif] *m* (–s;–tive** ['tivə]) private investigator; (coll) private eye

detonieren [dɛto'nirən] *intr* detonate; etw. **d. lassen** detonate s.th.

deuchte ['dɔɪçtə] *pret* of **dünken**

Deutelei [dɔɪtə'laɪ] *f* (–;–en) quibble

deuteln ['dɔɪtəln] *intr* (an *dat*) quibble (about), split hairs (over)

deuten ['dɔɪtən] *tr* interpret; **falsch d.** misinterpret || *intr* (auf *acc*) (& fig) point (to)

deutlich ['dɔɪtlɪç] *adj* clear, distinct

deutsch [dɔɪtʃ] *adj* German || **Deutsche** §5 *mf* German

Deu'tung *f* (–;–en) interpretation

Devise [dɛ'vizə] *f* (–;–n) motto; **Devisen** foreign currency

Devi'senbestand *m* foreign-currency reserve

Devi'senbilanz *f* balance of payments

Devi'senkurs *m* rate of exchange

Dezember [dɛ'tsɛmbər] *m* (–s;–) December

dezent [dɛ'tsɛnt] *adj* unobtrusive; (*Licht, Musik*) soft; (*anständig*) decent

Dezernat [dɛtsɛr'nat] *n* (-[e]s;–e) (administrative) department

dezimal [dɛtsi'mal] *adj* decimal || **Dezimale** [dɛtsi'malə] *f* (–;–n) decimal

Dezimal'bruch *m* decimal fraction

Dezimal'zahl *f* decimal

dezimieren [dɛtsi'mirən] *tr* decimate

Dia ['di·a] *n* (–s;–s) (coll) slide

Diadem [di·a'dem] *n* (–s;–e) diadem

Diagnose [dɪ·a'gnozə] *f* (–;–n) diagnosis

diagnostizieren [dɪ·agnɔstɪ'tsirən] *tr* diagnose

diagonal [dɪ·ago'nal] *adj* diagonal || **Diagonale** *f* (–;–n) diagonal

Diagramm [dɪ·a'gram] *n* (-[e]s;e) diagram; graph

Diakon [dɪ·a'kon] *m* (–s;–e & –en;–en) deacon

Dialekt [dɪ·a'lɛkt] *m* (-[e]s;–e) dialect

dialektisch [dɪ·a'lɛktɪʃ] *adj* dialectical

Dialog [dɪ·a'lok] *m* (–s;–e) dialogue

Diamant [dɪ·a'mant] *m* (–en;–en) diamond

Diaposi·tiv [dɪ·apɔzɪ'tif] *n* (–s;–tive** ['tivə]) slide, transparency

Diät [dɪ'et] *f* (–;–en) diet (*under medical supervision*); **Diäten** daily allowance; **diät leben** be on a diet

Diät– *comb.fm.* dietary

diätetisch [dɪe'tetɪʃ] *adj* dietetic

dich [dɪç] §11 *pers pron* you, thee || *reflex pron* yourself, thyself

dicht [dɪçt] *adj* dense; thick; heavy; leakproof; tight || **Dichte** ['dɪçtə] *f* (–;–en) density

dichten ['dıçtən] *tr* tighten; caulk; compose, write || *intr* write poetry
Dichter ['dıçtər] *m* (-s;-) (important) writer; poet
Dichterin ['dıçtərɪn] *f* (-;-nen) poetess
dichterisch ['dıçtərɪʃ] *adj* poetic(al)
dicht'gedrängt *adj* tightly packed
dicht'halten §90 *intr* keep mum
Dicht'heit *f* (-;), **Dich'tigkeit** *f* (-;) density; compactness; tightness
Dich'kunst *f* poetry
dicht'machen *tr* (coll) close up
Dich'tung *f* (-;-en) gasket; packing; imagination; fiction; poetry; poem; **Dich'tungsring** *m*, **Dich'tungsscheibe** *f* washer; gasket
dick [dɪk] *adj* thick; fat; big; (*Luft*, *Freunde*) close; **dicke Luft!** (coll) cheese it!; **sich d. tun** talk big ||
Dicke *f* (-;) thickness, stoutness
Dick'darm *m* (anat) colon
dickfellig ['dɪkfɛlıç] *adj* thick-skinned
dick'flüssig *adj* viscous
Dickicht ['dɪkıçt] *n* (-[e]s;-e) thicket
Dick'kopf *m* thick head
dickköpfig ['dɪkkœpfıç] *adj* thick-headed
dickleibig ['dɪklaɪbɪç] *adj* stout, fat
Dick'schädel *m* thick head
dick'schädelig ['dɪkʃedəlıç] *adj* thick-headed
die [di] §1 *def art* the || §1 *dem adj* & *dem pron* this, that; **die und die** such and such || §11 *rel pron* who, which, that
Dieb [dip] *m* (-[e]s;-e) thief
Dieberei [dibə'raɪ] *f* (-;-en) thievery; (*Diebstahl*) theft
Diebesbande ['dibəsbandə] *f* pack of thieves
Diebin ['dibɪn] *f* (-;-nen) thief
diebisch ['dibɪʃ] *adj* thievish || *adv*— **sich d. freuen** be tickled pink
Diebstahl ['dipʃtal] *m* (-[e]s;-̈) theft, larceny; **leichter D.** petty larceny; **schwerer D.** grand larceny
diejenige ['dijenıgə] §4,3 *dem adj* that || *dem pron* the one; she
Diele ['dilə] *f* (-;-n) floorboard; (*breiter Flur*) entrance hall; **Dielen** flooring
dienen ['dinən] *intr* (*dat*) serve; **damit ist mir nicht gedient** that doesn't help me any; **womit kann ich d.?** may I help you?
Diener –in ['dinər(ɪn)] §6 *mf* servant
die'nerhaft *adj* servile
dienern ['dinərn] *intr* bow and scrape
Die'nerschaft *f* (-;) domestics, help
dienlich ['dinlıç] *adj* useful
Dienst [dinst] *m* (-es;-e) service; job; employment; (adm, mil) grade; **außer D.** retired; **im. D.** on duty; **j-m e-n D. tun** do s.o. a favor
Dienstag ['dinstak] *m* (-[e]s;-e) Tuesday
Dienst'alter *n* seniority
dienstbar ['dinstbar] *adj* subservient
Dienst'barkeit *f* (-;) servitude, bondage; (jur) easement
dienst'beflissen *adj* eager to serve || *adv* eagerly

Dienst'bote *m* servant, domestic
Dienst'boteneingang *m* service entrance
Dienst'eid *m* oath of office
dienst'eifrig *adj* eager to serve || *adv* eagerly
Dienst'einteilung *f* work schedule; (mil) duty roster
Dienst'fahrt *f* official trip
dienst'frei *adj*—**d. haben** be off duty
Dienst'gebrauch *m*—**nur zum D.** for official use only
Dienst'gespräch *n* business call
Dienst'grad *m* (mil) rank, grade; (nav) rating
dienst'habend *adj* on duty
Dienst'herr *m* employer; (hist) lord
Dienst'leistung *f* service
dienst'lich *adj* official || *adv* officially; on official business
Dienst'mädchen *n* maid
Dienst'pflicht *f* official duty; compulsory military service
Dienst'plan *m* work schedule; (mil) duty roster
Dienst'sache *f* official business
dienst'tauglich *adj* fit for active service
diensttuend ['dinsttu·ənt] *adj* on duty; active; in charge
Dienst'weg *m* official channels
Dienst'wohnung *f* official residence
dies [dis] *dem adj* & *dem pron* var of **dieses**
diese ['dizə] §3 *dem adj* this || *dem pron* this one
dieselbe [di'zɛlbə] §4,3 *dem adj* & *dem pron* the same
Dieselmotor ['dizəlmotər] *m* diesel engine
dieser ['dizər] §3 *dem adj* this || *dem pron* this one
dieses ['dizəs] §3 *dem adj* this || *dem pron* this one
diesig ['dizıç] *adj* hazy, misty
dies'jährig *adj* this year's
dies'mal *adv* this time
diesseits ['diszaɪts] *prep* (*genit*) on this side of
Dietrich ['ditrıç] *m* (-s;-e) skeleton key; (*Einbrecherwerkzeug*) picklock
Differential [diferen'tsjal] *n* (-s;-e) (aut, math) differential
Differential– *comb.fm.* (econ, elec, mach, math, phys) differential
Differenz [dife'rents] *f* (-;-en) difference
Diktaphon [dikta'fon] *n* (-[e]s;-e) dictaphone
Diktat [dɪk'tat] *n* (-s;-e) dictation; **nach D. schreiben** take dictation
Dik·tator [dɪk'tatɔr] *m* (-s;-tatoren) [ta'torən]) dictator
diktatorisch [dikta'torıʃ] *adj* dictatorial
Diktatur [dɪkta'tur] *f* (-;-en) dictatorship
diktieren [dɪk'tirən] *tr* & *intr* dictate
Dilettant –in [dɪlɛ'tant(ɪn)] §7 *mf* dilettante, amateur
Diner [dɪ'ne] *n* (-s;-s) dinner
Ding [dɪŋ] *n* (-[e]s;-e) thing; **ein D. drehen** (coll) pull a job
dingen ['dɪŋən] §109 & §142 *tr* hire

ding′fest *adj*—**j–n d. machen** arrest s.o.

ding′lich *adj* real

Dings [dɪŋs] *n* (**-s;**) (coll) thing, doodad, thingamajig

Dings′bums *m & n* (**-;**) var of **Dingsda**

Dings′da *mfn* (**-s;**) what-d'ye-call-it

Diözese [dɪ·ø'tsezə] *f* (**-;–n**) diocese

Diphtherie [dɪfte'ri] *f* (**-;**) diphtheria

Dipl.-Ing. *abbr* (**Diplom-Ingenieur**) engineer holding a degree

Diplom [dɪ'plom] *n* (**-s;–e**) diploma

Diplom– *comb.fm.* holding a degree

Diplomat [dɪplə'mat] *m* (**-en;–en**) diplomat

Diplomatie [dɪpləma'ti] *f* (**-;**) diplomacy

Diplomatin [dɪplə'matɪn] *f* (**-;–nen**) diplomat

diplomatisch [dɪplə'matɪʃ] *adj* diplomatic

dir [dir] §11 *pers pron* to or for you, to or for thee ‖ *reflex pron* to or for yourself, to or for thyself

direkt [dɪ'rɛkt] *adj* direct

Direktion [dɪrɛk'tsjon] *f* (**-;**) direction; (*Verwaltung*) management

Direk·tor [dɪ'rɛktər] *m* (**-s;–toren** ['torən]) director; (*e–r Bank*) president; (*e–r Schule*) principal; (*e–s Gefängnisses*) warden

Direktorat [dɪrɛktə'rat] *n* (**-[e]s;–e**) directorship

Direktorin [dɪrɛk'torɪn] *f* (**-;–nen**) director; (*educ*) principal

Direkto·rium [dɪrɛk'torɪ·um] *n* (**-s; –rien** [rɪ·ən]) board of directors; executive committee

Direktrice [dɪrɛk'trisə] *f* (**-;–n**) directress, manager

Dirigent –in [dɪrɪ'gɛnt(ɪn)] §7 *mf* (mus) conductor

dirigieren [dɪrɪ'girən] *tr* direct, manage; (mus) conduct

Dirnd(e)l ['dɪrndəl] *n* (**-s;–**) girl; (*Tracht*) dirndle

Dirne ['dɪrnə] *f* (**-;–n**) girl; (pej) prostitute

Dis [dɪs] *n* (**-;–**) D sharp

disharmonisch [dɪshar'monɪʃ] *adj* discordant

Diskont [dɪs'kɔnt] *m* (**-[e]s;–e**) discount

diskontieren [dɪskən'tirən] *tr* discount

Diskothek [dɪskə'tek] *f* (**-;–en**) discotheque

diskret [dɪs'kret] *adj* discreet

Diskretion [dɪskrɛ'tsjon] *f* (**-;–en**) discretion

Diskussion [dɪsku'sjon] *f* (**-;–en**) discussion

diskutieren [dɪsku'tirən] *tr* discuss ‖ *intr*—**d. über** (*acc*) discuss

disponieren [dɪspə'nirən] *intr* (**über** *acc*) dispose (of)

Disposition [dɪspəzɪ'tsjon] *f* (**-;–en**) disposition; arrangement; disposal

Distanz [dɪs'tants] *f* (**-;–en**) distance

distanzieren [dɪstan'tsirən] *tr* (**mit**) beat (by, e.g., one meter) ‖ *ref* (**von**) dissociate oneself (from)

distanziert′ *adj* (fig) detached

Distel ['dɪstəl] *f* (**-;–n**) thistle

Dis′telfink *m* goldfinch

Distrikt [dɪs'trɪkt] *m* (**-[e]s;–e**) district

Disziplin [dɪstsɪ'plin] *f* (**-;–en**) discipline

disziplinarisch [dɪstsɪplɪ'narɪʃ] *adj* disciplinary

dito ['dito] *adv* ditto ‖ **Dito** *n* (**-s;–s**) ditto

Dividend [dɪvɪ'dɛnt] *m* (**-en;–en**), **Dividende** [dɪvɪ'dɛndə] *f* (**-;–n**) dividend

dividieren [dɪvɪ'dirən] *tr* divide

Division [dɪvɪ'zjon] *f* (**-;–en**) division

Diwan ['divan] *m* (**-s;–e**) divan

D-Mark ['demark] *f* (**-;–**) mark (*monetary unit of West Germany*)

doch [dɔx] *adv* yet; of course

Docht [dɔxt] *m* (**-[e]s;–e**) wick

Dock [dɔk] *n* (**-[e]s;–s & –e**) dock

docken ['dɔkən] *tr & intr* (naut, rok) dock

Dogge ['dɔgə] *f* (**-;–n**) mastiff; **deutsche D.** Great Dane

Dog·ma ['dɔgma] *n* (**-s;–men** [mən]) dogma

Dohle ['dolə] *f* (**-;–n**) jackdaw

Dok·tor ['dɔktər] *m* (**-s;–toren** ['torən]) doctor

Dok′torarbeit *f* dissertation

Dok′torvater *m* adviser (*for a doctoral dissertation*)

Dokument [dɔku'mɛnt] *n* (**-[e]s;–e**) document; (jur) instrument, deed

Dokumentarfilm [dɔkumɛn'tarfɪlm] *m* documentary

dokumentarisch [dɔkumɛn'tarɪʃ] *adj* documentary

Dolch [dɔlç] *m* (**-[e]s;–e**) dagger

Dolch′stoß *m* stab in the back

Dollar ['dɔlar] *m* (**-s;–**) dollar

dolmetschen ['dɔlmɛtʃən] *tr & intr* interpret

Dol′metscher –in §6 *mf* interpreter

Dom [dom] *m* (**-[e]s;–e**) cathedral; dome

Domäne [dɔ'mɛnə] *f* (**-;–n**) domain

Domino ['domino] *n* (**-s;–s**) domino

Donau ['donau] *f* (**-;**) Danube

Donner ['dɔnər] *m* (**-s;–**) thunder

Don′nerkeil *m* thunderbolt

donnern ['dɔnərn] *intr* thunder

Don′nerschlag *m* clap of thunder

Don′nerstag *m* (**-[e]s;–e**) Thursday

Don′nerwetter *n* thunderstorm; **zum D.!** confound it! ‖ *interj* geez!

doof [dof] *adj* (coll) goofy

dopen ['dopən] *tr* dope (*a racehorse*)

Doppel ['dɔpəl] *n* (**-s;–**) duplicate; (tennis) doubles

Doppel– *comb.fm.* double, two, bi-, twin

Dop′pelbelichtung *f* double exposure

Dop′pelbild *n* (telv) ghost

Dop′pelbruch *m* compound fracture

Dop′pelehe *f* bigamy

Dop′pelgänger *m* double; second self

Dop′pellaut *m* diphthong

doppeln ['dɔpəln] *tr* double

Dop′pelprogramm *n* double feature

Dop′pelpunkt *m* (typ) colon

doppelreihig ['dɔpəlraɪ·ɪç] *adj* double-breasted

Dop′pelrendezvous *n* double date

dop′pelseitig adj reversible; (*Lunge-nentzündung*) double
Dop′pelsinn m double entendre
dop′pelsinnig adj ambiguous
Dop′pelspiel n (fig) double-dealing; (sport) double-header; (tennis) doubles
doppelt ['dɔpəlt] adj double; **doppelter Boden** false bottom; **ein doppeltes Spiel spielen mit** doublecross; **in doppelter Ausführung** in duplicate || adv twice; **ein Buch d. haben** have two copies of a book
Dop′pelverdiener –in §6 mf moonlighter
Dop′pelvokal m diphthong
doppelzüngig ['dɔpəltsʏŋɪç] adj two-faced
Dorf [dɔrf] n (-[e]s;⸚er) village
Dorf′bewohner –in §6 mf villager
Dörfchen ['dœrfçən] n (-s;-) hamlet
Dorn [dɔrn] m (-[e]s;-en) thorn; tongue (*of a buckle*); (mach) pin; (sport) spike
Dorn′busch m briar, bramble
dornig ['dɔrnɪç] adj thorny
Dornröschen ['dɔrnrøsçən] n (-s;) Sleeping Beauty
Dörr– [dœr] comb.fm. dried
dorren ['dɔrən] intr (SEIN) dry (up)
dörren ['dœrən] tr dry
Dorschlebertran ['dɔrʃlebərtran] m (-[e]s;) cod-liver oil
dort [dɔrt] adv there, over there
dort′her adv from there
dort′hin adv there, to that place
dor′tig adj in that place, there
Dose ['dozə] f (-;-n) can; box
dösen ['døzən] intr doze
Do′senöffner m can opener
dosieren [dɔ'zirən] tr prescribe (the correct dosage of)
Dosie′rung f (-;-en) dosage
Do·sis ['dozɪs] f (-;-sen [zən]) dose
dotieren [dɔ'tirən] tr endow; **ein Preis mit 100 Mark dotiert** a prize worth 100 marks
Dotter ['dɔtər] m & n (-s;-) yolk
Double ['dubəl] m & n (-s;-s) (cin, theat) stand-in
Dozent –in [dɔ'tsɛnt(ɪn)] §7 (university) instructor, lecturer
Drache ['draxə] m (-n;-n) dragon; (*böses Weib*) battle-ax
Drachen ['draxən] m (-s;-) kite
Dra′chenfliegen n (-s;) hang gliding
Draht [drat] m (-[e]s;⸚e) wire; **auf D. sein** (coll) be on the beam
drahten ['dratən] tr telegraph, wire
draht′haarig adj wire-haired
Draht′hindernis n (mil) wire entanglement, barbed wire
drahtig ['dratɪç] adj wiry
draht′los adj wireless
Draht′seil n cable
Draht′seilbahn f cable car, funicular
Draht′zaun m wire fence
drall [dral] adj plump; (*Faden*) sturdy || **Drall** m (-s;-e) rifling
Dra·ma ['drama] n (-s;-men [mən]) drama
Dramatiker –in [dra'matɪkər(ɪn)] §6 mf dramatist, playwright

dramatisch [dra'matɪʃ] adj dramatic
dran [dran] adv var of **daran**
drang [draŋ] pret of **dringen** || **Drang** m (-[e]s;⸚e) pressure; urge
drängeln ['drɛŋəln] tr & intr shove
drängen ['drɛŋən] tr & intr push, shove; (*drücken*) press || ref crowd, crowd together; **force one's way**
Drangsal ['draŋzal] f (-;-e) distress, anguish; hardship
drangsalieren [draŋza'lirən] tr vex
drastisch ['drastɪʃ] adj drastic
drauf [drauf] adv var of **darauf**
Drauf′gänger m (-s;-) go-getter
drauf′gehen §82 intr (SEIN) (coll) go down the drain
drauflos′ adv—**d. arbeiten an** (dat) work away at
drauflos′gehen §82 intr (SEIN)—**d. auf** (acc) make straight for
drauflos′reden intr ramble on
drauflos′schlagen §132 intr (auf acc) let fly (at)
draußen ['drausən] adv outside; out of doors; (*in der Fremde*) abroad
drechseln ['drɛksəln] tr work (*on a lathe*); (fig) embellish
Dreck [drɛk] m (-[e]s;) dirt; mud; excrement; (*Abfälle*) trash
dreckig ['drɛkɪç] adj dirty; muddy
Dreh– [dre] comb.fm. revolving, rotary
Dreh′arbeiten pl (cin) shooting
Dreh′aufzug m dumb waiter
Dreh′bank f (-;⸚e) lathe
drehbar ['drebar] adj revolving
Dreh′buch n (mov) script, scenario
drehen ['dre·ən] tr turn; (*Zigaretten*) roll; (coll) wangle; (cin) shoot || ref turn; rotate
Dreh′kreuz n turnstile
Dreh′orgel f hurdy-gurdy
Dreh′orgelspieler m organ grinder
Dreh′punkt m fulcrum; (fig) pivotal point
Dreh′scheibe f potter's wheel; (rr) turntable
Dreh′stuhl m swivel chair
Dre′hung f (-;-en) turn
Dreh′zahl f revolutions per minute
Dreh′zahlmesser m tachometer
drei [draɪ] adj & pron three || **Drei** f (-;-en) three; (educ) C
dreidimensional ['draɪdɪmɛnzjɔnal] adj three-dimensional
Dreieck ['draɪ·ɛk] n (-[e]s;-e) triangle
drei′eckig adj triangular
drei′fach adj threefold, triple
dreifältig ['draɪfɛltɪç] adj threefold, triple
Dreifaltigkeit [draɪ'faltɪçkaɪt] f (-;) Trinity
Drei′fuß m tripod
Dreikäsehoch [draɪ'kezəhoç] m (-s;-) (coll) shrimp, runt
drei′mal adv three times, thrice
Drei′rad n tricycle
Drei′sprung m hop, step, and jump
dreißig ['draɪsɪç] adj & pron thirty || **Dreißig** f (-;- & -en) thirty
dreißiger ['draɪsɪgər] invar adj of the thirties, in the thirties
dreißigste ['draɪsɪçstə] §9 adj & pron thirtieth

dreist [draɪst] *adj* brazen, bold
dreistimmig ['draɪ/tɪmɪç] *adj* for three voices
drei'zehn *adj* & *pron* thirteen ‖ **Dreizehn** *f* (-;-) thirteen
drei'zehnte §9 *adj* & *pron* thirteenth
dreschen ['drɛ/ən] §67 *tr* thresh; (coll) thrash
Dresch'flegel *m* flail
Dresch'tenne *f* threshing floor
dressieren [drɛ'sirən] *tr* train; (*Pferd*) break in
Dressur [drɛ'sur] *f* (-;) training
dribbeln ['drɪbəln] *intr* (sport) dribble
drillen ['drɪlən] *tr* drill; train
Drillich ['drɪlɪç] *m* (-s;-e) denim
Dril'lichanzug *m* dungarees; (mil) fatigue uniform, fatigues
Dril lichhosen *pl* dungarees, jeans
Drilling ['drɪlɪŋ] *m* (-s;-e) triplet
drin [drɪn] *adv* var of **darin**
dringen ['drɪŋən] §142 *intr* (auf *acc*) press (for), insist (on); (in *acc*) pressure, urge ‖ *intr* (SEIN) (aus) break forth (from); (durch) penetrate, pierce; (durch) force one's way (through); (in *acc*) penetrate (into), get (into); **in die Öffentlichkeit d.** leak out; **in j–n d.** press the point with s.o.; **d. bis zu** get as far as
drin'gend *adj* urgent; (*Gefahr*) imminent; (*Verdacht*) strong
dring'lich *adj* urgent
Dring'lichkeit *f* (-;-en) urgency; priority
Drink [drɪŋk] *m* (-s;-s) alcoholic drink
drinnen ['drɪnən] *adv* inside
dritt [drɪt] *adv*—**zu d.** the three of
dritte ['drɪtə] §9 *adj* & *pron* third; **ein Dritter** a disinterested person; (com, jur) a third party
Drittel ['drɪtəl] *n* (-s;-) third (*part*)
drittens ['drɪtəns] *adv* thirdly
dritt'letzt *adj* third from last
droben ['drobən] *adv* above; up there
Droge ['drogə] *f* (-;-n) drug
Droge·rie [drogə'ri] *f* (-;-rien ['ri·ən]) drugstore
Drogist –**in** [dro'gɪst(ɪn)] §7 *mf* druggist
Droh'brief *m* threatening letter
drohen ['dro·ən] *intr* (*dat*) threaten
dro'hend *adj* threatening; impending
Drohne ['dronə] *f* (-;-n) drone
dröhnen ['drønən] *intr* boom, roar; (*Kopf, Motor*) throb
Dro'hung *f* (-;-en) threat
drollig ['drolɪç] *adj* amusing, funny
Dromedar [dromɛ'dar] *n* (-s;-e) dromedary
drosch [dro/] *pret* of **dreschen**
Droschke ['dro/kə] *f* (-;-n) cab, hackney; taxi
Drosch'kenkutscher *m* coachman
Drossel ['drosəl] *f* (-;-n) thrush; (aut) throttle
Dros'selhebel *m* (aut) throttle
drosseln ['drosəln] *tr* (coll) curb, cut; (aut) throttle; (elec) choke
drüben ['drybən] *adv* over there
Druck [druk] *m* (-[e]s;⁻e) (& fig) pressure; (*der Hand*) squeeze; (phys)

compression, pressure ‖ *m* (-[e]s-e) printing; print, type; (tex) print
Druck'anzug *m* (aer) pressurized suit
Druck'bogen *m* (printed) sheet
druck'dicht *adj* pressurized
Drückeberger ['drykəbergər] *m* (-s;-) shirker; absentee; (mil) goldbrick
drucken ['drukən] *tr* print
drücken ['drykən] *tr* press; squeeze; imprint; (*Preise*) lower; (cards) discard; **die Stimmung d.** be a kill-joy; **j–m die Hand d.** shake hands with s.o. ‖ *intr* (*Schuh*) pinch
Druck'entlastung *f* decompression
Drucker ['drukər] *m* (-s;-) printer
Drücker ['drykər] *m* (-s;-) push button; (*e–s Schlosses*) latch, latch key; (*e–s Gewehrs*) trigger
Druckerei [drukə'raɪ] *f* (-;-en) print shop, press
Druckerschwärze (**Druck'kerschwärze**) *f* printer's ink
Druck'fehler *m* misprint
druck'fertig *adj* ready for the press
druck'fest *adj* pressurized
Druck'kabine *f* pressurized cabin
Druck'knopf *m* push button; (*am Kleid*) snap
Druck'knopfbetätigung *f* push-button control
Druck'luft *f* compressed air
Druckluft– *comb.fm.* pneumatic, air
Druck'luftbremse *f* air brake
Druck'lufthammer *m* jackhammer
Druck'messer *m* pressure gauge
Druck'sache *f* printed matter; **Drucksachen** (com) literature
Druck'schrift *f* type; block letters; publication, printed work; leaflet
drucksen ['druksən] *intr* hem and haw
drum [drum] *adv* var of **darum**
Drüse ['dryzə] *f* (-;-n) gland
Drüsen– *comb.fm.* glandular
Dschungel ['dʒuŋəl] *m* (-s;-) jungle
du [du] §11 *per pron* you, thou
Dübel ['dybəl] *m* (-s;-) dowel
Dublette [du'blɛtə] *f* (-;-n) duplicate; imitation stone
ducken ['dukən] *tr* (*den Kopf*) duck; (coll) take down a peg or two ‖ *ref* duck
Duckmäuser ['dukmɔɪzər] *m* (-s;-) pussyfoot
dudeln ['dudəln] *tr* hum ‖ *intr* hum, drone; (mus) play the bagpipe
Dudelsack ['dudəlzak] *m* bagpipe
Duell [du'ɛl] *n* (-s;-e) duel
duellieren [du·ə'lirən] *recip* duel
Duett [du'ɛt] *n* (-[e]s;-e) duet
Duft [duft] *m* (-[e]s;⁻e) fragrance
duften ['duftən] *intr* be fragrant
duf'tend *adj* fragrant
duftig ['duftɪç] *adj* flimsy, dainty
dulden ['duldən] *tr* (*ertragen*) bear; (*leiden*) suffer; (*zulassen*) tolerate ‖ *intr* suffer
duldsam ['duldzam] *adj* tolerant
Duld'samkeit *f* (-;) tolerance
dumm [dum] *adj* stupid, dumb; foolish
Dumm'heit *f* (-;-en) stupidity; foolishness; (*Streich*) foolish prank
Dumm'kopf *m* dunderhead
dumpf [dumpf] *adj* dull, muffled;

(*schwül*) muggy; (*moderig*) musty, moldy; (*Ahnung*) vague
dumpfig ['dumpfıç] *adj* musty, moldy; muggy
Düne ['dynə] *f* (-;-n) sand dune
Dung [duŋ] *m* (-[e]s;) dung; (*künstlicher*) fertilizer
düngen ['dyŋən] *tr* manure; fertilize
Dünger ['dyŋər] *m* (-s;) var of **Dung**
dunkel ['duŋkəl] *adj* dark; vague; obscure ‖ **Dunkel** *n* (-s;) darkness
Dünkel ['dyŋkəl] *m* (-s;) conceit
dün'kelhaft *adj* conceited
Dun'kelheit *f* (-;) darkness; obscurity
Dun'kelkammer *f* (phot) darkroom
Dun'kelmann *m* (-[e]s;̈-er) shady character
dünn [dyn] *adj* thin
Dunst [dunst] *m* (-es;̈-e) vapor, mist, haze; (*Rauch*) smoke; (*Dampf*) steam; **in D. und Rauch aufgehen** (fig) go up in smoke; **sich in (blauen) D. auflösen** vanish in thin air
dünsten ['dynstən] *tr & intr* stew; steam
dunstig ['dunstıç] *adj* steamy; (*Wetter*) misty, hazy
Duplikat [duplı'kɑt] *n* (-[e]s;-e) duplicate; copy
Dur [dur] *invar n* (mus) major
durch [durç] *adv* throughout; **d. und d.** through and through ‖ *prep* (acc) through, by, by means of
durch'arbeiten *tr* work through ‖ *ref* (durch) work one's way (through); elbow one's way (through)
durchaus' *adv* throughout; entirely; quite, absolutely; **d. nicht** by no means
durch'backen §50 *tr* bake through and through
durch'blättern *tr* thumb through
durch'bleuen *tr* beat up
Durch'blick *m* vista
durch'blicken *intr* be apparent; (durch) look (through); **d. lassen** intimate
durchblutet [durç'blutət] *adj* supplied with blood
durch'bohren *tr* bore through ‖ **durchboh'ren** *tr* pierce
durch'braten §63 *tr* roast thoroughly
durchbre'chen §64 *tr* break through; (*Vorschriften*) violate; (mil) breach ‖ **durch'brechen** *tr* cut (*a hole*); break in half ‖ *intr* (SEIN) break through
durch'brennen §97 *tr* burn through; (*e-e Sicherung*) blow ‖ *intr* (SEIN) run away; (*Sicherung*) blow
durch'bringen §65 *tr* get through; (*Gesetz*) pass; (*Geld*) spend; (med) pull (*a patient*) through ‖ *ref* support oneself; **sich ehrlich d.** make an honest living
Durch'bruch *m* breakthrough; (*Öffnung*) breach, gap; (*der Zähne*) cutting
durch'denken §66 *tr* think through ‖ **durchden'ken** *tr* think out, think over
durch'drängen *ref* push one's way through
durch'drehen *tr* grind; (*Wäsche*) put

through the wringer ‖ *intr* (SEIN) (coll) go mad
durchdrin'gen §142 *tr* penetrate; pervade, imbue ‖ **durch'dringen** *intr* (SEIN) get through; penetrate
durch'drucken *tr* (parl) push through
durchdrungen [durç'druŋən] *adj* imbued
durchei'len *tr* rush through ‖ **durch'eilen** *intr* (SEIN) (durch) rush through
durcheinan'der *adj & adv* in confusion ‖**Durcheinander** *n* (-s;-) mess, muddle
durcheinan'derbringen §65 *tr* muddle
durcheinan'dergeraten §63 *intr* (SEIN) get mixed up
durcheinan'derlaufen §105 *intr* (SEIN) mill about
durcheinan'derreden *intr* speak all at once
durcheinan'derwerfen §160 *tr* throw into confusion, turn upside down
durchfah'ren §71 *tr* travel through; (*Gedanke, Schreck*) strike ‖ **durch'fahren** §71 *intr* (SEIN) go through without stopping
Durch'fahrt *f* passage; **keine D.!** no thoroughfare
Durch'fahrtshöhe *f* clearance
Durch'fall *m* diarrhea; (coll) flop; (educ) flunk, failure
durch'fallen §72 *intr* (SEIN) fall through; (educ) flunk; (theat) flop
durch'fechten §74 *tr* fight through
durch'finden §59 *ref* find one's way
durchflech'ten *tr* interweave
durchfor'schen *tr* examine, make an exhaustive study of
Durchfor'schung *f* exploration; search; thorough research
durch'fressen §70 *tr* eat through; corrode ‖ *ref* (bei) sponge (on); (durch) work one's way (through)
Durchfuhr ['durçfur] *f* (-;-en) transit
durchführbar ['durçfyrbɑr] *adj* feasible
durch'führen *tr* lead through or across; (*Auftrag*) carry out; (*Gesetz*) enforce
Durch'gang *m* passage; aisle; (fig) transition; (astr, com) transit; **D. verboten!** no thoroughfare, no trespassing
Durch'gänger *m* (-s;-) runaway
Durch'gangslager *n* transit camp
Durch'gangsverkehr *m* through traffic
Durch'gangszug *m* through train
durch'geben §80 *tr* pass on
durch'gebraten *adj* (culin) well done
durch'gehen §82 *tr* (SEIN) go through; (*durchlesen*) go over ‖ *intr* (SEIN) go through; (*Pferd*) bolt; (*heimlich davonlaufen*) run away; abscond; (*Vorschlag*) pass
durch'gehend(s) *adv* generally; (*durchaus*) throughout
durchgeistigt [durç'gaıstıçt] *adj* highly intellectual
durch'greifen §88 *intr* reach through; (fig) take drastic measures
durch'greifend *adj* vigorous; drastic
durch'halten §90 *tr* keep up ‖ *intr* hold out, stick it out
durch'hauen §93 *tr* chop through;

knock a hole through; (coll) thrash, beat

durch′hecheln *tr* (coll) run down

durch′helfen §96 *intr* (*dat*) (**durch**) help (through) || *ref* get by, manage

durch′kämmen *tr* (& fig) comb through

durch′kochen *tr* boil thoroughly

durch′kommen §99 *intr* (SEIN) come through; (*durch Krankheit*) pull through; (*sich durchhelfen*) get by; (educ) pass

durchkreu′zen *tr* cross; (*durchstreichen*) cross out; (fig) frustrate

Durch·laß ['durçlas] *m* (**–lasses;–lässe**) passage; outlet; culvert

durch′lassen §104 *tr* let through, let pass; (*Licht*) transmit; (educ) pass

durchlässig ['durçlɛsɪç] *adj* permeable

Durch′laßschein *m* pass

durchlau′fen §105 *tr* run through; look through; (*Schule*) go through; **seine Bahn d.** run its course || **durch′laufen** §105 *ref—sich* [*dat*] **die Schuhe d.** wear out one's shoes || §105 *intr* (SEIN) run through

durchle′ben *tr* live through

durch′lesen §107 *tr* read over, peruse

durchleuch′ten *tr* illuminate; (*Gesicht*) light up; (*Ei*) test; X-ray

durch′liegen §108 *ref* develop bedsores || **Durchliegen** *n* (**–s;**) bedsores

durchlo′chen *tr* punch

durch′löchern *tr* perforate; pierce; (*mit Kugeln*) riddle

durch′machen *tr* go through, undergo

Durch′marsch *m* marching through; (coll) diarrhea, runs

Durch′messer *m* diameter

durchnäs′sen *tr* soak, drench

durch′nehmen §116 *tr* (*in der Klasse*) do. have

durch′pausen *tr* trace

durch′peitschen *tr* whip soundly; (*Gesetzentwurf*) rush through

durchque′ren *tr* cross, traverse

durch′rechnen *tr* check, go over

Durch′reise *f* passage; **auf seiner D.** on his way through

durch′reisen *intr* (SEIN) travel through

Durch′reisende §5 *mf* transient, transit passenger

durch′reißen §53 *tr* tear in half || *intr* (SEIN) tear, break, snap

Durch′sage *f* special announcement

durch′sagen *tr* announce

durchschau′en *tr* (fig) see through || **durch′schauen** *intr* look through

durch′scheinen §128 *intr* shine through; show through; be seen

durch′scheuern *tr* rub through

durchschie′ßen §76 *tr* shoot through, riddle; (typ) lead || **durch′schießen** §76 *intr* (**durch**) shoot (through) || *intr* (SEIN) dash through

Durch′schlag *m* carbon copy; (*Sieb*) (large) strainer, separator; (elec) breakdown; (tech) punch

durchschla′gen §132 *tr* penetrate || **durch′schlagen** §132 *tr* knock a hole through; (*Holz*) split; (*Fensterscheibe*) smash; (*Nagel*) drive through; (*Kartoffeln, Früchte*) strain; (*mit Kohlepapier*) make a carbon copy of

|| *ref* fight one's way through; (*sich durchhelfen*) manage || *intr* come through; penetrate; take effect; show up || *intr* (SEIN) (*Sicherung*) blow

durch′schlagend *adj* effective; striking

Durch′schlagpapier *n* carbon paper

durch′schleichen §85 *ref* & *intr* (SEIN) creep through

durchschleu′sen *tr* pass (*a ship*) through a lock; (*Passagiere, Rekruten, usw.*) process; (fig) sneak (*s.o.*) through

durch′schneiden §106 *tr* cut through; cut in half || **durchschnei′den** §106 *tr* cut through, cut across || *ref* cross, intersect

Durch′schnitt *m* cutting through; average; cross section; **der große D.** der **Menschen** the majority of people; **im D.** on an average

durch′schnittlich *adj* average || *adv* on the average

Durchschnitts– *comb.fm.* average; mean

Durch′schnittsmensch *m* average person

durch′schreiben §62 *tr* make a carbon copy of

durch′sehen §138 *tr* look over, examine; (*flüchtig anschauen*) scan; (*Papiere, Post*) check || *intr* see through

durch′seihen *tr* filter; percolate

durchset′zen *tr* intersperse; penetrate || **durch′setzen** *tr* carry through; **d., daß** bring it about that, succeed in (*ger*) || *ref* get one's way

Durch′sicht *f* examination, inspection; (*auf acc*) view (of)

durch′sichtig *adj* transparent; clear

durch′sickern *intr* (SEIN) seep out; (*Wahrheit, Gerücht*) leak out

durch′sieben *tr* sift

durch′sprechen §64 *tr* talk over

durchste′chen §64 *tr* pierce || **durch′stechen** §64 *tr* (*Nadel*) stick through

durch′stehen §146 *tr* go through

durchstö′bern *tr* rummage through

durch′stoßen §150 *tr* push (*s.th.*) through; (*Tür*) knock down; (*Scheibe*) smash in; (*Ellbogen*) wear through; (mil) penetrate || **durchsto′ßen** §150 *tr* break through || **durch′stoßen** §150 *intr* (SEIN) break through

durchstrei′chen §85 *tr* roam through || **durch′streichen** §85 *tr* cross out

durchstrei′fen *tr* wander through

durchsu′chen *tr* go through, search

durch′treten §152 *tr* (*Sohle*) wear a hole in; (*Gashebel*) floor || *intr* (SEIN) go through, pass through

durchtrieben [durç′tribən] *adj* sly

durchwa′chen *tr* remain awake through

durchwach′sen *adj* gristly

durch′wählen *tr* & *intr* dial direct

durchwan′dern *tr* travel or walk through || **durch′wandern** *intr* (SEIN) (**durch**) walk (through), hike (through)

durchwe′ben *tr* interweave

durch′weg(s) *adv* throughout

durchwei′chen, durch′weichen *tr* soak

durchwüh′len *tr* burrow through; (*Ge–*

päck, Schränke) rummage through ||
durch'wühlen *ref* burrow through;
(fig) work one's way through
durch'wursteln *ref* muddle through
durchzie'hen §163 *tr* pass through,
cross; (*Zimmer*) permeate, fill;
streak; (sew) interweave || **durch'-**
ziehen §163 *tr* pull through || *intr*
(SEIN) pass through; flow through
durchzucken (**durchzuk'ken**) *tr* flash
through the mind of
Durch'zug *m* passage; (*Luftzug*) draft
durch'zwängen *tr* force through || *ref*
squeeze through
dürfen ['dʏrfən] §69 *aux* be allowed;
be likely; **darf ich?** may I?; **ich darf**
nicht I must not; **man darf wohl er-**
warten it is to be expected
durfte ['dʊrftə] *pret* of **dürfen**
dürftig ['dʏrftɪç] *adj* needy; poor,
wretched, miserable, scanty
dürr [dʏr] *adj* dry; (*Boden*) arid, barren; (*Holz*) dead, dry; (*Mensch*)
skinny || **Dürre** ['dʏrə] *f* (-;) dry-
ness; barrenness; leanness; drought
Durst [dʊrst] *m* (-[e]s;) (**nach**) thirst
(for); **D. haben** be thirsty

dursten ['dʊrstən], **dürsten** ['dʏr-
stən] *intr* be thirsty; (**nach**) thirst
(for)
durstig ['dʊrstɪç] *adj* thirsty
Dusche ['duʃə] *f* (-;-n) shower
duschen ['duʃən] *intr* take a shower
Düse ['dyzə] *f* (-;-n) nozzle, jet
Dusel ['duzəl] *m* (-s;-) (coll) fluke
Düsen– *comb.fm.* jet
Dü'senantrieb *m* jet propulsion
Dü'senjäger *m* jet fighter
düster ['dystər] *adj* gloomy; sad; dark
|| **Düster** *n* (-s;) gloom; darkness
Dutzend ['dʊtsənt] *n* (-s;- & -e) dozen
dut'zendmal *adv* a dozen times
dut'zendweise *adv* by the dozen
Duzbruder ['dutsbrudər] *m* buddy
duzen ['dutsən] *tr* say **du** to, be on in-
timate terms with
Dynamik [dy'namɪk] *f* (-s;) dynamics
dynamisch [dy'namɪʃ] *adj* dynamic
Dynamit [dyna'mit] *n* (-s;-e) dyna-
mite
Dynamo ['dynamo] *m* (-s;-s) dynamo
Dyna·stie [dynas'ti] *f* (-;-stien
['sti·ən] dynasty
D'-Zug *m* through train, express

E

E, e [e] *invar n* E, e; (mus) E
Ebbe ['ɛbə] *f* (-;-n) ebb tide
eben ['ebən] *adj* even, level, flat; **zu**
ebener Erde on the ground floor ||
adv just; a moment ago; exactly
|| *interj* exactly!; that's right!
E'benbild *n* image, exact likeness
ebenbürtig ['ebənbʏrtɪç] *adj* of equal
rank, equal
ebenda ['ebən'da] *adv* right there;
(*beim Zitieren*) ibidem
ebendersel'be §4,3 *adj* self-same
ebendes'wegen *adv* for that very reason
Ebene ['ebənə] *f* (-;-n) plain; (fig)
level; (geom) plane
e'benerdig *adj* ground-floor
e'benfalls *adv* likewise, too
E'benholz *n* ebony
E'benmaß *n* right proportions
e'benmäßig *adj* well-proportioned
e'benso *adv* just as; likewise
e'bensogut *adv* just as well
e'bensoviel *adv* just as much
e'bensowenig *adv* just as little
Eber ['ebər] *m* (-s;-) boar
E'beresche *f* mountain ash
ebnen ['ebnən] *tr* level, even; smooth
Echo ['ɛço] *n* (-s;-s) echo
echoen ['ɛçɔ·ən] *intr* echo
echt [ɛçt] *adj* genuine, real, true
Eck [ɛk] *n* (-[e]s;-e) corner; end
Eck– *comb.fm.* corner; end
Ecke ['ɛkə] *f* (-;-n) corner; edge
Ecker ['ɛkər] *f* (-;-n) beechnut
eckig ['ɛkɪç] *adj* angular; (fig) awkward; **eckige Klammer** bracket
Eck'stein *m* cornerstone; (cards) dia-
monds

Eck'stoß *m* (fb) corner kick
Eck'zahn *m* canine tooth
Eclair [ɛ'kler] *n* (-s;-s) éclair
edel ['edəl] *adj* noble; (*Metall*) pre-
cious; (*Pferd*) thoroughbred; **edle**
Teile vital organs
e'deldenkend *adj* noble-minded
e'delgesinnt *adj* noble-minded
E'del·mann *m* (-[e]s;-leute) noble
e'delmütig *adj* noble-minded
E'delstahl *m* high-grade steel
E'delstein *m* precious stone, gem
E'delweiß *n* (-[e]s;-e) edelweiss
Edikt [ɛ'dɪkt] *n* (-[e]s;-e) edict
Edle ['edlə] §5 *mf* noble
Efeu ['efɔɪ] *m* (-s;-e) ivy
Effekt [ɛ'fɛkt] *m* (-[e]s;-e) effect
Effekten [ɛ'fɛktən] *pl* property; ef-
fects; (fin) securities, stocks
Effek'tenmakler –in §6 *mf* stock broker
Effekthascherei [ɛfɛkthaʃə'raɪ] *f* (-;)
showiness
effektiv [ɛfɛk'tif] *adj* effective; (*wirk-*
lich) actual
Effektiv'lohn *m* take-home pay
Effet [ɛ'fe] *n* (-s;) spin, English
egal [ɛ'gal] *adj* equal; all the same
Egge ['ɛgə] *f* (-;-n) harrow
eggen ['ɛgən] *tr* harrow
Ego ['ego] *n* (-s;) ego
Egoismus [ego'ɪsmus] *m* (-;) egoism
Egoist –in [ego'ɪst(ɪn)] §7 *mf* egoist
egoistisch [ego'ɪstɪʃ] *adj* egoistic
Egotist –in [ego'tɪst(ɪn)] §7 *mf* egotist
eh [e] *adv* (Aust) anyhow, anyway
ehe ['e·ə] *conj* before || **Ehe** *f* (-;-n)
marriage; matrimony
E'hebrecher *m* (-s;-) adulterer

E'hebrecherin f (-;-nen) adulteress
e'hebrecherisch adj adulterous
E'hebruch m adultery, infidelity
ehedem ['eˑə'dem] adv formerly
E'hefrau f wife
E'hegatte m spouse
E'hegattin f spouse
E'hegelöbnis n marriage vow
E'hehälfte f (coll) better half
E'heleute pl married couple
e'helich adj marital; (Kind) legitimate
e'helos adj unmarried, single
E'helosigkeit f (-;) celibacy
ehemalig ['eˑəmɑlɪç] adj former; ex-; (verstorben) late
ehemals ['eˑəmɑls] adv formerly
E'hemann m husband
E'hepaar n married couple
eher ['eˑər] adv sooner; rather
E'hering m wedding band
ehern ['eˑərn] adj brass; (fig) unshakable
E'hescheidung f divorce
E'hescheidungsklage f divorce suit
E'heschließung f marriage
E'hestand m married state, wedlock
ehestens ['eˑəstəns] adv at the earliest; as soon as possible
E'hestifter –in §6 mf matchmaker
E'heversprechen n promise of marriage
Ehrabschneider –in ['erap/naɪdər(ɪn)] §6 mf slanderer
ehrbar ['erbɑr] adj honorable, respectable
Ehr'barkeit f (-;) respectability
Ehre ['erə] f (-;-n) honor; glory
ehren ['erən] tr honor; **Sehr geehrter Herr** Dear Sir
eh'renamtlich adj honorary
Eh'rendoktor m honorary doctor
Eh'renerklärung f apology
eh'renhaft adj honorable
ehrenhalber ['erənhalbər] invar adj—**Doktor e.** Doctor honoris causa
Eh'renmitglied n honorary member
Eh'renrechte pl—**bürgerliche E.** civil rights
Eh'rensache f point of honor
eh'renvoll adj honorable, respectable
eh'renwert adj honorable
Eh'renwort n word of honor; **auf E. entlassen** put on parole
chrerbietig ['ererbitɪç] adj respectful, reverent, deferential
Ehrerbietung ['ererbituŋ] f (-;), **Ehr-furcht** ['erfurçt] f (-;) respect, reverence; (vor dat) awe (of)
ehrfürchtig ['erfyrçtɪç], **ehrfurchtsvoll** ['erfurçtsfɔl] adj respectful
Ehr'gefühl n sense of honor
Ehr'geiz m ambition
ehr'geizig adj ambitious
ehrlich ['erlɪç] adj honest; sincere; fair; **j–n e. machen** restore s.o.'s good name
Ehr'lichkeit f (-;) honesty; candor
ehr'los adj dishonorable; (Frau) of easy virtue; infamous
Ehr'losigkeit f (-;) dishonesty; infamy
ehrsam ['erzɑm] adj respectable
Ehr'sucht f (-;) ambition
ehr'süchtig adj ambitious

Ehr'verlust m loss of civil rights
ehr'würdig adj venerable; (eccl) reverend
ei [aɪ] interj oh!; ah!; ei,ei! oho!; ei je! oh dear!; ei was! nonsense! ‖ **Ei** n (-[e]s;-er) egg
Eiche ['aɪçə] f (-;-n) oak
Eichel ['aɪçəl] f (-;-n) acorn; (cards) club
eichen ['aɪçən] adj oak ‖ tr gauge
Ei'chenlaub n oak leaf cluster
Eichhörnchen ['aɪçhœrnçən] n (-s;-), **Eichkätzchen** ['aɪçketsçən] n (-s;-) squirrel
Eichmaß ['aɪçmɑs] n gauge; standard
Eid [aɪt] m (-[e]s;-e) oath
Eid'bruch m perjury
eid'brüchig adj perjured
Eidechse ['aɪdeksə] f (-;-n) lizard
Eiderdaunen ['aɪdərdaunən] pl eider down
eidesstattlich ['aɪdəs/tatlɪç] adj in lieu of an oath, solemn
eid'lich adj sworn ‖ adv under oath
Ei'dotter m egg yolk
Ei'erkrem f custard
Ei'erkuchen m omelet; pancake
Ei'erlandung f three-point landing
Ei'erlikör m eggnog
Ei'erschale f eggshell
Ei'erstock m ovary
Eifer ['aɪfər] m (-;) zeal, eagerness
Eiferer –in ['aɪfərər(ɪn)] §6 mf zealot
Ei'fersucht f jealousy
ei'fersüchtig adj (auf acc) jealous (of)
eifrig ['aɪfrɪç] adj zealous; ardent
Ei'gelb n (-[e]s;-e) egg yolk
eigen ['aɪgən] adj own; of (my, your, etc.) own; (dat) peculiar (to), characteristic (of) ‖ invar pron—**etw mein e. nennen** call s.th. my own
ei'genartig adj peculiar; odd, queer
Eigenbrötler ['aɪgənbrøtlər] m (-s;-) (coll) lone wolf, loner; crank
Ei'gengewicht n dead weight
eigenhändig ['aɪgənhendɪç] adj & adv with or in one's own hand
Ei'genheit f (-;-en) peculiarity
Ei'genliebe f self-love, egotism
Ei'genlob n self-praise
ei'genmächtig adj arbitrary, high-handed
Ei'genname m proper name
Ei'gennutz m self-interest
ei'gennützig adj selfish
eigens ['aɪgəns] adv expressly
Ei'genschaft f (-;-en) quality, property; **in seiner E. als** in his capacity as
Ei'genschaftswort n (-[e]s;=er) adjective
Ei'gensinn m stubbornness
ei'gensinnig adj stubborn
eigentlich ['aɪgəntlɪç] adj actual ‖ adv actually, really
Eigentum ['aɪgəntum] n (-[e]s;=er) property, possession; ownership
Eigentümer –in ['aɪgəntymər(ɪn)] §6 mf (legal) owner ‖ m proprietor ‖ f proprietress
eigentümlich ['aɪgəntymlɪç] adj odd; (dat) peculiar (to)
Ei'gentümlichkeit f (-;-en) peculiarity

Ei′gentumsrecht *n* ownership, title

Ei′genwechsel *m* promissory note

ei′genwillig *adj* independent; *(Stil)* original

eignen [′aıgnən] *ref* (für) be suited (to); (als) be suitable (as); (zu) be cut out (for)

Eig′nung *f* (–;–en) qualification, aptitude

Ei′gnungsprüfung *f* aptitude test

Eilbrief [′aılbrif] *m* special delivery

Eile [′aılə] *f* (–;) hurry; **E. haben** or **in E. sein** be in a hurry

eilen [′aılən] *ref* hurry (up) ‖ *intr* be urgent ‖ *intr* (SEIN) hurry; **eilt!** *(Briefaufschrift)* urgent! ‖ *impers*—**es eilt mir nicht damit** I'm in no hurry about it

eilends [′aılənts] *adv* hurriedly

Eilgut [′aılgut] *n* express freight

eilig [′aılıç] *adj* quick, hurried; urgent ‖ *adv* hurriedly; **es e. haben** be in a hurry

Eilpost [′aılpost] *f* special delivery

Eilzug [′aıltsuk] *m* (rr) limited

Eimer [′aımər] *m* (–s;–) bucket, pail

ein [aın] §2,1 *indef art* a, an ‖ §2,1 *num adj* one ‖ *adv* in; **ein und aus in and out; nicht ein und aus wissen** not know which way to turn ‖ **einer** *indef pron & num pron* see **einer**

ein–, Ein– *comb.fm.* one–, single

einan′der *invar recip pron* each other; *(unter mehreren)* one another

ein′arbeiten *tr* train (for a job); **(in** *(acc)* work (into) ‖ *ref* **(in** *acc)* become familiar (with), get the hang (of)

einarmig [′aınarmıç] *adj* one-armed

einäschern [′aınɛʃərn] *tr* reduce to ashes, incinerate; *(Leiche)* cremate

ein′atmen *tr & intr* inhale

ein′äugig *adj* one-eyed

einbahnig [′aınbanıç] *adj* single-lane; single-line; one-way

Ein′bahnstraße *f* one-way street

ein′balsamieren *tr* embalm

Ein′band *m* (–[e]s;⸚e) binding; cover

ein′bauen *tr* build in, install

einbegriffen [′aınbəgrıfən] *adj* included. inclusive

ein′behalten §90 *tr* retain; *(Lohn)* withhold

ein′berufen §122 *tr* call, convene; (mil) call up, draft ‖ **Einberufene** §5 *mf* draftee

Ein′berufung *f* (–;–en) (mil) induction

ein′betten *tr* embed

ein′beziehen §163 *tr* include

ein′bilden *ref*—**sich** [*dat*] **etw e.** imagine s.th.

ein′binden §59 *tr* (bb) bind

ein′blenden *tr* (cin) fade in

Ein′blick *m* view; (fig) insight

ein′brechen §64 *tr* break in ‖ *intr* (SEIN) collapse; *(Nacht)* fall; *(Kälte)* set in; *(Dieb)* break in

Ein′brecher –in §6 *mf* burglar

ein′bringen §65 *tr* bring in; earn; yield

Ein′bruch *m* break-in, burglary; invasion; **E. der Nacht** nightfall

Ein′bruchsdiebstahl *m* burglary

ein′bruchssicher *adj* burglarproof

einbürgern [′aınbʏrgərn] *tr* naturalize ‖ *ref* (fig) take root, become accepted

Ein′bürgerung *f* (–;) naturalization

Ein′buße *f* loss, forfeiture

ein′büßen *tr* lose, forfeit

ein′dämmen *tr* check, contain

ein′decken *tr* cover ‖ *ref* **(mit)** stock up (on)

Eindecker [′aındɛkər] *m* (–s;–) monoplane

ein′deutig *adj* unequivocal, clear

eindeutschen [′aındoıtʃən] *tr* Germanize

ein′drängen *ref* squeeze in; interfere

ein′dringen §142 *intr* (SEIN) penetrate, come in; **e. auf** *(acc)* crowd in on; **e. in** *(acc)* rush into; penetrate; infiltrate; (mil) invade

ein′dringlich *adj* urgent

Eindringling [′aındrınlın] *m* (–s;–e) intruder, interloper; gate-crasher

Ein′druck *m* imprint; impression

ein′drücken *tr* press in; crash, flatten; imprint; *(Fenster)* smash in

Ein′druckskunst *f* impressionism

ein′drucksvoll *adj* impressive

ein′engen *tr* narrow; (fig) limit

einer [′aınər] §2,4 *indef pron & num pron* one ‖ **Einer** *m* (–s;–) (math) unit

einerlei [′aınərlaı] *invar adj* (nur attributiv) one kind of; (nur prädikativ) all the same ‖ **Einerlei** *n* (–;) monotony

einerseits [′aınərzaıts], **einersteils** [′aınəstaıls] *adv* on the one hand

ein′fach *adj* single; simple ‖ *adv* simply

einfädeln [′aınfedəln] *tr* thread; (fig) engineer

ein′fahren §71 *tr* *(Auto)* break in; *(Ernte)* bring in; (aer) retract ‖ *ref* get driving experience; **die Sache hat sich gut eingefahren** it's off to a good start ‖ *intr* (SEIN) drive in; (rr) arrive

Ein′fahrt *f* entrance; gateway

Ein′fall *m* inroad; (fig) idea; (mil) invasion

ein′fallen §72 *intr* (SEIN) fall in; cave in, collapse; *(in die Rede)* butt in; join in; **e. in** *(acc)* invade; **j–m e.** occur to s.o.; **sich** [*dat*] **etw e. lassen** take s.th. into one's head: think up s.th.; **sich** [*dat*] **nicht e. lassen** not dream of them; **was fällt dir ein?** what's the idea?

ein′fallslos *adj* unimaginative

ein′fallsreich *adj* imaginative

Ein′falt *f* simplicity; simple-mindedness

einfältig [′aınfeltıç] *adj* (pej) simple

Ein′faltspinsel *m* sucker, simpleton

ein′farbig *adj* one-colored; plain

ein′fassen *tr* edge, trim; *(einschließen)* enclose; *(Edelstein)* set

Ein′fassung *f* (–;–en) border; mounting

ein′fetten *tr* grease

ein′finden §59 *ref* show up

ein′flechten *tr* plait; *(Haar)* braid; (fig) insert

ein′fliegen §57 *tr* *(Truppen)* fly in;

(*Flugzeug*) flight-test ‖ *intr* (SEIN) fly in

ein'fließen §76 *intr* (SEIN) flow in; **e. in** (*acc*) flow into; **einige Bemerkungen e.** lassen slip in a few remarks

ein'flößen *tr* infuse, instill

Ein'fluß *m* influx; (fig) influence

ein'flußreich *adj* influential

ein'förmig *adj* monotonous

einfried(ig)en ['aɪnfrid(ɪg)ən] *tr* enclose, fence in

ein'frieren §77 *tr* (& fin) freeze ‖ *intr* (SEIN) freeze (up) ‖ **Einfrieren** *n* (-s;) (fin) freeze

ein'fügen *tr* insert, fit ‖ *ref* fit in; (in *acc*) adapt oneself (to)

ein'fühlen *ref* (in *acc*) relate (to)

Einfuhr ['aɪnfur] *f* (-;-en) importation; **Einfuhren** imports

ein'führen *tr* import; introduce; (in *ein Amt*) install

Ein'führung *f* (-;-en) introduction

Ein'fuhrwaren *pl* imports

Ein'fuhrzoll *m* import duty

ein'füllen *tr*—**e. in** (*acc*) pour into

Ein'gabe *f* petition; application

Ein'gang *m* entrance; entry; beginning; introduction; (*von Waren*) arrival; **Eingänge** (com) incoming goods; incoming mail; (fin) receipts

ein'geben §80 *tr* suggest, prompt; (med) administer, give

eingebildet ['aɪngəbɪldət] *adj* imaginary; self-conceited

eingeboren ['aɪngəborən] *adj* native; only-begotten; (*Eigenschaft*) innate ‖ **Eingeborene** §5 *mf* native

Ein'gebung *f* (-;-en) suggestion; (*höhere*) inspiration

eingedenk ['aɪngədɛŋk] *adj* (*genit*) mindful (of)

ein'gefallen *adj* (*Backen, Augen*) sunken

eingefleischt ['aɪngəflaɪʃt] *adj* inveterate

ein'gefroren *adj* icebound

ein'gehen §82 *tr* (HABEN & SEIN) enter into; (*Verpflichtungen*) incur; (*Wette, Geschäft*) make; (*Chance*) take; (*Versicherung*) take out; **e–n Vergleich e.** come to an agreement ‖ *intr* (SEIN) come in; arrive; (*aufhören*) come to an end; fizzle out; (*Stoff*) shrink; (bot, zool) die off; (com) close down; **e. auf** (*acc*) go into, consider; consent to; **e. lassen** drop, discontinue; **es geht mir nicht ein, daß** I can't accept the fact that

ein'gehend *adj* thorough

eingelegt ['aɪngəlegt] *adj* inlaid

Eingemachte ['aɪngəmaxtə] §5 *n* (-n;) preserves

eingemeinden ['aɪngəmaɪndən] *tr* (*Vorort*) incorporate

eingenommen ['aɪngənɔmən] *adj* prejudiced; **von sich e.** self-conceited

eingeschnappt ['aɪngəʃnapt] *adj* (coll) peeved

eingeschneit ['aɪngəʃnaɪt] *adj* snowed in

Eingesessene ['aɪngəzɛsənə] §5 *mf* resident

Ein'geständis *n* (-ses;-se) confession

ein'gestehen §146 *tr* confess, admit

Eingeweide ['aɪngəvaɪdə] *pl* viscera; intestines; (*von Vieh*) entrails

Eingeweihte ['aɪngəvaɪtə] §5 *mf* insider

ein'gewöhnen *tr* (in *acc*) accustom (to) ‖ *ref* (in *acc*) become accustomed (to)

eingewurzelt ['aɪngəvurtsəlt] *adj* deeprooted

ein'gießen §76 *tr* pour in, pour out

eingleisig ['aɪnglaɪzɪç] *adj* single-track

ein'gliedern *tr* integrate; annex

ein'graben §87 *tr* bury; engrave ‖ *ref* burrow; (mil) dig in

ein'greifen §88 *intr* take action; interfere; (in *j–s Rechte*) encroach; (mach) mesh, be in gear ‖ **Eingreifen** *n* (-s;) interference; (mach) meshing

Ein'griff *m* interference; encroachment; (mach) meshing; (surg) operation

ein'hacken *tr*—**e. auf** (*acc*) peck at; (fig) pick at

ein'haken *tr* (in *acc*) hook (into) ‖ *ref*—**sich bei j–m e.** link arms with s.o. ‖ *intr* (fig) cut in

Ein'halt *m* (-[e]s;) stop, halt; **E. gebieten** (*dat*) put a stop to

ein'halten §90 *tr* stick to; (*Verabredung*) keep; (*Zahlungen*) keep up; **die Zeit e.** be punctual ‖ *intr* stop

ein'händigen *tr* hand over

ein'hängen §92 *tr* (*Türe*) hang; (in *acc*) hook (into); (telp) hang up ‖ *ref*—**sich bei j–m e.** link arms with s.o. ‖ *intr* (telp) hang up

ein'heften *tr* sew in; baste on

ein'heimisch *adj* domestic; local; homegrown; **e. in** (*dat*) native to

einheimsen ['aɪnhaɪmzən] *tr* reap

Einheit ['aɪnhaɪt] *f* (-;-en) oneness, unity; (math, mil) unit

ein'heitlich *adj* uniform

Einheits– *comb.fm.* standard, uniform; unit; united

ein'heizen *intr* start a fire; **j–m tüchtig e.** (fig) burn s.o. up

einhellig ['aɪnhɛlɪç] *adj* unanimous

ein'holen *tr* bring in; (*Flagge*) hawl down; (*Segel*) hawl down; (*im Wettlauf*) catch up with; (*Erkundigungen lauf*) catch up with; (*Erkundigungen*) make; (*Rat, Nachricht, Erlaubnis*) get; (*Verlust*) make good; (*abholen und geleiten*) escort; (*Schiff, Tau*) tow in ‖ *intr* shop

Ein'horn *n* (myth) unicorn

ein'hüllen *tr* wrap up; enclose

einig ['aɪnɪç] *adj* united; of one mind; **sich** [*dat*] **e. sein** be in agreement

einige ['aɪnɪgə] §9 *indef adj & indef pron* some

einigen ['aɪnɪgən] *tr* unite ‖ *ref* come to terms, agree

einigermaßen ['aɪnɪgərmasən] *adv* to some extent; (*ziemlich*) somewhat

ei'niggehen §82 *intr* (SEIN) concur

Ei'nigkeit *f* (-;) unity; harmony; agreement

Ei′nigung *f* (–;–en) unification; agreement, understanding
ein′impfen *tr*—j–m **Impfstoff e.** inoculate s.o. with vaccine; **j–m e., daß** (fig) drive it into s.o. that
ein′jagen *tr* (*dat*) put (*e.g., a scare*) into
ein′jährig *adj* one-year-old; (bot) annual
ein′kassieren *tr* collect
Ein′kauf *m* purchase; **Einkäufe machen** go shopping
ein′kaufen *tr* purchase; **e. gehen** go shopping
Ein′käufer –in §6 *mf* shopper
Ein′kaufspreis *m* purchase price
Ein′kehr *f*—E. **bei sich halten** search one's conscience; **E. halten** stop off
ein′kehren *intr* (SEIN) stay overnight; (*im Gasthaus*) stop off, stay
ein′keilen *tr* wedge in
ein′kerben *tr* notch, cut a notch in
einkerkern [′aınkɛrkərn] *tr* imprison
einkesseln [′aınkɛsəln] *tr* encircle
ein′klagen *tr* sue for (*a bad debt*)
ein′klammern *tr* bracket, put in parentheses
Ein′klang *m* unison; accord
Ein′klebebuch *n* scrap book
ein′kleben *tr* (in *acc*) paste (into)
ein′kleiden *tr* clothe; vest; (mil) issue uniforms to
ein′klemmen *tr* jam in, squeeze in
ein′klinken *tr* & *intr* engage, catch
ein′knicken *tr* fold
ein′kochen *tr* thicken (*by boiling*); can || *intr* thicken
ein′kommen §99 *intr* (SEIN)—**bei j–m um etw e.** apply to s.o. for s.th. ||
Einkommen *n* (–s;) income, revenue
Ein′kommensteuer *f* income tax
Ein′kommensteuererklärung *f* income-tax return
Ein′kommenstufe *f* income bracket
ein′kreisen *tr* encircle
Einkünfte [′aınkynftə] *pl* revenue
ein′kuppeln *tr* let out the clutch
ein′laden §103 *tr* load; invite
Ein′ladung *f* (–;–en) invitation
Ein′lage *f* (–;–n) (*im Brief*) enclosure; (*im Schuh*) insole; arch support; (*Zwischenfutter*) padding; (*Kapital*–) investment; (*Sparkassen*–) deposit; (*beim Spiel*) bet; (culin) solids (*in soup*); (dent) temporary filling; (mus) musical extra
ein′lagern *tr* store, store up
Ein·laß [′aınlas] *m* (–lasses;) admission; admittance; (tech) intake
ein′lassen §104 *tr* let it, admit; (tech) (in *acc*) sink (into) || *ref* (auf *acc*, in *acc*) let oneself get involved (in)
Ein′laßkarte *f* admission ticket
Ein′lauf *m* incoming mail; (*e–s Schiffes*) arrival; **j–m e–n E. machen** give s.o. an enema
ein′laufen §105 *intr* (SEIN) come in, arrive; (*Stoff*) shrink; **das Badewasser e.** lassen run the bath; **j–m das Haus e.** keep running to s.o.'s house || *ref* warm up (*by running*)
ein′leben *ref* (in *acc*) accustom oneself (to)

Ein′legearbeit *f* inlaid work
Ein′legebrett *n* (*e–s Tisches*) leaf
ein′legen *tr* put in; (*Fleisch, Gurken*) pickle; (*Geld*) deposit; (*in e–n Brief*) enclose; (*Film, Kassette*) insert; (*Veto*) interpose; (*Beschwerde*) lodge; (*Protest*) enter; (*Berufung*) (jur) file; **Busse e.** put on extra buses
ein′leiten *tr* introduce; (*Buch*) write a preface to; (*beginnen, eröffnen*) start, open; **ein Verfahren e. gegen** institute proceedings against s.o.
Ein′leitung *f* (–;–en) introduction; initiation
ein′lenken *intr* (fig) give in
ein′leuchten *intr* be evident; (coll) sink in
ein′liefern *tr* deliver; (*ins Gefängnis*) put, commit; **ins Krankenhaus e.** take to the hospital
ein′lösen *tr* ransom; redeem; (*Scheck*) cash
ein′machen *tr* can, preserve
ein′mal *adv* once; (*künftig*) one day; **auf e.** suddenly; all at the same time; **einmal…einmal** now…now; **nicht e.** (unstressed) not even; (stressed) not even once
Ein′maleins′ *n* multiplication table
ein′malig *adj* unique
Einmann– *comb.fm.* one-man
Ein′marsch *m* entry
ein′marschieren *intr* (SEIN) march in
ein′mauern *tr* wall in
ein′mengen *ref*, **ein′mischen** *ref* (in *acc*) meddle (with), interfere (with)
Ein′mischung *f* (–;–en) interference
einmotorig [′aınmə′toriç] *adj* single-engine
einmummen [′aınmumən] *ref* bundle up
ein′münden *intr* (in *acc*) empty (into); (*Straßen*) run (into)
Ein′mündung *f* (–;–en) (*e–s Flusses*) mouth; (*e–r Straße*) junction
ein′mütig *adj* unanimous
ein′nähen *tr* sew in; (*Kleid*) take in
Ein′nahme *f* (–;–n) taking; capture; (fin) receipts; **Einnahmen** income
ein′nehmen §116 *tr* take; capture; (*Essen*) eat; (*Geld*) earn; (*Steuern*) collect; (*Stellung*) fill; (sew) take in; **e–e Haltung e.** assume an attitude; **e–e hervorragende Stelle e.** rank high; **j–n für sich e.** captivate s.o.; **j–n gegen sich e.** prejudice s.o. against oneself; **seinen Platz e.** take one's seat
ein′nicken *intr* (SEIN) doze off
ein′nisten *ref* (in *dat*) settle (in); (fig) find a home (at)
Ein′öde *f* desert, wilderness
ein′ordnen *tr* put in its place; file; classify || *ref* fit into place; (*sich anstellen*) get in line; **sich rechts (or links) e.** get into the right (or left) lane
ein′packen *tr* pack up
ein′passen *tr* (in *acc*) fit (into)
ein′pauken *tr*—j–m **etw e.** drum s.th. into s.o.'s head
ein′pferchen *tr* pen up; (fig) crowd together

ein'pflanzen *tr* plant; implant
ein'pökeln *tr* pickle; salt
ein'prägen *tr* imprint, impress
ein'quartieren *tr* billet, quarter
ein'rahmen *tr* frame
ein'rammen *tr* ram in, drive in
ein'räumen *tr* (*Recht, Kredit*) grant; (*zugeben*) concede, admit; **e. in** (*acc*) put into
ein'rechnen *tr* include, comprise
Ein'rede *f* objection; (jur) plea
ein'reden *tr*—j–m etw **e.** talk s.o. into s.th; **das lasse ich mir nicht e.** I can't believe that || *intr*—**auf j–n e.** badger s.o.
ein'reiben §62 *tr* rub
ein'reichen *tr* hand in, file; (*Rechnung*) present; (*Abschied*) tender; (*Gesuch*) submit; (*Beschwerde, Klage*) file
ein'reihen *tr* file; rank; enroll; (*Bücher*) shelve || *ref* fall into place; fall in line
ein'reihig *adj* single-breasted
Ein'reise *f* entry
ein'reißen §53 *tr* tear; demolish || *intr* (SEIN) tear; (fig) spread
ein'renken *tr* (*Knochen*) set; (fig) set right
ein'richten *tr* arrange; establish; (*Wohnung*) furnish; (surg) set || *ref* settle down; economize, make ends meet; (**auf** *acc*) make arrangements (for); (**nach**) adapt oneself (to)
Ein'richtung *f* (–;-en) setup; establishment; furniture; equipment
Ein'richtungsgegenstand *m* piece of furniture, piece of equipment
ein'rosten *intr* (SEIN) get rusty
ein'rücken *tr* (*Zeile*) indent; (*Anzeige*) put in || *intr* (SEIN) march in; **in j–s Stelle e.** succeed s.o.; **zum Militär e.** enter military service
Ein'rückung *f* (–;-en) indentation
ein'rühren *tr* (**in** *acc*) stir (into)
eins [aɪns] *pron* one; one o'clock; **es ist mir eins** it's all the same to me || **Eins** *f* (–;-en) one; (*auf Würfeln*) ace; (educ) A
einsam ['aɪnzɑm] *adj* lonely, lonesome
ein'sammlen *tr* gather; (*Geld*) collect
Ein'satz *m* insert, insertion; (*Wette*) bet; (*Risiko*) risk; (*Verwendung*) use; (*für Flaschen*) deposit; (aer) sortie; (mil) action; (mus) starting in, entry; **im E. stehen** be in action; **im vollen E.** in full operation; **unter E. seines Lebens** at the risk of one's life; **zum E. bringen** employ, use; (*Maschinen*) put into operation; (*Polizei*) call out; (mil) throw into action
ein'satzbereit *adj* combat-ready
Ein'satzstück *n* insert
ein'saugen *tr* suck in; (fig) imbibe
ein'säumen *tr* (sew) hem
ein'schalten *tr* insert; (elec) switch on, turn on || *ref* intervene
ein'schärfen *tr*—j–m etw **e.** impress s.th. on s.o.
ein'schätzen *tr* appraise, value
ein'schenken *tr* pour
ein'schicken *tr* send in
ein'schieben §130 *tr* push in; insert

ein'schießen §76 *tr* (*Gewehr*) test; (*Geld*) contribute; (*Brot in den Ofen*) shove; (fb) score || *ref* (**auf** *acc*) zero in (on)
ein'schiffen *tr* & *intr* embark
Ein'schiffung *f* (–;-en) embarkation
ein'schlafen §131 *intr* (SEIN) fall asleep; (*Glied*) go to sleep
ein'schläf(e)rig *adj* single (bed)
einschläfern ['aɪnʃlɛfərn] *tr* lull to sleep; (vet) put to sleep
Ein'schlag *m* striking; impact; explosion; (*Umschlag*) wrapper; (fig) admixture, element; (golf) putt; (sew) tuck; (tex) weft, woof
ein'schlagen §132 *tr* (*Nagel*) drive in; (*zerbrechen*) smash, bash in; (*einwickeln*) wrap; (*Weg*) take; (*Laufbahn*) enter upon; (*Pflanzen*) stick in the ground; (golf) putt; **die Richtung e. nach** go in the direction of || *intr* (*Blitz*) strike; (*Erfolg haben*) be a success; **nicht e.** fail
einschlägig ['aɪnʃlɛgɪç] *adj* relevant
Ein'schlagpapier *n* wrapping paper
ein'schleichen §85 *ref* (**in** *acc*) creep (into), slip (into); (**in j–s Gunst**) worm one's way
ein'schleppen *tr* tow in; (*e–e Krankheit*) bring in (*from abroad*)
ein'schleusen *tr* (*Schmuggelwaren*) sneak in; (*Spionen*) plant
ein'schließen §76 *tr* lock up; (**in e–m Brief**) enclose; (fig) include; (mil) encircle, surround
ein'schließlich *adv* inclusive(ly) || *prep* (*genit*) inclusive of
ein'schlummern *intr* (SEIN) doze off
Ein'schluß *m* encirclement; **mit E.** (*genit*) including
ein'schmeicheln *ref* (**bei**) ingratiate oneself (with)
ein'schmeichelnd *adj* ingratiating
ein'schmuggeln *tr* smuggle in
ein'schnappen *intr* (SEIN) snap shut; (fig) take offense
ein'schneidend *adj* (fig) incisive
Ein'schnitt *m* cut, incision; (*Kerbe*) notch; (geol) gorge; (pros) caesura
ein'schnüren *tr* tie up; pinch
ein'schränken *tr* (**auf** *acc*) restrict (to), confine (to); (*Ausgaben*) cut; (*Behauptung*) qualify || *ref* economize
Ein'schränkung *f* (–;-en) restriction; **ohne jede E.** without reservation
Ein'schreibebrief *m* registered letter
ein'schreiben §62 *tr* enroll; (*Brief*) register; (*eintragen*) enter; **e–n Brief e. lassen** send a letter by registered mail || *ref* register
ein'schreiten §86 *intr* (SEIN) step in, intervene; (**gegen**) take action (against)
ein'schrumpfen *intr* (SEIN) shrivel up
ein'schüchtern *tr* intimidate, overawe
Ein'schüchterung *f* (–;) intimidation
ein'schulen *tr* enroll in school
Ein'schuß *m* hit (*of a bullet*)
ein'schütten *tr* pour in
ein'segnen *tr* (*neues Gebäude*) consecrate; (*konfirmieren*) confirm
ein'sehen §138 *tr* inspect; (*Akten*) consult; (fig) realize; (mil) observe ||

Einsehen *n*—**ein E. haben** show (some) consideration
ein'seifen *tr* soap; (coll) softsoap
ein'seitig *adj* one-sided
ein'senden §140 *tr* send in, submit
Ein'sender –**in** §6 *mf* sender
ein'senken *tr* (**in** *acc*) sink (into)
ein'setzen *tr* insert, put in; (*Geld*) bet; (*Leben*) risk; (*Polizei*) call out; (*Truppen*) commit; (*Kräfte*) muster; (*Einfluß*) use; (*Beamten*) install; (*ernennen*) appoint; (*einpflanzen*) plant; (*Artillerie, Tanks, Bomber*) employ; (*Edelsteine*) mount || *ref* (**für**) stand up (for) || *intr* set in, begin; (mus) come in
Ein'sicht *f* inspection; (fig) insight
ein'sichtig *adj* understanding
ein'sichtsvoll *adj* understanding
ein'sickern *intr* (SEIN) seep in; (mil) infiltrate
Einsiedelei [aɪnzidə'laɪ] *f* (–;–en) hermitage
Einsiedler –**in** ['aɪnzidlər(ɪn)] §6 *mf* hermit, recluse
einsilbig ['aɪnzɪlbɪç] *adj* monosyllabic; (fig) taciturn
ein'sinken §143 *intr* (SEIN) sink in; (*Erdboden*) subside
ein'sparen *tr* economize on, save
ein'sperren *tr* lock up
ein'springen §142 *intr* (SEIN) jump in; (**für**) substitute (for); (tech) catch
ein'spritzen *tr* inject
Ein'spritzung *f* (–;–en) injection
Ein'spruch *m* objection; (jur) appeal
einspurig ['aɪnʃpurɪç] *adj* single-track
einst [aɪnst] *adv* once; (*künftig*) someday; **e. wie jezt** (now) as ever
Ein'stand *m* (tennis) deuce
ein'stecken *tr* insert, put in; stick in, pocket; (*Schwert*) sheathe; (*hinnehmen*) take; (coll) lock up, jail
ein'stehen §146 *intr* (SEIN) (**für**) vouch (for), stand up (for); **für die Folgen e.** take the responsibility
ein'steigen §148 *intr* (SEIN) get in; **alle e.!** all aboard!
Ein'steigkarte *f* (aer) boarding pass
Ein'steigloch *n* manhole
einstellbar ['aɪnʃtɛlbar] *adj* adjustable
ein'stellen *tr* put in; (*Arbeiter*) hire; (*Gerät*) set, adjust; (*beenden*) stop, quit; (*Sender*) tune in on; (*Fernglas, Kamera*) focus; **die Arbeit e.** go on strike; **etw bei j–m e.** leave s.th. at s.o.'s house; **in die Garage e.** put into the garage; **zum Heeresdienst e.** induct || *ref* show up, turn up; **sich e. auf** (*acc*) attune oneself to
Ein'stellung *f* (–;–en) adjustment; setting; focusing; stoppage; (*der Feindseligkeiten, Zahlungen*) suspension; hiring; (aut) timing; (mil) induction; **E. des Feuers** cease-fire; **geistige E.** mental attitude
einstig ['aɪnstɪç] *adj* former; (*verstorben*) late; (*künftig*) future
ein'stimmen *intr* join in; **e. in** (*acc*) agree to, consent to
einstimmig ['aɪnʃtɪmɪç] *adj* unanimous
ein'studieren *tr* study; rehearse
ein'stufen *tr* classify

ein'stürmen *intr* (SEIN) (**auf** *acc*) rush (at); (mil) charge
Ein'sturz *m* (–es;) collapse
ein'stürzen *intr* (SEIN) collapse; **e. auf** (*acc*) (fig) overwhelm
einstweilen ['aɪnstvaɪlən] *adv* for the present; temporarily
einstweilig ['aɪnstvaɪlɪç] *adj* temporary
Ein'tänzer *m* gigolo
ein'tauschen *tr* trade in; **e. gegen** exchange for
ein'teilen *tr* divide; (*austeilen*) distribute; (*einstufen*) classify; (*Geld, Zeit*) budget; (*Arbeit*) plan
eintönig ['aɪntønɪç] *adj* monotonous
Ein'tönigkeit *f* (–;) monotony
Ein'topf *m*, **Ein'topfgericht** *n* one-dish meal
Ein'tracht *f* (–;) harmony, unity
einträchtig ['aɪntrɛçtɪç] *adj* harmonious
Eintrag ['aɪntrɑk] *m* (–[e]s;⸚e) entry; **E. tun** (*dat*) hurt
ein'tragen §132 *tr* enter, register; (*Gewinn*) bring in, yield; **j–m etw e.** bring down s.th. on s.o. || *ref* register
einträglich ['aɪntreklɪç] *adj* profitable, lucrative
Ein'tragung *f* (–;–en) entry
ein'treffen §151 *intr* (SEIN) arrive; (*in Erfüllung gehen*) come true
ein'treiben §62 *tr* drive in; (*Geld*) collect || *intr* (SEIN) drift in, sail in
ein'treten §152 *tr* smash in || *ref*—**sich** [*dat*] **e–n Nagel e.** step on a nail || *intr* (SEIN) enter; (*geschehen*) occur; (*Fieber*) develop; (*Fall, Not*) arise; (*Dunkelheit*) fall; **e. für** stand up for, champion; **e. in** (*acc*) join, enter
Ein'tritt *m* (–s;) entry; (*Einlaß*) admittance; (*Anfang*) beginning, onset; (rok) re-entry; **E. frei** free admission; **E. verboten** no admittance
Ein'trittsgeld *n* admission fee
Ein'trittskarte *f* admission ticket
ein'trocknen *intr* (SEIN) dry up
ein'trüben *ref* become overcast
ein'tunken *tr* (**in** *acc*) dip (into)
ein'üben *tr* practice; train, coach
ein'verleiben *tr* incorporate
Einvernahme ['aɪnfɛrnɑmə] *f* (–;–n) interrogation
Ein'vernehmen *n* (–s;) agreement; **sich mit j–m ins E. setzen** try to come to an understanding with s.o.
einverstanden ['aɪnfɛr/tandən] *adj* in agreement || *interj* agreed!
Ein'verständnis *n* agreement; approval
ein'wachsen *tr* wax || *intr* (SEIN) (**in** *acc*) *grow* (into)
Ein'wand *m* (–s;⸚e) objection
Ein'wanderer –**in** §6 *mf* immigrant
ein'wandern *intr* (SEIN) immigrate
Ein'wanderung *f* (–;) immigration
ein'wandfrei *adj* unobjectionable; (*tadellos*) flawless; (*Alibi, Zustand*) perfect; (*Quelle*) unimpeachable
einwärts ['aɪnvɛrts] *adv* inward(s)
Einweg– *comb.fm.* disposable
ein'weichen *tr* soak
ein'weihen *tr* consecrate, dedicate; **e. in** (*acc*) initiate into; let in on

Ein'weihung *f* (-;-en) dedication; initiation
ein'weisen §118 *tr* install; (*Verkehr*) direct; **e. in** (*acc*) assign to; **j-n in seine Pflichten e.** brief s.o. in his duties; **j-n ins Krankenhaus e.** have s.o. admitted to the hospital
ein'wenden §140 *tr*—**etw e. gegen** raise an objection to; **nichts einzuwenden haben gegen** have no objections to
Ein'wendung *f* (-;-en) objection
ein'werfen §160 *tr* throw in; (*Fenster*) smash; (*Brief*) mail; (*Münze*) insert; (fig) interject
ein'wickeln *tr* wrap (up); (fig) trick
ein'willigen *intr* (**in** *acc*) agree (to)
ein'wirken *intr* (**auf** *acc*) have an effect (on), exercise infuence (on)
Ein'wirkung *f* (-;-en) effect, influence
Ein'wohner –**in** §6 *mf* inhabitant
Ein'wurf *m* (*Schlitz*) slot; (*e-r Münze*) insertion; (*Einwand*) objection
ein'wurzeln *ref* take root
Ein'zahl *f* (-;) singular
ein'zahlen *tr* pay in; (**in** *e-e Kasse*) deposit
Ein'zahlung *f* (-;-en) payment; deposit
Ein'zahlungsschein *m* deposit slip
einzäunen ['aɪntsɔɪnən] *tr* fence in
Einzel ['aɪntsəl] *n* (-s;-) singles
Einzel– *comb.fm.* individual; single; isolated; detailed; retail
Ein'zelbild *n* (cin) frame; (phot) still
Ein'zelfall *m* individual case
Ein'zelgänger *m* (coll) lone wolf
Ein'zelhaft *f* solitary confinement
Ein'zelhandel *m* retail trade
Ein'zelheit *f* (-;-en) item; detail, particular; **wegen näherer Einzelheiten** for further particulars
einzellig ['aɪntsɛlɪç] *adj* single-cell
einzeln ['aɪntsəln] *adj* single; particular, individual; separate
Ein'zelperson *f* individual
Ein'zelspiel *n* singles (match)
Ein'zelwesen *n* individual
Ein'zelzimmer *n* single room; (*im Krankenhaus*) private room
ein'ziehen §163 *tr* draw in; retract; (*Flagge*) hawl down; (*Segel*) take in; (*Münzen*) call in; (*eintreiben*) collect; (mil) draft || *intr* (SEIN) move in; **e. in** (*acc*) enter; penetrate
einzig ['aɪntsɪç] *adj & adv* only; **e. darstellen** be unique || *indef pron*—**ein einziger** one only; **kein einziger** not a single one
ein'zigartig *adj* unique; extraordinary
Ein'zug *m* entry; moving in; (*Beginn*) start; (tvp) indentation; **seinen E. halten** make one's entry
ein'zwängen *tr* (**in** *acc*) squeeze (into)
Eis [aɪs] *n* (-es;) ice; (*Speise*-) ice cream || ['e·ɪs] *n* (-;-s) (mus) E sharp
Eis'bahn *f* ice-skating rink
Eis'bär *m* polar bear
Eis'bein *n* (culin) pigs feet
Eis'berg *m* iceberg
Eis'beutel *m* (med) ice pack
Eis'blume *f* window frost
Eis'creme *f* ice cream
Eis'diehle *f* ice cream parlor

Eisen ['aɪzən] *n* (-s;-) iron; **altes E.** scrap iron; **heißes E.** (fig) hot potato; **zum alten E. werfen** (fig) scrap
Ei'senbahn *f* railroad; **mit der E.** by train, by rail
Ei'senbahndamm *m* railroad embankment
Ei'senbahner *m* (-s;-) railroader
Ei'senbahnknotenpunkt *m* railroad junction
Ei'senblech *n* sheet iron
Ei'senerz *n* iron ore
Ei'senhütte *f* ironworks
Ei'senwaren *pl* hardware, ironware
Ei'senwarenhandlung *f* hardware store
Ei'senzeit *f* iron age
eisern ['aɪzərn] *adj* iron; (*Fleiß*) unflagging; (*Rationen*) emergency
Eis'glätte *f* icy road conditions
eis'grau *adj* hoary
eisig ['aɪsɪç] *adj* icy; icy-cold
Eis'kappe *f* ice cap
Eis'kunstlauf *m* figure skating
Eis'lauf *m* ice skating
Eis'laufbahn *f* ice-skating rink
eis'laufen §105 *intr* (SEIN) ice-skate
Eis'läufer –**in** §6 *mf* skater
Eis'meer *n*—**Nördliches E.** Arctic Ocean; **Südliches E.** Antarctic Ocean
Eis'pickel *m* ice axe
Eis'schnellauf *m* speed skating
Eis'scholle *f* ice floe
Eis'schrank *m* icebox
Eis'vogel *m* kingfisher
Eis'würfel *m* ice cube
Eis'würfelschale *f* ice-cube tray
Eis'zapfen *m* icicle
Eis'zeit *f* ice age, glacial period
eitel ['aɪtəl] *adj* (*nutzlos*) vain, empty; (*selbstgefällig*) vain; || *invar adj* pure || *adv* merely
Ei'telkeit *f* (-;) vanity
Eiter ['aɪtər] *m* (-s;) pus
Ei'terbeule *f* boil, abscess
eitern ['aɪtərn] *intr* fester, suppurate
Ei'terung *f* (-;-en) festering
eitrig ['aɪtrɪç] *adj* pussy
Ei'weiß *n* (-es;-e) egg white; albumen
Ekel ['ekəl] *m* (-s;) (**vor** *dat*) disgust (at) || *n* (-s;) (coll) pest
ekelerregend ['ekələregənt] *adj* sickening, nauseating
e'kelhaft *adj* disgusting
ekeln ['ekəln] *impers*—**es eket mir** or **mich** I am disgusted || *ref* (**vor** *dat*) feel disgusted (at)
eklig ['eklɪç] *adj* disgusting, revolting; nasty, beastly
Ekzem [ɛk'tsem] *n* (-s;-e) eczema
elastisch [e'lastɪʃ] *adj* elastic
Elch [ɛlç] *m* (-[e]s;-e) elk, moose
Elefant [ele'fant] *m* (-en;-en) elephant
Elefan'tentreiber *m* mahout
Elefan'tenzahn *m* elephant's tusk
elegant [ele'gant] *adj* elegant
Eleganz [ele'gants] *f* (-;) elegance
Elektriker [e'lɛktrɪkər] *m* (-s;-) electrician
elektrisch [e'lɛktrɪʃ] *adj* electric(al)
elektrisieren [ɛlɛktrɪ'zirən] *tr* electrify
Elektrolyse [ɛlɛktro'lyzə] *f* (-;-) electricity

Elektrizitäts– comb.fm. electric, electro–
Elektro– [ɛlɛktrɔ] comb.fm. electrical, electro–
Elektrode [ɛlɛk'trodə] f (–;–n) electrode
Elek'trogerät n electrical appliance
Elektrizität [ɛlɛktrɪtsɪ'tet] f (–;) electricity
Elek·tron [ɛ'lɛktrɔn] n (–s;–tronen ['tronən]) electron
Elektronen– [ɛlɛktronən–] comb.fm. electronic
Elektronik [ɛlɛk'tronɪk] f (–;) electronics
Elektrotechnik f (–;) electrical engineering
Elektrotech'niker m (–s;–) electrical engineer
Element [ɛlɛ'mɛnt] n (–[e]s;–e) element; (elec) cell
elementar [ɛlɛmɛn'tar] adj elementary
Elementar'buch n primer
Elen ['elɛn] m & n (–s;–) elk
elend ['elənt] adj miserable || **Elend** n (–[e]s;) misery; extreme poverty; **das graue E.** the blues
E'lendsviertel n slums
elf [ɛlf] adj & pron eleven || **Elf** f (–;–en) eleven
Elfe ['ɛlfə] m (–n;–n), f (–;–n) elf
Elfenbein ['ɛlfənbaɪn] n (–s;) ivory
elfte ['ɛlftə] §9 adj & pron eleventh
Elftel ['ɛlftəl] n (–s;–) eleventh (part)
Elite [ɛ'litə] f (–;) elite, flower
Ellbogen ['ɛlbogən] m (–s;–) elbow
Ell'bogenfreiheit f elbowroom
Elsaß ['ɛlzas] n (–;) Elsace
elsässisch ['ɛlzɛsɪʃ] adj Alsatian
Elster ['ɛlstər] f (–;–n) magpie
elterlich ['ɛltərlɪç] adj parental
Eltern ['ɛltərn] pl parents; **nicht von schlechtern E.** (coll) terrific
El'ternbeirat m Parent-Teacher Association
El'ternhaus n home
el'ternlos adj orphaned; **elternlose Zeugung** spontaneous generation
El'ternschaft f parenthood
El'ternteil m parent
Email [ɛ'maj] n (–s;), **Emaille** [ɛ'maljə] f (–;) enamel
Email'geschirr n enamelware
Emai'llack m enamel paint
emaillieren [ɛma(l)'jirən] tr enamel
Email'waren pl enamelware
emanzipieren [ɛmantsɪ'pirən] tr emancipate
Embargo [ɛm'bargo] n (–s;–s) embargo
Embo·lie [ɛmbɔ'li] f (–;–lien ['li·ən]) embolism
Embry·o ['ɛmbry·o] m (–s;–onen ['onən]) embryo
Emigrant –in [ɛmɪ'grant(ɪn)] §7 mf emigrant
Emission [ɛmɪ'sjon] f (–;–en) emission; (fin) issuance; (rad) broadcasting
empfahl [ɛm'pfal] pret of **empfehlen**
Empfang [ɛm'pfaŋ] m (–[e]s;–̈e) reception; (Erhalten) receipt; (im Hotel) reception desk

empfangen [ɛm'pfaŋən] §73 tr receive; (Kind) conceive
Empfänger –in [ɛm'pfɛŋər(ɪn)] §6 mf receiver, recipient; addressee
empfänglich [ɛm'pfɛŋlɪç] adj (für) susceptible (to)
Empfängnis [ɛm'pfɛŋnɪs] f (–;) conception
empfängnis'verhütend adj contraceptive; **empfängnisverhütendes Mittel** contraceptive
Empfäng'nisverhütung f contraception
Empfangs'chef m desk clerk
Empfangs'dame f receptionist; (im Restaurant) hostess
Empfangs'schein m (com) receipt
empfehlen [ɛm'pfelən] §147 tr recommend; **e. Sie mich** (dat) remember me to || ref say goodbye
empfeh'lenswert adj commendable
Empfeh'lung f (–;–en) recommendation; (Gruß) compliments
empfinden [ɛm'pfɪndən] §59 tr feel
empfindlich [ɛm'pfɪntlɪç] adj sensitive; delicate, touchy; (Kälte) bitter; (gegen) susceptible (to)
Empfind'lichkeit f (–;–en) sensitivity, touchiness; susceptibility
empfindsam [ɛm'pfɪntzam] adj sensitive, touchy; sentimental
Empfind'samkeit f (–;–en) sensibility; sentimentality
Empfin'dung f (–;–en) sensation; feeling, sentiment
empfin'dunglos adj numb; (fig) callous
Empfin'dungswort n (gram) interjection
Emphysem [ɛmfy'zem] n (–s;) emphysema
empor [ɛm'por] adv up, upwards
empören [ɛm'pørən] tr anger, shock || ref rebel, revolt; (mil) mutiny
empor'fahren §71 intr (SEIN) jump up
empor'kommen §99 intr (SEIN) rise up; (in der Welt) get ahead
Emporkömmling [ɛm'porkœmlɪŋ] m (–s;–e) upstart, parvenu
empor'ragen intr tower, rise
empor'steigen §148 intr (SEIN) rise
empor'streben intr (SEIN) rise, soar; (fig) aspire
Empö'rung f (–;–en) revolt; (über acc) indignation (at)
emsig ['ɛmzɪç] adj industrious, busy
Em'sigkeit f (–;) industry; activity
End– [ɛnt] comb.fm. final, ultimate
Ende ['ɛndə] n (–s;–n) end; ending; outcome; **letzten Endes** in the final analysis; **zu E. gehen** end; **zu E. sein** be over
enden ['ɛndən] tr & intr end; **nicht e. wollend** unending
End'ergebnis n final result, upshot
End'gerade f (–;) home stretch
end'gültig adj final, definitive
endigen ['ɛndɪgən] tr & intr end; **e. auf** (acc) (gram) terminate in
Endivie [ɛn'divjə] f (–;–n) endive
End'lauf m (sport) final heat
end'lich adj final; limited, finite || adv finally, at last
end'los adj endless
End'runde f final round, finals

End'station *f* final stop, terminus
End'summe *f* sum total
End'termin *m* final date; closing date
En'dung *f* (-;-en) ending
Ener·gie [ɛnɛr'gi] *f* (-;-gien ['gi·ən]) energy
energisch [ɛ'nɛrgɪʃ] *adj* energetic
eng [ɛŋ] *adj* narrow; tight; (*Freunde*) close; (*innig*) intimate; **im engeren Sinne** strictly speaking
engagieren [ãga'zirən] *tr* engage, hire || *ref* commit oneself
Enge ['ɛŋə] *f* (-;-n) narrowness; tightness; (*Meer-*) strait; (fig) tight spot
Engel ['ɛŋəl] *m* (-s;-) angel
en'gelhaft *adj* angelic
eng'herzig *adj* stingy; petty
England ['ɛŋlant] *n* (-s;) England
Engländer ['ɛŋlendər] *m* (-s;-) Englishman; **die E.** the English
Engländerin ['ɛŋlendərɪn] *f* (-;-nen) Englishwoman
englisch ['ɛŋlɪʃ] *adj* English
Eng'paß *m* pass, defile; (fig) bottleneck
engros [ã'gro] *adv* wholesale
engstirnig ['ɛŋʃtɪrnɪç] *adj* narrowminded
Enkel ['ɛŋkəl] *m* (-s;-) grandson
Enkelin ['ɛŋkəlɪn] *f* (-;-nen) granddaughter
En'kelkind *n* grandchild
enorm [ɛ'nɔrm] *adj* enormous
Ensemble [ã'sãbl(ə)] *n* (-s;-s) (mus) ensemble; (theat) company, cast
ent- [ɛnt] *insep pref*
entarten [ɛnt'artən] *intr* (SEIN) degenerate
entartet [ɛnt'artət] *adj* degenerate; (fig) decadent
entäu'ßern *ref* (*genit*) divest oneself of
entbehren [ɛnt'berən] *tr* lack, miss; do without; spare; dispense with
entbehr'lich *adj* dispensable; needless, superfluous
Entbeh'rung *f* (-;-en) privation, need
entbin'den §59 *tr* release, absolve; (*Frau*) deliver || *intr* give birth
Entbin'dung *f* (-;-en) dispensation; (*Niederkunft*) delivery, childbirth
Entbin'dungsanstalt *f* maternity hospital
entblät'tern *tr* defoliate || *ref* defoliate; (coll) strip
entblößen [ɛnt'bløsən] *tr* bare; uncover; (mil) expose || *ref* strip; remove one's hat
entbren'nen §97 *intr* (SEIN) flare up
entdecken (entdek'ken) *tr* discover || *ref*—**sich j-m e.** confide in s.o.
Entdeckung (**Entdek'kung**) *f* (-;-en) discovery
Ente ['ɛntə] *f* (-;-n) duck; (coll) hoax
enteh'ren *tr* dishonor; (*Mädchen*) violate, deflower
enteh'rend *adj* disgraceful
Enteh'rung *f* (-;-en) disgrace; rape
enteig'nen *tr* dispossess
enteisen [ɛnt'aɪzən] *tr* defrost; deice
enter'ben *tr* disinherit
Enterich ['ɛntərɪç] *m* (-s;-e) drake
entern ['ɛntərn] *tr* (naut) board
entfachen [ɛnt'faxən] *tr* kindle; (fig) provoke

entfah'ren §71 *intr* (SEIN) (*dat*) slip out (on)
entfal'len §72 *intr* (SEIN) (*dat*) slip (from); **auf j-n e.** fall to s.o.'s share; **entfällt** not applicable
entfal'ten *tr* unfold; display; (mil) deploy || *ref* unfold; develop
entfernen [ɛnt'fɛrnən] *tr* remove || *ref* withdraw, move away; deviate
entfernt [ɛnt'fɛrnt] *adj* distant; **nicht weit davon e. zu** (*inf*) far from (*ger*)
Entfer'nung *f* (-;-en) removal; range; distance; absence
Entfer'nungsmesser *m* (phot) range finder
entfes'seln *tr* unleash
entflam'men *tr* inflame || *intr* (SEIN) ignite; flash; (fig) flare up
entflech'ten *tr* disentangle; (*Kartell*) break up; (mil) disengage
entflie'hen §75 *intr* (SEIN) flee, escape; (*Zeit*) fly
entfremden [ɛnt'fremdən] *tr* alienate
enfrosten [ɛnt'frɔstən] *tr* defrost
entführ'ren *tr* abduct; kidnap; (*Flugzeug*) hijack; (hum) steal
Entführ'rer **-in** §6 *mf* abductor, kidnaper; (aer) hijacker
Entführ'rung *f* (-;-en) abduction; kidnaping; (aer) hijacking
entge'gen *prep* (*dat*) contrary to; in the direction of, towards
entge'gengehen §82 *intr* (SEIN) (*dat*) go to meet; (*dat*) face, confront
entge'gengesetzt *adj* contrary, opposite
entge'genhalten §90 *tr* hold out; point out, say in answer
entge'genkommen §99 *intr* (SEIN) (*dat*) approach; (*dat*) come to meet; (*dat*) meet halfway || **Entgegenkommen** *n* (-s;) courtesy
entge'genkommend *adj* on-coming; (fig) accommodating
entge'genlaufen §105 *intr* (SEIN) (*dat*) run towards; (*dat*) run counter to
entge'gennehmen §116 *tr* accept, receive
entge'gensehen §138 *intr* (*dat*) look forward to; (*dat*) await; (*dat*) face
entge'gensetzen *tr* put up, offer
entge'genstehen §146 *intr* (*dat*) oppose
entge'genstellen *tr* set in opposition || *ref* (*dat*) oppose, resist
entge'genstrecken *tr* (*dat*) stretch out (toward)
entge'gentreten §152 *intr* (SEIN) (*dat*) walk toward; (fig) (*dat*) confront
entgegnen [ɛnt'gegnən] *tr* & *intr* reply
Entgeg'nung *f* (-;-en) reply
entge'hen §82 *intr* (SEIN) (*dat*) escape, elude; **sich** [*dat*] **etw e. lassen** let s.th. slip by
Entgelt [ɛnt'gɛlt] *n* (-[e]s;) compensation, payment
entgel'ten §83 *tr* pay for
entgeistert [ɛnt'gaɪstərt] *adj* aghast
entgleisen [ɛnt'glaɪzən] *intr* (SEIN) jump the track; (fig) make a slip
Entglei'sung *f* (-;-en) derailment; (fig) slip
entglei'ten §86 *intr* (SEIN) (*dat*) slip away (from)
entgräten [ɛnt'gretən] *tr* bone (*a fish*)

enthaaren [ɛnt'haːrən] *tr* remove the hair from
Enthaa'rungsmittel *n* hair remover
enthal'ten §90 *tr* contain; comprise || *ref* (*genit*) refrain (from); **sich der Stimme e.** (parl) abstain
enthaltsam [ɛnt'haltzɑm] *adj* abstinent
Enthalt'samkeit *f* (-;) abstinence
Enthal'tung *f* (-;-en) abstention
enthär'ten *tr* (*Wasser*) soften
enthaupten [ɛnt'hauptən] *tr* behead
enthäuten [ɛnt'hɔɪtən] *tr* skin
enthe'ben §94 *tr* (*genit*) exempt (from), relieve (of); (*e–s Amtes*) remove (*from office*)
enthei'ligen *tr* desecrate, profane
enthül'len *tr* unveil; reveal, expose
Enthül'lung *f* (-;-en) unveiling; (fig) exposé
enthül'sen *tr* shell; (*Mais*) husk
Enthusiasmus [ɛntuzi'asmus] *m* (-;) enthusiasm
enthusiastisch [ɛntuzi'astɪʃ] *adj* enthusiastic
entjungfern [ɛnt'juŋfərn] *tr* deflower
entkei'men *tr* sterilize; (*Milch*) pasteurize || *intr* (SEIN) escape
entkernen [ɛnt'kɛrnən] *tr* (*Obst*) pit
entklei'den *tr* undress; (*genit*) strip (of), divest (of) || *ref* undress
Entklei'dungsnummer *f* striptease act
Entklei'dungsrevué *f* striptease show
entkom'men §99 *intr* (SEIN) (*dat*) escape (from) || **Entkommen** *n* (-s;) escape
entkor'ken *tr* uncork, open
entkräften [ɛnt'krɛftən] *tr* weaken; (*Argument*) refute
entla'den §103 *tr* unload; (*Batterie*) discharge || *ref* (*Gewehr*) go off; (*Sturm*) break; (elec) discharge; **sein Zorn entlud sich** he vented his anger
Entla'dung *f* (-;-en) unloading; discharge; explosion; **zur E. bringen** detonate
entlang' *adv* along || *prep* (*dat* or *acc* or an *dat*; or after *genit* or *dat*) along
entlarven [ɛnt'larfən] *tr* expose
entlas'sen §104 *tr* dismiss, fire; set free; (mil) discharge
Entlas'sungspapiere *pl* discharge papers
entla'sten *tr* unburden; (**von**) relieve (of); (jur) exonerate
Entla'stungsstraße *f* bypass
Entla'stungszeuge *m* witness for the defense
entlauben [ɛnt'laubən] *tr* defoliate
entlaubt' *adj* leafless
entlau'fen §105 *intr* (SEIN) (*dat*) run away (from); (*mit e–m Liebhaber*) elope
entlausen [ɛnt'lauzən] *tr* delouse
entledigen [ɛnt'leːdɪgən] *tr* (*genit*) release (from) || *ref* (*genit*) get rid (of), rid oneself (of)
entlee'ren *tr* empty; drain
entle'gen *adj* distant, remote
entleh'nen *tr* borrow
entlei'hen §81 *tr* borrow
entlo'ben *ref* break the engagement
entlocken (**entlok'ken**) *tr* elicit
entloh'nen *tr* pay, pay off
entlüf'ten *tr* ventilate

entmannen [ɛnt'manən] *tr* castrate
entmilitarisieren [ɛntmɪlitarɪ'ziːrən] *tr* demilitarize
entmutigen [ɛnt'muːtɪgən] *tr* discourage
entneh'men §116 *tr* (*dat*) take (from); (*Geld*) (**aus**) withdraw (from); (*dat* or **aus**) infer (from), gather (from)
entnerven [ɛnt'nɛrfən] *tr* enervate
entpuppen [ɛnt'pupən] *ref* emerge from the cocoon; **sich e. als** (fig) turn out to be
enträtseln [ɛnt'rɛtsəln] *tr* solve; (*Schriftzeichen*) decipher
entrei'ßen §53 *tr* (*dat*) wrest (from)
entrich'ten *tr* pay
entrin'nen §121 *intr* (SEIN) escape (from)
entrol'len *tr* unroll; unfurl || *ref* unroll || *intr* (SEIN) roll down
entrüsten [ɛnt'rʏstən] *tr* anger || *ref*— **sich e. über** (*acc*) become incensed at; be shocked at
Entrü'stung *f* (-;) anger, indignation
entsa'gen *intr* (*dat*) renounce, forego; **dem Thron e.** abdicate
Entsatz' *m* (-es;) (mil) relief
entschä'digen *tr* compensate; reimburse
Entschä'digung *f* (-;) compensation
Entschä'digungsanspruch *m* damage claim
entschär'fen *tr* defuse
Entscheid [ɛnt'ʃait] *m* (-[e]s;-e) (jur) decision
entschei'den §112 *tr*, *ref* & *intr* decide
entschei'dend *adj* decisive
Entschei'dung *f* (-;-en) decision
Entschei'dungsbefugnis *f* jurisdiction
Entschei'dungskampf *m* (sport) finals
Entschei'dungsspiel *n* (cards) rubber game; (sport) finals
Entschei'dungsstunde *f* moment of truth
entschei'dungsvoll *adj* critical
entschieden [ɛnt'ʃiːdən] *adj* decided; decisive; firm, resolute
entschla'fen §131 *intr* (SEIN) fall asleep; (*sterben*) pass away, die
entschlei'ern *tr* unveil; (fig) reveal
entschlie'ßen §76 *ref* (**zu**) decide (on)
Entschlie'ßung *f* (-;-en) (parl) resolution
entschlossen [ɛnt'ʃlɔsən] *adj* resolute
entschlüp'fen *intr* (SEIN) (*dat*) slip away (from); (*dat*) slip out (on)
Entschluß' *m* resolve, decision
entschlüs'seln *tr* decipher
Entschluß'kraft *f* will power
entschulden [ɛnt'ʃuldən] *tr* free of debt
entschuldigen [ɛnt'ʃuldɪgən] *tr* excuse; exculpate || *ref* apologize; **es läßt sich e.** it's excusable; **sich e. lassen** beg to be excused; **sich mit Unwissenheit e.** plead ignorance
entschul'digend *adj* apologetic
Entschul'digung *f* (-;-en) excuse; apology; **ich bitte um E.** I beg your pardon
Entschul'digungsgrund *m* excuse
entseelt [ɛnt'zeːlt] *adj* lifeless, dead
entsen'den §140 *tr* send off
entset'zen *tr* horrify; (mil) relieve ||

ref (über *acc*) be horrified (at) || **Entsetzen** *n* (-s;) horror
entsetz'lich *adj* horrible, appalling || *adv* (coll) awfully
Entset'zung *f* (-;) dismissal; (mil) relief
entsi'chern *tr* take (*a gun*) off safety
entsie'geln *tr* unseal
entsin'nen §121 *ref* (*genit*) recall
entspan'nen *tr* & *ref* relax
Entspan'nung *f* (-;) relaxation; (pol) detente
entspre'chen §64 *intr* (*dat*) correspond (to); (*dat*) meet, suit; (*dat*) be equivalent (to); (*dat*) answer (*a description*)
entspre'chend *adj* corresponding; adequate; equivalent || *adv* accordingly || *prep* (*dat*) according to
entsprin'gen §142 *intr* (SEIN) rise, originate; (*entlaufen*) escape
entstaatlichen [ɛnt'ʃtɑtlɪçən] *tr* free from state control, denationalize
entstam'men *intr* (SEIN) (*dat*) descend (from), originate (from)
entste'hen §146 *intr* (SEIN) originate
Entste'hung *f* (-;) origin
entstel'len *tr* disfigure; deface; (*Tatsachen*) distort
enttäu'schen *tr* disappoint
entthronen [ɛnt'tronən] *tr* dethrone
entvölkern [ɛnt'fœlkərn] *tr* depopulate
entwach'sen §155 *intr* (SEIN) (*dat*) outgrow
entwaff'nen *tr* disarm
entwar'nen *intr* sound the all-clear
entwäs'sern *tr* drain; dehydrate
entweder [ɛnt'vedər] *conj*—**entweder ... oder** either ... or
entwei'chen §85 *intr* (SEIN) escape
entwei'hen *tr* desecrate, profane
entwen'den *tr* steal
entwer'fen §160 *tr* sketch; draft
entwer'ten *tr* (*Geld*) depreciate; (*Briefmarke*) cancel; (*Karten*) punch
entwickeln (entwik'keln) *tr* develop; evolve; (mil) deploy || *ref* develop
Entwick'lung *f* (-;-en) development; evolution; (mil) deployment
Entwick'lungsland *n* developing country
Entwick'lungslehre *f* theory of evolution
entwin'den §59 *tr* (*dat*) wrest (from) || *ref* extricate oneself
entwirren [ɛnt'vɪrən] *tr* & *ref* unravel
entwi'schen *intr* (SEIN) escape; (*dat* or *aus*) slip away (from)
entwöhnen [ɛnt'vønən] *tr* wean; **j–n e.** (*genit*) break s.o. of || *ref* (*genit*) give up
Entwurf' *m* (-s;-̈e) sketch; draft
entwur'zeln *tr* uproot
entzau'bern *tr* disenchant
entzie'hen §163 *tr* (*dat*) withdraw (from), take away (from); (chem) extract; **j–m das Wort e.** (parl) rule s.o. out of order || *ref* (*dat*) shirk, elude
Entzie'hungsanstalt *f* rehabilitation center
entziffern [ɛnt'tsɪfərn] *tr* decipher
entzücken (entzük'ken) *tr* delight

Entzückung (Entzük'kung) *f* (-;-en) delight, rapture
Entzug' *m* (-[e]s;) deprivation
entzündbar [ɛnt'tsʏntbɑr] *adj* inflammable
entzün'den *tr* set on fire; (fig) inflame || *ref* catch fire; (pathol) become inflamed
Entzün'dung *f* (-;) kindling; (pathol) inflammation
entzwei' *adv* in two, apart
entzwei'brechen §64 *tr* & *intr* break in two, snap
entzweien [ɛnt'tsvɑɪ·ən] *tr* divide
Enzykli·ka [ɛn'tsʏklɪkɑ] *f* (-;-ken [kən]) encyclicle
Enzyklopä·die [ɛntsʏkləpɛ'di] *f* (-; -dien ['di·ən]) encyclopedia
Enzym [ɛn'tsym] *n* (-[e]s;-e) enzyme
Epaulette [ɛpɔ'lɛtə] *f* (-;-n) epaulet
ephemer [ɛfɛ'mer] *adj* ephemeral
Epide·mie [ɛpɪdɛ'mi] *f* (-;-mien ['mi·ən] epidemic
epidemisch [ɛpɪ'demɪʃ] *adj* epidemic
Epigramm [ɛpɪ'gram] *n* (-s;-e) epigram
Epik ['epɪk] *f* (-;) epic poetry
Epilog [ɛpɪ'lok] *m* (-s;-e) epilogue
episch ['epɪʃ] *adj* epic
Episode [ɛpɪ'zodə] *f* (-;-n) episode
Epoche [ɛ'pɔxə] *f* (-;-n) epoch
Epos ['epɔs] *n* (-; **Epen** ['epən]) epic
Equipage [ɛk(v)ɪ'paʒə] *f* (-;-n) carriage; (naut) crew; (sport) team
Equipe [ɛ'k(v)ɪp(ə)] *f* (-;-n) team; group
er [er] §11 *pers pron* he; it
er- [ɛr] *insep pref*
erach'ten *tr* think || **Erachten** *n* (-s;) opinion; **meines Erachtens** in my opinion
erar'beiten *tr* acquire (*by working*)
Erb- [ɛrp] *comb.fm.* hereditary
Erb'anfall *m* inheritance
Erb'anlage *f* (biol) gene
erbarmen [ɛr'barmən] *tr* move to pity || *ref* (*genit*) pity; **erbarme Dich unser** have mercy on us || **Erbarmen** *n* (-s;) pity, mercy
erbar'menswert, erbar'menswürdig *adj* pitiable
erbärmlich [ɛr'bɛrmlɪç] *adj* pitiful; wretched, miserable || *adv* awfully
erbar'mungslos *adj* pitiless
erbau'en *tr* erect; (fig) edify || *ref* (*an dat*) be edified (by)
Erbau'er *m* (-s;-) builder
erbau'lich *adj* edifying
Erbau'ung *f* (-;) building; edification
Erbau'ungsbuch *n* book of devotions
erb'berechtigt *adj* eligible as heir
Erbe ['ɛrbə] *m* (-n;-n) heir; **ohne Leibliche Erben** without issue || *n* (-s;) inheritance, heritage; **väterliches E.** patrimony
erbe'ben *intr* (SEIN) tremble
erb'eigen *adj* hereditary
erben ['ɛrbən] *tr* inherit
erbet'teln *tr* get (by begging)
erbeuten [ɛr'bɔɪtən] *tr* capture
Erb'feind *m* traditional enemy
Erb'folge *f* succession
erbie'ten §58 *ref* volunteer

Erbin ['ɛrbɪn] *f* (-;-nen) heiress
erbit'ten §60 *ref*—**sich** [*dat*] **etw e.** ask for s.th., request s.th.
erbittern [ɛr'bɪtərn] *tr* embitter
Erb'krankheit *f* hereditary disease
erblassen [ɛr'blasən] *intr* (SEIN) turn pale
Erblasser –in ['ɛrplasər(ɪn)] §6 *mf* testator
erbleichen [ɛr'blaɪçən] §85 & §109 *intr* (SEIN) turn pale; (poet) die
erb'lich *adj* hereditary
Erb'lichkeit *f* (-;) heredity
erblicken (erblik'ken) *tr* spot, see
erblinden [ɛr'blɪndən] *intr* (SEIN) go blind
Erblin'dung *f* (-;) loss of sight
Erb'onkel *m* (coll) rich uncle
erbre'chen §64 *tr* break open || *ref* vomit
erbrin'gen §65 *tr* produce
Erb'schaft *f* (-;-en) inheritance
Erbse ['ɛrpsə] *f* (-;-n) pea
Erb'stück *n* heirloom
Erb'sünde *f* original sin
Erb'tante *f* (coll) rich aunt
Erb'teil *m* share (in an inheritance)
Erd– [ert] *comb.fm.* earth, of the earth; geo–; ground
Erd'anschluß *m* (elec) ground
Erd'arbeiten *pl* excavation work
Erd'bahn *f* orbit of the earth
Erd'ball *m* globe
Erd'beben *n* (-s;–) earthquake
Erd'bebenmesser *m* seismograph
Erd'beere *f* strawberry
Erd'boden *m* ground, earth; **dem E. gleichmachen** raze (to the ground)
Erde ['ɛrdə] *f* (-;-n) earth; ground, soil, land; (elec) ground wire; **zu ebener E.** on the ground floor
erden ['ɛrdən] *tr* (elec) ground
erdenk'en §66 *tr* think up
erdenk'lich *adj* imaginable
Erd'gas *n* natural gas
Erd'geschoß *n* ground floor
erdich'ten *tr* fabricate, think up
Erdich'tung *f* (-;-en) fabrication
erdig ['ɛrdɪç] *adj* earthy
Erd'innere §5 *n* interior of the earth
Erd'klumpen *m* clod
Erd'kreis *m* earth, world
Erd'kugel *f* globe, sphere; world
Erd'kunde *f* geography
Erd'leitung *f* (elec) ground wire
Erd'nuß *f* peanut
Erd'nußbutter *f* peanut butter
Erd'öl *n* petroleum, oil; **auf E. stoßen** strike oil
erdolchen [ɛr'dɔlçən] *tr* stab
Erd'reich *n* soil
erdreisten [ɛr'draɪstən] *ref* have the nerve, have the audacity
Erd'rinde *f* crust of the earth
erdros'seln *tr* strangle
erdrücken (erdrük'ken) *tr* crush to death
erdrückend (erdrük'kend) *adj* overwhelming
Erd'rutsch *m* land slide
Erd'schicht *f* stratum
Erd'spalte *f* fissure; chasm
Erd'teil *m* continent

erdul'den *tr* suffer
ereifern [ɛr'aɪfərn] *ref* get excited
ereignen [ɛr'aɪgnən] *ref* happen, occur
Ereignis [ɛr'aɪgnɪs] *n* (-ses;-se) event, occurrence
ereig'nislos *adj* uneventful
ereig'nisvoll *adj* eventful
Erektion [ɛrɛk'tsjon] *f* (-;-en) erection
Eremit [ɛrɛ'mit] *m* (-en;-en) hermit
erer'ben *tr* inherit
erfah'ren *adj* experienced || §71 *tr* find out; (*erleben*) experience; (*Pflege*) receive
Erfah'rung *f* (-;-en) experience
erfas'sen *tr* grasp; understand; include; register, list
erfin'den §59 *tr* invent
Erfin'der –in §6 *mf* inventor
erfinderisch [ɛr'fɪndərɪʃ] *adj* inventive
Erfin'dung *f* (-;-en) invention
Erfin'dungsgabe *f* inventiveness
erfle'hen *tr* obtain (by entreaty)
Erfolg [ɛr'fɔlk] *m* (-[e]s;-e) success; (*Wirkung*) result
erfol'gen *intr* (SEIN) ensue; occur
erfolg'los *adj* unsuccessful || *adv* in vain
erfolg'reich *adj* successful
Erfolgs'mensch *m* go-getter
erfolg'versprechend *adj* promising
erforderlich [ɛr'fɔrdərlɪç] *adj* required, necessary
erfor'derlichenfalls *adv* if need be
erfordern [ɛr'fɔrdərn] *tr* require
Erfordernis [ɛr'fɔrdərnɪs] *n* (-ses;-se) requirement; exigency
erfor'schen *tr* investigate; (*Land*) explore
Erfor'scher –in §6 *mf* explorer
Erfor'schung *f* (-;-en) investigation; exploration
erfra'gen *tr* ask for; find out
erfreu'en *tr* delight || *ref* (**an** *dat*) be delighted (at); **sich e.** (*genit*) enjoy
erfreulich [ɛr'frɔɪlɪç] *adj* delightful; (*Nachricht*) welcome, good
erfreut [ɛr'frɔɪt] *adj* (**über** *acc*) glad (about); **e. zu** (*inf*) pleased to (*inf*)
erfrie'ren §77 *intr* (SEIN) freeze to death; (*Pflanzen*) freeze
Erfrie'rung *f* (-;-en) frostbite
erfrischen [ɛr'frɪʃən] *tr* refresh
Erfri'schung *f* (-;-en) refreshment
erfül'len *tr* fill; fulfill; (*Aufgabe*) perform; (*Bitte*) comply with; (*Hoffnungen*) live up to || *ref* materialize
Erfül'lung *f* (-;) fulfillment; accomplishment; **in E. gehen** come true
erfunden [ɛr'fundən] *adj* made-up
ergänzen [ɛr'gɛntsən] *tr* complete; complement; (*Statue*) restore
ergän'zend *adj* complementary
ergattern [ɛr'gatərn] *tr* (coll) dig up
ergau'nern *tr*—**etw von j-m e.** cheat s.o. out of s.th.
erge'ben *adj* devoted || §80 *tr* yield; amount to; show || *ref* surrender; (*dat*) devote oneself (to); (**aus**) result (from); **sich dem Trunk e.** take to drinking; **sich e. in** (*acc*) resign oneself to
Erge'benheit *f* (-;) devotion; resignation

ergebenst [ɛr'geːbənst] *adv* respectfully
Ergebnis [ɛr'geːpnɪs] *n* (-ses;-se) result, outcome; (*Punktzahl*) score
Erge′bung *f* (-;) submission, resignation; (mil) surrender
erge′hen §82 *intr* (SEIN) come out, be published; **e. lassen** issue, publish; **etw über sich e. lassen** put up with s.th.; **Gnade vor Recht e. lassen** show leniency || *ref* take a stroll; **sich e. in** (*acc*) indulge in; **sich e. über** (*acc*) expatiate on || *impers*—**es ist ihm gut ergangen** things went well for him || **Ergehen** *n* (-s;) state of health
ergiebig [ɛr'giːbɪç] *adj* productive, fertile; rich, abundant
ergie′ßen §76 *ref* flow; pour out
ergötzen [ɛr'gœtsən] *tr* amuse || *ref* (an *dat*) take delight (in)
ergötz′lich *adj* delightful
ergrau′en *intr* (SEIN) turn gray
ergrei′fen §88 *tr* seize; (*Verbrecher*) apprehend; (*Gemüt*) move; (*Beruf, Waffen*) take up; (*Maßnahmen*) take
Ergrei′fung *f* (-;) seizure
ergriffen [ɛr'grɪfən] *adj* moved; **e. von** seized with
Ergrif′fenheit *f* (-;) emotion
ergrün′den *tr* get to the bottom of
Erguß′ *m* discharge; (fig) flood of words
erha′ben *adj* elevated, lofty; **erhabene Arbeit** relief work; **e. sein über** (*acc*) be above
Erhalt′ *m* (-es;) receipt
erhal′ten §90 *tr* get, receive; keep, keep up, maintain; conserve; (*Familie*) support; (*Gesundheit*) preserve; **Betrag dankend e.** (*stamped on bills*) paid; **gut e.** well preserved; **noch e. sein** survive || *ref* survive; (**von**) subsist (on)
erhältlich [ɛr'hɛltlɪç] *adj* obtainable
Erhal′tung *f* (-;) preservation; maintenance; support; (*der Energie, usw.*) conservation
erhän′gen *tr* hang
erhär′ten *tr* harden; (fig) substantiate || *intr* (SEIN) harden
erha′schen *tr* catch; **e–n Blick von ihr e.** catch her eye
erhe′ben §94 *tr* raise; (*erhöhen*) elevate; (*preisen*) exalt; (*Steuern*) collect; (*Anklage*) bring; (math) raise || *ref* get up, rise, start; arise
erheblich [ɛr'heːplɪç] *adj* considerable
Erhe′bung *f* (-;-en) elevation; promotion; uprising, revolt; **Erhebungen machen** make inquiries
erheitern [ɛr'haɪtərn] *tr* amuse || *ref* cheer up
erhellen [ɛr'hɛlən] *tr* light up; (fig) shed light on || *ref* grow light(er); light up || *impers*—**es erhellt** it appears
erhitzen [ɛr'hɪtsən] *tr* heat; (fig) inflame || *ref* grow hot; get angry
erhöhen [ɛr'hø·ən] *tr* raise; (fig) heighten || *ref* increase; be enhanced
Erhö′hung *f* (-;-en) rise
erho′len *ref* recover; relax
Erho′lung *f* (-;-en) recovery; relaxation; recreation

erho′lungsbedürftig *adj* in need of rest
Erho′lungsheim *n* convalescent home
erhö′ren *tr* (*Gebet*) hear; (*Bitte*) grant
erinnerlich [ɛr'ɪnərlɪç] *adj*—**das ist mir nicht e.** it slipped my mind; **soviel mir e. ist** as far as I can remember
erinnern [ɛr'ɪnərn] *tr* (**an** *acc*) remind (of) || *ref* (**an** *acc*) remember
Erin′nerung *f* (-;-en) recollection, remembrance; (*Mahnung*) reminder; **zur E. an** (*acc*) in memory of
Erin′nerungsvermögen *n* memory
erkalten [ɛr'kaltən] *intr* (SEIN) cool off; (fig) grow cool
erkälten [ɛr'kɛltən] *ref* catch cold
Erkäl′tung *f* (-;-en) cold
erkennbar [ɛr'kɛnbar] *adj* recognizable
erkennen [ɛr'kɛnən] §97 *tr* make out; recognize; detect; realize; **j–n e. für** (com) credit s.o. with; **sich zu e. geben** disclose one's identity; **zu e. geben, daß** indicate that || *intr*—**auf e–e Geldstrafe e.** impose a fine; **gegen j–n e.** judge against s.o.
erkenntlich [ɛr'kɛntlɪç] *adj* grateful
Erkennt′lichkeit *f* (-;) gratitude
Erkenntnis [ɛr'kɛntnɪs] *f* (-;-se) insight, judgment, realization, knowledge; (philos) cognition || *n* (-ses;-se) decision, finding
Erker ['ɛrkər] *m* (-s;-) (archit) oriel
Er′kerfenster *n* bay window
erklären [ɛr'kleːrən] *tr* explain, account for; (*aussprechen*) state
Erklä′rer -in §6 *mf* commentator
erklär′lich *adj* explicable
Erklä′rung *f* (-;-en) explanation; statement; commentary; (jur) deposition
erklin′gen §142 *intr* (SEIN) sound; (*widerhallen*) resound
erkor (ɛr'kor) *pret* of **erkiesen**
erkoren [ɛr'korən] *adj* chosen
erkranken [ɛr'kraŋkən] *intr* (SEIN) get sick; (*Pflanzen*) become diseased
erkühnen [ɛr'kynən] *ref* dare, venture
erkunden [ɛr'kundən] *tr* & *intr* reconnoiter
erkundigen [ɛr'kundɪgən] *ref* inquire
Erkun′digung *f* (-;-en) inquiry
Erkun′dung *f* (-;) reconnaissance
erlahmen [ɛr'laːmən] *intr* (SEIN) tire; (*Kraft*) give out
erlangen [ɛr'laŋən] *tr* reach; (*sich verschaffen*) get; **wieder e.** recover
Er·laß [ɛr'las] *m* (-lasses;-lässe) remission; exemption; edict, order
erlas′sen §104 *tr* release; (*Schulden*) cancel; (*Strafe*) remit; (*Sünden*) pardon; (*Verordnung*) issue; **e. Sie es mir zu** (*inf*) allow me not to (*inf*), don't ask me to (*inf*)
erläßlich [ɛr'lɛslɪç] *adj* pardonable
erlauben [ɛr'laubən] *tr* allow || *ref*—**sich** [*dat*] **e. zu** (*inf*) take the liberty to (*inf*); **sich** [*dat*] **nicht e.** not be able to afford
Erlaubnis [ɛr'laupnɪs] *f* (-;-se) permission
Erlaub′nisschein *m* permit, license
erlaucht [ɛr'lauxt] *adj* illustrious
erläutern [ɛr'lɔɪtərn] *tr* explain
Erläu′terung *f* (-;-en) explanation

Erle ['ɛrlə] *f* (-;-n) (bot) alder
erle'ben *tr* live to see; experience
Erlebnis [ɛr'lepnɪs] *n* (-ses;-se) experience, adventure; occurrence
erledigen [ɛr'ledɪgən] *tr* settle; (*Post, Einkäufe, Gesuch*) attend to, take care of; **j–n e.** (coll) do s.o. in
erledigt [ɛr'ledɪçt] *adj* (& fig) finished; (*Stellung*) open; (coll) bushed
erle'gen *tr* pay down; (*töten*) kill
erleichtern [ɛr'laɪçtərn] *tr* lighten; make easy; (*Not*) relieve, ease
Erleich'terung *f* (-;) alleviation
erlei'den §106 *tr* suffer
erler'nen *tr* learn
erle'sen *adj* choice ‖ §107 *tr* choose
erleuch'ten *tr* light up; enlighten
erlie'gen §108 *intr* (SEIN) (*dat*) succumb (to), fall victim (to)
erlogen [ɛr'logən] *adj* false
Erlös [ɛr'løs] *m* (-es;) proceeds
erlosch [ɛr'lɔʃ] *pret* of **erlöschen**
erloschen [ɛr'lɔʃən] *pp* of **erlöschen**
erlöschen [ɛr'lœʃən] §110 *intr* (SEIN) go out; (*Vertrag*) expire; (fig) become extinct
erlö'sen *tr* redeem; free; get (*by sale*)
Erlö'ser *m* (-s;-) deliverer; (relig) Redeemer
Erlö'sung *f* (-;) redemption
ermächtigen [ɛr'mɛçtɪgən] *tr* authorize
Ermäch'tigung *f* (-;-en) authorization
ermah'nen *tr* admonish
Ermah'nung *f* (-;-en) admonition
ermangeln [ɛr'maŋəln] *intr* (*genit*) lack; **es an nichts e.** lassen spare no pains; **nicht e. zu** (*inf*) not fail to (*inf*)
Erman'gelung *f*—**in E.** (*genit*) in default of
ermä'ßigen *tr* reduce
ermatten [ɛr'matən] *tr* tire ‖ *intr* (SEIN) tire; grow weak; slacken
Ermat'tung *f* (-;) fatigue
ermes'sen §70 *tr* judge, estimate; realize; **e. aus** infer from ‖ **Ermessen** *n* (-s;) judgment, opinion; **nach freiem E.** at one's discretion
ermitteln [ɛr'mɪtəln] *tr* ascertain ‖ *intr* conduct an investigation
Ermitt'lung *f* (-;-en) ascertainment; **Ermittlungen** investigation
Ermitt'lungsausschuß *m* fact-finding committee
Ermitt'lungsbeamte *m* investigator
Ermitt'lungsverfahren *n* judicial inquiry
ermöglichen [ɛr'møklɪçən] *tr* enable, make possible
ermorden [ɛr'mɔrdən] *tr* murder
ermüden [ɛr'mydən] *tr* tire ‖ *intr* (SEIN) tire, get tired
Ermü'dung *f* (-;) fatigue
ermuntern [ɛr'muntərn] *tr* cheer up; encourage ‖ *ref* cheer up
Ermun'terung *f* (-;) encouragement
ermutigen [ɛr'mutɪgən] *tr* encourage
ernäh'ren *tr* nourish; (fig) support
Ernäh'rer –**in** §6 *mf* supporter
Ernäh'rung *f* (-;) nourishment; support; (physiol) nutrition
ernen'nen §97 *tr* nominate, appoint
erneuern [ɛr'nɔɪ-ərn] *tr* renew; reno-

vate; (*Gemälde*) restore; (*Öl*) change; (*Reifen*) retread; (mach) replace
erneu'ert *adj* repeated ‖ *adv* anew
Erneu'erung *f* (-;-en) renewal; renovation; restoration; replacement
erniedrigen [ɛr'nidrɪgən] *tr* lower; (*demütigen*) humble; (*im Rang*) degrade ‖ *ref* humble oneself; debase oneself
ernst [ɛrnst] *adj* earnest; serious ‖ **Ernst** *m* (-[e]s;) seriousness; **im E.** in earnest
Ernst'fall *m*—**im E.** in case of emergency; (mil) in case of war
ernst'haft *adj* earnest, serious
ernst'lich *adj* earnest; serious
Ernte ['ɛrntə] *f* (-;-n) harvest; crop
ernten ['ɛrntən] *tr* reap, harvest
ernüch'tern *tr* sober; disallusion ‖ *ref* sober up; be disallusioned
Ero'berer –**in** §6 *mf* conqueror
erobern [ɛr'obərn] *tr* conquer
Ero'berung *f* (-;-en) conquest
eröff'nen *tr* open; (*feierlich*) inaugurate; disclose ‖ *ref* open; present itself; **sich j–m e.** unburden oneself to s.o.
Eröff'nung *f* (-;-en) (grand) opening; inauguration; announcement
erörtern [ɛr'œrtərn] *tr* discuss
erotisch [ɛ'rotɪʃ] *adj* erotic
Erpel ['ɛrpəl] *m* (-s;-) drake
erpicht [ɛr'pɪçt] *adj*—**e. auf** (*acc*) keen on, dead set on, hell bent on
erpres'sen *tr* extort; (*Person*) blackmail
Erpres'sung *f* (-;-en) extortion; blackmail
erpro'ben *tr* test, try out
erquicken [ɛr'kvɪkən] *tr* refresh
erquick'lich *adj* refreshing; agreeable
erra'ten §63 *tr* guess
errech'nen *tr* calculate
erregbar [ɛr'rekbar] *adj* excitable; irritable
erregen [ɛr'regən] *tr* excite; cause ‖ *ref* get excited, get worked up
Erre'gung *f* (-;) excitation; agitation; excitement; **E. öffentlichen Ärgernisses** disorderly conduct
erreichbar [ɛr'raɪçbar] *adj* reachable; available
errei'chen *tr* reach, attain; get to; (*Zug, Bus*) catch; **e., daß** bring it about that
erret'ten *tr* save, rescue
Erret'tung *f* (-;-en) rescue; (relig) Salvation
errich'ten *tr* erect; found
errin'gen §142 *tr* get; attain, achieve
errö'ten *intr* (SEIN) redden; blush
Errungenschaft [ɛr'ruŋənʃaft] *f* (-;-en) achievement; acquisition
Ersatz' *m* (-es;) substitute; replacement; compensation; (mil) recruitment
Ersatz– *comb.fm.* substitute, replacement; spare; alternative; recruiting
Ersatz'mann *m* substitute; alternate
Ersatz'stück *n*, **Ersatz'teil** *n* spare part, spare
erschaf'fen §126 *tr* create
Erschaf'fer –**in** §6 *mf* creator
Erschaf'fung *f* (-;-en) creation

erschal'len §127 *intr* (SEIN) begin to sound; ring out; resound

erschau'ern *intr* shudder

erschei'nen §128 *intr* (SEIN) appear; (*Buch*) come out, be published

Erschei'nung *f* (-;-en) appearance; apparition; phenomenon

erschie'ßen §76 *tr* shoot (dead)

Erschie'ßung *f* (-;-en) shooting, execution

Erschie'ßungskommando *n* firing squad

erschlaffen [ɛr'ʃlafən] *tr* relax; enervate || *intr* (SEIN) relax; weaken

erschla'gen §132 *tr* slay; **wie e. dead tired**

erschlie'ßen §76 *tr* open up; develop; **e.** aus infer from; derive from || *ref* —sich j-m e. unburden oneself to s.o.

erschöp'fen *tr* exhaust; (fig) deplete

erschrak [ɛr'ʃrak] *pret* of **erschrecken**

erschrecken (**erschrek'ken**) *tr* startle; shock || *ref* get scared || §134 *intr* (SEIN) be startled

erschreckend (**erschrek'kend**) *adj* terrifying; alarming; dreadful

erschüt'ten *tr* shake; upset; move deeply

Erschüt'terung *f* (-;-en) tremor; vibration; deep feeling; concussion

erschweren [ɛr'ʃverən] *tr* make more difficult; hamper, impede

erschwin'deln *tr*—etw von j-m e. cheat s.o. out of s.th.

erschwin'gen §142 *tr* afford

erschwing'lich *adj* within one's means

erse'hen §138 *tr* (aus) gather (from)

erseh'nen *tr* long for

ersetzbar [ɛr'zɛtsbar] *adj* replaceable

erset'zen *tr* replace; (*Schaden*) compensate for; (*Kräfte*) renew; **j-m etw e.** reimburse s.o. for s.th.; **sie ersetzte ihm die Eltern** she was mother and father to him

ersetz'lich *adj* replaceable

ersicht'lich *adj* evident

ersin'nen §121 *tr* think up

erspa'ren *tr* save

Ersparnis [ɛr'sparnıs] *f* (-;-se) (an *dat*) saving (in)

ersprießlich [ɛr'ʃpriːslɪç] *adj* useful

erst [ɛrst] *adv* first; at first; just; only; not until; **e. recht** really; **e. recht nicht** most certainly not

erstar'ren *intr* (SEIN) grow stiff; (*Finger*) grow numb; (*Blut*) congeal; (*Zement*) set; (fig) run cold; **vor Schreck e.** be paralyzed with fear

erstatten [ɛr'ʃtatən] *tr* refund, repay; (*Bericht*) file; **Meldung e.** report

Erstat'tung *f* (-;-en) refund; reimbursement; compensation

Erst'aufführung *f* primiere

erstau'nen *tr* astonish || *intr* (SEIN) (über *acc*) be astonished (at) || **Erstaunen** *n* (-s;) astonishment; **in E. setzen** astonish

erstaun'lich *adj* astonishing

Erst'ausfertigung *f* original

erste ['ɛrstə] §9 *adj* first; **der erste beste** the first that comes along; **fürs e.** for the time being; **zum ersten, zum zweiten, zum dritten** going, going, gone

erste'chen §64 *tr* stab

erste'hen §146 *tr* buy, get || *intr* (SEIN) rise; (*Städte*) spring up

erstei'gen §148 *tr* climb

erstel'len *tr* provide, supply; erect

erstens ['ɛrstəns] *adv* first; in the first place

erst'geboren *adj* first-born

ersticken [ɛr'ʃtɪkən] *tr* choke, stifle, smother; **im Keim e.** nip in the bud || *intr* (SEIN) choke; **in Arbeit e.** be snowed under

erstklassig ['ɛrstklasıç] *adj* first-class

Erstling ['ɛrstlıŋ] *m* (-s;-e) first-born child; (fig) first fruits

Erstlings- *comb.fm.* first

Erst'lingsausstattung *f* layette

erstmalig ['ɛrstmalıç] *adj* first

erstre'ben *tr* strive for

erstrecken (**erstrek'ken**) *ref* extend

ersu'chen *tr* request, ask

ertappen [ɛr'tapən] *tr* surprise, catch

ertei'len *tr* give; confer; (*Auftrag*) place; (*Audienz*, *Patent*) grant

ertö'nen *intr* (SEIN) sound; resound

ertö'ten *tr* (fig) stifle

Ertrag [ɛr'trak] *m* (-[e]s;-̈e) yield; proceeds; produce

ertra'gen §132 *tr* stand, bear

erträglich [ɛr'treklıç] *adj* bearable

ertränken [ɛr'trɛŋkən] *tr* drown

erträu'men *tr* dream of

ertrin'ken §143 *intr* (SEIN) drown

ertüchtigen [ɛr'tʏçtɪgən] *tr* train

erübrigen [ɛr'ybrɪgən] *tr* save; (*Zeit*) spare || *ref* be superfluous

erwa'chen *intr* (SEIN) wake up

erwach'sen *adj* adult || §155 *intr* (SEIN) grow, grow up; arise || **Erwachsene** §5 *mf* adult, grown-up

erwä'gen §156 *tr* weigh, consider

Erwä'gung *f* (-;-en) consideration

erwäh'len *tr* choose

erwäh'nen *tr* mention

erwäh'nenswert *adj* worth mentioning

Erwäh'nung *f* (-;) mention

erwär'men *tr* warm, warm up

erwar'ten *tr* expect, await; **etw zu e. haben** be in for s.th.

Erwar'tung *f* (-;-en) expectation

erwar'tungsvoll *adj* expectant

erwecken (**erwek'ken**) *tr* wake; (*Hoffnungen*) raise; (*Gefühle*) awaken; **den Anschein e.** give the impression

erweh'ren *ref* (*genit*) ward off; (*genit*) refrain from; (*der Tränen*) hold back

erwei'chen *tr* soften; (fig) move, touch; **sich e. lassen** relent

erwei'sen §118 *tr* prove; show; (*Achtung*) show; (*Dienst*) render; (*Ehre*, *Gunst*) do || *ref*—**sich e. als** prove

erweitern [ɛr'vaitərn] *tr & ref* widen; (*vermehren*) increase; extend, expand

Erwerb [ɛr'verp] *m* (-[e]s;-e) acquisition; (*Verdienst*) earnings; (*Unterhalt*) living

erwer'ben §149 *tr* acquire; gain; (*verdienen*) earn; (*kaufen*) purchase

erwerbs'behindert *adj* disabled

Erwerbs'betrieb *m* business enterprise

erwerbs'fählg *adj* capable of earning a living

erwerbs'los *adj* unemployed

Erwerbs'quelle *f* source of income
Erwerbs'sinn *m* acquisitiveness
erwerbs'tätig *adj* gainfully employed
erwerbs'unfähig *adj* unable to earn a living
Erwerbs'zweig *m* line of business
Erwer'bung *f* (-;-en) acquisition
erwidern [ɛr'vidərn] *tr* reply; reciprocate, return
Erwi'derung *f* (-;-en) reply; return; retaliation
erwir'ken *tr* secure, obtain
erwi'schen *tr* catch; **ihn hat's erwischt!** (coll) he's had it!
erwünscht [ɛr'vynʃt] *adj* desired; welcome; (*wünschenswert*) desirable
erwür'gen *tr* strangle
Erz [ɛrts] *n* (-es;-e) ore; brass; bronze
Erz-, erz- *comb.fm.* ore; bronze; utterly; (fig) arch-
erzählen [ɛr'tsɛlən] *tr* tell, narrate
Erzäh'lung *f* (-;-en) story, narrative
Erz'bischof *m* archbishop
Erz'engel *m* archangel
erzeu'gen *tr* beget; manufacture; produce; generate
Erzeugnis [ɛr'tsɔɪknɪs] *n* (-ses;-se) product; produce
Erzeu'gung *f* (-;-en) production; manufacture
erzie'hen §163 *tr* bring up, rear; (*geistig*) educate
Erzieher [ɛr'tsi·ər] *m* (-s;-) educator; private tutor
Erzieherin [ɛr'tsi·ərɪn] *f* (-;-nen) educator; governess
erzieherisch [ɛr'tsi·ərɪʃ] *adj* educational, pedagogical
Erzie'hung *f* (-;) upbringing; education; (*Lebensart*) breeding
Erzie'hungslehre *f* (educ) education
Erzie'hungswesen *n* educational system
erzie'len *tr* achieve, reach; (*Gewinn*) realize; (sport) score
Erz'lager *n* ore deposit
Erz'probe *f* assay
erzür'nen *tr* anger ‖ *ref* get angry
erzwin'gen §142 *tr* force; wring, obtain by force; (*Gehorsam*) exact
es [ɛs] *adv* (as expletive) there; **es gibt** there is, there are ‖ §11 *pers pron* it; he; she ‖ **Es** *n* (-;-) (mus) E flat; (psychol) id
Esche ['ɛʃə] *f* (-;-n) ash tree
Esel ['ezəl] *m* (-s;-) donkey, ass
Eselei [ezə'laɪ] *f* (-;-en) foolish act, foolish remark
E'selsbrücke *f* (educ) pony
E'selsohr *n* dog's-ear
eskalieren [ɛska'lirən] *tr & intr* escalate
Eskimo ['ɛskɪmo] *m* (-s;-s) Eskimo
Espe ['ɛspə] *f* (-;-n) (bot) aspen
eßbar ['ɛsbar] *adj* edible, eatable
Eßbesteck ['ɛsbəʃtɛk] *n* knife, fork, and spoon
Esse ['ɛsə] *f* (-;-n) chimney; forge
essen ['ɛsən] §70 *tr & intr* eat; **zu Mittag e.** eat lunch ‖ **Essen** *n* (-s;) eating; food, meal
Essenz [ɛ'sɛnts] *f* (-;-en) essence
Eßgeschirr ['ɛsgəʃɪr] *n* (-s;) tableware; table service; (mil) mess kit

Eßgier ['ɛsgir] *f* (-;) gluttony
Essig ['ɛsɪç] *m* (-s;-e) vinegar
Es'siggurke *f* pickle, gherkin
Es'sigsäure *f* acetic acid
Eßlöffel ['ɛslœfəl] *m* (-s;-) tablespoon
Eßnapf ['ɛsnapf] *m* dinner pail
Eßsaal ['ɛszal] *m* dining room
Eßstäbchen ['ɛs/tɛpçən] *n* chopstick
Eßwaren ['ɛsvarən] *pl* food, victuals
Eßzimmer ['ɛstsɪmər] *n* (-s;-) dining room
Estland ['ɛstlant] *n* (-s;) Estonia
Estrade [ɛs'tradə] *f* (-;-n) dais
etablieren [ɛta'blirən] *tr* establish
Etablissement [ɛtablɪs(ə)'mã] *n* (-s;-s) establishment
Etage [ɛ'taʒə] *f* (-;-n) floor, story
Eta'genbett *n* bunk bed
Eta'genwohnung *f* apartment
Etappe [ɛ'tapə] *f* (-;-n) (*Teilstrecke*) leg, stage; (mil) rear eschelon, rear
Etat [ɛ'ta] *m* (-s;-s) budget
Etats'jahr *n* fiscal year
etepetete [ɛtəpe'tetə] *adj* overly particular
Ethik ['etɪk] *f* (-;) ethics
ethisch ['etɪʃ] *adj* ethical
ethnisch ['etnɪʃ] *adj* ethnic
Ethnologie [ɛtnɔlɔ'gi] *f* (-;) ethnology
Etikett [ɛtɪ'kɛt] *n* (-s;-e) tab, label
Etikette [ɛtɪ'kɛtə] *f* (-;) etiquette
etikettieren [ɛtɪke'tirən] *tr* label
etliche [ɛt'lɪçə] *adj & pron* a few
Etui [ɛ'tvi] *n* (-s;-s) case (*for spectacles, cigarettes, etc.*)
etwa ['ɛtva] *adv* about, around; perhaps; by chance; for example
etwaig [ɛt'va·ɪç] *adj* eventual
etwas ['ɛtvas] *adj* some, a little ‖ *adv* somewhat ‖ *pron* something; anything ‖ **Etwas** *n*—**ein gewißes E.** a certain something
euch [ɔɪç] *pers pron* you; to you ‖ *reflex pron* yourselves
euer ['ɔɪ·ər] *adj* your
Eukalyp•tus [ɔɪka'lyptus] *m* (-;- & -ten [tən]) eucalyptus
Eule ['ɔɪlə] *f* (-;-n) owl
Euphorie [ɔɪfɔ'ri] *f* (-;) euphoria
euphorisch [ɔɪ'forɪʃ] *adj* euphoric
eurige ['ɔɪrɪgə] §2,5 *pron* yours
Europa [ɔɪ'ropa] *n* (-s;) Europe
Europäer -in [ɔɪrɔ'pe·ər(ɪn)] §6 *mf* European
europäisch [ɔɪrɔ'pe·ɪʃ] *adj* European
Euter ['ɔɪtər] *n* (-s;-) udder
evakuieren [ɛvaku'irən] *tr* evacuate
evangelisch [ɛvan'gelɪʃ] *adj* evangelical; Protestant
Evangelist [ɛvange'lɪst] *m* (-en;-en) Evangelist
Evange•lium [ɛvan'geljum] *n* (-s;-lien [ljən]) gospel
eventuell [ɛventu'ɛl] *adj* eventual ‖ *adv* possibly
ewig ['eviç] *adj* eternal; perpetual
E'wigkeit *f* (-;-en) eternity
e'wiglich *adv* forever
exakt [ɛ'ksakt] *adj* exact
Exa•men [ɛ'ksamən] *n* (-s;-s & -mina [mɪna]) examination
examinieren [ɛksamɪ'nirən] *tr* examine
exekutiv [ɛkseku'tif] *adj* executive

Exempel [ɛ'ksɛmpəl] *n* (-s;-) example; ein E. statuieren an (*dat*) make an example of
Exemplar [ɛksɛm'plɑr] *n* (-s;-e) sample, specimen; (*e-s Buches*) copy
exerzieren [ɛksɛr'tsirən] *tr & intr* exercise
Exil [ɛ'ksil] *n* (-s;-e) exile
Existenz [ɛksɪ'stɛnts] *f* (-;-en) existence; livelihood; personality
Existenz′minimum *n* living wage
existieren [ɛksɪs'tirən] *intr* exist
exklusiv [ɛkslʊ'zif] *adj* exclusive
Exkommunikation[ɛkskɔmʊnɪka'tsjon] *f* (-;-en) excommunication
exkommunizieren [ɛkskɔmʊnɪ'tsirən] *tr* excommunicate
Exkrement [ɛkskrɛ'mɛnt] *n* (-[e]s;-e) excrement
exmittieren [ɛksmɪ'tirən] *tr* evict
exotisch [ɛ'ksotɪʃ] *adj* exotic
expedieren [ɛkspɛ'dirən] *tr* send, ship
Expedition [ɛkspɛdɪ'tsjon] *f* (-;-en) forwarding; (mil) expedition
Experiment [ɛkspɛrɪ'mɛnt] *n* (-[e]s; -e) experiment
experimentieren [ɛkspɛrɪmɛn'tirən] *intr* experiment

explodieren [ɛksplɔ'dirən] *intr* (SEIN) explode; blow up
Explosion [ɛksplɔ'zjon] *f* (-;-en) explosion
exponieren [ɛkspɔ'nirən] *tr* expose; (*darlegen*) expound, set forth
Export [ɛks'pɔrt] *m* (-[e]s;-e) export
exportieren [ɛkspɔr'tirən] *tr* export
Ex·preß [ɛks'prɛs] *m* (-presses; -presse) express
Expreß′zug *m* express train
extra ['ɛkstrɑ] *adv* extra; (coll) on purpose, for spite
Ex′trablatt *n* (journ) extra
extrahieren [ɛkstra'hirən] *tr* extract
Extrakt [ɛks'trakt] *m* (-[e]s;-e) extract; (*aus Büchern*) excerpt
extravagant [ɛkstrava'gant] *adj* luxurious; wild, fantastic
Extravaganz [ɛkstrava'gants] *f* (-;-en) luxury
extrem [ɛks'trem] *adj* extreme ‖ **Extrem** *n* (-s;-e) extreme
Exzellenz [ɛkstsɛ'lɛnts] *f* (-;-en) Excellency
exzentrisch [ɛks'tsɛntrɪʃ] *adj* eccentric
Ex·zeß [ɛks'tsɛs] *m* (-zesses;-zesse) excess

F

F, f [ɛf] *invar n* F, f; (mus) F
Fabel ['fɑbəl] *f* (-;-n) fable; story; (*e-s Dramas*) plot
fa′belhaft *adj* fabulous
fabeln ['fɑbəln] *intr* tell stories
Fabrik [fa'brik] *f* (-;-en) factory, mill
Fabrik′anlage *f* manufacturing plant
Fabrikant [fabrɪ'kant(ɪn)] *§7 mf* manufacturer, maker
Fabrikat [fabrɪ'kɑt] *n* (-[e]s;-e) product; brand, make
Fabrikation [fabrɪka'tsjon] *f* (-;) manufacture, manufacturing
Fabrikations′fehler *m* flaw, defect
Fabrikations′nummer *f* serial number
Fabrik′marke *f* trademark
fabrik′mäßig *adj* mass
Fabrik′nummer *f* serial number
Fabrik′waren *pl* manufactured goods
Fabrik′zeichen *n* trademark
fabrizieren [fabrɪ'tsirən] *tr* manufacture
fabulieren [fabʊ'lirən] *tr* make up ‖ *intr* tell yarns
fabulös [fabʊ'løs] *adj* fabulous
Facette [fa'sɛtə] *f* (-;-n) facet
Fach [fax] *n* (-[e]s;⁼er) compartment; (*im Schreibtisch*) pigeonhole; (*Bücherbrett*) shelf; (*fig*) field, department; line, business; (educ) subject; vom F. sein be an expert
Fach′arbeiter -in §6 *mf* specialist
Fach′arzt *m*, **Fach′ärztin** *f* (med) specialist
Fach′ausbildung *f* professional training
Fach′ausdruck *m* technical term

fächeln ['fɛçəln] *tr* fan
Fächer ['fɛçər] *m* (-s;-) fan
Fä′cherpalme *f* palmetto
Fach′gebiet *n* field, line; department
Fach′gelehrte §5 *mf* expert
fach′gemäß *adj* expert, professional
Fach′genosse *m* colleague
Fach′kenntnisse *pl* specialized knowledge
Fach′kreis *m* experts, specialists
fach′kundig *adj* expert, experienced
fach′lich *adj* professional; technical, specialized
Fach′mann *m* (-es;⁼er & -leute) expert, specialist
fachmännisch ['faxmɛnɪʃ] *adj* expert
Fach′schule *f* vocational school
Fachsimpelei [faxzɪmpə'laɪ] *f* (-;-en) shoptalk
fachsimpeln ['faxzɪmpəln] *intr* talk shop
Fach′werk *n* framework; specialized book
Fach′zeitschrift *f* technical journal
Fackel ['fakəl] *f* (-;-n) torch
fackeln ['fakəln] *intr* flare; (fig) hesitate. dilly-dally
Fackelschein (**Fak′kelschein**) *m* torchlight
Fackelzug (**Fak′kelzug**) *m* torchlight procession
fade ['fɑdə] *adj* stale; (fig) dull
Faden ['fɑdən] *m* (-s;⁼) (& fig) thread; filament; (naut) fathom; keinen guten F. lassen an (*dat*) tear apart
Fa′denkreuz *n* crosshairs
Fa′dennudeln *pl* vermicelli

fadenscheinig ['fadənʃaınıç] *adj* threadbare
Fagott [fa'gɔt] *n* (-[e]s;-e) bassoon
fähig ['fe·ıç] *adj* capable, able
Fä'higkeit *f* (-;-en) ability; talent
fahl [fal] *adj* pale; faded, washed-out
fahnden ['fandən] *intr* (**nach**) search (for), hunt (for)
Fahn'dung *f* (-;-en) search, hunt
Fahne ['fanə] *f* (-;-n) flag; pennant; (mil) colors; (typ) galley proof
Fah'nenabzug *m* galley proof
Fah'neneid *m* (mil) swearing in
Fah'nenflucht *f* desertion
fah'nenflüchtig *adj*—**f. werden** desert || **Fahnenflüchtige** §5 *mf* deserter
Fah'nenmast *m* flagpole
Fah'nenträger **–in** §6 *mf* standard bearer
Fähnrich ['fenrıç] *m* (-s;-e) officer cadet; **F. zur See** midshipman
Fahrbahn ['farban] *f* (traffic) lane
fahrbar ['farbar] *adj* passable; navigable; mobile
fahrbereit ['farbəraıt] *adj* in running order
Fahr'bereitschaft *f* (-;-en) motor pool
Fähre ['ferə] *f* (-;-n) ferry
fahren ['farən] §71 *tr* haul; (*lenken*) drive; (*Boot*) sail || *intr* (SEIN) go; travel, drive; ride; **es fuhr mir durch den Sinn** it flashed across my mind; **f. lassen** run (*a boat, train*); let go; (fig) abandon, renounce; **gut f. bei** do well in; **mit der Hand f. über** (*acc*) run one's hand over; **rechts f.** (public sign) keep right; **was ist in ihn gefahren?** what's gotten into him?
fah'renlassen §104 *tr* let go of
Fah'rer **–in** §6 *mf* driver
Fah'rerflucht *f* hit-and-run case
Fahrgast ['fargast] *m* passenger
Fahrgeld ['fargelt] *n* fare
Fahrgelegenheit ['fargəleɡənhaıt] *f* transportation (facilities)
Fahrgestell ['farɡəʃtel] *n* (-[e]s;-e) (aer) landing gear; (aut) chassis
fahrig ['farıç] *adj* fidgety
Fahrkarte ['farkartə] *f* ticket
Fahr'kartenausgabe *f*, **Fahr'kartenschalter** *m* ticket window
fahrlässig ['farlesıç] *adj* negligent; **fahrlässige Tötung** involuntary manslaughter
Fahr'lässigkeit *f* (-;) negligence
Fahrlehrer **–in** ['farlerər(ın)] §6 *mf* driving instructor
Fahrnis ['farnıs] *f* (-;-se) movables
Fährnis ['fernıs] *f* (-;-se) (poet) danger
Fahrplan ['farplan] *m* schedule
fahr'planmäßig *adj* scheduled || *adv* on schedule, on time
Fahrpreis ['farpraıs] *m* fare
Fahrprüfung ['farpryfuŋ] *f* driver's test
Fahrrad ['farrad] *n* bicycle
Fahrrinne ['farrınə] *f* channel
Fahrschein ['farʃaın] *m* ticket
Fahrstuhl ['farʃtul] *m* elevator; (med) wheel chair
Fahr'stuhlführer **–in** §6 *mf* elevator operator

Fahr'stuhlschacht *m* elevator shaft
Fahrstunde ['farʃtundə] *f* driving lesson
Fahrt [fart] *f* (-;-en) ride, drive; trip; **auf F. gehen** go hiking; **F. verlieren** lose speed; **freie F. haben** have the green light; **in F. kommen** pick up speed; (fig) swing into action; **in F. sein** (coll) be keyed up; (coll) be on the warpath; (naut) be under way
Fährte ['fertə] *f* (-;-n) track, scent
Fahrt'unterbrechung *f* (-;-en) stopover
Fahrwasser ['farvasər] *n* navigable water; (& fig) wake
Fahrwerk ['farverk] *n* see **Fahrgestell**
Fahrzeug ['fartsɔık] *n* vehicle; vessel, craft
Fahr'zeugpark *m* (aut) fleet; (rr) rolling stock
fair [fer] *adj* fair
Fairneß ['fernes] *f* (-;) fairness
Fäkalien [fe'kaljən] *pl* feces
faktisch ['faktıʃ] *adj* actual, factual
Fak·tor ['faktər] *m* (-s;-toren) ['torən]) factor; foreman; (com) agent
Faktu·ra [fak'tura] *f* (-;-ren [rən]) invoice
Fakultät [fakʊl'tet] *f* (-;-en) (educ) department, school
falb [falp] *adj* claybank (*horse*)
Falke ['falkə] *m* (-;-n) falcon; (pol) hawk
Fal'kenjagd *f* falconry
Falkner ['falknər] *m* (-s;-) falconer
Fall [fal] *m* (-[e]s;⸗e) fall, drop; downfall; case; **auf alle Fälle** in any case; **auf keinen F.** in no case; **auf jeden F.** in any case; **gesetzt den F.** supposing; **im besten F.** at best; **im schlimmsten F.** if worst comes to worst; **von F. zu F.** according to circumstances; **zu F. bringen**; (fig) ruin; (parl) defeat; **zu F. kommen** (fig) collapse
Fall'brücke *f* drawbridge
Falle ['falə] *f* (-;-n) (& fig) trap; (fig) pitfall; (*Bett*) (coll) sack
fallen ['falən] §72 *intr* (SEIN) fall, drop; (*Schuß*) be heard; (mil) fall in battle; **j-m ins Wort f.** interrupt s.o. || **Fallen** *n* (-s;) fall, drop; (fig) downfall
fällen ['felən] *tr* (*Bäume*) fell; (*Urteil*) pass; (chem) precipitate
Fallensteller ['falənʃtelər] *m* (-s;-) trapper
Fall'grube *f* trap, pit; (fig) pitfall
fällig ['felıç] *adj* due; payable
Fäl'ligkeit *f* (-;-en) due date
Fall'obst *n* windfall
Fall'rohr *n* soil pipe; (*e–r Dachrinne*) down spout
falls [fals] *conj* in case, if
Fall'schirm *m* parachute
Fall'schirmabsprung *m* parachute jump
Fall'schirmjäger *m* paratrooper
Fall'schirmspringer **–in** §6 *mf* parachutist, sky diver
Fall'strick *m* snare
Fall'sucht *f* (pathol) epilepsy
fall'süchtig *adj* (pathol) epileptic
Fall'tür *f* trapdoor

falsch [falʃ] *adj* false; (*verkehrt*) wrong; (*unecht*) counterfeit; **falsches Spiel** double-dealing || *adv* wrongly; **f. gehen** (horol) be off; **f. schreiben** misspell; **f. schwören** perjure oneself; **f. singen** sing off key; **f. spielen** cheat; **f. verbunden** wrong number || **Falsch** *m*—**ohne F.** without guile
fälschen [ˈfɛlʃən] *tr* falsify; (*Geld*) counterfeit; (*Urkunde*) forge
Fäl'scher –in §6 *mf* forger; counterfeiter
Falsch'geld *n* counterfeit money
Falsch'heit *f* (–;–en) falsity; deceitfulness
fälschlich [ˈfɛlʃlɪç] *adv* falsely
Falsch'münzer *m* counterfeiter
Falsch'spieler –in §6 *mf* card sharp
Fäl'schung *f* (–;–en) falsification; forgery; fake
Faltboot [ˈfaltbot] *n* collapsible boat
Falte [ˈfaltə] *f* (–;–n) fold; (*Plissee*) pleat, crease; (*Runzel*) wrinkle
fälteln [ˈfɛltəln] *tr* pleat
falten [ˈfaltən] *tr* fold; wrinkle
Fal'tenrock *m* pleated skirt
Falter [ˈfaltər] *m* (–s;–) butterfly; (*Nacht–*) moth
faltig [ˈfaltɪç] *adj* creased; wrinkled
Falz [falts] *m* (–es;–e) fold; (*Kerbe*) notch; (carp) rabbet
familiär [famɪˈljer] *adj* intimate; familiar
Familie [faˈmiljə] *f* (–;–n) family
Fami'lienangehörige §5 *mf* member of the family
Fami'lienanschluß *m*—**F. haben** live as one of the family
Fami'lienname *m* last name
Fami'lienstand *m* marital status
Fami'lienstück *n* family heirloom
Fami'lienzuwachs *m* addition to the family
famos [faˈmos] *adj* excellent, swell
Fan [fɛn] *m* (–s;–s) (sport) fan
Fanatiker –in [faˈnatɪkər(ɪn)] §6 *mf* fanatic; (sport) fan
fanatisch [faˈnatɪʃ] *adj* fanatic
fand [fant] *pret* of **finden**
Fanfare [fanˈfarə] *f* (–;–n) (mus) fanfare
Fang [faŋ] *m* (–[e]s;–e) capture; (*Fisch–*) haul, catch; (*Falle*) trap; (*Kralle*) claw
Fang'arm *m* tentacle
Fang'eisen *n* steel trap
fangen [ˈfaŋən] §73 *tr* catch; trap; (*Ohrfeige*) get || *ref* get caught || **Fangen** *n*—**F. spielen** play catch
Fang'frage *f* loaded question
Fang'messer *n* hunting knife
Fang'zahn *m* fang; tusk
Farb– [farp] *comb.fm.* color
Farb'abzug *m* (phot) color print
Farb'aufnahme *f* color photograph
Farb'band *n* (–[e]s;–er) typewriter ribbon
Farbe [ˈfarbə] *f* (–;–n) color; dye; (*zum Malen*) paint; (*Gesichts–*) complexion; (cards) suit; **F. bekennen** folow suit; (fig) lay one's cards on the table
färben [ˈfɛrbən] *tr* color, dye, tint ||

ref take on color; change color; **sich rot f.** turn red; blush
far'benprächtig *adj* colorful
Fär'ber –in §6 *mf* dyer
Farb'fernsehen *n* color television
Farb'film *m* color film
farbig [ˈfarbɪç] *adj* colored; colorful
Farb'kissen *n* ink pad
Farb'körper *m* pigment
farb'los *adj* colorless
Farb'spritzpistole *f* paint sprayer
Farb'stift *m* colored pencil; crayon
Farb'stoff *m* dye
Farb'ton *m* tone, hue, shade
Fär'bung *f* (–;–en) coloring; hue
Farm [farm] *f* (–;–en) farm
Farmer –in [ˈfarmər(ɪn)] §6 *mf* farmer
Farn [farn] *m* (–[e]s;–e) fern
Farn'kraut *n* fern
Fasan [faˈzan] *m* (–s;–e & –en) pheasant
Fasching [ˈfaʃɪŋ] *m* (–s;) carnival
Faschismus [faˈʃɪsmʊs] *m* (–;) fascism
Faschist –in [faˈʃɪst(ɪn)] §7 *mf* fascist
Faselei [fazəˈlaɪ] *f* (–;–en) drivel
Faselhans [ˈfazəlhans] *m* (–ˈ;–e & –ˣe) blabberer; scatterbrain
faseln [ˈfazəln] *intr* talk nonsense
Faser [ˈfazər] *f* (–;–n) fiber; (*im Holz*) grain; (*Fädchen*) thread, string
Fa'serholzplatte *f* fiberboard
fasern [ˈfazərn] *tr* unravel || *ref* fray || *intr* unravel
Fa'serschreiber *m* felt pen
Faß [fas] *n* (**Fasses;Fässer**) barrel, keg; (*Bütte*) vat, tub
Fassade [faˈsadə] *f* (–;–n) façade
faßbar [ˈfasbar] *adj* comprehensible
Faß'bier *n* draft beer
fassen [ˈfasən] *tr* (*packen*) seize; (*erwischen*) apprehend; (*begreifen*) grasp; (*Edelstein*) mount; (*enthalten können*) hold, seat; (*Essen*) (mil) draw; **e–n Gedanken f.** form an idea; **in Worte f.** put into words; **j–n bei der Ehre f.** appeal to s.o.'s honor; **Tritt fassen** fall in step || *ref* get hold of oneself; **in sich f.** include; **sich f. an** (*acc*) put one's hand to, touch; **sich in Geduld f.** exercise patience; **sich kurz f.** be brief || *intr* take hold; (*nach*) grab (for); **es ist nicht zu f.** it is incomprehensible
Faß'hahn *m* tap, faucet
faß'lich *adj* conceivable
Fasson [faˈson] *f* (–;–en) style, cut
Fas'sung *f* (–;–en) composure; (*schriftlich*) draft; (*für Edelsteine*) setting, mounting; (*Brillenrand*) frame; (*Wortlaut*) wording; (*Lesart*) version; (elec) socket; **aus der F. bringen** upset; **außer F. sein** be beside oneself
Fas'sungskraft *f* comprehension
fas'sungslos *adj* disconcerted, shaken
Fas'sungsvermögen *n* capacity; (*geistliches*) (powers of) comprehension
fast [fast] *adv* almost, nearly
fasten [ˈfastən] *intr* fast || **Fasten** *n* (–s;) fasting
Fa'stenzeit *f* Lent, Lenten season
Fast'nacht *f* carnival
Fast'tag *m* day of fasting, fast day

faszinieren [fastsɪ'nirən] *tr* fascinate
fatal [fa'tɑl] *adj* disastrous; *(unangenehm)* unpleasant
fauchen ['fauxən] *intr* hiss; *(Person)* snarl; *(Katze)* spit
faul [faul] *adj* rotten; lazy; bad, nasty; *(verdächtig)* fishy; *(Ausrede, Witz)* lame, poor; (sport) foul ‖ **Faul** *n* (-s;-s) (sport) foul
Fäule ['fɔɪlə] *f* (-;) rot, decay
faulen ['faulən] *intr* rot, decay
faulenzen ['faulentsən] *intr* loaf
Faulenzer ['faulentsər] *m* (-s;-) loafer; *(Liegestuhl)* chaise longue; *(Linienblatt)* ruled sheet of paper
Faul'heit *f* (-;) laziness
faulig ['fauliç] *adj* rotten, putrid
Fäulnis ['fɔɪlnɪs] *f* (-;) rot; **in F. übergehen** begin to rot
Faul'pelz *m* (coll) loafer
Faust [faust] *f* (-;⁼e) fist; **auf eigene F.** on one's own
faust'dick' *adj* (coll) whopping
Faust'handschuh *m* mitten
Faust'kampf *m* boxing match
Fäustling ['fɔɪstlɪŋ] *m* (-[e]s;-e) mitten
Faust'schlag *m* punch, blow
Favorit –in [favə'rit(ɪn)] §7 *mf* favorite
Faxen ['faksən] *pl* antics; faces; **F. machen** fool around; make a fuss; **F. schneiden** make faces
Fazit ['fatsɪt] *n* (-s;-e & -s) result; **das F. ziehen** sum it up
Feber ['febər] *m* (-[s];-) (Aust) February
Februar ['febru·ɑr] *m* (-[s];-e) February
fechten ['feçtən] §74 *intr* fence; fight; *(betteln)* beg
Feder ['fedər] *f* (-;-n) feather; pen; quill; (mach) spring; **F. und Nut** (carp) tongue and groove
Fe'derball *m* shuttlecock
Fe'derballspiel *n* badminton
Fe'derbett *n* feather bed
Fe'derbusch *m* plume
Federfuchser ['fedərfuksər] *m* (-s;-) scribbler; hack writer
fe'derführend *adj* in charge
Fe'dergewicht *n* featherweight division
Federgewichtler ['fedərgəviçtlər] *m* (-s;-) featherweight (boxer)
Fe'derhubtor *n* overhead door
Fe'derkernmatratze *f* innerspring mattress
Fe'derkiel *m* quill
Fe'derkraft *f* springiness; tension
Fe'derkrieg *m* paper war, war of words
fe'derleicht' *adj* light as a feather
Fe'derlesen *n*—**ohne viel Federlesen(s)** without much ado
Fe'dermesser *n* penknife
federn ['fedərn] *tr* fit with springs ‖ *intr* be springy; *(Vogel)* moult; (gym) bounce
Fe'derring *m* lock washer
Fe'derstrich *m* stroke of the pen
Fe'derung *f* (-;) (aut) suspension
Fe'derzug *m* stroke of the pen
Fee [fe] *f* (-;Feen ['fe·ən]) fairy

Feg(e)feuer ['feg(ə)fɔɪ·ər] *n* (-s;) purgatory
fegen ['fegən] *tr* sweep; *(Laub)* tear off ‖ *intr* (SEIN) tear along
Fehde ['fedə] *f* (-;-n) feud
Feh'dehandschuh *m* gauntlet
fehl [fel] *adj*—**f. am Ort** out of place ‖ **Fehl** *m* (-[e]s;-e) blemish; fault
fehl- *comb.fm.* wide of the mark; mis-, incorrectly, wrongly ‖ **Fehl-** *comb. fm.* missing; vain, unsuccessful; incorrect, wrong; faulty; negative
Fehl'anzeige *f* negative report
Fehl'ball *m* (tennis) fault
fehlbar ['felbar] *adj* fallible
Fehl'betrag *m* shortage, deficit
Fehl'bitte *f* vain request; **e–e F. tun** meet with a refusal
fehlen ['felən] *tr* miss ‖ *intr* be absent; be missing; be lacking; fail, be unsuccessful; sin, err; *(dat)* miss, e.g., **er fehlt mir sehr** I miss him very much; *(dat)* lack, e.g., **ihm fehlt die Zeit** he lacks the time; **was fehlt Ihnen?** what's wrong with you? ‖ *impers*—**es fehlte nicht viel, und ich wäre gefallen** I came close to falling
Fehler ['felər] *m* (-s;-) mistake, error; flaw, imperfection; blunder
feh'lerfrei *adj* faultless, flawless
feh'lerhaft *adj* faulty
feh'lerlos *adj* faultless, flawless
Fehl'geburt *f* miscarriage
fehl'gehen §82 *intr* (SEIN) go wrong; *(Schuß)* miss
Fehl'gewicht *n* short weight
fehl'greifen §88 *intr* miss one's hold; (fig) make a mistake
Fehl'griff *m* mistake, blunder
Fehl'leistung *f* (Freudian) slip
fehl'leiten *tr* (& fig) misdirect
Fehl'schlag *m* miss; failure, disappointment; (baseball) foul
Fehl'schluß *m* false inference; fallacy
Fehl'spruch *m* miscarriage of justice
Fehl'start *m* false start
Fehl'tritt *m* false step; (fig) slip
Fehl'wurf *m* *(beim Würfeln)* crap
fehl'zünden *intr* backfire
feien ['faɪ·ən] *tr*—**gefeit sein gegen** be immune to; **j–n f. gegen** make s.o. immune to
Feier ['faɪ·ər] *f* (-;-n) celebration; ceremony
Fei'erabend *m* closing time
fei'erlich *adj* solemn
Fei'erlichkeit *f* (-;-en) solemnity; **Feierlichkeiten** festivities; ceremonies
feiern ['faɪ·ərn] *tr* celebrate, observe; honor ‖ *intr* rest from work
Fei'erstunde *f* commemorative ceremony
Fei'ertag *m* holiday; holy day
feig [faɪk] *adj* cowardly
feige ['faɪgə] *adj* cowardly ‖ **Feige** *f* (-;-n) fig
Feig'heit *f* (-;) cowardice
feig'herzig *adj* faint-hearted
Feigling ['faɪklɪŋ] *m* (-s;-e) coward
feil [faɪl] *adj* for sale
feil'bieten §58 *tr* offer for sale
Feile ['faɪlə] *f* (-;-n) file

feilen ['faɪlən] *tr* file
feilschen ['faɪl/ən] *intr* (**um**) haggle (over), dicker (about)
Feilspäne ['faɪl/penə] *pl* filings
fein [faɪn] *adj* fine; delicate; fancy
feind [faɪnt] *adj* hostile || **Feind** *m* (-[e]s;-e) enemy, foe
Feind- *comb.fm.* enemy, hostile; against the enemy
Feind'fahrt *f* (nav) operation against the enemy
Feind'flug *m* (aer) combat mission
Feindin ['faɪndɪn] *f* (-;-nen) enemy
feind'lich *adj* hostile
Feind'schaft *f* (-;-en) enmity
feind'selig *adj* hostile
Feind'seligkeit *f* (-;-en) hostility, animosity; hostile action
fein'fühlend, fein'fühlig *adj* sensitive
Fein'gefühl *n* sensitivity
Fein'heit *f* (-;-en) fineness, fine quality; delicacy; subtlety
Fein'mechanik *f* precision engineering
Feinschmecker ['faɪn/mɛkər] *m* (-s;-) gourmet, epicure
fein'sinnig *adj* sensitive; subtle
feist [faɪst] *adj* fat, plump
Feld [fɛlt] *n* (-[e]s;-er) field; panel, compartment; (checkers, chess) square; **auf dem Felde** in the field(s); **auf freiem Felde** in the open; **aufs F. gehen** go to (work in) the fields; **das F. behaupten** stand one's ground; **ins F. ziehen** take the field
Feld'bau *m* agriculture
Feld'becher *m* collapsible drinking cup
Feld'bett *n* army cot; camping cot
Feld'blume *f* wild flower
Feld'bluse *f* army jacket
feld'dienstfähig *adj* fit for active duty
Feld'flasche *f* canteen
Feld'geistliche *m* (-n;-n) army chaplain
Feld'gendarm *m* military police
Feld'gendarmerie *f* military police
Feld'geschrei *n* battle cry
Feld'geschütz *n* field gun, field piece
Feld'herr *m* general; commander in chief
Feld'lager *n* bivouac, camp
Feld'lazarett *n* evacuation hospital
Feld'lerche *f* skylark
Feld'marschall *m* field marshal
feld'marschmäßig *adj* with full field pack
Feld'messer *m* surveyor
Feld'meßkunst *f* (-;) surveying
Feld'mütze *f* (mil) overseas cap
Feld'postamt *n* army post office
Feld'schlacht *f* battle
Feld'stecher *m* field glasses
Feldwebel ['fɛltvebəl] *m* (-s;-) sergeant
Feld'zeichen *n* ensign, standard
Feld'zug *m* campaign
Felge ['fɛlgə] *f* (-;-n) rim
Fell [fɛl] *n* (-[e]s;-e) pelt, skin; fur; **ein dickes F. haben** be thick-skinned
Fels [fɛls] *m* (-es & -en;-en) rock; cliff; **zackige Felsen** crags
Fels'block *m* boulder
Felsen ['fɛlzən] *m* (-s;-) rock; cliff
fel'senfest *adj* firm as a rock

Fel'sengebirge *n* Rocky Mountains
Fel'senklippe *f* cliff
Fel'senriff *n* reef
felsig ['fɛlzɪç] *adj* rocky
Fenster ['fɛnstər] *n* (-s;-) window
Fen'sterbrett *n* window sill
Fen'sterflügel *m* casement
Fen'sterladen *m* window shutter
Fen'sterleder *n* chamois
Fen'sterplatz *m* (rr) window seat
Fen'sterrahmen *m* window frame; sash
Fen'sterrosette *f* rose window
Fen'sterscheibe *f* windowpane
Ferien ['ferjən] *pl* vacation; (parl) recess
Fe'rienreisende §5 *mf* vacationer
Fe'rienstimmung *f* holiday spirit
Ferkel ['fɛrkəl] *n* (-s;-) piglet
Ferkelei [fɛrkə'laɪ] *f* (-;-en) obscenity
fern [fɛrn] *adj* far, distant; (*entlegen*) remote; (*weit fort*) far away
Fern'amt *n* long-distance exchange
Fern'anruf *m* long-distance call
Fern'aufklärung *f* long-range reconnaissance
Fern'bedienung *f* remote control
fern'bleiben §62 *intr* (SEIN) (*dat*) stay away (from) || **Fernbleiben** *n* (-s;) absence; absenteeism
Fern'blick *m* distant view, vista
Ferne ['fɛrnə] *f* (-;-n) distance
ferner ['fɛrnər] *adj* remote, distant || *adv* further; moreover
Fern'fahrer *m* long-distance trucker
Fern'fahrt *f* long-distance trip
Fern'gang *m* (aut) overdrive
Fern'geschoß *n* long-range missile
Fern'geschütz *n* long-range gun
Fern'gespräch *n* long-distance call; toll call
Fern'glas *n* binoculars
fern'halten §90 *tr* & *ref* keep away
Fern'heizung *f* heating from a central heating plant
Fern'kursus *m* correspondence course
Fern'laster *m* long-distance truck
fern'lenken *tr* guide by remote control
Fern'lenkrakete *f* guided missile
Fern'lenkung *f* (-;-en) remote control
Fern'lenkwaffe *f* guided missile
Fern'licht *n* (aut) high beam
fern'liegen §108 *impers*—**es liegt mir fern zu** (*inf*) I'm far from (*ger*)
Fernmelde- [fɛrnmɛldə] *comb.fm.* communications, signal
Fern'meldetruppen *pl* signal corps
Fern'meldewesen *n* telecommunications system
fern'mündlich *adj* & *adv* by telephone
Fern'objektiv *n* telephoto lens
Fernost- *comb.fm.* Far Eastern
fern'östlich *adj* Far Eastern
Fern'rohr *n* telescope
Fern'rohraufsatz *m* telescopic gun sight
Fern'ruf *m* telephone call; telephone number
Fern'schnellzug *m* long-distance express
Fern'schreiber *m* teletype, telex
Fernseh- [fɛrnze] *comb.fm.* television
Fern'sehansager -in §6 *mf* television announcer
Fern'sehapparat *m* television set

Fern'sehbildröhre *f* picture tube
fern'sehen §138 *intr* watch television
|| **Fernsehen** *n* (-s;) television
Fern'seher *m* (-s;-) television set; television viewer
Fern'sehgerät *n* television set
Fern'sehkanal *m* television channel
Fern'sehschau *f* television show
Fern'sehsendung *f* telecast
Fern'sehteilnehmer -in §6 *mf* televiewer
Fern'sehübertragung *f* telecast
Fern'sicht *f* view, vista; panorama
fern'sichtig *adj* far-sighted
Fernsprech– [fɛrn∫prɛç] *comb.fm.* telephone
Fern'sprechauftragsdienst *m* answering service
Fern'sprechautomat *m* pay phone
Fern'sprecher *m* telephone
Fern'sprechzelle *f* telephone booth
fern'stehen §146 *intr* (*dat*) have no personal contact (with); (*dat*) not be close (to)
Fern'stehende §5 *mf* outsider; disinterested observer
fern'steuern *tr* guide by remote control
Fern'studium *n* correspondence course
Ferse ['fɛrzə] *f* (-;-n) heel
Fer'sengeld *n*—F. geben take to one's heels
fertig ['fɛrtɪç] *adj* finished; ready; (*kaputt*) ruined, done for
fertig–, Fertig– *comb.fm.* final; finished; finishing; prefabricated
fer'tigbringen §65 *tr* finish, get done; bring about; **es glatt f. zu** (*inf*) be capable of (*ger*); **es nicht f., ihm das zu sagen** not have the heart to tell him that
fertigen ['fɛrtɪgən] *tr* manufacture
Fer'tigkeit *f* (-;-n) skill
Fer'tigrasen *m* sod
fer'tigstellen *tr* complete; get ready
Fer'tigung *f* (-;-en) manufacture, production; copy, draft
Fes [fɛs] *n* (mus) F flat
fesch [fɛʃ] *adj* smart, chic
Fessel ['fɛsəl] *f* (-;-n) fetter, bond; (anat) ankle; (vet) fetlock
Fes'selballon *m* captive balloon
fesseln ['fɛsəln] *tr* chain, tie; (*bezaubern*) captivate, arrest; (mil) contain; **ans Bett gefesselt** confined to bed, bedridden
fes'selnd *adj* fascinating, gripping; (*Personalität*) magnetic
fest [fɛst] *adj* firm; solid; tight; stationary; steady; (*Preis, Kost, Einkommen, Gehalt*) fixed; (*Schlaf*) sound; (mil) fortified; **feste Straße** improved road || **Fest** *n* (-es;-e) feast; festival
fest'backen *intr* (SEIN) cake (on)
fest'besoldet *adj* with a fixed salary
fest'binden §59 *tr* (an *dat*) tie (to)
Fest'essen *n* banquet
fest'fahren §71 *tr* run aground || *ref* come to a standstill
fest'halten §90 *tr* hold on to || *ref* (an *dat*) cling (to), hold on (to)
festigen ['fɛstɪgən] *tr* strengthen; consolidate || *ref* grow stronger

Fe'stigkeit *f* (-;-en) firmness; steadiness; strength
Fe'stigung *f* (-;) strengthening; consolidation; stabilization
Fest'land *n* continent
fest'legen *tr* fix, determine, set; (*Anordnung*) lay down; (fin, naut) tie up; **j–n f. auf** (*acc*) pin s.o. down on || *ref* (auf *acc*) commit oneself (to)
fest'lich *adj* festive
Fest'lichkeit *f* (-;-en) festivity
fest'liegen §108 *intr* be stranded
fest'machen *tr* fix; (fig) settle || *intr* (naut) moor
Fest'mahl *n* feast
Fest'nahme *f* (-;-n) arrest
fest'nehmen §116 *tr* arrest, apprehend
Fest'rede *f* ceremonial speech
Fest'saal *m* grand hall, banquet hall
fest'schnallen *tr* buckle up || *ref* fasten one's seat belt
Fest'schrift *f* homage volume
fest'setzen *tr* fix, set || *ref* settle down (*in a town, etc.*)
fest'sitzen *intr* fit tight; be stuck
Fest'spiel *n* play for a festive occasion; **Festspiele** (mus, theat) festival
fest'stehen §146 *intr* stand firm; (*Tatsache*) be certain || *impers*—**es steht fest** it is a fact
fest'stehend *adj* stationary; (*Achse*) fixed; (*Tatsache*) established
feststellbar ['fɛst∫tɛlbɑr] ascertainable
Fest'stellbremse *f* hand brake
fest'stellen *tr* ascertain; (*unbeweglich machen*) lock, secure; (*Tatbestand*) find out, establish; (*angeben*) state; (*Schaden*) assess; (*Kurs*) (fin) set, fix
Fest'stellschraube *f* set screw
Fest'tag *m* feastday; holiday
Fe'stung *f* (-;-en) fortress
Fe'stungsgraben *m* moat
Fest'wagen *m* float
Fest'wert *m* standard value; (math, phys) constant
Fest'wiese *f* fairground
fest'ziehen §163 *tr* pull tight
Fest'zug *m* procession
Fetisch ['fetɪ∫] *m* (-[e]s;-e) fetish
fett [fet] *adj* fat; (*Boden, Milch, Gemisch*) rich; (*Zeiten, Leben*) of plenty || **Fett** *n* (-[e]s;-e) fat; (*Schmalz*) lard; (*Pflanzen–*) shortening; (*Schmier–*) grease
Fett'auge *n* speck of fat
Fett'druck *m* boldface type
fetten ['fetən] *tr* grease, lubricate
Fett'fleck *m* grease spot
fettig ['fetɪç] *adj* fatty, greasy, oily
Fett'kloß *m* (coll) fatso
Fett'kohle *f* bituminous coal
fettleibig ['fetlaɪbɪç] *adj* stout
Fettnäpfchen ['fetnɛpfçən] *n*—**bei j–m ins F. treten** hurt s.o.'s feelings; **ins F. treten** put one's foot in it
Fett'presse *f* (aut) grease gun
Fett'spritze *f* (aut) grease gun
Fett'sucht *f* obesity
Fett'wanst *m* (sl) fatso
Fetzen ['fetsən] *m* (-s;-) rag; bit, scrap; (Aust) dishcloth; **daß die F. fliegen** violently
feucht [fɔɪçt] *adj* moist, damp, humid

feuchten ['fɔɪçtən] *tr* moisten, dampen
Feuch'tigkeit *f* (-;) moisture, dampness, humidity
feudal [fɔɪ'dɑl] *adj* feudal; (fig) magnificent
Feudalismus [fɔɪda'lɪsmʊs] *m* (-;) feudalism
Feuer ['fɔɪ·ər] *n* (-s;-) fire
Feu'eralarm *m* fire alarm
Feu'eralarmübung *f* fire drill
feu'erbeständig *adj* fireproof
Feu'erbestattung *f* cremation
Feu'erbrand *m* firebrand
Feu'ereifer *m* enthusiasm, zeal
Feu'ereinstellung *f* cease-fire
feu'erfest *adj* fireproof
Feu'erfliege *f* firefly
feu'erflüssig *adj* molten
feu'ergefährlich *adj* inflammable
Feu'erhahn *m* hydrant, fireplug
Feu'erhaken *m* poker
Feu'erherd *m* fireplace
Feu'erkampf *m* fire fight, gun battle
Feu'erkraft *f* (mil) fire power
Feu'erleiter *f* fire ladder; (*Nottreppe*) fire escape
Feu'erlinie *f* firing line
Feu'erlöscher *m* fire extinguisher
Feu'ermelder *m* fire alarm
Feu'ermeldung *f* fire alarm
feuern ['fɔɪ·ərn] *tr* fire; (coll) fire, sack ‖ *intr* fire, shoot
Feu'erprobe *f* ordeal by fire; acid test
Feu'ersalve *f* fusillade
Feu'erschneise *f* firebreak
Feu'erspritze *f* fire engine
Feu'erstein *m* flint
Feu'ertaufe *f* baptism of fire
Feu'erversicherung *f* fire insurance
Feu'erwache *f* firehouse
Feu'erwalze *f* (mil) creeping barrage
Feu'erwehr *f* fire department
Feu'erwehrmann *m* (-[e]s;=er & -leute) fireman
Feu'erwerk *n* fireworks
Feu'erwerkskörper *m* firecracker
Feu'erzange *f* fire tongs
Feu'erzeug *n* cigarette lighter
Feu'erzeugbenzin *n* lighter fluid
feurig ['fɔɪrɪç] *adj* fiery; ardent
Fiasko [fɪ'asko] *n* (-s;-s) fiasco
Fibel ['fibəl] *f* (-;-n) primer; (archeol) fibula
Fiber ['fibər] *f* (-;-n) fiber
Fichte ['fɪçtə] *f* (-;-n) spruce; pine
Fich'tennadel *f* pine needle
fidel [fɪ'del] *adj* jolly, cheerful
Fieber ['fibər] *n* (-s;-) fever; **das F. messen** take the temperature
fie'berhaft *adj* feverish
fieberig ['fibərɪç] *adj* feverish
fie'berkrank *adj* running a fever
fiebern ['fibərn] *intr* be feverish
Fie'berphantasie *f* delirium
Fie'bertabelle *f* temperature chart
Fiedel ['fidəl] *f* (-;-n) fiddle
Fie'delbogen *m* fiddlestick
fiel [fil] *pret of* **fallen**
Figur [fɪ'gur] *f* (-;-en) figure; (cards) face card
figürlich [fɪ'gyrlɪç] *adj* figurative
fiktiv [fɪk'tif] *adj* fictitious
Filet [fɪ'le] *n* (-s;-s) (culin) fillet

Filiale [fɪl'jalə] *f* (-;-n) branch
Filia'lengeschäft *n* chain store
Filigran [fɪlɪ'gran] *n* (-s;-e), **Fili-gran'arbeit** *f* filigree
Film [fɪlm] *m* (-s;-e) film; (cin) movie
Film'atelier *n* motion-picture studio
Film'empfindlichkeit *f* film speed
Film'kulisse *f* (cin) movie set
Film'leinwand *f* movie screen
Film'probe *f* screen test
Film'regisseur *m* (cin) director
Film'wesen *n* motion-picture industry
Filter ['fɪltər] *m* & *n* (-s;-) filter
Fil'teranlage *f* filtration plant
Fil'terkaffee *m* drip-grind coffee
Fil'termundstück *n* filter tip
filtern ['fɪltərn] *tr* filter, strain
filtrieren [fɪl'trirən] *tr* filter
Filz [fɪlts] *m* (-es;-e) felt; (coll) miser, skinflint
Filz'schreiber *m* felt pen
Fimmel ['fɪməl] *m* (-s;-) craze, fad
-fimmel *m comb.fm.* mania for
Finanz [fɪ'nants] *f* (-;-en) finance
Finanz- *comb.fm.* financial, fiscal
Finanz'amt *n* internal revenue service
Finanz'ausschuß *m* (adm) ways and means committee
Finanzen [fɪ'nantsən] *pl* finances
finanziell [fɪnan'tsjel] *adj* financial
finanzieren [fɪnan'tsirən] *tr* finance
Finanz'minister *m* secretary of the treasury
Finanz'ministerium *n* treasury department
Finanz'wesen *n* finances
Finanz'wirtschaft *f* public finances
Findelkind ['fɪndəlkɪnt] *n* foundling
finden ['fɪndən] §59 *tr* find; **f. Sie nicht?** don't you think so? ‖ *ref* be found; **ach, das wird sich schon f.** oh, we'll see about that; **es fanden sich** there were; **es findet sich it** happens, it turns out; **sich f. in** (*acc*) resign oneself to; **sie haben sich gefunden** they were united ‖ *intr* find one's way
findig ['fɪndɪç] *adj* resourceful
Findling ['fɪntlɪŋ] *m* (-s;-e) foundling; (geol) boulder
fing [fɪŋ] *pret of* **fangen**
Finger ['fɪŋər] *m* (-s;-) finger
Fin'gerabdruck *m* fingerprint
fin'gerfertig *adj* deft
Fin'gerhut *m* thimble; (bot) foxglove
fingern ['fɪŋərn] *tr* finger
Fin'gerspitze *f* finger tip; **bis in die Fingerspitzen** through and through
Fin'gerspitzengefühl *n* sensitivity
Fin'gersprache *f* sign language
Fingerzeig ['fɪŋərtsaɪk] *m* (-s;-e) hint
fingieren [fɪŋ'girən] *tr* feign
fingiert [fɪŋ'girt] *adj* fictitious
Fink [fɪŋk] *m* (-en;-en) finch
Finne ['fɪnə] *m* (-n;-n) Finn ‖ *f* (-;-n) fin; (*Ausschlag*) pimple
Fin'nenausschlag *m* acne
Finnin ['fɪnɪn] *f* (-;-nen) Finn
finnisch ['fɪnɪʃ] *adj* Finnish
Finnland ['fɪnlant] *n* (-s;) Finland
finster ['fɪnstər] *adj* dark; gloomy
Finsternis ['fɪnstərnɪs] *f* (-;) darkness; gloom

Finte ['fɪntə] *f* (-;-n) feint; trick
Firlefanz ['fɪrləfants] *m* (-es;) junk;
F. treiben fool around
Fir·ma ['fɪrma] *f* (-;-men [mən]) firm
Firmament [fɪrma'mɛnt] *n* (-[e]s;-e)
firmament
firmen ['fɪrmən] *tr* (Cath) confirm
Fir'menschild *n* (com) name plate
Fir'menwert *m* (com) good will
Firmling ['fɪrmlɪŋ] *m* (-s;-e) (Cath)
person to be confirmed
Fir'mung *f* (-;-en) (Cath) confirmation
Fir·nis ['fɪrnɪs] *m* (-ses;-se) varnish;
mit **F.** streichen varnish
firnissen ['fɪrnɪsən] *tr* varnish
First [fɪrst] *m* (-es;-e) (archit) ridge
(*of roof*); (poet) mountain ridge
Fis [fɪs] *n* (-;-) (mus) F sharp
Fisch [fɪʃ] *m* (-es;-e) fish
fischen ['fɪʃən] *tr* fish for, catch ‖ *intr*
(nach) fish (for)
Fi'scher *m* (-s;-) fisherman
Fischerei [fɪʃə'raɪ] *f* (-;-en) fishing;
fishery; fishing trade
Fi'schergerät *n* fishing tackle
Fisch'fang *m* catch, haul
Fisch'gräte *f* fishbone
Fisch'grätenmuster *n* (tex) herringbone
Fisch'händler –in §6 *mf* fishmonger
fischig ['fɪʃɪç] *adj* fishy
Fisch'kunde *f* ichthyology
Fisch'laich *m* spawn, fish eggs
Fisch'otter *m* & *f* otter
Fisch'rogen *m* roe
Fisch'schuppe *f* scale (*of a fish*)
Fisch'zug *m* (& fig) catch
fiskalisch [fɪs'kalɪʃ] *adj* fiscal
Fis·kus ['fɪskus] *m* (-;-kusse & –ken
[kən]) treasury
Fistelstimme ['fɪstəl/tɪmə] *f* falsetto
Fittich ['fɪtɪç] *m* (-es;-e) (poet) wing
fix [fɪks] *adj* (*Idee, Preis*) fixed;
(*flink*) smart, sharp; **fix und fertig**
all set; all in; done for; **fix und
fertig** mił through with; **mach fix!**
make it snappy!
fixen ['fɪksən] *intr* sell short
fixieren [fɪ'ksirən] *tr* fix, decide upon;
stare fixedly at; (phot) fix
Fixier'mittel *n* (phot) fixer
flach [flax] *adj* flat, level; shallow;
(*Relief*) low; (fig) dull
Fläche ['flɛçə] *f* (-;-n) surface; plain;
expanse; facet; (geom) area
Flä'cheninhalt *m* (geom) area
Flä'chenraum *m* surface area
flach'fallen §72 *intr* (SEIN) (coll) fall
flat, flop
Flach'heit *f* (-;) flatness; shallowness
Flach'land *n* lowland
Flach'relief *n* low relief, bas-relief
Flach'rennen *n* flat racing
Flachs [flaks] *m* (-es;-e) flax
flachsen ['flaksən] *intr* (coll) kid
flächse(r)n ['flɛksə(r)n] *adj* flaxen
Flach'zange *f* pliers
flackern ['flakərn] *intr* flicker; (*Stimme*) quaver, shake
Flagge ['flagə] *f* (-;-n) flag (*esp. for
signaling or identification*)
Flag'genmast *m* flagpole
Flag'genstange *f* flagstaff

Flagg'schiff *n* flagship
Flak [flak] *abbr* (**Flugzeugabwehr-
kanone**) anti-aircraft gun
Flak'feuer *n* flak
Flakon [fla'kõ] *m* & *n* (-s;-s) perfume
bottle
Flamme ['flamə] *f* (-;-n) flame
flammen ['flamən] *intr* blaze; be in
flames
flam'mend *adj* passionate
Fla'mmenwerfer *m* flame thrower
Flandern ['flandərn] *n* (-s;) Flanders
flandrisch ['flandrɪʃ] *adj* Flemish
Flanell [fla'nɛl] *m* (-s;-e) flannel
Flanke ['flaŋkə] *f* (-;-n) flank
Flan'kenfeuer *n* (mil) enfilade; **mit F.**
bestreichen enfilade
flankieren [flaŋ'kirən] *tr* flank
Flansch [flanʃ] *m* (-es;-e) flange
Flasche ['flaʃə] *f* (-;-n) bottle; (coll)
flop; (mach) pulley
Fla'schengranate *f* Molotov cocktail
Fla'schenzug *m* block and tackle; (coll)
pulley
Flaschner ['flaʃnər] *m* (-s;-) plumber
flatterhaft ['flatərhaft] *adj* fickle
flattern ['flatərn] *intr* flutter, flap
flau [flau] *adj* stale; (*schwach*) feeble,
faint; (*fade*) dull, lifeless; (com)
slack; (phot) overexposed; **mir ist
f.** (im Magen) I feel queezy
Flaum [flaum] *m* (-[e]s;) down; (*am
Gesicht, am Pfirsich*) fuzz
flaumig ['flaumɪç] *adj* downy, fluffy
Flause ['flauzə] *f* (-;-n) fib; **Flausen**
funny ideas, nonsense
Flaute ['flautə] *f* (-;-n) (com) slack
period; (naut) dead calm
fläzen ['flɛtsən] *ref* sprawl out
Flechse ['flɛksə] *f* (-;-n) (dial) sinew,
tendon
Flechte ['flɛçtə] *f* (-;-n) plait; (bot)
lichen; (pathol) ringworm
flechten ['flɛçtən] §74 *tr* braid, plait;
(*Körbe*) weave
Fleck [flɛk] *m* (-[e]s;-e & -en) spot;
blemish; (*Flicken, Landstück*) patch
Flecken ['flɛkən] *m* (-s;-) spot; piece
of land; (*Markt-*) market town
fleckenlos (flek'kenlos) *adj* spotless
Fleck'fieber *n* spotted fever
fleckig ['flɛkɪç] *adj* spotty; splotchy
fleddern ['flɛdərn] *tr* (sl) rob
Fledermaus ['fledərmaus] *f* bat
Flegel ['flegəl] *m* (-s;-) flail; (coll)
lout, boor
Flegelei [flegə'laɪ] *f* (-;) rudeness
fle'gelhaft *adj* uncouth, boorish
Fle'geljahre *pl* awkward age
flehen ['fle·ən] *intr* plea; **zu j-m f.**
implore s.o. ‖ **Flehen** *n* (-s;-) supplication
Fleisch [flaɪʃ] *n* (-es;) flesh; meat;
sich ins eigene F. schneiden cut one's
own throat; **wildes F.** proud flesh
Fleisch'bank *f* (-;-ⁿe) meat counter
Fleisch'beil *n* cleaver
Fleisch'beschau *f* meat inspection
Fleisch'brühe *f* broth
Flei'scher *m* (-s;-) butcher
Flei'scheslust *f* (-;) lust
Fleisch'farbe *f* flesh color
fleisch'fressend *adj* carnivorous

Fleisch'hacker (-s;-) *m*, Fleisch'hauer *m* (-s;-) butcher
fleischig ['flaɪʃɪç] *adj* fleshy; meaty
fleisch'lich *adj* carnal
Fleisch'markt *m* meat market
Fleisch'pastete *f* meat pie
Fleisch'saft *m* meat juice, gravy
Fleisch'salat *m* diced-meat salad
Fleisch'speise *f* meat course
Fleisch'spieß *m* skewer
Fleischwerdung ['flaɪʃverdʊŋ] *f* (-;) incarnation
Fleisch'wolf *m* meat grinder
Fleisch'wunde *f* flesh wound, laceration
Fleisch'wurst *f* pork sausage
Fleiß [flaɪs] *m* (-es;) diligence, industry; mit F. intentionally
fleißig ['flaɪsɪç] *adj* diligent, hardworking
flektieren [flɛk'tirən] *tr* inflect
fletschen ['flɛtʃən] *tr* bare (*teeth*)
Flexion [flɛk'sjon] *f* (-;-en) (gram) inflection
flicken ['flɪkən] *tr* patch, repair || Flicken *m* (-s;-) patch
Flick'schuster *m* cobbler
Flick'werk *n* patchwork; hotchpotch; (*Pfuscherei*) bungling job
Flick'zeug *n* repair kit
Flieder ['flidər] *m* (-s;-) lilac
Fliege ['fligə] *f* (-;-n) fly; (coll) bow tie
fliegen ['fligən] §57 *tr* fly, pilot || *intr* (SEIN) fly; (coll) get sacked; in die Luft f. blow up
Flie'genfenster *n* window screen
Flie'gengewicht *n* flyweight division
Fliegengewichtler ['fligəngəvɪçtlər] *m* (-s;-) flyweight (boxer)
Flie'gengitter *n* screen
Flie'genklappe *f*, Flie'genklatsche *f* fly swatter
Flie'genpilz *m* toadstool
Flie'ger *m* (-s;-) flyer
Flieger– *comb.fm.* air-force; air, aerial; flying; airman's
Flie'gerabwehr *f* anti-aircraft defense
Flie'geralarm *m* air-raid alarm
Flie'gerangriff *m* air raid
Flie'gerheld *m* (aer) ace
Flie'gerhorst *m* air base
Flie'gerin *f* (-;-nen) flyer
Flie'gerschaden *m* air-raid damage
fliehen ['fli-ən] §75 *tr* run away from; avoid || *intr* (SEIN) flee
Flieh'kraft *f* (-;) centrifugal force
Fliese ['flizə] *f* (-;-n) tile
Flie'senleger *m* tiler, tile man
Fließband ['flisbant] *n* (-[e]s;⸚er) assembly line
fließen ['flisən] §76 *intr* (SEIN) flow
flie'ßend *adj* (*Wasser*) running; (fig) fluent
Fließheck ['flishɛk] *n* (aut) fastback
Fließpapier ['flispapir] *n* blotting paper
flimmern ['flɪmərn] *intr* glimmer; glisten, shimmer; flicker
flink [flɪŋk] *adj* nimble, quick; mach mal f.! get a move on!
Flinte ['flɪntə] *f* (-;-n) shotgun; gun
Flin'tenlauf *m* gun barrel

flirren ['flɪrən] *intr* shimmer
Flirt [flɪrt] *m* (-s;-s) flirtation; boyfriend, girlfriend
flirten ['flɪrtən] *intr* flirt
Flitter ['flɪtər] *m* (-s;-) sequins; (*Scheinglanz*) flashiness
Flit'terglanz *m* flashiness
Flit'tergold *m* gold tinsel
Flit'terkram *m* trinkets
Flit'terstaat *m* flashy clothes
Flit'terwochen *pl* honeymoon
flitzen ['flɪtsən] *intr* (SEIN) flit
flocht [flɔxt] *pret* of flechten
Flocke ['flɔkə] *f* (-;-n) flake; tuft
flog [flok] *pret* of fliegen
floh [flo] *pret* of fliehen || Floh *m* (-s;⸚e) flea; j–m e–n F. ins Ohr setzen put a bug in s.o.'s ear
Floh'hüpfspiel *n* tiddlywinks
Flor [flor] *m* (-s;-e) bloom || *m* (-s;-e & ⸚e) gauze; (tex) nap, pile
Flor'band *n* (-[e]s;⸚er) crepe; mourning band
Florett [flɔ'ret] *n* (-s;-e) foil
florieren [flɔ'rirən] *intr* flourish
Floskel ['flɔskəl] *f* (-;-n) rhetorical ornament, flowery phrase
Floß [flos] *n* (-es;⸚e) raft
Flosse ['flɔsə] *f* (-;-n) fin; (aer) stabilizer
flößen ['fløsən] *tr* float
Flöte ['fløtə] *f* (-;-n) flute; (cards) flush
flöten ['fløtən] *tr* play on the flute || *intr* play the flute; f. gehen (fig) go to the dogs
flott [flɔt] *adj* afloat; brisk, lively; gay; chic, dashing
Flotte ['flɔtə] *f* (-;-n) fleet
Flot'tenstützpunkt *m* naval base
flott'gehend *adj* (com) brisk, lively
Flottille [flɔ'tɪljə] *f* (-;-n) flotilla
flott'machen *tr* set afloat; (fig) get going again
Flöz [fløts] *n* (-es;-e) (min) seam
Fluch [flux] *m* (-[e]s;⸚e) curse
fluchen ['fluxən] *intr* curse
Flucht [fluxt] *f* (-;-en) flight; escape; straight line, alignment; (*Häuser–*) row; (*Spielraum*) space, leeway; (*Zimmer–*) suite; außerhalb der F. out of line; in die F. schlagen put to flight
flüchten ['flyçtən] *ref* (an *acc*, in *acc*) take refuge (in), have recourse (to) || *intr* (SEIN) flee; escape; (vor *dat*) run away (from)
flüchtig ['flyçtɪç] *adj* fugitive; fleeting; cursory, superficial; hurried; (chem) volatile; f. sein be on the run; f. werden escape, flee
Flüch'tigkeitsfehler *m* oversight, slip
Flüchtling ['flyçtlɪŋ] *m* (-s;-) fugitive; refugee
Flücht'lingslager *n* refugee camp
Flug [fluk] *m* (-[e]s;⸚e) flight
Flug'abwehr *f* anti-aircraft defense
Flugabwehr– *comb.fm.* anti-aircraft
Flug'anschluß *m* plane connection
Flug'aufgabe *f*, Flug'auftrag *m* (aer) mission
Flug'bahn *f* line of flight; trajectory
Flug'blatt *n* leaflet, flyer

Flügel ['flygəl] *m* (-s;-) wing; (*e-r Doppeltür*) leaf; (mus) grand piano
Flü'geladjutant *m* aide-de-camp
Flü'gelfenster *n* casement window
Flü'gelmutter *f* wing nut
Flü'gelschlag *m* flap of the wings
Flü'gelschraube *f* thumb screw
Flü'geschraubenmutter *f* wing nut
Flü'geltür *f* folding door
Flug'gast *m* (aer) passenger
flügge ['flygə] *adj* (*Vogel*) fledged (fig) ready to go on one's own
Flug'gesellschaft *f* airline company
Flug'hafen *m* airport
Flug'hafenbefeuerung *f* airport lights
Flug'kapitän *m* captain, pilot
Flug'karte *f* plane ticket; aeronautical chart
flug'klar *adj* ready for take-off
Flug'körper *m* missile; space vehicle
Flug'leitung *f* air-traffic control
Flug'linie *f* air route; airline
Flug'meldesystem *n* air-raid warning system
Flug'motor *m* aircraft engine
Flug'ortung *f* (aer) navigation
Flug'plan *m* flight schedule
Flug'platz *m* airfield, airport
Flug'post *f* air mail
Flug'preis *m* air fare
flugs [fluks] *adv* quickly; at once
Flug'schein *m* plane ticket
Flug'schneise *f* air lane
Flug'schrift *f* pamphlet
Flug'strecke *f* flying distance
Flug'stützpunkt *m* air base
flug'tauglich, flug'tüchtig *adj* airworthy
Flug'techniker –in §6 *mf* aeronautical engineer
Flug'verbot *n* (aer) grounding
Flug'verkehr *m* air traffic
Flug'wesen *n* aviation; aeronautics
Flug'wetter *n* flying weather
Flug'zeug *n* airplane, aircraft
Flug'zeugabwehrgeschütz *n,* **Flug'zeugabwehr** *f* anti-aircraft gun
Flug'zeug....hrer *m* pilot; zweiter F. co-pilot, second officer
Flug'zeugführerschein *m* pilot's license
Flug'zeuggeschwader *n* wing (*consisting of 3 squadrons of 9 planes each*)
Flug'zeugkreuzer *m,* **Flug'zeugmutterschiff** *n* seaplane tender, seaplane carrier
Flug'zeugrumpf *m* fuselage
Flug'zeugstaffel *f* squadron (*consisting of 9 planes*)
Flug'zeugträger *m* aircraft carrier
Flug'zeugwerk *n* aircraft factory
Flunder ['flundər] *f* (-;-n) flounder
Flunkerer ['fluŋkərər] *m* (-s;-) fibber
flunkern ['fluŋkərn] *intr* fib
Flunsch [flun∫] *m* (-es;-e) face; e-n F. ziehen (or machen) make a face
Fluor ['flu-ər] *n* (-s;) fluorine
Fluoreszenz [flu·ɔrɛs'tsɛnts] *f* (-;) fluorescence; fluorescent light
Fluorid [flu·ɔ'rit] *n* (-[e]s;-e) fluoride
Flur [flur] *m* (-[e]s;-e) entrance hall; hallway || *f* (-;-en) open farmland; meadow; community farmland

Flur'garderobe *f* hallway closet
Fluß [flus] *m* (**Flusses; Flüsse**) river; flow; (metal) fusion; (phys) flux
flußab'wärts *adv* downstream
flußauf'wärts *adv* upstream
Fluß'bett *n* riverbed, channel
Flüßchen ['flys̨çən] *n* (-s;-) rivulet
flüssig ['flysıç] *adj* liquid; fluid; (*Gelder*) ready; **f. machen** convert into cash || *adv* fluently
Flüs'sigkeit *f* (-;-en) liquid, fluid; (fig) fluency; (fin) liquidity
Flüs'sigkeitsmaß *n* liquid measure
Fluß'pferd *n* hypopotamus
flüstern ['flystərn] *tr & intr* whisper
Flü'sterparole *f* rumor
Flut [flut] *f* (-;-en) flood; waters; high tide
fluten ['flutən] *tr* flood || *intr* (SEIN) flow, pour
Flut'grenze *f* high-water mark
Flut'licht *n* floodlight
Flut'linie *f* high-water mark
Flut'wasser *n* tidewater
Flut'welle *f* tidal wave
Flut'zeit *f* flood tide, high tide
focht [fɔxt] *pret* of **fechten**
Focksegel ['fɔkzegəl] *n* (-s;-) foresail
fohlen ['folən] *intr* foal || **Fohlen** *n* (-s;-) foal
Folge ['fɔlgə] *f* (-;-n) sequence; consequence; succession; series; (*e-s Romans*) continuation; (*e-r Zeitschrift*) number; **die Folgen tragen** take the consequences; **in der F.** subsequently
folgen ['fɔlgən] *intr* (*dat*) obey || *intr* (SEIN) (*dat*) follow; (*dat*) succeed; (aus) ensue (from)
folgendermaßen ['fɔlgəndərmasən] *adv* in the following manner, as follows
fol'genschwer *adj* momentous, grave
fol'gerichtig *adj* logical, consistent
folgern ['fɔlgərn] *tr* infer, conclude
Fol'gerung *f* (-;-en) inference, conclusion
Fol'gesatz *m* (gram) result clause
fol'gewidrig *adj* inconsistent
Fol'gezeit *f*—in der F. in subsequent times
folglich ['fɔlklıç] *adv* consequently
folgsam ['fɔlkzam] *adj* obedient
Foliant [fol'jant] *m* (-en;-en) folio
Folie ['foljə] *f* (-;-n) (metal) foil
Folter ['fɔltər] *f* (-;-n) torture; rack; **auf die F. spannen** put to the rack; (fig) keep in suspense
Fol'terbank *f* (-;-̈e) rack
foltern ['fɔltərn] *tr* torture
Fol'terqual *f* torture
Fol'terverhör *n* third degree
Fön [føn] *m* (-[e]s;-e) hand hairdryer
Fond [fõ] *m* (-s;-s) background; rear, back; (culin) gravy
Fonds [fõ] *m* (-s [fõs];-s [fõs]) fund
Fontäne [fɔn'tɛnə] *f* (-;-n) fountain
foppen ['fɔpən] *tr* tease; bamboozle
Fopperei [fɔpə'raɪ] *f* (-;-en) teasing
forcieren [fɔr'sirən] *tr* force; speed up
Förderband ['fœdərbant] *n* (-;-̈er) conveyor belt

För'derer *m* (-s;-) promoter; patron
för'derlich *adj* useful; (*dat*) conducive (to)
fordern ['fərdərn] *tr* demand; (*Recht*) claim; (*zum Zweikampf*) challenge; (*vor Gericht*) summon
fördern ['fœrdərn] *tr* promote, back; (*Kohle*) produce; **förderndes Mitglied** social member; **zutage f.** bring to light
For'derung *f* (-;-en) demand, claim; debt; (*zum Zweikampf*) challenge
För'derung *f* (-;-en) promotion; support; encouragement; (min) output
Forelle [fɔ'rɛlə] *f* (-;-n) trout
Forke ['fɔrkə] *f* (-;-n) pitchfork
Form [fɔrm] *f* (-;-en) form; shape; mold; condition; (gram) voice; **die F. wahren** keep up appearances
formal [fɔr'mɑl] *adj* formal
Formalität [fɔrmalɪ'tet] *f* (-;-en) formality
Format [fɔr'mɑt] *n* (-[e]s;-e) size, format; distinction, stature
Formel ['fɔrməl] *f* (-;-n) formula
for'melhaft *adj* (*Wendung, Gebet*) set
formell [fɔr'mɛl] *adj* formal
formen ['fɔrmən] *tr* form, shape, mold
For'menlehre *f* morphology
Form'fehler *m* defect; flaw; (jur) irregularity
formieren [fɔr'mirən] *tr & ref* line up
-förmig [fœrmɪç] *comb.fm.* -shaped
förmlich ['fœrmlɪç] *adj* formal ‖ *adv* virtually; literally; formally
form'los *adj* shapeless; informal; unconventional; rude; (chem) amorphous
form'schön *adj* well-shaped, beautiful
Formular [fɔrmu'lɑr] *n* (-s;-e) form, blank
formulieren [fɔrmu'lirən] *tr* formulate; word, phrase
Formulie'rung *f* (-;-en) formulation; wording
form'vollendet *adj* perfectly shaped
forsch [fɔrʃ] *adj* dashing ‖ *adv* briskly
forschen ['fɔrʃən] *intr* do research; (nach) search (for)
For'scher -in §6 *mf* researcher; scholar; explorer
For'schung *f* (-;-en) research
For'schungsanstalt *f* research center
Forst [fɔrst] *m* (-[e]s;-e) forest
Förster ['fœrstər] *m* (-s;-) forester; forest ranger
Forst'fach *n* forestry
Forst'mann *m* (-es;-leute) forester
Forst'revier *n* forest range
Forst'wesen *n*, **Forst'wirtschaft** *f* forestry
fort [fɔrt] *adv* away; gone, lost; (*weiter*) on; (*vorwärts*) forward; **ich muß f.** I must be off; **in e-m f.** continuously; **und so f.** and so forth ‖ **Fort** [fɔr] *n* (-s;-s) (mil) fort
fortan' *adv* from now on, henceforth
Fort'bestand *m* continued existence
fort'bestehen §146 *intr* continue
fort'bewegen §56 *tr* move along ‖ *ref* get about
fort'bilden *ref* continue one's studies
Fort'bildung *f* continuing education

fort'bleiben §62 *intr* (SEIN) stay away
Fort'dauer *f* continuance
fort'dauern *intr* continue; last
fort'fahren §71 *tr* hawl away; continue (*to say*); **f. zu** (*inf*) continue to (*inf*), **go on** (*ger*) ‖ *intr* continue, **go on** ‖ *intr* (SEIN) drive off, leave
Fort'fall *m* omission; discontinuation; **in F. kommen** be discontinued
fort'fallen §72 *intr* (SEIN) drop out; be omitted; be discontinued
fort'führen *tr* lead away; continue; (*Geschäft*) carry on; (*Linie*) extend
Fort'gang *m* departure; continuation; progress
fort'gehen §82 *intr* (SEIN) go away
fort'geschritten *adj* advanced; late
fort'gesetzt *adj* incessant
fort'kommen §99 *intr* (SEIN) go on, make progress; get away; **in der Welt f.** get ahead in the world ‖ **Fortkommen** *n* (-s;) progress
fort'lassen §104 *tr* allow to go; omit
fort'laufen §105 *intr* (SEIN) run away
fort'laufend *adj* continuing; (*Nummer*) consecutive
fort'leben *intr* live on
fort'pflanzen *tr* propagate; spread ‖ *ref* reproduce; propagate; spread
Fort'pflanzung *f* (-;) propagation
fort'reißen §53 *tr* tear away; **j-n mit sich f.** sweep s.o. off his feet; **sich f. lassen** be caried away
fort'schaffen *tr* remove
fort'scheren *ref* (coll) scram
fort'schreiten §86 *intr* (SEIN) progress, advance
Fort'schritt *m* progress; improvement
fort'schrittlich *adj* progressive
fort'setzen *tr* continue; resume
Fort'setzung *f* (-;-en) continuation; sequel; installment; **F. folgt** to be continued
fort'während *adj* continual; lasting, permanent ‖ *adv* all the time, always
Fossil [fɔ'sil] *n* (-s;-ien [jən]) fossil
foul [faul] *adj* foul, dirty ‖ **Foul** *n* (-s;-) (sport) foul; **ein F. begehen an** (*dat*) commit a foul against
foulen ['faulən] *tr* (sport) foul
Foyer [fwa'je] *n* (-s;-s) foyer; (*im Hotel*) lobby
Fracht [fraxt] *f* (-;-en) freight, cargo
Fracht'brief *m* bill of lading
Frachter ['fraxtər] *m* (-s;-) freighter
Fracht'gut *n* freight, goods
Fracht'raum *m* cargo compartment; cargo capacity
Fracht'stück *n* package
Frack [frak] *m* (-[e]s;ː-e *&* -s) tails
Frack'schoß *m* coattail
Frage ['frɑgə] *f* (-;-n) question; **außer F. stehen** be out of the question; **e-e F. stellen** ask a question; **in F. stellen** call in question; **kommt nicht in F.!** nothing doing!
Fra'gebogen *m* questionnaire
fragen ['frɑgən] *tr* ask; **j-n f. nach** ask s.o. about; **j-n nach der Zeit f.** ask s.o. the time; **j-n f. um** ask s.o. for ‖ *ref* wonder ‖ *impers ref*—**es fragt sich, ob** the question is whether ‖ *intr* ask

Fra'gesatz *m* interrogative sentence; **abhängiger F.** indirect question
Fragesteller ['frɑgəʃtɛlər] *m* (**-s;-**) questioner
Fra'gewort *n* (**-es;ːer**) interrogative
Fra'gezeichen *n* question mark
fraglich ['frɑklıç] *adj* questionable
fraglos ['frɑklos] *adv* unquestionably
Fragment [frag'ment] *n* (**-[e]s;-e**) fragment
frag'würdig *adj* questionable
Fraktion [frak'tsjon] *f* (**-;-en**) (chem) fraction; (pol) faction
fraktionell [fraktsə'nɛl] *adj* factional
Fraktur [frak'tur] *f* (**-;-en**) fracture; Gothic type, Gothic lettering; **mit j-m F. reden** talk turkey with s.o.
frank [fraŋk] *adv*—**f. und frei** quite frankly
Franke ['fraŋkə] *m* (**-n;-n**) Franconian; (hist) Frank
Franken ['fraŋkən] *m* (**-[e]s;-**) (Swiss) franc || *n* (**-s;**) Franconia
frankieren [fraŋ'kirən] *tr* frank, put postage on
Fränkin ['frɛŋkın] *f* (**-;-nen**) Frank
franko ['fraŋko] *adv* postage paid; **f. Berlin** freight paid to Berlin; **f. verzollt** free of freight and duty
Frank'reich *n* (**-s;**) France
Franse ['franzə] *f* (**-;-n**) fringe
fransen ['franzən] *intr* fray
Franzband ['frantsbant] *m* (**-[e]s;ːe**) leather binding
Franz'branntwein *m* rubbing alcohol
Franzose [fran'tsozə] *m* (**-;-n**) Frenchman; **die Franzosen** the French
Französin [fran'tsøzın] *f* (**-;-nen**) Frenchwoman
französisch [fran'tsøzıʃ] *adj* French
frappant [fra'pant] *adj* striking
frappieren [fra'pirən] *tr* strike, astonish; (*Wein*) put on ice
fräsen ['frezən] *tr* mill
fraß [fras] *pret* of **fressen** || **Fraß** *m* (**-es;**) fodder, food; (pel) garbage
Fratz [frats] *m* (**-es;-e**) brat
Fratze ['fratsə] *f* (**-;-n**) grimace; (coll) face; **e-e F. schneiden** make a face
frat'zenhaft *adj* grotesque
Frau [frau] *f* (**-;-en**) woman; lady; wife; (*vor Namen*) Mrs; **zur F. geben** give in marriage
Frauen– *comb.fm.* of women
Frau'enarzt *m*, **Frau'enärztin** *f* gynecologist
Frau'enheld *m* ladykiller
Frau'enkirche *f* Church of Our Lady
Frau'enkleidung *f* women's wear
Frau'enklinik *f* women's hospital
Frau'enleiden *n* gynecological disorder
Frau'enzimmer *n* (pej) woman, female
Fräulein ['frɔilain] *n* (**-s;-**) young lady; (*vor Namen*) Miss
frau'lich *adj* womanly
frech [frɛç] *adj* brazen; fresh, smart
Frech'dachs *m* smart aleck
Frech'heit *f* (**-;-en**) impudence
Fregatte [fre'gatə] *f* (**-;-n**) frigate
frei [frai] *adj* free; (*Feld*) open; (*offen*) frank; **auf freien Fuß setzen** release; **auf freier Strecke** (rr) outside the station; **die freien Berufe** the professions; **freie Fahrt** (public sign) resume speed; **freies Spiel haben** have a free hand; **frei werden** (chem) be released; **ich bin so frei** thank you, I will have some; **sich frei machen** take off one's clothes; **Freie $5 n**—**im Freien** out of doors; **ins Freie** out of doors, into the open
Frei'bad *n* outdoor swimming pool
Frei'bank *f* (**-;ːe**) cheap-meat counter
frei'beruflich *adj* freelance
Frei'betrag *m* allowable deduction
Frei'brief *m* charter; (fig) license
Freier ['frai-ər] *m* (**-s;-**) suitor
Frei'frau *f* baroness
Frei'gabe *f* release
frei'geben §80 *tr* release; **für den Verkehr f.** open to traffic || *intr*—**j-m f. give s.o.** (*time*) off
freigebig ['fraigebiç] *adj* generous
Frei'gebigkeit *f* (**-;**) generosity
Frei'geist *m* freethinker
frei'geistig *adj* open-minded
frei'gestellt *adj* optional
frei'haben *intr* be off
Frei'hafen *m* free port
frei'halten §90 *tr* keep open; **j-n f. pay** the tab for s.o.
Frei'heit *f* (**-;-en**) freedom; **dichterische F.** poetic license
Frei'heitskrieg *m* war of liberation
Frei'heitsstrafe *f* imprisonment
Frei'herr *m* baron
Frei'karte *f* free ticket; (theat) complimentary ticket
Frei'korps *n* volunteer corps
frei'lassen §104 *tr* release, set free
Frei'lauf *m* coasting
frei'legen *tr* lay open, expose
frei'lich *adv* of course
Freilicht– *comb.fm.* open-air
frei'machen *tr* (*Platz*) vacate; (*Straße*) clear; (*Brief*) stamp; **den Arm f.** roll up one's sleeves || *ref* undress
Frei'marke *f* postage stamp
Frei'maurer *m* Freemason
Frei'maurerei *f* freemasonry
Frei'mut *m* frankness
frei'mütig *adj* frank, outspoken
frei'schaffend *adj* freelance
Frei'sinn *m* (pol) liberalism
frei'sinnig *adj* (pol) liberal
frei'sprechen §64 *tr* acquit
Frei'spruch *m* acquittal
frei'stehen §146 *intr*—**es steht Ihnen frei zu** (*inf*) you are free to (*inf*)
frei'stehend *adj* free-standing; (*Gebäude*) detached
Frei'stelle *f* scholarship
frei'stellen *tr* exempt; **j-m etw f.** leave it to s.o.'s discretion
Frei'stoß *m* (fb) free kick
Frei'tag *m* Friday
Frei'tod *m* suicide
Frei'treppe *f* outdoor stairway
Frei'wild *n* (& fig) fair game
frei'willig *adj* voluntary || **Freiwillige** $5 *mf* (& mil) volunteer
Frei'zeichen *n* (telp) dial tone
Frei'zeit *f* spare time, leisure
Frei'zeitgestaltung *f* planning one's leisure time
freizügig ['fraitsygiç] *adj* unhampered

fremd [frɛmt] *adj* foreign; strange; someone else's; (*Name*) assumed
fremd'artig *adj* strange, odd
Fremde ['frɛmdə] §5 *mf* foreigner; stranger || *f—aus der F.* from abroad; **in der F.** far from home; **in die F.** gehen go far from home; go abroad
Frem'denbuch *n* visitors' book
Frem'denführer –in §6 *mf* tour guide; (*Buch*) guidebook
Frem'denheim *n* boarding house
Frem'denlegion *f* foreign legion
Frem'denverkehr *m* tourism
Frem'denzimmer *n* guest room; spare room
Fremd'herrschaft *f* foreign domination
Fremd'körper *m* foreign body; (pol) alien element
fremdländisch ['frɛmtlendɪʃ] *adj* foreign
Fremdling ['frɛmtlɪŋ] *m* (-s;-) stranger
Fremd'sprache *f* foreign language
Fremd'wort *n* (-es;ːer) foreign word
frequentieren [frɛkvɛn'tirən] *tr* frequent
Frequenz [frɛ'kvɛnts] *f* (-;-en) frequency; (*Besucherzahl*) attendance
Freske ['frɛskə] *f* (-;-n), **Fres·ko** ['frɛsko] *n* (-s;-ken [kən]) fresco
Freßbeutel ['frɛsbɔɪtəl] *m* feed bag
Fresse ['frɛsə] *f* (-;-n) (sl) puss
fressen ['frɛsən] §70 *tr* (*von Tieren*) eat; feed on; (sl) devour; (*ätzen*) corrode, pit; (tech) freeze || *ref—sich satt f.* stuff oneself || *intr* (sl) eat; (an *dat*) gnaw (at)
Fresserei [frɛsə'raɪ] *f* (-;) gluttony
Freude ['frɔɪdə] *f* (-;-n) joy, pleasure
Freu'denbotschaft *f* glad tidings
Freu'denfeier *f,* **Freu'denfest** *n* celebration, happy occasion
Freu'denhaus *n* brothel
Freu'denmädchen *n* prostitute
freudig ['frɔɪdɪç] *adj* joyful, happy
freud'los *adj* joyless, sad
freuen ['frɔɪ·ən] *tr* please || *ref* be happy; (an *dat*) be delighted (by); (auf *acc*) look forward (to); (über *acc*) be glad (about) || *impers—es freut mich* I am glad
Freund [frɔɪnt] *m* (-[e]s;-e) friend; boyfriend; **F. der Musik** music lover
Freundin ['frɔɪndɪn] *f* (-;-nen) friend; girlfriend
freund'lich *adj* friendly; cheerful
Freund'lichkeit *f* (-;) friendliness
Freund'schaft *f* (-;-en) friendship
Frevel ['frefəl] *m* (-s;-) outrage; crime; sacrilege
fre'velhaft *adj* wicked
freveln ['frefəln] *intr* commit an outrage; **am Gesetz f.** violate the law
Fre'veltat *f* outrage
Friede ['fridə] *m* (-ns;), **Frieden** ['fridən] *m* (-s;) peace
Frie'densrichter *m* justice of the peace
Frie'densschluß *m* conclusion of peace
Frie'densstifter –in §6 *mf* peacemaker
Frie'densverhandlungen *pl* peace negotiations
Frie'densvertrag *m* peace treaty

friedfertig ['fritfɛrtɪç] *adj* peaceable
Friedhof ['frithof] *m* cemetery
friedlich ['fritlɪç] *adj* peaceful
friedliebend ['fritlibənt] *adj* peaceloving
frieren ['friːən] §77 *intr* be cold; freeze || *impers—es friert mich* I'm freezing
Fries [fris] *m* (-es;-e) frieze
Frikadelle [frɪka'dɛlə] *f* (-;-n) meatball
frisch [frɪʃ] *adj* fresh; (*kühl*) cool; (*munter*) brisk || *adv* freshly; **f. gestrichen** (public sign) wet paint; **f. zu!** on with it! || **Frische** *f* (-;) freshness; coolness; briskness
Frisch'haltepackung *f* vacuum package
Friseur [frɪ'zør] *m* (-s;-e) barber
Friseur'laden *m* barbershop
Friseur'sessel *m* barber chair
Friseuse [frɪ'zøzə] *f* (-;-n) hairdresser
frisieren [frɪ'zirən] *tr* (*Dokumente*) doctor; (aut) soup up; **j–m die Haare f.** do s.o.'s hair
Frisier'haube *f* hair dryer; hair net
Frisier'kommode *f,* **Frisier'tisch** *m* dresser
Frist [frɪst] *f* (-;-en) time, period, term; (com, jur) grace; **die F. einhalten** meet the deadline
fristen ['frɪstən] *tr—das Leben f.* eke out a living
Frisur [frɪ'zur] *f* (-;-en) hairstyle
frivol [frɪ'vol] *adj* frivolous
froh [fro] *adj* glad, happy, joyful
froh'gelaunt *adj* cheerful
fröhlich ['frølɪç] *adj* gay, merry
froh'locken *intr* rejoice
Froh'sinn *m* good humor
fromm [frɔm] *adj* pious, devout
Frömmelei [frœmə'laɪ] *f* (-;-en) sanctimoniousness; sanctimonious act
frommen ['frɔmən] *intr* (dat) profit
Frömmigkeit ['frœmɪçkaɪt] *f* (-;) piety
Frömmler –in ['frœmlər-ɪn] §6 *mf* hypocrite
Fron [fron] *f* (-;) drudgery; (hist) forced labor
frönen ['frønən] *intr* (dat) gratify
Fron'leichnam *m* Corpus Christi
Front [frɔnt] *f* (-;-en) (& mil) front
Front'abschnitt *m* (mil) sector
fror [fror] *pret* of **frieren**
Frosch [frɔʃ] *m* (-es;ːe) frog; (*Feuerwerkkörper*) firecracker; **sei kein F.!** don't be a party pooper
Frost [frɔst] *m* (-es;ːe) frost
Frost'beule *f* chilblain
frösteln ['frœstəln] *intr* feel chilly
Frosterfach ['frɔstərfax] *n* freezer compartment (*of refrigerator*)
frostig ['frɔstɪç] *adj* frosty; chilly
Frost'schutzmittel *n* antifreeze
Frottee [frɔ'te] *m & n* (-s;-s) terry cloth
frottieren [frɔ'tirən] *tr* rub down
Frottier'tuch *n* Turkish towel
Frucht [fruxt] *f* (-;ːe) fruit; foetus
fruchtbar ['fruxtbar] *adj* fruitful
frucht'bringend *adj* productive
Früch'tebecher *m* fruit cup (*as dessert*)
fruchten ['fruxtən] *intr* bear fruit; have effect; be of use

Frucht'folge *f* rotation of crops
Frucht'knoten *m* (bot) pistil
frucht'los *adj* fruitless
Frucht'saft *m* fruit juice
Frucht'wechsel *m* rotation of crops
frugal [fru'gɑl] *adj* frugal
früh [fry] *adj* early || *adv* early; in the morning; **von f. bis spät** from morning till night || **Frühe** *f* (-;) early morning; **in aller F.** very early
früher ['fry·ər] *adj* earlier; former || *adv* earlier; sooner; formerly
frühestens ['fry·əstəns] *adv* at the earliest
Früh'geburt *f* premature birth
Früh'jahr *n*, **Frühling** ['fryliŋ] *m* (-s; -e) spring
Früh'lingsmüdigkeit *f* spring fever
früh'reif *adj* precocious
Früh'schoppen *m* eye opener (*beer, wine*)
Früh'stück *n* breakfast; **zweites F.** lunch
frühstücken ['fry/tykən] *intr* eat breakfast
früh'zeitig *adj & adv* (too) early
Fuchs [fuks] *m* (-es;̈e) fox; (*Pferd*) sorrel, chestnut; (educ) freshman
Fuchsie ['fuksjə] *f* (-;-n) fuchsia
fuchsig ['fuksıç] *adj* red; (fig) furious, wild
Fuchs'jagd *f* fox hunt(ing)
fuchs'rot' *adj* sorrel
Fuchs'schwanz *m* foxtail; (bot) amaranth; (carp) hand saw (*with tapered blade*)
fuchs'teufelswild' *adj* hopping mad
Fuge ['fugə] *f* (-;-n) joint; (mus) fugue; **aus allen Fugen gehen** come apart; go to pieces, go to pot
fügen ['fygən] *tr* join; (*verhängen*) decree; (carp) joint || *ref* give in; **es fügte sich** it so happened
fügsam ['fykzɑm] *adj* compliant; (*Haar*) manageable
Fü'gung *f* (-;-en) (gram) construction; **F. des Himmels, F. Gottes** divine providence; **F. des Schicksals** stroke of fate; **göttliche F.** divine providence
fühlbar ['fylbɑr] *adj* tangible; noticeable; **sich f. machen** make itself felt
fühlen ['fylən] *tr* feel, touch; sense || *ref* feel; feel big || *intr*—**f. mit** feel for (*s.o.*); **f. nach** feel for, grope for
-fühlig [fylıç] *comb.fm.* –feeling
Füh'lung *f* (-;) touch, contact; **F. nehmen mit** get in touch with
fuhr [fur] *pret* of **fahren**
Fuhre ['furə] *f* (-;-n) wagon load
führen ['fyrən] *tr* lead; guide; (*Artikel*) carry, sell; (*Besprechungen*) hold, conduct; (*Bücher*) keep; (*Geschäft*) run, manage; (*Krieg*) carry on; (*Sprache*) use; (*Titel*) bear; (*Truppen*) command; (*Waffe*) wield; (*Fahrzeug*) drive; (aer) pilot; **den Beweis f.** prove; **de Aufsicht f. über** (*acc*) superintend; **j–m den Haushalt f.** keep house for s.o. || *ref* conduct oneself || *intr* lead; (sport) be in the lead
Füh'rer –in §6 *mf* leader, guide; (aer) pilot; (aut) driver; (com) manager; (sport) captain
Füh'rerschaft *f* (-;) leadership
Füh'rerschein *m* driver's license
Füh'rerscheinentzug *m* suspension of driver's license
Führhund ['fyrhʊnt] *m* Seeing Eye dog
Fuhr'park *m* (aut) fleet
Füh'rung *f* (-;-en) guidance; leadership; management; guided tour; behavior; (mil) command; (sport) lead
Füh'rungskraft *f* executive; **die Führungskräfte** management; (pol) authorities; **untere F.** junior executive
Füh'rungsschicht *f* (com) management
Füh'rungsspitze *f* top echelon
Fuhr'unternehmen *n* trucking
Fuhr'werk *n* cart, wagon; vehicle
Füllbleistift ['fylblaɪ/tıft] *m* mechanical pencil
Fülle ['fylə] *f* (-;) fullness; abundance, wealth; (*Körper–*) plumpness
füllen ['fylən] *tr* fill || *ref* fill up || **Füllen** *n* (-s;-) foal, colt, filly
Fül'ler *m* (-s;-) fountain pen
Füll'federhalter *m* fountain pen
Füll'horn *n* cornucopia
Füllsel ['fylzəl] *n* (-s;-) stopgap; (*beim Schreiben*) padding; (culin) stuffing
Fül'lung *f* (-;-en) (*Zahn–*) filling; (*Tür–*) panel; (culin) stuffing
Fund [funt] *m* (-[e]s;-e) find; discovery
Fundament [funda'mɛnt] *n* (-[e]s;-e) foundation
fundamental [fundamen'tɑl] *adj* fundamental
Fund'büro *n* lost-and-found department
Fund'grube *f* (fig) mine, storehouse
fundieren [fun'dirən] *tr* lay the foundations of; found; establish; (*Schuld*) fund; **fundiertes Einkommen** unearned income; **gut fundiert** well-established
fünf [fynf] *adj & pron* five || **Fünf** *f* (-;-en) five
Fünf'eck *n* pentagon
fünfte ['fynftə] §9 *adj & pron* fifth
Fünftel ['fynftəl] *n* (-s;-) fifth (*part*)
fünf'zehn *adj & pron* fifteen || **Fünfzehn** *f* (-;-en) fifteen
fünf'zehnte §9 *adj & pron* fifteenth
Fünf'zehntel *n* (-s;-) fifteenth (*part*)
fünfzig ['fynfzıç] *adj* fifty
fünf'ziger *invar adj* of the fifties; **die f. Jahre** the fifties
fünfzigste ['fynftsıçstə] §9 *adj & pron* fiftieth
fungieren [fuŋ'girən] *intr* function; **f. als** function as, act as
Funk [fuŋk] *m* (-s;) radio
Funk'amateur *m* (rad) ham
Funk'bastler –in §6 *mf* (rad) ham
Fünkchen ['fyŋkçən] *n* (-s;-) small spark; **kein F.** (fig) not an ounce
Funke ['fuŋkə] *m* (-ns;-n), **Funken** ['fuŋkən] *m* (-s;-) spark
funkeln ['fuŋkəln] *intr* sparkle; (*Sterne*) twinkle
fun'kelnagelneu' *adj* brand-new

funken ['fuŋkən] *tr* radio, broadcast || *intr* spark
Fun'ker *m* (-s;-) radio operator
Funk'feuer *n* (aer) radio beacon
Funk'leitstrahl *m* radio beam
Funk'meßanlage *f* radar installation
Funk'meßgerät *n* radar
Funk'netz *n* radio network
Funk'peilung *f* radio direction finding
Funk'spruch *m* radiogram
Funk'streifenwagen *m* squad car
Funktionär -in [fuŋktsjə'ner(ɪn)] §8 *mf* functionary
für [fyr] *prep (acc)* for || **Für** *n*—**das Für und Wider** the pros and cons
Für'bitte *f* intercession
Furche ['furçə] *f* (-;-n) furrow; *(Runzel)* wrinkle; *(Wagenspur)* rut
furchen ['furçən] *tr* furrow; wrinkle
Furcht [furçt] *f* (-;) fear, dread
furchtbar ['furçtbar] *adj* terrible
fürchten ['fyrçtən] *tr* fear, be afraid of || *ref* (**vor** *dat*) be afraid (of)
fürchterlich ['fyrçtərlıç] *adj* terrible, awful
furcht'erregend *adj* awe-inspiring
furcht'los *adj* fearless
furchtsam ['furçtzam] *adj* timid, shy
Furie ['furjə] *f* (-;-n) (myth) Fury
Furnier [fur'nir] *n* (-s;-e) veneer
Furore [fu'rorə] *f* (-;) & *n* (-s;) stir; **F. machen** cause a stir, be a big hit
Für'sorge *f* care; welfare
Für'sorgeamt *n* welfare department
Fürsorger -in ['fyrzɔrgər(ɪn)] §6 *mf* social worker; welfare officer
fürsorglich ['fyrzɔrklıç] *adj* thoughtful
Für'sprache *f* intercession; **F. einlegen** intercede
Für'sprecher -in §6 *mf* intercessor
Fürst [fyrst] *m* (-en;-en) prince
Fürstentum ['fyrstəntum] *n* (-s;-er) principality
Fürstin ['fyrstɪn] *f* (-;-nen) princess
fürst'lich *adj* princely
Furt [furt] *f* (-;-en) ford
Furunkel [fu'runkəl] *m* (-s;-) boil
Für'wort *n* (-[e]s;-er) pronoun

Furz [furts] *m* (-es;-e) (vulg) fart
Fusel ['fuzəl] *m* (-s;) (coll) booze
Fusion [fu'sjon] *f* (-;-en) (com) merger
Fuß [fus] *m* (-es;-e) foot; **auf freien Fuß setzen** set free; **zu Fuß** on foot; **zu Fuß gehen** walk
Fuß'abdruck *m* footprint
Fuß'ball *m* soccer; football
Fuß'bank *f* (-;-e) footstool
Fuß'bekleidung *f* footwear
Fuß'boden *m* floor; flooring
Fussel ['fusəl] *f* (-;-n) fuzz
fußen ['fusən] *intr*—**f. auf** *(dat)* be based on; rely on
Fuß'fall *m* prostration
fuß'fällig *adv* on one's knees
fuß'frei *adj* ankle-length
Fuß'freiheit *f* leg room
Fuß'gänger *m* (-s;-) pedestrian
Fuß'gelenk *n* ankle joint
Fuß'gestell *n* pedestal
-füßig [fysıç] *comb.fm.* -footed
Fuß'knöchel *m* ankle
Fuß'leiste *f* baseboard, washboard
Füßling ['fyslıŋ] *m* (-s;-e) foot *(of stocking, sock, etc.)*
Fuß'note *f* footnote
Fuß'pfad *m* footpath
Fuß'pilz *m* athlete's foot
Fuß'spur *f* footprint(s)
Fuß'stapfe *f* footstep
Fuß'steg *m* footbridge; footpath
Fuß'steig *m* footpath; sidewalk
Fuß'tritt *m* step; *(Stoß)* kick
futsch [futʃ] *adj* (coll) gone; (coll) ruined
Futter ['futər] *n* (-s;) fodder, feed; *(e-s Mantels)* lining
Futteral [futə'ral] *n* (-s;-e) case
Fut'terkrippe *f* crib; (sl) gravy train
Fut'terkrippensystem *n* (pol) spoils system
futtern ['futərn] *intr* (coll) eat heartily
füttern ['fytərn] *tr* feed; *(Kleid, Mantel, Pelz)* line
Fut'terneid *m* jealousy
Fut'terstoff *m* lining
Fut'tertrog *m* feed trough

G

G, g [ge] *invar n* G, g; (mus) G
gab [gap] *pret* of **geben**
Gabardine [gabar'dinə] *m* (-s;-) (tex) gabardine
Gabe ['gabə] *f* (-;-n) gift; donation; talent; (med) dose; **milde G.** alms
Gabel ['gabəl] *f* (-;-n) fork; (arti) bracket; (telp) cradle
Ga'belbein *n* wishbone
Ga'belbissen *m* tidbit
Ga'belfrühstück *n* brunch
gabelig ['gabəlıç] *adj* forked
gabeln ['gabəln] *tr* pick up with a fork || *ref* divide, branch off
Ga'belstapler *m* forklift
Ga'belung *f* (-;-en) fork *(in the road)*

gackeln ['gakəln], **gackern** ['gakərn], **gacksen** ['gaksən] *intr* cackle, cluck
Gage ['gaʒə] *f* (-;-n) salary, pay
gähnen ['genən] *intr* yawn
gaffen ['gafən] *intr* gape; stare
Gala ['gala] *invar adj* gala, Sunday best
galant [ga'lant] *adj* courteous; **galantes Abenteuer** love affair
Galante·rie [galantə'ri] *f* (-;-rien ['ri·ən]) courtesy; flattering word
Gala·xis [ga'laksıs] *f* (-;-xien [ksjən]) galaxy
Galeere [ga'lerə] *f* (-;-n) galley
Gale·rie [galə'ri] *f* (-;-rien ['ri·ən]) gallery
Galgen ['galgən] *m* (-s;-) gallows

Gal'genfrist *f* (coll) brief respite
Gal'genhumor *m* grim humor
Gal'genstrick *m*, **Gal'genvogel** *m* (coll) good-for-nothing
gälisch ['gɛlɪʃ] *adj* Gaelic
Galle ['galə] *f* (-;) gall, bile; (fig) bitterness
Gal'lenblase *f* gall bladder
Gal'lenstein *m* gallstone
Gallert ['galərt] *n* (-[e]s;-e), **Gallerte** [ga'lɛrtə] *f* (-;-n) gelatine; jelly
gallig ['galɪç] *adj* bitter; grouchy
Gallone [ga'lonə] *f* (-;-n) gallon
Galopp [ga'lɔp] *m* (-[e]s;-s & -e) gallop; **im G. reiten** gallop; **in gestrecktem G.** at full gallop; **in kurzem G.** at a canter
galoppieren [galə'pirən] *intr* (SEIN) gallop
galt [galt] *pret* of **gelten**
galvanisieren [galvanɪ'zirən] *tr* galvanize; electroplate
Gambe ['gambə] *f* (-;-n) bass viol
gammeln ['gaməln] *intr* bum around
Gammler ['gamlər] *m* (-s;-) hippie
Gamsbart ['gamsbart] *m* goatee
gang [gaŋ] *adj*—**g. und gäbe** customary || **Gang** *m* (-[e]s;-̈) walk, gait; (*e-r Maschine*) running, operation; (*im Hause*) hallway; (*zwischen Reihen*) aisle; (*Botengang*) errand; (*Röhre*) conduit; (*e-r Schraube*) thread; (anat) duct, canal; (aut) gear; (box) round; (culin) course; (min) vein, lode; (min) gallery; (mus) run; **außer G. setzen** stop; (aut) put in neutral; **erster G.** low gear; **es ist etw im G.** there is s.th. afoot; **im G. sein** be in operation; be in progress; **in G. bringen** (or **setzen**) set in motion; **in vollem G.** in full swing
Gang'art *f* gait
gangbar ['gaŋbar] *adj* passable; (*Münze*) current; (com) marketable
Gängelband ['gɛŋəlbant] *n*—**am G. führen** (fig) lead by the nose, dominate
-gänger [gɛŋər] *comb.fm.*, e.g., **Fußgänger** pedestrian
gängig ['gɛŋɪç] *adj* see **gangbar**
Gang'schaltung *f* (aut) gear shift
Gangster ['gɛŋstər] *m* (-s;-s) gangster
Ganove [ga'novə] *m* (-;-n) crook
Gans [gans] *f* (-;-̈e) goose
Gänseblümchen ['gɛnzəblymçən] *n* (-s;-) daisy
Gänsehaut ['gɛnzəhaut] *f* (coll) goose flesh, goose pimples
Gänseklein ['gɛnzəklain] *n* (-s;) (culin) giblets
Gänsemarsch ['gɛnzəmarʃ] *m* single file
Gänserich ['gɛnzərɪç] *m* (-s;-e) gander
ganz [gants] *adj* whole; all; total; intact; **im ganzen** in all || *adv* entirely, quite; **g. und gar** completely; **g. und gar nicht** not at all || **Ganze §5** *n* whole; **aufs G. gehen** go all the way
Ganz'aufnahme *f* full-length photograph
Gänze ['gɛntsə] *f* (-;)—**in G.** in its entirety; **zur G.** entirely
Ganz'fabrikat *n* finished product

Ganz'leinenband *m* (-[e]s;-̈e) cloth-bound volume
gänzlich ['gɛntslɪç] *adj* entire, total
ganz'seitig *adj* full-page
ganz'tägig *adj* full-time
gar [gar] *adj* (culin) well done; (metal) refined || *adv* quite, very; (*sogar*) even; **gar nicht** not at all
Garage [ga'raʒə] *f* (-;-n) garage
Garan∙tie [garan'ti] *f* (-;-tien ['ti∙ən]) guarantee
garantieren [garan'tirən] *tr* guarantee || *intr*—**g. dafür, daß** guarantee that
Garaus ['garaus] *m* (-;) finishing blow
Garbe ['garbə] *f* (-;-n) sheaf, shock
Garde ['gardə] *f* (-;-n) guard
Gardenie [gar'denjə] *f* (-;-n) gardenia
Garderobe [gardə'robə] *f* (-;-n) wardrobe; (*Kleiderablage*) cloakroom; (theat) dressing room
Gardero'benmarke *f* hat or coat check
Gardero'benständer *m* coatrack, hatrack
Garderobiere [gardərə'bjerə] *f* (-;-n) cloakroom attendant
Gardine [gar'dinə] *f* (-;-n) curtain
Gardi'nenhalter *m* tieback
Gardi'nenpredigt *f* (coll) dressing down
Gardi'nenstange *f* curtain rod
gären ['gerən] §78 *intr* ferment; bubble
Gärmittel ['germɪtəl] *n* ferment; leaven
Garn [garn] *n* (-[e]s;-e) yarn; thread; snare; (fig) trap; (fig) yarn
Garnele [gar'nelə] *f* (-;-n) shrimp
garnieren [gar'nirən] *tr* garnish; trim
Garnison [garnɪ'zon] *f* (-;-en) garrison
Garnitur [garnɪ'tur] *f* (-;-en) trimming; set (*of matching objects*); (mach) fittings, mountings; (mil) uniform
garstig ['garstɪç] *adj* ugly; nasty
Garten ['gartən] *m* (-s;-̈) garden
Gar'tenanlage *f* gardens, grounds
Gar'tenarbeit *f* gardening
Gar'tenarchitekt *m* landscape gardener
Gar'tenbau *m* gardening; horticulture
Gar'tenlaube *f* arbor
Gar'tenmesser *n* pruning knife
Gärtner ['gertnər] *m* (-s;-) gardener
Gärtnerei [gertnə'rai] *f* (-;-en) gardening; truck farm; nursery
Gä'rung *f* (-;) fermentation
Gas [gas] *n* (-es;-e) gas; **Gas geben** step on the gas
Gas'anstalt *f* gasworks
gas'artig *adj* gaseous
Gas'behälter *m* gas tank
gas'förmig *adj* gaseous
Gas'hebel *m* (aut) accelerator
Gas'heizung *f* gas heat(ing)
Gas'herd *m* gas range
Gas'krieg *m* chemical warfare
Gas'leitung *f* gas main
Gas'messer *m* gas meter
Gasse ['gasə] *f* (-;-n) side street; **über die G. verkaufen** sell takeouts
Gas'sendirne *f* streetwalker
Gas'senhauer *m* popular song
Gas'senjunge *m* urchin

Gast [gast] *m* (-[e]s;ᵘe) guest; boarder; (com) customer; (theat) guest performer; **zu Gast bitten** invite

Gästebuch ['gɛstəbux] *n* guest book; visitors' book

Gast'freund *m* guest

gast'freundlich *adj* hospitable

Gast'freundschaft *f* hospitality

Gast'geber *m* host

Gast'geberin *f* hostess

Gast'haus *n*, **Gast'hof** *m* inn

Gast'hörer –in §6 *mf* (educ) auditor

gastieren [gas'tirən] *intr* (telv, theat) appear as a guest

gast'lich *adj* hospitable

Gast'mahl *n* feast; banquet

Gast'professor *m* visiting professor

Gast'rolle *f* guest performance; **e-e G. geben** pay a flying visit

Gast'spiel *n* (theat) guest performance

Gast'stätte *f* restaurant

Gast'stube *f* dining room

Gast'wirt *m* innkeeper

Gast'wirtschaft *f* restaurant

Gas'uhr *f* gas meter

Gas'werk *n* gas works

Gas'zähler *m* gas meter

Gatte ['gatə] *m* (-n;-n) husband; **Gatten** married couple

Gatter ['gatər] *n* (-s;-) grating; latticework; iron gate

Gattin ['gatın] *f* (-;-nen) wife

Gattung ['gatuŋ] *f* (-;-en) kind, type, species; family; (biol) genus

Gat'tungsname *m* generic name; (gram) common noun

Gau [gau] *m* (-[e]s;-e) district

Gaukelbild ['gaukəlbɪlt] *n* illusion

gaukeln ['gaukəln] *intr* flit, flutter; perform hocus-pocus

Gau'kelspiel *n*, **Gau'kelwerk** *n* sleight of hand; delusion

Gaul [gaul] *m* (-[e]s;ᵘe) horse; nag

Gaumen ['gaumən] *m* (-s;-) palate

Gauner ['gaunər] *m* (-s;-) rogue; swindler

Gaunerei [gaunə'raɪ] *f* (-;-en) swindling, cheating

gaunern ['gaunərn] *intr* swindle

Gau'nersprache *f* thieves' slang

Gaze ['gazə] *f* (-;-n) gauze; cheesecloth

Gazelle [ga'tsɛlə] *f* (-;-n) gazelle

Geächtete [gə'ɛçtətə] §5 *mf* outlaw

Geächze [gə'ɛçtsə] *n* (-s;) moaning

geartet [gə'artət] *adj*—**anders g. sein** be of a different disposition

Gebäck [gə'bɛk] *n* (-s;) baked goods, cookies

geballt [gə'balt] *adj* concentrated; dense; (Schnee) hardened; (Faust) clenched; (Stil) succinct

gebannt [gə'bant] *adj* spellbound

gebar [gə'bar] *pret* of **gebären**

Gebärde [gə'bɛrdə] *f* (-;-n) gesture

gebärden [gə'bɛrdən] *ref* behave

Gebär'denspiel *n* gesticulation

gebaren [gə'barən] *ref* behave, act || **Gebaren** *n* (-s;) behavior

gebären [gə'bɛrən] §79 *tr* bear || **Gebären** *n* (-s;) childbirth; labor

Gebär'mutter *f* (anat) uterus

Gebär'mutterkappe *f* diaphragm

Gebäude [gə'bɔɪdə] *n* (-s;-) building

gebefreudig ['gebəfrɔɪdɪç] *adj* open-handed

Gebein [gə'baɪn] *n* (-[e]s;-e) bones; **Gebeine** bones; mortal remains

Gebell [gə'bɛl] *n* (-[e]s;), **Gebelle** [gə'bɛlə] *n* (-s;) barking

geben ['gebən] §80 *tr* give; yield; (Gelegenheit) afford; (Laut) utter; (Karten) deal; **Feuer g.** give (s.o.) a light; (mil) open fire; **viel g. auf** (acc) set great store by; **von sich g.** utter; throw up; (Rede) deliver; (chem) give off || *ref* give; (Kopfweh, usw.) get better; **sich g. als** pretend to be; **sich gefangen g.** surrender || *impers*—**es gibt there is, there are; es wird Regen geben** it's going to rain

Ge'ber –in §6 *mf* giver, donor

Gebet [gə'bet] *n* (-[e]s;-e) prayer

gebeten [gə'betən] *pp* of **bitten**

Gebiet [gə'bit] *n* (-[e]s;-e) district, territory; (Fläche) area; (Fach) line; (Bereich) field, sphere

gebieten [gə'bitən] §58 *tr* (Stillschweigen) impose; (Ehrfurcht) command; (verlangen) demand; **j–m g., etw zu tun** order s.o. to do s.th. || *intr* (über acc) have control (over); (dat) control

Gebieter [gə'bitər] *m* (-s;-) master; ruler; commander; governor

Gebieterin [gə'bitərin] *f* (-;-nen) mistress; (des Hauses) lady

gebieterisch [gə'bitərɪʃ] *adj* imperious

Gebilde [gə'bɪldə] *n* (-s;-) shape, form; structure; (geol) formation

gebildet [gə'bɪldət] *adj* educated

Gebirge [gə'bɪrgə] *n* (-s;-) mountain range, mountains; **festes G.** bedrock

gebirgig [gə'bɪrgɪç] *adj* mountainous

Gebirgs– [gəbɪrks] *comb.fm.* mountain

Gebirgs'bewohner –in §6 *mf* mountaineer

Gebirgs'kamm *m*, **Gebirgs'rücken** *m* mountain ridge

Gebirgs'zug *m* mountain range

Ge·biß [gə'bɪs] *n* (-bisses;-bisse) teeth; false teeth; (am Zaum) bit

gebissen [gə'bɪsən] *pp* of **beißen**

Gebläse [gə'blezə] *n* (-s;-) bellows; blower; (aut) supercharger

geblieben [gə'blibən] *pp* of **bleiben**

Geblök [gə'blók] *n* (-[e]s;) bleating

geblümt [gə'blymt] *adj* flowered

Geblüt [gə'blyt] *n* (-[e]s;) (& fig) blood

geboren [gə'borən] *pp* of **gebären** || *adj* born; native; **geborene nee**

geborgen [gə'bɔrgən] *pp* of **bergen** || *adj* safe

Gebor'genheit *f* (-;) safety, security

geborsten [gə'bɔrstən] *pp* of **bersten**

Gebot [gə'bot] *n* (-[e]s;-e) order, command; commandment; (Angebot) bid

geboten [gə'botən] *pp* of **bieten** || *adj* requisite; **dringend g.** imperative

Gebr. *abbr.* (**Gebrüder**) Brothers

gebracht [gə'braxt] *pp* of **bringen**

gebrannt [gə'brant] *pp* of **brennen**

Gebräu [gə'brɔɪ] *n* (-[e]s;-e) brew
Gebrauch [gə'braux] *m* (-s;-̈e) use; usage; (*Sitte*) custom
gebrauchen [gə'brauxən] *tr* use, employ
gebräuchlich [gə'brɔɪçlɪç] *adj* usual; in use; (*gemein*) common
Gebrauchs'anweisung *f* directions
gebrauchs'fertig *adj* ready for use; (*Kaffee, usw.*) instant
Gebrauchs'graphik *f* commercial art
Gebrauchs'gut *n* commodity
Gebrauchs'muster *n* registered pattern
gebraucht [gə'brauxt] *adj* second-hand
Gebraucht'wagen *m* used car
Gebrechen [gə'breçən] *n* (-s;-) physical disability, infirmity
gebrech'lich *adj* frail, weak; rickety
gebrochen [gə'brɔxən] *pp* of **brechen**
Gebrüder [gə'brydər] *pl* brothers
Gebrüll [gə'bryl] *n* (-[e]s;) roaring; bellowing; lowing
Gebühr [gə'byr] *f* (-;-en) charge, fee; due, what is due; **nach G.** deservedly; **über G.** excessively; **zu ermäßigter G.** at a reduced rate
gebühren [gə'byrən] *intr* (*dat*) be due to || *impers ref*—**es gebührt sich** it is proper
gebüh'rend *adj* due; (*entsprechend*) appropriate || *adv* duly
gebüh'renfrei *adj* free of charge
gebüh'renpflichtig *adj* chargeable
gebunden [gə'bundən] *pp* of **binden** || *adj* bound; (*Hitze*) latent; (*Preise*) controlled; (*Kapital*) tied-up; **g. an** (*acc*) (chem) combined with; **gebundene Rede** verse
Geburt [gə'burt] *f* (-;-en) birth
Gebur'tenbeschränkung *f* birth control
Gebur'tenregelung *f* birth control
Gebur'tenrückgang *m* decline in births
gebürtig [gə'byrtɪç] *adj* native
Geburts'anzeige *f* announcement of birth; registration of birth
Geburts'fehler *n* congenital defect
Geburts'helfer **-in** §6 *mf* obstetrician || *f* midwife
Geburts'hilfe *f* obstetrics
Geburts'mal *n* birth mark
Geburts'recht *n* birthright
Geburts'schein *m* birth certificate
Geburts'tag *m* birthday
Geburts'tagskind *n* person celebrating his or her birthday
Geburts'wehen *pl* labor pains
Geburts'zange *f* forceps
Gebüsch [gə'byʃ] *n* (-es;-e) thicket, underbrush; clump of bushes
Geck [gek] *m* (-en;-en) dude
geckenhaft [gek'kenhaft] *adj* flashy
gedacht [gə'daxt] *pp* of **denken**
Gedächtnis [gə'dɛçtnɪs] *n* (-ses;) memory; **aus dem G.** by heart; **im G. behalten** bear in mind; **zum G.** (*genit* or **an** *acc*) in memory of
Gedächt'nisfehler *m* lapse of memory
Gedächt'nisrede *f* memorial address
gedämpft [gə'dempft] *adj* muffled; hushed, quiet; (*Licht, Stimme*) subdued; (culin) stewed
Gedanke [gə'daŋkə] *m* (-ns;-n) thought; notion, idea; **etw in Ge-**

danken tun do s.th. absent-mindedly; **in Gedanken sein** be preoccupied; **sich** [*dat*] **Gedanken machen über** (*acc*) worry about
Gedan'kenblitz *m* (iron) brain wave
Gedan'kenfolge *f*, **Gedan'kengang** *m* train of thought
gedan'kenlos *adj* thoughtless; absent-minded; irresponsible
Gedan'kenpunkt *m* suspension point
Gedan'kenstrich *m* (typ) dash
Gedan'kenübertragung *f* telepathy
gedank'lich *adj* mental; intellectual
Gedärme [gə'dermə] *pl* intestines
Gedeck [gə'dɛk] *n* (-[e]s;-e) cover; table setting; menu
gedeihen [gə'daɪ.ən] §81 *intr* (SEIN) thrive; succeed || **Gedeihen** *n* (-s;) prosperity; success
Gedenk- [gədeŋk] *comb.fm.* memorial; commemorative
gedenken [gə'deŋkən] §66 *intr* (*genit*) think of, be mindful of; remember; mention; **g. zu** (*inf*) intend to (*inf*) || **Gedenken** *n* (-s;) memory
gedeucht [gə'dɔɪçt] *pp* of **dünken**
Gedicht [gə'dɪçt] *n* (-[e]s;-e) poem; (fig) dream
gediegen [gə'digən] *adj* (*Gold*) solid; (*Silber*) sterling; (*Arbeit*) excellent; (*Kenntnisse*) thorough; (*Möbel*) solidly made; (*Charakter*) sterling; (coll) very funny
gedieh [gə'di] *pret* of **gedeihen**
gediehen [gə'di.ən] *pp* of **gedeihen**
Gedränge [gə'drɛŋə] *n* (-s;-) pushing; crowd; difficulties; (fb) scrimmage
gedrängt [gə'drɛŋt] *adj* crowded, packed; (*Sprache*) concise
gedroschen [gə'drɔʃən] *pp* of **dreschen**
gedrückt [gə'drykt] *adj* depressed
gedrungen [gə'druŋən] *pp* of **dringen** || *adj* compact; stocky; squat; (*Sprache*) concise
Geduld [gə'dult] *f* (-;) patience
gedulden [gə'duldən] *ref* wait (patiently)
geduldig [gə'duldɪç] *adj* patient
Geduld'spiel *n* puzzle
gedungen [gə'duŋən] *pp* of **dingen**
gedunsen [gə'dunzən] *adj* bloated
gedurft [gə'durft] *pp* of **dürfen**
geehrt [gə'ert] *adj*—**Sehr geehrte Herren!** Dear Sirs; **Sehr geehrter Herr X!** Dear Mr. X
geeignet [gə'aɪgnət] *adj* suitable, right; qualified; appropriate
Gefahr [gə'far] *f* (-;-en) danger; (*Wagnis*) risk; **G. laufen zu** (*inf*) run the risk of (*ger*)
gefährden [gə'ferdən] *tr* jeopardize
gefährlich [gə'ferlɪç] *adj* dangerous
gefahr'los *adj* safe
Gefährt [gə'fert] *n* (-[e]s;-e) carriage
Gefährte [gə'fertə] *m* (-n;-n), **Gefährtin** [gə'fertɪn] *f* (-;-nen) companion; spouse
Gefälle [gə'felə] *n* (-s;-) pitch; slope
gefallen [gə'falən] *adj* fallen; (mil) killed in action || §72 *ref*—**sich g. in** (*dat*) take pleasure in || *intr* please; **das gefällt mir** I like this; **das lasse ich mir nicht g.** I won't stand for

this || **Gefallen** *m* (-;-) favor || *n* (-s;) (an *dat*) pleasure (in); **j-m etw zu G. tun** do s.th. to please s.o.; **nach G.** as one pleases; at one's descretion

gefällig [gə'fɛlɪç] *adj* pleasing; obliging; kind; **j-m g. sein** do s.o. a favor; **Kaffee g.?** would you care for coffee?; **was ist g.?** what can I do for you?; **würden Sie so g. sein zu** (*inf*)? would you be so kind as to (*inf*)?

Gefäl'ligkeit *f* (-;-en) favor

gefälligst [gə'fɛlɪçst] *adv* if you please; please

gefangen [gə'faŋən] *pp* of **fangen** || *adj* captive; **g. nehmen** take prisoner || **Gefangene** §5 *mf* captive, prisoner

Gefan'genenlager *n* prison camp; (mil) prisoner-of-war camp

Gefan'gennahme *f* (-;) capture; arrest

gefan'gennehmen §116 *tr* take prisoner

Gefan'genschaft *f* (-;) captivity; imprisonment; **in G. geraten** be taken prisoner

gefan'gensetzen *tr* imprison

Gefängnis [gə'fɛŋnɪs] *n* (-ses;-se) prison, jail; imprisonment

Gefäng'nisdirektor *m* warden

Gefäng'nisstrafe *f* prison term

Gefäng'niswärter –in §6 *mf* guard

Gefäß [gə'fɛs] *n* (-es;-e) vessel; jar

gefaßt [gə'fast] *adj* calm, composed; **g. auf** (*acc*) ready for

Gefecht [gə'fɛçt] *n* (-[e]s;-e) fight, battle, action

Gefechts'auftrag *m* (mil) objective

Gefechts'kopf *m* warhead

Gefechts'lage *f* tactical situation

Gefechts'stand *m* command post

gefeit [gə'faɪt] *adj* (**gegen**) immune (from), proof (against)

Gefieder [gə'fidər] *n* (-s;-) plumage

gefleckt [gə'flɛkt] *adj* spotted

geflissentlich [gə'flɪsəntlɪç] *adj* intentional, willful

geflochten [gə'flɔxtən] *pp* of **flechten**

geflogen [gə'flogən] *pp* of **fliegen**

geflohen [gə'flo·ən] *pp* of **fliehen**

geflossen [gə'flɔsən] *pp* of **fließen**

Geflügel [gə'flygəl] *n* (-s;) fowl; (*Federvieh*) poultry

Geflü'gelmagen *m* gizzard

Geflunker [gə'fluŋkər] *m* (-s;) (coll) fibbing

Geflüster [gə'flystər] *n* (-s;) whisper

Gefolge [gə'fɔlgə] *n* (-s;-) retinue; **in seinem G.** in its wake

Gefolgschaft [gə'fɔlkʃaft] *f* (-;-en) allegiance; followers

gefräßig [gə'frɛsɪç] *adj* gluttonous

Gefrä'ßigkeit *f* (-;) gluttony

Gefreite [gə'fraɪtə] §5 *m* private first class; lance corporal (Brit)

gefressen [gə'frɛsən] *pp* of **fressen**

Gefrieranlage [gə'friranlagə] *f* **Gefrierapparat** [gə'friraparat] *m* freezer

gefrieren [gə'frirən] §77 *intr* (SEIN) freeze

Gefrie'rer *m* (-s;-) freezer; deepfreeze

Gefrier'fach *n* freezing compartment

Gefrier'punkt *m* freezing point

Gefrier'schutz *m*, **Gefrier'schutzmittel** *n* antifreeze

gefroren [gə'frorən] *pp* of **frieren** || **Gefrorene** §5 *n* ice cream

Gefüge [gə'fygə] *n* (-s;-) structure, make-up; arrangement; texture

gefügig [gə'fygɪç] *adj* pliant, pliable

Gefühl [gə'fyl] *n* (-[e]s;-e) feeling; feel; touch; sense; sensation

gefühl'los *adj* numb; callous

gefühls-, Gefühls- [gəfyls] *comb.fm.* of the emotions; emotional; sentimental; (anat) sensory

gefühls'betont *adj* emotional

Gefühlsduselei [gə'fylsduzəlaɪ] *f* (-;) sentimentalism, mawkishness

gefühls'selig *adj* mawkish

gefühl'voll *adj* sensitive; tender-hearted || *adv* with feeling

gefunden [gə'fundən] *pp* of **finden**

gefurcht [gə'furçt] *adj* furrowed

gegangen [gə'gaŋən] *pp* of **gehen**

gegeben [gə'gebən] *pp* of **geben** || *adj* given; (*Umstände*) existing; **gegebene Methode** best approach; **zu gegebener Zeit** at the proper time

gege'benfalls *adv* if necessary

gegen ['gegən] *prep* (*acc*) towards; against; about, approximately; compared with; contrary to; in exchange for

gegen-, Gegen- *comb.fm.* anti–; counter–; contrary; opposite; back; in return

Ge'genantwort *f* rejoinder

Ge'genbeschuldigung *f* countercharge

Ge'genbild *n* counterpart

Gegend ['gegənt] *f* (-;-en) neighborhood, vicinity; region, district

gegeneinan'der *adv* against one another; towards one another

Ge'gengerade *f* back stretch

Ge'gengewicht *n* counterbalance; (am Rad) (aut) weight; **das G. halten** (*dat*) counterbalance

Ge'gengift *n* antidote

Ge'genkandidat –in §7 *mf* rival candidate

Ge'genklage *f* countercharge; counterclaim

Ge'genmittel *n* (**gegen**) remedy (for), antidote (against)

Ge'genrede *f* reply, rejoinder

Ge'gensatz *m* contrast; opposite, antithesis; (*Widerspruch*) opposition

gegensätzlich ['gegənzetslɪç] *adj* contrary, opposite, antithetical

Ge'genschlag *m* counterplot

ge'genseitig *adj* mutual, reciprocal

Ge'genstand *m* object, thing; subject

gegenständlich ['gegən/tɛntlɪç] *adj* objective; (fa) representational; (log) concrete

ge'genstandslos *adj* baseless; without purpose; irrelevant; (fa) non-representational

Ge'genstoß *m* (box) counterpunch; (mil) counterthrust

Ge'genstück *n* counterpart

Ge'genteil *n* contrary, opposite; **im G.** on the contrary

ge'genteilig *adj* contrary, opposite

gegenü'ber *prep* (*dat*) opposite to; across from; with regard to; compared with

gegenü'berstellen *tr* (*dat*) place opposite to; (*dat*) confront with; (*dat*) contrast with
Gegenü'berstellung *f* confrontation; comparison; (*auf e-r Wache*) line-up
Gegenwart ['gegənvart] *f* (–;) present; present time; (gram) present tense
gegenwärtig ['gegənvertıç] *adj* present, current || *adv* at present; nowadays
Ge'genwehr *f* defense, resistance
Ge'genwind *m* head wind
Ge'genwirkung *f* (**auf** *acc*) reaction (to)
ge'genzeichnen *tr* countersign
Ge'genzug *m* countermove
geglichen [gə'glıçən] *pp* of **gleichen**
geglitten [gə'glıtən] *pp* of **gleiten**
Gegner –in ['gegnər(ın)] §6 *mf* opponent, rival || *m* (mil) enemy
gegnerisch ['gegnərıʃ] *adj* adverse; antagonistic; opposing; (mil) enemy
gegolten [gə'gɔltən] *pp* of **gelten**
gegoren [gə'gorən] *pp* of **gären**
gegossen [gə'gɔsən] *pp* of **gießen**
gegriffen [gə'grıfən] *pp* of **greifen**
Gehabe [gə'habə] *n* (–s;) affectation
gehaben [gə'habən] *ref* fare; **gehab dich nicht so!** stop putting on!; **gehab dich wohl!** farewell!
Gehackte [gə'haktə] §5 *n* hamburger
Gehalt [gə'halt] *m* (–[e]s;–e) contents; capacity; standard; **G. an** (*dat*) percentage of || *n* (–[e]s;–er) salary
Gehalts'stufe *f* salary bracket
Gehalts'zulage *f* increment, raise
gehalt'voll *adj* substantial; profound
Gehänge [gə'heŋə] *n* (–s;–) slope; pendant; festoon; (*e-s Degens*) belt
gehangen [gə'haŋən] *pp* of **hängen**
gehässig [gə'hesıç] *adj* spiteful, nasty
Gehäuse [gə'hɔızə] *n* (–s;–) case, box; housing; (*e-r Schnecke*) shell; (*e-s Apfels*) core
Gehege [gə'hegə] *n* (–s;) enclosure
geheim [gə'haım] *adj* secret; **streng g.** top-secret
geheim'halten §90 *tr* keep secret
Geheimnis [gə'haımnıs] *n* (–ses;–se) secret, mystery
geheim'nisvoll *adj* mysterious
Geheim'schrift *f* code; coded message
Geheim'tinte *f* invisible ink
Geheim'vorbehalt *m* mental reservation
Geheiß [gə'haıs] *n* (–es;) bidding
gehen ['ge·ən] §82 *intr* (SEIN) go; walk; leave; (*Teig*) rise; (*Maschine*) work; (*Uhr*) go; (*Ware*) sell; (*Wind*) blow; **das geht nicht** that will not do; **das geht schon** it will be all right; **sich g. lassen** take it easy; **wieviel Zoll g. auf einen Fuß?** how many inches make a foot? || *impers*—**es geht mir gut** I am doing well; **es geht nichts über** (*acc*) there is nothing like; **es geht um...** is at stake; **wie geht es Ihnen?** how are you?
geheuer [gə'hɔı·ər] *adj*—**mir war nicht recht g. zumute** I didn't feel quite at ease; **nicht g.** spooky; suspicious; risky
Geheul [gə'hɔıl] *n* (–s;) howling; loud sobbing

Gehilfe [gə'hılfə] *m* (–n;–n), **Gehilfin** [gə'hılfın] *f* (–;–nen) assistant
Gehirn [gə'hırn] *n* (–[e]s;–e) brains, mind; (anat) brain; **sein G. anstrengen** rack one's brain
Gehirn– *comb.fm.* brain; cerebral
Gehirn'erschütterung *f* concussion
Gehirn'schlag *m* (pathol) stroke
Gehirn'wäsche *f* brainwashing
gehoben [gə'hobən] *pp* of **heben** || *adj* (*Stellung*) high; (*Stil*) lofty; **gehobene Stimmung** high spirits
Gehöft [gə'høft] *n* (–[e]s;–e) farm
geholfen [gə'hɔlfən] *pp* of **helfen**
Gehölz [gə'hœlts] *n* (–es;–e) grove; thicket
Gehör [gə'hør] *n* (–s;) hearing; ear
Gehör– *comb.fm.* of hearing; auditory
gehorchen [gə'hɔrçən] *intr* (*dat*) obey
gehören [gə'hørən] *ref* be proper, be right || *intr* (*dat* or **zu**) belong to; (**in** *acc*) go into, belong in
gehörig [gə'hørıç] *adj* proper, due; (*dat* or **zu**) belonging to || *adv* properly; duly; thoroughly
Gehörn [gə'hørn] *n* (–s;–e) horns; **Gehörne** sets of horns
gehorsam [gə'horzam] *adj* obedient || *adv* obediently; **gehorsamst** respectfully || **Gehorsam** *m* (–s;) obedience
Gehor'samverweigerung *f* disobedience
gehren ['gerən] *tr* (carp) miter
Gehrlade ['gerladə] *f* (–;–n) miter box
Gehrock ['gerɔk] *m* Prince Albert
Geh'rung *f*—**auf G., nach der G. on** the slant; **auf G. verbinden** miter
Geh'rungslade *f* (–;–n) miter box
Gehsteig ['geʃtaık] *m* sidewalk
Gehweg ['gewek] *m* sidewalk; footpath
Gehwerk ['geverk] *n* clockwork, works
Geier ['gaı·ər] *m* (–s;–) vulture; **zum Geier!** what the devil!
Geifer ['gaıfər] *m* (–s;) drivel; froth, slaver, foam; (fig) venom
geifern ['gaıfərn] *intr* slaver
Geige ['gaıgə] *f* (–;–n) violin, fiddle
geigen ['gaıgən] *intr* play the violin
Gei'genbogen *m* bow, fiddlestick
Gei'genharz *n* rosin
Gei'ger –in §6 *mf* violinist
geil [gaıl] *adj* lustful; in heat; (*Boden*) rich; (*üppig*) luxuriant
Geisel ['gaızəl] *f* (–;–n) hostage
Geiser ['gaızər] *m* (–s;–) geyser
Geiß [gaıs] *f* (–;–en) she-goat
Geißel ['gaısəl] *f* (–;–n) scourge
geißeln ['gaısəln] *tr* scourge; (fig) castigate
Geist [gaıst] *m* (–es;–er) spirit; (*Gespenst*) ghost; (*Verstand*) mind, intellect; **im Geiste** in one's imagination; in spirit
Gei'sterbeschwörung *f* (–;) necromancy
Gei'sterstadt *f* ghost town
Gei'sterstunde *f* witching hour
geistes– [gaıstəs] *comb.fm.* spiritually; mentally, intellectually || **Geistes–** *comb.fm.* spiritual; mental, intellectual
gei'stesabwesend *adj* absent-minded
Gei'stesanlagen *pl* natural gift
Gei'stesarbeit *f* brainwork
Gei'stesarmut *f* dullness, stupidity

Gei'stesblitz *m* brain wave; aphorism
Gei'stesflug *m* flight of the imagination
Gei'stesfreiheit *f* intellectual freedom
Gei'stesfrucht *f* brainchild
Gei'stesgegenwart *f* presence of mind
gei'stesgegenwärtig *adj* mentally alert
geistesgestört ['gaɪstəsgəʃtørt] *adj* mentally disturbed
Gei'steshaltung *f* mentality
gei'steskrank *adj* insane
gei'stesschwach *adj* feeble-minded
Gei'stesstörung *f* mental disorder
Gei'stes- und Natur'wissenschaften *pl* arts and sciences
Gei'stesverfassung *f* frame of mind
gei'stesverwandt *adj* (mit) spiritually akin (to); (mit) congenial (with)
Gei'stesverwirrung *f* derangement
Gei'steswissenschaften *pl* humanities
gei'steswissenschaftlich *adj* humanistic
Gei'steszustand *m* state of mind
geistig ['gaɪstɪç] *adj* mental, intellectual; spiritual
geist'lich *adj* spiritual; (*Orden*) religious; (*kirchlich*) sacred, ecclesiastical; der geistliche Stand holy orders; the clergy ‖ Geistliche §5 *m* clergyman
Geist'lichkeit *f* (-;) clergy
geist'los *adj* spiritless; dull; stupid
geist'reich *adj* witty; ingenious
Geiz [gaɪts] *m* (-es;) stinginess; avarice
geizen ['gaɪtsən] *intr*—g. mit be sparing with; nicht g. mit show freely
Geiz'hals *m* (coll) tightwad
geizig ['gaɪtsɪç] *adj* stingy, miserly
Geiz'kragen *m* (coll) tightwad
Gejammer [gə'jamər] *n* (-s;) wailing
gekannt [gə'kant] *pp* of kennen
Geklapper [gə'klapər] *n* (-s;) rattling
Geklatsche [gə'klatʃə] *n* (-s;) clapping; gossiping
Geklirr [gə'klɪr] *n* (-[e]s;) rattling
geklommen [gə'kləmən] *pp* of klimmen
geklungen [gə'kluŋən] *pp* of klingen
gekniffen [gə'knɪfən] *pp* of kneifen
gekonnt [gə'kənt] *pp* of können
Gekreisch [gə'kraɪʃ] *n* (-es;) screaming; screeching
Gekritzel [gə'krɪtsəl] *n* (-s;) scribbling
gekrochen [gə'krəxən] *pp* of kriechen
Gekröse [gə'krøzə] *n* (-s;) tripe
gekünstelt [gə'kynstəlt] *adj* affected
Gelächter [gə'lɛçtər] *n* (-s;) laughter
Gelage [gə'lɑgə] *n* (-s;) carousing
Gelände [gə'lɛndə] *n* (-s;-) terrain; site, lot; (educ) campus; (golf) fairway
Gelän'delauf *m* crosscountry running
Gelän'depunkt *m* landmark
Geländer [gə'lɛndər] *n* (-s;-) railing; guardrail; banister; parapet
gelang [gə'laŋ] *pret* of gelingen
gelangen [gə'laŋən] *intr* (SEIN) (an *acc*, in *acc*, zu) attain, reach
gelassen [gə'lasən] *pp* of lassen ‖ *adj* composed, calm
Gelatine [ʒɛla'tinə] *f* (-;) gelatin
geläufig [gə'ləɪfɪç] *adj* fluent; (*gemein*) common; (*Zunge*) glib

gelaunt [gə'launt] *adj*—gut gelaunt in good humor; zu etw g. sein be in the mood for s.th.
Geläut [gə'ləɪt] *n* (-es;), Geläute [gə-'ləɪtə] *n* (-s;) ringing; chimes
gelb [gɛlp] *adj* yellow ‖ Gelb *n* (-s;. yellow
gelb'lich *adj* yellowish
Gelb'sucht *f* jaundice
Geld [gɛlt] *n* (-[e]s;) money; bares G. cash
Geld– *comb.fm.* money, financial
-geld *n comb.fm.* money; fee(s); tax, toll; allowance
Geld'anlage *f* investment
Geld'anleihe *f* loan
Geld'anweisung *f* money order; draft
Geld'ausgabe *f* expense; expenditure
Geld'beutel *m* pocketbook
Geld'bewilligung *f* (parl) appropriation
Geld'buße *f* fine
Geld'einlage *f* deposit
Geld'einwurf *m* coin slot
Geld'entwertung *f* inflation
Geld'erwerb *m* moneymaking
Geld'geber *m* investor; mortgagee
Geld'gier *f* avarice
Geld'mittel *pl* funds, resources
Geld'onkel *m* sugar daddy
Geld'schein *m* bank note, bill
Geld'schrank *m* safe
Geld'schublade *f* till (*of cash register*)
Geld'sendung *f* remittance
Geld'sorte *f* (fin) denomination
Geld'spende *f* contribution, donation
Geld'strafe *f* fine
Geld'stück *n* coin
Geld'überhang *m* surplus (of money)
Geld'währung *f* currency; monetary standard
Geld'wechsel *m* money exchange
Geld'wesen *n* financial system, finance
Gelee [ʒɛ'le] *m & n* (-s;-s) jelly
gelegen [gə'legən] *pp* of liegen ‖ *adj* located; convenient; opportune; du kommst mir gerade g. you're just the person I wanted to see; es kommt mir gerade gelegen that suits me just fine; mir ist daran g. zu (*inf*) I'm anxious to (*inf*); was ist daran g.? what of it?
Gele'genheit *f* (-;-en) occasion; opportunity, chance; (com) bargain
Gelegenheits– *comb.fm.* occasional
Gele'genheitsarbeit *f* odd job
Gele'genheitskauf *m* good bargain
gele'gentlich *adj* occasional; casual; chance ‖ *adv* occasionally ‖ *prep* (*genit*) on the occasion of
gelehrig [gə'leriç] *adj* teachable; intelligent
gelehrsam [gə'lerzam] *adj* erudite
gelehrt [gə'lert] *adj* learned, erudite ‖ Gelehrte §5 *mf* scholar
Geleise [gə'laɪzə] *n* (-s;-) rut; (rr) track; totes G. blind alley, deadlock
Geleit [gə'laɪt] *n* (-[e]s;) escort; freies (or sicheres) G. safe-conduct; j-m das G. geben escort s.o., accompany s.o.; zum G. forward
geleiten [gə'laɪtən] *tr* escort, accompany; j-n zur Tür g. see s.o. to the door

Geleit'zug *m* convoy
Geleit'zugsicherung *f* convoy escort
Gelenk [gə'lɛŋk] *n* (-[e]s;-e) joint
Gelenk'entzündung *f* arthritis
gelenkig [gə'lɛŋkɪç] *adj* jointed; flexible; agile
gelernt [gə'lɛrnt] *adj* skilled
Gelichter [gə'lɪçtər] *n* (-s;) riffraff
Geliebte [gə'liptə] §6 *mf* beloved, sweetheart
geliehen [gə'li·ən] *pp* of **leihen**
gelieren [ʒɛ'lirən] *intr* jell, gel
gelinde [gə'lɪndə] *adj* soft; gentle, mild || *adv* gently, mildly; **g. gesagt** to put it mildly
gelingen [gə'lɪŋən] §142 *intr* (SEIN) succeed || *impers* (SEIN)—**es gelingt mir** I succeed || **Gelingen** *n* (-s;) success
gelitten [gə'lɪtən] *pp* of **leiden**
gell [gɛl] *adj* shrill || *interj* say!
gellen ['gɛlən] *intr* ring out; yell
gel'lend *adj* shrill, piercing
geloben [gə'lobən] *tr* solemnly promise, vow; take the vow of || *ref—* **sich** [*dat*] **g.** vow to oneself
gelogen [gə'logən] *pp* of **lügen**
gelt [gɛlt] *interj* say!
gelten ['gɛltən] §83 *tr* be worth; **wenig g.** mean little || *intr* be valid; (*Münze*) be legal tender; (*Gesetz*) be in force; (*Grund*) hold true; (*Regel*) apply; (*Mittel*) be allowable; (*beim Spiel*) count; **g. als** or **für** have the force of; **g.** ranked as; pass for, be considered; **g. lassen** acknowledge as correct; **j–m g.** be aimed at s.o. || *impers—***es gilt** (*acc*) be at stake; be a matter of; be worth (*s.th.*); **es gilt mir gleich, ob** it's all the same to me whether; **es gilt zu** (*inf*) it is necessary to (*inf*); **jetzt gilt's!** here goes!
Gel'tung *f* (-;) validity; value, importance; **zur G. bringen** make the most of; **zur G. kommen** show off well
Gel'tungsbedürfnis *n* need for recognition
Gelübde [gə'lʏpdə] *n* (-s;-) vow
gelungen [gə'luŋən] *pp* of **gelingen** || *adj* successful; (*Wendung*) wellturned; funny
Gelüst [gə'lʏst] *n* (-[e]s;-e) desire
gelüsten [gə'lʏstən] *impers—***es gelüstet mich nach** I could go for
gemach [gə'max] *adv* slowly, by degrees || **Gemach** *n* (-[e]s;⸚er) room; apartment; chamber
gemächlich [gə'mɛçlɪç] *adj* leisurely; comfortable
Gemahl [gə'mal] *m* (-[e]s;-e) husband
Gemahlin [gə'malɪn] *f* (-;-nen) wife
Gemälde [gə'mɛldə] *n* (-s;-) painting
gemäß [gə'mes] *prep* (*dat*) according to
gemäßigt [gə'mesɪçt] *adj* moderate
gemein [gə'maɪn] *adj* common; mean; vile; **sich g. machen mit** associate with || **Gemeine** §5 *m* (mil) private
Gemeinde [gə'maɪndə] *f* (-;-n) community; municipality; (eccl) parish
Gemein'deabgaben *pl* local taxes
Gemein'deanleihen *pl* municipal bonds

Gemein'dehaus *n* town hall
gemein'frei *adj* in the public domain
gemein'gefährlich *adj* constituting a public danger, dangerous
gemein'gültig *adj* generally accepted
Gemein'heit *f* (-;-en) meanness; dirty trick; vulgarity
gemein'hin *adv* commonly, usually
Gemein'kosten *pl* overhead
Gemein'nutz *m* public interest
gemein'nützig *adj* non-profit
Gemein'platz *m* platitude
gemeinsam [gə'maɪnzam] *adj* common, joint; mutual
Gemein'schaft *f* (-;-en) community; close association
gemein'schaftlich *adj* common, joint; mutual
Gemein'schaftsanschluß *m* (telp) party line
Gemein'schaftsarbeit *f* teamwork
Gemein'schaftsgeist *m* esprit de corps
Gemein'sinn *m* public spirit
gemein'verständlich *adj* popular; **g. darstellen** popularize
Gemein'wesen *n* community
Gemein'wohl *n* commonweal
Gemenge [gə'mɛŋə] *n* (-s;-) mixture; (*Kampfgewühl*) scuffle, melee
gemessen [gə'mɛsən] *pp* of **messen** || *adj* deliberate; precise; dignified; **g. an** (*dat*) compared with
Gemetzel [gə'mɛtsəl] *n* (-s;-) massacre
gemieden [gə'midən] *pp* of **meiden**
Gemisch [gə'mɪʃ] *n* (-es;-e) mixture
Gemischt'warenhandlung *f* general store
Gemme ['gɛmə] *f* (-;-n) gem
gemocht [gə'maxt] *pp* of **mögen**
gemolken [gə'malkən] *pp* of **melken**
Gemse ['gɛmzə] *f* (-;-n) chamois
Gemunkel [gə'muŋkəl] *n* (-s;-) gossip, whispering
Gemurmel [gə'murməl] *n* (-s;) murmur
Gemüse [gə'myzə] *n* (-s;-) vegetable; vegetables
Gemü'sebau *m* (-[e]s;) vegetable gardening
Gemü'sekonserven *pl* canned vegetables
gemüßigt [gə'mysɪçt] *adj—***sich g. fühlen** feel compelled
gemußt [gə'must] *pp* of **müssen**
Gemüt [gə'myt] *n* (-[e]s;-er) mind; disposition; person, soul; warmth of feeling; **j–m etw zu Gemüte führen** bring s.th. home to s.o.
gemütlich [gə'mytlɪç] *adj* goodnatured, easy-going; (*Wohnung*) cosy
Gemüt'lichkeit *f* (-;) easy-going nature; cosiness
Gemüts'art *f* disposition, nature
Gemüts'bewegung *f* emotion
gemüts'krank *adj* melancholy
Gemüts'mensch *m* warm-hearted person
Gemüts'ruhe *f—***in** (**aller**) **G.** in peace and quiet
Gemüts'stimmung *f* mood
Gemüts'verfassung *f* state of mind
Gemüts'zustand *m* frame of mind

gemüt′voll *adj* emotional
gen [gɛn] *prep* (*acc*) (poet) towards ‖ **Gen** [gɛn] *n* (-s;-e) (biol) gene
genannt [gə'nant] *pp* of **nennen**
genau [gə'nau] *adj* exact; fussy
genau′genommen *adv* strictly speaking
Genau′igkeit *f* (-;) exactness, accuracy; meticulousness
Gendarm [ʒã'darm] *m* (-en;-en) policeman
Gendarme·rie [ʒãdarmə'ri] *f* (-;-rien ['ri·ən]) rural police; rural police station
Genealo·gie [gɛnɛ·alə'gi] *f* (-;-gien ['gi·ən]) genealogy
genehm [gə'nem] *adj* agreeable; acceptable; (*dat*) convenient (for)
genehmigen [gə'nemɪgən] *tr* grant; approve; **sich** [*dat*] **etw g.** (coll) treat oneself to s.th.; **genehmigt O.K.**
Geneh′migung *f* (-;-en) grant; approval; permission; permit
geneigt [gə'naɪkt] *adj* sloping; (**zu**) inclined (to); (*dat*) well-disposed (towards)
Geneigt′heit *f* inclination; good will
General [gɛnɛ'ral] *m* (-[e]s;-e & ⸗e) general
General′feldmarschall *m* field marshal
General′inspekteur *m* chief of the joint chiefs of staff
Generalität [generalɪ'tet] *f* (-;) body of generals
General′konsul *m* consul general
General′leutnant *m* lieutenant general; (aer) air marshal
General′major *m* major general
General′nenner *m* common denominator
General′probe *f* dress rehearsal
General′stabskarte *f* strategic map
General′vollmacht *f* full power of attorney
Generation [genera'tsjon] *f* (-;-en) generation
generell [gɛnɛ'rɛl] *adj* general, blanket
genesen [gə'nezən] §84 *intr* (SEIN) convalesce; (**von**) recover (from)
Gene′sung *f* (-;-en) convalescence
Gene′sungsheim *n* convalescent home
genetisch [gɛ'netɪʃ] *adj* genetic
Genf [gɛnf] *n* (-s;) Geneva
Gen′forscher -in §6 *mf* genetic engineer
Gen′forschung *f* (-;) genetic engineering
genial [ge'njal] *adj* brilliant, gifted
Genick [gə'nɪk] *n* (-s;-e) nape of the neck
Genick′bruch *m* broken neck
Genick′schlag *m* (box) rabbit punch
Genie [ʒɛ'ni] *n* (-s;-s) (man of) genius
genieren [ge'nirən] *tr* bother; embarrass ‖ *ref* feel embarrassed
genießbar [gə'nisbar] *adj* edible; drinkable; (fig) agreeable
genießen [gə'nisən] §76 *tr* enjoy; eat; drink
Genie′streich *m* stroke of genius
Genitalien [genɪ'taljən] *pl* genitals
Geni·tiv ['genɪtif] *m* (-s;-tive ['tivə]) genitive
genommen [gə'nɔmən] *pp* of **nehmen**

genoß [gə'nɔs] *pret* of **genießen**
Genosse [gə'nɔsə] *m* (-n;-n) companion, buddy; (pol) comrade –**genosse** *m comb.fm.* fellow-, –mate
Genos′senschaft *f* (-;-en) association; coöperative
Genossin [gə'nɔsɪn] *f* (-;-nen) companion, buddy; (pol) comrade
genug [gə'nuk] *invar adj* & *adv* enough
Genüge [gə'nygə] *f—j—m* G. **tun** give s.o. satisfaction; **zur G.** enough; only too well
genügen [gə'nygən] *intr* suffice, do ‖ *ref—sich* [*dat*] **g. lassen an** (*dat*) be content with
genü′gend *adj* sufficient
genügsam [gə'nykzam] *adj* easily satisfied; frugal
genug′tun §154 *intr* (*dat*) satisfy
Genugtuung [gə'nuktu·ʊŋ] *f* (-;) satisfaction
Ge·nuß [gə'nus] *m* (-nusses;-nüsse) enjoyment; pleasure; (*Nutznießung*) use; (*von Speisen*) consumption
Genuß′mittel *n* semi-luxury (*as coffee, tobacco, etc.*)
genuß′reich *adj* thoroughly enjoyable
genuß′süchtig *adj* pleasure-seeking
Geographie [gɛ·ɔgra'fi] *f* (-;) geography
geographisch [gɛ·ɔ'grafɪʃ] *adj* geographical
Geologe [gɛ·ɔ'logə] *m* (-n;-n) geologist
Geologie [gɛ·ɔlɔ'gi] *f* (-;) geology
Geometer [gɛ·ɔ'metər] *m* (-s;-) surveyor
Geometrie [gɛ·ɔme'tri] *f* (-;) geometry
Geophysik [gɛ·ɔfy'zik] *f* (-;) geophysics
Geopolitik [gɛ·ɔpɔlɪ'tik] *f* (-;) geopolitics
Georgine [gɛ·ɔr'ginə] *f* (-;-n) dahlia
Gepäck [gə'pɛk] *n* (-[e]s;) luggage
Gepäck′abfertigung *f* luggage check-in; luggage counter
Gepäck′ablage *f* luggage rack
Gepäck′anhänger *m* tag; luggage trailer
Gepäck′aufbewahrung *f* baggage room
Gepäck′netz *n* baggage rack (*net type*)
Gepäck′raum *m* luggage compartment
Gepäck′schein *m* luggage check
Gepäck′träger *m* porter; (aut) roof rack
Gepäck′wagen *m* (rr) baggage car
gepanzert [gə'pantsərt] *adj* armored
gepfeffert [gə'pfefərt] *adj* peppered; (*Worte*) sharp; (*Preis*) exorbitant
Gepfeife [gə'pfaɪfə] *n* (-s;) whistling
gepfiffen [gə'pfɪfən] *pp* of **pfeifen**
gepflogen [gə'pflogən] *pp* of **pflegen**
Gepflo′genheit *f* (-;-en) custom, practice
Geplänkel [gə'plɛŋkəl] *n* (-s;) skirmish; (fig) exchange of words
Geplapper [gə'plapər] *n* (-s;) jabber
Geplärr [gə'pler] *n* (-s;) bawling
Geplauder [gə'plaudər] *n* (-s;) small talk, chat
Gepolter [gə'pɔltər] *n* (-s;) rumbling
Gepräge [gə'pregə] *n* (-s;) impression; stamp, character
Gepränge [gə'prɛŋə] *n* (-s;) pomp

gepriesen [gə'pri:zən] *pp* of **preisen**
gequollen [gə'kvɔlən] *pp* of **quellen**
gerade [gə'rɑ:də] *adj* straight; even; direct; (*Haltung*) erect; (*aufrichtig*) straightforward || *adv* straight; exactly; just; just now || **Gerade** *f* (**-n**; **-n**) straight line; straightaway; (box) straight; **rechte G.** straight right
gerade(n)wegs [gə'rɑ:də(n)veks] *adv* immediately, straightaway
geradezu' *adv* downright
Geranie [gɛ'rɑnjə] *f* (**-**;**-n**) geranium
gerannt [gə'rant] *pp* of **rennen**
Gerassel [gə'rasəl] *n* (**-s**;) clanking
Gerät [gə'rɛt] *n* (**-[e]s**;**-e**) device, instrument; tool; (rad, telv) set
geraten [gə'rɑtən] *pp* of **raten** || *adj* successful; (*ratsam*) advisable || §63 *intr* (SEIN) (*gut, schlecht, usw.*) turn out; **außer sich g.** be beside oneself; **g. an** (acc) come by; **g. auf** (acc) get into; get on to; **g. hinter** (acc) get behind; find out about; **g. in** (acc) get into, fall into; **g. nach** take after; **g. über** (acc) come across; **in Bewegung g.** begin to move; **in Brand g.** catch fire; **ins Schleudern g.** begin to skid; **ins Stocken g.** come to a standstill
Gerä'teschuppen *m* tool shed
Geratewohl [gə'rɑtəvol] *n* (**-s**;)—**aufs G.** at random
geraum [gə'raum] *adj* considerable
geräumig [gə'rɔimɪç] *adj* spacious
Geräusch [gə'rɔi∫] *n* (**-[e]s**;**-e**) noise
gerben ['gɛrbən] *tr* tan
Gerberei [gɛrbə'rai] *f* (**-**;**-en**) tannery
gerecht [gə'rɛçt] *adj* just, fair; justified; **g. werden** (*dat*) do justice to
Gerech'tigkeit *f* (**-**;) justice; fairness
Gerede [gə'redə] *n* (**-s**;) talk; hearsay
gereichen [gə'raiçən] *intr*—**es gereicht ihm zur Ehre** it does him justice; **es gereicht ihm zum Vorteil** it is to his advantage; **es gereicht mir zur Freude** it gives me pleasure
gereizt [gə'raitst] *adj* irritable; irritated
gereuen [gə'rɔi·ən] *tr* cause (s.o.) regret || *ref*—**sich keine Mühe g. lassen** spare no trouble || *impers*—**es gereut mich** I regret
Geriatrie [gɛrɪ·a'tri] *f* (**-**;) geriatrics
Gericht [gə'rɪçt] *n* (**-[e]s**;**-e**) court; courthouse; judgment; (culin) dish; **das Jüngste G.** the Last Judgment
gericht'lich *adj* legal, judicial, court
Gerichtsbarkeit [gə'rɪçtsbarkait] *f* (**-**;) jurisdiction
Gerichts'bote *m* (jur) bailiff
Gerichts'hof *m* law court; **Oberster G.** Supreme Court
Gerichts'medizin *f* forensic medicine
Gerichts'saal *m* courtroom
Gerichts'schreiber **-in** §6 *mf* (jur) clerk
Gerichts'stand *m* (jur) venue
Gerichts'verhandlung *f* hearing; trial
Gerichts'vollzieher *m* (jur) marshal
Gerichts'wesen *n* judicial system
gerieben [gə'ribən] *pp* of **reiben** || *adj* cunning, smart
Geriesel [gə'rizəl] *n* (**-s**;) purling
gering [gə'rɪŋ] *adj* slight, trifling;

small; (*niedrig*) low; (*ärmlich*) poor; (*minderwertig*) inferior; **nicht im geringsten** not in the least
gering'achten *tr* think little of
gering'fügig *adj* insignificant
gering'schätzen *tr* look down on
Gering'schätzung *f* contempt, disdain
gerinnen [gə'rɪnən] §121 *intr* coagulate, clot; (*Milch*) curdle
Gerinnsel [gə'rɪnzəl] *n* (**-s**;-) clot
Gerippe [gə'rɪpə] *n* (**-s**;-) skeleton; (*Gerüst*) framework
gerippt [gə'rɪpt] *adj* ribbed; (*Säule*) fluted; (*Stoff*) corded
gerissen [gə'rɪsən] *pp* of **reißen** || *adj* sly
geritten [gə'rɪtən] *pp* of **reiten**
gern(e) ['gern(ə)] *adv* gladly; **g. haben** or **mögen** like; **ich rauche g.** I like to smoke
gerochen [gə'rɔxən] *pp* of **riechen**
Geröll [gə'rœl] *n* (**-s**;) pebbles
geronnen [gə'rɔnən] *pp* of **gerinnen** & **rinnen**
Gerste ['gerstə] *f* (**-**;**-n**) barley
Ger'stenkorn *n* grain of barley; (pathol) sty
Gerte ['gertə] *f* (**-**;**-n**) switch, rod
Geruch [gə'rux] *m* (**-[e]s**;⁼e) smell
geruch'los *adj* odorless
Gerücht [gə'rʏçt] *m* (**-[e]s**;**-e**) rumor
geruhen [gə'ru·ən] *intr* deign
geruhsam [gə'ruzɑm] *adj* quiet; relaxed
Gerümpel [gə'rʏmpəl] *n* (**-s**;) junk
gerungen [gə'ruŋən] *pp* of **ringen**
Gerüst [gə'rʏst] *n* (**-s**;**-e**) scaffold; (*Tragewerk*) frame; (fig) outline
Ges [gɛs] *n* (**-**;-) (mus) G flat
gesamt [gə'zamt] *adj* entire, total
gesamt-, Gesamt- *comb.fm.* total, overall; all-; joint; collective
gesandt [gə'zant] *pp* of **senden**
Gesand'te §5 *mf* envoy
Gesandt'schaft *f* (**-**;**-en**) legation
Gesang [gə'zaŋ] *m* (**-[e]s**;⁼e) singing; song; (lit) canto
Gesang'verein *m* glee club
Gesäß [gə'zes] *n* (**-es**;**-e**) buttocks; (coll) behind
Geschäft [gə'∫eft] *n* (**-[e]s**;**-e**) business; deal, bargain; shop. store
Geschäftemacherei [gə'∫eftəmaxərai] *f* (**-**;) commercialism
geschäftig [gə'∫etɪç] *adj* busy
Geschäf'tigkeit *f* (**-**;) hustle, bustle
geschäft'lich *adj* business || *adv* on business
Geschäfts'abschluß *m* contract; deal
Geschäfts'aufsicht *f* receivership
Geschäfts'bedingungen *pl* terms
geschäfts'führend *adj* managing; executive; **geschäftsführende Regierung** caretaker government
Geschäfts'führer **-in** §6 *mf* manager
Geschäfts'haus *n* firm; office building
Geschäfts'inhaber **-in** §6 *mf* proprietor
geschäfts'kundig *adj* with business experience
Geschäfts'lokal *n* business premises; (*Laden*) shop; (*Büro*) office
Geschäfts'mann *m* (**-[e]s**;**-leute**) businessman

geschäfts'mäßig *adj* business-like
Geschäfts'ordnung *f* rules of procedure; zur G.! point of order!
Geschäfts'reise *f* business trip
Geschäfts'schluß *m* closing time
Geschäfts'stelle *f* office; branch
Geschäfts'träger *m* agent, representative; (pol) chargé d'affaires
geschäfts'tüchtig *adj* sharp
Geschäfts'verbindung *f* business connections
Geschäfts'verkehr *m* business transactions
Geschäfts'viertel *n* business district
Geschäfts'wert *m* (com) good will
Geschäfts'zweig *m* line of business
geschah [gə'ʃa] *pret* of geschehen
geschehen [gə'ʃe·ən] §138 *intr* (SEIN) happen; take place; be done; das geschieht dir recht! serves you right!
‖ Geschehen *n* (-s;) events
Geschehnis [gə'ʃenɪs] *n* (-ses;-se) event
gescheit [gə'ʃaɪt] *adj* clever; bright; sensible; er ist wohl nicht ganz g. he's not all there
Geschenk [gə'ʃɛŋk] *n* (-[e]s;-e) gift
Geschichte [gə'ʃɪçtə] *f* (-;-n) story; history; (coll) affair, thing
geschicht'lich *adj* historical
Geschichts'forscher –in §6 *mf*, Geschichts'schreiber –in §6 *mf* historian
Geschick [gə'ʃɪk] *n* (-[e]s;-e) fate, destiny; dexterity, skill
Geschick'lichkeit *f* (-;) skillfulness
geschickt [gə'ʃɪkt] *adj* skillful
geschieden [gə'ʃidən] *pp* of scheiden
geschienen [gə'ʃinən] *pp* of scheinen
Geschirr [gə'ʃɪr] *n* (-[e]s;-e) dishes; china; pot; (e–s Pferdes) harness
Geschirr'schrank *m* kitchen cabinet
Geschirrspülmaschine [gə'ʃɪrʃpylmaʃinə] *f* dishwasher
Geschirr'tuch *n* dishtowel
geschissen [gε'ʃɪsən] *pp* of scheißen
Geschlecht [gə'ʃlɛçt] *n* (-[e]s;-er) sex; race; family, line; generation; (gram) gender
geschlecht'lich *adj* sexual
Geschlechts'krankheit *f* venereal disease
Geschlechts'teile *pl* genitals
Geschlechts'trieb *m* sexual instinct
Geschlechts'verkehr *m* intercourse
Geschlechts'wort *n* (-[e]s;-¨) (gram) article
geschlichen [gə'ʃlɪçən] *pp* of schleichen
geschliffen [gə'ʃlɪfən] *pp* of schleifen ‖ *adj* (Glas) cut; (fig) polished
geschlissen [gə'ʃlɪsən] *pp* of schleißen
geschlossen [gə'ʃlɔsən] *pp* of schließen ‖ *adj* closed; enclosed; (Front) united; (Gesellschaft) private; (ling) close; (telv) closed-circuit ‖ *adv* unanimously; g. hinter j–m stehen be solidly behind s.o.
geschlungen [gə'ʃluŋən] *pp* of schlingen
Geschmack [gə'ʃmak] *m* (-s;-¨e & -¨er) taste
Geschmacks'richtung *f* vogue

geschmeidig [ge'ʃmaɪdɪç] *adj* pliant; flexible; lithe; (Haar) manageable
Geschmeiß [gə'ʃmaɪs] *n* (-es;) vermin; rabble
geschmissen [gə'ʃmɪsən] *pp* of schmeißen
geschmolzen [gə'ʃmɔltsən] *pp* of schmelzen
Geschnatter [gə'ʃnatər] *n* (-s;) cackle
geschniegelt [gə'ʃnigəlt] *adj* spruce
geschnitten [gə'ʃnɪtən] *pp* of schneiden
geschnoben [gə'ʃnobən] *pp* of schnauben
geschoben [gə'ʃobən] *pp* of schieben
gescholten [gə'ʃɔltən] *pp* of schelten
Geschöpf [gə'ʃœpf] *n* (-[e]s;-e) creature
geschoren [gə'ʃorən] *pp* of scheren
Ge·schoß [gə'ʃɔs] *n* (-schosses; -schosse) shot; missile; shell; floor, story
Geschoß'bahn *f* trajectory
geschossen [gə'ʃɔsən] *pp* of schießen
geschraubt [gə'ʃraʊbt] *adj* affected; (Stil) stilted
Geschrei [gə'ʃraɪ] *n* (-[e]s;) shouting
Geschreibsel [gə'ʃraɪpsəl] *n* (-s;) scribbling, scrawl
geschrieben [gə'ʃribən] *pp* of schreiben
geschrieen [gə'ʃri·ən] *pp* of schreien
geschritten [gə'ʃrɪtən] *pp* of schreiten
geschunden [gə'ʃundən] *pp* of schinden
Geschütz [gə'ʃyts] *n* (-es;-e) gun
Geschütz'bedienung *f* gun crew
Geschütz'legierung *f* gun metal
Geschütz'stand *m* gun emplacement
Geschwader [gə'ʃvadər] *n* (-s;-) (aer) group (consisting of 27 aircraft); (nav) squadron
Geschwätz [gə'ʃvɛts] *n* (-es;) chatter
geschweige [gə'ʃvaɪgə]—g. denn let alone, much less
geschwiegen [gə'ʃvigən] *pp* of schweigen
geschwind [gə'ʃvɪnt] *adj* quick
Geschwin'digkeit *f* (-;-en) speed; velocity; mit der G. von at the rate of
Geschwin'digkeitsbegrenzung *f* speed limit
Geschwin'digkeitsmesser *m* speedometer
Geschwind'schritt *m* (mil) double time
Geschwister [gə'ʃvɪstər] *pl* brother and sister, brothers, sisters, brothers and sisters; siblings
geschwollen [gə'ʃvɔlən] *pp* of schwellen ‖ *adj* turgid
geschwommen [gə'ʃvɔmən] *pp* of schwimmen
geschworen [gə'ʃvorən] *pp* of schwören ‖ Geschworene §5 *mf* juror; die Geschworenen the jury
Geschwo'renengericht *n* jury
Geschwulst [gə'ʃvulst] *f* (-;-¨e) swelling; tumor
geschwunden [gə'ʃvundən] *pp* of schwinden
geschwungen [gə'ʃvuŋən] *pp* of schwingen
Geschwür [gə'ʃvyr] *n* (-s;-e) ulcer

Geselle [gə'zɛlə] *m* (**-n;-n**) journeyman; companion; lad, fellow
gesellen [gə'zɛlən] *ref*—**sich zu j-m g.** join s.o.
gesellig [gə'zɛlɪç] *adj* gregarious, sociable
Gesell'schaft *f* (**-;-en**) society; company; (pej) bunch; (com) company; **j-m G. leisten** keep s.o. company
Gesell'schafter -in §6 *mf* companion; shareholder; (com) partner
gesell'schaftlich *adj* social
Gesell'schaftsspiel *n* party game
Gesell'schaftswissenschaft *f* social science; sociology
gesessen [gə'zɛsən] *pp* of **sitzen**
Gesetz [gə'zɛts] *n* (**-es;-e**) law
Gesetz'buch *n* legal code
Gesetz'entwurf *m* (parl) bill
Gesetzes- [gəzɛtsəs] *comb.fm.* legal, of law, of the law
Geset'zesantrag *m,* **Geset'zesvorlage** *f* (parl) bill
gesetz'gebend *adj* legislative
Gesetz'geber -in §6 *mf* legislator
Gesetz'gebung *f* (**-;**) legislation
gesetz'lich *adj* legal
gesetz'los *adj* lawless
gesetz'mäßig *adj* legal; legitimate
Gesetz'sammlung *f* code of laws
gesetzt [gə'zɛtst] *adj* sedate; (*Alter*) mature; **g. den Fall, daß** assuming that ‖ *adv* in a dignified manner
gesetz'widrig *adj* illegal, unlawful
Gesicht [gə'zɪçt] *n* (**-[e]s;-er**) face; sight; eyesight; (*Aussehen*) look
Gesichts'farbe *f* complexion
Gesichts'kreis *m* horizon; outlook
Gesichts'punkt *m* point of view, angle
Gesichts'spannung *f* face lift
Gesichts'zug *m* feature
Gesims [gə'zɪms] *n* (**-es;-e**) molding
Gesindel [gə'zɪndəl] *n* (**-s;**) rabble; lichtscheues G. shady characters
gesinnt [gə'zɪnt] *adj* disposed; **-minded**
Gesinnung [gə'zɪnʊŋ] *f* (**-;-en**) mind; character; convictions
gesin'nungslos *adj* without definite convictions
gesin'nungsmäßig *adv* according to one's convictions
gesin'nungstreu, gesin'nungstüchtig *adj* staunch
gesittet [gə'zɪtət] *adj* polite; civilized
gesoffen [gə'zɔfən] *pp* of **saufen**
gesogen [gə'zogən] *pp* of **saugen**
gesonnen [gə'zɔnən] *pp* of **sinnen** ‖ *adj*—**g. sein zu** (*inf*) have a mind to (*inf*), be inclined to (*inf*)
gesotten [gə'zɔtən] *pp* of **sieden**
Gespann [gə'ʃpan] *n* (**-[e]s;-e**) team; pair, combination
gespannt [gə'ʃpant] *adj* stretched; tense; (*Aufmerksamkeit*) close; (*Beziehungen*) strained; **ich bin g.** (coll) I wonder, I am anxious to know
Gespenst [gə'ʃpɛnst] *n* (**-[e]s;-er**) ghost, specter
gespen'sterhaft *adj* ghostly; spooky
gespenstisch [gə'ʃpɛnstɪʃ] *adj* ghostly
gespie(e)n [gə'ʃpi(ə)n] *pp* of **speien**
Gespiele [gə'ʃpilə] *m* (**-n;-n**), **Gespielin** [gə'ʃpilɪn] *f* (**-;-nen**) playmate

Gespinst [gə'ʃpɪnst] *n* (**-es;-e**) yarn; (*Gewebe*) web
gesponnen [gə'ʃpɔnən] *pp* of **spinnen**
Gespött [gə'ʃpœt] *n* (**-[e]s;**) ridicule; laughing stock
Gespräch [gə'ʃprɛç] *n* (**-[e]s;-e**) conversation; (telp) call; **Gespräche** (pol) talks; **G. mit Voranmeldung** person-to-person call
gesprächig [gə'ʃprɛçɪç] *adj* talkative
gespreizt [gə'ʃpraɪtst] *adj* outspread; affected ‖ *adv*—**g. tun** act big
gesprenkelt [gə'ʃprɛŋkəlt] *adj* spotted
gesprochen [gə'ʃprɔçən] *pp* of **sprechen**
gesprossen [gə'ʃprɔsən] *pp* of **sprießen**
gesprungen [gə'ʃprʊŋən] *pp* of **springen**
Gestade [gə'ʃtadə] *n* (**-s;-**) (river) bank; (sea)shore
Gestalt [gə'ʃtalt] *f* (**-;-en**) shape; figure; (*Wuchs*) stature
gestalten [gə'ʃtaltən] *tr* shape; form; arrange ‖ *ref* take shape; turn out
Gestal'tung *f* (**-;-en**) formation; development; arrangement; design
gestanden [gə'ʃtandən] *pp* of **stehen**
geständig [gə'ʃtɛndɪç] *adj*—**g. sein** admit one's guilt
Geständnis [gə'ʃtɛntnɪs] *n* (**-ses;-se**) confession, admission
Gestank [gə'ʃtaŋk] *m* (**-[e]s;**) stench
Gestapo [gə'ʃtapo] *f* (**-;**) (**Geheime Staatspolizei**) secret state police
gestatten [gə'ʃtatən] *tr* permit, allow
Geste ['gɛstə] *f* (**-;-n**) gesture
gestehen [gə'ʃte·ən] §146 *tr* admit
Gestein [gə'ʃtaɪn] *n* (**-[e]s;-e**) rock
Gestell [gə'ʃtɛl] *n* (**-[e]s;-e**) frame; rack; mounting; (coll) beanpole
Gestel'lungsbefehl *m* (mil) induction orders
gestern ['gɛstərn] *adv* yesterday; **g. abend** last evening, last night
gestiefelt [gə'ʃtifəlt] *adj* in boots
gestiegen [gə'ʃtigən] *pp* of **steigen**
gestikulieren [gɛstiku'lirən] *intr* gesticulate
Gestirn [gə'ʃtɪrn] *n* (**-[e]s;-e**) star; (*Sternbild*) constellation
gestirnt [gə'ʃtɪrnt] *adj* starry
gestoben [gə'ʃtobən] *pp* of **stieben**
Gestöber [gə'ʃtøbər] *n* (**-s;-**) snow flurry
gestochen [gə'ʃtɔxən] *pp* of **stechen**
gestohlen [gə'ʃtolən] *pp* of **stehlen**
gestorben [gə'ʃtɔrbən] *pp* of **sterben**
gestoßen [gə'ʃtosən] *pp* of **stoßen**
Gesträuch [gə'ʃtrɔɪç] *n* (**-[e]s;**) bushes, shrubbery
gestreift [gə'ʃtraɪft] *adj* striped
gestrichen [gə'ʃtrɪçən] *pp* of **streichen**
gestrig ['gɛstrɪç] *adj* yesterday's
gestritten [gə'ʃtrɪtən] *pp* of **streiten**
Gestrüpp [gə'ʃtrʏp] *n* (**-[e]s;**) underbrush
gestunken [gə'ʃtʊŋkən] *pp* of **stinken**
Gestüt [gə'ʃtyt] *n* (**-[e]s;-e**) stud farm
Gestüt'hengst *m* stallion, studhorse
Gesuch [gə'zux] *n* (**-[e]s;-e**) request; application; (jur) petition
gesucht [gə'zuxt] *adj* wanted; in demand; studied; (*Vergleich*) farfetched
Gesudel [gə'zudəl] *n* (**-s;**) messy job

Gesumme [gə'zumə] n (-s;) humming
gesund [gə'zunt] adj healthy; sound;
wholesome; **g. werden** get well
Gesund'beter –in §6 mf faith healer
Gesund'brunnen m mineral spring
gesunden [gə'zundən] intr (SEIN) get
well again, recover
Gesund'heit f (–;) health; **auf Ihre G.!**
to your health!; **G.!** (God) bless you!
Gesund'heitslehre f hygiene
Gesund'heitspflege f hygiene
Gesund'heitsrücksichten pl—**aus G.**
for reasons of health
Gesund'heitswesen n public health
gesungen [gə'zuŋən] pp of **singen**
gesunken [gə'zuŋkən] pp of **sinken**
Getäfel [gə'tɛfəl] n (-s;) wainscoting
getä'felt adj inlaid
getan [gə'tan] pp of **tun**
Getöse [gə'tøzə] n (-s;) din, noise
getragen [gə'tragən] pp of **tragen** || adj
solemn
Getrampel [gə'trampəl] n (-s;) trample
Getränk [gə'trɛŋk] n (-[e]s;-e) drink
getrauen [gə'trau·ən] ref dare
Getreide [gə'traɪdə] n (-s;-) grain
Getrei'deboden m granary
Getrei'despeicher m grain elevator
getreu [gə'trɔɪ] adj faithful, true
getreu'lich adv faithfully
Getriebe [gə'tribə] n (-s;-) hustle and
bustle; (adm) machinery; (aut) transmission
getrieben [gə'tribən] pp of **treiben**
getroffen [gə'trɔmən] pp of **treffen**
getrogen [gə'trogən] pp of **trügen**
getrost [gə'trost] adj confident
getrunken [gə'truŋkən] pp of **trinken**
Getto ['gɛto] n (-s;-s) ghetto
Getue [gə'tu·ə] n (-s;) fuss
Getümmel [gə'tyməl] n (-s;) turmoil
getupft [gə'tupft] adj polka-dot
Geviert [gə'firt] n (-[e]s;-e) square
Gewächs [gə'vɛks] n (-es;-e) growth;
plant
gewachsen [gə'vaksən] adj—**g. sein**
(dat) be equal to, be up to
Gewächs'haus n greenhouse, hothouse
gewagt [gə'vakt] adj risky; off-color
gewählt [gə'vɛlt] adj choice; refined
gewahr [gə'var] adj—**g. werden** (genit)
become aware of
Gewähr [gə'ver] f (–;) guarantee
gewahren [gə'varən] tr notice
gewähren [gə'verən] tr grant
gewähr'leisten tr guarantee, ensure
Gewähr'leistung f (-;-en) guarantee
Gewahrsam [gə'varzam] m (-[e]s;)
safekeeping, custody || n (-[e]s;-e)
prison
Gewährs'mann m (-[e]s;–er & –leute)
informant, source
Gewährs'pflicht f warranty
Gewalt [gə'valt] f (–;-en) force; violence; authority; (Aufsicht) control
Gewalt'haber m (-s;-) ruler; tyrant
Gewalt'herrschaft f tyranny
Gewalt'herrscher m tyrant
gewal'tig adj powerful; huge; (coll)
awful || adv terribly
Gewalt'kur f drastic measure; (coll)
crash program
gewalt'los adj nonviolent

Gewalt'marsch m forced march
Gewalt'mensch m brute, tyrant
gewaltsam [gə'valtzam] adj violent;
forcible; drastic || adv by force
Gewalt'samkeit f (–;) violence
Gewalt'streich m bold stroke
Gewalt'tat f act of violence
gewalt'tätig adj violent, brutal
Gewalt'verbrechen n felony
Gewalt'verbrecher –in §6 mf felon
Gewand [gə'vant] n (-[e]s;–er) robe;
appearance, guise; (eccl) vestment
gewandt [gə'vant] pp of **wenden** || adj
agile; clever
gewann [gə'van] pret of **gewinnen**
gewärtig [gə'vertiç] adj—**g. sein**
(genit) be prepared for
Gewäsch [gə've∫] n (-es;) nonsense
Gewässer [gə'vesər] n (-s;-) body of
water; waters
Gewebe [gə'vebə] n (-s;-) tissue; (tex)
fabric
geweckt [gə'vɛkt] adj bright, sharp
Gewehr [gə'ver] n (-[e]s;-e) rifle
Geweih [gə'vaɪ] n (-[e]s;-e) antlers
Gewerbe [gə'verbə] n (-s;-) trade,
business; calling, profession; industry
Gewer'bebetrieb m business enterprise
Gewer'beschule f trade school
gewerblich [gə'verpliç] adj industrial;
commercial, business
gebwerbs'mäßig adj professional
Gewerkschaft [gə'verk∫aft] f (-;-en)
labor union
gewerk'schaftlich adj union || adv—
sich g. organisieren unionize
Gewerk'schaftsbeitrag m union dues
gewesen [gə'vezən] pp of **sein**
gewichen [gə'viçən] pp of **weichen**
Gewicht [gə'viçt] n (-[e]s;-e) (& fig)
weight
gewichtig [gə'viçtiç] adj weighty
gewiegt [gə'vigt] adj experienced,
smart, shrewd
gewiesen [gə'vizən] pp of **weisen**
gewillt [gə'vilt] adj willing
Gewimmel [gə'viməl] n (-s;) swarm;
(Menschen–) throng
Gewimmer [gə'vimər] n (-s;) whim-
pering; whining
Gewinde [gə'vində] n (-s;-) thread
(of a screw); (Kranz) garland; skein
Gewinn [gə'vin] m (-[e]s;-e) win-
nings; profit; (Vorteil) advantage
Gewinn'anteil m profit
Gewinn'aufschlag m (com) markup
Gewinn'beteiligung f profit sharing
gewinn'bringend adj profitable
gewinnen [gə'vinən] §121 tr win, gain;
reach || intr win; make a profit;
improve; **g. an** (dat) gain in; **g. von**
or **durch** profit by
gewin'nend adj engaging
Gewinn'spanne f margin of profit
Gewinn'sucht f greed; profiteering
Gewinsel [gə'vinzəl] n (-s;) whim-
pering
Gewirr [gə'vir] n (-[e]s;-e) tangle;
entanglement; maze
gewiß [gə'vis] adj sure, certain || adv
certainly; **aber g.!** of course!
Gewissen [gə'visən] n (-s;-) conscience

gewis'senhaft adj conscientious
gewis'senlos adj unscrupulous
Gewis'sensbisse pl pangs of conscience
Gewis'sensnot f moral dilemma
gewis'sermaßen adv to some extent; so to speak
Gewiß'heit f (-;-en) certainty
gewiß'lich adv certainly
Gewitter [gə'vɪtər] n (-s;-) thunderstorm
gewittern [gə'vɪtərn] impers—es gewittert a storm is brewing
Gewit'terregen m thundershower
gewitzigt [gə'vɪtsɪçt] adj—g. sein to have learned from experience
gewitzt [gə'vɪtst] adj bright, smart
gewoben [gə'vobən] pp of **weben**
gewogen [gə'vogən] pp of **wägen** & **wiegen** || adj well disposed
Gewo'genheit f (-;) favorable attitude
gewöhnen [gə'vønən] tr (an acc) accustom (to) || ref (an acc) get used (to)
Gewohnheit [gə'vonhaɪt] f (-;-en) habit, custom
gewohn'heitsmäßig adj habitual
Gewohn'heitsmensch m creature of habit
gewöhnlich [gə'vønlɪç] adj usual; normal; common, ordinary
gewohnt [gə'vont] adj usual; g. sein (acc) be used to
Gewölbe [gə'vœlbə] n (-s;-) vault; arch
gewölbt [gə'vœlpt] adj vaulted
Gewölk [ge'vœlk] n (-[e]s;) clouds
gewonnen [gə'vɔnən] pp of **gewinnen**
geworben [gə'vɔrbən] pp of **werben**
geworden [gə'vɔrdən] pp of **werden**
geworfen [gə'vɔrfən] pp of **werfen**
gewrungen [gə'vruŋən] pp of **wringen**
Gewühl [gə'vyl] n (-[e]s;) milling crowd
gewunden [gə'vundən] pp of **winden**
gewürfelt [gə'vYrfəlt] adj checkered
Gewürm [gə'vYrm] n (-[e]s;) vermin
Gewürz [gə'vYrts] n (-[e]s;-e) spice
Gewürz'nelke f clove
gewußt [gə'vust] pp of **wissen**
Geysir ['gaɪzɪr] m (-s;-) geyser
gezackt [gə'tsakt] adj jagged; (bot) serrated
gezähnt [gə'tsent] adj toothed; (Rand) perforated; (bot) dentated
Gezänk [gə'tseŋk] n (-[e]s;) squabbling
Gezeiten [gə'tsaɪtən] pl tides
Gezeiten- comb.fm. tidal
Gezeter [gə'tsetər] n (-s;) yelling
geziehen [gə'tsi-ən] pp of **zeihen**
geziemen [gə'tsimən] intr (dat) be proper for || impers ref—es geziemt sich für j-n it is right for s.o.
geziert [gə'tsirt] adj affected, phoney
Gezisch [gə'tsɪʃ] n (-es;) hissing
gezogen [gə'tsogən] pp of **ziehen**
Gezücht [gə'tsYçt] n (-[e]s;-e) riffraff
Gezwitscher [gə'tsvɪtʃər] n (-s;) chirping
gezwungen [gə'tsvuŋən] pp of **zwingen** || adj forced; (Stil) labored || adv stiffly
Gicht [gɪçt] f (-;-en) gout

Giebel ['gibəl] m (-s;-) gable
Gier [gir] f (-;) greed
gierig ['girɪç] adj (nach) greedy (for)
Gießbach ['gisbax] m torrent
gießen ['gisən] §76 tr pour; (Blumen, usw.) water; (metal) cast, found || impers—es gießt it is pouring
Gießer ['gisər] m (-s;-) foundryman
Gießerei [gisə'raɪ] f (-;-en) foundry
Gieß'form f casting mold; (typ) matrix
Gieß'kanne f sprinkling can
Gift [gɪft] n (-[e]s;-e) poison
giftig ['gɪftɪç] adj poisonous; malicious
Gigant [gɪ'gant] m (-en;-en) giant
Gilde ['gɪldə] f (-;-n) guild
Gimpel ['gɪmpəl] m (-s;-) (coll) sucker
ging [gɪŋ] pret of **gehen**
Gipfel ['gɪpfəl] m (-s;-) top; peak
Gip'felkonferenz f summit meeting
Gips [gɪps] m (-es;-e) gypsum; plaster of Paris; (surg) cast
Gips'arbeit f plastering
Gips'diele f plasterboard
gipsen ['gɪpsən] tr plaster
Gips'verband m (surg) cast
Giraffe [gɪ'rafə] f (-;-n) giraffe
girieren [ʒɪ'rirən] tr endorse
Girlande [gɪr'landə] f (-;-n) garland
Giro ['ʒiro] n (-s;-s) endorsement
girren ['girən] intr coo
Gis [gɪs] n (-;-) (mus) G sharp
Gischt [gɪʃt] m (-es;) foam; spray
Gitarre [gɪ'tarə] f (-;-n) guitar
Gitter ['gɪtər] n (-s;-) grating, grille; bars; lattice; railing; trellis; (electron) grid
Git'terbett n baby crib
Git'ternetz n grid (on map)
Git'tertor n wrought-iron gate
Git'terwerk n latticework
Glacehandschuhe [gla'sehantʃu-ə] pl (& fig) kid gloves
Gladi·ator [gladɪ'atər] m (-s;-atoren [a'torən]) gladiator
Glanz [glants] m (-es;) shine; polish; luster; brilliance
glänzen ['glentsən] tr polish || intr shine; durch Abwesenheit g. be conspicuous by one's absence
glän'zend adj bright; glossy; polished; (fig) splendid, brilliant
Glanz'leder n patent leather
Glanz'licht n (paint) highlight
glanz'los adj dull; lackluster
Glanz'punkt m highlight
Glanz'stück n master stroke
glanz'voll adj brilliant, splendid
Glanz'zeit f heyday, golden age
Glas [glas] n (-es;-̈er) glass
Glaser ['glazər] m (-s;-) glazier
gläsern ['glezərn] adj glass; glassy
Glas'hütte f glassworks
glasieren [gla'zirən] tr glaze; (Kuchen) frost, ice
glasig ['glazɪç] adj glassy; vitreous
Glas'jalousie f jalousie window
Glas'scheibe f pane of glass
Glasur [gla'zur] f (-;-en) enamel (on pots); glaze; (culin) icing
glatt [glat] adj smooth; (eben) even; (poliert) glossy; (schlüpfrig) slippery; (Absage) flat; (Lüge) downright || adv smoothly; directly; entirely

Glätte ['glɛtə] f (-;) smoothness; slipperiness; (*Politur*) polish
Glatt'eis n sheet of ice; **bei G. fahren** drive in icy conditions
glätten ['glɛtən] tr smooth; smooth out || ref smooth out; become calm
glatt'streichen §85 tr smooth out
glatt'weg adv outright, point-blank
glattzüngig ['glattsYŋıç] adj smooth-talking
Glatze ['glatsə] f (-;-n) bald head
glatz'köpfig adj baldheaded
Glaube ['glaubə] m (-ns;), **Glauben** ['glaubən] m (-s;) belief; faith
glauben ['glaubən] tr believe; (*annehmen*) suppose || intr (dat) believe; **g. an** (acc) believe in; **j-m aufs Wort glauben** take s.o.'s word
Glau'bensbekenntnis n profession of faith; creed
Glau'benslehre f Christian doctrine
Glau'benssatz m dogma
gläubig ['glɔıbıç] adj believing || **Gläubige** §5 mf believer || **Gläubiger –in** §6 mf creditor
glaublich ['glauplıç] adj credible
glaub'würdig adj credible; reliable; plausible
Glaukom [glau'kom] n (-s;-e) glaucoma
gleich [glaıç] adj (dat) like; (an dat) equal (in); **es ist mir ganz g.** it's all the same to me || adv equally; immediately
gleichaltrig ['glaıçaltrıç] adj of the same age
gleich'artig adj similar, homogeneous
gleich'bedeutend adj synonymous
Gleich'berechtigung f (pol) equality
gleichen ['glaıçən] §85 intr (dat) resemble, look like, be like
glei'chermaßen adv equally, likewise
gleich'falls adv likewise; as well
gleich'förmig adj uniform; regular; monotonous
gleich'gesinnt adj like-minded
Gleich'gewicht n equilibrium
gleich'gültig adj indifferent; **es ist mir g.** it's all the same to me
Gleich'heit f (-;-en) equality; (*Ähnlichkeit*) likeness
Gleich'klang m consonance; unison
gleich'kommen §99 intr (SEIN) (dat) equal; (dat) be tantamount to
gleich'laufend adj (mit) parallel (to)
gleich'machen tr make equal; standardize; **dem Erdboden g.** raze
Gleich'maß n regularity; evenness; balance, equilibrium; proportion
gleich'mäßig adj symmetrical; regular
Gleich'mut m equanimity, calmness
gleich'mütig adj calm
gleichnamig ['glaıçnamıç] adj of the same name; (phys) like
Gleichnis ['glaıçnıs] n (-ses;-se) parable; figure of speech; simile
Gleich'richter m (elec) rectifier
gleichsam ['glaıçzam] adv so to speak; more or less, practically
gleichschenklig ['glaıç/eŋklıç] adj isosceles
Gleich'schritt m—**im G.** in cadence; **im G. marsch!** forward, march!

gleich'seitig adj equilateral
gleich'setzen tr (dat or mit) equate (with)
Gleich'setzung f (-;), **Gleich'stellung** f (-;) equalization
Gleich'strom m direct current
gleich'tun §154 tr—es j-m g. emulate s.o.
Glei'chung f (-;-en) (math) equation
gleichviel' adv—g. wer not matter who
gleich'wertig adj evenly matched
gleichwohl' adv nevertheless
gleich'zeitig adj simultaneous
gleich'ziehen §163 intr (mit) catch up (with or to)
Gleis [glaıs] n (-es;-e) (rr) track
Gleitboot ['glaıtbot] n hydrofoil
gleiten ['glaıtən] §86 intr (SEIN) glide; slip, slide
Gleitfläche ['glaıtfleçə] f (aer) hydroplane
Gleitflugzeug ['glaıtfluktsɔık] n (aer) glider
Gleitschutz– comb.fm. skid-proof
Gleit'zeit f flexitime
Gletscher ['glet/ər] m (-s;-) glacier
glich [glıç] pret of **gleichen**
Glied [glit] n (-[e]s;-er) limb; member; joint; link; (anat) penis; (log, math) term; (mil) rank, file
glie'derlahm adj paralyzed
gliedern ['glidərn] tr arrange; plan; divide, break down || ref (in acc) consist of
Glie'derung f (-;-en) arrangement; construction; division; organization
Gliedmaßen ['glitmasən] pl limbs
glimmen ['glımən] intr §136 & §109 intr glimmer; glow
Glim'mer m (-s;) glimmer; (min) mica
glimpflich ['glımpflıç] adj gentle; (*Strafe*) light, lenient
glitschen ['glıt/ən] intr (SEIN) slip
glitschig ['glıt/ıç] adj slippery
glitt [glıt] pret of **gleiten**
glitzern ['glıtsərn] intr glitter
global [glo'bal] adj global
Glo·bus ['globus] m (-bus & -busses; -busse & -ben [bən]) globe
Glöckchen ['glœkçən] n (-s;-) small bell
Glocke ['glɔkə] f (-;-n) bell; (e-s *Rocks*) flare
Glockenspiel (Glok'kenspiel) n carillon
Glockenstube (Glok'kenstube) f, **Glockenturm (Glok'kenturm)** m belfry
Glockenzug (Glok'kenzug) m bell rope
Glöckner ['glœknər] m (-s;-) bell ringer; sexton
glomm [glɔm] pret of **glimmen**
Glorie ['glorjə] f (-;-n) glory
Glo'rienschein m halo
glorreich ['glorraıç] adj glorious
glotzäugig ['glɔtsɔıgıç] adj popeyed
glotzen ['glɔtsən] intr stare, goggle
Glück [glyk] n (-[e]s;) luck; fortune; happiness; **auf gut G.** at random; **zum G.** luckily
glucken ['glukən] intr cluck
glücken ['glykən] intr (SEIN) succeed || impers—es glückt mir I succeed
gluckern ['glukərn] intr gurgle

glück'lich adj lucky, fortunate; happy; (günstig) auspicious
glück'licherweise adv fortunately
glück'selig adj blissful; blessed; joyful
Glück'seligkeit f (-;) bliss; joy
glucksen ['gluksən] intr gurgle; chuckle
Glücks'fall m stroke of luck; windfall
Glücks'güter pl earthly possessions
Glücks'hafen m raffle drum
Glücks'pilz m (coll) lucky dog
Glücks'spiel n game of chance
Glücks'topf m grab bag
glück'verheißend adj auspicious
Glück'wunsch m good wishes, congratulations
Glück'wunschkarte f greeting card
Glühbirne ['glybɪrnə] f light bulb
glühen ['gly·ən] tr make red-hot; (metal) anneal || intr glow
glü'hendheiß' adj red-hot
Glühfaden ['glyfadən] m filament
Glühwurm ['glyvurm] m firefly
Glut [glut] f (-;) embers; fire; scorching heat; (fig) ardor
Glyzerin [glytsə'rin] n (-s;) glycerine
GmbH abbr (Gesellschaft mit beschränkter Haftung) Inc.; Ltd. (Brit)
Gnade ['gnadə] f (-;-n) grace; favor; mercy; **von eigenen Gnaden** self-styled
Gna'denbeweis m token of favor
Gna'denbrot n—**bei j-m das G. essen** to live on s.o.'s charity
Gna'denfrist f grace, e.g., **e-e G. von zwei Monaten** two months' grace
Gna'dengesuch n plea for mercy
Gna'denstoß m coup de grâce, deathblow
gnädig ['gnedɪç] adj gracious, kind; merciful; **gnädige Frau** madam; **Sehr verehrte gnädige Frau** Dear Madam
Gold [gɔlt] n (-[e]s;) gold
Gold'blech n gold foil
Gold'fink m (orn) goldfinch
goldig ['gɔldɪç] adj (coll) cute
Gold'plombe f (dent) gold filling
Gold'schmied m goldsmith
Gold'schnitt m gilt edging
Golf [gɔlf] m (-[e]s;-e) gulf; bay || n (-s;) golf
Golf'platz m golf course
Golf'schläger m golf club
Gondel ['gɔndəl] f (-;-n) gondola
Gon'delführer m gondolier
gönnen ['gœnən] tr not begrudge; allow; **j-m etw nicht g.** begrudge s.o. s.th.
Gön'ner –in §6 mf patron
gön'nerhaft adj patronizing
Gön'nerschaft f (-;) patronage
gor [gor] pret of gären
Gorilla [gə'rɪla] m (-s;-s) gorilla
goß [gɔs] pret of gießen
Gosse ['gɔsə] f (-;-n) gutter
Gote ['gotə] m (-n;-n) Goth
gotisch ['gotɪʃ] adj Gothic
Gott [gɔt] m (-[e]s;̈er) god; God
gottbegnadet ['gɔtbəgnadət] adj gifted
gott'ergeben adj resigned to God's will
Got'tesdienst m divine service; Mass
got'tesfürchtig adj God-fearing
Got'tesgabe f godsend

got'teslästerlich adj blasphemous
Got'teslästerung f blasphemy
Got'tesurteil n ordeal
gott'gefällig adj pleasing to God
Gott'heit f (-;-en) deity, divinity
Göttin ['gœtɪn] f (-;-nen) goddess
göttlich ['gœtlɪç] adj godlike, divine; (fig) heavenly
gottlob' interj thank goodness!
Gott'mensch m God incarnate
gott'selig adj godly
gott'verlassen adj godforsaken
Götze ['gœtsə] m (-n;-n) idol
Göt'zenbild n idol
Göt'zendiener –in §6 mf idolater
Göt'zendienst m idolatry
Gouvernante [guver'nantə] f (-;-n) governess
Gouverneur [guver'nør] m (-s;-e) governor
Grab [grap] n (-[e]s;̈er) grave; tomb
graben ['grabən] §87 tr dig; burrow || **Graben** m (-s;̈) ditch; trench; moat
Grab'geläute n death knell
Grab'gesang m funeral dirge
Grab'hügel m burial mound
Grab'inschrift f epitaph
Grab'mal n tombstone; tomb, sepulcher
Grab'stätte f burial place
Grab'stelle f burial plot
Grad [grat] m (-[e]s;-e) degree; grade; (mil) rank
grade ['gradə] adv var of gerade
Grad'einteilung f gradation
Grad'messer m graduated scale; (fig) yardstick
grad'weise adv by degrees
Graf [graf] m (-en;-en) count; earl (Brit)
Gräfin ['grefɪn] f (-;-nen) countess
gräflich ['greflɪç] adj count's; earl's
Graf'schaft f (-;-en) county
gram [gram] adj—**j-m g. sein** be cross with s.o. || **Gram** m (-[e]s;) grief
grämen ['gremən] tr sadden, distress || ref (über acc) grieve (over)
grämlich ['gremlɪç] adj glum; crabby
Gramm [gram] n (-s;-& -e) gram
Grammatik [gra'matɪk] f (-;-en) grammar
grammatisch [gra'matɪʃ] adj grammatical
Gran [gran] n (-[e]s;) (fig) bit, jot
Granat [gra'nat] m (-[e]s;-e) garnet
Granat'apfel m pomegranate
Granate [gra'natə] f (-;-n) (arti) shell; (mil) grenade
Granat'feuer n shelling
Granat'hülse f shell case
Granat'splitter m shrapnel
Granat'werfer m (mil) mortar
grandios [grandi'os] adj grandiose
Granit [gra'nit] m (-[e]s;-e) granite
Graphik ['grafɪk] f (-;-en) graphic arts; print; engraving; woodcut
graphisch ['grafɪʃ] adj graphic
Graphit [gra'fit] m (-[e]s;) graphite
Gras [gras] n (-es;̈er) grass
grasen ['grazən] intr graze
Gras'halm m blade of grass
Grashüpfer ['grashypfer] m (-s;-) grasshopper

grasig ['grɑzɪç] *adj* grassy
Gras'mäher *m* lawn mower; grass cutter
Gras'mähmaschine *f* lawn mower
Gras'narbe *f* sod, turf
grassieren [gra'sirən] *intr* rage
gräßlich ['gresliç] *adj* grisly
Gras'weide *f* pasture
Grat [grat] *m* (-[e]s;-e) ridge; edge
Gräte ['gretə] *f* (-;-n) fishbone
Gratifikation [gratıfıka'tsjon] *f* (-; -en) bonus
grätig ['gretɪç] *adj* full of fishbones; (*mürrisch*) crabby
gratis ['grɑtıs] *adv* gratis; **g. und franko** (coll) for free
Gratulation [gratula'tsjon] *f* (-;-en) congratulations
gratulieren [gratu'lirən] *intr*—**j-m g. zu** congratulate s.o. on
grau [grau] *adj* gray; (*Vorzeit*) remote || **Grau** *n* (- & -s;-s) gray
Grau'bär *m* grizzly bear
grauen ['grau-ən] *intr* dawn || *impers* —**es graut** day is breaking; **es graut mir vor** (*dat*) I shudder at || **Grauen** *n* (-s;) (vor *dat*) horror (of)
grau'enhaft, grau'envoll *adj* horrible
gräulich ['grɔɪlıç] *adj* grayish
Graupe ['graupə] *f* (-;-n) peeled barley
graupeln ['graupəln] *impers*—**es graupelt** it is sleeting || **Graupeln** *pl* sleet
Graus [graus] *m* (-es;) dread, horror
grausam ['grauzam] *adj* cruel; (coll) awful
Grau'schimmel *m* gray horse
grausen ['grauzən] *impers*—**es graust mir vor** (*dat*) I shudder at
grausig ['grauzıç] *adj* gruesome
Graveur [gra'vør] *m* (-s;-e) engraver
gravieren [gra'virən] *tr* engrave
gravie'rend *adj* aggravating
gravitätisch [gravı'tetıʃ] *adj* stately
Grazie ['gratsjə] *f* (-;-n) grace, charm
graziös [gra'tsjøs] *adj* graceful
Greif [graıf] *m* (-[e]s;-e) griffin
greifbar ['graıfbar] *adj* tangible; at hand
greifen ['graıfən] §88 *tr* grasp; seize; (*Note*) strike || *intr* (*Anker*) catch; (*Zahnrad*) engage; **ans Herz g.** touch deeply; **an j-s Ehre g.** attack s.o.'s honor; **g. in** (*acc*) reach into; **g. nach** reach for; try to seize; **g. zu** reach for; (fig) resort to; **um sich g.** grope about; (*Feuer*) spread; **zu den Waffen g.** take up arms
Greis [graıs] *m* (-es;-e) old man
Grei'senalter *n* old age
grei'senhaft *adj* aged; senile
Greisin ['graızın] *f* (-;-nen) old lady
grell [grel] *adj* (*Ton*) shrill; (*Farbe, Kleider*) flashy; (*Licht*) glaring
Gre·mium ['gremjum] *n* (-s;-mien [mjən]) group, body; committee; corporation
Grenze ['grentsə] *f* (-;-n) boundary; frontier; borderline; limit
grenzen ['grentsən] *intr* (**an** *acc*) adjoin, border (on); (fig) verge (on)
gren'zenlos *adj* limitless
Grenz'fall *m* borderline case

Grenz'linie *f* boundary line
Grenz'sperre *f* ban on border traffic; frontier barricade
Grenz'stein *m* boundary stone
Greuel ['grɔɪ-əl] *m* (-s;-) abhorrence; horror, abomination
Greu'eltat *f* atrocity
greulich ['grɔɪlıç] *adj* horrible
Griebs ['grips] *m* (-es;-e) core
Grieche ['griçə] *m* (-n;-n) Greek
Grie'chenland *n* (-s;) Greece
Griechin ['griçın] *f* (-;-nen) Greek
griechisch ['griçıʃ] *adj* Greek
Griesgram ['grisgram] *m* (-[e]s;-e) (coll) grouch
Grieß [gris] *m* (-es;-e) grit; gravel
Grieß'mehl *n* farina
griff [grıf] *pret* of **greifen** || **Griff** *m* (-[e]s;-e) grip; handle; hilt; (mus) touch
Grill [grıl] *m* (-s;-s) grill; broiler
Grille ['grılə] *f* (-;-n) cricket; (fig) whim
grillen ['grılən] *tr* grill; broil
gril'lenhaft *adj* whimsical
Grimasse [grı'masə] *f* (-;-n) grimace
Grimm [grım] *m* (-[e]s;) anger, fury
grimmig ['grımıç] *adj* furious
Grind [grınt] *m* (-[e]s;-e) scab
grinsen ['grınzən] *intr* grin
Grippe ['grıpə] *f* (-;) grippe
grob [grop] *adj* coarse, rough; crude
Grobian ['grobjan] *m* (-s;-e) boor
gröblich ['grøplıç] *adj* gross
grölen ['grølən] *intr* shout raucously
Groll [grɔl] *m* (-[e]s;) resentment
grollen ['grɔlən] *intr* rumble; (**über** *acc*) be resentful (about); **j-m g.** have a grudge against s.o.
Grönland ['grønlant] *n* (-s;) Greenland
Gros [grɔs] *n* (-ses;-) gross || [gro] *n* (-;-) bulk; (mil) main forces
Groschen ['grɔʃən] *m* (-s;-) (Aust) penny (*one hundredth of a shilling*)
groß [gros] *adj* big, large; tall; great
groß'artig *adj* grand; magnificent
Groß'aufnahme *f* (phot) close-up
groß'äugig *adj* wide-eyed
Groß'betrieb *m* big company
Großbritan'nien *n* Great Britain
Größe ['grøsə] *f* (-;-n) size, greatness; celebrity; (astr) magnitude; (math) quantity
Groß'eltern *pl* grandparents
Groß'enkel *m* great-grandson
Groß'enkelin *f* great-granddaughter
großenteils ['grosəntaıls] *adv* largely
Größenwahn ['grøsənvan] *f* megalomania
Groß'grundbesitz *m* large estate
Groß'handel *m* wholesale trade; **im G. kaufen** buy wholesale
Großhandels- *comb.fm.* wholesale
Groß'händler -in §6 *mf* wholesaler
Groß'handlung *f* (-;-en) wholesale business
groß'herzig *adj* big-hearted
Grossist [grɔ'sıst] *m* (-en;-en) wholesaler
groß'jährig *adj* of legal age
Groß'maul *n* bigmouth
Groß'mut *m* magnanimity

groß'mütig *adj* big-hearted
Groß'mutter *f* grandmother
Groß'onkel *m* great-uncle
Groß'schreibung *f* capitalization
Groß'segel *n* main sail
Groß'sprecher *m* braggart
großspurig ['gros∫purɪç] *adj* pompous
Groß'stadt *f* large city (*with over 100,000 inhabitants*)
Großstädter ['gros∫tɛtər] *m* (*-s;-*) (coll) city slicker
Groß'tat *f* achievement
Groß'teil *m* major part
größtenteils ['grøstəntaɪls] *adv* mainly
groß'tun §154 *intr* brag; put on the dog
Groß'vater *m* grandfather
Groß'wild *n* big game
groß'ziehen §163 *tr* bring up, raise
großzügig ['grostsygɪç] *adj* broad-minded, liberal; generous; large-scale
grotesk [gro'tɛsk] *adj* grotesque
Grotte ['grɔtə] *f* (*-;-n*) grotto
grub [grup] *pret* of **graben**
Grübchen ['grypçən] *n* (*-s;-*) dimple
Grube ['grubə] *f* (*-;-n*) pit; mine
Grübelei [grybə'laɪ] *f* (*-;-en*) brooding
grübeln ['grybəln] *intr* brood
Gruben– [grubən] *comb.fm.* mine, miner's
Gruft [grʊft] *f* (*-;÷e*) tomb, vault
grün [gryn] *adj* green; **Grüne Minna** (sl) paddy wagon || **Grün** *n* (*-s;*) green
Grün'anlage *f* public park
Grund [grʊnt] *m* (*-[e]s;÷e*) ground; land; bottom; foundation, basis; cause, ground; **auf G. von** on the strength of; **G. und Boden** property; **im Grunde genommen** after all; **in G. und Boden** outright
–grund *m* *comb.fm.* bottom of; –ground; grounds for, reasons for
Grund'anstrich *m* first coat
Grund'ausbildung *f* (mil) basic training
Grund'bedeutung *f* primary meaning
Grund'begriff *m* fundamental principle
Grund'besitz *m* real estate
Grund'buch *n* land register
grund'ehr'lich *adj* thoroughly honest
gründen ['grʏndən] *tr* found; **g. auf** (*acc*) base on || *ref* (**auf** *acc*) be based (on)
Gründer –in ['grʏndər(ɪn)] §6 *mf* founder
grund'falsch' *adj* absolutely false
Grund'farbe *f* primary color
Grund'fläche *f* area; (geom) base
grundieren [grʊn'dirən] *tr* prime; size
Grundier'farbe *f* primer coat
Grundier'schicht *f* primer coat
Grund'kapital *n* capital stock
Grund'lage *f* basis, foundation
grund'legend *adj* basic, fundamental
Grund'legung *f* founding, foundation
gründlich ['grʏntlɪç] *adj* thorough
Grund'linie *f* (geom) base; **Grundlinien** basic features, outlines
Grundon'nerstag *m* Holy Thursday
Grund'riß *m* floor plan; outline

Grund'satz *m* principle
grundsätzlich ['grʊntzɛtslɪç] *adj* basic || *adv* as a matter of principle
Grund'schule *f* primary school
Grund'stein *m* cornerstone
Grund'stellung *f* position of attention; **die G. einnehmen** come to attention
Grund'steuer *f* real-estate tax
Grund'stoff *m* raw material; (chem) element
Grund'strich *m* downstroke
Grund'stück *n* lot, property
Grund'ton *m* (fig) prevailing mood; (mus) keynote; (paint) ground shade
Grün'dung *f* (*-;-en*) foundation
grund'verschie'den *adj* entirely different
Grund'wasserspiegel *m* water table
Grund'zahl *f* cardinal number
Grund'zug *m* main feature; **Grundzüge** fundamentals, essentials
Grüne ['grynə] *n—ins* **G.** into the country
grün'lich *adj* greenish
Grün'schnabel *m* know-it-all
Grünspan ['gryn∫pan] *m* (*-[e]s;*) verdigris
Grün'streifen *m* grass strip; (*auf der Autobahn*) median strip
grunzen ['grʊntsən] *tr* & *intr* grunt
Gruppe ['grʊpə] *f* (*-;-n*) group; (mil) squad
Grup'penführer *m* group leader; (hist) lieutenant general (*of S.S. troops*); (mil) squad leader
gruppieren [grʊ'pirən] *tr* & *ref* group
Gruppie'rung *f* (*-;-en*) grouping
gruselig ['gruzəlɪç] *adj* creepy
gruseln ['gruzəln] *intr—j-n* **g. machen** give s.o. the creeps || *ref* have a creepy feeling || *impers—es* **gruselt mir** (or **mich**) it gives me the creeps
Gruß [grus] *m* (*-es;÷e*) greeting; salute; greetings, regards; **mit freundlichem Gruß, Ihr ...** Sincerely yours
grüßen ['grysən] *tr* greet; salute, **grüß Gott!** hello!; *j-n* **g. lassen** send best regards to s.o.
Grütze ['grytsə] *f* (*-;-n*) groats; (coll) brains
gucken ['gʊkən] *intr* look; peep
Guck'loch *n* peephole
Guerilla [ge'rɪlja] *m* (*-s;-s*) guerilla
Gulasch ['gula∫] *n* (*-[e]s;-s*) goulash
gültig ['gʏltɪç] *adj* valid; legal
Gummi ['gumi] *m* & *n* (*-s;-s*) gum; rubber
gum'miartig *adj* gummy; rubbery
Gum'miband *n* (*-[e]s;÷er*) rubber band; elastic
Gum'mibaum *m* rubber plant
Gum'mibonbon *m* & *n* gumdrop
gummieren [gʊ'mirən] *tr* gum; rubberize
Gum'miknüppel *m* truncheon; billy club
Gummilinse *f* (phot) zoom lens
Gum'mimantel *m* mackintosh
Gum'mireifen *m* tire
Gum'mischuhe *pl* rubbers
Gum'mizelle *f* padded cell
Gunst [gʊnst] *f* (*-;*) favor, goodwill; kindness, good turn

Gunst'bezeigung *f* expression of good-will
günstig ['gʏnstɪç] *adj* favorable; (*Bedingungen*) easy
Günstling ['gʏnstlɪŋ] *m* (-s;-e) favorite; (pej) minion
Gurgel ['gʊrgəl] *f* (-;-n) gullet
gurgeln ['gʊrgəln] *intr* gurgle; gargle
Gurke ['gʊrkə] *f* (-;-n) cucumber
Gurt [gʊrt] *m* (-[e]s;-e) belt, strap
Gürtel ['gʏrtəl] *m* (-s;-) girdle; belt; (geog) zone
gürten ['gʏrtən] *tr* gird
Guß [gʊs] *m* (**Gusses; Güsse**) gush; (*Regen*) downpour; (*Gießen*) casting; (culin) icing; (typ) font
gut [gut] *adj* good; **es ist schon gut** it's all right; **mach's gut!** so long! || *adv* well || **Gut** *n* (-[e]s;=er) good; possessions; estate; (com) commodity; **Güter** goods; assets
Gut'achten *n* (-s;-) expert opinion
gut'artig *adj* good-natured; (pathol) benign
gut'aussehend *adj* good-looking
Gut'dünken *n* (-s;) judgment; discretion; **nach G.** at will, as one pleases; (culin) to taste
Gute ['gutə] §5 *n* good; **alles G!** best of everything!; **sein Gutes haben** have its good points
Güte ['gytə] *f* (-;) goodness
Güter- [gytər] *comb.fm.* freight; property; (com) of goods
Gü'terabfertigung *f* freight office
Gü'terbahnhof *m* (rr) freight yard
gut'erhalten *adj* in good condition

Gü'terwagen *m* freight car; **geschlossener G.** boxcar; **offener G.** gondola car
Gü'terzug *m* freight train
gut'gelaunt *adj* good-humored
gut'gesinnt *adj* well-disposed
gut'haben §89 *tr* have to one's credit || **Guthaben** *n* (-s;-) credit balance
gut'heißen §95 *tr* approve of
gut'herzig *adj* good-hearted
gütig ['gytɪç] *adj* kind, good
gütlich ['gytlɪç] *adj* amicable
gut'machen *tr*—**wieder g.** make good for
gut'mütig *adj* good-natured
gut'sagen *intr*—**für j-n g.** vouch for s.o.
Gut'schein *m* coupon; credit note
gut'schreiben §62 *tr*—**j-m e-n Betrag g.** credit s.o. with a sum
Gut'schrift *f* credit entry; credit item
Gut'schriftsanzeige *f* credit note
Guts'herr *m* landowner
gut'tun §154 *intr* do good; behave
gut'willig *adj* willing, obliging
Gymnasiast **-in** [gʏm'nazjast(ɪn)] §7 *mf* high school student
Gymna·sium [gʏm'nazjʊm] *n* (-s;-sien [zjən]) high school (*with academic course*)
Gymnastik [gʏm'nastɪk] *f* (-;) gymnastics
Gynäkologe [gʏnɛkɔ'logə] *m* (-n;-n), **Gynäkologin** [gʏnɛkɔ'login] *f* (-; nen) gynecologist
Gynäkologie [gʏnɛkɔlɔ'gi] *f* (-;) gynecology

H

H, h [hɑ] *invar n* H, h; (mus) B
Haar [hɑr] *n* (-[e]s;-e) hair; (tex) nap, pile; **aufs H.** exactly; **um ein H.** by a hair's breadth
Haar'büschel *n* tuft of hair
haaren ['hɑrən] *intr* lose hair
Haarfärbmittel ['hɑrfɛrpmɪtəl] *n* hair dye
Haar'feder *f* hairspring
haar'genau' *adj* exact, precise
haarig ['hɑrɪç] *adj* hairy
haar'klein *adj* (coll) in detail
Haar'locke *f* lock of hair
Haar'nadel *f* hairpin
haar'scharf' *adj* razor-sharp
Haar'schneider *m* barber
Haar'schnitt *m* haircut
Haar'spange *f* barrette
Haarspray ['hɑrspre] *m* (-s;-s) hair spray
haar'sträubend *adj* hair-raising
Haar'teil *m* hair piece
Haar'tolle *f* loose curl
Haar'tracht *f* hairdo
Haar'trockner *m*, **Haar'trockenhaube** *f* hair dryer
Haar'wäsche *f* shampoo
Haar'wasser *n* hair tonic

Haar'wickler *m* curler; hair roller
Haar'zwange *f* tweezers
Hab [hap] *invar n*—**Hab und Gut** possessions
Habe ['hɑbə] *f* (-;) possessions
haben ['hɑbən] §89 *tr & aux* have || **Haben** *n* (-s;) credit side
Habe'nichts *m* (-es;-e) have-not
Hab'gier *f* greed, avarice
hab'haft *adj*—**h. werden** (*genit*) get hold of; (*Diebes*) apprehend
Habicht ['hɑbɪçt] *m* (-[e]s;-e) hawk
Ha'bichtsnase *f* aquiline nose
Habilitation [hɑbɪlɪta'tsjon] *f* (-;-en) accreditation as a university lecturer
habilitieren [hɑbɪlɪ'tirən] *ref* be accredited as a university lecturer
Hab'seligkeiten *pl* belongings
Hab'sucht *f* greed, avarice
hab'süchtig *adj* greedy, avaricious
Hackbeil ['hakbaɪl] *n* cleaver
Hacke ['hakə] *f* (-;-n) heel; hoe; pick; pickax; hatchet; mattock
hacken ['hakən] *tr* hack, chop; peck || *intr* (nach) peck (at)
Häckerling ['hɛkərlɪŋ] *m* (-s;) chaff
Hackfleisch ['hakflaɪʃ] *n* ground meat
Häcksel ['hɛksəl] *n* (-s;) chaff

Hader ['hɑdər] m (-s;) strife || m (-s; -n) rag
hadern ['hɑdərn] intr quarrel
Hafen ['hɑfən] m (-s;ᐞ) harbor; port; (fig) haven
Ha'tenamt n port authority
Ha'fenanlagen pl docks
Ha'fenarbeiter m longshoreman
Ha'fendamm m jetty, mole
Ha'fensperre f blockade
Ha'fenstadt f seaport
Ha'fenviertel n dock area, waterfront
Hafer ['hɑfər] m (-s;-) oats; **ihn sticht der H.** he's feeling his oats
Ha'fergrütze f, **Ha'fermehl** n oatmeal
Hafner ['hɑfnər] m (-s;-) potter
Haft [haft] f (-;) arrest; custody; imprisonment; **in H.** under arrest; ın custody; in prison
haftbar ['haftbɑr] adj (jur) liable
Haft'befehl m warrant for arrest
haften ['haftən] intr (an dat) cling (to), stick (to); **h. für** vouch for; (jur) be held liable for; (jur) put up bail for
Haft'fähigkeit f, **Haft'festigkeit** f adhesion
Häftling ['heftlɪŋ] m (-s;-e) prisoner
Haft'lokal n (mil) guardhouse
Haft'pflicht f liability
haft'pflichtig adj (für) liable (for)
Haft'pflichtversicherung f liability insurance
Haft'richter m (jur) magistrate
Haft'schale f contact lens
Haf'tung f (-;-en) liability
Hag [hɑk] m (-[e]s;-e) enclosure; (Hain) grove; (Buschwerk) bushes
Hagedorn ['hɑgədɔrn] m hawthorn
Hagel ['hɑgəl] m (-s;) hail
Ha'gelkorn n hailstone
hageln ['hɑgəln] intr (SEIN) (fig) rain down || impers—es hagelt it is hailing
Ha'gelschauer m hailstorm
hager ['hɑgər] adj gaunt, haggard
Hagestolz ['hɑgə/tɔlts] m (-es;-e) confirmed bachelor
Häher ['he·ər] m (-s;-) (orn) jay
Hahn [hɑn] m (-[e]s;ᐞe) rooster; (Wasser-) faucet; **den H. spannen** cock the gun; **H. im Korbe sein** rule the roost
Hähnchen ['hençən] n (-s;-) young rooster
Hah'nenkamm m cockscomb
Hah'nenkampf m cock fight
Hah'nenschrei m crow of the cock
Hahnrei ['hɑnraɪ] m (-s;-e) cuckold
Hai [haɪ] m (-[e]s;-e), **Hai'fisch** m shark
Hain [haɪn] m (-[e]s;-e) grove
Haiti [ha'iti] n (-s;) Haiti
Häkelarbeit ['hekəlarbaɪt] f crocheting
häkeln ['hekəln] tr & intr crochet || **Häkeln** n (-s;) crocheting
Haken ['hɑkən] m (-s;-) hook; (Spange) clasp; (fig) snag, hitch
Ha'kenkreuz n swastika
Ha'kennase f hooknose
halb [halp] adj & adv half
halb-, Halb- comb.fm. half-, semi-
Halb'blut n half-breed

-halber [halbər] comb.fm. for the sake of; owing to
halb'fett adj (typ) bold
Halb'franzband m (bb) half leather
halb'gar adj (culin) (medium) rare
Halb'gott m demigod
Halbheit ['halphaɪt] f (-;) half-
Halb'kugel f hemisphere
halbieren [hal'birən] tr halve, bisect
Halb'insel f peninsula
Halb'kettenfahrzeug n half-track
Halb'kugel f hemisphere
halb'lang adj half-length; **halblange Ärmel** half sleeves
halb'laut adj low || adv in a low voice
Halb'leiter m (elec) semiconductor
halb'mast adv at half-mast; **auf h.** at half-mast
Halb'messer m radius
halbpart ['halppart] adv—**mit j–m h. machen** go fifty-fifty with s.o.
Halb'schuh m low shoe
Halb'schwergewicht n light-heavyweight division
Halb'schwergewichtler m light-heavyweight
halb'stündig adj half-hour
halb'stündlich adj half-hourly || adv every half hour
Halb'vers m hemistich
halbwegs ['halbveks] adv halfway
Halb'welt f demimonde
halbwüchsig ['halpvyksɪç] adj teenage || **Halbwüchsige** §5 mf teenager
Halb'zug m (mil) section
Halde ['haldə] f (-;-n) slope; (Schutt-) slag pile
half [half] pret of **helfen**
Hälfte ['helftə] f (-;-n) half
Halfter ['halftər] f (-;-n) holster || n (-s;-) halter
Hall [hal] m (-[e]s;-e) sound; clang
Halle ['halə] f (-;-n) hall; (e-s Hotels) lobby; (aer) hangar; (rr) concourse
hallen ['halən] intr sound, resound
Hal'lenbad n indoor pool
Hallo [ha'lo] n (-s;) hullabaloo || interj (to attract attention) hey!; (telp) hello
Halm [halm] m (-[e]s;-e) stem, stalk; blade (of grass)
Hals [hals] m (-es;ᐞe) neck; throat; **H. über Kopf** head over heels
Hals'abschneider m cutthroat
hals'abschneiderisch adj cutthroat
Hals'ader f jugular vein
Hals'ausschnitt m neckline, neck
Hals'band n (-[e]s;ᐞer) necklace, choker; (e-s Hundes) collar
halsbrecherisch ['halsbreçərɪʃ] adj breakneck
Hals'ent·ündung f sore throat
Hals'kette f necklace, chain
Hals'kragen m collar
Hals'krause f frilled collar
hals'starrig adj stubborn
Hals'weh n sore throat
halt [halt] adv just. simply || interj stop!; (mil) halt! || **Halt** m (-[e]s; -e) hold; foothold; support; stability; stop. halt
haltbar ['haltbɑr] adj durable; tenable

halten ['haltən] §90 *tr* hold; keep; detain; (*Rede*) deliver; (*Vorlesung*) give; (*feiern*) celebrate; **es h. mit** do with; have an affair with; **etw auf sich h.** have self-respect; **j-n h. für** take s.o. for; **viel h. von** think highly of ‖ *ref* keep, last; hold ones own; **an sich h.** restrain oneself; **auf sich h.** be particular about one's appearance; **sich an etw h.** (fig) stick to s.th.; **sich an j-n h.** hold s.o. liable; **sich gesund h.** keep healthy; **sich links h.** keep to the left ‖ *intr* stop; last; **h. auf** (*acc*) pay attention to; **h. nach** head for; **h. zu** stick by; **was das Zeug hält** with might and main

Hal'ter *m* (-s;-) holder; rack; owner
Hal'teriemen *m* strap (*on bus or trolley*)
Hal'testelle *f* bus stop, trolley stop; (rr) stop
Hal'teverbot *n* (public sign) no stopping
-haltig [haltıç] *comb.fm.* containing
halt'los *adj* without support; helpless; unprincipled
halt'machen *intr* stop, halt
Hal'tung *f* (-;-en) pose, posture; attitude
Halte'zeichen *n* stop sign
Halunke [ha'luŋkə] *m* (-;-n) rascal
hämisch ['hemıʃ] *adj* spiteful, malicious
Hammel ['haməl] *m* (-s;-e & ⸚) wether; (coll) mutton-head; (culin) mutton
Ham'melkeule *f* leg of mutton
Hammer ['hamər] *m* (-s;⸚) hammer; gavel; **unter den H. kommen** be auctioned off
hämmern ['hemərn] *tr & intr* hammer
Hämorrhoiden [hemərə'idən] *pl* hemorroids, piles
Hampelmann ['hampəlman] *m* (-[e]s; ⸚er) jumping jack
hamstern ['hamstərn] *tr* hoard
Hand [hant] *f* (-;⸚e) hand; **an H. von** with the help of; **auf eigene H.** of one's own accord; **aus erster H.** (*bei Verkauf*) one-owner; **aus erster H. haben** hear first-hand; **aus erster H. kaufen** buy directly; **bei der H.** at hand, handy; **die letzte H. finishing touches; die öffentliche H.** the state, public authorities; **es liegt auf der H.** it is obvious; **H. ans Werk legen** get down to work; **H. aufs Herz!** cross my heart!; **Hände hoch!** hands up!; **H. und Fuß haben** make sense; **in die H. (or Hände) bekommen** get one's hands on; **j-m an die H. gehen** lend s.o. a hand; **j-m die H. drücken** shake hands with s.o.; **j-m etw an (die) H. geben** quote s.o. a price on s.th.; **j-m zur H. gehen** lend s.o. a hand; **unter der H.** underhandedly; unofficially; **von der H. weisen** reject; **zu Händen Herrn X** Attention Mr. X; **zur H.** at hand, handy
Hand'arbeit *f* manual labor; needlework
Hand'aufheben *n*, **Hand'aufhebung** *f* show of hands

Hand'ausgabe *f* abridged edition
Hand'bedienung *f* manual control
Hand'betrieb *m*—**mit (or für) H.** hand-operated
Hand'bibliothek *f* reference library
hand'breit *adj* wide as a hand ‖ **Hand'breit** *f* (-;-) hand's breadth
Hand'bremse *f* (aut) hand brake
Hand'buch *n* handbook, manual
Händedruck ['hendədruk] *m* handshake
Händeklatschen ['hendəklatʃən] *n* clapping
Handel ['handəl] *m* (-s;⸚) trade; deal, bargain; business; affair; **e-n H. eingehen** conclude a deal; **e-n H. treiben** carry on business; **H. und Gewerbe** trade and industry; **Händel suchen** pick a quarrel; **im H. sein** be on the market; **in den H. bringen** put on the market
-handel *m comb.fm.* –trade, –business
handeln ['handəln] *intr* act; take action; proceed; **gegen das Gesetz h.** go against the law; **gut an j-m h.** treat s.o. well; **h. über** (*acc*) or **von** deal with; **h. mit** do business with; **im großen h.** do wholesale business ‖ *impers ref*—**es handelt sich um** it is a matter of; **darum handelt es sich nicht** that's not the point
Han'delsabkommen *n* trade agreement
Han'delsartikel *m* commodity
Han'delsbetrieb *m* commercial enterprise; business; firm
Han'delsbilanz *f* balance of trade; **aktive H.** favorable balance of trade
Han'delsdampfer *m* (naut) merchantman
han'delseinig *adj*—**h. werden mit** come to terms with
Han'delsgärtner *m* truck farmer
Han'delskammer *f* chamber of commerce
Han'delsmarine *f* merchant marine
Han'delsmarke *f* trademark
Han'delsminister *m* secretary of commerce
Han'delsministerium *n* department of commerce
Han'delsplatz *m* trade center
Han'delsschiff *n* merchantman
Han'delssperre *f* trade embargo
händelsüchtig ['hendəlzʏçtıç] *adj* quarrelsome
Han'delsvertrag *m* commercial treaty
Han'delswert *m* trade-in value
Han'delszeichen *n* trademark
Hand'exemplar *n* desk copy
Hand'fertigkeit *f* manual dexterity
Hand'fessel *f* handcuff
hand'fest *adj* sturdy; well-founded
Hand'fläche *f* palm of the hand
Hand'geld *n* advance payment; deposit
Hand'gelenk *n* wrist; **aus (or mit) dem H.** (coll) easy as pie
hand'gemein *adj*—**h. werden** come to blows
Hand'gemenge *n* scuffle
Hand'gepäck *n* hand luggage
Hand'gepäckschließfach *n* locker
Hand'granate *f* hand grenade
hand'greiflich *adj* tangible; obvious;

j–m etw h. **machen** make s.th. clear to s.o.; h. **werden** come to blows
Hand'griff m grip; handle; **keinen H. tun** not lift a finger
Hand'habe f (–;–n) handle; pretext; occasion; **er hat keine H. gegen mich** he has nothing on me
hand'haben tr handle; (*Maschine*) operate; (*Rechtspflege*) administer; (fig) manage
–hänaig [hɛndɪç] comb.fm. –handed
Hand'karren m hand cart, push cart
Hand'koffer m suitcase; attaché case
Handlanger ['hantlaŋər] m (–s;–) handyman; (pej) underling
Händler –in ['hɛndlər(ɪn)] §6 mf dealer, merchant; storekeeper
Hand'lesekunst f palmistry
Hand'leserin f (–;–nen) palm reader
hand'lich adj handy
Hand'lung f (–;–en) shop; act, action
–handlung f comb.fm. business; shop
Hand'lungsgehilfe m clerk, salesman
Hand'lungsweise f conduct
Hand'pflege f manicure
Hand'pflegerin f (–;–nen) manicurist
Hand'rücken m back of the hand
Hand'schaltung f manual shift
Hand'schelle f handcuff
Hand'schlag m handshake
Hand'schreiben n hand-written letter
Hand'schrift f handwriting; manuscript; (sl) slap, box on the ear
Hand'schriftenkunde f paleography
hand'schriftlich adj hand-written
Hand'schuh m glove
Hand'schuhfach n (aut) glove compartment
Hand'streich m (mil) raid
Hand'tasche f handbag, purse
Hand'tuch n towel; **schmales H.** (sl) beanpole
Hand'tuchhalter m towel rack
Hand'umdrehen n—im. **H.** in a jiffy
Hand'voll f (–;–) handful
Hand'werk n craft, trade; **j–m ins H. pfuschen** (sl) stick one's nose in s.o. else's business
Hand'werker m craftsman
Hand'werkszeug n tool kit
Hand'wörterbuch n pocket dictionary
Hand'wurzel f wrist
Hand'zettel m handbill
hanebüchen ['hɑnəbyçən] adj (coll) incredible; (coll) monstrous
Hanf [hanf] m (–[e]s;) hemp
Hang [haŋ] m (–[e]s;ᵙ) slope; hillside; (fig) inclination, tendency
Hangar ['haŋɑr] m (–s;–s) hangar
Hängebacken ['hɛŋəbakən] pl jowls
Hängebauch ['hɛŋəbaux] m potbelly
Hängebrücke ['hɛŋəbrykə] f suspension bridge
Hängematte ['hɛŋəmatə] f hammock
hängen ['hɛŋən] tr hang || ref—sich an j–n h. hang on to s.o.; **sich ans Telephon h.** be on the telephone || §92 intr hang; cling, stick
hän'genbleiben §62 intr (SEIN) stick; be detained, get stuck; (an dat) get caught (on); (educ) stay behind
Hans [hans] m (–' & –ens;) Johnny, Jack

Hans'dampf m (–[e]s;–e) busybody; **H. in allen Gassen** jack-of-all trades
Hänselei [hɛnzə'laɪ] f (–;–en) teasing
hänseln ['hɛnzəln] tr tease
Hans'narr m fool
Hans'wurst m (–es;–e & ᵙe) clown
Hantel ['hantəl] f (–;–n) dumbell
hantieren [han'tirən] intr (an acc) be busy (with); **mit etw h.** handle s.th.
hapern ['hɑpərn] impers—bei mir hapert es an (dat) (or mit) I am short of; bei mir hapert es in (dat) (or mit) I am weak in; damit hapert's that's the hitch
Happen ['hapən] m (–s;–) morsel; mouthful; (fig) good opportunity; **fetter H.** (coll) big hawl
happig ['hapɪç] adj greedy; (*Preis*) steep
Härchen ['hɛrçən] n (–s;–) tiny hair
Harem ['hɑrɛm] m (–s;–s) harem
Häre·sie [hɛrɛ'zi] f (–;–sien ['zi·ən]) heresy
Häretiker [hɛ'retɪkər] m (–s;–) heretic
Harfe ['harfə] f (–;–n) harp
Harke ['harkə] f (–;–n) rake
harken ['harken] tr & intr rake
Harm [harm] m (–[e]s;) harm; grief
härmen ['hɛrmən] ref (um) grieve (over)
harm'los adj harmless
Harmo·nie [harmə'ni] f (–;–nien ['ni·ən]) harmony
harmonieren [harmə'nirən] intr harmonize
Harmoni·ka [har'mɔnɪkɑ] f (–;–kas & –ken [kən]) accordion; harmonica
harmonisch [har'mɔnɪʃ] adj harmonious
Harn [harn] m (–[e]s;–e) urine; **H. lassen** pass water
Harn'blase f (anat) bladder
harnen ['harnən] intr urinate
Harn'glas n urinal
Harn'grieß m (pathol) gravel
Harnisch ['harnɪʃ] m (–es;–e) armor; **in H. geraten über** (acc) fly into a rage over; **j–n in H. bringen** get s.o. hopping mad
Harn'leiter m (anat) ureter; (surg) catheter
Harn'röhre f urethra
harn'treibend adj diuretic
Harpune [har'punə] f (–;–n) harpoon
harpunieren [harpu'nirən] tr harpoon
harren ['harən] intr tarry; hope; (genit or auf acc) wait (for)
harsch [harʃ] adj harsh || **Harsch** m (–es;), **Harsch'schnee** m crushed snow
hart [hart] adj hard; severe || adv— **h. an** (dat) close to, hard by
Härte ['hɛrtə] f (–;) hardness; severity
härten ['hɛrtən] tr, ref & intr harden
Hart'faserplatte f fiber board
Hart'geld n coins
hartgesotten ['hartgəzɔtən] adj hardboiled; (*Verbrecher*) hardened
hart'herzig adj hard-hearted
hart'köpfig adj thick-headed
hart'leibig adj constipated
Hart'leibigkeit f (–;) constipation
hart'löten tr braze

hartnäckig ['hartnεkıç] adj stubborn
Hart'platz m (tennis) hard court
Harz [harts] n (-es;-e) resin; rosin
harzig [hartsıç] adj resinous
Hasardspiel [ha'zart/pil] n gambling game; gamble
haschen ['ha/ən] tr snatch, grab || intr (nach) try to catch, snatch (at)
Hase ['hazə] m (-n;-n) hare; **alter H.** old-timer, veteran
Ha'selnuß ['hazəlnʊs] f hazelnut
Hasenfuß m (coll) coward
Ha'senherz n (coll) yellow belly
Ha'senmaus f chinchilla
Hasenpanier ['hazənpanir] n—**das H. ergreifen** take to ones heels
ha'senrein adj—**nicht ganz h.** (fig) a bit fishy, rather shady
Ha'senscharte f harelip
Haspe ['haspə] f (-;-n) hasp
Haspel ['haspəl] f (-;-n) & m (-s;-) reel, spool; winch, windlass
haspeln ['haspəln] tr reel, spool
Haß m (Hasses;) hatred
hassen ['hasən] tr hate
has'senswert, has'senswürdig adj hateful
häßlich ['hεslıç] adj ugly; nasty
Hast [hast] f (-;) haste
hasten ['hastən] intr be in a hurry, act quickly || intr (SEIN) hasten, rush
hastig ['hastıç] adj hasty
hätscheln ['het/əln] tr caress, cuddle; (verzärteln) coddle, spoil
hatte ['hatə] pret of **haben**
Haube ['haubə] f (-;-n) cap; (aer) cowling; (aut) hood; (orn) crest
Haubitze [hau'bıtsə] f (-;-n) howitzer
Hauch [haux] m (-[e]s;-e) breath; breeze; (Schicht) thin layer; (Spur) trace
hauch'dünn' adj paper-thin
hauchen ['hauxən] tr whisper; (ling) aspirate || intr breathe
Hauch'laut m (ling) aspirate
Haue ['hau·ə] f (-;-n) hoe; adze; **H. kriegen** get a spanking
hauen ['hau·ən] §93 tr hack, cut; strike; (Baum) fell; (Stein) hew || §109 tr beat (up) || intr—**h. nach** lash out at; **um sich h.** flail
Hauer ['hau·ər] m (-s;-) tusk
häufeln ['hɔɪfəln] tr hill
häufen ['hɔɪfən] tr & ref pile up
Haufen ['haufən] m (-s;-) pile, heap
Hau'fenwolke f cumulus cloud
häufig ['hɔɪfıç] adj frequent || adv frequently
Häu'figkeit f (-;) frequency
Häu'fung f (-;-en) accumulation
Haupt [haupt] n (-[e]s;¨er) head; top; chief, leader **aufs H. schlagen** vanquish
Haupt- comb.fm. head; chief; major; most important; prime; primary, leading
Haupt'altar m high altar
haupt'amtlich adj full-time
Haupt'bahnhof m main train station
Haupt'darsteller m leading man
Haupt'darstellerin f leading lady
Häuptel ['hɔɪptəl] n (-s;-) head
Haupt'fach n (educ) major

Haupt'farbe f primary color
Haupt'feldwebel m first sergeant
Haupt'film m (cin) feature
Haupt'gefreite §5 m private first class; lance corporal (Brit); seaman; airman second class
Haupt'geschäftsstelle f head office
Haupt'gewinn m first prize
Haupt'haar n hair (on the head)
Häuptling ['hɔɪptlıŋ] m (-s;-e) chief
häuptlings ['hɔɪptlıŋs] adv head first
Haupt'linie f (rr) trunk line
Haupt'mann m (-[e]s;-leute) captain
Haupt'masse f bulk
Haupt'mast m mainmast
Hauptnenner ['hauptnεnər] m (-s;-) (math) common denominator
Haupt'probe f dress rehearsal
Haupt'quartier n headquarters; **Großes H.** general headquarters
Haupt'rolle f leading role, lead
Haupt'sache f main thing; (jur) point at issue
haupt'sächlich adj main, principal
Haupt'satz m (gram) main clause; (phys) principle, law
Haupt'schalter m master switch
Haupt'schiff n (archit) nave
Haupt'schlagader f aorta
Haupt'schlüssel m master key, pass key
Haupt'schriftleiter m editor in chief
Haupt'spaß m great fun; great joke
Haupt'stadt f capital
Haupt'straße f main street; highway
Haupt'strecke f (rr) main line
Haupt'stütze f mainstay
Haupt'ton m primary accent
Haupt'treffer m first prize; jackpot
Haupt'verkehr m peak-hour traffic
Haupt'verkehrsstraße f main artery
Haupt'verkehrszeit f rush hour
Haupt'wort n (-[e]s;¨er) noun
Haus [haus] n (-es;¨er) house; **ein großes H. führen** do a lot of entertaining; **H. und Hof** house and home; **öffentliches H.** brothel; **nach Hause** home; **sich zu Hause fühlen** feel at home; **von zu Hause** from home
Haus'angestellte §5 mf domestic
Haus'apotheke f medicine cabinet
Haus'arbeit f housework; (educ) homework
Haus'arzt m family doctor
Haus'aufgabe f homework
haus'backen adj homemade; (Frau) plain; (fig) provincial
Haus'bedarf m household needs; **für den H.** for the home
Haus'brand m domestic fuel
Haus'bursche m porter
Haus'diener m porter
hausen ['hauzən] intr reside; (coll) make a mess; **schlimm h.** wreak havoc
Häuserblock ['hɔɪzərblɔk] m block of houses
Häusermakler –in ['hɔɪzərmaklər(ın)] §6 mf realtor
Haus'flur m entrance hall; hallway
Haus'frau f housewife; landlady
Haus'freund m friend of the family; (coll) wife's lover

Haus'gebrauch *m* family custom; household use
Haus'gehilfin *f* domestic
Haus'genosse *m*, **Haus'genossin** *f* occupant of the same house
Haus'gesinde *n* domestics
Haus'glocke *f* doorbell
Haus'halt *m* household; budget; **den H. führen** keep house
haus'halten §90 *intr* keep house; economize
Haushälter –in ['haʊshɛltər(ɪn)] §6 *mf* housekeeper
haushälterisch ['haʊshɛltərɪʃ] *adj* economical
Haus'haltsausschuß *m* ways and means committee
Haus'haltsgerät *n* household utensil
Haus'haltsjahr *n* fiscal year
Haus'haltsplan *m* budget
Haus'haltung *f* housekeeping; household; family budget; management
Haus'haltungslehre *f* home economics
Haus'herr *m* master of the house; landlord
Haus'herrin *f* lady of the house; landlady
haus'hoch' *adj* very high; vast
Haus'hofmeister *m* steward
hausieren [haʊ'zirən] *intr*—**mit etw h.** peddle s.th.; go around telling everyone about s.th.
Hausierer [haʊ'zirər] *m* (–s;–) door-to-door salesman
Haus'lehrer –in §6 *mf* private tutor
häuslich ['hɔɪslɪç] *adj* home, domestic; homey; thrifty
Häus'lichkeit *f* (–;) family life; home
Haus'mädchen *n* maid
Haus'meister *m* caretaker, janitor
Haus'mittel *n* home remedy
Haus'mutter *f* mother of the family
Haus'pflege *f* home nursing
Haus'schlüssel *m* front-door key
Haus'schuh *m* slipper
Hausse ['hoɛs] *f* (–;–n) (econ, st. exch.) boom
Haus'sespekulant *m* (st. exch.) bull
Haussier [hos'je] *m* (–s;–) (st. exch.) bull
haussieren [ho'sirən] *tr* (fin) raise || *intr* (fin) go up, rise
Haus'stand *m* household
Haus'suchungsbefehl *m* search warrant
Haus'tier *n* domestic animal; pet
Haus'vater *m* father of the family
Haus'verwalter *m* superintendent
Haus'wesen *n* household
Haus'wirt *m* landlord
Haus'wirtin *f* landlady
Haus'wirtschaft *f* housekeeping
haus'wirtschaftlich *adj* domestic; household
Haus'wirtschaftslehre *f* home economics
Haus'zins *m* house rent
Haut [haʊt] *f* (–;ˑe) skin; hide; **aus der H. fahren** fly off the handle
Haut'abschürfung *f* skin abrasion
Haut'arzt *m* dermatologist
Haut'ausschlag *m* rash
Häutchen ['hɔɪtçən] (–s;–) membrane; pellicle; film

häuten ['hɔɪtən] *tr* skin || *ref* slough the skin
haut'eng *adj* skin-tight
Haut'farbe *f* complexion
Haut'plastik *f* skin graft
Haut'reizung *f* skin irritation
Haut'transplantation *f*, **Haut'verpflanzung** *f* skin grafting
havariert [hava'rirt] *adj* damaged
H'-Bombe *f* H-bomb
Hebamme ['hepamə] *f* (–;–n) midwife
Hebebaum ['hebəbaʊm] *m* lever
Hebebühne ['hebəbynə] *f* car lift
Hebeeisen ['hebə·aɪzən] *n* crowbar
Hebel ['hebəl] *m* (–s;–) lever
heben ['hebən] §94 *tr* lift, raise; (steigern) increase; (fördern) further; (aut) jack up || *ref* rise
Heber ['hebər] *m* (–s;–) siphon; (aut) jack
Hebeschiff ['hebəʃɪf] *n* salvage ship
Hebräer –in [hɛ'bre·ər(ɪn)] §6 *mf* Hebrew
hebräisch [hɛ'bre·ɪʃ] *adj* Hebrew
He'bung *f* (–;–en) lifting; increase; improvement; (mus, pros) stress
Hecht [hɛçt] *m* (–[e]s;–e) (ichth) pike
hechten ['hɛçtən] *intr* dive
Hecht'sprung *m* flying leap; jacknife dive
Heck [hɛk] *n* (–[e]s;–e & –s) stern; (aer) tail; (aut) rear
Heck'antrieb *m* (aut) rear drive
Hecke ['hɛkə] *f* (–;–n) hedge; brood, hatch
hecken ['hɛkən] *tr & intr* breed
Heckenhüpfen (**Heck'kenhüpfen**) *n* (–s;) (aer) hedgehopping
Heckenschütze (**Heck'kenschütze**) *m* sniper
Heck'fenster *n* (aut) rear window
Heck'licht *n* (aer, aut) tail light
Heck'motor *m* rear engine
Heck'pfennig *m* lucky penny
Heck'schütze *m* (aer) tail gunner
heda ['heda] *interj* hey there!
Heer [her] *n* (–[e]s;–e) army; host
Heeres– [herəs] *comb.fm.* army
Hee'resbericht *m* official army communiqué
Hee'resdienst *m* military service
Hee'resdienstvorschriften *pl* army regulations
Hee'resgeistliche §5 *m* army chaplain
Hee'resmacht *f* armed forces; army
Hee'reszug *m* (mil) campaign
Heer'lager *n* army camp; (pol) faction
Heer'schar *f* host, legion
Heer'zug *m* (mil) campaign
Hefe ['hefə] *f* (–;–n) yeast; dregs
He'feteig *m* leavened dough
Heft [hɛft] *n* (–[e]s;–e) haft, handle; notebook; (e–r Zeitschrift) issue
heften ['hɛftən] *tr* fasten together; sew, stitch; tack, baste; (Blick) fix || *ref* (an acc) stick close (to)
heftig ['hɛftɪç] *adj* violent; (Regen) heavy; (Fieber) high; **h. werden** lose one's temper
Heft'klammer *f* paper clip; staple
Heft'maschine *f* stapler
Heft'stich *m* (sew) tack
Heft'zwecke *f* thumbtack

hegen ['heːgən] *tr* (*Wild*) preserve; (*Zweifel, Gedanken*) have; **h. und pflegen** lavish care on
Hehl [heːl] *n* (-[e]s;) secret
hehlen ['heːlən] *intr* receive stolen goods
Heh′ler –in §6 *mf* fence
hehr [heːr] *adj* sublime, noble
Heide ['haɪdə] *m* (-n;-n) heathen; (*Bib*) gentile ‖ *f* (-;-n) heath
Hei′dekraut *n* heather
Heidelbeere ['haɪdəlbeːrə] *f* blueberry
Hei′denangst *f* (coll) jitters
Hei′dengeld *n* (coll) piles of money
Hei′denlärm *m* hullabaloo
hei′denmäßig *adv*—**h. viel** tremendous amount of
Hei′denspaß *m* (coll) great fun
Heidentum ['haɪdəntum] *n* (-s;) heathendom
heidi [haɪ′di] *adj* gone; lost; **h. gehen** get lost; be all gone ‖ *interj* quick!
Heidin ['haɪdɪn] *f* (-;-nen) heathen
heidnisch ['haɪdnɪʃ] *adj* heathen
heikel ['haɪkəl] *adj* particular, fastidious; (*Sache*) ticklish
heil [haɪl] *adj* safe, sound; undamaged ‖ **Heil** *n* (-[e]s;) welfare, benefit; salvation ‖ **Heil** *interj* hail!
Heiland ['haɪlant] *m* (-[e]s;) Saviour
Heil′anstalt *f* sanitarium
Heil′bad *n* spa
heilbar ['haɪlbar] *adj* curable
heil′bringend *adj* beneficial, healthful
Heilbutt ['haɪlbut] *m* (-[e]s;-e) (ichth) halibut
heilen ['haɪlən] *tr* heal ‖ *intr* (HABEN & SEIN) heal
Heil′gehilfe *m* male nurse
Heil′gymnastik *f* physical therapy
heilig ['haɪlɪç] *adj* holy, sacred ‖ **Heilige** §5 *mf* saint
Hei′ligabend *m* Christmas Eve
heiligen ['haɪlɪgən] *tr* hallow
Hei′ligenschein *m* halo
Hei′ligkeit *f* (-;) holiness, sanctity
hei′ligsprechen §64 *tr* canonize
Heiligtum ['haɪlɪçtum] *n* (-[e]s;ː‥er) sanctuary; shrine; sacred relic
Hei′ligung *f* (-;) sanctification
Heil′kraft *f* healing power
Heil′kraut *n* medicinal herb
Heil′kunde *f* medical science
heil′los *adj* wicked; (coll) awful
Heil′mittel *n* remedy; medicine
Heil′mittellehre *f* pharmacology
heilsam ['haɪlzam] *adj* healthful
Heils′armee *f* Salvation Army
Heil′stätte *f* sanitarium
Hei′lung *f* (-;-en) cure
heim [haɪm] *adv* home ‖ **Heim** *n* (-[e]s;-e) home; (*Alters-*) old-age home
Heimat ['haɪmat] *f* (-;-en) home; hometown; homeland
hei′matlich *adj* native
hei′matlos *adj* homeless
Hei′matort *m* hometown, home village
Hei′matstadt *f* hometown, native city
heim′begeben §80 *ref* head home
Heimchen ['haɪmçən] *n* (-s;-) cricket
Heim′computer *m* home computer
Heim′fahrt *f* homeward journey

heim′finden §59 *intr* find one's way home
Heim′gang *m* going home; passing on
heimisch ['haɪmɪʃ] *adj* local; locally-produced; domestic; **heimische Sprache** vernacular; **h. werden** settle down; become established; **sich h. fühlen** feel at home
Heimkehr ['haɪmkeːr] *f* (-;) homecoming
heim′kehren *intr* (SEIN) return home
Heim′kunft *f* homecoming
heim′leuchten *intr* (sl) (*dat*) tell (*s.o.*) where to get off
heim′lich *adj* secret
Heim′lichkeit *f* (-;-en) secrecy; (*Geheimnis*) secret
Heim′reise *f* homeward journey
heim′suchen *tr* afflict, plague
Heim′tücke *f* treachery
heim′tückisch *adj* treacherous
heimwärts ['haɪmverts] *adv* homeward
Heim′weh *n* homesickness; nostalgia
heim′zahlen *tr*—**j-m etw h.** (coll) pay s.o. back for s.th.
Heini ['haɪni] *m* (-s;) Harry; guy
Heinzelmännchen ['haɪntsəlmençən] *pl* (myth) little people
Heirat ['haɪrat] *f* (-;-en) marriage
heiraten ['haɪratən] *tr & intr* marry
Hei′ratsantrag *m* marriage proposal
hei′ratsfähig *adj* marriageable
Hei′ratsgut *n* dowry
Hei′ratskandidat *m* eligible bachelor
Hei′ratsurkunde *f* marriage certificate
Hei′ratsvermittler –in §6 *mf* marriage broker
heischen ['haɪʃən] *tr* demand; beg
heiser ['haɪzər] *adj* hoarse
heiß [haɪs] *adj* hot; (fig) ardent
heißen ['haɪsən] §95 *tr* call; ask, bid; mean ‖ *intr* be called; **das heißt** that is, i.e.; **wie h. Sie?** what is your name?
heiß′geliebt *adj* beloved
heiter ['haɪtər] *adj* cheerful; hilarious; serene; (*Wetter*) clear
Heiz– [haɪts] *comb.fm.* heating
Heiz′anlage *f* heating system
Heiz′apparat *m* heater
hei•en ['haɪtsən] *tr* heat; **den Ofen mit Kohle h.** burn coal in the stove ‖ *intr* give off heat; heat; turn on the heating; light the fire (or stove)
Hei′zer *m* (-s;) boilerman; (naut) stoker; (rr) fireman
Heiz′faden *m* (elec) filament
Heiz′kissen *n* heating pad
Heiz′körper *m* radiator; heater
Heiz′material *n* fuel
Heiz′platte *f* hot plate
Heiz′raum *m* boiler room
Heiz′schlange *f* heating coil
Hei′zung *f* (-;) heating; (coll) central heating; radiator
Hei′zungskessel *m* boiler
Hei′zungsrohr *n* radiator pipe
Held [helt] *m* (-en;-en) hero
Hel′denalter *n* heroic age
Hel′dengedicht *n* epic
Hel′dengeist *m* heroism
hel′denhaft *adj* heroic
Hel′denmut *m* heroism

hel'denmütig *adj* heroic
Hel'dentat *f* heroic deed, exploit
Heldentum ['hɛldəntum] *n* (-[e]s;) heroism
Heldin ['hɛldɪn] *f* (-;-nen) heroine
helfen ['hɛlfən] *intr* (*dat*) help; **es hilft nichts** it's of no use
Hel'fer -in §6 *mf* helper
Hel'fershelfer *m* accomplice
Helikopter [helɪ'kɔptər] *m* (-s;-) helicopter
hell [hɛl] *adj* clear; bright; lucid; (*Haar*) fair; (*Bier*) light; (*Wahnsinn*, *usw.*) sheer || **Helle** §5 *f* brightness; lightness; clarity || *n* light; **ein Helles** a glass of light beer
hellenisch [hɛ'lenɪʃ] *adj* Hellenic
Heller ['hɛlər] *m* (-s;-) penny
hellhörig ['hɛlhørɪç] *adj* having sharp ears; **h. werden** prick up one's ears
hellicht ['hɛlɪçt] *adj*—**hellichter Tag** broad daylight
Hel'ligkeit *f* (-;-en) brightness; (astr) magnitude
hell'sehen §138 *intr* be clairvoyant || **Hellsehen** *n* (-s;) clairvoyance
Hell'seher -in §6 *mf* clairvoyant; (coll) mind reader
hell'sichtig *adj* clear-sighted
hell'wach' *adj* wide awake
Helm [hɛlm] *m* (-[e]s;-e) helmet; (archit) dome, spire; (naut) helm
Helm'busch *m* crest, plume
Hemd [hɛmt] *n* (-[e]s;-en) shirt
Hemd'brust *f* dickey, shirt front
Hemd'hose *f* union suit
hemmen ['hɛmən] *tr* slow up; stop; **gehemmt** inhibited
Hemmnis ['hɛmnɪs] *n* (-ses;-se) hindrance
Hemmschuh ['hɛmʃu] *m* (fig) hindrance; (rr) brake
Hem'mung *f* (-;-en) inhibition
hem'mungslos *adj* uninhibited
Hengst [hɛŋst] *m* (-es;-e) stallion
Henkel ['hɛŋkəl] *m* (-s;-) handle
henken ['hɛŋkən] *tr* hang (*s.o.*)
Henker ['hɛŋkər] *m* (-s;-) hangman
Henne ['hɛnə] *f* (-;-n) hen
her [her] *adv* hither, here; ago
herab [he'rap] *adv* down, downwards
herab- *comb.fm.* down; down here
herab'drücken *tr* press down; force down; **die Kurse h.** bear the market
herab'lassen §104 *ref* condescend
Herab'lassung *f* (-;) condescension
herab'sehen §138 *intr* (**auf** *acc*) look down (on)
herab'setzen *tr* put down; reduce; belittle, disparage
herab'steigen §148 *intr* (SEIN) climb down; (*vom Pferd*) dismount
herab'würdigen *tr* demean
Heraldik [he'raldɪk] *f* (-;) heraldry
heran [he'ran] *adv* near; up
heran'arbeiten *ref* (**an** *acc*) work one's way (towards)
heran'bilden *tr* (**zu**) train (as)
heran'brechen §64 *intr* (SEIN) (*Tag*) dawn, break; (*Nacht*) fall, come on
heran'gehen §82 *intr* (SEIN) go close; **h. an** (*acc*) approach, go up to
heran'kommen §99 *intr* (SEIN) come

near; **h. an** (*acc*) approach; get at; **h. bis an** (*acc*) reach as far as
heran'machen *ref*—**h. an** (*acc*) apply oneself to; approach
heran'nahen *intr* (SEIN) approach
heran'wachsen §155 *intr* (SEIN) (**zu**) grow up (to be)
heran'wagen *ref* (**an** *acc*) dare to approach
heran'ziehen §163 *tr* pull closer; call on for help; (*Quellen*) consult; (*zur Beratung*) call in; (*Pflanzen*) grow; (*Nachwuchs*) train || *intr* (SEIN) approach
herauf [he'rauf] *adv* up, up here; upstairs
herauf'arbeiten *ref* work one's way up
herauf'bemühen *ref* take the trouble to come up (or upstairs)
herauf'beschwören §137 *tr* conjure up; (*verursachen*) bring on, provoke
herauf'kommen §99 *intr* (SEIN) come up
herauf'setzen *tr* raise, increase
herauf'steigen §148 *intr* (SEIN) climb up; (*Tag*) dawn
herauf'ziehen §163 *tr* pull up || *intr* (SEIN) move upstairs; (*Sturm*) come up
heraus [he'raus] *adv* out, out here
heraus'bekommen §99 *tr* (**aus**) get out (of); (*Wort*) utter; (*Geld*) get back in change; (*Problem*) figure out
heraus'bringen §65 *tr* bring out; (*Wort*) utter; (*Lösung*) work out; (*Buch*) publish; (*Fabrikat*) bring out
heraus'drücken *tr* squeeze out; (*die Brust*) throw out
heraus'fahren §71 *intr* (SEIN) drive out; (*aus dem Bett*) jump out; (*Bemerkung*) slip out
heraus'finden §59 *tr* find out || *ref* (**aus**) find one's way out (of)
heraus'fordern *tr* challenge, call on
heraus'fordernd *adj* defiant || *adv* defiantly; **sich h. anziehen** dress provocatively
Heraus'forderung *f* (-;-en) challenge
heraus'fühlen *tr* sense
Heraus'gabe *f* surrender; (*e-s Buches*) publication; (jur) restitution
heraus'geben §80 *tr* surrender; give back; (*Buch*) publish || *intr* (*dat*) give (*s.o.*) his change; **h. auf** (*acc*) give change for
Heraus'geber *m* publisher; (*Redakteur*) editor
heraus'greifen §88 *tr* single out
heraus'haben §89 *tr* have (*s.th.*) figured out; **er hat den Bogen heraus** (coll) he has the knack of it
heraus'halten §90 *tr* hold out || *ref* (**aus**) keep out (of)
heraus'hängen §92 *tr* & *intr* hang out
heraus'kommen §99 *intr* (SEIN) come out
heraus'lesen §107 *tr* pick out; deduce; **zu viel aus e-m Gedicht h.** read too much into a poem
heraus'machen *tr* (*Fleck*) get out || *ref* (*Kinder*) turn out well; (*Geschäft*) make out well
heraus'nehmen §116 *tr* take out || *ref*

—sich [*dat*] **zu viel** (or **Freiheiten**) **h.** take liberties
heraus'platzen *intr* (SEIN)—**mit etw h.** blurt out s.th.
heraus'putzen *ref* dress up
heraus'reden *ref* (**aus**) talk one's way out (of)
heraus'rücken *tr* move out (here); (coll) (*Geld*) shell out ‖ *intr* (SEIN) —**mit dem Geld h.** shell out money; **mit der Sprache h.** reveal it, admit it
heraus'schälen *ref* become apparent
heraus'stehen §146 *intr* protrude
heraus'steigen §148 *intr* (SEIN) (**aus**) climb out (of), step out (of)
heraus'stellen *tr* put out; **groß h.** give a big build-up to; **klar h.** present clearly ‖ *ref* emerge, come to light; **sich h.** als prove to be
heraus'streichen §85 *tr* delete; (fig) praise
heraus'suchen *tr* pick out
heraus'treten §152 *intr* (SEIN) come out, step out; bulge, protrude
heraus'winden §59 *ref* extricate oneself
heraus'wirtschaften *tr* manage to save; (*Profit*) manage to make
heraus'ziehen §163 *tr* pull out
herb [herp] *adj* harsh; (*sauer*) sour; (*zusammenziehend*) tangy; (*Wein*) dry; (*Worte*) bitter; (*Schönheit*) austere ‖ **Herbe** *f* (—;) harshness; tang; bitterness; austerity
herbei' *adv* here (*toward the speaker*)
herbei— *comb.fm.* up, along, here (*toward the speaker*)
herbei'bringen §65 *tr* bring along
herbei'eilen *intr* (SEIN) hurry here
herbei'führen *tr* bring here; cause
herbei'kommen §99 *intr* (SEIN) come up
herbei'lassen §104 *ref* condescend
herbei'rufen §122 *tr* call over; summon
herbei'schaffen *tr* bring here; procure; (*Geld*) raise
herbei'sehnen *tr* long for
herbei'strömen *intr* (SEIN) come flocking, flock
herbei'winken *tr* beckon (*s.o.*) to come over
herbei'wünschen *tr* long for, wish for
Herberge ['herbergə] *f* (—;-n) lodging, shelter; hostel; (obs) inn
her'beten *tr* say mechanically
Herb'heit *f* (—;), **Her'bigkeit** *f* (—;) harshness; tang; bitterness; austerity
her'bringen §65 *tr* bring here
Herbst [herpst] *m* (—es;—e) autumn
herbst'lich *adj* autumn, fall
Herd [hert] *m* (—[e]s;—e) hearth, fireplace; home; kitchen range; center
Herde ['herdə] *f* (—;-n) herd, flock
herein [he'raɪn] *adv* in, in here; **h.!** come in!
herein— *comb.fm.* in, in here (*toward the speaker*)
herein'bemühen *tr* ask (*s.o.*) to come in ‖ *ref* trouble oneself to come in
herein'bitten §60 *tr* invite in
Herein'fall *m* disappointment, letdown
herein'fallen §72 *intr* (SEIN) fall in; **h. auf** (*acc*) fall for; **h. in** (*acc*) fall into

herein'legen *tr* fool, take in
herein'platzen *intr* (SEIN) burst in
her'fallen §72 *intr* (SEIN)—**h. über** (*acc*) fall upon, attack
her'finden §59 *ref* & *intr* find one's way here
Her'gang *m* background details
her'geben §80 *tr* hand over; give up ‖ *ref*—**sich h. zu** be a party to
her'halten §90 *tr* hold out, extend ‖ *intr*—**h. müssen** (*Person*) be the victim; (*Sache*) have to do (*as a makeshift*)
Hering ['herɪŋ] *m* (—s;—e) herring; **sitzen wie die Heringe** be packed in like sardines
her'kommen §99 *intr* (SEIN) come here; (*Wort*) originate; **wo kommst du denn her?** where have you come from? ‖ **Herkommen** *n* (—s;—) origin; custom, tradition, convention
herkömmlich ['herkœmlɪç] *adj* customary, usual; traditional, conventional
Herkunft ['herkʊnft] *f* (—;) origin; birth, family
her'laufen §105 *intr* (SEIN) walk here; **hinter j—m h.** follow s.o.
her'leiten *tr* derive; deduce, infer
Her'leitung *f* (—;-en) derivation
her'machen *tr*—**viel h. von** make a fuss over ‖ *ref*—**sich h. über** (*acc*) attack; (fig) tackle
Hermelin [hermə'lin] *m* (—s;—e) ermine ‖ *n* (—s;—e) (zool) ermine
hermetisch [her'metɪʃ] *adj* hermetic
hernach' *adv* afterwards
her'nehmen §116 *tr* get; **j—n scharf h.** give s.o. a good talking-to
hernie'der *adv* down, down here
Heroin [hero'in] *n* (—s;) (pharm) heroin
Heroine [hero'inə] *f* (—;-n) heroine
heroisch [he'ro·ɪʃ] *adj* heroic
Heroismus [hero'ɪsmʊs] *m* (—;) heroism
Herold ['herɔlt] *m* (—[e]s;—e) herald
Heros ['herɔs] *m* (—; **Heroen** [he'ro·ən]) hero
Herr [her] *m* (—n;—en) lord; master; gentleman; (*als Anrede*) Sir; (*vor Eigennamen*) Mr.; (*Gott*) Lord; **meine Herren!** gentlemen!
her'reichen *tr* hand, pass
Herren— [herən] *comb.fm.* man's, men's; gentlemen's
Her'renabend *m* stag party
Her'renbegleitung *f*—**in H.** accompanied by a gentleman
Her'rendoppel(spiel) *n* (tennis) men's doubles
Her'reneinzel(spiel) *n* (tennis) men's singles
Her'renfahrer *m* (aut) owner-driver
Her'renfriseur *m* barber
Her'rengesellschaft *f* male company; stag party
Her'rengröße *f* men's size
Her'rengut *n* domain, manor
Her'renhaus *n* mansion; House of Lords
Her'renhof *m* manor
Her'renleben *n* life of Riley

her'renlos *adj* ownerless
Her'renmensch *m* born leader
Her'renschnitt *m* woman's very short hairstyle
Her'renzimmer *n* study
Herr'gott *m* Lord, Lord God
her'richten *tr* arrange; get ready
Herrin ['hɛrɪn] *f* (-;-nen) lady
herrisch ['hɛrɪʃ] *adj* masterful
herr'lich *adj* splendid
Herr'lichkeit *f* (-;-en) splendor
Herr'schaft *f* (-;-en) rule, domination; mastery; control; lord, master; estate; **meine Herrschaften!** ladies and gentlemen!
herr'schaftlich *adj* ruler's; gentleman's; high-class
herrschen ['hɛrʃən] *intr* rule; prevail; exist
Herr'scher –in §6 *mf* ruler
Herrschsucht ['hɛrʃzuçt] *f* (-;) thirst for power; bossiness
herrsch'süchtig *adj* power-hungry; autocratic; domineering
her'rühren *intr*—**h. von** come from, originate with
her'sagen *tr* recite, say
her'schaffen *tr* get (here)
her'stammen *intr*—**h. von** come from, be descended from; (gram) be derived from
her'stellen *tr* put here; (*erzeugen*) produce; **fabrikmäßig h.** mass-produce; **Verbindung h.** establish contact; (telp) put a call through
Her'steller *m* (-s;-) manufacturer
Hèr'stellung *f* (-;-en) production
Her'stellungsbetrieb *m* factory
Her'stellungsverfahren *n* manufacturing process
herüber [hɛ'rybər] *adv* over, over here, in this direction (*toward the speaker*)
herum [hɛ'rum] *adv* around; about
herum'bringen §65 *tr* bring around; (*Zeit*) spend
herum'drehen *tr, ref & intr* turn around
herum'fragen *intr* make inquiries
herumfuchteln [hɛ'rumfuxtəln] *intr*— **mit den Händen h.** wave one's hands about
herum'führen *tr* show around
herum'greifen §88 *intr*—**h. um** reach around
herum'hacken *intr*—**h. auf** (*dat*) pick on, criticize
herum'kauen *intr* (**an** *dat*, **auf** *dat*) chew away (on)
herum'kommen §99 *intr* (SEIN) get around; **h. um** get around; evade
herum'lungern *intr* loaf around
herum'reiten §86 *intr* (SEIN) ride around; **h. auf** (*dat*) harp on (*s.th.*); pick on (*s.o.*)
herum'schnüffeln *intr* snoop around
herum'streichen §85 *intr* (SEIN) prowl about
herum'streiten §86 *ref* squabble
herum'treiben §62 *tr* drive around || *ref* roam around, knock about
Herum'treiber *m* (-s;-) loafer, tramp
herum'ziehen §163 *tr* pull around; **h. um** draw (*s.th.*) around || *ref*—**sich h. um** surround || *intr* (SEIN) wander

around; run around; **h. um** march around
herunter [hɛ'runtər] *adv* down, down here (*towards the speaker*); downstairs; **den Berg h.** down the mountain; **ins Tal h.** down into the valley
herun'terbringen §65 *tr* bring down; (fig) lower, reduce
herun'tergehen §82 *intr* (SEIN) go down; (*Preis, Temperatur*) fall, drop
herun'terhandeln *tr* (*Preis*) beat down
herun'terhauen §93 *tr* chop off; (*Brief*) dash off; **j–m eins h.** clout s.o.
herun'terkommen §99 *intr* (SEIN) come down; come downstairs; deteriorate
herun'terlassen §104 *tr* let down, lower
herun'terleiern *tr* drone
herun'terlesen §107 *tr* (*Liste*) read down; rattle off
herun'termachen *tr* take down; turn down; (coll) chew out; (coll) pan
herun'terschießen §76 *tr* shoot down
herun'tersein §139 *intr* (SEIN) be run-down
herun'terwirtschaften *tr* ruin (*through mismanagement*)
herun'terwürgen *tr* choke down
hervor [hɛr'for] *adv* out; forth
hervor'bringen §65 *tr* bring out; engender, produce; (*Wort*) utter
hervor'dringen §142 *intr* (SEIN) emerge
hervor'gehen §82 *intr* (SEIN)—**h. aus** come from; emerge from; to have been trained at
hervor'heben §94 *tr* highlight
hervor'holen *tr* produce
hervor'kommen §99 *intr* (SEIN) come out
hervor'lugen *intr* peep out
hervor'ragen *intr* jut out; be prominent; **h. über** (*acc*) tower over
hervor'ragend *adj* prominent
hervor'rufen §122 *tr* evoke, cause; (*Schauspieler*) recall
hervor'stechen §64 *intr* stick out; be conspicuous; be prominent
hervor'treten §152 *intr* (SEIN) emerge; come to the fore; become apparent; (*Augen*) bulge; (*Ader*) protrude
hervor'tun §154 *ref* distinguish oneself
hervor'wagen *ref* dare to come out; **sich mit e-r Antwort h.** venture an answer
hervor'zaubern *tr* produce by magic; **ein Essen h.** whip up a meal
Herweg ['hɛrvek] *m* way here; way home
Herz [hɛrts] *n* (–ens;–en) heart; (*als Anrede*) darling; (cards) heart(s); **ich bringe es nicht übers H. zu** (*inf*) I haven't the heart to (*inf*); **sich** [*dat*] **ein H. fassen** get up the courage; **seinem Herzen Luft machen** give vent to one's feelings
Herz– *comb.fm.* heart, cardiac
Herz'anfall *m* heart attack
Herz'beschwerden *pl* heart trouble
Herz'blume *f* (bot) bleeding heart
herzen ['hɛrtsən] *tr* hug, embrace
Her'zensgrund *m* bottom of one's heart
her'zensgut *adj* good-hearted

Her′zenslust *f*—**nach H.** to one's heart's content
herz′ergreifend *adj* moving, touching
Herz′geräusch *n* heart murmur
herz′haft *adj* hearty
herzig [′hɛrtsɪç] *adj* sweet, cute
–herzig *comb.fm.* –hearted
Herzinfarkt [′hɛrtsɪnfarkt] *m* (–[e]s; –e) cardiac infarction
herz′innig *adj* heartfelt
herz′inniglich *adv* sincerely
Herz′klappe *f* cardiac valve
Herz′klopfen *n* palpitations
Herz′kollaps *m* heart failure
herz′lich *adj* cordial; sincere ‖ *adv* very; **h. wenige** precious few
herz′los *adj* heartless
Herzog [′hɛrtsɔk] *m* (–[e]s; ̈e) duke
Herzogin [′hɛrtsɔgɪn] *f* (–; –nen) duchess
Herzogtum [′hɛrtsɔktum] *n* (–[e]s; ̈er) dukedom; duchy
Herz′schlag *m* heartbeat; heart failure
Herz′stück *n* heart, central point
Herz′verpflanzung *f* heart transplant
Herz′weh *n* (& fig) heartache
Hetzblatt [′hɛtsblat] *n* scandal sheet
Hetze [′hɛtsə] *f* (–; –n) hunting; hurry, rush; vicious campaign; baiting
hetzen [′hɛtsən] *tr* hunt; bait; rush; (fig) hound; **e–n Hund auf j–n h.** sic a dog on s.o. ‖ *ref* rush ‖ *intr* stir up trouble; **h. gegen** conduct a vicious campaign against ‖ *intr* (SEIN) race, dash
Het′zer **–in** §6 *mf* agitator
Hetz′hund *m* hound, hunting dog
Hetz′jagd *f* hunt; baiting; hurry
Hetz′rede *f* inflammatory speech
Heu [hɔɪ] *n* (–[e]s;) hay
Heu′boden *m* hayloft
Heuchelei [hɔɪçə′laɪ] *f* (–; –en) hypocrisy; piece of hypocrisy
heucheln [′hɔɪçəln] *tr* feign ‖ *intr* be hypocritical
Heuch′ler **–in** §6 *mf* hypocrite
heuchlerisch [′hɔɪçlərɪʃ] *adj* hypocritical
heuen [′hɔɪ·ən] *intr* make hay
heuer [′hɔɪ·ər] *adv* this year
heuern [′hɔɪ·ərn] *tr* hire
Heu′fieber *n* hayfever
Heu′gabel *f* pitchfork
heulen [′hɔɪlən] *intr* bawl; (*Wind*) howl
heurig [′hɔɪrɪç] *adj* this year's ‖ **Heurige** §5 *m* new wine
Heu′schnupfen *m* (–s;) hayfever
Heuschober [′hɔɪʃobər] *m* (–s;–) haystack
Heu′schrecke *f* (–;–n) locust
heute [′hɔɪtə] *adv* today; **h. abend** this evening; **h. früh** (or **h. morgen**) this morning; **h. vor acht Tagen** a week ago today; **h. in acht Tagen** today a week
heutig [′hɔɪtɪç] *adj* today's; present-day; **am heutigen Tage** (or **der heutige Tag** or **mit dem heutigen Tag**) today
heutzutage [′hɔɪttsutagə] *adv* nowadays
Hexe [′hɛksə] *f* (–;–n) witch; hag

hexen [′hɛksən] *intr* practice witchcraft
He′xenkessel *m* chaos, inferno
He′xenmeister *m* wizard; sorcerer
He′xenschuß *m* lumbago
Hexerei [hɛksə′raɪ] *f* (–;) witchcraft
Hiatus [hɪ′atus] *m* (–;–) (& pros) hiatus
Hibis·kus [hɪ′bɪskus] *m* (–;–ken [kən]) hibiscus
hieb [hip] *pret* of **hauen** ‖ **Hieb** *m* (–[e]s;–e) blow, stroke; **Hiebe** thrashing
hieb′–undstich′fest *adj* (fig) watertight
Hieb′wunde *f* gash
hielt [hilt] *pret* of **halten**
hier [hir] *adv* here
hieran′ *adv* at (by, in, on, to) it or them
Hierar·chie [hɪ·erar′çi] *f* (–;–chien [′çi·ən]) hierarchy
hierauf′ *adv* on it, on them; then
hieraus′ *adv* out of it (or them); from this (or these)
hierbei′ *adv* near here; here; in this case; in connection with this
hierdurch′ *adv* through it (or them); through here; hereby
hierfür′ *adv* for it (or them)
hierge′gen *adv* against it
hierher′ *adv* hither, here
hier′herum *adv* around here
hierhin′ *adv* here; **bis h.** up to here
hierin′ *adv* herein, in this
hiermit′ *adv* herewith, with it
hiernach′ *adv* after this, then; about this; according to this
Hieroglyphe [hɪ·ero′glyfə] *f* (–;–n) hieroglyph
hierorts [′hirɔrts] *adv* in this town
hierü′ber *adv* over it (or them); about it (or this)
hierzu′ *adv* to it; in addition to it; concerning this
hiesig [′hizɪç] *adj* local
hieß [his] *pret* of **heißen**
Hilfe [′hɪlfə] *f* (–;–n) help, aid; **zu H. nehmen** make use of
Hil′feleistung *f* assistance
Hil′feruf *m* cry for help
hilf′los *adj* helpless
hilf′reich *adj* helpful
Hilfs– [hɪlfs] *comb.fm.* auxiliary
Hilfs′arbeiter **–in** §6 *mf* unskilled laborer
Hilfs′arzt *m*, **Hilf′ärztin** *f* intern
hilfs′bedürftig *adj* needy
hilfs′bereit *adj* ready to help
Hilfs′dienst *m* help, assistance
Hilfs′gerät *n* labor-saving device
Hilfs′kraft *f* assistant, helper; (mach) auxiliary power
Hilfs′kraftbremse *f* power brake
Hilfs′kraftlenkung *f* power steering
Hilfs′lehrer **–in** §6 *mf* student teacher
Hilfs′maschine *f* auxiliary engine
Hilfs′mittel *n* aid, device; remedy; financial aid
Hilfs′quellen *pl* material; sources
Hilfs′rakete *f* booster rocket
Hilfs′schule *f* school for the mentally slow

Hilfs'truppen *pl* auxiliaries
Hilfs'werk *n* welfare organization
Hilfs'zeitwort *n* (-[e]s;-er) (gram) auxiliary (verb)
Himbeere ['hɪmbərə] *f* (-;-n) raspberry
Himmel ['hɪməl] *m* (-s;-) sky, skies; heaven(s); firmament; (eccl) baldachin; **ach du lieber H.!** good heavens!; **aus heiterem H.** out of the blue; **in den H. heben** praise to the skies
himmelan' *adv* skywards; heavenwards
him'melangst *invar adj*—**mir wird h.** I feel frightened to death
Him'melbett *n* canopy bed
him'melblau *adj* sky-blue
Him'melfahrt *f* ascension; assumption
Him'melfahrtstag *m* Ascension Day
Him'melreich *n* kingdom of heaven
Himmels- *comb.fm.* celestial
him'melschreiend *adj* atrocious
Him'melsgegend *f* region of the sky; point of the compass
Him'melskörper *m* celestial body
Him'melsrichtung *f* point of the compass; direction
Him'melsschrift *f* skywriting
Him'melswagen *m* (astr) Great Bear
Him'melszelt *n* canopy of heaven
himmelwärts ['hɪməlverts] *adv* skywards; heavenwards
himmlisch ['hɪmlɪʃ] *adj* heavenly, celestial; divine; (coll) gorgeous
hin [hɪn] *adv* there (*away from the speaker*); **ganz hin** (coll) bushed; (coll) quite carried away; **hin ist hin** what's done is done; **hin und her** up and down, back and forth; **hin und wieder** now and then; **vor sich hin** to oneself
hinab' *adv* down
hinan' *adv* up; **bis an etw h.** up to s.th., as far as s.th.
hinauf' *adv* up, up there; upstairs; **den Fluß h.** up the river
hinauf'reichen *tr* hand (*s.th.*) up ‖ *intr* reach up
hinauf'schrauben *tr* (*Preis*) jack up
hinauf'setzen *tr* raise, increase
hinauf'steigen §148 *tr* (SEIN) (*Treppe, Berg*) climb ‖ *intr* (SEIN) climb up; (*Temperatur*) rise
hinaus' *adv* out, out there; **auf viele Jahre h.** for many years to come
hinaus'beißen §53 *tr* (coll) edge out
hinaus'gehen §82 *intr* (SEIN) go out; **h. auf** (*acc*) look out over; lead to; drive at, imply; **h. über** (*acc*) exceed
hinaus'kommen §99 *intr* (SEIN) come out; **es kommt auf eins** (or **aufs gleiche**) **hinaus** it amounts to the same thing; **h. über** (*acc*) get beyond
hinaus'laufen §105 *intr* (SEIN) run out; **es läuft aufs eins** (or **aufs gleiche**) **hinaus** it amounts to the same thing
hinaus'schieben §130 *tr* push out; (*Termin, usw.*) postpone
hinaus'werfen §160 *tr* throw out; fire
hinaus'wollen §162 *intr* want to go out; **h. auf** (*acc*) be driving at; **hoch h.** aim high, be ambitious
hinaus'ziehen §163 *tr* prolong ‖ *ref*

take longer than expected ‖ *intr* (SEIN) go out; move out
Hin'blick *m*—**im H. auf** (*acc*) in view of
hin'bringen §65 *tr* bring (there); take (there); (*Zeit*) pass
hinderlich ['hɪndərlɪç] *adj* in the way
hindern ['hɪndərn] *tr* block; **h. an** (*dat*) prevent from (*ger*)
Hindernis ['hɪndərnɪs] *n* (-ses;-se) hindrance; obstacle
Hin'dernisbahn *f* obstacle course
Hin'dernislauf *m* (sport) hurdles
Hin'dernisrennen *n* steeplechase; hurdles
hin'deuten *intr* (auf *acc*) point (to)
hindurch' *adv* through; **den ganzen Sommer h.** throughout the summer
hinein' *adv* in, in there
hinein'arbeiten *ref*—**sich h. in** (*acc*) work one's way into
hinein'denken §66 *ref*—**sich h. in** (*acc*) imagine oneself in
hinein'geraten §63 *intr* (SEIN)—**h. in** (*acc*) get into, fall into
hinein'leben *intr*—**in den Tag h.** live for the moment
hinein'tun §154 *tr* put in
Hin'fahrt *f* journey there, out-bound passage
hin'fallen §72 *intr* (SEIN) fall down
hinfällig ['hɪnfɛlɪç] *adj* frail; (*Gesetz*) invalid
hinfort' *adv* henceforth
hing [hɪŋ] *pret* of **hängen**
Hin'gabe *f* (an *acc*) devotion (to)
hin'geben §80 *tr* give up ‖ *ref* (*dat*) abandon oneself (to)
Hin'gebung *f* (-;) devotion
hinge'gen *adv* on the other hand
hin'gehen §82 *intr* (SEIN) go there; pass
hin'halten §90 *tr* hold out; (*Person*) keep waiting, string along; **den Kopf h.** (fig) take the rap
hinken ['hɪŋkən] *intr* limp; **der Vergleich hinkt** that's a poor comparison ‖ *intr* (SEIN) limp
hin'länglich *adj* sufficient
hin'legen *tr* put down ‖ *ref* lie down
hin'nehmen §116 *tr* accept; take, put up with
hin'raffen *tr* snatch away
hin'reichen *tr* (*dat*) pass to, hand to ‖ *intr* reach; suffice
hin'reißen §53 *tr* enchant, carry away
hin'richten *tr* execute; **h. auf** (*acc*) direct towards
Hin'richtung *f* (-;-en) execution
Hin'richtungsbefehl *m* death warrant
hin'setzen *tr* put down ‖ *ref* sit down
Hin'sicht *f* respect, way; **in H. auf** (*acc*) regarding, in regard to
hin'sichtlich *prep* (*genit*) regarding
hin'stellen *tr* put there; put down
hintan'setzen, **hintan'stellen** *tr* put last, consider last
hinten ['hɪntən] *adv* at the back, in the rear; **h. im Zimmer** at the back of the room; **nach h.** to the rear; backwards; **von h.** from the rear
hinter ['hɪntər] *prep* (*dat*) behind; **j-m her sein** be after s.o. ‖ *prep* (*acc*) behind; **h. etw kommen** find

out about s.th., get to the bottom of s.th.

Hin'terachse *f* rear axle

Hin'terbacke *f* buttock

Hin'terbein *n* hind leg; **sich auf die Hinterbeine setzen** strain oneself

Hinterbliebene ['hɪntərblibənə] §5 *mf* survivor (*of a deceased*); **H.** *pl* next-of-kin

hinterbrin'gen §65 *tr—j–m etw h.* let s.o. in on s.th.

Hin'terdeck *n* quarter deck

hinterdrein [hɪntər'draɪn] *adv* after; subsequently, afterwards

hin'tere §9 *adj* back, rear ‖ **Hintere** §5 *m* (coll) behind

hintereinan'der *adv* one behind the other; in succession; one after the other

Hin'terfuß *m* hind foot

Hin'tergaumen *m* soft palate, velum

Hin'tergedanke *m* ulterior motive

hinterge'hen §82 *tr* deceive

Hin'tergrund *m* background

Hin'terhalt *m* ambush

hinterhältig ['hɪntərhɛltɪç] *adj* underhanded

Hin'terhand *f* hind quarters (*of horse*)

Hin'terhaus *n* rear building

hinterher' *adv* behind; afterwards

Hin'terhof *m* backyard

Hin'terkopf *m* back of the head

Hin'terland *n* hinterland

hinterlas'sen §104 *tr* leave behind

Hinterlas'senschaft *f* (–;–en) inheritance

Hin'terlauf *m* hind leg

hinterle'gen *tr* deposit

Hinterle'gung *f* (–;–en) deposit

Hin'terlist *f* deceit; trick, ruse

Hin'termann *m* (–[e]s;ːer) instigator; wheeler-dealer; (pol) backer

Hintern ['hɪntərn] *m* (–s;–) (coll) behind

Hin'terradantrieb *m* rear-wheel drive

hinterrücks ['hɪntərryks] *adv* from behind; (fig) behind one's back

Hin'tertreffen *n*—**ins H.** geraten fall behind; **im H.** sein be at a disadvantage

hintertrei'ben §62 *tr* frustrate

Hintertrei'bung *f* (–;–en) frustration

Hin'tertreppe *f* backstairs

Hin'tertür *f* backdoor

Hinterwäldler ['hɪntərvɛltlər] *m* (–s;–) hillbilly

hin'terwäldlerisch *adj* hillbilly

hinterzie'hen §163 *tr* evade

Hinterzie'hung *f* (–;) tax evasion

hinü'ber *adv* over, over there; across

hinun'ter *adv* down

hinun'tergehen §82 *tr* (SEIN) (*Treppe*) go down ‖ *intr* (SEIN) go down

hinweg [hɪn'wɛk] *adv* away; **über etw h.** over s.th., across s.th. ‖ **Hinweg** ['hɪnvɛk] *m* way there

hinweg'kommen §99 *intr* (SEIN)—**h. über** (*acc*) get over

hinweg'sehen §138 *intr*—**h. über** (*acc*) look over; overlook, ignore

hinweg'setzen *ref*—**sich h. über** (*acc*) ignore, disregard

hinweg'täuschen *tr* mislead, blind

Hinweis ['hɪnvaɪs] *m* (–es;–e) reference; hint; announcement

hin'weisen §118 *tr—j–m h. auf** (*acc*) point to; point out **s.th. out to s.o.** ‖ *intr*—**h. auf** (*acc*) point to; point out

hin'werfen §160 *tr* throw down; (coll) dash off, jot down

hin'wirken *intr*—**h. auf** (*acc*) work toward(s)

hin'ziehen §163 *tr* attract protract ‖ *ref* drag on; **sich h. an** (*dat*) run along; **sich h. bis zu** extend to

hin'zielen *intr*—**h. auf** (*acc*) aim at

hinzu' *adv* there, thither; in addition

hinzu'fügen *tr* add

hinzu'kommen §99 *intr* (SEIN) come (upon the scene); be added; **es kamen noch andere Gründe hinzu** besides, there were other reasons

hinzu'setzen *tr* add

hinzu'treten §152 *intr* (SEIN) (**zu**) walk up (to); **es traten noch andere Gründe hinzu** besides, there were other reasons

hinzu'tun §154 *tr* add

hinzu'ziehen §163 *tr* (*Arzt*) call in

Hirn [hɪrn] *n* (–[e]s;–e) brain; brains; **sein H.** anstrengen rack one's brains

Hirn– *comb.fm.* brain; cerebral; intellectual

Hirn'anhang *m* pituitary gland

Hirn'gespinst *n* figment of the imagination

Hirn'hautentzündung *f* meningitis

hirn'los *adj* brainless

Hirn'rinde *f* (anat) cortex

Hirn'schale *f* cranium

hirn'verbrannt *adj* (coll) crazy

Hirsch [hɪrʃ] *m* (–es;–e) deer, stag

Hirsch'fänger *m* hunting knife

Hirsch'kalb *n* fawn, doe

Hirsch'kuh *f* hind

Hirsch'leder *n* deerskin, buckskin

Hirt [hɪrt] *m* (–en;–en) shepherd

–hirte [hɪrtə] *m* (–n;–n) –herd

Hir'tenbrief *m* (eccl) pastoral letter

Hirtin ['hɪrtɪn] *f* (–;–nen) shepherdess

His [hɪs] *n* (–;) (mus) B sharp

hissen ['hɪsən] *tr* hoist

Historie [hɪs'torjə] *f* (–;–n) history; story

Historiker –in [hɪs'torɪkər(ɪn)] §6 *mf* historian

historisch [hɪs'torɪʃ] *adj* historical

Hitze ['hɪtsə] *f* (–;–n) heat

hit'zebeständig *adj* heat-resistant

Hit'zeferien *pl* school holiday (*because of hot weather*)

Hit'zeschild *m* (rok) heat shield

Hit'zewelle *f* heat wave

hitzig ['hɪtsɪç] *adj* hot-tempered

Hitz'kopf *m* hothead

hitz'köpfig *adj* hot-headed

Hitz'schlag *m* heatstroke

hob [hop] *pret* of **heben**

Hobel ['hobəl] *m* (–s;–) (carp) plane

Ho'belbank *f* carpenter's bench

hobeln ['hobəln] *tr* (carp) plane

hoch [hox], (höher ['hø·ər]; höchste ['høçstə] §9) high; noble; (*Alter*) advanced; **das ist mir zu h.** that's beyond me; **hohes Gericht!** your honor!; members of the jury!; **in höchster Not** in dire need ‖ *adv* high; highly, very; (math) up to the ... power ‖ **Hoch** *n* (-s;-s) (*Trinkspruch, Heilruf*) cheer; (meteor) high

hoch– *comb.fm.* up; upwards; highly, very; high, as high as

hoch′achten *tr* esteem

Hoch′actung *f* (-;) esteem; **mit vorzüglicher H., Ihr** ... or **Ihre** ... Very truly yours, Respectfully yours

hoch′achtungsvoll *adj* respectful ‖ *adv* —h., Ihr ... or Ihre ... Very truly yours, Respectfully yours

Hoch′amt *n* (eccl) High Mass

Hoch′antenne *f* outdoor antenna

hoch′arbeiten *ref* work one's way up

hoch′aufgeschossen *adj* tall, lanky

Hoch′bahn *f* el, elevated train

Hoch′bauingenieur *m* structural engineer

hoch′bäumen *ref* rear up

Hoch′behälter *m* water tower; reservoir

Hochbeiner [′hoxbaɪnər] *m* (-s;-) (ent) daddy-long-legs

hoch′beinig *adj* long-legged

hoch′betagt *adj* advanced in years

Hoch′betrieb *m* bustle, big rush

Hoch′blüte *f* high bloom; (fig) heyday

hoch′bringen §65 *tr* restore to health; (*Geschäft*) put on its feet; **es h.** (sport) get a high score

Hoch′burg *f* fortress, citadel

hoch′denkend *adj* noble-minded

hoch′deutsch *adj* High German

Hoch′druck *m* high pressure; (fig) great pressure; (meteor) high; **mit H.** (fig) full blast

Hoch′druckgebiet *n* (meteor) high, high-pressure area

Hoch′ebene *f* plateau

hoch′fahrend *adj* high-handed

hoch′fein *adj* very refined; high-grade

Hoch′flut *m* high tide; (fig) deluge

Hoch′form *f* top form

hochfrequent [′hoxfrekvɛnt] *adj* high-frequency

Hoch′frequenz *f* high-frequency

Hoch′frisur *f* upsweep

Hoch′gefühl *n* elation

hoch′gemut *adj* cheerful

Hoch′genuß *m* great pleasure

Hoch′gericht *n* place of execution

hoch′gesinnt *adj* noble-minded

hoch′gespannt *adj* (*Hoffnungen*) high; (elec) high-voltage

hoch′gestellt *adj* high-ranking

Hoch′glanz *m* high polish, high gloss

Hoch′haus *n* high rise (building)

hoch′herzig *adj* generous

hoch′jagen *tr* (*Wild*) ferret out; (*Motor*) race; (coll) blow up

hochkant [′hoxkant] *adv* on end

Hoch′konjunktur *f* (econ) boom

Hoch′land *n* highlands; plateau

Hoch′leistung *f* (-;-en) high output; (sport) first-class performance

Hochleistungs– *comb.fm.* high-powered; high-capacity; high-speed; heavy-duty

Hoch′mut *m* haughtiness, pride

hoch′mütig *adj* haughty, proud

hochnäsig [′hoxnezɪç] *adj* snooty

Hoch′ofen *m* blast furnace

hoch′ragend *adj* towering

hoch′rappeln *ref* (coll) get on one's feet again, pick up again

hoch′rollen *tr* roll up

Hoch′ruf *m* cheer

Hoch′saison *f* height of the season

Hoch′schule *f* university, academy

Hoch′schüler –in §6 *mf* university student

Hoch′seefischerei *f* deep-sea fishing

hoch′selig *adj* late, of blessed memory

Hoch′spannung *f* high voltage

Hoch′spannungsleitung *f* high-tension line

hoch′spielen *tr* play up; put into the limelight

Hoch′sprache *f* standard language; (die) **deutsche H.** standard German

höchst *adv* see **hoch**

Höchst– *comb.fm.* maximum, top

Hochstapelei [hoxʃtɑpə′laɪ] *f* (-;) false pretenses; fraud

Hochstapler [′hoxʃtɑplər] *m* (-s;) confidence man; imposter, swindler

Hoch′start *m* (sport) standing start

Höchst′belastung *f* (-;-en) maximum load; (elec) peak load

höchstens [′høçstəns] *adv* at best, at the very most

Höchst′form *f* (sport) top form

Höchst′frequenz *f* ultrahigh frequency

Höchst′geschwindigkeit *f* top speed; zulässige **H.** speed limit

Höchst′leistung *f* (-;-en) maximum output; highest achievement; (sport) record

Hoch′straße *f* overpass

Hoch′ton *m* (ling) primary stress

hoch′tönend *adj* bombastic

hochtourig [′hoxturɪç] *adj* high-revving

hoch′trabend *adj* pompous

Hoch′-und Tief′bau *m* (-[e]s;) civil engineering

hoch′verdient *adj* of great merit

Hoch′verrat *m* high treason

Hoch′verräter –in §6 *mf* traitor

Hoch′wasser *n* flood(s); **der Fluß führt H.** the river is swollen

hoch′wertig *adj* high-quality

Hoch′wild *n* big game

Hoch′würden *pl* (*als Anrede*) Reverend; **Seine H.** ... the Reverend ...

Hoch′zeit *f* wedding

hoch′zeitlich *adj* bridal; nuptial

Hoch′zeitsfeier *f* wedding ceremony; wedding reception

Hoch′zeitspaar *n* newly-weds

Hoch′zeitsreise *f* honeymoon

Hocke [′hokə] *f* (-;-n) crouch

hocken [′hokən] *ref* & *intr* squat; (coll) sit down

Hocker [′hokər] *m* (-s;-) stool

Höcker [′hœkər] *m* (-s;-) hump; bump

höckerig [′hœkərɪç] *adj* hunchbacked; (*Weg*) bumpy

Hockey [′hoki] *n* (-s;) hockey

Ho′ckeyschläger *m* hockey stick

Hode [′hodə] *f* (-;-n) testicle

Ho′densack *m* (anat) scrotum

Hof [hof] *m* (-[e]s;⁼e) courtyard;

yard; barnyard; (*e–s Königs*) court; (astr) halo; corona; **e–m Mädchen den Hof machen** court a girl
Hoffart ['hɔfart] *f* (–;) haughtiness
hoffärtig ['hɔfɛrtɪç] *adj* haughty
hoffen ['hɔfən] *tr*—**das Beste h.** hope for the best ‖ *intr* (auf *acc*) hope (for); **auf j–n h.** put one's hopes in s.o
hoffentlich ['hɔfəntlɪç] *adv* as I hope; **h. kommt er bald** I hope he comes soon
Hoffnung ['hɔfnʊŋ] *f* (–;–en) hope
hoff′nungslos *adj* hopeless
hoff′nungsvoll *adj* hopeful; promising
Hof′hund *m* watchdog
hofieren [hɔ'firən] *tr* court
höfisch ['høfɪʃ] *adj* court, courtly
höflich ['høflɪç] *adj* polite, courteous
Höf′lichkeit *f* (–;–en) politeness, courtesy
Höf′lichkeitsformel *f* complimentary close (*in a letter*)
Höfling ['høflɪŋ] *m* (–[e]s;–e) courtier
Hof′meister *m* steward; tutor
Hof′narr *m* court jester
Hof′staat *m* royal household; retinue
hohe ['ho·ə] *adj* see **hoch**
Höhe ['hø·ə] *f* (–;–en) height; altitude; (*Anhöhe*) hill; (mus) pitch; **auf der H. in good shape; das ist die H.!** that's the limit!; **in der H. von** in the amount of; **in die H. up; in die H. fahren** jump up; **wieder in die H. bringen** (com) put back on its feet
Hoheit ['hohart] *f* (–;–en) sovereignty; (*als Titel*) Highness
Ho′heitsbereich *m* (pol), **Ho′heitsgebiet** *n* (pol) territory
Ho′heitsgewässer *pl* territorial waters
Ho′heitsrechte *pl* sovereign rights
ho′heitsvoll *adj* regal, majestic
Ho′heitszeichen *n* national emblem
Hö′henmesser *m* altimeter
Hö′henruder *n* (aer) elevator
Hö′hensonne *f* ultra-violet lamp
Hö′henstrahlen *pl* cosmic rays
Hö′henzug *m* mountain range
Ho′hepriester *m* high priest
Hö′hepunkt *m* climax; height, acme
höher ['hø·ər] *adj* see **hoch**
hohl [hol] *adj* hollow
Höhle ['hølə] *f* (–;–n) cave; grotto; lair, den; hollow, cavity; socket
Höh′lenmensch *m* caveman
hohl′geschliffen *adj* hollow-ground
Hohl′heit *f* (–;) hollowness
Hohl′maß *n* dry measure; liquid measure
Hohl′raum *m* hollow, cavity
Hohl′saum *m* hemstitch
Hohl′weg *m* defile, narrow pass
Hohn [hon] *m* (–[e]s;) scorn; sarcasm; **etw j–m Hohn tun** do s.th. in defiance of s.o.
höhnen ['hønən] *intr* jeer; sneer
höhnisch ['hønɪʃ] *adj* scornful
hohn′sprechen §64 *intr* (*dat*) treat with scorn; defy; make a mockery of
Höker –in ['høkər(ɪn)] §6 *mf* huckster
hold [hɔlt] *adj* kindly; lovely, sweet
hold′selig *adj* lovely, sweet

holen ['holən] *tr* fetch; get; (*Atem, Luft*) draw; **h. lassen** send for; **sich** [*dat*] **etw h.** (coll) catch s.th.
Holland ['hɔlant] *n* (–s;) Holland
Holländer ['hɔlɛndər] *m* (–s;–) Dutchman
Holländerin ['hɔlɛndərɪn] *f* (–;–nen) Dutch woman
holländisch ['hɔlɛndɪʃ] *adj* Dutch
Hölle ['hœlə] *f* (–;) hell
Höl′lenangst *f* mortal fear
höllisch ['hœlɪʃ] *adj* hellish
Holm [hɔlm] *m* (–[e]s;–e) islet; (*Stiel*) handle; (aer) spar; (gym) parallel bar
holp(e)rig ['hɔlp(ə)rɪç] *adj* bumpy
holpern ['hɔlpərn] *intr* jolt, bump along; (*beim Lesen*) stumble
Holunder [hɔ'lʊndər] *m* (–s;–) (bot) elder
Holz [hɔlts] *n* (–es;≈er) wood; lumber; timber, trees; **ins H. gehen** go into the woods
Holz′apfel *m* crab apple
Holz′arbeit *f* woodwork; lumbering
Holz′arbeiter *m* woodworker; lumberjack
holz′artig *adj* woody
Holz′blasinstrumente *pl* wood winds
Holz′brei *m* wood pulp
holzen ['hɔltsən] *tr* fell; deforest; (coll) spank ‖ *intr* cut wood
hölzern ['hœltsərn] *adj* wooden; (fig) clumsy
Holzfäller ['hɔltsfɛlər] *m* (–s;–) lumberjack, logger
Holz′faser *f* wood fiber; wood pulp; grain; **gegen die H.** against the grain
Holz′faserstoff *m* wood pulp
Holzhacker ['hɔltshakər] *m* (–s;–), **Holzhauer** ['hɔltshau·ər] *m* (–s;–) lumberjack; wood chopper
holzig ['hɔltsɪç] *adj* woody, wooded; (*Gemüse*) stringy
Holz′knecht *m* lumberjack
Holz′kohle *f* charcoal
Holz′nagel *m* wooden peg
Holz′platz *m* lumber yard
holz′reich *adj* wooded
Holz′schnitt *m* woodcut; wood engraving
Holz′schuh *m* wooden shoe
Holz′schuppen *m* woodshed
Holz′wolle *f* excelsior
Homi·lie [homɪ'li] *f* (–;–lien ['li·ən]) homily
homogen [homo'gen] *adj* homogeneous
Homosexualität [homozɛksu·alɪ'tet] *f* (–;) homosexuality
homosexuell [homozɛksu·'ɛl] *adj* homosexual ‖ **Homosexuelle** §5 *mf* homosexual
Honig ['honɪç] *m* (–s;) honey
Ho′nigkuchen *m* gingerbread
ho′nigsüß *adj* sweet as honey
Ho′nigwabe *f* honeycomb
Honorar [hono'rɑr] *n* (–s;–e) fee
Honoratioren [honoratsi'orən] *pl* dignitaries
honorieren [hono'rirən] *tr* give an honorarium to; pay royalties to; (*Scheck*) honor
Hopfen ['hɔpfən] *m* (–s;) hops

hopp [hɔp] *interj* up!; quick!; **hopp, los!** get going!
hoppla ['hɔpla] *interj* whoops!; **jetzt aber h.!** come on!; look sharp!
hops [hɔps] *adj*—**h. gehen** go to pot; **h. sein** be done for
hopsasa ['hɔpsasa] *interj* upsy-daisy
hopsen ['hɔpsən] *intr* (SEIN) hop
Hop'ser *m* (-s;-) hop
Hörapparat ['hørˌaparɑt] *m* hearing aid
hörbar ['hørbɑr] *adj* audible
hörbehindert ['hørbəˌhɪndərt] *adj* hard of hearing
Hörbericht ['hørbərɪçt] *m* radio report; radio commentary
horchen ['hɔrçən] *intr* listen; eavesdrop
Hor'cher –*in* §6 *mf* eavesdropper
Horch'gerät *n* sound detector; (nav) hydrophone
Horch'posten *m* (mil) listening post
Horde ['hɔrdə] *f* (-;-n) horde
hören ['hørən] *tr* hear; listen to; (*Vorlesung*) attend || *intr* hear; **h. auf** (*acc*) pay attention to, obey
Hö'rer *m* (-s;-) listener; member of an audience; student; (telp) receiver
Hö'rerbrief *m* letter from a listener
Hö'rerkreis *m* listeners
Hö'rerschaft *f* (-;-en) audience; (educ) enrollment
Hör'folge *f* radio serial
Hör'gerät *n* hearing aid
hörig ['hørɪç] *adj* in bondage || **Hörige** §5 *mf* serf, thrall
Horizont [hɔrɪˈtsɔnt] *m* (-[e]s;-e) horizon
horizontal [hɔrɪtsɔnˈtɑl] *adj* horizontal || **Horizontale** §5 *f* horizontal line
Horn [hɔrn] *n* (-[e]s;ꞏꞌer) horn; (mil) bugle; (mus) horn, French horn
Hörnchen ['hœrnçən] *n* (-s;-) crescent roll
Horn'haut *f* (anat) cornea
Hornisse [hɔrˈnɪsə] *f* (-;-n) hornet
Hornist [hɔrˈnɪst] *m* (-en;-en) bugler
Horn'ochse *f* (coll) dumb ox
Horoskop [hɔrɔˈskop] *n* (-[e]s;-e) horoscope
horrend [hɔˈrɛnt] *adj* (coll) terrible
Hör'rohr *n* stethescope
Hör'saal *m* lecture room
Hör'spiel *n* radio play
Horst [hɔrst] *m* (-[e]s;-e) (eagle's) nest
Hort [hɔrt] *m* (-[e]s;-e) hoard, treasure; (place of) refuge; protector
Hör'weite *f*—**in H.** within earshot
Hose ['hozə] *f* (-;-n), **Hosen** ['hozən] *pl* pants, trousers; (*Unterhose*) shorts; panties; **sich auf die Hosen setzen** buckle down
Ho'senboden *m* seat (of trousers)
Ho'senklappe *f*, **Ho'senlatz** *m* fly
Ho'senrolle *f* (theat) male role
Ho'senträger *pl* suspenders
Hospitant [hɔspɪˈtant] *m* (-en;-en) (educ) auditor
hospitieren [hɔspɪˈtirən] *intr* (educ) audit a course
Hospiz [hɔsˈpits] *n* (-es;-e) hospice
Hostie ['hɔstjə] *f* (-;-n) host, wafer

Hotel [hoˈtɛl] *n* (-s;-s) hotel
Hotel'boy *m* bellboy, bellhop
Hotel'diener *m* hotel porter
Hotel'fach *n*, **Hotel'gewerbe** *n* hotel business
Hub [hup] *m* (-[e]s;ꞏꞌe) (mach) stroke
hübsch [hypʃ] *adj* prᴇtty; handsome; (coll) good-sized
Hubschrauber ['hupˌʃraubər] *m* (-s;-) helicopter
huckepack ['hukəpak] *adv* piggyback
hudeln ['hudəln] *intr* be sloppy
Huf [huf] *m* (-[e]s;-e) hoof
Huf'eisen *n* horseshoe
Huf'schlag *m* hoofbeat
Hüfte ['hʏftə] *f* (-;-n) hip; **die Arme in die Hüften gestemmt** with arms akimbo
Hüft'gelenk *n* hip joint
Hüft'gürtel *m*, **Hüft'halter** *m* garter belt
Hügel ['hygəl] *m* (-s;-) hill; mound
hügelab' *adv* downhill
hügelauf' *adv* uphill
hügelig ['hygəlɪç] *adj* hilly
Huhn [hun] *n* (-[e]s;ꞏꞌer) fowl; hen, chicken
Hühnchen ['hynçən] *n* (-s;-) young chicken; **ein H. zu rupfen haben mit** (fig) have a bone to pick with
Hüh'nerauge *n* (pathol) corn
Hüh'nerdraht *m* chicken wire
Hüh'nerhund *m* bird dog
Huld [hult] *f* (-;) grace, favor
huldigen ['huldɪgən] *intr* (*dat*) pay homage to
Hul'digung *f* (-;) homage
Hul'digungseid *m* oath of allegiance
huld'reich, huld'voll *adj* gracious
Hülle ['hʏlə] *f* (-;-n) cover; case; wrapper; envelope; (*e-s Buches*) jacket; (fig) cloak; **in H. und Fülle** in abundance; **sterbliche H.** mortal remains
hüllen ['hʏlən] *tr* cover; veil; wrap
Hülse ['hʏlzə] *f* (-;-n) pod, hull; cartridge case, shell case
Hül'senfrucht *f* legume
human [huˈman] *adj* humane
humanistisch [humaˈnɪstɪʃ] *adj* humanistic; classical
humanitär [humanɪˈter] *adj* humanitarian
Humanität [humanɪˈtet] *f* (-;) humanity; humaneness
Humanitäts'duselei *f* sentimental humanitarianism
Humanitäts'verbrechen *n* crime against humanity
Hummel ['huməl] *f* (-;-n) bumblebee
Hummer ['humər] *m* (-s;-) lobster
Humor [huˈmor] *m* (-s;) humor
humoristisch [humoˈrɪstɪʃ] *adj* humorous
humpeln ['humpəln] *intr* (SEIN) hobble
Hund [hunt] *m* (-[e]s;-e) dog
Hündchen ['hyntçən] *n* (-s;-) small dog; puppy
Hun'deangst *f*—**e-e H. haben** (coll) be scared stiff
Hun'dearbeit *f* drudgery
Hun'dehütte *f* doghouse
Hun'dekälte *f* severe cold

Hun′demarke *f* dog tag
hun′demü′de *adj* (coll) dog-tired
hundert [′hʊndərt] *invar adj & pron* hundred ‖ **Hundert** *n* (-s;-e) hundred; **drei von H.** three percent; **im H.** by the hundred ‖ *f* (-;-en) hundred
hun′dertfach *adj* hundredfold
Hundertjahr′feier *f* centennial
Hun′dertsatz *m* percentage
hundertste [′hʊndərtstə] §9 *adj & pron* hundredth
Hun′deschau *f* dog show
Hun′dezwinger *m* dog kennel
Hündin [′hʏndɪn] *f* (-;-nen) bitch
hündisch [′hʏndɪʃ] *adj* (*Benehmen*) servile; (*Angst*) deadly
hunds′gemein *adj* beastly
hunds′miserabel *adj* (sl) lousy
Hunds′stern *m* Dog Star
Hunds′tage *pl* dog days
Hüne [′hynə] *m* (-n;-n) giant
hü′nenhaft *adj* gigantic
Hunger [′hʊŋger] *m* (-s;) hunger; **H. haben** be hungry
Hun′gerkur *f* starvation diet
Hun′gerlohn *m* starvation wages
hungern [′hʊŋərn] *intr* be hungry; go without food; **h. nach** yearn for ‖ *impers*—**es hungert mich** I am hungry
Hun′gersnot *f* famine
Hun′gertod *m* death from starvation
Hun′gertuch *n*—**am H. nagen** go hungry; live in poverty
hungrig [′hʊŋrɪç] *adj* hungry; (*Jahre*) lean
Hunne [′hʊnə] *m* (-n;-n) (hist) Hun
Hupe [′hupə] *f* (-;-n) (aut) horn
hupen [′hupən] *intr* blow the horn
hüpfen [′hʏpfən], **hupfen** [′hʊpfən] *intr* (SEIN) hop, jump
Hürde [′hʏrdə] *f* (-;-n) hurdle
Hure [′hurə] *f* (-;-n) whore
huren [′hurən] *intr* whore around
hurtig [′hʊrtɪç] *adj* nimble, swift
huschen [′hʊʃən] *intr* (SEIN) scurry
hüsteln [′hʏstəln] *intr* clear the throat
husten [′hustən] *tr* cough up ‖ *intr* cough; **h. auf** (*acc*) (coll) not give a rap about

Hut [hut] *m* (-[e]s;̈-e) hat ‖ *f* (-;) protection, care; **auf der Hut sein** be on guard
hüten [′hytən] *tr* guard, protect; tend; **das Bett h.** be confined to bed; **das Haus h.** stay indoors; **Kinder h.** baby-sit ‖ *ref* (**vor** *dat*) be on guard (against), beware (of); **ich werde mich schön h.** (coll) I'll do no such thing
Hü′ter –**in** §6 *mf* guardian
Hut′krempe *f* brim of a hat
hut′los *adj* hatless
Hütte [′hʏtə] *f* (-;-n) hut; cabin; doghouse; glassworks; (Bib) tabernacle; (metal) foundry
Hüt′tenkunde *f*, **Hüt′tenwesen** *n* metallurgy
Hyäne [hy′enə] *f* (-;-n) hyena
Hyazinthe [hya′tsɪntə] *f* (-;-n) hyacinth
Hydrant [hy′drant] *m* (-en;-en) hydrant
Hydraulik [hy′draʊlɪk] *f* (-;) hydraulics; hydraulic system
hydraulisch [hy′draʊlɪʃ] *adj* hydraulic
hydrieren [hy′drirən] *tr* hydrogenate
Hygiene [hy′gjenə] *f* (-;) hygiene
hygienisch [hy′gjenɪʃ] *adj* hygienic
Hymne [′hymnə] *f* (-;-n) hymn; anthem
Hyperbel [hy′perbəl] *f* (-;-n) (geom) hyperbola; (rhet) hyperbole
Hypnose [hyp′nozə] *f* (-;-n) hypnosis
hypnotisch [hyp′notɪʃ] *adj* hypnotic
Hypothese [hypɔ′tezə] *f* (-;-n) hypothesis
Hypochonder [hypɔ′xɔndər] *m* (-s;-) hypochondriac
Hypothek [hypɔ′tek] *f* (-;-en) mortgage
Hypothe′kengläubiger *m* mortgagee
Hypothe′kenschuldner *m* mortgagor
Hypothese [hypɔ′tezə] *f* (-;-n) hypothesis
hypothetisch [hypɔ′tetɪʃ] *adj* hypothetical
Hysterektomie [hysterɛktɔ′mi] *f* (-;) hysterectomy
Hysterie [hystɛ′ri] *f* (-;) hysteria
hysterisch [hys′terɪʃ] *adj* hysterical

I

I, i [i] *invar n* I, i
iah [′i′a] *interj* heehaw!
iahen [′i′a·ən] *intr* heehaw, bray
iberisch [i′berɪʃ] *adj* Iberian
ich [ɪç] §11 *pers pron* I
ichbezogen [′ɪçbətsogən] *adj* self-centered, egocentric
Ich′sucht *f* egotism
ideal [ide′al] *adj* ideal ‖ **Ideal** *n* (-s; -e) deal
idealisieren [ide·alɪ′zirən] *tr* idealize
Idealismus [ide·a′lɪsmʊs] *m* (-;) idealism
Idealist –**in** [ide·a′lɪst(ɪn)] §7 *mf* idealist

idealistisch [ide·a′lɪstɪʃ] *adj* idealistic
I·dee [ɪ′de] *f* (-;-deen [′de·ən]) idea
Iden [′idən] *pl* Ides
identifizieren [ɪdɛntɪfɪ′tsirən] *tr* identify ‖ *ref*—**i. mit** identify with
identisch [ɪ′dɛntɪʃ] *adj* identical
Identität [ɪdɛntɪ′tet] *f* (-;-en) identity
Ideolo·gie [ide·olɔ′gi] *f* (-;-gien [′gi·ən]) ideology
Idiom [ɪ′djom] *n* (-s;-e) idiom, dialect, language
idiomatisch [ɪdjɔ′matɪʃ] *adj* idiomatic
Idiosynkra·sie [ɪdjɔzynkra′zi] *f* (-; -sien [′zi·ən]) idiosyncrasy
Idiot [ɪ′djot] *m* (-en;-en) idiot

Idio·tie [ɪdjɔ'ti] *f* (–;–tien ['ti·ən]) idiocy
Idiotin [ɪdjotɪn] *f* (–;–nen) idiot
Idol [ɪ'dol] *n* (–s;–e) idol
idyllisch [ɪ'dylɪʃ] *adj* idyllic
Igel ['igəl] *m* (–s;–) hedgehog
Ignorant [ɪgnɔ'rant] *m* (–en;–en) ignoramus
ignorieren [ɪgnɔ'rirən] *tr* ignore
ihm [im] §11 *pers pron* (dative of **er** and **es**) (to) him; (to) it
ihn [in] §11 *pers pron* (accusative of **er**) him
ihnen ['inən] §11 *pers pron* (dative of **sie**) (to) them || **Ihnen** §11 *pers pron* (dative of **Sie**) (to) you
ihr [ir] §2,2 *poss adj* her; their || §11 *pers pron* (dative of **sie**) (to) her || **Ihr** §2,2 *poss adj* your
ihrerseits ['irərzaɪts] *adv* on her (or their) part; **Ihrerseits** on your part
ihresgleichen ['irəs'glaɪçən] *pron* the likes of her (or them); her (or their) equal(s); **Ihresgleichen** the likes of you; your equal(s)
ihrethalben ['irət'halbən] *adv* var of **ihretwegen**
ihretwegen ['irət'vegen] *adv* because of her (or them); for her (or their) sake; **Ihretwegen** because of you, for your sake
ihretwillen ['irət'vɪlən] *adv* var of **ihretwegen**
ihrige ['irɪgə] §2,5 *poss pron* hers; theirs; **Ihrige** yours
Ikone [i'konə] *f* (–;–n) icon
illegal [ɪlɛ'gal] *adj* illegal
illegitim [ɪlɛgɪ'tim] *adj* illegitimate
illuminieren [ɪlumɪ'nirən] *tr* illuminate
Illusion [ɪlu'zjon] *f* (–;–en) illusion
illustrieren [ɪlus'trirən] *tr* illustrate
Illustrierte [ɪlus'trirtə] §5 *f* (illustrated) magazine
Iltis ['ɪltɪs] *m* (–ses;–se) polecat
im [ɪm] *contr* **in dem**
Image ['ɪmɪdʒ] *n* (–s;–s) (fig) image
imaginär [ɪmagɪ'ner] *adj* imaginary
Im·biß ['ɪmbɪs] *m* (–bisses;–bisse) snack
Im'bißhalle *f* luncheonette
Im'bißstube *f* snack bar
Imi·tator [ɪmɪ'tatɔr] *m* (–s;–tatoren [ta'torən]) imitator; impersonator
Imker ['ɪmkər] *m* (–s;–) beekeeper
immateriell [ɪmatɛ'rjɛl] *adj* immaterial, spiritual
immatrikulieren [ɪmatrɪku'lirən] *tr & intr* register; **sich i.** lassen get registered
immens [ɪ'mɛns] *adj* immense
immer ['ɪmər] *adv* always; **auf i. und ewig** for ever and ever; **für i.** for good; **i. langsam!** steady now!; **i. mehr** more and more; **i. wieder** again and again; **noch i.** still; **nur i. zu!** keep trying!; **was auch i.** whatever
immerdar' *adv* (Lit) forever
immerfort' *adv* all the time
im'mergrün *adj* evergreen || **Immergrün** *n* (–s;–e) evergreen
immerhin' *adv* after all, anyhow
immerwäh'rend *adj* perpetual
immerzu' *adv* all the time, constantly

Immobilien [ɪmɔ'biljen] *pl* real estate
Immobi'lienmakler –in §6 *mf* real-estate broker
immun [ɪ'mun] *adj* (gegen) immune (to)
immunisieren [ɪmunɪ'zirən] *tr* immunize
Imperativ [ɪmpera'tif] *m* (–s;–e) (gram) imperative
Imperfek·tum [ɪmper'fɛktum] *n* (–s; –ta [ta]) (gram) imperfect
Imperialismus [ɪmperɪ·a'lɪsmus] *m* (–;) imperialism
impfen ['ɪmpfen] *tr* vaccinate; inoculate
Impfling ['ɪmpflɪŋ] *m* (–s;–e) person to be vaccinated or inoculated
Impf'schein *m* vaccination certificate
Impf'stoff *m* vaccine
Imp'fung *f* (–;–en) vaccination; inoculation
imponieren [ɪmpɔ'nirən] *intr* (*dat*) impress
Import [ɪm'pɔrt] *m* (–[e]s;–e) import
importieren [ɪmpɔr'tirən] *tr* import
imposant [ɪmpɔ'zant] *adj* imposing
imprägnieren [ɪmprɛg'nirən] *tr* waterproof; creosote
Impresario [ɪmprɛ'zarjo] *m* (–s;–s) agent, business manager
Impres·sum [ɪm'prɛsum] *n* (–s;–sen [sən]) (journ) masthead
imstande [ɪm'/tandə] *adv*—**i. sein zu** (*inf*) be in a position to (*inf*)
in [ɪn] *prep* (*position*) (*dat*) in, at; (*direction*) (acc) in, into
Inangriffnahme [ɪn'angrɪfnamə] *f* (–;) starting; putting into action
Inanspruchnahme [ɪn'an/pruxnamə] *f* (–;) laying claim; demands; utilization
In'begriff *m* essence; embodiment
in'begriffen *adj* included
Inbrunst ['ɪnbrunst] *f* (–;) ardor
inbrünstig ['ɪnbrynstɪç] *adj* ardent
indem [ɪn'dem] *conj* while, as; by (*ger*)
Inder –in ['ɪndər(ɪn)] §6 *mf* Indian (*inhabitant of India*)
indes [ɪn'des], **indessen** [ɪn'dɛsən] *adv* meanwhile; however || *conj* while; whereas
Indianer –in [ɪn'djanər(ɪn)] §6 *mf* Indian (*of North America*)
Indien ['ɪndjən] *n* (–s;) India
Indio ['ɪndɪ·o] *m* (–s;–s) Indian (*of Central or South America*)
indisch ['ɪndɪʃ] *adj* Indian
indiskret [ɪndɪs'kret] *adj* indiscreet
indiskutabel [ɪndɪsku'tabəl] *adj* out of the question
individuell [ɪndɪvɪdu'ɛl] *adj* individual
Individu·um [ɪndɪ'vidu·um] *n* (–s;–en [ən]) individual; (pej) character
Indizienbeweis [ɪn'ditsjənbəvaɪs] *m* (piece of) circumstantial evidence
Indossament [ɪndɔsa'mɛnt] *n* (–[e]s; –e) indorsement
Indossat [ɪndɔ'sant] *m* (–en;–en) indorser
indossieren [ɪndɔ'sirən] *tr* indorse
industrialisieren [ɪndustrɪ·alɪ'zirən] *tr* industrialize

Indus·trie [ɪndʊs'tri] *f* (–;–**trien** ['tri·ən]) industry
Industrie'anlage *f* industrial plant
Industrie'betrieb *m* industrial establishment
Industrie'kapitän *m* tycoon
industriell [ɪndʊstri'ɛl] *adj* industrial || **Industrielle** §5 *m* industrialist
ineinan'der *adv* into one another; **i. übergehen** merge
ineinan'derfügen *tr* dovetail
ineinan'dergreifen §88 *intr* mesh
ineinan'derpassen *intr* dovetail
infam [ɪn'fam] *adv* (coll) frightfully
Infante·rie [ɪnfantə'ri] *f* (–;–**rien** ['ri·ən]) infantry
Infanterist [ɪnfantə'rɪst] *m* (–en;–en) infantryman
infantil [ɪnfan'til] *adj* infantile
Infektion [ɪnfɛk'tsjon] *f* (–;–en) infection
Infini·tiv [ɪnfɪnɪ'tif] *m* (–s;–**tive** ['tivə]) infinitive
infizieren [ɪnfi'tsirən] *tr* infect
infolge [ɪn'fɔlgə] *prep* (genit) in consequence of, owing to; according to
infolgedes'sen *adv* consequently
Information [ɪnfɔrma'tsjon] *f* (–;–en) (piece of) information
informieren [ɪnfɔr'mirən] *tr* inform
infrarot [ɪnfra'rot] *adj* infrared || **Infrarot** *n* (–s;–) infrared
Ingenieur [ɪnʒɛn'jør] *m* (–s;–e) engineer
Ingenieur'bau *m* (–[e]s;) civil engineering
Ingenieur'wesen *n* engineering
ingeniös [ɪnge'njøs] *adj* ingenious
Ingrimm ['ɪngrɪm] *m* inner rage
Ingwer ['ɪŋvər] *m* (–s;) ginger
Ing'werplätzchen *n* gingersnap
Inhaber –**in** ['ɪnhabər(ɪn)] §6 *mf* owner; bearer; occupant; holder
inhaftieren [ɪnhaf'tirən] *tr* arrest
Inhalierapparat [ɪnha'liraparat] *m* (med) inhalator
inhalieren [ɪnha'lirən] *tr & intr* inhale
Inhalt ['ɪnhalt] *m* (–[e]s;–e) contents; subject matter; (geom) area; volume
In'haltsangabe *f* summary; list of contents
in'haltsarm, in'haltsleer *adj* empty
in'haltsreich *adj* substantive; (*Leben*) full
in'haltsschwer *adj* pregnant with meaning; momentous
In'haltsverzeichnis *n* table of contents
in'haltsvoll *adj* full of meaning
inhibieren [ɪnhi'birən] *tr* inhibit
Initiative [ɪnɪtsja'tivə] *f* (–;–en) initiative
Injektion [ɪnjɛk'tsjon] *f* (–;–en) injection
Injektions'nadel *f* hypodermic needle
injizieren [ɪnjɪ'tsirən] *tr* inject
Inkasso [ɪn'kaso] *n* (–s;–s) bill collecting
Inkas'sobeamte *m* bill collector
inklusive [ɪnklu'zivə] *adj* inclusive || *prep* (genit) including
inkonsequent ['ɪnkɔnzɛkvɛnt] *adj* inconsistent; illogical
Inkraft'treten *n* going into effect

In'land *n* (–[e]s;) home country; interior
Inländer –**in** ['ɪnlɛndər(ɪn)] §6 *mf* native
inländisch ['ɪnlɛndɪʃ] *adj* home, domestic; inland
In'landspost *f* domestic mail
Inlett ['ɪnlɛt] *n* (–[e]s;–e) bedtick
in'liegend *adj* enclosed
inmit'ten *prep* (genit) in the middle of, among
innehaben ['ɪnəhabən] §89 *tr* (*Amt*) hold; (*Wohnung*) occupy, own
innehalten ['ɪnəhaltən] §90 *intr* stop
innen ['ɪnən] *adv* inside; indoors; **nach i.** inwards; **tief i.** deep down
Innen– *comb.fm.* inner, internal; inside, interior; home, domestic
In'nenarchitekt –**in** §7 *mf* interior decorator
In'nenaufnahme *f* (phot) indoor shot
In'nenhof *m* quadrangle
In'nenleben *n* inner life
In'nenminister *m* Secretary of the Interior; Secretary of State for Home Affairs (Brit)
In'nenpolitik *f* domestic policy
In'nenraum *m* interior (*of building*)
In'nenstadt *f* center of town, inner city
inner– [ɪnər] *comb.fm.* internal; intra-
innere ['ɪnərə] §9 *adj* inner, internal; inside; inward; domestic || **Innere** §5 *n* inside, interior
in'nerhalb *adv* on the inside; **i. von** within || *prep* (genit) inside, within
in'nerlich *adj* inner, inward || *adv* inwardly; mentally, emotionally
In'nerlichkeit *f* (–;–en) introspection; inner quality
innerste ['ɪnərstə] §9 *adj* innermost
innesein ['ɪnəzaɪn] §139 *intr* (SEIN) (genit) be aware of
innewerden ['ɪnəverdən] §159 *intr* (SEIN) (genit) become aware of
innig ['ɪnɪç] *adj* close; deep, heartfelt || *adv* deeply
In'nigkeit *f* (–;) intimacy; deep feeling; tender affection
Innung ['ɪnʊŋ] *f* (–;–en) guild
inoffiziell ['ɪnɔfɪtsjɛl] *adj* unofficial
ins *contr* **in das**
Insasse ['ɪnzasə] *m* (–n;–n), **Insassin** ['ɪnsasɪn] *f* (–;–nen) occupant; (*e–s Gefängnisses*) inmate; (*e–s Autos*) passenger
insbesondere [ɪnsbə'zɔndərə] *adv* in particular, especially
In'schrift *f* inscription
Insekt [ɪn'zɛkt] *n* (–[e]s;–en) insect
Insek'tenbekämpfungsmittel *n* insecticide
Insek'tenkunde *f* entomology
Insek'tenstich *m* insect bite
Insektizid [ɪnzɛkti'tsit] *n* (–[e]s;–e) insecticide
Insel ['ɪnzəl] *f* (–;–n) island
Inserat [ɪnzə'rɑt] *n* (–es;–e) classified advertisement, ad
inserieren [ɪnzə'rirən] *tr* insert || *intr* (in dat) advertise (in)
insgeheim [ɪnsgə'haɪm] *adv* secretly
insgemein [ɪnsgə'maɪn] *adv* as a whole; in general, generally

insgesamt [ɪnsgə'zamt] *adv* in a body, as a unit; in all, altogether
inso'fern *adv* to this extent || **insofern'** *conj* in so far as
insoweit' *adv* & *conj* var of **insofern**
Inspek·tor [ɪn'spɛktər] *m* (-s;-toren ['torən]) inspector
inspirieren [ɪnspɪ'rirən] *tr* inspire
inspizieren [ɪnspɪ'tsirən] *tr* inspect
Installation [ɪnstala'tsjon] *f* (-;-en) installation
installieren [ɪnsta'lirən] *tr* install
instand [ɪn'ʃtant] *adv*—**i. halten** keep in good condition; **i. setzen** repair
Instand'haltung *f* upkeep, maintenance
inständig [ɪn'ʃtendɪç] *adj* insistent
Instand'setzung *f* repair, renovation
Instanz [ɪn'stants] *f* (-;-en) (adm) authority; **e-e höhere I.** anrufen appeal to a higher court; **Gericht der ersten I.** court of primary jurisdiction; **Gericht der zweiten I.** court of appeal; **höchste I.** court of final appeal
Institut [ɪnstɪ'tut] *n* (-[e]s;-e) institute
instruieren [ɪnstru'irən] *tr* instruct
Instruktion [ɪnstruk'tsjon] *f* (-;-en) instruction
Instrument [ɪnstru'mɛnt] *n* (-[e]s;-e) instrument
Instrumentalist –in [ɪnstrumɛnta'lɪst (ɪn)] §7 *mf* instrumentalist
Insulaner –in [ɪnzu'lɑnər(ɪn)] §6 *mf* islander
insular [ɪnzu'lɑr] *adj* insular
Insulin [ɪnzu'lin] *n* (-s;) insulin
inszenieren [ɪnstse'nirən] *tr* stage
Intellekt [ɪntɛ'lɛkt] *m* (-[e]s;) intellect
intellektuell [ɪntɛlɛktu'ɛl] *adj* intellectual || **Intellektuelle** §5 *mf* intellectual
intelligent [ɪntɛlɪ'gɛnt] *adj* intelligent
Intelligenzler [ɪntɛlɪ'gɛntslər] *m* (-s;-) (pej) egghead
Intendant [ɪntɛn'dant] *m* (-en;-en) (theat) director
intensiv [ɪntɛn'zif] *adj* intense; intensive
–intensiv *comb.fm.*, e.g., **lohnintensive Güter** goods of which wages constitute a high proportion of the cost
interessant [ɪntere'sant] *adj* interesting
Interesse [ɪnte'resə] *n* (-s;-n) (**an** *dat*, **für**) interest (in)
interes'selos *adj* uninterested
Interes'sengemeinschaft *f* community of interest; (com) syndicate
Interessent –in [ɪntere'sɛnt(ɪn)] §7 *mf* interested party
interessieren [ɪntere'sirən] *tr* (**für**) interest (in) || *ref*—**sich i. für** be interested in
interimistisch [ɪnterɪ'mɪstɪʃ] *adj* provisional
intern [ɪn'tɛrn] *adj* internal
Internat [ɪntɛr'nat] *n* (-[e]s;-e) boarding school
international [ɪntɛrnatsjə'nɑl] *adj* international
Internat(s)'schüler –in §6 *mf*, **Interne** [ɪn'tɛrnə] §5 *mf* boarding student
internieren [ɪntɛr'nirən] *tr* intern

Internist –in [ɪntɛr'nɪst(ɪn)] §7 *mf* (med) internist
Interpret [ɪntɛr'pret] *m* (-en;-en) interpreter; exponent
interpunktieren [ɪntɛrpuŋk'tirən] *tr* punctuate
Interpunktion [ɪntɛrpuŋk'tsjon] *f* (-; -en) punctuation
Interpunktions'zeichen *n* punctuation mark
Intervall [ɪntɛr'val] *n* (-s;-e) interval
intervenieren [ɪntɛrve'nirən] *intr* intervene
Interview ['ɪntɛrvju] *n* (-s;-s) interview
interviewen [ɪntɛr'vju·ən] *tr* interview
intim [ɪn'tim] *adj* intimate
Intimität [ɪntɪmɪ'tet] *f* (-;-en) intimacy
intolerant [ɪntɔle'rant] *adj* intolerant
intonieren [ɪntɔ'nirən] *tr* intone
intransitiv ['ɪntransɪtif] *adj* intransitive
intravenös [ɪntrave'nøs] *adj* intravenous
intrigant [ɪntrɪ'gant] *adj* intriguing, scheming || **Intragant** –in §7 *mf* intriguer, schemer
Intrige [ɪn'trigə] *f* (-;-n) intrigue
introspektiv [ɪntrɔspɛk'tif] *adj* introspective
Introvertierte [ɪntrɔver'tirtə] §5 *mf* introvert
invalide [ɪnva'lidə] *adj* disabled || **Invalide** §5 *mf* invalid
Invalidität [ɪnvalɪdɪ'tet] *f* (-;) disability
Invasion [ɪnva'zjon] *f* (-;-en) invasion
Inventar [ɪnvɛn'tar] *n* (-s;-e) inventory
Inventur [ɪnvɛn'tur] *f* (-;-en) stock taking; **I. machen** take stock
inwärts ['ɪnvɛrts] *adv* inwards
inwendig ['ɪnvɛndɪç] *adj* inward, inner
inwiefern' *adv* how far; in what way
inwieweit' *adv* var of **inwiefern**
In'zucht *f* inbreeding
inzwi'schen *adv* meanwhile
Ion [ɪ'on] *n* (-s;-en) (phys) ion
ionisieren [ɪ·ɔnɪ'zirən] *tr* ionize
Irak [ɪ'rak] *m* (-s;) Iraq
Iraker –in [ɪ'rakər(ɪn)] §6 *mf* Iraqi
irakisch [ɪ'rakɪʃ] *adj* Iraqi
Iran [ɪ'ran] *n* (-s;) Iran
Iraner –in [ɪ'ranər(ɪn)] §6 *mf* Iranian
iranisch [ɪ'ranɪʃ] *adj* Iranian
irden ['ɪrdən] *adj* earthen
irdisch ['ɪrdɪʃ] *adj* earthly, worldly || **Irdische** §5 *n* earthly nature
Ire ['irə] *m* (-n;-n) Irishman; **die Iren** the Irish
irgend ['ɪrgənt] *adv*—**i. etwas** something, anything; **i. jemand** someone, anyone; **nur i.** possibly
ir'gendein *adj* some, any || **ingendeiner** *indef pron* someone, anyone
ir'gendeinmal *adv* at some time or other
ir'gendwann *adv* at some time or other
ir'gendwelcher *adj* any; any kind of
ir'gendwer *indef pron* someone
ir'gendwie *adv* somehow or other
ir'gendwo *adv* somewhere or other; anywhere

ir'gendwoher *adv* from somewhere or other
ir'gendwohin *adv* somewhere or other
Irin ['ɪrɪn] *f* (–;-nen) Irish woman
Iris ['iɾɪs] *f* (–;–) (anat, bot) iris
irisch ['iɾɪʃ] *adj* Irish
Irland ['ɪrlant] *n* (–s;) Ireland
Iro·nie [ɪɾə'ni] *f* (–;-nien ['ni·ən]) irony
ironisch [ɪ'ronɪʃ] *adj* ironic(al)
irre ['ɪrə] *adj* stray; confused; mad; **i.** werden go astray; get confused; **i.** werden an (*dat*) lose faith in ‖ **Irre** §5 *mf* lunatic ‖ *f* maze; wrong track; **in die I. führen** put on the wrong track; **in die I. gehen** go astray
ir'refahren §71 *intr* (SEIN) lose one's way, go wrong
ir'reführen *tr* mislead
ir'regehen §82 *intr* (SEIN) lose one's way; (fig) go wrong
ir'remachen *tr* confuse; **j–n i. an** (*dat*) make s.o. lose faith in
irren ['ɪrən] *intr* go astray; err ‖ *ref* (in *dat*) be mistaken (about); **sich in der Straße i.** take the wrong road; **sich in der Zeit i.** misjudge the time
Ir'renanstalt *f*, **Ir'renhaus** *n* insane asylum
Ir'renhäusler ['ɪrənhɔɪzlər] *m* (–s;–) inmate of an insane asylum
ir'rereden *intr* rave; talk deliriously
Irrfahrt ['ɪrfart] *f* odyssey
Irrgang ['ɪrgaŋ] *m* winding path
Irrgarten ['ɪrgartən] *m* labyrinth
Irrglaube ['ɪrglaʊbə] *m* heresy
irrgläubig ['ɪrglɔɪbɪç] *adj* heretical
irrig ['ɪrɪç] *adj* mistaken
Irri·gator [ɪrɪ'gatɔr] *m* (–s;-gatoren [ga·torən]) douche

irritieren [ɪrɪ'tirən] *tr* irritate; (coll) confuse
Irrlehre ['ɪrlerə] *f* false doctrine
Irrlicht ['ɪrlɪçt] *n* jack-o'-lantern
Irrsinn ['ɪrzɪn] *m* insanity
irr'sinnig *adj* insane
Irrtum ['ɪrtum] *n* (–s;-̈er) error
irrtümlich ['ɪrtymlɪç] *adj* erroneous
Irrweg ['ɪrvek] *m* wrong track
Irrwisch ['ɪrvɪʃ] *m* (–es;–e) jack-o'-lantern; (coll) fireball
Islam [ɪs'lam] *m* (–s;) Islam
Island ['islant] *n* (–s;) Iceland
Iso·lator [ɪzɔ'latɔr] *m* (–s;-latoren [la'torən]) (elec) insulator
Isolier– [ɪzɔlir] *comb.fm.* isolation; insulating; insulated
Isolier'band *n* (–[e]s;-̈er) friction tape
isolieren [ɪzɔ'lirən] *tr* (*Kranke*) isolate; (*abdichten*) insulate
Isolier'haft *f* solitary confinement
Insolier'station *f* isolation ward
Isolie'rung *f* (–;-en) isolation; (elec) insulation
Isotop [ɪzɔ'top] *n* (–[e]s;-e) isotope
Israel ['ɪsra·ɛl] *n* (– & –s;) Israel
Israeli [ɪsra'eli] *m* (–s;–s) Israeli
israelisch [ɪsra'eliʃ] *adj* Israeli
Israelit –in [ɪsra·ɛ'lit(ɪn)] §7 *mf* Israelite
israelitisch [ɪsra·ɛ'litɪʃ] *adj* Israelite
Ist– [ɪst] *comb.fm.* actual
Ist-'Bestand *m* actual stock; (fin) actual balance; (mil) actual stockpile
Ist-'Stand *m*, **Ist-'Stärke** *f* (mil) effective strength
Italien [ɪ'taljən] *n* (–s;) Italy
Italiener –in [ɪtal'jenər(ɪn)] §6 *mf* Italian
italienisch [ɪtal'jenɪʃ] *adj* Italian

J

J, j [jɔt] *invar n* J, j
ja [ja] *adv* yes; indeed, certainly; of course ‖ **Ja** *n* (–s;–s) yes
Jacht [jaxt] *f* (–;-en) yacht
Jacke ['jakə] *f* (–;-n) jacket, coat
Jackenkleid (**Jak'kenkleid**) *n* lady's two-piece suit
Jackett [ʒa'kɛt] *n* (–s;–s) jacket
Jagd [jakt] *f* (–;-en) hunt(ing); **auf die J. gehen** go hunting; **J. machen auf** (*acc*) hunt for
Jagd'abschirmung *f* (aer) fighter screen
Jagd'aufseher *m* gamewarden
jagdbar ['jaktbar] *adj* in season, fair (*game*)
Jagd'bomber *m* (aer) fighter-bomber
Jagd'flieger *m* fighter pilot
Jagd'flugzeug *n* (aer) fighter plane
Jagd'gehege *n* game preserve
Jagd'geleit *n* (aer) fighter escort
Jagd'hund *m* hunting dog, hound
Jagd'rennen *n* steeplechase
Jagd'revier *n* hunting ground
Jagd'schein *m* hunting license

Jagd'schutz *m* (aer) fighter protection
Jagd'verband *m* (aer) fighter unit
Jagd'wild *n* game; game bird
jagen ['jagən] *tr* hunt; pursue; chase; (fig) follow close on; **in die Luft j.** blow up ‖ *intr* go hunting; **j. nach** pursue ‖ *intr* (SEIN) rush
Jäger ['jegər] *m* (–s;–) hunter; (aer) fighter plane; (mil) rifleman
Jägerei [jegə'raɪ] *f* (–;) hunting
Jä'gerlatein *n* (coll) fish story
Jaguar ['jagu·ar] *m* (–s;–s) jaguar
jäh [je] *adj* sudden; steep ‖ **Jähe** *f* (–;) suddenness; steepness
jählings ['jelɪŋs] *adv* suddenly; steeply
Jahr [jar] *n* (–[e]s;-e) year
jahraus' *adv*—**j. jahrein** year in year out, year after year
Jahr'buch *n* almanac; yearbook; annual
jahrelang ['jarəlaŋ] *adj* long-standing ‖ *adv* for years
jähren ['jerən] *ref* be a year ago
Jahres– [jarəs] *comb.fm.* annual, yearly, of the year

Jah'resfeier *f* anniversary
Jah'resfrist *f* period of a year
Jah'resrente *f* annuity
Jah'restag *m* anniversary
Jah'reszahl *f* date, year
Jah'reszeit *f* season
jah'reszeitlich *adj* seasonal
Jahr'gang *m* age group; class, year; crop; vintage; **er gehört zu meinem J.** he was born in the same year as I
Jahrhun'dert *n* century
–jährig [jɛrɪç] *comb.fm.* –year–old
jährlich [ˈjɛrlɪç] *adj* yearly, annual
Jahr'markt *m* fair
Jahr'marktplatz *m* fairground
Jahrtau'send *n* millennium
Jahrzehnt [jɑrˈtsent] *n* (–[e]s;–e) decade
Jäh'zorn *m* fit of anger; hot temper
jäh'zornig *adj* quick-tempered
Jalou·sie [ʒaluˈzi] *f* (–;–sien [ˈzi·ən]) louvre; Venetian blind
Jammer [ˈjamər] *m* (–s;) misery; wailing; **es ist ein J., daß** it's a pity that
Jam'merlappen *m* (pej) jellyfish
jämmerlich [ˈjemərlɪç] *adj* miserable; pitiful; (*Anblick*) sorry
jammern [ˈjamərn] *tr* move to pity ‖ *intr* (über *acc*, **um**) moan (about); **j. nach** (or **um**) whimper for
jam'merschade *adj* deplorable
Jänner [ˈjenər] *m* (–s & –;–) (Aust) January
Januar [ˈjanʊ·ɑr] *m* (–s & –;–e) January
Japan [ˈjapan] *n* (–s;) Japan
Japaner –in [jaˈpanər(ɪn)] §6 *mf* Japanese
japanisch [jaˈpanɪʃ] *adj* Japanese
jappen [ˈjapən] *intr* pant, gasp
Jasager [ˈjɑzagər] *m* (–s;–) yes-man
jäten [ˈjetən] *tr* weed; **das Unkraut j.** pull out weeds ‖ *intr* weed
Jauche [ˈjaʊxə] *f* (–;–n) liquid manure; (sl) slop
jauchen [ˈjaʊxən] *tr* manure
Jau'chegrube *f* cesspool
jauchzen [ˈjaʊxtsən] *intr* rejoice; **vor Freude j.** shout for joy ‖ **Jauchzen** *n* (–s;) jubilation
Jauch'zer *m* (–s;–) shout of joy
jawohl [jaˈvol] *interj* yes, indeed!
Ja'wort *n* (–[e]s;) consent
Jazz [dʒez], [jats] *m* (–;) jazz
je [je] *adv* ever; **denn je** than ever; **je länger, je** (or **desto**) **besser** the longer the better; **je nach** according to, depending on; **je nachdem, ob** according to whether; **je Pfund per** pound; **je zwei** two each; two by two, in twos; **seit je** always
Jeans [dʒinz] *pl* jeans
jedenfalls [ˈjedənfals] *adv* at any rate; **ich j.** I for one
jeder [ˈjedər] §3 *indef adj* each, every ‖ *indef pron* each one, everyone
jederlei [ˈjedərˈlaɪ] *invar adj* every kind of
je'dermann *indef pron* everyone, everybody
je'derzeit *adv* at all times, at any time
je'desmal *adv* each time, every time
jedoch [jɛˈdɔx] *adv* however

jeglicher [ˈjeklɪçər] §3 *indef adj* each, every ‖ *indef pron* each one, everyone
je'her *adv*—**von j.** since time immemorial
Jelän'gerjelie'ber *m & n* honeysuckle
jemals [ˈjemals] *adv* ever
jemand [ˈjemant] *indef pron* someone, somebody; anyone, anybody
jener [ˈjenər] §3 *dem adj* that ‖ *dem pron* that one
jenseitig [ˈjenzaɪtɪç] *adj* opposite, beyond, otherworldly
jenseits [ˈjenzaɪts] *prep* (*genit*) on the other side of; beyond ‖ **Jenseits** *n* (–;) beyond
jetzig [ˈjetsɪç] *adj* present, current
jetzt [jetst] *adv* now
jeweilig [ˈjevaɪlɪç] *adj* at that time
jeweils [ˈjevaɪls] *adv* at that time
jiddisch [ˈjɪdɪʃ] *adj* Yiddish
Joch [jɔx] *n* (–[e]s;–e) yoke; yoke of oxen; (*e–r Brücke*) span; (*e–s Berges*) saddleback
Joch'bein *n* cheekbone
Joch'brücke *f* pile bridge
Jockei [ˈdʒɔki] *m* (–s;–s) jockey
Jod [jot] *n* (–s;) iodine
jodeln [ˈjodəln] *intr* yodel
Jodler –in [ˈjodlər(ɪn)] §6 *mf* yodeler ‖ *m* yodel
Jodtinktur [ˈjottɪŋktur] *f* (–;) (pharm) iodine
Johannisbeere [jɔˈhanɪsberə] *f* currant
johlen [ˈjolən] *intr* yell, boo
jonglieren [ʒɔŋˈ(g)lirən] *tr & intr* juggle
Journalist –in [ʒurnaˈlɪst(ɪn)] §7 *mf* journalist
jovial [joˈvjal] *adj* jovial
Jubel [ˈjubəl] *m* (–s;) jubilation
Ju'belfeier *f*, **Ju'belfest** *n* jubilee
Ju'beljahr *n* jubilee year
jubeln [ˈjubəln] *intr* rejoice; shout for joy
Jubilä·um [jubɪˈle·um] *n* (–s;–en [ən]) jubilee
juche [jʊxˈhe] *interj* hurray!
juchei [jʊxˈhaɪ] *interj* hurray!
juchzen [ˈjʊxtsən] *intr* shout for joy
jucken [ˈjʊkən] *tr* itch; scratch ‖ *ref* scratch ‖ *intr* itch ‖ *impers*—**es juckt mich** I feel itchy; **es juckt mir** (or **mich**) **in den Fingern zu** (*inf*) I am itching to (*inf*); **es juckt sie in den Beinen** she is itching to dance
Jude [ˈjudə] *m* (–n;–n) Jew
Ju'denschaft *f* (–;) Jewry
Ju'denstern *m* star of David
Judentum [ˈjudəntum] *n* (–s;) Judaism; **das J.** the Jews
Jüdin [ˈjydɪn] *f* (–;–nen) Jewish woman
jüdisch [ˈjydɪʃ] *adj* Jewish
Jugend [ˈjugənt] *f* (–;) youth
Ju'gendalter *n* youth; adolescence
Ju'gendgericht *n* juvenile court
Ju'gendherberge *f* youth hostel
Ju'gendkriminalität *f* juvenile delinquency
jugendlich [ˈjugəntlɪç] *adj* youthful ‖ **Jugendliche** §5 *mf* youth, teenager
Ju'gendliebe *f* puppy love
Ju'gendstrich *m* youthful prank

Jugoslawien [jugɔ'slavjən] *n* (-s;) Yugoslavia
jugoslawisch [jugɔ'slavɪʃ] *adj* Yugoslav
Juli ['juli] *m* (-[s];-s) July
jung [juŋ] *adj* (jünger ['jyŋər]; jüngste ['jyŋstə] §9) young; (*Erbsen*) green; (*Wein*) new || Junge §5 *m* boy || *n* newly born; young
jungen ['juŋən] *intr* produce young
jun'genhaft *adj* boyish
Jünger ['jyŋər] *m* (-s;-) disciple
Jungfer ['juŋfər] *f* (-;-n) maiden; virgin
jüngeferlich ['jyŋfərlɪç] *adj* maidenly
Jung'fernfahrt *f* maiden voyage
Jung'fernhäutchen *n* hymen
Jung'fernkranz *m* bridal wreath
Jung'fernschaft *f* virginity
Jung'frau *f* virgin
jungfräulich ['juŋfrɔɪlɪç] *adj* maidenly; virgin
Jung'fräulichkeit *f* virginity
Jung'geselle *m* bachelor
Jung'gesellenstand *m* bachelorhood
Jung'gesellin *f* single girl
Jüngling ['jyŋlɪŋ] *m* (-s;-e) young man
jüngst [jyŋst] *adv* recently
jüng'ste *adj* see jung

Juni ['juni] *m* (-[s];-s) June
Junker ['juŋkər] *m* (-s;-) young nobleman; nobleman
Jura ['jura] *pl*—J. studieren study law
Jurist –in [ju'rɪst(ɪn)] §7 *mf* lawyer; (educ) law student
Juristerei [jurɪstə'raɪ] *f* (-;) jurisprudence
juristisch [ju'rɪstɪʃ] *adj* legal, law; juristische Person legal entity, corporation
just [just] *adv* just, precisely
justieren [jus'tirən] *tr* adjust
Justiz [jus'tits] *f* (-;) justice; administration of justice
Justiz'irrtum *m* miscarriage of justice
Justiz'minister *m* minister of justice; attorney general; Lord Chancellor (Brit)
Jutesack ['jutəzak] *m* gunnysack
Juwel [ju'vel] *n* (-s;-en) jewel, gem; Juwelen jewelry
Juwe'lenkästchen *n* jewel box
Juwelier –in [juvɛ'lir(ɪn)] §6 *mf* jeweler
Juwelier'waren *pl* jewelry
Jux [juks] *m* (-es;-e) spoof, joke; aus Jux as a joke; sich [*dat*] e–n Jux mit j–m machen play a joke on s.o.

K

K, k [ka] *invar n* K, k
Kabale [ka'balə] *f* (-;-n) intrigue
Kabarett [kaba'rɛt] *n* (-[e]s;-e) cabaret; floor show; (*drehbare Platte*) lazy Suzan
Kabel ['kabəl] *n* (-s;-) cable
Ka'belgramm *n* (-es;-e) cablegram
Kabeljau ['kabəljau] *m* (-s;-e) codfish
kabeln ['kabəln] *tr* cable
Kabine [ka'binə] *f* (-;-n) cabin; booth; (aer) cockpit
Kabinett [kabɪ'nɛt] *n* (-s;-e) closet; small room; (& pol) cabinet
Kabriolett [kabrɪ·ɔ'lɛt] *n* (-[e]s;-e) (aut) convertible
Kachel ['kaxəl] *f* (-;-n) glazed tile
kacken ['kakən] *intr* (sl) defecate
Kadaver [ka'davər] *m* (-s;-) cadaver
Kada'vergehorsam *m* blind obedience
Kadenz [ka'dɛnts] *f* (-;-en) cadence
Kader ['kadər] *m* (-s;-) cadre
Kadett [ka'dɛt] *m* (-en;-en) cadet
Käfer ['kefər] *m* (-s;-) beetle
Kaffee ['kafe] *m* (-s;-s) coffee
Kaf'feebohne *f* coffee bean
Kaf'feeklatsch *m* coffee klatsch
Kaf'feemaschine *f* coffee maker
Kaf'feepflanzung *f*, Kaf'feeplantage *f* coffee plantation
Kaf'feesatz *m* coffee grounds
Kaf'feetante *f* coffee fiend
Käfig ['kefɪç] *m* (-[e]s;-e) cage
kahl [kal] *adj* bald; (*Baum*) bare; (*Landschaft*) bleak, barren
kahl'köpfig *adj* bald-headed
Kahm [kam] *m* (-[e]s;-e) mold; scum

kahmig ['kamɪç] *adj* moldy; scummy
Kahn [kan] *m* (-[e]s;-e) boat; barge
Kai [kaɪ], [ke] *m* (-s;-s) quay, wharf
Kaiser ['kaɪzər] *m* (-s;-) emperor
Kaiserin ['kaɪzərɪn] *f* (-;-nen) empress
kai'serlich *adj* imperial
Kai'serreich *n*, Kaisertum ['kaɪzərtum] *n* (-[e]s;-̈er) empire
Kai'serschnitt *m* Caesarian operation
Kai'serzeit *f* (*hist*) Empire
Kajüte [ka'jytə] *f* (-;-n) (naut) cabin
Kajü'tenjunge *m* cabin boy
Kajü'tentreppe *f* (naut) companionway
Kakao [ka'ka·ɔ] *m* (-s;-) cocoa; j–n durch den K. ziehen pull s.o.'s leg
Kaktee [kak'te·ə] *f* (-;-n), Kaktus ['kaktus] *m* (-;-se) cactus
Kalauer ['kalau·ər] *m* (-s;-) pun
Kalb [kalp] *n* (-[e]s;-̈er) calf
Kalbe ['kalbə] *f* (-;-n) heifer
kalbern ['kalbərn] *intr* be silly
Kalb'fell *n* calfskin
Kalb'fleisch *n* veal
Kalbs'braten *m* roast veal
Kalbs'kotelett *n* veal cutlet
Kalbs'schnitzel *n* veal cutlet
Kaleidoskop [kalaɪdɔ'skop] *n* (-s;-e) kaleidoscope
Kalender [ka'lɛndər] *m* (-s;-) calendar
Kali ['kalɪ] *n* (-s;) potash
Kaliber [ka'libər] *n* (-s;-) caliber
kalibrieren [kalɪ'brirən] *tr* calibrate; gauge
Kaliko ['kalɪko] *m* (-s;-s) calico
Kalium ['kaljum] *n* (-s;) potassium

Kalk [kalk] m (-[e]s;-e) lime; calcium
kalken ['kalkən] tr whitewash; lime
kalkig ['kalkıç] adj limy
Kalk'ofen m limekiln
Kalk'stein m limestone
Kalk'steinbruch m limestone quarry
Kalkül [kal'kyl] m & n (-s;-e) calculation; (math) calculus
kalkulieren [kalku'lirən] tr calculate
Kal·mar ['kalmar] m (-s;-mare ['marə]) squid
Kalo·rie [kalə'ri] f (-;-rien ['ri·ən]) calorie
Kalotte [ka'lɔtə] f (-;-n) skullcap
kalt [kalt] adj (kälter ['kɛltər); kälteste ['kɛltəstə] §9) cold
kaltblütig ['kaltblytıç] adj cold-blooded
Kälte ['kɛltə] f (-;) cold, coldness
käl'tebeständig adj cold-resistant
Käl'tegrad m degree below freezing
kälten ['kɛltən] tr chill
Käl'tewelle f (meteor) cold wave
Kalt'front f cold front
kalt'herzig adj cold-hearted
kalt'machen tr (sl) bump off
kaltschnäuzig ['kalt/nɔitsıç] adj (coll) callous; (coll) cool, unflappable
kalt'stellen tr render harmless
kam [kam] pret of **kommen**
Kambodscha [kam'bɔtʒa] n (-s;) Cambodia
kambodschanisch [kambɔ'dʒanı/] adj Cambodian
Kamel [ka'mel] n (-[e]s;-e) camel
Kamel'garn n mohair
Kamera ['kamera] f (-;-s) camera
Kamerad [kamə'rat] m (-en;-en), **Kameradin** [kamə'radın] f (-;-nen) comrade
Kamerad'schaft ((-;-en) comradeship
Kamin [ka'min] m (-s;-e) chimney; fireplace
Kamin'platte f hearthstone
Kamin'sims n mantelpiece
Kamm [kam] m (-[e]s;ːe) comb; (e-s Gebirges) ridge; (e-r Welle) crest
kämmen ['kɛmən] tr comb; (Wolle) card
Kammer ['kamər] f (-;-n) chamber; (adm) board; (anat) ventricle
Kam'merdiener m valet
Kämmerer ['kɛmərər] m (-s;-) chamberlain; (Schatzmeister) treasurer
Kam'mermusik f chamber music
Kamm'garn n (tex) worsted
Kamm'rad n cogwheel
Kampagne [kam'panjə] f (-;-n) campaign
Kämpe ['kɛmpə] m (-n;-n) warrior
Kampf [kampf] m (-[e]s;ːe) fight
Kampf'bahn f (sport) stadium, arena
kämpfen ['kɛmpfən] tr & intr fight
Kampfer ['kampfər] m (-s;) camphor
Kämpfer -in ['kɛmpfər(ın)] §6 mf fighter
kämpferisch ['kɛmpfərı/] adj fighting
kampf'erprobt adj battle-tested
kampf'fähig adj fit to fight; (mil) fit for active service
Kampf'hahn m gamecock; (fig) scrapper
Kampf'handlung f (mil) action

Kampf'müdigkeit f combat fatigue
Kampf'parole f (pol) campaign slogan
Kampf'platz m battleground
Kampf'raum m battle zone
Kampf'richter m referee, umpire
Kampf'schwimmer m (nav) frogman
Kampf'spiel n (sport) competition
Kampf'staffel f tactical squadron
kampf'unfähig adj disabled; **k. machen** put out of action
Kampf'veranstalter m (sport) promotor
Kampf'verband m combat unit
Kampf'wert m fighting efficiency
Kampf'ziel n (mil) objective
kampieren [kam'pirən] intr camp
Kanada ['kanada] n (-s;) Canada
Kanadier -in [ka'nadjər(ın)] §6 mf Canadian || n canoe
kanadisch [ka'nadı/] adj Canadian
Kanaille [ka'naljə] f (-;-n) bum; (Pöbel) riffraff
Kanal [ka'nal] m (-s;ːe) canal; (für Abwasser) drain, sewer; (agr) irrigation ditch; (anat, elec) duct; (geol, telv) channel
Kanalisation [kanalıza'tsjon] f (-;) drainage; sewerage system
Kanalräumer [ka'nalrɔimər] m (-s;-) sewer worker
Kanal'wähler m (telv) channel selector
Kanapee ['kanape] n (-s;-s) sofa
Kanarienvogel [ka'narjənfogəl] m canary
Kandare [kan'darə] f (-;-n) bit, curb; **j-n an die K. nehmen** take s.o. in hand
Kanda'renkette f curb chain
Kandelaber [kandɛ'labər] m (-s;-) candelabrum
Kandidat -in [kandı'dat(ın)] §7 mf candidate
Kandidatur [kandıda'tur] f (-;-en) candidacy
kandideln [kan'didəln] ref get drunk
kandidieren [kandı'dirən] intr be a candidate, run for office
Kandis ['kandıs] m (-;) rock candy
Kaneel [ka'nel] m (-s;-e) cinnamon
Känguruh ['kɛŋguru] n (-s;-s) kangaroo
Kaninchen [ka'nınçən] n (-s;-) rabbit
Kanister [ka'nıstər] m (-s;-) canister
Kanne ['kanə] f (-;-n) can; pot; jug
Kannelüre [kanə'lyrə] f (-;-n) (archit) flute
Kannibale [kanı'balə] m (-n;-n), **Kannibalin** [kanı'balın] f (-;-nen) cannibal
kannte ['kantə] pret of **kennen**
Ka·non ['kanɔn] m (-s;-s) (Maßstab; Gebet bei der Messe) canon; (mus) round || m (-s;-nones ['nonəs] canon (of Canon Law)
Kanone [ka'nonə] f (-;-n) (arti) gun; (hist) canon; (coll) expert; **unter aller K.** indescribably bad
Kano'nenboot n gunboat
Kano'nenrohr n gun barrel; **heiliges K.!** holy smokes!
kanonisieren [kanɔnı'zirən] tr canonize
Kante ['kantə] f (-;-n) edge

kanten ['kantən] *tr* set on edge; (*beim Schifahren*) cant || **Kanten** *m* (-s;-) end of a loaf, crust
Kanthaken ['kanthɑkən] *m* grappling hook
kantig ['kantɪç] *adj* angular; squared
Kantine [kan'tinə] *f* (-;-n) canteen; (mil) post exchange
Kanton [kan'ton] *m* (-s;-e) canton
Kan·tor ['kantər] *m* (-s;-toren ['torən]) choir master; organist
Kanu [ka'nu] *n* (-s;-s) canoe
Kanzel ['kantsəl] *f* (-;-n) pulpit; (aer) cockpit
Kanzlei [kants'laɪ] *f* (-;-en) office; chancellery
Kanzlei'papier *n* official foolscap
Kanzlei'sprache *f* legal jargon
Kanzler ['kantslər] *m* (-s;-) chancellor
Kap [kap] *n* (-s;-s) cape, headland
Kapaun [ka'paun] *m* (-s;-e) capon
Kapazität [kapatsɪ'tet] *f* (-;-en) capacity; (*Könner*) authority
Kapelle [ka'pelə] *f* (-;-n) chapel; (mus) band
Kapell'meister *m* band leader; orchestra conductor
kapern ['kapərn] *tr* capture; (coll) nab
kapieren [ka'pirən] *tr* get, understand || *intr* get it; **kapiert?** got it?
kapital [kapɪ'tɑl] *adj* excellent || **Kapital** *n* (-s;-e & -ien [jən]) (fin) capital; **K. schlagen aus** capitalize on; **K. und Zinsen** principal and interest
Kapital'anlage *f* investment
Kapital'ertragssteuer *f* tax on unearned income
kapitalisieren [kapɪtalɪ'zirən] *tr* (fin) capitalize
Kapitalismus [kapɪta'lɪsmus] *m* (-s;) capitalism
Kapitalist -in [kapɪta'lɪst(ɪn)] *m* §7 capitalist
Kapital'verbrechen *n* capital offense
Kapitän [kapɪ'ten] *m* (-s;-e) captain, skipper; **K. zur See** (nav) captain
Kapitän'leutnant *m* (nav) lieutenant
Kapitel [ka'pɪtəl] *n* (-s;-) chapter
Kapitell [kapɪ'tɛl] *n* (-s;-e) (archit) capital
kapitulieren [kapɪtu'lirən] *intr* capitulate, surrender; reenlist
Kaplan [ka'plɑn] *m* (-s;≃e) chaplain; (R.C.) assistant (pastor)
Kapo ['kapo] *m* (-s;-s) prisoner overseer; (mil) (coll) N.C.O.
Kappe ['kapə] *f* (-;-n) cap; hood, cover; **etw auf seine eigene K. nehmen** take the responsibility for s.th.
Käppi ['kɛpɪ] *n* (-s;-s) garrison cap
Kaprice [ka'prisə] *f* (-;-n) caprice
Kapriole [kaprɪ'olə] *f* (-;-n) caper
kaprizieren [kaprɪ'tsirən] *ref*—**sich k. auf** (*acc*) be dead set on
kapriziös [kaprɪ'tsjøs] *adj* capricious
Kapsel ['kapsəl] *f* (-;-n) capsule; (*e–r Flasche*) cap; (*e–s Sprengkörpers*) detonator
kaputt [ka'put] *adj* (sl) broken; (sl) ruined; (sl) exhausted; (sl) dead
kaputt'gehen §82 *intr* (SEIN) get ruined
kaputt'machen *tr* ruin

Kapuze [ka'putsə] *f* (-;-n) hood; (eccl) cowl
Kapuziner [kapu'tsinər] *m* (-s;-) Capuchin
Kapuzi'nerkresse *f* Nasturtium
Karabiner [kara'binər] *m* (-s;-) carbine
Karabi'nerhaken *m* snap
Karaffe [ka'rafə] *f* (-;-n) carafe
Karambolage [karambo'laʒə] *f* (-;-n) (coll) collision
karambolieren [karambo'lirən] *intr* (coll) collide
Karamelle [kara'melə] *f* (-;-n) caramel
Karat [ka'rɑt] *n* (-[e]s;) carat
-karätig [karetɪç] *comb.fm.* -carat
Karawane [kara'vɑnə] *f* (-;-n) caravan
Karbid [kar'bit] *n* (-[e]s;-e) carbide
Karbolsäure [kar'bolzɔɪrə] *f* (-;) carbolic acid
Karbon [kar'bon] *n* (-s;) (geol) carbon
Karbunkel [kar'buŋkəl] *n* (-s;-) carbuncle
Kardinal– [kardɪnɑl] *comb.fm.* cardinal, principal || **Kardinal** *m* (-s;≃e) (eccl, orn) cardinal
Karenzzeit [ka'rentstsaɪt] *f* (ins) waiting period
Karfreitag [kɑr'fraɪtɑk] *m* Good Friday
karg [kark] *adj* (**karger** & **kärger** ['kergər]; **kargste** & **kärgste** ['kerstə] §9) (*ärmlich*) meager; (*Boden*) poor; (*Landschaft*) bleak
kargen ['kargən] *intr* be sparing
Karg'heit *f* (-;) bleakness; meagerness; frugality
kärglich ['kerlɪç] *adj* meager, poor
kariert [ka'rirt] *adj* checked, squared
Karikatur [karɪka'tur] *f* (-;-en) caricature; cartoon
karikieren [karɪ'kirən] *tr* caricature
Karl [karl] *m* (-s;) Charles; **Karl der Große** Charlemagne
Karmeliter [karme'litər] *m* (-s;-) Carmelite Friar
Karmelitin [karme'litɪn] *f* (-;-nen) Carmelite nun
karmesinrot [karme'zinrot], **karminrot** [kar'mɪnrot] *adj* crimson
Karneval ['karnəval] *m* (-s;-s & -e) carnival
Karnickel [kar'nɪkəl] *n* (-s;-) (coll) rabbit; (*Sündenbock*) (coll) scapegoat; (*Einfaltspinsel*) simpleton
Karo ['kɑrə] *n* (-s;-s) diamond; check, square; (cards) diamond(s)
Karosse [ka'rɔsə] *f* (-;-n) state carriage
Karosse·rie [karosə'ri] *f* (-;-rien ['ri·ən] (aut) body
Karotte [ka'rɔtə] *f* (-;-n) carrot
Karpfen ['karpfən] *m* (-s;-) carp
Karre ['karə] *f* (-;-n), **Karren** ['karən] *m* (-s;-) cart; wheelbarrow; **die alte K.** the old rattletrap
Karriere [ka'rjerə] *f* (-;-n) career; gallop; **K. machen** get ahead
Karte ['kartə] *f* (-;-n) card; ticket; (*Landkarte*) map; (*Speise-*) menu
Kartei [kar'taɪ] *f* (-;-en) card file
Kartei'karte *f* index card

Kartell [kar'tɛl] *n* (-s;-e) cartel
Kar'tenkunststück *n* card trick
Kartenlegerin ['kartənlegərɪn] *f* (-;
-nen) fortuneteller
Kar'tenstelle *f* ration board
Kartoffel [kar'tɔfəl] *f* (-;-n) potato
Kartof'felbrei *m* mashed potatoes
Kartoffelpuffer [kar'tɔfəlpufər] *m* (-s;
-) potato pancake
Karton [kar'tɔn] *m* (-s;-s) cardboard;
carton; (paint) cartoon
Kartonage [kartɔ'naʒə] *f* (-;-n) card-
board box
kartoniert [kartɔ'nirt] *adj* (bb) soft-
cover
Karton'papier *n* (thin) cardboard
Kartothek [kartɔ'tek] *f* (-;-en) card
index; card filing system
Kartothek'ausgabe *f* loose-leaf edition
Karussell [karu'sɛl] *n* (-s;-e) merry-
go-round
Karwoche ['karvɔxə] *f* Holy Week
Karzer ['kartsər] *m* (-s;-) (educ) detention room; **K. bekommen** get a
detention
Kaschmir ['kaʃmɪr] *m* (-s;-e) cashmere
Käse ['kezə] *m* (-s;-) cheese; (sl)
baloney
Kaserne [ka'zɛrnə] *f* (-;-n) barracks
käsig ['kezɪç] *adj* cheesy; (*Gesichtsfarbe*) pasty
Kasino [ka'zino] *n* (-s;-s) casino;
(mil) officer's mess
Kas'pisches Meer' ['kaspɪʃəs] *n* Cas-
pian Sea
Kassa ['kasa] *f*—**per K.** in cash
Kassa– *comb.fm.* cash, spot
Kasse ['kasə] *f* (-;-n) money box; till;
cash register; cashiers desk; (*Bar-
geld*) cash; (adm) finance depart-
ment; (educ) bursars office; (sport)
ticket window; (theat) box office;
gegen (or **per**) **K.** cash, for cash;
gut bei K. sein (coll) be flush
Kas'senabschluß *m* balancing of ac-
counts
Kas'senbeamte *m* cashier; teller
Kas'senbeleg *m* sales slip
Kas'senbestand *m* cash on hand
Kas'senerfolg *m* (theat) hit
Kas'senführer –**in** §6 *mf* cashier
Kas'senschalter *m* teller's window
Kas'senschrank *m* safe
Kas'senzettel *m* sales slip
Kasserolle [kasə'rɔlə] *f* (-;-n) casse-
role
Kassette [ka'sɛtə] *f* (-;-n) base, box;
(cin, phot) cassette
kassieren [ka'sirən] *tr* (*Geld*) take in;
get; (*Urteil*) annul; (coll) confiscate;
(coll) arrest; (mil) break
Kassie'rer –**in** §6 *mf* cashier; teller
Kastagnette [kastan'jetə] *f* (-;-n)
castanet
Kastanie [kas'tanjə] *f* (-;-n) chestnut
Kästchen ['kɛstçən] *n* (-s;-) case, box
Kaste ['kastə] *f* (-;-n) caste
kasteien [kas'tai·ən] *tr & ref* mortify;
sein Leib k. mortify the flesh
Kastell [kas'tɛl] *n* (-s;-e) small fort
Kasten ['kastən] *m* (-s;∺ & -) chest,
case, box; cupboard, cabinet; (*Auto*)

(coll) crate; (*Boot*) (coll) tub; (*Gefängnis*) (coll) jug
Ka'stengeist *m* snobbishness
Ka'stenwagen *m* (aut) panel truck; (rr)
boxcar
Ka'stenwesen *n* caste system
Kastrat [kas'trat] *m* (-en;-en) eunuch
kastrieren [kas'trirən] *tr* castrate
Katakomben [kata'kɔmbən] *pl* cata-
combs
Katalog [kata'lok] *m* (-[e]s;-e) catalogue
katalogisieren [katalɔgɪ'zirən] *tr* catalogue
Katapult [kata'pult] *m & n* (-[e]s;-e)
catapult
katapultieren [katapul'tirən] *tr* catapult
Katarakt [kata'rakt] *m* (-[e]s;-e) cataract, rapids; (pathol) cataract
Katasteramt [ka'tastəramt] *n* land-
registry office
katastrophal [katastrɔ'fal] *adj* cata-
strophic, disastrous
Katastrophe [kata'strofə] *f* (-;-n)
catastrophe, disaster
Katastro'phengebiet *n* disaster area
Katego·rie [katego'ri] *f* (-;-rien)
['ri·ən] category
kategorisch [kate'gorɪʃ] *adj* categori-
cal
Kater ['katər] *m* (-s;-) tomcat; (coll)
hangover
Katheder [ka'tedər] *n & m* (-s;-)
teacher's desk
Kathe'derblüte *f* teacher's blunder
Kathedrale [kate'dralə] *f* (-;-n) cathe-
dral
Kathode [ka'todə] *f* (-;-n) cathode
Katholik –**in** [katɔ'lik(ɪn)] §7 *mf*
Catholic
katholisch [ka'tolɪʃ] *adj* Catholic
Kattun [ka'tun] *m* (-s;-e) calico
Kätzchen ['kɛtsçən] *n* (-s;-) kitten
Katze ['katsə] *f* (-;-n) cat; **für die K.**
(coll) for the birds
kat'zenartig *adj* cat-like, feline
Kat'zenauge *n* reflector
Kat'zenbuckel *m* cat's arched back;
vor j-m K. machen lick s.o.'s boots
kat'zenfreundlich *adj* overfriendly
Kat'zenjammer *m* hangover; blues
Kat'zenkopf *m* (coll) cobblestone;
(box) rabbit punch
Kat'zensprung *m* stone's throw
Kauderwelsch ['kaudərvɛlʃ] *n* (-es;)
gibberish
kauen ['kau·ən] *tr* chew
kauern ['kau·ərn] *ref & intr* cower
Kauf [kauf] *m* (-[e]s;∺e) purchase;
in K. nehmen (fig) take, put up with;
leichten Kaufes davonkommen get
off cheaply; **zum K. stehen** be for
sale
Kauf'auftrag *m* (com) order
kaufen ['kaufən] *tr* purchase, buy
Käufer –**in** ['kɔrfər(ɪn)] §6 *mf* buyer
Kauf'haus *n* department store
Kauf'kraft *f* purchasing power
käuflich ['kɔrflɪç] *adj* for sale; (*bestechlich*) open to bribes
Kauf'mann *m* (-[e]s;-leute) businessman; salesman

kaufmännisch ['kaufmɛnɪʃ] *adj* commercial, business
Kauf'mannsdeutsch *n* business German
Kauf'zwang *m* obligation to buy
Kaugummi ['kaugumɪ] *m* chewing gum
kaukasisch [kau'kɑzɪʃ] *adj* Caucasian
Kaulquappe ['kaulkvapə] *f* (-;-n) tadpole, poiliwog
kaum [kaum] *adv* hardly, scarcely
Kautabak ['kautabak] *m* chewing tobacco
Kaution [kau'tsjon] *f* (-;-en) (jur) bond; (*Bürgschaft*) (jur) bail; **gegen K.** on bail
Kautschuk ['kautʃuk] *m* (-s;-e) rubber
Kauz [kauts] *m* (-es;-e) owl; (sl) crackpot
Kavalier [kava'lir] *m* (-s;-e) cavalier; gentleman; beau
Kavalkade [kaval'kadə] *f* (-;-n) cavalcade
Kavalle•rie [kavalə'ri] *f* (-;-rien ['ri-ən]) cavalry
Kavallerist [kavalə'rɪst] *m* (-en;-en) cavalryman, trooper
Kaviar ['kɑvjar] *m* (-[e]s;-e) caviar
keck [kɛk] *adj* bold; impudent; cheeky
Kegel ['kegəl] *m* (-s;-) tenpin; (geom) cone; **K. schieben** bowl
Ke'gelbahn *f* bowling alley
kegeln ['kegəln] *intr* bowl
Keg'ler –in §6 *mf* bowler
Kehle ['kelə] *f* (-;-n) throat
kehlig ['kelɪç] *adj* throaty
Kehlkopf ['kelkɔpf] *m* larynx
Kehl'kopfentzündung *f* laryngitis
Kehre ['kerə] *f* (-;-n) turn, bend
kehren ['kerən] *tr* sweep; (*wenden*) turn; **alles zum besten k.** make the best of it; **j-m den Rücken k.** turn one's back on s.o. ‖ *ref* turn; **in sich gekehrt sein** be lost in thought; **sich an nichts k.** not care about anything; **sich k. an** (*acc*) heed ‖ *intr* sweep
Kehricht ['kerɪçt] *m & n* (-[e]s;) sweepings: trash, rubbish
Keh'richteimer *m* trash can
Keh'richtschaufel *f* dustpan
Kehr'maschine *f* street cleaner
Kehr'reim *m* refrain, chorus
Kehr'seite *f* reverse; (fig) seamy side
kehrtmachen ['kertmaxən] *intr* turn around; (mil) about-face
Kehrt'wendung *f* about-face
keifen ['kaɪfən] *intr* nag
Keiferei [kaɪfə'raɪ] *f* (-;-en) nagging; squabble
Keil [kaɪl] *m* (-[e]s;-e) wedge
keilen ['kaɪlən] *tr* wedge; (*coll*) recruit ‖ *recip* scrap
Keilerei [kaɪlə'raɪ] *f* (-;-en) scrap
keil'förmig *adj* wedge-shaped; tapered
Keil'hammer *m* sledgehammer
Keil'hose *f* tapered trousers
Keil'schrift *f* cuneiform writing
Keim [kaɪm] *m* (-[e]s;-e) germ; embryo; (fig) seeds; (bot) bud, sprout; **im K. ersticken** nip in the bud; **im K. vorhanden** at an embryonic stage; **Keime treiben** germinate
keimen ['kaɪmən] *intr* germinate;

sprout ‖ **Keimen** *n*—**zum K. bringen** cause to germinate
keim'frei *adj* germ-free, sterile
Keimling ['kaɪmlɪŋ] *m* (-s;-e) embryo; sprout; seedling
keimtötend ['kaɪmtøtənt] *adj* germicidal; antiseptic, sterilizing
Keim'zelle *f* germ cell, sex cell
kein [kaɪn] §2,2 *adj* no, not any
keiner ['kaɪnər] §2,4 *indef pron* none; no one, nobody, not one; **k. von beiden** neither of them
keinerlei ['kaɪnər'laɪ] *invar adj* no... of any kind, no...whatsoever
keineswegs ['kaɪnəs'veks] *adv* by no means, not at all
Keks [keks] *m & n* (-es;-e) biscuit, cracker; cookie
Kelch [kɛlç] *m* (-[e]s;-e) cup; (bot) calyx; (eccl) chalice
Kelch'blatt *n* (bot) sepal
Kelle ['kelə] *f* (-;-n) ladle; (hort, mas) trowel
Keller ['kelər] *m* (-s;-) cellar
Kel'lergeschoß *n* basement
Kel'lergewölbe *n* underground vault
Kellner ['kɛlnər] *m* (-s;-) waiter
Kellnerin ['kɛlnərɪn] *f* (-;-nen) waitress
Kelte ['kɛltə] *m* (-n;-n) Celt
Kelter ['kɛltər] *f* (-;-n) wine press
keltern ['kɛltərn] *tr* press
Keltin ['kɛltɪn] *f* (-;-nen) Celt
keltisch ['kɛltɪʃ] *adj* Celtic
kennbar ['kɛnbar] *adj* recognizable
kennen ['kɛnən] §97 *tr* be acquainted with, know
ken'nenlernen *tr* get to know, meet
Ken'ner –in §6 *mf* expert
Ken'nerblick *m* knowing glance
Ken'ner –in §6 *mf* expert
Kennkarte ['kɛnkartə] *f* identity card
kenntlich ['kɛntlɪç] *adj* identifiable, recognizable; conspicuous
Kenntnis ['kɛntnɪs] *f* (-;-se) knowledge; **gute Kenntnisse haben in** (*dat*) be well versed in; **j-n von etw in K. setzen** apprise s.o. of s.th.; **Kenntnisse** knowledge; skills; know-how; **oberflächliche Kenntnisse** a smattering; **von etw K. nehmen** take note of s.th.; **zur K. nehmen** take note of s.th.
Kennwort ['kɛnvɔrt] *n* (-[e]s;-̈er) code word; (mil) password
Kennzeichen ['kɛntsaɪçən] *n* distinguishing mark; hallmark; criterion; (aer) marking; (aut) license number
kennzeichnen ['kɛntsaɪçnən] *tr* characterize; identify; brand
Kennziffer ['kɛntsɪfər] *f* code number
kentern ['kɛntərn] *intr* (SEIN) capsize
Keramik [ke'ramɪk] *f* (-;) ceramics; pottery
keramisch [ke'ramɪʃ] *adj* ceramic
Kerbe ['kɛrbə] *f* (-;-n) notch, groove
kerben ['kɛrbən] *tr* notch, nick; make a groove in; serrate
Kerbholz ['kɛrphɔlts] *n*—**etw auf dem K. haben** have a crime chalked up against one
Kerbtier ['kɛrptir] *n* insect
Kerker ['kɛrkər] *m* (-s;-) jail

Kerl [kɛrl] *m* (-s;-e) fellow, guy; (*Mädchen*) lass

Kern [kɛrn] *m* (-[e]s;-e) kernel; (*im Obst*) pit, stone, pip; hard core; (*e-s Problems*) crux; (phys) nucleus

Kern- *comb.fm.* core; central, basic; through and through; (phys) nuclear

Kern'aufbau *m* nuclear structure

kern'deutsch' *adj* German through and through

Kern'energie *f* nuclear energy

Kern'fächer *pl* core curriculum

kern'gesund' *adj* perfectly sound

Kern'holz *n* heartwood

kernig ['kɛrnɪç] *adj* full of seeds; robust, vigorous

kern'los *adj* seedless

Kern'physik *f* nuclear physics

Kern'punkt *m* gist, crux; focal point

Kern'schußweite *f*—auf K. at point-blank range

Kern'spaltung *f* nuclear fission

Kern'truppen *pl* crack troops

Kern'verschmelzung *f* nuclear fusion

Kern'waffe *f* nuclear weapon

Kerosin [kɛro'zin] *n* (-s;) kerosene

Kerze ['kɛrtsə] *f* (-;-n) candle; (aut) plug

ker'zengera'de *adj* straight as an arrow || *adv* bolt upright

Kessel ['kɛsəl] *m* (-s;-) kettle; cauldron; boiler; (geog) basin-shaped valley; (mil) pocket

Kes'selpauke *f* kettledrum

Kes'selraum *m* boiler room

Kes'selschmied *m* boilermaker

Kes'selwagen *m* (aut) tank truck; (rr) tank car

Kette ['kɛtə] *f* (-;-n) chain; (*e-s Panzers*) track

ketten ['kɛtən] *tr* (an *acc*) chain (to)

Ket'tengeschäft *n* chain store

Ket'tenglied *n* chain link

Ket'tenhund *m* watch dog

Ket'tenrad *n* sprocket

Ket'tenraucher –in §6 *mf* chain smoker

Ket'tenstich *m* chain stitch, lock stitch

Ketzer –in ['kɛtsər(ɪn)] §6 *mf* heretic

Ketzerei [kɛtsə'raɪ] *f* (-;-en) heresy

ketzerisch ['kɛtsərɪʃ] *adj* heretical

keuchen ['kɔɪçən] *intr* pant, gasp

Keuch'husten *m* (-s;) whooping cough

Keule ['kɔɪlə] *f* (-;-n) club; (culin) leg. drumstick

keusch [kɔɪʃ] *adj* chaste

Keusch'heit *f* (-;) chastity

KG *abbr* (**Kommanditgesellschaft**) Ltd.

Khaki ['kɑki] *m* (-;) (tex) khaki

kichern ['kɪçərn] *intr* giggle

kicken ['kɪkən] *tr* (fb) kick

Kicker ['kɪkər] *m* (-s;-) soccer player

Kiebitz ['kibɪts] *m* (-[e]s;-e) (orn) lapwing; (*Zugucker*) kibitzer

kiebitzen ['kibɪtsən] *intr* kibitz

Kiefer ['kifər] *m* (-s;-) jaw(bone) || *f* (-;-n) pine; **gemeine K.** Scotch pine

Kiel [kil] *m* (-[e]s;-e) (*Feder*) quill; (naut) keel

Kiel'raum *m* hold

Kiel'wasser *n* wake

Kieme ['kimə] *f* (-;-n) gill

Kien ['kin] *m* (-[e]s;-e) pine cone

Kien'span *m* pine torch

Kiepe ['kipə] *f* (-;-n) basket (*carried on one's back*)

Kies [kis] *m* (-es;-e) gravel

Kiesel ['kizəl] *m* (-s;-) pebble

Kilo ['kilo] *n* (-s;-s & -) kilogram

Kilogramm [kilo'gram] *n* (-s;-e & -) kilogram

Kilometer [kilo'metər] *m* & *n* (-s;-) kilometer

Kilome'terfresser *m* (coll) speedster

Kilowatt [kilo'vat] *n* (-s;-) kilowatt

Kimm [kɪm] *m* (-es;-e) horizon || *f* (-;-e) (naut) bilge

Kimme ['kɪmə] *f* (-;-n) notch; groove; (*e-s Gewehrs*) sight

Kind [kɪnt] *n* (-[e]s;-er) child; baby

Kinder- [kɪndər] *comb.fm.* child's, children's

Kin'derarzt *m*, **Kin'derärztin** *f* pediatrician

Kinderei [kɪndə'raɪ] *f* (-;-en) childish behavior, childish prank

Kin'derfrau *f* nursemaid

Kin'derfräulein *n* governess

Kin'derfürsorge *f* child welfare

Kin'dergarten *m* nursery school, playschool

Kin'dergärtnerin *f* nursery school attendant

Kin'dergeld *n* see **Kinderzulage**

Kin'derheilkunde *f* pediatrics

Kin'derheim *n* children's home

Kin'derhort *m* day nursery

Kin'derlähmung *f* polio

kin'derleicht *adj* easy as pie

Kin'derlied *n* nursery rhyme

kin'derlos *adj* childless

Kin'dermädchen *n* nursemaid

Kin'derpuder *m* baby powder

Kin'derreim *m* nursery rhyme

Kin'derschreck *m* bogeyman

Kin'dersportwagen *m* stroller

Kin'derstube *f* nursery; (*Erziehung*) upbringing

Kin'derstuhl *m* highchair

Kin'derwagen *m* baby carriage

Kin'derzulage *f* family allowance (*paid by the employer*)

Kin'desalter *n* childhood; infancy

Kin'desannahme *f* adoption

Kin'desbeine *pl*—**von Kindesbeinen an** from childhood on

Kin'desentführer –in §6 *mf* kidnaper

Kin'desentführung *f*, **Kin'desraub** *m* kidnaping

Kind'heit *f* (-;) childhood

kindisch ['kɪndɪʃ] *adj* childish

kindlich ['kɪntlɪç] *adj* childlike

Kinetik [kɪ'netɪk] *f* (-;) kinetics

kinetisch [kɪ'netɪʃ] *adj* kinetic

Kinkerlitzchen ['kɪŋkərlɪtsçən] *pl* trifles; gimmicks

Kinn [kɪn] *n* (-[e]s;-e) chin

Kinn'backen *m* jawbone

Kinn'haken *m* (box) uppercut

Kinn'kette *f* curb chain

Kino ['kino] *n* (-s;-s) movie theater

Ki'nobesucher –in §6 *mf* moviegoer

Ki'nokamera *f* movie camera

Ki'nokasse *f* box office

Kiosk [kɪ'ɔsk] *m* (-[e]s;-e) stand

Kipfel ['kɪpfəl] *n* (-s;-) (Aust) (culin) crescent roll

Kippe ['kɪpə] *f* (-;-n) edge; (*Zigarettenstummel*) butt; **auf der K.** stehen stand on edge; (fig) be touch and go
kippen ['kɪpən] *tr* tilt, tip over; dump || *intr* (SEIN) tilt; overturn
Kipper ['kɪpər] *m* (-s;-) dump truck
Kirche ['kɪrçə] *f* (-;-n) church
Kirchen- [kɪrçən] *comb.fm.* church, ecclesiastical
Kir'chenbann *m* excommunication; **in den K.** tun excommunicate
Kir'chenbau *m* (-[e]s;) building of churches || *m* (-[e]s;-ten) church
Kir'chenbesuch *m* church attendance
Kir'chenbuch *n* parish register
Kir'chendiener *m* sacristan, sexton
Kir'chengut *n* church property
Kir'chenlied *n* hymn
Kir'chenschändung *f* desecration of a church
Kir'chenschiff *n* (archit) nave
Kir'chenspaltung *f* schism
Kir'chenstaat *m* Papal States
Kir'chenstuhl *m* pew
Kir'chentag *m* Church congress
Kirchgang ['kɪrçgaŋ] *m* going to church
Kirch'gänger –in §6 *mf* church-goer
Kirch'hof *m* churchyard
kirch'lich *adj* church, ecclesiastical
Kirch'spiel *n* parish
Kirch'turm *m* steeple
Kirch'turmpolitik *f* (pej) parochialism
Kirch'turmspitze *f* spire
Kirchweih ['kɪrçvaɪ] *f* (-;-en) church picnic
Kirch'weihe *f* dedication of a church
Kirch'weihfest *n* church picnic
Kirsch [kɪrʃ] *m* (-es;-) cherry brandy
Kirsche ['kɪrʃə] *f* (-;-n) cherry
Kirsch'wasser *n* cherry brandy
Kissen ['kɪsən] *n* (-s;-) cushion, pillow; (*Polster*) pad
Kis'senbezug *m* pillowcase
Kiste ['kɪstə] *f* (-;-n) box, crate, case; (aer) crate; (aut) rattletrap; (naut) tub
Kitsch [kɪtʃ] *m* (-es;) kitsch
kitschig ['kɪtʃɪç] *adj* trashy; mawkish
Kitt [kɪt] *m* (-[e]s;-e) putty; cement; **der ganze Kitt** the whole caboodle
Kittchen ['kɪtçən] *n* (-s;-) (coll) jail
Kittel ['kɪtəl] *m* (-s;-) smock, coat; (Aust) skirt
Kit'telkleid *n* house dress
kitten ['kɪtən] *tr* putty; cement, glue; (fig) patch up
Kit'zel ['kɪtsəl] *m* (-s;) tickle; (fig) itch
kitzeln ['kɪtsəln] *tr* tickle
kitzlig ['kɪtslɪç] *adj* ticklish
Kladderadatsch [kladəra'datʃ] *m* (-es;) crash, bang; mess, muddle
klaffen ['klafən] *intr* gape, yawn
kläffen ['klɛfən] *intr* yelp
Klafter ['klaftər] *f* (-;- & -n), *m* & *n* (-s;-) fathom; (*Holz*-) cord
klagbar ['klakbar] *adj* (jur) actionable
Klage ['klagə] *f* (-;-n) complaint; (jur) (civil) suit
Kla'gelied *n* dirge, threnody
klagen ['klagən] *tr*—j-m seinen **Kummer k.** pour out one's troubles to s.o.

|| *intr* complain; **auf Scheidung k.** sue for divorce; **k. über** (*acc*) complain about; **k. um** lament
Kläger –in ['klegər(ɪn)] §6 *mf* (jur) plaintiff
Kla'geweib *n* hired mourner
kläglich ['kleklɪç] *adj* plaintive, pitiful; (*Zustand*) sorry; (*Ergebnis, Ende*) miserable
klaglos ['klaklos] *adv* uncomplainingly
klamm [klam] *adj* (*erstarrt*) numb; (*feuchtkalt*) clammy; **k. an Geld** (coll) short of dough || **Klamm** *f* (-;-en) gorge
Klammer ['klamər] *f* (-;-n) clamp; clip; paper clip; (*Schließe*) clasp; clothespin; hair clip, bobby pin; **eckige K.** bracket; **runde K.** parenthesis
klammern ['klamərn] *tr* clamp; clasp || *ref*—**sich k. an** (*acc*) cling to
Klamotte [kla'mɔtə] *f* (-;-n)—**alte K.** oldy; (aer, aut) old crate; **Klamotten** things, clothes
Klampfe ['klampfə] *f* (-;-n) guitar
klang [klaŋ] *pret* of **klingen** || **Klang** *m* (-[e]s;-̈e) tone, sound
Klang'farbe *f* timbre
klang'getreu *adj* high-fidelity
Klang'regler *m* (rad) tone-control knob
Klang'taste *f* tone-control push button
klang'voll *adj* sonorous
Klappe ['klapə] *f* (-;-n) flap; (*Mund*) (sl) trap; (anat, mach) valve; **in die K.** gehen (sl) hit the sack
klappen ['klapən] *tr* flip || *intr* flap, fold || *impers*—**es klappt** (coll) it clicks, it turns out well
Klapper ['klapər] *f* (-;-n) rattle
klap'perdürr' *adj* skinny
Klap'pergestell *n* (coll) beanpole; (*Kiste*) (coll) rattletrap
klappern ['klapərn] *intr* rattle, clatter; (*Zähne*) chatter
Klap'perschlange *f* rattlesnake
Klap'perstorch *m* stork
Klappflügel ['klapflygəl] *m* (aer) folding wing (*of carrier plane*)
Klappmesser ['klapmesər] *n* jackknife
klapprig ['klaprɪç] *adj* rickety
Klappstuhl ['klapʃtul] *m* folding chair
Klapptisch ['klaptɪʃ] *m* drop-leaf table
Klapptür ['klaptyr] *f* trap door
Klaps [klaps] *m* (-es;-e) smack, slap; **e-n K.** kriegen (sl) go nuts
klapsen ['klapsən] *tr* smack, slap
Klaps'mühle *f* (coll) booby hatch
klar [klar] *adj* clear; **klar zum Start** ready for take-off
Kläranlage ['kleranlagə] *f* sewage-disposal plant
klären ['kleran] *tr* clear; (*Mißverständnis*) clear up || *ref* become clear
Klar'heit *f* (-;) clearness, clarity
Klarinette [klarɪ'netə] *f* (-;-n) clarinet
klar'legen, klar'stellen *tr* clear up
Klärung ['kleruŋ] *f* (-;) clarification
Klasse ['klasə] *f* (-;-n) class; (educ) grade, class
Klas'senarbeit *f* test
Klas'senaufsatz *m* composition (*written in class*)
klas'senbewußt *adj* class-conscious

Klas′seneinteilung *f* classification
Klas′senkamerad –**in** §7 *mf* classmate
Klas′sentreffen *n* (–s;–) class reunion
klassifizieren [klasıfı'tsirən] *tr* classify
Klassifizie′rung *f* (–;–en) classification
–**klassig** [klasıç] *comb.fm.* –class,
 –grade
Klassik ['klasık] *f* (–;) classical antiquity, classical period
Klas′siker –**in** §6 *mf* classical author
klassisch ['klasıʃ] *adj* classic(al)
Klatsch [klatʃ] *m* (–es;) clap; gossip
Klatsch′base *f* gossipmonger; tattletale
Klatsch′blatt *n* scandal sheet
Klatsche ['klatʃə] *f* (–;–n) fly swatter;
 tattletale; (educ) pony
klatschen ['klatʃən] *tr* smack, slap;
 dem Lehrer etw k. tattletale to the
 teacher about s.th.; **j–m Beifall k.**
 applaud s.o. ‖ *intr* clap; (*Regen*)
 patter; (fig) gossip; **in die Hände** (or
 mit den Händen) k. clap the hands
Klatscherei [klatʃə'raı] *f* (–;–en) gossip
klatsch′naß′ *adj* soaking wet
Klatsch′spalte *f* glossip column
klauben ['klaubən] *tr* pick
Klaue ['klau·ə] *f* (–;–n) claw, talon;
 (*Spalthuf*) hoof; (coll) scrawl
klauen ['klau·ən] *tr* (coll) snitch
Klause ['klauzə] *f* (–;–n) hermitage;
 (*Schlucht*) defile; (coll) den, pad
Klausel ['klauzəl] *f* (–;–n) clause; (*Abmachung*) stipulation
Klausner ['klauznər] *m* (–s;–) hermit
Klausur [klau'zur] *f* (–;–en) seclusion;
 (educ) final examination
Klausur′arbeit *f* final examination
Klaviatur [klavja'tur] *f* (–;–en) keyboard
Klavier [kla'vir] *n* (–[e]s;–e) piano
Klavier′auszug *m* piano score
Klebemittel ['klebəmıtəl] *n* (–s;–) adhesive, glue
kleben ['klebən] *tr & intr* stick
Kleberolle ['klebərələ] *f* roll of
 gummed tape
Klebestreifen ['klebə/traıfən] *m* adhesive tape; Scotch tape (*trademark*)
Klebezettel ['klebətsetəl] *m* label,
 sticker
klebrig ['klebrıç] *adj* sticky
Klebstoff ['klep/tɔf] *m* adhesive
Klecks [klɛks] *m* (–es;–e) stain; dab
klecksen ['klɛksən] *tr* splash ‖ *intr*
 make blotches
Kleckser –**in** ['klɛksər(ın)] §6 *mf*
 scribbler; dauber
Klee [kle] *m* (–s;) clover
Klee′blatt *n* cloverleaf; (fig) trio
Kleid [klaıt] *n* (–[e]s;–er) garment;
 dress; robe; **Kleider** clothes
kleiden ['klaıdən] *tr* dress; **j–n gut k.**
 look good on s.o.
Klei′derablage *f* cloakroom; (*Kleiderständer*) clothes rack
Klei′derbestand *m* wardrobe
Klei′derbügel *m* coat hanger
Klei′dersack *m* (mil) duffle bag
Klei′derschrank *m* clothes closet
Klei′derständer *m* clothes rack
kleidsam ['klaıtzam] *adj* well-fitting,
 becoming

Klei′dung *f* (–;) clothing
Kleie ['klaı·ə] *f* (–;–n) bran
klein [klaın] *adj* small, little; short;
 ein k. wenig a little bit ‖ **Kleine** §5
 m little boy ‖ *f* little girl ‖ *n* little
 one
Klein′anzeigen *pl* classified ads
Klein′arbeit *f* detailed work
Klein′asien *n* Asia Minor
Klein′bahn *f* narrow-gauge railroad
Klein′bauer *m* small farmer
Klein′betrieb *m* small business
Kleinbild– *comb.fm.* (phot) 35mm
klein′bürgerlich *adj* lower middle-class
Klein′geld *n* change
klein′gläubig *adj* of little faith
Klein′handel *m* retail business
Klein′händler –**in** §6 *mf* retailer
Klein′hirn *n* (anat) cerebellum
Klein′holz *n* kindling; **K. aus j–m machen** (coll) beat s.o. to a pulp
Klei′nigkeit *f* small object; trifle,
 minor detail; small matter
Klei′nigkeitskrämer *m* fusspot
kleinkalibrig ['klaınkalibrıç] *adj* small-bore
Klein′kind *n* infant
Klein′kinderbewahranstalt *f* day care
 center
Klein′kram *m* odds and ends; details
klein′laut *adj* subdued
klein′lich *adj* stingy; (*Betrag*) paltry;
 (*engstirnig*) narrow-minded, pedantic
Klein′mut *m* despondency; faintheartedness
klein′mütig *adj* despondent; fainthearted
Klei′nod ['klaınot] *n* (–[e]s;–node &
 –nodien ['nodjən] jewel, gem
klein′schneiden §106 *tr* chop up
Klein′schreibmaschine *f* portable typewriter
Kleister ['klaıstər] *m* (–s;–) paste
Klemme ['klemə] *f* (–;–n) clamp, clip;
 (coll) tight spot, fix; (elec) terminal;
 (surg) clamp
klemmen ['klemən] *tr* tuck, put; (*stehlen*) pinch, swipe ‖ *ref*—**sich** [*dat*]
 den Finger k. smash one's finger;
 sich hinter die Arbeit k. get down to
 business; **sich k. hinter** (*acc*) get after
 ‖ *intr* be stuck
Klempner ['klempnər] *m* (–s;–) tinsmith; plumber
Klempnerei [klempnə'raı] *f* (–;)
 plumbing
Kleptomane [klepto'manə] §5 *mf* kleptomaniac
klerikal [klerı'kal] *adj* clerical
Kleriker ['klerıkər] *m* (–s;–) clergyman, priest
Klerus ['klerus] *m* (–;) clergy
Klette ['kletə] *f* (–;–n) (bot) burr;
 (coll) pain in the neck
Klet′tergarten *m* training area (*for
 mountain climbing*)
klettern ['kletərn] *intr* (SEIN) climb
Klet′terpflanze *f* (bot) creeper
Klet′terrose *f* rambler
Klet′tertour *f* climbing expedition
Klient [klı'ent] *m* (–en;–en) client
Klientel [klı·ɛn'tel] *f* (–;–en) clientele
 (*of a lawyer*)

Klientin [klɪ'entɪn] *f* (-;-nen) client
Klima ['klima] *n* (-s;-s) climate
Kli'maanlage *f* air conditioner
kli'magerecht *adj* air-conditioned
klimatisch [klɪ'matɪʃ] *adj* climatic
klimatisieren [klɪmatɪ'zirən] *tr* air-condition
Klimatisie'rung *f* (-;) air conditioning
Klimbim [klɪm'bɪm] *m* (-s;) (coll) junk; (coll) racket; (coll) fuss
klimmen ['klɪmən] §164 *intr* (SEIN) climb
klimpern ['klɪmpərn] *intr* jingle; *(auf der Gitarre)* strum; **mit den Wimpern k.** flutter one's eyelashes
Klinge ['klɪŋə] *f* (-;-n) blade; sword, saber; **über die K. springen lassen** put to the sword
Klingel ['klɪŋəl] *f* (-;-n) bell
Klin'gelbeutel *m* collection basket
Klin'gelknopf *m* doorbell button
klingeln ['klɪŋəln] *intr* ring, tinkle; *(Vers, Reim)* jingle ‖ *impers*—**es klingelt** the doorbell is ringing; there goes the (school) bell; the phone is ringing
kling'klang *interj* ding-dong!
Klinik ['klinɪk] *f* (-;-en) teaching hospital *(of a university)*; private hospital; nursing home
klinisch ['klinɪʃ] *adj* clinical; hospital
Klinke ['klɪŋkə] *f* (-;-n) door handle; (telp) jack; **Klinken putzen** beg or peddle from door to door
Klippe ['klɪpə] *f* (-;-n) rock, reef
klirren ['klɪrən] *intr* rattle, clang; *(Gläser)* clink; *(Waffen)* clash
Klischee [klɪ'ʃe] *n* (-s;-s) cliché
Klistier [klɪs'tir] *n* (-s;-e) enema
klistieren [klɪs'tirən] *tr* give an enema to
klitschig ['klɪtʃɪç] *adj* doughy
Klo [klo] *n* (-s;-s) (coll) john
Kloake [klo'akə] *f* (-;-n) sewer
Kloben ['klobən] *m* (-s;-) pulley; *(Holz)* block; *(Schraubenstock)* vise
klobig ['klobɪç] *adj* clumsy; bulky
klomm [klɔm] *pret* of **klimmen**
klopfen ['klɔpfən] *tr (Nagel)* drive; *(Teppich)* beat; *(Fleisch)* pound ‖ *intr* knock; *(Herz)* beat, pound; *(Motor)* ping; **j-m auf die Schulter k.** pat s.o. on the back ‖ *impers*—**es klopft** s.o. is knocking
klopffest ['klɔpffest] *adj* antiknock
Klöppel ['klœpəl] *m* (-s;-) bobbin; *(e-r Glocke)* clapper; (mus) mallet
klöppeln ['klœpəln] *tr* make *(lace)* with bobbins
Klops [klɔps] *m* (-es;-e) meatball
Klosett [klo'zet] *n* (-s;-e & -s) (flush) toilet
Klosett'becken *n* toilet bowl
Klosett'brille *f* toilet seat
Klosett'deckel *m* toilet-seat lid
Klosett'papier *n* toilet paper
Kloß [klos] *m* (-es;ⁿe) dumpling; **e-n K. im Hals haben** have a lump in one's throat
Kloster ['klostər] *n* (-s;ⁿ) monastery; convent
Kloster- *comb.fm.* monastic
Klo'sterbruder *m* lay brother, friar

Klo'sterfrau *f* nun
klösterlich ['kløstərlɪç] *adj* monastic
Klotz [klɔts] *m* (-es;ⁿe) block; toy building block; (coll) blockhead; **ein K. am Bein** (coll) a drag; **wie ein K.** schlafen sleep like a log
klotzig ['klɔtsɪç] *adj* clumsy; uncouth ‖ *adv*—**k. reich** filthy rich
Klub [klup] *m* (-s;-s) club
Klub'jacke *f* blazer
Klub'sessel *m* easy chair
Kluft [kluft] *f* (-;ⁿe) gorge, ravine; (fig) gulf; (poet) chasm ‖ *f* (-;-en) outfit, uniform
klug [kluk] *adj* (**klüger** ['klygər]; **klügste** ['klygstə] §9) clever, bright; wise; **aus Schaden k. werden** learn the hard way; **nicht k. werden können aus** be unable to figure out
klügeln ['klygəln] *intr* quibble
Klug'heit *f* (-;) cleverness; intelligence; wisdom
klüglich ['klyklɪç] *adv* wisely
Klug'redner *m* wise guy, know-it-all
Klumpen ['klumpən] *m* (-s;-) lump, clod; *(Haufen)* heap; (min) nugget
Klumpfuß ['klumpfus] *m* clubfoot
klumpig ['klumpɪç] *adj* lumpy
Klüngel ['klyŋəl] *m* (-s;-) clique
knabbern ['knabərn] *intr* nibble
Knabe ['knabə] *m* (-n;-n) boy
Kna'benalter *n* boyhood
kna'benhaft *adj* boyish
knack [knak] *interj* crack!; snap!; click!
knacken ['knakən] *tr* crack ‖ *intr* crack; *(Schloß)* click; *(Feuer)* crackle
Knacks [knaks] *m* (-es;-e) crack; snap; click; **e-n K. kriegen** get a crack; **e-n K. weg haben** be badly hit; **sich** *[dat]* **e-n K. holen** suffer a blow
Knack'wurst *f* pork sausage; smoked sausage
Knall [knal] *m* (-[e]s;-e) crack, bang; **K. und Fall** on the spot, at once
Knallblättchen ['knalbletçən] *n* (-s;-) cap *(for a toy pistol)*
Knall'bonbon *m & n* noise maker
Knall'büchse *f* popgun
Knall'dämpfer *m* silencer
Knall'effekt *m* big surprise
knall'rot *adj* fiery red
knapp [knap] *adj* *(eng)* close, tight; *(Mehrheit)* bare; *(Zeit)* short; *(Stil)* concise; **k. werden** run short, run low
Knappe ['knapə] *m* (-n;-n) (hist) squire; (min) miner
Knapp'heit *f* (-;) closeness, tightness; shortage; conciseness
Knapp'schaft *f* (-;-en) miner's union
Knapp'schaftskasse *f* miner's insurance
knarren ['knarən] *intr* creak
Knaster ['knastər] *m* (-s;-) tobacco
knattern ['knatərn] *intr* crackle; *(Maschinengewehr)* rattle ‖ *intr* (SEIN) put-put along
Knäuel ['knɔɪ-əl] *m & n* (-s;-) *(Garn-)* ball; *(Menschen-)* throng
Knauf [knauf] *m* (-[e]s;ⁿ) knob
Knauser **-in** ['knauzər(ɪn)] §6 *mf* tightwad

Knauserei [knauzə'raɪ] *f* (-;) stinginess
knauserig ['knauzərɪç] *adj* stingy
knausern ['knauzərn] *intr* be stingy
knautschen ['knautʃən] *tr* crumple || *intr* crumple; (coll) wimper
Knebel ['knebəl] *m* (-s;-) gag
Kne'belbart *m* handlebar moustache
knebeln ['knebəln] *tr* gag; (fig) muzzle
Kne'belpresse *f* tourniquet
Kne'belung *f*—**K. der Presse** muzzling of the press
Knecht [knɛçt] *m* (-[e]s;-e) servant; farmhand; serf; slave
knechten ['knɛçtən] *tr* enslave; oppress
knechtisch ['knɛçtɪʃ] *adj* servile
Knecht'schaft *f* (-;) servitude
kneifen ['knaɪfən] §88 & §109 *tr* pinch || §88 *intr* (*Kleid*) be too tight; back out, back down; (fencing) retreat; **k. vor** (*dat*) shirk, dodge
Kneifzange ['knaɪftsaŋə] *f* (pair of) pincers
Kneipe ['knaɪpə] *f* (-;-n) saloon
kneipen ['knaɪpən] *intr* (coll) booze
Knei'penwirt *m* saloon keeper
Kneiperei [knaɪpə'raɪ] *f* (-;-en) drinking bout
kneten ['knetən] *tr* knead; massage
Knick [knɪk] *m* (-[e]s;-e) bend; (*Bruch*) break; (*Falte*) fold, crease
knicken ['knɪkən] *tr* bend; break; fold; (*Hoffnungen*) dash || *intr* (SEIN) snap
Knicker ['knɪkər] *m* (-s;-) tightwad
Knicks [knɪks] *m* (-es;-e) curtsy
knicksen ['knɪksən] *intr* curtsy
Knie [kni] *n* (-s;- ['kni·ə]) knee
Knie'beuge *f* knee bend
Knie'beugung *f* genuflection
knie'fällig *adj* on one's knees
knie'frei *adj* above-the-knee
Knie'freiheit *f* legroom
Knie'kehle *f* hollow of the knee
knien ['kni·ən] *intr* kneel
Knie'scheibe *f* kneecap
Knie'schützer *m* (sport) kneepad
kniff ['knɪf] *pret* of **kneifen** || **Kniff** *m* (-[e]s;-e) crease, fold; (*Kunstgriff*) knack
kniff(e)lig ['knɪf(ə)lɪç] *adj* tricky
kniffen ['knɪfən] *tr* crease, fold
Knigge ['knɪgə] *m* (-;) (fig) Emily Post
knipsen ['knɪpsən] *tr* (*Karte*) punch; (phot) snap || *intr* snap a picture; **mit den Fingern k.** snap one's fingers
Knirps [knɪrps] *m* (-es;-e) (coll) shrimp
knirschen ['knɪrʃən] *intr* crunch; **mit den Zähnen k.** gnash one's teeth
knistern ['knɪstərn] *intr* crackle; (*Seide*) rustle
knitterfest ['knɪtərfɛst] *adj* wrinkle-proof
knittern ['knɪtərn] *tr* wrinkle; crumple
knobeln ['knobəln] *intr* play dice; **an e-m Problem k.** puzzle over a problem
Knoblauch ['knoblaux] *m* (-[e]s;) garlic
Knöchel ['knœçəl] *m* (-s;-) knuckle, joint; ankle
Knochen ['knɔxən] *m* (-s;-) bone

Kno'chenbruch *m* fracture
Kno'chengerüst *n* skeleton
Kno'chenmark *n* marrow
Kno'chenmühle *f* (coll) sweat shop
knöchern ['knœçərn] *adj* bone; bony
knochig ['knɔxɪç] *adj* bony
Knödel ['knødəl] *m* (-s;-) dumpling; **e-n K. im Hals haben** have a lump in one's throat
Knolle ['knɔlə] *f* (coll) bulbous nose; (bot) tuber
Knollen ['knɔlən] *m* (-s;-) lump; (coll) bulbous nose
knollig ['knɔlɪç] *adj* bulbous
Knopf [knɔpf] *m* (-[e]s;ːe) button; knob; (*e-r Stechnadel*) head; **alter K.** old fogey
knöpfen ['knœpfən] *tr* button
Knopf'loch *n* buttonhole
knorke ['knɔrkə] *adj* (coll) super
Knorpel ['knɔrpəl] *m* (-s;-) cartilage
Knorren ['knɔrən] *m* (-s;-) knot, gnarl
knorrig ['knɔrɪç] *adj* gnarled, knotty
Knospe ['knɔspə] *f* (-;-n) bud
knospen ['knɔspən] *intr* bud
knoten ['knotən] *tr* & *intr* knot || **Knoten** *m* (-s;-) knot; (*Schwierigkeit*) snag; (*Haarfrisur*) chignon; (*Seemeile*) knot; (astr, med, phys) node; (theat) plot
Kno'tenpunkt *m* intersection, interchange; (rr) junction
knotig ['knotɪç] *adj* knotty
Knuff [knuf] *m* (-[e]s;ːe) (coll) poke
knuffen ['knufən] *tr* (coll) poke
knüllen ['knylən] *tr* crumple
Knüller ['knylər] *m* (-s;-) (coll) hit
knüpfen ['knypfən] *tr* tie, knot; (*Teppich*) weave; (*Bündnis*) form; (*befestigen*) fasten; **k. an** (*acc*) tie in with || *ref*—**sich k. an** (*acc*) be tied in with
Knüppel ['knypəl] *m* (-s;-) cudgel; (*e-s Polizisten*) blackjack; (aer) control stick
knurren ['knurən] *intr* growl, snarl; (*Magen*) rumble; (fig) grumble
knurrig ['knurɪç] *adj* grumpy
knusprig ['knusprɪç] *adj* crisp; (*Mädchen*) attractive
Knute ['knutə] *f* (-;-n) whip; (*Gewalt*) power; (*Gewaltherrschaft*) tyranny
knutschen ['knutʃən] *tr, recip & intr* (coll) neck, pet
Knüttel ['knytəl] *m* (-s;-) cudgel
Knüt'telvers *m* doggerel
k.o. ['ka'o] *adj* knocked out || *adv*—**k.o. schlagen** knock out || **K.O.** *m* (-[s];-s) knockout
Koalition [ko·alɪ'tsjon] *f* (-;-en) coalition
Kobalt ['kobalt] *n* (-es;) cobalt
Koben ['kobən] *m* (-s;-) pigsty
Kobold ['kobɔlt] *m* (-[e]s;-e) goblin
Kobolz [ko'bɔlts] *m*—**e-n K. schießen** do a somersault
Koch [kɔx] *m* (-[e]s;ːe) cook
Koch'buch *n* cookbook
kochen ['kɔxən] *tr* & *intr* cook; boil
Kocher ['kɔxər] *m* (-s;-) cooker; boiler

Köcher ['kœçər] *m* (-s;-) quiver; golf bag
Koch'fett *n* shortening
Koch'geschirr *n* (mil) mess kit
Koch'herd *m* kitchen range
Köchin ['kœçɪn] *f* (-;-nen) cook
Koch'löffel *m* wooden spoon
Koch'salz *n* table salt
Köder ['kødər] *m* (-s;-) bait; lure
ködern ['kødərn] *tr* bait; lure
Kodex ['kodɛks] *m* (-es;-e) codex; (jur) code
kodifizieren [kodɪfɪ'tsirən] *tr* codify
Koffein [kɔfɛ'in] *n* (-s;) caffeine
Koffer ['kɔfər] *m* (-s;-) suitcase; trunk; case (*for portable items*)
Kof'ferfernseher *m* portable television
Kof'fergerät *n* (rad, telv) portable set
Kof'ferraum *m* (aut) trunk
Kof'ferschreibmaschine *f* portable typewriter
Kognak ['kɔnjak] *m* (-s;-s) cognac
Kohl [kol] *m* (-s;) cabbage; nonsense
Kohle ['kolə] *f* (-;-n) coal; (*Holzkohle*) charcoal
Kohlehydrat ['koləhʏdrɑt] *n* (-[e]s; -e) carbohydrate
kohlen ['kolən] *tr & intr* carbonize
Koh'lenbergbau *m* coal mining
Koh'lenbergwerk *n* coal mine
Koh'lendioxyd *n* carbon dioxide
Koh'lenoxyd *n* carbon monoxide
Koh'lenrevier *n* coal field
Koh'lensäure *f* carbonic acid
Koh'lenstoff *m* carbon
Koh'lenwagen *m* coal truck; (rr) coal car
Koh'lepapier *n* carbon paper
Koh'leskizze *f* charcoal sketch
kohl'ra'benschwarz' *adj* jet black
Koitus ['ko·ɪtus] *m* (-;) coitus
Koje ['kojə] *f* (-;-n) bunk, berth
Kojote [kɔ'jotə] *m* (-;-n) coyote
Kokain [kɔka'in] *n* (-s;) cocaine
Kokerei [kɔkə'raɪ] *f* (-;-en) coking plant
kokett [kɔ'kɛt] *adj* flirtatious || **Kokette** *f* (-;-n) flirt
kokettieren [kɔkɛ'tirən] *intr* flirt
Kokon [ko'kõ] *m* (-s;-s) cocoon
Kokosnuß ['kokɔsnus] *f* coconut
Kokospalme ['kokɔspalmə] *f* coconut palm, coconut tree
Koks [koks] *m* (-es;-e) coke; (coll) nonsense; (*Geld*) (coll) dough
Kolben ['kɔlbən] *m* (-s;-) butt; (*Keule*) mace; (*Löt-*) soldering iron; (aut) piston; (chem) flask; (culin) cob; (elec) bulb
Kol'benhub *m* piston stroke
Kol'benring *m* piston ring
Kol'benstange *f* piston rod
Kolchose [kɔl'çozə] *f* (-;-n) collective farm
Kolibri ['kolɪbrɪ] *m* (-s;-s) humming bird
Kolik ['kolɪk] *f* (-;-en) colic
Kolkrabe ['kɔlkrɑbə] *m* (-n;-n) raven
Kollaborateur [kɔlabɔra'tør] *m* (-s;-) collaborator (*with the enemy*)
kollaborieren [kɔlabɔ'rirən] *intr* collaborate
Kollaps [kɔ'laps] *m* (-es;-e) collapse

kollationieren [kɔlatsjɔ'nirən] *tr* collate
Kol·leg [kɔ'lek] *n* (-s;-s & -legien ['legjən]) lecture; course of lectures; theological college
Kollege [kɔ'legə] *m* (-n;-n) colleague
Kolleg'heft *n* lecture notes
Kollegin [kɔ'legɪn] *f* (-;-nen) colleague
Kollekte [kɔ'lɛktə] *f* (-;-n) collection; (eccl) collect
Kollektion [kɔlɛk'tsjon] *f* (-;-en) collection
kollektiv [kɔlɛk'tif] *adj* collective || **Kollektiv** *n* (-s;-e) collective
Koller ['kɔlər] *m* (-s;) rage, temper
kollern ['kɔlərn] *ref* roll about; (*vor Lachen*) double over || *intr* (*Puter*) gobble; (*Magen*) rumble || *intr* (SEIN) roll
kollidieren [kɔlɪ'dirən] *intr* (SEIN) collide
Kollier [kɔ'lir] *n* (-s;-s) necklace
Kollision [kɔlɪ'zjon] *f* (-;-en) collision
Köln [kœln] *n* (-s;) Cologne
Kölnischwasser [kœlnɪʃ'vasər] *n* cologne
kolonial [kɔlɔ'njal] *adj* colonial
Kolonial'waren *pl* groceries
Kolonial'warengeschäft *n* grocery store
Kolo·nie [kɔlɔ'ni] *f* (-;-nien ['ni·ən]) colony
Kolonnade [kɔlɔ'nadə] *f* (-;-n) colonnade
Kolonne [kɔ'lɔnə] *f* (-;-n) column; (mil) convoy (*of vehicles*)
kolorieren [kɔlɔ'rirən] *tr* color
Kolorit [kɔlɔ'rit] *n* (-[e]s;-e) coloring
Ko·loß [kɔ'lɔs] *m* (-losses;-losse) colossus; giant
kolossal [kɔlɔ'sal] *adj* colossal
Kolportage [kɔlpɔr'taʒə] *f* (-;-n) trashy literature; spreading of rumors
kolportieren [kɔlpɔr'tirən] *tr* peddle; (*Gerüchte*) spread
Kolumnist **-in** [kɔlum'nɪst(ɪn)] §7 *mf* columnist
Kombi ['kɔmbi] *m* (-s;-s) (coll) station wagon
Kombination [kɔmbɪna'tsjon] *f* (-; -en) combination; (*Flieger-*) flying suit; (*e-s Monteurs*) coveralls; sport suit; reasoning, deduction; conjecture
kombinieren [kɔmbɪ'nirən] *tr* combine || *intr* reason
Kom'biwagen *m* station wagon
Kombüse [kɔm'byzə] *f* (-;-n) (naut) galley, kitchen
Komik ['komɪk] *f* (-;) humor
Komiker ['komɪkər] *m* (-s;-) comedian
Komikerin ['komɪkərɪn] *f* (-;-nen) comedienne
komisch ['komɪʃ] *adj* funny
Komitee [komɪ'te] *n* (-s;-s) committee
Komma ['koma] *n* (-s;-s) comma; (*Dezimalzeichen*) decimal point
Kommandant [koman'dant] *m* (-en; -en) commanding officer; commandant

Kommandantur [kɔmandan'tur] *f* (-;
-en) headquarters
Kommandeur [kɔman'dør] *m* (-s;-e)
commanding officer, commander
kommandieren [kɔman'dirən] *tr* command, order; be in command of;
(mil) detail; (mil) detach || *intr* command, be in command
Kommanditgesellschaft [kɔman'ditgəzɛlʃaft] *f* limited partnership; **K.**
auf Aktien partnership limited by shares
Kommando [kɔ'mando] *n* (-s;-s) command, order; (mil) command; (mil)
detachment, detail; **K. zurück!** as
you were!
Komman'dobrücke *f* (nav) bridge
Komman'doraum *m* control room
Komman'dostab *m* baton
Komman'dostand *m*, **Komman'dostelle**
f command post; (nav) bridge
Komman'dotruppe *f* commando unit
Komman'doturm *m* conning tower;
control tower (*of an aircraft carrier*)
kommen ['kɔmən] §99 *intr* (SEIN)
come; (*geschehen*) happen; **auf etw**
[*acc*] **k.** hit on s.th.; **auf jeden k.**
drei Mark each one gets three marks; **das**
kommt bloß daher, daß that's entirely due to; **dazu k.** get around to
it; get hold of it; **hinter etw** [*acc*] **k.**
find s.th. out; **j-m grob k.** be rude
to s.o.; **k. lassen** send for; **nichts k.**
lassen auf (*acc*) defend; **so weit k.**,
daß reach the point where; **ums**
Leben k. lose one's life; **wenn Sie**
mir so k. if you talk like that to me;
weit k. get far; **wieder zu sich k.**
come to, regain consciousness; **wie**
kam er denn dazu? how come he did
it? **wie komme ich zum Bahnhof?**
how do I get to the train station?
Kommentar [kɔmɛn'tar] *m* (-s;-e)
commentary; **kein K.!** no comment!
Kommen·tator [kɔmɛn'tator] *m* (-s;
-tatoren [ta'torən]) commentator
kommentieren [kɔmɛn'tirən] *tr* comment on
Kommers [kɔ'mɛrs] *m* (-es;-e) drinking party
Kommers'buch *n* students' song book
kommerziell [kɔmɛr'tsjɛl] *adj* commercial
Kommilitone [kɔmɪlɪ'tonə] *m* (-n;-n)
fellow student
Kom·mis [kɔ'mi] *m* (-mis ['mis];
-mis ['mis]) clerk
Kom·miß [kɔ'mɪs] *m* (-misses;) (coll)
army; (coll) army life
Kommissar [kɔmɪ'sar] *m* (-s;-e) commissioner; (pol) commissar
kommissarisch [kɔmɪ'sariʃ] *adj* provisional, temporary
Kommission [kɔmɪ'sjon] *f* (-;-en)
commission, board; **in K.** (com) on
consignment; on a commission basis
Kommissionär [kɔmɪsjɔ'ner] *m* (-s;-e)
agent; wholesale bookseller
Kommissions'gebühr *f* (com) commission
kommissions'weise *adv* on a commission basis
Kommiß'stiefel *m* army boot
kommod [kɔ'mot] *adj* comfortable

Kommode [kɔ'modə] *f* (-;-n) bureau,
chest of drawers
kommunal [kɔmu'nal] *adj* municipal,
local
Kommunal'politik *f* local politics
Kommune [kɔ'munə] *f* (-;-n) municipality; **die K.** the Commies
Kommunikant -in [kɔmunɪ'kant(ɪn)]
§7 *mf* communicant
Kommunion [kɔmu'njon] *f* (-;-en)
Communion
Kommuniqué [kɔmynɪ'ke] *n* (-s;-s)
communiqué
Kommunismus [kɔmu'nɪsmus] *m* (-;)
communism
Kommunist -in [kɔmu'nɪst(ɪn)] §7 *mf*
communist
kommunistisch [kɔmu'nɪstɪʃ] *adj* communist(ic)
Komödiant [kɔmø'djant] *m* (-en;-en)
comedian; (pej) ham
Komödie [kɔ'mødjə] *f* (-;-n) comedy;
K. spielen (coll) put on an act
Kompagnon [kɔmpan'jõ] *m* (-s;-s)
(business) partner; associate
kompakt [kɔm'pakt] *adj* compact
Kompa·nie [kɔmpa'ni] *f* (-;-nien
['ni-ən]) company
Kompanie'chef *m* company commander
komparativ [kɔmpara'tif] *adj* comparative || **Komparativ** *m* (-s;-e)
comparative
Komparse [kɔm'parzə] *m* (-n;-n)
(theat) extra
Kom·paß ['kɔmpas] *m* (-passes;
-passe) compass
Kompen·dium [kɔm'pɛndjum] *n* (-s;
-dien [djən]) compendium
Kompensation [kɔmpɛnza'tsjon] *f* (-;
-en) compensation
Kompensations'geschäft *n* fair-value
exchange
kompensieren [kɔmpɛn'zirən] *tr* compensate for, offset
Kompetenz [kɔmpɛ'tɛnts] *f* (-;-en)
(jur) jurisdiction
komplementär [kɔmplɛmɛn'ter] *adj*
complementary
Komplet [kɔ'ple] *n* (-s;-s) dress with
matching coat
komplett [kɔm'plɛt] *adj* complete;
everything included
komplex [kɔm'plɛks] *adj* complex ||
Komplex *m* (-es;-e) complex
Komplice [kɔm'plitsə] *m* (-n;-n) accomplice
komplizieren [kɔmplɪ'tsirən] *tr* complicate
Komplott [kɔm'plɔt] *n* (-[e]s;-e) plot
Komponente [kɔmpə'nɛntə] *f* (-;-n)
component
komponieren [kɔmpə'nirən] *tr* compose
Komponist -in [kɔmpə'nɪst(ɪn)] §7 *mf*
composer
Komposition [kɔmpɔzɪ'tsjon] *f* (-;-en)
composition
Komposi·tum [kɔm'pozɪtum] *n* (-s;
-ta [ta] & -ten [tən]) compound
(word)
Kompott [kɔm'pɔt] *n* (-[e]s;-e) stewed fruit

Kompres·sor [kɔm'prɛsɔr] *m* (–s; –soren ['sorən]) compressor; (aut) supercharger
komprimieren [kɔmprɪ'mirən] *tr* compress
Kompro·miß [kɔmprɔ'mɪs] *m* (–misses; –misse) compromise
kompromittieren [kɔmprɔmɪ'tirən] *tr* compromise
kondensieren [kɔndɛn'zirən] *tr*, *ref* & *intr* (SEIN) condense
Kondensmilch [kɔn'dɛnsmɪlç] *f* evaporated milk
Kondens'streifen [kɔn'dɛnsftraɪfən] *m* contrail
Konditorei [kɔndɪtə'raɪ] *f* (–;–en) pastry shop
Konfekt [kɔn'fɛkt] *n* (–[e]s;) candy, chocolates; fancy cookies
Konfektion [kɔnfɛk'tsjon] *f* (–;) readymade clothes; manufacture of readymade clothes
Konfektionär [kɔnfɛktsjɔ'ner] *m* (–s; –e) clothing manufacturer; clothing retailer
konfektionieren [kɔnfɛktsjɔ'nirən] *tr* manufacture (*clothes*)
Konferenz [kɔnfɛ'rɛnts] *f* (–;–en) conference
konferieren [kɔnfɛ'rirən] *intr* confer, hold a conference
Konfession [kɔnfɛ'sjon] *f* (–;–en) religious denomination; (eccl) confession; confession of faith, creed
konfessionell [kɔnfɛsjɔ'nɛl] *adj* denominational
konfessions'los *adj* nondenominational
Konfessions'schule *f* denominational school, parochial school
konfirmieren [kɔnfɪr'mirən] *tr* (eccl) (Prot) confirm
konfiszieren [kɔnfɪs'tsirən] *tr* confiscate
Konfitüre [kɔnfɪ'tyrə] *f* (–;–n) jam
Konflikt [kɔn'flɪkt] *m* (–[e]s;–e) conflict
konform [kɔn'fɔrm] *adj* concurring; **mit j–m k. gehen** agree with s.o.
Konfrontation [kɔnfrɔnta'tsjon] *f* (–; –en) confrontation
konfrontieren [kɔnfrɔn'tirən] *tr* confront
konfus [kɔn'fus] *adj* confused, puzzled
Kongruenz [kɔngru'ɛnts] *f* (–;) (geom) congruence; (gram) agreement
König ['kønɪç] *m* (–[e]s;–e) king
Königin ['kønɪgɪn] *f* (–;–nen) queen
kö'niglich *adj* kingly, royal
Kö'nigreich *n* kingdom
Kö'nigsadler *m* golden eagle
Kö'nigsrose *f* (bot) peony
Kö'nigsschlange *f* boa constrictor
kö'nigstreu *adj* royalist
Kö'nigswürde *f* kingship
Königtum ['kønɪçtum] *n* (–s;) royalty, kinship; monarchy
konisch ['konɪf] *adj* conical
konjugieren [kɔnju'girən] *tr* conjugate
Konjunktion [kɔnjuŋk'tsjon] *f* (–;–en) conjunction
Konjunktiv [kɔnjuŋk'tif] *m* (–s;–e) subjunctive mood
Konjunktur [kɔnjuŋk'tur] *f* (–;–en)

economic situation; business trend; (*Hochstand*) boom
konkav [kɔn'kaf] *adj* concave
konkret [kɔn'kret] *adj* concrete
Konkurrent –in [kɔnku'rɛnt(ɪn)] §7 *mf* competitor
Konkurrenz [kɔnku'rɛnts] *f* (–;–en) competition; **K. machen** (*dat*) compete with
konkurrenz'fähig *adj* competitive
konkurrieren [kɔnku'rirən] *intr* compete
Konkurs [kɔn'kurs] *m* (–es;–e) bankruptcy; **in K. gehen** (or geraten) go bankrupt; **K. anmelden** declare bankruptcy
Konkurs'masse *f* bankrupt company's assets
können ['kœnən] §100 *tr* able to do; know; **ich kann nichts dafür** I can't help it ‖ *intr*—**ich kann nicht hinein** I can't get in ‖ *mod aux* be able to; know how to; be allowed; **das kann sein** that may be; **ich kann nicht sehen** I can't see ‖ **Können** *n* (–s;) ability
Könner ['kœnər] *m* (–s;–) expert
konnte ['kɔntə] *pret* of **können**
konsequent [kɔnze'kvɛnt] *adj* consistent
Konsequenz [kɔnze'kvɛnts] *f* (–;–en) consistency; (*Folge*) consequence
konservativ [kɔnzɛrva'tif] *adj* conservative
Konservato·rium [kɔnzɛrva'torjum] *n* (–s;–rien [rjən]) conservatory
Konserve [kɔn'zɛrvə] *f* (–;–n) canned food
Konser'venbüchse *f*, **Konser'vendose** *f* can
Konser'venfabrik *f* cannery
Konser'venöffner *m* can opener
konservieren [kɔnzɛr'virən] *tr* preserve
Konservie'rung *f* (–;) preservation
Konsisto·rium [kɔnzɪs'torjum] *n* (–s; –rien [rjən]) (eccl) consistory
Konsole [kɔn'zolə] *f* (–;–n) bracket; (archit) console
konsolidieren [kɔnzɔlɪ'dirən] *tr* consolidate
Konsonant [kɔnzɔ'nant] *m* (–en;–en) consonant
Konsorte [kɔn'zɔrtə] *m* (–n;–n) (pej) accomplice; (fin) member of a syndicate
Konsor·tium [kɔn'zɔrtjum] *n* (–s;–tien [tjən]) (fin) syndicate
konstant [kɔn'stant] *adj* constant ‖ **Konstante** §5 *f* (math, phys) constant
konstatieren [kɔnsta'tirən] *tr* ascertain; state; (med) diagnose
konsterniert [kɔnstɛr'nirt] *adj* stunned
konstituieren [kɔnstɪtu'irən] *tr* constitute ‖ *ref* be established; **sich als Ausschuß k. form** a committee of the whole
konstitutionell [kɔnstɪtutsjɔ'nɛl] *adj* constitutional
konstruieren [kɔnstru'irən] *tr* construct; (*entwerfen*) design; (gram) construe
Konsul ['kɔnzul] *m* (–s;–n) consul

konsularisch [kɔnzu'larɪʃ] *adj* consular

Konsulat [kɔnzu'lat] *n* (-[e]s;-e) consulate; (hist) consulship

Konsulent –in [kɔnzu'lɛnt(ɪn)] §7 *mf* (jur) counsel

konsultieren [kɔnzul'tirən] *tr* consult

Konsum [kɔn'zum] *m* (-s;-s) cooperative store; (com) consumption

Konsument –in [kɔnzu'mɛnt(ɪn)] §7 *mf* consumer

Konsum'güter *pl* consumer goods

konsumieren [kɔnzu'mirən] *tr* consume

Konsum'verein *m* cooperative society

Kontakt [kɔn'takt] *m* (-[e]s;-e) contact

Kontakt'glas *n*, **Kontakt'schale** *f* contact lens

Konteradmiral ['kɔntəratmiral] *m* rear admiral

Konterfei [kɔntər'faɪ] *n* (-s;-e) portrait, likeness

kontern ['kɔntərn] *tr* counter

Kontinent ['kɔntɪnənt] *m* (-[e]s;-e) continent

Kontingent [kɔntɪŋ'gɛnt] *n* (-[e]s;-e) quota; (mil) contingent

Kon·to ['kɔnto] *n* (-s;-s & -ten [tən]) account

Kon'toauszug *m* bank statement

Kontor [kɔn'tor] *n* (-s;-e) (com) office

Kontorist –in [kɔntə'rɪst(ɪn)] §7 *mf* clerk (*in an office*)

Kontrahent [kɔntra'hɛnt] *m* (-en;-en) contracting party; dueller

kontrahieren [kɔntra'hirən] *tr & intr* contract

Kontrakt [kɔn'trakt] *m* (-[e]s;-e) contract

Kontrapunkt ['kɔntrapʊŋkt] *m* (mus) counterpoint

konträr [kɔn'trer] *adj* contrary

Kontrast [kɔn'trast] *m* (-[e]s;-e) contrast

konstrastieren [kɔntras'tirən] *intr* contrast

Kontrast'regelung *f* (telv) contrast button

Kontroll– [kɔntrɔl] *comb.fm.* checking; control

Kontroll'abschnitt *m* stub (*of ticket*)

Kontrolle [kɔn'trɔlə] *f* (-;-n) control; check, inspection

Kontrolleur [kɔntrɔ'lør] *m* (-s;-e) inspector, supervisor; (aer) air-traffic controller; (indust) timekeeper

kontrollieren [kɔntrɔ'lirən] *tr* control; check, inspect; (*Bücher*) audit

Kontroll'kasse *f* cash register

Kontroll'leuchte *f* (aut) warning light (*on dashboard*)

Kontroll'turm *m* (aer) control tower

Kontroverse [kɔntrə'vɛrzə] *f* (-;-n) controversy

Kontur [kɔn'tur] *f* (-;-en) contour

Konvent [kɔn'vɛnt] *m* (-[e]s;-e) convent; monastery; (*Versammlung*) convention

Konvention [kɔnvɛn'tsjon] *f* (-;-en) convention

konventionell [kɔnvɛntsjɔ'nɛl] *adj* conventional

Konversation [kɔnvɛrza'tsjon] *f* (-;-en) conversation

Konversations'lexikon *n* encyclopedia; **wandelndes K.** (coll) walking encyclopedia

konvertieren [kɔnvɛr'tirən] *tr* convert || *intr* be converted

Konvertit –in [kɔnvɛr'tit(ɪn)] §7 *mf* convert

konvex [kɔn'vɛks] *adj* convex

Konvikt [kɔn'vɪkt] *n* (-s;-e) minor seminary

Konvoi ['kɔnvɔɪ] *m* (-s;-s) convoy

Konvolut [kɔnvə'lut] *n* (-[e]s;-e) bundle, roll

Konzentration [kɔntsɛntra'tsjon] *f* (-; -en) concentration

Konzentrations'lager *n* concentration camp

konzentrieren [kɔntsɛn'trirən] *tr & ref* (auf *acc*) concentrate (*on*)

konzentrisch [kɔn'tsɛntrɪʃ] *adj* concentric

Konzept [kɔn'tsɛpt] *n* (-[e]s;-e) rough draft; **aus dem K. bringen** confuse, throw off; **aus dem K. kommen** lose one's train of thought

Konzept'papier *n* scribbling paper

Konzern [kɔn'tsɛrn] *m* (-s;-e) (com) combine

Konzert [kɔn'tsɛrt] *n* (-[e]s;-e) concert

Konzert'flügel *m* grand piano

Konzession [kɔntsɛ'sjon] *f* (-;-en) concession; license

konzessionieren [kɔntsɛsjɔ'nirən] *tr* (com) license

Kon·zil [kɔn'tsil] *n* (-[e]s;-e & -zilien ['tsiljən]) (eccl) council

konziliant [kɔntsɪ'ljant] *adj* conciliatory; understanding

konzipieren [kɔntsɪ'pirən] *tr* conceive

koordinieren [kɔ·ɔrdɪ'nirən] *tr* coordinate

Kopf [kɔpf] *m* (-es;ꞏe) head; **aus dem Kopfe** by heart; **j–m über den K. wachsen** be taller than s.o.; (fig) be too much for s.o.; **mit dem K. voran** head first; **seinen eigenen K. haben** have a mind of one's own; **seinen K. lassen müssen** lose one's life

Kopf'bedeckung *f* headgear, head wear

Kopf'brett *n* headboard

köpfen ['kœpfən] *tr* behead; (*Baum*) top; (fb) head

Kopf'ende *n* head (*of bed, etc.*)

Kopf'geld *n* reward (*for capture of criminal*)

Kopf'haut *f* scalp

Kopf'hörer *m* headset, earphones

-köpfig [kœpfɪç] *comb.fm.* –headed; –man

Kopf'kissen *n* pillow

Kopf'kissenbezug *m* pillowcase

kopf'lastig *adj* top-heavy

Kopf'lehne *f* headrest

Kopf'rechnen *n* (-s;) mental arithmetic

Kopf'salat *m* head lettuce

kopf'scheu *adj* (*Pferd*) nervous; (*Person*) shy; **k. werden** become alarmed

Kopf'schmerzen *pl* headache

Kopf'schuppen *pl* dandruff

Kopf'sprung *m* dive; **e–n K. machen** dive
Kopf'stand *m* handstand; **e–n K. machen** (aer) nose over
Kopf'stärke *f* (mil) strength
kopf'stehen §146 *intr* stand on one's head; (fig) be upside down
Kopf'steinpflaster *n* cobblestones
Kopf'steuer *f* poll tax
Kopf'stimme *f* falsetto
Kopf'stoß *m* butt; (fb) header
Kopf'tuch *n* kerchief, babushka
kopfü'ber *adv* head over heels
kopfun'ter *adv*—**kopfüber k.** head over heels
Kopf'weh *n* headache
Kopf'wellenknall *m* sonic boom
Ko•pie [ko'pi] *f* (–;–pien ['pi·ən]) copy, duplicate; (phot) print
kopieren [ko'pirən] *tr* copy; (phot) print
Kopier'maschine *f* copier, photocopying machine
Kopier'papier *n* tracing paper; carbon paper; (phot) printing paper
Kopier'stift *m* indelible pencil
Koppel ['kopəl] *f* (–;–n) leash; (*Gehege*) enclosure, paddock || *n* (–s;–) (mil) belt
koppeln ['kopəln] *tr* tie together, yoke; (fig) tie in; (elec) connect; (rad, rr) couple; (rok) dock || **Koppeln** *n* (–s;) (aer, naut) dead reckoning; (rok) docking
Kopplungsgeschäft ['kopluŋsgəʃɛft] *n* package deal
Koralle [ko'ralə] *f* (–;–n) coral
Korb [korp] *m* (–[e]s;ːe) basket; **j–m den K. geben** (fig) give s.o. the brush-off
Korb'ball *m* basketball
Körbchen ['kœrpçən] *n* (–s;–) little basket; (*e–s Büstenhalters*) cup
Korb'flasche *f* demijohn
Korb'geflecht *n* wickerwork
Korb'möbel *pl* wicker furniture
Korb'weide *f* (bot) osier
Kordel ['kordəl] *f* (–;–n) cord
Kordon [kor'dõ] *m* (–s;–s) cordon; (*Ordensband*) ribbon
Korea [ko're·a] *n* (–s;) Korea
koreanisch [kore'aniʃ] *adj* Korean
Korinthe [ko'rintə] *f* (–;–n) currant
Kork [kork] *m* (–[e]s;–e) cork
Korken ['korkən] *m* (–s;–) cork, stopper
Korkenzieher ['korkəntsi·ər] *m* (–s;–) corkscrew
Korn [korn] *n* (–[e]s;ːer) grain; seed; (*am Gewehr*) bead; (*Getreide*) rye; (*e–r Münze*) fineness; (phot) graininess; **j–n aufs K. nehmen** draw a bead on s.o.
Korn'ähre *f* ear of grain
Korn'branntwein *m* whiskey
Kornett [kor'nɛt] *n* (–[e]s;–e) (mus) cornet
körnig ['kœrnıç] *adj* granular
Korn'kammer *f* granary; (fig) breadbasket
koronar [koro'nar] *adj* coronary
Körper ['kœrpər] *m* (–s;–) body; (geom, phys) solid

Kör'perbau *m* (–[e]s;) build, physique
kör'perbehindert *adj* physically handicapped
Kör'perbeschaffenheit *f* constitution
Körperchen [kœrpərçən] *n* (–s;–) corpuscle
Kör'perfülle *f* plumpness, corpulence
Kör'pergeruch *m* body odor
Kör'perhaltung *f* posture, bearing
Kör'perkraft *f* physical strength
kör'perlich *adj* physical; (*stofflich*) corporeal
Kör'perpflege *f* personal hygiene
Kör'perpuder *m* talcum powder
Kör'perschaft *f* (–;–en) body (*of persons*); corporation
Kör'perverletzung *f* bodily injury
Korporation [korpora'tsjon] *f* (–;–en) corporation
Korps [kor] *n* (– [kors];– [kors]) corps
Korps'geist *m* esprit de corps
Korps'student *m* member of a fraternity
korrekt [ko'rɛkt] *adj* correct, proper
Korrek•tor [ko'rɛktor] *m* (–s;–toren** ['torən]) proofreader
Korrektur [korɛk'tur] *f* (–;–en) correction; proofreading
Korrektur'bogen *m* page proof
Korrektur'fahne *f* galley proof
Korrelat [korɛ'lat] *n* (–[e]s;–e) correlative
Korrespondent –in [korɛspon'dɛnt(ın)] §7 *mf* correspondent
Korrespondenz [korɛspon'dɛnts] *f* (–; –en) correspondence
Korrespondenz'karte *f* (Aust) postcard
Korridor ['koridor] *m* (–s;–e) corridor
korrigieren [kori'girən] *tr* correct
korrodieren [koro'dirən] *tr* & *intr* corrode
Korse ['korzə] *m* (–n;–n) Corsican
Korsett [kor'zɛt] *n* (–[e]s;–e & –s) corset
Korsika ['korzıka] *n* (–s;) Corsica
Korvette [kor'vɛtə] *f* (–;–n) corvette
Kosak [ko'zak] *m* (–en;–en) Cossack
K.–o.–Schlag [ka'o/lak] *m* knockout punch
kosen ['kozən] *tr* fondle, caress
Kosename ['kozənamə] *m* pet name
Kosmetik [kos'metık] *f* (–;) beauty treatment; **chirugische K.** cosmetic surgery. plastic surgery
Kosme'tikartikel *m* cosmetic
Kosmeti•kum [kos'metıkum] *n* (–s;–ka [ka]) cosmetic
kosmisch ['kozmıʃ] *adj* cosmic
kosmopolitisch [kosmopo'litıʃ] *adj* cosmopolitan
Kosmos ['kosmos] *m* (–;) cosmos
Kost [kost] *f* (–;) food, board
kostbar ['kostbar] *adj* valuable; costly
Kost'barkeit *f* (–;–en) costliness; (fig) precious thing
kosten ['kostən] *tr* cost; taste, sip || **Kosten** *pl* costs; **auf K.** (*genit*) at the expense of; **auf seine K. kommen** get one's money's worth; **sich in K. stürzen** go to great expense
Ko'stenanschlag *m* estimate
Ko'stenaufwand *m* expenditure, outlay
Ko'stenberechnung *f* cost accounting

Ko'stenersatz *m*, **Ko'stenerstattung** *f* reimbursement of expenses
ko'stenlos *adj* free of charge
Ko'stenvoranschlag *m* estimate
Kost'gänger –in §6 *mf* boarder
köstlich ['kœstlıç] *adj* delicious; delightful || *adv*—**sich k.** amüsieren have a grand time
Kost'probe *f* sample (*to taste*)
kostspielig ['kɔst/pilıç] *adj* expensive
Kostüm [kɔs'tym] *n* (-s;-e) costume; woman's suit; fancy dress
kostümieren [kɔsty'mirən] *tr & ref* dress up
Kostüm'probe *f* dress rehearsal
Kot [kot] *m* (-[e]s;) mud, dirt; (*tierischer*) dirt, dung; excrement
Kotelett [kɔtə'lɛt] *n* (-[e]s;-e & -s) pork chop; cutlet
Köter ['køtər] *m* (-s;-) mut, mongrel
Kot'flügel *m* (aut) fender
kotig ['kotıç] *adj* muddy, dirty
kotzen ['kɔtsən] *intr* (sl) puke || **Kotzen** *n*—**es ist zum K.** it's enough to make you throw up
Krabbe ['krabə] *f* (-;-n) crab; shrimp; (*niedliches Kind*) little darling
krabbeln ['krabəln] *tr & intr* tickle || *intr* (SEIN) crawl
Krach [krax] *m* (-[e]s;-s & -e) crash, bang; (*Lärm*) racket; (*Streit*) row; (fin) crash; **K. machen** kick up a row
krachen ['kraxən] *intr* crash, crack
krächzen ['krɛçtsən] *intr* croak, caw
kraft [kraft] *prep* (*genit*) by virtue of || **Kraft** *f* (-;-e) strength, power, force; **außer K. setzen** repeal; **in K. sein** be in force; **in K. treten** come into force
Kraft'anlage *f* (elec) power plant
Kraft'anstrengung *f* strenuous effort
Kraft'aufwand *m* effort
Kraft'ausdruck *m* swear word; **Kraftausdrücke** strong language
Kraft'brühe *f* concentrated broth
Kraft'fahrer –in §6 *mf* motorist
Kraft'fahrzeug *n* motor vehicle
kräftig ['krɛftıç] *adj* strong, powerful; (*Speise*) nutritious || *adv* hard; heartily
kräftigen ['krɛftıgən] *tr* strengthen
Kraft'leistung *f* feat of strength
kraft'los *adj* powerless; weak
Kraft'meier *m* (coll) bully; (coll) muscle man
Kraft'probe *f* test of strength
Kraft'protz *m* (coll) powerhouse
Kraft'rad *n* motorcycle
Kraft'stoff *m* fuel
Kraft'stoffleitung *f* fuel line
kraftstrotzend ['kraft/trɔtsənt] *adj* strapping
Kraft'übertragung *f* (aut) transmission
Kraft'wagen *m* motor vehicle
Kraft'werk *n* generating plant
Kraft'wort *n* (-[e]s;-er) swear word
Kragen ['kragən] *m* (-s;-) collar
Krähe ['krɛ·ə] *f* (-;-n) crow
krähen ['krɛ·ən] *intr* crow
Krähenfüße ['krɛ·ənfysə] *pl* crow's feet (*wrinkles*)
Krakeel [kra'kel] *m* (-s;-e) (coll) rumpus; (*lauter Streit*) brawl

krakeelen [kra'kelən] *intr* (coll) kick up a storm
Kralle ['kralə] *f* (-;-n) claw
Kram [kram] *m* (-[e]s;) (coll) things, stuff; (coll) business, affairs
kramen ['kramən] *intr* rummage
Krämer –in ['kremər(ın)] §6 *mf* shopkeeper || *m* (pej) philistine
Krä'merseele *f* philistine
Kram'laden *m* general store
Krampe ['krampə] *f* (-;-n) staple
Krampf [krampf] *m* (-[e]s;-e) cramp; spasm; convulsion; (*Unsinn*) nonsense
Krampf'ader *f* varicose vein
krampf'artig *adj* spasmodic
krampf'haft *adj* convulsive
Kran [kran] *m* (-[e]s;-e & -e) (mach) crane
Kranich ['kranıç] *m* (-s;-e) (orn) crane
krank [kraŋk] *adj* sick, ill || **Kranke** §5 *mf* patient
–krank *comb.fm.* suffering from
kränkeln ['krɛŋkəln] *intr* be sickly
kranken ['kraŋkən] *intr*—**k. an** (*dat*) suffer from
kränken ['krɛŋkən] *tr* hurt, offend || *ref* (*über acc*) feel hurt (at)
Kran'kenanstalt *f* hospital
Kran'kenbahre *f* stretcher
Kran'kenbett *n* sickbed
Kran'kenfahrstuhl *m* wheel chair
Kran'kengeld *n* sick benefit
Kran'kenhaus *n* hospital; **ins K. einweisen** hospitalize
Kran'kenkasse *f* medical insurance plan
Kran'kenlager *n* sickbed
Kran'kenpflege *f* nursing
Kran'kenpfleger –in §6 *mf* nurse
Kran'kenrevier *n* (mil) sick quarters; (nav) sick bay
Kran'kensaal *m* hospital ward
Kran'kenschwester *f* nurse
Kran'kenstube *f* infirmary
Kran'kenstuhl *m* wheel chair
Kran'kenurlaub *m* sick leave
Kran'kenversicherung *f* health insurance
Kran'kenwagen *m* ambulance
krank'feiern *intr* (coll) play sick
krank'haft *adj* morbid, pathological
Krank'heit *f* (-;-en) sickness, disease
Krank'heitsbericht *m* medical bulletin
Krank'heitserscheinung *f* symptom
kränklich ['krɛŋklıç] *adj* sickly
Kränk'lichkeit *f* (-;) poor health
Kränkung ['krɛŋkʊŋ] *f* (-;-en) offense
Kran'wagen *m* (aut) wrecker, tow truck
Kranz [krants] *m* (-[e]s;-e) wreath
Kränzchen ['krɛntsçən] *n* (-s;-) small wreath; ladies' circle; informal dance
kränzen ['krɛntsən] *tr* wreathe
Krapfen ['krapfən] *m* (-s;-) doughnut
kraß [kras] *adj* crass, gross
Krater ['kratər] *m* (-s;-) crater
Kratzbürste ['kratsbʏrstə] *f* wire brush; (fig) stand-offish woman
Krätze ['krɛtsə] *f* (-;) itch, scabies
kratzen ['kratsən] *tr & intr* scratch
Krat'zer *m* (-s;-) scratch; scraper

krauen ['kraʊ·ən] *tr* scratch gently
kraus [kraʊs] *adj* (*Haar*) frizzy; (*Gedanken*) confused; **die Stirn k. ziehen** knit one's brows
Krause ['kraʊzə] *f* (-;-n) ruffle
kräuseln ['krɔɪzəln] *tr* & *ref* curl
Krau'seminze *f* (bot) spearmint
Kraus'haar *n* frizz
Kraut [kraʊt] *n* (-[e]s;⁼er) herb, plant; leafy top; (*Kohl*) cabbage; **ins K. schießen** run wild
Krawall [kra'val] *m* (-[e]s;-e) riot; (coll) rumpus
Krawatte [kra'vatə] *f* (-;-n) necktie
Krawat'tenhalter *m* tie clip
kraxeln ['kraksəln] *intr* (SEIN) climb
Kreatur [kre·a'tur] *f* (-;-en) creature
Krebs [kreps] *m* (-es;-e) crawfish, crab; (pathol) cancer
krebs'artig *adj* (pathol) cancerous
Kredenz [kre'dents] *f* (-;-en) buffet, credenza, sideboard
kredenzen [kre'dentsən] *tr* (*Wein*) serve
Kredit [kre'dit] *m* (-[e]s;-e) credit
Kredit'bank *f* commercial bank
kreditieren [kredɪ'tirən] *tr* credit || *intr* give credit
Kredit'karte *f* credit card
Kredit'würdigkeit *f* trustworthiness; (com) credit rating
Kreide ['kraɪdə] *f* (-;-n) chalk, piece of chalk, crayon
kreieren [kre'irən] *tr* create
Kreis [kraɪs] *m* (-es;-e) circle; (*Bereich*) field; (*Bezirk*) district; (adm) county; (elec) circuit
Kreis'abschnitt *m* segment
Kreis'amt *n* district office
Kreis'ausschnitt *m* sector
Kreis'bahn *f* orbit
Kreis'bogen *m* (geom) arc
kreischen ['kraɪʃən] *intr* shriek
Kreisel ['kraɪzəl] *m* (-s;-) gyroscope; top (toy)
Krei'selbewegung *f* gyration
Krei'selhorizont *m* artificial horizon
kreiseln ['kraɪzəln] *intr* spin, rotate, gyrate; spin the top
Krei'selpumpe *f* centrifugal pump
kreisen ['kraɪzən] *intr* circle; revolve; (*Blut*) circulate
kreis'förmig *adj* circular
Kreis'lauf *m* circulation; cycle
Kreis'laufsstörung *f* circulatory disorder
kreis'rund *adj* circular
Kreis'säge *f* circular saw, buzz saw
kreißen ['kraɪsən] *intr* be in labor
Kreißsaal ['kraɪszal] *m* delivery room
Kreis'stadt *f* (rural) county seat
Kreis'umfang *m* circumference
Kreis'verkehr *m* traffic circle
Krem [krem] *f* (-;-s) & *m* (-s;-s) cream
Kreml ['kreməl] *m* (-[e]s;) Kremlin
Krempe ['krempə] *f* (-;-n) brim, rim
Krempel ['krempəl] *m* (-s;) (coll) stuff, junk || *f* (-;-n) (tex) card
Kren [kren] *m* (-[e]s;) horseradish
krepieren [kre'pirən] *intr* (SEIN) (*Tiere*) die; (*Granate*) explode, burst; (sl) kick the bucket

Krepp [krep] *m* (-s;-s) crepe
Kreta ['kreta] *n* (-s;) Crete
Kretonne [kre'tɔnə] *f* (-;-n) cretonne
kreuz [krɔɪts] *adv*—**k. und quer** crisscross** || **Kreuz** *n* (-es;-e) cross; (anat) small of the back; (cards) club(s)
Kreuz'abnahme *f* deposition
Kreuz'band *n* (-[e]s;⁼er) mailing wrapper (for newspapers, etc.)
kreuz'brav' *adj* (coll) very honest; (coll) very well-behaved
kreuzen ['krɔɪtsən] *tr* cross || *recip* cross; interbreed || *intr* cruise
Kreuzer ['krɔɪtsər] *m* (-s;-) penny; (nav) cruiser
Kreuz'fahrer *m* crusader
Kreuz'fahrt *f* cruise; (hist) crusade
Kreuz'feuer *n* crossfire
kreuz'fidel' *adj* very cheerful
Kreuz'gang *m* (archit) cloister(s)
kreuzigen ['krɔɪtsɪgən] *tr* crucify
Kreu'zigung *f* (-;-en) crucifixion
Kreuz'otter *f* adder
Kreuz'ritter *m* crusader; Knight of the Teutonic Order
Kreuz'schiff *m* transept (of church)
Kreuz'schlitzschraubenzieher *m* Phillips screwdriver
Kreu'zung *f* (-;-en) intersection; crossbreeding; hybrid; (rr) crossing
Kreuz'verhör *n* cross-examination; **j-n ins K. nehmen** cross-examine s.o.
Kreuz'verweis *m* cross reference
Kreuz'weg *m* crossroad; (eccl) stations of the cross
Kreuz'worträtsel *n* crossword puzzle
Kreuz'zeichen *n* (eccl) sign of the cross; (typ) dagger
Kreuz'zug *m* crusade
kribbelig ['krɪbəlɪç] *adj* irritable; (nervös) edgy, on edge
kribbeln ['krɪbəln] *intr* tickle
kriechen ['kriçən] §102 *intr* (SEIN) creep, crawl
kriecherisch ['kriçərɪʃ] *adj* fawning
Kriechtier ['kriçtir] *n* reptile
Krieg [krik] *m* (-[e]s;-e) war
kriegen ['krigən] *tr* (coll) get, catch
Krie'ger *m* (-s;-) warrior
kriegerisch ['krigərɪʃ] *adj* warlike; (*Person*) belligerent
krieg'führend *adj* warring
Kriegs'akademie *f* war college
Kriegs'bemalung *f* war paint
Kriegs'berichter *m*, **Kriegs'berichterstatter** *m* war correspondent
Kriegs'dienst *m* military service
Kriegs'dienstverweigerer *m* conscientious objector
Kriegs'einsatz *m* (mil) action
Kriegs'entschädigung *f* reparations
Kriegs'fall *m*—**im K.** in case of war
Kriegs'flotte *f* fleet; naval force
Kriegs'fuß *m*—**mit j-m auf K. stehen** be at loggerheads with s.o.
Kriegs'gebiet *n* war zone
Kriegs'gefangene §5 *mf* prisoner of war
Kriegs'gericht *n* court martial
Kriegsgewinner ['kriksgəvɪnlər] *m* (-s;-) war profiteer
Kriegs'hafen *m* naval base
Kriegs'hetzer *m* warmonger

Kriegs'kamerad m fellow soldier
Kriegs'lazarett n base hospital
Kriegs'list f stratagem
Kriegs'marine f navy
Kriegs'ministerium n war department
Kriegs'opfer n war victim
Kriegs'pfad m warpath
Kriegs'rat m council of war
Kriegs'recht n martial law
Kriegs'rüstung f arming for war; war production
Kriegs'schauplatz m theater of war
Kriegs'schuld f war debt; war guilt
Kriegs'teilnehmer m combatant; (ehemaliger) ex-serviceman, veteran
Kriegs'verbrechen n war crime
Kriegs'versehrte §5 m disabled veteran
kriegs'verwendungsfähig adj fit for active duty
Kriegs'wesen n warfare, war
Kriegs'zug m (mil) campaign
Kriegs'zustand m state of war
Krim [krım] f (-;) Crimea
Krimi ['krimi] m (-s;-s) & (-;-) (coll) murder mystery; (telv) thriller
kriminal [krımı'nɑl] adj criminal
Kriminal- comb.fm. criminal, crime
Kriminal'beamte m criminal investigator
Kriminal'roman m detective novel
Kriminal'stück n (telv) thriller
kriminell [krımı'nel] adj criminal ‖
Kriminelle §5 mf criminal
Krimskrams ['krımskrams] m (-es;) (coll) junk
Kripo ['kripo] abbr (**Kriminalpolizei**) crime squad
Krippe ['krıpə] f (-;-n) crib, manger; day nursery (for infants up to 3 years)
Krise ['krizə] f (-;-n) crisis
kriseln ['krizəln] impers—es **kriselt** there's a crisis, trouble is brewing
Kristall [krıs'tal] m (-s;-e) crystal
Kristalleuchter (**Kristall'leuchter**) m crystal chandelier
Kristall'glas n crystal
kristallisieren [krıstalı'zirən] ref & intr crystallize
Kristall'zucker m granulated sugar
Krite·rium [krı'terjum] n (-s;-rien [rjən]) criterion
Kritik [krı'tik] f (-;-en) criticism; critique; **unter aller K.** abominable
Kritikaster [krıtı'kaster] m (-s;-) (pej) faultfinder
Kritiker -in ['kritıkər(ın)] §6 mf critic; reviewer
kritik'los adj uncritical
kritisch ['kritıʃ] adj critical
kritisieren [krıtı'zirən] tr criticize; (werten) review
Krittelei [krıtə'laı] f (-;-en) faultfinding; petty criticism
kritteln ['krıtəln] intr (an dat) find fault (with), grumble (about)
Kritzelei [krıtsə'laı] f (-;-en) scribbling, scrawling; scribble, scrawl
kritzeln ['krıtsəln] tr & intr scribble
kroch [krox] pret of **kriechen**
Krokodil [krɔkə'dil] n (-[e]s;-e) crocodile
Krokus ['krokus] m (-;- & -se) crocus

Krone ['kronə] f (-;-n) crown
krönen ['krønən] tr crown
Kronerbe ['kronɛrbə] m, **Kronerbin** ['kronɛrbın] f heir apparent
Kronleuchter ['kronlɔıçtər] m chandelier
Kronprinz ['kronprınts] m crown prince
Kronprinzessin ['kronprıntsɛsın] f crown princess
Krö'nung f (-;-en) coronation
Kropf [krɔpf] m (-[e]s;⸚e) crop (of bird); (pathol) goiter
Kröte ['krøtə] f (-;-n) toad; **Kröten** (coll) coins, coppers
Krücke ['krykə] f (-;-n) crutch
Krückstock ['kryk/tɔk] m walking stick
Krug [kruk] m (-[e]s;⸚e) jar, jug; mug; pitcher; (Wirtshaus) tavern
Krume ['krumə] f (-;-n) crumb; topsoil
Krümel ['kryməl] m (-s;-) crumb
krümeln ['kryməln] tr & intr crumble
krumm [krum] adj (**krummer** & **krümmer** ['krymər]; **krummste** & **krümmste** ['krymstə] §9) bent, stooping; crooked
krumm'beinig adj bowlegged
krümmen ['krymən] tr bend, curve ‖ ref (vor Schmerzen) writhe; (vor Lachen) double up; (Wurm) wriggle; (Holz) warp; (Fluß, Straße) wind
Krümmer ['krymər] m (-s;-) (tech) elbow
krumm'nehmen §116 tr (coll) take the wrong way, take amiss
Krumm'stab m (eccl) crozier
Krüm'mung f (-;-en) bend, curve; winding
krumpeln ['krumpəln] tr & intr (coll) crumple, crease
Krüppel ['krypəl] m (-s;-) cripple; **zum K. machen** cripple
krüp'pelhaft adj deformed
krüp'pelig adj crippled; stunted
Kruste ['krustə] f (-;-n) crust
Kru'stentier n crustacean
krustig ['krustıç] adj crusty
Kruzifix [krutsı'fıks] n (-es;-e) crucifix
Kryp·ta ['krypta] f (-;-ten [tən]) crypt
Kübel ['kybəl] m (-s;-) tub; bucket
Kü'belwagen m jeep
kubieren [ku'birən] tr (math) cube
Kubik- [kubik] comb.fm. cubic
Kubik'maß n cubic measure
kubisch ['kubıʃ] adj cubic
Kubismus [ku'bısmus] m (-;) cubism
Küche ['kyçə] f (-;-n) kitchen; (culin) cuisine
Kuchen ['kuxən] m (-s;-) cake, pie
Ku'chenblech n cookie sheet
Küchenchef m chef
Kü'chendienst m (mil) K.P.
Ku'chenform f cake pan
Kü'chengerät n kitchen utensil
Kü'chengeschirr n kitchen utensils
Kü'chenherd m kitchen range, stove
Kü'chenmaschine f electric kitchen appliance
Kü'chenmeister m chef

Kü′chenzettel *m* menu
Küchlein ['kyçlaın] *n* (**-s;-**) chick; (culin) small cake
Kuckuck ['kʊkʊk] *m* (**-s;-e**) cuckoo; **zum K.** gehen (coll) go to hell
Kufe ['kuːə] *f* (**-;-n**) vat; (*Schlitten-*) runner
Küfer ['kyfər] *m* (**-s;-**) cooper
Kugel ['kugəl] *f* (**-;-n**) ball; sphere; (*Geschoß*) bullet; (sport) shot
ku′gelfest *adj* bulletproof
ku′gelförmig *adj* spherical
Ku′gelgelenk *n* (mach) ball-and-socket joint; (anat) socket joint
Ku′gellager *n* ball bearing
kugeln ['kugəln] *tr* roll || *ref* roll around; **sich vor Lachen k.** double over with laughter || *intr* (SEIN) roll
Ku′gelregen *m* hail of bullets
ku′gelrund′ *adj* round; (coll) tubby
Ku′gelschreiber *m* ball-point pen
Ku′gelstoßen *n* (sport) shot put
Kuh [ku] *f* (**-;⸗e**) cow
Kuh′dorf *n* hick town
Kuh′fladen *m* cow dung
Kuh′handel *m* (pol) horse trading
Kuh′haut *f* cowhide; **das geht auf keine K.** but that's a long story
kühl [kyl] *adj* cool
Kühl′anlage *f* refrigerator; cooling system; cold storage (room)
Kühle ['kylə] *f* (**-;**) cool, coolness
kühlen ['kylən] *tr* cool; (*Wein*) chill
Küh′ler *m* (**-s;-**) cooler; (aut) radiator
Küh′lerverschluß *m* radiator cap
Kühl′mittel *n* coolant
Kühl′schrank *m* refrigerator
Kühl′truhe *f* freezer
Kühl′wagen *m* refrigerator truck; (rr) refrigerator car
Kuh′magd *f* milkmaid
Kuh′mist *m* cow dung
kühn [kyn] *adj* bold, daring
Kühn′heit *f* (**-;**) boldness, daring
Kuhpocken ['kupɔkən] *pl* cowpox
Kuh′stall *m* cowshed, cow barn
Kujon [ku'jon] *m* (**-s;-e**) (pej) louse
kujonieren [kujo'nirən] *tr* bully
Küken ['kykən] *n* (**-s;-**) chick
Kukuruz ['kukurʊts] *m* (**-es;**) (Aust) corn
kulant [ku'lant] *adj* obliging; generous
Kuli ['kulɪ] *m* (**-s;-s**) coolie
kulinarisch [kulɪ'narɪʃ] *adj* culinary
Kulisse [ku'lɪsə] *f* (**-;-n**) (theat) wing; **hinter den Kulissen** behind the scenes; **Kulissen** scenery
Kulis′senfieber *n* stage fright
kullern ['kulərn] *intr* (SEIN) roll
kulminieren [kulmɪ'nirən] *intr* culminate
Kult [kʊlt] *m* (**-[e]s;-e**) cult
kultivieren [kʊltɪ'virən] *tr* cultivate
Kultur [kʊl'tur] *f* (**-;-en**) culture, civilization; (agr) cultivation; (bact, chem) culture
Kultur′austausch *m* cultural exchange
kulturell [kʊltu'rel] *adj* cultural
Kultur′erbe *n* cultural heritage
Kultur′film *m* educational film
Kultur′geschichte *f* history of civilization; cultural history
Kultur′volk *n* civilized people

Kul·tus ['kʊltʊs] *m* (**-;-te** [tə]) cult
Kümmel ['kymɐl] *m* (**-s;-**) caraway seed; caraway brandy
Küm′melbrot *n* seeded rye bread
Kummer ['kumər] *m* (**-s;**) grief, sorrow; worry, concern, trouble; **j-m** großen **K.** bereiten cause s.o. a lot of worry; **sich** [*dat*] **K.** machen über (*acc*) worry about
kümmerlich ['kymɐrlɪç] *adj* wretched; (*dürftig*) needy
Kümmerling ['kymɐrlɪŋ] *m* (**-s;-e**) stunted animal; stunted plant
kümmern ['kymɐrn] *tr* trouble, worry; concern || *ref*—**sich k. um** worry about; take care of; **sich nicht k. um** not bother about; neglect
Kümmernis ['kymɐrnɪs] *f* (**-;-se**) worry, trouble
kum′mervoll *adj* grief-stricken
Kumpan [kum'pan] *m* (**-s;-e**) companion; buddy
Kumpel ['kumpəl] *m* (**-s;-**) buddy, sidekick; (min) miner
kund [kʊnt] *adj* known
kündbar ['kyntbar] *adj* (*Vertrag*) terminable; (fin) redeemable
Kunde ['kundə] *m* (**-n;-n**) customer; **übler K.** (fig) tough customer || *f* (**-;**) news, information; lore
-kunde *f* *comb.fm.* –ology; –graphy; science of; guide to, study of
Kun′dendienst *m* customer service; warranty service
Kun′denkreis *m* clientele
kund′geben §80 *tr* make known, announce
Kundgebung ['kuntgebuŋ] *f* (**-;-en**) manifestation; (pol) rally
kundig ['kundɪç] *adj* well-informed; **k. sein** (*genit*) know
-kundig *comb.fm.* well versed in; able to
kündigen ['kyndɪgən] *tr* (*Vertrag*) give notice to terminate; (*Wohnung*) give notice to vacate; (*Stellung*) give notice of quitting; (*Kapital*) call in; (*Hypothek*) foreclose on; **j-n fristlos k.** (coll) sack s.o. || *intr* (*dat*) given notice to, release
Kün′digung *f* (**-;-en**) (*seitens des Arbeitnehmers*) resignation; (*seitens des Arbeitgebers*) notice (*of termination*); **mit monatlicher K.** subject to a month's notice
Kün′digungsfrist *f* period of notice
kund′machen *tr* make known, announce
Kund′machung *f* (**-;-en**) announcement
Kund′schaft *f* (**-;**) clientele, customer(s); (mil) reconnaissance
kundschaften ['kuntʃaftən] *intr* go on reconnaissance
Kund′schafter *m* (**-s;-**) scout, spy
kund′tun §154 *tr* make known, announce
kund′werden §159 *intr* (SEIN) become known
künftig ['kynftɪç] *adj* future, to come, next || *adv* in the future, from now on
künf′tighin′ *adv* from now on, hereafter

Kunst [kʊnst] *f* (-;=e) art; skill; **das ist keine K.** it's easy
Kunstbanause ['kʊnstbanaʊzə] *m* (-n; -n) philistine
Kunst'dünger *m* chemical fertilizer
Künstelei [kʏnstə'laɪ] *f* (-;-en) affectation
Kunst'faser *f* synthetic fiber
Kunst'fehler *m*—**ärztlicher K.** malpractice
kunst'fertig *adj* skillful, skilled
Kunst'flieger *m* stunt pilot
Kunst'flug *m* stunt flying
Kunst'freund –**in** §8 *mf* art lover; patron of the arts
Kunst'gegenstand *m* objet d'art
kunst'gerecht *adj* skillful; expert
Kunst'gewerbe *n* arts and crafts
Kunst'glied *n* artificial limb
Kunst'griff *m* trick
Kunst'händler –**in** §6 *mf* art dealer
Kunst'kenner –**in** §6 *mf* art connoisseur
Kunst'laufen *n* figure skating
Künstler –**in** ['kʏnstlər(ɪn)] §6 *mf* artist; performer
künstlerisch ['kʏnstlərɪʃ] *adj* artistic
künstlich ['kʏnstlɪç] *adj* artificial; (chem) synthetic
Kunst'liebhaber –**in** §6 *mf* art lover
kunst'los *adj* unaffected
Kunst'maler –**in** §6 *mf* painter, artist
Kunst'pause *f* pause for effect
kunst'reich *adj* ingenious
Kunst'reiter *m* equestrian
Kunst'seide *f* rayon
Kunst'springen *n* (sport) diving
Kunst'stoff *m* plastic material; synthetic material; (tex) synthetic fiber
Kunststoff– *comb.fm.* plastic; plastics
Kunst'stopfen *n* invisible mending
Kunst'stück *n* trick, feat
Kunst'tischler *m* cabinet maker
Kunstverständige ['kʊnstfer/tendɪgə] §5 *mf* art expert
kunst'voll *adj* elaborate, ornate
Kunst'werk *n* work of art
kunterbunt ['kʊntərbʊnt] *adj* chaotic
Kupfer ['kʊpfər] *n* (-s;) copper
kupfern ['kʊpfərn] *adj* copper
kupieren [kʊ'piːrən] *tr* (*Schwanz, Ohren*) cut off; (*Spielkarten*) cut; (*Fahrkarten*) punch
Kuppe ['kʊpə] *f* (-;-n) top, summit
Kuppel ['kʊpəl] *f* (-;-n) cupola
Kuppelei [kʊpə'laɪ] *f* (-;) procuring
kuppeln ['kʊpəln] *tr* couple, connect ‖ *intr* be a pimp; be a procuress; (aut) operate the clutch
Kuppler ['kʊplər] *m* (-s;-) pimp
Kupplerin ['kʊplərɪn] *f* (-;-nen) procuress
Kupplung ['kʊplʊŋ] *f* (-;-en) (aut) clutch; (rr) coupling
Kur [kuːr] *f* (-;-en) cure (*at a spa*); **j–n in die Kur nehmen** give s.o. a talking to
Kuratel [kʊra'tel] *f* (-;) guardianship; **j–n unter K. stellen** appoint a guardian for s.o.
Ku·rator [kʊ'rɑtər] *m* (-s;-ratoren [ra'torən]) (*e–s Museums*) curator; (educ) trustee; (jur) guardian

Kurato·rium [kʊra'torjʊm] *n* (-s;-rien [rjən]) (educ) board of trustees
Kurbel ['kʊrbəl] *f* (-;-n) crank, handle, winch
Kurbelei [kʊrbə'laɪ] *f* (-;-en) shooting a film; (aer) dogfight
Kur'belgehäuse *n* (aut) crankcase
kurbeln ['kʊrbəln] *tr* crank; (*Film*) shoot ‖ *intr* engage in a dogfight
Kur'belstange *f* (mach) connecting rod
Kur'belwelle *f* (mach) crankshaft
Kürbis ['kʏrbɪs] *m* (-ses;-se) pumpkin; (*Kopf*) (sl) bean
küren ['kyːrən] §165 & §109 *tr* elect
Kurfürst ['kʊrfʏrst] *m* (-en;-en) elector (*of the Holy Roman Empire*)
Kur'haus *n* spa; hotel
Kurie ['kʊrjə] *f* (-;-n) (eccl) curia
Kurier [kʊ'riːr] *m* (-s;-e) courier
kurieren [kʊ'riːrən] *tr* cure
kurios [kʊ'rjos] *adj* odd, curious
Kuriosität [kʊrjozɪ'tet] *f* (-;-en) quaintness; curio, curiosity
Kur'ort *m* health resort, spa
Kurpfuscher ['kʊrpfuʃər] *m* (-s;-) quack
Kurrentschrift [kʊ'rentʃrɪft] *f* cursive script
Kurs [kʊrs] *m* (-es;-e) (educ) course; (fin) rate of exchange; (fin) circulation; (naut) course;(st. exch.) price; **außer K. setzen** take out of circulation; **hoch im K. stehen** be at a premium; (fig) rate high; **zum Kurse von** at the rate of
Kurs'bericht *m* (st. exch.) market report
Kurs'buch *n* (rr) timetable
Kürschner ['kʏrʃnər] *m* (-s;-) furrier
Kurs'entwicklung *f* price trend
Kurs'gewinn *m* (st. exch.) gain
kursieren [kʊr'ziːrən] *intr* circulate
Kursive [kʊr'zivə] *f* (-;), **Kursivschrift** [kʊr'zifʃrɪft] *f* (-;) italics
Kurs'stand *m* (st. exch.) price level
Kur·sus ['kʊrzus] *m* (-;-se [zə]) (educ) course
Kurs'veränderung *f* (fin) change in exchange rates; (naut) change of course; (pol) change of policy; (st. exch.) price change
Kurs'wert *m* (st. exch.) market value
Kurve ['kʊrvə] *f* (-;-n) curve; **in die K. gehen** (aer) bank
kurz [kʊrts] *adj* (**kürzer** ['kʏrtsər]; **kürzeste** ['kʏrtsəstə] §9) short, brief; **auf das kürzeste** very briefly; **binnen kurzem** within a short time; **in kurzem** before long; **k. und gut in a word; seit kurzem** for the last few days or weeks; **über k. oder lang** sooner or later; **zu k. kommen** (coll) get the short end of it ‖ *adv* shortly; briefly; curtly
kurzatmig ['kʊrtsatmɪç] *adj* shortwinded; (*Pferd*) broken-winded
Kürze ['kʏrtsə] *f* (-;) shortness; brevity; **in K.** shortly; briefly
kürzen ['kʏrtsən] *tr* shorten; (*Gehalt*) cut; (math) reduce
kurzerhand' *adv* offhand
Kurz'fassung *f* abridged version
Kurz'film *m* (cin) short

kurzfristig ['kurtsfrɪstɪç] *adj* short-term
Kurz'geschichte *f* short story
kurzlebig ['kurtslebɪç] *adj* short-lived
kürzlich ['kʏrtslɪç] *adj* lately, recently
Kurz'meldung *f* news flash
Kurz'nachrichten *pl* news summary
kurz'schließen §76 *tr* short-circuit
Kurz'schluß *m* short circuit
Kurz'schlußbrücke *f* (elec) jumper
Kurz'schrift *f* shorthand
kurz'sichtig *adj* near-sighted; (fig) short-sighted
Kurz'streckenlauf *m* sprint
Kurz'streckenläufer –in §6 *mf* sprinter
kurzum' *adv* in short, in a word
Kür'zung *f* (–;–en) reduction; curtailment; (*e–s Buches*) abridgment
Kurz'waren *pl* sewing supplies
kurz'weg *adv* bluntly, flatly
Kurzweil ['kurtsvaɪl] *f* (–;) pastime
kurzweilig ['kurtsvaɪlɪç] *adj* amusing
kusch [kuʃ] *interj* lie down! (*to a dog*)
kuschen ['kuʃən] *ref* lie down; crouch ‖ *intr* lie down; crouch, cringe; (*Person*) knuckle under, submit
Kusine [ku'zinə] *f* (–;–n) female cousin
Kuß [kus] *m* (**Kusses; Küsse**) kiss; **kalter K.** popsicle

küssen ['kʏsən] *tr & intr* kiss
Kuß'hand *f*—j–m e–e **K. zuwerfen** throw s.o. a kiss; **mit K.** with pleasure
Küste ['kʏstə] *f* (–;–n) coast, shore
Kü'stenfahrer *m* coasting vessel
Kü'stenfischerei *f* inshore fishing
Kü'stengewässer *n* coastal waters
Kü'stenlinie *f* coastline, shoreline
kü'stennah *adj* offshore; coastal
Kü'stenschiffahrt *f* coastal shipping
Kü'stenstreife *f* shore patrol
Küster ['kʏstər] *m* (–s;–) sexton
Kustos ['kustɔs] *m* (–; **Kustoden** [kus-'todən]) custodian
Kutsche ['kutʃə] *f* (–;–n) coach
Kut'scher *m* (–s;–) coachman
kutschieren [ku'tʃirən] *intr* drive a coach ‖ *intr* (SEIN) ride in a coach
Kutte ['kutə] *f* (–;–n) (eccl) cowl
Kutteln ['kutəln] *pl* tripe
Kutter ['kutər] *m* (–s;–) (naut) cutter
Kuvert [ku'vert] *n* (–s;–s) & (–[e]s;–e) envelope; table setting
kuvertieren [kuver'tirən] *tr* put into an envelope
Kux [kuks] *m* (–es;–e) mining share
Kyklon [ky'klon] *m* (–s;–e) cyclone
Kyniker ['kynɪkər] *m* (–s;–) (philos) cynic

L

L, l [ɛl] *invar n* L, l
laben ['labən] *tr* refresh
Labial [la'bjal] *m* (–s;–e) labial
labil [la'bil] *adj* unstable
Labor [la'bor] *n* (–s;–s) (coll) lab
Laborant [labɔ'rant] (**in**)] §7 *mf* laboratory technician
Laborato·rium [labɔra'torjum] *n* (–s; **rien** [rjən]) laboratory
laborieren [labɔ'rirən] *intr* experiment; **l. an** (*dat*) suffer from
Labsal ['lapzal] *n* (–[e]s;–e) refreshment
La'bung *f* (–;–en) refreshment
Labyrinth [laby'rɪnt] *n* (–[e]s;–e) labyrinth
Lache ['laxə] *f* (–;–n) puddle, pool; laugh; **e–e gellende L. anschlagen** break out in laughter
lächeln ['leçəln] *intr* (über *acc*) smile (at) ‖ **Lächeln** *n* (–s;) smile; **höhnisches L.** sneer
lachen ['laxən] *intr* laugh; **daß ich nicht lache!** don't make me laugh! ‖ **Lachen** *n* (–s;) laugh, laughter; **du hast gut L.!** you can laugh!
lächerlich ['leçərlɪç] *adj* ridiculous; **l. machen** ridicule; **sich l. machen** make a fool of oneself
lachhaft ['laxhaft] *adj* ridiculous
Lachkrampf ['laxkrampf] *m* fit of laughter
Lachs [laks] *m* (–es;–e) salmon
Lachsalve ['laxzalvə] *f* (–;–n) peal of laughter

Lachs'schinken *m* raw, lightly smoked ham
Lack [lak] *m* (–[e]s;–e) lacquer, varnish
Lackel ['lakəl] *m* (–s;–) (coll) dope
lackieren [la'kirən] *tr* lacquer, varnish; (*Autos*) paint
Lack'leder *n* patent leather
Lackmuspapier ['lakmuspapir] *n* litmus paper
Lack'schuhe *pl* patent-leather shoes
Lade ['ladə] *f* (–;–n) box, case; (*Schublade*) drawer
La'dearbeiter *m* loader
La'debaum *m* derrick
La'defähigkeit *f* loading capacity
La'dehemmung *f* jamming (*of a gun*); **L. haben** jam
La'deklappe *f* tailgate
La'delüke *f* (naut) hatch
laden ['ladən] §103 *tr* load; (*Gast*) invite; (elec) charge; (jur) summon; **geladen sein** (coll) be burned up ‖ **Laden** *m* (–s;⁼) store, shop; (*Fenster-*) shutter; **den L. schmeißen** pull it off, lick it
La'dendieb *m*, **La'dendiebin** *f* shoplifter
La'dendiebstahl *m* shoplifting
La'denhüter *m* drug on the market
La'deninhaber –in §6 *mf* shopkeeper
La'denkasse *f* till
Lä'denmädchen *n* salesgirl
La'denpreis *m* retail price
La'denschluß *m* closing time

La'denschwengel *m* (pej) stupid shop clerk
La'dentisch *m* counter
La'derampe *f* loading platform
La'deschein *m* bill of lading
La'destock *m* ramrod
La'destreifen *m* cartridge clip
La'dung *f* (-;-en) loading; load; (*Güter*) freight; (elec) charge; (jur) summons; (mil) charge; (naut) cargo
Lafette [la'fɛtə] *f* (-;-n) gun mount
Laffe ['lafə] *m* (-n;-n) jazzy dresser
lag [lak] *pret* of **liegen**
Lage ['lagə] *f* (-;-n) site, location; situation; (*Zustand*) condition, state; (*Haltung*) posture; (*Schicht*) layer, deposit; (*Salve*) volley; (*Bier*) round; (bb) quire; (mil) position; (mus) pitch; **mißliche L.** predicament; **versetzen Sie sich in meine L.** put yourself in my position
Lager ['lagər] *n* (-s;-) bed; (*e-s Wildes*) lair; (*Stapelplatz*) dump; (*Partei*) side, camp; (*von Waffen*) cache; (*Vorrat*) stock; (*Warenlager*) stockroom; (geol) stratum, vein; (mach) bearing; (mil) camp; **auf L.** in stock; (fig) up one's sleeve; **ein L. halten von** keep stock of
La'geraufnahme *f* inventory
La'gerbier *n* lager beer
La'gerfähigkeit *f* shelf life
La'gerfeuer *n* campfire
La'gergebühr *f* storage charges
La'gerhalter *m* stock clerk
La'gerhaus *n* warehouse
Lagerist –in [lagə'rɪst(ɪn)] §7 *mf* warehouse clerk
La'gerleben *n* camp life
lagern ['lagərn] *tr* lay down; (*Waren*) stock, store; (*altern*) season; (mach) mount on bearings || *ref* lie down, rest || *intr* lie down, rest; (*Waren*) be stored; (*Wein*) season; (geol) be deposited; (mil) camp
La'gerort *m*, **La'gerplatz** *m* resting place; (*Stapelplatz*) dump; (mil) camp site
La'gerraum *m* storeroom, stockroom
La'gerstand *m* stock on hand, inventory
La'gerstätte *f*, **La'gerstelle** *f* resting place; (geol) deposit; (mil) camp site
La'gerung *f* (-;-en) storage; (*Alterung*) seasoning; (geol) stratification
La'gervorrat *m* stock, supply
Lagune [la'gunə] *f* (-;-n) lagoon
lahm [lam] *adj* lame; paralyzed || **Lahme** §5 *mf* paralytic
lahmen ['lamən] *intr* be lame, limp
lähmen ['lɛmən] *tr* paralyze; (*Verkehr*) tie up; (fig) cripple
lahm'legen *tr* cripple, paralyze; (mil) neutralize
Läh'mung *f* (-;-en) paralysis
Laib [laɪp] *m* (-[e]s;-e) loaf
Laich [laɪç] *m* (-[e]s;-e) spawn
laichen ['laɪçən] *intr* spawn
Laie ['laɪ·ə] *m* (-n;-n) layman; **Laien** laity
Lai'enbruder *m* lay brother
lai'enhaft *adj* layman's
Lakai [la'kaɪ] *m* (-en;-en) lackey

Lake ['lakə] *f* (-;-n) brine, pickle
Laken ['lakən] *n* (-s;-) sheet
lakonisch [la'konɪʃ] *adj* laconic
Lakritze [la'krɪtsə] *f* (-;-n) licorice
Lakune [la'kunə] *f* (-;-n) lacuna
lallen ['lalən] *tr & intr* stammer
lamellenförmig [la'mɛlənfœrmɪç] *adj* laminate
lamentieren [lamen'tirən] *intr* wail
Lametta [la'mɛta] *n* (-s;) tinsel
Lamm [lam] *n* (-[e]s;⸚er) lamb
Lamm'braten *m* roast lamb
Lämmerwolke ['lɛmərvɔlkə] *f* cirrus
Lamm'fleisch *n* (culin) lamb
lamm'fromm' *adj* meek as a lamb
Lampe ['lampə] *f* (-;-n) lamp; light
Lam'penfieber *n* stage fright
Lam'penschirm *m* lamp shade
Lampion [lam'pjõ] *m* (-s;-s) Chinese lantern
lancieren [lã'sirən] *tr* launch, promote; (*Kandidaten*) (pol) groom
Land [lant] *n* (-[e]s;⸚er & -e) land; (*Ackerboden*) ground, soil; (*Staat*) country; (*Provinz*) state; (*Gegensatz: Stadt*) country; **ans L.** ashore; **auf dem Lande** in the country; **aufs L.** into the country; **aus aller Herren Ländern** from everywhere; **außer Landes gehen** go abroad; **zu Lande** by land
Land'arbeiter *m* farm hand
Land'armee *f* land forces
Land'bau *m* farming, agriculture
Land'besitz *m* landed property
Land'besitzer –in §6 *mf* landowner
Landebahn ['landəban] *f* runway
Landedeck ['landədɛk] *n* flight deck
Land'edel•mann *m* (-es;-leute) country gentleman
Landefeuer ['landəfɔɪ·ər] *n* runway lights
land'einwärts *adv* inland
Landekopf ['landəkɔpf] *m* beachhead
landen ['landən] *tr & intr* (SEIN) land
Land'enge *f* isthmus, neck of land
Landeplatz ['landəplats] *m* wharf; (aer) landing field
Länderei [lɛndə'raɪ] *f* (-;-en) or **Ländereien** *pl* lands, estates
Länderkunde ['lɛndərkundə] *f* geography
Landes– [landəs] *comb.fm.* national, native, of the land
Lan'desaufnahme *f* land survey
Lan'desbank *f* national bank
Lan'desbeschreibung *f* topography
lan'deseigen *adj* state-owned
Lan'deserzeugnis *n* domestic product
Lan'desfarben *pl* national colors
Lan'desfürst *m* sovereign
Lan'desgesetz *n* law of the land
Lan'desherr *m* sovereign
Lan'desherrschaft *f*, **Lan'deshoheit** *f* sovereignty
Lan'dessprache *f* vernacular
Lan'destracht *f* national costume
Lan'destrauer *f* public mourning
lan'desüblich *adj* customary
Lan'desvater *m* sovereign
Lan'desverrat *m* high treason
Lan'desverräter –in §6 *mf* traitor
Lan'desverteidigung *f* national defense

Land'flucht f rural exodus
land'flüchtig adj exiled, fugitive
Land'friedensbruch m disturbance of the peace
Land'gericht n district court, superior court
Land'gewinnung f land reclamation
Land'gut n country estate
Land'haus n country house
Land'jäger m rural policeman; (culin) sausage
Land'junker m country squire
Land'karte f map
Land'kreis m rural district
land'läufig adj customary
Ländler ['lɛntlər] m (-s;-) waltz
Land'leute pl country folk
ländlich ['lɛntlɪç] adj rural, rustic
Land'luft f country air
Land'macht f land forces
Land'mann m (-[e]s;-leute) farmer
Land'marke f landmark (for travelers and sailors)
Land'maschinen pl farm machinery
Land'messer m surveyor
Land'partie f outing, picnic
Land'plage f nation-wide plague; (coll) big nuisance
Land'rat m regional governor
Land'ratte f (fig) landlubber
Land'recht n common law
Land'regen m steady rain
Land'rücken m ridge
Land'schaft f (-;-en) landscape, scenery; (Bezirk) district, region
land'schaftlich adj scenic; regional
Landser ['lantsər] m (-s;-) G.I.
Lands'knecht m mercenary
Lands'mann m (-[e]s;-leute) fellow countryman
Land'spitze f promontory
Land'straße f highway
Land'streicher m (-s;-) tramp, hobo
Land'strich m tract of land
Land'sturm m home guard
Land'tag m state assembly
landumschlossen ['lantʊmʃlɔsən] adj landlocked
Lan'dung f (-;-en) landing
Lan'dungsboot n landing craft
Lan'dungsbrücke f jetty, pier
Lan'dungsgestell n landing gear
Lan'dungssteg m gangplank
Land'vermessung f surveying
Land'volk n country folk
Land'weg m overland route
Land'wehr f militia, home guard
Land'wirt m farmer
Land'wirtschaft f agriculture; **L. betreiben** farm
land'wirtschaftlich adj farm, agricultural
Land'zunge f spit of land
lang [laŋ] adj (länger ['lɛŋər]; längste ['lɛŋstə] §9) long; (Person) tall || adv—**die ganze Woche l.** all week; **e-e Stunde l.** for an hour
langatmig ['laŋatmɪç] adj long-winded
lang'beinig adj long-legged
lange ['laŋə] adv long, a long time; **es ist noch l. nicht fertig** it is far from ready; **schon l. her** long ago; **schon l. her, daß** a long time since;

so l. bis until; **so l. wie** as long as; **wie l.?** how long?
Länge ['lɛŋə] f (-;-n) length; long syllable; (geog) longitude; (pros) quantity; **auf die L. in** the long run; **der L. nach** lengthwise; **in die L. ziehen** drag out
langen ['laŋən] tr reach, hand; **j-m eine l.** (coll) give s.o. a smack || intr be enough; **l. nach** reach for || impers—**es langt mir I have enough; jetzt langt's mir aber! I've had it!**
Län'gengrad m degree of longitude
Län'genkreis m meridian
Län'genmaß n linear measure
Lan'geweile f boredom; **sich** [dat] **die L. vertreiben** (coll) kill time
Lang'finger m pickpocket
langfingerig ['laŋfɪŋərɪç] adj (fig) thievish
langfristig ['laŋfrɪstɪç] adj long-term
lang'jährig adj long-standing
Lang'lauf m crosscountry skiing
langlebig ['laŋlebɪç] adj long-lived
Lang'lebigkeit f (-;) longevity
lang'legen ref lie down, stretch out
länglich ['lɛŋlɪç] adj oblong
läng'lichrund adj oval, elliptical
Lang'mut f patience
lang'mütig adj patient
Lang'mütigkeit f patience
längs [lɛŋs] prep (genit or dat) along
langsam ['laŋzam] adj slow
Lang'spielplatte f long-playing record
längst [lɛŋst] adv long since, long ago
längstens ['lɛŋstəns] adv at the latest; (höchstens) at the most
Langstrecken– comb.fm. long-range; (sport) long-distance
langweilen ['laŋvaɪlən] tr bore || ref feel bored
Lang'weiler m (-s;-) slowpoke
langweilig ['laŋvaɪlɪç] adj boring
langwierig ['laŋvirɪç] adj lengthy
Lanolin [lano'lin] n (-s) lanolin
Lanze ['lantsə] f (-;-n) lance, spear
Lan'zenstechen n (-s;) jousting
Lanzette [lan'tsetə] f (-;-n) lancet
Lappalie [la'paljə] f (-;-n) trifle
Lappen ['lapən] m (-s;-) rag; (anat) lobe
läppisch ['lɛpɪʃ] adj silly, trifling
Lappland ['laplant] n (-s;) Lapland
Lärche ['lɛrçə] f (-;-n) (bot) larch
Lärm [lɛrm] m (-[e]s;) noise; **L. schlagen** (fig) make a fuss
lärmen ['lɛrmən] intr make noise
lär'mend adj noisy
Larve ['larfə] f (-;-n) mask; larva
las [las] pret of lesen
lasch [laʃ] adj limp; (Speise) insipid
Lasche ['laʃə] f (-;-n) (Klappe) flap; (Schuh–) tongue; (rr) fishplate
lasieren [la'zirən] tr glaze
lassen ['lasən] §104 tr let; (erlauben) allow; (bewirken) have, make; leave (behind, undone, open, etc.); **den Film entwickeln l.** have the film developed; **etw fallen l.** drop s.th.; **ich kann es nicht l.** I can't help it; **j-n warten l.** keep s.o. waiting; **kommen l.** send for; **laß den Lärm!** stop

the noise!; **laß es!** cut it out!; **laßt uns gehen** let us go; **sein Leben l.** lose one's life; **sein Leben l. für** sacrifice one's life for || *ref*—**das läßt sich denken** I can imagine; **das läßt sich hören!** now you're talking!; **es läßt sich nicht beschreiben** it defies description; **es läßt sich nicht leugnen, daß** it cannot be denied that; **sich** [*dat*] **Zeit l.** take one's time

lässig ['lɛsɪç] *adj* (*faul*) lazy; (*träge*) sluggish; (*nachlässig*) remiss

Läs'sigkeit *f* (–;) laziness; negligence

läßlich ['lɛslɪç] *adj* venial

Last [last] *f* (–;–en) load, weight; (*Bürde*) burden; (*Hypotek*) encumbrance; (aer, naut) cargo, freight; **j–m etw zur L.** legen blame s.o. for s.th.; **L. der Beweise** weight of evidence; **ruhende L.** dead weight; **zur L. fallen** (*dat*) become a burden for

Last'auto *n* truck

lasten ['lastən] *intr* (**auf** *dat*) weigh (on)

la'stenfrei *adj* unencumbered

La'stensegler *m* transport glider

Laster ['lastər] *m* (–s;–) (coll) truck || *n* (–s;–) vice

Lästerer –in ['lɛstərər(ɪn)] §6 *mf* slanderer; blasphemer

la'sterhaft *adj* vicious

La'sterleben *n* life of vice

lästerlich ['lɛstərlɪç] *adj* slanderous; blasphemous

Lästermaul ['lɛstərmaul] *n* scandalmonger

lästern ['lɛstərn] *tr* slander; blaspheme

Lä'sterung *f* (–;–en) slander; blasphemy

lästig ['lɛstɪç] *adj* troublesome; **j–m l. fallen** bother s.o.

Last'kahn *m* barge

Last'kraftwagen *m* truck

Last'schrift *f* (acct) debit

Last'tier *n* beast of burden

Last'träger *m* porter

Last'wagen *m* truck

Last'zug *m* tractor-trailer (*consisting of several trailers*)

Lasur [la'zur] *f* (–;) glaze

Latein [la'tain] *n* (–s;) Latin

lateinisch [la'tainiʃ] *adj* Latin

Laterne [la'tɛrnə] *f* (–;–n) lantern; lamp

Latrine [la'trinə] *f* (–;–n) latrine

Latri'nenparole *f* scuttlebut

Latsche ['lɑt/ə] *f* (–;–n) (coll) slipper || ['lat/ə] *f* (–;–n) (bot) dwarf pine

latschen ['lɑt/ən] *intr* (SEIN) shuffle along

Latte ['latə] *f* (–;–n) lath

Lat'tenkiste *f* crate

Lat'tenzaun *m* picket fence

Lattich ['latɪç] *m* (–[e]s;–e) lettuce

Latz [lats] *m* (–es;ᵘe) bib; (*Klappe*) flap; (*Schürzchen*) pinafore

Lätzchen ['lɛtsçən] *n* (–s;–) bib

lau [lau] *adj* lukewarm; (*Wetter*) mild; (fig) half-hearted

Laub [laup] *n* (–[e]s;) foliage

Laub'baum *m* deciduous tree

Laube ['laubə] *f* (–;–n) arbor; (*Säulen-*gang) portico; (*Bogengang*) arcade; (theat) box

Lau'bengang *m* arcade

Laub'säge *f* fret saw

Laub'sägearbeit *f* fretwork

Laub'werk *n* foliage

Lauer ['lau·ər] *f* (–;) ambush; **auf der L. liegen** lie in wait

lauern ['lau·ərn] *intr* lurk; **l. auf** (*acc*) lie in wait for, watch for

lau'ernd *adj* (*Blick*) wary; (*Gefahr*) lurking

Lauf [lauf] *m* (–[e]s;ᵘe) running; run; (*e–s Flusses*) course; (*Strömung*) current; (*Wettlauf*) race; (*e–s Gewehrs*) barrel; (astr) path, orbit; **den Dingen freien L. lassen** let things take their course; **im Laufe der Zeit** in the course of time; **im vollen Laufe** at full speed

Lauf'bahn *f* career; (astr) orbit; (sport) lane

Lauf'bursche *m* errand boy; office boy

laufen ['laufən] §105 *intr* (SEIN) run; (*zu Fuß gehen*) walk; (*leck sein*) leak; (*Zeit*) pass; **die Dinge l. lassen** let things slide; **j–n l. lassen** let s.o. go; (*straflos*) let s.o. off

lau'fend *adj* (*ständig*) steady; (*Jahr, Preis*) current; (*Nummern*) consecutive; (*Wartung, Geschäft*) routine; (*Meter, usw.*) running; **auf dem laufenden** up to date; **laufendes Band** conveyor belt; assembly line

Läufer ['lɔifər] *m* (–s;–) runner; (*Teppich*) runner; (chess) bishop; (fb) halfback; (mach) rotor; (mus) run

Lauferei [laufə'rai] *f* (–;–en) running around

Lauf'feuer *n* (–s) wildfire

Lauf'fläche *f* tread (*on tire*)

Lauf'gewicht *n* sliding weight

Lauf'gitter *n* playpen

Lauf'graben *m* trench

läufig ['lɔifɪç] *adj* in heat

Läu'figkeit *f* (–;) heat

Lauf'junge *m* errand boy; office boy

Lauf'kran *m* (mach) traveling crane

Lauf'kunde *m* chance customer

Lauf'masche *f* run (*in stocking*)

lauf'maschenfrei *adj* runproof

Lauf'paß *m* (coll) walking papers; (coll) brush-off

Lauf'planke *f* gangplank

Lauf'rad *n* (*e–r Turbine*) rotor; (aer) landing wheel

Lauf'schritt *m* double-quick time

Lauf'steg *m* footbridge

Laufställchen ['lauf/tɛlçən] *n* (–s;–) playpen

Lauf'zeit *f* rutting season; (*e–s Vertrags*) term; (cin) running time; (mach) (service) life

Lauge ['laugə] *f* (–;–n) lye; (*Salzlauge*) brine; (*Seifenlauge*) suds

Lau'gensalz *n* alkali

lau'gensalzig *adj* alkaline

Laune ['launə] *f* (–;–n) mood, humor; (*Grille*) whim

lau'nenhaft *adj* capricious

launig ['launɪç] *adj* humorous, witty

lau'nisch *adj* moody

Laus [laus] *f* (–;ᵘe) louse

Laus'bub *m* rascal

lauschen ['lauʃən] *intr* listen; eavesdrop; **l. auf** (*acc*) listen to

Lau'scher –in §6 *mf* eavesdropper

lauschig ['lauʃɪç] *adj* cosy, peaceful

Lau'sebengel *m*, **Lau'sejunge** *m*, **Lau'sekerl** *m* (coll) rascal, brat

lausen ['lauzən] *tr* pick lice from; **ich denke, mich laust der Affe** (coll) I couldn't believe my eyes

lausig ['lauzɪç] *adj* lousy

laut [laut] *adj* loud; (*lärmend*) noisy; **l. werden** become public; **l. lassen** divulge || *prep* (*genit & dat*) according to; (com) as per; **l. Bericht** according to the report || **Laut** *m* (-[e]s;-e) sound

Laute ['lautə] *f* (-;-n) lute

lauten ['lautən] *intr* sound; (*Worte*) read, go, say; **das Urteil lautet auf Tod** the sentence is death

läuten ['lɔɪtən] *tr & intr* ring, toll || *impers*—**es läutet** the bell is ringing || **Läuten** *n* (-s;) toll

lauter ['lautər] *adj* pure; (*aufrecht*) sincere || *invar adj* (*nichts als*) nothing but

Lau'terkeit *f* (-;) purity; sincerity

läutern ['lɔɪtərn] *tr* purify; (*Metall, Zucker*) refine; (*veredeln*) ennoble

Laut'gesetz *n* phonetic law

Laut'lehre *f* phonetics, phonology

laut'lich *adj* phonetic

laut'los *adj* soundless

Laut'malerei *f* onomatopoeia

Laut'schrift *f* phonetic spelling

Laut'sprecher *m* loudspeaker

Laut'sprecheranlage *f* public address system

Laut'sprecherwagen *m* sound truck

Laut'stärke *f* volume

Laut'stärkeregler *m* volume control

Laut'system *n* phonetic system

Laut'zeichen *n* phonetic symbol

lau'warm *adj* lukewarm

Lava ['lava] *f* (-;) lava

Lavendel [la'vɛndəl] *m* (-s;) (bot) lavender

laven'delfarben *adj* lavender

lavieren [la'virən] *intr* (fig) maneuver; (naut) tack

Lawine [la'vinə] *f* (-;-n) avalanche

lax [laks] *adj* lax

Lax'heit *f* (-;) laxity

Laxiermittel [la'ksirmɪtəl] *n* laxative

Layout ['le·aut] *n* (-s;-s) layout

Lazarett [latsa'rɛt] *n* (-[e]s;-e) (mil) hospital

Lebedame ['lebədamə] *f* woman of leisure

Lebehoch [lebə'hox] *n* (-s;-s) cheer; toast; **ein dreimaliges L.** three cheers

Lebemann ['lebəman] *m* playboy

leben ['lebən] *tr & intr* live || **Leben** *n* (-s;-) life; existence; **am L. bleiben** survive; **am L. erhalten** keep alive; **ins L. rufen** bring into being; **sein L. lang** all his life; **ums L. kommen** lose one's life

lebendig [le'bɛndɪç] *adj* living, alive; (*lebhaft*) lively; (*Darstellung*) vivid

Le'bensalter *n* age, period of life

Le'bensanschauung *f* outlook on life

Le'bensart *f* manners

Le'bensaufgabe *f* mission in life

Le'bensbaum *m* (bot) arbor vitae

Le'bensbedingungen *pl* living conditions

Le'bensbeschreibung *f* biography

Le'bensdauer *f* life span

Le'benserwartung *f* life expectancy

le'bensfähig *adj* viable

Le'bensfrage *f* vital question

Le'bensgefahr *f* mortal danger

le'bensgefährlich *adj* perilous

Le'bensgefährte *m*, **Le'bensgefährtin** *f* life companion, spouse

le'bensgroß *adj* life-size

Le'benshaltung *f* standard of living

Le'benshaltungskosten *pl* cost of living

Le'bensinteressen *pl* vital interests

Le'benskraft *f* vitality

Le'benskünstler *m*—**er ist ein L.** nothing can get him down

lebenslänglich ['lebənslɛŋlɪç] *adj* life

Le'benslauf *m* curriculum vitae

Le'bensmittel *pl* groceries

Le'bensmittelgeschäft *n* grocery store

Le'bensmittelkarte *f* food ration card

Le'bensmittellieferant *m* caterer

le'bensmüde *adj* weary of life

le'bensnotwendig *adj* vital, essential

Le'bensprozeß *m* vital function

Le'bensstandard *m* standard of living

Le'bensstellung *f* lifetime job; tenure

Le'bensstil *m* life style

Le'bensunterhalt *m* livelihood

le'bensuntüchtig *adj* impractical

Le'bensversicherung *f* life insurance

Le'benswandel *m* conduct; life

Le'bensweise *f* way of life

Le'bensweisheit *f* worldly wisdom

le'benswichtig *adj* vital, essential

Le'benszeichen *n* sign of life

Le'benszeit *f* lifetime; **auf L.** for life

Leber ['lebər] *f* (-;-n) liver; **frei von der L. weg reden** speak frankly

Le'berfleck *m* mole

Leberkäs ['lebərkes] *m* (-es;) meat loaf (*made with liver*)

Le'bertran *m* cod-liver oil

Lebewesen ['lebəvezən] *n* living being

Lebewohl [lebə'vol] *n* (-[e]s;-e) farewell

lebhaft ['lephaft] *adj* lively; full of life; (*Farbe*) bright; (*Straße*) busy; (*Börse*) brisk; (*Interesse*) keen

Lebkuchen ['lepkuxən] *m* gingerbread

leblos ['leplos] *adj* lifeless

Lebtag ['leptak] *m*—**mein L.** in all my life

Lebzeiten ['leptsaɪtən] *pl*—**zu meinen L.** in my lifetime

lechzen ['lɛçtsən] *intr* (**nach**) thirst (for)

leck [lɛk] *adj* leaky || **Leck** *n* (-[e]s;-e) leak; **ein L. bekommen** spring a leak

lecken ['lɛkən] *tr* lick || *intr* leak; (naut) have sprung a leak

lecker ['lɛkər] *adj* dainty; (*köstlich*) delicious

Leckerbissen (**Lek'kerbissen**) *m* delicacy, dainty

Leckerei [lɛkə'raɪ] *f* (-;-en) daintiness; sweets

leckerhaft (**lek'kerhaft**) *adj* dainty

Leckermaul (Lek′kermaul) *n*—**ein L. sein** have a sweet tooth
Leder [′ledər] *n* (-s;) leather
ledern [′ledərn] *adj* leather; (fig) dull, boring
ledig [′ledɪç] *adj* single; (*Kind*) illegitimate; **l.** (*genit*) free of; **lediger Stand** single state; celibacy
le′diglich *adv* merely, only
leer [ler] *adj* empty, void; (fig) vain ||
Leere *f* (-;) emptiness, void; vacuum || *n*—**der Schlag ging ins L.** the blow missed; **ins L.** starren stare into space
leeren [′lerən] *tr* empty
Leer′gut *n* empties (*bottles, cases*)
Leer′lauf *m* (aut) idling, idle; (*Gang*) (aut) neutral
leer′laufen §105 *intr* (SEIN) idle
leer′stehend *adj* unoccupied, vacant
Leer′taste *f* (typ) space bar
legal [le′gɑl] *adj* legal
legalisieren [legali′zirən] *tr* legalize
Legat [le′gɑt] *m* (-en;-en) legate || *n* (-[e]s;-e) legacy, bequest
legen [′legən] *tr* lay, put; **auf die Kette l.** chain, tie up; **j–m ans Herz l.** recommend warmly to s.o.; **Nachdruck l. auf** (*acc*) emphasize; **Wert l. auf** (*acc*) attach importance to || *ref* lie down; go to bed; (*Wind*) die down; **die Krankheit hat sich ihm auf die Lungen gelegt** his sickness affected his lungs
legendär [legen′der] *adj* legendary
Legende [le′gendə] *f* (-;-n) legend
legieren [le′girən] *tr* alloy
Legie′rung *f* (-;-en) alloy
Legion [le′gjon] *f* (-;-en) legion
Legionär [legjo′ner] *m* (-s;-e) legionnaire, legionary
legislativ [legɪsla′tif] *adj* legislative ||
Legislative [legɪsla′tivə] *f* (-;-n) legislature
Legis·lator [legɪs′lɑtor] *m* (-s;-latoren [la′torən]) legislator
Legislatur [legɪsla′tur] *f* (-;-en) legislature
legitim [legi′tim] *adj* legitimate
Legitimation [legɪtɪma′tsjon] *f* (-;-en) proof of identity
legitimieren [legɪtɪ′mirən] *tr* legitimize; (*berechtigen*) authorize || *ref* prove one's identity
Lehen [′le·ən] *n* (-s;-) (hist) fief
Le′hensherr *m* liege lord
Le′hens·mann *m* (-[e]s;-leute) vassal
Lehm [lem] *m* (-[e]s;-e) clay, loam
lehmig [′lemɪç] *adj* clayey, loamy
Lehne [′lenə] *f* (-;-n) support; (*e–s Stuhls*) arm, back; (*Abhang*) slope
lehnen [′lenən] *tr, ref & intr* lean
Lehnsessel [′lenzesəl] *m*, **Lehnstuhl** [′len/tul] *m* armchair, easy chair
Lehn′wort [′lenvɔrt] *n* (-[e]s;-̈er) loan word
Lehramt [′leramt] *n* teaching profession; professorship
Lehranstalt [′leran/talt] *f* educational institution
Lehrbrief [′lerbrif] *m* apprentice's diploma
Lehrbube [′lerbubə] *m* apprentice

Lehrbuch [′lerbux] *n* textbook
Lehrbursche [′lerbur/ə] *m* apprentice
Lehre [′lerə] *f* (-;-n) doctrine, teaching; (*Wissenschaft*) science; (*Theorie*) theory; (*Unterweisung*) instruction; (*Warnung*) lesson; (*e–r Fabel*) moral; (*Richtschnur*) rule, precept; (*e–s Lehrlings*) apprenticeship; (tech) gauge; **in der L. sein** be serving one's apprenticeship
lehren [′lerən] *tr* teach, instruct
Lehrer –in [′lerər(ɪn)] §6 *mf* teacher
Leh′rerbildungsanstalt *f* teacher's college
Leh′rerkollegium *n* teaching staff
Lehrfach [′lerfax] *n* subject
Lehrfilm [′lerfɪlm] *m* educational film
Lehrgang [′lergaŋ] *m* (educ) course
Lehrgedicht [′lergədɪçt] *n* didactic poem
Lehrgegenstand [′lergegən/tant] *m* (educ) subject
Lehrgeld [′lergelt] *n*—**L. zahlen** (fig) learn the hard way
lehrhaft [′lerhaft] *adj* didactic
Lehrjunge [′lerjuŋə] *m* apprentice
Lehrkörper [′lerkørpər] *m* teaching staff; faculty (*of a university*)
Lehrling [′lerlɪŋ] *m* (-s;-e) apprentice
Lehrmädchen [′lermetçən] *n* girl apprentice
Lehrmeister [′lermaɪstər] *m* master, teacher, instructor
Lehrmittel [′lermɪtəl] *n* teaching aid
Lehrplan [′lerplan] *m* curriculum
lehrreich [′lerraɪç] *adj* instructive
Lehrsaal [′lerzal] *m* lecture hall
Lehrsatz [′lerzats] *m* (eccl) dogma; (math) theorem
Lehrspruch [′ler/prux] *m* maxim
Lehrstelle [′ler/telə] *f* position as an apprentice
Lehrstoff [′ler/tɔf] *m* subject matter
Lehrstuhl [′ler/tul] *m* (educ) chair
Lehrstunde [′ler/tundə] *f* lesson
Lehrzeit [′lertsaɪt] *f* apprenticeship
Leib [laɪp] *m* (-[e]s;-er) body; (*Bauch*) belly, abdomen; (*Taille*) waist; (*Mutterleib*) womb; **am ganzen L.** zittern tremble all over; **bleib mir nur damit vom Leibe!** (coll) don't bother me with that: **e–n harten L. haben** be constipated; **gesegneten Leibes** with child; **L. und Leben** life and limb; **mit L. und Seele** through and through; **sich** [*dat*] **j–n vom Leibe halten** keep s.o. at arm's length; **zu Leibe gehen** (*dat*) tackle (*s.th.*), attack (*s.o.*)
Leib′arzt *m* personal physician
Leib′binde *f* sash
Leibchen [′laɪpçən] *n* (-s;-) bodice; vest
leib′eigen *adj* in bondage || **Leibeigene** §5 *mf* serf
Leib′eigenschaft *f* (-;) serfdom, bondage
Lei′besbeschaffenheit *f* (-;-en) constitution
Lei′beserbe *m* (-n;-n) offspring
Lei′beserziehung *f* physical education
Lei′besfrucht *f* fetus
Lei′beskräfte *pl*—**aus Leibeskräften**

schreien scream at the top of one's lungs
Lei'besübungen *pl* physical education
Lei'besvisitation *f* body search
Leib'garde *f* bodyguard
Leibgardist ['laɪpgardɪst] *m* (**-en;-en**) bodyguard
Leib'gericht *n* favorite dish
leibhaft(ig) ['laɪphaft(ɪç)] *adj* incarnate, real
leib'lich *adj* bodily, corporal; **leiblicher Vetter** first cousin; **sein leiblicher Sohn** his own son
Leib'rente *f* annuity for life
Leib'schmerzen *pl*, **Leib'schneiden** *n* abdominal pains
Leibstandarte ['laɪpʃtandartə] *f* (**-;-n**) (hist) SS bodyguard
Leib'wache *f* bodyguard
Leib'wäsche *f* underwear
Leiche ['laɪçə] *f* (**-;-n**) corpse, body; carcass; (dial) funeral
Leichenbegängnis ['laɪçənbəgeŋnɪs] *n* (**-ses;-se**) funeral, interment
Leichenbeschauer ['laɪçənbəʃau·ər] *m* (**-s;-**) coroner
Leichenbestatter ['laɪçənbəʃtatər] *m* (**-s;-**) undertaker
Lei'chenbittermiene *f* woe-begone look
Leichenfledderer ['laɪçənfledərər] *m* (**-s;-**) body stripper
Lei'chengift *n* ptomaine poison
lei'chenhaft *adj* corpse-like
Lei'chenhalle *f* mortuary
Lei'chenöffnung *f* autopsy
Lei'chenräuber *m* body snatcher
Lei'chenrede *f* eulogy
Lei'chenschau *f* post mortem
Lei'chenschauhaus *m* morgue
Lei'chenstarre *f* rigor mortis
Lei'chenträger *m* pallbearer
Lei'chentuch *n* shroud
Lei'chenverbrennung *f* cremation
Lei'chenwagen *m* hearse
Lei'chenzug *m* funeral cortege
Leichnam ['laɪçnam] *m* (**-[e]s;-e**) corpse
leicht [laɪçt] *adj* light; (*nicht schwierig*) easy; (*gering*) slight; **leichten Herzens** light-heartedly
Leicht'atletik *f* track and field
Leicht'bauweise *f* lightweight construction
Leicht'benzin *n* cleaning fluid
leichtbeschwingt ['laɪçtbəʃvɪŋt] *adj* gay
leicht'blütig *adj* light-hearted
leicht'entzündlich *adj* highly flammable
Leichter ['laɪçtər] *m* (**-s;-**) (naut) lighter
leicht'fertig *adj* frivolous, flippant; careless
leicht'flüchtig *adj* highly volatile
leicht'flüssig *adj* thin
Leicht'gewicht *n* lightweight division
Leichtgewichtler ['laɪçtgəvɪçtlər] *m* (**-s;-**) lightweight boxer
leicht'gläubig *adj* gullible
leicht'hin' *adv* lightly, casually
Leich'tigkeit *f* (**-;**) ease
leichtlebig ['laɪçtlebɪç] *adj* easygoing
Leicht'sinn *m* frivolity, irresponsibility;

(*Sorglosigkeit*) carelessness; (*Unbedachtsamkeit*) imprudence
leicht'sinnig *adj* frivolous, irresponsible
leicht'verdaulich *adj* easy to digest
leicht'verderblich *adj* perishable
leid [laɪt] *adj—er* **tut mir l. I** feel sorry for him; **es tut mir l., daß I** am sorry that; **es ist** (or **tut**) **mir l. um** I feel sorry for, I regret; **ich bin es l.** I'm fed up with it || **Leid** *n* (**-[e]s;**) (*Betrübnis*) sorrow; (*Schaden*) harm; (*Unrecht*) wrong; **j-m ein L. antun** harm s.o.
Leideform ['laɪdəfɔrm] *f* (gram) passive voice
leiden ['laɪdən] §106 *tr* suffer; (*ertragen*) stand || *intr* (**an** *dat*) suffer (*from*) || **Leiden** *n* (**-s;-**) suffering; (*Krankheit*) ailment
Lei'denschaft *f* (**-;-en**) passion
lei'denschaftlich *adj* passionate
lei'denschaftslos *adj* dispassionate
Lei'densgefährte *m*, **Lei'densgefährtin** *f* fellow sufferer
Lei'densgeschichte *f* tale of woe; (relig) Passion
Lei'densweg *m* way of the cross
leider ['laɪdər] *adv* unfortunately
leiderfüllt ['laɪterfʏlt] *adj* sorrowful
leidig ['laɪdɪç] *adj* tiresome
leidlich ['laɪtlɪç] *adv* tolerable; (*halbwegs gut*) passable || *adv* so–so
leidtragend ['laɪttragənt] *adj* in mourning || **Leidtragende** §5 *mf* mourner; **er ist der L. dabei** he is the one that suffers for it
Leid'wesen *n—***zu meinem L.** to my regret
Leier ['laɪ·ər] *f* (**-;-n**) (mus) lyre
Lei'erkasten *m* hand organ, hurdygurdy
Lei'ermann *m* (**-[e]s;⁼er**) organ grinder
leiern ['laɪ·ərn] *tr* (*winden*) crank; (*Gebete, Verse*) drone || *intr* drone
Leih- [laɪ] *comb.fm.* loan, rental
Leih'amt *n*, **Leih'anstalt** *f* loan office
Leih'bibliothek *f* rental library
leihen ['laɪ·ən] *tr* lend, loan out; (*entleihen*) (**von**) borrow (*from*)
Leih'gebühr *f* rental fee
Leih'haus *n* pawnshop
Leim [laɪm] *m* (**-[e]s;-e**) glue; birdlime; **aus dem L. gehen** fall apart; **j-m auf den L. gehen** be taken in by s.o.
leimen ['laɪmən] *tr* glue; (*betrügen*) take in, fool
Leim'farbe *f* distemper
leimig ['laɪmɪç] *adj* gluey
Lein [laɪn] *m* (**-[e]s;-e**) flax
Leine ['laɪnə] *f* (**-;-n**) line, cord; (*Hunde-*) leash
Leinen ['laɪnən] *n* (**-s;-**) linen
Lei'neneinband *m* (**-[e]s;⁼e**) (bb) cloth binding
Lei'nenschuh *m* sneaker, canvas shoe
Lei'nenzeug *n* linen fabric
Lein'öl *n* linseed oil
Lein'tuch *n* sheet
Lein'wand *f* linen cloth; canvas; (cin) screen
leise ['laɪzə] *adj* soft, low; (*sanft*) gentle; (*gering*) faint; (*Schlaf*) light

lei'sestellen *tr* (rad) turn down
Lei'setreter *m* (-s;-) pussyfoot
Leiste ['laɪstə] *f* (-;-n) (*Rand*) border; (anat) groin; (carp) molding
leisten ['laɪstən] *tr* do, perform, accomplish; (*Dienst*) render; (*Eid*) take; (*Abbitte, Hilfe, Widerstand*) offer; **Bürgschaft l. für** put up bail for; **Folge l.** (*dat*), **Gehorsam l.** (*dat*) obey; **Genüge l.** (*dat*) satisfy; **j-m Gesellschaft l.** keep s.o. company; **sich** [*dat*] **etw l. können** be able to afford s.th. ‖ **Leisten** *m* (-s;-) last; **alles über e-n L. schlagen** (fig) be undiscriminating
Lei'stenbruch *m* hernia, rupture
Lei'stung *f* (-;-en) performance; efficiency; ability; feat, achievement; (*Ergebnis*) result; (*Erzeugung*) production; (*Abgabe, Ausstoß*) output; (*Beitrag*) contribution; (*Dienstleistungen*) services rendered; (elec) power, wattage; (indust) output, production; (insur) benefits; (mach) capacity
Lei'stungsanreiz *m* incentive
lei'stungsfähig *adj* (*Person*) efficient; (*Motor*) powerful; (*Fabrik*) productive; (phys) efficient
Lei'stungsfähigkeit *f* efficiency; proficiency; (*e-s Autos*) performance; (*e-s Motors*) power; (mach) output
lei'stungsgerecht *auj* based on merit
Lei'stungsgrenze *f* peak of performance
Leis'tungslohn *m* pay based on performance
Lei'stungszulage *f* bonus
Leit- [laɪt] *comb.fm.* leading, dominant, guiding
Leit'artikel *m* editorial
Leit'bild *n* (good) example, ideal
leiten ['laɪtən] *tr* lead, guide; (*Verkehr*) route; (*Betrieb*) direct, run; (*Versammlung*) preside over; (arti) direct; (elec, mus, phys) conduct
Lei'ter *m* (-s;-) leader; director; (educ) principal; (elec, mus) conductor ‖ *f* (-;-n) ladder
Lei'terin *f* (-;-nen) leader; director
Leit'faden *m* manual, guide
Leit'fähigkeit *f* conductivity
Leit'gedanke *m* main idea, main theme
Leit'hammel *m* (fig) boss, leader
Leit'motiv *n* keynote; (mus) leitmotiv
Leit'satz *m* basic point
Leit'spruch *m* motto
Leit'stelle *f* head office
Leit'stern *m* polestar, lodestar
Lei'tung *f* (-;-en) direction, guidance; (*Beaufsichtigung*) management; (*Rohr*) pipeline; (*für Gas, Wasser*) main; (elec) lead; (phys) conduction; (telp) line; **e-e lange L. haben** be rather dense; **L. besetzt!** line is busy!
Lei'tungsdraht *m* (elec) lead
Lei'tungsmast *m* telephone pole
Lei'tungsnetz *n* (elec) power lines
Lei'tungsrohr *n* pipe, main
Lei'tungsvermögen *n* conductivity
Lei'tungswasser *n* tap water
Leit'werk *n* (aer) tail assembly
Leit'zahl *f* code number

Lektion [lɛk'tsjon] *f* (-;-en) lesson; (fig) lecture, rebuke
Lek·tor ['lɛktɔr] *m* (-s;-toren ['torən]) lecturer; (*e-s Verlags*) reader
Lektüre [lɛk'tyrə] *f* (-;) reading matter, literature
Lende ['lɛndə] *f* (-;-n) loin; (*Hüfte*) hip
Len'denbraten *m* roast loin, sirloin
len'denlahm *adj* stiff; (*Ausrede*) lame
Len'denschurz *m* loincloth
Len'denstück *n* tenderloin, sirloin
lenkbar ['lɛŋkbar] *adj* manageable; steerable, maneuverable; **lenkbares Luftschiff** dirigible
lenken ['lɛŋkən] *tr* guide, control; (*Wagen*) drive; (*wenden*) turn; (*steuern*) steer; **Aufmerksamkeit l. auf** (acc) call attention to
Len'ker **–in** §6 *mf* ruler; (aut) driver
Lenkrad ['lɛŋkrat] *n* steering wheel
Lenksäule ['lɛŋkzɔɪlə] *f* steering column
Lenkstange ['lɛŋkʃtaŋə] *f* handlebar; (aut) connecting rod
Len'kung *f* (-;-en) guidance, control; (aut) steering mechanism
Lenz [lɛnts] *m* (-es;-e) (fig) prime of life; (poet) spring
Lenz'pumpe *f* bilge pump
Lepra ['lepra] *f* (-;) leprosy
Lerche ['lɛrçə] *f* (-;-n) (orn) lark
lernbegierig ['lɛrnbəgiriç] *adj* eager to learn, studious
lernen [,'lɛrnən] *tr* & *intr* learn; study
Lesart ['lezart] *f* version
lesbar ['lezbar] *adj* legible; readable
Lesbierin ['lesbɪ·ərɪn] *f* (-;-nen) lesbian
lesbisch ['lesbɪʃ] *adj* lesbian; **lesbische Liebe** lesbianism
Lese ['lezə] *f* (-;-n) gathering, picking; (*Wein–*) vintage
Lese– [lezə] *comb.fm.* reading; lecture
Le'sebrille *f* reading glasses
Le'sebuch *n* reader
Le'sehalle *f* reading room
lesen ['lezən] §107 *tr* read; gather; (*Messe*) say ‖ *intr* read; lecture; **l. über** (acc) lecture on
le'senswert *adj* worth reading
Le'seprobe *f* specimen from a book; (theat) reading rehearsal
Le'ser –in §6 *mf* reader; picker
Le'seratte *f* (coll) bookworm
le'serlich *adj* legible
Le'serzuschrift *f* letter to the editor
Le'sestoff *m* reading matter
Le'sezeichen *n* bookmark
Le'sung *f* (-;-en) reading
Lette ['lɛtə] *m* (-n;-n), **Lettin** ['lɛtɪn] *f* (-;-nen) Latvian
lettisch ['lɛtɪʃ] *adj* Latvian
Lettland ['lɛtlant] *n* (-[e]s;) Latvia
letzte ['lɛtstə] §9 *adj* last; (*endgültig*) final, ultimate; (*neueste*) latest; (*Ausweg*) last; **bis ins l.** to the last detail; **in den letzten Jahren** in recent years; **in der letzten Zeit** lately; **letzten Endes** in the final analysis ‖ **Letzte** §5 *pron* last, last one; **am Letzten** on the last of the month; **sein Letztes hergeben** do one's ut-

most; **zu guter Letzt** finally, last but not least
letztens ['lɛtstəns] *adv* lately
letztere ['lɛtstərə] §5 *mfn* latter
letzthin [lɛtst'hɪn] *adv* lately
letztlich ['lɛtstlɪç] *adv* lately, recently; **in the final analysis**
letztwillig ['lɛtstvɪlɪç] *adj* testamentary
Leucht– [lɔɪçt] *comb.fm.* luminous; illuminating
Leucht′bombe *f* flare bomb
Leuchte ['lɔɪçtə] *f* (–;–n) light, lamp; lantern; (fig) luminary
leuchten ['lɔɪçtən] *intr* shine
leuch′tend *adj* shining, bright; luminous
Leuchter ['lɔɪçtər] *m* (–s;–) candlestick; chandelier
Leucht′farbe *f* luminous paint
Leucht′feuer *n* (aer) flare; (naut) beacon
Leucht′käfer *m* lightning bug
Leucht′körper *m* light bulb; light fixture
Leucht′kugel *n* tracer bullet; flare
Leucht′pistole *f* Very pistol
Leucht′rakete *f* (aer) flare
Leucht′reklame *f* neon sign
Leucht′röhre *f* fluorescent lamp
Leucht′spurgeschoß *n* tracer bullet
Leucht′turm *m* lighthouse
Leucht′zifferblatt *n* luminous dial
leugnen ['lɔɪgnən] *tr* deny; disclaim
Leukoplast [lɔɪkə'plast] *n* (–[e]s;–e) adhesive tape
Leumund ['lɔɪmʊnt] *m* (–[e]s;) reputation
Leu′mundszeugnis *n* character reference
Leute ['lɔɪtə] *pl* people, persons, men; (*Dienstleute*) servants
Leu′teschinder *m* oppressor; slave driver
Leutnant ['lɔɪtnant] *m* (–s;–s) lieutenant
Leut′priester *m* secular priest
leut′selig *adj* affable
Lexikograph [lɛksɪkə'graf] *m* (–en;–en) lexicographer
Lexikon ['lɛksɪkɔn] *n* (–s;–s) encyclopedia
Libanon ['libanɔn] *n* (–s;) Lebanon
Libelle [lɪ'bɛlə] *f* (–;–n) dragonfly; (carp) level
liberal [libe'ral] *adj* liberal
Liberalismus [lɪbera'lɪsmʊs] *m* (–s;) liberalism
Libyen ['libY.ən] *n* (–s;) Libya
licht [lɪçt] *adj* light, bright; (*durchsichtig*) clear || **Licht** *n* (–[e]s;–er) light; (*Kerze*) candle
licht′beständig *adj* non-fading
Licht′bild *n* photograph
Licht′bildervortrag *m* illustrated lecture
licht′blau *adj* light-blue
Licht′blick *m* (fig) bright spot
Licht′bogen *m* (elec) arc
Licht′bogenschweißung *f* arc welding
Licht′brechung *f* (–;–en) refraction of light
Licht′druck *m* phototype
licht′durchlässig *adj* translucent

licht′echt *adj* non-fading
licht′empfindlich *adj* sensitized; **l. machen** sensitize
Licht′empfindlichkeit *f* (phot) speed
lichten ['lɪçtən] *tr* clear; thin; (*Anker*) weigh
lichterloh ['lɪçtərlo] *adv* ablaze; **l. brennen** be ablaze
Licht′hof *m* (archit) light well, inner court; (phot) halo
Licht′kegel *m* beam of light
Licht′maschine *f* generator, dynamo
Licht′pause *f* blueprint
Licht′punkt *m* (fig) ray of hope
Licht′schacht *m* light well
Licht′schalter *m* light switch
licht′scheu *adj*—**lichtscheues Gesindel** shady characters
Licht′schirm *m* lamp shade
Licht′seite *f* (fig) bright side
Licht′spiele *pl*, **Licht′spielhaus** *n*, **Licht′spieltheater** *n* movie theater
licht′stark *adj* (*Objektiv*) high-powered; (phot) high-speed
Lich′tung *f* (–;–en) clearing
Lid [lit] *n* (–[e]s;–er) eyelid
Lid′schatten *m* eye shadow
lieb [lip] *adj* dear; (*nett*) nice; **der liebe Gott** the good Lord; **es ist mir l., daß** I am glad that; **seien Sie so l. und** please; **sich lieb Kind machen bei** ingratiate oneself with
lieb′äugeln *intr*—**l. mit** (& *fig*) flirt with
Liebchen ['lipçən] *n* (–s;–) darling
Liebe ['libə] *f* (–;) (zu) love (*for, of*)
liebedienerisch ['libədinərɪʃ] *adj* fawning
Liebelei [libə'laɪ] *f* (–;–en) flirtation
lie′ben ['libən] *tr* love, be fond of
lie′bend *adj* loving || *adv*—**l. gern** gladly || **Liebende** §5 *mf* lover
lie′benswert *adj* lovable
lie′benswürdig *adj* lovable; charming; **das ist sehr l. von Ihnen** that's very kind of you
lieber ['libər] *adv* rather, sooner; **l. haben** prefer
Liebes– [libəs] *comb.fm.* love, of love
Lie′besdienst *m* favor, good turn
Lie′beserlebnis *n* romance
Lie′besgabe *f* charitable gift
Lie′beshandel *m* love affair
Lie′besmahl *n* love feast
Lie′besmühe *f*—**verlorene L.** wasted effort
Lie′bespaar *n* couple (of lovers)
Lie′bespfand *n* token of love
Lie′bestrank *m* love potion
Lie′beswerben *n* advances
lie′bevoll *adj* loving, affectionate
Lieb′frauenkirche *f* Church of Our Lady
lieb′gewinnen §121 *tr* grow fond of
lieb′haben §89 *tr* love, be fond of
Liebhaber ['liphabər] *m* (–s;–) lover, beau; amateur; fan, buff; **erster L.** leading man
lieb′kosen *tr* caress, fondle
lieb′lich *adj* lovely, sweet; charming
Liebling ['liplɪŋ] *m* (–s;–e) darling; (*Haustier*) pet; (*Günstling*) favorite
Lieblings– *comb.fm.* favorite

Lieb'lingsgedanke *m* pet idea
Lieb'lingswunsch *m* dearest wish
lieb'los *adj* unkind
lieb'reich *adj* kind, affectionate
Lieb'reiz *m* charm, attractiveness
lieb'reizend *adj* charming
Lieb'schaft *f* (-;-en) love affair
liebste ['lipstə] §9 *adj* favorite; **am liebsten trinke ich Wein** I like wine best of all
Lied [lit] *n* (-[e]s;-er) song; **er weiß ein L. davon zu singen** he can tell you all about it; **geistliches L.** hymn
liederlich ['lidərlıç] *adj* dissolute; (*unordentlich*) disorderly
lief [lif] *pret* of **laufen**
Lieferant –in [lifə'rant(ın)] §7 *mf* supplier; (*Verteiler*) distributor; (*von Lebensmitteln*) caterer
Lieferauto ['lifərauto] *n* delivery truck
lieferbar ['lifərbar] *adj* available, deliverable
Liefergebühr ['lifərgə'byr] *f* delivery charge
liefern ['lifərn] *tr* deliver; (*beschaffen*) supply, furnish; (*Ertrag*) yield; **ich bin geliefert** (coll) I'm done for
Lieferschein ['lifər∫aın] *m* delivery receipt
Lie'ferung *f* (-;-en) delivery, shipment; supply; (*e-s Werkes*) installment, number; **zahlbar bei L.** cash on delivery
Lieferwagen ['lifərvagən] *m* delivery truck
Liege ['ligə] *f* (-;-n) couch
Lie'gekur *f* rest cure
liegen ['ligən] §108 *intr* lie, be situated; **gut auf der Straße l.** hug the road; **l. an** (*dat*) lie near; (fig) be due to; **wie die Sache jetzt liegt** as matters now stand ‖ *impers*—**es liegt an ihm zu** (*inf*) it's up to him to (*inf*); **es liegt auf der Hand** it is obvious; **es liegt mir nichts daran** it doesn't matter to me; **es liegt mir (sehr viel) daran** it matters (a great deal) to me
lie'genbleiben §62 *intr* (SEIN) stay in bed; (*Waren*) remain unsold; (*stekkenbleiben*) have a breakdown; (*Arbeit*) be left undone
lie'genlassen §104 *tr* let lie; leave alone; (*Arbeit*) leave undone
Lie'genschaft *f* (-;-en) real estate
Lie'gestuhl *m* deck chair
Lie'gestütz *m* (gym) pushup
lieh [li] *pret* of **leihen**
ließ [lis] *pret* of **lassen**
Li·ga ['ligɑ] *f* (-;-gen [gən)] league
Liguster [li'gustər] *m* (-s;-) privet
liieren [li'irən] *ref*—**sich l. mit** ally oneself with
Likör [li'kør] *m* (-s;-e) liqueur
lila ['lila] *adj* lilac
Lilie ['liljə] *f* (-;-n) lily
Limonade [limɔ'nɑdə] *f* (-;-n) soft drink, soda
lind [lınt] *adj* mild, gentle
Linde ['lındə] *f* (-;-n) (bot) linden
lindern ['lındərn] *tr* alleviate; (*Übel*) mitigate; (*mildern*) soften

Lindwurm ['lıntvurm] *m* dragon
Lineal [line'al] *n* (-s;-e) ruler
Linguist –in [lıŋgu'ıst(ın)] §7 *mf* linguist
Linie ['linjə] *f* (-;-n) line; **auf gleicher L. mit** on a level with; **in erster L.** in the first place
Li'nienpapier *n* lined paper
Li'nienrichter *m* (sport) linesman
Li'nienschiff *n* ship of the line
li'nientreu *adj*—**l. sein** follow the party line
linieren [lı'nirən] *tr* line, rule
linke ['lıŋkə] §9 *adj* left; (*Seite*) wrong, reverse ‖ §5 **Linke** *m* (box) left ‖ §5 *f* left side; left hand; **die L.** (pol) the left
linkisch ['lıŋkı∫] *adj* clumsy, awkward
links [lıŋks] *adv* left; to the left; on the left; (*verkehrt*) inside out; **l. liegenlassen** bypass, ignore; **links um!** left, face!
links'drehend *adj* counterclockwise
linksgängig ['lıŋksgɛŋıç] *adj* counterclockwise
Linkshänder ['lıŋkshɛndər] *m* (-s;-) left-hander
links'läufig *adj* counterclockwise
links'stehend *adj* (pol) leftist
Linnen ['lınən] *n* (-s;) linen
Linse ['lınzə] *f* (-;-n) (bot) lentil; (opt) lens
Lippe ['lıpə] *f* (-;-n) lip; **e-e L. riskieren** (fig) speak out of turn
Lip'penbekenntnis *n* lip service
Lip'penlaut *m* labial
Lip'penstift *m* lipstick
liquid [li'kvit] *adj* (*Geldmittel*) liquid; (*Gesellschaft*) solvent
Liquidation [lıkvida'tsjon] *f* (-;-en) liquidation; (*Kostenrechnung*) bill
liquidieren [lıkvı'dirən] *tr* liquidate; (*Geschäft*) wind up; (*Honorar*) charge
lispeln ['lıspəln] *tr & intr* lisp; (*flüstern*) whisper
Lissabon [lısa'bon] *n* (-s;) Lisbon
List [lıst] *f* (-;-en) cunning; trick
Liste ['lıstə] *f* (-;-n) list; **schwarze L.** blacklist
Lis'tenwahl *f* block voting
listig ['lıstıç] *adj* cunning, sly
Litanei [lita'naı] *f* (-;-en) litany
Litauen ['litau·ən] *n* (-s;) Lithuania
litauisch ['litau·ı∫] *adj* Lithuanian
Liter ['litər] *m & n* (-s;-) liter
literarisch [lıta'rarı∫] *adj* literary
Literatur [lıtera'tur] *f* (-;-en) literature
Litfaßsäule ['lıtfaszɔılə] *f* advertising pillar
Litur·gie [lıtur'gi] *f* (-;-gien ['gi·ən]) liturgy
Litze ['lıtsə] *f* (-;-n) cord; (elec) strand
Li·vree [li'vre] *f* (-;-vreen ['vre·ən]) uniform, livery
Lizenz [li'tsɛnts] *f* (-;-en) license
Lob [lop] *n* (-[e]s;) praise
loben ['lobən] §109 *tr* praise
lo'benswert *adj* praiseworthy
Lobhudelei [lophudə'laı] *f* (-;-en) flattery

lob'hudeln *tr* heap praise on
löblich ['løplɪç] *adj* commendable
lob'preisen *tr* extol, praise
Lob'rede *f* panegyric
Loch [lɔx] *n* (-es;⸗er) hole
Loch'bohrer *m* auger
lochen ['lɔxən] *tr* punch, perforate
Locher ['lɔxər] *m* (-s;-) punch
löcherig ['lœçərɪç] *adj* full of holes
Loch'karte *f* punch card
Lo'chung *f* (-;-en) perforation
Locke ['lɔkə] *f* (-;-n) lock, curl
locken ['lɔkən] *tr* allure, entice; decoy; (*Hund*) whistle to
locker ['lɔkər] *adj* loose; (*nicht straff*) slack; spongy; (*moralisch*) loose
lockern ['lɔkərn] *tr* loosen
lockig ['lɔkɪç] *adj* curly, curled
Lock'mittel *n*, **Lock'speise** *f* (& fig) bait
Lockspitzel ['lɔkʃpɪtsəl] *m* stoolpigeon
Lo'ckung *f* (-;-en) allurement
Lock'vogel *m* (& fig) decoy
Loden ['lodən] *m* (-s;-) coarse woolen cloth
lodern ['lodərn] *intr* blaze; (fig) glow
Löffel ['lœfəl] *m* (-s;-) spoon; (culin) spoonful; (coll & hunt) ear; **über den L.** balbieren hoodwink
Löf'felbagger *m* power shovel
löffeln ['lœfəln] *tr* spoon out
log [lok] *pret* of **lügen**
Logbuch ['lɔkbux] *n* logbook
Loge ['loʒə] *f* (-;-n) (*der Freimaurer*) lodge; (theat) box
Lo'genbruder *m* freemason
Logierbesuch [lɔ'ʒirbəzux] *m* houseguest(s)
logieren [lɔ'ʒirən] *intr* (bei) stay (*with*)
Logik ['logɪk] *f* (-;) logic
Logis [lɔ'ʒi] *invar n* lodgings
logisch ['logɪʃ] *adj* logical
Lohe ['lo·ə] *f* (-;-n) blaze, flame
Lohgerber ['logɛrbər] *m* (-s;-) tanner
Lohn [lon] *m* (-[e]s;⸗e) pay, wages; (fig) reward
Lohn'abbau *m* wage cut
lohnen ['lonən] *tr* compensate, reward; (*Arbeiter*) pay; **j-m etw l.** reward s.o. for s.th. || *ref* pay, be worthwhile
löhnen ['lønən] *tr* pay, pay wages to
Lohn'erhöhung *f* raise, wage increase
Lohn'gefälle *n* wage differential
Lohn'herr *m* employer
lohn'intensiv *adj* with high labor costs
Lohn'liste *f* payroll
Lohn'satz *m* pay rate
Lohn'stopp *m* wage freeze
Lohn'tag *m* payday
Lohn'tüte *f* pay envelope
Löh'nung *f* (-;-en) payment
lokal [lɔ'kɑl] *adj* local || **Lokal** *n* (-[e]s;-e) locality, premises; (*Wirtshaus*) restaurant, pub, inn
lokalisieren [lɔkɑlɪ'zirən] *tr* localize
Lokalität [lɔkɑlɪ'tet] *f* (-;-en) locality
Lokomotive [lɔkɔmɔ'tivə] *f* (-;-n) locomotive
Lokomotiv'führer *m* (rr) engineer
Lokus ['lokʊs] *m* (-;-se) (coll) john
Lorbeer ['lɔrbər] *m* (-s;-en) laurel

los [los] *adj* loose; **es ist etw los** there is s.th. going on; **es ist nichts los** there is nothing going on; **etw los haben** have s.th. on the ball; **j-n** (or etw) **los sein** be rid of s.o. (or s.th.); **los!** go on!, scram!; (*sprich!*) fire away!; (*mach schnell!*) let's go!; (sport) play ball!; **mit ihm ist nicht viel los** he's no great shakes; **was ist los?** what's the matter? || **Los** *n* (-[e]s;-e) lot; (*Lotterie-*) ticket; (*Anteil*) lot, portion; (*Schicksal*) fate; **das Große Los** first prize; **das Los ziehen** draw lots; **die Lose sind gefallen** the die is cast
los- *comb.fm.* un–, e.g., **losmachen** undo
los'arbeiten *tr* extricate || *ref* get loose, extricate oneself || *intr* (auf acc) work away (at)
lösbar ['løsbar] *adj* solvable
los'binden §59 *tr* loosen, untie
los'brechen §64 *tr* break off || *intr* (SEIN) break loose
Löschblatt ['lœʃblat] *n* blotter
Löscheimer ['lœʃaimər] *m* fire bucket
löschen ['lœʃən] *tr* put out; (*Durst*) quench; (*Schuld*) cancel; (*Schrift*) blot; (*Bandaufnahme*) erase; (*Firma*) liquidate; (*Hypotek*) pay off; (naut) unload
Lö'scher *m* (-s;-) blotter; (*Feuer-*) fire extinguisher
Löschgerät ['lœʃgəret] *n* fire extinguisher
Löschmannschaft ['lœʃmanʃaft] *f* fire brigade
Löschpapier ['lœʃpapir] *n* blotting paper
Lö'schung *f* (-;-en) extinction; (*Tilgung*) cancellation; (naut) unloading
los'drehen *tr* unscrew, twist off
los'drücken *tr* fire || *intr* pull the trigger
lose ['lozə] §9 *adj* loose
Lösegeld ['løzəgɛlt] *n* ransom
loseisen ['losaizən] *tr—Geld l.* **von** wangle money out of; **j-n l. aus** get s.o. out of; **j-n l. von** get s.o. away from || *ref* (von) worm one's way (*out of*)
losen ['lozən] *intr* draw lots
lösen ['løzən] *tr* loosen, untie; (*abtrennen*) sever; (*Bremse*) release; (*Fahrkarte*) buy; (*loskaufen*) ransom; (*lossprechen*) absolve; (*Rätsel*) solve; (*Schuß*) fire; (*Verlobung*) break off || *ref* come loose, come undone; dissolve; (*sich befreien*) free oneself
los'fahren §71 *intr* (SEIN) drive off; **l. auf** (*acc*) head for; rush at; attack (verbally)
los'gehen §82 *intr* (SEIN) (coll) begin; (*Gewehr*) go off; (*sich lösen*) come loose; **auf j-n l.** attack s.o.
los'haken *tr* unhook
los'kaufen *tr* ransom
los'ketten *tr* unchain
los'kommen §99 *intr* (SEIN) come loose, come off; **ich komme nicht davon los** I can't get over it; **l. von** get away from; get rid of
los'lachen *intr* burst out laughing

los'lassen §104 *tr* let go; release; **den Hund l. auf** (*acc*) sic the dog on
los'legen *intr* (coll) start up, let fly; (*reden*) (coll) open up; **leg los!** (*coll*) fire away!
löslich ['løslɪç] *adj* soluble
los'lösen *tr* detach
los'machen *tr* undo, untie; (*freimachen*) free || *ref* disengage onself
los'platzen *intr* (SEIN) burst out laughing; **l. mit** blurt out
los'reißen §53 *tr* & *ref* break loose
los'sagen *ref*—**sich l. von** renounce
los'schlagen §132 *tr* knock off; (*verkaufen*) dispose of, sell cheaply || *intr* open the attack; **l. auf** (*acc*) let fly at
los'schnallen *tr* unbuckle
los'schrauben *tr* unscrew
los'sprechen §64 *tr* absolve
los'steuern *intr*—**l. auf** (*acc*) head for
Lo'sung *f* (-;-en) (*Kot*) dung; (mil) password; (pol) slogan
Lö'sung *f* (-;-en) solution
Lö'sungsmittel *n* solvent; thinner
los'werden §159 *tr* (SEIN) get rid of
los'ziehen §163 *intr* (SEIN) set out, march away; **l. auf** (*acc*) talk about, run down
Lot [lot] *n* (-[e]s;-e) plummet; plumb line; (*Lötmetall*) solder; (geom) perpendicular; **im Lot** perpendicular; (fig) in order; **ins Lot bringen** (fig) set right
Löteisen ['løtaɪzən] *n* soldering iron
loten ['lotən] *tr* (naut) plumb || *intr* (naut) take soundings
löten ['løtən] *tr* solder
Lötkolben ['løtkɔlbən] *m* soldering iron
Lötlampe ['løtlampə] *f* blowtorch
Lötmetall ['løtmetal] *n* solder
lot'recht *adj* perpendicular
Lotse ['lotsə] *m* (-n;-n) (aer) air traffic controller; (naut) pilot
lotsen ['lotsən] *tr* (*Flugzeuge*) guide in; (naut) pilot
Lotte·rie [lɔtə'ri] *f* (-;-rien* ['ri·ən]) lottery, sweepstakes
Lotterie'los *n* lottery ticket
lotterig ['lɔtərɪç] *adj* sloppy
Lotterleben ['lɔtərlebən] *n* dissolute life
Lotto ['lɔto] *n* (-s;-s) state-owned numbers game
Löwe ['løvə] *m* (-n;-n) lion
Lö'wenanteil *m* lion's share
Lö'wenbändiger –**in** §6 *mf* lion tamer
Lö'wengrube *f* lion's den
Lö'wenmaul *n* (bot) snapdragon
Lö'wenzahn *m* (bot) dandelion
Löwin ['løvɪn] *f* (-;-nen) lioness
loyal [lɔ·a'jal] *adj* loyal
Luchs [luks] *m* (-es;-e) lynx
Lücke ['lʏkə] *f* (-;-n) gap, hole; (*Mangel*) deficiency; (*im Gesetz*) loophole; (*Zwischenraum*) interval; **auf L. stehend** staggered
Lückenbüßer ['lʏkənbysər] *m* (-s;-) stop-gap
lückenhaft (lük'kenhaft) *adj* defective, fragmentary
Luder ['ludər] *n* (-s;-) carrion; (coll)

cad; (*Weibsbild*) slut; **das arme L.!** the poor thing!; **dummes L.!** fathead!
Lu'derleben *n* dissolute life
ludern ['ludərn] *intr* lead a dissolute life
Luft [luft] *f* (-;⁼e) air; (*Atem*) breath; (*Brise*) breeze; **die L. ist rein** the coast is clear; **es ist dicke L.** there is trouble brewing; **es liegt etw in der L.** (fig) there's s.th. in the air; **frische L.** schöpfen get a breath of fresh air; **in die L. fliegen** be blown up; **in die L. gehen** blow one's top; **in die L. sprengen** blow up; **j–n an die L. setzen** give s.o. the air; **nach L. schnappen** gasp for breath; **seinem Zorn L. machen** give vent to one's anger; **tief L. holen** take a deep breath
Luft'alarm *m* air-raid alarm
Luft'angriff *m* air raid
Luft'ansicht *f* aerial view
Luft'aufklärung *f* air reconnaissance
Luft'bild *n* aerial photograph
Luft'bremse *f* air brake
Luft'brücke *f* airlift
Lüftchen ['lʏftçən] *n* (-s;-) gentle breeze
luft'dicht' *adj* airtight
Luft'druck *m* atmospheric pressure; (*e–r Explosion*) blast; (aut) air pressure
Luft'druckbremse *f* air brake
Luft'druckmesser *m* barometer
Luft'druckprüfer *m* tire gauge
Luft'düse *f* air nozzle, air jet
lüften ['lʏftən] *tr* air, ventilate; **den Hut l.** tip one's hat
Luft'fahrt *f* aviation
Luft'fahrzeug *n* aircraft
Luft'flotte *f* air force
luft'förmig *adj* gaseous
Luft'hafen *m* airport
Luft'heizung *f* hot-air heating
Luft'herrschaft *f* air supremacy
Luft'hülle *f* atmosphere
luftig ['lʊftɪç] *adj* airy; (*windig*) windy; (*Person*) flighty; (*Kleidung*) loosely woven, light
Luftikus ['luftɪkus] *m* (-;-se) light-headed person
Luft'klappe *f* air valve
luft'krank *adj* airsick
Luft'kurort *m* mountain resort
Luft'landetruppen *pl* airborne troops
luft'leer *adj* vacuous; **luftleerer Raum** vacuum
Luft'linie *f* beeline; **fünfzig Kilometer L.** 50 kilometers as the crow flies
Luft'loch *n* vent; (aer) air pocket
Luft'parade *f* flyover
Luft'post *f* airmail
Luft'raum *m* atmosphere; air space
Luft'reifen *m* tire
Luft'reklame *f* sky writing
Luft'röhre *f* (anat) windpipe
Luft'schiff *n* airship
Luft'schiffahrt *f* aviation
Luft'schloß *n* castle in the air
Luft'schutz *m* air-raid protection
Luft'schutzkeller *m* air-raid shelter
Luft'schutzwart *m* air-raid warden
Luft'spiegelung *f* mirage

Luft'sprung *m* caper
Luft'streitkräfte *pl* air force
Luft'strom *m* air current
Luft'strudel *m* (aer) wash
Luft'stützpunkt *m* air base
luft'tüchtig *adj* air-worthy
Lüf'tung *f* (-;) airing, ventilation
Luft'veränderung *f* change of climate
Luft'verkehrsgesellschaft *f*, **Luft'verkehrslinie** *f* airline
Luft'vermessung *f* aerial survey
Luft'verpestung *f* (-;), **Luft'verschmutzung** *f* (-;), **Luft'verunreinigung** *f* (-;) air pollution
Luft'waffe *f* air force
Luft'warnung *f* air-raid warning
Luft'weg *m* air route; **auf dem Luftwege** by air
Luft'widerstand *m* (phys) air resistance
Luft'zug *m* draft
Lug [luk] *m* (-[e]s;) lie; **Lug und Trug** pack of lies
Lüge ['lygə] *f* (-;-n) lie; **fromme L.** white lie; **j-n Lügen strafen** prove s.o. a liar
lugen ['lugən] *intr* peep
lügen ['lygən] §111 *tr*—**das Blaue vom Himmel herunter l.** lie like mad ‖ *intr* lie, tell a lie
Lügendetek·tor ['lygəndetɛktɔr] *m* (-s; -toren** ['torən]) lie detector
Lü'gengeschichte *f* cock-and-bull story
Lü'gengespinst *n*, **Lü'gengewebe** *n* tissue of lies
lü'genhaft *adj* (*Person*) dishonest, lying; (*Nachricht*) untrue
Lügner –in ['lygnər(ɪn)] §6 *mf* liar
lügnerisch ['lygnərɪʃ] *adj* dishonest
Luke ['lukə] *f* (-;-n) (*am Dach*) dormer window; (naut) hatch
Lümmel ['lyməl] *m* (-s;-) lout
Lump [lump] *m* (-en;-en) scoundrel
lumpen ['lumpən] *intr* lead a wild life; **sich nicht l. lassen** (coll) be generous ‖ **Lumpen** *m* (-s;-) rag
Lum'pengeld *n* measly sum; **für ein L.** dirtcheap
Lum'pengesindel *n* mob, rabble
Lum'penhändler *m* ragman
Lum'penkerl *m* (coll) bum
Lum'penpack *n* rabble, riffraff
Lumperei [lumpə'raɪ] *f* (-;-en) shady deal; dirty trick; (*Kleinigkeit*) trifle
lumpig ['lumpɪç] *adj* ragged; shabby

Lunge ['luŋə] *f* (-;-n) lung
Lungen– *comb.fm.* pulmonary
Lun'genentzündung *f* pneumonia
Lun'genflügel *m* lung
lun'genkrank *adj* consumptive ‖ **Lungenkranke** §5 *mf* consumptive
Lun'genschwindsucht *f* tuberculosis
lungern ['luŋərn] *intr* (HABEN & SEIN) loiter about, lounge about
Lunte ['luntə] *f* (-;-n) fuse; **L. riechen** smell a rat
Lupe ['lupə] *f* (-;-n) magnifying glass; **unter die L. nehmen** examine closely
lüpfen ['lypfən] *tr* lift gently
Lust [lust] *f* (-;̈e) pleasure; (*Verlangen*) desire; (*Wollust*) lust; **L. haben zu** (*inf*) feel like (*ger*); **mit L. und Liebe** with heart and soul
Lust'barkeit *f* (-;-en) amusement, entertainment
Lüster ['lystər] *m* (-s;-) luster
lüstern ['lystərn] *adj* desirous (*of*); lustful; (*Bilder, Späße*) lewd
Lü'sternheit *f* (-;) greediness; lustfulness; lewdness
Lust'fahrt *f* pleasure ride
lustig ['lustɪç] *adv* gay, jolly; (*belustigend*) amusing; **du bist vielleicht l.!** you must be joking!; **l. sein** have a gay time; **sich l. machen über** (*acc*) poke fun at
Lüstling ['lystlɪŋ] *m* (-s;-e) lecher
lust'los *adj* listless; (*Börse*) inactive
Lustmolch ['lustmɔlç] *m* (-[e]s;-e) sex fiend
Lust'mord *m* sex murder
Lust'reise *f* pleasure trip
Lust'seuche *f* venereal disease
Lust'spiel *n* comedy
lust'wandeln *intr* (SEIN) stroll
Lutheraner –in [lutə'ranər(ɪn)] §6 *mf* Lutheran
lutherisch ['lutərɪʃ] *adj* Lutheran
lutschen ['lutʃən] *tr* & *intr* suck
Lut'scher *m* (-s;-) nipple, pacifier
Luxus ['luksus] *m* (-;) luxury
Lu'xusausgabe *f* deluxe edition
Luzerne [lu'tsɛrnə] *f* (-;-n) alfalfa
Lymphe ['lymfə] *f* (-;-n) lymph
lynchen ['lynçən] *tr* lynch
Lyrik ['lyrɪk] *f* (-;) lyric poetry
lyrisch ['lyrɪʃ] *adj* lyric(al)
Lyze·um [ly'tse·um] *n* (-s;-en [ən]) girls' high school

M

M, m [ɛm] *invar n* M, m
M *abbr* (**Mark**) (fin) mark
Maar [mɑr] *n* (-[e]s;-e) crater lake
Maat [mɑt] *m* (-[e]s;-e) (naut) mate
Machart ['maxɑrt] *f* make, type
Mache ['maxə] *f* (-;) (coll) make-believe; **er hat es schon in der M.** he is working on it
machen ['maxən] *tr* make; (*tun*) do; (*bewirken*) produce; (*verursachen*) cause; (*Prüfung, Reise, Spaziergang*)

take; (*Begriff*) form; (*Besuch*) pay; (*Freude*) give; (*Holz*) chop; (*Konkurrenz*) offer; **das macht mir zu schaffen** that causes me trouble; **das macht nichts** it doesn't matter; never mind; **das macht Spaß** that's fun; **Dummheiten m.** behave foolishly; **Ernst m.** be in earnest; **gemacht!** right!; O.K.!; **Geschäfte m.** do business; **Geschichten m.** make a fuss; **Hochzeit m.** get married; **ich mache**

Spaß I'm joking; **mach dir nichts daraus!** don't worry about it; **mach's gut!** so long!; **wieviel macht es?** how much is it? || *ref* make progress, be all right; **sich auf den Weg m.** set out; **sich** [*dat*] **etw m.** lassen have s.th. made to order; **sich m.** **an** (*acc*) get down to; **sich** [*dat*] **nichts daraus m.** not care for (or about) || *intr*—**laß mich nur m.!** just leave it to me; **mach, daß . . . !** see to it that . . . !; **m. in** (*dat*) deal in; dabble in; **mach schon** (or **zu**)! get going!; **nichts zu m!** (coll) nothing doing! no dice!

Machenschaften ['maxən∫aftən] *pl* intrigues

Macher ['maxər] *m* (-s;-) instigator; (coll) big shot

Macht [maxt] *f* (-;̈e) might, power; (*Kraft*) force, strength; **aus eigener M.** on one's own responsibility; **an der Macht** in power; **an die M. kommen** come to power

Macht'ausgleich *m* balance of power

Macht'befugnis *f* authority

Machthaber ['maxthabər] *m* (-s;-) ruler; dictator

machthaberisch ['maxthabərɪ∫] *adj* dictatorial

mächtig ['mɛçtɪç] *adj* mighty, powerful; (*riesig*) huge

macht'los *adj* powerless

Macht'losigkeit *f* (-;) impotence

Macht'politik *f* power politics

Macht'vollkommenheit *f* absolute power; **aus eigener M.** on one's own authority

Macht'wort *n* (-[e]s;-e)—**ein M.** sprechen put one's foot down

Machwerk ['maxverk] *n* bad job

Mädchen ['mɛtçən] *n* (-s;-) girl; maid

mäd'chenhaft *adj* girlish; maidenly

Mäd'chenhandel *m* white slavery

Mäd'chenname *m* maiden name; girl's name

Made ['madə] *f* (-;-n) maggot

Mädel ['mɛdəl] *n* (-s;-) (coll) girl

madig ['madɪç] *adj* wormy

Magazin [maga'tsin] *n* (-s;-e) warehouse; (*Zeitschrift; Fernsehprogramm; am Gewehr*) magazine

Magd [makt] *f* (-;̈e) maid; (poet) maiden

Magen ['magən] *m* (-s;̈ & -) stomach; **auf nüchternen M.** on an empty stomach

Ma'genbeschwerden *pl* stomach trouble

Ma'gengrube *f* pit of the stomach

Ma'gensaft *m* gastric juice

Ma'genweh *n* stomach ache

mager ['magər] *adj* lean; (*Ernte*) poor

Magie [ma'gi] *f* (-;) magic

Magier –in ['magjər(ɪn)] §6 *mf* magician

magisch ['magɪ∫] *adj* magic(al)

Magister [ma'gɪstər] *m* (-s;-) school teacher; **M. der freien Künste** Master of Arts

Magistrat [magɪs'trat] *m* (-[e]s;-e) city council; (hist) magistracy

Magnat [mag'nat] *m* (-en;-en) magnate

Magnet [mag'net] *m* (-[e]s;-e) or (-en;-en) magnet

magnetisch [mag'netɪ∫] *adj* magnetic

magnetisieren [magnetɪ'zirən] *tr* magnetize

Magnetismus [magne'tɪsmʊs] *m* (-;) magnetism

Mahagoni [maha'goni] *n* (-s;) mahogony

Mahd [mat] *f* (-;-en) mowing

Mähdrescher ['medrɛ∫ər] *m* (agr) combine

mähen ['me·ən] *tr* mow; (*Getreide*) reap

Mä'her *m* (-s;-) mower; reaper

Mahl [mal] *n* (-[e]s;̈er) meal

mahlen ['malən] (*pp* **gemahlen**) *tr* grind || *intr* spin

Mahl'zahn *m* molar

Mahl'zeit *f* meal; **prost M.!** that's a nice mess!

Mähmaschine ['mema∫inə] *f* reaper; (*Rasen-*) lawn mower

Mähne ['menə] *f* (-;-n) mane

mahnen ['manən] *tr* (an *acc*) remind (of); (an *acc*) warn (about or of)

Mahnmal ['manmal] *n* (-s;-e) monument

Mah'nung *f* (-;-en) admonition; (com) reminder, notice

Mähre ['merə] *f* (-;-n) old nag

Mähren ['merən] *n* (-s;) Moravia

Mai [mai] *m* (-[e]s;-e) May

Mai'baum *m* maypole

Mai'blume *f* lily of the valley

Maid [mait] *f* (-;-en) (poet) maiden

Mai'glöckchen *n* lily of the valley

Mai'käfer *m* June bug

Mailand ['mailant] *n* (-[e]s;) Milan

Mais [mais] *m* (-es;) Indian corn

Maische ['mai∫ə] *f* (-;) mash

Mais'hülse *f* corn husk

Mais'kolben *m* corncob

Majestät [majes'tet] *f* (-;-en) majesty

majestätisch [majes'tetɪ∫] *adj* majestic

Maior [ma'jor] *m* (-s;-e) major

Majoran [majo'ran] *m* (-s;-e) marjoram

maiorenn [majo'ren] *adj* of age

Majorität [majorɪ'tet] *f* (-;-en) majority

Makel ['makəl] *m* (-s;-) spot, stain

Mäkelei [mekə'lai] *f* (-;-en) carping

mäkelig ['mekalɪç] *adj* critical; (*im Essen*) picky

ma'kellos *adj* spotless; (fig) impeccable

mäkeln ['mekəln] *intr* (an *dat*) carp (at), find fault (with)

Makkaroni [maka'roni] *pl* macaroni

Makler –in ['maklər(ɪn)] §6 *mf* agent, broker

Mäkler –in ['meklər(ɪn)] §6 *mf* faultfinder

Mak'lergebühr *f* brokerage

Makrele [ma'krelə] *f* (-;-n) mackerel

Makrone [ma'kronə] *f* (-;-n) macaroon

Makulatur [makula'tur] *f* (-;) waste

mal [mal] *adv* (coll) once; (arith) times; **komm mal her!** come here once!; **zwei mal drei** two times three; **zwei mal Spinat** two (orders of)

spinach ‖ **Mal** *n* (-[e]s;-e) mark, sign; (*Mutter-*) birthmark, mole; (*Fleck*) stain; time; **dieses Mal** this time; **manches liebe Mal** many a time; **mit e-m Male** all at once
Malbuch ['mɑlbux] *n* coloring book
malen ['mɑlən] *tr & intr* paint
Ma'ler –in §6 *mf* painter
Malerei [mɑlə'raɪ] *f* (-;-en) painting
malerisch ['mɑlərɪʃ] *adj* picturesque
Ma'lerleinwand *f* canvas
Malkunst ['mɑlkʊnst] *f* art of painting
Malstrom ['mɑlʃtrom] *m* maelstrom
malträtieren [mɑltrɛ'tirən] *tr* maltreat
Malve ['mɑlvə] *f* (-;-n) mallow
Malz [mɑlts] *n* (-es;) malt
Malz'bonbon *m* cough drop
Mal'zeichen *n* multiplication sign
Mama [ma'mɑ], ['mɑma] *f* (-;-s) mom, ma
Mamsell [mam'zɛl] *f* (-;-en) miss; (*Wirtschafterin*) housekeeper
man [man] *indef pron* one, they, people, you; **man hat mir gesagt** I have been told
manch [manç] *invar adj*—**manch ein** many a ‖ **mancher** §3 *adj* many a; **manche** *pl* some, several ‖ *pron* many a person; many a thing
mancherlei ['mançərlaɪ] *invar adj* all sorts of, various
Manchester [man'ʃestər] *m* (-s;) corduroy
manch'mal *adv* sometimes
Mandant –in [man'dant(ɪn)] §7 *mf* client
Mandarine [manda'rinə] *f* (-;-n) tangerine
Mandat [man'dɑt] *n* (-[e]s;-e) mandate
mandatieren [manda'tirən] *tr* mandate
Mandel ['mandəl] *f* (-;-n) almond; (*15 Stück*) fifteen; (anat) tonsil
Man'delentzündung *f* tonsilitis
Mandoline [mandɔ'linə] *f* (-;-n) mandolin
Mandschurei [mantʃu'raɪ] *f* (-;) Manchuria
Mangan [maŋ'gan] *n* (-s;) manganese
Mangel ['maŋəl] *m* (-s;⸗) lack, deficiency; (*Knappheit*) shortage; (*Fehler*) shortcoming; **aus M. an** (*dat*) for lack of; **M. haben an** (*dat*) be deficient in; **M. leiden an** (*dat*) be short of ‖ *f* (-;-n) mangle
Mangel- *comb.fm.* in short supply
Man'gelberuf *m* undermanned profession
man'gelhaft *adj* defective; faulty; unsatisfactory, deficient
Man'gelkrankheit *f* nutritional deficiency
mangeln ['maŋəln] *tr* (*Wäsche*) mangle ‖ *intr* (**an** *dat*) be short of, lack ‖ *impers*—**es mangelt mir an** (*dat*) I lack
Mängelrüge ['mɛŋəlrygə] *f* (-;-n) (com) complaint (*about a shipment*)
mangels ['maŋəls] *prep* (*genit*) for want of, for lack of
Ma·nie [ma'ni] *f* (-;-nien* ['ni·ən]) mania
Manier [ma'nir] *f* (-;-en) manner

manieriert [manɪ'rirt] *adj* affected
Manieriert'heit *f* (-;-en) mannerism
manier'lich *adj* mannerly, polite
Manifest [manɪ'fɛst] *n* (-es;-e) (aer, naut) manifest; (pol) manifesto
Maniküre [manɪ'kyrə] *f* (-;-n) manicure; manicurist
maniküren [manɪ'kyrən] *tr* manicure
manipulieren [manɪpu'lirən] *tr* manipulate
manisch ['manɪʃ] *adj* maniacal
Manko ['maŋko] *n* (-s;-s) deficit; (com) shortage
Mann [man] *m* (-[e]s;⸗er) man; (*Gatte*) husband; **an den M. bringen** manage to get rid of; **der M. aus dem Volke** the man in the street; **seinen M. stehen** hold one's own
mannbar ['manbɑr] *adj* marriageable
Mann'barkeit *f* (-;) puberty; marriageable age (*of girls*)
Männchen ['mɛnçən] *n* (-s;-) little man; (*Ehemann*) hubby; (zool) male; **M. machen** sit on its hind legs
Männerchor ['mɛnərkor] *m* men's choir
Mannesalter ['manəsaltər] *n* manhood
Manneszucht ['manəstsʊxt] *f* discipline
mann'haft *adj* manly, valiant
mannigfaltig ['manɪçfaltɪç] *adj* manifold
Man'nigfaltigkeit *f* (-;) diversity
männlich ['mɛnlɪç] *adj* male; (fig) manly; (gram) masculine
Männ'lichkeit *f* (-;) manhood; virility
Mannsbild ['mansbɪlt] *n* (pej) man
Mann'schaft *f* (-;-en) crew; (sport) team, squad; **Mannschaften** (mil) enlisted men
Mann'schaftsführer –in §6 *mf* (sport) captain
Mann'schaftswagen *m* (mil) personnel carrier
Mannsleute ['manslɔɪtə] *pl* menfolk
mannstoll ['manstɔl] *adj* man-crazy
Manns'tollheit *f* (-;) nymphomania
Mann'weib *n* mannish woman
Manometer [manɔ'metər] *n* pressure gauge
Manöver [ma'nøvər] *n* (-s;-) maneuver
manövrieren [manø'vrirən] *intr* maneuver
manövrier'fähig *adj* maneuverable
Mansarde [man'zardə] *f* (-;-n) attic
manschen ['manʃən] *tr & intr* splash
Manschette [man'ʃetə] *f* (-;-n) cuff
Manschet'tenknopf *m* cuff link
Mantel ['mantəl] *m* (-s;⸗) overcoat; (*Fahrrad-*) tire; (*e-s Kabels*) sheathing; (*Geschoß-*) jacket, case; (geol, orn) mantle
manuell [manu'ɛl] *adj* manual
Manufaktur [manufak'tur] *f* (-;-en) manufacture
Manufaktur'waren *pl* manufactured goods
Manuskript [manu'skrɪpt] *n* (-[e]s;-e) manuscript
Mappe ['mapə] *f* (-;-n) briefcase; (*Aktendeckel*) folder
Märchen ['mɛrçən] *n* (-s;-) fairy tale
mär'chenhaft *adj* legendary; (*fig*) fabulous

Mär'chenland n fairyland
Marchese [mar'keza] m (-;-n) marquis
Marder ['mardər] m (-s;-) marten; (fig) thief
Margarine [marga'rinə] ƒ (-;) margarine
Marienbild [ma'ri·ənbɪlt] n image of the Virgin
Marienfäden [ma'ri·ənfedən] pl gossamer(s)
Marienglas [ma'ri·ənglas] n mica
Marienkäfer [ma'ri·ənkefər] m ladybug
Marine [ma'rinə] ƒ (-;-n) (Kriegs-) navy; (Handels-) merchant marine
mari'neblau adj navy-blue
Mari'neflugzeug n seaplane
Mari'neinfanterie ƒ marines
Mari'neminister m secretary of the navy
Mari'neoffizier –in §6 mƒ naval officer
Mari'nesoldat m marine
marinieren [marɪ'nirən] tr marinate
Marionette [marɪ·ə'netə] ƒ (-;-n) puppet
Marionet'tentheater n puppet show
Mark [mark] ƒ (-;-) (fin) mark; (hist) borderland, march ‖ n (-[e]s;) marrow; (im Holz) pith; **bis ins M.** to the quick; **er hat M.** (fig) he has guts; **j-m durch M. und Bein gehen** (fig) go right through s.o.
markant [mar'kant] adj (einprägsam) marked; (außergewöhnlich) striking; (Geländepunkt) prominent
Marke ['markə] ƒ (-;-n) mark; (Brief-) stamp; (Handelszeichen) trademark; (Sorte) brand; (Fabrikat) make; (Spiel-) counter
mark'erschütternd adj piercing
Marketenderei [markətendə'raɪ] ƒ (-;-en) post exchange, PX
Marketing ['markɪtɪŋ] n (-s;) (com) marketing
markieren [mar'kirən] tr mark; (spielen) pretend to be
Markise [mar'kizə] ƒ (-;-n) awning
Mark'stein m landmark
Markt [markt] m (-[e]s;∺e) market; (Jahrmarkt) fair
Markt'bude ƒ booth, stall
markten ['marktən] intr (um) bargain (for)
markt'fähig adj marketable
Markt'flecken m market town
marktgängig ['marktgɛŋɪç] adj marketabⁱe
Markt'platz m market place
Markt'schreier m quack
Marmelade [marmə'ladə] ƒ (-;-n) jam
Marmor ['marmɔr] m (-s;-e) marble
Mar'morbruch m marble quarry
marmorn ['marmɔrn] adi marble
marode [ma'rodə] adj (coll) tired out
Marodeur [marɔ'dǿr] m (-s;-e) marauder
marodieren [marɔ'dirən] intr maraud
Marone [ma'ronə] ƒ (-;-n) chestnut
Maroquin [marɔ'kɛ̃] m (-s;) morocco
Marotte [ma'rɔtə] ƒ (-;-n) whim
marsch [marʃ] interj march!; be off!; **m., m.!** on the double ‖ **Marsch** m (-es; ∺e) march; **in M. setzen** get

going; **j–m den M. blasen** (coll) chew s.o. out; (sich) **in M. setzen** set out
Marschall ['marʃal] m (-s;∺e) marshal
Mar'schallstab m marshal's baton
Marsch'gepäck n full field pack
marschieren [mar'ʃirən] intr (SEIN) march
Marsch'kompanie ƒ replacement company
Marsch'lied n marching song
Marsch'verpflegung ƒ field rations
Marter ['martər] ƒ (-;-n) torture
martern ['martərn] tr torture, torment
Mar'terpfahl m stake
Märtyrer –in ['mɛrtYrər(ɪn)] §6 mƒ martyr
Märtyrertum ['mɛrtYrərtum] n (-s;) martyrdom
März [mɛrts] m (-[es];-e) March
Masche ['maʃə] ƒ (-;-n) mesh; stitch; (fig) trick
Ma'schendraht m chicken wire; screen; wire mesh
ma'schenfest adj runproof
Maschine [ma'ʃinə] ƒ (-;-n) machine; (aer) airplane
maschinell [maʃɪ'nɛl] adj mechanical ‖ adv by machine
Maschi'nenantrieb m—mit M. machine-driven
Maschi'nenbau m (-[e]s;) mechanical engineering
Maschi'nengewehr n machine gun
Maschi'nengewehrschütze m machine gunner
maschi'nenmäßig adj mechanical
Maschi'nenpistole ƒ tommy gun
Maschi'nenschaden m engine trouble
Maschi'nenschlosser m machinist
maschi'nenschreiben tr type ‖ **Maschinenschreiben** n (-s;-) typing; typewritten letter
Maschi'nenschrift ƒ typescript
Maschi'nensprache ƒ computer language
Maschinerie [maʃɪnə'ri] ƒ (-;) (& fig) machinery
Maschinist –in [maʃɪ'nɪst(ɪn)] §7 mƒ machinist
Masern ['mɑzərn] pl measles
Maserung ['mɑzəruŋ] ƒ (-;) grain (in wood)
Maske ['maskə] ƒ (-;-n) mask; (fig) disguise; (theat) make-up
Ma'skenball m masquerade
Maskerade [mas'radə] ƒ (-;-n) masquerade
maskieren [mas'kirən] tr mask
Maskotte [mas'kɔtə] ƒ (-;-n) mascot
maskulin [masku'lin] adj masculine
Maskuli·num [masku'linum] n (-s;-na [na]) masculine noun
maß [mɑs] pret of **messen** ‖ **Maß** n (-es;-e) measure; (Messung) measurement; (Ausdehnung) extent, dimension; (Verhältnis) rate, proportion; (Grad) degree; (Mäßigung) moderation; **das Maß ist voll!** I've had it!; **das Maß überschreiten** go too far; **er hat sein gerütteltes Maß an Kummer gehabt** he had his full share of trouble; **in gewissem Maße** to a certain extent; **in hohem Maße**

highly; **j-m Maß nehmen zu** take s.o.'s measurements for; **Maß halten** observe moderation; **mit Maße in** moderation; **nach Maß angefertigt** custom-made; **ohne Maß und Ziel** without limit; **weder Maß noch Ziel kennen** know no bounds; **zweierlei Maß** double standard || *f* (-;- & -e) quart (*of beer*), stein

massakrieren [masa'krirən] *tr* massacre

Maß'anzug *m* tailor-made suit

Maß'arbeit *f* work made to order

Masse ['masə] *f* (-;-n) mass; bulk; (*Menge*) volume; (*Volk*) crowd; (*Hinterlassenschaft*) estate; (elec) ground; **die breite M.** the masses; the rank and file; **e-e Masse...**(coll) lots of

Maß'einheit *f* unit of measure

Masseleisen ['masəlaɪzən] *n* pigiron

Massen– *comb.fm.* mass, bulk, wholesale

Mas'senabsatz *m* wholesale selling

Mas'senangriff *m* mass attack

Mas'senanziehung *f* gravitation

mas'senhaft *adj* in large quantities

Maß'gabe *f*—**mit der M.**, **daß** with the understanding that; **nach M.** (*genit*) in proportion to; according to; (jur) as provided in

maß'gebend, maßgeblich ['masgeplıç] *adj* standard; authoritative; (*Kreise*) leading, influential; **das ist nicht maßgebend für** that is no criterion for

maß'gerecht *adj* to scale

maß'halten §90 *intr* observe moderation

maß'haltig *adj* precise

massieren [ma'sirən] *tr* massage; (*Truppen*) mass

massig ['masıç] *adj* bulky; solid; (*Person*) stout || *adv*—**m. viel** (coll) very much

mäßig ['mesıç] *adj* moderate; frugal; (*Leistung*) mediocre

mäßigen ['mesıgən] *tr* moderate, tone down || *ref* control oneself

Mä'ßigkeit *f* moderation; frugality; temperance

Mä'ßigung *f* (-;) moderation

massiv [ma'sif] *adj* massive; solid

Maß'krug *m* beer mug, stein

Maß'liebchen *n* daisy

maß'los *adj* immoderate || *adv* extremely

Maß'nahme *f* (-;-n), **Maß'regel** *f* (-; -n) measure, step, move

maß'regeln *tr* reprimand

Maß'schneider *m* custom tailor

Maß'stab *m* ruler; (fig) yardstick, standard; (*auf Landkarten*) scale; **jeden M. verlieren** lose all sense of proportion

maß'voll *adj* moderate; (*Benehmen*) discreet

Mast [mast] *m* (-es;-en & -e) pole; (naut) mast || *f* (-;) (*Schweinfutter*) mast

Mast'baum *m* (naut) mast

Mast'darm *m* rectum

mästen ['mestən] *tr* fatten

Mast'korb *m* masthead, crow's nest

Material [materı'al] *n* (-s;-ien [ı·ən]) material

Materialismus [materı·a'lısmus] *m* (-;) materialism

materialistisch [materı·a'lıstıʃ] *adj* materialistic

Material'waren *pl* (Aust) medical supplies

Materie [ma'terı·ə] *f* (-;-n) matter

materiell [materı'el] *adj* material; (*Schwierigkeiten*) financial; (*Recht*) substantive

Mathe ['matə] *f* (-;) (coll) math

Mathematik [matema'tik] *f* (-;) mathematics

Mathematiker –in [matɛ'matıkər(ın)] §6 *mf* mathematician

mathematisch [mate'matıʃ] *adj* mathematical

Matratze [ma'tratsə] *f* (-;-n) mattress

Mätresse [mɛ'trɛsə] *f* (-;-n) mistress

Matrize [ma'tritsə] *f* (-;-n) stencil; (*Stempel*) die, matrix

Matrone [ma'tronə] *f* (-;-n) matron

matro'nenhaft *adj* matronly

Matrose [ma'trozə] *m* (-n;-n) sailor

Matro'senzug *m* sailor's uniform

Matro'senjacke *f* (nav) peacoat

Matsch [matʃ] *m* (-es;) (*Brei*) mush; (*Schlamm*) mud; (*halbgetauter Schnee*) slush

matschig ['matʃıç] *adj* mushy; muddy; slushy

matt [mat] *adj* dull; weak; limp; (*Glas, Birne*) frosted; (*Börse*) slack; (*erschöpft*) exhausted; (*Kugel*) spent; (*Licht*) dim; (*Metall*) tarnished; (phot) matt; **m. machen** dull; tarnish; **m. setzen** checkmate

Matte ['matə] *f* (-;-n) mat; (*Wiese*) Alpine meadow; (poet) mead

Matt'glas *n* frosted glass

Matt'gold *n* dull gold

Matt'heit *f* dullness; fatigue

matt'herzig *adj* faint-hearted

Mat'tigkeit *f* (-;) fatigue

Matura [ma'tura] *f* (-;) (Aust) final examination (*before graduation*)

Mätzchen ['metsçən] *n* (-s;-) trick; **M. machen** play tricks; put on airs

Mauer ['mau·ər] *f* (-;-n) wall

Mau'erblümchen *n* (fig) wallflower

Mau'erkalk *m* mortar

mauern ['mau·ərn] *tr* build (*in stone or brick*)

Mau'erstein *m* brick

Mau'erwerk *n* brickwork; masonry

Mau'erziegel *m* brick

Maul [maul] *n* (-[e]s;̈er) mouth; maw; **halt's M.!** (sl) shut up!

Maul'affe *m* gaping fool

Maul'beerbaum *m* mulberry tree

Maul'beere *f* mulberry

maulen ['maulən] *intr* gripe

Maul'esel *m* mule

maul'faul *adj* too lazy to talk

Maul'held *m* braggart

Maul'korb *m* muzzle

Maul'schelle *f* slap in the face

Maul'sperre *f* lock jaw

Maul'tier *n* mule

Maul'trommel *f* Jew's-harp

Maul'– und Klau'enseuche *f* hoof and mouth disease
Maul'werk *n*—**ein großes M. haben** have the gift of gab
Maul'wurf *m* (zool) mole
Maul'wurfshaufen *m*, **Maul'wurfshügel** *m* molehill
Maure ['maurə] *m* (-n;-n) Moor
Maurer ['maurər] *m* (-s;-) mason; bricklayer
Mau'rerkelle *f* trowel
Mau'rerpolier *m* bricklayer foreman
Maus [maus] *f* (-;̈e) mouse
Mäuschen ['mɔɪsçən] *n* (-s;-) little mouse; (fig) pet, darling; wench
Mau'sefalle *f* mousetrap
mausen ['mauzən] *tr* pilfer, swipe || *intr* catch mice
Mauser ['mauzər] *f* (-;) molting season; **in der M. sein** be molting
mausern ['mauzərn] *ref* molt
mau'setot' *adj* dead as a doornail
mausig ['mauzɪç] *adj*—**sich m. machen** put on airs, be stuck-up
Mauso·leum [mauzɔ'le·um] *n* (-s; -leen ['le·ən]) mausoleum
Maxime [ma'ksimə] *f* (-;-n) maxim
Mayonnaise [majɔ'nezə] *f* (-;) mayonnaise
Mechanik [me'çanɪk] *f* (-;-en) mechanics; (*Triebwerk*) mechanism
Mechaniker [me'çanɪkər] *m* (-s;-) mechanic
mechanisch [me'çanɪʃ] *adj* mechanical; power–
mechanisieren [meçanɪ'zirən] *tr* mechanize
Mechanis·mus [meça'nɪsmus] *m* (-; -men [mən]) mechanism; (*Uhrwerk*) works
Meckerer ['mɛkərər] *m* (-s;-) (coll) grumbler
meckern ['mɛkərn] *intr* bleat; (coll) grumble
Medaille [me'daljə] *f* (-;-n) medal
Medaillon [medal'jõ] *n* (-s;-s) medallion; locket
Medikament [medɪka'ment] *n* (-s;-e) medication
Meditation [medɪta'tsjon] *f* (-;-en) meditation
meditieren [medɪ'tirən] *intr* meditate
Medizin [medɪ'tsin] *f* (-;-en) medicine
Medizinalassistant [medɪtsɪ'nalasɪstant(ɪn)] §7 *mf* intern
Medizinalbeamte [medɪtsɪ'nalbə·amtə] *m* health officer
Medizinalbehörde [medɪtsɪ'nalbəhørdə] *f* board of health
Mediziner –in [medɪ'tsinər(ɪn)] §6 *mf* physician; medical student
medizinisch [medɪ'tsinɪʃ] *adj* medical, medicinal; medicated; **medizinische Fakultät** medical school
Meer [mer] *n* (-[e]s;-e) sea; **am Meere** at the seashore; **übers M.** overseas
Meer'busen *m* bay, gulf
Meer'enge *f* straits
Meeres– [merəs] *comb.fm.* sea, marine
Mee'resarm *m* inlet
Mee'resboden *m* bottom of the sea
Mee'resbucht *f* bay

Mee'resgrund *m* bottom of the sea
Mee'reshöhe *f* sea level
Mee'resküste *f* seacoast
Mee'resleuchten *n* phosphorescence
Mee'resspiegel *m* sea level
meer'grün *adj* sea-green
Meer'rettich *m* horseradish
Meer'schaum *m* meerschaum
Meer'schwein *n* porpoise
Meer'schweinchen *n* guinea pig
Meer'ungeheuer *n* sea monster
Meer'weib *n* mermaid
Mehl [mel] *n* (-[e]s;) (*grobes*) meal; (*feines*) flour; (*Staub*) dust, powder
Mehl'kloß *m* dumpling
Mehl'speise *f* pastry; pudding
Mehl'suppe *f* gruel
Mehl'tau *m* mildew
mehr [mer] *invar adj & adv* more; **immer m.** more and more; **kein Wort m.!** not another word!; **m. oder weniger** more or less, give or take; **nicht m.** no more, no longer; **nie m.** never again || **Mehr** *n* (-s;) majority; (*Zuwachs*) increase; (*Überschuß*) surplus
Mehr'arbeit *f* extra work; (*Überstunden*) overtime
Mehr'aufwand *m*, **Mehr'ausgabe** *f* additional expenditure
Mehr'betrag *m* surplus; extra charge
mehr'deutig *adj* ambiguous
mehren ['merən] *tr & ref* increase
mehrere ['merərə] *adj & pron* several
mehr'fach *adj* manifold; repeated, multiple
mehr'farbig *adj* multicolored
Mehr'gebot *n* higher bid
Mehr'gepäck *n* excess luggage
Mehr'gewicht *n* excess weight
Mehr'heit *f* (-;-en) majority; (pol) plurality
Mehr'heitsbeschluß *m*, **Mehr'heitsentscheidung** *f* plurality vote
mehr'jährig *adj* (bot) perennial
Mehr'kosten *pl* extra charges
Mehr'ladegewehr *n* repeater
Mehr'leistung *f* increased performance; (ins) extended benefits
mehrmalig ['mermalɪç] *adj* repeated
mehrmals ['mermals] *adv* several times, on several occasions; repeatedly
Mehr'porto *n* additional postage
Mehr'preis *m* extra charge
mehr'seitig *adj* multilateral; many-sided; (*Brief*) of many pages
mehrsilbig ['merzɪlbɪç] *adj* polysyllabic
mehrsprachig ['merʃpraxɪç] *adj* polyglot
mehrstöckig ['merʃtœkɪç] *adj* multistory
mehrstufig ['merʃtufɪç] *adj* multistage
Meh'rung *f* (-;) increase, multiplication
Mehr'verbrauch *m* increased consumption
Mehr'wertsteuer *f* added value tax
Mehr'zahl *f* majority; (gram) plural
meiden ['maɪdən] §112 *tr* avoid, shun
Meier ['maɪ·ər] *m* (-s;-) tenant farmer; dairy farmer
Meierei [maɪ·ə·'raɪ] *f* (-;-en) dairy

Mei'ergut *n*, **Mei'erhof** *m* dairy farm
Meile ['maɪlə] *f* (-;-n) mile
mei'lenweit *adj* extending for miles, miles and miles of || *adv* far away; **m. auseinander** miles apart
Mei'lenzahl *f* mileage
mein [maɪn] §2,2 *poss adj* my || §2,4,5 *pron* mine; **das Meine** my share; my due; **die Meinen** my family
Meineid ['maɪnaɪt] *m* (-[e]s;) perjury; **e-n M. schwören** (or **leisten**) commit perjury
meineidig ['maɪnaɪdɪç] *adj* perjured; **m. werden** perjure oneself
meinen ['maɪnən] *tr* think; (*im Sinne haben*) mean, intend; **das will ich m.** I should think so; **die Sonne meint es heute gut** the sun is very warm today; **es ehrlich m.** have honorable intentions; **es gut m.** mean well; **ich meinte dich im Recht** I thought you were in the right; **m. Sie das ernst** (or **im Ernst**)? do you really mean it?; **was m. Sie damit?** what do you mean by that?; **was m. Sie dazu?** what do you think of that? || *intr* think; **m. Sie?** do you think so?; **m. Sie nicht auch?** don't you agree?; **wie m. Sie?** I beg your pardon?
meinerseits ['maɪnər'zaɪts] *adv* for my part
meinesgleichen ['maɪnəs'glaɪçən] *pron* people like me, the likes of me
meinethlben ['maɪnət'halbən], **meinetwegen** ['maɪnət'vegən] *adv* for my sake, on my account; for all I care
meinetwillen ['maɪnət'vɪlən] *adv*—**um m.** for my sake, on my behalf
meinige ['maɪnɪgə] §2,5 *pron* mine
Mei'nung *f* (-;-en) opinion; **anderer M. mit j-m sein über** (*acc*) disagree with s.o. about; **der M. sein** be of the opinion; **geteilter M. sein** be of two minds; **j-m die** (or **seine**) **M. sagen** give s.o. a piece of one's mind; **meiner M. nach** in my opinion; **vorgefaßte M.** preconceived idea
Mei'nungsäußerung *f* expression of opinion
Mei'nungsaustausch *m* exchange of views
Mei'nungsbefragung *f*, **Mei'nungsforschung** *f* public opinion poll
Mei'nungsumfrage *f* public opinion poll
Mei'nungsverschiedenheit *f* difference of opinion, disagreement
Meise ['maɪzə] *f* (-;-n) titmouse
Meißel ['maɪsəl] *m* (-s;-) chisel
meißeln ['maɪsəln] *tr* & *intr* chisel
meist [maɪst] *adj* most; **am meisten** most; **das meiste** the most; **die meisten Menschen** most people; **die meiste Zeit** most of the time; **die meiste Zeit des Jahres** most of the year || *adv* usually, generally
Meist'begünstigungsklausel *f* most-favored nation clause
Meist'bietende §5 *mf* highest bidder
meistens ['maɪstəns] *adv* mostly
Meister ['maɪstər] *m* (-s;-) master; boss; (*im Betrieb*) foreman; (sport) champion
mei'sterhaft *adj* masterly

Meisterin ['maɪstərɪn] *f* (-;-nen) master's wife; (sport) champion
mei'sterlich *adj* masterly
meistern ['maɪstərn] *tr* master
Mei'sterschaft *f* (-;-en) mastery; (sport) championship
Mei'sterstück *n*, **Mei'sterwerk** *n* masterpiece
Mei'sterzug *m* master stroke
Melancholie [melaŋko'li] *f* (-;) melancholy
melancholisch [melaŋ'kolɪʃ] *adj* melancholy
Melasse [me'lasə] *f* (-;-n) molasses
Meldeamt ['meldə·amt] *n.* **Meldebüro** ['meldəbyro] *n* registration office
Meldefahrer ['meldəfarər] *m* (mil) dispatch rider
Meldegänger ['meldəgɛŋər] *m* (mil) messenger, runner
melden ['meldən] *tr* report; (*polizeilich*) turn (*s.o.*) in; **den Empfang m.** (*genit*) acknowledge the receipt of; **er hat nichts zu m.** he has nothing to say in the matter; **gemeldet werden zu** (sport) be entered in; **j-m m. lassen, daß** send s.o. word that || *ref* report; (*Alter*) begin to show; (*Gläubiger*) come forward; (*Kind*) cry; (*Magen*) growl; (*polizeilich*) register; (*Winter*) set in; (telp) answer; **sich auf e-e Anzeige m.** answer an ad; **sich krank m.** (mil) go on sick call; **sich m. zu** apply for; (*freiwillig*) volunteer for; (mil) enlist in; (sport) enter; **sich zum Dienst m.** (mil) report for duty; **sich zum Wort m.** ask to speak; (*in der Schule*) hold up the hand
Mel'der *m* (-s;-) (mil) runner
Meldezettel ['meldətsetəl] *m* registration form
Mel'dung *f* (-;-en) report; message, notification; (*Bewerbung*) application
Melkeimer ['melkaɪmər] *m* milk pail
melken ['melkən] §113 *tr* milk
Melo·die [melo'di] *f* (-;-dien ['di·ən]) melody
melodisch [me'lodɪʃ] *adj* melodious
Melone [me'lonə] *f* (-;-n) melon; (coll) derby
Meltau ['meltau] *m* (-[e]s;) honeydew
Membran [mem'bran] *f* (-;-en), **Membrane** [mem'branə] *f* (-;-n) membrane
Memme ['memə] *f* (-;-n) coward
Memoiren [memo'arən] *pl* memoirs
memorieren [memo'rirən] *tr* memorize
Menge ['mɛŋə] *f* (-;-n) quantity, amount; crowd; **e-e M.** a lot of
mengen ['mɛŋən] *tr* mix || *ref* (*unter acc*) mingle (with); (**in** *acc*) meddle (**in**)
Men'genlehre *f* (math) theory of sets
men'genmäßig *adj* quantitative
Mengsel ['mɛŋzəl] *n* (-s;-) hodgepodge
Mennige ['mɛnɪgə] *f* (-;) rust-preventive paint
Mensch [mɛnʃ] *m* (-en;-en) human being, man; person, individual; **die Menschen** the people; **kein M.** no one || *n* (-es; -er) hussy, slut

Menschen– [menʃən] *comb.fm.* man, of men; human
Men'schenalter *n* generation, age
Men'schenfeind –in §8 *mf* misanthropist
Men'schenfresser *m* cannibal
Men'schenfreund –in §8 *mf* philanthropist
men'schenfreundlich *adj* philanthropic, humanitarian
Men'schengedenken *n*—seit M. since time immemorial
Men'schengeschlecht *n* mankind
Men'schengewühl *n* milling crowd
Men'schenglück *n* human happiness
Men'schenhandel *m* slave trade
Men'schenhaß *m* misanthropy
Men'schenjagd *f* manhunt
Men'schenkenner –in §6 *mf* judge of human nature
Men'schenkind *n* human being; armes M. poor soul
men'schenleer *adj* deserted
Men'schenliebe *f* philanthropy
Men'schenmaterial *n* manpower
men'schenmöglich *adj* humanly possible
Men'schenraub *m* kidnaping
Men'schenräuber –in §6 *mf* kidnaper
Men'schenrechte *pl* human rights
men'schenscheu *adj* shy, unsociable
Men'schenschinder *m* oppressor, slave driver
Men'schenschlag *m* race
Men'schenseele *f* human soul; keine M. not a living soul
Men'schenskind *interj* man alive!
Men'schensohn *m* (Bib) Son of man
men'schenunwürdig *adj* degrading
Men'schenverächter –in §6 *mf* cynic
Men'schenverstand *m*—guter M. common sense
Men'schenwürde *f* human dignity
men'schenwürdig *adj* decent
Mensch'heit *f* (–;) mankind, humanity
mensch'lich *adj* human; (*human*) humane
Mensch'lichkeit *f* (–;) humanity
Menschwerdung ['menʃverdʊŋ] *f* (–;) incarnation
Menstruation [mentru·a'tsjon] *f* (–;–en) menstruation
Mensur [men'zur] *f* (–;–en) measure; (*Meßglas*) measuring glass; students' duel
Mentalität [mentalɪtet] *f* (–;) mentality
Menuett [menu'et] *n* (–[e]s;–e) minuet
Meridian [merɪ'djan] *m* (–s;–e) (astr) meridian
merkbar ['merkbar] *adj* noticeable
Merkblatt ['merkblat] *n* instruction sheet
Merkbuch ['merkbux] *n* notebook
merken ['merkən] *tr* notice; realize; etw m. lassen show s.th., betray s.th.; man merkte es sofort an ihrem Ausdruck, daß one noticed immediately by her expression that ‖ *ref*—m. Sie sich [*dat*], was ich sage! mark my word!; sich [*dat*] etw m. bear s.th. in mind; sich [*dat*] nichts m. lassen not give oneself away ‖ *intr*—m. auf (*acc*) pay attention to, heed
merk'lich *adj* noticeable

Merkmal ['merkmal] *n* (–[e]s;–e) mark, feature, characteristic
Merkur [mer'kur] *m* & *n* (–s;) mercury
Merk'wort *n* (–[e]s;–̈er) catchword; (theat) cue
merk'würdig *adj* remarkable; (*seltsam*) curious, strange
merkwürdigerweise ['merkvɥrdɪgər-vaɪzə] *adv* strange to say
Merk'würdigkeit *f* (–;–en) strange thing
Merk'zeichen *n* mark
meschugge [me'ʃugə] *adj* (coll) nuts
Mesner ['mesnər] *m* (–s;–) sexton
Meß– [mes] *comb.fm.* measuring; (eccl) mass
Meß'band *n* (–[e]s;–̈er) measuring tape
meßbar ['mesbar] *adj* measurable
Meß'buch *n* (relig) missal
Meß'diener *m* acolyte
Messe ['mesə] *f* (–;–n) fair; (eccl) mass; (nav) officers' mess
messen ['mesən] §70 *tr* measure; (*Zeit*) time, clock; (*mustern*) size up ‖ *ref*—sich m. mit cope with; (*geistig*) match wits with; sich nicht m. können mit be no match for ‖ *intr* measure
Messer ['mesər] *m* (–s;–) gauge; meter ‖ *n* (–s;–) knife; (surg) scalpel; bis aufs M. to the death
Mes'serheld *m* (coll) cutthroat
mes'serscharf' *adj* razor-sharp
Mes'serschmied *m* cutler
Messerschmiedewaren ['mesərʃmidəva-rən] *pl* cutlery
Mes'serschneide *f* knife edge
Meß'gewand *n* (eccl) vestment; chasuble
Meß'hemd *n* (eccl) alb
Messias [me'si·as] *invar m* Messiah
Messing ['mesɪŋ] *n* (–s;) brass
messingen ['mesɪŋən] *adj* brass
Meß'opfer *n* sacrifice of the mass
Mes'sung *f* (–;–en) measurement
Metall [me'tal] *n* (–s;–e) metal
Metall'baukasten *m* erector set
metallen [me'talən], metallisch [me-'talɪʃ] *adj* metallic
Mettall'säge *f* hacksaw
Metallurgie [metalur'gi] *f* (–;) metallurgy
metall'verarbeitend *adj* metal-processing
Metall'waren *pl* hardware
Metapher [me'tafər] *f* (–;–n) metaphor
Meteor [mete'or] *m* (–s;–e) meteor
Meteorologe [mete·orə'logə] *m* (–n;–n) meteorologist
Meteorologie [mete·orolə'gi] *f* (–;) meteorolgy
Meteorologin [mete·orə'login] *f* (–;–nen) meteorologist
meteorologisch [mete·orə'logɪʃ] *adj* meteorological
Meteor'stein *m* meteorite, aerolite
Meter ['metər] *m* & *n* (–s;–) meter
Me'termaß *n* tape measure
Methode [me'todə] *f* (–;–n) method
methodisch [me'todɪʃ] *adj* methodical
Metrik ['metrɪk] *f* (–;) metrics
metrisch ['metrɪʃ] *adj* metrical

Metropole [metrɔ'polə] *f* (-;-n) metropolis
Mette ['metə] *f* (-;-n) matins
Mettwurst ['metvurst] *f* soft sausage
Metzelei [metsə'laɪ] *f* (-;-en) massacre, slaughter
metzeln ['metsəln] *tr* massacre
Metzger ['metsgər] *m* (-s;-) butcher
Metzgerei [metsgə'raɪ] *f* (-;-en) butcher shop
Meuchelmord ['mɔɪçəlmɔrt] *m* assassination
Meuchelmörder –in ['mɔɪçəlmœrdər (ɪn)] §6 *mf* assassin
meucheln ['mɔɪçəln] *tr* murder
meuchlerisch ['mɔɪçlərɪʃ] *adj* murderous
meuchlings ['mɔɪçlɪŋs] *adv* treacherously
Meute ['mɔɪtə] *f* (-;-n) pack (*of hounds*); (fig) horde, gang
Meuterei [mɔɪtə'raɪ] *f* (-;-en) mutiny
meuterisch ['mɔɪtərɪʃ] *adj* mutinous
meutern ['mɔɪtərn] *intr* mutiny
Mexikaner –in [meksɪ'kanər(ɪn)] §6 *mf* Mexican
mexikanisch [meksɪ'kanɪʃ] *adj* Mexican
Mexiko ['meksɪko] *n* (-s;) Mexico
miauen [mɪ'au·ən] *intr* meow
mich [mɪç] §11 *pers pron* me || §11 *reflex pron* myself
mied [mit] *pret* of **meiden**
Mieder ['midər] *n* (-s;-) bodice
Mie'derwaren *pl* foundation garments
Mief [mif] *n* (-s;) foul air
Miene ['minə] *f* (-;-n) mien; facial expression; **M. machen zu** (*inf*) make a move to (*inf*); **ohne die M. zu verziehen** without flinching
mies [mis] *adj* (coll) miserable, lousy
Mies'macher *m* (-s;-) alarmist
Miet– [mit] *comb.fm.* rental, rented; rent
Miet'auto *n* rented car
Miete ['mitə] *f* (-;-n) rent; (*Zins*) rental; (*Erd-*) pit (*for storing vegetables*); **in M. geben** rent out; **in M. nehmen** rent; **kalte M.** rent not including heat; **zur M. wohnen** live in a rented apartment (or home)
mieten ['mitən] *tr* rent, hire; (*Flugzeug*) charter
Miet'entschädigung *f* allowance for house rent
Mie'ter –in §6 *mf* tenant
Miet'ertrag *m* rent, rental
Miet'kontrakt *m* lease
Mietling ['mitlɪŋ] *m* (-s;-e) hireling
Miets'haus *n* apartment building
Miets'kaserne *f* tenement house
Miet'vertrag *m* lease
Miet'wagen *m* rented car
Miet'wohung *f* apartment
Miet'zins *m* rent
Mieze ['mitsə] *f* (-;-n) pussy
Migräne [mɪ'grenə] *f* (-;-n) migraine
Mikrobe [mɪ'krobə] *f* (-;-n) microbe
Mikrofilm ['mikrofɪlm] *m* microfilm
Mikrophon [mɪkrɔ'fon] *n* (-s;-e) microphone
Mikroskop [mɪkrɔ'skop] *n* (-s;-e) microscope

mikroskopisch [mɪkrɔ'skopɪʃ] *adj* microscopic
Milbe ['mɪlbə] *f* (-;-n) (ent) mite
Milch [mɪlç] *f* (-;) milk
Milch'bart *m* sissy
Milch'brot *n*, **Milch'brötchen** *n* French roll
Milch'bruder *m* foster brother
Milch'drüse *f* mammary gland
Milch'eimer *m* milk pail
Milch'geschäft *n* creamery, dairy
Milch'glas *m* milk glass
milchig ['mɪlçɪç] *adj* milky
Milch'mädchen *n* milkmaid
Milch'mädchenrechnung *f* oversimplification
Milch'mixgetränk *n* milkshake
Milch'pulver *n* powdered milk
Milch'reis *m* rice pudding
Milch'schwester *f* foster sister
Milch'straße *f* Milky Way
Milch'tüte *f* carton of milk
Milch'wirtschaft *f* dairy
Milchzähne ['mɪlçtsenə] *pl* baby teeth
mild [mɪlt] *adj* mild; (*nicht streng*) lenient; (*Stiftung*) charitable; (*Wein*) smooth; (*Lächeln*) faint || **Milde** *f* (-;) mildness; leniency; kindness
mildern ['mɪldərn] *tr* soften, alleviate; **mildernde Umstände** extenuating circumstances
Mil'derung *f* (-;) softening, alleviation, mitigation
mild'herzig, mild'tätig *adj* charitable
Militär [mɪlɪ'ter] *n* (-s;) military, army; **zum M. gehen** join the army || *m* (-s;-s) professional soldier
Militär'dienst *m* military service
Militär'geistliche §5 *m* chaplain
Militär'gericht *n* military court
militärisch [mɪlɪ'terɪʃ] *adj* military
Militarismus [mɪlɪta'rɪsmus] *m* (-;) militarism
Miliz [mɪ'lits] *f* (-;) militia
Miliz'soldat *m* militiaman
Milliardär –in [mɪljar'der(ɪn)] §8 *mf* multimillionaire
Milliarde [mɪl'jardə] *f* (-;-n) billion
Milligramm [mɪlɪ'gram] *n* milligram
Millimeter [mɪlɪ'metər] *n* & *m* millimeter
Millime'terpapier *n* graph paper
Million [mɪl'jon] *f* (-;-en) million
Millionär –in [mɪljɔ'ner(ɪn)] §8 *mf* millionaire
millionste [mɪl'jonstə] §9 *adj* & *pron* millionth
Milz [mɪlts] *f* (-;) spleen
Mime ['mimə] *m* (-n;-n) mime
Mimiker –in ['mimɪkər(ɪn)] §6 *mf* mimic
Mimose [mɪ'mozə] *f* (-;-n) mimosa
minder ['mɪndər] *adj* lesser, smaller; (*geringer*) minor, inferior || *adv* less; **m. gut** inferior; **nicht m.** likewise
min'derbedeutend *adj* less important
min'derbegabt *adj* less talented
min'derbemittelt *adj* of moderate means
Min'derbetrag *m* shortage, deficit
Min'derheit *f* (-;-en) minority
min'derjährig *adj* underage || **Minderjährige** §5 *mf* minor

mindern ['mɪndərn] *tr* lessen, diminish
Min'derung *f* (-;-en) diminution
min'derwertig *adj* inferior
Min'derwertigkeit *f* inferiority
Min'derwertigkeitskomplex *m* inferiority complex
Min'derzahl *f* minority
Mindest– [mɪndəest] *comb.fm.* minimum
mindeste ['mɪndəstə] §9 *adj* least; (*kleinste*) smallest; **nicht die mindesten Aussichten** not the slightest chance; **nicht im mindesten** not in the least; **zum mindesten** at the very least
mindestens ['mɪndəstəns] *adv* at least
Min'destgebot *n* lowest bid
Min'destlohn *m* minimum wage
Mine ['minə] *f* (-;-n) (*im Bleistift*) lead; (mil, min) mine; **alle Minen springen lassen** (fig) pull out all the stops
Minenleger ['minənlegər] *m* (-s;-) minelayer
Minenräumboot ['minənrɔɪmbot] *n* minesweeper
Mineral [minə'ral] *n* (-s;-e & -ien [jən]) mineral
mineralisch [minə'ralɪʃ] *adj* mineral
Mineralogie [minəralə'gi] *f* (-;) mineralogy
Miniatur [minja'tur] *f* (-;-en) miniature
minieren [mi'nirən] *tr* (fig) undermine; (mil) mine
minimal [mini'mal] *adj* minimal
Minirock ['minirɔk] *m* miniskirt
Minister [mi'nɪstər] *m* (-s;-) minister, secretary
Ministe·rium [minɪs'terjum] *n* (-s; -rien [rjən]) ministry, department
Mini'sterpräsident *m* prime minister
Mini'sterrat *m* (-[e]s;-̈e) cabinet
Ministrant [minɪs'trant] *m* (-en;-en) altar boy, acolyte
Minne ['minə] *f* (-;) (obs) love
Min'nesänger *m* minnesinger; troubadour
minorenn [minə'ren] *adj* underage
minus ['minus] *adv* minus || **Minus n** (-;-) minus; (com) deficit
Minute [mi'nutə] *f* (-;-n) minute
Minu'tenzeiger *m* minute hand
-minutig [minutɪç] *comb.fm.* –minute
Minze ['mɪntsə] *f* (-;-n) (bot) mint
mir [mir] §11 *pers pron* me, to me, for me; **mir ist kalt** I am cold; **mir nichts, dir nichts** suddenly; **von mir aus** for all I care || §11 *reflex pron* myself, to myself, for myself
Mirabelle [mira'belə] *f* (-;-n) yellow plum
Mirakel [mi'rakəl] *n* (-s;-) miracle
Mira'kelspiel *n* miracle play
Mischehe ['mɪʃe·ə] *f* mixed marriage
mischen ['mɪʃən] *tr* mix, blend; (cards) shuffle
Mischling ['mɪʃlɪŋ] *m* (-es;-e) half-breed; mongrel
Mischmasch ['mɪʃmaʃ] *m* (-es;-e) hodgepodge
Mischpult ['mɪʃpʊlt] *n* (rad, telv) master console

Mischrasse ['mɪʃrasə] *f* cross-breed
Mi'schung *f* (-;-en) mixture, blend
Misere [mi'zerə] *f* (-;-n) misery
Miß–, miß– [mɪs] *comb.fm.* mis–, dis–, amiss; bad, wrong, false
mißach'ten *tr* disregard; (*geringschätzen*) slight
mißartet [mɪs'artət] *adj* degenerate
miß'behagen *intr* (*dat*) displeasure || **Mißbehagen n** (-s;) displeasure
miß'bilden *tr* misshape, deform
Miß'bildung *f* (-;-en) deformity
miß'billigen *tr* disapprove
Miß'billigung *f* (-;-en) disapproval
Miß'brauch *m* abuse; (*falsche Anwendung*) misuse
mißbrau'chen *tr* abuse; misuse
mißbräuchlich ['mɪsbrɔɪçlɪç] *adj* improper
mißdeu'ten *tr* misinterpret
missen ['mɪsən] *tr* miss; do without
Miß'erfolg *m* failure, flop
Miß'ernte *f* bad harvest
Missetat ['mɪsətat] *f* misdeed; (*Verstoß*) offense; (*Verbrechen*) felony; (*Sünde*) sin
Missetäter –in ['mɪsətetər(ɪn)] §6 *mf* wrongdoer; offender; felon; sinner
mißfal'len §72 *intr* (*dat*) displease || **Mißfallen n** (-s;) displeasure
miß'fällig *adj* displeasing; (*anstößig*) shocking; (*verächtlich*) disparaging
miß'farben, miß'farbig *adj* discolored
Miß'geburt *f* freak
mißgelaunt ['mɪsgəlaunt] *adj* in bad humor, sour
Miß'geschick *n* (-s;) mishap; misfortune
Miß'gestalt *f* deformity; monster
miß'gestaltet *adj* deformed, misshapen
mißgestimmt ['mɪsgəʃtɪmt] *adj* grumpy
mißglücken (**mißglük'ken**) *intr* (SEIN) fail, not succeed
mißgön'nen *tr* begrudge
Miß'griff *m* mistake
Miß'gunst *f* grudge, jealousy
mißhan'deln *tr* mistreat
Miß'heirat *f* mismarriage
Mißhelligkeit ['mɪshelɪçkaɪt] *f* (-;-en) friction, disagreement
Mission [mi'sjon] *f* (-;-en) mission
Missionar [misjə'nar] *m*, **Missionär** [misjə'ner] *m* (-s;-e) missionary
Miß'klang *m* dissonance; (fig) sour note
Miß'kredit *m* discredit, disrepute
mißlang [mɪs'laŋ] *pret* of **mißlingen**
miß'lich *adj* awkward; (*gefährlich*) dangerous; (*bedenklich*) critical
miß'liebig *adj* unpopular
mißlingen [mɪs'lɪŋən] §142 *intr* (SEIN) go wrong, misfire, prove a failure || **Mißlingen n** (-s;) failure
Miß'mut *m* bad humor; discontent
miß'mutig *adj* sullen; discontented
mißra'ten §63 *intr* (SEIN) go wrong, misfire; **mißratene Kinder** spoiled children
Miß'stand *m* bad state of affairs; **Mißstände abschaffen** remedy abuses
Miß'stimmung *f* dissension; (*Mißmut*) bad humor
Miß'ton *m* dissonance; (fig) sour note

mißtrau'en *intr* (*dat*) mistrust, distrust || **Miß'trauen** *n* (*-s*;) mistrust
mißtrauisch ['mistrau·iʃ] *adj* distrustful
Miß'vergnügen *n* displeasure
miß'vergnügt *adj* cross; discontented
Miß'verhältnis *n* disproportion
Miß'verständnis *n* misunderstanding
miß'verstehen §146 *tr* & *intr* misunderstand
Miß'wirtschaft *f* mismanagement
Mist [mist] *m* (*-es*;) dung, manure; (*Schmutz*) dirt; (fig) mess, nonsense; **M. machen** (coll) blow the job; (*Spaß machen*) (coll) horse around; **viel M. verzapfen** talk a lot of nonsense
Mist'beet *n* hotbed
Mistel ['mistəl] *f* (*-;-n*) mistletoe
misten ['mistən] *tr* (*Stall*) muck; (*Acker*) fertilize
Mist'fink *m* (coll) dirty brat
Mist'haufen *m* manure pile
mistig ['mistiç] *adj* dirty; (*sehr unangenehm*) very unpleasant
mit [mit] *adv* along; also, likewise; simultaneously || *prep* (*dat*) with; **mit 18 Jahren** at the age of eighteen
Mit'angeklagte §5 *mf* codefendant
Mit'arbeit *f* cooperation, collaboration
mit'arbeiten *intr* cooperate, collaborate; **m. an** (*dat*) contribute to
Mit'arbeiter –in §6 *mf* co-worker
Mit'arbeiterstab *m* staff
mit'bekommen §99 *tr* receive when leaving; (*verstehen*) get, catch
mit'benutzen *tr* use jointly
Mit'bestimmung *f* share in decision making
mit'bewerben *ref* (um) compete (for)
Mit'bewerber –in §6 *mf* competitor
mit'bringen §65 *tr* bring along
Mitbringsel ['mitbriŋzəl] *n* (*-s*;-) little present
Mit'bürger –in §6 *mf* fellow citizen
Mit'eigentümer –in §6 *mf* co-owner
miteinan'der *adv* together
mit'empfinden §59 *tr* sympathize with
Mit'erbe *m*, **Mit'erbin** *f* coheir
Mitesser ['mitesər] *m* (*-s*;-) pimple, blackhead
mit'fahren §71 *intr* (SEIN) ride along; **j–n m. lassen** give s.o. a lift
mit'fühlen *tr* share, sympathize with
mit'fühlend *adj* sympathetic
mit'gehen §82 *intr* (SEIN) (**mit**) go along (with)
Mit'gift *f* dowry
Mit'giftjäger *m* fortune hunter
Mit'glied *n* member; **M. auf Lebenszeit** life member
Mit'gliederversammlung *f* general meeting
Mit'gliederzahl *f* membership
Mit'gliedsbeitrag *m* dues
Mit'gliedschaft *f* (*-;-en*) membership
Mit'gliedskarte *f* membership card
Mit'gliedstaat *m* member nation
Mit'haftung *f* joint liability
mit'halten §90 *intr* be one of a party; **ich halte mit** I'll join you
mit'helfen §96 *intr* help along, pitch in

Mit'helfer –in §6 *mf* assistant
Mit'herausgeber –in §6 *mf* coeditor
Mit'hilfe *f* assistance
mithin' *adv* consequently
mit'hören *tr* listen in on; (*zufällig*) overhear; (rad, telp) monitor
Mit'inhaber –in §6 *mf* copartner
Mit'kämpfer –in §6 *mf* fellow fighter
mit'klingen §142 *intr* resonate
mit'kommen §99 *intr* (SEIN) come along; (fig) keep up
mit'kriegen *tr* (coll) see **mitbekommen**
Mit'läufer –in §6 *mf* (pol) fellow traveler
Mit'laut *m* consonant
Mit'leid *n* compassion, pity
Mit'leidenschaft *f*—j–n in M. ziehen affect s.o.
mit'leidig *adj* compassionate; pitiful
Mit'leidsbezeigung *f* condolences
mit'leidslos *adj* pitiless
mit'leidsvoll *adj* full of pity
mit'machen *tr* participate in, join in on; (*ertragen*) suffer, endure
Mit'mensch *m* fellow man
mit'nehmen §116 *tr* take along; (*erschöpfen*) wear out, exhaust; (*abholen*) pick ,up; (*Ort, Museum*) visit, take in; **j–n arg m.** treat s.o. roughly
mitnichten [mit'niçtən] *adv* by no means, not at all
mit'rechnen *tr* include || *intr* count
mit'reden *tr*—**ein Wort mitzureden haben bei** have a say in || *intr* join in a conversation
Mit'reisende §5 *mf* travel companion
mit'reißen §53 *tr* (& fig) carry away
mit'reißend *adj* stirring
mitsamt [mit'zamt] *prep* (*dat*) together with
mit'schreiben §62 *intr* take notes
Mit'schuld *f* (an *dat*) complicity (in)
mit'schuldig *adj* (an *dat*) accessory (to) || **Mitschuldige** §5 *mf* accomplice
Mit'schüler –in §6 *mf* schoolmate
mit'singen §142 *intr* sing along
mit'spielen *intr* play along; (fig) be involved; **j–m arg** (or **übel**) **m.** play s.o. dirty
Mit'spieler –in §6 *mf* partner
Mit'spracherecht *n* right to share in decision making
mit'sprechen §64 *tr* say with (*s.o.*) || *intr* be involved; (*an e–r Entscheidung beteiligt sein*) share in decision making
Mit'tag *m* noon; (poet) South; **M. machen** stop for lunch; **zu M. essen** eat lunch
Mittag– *comb.fm.* midday, noon; lunch
mit'tägig *adj* midday, noontime
mittags ['mitaks] *adv* at noon
Mit'tagskreis *m*, **Mit'tagslinie** *f* meridian
Mit'tagsruhe *f* siesta
Mit'tagsstunde *f* noon; lunch hour
Mit'tagstisch *m* lunch table; lunch; **gut bürglicher M.** good home cooking
Mit'tagszeit *f* noontime; lunch time
Mit'täter –in §6 *mf* accomplice
Mit'täterschaft *f* complicity

Mitte ['mɪtə] *f* (-;-n) middle, midst; (*Mittelpunkt*) center; **ab durch die M.!** (coll) scram!; **aus unserer M.** from among us; **die goldene M.** the golden mean; **die richtige M. treffen** hit a happy medium; **er ist M. Vierzig** he is in his mid-forties; **in die M. nehmen** take by both arms; (sport) sandwich in; **j-m um die M. fassen** put one's arms around s.o.'s waist

mit'teilbar *adj* communicable

mit'teilen *tr* tell; (*im Vertrauen*) intimate; **ich muß Ihnen leider m., daß** I regret to inform you that

mitteilsam ['mɪttaɪlzɑm] *adj* communicative

Mit'teilung *f* (-;-en) communication; information; (*amtliche*) communiqué; (*an die Presse*) release

mittel ['mɪtəl] *adj* medium, average ‖ **Mittel** *n* (-s;-) middle; means; (*Heil-*) remedy; (*Maßnahme*) measure; (*Ausweg*) expedient; (*Durchschnitt*) average; (math) mean; (phys) medium; **im M.** on the average; **ins M. treten** (or **sich ins M. legen**) intervene, intercede; **letztes M.** last resort; **mit allen Mitteln** by every means; **Mittel** *pl* resources, means; funds; **M. und Wege** ways and means; **M. zum Zweck** means to an end; **sicheres M.** reliable method

Mit'telalter *n* Middle Ages

mittelalterlich ['mɪtəlaltərlɪç] *adj* medieval

Mit'telamerika *n* Central America

mittelbar ['mɪtəlbɑr] *adj* indirect

Mit'telgang *m* center aisle

Mit'telgebirge *n* highlands

Mit'telgewicht *n* (box) middleweight class

Mittelgewichtler ['mɪtəlgəvɪçtlər] *m* (-s;-) middleweight boxer

Mit'telgröße *f* medium size

mit'telhochdeutsch *adj* Middle High German ‖ **Mittelhochdeutsch** *n* (-es;) Middle High German

Mit'tellage *f* central position; (mus) middle range

mittelländisch ['mɪtəllɛndɪʃ] *adj* Mediterranean

Mit'telläufer *m* (fb) center halfback

mit'tellos *adj* penniless, destitute

Mit'telmaß *n* medium; balance; average

mitt'telmäßig *adj* medium, mediocre; (*leidlich*) indifferent, so-so

Mit'telmäßigkeit *f* mediocrity

Mit'telmast *m* mainmast

Mit'telmeer *n* Mediterranean

Mit'telohr *n* middle ear

Mit'telpreis *m* average price

Mit'telpunkt *m* center

mittels ['mɪtəls] *prep* (*genit*) by means of

Mit'telschiff *n* (archit) nave

Mit'telschule *f* secondary school

Mit'tels·mann *m* (-[e]s;-er & -leute) go-between; (com) middleman

Mit'telsorte *f* medium quality

Mit'telsperson *f* see **Mittelsmann**

Mit'telstand *m* middle class

Mit'telstürmer *m* (fb) center forward

Mit'telweg *m* middle course; **der goldene M.** the golden mean; **e-n M. einschlagen** steer a middle course

Mit'telwort *n* (-[e]s;-er) (gram) participle

mitten ['mɪtən] *adv*—**m. am Tage** in broad daylight; **m. auf dem Wege** well on the way; **m. auf der Straße**; right in the middle of the street; **m. aus** from the midst of, from among; **m. darin** right in the very center (of it, of them); **m. entzwei brechen** break right in two; **m. im Winter** in the dead of winter; **m. in der Luft** in midair; **m. ins zwanzigste Jahrhundert** well into the twentieth century

Mitternacht ['mɪtərnaxt] *f* midnight

mitternächtig ['mɪtərnɛçtɪç], **mitternächtlich** ['mɪtərnɛçtlɪç] *adj* midnight

Mittler -in ['mɪtlər(ɪn)] §6 *mf* mediator; (com) middleman

mittlere ['mɪtlərə] §9 *adj* middle, central; (*durchschnittlich*) average; (*mittelmäßig*) medium; (math) mean; **der Mittlere Osten** the Middle East; **in mittleren Jahren sein** be middle-aged; **von mittlerer Größe** medium-sized

mitt'lerweile *adv* in the meantime

mittschiffs ['mɪtʃɪfs] *adv* amidships

Mittwoch ['mɪtvɔx] *m* (-[e]s;-e) Wednesday

mitun'ter *adv* now and then

mit'unterzeichnen *tr* & *intr* countersign

mit'verantwortlich *adj* jointly responsible

Mit'verantwortung *f* joint responsibility

Mit'verschworene §5 *mf* co-conspirator

Mit'welt *f* present generation; our (his, etc.) contemporaries

mit'wirken *intr* (**an** *dat* or **bei**) cooperate (in)

Mit'wirkung *f* cooperation

Mit'wissen *n*—**ohne mein M.** without my knowledge

Mitwisser -in ['mɪtvɪsər(ɪn)] §6 *mf* accessory; one in the know

mit'zählen *tr* include ‖ *intr* count along

mixen ['mɪksən] *tr* mix

Mixgetränk ['mɪksgətrɛŋk] *n* mixed drink

Mixtur ['mɪks'tur] *f* (-;-en) mixture

Möbel ['møbəl] *n* (-s;-) piece of furniture; **Möbel** *pl* furniture

Mö'belstück *n* piece of furniture

Möbeltransporteur ['møbəltransportør] *m* (-s;-e) mover

Mö'belwagen *m* moving van

mobil [mo'bil] *adj* movable; (*flink*) chipper; (mil) mobile

Mobiliar [mobi'ljar] *n* (-[e]s;) furniture

Mobilien [mo'biljən] *pl* movables

mobilisieren [mobili'zirən] *tr* mobilize

Mobilisierung [mobili'zirʊŋ] *f* (-;) mobilization

mobil'machen *tr* mobilize
Mobilmachung [mɔ'bilmaxuŋ] *f* (-;) mobilization
möblieren [mø'blirən] *tr* furnish; **möbliert wohnen** (coll) live in a furnished room; **neu m.** refurnish
mochte ['mɔxtə] *pret* of **mögen**
Mode ['modə] *f* (-;-n) fashion, style
Mo'debild *n* fashion plate
Modell [mɔ'dɛl] *n* (-[e]s;-e) model; (*Muster*) pattern; (fig) prototype; **M. stehen zu** (*dat*) model for
modellieren [mɔdɛ'lirən] *tr* fashion, shape
Modell'puppe *f* mannequin
modeln ['modəln] *tr* fashion, shape; (nach) model (on) ‖ *ref*—**zu alt sein, um sich m. zu lassen** be too old to change
Mo'dengeschäft *n* dress shop
Mo'denschau *f* fashion show
Mo'denzeitung *f* fashion magazine
Moder ['modər] *m* (-;) mold; mustiness; (*Schlamm*) mud
Mo'derduft *m*, **Mo'dergeruch** *m* musty smell
moderig ['modərɪç] *adj* moldy, musty
modern [mɔ'dɛrn] *adj* modern ‖ ['modərn] *intr* rot, decay ‖ **Modern** *n* (-s;) decay
modernisieren [modɛrnɪ'zirən] *tr* modernize; bring up to date
Mo'deschmuck *m* costume jewelry
Mo'deschriftsteller –in §6 *mf* popular writer
Mo'dewaren *pl* (com) novelties
modifizieren [mɔdɪfɪ'tsirən] *tr* modify
modisch ['modɪʃ] *adj* fashionable
Modistin [mɔ'dɪstɪn] *f* (-;-nen) milliner
modrig ['modrɪç] *adj* moldy
modulieren [mɔdu'lirən] *tr* modulate; (*Stimme*) inflect
Mo·dus ['modus] *m* (-;-di [di]) mode, manner; (gram) mood
mogeln ['mogəln] *intr* cheat ‖ **Mogeln** *n* (-s;) cheating
mögen ['møgən] §114 *tr* like, care for; **ich mag lieber** I prefer ‖ *mod aux* may; can; care to; **er mag nicht nach Hause gehen** he doesn't care to go home; **ich möchte lieber bleiben** I'd rather stay; **ich möchte wissen** I should like to know; **mag kommen was da will** come what may; **wer mag das nur sein?** who can that be?; **wie mag das geschehen sein?** how could this have happened?
möglich ['møklɪç] *adj* possible; (*ausführbar*) feasible; **sein möglichstes tun** do one's utmost ‖ **Mögliche** §5 *n* possibility; **er muß alles Mögliche bedenken** he must consider every possibility; **im Rahmen des Möglichen** within the realm of possibility
möglichenfalls ['møklɪçənfals], **möglicherweise** ['møklɪçərvaizə] *adv* possibly, if possible
Mög'lichkeit *f* (-;-en) possibility; potentiality; **ist es die M.!** well, I never!; **finanzielle Möglichkeiten** financial means; **nach M.** as far as possible

möglichst ['møklɪçst] *adv* as ... as possible
Mohn [mon] *m* (-[e]s;-e) poppyseed; (bot) poppy
Mohn'samen *m* poppyseed
Mohr [mor] *m* (-en;-en) Moor
Möhre ['mørə] *f* (-;-n) carrot
Mohr'rübe *f* carrot
Mokka ['mɔka] *m* (-s;-s) mocha (*coffee*)
Molch [mɔlç] *m* (-[e]s;-e) salamander
Mole ['molə] *f* (-;-n) mole, breakwater
Molekül [mɔlɛ'kyl] *n* (-s;-e) molecule
molekular [mɔlɛku'lar] *adj* molecular
Molke ['mɔlkə] *f* (-;) whey
Molkerei [mɔlkə'rai] *f* (-;-en) dairy
Moll [mɔl] *invar n* (mus) minor
mollig ['mɔlɪç] *adj* plump; (*Frau*) buxom; (*behaglich*) snug, cozy
Moll'tonart *f* (mus) minor key
Moment [mo'mɛnt] *m* (-[e]s;-e) moment ‖ *n* (-[e]s;-e) momentum; (*Antrieb*) impulse, impetus; (*Faktor*) factor, point; (*Beweggrund*) motive
momentan [mɔmɛn'tan] *adj* momentary
Moment'aufnahme *f* snapshot; (*Bewegungsaufnahme*) action shot
Monarch [mo'narç] *m* (-en;-en) monarch
Monar·chie [mɔnar'çi] *f* (-;-chien ['çi·ən]) monarchy
Monat ['monat] *m* (-[e]s;-e) month
monatelang ['monatəlaŋ] *adj* lasting for months ‖ *adv* for months
mo'natlich *adj* monthly
Mo'natsbinde *f* sanitary napkin
Mo'natsfluß *m* menstruation
mo'natsweise *adv* monthly
Mönch [mœnç] *m* (-[e]s;-e) monk, friar
Mönchs'kappe *f* monk's cowl
Mönchs'kloster *n* monastery
Mönchs'kutte *f* monk's habit
Mönchs'orden *m* monastic order
Mönchs'wesen *n* monasticism
Mond [mont] *m* (-[e]s;-e) moon; **abnehmender M.** waning moon; **zunehmender M.** waxing moon
mondän [mɔn'den] *adj* sophisticated
Mond'fähre *f* (rok) lunar lander
Mond'finsternis *f* lunar eclipse
mond'hell' *adj* moonlit
Mond'jahr *n* lunar year
Mond'kalb *n* (fig) born fool
Mond'schein *m* moonlight
Mond'sichel *f* crescent moon
Mond'sucht *f* lunacy; somnambulism
mond'süchtig *adj* moonstruck
Moneten [mo'neten] *pl* (coll) dough
monieren [mo'nirən] *tr* criticize; remind
Monogramm [mɔnɔ'gram] *n* (-s;-e) monogram
Monolog [mɔnɔ'lok] *m* (-s;-e) monologue
Monopol [mɔnɔ'pol] *n* (-s;-e) monopoly
monopolisieren [mɔnɔpɔlɪ'zirən] *tr* monopolize
monoton [mɔnɔ'ton] *adj* monotonous
Monotonie [mɔnɔtɔ'ni] *f* (-;) monotony

Monsterfilm ['mɔnstərfɪlm] *m* (cin) spectacular
Monstranz [mɔn'strants] *f* (-;-en) monstrance
monströs [mɔn'strøs] *adj* monstrous
Monstrosität [mɔnstrɔzı'tet] *f* (-;-en) monstrosity
Mon·strum ['mɔnstrʊm] *n* (-;-stra [stra]) monster
Monsun [mɔ'zun] *m* (-s;-e) monsoon
Montag ['mɔntɑk] *m* (-[e]s;-e) Monday
Montage [mɔn'tɑʒə] *f* (-;-n) mounting, fitting; (mach) assembly
Monta'gebahn *f*, **Monta'geband** *n* assembly line
Monta'gehalle *f* assembly room
montags ['mɔntɑks] *adv* Mondays
Montan- [mɔntɑn] *comb.fm.* mining
Monteur [mɔn'tør] *m* (-s;-e) assembly-man, mechanic
Monteur'anzug *m* coveralls
montieren [mɔn'tirən] *tr* mount, fit; (*zusammenbauen*) assemble; (*einrichten*) install; (*aufstellen*) set up
Montur [mɔn'tur] *f* (-;-en) uniform
Moor [mor] *n* (-[e]s;-e) swamp
Moor'bad *n* mud bath
moorig ['morɪç] *adj* swampy
Moos [mos] *n* (-es;) moss; (*Geld*) (coll) dough
Mop [mɔp] *m* (-s;-s) mop
Moped ['mopɛd] *n* (-s;-s) motor bike, moped
moppen ['mɔpən] *tr* mop
mopsen ['mɔpsən] *tr* (coll) swipe || *ref* be bored stiff; be upset
Moral [mo'rɑl] *f* (-;) morality; (*Nutzwendung*) moral; (mil) morale
moralisch [mo'rɑlıʃ] *adj* moral
moralisieren [mɔralı'zirən] *intr* moralize
Moralität [mɔralı'tet] *f* (-;) morality
Morast [mo'rast] *m* (-es;-e & ̈e) mire; morass, quagmire
Mord [mɔrt] *m* (-[e]s;-e) murder
Mord'anschlag *m* murder attempt; (pol) assassination attempt
Mord'brennerei *f* arson and murder
Mord'bube *m* murderer, assassin
morden ['mɔrdən] *tr* & *intr* murder
Mörder **-in** ['mœrdər(ın)] §6 murderer
möderisch ['mœrdərıʃ] *adj* murderous; (coll) awful, terrible
mord'gierig *adj* bloodthirsty
Mord'kommission *f* homicide squad
mord'lustig *adj* bloodthirsty
Mords- [mɔrts] *comb.fm.* huge; terrible, awful; fantastic, incredible
Mords'angst *f* mortal fear
Mords'geschichte *f* tall story
Mords'geschrei *n* loud shouting
Mords'kerl *m* (coll) great guy
mords'mäßig *adv* (coll) awfully
Mords'spektakel *n* awful din
Mord'tat *f* murder
Mord'waffe *f* murder weapon
Mores ['morɛs] *pl—*j*-n* **M. lehren** teach s.o. manners
morgen ['mɔrgən] *adv* tomorrow; **m. abend** tomorrow evening (or night); **m. früh** tomorrow morning; **m. in**

acht Tagen (or **über acht Tage**) a week from tomorrow; **m. mittag** tomorrow noon || **Morgen** *m* (-s;-) morning; acre; **des Morgens** in the morning || *n* (-;) tomorrow
Mor'genblatt *n* morning paper
Mor'gendämmerung *f* dawn, daybreak
mor'gendlich *adj* morning
Mor'gengabe *f* wedding present
Mor'gengrauen *n* dawn, daybreak
Mor'genland *n* Orient
Morgenländer **-in** ['mɔrgənlɛndər(ın)] §6 *mf* Oriental
Mor'genrock *m* house robe
Mor'genrot *n*, **Mor'genröte** *f* dawn, sunrise; (fig) dawn, beginning
morgens ['mɔrgəns] *adv* in the morning
Mor'genstern *m* morning star
Mor'genstunde *f* morning hour
Mor'genzeitung *f* morning paper
morgig ['mɔrgɪç] *adj* tomorrow's
Morphium ['mɔrfjum] *n* (-s;) morphine
morsch [mɔrʃ] *adj* rotten; (*baufällig*) dilapidated; (*brüchig*) brittle; (fig) decadent
Morsealphabet ['mɔrzə·alfabet] *n* Morse code
Mörser ['mœrzər] *m* (-s;-) (& mil) mortar
Mör'serkeule *f* pestle
Mörtel ['mœrtal] *m* (-s;-) mortar; plaster; **mit M. bewerfen** roughcast
Mör'telkelle *f* trowel
Mör'teltrog *m* hod
Mosaik [moza'ik] *n* (-s;-en) mosaic
mosaisch [mo'za·ıʃ] *adj* Mosaic
Moschee [mo'ʃe] *f* (-;-n) mosque
Moskau ['mɔskau] *n* (-s;) Moscow
Moslem ['mɔsləm] *m* (-s;-s) Moslem
moslemisch [mɔs'lemıʃ] *adj* Moslem
Most [mɔst] *m* (-es;-e) must, grape juice; new wine
Mostrich ['mɔstrɪç] *m* (-[e]s;-e) mustard
Motel [mo'tɛl] *n* (-s;-s) motel
Motiv [mo'tif] *n* (-[e]s;-e) (*Beweggrund*) motive; (mus, paint) motif
motivieren [mɔtı'virən] *tr* justify
Mo·tor ['motor], [mo'tor] *m* (-s; -toren ['torən] & -tore ['torə]) motor
Mo'tordefekt *m* motor trouble
Mo'torhaube *f* (aer) cowl; (aut) hood
-motorig [motorɪç] *comb.fm.* -motor, -engine
Mo'torpanne *f* (aut) breakdown
Mo'torpflug *m* tractor plow
Mo'torrad *n* motorcycle
Mo'torradfahrer **-in** §6 *mf* motorcyclist
Mo'torrasenmäher *m* power mower
Mo'torroller *m* motor scooter
Mo'torsäge *f* power saw
Mo'torschaden *m* engine trouble
Motte ['mɔtə] *f* (-;-n) moth
mot'tenfest *adj* mothproof
Mot'tenkugel *f* mothball
Motto ['mɔto] *n* (-s;-s) motto
moussieren [mu'sirən] *intr* fizz; (*Wein*) sparkle
Möwe ['møvə] *f* (-;-n) sea gull

Mucke ['mʊkə] *f* (-;-n) whim; (dial) gnat; **Mucken haben** have moods
Mücke ['mykə] *f* (-;-n) gnat; mosquito; (dial) fly
Mucker ['mʊkər] *m* (-s;-) hypocrite; bigot; grouch; (coll) awkward guy
Muckerei [mʊkə'raɪ] *f* (-;) hypocrisy
muckerhaft ['mʊkərhaft] *adj* hypocritical, bigoted
Mucks [mʊks] *m* (-es;-e) faint sound; **keinen M. mehr!** not another sound!
mucksen ['mʊksən] *ref* & *intr* stir, say a word; **nicht gemuckst!** stay pat!
müde ['mydə] *adj* tired; **zum Umfallen m.** ready to drop
Mü'digkeit *f* (-;) weariness
Muff [mʊf] *m* (-[e]s;-e) (*Handwärmer*) muff; (*Schimmel*) mold; musty smell
Muffe ['mʊfə] *f* (-;-n) (mach) sleeve
muffeln ['mʊfəln] *intr* sulk, be grouchy; (*anhaltend kauen*) munch; mumble
muffig ['mʊfɪç] *adj* musty; (*Person*) sulky; (*Luft*) stale, frowzy
Mühe ['my·ə] *f* (-;-n) trouble, pains; (*Anstrengung*) effort; **geben Sie sich keine M.!** don't bother; **j-m M. machen** cause s.o. trouble; **mit M.** with difficulty; **mit M. und Not** barely; **nicht der M. wert** not worthwhile; **sich** [*dat*] **große M. machen** go to great pains; **verlorene M.** wasted effort
mü'helos *adj* easy, effortless
muhen ['mu·ən] *intr* moo, low
mühen ['my·ən] *ref* take pains
mü'hevoll *adj* hard, troublesome
Mühewaltung ['my·əvaltʊŋ] *f* (-;) trouble, efforts; **für Ihre M. dankend, verbleiben wir** ... thanking you for your cooperation, we remain ...
Mühle ['mylə] *f* (-;-n) mill
Mühlrad ['mylrɑt] *n* water wheel
Mühlstein ['myl/taɪn] *m* millstone
Muhme ['mumə] *f* (-;-n) aunt; cousin
Mühsal ['myzɑl] *f* (-;-e) trouble
mühsam ['myzɑm] *adj* wearisome; (*Leben*) hard; (*Arbeit*) painstaking || *adv* with effort, with difficulty
mühselig ['myzelɪç] *adj* (*Arbeit*) hard; (*Leben*) miserable, tough
Mulatte [mu'latə] *m* (-n;-n), **Mulattin** [mu'latɪn] *f* (-;-nen) mulatto
Mulde ['mʊldə] *f* (-;-n) trough; (geol) depression, basin
Mull [mʊl] *m* (-[e]s;) gauze
Müll [myl] *m* (-[e]s;) dust, ashes; (*Abfälle*) trash, garbage
Müll'abfuhr *f* garbage disposal
Müll'abfuhrwagen *m* garbage truck
Müll'eimer *m* trash can, garbage can
Müller ['mylər] *m* (-s;-) miller
Müllerin ['mylərɪn] *f* (-;-nen) miller's wife; miller's daughter
Müll'fahrer *m* garbage man
Müll'haufen *m* scrap heap
Müll'platz *m* garbage dump
Müll'schaufel *f* dustpan
Mulm [mʊlm] *m* (-[e]s;) rotten wood
mul'mig *adj* rotten; dusty; (*Luft*) sticky; (*Lage*) ticklish

Multiplikation [mʊltɪplɪka'tsjon] *f* (-;) multiplication
multiplizieren [mʊltɪplɪ'tsirən] *tr* multiply
Mumie ['mumjə] *f* (-;-n) mummy
Mumm [mʊm] *m* (-s;) (coll) drive, grit
Mummelgreis ['mʊməlgraɪs] *m* (coll) old fogey
mummeln ['mʊməln] *tr* & *intr* mumble
Mund [mʊnt] *m* (-[e]s;ːer) mouth; **den M. aufreißen** brag; **den M. halten** shut up; **den M. vollnehmen** talk big; **e–n losen M. haben** answer back; **sich** [*dat*] **den Mund verbrennen** put one's foot into it; **wie auf den M. geschlagen** dumbfounded
Mund'art *f* dialect
Mündel ['myndəl] *m* & *n* (-s;-) & *f* (-;-n) ward
Mündelgelder ['myndəlgeldər] *pl* trustfund
mün'delsicher *adj* gilt-edged; absolutely safe
munden ['mʊndən] *intr* taste good
münden ['myndən] *intr*—**m. in** (*acc*) empty into, flow into
mund'faul *adj* too lazy to talk
mund'gerecht *adj* palatable
Mund'geruch *m* halitosis
Mund'harmonika *f* mouth organ
Mund'höhle *f* oral cavity
mündig ['myndɪç] *adj* of age
Mün'digkeit *f* (-;) majority, full age
mündlich ['myntlɪç] *adj* oral, verbal
Mund'pflege *f* oral hygiene
Mund'sperre *f* lockjaw
Mund'stück *n* mouthpiece; (*Zigaretten*–) tip; (*Düse*) nozzle
mund'tot *adj*—**j–n m. machen** (fig) silence s.o.
Mund'tuch *n* table napkin
Mün'dung *f* (*e–s Flusses*) mouth; (*e–r Feuerwaffe*) muzzle
Mün'dungsfeuer *n* muzzle flash
Mün'dungsweite *f* (arti) bore
Mund'vorrat *m* provisions
Mund'wasser *n* mouthwash
Mund'werk *n* (fig) mouth, tongue
Mund'winkel *m* corner of the mouth
Munition [mʊni'tsjon] *f* (-;) ammunition
Munitions'lager *n* ammunition dump
munkeln ['mʊŋkəln] *tr* & *intr* whisper
Münster ['mynstər] *n* (-s;-) cathedral
munter ['mʊntər] *adj* awake; (*lebhaft*) lively; (*rüstig*) vigorous; gay
Münz– [mʏnts] *comb.fm.* monetary; of the mint; coin; coinage; coin-operated
Münz'anstalt *f* mint
Münze ['mʏntsə] *f* (-;-n) coin; change; (*Münzanstalt*) mint; (*Denkmünze*) medal; bare **M.** hard cash; **für bare Münze nehmen** take at face value
Münz'einheit *f* monetary unit
Münz'einwurf *m* coin slot
münzen ['mʏntsən] *tr* coin, mint; **das ist auf ihn gemünzt** that is meant for him || **Münzen** *n* (-s;) mintage, coinage
Münz'fälscher *m* counterfeiter
Münz'fernsprecher *m* public telephone

Münz'kunde *f* numismatics
Münz'wesen *n* monetary system
Münz'wissenschaft *f* numismatics
mürb [myrp], **mürbe** ['mYrbə] *adj*
(*Fleisch*) tender; (*sehr reif*) mellow;
(*gut durchgekocht*) well done; (*Gebäck*) crisp and flaky; (*brüchig*)
brittle; (*erschöpft*) worn out; (mil)
demoralized; **j-n mürbe machen** (fig)
break s.o. down; **mürbe werden**
soften, give in
Murks [murks] *m* (-es;) bungling job
murksen ['murksən] *intr* bungle
Murmel ['murməl] *f* (-;-n) marble
murmeln ['murməln] *tr & intr* murmur
Mur'meltier *n* ground hog, woodchuck
murren ['murən] *intr* grumble
mürrisch ['mYrɪʃ] *adj* grouchy, crabby
Mus [mus] *n* (-es;-e) purée; sauce
Muschel ['muʃəl] *f* (-;-n) mussel;
(*Schale*) shell; (anat) concha
Muse ['muzə] *f* (-;-n) (myth) Muse
Muse·um [mu'ze·um] *n* (-s;-en) museum
Musik [mu'zik] *f* (-;) music
Musikalien [muzɪ'kaljən] *pl* music
book
musikalisch [muzɪ'kalɪʃ] *adj* musical
Musikant [muzɪ'kant] *m* (-en;-en)
musician
Musikan'tenknochen *m* funny bone
Musik'automat *m*, **Musikbox** ['mjuzɪkbɔks] *f* (-;-en) juke box
Musiker -in ['muzɪkər(ɪn)] §6 *mf*
musician
Musik'hochschule *f* conservatory
Musik'kapelle *f* band
Musik'korps *n* military band
Musik'pavillon *m* bandstand
Musik'schrank *m*, **Musik'truhe** *f* radiophonograph console
Musi·kus ['muzɪkus] *m* (-;-zi [tsi])
(hum) musician
Musik'wissenschaft *f* musicology
musisch ['muzɪʃ] *adj* artistic
musizieren [muzɪ'tsirən] *intr* play
music
Muskat [mus'kat] *m* (-[e]s;-e) nutmeg
Muskateller [muska'tɛlər] *m* (-s;)
muscatel
Muskat'nuß *f* nutmeg
Muskel ['muskəl] *m* (-s;-n) muscle
Mus'kelkater *m* (coll) charley horse
Mus'kelkraft *f* brawn
Mus'kelriß *m* torn muscle
Mus'kelschwund *m* muscular distrophy
Mus'kelzerrung *f* pulled muscle
Muskete [mus'ketə] *f* (-;-n) musket
Muskulatur [muskula'tur] *f* (-;-en)
muscles, muscular system
muskulös [musku'lØs] *adj* muscular
Muß [mus] *invar n* must, necessity
Muße ['musə] *f* (-;) leisure; **mit M.**
at leisure
Muß'ehe *f* shotgun wedding
Musselin [musə'lin] *m* (-s;-e) muslin
müssen ['mYsən] *intr*—**ich muß nach
Hause** I must go home || *mod aux*—
ich muß (*inf*) I must (*inf*), I have to
(*inf*); **ich muß nicht** I don't have to;
muß das wirklich sein? is it really
neecessary?; **sie hätten hier sein m.**

they ought to have been here; **sie
müssen bald kommen** they are bound
to come soon
müßig ['mysɪç] *adj* idle; (*unnütz*) unprofitable; (*zwecklos*) useless; (*überflüssig*) superfluous
Mü'ßiggang *m* idleness
Müßiggänger *m* loafer
mußte ['mustə] *pret* of **müssen**
Muster ['mustər] *n* (-s;-) pattern;
(*Probestück*) sample; (*Vorbild*) example, model; **das M. e-r Hausfrau**
a model housewife; **nach dem M.
von** along the lines of; **sich** [*dat*]
ein M. nehmen an (*dat*) model oneself on
Mu'sterbeispiel *n* typical example
Mu'sterbild *n* ideal, paragon
Mu'stergatte *m* model husband
Mu'stergattin *f* model wife
mu'stergültig *adj* model, ideal
Mu'stergut *n* model farm
mu'sterhaft *adj* model, ideal
Mu'sterknabe *m* (pej) sissy
Mu'sterkollektion *f* (kit of) samples
mustern ['mustərn] *tr* examine, eye,
size up; (mil) inspect, review
Mu'sterprozeß *m* test case
Mu'sterschüler -in §6 *mf* model pupil
Mu'sterstück *n* specimen, sample
Mu'sterstudent -in §7 *mf* model student
Mu'sterung *f* (-;-en) inspection; examination; (mil) review
Mu'sterungsbescheid *m* induction notice
Mu'sterungskommission *f* draft board
Mu'sterwerk *n* standard work
Mu'sterwort *n* (-[e]s;-er) (gram) paradigm
Mut [mut] *m* (-[e]s) courage; **den
Mut sinken lassen** lose heart; **guten
Mutes sein** feel encouraged; **j-m
den Mut nehmen** discourage s.o.;
nur Mut! cheer up!
Mutation [muta'tsjon] *f* (-;-en) (biol)
mutation, sport
Mütchen ['mytçən] *n*—**sein M. kühlen
an** (*dat*) take it out on
mutieren [mu'tirən] *intr* (*Stimme*)
change
mutig ['mutɪç] *adj* courageous, brave
–**mütig** [mytɪç] *comb.fm.* –minded,
–feeling
mut'los *adj* discouraged
Mut'losigkeit *f* (-;) discouragement
mutmaßen ['mutmasən] *tr* suppose,
conjecture
mutmaßlich ['mutmaslɪç] *adj* supposed, alleged; **mutmaßlicher Erbe**
heir presumptive || *adv* presumably
Mut'maßung *f* (-;-en) conjecture,
guesswork; **Mutmaßungen anstellen**
conjecture
Mutter ['mutər] *f* (-;⁼) mother; **werdende M.** expectant mother || *f* (-;
-n) nut
Mut'terboden *m* rich soil
Mütterchen ['mytərçən] *n* (-s;-)
mummy; little old lady
Mut'tererde *f* rich soil; native soil
Mut'terfürsorge *f* maternity welfare
Mut'terkuchen *m* (anat) placenta

Mut'terleib *m* womb
Mütterlich ['mʏtərlıç] *adj* motherly, maternal; **m.** **verwandt** related on the mother's side
mut'terlos *adj* motherless
Mut'termal *n* birthmark
Mut'terpferd *n* mare
Mut'terschaf *n* ewe
Mut'terschaft *f* (-;) motherhood, maternity
Mut'terschlüssel *m* (mach) wrench
mut'terseelenallein' *adj* all alone
Muttersöhnchen ['mutərzønçən] *n* (-s;-) mamma's boy
Mut'tersprache *f* mother tongue
Mut'terstelle *f*—bei j–m die M. vertreten be a mother to s.o.
Mut'terstute *f* mare
Mut'tertier *n* (zool) dam
Mut'terwitz *m* common sense
Mutti ['muti] *f* (-;-s) (coll) mom
mut'voll *adj* courageous
Mut'wille *m* mischievousness

mut'willig *adj* mischievous, willful
Mütze ['mʏtsə] *f* (-;-n) cap
Myriade [mʏrı'adə] *f* (-;-n) myriad
Myrrhe ['mʏrə] *f* (-;-n) myrrh
Myrte ['mʏrtə] *f* (-;-n) myrtle
Mysterienspiel [mʏs'terjənʃpil] *n* (theat) mystery play
mysteriös [mʏste'rjøs] *adj* mysterious
Myste·rium [mʏs'terjum] *n* (-s;-rien [rjən]) mystery
mystifizieren [mʏstıfı'tsirən] *tr* mystify; (*täuschen*) hoax
Mystik ['mʏstık] *f* (-;) mysticism
My'stiker –in §6 *mf* mystic
mystisch ['mʏstıʃ] *adj* mystic(al)
Mythe ['mytə] *f* (-;-n) myth
mythisch ['mytıʃ] *adj* mythical
Mytholo·gie [mytɔlɔ'gi] *f* (-;-gien ['gi·ən]) mythology
mythologisch [mytə'logıʃ] *adj* mythological
My·thus ['mytus] *m* (-;-then [tən]) myth

N

N, n [ɛn] *invar n* N, n
na [na] *interj* well!; **na also!** there you are!; **na, so was!** don't tell me!; **na, und ob!** I'll say!; **na, warte!** just you wait!
Nabe ['nabə] *f* (-;-n) hub
Nabel ['nabəl] *m* (-s;-) navel
Na'belschnur *f* umbilical cord
nach [nax] *adv* after; **n. und n.** little by little; **n. wie vor** now as ever || *prep* (*dat*) (*Zeit*) after; (*Reihenfolge*) after, behind; (*Ziel, Richtung*) to, towards, for; (*Art, Maß, Vorbild, Richtschnur*) according to, after
Nach-, nach- *comb.fm.* subsequent, additional, supplementary; post-; over, over again, re-; after
nach'äffen *tr* ape, imitate
nachahmen ['naxamən] *tr* imitate, copy
Nach'ahmer –in §6 *mf* imitator
Nach'ahmung *f* (-;-en) imitation, copy
nach'arbeiten *tr* copy; (*ausbessern*) touch up; (*Versäumtes*) make up for
nach'arten *intr* (SEIN) (*dat*) take after
Nachbar ['naxbar] *m* (-s & -n;-n), **Nachbarin** ['naxbarın] *f* (-;-nen) neighbor
nach'barlich *adj* neighborly; neighboring
Nach'barschaft *f* (-;-en) neighborhood; **gute N. halten** be on friendly terms with neighbors
Nach'bau *m* (-s;) imitation, duplication; licensed manufacture; **unerlaubter N.** illegal manufacture
Nach'behandlung *f* (med) follow-up treatment
nach'bestellen *tr* reorder, order more of
Nach'bestellung *f* (-;-en) repeat order
nach'beten *tr & intr* repeat mechanically

nach'bezahlen *tr* pay afterwards; pay the rest of || *intr* pay afterwards
Nach'bild *n* copy
nach'bilden *tr* copy
Nach'bildung *f* (-;-en) copying; (*Kopie*) copy, reproduction; (*Modell*) mock-up; (*Attrappe*) dummy
nach'bleiben §62 *intr* (SEIN) remain behind; (educ) stay in; **hinter j–m n.** lag behind s.o.
nach'blicken *intr* (*dat*) look after
nach'brennen §97 *intr* smolder || **Nachbrennen** *n* (-s;) (rok) afterburn
Nach'brenner *m* (aer) afterburner
nach'datieren *tr* postdate
nachdem [nax'dem] *adv* afterwards; **je n.** as the case may be, it all depends || *conj* after, when; **je n.** according to how, depending on how
nach'denken §66 *intr* think it over; **n. über** (*acc*) think over, reflect on || **Nachdenken** *n* (-s;) reflection; **bei weiterem N.** on second thought
nach'denklich *adj* reflective, thoughtful; (*Buch*) thought-provoking; (*abwesend*) lost in thought
Nach'dichtung *f* (-;-en) free poetical rendering
nach'drängen *intr* (SEIN) (*dat*) crowd after; pursue
nach'dringen §142 *intr* be in hot pursuit; (*dat*) pursue
Nach'druck *m* (*Betonung*) stress, emphasis; energy; (*Raubdruck*) pirated edition; (typ) reprint; **mit N.** emphatically; **N. verboten** all rights reserved
nach'drucken *tr* reprint
nach'drücklich *adj* emphatic; **n. betonen** emphasize
nach'dunkeln *intr* get darker
nach'eifern *intr* (*dat*) emulate

nach'eilen *intr* (SEIN) (*dat*) hasten after, rush after
nacheinan'der *adv* one after another
nach'empfinden §59 *tr* have a feeling for; **j—m etw n.** sympathize with s.o. about s.th.
Nachen ['naxən] *m* (-s;-) (poet) boat
nach'erzählen *tr* repeat, retell
Nachfahr ['naxfar] *m* (-s;-en) descendant
nach'fahren §71 *intr* (SEIN) (*dat*) drive after, follow
nach'fassen *tr* (mil) get a second helping of ‖ *intr* (econ) do a follow-up
Nach'folge *f* succession
nach'folgen *intr* (*dat*) succeed, follow; follow in the footsteps of
nach'folgend *adj* following, subsequent
Nach'folger **-in** §6 *mf* follower; successor
nach'fordern *tr* charge extra; claim subsequently
nach'forschen *intr* (*dat*) investigate
Nach'frage *f* inquiry; (com) demand
nach'fragen *intr* (**nach**) ask (about)
Nach'frist *f* time extension
nach'fühlen *tr*—**j—m etw n.** sympathize with s.o. about s.th.
nach'füllen *tr* refill, fill up
nach'geben §80 *tr* give later; (*beim Essen*) give another helping of; **j—m nichts an Eifer n.** not be outdone by s.o. in zeal ‖ *intr* give way, give; (*schlaff werden*) slacken, give; (*dat*) give in to, yield to
nach'geboren *adj* younger; posthumous
Nach'gebühr *f* postage due
nach'gehen §82 *intr* (SEIN) (*dat*) follow; (*Geschäften*) attend to; (*untersuchen*) investigate, check on
nachgemacht ['naxgəmaxt] *adj* false, imitation; (*künstlich*) artificial
nachgeordnet ['naxgə·ɔrdnət] *adj* subordinate
nach'gerade *adv* by now; (*allmählich*) gradually; (*wirklich*) really
Nach'geschmack *m* aftertaste, bad taste
nachgewiesenermaßen ['naxgəvizənərmasən] *adv* as has been shown (or proved)
nachgiebig ['naxgibɪç] *adj* elastic, yielding, compliant; (*nachsichtig*) indulgent; (st. exch.) declining
nach'gießen §76 *tr* fill up, refill ‖ *intr* add more
nach'glühen *tr* (tech) temper ‖ *intr* smolder
nach'grübeln *intr* (*dat* or **über** *acc*) mull (over), ponder (on)
Nach'hall *m* echo, reverberation
nach'hallen *intr* echo, reverberate
nachhaltig ['naxhaltɪç] *adj* lasting
nach'hängen §92 *intr* (*dat*) give free rein to ‖ *impers*—**es hängt mir nach** I still feel the effects of it
nach'helfen §96 *intr* (*dat*) help along
nach'her *adv* afterwards, later, then; **bis n.!** so long!
nachherig ['naxherɪç] *adj* later
Nach'hilfe *f* assistance, help
Nach'hilfelehrer **-in** §6 *mf* tutor
Nach'hilfestunde *f* tutoring lesson

Nach'hilfeunterricht *m* tutoring
nach'hinken *intr* (*dat*) lag behind
Nachholbedarf ['naxholbədarf] *m* backlog of unsatisfied demands
nach holen *tr* make up for
Nach'hut *f* (mil) rear guard
nach'jagen *tr*—**j—m etw n.** send s.th. after s.o. ‖ *intr* (SEIN) (*dat*) pursue
Nach'klang *m* echo; (fig) reminiscence
nach'klingen §142 *intr* reecho, resound
Nachkomme ['naxkɔmə] *m* (-n;-n) offspring, descendant
nach'kommen §99 *intr* (SEIN) (*dat*) follow; join (*s.o.*) later; (*Vorschriften, e—m Gesetz*) obey; (*e—m Versprechen*) keep; (*e—r Pflicht*) live up to
Nach'kommenschaft *f* (-;) posterity
Nachkömmling ['naxkœmlɪŋ] *m* (-s; -e) offspring, descendant
Nach·laß ['naxlas] *m* (-lasses;-lässe) remission; (*am Preis*) reduction; (*Erbschaft*) estate; **literarischer N.** unpublished works
nach'lassen §104 *tr* leave behind; (*lockern*) slacken; **j—m 15% vom Preise n.** give s.o. a fifteen percent reduction in price ‖ *intr* (*sich lokkern*) slacken; (*sich vermindern*) diminish; (*milder werden*) relent; (*Regen*) let up; (*Kräfte*) give out; (*Wind, Sturm*) die down; (*schlechter werden*) get worse
Nach'laßgericht *n* probate court
nach'lässig *adj* careless, negligent
Nach'lässigkeit *f* carelessness, negligence
nach'laufen §105 *intr* (SEIN) (*dat*) run after, pursue
nach'leben *intr* (*dat*) live up to ‖ **Nachleben** *n* afterlife
Nach'lese *f* gleanings
nach'lesen §107 *tr* glean; (*Stelle im Buch*) reread, look up
nach'liefern *tr* deliver subsequently
nach'machen *tr* imitate; (*fälschen*) counterfeit; **j—m alles n.** imitate s.o. in everything
nach'malen *tr* copy
nachmalig ['naxmalɪç] *adj* later
nachmals ['naxmals] *adv* afterwards
nach'messen §70 *tr* measure again
Nach'mittag *m* afternoon
nach'mittags *adv* in the afternoon
Nach'mittagsvorstellung *f* matinée
Nach'nahme *f* (-;) C.O.D.
Nach'name *m* last name, family name
nach'plappern *tr* repeat mechanically
Nach'porto *n* postage due
nachprüfbar ['naxpryfbar] *adj* verifiable
nach'prüfen *tr* verify, check out
nach'rechnen *tr* (acct) check
Nach'rede *f* epilogue; **j—n in üble N. bringen** bring s.o. into bad repute; **üble N.** slander; **üble N. verbreiten** spread nasty rumors
nach'reden *tr*—**j—m etw n.** say s.th. behind s.o.'s back
Nachricht ['naxrɪçt] *f* (-;-en) news; (*Bericht*) report; (*kurzer Bericht*) notice; (*Auskunft*) information; **e—e N. verbreiten** spread the news; **geben Sie mir von Zeit zu Zeit N.!** keep me

advised; **Nachrichten** (rad, telv) news, news report; **Nachrichten einholen** make inquiries; **Nachrichten einziehen** gather information; **zur N.!** for your information

Nach'richtenabteilung ƒ (mil) intelligence section

Nach'richtenagentur ƒ news agency

Nach'richtenbüro n news room; news agency

Nach'richtendienst m news service; (mil) army intelligence

Nach'richtensatellit m communications satellite

Nach'richtensendung ƒ newscast

Nach'richtenwesen n communications

nach'rücken intr (SEIN) (im Rang) move up; (mil) (dat) follow up; **j–m n.** move up into s.o.'s position

Nach'ruf m obituary

nach'rufen §122 tr (dat) call after

Nach'ruhm m posthumous fame

nach'rühmen tr—j–m etw n. say s.th. nice about s.o.

nach'sagen tr—j–m etw n. repeat s.th. after s.o.; say s.th behind s.o.'s back; **das lasse ich mir nicht n.** I won't let that be said of me

Nach'satz m concluding clause

nach'schaffen tr replace

nach'schauen intr (dat) gaze after

nach'schicken tr forward

Nachschlagebuch ['naxʃlɑgəbux] n reference book

nach'schlagen §132 tr look up; (Buch) consult || intr (box) counter

Nachschlagewerk ['naxʃlɑgəverk] n reference work

Nach'schlüssel m skeleton key

nach'schreiben §62 tr copy; take down from dictation

Nach'schrift ƒ postscript

Nach'schub m (mil) supply, fresh supplies; (mil) supply lines

Nach'schublinie ƒ (mil) supply line

Nach'schubstützpunkt m (mil) supply base

Nach'schubweg m supply line

nach'sehen §138 tr (nachschlagen) look up; (nachprüfen) check; (acct) audit; (mach) overhaul; **j–m vieles n.** overlook much in s.o. || intr (dat) gaze after || **Nachsehen** n—das N. haben get the short end

nach'senden §140 tr send after, forward

nach'setzen intr (dat) run after

Nach'sicht ƒ patience; **mit j–m N. üben** have patience with s.o.

nach'sichtig, nach'sichtsvoll adj lenient, considerate

Nach'silbe ƒ suffix

nach'sinnen §121 intr (über acc) reflect (on). muse (over)

nach'sitzen intr be kept in after school

Nach'sommer m Indian summer

Nach'speise ƒ dessert

Nach'spiel n (fig) sequel

nach'spüren intr (dat) track down

nächst [neçst] prep (dat) next to

nächst'beste §9 adj second-best

nächstdem' adv thereupon

nächste ['neçstə] §9 adj (super of

nahe) next; (Weg) shortest; (Beziehungen) closest || **Nächste** §5 mƒ neighbor, fellow man, fellow creature

nach'stehen §146 intr (dat) be inferior to

nach'stehend adj following || adv (mentioned) below

nach'stellen tr (Schraube) reset, adjust; (Uhr) set back || intr (dat) be after; (e–m Mädchen) run after

Nach'stellung ƒ (–;–en) persecution; ambush; (gram) postposition

nächsten ['neçstən] adv one of these days, before long; next time

Näch'stenliebe ƒ charity

nächst'liegend adj nearest

nach'stöbern intr rummage about

nach'stoßen §150 intr (SEIN) (dat) (mil) follow up

nach'streben intr (dat) strive after; (e–r Person) emulate

nach'strömen, nach'strümen, nach'stürzen intr (SEIN) (dat) crowd after

nach'suchen tr search for || intr—n. um apply for

Nach'suchung ƒ (–;–en) search, inquiry; petition

Nacht [naxt] ƒ (–;ᵂe) night; **bei N. und Nebel** under cover of night

Nacht'ausgabe ƒ final (edition)

Nacht'teil m disadvantage

nach'teilig adj disadvantageous

Nacht'essen n supper

Nacht'eule ƒ night owl

Nacht'falter m (ent) moth

Nacht'geschirr n chamber pot

Nacht'gleiche ƒ equinox

Nacht'hemd n nightgown

Nachtigall ['naxtɪgal] ƒ (–;–n) nightingale

nächtigen ['neçtɪgən] intr pass the night

Nach'tisch m dessert

Nacht'klub m, **Nacht'lokal** n nightclub

Nacht'lager n accommodations for the night

nächtlich ['neçtlɪç] adj night, nightly

Nacht'mal n supper

Nacht'musik ƒ serenade

nach'tönen intr resound; (Note) linger

Nacht'quartier n accommodations for the night

Nachtrag ['naxtrak] m (–[e]s;ᵂe) supplement, addition

nach'tragen §132 tr add; **j–m etw n.** carry s.th. after s.o.; (fig) hold s.th. against s.o.

nachträgerisch ['naxtregərɪʃ] adj resentful. vindictive

nachträglich ['naxtreklɪç] adj supplementary; (später) subsequent

Nachtrags– comb.fm. supplementary

Nacht'trupp m (–s;) rear guard

nachts [naxts] adv at night

Nacht'schicht ƒ night shift

nacht'schlafend adj—bei (or zu) **nachtschlafender Zeit** late at night

Nacht'schwärmer –in §6 mƒ reveler

Nacht'tisch m night table

Nacht'topf m chamber pot

nach'tun §154 tr—j–m etw n. imitate s.o. in s.th.

Nacht'wache ƒ night watch, vigil

Nacht'wächter m night watchman

Nachtwandler –in [ˈnaxtvandlər(ɪn)] §6 *mf* sleepwalker, somnambulist
Nacht'zeug *n* overnight things
Nach'urlaub *m* extended leave
nach'wachsen §155 *intr* (SEIN) grow again
Nach'wahl *f* special election
Nachwehen [ˈnaxveˑən] *pl* afterpains; (fig) painful consequences
nach'weinen *tr*—keine Tränen n. (*dat*) waste no tears over ‖ *intr* (*dat*) cry over
Nachweis [ˈnaxvaɪs] *m* (–es;–e) proof; den N. bringen (or führen) furnish proof
nach'weisbar *adj* demonstrable
nach'weisen §118 *tr* point, show; (*beweisen*) prove; (*begründen*) substantiate; (*verweisen*) refer to
nach'weislich *adj* demonstrable
Nach'welt *f* posterity
nach'wiegen §57 *tr* verify the weight of
nach'wirken *intr* have an aftereffect
Nach'wirkung *f* (–;–en) aftereffect
Nach'wort *n* (–[e]s;–e) epilogue
Nach'wuchs *m* younger generation; younger set; children
nach'zahlen *tr & intr* pay extra
nach'zählen *tr* count over, check
nach'zeichnen *tr* draw a copy of ‖ *intr* copy
nach'ziehen §163 *tr* drag; tow; (*Linien*) trace; (*Schraube*) tighten ‖ *intr* (SEIN) (*dat*) follow after
nach'zoteln *intr* (SEIN) (coll) trot after
Nachzügler –in [ˈnaxtsyklər(ɪn)] §6 *mf* straggler; latecomer
Nackedei [ˈnakədaɪ] *m* (–[e]s;–e) naked child; nude
Nacken [ˈnakən] *m* (–s;–) nape of the neck
nackend [ˈnakənt] *adj* var of **nackt**
Nackenschlag (Nak'kenschlag) *m* rabbit punch; (fig) hard blow
–nackig [nakɪç] *comb.fm.* –necked
nackt [nakt] *adj* nude, bare; (*Tatsache*) hard; **sich n. ausziehen** strip bare
Nackt'heit *f* (–;) nudity, nakedness
Nadel [ˈnadəl] *f* (–;–n) needle; pin; **wie auf Nadeln sitzen** be on pins and needles
Na'delbaum *m* coniferous tree
Na'delkissen *n* pin cushion
Nadelöhr [ˈnadəløːr] *n* (–s;–e) eye of a needle
Na'delstich *m* pinprick; (sew) stitch
Nagel [ˈnagəl] *m* (–s;⁼) nail; **an den N. hängen** (fig) shelve; **an den Nägeln kauen** bite one's nails
Na'gelhaut *f* cuticle
nageln [ˈnagəln] *tr & intr* nail
na'gelneu' *adj* brand-new
nagen [ˈnagən] *tr* gnaw; **das Fleisch vom Knochen n.** pick the meat off the bone ‖ *intr* (**an** *dat*) gnaw (at), nibble (at); (fig) (**an** *dat*) rankle
Nagetier [ˈnagətir] *n* rodent
Nah– [na] *comb.fm.* close-range, short-range
Näh– [ne] *comb.fm.* sewing, needlework
Näh'arbeit *f* sewing, needlework
Näh'aufnahme *f* (phot) close-up

nahe [ˈnaˑə] *adj* (näher [ˈneˑər]; nächste [ˈneçstə] §9) near, close; nearby; (*bevorstehend*) forthcoming; (*Gefahr*) imminent ‖ *adv*—j–m zu n. treten hurt s.o.'s feelings; **n. an.** (*dat* or *acc*), **n. bei** close to; **n. daran sein zu** (*inf*) be on the point of (*ger*)
Nähe [ˈneˑə] *f* (–;–n) nearness; vicinity; **in der N.** close by
na'hebei *adv* nearby
na'hebringen §65 *tr* drive home
na'hegehen §82 *intr* (SEIN) (*dat*) affect, touch, grieve
na'hekommen §99 *intr* (SEIN) approach; (*dat*) come near to; **der Wahrheit n.** get at the truth
na'helegen *tr* suggest
na'heliegen §108 *intr* be close by; be obvious; be easy
na'heliegend *adj* obvious
nahen [ˈnaˑən] *ref & intr* (SEIN) approach; (*dat*) draw near to
nähen [ˈneˑən] *tr & intr* sew, stitch
näher [ˈneˑər] *adj* (*comp* of **nahe**) nearer; **bei näherer Betrachtung** upon further consideration ‖ *adv* closer; **immer n. kommen** close in; **treten Sie n.!** this way, please! ‖ **Nähere** §5 *n* details, particulars; **das N. auseinandersetzen** explain fully; **Näheres erfahren** learn further particulars; **sich des Näheren entsinnen** remember all particulars; **wenn Sie Näheres wissen wollen** if you want details
Näherin [ˈneˑərɪn] *f* (–;–nen) seamstress
nähern [ˈneˑərn] *ref* approach; (*dat*) draw near to, approach
Nä'herungswert *m* approximate value
na'hestehen §146 *intr* (*dat*) share the view of
na'hetreten §152 *intr* (SEIN) (*dat*) come into close contact with
na'hezu *adv* almost, nearly
Näh'garn *n* thread
Nah'kampf *m* hand-to-hand fighting; (box) in-fighting
nahm [nam] *pret* of **nehmen**
Näh'maschine *f* sewing machine
–nahme [namə] *f* (–;–n) *comb.fm.* taking
Nähr– [ner] *comb.fm.* nutritive
Nähr'boden *m* rich soil; (fig) breeding ground; (biol) culture medium
nähren [ˈnerən] *tr* nourish, feed; (*Kind*) nurse ‖ *ref* make a living; **sich n. von** subsist on ‖ *intr* be nutritious
nahrhaft [ˈnarhaft] *adj* nourishing, nutritious, nutritive
Nähr'mittel *pl* (*Teigwaren*) noodles; (*Hülsenfrüchte*) beans and peas
Nahrung [ˈnaruŋ] *f* (–;) nourishment; (*Kost*) diet; (*Unterhalt*) livelihood
Nah'rungsmittel *pl* food
Nah'rungsmittelvergiftung *f* food poisoning
Nah'rungssorgen *pl* difficulty in making ends meet
Nähr'wert *m* nutritive value
Näh'stube *f* sewing room
Naht [nat] *f* (–;⁼e) seam

Nah'verkehr *m* local traffic
Näh'zeug *n* sewing kit
naiv [na'if] *adj* naive
Name ['namə] *m* (-ns;-n), **Namen** ['namən] *m* (-s;-) name
na'menlos *adj* nameless; (*unsäglich*) indescribable
namens ['namens] *adv* named, called ‖ *prep* (*genit*) in the name of, on behalf of
Na'mensschild *n* nameplate
Na'menstag *m* name day
Na'mensvetter *m* namesake
namentlich ['namentlıç] *adj*—**namentliche Abstimmung** roll-call vote ‖ *adv* by name, individually; (*besonders*) especially
Na'menverzeichnis *n* index of names; nomenclature
namhaft ['namhaft] *adj* distinguished; (*beträchtlich*) considerable; **n. machen** name, specify
nämlich ['nemlıç] *adv* namely, that is; (coll) you know, you see
nannte ['nantə] *pret* of **nennen**
nanu [na'nu] *interj* gee!
Napf [napf] *m* (-es;⁻e) bowl
Narbe ['narbə] *f* (-;-n) scar; (*des Leders*) grain; (agr) topsoil
narbig ['narbıç] *adj* scarred
Narkose [nar'kozə] *f* (-;-n) anesthesia
Narkoti·kum [nar'kotıkum] *n* (-s;-ka [ka]) narcotic, dope
narkotisch [nar'kotıʃ] *adj* narcotic
Narr [nar] *m* (-en;-en) fool; (hist) jester; **j-n zum Narren halten** make a fool of s.o.
Närrchen ['nerçən] *n* (-s;-) silly little goose
narren ['narən] *tr* make a fool of
Narrenfest ['narənfest] *n* masquerade
Narrenhaus ['narənhaus] *n* madhouse
Narrenkappe ['narənkapə] *f* cap and bells
narrensicher ['narənzıçər] *adj* (coll) foolproof
Narren(s)possen ['narən(s)posən] *pl* horseplay; **laß die N.!** stop horsing around!
Narr'heit *f* (-;-en) folly
närrisch ['nerıʃ] *adj* foolish; (*verrückt*) crazy; (*Kauz*) eccentric; **n. sein auf** (*acc*) be crazy about
Narzisse [nar'tsısə] *f* (-;-n) (bot) narcissus; **gelbe N.** daffodil
naschen ['naʃən] *tr* nibble at ‖ *intr* (**an** *dat*, **von**) nibble (on); **gern n. haben** have a sweet tooth
Näscher –in ['neʃər(ın)] §6 *mf* nibbler
Näscherei [neʃə'raɪ] *f* (-;-en) snack
naschhaft ['naʃhaft] *adj* sweet-toothed
Naschkatze ['naʃkatsə] *f* nibbler
Naschmaul ['naʃmaul] *n* nibbler
Naschwerk ['naʃverk] *n* sweets, tidbits
Nase ['nazə] *f* (-;-n) nose; **auf der N. liegen** be laid up in bed; **aufgeworfene N.** turned-up nose; **das sticht ihm in die N.** it annoys him; he's itching to have it; **daß du die N. im Gesicht behältst!** keep your shirt on!; **dem Kind die N. putzen** wipe the child's nose; **die N. läuft ihm blau an** his nose is getting red; **die N. rüm-**

pfen über (*acc*) turn up one's nose at; **die N. voll haben von** be fed up with; **e–e tüchtige N. voll bekommen** (or **einstecken müssen**) get chewed out; **faß dich an deine eigene N.!** mind your own business!; **feine N. für** flair for; **immer der N. nach!** follow your nose!; **in der N. bohren** poke one's nose; **j–m e–e lange N. machen** thumb one's nose at s.o.; **j–m e–e N. drehen** outwit s.o.; **j–m die Würmer aus der N. ziehen** worm it out of s.o.; **j–m etw auf die N. binden** divulge s.th. to s.o.; **j–m in die N. fahren** (or **steigen**) annoy s.o.; **j–n an der N. herumführen** lead s.o. by the nose; **man kann es ihm an der N. ansehen** it's written all over his face; **mit langer N. abziehen** be the loser; **pro N. per head**; **sich** [*dat*] **die N. begießen** wet one's whistle
näseln ['nezəln] *intr* speak through the nose ‖ **Näseln** *n* (-s;) nasal twang
nä'selnd *adj* nasal
Na'senbein *n* nasal bone
Na'senbluten *n* (-s;) nosebleed
na'senlang *adv*—**alle n.** constantly
Na'senlänge *f*—**um e–e N.** by a nose
Na'senlaut *m* (phonet) nasal
Na'senloch *n* nostril
Na'senrücken *m* bridge of the nose
Na'senschleim *m* mucus
Na'senschleimhaut *f* mucous membrane
Nasenspray ['nazənspre] *m* (-s;-s) nose spray
Na'sentropfen *m* nose drop
na'seweis *adj* fresh, wise ‖ **Naseweis** *m* (-es;-e) wise guy
Na'seweisheit *f* freshness
nasführen ['nasfyrən] *tr* lead by the nose; (*foppen*) fool
Nashorn ['nashorn] *n* (-[e]s;⁻er) rhinoceros
naß [nas] *adj* (**nasser** ['nasər] or **nässer** ['nesər]; **nasseste** ['nasəstə] or **nässeste** ['nesəstə] §9) wet; (*feucht*) moist ‖ **Naß** *n* (Nasses;) (poet) liquid
Nassauer ['nasau·ər] *m* (-s;-) sponger, chiseler
nassauern ['nasau·ərn] *intr* (coll) sponge
Nässe ['nesə] *f* (-;) wetness; moisture
nässen ['nesən] *tr* wet; moisten ‖ *intr* ooze
naß'forsch *adj* rash, bold
naß'kalt *adj* raw, cold and damp
Nation [na'tsjon] *f* (-;-en) nation
national [natsjo'nal] *adj* national
National'hymne *f* national anthem
nationalisieren [natsjonalı'zirən] *tr* nationalize
Nationalismus [natsjona'lısmus] *m* (-;) nationalism
Nationalität [natsjonalı'tet] *f* (-;-en) nationality; ethnic minority
National'sozialismus *m* national socialism, Nazism
National'sozialist –in §7 *mf* national socialist, Nazi
National'tracht *f* national costume
Nativität [natıvı'tet] *f* (-;-en) horoscope

Natrium ['nɑtrɪ·um] *n* (-s;) sodium
Natter ['natər] *f* (-;-n) adder, viper
Natur [na'tur] *f* (-;-en) nature; (*Körperbeschaffenheit*) constitution; (*Gemütsart*) disposition; (*Art*) character; (*Person*) creature; **von N.** by nature
Natura [na'tura] *f*—**in N.** in kind
Naturalien [natu'raljən] *pl* produce
naturalisieren [naturalɪ'zirən] *tr* naturalize ‖ *ref*—**sich n.** lassen become naturalized
Natur'anlage *f* disposition
Natur'arzt *m* naturopath
Naturell [natu'rɛl] *n* (-[e]s;-e) nature, temperament
Natur'erscheinung *f* phenomenon
Natur'forscher –in §6 *mf* naturalist
Natur'gabe *f* natural gift, talent
natur'gemäß *adv* naturally
Natur'geschichte *f* natural history
Natur'gesetz *n* natural law
natur'getreu *adj* life-like
Natur'kunde *f*, **Natur'lehre** *f* natural science
natürlich [na'tyrlɪç] *adj* natural; (*echt*) real; (*ungezwungen*) natural; **das geht aber nicht mit natürlichen Dingen zu** there is s.th. fishy about it; **das geht ganz n. zu** there is nothing strange about it ‖ *adv* naturally, of course
Natur'mensch *m* primitive man; nature enthusiast
Natur'philosoph *m* natural philosopher
Natur'recht *n* natural right
Natur'schutz *m* preservation of natural beauty
Natur'schutzgebiet *n* wildlife preserve
Natur'schutzpark *m* national park
Natur'spiel *n* freak of nature
Natur'theater *n* outdoor theater
Natur'trieb *m* instinct
Natur'verehrung *f* natural religion
Natur'volk *n* primitive people
natur'widrig *adj* contrary to nature
Natur'wissenschaft *f* natural science
Natur'wissenschaftler –in §6 *mf* scientist
naturwüchsig [na'turvyksɪç] *adj* unspoiled by civilization
Natur'zustand *m* natural state
nautisch ['nautɪʃ] *adj* nautical
Navigation [navɪga'tsjon] *f* (-;) navigation
navigieren [navɪ'girən] *intr* navigate
Nazi ['natsi] *m* (-s;-s) Nazi
Nazismus [na'tsɪmus] *m* (-;) Nazism
nazistisch [na'tsɪstɪʃ] *adj* Nazi
Nebel ['nebəl] *m* (-s;-) fog, mist; (*Dunst*) haze
Ne'belbank *f* (-;̈e) fog bank
Ne'belfeld *n* patch of fog
Ne'belferne *f* hazy distance; (fig) dim future
Ne'belfleck *m* (astr) nebula
ne'belhaft *adj* foggy, hazy; (*Ferne*) dim
Ne'belhorn *n* foghorn
nebeln ['nebəln] *intr* be foggy
Ne'belscheinwerfer *m* (aut) fog light
Ne'belschicht *f* fog bank
Ne'belschirm *m* smoke screen
Ne'belvorhang *m* smoke screen
neben ['nebən] *prep* (*dat & acc*) by,

beside; side by side with, alongside, close to, next to; (*verglichen mit*) compared with; (*außer*) besides, aside from; in addition to; extra
Neben– *comb.fm.* secondary, accessory, by–, side–, subordinate
Ne'benabsicht *f* ulterior motive
Ne'benaltar *m* side altar
Ne'benamt *n* additional duties
nebenan' *adv* close by; next-door
Ne'benanschluß *m* (telp) extension; (telp) party line
Ne'benarbeit *f* extra work
Ne'benarm *m* tributary, branch
Ne'benausgaben *pl* incidentals, extras
Ne'benausgang *m* side exit
Ne'benbahn *f* (rr) branch line
Ne'benbedeutung *f* (-;-en) secondary meaning
nebenbei' *adv* close by; (*außerdem*) besides, on the side; (*beiläufig*) incidentally
Ne'benberuf *m* sideline, side job
ne'benberuflich *adj* sideline, spare-time
Ne'benbeschäftigung *f* sideline
Nebenbuhler –in ['nebənbulər(ɪn)] §6 *mf* competitor, rival
ne'benbuhlerisch *adj* rival
Ne'bending *n* secondary matter
nebeneinan'der *adv* side by side; neck and neck; (*gleichzeitig*) simultaneously; **n. bestehen** coexist
Nebeneinan'derleben *n* coexistence
nebeneinan'derstellen *tr* juxtapose
Ne'beneingang *m* side entrance
Ne'beneinkünfte *pl*, **Ne'beneinnahmen** *pl* extra income
Ne'benerzeugnis *n* by-product
Ne'benfach *n* (educ) minor; **als N. studieren** minor in
Ne'benflügel *m* (archit) wing
Ne'benfluß *m* tributary
Ne'benfrage *f* side issue
Ne'benfrau *f* concubine
Ne'bengang *m* side aisle
Ne'bengasse *f* side street, alley
Ne'bengebäude *n* annex, wing
Ne'bengedanke *m* ulterior motive
Ne'bengericht *n* side dish
Ne'bengeschäft *n* (com) branch
Ne'bengleis *n* (rr) siding, sidetrack
Ne'benhandlung *f* (-;-en) subplot
nebenher' *adv* on the side; besides; along
nebenhin' *adv* incidentally, by the way
Ne'benkosten *pl* incidentals, extras
Ne'benlinie *f* (rr) branch line
Ne'benmann *m* (-[e]s;̈er) neighbor
Ne'benprodukt *n* by-product
Ne'benpunkt *m* minor point
Ne'benrolle *f* supporting role
Ne'bensache *f* side issue
ne'bensächlich *adj* subordinate; incidental; (*unwesentlich*) unimportant
Ne'bensächlichkeit *f* unimportance; triviality
Ne'bensatz *m* subordinate clause
Ne'benschaltung *f* (-;-en) (elec) shunt
Ne'benschluß *m* (elec) shunt
Ne'benspesen *pl* additional charges
ne'benstehend *adj* marginal, in the margin ‖ **Nebenstehende** §5 *mf* bystander

Ne'benstelle *f* branch; (telp) extension
Ne'benstraße *f* side street
Ne'bentisch *m* next table
Ne'bentür *f* side door
Ne'benverdienst *m* extra pay; side job
Ne'benvorstellung *f* side show
Ne'benweg *m* side road
Ne'benwirkung *f* (-;-en) side effect
Ne'benzimmer *n* adjoining room
Ne'benzweck *m* secondary aim
neblig ['nebliç] *adj* foggy, misty
nebst [nepst] *prep* (*dat*) including
necken ['nɛkən] *tr & recip* tease, kid
Neckerei [nɛkə'raɪ] *f* (-;-en) teasing
neckisch ['nɛkɪʃ] *adj* fond of teasing; (coll) cute
nee [ne] *adv* (dial) no
Neffe ['nɛfə] *m* (-n;-n) nephew
Negation [nɛga'tsjon] *f* (-;-en) negation
negativ [nɛga'tif] *adj* negative || **Negativ** *n* (-s;-e) negative
Neger –**in** ['negər(ɪn)] §6 *mf* black, Negro
Negligé [neglɪ'ʒe] *n* (-s;-s) negligee
nehmen ['nemən] §116 *tr* take; (*weg–*) take away; (*anstellen*) take on, hire; (*Anwalt*) retain; (*Hindernis*) clear, take; (*Kurve*) negotiate; (*Schaden*) suffer; **Anfang n.** begin; **Anstand n.** hesitate; **an sich n.** pocket, misappropriate; collect; retrieve; **Anstoß n. an** (*dat*) take offense at; **auf sich n.** assume, take upon oneself; **das Wort n.** begin to speak; **den Mund voll n.** (coll) talk big; **die Folgen auf sich n.** bear the consequences; **ein Ende n.** come to an end; **ein gutes Ende n.** turn out all right; **er versteht es, die Kunden richtig zu n.** he knows how to handle customers; **etw genau n.** take s.th. literally; **ich lasse es mir nicht n. zu** (*inf*) I insist on (*ger*); **im Grunde genommen** basically; **in Angriff n.** begin; **in Arbeit n.** start making; **in die Hand n.** pick up; (fig) take in hand; **j–m etw n.** take s.th. away from s.o.; deprive s.o. of s.th.; **kein Ende n.** go on endlessly; **man nehme zwei Eier, usw.** (*im Kochbuch*) take two eggs, etc.; **n. Sie bitte Platz!** please sit down; **n. wir den Fall, daß** let's suppose that; **Rücksicht n. auf** (*acc*) show consideration for; **sich** [*dat*] **das Leben n.** take one's life; **sich** [*dat*] **nichts von seinen Rechten n.** lassen insist on one's rights; **streng genommen** strictly speaking; **Stunden n.** take lessons; **Urlaub n.** take a vacation; (mil) go on furlough; **wie man's nimmt** it all depends; **zu Hilfe n.** use; **zur Ehe n.** marry; **zu sich** [*dat*] **n.** put into one's pocket; (*Speise*) eat; (*Kind*) take charge of
Neid [naɪt] *m* (-es;) envy; **blasser** (or **gelber**) **N.** pure envy; **vor N. vergehen** die of envy
neiden ['naɪdən] *tr*—**j–m etw n.** envy s.o. for s.th.
Neid'hammel *m* envious person
nei'dig *adj* (dial) var of **neidisch**
neidisch ['naɪdɪʃ] *adj* (**auf** *acc*) envious (of)

neid'los *adj* free of envy
Neid'nagel *m* hangnail
Neige ['naɪgə] *f* (-;-n) slope; (*Abnahme*) decline; (*Überbleibsel*) sediment, dregs; **zur N. gehen** (*Geld, Vorräte*) run low; (*Sonne*) go down; (*Tag, Jahr*) draw to a close
neigen ['naɪgən] *tr* incline, bend; **geneigt** sloping; (fig) friendly, favorable || *ref* (**vor** *dat*) bow (to); (*Abhang*) slope; **sich zum Ende n.** draw to a close || *intr*—**n. zu** be inclined to
Nei'gung *f* (-;-en) slope, incline; (*des Hauptes*) bowing; (*e–s Schiffes*) list; (*in der Straße*) dip; (*Gefälle*) gradient; (*Hang*) inclination; (*Anlage*) tendency; (*Vorliebe*) taste, liking; (*Zuneigung*) affection; **e–e N. nach rechts haben** lean towards the right; **N. fassen zu** take (a fancy) to
nein [naɪn] *adv* no || **Nein** *n* (-s;) no
Nein'stimme *f* (parl) nay
Nekrolog [nɛkro'lok] *m* (-[e]s;-e) obituary
Nektar ['nɛktar] *m* (-s;) nectar
Nelke ['nɛlkə] *f* (-;-n) carnation; (*Gewürz*) clove
Nel'kenöl *n* oil of cloves
Nel'kenpfeffer *m* allspice
Nemesis ['nɛmezɪs] *f* (-;) Nemesis
nennbar ['nɛnbar] *adj* mentionable
nennen ['nɛnən] §97 *tr* name, call; (*erwähnen*) mention; (*benennen*) term || *ref* be called, be named
nen'nenswert *adj* worth mentioning
Nenner ['nɛnər] *m* (-s;-) (math) denominator; **auf e–n gemeinsamen N. bringen** reduce to a common denominator
Nennform ['nɛnfɔrm] *f* (gram) infinitive
Nenngeld ['nɛngelt] *n* entry fee
Nen'nung *f* (-;) naming; mentioning
Nennwert ['nɛnvert] *m* face value
Neologis·mus [nɛ·olo'gɪsmʊs] *m* (-; -men [mən]) neologism
Neon ['ne·on] *n* (-s;) neon
Ne'onlicht *n* neon light
Nepotismus [nɛpo'tɪsmʊs] *m* (-;) nepotism
neppen ['nɛpən] *tr* (coll) gyp, clip
Nepplokal ['nɛplokal] *n* (sl) clip joint
Neptun [nɛp'tun] *m* (-s;) Neptune
Nerv [nɛrf] *m* (-s;-en) nerve; **die Nerven behalten** keep cool; **die Nerven verlieren** lose one's head; **j–m auf die Nerven gehen** get on s.o.'s nerves; **mit den Nerven herunter sein** be a nervous wreck
Nerven–, nerven– [nɛrfən] *comb.fm.* nervous, neuro–, of nerves
Ner'venarzt *m*, **Ner'venärztin** *f* neurologist
ner'venaufreibend *adj* nerve-racking
Ner'venberuhigungsmittel *n* sedative
Ner'venbündel *n* (fig) bundle of nerves
Ner'venentzündung *f* neuritis
Ner'venfaser *f* nerve fiber
Ner'venheilanstalt *f* mental institution
Ner'venheilkunde *f* neurology
Ner'venkitzel *m* thrill, suspense
Ner'venknoten *m* ganglion
ner'venkrank *adj* neurotic

Ner'venkrieg *m* war of nerves
Ner'venlehre *f* neurology
Ner'vensäge *f* (coll) pain in the neck
Ner'venschmerz *m* neuralgia
Ner'venschwäche *f* nervousness
Ner'venzentrum *n* (fig) nerve center
Ner'venzusammenbruch *m* nervous breakdown
nervig [ˈnɛrvɪç], [ˈnɛrfɪç] *adj* sinewy
nervös [nɛrˈvøs] *adj* nervous
Nervosität [nɛrvɔziˈtet] *f* (-;) nervousness
Nerz [nɛrts] *m* (-es;-e) (zool) mink
Nerz'mantel *m* mink coat
Nessel [ˈnɛsəl] *f* (-;-n) nettle; **sich in die Nesseln setzen** (fig) get oneself into hot water
Nest [nɛst] *n.* (-es;-er) nest; (*Schlupfwinkel*) hideout; small town; dead town; (*Bett*) (coll) bed
nesteln [ˈnɛstəln] *tr* lace, tie ‖ *intr*
—*n.* an (*dat*) fiddle with, fuss with
Nesthäkchen [ˈnɛsthekçən] *n* (-s;-), **Nestküken** [ˈnɛstkykən] *n* (-s;-) baby (*of the family*)
nett [nɛt] *adj* nice; (*sauber*) neat; (*niedlich*) cute; **das kann ja n. werden!** (iron) that's going to be just dandy!
netto [ˈnɛto] *adv* net; clear
Net'togewicht *n* net weight
Net'togewinn *m* clear profit
Net'tolohn *m* take-home pay
Net'topreis *m* net price
Netz [nɛts] *n* (-es;-e) net; network; grid
netzen [ˈnɛtsən] *tr* wet, moisten
Netz'haut *f* retina
Netz'werk *n* netting, webbing
neu [nɔɪ] *adj* new; (*frisch*) fresh; (*unlängst geschehen*) recent; **aufs neue** anew; **neuere Geschichte** modern history; **neuere Sprachen** modern languages; **von neuem** all over again ‖ *adv* newly; recently; anew; afresh ‖ **Neue** §5 *mf* newcomer ‖ §5 *n*— **was gibt es Neues?** what's new?
Neu-, neu- *comb.fm.* new-, newly; re-; neo-
Neu'anlage *f* new installation; (fin) reinvestment
Neu'anschaffung *f* recent acquisition
neu'artig *adj* novel; modern
Neu'aufführung *f* (-;-en) (theat) revival
Neu'ausgabe *f* new edition, republication; (*Neudruck*) reprint
Neu'bau *m* (-[e]s;-bauten) new building
neu'bearbeiten *tr* revise
Neubelebung [ˈnɔɪbəlebuŋ] *f* (-;-en) revival
Neu'bildung *f* (-;-en) new growth; (gram) neologism
Neu'druck *m* reprint
neuerdings [ˈnɔɪ·ərdɪŋs] *adv* recently; (*vom neuem*) anew
Neuerer -in [ˈnɔɪ·ərər(ɪn)] §6 *mf* innovator
Neuerung [ˈnɔɪ·əruŋ] *f* (-;-en) innovation
neuestens [ˈnɔɪ·əstəns] *adv* recently
Neu'fassung *f* revision

Neufundland [nɔɪˈfuntlant] *n* (-s;) Newfoundland
neu'gebacken *adj* fresh-baked; brand-new
neu'geboren *adj* new-born
neu'gestalten *tr* reorganize
Neu'gier *f*, **Neugierde** [ˈnɔɪgirdə] *f* (-;) curiosity, inquisitiveness
neu'gierig *adj* curious, nosey
Neu'gründung *f* (-;-en) reestablishment
Neu'gruppierung *f* (-;-en) regrouping; reshuffling
Neu'heit *f* (-;-en) novelty
neu'hochdeutsch *adj* modern High German
Neu'igkeit *f* (-;-en) news, piece of news
Neu'jahr *n* New Year
Neu'land *n* virgin soil; (fig) new ground
neu'lich *adv* lately
Neuling [ˈnɔɪlɪŋ] *m* (-[e]s;-e) beginner
neu'modisch *adj* fashionable; newfangled
neun [nɔɪn] *invar adj* & *pron* nine ‖ **Neun** *f* (-;-en) nine
Neunmalkluge [ˈnɔɪnmɑlklugə] §5 *mf* wiseacre
neunte [ˈnɔɪntə] §9 *adj* & *pron* ninth
Neuntel [ˈnɔɪntəl] *n* (-s;-) ninth
neun'zehn *invar adj* & *pron* nineteen ‖
neun'zehnte §9 *adj* & *pron* nineteenth
neunzig [ˈnɔɪntsɪç] *invar adj* & *pron* ninety ‖ **Neunzig** *f* (-;-en) ninety
neunziger [ˈnɔɪntsɪgər] *invar adj* of the nineties; **die n. Jahre** the nineties ‖ **Neunziger -in** §6 *mf* nonagenarian
neunzigste [ˈnɔɪntsɪçstə] §9 *adj* & *pron* ninetieth
Neu'ordnung *f* (-;-en) reorganization
Neural·gie [nɔɪralˈgi] *f* (-;-gien) [ˈgi·ən]) neuralgia
Neu'regelung *f* (-;-en) rearrangement
Neu·ron [ˈnɔɪrɔn] *n* (-;-ronen [ˈronən]) neuron
Neurose [nɔɪˈrozə] *f* (-;-n) neurosis
Neurotiker -in [nɔɪˈrotɪkər(ɪn)] §6 *mf* neurotic
neurotisch [nɔɪˈrotɪʃ] *adj* neurotic
Neusee'land *n* (-s;) New Zealand
Neu'silber *n* German silver
Neusprachler -in [ˈnɔɪʃpraxlər(ɪn)] §6 *mf* modern-language teacher
Neu'stadt *f* new section of town
Neu'steinzeit *f* neolithic age
neu'steinzeitlich *adj* neolithic
neutral [nɔɪˈtrɑl] *adj* neutral
neutralisieren [nɔɪtraliˈzirən] *tr* neutralize
Neutralität [nɔɪtraliˈtet] *f* (-;) neutrality
Neu·tron [ˈnɔɪtrɔn] *n* (-;-tronen [ˈtronən]) neutron
Neu·trum [ˈnɔɪtrum] *n* (-s;-tra [tra] & -tren [trən]) (gram) neuter
neuvermählt [ˈnɔɪfermelt] *adj* newly married ‖ **Neuvermählte** §5 *pl* newlyweds
Neu'zeit *f* recent times
Nibelung [ˈnibəluŋ] *m* (-s;) (myth)

(King) Nibelung ‖ *m* (**-en;-en**) Nibelung

nicht [nɪçt] *adv* not; **auch...nicht** not ...either; **n. doch!** please don't; **n. einmal** not even, not so much as; **n. mehr** no longer, no more; **n. um die Welt** not for the world; **n. wahr?** isn't it so?, no?, right?

Nicht-, nicht- *comb.fm.* in-, im-, un-, non-

Nicht'achtung *f* disregard, disrespect; **N. des Gerichts** contempt of court

nicht'amtlich *adj* unofficial

Nicht'angriffspakt *m* nonaggression pact

Nicht'annahme *f* nonacceptance

Nichte ['nɪçtə] *f* (**-;-n**) niece

Nicht'einmischung *f* noninterference

Nicht'eisenmetall *n* nonferrous metal

nichtig ['nɪçtɪç] *adj* invalid; void; (*eitel*) vain; (*vergänglich*) transitory; **für n. erklären** annul

Nich'tigkeit *f* (**-;-en**) invalidity; futility; (*Kleinigkeit*) trifle; **Nichtigkeiten** trivia

Nich'tigkeitserklärung *f* annulment

Nicht'kämpfer *m* noncombatant

nicht'öffentlich *adj* private; (*Sitzung*) closed

nicht'rostend *adj* rustproof; (*Stahl*) stainless

nichts [nɪçts] *indef pron* nothing; **gar n.** nothing at all; **n. als** nothing but; **n. mehr davon!** not another word about it!; **n. und wieder n.** absolutely nothing; **soviel wie n.** next to nothing; **um n.** for nothing, to no avail; **weiter n.?** is that all?; **wenn es weiter n. ist!** if it's nothing worse than that ‖ **Nichts** *n* (**-s;**) nothingness; nonentity; (*Leere*) void; (*Kleinigkeit*) trifle; **vor dem N. stehen** be faced with utter ruin

nichtsdestowe'niger *adv* nevertheless

Nichts'könner *m* incompetent person; ignoramus

Nichts'nutz *m* good-for-nothing

nichts'nutzig *adj* good-for-nothing

nichts'sagend *adj* insignificant; (*Antwort*) vague; noncommittal; (*Gesicht*) vacuous; (*Redensart*) trite

Nichts'tuer -in ₰6 *mf* loafer

Nichts'wisser -in ₰6 *mf* ignoramus

nichts'würdig *adj* contemptible

Nicht'zutreffende ₰5 *n*—**Nichtzutreffendes streichen!** delete if not applicable

Nickel ['nɪkəl] *n* (**-;-**) (metal) nickel

nicken ['nɪkən] *intr* nod; (*schlummern*) nap

Nickerchen ['nɪkərçən] *n* (**-s;-**) nap

nie [ni] *adv* never, at no time

nieder ['nidər] *adj* low; (*gemein*) base ‖ *adv* down

nie'derbrechen ₰64 *tr & intr* (SEIN) break down

nie'derbrennen ₰97 *tr & intr* (SEIN) burn down

nie'derdeutsch *adj* Low German ‖ **Niederdeutsch** *n* Low German ‖ **Niederdeutsche** ₰5 *mf* North German

nie'derdonnern *tr* (coll) shout down ‖ *intr* go (or come) crashing down

Nie'derdruck *m* low pressure

nie'derdrücken *tr* press down (fig) weigh down; (*unterdrücken*) oppress; (*entmutigen*) depress

nie'derfallen ₰72 *intr* (SEIN) fall down

Nie'derfrequenz *f* low frequency; audio frequency

Nie'dergang *m* descent; (*der Sonne*) setting; (fig) decline, fall

nie'dergehen ₰82 *intr* (SEIN) go down; (*Flugzeug*) land; (*Regen*) fall; (*Vorhang*) drop

nie'dergeschlagen *adj* dejected

nie'derhalten ₰90 *tr* hold down, keep down

nie'derholen *tr* lower, haul down

Nie'derholz *n* underbrush

nie'derkämpfen *tr* (& fig) overcome

nie'derkommen ₰99 *intr* (SEIN) (**mit**) give birth (to)

Niederkunft ['nidərkʊnft] *f* (**-;**) confinement, childbirth

Nie'derlage *f* defeat; (*Lager*) warehouse; (*Filiale*) branch

Niederlande, die ['nidərlandə] *pl* The Netherlands, Holland

Niederländer ['nidərlɛndər] *m* (**-s;-**) Dutchman

niederländisch ['nidərlɛndɪʃ] *adj* Dutch

nie'derlassen ₰104 *tr* let down ‖ *ref* sit down, recline; (*Wohnsitz nehmen*) settle; (*ein Geschäft eröffnen*) set oneself up in business; (*Vogel, Flugzeug*) land

Nie'derlassung *f* (**-;-en**) settlement, colony; establishment; (*e-r Bank*) branch; (com) plant

nie'derlegen *tr* lay down, put down; (*Amt*) resign; (*Geschäft*) give up; (*Krone*) abdicate; (*schriftlich*) set down in writing; **die Arbeit n.** go on strike ‖ *ref* lie down; go to bed

nie'dermachen *tr* butcher, massacre

nie'dermähen *tr* mow down

nie'dermetzeln *tr* butcher, massacre

Nie'derschlag *m* (*Bodensatz*) sediment; (box) knockdown; (chem) precipitate; (meteor) precipitation; **radioaktiver N.** fallout

nie'derschlagen ₰132 *tr* knock down; (*Augen*) cast down; (*Aufstand*) put down; (*vertuschen*) hush up; (*Verfahren*) quash; (*Forderung*) waive; (*Hoffnungen*) dash; (chem) precipitate

nie'derschmettern *tr* knock to the ground; (fig) crush

nie'derschreiben ₰62 *tr* write down

nie'dersetzen *tr* set down ‖ *ref* sit down

nie'dersinken ₰143 *intr* (SEIN) sink down

nie'derstimmen *tr* vote down

Nie'dertracht *f* nastiness, meanness

nie'derträchtig *adj* nasty; underhand

Nie'derung *f* (**-;-en**) low ground, depression

niederwärts ['nidərvɛrts] *adv* downward

nie'derwerfen ₰160 *tr* knock down; (*Aufstand*) put down ‖ *ref* fall down

Nie'derwild *n* small game

niedlich ['nitlɪç] *adj* nice, cute

Niednagel ['nitnagəl] *m* hangnail

niedrig ['nidrɪç] *adj* low; *(Herkunft)* humble; *(gemein)* mean, base
niemals ['nimals] *adv* never
niemand ['nimant] *indef pron* no one, nobody
Nie′mandsland *n* no man's land
Niere ['nirə] *f* (–;–n) kidney; **das geht mir an die Nieren** (fig) that cuts me deep
nieseln ['nizəln] *impers*—**es nieselt** it is drizzling
Nie′selregen *m* drizzle
niesen ['nizən] *intr* sneeze
Niet [nit] *m* (–[e]s;–e) rivet
Niete ['nitə] *f* (–;–n) rivet; *(in der Lotterie)* blank; *(Versager)* flop
nieten ['nitən] *tr* rivet
niet–′ und na′gelfest *adj* nailed down
Nihilismus [nihi′lɪsmɪs] *m* (–;) nihilism
Nikotin [nɪko′tin] *n* (–s;) nicotine
nikotin′arm *adj* low in nicotine
Nil [nil] *m* (–s;) Nile
Nil′pferd *n* hippopotamus
Nimbus ['nɪmbʊs] *m* (–;–se) halo; aura; *(Ansehen)* prestige; (meteor) nimbus
nimmer ['nɪmər] *adv* never; (dial) no more
nim′mermehr *adv* never more; by no means
Nippel ['nɪpəl] *m* (–s;–) (mach) nipple
nippen ['nɪpən] *tr & intr* sip
Nippsachen ['nɪpzaxən] *pl* knicknacks
nirgends ['nɪrgənts] *adv* nowhere
nirgendwo ['nɪrgəntvo] *adv* nowhere
Nische ['nɪʃə] *f* (–;–n) niche
nisten ['nɪstən] *intr* nest
Nitrat [nɪ′trat] *n* (–[e]s;–e) nitrate
Nitrid [nɪ′trit] *n* (–[e]s;–e) nitride
Nitroglyzerin [nɪtroglytsə′rin] *n* (–s;) nitroglycerin
Niveau [nɪ′vo] *n* (–s;–s) level; **N. haben** have class; **unter dem N. sein** be substandard
Niveau′übergang *m* (rr) grade crossing
nivellieren [nɪvɛ′lirən] *tr* level
nix [nɪks] *indef pron* (dial) nothing ‖ **Nix** *m* (–[e]s;–e) water sprite
Nixe ['nɪksə] *f* (–;–n) water nymph
nobel ['nobəl] *adj* noble; elegant; *(freigebig)* generous
noch [nɔx] *adv* still, yet; even; else; **heute n.** this very day; **n. besser** even bettter; **n. dazu** over and above that; **n. einer** one more, still another; **n. einmal** once more; **n. einmal so viel** twice as much; **n. etwas** one more thing; **n. etwas?** anything else?; **n. heute** even today; **n. immer** still; **n. nicht** not yet; **n. nie** never before; **n. und n.** (coll) over and over; **sei es n. so klein** now matter how small it is; **was denn n. alles?** what next? **wer kommt n.?** who else is coming?
noch′mal *adv* once more
nochmalig ['nɔxmalɪç] *adj* repeated
nochmals ['nɔxmals] *adv* once more
Nocke ['nɔkə] *f* (–;–n) (mach) cam
Nockenwelle (Nok′kenwelle) *f* camshaft
Nockerl ['nɔkərl] *n* (–s;– & –n) (Aust) dumpling

Nomade [nɔ′madə] *m* (–n;–n) nomad
nominell [nɔmi′nel] *adj* nominal
nominieren [nɔmi′nirən] *tr* nominate
Nonne ['nɔnə] *f* (–;–n) nun
Non′nenkloster *n* convent
Noppe ['nɔpə] *f* (–;–n) (tex) nap
Nord [nɔrt] *m* (–[e]s;) North; (poet) north wind
Norden ['nɔrdən] *m* (–s;) North; **im N. von** north of
nordisch ['nɔrdɪʃ] *adj* northern; *(Rasse)* Nordic; *(skandinavisch)* Norse
nördlich ['nœrtlɪç] *adj* northern
Nord′licht *n* northern lights
nordwärts ['nɔrtverts] *adv* northward
Nörgelei [nœrgə′laɪ] *f* (–;–en) griping
nörgelig ['nœrgəlɪç] *adj* nagging
nörgeln ['nœrgəln] *intr*—**n. an** *(dat)* gripe about, kick about
Norm [nɔrm] *f* (–;–en) norm, standard
normal [nɔr′mal] *adj* normal, standard
normalisieren [nɔrmalɪ′zirən] *tr* normalize
Normal′zeit *f* standard time
Normanne [nɔr′manə] *m* (–n;–n) Norman
normen ['nɔrmən], **normieren** [nɔr′mirən] *tr* normalize, standardize
Norwegen ['nɔrvegən] *n* (–s;) Norway
Norweger –in ['nɔrvegər(ɪn)] §6 *mf* Norwegian
norwegisch ['nɔrvegɪʃ] *adj* Norwegian
Not [not] *f* (–;˝e) need, want; *(Notlage)* necessity; *(Gefahr)* distress; *(Dringlichkeit)* emergency; **es hat keine Not** there's no hurry about it; **es tut not** it is necessary; **in der Not** in a pinch; **in Not geraten** fall upon hard times; **j–m große Not machen** give s.o. a lot of trouble; **j–m seine Not klagen** cry on s.o.'s shoulders; **mit knapper Not** narrowly; **mit Not** scarcely; **Not haben zu** *(inf)* be scarcely able to *(inf)*; **Not leiden** suffer want; **ohne Not** needlessly; **seine liebe Not haben mit** have a lot of trouble with; **sie haben Not auszukommen** they have difficulty making ends meet; **zur Not** if need be, in a pinch
Nota ['nota] *f* (–;–s) note; **etw in N. geben** place an order for s.th.; **etw in N. nehmen** make a note of s.th.
Notar –in [nɔ′tar(ɪn)] §8 *mf* notary public
Notariat [nɔta′rjat] *n* (–[e]s;–e) notary office
notariell [nɔta′rjɛl] *adv*—**n. beglaubigen** notarize
Not′ausgang *m* emergency exit
Not′ausstieg *m* escape hatch
Not′behelf *m* makeshift, stopgap
Not′bremse *f* (rr) emergency brake
Not′durft ['notdurft] *f* (–;) want; necessities of life; **seine N. verrichten** relieve oneself
not′dürftig *adj* scanty, poor; hard up; *(behelfsmäßig)* temporary
Note ['notə] *f* (–;–n) note; *(Banknote)* bill; *(Eigenart)* trait; (educ) mark; (mus) note; **in Noten setzen** set to music; **nach Noten** (fig) thoroughly; **persönliche Note** personal

touch; **wie nach Noten** like clock-work
No'tenblatt *n* sheet music
No'tenbuch *n*, **No'tenheft** *n* music book
No'tenlinie *f* (mus) line
No'tenschlüssel *m* (mus) clef
No'tenständer *m* music stand
No'tensystem *n* (mus) staff
Not'fall *m* emergency
notfalls ['notfals] *adv* if necessary
notgedrungen ['notgədruŋən] *adj* compulsory || *adv* of necessity
notieren [nɔ'tirən] *tr* note down; jot down; (*Preise*) quote
Notie'rung *f* (–;–en) noting; (st. exch.) quotation
nötig ['nøtɪç] *adj* necessary; **das habe ich nicht n.!** I don't have to stand for that!; **n. haben** need
nötigen ['nøtɪgən] *tr* urge; (*zwingen*) force || *ref*—**lassen Sie sich nicht n.!** don't wait to be asked; **sich genötigt sehen zu** (*inf*) feel compelled to (*inf*)
nö'tigenfalls *adv* in case of need
Nö'tigung *f* (–;) compulsion; urgent request; (jur) duress
Notiz [nɔ'tits] *f* (–;–en) notice; (*Vermerk*) note, memorandum; **keine N. nehmen von** take no notice of; **sich** [*dat*] **Notizen machen** jot down notes
Notiz'block *m* scratch pad
Not'lage *f* predicament; emergency
Not'landung *f* emergency landing
Not'lüge *f* white lie
Not'maßnahme *f* emergency measure
Not'nagel *m* (fig) stopgap
notorisch [nɔ'torɪʃ] *adj* notorious
Not'pfennig *m* savings; **sich e–n N. aufsparen** save up for a rainy day
Not'ruf *m* (telp) emergency
Not'signal *n* distress signal
Not'stand *m* state of emergency
Not'standsgebiet *n* disaster area
Not'treppe *f* fire escape
Not'wehr *f*—**aus N.** in self-defense
notwendig ['notvendɪç] *adj* necessary
Not'wendigkeit *f* (–;–en) necessity
Not'zeichen *n* distress signal
Not'zucht *f* rape
not'züchtigen *tr* rape, ravish
Nougat ['nugat] *m & n* (–s;–s) nougat
Novelle [nɔ'vɛlə] *f* (–;–n) short story; (parl) amendment, rider
November [nɔ'vɛmbər] *m* (–s;–) November
Novität [nɔvɪ'tet] *f* (–;–en) novelty
Novize [nɔ'vitsə] *m* (–n;–n), **Novizin** [nɔ'vitsɪn] *f* (–;–nen), novice
Noviziat [nɔvɪ'tsjat] *n* (–[e]s;–e) noviatiate
Nu [nu] *invar m*—**im Nu** in a jiffy
Nuance [nʏ'ɑ̃sə] *f* (–;–n) nuance
nüchtern ['nʏçtərn] *adj* fasting; not having had breakfast; (*Magen*) empty; (*nicht betrunken*) sober; (*leidenschaftlos*) cool; (*geistlos*) dry, dull; (*unsentimental*) matter-of-fact
Nudel ['nudəl] *f* (–;–n) noodle; **e–e komische N.** (coll) a funny person
Nu'delholz *n* rolling pin

nudeln ['nudəln] *tr* force-feed
Nugat ['nugat] *m* (–s;–s) nougat
nuklear [nukle'ar] *adj* nuclear
Nukle·on ['nukle·ɔn] *n* (–s;–onen) ['onən]) nucleon
null [nul] *adj* null; **n. und nichtig** null and void; **n. und nichtig machen** annul || **Null** *f* (–;–en) naught; zero; (fig) nobody; **in N. Komma nichts** in less than no time, in no time
Null'punkt *m* zero; freezing point; **auf dem N. angekommen sein** hit bottom
Numera·le [nume'ralə] *n* (–s;–lien [ljən] & –lia [lja]) numeral
numerieren [nume'rirən] *tr* number; **numerierten Platz** reserved seat
numerisch [nu'merɪʃ] *adj* numerical
Nummer ['numər] *f* (–;–n) number; (*Größe*) size; (*e–r Zeitung*) issue; **auf N. Sicher sitzen** (sl) be in jail; **bei j–m e–e gute N. haben** (coll) be in good with s.o.; **e–e bloße N.** a mere figurehead; **er ist e–e N.** he's quite a character; **laufende N.** serial number; **N. besetzt!** line is busy!
Num'mernfolge *f* numerical order
Num'mernscheibe *f* (telp) dial
Num'mernschild *n* (aut) license plate
nun [nun] *adv* now; **nun? well?; nun aber now; nun also!** well now!; **nun gut!** all right then!; **nun und nimmer(mehr)** never more; **von nun ab** from now on; **wenn er nun käme?** what if he came?
nun'mehr' *adv* now; from now on
nur [nur] *adv* only, merely, but; (*lauter*) nothing but; **nicht nur . . . sondern auch** not only . . . but also; **nur daß** except that; **nur eben** scarcely; (*zeitlich*) a moment ago; **nur zu!** go to it!; **wenn nur** if only, provided that
Nürnberg ['nʏrnberk] *n* (–s;) Nuremberg
nuscheln ['nuʃəln] *intr* (coll) mumble
Nuß [nus] *f* (–; Nüsse) nut
nuß'braun *adj* nut-brown; (*Augen*) hazel
Nuß'kern *m* kernel
Nußknacker ['nusknakər] *m* (–s;–) nutcracker
Nuß'schale *f* nutshell
Nüster ['nystər] *f* (–;–n) nostril
Nut [nut] *f* (–;–en), **Nute** ['nutə] *f* (–;–n) groove, rabbet
Nutte ['nutə] *f* (–;–n) whore
nutz [nuts] *adj* useful; **zu nichts n. sein** be good for nothing || **Nutz** *m* (–es;) use; benefit; profit; **zu j–s N. und Frommen** for s.o.'s benefit
Nutz'anwendung *f* utilization
nutzbar ['nutsbar] *adj* useful; **sich** [*dat*] **etw n. machen** utilize s.th.
nutz'bringend *adj* useful, profitable
nütze ['nʏtsə] *adj* useful; **nichts n. of** no use; **zu nichts n. sein** be good for nothing
Nutz'effekt *m* efficiency
nutzen ['nutsən], **nützen** ['nʏtsən] *tr* make use of; **das kann mir viel** (**wenig, nichts**) **n.** this can do me much (little, no) good; **was nützt das**

alles? what's the good of all this? ||
intr do good || *impers*—es nützt
nichts it's no use || Nutzen *m* (-s;-)
use; benefit; (*Gewinn*) profit; (*Vor-
teil*) advantage; von N. sein be of use
Nutz'fahrzeug *n* commercial vehicle
Nutz'garten *m* vegetable garden
Nutz'holz *n* lumber
Nutz'leistung *f* (mech) output

nützlich ['nʏtslɪç] *adj* useful
nutz'los *adj* useless
Nutz'losigkeit *f* (-;) uselessness
Nutz'schwelle *f* break-even point
Nut'zung *f* (-;) use
Nylon ['naɪlən] *n* (-s;) nylon
Nymphe ['nʏmfə] *f* (-;-n) nymph
Nymphomanin [nʏmfə'manɪn] *f* (-;
-nen) nymphomaniac

O

O, o [o] *invar n* O, o
Oase [ɔ'azə] *f* (-;-n) oasis
ob [ɔp] *prep* (*dat*) above; (*genit*) on
account of || *conj* whether; als ob
as if; na ob! rather!; und ob! and
how!
Obacht ['obaxt] *f* (-;)—in O. nehmen
take care of; O.! watch out!; O.
geben auf (*acc*) pay attention to;
take care of
Obdach ['ɔpdax] *n* (-[e]s;) shelter
ob'dachlos *adj* homeless
Obduktion [ɔpdʊk'tsjon] *f* (-;-en)
autopsy
obduzieren [ɔpdʊ'tsirən] *tr* perform
an autopsy on
O-Beine ['obaɪnə] *pl* bow legs
O'-beinig *adj* bowlegged
Obelisk [ɔbe'lɪsk] *m* (-en;-en) obelisk
oben ['obən] *adv* above; (*in der Höhe*)
up; (*im Himmelsraum*) on high; (*im
Hause*) upstairs; (*auf der Spitze*) at
the top; (*auf der Oberfläche*) on the
surface; (*Aufschrift auf Kisten*) this
side up; da o. up there; nach o.
gehen go up, go upstairs; o. am
Tische sitzen sit at the head of the
table; o. auf (*dat*) at the top of, on
the top of; von o. from above; von
o. bis unten from top to bottom;
from head to foot; von o. herab (fig)
condescendingly; wie o. angegeben
as stated above
obenan' *adv* at the top, at the head
obenauf' *adv* on top; immer o. sein
be always in top spirits
obendrein [obən'draɪn] *adv* on top of
it, into the bargain
o'benerwähnt, o'bengennant *adj* above-
mentioned
o'bengesteuert *adj* (aut) overhead
obenhin' *adv* superficially; perfunctorily
obenhinaus' *adv*—o. wollen have big
ideas
o'ben-oh'ne *adj* (coll) topless
o'benstehend *adj* given above
Ober ['obər] *m* (-s;-) (coll) waiter;
Herr O.! waiter!
Ober- *comb.fm.* upper, higher; superior; chief, supreme, head; southern
O'berägypten *n* Upper Egypt
O'berarm *m* upper arm
O'beraufseher *m* inspector general;
superintendent
O'beraufsicht *f* superintendence

O'berbau *m* (-[e]s;-ten) superstructure
O'berbefehl *m* supreme command; O.
führen have supreme command
O'berbefehlshaber *m* commander in
chief
O'berbegriff *m* wider concept
O'berdeck *n* upper deck
O'berdeckomnibus *m* double-decker
bus
o'berdeutsch *adj* of southern Germany
obere ['obərə] §9 *adj* higher, upper;
chief, superior; supreme || Obere §5
m (eccl) father superior || *n* top
o'berfaul *adj* (fig) fishy
O'berfeldwebel *m* sergeant first class
O'berfläche *f* surface
o'berflächlich *adj* superficial
O'bergefreite §5 *m* corporal
O'bergeschoß *n* upper floor
O'bergewalt *f* supreme authority
o'berhalb *prep* (*genit*) above
O'berhand *f* (fig) upper hand; die O.
gewinnen über (*acc*) get the better
of
O'berhaupt *n* head, chief
O'berhaus *n* upper house
O'berhaut *f* epidermis
O'berhemd *n* shirt, dress shirt
O'berherr *m* sovereign
O'berherrschaft *f* sovereignty; suprem-
acy
O'berhirte *m* prelate
O'berhofmeister *m* Lord Chamberlain
O'berhoheit *f* supreme authority
Oberin ['obərɪn] *f* (-;-nen) mother
superior; (med) head nurse
O'beringenieur *m* chief engineer
o'berirdisch *adj* above-ground; over-
head
O'berkellner *m* head waiter
O'berkiefer *m* upper jaw
O'berkleidung *f* outer wear
O'berkommando *n* general headquar-
ters
O'berkörper *m* upper part of the body
O'berland *n* highlands
Oberländer -in ['obərlɛndər(ɪn)] §6
mf highlander
o'berlastig *adj* top-heavy
O'berleder *n* uppers
O'berlehrer -in §6 *mf* secondary school
teacher, high school teacher
O'berleitung *f* supervision; (elec) over-
head line (*of trolley, etc.*)
O'berleutnant *m* first lieutenant

O'berlicht *n* skylight
O'berliga *f* (sport) upper division
O'berlippe *f* upper lip
O'berpostamt *n* general post office
O'berprima *f* senior class
Obers ['obərs] *m* (–;) (Aust) cream
O'berschenkel *m* thigh
O'berschicht *f* upper layer; (*der Be-völkerung*) upper classes; geistige O. intelligentsia
O'berschule *f* high school
O'berschwester *f* (med) head nurse
O'berseite *f* topside, right side
Oberst ['obərst] *m* (–en;–en) colonel
O'berstaatsanwalt *m* attorney general
oberste ['obərstə] §9 *adj* (*super* of obere) uppermost, highest, top ‖ Oberste §5 *mf* senior, chief
O'berstimme *f* treble, soprano
O'berstleutnant *m* lieutenant colonel
O'berstock *m* upper floor
O'berwasser *n*—O. haben (fig) have the upper hand
O'berwelt *f* upper world
O'berwerk *n* upper manual (*of organ*)
obgleich' *conj* though, although
Ob'hut *f* (–;) care, protection
obig ['obɪç] *adj* above, above-mentioned
Objekt [ɔp'jɛkt] *n* (–[e]s;–e) object
objektiv [ɔpjɛk'tif] *adj* objective; (*un-parteiisch*) impartial ‖ Objektiv *n* (–s;–e) objective lens
Objektivität [ɔpjɛktɪvɪ'tɛt] *f* (–;) objectivity; impartiality
Objekt'träger *m* slide (*of microscope*)
Oblate [ɔ'blɑtə] *f* (–;–n) wafer; (eccl) host
obliegen [ɔp'ligən] §108 *intr* (*dat*) apply oneself to, devote oneself to; (*dat*) be incumbent upon ‖ *impers*—es obliegt mir zu (*inf*) it's up to me to (*inf*)
Ob'liegenheit *f* (–;–en) obligation
obligat [ɔblɪ'gat] *adj* obligatory; (*unerläßlich*) indispensable; (*unvermeidlich*) inevitable
Obligation [ɔblɪga'tsjon] *f* (–;–en) bond; obligation
obligatorisch [ɔblɪga'torɪʃ] *adj* obligatory
Ob·mann ['ɔpman] *m* (–[e]s;–er & –leute) chairman; (jur) foreman
Oboe [ɔ'bo·ə] *f* (–;–n) oboe
Obrigkeit ['obrɪçkaɪt] *f* (–;–en) authority; (coll) authorities
o'brigkeitlich *adj* government(al)
obschon' *conj* though, although
Observato·rium [ɔpzɛrva'torjʊm] *n* (–s;–rien) [rjən] observatory
obsiegen ['ɔpzigən] *intr* be victorious; (*dat*) triumph over
obskur [ɔps'kur] *adj* obscure
Obst [opst] *n* (–es;) (*certain kinds of*) fruit (*mainly central-European, e.g., apples, plums; but not bananas, oranges*); O. und Südfrüchte European and (sub)tropical fruit
Obst'garten *m* orchard
Obst'kern *m* stone; seed, pip
Obstruktion [ɔpstruk'tsjon] *f* (–;–en) obstruction; (pol) filibuster; O. treiben filibuster

obszön [ɔps'tsøn] *adj* obscene
Obszönität [ɔpstsønɪ'tet] *f* (–;–en) obscenity
ob'walten, obwal'ten *intr* exist; prevail; hold sway
obwohl' *conj* though, although
Ochse ['ɔksə] *m* (–n;–n) ox
ochsen ['ɔksən] *intr* (educ) cram
O'chsenfleisch *n* beef
O'chsenfrosch *m* bullfrog
öde ['ødə] *adj* bleak ‖ Öde *f* (–;–n) wasteland; (fig) bleakness
Ödem [ø'dem] *n* (–s;–e) edema
oder ['odər] *conj* or
Öd·land ['øtlant] *n* (–[e]s;–ländereien [lɛndə'raɪ·ən]) wasteland
Ofen ['ofən] *m* (–s;ː) stove; (*Back-*) oven; (*Hoch-*) furnace; (*Brenn-, Dürr-*) kiln
O'fenklappe *f* damper
O'fenrohr *n* stovepipe
O'fenröhre *f* warming oven
offen ['ɔfən] *adj* open; (*öffentlich*) public; (fig) frank, open
offenbar ['ɔfənbar] *adj* obvious, manifest
offenbaren [ɔfən'barən] *tr* reveal
Offenba'rung *f* (–;–en) revelation
Of'fenheit *f* (–;) openness
of'fenherzig *adj* forthright; (*Kleid*) (hum) low-cut
of'fenkundig *adj* well-known; (*offensichtlich*) obvious; (*Beweis*) clear
of'fensichtlich *adj* obvious
offensiv [ɔfɛn'zif] *adj* offensive ‖ Offensive [ɔfɛn'zivə] *f* (–;–n) offensive
öffentlich ['œfəntlɪç] *adj* public; (*Dienst*) civil; öffentliches Haus brothel
Öf'fentlichkeit *f* (–;) public; publicity; an die Ö. treten appear in public; im Licht der Ö. in the limelight; in aller Ö. in public; sich in die Ö. flüchten rush into print
offerieren [ɔfə'rirən] *tr* offer
Offerte [ɔ'fɛrtə] *f* (–;–n) offer
Offerto·rium [ɔfɛr'torjʊm] *n* (–s;–rien [rjən]) offertory
Offiziant [ɔfɪ'tsjant] *m* (–en;–en) officiating priest
offiziell [ɔfɪ'tsjɛl] *adj* official
Offizier [ɔfɪ'tsir] –in [ɔfɪ'tsir(ɪn)] §6 *mf* officer
Offiziers'anwärter –in §6 *mf* officer candidate
Offiziers'bursche *m* orderly
Offiziers'deck *n* quarter deck
Offiziers'kasino *n* officers' club
Offiziers'patent *n* officer's commission
Offizin [ɔfɪ'tsin] *f* (–;–en) drugstore; (*Druckerei*) print shop, press
offiziös [ɔfɪ'tsjøs] *adj* semiofficial
öffnen ['œfnən] *tr* & *ref* open
Öff'ner *m* (–s;–) opener
Öff'nung *f* (–;–en) opening
oft [oft], öfter(s) ['œftər(s)] *adv* often
oftmals ['ɔftmals] *adv* often(times)
oh [o] *interj* oh!, O!
Oheim ['ohaɪm] *m* (–s;–e) uncle
Ohm [om] *m* (–s;–e) (poet) uncle ‖ *n* (–s;–) (elec) ohm
ohne ['onə] *prep* (*acc*) without; o. daß (*ind*) without (*ger*); o. mich! count

me out!; **o. weiteres** right off; **o. zu** (*inf*) without (*ger*)
ohnedies' *adv* anyhow, in any case
ohneglei'chen *adj* unequaled
ohnehin' *adv* anyhow, as it is
Ohnmacht ['ɔnmaxt] *f* (–;) faint, unconsciousness; helplessness; **in O. fallen** (or **sinken**) faint, pass out
ohnmächtig ['ɔnmɛçtɪç] *adj* unconscious; helpless; **o. werden** faint
Ohr [or] *n* (–[e]s;–en) ear; (*im Buch*) dog-ear; **die Ohren spitzen** prick up the ears; **es dick hinter den Ohren haben** be sly; **ganz Ohr sein** be all ears; **j–m in den Ohren liegen** keep dinning it into s.o.'s ears; **j–n hinter die Ohren hauen** box s.o.'s ears; **j–n übers Ohr hauen** cheat s.o.; **sich aufs Ohr legen** take a nap; **zum e–n Ohr hinein, zum anderen wieder hinaus** in one ear and out the other
Öhr [ør] *n* (–(e)s;–e) eye (*of needle*); ax hole, hammer hole
ohrenbetäubend *adj* earsplitting
Oh'renklingen *n* ringing in the ears
Oh'rensausen *n* buzzing in the ear
Oh'renschmalz *n* earwax
Oh'renschmaus *m* treat for the ears
Ohrenschützer *m* earmuff
Ohr'feige *f* (–;–n) box on the ear
ohrfeigen ['orfaɪgən] *tr* box on the ear
Ohrläppchen ['orlɛpçən] *n* (–s;–) earlobe
Ohr'muschel *f* auricle
okkult [ɔ'kʊlt] *adj* occult
Ökologie [økɔlɔ'gi] *f* (–;) ecology
ökologisch [økɔ'logɪʃ] *adj* ecological
Ökonom [økɔ'nom] *m* (–en;–en) economist
Ökono·mie [økɔnɔ'mi] (–;–mien ['mi·ən]) economy; economics
ökonomisch [økɔ'nomɪʃ] *adj* economical
Oktav [ɔk'taf] *n* (–s;–e) octavo
Oktave [ɔk'tavə] *f* (–;–n) octave
Oktober [ɔk'tobər] *m* (–s;–) October
oktroyieren [ɔktrwa'jirən] *tr* impose
Okular [ɔkʊ'lar] *n* (–s;–e) eyepiece
okulieren [ɔkʊ'lirən] *tr* inoculate
Ökumene [øku'menə] *f* (–;) ecumenism
ökumenisch [øku'menɪʃ] *adj* ecumenical
Okzident ['ɔktsɪdɛnt] *m* (–s;) Occident
Öl [øl] *n* (–[e]s;–e) oil; **Öl ins Feuer gießen** (fig) add fuel to the fire
Öl'baum *m* olive tree
Öl'berg *m* Mount of Olives
Oleander [ɔle'andər] *m* (–s;–) oleander
ölen ['ølən] *tr* oil; (mach) lubricate
Öl'götze *m* (coll) dummy, lout
Öl'heizung *f* oil heat
ölig ['ølɪç] *adj* oily
Oligar·chie [ɔligar'çi] *f* (–;–chien ['çi·ən]) oligarchy
Olive [ɔ'livə] *f* (–;–n) olive
Oli'venöl *n* olive oil
Öl'leitung *f* pipeline
Öl'quelle *f* oil well
Öl'schlick *m* oil slick
Öl'stand *m* (aut) oil level
Öl'standanzeiger *m* oil gauge

Öl'standmesser *m* (aut) oil gauge; dip stick
Ö'lung *f* (–;–en) oiling; anointing; **die Letzte Ö.** extreme unction
Olymp [ɔ'lymp] *m* (–s;) Mt. Olympus
Olympiade [ɔlym'pjadə] *f* (–;–n) olympiad
olympisch [ɔ'lympɪʃ] *adj* Olympian; Olympic; **die Olympischen Spiele** the Olympics
öl'zweig *m* olive branch
Oma ['oma] *f* (–;–s) (coll) grandma
Omelett [ɔm(ə)'lɛt] *n* (–[e]s;–e & –s) omelette
O·men ['omɛn] *n* (–s;–mina ['mɪna]) omen
ominös [ɔmi'nøs] *adj* ominous
Omnibus ['ɔmnɪbʊs] *m* (ses;–se) bus
Onanie [ɔna'ni] *f* (–;) masturbation
ondulieren [ɔndu'lirən] *tr* (*Haar*) wave
Onkel ['ɔŋkəl] *m* (–s;– & –s) uncle; **der große O.** (coll) the big toe
Opa ['opa] *m* (–s;–s) (coll) grandpa
Oper ['opər] *f* (–;–n) opera
Operateur [ɔpera'tør] *m* (–s;–s) operator; (cin) projectionist; (surg) operating surgeon
Operation [ɔpera'tsjon] *f* (–;–en) operation
Operations'gebiet *n* theater of operations
Operations'saal *m* operating room
operativ [ɔpera'tif] *adj* surgical; operational, strategic
operieren [ɔpe'rirən] *tr* operate on; **sich o. lassen** undergo an operation
O'pernglas *n*, **O'perngucker** *m* opera glasses
O'pernhaus *n* opera house, opera
Opfer ['ɔpfər] *n* (–s;–) sacrifice; victim; **zum O. fallen** (*dat*) fall victim to
op'ferfreudig *adj* self-sacrificing
Op'fergabe *f* offering
Op'ferkasten *m* poor box
Op'ferlamm *n* sacrificial lamb; Lamb of God; (fig) victim
Op'fermut *m* spirit of sacrifice
opfern ['ɔpfərn] *tr* sacrifice, offer up
Op'ferstock *m* poor box
Op'fertier *n* victim
Op'fertod *m* sacrifice of one's life
Op'fertrank *m* libation
Op'ferung *f* (–;–en) offering, sacrifice
op'ferwillig *adj* willing to make sacrifices
opponieren [ɔpɔ'nirən] *intr* (*dat*) oppose
opportun [ɔpɔr'tun] *adj* opportune
optieren [ɔp'tirən] *intr*—**o. für** opt for
Optik ['ɔptɪk] *f* (–;) optics
Optiker –in ['ɔptɪkər(ɪn)] §6 *mf* optician
optimistisch [ɔpti'mɪstɪʃ] *adj* optimistic
optisch ['ɔptɪʃ] *adj* optic(al)
Orakel [ɔ'rakəl] *n* (–s;–) oracle
ora'kelhaft *adj* oracular
orange [ɔ'rãʒə] *adj* orange ‖ **Orange** *f* (–;–n) orange
oran'genfarben, oran'genfarbig *adj* orange-colored
oratorisch [ɔra'torɪʃ] *adj* oratorical

Orchester [ɔr'kɛstər] *n* (-s;-) orchestra

orchestral [ɔrçɛs'trɑl] *adj* orchestral

orchestrieren [ɔrkɛs'trirən] *tr* orchestrate

Orchidee [ɔrçɪ'de·ə] *f* (-;-n) orchid

Orden ['ɔrdən] *m* (-s;-) medal, decoration; (eccl) order

Or'densband *n* (-[e]s;-er) ribbon

Or'densbruder *m* monk, friar

Or'denskleid *n* (eccl) habit

Or'densschwester *f* nun, sister

ordentlich ['ɔrdəntlɪç] *adj* orderly; *(aufgeräumt)* tidy; *(anständig)* decent, respectable; *(regelrecht)* regular; *(tüchtig)* sound; *(Frühstück)* solid; *(Mitglied)* active; *(Professor)* full; **e-e ordentliche Leistung** a pretty good job; **in ordentlichem Zustand** in good condition || *adv* thoroughly, properly; *(sehr)* (coll) awfully, very; really

Order ['ɔrdər] *f* (-;-n) (com, mil) order

ordinär [ɔrdɪ'ner] *adj* ordinary; vulgar; rude

Ordina·rius [ɔrdɪ'narjʊs] *m* (-;-rien [rjən]) professor; (eccl) ordinary

Ordinär'preis *m* retail price

ordinieren [ɔrdɪ'nirən] *tr* ordain || *intr* (med) have office hours

ordnen ['ɔrdnən] *tr* arrange; *(regeln)* put in order; *(säubern)* tidy up

Ord'nung *f* (-;-en) order, arrangement; classification; system; class; rank; regulation; (mil) formation; **aus der O. bringen** disturb; **in bester O.** in tiptop shape; **in O. bringen** set in order; **in O. sein** be all right; **nicht in O. sein** be out of order; be wrong; be out of sorts

ord'nungsgemäß *adv* duly

Ord'nungsliebe *f* tidiness, orderliness

ord'nungsmäßig *adj* orderly, regular || *adv* duly

Ord'nungsruf *m* (parl) call to order

Ord'nungssinn *m* sense of order

Ord'nungsstrafe *f* fine

ord'nungswidrig *adj* irregular, illegal

Ord'nungszahl *f* ordinal number

Ordonnanz [ɔrdə'nants] *f* (-;-en) (mil) orderly

Organ [ɔr'gɑn] *n* (-s;-e) organ

Organisation [ɔrganɪza'tsjon] *f* (-;-en) organization

organisch [ɔr'gɑnɪʃ] *adj* organic; *(Gewebe)* structural || *adv* organically

organisieren [ɔrganɪ'zirən] *tr* organize; (mil) scrounge || *ref* unionize; **organisierter Arbeiter** union worker

Organis·mus [ɔrga'nɪsmʊs] *m* (-;-men [mən]) organism

Organist –in [ɔrga'nɪst(ɪn)] §7 *mf* organist

Orgas·mus [ɔr'gasmʊs] *m* (-;-men [mən]) orgasm

Orgel ['ɔrgəl] *f* (-;-n) organ

Or'gelzug *m* organ stop

Orgie ['ɔrgjə] *f* (-;-n) orgy

Orient ['ɔrjɛnt] *m* (-s;) Orient

Orientale [ɔrjɛn'talə] *m* (-n;-n) Orientalin [ɔrjɛn'talɪn] *f* (-;-nen) Oriental

orientalisch [ɔrjɛn'talɪʃ] *adj* oriental

orientieren [ɔrjɛn'tirən] *tr* orient; (fig) inform, instruct; (mil) brief

Orientie'rung *f* (-;-en) orientation; information, instruction; **die O. verlieren** lose one's bearings

Orientie'rungssinn *m* sense of direction

original [ɔrigi'nɑl] *adj* original || **Original** *n* (-s;-e) original; (typ) copy

Original'ausgabe *f* first edition

Originalität [ɔriginalɪ'tet] *f* (-;) originality

Original'sendung *f* live broadcast

originell [ɔrigi'nɛl] *adj* original

Orkan [ɔr'kɑn] *m* (-[e]s;-e) hurricane

Ornament [ɔrna'mɛnt] *n* (-[e]s;-e) ornament

Ornat [ɔr'nɑt] *m* (-[e]s;-e) robes

Ort [ɔrt] *m* (-[e]s;-e) place, spot; *(Örtlichkeit)* locality; *(Dorf)* village; **am Ort sein** be appropriate; **an allen Orten** everywhere; **an Ort und Stelle** on the spot; **an Ort und Stelle gelangen** reach one's destination; **höheren Ortes** at higher levels; **Ort der Handlung** scene of action; **vor Ort** on location; **vor Ort arbeiten** (min) work at the face || *m* (-[e]s; -er) position, locus

Örtchen ['œrtçən] *n* (-s;-) toilet

orten ['ɔrtən] *tr* get the bearing on, locate || *intr* take a bearing

orthodox [ɔrto'dɔks] *adj* orthodox

Orthographie [ɔrtɔgra'fi] *f* (-;) orthography

Orthopäde [ɔrtɔ'pedə] *m* (-n;-n), **Orthopädin** [ɔrtɔ'pedɪn] *f* (-;-nen) orthopedist

orthopädisch [ɔrtɔ'pedɪʃ] *adj* orthopedic

örtlich ['œrtlɪç] *adj* local, topical

Ört'lichkeit *f* (-;-en) locality

Orts-, orts- [ɔrts] *comb.fm.* local

Orts'amt *n* (telp) local exchange

Orts'angabe *f* address

orts'ansässig *adj* resident || **Ortsansässige** §5 *mf* resident

Orts'behörde *f* local authorities

Orts'beschreibung *f* topography

Ort'schaft *f* (-;-en) place; *(Dorf)* village

orts'fremd *adj* nonlocal, out-of-town

Orts'gespräch *n* (telp) local call

Orts'kenntnis *f* familiarity with a place

orts'kundig *adj* familiar with the locality

Orts'name *m* place name

Orts'sinn *m* sense of direction

Orts'veränderung *f* change of scenery

Orts'verkehr *m* local traffic

Orts'zeit *f* local time

Orts'zustellung *f* local delivery

Or'tung *f* (-;-en) (aer, naut) taking of bearings, navigation

Öse ['øzə] *f* (-;-n) loop, eye; *(des Schuhes)* eyelet

Ost [ɔst] *m* (-es;-e) East; (poet) east wind

Ost- *comb.fm.* eastern, East

Osten ['ɔstən] *m* (-s;) East; **der Ferne O.** the Far East; **der Nahe O.** the Near East; **nach O.** eastward

ostentativ [ɔstɛnta'tif] *adj* ostentatious

Oster– [ostər] *comb.fm.* Easter
O'sterei *n* Easter egg
O'sterfest *n* Easter
O'sterhase *m* Easter bunny
O'sterlamm *m* paschal lamb
Ostern ['ostərn] *n* (–;–) & *pl* Easter
österreich ['østəraɪç] *n* (–s;) Austria
österreicher –**in** ['østəraɪçər(ɪn)] §6 *mf* Austrian
österreichisch ['østəraɪçɪʃ] *adj* Austrian
O'sterzeit *f* Eastertide
Ost'front *f* eastern front
Ost'gote *m* Ostrogoth
östlich ['œstlɪç] *adj* eastern, easterly; Oriental; **ö. von** east of
Ost'mark *f* East-German mark
Ost'see *f* Baltic Sea
ostwärts ['ostverts] *adv* eastward

Otter ['otər] *m* (–s;–) otter || *f* (–;–n) (*Schlange*) adder
Ouvertüre [uvɛr'tyrə] *f* (–;–n) (mus) overture
oval [o'val] *adj* oval || **Oval** *n* (–s;–e) oval
Ovar [o'var] *n* (–s;–e & –ien [jən]) ovary
Overall ['ovərol] *m* (–s;–s) overalls
Oxyd [o'ksyt] *n* (–[e]s;–e) oxide
Oxydation [oksyda'tsjon] *f* (–;) oxidation
oxydieren [oksy'dirən] *tr* & *intr* (SEIN) oxidize
Ozean ['otse·an] *m* (–s;–e) ocean; **der Große** (*or* **Stille**) **O.** the Pacific
Ozeanographie [otse·anəgra'fi] *f* (–;) oceanography
Ozon [o'tson] *n* (–s;) ozone

P

P, p [pe] *invar n* P, p
paar [par] *adj* even || *invar adj*—**ein p.** a couple of, a few || **Paar** *n* (–[e]s; –e) pair, couple; **zu Paaren treiben** rout
paaren ['parən] *tr* match, mate || *ref* mate
paarig ['parɪç] *adj* in pairs
paar'laufen §105 *intr* (SEIN) skate as a couple
paar'mal *adv*—**ein p.** a couple of times
Paa'rung *f* (–;) pairing, matching; (*Begattung*) mating
Paa'rungszeit *f* mating season
paar'weise *adv* in pairs, two by two
Pacht [paxt] *f* (–;–en) lease; (*Geld*) rent; **in P. geben** lease out; **in P. nehmen** lease, rent
Pacht'brief *m* lease
pachten ['paxtən] *tr* take a lease on
Pächter –**in** ['pɛçtər(ɪn)] §6 *mf* tenant
Pacht'ertrag *m*, **Pacht'geld** *n* rent
Pacht'gut *n*, **Pacht'hof** *m* leased farm
Pacht'kontrakt *m* lease
Pach'tung *f* (–;–en) leasing; leasehold
Pacht'vertrag *m* lease
Pacht'zeit *f* term of lease
Pacht'zins *m* rent
Pack [pak] *m* (–[e]s;–e & ⸚e) pack; (*Paket*) parcel; (*Ballen*) bale; **ein P. Spielkarten** a pack of cards || *n* (–[e]s;) rabble; **ein P. von Lügnern** a pack of liars
Päckchen ['pɛkçən] *n* (–s;–) small package; (*Zigaretten–*) pack
packen ['pakən] *tr* pack, pack up; (*fassen*) seize, grab; (fig) grip, thrill; **pack dich!** scram! || **Packen** *m* (–s;–) pack; (*Ballen*) bale || *n* (–s;) packing
Pack'esel *m* (fig) drudge
Pack'papier *n* wrapping paper
Pack'pferd *n* packhorse
Pack'tier *n* pack animal
Packung (Pak'kung) *f* (–;–en) packing; (*Paket*) packet; **P. Zigaretten** pack of cigarettes

Pack'wagen *m* (rr) baggage car
Pädadoge [pɛda'gogə] *m* (–n;–n) pedagogue
Pädagogik [pɛda'gogɪk] *f* (–;) pedagogy
pädagogisch [pɛda'gogɪʃ] *adj* pedagogical, educational
Paddel ['padəl] *n* (–s;–) paddle
Pad'delboot *n* canoe
paddeln ['padəln] *intr* paddle, canoe
Pädiatrie [pedɪ·a'tri] *f* (–;) pediatrics
paff [paf] *interj* bang!
paffen ['pafən] *tr* & *intr* puff
Page ['paʒə] *m* (–n;–n) page
Pa'genfrisur *f*, **Pa'genkopf** *m* pageboy
Pagode [pa'godə] *f* (–;–n) pagoda
Pair [per] *m* (–s;–s) peer
Pak [pak] *f* (–;– & –s) (**Panzerabwehrkanone**) antitank gun
Paket [pa'ket] *n* (–[e]s;–e) parcel; (*Bücher–, Post–*) bundle
Paket'adresse *f* gummed label
Paket'post *f* parcel post
Pakt [pakt] *m* (–[e]s;–e) pact
paktieren [pak'tirən] *intr* make a pact
Paläontologie [pale·ontolo'gi] *f* (–;) paleontology
Palast [pa'last] *m* (–es;⸚e) palace
palast'artig *adj* palatial
Palästina [pale'stina] *n* (–s;) Palestine
Palette [pa'letə] *f* (–;–n) palette
Palisade [palɪ'zadə] *f* (–;–n) palisade
Palme ['palmə] *f* (–;–n) palm tree; palm branch; **j–n auf die P. bringen** (coll) drive s.o. up the wall
Palm'wedel *m*, **Palm'zweig** *m* palm branch
Pampelmuse ['pampəlmuzə] *f* (–;–n) grapefruit
Pamphlet [pam'flet] *n* (–[e]s;–e) lampoon
Panama ['panama] *n* (–s;) Panama
Paneel [pa'nel] *n* (–s;–e) panel
paneelieren [pane'lirən] *tr* panel
Panier [pa'nir] *n* (–s;–e) slogan
panieren [pa'nirən] *tr* (culin) bread

Panik ['pɑnɪk] f (-;) panic
panisch ['pɑnɪʃ] adj panic-stricken
Panne ['panə] f (-;-n) breakdown;
(Reifenpanne) blowout; (fig) mishap
Panora·ma [panɔ'rɑma] n (-s;-men
[mən]) panorama
panschen ['panʃən] tr adulterate, water
down || intr splash about; mix
Panther ['pantər] m (-s;-) panther
Pantine [pan'tinə] f (-;-n) clog
Pantoffel [pan'tɔfəl] m (-s;-n) slipper;
unter dem P. stehen be henpecked
Pantof'felheld m henpecked husband
Panzer ['pantsər] m (-s;-) armor; ar-
mor plating; (mil) tank; (zool) shell
Pan'zerabwehrkanone f antitank gun
pan'zerbrechend adj armor-piercing
Pan'zerfalle f tank trap
Pan'zerfaust f bazooka
Pan'zergeschoß n, Pan'zergranate f
armor-piercing shell
Pan'zerhandschuh m gauntlet
Pan'zerhemd n coat of mail
Pan'zerkreuzer m battle cruiser
panzern ['pantsərn] tr armor || ref
arm oneself
Pan'zerschrank m safe
Panzerspähwagen ['pantsər/pevagən]
m (mil) armored car
Pan'zersperre f antitank obstacle
Pan'zerung f (-;-en) armor plating
Pan'zerwagen m armored car
Papagei [papa'gaɪ] m (-en;-en) &
(-[e]s;-e) parrot
Papier [pa'pir] n (-[e]s;-e) paper
Papier'bogen m sheet of paper
Papier'brei m paper pulp
papieren [pa'pirən] adj paper
Papier'fabrik f paper mill
Papier'format n size of paper
Papier'korb m wastebasket
Papier'krieg m (fig) red tape
Papier'mühle f paper mill
Papier'schlange f paper streamer
Papier'tüte f paper bag
Papier'waren pl stationery
Papp [pap] m (-[e]s;-e) (Brei) pap;
(Kleister) paste
Papp- [pap] comb.fm. sticky; card-
board
Papp'band m (-[e]s;ːe) paperback
Papp'deckel m piece of cardboard
Pappe ['papə] f (-;) cardboard
Pappel ['papəl] f (-;-n) poplar
päppeln ['pepəln] tr feed lovingly
pappen ['papən] tr paste, glue || intr
stick
Papp'penstiel m (coll) trifle; das ist
keinen P. wert (coll) this isn't worth
a thing
papperlapapp [papərla'pap] interj non-
sense!
pap'pig adj sticky
Papp'karton m, Papp'schachtel f card-
board box, cardboard carton
Papp'schnee m sticky snow (for skiing)
Paprika ['paprika] m (-s;) paprika
Pap'rikaschote f (green) pepper
Papst [papst] m (-es;ːe) pope
päpstlich ['pepstlɪç] adj papal
Papsttum ['papsttum] n (-s;) papacy
Papy·rus [pa'pyrus] m (-;-ri [ri])
papyrus

Parabel [pa'rabəl] f (-;-n) parable;
(geom) parabola
Parade [pa'radə] f (-;-n) parade;
(fencing) parry; (mil) review; (fb)
save
Para'deanzug m (mil) dress uniform
Paradeiser [para'daɪzər] m (-s;-)
(Aust) tomato
Para'depferd n (fig) show-off
Para'deplatz m parade ground
Para'deschritt m goose step
paradieren [para'dirən] intr parade;
(fig) show off
Paradies [para'dis] n (-es;-e) paradise
Paradies'apfel m tomato
paradox [para'dɔks] adj paradoxical ||
Paradox n (-es;-e) paradox
Paraffin [para'fin] n (-s;-e) paraffin
Paragraph [para'graf] m (-en & -s;
-en) paragraph; (jur) section
parallel [para'lel] adj parallel || Paral-
lele f (-;-n) parallel
Paralyse [para'lyzə] f (-;-n) paralysis
paralysieren [paraly'zirən] tr paralyze
Paralytiker -in [para'lytɪkər(ɪn)] §6
mf paralytic
Paranuß ['paranus] f Brazil nut
Parasit [para'zit] m (-en;-en) parasite
parat [pa'rat] adj ready
Pardon [par'dɔ̃] m (-s;) pardon; kei-
nen P. geben (mil) given no quarter
Parenthese [parɛn'tezə] f (-;-n) parenthesis
Parfüm [par'fym] n (-[e]s;-e) perfume
Parfüme·rie [parfymə'ri] f (-;-rien
['ri·ən]) perfume shop
parfümieren [parfY'mirən] tr perfume
pari ['pari] adv at par || Pari m (-
[s];) par; auf P. at par
Paria ['parja] m (-s;-s) pariah
parieren [pa'rirən] tr (Pferd) rein in;
(Hieb) parry || intr (dat) obey
Pa'rikurs m (com) parity
Paris [pa'ris] n (-;) Paris
Pariser -in [pa'rizər(ɪn)] §6 mf Pari-
sian
Parität [pari'tet] f (-;) equality; (fin,
st. exch.) parity
paritätisch [pari'tetɪʃ] adj on a footing of equality
Park [park] m (-s;-s & -e) park
Park'anlage f park; Parkanlagen
grounds
parken ['parkən] tr & intr park
Parkett [par'ket] n (-[e]s;-e) (Fußboden) parquet; (theat) parquet
Parkett'fußboden m parquet flooring
Park'licht n parking light
Park'platz m parking lot
Park'platzwärter m parking lot attendant
Park'uhr f parking meter
Parlament [parla'mɛnt] n (-[e]s;-e)
parliament
Parlamentär [parlamɛn'ter] m (-s;-e)
truce negotiator
parlamentarisch [parlamɛn'tarɪʃ] adj
parliamentary
parlamentieren [parlamɛn'tirən] intr
(coll) parley
Paro·die [parɔ'di] f (-;-dien ['di·ən])
parody
parodieren [parɔ'dirən] tr parody

Parole [pa'rolə] *f* (**-;-n**) (mil) password; (pol) slogan
Partei [par'taɪ] *f* (**-;-en**) party; (*Mieter*) tenant(s); (jur, pol) party; (sport) side; **j-s P. ergreifen** or **P. nehmen für j-n** side with s.o.
Partei'bonze *m* (pol) party boss
Partei'gänger –in §6 *mf* (pol) party sympathizer
Partei'genosse *m*, **Partei'genossin** *f* party member
Partei'grundsatz *m* party plank
parteiisch [par'taɪ·ɪʃ] *adj* partial, biased; (pol) partisan
partei'lich *adj* partisan
Partei'lichkeit *f* (**-;**) partiality
partei'los *adj* (pol) independent ‖ **Parteilose** §5 *mf* independent
Partei'losigkeit *f* (**-;**) impartiality; political independence
Partei'nahme *f* (**-;**) taking sides
Partei'programm *n* party platform
Partei'tag *m* party rally
Partei'zugehörigkeit *f* party affiliation
Parterre [par'tɛr] *n* (**-s;-s**) ground floor; (theat) parterre
Par·tie [par'ti] *f* (**-;-tien** ['ti·ən]) part; (*Gesellschaft*) party; (*Spiel*) game; (*Ausflug*) outing; (com) lot; (theat) role; **e-e gute P. machen** (coll) marry rich; **ich bin mit von der P.!** count me in!
partiell [par'tsjɛl] *adj* partial ‖ *adv* partly, partially
Partikel [par'tikəl] *f* (**-;-n**) particle
Partisan –in [partɪ'zɑn(ɪn)] §7 *mf* partisan
Partitur [partɪ'tur] *f* (**-;-en**) (mus) score
Partizip [partɪ'tsip] *n* (**-s;-ien** [jən]) participle
Partner –in ['partnər(ɪn)] §6 *mf* partner
Part'nerschaft *f* (**-;-en**) partnership
Parzelle [par'tsɛlə] *f* (**-;-n**) lot
parzellieren [partsɛ'lirən] *tr* parcel out, allot
paschen ['paʃən] *tr* smuggle ‖ *intr* smuggle; (*würfeln*) play dice
Paß [pas] *m* (**Passes; Pässe**) pass; passport; (geog) mountain pass
passabel [pa'sabəl] *adj* tolerable
Passage [pa'saʒə] *f* (**-;-n**) passage; (mus) run
Passagier [pasa'ʒir] *m* (**-s;-e**) passenger; **blinder P.** stowaway
Passagier'dampfer *m* passenger liner
Passagier'gut *n* luggage
Passah ['pasa] *n* (**-s;**), **Pas'sahfest** *n* Passover
Paß'amt *n* passport office
Passant –in [pa'sant(ɪn)] §7 *mf* passerby
Paß'ball *m* (sport) pass
Paß'bild *n* passport photograph
passen ['pasən] *ref* be proper ‖ *intr* fit; (*dat*) suit; (cards, fb) pass; **p. auf** (*acc*) watch for, wait for; **p. zu** suit, fit; **sie p. zueinander** they are a good match
pas'send *adj* suitable; convenient; (*Kleidungsstück*) matching; **für p. halten** think it proper

Paß'form *f*—**e-e gute P. haben** be form-fitting
passierbar [pa'sirbɑr] *adj* passable
passieren [pa'sirən] *tr* pass, cross; (culin) sift, sieve ‖ *intr* (SEIN) happen
Passier'schein *m* pass, permit
Passion [pa'sjon] *f* (**-;-en**) passion
passioniert [pasjo'nirt] *adj* ardent
Passions'spiel *n* passion play
passiv [pa'sif] *adj* passive; (*Handelsbilanz*) unfavorable; **passives Wahlrecht** eligibility ‖ **Passiv** *n* (**-s;-e**) (gram) passive
Passiva [pa'siva] *pl*, **Passiven** [pa'sivən] *pl* debts, liabilities
Paß'kontrolle *f* passport inspection
Paste ['pastə] *f* (**-;-n**) paste
Pastell [pa'stɛl] *n* (**-s;-e**) pastel; crayon
pastell'farben *adj* pastel
Pastell'stift *m* crayon
Pastete [pas'tetə] *f* (**-;-n**) meat pie, fish pie
pasteurisieren [pastœrɪ'zirən] *tr* pasteurize
Pastille [pa'stɪlə] *f* (**-;-n**) lozenge
Pa·stor ['pastɔr] *m* (**-s;-storen** ['tɔrən]) pastor, minister, vicar
Pate ['patə] *m* (**-n;-n**) godfather ‖ *f* (**-;-n**) godmother
Pa'tenkind *n* godchild
patent [pa'tent] *adj* neat; smart; **ein patenter Kerl** quite a fellow ‖ **Patent** *n* (**-[e]s;-e**) patent; (mil) commission; **P. angemeldet** patent pending
Patent'amt *n* patent office
patentieren [paten'tirən] *tr* patent
Pater ['patər] *m* (**-s; Patres** ['patrɛs]) (eccl) Father
pathetisch [pa'tetɪʃ] *adj* impassioned; solemn
Pathologe [pato'logə] *m* (**-n;-n**) pathologist
Pathologie [patolo'gi] *f* (**-;**) pathology
Pathologin [pato'login] *f* (**-;-nen**) pathologist
Patient –in [pa'tsjent(ɪn)] §7 *mf* patient
Patin ['patɪn] *f* (**-;-nen**) godmother
Patriarch [patrɪ'arç] *m* (**-en;-en**) patriarch
Patriot –in [patrɪ'ot(ɪn)] §7 *mf* patriot
patriotisch [patrɪ'otɪʃ] *adj* patriotic
Patrize [pa'tritsə] *f* (**-;-n**) die, stamp
Patrizier –in [pa'tritsjər(ɪn)] §6 *mf* patrician
Patron [pa'tron] *m* (**-s;-e**) patron; (pej) guy
Patronat [patro'nat] *n* (**-[e]s;-e**) patronage
Patrone [pa'tronə] *f* (**-;-n**) cartridge
Patro'nengurt *m* cartridge belt
Patro'nenhülse *f* cartridge case
Patronin [pa'tronɪn] *f* (**-;-nen**) patroness
Patrouille [pa'trʊljə] *f* (**-;-n**) patrol
patrouillieren [patru'ljirən] *tr & intr* patrol
Patsche ['patʃə] *f* (**-;-en**) (*Pfütze*) puddle; (coll) jam, scrape; **in der P. lassen** leave in a lurch; **in e-e P. geraten** get into a jam

patschen ['patʃən] *tr* slap || *intr* splash; in die Hände p. clap hands
patsch'naß' *adj* soaking wet
patzig ['patsɪç] *adj* snappy, sassy
Pauke ['paukə] *f* (-;-n) kettledrum; j-m e-e P. halten give s.o. a lecture
pauken ['paukən] *tr* (educ) cram || *intr* beat the kettledrum; (educ) cram
Pau'ker *m* (-s;-) (coll) martinet
pausbackig ['pausbakɪç], **pausbäckig** ['pausbɛkɪç] *adj* chubby-faced
pauschal [pau'ʃal] *adj* (*Summe*) flat
Pauschal'betrag *m* flat rate
Pauscha·le [pau'ʃalə] *n* (-s;-lien [ljən]) lump sum
Pauschal'preis *m* package price
Pauschal'reise *f* all-inclusive tour
Pauschal'summe *f* flat sum
Pause ['pauzə] *f* (-;-n) pause; (*Pauszeichnung*) tracing; (educ) recess, break; (mus) rest; (theat) intermission; e-e P. machen take a break
pausen ['pauzən] *tr* trace
pau'senlos *adj* continuous
Pau'senzeichen *n* (rad) station identification
pausieren [pau'zirən] *intr* pause; rest
Pauspapier ['pauzpapir] *n* tracing paper
Pavian ['pavjan] *m* (-s;-e) baboon
Pavillon ['pavɪljõ] *m* (-s;-s) pavilion
Pazifik [pa'tsifɪk] *m* (-s;) Pacific
pazifisch [pa'tsifɪʃ] *adj* Pacific
Pazifist –in [patsɪ'fɪst(ɪn)] §7 *mf* pacifist
Pech [pɛç] *n* (-[e]s;-e) pitch; **P. haben** (coll) have tough luck
Pech'fackel *f* torch
Pech'kohle *f* bituminous coal
pech'ra'benschwarz' *adj* pitch-black
pech'schwarz' *adj* pitch-dark
Pech'strähne *f* streak of bad luck
Pech'vogel *m* (coll) unlucky fellow
Pedal [pe'dal] *n* (-s;-e) pedal
Pedant [pe'dant] *m* (-en;-en) pedant
pedantisch [pe'dantɪʃ] *adj* pedantic
Pegel ['pegəl] *m* (-s;-) water gauge
Pe'gelstand *m* water level
Peil- [paɪl] *comb.fm.* direction-finding, sounding
peilen ['paɪlən] *tr* take the bearings of; (*Tiefe*) sound; über den Daumen p. (coll) estimate roughly || *intr* take bearings
Pei'lung *f* (-;-en) bearings; taking of bearings; sounding
Pein [paɪn] *f* (-;) pain, torment
peinigen ['paɪnɪɡən] *tr* torment
pein'lich *adj* painful; embarrassing; (*genau*) painstaking; (*sorgfältig*) scrupulous || *adv* scrupulously; carefully
Peitsche ['paɪtʃə] *f* (-;-n) whip; mit der P. knallen crack the whip
peitschen ['paɪtʃən] *tr* whip
Peit'schenhieb *m* whiplash
Peit'schenknall *m* crack of the whip
Pelerine [pelə'rinə] *f* (-;-n) cape
Pelikan ['pelɪkan] *m* (-s;-e) pelican
Pelle ['pelə] *f* (-;-n) peel, skin
pellen ['pelən] *tr* peel, skin
Pellkartoffeln ['pelkartɔfəln] *pl* potatoes in their jackets

Pelz [pelts] *m* (-es;-e) fur; (*Fell*) pelt; fur coat
Pelz'besatz *m* fur trimming
Pelz'futter *n* fur lining
Pelz'händler –in §6 *mf* furrier
pel'zig *adj* furry; (*Gefühl im Mund*) cottony
Pelz'tier *n* fur-bearing animal
Pelz'tierjäger *m* trapper
Pelz'werk *n* furs
Pendel ['pendəl] *n* (-s;-) pendulum
pendeln ['pendəln] *intr* swing, oscillate; (*zwischen zwei Orten*) commute
Pen'deltür *f* swinging door
Pen'delverkehr *m* commuter traffic; shuttle service
Pen'delzug *m* shuttle train
Pendler ['pendlər] *m* (-s;-) commuter
Penizillin [penɪtsɪ'lin] *n* (-s;) penicillin
Pension [pen'zjon] *f* (-;-en) pension, retirement pay; (*Fremdenhaus*) boarding house; (*Unterkunft und Verpflegung*) room and board; (*Pensionat*) girls' boarding school; in P. gehen go on pension
Pensionär [penzjo'ner] *m* (-s;-e) pensioner; boarder
Pensionat [penzjo'nat] *n* (-[e]s;-e) girls boarding school
pensionieren [penzjo'nirən] *tr* put on pension; (mil) retire on half pay; sich p. lassen retire
Pensions'kasse *f* pension fund
Pensions'preis *m* price of room and board
Pen·sum ['penzum] *n* (-s;-sen [zən] & -sa [za]) task, assignment; quota
per [per] *prep* (*acc*) per, by, with; (*zeitlich*) by, until; per Adresse care of, c/o; per sofort at once
perfekt [per'fekt] *adj* perfect; concluded || **Perfekt** *n* (-[e]s;-e) perfect
Pergament [perga'ment] *n* (-[e]s;-e) parchment
Periode [per'jodə] *f* (-;-n) period
periodisch [per'jodɪʃ] *adj* periodic
Periphe·rie [perɪfe'ri] *f* (-;-rien ['ri·ən]) periphery
Periskop [perɪ'skop] *n* (-s;-e) periscope
Perle ['perlə] *f* (-;-n) pearl; (*aus Glas*) bead; (*Tropfen*) drop, bead; (*Bläschen*) bubble; (fig) gem
perlen ['perlən] *intr* sparkle
Per'lenauster *f* pearl oyster
Per'lenkette *f*, **Per'lenschnur** *f* pearl necklace, string of pearls
Perlhuhn ['perlhun] *n* guinea fowl
perlig ['perlɪç] *adj* pearly
Perl'muschel *f* pearl oyster
Perlmutt ['perlmut] *n* (-s;), **Perl'mutter** *f* mother of pearl
perplex [per'pleks] *adj* perplexed
Persenning [per'zenɪŋ] *f* (-;-en) tarpaulin
Persien ['perzjən] *n* (-s;) Persia
persisch [perzɪʃ] *adj* Persian
Person [per'zon] *f* (-;-en) person; (theat) character; ich für meine P. I for one; klein von P. small of stature
Personal [perzo'nal] *n* (-s;) personnel
Personal'akte *f* personal file, dossier

Personal'angaben *pl* personal data
Personal'aufzug *m* passenger elevator
Personal'ausweis *m* identity card
Personal'chef *m* personnel manager
Personalien [pɛrzɔ'naljən] *pl* personal data, particulars
Personal'pronomen *n* personal pronoun
Perso'nengedächtnis *n* good memory for names
Perso'nenkraftwagen *m* passenger car
Perso'nenschaden *m* personal injury
Perso'nenverzeichnis *n* list of persons; (theat) dramatis personae, cast
Perso'nenwagen *m* passenger car
Perso'nenzug *m* passenger train; (rr) local
personifizieren [pɛrzɔnifɪ'tsirən] *tr* personify
persönlich [pɛr'zønlɪç] *adj* personal || *adv* personally, in person
Persön'lichkeit *f* (-;-en) personality
Perspektiv [pɛrspɛk'tif] *n* (-s;-e) telescope
Perücke [pɛ'rʏkə] *f* (-;-n) wig
pervers [pɛr'vɛrs] *adj* perverse
pessimistisch [pɛsɪ'mɪstɪʃ] *adj* pessimistic
Pest [pɛst] *f* (-;) plague
pest'artig *adj* pestilential
Pestilenz [pɛstɪ'lɛnts] *f* (-;-en) pestilence
Petersilie [pɛtər'ziljə] *f* (-;) parsley
Petroleum [pɛ'trole·ʊm] *n* (-s;) petroleum
Petschaft ['pɛtʃaft] *n* (-s;-e) seal
Petting ['pɛtɪŋ] *n* (-s;) petting
petto ['peto]—**in p. haben** have in reserve; (coll) have up one's sleeve
Petunie [pɛ'tunjə] *f* (-;-n) petunia
Petze ['pɛtsə] *f* (-;-n) tattletale
petzen ['pɛtsən] *intr* tattle, squeal
Pfad [pfat] *m* (-[e]s;-e) path, track
Pfadfinder ['pfatfɪndər] *m* (-s;-) boy scout
Pfadfinderin ['pfatfɪndərɪn] *f* (-;-nen) girl scout
Pfaffe ['pfafə] *m* (-n;-n) (pej) priest
Pfahl [pfal] *m* (-[e]s;⸚e) stake; post
Pfahl'bau *m* (-[e]s;-bauten) lake dwelling
Pfahl'werk *n* palisade, stockade
Pfahl'wurzel *f* taproot
Pfahl'zaun *m* palisade, stockade
Pfälzer -in ['pfɛltsər(ɪn)] §6 *mf* inhabitant of the Palatinate
Pfand [pfant] *n* (-[e]s;⸚er) pledge; deposit; (*Bürgschaft*) security, pawn (*auf Immobilien*) mortgage; **zum Pfande geben** (or **setzen**) pawn, mortgage
pfändbar ['pfɛntbar] *adj* (jur) attachable
Pfand'brief *m* mortgage papers
pfänden ['pfɛndən] *tr* attach, impound
Pfand'geber *m* mortgagor
Pfand'gläubiger *m* mortgagee
Pfand'haus *n*, **Pfand'leihe** *f* pawnshop
Pfand'leiher -in §6 *mf* pawnbroker
Pfand'recht *n* lien
Pfand'schein *m* pawn ticket
Pfand'schuldner *m* mortgagor
Pfän'dung *f* (-;-en) attachment, confiscation

Pfanne ['pfanə] *f* (-;-n) pan; (anat) socket; **etw auf der P. haben** (fig) have s.th. up one's sleeve; **in die P. hauen** (fig) make mincemeat of
Pfan'nenstiel *m* panhandle
Pfann'kuchen *m* pancake; **Berliner P.** doughnut
Pfarr- [pfar] *comb.fm.* parish, parochial
Pfarr'amt *n* rectory
Pfarr'bezirk *m* parish
Pfarr'dorf *n* parish seat
Pfarre ['pfarə] *f* (-;-n) parish; (*Pfarrhaus*) rectory
Pfarrei [pfa'raɪ] *f* (-;-en) parish; (*Pfarrhaus*) rectory
Pfarrer ['pfarər] *m* (-s;-) pastor
Pfarr'gemeinde *f* parish
Pfarr'haus *n* rectory
Pfarr'kind *n* parishioner
Pfarr'kirche *f* parish church
Pfarr'schule *f* parochial school
Pfau [pfaʊ] *m* (-[e]s;-en) peacock
Pfau'enhenne *f* peahen
Pfeffer ['pfɛfar] *m* (-s;) pepper
pfefferig ['pfɛfarɪç] *adj* peppery
Pfef'ferkorn *n* peppercorn
Pfef'ferkuchen *m* gingerbread
Pfef'ferminze *f* (bot) peppermint
Pfef'ferminzplätzchen *n* peppermint cookie
pfeffern ['pfɛfarn] *tr* pepper
Pfef'fernuß *f* ginger nut
Pfeife ['pfaɪfə] *f* (-;-n) whistle; (*Orgel-*) pipe; (*zum Rauchen*) (tobacco) pipe
pfeifen ['pfaɪfən] *tr* whistle; **ich pfeife ihm was** he can whistle for it || *intr* whistle; (*Schiedsrichter*) blow the whistle; (*Maus*) squeak; (*Vogel*) sing; (*dat*) whistle for or to; **auf dem letzten Loche p.** be on one's last legs; **ich pfeife darauf!** I couldn't care less!
Pfei'fenkopf *m* pipe bowl
Pfei'fenrohr *n* pipestem
Pfei'fer -in §6 *mf* whistler; (mus) piper, fife player
Pfeif'kessel *m*, **Pfeif'topf** *m* whistling kettle
Pfeil [pfaɪl] *m* (-[e]s;-e) arrow, dart; **P. und Bogen** bow and arrow
Pfei'ler *m* (-s;-) (& fig) pillar; (*e-r Brücke*) pier
pfeil'gera'de *adj* straight as an arrow
pfeil'schnell' *adj* swift as an arrow || *adv* like a shot
Pfeil'schütze *m* archer
Pfeil'spitze *f* arrowhead
Pfennig ['pfɛnɪç] *m* (-[e]s;-e & -) pfennig, penny (*one hundredth of a mark*)
Pfennigfuchser ['pfɛnɪçfʊksər] *m* (-s; -) penny pincher
Pferch [pfɛrç] *m* (-[e]s;-e) fold, pen
pferchen ['pfɛrçən] *tr* herd together, pen in
Pferd [pfert] *n* (-[e]s;-e) horse; **zu Pferde** on horseback
Pferde- [pferdə] *comb.fm.* horse
Pfer'deapfel *m* horse manure
Pfer'debremse *f* horsefly
Pfer'dedecke *f* horse blanket

Pfer′defuß m (*Kennzeichen des Teufels*) cloven hoof; (pathol) clubfoot
Pfer′degeschirr n harness
Pfer′degespann n team of horses
Pfer′deknecht m groom
Pfer′dekoppel f corral
Pfer′delänge f (*beim Rennen*) length
Pfer′derennbahn f race track
Pfer′derennen n horse racing
Pfer′destärke f horsepower
Pfer′dezucht f horse breeding
pfiff [pfɪf] *pret* of **pfeifen** ‖ **Pfiff** m (-[e]s;-e) whistle; **den P. heraushaben** (fig) know the ropes
Pfifferling [′pfɪfərlɪŋ] m (-s;-e) (bot) chanterelle; **keinen P. wert** not worth a thing
pfiffig [′pfɪfɪç] *adj* shrewd, sharp
Pfiffikus [′pfɪfɪkʊs] m (-;-), (-ses;-se) (coll) sly fox
Pfingsten [′pfɪŋstən] n (-s;) Pentecost
Pfingst′rose f (bot) peony
Pfingst′son′ntag m Whitsunday
Pfirsich [′pfɪrzɪç] m (-[e]s;-e) peach
Pflanze [′pflantsə] f (-;-n) plant
pflanzen [′pflantsən] *tr* plant
Pflan′zenfaser f vegetable fiber
Pflan′zenfett n vegetable shortening
pflan′zenfressend *adj* herbivorous
Pflan′zenkost f vegetable diet
Pflan′zenkunde f botany
Pflan′zenleben n plant life, vegetation
Pflan′zenlehre f botany
Pflan′zenöl n vegetable oil
Pflan′zenreich n vegetable kingdom
Pflan′zensaft m sap, juice
Pflan′zenschutzmittel n pesticide
Pflan′zenwelt f flora
Pflan′zer –in §6 mf planter
pflanz′lich *adj* vegetable
Pflanz′schule f, **Pflanz′stätte** f nursery; (fig) hotbed
Pflan′zung f (-;-en) plantation
Pflaster [′pflastər] n (-s;-) pavement; (*Fleck*) patch; (med) Band-Aid; **als P.** (fig) in compensation; **ein teueres P.** (fig) an expensive place; **P. treten** (fig) pound the sidewalks
Pflasterer [′pflastərər] m (-s;-) paver
pfla′stermüde *adj* tired of walking the streets
pflastern [′pflastərn] *tr* pave
Pfla′sterstein m paving stone; (*Kopfstein*) cobblestone
Pfla′stertreter m (-s;-) loafer
Pfla′sterung f (-;) paving
Pflaume [′pflaumə] f (-;-n) plum; (*spitze Bemerkung*) dig
pflaumen [′pflaumən] *intr* (coll) tease
pflau′menweich *adj* (fig) spineless
Pflege [′pfleɡə] f (-;-n) care; (*e-s Kranken*) nursing; (*Wartung*) tending; (*e-s Gartens, der Künste*) cultivation; **gute P. haben** be well cared for; **in P. nehmen** take charge of
Pflegebefohlene [′pfleɡəbəfoːlənə] §5 mf charge; fosterchild
Pfle′geeltern pl foster parents
Pfle′geheim n nursing home
Pfle′gekind n foster child
pflegen [′pfleɡən] *tr* take care of, look after; (*Kranken*) nurse; (*Garten, Kunst*) cultivate; (*Freundschaft*) fos-

ter; **Geselligkeit p.** lead an active social life; **Umgang p. mit** associate with ‖ *intr*—**p. zu** (*inf*) be wont to (*inf*), be in the habit of (*ger*); **sein Vater pflegte zu sagen** his father used to say; **sie pflegt morgens zeitig aufzustehen** she usually gets up early in the morning ‖ *intr* (pp **gepflegt** & **gepflogen**) (*genit*) carry on; **der Liebe p.** enjoy the pleasures of love; **der Ruhe p.** take a rest; **Rats p. mit** consult with
Pfle′ger –in §6 mf nurse; (jur) guardian
Pfle′gesohn m foster son
Pfle′gestelle f foster home
Pfle′getocher f foster daughter
Pfle′gevater m foster father
pfleglich [′pfleːklɪç] *adj* careful
Pflegling [′pfleːklɪŋ] m (-s;-e) foster child; (*Pflegebefohlener*) charge
Pflegschaft [′pfleːkʃaft] f (-;-en) (jur) guardianship
Pflicht [pflɪçt] f (-;-en) duty; **sich seiner P. entziehen** evade one's duty
pflicht′bewußt *adj* conscientious
Pflicht′bewußtsein n conscientiousness
Pflicht′eifer m zeal
pflicht′eifrig *adj* zealous
Pflicht′erfüllung f performance of duty
Pflicht′fach n (educ) required course
Pflicht′gefühl n sense of duty
pflicht′gemäß *adj* dutiful
–pflichtig [pflɪçtɪç] *comb.fm.* obligated, e.g., **schulpflichtig** obligated to attend school
pflicht′schuldig *adj* duty-bound
pflicht′treu *adj* dutiful, loyal
pflicht′vergessen *adj* forgetful of one's duty; (*untreu*) disloyal
Pflicht′vergessenheit f dereliction of duty; disloyalty
Pflicht′verletzung f, **Pflicht′versäumnis** n neglect of duty
Pflock [pflɔk] m (-[e]s;-̈e) peg; **e-n P. zurückstecken** (fig) come down a peg
pflog [pfloːk] *pret* of **pflegen**
pflücken [′pflʏkən] *tr* pluck, pick
Pflug [pfluːk] m (-[e]s;-̈e) plow
pflügen [′pflyːɡən] *tr* & *intr* plow
Pflug′schar f plowshare
Pforte [′pfɔrtə] f (-;-n) gate
Pförtner –in [′pfœrtnər(ɪn)] §6 mf gatekeeper ‖ m doorman; (anat) pylorus
Pfosten [′pfɔstən] m (-s;-) post; (carp) jamb
Pfote [′pfoːtə] f (-;-n) paw; **j-m eins auf die Pfoten geben** rap s.o.'s knuckles
Pfriem [pfriːm] m (-[e]s;-e) awl
Pfropf [pfrɔpf] m (-[e]s;-e) stopper, plug, cork
pfropfen [′pfrɔpfən] *tr* cork, plug; (*stopfen*) cram; (hort) graft ‖ **Pfropfen** m (-s;-) stopper, plug, cork
Pfrop′fenzieher m corkscrew
Pfropf′reis n (hort) graft
Pfründe [′pfryndə] f (-;-n) benefice; (*ohne Seelsorge*) sinecure; **fette P.** (fig) cushy, well-paying job
Pfuhl [pfuːl] m (-[e]s;-e) pool, puddle; (fig) pit

Pfühl [pfyl] *m* (-[e]s;-e) (poet) cushion

pfui ['pfu·ɪ] *interj* phooey!; **p. über dich!** shame on you!

Pfund [pfʊnt] *n* (-[e]s;-e) pound

pfundig ['pfʊndɪç] *adj* (coll) great

-pfündig [pfʏndɪç] *comb.fm.* -pound

Pfundskerl ['pfʊntskerl] *m* (coll) great guy

pfund'weise *adv* by the pound

Pfuscharbeit ['pfuʃarbaɪt] *f* bungling

pfuschen ['pfuʃən] *tr & intr* bungle; **j-m ins Handwerk p.** meddle in s.o.'s business

Pfuscherei [pfuʃə'raɪ] *f* (-;-en) bungling

Pfütze ['pfʏtsə] *f* (-;-n) puddle

Phänomen [fɛnə'men] *n* (-s;-e) phenomenon

phänomenal [fɛnəmɛ'nal] *adj* phenomenal

Phanta·sie [fanta'zi] *f* (-;-sien ['zi·ən]) imagination

Phantasie'gebilde *n* daydream

phantasieren [fanta'zirən] *intr* daydream; (mus) improvise; (pathol) be delirious

phantasie'voll *adj* imaginative

Phantast -in [fan'tast(ɪn)] §7 *mf* visionary

phantastisch [fan'tastɪʃ] *adj* fantastic

Phantom [fan'tom] *n* (-s;-e) phantom

Pharisäer [farɪ'ze·ər] *m* (-s;-) Pharisee; (fig) pharisee

pharmazeutisch [farma'tsɔɪtɪʃ] *adj* pharmaceutical

Pharmazie [farma'tsi] *f* (-;) pharmacy

Phase ['fazə] *f* (-;-n) phase

Philantrop -in [fɪlan'trop(ɪn)] §7 *mf* philanthropist

philanthropisch [fɪlan'tropɪʃ] *adj* philanthropic

Philister [fɪ'lɪstər] *m* (-s;-) Philistine

Phiole [fɪ'olə] *f* (-;-n) vial, phial

Philologe [fɪlo'logə] *m* (-n;-n) philologist

Philologie [fɪlolo'gi] *f* (-;) philology

Philologin [fɪlo'login] *f* (-;-nen) philologist

Philosoph [fɪlo'zof] *m* (-en;-en) philosopher

Philoso·phie [fɪlozo'fi] *f* (-;-fien ['fi·ən]) philosophy

philosophieren [fɪlozo'firən] *intr* philosophize

philosophisch [fɪlo'zofɪʃ] *adj* philosophic(al)

Phlegma ['flɛgma] *n* (-s;) indolence

Phonetik [fo'netɪk] *f* (-;) phonetics

phonetisch [fo'netɪʃ] *adj* phonetic

Phönix ['følnɪks] *m* (-[e]s;-e) phoenix

Phönizien [fø'nitsjən] *n* (-s;) Phoenicia

Phönizier -in [fø'nitsjər[ɪn)] §6 *mf* Phoenician

Phosphor ['fɔsfor] *m* (-s;) phosphorus

phos'phorig *adj* phosphorous

Photo ['foto] *n* (-s;-) photo

Pho'toapparat *m* camera

photogen [fɔto'gen] *adj* photogenic

Photograph [fɔto'graf] *m* (-en;-en) photographer

Photogra·phie [fɔtogra'fi] *f* (-;-fien ['fi·ən]) photography

photographieren [fɔtogra'firən] *tr & intr* photograph; **sich p. lassen** have one's photograph taken

Photographin [fɔto'grafin] *f* (-;-nen) photographer

photographisch [fɔto'grafɪʃ] *adj* photographic

Photokopie' *f* photocopy

photokopie'ren *tr* photocopy

Pho'tozelle *f* photoelectric cell

Phrase ['frazə] *f* (-;-n) phrase; (fig) platitude; **das sind nur Phrasen** that's just talk

phra'senhaft *adj* empty, trite; windy

Physik [fʏ'zik] *f* (-;) physics

physikalisch [fʏzɪ'kalɪʃ] *adj* physical

Physiker -in ['fʏsɪkər(ɪn)] §6 *mf* physicist

Physiogno·mie [fʏzjɔgno'mi] *f* (-; -mien ['mi·ən]) physiognomy

Physiologie [fʏzjɔlo'gi] *f* (-;) physiology

physiologisch [fʏzjo'logɪʃ] *adj* physiological

physisch ['fyzɪʃ] *adj* physical

Pianino [pɪ·a'nino] *n* (-s;-s) small upright piano

Pianist -in [pɪ·a'nɪst(ɪn)] §7 *mf* pianist

picheln ['pɪçəln] *tr & intr* tipple

pichen ['pɪçən] *tr* pitch, cover with pitch

Pichler -in ['pɪçlər(ɪn)] §6 *mf* tippler

Picke ['pɪkə] *f* (-;-n) pickax

Pickel ['pɪkəl] *m* (-s;-) pimple; *(Picke)* pickax; *(Eispicke)* ice ax

Pickelhaube (Pik'kelhaube) *f* spiked helmet

Pickelhering (Pik'kelhering) *m* pickled herring

pickelig (pik'kelig) *adj* pimply

picken ['pɪkən] *tr & intr* peck

picklig ['pɪklɪç] *adj* var of pickelig

Picknick ['pɪknɪk] *n* (-s;-s) picnic

pieken ['pikən] *tr* sting; (coll) prick

piekfein ['pik'faɪn] *adj* tiptop

pieksauber ['pik'zaubər] *adj* spick and span

piepen ['pipən] *intr* chirp; *(Maus)* squeal; **bei dir piept's wohl?** are you quite all there? || **Piepen** *n*— **das ist zum P.!** that's ridiculous

Pier [pir] *m* (-s;-e) pier

piesacken ['pizakən] *tr* (coll) pester

Pietät [pɪ·e'tet] *f* (-;) piety

pietät'los *adj* irreverent

pietät'voll *adj* reverent(ial)

Pigment [pɪg'ment] *n* (-[e]s;-e) pigment

Pik [pik], [pɪk] *m* (-s;-s & -e) *(Bergspitze)* peak || *m* (-s;-e) (coll) grudge; **e-n Pik auf j-n haben** hold a grudge against s.o. || *n* (-s;-e) (cards) spade(s)

pikant [pɪ'kant] *adj* piquant, pungent; *(Bemerkung)* suggestive

Pikante·rie [pɪkantə'ri] *f* (-;-rien ['ri·ən]) piquancy; spicy story, suggestive remark

Pike ['pikə] *f* (-;-n) pike, spear; **von der P. auf dienen** (fig) rise through the ranks

pikiert [pɪ'kirt] *adj* (**über** *acc*) piqued (at)

Pikkolo ['pɪkɔlo] *m* (-s;-s) apprentice waiter; (mus) piccolo
Pik'koloflöte *f* (mus) piccolo
Pilger ['pɪlgər] *m* (-s;-) pilgrim
Pil'gerfahrt *f* pilgrimage
Pilgerin ['pɪlgərɪn] *f* (-;-nen) pilgrim
pilgern ['pɪlgərn] *intr* (SEIN) go on a pilgrimage, make a pilgrimage
Pille ['pɪlə] *f* (-;-n) pill; **P. danach** morning-after pill
Pilot –**in** [pɪ'lot(ɪn)] §7 *mf* pilot
Pilz [pɪlts] *m* (-es;-e) fungus; mushroom
pimp(e)lig ['pɪmp(ə)lɪç] *adj* sickly, delicate; (*verweichlicht*) effeminate
Pinguin [pɪngu'in] *m* (-s;-e) penguin
Pinie ['pinjə] *f* (-;-n) umbrella pine
Pinke ['pɪŋkə] *f* (-;) (coll) dough
Pinkel ['pɪŋkəl] *m* (-s;-) (coll) dude
pinkeln ['pɪŋkəln] *intr* (sl) pee
Pinne ['pɪnə] *f* (-;-n) pin; tack; (naut) tiller
Pinscher ['pɪnʃər] *m* (-s;-) terrier
Pinsel ['pɪnzəl] *m* (-s;-) brush; (fig) simpleton, dope
Pinselei [pɪnzə'laɪ] *f* (-;-en) daubing; (*schlechte Malerei*) daub
pinseln ['pɪnzəln] *tr & intr* paint
Pinzette [pɪn'tsetə] *f* (-;-n) pair of tweezers, tweezers
Pionier [pɪ·ə'nir] *m* (-s;-e) (fig) pioneer; (mil) engineer
Pionier'arbeit *f* (fig) spadework
Pionier'truppe *f* (mil) engineers
Pirat [pɪ'rat] *m* (-en;-en) pirate
Piraterie [pɪratə'ri] *f* (-;) piracy
Pirol [pɪ'rol] *m* (-s;-e) oriole
Pirsch [pɪrʃ] *f* (-;) hunt
pirschen ['pɪrʃən] *intr* stalk game
Pirsch'jagd *f* hunt
Pistazie [pɪs'tatsjə] *f* (-;-n) pistachio
Piste ['pɪstə] *f* (-;-n) beaten track; ski run; toboggan run; (aer) runway
Pistole [pɪs'tolə] *f* (-;-n) pistol
Pisto'lentasche *f* holster
pitsch(e)naß ['pɪtʃ(ə)'nas] *adj* soaked to the skin
pittoresk [pɪtə'resk] *adj* picturesque
Pkw., PKW *abbr* (**Personenkraftwagen**) passenger car
placieren [pla'sirən] *tr* place
placken ['plakən] *tr* pester, plague ‖ *ref* toil, drudge
Plackerei [plakə'raɪ] *f* (-;) drudgery
plädieren [plɛ'dirən] *intr* plead
Plädoyer [plɛdwa'je] *n* (-s;-s) plea
Plage ['plagə] *f* (-;-n) trouble, bother; torment; (*Seuche*) plague
Pla'gegeist *m* pest, pain in the neck
plagen ['plagən] *tr* trouble, bother; (*mit Fragen, usw.*) pester
Plagiat [pla'gjat] *n* (-[e]s;-e) plagiarism
Pla'giator [pla'gjatər] *m* (-s;-giatoren [gja'torən]) plagiarist
Plakat [pla'kat] *n* (-[e]s;-e) poster
Plakat'träger *m* sandwich man
Plakette [pla'ketə] *f* (-;-n) plaque
plan [plan] *adj* plain, clear; (*eben*) level ‖ **Plan** *m* (-[e]s;ˑe) plan; (*Stadt-*) map; (poet) battlefield; **auf den P. treten** appear on the scene
Plane ['planə] *f* (-;-n) tarpaulin

Plänemacher ['plenəmaxər] *m* (-s;-) schemer
planen ['planən] *tr* plan
Pläneschmied ['plenəʃmit] *m* schemer
Planet [pla'net] *m* (-en;-en) planet
Planeta·rium [plane'tarjum] *n* (-s; -rien [rjən]) planetarium
Planeten– [planetən] *comb.fm.* planetary
Plane'tenbahn *f* planetary orbit
plan'gemäß *adv* according to plan
planieren [pla'nirən] *tr* level, grade
Planier'raupe *f* bulldozer
Planimetrie [planime'tri] *f* (-;) plane geometry
Planke ['plaŋkə] *f* (-;-n) plank
Plänkelei [plɛŋkə'laɪ] *f* (-;-en) skirmish, skirmishing
plänkeln ['plɛŋkəln] *intr* skirmish
plan'los *adj* aimless; indiscriminate
plan'mäßig *adj* systematic; fixed, regular; (*Verkehr*) scheduled ‖ *adv* according to plan
planschen ['planʃən] *intr* splash
Plantage [plan'taʒə] *f* (-;-n) plantation
Pla'nung *f* (-;) planning
plan'voll *adj* systematic, methodical
Plan'wagen *m* covered wagon
Plan'wirtschaft *f* planned economy
Plapperei [plapə'raɪ] *f* (-;) chatter
Plappermaul ['plapərmaʊl] *n* chatterbox
plappern ['plapərn] *intr* chatter; prattle
plärren ['plerən] *intr* (coll) bawl
Plas·ma ['plasma] *n* (-s;-men [mən]) plasma
Plastik ['plastɪk] *f* (-;-en) (*Bildwerk*) sculpture; (surg) plastic surgery ‖ *n* (-s;) plastic
plastisch ['plastɪʃ] *adj* plastic; (*anschaulich*) graphic
Platane [pla'tanə] *f* (-;-n) sycamore
Plateau [pla'to] *n* (-s;-s) plateau
Plateau'schuhe *pl* platform shoes
Platin [pla'tin] *n* (-s;) platinum
platin'blond *adj* platinum-blonde
Platoniker [pla'tonɪkər] *m* (-s;-) Platonist
platonisch [pla'tonɪʃ] *adj* Platonic
plätschern ['plɛtʃərn] *intr* splash; (*Bach*) babble
platt [plat] *adj* flat; (*nichtssagend*) trite; (coll) flabbergasted
Plättbrett ['plɛtbret] *n* ironing board
platt'deutsch *adj* Low German
Platte ['platə] *f* (-;-n) plate; top, surface; slab; (*Präsentierteller*) tray; (*Speise*) dish; (fig) pate, bean; (mus) record; (phot) plate
Plätteisen ['plɛtaɪzən] *n* flatiron
plätten ['plɛtən] *tr & intr* iron
Plat'tenjockey *m* disc jockey
Plat'tenspieler *m* record player
Plat'tenteller *m* turntable
Plat'tenwechsler *m* record changer
Platt'form *f* platform
Platt'fuß *m* (aut) flat; **Plattfüße** flat feet
platt'füßig *adj* flat-footed
Platt'heit *f* (-;-en) flatness; (fig) banality

plattieren [pla'tirən] *tr* plate
Plättwäsche ['plɛtvɛʃə] *f* ironing
Platz [plats] *m* (**-es;**ᴇe) place; spot; locality; square; (*Sitz*) seat; (*Raum*) room, space; (*Stellung*) position; (sport) ground, field; (tennis) court; **auf die Plätze, fertig, los!** on your marks, get set, go! **fester P.** (mil) fortified position; **freier P.** open space; **immer auf dem Platze sein** be always on the alert; **nicht am P. sein** be out of place; be irrelevant; **P. da!** make way; **P. greifen** (fig) take effect, gain ground; **P. machen** make room; **P. nehmen** sit down; **seinen P. behaupten** stand one's ground
Platz'anweiser –in §6 *mf* usher
Plätzchen ['plɛtsçən] *n* (**-s;-**) little place; little square; (*Süßware*) candy wafer; (*Gebäck*) cookie, cracker
platzen ['platsən] *intr* (SEIN) burst; split; crack; (*Granate*) explode; (*Luftreifen*) blow out; (fig) come to nothing; **da platzte ihm endlich der Kragen** he finally blew his top; **der Wechsel ist geplatzt** the check bounced
Platz'karte *f* reserved-seat ticket
Platz'kommandant *m* commandant
Platz'konzert *n* open-air concert
Platz'patrone *f* blank cartridge; **mit Platzpatronen schießen** fire blanks
Platz'regen *m* cloudburst
Platz'runde *f* (aer) circuit of a field
Platz'wechsel *m* change of place; (sport) change in lineup
Platz'wette *f* betting on a horse to finish in first, second, or third place, bet to place
Plauderei [plaudə'raɪ] *f* (**-;-en**) chat; small talk
Plau'derer –in §6 *mf* talker, chatterer
plaudern ['plaudərn] *intr* chat, chatter; **aus der Schule p.** tell tales out of school
Plaudertasche ['plaudərtaʃə] *f* chatterbox
Plauderton ['plaudərton] *m* conversational tone
plausibel [plau'zibəl] *adj* plausible
plauz [plauts] *interj* crash!
pleite ['plaɪtə] *adj* (coll) broke ‖ *adv* **—p. gehen** go broke ‖ **Pleite** *f* (**-;**) (coll) bankruptcy; **P. machen** (coll) go broke
Plenarsitzung [plə'narʦɪtsʊŋ] *f* (**-;-en**) plenary session
Plenum ['plenʊm] *n* (**-s;**) plenary session
Pleuelstange ['plɔɪ·əlʃtaŋə] *f* (mach) connecting rod
Plexiglas ['plɛksɪglas] *n* (**-es;**) plexiglass
Plinse ['plɪnzə] *f* (**-;-n**) pancake; fritter
Plissee [plɪ'se] *n* (**-s;-s**) pleat
Plissee'rock *m* pleated skirt
plissieren [plɪ'sirən] *tr* pleat
Plombe ['plɔmbə] *f* (**-;-n**) lead seal; (dent) filling
plombieren [plɔm'birən] *tr* seal with lead; (dent) fill

plötzlich ['plœtslɪç] *adj* sudden ‖ *adv* suddenly, all of a sudden
plump [plump] *adj* (*unförmig*) shapeless; (*schwerfällig*) heavy, slow; (*derb*) coarse; (*unbeholfen*) ungainly; (*taktlos*) tactless, blunt
plumps [plumps] *interj* plop! thump!
plumpsen ['plumpsən] *intr* (HABEN & SEIN) plop, flop
Plunder ['plundər] *m* (**-s;**) junk
plündern ['plyndərn] *tr* & *intr* plunder
Plural ['plural] *m* (**-s;-e**) plural
plus [plus] *adv* plus ‖ **Plus** *n* (**-;-**) plus; (*Überschuß*) surplus; (*Vorteil*) advantage, edge
Plus'pol *m* (elec) positive pole
Plutokrat [pluto'krat] *m* (**-en;-en**) plutocrat
Plutonium [plu'tonjum] *n* (**-s;**) plutonium
pneumatisch [pnɔɪ'matɪʃ] *adj* pneumatic
Pöbel ['pøbəl] *m* (**-s;**) mob, rabble
pö'belhaft *adj* rude, rowdy
Pö'belherrschaft *f* mob rule
pochen ['pɔxən] *tr* (min) crush ‖ *intr* knock; (*Herz*) pound; **p. an** (*dat*) knock on; **p. auf** (*acc*) pound on; (fig) insist on
Pochmüle ['pɔxmylə] *f,* **Pochwerk** ['pɔxverk] *n* crushing mill
Pocke ['pɔkə] *f* (**-;-n**) pockmark; **Pocken** (pathol) smallpox
Pockennarbe [Pok'kennarbe] *f* pockmark
pockennarbig (pok'kennarbig) *adj* pockmarked
Podest [pɔ'dɛst] *m* & *n* (**-es;-e**) pedestal; (*Treppenabsatz*) landing; podium
Po·dium ['podjum] *n* (**-s;-dien** [djən]) podium, platform
Poesie [pɔ·ε'zi] *f* (**-;**) poetry
Poet [pɔ'et] *m* (**-en;-en**) poet
Poetik [pɔ'etɪk] *f* (**-;**) poetics
poetisch [pɔ'etɪʃ] *adj* poetic
Pointe [pɔ'ɛ̃tə] *f* (**-;**) point (*of joke*)
Pokal [pɔ'kal] *m* (**-s;-e**) goblet; (sport) cup
Pökel ['pøkəl] *m* (**-s;**) brine
Pö'kelfleisch *n* salted meat
Pö'kelhering *m* pickled herring
pökeln ['pøkəln] *tr* pickle, salt
Poker ['pokər] *n* (**-s;**) poker
Pol [pol] *m* (**-s;-e**) pole
Polar- [pɔlar] *comb.fm.* polar
polarisieren [pɔlarɪ'zirən] *tr* polarize
Polarität [pɔlarɪ'tet] *f* (**-;-en**) polarity
Polar'kreis *m* polar circle; **nördlicher P.** Arctic Circle; **südlicher P.** Antarctic Circle
Polar'licht *n* polar lights
Polar'stern *m* polestar
Polar'zone *f* frigid zone
Pole ['polə] *m* (**-n;-n**) Pole
Polemik [pɔ'lemɪk] *f* (**-;**) polemics
polemisch [pɔ'lemɪʃ] *adj* polemical
Polen ['polən] *n* (**-s;**) Poland
Police [pɔ'lisə] *f* (**-;-n**) (ins) policy
Polier [pɔ'lir] *m* (**-s;-e**) foreman
polieren [pɔ'lirən] *tr* polish
Polin ['polɪn] *f* (**-;-nen**) Pole
Politik [pɔlɪ'tik] *f* (**-;-en**) policy; (*Staatsangelegenheiten*) politics

Politiker -in [pɔ'litɪkər(ɪn)] §6 *mf* politician
Politi·kum [pɔ'litɪkʊm] *n* (-s;-ka [ka]) political issue, political matter
politisch [pɔ'litɪʃ] *adj* political
politisieren [pɔlɪtɪ'zirən] *intr* talk politics
Politur [pɔlɪ'tur] *f* (-;-en) polish
Polizei [pɔlɪ'tsaɪ] *f* (-;) police
Polizei'aufgebot *n* posse
Polizei'aufsicht *f*—**unter P. stehen** have to report periodically to the police
Polizei'beamte §5 *m* police officer
Polizei'büro *n*, **Polizei'dienststelle** *f* police station
Polizei'knüppel *m* billy club
Polizei'kommissar *m* police commissioner
polizei'lich *adj* police
Polizei'präsident *m* chief of police
Polizei'revier *n* police station
Polizei'spion *m*, **Polizei'spitzel** *m* stoolpigeon
Polizei'streife *f* raid; police patrol
Polizei'streifenwagen *m* squad car
Polizei'stunde *f* closing time; curfew
Polizei'wache *f* police station
polizei'widrig *adj* against police regulations
Polizist [pɔlɪ'tsɪst] *m* (-en;-en) policeman
Polizistin [pɔlɪ'tsɪstɪn] *f* (-;-nen) policewoman
Polizze [pɔ'lɪtsə] *f* (-;-n) (Aust) insurance policy
Polka ['pɔlka] *f* (-;-s) polka
polnisch ['pɔlnɪʃ] *adj* Polish
Polo ['polo] *n* (-s;) (sport) polo
Polster ['pɔlstər] *m & n* (-s;-) cushion
Pol'stergarnitur *f* living-room suite
Pol'stermöbel *pl* upholstered furniture
polstern ['pɔlstərn] *tr* upholster
Pol'stersessel *m* upholstered chair
Pol'sterstuhl *m* padded chair
Pol'sterung *f* (-;) padding, stuffing
Polterabend ['pɔltərabənt] *m* eve of the wedding day
Poltergeist ['pɔltərgaɪst] *m* poltergeist
poltern ['pɔltərn] *intr* make noise; *(rumpeln)* rumble; *(zanken)* bluster
Polyp [pɔ'lyp] *m* (-en;-en) (pathol, zool) polyp; *(Polizist)* (sl) cop
Polytechni·kum [pɔly'teçnɪkʊm] *n* (-s; -ka [ka]) polytechnic institute
Pomade [pɔ'madə] *f* (-;-n) pomade
Pomeranze [pɔmə'rantsə] *f* (-;-n) bitter orange
Pommern ['pɔmərn] *n* (-s;) Pomerania
Pommes frites [pɔm'frɪt] *pl* French fries
Pomp [pɔmp] *m* (-es;) pomp
Pompadour ['pɔmpadur] *m* (-s;-e & -s) lady's string-drawn bag
pomp'haft, pompös [pɔm'pøs] *adj* pompous
pontifikal [pɔntɪfɪ'kal] *adj* pontifical
Pontifikat [pɔntɪfɪ'kat] *n* (-s;) pontificate
Pontius ['pɔntsjʊs] *m*—**von P. zu Pilatus geschickt werden** (coll) get the run-around
Pony ['pɔnɪ] *m* (-s;-s) *(Damenfrisur)* pony ‖ *n* (-s;-s) *(Pferd)* pony

Popo [pɔ'po] *m* (-s;-s) (coll) backside
populär [pɔpu'ler] *adj* popular
Popularität [pɔpularɪ'tet] *f* (-;) popularity
Pore ['porə] *f* (-;-n) pore
porig ['porɪç] *adj* porous
Pornofilm ['pɔrnofɪlm] *m* (coll) smoker, pornographic movie
Pornoladen ['pɔrnoladən] *m* (coll) porn shop
Pornographie [pɔrnogra'fi] *f* (-;) pornography
poros [pɔ'ros] *adj* porous
Porphyr ['pɔrfyr] *m* (-s;) porphyry
Porree ['pɔre] *m* (-s;-s) (bot) leek
Portal [pɔr'tal] *n* (-s;-e) portal
Portemonnaie [pɔrtmɔ'ne] *n* (-s;-s) wallet
Portier [pɔr'tje] *m* (-s;-s) doorman
Portion [pɔr'tsjon] *f* (-;-en) portion; (culin) serving, helping; **halbe P.** (coll) half pint; **zwei Portionen Kaffee** two cups of coffee
Por·to ['pɔrto] *n* (-s;-ti [ti]) postage
Por'togebühren *pl* postage
Por'tokasse *f* petty cash
Porträt [pɔr'tret] *n* (-s;-s), (-[e]s;-e) portrait
porträtieren [pɔrtre'tirən] *tr* portray
Portugal ['pɔrtugal] *n* (-s;) Portugal
Portugiese [pɔrtu'gizə] *m* (-n;-n), **Portugiesin** [pɔrtu'gizɪn] *f* (-;-nen) Portuguese
portugiesisch [pɔrtu'gizɪʃ] *adj* Portuguese
Porzellan [pɔrtsə'lan] *n* (-s;-e) porcelain; china; **Meißener Porzellan** Dresden china
Porzellan'brennerei *f* porcelain factory
Posament [pɔza'mɛnt] *n* (-[e]s;-en) trimming, lace
Posaune [pɔ'zaunə] *f* (-;-n) trombone
posaunen [pɔ'zaunən] *intr* play the trombone
Pose ['pozə] *f* (-;-n) pose
posieren [pɔ'zirən] *intr* pose
Position [pɔzɪ'tsjon] *f* (-;-en) position
Positions'lampe *f* **Positions'licht** *n* (aer, naut) navigation light
positiv [pɔzɪ'tif] *adj* *(bejahend)* affirmative; *(Kritik)* favorable; (elec, math, med) positive ‖ *adv* in the affirmative; (coll) for certain ‖ **Positiv** *m* (-s;-e) (gram) positive degree ‖ *n* (-s;-e) (mus) small organ; (phot) positive
Positur [pɔzɪ'tur] *f* (-;-en) posture, attitude; **sich in P. setzen** (or **stellen** or **werfen**) strike a pose
Posse ['pɔsə] *f* (-;-n) (theat) farce
Possen ['pɔsən] *m* (-s;-) trick, practical joke; **j-m e-n P. spielen** play a practical joke on s.o.; **laß die P.!** cut out the nonsense; **P. treiben** (or **reißen**) crack jokes
pos'senhaft *adj* farcical, comical
Possenreißer ['pɔsənraɪsər] *m* (-s;-) joker
Pos'senspiel *n* farce, burlesque
possierlich [pɔ'sirlɪç] *adj* funny
Post [pɔst] *f* (-;-en) mail; *(Postgebäude)* post office
postalisch [pɔs'talɪʃ] *adj* postal

Postament [pɔsta'mɛnt] *n* (-[e]s;-e) pedestal
Post'amt *n* post office
Post'anweisung *f* money order
Post'auto *n* mail truck
Post'beamte *m* postal clerk
Post'beutel *m* mailbag
Post'bote *m* mailman
Post'direktor *m* postmaster
Posten ['pɔstən] *m* (-s;-) post; (*Stellung*) position; (acct) entry, item; (com) line, lot; (mil) guard, sentinel; **auf dem P. sein** (fig) be on guard; **auf verlorenem P. kämpfen** (coll) play a losing game; **nicht recht auf dem P. sein** be out of sorts; **P. aufstellen** post sentries; **P. stehen** stand guard; **ruhiger P.** (mil) soft job
Po'stenjäger –in §6 *mf* job hunter
Po'stenkette *f* line of outposts
Post'fach *n* post-office box
Post'gebühr *f* postage
posthum [pɔst'hum] *adj* posthumous
postieren [pɔs'tirən] *tr* post, place
Postille [pɔs'tilə] *f* (-;-n) devotional book
Post'karte *f* post card
Post'kasten *m* mail box
Post'kutsche *f* stagecoach
post'lagernd *adj* general-delivery || *adv* general delivery
Postleitzahl ['pɔstlaɪttsal] *f* zip code
Post'minister *m* postmaster general
Post'nachnahme *f* (-;-n) C.O.D.
Post'sack *m* mailbag
Post'schalter *m* post-office window
Post'scheck *m* postal check
Postschließfach ['pɔst/lisfax] *n* post-office box
Postskript [pɔst'skrɪpt] *n* (-[e]s;-e) postscript
Post'stempel *m* postmark
Post'überweisung *f* money order
post'wendend *adj & adv* by return mail
Post'wertzeichen *n* postage stamp
Post'wesen *n* postal system
potent [po'tent] *adj* potent
Potential [pɔtɛn'tsjal] *n* (-s;-e) potential
Potenz [po'tents] *f* (-;-en) potency; (math) power; **dritte P.** (math) cube; **zweite P.** (math) square
potenzieren [pɔtɛn'tsirən] *tr* raise to a higher power; (fig) intensify
Pottasche ['pɔta/ə] *f* (-;) potash
Pottwal ['pɔtval] *m* sperm whale
potz [pɔts] *interj*—**p. Blitz!** holy smoke!
potztau'send *interj* holy smoke!
poussieren [pu'sirən] *tr* (coll) flirt with; (coll) butter up || *intr* flirt
Pracht [praxt] *f* (-;) splendor, magnificence
Pracht'ausgabe *f* deluxe edition
Pracht'exemplar *n* beauty, beaut
prächtig ['prɛçtɪç] *adj* splendid
Pracht'kerl *m* (coll) great guy
Pracht'stück *n* (coll) beauty, beaut
pracht'voll *adj* gorgeous
Pracht'zimmer *n* stateroom (*in palace*)
Prädikat [prɛdɪ'kat] *n* (-[e]s;-e) title; (educ) mark, grade; (gram) predicate

Prädikatsnomen [prɛdɪ'katsnomən] *n* (-s;-s) (gram) complement
Präfix [prɛ'fɪks] *n* (-es;-e) prefix
Prag [prak] *n* (-s;) Prague
Prägeanstalt ['prɛgə·anstalt] *f* mint
prägen ['prɛgən] *tr* stamp, coin || *ref* —**das hat sich mir tief in das Gedächtnis geprägt** that made a lasting impression on me
Prä'gestempel *m* (mach) die
pragmatisch [prag'matɪ/] *adj* pragmatic
prägnant [prɛ'gnant] *adj* pithy, terse
Prä'gung *f* (-;-en) coining, minting; (fig) coinage
prahlen ['pralən] *intr* (**mit**) brag (about); (**mit**) show off (with)
Prah'ler *m* (-s;-) braggart; show-off
Prahlerei [pralə'raɪ] *f* (-;-en) bragging, boasting; (*Prunken*) showing off
Prah'lerin *f* (-;-nen) braggart; show-off
prahlerisch ['pralərɪ/] *adj* bragging
Prahlhans ['pralhans] *m* (-es;̈e) braggart
Prahm [pram] *m* (-[e]s;-e) flat-bottomed lighter
Praktik ['praktɪk] *f* (-;-en) practice; (*Kniff*) trick
Praktikant –in [praktɪ'kant(ɪn)] §7 *mf* student in on-the-job training
Praktiker ['praktɪkər] *m* (-s;-) practical person
Prakti·kum ['praktɪkum] *n* (-s;-ka [ka]) practical training
Praktikus ['praktɪkus] *m* (-;-se) old hand
praktisch ['praktɪ/] *adj* practical; **praktischer Arzt** general practitioner
praktizieren [praktɪ'tsiren] *tr* practice; **etw in die Tasche p.** manage to slip s.th. into the pocket
Prälat [prɛ'lat] *m* (-en;-en) prelate
Praline [pra'linə] *f* (-;-n) chocolate
prall [pral] *adj* (*straff*) tight; (*Brüste*) full; (*Backen*) chubby; (*Arme, Beine*) shapely; (*Sonne*) blazing || **Prall** *m* (-[e]s;-e) impact; collision
prallen ['pralən] *intr* (SEIN) bounce, rebound; (*Sonne*) beat down
Prämie ['premjə] *f* (-;-n) award, prize; premium; bonus
prämiieren [premi'irən] *tr* award a prize to
prangen ['praŋən] *intr* shine; look beautiful
Pranger ['praŋər] *m* (-s;-) pillory
Pranke ['praŋkə] *f* (-;-n) claw
pränumerando [prenumə'rando] *adv* in advance, beforehand
Präparat [prepa'rat] *n* (-[e]s;-e) preparation
präparieren [prepa'rirən] *tr* prepare
Präposition [prepɔzɪ'tsjon] *f* (-;-en) preposition
Prä·rie [prɛ'ri] *f* (-;-rien ['ri·ən]) prairie
Präsens ['prezens] *n* (-; **Präsentia** [prɛ'zentsɪ·a]) (gram) present
präsent [prɛ'zent] *adj* present || **Präsent** *n* (-s;-e) present, gift
präsentieren [prezen'tirən] *tr* present
Präsentier'teller *m* tray

Präsenzstärke [prɛ'zɛnts/tɛrkə] *f* effective strength
Präservativ [prezɛrva'tif] *m* (-s;-e) prophylactic, condom
Präsident [prɛzɪ'dɛnt] *m* (-en;-en) president
Präsidenten- [prezɪdɛntən] *comb.jm.* presidential
Präsident'schaft *f* (-;-en) presidency
präsidieren [prɛzɪ'dirən] *intr* preside
Präsi·dium [prɛ'zidjʊm] *n* (-s;-dien [djən]) presidency; chairmanship
prasseln ['prasəln] *intr* crackle; (*Regen*) patter
prassen ['prasən] *intr* lead a dissipated life
Prasserei [prasə'raɪ] *f* (-;) luxurious living, high life
Prätendent [prɛten'dɛnt] *m* (-en;-en) (auf *acc*) pretender (to)
Pra·xis ['praksɪs] *f* (-;-xen [ksən]) practice; experience; doctor's office; law office; (jur) clientele; (med) patients
Präzedenzfall [prɛtsɛ'dɛntsfal] *m* precedent
präzis [prɛ'tsis] *adj* precise
Präzision [prɛtsɪ'zjon] *f* (-;) precision
predigen ['predɪgən] *tr* & *intr* preach
Prediger ['predɪgər] *m* (-s;-) preacher
Predigt ['predɪçt] *f* (-;-en) sermon
Preis [praɪs] *m* (-es;-e) price, rate, cost; (poet) praise, glory; **äußerster P.** (coll) rock-bottom price; **um jeden P.** (fig) at all costs; **um keinen P.** (fig) on no account; **zum P. von** at the rate of
Preis'aufgabe *f* project in a competition
Preis'aufschlag *m* extra charge
Preis'ausschreiben *n* competition
Preisdrückerei ['praɪsdrYkəraɪ] *f* (-; -en) price cutting
Preiselbeere ['praɪzəlberə] *f* cranberry
preisen ['praɪzən] *tr* praise
Preis'ermäßigung *f* price reduction
Preis'frage *f* question in a competition; question of price (coll) sixty-four-dollar question
Preis'gabe *f* abandonment, surrender
preis'geben $80 *tr* abandon, surrender; (*Geheimnis*) betray; **j-n dem Spott p.** hold s.o. up to ridicule
preisgekrönt ['praɪsgəkrønt] *adj* prize-winning
Preis'gericht *n* jury
Preis'grenze *f* price limit; **obere P.** ceiling; **untere P.** minimum price
preis'günstig *adj* worth the money
Preis'lage *f* price range
Preis'niveau *n* price level
Preis'notierung *f* rate of exchange
Preis'richter *m* judge (*in competition*)
Preis'schießen *n* shooting competition
Preis'schild *n* price tag
Preis'schlager *m* bargain price
Preis'schrift *f* prize-winning essay
Preis'stopp *m* price freezing
Preis'sturz *m* drop in prices
Preis'träger –in $6 *mf* prize winner
Preistreiberei [praɪstraɪbə'raɪ] *f* (-;) price rigging
Preis'überwachung *f* price control

Preis'verzeichnis *n* price list
preis'wert, preis'würdig *adj* worth the money, reasonable
Preis'zuschlag *m* markup
prekär [prɛ'kɛr] *adj* precarious
Prellbock ['prɛlbɔk] *m* (rr) buffer
prellen ['prɛlən] *tr* bump; bounce; toss up (*in a blanket*); (**um**) cheat (out of) || *ref*—**sich** [*dat*] **den Arm p.** bruise one's arm
Prel'ler *m* (-s;-) bump; ricochet; bilker, cheat
Prellerei [prɛlə'raɪ] *f* (-;-en) (act of) cheating
Prell'schuß *m* ricochet
Prell'stein *m* curbstone
Prel lung *f* (-;-en) bruise
Premier [prə'mje] *m* (-s;-s) premier
Premiere [prə'mjerə] *f* (-;-n) (theat) premiere, first night, opening
Premier'minister *m* prime minister
Presbyterianer –in [presbYtə'rjanər (ɪn)] $6 *mf* Presbyterian
presbyterianisch [presbYtə'rjanɪʃ] *adj* Presbyterian
preschen ['prɛʃən] *intr* charge
pressant [prɛ'sant] *adj* pressing
Presse ['prɛsə] *f* (-;-n) (& journ) press; (educ) cram class
Pres'seagentur *f* press agency
Pres'seamt *n* public-relations office
Pres'seausweis *m* press card
Pres'sebericht *m* press report
Pres'sechef *m* press secretary
Pres'sekonferenz *f* press conference
Pres'semeldung *f* news item
Pres'sestelle *f* public-relations office
Pres'severtreter *m* reporter; public-relations officer
Preßkohle ['prɛskolə] *f* briquette
Preßluft ['prɛslʊft] *f* compressed air
Preß'lufthammer *m* jackhammer
Preuße ['prɔɪsə] *m* (-n;-n) Prussian
Preußen ['prɔɪsən] *n* (-;) Prussia
Preußin ['prɔɪsɪn] *f* (-;-nen) Prussian
preußisch ['prɔɪsɪʃ] *adj* Prussian
prickeln ['prɪkəln] *intr* tingle
Priem [prim] *m* (-[e]s;-e) plug (*of tobacco*)
priemen ['primən] *intr* chew tobacco
pries [pris] *pret* of **preisen**
Priester ['pristər] *m* (-s;-) priest
Prie'steramt *n* priesthood
Priesterin ['pristərɪn] *f* (-;-nen) priestess
prie'sterlich *adj* priestly
Prie'sterrock *m* cassock
Priestertum ['pristərtum] *n* (-s;) priesthood
Prie'sterweihe *f* (eccl) ordination
prima ['prima] *invar adj* first-class; terrific, swell
primär [prɪ'mer] *adj* primary || *adv* primarily
Primat [prɪ'mat] *m* & *n* (-[e]s;-e) primacy, priority || *m* (-en;-en) primate
Primel ['priməl] *f* (-;-n) primrose
primitiv [prɪmi'tif] *adj* primitive
Prinz [prɪnts] *m* (-en;-en) prince
Prinzessin [prɪn'tsɛsɪn] *f* (-;-nen) princess
Prinz'gemahl *m* prince consort

Prin·zip [prɪn'tsip] n (-s;-zipien ['tsipjən]) principle
prinzipiell [prɪntsɪ'pjɛl] adj in principle, fundamentally
Prinzi'pienreiter m (coll) pedant
prinz'lich adj princely
Pri·or ['pri·ɔr] m (-s;-oren ['orən]) (eccl) prior
Priorität [prɪ·ɔrɪ'tɛt] f (-;-en) priority
Prise ['prizə] f (-;-n) pinch (of salt, etc.); (nav) prize
Pris·ma ['prɪsma] n (-s;-men [mɛn]) prism
privat [prɪ'vat] adj private; personal
Privat'adresse f, **Privat'anschrift** f home address
Privat'dozent –in §7 mf non-salaried university lecturer
Privat'druck m private printing
Privat'eigentum n private property
Privat'gespräch n (telp) personal call
privatim [prɪ'vatɪm] adv privately; confidentially
privatisieren [prɪvatɪ'zirən] intr be financially independent
Privat'lehrer –in §6 mf tutor
Privat'recht n civil law
privat'rechtlich adj (jur) civil
Privi·leg [prɪvɪ'lek] n (-[e]s;-legien ['legjən]) privilege
privilegiert [prɪvɪlɛ'girt] adj privileged
probat [prɔ'bat] adj tried, tested
Probe ['probə] f (-;-n) (Versuch) trial, experiment; (Prüfung) test; (Muster) sample; (Beweis) proof; (theat) rehearsal; **auf die P. stellen** put to the test; **auf** (or **zur**) **P.** on approval
Pro'beabdruck m, **Pro'beabzug** m (typ) proof
Pro'bebild n (phot) proof
Pro'bebogen m proof sheet
Pro'bedruck m (typ) proof
Pro'befahrt f road test, trial run
Pro'beflug m test flight
Pro'belauf m trial run; dry run
Pro'besendung f sample sent on approval
Pro'bestück n sample, specimen
pro'beweise adv on trial; on approval
Pro'bezeit f probation period
probieren [prɔ'birən] tr try out, test; try, taste; (metal) assay
Probier'glas n test tube
Probier'stein m touch-stone
Problem [prɔ'blem] n (-s;-e) problem
Produkt [prɔ'dukt] n (-[e]s;-e) product; (des Bodens) produce
Produktion [prɔduk'tsjon] f (-;-en) production; (indust) output
produktiv [prɔduk'tif] adj productive
Produzent [prɔdu'tsɛnt] m (-en;-en) (& cin) producer
produzieren [prɔdu'tsirən] tr produce || ref perform; (pej) show off
profan [prɔ'fan] adj profane
profanieren [prɔfa'nirən] tr profane
Profession [prɔfɛ'sjon] f (-;-en) profession
Professional [prɔfɛsjɔ'nal] m (-s;-e) (sport) professional
professionell [prɔfɛsjɔ'nɛl] adj professional
Profes·sor [prɔ'fɛsɔr] m (-s;-soren ['sorən]), **Professorin** [prɔfɛ'sorɪn] f (-;-nen) professor; **außerordentlicher P.** associate professor; **ordentlicher P.** full professor
Professur [prɔfɛ'sur] f (-;-en) professorship
Profi ['profi] m (-s;-s) (coll) pro
Profil [prɔ'fil] n (-s;-e) profile; (aut) tread; **im P.** in profile
profiliert [prɔfɪ'lirt] adj outstanding
Profit [prɔ'fit] m (-[e]s;-e) profit
profitabel [prɔfɪ'tabəl] adj profitable
Profit'gier f profiteering
profitieren [prɔfɪ'tirən] tr & intr profit
Prognose [prɔ'gnozə] f (-;-n) (med) prognosis; (meteor) forecast
Programm [prɔ'gram] n (-s;-e) program; (pol) platform
programmieren [prɔgra'mirən] tr (data proc) program
Projekt [prɔ'jɛkt] n (-[e]s;-e) project
Projektil [prɔjɛk'til] n (-s;-e) projectile
Projektion [prɔjɛk'tsjon] f (-;-en) projection
Projektions'apparat m, **Projektions' gerät** n, **Projek·tor** [prɔ'jɛktɔr] m (-s;-toren ['torən]) projector
projizieren [prɔjɪ'tsirən] tr project
proklamieren [prɔkla'mirən] tr proclaim
Prokura [prɔ'kura] f (-;) power of attorney; **per P.** by proxy
Prolet [prɔ'let] m (-en;-en) (pej) cad
Proletariat [prɔleta'rjat] n (-[e]s;-e) proletariat
Proletarier –in [prɔle'tarjər(ɪn)] §6 mf proletarian
proletarisch [prɔle'tarɪʃ] adj proletarian
Prolog [prɔ'lok] m (-[e]s;-e) prologue
prolongieren [prɔlɔŋ'girən] tr extend; (cin) hold over
Promenade [prɔmə'nadə] f (-;-n) avenue; (Spaziergang) promenade
promenieren [prɔmə'nirən] intr stroll
prominent [prɔmɪ'nɛnt] adj prominent
Promotion [prɔmɔ'tsjon] f (-;-en) awarding of the doctor's degree
promovieren [prɔmɔ'virən] intr attain a doctor's degree
prompt [prɔmpt] adj prompt, quick
Prono·men [prɔ'nomən] n (-s;-mina [mina]) pronoun
Propaganda [prɔpa'ganda] f (-;) propaganda
propagieren [prɔpa'girən] tr propagate
Propeller [prɔ'pɛlər] m (-s;-) propeller
Prophet [prɔ'fet] m (-en;-en) prophet
Prophetin [prɔ'fetɪn] f (-;-nen) prophetess
prophetisch [prɔ'fetɪʃ] adj prophetic
prophezeien [prɔfe'tsai·ən] tr prophesy
Prophezei'ung f (-;-en) prophecy
Proportion [prɔpɔr'tsjon] f (-;-en) proportion
proportional [prɔpɔrtsjɔ'nal] adj proportional
proportioniert [prɔpɔrtsjɔ'nirt] adj proportionate
Propst [propst] m (-es;-̈e) provost

Prosa ['proza] *f* (-;) prose
prosaisch [pro'za·ıʃ] *adj* prosaic
prosit ['prozıt] *interj* to your health!
|| **Prosit** *n* (-s;-s) toast
Prospekt [pro'spɛkt] *m* (-[e]s;-e) prospect, view; brochure, folder
prostituieren [prostıtu'irən] *tr* prostitute
Prostituierte [prostıtu'irtə] §5 *f* prostitute
protegieren [protɛ'girən] *tr* patronize; (*schützen*) protect
Protektion [protɛk'tsjon] *f* (-;) pull, connections
Protest [pro'tɛst] *m* (-es;-e) protest
Protestant –in [protɛs'tant(ın)] §7 *mf* Protestant
protestantisch [protɛs'tantıʃ] *adj* Protestant
protestieren [protɛs'tirən] *tr & intr* protest
Protokoll [proto'kɔl] *n* (-s;-e) protocol; record, minutes; **P. führen** take the minutes; **zu P. nehmen** take down
Protokoll'führer –in §6 *mf* recording secretary; (jur) clerk
protokollieren [protoko'lirən] *tr* record
Pro·ton ['proton] *n* (-s;-tonen ['tonən]) (phys) proton
Protz [prots] *m* (-en;-en) show-off
protzen ['protsən] *intr* show off
prot'zenhaft, protzig ['protsıç] *adj* show-offish
Prozedur [protsɛ'dur] *f* (-;-en) procedure; (jur) proceeding
Prozent [pro'tsɛnt] *n* (-[e]s;-e) percent
Prozent'satz *m* percentage
Pro·zeß [pro'tsɛs] *m* (-zesses;-zesse) process; (jur) case, suit; (jur) proceedings; **e-en P. anstrengen** (or **führen**) **gegen** sue; **kurzen P. machen mit** make short work of
Prozeß'akten *pl* (jur) record
Prozeß'führer –in §6 *mf* litigant
prozessieren [protsɛ'sirən] *intr* go to court; **p. gegen** sue
Prozession [protsɛ'sjon] *f* (-;-en) procession
Prozeß'kosten *pl* (jur) court costs
Prozeß'vollmacht *f* power of attorney
prüde ['prydə] *adj* prudish
prüfen ['pryfən] *tr* test; (*nachprüfen*) check, verify; (*untersuchen*) examine; (*kosten*) taste; (acct) audit
Prüfer –in §6 *mf* examiner; (acct) auditor
Prüfling ['pryflıŋ] *m* (-s;-e) examinee
Prüfstein ['pryfʃtaın] *m* touchstone
Prü'fung *f* (-;-en) test; examination; check, verification; (acct) audit; (jur) review
Prü'fungsarbeit *f* test paper
Prü'fungsausschuß *m*, **Prü'fungskommission** *f* examining board
Prügel ['prygəl] *m* (-s;-) stick, cudgel; **Prügel** *pl* whipping
Prügelei [prygə'laı] *f* (-;-en) brawl; free-for-all
Prü'gelknabe *m* whipping boy, scapegoat
prügeln ['prygəln] *tr* beat, whip || *ref* have a fight

Prü'gelstrafe *f* corporal punishment
Prunk [pruŋk] *m* (-[e]s;) pomp, show
prunken ['pruŋkən] *intr* show off
Prunk'gemach *n* stateroom
prunk'haft *adj* showy
Prunk'sucht *f* ostentatiousness
prunk'süchtig *adj* ostentatious
prunk'voll *adj* gorgeous
Prunk'zimmer *n* stateroom
prusten ['prustən] *intr* snort
Psalm [psalm] *m* (-s;-en) psalm
Psalter ['psaltər] *m* (-s;-) psalter
Pseudonym [psoıdo'nym] *n* (-s;-e) pseudonym
Psychiater (psʏçi'atər] *m* (-s;-) psychiatrist
Psychiatrie [psʏçi·a'tri] *f* (-;) psychiatry
psychiatrisch [psʏçi'atrıʃ] *adj* psychiatric
psychisch ['psʏçıʃ] *adj* psychic(al)
Psychoanalyse [psʏço·ana'lyzə] *f* (-;) psychoanalysis
Psychoanalytiker –in [psʏço·ana'lytıkər(ın)] §6 *mf* psychoanalyst
Psychologe [psʏço'logə] *m* (-n;-n) psychologist
Psychologie [psʏçolo'gi] *f* (-;) psychology
Psychologin [psʏço'login] *f* (-;-nen) psychologist
psychologisch [psʏço'logıʃ] *adj* psychological
Psychopath –in [psʏço'pat(ın)] §7 *mf* psychopath
Psychose [psʏ'çozə] *f* (-;-n) psychosis
Psychotherapie [psʏçotera'pi] *f* (-;) psychotherapy
Pubertät [puber'tɛt] *f* (-;) puberty
publik [pub'lik] *adj* public
Publi·kum ['publıkum] *n* (-s;-ka [ka]) public; (theat) audience
publizieren [publı'tsirən] *tr* publish
Publizist –in [publı'tsıst(ın)] §7 *mf* (journ) writer on public affairs; teacher or student of journalism
Publizität [publıtsı'tɛt] *f* (-;) publicity
Pudel ['pudəl] *m* (-s;-) poodle; **des Pudels Kern** (fig) gist of the matter
Pu'delmütze *f* fur cap; woolen cap
pu'delnaß *adj* (coll) soaking wet
Puder ['pudər] *m* (-s;) powder
Pu'derdose *f* powder box; compact
Pu'derquaste *f* powder puff
Pu'derzucker *m* powdered sugar
Puff [puf] *m* (-[e]s;=e & -e) (*Stoß*) poke; (*Knall*) pop; (*Bausch*) puff; || *m* (-s;-s) (coll) brothel
Puff'ärmel *m* puffed sleeve
puffen ['pufən] *tr* poke; (coll) prod || *intr* puff; (*knallen*) pop, bang away
Puffer ['pufər] *m* (-s;-) buffer; popgun; (culin) potato pancake
Puf'ferbatterie *f* booster battery
Puf'ferstaat *m* buffer state
Puff'mais *m* popcorn
Puff'reis *m* (-es) puffed rice
Pulli ['puli] *m* (-s;-s) (coll) sweater
Pullover [pu'lovər] *m* (-s;-) sweater
Puls [puls] *m* (-es;-e) pulse
Puls'ader *f* artery
pulsieren [pul'zirən] *intr* pulsate
Puls'schlag *m* pulse beat

Pult [pʊlt] n (-[e]s;-e) desk
Pulver ['pʊlfər] n (-s;-) powder; (Schieß-) gunpowder; (coll) dough
pul'verig adj powdery
pulverisieren [pʊlfərɪ'zirən] tr pulverize
Pul'verschnee m powdery snow
Pummel ['pʊməl] m (-s;-) butterball (chubby child)
pummelig ['pʊməlɪç] adj (coll) chubby
Pump [pʊmp] m—**auf P.** (coll) on tick
Pumpe ['pʊmpə] f (-;-n) pump
pumpen ['pʊmpən] tr pump; (coll) give on tick; (coll) get on tick ‖ intr pump
Pum'penschwengel m pump handle
Pumpernickel ['pʊmpərnɪkəl] m (-s; -) pumpernickel
Pump'hosen f pair of knickerbockers
Punkt [pʊŋkt] m (-[e]s;-e) point; (Tüpfelchen) dot; (Stelle) spot; (Einzelheit) item; (gram) period; **der tote P.** a deadlock; **dunkler P.** (fig) skeleton in the closet; **nach Punkten siegen** win on points; **P. sechs Uhr** at six o'clock sharp; **springender P.** crux; **strittiger P.** point at issue; **wunder P.** (fig) sore spot
Punkt'gleichheit f (sport) tie
punktieren [pʊŋk'tirən] tr dot, stipple; **punktierte Linie** dotted line
pünktlich ['pʏŋktlɪç] adj punctual
Punkt'sieg m (box) winning on points
punktum ['pʊŋktʊm] interj—**und damit p.!** and that's it!; period!
Punkt'zahl f (sport) score
Punsch [pʊnʃ] m (-es;) punch (drink)
Punze ['pʊntsə] f (-;-n) punch, stamp
punzen ['pʊntsən] tr punch, stamp
Pupille [pu'pɪlə] f (-;-n) (anat) pupil
Puppe ['pʊpə] f (-;-n) doll; puppet; (Schneider-) dummy; (zool) pupa
Pup'penspiel n puppet show
Pup'penwagen m doll carriage
pur [pur] adj pure, sheer

Püree [pʏ're] n (-s;-s) mashed potatoes; puree
purgieren [pʊr'girən] tr & intr purge
Purpur ['pʊrpʊr] m (-s;) purple
pur'purfarben adj purple
purpurn [pʊrpʊrn] adj purple
Purzelbaum ['pʊrtsəlbaum] m somersault; **e-en P. schlagen** do a somersault
purzeln ['pʊrtsəln] intr (SEIN) tumble
pusselig ['pʊsəlɪç] adj fussy
Puste ['pʊstə] f (-;) (coll) breath
Pustel ['pʊstəl] f (-;-n) pustule
pusten ['pʊstən] tr—**ich puste dir was!** (coll) you may whistle for it! ‖ intr puff, pant
Pu'sterohr n peashooter
Pute ['pʊtə] f (-;-n) turkey (hen)
Puter ['pʊtər] m (-s;-) turkey (cock)
Putsch [pʊtʃ] m (-es;-e) putsch, uprising
Putz [pʊts] m (-es;) finery; trimming; ornaments; plaster
putzen ['pʊtsən] tr (reinigen) clean; (Schuhe) polish; (Zähne) brush; (Person) dress; (schmücken) adorn ‖ ref dress; **sich** [dat] **die Nase p.** blow one's nose
Put'zer m (-s;-) cleaner; (mil) orderly
Putzerei [pʊtsə'raɪ] f (-;-en) (Aust) dry cleaner's; (Aust) laundry
Putz'frau f cleaning woman
putzig ['pʊtsɪç] adj funny
Putz'lappen m cleaning cloth
Putz'mittel n cleaning agent
Putz'wolle f cotton waste
Putz'zeug n cleaning things
Pygmäe [pʏg'me·ə] m (-n;-n) pygmy
Pyjama [pɪ'dʒɑma] m (-s;-s) pajamas
Pyramide [pʏra'midə] f (-;-n) pyramid; (mil) stack
Pyrenäen [pʏrɛ'ne·ən] pl Pyrenees
Pyrotechnik [pʏro'tɛçnɪk] f (-;) pyrotechnics
Pythonschlange ['pytɔnʃlaŋə] f python

Q

Q, q [ku] invar n Q, q
quabbelig ['kvabəlɪç] adj flabby; quivering, jelly-like
quabbeln ['kvabəln] intr quiver
Quackelei [kvakə'laɪ] f (-;-en) silly talk; (unnützes Zeug) rubbish
Quacksalber ['kvakzalbər] m (-s;-) quack
Quader ['kvɑdər] m (-s;-) ashlar
Quadrant [kva'drant] m (-en;-en) quadrant
Quadrat [kva'drɑt] n (-[e]s;-e) square; **e-e Zahl ins Q. erheben** square a number; **zwei Fuß im Q.** two feet square
quadratisch [kva'drɑtɪʃ] adj square; quadratic
Quadrat'meter n square meter
Quadrat'wurzel f square root
quadrieren [kva'drirən] tr square

quaken ['kvakən] intr (Ente) quack; (Frosch) croak
quäken ['kvekən] intr bawl
Qual [kvɑl] f (-;-en) torment, agony
quälen ['kvelən] tr torment; worry; (ständig bedrängen) pester ‖ ref— **sich mit e-r Arbeit q.** slave at a job; **sich umsonst q.** labor in vain; **sich zu Tode q.** worry oneself to death
Quälgeist ['kvelgaɪst] m pest
Qualifikation [kvalɪfɪka'tsjon] f (-; -en) qualification
qualifizieren [kvalɪfɪ'tsirən] tr & ref (zu) qualify (for)
Qualität [kvalɪ'tet] f (-;-en) quality
Qualitäts- comb.fm. high-quality, high-grade, quality
Qualle ['kvalə] f (-;-n) jellyfish
Qualm [kvalm] m (-[e]s;) smoke; vapor

qualmen ['kvalmən] *tr* smoke || *intr* smoke; (coll) smoke like a chimney
qual'mig *adj* smoky
qual'voll *adj* agonizing
Quantentheorie ['kvantəntɛ·ɔri] *f* quantum theory
Quantität [kvantɪ'tet] *f* (-;-en) quantity
Quan·tum ['kvantʊm] *n* (-s;-ten [tən]) quantum; quantity; (*Anteil*) portion
Quappe ['kvapə] *f* (-;-n) tadpole
Quarantäne [kvaran'tenə] *f* (-;-n) quarantine
Quark [kvark] *m* (-[e]s;) curds; cottage cheese; (fig) nonsense
Quark'käse *m* cottage cheese
quarren ['kvarən] *intr* (*Frosch*) croak; (fig) groan
Quart [kvart] *n* (-s;-e) quart; quarto || *f* (-;-en) (mus) fourth
Quartal [kvar'tɑl] *n* (-s;-e) quarter (*of a year*)
Quartals'abrechnung *f* (fin) quarterly statement
Quartals'säufer *m* periodic drunkard
Quart'band *m* (-[e]s;⸚e) quarto volume
Quarte ['kvartə] *f* (-;-n) (mus) fourth
Quartett [kvar'tet] *n* (-[e]s;-e) quartet
Quart'format *n* quarto
Quartier [kvar'tir] *n* (-s;-e) (*Stadtviertel*) quarter; (*Unterkunft*) quarters; (mil) quarters, billet
Quartier'meister *m* (mil) quartermaster
Quarz [kvarts] *m* (-es;-e) quartz
quasseln ['kvasəln] *tr* (coll) talk || *intr* talk nonsense
Quast [kvast] *m* (-[e]s;-e) brush
Quaste ['kvastə] *f* (-;-n) tassel
Quatsch [kvat/] *m* (-es;) (coll) baloney
quatschen ['kvat/ən] *intr* chatter; talk nonsense; (*durch Schlamm*) slog
Quecksilber ['kvɛkzɪlbər] *n* mercury
queck'silbrig *adj* fidgety
Quell [kvɛl] *m* (-[e]s;-e) (poet) var of **Quelle**
Quelle ['kvɛlə] *f* (-;-n) fountainhead; source; spring
quellen ['kvɛlən] §119 *tr* cause to swell; soak || *intr* (SEIN) spring, gush; (*Tränen*) well up; (*anschwellen*) swell; **ihm quollen die Augen fast aus dem Kopf** his eyes almost popped out
Quel'lenangabe *f* citation; bibliography
quel'lenmäßig *adj* according to the best authorities, authentic
Quel'lenmaterial *n* source material
Quel'lenstudium *n* original research

Quell'fluß *m* source
Quell'gebiet *n* headwaters
Quell'wasser *n* spring water
Quengelei [kvɛŋə'laɪ] *f* (-;-en) nagging
quengeln ['kvɛŋəln] *intr* nag
quer [kver] *adj* cross, transverse || *adv* crosswise; **q. über** (*acc*) across
Quer'balken *m* crossbeam
Quere ['kverə] *f* (-;) diagonal direction; **j–m in die Q. kommen** run across s.o.; (fig) disturb s.o.
queren ['kverən] *tr* traverse, cross
querfeldein' *adv* cross-country
Quer'kopf *m* contrary person
quer'köpfig *adj* contrary
Quer'pfeife *f* (mus) fife
Quer'ruder *n* (aer) aileron
Quer'schiff *n* (archit) transept
Quer'schläger *m* ricochet
Quer'schnitt *m* cross section
Quer'treiber *m* schemer, plotter
querü'ber *adv* straight across
Querulant –in [kverʊ'lant(ɪn)] §7 *mf* grumbler, grouch
Quetsche ['kvɛt/ə] *f* (-;-n) squeezer; (pej) joint
quetschen ['kvɛt/ən] *tr* squeeze, pinch; bruise; (*zerquetschen*) crush, mash
Quetsch'kartoffeln *pl* mashed potatoes
Quetsch'ung *f* (-;-en) bruise, contusion
Quetsch'wunde *f* bruise
quick [kvɪk] *adj* brisk, lively
quick'lebendig *adj* (coll) very lively
quieken ['kvikən] *intr* squeal, squeak
quietschen ['kvit/ən] *intr* (*Tür*) creak; (*Ferkel*) squeal; (*Bremsen*) screech
Quintessenz ['kvɪntesɛnts] *f* (-;) quintessence
Quintett [kvɪn'tet] *n* (-[e]s;-e) quintet
Quirl [kvɪrl] *m* (-[e]s;-e) (fig) fidgeter; (culin) whisk, mixer
quirlen ['kvɪrlən] *tr* beat, mix
quitt [kvɪt] *adj* even, square
Quitte ['kvɪtə] *f* (-;-n) quince
quittieren [kvɪ'tirən] *tr* give a receipt for; (*aufgeben*) quit
Quit'tung *f* (-;-en) receipt
Quiz [kvɪs] *n* (-;-) quiz
quoll [kvɔl] *pret* of **quellen**
Quotation [kvɔta'tsjon] *f* (-;-en) (st. exch.) quotation
Quote ['kvotə] *f* (-;-en) quota
Quotient [kvɔ'tsjɛnt] *m* (-en;-en) quotient
quotieren [kvɔ'tirən] *tr* quote

R

R, r [ɛr] *invar n* R, r
Rabatt [ra'bat] *m* (-[e]s;-e) reduction, discount
Rabatt'marke *f* trading stamp
Rabatz [ra'bats] *m*—**R. machen** (coll) raise Cain
Rab·bi ['rabi] *m* (-[s];-s & –binen

['binən]), **Rabbiner** [ra'binər] *m* (-s;-) rabbi
Rabe ['rabə] *m* (-n;-n) raven; **weißer R.** (fig) rare bird
Ra'benaas *n* (coll) beast
Ra'benmutter *f* hard-hearted mother
ra'benschwarz' *adj* jet-black

rabiat [ra'bjɑt] *adj* rabid, raving
Rache ['raxə] *f* (-;) revenge
Rachen ['raxən] *m* (-s;-) throat; mouth; (fig) jaws
rächen ['rɛçən] *tr* avenge ‖ *ref* (*an dat*) avenge oneself (on)
Ra'chenhöhle *f* pharynx
Ra'chenkatarrh *m* sore throat
Rä'cher –in §6 *mf* avenger
Rachgier ['raxgir] *f* revengefulness
rach'gierig, rach'süchtig *adj* vengeful
Rad [rɑt] *n* (-[e]s;⁼er) wheel; bike; **ein Rad schlagen** turn a cartwheel; (*Pfau*) fan the tail
Radar ['radɑr], [ra'dɑr] *n* (-s;) radar
Ra'dargerät *n* radar
Ra'darschirm *m* radarscope
Radau [ra'dau] *m* (-s;-) (coll) row
Radau'macher *m* rowdy
Rädchen ['rɛtçən] *n* (-s;-) little wheel
Rad'dampfer *m* river boat
radebrechen ['radəbrɛçən] §64 *tr* murder (*a language*)
radeln ['radəln] *intr* (SEIN) (coll) ride a bike
Rädelsführer ['redəlsfyrər] *m* ringleader
rädern ['redərn] *tr* torture; **wie gerädert sein** (coll) be bushed
Räderwerk ['redərverk] *n* gears; (fig) clockwork
rad'fahren §71 *intr* (SEIN) ride a bicycle
radieren [ra'dirən] *tr* erase; etch
Radie'rer *m* (-s;-) eraser; etcher
Radier'gummi *m* eraser
Radier'kunst *f* art of etching
Radier'messer *n* scraper, eraser
Radie'rung *f* (-;-en) erasure; etching
Radieschen [ra'disçən] *n* (-s;-) radish
radikal [radɪ'kal] *adj* radical ‖ **Radikale** §5 *mf* radical, extremist
Radio ['radjo] *n* (-s;-s) radio; **im R.** on the radio; **R. hören** listen to the radio
Ra'dioamateur *m* (rad) ham
Ra'dioapparat *m*, **Ra'diogerät** *n* radio set
Radiologe [radjo'logə] *m* (-n;-n) radiologist
Radiologie [radjolo'gi] *f* (-;) radiology
Ra'dioröhre *f* radio tube
Ra'diosender *m* radio transmitter
Radium ['radium] *n* (-s;) radium
Ra·dius ['radjus] *m* (-;-dien [djən]) radius
Rad'kappe *f* hubcap
Rad'kranz *m* rim
Radler –in ['radlər(ɪn)] §6 *mf* cyclist
Rad'nabe *f* hub
Rad'rennen *n* bicycle race
–rädrig [redrɪç] *comb.fm.* –wheeled
rad'schlagen §132 *intr* turn a cartwheel
Rad'spur *f* rut, track
Rad'stand *m* wheelbase
Rad'zahn *m* cog
raffen ['rafən] *tr* snatch up, gather up; (sew) take up
Raffgier ['rafgir] *f* rapacity
raffgierig ['rafgirɪç] *adj* rapacious
Raffine·rie [rafɪnə'ri] *f* (-;-rien ['ri·ən]) refinery
raffinieren [rafɪ'nirən] *tr* refine

raffiniert [rafɪ'nirt] *adj* refined; (fig) shrewd, cunning
Raffzahn ['raftsan] *m* canine tooth
ragen ['ragən] *intr* tower, loom
Ragout [ra'gu] *n* (-s;-s) (culin) stew
Rahe ['ra·ə] *f* (-;-n) (naut) yard
Rahm [ram] *m* (-[e]s;) cream
Rahmen ['ramən] *m* (-s;-) frame; (*Gefüge*) framework; (*Bereich*) scope, limits; (fig) setting; (aut) chassis; **aus dem R. fallen** be out of place; **e-n R. abgeben für** form a setting for; **im R.** (*genit*) in the course of; **im R. von** (or *genit*) within the scope of; within the framework of
Rah'menerzählung *f* story within a story
rahmig ['ramɪç] *adj* creamy
Rakete [ra'ketə] *f* (-;-n) rocket
Rake'tenabschußrampe *f* launch pad
Rake'tenbunker *m* silo
Rake'tenstart *m* rocket launch
Rake'tenwerfer *m* rocket launcher
Rake'tenwesen *n* rocketry
Rakett [ra'ket] *n* (-[e]s;-e & -s) (tennis) racket
Rammbär ['ramber] *m*, **Rammbock** ['rambɔk] *m*, **Ramme** ['ramə] *f* (-;-n) rammer; pile driver
rammeln ['raməln] *tr* shove; (*zusammenpressen*) pack; (*belegen*) copulate with ‖ *intr* copulate
rammen ['ramən] *tr* ram; (*Beton*) tamp
Rampe ['rampə] *f* (-;-n) ramp; (rok) launch pad; (rr) platform; (theat) apron
Ram'penlicht *n* footlights; (fig) limelight
Ramsch [ramʃ] *m* (-es;) odds and ends; junk; (com) rummage
Ramsch'verkauf *m* rummage sale
Ramsch'waren *pl* junk
Rand [rant] *m* (-[e]s;⁼er) edge, border; (*e-s Druckseite*) margin; **am Rande bemerken** note in passing; **außer R. und Band** completely out of control; **bis zum Rande** to the brim; **e-n R. hinterlassen** leave a ring (*e.g., from a wet glass*); **Ränder unter den Augen** circles under the eyes
Rand'auslöser *m* (typ) margin release
Rand'bemerkung *f* marginal note; (fig) snide remark
rändeln ['rendəln], **rändern** ['rendərn] *tr* border, edge; (*Münzen*) mill
Rand'gebiet *n* borderland; (*e–r Stadt*) outskirts
rand'los *adj* rimless
Rand'staat *m* border state
Ranft [ranft] *m* (-[e]s;⁼e) crust
rang [raŋ] *pret* of **ringen** ‖ **Rang** *m* (-[e]s;⁼e) rank; (theat) balcony; **j–m den R. ablaufen** (fig) run rings around s.o.
Rang'abzeichen *n* insignia of rank
Rang'älteste §5 *mf* ranking officer
Range ['raŋə] *m* (-n;-n) & *f* (-;-n) brat
Rangier'bahnhof *m* (rr) marshaling yard
rangieren [rã'ʒirən] *tr* rank; (rr) shunt, switch ‖ *intr* rank

Rang'ordnung *f* order of precedence
Rang'stufe *f* rank
rank [raŋk] *adj* slender
Ranke ['raŋkə] *f* (-;-n) tendril
Ränke ['reŋkə] *pl* schemes; **R. schmieden** scheme
ranken ['raŋkən] *ref & intr* creep, climb; **sich r. um** wind around
rän'kevoll *adj* scheming
rann [ran] *pret* of **rinnen**
rannte ['rantə] *pret* of **rennen**
Ranzen ['rantsən] *m* (-s;-) knapsack; school bag; (*Bauch*) belly; (mil) field pack
ranzig ['rantsıç] *adj* rancid
rapid [ra'pit], **rapide** [ra'pidə] *adj* rapid
Rappe ['rapə] *m* (-n;-n) black horse
rar [rar] *adj* rare, scarce
Rarität [rarı'tet] *f* (-;-en) rarity
rasant [ra'zant] *adj* grazing, point-blank (*fire*); (fig) impetuous
Rasanz [ra'zants] *f* (-;) flat trajectory; (fig) impetuosity
rasch [raʃ] *adj* quick; (*hastig*) hasty
rascheln ['raʃəln] *intr* rustle
Rasch'heit *f* (-;) haste, speed
rasen ['razən] *intr* rage, rave ‖ *intr* (SEIN) rush; (aut) speed ‖ **Rasen** *m* (-s;-) lawn, grass
ra'send *adj* raging, raving; wild, mad; (*Hunger*) ravenous; (*Wut*) towering; (*Tempo*) break-neck; **r. werden** see red
Ra'sendecke *f* turf
Ra'senmäher *m* lawn mower
Ra'senplatz *m* lawn
Ra'sensprenger *m* lawn sprinkler
Raserei [razə'raı] *f* (-;) rage, madness; (aut) reckless driving
Rasier– [razir] *comb.fm.* shaving, razor
Rasier'apparat *m* safety razor
rasieren [ra'zirən] *tr & ref* shave
Rasier'klinge *f* razor blade
Rasier'messer *n* straight razor
Rasier'napf *m* shaving mug
Rasier'pinsel *m* shaving brush
Rasier'wasser *n* after-shave lotion
Rasier'zeug *n* shaving outfit
Raspel ['raspəl] *f* (-;-n) rasp; (culin) grater
raspeln ['raspəln] *tr* rasp; grate
Rasse ['rasə] *f* (-;-n) race; (*Zucht*) breed, blood, stock; (fig) good breeding
Rassel ['rasəl] *f* (-;-n) rattle
rasseln ['rasəln] *intr* rattle; **durchs Examen r.** (coll) flunk the exam
Rassen– [rasən] *comb.fm.* racial
Ras'senfrage *f* racial problem
Ras'senhaß *m* racism, race hatred
Ras'senkreuzung *f* miscegenation; crossbreeding
Ras'senkunde *f* ethnology
ras'senmäßig *adi* racial
Ras'senmerkmal *n* racial characteristic
Ras'sentrennung *f* segregation
Ras'senunruhen *pl* racial disorders
Ras'sepferd *n* thoroughbred (horse)
ras'serein *adj* racially pure; thoroughbred
Ras'sevieh *n* purebred cattle

rassig ['rasıç] *adj* racy; thoroughbred
rassisch ['rasıʃ] *adj* racial
Rast [rast] *f* (-;-en) rest; station, stage; (mach) notch, groove; (mil) halt; **e–e R. machen** take a rest
rasten ['rastən] *intr* rest; (mil) halt
rast'los *adj* restless
Rast'losigkeit *f* (-;) restlessness
Rast'platz *m*, **Rast'stätte** *f* resting place
Rast'tag *m* day of rest
Rasur [ra'zur] *f* (-;-en) shave
Rat [rat] *m* (-[e]s; **Ratschläge** ['ratʃlegə]) advice, piece of advice, counsel; (*Beratung*) deliberation; (*Ausweg*) means, solution; **auf e–n Rat hören** listen to reason; **sich** [*dat*] **keinen Rat mehr wissen** be at one's wits' end; **zu Rate ziehen** consult (*a person, dictionary, etc.*) ‖ *m* (-[e]s; ≃e) council, board; (*Person*) councilor, alderman; advisor; (jur) counsei
Rate ['ratə] *f* (-;-n) installment; **auf Raten** on the installment plan
raten ['ratən] §63 *tr* guess; (*Rätsel*) solve; **das will ich dir nicht geraten haben!** you had better not!; **geraten!** you guessed it!; **j–m etw r.** advise s.o. about s.th.; **komm nicht wieder. das rate ich dir!** take my advice and don't come back! ‖ *intr* guess; give advice; (*dat*) advise; **gut r.** take a good guess; **hin und her r.** make random guesses; **j–m gut r.** give s.o. good advice; **j–m zu etw r.** recommend s.th. to s.o. ‖ **Raten** *n* (-s;) guesswork; advice
ra'tenweise *adv* by installments
Ra'tenzahlung *f* payment in installments; **auf R.** on the installment plan
Räterepublik ['retərepublık] *f* Soviet Union, Soviet Republic
Rat'geber –in §6 *mf* adviser, counselor
Rat'haus *n* city hall
ratifizieren [ratıfı'tsirən] *tr* ratify
Ratifizie'rung *f* (-;-en) ratification
Ration [ra'tsjon] *f* (-;-en) ration
rational [ratsjo'nal] *adj* rational
rationalisieren [ratsjonalı'zirən] *tr* streamline (*operations in industry*)
rationell [ratsjo'nel] *adj* rational
rationieren [ratsjo'nirən] *tr* ration
rätlich ['retlıç] *adj* advisable
rat'los *adj* helpless, perplexed
ratsam ['ratzam] *adj* advisable
Ratsche ['ratʃə] *f* (-;-n) rattle; (coll) chatterbox; (tech) ratchet
ratschen ['ratʃən] *intr* make noise with a rattle; (coll) chat
Rat'schlag *m* advice, piece of advice
rat'schlagen §132 *intr* deliberate, consult
Rat'schluß *m* decision, decree, resolution
Rätsel ['retsəl] *n* (-s;-) puzzle; (fig) riddle, enigma, mystery
rät'selhaft *adj* puzzling; mysterious
Ratte ['ratə] *f* (-;-n) rat
Rat'tenschwanz *m* rat tail; (fig) tangle; (coll) whole string (*of questions, etc.*); (*Haarzopf*) (coll) pigtail
rattern ['ratərn] *intr* rattle
ratzekahl ['ratsə'kal] *adj* (*Person*)

completely bald; (*Landschaft*) completely barren ‖ *adv* completely
Raub [raup] *m* (-[e]s;) robbery; plunder; (*Beute*) prey, spoils; **zum Raube fallen** fall prey, fall victim
Raub- *comb.fm.* predatory, rapacious
Raub'bau *m* (-[e]s;) excessive exploitation (*of natural resources*)
rauben ['raubən] *tr*—j—m *etw* **r.** rob s.o. of s.th.; **e-m Mädchen die Unschuld r.** seduce a girl; **e-n Kuß r.** steal a kiss ‖ *intr* rob
Räuber ['rɔɪbər] *m* (-s;-) robber; **R. und Gendarm spielen** play cops and robbers
Räu'berbande *f* gang of robbers
Räu'berhauptmann *m* gang leader
räuberisch ['rɔɪbərɪʃ] *adj* predatory
Raub'fisch *m* predatory fish
Raub'gesindel *n* gang of robbers
Raub'lust *f* rapacity
raub'gierig *adj* rapacious
Raub'lust *f* rapacity
Raub'mord *m* murder with robbery
Raub'mörder *m* robber and murderer
Raub'schiff *n* corsair, pirate ship
Raub'tier *n* beast of prey
Raub'überfall *m* holdup, robbery
Raub'vogel *m* bird of prey
Raub'zug *m* plundering raid
Rauch [raux] *m* (-[e]s;) smoke
rauchen ['rauxən] *tr & intr* smoke
Raucher ['rauxər] *m* (-s;-) smoker
Räucher- [rɔɪxər] *comb.fm.* smoked
Rau'cherabteil *n* smoking section
Räu'cherfaß *n* (eccl) censer
Räu'cherhering *m* smoked herring
Rau'cherhusten *m* cigarette cough
Räu'cherkammer *f* smokehouse
räuchern ['rɔɪxərn] *tr* smoke, cure; (*desinzieren*) fumigate
Räu'cherschinken *m* smoked ham
Räu'cherung *f* (-;) smoking; fumigation
Rau'cherwagen *m* (rr) smoker
Rauch'fahne *f* trail of smoke
Rauch'fang *m* (*über dem Herd*) hood; (*im Schornstein*) flue
Rauch'fleisch *n* smoked meat
rauchig ['rauxɪç] *adj* smoky
rauch'los *adj* smokeless
Rauch'schleier *m* (mil) smoke screen
Rauch'waren *pl* (*Pelze*) furs; (*Tabakwaren*) tobacco supplies
Räude ['rɔɪdə] *f* (-;) mange
räudig ['rɔɪdɪç] *adj* mangy; **räudiges Schaf** (fig) black sheep
Raufbold ['raufbɔlt] *m* (-[e]s;-e) roughneck, bully
Raufe ['raufə] *f* (-;-n) hayrack
raufen ['raufən] *tr* tear, pull out ‖ *recip & intr* fight, brawl, scuffle
Rauferei [raufə'raɪ] *f* (-;-en) fight, scuffle
Rauf'handel *m* fight, scuffle
rauf'lustig *adj* scrappy, belligerent
rauh [rau] *adj* rough; (*Hals*) hoarse; (*Behandlung*) harsh; **rauhe Wirklichkeit** hard facts
Rauh'bein *n* (fig) roughneck, churl
rauh'beinig *adj* tough, churlish
Rau'heit *f* (-;) roughness; hoarseness
rauhen ['rau·ən] *tr* roughen

Rauh'futter *n* roughage
rauh'haarig *adj* shaggy, hirsute
Rauh'reif *m* hoarfrost
Raum [raum] *m* (-[e]s;-̈e) room, space; (*Zimmer*) room; (*Bereich*) area; (*e-s Schiffes*) hold; **am Rande R. lassen** (typ) leave a margin; **freier R.** open space; **gebt R.!** make way! **luftleerer R.** vacuum; **R. bieten für** accommodate; **R. einnehmen** take up space; **R. geben** (*dat*) give way to; comply with
Raum'anzug *m* space suit
Räumboot ['rɔɪmbot] *n* minesweeper
Raum'dichte *f* (phys) density by volume
räumen ['rɔɪmən] *tr* clear; (*Wohnung*) vacate; (*Minen*) sweep; (mil) evacuate; **den Saal r.** clear the room; **das Lager r.** (com) clear out the stock; **j-n aus dem Wege r.** (fig) finish s.o. off
Raum'ersparnis *f* economy of space; **der R. wegen** to save space
Raum'fahrer *m* spaceman
Raum'fahrt *f* space travel
Raum'flug *m* space flight
Raum'gestaltung *f* interior decorating
Raum'inhalt *m* volume, capacity
Raum'kunst *f* interior decorating
Raum'lehre *f* geometry
räumlich ['rɔɪmlɪç] *adj* spatial
Räum'lichkeit *f* (-;-en) room
Raum'mangel *m* lack of space
Raum'medizin *f* space medicine
Raum'meter *n* cubic meter
Raum'schiff *n* space ship
Raum'schiffart *f* space travel
Raum'schiffkapsel *f* space capsule
Raum'sonde *f* unmanned space explorer
Raum'ton *m* stereophonic sound
Räu'mung *f* (-;-en) clearing, removal; (com) clearance; (mil) evacuation
Räu'mungsausverkauf *m* clearance sale
Räu'mungsbefehl *m* eviction notice; (mil) evacuation order
raunen ['raunən] *tr & intr* whisper
raunzen ['rauntsən] *intr* grumble
Raupe ['raupə] *f* (-;-n) (ent, mach) caterpillar
Rau'penfahrzeug *n* full-track vehicle
Rau'penkette *f* caterpillar track
Rau'penschlepper *m* caterpillar tractor
Rausch [rauʃ] *m* (-es;-e) drunkenness; (fig) intoxication, ecstasy; **e-n R. haben** be drunk; **sich** [*dat*] **e-n R. antrinken** get drunk
rauschen ['rau·ən] *intr* (*Blätter, Seide*) rustle; (*Bach*) murmur; (*Brandung, Sturm*) roar ‖ *intr* (SEIN) strut; rush
rau'schend *adj* rustling; (*Fest*) uproarious; (*Beifall*) thunderous
Rausch'gift *n* drug, dope
Rausch'gifthandel *m* drug traffic
Rausch'giftschieber –in §6 *mf* pusher
Rausch'giftsucht *f* drug addiction
Rausch'giftsüchtige §5 *mf* dope addict
Rausch'gold *n* tinsel
räuspern ['rɔɪspərn] *ref* clear one's throat
Rausschmeißer ['rausʃmaɪsər] *m* (-s;-) (coll) bouncer

Raute ['raυtə] ƒ (-;-n) (cards) diamond; (geom) rhombus
Rayon [rɛ'jō] m (-s;-s) (Bezirk) district, region; (im Warenhaus) department
Raz·zia ['ratsja] ƒ (-;-zien [tsjən]) police raid
Reagenzglas [re·a'gɛntsglɑs] n test tube
reagieren [re·a'girən] intr (auf acc) react (to)
Reaktion [re·ak'tsjon] ƒ (-;-en) reaction
reaktionär [re·aktsjɔ'ner] adj reactionary || **Reaktionär** m (-s;-e) reactionary
Reak·tor [rɛ'aktɔr] m (-s;-toren ['torən]) (phys) reactor
real [re'ɑl] adj real
Real'gymnasium n high school (where modern languages, mathematics, or sciences are stressed)
Realien [re'aljən] pl real facts, realities; exact sciences
realisieren [re·alɪ'zirən] tr realize
Realist -in [re·a'lɪst(ɪn)] §7 mƒ realist
realistisch [re·a'lɪstɪʃ] adj realistic
Realität [re·alɪ'tet] ƒ (-;-en) reality; **Realitäten** real property
Real'lexikon n encyclopedia
Real'lohn m purchasing power of wages
Real'schule ƒ non-classical secondary school
Rebe ['rebə] ƒ (-;-n) vine; tendril
Rebell [rɛ'bɛl] m (-en;-en) rebel
rebellieren [rebe'lirən] intr rebel
Rebellin [rɛ'bɛlɪn] ƒ (-;-nen) rebel
Rebellion [rebɛl'jon] ƒ (-;-en) rebellion
rebellisch [re'bɛlɪʃ] adj rebellious
Re'bensaft m (poet) juice of the grape
Rebhuhn ['rephun] n partridge
Rebstock ['rep/tɔk] m vine
rechen ['rɛçən] tr rake || **Rechen** m (-s;-) rake; grate
Re'chenaufgabe ƒ arithmetic problem
Re'chenautomat m computer
Re'chenbrett n abacus
Re'chenbuch n arithmetic book
Re'chenexemplar n arithmetic problem
Re'chenkunst ƒ arithmetic
Re'chenmaschine ƒ calculator
Re'chenpfennig m counter
Re'chenschaft ƒ (-;) account; **ʃ-n zur R. ziehen** call s.o. to account
Re'chenschaftsbericht m report
Re'chenschieber m slide rule
rechnen ['rɛçnən] tr reckon, calculate, figure out || intr reckon; calculate; **falsch r.** miscalculate; **r. auf** (acc) count on; **r. mit** be prepared for; expect; take into account; **r. zu** be counted among || **Rechnen** n (-s;) arithmetic; calculation
Rech'ner m (-s;-) calculator, computer; **er ist ein guter R.** he is good at numbers
rechnerisch ['rɛçnərɪʃ] adj arithmetical
Rech'nung ƒ (-;-en) calculation; account; bill; (Warenrechnung) invoice; (im Restaurant) check; **auf ʃ-s R. setzen** (or **stellen**) charge to s.o.'s

account; **auf R. kaufen** buy on credit; **auf seine R. kaufen** get one's money's worth; **außer R. lassen** overlook; **das geht auf meine R.** this is on me; **die R. begleichen** settle an account (or bill); **j-m in R. stellen** charge to s.o.'s account; **in R. ziehen** take into account; **R. tragen** (dat) make allowance for
Rech'nungsabschluß m closing of accounts
Rech'nungsauszug m (com) statement
Rech'nungsführer -in §6 mƒ accountant
Rech'nungsführung ƒ accounting
Rech'nungsjahr n fiscal year
Rech'nungsprüfer -in §6 mƒ auditor
Rech'nungswesen n accounting
recht [rɛçt] adj right; (richtig) correct; (echt) real; (gerecht) all right, right; (geziemend) suitable, proper; **es ist mir nicht r.** I don't like it; **es ist schon r.** that's all right; **mir soll's r. sein** I don't mind; **zur rechten Zeit** at the right moment || adv right; quite; (sehr) very; **das kommt mir gerade r.** that comes in handy; **erst r.** all the more; **es j-m r. machen** please s.o.; **es geschieht ihm r. it** serves him right; **j-m r. geben** agree with s.o.; **nun erst r. nicht** now less than ever; **r. daran tun zu** (inf) do right to (inf); **r. haben** be right || **Recht** n (-[e]s;-e) right; (Vorrecht) privilege; (jur) law; **alle Rechte vorbehalten** all rights reserved; **die Rechte studieren** study law; **mit R.** with good reason; **R. sprechen** dispense justice; **sich** [dat] **selbst R. verschaffen** take the law into one's hands; **von Rechts wegen** by rights; **wieder zu seinem Rechte kommen** come into one's own again; **zu R. bestehen** be justified || **Rechte §5** mƒ right person; **an den Rechten kommen** meet one's match; **du bist mir der R.!** you're a fine fellow! || ƒ right hand; (box) right; **die R.** (pol) the right || n right; **er dünkt sich** [dat] **was Rechtes** he thinks he's somebody; **nach dem Rechten sehen** look after things
Recht'eck n rectangle, oblong
recht'eckig adj rectangular
recht'fertigen tr justify, vindicate
Recht'fertigung ƒ (-;-en) justification
recht'gläubig adj orthodox
rechthaberisch ['rɛçthabərɪʃ] adj dogmatic
recht'lich adj legal, lawful; (ehrlich) honest, honorable
Recht'lichkeit ƒ (-;) legality; (Redlichkeit) honesty
recht'los adj without rights
recht'mäßig adj legal; legitimate
Recht'mäßigkeit ƒ (-;) legality; legitimacy
rechts [rɛçts] adv on the right; right, to the right
Rechts- comb.fm. legal
Rechts'angelegenheit ƒ legal matter
Rechts'anspruch m legal claim
Rechts'anwalt m lawyer, attorney

Rechts'ausdruck m legal term
Rechts'auskunft f legal advice
Rechts'außen m (-;-) (fb) right wing
Rechts'beistand m legal adviser
recht'schaffen adj honest
Recht'schaffenheit f (-;) honesty
Recht'schreibung f orthography
Rechts'fall m case, legal case
Rechts'gang m legal procedure
Rechts'gefühl sense of justice
Rechts'gelehrsamkeit f jurisprudence
Rechts'grund m legal grounds; (Anspruch) title, claim
rechts'gültig adj legal, valid
Rechts'gültigkeit f legality
Rechts'gutachten n legal opinion
Rechts'handel m lawsuit
rechtshändig ['rɛçtshɛndɪç] adj right-handed
rechts'herum adv clockwise
Rechts'kraft f legal force
rechts'kräftig adj valid
Rechts'lage f legal status
Rechts'lehre f jurisprudence
Rechts'mittel n legal remedy
Rechts'pflege f administration of justice
Recht'sprechung f (-;) administration of justice; **die R.** (coll) the judiciary
Rechts'schutz m legal protection
Rechts'spruch m verdict
Rechts'streit m legal dispute; pending case; difference of opinion in the interpretation of the law
rechtsum' interj (mil) right face!
rechts'ungültig adj illegal, invalid
rechts'verbindlich adj legally binding
Rechtsverdreher –in ['rɛçtsfɛrdre·ər(ɪn)] §6 mf pettifogger
Rechts'verletzung f (-;-en) violation of the law; infringement of another's rights
Rechts'weg m recourse to the law; **auf dem Rechtswege** by the courts; **den R. beschreiten** take legal action
Rechts'wissenschaft f jurisprudence
Reck [rɛk] n (-[e]s;-e) horizontal bar
recken ['rɛkən] tr stretch; **den Hals r.** crane one's neck
Redakteur [rɛdak'tør] m (-s;-e) editor
Redaktion [rɛdak'tsjon] f (-;-en) editorship; (Arbeitskräfte) editorial staff; (Arbeitsraum) editorial office
redaktionell [rɛdaktsjo'nɛl] adj editorial
Redaktions'schluß m press time, deadline
Rede ['redə] f (-;-n) speech; (Gespräch) conversation; (Gerücht) rumor; **das ist nicht der R. wert** that is not worth mentioning; **davon kann keine R. sein** that's out of the question; **die in R. stehende Person** the person in question; **e–e R. halten** give a speech; **es geht die R., daß** it is rumored that; **gebundene R.** verse; **gehobene R.** lofty language; **j–m in die R. fallen** interrupt s.o.; **j–m R. und Antwort stehen** explain oneself to s.o.; **j–n zur R. stellen** take s.o. to task; **keine R.!** absolutely not!; **lose Reden führen** engage in loose talk; **ungebundene R.** prose

Re'defigur f figure of speech
Re'defluß m flow of words
Re'defreiheit f freedom of speech
Re'degabe f eloquence, fluency
re'degewandt adj fluent; (iron) glib
Re'degewandtheit f fluency, eloquence
Re'dekunst f eloquence
reden ['redən] tr speak, talk ‖ ref— **mit sich r. lassen** listen to reason; **sich heiser r.** talk oneself hoarse; **von sich r. machen** cause a lot of talk ‖ intr speak, talk; converse; **du hast gut r.!** it's easy for you to talk; **j–m ins Gewissen r.** appeal to s.o.'s conscience; **j–m nach dem Munde r.** humor s.o.; **mit j–m deutsch r.** (fig) talk turkey to s.o.
Re'densart f phrase, expression; idiom
Rederei [redə'raɪ] f (-;-en) empty talk
Re'deschwall m verbosity
Re'deteil m part of speech
Re'deweise f style of speaking
Re'dewendung f phrase, expression
redigieren [redɪ'girən] tr edit
redlich ['retlɪç] adj upright, honest ‖ adv—**es r. meinen** mean well; **sich r. bemühen** make an honest effort
Red'lichkeit f (-;) honesty, integrity
Redner –in ['rednər(ɪn)] §6 mf speaker
Red'nerbühne f podium, platform
Red'nergabe f (gift of) eloquence
rednerisch ['rednərɪʃ] adj rhetorical
Redoute [re'dutə] f (-;-n) masquerade; (mil) redoubt
redselig ['retzelɪç] adj talkative
Reduktion [reduk'tsjon] f (-;-en) reduction
reduplizieren [reduplɪ'tsirən] tr reduplicate
reduzieren [redu'tsirən] tr (auf acc) reduce (to)
Reede ['redə] f (-;-n) (naut) roadstead
Reeder ['redər] m (-s;-) shipowner
Reederei [redə'raɪ] f (-;-en) shipping company; shipping business
reell [re'ɛl] adj honest; (Preis) fair; (Geschäft) sound ‖ adv—**r. bedient werden** get one's money's worth
Reep [rep] n (-[e]s;-e) (naut) rope
Referat [refə'rat] n (-[e]s;-e) report; (Vortrag) paper; **ein R. halten** give a paper
Referendar [referen'dar] m (-s;-e) junior lawyer; in-service teacher
Referent –in [refe'rent(ɪn)] §7 mf reader of a paper; (Berichterstatter) reporter; (Gutachter) official adviser
Referenz [refe'rents] f (-;-en) reference; **j–n als R. angeben** give s.o. as a reference; **gute Referenzen verfügen** have good references
referieren [refe'rirən] intr (über acc) give a report (on); (über acc) read a paper (on)
reffen ['refən] tr (naut) reef
reflektieren [reflek'tirən] tr reflect ‖ intr reflect; **r. auf** (acc) reflect on; (com) think of buying
Reflek·tor [re'flektor] m (-s;-toren) ['torən]) reflector
Reflex [re'flɛks] m (-es;-e) reflex
Reflex'bewegung f reflex action

Reflexion [reflɛ'ksjon] *f* (-;-en) reflection

reflexiv [reflɛ'ksif] *adj* reflexive

Reform [re'form] *f* (-;-en) reform

Reformation [reforma'tsjon] *f* (-;-en) reformation

Refor·mator [refor'mator] *m* (-s; [ma'toren]) reformer

Reform'haus *n* health-food store

reformieren [refor'miren] *tr* reform

Reform'kost *f* health food

Refrain [rə'frɛ̃] *m* (-s;-s) refrain; **den R.** mitsingen join in the refrain

Regal [re'gal] *n* (-s;-e) shelf

Regat·ta [re'gata] *f* (-;-ten [tən]) regatta

rege ['regə] *adj* brisk, lively

Regel ['regəl] *f* (-;-n) rule, regulation; (pathol) menstruation; **in der R.** as a rule

re'gellos *adj* irregular; disorderly

Re'gellosigkeit *f* (-;-en) irregularity

re'gelmäßig *adj* regular

Re'gelmäßigkeit *f* regularity

regeln ['regəln] *tr* regulate; arrange; control

re'gelrecht *adj* regular; downright

Re'gelung *f* (-;-en) regulation; control

re'gelwidrig *adj* against the rules; (sport) foul

regen ['regən] *tr & ref* move, stir ‖ **Regen** *m* (-s;-) rain; **vom R. unter die Traufe kommen** jump out of the frying pan into the fire

re'genarm *adj* rainless, dry

Re'genbö *f* rain squall

Re'genbogen *m* rainbow

Re'genbogenhaut *f* (anat) iris

re'gendicht *adj* rainproof

Re'genfall *m* rainfall

re'genfest *adj* rainproof

Re'genguß *m* downpour

Re'genhaut *f* oilskin coat

Re'genmantel *m* raincoat

Re'genmenge *f* amount of rainfall

Re'genmesser *m* rain gauge

Re'genpfeifer *m* (orn) plover

Re'genschauer *m* shower

Re'genschirm *m* umbrella

Regent –in [re'gent(ın)] §7 *mf* regent

Re'gentag *m* rainy day

Re'gentropfen *m* raindrop

Re'genumhang *m* cape

Re'genwetter *n* rainy weather

Re'genwurm *m* earthworm

Re'genzeit *f* rainy season

Re·gie [re'ʒi] *f* (-;-gien ['ʒi·ən]) management, administration; (com) state monopoly; (cin, theat) direction

Regie'assistent –in §7 *mf* (cin, theat) assistant director

Regie'pult *n* (rad) control console

Regie'raum *m* (rad) control room

regieren [re'girən] *tr* govern, rule; (gram) govern, take ‖ *intr* reign; (fig) predominate

Regie'rung *f* (-;-en) government, rule; administration; reign

Regie'rungsanleihe *f* government loan

Regie'rungsantritt *m* accession

Regie'rungsbeamte §5 *m* government official

Regie'rungssitz *m* seat of government

Regie'rungszeit *f* reign; administration

Regime [re'ʒim] *n* (-s;-s) regime

Regiment [regɪ'ment] *n* (-[e]s;-e) rule, government ‖ *n* (-[e]s;-er) (mil) regiment

Regiments– *comb.fm.* regimental

Regiments'kommandeur *m* regimental commander

Region [re'gjon] *f* (-;-en) region

regional [regjo'nal] *adj* regional

Regisseur [reʒɪ'sør] *m* (-s;-e) (cin, theat) director

Register [re'gɪstər] *n* (-s;-) file clerk; (*Inhaltsverzeichnis*) index; (*Orgel*–) stop

Regi·strator [regɪs'trator] *m* (-s; –stratoren [stra'torən]) registrar

Registratur [regɪstra'tur] *f* (-;-en) filing; filing cabinet

registrieren [regɪs'trirən] *tr* register; (*Betrag*) ring up

Registrier'kasse *f* cash register

Registrie'rung *f* (-;-en) registration

Reglement [reglə'mã] *n* (-s;-s) regulation(s), rule(s)

Regler ['reglər] *m* (-s;-) regulator; (mach) governor

reglos ['reklos] *adj* motionless

regnen ['regnən] *impers*—**es regnet** it is raining; **es regnet Bindfäden** it's raining cats and dogs; **es regnete Püffe** blows came thick and fast

regnerisch ['regnərɪʃ] *adj* rainy

Re·greß [re'grɛs] *m* (-gresses;-gresse) recourse, remedy; **R. nehmen zu** have recourse to

regsam ['rekzam] *adj* lively; quick

regulär [regu'lɛr] *adj* regular

regulierbar [regu'lirbar] *adj* adjustable

regulieren [regu'lirən] *tr* regulate; adjust

Regung ['reguŋ] *f* (-;-en) motion, stirring; emotion; impulse

Reh [re] *n* (-[e]s;-e) deer

rehabilitieren [rehabɪlɪ'tirən] *tr* rehabilitate

Rehabilitie'rung *f* (-;-en) rehabilitation

Reh'bock *m* roebuck

Reh'braten *m* roast venison

Reh'kalb *n* fawn

Reh'keule *f* leg of venison

Rehkitz ['rekɪts] *n* (-es;-e) fawn

Reh'leder *n* doeskin

Reibahle ['raɪpalə] *f* (-;-n) reamer

Reibe ['raɪbə] *f* (-;-n) (coll) grater

Reibeisen ['raɪpaɪzən] *n* (culin) grater

reiben ['raɪbən] §62 *tr* rub; grate; grind ‖ *ref*—**sich r. an** (*dat*) take offense at ‖ *intr* rub

Reiberei [raɪbə'raɪ] *f* (-;-en) (coll) friction, squabble

Rei'bung *f* (-;-en) friction

rei'bungslos *adj* frictionless; (fig) smooth

reich [raɪç] *adj* wealthy; (**an** *dat*) rich (in); (*Fang*) big; (*Phantasie*) fertile; (*Mahlzeit*) lavish ‖ **Reich** *n* (-[e]s; -e) empire, realm; kingdom

reichen ['raɪçən] *tr* reach; hand, pass ‖ *intr* reach, extend; do, manage; **das reicht!** that will do!

reich'haltig *adj* rich; abundant

reich'lich adj plentiful, abundant || adv pretty, fairly
Reichs'kanzlei f chancellery
Reichs'kanzler m chancellor
Reichs'mark f reichsmark
Reichs'tag m (hist) diet; (hist) Reichstag (lower house)
Reichtum ['raɪçtum] n (-s;ⁿer) riches
Reich'weite f reach, range
reif [raɪf] adj ripe; (fig) mature || **Reif** m (-[e]s;) frost
Reife ['raɪfə] f (-;) ripeness; (fig) maturity
reifen ['raɪfən] intr (SEIN) ripen; mature || impers—es reift there is frost || **Reifen** m (-s;-) tire; hoop
Rei'fendruckmesser m tire gauge
Rei'fenpanne f, **Rei'fenschaden** m flat tire, blowout
Rei'feprüfung f final examination (as prerequisite for entering university)
Rei'fezeugnis n high school diploma
reif'lich adj careful
Reigen ['raɪgən] m (-s;-) square dance
Reihe ['raɪ·ə] f (-;-n) row, string; set, series; rank, file; turn; **an der R. sein** be next; **an die R. kommen** get one's turn; **aus der R. tanzen** (fig) go one's own way; **die R. ist an mir** it's my turn; **nach der R.** in succession
reihen ['raɪ·ən] tr range, rank; (Perlen) string
Rei'hendorf n one-street village
Rei'henfabrikation f assembly-line production
Rei'henfolge f succession, sequence
Rei'henhaus n row house
Rei'henschaltung f (elec) series connection
reih'enweise adv in rows
Reiher ['raɪ·ər] m (-s;-) heron
Reim [raɪm] m (-[e]s;-e) rhyme
reimen ['raɪmən] tr (auf acc) make rhyme (with) || ref rhyme; (fig) make sense; (auf acc) rhyme (with) || intr rhyme
reim'los adj unrhymed, blank
rein [raɪn] adj pure; (sauber) clean; (klar) clear; (Gewinn) net; (Wahrheit) simple; (Wahnsinn) sheer, absolute; **etw ins reine bringen** clear up s.th.; **etw ins reine schreiben** write (or type) a final copy of s.th.; **mit j-m ins reine kommen** come to an understanding with s.o. || adv quite, downright; **r. alles** almost everything || **Rein** f (-;-en) pan
Reindl ['raɪndəl] n (-s;- & -n) pan
Rei'nemachen n (-s;) housecleaning
Rein'ertrag m clear profit
Rein'fall m flop, disappointment
Rein'gewicht n net weight
Rein'gewinn m net profit
Rein'heit f (-;) purity; cleanness
reinigen ['raɪnɪgən] tr clean, cleanse; (fig) purify, refine
Rei'nigung f (-;-en) cleaning; purification; dry cleaning
Rei'nigungsanstalt f dry cleaner's
Rei'nigungsmittel n cleaning agent
Reinmachefrau ['raɪnmaxəfrau] f cleaning woman
Rein'schrift f final copy

reinweg ['raɪn'vɛk] adv (coll) flatly, absolutely
rein'wollen adj all-wool
Reis [raɪs] m (-es;) rice || n (-es;-er) twig; (fig) scion
Reis'brei m rice pudding
Reise ['raɪzə] f (-;-n) trip, tour; (aer) flight; (naut) voyage; **auf der R. while traveling; auf Reisen sein** be traveling
Rei'sebericht m travelogue
Rei'sebeschreibung f travel book
Rei'sebüro n travel agency
rei'sefertig adj ready to leave
Rei'seführer m guidebook
Rei'segefährte m, **Rei'segefährtin** f travel companion
Rei'segenehmigung f travel permit
Rei'segepäck n luggage; (rr) baggage
Rei'segesellschaft f tour operator(s); travel group
Rei'sehandbuch n guidebook
Rei'seleiter –in §6 mf courier, guide
rei'selustig adj fond of traveling
reisen ['raɪzən] intr (SEIN) travel
Reisende ['raɪzəndə] §5 mf traveler
Rei'sepaß m passport
Rei'seplan m itinerary
Rei'seprospekt m travel folder
Rei'seroute f itinerary
Rei'sescheck m traveler's check
Rei'seschreibmaschine f portable typewriter
Rei'sespesen pl travel expenses
Rei'setasche f overnight bag, flight bag
Rei'seziel n destination
Reisig ['raɪzɪç] n (-s;) brushwood
Rei'sigbündel n faggot
Reisige ['raɪzɪgə] §5 m cavalryman
Reißaus [raɪs'aus] —**R. nehmen** (coll) take to one's heels
Reißbrett ['raɪsbrɛt] n drawing board
reißen ['raɪsən] §53 tr tear, rip; (ziehen) pull, yank; (wegschnappen) wrest, snatch || intr tear; pull, tug; break, snap; (sich spalten) split, burst; **das reißt ins Geld** this is running into money; **mir reißt die Geduld** I am losing all patience || ref—**an sich r.** seize; (com) monopolize; **die Führung an sich r.** take the lead; **sich an e-m Nagel r.** scratch oneself on a nail: **sich um etw r.** scramble for s.th. || **Reißen** n (-s;) tearing; bursting; sharp pains: rheumatism
rei'ßend adj rapid; (Schmerz) sharp; (Tier) rapacious; **reißenden Absatz finden** (coll) sell like hotcakes
Reißer ['raɪsər] m (-s;-) bestseller; (cin) box-office hit; (com) good seller
Reißfeder ['raɪsfedər] f drawing pen
Reißleine ['raɪslaɪnə] f rip cord
Reißnagel ['raɪsnagəl] m thumbtack
Reißschiene ['raɪsʃinə] f T-square
Reißverschluß ['raɪsfɛrʃlus] m zipper
Reißzahn ['raɪstsan] m canine tooth
Reißzeug ['raɪstsɔɪk] n mechanical-drawing tools
Reißzwecke ['raɪstsvɛkə] f thumbtack
Reit- [raɪt] comb.fm. riding
Reit'anzug m riding habit

Reit'bahn f riding ring
reiten ['raɪtən] §86 tr ride; **e—n Weg r.** ride along a road; **ihn reitet der Teufel** (coll) he is full of the devil; **krumme Touren r.** (coll) pull shady deals; **Prinzipien r.** (fig) stick rigidly to principles; **über den Haufen r.** knock down ‖ intr (SEIN) go horseback riding; **geritten kommen** come on horseback; **vor Anker r.** ride at anchor
Rei'ter –in §6 mf rider
Rei'terstandbild n equestrian statue
Reit'gerte f riding crop
Reit'hose f riding breeches
Reit'knecht m groom
Reit'kunst m horsemanship
Reit'peitsche f riding crop
Reit'pferd n saddle horse
Reit'schule f riding academy
Reit'stiefel m riding boot
Reit'weg m bridle path
Reiz [raɪts] m (–es;–e) charm, appeal; (Erregung) irritation; (physiol, psychol) stimulus; **e—n R.** ausüben auf (acc) attract; **sie läßt ihre Reize spielen** she turns on the charm
reizbar ['raɪtsbɑr] adj irritable; (empfindlich) sensitive, touchy
reizen ['raɪtsən] tr (entzünden, ärgern) irritate; (locken) allure; (anziehen) attract; (anregen) excite, stimulate; (aufreizen) provoke; (Appetit) whet ‖ intr (cards) bid ‖ impers—**es reizt mich zu** (inf) I'm itching to (inf)
rei'zend adj charming; cute, sweet; (pathol) irritating
Reiz'entzug m sensory deprivation
Reiz'husten m (–s;) constant cough
reiz'los adj unattractive; (Kost) bland
Reiz'mittel n stimulant; (fig) incentive
Reiz'stoff m irritant
Rei'zung f (–;–en) irritation; (Lokkung) allurement; (Anregung) stimulation; (Aufreizung) provocation
reiz'voll adj charming, attractive; fascinating; (verlockend) tempting
rekeln ['rekəln] ref (coll) lounge
Reklamation [reklama'tsjon] f (–;–en) complaint, protest
Reklame [re'klɑmə] f (–;–n) advertisement, ad; publicity; **R. machen für** advertise
Rekla'mebüro n advertising agency
Rekla'mefeldzug m advertising campaign
reklamieren [rekla'mirən] tr claim ‖ intr (gegen) protest (against); (wegen) complain (about)
rekognoszieren [rekɔs'tsirən] tr & intr reconnoiter
Rekonvaleszent –in [rekɔnvales'tsent (ɪn)] §7 mf convalescent
Rekonvaleszenz [rekɔnvales'tsents] f (–;) convalescence
Rekord [re'kɔrt] m (–[e]s;–e) record
Rekord'ernte f bumper crop, record crop
Rekordler –in [re'kɔrtlər(ɪn)] §6 mf (coll) record holder
Rekord'versuch m attempt to break the record

Rekrut [re'krut] m (–en;–en) recruit
Rekru'tenausbildung f basic training
Rekru'tenaushebung f recruitment
rekrutieren [rekru'tirən] tr recruit ‖ ref—**sich r.** aus be recruited from
Rek·tor ['rektər] m (–s;–toren ['torən]) principal; (e—r Universität) president
Relais [rə'le] n (–lais ['le(s)];–lais ['les]) relay
relativ [rela'tif] adj relative
Relegation [relega'tsjon] f (–;–en) expulsion
relegieren [rele'girən] tr expel
Relief [re'ljef] n (–s;–s & –e) relief
Religion [reli'gjon] f (–;–en) religion
Religions'ausübung f practice of religion
Religions'bekenntnis n religious denomination
religiös [reli'gjøs] adj religious
Reling ['relɪŋ] f (–s;–s) (naut) rail
Reliquie [re'likvjə] f (–;–n) relic
Reli'quienschrein m reliquary
remis [re'mi] adj (cards) tied ‖ **Remis** n (–;–) (chess) tie, draw
remittieren [remɪ'tirən] tr (Geld) remit; (Waren) return ‖ intr (Fieber) go down
rempeln ['rempəln] tr bump, jostle ‖ intr (fb) block
Remter ['remtər] m (–s;–) refectory; assembly hall
Ren [ren] (–s;–e) reindeer
Renaissance [rəne'sɑs] f (–;–n) renaissance
Rendite [ren'ditə] f (–;–n) return
Renn– [ren] comb.fm. race, racing
Renn'bahn f race track; (aut) speedway
Renn'boot n racing boat
rennen ['renən] §97 tr run; **j—m den Degen durch den Leib r.** run s.o. through with a sword; **über den Haufen r.** run over; **zu Boden r.** knock down ‖ intr (SEIN) run; race ‖ **Rennen** n (–s;–) running; race; (Einzelrennen) heat; **das R. machen** win the race; **totes R.** dead heat, tie
Ren'ner m (–s;–) (good) race horse
Renn'fahrer m (aut) race driver
Renn'pferd n race horse
Renn'platz m race track; (aut) speedway
Renn'rad n racing bicycle, racer
Renn'sport m racing
Renn'strecke f race track; distance (to be raced); (aut) speedway
Renn'wagen m racing car, racer
Renommee [renɔ'me] n (–s;–s) reputation
renommieren [renɔ'mirən] intr (mit) brag (about), boast (about)
renommiert' adj (wegen) renowned (for)
Renommist [renɔ'mɪst] m (–en;–en) braggart
renovieren [renɔ'virən] tr renovate; redecorate
rentabel [ren'tɑbəl] adj profitable
Rentabilität [rentabɪli'tet] f (–;–en) (e–r Investition) return; (fin) productiveness

Rente ['rɛntə] ƒ (-;-n) income, revenue; pension; annuity
Ren'tenbrief *m* annuity bond
Ren'tenempfänger –in §6 *mƒ* pensioner
Rentier [rɛn'tje] *m* (-s;-s) person of independent means || ['rɛntir] *n* (-s; -s;) reindeer
rentieren [rɛn'tirən] *reƒ* pay
Rentner –in ['rɛntnər(ɪn)] §6 *mƒ* person on pension
Reparatur [rɛpara'tur] ƒ (-;-en) repair
Reparatur'werkstatt ƒ repair shop; (aut) garage
reparieren [rɛpa'rirən] *tr* repair, fix
Reportage [rɛpɔr'taʒə] ƒ (-;-n) report; coverage
Reporter –in [rɛ'pɔrtər(ɪn)] §6 *mƒ* reporter
Repräsentant –in [rɛprɛzen'tant(ɪn)] §7 *mƒ* representative
repräsentieren [rɛprɛzen'tirən] *tr* represent || *intr* be a socialite
Repressalie [rɛprɛ'saljə] ƒ (-;-n) reprisal
Reprise [rɛ'prizə] ƒ (-;-n) (cin) rerun; (mus) repeat; (theat) revival
reproduzieren [rɛprodu'tsirən] *tr* reproduce
Reptil [rɛp'til] *n* (-s;-ien [jən] & -e) reptile
Republik [rɛpu'blik] ƒ (-;-en) republic
Republikaner –in [rɛpublɪ'kanər(ɪn)] §6 *mƒ* republican
republikanisch [rɛpublɪ'kanɪʃ] *adj* republican
Requisit [rɛkvɪ'zit] *n* (-[e]s;-en) requisite; **Requisiten** (theat) props
Reservat [rɛzɛr'vat] *n* (-[e]s;-e) reservation
Reserve [rɛ'zɛrvə] ƒ (-;-n) reserve
Reser'vebank ƒ (-;̈-e) (sport) bench
Reser'vereifen *m* spare tire
Reser'veteil *m* spare part
Reser'vetruppen *pl* (mil) reserves
reservieren [rɛzɛr'virən] *tr* reserve
Reservie'rung ƒ (-;-en) reservation
Residenz [rɛzɪ'dɛnts] ƒ (-;-en) residence
Residenz'stadt ƒ capital
residieren [rɛzɪ'dirən] *intr* reside
resignieren [rɛzɪg'nirən] *intr* resign
Respekt [rɛ'spɛkt] *m* (-[e]s;) respect
respektabel [rɛspɛk'tabəl] *adj* respectable
respektieren [rɛspɛk'tirən] *tr* respect
respekt'los *adj* disrespectful
respekt'voll *adj* respectful
Ressort [rɛ'sor] *n* (-s;-s) department
Rest [rɛst] *m* (-es;-e & -er) rest; (*Stoff-*) remnant; (*Zahlungs-*) balance; (*Bodensatz*) residue; (math) remainder; (*irdische* (or *sterbliche*) **Reste** earthly (or mortal) remains; **j–m den R. geben** (coll) finish s.o. off
Rest'auflage ƒ remainders
Restaurant [rɛstɔ'rɑ̃] *n* (-s;-s) restaurant
Restauration [rɛstaura'tsjon] ƒ (-;-en) restoration; (Aust) restaurant
Rest'bestand *m* remainder
Rest'betrag *m* balance, remainder
Re'steverkauf *m* remnant sale

rest'lich *adj* remaining
rest'los *adj* complete
Resultat [rɛzul'tɑt] *n* (-[e]s;-e) result; upshot; (sport) score
retten ['rɛtən] *tr* save, rescue
Ret'ter *m* (-s;-) rescuer; (*Heiland*) Savior
Rettich ['rɛtɪç] *m* (-s;-e) radish
Ret'tung ƒ (-;-en) rescue; salvation
Ret'tungsaktion ƒ rescue operation
Ret'tungsboot *n* lifeboat
Ret'tungsfloß *n* life raft
Ret'tungsgürtel *m* life preserver
Ret'tungsleine ƒ life line
ret'tungslos *adj* irretrievable
Ret'tungsmannschaft ƒ rescue party
Ret'tungsring *m* life preserver
Ret'tungsstation ƒ first-aid station
retuschieren [rɛtu'ʃirən] *tr* retouch
Reue ['rɔɪə] ƒ (-;) remorse
reu'elos *adj* remorseless, impenitent
reuen ['rɔɪ-ən] *tr*—**die Tat reut mich** I regret having done it; **die Zeit reut mich** I regret wasting the time || *impers*—**es reut mich, daß I regret** that, I am sorry that
reu'evoll *adj* repentant, contrite
Reugeld ['rɔɪgɛlt] *n* forfeit
reumütig ['rɔɪmytɪç] *adj* repentant
Revanche [re'vɑ̃ʃə] ƒ (-;) revenge
Revan'chekrieg *m* punitive war
revan'chelustig *adj* vengeful
Revan'chepartie ƒ (sport) return game
revanchieren [revɑ̃'ʃirən] *reƒ* (**an** *dat*) take revenge (on); **sich für e–en Dienst r.** return a favor
Revers [re'vɛrs] *m* (-es;-e) (*e–r Münze*) reverse; (*Erklärung*) statement || (rɛ'ver] *m* (Aust) & *n* (-;-) lapel; cuff
revidieren [revɪ'dirən] *tr* revise; (*nachprüfen*) check; (com) audit
Revier [re'vir] *n* (-s;-e) district; quarter; hunting ground; police station; (mil) sick quarters
Revier'stube ƒ (mil) sickroom
Revision [revɪ'zjon] ƒ (-;-en) revision; (com) audit; (jur) appeal
Re·visor [re'vizɔr] *m* (-s;-visoren [vɪ'zorən]) reviser; (com) auditor
Revolte [re'vɔltə] ƒ (-;-n) revolt
revoltieren [revɔl'tirən] *intr* revolt
Revolution [revolu'tsjon] ƒ (-;-en) revolution
revolutionär [revolutsjɔ'ner] *adj* revolutionary || **Revolutionär** –in §8 *mƒ* revolutionary
Revolver [re'vɔlvər] *m* (-s;-) revolver
Revol'verblatt *n* (coll) scandal sheet
Revol'verschnauze ƒ (coll) lip, sass
Re·vue [re'vy] ƒ (-;-vuen ['vy·ən]) review; (theat) revue
Rezensent –in [retsen'zɛnt(ɪn)] §7 *mƒ* reviewer, critic
rezensieren [retsen'zirən] *tr* review
Rezension [retsen'zjon] ƒ (-;-en) review
Rezept [re'tsɛpt] *n* (-[e]s;-e) (culin) recipe; (med) prescription
rezitieren [retsɪ'tirən] *tr* recite
Rhabarber [ra'barbər] *m* (-s;) rhubarb
Rhapso·die [rapsɔ'di] ƒ (-;-dien ['di·ən]) rhapsody

Rhein [raɪn] *m* (-[e]s;) Rhine
Rhesusfaktor ['rezusfaktər] *m* (-s;) Rh factor
Rhetorik [rɛ'torɪk] *f* (-;) rhetoric
rhetorisch [rɛ'torɪʃ] *adj* rhetorical
rheumatisch [rɔɪ'matɪʃ] *adj* rheumatic
Rheumatismus [rɔɪma'tɪsmʊs] *m* (-;) rheumatism
rhythmisch ['rytmɪʃ] *adj* rhythmical
Rhyth‧mus ['rytmʊs] *m* (-;-men [mən]) rhythm
Richtbeil ['rɪçtbaɪl] *n* executioner's ax
Richtblei ['rɪçtblaɪ] *n* plummet
richten ['rɪçtən] *tr* arrange, adjust; put in order; *(lenken)* direct; *(Waffe, Fernrohr)* (auf *acc*) point (at), aim (at); *(Bitte, Brief, Frage, Rede)* (an *acc*) address (to); *(Augenmerk, Streben)* (auf *acc*) concentrate (on), focus (on); *(Bett)* make; *(Essen)* prepare; *(ausbessern)* fix; *(gerade biegen)* straighten; *(jur)* judge, sentence; *(mil)* dress; **zugrunde r.** ruin || *ref* (auf *acc*, gegen) be directed (at); **das richtet sich ganz danach, ob** it all depends on whether; **sich** [*dat*] **die Haare r.** do one's hair; **sich r. nach** follow the example of; **sich selbst r.** commit suicide || *intr* judge, sit in judgment
Rich'ter *m* (-s;-) judge
Rich'teramt *n* judgeship
Rich'terin *f* (-;-nen) judge
Rich'terkollegium *n* (jur) bench
rich'terlich *adj* judicial
Rich'terspruch *m* judgment; sentence
Rich'terstand *m* judiciary
Rich'terstuhl *m* tribunal, bench
richtig ['rɪçtɪç] *adj* right, correct; *(echt)* real, genuine; *(genau)* exact; *(Zeit)* proper || *adv* right, really, downright; **die Uhr geht r.** the clock keeps good time; **und r., da kam sie!** and sure enough, there she was!
rich'tiggehend *adj* *(Uhr)* keeping good time; (fig) regular
Rich'tigkeit *f* (-;) correctness; accuracy
rich'tigstellen *tr* rectify
Richtlinien ['rɪçtlinjən] *pl* guidelines
Richtlot ['rɪçtlot] *n* plumbline
Richtmaß ['rɪçtmas] *n* standard, gauge
Richtplatz ['rɪçtplats] *m* place of execution
Richtpreis ['rɪçtpraɪs] *n* standard price
Richtschnur ['rɪçtʃnur] *f* plumbline; (fig) guiding principle
Richtschwert ['rɪçtʃvert] *n* executioner's sword
Richtstätte ['rɪçtʃtɛtə] *f* place of execution
Rich'tung *f* (-;-en) direction; *(Weg)* course; *(Entwicklung)* trend; *(Einstellung)* slant, view
Rich'tungsanzeiger *m* (aut) direction signal
Richtwaage ['rɪçtvagə] *f* level
rieb [rip] *pret* of **reiben**
riechen ['riçən] §102 *tr* smell; (fig) stand; **kein Pulver r. können** have no guts || *intr* smell; **r. an** (*dat*) sniff at; **r. nach** smell of
Riechsalz ['riçzalts] *n* smelling salts

rief [rif] *pret* of **rufen**
Riefe ['rifə] *f* (-;-n) groove; (archit) flute
Riege ['rigə] *f* (-;-n) (gym) squad
Riegel ['rigəl] *m* (-s;-) bolt; *(Seife)* cake; *(Schokolade)* bar
riegeln ['rigəln] *tr* bolt, bar
Riemen ['rimən] *m* (-s;-) strap; *(Leib-, Trieb-)* belt; *(Ruder)* oar; *(e-s Gewehrs)* sling
Rie'menscheibe *f* pulley
Ries [ris] *n* (-es;-e) ream *(of one thousand sheets)*
Riese ['rizə] *m* (-;-n) giant
rieseln ['rizəln] *intr* (HABEN & SEIN) trickle; *(Bach)* purl || *impers—es* **rieselt** it is drizzling
Rie'selregen *m* drizzle
Rie'senbomber *m* superbomber
Rie'senerfolg *m* smash hit
rie'sengroß' *adj* gigantic
rie'senhaft *adj* gigantic
Rie'senrad *n* Ferris wheel
Rie'senschlange *f* boa constrictor
Rie'sentanne *f* (bot) sequoia
riesig ['rizɪç] *adj* gigantic, huge || *adv* (coll) awfully
Riesin ['rizɪn] *f* (-;-nen) giant
riet [rit] *pret* of **raten**
Riff [rɪf] *n* (-[e]s;-e) reef
Rille ['rɪlə] *f* (-;-n) groove; small furrow; (archit) flute
Rimesse [rɪ'mɛsə] *f* (-;-n) (com) remittance
Rind [rɪnt] *n* (-[e]s;-er) head of cattle; **Rinder** cattle
Rinde ['rɪndə] *f* (-;-n) rind; *(Baum-)* bark; *(Brot-)* crust; (anat) cortex
Rin'derbraten *m* roast beef
Rin'derbremse *f* horsefly
Rin'derherde *f* herd of cattle
Rin'derhirt *m* cowboy
Rind'fleisch *n* beef
Rinds'leder *n* cowhide
Rinds'lendenstück *n* rump steak, tenderloin
Rinds'rückenstück *n* sirloin of beef
Rind'vieh *n* cattle; (sl) idiot
Ring [rɪŋ] *m* (-[e]s;-e) ring; *(Kreis)* circle; *(Kettenglied)* link; *(Kartell)* combine; (astr) halo
Ringel ['rɪŋəl] *m* (-s;) small ring; *(Locke)* ringlet, curl
Rin'gelblume *f* marigold
ringeln ['rɪŋəln] *tr* & *ref* curl
Rin'gelreihen *m* ring-around-the-rosy
Rin'gelspiel *n* merry-go-round
ringen [rɪŋən] §142 *tr* wrestle; *(Wäsche, Hände)* wring; *(herauswinden)* wrest || *intr* wrestle; (fig) struggle
Rin'ger –in §6 *mf* wrestler
Ring'kampf *m* wrestling match
Ring'mauer *f* town wall, city wall
Ring'richter *m* (box) referee
rings [rɪŋs] *adv* around; **r. um all** around
Ring'schlüssel *m* socket wrench
rings'herum', rings'um', rings'umher' *adv* all around
Rinne ['rinə] *f* (-;-n) groove; *(Strombett)* channel; *(Leitung)* duct; *(Gosse)* gutter; *(Erdfurche)* furrow

rinnen ['rɪnən] §121 *intr* (SEIN) run, flow; trickle || *intr* (HABEN) leak
Rinnsal ['rɪnzɑl] *n* (-[e]s;-e) little stream
Rinn'stein *m* gutter; (*Ausgußbecken*) sink; (*unterirdisch*) culvert
Rippchen ['rɪpçən] *n* (-s;-) cutlet
Rippe ['rɪpə] *f* (-;-n) rib; (*Schokolade*) bar; (archit) groin
rippen ['rɪpən] *tr* rib, flute
Rip'penfellentzündung *f* pleurisy
Rip'penstoß *m* nudge (in the ribs)
Rip'penstück *n* loin end
Risi•ko ['rizɪko] *n* (-s;-s & -ken [kən]) risk; **ein R.** eingehen take a risk
riskant [rɪs'kant] *adj* risky
riskieren [rɪs'kirən] *tr* risk
riß [rɪs] *pret* of **reißen** || **Riß** *m* (Risses; Risse) tear, rip; (*Bruch*) fracture; (*Lücke*) gap; (*Kratzer*) scratch; (*Spalt*) split, cleft; (*Spaltung*) fissure; (*Sprung*) crack; (*Zeichnung*) sketch; (eccl) schism; (geol) crevasse
rissig ['rɪsɪç] *adj* torn; cracked; split; (*Haut*) chapped
Rist [rɪst] *m* (-es;-e) wrist; (*des Fußes*) instep
ritt [rɪt] *pret* of **reiten** || **Ritt** *m* (-[e]s; -e) ride
Ritter ['rɪtər] *m* (-s;-) knight; cavalier; **zum R.** schlagen knight
Rit'tergut *n* manor
Rit'terkreuz *n* (mil) Knight's Cross (*of the Iron Cross*)
rit'terlich *adj* knightly; (fig) chivalrous
Rit'terlichkeit *f* (-;) chivalry
Rit'terzeit *f* age of chivalry
rittlings ['rɪtlɪŋs] *adv*—**r. auf** (*dat* or *acc*) astride
Ritual [rɪtu'al] *n* (-s;-e & -ien [jən]) ritual
rituell [rɪtu'el] *adj* ritual
Ri•tus ['ritus] *m* (-;-ten [tən]) rite
Ritz [rɪts] *m* (-es;-e), **Ritze** ['rɪtsə] *f* (-;-en) crack, crevice; (*Schlitz*) slit; (*Schramme*) scratch
ritzen ['rɪtsən] *tr* scratch; (*Glas*) cut
Rivale [rɪ'valə] *m* (-n;-n), **Rivalin** [rɪ'valɪn] *f* (-;-nen) rival
rivalisieren [rɪvalɪ'zirən] *intr* be in rivalry; **r. mit** rival
Rivalität [rɪvalɪ'tɛt] *f* (-;-en) rivalry
Rizinusöl ['ritsɪnusøl] *n* castor oil
Robbe ['rɔbə] *f* (-;-n) seal
robben ['rɔbən] *intr* (HABEN & SEIN) (mil) crawl (*using one's elbows*)
Rob'benfang *m* seal hunt
Robe ['robə] *f* (-;-n) robe, gown
Roboter ['robotər] *m* (-s;-) robot
robust [ro'bust] *adj* robust
roch [rɔx] *pret* of **riechen**
röcheln ['rœçəln] *tr* gasp out || *intr* rattle (*in one's throat*)
rochieren [rɔ'ʃirən] *intr* (chess) castle
Rock [rɔk] *m* (-[e]s;⁀e) skirt; jacket
Rock'schoß *m* coattail
Rodel ['rodəl] *m* (-s;-) & *f* (-;-n) toboggan; (*mit Steuerung*) bobsled
Ro'delbahn *f* toboggan slide
rodeln ['rodəln] *intr* (HABEN & SEIN) toboggan
Ro'delschlitten *m* toboggan; bobsled

roden ['rodən] *tr* root out; (*Wald*) clear; (*Land*) make arable
Rogen ['rogən] *m* (-s;) roe, spawn
Roggen ['rɔgən] *m* (-s;) rye
roh [ro] *adj* raw; crude; (*Steine*) unhewn; (*Dielen*) bare; (fig) uncouth, brutal
Roh'bau *m* (-[e]s;-ten) rough brickwork
Roh'diamant *m* uncut diamond
Roh'einnahme *f* gross receipts
Roh'eisen *n* pig iron
Ro'heit *f* (-;) rawness, raw state; crudeness; brutality
Roh'entwurf *m* rough sketch
Roh'gewicht *n* gross weight
Roh'gewinn *m* gross profit
Roh'gummi *m* crude rubber
Roh'haut *f* rawhide
Roh'kost *f* uncooked vegetarian food
Rohling ['rolɪŋ] *m* (-s;-e) blank; slug; (fig) thug, hoodlum
Roh'material *n* raw material
Roh'öl *n* crude oil
Rohr [ror] *n* (-[e]s;-e) reed, cane; (*Röhre*) pipe, tube; (*Kanal*) duct, channel; (*Gewehrlauf*) barrel
Rohr'anschluß *m* pipe joint
Rohr'bogen *m* elbow
Röhre ['rørə] *f* (-;-n) tube, pipe; (electron) tube
Röh'renblitz *m* electronic flash
Röh'renblitzgerät *n* electronic flash unit
Rohr'leger *m* pipe fitter
Rohr'leitung *f* pipeline, main
Rohr'schäftung *f* sleeve joint
Rohr'schelle *f* pipe clamp
Rohr'zange *f* pipe wrench
Rohr'zucker *m* cane sugar
Roh'stoff *m* raw material
Rolladen (**Roll'laden**) *m* sliding shutter; sliding cover
Rollbahn ['rɔlban] *f* (aer) runway; (mil) road leading up to the front
Röllchen ['rœlçən] *n* (-s;-) caster
Rolldach ['rɔldax] *n* (aut) sun roof
Rolle ['rɔlə] *f* (-;-n) roll; (*Walze*) roller; (*Flaschenzug*) pulley; (*Spule*) spool, reel; (*unter Möbeln*) caster; (*Mangel*) mangle; (*Liste*) list, register; (theat) role; **aus der R.** fallen (fig) misbehave; **spielt keine R.!** never mind!, forget it!
rollen ['rɔlən] *tr* roll; (*auf Rädern*) wheel; (*Wäsche*) mangle; || *ref* curl up || *intr* (HABEN & SEIN) roll; (*Flugzeug*) taxi; (*Geschütze*) roar || **Rollen** *n*—**ins. R.** kommen get going
Rol'lenbesetzung *f* (theat) cast
Rol'lenlager *n* roller bearing
Rol'lenzug *m* block and tackle
Rol'ler *m* (-s;-) scooter; motor scooter
Roll'feld *n* (aer) runway
Roll'kragen *m* turtleneck
Roll'mops *m* pickled herring
Rollo ['rɔlo] *n* (-s;-s) (coll) blind, shade
Roll'schuh *m* roller skate; **R. laufen** roller-skate
Roll'schuhbahn *f* roller-skating rink
Roll'stuhl *m* wheelchair
Roll'treppe *f* escalator

Roll'wagen *m* truck
Rom [rom] *n* (-s;) Rome
Roman [rɔ'man] *m* (-s;-e) novel
Roman'folge *f* serial
roman'haft *adj* fictional
romanisch [rɔ'manɪʃ] *adj* (*Sprache*) Romance; (archit) Romanesque
Romanist -in [rɔma'nɪst(ɪn)] §7 *mf* scholar of Romance languages
Roman'schriftsteller -in §6 *mf* novelist
Romantik [rɔ'mantɪk] *f* (-;) Romanticism
romantisch [rɔ'mantɪʃ] *adj* romantic
Romanze [rɔ'mantsə] (-;-n) romance
Römer -in ['rømər(ɪn)] §6 *mf* Roman
römisch ['rømɪʃ] *adj* Roman
rö'misch-katho'lisch *adj* Roman Catholic
röntgen ['rœntgən] *tr* x-ray
Rönt'genapparat *m* x-ray machine
Rönt'genarzt *m*, **Rönt'genärztin** *f* radiologist
Rönt'genaufnahme *f*, **Rönt'genbild** *n* x-ray
Rönt'genstrahlen *pl* x-rays
rosa ['roza] *adj* pink ‖ **Rosa** *n* (-s; & -s) pink
Rose ['rozə] *f* (-;-n) rose
Ro'senkohl *m* Brussels sprouts
Ro'senkranz *m* (eccl) rosary
ro'senrot *adj* rosy, rose-colored
Ro'senstock *m* rosebush
rosig ['rozɪç] *adj* (& fig) rosy; (*Laune*) happy
Rosine [rɔ'zinə] *f* (-;-n) raisin
Roß [rɔs] *n* (**Rosses; Rosse**) horse; (sl) jerk; (poet) steed
Rost [rɔst] *m* (-es;) rust; mildew ‖ *m* (-es;-e) grate; grill; **auf dem R. braten** grill
Rost'braten *m* roast beef
Röstbrot ['røstbrot] *n* toast
rosten ['rɔstən] *intr* rust
rösten ['røstən] *tr* (*auf dem Rost*) grill; (*in der Pfanne*) roast; (*Brot*) toast; (*Mais*) pop; (*Kaffee*) roast
Rö'ster *m* (-s;-) roaster; toaster
Rost'fleck *m* rust stain
rost'frei *adj* rust-proof; (*Stahl*) stainless
rostig ['rɔstɪç] *adj* rusty, corroded
rot [rot] *adj* (**röter** ['røtər]; **röteste** ['røtəstə] §9) red ‖ **Rot** *n* (-es;) red; (*Schminke*) rouge
Rotation [rɔta'tsion] *f* (-;-en) rotation
Rotations'maschine *f* rotary press
rotbäckig ['rotbɛkɪç] *adj* red-cheeked
Rot'dorn *m* (bot) pink hawthorn
Röte ['røtə] *f* (-;) red(ness); blush
Röteln ['røtəln] *pl* German measles
rotieren [rɔ'tirən] *intr* rotate
Rotkäppchen ['rotkɛpçən] *n* (-s;) Little Red Riding Hood
Rotkehlchen ['rotkelçən] *n* (-s;-) robin
rötlich ['røtlɪç] *adj* reddish
Ro·tor ['rotɔr] *m* (-s;-toren ['torən]) (aer) rotor; (elec) armature
Rot'schimmel *m* roan (*horse*)
Rot'tanne *f* spruce
Rotte ['rɔtə] *f* (-;-n) gang, mob
Rotz [rɔts] *m* (-es;-e) (sl) snot
rot'zig *adj* (sl) snotty

Rouleau [ru'lo] *n* (-s;-s) window shade
Route ['rutə] *f* (-;-n) route
Routine [ru'tinə] *f* (-;) routine; practice, experience
routiniert [rutɪ'nirt] *adj* experienced
Rübe ['rybə] *f* (-;-n) beet; **gelbe R.** carrot; **weiße R.** turnip
Rubin [ru'bin] *m* (-s;-e) ruby
Rubrik [ru'brik] *f* (-;-en) rubric; heading; (*Spalte*) column
ruchbar ['ruxbar] *adj* known, public
ruchlos ['ruxlos] *adj* wicked
Ruck [ruk] *m* (-[e]s;-e) jerk; yank; jolt; **auf e-n R.** at once; **mit e-m R.** in one quick move
Rück-, rück- [ryk] *comb.fm.* re-, back, rear; return
Rück'ansicht *f* rear view
Rück'antwort *f* reply; **Postkarte mit R.** prepaid reply postcard
rück'bezüglich *adj* (gram) reflexive
Rück'bleibsel *n* remainder
rücken ['rykən] *tr* move, shove ‖ *intr* (SEIN) move; (*Platz machen*) move over; (*marschieren*) march; **höher r.** be promoted; **näher r.** approach ‖ **Rücken** *m* (-s;-) back; (*Rückseite*) rear; (*der Nase*) bridge
Rückendeckung (Rük'kendeckung) *f* (fig) backing, support
Rückenlehne (Rük'kenlehne) *f* back rest
Rückenmark (Rük'kenmark) *n* spinal cord
Rückenschwimmen (Rük'kenschwimmen) *n* backstroke
Rückenwind (Rük'kenwind) *m* tail wind
Rückenwirbel (Rük'kenwirbel) *m* (anat) vertebra
rück'erstatten *tr* reimburse, refund
Rück'fahrkarte *f*, **Rück'fahrschein** *m* round-trip ticket
Rück'fahrt *f* return trip
Rück'fall *m* relapse
rück'fällig *adj* habitual, relapsing
rück'federnd *adj* resilient
Rück'flug *m* return flight
Rück'frage *f* further question
Rück'führung *f* repatriation
Rück'gabe *f* return, restitution
Rück'gang *m* return; regression; (*der Preise*) drop; (econ) recession
rückgängig ['rykgɛnɪç] *adj* retrogressive; dropping; **r. machen** cancel
rück'gewinnen §121 *tr* recover
Rück'grat *n* backbone, spine
Rück'griff *m* (auf *acc*) recourse (to)
Rück'halt *m* backing; (mil) reserves; **e-n R. an j-m haben** have s.o.'s backing; **ohne R.** without reservation
rück'haltlos *adj* frank, unreserved ‖ *adv* without reserve
Rück'handschlag *m* (tennis) back-hand stroke
Rück'kauf *m* repurchase
Rück'kehr *f* return; (fig) comeback
Rück'kopplung *f* (electron) feedback
Rück'lage *f* reserves, savings
Rück'lauf *m* reverse; (mil) recoil
Rück'läufer *m* letter returned to sender
rückläufig ['ryklɔɪfɪç] *adj* retrograde

Rück'licht n (aut) taillight
rücklings ['rʏklɪŋs] adv backwards
Rück'nahme f withdrawal, taking back
Rück'porto n return postage
Rück'prall m bounce, rebound, recoil
Rück'reise f return trip
Ruck'sack m knapsack
Rück'schau m—**R. halten auf** (acc) look back on
Rück'schlag m back stroke; (e–s Balles) bounce; (fig) setback
Rück'schluß m conclusion, inference
Rück'schritt m backward step; (fig) falling off, retrogression
Rück'seite f back; reverse; wrong side
Rück'sicht f regard, respect, consideration; **aus R. auf** (acc) out of consideration for; **in** (or **mit**) **R. auf** (acc) in regard to; **ohne R. auf** (acc) irrespective of; **R. nehmen auf** (acc) take into account, show consideration for
rück'sichtlich prep (genit) considering
rück'sichtslos adj inconsiderate; reckless; ruthless
rück'sichtsvoll adj considerate
Rück'sitz m (aut) rear seat
Rück'spiegel m (aut) rear-view mirror
Rück'spiel n return match
Rück'sprache f discussion; conference; **R. nehmen mit** consult with
Rück'stand m arrears; (Satz) sediment; (Rest) remainder; (von Aufträgen, usw.) backlog; (chem) residue
rück'ständig adj behind, in arrears; (Geld) outstanding; (Raten) delinquent; (altmodisch) backward
Rück'stau m back-up water
Rück'stelltaste f backspace key
Rück'stoß m repulsion; recoil, kick
Rückstrahler ['rʏkstralər] m (-s;-) reflector
Rück'strahlung f reflection
Rück'tritt m resignation
Rück'trittbremse f coaster brake
Rück'umschlag m return envelope
rückwärts ['rʏkverts] adv backward(s)
Rück'wärtsgang m (aut) reverse
Rück'weg m way back, return
ruck'weise adv by fits and starts
rück'wirken intr react
rück'wirkend adj retroactive
Rück'wirkung f (-;-en) reaction; repercussion
rück'zahlen tr repay, refund
Rück'zug m withdrawal; retreat; **zum R. blasen** sound the retreat
Rück'zugsgefecht n running fight
rüde ['rydə] adj rude, coarse || **Rüde** m (-n;-n) male (wolf, fox, etc.)
Rudel ['rudəl] n (-s;-) herd; flock; (von Wölfen, U-Booten) wolf pack
Ruder ['rudər] n (-s;-) (aer, naut) rudder; (naut) oar
Ru'derblatt n blade of an oar
Ru'derboot n rowboat
Ru'derer –in §6 mf rower
Ru'derklampe f oarlock
rudern ['rudərn] tr & intr row
Ru'derschlag m stroke of the oar
Ru'dersport m (sport) crew
Ruf [ruf] m (-[e]s;-e) call; shout, yell; (Berufung) vocation; (Nach-

rede) reputation; appointment; (com) credit
rufen ['rufən] §122 tr call; shout; **r. lassen** send for || intr call; shout
Ruf'mord m character assassination
Ruf'name m first name
Ruf'nummer f telephone number
Ruf'weite f—**in R. within** earshot
Ruf'zeichen n (rad) station identification; (telp) call sign
Rüge ['rygə] f (-;-n) reprimand
rügen ['rygən] tr reprimand
Ruhe ['ru·ə] f (-;) rest; quiet, calm; (Frieden) peace; (Stille) silence; **immer mit der R.!** (coll) take it easy!
ru'hebedürftig adj in need of rest
Ru'hegehalt n pension
Ru'hekur f rest cure
ru'helos adj restless
ruhen ['ru·ən] intr rest; sleep
Ru'hepause f pause, break
Ru'heplatz m resting place
Ru'hestand m retirement
Rü'hestätte f resting place
Ru'hestörer –in §6 mf disturber of the peace
Ru'hetag m day of rest, day off
Ru'hezeit f leisure
ruhig ['ru·ɪç] adj still, quiet; calm
Ruhm [rum] m (-[e]s;) glory, fame
rühmen ['rymən] tr praise || ref (genit) boast (about)
rühmlich ['rymlɪç] adj praiseworthy
ruhm'los adj inglorious
ruhmredig ['rumredɪç] adj vainglorious
ruhm'reich adj glorious
ruhm'voll adj famous, glorious
ruhm'würdig adj praiseworthy
Ruhr [rur] f (-;) dysentery; **Ruhr** (river)
Rührei ['ryraɪ] n scrambled egg
rühren ['ryrən] tr stir; touch; move; (Trommel) beat; **alle Kräfte r.** exert every effort || ref stir, move; get a move on; **rührt euch!** (mil) at ease! || intr stir, move; **r. an** (acc) touch; (fig) mention; **r. von** originate in
rührig ['ryrɪç] adj active; agile
Rührlöffel ['ryrlœfəl] m ladle
rührselig ['ryrzelɪç] adj sentimental
Rührstück ['ryrʃtʏk] n soap opera
Rüh'rung f (-;-en) emotion
Ruin [ru'in] m (-s;) ruin; decay
Ruine [ru'inə] f (-;-n) ruins; (fig) wreck
rui'nenhaft adj ruinous
ruinieren [ru·i'nirən] tr ruin
Rülps [rʏlps] m (-es;-e) belch
rülpsen ['rʏlpsən] intr belch
Rülp'ser m (-s;-) belch
Rum [rum] m (-s;-s) rum
Rumäne [ru'menə] m (-n;-n) Rumanian
Rumänien [ru'menjən] n (-s;) Rumania
Rumänin [ru'menɪn] f (-;-nen) Rumanian
rumänisch [ru'menɪʃ] adj Rumanian
Rummel ['ruməl] m (-s;) row; racket; hustle and bustle; **auf den R. gehen** go to the fair; **den ganzen R. kaufen** (coll) buy the works
Rum'melplatz m amusement park, fair
Rumor [ru'mor] m (-s;) noise, racket

Rumpel ['rumpəl] *f* (-;-n) scrub board
Rum'pelkammer *f* storage room, junk room
Rum'pelkasten *m* (aut) jalopy
rumpeln ['rumpəln] *tr* (*Wäsche*) scrub || *intr* rumble, rattle
Rumpf [rumpf] *m* (-[e]s;ᵕe) trunk, body; torso; (aer) fuselage; (naut) hull
rümpfen ['rympfən] *tr*—**die Nase r. über** (*acc*) turn up one's nose at
rund [runt] *adj* round; (*Absage*) flat || *adv* around; about, approximately; **r. um** around
Rund'blick *m* panorama
Rund'brief *m* circular letter
Runde ['rundə] *f* (-;-n) round; (box) round; (*beim Rennsport*) lap
runden ['rundən] *tr* make round; round off || *ref* become round
Rund'erlaß *m* circular
rund'erneuern *tr* (aut) retread; **runderneuerter Reifen** *m* retread
Rund'fahrt *f* sightseeing tour
Rund'flug *m* (aer) circuit
Rund'frage *f* questionnaire, poll
Rund'funk *m* radio; **im R.** on the radio
Rund'funkansage *f* radio announcement
Rund'funkansager –**in** §6 *mf* radio announcer
Rund'funkgerät *n* radio set
Rund'funkgesellschaft *f* broadcasting company
Rund'funkhörer –**in** §6 *mf* listener
Rund'funknetz *n* radio network
Rund'funksender *m* broadcasting station
Rund'funksendung *f* radio broadcast
Rund'funksprecher –**in** §6 *mf* announcer
Rund'funkwerbung *f* (rad) commercial
Rund'gang *m* tour; stroll
rund'heraus' *adv* plainly, flatly
rundherum' *adv* all around
rund'lich *adj* round; (*dick*) plump
Rund'reise *f* sightseeing tour
Rund'schau *f* panorama; (journ) news in brief
Rund'schreiben *n* circular letter
rundweg ['runt'vɛk] *adv* bluntly, flatly

Runzel ['runtsəl] *f* (-;-n) wrinkle
runzelig ['runtseliç] *adj* wrinkled
runzeln ['runtsəln] *tr* wrinkle; **die Brauen r.** knit one's brows; **die Stirn r.** frown || *ref* wrinkle
Rüpel ['rypəl] *m* (-s;-) boor
rü'pelhaft *adj* rude, boorish
rupfen ['rupfən] *tr* pluck; (fig) fleece
ruppig ['rupiç] *adj* shabby; (fig) rude
Ruprecht ['rupreçt] *m* (-s;)—**Knecht R.** Santa Claus
Ruß [rus] *m* (-es;) soot
Russe ['rusə] *m* (-n;-n) Russian
Rüssel ['rysəl] *m* (-s;-) snout; (*Elephanten-*) trunk; (coll) snout; (ent) proboscis
rußig ['rusiç] *adj* sooty
Russin ['rusin] *f* (-;-nen) Russian
russisch ['rusiʃ] *adj* Russian
Rußland ['ruslant] *n* (-s;) Russia
Rüst- [ryst] *comb.fm.* scaffolding; armament, munition
rüsten ['rystən] *tr* arm, equip; prepare || *ref* get ready || *intr* (zu) get ready (for); **zum Krieg r.** mobilize
Rüster ['rystər] *f* (-;-n) elm
rüstig ['rystiç] *adj* vigorous; alert
Rüst'kammer *f* armory, arsenal
Rü'stung *f* (-;-en) preparation; equipment; armament; mobilization; armor; implements; (archit) scaffolding
Rü'stungsbetrieb *m* munitions factory
Rü'stungsfertigung *f* war production
Rü'stungsindustrie *f* war industry
Rü'stungskontrolle *f* arms control
Rü'stungsmaterial *n* war materiel
Rü'stungsstand *m* state of preparedness
Rüst'zeug *n* kit; (fig) knowledge
Rute ['rutə] *f* (-;-n) rod; twig; tail; (anat) penis
Rutsch [rutʃ] *m* (-es;-e) slip, slide
Rutsch'bahn *f* slide; chute
Rutsche ['rutʃə] *f* (-;-n) slide; chute
rutschen ['rutʃən] *intr* (SEIN) slip, slide; (aut) skid
rutschig ['rutʃiç] *adj* slippery
rütteln ['rytəln] *tr* shake; jolt; (*Getreide*) winnow; (*aus dem Schlafe*) rouse || *intr*—**r. an** (*acc*) cause to rattle; (fig) try to undermine

S

S, s [ɛs] *invar n* S, s
SA *abbr* (mil) (*Sturmabteilung*) storm troopers
Saal [zɑl] *m* (-[e]s; **Säle** ['zɛlə]) hall
Saat [zɑt] *f* (-;-en) seed; (*Säen*) sowing; (*Getreide auf dem Halm*) crop(s); **die S. bestellen** sow
Saat'bestellung *f* sowing
Saat'kartoffel *f* seed potato
Sabbat ['zabat] *m* (-s;-e) Sabbath
Sabberei [zabə'rai] *f* (-;-en) drooling; (*Geschwätz*) drivel
sabbern ['zabərn] *intr* drool, drivel

Säbel ['zebəl] *m* (-s;) saber; **mit dem S. rasseln** (pol) rattle the saber
sä'belbeinig *adj* bowlegged
säbeln ['zebəln] *tr* (coll) hack
Sä'belrasseln *n* (pol) saber rattling
Sabotage [zabo'tɑʒə] *f* (-;-n) sabotage
Saboteur [zabo'tør] *m* (-s;-e) saboteur
sabotieren [zabo'tirən] *tr* sabotage
Saccharin [zaxa'rin] *n* (-s;) saccharin
Sach- [zax] *comb.fm.* of facts, factual
Sach'anlagevermögen *n* tangible fixed assets
Sach'bearbeiter –**in** §6 *mf* specialist

Sach'beschädigung *f* property damage
Sach'bezüge *pl* compensation in kind
Sach'buch *n* nonfiction (work)
Sach'darstellung *f* statement of facts
sach'dienlich *adj* relevant, pertinent
Sache ['zaxə] *f* (-;-n) thing, matter;
cause; (jur) case; bei der S. sein be
on the ball; beschlossene S. foregone
conclusion; die S. der Freiheit the
cause of freedom; große S. big affair; gute S. good cause; heikle S.
delicate point; in eigner S. on one's
own behalf; in Sachen X gegen Y
(jur) in the case of X versus Y;
meine sieben Sachen all my belongings; nicht bei der S. sein not be with
it; nicht zur S. gehörig irrelevant;
von der S. abkommen get off the
subject; zur S.! come to the point!
(parl) question!
sach'gemäß *adj* proper, pertinent || *adv*
in a suitable manner
Sach'kenner –in §6 *mf* expert
Sach'kenntnis *f,* Sach'kunde *f* expertise
sach'kundig *adj* expert || Sach'kundige
§5 *mf* expert
Sach'lage *f* state of affairs, circumstances
Sach'leistung *f* payment in kind
sach'lich *adj* (*treffend*) to the point;
(*gegenständlich*) objective; (*tatsächlich*) factual; (*unparteiisch*) impar-
tial; (*nüchtern*) matter-of-fact || *adv*
to the point
sächlich ['zeçlıç] *adj* (gram) neuter
Sach'lichkeit *f* (-;) objectivity; reality;
impartiality; matter-of-factness
Sach'register *n* index
Sach'schaden *m* property damage
Sach'schadenersatz *m* indemnity (*for
property damage*)
Sachse ['zaksə] *m* (-n;-n) Saxon
Sachsen ['zaksən] *n* (-s;) Saxony
sächsisch ['zeksıʃ] *adj* Saxon
sacht(e) ['zaxt(ə)] *adj* soft, gentle;
(*langsam*) slow || *adv* gingerly; im-
mer sacht! easy does it!
Sach'verhalt *m* facts of the case
Sach'vermögen *n* real property
sach'verständig *adj* experienced ||
Sachverständige §5 *mf* expert
Sach'wert *m* actual value; Sachwerte
material assets
Sach'wörterbuch *n* encyclopedia
Sack [zak] *m* (-[e]s;≃e) sack, bag;
pocket; j–n in den S. stecken (coll)
be way above s.o.; mit S. und Pack
bag and baggage
Säckel ['zekəl] *m* (-s;-) little bag;
pocket; purse
sacken ['zakən] *tr* bag || *ref* be baggy
|| *intr* (SEIN) sag; (archit) settle;
(naut) founder
Sack'gasse *f* blind alley, dead end;
(fig) stalemate, dead end
Sack'leinwand *f* burlap
Sack'pfeife *f* bagpipe
Sack'tuch *n* handkerchief
Sadist –in [za'dıst(ın)] §7 *mf* sadist
sadistisch [za'dıstıʃ] *adj* sadistic
säen ['ze·ən] *tr & intr* sow
Saffian ['zafjan] *m* (-s;) morocco

Safran ['zafran] *m* (-s;-e) saffron
Saft [zaft] *m* (-[e]s;≃e) juice; sap;
(culin) gravy
saftig ['zaftıç] *adj* juicy; (*Witze*) spicy
saft'los *adj* juiceless; (fig) wishy-washy
saft'reich *adj* juicy, succulent
Sage ['zagə] *f* (-;-n) legend, saga
Säge ['zegə] *f* (-;-n) saw
Sä'geblatt *n* saw blade
Sä'gebock *m* sawhorse, sawbuck
Sä'gefisch *m* sawfish
Sä'gemehl *n* sawdust
sagen ['zagən] *tr* say; (*mitteilen*) tell;
das hat nichts zu s. that's neither
here nor there; das will nicht s. that
is not to say; gesagt, getan no sooner
said than done; j–m s. lassen send
s.o. word; laß dir gesagt sein let it
be a warning to you; sich [*dat*]
nichts s. lassen not listen to reason
sägen ['zegən] *tr* saw || *intr* saw; (coll)
snore, cut wood
sa'genhaft *adj* legendary
Sägespäne ['zegəʃpenə] *pl* sawdust
Sä'gewerk *n* sawmill
sah [za] *pret* of sehen
Sahne ['zanə] *f* (-;) cream
Saison [se'zõ] *f* (-;-s) season
Saison– *comb.fm.* seasonal
saison'bedingt, saison'mäßig *adj* seasonal
Saite ['zaıtə] *f* (-;-n) string, chord
Sai'teninstrument *n* string instrument
Sakko ['zako] *m & n* (-s;-s) suit coat
Sak'koanzug *m* sport suit
Sakrament [zakra'ment] *n* (-[e]s;-e)
sacrament; das S. des Altars the
Eucharist || *interj* (sl) dammit!
Sakrileg [zakrı'lek] *n* (-s;-e) sacrilege
Sakristan [zakrıs'tan] *m* (-s;-e) sac-
ristan
Sakristei [zakrıs'taı] *f* (-;-en) sacristy
Säkular– [zekular] *comb.fm.* secular;
centennial
säkularisieren [zekuları'zirən] *tr* secu-
larize
Salami [za'lami] *f* (-;-s) salami
Salat [za'lat] *m* (-[e]s;-e) salad; let-
tuce; gemischter S. tossed salad
Salat'soße *f* salad dressing
salbadern [zal'badərn] *intr* talk hypo-
critically, put on the dog
Salbe ['zalbə] *f* (-;-n) salve
salben ['zalbən] *tr* put salve on; anoint
Sal'bung *f* (-;-en) anointing
sal'bungsvoll *adj* unctuous
saldieren [zal'dirən] *tr* (com) balance
Sal·do ['zaldo] *m* (-s;-s & di [di])
(acct) balance; e–n S. aufstellen (or
ziehen) strike a balance; e–n S. ausweisen show a balance
Saline [za'linə] *f* (-;-n) saltworks
Salmiak [zal'mjak] *m* (-s;) ammonium
chloride, sal ammoniac
Salmiak'geist *m* ammonia
Salon [za'lõ] *m* (-s;-s) salon; parlor,
living room
salon'fähig *adj* (*Aussehen*) presentable;
(*Ausdruck*) fit for polite company
Salon'held *m,* Salon'löwe *m* ladies' man
salopp [za'lɔp] *adj* sloppy; (*ungezwungen*) casual
Salpeter [zal'petər] *m* (-s;) saltpeter

salpeterig [zal'petərıç] *adj* nitrous
Salpe'tersäure *f* nitric acid
Salto ['zalto] *m* (-s;-s) somersault
Salut [za'lut] *m* (-[e]s;-e) salute; **S.**
 schießen fire a salute
salutieren [zalu'tirən] *tr & intr* salute
Salve ['zalvə] *f* (-;-n) volley, salvo
Salz [zalts] *n* (-es;-e) salt
Salz'bergwerk *n* salt mine
Salz'brühe *f* brine
salzen ['zaltsən] *tr* salt
Salz'faß *n* salt shaker
Salz'fleisch *n* salted meat
Salz'gurke *f* pickle
salz'haltig *adj* saline
Salz'hering *m* pick.ed herring
salzig ['zaltsıç] *adj* salty; saline
Salz'kartoffeln *pl* boiled potatoes
Salz'lake *f* brine
Salz'säure *f* hydrochloric acid, muriatic
 acid
Salz'sole *f* brine
Salz'werk *n* salt works
Samariter –in [zama'ritər(ın)] §6 *mf*
 Samaritan
Same ['zamə] *m* (-ns;-n), **Samen**
 ['zamən] *m* (-s;-) seed; (biol) semen
Sa'menkorn *n* grain of seed
Sa'menstaub *m* pollen
Samentierchen ['zaməntirçən] *n* (-s;-)
 spermatozoon
sämig ['zemıç] *adj* (culin) thick,
 creamy
Sämischleder ['zemıʃledər] *n* chamois
Sämling ['zemlıŋ] *m* (-s;-e) seedling
Sammel– [zaməl] *comb.fm.* collecting,
 collective
Sam'melbatterie *f* storage battery
Sam'melbecken *n* reservoir; storage
 tank
Sam'melbegriff *m* collective noun
Sam'melbüchse *f* poor box
Sam'mellinse *f* convex lens
sammeln ['zaməln] *tr* gather; collect;
 (*Aufmerksamkeit, Truppen*) concen-
 trate || *ref* gather; compose oneself;
 sich wieder s. (mil) reassemble
Sam'melname *m* collective noun
Sam'melplatz *m* collecting point; meet-
 ing place; (mil) rendezvous
Sam'melverbindung *f* conference call
Sam'melwerk *n* compilation
Sammler ['zamlər] *m* (-s;-) collector;
 compiler; (elec) storage cell
Samm'lung *f* (-;-en) collection; (*Zusammenstellung*) compilation; (*Fassung*) composure; concentration
Samstag ['zamstak] *m* (-[e]s;-e) Sat-
 urday
samt [zamt] *adv—s.* **und sonders** each
 and everyone, without exception ||
 prep (*dat*) together with || **Samt** *m*
 (-[e]s;-e) velvet
samt'artig *adj* velvety
sämtlich ['zemtlıç] *adj* all, complete ||
 adv all together
Sanato•rium [zana'torjum] *n* (-s;-rien
 [rjən]) sanitarium
Sand [zant] *m* (-[e]s;-e) sand; **im
 Sande verlaufen** (fig) peter out
Sandale [zan'dalə] *f* (-;-n) sandal
Sand'bahn *f* (sport) dirt track
Sand'bank *f* (-;ᵋe) sandbank

Sand'boden *m* sandy soil
Sand'düne *f* sand dune
Sand'grube *f* sand pit
sandig ['zandıç] *adj* sandy
Sand'kasten *m* sand box
Sand'korn *n* grain of sand
Sand'mann *m* (-[e]s;) (*fig*) sandman
Sand'papier *n* sandpaper; **mit S. ab-
 schleifen** sand, sandpaper
Sand'sack *m* sandbag
Sand'stein *m* sandstone
Sand'steingebäude *n* brownstone
sand'strahlen *tr* sandblast
Sand'sturmgebiet *n* dust bowl
sandte ['zantə] *pret* of **senden**
Sand'torte *f* sponge cake
Sand'uhr *f* hour glass
Sand'wüste *f* sandy desert
sanft [zanft] *adj* soft, gentle
Sänfte ['zenftə] *f* (-;-n) sedan chair
Sanft'mut *f* gentleness, meekness
sanft'mütig *adj* gentle, meek, mild
sang [zaŋ] *pret* of **singen** || **Sang** *m*
 (-[e]s;ᵋe) song; **mit S. und Klang**
 (fig) with great fanfare
sang-'und klang'los *adv* unceremoni-
 ously
Sänger ['zeŋər] *m* (-s;-) singer
Sän'gerchor *m* glee club
Sängerin ['zeŋərın] *f* (-;-nen) singer
Sanguiniker [zaŋ'gwinıkər] *m* (-s;-)
 optimist
sanguinisch [zaŋ'gwinıʃ] *adj* sanguine
sanieren [za'nirən] *tr* cure; improve
 the sanitary conditions of; disinfect;
 (fin) put on a firm basis
Sanie'rung *f* (-;-en) restoration; reorganization
sanitär [zanı'ter] *adj* sanitary
Sanitäter [zanı'tetər] *m* (-s;-) first-
 aid-man; (mil) medic
Sanitäts– [zanıtets] *comb.fm.* first-aid,
 medical
Sanitäts'korps *n* army medical corps
Sanitäts'soldat *m* medic
Sanitäts'wache *f* first-aid station
Sanitäts'wagen *m* ambulance
Sanitäts'zug *m* hospital train
sank [zaŋk] *pret* of **sinken**
Sanka ['zaŋka] *m* (-s;-s) (**Sanitäts-
 kraftwagen**) field ambulance
Sankt [zaŋkt] *invar mf* Saint
Sanktion [zaŋk'tsjon] *f* (-;-en) sanc-
 tion
sanktionieren [zaŋktsjo'nirən] *tr* sanc-
 tion
sann [zan] *pret* of **sinnen**
Saphir ['zafir] *m* (-s;-e) sapphire
sapperment [zapər'ment] *interj* the
 deuce!
Sardelle [zar'delə] *f* (-;-n) anchovy
Sardine [zar'dinə] *f* (-;-n) sardine
Sardinien [zar'dinjən] *n* (-s;) Sardinia
sardinisch [zar'dinıʃ] *adj* Sardinian
Sarg [zark] *m* (-[e]s;ᵋe) coffin
Sarg'tuch *n* pall
Sarkasmus [zar'kasmus] *m* (-;) sarcasm
sarkastisch [zar'kastıʃ] *adj* sarcastic
Sarkophag [zarko'fak] *m* (-s;-e) sar-
 cophagus
saß [zas] *pret* of **sitzen**
Satan ['zatan] *m* (-s;-e) Satan

satanisch [za'tɑnɪʃ] *adj* satanic(al)
Satellit [zatɛ'lit] *m* (-en;-en) satellite
Satin [sa'tē] *m* (-s;-s) satin
Satire [za'tirə] *f* (-;-n) satire
Satiriker –**in** [za'tirɪkər(ɪn)] §6 *mf* satirist
satirisch [za'tirɪʃ] *adj* satirical
satt [zat] *adj* satisfied; satiated; (*Farben*) deep, rich; (chem) saturated; **etw s. bekommen** (or **haben**) be fed up with s.th.; **ich bin s.** I've had enough; **sich s. essen** eat one's fill
Sattel ['zatəl] *m* (-s;⁼) saddle
sat'telfest *adj* (fig) well-versed
Sat'telgurt *m* girth
satteln ['zatəln] *tr* saddle
Sat'telschlepper *m* semi-trailer
Sat'teltasche *f* saddlebag
Satt'heit *f* (-;) saturation; (*der Farben*) richness
sättigen ['zetɪgən] *tr* satisfy, satiate; saturate
Sät'tigung *f* (-;) satiation; saturation
Sattler ['zatlər] *m* (-s;-) harness maker
sattsam ['zatzɑm] *adv* sufficiently
saturieren [zatʊ'rirən] *tr* saturate
Satz [zats] *m* (-es;⁼e) sentence; clause; phrase; (*Behauptung*) proposition; (*Bodensatz*) grounds; sediment; (*Betrag*) amount; (*Tarif*) rate; (*Gebühr*) fee; (*Garnitur*) set; (*Sprung*) leap; (*Wette*) stake; (*Menge*) batch; (math) theorem; (mus) movement; (tennis) set; (typ) typesetting, composition; **e–en S. machen** jump; **e–n S. aufstellen** set down an article of faith; **einfacher S.** simple sentence; **hauptwörtlicher S.** substantive clause; **in S. gehen** go to press; **verkürzter S.** phrase; **zum S. von** at the rate of; **zusammengesetzter S.** compound sentence
Satz'aussage *f* gram) predicate
Satz'bau *m* (-[e]s;) (gram) construction
Satz'gefüge *n* complex sentence
Satz'gegenstand *m* (gram) subject
Satz'lehre *f* syntax
Satz'teil *m* (gram) part of speech
Sat'zung *f* (-;-en) rule, regulation; (*Vereins-*) bylaw; statute
sat'zungsgemäß, sat'zungsmäßig *adj* statutory, according to the bylaws
Satz'zeichen *n* punctuation mark
Sau [zau] *f* (-;⁼e) sow; (pej) pig; **wie e–e gesengte Sau fahren** drive like a maniac
Sau'arbeit *f* (coll) sloppy work; (coll) tough job; (coll) dirty job
sauber ['zaubər] *adj* clean; exact
säuberlich ['zɔibərlɪç] *adj* clean, neat; (*anständig*) decent
sau'bermachen *tr* clean, clean up
säubern ['zɔibərn] *tr* clean; (*freimachen*) clear; (*Buch*) expurgate; (mil) mop up; (pol) purge
Säu'berungsaktion *f* (mil) mopping-up operation; (pol) purge
Sau'borste *f* hog bristle
Sauce ['zosə] *f* (-;-n) sauce; gravy; (*Salat-*) dressing
sau'dumm' *adj* (coll) awfully dumb
sauer ['zaʊ·ər] *adj* sour

Sau'erbraten *m* braised beef soaked in vinegar
Sauerei [zaʊ·ə'raɪ] *f* (-;-en) filth, filthy joke
Sau'erkohl *m*, **Sau'erkraut** *n* sauerkraut
säuerlich ['zɔɪ·ərlɪç] *adj* sourish, acidulous; (*Lächeln*) forced
säuern ['zɔɪ·ərn] *tr* sour; (*Teig*) leaven || *intr* turn sour, acidify
Sau'erstoff *m* (-[e]s;) oxygen
Sau'erstofflasche *f* oxygen tank
Sau'erteig *m* leaven
Sau'ertopf *m* (coll) sourpuss
Sau'erwasser *n* sparkling water
Saufaus ['zaufaus] *m* (-;-), **Saufbold** ['zaufbɔlt] *m* (-[e]s;-e), **Saufbruder** ['zaufbrudər] *m* (coll) booze hound
saufen ['zaufən] §124 *tr* drink, guzzle || *intr* drink; (sl) booze
Säufer –**in** ['zɔɪfər(ɪn)] §6 *mf* drunkard
Saufgelage ['zaufgəlɑgə] *n* booze party
Sau'fraß *m* terrible food, slop
Säugamme ['zɔɪkamə] *f* wet nurse
saugen ['zaugən] §109 & §125 *tr* suck || *ref*—**sich** [*dat*] **etw aus den Fingern s.** invent s.th., make up s.th.
säugen ['zɔɪgən] *tr* suckle, nurse
Sauger ['zaugər] *m* (-s;-) sucker; nipple; pacifier
Säuger ['zɔɪgər] *m* (-s;-), **Säugetier** ['zɔɪgətir] *n* mammal
Saug'flasche *f* baby bottle
Säugling ['zɔɪklɪŋ] *m* (-s;-e) baby
Säug'lingsausstattung *f* layette
Säug'lingsheim *n* nursery
Sau'glück *n* (coll) dumb luck
Saug'napf *m* suction cup
Saug'pumpe *f* suction pump
Saug'watte *f* absorbent cotton
Saug'wirkung *f* suction
Sau'hund *m* (sl) louse, dirty dog
Sau'igel *m* (sl) dirty guy
sauigeln ['zau·igəln] *intr* (sl) tell dirty jokes
Sau'kerl *m* (sl) cad, skunk
Säule ['zɔɪlə] *f* (-;-n) column; (& fig) pillar; (elec) dry battery; (phys) pile
Säu'lenfuß *m* base of a column
Säu'lengang *m* colonnade, peristyle
Säu'lenhalle *f* portico, gallery
Säu'lenkapitell *n*, **Säu'lenknauf** *m*, **Säu'lenknopf** *m* (archit) capital
Säu'lenschaft *m* shaft of a column
Säu'lenvorbau *m* portico, (front) porch
Saum [zaum] *m* (-[e]s;⁼e) seam, hem; (*Rand*) border; (*e–r Stadt*) outskirts
säumen ['zɔɪmən] *tr* hem; border; (*Straßen*) line || *intr* tarry
Sau'mensch *n* (vulg) slut
säumig ['zɔɪmɪç] *adj* tardy
Säumnis ['zɔɪmnɪs] *f* (-;-nisse) dilatoriness; (*Verzug*) delay; (*Nichter-füllung*) default
Saum'pfad *m* mule track
Saum'tier *n* beast of burden
Sau'pech *n* (coll) rotten luck
Säure ['zɔɪrə] *f* (-;-n) sourness; acidity; tartness; (chem) acid
Säuregur'kenzeit *f* slack season
Säu'remesser *m* (aut) battery tester
Saures ['zaʊrəs] *n*—**gib ihm S.** (coll) give it to 'im!

Saus [zaʊs] *m*—in S. und Braus leben live high

säuseln ['zɔɪzəln] *intr* rustle; **mit säuselnder Stimme** in whispers

sausen ['zaʊsən] *intr* (*Wind, Kugel*) whistle; (*Wasser*) gush ‖ *intr* (SEIN) rush, whiz ‖ *impers*—**mir saust es in den Ohren** my ears are ringing ‖ **Sausen** *n* (–s;) rush and roar; humming, ringing (*in the ears*)

Sau'stall *m* pigsty; (fig) terrible mess

Sau'wetter *n* (coll) nasty weather

Sau'wirtschaft *f* (coll) helluva mess

sau'wohl' *adj* (coll) in great shape

Saxophon [zaksɔ'fon] *n* (–s;–e) saxophone

Schabe ['ʃabə] *f* (–;–n) cockroach

Schabeisen ['ʃapaɪzən] *n* scraper

schaben ['ʃabən] *tr* scrape; grate, rasp

Scha'ber *m* (–s;–) scraper

Schabernack ['ʃabərnak] *m* (–[e]s;–e) practical joke

schäbig ['ʃebɪç] *adj* shabby; (fig) mean

Schablone [ʃa'blonə] *f* (–;–n) (*Muster*) pattern, model; (*Matrize*) stencil; (*mechanische Arbeit*) routine; **nach der S.** mechanically

schablo'nenhaft, schablo'nenmäßig *adj* mechanical; (*Arbeit*) routine

Schach [ʃax] *n* (–[e]s;) chess; **in S. halten** (fig) keep in check; **S. bieten** (or **geben**) check; (fig) defy; **S. dem König!** check!

Schach'brett *n* chessboard

Schacher ['ʃaxər] *m* (–s;) haggling; **S. treiben** haggle, huckster

Schach'feld *n* (chess) square

Schach'figur *f* chessman; (fig) pawn

schach'matt' *adj* checkmated; (fig) beat

Schach'partie *f*, **Schach'spiel** *n* game of chess

Schacht [ʃaxt] *m* (–[e]s;–e) shaft; manhole

Schacht'deckel *m* manhole cover

Schachtel ['ʃaxtəl] *f* (–;–n) box; (*von Zigaretten*) pack; (fig) frump

Schach'zug *m* (chess & fig) move

schade ['ʃadə] *adj* too bad

Schädel ['ʃedəl] *m* (–s;–) skull; **mir brummt** (or **dröhnt**) **der S.** my head is throbbing

Schä'delbruch *m*, **Schä'delfraktur** *f* skull fracture

Schä'delhaut *f* scalp

Schä'delknochen *m* cranium

Schä'dellehre *f* phrenology

schaden ['ʃadən] *intr* do harm; (*dat*) harm, damage; **das wird ihr nichts s.** it serves her right; **ein Versuch kann nichts s.** there's no harm in trying ‖ *impers*—**es schadet nichts** it doesn't matter ‖ **Schaden** *m* (–s;–) damage, injury; (*Verlust*) loss; (*Nachteil*) disadvantage; **er will deinen S. nicht** he means you no harm; **j–m S. zufügen** inflict loss on s.o.; (coll) give s.o. a black eye; **mit S. verkaufen** sell at a loss; **S. nehmen** come to grief; **zu meinem S.** to my detriment

Scha'denersatz *m* compensation, damages; (*Wiedergutmachen*) reparation; **S. leisten** pay damages; make amends

Scha'denersatzklage *f* damage suit

Scha'denfreude *f* gloating

scha'denfroh *adj* gloating, malicious

Scha'denversicherung *f* comprehensive insurance

schadhaft ['ʃathaft] *adj* damaged; (*Material*) faulty; (*Zähne*) decayed; (*baufällig*) dilapidated

schädigen ['ʃedɪgən] *tr* inflict financial damage on; (*benachteiligen*) wrong; (*Ruf*) damage; (*Rechte*) infringe on

Schä'digung *f* (–;) damage

schädlich ['ʃetlɪç] *adj* harmful; (*nachteilig*) detrimental; (*verderblich*) noxious; (*Speise*) unwholesome

Schädling ['ʃetlɪŋ] *m* (–s;–e) (*Person*) parasite; (ent) pest; **Schädlinge** vermin

Schäd'lingsbekämpfung *f* pest control

schadlos ['ʃatlos] *adj*—**sich an j–m s. halten** make s.o. pay (*for an injury done to oneself*); **sich für etw s. halten** compensate oneself for s.th., make up for s.th.

Schaf [ʃaf] *n* (–[e]s;–e) sheep; (fig) blockhead, dope

Schaf'bock *m* ram

Schäfchen ['ʃefçən] *n* (–s;–) lamb; (*Wolken*) fleecy clouds

Schäf'chenwolke *f* fleecy cloud

Schäfer ['ʃefər] *m* (–s;–) shepherd

Schä'ferhund *m* sheep dog; **deutscher S.** German shepherd

Schaf'fell *n* sheepskin

schaffen ['ʃafən] §109 *tr* do; get; put; manage, manage to do; (*erreichen*) accomplish; (*liefern*) supply; (*erschaffen*) bring, cause; (*wegbringen*) take; **auf die Seite s.** put aside; (*betrügerisch*) embezzle; **ich schaffe es noch, daß I'll** see to it that; **Rat s.** know what to do; **vom Halse s.** get off one's neck ‖ §126 *tr* create; produce; **wie geschaffen sein** für cut out for ‖ §109 *intr* do; (*arbeiten*) work; **j–m viel zu s. machen** cause s.o. a lot of trouble; **sich zu s. machen** be busy, putter around

schaf'fend *adj* working; (*schöpferisch*) creative; (*produktiv*) productive

Schaf'fensdrang *m* creative urge

Schaf'fenskraft *f* creative power

Schaffner ['ʃafnər] *m* (–s;–) (rr) conductor

Schaf'fung *f* (–;–en) creation

Schaf'hirt *m* shepherd

Schaf'pelz *m* sheepskin coat

Schaf'pferch *m* sheepfold

Schafs'kopf *m* (sl) mutton-head

Schaf'stall *m* sheepfold

Schaft [ʃaft] *m* (–[e]s;–e) shaft; (*e–r Feder*) stem; (*e–s Gewehrs*) stock; (*e–s Ankers*) shank; (bot) stem, stalk

Schaft'stiefel *m* high boot

Schaf'zucht *f* sheep raising

Schakal [ʃa'kal] *m* (–s;–e) jackal

schäkern ['ʃekərn] *intr* joke around; flirt

schal [ʃal] *adj* stale; insipid; (fig) flat ‖ **Schal** *m* (–s;–e & –s) scarf; shawl

Schale ['ʃalə] *f* (–;–n) bowl; (*Tasse*) cup; (*von Obst*) peel, skin; (*Hülse*) shell; (*Schote*) pod; (*Rinde*) bark;

(*Waagschale*) scale; (zool) shell; **sich in S. werfen** (coll) doll up
schälen ['ʃɛlən] *tr* peel; (*Mais*) husk; (*Baumrinde*) bark || *ref* peel off
Scha'lentier *n* (zool) crustacean
Schalk [ʃalk] *m* (-[e]s;-e & ̈e) rogue
schalk'haft *adj* roguish
Schall [ʃal] *m* (-[e]s;-e & ̈e) sound; (*Klang*) ring; (*Lärm*) noise
Schall'boden *m* sounding board
Schall'dämpfer *m* (*an Schußwaffen*) silencer; (aut) muffler; (mus) soft pedal
schall'dicht *adj* soundproof
Schall'dose *f* (electron) pickup
Schall'druck *m* sonic boom
Schallehre (Schall'lehre) *f* acoustics
schallen ['ʃalən] *intr* sound, resound
Schall'grenze *f* sound barrier
Schall'mauer *f* sound barrier
Schall'meßgerät *n* sonar
Schall'pegel *m* sound level
Schall'platte *f* phonograph record
Schall'plattenaufnahme *f* recording
Schall'wand *f* baffle
Schall'welle *f* sound wave
Schalotte [ʃa'lɔtə] *f* (-;-n) (bot) scallion
schalt [ʃalt] *pret* of **schelten**
Schalt– *comb.fm.* switch; connecting; breaking; shifting
Schalt'bild *n* circuit diagram
Schalt'brett *n* switchboard; control panel; (aut) dashboard
Schalt'dose *f* switch box
schalten ['ʃaltən] *tr* switch; (*anlassen*) start; (*Gang*) (aut) shift || *intr* switch; (*regieren*) be in command; (aut) shift gears; **s. und walten mit** do as one pleases with
Schal'ter *m* (-s;-) switch; (*Ausschalter*) circuit breaker; (*für Kundenverkehr*) window, ticket window
Schal'terdeckel *m* switch plate
Schalt'hebel *m* (aut) gearshift; (elec) switch lever
Schalt'jahr *n* leap year
Schalt'kasten *m* switch box
Schalt'pult *n* (rad, telv) control desk
Schalt'tafel *f* switchboard, instrument panel; (aut) dashboard
Schalt'uhr *f* timer
Schal'tung *f* (-;-en) switching; (elec) connection; (elec) circuit
Schaluppe [ʃa'lupə] *f* (-;-n) sloop
Scham [ʃam] *f* (-;) shame; (anat) genitals
Scham'bein *n* (anat) pubis
schämen ['ʃɛmən] *ref* (**über** *acc*) feel ashamed (of)
Scham'gefühl *n* sense of shame
Scham'haar *n* pubic hair
scham'haft *adj* modest, bashful
scham'los *adj* shameless
Schampun [ʃam'pun] *n* (-s;-s) shampoo
schampunieren [ʃampu'nirən] *tr* shampoo
scham'rot *adj* blushing; **s. werden** blush
Scham'teile *pl* genitals
Schand– [ʃant] *comb.fm.* of shame
schandbar ['ʃantbar] *adj* shameful; infamous

Schande ['ʃandə] *f* (-;) shame, disgrace
schänden ['ʃɛndən] *tr* disgrace; (*entweihen*) desecrate; (*Mädchen*) rape
Schän'der *m* (-s;-) violator; rapist
Schand'fleck *m* stain; (fig) blemish; (fig) good-for-nothing; **der S. der Familie** the disgrace of the family
schändlich ['ʃɛntlɪç] *adj* shameful, disgraceful; scandalous || *adv* (coll) awfully
Schand'mal *n* stigma
Schand'tat *f* shameful deed, crime
Schän'dung *f* (-;-en) desecration; disfigurement; rape
Schank [ʃaŋk] *m* (-[e]s;̈e) bar, saloon
Schank'bier *n* draft beer
Schank'erlaubnis *f*, **Schank'gerechtigkeit** *f*, **Schank'konzession** *f* liquor license
Schank'stätte *f* bar, tavern
Schank'tisch *m* bar
Schank'wirt *m* bartender
Schank'wirtschaft *f* bar, saloon
Schanzarbeit ['ʃantsarbaɪt] *f* earthwork; **Schanzarbeiten** entrenchments
Schanze ['ʃantsə] *f* (-;-n) entrenchments, trenches; (naut) quarter-deck; (sport) take-off ramp (*of ski jump*)
Schanz'gerät *n* entrenching tool
Schar [ʃar] *f* (-;-en) group, bunch; crowd; (*von Vögeln*) flock, flight
Scharade [ʃa'radə] *f* (-;-n) charade
scharen ['ʃarən] *ref* (**um**) gather (around)
scharf [ʃarf] *adj* (**schärfer** ['ʃɛrfər]; **schärfste** ['ʃɛrfstə] §9) sharp; (*Tempo*) fast; (*Bemerkung*) cutting; (*Blick*) hard; (*Brille*) strong; (*Fernrohr*) powerful; (*Geruch*) pungent; (*Munition*) live; (*Pfeffer, Senf*) hot; (*streng*) severe; (*genau*) exact; (*Ton*) shrill; (*wahrnehmend*) keen; **s. machen** sharpen; **s. sein auf** (acc) be keen on || *adv* hard; fast; **j–n s. nehmen** be very strict with s.o.; **s. ansehen** look hard at; **s. geladen** loaded; **s. schießen** shoot with live ammunition; **s. umreißen** define clearly
Scharf'blick *m* (fig) sharp eye
Schärfe ['ʃɛrfə] *f* (-;-n) sharpness; keenness; pungency; severity; accuracy
Scharf'einstellung *f* (phot) focusing
schärfen ['ʃɛrfən] *tr* sharpen, whet; make pointy; (fig) intensify
scharf'kantig *adj* sharp-edged
scharf'machen *tr* stir up; (*Bomben*) arm; (*Zünder*) activate
Scharf'macher *m* demagogue, agitator
Scharf'richter *m* executioner
Scharf'schütze *m* (mil) sharpshooter
scharf'sichtig *adj* sharp-eyed; (fig) clear-sighted
Scharf'sinn *m* sagacity, acumen
scharf'sinnig *adj* sharp, sagacious
Scharlach ['ʃarlax] *m* (-s;-e) scarlet; (pathol) scarlet fever
schar'lachfarben *adj* scarlet
schar'lachrot *adj* scarlet
Scharlatan ['ʃarlatan] *m* (-s;-e) charlatan, quack

scharmant [ʃar'mant] *adj* charming
Scharmützel [ʃar'mʏtsəl] *n* (-s;-) skirmish
Scharnier [ʃar'nir] *n* (-s;-e) hinge; joint
Schärpe ['ʃɛrpə] *f* (-;-n) sash
Scharre ['ʃarə] *f* (-;-n) scraper
Scharreisen ['ʃaraɪzən] *n* scraper
scharren ['ʃarən] *tr* scrape, paw ‖ *intr* scrape; (an *acc*) scratch (on); **auf den Boden s.** paw the ground; **mit den Füßen** scrape the feet (*in disapproval*)
Scharte ['ʃartə] *f* (-;-n) nick, dent; (*Kerbe*) notch; (*Kratzer*) scratch; (*Riß*) crack; (*Bergsattel*) gap; (fig) mistake; **e-e S. auswetzen** (fig) make amends
Scharteke [ʃar'tekə] *f* (-;-n) worthless old book; (fig) frump
schartig ['ʃartɪç] *adj* jagged; notched
Schatten ['ʃatən] *m* (-s;-) shade; shadow; **in den S. stellen** throw into the shade
Schat'tenbild *n* silhouette; (fig) phantom
Schat'tendasein *n* shadowy existence
Schat'tengestalt *f* shadowy figure
schat'tenhaft *adj* shadowy
Schat'tenriß *m* silhouette
Schat'tenseite *f* shady side; dark side; (fig) seamy side
schattieren [ʃa'tirən] *tr* shade; (*schraffieren*) hatch; (*abtönen*) tint
Schattie'rung *f* (-;-en) shading; (*Farbton*) shade, tint
schattig ['ʃatɪç] *adj* shadowy; shady
Schatulle [ʃa'tulə] *f* (-;-n) cash box; (*für Schmuck*) jewelry box; (hist) private funds (*of a prince*)
Schatz [ʃats] *m* (-es;-̈e) treasure; (*Vorrat*) store; (fig) sweetheart
Schatz'amt *n* treasury department
Schatz'anweisung *f* treasury bond
schätzbar ['ʃɛtsbar] *adj* valuable
schätzen ['ʃɛtsən] *tr* (*Grundstücke, Häuser, Schaden*) estimate, appraise; (*urteilen, vermuten*) guess; (*achten*) esteem, value; (*würdigen*) appreciate; **er schätzte mich auf 20 Jahre** he took me for 20 years old; **zu hoch s.** overestimate, overrate; **zu s. wissen** appreciate ‖ *ref*—**sich** [*dat*] **es zu Ehre s.** consider it an honor; **sich glücklich s.** consider oneself lucky ‖ *recip*—**sie s. sich nicht** there's no love lost between them
schät'zenswert *adj* valuable
Schät'zer –**in** §6 *mf* appraiser; (*zur Besteuerung*) assessor
Schatz'kammer *f* treasury; (fig) storehouse
Schatz'meister –**in** §6 *mf* treasurer
Schät'zung *f* (-;-en) estimate; (*Meinung*) estimation; (*Hochachtung*) esteem; (*Hochschätzung*) appreciation; (*zur Besteuerung*) assessment
schät'zungsweise *adv* approximately
Schät'zungswert *m* estimated value; assessed value; (*des Schadens*) appraisal
Schatz'wechsel *m* treasury bill
Schau [ʃau] *f* (-;-en) view; (*Ausstellung*) exhibition, show; (mil) review; (telv) show; **zur S. stehen** be on display; **zur S. stellen** put on display; **zur S. tragen** feign
Schau'bild *n* diagram, chart
Schauder ['ʃaudər] *m* (-s;-) shudder, shiver; (*Schrecken*) horror, terror
schauderbar ['ʃaudərbar] *adj* terrible
schau'dererregend *adj* horrifying
schau'derhaft *adj* horrible, awful
schaudern ['ʃaudərn] *intr* (**vor** *dat*) shudder (at) ‖ *impers*—**es schaudert mich** I shudder
schauen ['ʃau·ən] *tr* look at; (*beobachten*) observe ‖ *intr* look
Schauer ['ʃau·ər] *m* (-s;-) shower, downpour; (*Schauder*) shudder, chill; thrill; (*Anfall*) fit, attack; **einzelne S.** scattered showers
Schau'erdrama *n* (theat) thriller
schau'erlich *adj* dreadful, horrible
schauern ['ʃau·ərn] *intr* shudder ‖ *impers*—**es schauert** it is pouring; **es schauert mich** (**or mir**) **vor** (*dat*) **I** shudder at; I shiver with
Schau'erroman *m* thriller
Schaufel ['ʃaufəl] *f* (-;-n) shovel; scoop; (*Rad-*) paddle; (*Turbinen-*) blade, vane
schaufeln ['ʃaufəln] *tr* shovel; (*Grab*) dig ‖ *intr* shovel
Schau'felrad *n* paddle wheel
Schau'fenster *n* display window; **die S. ansehen** go window-shopping
Schau'fensterauslage *f* window display
Schau'fensterbummel *m* window-shopping
Schau'fensterdekoration *f* window dressing
Schau'fliegen *n* stunt flying
Schau'flug *m* air show
Schau'gepränge *n* pageantry
Schau'gerüst *n* grandstand
Schau'kampf *m* (box) exhibition fight
Schau'kasten *m* showcase
Schaukel ['ʃaukəl] *f* (-;-n) swing
schaukeln ['ʃaukəln] *tr* swing; rock ‖ *intr* swing; rock; sway
Schau'kelpferd *n* rocking horse
Schau'kelreck *n* trapeze
Schau'kelstuhl *m* rocking chair
Schau'loch *n* peephole
Schaum [ʃaum] *m* (-[e]s;-̈e) foam, froth; (*Abschaum*) scum; (*Geifer*) slaver; **zu S. schlagen** whip; **zu S. werden** (fig) come to nothing
Schaum'bad *n* bubble bath
schäumen ['ʃɔɪmən] *intr* foam; (*Wein*) sparkle; (*aus Wut*) fume, boil
Schaum'gummi *n* & *m* foam rubber
Schaum'haube *f* head (*on beer*)
schaumig ['ʃaumɪç] *adj* foamy
Schaum'krone *f* whitecap (*on wave*)
Schau'modell *n* mock-up
Schaum'wein *m* sparkling wine
Schau'platz *m* scene, theater
Schau'prozeß *m* mock trial
schaurig ['ʃaurɪç] *adj* horrible
Schau'spiel *n* play, drama; spectacle
Schau'spieler *m* actor
Schau'spielerin *f* actress
schau'spielerisch *adj* theatrical

schauspielern ['ʃauʃpilərn] *intr* act; (*schwindeln*) act, make believe
Schau'spielhaus *n* theater
Schau'spielkunst *f* dramatic art
Schau'stück *n* show piece; (*Muster*) sample
Scheck [ʃɛk] *m* (–s;–s & –e) check; e–n S. ausstellen an (*acc*) über (*acc*) write out a check to (*s.o.*) in the amount of; e–n S. einlösen cash a check; e–n S. sperren lassen stop payment on a check; offener S. blank check
Scheck'abschnitt *m* check stub
Scheck'formular *n* blank check
Scheck'heft *n* check book
scheckig ['ʃɛkiç] *adj* dappled
Scheck'konto *n* checking account
scheel [ʃel] *adj* squinting; squint-eyed; (fig) envious, jealous
Scheffel ['ʃɛfəl] *m* (–s;–) bushel
scheffeln ['ʃɛfəln] *tr* amass
Scheibe ['ʃaɪbə] *f* (–;–n) disk; sheet; plate; (*Glas–*) pane; (*Honig–*) honeycomb; (*Ziel*) target; (*Schnitte*) slice; (astr) orb, disk; (mach) washer; (telp) dial
Schei'benbremse *f* disk brake
Schei'benkönig *m* top marksman
Schei'benschießen *n* target practice
Schei'benwäscher *m* windshield washer
Schei'benwischer *m* windshield wiper
Scheide ['ʃaɪdə] *f* (–;–n) sheath; border, boundary; (anat) vagina
Schei'debrief *m* farewell letter
Schei'degruß *m* goodbye
scheiden ['ʃaɪdən] §112 *tr* separate, divide; (*zerlegen*) decompose; (*Ehe*) dissolve; (*Eheleute*) divorce; (chem) analyze; (chem) refine ‖ *ref* part; sich s. lassen get a divorce ‖ *intr* (SEIN) part; depart; (*aus dem Amt*) resign, retire
schei'dend *adj* (*Tag*) closing; (*Sonne*) setting
Schei'dewand *f* partition
Schei'deweg *m* fork, crossroad; (fig) moment of decision
Schei'dung *f* (–;–en) separation; (*Ehe–*) divorce
Schein [ʃaɪn] *m* (–[e]s;–e) shine; (*Licht*) light; (*Schimmer*) gleam, glitter; (*Strahl*) flash; (*Erscheinung*) appearance; (*Anschein*) pretense, show; (*Urkunde*) certificate, papers, license, ticket; (*Geldschein*) bill; (*Quittung*) receipt; dem Scheine nach apparently; den äußeren S. wahren save face; sich [*dat*] den S. geben make believe; zum S. pro forma
Schein– *comb.fm.* sham, mock, make-believe
scheinbar ['ʃaɪnbar] *adj* seeming, apparent; likely; (*vorgeblich*) make-believe
Schein'bild *n* illusion; phantom
scheinen ['ʃaɪnən] §128 *intr* shine; seem, appear ‖ *impers*—es scheint it seems
Schein'grund *n* pretext
schein'heilig *adj* sanctimonious, hypocritical
Schein'tod *m* suspended animation

Schein'werfer *m* flashlight; (aer) beacon; (aut) headlight
Scheit [ʃaɪt] *n* (–[e]s;–e) piece of chopped wood; Holz in Scheite hakken chop wood
Scheitel ['ʃaɪtəl] *m* (–s:–) apex, top; top of the head; (*des Haares*) part; e–n S. ziehen make a part
scheiteln ['ʃaɪtəln] *tr & ref* part
Schei'telpunkt *m* (fig) summit; (astr) zenith; (math) vertex
Schei'telwinkel *m* opposite angle
Scheiterhaufen ['ʃaɪtərhaufən] *m* funeral pile; auf dem S. sterben die at the stake
scheitern ['ʃaɪtərn] *intr* (SEIN) run aground, be wrecked; (*Plan*) miscarry ‖ **Scheitern** *n* (–s;) shipwreck; (fig) failure
Schelle ['ʃɛlə] *f* (–;–n) bell; (*Fessel*) handcuff; (*Ohrfeige*) box on the ear
schellen ['ʃɛlən] *tr & intr* ring
Schel'lenkappe *f* cap and bells
Schellfisch ['ʃɛlfɪʃ] *m* haddock
Schelm [ʃɛlm] *m* (–[e]s;–e) rogue; (Lit) knave; armer S. poor devil
Schel'menstreich *m* prank
schelmisch ['ʃɛlmɪʃ] *adj* roguish, impish
Schelte ['ʃɛltə] *f* (–;–n) scolding
schelten ['ʃɛltən] *tr & intr* scold
Scheltwort ['ʃɛltvɔrt] *n* (–[e]s;–e & ̈–er) abusive word; word of reproof
Sche•ma ['ʃema] *n* (–s;–s & –mata [mata] & –men [mən]) scheme; diagram; (*Muster*) pattern, design
Schemel ['ʃemal] *m* (–s;–) stool
Schemen ['ʃemən] *m* (–s;–) phantom, shadow
sche'menhaft *adj* shadowy
Schenk [ʃɛŋk] *m* (–en;–en) bartender
Schenke ['ʃɛŋkə] *f* (–;–n) bar, tavern
Schenkel ['ʃɛŋkəl] *m* (–s;–) thigh; (*e–s Winkels*) side; (*e–r Schere*) blade; (*e–s Zirkels*) leg
schenken ['ʃɛŋkən] *tr* give, offer; pour (out); (*Aufmerksamkeit*) pay; (*Schuld*) remit; das ist geschenkt that's dirt cheap; das kann ich mir s. I can pass that up; das kannst du dir s.! keep it to yourself! j–m Beifall s. applaud s.o.; j–m das Leben s. grant s.o. pardon
Schenk'stube *f* taproom, barroom
Schenk'tisch *m* bar
Schen'kung *f* (–;–en) donation
Schenk'wirt *m* bartender
scheppern ['ʃɛpərn] *intr* (coll) rattle
Scherbe ['ʃɛrbə] *f* (–;–n), **Scherben** ['ʃɛrbən] *m* (–s;–) broken piece; potsherd; in Scherben gehen go to pieces
Scher'bengericht *n* ostracism
Scherbett [ʃɛr'bɛt] *m* (–[e]s;–e) sherbe(r)t
Schere ['ʃerə] *f* (–;–n) (pair of) scissors; shears; (*Draht–*) cutter; (zool) claw
scheren ['ʃerən] *tr* bother; was schert dich das? what's that to you? ‖ §129 *tr* cut, clip, trim; (*Schafe*) shear; ‖ §109 *ref*—scher dich ins Bett! off to bed with you!; scher dich zum Teu-

fel! the devil with you!; **sich um etw s.** trouble oneself about s.th.

Schererei [ʃerə'raı] *f* (-;-en) trouble

Scherflein ['ʃerflaın] *n* (-s;-) bit; **sein S.** beitragen contribute one's bit

Scherz [ʃɛrts] *m* (-es;-e) joke; **im** (or **zum**) **S.** for fun; **S. treiben mit** make fun of

scherzen ['ʃɛrtsən] *intr* joke, kid

scherz'haft *adj* joking, humorous

Scherz'name *m* nickname

scherz'weise *adv* in jest, as a joke

scheu [ʃɔı] *adj* shy; **s. machen** frighten; startle ‖ **Scheu** *f* (-;) shyness

Scheuche ['ʃɔıçə] *f* (-;-n) scarecrow

scheuchen ['ʃɔıçən] *tr* scare (away)

scheuen ['ʃɔı·ən] *tr* shun; shrink from; fear; (*Mühen, Kosten*) spare; **ohne die Kosten zu s.** regardless of expenses ‖ *ref* (**vor** *dat*) be afraid (of); **ich s. mich zu** (*inf*) I am reluctant to (*inf*) ‖ *intr—s.* **vor** (*dat*) shy at

Scheuer ['ʃɔı·ər] *f* (-;-n) barn

Scheu'erbürste *f* scrub brush

Scheu'erfrau *f* scrubwoman

Scheu'erlappen *m* scrub rag

scheuern ['ʃɔı·ərn] *tr* scrub, scour; (*reiben*) rub

Scheu'erpulver *n* scouring powder

Scheu'klappe *f* blinder (*for horses*)

Scheune ['ʃɔınə] *f* (-;-n) barn

Scheu'nendrescher *m*—**er ißt wie ein S.** (coll) he eats like a horse

Scheusal ['ʃɔızal] *n* (-s;-e) monster

scheußlich ['ʃɔıslıç] *adj* dreadful, atrocious; (coll) awful, rotten

Scheuß'lichkeit *f* (-;-en) hideousness; (*Tat*) atrocity

Schi [ʃi] *m* (-s;- & -er) ski; **Schi fahren** (or **laufen**) ski

Schicht [ʃıçt] *f* (-;-en) layer, film; (*Farb-*) coat; (*Arbeiter-*) shift; (*Gesellschafts-*) class; (geol) stratum; (phot) emulsion; **Leute aus allen Schichten** people from all walks of life; **S. machen** (coll) knock off from work

Schicht'arbeit *f* shift work

schichten ['ʃıçtən] *tr* arrange in layers; laminate; (*Holz*) stack (up); (*in Klassen einteilen*) classify; (geol) stratify; (*Ladung*) (naut) stow

Schich'tenaufbau *m*, **Schich'tenbildung** *f* (geol) stratification

-schichtig [ʃıçtıç] *comb.fm.* -layer, -ply

Schicht'linie *f* contour

Schicht'linienplan *m* contour map

Schicht'meister *m* shift foreman

schicht'weise *adv* in layers; in shifts

schick [ʃık] *adj* chic, swank ‖ **Schick:** *m* (-[e]s;) stylishness; (*Geschick*) skill; (*Geschmack*) tact, taste; **S. haben für** have a knack for

schicken ['ʃıkən] *tr* send ‖ *ref—sich* **s. für** (or **zu**) be suitable for; **sich s. in** (*acc*) adapt oneself to; resign oneself to ‖ *intr—nach* j-m **s.** send for s.o. ‖ *impers—es schickt sich* it is proper; (*sich ereignen*) come to pass

schick'lich *adj* proper; decent

Schick'lichkeit *f* (-;) propriety

Schick'lichkeitsgefühl *n* sense of propriety

Schicksal ['ʃıkzal] *n* (-[e]s;-e) destiny, fate

Schich'salsgefährte *m* fellow sufferer

Schick'salsglaube *m* fatalism

Schick'salsgöttinnen *pl* (myth) Fates

Schick'salsschlag *m* stroke of fate

Schickung (**Schik'kung**) *f* (-;-en) (divine) dispensation

Schiebe- [ʃibə] *comb.fm.* sliding, push

Schie'beleiter *f* extension ladder

schieben ['ʃibən] §130 *tr* push, shove; traffic in; **auf die lange Bank s.** put off; **e-e ruhige Kugel s.** have a cushy job; **Kegel s.** bowl; **Wache s.** (mil) pull guard duty ‖ *ref* move, shuffle ‖ *intr* shuffle along; profiteer

Schieber ['ʃibər] *m* (-s;-) slide valve; (*Riegel*) bolt; (*am Schornstein*) damper; (fig) racketeer

Schie'bergeschäft *f* (com) racket

Schiebertum ['ʃibərtum] *n* (-s;) (com) racketeering

Schie'betür *f* sliding door

schied [ʃit] *pret* of **scheiden**

Schieds- [ʃits] *comb.fm.* of arbitration

Schieds'gericht *n* board of arbitration; **an ein S. verweisen** refer to arbitration

Schieds'mann *m* (-[e]s;-̈er) arbitrator

Schieds'richter *m* arbitrator; (sport) referee, umpire

schieds'richterlich *adj* of an arbitration board ‖ *adv* by arbitration

Schieds'spruch *m* decision; **e-n S. fällen** render a decision

schief [ʃif] *adj* (*abfallend*) slanting; (*krumm*) crooked; (*einseitig*) lopsided; (*geneigt*) inclined; (*Winkel*) oblique; (*falsch*) false, wrong; **auf die schiefe Ebene geraten** (fig) go downhill; **schiefe Lage** (fig) tight spot; **schiefes Licht** (fig) bad light ‖ *adv* at an angle; awry; obliquely; wrong; **s. ansehen** look askance at; **s. halten** tip, tilt; **s. nehmen** take amiss

Schiefer ['ʃifər] *m* (-s;-) slate; (*Splitter*) splinter

Schie'ferbruch *m* slate quarry

Schie'feröl *n* shale oil

Schie'fertafel *f* (educ) slate

schief'gehen §82 *intr* (SEIN) go wrong

schief'treten §152 *tr—die Absätze s.** wear down the heels

schieläugig ['ʃilɔıgıç] *adj* squint-eyed; cross-eyed

schielen ['ʃilən] *intr* squint; **s. nach** squint at; leer at

schie'lend *adj* squinting; cross-eyed; furtive

schien [ʃin] *pret* of **scheinen**

Schienbein ['ʃinbaın] *n* shinbone, tibia

Schien'beinschützer *m* shinguard

Schiene ['ʃinə] *f* (-;-n) (rr) rail, track; (surg) splint; **aus den Schienen springen** jump the track

schienen ['ʃinən] *tr* put in splints

Schie'nenbahn *f* track, rails; streetcar; railroad

Schie'nenfahrzeug *n* rail car

Schie'nengleis *n* track

schier [ʃir] *adj* sheer ‖ *adv* almost
Schierling [ˈʃirlɪŋ] *m* (-s;-e) (bot) hemlock
Schieß- [ʃis] *comb.fm.* shooting
Schieß'baumwolle *f* guncotton
Schieß'bedarf *m* ammunition
Schieß'bude *f* shooting gallery
Schieß'eisen *n* (hum) shooting iron
schießen [ˈʃisən] §76 *tr* shoot, fire; **e-n Bock s.** (coll) pull a boner; **ein Tor s.** make a goal ‖ *intr* (auf *acc*) shoot (at); **aus dem Hinterhalt s.** snipe; **gut s.** be a good shot; **scharf s.** shoot with live ammunition ‖ *intr* (SEIN) shoot up; spurt; zig, fly; **das Blut schoß ihm ins Gesicht** his face got red; **in Samen s.** go to seed; **ins Kraut s.** sprout ‖ **Schießen** *n* (-s;) shooting; **das ist ja zum s.!** (coll) that's a riot!
Schießerei [ʃisəˈrai] *f* (-;-en) gun fight; pointless firing
Schieß'gewehr *n* firearm
Schieß'hund *m* (hunt) pointer
Schieß'lehre *f* ballistics
Schieß'platz *m* firing range
Schieß'prügel *m* (hum) shooting iron
Schieß'pulver *n* gunpowder
Schieß'scharte *f* loophole
Schieß'scheibe *f* target
Schieß'stand *m* shooting gallery; (mil) firing range, rifle range
Schieß'übung *f* firing practice
Schi'fahrer **-in** §6 *mf* skier
Schiff [ʃif] *n* (-[e]s;-e) ship; (archit) nave; (typ) galley
Schiffahrt (**Schiff'fahrt**) *f* navigation
Schiffahrtslinie (**Schiff'fahrtslinie**) *f* steamship line
Schiffahrtsweg (**Schiff'fahrtsweg**) *m* shipping lane
schiffbar [ˈʃifbar] *adj* navigable
Schiff'bau *m* (-[e]s;) shipbuilding
Schiff'bruch *m* shipwreck
schiff'brüchig *adj* shipwrecked
Schiff'brücke *f* pontoon bridge; (naut) bridge
Schiffchen [ˈʃifçən] *n* (-s;-) little ship; (mil) overseas cap; (tex) shuttle
schiffen [ˈʃifən] *intr* (vulg) pee ‖ *impers*—**es schifft** (vulg) it's pouring
Schiffer [ˈʃifər] *m* (-s;-) seaman; skipper; (*Schiffsführer*) navigator
Schif'ferklavier *n* (coll) concertina
Schiffs'journal *n* log, logbook
Schiffs'junge *m* cabin boy
Schiffs'küche *f* galley
Schiffs'ladung *f* cargo
Schiffs'luke *f* hatch
Schiffs'mannschaft *f* crew
Schiffs'ortung *f* dead reckoning
Schiffs'raum *m* hold; tonnage
Schiffs'rumpf *m* hull
Schiffs'schraube *f* propeller
Schiffs'tau *n* hawser
Schiffs'taufe *f* christening of a ship
Schiffs'werft *f* shipyard, dockyard
Schiffs'winde *f* winch, capstan
Schiffs'zimmermann *m* ship's carpenter; (*bei e-r Werft*) shipwright
Schikane [ʃiˈkanə] *f* (-;-n) chicanery; **mit allen Schikanen** with all the frills; (aut) fully loaded

schikanieren [ʃikaˈnirən] *tr* harass
schikanös [ʃikaˈnøs] *adj* annoying
Schi'langlauf *m* cross-country skiing
Schi'lauf *m* skiing
schi'laufen §105 *intr* (SEIN) ski ‖ **Schilaufen** *n* (-s;) skiing
Schi'läufer **-in** §6 *mf* skier
Schild [ʃilt] *m* (-[e]s;-e) shield; (heral) coat of arms; **etw im Schilde führen** have s.th. up one's sleeve ‖ *n* (-[e]s;-er) sign; road sign; name-plate; (*e-s Arztes, usw.*) shingle; (*Etikett*) label; (*Mützenschirm*) visor, shade
Schild'bürger *m* (fig) dunce
Schild'bürgerstreich *m* boner
Schild'drüse *f* thyroid gland
Schilderhaus [ˈʃildərhaus] *n* sentry box
Schil'dermaler *m* sign painter
schildern [ˈʃildərn] *tr* depict, describe
Schil'derung *f* (-;-en) description
Schild'kröte *f* tortoise, turtle
Schildpatt [ˈʃiltpat] *n* (-[e]s;) tortoise shell, turtle shell
Schilf [ʃilf] *n* (-[e]s;-e) reed
Schilf'rohr *n* reed
Schi'lift *m* ski lift
Schiller [ˈʃilər] *m* (-s;) luster; iridescence
schillern [ˈʃilərn] *intr* be iridescent
Schil'lerwein *m* bright-red wine
Schilling [ˈʃilɪŋ] *m* (-s;- & -e) shilling; (Aust) schilling
Schimäre [ʃiˈmerə] *f* (-;-n) chimera
Schimmel [ˈʃiməl] *m* (-s;-) white horse; mildew, mold
schimmelig [ˈʃiməlɪç] *adj* moldy
schimmeln [ˈʃiməln] *intr* (HABEN & SEIN) get moldy
Schimmer [ˈʃimər] *m* (-s;) glimmer
schimmern [ˈʃimərn] *intr* glimmer
schimmlig [ˈʃimlɪç] *adj* moldy
Schimpanse [ʃimˈpanzə] *m* (-n;-n) chimpanzee
Schimpf [ʃimpf] *m* (-[e]s;-e) insult, abuse
schimpfen [ˈʃimpfən] *tr* scold, abuse ‖ *intr* be abusive; (über *acc* or auf *acc*) curse (at), swear (at)
schimpf'lich *adj* disgraceful
Schimpf'name *m* nickname; **j-m Schimpfnamen geben** call s.o. names
Schimpf'wort *n* (-[e]s;-e & ̈-er) swear word
Schindaas [ˈʃintas] *n* carrion
Schindel [ˈʃindəl] *f* (-;-n) shingle
schindeln [ˈʃindəln] *tr* shingle
schinden [ˈʃindən] §167 *tr* skin; torment; oppress; exploit; **Eindruck s.** try to make an impression; **Eintrittsgeld s.** crash the gate; **Zeilen s.** pad the writing; **Zigaretten s.** bum cigarettes ‖ *ref* break one's back
Schin'der *m* (-s;-) slave driver
Schinderei [ʃindəˈrai] *f* (-;-en) drudgery, grind
Schindluder [ˈʃintludər] *n* carrion; **mit j-m S. treiben** treat s.o. outrageously
Schindmähre [ˈʃintmerə] *f* old nag
Schinken [ˈʃiŋkən] *m* (-s;-) ham; (hum) tome; (hum) huge painting
Schinnen [ˈʃinən] *pl* dandruff

Schippe ['ʃɪpə] *f* (-;-n) shovel, scoop; (cards) spade(s); **e-e S. machen** (or **ziehen**) pout; **j-n auf die S. nehmen** (coll) pull s.o.'s leg
schippen ['ʃɪpən] *tr & intr* shovel
Schirm [ʃɪrm] *m* (-[e]s;-e) screen; umbrella; x-ray screen; lampshade; visor; (fig) protection, shelter; (hunt) blind
Schirm'bild *n* x-ray
Schirm'bildaufnahme *f* x-ray
Schirm'dach *n* lean-to
schirmen ['ʃɪrmən] *tr* protect
Schirm'futteral *n* umbrella case
Schirm'herr *m* protector, patron
Schirm'herrin *f* protectress, patroness
Schirm'herrschaft *f* protectorate; patronage
Schirm'ständer *m* umbrella stand
Schir'mung *f* (-;-en) (elec) shielding
schirren ['ʃɪrən] *tr* harness
Schis·ma ['ʃɪsma] *n* (-;-mata [mata] & -men [mən]) schism
Schi'sprung *m* ski jump
Schi'stock *m* ski pole
schizophren [sçɪtsə'fren] *adj* schizophrenic
Schizophrenie [sçɪtsəfre'ni] *f* (-;) schizophrenia
schlabbern ['ʃlabərn] *tr* lap up ‖ *intr* (*geifern*) slobber; (fig) babble
Schlacht [ʃlaxt] *f* (-;-en) battle; **die S. bei** the battle of
schlachten ['ʃlaxtən] *tr* slaughter
Schlach'tenbummler *m* camp follower; (sport) fan
Schlächter ['ʃlɛçtər] *m* (-s;-) butcher
Schlacht'feld *n* battlefield
Schlacht'flieger *m* combat pilot; close-support fighter
Schlacht'geschrei *n* battle cry
Schlacht'haus *n* slaughterhouse
Schlacht'kreuzer *m* heavy cruiser
Schlacht'opfer *n* sacrifice; (fig) victim
Schlacht'ordnung *f* battle array
Schlacht'roß *n* (hist) charger
Schlacht'ruf *m* battle cry
Schlacht'schiff *n* battleship
Schlach'tung *f* (-;-en) slaughter
Schlacke ['ʃlakə] *f* (-;-n) cinder; lava; (metal) slag, dross
schlackig ['ʃlakɪç] *adj* sloppy (*weather*)
Schlaf [ʃlaf] *m* (-[e]s;) sleep
Schlaf'abteil *m* sleeping compartment
Schlaf'anzug *m* pajamas
Schläfchen ['ʃlɛfçən] *n* (-s;-) nap; **ein S. machen** take a nap
Schläfe ['ʃlɛfə] *f* (-;-n) temple
schlafen ['ʃlafən] §131 *tr* sleep ‖ *intr* sleep; **sich s. legen** go to bed
Schla'fenszeit *f* bedtime
Schläfer -in ['ʃlɛfər(ɪn)] §6 *mf* sleeper
schläfern ['ʃlefərn] *impers*—**es schläfert mich** I'm sleepy
schlaff [ʃlaf] *adj* slack; limp; flabby; (*locker*) loose
Schlaf'gelegenheit *f* sleeping accommodations
Schlaf'kammer *f* bedroom
Schlaf'krankheit *f* sleeping sickness
schlaf'los *adj* sleepless
Schlaf'losigkeit *f* (-;) sleeplessness
Schlaf'mittel *n* sleeping pill

Schlaf'mütze *f* nightcap; (fig) sleepyhead
schläfrig ['ʃlefrɪç] *adj* sleepy, drowsy
Schläf'rigkeit *f* (-;) sleepiness, drowsiness
Schlaf'rock *m* housecoat
Schlaf'saal *m* dormitory
Schlaf'sack *m* sleeping bag
Schlaf'stätte *f*, **Schlaf'stelle** *f* place to sleep
Schlaf'stube *f* bedroom
Schlaf'trunk *m* (hum) nightcap
schlaf'trunken *adj* still half-asleep
Schlaf'wagen *m* (rr) sleeping car
schlaf'wandeln *intr* (SEIN) walk in one's sleep
Schlafwandler -in ['ʃlafvandlər(ɪn)] §6 *mf* sleepwalker
Schlaf'zimmer *n* bedroom
Schlag [ʃlak] *m* (-[e]s;ꞏe) blow; stroke; (*Puls-*) beat; (*Faust-*) punch; (*Hand-*) slap; (*Donner-*) clap; (*Tauben-*) loft; (*Art, Sorte*) kind, sort, breed; (*e-s Taues*) coil; (*der Vögel*) song; (*vom Pferd*) kick; (*e-r Kutsche*) door; (*Holz-*) cut; (*Pendel*) swing; (agr) field; (elec) shock; (mil) scoop, ladleful; (pathol) stroke; **ein S. ins Wasser** a vain attempt; **Leute seines Schlages** the likes of him; **S. zwölf Uhr** at the stroke of twelve; **von gutem S.** of the right sort
Schlag'ader *f* artery
Schlag'anfall *m* (pathol) stroke
schlag'artig *adj* sudden, surprise; (*heftig*) violent ‖ *adv* all of a sudden; with a bang
Schlag'baum *m* barrier
Schlag'besen *m* eggbeater
Schlag'bolzen *m* firing pin
Schlägel ['ʃlegəl] *m* (-s;-) sledge hammer
schlagen ['ʃlagən] §132 *tr* hit; strike; beat; (*besiegen*) defeat; (*strafen*) spank; (*Alarm*) sound; (*Brücke*) build; (*Eier*) beat; (*Geld*) coin; (*Holz*) fell; (*Saiten*) strike; (*Schlacht*) fight; **die Augen zu Boden s.** cast down the eyes; **durch ein Sieb s.** strain, sift; **e-e geschlagene Stunde** (coll) a solid hour; **in die Flucht s.** put to flight; **in Fesseln s.** put in chains; **in Papier s.** wrap in paper; **Wurzel s.** take root; **zu Boden s.** knock down ‖ *ref* come to blows; fight a duel; fence; **sich gut s.** stand one's ground; **sich s. zu** side with; **um sich s.** flail about ‖ *intr* strike; beat; (*Pferd*) kick; (*Vogel*) sing; **mit den Flügeln s.** flap the wings; **nach j-m s.** take a swing at s.o.; (fig) be like s.o., take after s.o.
schla'gend *adj* striking, impressive; convincing; **schlagende Verbindung** dueling fraternity; **schlagende Wetter** firedamp
Schla'ger *m* (-s;-) (*tolle Sache*) hot item; (mus, theat) hit
Schläger ['ʃlegər] *m* (-s;-) beater; hitter; batter; baseball bat; golf club; tennis racket; eggbeater; mallet; (*Singvogel*) warbler; (*Raufbold*) bully

Schlägerei [ʃlegəˈraɪ] *f* (-;-en) fight, fighting; brawl
Schla'gerpreis *m* rock-bottom price
Schla'gersänger -in §6 *mf* pop singer
schlag'fertig *adj* quick with an answer; (*Antwort*) ready
Schlag'holz *n* club, bat
Schlag'instrument *n* percussion instrument
Schlag'kraft *f* striking power
schlag'kräftig *adj* (*Armee*) powerful; (*Beweis*) conclusive
Schlag'licht *n* strong light; glare
Schlag'loch *n* pothole
Schlag'mal *n* (baseball) home plate
Schlag'ring *m* brass knuckles
Schlag'sahne *f* whipped cream
Schlag'schatten *m* deep shadow
Schlag'seite *f* (naut) list; **S. haben** have a list; (hum) be drunk
Schlag'uhr *f* striking clock
Schlag'weite *f* striking distance
Schlag'welle *f* breaker, comber
Schlag'wetter *pl* (min) firedamp
Schlag'wort *n* (-[e]s;-̈er & -e) slogan; key word, subject (*in cataloguing*); (*Phrasendrescherei*) claptrap
Schlag'wörterkatalog *m* (libr) subject index
Schlag'zeile *f* headline
Schlag'zeug *n* percussion instruments
Schlaks [ʃlaks] *m* (-es;-e) lanky person
schlaksig [ˈʃlaksɪç] *adj* lanky
Schlamassel [ʃlaˈmasəl] *m & n* (-s;-) (coll) jam, pickle, mess
Schlamm [ʃlam] *m* (-[e]s;-e) mud, slime; (*im Motor*) sludge; (fig) mire
Schlamm'bad *n* mud bath
schlämmen [ˈʃlɛmən] *tr* dredge; (metal) wash
schlammig [ˈʃlamɪç] *adj* muddy
Schlampe [ˈʃlampə] *f* (-;-n) frump; (sl) slut
Schlamperei [ʃlampəˈraɪ] *f* (-;-en) slovenliness; untidiness, mess
schlampig [ˈʃlampɪç] *adj* sloppy
schlang [ʃlaŋ] *pret* of **schlingen**
Schlange [ˈʃlaŋə] *f* (-;-n) snake; queue, waiting line; (*Wasserschlauch*) hose; **Schlange stehen nach** line up for
schlängeln [ˈʃlɛŋəln] *ref* wind; (*Fluß*) meander; (*sich krümmen*) squirm; wriggle; (fig) worm one's way
Schlan'genbeschwörer -in §6 *mf* snake charmer
Schlan'genlinie *f* wavy line
schlank [ʃlaŋk] *adj* slender, slim; **im schlanken Trabe** at a fast clip
Schlank'heit *f* (-;) slenderness
Schlank'heitskur *f*—e-e S. **machen** diet
schlankweg [ˈʃlaŋkvɛk] *adv* flatly; downright
schlapp [ʃlap] *adj* slack, limp; flabby; (*müde*) washed out || **Schlappe** *f* (-;-n) setback; (*Verlust*) loss
schlappen [ˈʃlapən] *intr* flap; shuffle along || **Schlappen** *m* (-s;-) slipper
schlappern [ˈʃlapərn] *tr* lap up
schlapp'machen *intr* (*zusammenbrechen*) collapse; (*ohnmächtig werden*) faint; (*nicht durchhalten*) call it quits

Schlapp'schwanz *m* (coll) weakling, sissy; (*Feigling*) coward
Schlaraffenland [ʃlaˈrafənlant] *n* paradise
Schlaraffenleben [ʃlaˈrafənlebən] *n* life of Riley
schlau [ʃlau] *adj* sly; clever
Schlauch [ʃlaux] *m* (-[e]s;-̈e) hose; tube; (fig) souse; (aut) inner tube; (educ) pony
Schlauch'boot *n* rubber dinghy
schlauchen [ˈʃlauxən] *tr* drive hard; (mil) drill mercilessly
Schlauch'ventil *n* (aut) valve
Schläue [ˈʃlɔɪ·ə] *f* (-;) slyness
schlau'erweise *adv* prudently
Schlaufe [ˈʃlaufə] *f* (-;-n) loop
Schlau'kopf *m*, **Schlau'meier** *m* sly fox
schlecht [ʃlɛçt] *adj* bad, poor; **mir wird s.** I'm getting sick; **schlechter werden** get worse; **s. werden** go bad || *adv* poorly; **die Uhr geht s.** the clock is off; **s. daran sein** be badly off; **s. und recht** somehow; **s. zu sprechen sein auf** (*acc*) have it in for
schlechterdings [ˈʃlɛçtərdɪŋs] *adv* utterly, absolutely
schlecht'gelaunt *adj* in a bad mood
schlecht'hin' *adv* simply, downright
schlecht'machen *tr* talk behind the back of
schlechtweg [ˈʃlɛçtvɛk] *adv* simply, downright
schlecken [ˈʃlɛkən] *tr* lick || *intr* eat sweets, nibble
Schleckerei [ʃlɛkəˈraɪ] *f* (-;-en) sweets
schleckern [ˈʃlɛkərn] *intr* have a sweet tooth || *impers*—**mich schleckert es nach** I have a yen for
Schlegel [ˈʃlegəl] *m* (-s;-) sledge hammer; (*Holz-*) mallet; (culin) leg; (mus) drumstick
schleichen [ˈʃlaɪçən] §85 *ref & intr* (SEIN) sneak
schlei'chend *adj* creeping; furtive; (*Krankheit*) lingering; (*Gift*) slow
Schlei'cher *m* (-s;-) sneak, hypocrite
Schleicherei [ʃlaɪçəˈraɪ] *f* (-;-en) sneaking; underhand dealing
Schleich'gut *n* contraband
Schleich'handel *m* underhand dealing; smuggling; black-marketing
Schleich'weg *m* secret path; **auf Schleichwegen** in a roundabout way
Schleier [ˈʃlaɪ·ər] *m* (-s;-) veil; haze; gauze
schlei'erhaft *adj* hazy; mysterious; (fig) veiled; **das ist mir s.** I don't know what to make of it
Schleif- [ʃlaɪf] *comb.fm.* sliding; grinding, abrasive
Schleif'bürste *f* (elec) brush
Schleife [ˈʃlaɪfə] *f* (-;-n) (am Kleid, im Haar) bow; (in Schnüren) slipknot; (e-r Straße) hairpin curve; (e-s Flusses) bend; (Wende-) loop; (mit langen Bändern) streamer; (Rutschbahn) slide, chute; (aer) loop
schleifen [ˈʃlaɪfən] *tr* drag; (Kleid) trail along; demolish; raze; (mus) slur || §88 *tr* grind; whet; polish; (Glas, Edelstein) cut; (mil) drill hard || §109 *intr* drag, trail

Schleif'mit'tel n abrasive
Schleif'papier n sandpaper
Schleif'rad n emery wheel
Schleif'stein m whetstone
Schleim [ʃlaɪm] m (-[e]s;-e) slime; mucus, phlegm
Schleim'haut f mucous membrane
schleimig ['ʃlaɪmɪç] adj slimy; mucous
schleißen ['ʃlaɪsən] §53 tr split; slit; (Federkiele) strip || intr wear out
Schlemm [ʃlɛm] m (-s;-e) (cards) slam
schlemmen ['ʃlɛmən] intr carouse; gorge oneself; live high
Schlem'mer –in §6 mf glutton, guzzler; gourmet
schlem'merhaft adj gluttonous; (üppig) plentiful, luxurious
Schlem'merlokal n gourmet restaurant
Schlempe ['ʃlɛmpə] f (-;-n) slop
schlendern ['ʃlɛndərn] intr (SEIN) stroll
Schlendrian ['ʃlɛndri·ɑn] m (-s;) routine
schlenkern ['ʃlɛŋkərn] tr dangle, swing || intr dangle; **mit den Armen s.** swing the arms
Schlepp– [ʃlɛp] comb.fm. towing, drag
Schlepp'dampfer m tugboat
Schlepp'dienst m towing service
Schleppe ['ʃlɛpə] f (-;-n) train
schleppen ['ʃlɛpən] tr drag; lug, tote; (aer, naut) tow || ref drag along; **sich mit etw s.** be burdened with s.th.
Schlep'penkleid n dress with a train
Schlep'per m (-s;-) hauler; tractor; tugboat; tender, lighter
Schlepp'fischerei f trawling
Schlepp'netz n dragnet, dredge; trawling net
Schlepp'netzboot n trawler
Schlepp'schiff n tugboat
Schlepp'tau n towline; **ins S. nehmen** take in tow
Schleuder ['ʃlɔɪdər] f (-;-n) sling; slingshot; (aer) catapult; (mach) centrifuge
schleudern ['ʃlɔɪdərn] tr fling; sling; (aer) catapult || intr (aut) skid; (com) undersell
Schleu'derpreis m cutrate price
Schleu'dersitz m (aer) ejection seat
schleunig ['ʃlɔɪnɪç] adj speedy || adv in all haste; (sofort) at once
schleunigst ['ʃlɔɪnɪçst] adv as soon as possible; right away
Schleuse ['ʃlɔɪzə] f (-;-n) lock, sluice, sluice way; drain, sewer
schleusen ['ʃlɔɪzən] tr (fig) maneuver
schlich [ʃlɪç] pret of **schleichen** || **Schlich** [ʃlɪç] m (-[e]s;-e) trick; **alle Schliche kennen** know all the ropes; **j-m auf die Schliche** (or **hinter j-s Schliche**) **kommen** be on to s.o.
schlicht [ʃlɪçt] adj smooth; plain
schlichten ['ʃlɪçtən] tr smooth; (fig) settle, arbitrate
Schlich'ter –in §6 mf arbitrator
Schlich'tung f (-;-en) arbitration; settlement
schlief [ʃlif] pret of **schlafen**
Schließe ['ʃlisə] f (-;-n) clasp; pin
schließen ['ʃlisən] §76 tr shut, close; lock; end, conclude; (Betrieb) shut

down; (Bücher) balance; (Konto; Klammer) close; (Bündnis) form; (Frieden; Rede) conclude; (Kompromiß) reach; (Heirat) form; (Geschäft, Handel) strike; (Versammlung) adjourn; (Wette) make; (Reihen) (mil) close; **ans Herz s.** press to one's heart; **aus etw. s., daß** conclude from s.th. that; **den Zug s.** (mil) bring up the rear; **e–n Vergleich s.** come to an agreement; **ins Herz s.** take a liking to; **kurz s.** (elec) short || ref shut, close; **in sich s.** comprise, include; (bedeuten) imply; (umfassen) involve; **von sich auf andere s.** judge others by oneself || intr shut, close; end
Schließ'fach n post office box; safe-deposit box
schließlich ['ʃlislɪç] adj final, eventual || adv finally
schliff [ʃlɪf] pp of **schleifen** || **Schliff** m (-[e]s;-e) polish; (e–s Diamanten) cut; (fig) polish; (mil) rigorous training
schlimm [ʃlɪm] adj bad; (bedenklich) serious; (traurig) sad; (wund) sore; (eklig) nasty; **am schlimmsten** worst; **immer schlimmer** worse and worse; **s. daran sein** be badly off
schlimmstenfalls ['ʃlɪmstənfals] adv at worst
Schlinge ['ʃlɪŋə] f (-;-n) loop; coil; (fig) trap, difficulty; (bot) tendril; (hunt) snare; (surg) sling; **in die S. gehen** (fig) fall into a trap
Schlingel ['ʃlɪŋəl] m (-s;-) rascal; **fauler S.** lazybones
schlingen ['ʃlɪŋən] §142 tr tie; twist; wind; wrap; gulp || ref wind, coil; climb, creep || intr gulp down food
Schlingerbewegung ['ʃlɪŋərbəveguŋ] f (naut) roll
schlingern ['ʃlɪŋərn] intr (naut) roll
Schlinggewächs ['ʃlɪŋgəvɛks] n,
Schlingpflanze ['ʃlɪŋpflantsə] f climber
Schlips [ʃlɪps] m (-es;-e) necktie
Schlitten ['ʃlɪtən] m (-s;-) sled; (an der Schreibmaschine) carriage
schlit'tenfahren §71 intr go sleigh riding; **mit j-m s.** make life miserable for s.o.
schlittern ['ʃlɪtərn] intr (HABEN & SEIN) slide; (Wagen) skid
Schlittschuh ['ʃlɪtʃu] m ice skate; **S. laufen** skate, go ice-skating
Schlitt'schuhläufer –in §6 mf ice skater
Schlitz [ʃlɪts] m (-es;-e) slit, slot; (Hosen-) fly
schlitz'äugig adj slit-eyed, sloe-eyed
schlitzen ['ʃlɪtsən] tr slit; rip
Schloß [ʃlɔs] n (Schlosses; Schlösser) castle; country mansion; lock; snap, clasp; **hinter S. und Riegel** behind bars; **unter S. und Riegel** under lock and key
Schloße ['ʃlɔsə] f (-;-n) hailstone
Schlosser ['ʃlɔsər] m (-s;-) mechanic; locksmith
Schloß'graben m moat
Schlot [ʃlot] m (-[e]s;-e & ⸚e) chimney, smokestack; (fig) louse

Schlot′baron *m* (coll) tycoon
Schlot′feger *m* chimney sweep
schlotterig [′ʃlɔtərɪç] *adj* loose, dangling; wobbly; (*liederlich*) slovenly
schlottern [′ʃlɔtərn] *intr* fit loosely; (*baumeln*) dangle; (*zittern*) tremble; (*wackeln*) wobble
Schlucht [ʃluçt] *f* (-;-en) gorge; ravine
schluchzen [′ʃluxtsən] *intr* sob
Schluck [ʃluk] *m* (-[e]s;-e) gulp; sip
Schluck′auf *m* (-s;) hiccups
schlucken [′ʃlukən] *tr & intr* gulp
Schlucker [′ʃlukər] *m* (-s;-)—**armer S.** (coll) poor devil
schlucksen [′ʃluksən] *intr* have the hiccups
schluderig [′ʃludərɪç] *adj* slipshod
schludern [′ʃludərn] *intr* do slipshod work
Schlummer [′ʃlumər] *m* (-s;) slumber
Schlum′merlied *n* lullaby
schlummern [′ʃlumərn] *intr* slumber
schlum′mernd *adj* latent
Schlum′merrolle *f* cushion
Schlund [ʃlunt] *m* (-[e]s;-e) gullet; pharynx; (*e-s Vulcans*) crater; (fig) abyss
Schlund′röhre *f* esophagus
Schlupf [ʃlupf] *m* (-[e]s;ːe) hole; (elec, mach) slip
schlüpfen [′ʃlypfən] *intr* (SEIN) slip; sneak
Schlüp′fer *m* (-s;-) (pair of) panties; (pair of) bloomers
Schlupf′jacke *f* sweater
Schlupf′loch *n* hiding place; loophole
schlüpfrig [′ʃlypfrɪç] *adj* slippery; (*obszön*) off-color
Schlupf′winkel *m* hiding place; haunt
schlurfen [′ʃlurfən] *intr* (SEIN) shuffle
schlürfen [′ʃlyrfən] *tr* slurp; lap up
Schluß [ʃlus] *m* (**Schlusses; Schlüsse**) end, close; (*Ablauf*) expiration; (*Folgerung*) conclusion; **S. damit!** time!; cut it out!; **S. folgt** to be concluded; **S. machen mit** put an end to; knock off from (*work*); break up with (*s.o.*); **zum S.** in conclusion
Schluß′effekt *m* upshot
Schlüssel [′ʃlysəl] *m* (-s;-) key; wrench; quota; code key; (fig) key, clue
Schlüs′selbein *n* collarbone, clavicle
Schlüs′selblume *f* cowslip; **helle S.** primrose
Schlüs′selbrett *n* keyboard
Schlüs′selbund *m* bunch of keys
schlüs′selfertig *adj* ready for occupancy
Schlüs′selloch *n* keyhole
Schluß′ergebnis *n* final result
Schluß′folge *f*, **Schluß′folgerung** *f* conclusion, deduction
Schluß′formel *f* complimentary close
schlüssig [′ʃlysɪç] *adj* determined; logical; (*Beweis*) conclusive; **sich** [*dat*] **noch nicht s. sein, ob** be undecided whether
Schluß′licht *n* (aut) taillight
Schluß′linie *f* (typ) dash
Schluß′rennen *n* (sport) final heat
Schluß′runde *f* (sport) finals
Schluß′schein *m* sales agreement

Schluß′verkauf *m* clearance sale
Schmach [ʃmax] *f* (-;) disgrace, shame; insult; humiliation
schmachten [′ʃmaxtən] *intr* (**vor** *dat*) languish (with); **s. nach** long for
Schmachtfetzen [′ʃmaxtfetsən] *m* sentimental song or book; melodrama
schmächtig [′ʃmeçtɪç] *adj* scrawny
Schmachtriemen [′ʃmaxtrimən] *m*—**den S. enger schnallen** (fig) tighten one's belt
schmach′voll *adj* disgraceful; humiliating
schmackhaft [′ʃmakhaft] *adj* tasty
schmähen [′ʃme·ən] *tr* revile, abuse; speak ill of
schmählich [′ʃmelɪç] *adj* disgraceful, scandalous; humiliating
Schmährede [′ʃmeredə] *f* abuse; diatribe
Schmähschrift [′ʃmeʃrɪft] *f* libel
schmähsüchtig [′ʃmezyçtɪç] *adj* abusive
Schmä′hung *f* (-;-en) abuse; slander
schmal [ʃmal] *adj* narrow; slim; meager
schmälern [′ʃmelərn] *tr* curtail; belittle
Schmal′spurbahn *f* narrow-gauge railroad
Schmalz [ʃmalts] *n* (-[e]s;) lard, grease; (fig) schmaltz
schmalzen [′ʃmaltsən] *tr* lard, grease
schmalzig [′ʃmaltsɪç] *adj* greasy; fatty; (fig) schmaltzy
schmarotzen [ʃma′rɔtsən] *intr* (**bei**) sponge (on)
Schmarot′zer *m* (-s;-) sponger; (zool) parasite
schmarotzerisch [ʃma′rɔtsərɪʃ] *adj* sponging; (zool) parasitic(al)
Schmarre [′ʃmarə] *f* (-;-n) scar; scratch
schmarrig [′ʃmarɪç] *adj* scary
Schmatz [ʃmats] *m* (-es;-e) hearty kiss
schmatzen [′ʃmatsən] *tr* (coll) kiss loudly || *intr* smack one's lips
Schmaus [ʃmaus] *m* (-es;ːe) feast; treat
schmausen [′ʃmauzən] *intr* (**von**) feast (on)
schmecken [′ʃmekən] *tr* taste, sample; (fig) stand || *intr* taste good; **s. nach** taste like
Schmeichelei [ʃmaiçə′lai] *f* (-;-en) flattery; coaxing
schmeichelhaft [′ʃmaiçəlhaft] *adj* flattering
schmeicheln [′ʃmaiçəln] *ref*—**sich** [*dat*] **s. zu** (*inf*) pride oneself on (*ger*) || *intr* be flattering; (*dat*) flatter
Schmeich′ler **-in** §6 *mf* flatterer
schmeichlerisch [′ʃmaiçlərɪʃ] *adj* flattering; complimentary; fawning
schmeißen [′ʃmaisən] §53 *tr* (coll) throw; (coll) manage; **e-e Runde Bier s.** set up a round of beer || *ref*—**mit Geld um sich s.** throw money around
Schmelz [ʃmelts] *m* (-es;-e) enamel; glaze; melodious ring; (fig) bloom
schmelzen [′ʃmeltsən] §133 *tr* melt; smelt || *intr* (SEIN) melt; (fig) soften

schmel'zend *adj* mellow; melodious
Schmelzerei [ʃmɛltsə'raɪ] *f* (-;-en) foundry
schmelz'flüssig *adj* molten
Schmelz'hütte *f* foundry
Schmelz'käse *m* soft cheese
Schmelz'ofen *m* smelting furnace
Schmelz'punkt *m* melting point
Schmelz'tiegel *m* crucible, melting pot
Schmer [ʃmer] *m & n* (-s;) fat, grease
Schmer'bauch *m* (coll) potbelly
Schmerz [ʃmerts] *m* (-es;-en) pain, ache; **mit Schmerzen** (coll) anxiously, impatiently
schmerzen [ˈʃmɛrtsən] *tr & intr* hurt
schmer'zend *adj* aching, sore
Schmer'zensgeld *n* damages (*for pain or anguish*)
Schmer'zenskind *n* problem child
schmerz'haft *adj* painful, aching
schmerz'lich *adj* painful, severe
schmerz'lindernd *adj* soothing
schmerz'los *adj* painless
Schmerz'schwelle *f* threshold of pain
Schmetterling [ˈʃmɛtərlɪŋ] *m* (-s;-e) butterfly
Schmet'terlingsstil *m* (sport) butterfly
schmettern [ˈʃmɛtərn] *tr* smash; **zu Boden s.** knock down ‖ *intr* (*Trompete*) blare; (*Vogel*) warble
Schmied [ʃmit] *m* (-[e]s;-e) smith
Schmiede [ˈʃmidə] *f* (-;-n) forge; blacksmith shop
Schmie'deeisen *n* wrought iron
Schmie'dehammer *m* sledge hammer
schmieden [ˈʃmidən] *tr* forge; hammer; (*Pläne, usw.*) devise, concoct
schmiegen [ˈʃmigən] *tr*—**das Kinn** (or **die Wange**) **in die Hand s.** prop one's chin (or cheek) in one's hand ‖ *ref* (**an** *acc*) snuggle up (to); **sich s. und biegen vor** (*dat*) bow and scrape before
schmiegsam [ˈʃmikzam] *adj* flexible
Schmier- [ʃmir] *comb.fm.* grease, lubricating; smearing
Schmiere [ˈʃmirə] *f* (-;-n) grease; lubricant; salve; (*Schmutz*) muck; (fig) mess; (fig) spanking; (theat) barnstormers; **S. stehen** be the lookout man
schmieren [ˈʃmirən] *tr* grease, lubricate; smear; (*Butter*) spread; (*Brot*) butter; (*bestechen*) bribe; **j-m e-e s.** (coll) paste s.o.; **wie geschmiert** like greased lightning ‖ *ref*—**sich** [*dat*] **die Kehle s.** (coll) wet one's whistle ‖ *intr* scribble
Schmie'renkomödiant -**in** §7 *mf* (theat) barnstormer, ham
Schmiererei [ʃmirə'raɪ] *f* (-;-en) greasing; smearing; scribbling
Schmier'fink *m* scrawler; (*Schmutzkerl*) dirty fellow
Schmier'geld *n* (coll) bribe; (coll) hush money; (coll) slush fund
schmierig [ˈʃmirɪç] *adj* smeary, greasy; oily; (*Geschäfte*) dirty
Schmier'käse *m* cheese spread
Schmier'mittel *n* lubricant
Schmier'pistole *f*, **Schmier'presse** *f* grease gun
Schmie'rung *f* (-;-en) lubrication

Schminke [ˈʃmɪŋkə] *f* (-;-n) rouge; make-up
schminken [ˈʃmɪŋkən] *tr* apply make-up to; rouge; **die Lippen s.** put on lipstick ‖ *ref* put on make-up
Schminkunterlage [ˈʃmɪŋkʊntərlagə] *f* base
Schmirgel [ˈʃmɪrgəl] *m* (-s;) emery
Schmir'gelleinen *n*, **Schmir'gelleinwand** *f* emery cloth
Schmir'gelpapier *n* emery paper
Schmir'gelscheibe *f* emery wheel
Schmiß [ʃmɪs] *m* (Schmisses; Schmisse) (coll) stroke, blow; (coll) gash; (coll) dueling scar; (coll) zip
schmissig [ˈʃmɪsɪç] *adj* (coll) snazzy
schmollen [ˈʃmɔlən] *intr* pout, sulk
schmolz [ʃmɔlts] *pret* of **schmelzen**
Schmorbraten [ˈʃmorbratən] *m* braised meat
schmoren [ˈʃmorən] *tr* braise, stew ‖ *intr* (fig) swelter; **laß ihn s.!** let him stew!
schmuck [ʃmʊk] *adj* nice, cute; smart, dapper; (*sauber*) neat ‖ **Schmuck** *m* (-[e]s;) ornament; decoration; trimmings; trinket(s); jewelry
schmücken [ˈʃmʏkən] *tr* adorn; decorate, trim; (*Aufsatz*) embellish ‖ *ref* spruce up, dress up
Schmuck'kästchen *n* jewel box
schmuck'los *adj* unadorned, plain
Schmuck'waren *pl* jewelry
Schmuddel [ˈʃmʊdəl] *m* (-s;-) slob
schmuddelig [ˈʃmʊdəlɪç] *adj* dirty
Schmuggel [ˈʃmʊgəl] *m* (-s;), **Schmuggelei** [ʃmʊgə'laɪ] *f* (-;-en) smuggling
schmuggeln [ˈʃmʊgəln] *tr & intr* smuggle
Schmug'gelware *f* contraband
Schmuggler -**in** [ˈʃmʊglər(ɪn)] §6 *mf* smuggler
schmunzeln [ˈʃmʊntsəln] *intr* grin ‖ **Schmunzeln** *n* (-s;) big grin
Schmutz [ʃmʊts] *m* (-es;) dirt, filth; (*Zote*) smut
schmutzen [ˈʃmʊtsən] *tr & intr* soil
Schmutz'fink *m* (coll) slob
Schmutz'fleck *m* stain, smudge, blotch
schmutz'ig *adj* dirty
Schnabel [ˈʃnabəl] *m* (-s;ː) beak, bill; **halt den S.!** (sl) shut up!
Schna'belhieb *m* peck
schnäbeln [ˈʃnebəln] *tr & intr* peck; (fig) kiss
Schnalle [ˈʃnalə] *f* (-;-n) buckle; (vulg) whore
schnallen [ˈʃnalən] *tr* buckle, fasten
schnalzen [ˈʃnaltsən] *intr*—**mit den Fingern s.** snap one's fingers; **mit der Zunge s.** click one's tongue
schnapp [ʃnap] *interj* snap!
schnappen [ˈʃnapən] *tr* grab; (*Dieb*) nab ‖ *intr* snap; **ins Schloß s.** snap shut; **mit den Fingern s.** snap one's fingers; **nach Luft s.** gasp for air; **s. nach** snap at
Schnapp'messer *n* jackknife
Schnapp'schuß *m* (phot) snapshot
Schnaps [ʃnaps] *m* (-es;ː) hard liquor
Schnaps'brennerei *f* distillery
Schnaps'bruder *m* (coll) booze hound

Schnaps'idee *f* (coll) crazy idea
schnarchen [ˈʃnarçən] *intr* snore
Schnarre [ˈʃnarə] *f* (-;-n) rattle
schnarren [ˈʃnarən] *intr* rattle; (*Säge*)
buzz; (*Insekten*) drone, buzz
schnattern [ˈʃnatərn] *intr* (*Enten*)
cackle; (*Zähne*) chatter; (fig) gab
schnauben [ˈʃnaubən] *intr* pant, puff;
(*Pferd*) snort; **nach Rache s.** breathe
revenge; **vor Wut s.** fume with rage
‖ *ref* blow one's nose
schnaufen [ˈʃnaufən] *intr* pant;
wheeze
Schnau'fer *m* (-s;-) (coll) deep breath
Schnauzbart [ˈʃnautsbart] *m* mustache
Schnauze [ˈʃnautsə] *f* (-;-n) snout,
muzzle; spout; (sl) snoot; (sl) big
mouth
Schnauzer [ˈʃnautsər] *m* (-s;-) schnauzer
schnauzig [ˈʃnautsɪç] *adj* rude
Schnecke [ˈʃnɛkə] *f* (-;-n) snail;
(*Nacht-*) slug; (*e-r Säule*) volute;
spiral; (anat) cochlea; (mach) worm;
(*e-r Violine*) (mus) scroll
Schneckenhaus (Schnek'kenhaus) *n*
snail shell
Schneckentempo (Schnek'kentempo) *n*
(fig) snail's pace
Schnee [ʃne] *m* (-s;) snow; whipped
egg white
Schnee'besen *m* eggbeater
Schnee'brett *n* snow slide, avalanche
Schnee'brille *f* snow goggles
Schnee'decke *f* blanket of snow
Schnee'flocke *f* snowflake
Schnee'gestöber *n* snow flurry
schneeig [ˈʃne·ɪç] *adj* snowy
Schnee'matsch *m* slush
Schnee'pflug *m* snowplow
Schnee'schaufel *f*, **Schnee'schippe** *f*
snow shovel
Schnee'schläger *m* eggbeater
Schnee'schmelze *f* thaw
Schnee'treiben *n* blizzard
schneeverweht [ˈʃnefervet] *adj* snow-
bound
Schnee'verwehung *f* snowdrift
Schnee'wehe *f* snowdrift
Schneewittchen [ˈʃnevɪtçən] *n* (-s;)
Snow White
Schneid [ʃnaɪt] *m* (-[e]s;) (coll)
pluck; (*Mut*) (coll) guts
Schneid'brenner *m* cutting torch
Schneide [ˈʃnaɪdə] *f* (-;-n) (cutting)
edge; (*e-s Hobels*) blade; **auf des
Messers S.** (fig) on the razor's edge
Schnei'debrett *n* cutting board
Schnei'demaschine *f* cutter, slicer
Schnei'demühle *f* sawmill
schneiden [ˈʃnaɪdən] §106 *tr* cut;
(*Baum*) prune; (*Fingernägel*) pare;
(*Hecke*) trim; (*nicht grüßen*) snub;
(surg) operate on; (tennis) slice;
Gesichter s. make faces; **klein s.** cut
up ‖ *ref* (fig) be mistaken; (fig) be
disappointed; (math) intersect; **sich
in den Finger s.** cut one's finger ‖
intr cut
Schnei'der (-s;-) *m* cutter; tailor
Schneiderei [ʃnaɪdəˈraɪ] *f* (-;-en)
tailoring; (*Werkstatt*) tailorshop
Schnei'derin *f* (-;-nen) dressmaker

schneidern [ˈʃnaɪdərn] *tr* make ‖ *intr*
do tailoring; be a dressmaker
Schnei'derpuppe *f* dummy
Schnei'dezahn *m* incisor
schneidig [ˈʃnaɪdɪç] *adj* sharp-edged;
energetic; smart, sharp
schneien [ˈʃnaɪ·ən] *impers*—**es schneit**
it is snowing
Schneise [ˈʃnaɪzə] *f* (-;-n) lane (*between rows of trees*)
schnell [ʃnɛl] *adj* fast, quick
Schnellauf (Schnell'lauf) *m* race;
sprint; speed skating
Schnell'bahn *f* high-speed railroad
Schnelle [ˈʃnɛlə] *f* (-;-n) speed;
(*Strom-*) rapids; **auf die S.** (coll)
in a hurry, very briefly
schnellen [ˈʃnɛlən] *tr* let fly ‖ *intr*
(SEIN) spring, jump up; (*Preise*)
shoot up; **mit dem Finger s.** snap
one's fingers
Schnell'gang *m* (aut) overdrive
Schnellhefter [ˈʃnɛlheftər] *m* (-s;-)
folder, file
Schnell'imbiß *m* snack
Schnell'kraft *f* elasticity
schnellstens [ˈʃnɛlstəns] *adv* as fast as
possible
Schnell'verfahren *n* quick process;
(jur) summary proceeding
Schnell'zug *m* express train
Schneppe [ˈʃnɛpə] *f* (-;-n) spout; (sl)
prostitute
schneuzen [ˈʃnɔɪtsən] *ref* blow one's
nose
schniegeln [ˈʃnigəln] *ref* dress up; **geschniegelt und gebügelt** dressed to
kill
schnipfeln [ˈʃnɪpfəln] *tr* & *intr* snip
Schnippchen [ˈʃnɪpçən] *n*—**j-m ein S.
schlagen** (coll) pull a fast one on
s.o.; outwit s.o.
Schnippel [ˈʃnɪpəl] *m* & *n* (-s;-) chip
schnippeln [ˈʃnɪpəln] *tr* & *intr* snip
schnippen [ˈʃnɪpən] *intr*—**mit den Fingern s.** (coll) snap one's fingers
schnippisch [ˈʃnɪpɪʃ] *adj* fresh ‖ *adv*
pertly; **s. erwidern** snap back
schnitt [ʃnɪt] *pret* of **schneiden** ‖
Schnitt *m* (-[e]s;-e) cut, incision;
(*Kerbe*) notch; (*Schnitte*) slice;
(*Quer-*) profile, cross section;
(*Durch-*) average; (*e-s Anzuges*) cut,
style; (*Gewinn*) cut; (agr) reaping;
(bb) edge; (cin) editing; (geom)
intersection; **weicher Schnitt** (cin)
dissolve
Schnitt'ansicht *f* sectional view
Schnitt'ball *m* (tennis) slice
Schnitt'blumen *pl* cut flowers
Schnitt'bohnen *pl* string beans
Schnittchen [ˈʃnɪtçən] *n* (-s;-) thin
slice; sandwich
Schnitte [ˈʃnɪtə] *f* (-;-n) slice
Schnit'ter -in §6 *mf* reaper, mower
Schnitt'fläche *f* (geom) plane
Schnitt'holz *n* lumber
schnittig [ˈʃnɪtɪç] *adj* smart-looking;
(aut) streamlined
Schnitt'lauch [ˈʃnɪtlaux] *m* (-[e]s;)
(bot) chive
Schnitt'linie *f* (geom) secant
Schnitt'meister *m* (cin) editor

Schnitt'muster *n* pattern (*of dress, etc.*)

Schnitt'punkt *m* intersection

Schnitt'waren *pl* dry goods

Schnitt'wunde *f* cut, gash

Schnitz [ʃnɪts] *m* (**-es;-e**) cut; slice; chop; chip

Schnitzel [ˈʃnɪtsəl] *n* (**-s;-**) chip; slice; shred; (*Abfälle*) parings; (culin) cutlet

schnitzeln [ˈʃnɪtsəln] *tr* cut up; shred; (*Holz*) whittle

schnitzen [ˈʃnɪtsən] *tr* carve

Schnit'zer *m* (**-s;-**) carver; (*Fehler*) blunder; **grober S.** boner

Schnitzerei [ʃnɪtsəˈraɪ] *f* (**-;-en**) wood carving, carved work

schnob [ʃnop] *pret* of **schnauben**

schnodderig [ˈʃnɔdərɪç] *adj* brash

schnöde [ˈʃnøːdə] *adj* vile; disdainful; (*Gewinn*) filthy

Schnorchel [ˈʃnɔrçəl] *m* (**-s;-**) snorkel

Schnörkel [ˈʃnœrkəl] *m* (**-s;-**) (*beim Schreiben*) flourish; (fig) frills; (archit) scroll

schnorren [ˈʃnɔrən] *tr* (coll) chisel, bum ‖ *intr* (coll) sponge, chisel

Schnösel [ˈʃnøːzəl] *m* (**-s;-**) wise guy

schnüffeln [ˈʃnʏfəln] *intr* snoop around; (**an** *dat*) sniff (at)

Schnüff'ler **-in** §6 *mf* (coll) snoop

Schnuller [ˈʃnʊlər] *m* (**-s;-**) pacifier

Schnultze [ˈʃnʊltsə] *f* (**-;-n**) (coll) tear-jerker

schnultzig [ˈʃnʊltsɪç] *adj* (coll) corny, mawkish

schnupfen [ˈʃnʊpfən] *tr* snuff ‖ *intr* take snuff ‖ **Schnupfen** *m* (**-s;-**) cold; **den S. bekommen** catch a cold

Schnupftabak [ˈʃnʊpftabak] *m* snuff

schnuppe [ˈʃnʊpə] *adj*—**das ist mir s.** it's all the same to me ‖ **Schnuppe** *f* (**-;-n**) shooting star; (*e-r Kerze*) snuff

Schnur [ʃnur] *f* (**-;̈e** & **-en**) string; (*Band*) braid; (elec) flexible cord; **nach der S.** regularly

Schnürband [ˈʃnyːrbant] *n* (**-[e]s;̈er**) shoestring; corset lace

Schnürchen [ˈʃnyːrçən] *n* (**-s;-**) string; **etw am S. haben** have at one's finger-tips; **wie am S.** like clockwork

schnüren [ˈʃnyːrən] *tr* tie; lace; (*Perlen*) string ‖ *ref* put on a corset

schnur'gerade *adj* straight ‖ *adv* straight, as the crow flies

schnurr [ʃnʊr] *interj* purr!; buzz!

Schnurrbart [ˈʃnʊrbart] *m* mustache

schnurren [ˈʃnʊrən] *intr* (*Katze*) purr; (*Rad*) whir; (*Maschine*) hum; (*schnorren*) sponge, chisel

schnurrig [ˈʃnʊrɪç] *adj* funny; queer

Schnürschuh [ˈʃnyːrʃu] *m* oxford shoe

Schnürsenkel [ˈʃnyːrzɛŋkəl] *m* shoe-string

schnurstracks [ˈʃnʊrʃtraks] *adv* right away; directly; **s. entgegengesetzt** diametrically opposite; **s. losgehen auf** (*acc*) make a beeline for

schob [ʃop] *pret* of **schieben**

Schober [ˈʃoːbər] *m* (**-s;-**) stack

Schock [ʃɔk] *m* (**-[e]s;-s**) shock ‖ *n* (**-[e]s;-e**) threescore

schockant [ʃɔˈkant] *adj* shocking

schockieren [ʃɔˈkirən] *tr* shock

schofel [ˈʃoːfəl] *adj* mean; miserable; (*schäbig*) shabby; (*geizig*) stingy

Schöffe [ˈʃœfə] *m* (**-n;-n**) juror

Schokolade [ʃɔkɔˈladə] *f* (**-;-n**) chocolate

schokoladen [ʃɔkɔˈladən] *adj* chocolate

Schokola'dentafel *f* chocolate bar

scholl [ʃɔl] *pret* of **schallen**

Scholle [ˈʃɔlə] *f* (**-;-n**) clod; sod; stratum; ice floe; (ichth) sole; **heimatliche S.** native soil

schon [ʃon] *adv* already; as early as; yet, as yet; (*sogar*) even; (*bloß*) the bare, the mere; **ich komme s.!** all right, I'm coming!; **s. am folgenden Tage** on the very next day; **s. der Gedanke** the mere thought; **s. früher** before now; **s. gut!** all right!; **s. immer** always; **s. lange** long since, for a long time; **s. wieder** again

schön [ʃøn] *adj* beautiful; nice; (*Künste*) fine; (*Mann*) handsome; (*Summe*) nice round; (*Geschlecht*) fair; **schönen Dank!** many thanks!; **schönen Gruß an** (*acc*) best regards to ‖ *adv* nicely; **der Hund macht s.** the dog sits up and begs; **s. warm** nice and warm

schonen [ˈʃonən] *tr* spare; take it easy on; treat with consideration ‖ *ref* take care of oneself

scho'nend *adj* careful; considerate

schön'färben *tr* gloss over

Schon'frist *f* period of grace

Schon'gang *m* (aut) overdrive

Schön'heit *f* (**-;-en**) beauty

Schön'heitsfehler *m* flaw

Schön'heitskönigin *f* beauty queen

Schön'heitspflege *f* beauty treatment

schön'tun §154 *intr* (*dat*) flatter; (*dat*) flirt (with)

Scho'nung *f* (**-;-en**) care, careful treatment; mercy; consideration; tree nursery; wild-game preserve

scho'nungslos *adj* unsparing; merciless; relentless

scho'nungsvoll *adj* considerate

Schon'zeit *f* (hunt) closed season

Schopf [ʃɔpf] *m* (**-[e]s;̈e**) tuft of hair; (orn) crest

schöpfen [ˈʃœpfən] *tr* draw; bail; scoop, ladle; (*frische Luft*) breathe; (*Mut*) take: **Verdacht s.** become suspicious; **wieder Atem** (or **Luft**) **s.** (fig) breathe freely again

Schöp'fer *m* (**-s;-**) creator; author; composer; master; sculptor; dipper, ladle

schöpferisch [ˈʃœpfərɪʃ] *adj* creative

Schöp'ferkraft *f* creative power

Schöpf'kelle *f* scoop

Schöpf'löffel *m* ladle

Schöp'fung *f* (**-;-en**) creation

Schoppen [ˈʃɔpən] *m* (**-s;-**) pint; glass of beer, glass of wine

schor [ʃor] *pret* of **scheren**

Schorf [ʃɔrf] *m* (**-[e]s;-e**) scab

Schornstein [ˈʃɔrnʃtaɪn] *m* chimney; smokestack

Schorn'steinfeger *m* chimney sweeper

Schoß [ʃɔs] *m* (**Schosses; Schosse**)

sprout ‖ [ʃos] m (-es;⁓e) lap; womb; (fig) bosom; **die Hände in den S. legen** cross one's arms; (fig) be idle
Schößling [ˈʃœslɪŋ] m (-s;-e) shoot
Schote [ˈʃotə] f (-;-n) pod, shell
Schotte [ˈʃɔtə] m (-n;-n) Scotchman ‖ f (-;-n) (naut) bulkhead
Schotter [ˈʃɔtər] m (-s;-) gravel; macadam, crushed stone; (rr) ballast
Schottin [ˈʃɔtɪn] f (-;-nen) Scotchwoman
schottisch [ˈʃɔtɪʃ] adj Scotch
schraffieren [ʃraˈfirən] tr hatch
schräg [ʃrek] adj oblique; (abfallend) slanting, sloping; diagonal ‖ adv obliquely; **s. gegenüber von** diagonally across from; **s. geneigt** sloping
Schräg'linie f diagonal
schrak [ʃrak] pret of schrecken
Schramme [ˈʃramə] f (-;-n) scratch, abrasion; scar
schrammen [ˈʃramən] tr scratch; skin
Schrank [ʃraŋk] m (-[e]s;⁓e) closet
Schranke [ˈʃraŋkə] f (-;-n) barrier; (fig) bounds, limit; (jur) bar; (rr) gate; (sport) starting gate
schran'kenlos adj boundless; exaggerated
Schran'kenwärter m (rr) signalman
Schrank'fach n compartment
Schrank'koffer m wardrobe trunk
Schrapnell [ʃrapˈnɛl] n (-s;-e & -s) shrapnel, piece of shrapnel
Schraubdeckel [ˈʃraupdɛkəl] m screw-on cap
Schraube [ˈʃraubə] f (-;-n) screw; bolt; (aer, naut) propeller
schrauben [ˈʃraubən] tr screw; **in die Höhe s.** raise ‖ ref—**sich in die Höhe s.** circle higher and higher
Schrau'benflügel m propeller blade
Schrau'bengang m, **Schrau'bengewinde** n thread (of a screw)
Schrau'benmutter f (-;-n) nut
Schrau'benschlüssel m wrench; **verstellbarer S.** monkey wrench
Schrau'benstrahl m, **Schrau'benstrom** m (aer) slipstream
Schraubenzieher [ˈʃraubəntsi·ər] m (-s;-) screwdriver
Schraubstock [ˈʃraupʃtɔk] m vice
Schrebergarten [ˈʃrebərgartən] m garden plot (at edge of town)
Schreck [ʃrek] m (-[e]s;-e) var of Schrecken
Schreck'bild n frightful sight; boogeyman
schrecken [ˈʃrekən] tr frighten, scare ‖ **Schrecken** m (-s;-) fright, fear
Schreckensbotschaft (**Schrek'kensbotschaft**) f alarming news
Schreckensherrschaft (**Schrek'kensherrschaft**) f reign of terror
Schreckenskammer (**Schrek'kenskammer**) f chamber of horrors
Schreckensregiment (**Schrek'kensregiment**) n reign of teror, terrorism
Schreckenstat (**Schrek'kenstat**) f atrocity
schreck'haft adj timid
schreck'lich adj frightful, terrible
Schrecknis [ˈʃrekms] n (-ses;-se) horror

Schreck'schuß m warning shot
Schreck'sekunde f reaction time
Schrei [ʃraɪ] m (-[e]s;-e) cry, shout; **letzter S.** latest fashion
Schreib- [ʃraɪp] comb.fm. writing
Schreib'art f style; spelling
Schreib'bedarf m stationery
Schreib'block m writing pad, note pad
schreiben [ˈʃraɪbən] §62 tr write; spell; type; **ins Konzept s.** make a rough draft of; **ins reine s.** make a clean copy; **Noten s.** copy music ‖ ref spell one's name ‖ intr write; spell; type ‖ **Schreiben** n (-s;-) writing; (com) letter
Schrei'ber m (-s;-) writer; clerk; recording instrument, recorder
schreib'faul adj too lazy to write
Schreib'feder f pen
Schreib'fehler m slip of the pen
Schreib'heft n copybook, exercise book
Schreib'mappe f portfolio
Schreib'maschine f typewriter; **mit der S. geschrieben** typed; **S. schreiben** type
Schreib'maschinenfarbband n (-[e]s; ⁓er) typewriter ribbon
Schreib'maschinenschreiber –in §6 mf typist
Schreib'maschinenschrift f typescript
Schreib'materialien pl, **Schreib'papier** n stationery
Schreib'schrift f (typ) script
Schreib'stube f (mil) orderly room
Schreib'tisch m desk
Schrei'bung f (-;-en) spelling
Schreib'unterlage f desk pad
Schreib'waren pl stationery
Schreib'warenhandlung f stationery store
Schreibweise f style; spelling
Schreib'zeug n writing materials
schreien [ˈʃraɪ·ən] §135 tr cry, shout, scream, howl ‖ ref—**sich heiser s.** shout oneself hoarse; **sich tot s.** yell one's lungs out ‖ intr cry, shout, scream, howl; (Esel) bray; (Eule) screech; (Schwein) squeal; **s. nach** clamor for; **s. über** (acc) cry out against; **s. vor** (dat) shout for (joy); cry out in (pain); roar with (laughter) ‖ **Schreien** n (-s;) shouting; **das ist zum S.!** that's a scream!
schrei'end adj shrill; (Farbe) loud; (Unrecht) flagrant
Schrei'hals m (coll) crybaby
Schrei'krampf m crying fit
Schrein [ʃraɪn] m (-[e]s;-e) reliquary
Schreiner [ˈʃraɪnər] m (-s;-) carpenter; cabinetmaker
schreiten [ˈʃraɪtən] §86 intr (SEIN) step; stride; **zur Abstimmung s.** proceed to vote; **zur Tat s.** proceed to act
schrie [ʃri] pret of schreien
schrieb [ʃrip] pret of schreiben
Schrift [ʃrift] f (-;-en) writing; handwriting; letter, character; document; book; publication; periodical; (auf Münzen) legend; (typ) type, font; **die Heilige S.** Holy Scripture; **nach der S. sprechen** speak standard German

Schrift'art f type, font
Schrift'auslegung f exegesis
Schrift'bild n type face
Schrift'deutsch n literary German
Schrift'führer –in §6 mf secretary
Schrift'leiter –in §6 mf editor
schrift'lich adj written || adv in writing; s. wiedergeben transcribe
Schrift'satz m (jur) brief; (typ) composition
Schrift'setzer m typesetter
Schrift'sprache f literary language
Schriftsteller –in ['ʃrɪftʃtelər(ɪn)] §6 mf writer, author
Schrift'stück n piece of writing; document
Schrifttum ['ʃrɪftum] n (–s;) literature
Schrift'verkehr m, **Schrift'wechsel** m correspondence
Schrift'zeichen n letter, character
schrill [ʃrɪl] adj shrill
schrillen ['ʃrɪlən] intr ring loudly
schritt [ʃrɪt] pret of **schreiten** ||
Schritt m (–[e]s;–e) step; pace; stride; (e–r Hose) crotch; (fig) step
Schritt'macher m pacemaker
schritt'weise adv gradually; step by step
schroff [ʃrɔf] adj steep; rugged; rude, uncouth; rough, harsh; (Ablehnung, Widerspruch) flat
schröpfen ['ʃrœpfən] tr (fig) milk, fleece; (med) bleed, cup
Schrot [ʃrot] m & n (–[e]s;–e) scrap; (Getreide) crushed grain, grits; (zum Schießen) buckshot
Schrot'brot n whole grain bread
Schrot'flinte f shotgun
Schrot'korn n, **Schrot'kugel** f pellet
Schrott [ʃrɔt] m (–[e]s;) scrap metal
Schrott'platz m junk yard
schrubben ['ʃrubən] tr scrub
Schrulle ['ʃrulə] f (–;–n) (coll) nutty idea
schrul'lenhaft, schrullig ['ʃrulɪç] adj whimsical
schrumpelig ['ʃrumpəlɪç] adj crumpled; wrinkled, shriveled
schrumpeln ['ʃrumpəln] intr shrivel
schrumpfen ['ʃrumpfən] intr (SEIN) shrink; shrivel; (pathol) atrophy
Schub [ʃup] m (–[e]s;–e) shove, push; batch; (phys) thrust
Schub'fach n drawer
Schub'karre f, **Schub'karren** m wheelbarrow
Schub'kasten m drawer
Schub'kraft f thrust
Schub'lade f drawer
Schub'leistung f thrust
Schubs [ʃups] m (–es;–e) (coll) shove
schubsen ['ʃupsən] tr & intr shove
Schub'stange f (aut) connecting rod
schüchtern ['ʃʏçtərn] adj shy, bashful
schuf [ʃuf] pret of **schaffen**
Schuft [ʃuft] m (–[e]s;–e) cad
schuften ['ʃuftən] intr drudge, slave
Schufterei [ʃuftə'raɪ] f (–;) drudgery; (Schuftigkeit) meanness
schuftig ['ʃuftɪç] adj (fig) rotten
Schuh [ʃu] m (–[e]s;–e) shoe; boot
Schuh'band n (–[e]s;–̈er) shoestring

Schuhflicker ['ʃuflɪkər] m (–s;–) shoe repairman, shoemaker
Schuh'krem m shoe polish
Schuh'laden m shoe store
Schuh'leisten m last
Schuh'löffel m shoehorn
Schuh'macher m shoemaker
Schuhplattler ['ʃuplatlər] m (–s;–) Bavarian folk dance
Schuh'putzer m shoeshine boy
Schuh'sohle f sole
Schuhspanner ['ʃuʃpanər] m (–s;–) shoetree
Schuh'werk n footwear
Schuh'wichse f shoe polish
Schuh'zeug n footwear
Schul– [ʃul] comb.fm. school
Schul'amt n school board
Schul'arbeit f homework; (Aust) classroom work
Schul'aufsicht f school board
Schul'bank f (–;–̈e) school desk
Schul'behörde f school board; board of education
Schul'beispiel n (fig) test case
Schul'besuch m attendance at school
Schul'bildung f schooling, education
schuld [ʃult] adj at fault, to blame ||
Schuld f (–;–en) debt; fault; guilt
schuld'bewußt adj conscious of one's guilt
schulden ['ʃuldən] tr owe
schuld'haft adj culpable || **Schuld'haft** f imprisonment for debt
Schul'diener m school janitor
schuldig ['ʃuldɪç] adj guilty; responsible; j–m etw s. sein owe s.o. s.th. ||
Schuldige §5 mf culprit; guilty party
Schul'digkeit f (–;–en) duty, obligation; seine S. tun do one's duty
Schul'direktor –in §7 mf principal
schuld'los adj innocent
Schuld'losigkeit f (–;) innocence
Schuldner –in ['ʃuldnər(ɪn)] §6 mf debtor
Schuld'schein m promissory note, IOU
Schuld'spruch m verdict of guilty
Schuld'verschreibung f promissory note, IOU; (Obligation) bond
Schule ['ʃulə] f (–;–n) school; auf der S. in school; S. machen (fig) set a precedent; von der S. abgehen quit school
schulen ['ʃulən] tr train; (pol) indoctrinate
Schüler ['ʃylər] m (–s;–) pupil (in grammar school or high school); trainee; (Jünger) disciple
Schü'leraustausch m student exchange
Schülerin ['ʃylərɪn] f (–;–nen) pupil
Schul'film m educational film
Schul'flug m training flight
schul'frei adj—schulfreier Tag holiday; s. haben have off
Schul'gelände n school grounds; campus
Schul'geld n tuition
Schul'gelehrsamkeit f book learning
Schul'hof m schoolyard, playground
Schul'kamerad m school chum
Schul'lehrer –in §6 mf schoolteacher
Schul'mappe f schoolbag
Schul'meister m schoolmaster; pedant
schul'meistern intr criticize

Schul'ordnung *f* school regulation
Schul'pflicht *f* compulsory school attendance
schul'pflichtig *adj* of school age; **schulpflichtiges Alter** school age
Schul'plan *m* curriculum
Schul'ranzen *m* schoolbag
Schul'rat *m* (-[e]s;-̈e) (educ) superintendent
Schul'reise *f* field trip
Schul'schiff *n* training ship
Schul'schluß *m* close of school
Schul'schwester *f* teaching nun
Schul'stunde *f* lesson, period
Schul'tasche *f* schoolbag
Schulter ['ʃʊltər] *f* (-;-n) shoulder
Schul'terblatt *n* shoulder blade
schul'terfrei *adj* off-the-shoulder; (*trägerfrei*) strapless
schultern ['ʃʊltərn] *tr* shoulder
Schul'terstück *n* epaulet
Schul'unterricht *m* instruction; schooling; **im S.** in school
Schul'wesen *n* school system
Schul'zeugnis *n* report card
Schul'zimmer *n* classroom
Schul'zwang *m* compulsory education
schummeln ['ʃʊməln] *intr* (coll) cheat
schund [ʃʊnt] *pret* of **schinden** ‖ **Schund** *m* (-[e]s;) junk, trash
Schund'literatur *f* trashy literature
Schund'roman *m* dime novel
Schupo ['ʃupo] *m* (-s;-s) (**Schutzpolizist**) policeman, copy ‖ *f* (-;) (**Schutzpolizei**) police
Schuppe [ʃʊpə] *f* (-;-n) scale; **Schuppen** dandruff
schuppen ['ʃʊpən] *tr* scale; scrape ‖ **Schuppen** *m* (-s;-) shed; (aer) hangar; (aut) garage
schuppig ['ʃʊpɪç] *adj* scaly, flaky
Schups [ʃʊps] *m* (-es;-e) shove
schupsen ['ʃʊpsən] *tr* shove
Schüreisen ['ʃyraɪzən] *n* poker
schüren ['ʃyrən] *tr* poke, stir; (fig) stir up, foment
schürfen ['ʃyrfən] *tr* scratch, scrape; dig for ‖ *intr* (**nach**) prospect (for)
schurigeln ['ʃurigəln] *tr* (coll) bully
Schurke ['ʃʊrkə] *m* (-n;-n) bum, punk
Schur'kenstreich *m*, **Schur'kentat** *f*, **Schurkerei** [ʃʊrkə'raɪ] *f* (-;-en) mean trick
schurkisch ['ʃurkɪʃ] *adj* mean, low-down
Schürze ['ʃyrtsə] *f* (-;-n) apron
schürzen ['ʃyrtsən] *tr* tuck up; tie
Schür'zenband *n* (-[e]s;-̈er) apron
Schür'zenjäger *m* skirt chaser, wolf
Schuß [ʃus] *m* (**Schusses; Schüsse**) shot; (*Ladung*) round; (*Schußwunde*) gunshot wound; (*rasche Bewegung*) rush; (*Brot*) batch; (bot) shoot; (culin) dash; (sport) shot; **blinder S.** blank; **e-n S. abgeben** fire a shot; **ein S. ins Blaue** a wild shot; **ein S. ins Schwarze** a bull's-eye; **im S. haben** have under control; **im vollen S.** in full swing; **in S. bekommen** get going; **in S. bringen** get (*s.th.*) going; **j-m vor den S. kommen** come within s.o.'s range; (fig) come across s.o.; **scharfer S.**

live round; **weit vom S.** out of harm's way
Schüssel ['ʃysəl] *f* (-;-n) bowl; (fig) dish
schuß'fest, schuß'sicher *adj* bulletproof
Schuß'waffe *f* firearm
Schuß'weite *f* range
Schuster ['ʃustər] *m* (-s;-) shoemaker; (fig) bungler
schustern ['ʃustərn] *intr* bungle
Schutt [ʃut] *m* (-es;) rubbish; rubble
Schutt'abladeplatz *m* dump
Schüttboden ['ʃytbodən] *m* granary
Schüttelfrost ['ʃytəlfrɔst] *m* shivers
schütteln ['ʃytəln] *tr* shake; **j-m die Hand s.** shake hands with s.o.
schütten ['ʃytən] *tr* pour, spill ‖ *impers* —**es schüttet** it is pouring
Schutz [ʃuts] *m* (-es;) protection, defense; (*Obdach*) shelter; (*Deckung*) cover; (*Schirm*) screen; (*Schutzgeleit*) safeguard; **zu S. und Trutz** defensive and offensive
Schutz'brille *f* safety goggles
Schütze ['ʃytsə] *m* (-n;-n) marksman, shot; (astr) Sagittarius; (mil) rifleman ‖ *f* (-;-n) sluice gate
schützen ['ʃytsən] *tr* (**gegen**) protect (against), defend (against); (**vor** *dat*) preserve (from) ‖ **Schützen** *m* (-s;-) (tex) shuttle
schüt'zend *adj* protective; tutelary
Schutz'engel *m* guardian angle
Schüt'zengraben *m* (mil) foxhole
Schüt'zenkompanie *f* rifle company
Schüt'zenkönig *m* crack shot
Schüt'zenloch *n* (mil) foxhole
Schüt'zenmine *f* anti-personnel mine
Schutz'geleit *n* escort; safe conduct; (aer) air cover; (nav) convoy
Schutz'glocke *f* (aer) umbrella
Schutz'gott *m*, **Schutz'göttin** *f* tutelary deity
Schutz'haft *f* protective custody
Schutzheilige §5 *mf* patron saint
Schutz'herr *m* protector; patron
Schutz'herrin *f* protectress; patroness
Schutz'impfung *f* immunization
Schutz'insel *f* traffic island
Schützling ['ʃytslɪŋ] *m* (-s;-e) ward
schutz'los *adj* defenseless
Schutz'mann *m* (-[e]s;-̈er & -leute) policeman
Schutz'marke *f* trademark
Schutz'mittel *n* preservative; preventive
Schutz'patron –in §8 *mf* patron saint
Schutz'polizei *f* police
Schutz'polizist *m* policeman, cop
Schutz'scheibe *f* (aut) windshield
Schutz'staffel *f* SS troops
Schutz'umschlag *m* dust jacket
Schutz–'und–Trutz–'Bündnis *f* defensive and offensive alliance
Schutz'waffe *f* defensive weapon
Schutz'zoll *m* protective tariff
Schwabe ['ʃvabə] *m* (-n;-n) Swabian
Schwaben ['ʃvabən] *n* (-s;) Swabia
Schwäbin ['ʃvebɪn] *f* (-;-nen) Swabian
schwäbisch ['ʃvebɪʃ] *adj* Swabian; **das Schwäbische Meer** Lake Constance
schwach [ʃvax] *adj* (**schwächer** ['ʃveçər]; **schwächste** ['ʃveçstə] §9)

weak; (*Hoffnung, Ton, Licht*) faint;
(*unzureichend*) scanty; sparse; (*armselig*) poor
Schwäche ['ʃvɛçə] *f* (-;-n) weakness
Schwach'kopf *m* dunce; sap, dope
schwächlich ['ʃvɛçlıç] *adj* feeble, delicate
Schwächling ['ʃvɛçlıŋ] *m* (-s;-e) weakling
schwach'sinnig *adj* feeble-minded ‖ **Schwachsinnige** §5 *mf* dimwit, moron
Schwach'strom *m* low-voltage current
Schwaden ['ʃvɑdən] *m* (-s;-) swath; cloud (*of smoke, etc.*)
Schwadron [ʃvaˈdron] *f* (-;-en) squadron
schwadronieren [ʃvadroˈnirən] *intr* (coll) brag
schwafeln ['ʃvɑfəln] *intr* talk nonsense
Schwager ['ʃvɑgər] *m* (-s;-͞) brother-in-law
Schwägerin ['ʃvegərın] *f* (-;-nen) sister-in-law
Schwalbe ['ʃvalbə] *f* (-;-n) swallow
Schwal'bennest *n* (aer) gun turret
Schwal'benschwanz *m* (*Frack*) tails; (carp) dovetail
Schwall [ʃval] *m* (-[e]s;-e) flood; (*von Worten*) torrent
schwamm [ʃvam] *pret* of **schwimmen** ‖ **Schwamm** *m* (-[e]s;-͞e) sponge; mushroom; fungus; dry rot; **S. darüber!** skip it!
schwammig ['ʃvamıç] *adj* spongy
Schwan [ʃvan] *m* (-[e]s;-͞e) swan
schwand [ʃvant] *pret* of **schwinden**
schwang [ʃvaŋ] *pret* of **schwingen**
schwanger ['ʃvaŋər] *adj* pregnant
schwängern ['ʃveŋərn] *tr* make pregnant; (fig) impregnate
Schwan'gerschaft *f* (-;-en) pregnancy
Schwan'gerschaftsverhütung *f* contraception
schwank [ʃvaŋk] *adj* flexible; unsteady ‖ **Schwank** *m* (-[e]s;-͞e) prank; joke; funny story; (theat) farce
schwanken ['ʃvaŋkən] *intr* stagger; (*schaukeln*) rock; (*schlingern*) roll; (*stampfen*) pitch; (*Flamme*) flicker; (*pendeln*) oscillate; (*vibrieren*) vibrate; (*wellenartig*) undulate; (*zittern*) shake; (*Preise*) fluctuate; (*zögern*) vacillate, hesitate
Schwanz [ʃvants] *m* (-es;-͞e) tail; (*Gefolge*) train; (*vulg*) pecker; **kein S.** not a living soul; **mit dem S. wedeln** (or **wippen**) wag its tail
schwänzeln ['ʃvɛntsəln] *intr* wag its tail; **s. um** fawn on
schwänzen ['ʃvɛntsən] *tr*—**die Schule s.** play hooky from school; **e-e Stunde s.** cut a class ‖ *intr* play hooky
schwappen ['ʃvapən] *intr* slosh around; **s. über** (*acc*) spill over
schwapps [ʃvaps] *interj* slap!; splash!
Schwäre ['ʃverə] *f* (-;-n) abscess
schwären ['ʃverən] *intr* fester
Schwarm [ʃvarm] *m* (-[e]s;-͞e) swarm; flock, herd; (*von Fischen*) school; (fig) idol; (fig) craze; (aer) flight of five aircraft; **sie ist mein S.** (coll) I have a crush on her

schwärmen ['ʃvɛrmən] *intr* swarm; stray; daydream; go out on the town; **s. für** (or **über** *acc* or **von**) rave about
Schwär'mer *m* (-s;-) enthusiast; reveler; daydreamer; firecracker; (religious) fanatic; (ent) hawk moth
Schwärmerei [ʃvɛrməˈraı] *f* (-;-en) enthusiasm; daydreaming; revelry; fanaticism
schwärmerisch ['ʃvɛrmərıʃ] *adj* enthusiastic; gushy; fanatic; fanciful
Schwarte ['ʃvartə] *f* (-;-n) rind, skin; (coll) old book
schwarz [ʃvarts] *adj* black; dark; (*ungesetzlich*) illegal; (*schmutzig*) dirty; (*düster*) gloomy; (*von der Sonne*) tanned; **schwarze Kunst** black magic; **schwarzes Brett** bulletin board ‖ *adv* illegally
Schwarz'arbeit *f* moonlighting; non-union work; illicit work
Schwarz'brenner *m* moonshiner
Schwärze ['ʃvertsə] *f* (-;-n) blackness; darkness; printer's ink
schwärzen ['ʃvertsən] *tr* darken; blacken
schwarz'fahren §71 *intr* (SEIN) drive without a license; ride without a ticket
Schwarz'fahrer -in §6 *mf* unlicensed driver; rider without a ticket
Schwarz'fahrt *f* joy ride; ride without a ticket
Schwarz'handel *m* black-marketing
Schwarz'händler -in §6 *mf* black marketeer; (*mit Eintrittskarten*) scalper
schwärzlich ['ʃvertslıç] *adj* blackish
Schwarz'markt *m* black market
Schwarz'seher -in §6 *mf* pessimist
Schwarz'sender *m* illegal transmitter
schwatzen ['ʃvatsən], **schwätzen** ['ʃvɛtsən] *tr* (coll) talk ‖ *intr* (coll) yap, talk nonsense; (coll) gossip
Schwät'zer -in §6 *mf* windbag; gossip
schwatz'haft *adj* talkative
Schwatz'maul *n* blabber mouth
Schwebe ['ʃvebə] *f* (-;) suspense; **in der S. sein** be undecided; be pending
Schwe'bebahn *f* cablecar
Schwe'beflug *m* hovering, soaring
schweben ['ʃvebən] *intr* (HABEN & SEIN) be suspended, hang; float; (*Hubschrauber*) hover; (*Segelflugzeug*) soar; glide; (fig) waver, be undecided; **in Gefahr s.** be in danger; **in Ungewißheit s.** be in suspense
Schwede ['ʃvedə] *m* (-n;-n) Swede
Schweden ['ʃvedən] *n* (-s;) Sweden
Schwedin ['ʃvedın] *f* (-;-nen) Swede
schwedisch ['ʃvedıʃ] *adj* Swedish
Schwefel ['ʃvefəl] *m* (-s;) sulfur
Schwe'felsäure *f* sulfuric acid
Schweif [ʃvaıf] *m* (-[e]s;-e) tail; (fig) train
schweifen ['ʃvaıfən] *tr* curve; (*spülen*) rinse ‖ *intr* (SEIN) roam, wander
Schweigegeld ['ʃvaıgəgelt] *n* hush money
schweigen ['ʃvaıgən] §148 *intr* be silent, keep silent; (*aufhören*) stop; **ganz zu s. von** to say nothing of; **s. zu** make no reply to

schwei'gend *adj* silent || *adv* in silence
schweigsam ['ʃvaɪkzɑm] *adj* taciturn
Schwein [ʃvaɪn] *n* (-[e]s;-e) pig, hog; **S. haben** be lucky, have luck
Schwei'nebraten *m* roast pork
Schwei'nefleisch *n* pork
Schwei'nehund *m* (pej) filthy swine
Schwei'nekoben *m* pigsty, pig pen
Schweinerei [ʃvaɪnə'raɪ] *f* (-;-en) mess; dirty business
Schwei'nerippchen *pl* pork chops
Schwei'newirtschaft *f* dirty mess
Schweins'kotelett *n* pork chop
Schweiß [ʃvaɪs] *m* (-es;) perspiration
schweißen ['ʃvaɪsən] *tr* weld || *intr* begin to melt, fuse; (hunt) bleed
Schwei'ßer -in §6 *mf* welder
Schweißfüße ['ʃvaɪsfysə] *pl* sweaty feet
schweißig ['ʃvaɪsɪç] *adj* sweaty; (hunt) bloody
Schweiß'perle *f* bead of sweat
Schweiz [ʃvaɪts] *f* (-;)—**die S.** Switzerland
Schwei'zer *m* Swiss; dairyman
schweizerisch ['ʃvaɪtsərɪʃ] *adj* Swiss
schwelen ['ʃvelən] *intr* smolder
schwelgen ['ʃvelgən] *intr* feast; **s. in** (*dat*) (fig) revel in; wallow in
Schwelgerei [ʃvelgə'raɪ] *f* (-;-en) feasting, carousing
schwelgerisch ['ʃvelgərɪʃ] *adj* riotous; luxurious
Schwelle ['ʃvelə] *f* (-;-n) sill; doorstep; (fig) verge; (psychol) threshold; (rr) railroad tie
schwellen ['ʃvelən] §119 *tr* swell || *intr* (SEIN) swell; (*Wasser*) rise; (*anwachsen*) increase
Schwel'lung *f* (-;-en) swelling
Schwemme ['ʃvemə] *f* (-;-n) watering place; (coll) taproom; (com) glut
schwemmen ['ʃvemən] *tr* wash off, rinse; (*Vieh*) water; (*Holz*) float
Schwengel ['ʃveŋəl] *m* (-s;-) pump handle; (*e-r Glocke*) hammer
schwenkbar ['ʃveŋkbɑr] *adj* rotating
schwenken ['ʃveŋkən] *tr* swing; shake; (*drohend*) brandish; (*Hut*) wave; (*spülen*) rinse || *intr* (SEIN) turn; swivel, pivot; (*Geschütz*) traverse; (mil) wheel; (pol) change sides
Schwen'kung *f* (-;-en) turn; wheeling; traversing; (fig) change of mind
schwer [ʃver] *adj* heavy; difficult, hard; serious; (*schwerfällig*) ponderous; (*Strafe*) severe; (*Wein*) strong; (*Speise*) rich; (*unbeholfen*) clumsy; (*Kompanie*) heavy-weapons; **drei Pfund s. sein** weigh three pounds; **schweres Geld bezahlen** pay a stiff price || *adv* hard; with difficulty; (coll) very
Schwere ['ʃverə] *f* (-;) weight; seriousness; (*des Weines*) body; difficulty; significance; (phys) gravity
schwe'relos *adj* weightless
schwer'fällig *adj* heavy; clumsy, slow
Schwer'gewicht *n* heavyweight class; (*Nachdruck*) emphasis
Schwergewichtler -in ['ʃvergəvɪçtlər (ɪn)] §6 *mf* (sport) heavyweight
schwer'hörig *adj* hard of hearing

Schwer'industrie *f* heavy industry
Schwer'kraft *f* gravity
schwer'lich *adv* hardly
Schwer'mut *f* melancholy, depression
schwer'mütig *adj* melancholy, depressed
schwer'nehmen §116 *tr* take hard
Schwer'punkt *m* center of gravity; crucial point, focal point
Schwert [ʃvert] *n* (-[e]s;-er) sword
Schwer'verbrecher -in §6 *mf* felon
schwer'verdient *adj* hard-earned
schwer'wiegend *adj* weighty
Schwester ['ʃvestər] *f* (-;-n) sister; nurse; nun
Schwe'sterhelferin *f* nurse's aide
schwieg [ʃvik] *pret* of **schweigen**
Schwieger- [ʃvigər] *comb.fm.* -in-law
Schwie'germutter *f* mother-in-law
Schwie'gersohn *m* son-in-law
Schwie'gertochter *f* daughter-in-law
Schwie'gervater *m* father-in-law
Schwiele ['ʃvilə] *f* (-;-n) callus
schwielig ['ʃvilɪç] *adj* callous
schwierig ['ʃvirɪç] *adj* hard, difficult
Schwie'rigkeit *f* (-;-en) difficulty
Schwimm- [ʃvɪm] *comb.fm.* swimming
Schwimm'anstalt *f*, **Schwimm'bad** *n*, **Schwimm'bassin** *n*, **Schwimm'becken** *n* swimming pool
schwimmen ['ʃvɪmən] §136 *intr* (HABEN & SEIN) swim; float
Schwimm'gürtel *m* life belt
Schwimm'haut *f* web
Schwimm'hose *f* bathing trunks
Schwimm'kraft *f* buoyancy
Schwimm'panzer *m* amphibious tank
Schwimm'weste *f* life jacket
Schwindel ['ʃvɪndəl] *m* (-s;-) dizziness; swindle, gyp; (*Unsinn*) bunk; (pathol) vertigo; **der ganze S.** the whole caboodle
Schwin'delanfall *m* dizzy spell
Schwin'delfirma *f* fly-by-night
schwin'delhaft *adj* fraudulent, bogus
schwindelig ['ʃvɪndəlɪç] *adj* dizzy
schwindeln ['ʃvɪndəln] *tr* swindle || *intr* fib || *impers*—**mir schwindelt** I feel dizzy
Schwin'delunternehmen *n* fly-by-night
schwinden ['ʃvɪndən] §59 *intr* (SEIN) dwindle; decline; (*Farbe*) fade
Schwind'ler -in §6 *mf* swindler; fibber
schwindlig ['ʃvɪntlɪç] *adj* dizzy
Schwindsucht ['ʃvɪntzuçt] *f* tuberculosis
Schwinge ['ʃvɪŋə] *f* (-;-n) wing; fan; winnow; (poet) pinion
schwingen ['ʃvɪŋən] §142 *tr* swing; wave; brandish; (agr) winnow; (tex) swingle || *ref* vault; soar || *intr* swing; sway; oscillate; vibrate
Schwin'ger *m* (-s;-) oscillator; (box) haymaker
Schwin'gung *f* (-;-en) oscillation; vibration; swinging
Schwips [ʃvɪps] *m*—**e-n S. haben** (coll) be tight, be tipsy
schwirren ['ʃvirən] *intr* (HABEN & SEIN) whiz, whir; buzz; (*Gerüchte*) fly
Schwitzbad ['ʃvɪtsbɑt] *n* Turkish bath
schwitzen ['ʃvɪtsən] *tr* & *intr* sweat

schwoll [ʃvɔl] *pret* of **schwellen**
schwor [ʃvor] *pret* of **schwören**
schwören ['ʃvørən] §137 *tr & intr*
swear; **auf j-n** (or **etw**) **s.** swear by
s.o. (or s.th.)
schwul [ʃvul] *adj* (vulg) homosexual
schwül [ʃvyl] *adj* sultry, muggy
Schwulität [ʃvulɪ'tet] *f* (-;-en) trouble
Schwulst [ʃvulst] *m* (-es;-̈e) bombast
schwülstig ['ʃvylstɪç] *adj* bombastic
schwummerig ['ʃvumərɪç] *adj* (coll)
shaky
Schwund [ʃvunt] *m* (-[e]s;) dwin-
dling; shrinkage; loss; leakage; (*des
Haares*) falling out; (rad) fading;
(pathol) atrophy
Schwung [ʃvuŋ] *m* (-[e]s;-̈e) swing;
vault; (*Tatkraft*) zip, go; (*der Phantasie*) flight; **in S. bringen** start; **S.
bekommen** gather momentum
schwung'haft *adj* brisk, lively
Schwung'kraft *f* centrifugal force; (fig)
zip, pep; (phys) momentum
Schwung'rad *n* (mach) flywheel
schwung'voll *adj* enthusiastic, lively
schwur [ʃvur] *pret* of **schwören** ‖
Schwur *m* (-[e]s;-̈e) oath
Schwur'gericht *n* jury
sechs [zɛks] *invar adj & pron* six ‖
Sechs *f* (-;-en) six
Sechs'eck *n* hexagon
Sechser ['zɛksər] *m* (-s;-) six; (*in der
Lotterie*) jackpot
Sechsta'gerennen *n* six-day bicycle race
sechste ['zɛkstə] §9 *adj & pron* sixth
Sechstel ['zɛkstəl] *n* (-s;-) sixth
sech'zehn *invar adj & pron* sixteen ‖
Sech'zehn *f* (-;-en) sixteen
sech'zehnte §9 *adj & pron* sixteenth
Sech'zehntel *n* (-s;-) sixteenth
sechzig ['zɛçtsɪç] *invar adj & pron*
sixty ‖ Sechzig *f* (-;-en) sixty
sechziger ['zɛçtsɪgər] *invar adj* of the
sixties; **die s. Jahre** the sixties ‖
Sechziger *m* (-s;-) sexagenarian
sechzigste ['zɛçtsɪçstə] §9 *adj & pron*
sixtieth
See [ze] *m* (Sees; Seen ['ze·ən] lake ‖
f (See; Seen ['ze·ən]) sea; ocean;
an der See at the seashore; **an die
See gehen** go to the seashore; **auf
See** at sea; **in See gehen** (or **stechen**)
put out to sea; **in See sein** be in open
water; **Kapitän zur See** navy captain;
zur See gehen go to sea
See'bad *n* seashore resort
See'bär *m* (fig) sea dog
see'fähig *adj* seaworthy
See'fahrer *m* seafarer
See'fahrt *f* seafaring; voyage
see'fest *adj* seaworthy; **s. werden** get
one's sea legs
See'gang *m*—**hoher** (or **schwerer** or
starker) **S.** heavy seas
See'hafen *m* seaport
See'handel *m* maritime trade
See'hund *m* (zool) seal
See'jungfer *f*, See'jungfrau *f* mermaid
See'kadett *m* naval cadet
See'karte *f* (naut) chart
see'krank *adj* seasick
See'krebs *m* lobster
Seele ['zelə] *f* (-;-n) soul; mind; (*Ein-*

wohner) inhabitant, soul; (*e-s Ge-
schützes*) bore; (*e-s Kabels*) core
See'lenangst *f* mortal fear
See'lenfriede *m* peace of mind
See'lenheil *n* salvation
See'lennot *f* mental distress
See'lenpein *f*, See'lenqual *f* mental
anguish
See'lenruhe *f* peace of mind; compo-
sure
see'lensgut *adj* good-hearted
seelisch ['zelɪʃ] *adj* mental, psychic
Seel'sorge *f* (-;) ministry
Seel'sorger *m* (-s;-) minister, pastor
See'macht *f* sea power
See'mann *m* (-[e]s;-leute) seaman
See'meile *f* nautical mile
See'möwe *f* sea gull
See'not *f* (naut) distress
See'ratte *f* (fig) old salt
See'raub *m* piracy
See'räuber *m* pirate; corsair
See'räuberei *f* piracy
See'recht *n* maritime law
See'reise *f* voyage; cruise
See'sperre *f* naval blockade
See'stadt *f* seaport town; coastal town
See'straße *f* shipping lane
See'streitkräfte *pl* naval forces
See'tang *m* seaweed
see'tüchtig *adj* seaworthy
See'warte *f* oceanographic institute
See'weg *m* sea route; **auf dem S. by
sea**
See'wesen *n* naval affairs
Segel ['zegəl] *n* (-s;-) sail
Se'gelboot *n* sailboat; (sport) yacht
Se'gelfliegen *n* gliding
Se'gelflieger –in §6 *mf* glider pilot
Se'gelflug *m* glide, gliding
Se'gelflugzeug *n* glider
Se'gelleinwand *f* sailcloth, canvas
segeln ['zegəln] *intr* (HABEN & SEIN)
sail; (aer) glide
Se'gelschiff *n* sailing vessel
Se'gelsport *m* sailing
Se'geltuch *n* sailcloth, canvas
Se'geltuchhülle *f*, Se'geltuchplane *f*
tarpaulin
Segen ['zegən] *m* (-s;-) blessing
se'gensreich *adj* blessed, blissful
Segler ['zeglər] *m* (-s;-) yachtsman;
(aer) glider; (naut) sailing vessel
segnen ['zegnən] *tr* bless
Seh– [ze] *comb.fm.* visual, of vision
sehen ['ze·ən] §138 *tr* see ‖ *intr* see;
look; **s. auf** (*acc*) look at; take care
of; face (*a direction*); **s. nach** look
for, look around for; **schlecht s.**
have poor eyes ‖ **Sehen** *n* (-s;) sight;
eyesight, vision; **vom S.** by sight
se'henswert *adj* worth seeing
Se'henswürdigkeit *f* object of interest;
Sehenswürdigkeiten sights
Seher ['ze·ər] *m* (-s;-) seer, prophet
Se'hergabe *f* gift of prophecy
Seh'feld *n* field of vision
Seh'kraft *f* eyesight
Sehne ['zenə] *f* (-;-n) tendon, sinew;
(*Bogen–*) string; (geom) secant
sehnen ['zenən] *ref*—**sich s. nach** long
for, crave ‖ **Sehnen** *n* (-s;) longing
Seh'nerv *m* optic nerve

sehnig ['zeniç] *adj* sinewy; *(Fleisch)* stringy
sehnlich ['zenliç] *adj* longing; ardent
Sehnsucht ['zenzuçt] *f* (-;) yearning
sehr [zer] *adv* very; very much
Seh'rohr *n* periscope
Seh'vermögen *n* sight, vision
Seh'weite *f* visual range; **in S.** within sight
seicht [zaiçt] *adj* (& fig) shallow
Seide ['zaidə] *f* (-;-n) silk
seiden ['zaidən] *adj* silk, silky
Sei'denatlas *m* satin
Sei'denpapier *n* tissue paper
Sei'denraupe *f* silkworm
Sei'denspinnerei *f* silk mill
Sei'denstoff *m* silk cloth
seidig ['zaidiç] *adj* silky
Seife ['zaifə] *f* (-;-n) soap
Sei'fenblase *f* soap bubble
Sei'fenbrühe *f* soapsuds
Sei'fenflocken *pl* soap flakes
Sei'fenlauge *f* soapsuds
Sei'fenpulver *n* soap powder
Sei'fenschale *f* soap dish
Sei'fenschaum *m* lather
seifig ['zaifiç] *adj* soapy
seihen ['zai·ən] *tr* strain, filter
Sei'her *m* (-s;-) strainer, filter
Seil [zail] *n* (-[e]s;-e) rope; cable
Seil'bahn *f* cable railway; cable car
seil'springen *intr* jump rope
Seil'tänzer **-in** §6 *mf* ropewalker
sein [zain] §139 *intr* (SEIN) be; exist; **es ist mir, als wenn** I feel as if; **es sei denn, daß** unless; **lassen Sie das s.!** stop it!; **wenn dem so ist** if that is the case; **wie dem auch sein mag** however that may be ‖ *aux* (to form compound past tenses of intransitive verbs of motion, change of condition, etc.) have, e.g., **ich bin gegangen** I have gone, I went ‖ §2.2 *poss adj* his; its; one's; her ‖ §2.4,5 *poss pron* his; hers; **die Seinen** his family; **er hat das Seine getan** he did his share; **jedem das Seine** to each his own ‖ **Sein** *n* (-s;) being; existence; reality
seinerseits ['zainər'zaits] *adv* for his part
seinerzeit ['zainər'tsait] *adv* in its time: in those days; in due time
seinesgleichen ['zainəs'glaiçən] *pron* people like him, the likes of him
seinethalben ['zainət'halbən], **seinetwegen** ['zainət'vegən] *adv* for his sake; on his account; *(von ihm aus)* for all he cares
seinetwillen ['zainət'vilən] *adv*—**um s.** for his sake, on his behalf
Seinige ['zainigə] §2,5 *pron* his; **das S.** his property, his own; his due; his share; **die Seinigen** his family
seit [zait] *prep* (*dat*) since, for; **s. e-m Jahr** for one year; **s. einiger Zeit** for some time past; **s. kurzem** lately; **s. langem** for a long time; **s. wann** since when ‖ *conj* since
seitdem [zait'dem] *adv* since that time ‖ *conj* since
Seite ['zaitə] *f* (-;-n) side; page; direction; *(Quelle)* source; (mil) flank
Sei'tenansicht *f* side view, profile

Sei'tenbau *m* (-[e]s;-ten) annex
Sei'tenblick *m* side glance
Sei'tenflosse *f* (aer) horizontal stabilizer
Sei'tenflügel *m* (archit) wing
Sei'tengang *m* side aisle
Sei'tengeleise *n* sidetrack
Sei'tenhieb *m* snide remark, dig
sei'tenlang *adj* pages of
Sei'tenriß *m* profile
sei'tens *prep* (*genit*) on the part of
Sei'tenschiff *n* (archit) aisle
Sei'tenschwimmen *n* sidestroke
Sei'tensprung *m* (fig) escapade
Sei'tenstück *n* (fig) counterpart
Sei'tenwind *m* cross wind
seither [zait'her] *adv* since then
–seitig [zaitiç] *comb.fm.* –sided
seit'lich *adj* lateral
seitwärts ['zaitverts] *adv* sideways, sidewards; aside
Sekretär **-in** [zekre'ter(in)] §8 *mf* secretary
Sekt [zekt] *m* (-[e]s;-e) champagne
Sekte ['zektə] *f* (-;-n) sect
Sek·tor ['zektər] *m* (-s;-toren ['torən]) sector; (fig) field
Sekundant [zekun'dant] *m* (-en;-en) (box) second
sekundär [zekun'der] *adj* secondary
Sekunde [ze'kundə] *f* (-;-n) second
Sekun'denbruchteil *m* split second
Sekun'denzeiger *m* second hand
Sekurit [zeku'rit] *n* (-s;) safety glass
selber ['zelbər] *invar pron* (coll) var of selbst
selbst [zelpst] *invar pron* self; in person, personally; (*sogar*) even; by oneself; **ich s.** I myself; **von s.** voluntarily; spontaneously; automatically ‖ *adv* even; **s. ich** even I; **s. wenn** even if, even when
Selbst'achtung *f* self-respect
selbständig ['zelpʃtendiç] *adj* independent
Selbst'bedienung *f* self-service
Selbst'beherrschung *f* self-control
Selbst'beobachtung *f* introspection
Selbst'bestimmung *f* self-determination
Selbst'betrug *m* self-deception
selbst'bewußt *adj* self-confident
Selbst'binder *m* necktie; (agr) combine
Selbst'erhaltung *f* self-preservation
selbst'gebacken *adj* homemade
selbst'gefällig *adj* complacent, smug
Selbst'gefühl *n* self-confidence
selbst'gemacht *adj* homemade
selbst'gerecht *adj* self-righteous
Selbst'gespräch *n* soliloquy
selbst'gezogen *adj* home-grown
selbst'herrlich *adj* high-handed
Selbst'herrschaft *f* autocracy
Selbst'herrscher *m* autocrat
Selbst'kosten *pl* production costs
Selbst'kostenpreis *m* factory price; **zum S. abgeben** sell at cost
Selbstlader ['zelpstladər] *m* (-s;-) automatic (weapon)
Selbst'laut *m* vowel
selbst'los *adj* unselfish
Selbst'mord *m* suicide
selbst'sicher *adj* self-confident
Selbst'steuer *n* automatic pilot

Selbst'sucht f egotism, selfishness
selbst'süchtig adj egotistical
selbst'tätig adj automatic
Selbst'täuschung f self-deception
Selbstüberhebung ['zɛlpstybərhebʊŋ] f (-;) self-conceit, presumption
Selbst'verbrennung f spontaneous combustion; self-immolation
Selbst'verlag m—**im S.** printed privately
Selbst'verleugnung f self-denial
Selbst'versorger m (-s;-) self-supporter
selbst'verständlich adj obvious; natural || adv of course
Selbst'verständlichkeit f foregone conclusion, matter of course
Selbst'verteidigung f self-defense
Selbst'vertrauen n self-confidence
Selbst'verwaltung f autonomy
Selbst'wähler m (-s;-) dial telephone
Selbst'zucht f self-discipline
selbst'zufrieden adj self-satisfied
Selbst'zufriedenheit f self-satisfaction
Selbst'zweck m end in itself
selig ['zeliç] adj blessed; (verstorben) late; (fig) ecstatic; (fig) tipsy; **seligen Angedenkens** of blessed memory; **s. werden** attain salvation, be saved
Se'ligkeit f (-;) happiness; salvation
Se'ligpreisung f (Bib) beatitude
se'ligsprechen §64 tr beatify
Sellerie ['zɛləri] m (-s;) & f (-;) celery (bulb)
selten ['zɛltən] adj rare, scarce || adv seldom, rarely
Selterswasser ['zɛltərsvasər] n seltzer, soda water
seltsam ['zɛltzam] adj odd, strange
Semester [zɛ'mɛstər] n (-s;-) semester
Semikolon ['zɛmɪkolɔn] n semicolon
Seminar [zɛmɪ'nɑr] n (-s;-e) seminary; (educ) seminar
Seminarist [zɛmɪnɑ'rɪst] m (-en;-en) seminarian
semitisch [zɛ'mɪtɪʃ] adj Semitic
Semmel ['zɛməl] f (-;-n) roll
Senat [zɛ'nat] m (-[e]s;-e) senate
Se-nator [zɛ'natɔr] m (-s;-natoren [na'torən]) senator
Sende- [zɛndə] comb.fm. transmitting, transmitter, broadcasting
senden ['zɛndən] tr & intr transmit, broadcast; telecast || §120 & §140 tr send || intr—**s. nach** send for
Sen'der m (-s;-) (rad, telv) transmitter; (rad) broadcasting station
Sen'deraum m broadcasting studio
Sen'dezeichen n station identification
Sen'dezeit f air time
Sen'dung f (-;-en) sending; (fig) mission; (com) shipment; (rad) broadcast; (telv) telecast
Senf [zɛnf] m (-[e]s;-e) mustard
sengen ['zɛŋən] tr singe, scorch
seng(e)rig ['zɛŋ(ə)rɪç] adj burnt; (fig) suspicious, fishy
senil [zɛ'nil] adj senile
Senilität [zɛnɪlɪ'tet] f (-;) senility
senior ['zɛnjɔr] adj senior
Senkblei ['zɛŋkblaɪ] n plummet; (naut) sounding lead
Senke ['zɛŋkə] f (-;-n) depression
senken ['zɛŋkən] tr lower; sink; (Kopf)

bow || ref sink, settle; dip, slope; (Mauer) sag
Senkfüße ['zɛŋkfysə] pl flat feet, fallen arches
Senk'fußeinlage f arch support
Senkgrube ['zɛŋkgrubə] f cesspool
Senkkasten ['zɛŋkkastən] m caisson
senkrecht ['zɛŋkrɛçt] adj vertical; (geom) perpendicular
Sen'kung f (-;-en) sinking; depression; dip, slope; sag; (der Preise) lowering
Sensation [zɛnza'tsjon] f (-;-en) sensation
sensationell [zɛnzatsjɔ'nɛl] adj sensational
Sensations'blatt n (pej) scandal sheet
Sensations'lust f sensationalism
Sensations'meldung f, **Sensations'nachricht** f (journ) scoop
Sensations'presse f yellow journalism
Sense ['zɛnzə] f (-;-n) scythe
sensibel [zɛn'zibəl] adj sensitive; (Nerven) sensory
Sensibilität [zɛnzɪbɪlɪ'tet] f (-;) sensitivity, sensitiveness
sentimental [zɛntɪmɛn'tal] adj sentimental
separat [zɛpa'rat] adj separate
September [zɛp'tɛmbər] m (-[s];) September
Serenade [zɛrɛ'nadə] f (-;-n) serenade
Serie ['zɛrjə] f (-;-n) series; line
Se'rienanfertigung f, **Se'rienbau** m, **Se'rienfabrikation** f, **Se'rienherstellung** f mass production
se'rienmäßig adj—**serienmäßige Herstellung** mass production || adv—**s. herstellen** mass-produce
Se'riennummer f serial number
Se'rienproduktion f mass production
seriös [zɛ'rjøs] adj serious; reliable
Se-rum ['zerʊm] n (-s;-ren [rən] & -ra [ra]) serum
Service ['zørvɪs(əs)];) (Kundendienst) service || [zɛr'vis] n (Services [zɛr'vis]; Service [zɛr'vis(ə)]) (Tafelgeschirr) service
Servierbrett [zɛr'virbrɛt] n tray
servieren [zɛr'virən] tr serve; **es ist serviert!** dinner is ready! || intr wait at table
Serviertisch [zɛr'virtɪʃ] m sideboard
Servierwagen [zɛr'virvagən] m serving cart
Serviette [zɛr'vjetə] f (-;-n) napkin
Servo- [zɛrvə] comb.fm. booster, auxiliary, servo, power, automatic
Ser'vobremsen pl power brakes
Ser'vokupplung f automatic transmission
Ser'volenkung f power steering
Servus ['zɛrvʊs] interj (Aust) hello!; (coll) so long!
Sessel ['zɛsəl] m (-s;-) easy chair
Ses'sellift m chair lift
seßhaft ['zɛshaft] adj settled; **sich s. machen** settle down
Setzei ['zɛtsaɪ] n fried egg
setzen ['zɛtsən] tr set, put, place; seat; (beim Spiel) bet; (Denkmal) erect; (Frist) fix; (Junge) breed; (Fische) stock; (Pflanzen) plant; (mus) com-

pose; (typ) set ‖ *ref* sit down; (*Kaffee*) settle ‖ *intr* set type; **s. auf** (*acc*) bet on ‖ *intr* (SEIN)—**s. über** (*acc*) jump over
Set′zer *m* (-s;-) typesetter, compositor
Setz′fehler *m* typographical error
Seuche [′zɔɪçə] *f* (-;-n) epidemic
seufzen [′zɔɪftsən] *intr* sigh
Seuf′zer *m* (-s;-) sigh
Sex [zɛks] *m* (-es;) sex
Sex-Appeal [′zɛks ə′pil] *m* (-s;) sex appeal
Sex′-Bombe *f* (coll) sex pot
Sexual- [zɛksʊɑl] *comb.fm.* sex
sexuell [zɛksʊ′ɛl] *adj* sexual
Sexus [′zɛksʊs] *m* (-;-) sex
sezieren [zɛ′tsirən] *tr* dissect
Shampoo [ʃam′pu] *n* (-s;-s) shampoo
Sibirien [zɪ′birjən] *n* (-s;) Siberia
sich [zɪç] §11 *reflex pron* oneself; himself; herself; itself; themselves; **an** (**und für**) **s.** in itself; **außer s.** sein be beside oneself ‖ *recip pron* each other, one another
Sichel [′zɪçəl] *f* (-;-n) sickle
sicher [′zɪçər] *adj* sure; positive; reliable; (**vor** *dat*) safe (from), secure (from) ‖ *adv* surely, certainly
Si′cherheit *f* (-;-en) safety, security; (*Gewißheit*) certainty; (*Zuverlässigkeit*) reliability; (*im Auftreten*) assurance; (com) security; (jur) bail
Si′cherheitsgurt *m*, **Si′cherheitsgürtel** *m* (aer, aut) seat belt
Si′cherheitsnadel *f* safety pin
Si′cherheitspolizei *f* security police
Si′cherheitsspielraum *m* margin of safety, leeway
si′cherlich *adv* surely, certainly
sichern [′zɪçərn] *tr* secure; fasten; guarantee; (*Gewehr*) put on safety
Si′cherstellung *f* safekeeping; guarantee
Si′cherung *f* (-;-en) protection; guarantee; (*an Schußwaffe*) safety catch; (elec) fuse; **durchgebrannte S.** blown fuse
Si′cherungskasten *m* fuse box
Sicht [zɪçt] *f* (-;) sight; (*Aussicht*) view; (*Sichtigkeit*) visibility; **auf kurze S.** short-range; **auf S.** at sight
sichtbar [′zɪçtbar] *adj* visible
sichten [′zɪçtən] *tr* sight; (fig) sift
sichtig [′zɪçtɪç] *adj* clear
sicht′lich *adj* visible
Sicht′vermerk *m* visa
sickern [′zɪkərn] *intr* (HABEN & SEIN) trickle, seep, leak
sie [zi] §11 *pers pron* she, her; it; they, them ‖ §11 **Sie** *pers pron* you
Sieb [zip] *n* (-[e]s;-e) sieve, colander; screen; (rad) filter
sieben [′zibən] *invar adj & pron* seven ‖ *tr* sift, strain; (fig) screen; (rad) filter ‖ **Sieben** *f* (-;-en) seven
siebente [′zibəntə] §9 *adj & pron* seventh
Siebentel [′zibəntəl] *n* (-s;-) seventh
siebte [′ziptə] §9 *adj & pron* seventh
Siebtel [′ziptəl] *n* (-s;-) seventh
siebzehn [′ziptsen] *invar adj & pron* seventeen ‖ **Siebenzehn** *f* (-;-en) seventeen

siebzehnte [′ziptsentə] §9 *adj & pron* seventeenth
Siebzehntel [′ziptsentəl] *n* (-s;-) seventeenth
siebzig [′ziptsɪç] *invar adj & pron* seventy ‖ **Siebzig** *f* (-;-en) seventy
siebziger [′ziptsɪgər] *invar adj* of the seventies; **die s. Jahre** the seventies ‖ **Siebziger** *m* (-s;-) septuagenarian
siebzigste [′ziptsɪçstə] §9 *adj & pron* seventieth
siech [ziç] *adj* sickly
siechen [′ziçən] *intr* be sickly
Siechtum [′ziçtum] *n* (-s;) lingering illness
siedeheiß [′zidə′haɪs] *adj* piping hot
siedeln [′zidəln] *intr* settle
sieden [′zidən] §141 *tr & intr* boil
Siedepunkt [′zidəpuŋkt] *m* boiling point
Siedler –in [′zidlər(ɪn)] §6 *mf* settler
Sied′lerstelle *f* homestead
Sied′lung *f* (-;-en) settlement; colony; housing development
Sieg [zik] *m* (-[e]s;-e) victory
Siegel [′zigəl] *n* (-s;-) seal
siegeln [′zigəln] *tr* seal
Sie′gelring *m* signet ring
siegen [′zigən] *intr* win, be victorious
Sie′ger –in §6 *mf* winner, victor; **zweiter Sieger** runner-up
Sieges- [zigəs] *comb.fm.* victory, of victory, triumphal
Sie′gesbogen *m* triumphal arch
sieg′reich *adj* victorious
Signal [zɪg′nal] *n* (-s;-e) signal
signalisieren [zɪgnalɪ′zirən] *tr* signal
Silbe [′zɪlbə] *f* (-;-n) syllable
Sil′bentrennung *f* syllabification
Silber [′zɪlbər] *n* (-s;) silver
silbern [′zɪlbərn] *adj* silver, silvery
Sil′berzeug *n* silver, silverware
Silhouette [zɪlu′ɛtə] *f* (-;-n) silhouette
Silo [′zilo] *m* (-s;-s) silo
Silvester [zɪl′vɛstər] *m* (-s;-), **Silve′sterabend** *m* New Year's Eve
simpel [′zɪmpəl] *adj* simple ‖ **Simpel** *m* (-s;-) simpleton
Sims [zɪms] *m & n* (-es;-e) ledge; (*Fenster-*) sill; (*Kamin-*) mantelpiece
Simulant –in [zɪmu′lant(ɪn)] §7 *mf* faker; (mil) goldbrick
simulieren [zɪmu′lirən] *tr* simulate, fake ‖ *intr* loaf
simultan [zɪmul′tan] *adj* simultaneous
Sinfo-nie [zɪnfɔ′ni] *f* (-;-nien [′ni-ən]) symphony
singen [′zɪŋən] §142 *tr & intr* sing
Singsang [′zɪŋzaŋ] *m* (-[e]s;) singsong
Sing′spiel *n* musical comedy, musical
Sing′stimme *f* vocal part
Singular [′zɪŋgular] *m* (-s;-e) singular
sinken [′zɪŋkən] §143 *intr* (SEIN) sink, slump, sag; (*Preise*) drop; **s. lassen** lower; (*Mut*) lose
Sinn [zɪn] *m* (-[e]s;-e) sense; mind; meaning; liking, taste
Sinn′bild *n* emblem, symbol
sinn′bildlich *adj* symbolic(al) ‖ *adv* symbolically; **s. darstellen** symbolize
sinnen [′zɪnən] §121 *tr* plan; plot ‖ *intr* (**auf** *acc*) plan, plot; (**über** *acc*)

think (about) ‖ **Sinnen** *n* (**-s;**) reflection, meditation, reverie
sin'nend *adj* pensive, reflective
Sin'nenlust *f* sensuality
Sin'nenmensch *m* sensualist
Sin'nenwelt *f* material world
Sin'nesänderung *f* change of mind
Sin'nesart *f* character, disposition
Sin'nestäuschung *f* illusion, hallucination, mirage
sinn'lich *adj* sensual; material
sinn'los *adj* senseless
sinn'reich *adj* ingenious, bright
sinn'verwandt *adj* synonymous
sinn'voll *adj* meaningful; sensible
Sintflut ['zɪntflut] *f* deluge, flood
Sippe ['zɪpə] *f* (**-;-n**) kin; clan
Sipp'schaft *f* (**-;-en**) clique, set
Sirup ['zirup] *m* (**-s;-e**) syrup
Sitte ['zɪtə] *f* (**-;-n**) custom; habit; usage; **die Sitten** the morals
Sit'tenbild *n*, **Sit'tengemälde** *n* description of the manners (*of an age*)
Sit'tengesetz *n* moral law
Sit'tenlehre *f* ethics
sit'tenlos *adj* immoral
Sit'tenpolizei *f* vice squad
sit'tenrein *adj* chaste
Sit'tenrichter *m* censor
sit'tenstreng *adj* puritanical, prudish
Sittich ['zɪtɪç] *m* (**-s;-e**) parakeet
sittlich ['zɪtlɪç] *adj* moral, ethical
Sittlichkeit *f* (**-;**) morality
Sitt'lichkeitsverbrechen *n* indecent assault
sittsam ['zɪtzam] *adj* modest, decent
Situation [zɪtu·a'tsjon] *f* (**-;-en**) situation
situiert [zɪtu'irt] *adj*—**gut s.** well-to-do
Sitz [zɪts] *m* (**-es;-e**) seat; residence; (*e-s Kleides*) fit; (*eccl*) see
sitzen ['zɪtsən] §144 *intr* sit; dwell; (*Vögel*) perch; (*Kleider*) fit; (*Hieb*) hit home; (*coll*) be in jail
sit'zenbleiben §62 *intr* (SEIN) remain seated; (*beim Tanzen*) be a wallflower; (*bei der Heirat*) remain unmarried; (*educ*) stay behind, flunk
sit'zenlassen §104 *tr* leave, abandon; (*Mädchen*) jilt
Sitz'gelegenheit *f* seating accommodation
Sitz'ordnung *f* seating arrangement
Sitz'platz *m* seat
Sitz'streik *m* sit-down strike
Sit'zung *f* (**-;-en**) session
Sit'zungsbericht *m* minutes
Sit'zungsperiode *f* session; (jur) term
Sizilien [zɪ'tsiljən] *n* (**-s;**) Sicily
Ska·la ['skɑla] *f* (**-;-len** [lən]) scale
Skandal [skan'dal] *m* (**-s;-e**) scandal
skandalös [skanda'løs] *adj* scandalous
Skandinavien [skandɪ'nɑvjən] *n* (**-s;**) Scandinavia
Skelett [skɛ'lɛt] *n* (**-[e]s;-e**) skeleton
Skepsis ['skɛpsɪs] *f* (**-;**) skepticism
Skeptiker –in ['skɛptɪkər(ɪn)] §6 *mf* skeptic
skeptisch ['skɛptɪʃ] *adj* skeptical
Ski [ʃi] *m* (**-s; Skier** ['ʃi·ər]) ski
Skizze ['skɪtsə] *f* (**-;-n**) sketch
skizzieren [skɪ'tsirən] *tr* & *intr* sketch
Sklave ['sklɑvə] *m* (**-n;-n**) slave

Sklaverei [sklɑvə'raɪ] *f* (**-;**) slavery
sklavisch ['sklɑvɪʃ] *adj* slavish
Skonto ['skɔnto] *m* & *n* (**-s;-s**) discount
Skrupel ['skrupəl] *m* (**-s;-**) scruple
skru'pellos *adj* unscrupulous
skrupulös [skrupu'løs] *adj* scrupulous
Skulptur [skʊlp'tur] *f* (**-;-en**) sculpture
Slalom ['slɑlɔm] *m* & *n* (**-s;-s**) slalom
Slawe ['slɑvə] *m* (**-n;-n**), **Slawin** ['slɑvɪn] *f* (**-;-nen**) Slav
slawisch ['slɑvɪʃ] *adj* Slavic
Smaragd [sma'rakt] *m* (**-[e]s;-e**) emerald
Smoking ['smokɪŋ] *m* (**-s;-s**) tuxedo
so [zo] *adv* so; this way, thus; **so ein** such a; **so oder so** by hook or by crook; **so...wie** as...as
sobald' *conj* as soon as
Socke ['zɔkə] *f* (**-;-n**) sock
Sockenhalter (**Sok'kenhalter**) *m* garter
Soda ['zoda] *f* (**-;**) & *n* (**-s;**) soda
sodann' *adv* then
Sodbrennen ['zotbrɛnən] *n* (**-s;**) heartburn
soeben [zo'ebən] *adv* just now, just
Sofa ['zofa] *n* (**-s;-s**) sofa
sofern' *conj* provided, if
soff [zɔf] *pret* of **saufen**
sofort' *adv* at once, right away
sofortig [zo'fɔrtɪç] *adj* immediate
sog [zok] *pret* of **saugen** ‖ **Sog** *m* (**-[e]s;**) suction; undertow; (aer) wash
sogar' *adv* even
so'genannt *adj* so-called; would-be
sogleich' *adv* at once, right away
Sohle ['zolə] *f* (**-;-n**) sole; bottom
Sohn [zon] *m* (**-[e]s;‍=e**) son
solan'ge *conj* as long as
solch [zɔlç] *adj* such
Sold [zɔlt] *m* (**-[e]s;-e**) pay
Soldat [zɔl'dat] *m* (**-en;-en**) soldier
Söldner ['zœldnər] *m* (**-s;-**) mercenary
Sole ['zolə] *f* (**-;-n**) brine
solid [zo'lit] *adj* solid; sound; reliable; steady; respectable; (*Preis*) reasonable; (com) sound, solvent
solide [zo'lidə] *adj* var of **solid**
Solist –in [zo'lɪst(ɪn)] §7 *mf* soloist
Soll [zɔl] *n* (**-s;-e**) quota; (acct) debit side; **S. und Haben** debit and credit
Soll– *comb.fm.* estimated; debit
sollen ['zɔlən] §145 *mod* (*inf*) be obliged to (*inf*), have to (*inf*); (*inf*) be supposed to (*inf*); (*inf*) be said to (*inf*)
Soll'wert *m* face value
solo ['zolo] *adv* (mus) solo ‖ **So·lo** *n* (**-s;-s** & **-li** [li]) solo
somit' *adv* so, consequently
Sommer ['zɔmər] *m* (**-s;-**) summer
Som'merfrische *f* health resort; **in die S. fahren** go to the country
Sommerfrischler ['zɔmərfrɪʃlər] *m* (**-s;-**) vacationer
som'merlich *adj* summery
Som'mersprosse *f* freckle
sonach' *adv* consequently, so
Sonate [zo'natə] *f* (**-;-n**) sonata
Sonde ['zɔndə] *f* (**-;-n**) probe
Sonder– [zɔndər] *comb.fm.* special, extra; separate

sonderbar ['zɔndərbɑr] *adj* strange, odd; peculiar
son'derlich *adj* special, particular
Sonderling ['zɔndərlıŋ] *m* (-s;-e) odd person, strange character
sondern ['zɔndərn] *tr* separate; sever; part; sort out; classify ‖ *conj* but
Son'derrecht *n* privilege
Son'derung *f* (-;-en) separation; sorting, sifting; classifying
Son'derverband *m* (mil) task force
Son'derzug *m* (rr) special
sondieren [zɔn'dirən] *tr* probe; (fig) sound out; (naut) sound
Sonnabend ['zɔnɑbənt] *m* (-s;-e) Saturday
Sonne ['zɔnə] *f* (-;-n) sun
sonnen ['zɔnən] *tr* sun ‖ *ref* sun oneself
Son'nenaufgang *m* sunrise
Son'nenbad *n* sun bath
Son'nenblende *f* (aut) sun visor; (phot) lens shade
Sonnenbrand *m* sunburn
Son'nenbräune *f* suntan
Son'nenbrille *f* (pair of) sun glasses
Son'nendach *n* awning
Son'nenenergie *f* solar energy
Son'nenfinsternis *f* eclipse of the sun
Son'nenfleck *m* sunspot
Son'nenjahr *n* solar year
son'nenklar' *adj* sunny; (fig) clear as day
Son'nenlicht *n* sunlight
Son'nenschein *m* sunshine
Son'nenschirm *m* parasol
Son'nensegel *n* awning
Son'nenseite *f* sunny side
Son'nenstich *m* sunstroke
Son'nenstrahl *m* sunbeam
Son'nensystem *n* solar system
Son'nenuhr *f* sundial
Son'nenuntergang *m* sunset
son'nenverbrannt *adj* sunburnt, tanned
Son'nenwende *f* solstice
sonnig ['zɔnıç] *adj* sunny
Sonntag ['zɔntɑk] *m* (-s;-e) Sunday
Sonn'tagsfahrer **-in** §6 *mf* Sunday driver
Sonn'tagskind *n* person born under a lucky star
Sonn'tagsstaat *m* Sunday clothes
sonor [zɔ'nor] *adj* sonorous
sonst [zɔnst] *adv* otherwise; else; (*ehemals*) formerly; **s. etw** something else; **s. keiner** no one else; **s. nichts** nothing else; **s. noch was?** anything else?; **wie s.** as usual; **wie s. was** (coll) like anything
sonstig ['zɔnstıç] *adj* other
sonst'wer *pron* someone else
sonst'wie *adv* in some other way
sonst'wo *adv* somewhere else
Sopran [zɔ'prɑn] *m* (-s;-e) soprano; treble
Sopranist **-in** [zɔpra'nıst(ın)] §7 *mf* soprano
Sorge ['zɔrgə] *f* (-;-n) care; worry; **außer S. sein** be at ease; **keine S.!** don't worry; **sich** [*dat*] **Sorgen machen über** (*acc*) or **um** be worried about

sorgen ['zɔrgən] *intr*—**dafür s., daß** take care that, see to it that; **s. für** take care of ‖ *ref* be uneasy; **sich s. über** (*acc*) grieve over; **sich s. um** be worried about
sor'genfrei *adj* carefree; untroubled
Sor'genkind *n* problem child
sor'genlos *adj* carefree
sor'genvoll *adj* uneasy, anxious
Sor'gerecht *n* (für) custody (of)
Sorgfalt ['zɔrkfalt] *f* (-;) care, carefulness; accuracy
sorgfältig ['zɔrkfɛltıç] *adj* careful
sorglich ['zɔrklıç] *adj* careful
sorglos ['zɔrklos] *adj* careless; thoughtless; carefree
sorgsam ['zɔrkzɑm] *adj* careful; cautious
Sorte ['zɔrtə] *f* (-;-n) sort, kind
sortieren [zɔr'tirən] *tr* sort out
Sortiment [zɔrtı'mɛnt] *n* (-[e]s;-e) assortment
Soße ['zosə] *f* (-;-n) sauce; gravy
sott [zɔt] *pret* of **sieden**
Souffleur [zu'fl⌀r] *m* (-s;-s), **Souffleuse** [zu'fl⌀zə] *f* (-;-n) prompter
soufflieren [zu'flirən] *intr* (*dat*) prompt
Soutane [zu'tɑnə] *f* (-;-n) cassock
Souvenir [zuvə'nir] *n* (-s;-s) souvenir
souverän [zuvə'ren] *adj* sovereign ‖ **Souverän** *m* (-s;-e) sovereign
Souveränität [zuvərenı'tet] *f* (-;) sovereignty
soviel' *adv* so much; **noch einmal s.** twice as much ‖ *conj* as far as
soweit' *conj* as far as
sowie' *conj* as well as
sowieso' *adv* in any case, anyhow
Sowjet [zɔv'jet] *m* (-s;-s) Soviet
sowjetisch [zɔv'jetıʃ] *adj* Soviet
sowohl' *conj*—**sowohl...als auch** as well as, both...and
sozial [zɔ'tsjal] *adj* social
Sozial'fürsorge *f* social welfare
sozialisieren [zɔtsjalı'zirən] *tr* nationalize
Sozialismus [zɔtsja'lısmus] *m* (-;) socialism
Sozialist **-in** [zɔtsja'lıst(ın)] §7 *mf* socialist
sozialistisch [zɔtsja'lıstıʃ] *adj* socialistic
Sozial'wissenschaft *f* social science
Soziologie [zɔtsjɔlɔ'gi] *f* (-;) sociology
Sozius ['zotsjus] *m* (-;-se) associate, partner; (*auf dem Motorrad*) rider
sozusa'gen *adv* so to speak, as it were
Spachtel ['ʃpaxtəl] *m* (-s;-) & *f* (-;-n) spatula; putty knife
Spach'telmesser *n* putty knife
Spagat [ʃpa'gɑt] *m* (-[e]s;-e) (gym) split; (dial) string
spähen ['ʃpe·ən] *intr* peer; spy
Spä'her *m* (-s;-) lookout; (mil) scout
Spä'herblick *m* searching glance
Spähtrupp ['ʃpetrup] *m* reconnaissance squad
Späh'wagen *m* reconnaissance car
Spalier [ʃpa'lir] *n* (-s;-e) trellis; double line (*of people*)
Spalt [ʃpalt] *m* (-[e]s;-e) split; crack; slit; (geol) cleft

Spalte ['ʃpaltə] ƒ (-;-n) split; crack; slit; (typ) column
spalten ['ʃpaltən] tr (pp **gespaltet** or **gespalten**) split; slit; crack; (Holz) chop
Spal'tung ƒ (-;-en) split; (der Meinungen) division; (chem) decomposition; (eccl) schism; (phys) fission
Span [ʃpan] m (-[e]s;ᵘe) chip; splinter; **Späne** shavings
Span'ferkel n suckling pig
Spange ['ʃpaŋə] ƒ (-;-n) clasp; hair clip; (Schnalle) buckle
Spanien ['ʃpanjən] n (-s;) Spain
Spanier **-in** ['ʃpanjər(ɪn)] §6 mƒ Spaniard
spanisch ['ʃpanɪʃ] adj Spanish; **das kommt mir s. vor** (coll) that's Greek to me; **spanischer Pfeffer** paprika; **spanische Wand** folding screen
spann [ʃpan] pret of **spinnen** ‖ **Spann** m (-s;-e) instep
Spanne ['ʃpanə] ƒ (-;-n) span; (com) margin
spannen ['ʃpanən] tr stretch; strain; make tense; (Bogen) bend; (Feder) tighten; (Flinte) cock; (Erwartungen) raise; (Pferde) hitch; **straff s.** tighten; ‖ intr be (too) tight; **s. auf** (acc) wait eagerly for; listen closely to
span'nend adj tight; exciting
Spann'kraft ƒ tension; elasticity; (fig) resiliency
spann'kräftig adj elastic
Span'nung ƒ (-;-en) stress; strain; pressure; close attention; suspense; excitement; strained relations; (elec) voltage
Spar- [ʃpar] comb.fm. savings
Spar'buch n bank book, pass book
Spar'büchse ƒ piggy bank
sparen ['ʃparən] tr & intr save
Spar'flamme ƒ pilot light
Spargel ['ʃpargəl] m (-s;-) asparagus
Spar'kasse ƒ savings bank
Spar'konto n savings account
spärlich ['ʃperlɪç] adj scanty; scarce; sparse; frugal; (Haar) thin ‖ adv poorly; scantily; sparsely
Sparren ['ʃparən] m (-s;-) rafter
sparsam ['ʃparzam] adj thrifty
Spaß [ʃpas] m (-es;ᵘe) joke; fun; **aus S. in fun; S. beiseite!** all joking aside; **S. haben an** (dat) enjoy; **S. machen** be joking; be fun; **viel S.!** have fun!; **zum S.** for fun
spaß'haft, spaßig ['ʃpasɪç] adj funny, facetious
Spaß'macher m joker
Spaßverderber ['ʃpasverderbər] m (-s;-) (coll) kill-joy
Spaß'vogel m joker
spät [ʃpet] adj late; **wie s. ist es?** what time is it? ‖ adv late
Spaten ['ʃpatən] m (-s;-) spade
später ['ʃpetər] adv later
späterhin' adv later on
spätestens ['ʃpetəstəns] adv at the latest
Spät'jahr n autumn, fall
Spatz [ʃpats] m (-es & -en;-en) sparrow
spazieren [ʃpa'tsirən] intr (SEIN) stroll, take a walk

spazie'renfahren §71 intr (SEIN) go for a drive
spazie'renführen tr walk (e.g., a dog)
spazie'rengehen §82 intr (SEIN) go for a walk
Spazier'fahrt ƒ drive
Spazier'gang m stroll, walk; **e-n S. machen** take a walk
Spazier'gänger **-in** §6 mƒ stroller
Spazier'weg m walk
Specht [ʃpeçt] m (-[e]s;-e) woodpecker
Speck [ʃpek] m (-[e]s;) fat; bacon; (beim Wal) blubber
Speck'bauch m (coll) potbelly
speckig ['ʃpekɪç] adj greasy, dirty
spedieren [ʃpe'dirən] tr dispatch, ship
Spediteur [ʃpedɪ'tør] m (-s;-e) shipper; furniture mover
Spedition [ʃpedɪ'tsjon] ƒ (-;-en) shipment; moving company, movers
Speer [ʃper] m (-[e]s;-e) spear; (sport) javelin
Speiche ['ʃpaiçə] ƒ (-;-n) spoke
Speichel ['ʃpaiçəl] m (-s;) saliva
Spei'chellecker m brown-noser
speicheln ['ʃpaiçəln] intr drool
Speicher ['ʃpaiçər] m (-s;-) warehouse; grain elevator; attic, loft
speichern ['ʃpaiçərn] tr store
speien ['ʃpai.ən] §135 tr vomit; spit; (Feuer) belch; (Wasser) spurt ‖ intr vomit, throw up; spit
Speise ['ʃpaizə] ƒ (-;-n) food; meal; (Gericht) dish
Spei'seeis n ice cream
Spei'sekammer ƒ pantry
Spei'sekarte ƒ menu
speisen ['ʃpaizən] tr feed; (fig) supply ‖ intr eat; **auswärts s.** dine out
Spei'senfolge ƒ menu
Spei'sereste pl leftovers
Spei'serohr n (mach) feed pipe
Spei'seröhre ƒ esophagus
Spei'sesaal m dining room
Spei'seschrank m cupboard
Spei'sewagen m (rr) diner
Spei'sezimmer n dining room
Spektakel [ʃpek'takəl] m (-s;-) noise, racket
Spekulant **-in** [ʃpeku'lant(ɪn)] §7 mƒ speculator
Spekulation [ʃpekula'tsjon] f (-;-en) speculation; venture
spekulieren [ʃpeku'lirən] intr speculate, reflect; (fin) speculate
Spelunke [ʃpe'luŋkə] ƒ (-;-n) (coll) drive, joint
Spende ['ʃpendə] ƒ (-;-n) donation
spenden ['ʃpendən] tr give; donate; (Sakramente) administer; (Lob) bestow; **j-m Trost s.** comfort s.o.
spendieren [ʃpen'dirən] tr—j-m etw s. treat s.o. to s.th.
Sperling ['ʃperlɪŋ] m (-s;-e) sparrow
Sperr- [ʃper] comb.fm. barrage; barred
Sperr'baum m barrier, bar
Sperre ['ʃperə] ƒ (-;-n) shutting; close; blockade; embargo; barricade; catch; lock; (rr) gate
sperren ['ʃperən] tr shut; (Gas, Licht) cut off; (Straße) block off; cordon

off; (*blockieren*) blockade; (*mit Schloß*) lock; (*verriegeln*) bolt; (*Konto, Gelder*) freeze; (*Scheck*) stop payment on; (*verbieten*) stop; (sport) block; (sport) suspend; (typ) space ‖ *intr* jam, be stuck
Sperr'feuer *n* barrage
Sperr'gebiet *n* restricted area
Sperr'holz *n* plywood
sperrig ['ʃpɛrɪç] *adj* bulky
Sperr'sitz *m* (*im Kino*) rear seat; (*im Zirkus*) front seat
Sperr'stunde *f* closing time; curfew
Sper'rung *f* (-;-en) stoppage; blocking; blockade; embargo; suspension (*of telephone service, etc.*)
Spesen ['ʃpezən] *pl* costs, expenses
Spezi ['ʃpetsi] *m* (-s;-s) (coll) buddy
spezial [ʃpe'tsjal] *adj* special
Spezial'arzt *m*, **Spezial'ärztin** *f* specialist
Spezial'fach *n* specialty
Spezial'geschäft *n* specialty shop
spezialisieren [ʃpetsjalɪ'zirən] *ref* (auf *acc*) specialize (in)
Spezialist –in [ʃpetsja'lɪst(ɪn)] §7 *mf* specialist
Spezialität [ʃpetsjalɪ'tet] *f* (-;-en) specialty
speziell [ʃpe'tsjɛl] *adj* special
spezifisch [ʃpe'tsifɪʃ] *adj* specific
Sphäre ['sferə] *f* (-;-n) sphere
sphärisch ['sferɪʃ] *adj* spherical
Spickaal ['ʃpɪkɑl] *m* smoked eel
spicken ['ʃpɪkən] *tr* lard; (fig) bribe
spie [ʃpi] *pret* of **speien**
Spiegel ['ʃpigəl] *m* (-s;-) mirror
Spie'gelbild *n* reflection (*in mirror*)
spie'gelblank' *adj* spick and span
Spie'gelei *n* fried egg
spie'gelglatt' *adj* glassy
spiegeln ['ʃpigəln] *tr* reflect; mirror ‖ *ref* be reflected ‖ *intr* shine
Spiel [ʃpil] *n* (-[e]s;-e) game; play; set (*of chessmen or checkers*); (cards) deck; (mach) play; (mus) playing; (sport) match; (theat) acting, performance; **auf dem S. stehen** be at stake; **aufs S. setzen** risk; **bei etw im S. sein** be at the bottom of s.th.; **leichtes S. haben mit** have an easy time with; **S. der Natur** freak of nature
Spiel'art *f* (biol) variety
Spiel'automat *m* slot machine
Spiel'bank *f* (-;-en) gambling table; gambling casino
Spiel'dose *f* music box
spielen ['ʃpilən] *tr & intr* play
Spielerei [ʃpilə'raɪ] *f* (-;-en) fooling around; child's play
Spiel'ergebnis *n* (sport) score
spielerisch ['ʃpilərɪʃ] *adj* playful
Spiel'feld *n* (sport) playing field
Spiel'film *m* feature film
Spiel'folge *f* program
Spiel'gefährte *m*, **Spiel'gefährtin** *f* playmate
Spiel'karten *pl* (playing) cards
Spiel'leiter *m* (cin, theat) director
Spiel'marke *f* chip, counter
Spiel'plan *m* program
Spiel'platz *m* playground; playing field

Spiel'raum *m* (fig) elbowroom; (mach) play
Spiel'sachen *pl* toys
Spiel'tisch *m* gambling table
Spiel'verderber *m* kill-joy
Spiel'verlängerung *f* overtime
Spiel'waren *pl* toys
Spiel'zeug *n* toy(s)
Spieß [ʃpis] *m* (-es;-e) spear, pike; (sl) top kick; (culin) spit; **den S. umdrehen gegen** turn the tables on
Spieß'bürger *m* Philistine, lowbrow
spieß'bürgerlich *adj* narrow-minded
spießen ['ʃpisən] *tr* spear; spit
Spie'ßer *m* (-s;-) Philistine, lowbrow
Spieß'gesell *m* accomplice
Spießruten ['ʃpisrutən] *pl*—**S. laufen** run the gauntlet
spinal [ʃpi'nal] *adj* spinal; **spinale Kinderlähmung** infantile paralysis
Spinat [ʃpi'nat] *m* (-[e]s;-e) spinach
Spind [ʃpɪnt] *m & n* (-[e]s;-e) wardrobe; (mil) locker
Spindel ['ʃpɪndəl] *f* (-;-n) spindle; (*Spinnrocken*) distaff
spin'deldürr' *adj* skinny, scrawny
Spinne ['ʃpɪnə] *f* (-;-n) spider
spinnen ['ʃpɪnən] *tr* spin; **Ränke s.** hatch plots ‖ *intr* purr; (*im Gefängnis sitzen*) do time; (sl) be looney
Spin'nengewebe *n* spider web
Spin'ner *m* (-s;-) spinner; (sl) nut
Spinnerei [ʃpɪnə'raɪ] *f* (-;-en) spinning; spinning mill
Spinn'faden *m* spider thread; **Spinnfäden** gossamer
Spinn'gewebe *n* (-s;-) cobweb
Spinn'rad *n* spinning wheel
Spinn'webe *f* (-;-n) (Aust) cobweb
Spion [ʃpi'on] *m* (-[e]s;-e) spy
Spionage [ʃpi·o'naʒə] *f* (-;) spying, espionage
Spiona'geabwehr *f* counterintelligence
spionieren [ʃpi·o'nirən] *intr* spy
Spirale [ʃpi'ralə] *f* (-;-n) spiral
Spirituosen [ʃpɪritu'ozən] *pl* liquor
Spiritus ['ʃpiritʊs] *m* (-;-se) alcohol
Spital [ʃpi'tal] *n* (-s;-̈er) hospital
spitz [ʃpɪts] *adj* pointed; sharp; (*Winkel*) acute
Spitz'bart *m* goatee
Spitz'bube *m* rascal; thief; swindler
Spitze ['ʃpɪtsə] *f* (-;-n) point; tip; top, summit; (tex) lace; **an der S. liegen** be in the lead; **auf die S. treiben** carry to extremes
Spitzel ['ʃpɪtsəl] *m* (-s;-) spy; stool pigeon; plain-clothes man
spitzen ['ʃpɪtsən] *tr* point; sharpen; (*Ohren*) prick up; **den Mund s.** purse the lips ‖ *ref*—**sich s. auf** (*acc*) look forward to ‖ *intr* be on one's toes
Spitzen– *comb.fm.* top; peak; leading; topnotch; maximum; (tex) lace
Spit'zenform *f* (sport) top form
Spit'zenleistung *f* top performance
Spit'zenmarke *f* (com) top brand
Spit'zer *m* (-s;-) pencil sharpener
spitz'findig *adj* subtle; sharp
Spitz'hacke *f*, **Spitz'haue** *f* pickax
spitzig ['ʃpɪtsɪç] *adj* pointed; (& fig) sharp

Spitz'marke *f* (typ) heading
Spitz'name *m* nickname; pet name
Spitz'nase *f* pointed nose
spleißen ['ʃplaɪsən] §53 *tr* splice
spliß [ʃplɪs] *pret* of **spleißen**
Splitter ['ʃplɪtər] *m* (-s;-) splinter; chip; fragment
split'ternackt' *adj* stark-naked
Split'terpartei *f* splinter party
split'tersicher *adj* shatterproof
spontan [ʃpɔn'tɑn] *adj* spontaneous
Spore ['ʃporə] *f* (-;-n) spore
Sporn [ʃpɔrn] *m* (-[e]s; **Sporen** ['ʃporən]) spur; (fig) stimulus; (aer) tail skid; (naut) ram
spornen ['ʃpɔrnən] *tr* spur
Sport [ʃpɔrt] *m* (-[e]s;-e) sport(s); **S. ausüben** (or **treiben**) play sports
Sport'freund –in §8 *mf* sports fan
Sport'hose *f* shorts, trunks
Sport'jacke *f* sport jacket, blazer
Sport'kleidung *f* sportswear
Sportler –in ['ʃpɔrtlər(ɪn)] §6 *mf* athlete
sport'lich *adj* sportsmanlike; (*Figur*) athletic; (*Kleidung*) sport
Sport'wagen *m* sports car; (*Kinderwagen*) stroller
Sport'wart *m* trainer
Spott [ʃpɔt] *m* (-[e]s;) mockery; scorn
Spott'bild *n* caricature
spott'bil'lig *adj* dirt-cheap
Spott'drossel *f* mockingbird
Spöttelei [ʃpœtə'laɪ] *f* (-;-en) mockery
spotten ['ʃpɔtən] *intr* (**über** *acc*) scoff (at), ridicule; **das spottet jeder Beschreibung** that defies description
Spötterei [ʃpœtə'raɪ] *f* (-;-en) mockery
Spott'gebot *n* (com) ridiculous offer
spöttisch ['ʃpœtɪʃ] *adj* mocking, satirical; sneering
Spott'name *m* nickname
Spott'schrift *f* satire
sprach [ʃprɑx] *pret* of **sprechen**
Sprach– *comb.fm.* speech; grammatical; linguistic; philological
Sprache ['ʃprɑxə] *f* (-;-n) language, tongue; speech; diction; style; idiom
Sprach'eigenheit *f*, **Sprach'eigentümlichkeit** *f* idiom, idiomatic expression
Sprach'fehler *m* speech defect
Sprach'forschung *f* linguistics
Sprach'führer *m* phrase book
Sprach'gebrauch *m* usage
Sprach'gefühl *n* feeling for a language
sprach'gewandt *adj* fluent
sprach'kundig *adj* proficient in languages
Sprach'lehre *f* grammar
Sprach'lehrer –in §6 *mf* language teacher
sprach'lich *adj* grammatical; linguistic
sprach'los *adj* speechless
Sprach'rohr *n* megaphone; (fig) mouthpiece
Sprach'schatz *m* vocabulary
Sprach'störung *f* speech defect
Sprach'wissenschaft *f* philology; linguistics
sprang [ʃpraŋ] *pret* of **springen**
Sprech– [ʃprɛç] *comb.fm.* speaking
Sprech'art *f* way of speaking

Sprech'bühne *f* legitimate theater
sprechen ['ʃprɛçən] §64 *tr* speak; talk; (*Gebet*) say; (*Urteil*) pronounce; speak to, see ǁ *intr* (**über** *acc*, **von**) speak (about), talk (about); **er ist nicht zu s.** he's not available
Spre'cher –in §6 *mf* speaker, talker
Sprech'fehler *m* slip of the tongue
Sprech'funkgerät *n* walkie-talkie
Sprech'probe *f* audition
Sprech'sprache *f* spoken language
Sprech'stunde *f* office hours
Sprech'stundenhilfe *f* receptionist
Sprech'zimmer *n* office (*of doctor, etc.*)
Spreize ['ʃpraɪtsə] *f* (-;-n) prop, strut; (gym) split
spreizen ['ʃpraɪtsən] *tr* spread, stretch out ǁ *ref* sprawl out; (fig) (**mit**) boast (of); **sich s. gegen** resist
Spreng– [ʃprɛŋ] *comb.fm.* high-explosive
Sprengel ['ʃprɛŋəl] *m* (-s;-) diocese; parish
sprengen ['ʃprɛŋən] *tr* break, burst; (*mit Sprengstoff*) blow up; (*Tür*) force; (*Versammlung*) break up; (*Mine*) set off; (*bespritzen*) sprinkle; (*Garten*) water ǁ *intr* (SEIN) gallop
Spreng'kommando *n* bomb disposal unit
Spreng'kopf *m* warhead
Spreng'körper *m*, **Spreng'stoff** *m* explosive
Spreng'wagen *m* sprinkling truck
Sprenkel ['ʃprɛŋkəl] *m* (-s;-) speck
sprenkeln ['ʃprɛŋkəln] *tr* speckle
Spreu [ʃprɔɪ] *f* (-;) chaff
Sprichwort ['ʃprɪçvɔrt] *n* (-[e]s;ˉer) proverb, saying
sprichwörtlich ['ʃprɪçvœrtlɪç] *adj* proverbial
sprießen ['ʃprisən] §76 *intr* (SEIN) sprout
Springbrunnen ['ʃprɪŋbrunən] *m* (-s;-) fountain
springen ['ʃprɪŋən] §142 *intr* (SEIN) jump; dive; burst; (*Eis*) crack; (coll) rush, hurry
Sprin'ger –in *m* (-s;-) jumper; (chess) knight; (sport) diver
Spring'insfeld *m* (-[e]s;-e) (coll) live wire
Spring'kraft *f* (& fig) resiliency
Spring'seil *n* jumping rope
Sprint [ʃprɪnt] *m* (-s;-s) sprint
Sprit [ʃprɪt] *m* (-[e]s;-e) alcohol; (coll) gasoline
Spritze ['ʃprɪtsə] *f* (-;-n) squirt; (*Feuerwehr*) fire engine; (med) injection, shot; (med) syringe
spritzen ['ʃprɪtsən] *tr* squirt; splash; (*sprühen*) spray; (*sprengen*) sprinkle; (*Wein*) mix with soda water; (med) inject ǁ *intr* spurt, spout ǁ *impers—* **es spritzt** it is drizzling ǁ *intr* (SEIN) dash, flit
Spritz'tour *f* (coll) side trip
spröde ['ʃprødə] *adj* brittle; (*Haut*) chapped; (fig) prudish, coy
sproß [ʃprɔs] *pret* of **sprießen** ǁ **Sproß** *m* (Sprosses; Sprosse) offspring, descendant; (bot) shoot

Sprosse ['ʃprɔsə] *f* (-;-n) rung; prong
sprossen ['ʃprɔsən] *intr* (HABEN & SEIN) sprout
Sprößling ['ʃprœslɪŋ] *m* (-s;-e) offspring, descendant; (bot) sprout
Spruch [ʃprux] *m* (-[e]s;Ꞙe) saying; motto; text, passage; (jur) sentence; (jur) verdict; **e-n S. fällen** give the verdict
Spruch'band *n* (-[e]s;Ꞙer) banderole
Sprudel ['ʃprudəl] *m* (-s;-) mineral water
sprudeln ['ʃprudəln] *intr* bubble
sprühen ['ʃpry·ən] *tr* emit ‖ *intr* spray; sparkle; (fig) flash ‖ *impers—* **es sprüht** it is drizzling
Sprüh'regen *m* drizzle
Sprüh'teufel *m* (coll) spitfire
Sprung [ʃprʊŋ] *m* (-[e]s;Ꞙe) jump; crack; (sport) dive
Sprung'brett *n* diving board; (fig) stepping stone
Spucke ['ʃpʊkə] *f* (-;) (coll) spit
spucken ['ʃpʊkən] *tr* spit ‖ *intr* spit; (*Motor*) sputter
Spuk [ʃpuk] *m* (-[e]s;-e) ghost, spook; (*Lärm*) racket; (*Alptraum*) nightmare
spuken ['ʃpukən] *intr* linger on ‖ *impers—***es spukt hier** this place is haunted
spuk'haft *adj* spooky
Spülabort ['ʃpylabɔrt] *m* flush toilet
Spül'becken *n* sink
Spule ['ʃpulə] *f* (-;-n) spool, reel; (elec) coil
Spüle ['ʃpylə] *f* (-;-n) wash basin
spulen ['ʃpulən] *tr* reel, wind
spülen ['ʃpylən] *tr* wash, rinse; (*Abort*) flush; **an Land s.** wash ashore ‖ *intr* flush the toilet; undulate
Spü'ler *m* (-s;-) dishwasher
Spülicht ['spylɪçt] *n* (-[e]s;-e) dishwater; swill, slop
Spül'maschine *f* dishwasher
Spül'mittel *n* detergent
Spülwasser *n* dishwater
Spund [ʃpunt] *m* (-[e]s;Ꞙe) bung, plug; (carp) feather, tongue
Spur [ʃpur] *f* (-;-en) trace; track, rut; (hunt) scent; **S. Salz** pinch of salt
spürbar ['ʃpyrbar] *adj* perceptible
spüren ['ʃpyrən] *tr* trace; track, trail; (*fühlen*) feel; (*wahrnehmen*) perceive
spur'los *adj* trackless ‖ *adv* without a trace
Spür'nase *f* (coll) good nose
Spür'sinn *m* flair
Spur'weite *f* (aut) tread; (rr) gauge
sputen ['ʃputən] *ref* hurry up
SS ['ɛs'ɛs] *f* (-;) (Schutzstaffel) S.S.
Staat [ʃtat] *m* (-[e]s;-en) state; government; (*Aufwand*) show; (*Putz*) finery
Staats— *comb.fm.* state; government; national; public; political
Staatsangehörigkeit ['ʃtatsangəhørɪçkait] *f* (-;) nationality
Staats'anwalt *m* district attorney
Staats'bauten *pl* public works
Staats'beamte *m* civil servant

Staats'bürger –in §6 *mf* citizen
Staats'bürgerkunde *f* civics
Staats'bürgerschaft *f* citizenship
Staats'dienst *m* civil service
staats'eigen *adj* state-owned
Staats'feind *m* public enemy
staats'feindlich *adj* subversive
Staats'form *f* form of government
Staats'gewalt *f* supreme power
Staats'hoheit *f* sovereignty
staats'klug *adj* politic, diplomatic
Staats'klugheit *f* statecraft
Staats'kunst *f* statesmanship
Staats'mann *m* (-[e]s;Ꞙer) statesman
staats'männisch *adj* statesmanlike
Staats'oberhaupt *n* head of state
Staats'papiere *pl* government bonds
Staats'recht *n* public law
Staats'streich *m* coup d'état
Staats'wirtschaft *f* political economy
Staats'wissenschaft *f* political science
Stab [ʃtap] *m* (-[e]s;Ꞙe) staff; rod; bar; (*e–r Jalousie*) slat; (eccl) crozier; (mil) staff; (mil) headquarters; (mus, sport) baton
stab'hochspringen §142 *intr* (SEIN) pole-vault
stabil [ʃta'bil] *adj* stable, steady
stabilisieren [ʃtabɪlɪ'zirən] *tr* stabilize
stach [ʃtax] *pret* of **stechen**
Stachel ['ʃtaxəl] *m* (-s;-n) prick; quill; (bot) thorn; (ent) sting
Sta'chelbeere *f* gooseberry
Sta'cheldraht *m* barbed wire
stachelig ['ʃtaxəlıç] *adj* prickly; (& fig) thorny
Sta'chelschwein *n* porcupine
Sta·dion ['ʃtadjɔn] *n* (-s;-dien [djən]) stadium
Sta·dium ['ʃtadjʊm] *n* (-s;-dien [djən]) stage
Stadt [ʃtat] *f* (-;Ꞙe) city, town
Städtchen ['ʃtɛtçən] *n* (-s;-) town
Städtebau ['ʃtetəbau] *m* (-[e]s;) city planning
Stadt'gemeinde *f* township
Stadt'gespräch *n* talk of the town
städtisch ['ʃtɛtıʃ] *adj* municipal
Stadt'plan *m* map of the city
Stadt'rand *m* outskirts
Stadt'rat *m* (-[e]s;Ꞙe) city council; (*Person*) city councilor
Stadt'teil *m* **Stadt'viertel** *n* quarter (of the city)
Stafette [ʃta'fetə] *f* (-;-n) courier; (sport) relay
Staffel ['ʃtafəl] *f* (-;-n) step, rung; (*Stufe*) degree; (aer) squadron (*of nine aircraft*); (sport) relay team
Staffelei [ʃtafə'lai] *f* (-;-en) easel
Staf'felkeil *m* (aer) V-formation
Staf'fellauf *m* relay race
staffeln ['ʃtafəln] *tr* graduate; (*Arbeitszeit, usw.*) stagger
stahl [ʃtal] *pret* of **stehlen** ‖ **Stahl** *m* (-[e]s;Ꞙe) steel
Stahl'beton *m* reinforced concrete
stählen ['ʃtelən] *tr* temper; (fig) steel
Stahl'kammer *f* steel vault
Stahlspäne ['ʃtalʃpenə] *pl* steel wool
stak [ʃtak] *pret* of **stecken**
Stalag ['ʃtalak] *n* (-s;-s) (Stammlager) main camp (*for P.O.W.'s*)

Stall [ʃtal] m (-[e]s;⸚e) stable; shed
Stall'knecht m groom
Stamm [ʃtam] m (-[e]s;⸚e) stem;
stalk; trunk; stock, race; tribe; breed
Stamm'aktie f common stock
Stamm'baum m family tree; pedigree
stammeln ['ʃtaməln] tr & intr stammer
Stamm'eltern pl ancestors
stammen ['ʃtamən] intr (SEIN) (aus,
von) come (from); (von) date
(from); (gram) (von) be derived
(from)
Stamm'gast m regular customer
stämmig ['ʃtemɪç] adj stocky; husky
Stamm'kneipe f favorite bar
Stamm'kunde m, Stamm'kundin f regular customer
Stamm'personal n skeleton staff
Stamm'tisch m reserved table
Stammutter (Stamm'mutter) f ances-
tress
Stamm'vater m ancestor
stampfen ['ʃtampfən] tr tamp, pound;
(Kartoffeln) mash; (Boden) paw ||
intr stamp the ground; (durch
Schnee) trudge; (naut) pitch
stand [ʃtant] pret of stehen || Stand m
(-[e]s;⸚e) stand; footing, foothold;
level, height; condition; status, rank;
class, caste; booth; profession; trade;
(sport) score; seinen S. behaupten
hold one's ground
Standard ['ʃtandart] m (-s;-s) standard
Standarte [ʃtan'dartə] f (-;-n) banner;
standard
Stand'bild n statue
Ständchen ['ʃtentçən] n (-s;-) serenade; j-m ein S. bringen serenade
s.o.
Ständer ['ʃtendər] m (-s;-) stand,
rack; pillar; stud; (mach) column
Stan'desamt n bureau of vital statistics
stan'desamtlich adj & adv before a
civil magistrate
stan'desgemäß adj according to rank
Stan'desperson f dignitary
stand'fest adj stable, steady, sturdy
stand'haft adj steadfast
stand'halten §90 intr hold out; (dat)
withstand
ständig ['ʃtendɪç] adj permanent;
steady, constant
Stand'licht n parking light
Stand'ort m position; station; (mil)
base; (mil) garrison
Stand'pauke f (coll) lecture
Stand'punkt m standpoint
Stand'recht n martial law
Stand'uhr f grandfather's clock
Stange ['ʃtaŋə] f (-;-n) pole; rod, bar;
perch, roost; e-e S. Zigaretten a carton of cigarettes; von der S. readymade (clothes)
stank [ʃtaŋk] pret of stinken
stänkern ['ʃteŋkərn] intr (coll) stink;
(coll) make trouble
Stanniol [ʃta'njol] n (-s;-e), Stanniol'papier n tinfoil
Stanze ['ʃtantsə] f (-;-n) stanza;
punch, die, stamp
stanzen ['ʃtantsən] tr (mach) punch
Stapel ['ʃtapəl] m (-s;-) stack; depot;

stock; (naut) slip; (tex) staple; auf
S. liegen be in drydock; vom S.
laufen lassen launch
Sta'pellauf m launching
stapeln ['ʃtapəln] tr stack, pile up
Sta'pelplatz m lumberyard; depot
stapfen ['ʃtapfən] intr (SEIN) slog
Star [ʃtar] m (-[e]s;-e) (orn) starling;
(pathol) cataract; grauer S. cataract;
grüner S. glaucoma || m (-s;-s) (cin,
theat) star
starb [ʃtarp] pret of sterben
stark [ʃtark] adj (stärker ['ʃterkər];
stärkste ['ʃterkstə] §9) strong; stout;
(Erkältung) bad; (Familie) big;
(Kälte) severe; (Frost, Verkehr)
heavy; (Wind) high; (Stunde) full ||
adv much; hard; very
Stärke ['ʃterkə] f (-;-n) strength;
force; stoutness; thickness; might;
violence; intensity; (Anzahl) number; (fig) forte; (chem) starch
stärken ['ʃterkən] tr strengthen;
(Wäsche) starch || ref take some
refreshment
Stark'strom m high-voltage current
Stär'kung f (-;-en) strengthening; refreshment; (Imbiß) snack
starr [ʃtar] adj stiff, rigid; fixed; inflexible; obstinate; dumbfounded;
numb || adv—s. ansehen stare at
starren ['ʃtarən] intr (auf acc) stare
(at); s. von be covered with
Starr'kopf m stubborn fellow
starr'köpfig adj stubborn
Starr'krampf m (-es;) tetanus
Starr'sinn m (-[e]s;) stubbornness
Start [ʃtart] m (-[e]s;-s & -e) start;
(aer) take-off; (rok) launching
Start'bahn f (aer) runway
starten ['ʃtartən] tr start; launch ||
intr (SEIN) start; (aer) take off; (rok)
lift off, be launched
Start'rampe f (rok) launch pad
Station [ʃta'tsjon] f (-;-en) station;
(med) ward; freie S. free room and
board
statisch ['ʃtatɪʃ] adj static
Statist -in [ʃta'tɪst(ɪn)] §7 mf (cin)
extra; (theat) supernumerary
Statistik [ʃta'tɪstɪk] f (-;-en) statistic;
(Wissenschaft) statistics
statistisch [ʃta'tɪstɪʃ] adj statistical
Stativ [ʃta'tif] n (-s;-e) stand; (phot)
tripod
statt [ʃtat] prep (genit) instead of; s.
zu (inf) instead of (ger) || Statt f
(-;) place, stead; an Kindes S. annehmen adopt
Stätte ['ʃtetə] f (-;-n) place, spot;
(Wohnung) abode; room
statt'finden §59 intr take place
statt'haft adj admissible; legal
Statthalter ['ʃtathaltər] m (-s;-) governor
statt'lich adj stately; imposing
Statue ['ʃtatu·ə] f (-;-n) statue
statuieren [ʃtatu'irən] tr establish; ein
Exempel s. an (dat) make an example of
Statur [ʃta'tur] f (-;-en) stature
Statut [ʃta'tut] n (-[e]s;-en) statute;
Statuten bylaws

Stau [ʃtaʊ] *m* (-[e]s;-e) dammed-up water; updraft; (aut) tie-up
Staub [ʃtaʊp] *m* (-[e]s;) dust
Stau'becken *n* reservoir
stauben [ˈʃtaʊbən] *intr* make dust
stäuben [ˈʃtɔɪbən] *tr* dust; sprinkle, powder; (*Flüssigkeit*) spray ‖ *intr* make dust; throw off spray
staubig [ˈʃtaʊbɪç] *adj* dusty
staub'saugen *tr & intr* vacuum
Staub'sauger *m* vacuum cleaner
Staub'wedel *m* feather duster
Staub'zucker *m* powdered sugar
stauchen [ˈʃtaʊçən] *tr* knock, jolt; compress; (sl) chew out
Stau'damm *m* dam
Staude [ˈʃtaʊdə] *f* (-;-n) perennial
stauen [ˈʃtaʊ·ən] *tr* dam up; (*Waren*) stow away; (*Blut*) stanch ‖ *ref* be blocked, jam up
Stau'er *m* (-s;-) stevedore
staunen [ˈʃtaʊnən] *intr* (**über** *acc*) be astonished (at) ‖ **Staunen** *n* (-s;) astonishment
stau'nenswert *adj* astonishing
Staupe [ˈʃtaʊpə] *f* (-;) (vet) distemper
Stau'see *m* reservoir
Stau'ung *f* (-;-en) damming up; blockage; (*Engpaß*) bottleneck; (*Verkehrs-*) jam-up; (pathol) congestion
stechen [ˈʃtɛçən] §64 prick; sting, bite; (*mit e-r Waffe*) stab; (*Torf*) cut; (*Star*) remove; (*Kontrolluhr*) punch; (*Wein*) draw; (*Näherei*) stitch; (*gravieren*) engrave; (cards) trump; (cards) take (*a trick*) ‖ *intr* sting, bite; (*Sonne*) be hot; (cards) be trump; **j-m in die Augen s.** catch s.o.'s eye ‖ *impers*—**es sticht mich in der Brust** I have a sharp pain in my chest
ste'chend *adj* (*Blick*) piercing; (*Geruch*) strong; (*Schmerz*) sharp, stabbing
Stech'karte *f* timecard
Stech'schritt *m* goosestep
Stech'uhr *f* time clock
Steckbrief [ˈʃtɛkbrif] *m* warrant for arrest
steck'brieflich *adv*—**s. verfolgen** put out a "wanted" notice for
Steckdose [ˈʃtɛkdozə] *f* (elec) outlet
stecken [ˈʃtɛkən] *tr & intr* stick ‖ **Stecken** *m* (-s;-) stick
steckenbleiben (**stek'kenbleiben**) §62 *intr* (SEIN) get stuck
Steckenpferd (**Stek'kenpferd**) hobbyhorse; (fig) hobby
Stecker (**Stek'ker**) *m* (-s;-) (elec) plug
Steck'kontakt *m* (elec) plug
Steck'nadel *f* pin
Steg [ʃtek] *m* (-[e]s;-e) footpath; footbridge; (*e-r Brille, Geige*) bridge; (*Landungs-*) jetty; (naut) gangplank
Steg'reif *m*—**aus dem S.** extempore
stehen [ˈʃte·ən] §146 *tr*—**e-m Maler Modell s.** sit for a painter; **Schlange s.** stand in line; **Schmiere s.** (coll) be a lookout; **Wache s.** stand guard ‖ *intr* (HABEN & SEIN) stand; stop; be; (gram) occur, be used; (*Kleider*) fit; **das steht bei Ihnen** that depends

on you; **gut s.** (*dat*) fit, suit; **gut s. mit** be on good terms with; **wie steht's?** (coll) how is it going?
ste'henbleiben §62 *intr* (SEIN) stop
ste'henlassen §104 *tr* leave standing; (*nicht anrühren*) leave alone; (*Fehler*) leave uncorrected; (*vergessen*) forget; (culin) allow to stand or cool
Ste'her *m* (-s;-) long-distance cyclist
Stehlampe [ˈʃtelampə] *f* floor lamp
Stehleiter [ˈʃtelaɪtər] *f* stepladder
stehlen [ˈʃtelən] §147 *tr & intr* steal
Stehplatz [ˈʃteplats] *m* standing room
steif [ʃtaɪf] *adj* stiff; rigid; (*Lächeln*) forced; (*förmlich*) formal; (*starr*) numb
steifen [ˈʃtaɪfən] *tr* stiffen; (*Wäsche*) starch
Steig [ʃtaɪk] *m* (-[e]s;-e) path
Steig'bügel *m* stirrup
steigen [ˈʃtaɪgən] §148 *tr* (*Treppen*) climb ‖ *intr* (SEIN) climb; rise; go up; (*Nebel*) lift; (*Blut in den Kopf*) rush ‖ **Steigen** *n* (-s;) rise; increase
steigern [ˈʃtaɪgərn] *tr* raise, increase; (*verstärken*) enhance; (gram) compare ‖ *ref* increase, go up
Stei'gerung *f* (-;-en) rising; increase; intensification; (gram) comparison
Stei'gerungsgrad *m* (gram) degree of comparison
Stei'gung *f* (-;-en) rise; (*Hang*) slope; (*e-s Propellers*) pitch
steil [ʃtaɪl] *adj* steep
Stein [ʃtaɪn] *m* (-[e]s;-e) stone; rock; (horol) jewel; (pathol) stone
stein'alt' *adj* old as the hills
Stein'bruch *m* quarry
Stein'druck *m* lithography; (*Bild*) lithograph
steinern [ˈʃtaɪnərn] *adj* stone
Stein'gut *n* earthenware
steinig [ˈʃtaɪnɪç] *adj* stony, rocky
steinigen [ˈʃtaɪnɪgən] *tr* stone
Stein'kohle *f* hard coal
Stein'metz *m* stonemason
stein'reich' *adj* (coll) filthy rich
Stein'salz *n* rock salt
Stein'schlag *m* (public sign) falling rocks
Stein'wurf *m* stone's throw
Stein'zeit *f* stone age
Steiß [ʃtaɪs] *m* (-es;-e) buttocks
Stelldichein [ˈʃteldɪçaɪn] *n* (-[s]; -[s]) (coll) date
Stelle [ˈʃtelə] *f* (-;-n) place, spot; position; job; agency, department; quotation; (math) digit; **an S. von** in place of; **auf der S.** on the spot; **auf der S. treten** (fig & mil) mark time; **freie** (or **offene**) **S.** opening; **zur S. sein** be on hand
stellen [ˈʃtelən] *tr* put, place; set; stand; (*ein-*) regulate, adjust; (*anordnen*) fix, arrange; (*Frage*) ask; (*Horoskop*) cast; (*Diagnose*) give; (*Falle, Wecker*) set; (*Kaution*) put up; (*Zeugen*) produce; **e-n Antrag s.** make a motion; **in Dienst s.** appoint; put into service ‖ *ref* place oneself; stand; give oneself up; **der Preis stellt sich auf...the price is...; sich s., als ob** act as if

Stel′lenangebot n help wanted
Stel′lenbewerber –in §6 mf applicant
Stel′lengesuch n situation wanted
Stel′lenjagd f job hunting
Stel′lennachweis m, **Stel′lenvermitt-lungsbüro** n employment agency
stel′lenweise adv here and there
–stellig [ʃtelɪç] comb.fm. –digit
Stell′schraube f set screw
Stel′lung f (–;–en) position; situation; job; standing; status; rank; posture; (mil) line, position; (mil) emplacement; **S. nehmen zu** express one's opinion on; (erklären) explain; (beantworten) answer
Stel′lungnahme f (–;–n) attitude, point of view; (Erklärung) comment; (Gutachten) opinion; (Bericht) report; (Beantwortung) answer; (Entscheid) decision; **sich** [dat] **e–e S. vorbehalten** not commit oneself
Stel′lungsgesuch n (job) application
stel′lungslos adj jobless
stell′vertretend adj acting
Stell′vertreter –in §6 mf representative; deputy; proxy; substitute
Stell′vertretung f (–;–en) representation; substitution; **in S. by proxy**
Stelzbein [ʃteltsbaɪn] n wooden leg
Stelze [ʃteltsə] f (–;–n) stilt
stelzen [ʃteltsən] intr (SEIN) stride
Stemmeisen [ʃtemaɪzən] n crowbar
stemmen [ʃtemən] tr support; (Gewicht) lift; (Loch) chisel ‖ ref—**sich s. gegen** oppose
Stempel [ʃtempəl] m (–s;–) stamp; prop; (Kolben) piston; (bot) pistil
Stem′pelkissen n ink pad, stamp pad
stempeln [ʃtempəln] tr stamp ‖ intr—**s. gehen** (coll) collect unemployment insurance
Stengel [ʃteŋəl] m (–s;–) stalk
Steno [ʃteno] f (–;) stenography
Stenograph [ʃtenoˈɡraf] m (–en;–en) stenographer
Stenographie [ʃtenoɡraˈfi] f (–;) stenography, shorthand
stenographieren [ʃtenoɡrˈfirən] tr take down in shorthand ‖ intr do shorthand
Stenographin [ʃtenoˈɡrafɪn] f (–;–nen) stenographer
Stenotypistin [ʃtenotyˈpɪstɪn] f (–;–nen) stenographer
Step [ʃtep] m (–s;–) tap dance; **S. tanzen** tap-dance
Steppdecke [ʃtepdɛkə] f comforter
Steppe [ʃtepə] f (–;–n) steppe
steppen [ʃtepən] tr quilt ‖ intr tap-dance ‖ **Steppen** n (–s;) tap-dancing
Sterbe– [ʃterbə] comb.fm. dying, death
Ster′befall m death
Ster′begeld n death benefit
Ster′behilfe f euthanasia
sterben [ʃterbən] §149 intr (SEIN) (an dat) die (of)
sterb′lich adj mortal ‖ adv—**s. verliebt in** (acc) head over heals in love with
Sterb′lichkeit f (–;) mortality
Sterb′lichkeitsziffer f death rate
stereotyp [stereoˈtyp] adj stereotyped
steril [ʃteˈril] adj sterile
sterilisieren [ʃterɪliˈzirən] tr sterilize

Stern [ʃtern] m (–[e]s;–e) star; (typ) asterisk
Stern′bild n constellation
Stern′blume f aster
Sterndeuter [ʃterndɔɪtər] m (–s;–) astrologer
Sterndeuterei [ʃterndɔɪtəˈraɪ] f (–;) astrology
Ster′nenbanner n Stars and Stripes
stern′ha′gelvoll′ adj (sl) dead drunk
stern′hell′ adj starlit
Stern′himmel m starry sky
Stern′kunde f astronomy
Stern′schuppe f shooting star
Stern′warte f observatory
stet [ʃtet], **stetig** [ʃtetɪç] adj steady
stets [ʃtets] adv constantly, always
Steuer [ʃtɔɪ.ər] f (–;–n) tax; duty ‖ n (–s;–) rudder, helm; (aer) controls; (aut) steering wheel; **am S. at the helm**; (aut) behind the wheel
Steu′eramt n tax office
Steu′erbord n (naut) starboard
Steu′ererhebung f levy of taxes
Steu′ererklärung f tax return
Steu′erflosse f vertical stabilizer
Steu′erhinterziehung f tax evasion
Steu′erjahr n fiscal year
Steu′erknüppel m control stick
Steu′er·mann m (–[e]s;∺er & –leute)** helmsman
steuern [ʃtɔɪ.ərn] tr steer; control; regulate; (aer, naut) pilot; (aut) drive ‖ intr (dat) curb, check
steu′erpflichtig adj taxable; dutiable
Steu′errad n steering wheel
Steu′erruder n rudder, helm
Steu′ersatz m tax rate
Steu′ersäule f (aer) control column; (aut) steering column
Steu′erstufe f tax bracket
Steu′erung f (–;–en) steering; (Bekämpfung) control; (Verhinderung) prevention; (aer) piloting; (aut) steering mechanism
Steu′erveranlagung f tax assessment
Steu′erwerk n (aer) controls
Steu′erzahler –in §6 mf tax payer
Steu′erzuschlag m surtax
Steven [ʃtevən] m (–s;–) (naut) stem
Stewar·deß [ˈst(j)u.ərdɛs] f (–;–dessen [dɛsən]) (aer) stewardess
stibitzen [ʃtɪˈbɪtsən] tr snitch
Stich [ʃtɪç] m (–[e]s;–e) prick; (Messer–) stab; (Insekten–) sting, bite; (Stoß) thrust; (Seitenstechen) sharp pain; (Kupfer–) engraving; (cards) trick; (naut) knot; (sew) stitch; **im S. lassen** abandon
Stichelei [ʃtɪçəˈlaɪ] f (–;–en) taunt
sticheln [ʃtɪçəln] intr—**gegen j-n s.** (fig) needle s.o.
Stich′flamme f flash
stich′haltig adj valid, sound
Stich′probe f spot check
Stich′tag m effective date; due date
Stich′wahl f run-off election
Stich′wort n (–[e]s;∺er) key word; dictionary entry ‖ n (–[e]s;–e) (theat) cue
Stich′wunde f stab wound
sticken [ʃtɪkən] tr embroider ‖ intr embroider

Stickerei [ʃtɪkə'raɪ] *f* (-;-en) embroidery
Stick'husten *m* whooping cough
stickig ['ʃtɪkɪç] *adj* stuffy, close
Stick'stoff *m* nitrogen
stieben ['ʃtibən] §130 *intr* (HABEN & SEIN) fly; (*Menge*) disperse
Stief [ʃtif] *comb.fm.* step–
Stief'bruder *m* stepbrother
Stiefel ['ʃtifəl] *m* (-s;-) boot
Stie'felknecht *m* bootjack
Stief'mutter *f* stepmother
Stief'mütterchen *n* (bot) pansy
Stief'vater *m* stepfather
stieg [ʃtik] *pret* of steigen
Stiege ['ʃtigə] *f* (-;-n) staircase
Stiel [ʃtil] *m* (-[e]s;-e) handle; (bot) stalk
stier [ʃtir] *adj* staring, glassy ‖ **Stier** *m* (-[e]s;-e) bull; (astr) Taurus
stieren ['ʃtirən] *intr* (**auf** *acc*) stare (at)
Stier'kampf *m* bullfight
stieß [ʃtis] *pret* of stoßen
Stift [ʃtɪft] *m* (-[e]s;-e) pin; peg; pencil; crayon; (*Zwecke*) tack; (coll) apprentice ‖ *n* (-[e]s;-e & -er) charitable foundation or institution
stiften ['ʃtɪftən] *tr* (*gründen*) found; (*spenden*) donate; (*verursachen*) cause; (*Unruhe*) stir up; (*Frieden*) make; (*Brand*) start; (*e-e Runde Bier*) set up
Stif'ter –in §6 *mf* founder; donor; (fig) author, cause
Stif'tung *f* (-;-en) foundation; donation; grant; **fromme S.** religious establishment; **milde S.** charitable institution
Stif'tungsfest *n* founder's day
Stil [ʃtil] *m* (-[e]s;-e) style
stil'gerecht *adj* in good taste
stilisieren [ʃtilɪ'zirən] *tr* word
stilistisch [ʃtɪ'lɪstɪʃ] *adj* stylistic
still [ʃtɪl] *adj* still; calm; silent; (com) slack; **im stillen** in secret; **Stiller Ozean** Pacific Ocean ‖ **Stille** *f* (-;) stillness; silence
still'bleiben §62 *intr* (SEIN) keep still
Stilleben (**Still'leben**) *n* still life
stillegen (**still'legen**) *tr* (*Betrieb*) shut down; (*Verkehr*) stop; (*Schiff*) put into mothballs
stillen ['ʃtɪlən] *tr* still; (*Hunger*) appease; (*Durst*) quench; (*Blut*) stanch; (*Begierde*) gratify
stilliegen (**still'liegen**) §108 *intr* lie still; (*Betrieb*) lie idle; (*Verkehr*) be at a standstill
still'schweigen §148 *intr* be silent; **s. zu** acquiesce in ‖ **Stillschweigen** *n* (-s;) silence; secrecy
still'schweigend *adj* silent; (fig) tacit
Still'stand *m* standstill; (*Sackgasse*) stalemate, deadlock
still'stehen §146 *intr* stand still; (*Betrieb*) be idle; (mil) stand at attention; **stillgestanden!** (mil) attention!
Stil'möbel *pl* period furniture
stil'voll *adj* stylish
Stimm– [ʃtɪm] *comb.fm.* vocal; voting
Stimm'abgabe *f* vote, voting
Stimm'band *n* (-[e]s;-̈er) vocal cord

Stimm'block *m* (parl) bloc
Stimm'bruch *m* change of voice
Stimme ['ʃtɪmə] *f* (-;-n) voice; vote
stimmen ['ʃtɪmən] *tr* make feel (*happy, etc.*); (mus) tune ‖ *intr* be right; vote; (mus) be in tune
Stim'menrutsch *m* (pol) landslide
Stimm'enthaltung *f* abstention
Stimm'gabel *f* tuning fork
Stimm'recht *n* right to vote, suffrage
Stim'mung *f* (-;-en) tone; (*Laune*) mood; (mil) morale; (mus) tuning; (st.exch.) trend
stim'mungsvoll *adj* cheerful
Stimm'zettel *m* ballot
stinken ['ʃtɪŋkən] §143 *intr* stink
Stink'tier *n* skunk
Stipen·dium [ʃtɪ'pɛndjʊm] *n* (-s;-dien [djən]) scholarship, grant
stippen ['ʃtɪpən] *tr* (coll) dunk
Stippvisite ['ʃtɪpvɪzitə] *f* (-;-n) short visit
Stirn [ʃtɪrn] *f* (-;-en), **Stirne** ['ʃtɪrnə] *f* (-;-n) forehead, brow; (fig) insolence, gall; **die S. runzeln** frown
Stirn'runzeln *n* (-s;) frown(ing)
stob [ʃtop] *pret* of stieben
stöbern ['ʃtøbərn] *tr* (*Wild*) flush; (*aus dem Bett*) yank ‖ *intr* poke around; browse; (*Schnee*) drift
stochern ['ʃtoxərn] *intr* poke around; **im Essen s.** pick at one's food; **im Feuer s.** stoke the fire; **in den Zähnen s.** pick one's teeth
Stock [ʃtok] *m* (-[e]s;-̈e) stick; cane; wand; baton; stem; vine; tree stump; cleaning rod; beehive; massif; story, floor; **im ersten S.** on the second floor
Stock–, stock– *comb.fm.* thoroughly
stock'blind' *adj* stone-blind
stock'dun'kel *adj* pitch-dark
Stöckel ['ʃtœkəl] *m* (-s;-) high heel
stocken ['ʃtokən] *intr* stop; (*Geschäft*) slack off; (*Blut*) coagulate; (*in der Rede*) get stuck; (*Milch*) curdle; (*Stimme*) falter; (*schimmeln*) become moldy; (*Unterhandlungen*) become deadlocked; (*Verkehr*) get tied up; (*zögern*) hesitate ‖ **Stocken** *n* (-s;) stopping; hesitation; **ins S. bringen** tie up
stock'fin'ster *adj* pitch-black
Stock'fleck *m* mildew
stock'fleckig *adj* mildewy
stockig ['ʃtokɪç] *adj* moldy
–stöckig [ʃtœkɪç] *comb.fm.* –story
stock'nüch'tern *adj* dead-sober
stock'steif' *adj* stiff as a board
stock'taub' *adj* stone-deaf
Stockung (**Stok'kung**) *f* (-;-en) stoppage; (*des Verkehrs*) tie-up; (*des Blutes*) congestion; (*Unterbrechung*) interruption; (*Verlangsamung*) slowdown; (*Zeitverlust*) delay; (*Pause*) pause; (*Zögern*) hesitation; (*der Unterhandlungen*) deadlock
Stock'werk *n* story, floor
Stoff [ʃtof] *m* (-[e]s;-e) stuff, matter; fabric, material; cloth; subject, topic; (chem) substance
stoff'lich *adj* material
Stoff'rest *m* (tex) remnant

Stoff'wechsel *m* metabolism
stöhnen ['stønən] *intr* groan, moan
Stolle ['stɔlə] *f* (-;-n) fruit cake
Stollen ['stɔlən] *m* (-s;-) fruit cake; tunnel; (*Pfosten*) post; (*Stütze*) prop
stolpern ['stɔlpərn] *intr* (SEIN) stumble, trip
stolz [stɔlts] *adj* (auf *acc*) proud (of) || **Stolz** *m* (-es;) pride
stolzieren [stɔl'tsirən] *intr* (SEIN) strut; (*Pferd*) prance
stopfen ['stɔpfən] *tr* stuff, cram; (*Pfeife*) fill; (*Strumpf*) darn; (mus) mute; **j-m den Mund s.** shut s.o. up || *intr* be filling; cause constipation
Stopf'garn *n* darning yarn
Stoppel ['stɔpəl] *f* (-;-n) stubble
stoppelig ['stɔpəliç] *adj* stubbly
stoppeln ['stɔpəln] *tr* glean; (fig) patch
stoppen ['stɔpən] *tr* stop; clock, time || *intr* stop
Stopp'licht *n* tail light; stoplight
Stopp'uhr *f* stopwatch
Stöpsel ['stœsəl] *m* (-s;-) stopper, cork; (coll) squirt; (elec) plug
stöpseln ['stœpsəln] *tr* plug; cork
Storch [stɔrç] *m* (-[e]s;-e) stork
stören ['størən] *tr* disturb, bother; (*Pläne*) cross; (*Vergnügen*) spoil; (mil) harass; (rad) jam
Störenfried ['størənfrit] *m* (-[e]s;-e) pain in the neck
störrig ['stœriç], **störrisch** ['stœrɪʃ] *adj* stubborn
Stö'rung *f* (-;-en) disturbance, trouble; breakdown; interruption; annoyance; intrusion; (rad) static; (rad) jamming
Stoß [stos] *m* (-es;-e) push, shove; hit, blow; nudge, poke; (*Einschlag*) impact; (*Erschütterung*) shock; (*Fecht-*) pass; (*Feuer-*) burst (of fire); (*Fuß-*) kick; (*Haufen*) pile, bundle; (*Rück-*) recoil; (*Saum*) seam, hem; (*Schwimm-*) stroke; (*Trompeten-*) blast; (*Wind-*) gust; (mil) thrust; (orn) tail
Stoß'dämpfer *m* shock absorber
Stößel ['støsəl] *m* (-s;-) pestle
stoßen ['stosən] §150 *tr* push, shove; hit, knock; kick; punch; jab, nudge, poke; ram; pound; pulverize; oust || *ref* bump oneself; **sich s. an** (*dat*) take offense at; take exception to || *intr* kick; (*mit den Hörnen*) butt; (*Gewehr*) recoil, kick; (*Wagen*) jolt (*Schiff*) toss; **in die Trompete s.** blow the trumpet; **s. auf** (*acc*) swoop down on || *intr* (SEIN)—**s. an** (*acc*) bump against; adjoin; be next-door to; **s. auf** (*acc*) run into; come across; (naut) dash against; **s. durch** (mil) smash through; **vom Lande s.** shove off; **zu j-m s.** side with s.o.
Stoß'stange *f* (aut) bumper
Stoß'trupp *m* assault party; **Stoßtruppen** shock troops; commandos, rangers
Stoß'zahn *m* tusk
stottern ['stɔtərn] *tr* stutter, stammer || *intr* stutter, stammer; (aut) sputter
stracks [straks] *adv* immediately; (*geradeaus*) straight ahead
Straf- [straf] *comb.fm.* penal; criminal

Straf'anstalt *f* penal institution
Straf'arbeit *f* (educ) extra work
Straf'aufschub *m* reprieve
strafbar ['strafbar] *adj* punishable
Strafe ['strafə] *f* (-;-n) punishment; penalty; (*Geld-*) fine; **bei S. von** under pain of; **zur S.** as punishment
strafen ['strafən] *tr* punish
straff [straf] *adj* tight; (*Seil*) taut; (*gespannt*) tense; (*aufrecht*) erect; (fig) strict; **s. spannen** tighten
straf'fällig *adj* punishable; culpable
Straf'geld *n* fine
Straf'gesetzbuch *n* penal code
sträflich ['strefliç] *adj* culpable
Sträfling ['streflɪŋ] *m* (-s;-e) convict
straf'los *adj* unpunished
Straf'porto *n* postage due
Straf'predigt *f* talking-to, lecture
Straf'raum *m* (sport) penalty box
Straf'recht *n* criminal law
Straf'stoß *m* (sport) penalty kick
Straf'umwandlung *f* (jur) commutation
Straf'verfahren *n* criminal proceedings
Strahl [stral] *m* (-[e]s;-en) ray; beam; flash; jet; (geom) radius
Strahl'antrieb *m* jet propulsion
strahlen ['stralən] *intr* beam, shine
Strahl'motor *m*, **Strahl'triebwerk** *n* jet engine
Strah'lung *f* (-;-en) radiation
Strähne ['strenə] *f* (-;-n) strand; lock; hank, skein
strähnig ['streniç] *adj* wispy
stramm [stram] *adj* tight; (*kräftig*) strapping; (*Zucht*) strict; (*Arbeit*) hard; (*Soldat*) smart; (*Mädel*) buxom || *adv*—**s. stehen** stand at attention
stramm'ziehen §183 *tr* draw tight
strampeln ['strampəln] *intr* kick
Strand [strant] *m* (-[e]s;-e) beach, seashore, shore
stranden ['strandən] *intr* (SEIN) be beached, run aground; be stranded
Strand'gut *n* flotsam, jetsam
Strand'gutjäger **-in** §6 *mf* beachcomber
Strand'korb *m* hooded beach chair
Strand'schirm *m* beach umbrella
Strang [straŋ] *m* (-[e]s;-e) rope; (*Strähne*) hank; (*Zugseil*) trace; (rr) track; **wenn alle Stränge reißen** (fig) if worse comes to worst
Strapaze [stra'patsə] *f* (-;-n) fatigue; exertion, strain
strapazieren [strapa'tsirən] *tr* tire out; (*Kleider*) wear hard
strapazier'fähig *adj* heavy-duty
strapaziös [strapa'tsjøs] *adj* tiring
Straße ['strasə] *f* (-;-n) street; road, highway; (*Meerenge*) strait
Stra'ßenanzug *m* business suit
Stra'ßenbahn *f* streetcar, trolley; trolley line
Stra'ßenbahnwagen *m* streetcar
Stra'ßendirne *f* streetwalker
Stra'ßengraben *m* ditch, gutter
Stra'ßenhändler **-in** §6 *mf* street vendor
Stra'ßenjunge *m* urchin
Stra'ßenkarte *f* street map
Stra'ßenkreuzung *f* intersection
Stra'ßenlage *f* (aut) roadability
Stra'ßenrennen *n* drag race

Stra'ßenrinne f gutter
Stra'ßenschild n street sign
Stra'ßensperrung f (public sign) road closed
Stra'ßenstreife f highway patrol
strategisch [ʃtraˈteɡiʃ] adj strategic
sträuben [ˈʃtrɔibən] tr ruffle || ref bristle, stand on end; **sich s. gegen** resist, struggle against
Strauch [ʃtraux] m (-[e]s;ꞋꞋer) shrub
straucheln [ˈʃtrauxəln] intr (SEIN) stumble, trip; (fig) go wrong
Strauß [ʃtraus] m (-[e]s;ꞋꞋe) bouquet || m (-[e]s;-e) ostrich
Strebe [ˈʃtrebə] f (-;-n) prop, strut
Stre'bebogen m flying buttress
streben [ˈʃtrebən] intr (nach) strive (after); (nach) tend (toward) || **Streben** n (-s;-) striving; pursuit; (Hang) tendency; (Anstrengung) endeavor
Stre'ber m (-s;-) go-getter, eager beaver; social climber; (in der Schule) grind
strebsam [ˈʃtrepzɑm] adj zealous
Streb'samkeit f (-;) zeal; industry
Strecke [ˈʃtrekə] f (-;-n) stretch; extent; distance; stage, leg; (geom) straight line; (hunt) bag; (rr) section; **zur S. bringen** catch up with; (box) defeat; (hunt) bag
strecken [ˈʃtrekən] tr stretch; (Metalle) laminate; (Wein) dilute; (fig) make last; **die Waffen s.** lay down one's arms || ref stretch (oneself)
Streich [ʃtraiç] m (-[e]s;-e) blow; (fig) trick, prank
streicheln [ˈʃtraiçəln] tr stroke; pat
streichen [ˈʃtraiçən] §85 tr stroke; (Butter, usw.) spread; (an-) paint; (Geige) play; (Messer) whet; (Rasiermesser) strop; (Streichholz) strike; (Flagge, Segel) lower; (Ärmel) roll down; (Ziegel) make; (mit Ruten) flog; delete; (sport) scratch || intr—**mit der Hand s. über** (acc) pass one's hand over || intr (SEIN) stretch, extend; wander; pass, move; rush
Streich'holz n match
Streich'holzbrief m matchbook
Streich'instrument n stringed instrument
Streich'orchester n string band
Streich'riemen m razor strop
Streif [ʃtraif] m (-[e]s;-e) streak, stripe; strip
Streif'band n (-[e]s;ꞋꞋer) wrapper
Streife [ˈʃtraifə] f (-;-n) raid; (Runde) beat; (mil) patrol
streifen [ˈʃtraifən] tr stripe; streak; graze; skim over; (abziehen) strip; (grenzen an) verge on; (Thema) touch on || intr (SEIN) roam; (mil) patrol; **s. an** (acc) brush against; (fig) verge on; **s. über** (acc) scan || **Streifen** m (-s;-) stripe; streak; strip; slip; (cin) movie
Strei'fendienst m patrol duty
Strei'fenwagen m patrol car, squad car
streifig [ˈʃtraifiç] adj striped
Streif'licht n flash, streak of light; **S. werfen auf** (acc) shed light on
Streif'wunde f scratch

Streif'zug m exploratory trip, looksee
Streik [ʃtraik] m (-[e]s;-s) strike, walkout; **wilder S.** wildcat strike
streiken [ˈʃtraikən] intr go on strike
Strei'kende §5 mf striker
Streik'posten m picket; **S. stehen** picket
Streit [ʃtrait] m (-[e]s;-e) fight; argument, quarrel; (jur) litigation
Streit'axt f battle-ax; **die S. begraben** (fig) bury the hatchet
streitbar [ˈʃtraitbɑr] adj belligerent
streiten [ˈʃtraitən] §86 recip & intr quarrel
Streit'frage f point at issue
streitig [ˈʃtraitiç] adj controversial; at issue
Streit'kräfte pl (mil) forces, troops
streit'lustig adj belligerent, scrappy
Streit'objekt n bone of contention
Streit'punkt m issue, point at issue
streit'süchtig adj quarrelsome
streng [ʃtreŋ] adj severe, stern; austere; strict; (Geschmack) sharp || **Strenge** f (-;) severity, sternness; austerity; strictness; sharpness
streng'genommen adv strictly speaking
streng'gläubig adj orthodox
Streu [ʃtrɔi] f (-;-en) straw bed
Streu'büchse f shaker
streuen [ˈʃtrɔi·ən] tr strew, sprinkle; (ausbreiten) spread; (verbreiten) scatter || intr spread, scatter
strich [ʃtriç] pret of **streichen** || **Strich** m (-[e]s;-e) stroke; line; (Streif) stripe; (Landstrich) tract; (carp) grain; (tex) nap; (typ) dash; **auf den S. gehen** walk the streets (as prostitute); **gegen den S. gehen** go against the grain; (fig) rub the wrong way
Strich'mädchen n streetwalker
Strich'punkt m semicolon
Strich'regen m local shower
strich'weise adv here and there
Strick [ʃtrik] m (-[e]s;-e) rope, cord; (fig) rogue, good-for-nothing
stricken [ˈʃtrikən] tr & intr knit
Strick'garn n knitting yarn
Strick'jacke f cardigan
Strick'kleid n knitted dress
Strick'leiter f rope ladder
Strick'waren pl knitwear
Strick'zeug n knitting things
Striemen [ˈʃtrimən] m (-s;-) stripe, streak; (in der Haut) weal
Strippe [ˈʃtripə] f (-;-n) string; strap; shoestring; (telp) line
stritt [ʃtrit] pret of **streiten**
strittig [ˈʃtritiç] adj controversial
Stroh [ʃtro] n (-[e]s;) straw
Stroh'dach n thatched roof
Stroh'halm m straw; drinking straw
Stroh'mann m (-[e]s;ꞋꞋer) scarecrow; (cards) dummy
Stroh'puppe f scarecrow
Stroh'sack m straw mattress; **heiliger S.!** holy smokes!
Strolch [ʃtrolç] m (-[e]s;-e) bum
strolchen [ˈʃtrolçən] intr bum around
Strom [ʃtrom] m (-[e]s;ꞋꞋe) river; stream; (von Worten) torrent; (& elec) current

stromab'wärts adv downstream
stromauf'wärts adv upstream
Strom'ausfall m (elec) power failure
strömen ['ʃtrømən] intr (HABEN & SEIN) stream; (Regen) pour (down)
Stro'mer m (-s;-) (coll) tramp
Strom'kreis m (elec) circuit
strom'linienförmig adj streamlined
Strom'richter m (elec) converter
Strom'schnelle f rapids
Strom'spannung f voltage
Strom'stärke f (elec) amperage
Strö'mung f (-;-en) current; trend
Strom'unterbrecher m circuit breaker
Strom'wandler m (elec) transformer
Strom'zähler m electric meter
Strophe ['ʃtrofə] f (-;-n) stanza
strotzen ['ʃtrɔtsən] intr—s. von or vor (dat) abound in, teem with
Strudel ['ʃtrudəl] m (-s;-) eddy, whirlpool; (fig) maelstrom; (culin) strudel
strudeln ['ʃtrudəln] intr eddy, whirl
Struktur [ʃtrʊk'tur] f (-;-en) structure; (tex) texture
Strumpf [ʃtrʊmpf] m (-[e]s;ˬe) stocking
Strumpf'band n (-[e]s;ˬer), **Strumpfhalter** m garter
Strumpf'waren pl hosiery
struppig ['ʃtrʊpɪç] adj shaggy, unkempt
Stube ['ʃtubə] f (-;-n) room
Stu'benmädchen n chambermaid
stu'benrein adj housebroken
Stubsnase ['ʃtupsnazə] f snub nose
Stuck [ʃtʊk] m (-[e]s;) stucco
Stück [ʃtʏk] n (-[e]s;-e) piece; lot; plot; stretch distance; (Butter) pat; (Zucker) lump; (Seife) cake; (Vieh) head; (mus) piece, number; (theat) play, show; **pro S.** apiece
stückeln ['ʃtʏkəln] tr cut or break into small pieces; piece together
stück'weise adv piecemeal
Stück'werk n patchwork
Student [ʃtu'dɛnt] m (-en;-en) college student
Studen'tenheim n dormitory
Studen'tenverbindung f fraternity
Studentin [ʃtu'dɛntɪn] f (-;-nen) college student, coed
Studie ['ʃtudjə] f (-;-n) (Lit) essay; (paint) study, sketch
Stu'diengang m (educ) course
Stu'dienplan m curriculum
Stu'dienrat m (-[e]s;ˬe) high school teacher
Stu'dienreferendar –in §8 mf practice teacher
Stu'dienreise f (educ) field trip
studieren [ʃtu'dirən] tr & intr study (at college); examine
studiert [ʃtu'dirt] adj college-educated; (gekünstelt) affected
Studier'zimmer n study
Stu-dium ['ʃtudjʊm] n (-s;-dien [djən]) study (at college); studies
Stufe ['ʃtufə] f (-;-n) step, stair; (e-r Leiter) rung; (Grad) degree; (Niveau) level; stage; (mus) interval
Stu'fenfolge f graduation; succession
Stu'fenleiter f stepladder; (fig) gamut
stu'fenweise adv by degrees

Stuhl [ʃtul] m (-[e]s;ˬe) chair; (Stuhlgang) stool, feces; **der Heilige S.** the Holy See
Stuhl'bein n leg of a chair
Stuhl'drang m urgent call of nature
Stuhl'gang m stool, feces; **S. haben** have a bowel movement
Stuhl'lehne f back of a chair
Stulpe ['ʃtʊlpə] f (-;-n) cuff
Stülpnase ['ʃtʏlpnazə] f snub nose
stumm [ʃtʊm] adj dumb, mute; (schweigend) silent; (gram) mute
Stummel ['ʃtʊməl] m (-s;-) (e-s Armes, Baumes, e-r Zigarette) stump
Stümper ['ʃtʏmpər] m (-s;-) bungler
Stümperei [ʃtʏmpə'raɪ] f (-;-en) bungling
stüm'perhaft adj bungling
stümpern ['ʃtʏmpərn] tr & intr bungle
stumpf [ʃtʊmpf] adj blunt; (& fig) obtuse || **Stumpf** m (-[e]s;ˬe) stump
Stumpf'sinn m apathy, dullness
stumpf'sinnig adj dull, stupid
Stunde ['ʃtʊndə] f (-;-n) hour; (educ) class, lesson, period
stunden ['ʃtʊndən] tr grant postponement of
Stun'dengeld n tutoring fee
Stun'dengeschwindigkeit f miles per hour
Stun'denkilometer pl kilometers per hour
stun'denlang adv for hours
Stun'denlohn m hourly wage(s)
Stun'denplan m roster, schedule
stun'denweise adv by the hour
Stun'denzeiger m hour hand
–stündig [ʃtʏndɪç] comb fm. –hour
stündlich ['ʃtʏntlɪç] adj hourly
Stun'dung f (-;-en) period of grace
Stunk [ʃtʊŋk] m (-[e]s;) stink; **S. machen** (sl) raise a stink
Stups [ʃtʊps] m (-es;-e) nudge
stupsen ['ʃtʊpsən] tr nudge
Stups'nase f snub nose
stur [ʃtur] adj stubborn; (Blick) fixed
Sturm [ʃtʊrm] m (-[e]s;ˬe) storm; gale
Sturm'abteilung f storm troopers
stürmen ['ʃtʏrmən] tr storm || intr rage, roar || intr (SEIN) rush || impers —es stürmt it is stormy
Stürmer ['ʃtʏrmər] m (-s;-) (fb) forward
stürmisch ['ʃtʏrmɪʃ] adj stormy; impetuous || adv—**nicht so s.!** not so fast!
Sturm'schritt m (mil) double time
Sturm'trupp m assault party
Sturm'welle f (mil) assault wave
Sturm'wind m gale, hurricane
Sturz [ʃtʊrts] m (-es;-e) fall, sudden drop; overthrow; collapse; (archit) lintel; (aut) camber; (com) slump
Sturz'bach m torrent
Sturz'bomber m dive bomber
Stürze ['ʃtʏrtsə] f (-;-n) lid
stürzen ['ʃtʏrtsən] tr throw down; upset, overturn; overthrow; (tauchen) plunge; **nicht s.!** this side up! || ref rush; plunge || intr (SEIN) fall, tumble; rush; (Tränen) pour; (aer) dive
Sturz'flug m (aer) dive
Sturz'helm m crash helmet

Sturz'regen *m* downpour
Sturz'see *f* heavy seas
Stute ['ʃtutə] *f* (-;-n) mare
Stütze ['ʃtʏtsə] *f* (-;-n) support, prop; (fig) help, support
stutzen ['ʃtutsən] *tr* cut short; (*Flügel*) clip; (*Bäume*) prune; (*Ohren*) crop; (*Bart*) trim || *intr* stop short; be startled; (*Pferd*) shy
stützen ['ʃtʏtsən] *tr* support; prop; shore up; (fig) support || *ref*—**sich s. auf** (*acc*) lean on; (fig) depend on
Stutzer ['ʃtutsər] *m* (-s;-) car coat; (coll) snazzy dresser
Stutz'flügel *m* baby grand piano
stutzig ['ʃtutsɪç] *adj* suspicious
Stütz'pfeiler *m* abutment
Stütz'punkt *m* footing; (mil) base; (phys) fulcrum
Subjekt [zup'jɛkt] *n* (-[e]s;-e) (coll) guy, character; (gram) subject
subjektiv [zupjɛk'tif] *adj* subjective
Substantiv [zupstan'tif] *n* (-[e]s;-e) (gram) substantive, noun
Substanz [zup'stants] *f* (-;-en) substance
subtil [zup'til] *adj* subtle
subtrahieren [zuptra'hirən] *tr* subtract
Subtraktion [zuptrak'tsjon] *f* (-;-en) subtraction
Subvention [zupvɛn'tsjon] *f* (-;-en) subsidy
Such– [zux] *comb.fm.* search
Such'anzeige *f* want ad
Such'büro *n,* **Such'dienst** *m* missing-persons bureau
Suche ['zuxə] *f* (-;-en) search; **auf der S. nach** in search of, in quest of
suchen ['zuxən] *tr* search for, look for; (*erstreben*) seek; want, desire; (*in der Zeitung*) advertise for; (*Gefahr*) court; **das Weite s.** run away || *intr* search; **nach etw s.** look for s.th.
Sucht [zuxt] *f* (-;⸗e) passion, mania; (*nach*) addition (to)
süchtig ['zʏçtɪç] *adj* addicted || **Süchtige §5** *mf* addict
Sud [zut] *m* (-[e]s;-e) brewing; brew
Süd [zyt] *m* (-[e]s;) south
sudelhaft ['zudəlhaft], **sudelig** ['zudəlɪç] *adj* slovenly, sloppy
sudeln ['zudəln] *tr & intr* mess up
Süden ['zydən] *m* (-s;) south
Sudeten [zu'detən] *pl* Sudeten mountains (*along northern border of Czechoslovakia*)
Süd'früchte *pl* (*tropical and subtropical*) fruit (*e.g., bananas, oranges*)
süd'lich *adj* south, southern, southerly; **s. von** south of || *adv* south
Südost' *m,* **Südo'sten** *m* southeast
südöst' lich *adj* southeast(ern)
Süd'pol *m* (-s;) South Pole
südwärts ['zytvɛrts] *adv* southward
Südwest' *m,* **Südwe'sten** *m* southwest
süffig ['zʏfɪç] *adj* tasty
suggerieren [zugɛ'rirən] *tr* suggest
suggestiv [zugɛs'tif] *adj* suggestive
Suggestiv'frage *f* leading question
suhlen ['zulən] *ref* wallow
Sühne ['zynə] *f* (-;) atonement
sühnen ['zynən] *tr* atone for, expiate
Sülze ['zʏltsə] *f* (-;-n) jellied meat

summarisch [zu'marɪʃ] *adj* summary
Summe ['zumə] *f* (-;-n) sum, total
summen ['zumən] *tr* hum || *intr* hum; buzz
Sum'mer *m* (-s;-) buzzer
summieren [zu'mirən] *tr* sum up, total || *ref* run up, pile up
Summton ['zumton] *m* (telp) dial tone
Sumpf [zumpf] *m* (-[e]s;⸗e) swamp
sumpfig ['zumpfɪç] *adj* swampy, marshy
Sünde ['zʏndə] *f* (-;-n) sin
Sün'denbock *m* scapegoat
Sün'denerlaß *m* absolution
Sün'denfall *m* original sin
Sün'der *m* (-s;-) sinner
Sünd'flut ['zʏntflut] *f* Deluge
sünd'haft, sündig ['zʏndɪç] *adj* sinful
sündigen ['zʏndɪgən] *intr* sin
Superlativ ['zuperlatif] *m* (-s;-e) (gram) superlative
Su'permarkt *m* supermarket
Suppe ['zupə] *f* (-;-n) soup
Sup'penschüssel *f* tureen
surren ['zurən] *intr* buzz
Surrogat [zurɔ'gat] *n* (-[e]s;-e) substitute
suspendieren [zuspɛn'dirən] *tr* suspend
süß [zys] *adj* sweet || **Süße** *f* (-;) sweetness
süßen ['zysən] *tr* sweeten
Sü'ßigkeit *f* (-;-en) sweetness; **Süßigkeiten** sweets, candy
Süß'kartoffel *f* sweet potato
süß'lich *adj* sweetish; (fig) mawkish
Süß'stoff *m* artificial sweetener
Süß'waren *pl* sweets, candy
Süß'wasser *n* fresh water
Symbol [zʏm'bol] *n* (-s;-e) symbol
Symbolik [zʏm'bolɪk] *f* (-;) symbolism
symbolisch [zʏm'bolɪʃ] *adj* symbolic(al)
Symme·trie [zʏmɛ'tri] *f* (-;-trien) ['tri·ən] symmetry
symmetrisch [zʏ'metrɪʃ] *adj* symmetrical
Sympa·thie [zʏmpa'ti] *f* (-;-thien) ['ti·ən] liking
sympathisch [zʏm'patɪʃ] *adj* likeable; **er ist mir s.** I like him
sympathisieren [zʏmpatɪ'zirən] *intr*—**s. mit** sympathize with; like
Sympho·nie [zʏmfɔ'ni] *f* (-;-nien) ['ni·ən] symphony
Symptom [zʏmp'tom] *n* (-s;-e) symptom
symptomatisch [zʏmptɔ'matɪʃ] *adj* (*für*) symptomatic (of)
Synagoge [zyna'gogə] *f* (-;-n) synagogue
synchronisieren [zʏnkrɔnɪ'zirən] *tr* synchronize
Syndikat [zʏndɪ'kat] *n* (-[e]s;-e) syndicate
Syndi·kus ['zʏndɪkus] *m* (-;-kusse & -ki [ki]) corporation lawyer
synonym [zyno'nym] *adj* synonymous || **Synonym** *n* (-s;-e) synonym
Syntax ['zʏntaks] *f* (-;) syntax
synthetisch [zʏn'tetɪʃ] *adj* synthetic
Syrien ['zyrjən] *n* (-s;) Syria

System [zʏs'tem] *n* (-s;-e) system
systematisch [zʏste'mɑtɪʃ] *adj* systematic
Szene ['stsenə] *f* (-;-n) scene; in S.
setzen stage; sich in S. setzen put on an act
Sze'nenaufnahme *f* (cin) take
Szenerie [stenə'ri] *f* (-;) scenery

T

T, t [te] *invar n* T, t
Tabak [ta'bak], ['tabak] *m* (-[e]s;-e) tobacco
Tabaks'beutel *m* tobacco pouch
Tabak'trafik *f* (Aust) cigar store
Tabak'waren *pl* tobacco products
tabellarisch [tabɛ'larɪʃ] *adj* tabular
tabellarisieren [tabɛlarɪ'zirən] *tr* tabulate
Tabelle [ta'bɛlə] *f* (-;-n) table, chart; graph
Tabernakel [taber'nakəl] *m & n* (-s;-) tabernacle
Tablett [ta'blet] *n* (-[e]s;-e) tray
Tablette [ta'bletə] *f* (-;-n) tablet, pill
tabu [ta'bu] *adj* taboo || Tabu *n* (-s; -s) taboo
Tachometer [taxo'metər] *n* speedometer
Tadel ['tadəl] *m* (-s;-) scolding; (Schuld) blame; (educ) demerit
ta'dellos *adj* blameless; flawless
tadeln ['tadəln] *tr* scold, reprimand; blame, find fault with
Tafel ['tafəl] *f* (-;-n) (Tisch, Diagramm) table; (Anschlag-) billboard; (Glas-) pane; (Holz-, Schalt-) panel; (Mahlzeit) meal, dinner; (Metall-) sheet, plate; (Platte) slab; (Schiefer-) slate; (Schreib-) tablet; (Schokolade) bar; (Wand-) blackboard; bei T. at dinner; die T. decken set the table; offene T. halten have open house
Ta'felaufsatz *m* centerpiece
Ta'felbesteck *n* knife, fork, and spoon
ta'felförmig *adj* tabular
Ta'felgeschirr *n* table service
Ta'felland *n* tableland, plateau
Ta'felmusik *f* dinner music
tafeln ['tafəln] *intr* dine, feast
täfeln ['tefəln] *tr* (Wand) wainscot, panel; (Fußboden) parquet
Ta'felöl *n* salad oil
Ta'felservice *n* tableware
Tä'felung *f* (-;-en) inlay; paneling
Taft [taft] *m* (-[e]s;-e) taffeta
Tag [tak] *m* (-[e]s;-e) day; daylight; am Tage by day; am Tage nach the day after; an den Tag bringen bring to light; bei Tage by day, in the daytime; den ganzen Tag all day long; e-n Tag um den andern every other day; e-s Tages someday; es wird Tag day is breaking; guten Tag! hello!; how do you do?; (bei Verabschiedung) good day!; goodby!; Tag der offenen Tür open house; unter Tage (min) underground, below the surface
tagaus', tagein' *adv* day in and day out
Tage- [tagə] *comb.fm.* day-, daily
Ta'geblatt *n* daily, daily paper
Ta'gebuch *n* diary, journal
Ta'gegeld *n* per diem allowance
ta'gelang *adv* for days
Ta'gelohn *m* daily wage
Tagelöhner -in ['tagəløner(ın)] §6 *mf* day laborer
tagen ['tagən] *intr* dawn; (beraten) meet; (jur) be in session
Ta'gesanbruch *m* daybreak
Ta'gesangriff *m* (aer) daylight raid
Ta'gesbefehl *m* (mil) order of the day
Ta'gesbericht *m* daily report
Ta'geseinnahme *f* daily receipts
Ta'gesgespräch *n* topic of the day
ta'geshell *adj* as light as day
Ta'geskasse *f* (theat) box office
Ta'gesleistung *f* daily output
Ta'geslicht *n* daylight
Ta'geslichtaufnahme *f* (phot) daylight shot
Ta'gesordnung *f* agenda; (coll) order of the day
Ta'gespreis *m* market price
Ta'gespresse *f* daily press
Ta'gesschau *f* (telv) news
Ta'geszeit *f* time of day; daytime; zu jeder T. at any hour
Ta'geszeitung *f* daily paper
ta'geweise *adv* by the day
Ta'gewerk *n* day's work
-tägig [tegıç] *comb.fm.* -day
täglich ['teklıç] *adj* daily
tags [taks] *adv*—t. darauf the following day; t. zuvor the day before
Tag'schicht *f* day shift
tags'über *adv* during the day, in the daytime
Tagung ['tagʊŋ] *f* (-;-en) convention, conference, meeting
Ta'gungsort *m* meeting place
Taifun [tai'fun] *m* (-s;-e) typhoon
Taille ['taljə] *f* (-;-n) waist; (Mieder) bodice
Takel ['takəl] *n* (-s;-) tackle
Takelage [takə'laʒə] *f* (-;-n) rigging
takeln ['takəln] *tr* rig
Ta'kelwerk *n* var of Takelage
Takt [takt] *m* (-[e]s;-e) tact; (mach) stroke; (mus) time, beat; (mus) bar; den T. schlagen mark time; im T. in time; in step; T. halten mark time
takt'fest *adj* keeping good time; (fig) reliable
Taktik ['taktɪk] *f* (-;-en) (& fig) tactics
Tak'tiker *m* (-s;-) tactician
taktisch ['taktɪʃ] *adj* tactical
takt'los *adj* tactless
Takt'messer *m* metronome
Takt'stock *m* baton

Takt'strich m (mus) bar
takt'voll adj tactful
Tal [tɑl] n (-[e]s;ᵂer) valley
Talar [ta'lɑr] m (-s;-e) robe, gown
Tal'boden m valley floor
Talent [ta'lɛnt] n (-[e]s;-e) talent
talentiert [talɛn'tirt] adj talented
Tal'fahrt f descent
Talg [talk] m (-[e]s;-e) suet; tallow
Talg'kerze f, **Talg'licht** n tallow candle
Talisman ['talɪsman] m (-s;-e) talisman
Talk(um)puder ['talk(ʊm)pudər] m talcum powder
Talmi ['talmi] n (-s;) (fig) imitation
Tal'sperre f dam
Tamburin [tambʊ'rin] n (-s;-e) tambourine
Tampon [tã'põ] m (-s;-s) (med) tampon
Tamtam [tam'tam] n (-s;-s) gong; (fig) fanfare, drum beating
Tand [tant] m (-[e]s;) trifle; bauble
tändeln ['tɛndəln] intr trifle; flirt
Tang [taŋ] m (-[e]s;-e) seaweed
Tangente [taŋ'gɛntə] f (-;-n) (geom) tangent
tangieren [taŋ'girən] tr concern
Tango ['taŋgo] m (-s;-s) tango
Tank [taŋk] m (-[e]s;-e & -s) tank
tanken ['taŋkən] intr get gas; refuel
Tan'ker m, **Tank'schiff** n tanker
Tank'stelle f gas (or service) station
Tank'wagen m tank truck; (rr) tank car
Tankwart ['taŋkvart] m (-[e]s;-e) gas station attendant
Tanne ['tanə] f (-;-n) fir (tree)
Tan'nenbaum m fir tree
Tan'nenzapfen m fir cone
Tante ['tantə] f (-;-n) aunt; **T. Meyer** (coll) john
Tantieme [tã'tjemə] f (-;-n) dividend; (com) royalty
Tanz [tants] m (-es;ᵂe) dance
Tanz'bein n—**das T. schwingen** (coll) cut a rug
Tanz'diele f dance hall
tänzeln ['tɛntsəln] intr (HABEN & SEIN) skip about; (Pferd) prance
tanzen ['tantsən] tr & intr dance
Tänzer –in ['tɛntsər(ɪn)] §6 mf dancer
Tanz'fläche f dance floor
Tanz'kapelle f dance band
Tanz'lokal n dance hall
Tanz'saal m ballroom
Tanz'schritt m dance step
Tanz'stunde f dancing lesson
Tapete [ta'petə] f (-;-n) wallpaper
Tape'tenpapier n wallpaper (in rolls)
Tape'tentür f wallpapered door
Tapezierarbeit [tape'tsirarbaɪt] f paperhanging
tapezieren [tape'tsirən] tr wallpaper
Tapezie'rer m (-s;-) paperhanger
tapfer ['tapfər] adj brave, valiant
Ta'pferkeit f (-;) bravery, valor
tappen ['tapən] intr (HABEN & SEIN) grope about; **t. nach** grope for
täppisch ['tepɪʃ] adj clumsy
tapsen ['tapsən] intr (SEIN) clump along

Tara ['tɑra] f (-;) (com) tare
Tarif [ta'rif] m (-s;-e) tariff; price list; wage scale; postal rates
Tarif'lohn m standard wages
Tarif'verhandlung f collective bargaining
Tarif'vertrag m wage agreement
Tarn– [tarn] comb.fm. camouflage
tarnen ['tarnən] tr camouflage
Tarn'kappe f (myth) magic cap (rendering wearer invisible)
Tar'nung f (-;) camouflage
Tasche ['taʃə] f (-;-n) pocket; handbag; pocketbook; schoolbag; flight bag; pouch; briefcase
Ta'schenausgabe f pocket edition
Ta'schenbuch n paperback
Ta'schendieb m pickpocket
Ta'schendiebstahl m pickpocketing
Ta'schengeld n pocket money
Ta'schenlampe f flashlight
Ta'schenmesser n pocketknife
Ta'schenrechner m pocket calculator
Ta'schenspieler –in §6 mf magician
Ta'schenspielerei f sleight of hand
Ta'schentuch n handkerchief
Ta'schenuhr f pocket watch
Ta'schenwörterbuch n pocket dictionary
Tasse ['tasə] f (-;-n) cup
Tastatur [tasta'tur] f (-;-en) keyboard
Taste ['tastə] f (-;-n) key
tasten ['tastən] tr feel, touch; (telg) send || ref feel one's way || intr (nach) grope (for)
Tastsinn ['tastzɪn] m sense of touch
tat [tɑt] pret of **tun** || **Tat** f (-;-en) deed, act; (Verbrechen) crime; **auf frischer Tat ertappen** catch redhanded; **in der Tat** in fact; **in die Tat umsetzen** implement
Tat'bestand m facts of the case
Tat'bestandsaufnahme f factual statement
tatenlos ['tɑtənlos] adj inactive
Ta'tenlosigkeit f (-;) inactivity
Täter –in ['tɛtər(ɪn)] §6 mf doer, perpetrator; culprit
Tat'form f (gram) active voice
tätig ['tetɪç] adj active; busy; **t. sein bei** be employed by
tätigen ['tetɪgən] tr conclude
Tä'tigkeit f (-;-en) activity; occupation, job, profession
Tä'tigkeitsbericht m progress report
Tä'tigkeitsfeld n field, line
Tä'tigung f (-;-en) transaction
Tat'kraft f energy, strength; vigor
tat'kräftig adj energetic; vigorous
tätlich ['tetlɪç] adj violent; **tätliche Beleidigung** (jur) assault and battery; **t. werden gegen** assault || adv —**t. beleidigen** (jur) assault
Tät'lichkeit f (-;-en) (act of) violence; **es kam zu Tätlichkeiten** it came to blows
Tat'ort m scene of the crime
tätowieren [tetə'virən] tr tattoo
Tätowie'rung f (-;-en) tattoo
Tat'sache f fact
Tat'sachenbericht m factual report
tat'sächlich adj actual, real, factual
tätscheln ['tetʃəln] tr pet, stroke

Tatterich ['tatəriç] *m* (–s;) shakes
Tatze ['tatsə] *f* (–;-n) paw
Tau [tau] *m* (–[e]s;) dew ‖ *n* (–[e]s; –e) rope; (naut) hawser
taub [taup] *adj* deaf; (*betäubt*) numb; (*unfruchtbar*) barren; (*Gestein*) not containing ore; (*Nuß*) hollow; (*Ei*) unfertile; (*Hafer*) wild; **t. gegen** deaf to; **t. vor Kälte** numb with cold
Taube ['taubə] *f* (–;-n) pigeon; (pol) dove
Tau'benhaus *n*, **Tau'benschlag** *m* dovecote
Taub'heit *f* (–;) deafness; numbness
taub'stumm *adj* deaf and dumb ‖ **Taubstumme** §5 *mf* deaf-mute
Tauchboot ['tauxbot] *n* submarine
tauchen ['tauxən] *tr* dip, duck, immerse ‖ *intr* (HABEN & SEIN) dive, plunge; (naut) submerge, dive
Tau'cher –in §6 *mf* (& orn) diver
Tau'cheranzug *m* diving suit
Tau'chergerät *n* aqualung
Tau'cherglocke *f* diving bell
Tauch'krankheit *f* bends
Tauch'schwimmer *m* (nav) frogman
tauen ['tau·ən] *tr* thaw, melt; (*schleppen*) tow ‖ *intr* (HABEN & SEIN) thaw ‖ *impers*—**es taut** dew is falling ‖ *impers* (HABEN & SEIN)—**es taut** it is thawing ‖ **Tauen** *n* (–s;) thaw
Tauf– [tauf] *comb.fm.* baptismal
Tauf'becken *n* baptismal font
Tauf'buch *n* parish register
Taufe ['taufə] *f* (–;-n) baptism, christening
taufen ['taufən] *tr* baptize, christen
Täufer ['tɔɪfər] *m*—**Johannes der T.** John the Baptizer
Täufling ['tɔɪflɪn] *m* (–s;-e) child (or person) to be baptized
Tauf'name *m* Christian name
Tauf'pate *m* godfather
Tauf'patin *f* godmother
Tauf'schein *m* baptismal certificate
taugen ['taugən] *intr* be of use; **zu etw t.** be good for s.th.
Taugenichts ['taugəniçts] *m* (–es;-e) good-for-nothing
tauglich ['taukliç] *adj* (**für, zu**) good (for), fit (for), suitable (for); (mil) able-bodied; **t. zu** (*inf*) able to (*inf*)
Taumel ['tauməl] *m* (–s;) giddiness; (*Überschwang*) ecstasy
taumelig ['tauməliç] *adj* giddy; reeling
taumeln ['tauməln] *intr* (SEIN) reel, stagger; be giddy; be ecstatic
Tausch [tauʃ] *m* (–es;-e) exchange
tauschen ['tauʃən] *tr* (gegen) exchange (for) ‖ *intr*—**mit j-m t.** exchange places with s.o.
täuschen ['tɔɪʃən] *tr* deceive, fool; (*betrügen*) cheat; (*Erwartungen*) disappoint ‖ *ref* be mistaken
täu'schend *adj* deceptive, illusory; (*Ähnlichkeit*) striking
Tausch'geschäft *n* exchange, swap
Tausch'handel *m* barter; **T. treiben** barter
Täu'schung *f* (–;-en) deception, deceit; fraud; **optische T.** optical illusion
Täu'schungsangriff *m* (mil) feint attack
Täu'schungsmanöver *n* feint

Tausch'wert *m* trade-in value
tausend ['tauzənt] *invar adj & pron* thousand ‖ **Tausend** *m*—**ei der T.!** (or **potz T.!**) holy smokes! ‖ *f* (–; –en) thousand ‖ *n* (–s;-e) thousand
Tau'sendfuß *m*, **Tausendfüß(l)er** ['tauzəntfys(l)ər] *m* (–s;–) centipede
tausendste ['tauzəntstə] §9 *adj & pron* thousandth
Tausendstel ['tauzəntstəl] *n* (–s;-) thousandth
Tau'tropfen *m* dewdrop
Tau'werk *n* (naut) rigging
Tau'wetter *n* thaw
Tau'ziehen *n* tug of war
Taxameter [taksa'metər] *m* taxi meter
Taxe ['taksə] *f* (–;-n) tax; (*Schätzung*) appraisal; (*Gebühr*) fee; (*Taxi*) taxi
Taxi ['taksi] *n* (–s;-s) taxi, cab
taxieren [ta'ksirən] *tr* appraise; rate
Taxifahrer –in §6 *mf* taxi driver
Ta'xistand *m* taxi stand
Taxus ['taksus] *m* (–;–) (bot) yew
Team [tim] *n* (–s;-s) team
Technik ['tɛçnɪk] *f* (–;-en) technique; workmanship; technology
Tech'niker –in §6 *mf* technician; engineer
Techni·kum ['tɛçnɪkum] *n* (–s;-ka [ka] & –ken [kən]) technical school; school of engineering
technisch ['tɛçnɪʃ] *adj* technical; **technische Angelegenheit** technicality; **technische Hochschule** technical institute
Technologie [tɛçnɔlɔ'gi] *f* (–;) technology
technologisch [tɛçnɔ'logɪʃ] *adj* technological
Tee [te] *m* (–s;-s) tea
Tee'gebäck *n* tea biscuit, cookie
Tee'kanne *f* teapot
Tee'kessel *m* teakettle
Tee'löffel *m* teaspoon; teaspoonful
Teenager ['tined₃ər] *m* (–s;–) teenager
Teer [ter] *m* (–[e]s;-e) tar
Teer'decke *f* tar surface, blacktop
teeren ['terən] *tr* tar
Teer'pappe *f* tar paper
Tee'satz *m* tealeaves
Teich [taiç] *m* (–[e]s;-e) pond, pool
Teig [taik] *m* (–[e]s;-e) dough
teigig ['taigiç] *adj* doughy
Teig'mulde *f* kneading trough
Teig'waren *pl* noodles; pastries
Teil [tail] *m & n* (–[e]s;-e) part; piece; portion; (*Abschnitt*) section; (jur) party; **der dritte T. von** one third of; **edle Teile des Körpers** vital parts; **zu gleichen Teilen** fifty-fifty; **zum größten T.** for the most part; **zum T.** partly, in part
Teil– *comb.fm.* partial
teilbar ['tailbar] *adj* divisible
Teilchen ['tailçən] *n* (–s;–) particle
teilen ['tailən] *tr* divide; (mit) share (with) ‖ *ref* (*Weg*) divide; (*Ansichten*) differ; **sich t. in** (*acc*) share
teil'haben §89 *intr* (**an** *dat*) participate (in), share (in)
Teilhaber –in ['tailhabər(in)] §6 *mf* participant; (com) partner
Teil'haberschaft *f* (–;-en) partnership

-teilig ['taɪlɪç] comb.fm. -piece
Teil'nahme f (-;) participation; sympathy; interest
teilnahmslos ['taɪlnɑmslos] adj indifferent; apathetic
Teil'nahmslosigkeit f (-;) indifference; apathy
teilnahmsvoll ['taɪlnɑmsfɔl] adj sympathetic; (besorgt) solicitous
teil'nehmen §116 intr (an dat) participate (in), take part (in); (an dat) attend; (fig) (an dat) sympathize (with)
Teil'nehmer -in §6 mf participant; (Mitglied) member; (sport) competitor; (telp) customer, party
teils [taɪls] adv partly
Teil'strecke f section, stage
Tei'lung f (-;-en) division; partition; separation; (Grade) graduation, scale; (Anteile) sharing
teil'weise adv partly
Teil'zahlung f partial payment; auf T. kaufen buy on the installment plan
Teint [tẽ] m (-s;-s) complexion
Telefon [tele'fon] n (-s;-e) telephone
Telegramm [tele'gram] n (-s;-e) telegram
Telegraph [tele'grɑf] m (-en;-en) telegraph
Telegra'phenstange f telegraph pole
telegraphieren [telegra'firən] tr & intr telegraph; (nach Übersee) cable
Teleobjektiv ['tele-ɔbjektif] n telephoto lens
Telephon [tele'fon] n (-s;-e) telephone, phone; ans T. gehen answer the phone
Telephon'anruf m telephone call
Telephon'anschluß m telephone connection
Telephon'gespräch n telephone call
Telephon'hörer m receiver
telephonieren [telefo'nirən] intr telephone; mit j-m t. phone s.o.
telephonisch [tele'foniʃ] adj telephone || adv by telephone
Telephonist -in [telefo'nɪst(ɪn)] §7 mf telephone operator
Telephon'vermittlung f telephone exchange
Telephon'zelle f telephone booth
Telephon'zentrale f telephone exchange
Teleskop [tele'skop] n (-s;-e) telescope
Television [televɪ'zjon] f (-;) television
Teller ['telər] m (-s;-) plate
Tel'lereisen n trap
Tel'lermine f antitank mine
Tel'lertuch n dishtowel
Tempel ['tempəl] m (-s;-) temple
Temperament [tempəra'ment] n (-[e]s;-e) temperament; enthusiasm; er hat kein T. he has no life in him; hitziges T. hot temper
temperament'los adj lifeless, boring
temperament'voll adj lively, vivacious
Temperatur [tempera'tur] f (-;-en) temperature
Temperenzler [tempe'rentslər] m (-s; -) teetotaler
temperieren [tempe'rirən] tr temper; cool; air-condition; (mus) temper

Tempo ['tempo] n (-s;-s & pl [pi]) tempo; speed; (mus) movement
Tempus ['tempʊs] n (-; -pora [pɔra]) (gram) tense
Tendenz [ten'dents] f (-;-en) tendency
Tender ['tendər] m (-s;-) (nav, rr) tender
Tenne ['tenə] f (-;-n) threshing floor
Tennis ['tenɪs] n (-;) tennis
Ten'nisplatz m tennis court
Ten'nisschläger m tennis racket
Ten'nistournier n tennis tournament
Tenor ['tenɔr] m (-s;) (Wortlaut) tenor, purport || [te'nor] m (-[e]s; ≈e) tenor
Teppich ['tepɪç] m (-s;-e) rug, carpet
Teppichkehrmaschine ['tepɪçkerma-ʃinə] f carpet sweeper
Termin [ter'min] m (-s;-e) date, time, day; deadline; (com) due date; er hat heute T. he is to appear in court today; äußerster T. deadline
termin'gemäß adv on time, punctually
Termin'geschäft n futures
Termin'kalender m appointment book; (jur) court calendar
Terminolo·gie [termɪnolo'gi] f (-; -gien ['gi·ən]) terminology
termin'weise adv (com) on time
Terpentin [terpen'tin] m (-s;) terpentine
Terrain [te'rẽ] n (-s;-s) ground; (Grundstück) lot; (mil) terrain; T. gewinnen (fig & mil) gain ground
Terrasse [te'rasə] f (-;-n) terrace
terras'senförmig adj terraced
Terrine [te'rinə] f (-;-n) tureen
Territo·rium [teri'torjʊm] n (-s;-rien [rjən]) territory
Terror ['terɔr] m (-s;) terror
terrorisieren [terɔrɪ'zirən] tr terrorize
Terrorist -in [terɔ'rɪst(ɪn)] §7 mf terrorist
Terz [terts] f (-;-en) (mus) third
Terzett [ter'tset] n (-[e]s;-e) trio
Test [test] m (-[e]s;-e & -s) test
Testament [testa'ment] n (-[e]s;-e) will; (eccl) Testament
testamentarisch [testamen'tarɪʃ] adj testamentary || adv by will; t. bestimmen will
Testaments'vollstrecker -in §6 mf executor
testen ['testən] tr test
teuer ['tɔɪ·ər] adj dear, expensive; (Preis) high
Teu'erung f (-;-en) rise in price
Teu'erungswelle f rise in prices
Teu'erungszulage f cost-of-living increase
Teufel ['tɔɪfəl] m (-s;-) devil; des Teufels sein be mad; wer zum T.? who the devil?
Teufelei [tɔɪfa'laɪ] f (-;-en) deviltry
Teufelsbanner ['tɔɪfəlsbanər] m (-s;-) exorcist
Teu'felskerl m helluva fellow
teuflisch ['tɔɪflɪʃ] adj devilish
Teutone [tɔɪ'tonə] m (-n;-n) Teuton
teutonisch [tɔɪ'toniʃ] adj Teutonic
Text [tekst] m (-[e]s;-e) text, words; (cin) script; (mus) libretto; (typ) double pica; aus dem T. kommen

lose the train of thought; **j–m den
T. lesen** give s.o. a lecture
Text'buch n (mus) libretto
Texter –in ['tɛkstər(ın)] §6 mf ad
writer, ad man; (mus) lyricist
Textil– [tɛkstil] comb.fm. textile
Textilien [tɛks'tiljən] pl, **Textil'waren**
pl textiles
text'lich adj textual
Theater [tɛ'atər] n (–s;–) theater; **T.
machen** (fig) make a fuss; **T. spielen**
(fig) make believe, put on
Thea'terbesucher –in §6 mf theater-
goer
Thea'terdichter –in §6 mf playwright
Thea'terkarte f theater ticket
Thea'terkasse f box office
Thea'terprobe f rehearsal
Thea'terstück n play
Thea'terzettel m program
theatralisch [tɛ·a'tralıʃ] adj theater;
(fig) theatrical
Theke ['tekə] f (–;–n) counter; bar
The·ma ['tema] n (–s;–men [mən] &
–mata [mata]) theme, subject
Theologe [tɛ·ɔ'logə] m (–n;–n) theolo-
gian
Theologie [tɛ·ɔlɔ'gi] f (–;) theology
theologisch [tɛ·ɔ'logıʃ] adj theological
theoretisch [tɛ·ɔ'retıʃ] adj theoreti-
ic(al)
Theo·rie [tɛ·ɔ'ri] f (–;–rien ['ri·ən])
theory
Thera·pie [tɛra'pi] f (–;–pien ['pi·ən])
therapy
Thermalbad [ter'malbat] n thermal
bath
Thermometer [termɔ'metər] n ther-
mometer
Thermome'terstand m thermometer
reading
Thermosflasche ['tɛrmɔsflaʃə] f ther-
mos bottle
Thermostat [termɔ'stat] m (–[e]s;–e)
& (–en;–en) thermostat
These ['tezə] f (–;–n) thesis
Thrombose [trɔm'bozə] f (–;–n)
thrombosis
Thron [tron] m (–[e]s;–e) throne
Thron'besteigung f accession to the
throne
Thron'bewerber m pretender to the
throne
Thron'folge f succession to the throne
Thron'folger m successor to the throne
Thron'himmel m canopy, baldachin
Thron'räuber m usurper
Thunfisch ['tunfıʃ] m tuna
Tick [tık] m (–[e]s;–s & –e) tic; (fig)
eccentricity; **e–n T. auf j–n haben**
have a grudge against s.o.; **e–n T.
haben** (coll) be balmy
ticken ['tıkən] intr tick
ticktack ['tık'tak] adv ticktock ‖
Ticktack n (–s;) ticktock
tief [tif] adj deep; profound; (niedrig)
low; (Schlaf) sound; (Farbe) dark;
(äußerst) extreme; **aus tiefstem Herzen** from the bottom of one's heart;
im tiefsten Winter in the dead of
winter ‖ adv deeply; **zu t. singen** be
flat ‖ **Tief** n (–[e]s;–e) (meteor) low
Tief'angriff m low-level attack

Tief'bau m (–[e]s;) underground engi-
neering; underground work
tief'betrübt adj deeply grieved
Tief'druckgebiet n (meteor) low
Tiefe ['tifə] f (–;–n) depth; profundity
Tief'ebene f lowlands, plain
teif'empfunden adj heartfelt
Tie'fenanzeiger m (naut) depth gauge
Tie'fenschärfe f (phot) depth of field
Tief'flug m low-level flight
Tief'gang m (fig) depth; (naut) draft
tief'gekühlt adj deep-freeze
tief'greifend adj far-reaching; radical;
deep-seated
Tief'kühlschrank m deep freeze
Tief'land n lowlands
tief'liegend adj low-lying; deep-seated;
(Augen) sunken
Tief'punkt m (& fig) low point
Tief'schlag m (box) low blow
Tiefsee– [tifze] comb.fm. deep-sea
tief'sinnig adj pensive; melancholy
Tief'stand m low level
Tiegel ['tigəl] m (–s;–) saucepan; (zum
Schmelzen) crucible; (typ) platen
Tier [tir] n (–[e]s;–e) animal; (& fig)
beast; **großes** (or **hohes**) **T.** (coll)
big shot, big wheel
Tier'art f species (of animal)
Tier'arzt m veterinarian
Tier'bändiger –in §6 mf wild-animal
tamer
Tier'garten m zoo
Tier'heilkunde f veterinary medicine
tierisch ['tirıʃ] adj animal (fig) brut-
ish, bestial
Tier'kreis m zodiac
Tier'kreiszeichen n sign of the zodiac
Tier'quälerei f cruelty to animals
Tier'reich n animal kingdom
Tier'schutzverein m society for the pre-
vention of cruelty to animals
Tier'wärter m keeper (at zoo)
Tier'welt f animal kingdom
Tiger ['tigər] m (–s;–) tiger
Tigerin ['tigərın] f (–;–nen) tigress
tilgen ['tılgən] tr wipe out; (ausrotten)
eradicate; (Schuld) pay off; (Sünden)
expiate; (streichen) delete
Til'gung f (–;–en) eradication, extinc-
tion; payment; deletion
Til'gungsfonds m sinking fund
Tingeltangel ['tıŋəltaŋəl] m & n (–s;–)
honky-tonk
Tinktur [tıŋk'tur] f (–;–en) tincture
Tinte ['tıntə] f (–;–n) ink; **in der T.
sitzen** (coll) be in a pickle
Tin'tenfaß n inkwell
Tin'tenfisch m cuttlefish
Tin'tenfleck m, **Tin'tenklecks** m ink
spot
Tin'tenstift m indelible pencil
Tip [tıp] m (–s;–s) tip, hint
Tippelbruder ['tıpəlbrudər] m tramp
tippeln ['tıpəl] intr (SEIN) (coll) tramp;
(coll) toddle
tippen ['tıpən] tr type ‖ intr type; tap;
(wetten) bet; **an j–n nicht t. können**
not be able to come near s.o. (in
performance); **daran kannst du nicht
t.** that's beyond your reach; **t. auf**
(acc) predict ‖ ref**—sich an die Stirn
t.** tap one's forehead

Tippfehler ['tɪpfelər] *m* typographical error

Tippfräulein ['tɪpfrɔɪlaɪn] *n* (coll) typist

tipptopp ['tɪp'tɔp] *adj* tiptop

Tirol [tɪ'rol] *n* (-s;) Tyrol

Tiroler **-in** [tɪ'rolər(ɪn)] §6 *mf* Tyrolean

tirolerisch [tɪ'rolərɪʃ] *adj* Tyrolean

Tisch [tɪʃ] *m* (-es;-e) table; (*Mahlzeit*) meal, dinner, supper; **bei T.** during the meal; **nach T.** after the meal; **reinen T.** machen make a clean sweep of it; **unter den T. fallen** be ignored; **vom grünen T.** arm-chair; bureaucratic; **vor T.** before the meal; **zu T., bitte!** dinner is ready

Tisch'aufsatz *m* centerpiece

Tisch'besen *m* crumb brush

Tisch'besteck *n* knife, fork, and spoon

Tisch'blatt *n* leaf of a table

Tisch'decke *f* tablecloth

Tisch'gast *m* dinner guest

Tisch'gebet *n*—**T.** sprechen say grace

Tisch'gesellschaft *f* dinner party

Tisch'glocke *f* dinner bell

Tisch'karte *f* name plate

Tisch'lampe *f* table lamp; desk lamp

Tischler ['tɪʃlər] *m* (-s;-) cabinet maker

Tisch'platte *f* table top

Tisch'rede *f* after-dinner speech

Tisch'tennis *n* Ping-Pong

Tisch'tuch *n* tablecloth

Tisch'zeit *f* mealtime, dinner time

Tisch'zeug *n* table linen and tableware

Titan [tɪ'tan] *m* (-en;-en) Titan ‖ *n* (-s;) (chem) titanium

titanisch [tɪ'tanɪʃ] *adj* titanic

Titel ['titəl] *m* (-s;-) title; (*Anspruch*) claim; **e-n T. innehaben** (sport) hold a title

Ti'telbild *n* frontispiece; (*e-r Illustrierten*) cover picture

Ti'telblatt *n* title page

Ti'telkampf *m* (box) title bout

Ti'telrolle *f* title role

titulieren [tɪtu'lirən] *tr* title

Toast [tost] *m* (-es;-e & -s) toast

toasten ['tostən] *tr* (*Brot*) toast ‖ *intr* propose a toast, drink a toast; **auf j-n t.** toast s.o.

toben ['tobən] *intr* rage; (*Kinder*) raise a racket ‖ **Toben** *n* (-s;) rage, raging; racket, noise

Tob'sucht *f* frenzy, madness

tob'süchtig *adj* raving, mad; frantic

Tochter ['tɔxtər] *f* (-;-̈) daughter

Toch'terfirma *f*, **Toch'tergesellschaft** *f* (com) subsidiary, affiliate

Tod [tot] *m* (-es;-e) death; (jur) decease; **des Todes sein** be a dead man; **sich** [*dat*] **den Tod holen** catch a death of a cold

tod'ernst *adj* dead serious

Todes– [todəs] *comb.fm.* of death; deadly

To'desanzeige *f* obituary

To'desfall *m* death

To'desgefahr *f* mortal danger

To'deskampf *m* death struggle

To'deskandidat *m* one at death's door

To'desstoß *m* coup de grâce

To'desstrafe *f* death penalty; **bei T.** on pain of death

To'destag *m* anniversary of death

To'desursache *f* cause of death

To'desurteil *n* death sentence

Tod'feind **-in** §8 *mf* mortal enemy

todgeweiht ['totgəvaɪt] *adj* doomed

tödlich ['tøtlɪç] *adj* deadly, fatal

tod'mü'de *adj* dead tired

tod'schick' *adj* (coll) very chic

tod'si'cher *adj* (coll) dead sure

Tod'sünde *f* mortal sin

Toilette [twa'lɛtə] *f* (-;-n) toilet

Toilet'tentisch *m* dressing table

tolerant [tolɛ'rant] *adj* (gegen) tolerant (toward)

Toleranz [tolɛ'rants] *f* (-;-en) toleration; (mach) tolerance

tolerieren [tolɛ'rirən] *tr* tolerate

toll [tɔl] *adj* mad, crazy; fantastic, terrific; **das wird noch toller kommen** the worst is yet to come; **er ist nicht so t.** (coll) he's not so hot; **es zu t. treiben** carry it a bit too far; **t. nach** crazy about

tollen ['tɔlən] *intr* (HABEN & SEIN) romp about

Toll'haus *n* (fig) bedlam

Toll'heit *f* (-;) madness

Toll'kopf *m* (coll) crackpot

toll'kühn *adj* foolhardy, rash

Toll'wut *f* rabies

Tolpatsch ['tɔlpatʃ] *m* (-es;-e), **Tölpel** ['tœlpəl] *m* (-s;-) (coll) clumsy ox

töl'pelhaft *adj* clumsy

Tomate [to'matə] *f* (-;-n) tomato

Ton [ton] *m* (-[e]s;-̈e) tone; sound; tint, shade; (*Betonung*) accent, stress; (fig) fashion; **den Ton angeben** (fig) set the tone; (mus) give the keynote; **e-n anderen Ton anschlagen** change one's tune; **große Töne reden** talk big; **guter Ton** (fig) good taste; **hast du Töne!** can you beat that! ‖ *m* (-s;-e) clay

Ton'abnehmer *m* (electron) pickup

ton'angebend *adj* leading

Ton'arm *m* pickup arm

Ton'art *f* type of clay; (mus) key

Ton'atelier *n* (cin) sound studio

Ton'band *n* (-[e]s;-̈er) (cin) sound track; (electron) tape

Ton'bandgerät *n* tape recorder

tönen ['tønən] *tr* tint, shade ‖ *intr* sound; (*läuten*) ring

tönern ['tønərn] *adj* clay, of clay

Ton'fall *m* intonation, accent

Ton'farbe *f* timbre

Ton'film *m* sound film

Ton'folge *f* melody

Ton'frequenz *f* audio frequency

Ton'geschirr *n* earthenware

Ton'höhe *f*, **Ton'lage** *f* pitch

Ton'leiter *f* (mus) scale

ton'los *adj* voiceless; unstressed

Ton'malerei *f* onomotopoeia

Ton'meister *m* sound engineer

Tonnage [to'naʒə] *f* (-;-n) (naut) tonnage

Tonne ['tɔnə] *f* (-;-n) barrel; ton

Ton'silbe *f* accented syllable

Ton'spur *f* groove (*of record*)

Ton'streifen *m* (cin) sound track

Tonsur [tɔn'zur] *f* (-;-en) tonsure
Ton'taube *f* clay pigeon
Ton'taubenschießen *n* trapshooting
Tö'nung *f* (-;-en) tint; (phot) tone
Ton'verstärker *m* amplifier
Ton'waren *pl* earthenware
Topas [tɔ'pɑs] *m* (-es;-e) topaz
Topf [tɔpf] *m* (-[e]s;ːe) pot
Topf'blume *f* potted flower
Töpfer ['tœpfər] *m* (-s;-) potter
Töpferei [tœpfə'raɪ] *f* (-;-en) potter's shop
Töp'ferscheibe *f* potter's wheel
Töp'ferwaren *pl* pottery
Topf'lappen *m* potholder
Topf'pflanze *f* potted plant
Topp [tɔp] *m* (-s;-e) (naut) masthead
‖ **topp** *interj* it's a deal
Tor [tor] *m* (-en;-en) fool ‖ *n* (-[e]s; -e) gate; gateway; (sport) goal
Torbogen *m* archway
Torf [tɔrf] *m* (-[e]s;) peat
Tor'flügel *m* door (*of double door*)
Torf'moos *n* peat moss
Tor'heit *f* (-;-en) foolishness, folly
Tor'hüter *m* gatekeeper; (sport) goalie
töricht ['tørɪçt] *adj* foolish, silly
Törin ['tørɪn] *f* (-;-nen) fool
torkeln ['tɔrkəln] *intr* (HABEN & SEIN) (coll) stagger
Tor'latte *f* (sport) crossbar
Tor'lauf *m* slalom
Tor'linie *f* (sport) goal line
Tornister [tɔr'nɪstər] *m* (-s;-) knapsack; school bag; (mil) field pack
torpedieren [tɔrpe'dirən] *tr* torpedo
Torpedo [tɔr'pedo] *m* (-s;-s) torpedo
Tor'pfosten *m* doorpost; (fb) goal post
Tor'schluß *m*—**kurz vor T.** (fig) at the eleventh hour
Torte ['tɔrtə] *f* (-;-n) cake; pie
Tortur [tɔr'tur] *f* (-;-en) torture
Tor'wächter *m*, **Torwart** ['tɔrvart] *m* (-[e]s;-e) (sport) goalie
Tor'weg *m* gateway
tosen ['tozən] *intr* (HABEN & SEIN) rage, roar ‖ **Tosen** *n* (-s;) rage, roar
tot [tot] *adj* dead; (*Kapital*) idle; (*Wasser*) stagnant; **toter Punkt** dead center; (fig) snag; **totes Rennen** dead heat; **tote Zeit** dead season
total [to'tal] *adj* total; all-out
totalitär [totalɪ'ter] *adj* totalitarian
tot'arbeiten *ref* work oneself to death
Tote ['totə] §5 *mf* dead person
töten ['tøtən] *tr* kill; (*Nerv*) deaden
To'tenacker *m* churchyard
To'tenbett *n* deathbed
to'tenblaß' *adj* deathly pale
To'tenblässe *f* deathly pallor
to'tenbleich' *adj* deathly pale
To'tengräber *m* gravedigger
To'tengruft *f* crypt
To'tenhemd *n* shroud, winding sheet
To'tenklage *f* lament
To'tenkopf *m* skull
To'tenkranz *m* funeral wreath
To'tenmaske *f* death mask
To'tenmesse *f* requiem
To'tenreich *n* (myth) underworld
To'tenschau *f* coroner's inquest
To'tenschein *m* death certificate
To'tenstadt *f* necropolis

To'tenstarre *f* rigor mortis
To'tenstille *f* dead silence
To'tenwache *f* wake
tot'geboren *adj* stillborn
Tot'geburt *f* stillbirth
tot'lachen *ref* die laughing
Toto ['toto] *m* (-s;-s) football pool
tot'schießen §76 *tr* shoot dead
Tot'schlag *m* manslaughter
tot'schlagen §132 *tr* strike dead; (*Zeit*) kill
tot'schweigen §148 *tr* hush up; keep under wraps ‖ *intr* hush up
tot'stellen *ref* feign death, play dead
tot'treten §152 *tr* trample to death
Tö'tung *f* (-;-en) killing
Tour [tur] *f* (-;-en) tour; turn; (*Umdrehung*) revolution; **auf die krumme T.** by hook or by crook; **auf die langsame T.** very leisurely; **auf höchsten Touren** at full spead; (fig) full blast; **auf Touren bringen** (aut) rev up; **auf Touren kommen** pick up speed; (fig) get worked up; **auf Touren sein** (coll) be in good shape
Tou'renzahl *f* revolutions per minute
Tourismus [tu'rɪsmus] *m* (-;) tourism
Tourist [tu'rɪst] *m* (-en;-en) tourist
Touri'stenverkehr *m*, **Touristik** [tu'rɪstɪk] *f* (-;) tourism
Touristin [tu'rɪstɪn] *f* (-;-nen) tourist
Tour·nee [tur'ne] *f* (-;-neen ['ne·ən]) (mus, theat) tour
Trab [trap] *m* (-[e]s;) trot; **im T.** at a trot
Trabant [tra'bant] *m* (-en;-en) satellite
traben ['trabən] *intr* (HABEN & SEIN) trot
Tra'ber *m* (-s;-) trotter
Tra'berwagen *m* sulky
Trab'rennen *n* harness racing
Tracht [traxt] *f* (-;-en) costume; (*Last*) load; (*Ertrag*) yield
trachten ['traxtən] *intr*—**t. nach** strive for; **t. zu** (*inf*) endeavor to (*inf*)
trächtig ['treçtɪç] *adj* pregnant
Tradition [tradɪ'tsjon] *f* (-;-en) tradition
traditionell [tradɪtsjə'nel] *adj* traditional
traf [traf] *pret of* **treffen**
Trafik [tra'fɪk] *f* (-;-en) (Aust) cigar store
träg [trek] *adj* var of **träge**
Tragbahre ['trakbarə] *f* (-;-n) stretcher, litter
Trag'balken ['trakbalkən] *m* supporting beam; girder; joist
Tragband ['trakbant] *n* (-[e]s;ːer) strap; shoulder strap
tragbar ['trakbar] *adj* portable; (*Kleid*) wearable; (fig) bearable
Trage ['tragə] *f* (-;-n) litter
träge ['tregə] *adj* lazy; slow; inert
tragen ['tragən] §132 *tr* carry; bear; endure; support; (*Kleider*) wear, have on; (*hervorbringen*) produce, yield; (*Bedenken*) have; (*Folgen*) take; (*Risiko*) run; (*Zinsen*) yield; **bei sich t.** have on one's person; **getragen sein von** be based on; **zur Schau t.** show off ‖ *ref* dress; **sich**

gut t. wear well ‖ *intr (Stimme)* carry; *(Schußwaffe)* have a range; *(Baum, Feld)* bear, yield; *(Eis)* be thick enough

Träger ['trɛgər] *m (-s;-)* carrier; porter; *(Inhaber)* bearer; shoulder strap; (archit) girder, beam

Trä'gerflugzeug *n* carrier plane

trä'gerlos *adj* strapless

tragfähig ['trɑkfe·ɪç] *adj* strong enough, capable of carrying; **tragfähige Grundlage** (fig) sound basis

Trag'fähigkeit *f (-;-en)* capacity, load limit; (naut) tonnage

Tragfläche ['trɑkfleçə] *f,* **Tragflügel** ['trɑkflygəl] *m* airfoil

Träg'heit ['trekhaɪt] *f (-;)* laziness; (phys) inertia

Traghimmel ['trɑkhɪməl] *m* canopy

Tragik ['trɑgɪk] *f (-;)* tragedy

tragisch ['trɑgɪʃ] *adj* tragic

Tragödie [tra'gødjə] *f (-;-n)* tragedy

Tragriemen ['trɑkrimən] *m* strap

Tragsessel ['trɑkzesəl] *m* sedan chair

Tragtasche ['trɑktaʃə] *f* shopping bag

Tragtier ['trɑktir] *n* pack animal

Tragweite ['trɑkvaɪtə] *f* range; *(Bedeutung)* significance, moment

Tragwerk ['trɑkverk] *n* (aer) airfoil

Trainer ['trɛnər] *m (-s;-)* coach

trainieren [tre'nirən] *tr & intr* train; coach

Training ['trenɪŋ] *n (-s;)* training

Trai'ningsanzug *m* sweat suit

traktieren [trak'tirən] *tr* treat; treat rougly

Trak·tor ['traktɔr] *m (-s;-toren* ['torən]) tractor

trällern ['trelərn] *tr & intr* hum

trampeln ['trampəln] *tr* trample

Tram'pelpfad *m* beaten path

Tran [tran] *m (-[e]s;-e)* whale oil; **im T. sein** be drowsy; be under the influence of alcohol

tranchieren [trã'ʃirən] *tr* carve

Träne ['trenə] *f (-;-n)* tear

tränen ['trenən] *intr* water

Trä'nengas *n* tear gas

trank [traŋk] *pret* of **trinken** ‖ **Trank** *m (-[e]s;ⁿe)* drink, beverage; potion

Tränke ['treŋkə] *f (-;-n)* watering hole

tränken ['treŋkən] *tr* give *(s.o.)* a drink; *(Tiere)* water; soak

Transfor·mator [transfɔr'matɔr] *m (-s; -matoren* [ma'torən] transformer

transformieren [transfɔr'mirən] *tr* transform; step up; step down

Transfusion [transfu'zjon] *f (-;-en)* transfusion

Tran·sistor [tran'zɪstɔr] *m (-s;-sistoren* [zɪs'torən]) transistor

transitiv [tranzɪ'tif] *adj* transitive

Transmission [transmɪ'sjon] *f (-;-en)* transmission

transparent [transpa'rent] *adj* transparent ‖ **Transparent** *n (-[e]s;-e)* transparency; *(Spruchband)* banderol

transpirieren [transpɪ'rirən] *intr* perspire

Transplantation [transplanta'tsjon] *f (-;-en)* (surg) transplant

Transport [trans'pɔrt] *m (-[e]s;-e)* transportation

transportabel [transpɔr'tabəl] *adj* transportable

Transporter [trans'pɔrtər] *m (-s;-)* troopship; transport plane

transport'fähig *adj* transportable

transportieren [transpɔr'tirən] *tr* transport, ship

Transport'unternehmen *n* carrier

Trapez [tra'pets] *n (-es;-e)* trapeze; (geom) trapezoid

trappeln ['trapəln] *intr* (SEIN) clatter; *(Kinder)* patter

Trassant [tra'sant] *m (-en;-en)* (fin) drawer

Trassat [tra'sat] *m (-en;-en)* drawee

trassieren [tra'sirən] *tr* trace, lay out; **e-n Wechsel b. auf** *(acc)* write out a check to

trat [trat] *pret* of **treten**

Tratsch [tratʃ] *m (-es;)* gossip

tratschen ['tratʃən] *intr* gossip

Tratte ['tratə] *f (-;-n)* (fin) draft

Trau– [trau] *comb.fm.* wedding, marriage

Traube ['traubə] *f (-;-n)* grape; bunch of grapes; (fig) bunch

Trau'bensaft *m* grape juice

Trau'benzucker *m* glucose

trauen ['trau·ən] *tr (Brautpaar)* marry; **sich t. lassen** get married ‖ *ref* dare ‖ *intr (dat)* trust (in), have confidence (in)

Trauer ['trau·ər] *f (-;)* grief, sorrow; mourning; *(Trauerkleidung)* mourning clothes; **T. anlegen** put on mourning clothes; **T. haben** be in mourning

Trau'eranzeige *f* obituary

Trau'erbotschaft *f* sad news

Trau'erfall *m* death

Trau'erfeier *f* funeral ceremony

Trau'erflor *m* mourning crepe

Trau'ergefolge *n,* **Trau'ergeleit** *n* funeral procession

Trau'ergottesdienst *m* funeral service

Trau'erkloß *m* (coll) sad sack

Trau'ermarsch *m* funeral march

trauern ['trau·ərn] *intr* (um) mourn (for); (um) wear mourning (for)

Trau'erspiel *n* tragedy

Trau'erweide *f* weeping willow

Trau'erzug *m* funeral cortege

Traufe ['traufə] *f (-;-n)* eaves

träufeln ['trɔɪfəln] *tr & intr* drip

Trauf'rinne *f* rain gutter

Trauf'röhre *f* rain pipe

traulich ['traulɪç] *adj* intimate; cozy

Traum [traum] *m (-[e]s;ⁿe)* dream; (fig) daydream, reverie

Traum'bild *n* vision, phantom

Traum'deuter –in §6 *mf* interpreter of dreams

träumen ['trɔɪmən] *tr & intr* dream

Träu'mer *m (-s;-)* dreamer

Träumerei [trɔɪmə'raɪ] *f (-;-en)* dreaming; daydream

Träumerin ['trɔɪmərɪn] *f (-;-nen)* dreamer

träumerisch ['trɔɪmərɪʃ] *adj* dreamy; absent-minded

Traum'gesicht *n* vision, phantom

traum'haft *adj* dream-like

traurig ['traurɪç] *adj* sad

Trau'ring *m* wedding ring (or band)

Trau'schein *m* marriage certificate
traut [traut] *adj* dear; cozy; intimate
Trau'ung *f* (-;-en) marriage ceremony; **kirchliche T.** church wedding; **standesamtliche T.** civil ceremony
Trau'zeuge *m* best man
Trecker ['trɛkər] *m* (-s;-) tractor
Treff [trɛf] *n* (-s;-s) (cards) club(s)
treffen ['trɛfən] §151 *tr* hit; (*begegnen*) meet; (*betreffen*) concern || *ref* meet; assemble; **sich t. mit** meet with || *intr* hit home; (box) land, connect || **Treffen** *n* (-s;-) meeting; (mil) encounter; (sport) meet
tref'fend *adj* pertinent; to the point; (*Ähnlichkeit*) striking
Tref'fer *m* (-s;-) hit; winner; prize
treff'lich *adj* excellent
Treff'punkt *m* rendezvous, meeting place
Treib- [traɪp] *comb.fm.* moving; driving
treiben ['traɪbən] §62 *tr* drive; propel; chase, expel; (*Beruf*) pursue; (*Blätter, Blüten*) put forth; (*Geschäft*) run, carry on; (*Metall*) work; (*Musik, Sport*) go in for; (*Sprachen*) study; (*Pflanzen*) force; **es zu weit t.** go too far; **was treibst du denn?** (coll) what are you doing? || *intr* blossom; sprout; (*Teig*) ferment || *intr* (SEIN) drift, float || **Treiben** *n* (-s;) doings, activity; drifting, floating
Treib'haus *n* hothouse
Treib'holz *n* driftwood
Treib'kraft *f* driving force
Treib'mine *f* floating mine
Treib'rakete *f* booster rocket
Treib'riemen *m* drive belt
Treib'sand *m* drifting sand; quicksand
Treib'stange *f* connecting rod
Treib'stoff *m* fuel; propellant
Treib'stoffbehälter *m* fuel tank
trennbar ['trɛnbɑr] *adj* separable
trennen ['trɛnən] *tr* separate; sever; (*Naht*) undo; (*Ehe*) dissolve; (elec, telp) cut off || *ref* part; separate; (*Weg*) branch off
Tren'nung *f* (-;-en) separation; parting; dissolution
Tren'nungsstrich *m* dividing line; hyphen
Trense ['trɛnzə] *f* (-;-n) snaffle
Treppe ['trɛpə] *f* (-;-n) stairs, stairway; flight of stairs; **die T. hinauffallen** (coll) be kicked upstairs; **zwei Treppen hoch wohnen** live two flights up
Trep'penabsatz *m* landing
Trep'penflucht *f* flight of stairs
Trep'pengeländer *n* banister
Trep'penhaus *n* staircase
Trep'penläufer *m* stair carpet
Trep'penstufe *f* step, stair
Tresor [trɛ'zor] *m* (-s;-e) safe; vault
Tresse ['trɛsə] *f* (-;-n) (mil) stripe
treten ['tretən] §152 *tr* tread; tread on; trample; (*Fußhebel*) work; (*Orgel*) pump; **mit Füßen t.** (fig) trample under foot || *intr* (SEIN) step, walk; tread; **an j-s Stelle t.** succeed s.o.; **auf der Stelle t.** (mil) mark time; **in**

Kraft t. go into effect; **j-m zu nahe t.** offend s.o.; **t. in** (*acc*) enter (into)
Tretmühle ['tretmylə] *f* treadmill
treu [trɔɪ] *adj* loyal, faithful, true
Treu'bruch *m* breach of faith
Treue ['trɔɪ·ə] *f* (-;) loyalty, fidelity; allegiance; **j-m die T. halten** remain loyal to s.o.
Treu'eid *m* oath of allegiance
Treu'hand *f* (jur) trust
Treuhänder -in ['trɔɪhɛndər(ɪn)] §6 *mf* trustee
Treu'handfonds *m* trust fund
treu'herzig *adj* trusting; sincere
treu'los *adj* unfaithful; (**gegen**) disloyal (to)
Tribüne [tri'bynə] *f* (-;-n) rostrum; (mil) reviewing stand; (sport) grandstand
Tribut [tri'but] *m* (-[e]s;-e) tribute
Trichter ['trɪçtər] *m* (-s;-) funnel; (*Bomben-*) crater, pothole; (mus) bell (*of wind instrument*); **auf den T. kommen** (coll) catch on
Trick [trɪk] *m* (-s;-s & -e) trick
Trick'film *m* animated cartoon
trieb [trip] *pret* of **treiben** || **Trieb** *m* (-[e]s;-e) sprout, shoot; urge, drive; instinct
Trieb'feder *f* (horol) mainspring
Trieb'kraft *f* motive power
trieb'mäßig *adj* instinctive
Trieb'werk *n* motor, engine
triefäugig ['trifɔɪgɪç] *adj* bleary-eyed
triefen ['trifən] §153 *intr* drip; (*Augen*) water; (*Nase*) run
triezen ['tritsən] *tr* (coll) tease
Trift [trɪft] *f* (-;-en) pasture land; cattle track; log-running
triftig ['trɪftɪç] *adj* cogent; valid
Trigonometrie [trɪgɔnɔmeˈtri] *f* (-;) trigonometry
Trikot [tri'ko] *m* & *n* (-s;-s) knitted cloth; (sport) trunks, tights
Triller ['trɪlər] *m* (-s;-) trill; (mus) quaver
trillern ['trɪlərn] *intr* trill; (*Vogel*) warble
Tril'lerpfeife *f* whistle
Trink- [trɪŋk] *comb.fm.* drinking
trinkbar ['trɪŋkbɑr] *adj* drinkable
Trink'becher *m* drinking cup
trinken ['trɪŋkən] §143 *tr* & *intr* drink
Trin'ker -in §6 *mf* drinker
trink'fest *adj* able to hold one's liquor
Trink'gelage *n* drinking party
Trink'geld *n* tip, gratuity
Trink'glas *n* drinking glass
Trink'halm *m* straw
Trink'spruch *m* toast
Trink'wasser *n* drinking water
Trio ['tri·o] *n* (-s;-s) trio
trippeln ['trɪpəln] *intr* (SEIN) patter
Tripper ['trɪpər] *m* (-s;) gonorrhea
trist [trɪst] *adj* dreary
tritt [trɪt] *pret* of **treten** || *m* (-[e]s; -e) step; kick; pace; footstep; footprint; small stepladder; pedal; **j-m e-n T. versetzen** give s.o. a kick
Tritt'brett *n* running board
Tritt'leiter *f* stepladder
Triumph [tri'umf] *m* (-[e]s;-e) triumph

Triumph'bogen *m* triumphal arch
triumphieren [trɪ·um'firən] *intr* triumph
Triumph'zug *m* triumphal procession
trocken ['trɔkən] *adj* dry; arid; **trockenes Brot** plain bread
Trockenbagger (Trok'kenbagger) *m* (mach) excavator
Trockendock (Trok'kendock) *n* drydock
Trockenei (Trok'kenei) *n* dehydrated eggs
Trockeneis (Trok'keneis) *n* dry ice
Trockenhaube (Trok'kenhaube) *f* hair drier
Trockenheit (Trok'kenheit) *f* (-;) dryness, aridity
trockenlegen (trok'kenlegen) *tr* (*Sumpf*) drain; (*Säugling*) change (the diapers of)
Trockenmaß (Trok'kenmaß) *n* dry measure
Trockenmilch (Trok'kenmilch) *f* powdered milk
Trockenschleuder (Trok'kenschleuder) *f* spin-drier, clothes drier
Trockenübung (Trok'kenübung) *f* dry run
trocknen ['trɔknən] *tr* dry ‖ *intr* (SEIN) dry, dry up
Troddel ['trɔdəl] *f* (-;-n) tassel
Trödel ['trødəl] *m* (-s;) secondhand goods; old clothes; junk; (fig) nuisance, waste of time
Trö'delkram *m* junk
trödeln ['trødəln] *intr* waste time
Tröd'ler -in §6 *mf* secondhand dealer
troff [trɔf] *pret* of **triefen**
trog [trok] *pret* of **trügen** **Trog** *m* (-[e]s;ꞌe) trough
Trommel ['trɔməl] *f* (-;-n) drum
Trom'melfell *n* drumhead; (anat) eardrum
trommeln ['trɔməln] *tr & intr* drum
Trom'melschlag *m* drumbeat
Trom'melschlegel *m*, **Trom'melstock** *m* drumstick
Trom'melwirbel *m* drum roll
Trommler ['trɔmlər] *m* (-s;-) drummer
Trompete [trɔm'petə] *f* (-;-n) trumpet
trompeten [trɔm'petən] *intr* blow the trumpet; (*Elefant*) trumpet
Trompe'ter -in §6 *mf* trumpeter
Tropen ['tropən] *pl* tropics
Tropf [trɔpf] *m* (-[e]s;ꞌe) simpleton; **armer T.** poor devil
tröpfeln ['trœpfəln] *tr & intr* drip ‖ *intr* (SEIN) trickle ‖ *impers—es* **tröpfelt** it is sprinkling
tropfen ['trɔpfən] *tr & intr* drip ‖ *intr* (SEIN) trickle ‖ **Tropfen** *m* (-s;-) drop; **ein T. auf den heißen Stein** a drop in the bucket
trop'fenweise *adv* drop by drop
Trophäe [tro'fɛ·ə] *f* (-;-n) trophy
tropisch ['tropɪʃ] *adj* tropical
Troß [trɔs] *m* (Trosses; Trosse) (coll) load, baggage; (coll) hangers-on
Trosse ['trɔsə] *f* (-;-n) cable; (naut) hawser
Trost [trost] *m* (-es;) consolation, comfort; **geringer T.** cold comfort;

wohl nicht bei T. sein not be all there
trösten ['trøstən] *tr* console, comfort ‖ *ref* cheer up; feel consoled
tröstlich ['trøstlɪç] *adj* comforting
trost'los *adj* disconsolate; bleak
Trost'preis *m* consolation prize
trost'reich *adj* comforting
Trö'stung *f* (-;-en) consolation
Trott [trɔt] *m* (-[e]s;-e) trot; (coll) routine
Trottel ['trɔtəl] *m* (-s;-) (coll) dope
trotten ['trɔtən] *intr* (SEIN) trot
Trottoir [trɔ'twar] *n* (-s;-e & -s) sidewalk
trotz [trɔts] *prep* (*genit*) in spite of; **t. alledem** for all that ‖ **Trotz** *m* (-es;) defiance; **j–m T. bieten** defy s.o.
trotz'dem *adv* nevertheless ‖ *conj* although
trotzen ['trɔtsən] *intr* be stubborn; (*schmollen*) sulk; (*dat*) defy
trotzig ['trɔtsɪç] *adj* defiant; sulky; obstinate
Trotz'kopf *m* defiant child (or adult)
trüb [tryp], **trübe** ['trybə] *adj* turbid, muddy; (*Wetter*) dreary; (*glanzlos*) dull; (*Erfahrung*) sad
Trubel ['trubəl] *m* (-s;) bustle
trüben ['trybən] *tr* make turbid, muddy; dim; dull; disturb, trouble (*Freude, Stimmung*) spoil ‖ *ref* grow cloudy; become muddy; become strained
Trübsal ['trypzal] *f* (-;-en) distress, misery; **T. blasen** be in the dumps
trüb'selig *adj* gloomy, sad
Trüb'sinn *m* (-[e]s;) gloom
trüb'sinnig *adj* gloomy
Trü'bung *f* (-;) muddiness; blurring
trudeln ['trudəln] *intr* go into a spin ‖ **Trudeln** *n* (-s;) spin; **ins T. kommen** (aer) go into a spin
trug [truk] *pret* of **tragen** ‖ **Trug** *m* (-[e]s;) deceit, fraud; delusion
Trug'bild *n* phantom; illusion
trügen ['trygən] §111 *tr & intr* deceive
trügerisch ['trygərɪʃ] *adj* deceptive, illusory; (*verräterisch*) treacherous
Trug'schluß *m* fallacy
Truhe ['tru·ə] *f* (-;-n) trunk, chest
Trulle ['trulə] *f* (-;-n) slut
Trümmer ['trʏmər] *pl* ruins; rubble
Trumpf [trumpf] *m* (-[e]s;ꞌe) trump
Trunk [truŋk] *m* (-[e]s;ꞌe) drinking; **im T.** when drunk
trunken ['truŋkən] *adj* drunk; **t. vor** (*dat*) elated with
Trunkenbold ['truŋkənbɔlt] *m* (-[e]s; -e) drunkard
Trun'kenheit *f* (-;) drunkenness; **T. am Steuer** (jur) drunken driving
trunk'süchtig *adj* alcoholic ‖ **Trunksüchtige** §5 *mf* alcoholic
Trupp [trup] *m* (-s;-s) troop, gang; (mil) detail, detachment
Truppe ['trupə] *f* (-;-n) (mil) troop; (theat) troupe; **Truppen** (mil) troops
Trup'peneinheit *f* unit
Trup'penersatz *m* reserves
Trup'pengattung *f* branch of service
Trup'penschau *f* (mil) review, parade

Trup′pentransporter *m* (aer) troop carrier; (nav) troopship
Trüp′penübung *f* field exercise
Trup′penverband *m* unit; task force
Trup′penverbandplatz *m* (mil) first-aid station
Trust [trʊst] *m* (-[e]s;-e & -s) (com) trust
Truthahn ['truthɑn] *m* turkey (cock)
Truthenne ['truthɛnə] *f* turkey (hen)
trutzig ['trʊtsɪç] *adj* defiant
Tscheche ['tʃɛçə] *m* (-n;-n), **Tschechin** ['tʃɛçɪn] *f* (-;-nen) Czech
tschechisch ['tʃɛçɪʃ] *adj* Czech
Tschechoslowakei [tʃɛçəsləva'kaɪ] *f* (-;)—**die T.** Czechoslovakia
Tube ['tubə] *f* (-;-n) tube; **auf die T. drücken** (aut) step on it
Tuberkulose [tubɛrkʊ'lozə] *f* (-;) tuberculosis
Tuch [tux] *n* (-[e]s;-e) cloth; fabric ‖ *n* (-[e]s;̈er) kerchief; shawl; scarf
tuchen ['tuxən] *adj* cloth, fabric
Tuch′fühlung *f*—**T. haben mit** (mil) stand shoulder to shoulder with; **T. halten mit** keep in close touch with
Tuch′seite *f* right side (*of cloth*)
tüchtig ['tʏçtɪç] *adj* able, capable, efficient; sound, thorough; excellent; good; (*Trinker*) hard; **t. in** (*dat*) good at; **t. zu** qualified for ‖ *adv* very much; hard; soundly, throughly; (sl) awfully
Tüch′tigkeit *f* (-;) ability, efficiency; soundness, thoroughness; excellency
Tuch′waren *pl* dry goods
Tücke ['tʏkə] *f* (-;-n) malice; **mit List und T.** by cleverness
tückisch ['tʏkɪʃ] *adj* insidious
tüfteln ['tʏftəln] *intr*—**t. an** (*dat*) (coll) puzzle over
Tugend ['tugənt] *f* (-;-en) virtue
Tugendbold ['tugəntbɔlt] *m* (-[e]s;-e) (pej) paragon of virtue
tu′gendhaft *adj* virtuous
Tulpe ['tʊlpə] *f* (-;-n) tulip
tummeln ['tuməln] *tr* (*Pferd*) exercise ‖ *ref* hurry; (*Kinder*) romp about
Tum′melplatz *m* playground; (fig) arena
Tümmler ['tʏmlər] *m* (-s;-) dolphin; (*Taube*) tumbler
Tumor ['tumɔr] *m* (-s; **Tumoren** [tʊ'morən]) tumor
Tümpel ['tʏmpəl] *m* (-s;-) pond
Tumult [tʊ'mʊlt] *m* (-[e]s;-e) uproar; uprising
tun [tun] §154 *tr* do; make; take; **dazu tun** add to it; **e-n Zug tun** take a swig; **es zu tun bekommen mit** have trouble with; **j-n in ein Internat tun** send s.o. to a boarding school ‖ *intr* do; be busy; **alle Hände voll zu tun haben** have one's hands full; **es ist mir darum zu tun** I am anxious about it; **groß tun** talk big; **mir ist sehr darum zu tun zu** (*inf*) it is very important for me to (*inf*); **nur so tun, als ob** pretend that; **spröde tun** be prudish; **stolz tun** be proud; **weh tun** hurt; **zu t. haben** be busy; have one's work cut out; **zu tun haben mit** have trouble with ‖ *impers*—**es tut mir**

leid I am sorry; **es tut nichts** it doesn't matter ‖ **Tun** *n* (-s;) doings; action; **Tun und Treiben** doings
Tünche ['tʏnçə] *f* (-;-n) whitewash
tünchen ['tʏnçən] *tr* whitewash
Tunichtgut ['tunɪçtgut] *m* (- & -[e]s; -e) good-for-nothing
Tunke ['tʊŋkə] *f* (-;-n) sauce; gravy
tunken ['tʊŋkən] *tr* dip, dunk
tunlichst ['tunlɪçst] *adv*—**das wirst du t. bleiben lassen** you had better leave it alone
Tunnel ['tunəl] *m* (-s;- & -s) tunnel
Tüpfchen ['tʏpfçən] *n* (-s;-) dot
Tüpfel ['tʏpfəl] *m* & *n* (-s;-) dot
tupfen ['tʊpfən] *tr* dab; dot ‖ **Tupfen** *m* (-s;-) dot, spot
Tür [tyr] *f* (-;-en) door
Tür′angel *f* door hinge
Tür′anschlag *m* doorstop
Turbine [tʊr'binə] *f* (-;-n) turbine
Turboprop ['turbɔprɔp] *m* (-s;-s) turboprop
Tür′drücker *m* latch
Tür′flügel *m* door (*of double door*)
Tür′griff *m* door handle; door knob
Türke ['tʏrkə] *m* (-n;-n) Turk
Türkei [tʏr'kaɪ] *f* (-;)—**die T.** Turkey
Türkin ['tʏrkɪn] *f* (-;-nen) Turk
Türkis [tʏr'kis] *m* (-es;-e) turquoise
türkisch ['tʏrkɪʃ] *adj* Turkish
türkisen [tʏr'kizən] *adj* turquoise
Tür′klingel *f* doorbell
Tür′klinke *f* door handle
Turm [tʊrm] *m* (-[e]s;̈e) tower; steeple; turret; (chess) castle
Türmchen ['tʏrmçən] *n* (-s;-) turret
türmen ['tʏrmən] *tr* & *ref* pile up ‖ *intr* (SEIN) run away, bolt
turm′hoch′ *adj* towering ‖ *adv* (by) far
Turm′spitze *f* spire
Turm′springen *n* high diving
Turn- [tʊrn] *comb.fm.* gymnastic, gym, athletic
turnen ['tʊrnən] *intr* do exercises ‖ **Turnen** *n* (-s;) gymnastics
Tur′ner *-in* §6 *mf* gymnast
turnerisch ['tʊrnərɪʃ] *adj* gymnastic
Turn′gerät *n* gymnastic apparatus
Turn′halle *f* gymnasium, gym
Turn′hemd *n* gym shirt
Turn′hose *f* trunks
Turnier [tʊr'nir] *n* (-s;-e) tournament
Turn′schuhe *pl* sneakers
Tür′pfosten *m* doorpost
Tür′rahmen *m* doorframe
Tür′schild *n* doorplate
Tür′schwelle *f* threshold
Tusche ['tʊ/ə] *f* (-;-n) (paint) wash; **chinesische T.** India ink
tuscheln ['tʊʃəln] *intr* whisper
Tute ['tutə] *f* (-;-n) (aut) horn
Tüte ['tytə] *f* (-;-n) paper bag; paper cone; ice cream cone
tuten ['tutən] *intr* blow the horn; (coll) blare away
Twen [tvɛn] *m* (-s;-s) young man (*in his twenties*)
Typ [typ] *m* (-s;-en) type; (*Bauart*) model
Type ['typə] *f* (-;-n) type; (coll) strange character
Ty′pennummer *f* model number

Typhus ['tyfʊs] *m* (–;) typhoid
typisch ['typɪʃ] *adj* (**für**) typical (of)
Tyrann [tʏ'ran] *m* (–en;–en) tyrant
Tyrannei [tʏra'naɪ] *f* (–;–en) tyranny

tyrannisch [tʏ'ranɪʃ] *adj* tyrannical
tyrannisieren [tʏranɪ'zirən] *tr* tyrannize, oppress
Tz ['tetsɛt] *n*—**bis ins Tz** thoroughly

U

U, u [u] *invar n* U, u
u.A.w.g. *abbr* (**um Antwort wird gebeten**) R.S.V.P.
U-Bahn ['uban] *f* (**Untergrundbahn**) subway
übel ['ybəl] *adj* evil; (*schlecht*) bad; (*unwohl*) queasy, sick; (*Geruch, usw.*) nasty, foul; **er ist ein übler Geselle** he's a bad egg; **mir ist ü. I feel sick; ü. daran sein** have it rough || *adv* badly; **est steht ü. mit** things don't look good for; **ü. auslegen** misconstrue; **ü. deuten** misinterpret; **ü. ergehen** fare badly; **ü. gelaunt** in bad humor || **Übel** *n* (–s;–) evil; ailment
ü'belgelaunt *adj* ill-humored
ü'belgesinnt *adj* evil-minded
Ü'belkeit *f* (–;) nausea
ü'belnehmen §116 *tr* take amiss; take offense at, resent
ü'belnehmend *adj* resentful
ü'belriechend *adj* foul-smelling
Ü'belstand *m* evil; bad state of affairs
Ü'beltat *f* misdeed, crime, offense
Ü'beltäter –in §6 *mf* wrongdoer; criminal
ü'belwollen §162 *intr* (*dat*) be ill-disposed towards || **Übelwollen** *n* (–s;) ill will, malevolence
ü'belwollend *adj* malevolent
üben ['ybən] *tr* practice, exercise; (*e–e Kunst*) cultivate; (*Handwerk*) pursue; (*Gewalt*) use; (*Verrat*) commit; (mil) drill; (sport) train; **Barmherzigkeit ü. an** (*dat*) have mercy on; **Gerechtigkeit ü. gegen** be fair to; **Nachsicht ü. gegen** be lenient towards; **Rache ü. an** (*dat*) take revenge on || *ref*—**sich im Schifahren ü.** practice skiing
über ['ybər] *adv*—**j–m ü. sein in** (*dat*) be superior to s.o. in; **ü. und ü.** over and over || *prep* (*dat*) over; above, on top of || *prep* (*acc*) by way of, via; (*bei, während*) during; (*nach*) past; over; across; (*betreffend*) about, concerning; **Briefe ü. Briefe** letter after letter; **ein Scheck ü. 10 DM** a check for 10 marks; **es geht nichts ü.** there is nothing better than; **heute übers Jahr** a year from today; **ü. Gebühr** more than was due; **ü. kurz oder lang** sooner or later; **ü. Land** crosscountry
überall' *adv* everywhere, all over
überallher' *adv* from all sides
überallhin' *adv* in every direction
Ü'berangebot *n* over-supply
überan'strengen *tr* overexert, strain || *ref* overexert oneself, strain oneself

überar'beiten *tr* revise, touch up || *ref* —**sich ü.** overwork oneself
Überar'beitung *f* (–;–en) revision, touching up; revised text
ü'beraus *adv* extremely, very
überbacken (überbak'ken) §50 *tr* bake lightly
Ü'berbau *m* (–[e]s; –e & –ten [tən]) superstructure
ü'berbeanspruchen *tr* overwork
ü'berbelasten *tr* overload
ü'berbelegt *adj* overcrowded
ü'berbelichten *tr* (phot) overexpose
ü'berbetonen *tr* overemphasize
überbie'ten §58 *tr* outbid; (fig) outdo
Überbleibsel ['ybərblaɪpsəl] *n* (–s;–) remains; leftovers
Überblen'dung *f* (cin) dissolve
Ü'berblick *m* survey; (fig) synopsis
überblicken (überblik'ken) *tr* survey
überbrin'gen §65 *tr* deliver; convey
Überbrin'ger –in §6 *mf* bearer
überbrücken (überbrük'ken) *tr* (& fig) bridge
Überbrückung (Überbrük'kung) *f* (–; –en) bridging; (rr) overpass
Überbrückungs– *comb.fm.* emergency, stop-gap
überdachen [ybər'daxən] *tr* roof over
überdau'ern *tr* outlast
überdecken (überdek'ken) *tr* cover
überden'ken §66 *tr* think over
überdies' *adv* moreover, besides
überdre'hen *tr* (*Uhr*) overwind
Ü'berdruck *m* excess pressure
Ü'berdruckanzug *m* space suit
Ü'berdruckkabine *f* pressurized cabin
Über·druß ['ybərdrʊs] *m* (–drusses;) boredom; (*Übersättigung*) satiety; (*Ekel*) disgust; **bis zum Ü.** ad nauseam
überdrüssig ['ybərdrʏsɪç] *adj* (*genit*) sick of, disgusted with
ü'berdurchschnittlich *adj* above the average
Ü'bereifer *m* excessive zeal
ü'bereifrig *adj* overzealous
überei'len *tr* precipitate; rush || *ref* be in too big a hurry; act rashly
übereilt [ybər'aɪlt] *adj* hasty, rash
übereinan'der *adv* one on top of the other
übereinan'derschlagen §132 *tr* cross
überein'kommen §99 *intr* (SEIN) come to an agreement || **Übereinkommen** *n* (–s;–) agreement
Überein'kunft *f* agreement
überein'stimmen *intr* be in agreement; concur; (*Farben, usw.*) harmonize
Überein'stimmung *f* agreement; accord; (*Gleichförmigkeit*) conformity;

(*Einklang*) harmony; **in Ü. mit** in line with

ü′berempfindlich *adj* oversensitive

überfah′ren §71 *tr* run over, run down; (*Fluß, usw.*) cross; **ein Signal ü.** go through a traffic light; **ü. werden** (coll) be taken in ‖ **ü′berfahren** §71 *tr* (*über e–n Fluß, usw.*) take across ‖ *intr* (SEIN) drive over, cross

Ü′berfahrt *f* crossing

Ü′berfall *m* surprise attack, assault; (*Raubüberfall*) holdup; (*Einfall*) raid

überfal′len §72 *tr* (*räuberisch*) hold up; assault; (mil) surprise; (mil) invade, raid; **ü. werden** be overcome (*by sleep*); be seized (*with fear*)

ü′berfällig *adj* overdue

Ü′berfallkommando *n* riot squad

überflie′gen §57 *tr* fly over; (*Buch*) skim through

ü′berfließen §76 *intr* (SEIN) overflow

überflügeln [ybər′flygəln] *tr* outflank; (fig) outstrip

Ü′berfluß *m* abundance; excess; **im Ü. vorhanden sein** be plentiful

ü′berflüssig *adj* superfluous

überflu′ten *tr* overflow, flood, swamp ‖ **ü′berfluten** *intr* (SEIN) overflow

überfor′dern *tr* demand too much of; overwork

Ü′berfracht *f* excess luggage

ü′berführen *tr* carry across; (*Leiche*) transport in state ‖ **überführ′ren** *tr* (*genit*) convince of; (*genit*) convict of

Überführ′rung *f* (–;–en) overpass; (*e–s Verbrechers*) conviction

Ü′berfülle *f* superabundance

überfül′len *tr* stuff, jam, pack

Ü′bergabe *f* delivery; (& mil) surrender

Ü′bergang *m* passage; crossing; transition; (jur) transfer; (mil) desertion; (paint) blending; (rr) crossing

Ü′bergangsbeihilfe *f* severance pay

Ü′bergangsstadium *n* transition stage

Ü′bergangszeit *f* transitional period

überge′ben §80 *tr* hand over; give up; (*einreichen*) submit; (& mil) surrender; **dem Verkehr ü.** open to traffic ‖ *ref* vomit, throw up

überge′hen §82 *tr* omit; overlook; **mit Stillschweigen ü.** pass over in silence ‖ **ü′bergehen** §82 *intr* (SEIN) go over, cross; (*sich verändern*) (**in** *acc*) change (into); **auf j–n ü.** devolve upon s.o.; **in andere Hände ü.** change hands; **in Fäulnis ü.** become rotten

Ü′bergewicht *n* overweight; (fig) preponderance; **das Ü. bekommen** become top-heavy; (fig) get the upper hand

ü′bergießen §76 *tr* spill ‖ **übergie′ßen** §76 *tr* pour over, pour on; (*Braten*) baste; **mit Zuckerguß ü.** (culin) ice

ü′bergreifen §88 *intr* (**auf** *acc*) spread (to); (**auf** *acc*) encroach (on)

Ü′bergriff *m* encroachment

ü′bergroß *adj* huge, colossal; oversize

ü′berhaben §89 *tr* have left; (*Kleider*) have on; (fig) be fed up with

überhand′nehmen §116 *intr* get the upper hand; run riot

ü′berhängen §92 *tr* (*Mantel*) put on;

(*Gewehr*) sling over the shoulders ‖ *intr* overhang, project

überhäu′fen *tr* overwhelm, swamp

überhaupt′ *adv* really; anyhow; (*besonders*) especially; (*überdies*) besides; at all; **ü. kein** no...whatever; **ü. nicht** not at all; **wenn ü.** if...at all; if...really

überheblich [ybər′hepliç] *adj* arrogant

überhei′zen, übzerhit′zen *tr* overheat

überhöhen [ybər′hø·ən] *tr* (*Kurve*) bank; (*Preise*) raise too high

ü′berholen *tr* take across; **die Segel ü.** shift sails ‖ *intr* (naut) heel ‖ **überho′len** *tr* outdistance, outrun; (*ausbessern*) overhaul; (*Fahrzeug*) pass; (fig) outstrip

überholt [ybər′hɔlt] *adj* obsolete, out of date; (*repariert*) reconditioned

überhö′ren *tr* not hear, miss; ignore; misunderstand

ü′berirdisch *adj* supernatural

überkandidelt [′ybərkandidəlt] *adj* (coll) nutty, wacky

ü′berkippen *intr* (SEIN) tilt over

überkle′ben *tr* paper over; **ü. mit** cover with

Ü′berkleid *n* outer garment; overalls

ü′berklug *adj* (pej) wise, smart

ü′berkochen *intr* (SEIN) boil over

überkom′men *adj* traditional ‖ §99 *tr* overcome ‖ *intr* (SEIN) be handed down to

überla′den *adj* overdone ‖ §103 *tr* overload

Ü′berlandbahn *f* interurban trolley line

Ü′berlandleitung *f* (elec) high-tension line; (telp) long-distance line

überlas′sen §104 *tr* yield, leave, relinquish; entrust; (com) sell; **das bleibt ihm ü.** he is free to do as he pleases ‖ *ref* (*dat*) give way to

Ü′berlast *f* overload; overweight

überla′sten *tr* overload

überlau′fen *adj* overcrowded; (fig) swamped ‖ §105 *tr* overrun; (*belästigen*) pester; **Angst überlief ihn** fear came over him ‖ **ü′berlaufen** §105 *intr* (SEIN) run over, overflow; boil over; (fig & mil) desert; **die Galle läuft mir über** (fig) my blood boils ‖ *impers*—**mich überläuft es kalt** I shudder

Ü′berläufer –**in** §6 *mf* (mil) deserter; (pol) turncoat

ü′berlaut *adj* too noisy

überle′ben *tr* outlive, survive ‖ *ref* go out of style

überle′bend *adj* surviving ‖ **Überlebende** §5 *mf* survivor

ü′berlebensgroß *adj* bigger than life

überlebt [ybər′lept] *adj* antiquated

überle′gen *adj* (*dat*) superior (to); (an *dat*) superior (in) ‖ *tr* consider, think over ‖ *ref*—**sich** [*dat*] **anders ü.** change one's mind; **sich** [*dat*] **ü.** consider, think over ‖ *intr* think it over ‖ **ü′berlegen** *tr* lay across; (*Mantel*) put on

Überle′genheit *f* (–;) superiority

überlegt′ *adj* well considered; (jur) willful

Überle'gung _f_ (-;-en) consideration
überle'sen §107 _tr_ read over, peruse
überlie'fern _tr_ deliver; hand down, transmit; (mil) surrender
Überlie'ferung _f_ (-;-en) delivery; (fig) tradition; (mil) surrender
überli'sten _tr_ outwit, outsmart
überma'chen _tr_ bequeath
Ü'bermacht _f_ superiority; (fig) predominance
ü'bermächtig _adj_ overwhelming; predominant
überma'len _tr_ paint over
übermannen [ybər'manən] _tr_ overpower
Ü'bermaß _n_ excess; bis zum Ü. to excess
ü'bermäßig _adj_ excessive ‖ _adv_ excessively; overly
Ü'bermensch _m_ superman
ü'bermenschlich _adj_ superhuman
übermitteln [ybər'mɪtəln] _tr_ transmit, convey, forward
Übermitt'lung _f_ (-;-en) transmission, conveyance, forwarding
ü'bermorgen _adv_ the day after tomorrow
übermüdet [ybər'mydət] _adj_ overtired
Ü'bermut _m_ exuberance, mischievousness
ü'bermütig _adj_ exuberant; haughty
ü'bernächste §9 _adj_ next but one; am übernächsten Tag the day after tomorrow; ü. Woche week after next
übernach'ten _intr_ spend the night
Übernach'tung _f_ (-;-en) accommodations for the night; spending the night
Ü'bernahme _f_ taking over, takeover
ü'bernatürlich _adj_ supernatural
überneh'men §116 _tr_ take over; assume; undertake; take upon oneself; accept, receive ‖ ü'bernehmen §116 _tr_ (Mantel, Schal) put on; (Gewehr) shoulder ‖ überneh'men §116 _ref_ overreach oneself; sich beim Essen ü. overeat
ü'berordnen _tr_ place over, set over
ü'berparteilich _adj_ nonpartisan
Ü'berproduktion _f_ overproduction
überprü'fen _tr_ examine again, check; verify; (Personen) screen
Überprü'fung _f_ (-;-en) checking; checkup
ü'berquellen §119 _intr_ (SEIN) (Teig) run over; überquellende Freude irrepressible joy
überqueren [ybər'kverən] _tr_ cross
überra'gen _tr_ tower over; (fig) surpass
überraschen [ybər'raʃən] _tr_ surprise
Überra'schung _f_ (-;-en) surprise
überrech'nen _tr_ count over
überre'den _tr_ persuade; j-n zu etw ü. talk a person into s.th.
Überre'dung _f_ (-;) persuasion
ü'berreich _adj_ (an _dat_) abounding (in) ‖ _adv_—ü. ausgestattet well equipped
überrei'chen _tr_ hand over, present
ü'berreichlich _adj_ superabundant
ü'berreif _adj_ overripe
überrei'zen _tr_ overexcite; (Augen, Nerven) strain
überreizt' _adj_ overwrought

überren'nen §97 _tr_ overrun; (fig) overwhelm
Ü'berrest _m_ rest, remainder; irdische Überreste mortal remains
Ü'berrock _m_ topcoat, overcoat
überrum'peln _tr_ take by surprise
Überrum'pelung _f_ (-;-en) surprise
überrun'den _tr_ (sport) lap
übersät [ybər'zet] _adj_ (fig) strewn, dotted
übersät'tigen _tr_ stuff; cloy; (chem) saturate, supersaturate
Übersät'tigung _f_ (chem) supersaturation
Überschall– _comb.fm._ supersonic
überschat'ten _tr_ overshadow
überschät'zen _tr_ overestimate
Ü'berschau _f_ survey
überschau'en _tr_ look over, survey; overlook (a scene)
überschla'fen §131 _tr_ (fig) sleep on
Ü'berschlag _m_ rough estimate; (aer) loop; (gym) somersault
überschla'gen _adj_ lukewarm ‖ §132 _tr_ skip, omit; estimate roughly; consider ‖ _ref_ go head over heels; do a somersault; (Auto) overturn; (Boot) capsize; (Flugzeug) do a loop; (beim Landen) nose over; (Stimme) break; (fig) (vor _dat_) outdo oneself (in) ‖ ü'berschlagen §132 _tr_ (Beine) cross; flip over; ü. in (acc) (fig) change suddenly to
ü'berschnappen _intr_ (SEIN) (Stimme) squeak; (coll) flip one's lid
überschnei'den §106 _ref_ (Linien) intersect; (& fig) overlap
überschrei'ben §62 _tr_ sign over
überschrei'ten §135 _tr_ shout down ‖ _ref_ strain one's voice
überschrei'ten §86 _tr_ cross, step over; (Kredit) overdraw; (Gesetz) violate, transgress; (fig) exceed, overstep
Ü'berschrift _f_ heading, title
Ü'berschuh _m_ overshoe
Ü'berschuß _m_ surplus, excess; profit
ü'berschüssig _adj_ surplus, excess
überschüt'ten _tr_ shower; (& fig) overwhelm, flood
Ü'berschwang _m_ (-[e]s;) rapture
überschwem'men _tr_ flood, inundate
Überschwem'mung _f_ (-;-en) flood, inundation
überschwenglich ['ybərʃveŋlɪç] _adj_ effusive, gushing
Ü'bersee _f_ (-;) overseas
Ü'berseedampfer _m_ ocean liner
Ü'berseehandel _m_ overseas trade
übersehbar [ybər'zebɑr] _adj_ visible at a glance
überse'hen §138 _tr_ survey, look over; (nicht bemerken) overlook; (absichtlich) ignore; (erkennen) realize
übersen'den §140 _tr_ send, forward; transmit; (Geld) remit
Übersen'dung _f_ (-;-en) forwarding; transmission; consignment
ü'bersetzen _tr_ ferry across ‖ überset'zen _tr_ translate
Überset'zung _f_ (-;-en) translation; (mach) gear, transmission
Ü'bersicht _f_ survey, review; (Abriß) abstract; (Zusammenfassung) sum-

mary; (*Umriß*) outline; (*Ausblick*) perspective; **jede Ü. verlieren** lose all perspective
ü'bersichtlich *adj* clear; (*Gelände*) open
Ü'bersichtsplan *m* general plan
ü'bersiedeln *intr* (SEIN) move; emigrate
ü'bersinnlich *adj* transcendental
überspan'nen *tr* span; cover; overstrain; (fig) exaggerate
überspannt [ybər'ʃpant] *adj* eccentric; extravagant
Überspannt'heit *f* (-;-en) eccentricity
Überspan'nung *f* (-;-en) overstraining; (fig) exaggeration; (elec) excess voltage
überspie'len *tr* outplay; outwit; (*Tonbandaufnahme*) transcribe; (*Schüchternheit*) hide
überspitzt [ybər'ʃpɪtst] *adj* oversubtle
übersprin'gen §142 *tr* jump; (*auslassen*) omit, skip || **ü'berspringen** §142 *intr* (SEIN) jump
ü'bersprudeln *intr* (SEIN) bubble over
ü'berständig *adj* leftover; (*Bier*) flat; (*Obst*) overripe
überste'hen §146 *tr* stand, endure; (*Krankheit, usw.*) get over; (*Operation*) pull through; (*überleben*) survive || **ü'berstehen** §146 *intr* jut out
überstei'gen §148 *tr* climb over; (*Hindernisse*) overcome; (*Erwartungen*) exceed || **ü'bersteigen** §148 *intr* (SEIN) step over
überstim'men *tr* vote down, defeat
überstrah'len *intr* shine upon; (*verdunkeln*) outshine, eclipse
überstrei'chen §85 *tr* paint over
ü'berstreifen *tr* slip on
überströ'men *tr* flood, inundate || **ü'berströmen** *intr* (SEIN) overflow
Ü'berstunde *f* hour of overtime; **Überstunden machen** work overtime
überstür'zen *tr* rush, hurry || *ref* be in too big a hurry; act rashly; (*Ereignisse*) follow one another rapidly
überstürzt [ybər'ʃtʏrtst] *adj* hasty
übertEuern [ybər'tɔɪ·ərn] *tr* overcharge
übertölpeln [ybər'tœpəln] *tr* dupe
übertö'nen *tr* drown out
Übertrag ['ybərtrak] *m* (-[e]s;⁼e) (acct) carryover, balance
übertragbar [ybər'trakbar] *adj* transferable; (pathol) contagious
übertra'gen *adj* figurative, metaphorical || §132 *tr* carry over, transfer; (*Amt, Titel*) confer; (*Aufgabe*) assign; (*Vollmacht*) delegate; (*Kurzschrift*) transcribe; (**in** *acc*) translate (into); (acct) transfer; (pathol) spread, communicate; (rad) broadcast, transmit; (*mit Relais*) relay; (telv) televise
Übertra'gung *f* (-;-en) carrying over; transfer; assignment; delegation; conferring; transcription; translation; copy; (pathol) spread; (rad) broadcast; relay; (telv) televising
übertref'fen §151 *tr* surpass, outdo
übertrei'ben §62 *tr* overdo; exaggerate; (theat) overact
Übertrei'bung *f* (-;-en) overdoing; exaggeration; (theat) overacting

übertre'ten §152 *tr* (*Gesetz*) transgress, break || *ref*—**sich** [*dat*] **den Fuß ü.** sprain one's ankle || **ü'bertreten** §152 *intr* (SEIN) (sport) go off sides; **ü. zu** (fig) go over to; (relig) be converted to
Übertre'tung *f* (-;-en) violation
Ü'bertritt *m* change, going over; (relig) conversion
übervölkern [ybər'fœlkərn] *tr* overpopulate
Übervöl'kerung *f* (-;) overpopulation
ü'bervoll *adj* brimful; crowded
übervorteilen [ybər'fortaɪlən] *tr* take advantage of, get the better of
überwa'chen *tr* watch over; supervise; (*kontrollieren*) inspect, check; (*polizeilich*) shadow; (rad, telv) monitor
Überwa'chung *f* (-;-en) supervision; inspection; control; surveillance
Überwa'chungsausschuß *m* watchdog committee
überwältigen [ybər'vɛltɪgən] *tr* overpower (fig) overwhelm
überwei'sen §118 *tr* (*Geld*) send; (*zu e-m Spezialisten*) refer
Überwei'sung *f* (-;-en) sending, remittance; referral
ü'berweltlich *adj* otherworldly
ü'berwerfen §160 *tr* throw over || **überwer'fen** §160 *ref* (**mit**) have a run-in (with)
überwie'gen §57 *tr* outweigh || *intr* prevail, preponderate || **Überwiegen** *n* (-s;) prevalence, preponderance
überwie'gend *adj* prevailing; (*Mehrheit*) vast || *adv* predominantly
überwin'den §59 *tr* conquer, overcome || *ref*—**sich ü. zu** (*inf*) bring oneself to (*inf*)
überwintern [ybər'vɪntərn] *intr* pass the winter; (bot) survive the winter
überwu'chern *tr* overrun; (fig) stifle
Ü'berwurf *m* wrap; shawl
Ü'berzahl *f* numerical superiority; majority
überzah'len *tr & intr* overpay
überzäh'len *tr* count over, recount
überzählig ['ybərtseliç] *adj* surplus
überzeu'gen *tr* convince || *ref*—**ü. Sie sich selbst davon!** go and see for yourself!
Überzeu'gung *f* (-;-en) conviction
überzie'hen §163 *tr* cover; (*mit Farbe*) coat; (*Bett*) put fresh linen on; (*Konto*) overdraw; **ein Land mit Krieg ü.** invade a country || **ü'berziehen** §163 *tr* (*Mantel, usw.*) slip on; **j-m eins ü.** (coll) give s.o. a whack
Ü'berzieher *m* (-s;-) overcoat
überzuckern (überzuk'kern) *tr* (& fig) sugarcoat
Ü'berzug *m* coat, film; (*Decke*) cover; (*Hülle*) case; pillow case; (*Kruste*) crust; (*Schale, Rinde*) skin
üblich ['ypliç] *adj* usual, customary
U'-Boot *n* (**Unterseeboot**) submarine
U'-Bootbunker *m* submarine pen
U'-Bootjäger *m* (aer) antisubmarine aircraft; (nav) subchaser
U'-Bootortungsgerät *n* sonar
U'-Bootrudel *n* (nav) wolf pack
übrig ['ybrɪç] *adj* left (over), remain-

ing, rest (of); **die übrigen** the others, the rest; **ein übriges tun** do more than is necessary; **etw ü. haben für** have a soft spot for; **im übrigen** for the rest, otherwise
ü'brigbehalten §90 *tr* keep, spare
ü'brigbleiben §62 *intr* (SEIN) be left (over) ‖ *impers*—**es blieb mir nichts anderes ü. als zu** (*inf*) I had no choice but to (*inf*)
übrigens ['ybrɪgəns] *adv* moreover; after all; by the way
ü'briglassen §104 *tr* leave, spare
Übung ['ybuŋ] *f* (-;-en) exercise; practice; (*Gewohnheit*) use; (*Ausbildung*) training; (mil) drill
Ü'bungsbeispiel *n* practical example
Ü'bungsbuch *n* composition book; workbook
Ü'bungsgelände *n* training ground; (*für Bomben*) target area
Ü'bungshang *m* (sport) training slope
Ü'bungsheft *n* composition book; workbook
Ufer ['ufər] *n* (-s;-) (*e-s Flusses*) bank; (*e-s Meers*) shore
U'ferdamm *m* embankment, levee
u'ferlos *adj* fruitless
Uhr [ur] *f* (-;-en) clock; watch; o'clock; **um wieviel Uhr?** at what time; **um zwölf Uhr** at twelve o'clock; **wieviel Uhr ist es?** what time is it?
Uhr'armband *n* (-[e]s;=er) watchband
Uhr'feder *f* watch spring
Uhr'glas *n* watch crystal
Uhr'macher *m* watchmaker
Uhr'werk *n* works, clockwork
Uhr'zeiger *m* hand
Uhr'zeigerrichtung *f*—**entgegen der U.** counterclockwise; **in der U.** clockwise
Uhr'zeigersinn *m*—**im U.** clockwise
Uhu ['uhu] *m* (-s;-s) owl
Ukraine [u'kraɪnə] *f* (-;)—**die U.** the Ukraine
ukrainisch [u'kraɪnɪʃ] *adj* Ukrainian
UK-Stellung [u'ka/teluŋ] *f* (-;-en) military deferment
Ulk [ulk] *m* (-[e]s;-e) joke, fun
ulken ['ulkən] *intr* (coll) make fun
ulkig ['ulkɪç] *adj* funny
Ulme ['ulmə] *f* (-;-n) elm
Ultima·tum [ultɪ'matum] *n* (-s;-ten [tən] & -ta [ta]) ultimatum
Ultra-, ultra- [ultra] *comb.fm.* ultra-
Ul'trakurzfrequenz *f* ultrashort frequency
ultramontan [ultramɔn'tan] *adj* strict Catholic
ul'trarot *adj* infrared
Ultraschall- *comb.fm.* supersonic
ul'traviolett *adj* ultraviolet
um [um] *adv*—**deine Zeit ist um** your time is up; **je…um so** the…the; **um so besser** all the better; **um so weniger** all the less; **um und um** round and round ‖ *prep* (*acc*) around, about; for; at; **um die Hälfte** half as much again; **um die Wette laufen** race; **um ein Jahr älter** one year older; **um etw eintauschen** exchange for s.th.; **um jeden Preis** at

any price; **um…Uhr** at…o'clock; **um…zu** (*inf*) in order to (*inf*)
um'ackern *tr* plow up, turn over
um'adressieren *tr* readdress
um'ändern *tr* change (around)
Um'änderung *f* (-;-en) change, alteration
um'arbeiten *tr* rework; (*Metall*) recast; (*Buch*) revise; (*Haus*) remodel; (*berichtigen*) emend, correct; (*verbessern*) improve
umar'men *tr* embrace, hug
Umar'mung *f* (-;-en) embrace, hug
Um'bau *m* (-[e]s;-e & -ten) rebuilding; alterations, remodeling; reorganization
um'bauen *tr* remodel; reorganize ‖ umbau'en *tr* build around; **umbauter Raum** floor space
um'besetzen *tr* (*Stellungen*) switch around; (pol) reshuffle; (theat) recast
um'biegen §47 *tr* bend (over); bend up, bend down
um'bilden *tr* remodel; reconstruct; (adm) reorganize, (pol) reshuffle
Um'bildung *f* (-;-en) remodeling; reconstruction; reorganization; reshuffling
um'binden §59 *tr* (*Schürze, usw.*) put on ‖ umbin'den §59 *tr* (*verletztes Glied, usw.*) bandage
um'blättern *tr* turn ‖ *intr* turn the page(s)
um'brechen §64 *tr* (*Bäume, usw.*) knock down; (*Acker*) plow up ‖ umbre'chen *tr* make into page proof
um'bringen §65 *tr* kill
Um'bruch *m* upheaval; (typ) page proof
um'buchen *tr* transfer to another account; book for another date
um'denken §66 *tr* rethink
um'dirigieren *tr* redirect
um'disponieren *tr* rearrange
umdrän'gen *tr* crowd around
um'drehen *tr* turn around; (*Hals*) wring; (*j-s Worte*) twist ‖ *ref* turn around ‖ *intr* turn around
Umdre'hung *f* (-;-en) turn; revolution
Um'druck *m* reprint; (typ) transfer
umeinan'der *adv* around each other
um'erziehen §163 *tr* reeducate
um'fahren §71 *tr* run down ‖ umfah'ren §71 *tr* drive around; sail around
um'fallen §72 *intr* (SEIN) fall over, fall down; collapse; give in
Um'fang *m* circumference; perimeter; (*Bereich*) range; (*Ausdehnung*) extent; (*des Leibes*) girth; (fig) scope; (mus) range; **im großen U.** on a large scale
umfan'gen §73 *tr* surround; embrace
um'fangreich *adj* extensive; (*körperlich*) bulky; (*geräumig*) spacious
umfas'sen *tr* embrace; clasp; comprise, cover; include; contain; (mil) envelop
umfas'send *adj* comprehensive; extensive
Umfas'sung *f* (-;-en) embrace; clasp; enclosure, fence; (mil) envelopment

Umfas'sungsmauer *f* enclosure
umflat'tern *tr* flutter around
umflech'ten §74 *tr* braid
umflie'gen §57 *tr* fly around || **um'fliegen** §57 *intr* (SEIN) (coll) fall down
umflie'ßen §76 *tr* flow around
um'formen *tr* reshape; (elec) convert
Um'former *m* (−s;−) (elec) converter
Um'frage *f* inquiry, poll; **öffentliche U.** public opinion poll
umfrieden [ʊm'fridən] *tr* enclose
Um'gang *m* round, circuit; revolution, rotation; (*Zug*) procession; association, company; (archit) gallery; **geschlechtlicher U.** sexual intercourse; **schlechter U.** bad company; **U. mit j-m haben** (or **pflegen**) associate with s.o.
umgänglich [ʊm'gɛŋlɪç] *adj* sociable
Um'gangsformen *pl* social manners
Um'gangssprache *f* colloquial speech
um'gangssprachlich *adj* colloquial
umgar'nen *tr* (fig) trap
umge'ben §80 *tr* surround
Umgebung [ʊm'gebʊŋ] *f* (−;−en) surroundings, environs, neighborhood; company, associates; background, environment
Umgegend ['ʊmgegənt] *f* (−;) (coll) neighborhood
umgehen §82 *tr* go around; evade; bypass; (mil) outflank || **um'gehen** §82 *intr* (SEIN) go around; (*Gerücht*) circulate; **an** (or **in**) **e-m Ort u.** haunt a place; **mit dem Gedanken** (or **Plan**) **u. zu** (*inf*) be thinking of (*ger*); **u. mit** deal with, handle; manage; be occupied with; hang around with
um'gehend *adj* immediate; **mit umgehender Post** by return mail; **umgehende Antwort erbeten!** please answer at your earliest convenience || *adv* immediately
Umge'hung *f* (−;−en) going around; bypassing; (fig) evasion; (mil) flanking movement
Umge'hungsstraße *f* bypass
umgekehrt ['ʊmgəkert] *adj* reverse; contrary || *adv* on the contrary; vice versa; upside down; inside out
um'gestalten *tr* alter; remodel
um'graben §87 *tr* dig up
umgren'zen *tr* fence in; (fig) limit
Umgren'zung *f* (−;−en) enclosure; (fig) limit, boundary
um'gruppieren *tr* regroup; (pol) reshuffle
um'gucken *ref* look around
um'haben §89 *tr* have on, be wearing
Um'hang *m* wrap; cape; shawl
um'hängen *tr* put on; (*Gewehr*) sling; (*Bild*) hang elsewhere
Um'hängetasche *f* shoulder bag
um'hauen §93 *tr* cut down; (coll) bowl over
umher' *adv* around, about
umher'blicken *tr* look around
umher'fuchteln *intr* gesticulate
umher'schweifen, umher'streifen *intr* (SEIN) rove, roam about
umhin' *adv*—**ich kann nicht u.** I can't do otherwise; **ich kann nicht u. zu** (*inf*) I can't help (*ger*)

umhül'len *tr* wrap up, cover; envelop
Umhül'lung *f* (−;−eu) wrapping
Umkehr ['ʊmker] *f* (−;) return; change; conversion; (elec) reversal
um'kehren *tr* turn around; overturn; (*Tasche*) turn out; (elec) reverse; (gram, math, mus) invert || *intr* (SEIN) turn back, return
Um'kehrung *f* (−;−en) overturning; reversal; conversion; inversion
um'kippen *tr* upset || *intr* (SEIN) tilt over
umklam'mern *tr* clasp; cling to; (mil) envelop; **einander u.** (box) clinch
Umklam'merung *f* (−;−en) embrace; (box) clinch; (mil) envelopment
umklei'den *tr* clothe || *ref* change around || **um'kleiden** *tr* change the clothes of
Um'kleideraum *m* dressing room
um'kommen §99 *intr* (SEIN) perish; (*Essen*) spoil
Um'kreis *m* circuit; vicinity; (geom) circumference; **5 km im U.** within a radius of 5 km
umkrei'sen *tr* circle, revolve around
um'krempeln *tr* (*Ärmel*) roll up; **völlig u.** (coll) change completely
um'laden §103 *tr* reload; transship
Um'lauf *m* circulation; (*Umdrehung*) revolution, rotation; (*Flugblatt*) circular; (*Rundschreiben*) circular letter; **in U.** setzen circulate
Um'laufbahn *f* orbit
um'laufen §105 *tr* run down || *intr* (SEIN) circulate || **umlau'fen** §105 *tr* walk around
Um'laut *m* (−es;−e) umlaut, vowel mutation; mutated vowel
umlegbar ['ʊmlekbar] *adj* reversible
um'legen *tr* lay down; turn down; (*anders legen*) shift; (*Kragen*) put on; (*gleichmäßig verteilen*) apportion; (coll) knock down; (vulg) lay
um'leiten *tr* detour, divert
Um'leitung *f* (−;−en) detour
um'lenken *tr* turn back
um'lernen *tr* relearn, learn anew
um'liegend *adj* surrounding
ummau'ern *tr* wall in
um'modeln *tr* remodel
umnachtet [ʊm'naxtət] *adj* deranged
Umnach'tung *f* (−;)—**geistige U.** mental derangement
um'nähen *tr* hem
umne'beln *tr* fog; (fig) dull; **umnebelter Blick** glassy eyes
um'nehmen §116 *tr* put on
um'packen *tr* repack
um'pflanzen *tr* transplant || **umpflan'zen** *tr*—**etw mit Blumen u.** plant flowers around s.th.
um'pflügen *tr* plow up, turn over
umrah'men *tr* frame
umranden [ʊm'randən] *tr* edge, border
Umran'dung *f* (−;−en) edging, edge
umran'ken *tr* twine around; **mit Efeu umrankt** ivy-clad
um'rechnen *tr* convert; **umgerechnet auf** (*acc*) expressed in
Um'rechnungskurs *m* rate of exchange
Um'rechnungstabelle *f* conversion table
Um'rechnungswert *m* exchange value

um'reißen §53 *tr* pull down; knock down ‖ **umrei'ßen** §53 *tr* outline
umrin'gen *tr* surround
Um'riß *m* outline
Um'rißzeichnung *f* sketch
um'rühren *tr* stir, stir up
um'satteln *tr* resaddle ‖ *intr* change jobs; (*educ*) change one's course or major; (*pol*) switch parties
Um'satz *m* turnover, sales
Um'satzsteuer *f* sales tax
umsäu'men *tr* enclose, hem in
um'schalten *tr* switch; (*Strom*) convert ‖ *intr* (auf *acc*) switch back (to)
Um'schalter *m* (elec) switch; (typ) shift key
Um'schaltung *f* (-;-en) switching; shifting
Um'schau *f* look around; **U. halten** have a look around
um'schauen *ref* look around
um'schichten *tr* regroup, reshuffle
umschichtig ['ʊmʃɪçtɪç] *adv* alternately
umschif'fen *tr* circumnavigate; (*ein Kap*) double
Um'schlag *m* (sudden) change, shift; envelope; (*e-s Buches*) cover, jacket; cuff; hem; transshipment; (med) compress
um'schlagen §132 *tr* knock down; (*Ärmel*) roll up; (*Bäume*) fell; (*Saum*) turn up; (*Seite*) turn; (*umladen*) transship ‖ *intr* (SEIN) (*Laune, Wetter*) change; (*Wind*) shift; (*kentern*) capsize
Um'schlagpapier *n* wrapping paper
umschlie'ßen §76 *tr* surround, enclose
umschlin'gen §142 *tr* clasp; embrace; wind around
um'schmeißen §53 *tr* (coll) throw over
um'schnallen *tr* buckle on
um'schreiben §62 *tr* rewrite; (*abschreiben*) transcribe; (*Wechsel*) re-endorse; **u. auf** (*acc*) transfer to ‖ **umschrei'ben** §62 *tr* circumscribe; paraphrase
Um'schreibung *f* (-;-en) transcription; transfer ‖ **Umschrei'bung** *f* (-;-en) paraphrase
Um'schrift *f* transcription; (*e-r Münze*) legend
um'schulen *tr* retrain
um'schütteln *tr* shake (up)
um'schütten *tr* spill; pour into another container
umschwär'men *tr* swarm around; (fig) idolize
Um'schweif *m* digression; **ohne Umschweife** point-blank; **Umschweife machen** beat around the bush
umschweifig [ʊm'ʃvaɪfɪç] *adj* round-about
um'schwenken *intr* wheel around; (fig) change one's mind
Um'schwung *m* change; (*Drehung*) revolution; (*Umkehrung*) reversal; (*der Gesinnung*) revulsion
umse'geln *tr* sail around; (*Kap*) double
Umse'gelung *f* (-;-en) circumnavigation
um'sehen §138 *ref* (nach) look around (for); (fig) (nach) look out (for)

um'sein §139 *intr* (SEIN) (*Zeit*) be up; (*Ferien*) be over
um'setzen *tr* shift; transplant; (*Nährstoffe*) assimilate; (*Schüler*) switch around; (*Ware*) sell; (*verwandeln*) convert; (mus) transpose; **Geld u. in** (*acc*) spend money on; **in die Tat u.** translate into action ‖ *ref*—**sich u. in** (*acc*) (biochem) be converted into
Um'sicht *f* (-;) circumspection
umsichtig ['ʊmzɪçtɪç] *adj* circumspect
um'siedeln *tr* & *intr* (SEIN) resettle
Um'siedlung *f* (-;-en) resettlement
umsonst' *adv* for nothing, gratis; (*vergebens*) in vain
um'spannen *tr* (*Wagenpferde*) change; (elec) transform ‖ **umspan'nen** *tr* span; encompass; include
Um'spanner *m* (-s;-) (elec) transformer
um'springen §142 *intr* (SEIN) (*Wind*) shift; **mit j-m rücksichtslos u.** (coll) treat s.o. thoughtlessly
Um'stand *m* circumstance; factor; fact; (*Einzelheit*) detail; (*Aufheben*) fuss; **in anderen Umständen** (coll) pregnant; **sich** [*dat*] **Umstände machen** go to the trouble; **Umstände machen** be formal; **unter Umständen** under certain conditions
umständehalber ['ʊmʃtɛndəhalbər] *adv* owing to circumstances
umständlich ['ʊmʃtɛntlɪç] *adj* detailed; (*förmlich*) formal; (*zu genau*) fussy; (*verwickelt*) complicated; (*Erzählung*) long-winded, round-about
Um'standskleid *n* maternity dress
Um'standskrämer *m* fusspot
Um'standswort *n* (-[e]s;-̈er) adverb
um'stehend *adj* (*Seite*) next ‖ **Umstehende** §5 *mf* bystander
Um'steige(fahr)karte *f* transfer
um'steigen §148 *intr* (SEIN) transfer
um'stellen *tr* put into a different place, shift; (*Möbel*) rearrange; (auf *acc*) convert (to) ‖ *ref* (auf *acc*) adjust (to) ‖ **umstel'len** *tr* surround
Um'stellung *f* (-;-en) change of position, shift; conversion; readjustment
um'stimmen *tr* tune to another pitch; **make** (*s.o.*) change his mind
um'stoßen §150 *tr* knock down; (*Pläne*) upset; (*Vertrag*) annul; (*Urteil*) reverse
umstricken (umstrik'ken) *tr* ensnare
umstritten [ʊm'ʃtrɪtən] *adj* contested; controversial
Um'sturz *m* overthrow
um'stürzen *tr* overturn; overthrow; (*Mauer*) tear down; (*Plan*) change, throw out ‖ *intr* (SEIN) fall down
Umstürzler –in ['ʊmʃtʏrtslər(ɪn)] §6 *mf* revolutionary, subversive
umstürzlerisch ['ʊmʃtʏrtslərɪʃ] *adj* revolutionary; subversive
Um'tausch *m* exchange
um'tauschen *tr* (gegen) exchange (for)
um'tun §154 *tr* (*Kleider*) put on ‖ *ref*—**sich u. nach** look around for
um'wälzen *tr* roll around; (fig) revolutionize ‖ *ref* roll around
umwäl'zend *adj* revolutionary
Umwäl'zung *f* (-;-en) revolution

umwandelbar ['ʊmvandəlbɑr] *adj* (com) convertible
um'wandeln *tr* change; (elec, fin) convert; (jur) commute
Um'wandlung *f* (-;-en) change; (elec, fin) conversion; (jur) commutation
um'wechseln *tr* exchange; (fin) convert
Um'weg *m* detour; **auf Umwegen** indirectly
um'wehen *tr* knock down ‖ **umwe'hen** *tr* blow around
Um'welt *f* environment
Um'weltverschmutzung *f* ecological pollution
um'wenden §140 *tr* turn over ‖ *ref & intr* turn around
umwer'ben §149 *tr* court, go with
um'werfen §160 *tr* throw down; upset; (*Plan*) ruin; (*Kleider*) throw about one's shoulders
umwickeln (**umwik'keln**) *tr* (*mit Band*) tape
umwin'den *tr* wreathe
umwölken [ʊm'vœlkən] *ref & intr* cloud over
umzäunen [ʊm'tsɔɪnən] *tr* fence in
um'ziehen §163 *ref* change one's clothes ‖ *intr* (SEIN) move ‖ **umzie'hen** §163 *ref*—**der Himmel hat sich umzogen** the sky has become overcast
umzingeln [ʊm'tsɪŋəln] *tr* encircle
Um'zug *m* procession, parade; (*Wohnungswechsel*) moving; (pol) march
un– [ʊn] *comb.fm.* un-, in-, ir-, non-
unabän'derlich *adj* unalterable
un'abhängig *adj* (von) independent (of) ‖ **Unabhängige** §5 *mf* (pol) independent
Un'abhängigkeit *f* independence
unabkömm'lich *adj* unavailable; indispensable; (mil) essential (*on the homefront*); **ich bin augenblicklich u.** I can't get away at the moment
unablässig ['ʊnaplɛsɪç] *adj* incessant
unablösbar [ʊnap'løsbɑr], **unablöslich** [ʊnap'løslɪç] *adj* unpayable
unabseh'bar *adj* unforeseeable; immense
unabsetz'bar *adj* irremovable
unabsicht'lich *adj* unintentional
unabwendbar [ʊnap'vɛntbɑr] *adj* inevitable
un'achtsam *adi* careless, inattentive
um'ähnlich *adj* dissimilar, unlike
unanfecht'bar *adi* indisputable
un'angebracht *adj* out of place
un'angefochten *adj* undisputed
un'angemessen *adj* improper; inadequate; unsuitable
un'angenehm *adj* unpleasant, disagreeable; awkward
un'annehmbar *adj* unacceptable
Un'annehmlichkeit *f* unpleasantness; annoyance, inconvenience; **Unannehmlichkeiten** trouble
un'ansehnlich *adj* unsightly; (*unscheinbar*) plain, inconspicuous
un'anständig *adj* indecent; obscene
un'antastbar *adj* unassailable
un'appetitlich *adj* unappetizing; (*ekelhaft*) unsavory
Un'art *f* bad habit; (*Ungezogenheit*)

naughtiness; (*schlechte Manieren*) bad manners
un'artig *adj* ill-behaved, naughty
un'aufdringlich *adj* unostentatious; unobtrusive
un'auffällig *adj* inconspicuous
unauffindbar ['ʊnaʊffɪntbɑr] *adj* not to be found
unaufgefordert ['ʊnaʊfgəfɔrdərt] *adj* unasked, uncalled for ‖ *adv* spontaneously
unaufhaltbar ['ʊnaʊfhaltbɑr], **unaufhaltsam** ['ʊnaʊfhaltzam] *adj* irresistible; relentless
unaufhörlich ['ʊnaʊfhørlɪç] *adj* incessant
un'aufmerksam *adj* inattentive
un'aufrichtig *adj* insincere
unaufschiebbar ['ʊnaʊf/ipbɑr] *adj* not to be postponed, urgent
unausbleiblich ['ʊnaʊsblaɪplɪç] *adj* inevitable
unausführbar ['ʊnaʊsfyrbɑr] *adj* unfeasible, impracticable
unausgeglichen ['ʊnaʊsgəglɪçən] *adj* uneven; (fig) unbalanced
unauslöschbar ['ʊnaʊslœ/bɑr], **unauslöschlich** ['ʊnaʊslœ/lɪç] *adj* inextinguishable; (*Tinte*) indelible
unaussprechlich ['ʊnaʊs/preçlɪç] *adj* unspeakable, ineffable
unausstehlich ['ʊnaʊs/telɪç] *adj* intolerable, insufferable
unbändig ['ʊnbɛndɪç] *adj* wild
un'barmherzig *adj* unmerciful
un'beabsichtigt *adj* unintentional
un'beachtet *adj* unobserved, unnoticed
unbeanstandet ['ʊnbə·an/tandət] *adj* unopposed, unhampered
unbearbeitet ['ʊnbə·arbaɪtət] *adj* unworked; (*roh*) raw; (*Land*) untilled; (mach) unfinished
unbebaut ['ʊnbəbaʊt] *adj* uncultivated; (*Gelände*) undeveloped
unbedacht ['ʊnbədaxt] *adj* thoughtless
un'bedenklich *adj* unhesitating; unswerving; unobjectionable, harmless ‖ *adv* without hesitation
un'bedeutend *adj* unimportant; slight
un'bedingt *adj* unconditional, unqualified; implicit
un'befahrbar *adj* impassable
un'befangen *adj* unembarrassed; (*unparteiisch*) impartial; natural, unaffected
unbefleckt ['ʊnbəflɛkt] *adj* immaculate
un'befriedigend *adj* unsatisfactory
un'befriedigt *adj* unsatisfied
un'befugt *adj* unauthorized; (jur) incompetent ‖ **Unbefugte** §5 *mf* unauthorized person
un'begabt *adi* untalented
unbegreif'lich *adj* incomprehensible
un'begrenzt *adj* unlimited
un'begründet *adj* unfounded
Un'behagen *n* discomfort, uneasiness
un'behaglich *adj* uncomfortable
unbehelligt ['ʊnbəhɛlɪçt] *adj* undisturbed, unmolested
unbehindert ['ʊnbəhɪndərt] *adj* unhindered; unrestrained
unbeholfen ['ʊnbəhɔlfən] *adj* clumsy

unbeirrbar ['ʊnbə·ɪrbɑr] *adj* unwavering
unbeirrt ['ʊnbə·ɪrt] *adj* unswerving
un'bekannt *adj* unknown; unfamiliar; unacquainted; (*Ursache*) unexplained || **Unbekannte** §5 *mf* stranger || *f* (math) unknown quantity
unbekümmert ['ʊnbəkʏmərt] *adj* (**um**) unconcerned (about)
un'beladen *adj* unloaded
unbelastet ['ʊnbəlastət] *adj* unencumbered; (*Wagen*) unloaded; carefree
un'belebt *adj* inanimate; (*Straße*) quiet; (com) slack
unbelichtet ['ʊnbəlɪçtət] *adj* (*Film*) unexposed
un'beliebt *adj* unpopular, disliked
unbemannt ['ʊnbəmant] *adj* unmanned
un'bemerkbar *adj* imperceptible
un'bemittelt *adj* poor
un'benommen *adj*—**es bleibt Ihnen u. zu** (*inf*) you are free to (*inf*); **es ist mir u., ob** it's up to me whether
unbenutzbar ['ʊnbənutsbɑr] *adj* unusable
unbenutzt ['ʊnbənutst] *adj* unused
un'bequem *adj* inconvenient; uncomfortable
unberechenbar ['ʊnbəreçənbɑr] *adj* incalculable; unpredictable
un'berechtigt *adj* unauthorized; unjustified
unbeschadet ['ʊnbəʃadət] *prep* (*genit*) without prejudice to
unbeschädigt ['ʊnbəʃedɪçt] *adj* unhurt; undamaged
un'bescheiden *adj* pushy
unbescholten ['ʊnbəʃɔltən] *adj* of good reputation
un'beschränkt *adj* unlimited; absolute
unbeschreiblich ['ʊnbəʃraɪplɪç] *adj* indescribable
unbesehen ['ʊnbəze·ən] *adv* sight unseen
un'besetzt *adj* unoccupied, vacant
unbesiegbar ['ʊnbəzikbɑr] *adj* invincible
unbesoldet ['ʊnbəzɔldət] *adj* unsalaried
un'besonnen *adj* thoughtless; careless; rash
un'besorgt *adj* unconcerned; carefree
un'beständig *adj* unsteady, inconstant; (*Preise*) fluctuating; (*Wetter*) changeable; (*Person*) fickle, unstable
unbestätigt ['ʊnbəʃtetɪçt] *adj* unconfirmed
un'bestechlich *adj* incorruptible
un'bestimmt *adj* indeterminate; vague; (*unsicher*) uncertain; (*unentschieden*) undecided; (gram) indefinite
unbestraft ['ʊnbəʃtraft] *adj* unpunished
unbestreit'bar *adj* indisputable
unbestritten ['ʊnbəʃtrɪtən] *adj* undisputed, uncontested
unbeteiligt ['ʊnbətaɪlɪçt] *adj* uninterested; indifferent; impartial
un'beträchtlich *adj* trifling, slight
unbeugsam ['ʊnbɔɪkzɑm] *adj* inflexible
unbewacht ['ʊnbəvaxt] *adj* unguarded
unbewaffnet ['ʊnbəvafnət] *adj* unarmed; (*Auge*) naked

un'beweglich *adj* immovable; motionless
unbewiesen ['ʊnbəvizən] *adj* unproved
unbewohnt ['ʊnbəvont] *adj* uninhabited
un'bewußt *adj* unconscious; involuntary
unbezähmbar [ʊnbə'tsembɑr] *adj* untamable; (fig) uncontrollable
Un'bilden *pl*—**U. der Witterung** inclement weather
Un'bildung *f* lack of education
un'billig *adj* unfair
unbotmäßig ['ʊnbotmesɪç] *adj* unruly; insubordinate
unbrauch'bar *adj* useless, of no use
un'bußfertig *adj* unrepentant
un'christlich *adj* unchristian
und [ʊnt] *conj* and; **und?** so what? **und wenn** even if
Un'dank *m* ingratitude
un'dankbar *adj* ungrateful; thankless
Un'dankbarkeit *f* ingratitude
undatiert ['ʊndatirt] *adj* undated
undenk'bar *adj* unthinkable
undenklich [ʊn'deŋklɪç] *adj*—**seit undenklichen Zeiten** from time immemorial
un'deutlich *adj* unclear, indistinct
un'deutsch *adj* un-German
un'dicht *adj* not tight; leaky
Un'ding *n* nonsense, absurdity
un'duldsam *adj* intolerant
undurchdring'lich *adj* (**für**) impervious (to); **undurchdringliche Miene** poker face
undurchführ'bar *adj* not feasible
un'durchlässig *adj* (**für**) impervious (to)
un'durchsichtig *adj* opaque; (*Beweggründe*) hidden; (*Machenschaften*) shady
un'eben *adj* uneven; bumpy; **nicht u.!** (coll) not bad!
un'echt *adj* false, spurious; artificial, imitation; (*Farbe*) fading
un'edel *adj* ignoble; (*Metall*) base
un'ehelich *adj* illegitimate
Un'ehre *f* dishonor
un'ehrenhaft *adj* dishonorable
un'ehrerbietig *adj* disrespectful
un'ehrlich *adj* dishonest; underhand
un'eigennützig *adj* unselfish
un'einig *adj* disunited; at odds
Un'einigkeit *f* disagreement
uneinnehm'bar *adj* impregnable
un'eins *adj* at odds, at variance
un'empfänglich *adj* (**für**) insusceptible (to)
un'empfindlich *adj* (**gegen**) insensitive (to); (**gegen**) insensible (to)
unend'lich *adj* endless; infinite; **auf u. einstellen** (phot) set at infinity || *adv* endlessly; infinitely; **u. viele** an endless number of
unentbehr'lich *adj* indispensible
unentrinnbar [ʊnent'rɪnbɑr] *adj* inescapable
un'entschieden *adj* undecided; (*schwankend*) indecisive; (sport) tie || **Unentschieden** *n* (**-s;-**) (sport) tie
Un'entschiedenheit *f* indecision
un'entschlossen *adj* irresolute

Un'entschlossenheit *f* indecision
unentschuld'bar *adj* inexcusable
unentwegt ['unentvekt] *adj* staunch; unswerving || *adv* continuously; untiringly || **Unentwegte** §5 *mf* die-hard
unentwirrbar ['unentvɪrbɑr] *adj* inextricable
unerbittlich [unɛr'bɪtlɪç] *adj* inexorable; (*Tatsache*) hard
un'erfahren *adj* inexperienced
unerfindlich [unɛr'fɪntlɪç] *adj* incomprehensible, mysterious
unerforschlich [unɛr'fɔrʃlɪç] *adj* inscrutable
unerfreulich ['unɛrfrɔɪlɪç] *adj* unpleasant
unerfüllbar [unɛr'fylbɑr] *adj* unattainable
un'ergiebig *adj* unproductive
un'ergründlich *adj* unfathomable
un'erheblich *adj* insignificant; (**für**) irrelevant (to)
unerhört [unɛr'hørt] *adj* unheard-of, unprecedented; outrageous || **un'erhört** *adj* (*Bitte*) unanswered
un'erkannt *adj* unrecognized || *adv* incognito
unerklär'lich *adj* inexplicable
unerläßlich [unɛr'lɛslɪç] *adj* indispensable
un'erlaubt *adj* illicit, unauthorized
un'erledigt *adj* unsettled, unfinished
unermeßlich [unɛr'meslɪç] *adj* immense
unermüdlich [unɛr'mydlɪç] *adj* untiring; (*Person*) indefatigable
unerquicklich [unɛr'kvɪklɪç] *adj* unpleasant
unerreich'bar *adj* unattainable, out of reach
unerreicht ['unɛrraɪçt] *adj* unrivaled
unersättlich [unɛr'zɛtlɪç] *adj* insatiable
unerschlossen ['unɛrʃlɔsən] *adj* undeveloped; (*Boden*) unexploited
unerschöpflich [unɛr'ʃøpflɪç] *adj* inhaustible
unerschrocken ['unɛrʃrɔkən] *adj* intrepid, fearless
unerschütterlich [unɛr'ʃytərlɪç] *adj* unshakable; imperturbable
unerschwing'lich *adj* unattainable; beyond one's means; exorbitant
unersetz'bar, unersetz'lich *adj* irreplaceable; (*Schaden*) irreparable
unerträg'lich *adj* intolerable
unerwähnt ['unɛrvɛnt] *adj* unmentioned; **u. lassen** pass over in silence
unerwartet ['unɛrvartət] *adj* unexpected, sudden
unerweis'lich *adj* unprovable
un'erwünscht *adj* undesired; unwelcome
unerzogen ['unɛrtsogən] *adj* ill-bred
un'fähig *adj* incapable, unable; unqualified, inefficient
Un'fähigkeit *f* inability; inefficiency
Un'fall *m* accident, mishap
Un'fallflucht *f* hit-and-run offense
Un'fallstation *f* first-aid station
Un'falltod *m* accidental death
Un'fallversicherung *f* accident insurance
Un'fallziffer *m* accident rate

unfaß'bar, unfaß'lich *adj* incomprehensible; inconceivable
unfehl'bar *adj* infallible; unfailing
Unfehl'barkeit *f* infallibility
un'fein *adj* coarse; indelicate
un'fern *adj* near; **u. von** not far from || *prep* (*genit*) not far from
un'fertig *adj* not ready; not finished; immature
Unflat ['unflɑt] *m* (**-s;**) dirt, filth
unflätig ['unfletɪç] *adj* dirty, filthy
un'folgsam *adj* disobedient
Un'folgsamkeit *f* disobedience
unförmig ['unfœrmɪç] *adj* shapeless
un'förmlich *adj* informal
unfrankiert ['unfraŋkirt] *adj* unfranked, unstamped
un'frei *adj* not free; unstamped || *adv* **—u. schicken** send c.o.d.
un'freiwillig *adj* involuntary
un'freundlich *adj* unfriendly, unkind
Un'friede *m* dissension, discord
un'fruchtbar *adj* unfruitful, sterile; (fig) fruitless
Unfug ['unfuk] *m* (**-[e]s;**) nuisance, disturbance; mischief; misdemeanor; **U. treiben** cause mischief
ungang'bar *adj* impassable; unsalable
Ungar ['uŋgar] *m* (**-;–n**), **Ungarin** ['uŋgarɪn] *f* (**-;–nen**) Hungarian
ungarisch ['uŋgarɪʃ] *adj* Hungarian
Ungarn ['uŋgarn] *n* (**-s;**) Hungary
un'gastlich *adj* inhospitable
ungeachtet ['unɡə·axtət] *adj* not esteemed || *prep* (*genit*) regardless of
ungeahnt ['uŋɡə·ɑnt] *adj* unexpected
ungebärdig ['uŋɡəberdɪç] *adj* unruly
ungebeten ['uŋɡəbetən] *adj* unbidden
ungebeugt ['uŋɡəbɔɪkt] *adj* unbowed; (gram) uninflected
un'gebildet *adj* uneducated
un'gebräuchlich *adj* unusual; (*veraltet*) obsolete
un'gebraucht *adj* unused
Un'gebühr *f* indecency, impropriety
un'gebührlich *adj* indecent, improper
ungebunden ['uŋɡəbundən] *adj* unbound; (*ausschweifend*) loose, dissolute; (*frei*) unrestrained; **ungebundene Rede** prose
ungedeckt ['uŋɡədɛkt] *adj* uncovered; (*Tisch*) unset; (*Haus*) roofless; (*Kosten*) unpaid; (*Scheck*) overdrawn
Un'geduld *f* impatience
un'geduldig *adj* impatient
un'geeignet *adj* unfit, unsuitable; unqualified
ungefähr ['uŋɡəfer] *adj* approximate || *adv* approximately, about; **nicht von u.** on purpose
ungefährdet ['uŋɡəferdət] *adj* safe, unendangered
un'gefährlich *adj* not dangerous
un'gefällig *adj* discourteous
un'gefüge *adj* monstrous; clumsy
un'gefügig *adj* unyielding, inflexible
ungefüttert ['uŋɡəfytərt] *adj* unlined
un'gehalten *adj* (*Versprechen*) unkept, broken; (**über** *acc*) indignant (at)
ungeheißen ['uŋɡəhaɪsən] *adv* of one's own accord
ungehemmt ['uŋɡəhemt] *adj* unchecked

ungeheuer ['ʊngəhɔɪ·ər] *adj* huge; monstrous ‖ *adv* tremendously ‖ **Ungeheuer** *n* (−s;−) monster
un'geheuerlich *adj* monstrous ‖ *adv* (coll) tremendously
ungehobelt ['ʊngəhobəlt] *adj* unplaned; (fig) uncouth
un'gehörig *adj* improper; (*Stunde*) ungodly
Un'gehörigkeit *f* (−;−en) impropriety
un'gehorsam *adj* disobedient ‖ **Ungehorsam** *m* (−s;) disobedience
un'gekünstelt *adj* unaffected, natural
un'gekürzt *adj* unabridged
un'gelegen *adj* inconvenient
Un'gelegenheiten *pl* inconvenience
un'gelehrig *adj* unteachable
un'gelenk *adj* clumsy; stiff
un'gelernt *adj* (coll) unskilled
Un'gemach *n* discomfort; trouble
un'gemein *adj* uncommon
un'gemütlich *adj* uncomfortable; (*Zimmer*) dreary; (*Person*) disagreeable
un'genannt *adj* anonymous
un'genau *adj* inaccurate, inexact
ungeniert ['ʊnʒenirt] *adj* informal ‖ *adv* freely
ungenieß'bar *adj* inedible; undrinkable; (& fig) unpalatable
un'genügend *adj* insufficient; **u. bekommen** get a failing grade
ungepflastert ['ʊngəpflastərt] *adj* unpaved, dirt
un'gerade *adj* uneven; crooked; (*Zahl*) odd
un'geraten *adj* spoiled
un'gerecht *adj* unjust, unfair
Un'gerechtigkeit *f* injustice
ungereimt ['ʊngəraɪmt] *adj* unrhymed; (*unvernünft*) absurd; **ungereimtes Zeug reden** talk nonsense
un'gern *adv* unwillingly, reluctantly
ungerührt ['ʊngəryrt] *adj* (fig) unmoved
un'geschehen *adj* undone; **u. machen** undo
ungescheut ['ʊngəʃɔɪt] *adv* without fear
Un'geschick *n*, **Un'geschicklichkeit** *f* awkwardness
un'geschickt *adj* awkward, clumsy
ungeschlacht ['ʊngəʃlaxt] *adj* uncouth
ungeschliffen ['ʊngəʃlɪfən] *adj* unpolished; (*Messer*) blunt; (*Edelstein*) uncut; (fig) rude
ungeschminkt ['ʊngəʃmɪŋkt] *adj* without makeup; (*Wahrheit*) unvarnished
un'gesellig *adj* unsociable
un'gesetzlich *adj* illegal
ungesittet ['ʊngəzɪtət] *adj* unmannerly; uncivilized
ungestört ['ʊngəʃtørt] *adj* undisturbed
ungestraft ['ʊngəʃtraft] *adj* unpunished ‖ *adv* scot-free
ungestüm ['ʊngəʃtym] *adj* impetuous, violent ‖ **Ungestüm** *n* (−[e]s;) impetuosity, violence
un'gesund *adj* unhealthy; unwholesome
ungeteilt ['ʊngətaɪlt] *adj* undivided
un'getreu *adj* disloyal, untrue
ungetrübt ['ʊngətrypt] *adj* cloudless, clear; (fig) untroubled

Ungetüm ['ʊngətym] *n* (−[e]s;−e) monster
ungeübt ['ʊngə·ypt] *adj* untrained; (*Arbeiter*) inexperienced
un'gewandt *adj* unskillful; clumsy
un'gewiß *adj* uncertain; **j−n im ungewissen lassen** keep s.o. in suspense
Un'gewißheit *f* uncertainty
Un'gewitter *n* storm
un'gewöhnlich *adj* unusual
un'gewohnt *adj* unusual; (*genit*) unaccustomed (to)
ungezählt ['ʊngətselt] *adj* countless
Ungeziefer ['ʊngətsifər] *n* (−s;) vermin, bugs
ungeziemend ['ʊngətsimənt] *adj* improper; (*frech*) impudent
un'gezogen *adj* rude; naughty
ungezügelt ['ʊngətsygəlt] *adj* unbridled
un'gezwungen *adj* unforced; natural, easy-going
Un'glaube *m* disbelief, unbelief
un'gläubig *adj* incredulous; (*heidnisch*) infidel ‖ **Ungläubige** §5 *mf* infidel
unglaub'lich *adj* incredible
un'glaubwürdig *adj* untrustworthy; incredible
un'gleich *adj* uneven, unequal; (*unähnlich*) unlike, dissimilar; (*Zahl*) odd ‖ *adv* much, far, by far
un'gleichartig *adj* heterogeneous
un'gleichförmig *adj* unequal; irregular
Un'gleichheit *f* inequality; difference, dissimilarity; unevenness
un'gleichmäßig *adj* disproportionate
Unglimpf ['ʊnglɪmpf] *m* (−[e]s;−e) harshness; wrong, insult
un'glimpflich *adj* harsh
Un'glück *n* (−s;) bad luck; (*Unfall*) accident; disaster, calamity
un'glücklich *adj* unlucky; unfortunate; unhappy
un'glücklicherweise *adv* unfortunately
Un'glücksbote *m* bearer of bad news
Un'glücksbringer *m* (−s;−) jinx
un'glückselig *adj* miserable; disastrous
Un'glücksfall *m* accident, misfortune
Un'glücksmensch *m* unlucky person
Un'glücksrabe *m*, **Un'glücksvogel** *m* unlucky fellow
Un'gnade *f* (−;) disfavor, displeasure
un'gnädig *adj* ungracious; **etw u. aufnehmen** take s.th. amiss
un'gültig *adj* null and void, invalid; **für u. erklären** nullify, void
Un'gültigkeit *f* invalidity
Un'gültigkeitserklärung *f* annulment
Un'gunst *f* disfavor; **zu meinen Ungunsten** to my disadvantage
un'günstig *adj* unfavorable, bad, adverse
un'gut *adj* unkind; **nichts für u.!** no offense!; **ungutes Gefühl** misgivings
un'haltbar *adj* not durable; untenable
un'handlich *adj* unwieldy, unhandy
Un'heil *n* disaster; mischief; **U. anrichten** cause mischief; **U. heraufbeschwören** ask for trouble
unheil'bar *adj* incurable; irreparable
un'heilvoll *adj* ominous; disastrous
un'heimlich *adj* uncanny; sinister
un'höflich *adj* impolite, uncivil

Un'höflichkeit *f* impoliteness
un'hold *adj* unkind || Unhold *m* (-[e]s;
-e) fiend
un'hörbar *adj* inaudible
un'hygienisch *adj* unsanitary
Uni ['uni] *f* (-;-s) (Universität) (coll)
university
uniform [unɪ'fɔrm] *adj* uniform || Uni-
form *f* (-;-en) uniform
Uni·kum ['unɪkum] *n* (-s;-s & -ka
[ka]) unique example; (coll) queer
duck
un'interessant *adj* uninteresting
un'interessiert *adj* (an *dat*) uninterested (in)
Union [un'jon] *f* (-;-en) union
universal [unɪver'zal] *adj* universal
Universal'mittel *n* panacea, cure-all
Universal'schlüssel *m* monkey wrench
Universität [unɪverzɪ'tet] *f* (-;-en)
university
Universitäts'auswahlmannschaft *f* varsity (team)
Universum [unɪ'vɛrzum] *n* (-s;) universe
Unke ['uŋkə] *f* (-;-n) toad
unken ['uŋkən] *intr* (coll) be a prophet
of doom
un'kenntlich *adj* unrecognizable; **u.**
machen disguise
Un'kenntnis *f* (-;) ignorance
Un'kenruf *m* croak
un'keusch *adj* unchaste
un'kindlich *adj* precocious; (*Verhalten*) disrespectful
un'kirchlich *adj* secular, worldly
un'klar *adj* unclear; muddy; misty; **im
unklaren sein über** (*acc*) be in the
dark about
Un'klarheit *f* obscurity
un'kleidsam *adj* unbecoming
un'klug *adj* unwise, imprudent
Un'klugheit *f* imprudence; foolish act
un'kontrollierbar *adj* unverifiable
un'körperlich *adj* incorporeal
Un'kosten *pl* expenses, costs; overhead; **sich in U. stürzen** go to great
expense
Un'kraut *n* weed, weeds; **U. jäten** pull
weeds
Un'krautvertilgungsmittel *n* weed
killer
un'kündbar *adj* binding; (*Darlehen*)
irredeemable; (*Stellung*) permanent
un'kundig *adj* (*genit*) ignorant (of),
unacquainted (with)
unlängst ['unlɛŋst] *adv* recently, the
other day
un'lauter *adj* unfair
un'leidlich *adj* intolerable
un'lenksam *adj* unruly
unles'bar, unle'serlich *adj* illegible
unleugbar ['unlɔɪkbar] *adj* indisputable, undeniable
un'lieb *adj* disagreeable; **es ist mir u.**
I am sorry
un'logisch *adj* illogical
unlös'bar *adj* (*Problem*) unsolvable;
(*untrennbar*) inseparable; (chem) insoluble
unlös'lich *adj* (chem) insoluble
Un'lust *f* reluctance; listlessness
un'lustig *adj* reluctant; listless

un'manierlich *adj* impolite
un'männlich *adj* unmanly
Un'maß *n* excess; **im U. to excess**
Un'masse *f* (coll) vast amount, lots
un'maßgeblich *adj* unauthoritative; irrelevant; **nach meiner unmaßgebli-
chen Meinung** in my humble opinion
un'mäßig *adj* immoderate; excessive
Un'menge *f* (coll)—e-e U. von lots of
Un'mensch *m* brute, monster
un'menschlich *adj* inhuman, brutal
Un'menschlichkeit *f* brutality
un'merklich *adj* imperceptible
un'methodisch *adj* unmethodical
un'mißverständlich *adj* unmistakable
un'mittelbar *adj* direct, immediate
un'möbliert *adj* unfurnished
un'modern *adj* outmoded
un'möglich, unmög'lich *adj* impossible
Un'möglichkeit *f* impossibility
Un'moral *f* immorality
un'moralisch *adj* immoral
un'mündig *adj* underage
un'musikalisch *adj* unmusical
Un'mut *m* (über *acc*) displeasure (at)
un'mutig *adj* displeased, annoyed
unnachahmlich ['unnaxamlɪç] *adj* in-
imitable
un'nachgiebig *adj* unyielding
un'nachsichtig *adj* unrelenting, inexorable; strict
unnahbar [un'nabar] *adj* inaccessible
un'natürlich *adj* unnatural
unnenn'bar *adj* inexpressible
un'nötig *adj* unnecessary
unnütz ['unnʏts] *adj* useless; vain
un'ordentlich *adj* disorderly; untidy
Un'ordnung *f* disorder; mess; **in U.
bringen** throw into disorder
un'organisch *adj* inorganic
un'paar, un'paarig *adj* unpaired, odd
un'parteiisch, un'parteilich *adj* impartial, disinterested
Un'parteilichkeit *f* impartiality
un'passend *adj* unsuitable; (*unschik-
klich*) improper; (*unzeitgemäß*) untimely
un'passierbar *adj* impassable
unpäßlich ['unpɛslɪç] *adj* indisposed,
ill
un'patriotisch *adj* unpatriotic
un'persönlich *adj* impersonal
un'politisch *adj* nonpolitical
un'populär *adj* unpopular
un'praktisch *adj* impractical; (*unerfahren*) unskillful
Un'rast *f* restlessness
Un'rat *m* (-[e]s;) garbage; dirt; **U.
wittern** (coll) smell a rat
un'rätlich, un'ratsam *adj* inadvisable
um'recht *adj* wrong || Unrecht *n* (-[e]s;)
—**im U. sein** be in the wrong; **j-m
U. geben** decide against s.o.; **mit (or
zu) U.** wrongly; unjustly; illegally
un'redlich *adj* dishonest
Un'redlichkeit *f* dishonesty
un'reell *adj* unfair
un'regelmäßig *adj* irregular
Un'regelmäßigkeit *f* irregularity
un'reif *adj* unripe, green; (fig) immature
Un'reife *f* unripeness; immaturity
un'rein *adj* unclean; (& fig) impure;

ins u. schreiben make a rough copy of
Un'reinheit f uncleanness; (& fig) impurity
un'reinlich adj dirty
un'rentabel adj unprofitable
un'rettbar adj irrecoverable
un'richtig adj incorrect, wrong
un'ritterlich adj unchivalrous
Un'ruh f (-;-en) (horol) balance wheel
Un'ruhe f restlessness; uneasiness; (Aufruhr) commotion, riot; (Störung) disturbance; (Besorgnis) anxiety
un'ruhig adj restless; uneasy; (laut) noisy; (Pferd) restive; (Meer) choppy; (nervös) jumpy
un'rühmlich adj inglorious
Un'ruhstifter -in §6 mf agitator, troublemaker; (Wirrkopf) screwball
uns [uns] pers pron us; to us || reflex pron ourselves; **wir sind doch unter uns** we are by ourselves || recip pron each other, one another; **wir sehen uns später** we'll meet later
un'sachgemäß adj inexpert
un'sachlich adj subjective; personal
unsagbar [un'zakbar], **unsäglich** [un-'zekliç] adj unspeakable; (fig) immense
un'sauber adj unclean; (unlauter) unfair, dirty
un'schädlich adj harmless
un'scharf adj (Apparat) out of focus; (Bild) blurred; (Begriff) poorly defined
un'schätzbar adj inestimable, invaluable
un'scheinbar adj inconspicuous, insignificant
un'schicklich adj unbecoming; indecent
Un'schicklichkeit f impropriety
un'schlüssig adj indecisive
Un'schlüssigkeit f indecision, hesitation
un'schmackhaft adj insipid, unpalatable
un'schön adj unlovely; plain, homely; (Angelegenheit) unpleasant
Un'schuld f innocence; **ich wasche meine Hände in U.** I wash my hands of it
un'schuldig adj innocent; (keusch) chaste; harmless; **sich für u. erklären** (jur) plead not guilty
un'schwer adj not difficult
Un'segen m adversity; (Fluch) curse
un'selbständig adj dependent, helpless
un'selig adj unfortunate; (Ereignis) fatal
unser ['unzər] §2,3 poss adj our || §2,4 poss pron ours || pers pron us; of us; **erinnerst du dich unser noch?** do you still remember us?; **es waren unser vier** there were four of us
unseresgleichen ['unzərəs'glaiçən] pron people like us; the likes of us
unserige ['unzəriɡə] §2,5 pron ours
unserthalben ['unzərt'halbən], **unsert-wegen** ['unzərt'veɡən] adv for our sake, on our behalf, on our account
un'sicher adj unsafe; shaky; precarious

Un'sicherheit f unsafeness; shakiness; insecurity; precariousness
un'sichtbar adj invisible
Un'sinn m (-[e]s;) nonsense, rubbish; **U. machen** fool around
un'sinnig adj nonsensical
Un'sitte f bad habit
un'sittlich adj immoral, indecent
Un'sittlichkeit f immorality
un'solid(e) adj unsolid; (Person) loose; (Firma) unreliable, shaky
unsortiert ['unzərtirt] adj unsorted
un'sozial adj antisocial
un'sportlich adj unsportsmanlike
unsrerseits ['unzrər'zaits] adv as for us, for our part
unsrige ['unzriɡə] §2,5 poss pron ours
un'ständig adj impermanent, temporary
un'statthaft adj inadmissible; forbidden
unsterb'lich adj immortal
Unsterb'lichkeit f immortality
Un'stern m unlucky star; (fig) disaster
un'stet adj unsteady; restless; changeable
un'stillbar adj unappeasable; (Durst) unquenchable; (Hunger) unsatiable
unstimmig ['unʃtimiç] adj discrepant; inconsistent
Un'stimmigkeit f (-;-en) discrepancy; inconsistency; (Widerspruch) disagreement
un'sträflich adj blameless; guileless
un'streitig adj indisputable
Un'summe f enormous sum
un'symmetrisch adj asymmetrical
un'sympathisch adj unpleasant; **er ist mir u.** I don't like him
un'tadelhaft adj blameless; flawless
Un'tat f crime
un'tätig adj inactive
un'tauglich adj unfit, unsuitable; useless; (Person) incompetent; **u. machen** disqualify
un'teilbar adj indivisible
unten ['untən] adv below, beneath; downstairs; **da u.** down there; **er ist bei ihnen u. durch** they are through with him; **nach u.** downstairs; downwards; **tief u.** far below; **u. am Berge** at the foot of the mountain; **u. an der Seite** at the bottom of the page; **von u. her** from underneath
unter ['untər] prep (dat) under, below; beneath, underneath; (zwischen) among; (während) during; **ganz u. uns gesagt** just between you and me; **u. aller Kritik** beneath contempt; **u. anderem** among other things; **u. diesem Gesichtspunkt** from this point of view; **u. Null** below zero; **was versteht man unter...?** what is meant by...? || prep (acc) under, below; beneath, underneath; among || **Unter** m (-s;-) (cards) jack
Unter-, unter- comb.fm. under-, sub-; lower
Un'terabteilung f subdivision
Un'terarm m forearm
Un'terart f subspecies
Un'terausschuß m subcommittee
Un'terbau m (-[e]s;-ten) foundation

un'terbelichten *tr* underexpose
un'terbewußt *adj* subconscious
Un'terbewußtsein *n* subconscious
unterbie'ten §58 *tr* undercut, undersell; underbid
un'terbinden §59 *tr* tie underneath ‖ unterbin'den §59 *tr* (*Verkehr*) tie up; (*Blutgefäß*) tie off; (*verhindern*) prevent; (*Angriff*) neutralize
Unterbin'dung *f* stoppage; (surg) ligature
unterblei'ben §62 *intr* (SEIN) remain undone; not take place; be discontinued; das muß u. that must be stopped
unterbre'chen §64 *tr* interrupt; (*einstellen*) suspend; (*Schweigen, Stille, Kontakt*) break; (*Verkehr*) hold up; (telp) disconnect; die Reise in München u. have a stopover in Munich ‖ *ref* stop short
Unterbre'cher *m* (elec) circuit breaker
Unterbre'chung *f* interruption; disconnection; (*e-r Fahrt*) stopover
unterbrei'ten *tr* submit
un'terbringen §65 *tr* provide a place for; find room for; (*Gäste*) accommodate, put up; (*Stapeln*) store; (*Anleihe*) place; (*Geld*) invest; (*Pferde*) stable; (*Wagen*) park; (*Truppe*) billet; e-n Artikel bei e-r Zeitung u. have an article published in a newspaper; j-n auf e-m Posten (or in e-r Stellung) u. find s.o. a job, place s.o.
Un'terbringung *f* (-;-en) accommodations, housing; billet; storage; investment; placement
Un'terbringungsmöglichkeiten *pl* accommodations
unterdes [untər'dɛs], unterdessen [untər'dɛsən] *adv* meanwhile
Un'terdruck *m* low pressure
unterdrücken (unterdrük'ken) *tr* suppress; (*Aufstand*) quell; (*bedrücken*) oppress; (*ersticken*) stifle; (*Seufzer*) repress
Un'terdruckgebiet *n* low-pressure area
Unterdrückung (Unterdrük'kung) *f* (-;) oppression; suppression
untere ['untərə] §9 *adj* lower, inferior
untereinan'der *adv* among one another; mutually; reciprocally
unterentwickelt ['untərɛntvɪkəlt] *adj* underdeveloped
unterernährt ['untərɛrnert] *adj* undernourished
Un'terernährung *f* (-;) undernourishment
Un'terfamilie *f* subfamily
unterfer'tigen *tr* sign
Unterfüh'rung *f* (-;-en) underpass
unterfüt'tern *tr* line
Un'tergang *m* setting; (fig) decline, fall; (naut) sinking
unterge'ben *adj* (*dat*) subject (to), inferior (to) ‖ Untergebene §5 *mf* subordinate
un'tergehen §82 *intr* (SEIN) go down, sink; (fig) perish; (astr) set
untergeordnet ['untərgə·ɔrdnət] *adj* subordinate ‖ Untergeordnete §5 *mf* subordinate

Un'tergeschoß *n* ground floor; (*Kellergeschoß*) basement
Un'tergestell *n* undercarriage
Un'tergewand *n* underwear
un'tergliedern *tr* subdivide
untergra'ben §87 *tr* undermine
Un'tergrund *m* subsoil
Un'tergrundbahn *f* subway
Un'tergrundbewegung *f* underground movement
un'terhalb *prep* (*genit*) below
Un'terhalt *m* (-[e]s;) support; maintenance, upkeep; livelihood
un'terhalten §90 *tr* hold under ‖ unterhal'ten §90 *tr* maintain; support; (*Briefwechsel*) keep up; (*Feuer*) feed; entertain, amuse ‖ *ref* enjoy oneself, have a good time; amuse oneself; sich u. mit talk with
unterhaltsam [untər'haltzam] *adj* entertaining, amusing, enjoyable
Un'terhaltsbeitrag *m* alimony; (*für Kinder*) support
Unterhaltsberechtigte ['untərhaltsbəreçtigtə] §5 *mf* dependent
Un'terhaltskosten *pl* living expenses
Unterhal'tung *f* (-;-en) entertainment, amusement; (*Gespräch*) conversation; (*Aufrechterhaltung*) upkeep; (*Unterstützung*) support
Unterhal'tungskosten *pl* maintenance cost, maintenance
Unterhal'tungslektüre *f* light reading
unterhan'deln *intr* negotiate
Un'terhändler -in §6 *mf* negotiator; (*Vermittler*) mediator
Unterhand'lung *f* (-;-en) negotiation
Un'terhaus *n* (parl) lower house
Un'terhemd *n* undershirt
unterhöh'len *tr* undermine
Un'terholz *n* undergrowth, underbrush
Un'terhose *f* shorts; panties; in Unterhosen zeigen (coll) debunk
un'terirdisch *adj* underground, subterranean; (myth) of the underworld
Un'terjacke *f* vest
unterjo'chen *tr* subjugate
Unterjo'chung *f* (-;) subjugation
Un'terkiefer *m* lower jaw
Un'terkinn *n* double chin
Un'terkleid *n* slip
Un'terkleidung *f* (-;) underwear
un'terkommen §99 *intr* (SEIN) find accommodations; find employment ‖ Unterkommen *n* (-s;) accommodations; (*Stellung*) job
Un'terkörper *m* lower part of the body
un'terkriegen *tr* (coll) get the better of; er läßt sich nicht u. he won't knuckle under
Unterkunft ['untərkunft] *f* (-;-̈e) accommodations; apartment; (*Obdach*) shelter, place to stay; (mil) quarters; U. und Verpflegung room and board
Un'terlage *f* foundation; base; pad; desk pad; rubber pad (*for a bed*); (*Teppich-*) underpad; (*Beleg*) voucher; (*Urkunde*) document; (archit) support; (geol) substratum; keine Unterlagen haben have nothing to go on; Unterlagen documentation; data
Un'terland *n* lowland

Unterlaß ['untərlas] *m*—**ohne U.** without letup

unterlas'sen §104 *tr* omit; neglect; skip; stop, cut out

Unterlas'sung *f* (-;-en) omission; neglect; failure

Unterlas'sungssünde *f* sin of omission

unterlau'fen *adj*—**blau u.** black-and-blue; **mit Blut u.** bloodshot || **un'terlaufen** §105 *intr* (SEIN) (*Fehler*) slip in

un'terlegen *tr* lay under, put under; (*Bedeutung, Sinn*) attach; **der Musik Worte u.** set words to music || **unterle'gen** *adj* defeated; (*dat*) inferior (to) || **Unterlegene** §5 *mf* loser

Unterle'genheit *f* (-;) inferiority

Unterlegring ['untərlekriŋ] *m*, **Unterlegscheibe** ['untərlekʃaɪbə] *f* washer

Un'terleib *m* abdomen

Unterleibs- *comb.fm.* abdominal

unterlie'gen §108 *intr* (SEIN) (*dat*) be beaten (by), lose (to); **e-m Rabatt u.** be subject to discount || *impers* (SEIN)—**es unterliegt keinem Zweifel, daß** there is no doubt that

Un'terlippe *f* lower lip

unterma'len *tr* put the primer on; **mit Musik u.** accompany with music

untermau'ern *tr* support

Un'termiete *f* (-;) subletting; **in U. abgeben** sublet; **in U. wohnen bei** sublet from

Un'termieter –in §6 *mf* subtenant

unterminie'ren *tr* (fig) undermine

unterneh'men §116 *tr* undertake; (*versuchen*) attempt; **Schritte u.** (fig) take steps || **Unternehmen** *n* (-s;-) undertaking; venture; enterprise; (mil) operation

unterneh'mend *adj* enterprising

Unterneh'mensberater *m* management consultant

Unterneh'mer –in §6 *mf* entrepreneur; (*Arbeitgeber*) employer; (*Bau–*) contractor

Unterneh'mung *f* (-;-en) undertaking; enterprise, business; (mil) operation

Unterneh'mungsgeist *m* initiative

unterneh'mungslustig *adj* enterprising

Un'teroffizier *m* noncommissioned officer, N.C.O.

un'terordnen *tr* (*dat*) subordinate (to) || *ref* (*dat*) submit (to)

unterre'den *ref* (mit) confer (with)

Unterre'dung *f* (-;-en) conference

Unterricht ['untərrɪçt] *m* (-[e]s;-e) instruction, lessons

unterrich'ten *tr* instruct; **u. von** (or **über** *acc*) inform (of, about)

Un'terrichtsfach *n* subject, course

Un'terrichtsfilm *m* educational film; (mil) training film

Un'terrichtsministerium *n* department of public instruction

Un'terrichtsstunde *f* (educ) period

Un'terrichtswesen *n* education; teaching

Un'terrock *m* slip

untersa'gen *tr* forbid, prohibit

Un'tersatz *m* saucer; support; (*Gestell*) stand; (archit) socle; (log) minor premise

unterschät'zen *tr* underrate, underestimate; undervalue

unterschei'den §112 *tr* distinguish || *ref* (**von**) differ (from)

Unterschei'dung *f* (-;-en) difference, distinction

Un'terschenkel *m* shank

un'terschieben §130 *tr* shove under; (statt *genit*) substitute (for); (*dat*) impute (to), foist (on)

Unterschied ['untərʃit] *m* (-[e]s;-e) difference, distinction; **zum U. von** as distinct from, unlike

un'terschiedlich *adj* different; varying

un'terschiedslos *adj* indiscriminate

unterschla'gen §132 *tr* embezzle; (*Nachricht*) suppress; (*Brief*) intercept

Unterschla'gung *f* (-;-en) embezzlement; suppression; interception

Unterschlupf ['untərʃlupf] *m* (-[e]s;) shelter; hide-out

unterschrei'ben §62 *tr* sign; (fig) subscribe to, agree to

Un'terschrift *f* signature

Un'terseeboot *n* submarine

unterseeisch ['untərze·iʃ] *adj* submarine

Un'terseekabel *n* transoceanic cable

Un'terseite *f* underside

untersetzt [untər'zetst] *adj* stocky

Un'tersetzung *f* (-;-en) (mech) reduction

un'tersinken §143 *intr* (SEIN) go down

Un'terstand *m* (mil) dugout

unterste ['untərstə] §9 *adj* lowest, bottom

unterste'hen §146 *ref* dare; **untersteh dich!** don't you dare! || *intr* (*dat*) be under (*s.o.*) || **un'terstehen** §146 *intr* take shelter

un'terstellen *tr* place under; (*Auto*) put into the garage || *ref* take cover || **unterstel'len** *tr* assume, suppose; (*dat*) impute (to); (mil) (*dat*) put under the command (of)

Unterstel'lung *f* (-;-en) assumption; imputation

unterstrei'chen §85 *tr* underline

unterstüt'zen *tr* support, back; help

Unterstüt'zung *f* (-;-en) support, backing; assistance; (*Beihilfe durch Geld*) relief; (ins) benefit

untersu'chen *tr* examine, inspect; investigate; study, do research on; (chem) analyze

Untersu'chung *f* (-;-en) examination; inspection; investigation; study, research; (chem) analysis

Untersu'chungsausschuß *m* fact-finding committee

Untersu'chungsgericht *n* court of inquiry

Untersu'chungshaft *f* (jur) detention

Untersu'chungsrichter *m* examining judge

Untertagebau [untər'tagəbau] *m* (-[e]s;) mine

Untertan ['untərtan] *m* (-s & -en;-en) subject

untertänig [untər'tenɪç] *adj* submissive

Un'tertasse *f* saucer; **fliegende U.** flying saucer

un′tertauchen *tr* submerge; duck || *intr* (SEIN) dive; (fig) disappear || **Unter-tauchen** *n* (–s;) dive; disappearance
Un′terteil *m* & *n* lower part, bottom
untertei′len *tr* subdivide
Untertei′lung *f* (–;–en) subdivision
Un′tertitel *m* subtitle; caption
Un′terton *m* undertone
un′tertreten §152 *intr* (SEIN) take cover
un′tervermieten *tr* sublet
Un′tervertrag *m* subcontract
unterwan′dern *tr* infiltrate
Un′terwäsche *f* underwear
Unterwasser– *comb.fm.* underwater, submarine
Un′terwasserbombe *f* depth charge
Un′terwasserhorchgerät *n* hydrophone
Un′terwasserortungsgerät *n* sonar
unterwegs [ʊntərˈveks] *adv* on the way; (com) in transit
unterwei′sen §118 *tr* instruct
Unterwei′sung *f* (–;–en) instruction
Un′terwelt *f* underworld; (myth) lower world
unterwer′fen §160 *tr* subjugate; (*dat*) subject (to) || *ref* (*dat*) submit to, subject oneself to; **sich** [*dat*] **ein Volk u.** subjugate a people
Unterwer′fung *f* (–;) subjugation; submission
unterworfen [ʊntərˈvɔrfən] *adj* subject
unterwürfig [ˈʊntərvʏrfɪç] *adj* submissive, subservient
unterzeich′nen *tr* sign
Unterzeich′ner –in §6 *mf* signer; signatory
Unterzeichnete [ʊntərˈtsaɪçnətə] §5 *mf* undersigned
Unterzeich′nung *f* (–;–en) signing; signature
un′terziehen §163 *tr* put on underneath || **unterzie′hen** §163 *tr* (*dat*) subject (to) || *ref*—**sich der Mühe u. zu** (*inf*) take the trouble to (*inf*); **sich e–r Operation u.** have an operation; **sich e–r Prüfung u.** take an examination
un′tief *adj* shallow || **Untiefe** *f* (–;–n) shoal
Un′tier *n* (& fig) monster
untilg′bar *adj* inextinguishable; (*Tinte*) indelible; (*Anleihe*) irredeemable
untrag′bar *adj* unbearable; (*Kleidung*) unwearable; (*Kosten*) prohibitive
untrenn′bar *adj* inseparable
un′treu *adj* unfaithful || **Untreue** *f* unfaithfulness; infidelity
untröst′lich *adj* inconsolable
untrüg′lich *adj* unerring, infallible
un′tüchtig *adj* incapable; inefficient
Un′tugend *f* bad habit, vice
un′überlegt *adj* thoughtless; rash
unüberseh′bar *adj* vast, huge; incalculable || *adv* very
unübersetz′bar *adj* untranslatable
un′übersichtlich *adj* unclear; (*Kurve*) blind
unübersteig′bar, unübersteig′lich *adj* insurmountable
unübertreff′lich *adj* unsurpassable
unübertroffen [ʊnybərˈtrɔfən] *adj* unsurpassed
unüberwind′lich *adj* invincible; (*Schwierigkeiten*) insurmountable

unumgäng′lich *adj* indispensable
unumschränkt [ˈʊnʊm/rɛŋkt] *adj* unlimited; (pol) absolute
unumstößlich [ˈʊnʊm/tøslɪç] *adj* irrefutable; (*unwiderruflich*) irrevocable
unumwunden [ˈʊnʊmvʊndən] *adj* blunt
un′unterbrochen *adj* continuous
unverän′derlich *adj* unchangeable, invariable
unverant′wortlich *adj* irresponsible
unveräu′ßerlich *adj* inalienable
unverbesserlich [ʊnfɛrˈbesərlɪç] *adj* incorrigible
unverbind′lich *adj* without obligation; (*Verhalten*) proper, formal; (*Antwort*) noncommittal
un′verblümt *adj* blunt, plain
unverbürgt [ʊnfɛrˈbʏrkt] *adj* unwarranted; (*Nachricht*) unconfirmed
un′verdächtig *adj* unsuspected
un′verdaulich *adj* indigestible
unverderbt [ˈʊnfɛrdɛrpt], **unverdorben** [ˈʊnfɛrdɔrbən] *adj* unspoiled
unverdient [ˈʊnfɛrdint] *adj* undeserved
un′verdrossen *adj* indefatigable
unverdünnt [ˈʊnfɛrdʏnt] *adj* undiluted
unverehelicht [ˈʊnfɛre·əlɪçt] *adj* unmarried, single
un′vereinbar *adj* incompatible; contradictory
unverfälscht [ˈʊnfɛrfɛl/t] *adj* genuine; (*Wein*) undiluted
un′verfänglich *adj* innocent
un′verfroren *adj* brash
un′vergänglich *adj* imperishable
un′vergeßlich *adj* unforgettable
unvergleich′bar *adj* incomparable
unvergleichlich [ˈʊnfɛrglaɪçlɪç] *adj* incomparable
un′verhältnismäßig *adj* disproportionate
un′verheiratet *adj* unmarried
unvergolten [ˈʊnfɛrgɔltən] *adj* unrewarded
unverhofft [ˈʊnfɛrhɔft] *adj* unhoped-for
unverhohlen [ˈʊnfɛrholən] *adj* unconcealed; (fig) open
un′verkäuflich *adj* unsalable
unverkennbar [ˈʊnfɛrkɛnbɑr] *adj* unmistakable
unverkürzt [ˈʊnfɛrkʏrtst] *adj* unabridged
unverlangt [ˈʊnfɛrlaŋt] *adj* unsolicited
un′verletzbar, un′verletzlich *adj* undamageable; (fig) inviolable
unverletzt [ˈʊnfɛrlɛtst] *adj* safe and sound, unharmed; (*Sache*) undamaged
unvermeid′lich *adj* inevitable
unvermindert [ˈʊnfɛrmɪndərt] *adj* undiminished
unvermittelt [ˈʊnfɛrmɪtəlt] *adj* sudden
Un′vermögen *n* inability; impotence
un′vermögend *adj* poor; impotent
unvermutet [ˈʊnfɛrmutət] *adj* unexpected
un′vernehmlich *adj* imperceptible
Un′vernunft *f* unreasonableness; folly
un′vernünftig *adj* unreasonable; foolish
un′verschämt *adj* brazen, shameless

unverschuldet ['ʊnferʃʊldət] *adj* unencumbered; (*unverdient*) undeserved
un'versehens *adv* unawares, suddenly
unversehrt ['ʊnferzert] *adj* undamaged (*Person*) unharmed
unversichert ['ʊnferzɪçərt] *adj* uninsured
unversiegbar [ʊnfer'zikbɑr] **unversieglich** [ʊnfer'ziklɪç] *adj* inexhaustible
unversiegelt ['ʊnferzigəlt] *adj* unsealed
un'versöhnlich *adj* irreconcilable
unversorgt ['ʊnferzɔrkt] *adj* unprovided for
Un'verstand *m* lack of judgment
un'verständig *adj* foolish
un'verständlich *adj* incomprehensible
unversucht ['ʊnferzuxt] *adj* untried
un'verträglich *adj* unsociable; quarrelsome; incompatible, contradictory
un'verwandt *adj* steady, unflinching
unverwelklich [ʊnfer'vɛlklɪç] *adj* unfading
un'verwendbar *adj* unusable
unverweslich ['ʊnfervezlɪç] *adj* incorruptible
unverwindbar [ʊnfer'vɪntbɑr] *adj* irreparable; (*Entäuschung*) lasting
un'verwundbar *adj* invulnerable
unverwüstlich ['ʊnfervystlɪç] *adj* indestructible; (*Stoff*) durable; (fig) irrepressible
unverzagt ['ʊnfertsɑkt] *adj* undaunted
un'verzeihlich *adj* unpardonable
unverzerrt ['ʊnfertsert] *adj* undistorted
unverzinslich ['ʊnfertsɪnslɪç] *adj* (fin) without interest
unverzüglich ['ʊnfertsyklɪç] *adj* prompt, immediate || *adv* without delay
unvollendet ['ʊnfɔlendət] *adj* unfinished
un'vollkommen *adj* imperfect
Un'vollkommenheit *f* imperfection
un'vollständig *adj* incomplete; (gram) defective
un'vorbereitet *adj* unprepared; (*Rede*) extemporaneous || *adv* extempore
un'voreingenommen *adj* unbiased
un'vorhergesehen *adi* unforeseen
un'vorsätzlich *adj* unintentional
un'vorsichtig *adj* incautious; careless
un'vorteilhaft *adj* disadvantageous; unprofitable; (*Kleid*) unflattering
un'wahr *adi* untrue
un'wahrhaftig *adj* untruthful
Un'wahrheit *f* untruth, falsehood
un'wahrnehmbar *adj* imperceptible
un'wahrscheinlich *adj* unlikely, improbable
unwan'delbar *adj* unchangeable
unwegsam ['ʊnvekzɑm] *adj* impassable
unweigerlich [ʊn'vaɪgərlɪç] *adj* unhesitating; (*Folge*) necessary || *adv* without fail
un'weit *adj*—**u. von** not far from || *prep* (*genit*) not far from
Un'wesen *n* mischief; **sein U. treiben** be up to one's old tricks
un'wesentlich *adj* unessential; unimportant; (**für**) immaterial (to)
Un'wetter *n* storm

un'wichtig *adj* unimportant
unwiederbringlich [ʊnvidər'brɪŋlɪç] *adj* irretrievable, irreparable
unwiderleg'bar *adj* irrefutable
unwiderruf'lich *adj* irrevocable
unwidersteh'lich *adj* irresistible
Un'wille *m*, **Un'willen** *m* indignation, displeasure; reluctance
un'willig *adj* (**über** *acc*) indignant (at), displeased (at); **u. zu** (*inf*) reluctant to (*inf*)
un'willkommen *adj* unwelcome
un'willkürlich *adj* involuntary
un'wirklich *adj* unreal
un'wirksam *adj* ineffective; inefficient; (chem) inactive; (jur) null and void
Un'wirksamkeit *f* ineffectiveness; inefficiency; (chem) inactivity
unwirsch ['ʊnvɪrʃ] *adj* surly
un'wirtlich *adj* inhospitable
un'wirtschaftlich *adj* uneconomical
unwissend ['ʊnvɪsənt] *adj* ignorant
Unwissenheit ['ʊnvɪsənhaɪt] *f* (–;) ignorance
un'wissenschaftlich *adj* unscientific
un'wissentlich *adv* unwittingly
un'wohl *adj* sickish; **ich fühle mich u.** I don't feel well
un'wohnlich *adj* uninhabitable; (*unbehaglich*) uncomfortable
un'würdig *adj* unworthy
Un'zahl *f* (**von**) huge number (of)
unzähl'bar, unzählig [ʊn'tselɪç] *adj* countless, innumerable
un'zart *adj* indelicate
Unze ['ʊntsə] *f* (–;–n) ounce
Un'zeit *f* wrong time
un'zeitgemäß *adj* out-of-date
un'zeitig *adi* untimely; (*Obst*) unripe
unzerbrech'lich *adj* unbreakable
unzerstör'bar *adj* indestructible
unzertrennlich [ʊntser'trenlɪç] *adj* inseparable
unziemend ['ʊntsimənt], **un'ziemlich** *adi* unbecoming, unseemly
Un'zucht *f* unchastity; lewdness
un'züchtig *adj* unchaste; lewd
un'zufrieden *adj* dissatisfied
un'zuänglich *adi* inaccessible; aloof
un'zulänglich *adj* inadequate
un'zulässig *adj* inadmissible; (*Beeinflussung, Einmischung*) undue
un'zurechnungsfähig *adj* unaccountable
un'zureichend *adj* inadequate
un'zusammenhängend *adi* incoherent
un'zuträglich *adi* (*dat*) bad (for)
un'zutreffend *adj* not applicable
un'zuverlässig *adj* unreliable
un'zweckmäßig *adj* inappropriate; unsuitable; impractical
un'zweideutig *adj* unambiguous
un'zweifelhaft *adj* undoubted
üppig ['ʏpɪç] *adj* luxurious, plush; (*Mahl*) sumptuous; (*Pflanzenwuchs*) luxuriant; (*sinnlich*) voluptuous
Ur-, ur- [ur] *comb.fm.* original; very
ur'alt *adj* very old, ancient
Uran [u'rɑn] *n* (–s;) uranium
Ur'aufführung *f* world première
urbar ['ʊrbɑr] *adj* arable; **u. machen** reclaim
Urbarmachung ['ʊrbɑrmaxʊŋ] *f* (–;) reclamation

Ur'bewohner *pl* aborigines
Ur'bild *n* prototype; original
ur'deutsch *adj* hundred-percent German
ur'eigen *adj* one's very own; original
Ur'einwohner *pl* aborigines
Ur'eltern *pl* ancestors
Ur'enkel *m* great-grandson
Ur'geschichte *f* prehistory
Ur'großmutter *f* great-grandmother
Ur'großvater *m* great-grandfather
Urheber –in ['urhebər(ɪn)] §6 *mf* originator, author
Ur'heberrecht *n* copyright
Ur'heberschaft *f* (–;–e) authorship
Urin [u'rin] *m* (–s;) urine
urinieren [urɪ'nirən] *intr* urinate
ur'ko'misch *adj* very funny
Urkunde ['urkundə] *f* (–;–n) document; deed; (*Vertrag*) instrument
Ur'kundenmaterial *n* documentation
urkundlich ['urkuntlıç] *adj* documentary; (*verbürgt*) authentic
Urlaub ['urlaup] *m* (–[e]s;–e) vacation; (mil) furlough
Ur'lauber –in §6 *mf* vacationer
Ur'laubsschein *m* (mil) pass
Ur'laubstag *m* day off
Urne ['urnə] *f* (–;–n) urn; ballot box; zur U. gehen go to the polls
Ur'nengang *m* balloting

ur'plötz'lich *adj* sudden ‖ *adv* all of a sudden
Ur'sache *f* cause, reason; keine U.! don't mention it!
ur'sächlich *adj* causal
Ur'schleim *m* (–es;) protoplasm
Ur'schrift *f* original text, original
Ur'sprung *m* origin, source; beginning; (*Ursache*) cause
ursprünglich ['ur∫prʏŋlıç] *adj* original
Ur'stoff *m* primary matter; (chem) element
Ur'teil *n* judgment; (*Ansicht*) view, opinion; (jur) verdict; (*Strafmaß*) (jur) sentence
urteilen ['urtaɪlən] *intr* judge; **u. nach** judge by
Ur'teilskraft *f* discernment
Ur'teilsspruch *m* verdict; sentence
Ur'text *m* original text
Ur'tier *n* protozoon
Ur'volk *n* aborigines
Ur'wald *m* virgin forest; jungle
ur'weltlich *adj* primeval
urwüchsig ['urvyksıç] *adj* original; (fig) rough
Ur'zeit *f* remote antiquity
Utensilien [uten'ziljən] *pl* utensils
Uto·pie [utɔ'pi] *f* (–;–pien ['pi·ən]) utopia; pipe dream
uzen ['utsən] *tr* tease, kid

V

V, v [faʊ] *invar n* V, v
vag [vɑk] *adj* vague
Vagabund [vaga'bunt] *m* (–en;–en) vagabond, tramp, bum
vagabundieren [vagabun'dirən] *intr* (HABEN & SEIN) bum around
vage ['vɑgə] *adj* vague
vakant [va'kant] *adj* vacant
Vakanz [va'kants] *f* (–;–en) vacancy
Vaku·um ['vɑku·um] *n* (–s;–ua [u·a]) vacuum
Vakzine [vak'tsinə] *f* (–;–n) vaccine
vakzinieren [vaktsɪ'nirən] *tr* vaccinate
Valet [va'let] *n* (–s;–s) farewell
Valu·ta [va'luta] *f* (–;–ten [tən]) value; (foreign) currency
Vampir ['vampir] *m* (–s;–e) vampire
Vandale [van'dɑlə] *m* (–n;–n) Vandal; (fig) vandal
Vanille [va'nɪljə] *f* (–;) vanilla
Variante [varɪ'antə] *f* (–;–n) variant
Varietät [varɪ·ɛ'tet] *f* (–;–en) variety
Varieté [varɪ·ɛ'te] *n* (–s;–s) vaudeville; vaudeville stage
variieren [varɪ'irən] *tr & intr* vary
Vase ['vɑzə] *f* (–;–n) vase
Vaselin [vazɛ'lin] *n* (–s;–e), Vaseline [vazɛ'linə] *f* (–;–n) vaseline
Vater ['fɑtər] *m* (–s;⸚) father
Va'terland *n* (native) country
vaterländisch ['fɑtərlɛndɪʃ] *adj* national ‖ *adv*—v. gesinnt patriotic
Va'terlandsliebe *f* patriotism
väterlich ['fetərlıç] *adj* fatherly

väterlicherseits ['fetərlıçər'zaɪts] *adv* on the father's side
Va'terliebe *f* paternal love
Va'terschaft *f* (–;) fatherhood
Va'terschaftsklage *f* paternity suit
Va'tersname *m* family name, last name
Va'terstadt *f* home town
Va'terstelle *f*—bei j–m V. vertreten be a father to s.o.
Vaterun'ser *n* (–s;–) Lord's Prayer
Vati ['fɑti] *m* (–s;–s) dad, daddy
Vatikan [vatɪ'kɑn] *m* (–s;) Vatican
v. Chr. *abbr* (vor Christus) B.C.
Vegetarier –in [vɛgɛ'tɑrjər(ɪn)] §6 *mf* vegetarian
Vegetation [vɛgɛta'tsjon] *f* (–;) vegetation
vegetieren [vɛgɛ'tirən] *intr* vegetate
Veilchen ['faɪlçən] *n* (–s;–) (bot) violet
Vene ['venə] *f* (–;–n) (anat) vein
Venedig [vɛ'nedıç] *n* (–s;) Venice
venerisch [vɛ'nerıʃ] *adj* venereal; venerisches Leiden venereal disease
Ventil [vɛn'til] *n* (–s;–e) valve; (bei der Orgel) stop; (fig) outlet
Ventilation [vɛntɪla'tsjon] *f* (–;) ventilation
Venti·lator [vɛntɪ'lɑtər] *m* (–s;–latoren [la'torən]) ventilator; fan
ver– [fɛr] *pref* up, e.g., verbrauchen use up; away, e.g., verjagen chase away; mis–, wrongly, e.g., verstellen misplace, verdrehen turn the wrong

way; (to form verbs from other parts of speech) **verwirklichen** realize, **vergöttern** deify; (to express a sense opposite that of the simple verb) **verlernen** forget, **verkaufen** sell; (to indicate consumption or waste through the action of the verb) **verschreiben** use up in writing; (to indicate intensification or completion) **verhungern** die of hunger; (to indicate cessation of action) **vergären** cease to ferment; (to indicate conversion to another state) **verflüssigen** liquify

verabfolgen [fɛr'apfɔlgən] *tr* hand over; deliver; (*Arznei*) give, administer

verabreden [fɛr'apredən] *tr* agree upon; **schon anderweitig verabredet sein** have a prior engagement ‖ *ref* make an appointment

Verab'redung *f* (-;-en) agreement; appointment

verabreichen [fɛr'apraɪçən] *tr* give

verabsäumen [fɛr'apzɔɪmən] *tr* var of **versäumen**

verabscheuen [fɛr'apʃɔɪ·ən] *tr* detest, loath, abhor

verab'scheuenswert, **verab'scheuenswürdig** detestable

verabschieden [fɛr'apʃidən] *tr* dismiss; (*Beamte*) put on pension; (*Gesetz*) pass; (mil) disband ‖ *ref* (**von**) take leave (of), say goodbye (to)

Verab'schiedung *f* (-;-en) dismissal; pensioning; (mil) disbanding; (parl) passing, enactment

verach'ten *tr* despise; **nicht zu v.** not to be sneezed at

verächtlich [fɛr'ɛçtlɪç] *adj* contemptuous; (*verachtungswert*) contemptible

Verach'tung *f* (-;) contempt

veralbern [fɛr'albərn] *tr* tease

verallgemeinern [fɛralgə'maɪnərn] *tr* & *intr* generalize

Verallgemei'nerung *f* (-;-en) generalization

veralten [fɛr'altən] *intr* become obsolete; (*Kleider*) go out of style

veraltet [fɛr'altət] *adj* obsolete; out of date, old-fashioned

Veran·da [vɛ'randa] *f* (-;-den [dən]) veranda, porch

veränderlich [fɛr'ɛndərlɪç] *adj* changeable; (math) variable

Verän'derlichkeit *f* (-;-en) changeableness; fluctuation; instability

verän'dern [fɛr'ɛndərn] *tr* change; vary ‖ *ref* change; look for a new job

Verän'derung *f* (-;-en) change

verängstigt [fɛr'ɛŋstɪçt] *adj* intimidated

verankern [fɛr'aŋkərn] *tr* anchor, moor

Veran'kerung *f* (-;-en) anchorage, mooring

veranlagen [fɛr'anlagən] *tr* (*zu e–r Steuer*) assess; **gut veranlagt** highly talented; **künstlerisch veranlagt** artificially inclined; **schlecht veranlagt** poorly endowed

Veran'lagung *f* (-;-en) talents; disposition; (fin) assessment

veran'lassen *tr* cause, occasion, make; (*bereden*) induce

Veran'lassung *f* (-;-en) cause, occasion; **auf V. von** at the suggestion of; **ohne jede V.** without provocation; **V. geben zu** give rise to

veranschaulichen [fɛr'anʃaʊlɪçən] *tr* make clear, illustrate

veran'schlagen §132 *tr* rate, value; (*im voraus berechnen*) estimate; **zu hoch v.** overrate

Veran'schlagung *f* (-;) estimate

veranstalten [fɛr'anʃtaltən] *tr* organize, arrange; (*Empfang*) give; (*Sammlung*) take up; (*Versammlung*) hold

Veran'stalter –in §6 *mf* organizer

Veran'staltung *f* (-;-en) organization, arrangement; affair; performance, show; meeting; (sport) event, meet

veran'tworten *tr* answer for, account for; (*verteidigen*) defend ‖ *ref* defend oneself, justify oneself

verantwortlich [fɛr'antvɔrtlɪç] *adj* responsible, answerable; **für etw v. zeichnen** sign for s.th.

Verant'wortlichkeit *f* (-;) responsibility; (jur) liability

Verant'wortung *f* (-;-en) responsibility; (*Rechtfertigung*) justification; **auf eigene V.** at one's own risk; **die V. abwälzen auf** (*acc*) pass the buck to; **zur V. ziehen** call to account

Verant'wortungsbewußtsein *n* sense of responsibility

verant'wortungsfreudig *adj* willing to assume responsibility

verant'wortungsvoll *adj* responsible

veräppeln [fɛr'ɛpəln] *tr* (coll) tease

verar'beiten *tr* manufacture, process; (**zu**) make (into); (*verdauen*) digest; (fig) assimilate

verar'beitend *adj* manufacturing

Verar'beitung *f* (-;-en) manufacturing; digestion; (fig) assimilation

verargen [fɛr'argən] *tr*—**j-m etw v.** blame s.o. for s.th.

verär'gern *tr* annoy

verarmen [fɛr'armən] *intr* (SEIN) grow poor

verästeln [fɛr'ɛstəln] *ref* branch out

verausgaben [fɛr'aʊsgabən] *tr* pay out ‖ *ref* run short of money

veräußern [fɛr'ɔɪsərn] *tr* sell

Verb [vɛrp] *n* (-s;-en) verb

verbal [vɛr'bal] *adj* verbal

Verband [fɛr'bant] *m* (-[e]s;Ꞌe) association, union, federation; (aer, nav) formation; (mil) unit; (surg) bandage, dressing; **sich aus dem V. lösen** (aer) peel off

Verband'kasten *m* first-aid kit

Verband'päckchen *n* first-aid pack

Verband'platz *m* first-aid station

Verband'stoff *m* bandage, dressing

verbannen [fɛr'banən] *tr* banish, exile

Verbannte [fɛr'bantə] §5 *mf* exile

Verban'nung *f* (-;-en) banishment; place of exile

verbarrikadie'ren *tr* barricade

verbau'en *tr* (*Gelände*) build up; use up (*in building*); (*Geld*) spend (*in building*); build poorly; **j-m den Weg v. zu** bar s.o.'s way to

verbei'ßen §53 *tr* swallow, suppress || *ref* (in *acc*) stick (to)
verber'gen §54 *tr & ref* hide
verbes'sern *tr* improve; correct; (*Aufsatz*) grade; (*Gesetz*) amend; (*Tatsache*) rectify || *ref* improve; better oneself
Verbes'serung *f* (-;-en) improvement; correction; amendment
verbeu'gen *ref* bow
Verbeu'gung *f* (-;-en) bow; curtsy
verbeulen [fɛr'bɔɪlən] *tr* dent; batter
verbie'gen §57 *tr* bend || *ref* warp
verbie'ten §58 *tr* forbid
verbil'den *tr* spoil; educate badly
verbil'ligen *tr* reduce the price of
Verbil'ligung *f* (-;-en) reduction
verbin'den §59 *tr* tie, tie up; join, unite; (*verketten*) link; (*zu Dank verpflichten*) obligate; (chem) combine; (med) bandage; (telp) (**mit**) connect (with), put through (to); **j-m die Augen v.** blindfold s.o. || *ref* unite
verbindlich [fɛr'bɪntlɪç] *adj* obliging; binding; **verbindlichsten Dank!** thank you ever so much!
Verbind'lichkeit *f* (-;-en) obligation; commitment; polite way; (*e-s Vertrags*) binding force
Verbin'dung *f* (-;-en) union; association; alliance; combination; contact; touch; (*Fuge, Gelenk*) joint; (chem) compound; (educ) fraternity; (mach, rr, telp) connection; (mil) liaison; **die V. verlieren mit** lose touch with; **e-e V. eingehen** (chem) form a compound; **er hat gute Verbindungen** he has good connections; **in V. mit** in conjunction with; **sich in V. setzen mit** get in touch with; **unmittelbare V.** (telp) direct call
Verbin'dungsbahn *f* connecting train
Verbin'dungsleitung *f* (telp) trunk line
Verbin'dungslinie *f* line of communication
Verbin'dungsoffizier *m* liaison officer
Verbin'dungspunkt *m*, **Verbin'dungsstelle** *f* joint, juncture
Verbin'dungsstück *n* joint, coupling
verbissen [fɛr'bɪsən] *adj* dogged, grim; (*Zorn*) suppressed; **v. sein in** (*dat*) stick doggedly to
Verbis'senheit *f* (-;) doggedness, grimness
verbitten [fɛr'bɪtən] §60 *ref*—**sich** [*dat*] **etw v.** not stand for s.th.
verbittern [fɛr'bɪtərn] *tr* embitter
Verbit'terung *f* (-;) bitterness
verblassen [fɛr'blasən] *intr* (SEIN) grow pale; (fig) fade
verblättern [fɛr'blɛtərn] *tr*—**die Seite v.** lose the page
Verbleib [fɛr'blaɪp] *m* (-[e]s;) whereabouts
verblei'ben §62 *intr* (SEIN) remain, be left; (**bei**) persist (in); **wir sind so verblieben, daß** we finally agreed that
verblei'chen §85 *intr* (SEIN) fade
verblen'den *tr* blind; dazzle; (*Mauer*) face; (*Fenster*) wall up
Verblen'dung *f* (-;-en) blindness, infatuation; (archit) facing

verblichen [fɛr'blɪçən] *adj* faded
verblödet [fɛr'blødət] *adj* idiotic
verblüffen [fɛr'blʏfən] *tr* dumbfound, flabbergast; bewilder, perplex
Verblüff'fung *f* (-;) bewilderment
verblü'hen *intr* (SEIN) wither; fade
verblümt [fɛr'blymt] *adj* euphemistic
verblu'ten *ref & intr* (SEIN) bleed to death
verbocken [fɛr'bɔkən] *tr* bungle
verboh'ren *ref*—**sich v. in** (*acc*) stick stubbornly to
verbohrt [fɛr'bort] *adj* stubborn; odd
verbolzen [fɛr'bɔltsən] *tr* bolt
verbor'gen *adj* secret; latent; hidden || *tr* lend out || **Verborgene** §5 *n*—**im Verborgenen** in secret, on the sly
Verbor'genheit *f* (-;) secrecy; concealment; seclusion
Verbot [fɛr'bot] *n* (-[e]s;-e) prohibition; (jur) injunction
verboten [fɛr'botən] *adj* forbidden; **Eintritt v.!** no admittance; **Plakatankleben v.!** post no bills!; **Stehenbleiben v.!** no loitering
verbrämen [fɛr'brɛmən] *tr* trim, edge; (fig) sugar-coat
verbrannt [fɛr'brant] *adj* burnt; torrid; **Politik der verbrannten Erde** scorched-earth policy
Verbrauch' *m* (-[e]s;) use, consumption
verbrau'chen *tr* use up, consume; waste; (*abnutzen*) wear out
Verbrau'cher *m* (-s;-) consumer; (*Benützer*) user; (*Kunde*) customer
Verbrau'chergenossenschaft *f* co-op
Verbrauchs'güter *pl* consumer goods
verbraucht' *adj* used up, consumed; worn out; (*Geld*) spent; (*Luft*) stale
verbre'chen §64 *tr* commit, do || **Verbrechen** *n* (-s;-) crime
Verbre'cher *m* (-s;-) criminal
Verbre'cheralbum *n* rogues' gallery
Verbre'cherin *f* (-;-nen) criminal
verbrecherisch [fɛr'breçərɪʃ] *adj* criminal
Verbre'cherkolonie *f* penal colony
verbreiten [fɛr'braɪtən] *tr* spread; (*Frieden, Licht*) shed || *ref* spread; **sich v. über** (*acc*) expatiate on
verbreitern [fɛr'braɪtərn] *tr & ref* widen, broaden
Verbrei'terung *f* (-;) widening, broadening
Verbrei'tung *f* (-;) spreading; dissemination; diffusion
verbren'nen §97 *tr* burn; scorch; (*bräunen*) tan; (*Leichen*) cremate || *ref* burn oneself; **sich** [*dat*] **die Finger v.** (& fig) burn one's fingers
Verbren'nung *f* (-;-en) burning, combustion; cremation; (*Brandwunde*) burn
Verbren'nungskraftmaschine *f*, **Verbren'nungsmotor** *m* internal combustion engine
Verbren'nungsraum *m* combustion chamber
verbrin'gen §65 *tr* spend, pass; (*wegbringen*) take away
verbrüdern [fɛr'brydərn] *ref* (**mit**) fraternize (with)

Verbrü′derung *f* (-;) fraternizing
verbrü′hen *tr* scald
verbu′chen *tr* book; **etw als Erfolg v.** chalk s.th. up as a success
Ver·bum ['vɛrbʊm] *n* (-s;-ba [ba]) verb
verbunden [fɛr'bʊndən] *adj* connected; **falsch v.!** sorry, wrong number!; **untereinander v.** interconnected; **zu Dank v.** obligated
verbünden [fɛr'bʏndən] *ref*—**sich mit j-m v.** ally oneself with s.o.
Verbun′denheit *f* (-;) connection, ties; solidarity, union
Verbündete [fɛr'bʏndətə] §5 *mf* ally
verbür′gen *tr* guarantee, vouch for ‖ *ref*—**sich v. für** vouch for
verbürgt [fɛr'bʏrkt] *adj* authenticated
verbüßen [fɛr'bysən] *tr* atone for, pay for; **seine Strafe v.** serve one's time
verchromen [fɛr'kromən] *tr* chrome-plate
Verchro′mung *f* (-;-en) chromeplating
Verdacht [fɛr'daxt] *m* (-[e]s;) suspicion; **in V. kommen** come under suspicion; **V. hegen gegen** have suspicions about; **V. schöpfen** get suspicious
verdächtig [fɛr'dɛçtɪç] *adj* suspicious; *(genit)* suspected (of)
verdächtigen [fɛr'dɛçtɪgən] *tr* cast suspicion on; *(genit)* suspect (of)
Verdäch′tigung *f* (-;-en) insinuation
verdammen [fɛr'damən] *tr* condemn; damn
Verdammnis [fɛr'damnɪs] *f* (-;) damnation, perdition
verdammt′ *adj* (sl) damn ‖ *interj* (sl) damn it!
verdamp′fen *tr & intr* (SEIN) evaporate
Verdamp′fung *f* (-;) evaporation
verdan′ken *tr*—**j-m etw v.** be indebted to s.o. for s.th.
verdarb [fɛr'darp] *pret* of **verderben**
verdattert [fɛr'datərt] *adj* (coll) shook up
verdauen [fɛr'dau·ən] *tr* digest
verdaulich [fɛr'daulɪç] *adj* digestible
Verdau′ung *f* (-;) digestion
Verdau′ungsbeschwerden *pl* **Verdau′-ungsstörung** *f* indigestion
Verdau′ungswerkzeug *n* digestive track
Verdeck [fɛr'dɛk] *n* (-[e]s;-e) hood *(of baby carriage)*; (aut) convertible top; (naut) deck
verdecken (verdek′ken) *tr* cover; hide
verden′ken §66 *tr*—**j-m etw v.** blame s.o. for s.th.
Verderb [fɛr'dɛrp] *m* (-[e]s;) ruin; decay
verderben [fɛr'dɛrbən] §149 *tr* spoil; ruin; *(Magen)* upset; *(verführen)* corrupt ‖ *intr* (SEIN) spoil, go bad; (fig) go to pot ‖ **Verderben** (-s;) ruin; **j-n ins V. stürzen** ruin s.o.
verderblich [fɛr'dɛrplɪç] *adj* ruinous; *(Lebensmittel)* perishable
Verderbnis [fɛr'dɛrpnɪs] *f* (-;) depravity
verderbt [fɛr'dɛrpt] *adj* depraved
Verderbt′heit *f* (-;) depravity
verdeutlichen [fɛr'dɔɪtlɪçən] *tr* make plain, explain

verdeutschen [fɛr'dɔɪt∫ən] *tr* translate into (or express in) German
verdich′ten *tr* condense, thicken ‖ *ref* condense; solidify; thicken; *(Nebel, Rauch)* grow thicker; *(Verdacht)* become stronger, grow
verdicken [fɛr'dɪkən] *tr & ref* thicken
verdie′nen *tr* deserve; *(Geld)* earn
Verdienst [fɛr'dinst] *m* (-es;-e) earnings; gain, profit ‖ *n* (-es;-e) merit; deserts; **es ist dein V., daß** it is owing to you that; **nach V.** deservedly; **nach V. behandelt werden** get one's due; **sich** [*dat*] **als** (or **zum**) **V. anrechnen** take credit for it; **V. um** services to
Verdienst′ausfall *m* loss of wages
verdienst′lich *adj* meritorious
Verdienst′spanne *f* margin of profit
verdienst′voll *adj* meritorious
verdient [fɛr'dint] *adj* —**sich um j-n v. machen** serve s.o. well
verdol′metschen *tr* translate orally; interpret
Verdol′metschung *f* (-;) oral translation; interpretation
verdonnern [fɛr'dɔnərn] *tr* (coll) condemn
verdop′peln *tr & ref* double
verdorben [fɛr'dɔrbən] *adj* spoiled; *(Luft)* foul; *(Magen)* upset; *(moralisch)* depraved
verdorren [fɛr'dɔrən] *intr* (SEIN) dry up, wither
verdrän′gen *tr* push aside, crowd out; dislodge; (phys) displace; (psychol) repress, inhibit
Verdrän′gung *f* (-;-en) (phys) displacement; (psychol) repression, inhibition
verdre′hen *tr* twist; *(Augen)* roll; *(Glied)* sprain; (fig) distort; **j-m den Kopf v.** make s.o. fall in love with one
verdreht′ *adj* twisted; (fig) distorted; (fig) *(verrückt)* cracked
verdreifachen [fɛr'draɪfaxən] *tr* triple
verdre′schen §67 *tr* (coll) spank
verdrießen [fɛr'drisən] §76 *tr* bother, annoy, get down; **laß es dich nicht v.!** don't let it get you down; **sich keine Mühe v. lassen** spare no pains ‖ *impers*—**es verdrießt mich, daß** it bothers me that
verdrießlich [fɛr'drislɪç] *adj* glum; tiresome; depressing; annoyed
verdroß [fɛr'drɔs] *pret* of **verdrießen**
verdro′ßen *adj* cross; *(mürrisch)* surly; *(lustlos)* listless
verdrucken (verdruk′ken) *tr* misprint
verdrücken (verdrük′ken) *tr* wrinkle; (coll) eat up, polish off ‖ *ref* (coll) sneak away
Ver·druß [fɛr'drʊs] *m* (-drusses; -drusse) annoyance, vexation; **j-m etw zum V. tun** do s.th. to spite s.o.
verduften [fɛr'dʊftən] *intr* (SEIN) lose its aroma; (coll) take off, scram
verdummen [fɛr'dʊmən] *tr* make stupid ‖ *intr* (SEIN) become stupid
verdunkeln [fɛr'dʊŋkəln] *tr* darken; obscure; *(Glanz)* dull; (fig) cloud; (astr) eclipse; (mil) black out ‖ *ref* darken; *(Himmel)* cloud over

Verdun'kelung *f* (-;-en) darkening; (astr) eclipse; (mil) blackout

verdünnen [fɛr'dʏnən] *tr* thin; dilute; (*Case*) rarefy

verdun'sten *intr* (SEIN) evaporate

Verdun'stung *f* (-;) evaporation

verdur'sten *intr* (SEIN) die of thirst

verdutzen [fɛr'dutsən] *tr* bewilder

veredeln [fɛr'edəln] *tr* ennoble; (*verfeinen*) refine; (*Rohstoff*) process; (*Boden*) enrich; (*Pflanze, Tier*) improve

Vere'delung *f* (-;) refinement; processing; enrichment; improvement

verehelichen [fɛr'e·əlɪçən] *ref* get married

verehren [fɛr'erən] *tr* revere; worship; (fig) adore; **j-m etw v.** present s.o. with s.th.

Vereh'rer –in §6 *mf* worshiper; (*Liebhaber*) admirer

verehrt [fɛr'ert] *adj*—**Sehr verehrte gnädige Frau!** Dear Madam; **Sehr verehrter Herr!** Dear Sir; **Verehrte Anwesende** (or **Gäste)!** Ladies and Gentlemen!

Vereh'rung *f* (-;) reverence, veneration; worship; adoration

vereiden [fɛr'aɪdən], **vereidigen** [fɛr'aɪdɪgən] *tr* swear in

Verein [fɛr'aɪn] *m* (-[e]s;-e) society

vereinbar [fɛr'aɪnbar] *adj* compatible

vereinbaren [fɛr'aɪnbarən] *tr* agree to, agree upon ‖ *ref*—**das läßt sich mit meinen Grundsätzen nicht v.** that is inconsistent with my principles

Verein'barkeit *f* (-;) compatibility

Verein'barung *f* (-;) agreement, arrangement; terms; **nur nach V.** by appointment only

vereinen [fɛr'aɪnən] *tr* unite, join

vereinfachen [fɛr'aɪnfaxən] *tr* simplify

Verein'fachung *f* (-;-en) simplification

vereinheitlichen [fɛr'aɪnhaɪtlɪçən] *tr* standardize

vereinigen [fɛr'aɪnɪgən] *tr* unite, join; (*verbinden*) combine; (*verschmelzen*) merge; (*versammeln*) assemble ‖ *ref* unite, join; (*Flüsse*) meet; **sich v. mit** team up with; **sich v. lassen mit** be compatible with, square with

Verei'nigten Staa'ten *pl* United States

Verein'igung *f* (-;-en) union; combination; society, association

vereinnahmen [fɛr'aɪnnamən] *tr* take in

vereinsamen [fɛr'aɪnzamən] *intr* (SEIN) become lonely; become isolated

Verein'samung *f* (-;) loneliness; isolation

Vereins'meier –in §6 *mf* (coll) joiner

vereinzeln [fɛr'aɪntsəln] *tr* isolate

verein'zelt *adj* isolated; sporadic

vereisen [fɛr'aɪsən] *tr* (surg) freeze ‖ *intr* (SEIN) become covered with ice; (aer) ice up

vereiteln [fɛr'aɪtəln] *tr* frustrate; baffle

verekeln [fɛr'ɛkəln] *tr*—**j-m etw v.** spoil s.th. for s.o.

veren'den *intr* (SEIN) die

verengen [fɛr'ɛŋən] *tr & ref* narrow

verer'ben *tr* bequeath, leave; (*über-*

mitteln) hand down; (*Krankheit*) transmit ‖ *ref* run in the family

Verer'bung *f* (-;-en) inheritance; transmission; heredity

Verer'bungslehre *f* genetics

verewigen [fɛr'evɪgən] *tr* perpetuate

verewigt [fɛr'evɪçt] *adj* late, deceased

verfah'ren *adj* bungled, messed up ‖ §71 *tr* bungle; (*Geld, Zeit*) spend (*on travel*) ‖ *ref* lose one's way, take a track ‖ *intr* (SEIN) proceed; act ‖ wrong turn; (fig) be on the wrong

Verfahren *n* (-s;-) procedure, method; system; (chem) process; (jur) proceedings, case

Verfall *m* (-[e]s;) deterioration, decay; decline, downfall; (*Fristablauf*) expiration; (*von Wechseln*) maturity; **in V. geraten** become dilapidated

verfal'len *adj* delapidated; **e-m Rauschgift v. sein** be addicted to a drug ‖ §72 *intr* (SEIN) decay, go to ruin, decline; (*ablaufen*) expire; (*Kranker*) waste away; (*Recht*) lapse; (*Pfand*) be forfeited; (*Wechsel*) mature

Verfall'tag *m* due date; date of maturity

verfäl'schen *tr* falsify; (*Geld*) counterfeit; (*Wein*) adulterate; (*Urkunde*) forge

Verfäl'schung *f* (-;-en) falsification; forging; adulteration

verfan'gen §73 *ref* become entangled ‖ *intr* (bei) have an effect (on)

verfänglich [fɛr'fɛŋlɪç] *adj* (*Frage*) loaded; (*Situation*) awkward

verfär'ben *ref* change color

verfas'sen *tr* compose, write

Verfas'ser –in §6 *mf* author

Verfas'sung *f* (-;-en) constitution; (*Zustand*) condition; frame of mind, mood

verfas'sungsgemäß, verfas'sungsmäßig *adj* constitutional

verfas'sungswidrig *adj* unconstitutional

verfau'len *intr* (SEIN) rot

verfech'ten §74 *tr* defend, stand up for

Verfech'ter *m* (-s;-) champion

verfeh'len *tr* (*Abzweigung, Ziel, Zug*) miss; (*Wirkung*) fail to achieve, not have; **ich werde nicht v. zu** (*inf*) I will not fail to (*inf*) ‖ *recip*—**wir haben uns verfehlt** we missed each other

verfehlt [fɛr'felt] *adj* wrong

Verfeh'lung *f* (-;-en) offense; mistake

verfeinden [fɛr'faɪndən] *recip* become enemies

verfeinern [fɛr'faɪnərn] *tr* refine, improve ‖ *ref* become refined, improve

verfertigen [fɛr'fɛrtɪgən] *tr* manufacture, make

Verfer'tigung *f* (-;) manufacture

verfilmen [fɛr'fɪlmən] *tr* adapt to the screen, make into a movie

Verfil'mung *f* (-;-en) film version

verfilzen [fɛr'fɪltsən] *ref* get tangled

verfinstern [fɛr'fɪnstərn] *ref* get dark

verflachen [fɛr'flaxən] *tr* flatten ‖ *ref & intr* (SEIN) flatten out

verflech'ten §74 *tr* interweave; (fig) implicate, involve

verflie'gen §57 *ref* (aer) lose one's

bearings || *intr* (SEIN) fly away; (*Zeit*) fly; evaporate; (fig) vanish
verflie'ßen §76 *intr* (SEIN) flow off; (*Frist*) run out, expire; (*Farben*) blend; (*Begriffe, Grenzen*) overlap
verflixt [fɛr'flɪkst] *adj* (sl) darn
verflossen [fɛr'flɔsən] *adj* past; former
verflu'chen *tr* curse, damn
verflucht' *adj* (sl) damn || *interj* (sl) damn it!
verflüchtigen [fɛr'flʏçtɪgən] *tr* volatilize || *ref* evaporate; (fig) disappear
verflüssigen [fɛr'flʏsɪgən] *tr* & *ref* liquefy
Verfolg [fɛr'fɔlk] *m* (-s;) course; **im V.** (*genit*) in pursuance of
verfol'gen *tr* pursue; follow up; persecute; haunt; (hunt) track; (jur) prosecute; **j-n steckbrieflich v.** send out a warrant for the arrest of s.o.
Verfol'ger –in §6 *mf* pursuer; persecutor
Verfol'gung *f* (-;-en) pursuit; persecution; (jur) prosecution
Verfol'gungswahn *m*, **Verfol'gungswahnsinn** *m* persecution complex
verfrachten [fɛr'fraxtən] *tr* ship; (coll) bundle off
Verfrach'ter –in §6 *mf* shipper
verfrühen [fɛr'fry·ən] *ref* be too early
verfügbar [fɛr'fykbɑr] *adj* available, at one's disposal
verfü'gen *tr* decree, order || *ref*—**sich v. nach** betake oneself to || *intr*—**v. über** (*acc*) have at one's disposal, have control over
Verfü'gung *f* (-;-en) decree, order; disposal; **einstweilige V.** (jur) injunction; **j-m zur V. stehen** be at s.o.'s disposal; **j-m zur V. stellen** put at s.o.'s disposal; **letztwillige V.** last will and testament
verfüh'ren *tr* mislead; (*zum Irrtum*) lead; (*verlocken*) seduce
Verfüh'rer –in §6 *mf* seducer
verführerisch [fɛr'fyrərɪʃ] *adj* seductive, tempting
Verfüh'rung *f* (-;-en) seduction
vergaffen [fɛr'gafən] *ref* (coll) (**in** *acc*) fall in love (with)
vergammeln [fɛr'gaməln] *intr* (SEIN) (coll) go to the dogs
vergangen [fɛr'gaŋən] *adj* past; (*Schönheit*) faded
Vergan'genheit *f* (-;) past; background; (gram) past tense
vergänglich [fɛr'gɛŋlɪç] *adj* transitory
vergasen [fɛr'gazən] *tr* gas
Verga'ser *m* (-s;-) carburetor
vergaß [fɛr'gas] *pret* of **vergessen**
verge'ben §80 *tr* forgive (*s.th.*); give away; (*Chance*) miss, pass up; (*Amt, freie Stelle*) fill; (*Auftrag*) place; (*Karten*) misdeal; (*verleihen*) confer; **v. sein** have a previous engagement; be engaged (*to a man*) || *ref*—**sich** [*dat*] **etw v.** compromise on s.th. || *intr* (*dat*) forgive (*s.o.*)
verge'bens [fɛr'gebəns] *adv* in vain
vergeb'lich [fɛr'geplɪç] *adj* vain, futile
Verge'bung *f* (-;) forgiveness; bestowal
vergegenwärtigen [fɛr'gegənvɛrtɪgən] *ref*—**sich** [*dat*] **etw. v.** visualize s.th.

verge'hen §82 *ref*—**sich an j-m v.** offend s.o.; (*sexuell*) violate s.o. || *intr* (SEIN) pass, go away; fade || **Vergehen** *n* (-s;-) offense, misdemeanor
vergel'ten §83 *tr* requite; **vergelt's Gott!** (coll) thank you!
Vergel'tung *f* (-;) repayment; retaliation, reprisal
Vergel'tungswaffe *f* V-1 or V-2
vergesellschaften [fɛrgə'zɛlʃaftən] *tr* socialize; nationalize
vergessen [fɛr'gɛsən] §70 *tr* forget
Verges'senheit *f* (-;)—**in V. geraten** fall (or sink) into oblivion
vergeßlich [fɛr'geslɪç] *adj* forceful
Vergeß'lichkeit *f* (-;) forgetfulness
vergeuden [fɛr'gɔɪdən] *tr* waste
Vergeu'dung *f* (-;) waste, squandering
vergewaltigen [fɛrgə'valtɪgən] *tr* do violence to; (*Mädchen*) rape
Vergewal'tigung *f* (-;-en) rape
vergewerkschaften [fɛrgə'vɛrkʃaftən] *tr* unionize
vergewissern [fɛrgə'vɪsərn] *ref* (*genit*) make sure of, ascertain
vergie'ßen §76 *tr* spill; (*Tränen*) shed
vergiften [fɛr'gɪftən] *tr* (& fig) poison; (*verseuchen*) contaminate || *ref* take poison
Vergif'tung *f* (-;-en) poisoning; contamination
vergipsen [fɛr'gɪpsən] *tr* plaster
Vergißmeinnicht [fɛr'gɪsmaɪnnɪçt] *n* (-[e]s;-e) forget-me-not
vergittern [fɛr'gɪtərn] *tr* bar up
Vergleich [fɛr'glaɪç] *m* (-[e]s;-e) comparison; (*Verständigung*) agreement; (*Ausgleich*) settlement; **e–n V. anstellen zwischen** make a comparison between; **e–n V. treffen** reach a settlement, come to an agreement
vergleichbar [fɛr'glaɪçbɑr] *adj* comparable
verglei'chen [fɛr'glaɪçən] §85 *tr* (**mit**) compare (with, to) || *ref* (**mit**) come to an agreement (with)
Vergleichs'grundlage *f* basis for comparison
vergleichs'weise *adv* by way of comparison
Verglei'chung *f* (-;-en) comparison; matching; contrasting
verglü'hen *intr* (SEIN) cease to glow
vergnügen [fɛr'gnygən] *tr* amuse, delight || *ref* enjoy oneself, amuse oneself || **Vergnügen** *n* (-s;-) delight, pleasure; **mit V.** with pleasure; **V. finden an** (*dat*) take delight in; **viel V.!** (coll) have fun!; **zum V.** for fun
vergnügt [fɛr'gnykt] *adj* cheerful, gay; (*über acc*) delighted (with)
Vergnü'gung *f* (-;-en) pleasure, amusement
Vergnü'gungspark *m* amusement park
Vergnü'gungsreise *f* pleasure trip
Vergnü'gungssteuer *f* entertainment tax
vergnü'gungssüchtig *adj* pleasure-loving
vergolden [fɛr'gɔldən] *tr* gild
Vergol'dung *f* (-;-en) gilding
vergönnen [fɛr'gœnən] *tr* not begrudge
vergöttern [fɛr'gœtərn] *tr* deify; (fig) idolize
vergra'ben §87 *tr* (& fig) bury

vergrämen [fɛr'grɛmən] *tr* annoy, anger
vergrämt [fɛr'grɛmt] *adj* haggard
vergrei'fen §88 *ref* (mus) hit the wrong note; **sich v. an** (*dat*) lay violent hands on; (*fremdem Gut*) encroach on; (*Geld*) misappropriate; (*Mädchen*) assault; **sich im Ausdruck v.** express oneself poorly
vergreisen [fɛr'graɪzən] *intr* (SEIN) age; become senile
vergriffen [fɛr'grɪfən] *adj* sold out; (*Buch*) out of print
vergröbern [fɛr'grøbərn] *tr* roughen || *ref* become coarser
vergrößern [fɛr'grøsərn] *tr* enlarge; increase; (*ausdehnen*) expand; (opt) magnify || *ref* become larger
Vergrö'ßerung *f* (–;–en) enlargement; increase; expansion; (opt) magnification
Vergrö'ßerungsapparat *m* (phot) enlarger
Vergrö'ßerungsglas *m* magnifying glass
Vergünstigung [fɛr'gʏnstɪguŋ] *f* (–; –en) privilege; (*bevorzugte Behandlung*) preferential treatment
vergüten [fɛr'gytən] *tr* make good; (*Stahl*) temper; **j-m etw v.** reimburse (or compensate) s.o. for s.th.
Vergü'tung *f* (–;–en) reimbursement, compensation; tempering
verhaften [fɛr'haftən] *tr* apprehend
Verhaf'tung *f* (–;–en) apprehension
verhal'ten *adj* (*Atem*) bated; (*Stimme*) low || §90 *tr* hold back; (*Atem*) hold; (*Lachen*) suppress; (*Stimme*) keep down; **den Schritt v.** slow down; (*stehenbleiben*) stop || *ref* behave, act; be; **A verhält sich zu B wie X zu Y** A is to B as X is to Y; **sich anders v.** be different; **sich ruhig v.** keep quiet || *impers ref*—**wenn es sich so verhält** if that's the case || **Verhalten** *n* (–s;) conduct, behavior; attitude
Verhältnis [fɛr'hɛltnɪs] *n* (–ses;–se) proportion, ratio; (*Beziehung*) relation; (*Liebes–*) love affair; **aus kleinen Verhältnissen** of humble birth; **bei sonst gleichen Verhältnissen** other things being equal; **das steht in keinem V. zu** that is all out of proportion to; **Verhältnisse** circumstances, conditions; matters; means
verhält'nismäßig *adj* proportionate || *adv* relatively, comparatively
Verhält'nismaßregeln *pl* instructions
Verhält'niswahl *f* proportional representation
verhält'niswidrig *adj* disproportionate
Verhält'niswort *n* (–[e]s;–̈er) preposition
verhan'deln *tr* discuss; (*Waren*) sell || *intr* negotiate; argue; (*beraten*) confer; (jur) plead a case; **gegen j-n wegen etw v.** (jur) try s.o. for s.th.
Verhand'lung *f* (–;–en) negotiation; discussion; proceedings, trial
verhangen [fɛr'haŋən] *adj* overcast
verhän'gen *tr* (*Fenster*) put curtains on; (*Strafe*) impose; (*Untersuchung*) order; (*Belagerungszustand*) pro-

claim; **mit verhängtem Zügel** at full speed
Verhängnis [fɛr'hɛŋnɪs] *n* (–ses;–se) destiny, fate; (*Unglück*) disaster
verhäng'nisvoll *adj* fateful; disastrous
verhärmt [fɛr'hɛrmt] *adj* haggard
verharren [fɛr'harən] *intr* (HABEN & SEIN) remain; (**auf** *dat*, **in** *dat*, **bei**) stick (to)
verhärten [fɛr'hɛrtən] *tr* & *ref* harden
verhaßt [fɛr'hast] *adj* hated, hateful
verhätscheln [fɛr'hɛtʃəln] *tr* pamper
Verhau [fɛr'haʊ] *m* (–[e]s;–e) barbwire entanglement
verhau'en §93 *tr* lick, beat up; (*Kind*) spank; (*Auftrag, Ball, usw.*) muff || *ref* make a blunder
verheddern [fɛr'hɛdərn] *ref* get tangled up
verheeren [fɛr'herən] *tr* devastate
verhee'rend *adj* terrible; (coll) awful
Verhee'rung *f* (–;) devastation
verhehlen [fɛr'helən] *tr* conceal
verhei'len *intr* (SEIN) heal up
verheimlichen [fɛr'haɪmlɪçən] *tr* keep secret, conceal
Verheim'lichung *f* (–;) concealment
verhei'raten *tr* marry; (*Tocher*) give away || *ref* (**mit**) get married (to)
Verhei'ratung *f* (–;) marriage
verhei'ßen §95 *tr* promise
Verhei'ßung *f* (–;–en) promise
verhei'ßungsvoll *adj* promising
verhel'fen §96 *intr*—**j-m zu etw v.** help s.o. to acquire s.th.
verherrlichen [fɛr'hɛrlɪçən] *tr* glorify
Verherr'lichung *f* (–;) glorification
verhet'zen *tr* instigate
verhexen [fɛr'hɛksən] *tr* bewitch, hex
verhimmeln [fɛr'hɪməln] *tr* praise to the skies; (*Schauspieler*) idolize
verhin'dern *tr* prevent
Verhin'derung *f* (–;) prevention; **im Falle seiner V.** in case he's unavailable
verhohlen [fɛr'holən] *adj* hidden
verhöh'nen *tr* jeer at; make fun of
Verhöh'nung *f* (–;) jeering; ridicule
Verhör [fɛr'hør] *n* (–s;–e) interrogation, questioning, hearing
verhö'ren *tr* interrogate, question || *ref* hear wrong
verhudeln [fɛr'hudəln] *tr* (coll) bungle
verhüllen [fɛr'hʏlən] *tr* cover, veil; wrap up; disguise
Verhül'lung *f* (–;–en) cover; disguise
verhun'gern *intr* (SEIN) starve to death
verhunzen [fɛr'huntsən] *tr* (coll) botch
verhü'ten *tr* prevent, avert
verinnerlicht [fɛr'ɪnərlɪçt] *adj* introspective
verir'ren *ref* lose one's way; (*Augen, Blick*) wander; (*fig*) make a mistake
verirrt [fɛr'ɪrt] *adj* stray
verja'gen *tr* chase away
verjähren [fɛr'jerən] *intr* (SEIN) fall under the statute of limitations
verjubeln [fɛr'jubəln] *tr* squander
verjüngen [fɛr'jʏŋən] *tr* rejuvenate; reduce in scale; taper || *ref* be rejuvenated; taper, narrow
Verjün'gung *f* (–;) rejuvenation; tapering; scaling down

verkatert [fɛr'kɑtərt] *adj* suffering from a hangover

Verkauf' *m* (-[e]s;ᵉe) sale

verkau'fen *tr* sell

Verkäu'fer -in §6 *mf* seller; salesclerk; vendor ‖ *m* salesman ‖ *f* salesgirl, saleswoman

verkäuf'lich *adj* salable

Verkaufs'anzeige *f* for-sale ad

Verkaufs'automat *m* vending machine

Verkaufs'leiter -in §6 *mf* sales manager

Verkaufs'schlager *m* good seller

Verkaufs'steigerung *f* sales promotion

Verkaufs'vertrag *m* agreement of sale

Verkehr [fɛr'ker] *m* (-s;) traffic; commerce; company, association; (*sexuell*) intercourse; (aer, rr) service; (fin) circulation

verkeh'ren *tr* reverse, invert; turn upside down; convert, change; (*Sinn, Worte*) twist ‖ *intr* (*Fahrzeug*) run, run regularly; **mit j-m geschlechtlich v.** have intercourse with s.o.; **mit j-m v.** associate with s.o.

Verkehrs'ader *f* main artery

Verkehrs'ampel *f* traffic light

Verkehrs'andrang *m* heavy traffic

Verkehrs'betrieb *m* public transportation company

Verkehrs'delikt *n* traffic violation

Verkehrs'flugzeug *n* airliner

Verkehrs'insel *f* traffic island

Verkehrs'mittel *n* means of transportation

Verkehrs'ordnungen *pl* traffic regulations

Verkehrs'polizist -in §7 *mf* traffic cop

verkehrs'reich *adj* crowded, congested

verkehrs'stark *adj* busy

Verkehrs'stockung *f*, **Verkehrs'störung** *f* traffic jam

Verkehrs'unfall *m* traffic accident

Verkehrs'unternehmen *n* transportation company

Verkehrs'vorschrift *f* traffic regulation

Verkehrs'wesen *n* traffic, transportation

Verkehrs'zeichen *n* traffic sign

verkehrt [fɛr'kert] *adj* reversed; upside down; inside out; wrong

verken'nen §97 *tr* misunderstand; (*Person*) misjudge, mistake

verketten [fɛr'ketən] *tr* chain together; (fig) link

Verket'tung *f* (-;) chaining; (fig) concatenation; (fig) coincidence

verkit'ten *tr* cement; putty; seal, bond

verkla'gen *tr* accuse; (jur) sue

Verklagte [fɛr'klɑktə] §5 *mf* defendant

verklat'schen *tr* (coll) slander; (educ) squeal on

verkle'ben *tr* glue, cement; **v. mit** cover with

verklei'den *tr* disguise, dress up; (*täfeln*) panel; line, face; (mil) camouflage

Verklei'dung *f* (-;-en) disguise; paneling; lining, facing; (mil) camouflage

verkleinern [fɛr'klaɪnərn] *tr* lessen, diminish; (fig) disparage; (math) reduce; **maßstäblich v.** scale down

Verklei'nerung *f* (-;-en) diminution, reduction; (fig) detraction

Verklei'nerungsform *f* diminutive

verklin'gen §142 *intr* (SEIN) die away

verkloppen [fɛr'klɔpən] *tr* (coll) beat up

verknacken [fɛr'knakən] *tr* (coll) sentence

verknallt [fɛr'knalt] *adj*—**in j-n v. sein** (coll) have a crush on s.o.

verknappen [fɛr'knapən] *intr* (SEIN) run short, run low

Verknap'pung *f* (-;) shortage

verknei'fen §88 *ref*—**sich** [*dat*] **etw v.** deny oneself s.th.

verkniffen [fɛr'knɪfən] *adj* wry

verknip'sen *tr* (*Film*) waste

verknöchern [fɛr'knœçərn] *intr* (SEIN) ossify; (*Glieder*) become stiff

verknöchert [fɛr'knœçərt] *adj* pedantic; (*Junggeselle*) inveterate

verknoten [fɛr'knotən] *tr* snarl, tie up

verknüp'fen *tr* tie together; (fig) connect, combine, relate

verknusen [fɛr'knuzən] *tr* (coll) stand

verkohlen [fɛr'kolən] *tr* carbonize; char; **j-n v.** (coll) pull s.o.'s leg

verkom'men *adj* decayed; degenerate; (*Gebäude*) squalid ‖ §99 *intr* (SEIN) decay, spoil; (fig) go to the dogs; **v. zu** degenerate into

Verkom'menheit *f* (-;) depravity

verkop'peln *tr* couple; (*Interessen*) (com) consolidate

verkorken [fɛr'kɔrkən] *tr* cork up

verkorksen [fɛr'kɔrksən] *tr* (coll) bungle ‖ *ref*—**sich** [*dat*] **den Magen v.** (coll) upset one's stomach

verkörpern [fɛr'kœrpərn] *tr* embody, personify; (*Rolle*) play

Verkör'perung *f* (-;-en) embodiment, incarnation

verkra'chen *ref*—**sich mit j-m v.** have an argument with s.o. ‖ *intr* (SEIN) (coll) go bankrupt

verkrampft [fɛr'krampft] *adj* cramped

verkrie'chen §102 *ref* hide; (& fig) crawl into a hole; **neben ihm kannst du dich v.!** you're no match for him!

verkrümeln [fɛr'kryməln] *tr* crumble ‖ *ref* (fig) disappear

verkrüm'men *tr* & *ref* bend

Verkrüm'mung *f* (-;) bend, crookedness; curvature

verkrüppeln [fɛr'krypəln] *tr* cripple ‖ *intr* (SEIN) become crippled; (*verkümmern*) become stunted

verkrustet [fɛr'krustət] *adj* caked

verküh'len *ref* catch a cold

verküm'mern *intr* (SEIN) become stunted; (pathol) atrophy

Verküm'merung *f* (-;) atrophy

verkünden [fɛr'kʏndən], **verkündigen** [fɛr'kʏndɪgən] *tr* announce, proclaim; (*Urteil*) pronounce

Verkün'digung *f* (-;-en), **Verkün'dung** *f* (-;-en) announcement, proclamation; pronouncement; **Mariä Verkündigung** (feast of the) Annunciation

verkup'peln *tr* couple; (*Mädchen, Mann*) procure; (*Tochter*) sell into prostitution

verkür'zen *tr* shorten; abridge; (*beschränken*) curtail; (*Zeit*) pass

Verkür'zung *f* (−;−en) shortening; abridgement; curtailment

verla'chen *tr* laugh at

verla'den §103 *tr* load, ship

Verlag [fer'lɑk] *m* (−[e]s;−e) publisher; **im V. von** published by

verla'gern *tr* shift; (*aus Sicherheitsgründen*) evacuate || *ref* shift

Verla'gerung *f* (−;−en) shift, shifting; evacuation

Verlags'anstalt *f* publisher

Verlags'buchhandlung *f* publisher and dealer

Verlags'recht *n* copyright

verlangen [fer'laŋən] *tr* demand, require; want, ask || *intr*—**v. nach** ask for; long for || **Verlangen** *n* (−s;) demand; request; wish; claim; (*Sehnsucht*) longing, yearning; **auf V.** upon demand, upon request

verlängern [fer'lɛŋərn] *tr* lengthen; prolong, extend; **seinen Paß v. lassen** have one's passport renewed

Verlän'gerung *f* (−;−en) lengthening; prolongation, extension; (sport) overtime

Verlän'gerungsschnur *f* extension cord

verlangsamen [fer'laŋzamən] *tr* slow down

verläppern [fer'lɛpərn] *tr* (coll) fritter away

Ver·laß [fer'las] *m* (−lasses;) reliance; **es ist kein V. auf ihn** you can't rely on him

verlas'sen *adj* abandoned, deserted; lonesome || §104 *tr* leave; forsake, desert || *ref*—**sich v. auf** (*acc*) rely on

Verlas'senheit *f* (−;) loneliness

verläßlich [fer'lɛslɪç] *adj* reliable

verlästern [fer'lɛstərn] *tr* slander

Verlä'sterung *f* (−;−en) slander

Verlaub [fer'laup] *m*—**mit V.** with your permission; **mit V. zu sagen** if I may say so

Verlauf' *m* (−[e]s;) course; **e−n guten V. haben** turn out well; **nach V. von** after a lapse of

verlau'fen §105 *intr* (SEIN) (*Zeit*) pass, lapse; (*ablaufen*) turn out, come off; (*vorgehen*) proceed, run || *ref* lose one's way; (*Wasser*) run off; (*Menschenmenge*) disperse

verlau'ten *intr* (SEIN) become known, be reported; **kein Wort davon v. lassen** not breathe a word about it; **wie verlautet** as reported || *impers*—**es verlautet** it is reported

verle'ben *tr* spend, pass

verlebt [fer'lept] *adj* haggard

verle'gen *adj* embarrassed; confused; **v. um** (*e−e Antwort*) at a loss for; (*Geld*) short of || *tr* move, shift; transfer; misplace; (*Buch*) publish; (*Geleise, Kabel, Rohre*) lay; (*sperren*) block; (*vertagen*) postpone || *ref*—**sich v. auf** (*acc*) apply onself to; devote oneself to; resort to

Verle'genheit *f* (−;) embarrassment; difficulties; predicament; **in V. bringen** embarrass

Verle'ger *m* (−s;−) publisher

Verle'gung *f* (−;−en) move, shift; transfer; postponement; (*von Kabeln, usw.*) laying

verlei'den *tr* spoil, take the joy out of

Verleih [fer'laɪ] *m* (−s;−e) rental service

verlei'hen §81 *tr* lend out, loan; rent out; (*Gunst*) grant; (*Titel*) confer; (*Auszeichnung*) award

Verlei'her −**in** §6 *mf* lender; grantor; (*von Filmen*) distributor

Verlei'hung *f* (−;−en) lending out; rental; grant; bestowal

verlei'nen *tr* mislead; (*zur Sünde, zum Trunk*) lead; (jur) suborn

verler'nen *tr* unlearn, forget

verle'sen §107 *tr* read out; (*Namen*) read off; (*Salat*) clean; (*Gemüse*) sort out || *ref* misread

verletzen [fer'lɛtsən] *tr* (& fig) injure, hurt; (*kränken*) offend; (*Gesetz*) break; (*Recht*) violate

verlet'zend *adj* offensive

Verletzte [fer'lɛtstə] §5 *mf* injured party

Verlet'zung *f* (−;−en) injury; offense; (*e−s Gesetzes*) breaking; (*e−s Rechtes*) violation

verleug'nen *tr* deny; (*Kind*) disown; (*Glauben*) renounce || *ref*—**sich selbst v.** act contrary to one's nature; **sich vor Besuchern v. lassen** refuse to see visitors

Verleug'nung *f* (−;−en) denial; renunciation; disavowal

verleumden [fer'lɔɪmdən] *tr* slander

verleumderisch [fer'lɔɪmdərɪʃ] *adj* slanderous, libelous

Verleum'dung *f* (−;−en) slander

verlie'ben *ref*—**sich in j−n v.** fall in love with s.o.

verliebt [fer'lipt] *adj* in love

verlieren [fer'lirən] §77 *tr* lose || *ref* lose one's way; disappear; disperse

Verlies [fer'lis] *n* (−es;−e) dungeon

verlo'ben *ref* (**mit**) become engaged (to)

Verlöbnis [fer'løpnɪs] *n* (−ses;−se) engagement

Verlobte [fer'loptə] §5 *m* fiancé; **die Verlobten** the engaged couple || *f* fiancée

Verlo'bung *f* (−;−en) engagement

verlocken (**verlok'ken**) *tr* lure, tempt; (*verführen*) seduce

verlockend (**verlok'kend**) *adj* tempting

Verlockung (**Verlok'kung**) *f* (−;−en) allurement, temptation

verlogen [fer'logən] *adj* dishonest

verloh'nen *impers ref*—**es verlo̊nt sich nicht** it doesn't pay || *impers*—**es verlohnt der Mühe nicht** it is not worth the trouble

verlor [fer'lor] *pret* of **verlieren**

verloren [fer'lorən] *pp* of **verlieren** || *adj* lost; (*hilflos*) forlorn; (*Ei*) poached; **der verlorene Sohn** the prodigal son

verlo'rengeben §80 *tr* give up for lost

verlo'rengehen §82 *intr* (SEIN) be lost

verlö'schen §110 *tr* extinguish; (*Schrift*) erase || *intr* (SEIN) (*Licht, Kerze*) go out; (*Zorn*) cease

verlo'sen *tr* raffle off, draw lots for
verlö'ten *tr* solder; **e–n v.** (coll) belt one down
verlottern [fɛr'lɔtərn] *intr* (coll) go to the dogs
verlumpen [fɛr'lυmpən] *tr* (coll) blow, squander ‖ *intr* (coll) go to the dogs
Verlust [fɛr'lυst] *m* (-[e]s;-e) loss; **in V. geraten** get lost; **Verluste** (mil) casualties
Verlust'liste *f* (mil) casualty list
verma'chen *tr* bequeath, leave
Vermächtnis [fɛr'mɛçtnɪs] *n* (-ses;-se) bequest, legacy
vermählen [fɛr'mɛlən] *tr* marry ‖ *ref* (mit) get married (to)
Vermäh'lung *f* (-;-en) marriage, wedding
vermah'nen *tr* admonish, warn
Vermah'nung *f* (-;-en) admonition
vermaledeien [fɛrmalɛ'daɪ·ən] *tr* curse
vermanschen [fɛr'manʃən] *tr* (coll) make a mess of
vermasseln [fɛr'masəln] *tr* (coll) bungle, muff
vermassen [fɛr'masən] *intr* (SEIN) lose one's individuality
vermauern [fɛr'maυ·ərn] *tr* wall up
vermehren [fɛr'merən] *tr & ref* increase; *(an Zahl)* multiply; **vermehrte Auflage** enlarged edition
vermei'den *tr* avoid
vermeidlich [fɛr'maɪtlɪç] *adj* avoidable
Vermei'dung *f* (-;) avoidance
vermei'nen *tr* suppose; presume, allege
vermeintlich [fɛr'maɪntlɪç] *adj* supposed, alleged; *(erdacht)* imaginary
vermel'den *tr* (poet) announce
vermen'gen *tr* mix, mingle; confound ‖ *ref* (mit) meddle (with)
Vermerk [fɛr'mɛrk] *m* (-[e]s;-e) note
vermer'ken *tr* note, record
vermes'sen *adj* daring, bold ‖ §70 *tr* measure; *(Land)* survey ‖ *ref* measure wrong; **sich v. zu** *(inf)* have the nerve to *(inf)*
Vermes'sung *f* (-;-en) surveying
vermie'ten *tr* rent out; lease out
Vermie'ter –in §6 *mf* (jur) lessor ‖ *m* landlord ‖ *f* landlady
vermindern [fɛr'mɪndərn] *tr* diminish, lessen; *(beschränken)* reduce, cut ‖ *ref* diminish, decrease
Vermin'derung *f* (-;-en) diminution, decrease; reduction, cut
verminen [fɛr'minən] *tr* (mil) mine
vermi'schen *tr & ref* mix
Vermi'schung *f* (-;-en) mixture
vermissen [fɛr'mɪsən] *tr* miss
vermißt [fɛr'mɪst] *adj* (mil) missing in action ‖ **Vermißte** §5 *mf* missing person
vermitteln [fɛr'mɪtəln] *tr* negotiate; arrange, bring about; *(beschaffen)* get, procure ‖ *intr* mediate; intercede
vermittels [fɛr'mɪtəls] *prep* (genit) by means of, through
Vermitt'ler –in §6 *mf* mediator, go-between; (com) agent
Vermitt'lung *f* (-;-en) negotiation; mediation; procuring, providing; intercession; *(Mittel)* means; agency;

brokerage; (telp) exchange; **durch gütige V.** *(genit)* through the good offices of
Vermitt'lungsamt *n* (telp) exchange
Vermitt'lungsgebühr *f*, **Vermitt'lungsprovision** *f* commission; brokerage
vermo'dern *intr* (SEIN) rot, decay
vermöge [fɛr'mø̜gə] *prep* (genit) by virtue of
vermö'gen §114 *tr* be able to do; **j–n v. zu** *(inf)* induce s.o. to *(inf)*; **sie vermag bei ihm viel** (or **wenig**) she has great (or little) influence with him; **v. zu** *(inf)* be able to *(inf)*, have the power to *(inf)* ‖ **Vermögen** *n* (-s;-) ability; capacity, power; fortune, means; property; (fin) capital, assets; **nach bestem V.** to the best of one's ability
vermö'gend *adj* well-to-do, well-off
Vermö'genslage *f* financial situation
Vermö'genssteuer *f* property tax
vermorscht [fɛr'mɔrʃt] *adj* rotten
vermottet [fɛr'mɔtət] *adj* moth-eaten
vermummen [fɛr'mυmən] *tr* disguise ‖ *ref* disguise oneself
vermuten [fɛr'mutən] *tr* suppose, presume
vermutlich [fɛr'mutlɪç] *adj* presumable ‖ *adv* presumably, I suppose
Vermu'tung *f* (-;-en) guess, conjecture
vernachlässigen [fɛr'naxlɛsɪgən] *tr* neglect
Vernach'lässigung *f* (-;) neglect
verna'geln *tr* nail up; board up
vernä'hen *tr* sew up
vernarben [fɛr'narbən] *intr* (SEIN) heal up
vernarren [fɛr'narən] *ref*—**sich v. in** *(acc)* be crazy about, be stuck on
verna'schen *tr* spend on sweets; *(Mädchen)* make love to
vernebeln [fɛr'nebəln] *tr* (mil) screen with smoke; (fig) hide, cover over
vernehmbar [fɛr'nembar] *adj* perceptible
verneh'men §116 *tr* perceive; *(erfahren)* hear, learn; (jur) question; **sich v. lassen** be heard, express an opinion ‖ **Vernehmen** *n* (-s;-)—**dem V. nach** reportedly, according to the report
vernehmlich [fɛr'nemlɪç] *adj* perceptible, audible; distinct
Verneh'mung *f* (-;-en) interrogation
vernei'gen *ref* bow; curtsy
Vernei'gung *f* (-;-en) bow; curtsy
verneinen [fɛr'naɪnən] *tr* say no to; reject, refuse; disavow
vernei'nend *adj* negative
Vernei'nung *f* (-;-en) negation; denial
vernichten [fɛr'nɪçtən] *tr* destroy, annihilate; *(Hoffnung)* dash
vernich'tend *adj* *(Kritik)* scathing; *(Niederlage)* crushing
Vernich'tung *f* (-;) destruction
vernickeln [fɛr'nɪkəln] *tr* nickel-plate
vernie'ten *tr* rivet
Vernunft [fɛr'nυnft] *f* (-;) reason; good sense; senses; **die gesunde V.** common sense; **V. annehmen** listen to reason; **zur V. bringen** bring to one's senses

Vernunft'ehe *f* marriage of convenience

vernunft'gemäß *adj* reasonable

vernünftig [fɛr'nʏnftɪç] *adj* rational; reasonable; sensible, level-headed

vernunft'los *adj* senseless

vernunft'mäßig *adj* rational; reasonable

veröden [fɛr'ødən] *intr* (SEIN) become desolate

veröffentlichen [fɛr'œfəntlɪçən] *tr* publish; announce

Veröf'fentlichung *f* (-;-en) publication; announcement

verord'nen *tr* decree; (med) prescribe

Verord'nung *f* (-;-en) decree, order; (med) prescription

verpach'ten *tr* farm out; lease, rent out

Verpäch'ter **-in** §6 *mf* lessor

verpacken (**verpak'ken**) *tr* pack up

Verpackung (**Verpak'kung**) *f* (-;-en) packing (material); wrapping

verpas'sen *tr* (*Gelegenheit, Anschluß, usw.*) miss; **j-m e-n Anzug v.** fit s.o. with a suit; **j-m e-e v.** (coll) give s.o. a smack

verpatzen [fɛr'patsən] *tr* (coll) make a mess of

verpesten [fɛr'pɛstən] *tr* infect, contaminate

verpet'zen *tr* (coll) squeal on

verpfän'den *tr* pawn; mortgage; **sein Wort v.** give one's word of honor

verpflan'zen *tr* (bot, surg) transplant

Verpflan'zung *f* (-;-en) (bot, surg) transplant

verpfle'gen *tr* feed; (mil) supply

Verpfle'gung *f* (-;) feeding; board; (mil) rations, supplies

verpflichten [fɛr'pflɪçtən] *tr* obligate, bind; **zu Dank v.** put under obligation

Verpflich'tung *f* (-;-en) obligation; commitment; (jur) liability

verpfuschen [fɛr'pfuʃən] *tr* (coll) botch, bungle, muff

verplap'pern *ref* blab out a secret

verplau'dern *tr* waste in chatting

verpönt [fɛr'pønt] *adj* taboo

verprü'geln *tr* (coll) wallop, thrash

verpuf'fen *intr* (SEIN) fizzle; (fig) fizzle out

verpulvern [fɛr'pulfərn] *tr* (coll) waste, fritter away

verpum'pen *tr* (coll) loan

verpusten [fɛr'pustən] *ref* (coll) catch one's breath

Verputz [fɛr'puts] *m* (-es;-e) finishing coat (of plaster)

verput'zen *tr* plaster; (*aufessen*) polish off; (coll) stand

verquicken [fɛr'kvɪkən] *tr* interrelate

verquollen [fɛr'kvɔlən] *adj* (*Augen*) swollen; (*Gesicht*) puffy; (*Holz*) warped

verrammeln [fɛr'raməln] *tr* barricade

verramschen [fɛr'ramʃən] *tr* (coll) sell dirt-cheap

verrannt [fɛr'rant] *adj*—**v. sein in** (*acc*) be stuck on

Verrat' *m* (-[e]s;) betrayal; treason

verra'ten §63 *tr* betray

Verräter **-in** [fɛr'retər(ɪn)] §6 *mf* traitor; betrayer

verräterisch [fɛr'retərɪʃ] *adj* treacherous; (*Spur, usw.*) telltale

verrau'chen *tr* spend on smokes

verräu'chern *tr* fill with smoke

verrech'nen *tr* (*ausgleichen*) balance; (*Scheck*) deposit; (fin) clear ‖ *ref* miscalculate; (fig) be mistaken

Verrech'nung *f* (-;-en) miscalculation; (fin) clearing; **nur zur V.** for deposit only

Verrech'nungsbank *f*, **Verrech'nungskasse** *f* clearing house

verrecken [fɛr'rɛkən] *intr* (SEIN) die; (sl) croak; **verrecke!** drop dead!

verreg'nen *tr* spoil with too much rain

verrei'sen *intr* (SEIN) go on a trip; **v. nach** depart for

verreist [fɛr'raɪst] *adj* out of town

verren'ken *tr* wrench, dislocate ‖ *ref*— **sich** [*dat*] **den Arm v.** wrench one's arm; **sich** [*dat*] **den Hals v.** (coll) crane one's neck

Verren'kung *f* (-;-en) dislocation

verrich'ten *tr* do; (*Gebet*) say; **seine Notdurft v.** ease oneself

Verrich'tung *f* (-;-en) performance; task, duty

verrie'geln *tr* bolt, bar

verringern [fɛr'rɪŋərn] *tr* diminish, reduce ‖ *ref* diminish; be reduced

Verrin'gerung *f* (-;-en) diminution; reduction

verrin'nen §121 *intr* (SEIN) run off; (*Zeit*) pass

verro'sten *intr* (SEIN) rust

verrotten [fɛr'rɔtən] *intr* (SEIN) rot

verrucht [fɛr'ruxt] *adj* wicked

verrücken (**verrük'ken**) *tr* move, shift

verrückt [fɛr'rʏkt] *adj* crazy; **v. auf** *etw* crazy about s.th.; **v. nach j-m** crazy about s.o. ‖ **Verrückte** §5 *mf* lunatic

Verrückt'heit *f* (-;-en) craziness, madness; crazy action or act

Verruf' *m* (-[e]s;) discredit, disrepute

verru'fen *adj* disreputable

verrüh'ren *tr* stir thoroughly

verrut'schen *intr* (SEIN) slip

Vers [fɛrs] *m* (-es;-e) verse

versa'gen *tr* refuse; **versagt sein** have a previous engagement ‖ *ref*—**sich** [*dat*] **etw v.** deny oneself s.th.; **ich kann es mir nicht v. zu** (*inf*) I can't refrain from (*ger*) ‖ *intr* fail; (*Beine, Stimme, usw.*) give out; (*Gewehr*) misfire; (*Motor*) fail to start; **bei e-r Prüfung v.** flunk a test ‖ **Versagen** *n* (-s;-) failure, flop; misfire

Versa'ger *m* (-s;-) failure, flop; (*Patrone*) dud

versal'zen *tr* oversalt; (fig) spoil

versam'meln *tr* gather together, assemble; convoke ‖ *ref* gather, assemble

Versamm'lung *f* (-;-en) assembly, meeting

Versand [fɛr'zant] *m* (-[e]s;) shipment; mailing

Versand'abteilung *f* shipping department

versanden [fɛr'zandən] *intr* (SEIN) silt up; (fig) bog down

Versand'geschäft n, **Versand'haus** n mail-order house

versäu'men tr (Gelegenheit, Schule, Zug) miss; (Geschäft, Pflicht) neglect; **v. zu** (inf) fail to (inf)

Versäumnis [fɛr'zɔɪmnɪs] f (-;-se), n (-ses;-se) omission, neglect; (educ) absence; (jur) default

verschaf'fen tr get, obtain ‖ ref—**sich** [dat] **etw v.** get; **sich** [dat] **Geld v.** raise money; **sich** [dat] **Respekt v.** gain respect

verschämt [fɛr'ʃɛmt] adj bashful, coy

Verschämt'heit f (-;) bashfulness

verschandeln [fɛr'ʃandəln] tr deface

verschan'zen tr fortify ‖ ref entrench oneself; **sich v. hinter** (dat) (fig) hide behind

Verschan'zung f (-;-en) entrenchment

verschär'fen tr intensify; aggravate; **verschärfter Arrest** detention on a bread-and-water diet ‖ ref get worse

verschei'den §112 tr (SEIN) pass away

verschen'ken tr give away

verscher'zen ref—**sich** [dat] **etw v.** throw away, lose (frivolously)

verscheu'chen tr scare away

verschicken (verschik'ken) tr send away; (deportieren) deport

Verschie'bebahnhof m marshaling yard

verschie'ben §130 tr postpone; shift; displace; black-market; (rr) shunt, switch ‖ ref shift

Verschie'bung f (-;-en) postponement; shift, shifting

verschieden [fɛr'ʃidən] adj different, various; distinct

verschie'denartig adj of a different kind

verschiedenerlei [fɛr'ʃidənərlaɪ] invar adj different kinds of

Verschie'denheit f (-;-en) difference; variety, diversity

verschiedentlich [fɛr'ʃidəntlɪç] adv repeatedly; at times, occasionally

verschie'ßen §76 tr (Schießvorrat) use up, expend ‖ intr (SEIN) (Farbe) fade

verschif'fen tr ship

Verschif'fung f (-;) shipment

verschim'meln intr (SEIN) get moldy

verschla'fen adj sleepy, drowsy ‖ §131 tr miss by sleeping; (Zeit) sleep away ‖ intr oversleep

Verschla'fenheit f (-;) sleepiness

Verschlag' m partition; crate

verschla'gen adj sly; (lau) lukewarm ‖ §132 tr partition off; board up; (Kisten) nail shut; (Seite im Buch) lose; (naut) drive off course; (tennis) misserve; **j-m den Atem v.** take s.o.'s breath away; **j-m die Sprache** (or **Rede, Stimme**) **v.** make s.o. speechless; **v. werden auf** (acc) (or **in** acc) be driven to ‖ impers—**es verschlägt nichts** it doesn't matter

verschlammen [fɛr'ʃlamən] intr (SEIN) silt up

verschlampen [fɛr'ʃlampən] tr ruin (through neglect); (verlegen) misplace ‖ intr get slovenly

verschlechtern [fɛr'ʃlɛçtərn] tr make worse ‖ ref get worse, deteriorate

Verschlech'terung f (-;) deterioration

verschleiern [fɛr'ʃlaɪ·ərn] tr veil; (Tatsachen) cover up; (Stimme) disguise; (mil) screen; **die Bilanz v.** juggle the books ‖ ref cloud up

verschleiert [fɛr'ʃlaɪ·ərt] adj hazy; (Stimme) husky; (Augen) misty

Verschlei'erung f (-;) coverup; camouflaging; (jur) suppression of evidence

verschlei'fen §88 tr slur, slur over

Verschleiß [fɛr'ʃlaɪs] m (-es;) wear and tear; (Aust) retail trade

verschlei'ßen §53 tr wear out; (Aust) retail ‖ ref wear out

verschleiß'fest adj durable

verschlep'pen tr drag off; abduct; (im Krieg) displace; (Verhandlungen) drag out; (Seuche) spread; (verzögern) delay

verschleu'dern tr waste, squander; (Waren) sell dirt-cheap

verschlie'ßen §76 tr shut; lock; put under lock and key ‖ ref (dat) close one's mind to

verschlimmern [fɛr'ʃlɪmərn] tr make worse; (fig) aggravate ‖ ref get worse

verschlin'gen §142 tr devour, wolf down; (verflechten) intertwine

verschlissen [fɛr'ʃlɪsən] adj frayed

verschlossen [fɛr'ʃlɔsən] adj shut; (fig) reserved, tight-lipped

verschlucken (verschluk'ken) tr swallow ‖ ref swallow the wrong way

verschlungen [fɛr'ʃluŋən] adj (Weg) winding; (fig) intricate

Ver·schluß' m (-schlusses;-schlüsse) fastener; (Schnapp-) catch; (Schloß) lock; (e-r Flasche) stopper; (Stöpsel) plug; (Plombe) seal; (e-s Gewehrs) breechlock; (phot) shutter; **unter V.** under lock and key

verschlüsseln [fɛr'ʃlʏsəln] tr code

Verschluß'laut m (ling) stop, plosive

verschmach'ten intr (SEIN) pine away; **vor Durst v.** be dying of thirst

verschmä'hen tr disdain

verschmel'zen §133 tr & intr (SEIN) fuse, merge; blend

Verschmel'zung f (-;-en) fusion; (com) merger

verschmer'zen tr get over

verschmie'ren tr smear; soil, dirty; (verwischen) blur

verschmitzt [fɛr'ʃmɪtst] adj crafty

verschmut'zen tr dirty ‖ intr (SEIN) get dirty

verschnap'pen ref give oneself away

verschnau'fen ref & intr stop for breath

verschnei'den §106 tr clip, trim; cut wrong; castrate; (Branntwein, Wein) blend

verschneit [fɛr'ʃnaɪt] adj snow-covered

Verschnitt' m (-[e]s;) blend

verschnup'fen tr annoy; **verschnupft sein** have a cold; (coll) be annoyed

verschnü'ren tr tie up

verschollen [fɛr'ʃɔlən] adj missing, never heard of again; (jur) presumed dead

verscho'nen tr spare; **j-n mit etw v.** spare s.o. s.th.

verschönern [fɛr'ʃønərn] tr beautify

verschossen [fɛr'ʃɔsən] *adj* faded, discolored; **(in** *acc)* (coll) be madly in love (with)
verschränken [fɛr'ʃrɛŋkən] *tr* fold (*one's arms*)
verschrau'ben *tr* screw tight
verschrei'ben §62 *tr* use up (*in writing*); (jur) make over; (med) prescribe ‖ *ref* make a mistake (*in writing*)
Verschrei'bung *f* (-;-en) prescription
verschrei'en §135 *tr* decry
verschrien [fɛr'ʃri·ən] *adj*—**v. sein als** have the reputation of being
verschroben [fɛr'ʃrobən] *adj* eccentric
Verschro'benheit *f* (-;-en) eccentricity
verschrotten [fɛr'ʃrɔtən] *tr* scrap
verschüch'tern *tr* intimidate
verschul'den *tr* encumber with debts; **etw v.** be guilty of s.th.; be the cause of s.th. ‖ **Verschulden** *n* (-s;) fault
verschuldet [fɛr'ʃuldət] *adj* in debt
Verschul'dung *f* (-;-en) indebtedness; encumbrance
verschüt'ten *tr* spill; (*ausfüllen*) fill up; (*Person*) bury alive
verschwägert [fɛr'ʃvegərt] *adj* related by marriage
verschwei'gen §148 *tr* keep secret; **j–m etw v.** keep s.th. from s.o.
Verschwei'gung *f* (-;) concealment
verschwei'ßen *tr* weld (together)
verschwenden [fɛr'ʃvendən] *tr* **(an** *acc)* waste (on), squander (on)
Verschwen'der **–in** §6 *mf* spendthrift
verschwenderisch [fɛr'ʃvendərɪʃ] *adj* wasteful; lavish, extravagant
Verschwen'dung *f* (-;) waste; extravagance
verschwiegen [fɛr'ʃvigən] *adj* discreet; reserved, reticent
Verschwie'genheit *f* (-;) discretion; reticence; secrecy
verschwim'men §136 *intr* (SEIN) become blurred; (fig) fade
verschwin'den §59 *intr* (SEIN) disappear; **ich muß mal v.** (coll) I have to go (to the toilet); **v. lassen** put out of the way; spirit off ‖ **Verschwinden** *n* (-s;) disappearance
verschwistert [fɛr'ʃvɪstərt] *adj* closely related
verschwit'zen *tr* sweat up; (coll) forget
verschwollen [fɛr'ʃvɔlən] *adj* swollen
verschwommen [fɛr'ʃvɔmən] *adj* hazy, indistinct; (*Bild*) blurred
Verschwom'menheit *f* (-;) haziness
verschwö'ren §137 *tr* forswear ‖ *ref* **(gegen)** plot (against); **sich zu etw v.** plot s.th.
Verschwö'rer **–in** §6 *mf* conspirator
Verschwö'rung *f* (-;-en) conspiracy
verse'hen §138 *tr* (*Amt, Stellung*) hold; (*Dienst, Pflicht*) perform; (*Haushalt, usw.*) look after; **(mit)** provide (with); (eccl) administer the last rites to; **j–s Dienst v.** fill in for s.o.; **mit e–m Saum v.** hem; **mit Giro v.** endorse; **mit Unterschrift v.** sign ‖ *ref* make a mistake; **ehe man es sich versieht** before you know it; **sich v.** (*genit*) expect ‖ **Versehen** *n* (-s;-) mistake, slip; oversight; **aus V.** by mistake

versehentlich [fɛr'ze·əntlɪç] *adv* by mistake, erroneously, inadvertently
versehren [fɛr'zerən] *tr* injure
Versehrte [fɛr'zertə] §5 *mf* disabled person
versen'den §140 *tr* send, ship; **ins Ausland v.** export
versen'gen *tr* scorch; (*Haar*) singe
versen'ken *tr* sink; submerge; lower; (*Kabel*) lay; (*Schraube*) countersink; (naut) scuttle ‖ *ref*—**sich v. in** (*acc*) become engrossed in
Versen'kung *f* (-;-en) sinking; (theat) trapdoor; **in der V. verschwinden** (fig) vanish into thin air
versessen [fɛr'zesən] *adj*—**v. auf** (*acc*) crazy about, obsessed with
verset'zen *tr* move, shift; (*Pflanze*) transplant; (*Schulkind*) promote; (*Beamte*) transfer; (*Schlag*) deal, give; (*verpfänden*) pawn; (*vermischen*) mix; (*Metall*) alloy; (*erwidern*) reply; (*vergeblich warten lassen*) (coll) stand up; (mus) transpose; **in Angst v.** terrify; **in Erstaunen v.** amaze; **in den Ruhestand v.** retire; **in Zorn v.** anger ‖ *ref*—**v. Sie sich in meine Lage** put yourself in my place
Verset'zung *f* (-;-en) moving, shifting; transplanting; transfer; mixing; alloying; (educ) promotion
Verset'zungszeichen *n* (mus) accidental
verseuchen [fɛr'zɔɪçən] *tr* infect, contaminate
Verseu'chung *f* (-;) infection; contamination
Vers'fuß *m* (pros) foot
versicherbar [fɛr'zɪçərbar] *adj* insurable
versichern [fɛr'zɪçərn] *tr* assure; assert, affirm; insure ‖ *ref* **(genit)** assure oneself of
Versicherte [fɛr'zɪçərtə] §5 *mf* insured
Versi'cherung *f* (-;-en) assurance; affirmation; insurance
Versi'cherungsanstalt *f* insurance company
Versi'cherungsbeitrag *m* premium
versi'cherungsfähig *adj* insurable
Versi'cherungsgesellschaft *f* insurance company
Versi'cherungsleistung *f* insurance benefit
Versi'cherungsmathematiker **–in** §6 *mf* actuary
Versi'cherungsnehmer **–in** §6 *mf* insured
versi'cherungspflichtig *adj* subject to mandatory insurance
Versi'cherungspolice *f*, **Versi'cherungsschein** *m* insurance policy
Versi'cherungsträger *m* underwriter
Versi'cherungszwang *m* compulsory insurance
versickern (**versik'kern**) *intr* (SEIN) seep out, trickle away
versie'geln *tr* seal (up); (jur) seal off
Versie'gelung *f* (-;) sealing (off)
versie'gen *intr* (SEIN) dry up
versil'bern *tr* silver-plate; (coll) sell
Versil'berung *f* (-;) silver-plating

versin'ken §143 *intr* (SEIN) (**in** *acc*) sink (into); (fig) (**in** *acc*) lapse (into)
versinnbildlichen [fɛr'zɪnbɪltlɪçən] *tr* symbolize
Version [vɛr'zjon] *f* (–;–en) version
versippt [fɛr'zɪpt] *adj* (**mit**) related (to)
versklaven [fɛr'sklɑvən] *tr* enslave
Vers'kunst *f* versification
Vers'macher –in §6 *mf* versifier
Vers'maß *n* meter
versoffen [fɛr'zɔfən] *adj* (coll) drunk
versohlen [fɛr'zolən] *tr* (coll) give (*s.o.*) a good licking
versöhnen [fɛr'zønən] *tr* (**mit**) reconcile (with) || *ref* become reconciled
versöhnlich [fɛr'zønlɪç] *adj* conciliatory
Versöh'nung *f* (–;) reconciliation
Versöh'nungstag *m* Day of Atonement
versonnen [fɛr'zɔnən] *adj* wistful
versor'gen *tr* look after; provide for; (**mit**) supply (with), provide (with)
Versor'ger –in §6 *mf* provider, breadwinner
Versor'gung *f* (–;) providing, supplying; (*Unterhalt*) maintenance; (*Alters– und Validen–*) social security
Versor'gungsbetrieb *m* public utility
Versor'gungstruppen *pl* service troops
Versor'gungswege *pl* supply lines
verspan'nen *tr* guy, brace
verspäten [fɛr'ʃpɛtən] *ref* come late; (rr) be behind schedule
verspätet [fɛr'ʃpɛtət] *adj* belated, late
Verspä'tung *f* (–;–en) lateness, delay; **mit e–r Stunde V.** one hour behind schedule; **V. haben** be late
verspei'sen *tr* eat up
verspekulie'ren *tr* lose on a gamble || *ref* lose all through speculation
versper'ren *tr* bar, block, obstruct; (*Tür*) lock
verspie'len *tr* lose, gamble away || *intr* —**bei j–m v.** lose favor with s.o.
verspielt [fɛr'ʃpilt] *adj* playful; frivolous
versponnen [fɛr'ʃpɔnən] *adj*—**in Gedanken versponnen** lost in thought
verspot'ten *tr* mock, deride
Verspot'tung *f* (–;) mockery, derision
verspre'chen §64 *tr* promise || *ref* make a mistake in speaking; **ich verspreche mir viel davon** I expect a lot from that || **Versprechen** *n* (–s;–) promise; slip of the tongue
Verspre'chung *f* (–;–en) promise
verspren'gen *tr* scatter, disperse
Versprengte [fɛr'ʃprɛŋtə] §5 *mf* (mil) straggler
versprit'zen *tr* squirt, spatter
versprü'hen *tr* spray
verspü'ren *tr* feel, sense
verstaatlichen [fɛr'ʃtatlɪçən] *tr* nationalize
Verstaat'lichung *f* (–;) nationalization
verstädtern [fɛr'ʃtɛtərn] *tr* urbanize
Verstäd'terung *f* (–;) urbanization
Verstand' *m* (–[e]s;) understanding; intellect; intelligence, brains; (*Vernunft*) reason; (*Geist*) mind; senses; sense; **den V.** verlieren lose one's

mind; **gesunder V.** common sense; **klarer V.** clear head; **nicht bei V. sein** be out of one's mind
Verstan'deskraft *f* intellectual power
verstan'desmäßig *adj* rational
Verstan'desmensch *m* matter-of-fact person
verstän'dig *adj* intelligent; sensible, reasonable; wise
verständigen [fɛr'ʃtɛndɪɡən] *tr* (**von**) inform (about), notify (of) || *ref*— **sich v. mit** make oneself understood to; come to an understanding with
Verstän'digung *f* (–;) understanding; information; communication; (telp) quality of reception
verständlich [fɛr'ʃtɛntlɪç] *adj* understandable, intelligible; **sich v. machen** make oneself understood
Verständnis [fɛr'ʃtɛntnɪs] *n* (–ses;–se) (**für**) understanding (of), appreciation (for)
verständ'nislos *adj* uncomprehending
verständ'nisinnig *adj* with deep mutual understanding; (*Blick*) knowing
verständ'nisvoll *adj* understanding; appreciative; (*Blick*) knowing
verstär'ken *tr* stink up
verstär'ken *tr* strengthen; (*steigern*) intensify; (elec) boost; (mil) reinforce; (rad) amplify
Verstär'ker *m* (–s;–) (rad) amplifier
Verstär'kung *f* (–;–en) strengthening; intensification; (mil) reinforcement; (rad) amplification
verstatten [fɛr'ʃtatən] *tr* permit
verstau'ben *intr* (SEIN) get dusty
verstäu'ben *intr* atomize
verstaubt [fɛr'ʃtaupt] *adj* dusty; (fig) antiquated
verstau'chen *tr* sprain
Verstau'chung *f* (–;–en) sprain
verstau'en *tr* stow away
Versteck [fɛr'ʃtɛk] *m* (–[e]s;–e) hiding place; hideout; **V. spielen** play hide-and-seek
verstecken (**verstek'ken**) *tr & ref* hide
versteckt [fɛr'ʃtɛkt] *adj* hidden, veiled; (*Absicht*) ulterior
verste'hen §146 *tr* understand, see; make out; realize; (*Sprache*) know; **e–n Spaß v.** take a joke; **ich verstehe es zu** (*inf*) I know how to (*inf*); **falsch v.** misunderstand; **verstanden?** get it?; **v. Sie mich recht!** don't get me wrong!; **was v. Sie unter** (*dat*)? what do you mean by? || *ref*—(**das**) **versteht sich!** that's understood!; **das versteht sich von selbst!** that goes without saying; **sich gut v. mit** get along well with; **sich v. auf** (*acc*) be skilled in; **sich v. zu etw v.** (*sich zu etw entschließen*) bring oneself to do s.th.; (*in etw einwilligen*) agree to s.th. || *recip* understand each other
verstei'fen *tr* stiffen; strut, brace, reinforce || *ref* stiffen; **sich v. auf** (*acc*) insist on
verstei'gen §148 *ref* lose one's way in the mountain; **sich dazu v., daß** go so far as to (*inf*)
Verstei'gerer *m* (–s;–) auctioneer
verstei'gern *tr* auction off

Verstei'gerung *f* (–;–en) auction
verstei'nern *intr* (SEIN) become petrified; (fig) be petrified
verstell'bar *adj* adjustable
verstel'len *tr* (*regulieren*) adjust; (*versperren*) block; (*Stimme, usw.*) disguise; (*Weiche*) throw; (*Verkehrsampel*) switch; (*Zeiger e–r Uhr*) move; misplace; **j–m den Weg v.** block s.o.'s way ‖ *ref* put on an act
Verstel'lung *f* (–;–en) adjusting; disguise
versteu'ern *tr* pay taxes on
Versteu'erung *f* (–;) paying of taxes
verstiegen [fɛr'ʃtigən] *adj* (*Idee, Plan*) extravagant, fantastic
verstim'men *tr* put out of tune; (fig) put out of humor
verstimmt [fɛr'ʃtɪmt] *adj* out of tune; (*Magen*) upset; **v. über** (*acc*) upset over
Verstim'mung *f* (–;) bad humor; (*zwischen zweien*) bad feeling, bad blood
verstockt [fɛr'ʃtɔkt] *adj* stubborn; (*Verbrecher*) hardened; (eccl) impenitent
Verstockt'heit *f* (–;) stubbornness; (eccl) impenitence
verstohlen [fɛr'ʃtolən] *adj* furtive
verstop'fen *tr* stop up, clog; (*Straße*) block, jam; (*Leib*) constipate
Verstop'fung *f* (–;) stopping up, clogging; congestion; (pathol) constipation
verstorben [fɛr'ʃtɔrbən] *adj* late, deceased ‖ **Verstorbene** §5 *mf* deceased
verstört [fɛr'ʃtørt] *adj* shaken, bewildered, distracted
Verstört'heit *f* (–;) bewilderment
Verstoß' *m* (gegen) violation (of), offense (against)
versto'ßen §150 *tr* disown ‖ *intr*—**v. gegen** violate, break
verstre'ben *tr* prop, brace
verstrei'chen §85 *tr* (*Butter*) spread; (*Risse*) plaster up ‖ *intr* (SEIN) pass, elapse; (*Gelegenheit*) slip by; (*Frist*) expire
verstreu'en *tr* scatter, disperse, strew
verstricken (**verstrik'ken**) *tr* use up in knitting; (fig) involve, entangle ‖ *ref* get entangled
verstümmeln [fɛr'ʃtyməln] *tr* mutilate; (*Funkspruch*) garble
Verstüm'melung *f* (–;–en) mutilation; (rad) garbling
verstummen [fɛr'ʃtumən] *intr* (SEIN) become silent; (*vor Erstaunen*) be dumbstruck; (*Geräusch*) cease
Versuch [fɛr'zux] *m* (–[e]s;–e) try, attempt; (*Probe*) test, trial; (*wissenschaftlich*) experiment; **e–n V. machen mit** have a try at
versu'chen *tr* try; tempt; (*kosten*) taste
Versuchs'anstalt *f* research institute
Versuchs'ballon *m* (& fig) trial balloon
Versuchs'flieger *m* test pilot
Versuchs'flug *m* test flight
Versuchs'kaninchen *n* (fig) guinea pig
Versuchs'reihe *f* series of tests
versuchs'weise *adv* by way of a test; on approval
Versu'chung *f* (–;–en) temptation

versumpfen [fɛr'zumpfən] *intr* (SEIN) become marshy; (coll) go to the dogs
versün'digen *ref* (an *dat*) sin (against)
versunken [fɛr'zuŋkən] *adj* sunk; **v. in** (*acc*) (fig) lost in
versü'ßen *tr* sweeten
verta'gen *tr* & *ref* (**auf** *acc*) adjourn (till), recess (till)
Verta'gung *f* (–;–en) adjournment
vertändeln [fɛr'tɛndəln] *tr* trifle away
vertäuen [fɛr'tɔɪ·ən] *tr* (naut) moor
vertau'schen *tr* (gegen) exchange (for)
Vertau'schung *f* (–;–en) exchange
verteidigen [fɛr'taɪdɪgən] *tr* defend
Vertei'diger –**in** §6 *mf* defender; (*Befürworter*) advocate; (jur) counsel for the defense ‖ *m* (fb) back
Vertei'digung *f* (–;–en) defense
Vertei'digungsbündnis *n* defensive alliance
Vertei'digungsminister *m* secretary of defense
Vertei'digungsministerium *n* department of defense
Vertei'digungsschrift *f* written defense
Vertei'digungsstellung *f* defensive position
vertei'len *tr* distribute; (*zuteilen*) allot; (*über e–e große Fläche*) scatter; (*steuerlich*) spread out; (*Rollen*) (theat) cast ‖ *ref* spread out
Vertei'ler *m* (–s;–) distributer; (*Anschriftenliste*) mailing list; (*von Durchschlägen*) distribution; (aut) distributor
Vertei'lung *f* (–;–en) distribution; allotment; (theat) casting
verteuern [fɛr'tɔɪ·ərn] *tr* raise the price of
verteufelt [fɛr'tɔɪfəlt] *adj* devilish; a devil of a
vertiefen [fɛr'tifən] *tr* make deeper; (fig) deepen ‖ *ref*—**sich v. in** (*acc*) become absorbed in
Vertie'fung *f* (–;–en) deepening; (*Höhlung*) hollow, depression; (*Nische*) niche; (*Loch*) hole; (fig) absorption
vertiert [fɛr'tirt] *adj* bestial
vertikal [vɛrtɪ'kal] *adj* vertical ‖ **Vertikale** *f* (–;–n) vertical
vertil'gen *tr* exterminate, eradicate; (*aufessen*) (coll) eat, polish off
Vertil'gung *f* (–;) extermination
vertip'pen *tr* type incorrectly ‖ *ref* make a typing error
verto'nen *tr* set to music
Verto'nung *f* (–;–en) musical arrangement
vertrackt [fɛr'trakt] *adj* (coll) odd, strange; (coll) blooming
Vertrag [fɛr'trak] *m* (–[e]s;–̈e) contract, agreement; (dipl) treaty
vertra'gen §132 *tr* stand, take; tolerate ‖ *recip* agree, be compatible; (*Farben*) harmonize; (*Personen*) get along
vertrag'lich *adj* contractual ‖ *adv* by contract, as stipulated; **sich v. verpflichten zu** (*inf*) contract to (*inf*)
verträglich [fɛr'treklɪç] *adj* sociable, personable; (*Speise*) digestible
Vertrags'bruch *m* breach of contract
vertragsbrüchig [fɛr'traksbryçɪç] *adj* —**v. werden** break a contract

vertrags'gemäß *adj* contractual
vertrags'widrig *adj* contrary to the terms of a contract or treaty
vertrau'en *intr* (*dat*) trust; **v. auf** (*acc*) trust in, have confidence in || **Vertrauen** *n* (-s;) trust, confidence; **ganz im V.** just between you and me; **im V.** confidentially
vertrau'enerweckend *adj* inspiring confidence
Vertrau'ensbruch *m* breach of trust
Vertrau'ens·mann *m* (-[e]s;ⁿer & -leute) confidential agent; (*Vertrauter*) confidant; (*Sprecher*) spokesman; (*Gewährsmann*) informant
Vertrau'ensposten *m,* **Vertrau'ensstellung** *f* position of trust
vertrau'ensvoll *adj* confident; trusting
Vertrau'ensvotum *n* vote of confidence
vertrau'enswürdig *adj* trustworthy
vertrauern [fɛr'trauˑərn] *tr* spend in mourning
vertraulich [fɛr'traulɪç] *adj* confidential; intimate
Vertrau'lichkeit *f* (-;-en) intimacy, familiarity; **sich** [*dat*] **Vertraulichkeiten herausnehmen** take liberties
verträu'men *tr* dream away
verträumt [fɛr'trɔɪmt] *adj* dreamy
vertraut [fɛr'traut] *adj* familiar; friendly, intimate || **Vertraute** §5 *mf* intimate friend || *m* confidant || *f* confidante
Vertraut'heit *f* (-;) familiarity
vertrei'ben §62 *tr* drive away, expel; (*aus dem Hause*) chase out; (*aus dem Lande*) banish; (*Ware*) sell, market; (*Zeit*) pass, kill
Vertrei'bung *f* (-;) expulsion
vertre'ten §152 *tr* represent; substitute for; (*Ansicht, usw.*) advocate || *ref* —**sich** [*dat*] **den Fuß v.** sprain one's ankle; **sich** [*dat*] **die Beine v.** (coll) stretch one's legs
Vertre'ter –**in** §6 *mf* representative; substitute; (*Bevollmächtigte*) proxy; (*im Amt*) deputy; (*Fürsprecher*) advocate; (com) agent
Vertre'tung *f* (-;-en) representation; substitution; (com) agency; (pol) mission; **in V.** by proxy; **in V.** (*genit*) signed for
Vertrieb' *m* (-[e]s;-e) sale, turnover; retail trade; sales department
Vertriebs'abkommen *n* franchise agreement
Vertriebs'abteilung *f* sales department
Vertriebs'kosten *pl* distribution costs
Vertriebs'leiter –**in** §6 *mf* sales manager
Vertriebs'recht *n* franchise
vertrin'ken §143 *tr* drink up
vertrock'nen *intr* (SEIN) dry up
vertrödeln [fɛr'trødəln] *tr* fritter away
vertrö'sten *tr* string along; **auf später v.** put off till later
vertun' §154 *tr* waste || *ref* (coll) make a mistake
vertu'schen *tr* hush up
verübeln [fɛr'ybəln] *tr* take (*s.th.*) the wrong way; **j-m etw v.** blame s.o. for s.th.
verü'ben *tr* commit, perpetrate

verul'ken *tr* (coll) kid
verunehren [fɛr'unerən] *tr* dishonor
veruneinigen [fɛr'unaɪnɪgən] *tr* disunite || *recip* fall out, quarrel
verunglimpfen [fɛr'unglɪmpfən] *tr* slander, defame
verunglücken [fɛr'unglʏkən] *intr* (SEIN) have an accident; (coll) fail
Verunglückte [fɛr'unglʏktə] §5 *mf* victim, casualty
verunreinigen [fɛr'unraɪnɪgən] *tr* soil, dirty; (*Luft, Wasser*) pollute
Verun'reinigung *f* (-;) pollution
verunstalten [fɛr'unʃtaltən] *tr* disfigure, deface
veruntreuen [fɛr'untrɔɪ-ən] *tr* embezzle
Verun'treuung *f* (-;) embezzlement
verunzieren [fɛr'untsirən] *tr* mar
verursachen [fɛr'urzaxən] *tr* cause
verur'teilen *tr* condemn; sentence
Verur'teilung *f* (-;-en) condemnation; sentence
vervielfachen [fɛr'filfaxən] *tr* multiply || *ref* increase considerably
vervielfältigen [fɛr'filfɛltɪgən] *tr* multiply; duplicate; mimeograph; (*nachbilden*) reproduce
Verviel'fältigung *f* (-;-en) duplication; mimeographing; reproduction; (phot) printing
Verviel'fältigungsapparat *m* duplicator
vervollkommnen [fɛr'fɔlkɔmnən] *tr* improve on, perfect
Vervoll'kommnung *f* (-;) improvement, perfection
vervollständigen [fɛr'fɔlʃtɛndɪgən] *tr* complete
Vervoll'ständigung *f* (-;) completion
verwach'sen *adj* overgrown; deformed; hunchbacked; **mit etw v. sein** (fig) be attached to s.th. || *intr* (SEIN) grow together; become deformed; (*Wunde*) heal up; **zu e-r Einheit v.** form a whole
Verwach'sung *f* (-;-en) deformity
verwackelt [fɛr'vakəlt] *adj* (phot) blurred
verwah'ren *tr* keep; **v. vor** (*dat*) protect against || *ref*—**sich v. gegen** protest against
verwahrlosen [fɛr'varlozən] *tr* neglect || *intr* (SEIN) (*Gebäude*) deteriorate; (*Kinder*) run wild; (*Personen*) go to the dogs
verwahrlost [fɛr'varlost] *adj* uncared-for; (*Person*) unkempt; (*sittlich*) degenerate; (*Garten*) overgrown with weeds
Verwahr'losung *f* (-;) neglect
Verwah'rung *f* (-;) care, safekeeping, custody; (fig) protest; **etw in V. nehmen** take care of s.th.; **j-m in V. geben** entrust to s.o.'s care
verwaisen [fɛr'vaɪzən] *intr* (SEIN) become an orphan, be orphaned
verwaist [fɛr'vaɪst] *adj* orphaned; (fig) deserted
verwalten [fɛr'valtən] *tr* administer, manage
Verwal'ter –**in** §6 *mf* administrator, manager
Verwal'tung *f* (-;-en) administration, management

Verwal'tungsapparat *m* administrative machinery

Verwal'tungsbeamte *m* civil service worker; administrative official

Verwal'tungsdienst *m* civil service

Verwal'tungsrat *m* advisory board; (*e-r Aktiengesellschaft*) board of directors; (*e-s Instituts*) board of trustees

verwan'deln *tr* change, turn, convert; (*Strafe*) commute || *ref* change, turn

Verwand'lung *f* (-;-en) change, transformation; (jur) commutation

verwandt [fɛr'vant] *adj* (mit) related (to); (*Wissenschaften*) allied; (*Wörter*) cognate; (*Seelen*) kindred || **Verwandte** §5 *mf* relative, relation

Verwandt'schaft *f* (-;-en) relationship; relatives; (chem) affinity

verwandt'schaftlich *adj* kindred

Verwand'schaftsgrad *m* degree of relationship

verwanzt [fɛr'vantst] *adj* (coll) full of bugs, lousy

verwar'nen *tr* warn, caution

Verwar'nung *f* (-;-en) warning, caution

verwa'schen *adj* washed-out, faded; (*verschwommen*) vague, fuzzy

verwäs'sern *tr* dilute; (fig) water down

verwe'ben §94 *tr* interweave

verwe'chseln *tr* confuse, get (*various items*) mixed up; (*Hüte, Mäntel*) take by mistake || **Verwechseln** *n* (-s;)—**sie sehen sich zum V. ähnlich** they are as alike as two peas

Verwechs'lung *f* (-;-en) mix-up

verwegen [fɛr'vegən] *adj* bold, daring

verwe'hen *tr* (*Blätter*) blow away; (*Spur*) cover up (with snow) || *intr* (SEIN) be blown in all directions; (*Spur*) be covered up; (*Worte*) drift away

verweh'ren *tr*—**j-m etw v.** refuse s.o. s.th.; prevent s.o. from getting s.th.

Verwe'hung *f* (-;-en) (snow)drift

verweichlichen [fɛr'vaɪçlɪçən] *tr* make effeminate; (*Kind*) coddle || *ref & intr* become effeminate; grow soft

verweichlicht [fɛr'vaɪçlɪçt] *adj* effeminate; soft, flabby

Verweich'lichung *f* (-;) effeminacy

verwei'gern *tr* refuse, deny, turn down

Verwei'gerung *f* (-;-en) refusal

verweilen [fɛr'vaɪlən] *intr* linger, tarry; (fig) dwell

verweint [fɛr'vaɪnt] *adj* red with tears

Verweis [fɛr'vaɪs] *m* (-es;-e) reprimand, rebuke; (*Hinweis*) reference

verwei'sen §118 *tr* banish; (*Schüler*) expel; **j-m etw v.** reprimand s.o. for s.th.; **j-n an j-n v.** refer s.o. to s.o.; **j-n auf etw v.** refer s.o. to s.th.

Verwei'sung *f* (-;-en) banishment; expulsion; (**an** *acc*) referral (to); (**auf** *acc*) reference (to)

verwel'ken *intr* (SEIN) wither, wilt

verweltlichen [fɛr'vɛltlɪçən] *tr* secularize

verwendbar [fɛr'vɛntbɑr] *adj* applicable; available; usable

Verwend'barkeit *f* (-;) availability; usefulness

verwen'den §140 *tr* use, employ; (**auf** *acc*, **für**) apply (to); **Zeit und Mühe v. auf** (*acc*) spend time and effort on || *ref*—**sich bei j-m v. für** intercede with s.o. for

Verwen'dung *f* (-;-en) use, employment; application; **keine V. haben für** have no use for; **vielseitige V.** versatility

verwen'dungsfähig *adj* usable

verwer'fen §160 *tr* reject; (*Plan*) discard; (*Berufung*) turn down; (*Klage*) dismiss; (*Urteil*) overrule || *ref* (*Holz*) warp; (geol) fault

verwerf'lich *adj* objectionable

Verwer'fung *f* (-;-en) rejection; warping; (geol) fault

verwer'ten *tr* utilize

Verwer'tung *f* (-;-en) utilization

verwesen [fɛr'vezən] *intr* (SEIN) rot

verweslich [fɛr'vezlɪç] *adj* perishable

Verwe'sung *f* (-;) decay

verwet'ten *tr* lose (*in betting*)

verwich'sen *tr* (coll) clobber

verwickeln (verwik'keln) *tr* snarl, entangle; complicate; (fig) involve || *ref*—**sich v. in** (*acc*) get entangled in; (fig) get involved in

Verwick'lung *f* (-;-en) snarl, tangle; involvement; complexity; complication

verwil'dern *intr* become overgrown; (*Person*) become depraved; (*Kind*) run wild, go wild

verwildert [fɛr'vɪldərt] *adj* wild, savage; weed-grown

verwin'den §59 *tr* get over; (*Verlust*) recover from

verwir'ken *tr* forfeit; (*Strafe*) incur || *ref*—**sich** [*dat*] **j-s Gunst v.** lose favor with s.o.

verwirklichen [fɛr'vɪrklɪçən] *tr* realize, make come true || *ref* come true

Verwirk'lichung *f* (-;) realization

Verwir'kung *f* (-;-en) forfeiture

verwirren [fɛr'vɪrən] *tr* throw into disorder; (*Haar*) muss up; confuse

verwirrt [fɛr'vɪrt] *adj* confused

Verwir'rung *f* (-;-en) confusion; **in V. geraten** become confused

verwirt'schaften *tr* squander

verwi'schen *tr* wipe out; (*teilweise*) blur; (*verschmieren*) smear; (*Spuren*) cover || *ref* become blurred

verwit'tern *intr* (SEIN) become weatherbeaten; (*zerfallen*) crumble away

verwittert [fɛr'vɪtərt] *adj* weatherbeaten

verwitwet [fɛr'vɪtvət] *adj* widowed

verwöhnen [fɛr'vøːnən] *tr* pamper, spoil

verworfen [fɛr'vɔrfən] *adj* depraved

Verwor'fenheit *f* (-;) depravity

verworren [fɛr'vɔrən] *adj* confused

verwundbar [fɛr'vʊntbɑr] *adj* vulnerable

verwun'den *tr* wound

verwunderlich [fɛr'vʊndərlɪç] *adj* remarkable, astonishing

verwun'dern *tr* astonish || *ref* (**über** *acc*) be astonished (at), wonder (at)

Verwun'derung *f* (-;) astonishment; **j-n in V. setzen** astonish s.o.

verwundet [fɛr'vʊndət] *adj* wounded

|| **Verwundete** §5 *mf* wounded person

verwunschen [fɛr'vʊnʃən] *adj* enchanted

verwün′schen *tr* damn, curse; (*in Märchen*) bewitch, put a curse on

verwünscht [fɛr'vʏnʃt] *adj* confounded, darn || *interj* darn it!

Verwün′schung *f* (–;–en) curse

verwurzelt [fɛr'vʊrtsəlt] *adj* deeply rooted

verwüsten [fɛr'vystən] *tr* devastate

Verwü′stung *f* (–;–en) devastation

verzagen [fɛr'tsɑgən] *intr* (SEIN) lose heart, despair; **v. an** (*dat*) give up on

verzagt [fɛr'tsɑkt] *adj* despondent

Verzagt′heit *f* (–;) despondency

verzäh′len *ref* miscount

verzärteln [fɛr'tsɛrtəln] *tr* pamper

verzau′bern *tr* bewitch, charm; **v. in** (*acc*) change into

Verzehr [fɛr'tser] *m* (–[e]s;) consumption

verzeh′ren *tr* consume; (*Geld*) spend; (*Mahlzeit*) eat || *ref* (in *dat*, **vor** *dat*) pine away (with); (**nach**) yearn (for)

verzeh′rend *adj* (*Blick*) longing; (*Fieber*) wasting; (*Leidenschaft*) burning

Verzeh′rung *f* (–;) consumption

verzeich′nen *tr* draw wrong; make a list of; register; catalogue; (opt) distort

Verzeichnis [fɛr'tsaɪçnɪs] *n* (–ses;–se) list; catalogue; (*im Buch*) index; (*Inventar*) inventory; (*Tabelle*) table; (telp) directory

verzeihen [fɛr'tsaɪ·ən] §81 *tr* forgive, pardon (*s.th.*); condone || *intr* (*dat*) forgive, pardon (*s.o.*)

verzeihlich [fɛr'tsaɪlɪç] *adj* pardonable

Verzei′hung *f* (–;) pardon

verzer′ren *tr* distort; contort

Verzer′rung *f* (–;–en) distortion; contortion; grimace

verzetteln [fɛr'tsɛtəln] *tr* fritter away; catalogue || *ref* spread oneself too thin

Verzicht [fɛr'tsɪçt] *m* (–[e]s;) renunciation; **V. leisten auf** (*acc*) waive

verzichten [fɛr'tsɪçtən] *intr*—**v. auf** (*acc*) do without; (*verabsäumen*) pass up; (*aufgeben*) give up, renounce; (*Rechte*) waive

verzieh [fɛr'tsi] *pret of* **verzeihen**

verzie′hen §163 *tr* distort; (*Kind*) spoil; **den Mund v.** make a face; **ohne e-e Miene zu v.** without batting an eye || *ref* disappear; (*Schmerz*) go away; (*Menge, Wolken*) disperse; (*Holz*) warp; (*durch Druck*) buckle; (coll) sneak off

verzie′ren *tr* decorate

Verzie′rung *f* (–;–en) decoration; (*Schmuck*) ornament

verzinsen [fɛr'tsɪnzən] *tr* pay interest on; **e-e Summe zu 6% v.** pay 6% interest on a sum || *ref* yield interest; **sich mit 6% v.** yield 6% interest

verzinslich [fɛr'tsɪnslɪç] *adj* bearing interest || *adv*—**v. anlegen** put out at interest

Verzin′sung *f* (–;) interest

verzog [fɛr'tsok] *pret of* **verziehen**

verzogen [fɛr'tsogən] *adj* distorted; (*Kind*) spoiled; (*Holz*) warped

verzö′gern *tr* delay; put off, postpone || *ref* be late

Verzö′gerung *f* (–;–en) delay; postponement

verzollen [fɛr'tsɔlən] *tr* pay duty on; (naut) clear; **haben Sie etw zu v.?** do you have anything to declare?

verzückt [fɛr'tsʏkt] *adj* ecstatic

Verzückung [fɛr'tsʏkʊŋ] *f* (–;) ecstasy

Verzug′ *m* (–[e]s;) delay; (*in der Leistung*) default; **in V. geraten mit** fall behind in; **ohne V.** without delay

verzwei′feln *intr* (HABEN & SEIN) (**an** *dat*) despair (of) || **Verzweifeln** *n*— **es ist zum V.** it's enough to drive one to despair

verzweifelt [fɛr'tsvaɪfəlt] *adj* desperate

Verzweif′lung *f* (–;) despair

verzweigen [fɛr'tsvaɪgən] *ref* branch out

verzweigt [fɛr'tsvaɪkt] *adj* having many branches; (fig) complex

verzwickt [fɛr'tsvɪkt] *adj* (coll) tricky, ticklish

Vestibül [vɛstɪ'byl] *n* (–s;–e) vestibule; (theat) lobby

Veteran [vetɛ'rɑn] *m* (–en;–en) veteran, ex-serviceman

Veterinär –**in** [vetɛrɪ'ner(ɪn)] §8 *mf* veterinarian

Veto ['veto] *n* (–s;–s) veto

Vetter ['fɛtər] *m* (–s;–) cousin

Vet′ternwirtschaft *f* nepotism

Vexierbild [vɛ'ksirbɪlt] *n* picture puzzle

vexieren [vɛ'ksirən] *tr* tease; pester

V-förmig ['fauførmɪç] *adj* V-shaped

vibrieren [vɪ'brirən] *intr* vibrate

Vieh [fi] (–[e]s;) livestock; cattle; animal, beast

Vieh′bestand *m* livestock

Vieh′bremse *f* horsefly

viehisch ['fi·ɪʃ] *adj* brutal

Vieh′tränke *f* water hole

Vieh′wagen *m* (rr) cattle car

Vieh′weide *f* cow pasture

Vieh′zucht *f* cattle breeding

Vieh′züchter –**in** §6 *mf* rancher

viel [fil] *adj* much; many; a lot of || *adv* much; a lot || *pron* much; many

viel′beschäftigt *adj* very busy

viel′deutig *adj* ambiguous

Viel′eck *n* polygon

vielerlei ['filər'laɪ] *invar adj* many kinds of

viel′fach *adj* multiple; manifold || *adv* (coll) often

Vielfach– *comb.fm.* multiple

viel′fältig *adj* manifold, various

Viel′fältigkeit *f* (–;) multiplicity; variety

vielleicht′ *adv* maybe, perhaps

vielmalig ['filmɑlɪç] *adj* oft repeated

vielmals ['filmɑls] *adv* frequently; **danke v.!** many thanks!

vielmehr′ *adv* rather, on the contrary

viel′sagend *adj* suggestive

viel′seitig *adj* many-sided, versatile

vielstufig ['fil∫tufɪç] *adj* multistage

viel′teilig *adj* of many parts

viel′versprechend *adj* very promising

vier [fir] *adj* four; **unter vier Augen** confidentially ‖ *pron* four; **auf allen vieren** on all fours ‖ **Vier** *f* (–;–en) four
vier'beinig *adj* four-legged
Vier'eck *n* quadrangle
vier'eckig *adj* quadrangular
viererlei ['firər'laı] *invar adj* four different kinds of
vier'fach, vier'fältig *adv* fourfold, quadruple
Vierfüßer ['firfysər] *m* (–s;–) quadruped
vierhändig ['firhendıç] *adv*—**v. spielen** (mus) play a duet
Vierlinge ['firlıŋə] *pl* quadruplets
vier'mal *adv* four times
vierschrötig ['fir∫røtıç] *adj* stocky
vierstrahlig ['fir∫tralıç] *adj* four-engine (jet)
viert [firt] *pron*—**zu v.** in fours; **wir gehen zu v.** the four of us are going
Viertakter ['firtaktər] *m* (–s;–), **Viertaktmotor** ['firtaktmotər] *m* four-cycle engine
Vierte ['firtə] §9 *adj & pron* fourth
vier'teilen *tr* quarter
Viertel ['fırtəl] *n* (–s;–) quarter; fourth (*part*); (*Stadtteil*) quarter, section
Vierteljahr' *n* quarter (*of a year*)
vierteljäh'rig, vierteljähr'lich *adj* quarterly
vierteln ['fırtəln] *tr* quarter
Vier'telnote *f* (*mus*) quarter note
Viertelpfund' *n* quarter of a pound
Viertelstun'de *f* quarter of an hour
viertens ['firtəns] *adv* fourthly
vier'zehn *invar adj & pron* fourteen ‖ **Vierzehn** *f* (–;–en) fourteen
vier'zehnte §9 *adj & pron* fourteenth
Vier'zehntel *n* (–s;–) fourteenth (*part*)
vierzig ['fırtsıç] *invar adj & pron* forty ‖ **Vierzig** *f* (–;–en) forty
vierziger ['fırtsıgər] *invar adj* of the forties; **die v. Jahre** the forties
vierzigste ['fırtsıçstə] §9 *adj & pron* fortieth
Vikar [vı'kar] *m* (–s;–e) vicar
Vil·la ['vıla] *f* (–;–len [lən]) villa
violett [vı·ɔ'let] *adj* violet
Violine [vı·ɔ'linə] *f* (–;–n) violin
Violin'schlüssel *m* treble clef
Viper ['vipər] *f* (–;–n) viper
viril [vı'ril] *adj* virile
virtuos [vırtu'os] *adj* masterly ‖ **Virtuose** [vırtu'ozə] *m* (–n;–n), **Virtuosin** [vırtu'ozın] *f* (–;–nen) virtuoso
Vi·rus ['virus] *n* (–;–ren [rən]) virus
Visage [vı'zaʒə] *f* (–;–n) (coll) mug
Visier [vı'zir] *n* (–s;–e) visor; (*am Gewehr*) sight
visieren [vı'zirən] *tr* (*eichen*) gauge; (*Paß*) visa
Vision [vı'zjon] *f* (–;–en) vision
visionär [vızjɔ'ner] *adj* visionary ‖ **Visionär** *m* (–s;–e) visionary
Visitation [vızıta'tsjon] *f* (–;–en) inspection; search
Visite [vı'zitə] *f* (–;–n) formal call; **Visiten machen** (med) make the rounds
Visi'tenkarte *f* calling card

visuell [vizu'ɛl] *adj* visual
Vi·sum ['vizum] *n* (–s;–sa [za]) visa
vital [vı'tal] *adj* energetic
Vitalität [vıtalı'tet] *f* (–;) vitality
Vitamin [vıta'min] *n* (–s;–e) vitamin
Vitamin'mangel *m* vitamin deficiency
Vitrine [vı'trinə] *f* (–;–n) showcase
Vize- [fitsə], [vitsə] *comb.fm.* vice-
Vi'zekönig *m* viceroy
Vlies [flis] *n* (–es;–e) fleece
Vogel ['fogəl] *m* (–s;–) bird; (coll) chap, bird; **den V. abschießen** (coll) bring down the house; **du hast e-n V.!** (coll) you're cuckoo!
Vo'gelbauer *n* birdcage
Vogelbeerbaum ['fogəlberbaum] *m* mountain ash
vo'gelfrei *adj* outlawed
Vo'gelfutter *n* birdseed
Vo'gelkunde *f* ornithology
Vo'gelmist *m* bird droppings
vögeln ['føgəln] *tr & intr* (vulg) screw
Vo'gelperspektive *f*, **Vo'gelschau** *f* bird's-eye view
Vo'gelpfeife *f* bird call
Vo'gelscheuche *f* scarecrow
Vo'gelstange *f* perch
Vogel-Strauß'-Politik *f* burying one's head in the sand; **V. betreiben** bury one's head in the sand
Vo'gelstrich *m*, **Vo'gelzug** *m* migration of birds
Vöglein ['føglaın] *n* (–s;–) little bird
Vogt [fokt] *m* (–[e]s;–e) (obs) steward; (obs) governor, prefect, magistrate
Vokabel [vɔ'kabəl] *f* (–;–n) vocabulary word
Vokal [vɔ'kal] *m* (–s;–e) vowel
Volk [folk] *n* (–[e]s;–er) people, nation; lower classes; (*von Bienen*) swarm; (*von Rebhühnern*) covey
Völker– [fœlkər] *comb.fm.* international
Völ'kerbund *m* League of Nations
Völ'kerfriede *m* international peace
Völ'kerkunde *f* ethnology
Völ'kermord *m* genocide
Völ'kerrecht *n* international law
Völ'kerschaft *f* (–;–en) tribe
Völ'kerwanderung *f* barbarian invasions
volk'reich *adj* populous
Volks'abstimmung *f* plebiscite
Volks'aufwiegler *m* rabble rouser
Volks'ausdruck *m* household expression
Volks'befragung *f* public opinion poll
Volks'begehren *n* national referendum
Volks'bibliotek *f* free library
Volks'charakter *m* national character
Volks'deutsche §5 *mf* German national
Volks'dichter *m* popular poet
volks'eigen *adj* state-owned
Volks'entscheid *m* referendum
Volks'feind *m* public enemy
Volks'gunst *f* popularity
Volks'haufen *m* crowd, mob
Volks'herrschaft *f* democracy
Volks'hochschule *f* adult evening school
Volks'justiz *f* lynch law

Volks'küche *f* soup kitchen
Volks'kunde *f* folklore
Volks'lied *n* folksong
volks'mäßig *adj* popular
Volks'meinung *f* popular opinion
Volks'menge *f* populace, crowd of people
Volks'musik *f* popular music
Volks'partei *f* people's party
Volks'republik *f* people's republic
Volks'schule *f* grade school
Volks'sitte *f* national custom
Volks'sprache *f* vernacular
Volks'stamm *m* tribe; race
Volks'stimme *f* popular opinion
Volks'stimmung *f* mood of the people
Volks'tracht *f* national costume
Volkstum ['fɔlkstum] *n* (-s;) nationality
volkstümlich ['fɔlkstymlıç] *adj* national; popular
Volks'verführer –in §6 *mf* demagogue
Volks'versammlung *f* public meeting
Volks'vertreter –in §6 *mf* representative
Volks'wirt *m* political economist
Volks'wirtschaft *f* national economy
Volks'wirtschaftslehre *f* (educ) political economy
Volks'wohl *n* public good
Volks'wohlfahrt *f* public welfare
Volks'zählung *f* census
voll [fɔl] *adj* full, filled; whole, entire; (*Tageslicht*) broad; (coll) drunk; **aus dem vollen schöpfen** have unlimited resources; **j–n für v. ansehen** (or **nehmen**) take s.o. seriously || *adv* fully, in full; **v. und ganz** fully
vollauf' *adv*—**das genügt v.** that's quite enough; **v. beschäftigt** plenty busy; **v. zu tun haben** have plenty to do
Voll'beschäftigung *f* full employment
Voll'besitz *m* full possession
Voll'blut *n*, **Voll'blutpferd** *n* thoroughbred
vollblütig ['fɔlblytıç] *adj* full-blooded
vollbrin'gen §65 *tr* achieve
vollbusig ['vɔlbuzıç] *adj* big-breasted
Voll'dampf *m* full steam; **mit V.** (fig) at full blast, full speed
vollenden [fɔl'ɛndən] *tr* bring to a close, finish, complete; (*vervollkommnen*) perfect; **er hat sein Leben vollendet** (poet) he died
vollendet [fɔl'ɛndət] *adj* perfect
vollends ['fɔlɛnts] *adv* completely
Vollen'dung *f* (–;) finishing, completing; (*Vollkommenheit*) perfection
Völlerei [fœlə'raɪ] *f* (–;) gluttony
voll'führen *tr* carry out, execute
voll'füllen *tr* fill up
Voll'gas *n* full throttle
Voll'gefühl *n*—**im V.** (*genit*) fully conscious of
Voll'genuß *m* full enjoyment
vollgepfropft ['fɔlgəpfrɔpft] *adj* jammed, packed
voll'gießen §76 *tr* fill up
völlig ['fœlıç] *adj* full, complete
voll'jährig *adj* of age
Voll'jährigkeit *f* legal age, majority
vollkom'men, **voll'kommen** *adj* perfect || *adv* (coll) absolutely

Vollkom'menheit *f* (–;) perfection
Voll'kornbrot *n* whole-grain bread
Voll'kraft *f* full vigor, prime
voll'machen *tr* fill up; (coll) dirty
Voll'macht *f* full authority; (jur) power of attorney; **in V. for...** (*prefixed to the signature of another at end of letter*)
Voll'matrose *m* able-bodied seaman
Voll'milch *f* whole milk
Voll'mond *m* full moon
Voll'pension *f* full board and lodging
voll'saftig *adj* juicy, succulent
voll'schenken *tr* fill up
voll'schlagen §132 *ref*—**sich** [*dat*] **den Bauch v.** (coll) stuff oneself
voll'schlank *adj* well filled out
Voll'sitzung *f* plenary session
Voll'spur *f* (rr) standard-gauge track
voll'ständig *adj* full; complete, entire || *adv* completely, quite
Voll'ständigkeit *f* (–;) completeness
voll'stopfen *tr* stuff, cram
vollstrecken (vollstrek'ken) *tr* (*Urteil*) carry out; (*Testament*) execute; **ein Todesurteil an j–m v.** execute s.o.
Vollstreckung (Vollstrek'kung) *f.* (–;) execution
voll'tanken *tr* (aut) fill up || *intr* (aut) fill it up
volltönend ['fɔltønənt] *adj* (*Stimme*) rich; (*Satz*) well-rounded
Voll'treffer *m* direct hit
Voll'versammlung *f* plenary session
Voll'waise *f* (full) orphan
voll'wertig *adj* of full value; complete, perfect
vollzählig ['fɔltselıç] *adj* complete; **sind wir v.?** are we all here? || *adv* in full force
vollzie'hen §163 *tr* execute, carry out, effect; (*Vertrag*) ratify; (*Ehe*) consummate || *ref* take place
voll'zie'hend *adj* executive
Vollzie'hung *f*, **Vollzug'** *m* execution, carrying out
Vollzugs'ausschuß *m* executive committee
Volontär –in [vɔlɔn'ter(ın)] §8 *mf* volunteer; trainee
volontieren [vɔlɔn'tirən] *intr* work as a trainee
Volt [vɔlt] *n* (–[e]s;–) (elec) volt
Volu·men [vɔ'lumən] *n* (–s;– & –mina [mına]) (*Band; Rauminhalt*) volume
vom [fɔm] *abbr* **von dem**
von [fɔn] *prep* (*dat*) (*beim Passiv*) by; **für den Genitiv**) of; (*räumlich, zeitlich*) from; (*über*) about, of; **von... an** from...on; **von Holz** (made) of wood; **von Kindheit auf** from earliest childhood; **von mir aus** as far as **I** am concerned; **von selbst** automatically
voneinan'der *adv* from each other; of each other; apart
vonnöten [fɔn'nøtən] *invar adj*—**v. sein** be necessary
vonstatten [fɔn'tatən] *adv*—**gut v. gehen** go well; **v. gehen** take place
vor [for] *prep* (*dat*) (*örtlich*) in front of, before; (*zeitlich*) before, prior to; (*Abwehr*) against, from; (*wegen*) of,

with, for; **etw vor sich haben** face s.th.; **heute vor acht Tagen** today a week ago; **vor sich gehen** take place, occur; **vor sich hin** to oneself || *prep* (*acc*) in front of
vorab' *adv* in advance
Vor'abend *m*—**am V.** (*genit*) on the eve of
Vor'ahnung *f* (coll) hunch, idea
voran' *adv* in front, out ahead || *interj* go ahead!, go on!
voran'gehen §82 *intr* (SEIN) go on ahead, take the lead; (fig) set an example; **die Arbeit geht gut voran** the work is coming along well
voran'kommen §99 *intr* (SEIN) make progress; **gut v.** come along well
Vor'anschlag *m* rough estimate
Vor'anzeige *f* preliminary announcement; (cin) preview of coming attractions
Vor'arbeit *f* preliminary work
vor'arbeiten *intr* do the work in advance; do the preliminary work
vorauf' *adv* ahead, in front
voraus' *adv* in front; (*dat*) ahead (of) || **vor'aus** *adv*—**im v.** in advance
Voraus'abteilung *f* (mil) vanguard
voraus'bedingen §142 *tr* stipulate beforehand
voraus'bestellen *tr* reserve
voraus'bestimmen *tr* predetermine
voraus'bezahlen *tr* pay in advance
voraus'eilen *intr* (SEIN) rush ahead
vorausgesetzt [fɔ'rausgəzɛtst] *adj*—**v., daß** provided that
Voraus'sage *f* prediction; prophecy; (*des Wetters*) forecast; (*Wink*) tip
voraus'sagen *tr* predict; prophesy; (*Wetter*) forecast
Voraus'sagung *f* var of **Voraussage**
voraus'schauen *intr* look ahead
voraus'schicken *tr* send ahead; (fig) mention beforehand
voraus'sehen §138 *tr* foresee
voraus'setzen *tr* presume, presuppose
Voraus'setzung *f* assumption; prerequisite; premise
Voraus'sicht *f* foresight
voraus'sichtlich *adj* probable, presumable || *adv* probably, presumably, the way it looks
Voraus'zahlung *f* advance payment
Vor'bau *m* (-[e]s;-ten) projection; balcony, porch
vor'bauen *tr* build out || *intr* (*dat*) take precautions against
vor'bedacht *adj* premeditated || **Vorbedacht** *m* (-[e]s;)—**mit V.** on purpose; **ohne V.** unintentionally
vor'bedeuten *tr* forebode
Vor'bedeutung *f* (-;-en) foreboding; omen, portent
Vor'bedingung *f* (-;-en) precondition
Vorbehalt ['fɔrbəhalt] *m* (-[e]s;-e) reservation; proviso; **mit allem V. hinnehmen!** take it for what it's worth!; **mit** (*or* **unter**) **dem V., daß** with the proviso that; **stiller** (*or* **innerer**) **V.** mental reservation; **unter V. aller Rechte** all rights reserved
vor'behalten §90 *tr* reserve; **Änderungen v.!** subject to change without

notice || *ref*—**sich** [*dat*] **etw v.** reserve s.th. for oneself
vor'behaltlich *prep* (*genit*) subject to
vor'behaltlos *adj* unreserved, unconditional
vorbei' *adv* over, past, gone; **es ist drei Uhr v.** it's past three o'clock; **v. an** (*dat*) past, by; **v. ist v.** done is done; **v. können** be able to pass
vorbei'eilen *intr* (SEIN)—**an j-m v.** rush past s.o.
vorbei'fahren §71 *intr* (SEIN) drive by
vorbei'fliegen §57 *intr* (SEIN) fly past
vorbei'fließen §76 *intr* (SEIN) flow by
vorbei'gehen §82 *intr* (SEIN) pass; **an j-m v.** pass by s.o. || **Vorbeigehen** *n* —**im V.** in passing
vorbei'gelingen §142 *intr* (SEIN) fail
vorbei'kommen §99 *intr* (SEIN) pass by; (coll) stop in
vorbei'lassen §104 *tr* let pass
Vorbei'marsch *m* parade
vorbei'marschieren *intr* (SEIN) march by
Vor'bemerkung *f* (-;-en) preliminary remark; (parl) preamble
vorbenannt ['forbənant] *adj* aforementioned
vor'bereiten *tr* prepare || *ref* (**auf** *acc*, **für**) get ready (for)
vor'bereitend *adj* preparatory
Vor'bereitung *f* (-;-en) preparation
Vor'bericht *m* preliminary report
Vor'besprechung *f* (-;-en) preliminary discussion
vor'bestellen *tr* order in advance; (*Zimmer, usw.*) reserve
Vor'bestellung *f* (-;-en) advance order; reservation
vor'bestraft *adj* previously convicted
vor'beten *tr* keep repeating || *intr* lead in prayer
vor'beugen *ref* bend forward || *intr* (*dat*) prevent
vor'beugend *adj* preventive
Vor'beugung *f* (-;-en) prevention
Vor'beugungsmittel *n* preventive
Vor'bild *n* model; (*Beispiel*) example
vor'bildlich *adj* exemplary, model
Vor'bildung *f* (-;-en) educational background
Vor'bote *m* forerunner; (fig) harbinger
vor'bringen §65 *tr* bring forward, produce; (*Gründe*) give; (*Plan*) propose; (*Klagen*) prefer; (*Wunsch*) express
vor'buchstabieren *tr* spell out
Vor'bühne *f* apron, proscenium
vor'datieren *tr* antedate
vordem [for'dem] *adv* formerly
Vorder- [fɔrdər] *comb.fm.* front, fore-
Vor'derachse *f* front axle
Vor'derarm *m* forearm
Vor'derbein *n* foreleg
vordere ['fɔrdərə] §9 *adj* front
Vor'derfront *f* front; (fig) forefront
Vor'derfuß *m* front foot
Vor'dergrund *m* foreground
vor'derhand *adv* for the time being
vor'derlastig *adj* (aer) nose-heavy
Vor'derlauf *m* (hunt) foreleg
Vor'dermann *m* (-[e]s;-̈er) man in front; **j-n auf V. bringen** (coll) put s.o. straight; **V. halten** keep in line

Vor'derpfote f front paw
Vor'derrad n front wheel
Vor'derradantrieb m front-wheel drive
Vor'derreihe f front row; front rank
Vor'dersicht f front view
Vor'derseite f front side, front; (e-r Münze) obverse, heads
Vor'dersitz m front seat
vorderste ['fɔrdərstə] §9 adj farthest front
Vor'dersteven m (naut) stem
Vor'derteil m & n front section; (naut) prow
Vor'dertür f front door
Vor'derzahn m front tooth
Vor'derzimmer n front room
vor'drängen tr & ref press forward
vor'dringen §142 intr (SEIN) forge ahead, advance
vor'dringlich adj urgent
Vor'druck m printed form, blank
vor'ehelich adj premarital
vor'eilig adj hasty, rash
Vor'eiligkeit f (-;) haste, rashness
vor'eingenommen adj biased, prejudiced
Vor'eingenommenheit f (-;-en) bias, prejudice
Vor'eltern pl ancestors, forefathers
vor'enthalten §90 tr—j-m etw v. withhold s.th. from s.o.
Vor'entscheidung f (-;-en) preliminary decision
vor'erst adv first of all; for the time being, for the present
vorerwähnt ['fɔrervent] adj aforesaid
Vorfahr ['fɔrfɑr] m (-en;-en) forebear
vor'fahren §71 intr (SEIN) (bei) drive up (to)
Vor'fahrt f, **Vor'fahrt(s)recht** n right of way
Vor'fall m incident; event
vor'fallen §72 intr (SEIN) happen
Vor'feld n (aer) apron (of airport); (mil) approaches
vor'finden §59 tr find there
Vor'freude f anticipation
Vor'frühling m early spring
vor'fühlen intr—bei j-m v. feel s.o. out, put out feelers to s.o.
Vorführdame ['fɔrfyrdɑmə] f mannequin
vor'führen tr bring forward, produce; display, demonstrate; (Kleider) model; (Film) show; (Stück) (theat) present
Vor'führer –in §6 mf projectionist
Vor'führung f (-;-en) production; demonstration; showing; show, performance
Vor'gabe f points, handicap
Vor'gaberennen n handicap (race)
Vor'gabespiel n handicap
Vor'gang m event, incident, phenomenon; (Verfahren) process, procedure; (Präzedenzfall) precedent; (in den Akten) previous correspondence
Vor'gänger –in §6 mf predecessor
Vor'garten m front yard
vor'geben §80 tr pretend; give as an excuse; j-m zehn Punkte v. give s.o. ten points odds || intr—j-m v. give

s.o. odds || **Vorgeben** n (-s;-) pretext
Vor'gebirge n foothills; (Kap) cape
vorgeblich ['fɔrgepliç] adj ostensible
vorgefaßt ['fɔrgəfast] adj preconceived
Vor'gefühl n inkling; **banges V.** misgivings; **im V. von** or genit in anticipation of
vor'gehen §82 intr (SEIN) advance; go first; act; take action, proceed; (sich ereignen) go on, happen; (Uhr) be fast; (dat) take precedence (over); **die Arbeit geht vor** work comes first; **was geht hier vor?** what's going on here? || **Vorgehen** n (-s;) advance; action, proceeding; **gemeinschaftliches V.** concerted action
vorgelagert ['fɔrgəlɑgərt] adj offshore
Vor'gelände n foreground
vorgenannt ['fɔrgənant] adj aforementioned
Vor'gericht n appetizer
Vor'geschichte f previous history; (Urgeschichte) prehistory
vor'geschichtlich adj prehistoric
Vor'geschmack m foretaste
Vorgesetzte ['fɔrgəzetstə] §5 mf superior; boss; (mil) senior officer
vor'gestern adv day before yesterday
vor'gestrig adj of the day before yesterday
vorgetäuscht ['fɔrgətɔɪʃt] adj make-believe
vor'greifen §88 intr (dat) anticipate
Vor'griff m anticipation
vor'gucken intr (Unterkleid) show
vor'haben §89 tr have in mind, plan; intend to do; (ausfragen) question; (schelten) scold; (Schürze) (coll) have on || **Vorhaben** n (-s;-) intention, plan; project
Vor'halle f entrance hall; lobby
vor'halten §90 tr—j-m etw v. hold s.th. in front of s.o.; (fig) reproach s.o. with s.th. || intr last
Vor'haltung f (-;-en) reproach; j-m **Vorhaltungen machen über** (acc) reproach s.o. for
Vor'hand f (cards) forehand; (tennis) forehand stroke; **die V. haben** (cards) lead off
vorhanden [for'handən] adj present, at hand, available; (com) in stock; **v. sein** exist
Vorhan'densein n existence; presence
Vor'hang m (-[e]s;⸗e) curtain; (theat) (coll) curtain call; **Eiserner V.** iron curtain
Vorhängeschloß ['fɔrhɛŋəʃlɔs] n padlock
Vor'hangstange f curtain rod
Vor'hangstoff m drapery material
Vor'haut f foreskin
Vor'hemd n dicky, shirt front
vor'her adv before, previously; (im voraus) in advance
vorher'bestellen tr reserve
vorher'bestimmen tr predetermine; (eccl) predestine
Vorher'bestimmung f predestination
vorher'gehend, vorherig [for'heriç] adj preceding, previous; prior
Vor'herrschaft f predominance

vor'herrschen *intr* predominate, prevail

vor'herrschend *adj* predominant, prevailing

Vorher'sage *f* prediction; forecast

vorher'sagen *tr* predict, foretell; *(Wetter)* forecast

vorhin' *adv* a little while ago

vor'historisch *adj* prehistoric

Vor'hof *m* front yard; (anat) auricle

Vor'hut *f* (mil) vanguard

vorige ['forɪgə] §9 *adj* previous, former; **voriges Jahr** last year

Vor'jahr *n* preceding year

vor'jährig *adj* last year's

Vor'kammer *f* (anat) auricle; (aut) precombustion chamber

Vor'kampf *m* (box) preliminary bout; (sport) heat

Vor'kämpfer –in §6 *mf* pioneer

Vorkehrung ['forkerʊŋ] *f* (-;-en) precaution; **Vorkehrungen treffen** take precautions

Vor'kenntnis *f* (von) basic knowledge (of); **Vorkenntnisse** rudiments, basics; **Vorkenntnisse nicht erforderlich** no previous experience necessary

vor'knöpfen *ref*—**sich** [*dat*] **j-n v.** (coll) chew s.o. out

Vor'kommando *n* (mil) advance party

vor'kommen §99 *intr* (SEIN) happen; *(Fall)* come up; *(als Besucher)* be admitted; *(scheinen)* seem, look; *(sich finden)* be found; *(zu Besuch)* call on ‖ *ref*—**er kam sich** [*dat*] **dumm vor** he felt silly ‖ *impers*—**es kommt dir nur so vor** you are just imagining it; **es kommt mir vor** it seems to me ‖ **Vorkommen** *n* (-s;-) occurrence; (min) deposit

Vorkommnis ['forkɔmnɪs] *n* (-ses;-se) event, occurrence

Vorkriegs– *comb.fm.* prewar

vor'laden §103 *tr* (jur) summon; *(unter Strafandrohung)* (jur) subpoena

Vor'ladung *f* (-;-en) (jur) summons; *(unter Strafandrohung)* (jur) subpoena

Vor'lage *f* submission, presentation; proposal; *(Muster)* pattern; bedside carpet; (fb) forward pass; (parl) bill

vor'lassen §104 *tr* let go ahead; *(Auto)* let pass; *(zulassen)* admit

Vor'lauf *m* (sport) qualifying heat

Vor'läufer –in §6 *mf* forerunner

vor'läufig *adj* preliminary; temporary ‖ *adv* provisionally; temporarily, for the time being

vor'laut *adj* forward, fresh

Vor'leben *n* past life, former life

Vorlegebesteck ['forlegəbəʃtɛk] *n* carving set

Vorlegegabel ['forlegəgɑbəl] *f* carving fork

Vor'legelöffel ['forlegəlœfəl] *m* serving spoon

Vorlegemesser ['forlegəmɛsər] *n* carving knife

vor'legen *tr* put forward; propose; *(Ausweis, Paß)* show; *(Essen)* serve; *(zur Prüfung, usw.)* submit, present; **den Ball v.** (fb) pass the ball; **ein scharfes Tempo v.** (coll) speed it up;

j-m e-e Frage v. ask s.o. a question ‖ *ref* lean forward

Ver'leger *m* (-s;-) throw rug

Vorlegeschloß ['forlegəʃlɔs] *n* padlock

vor'lesen §107 *tr*—**j-m etw v.** read s.th. to s.o.

Vor'lesung *f* (-;-en) reading; lecture; **e-e V. halten über** *(acc)* give a lecture on

Vor'lesungsverzeichnis *n* university catalogue

vor'letzte §9 *adj* second last; (gram) penultimate

Vor'liebe *f* preference

vorliebnehmen [for'lipnemən] §116 *intr* take pot luck; **v. mit** put up with

vor'liegen §108 *intr* be present; exist; be under consideration; **dem Richter v.** be up before the judge; **heute liegt nichts vor** there's nothing doing today; **mir liegt e-e Beschwerde vor** I have a complaint here; **was liegt gegen ihn vor?** what is the charge against him?

vor'liegend *adj* present, at hand

vor'lügen §111 *tr*—**j-m etw v. über** *(acc)* tell s.o. lies about

vor'machen *tr*—**du kannst mir doch nichts v.** you can't put anything over on me; **j-m etw v.** show s.o. how to do s.th. ‖ *ref*—**er läßt sich** [*dat*] **nichts v.** he's nobody's fool; **sich** [*dat*] **selbst etw v.** fool oneself

Vor'macht *f* leading power; supremacy

Vor'machtstellung *f* (position of) supremacy

vormalig ['formɑlɪç] *adj* former

vormals ['formɑls] *adv* formerly

Vor'marsch *m* advance

vor'merken *tr* note down; reserve; **sich v. lassen für** put in for

Vor'mittag *m* forenoon, morning

vor'mittags *adv* in the forenoon

Vor'mund *m* guardian

Vor'mundschaft *f* (-;-en) guardianship

vor'mundschaftlich *adj* guardian's

Vor'mundschaftsgericht *n* orphans' court

vorn [fɔrn] *adv* in front; ahead; **ganz v.** all the way up front; **nach v.** forward; **nach v. heraus wohnen** live in the front part of the house; **nach v. liegen** face the front; **von v.** from the front; **von v. anfangen** begin at the beginning

Vor'nahme *f* undertaking

Vor'name *m* first name

vorne ['fɔrnə] *adv* (coll) var of **vorn**

vornehm ['fornem] *adj* distinguished, high-class; **vornehme Welt** high society; **vornehmste Aufgabe** principal task ‖ *adv*—**v. tun** put on airs

vor'nehmen §116 *tr* *(umbinden)* put on; undertake, take up; *(Änderungen)* make; **wieder v.** resume ‖ *ref*—**sich** [*dat*] **ein Buch v.** take up a book; **sich** [*dat*] **etw v.** decide upon s.th.; **sich** [*dat*] **j-n v.** take s.o. to task; **sich** [*dat*] **v. zu** (*inf*) make up one's mind to (*inf*); **sich** [*dat*] **zuviel v.** bite off more than one can chew

Vor'nehmheit *f* (-;) distinction, high rank; distinguished bearing

vor'nehmlich *adv* especially
vor'neigen *ref* bend forward
vorn'herein *adv*—**von v.** from the first
vornweg ['fɔrnvɛk], (fɔrn'vɛk] *adv*—
er ist weit v. he is way out in front;
mit dem Kopf v. head first; **mit dem
Mund v.** sein be fresh
Vor'ort *m* suburb
Vorort- *comb.fm.* suburban
Vor'ortbahn *f* (rr) suburban line
Vor'ortzug *m* commuter train
Vor'platz *m* front yard; (*Diele*) entrance hall; (*Vorfeld*) (aer) apron
Vor'posten *m* (mil) outpost
Vor'rang *m* precedence; priority; pre-
eminence; **den V. vor j-m haben**
have precedence over s.o.
Vor'rat *m* (-[e]s;ᵕe) (an *dat*) stock
(of), supply (of); **auf V. kaufen** buy
in quantity; **e-n V. anlegen an** (*dat*)
stock
vorrätig ['fɔrretɪç] *adj* in stock
Vor'ratskammer *f* pantry, storeroom
Vor'ratsraum *m* storeroom
Vor'ratsschrank *m* pantry
Vor'raum *m* anteroom
vor'rechnen *tr*—**j-m etw v.** figure out
s.th. for s.o.; **j-m seine Fehler v.**
enumerate s.o.'s mistakes to s.o.
Vor'recht *n* privilege, prerogative
Vor'rede *f* preface, introduction
vor'reden *tr*—**j-m etw v.** try to make
s.o. believe s.th.
Vor'redner **-in** §6 *mf* previous speaker
Vor'richtung *f* (-;-en) preparation;
(*Gerät*) device, appliance, mechanism; (mach) fixture
vor'rücken *tr* move forward || *intr*
(SEIN) (*Truppen*) advance; (*Polizei*)
move in; (*im Dienst*) be promoted
Vor'runde *f* (sport) play-offs
vors [fɔrs] *abbr* **vor das**
vor'sagen *tr*—**j-m etw v.** recite s.th.
to s.o. || *intr* (*dat*) prompt
Vor'sager **-in** §6 *mf* prompter
Vor'satz *m* purpose, intention; (jur)
premeditation; **den V. fassen zu** (*inf*)
make up one's mind to (*inf*); **mit V.**
on purpose; **seinen V. ausführen**
gain one's ends
Vor'satzblatt *n* (bb) end paper
Vor'satzgerät *n* adapter
vorsätzlich ['fɔrzetslɪç] *adj* deliberate;
(*Mord*) premeditated
Vor'schau *f* (cin) preview
vor'schieben §130 *tr* push forward;
offer as an excuse; (fig) plead; **den
Riegel v.** (*dat*) (fig) prevent; **Truppen v.** move troops forward
vor'schießen §76 *tr* (*Geld*) (coll) ad-
vance || *intr* (SEIN) dart ahead
Vor'schiff *n* (naut) forecastle
Vor'schlag *m* proposal; (*Angebot*)
offer; (*Anregung*) suggestion; (*Empfehlung*) recommendation; (mus)
grace note; (parl) motion; **in V. bringen** propose; (parl) move
vor'schlagen §132 *tr* propose; suggest;
recommend; **zur Wahl v.** nominate
Vor'schlagsliste *f* slate of candidates
Vor'schlußrunde *f* (sport) semifinal
vor'schnell *adj* rash, hasty
vor'schreiben §62 *tr* prescribe, order;

specify; write out; **ich lasse mir
nichts v.** I take orders from no one
vor'schreiten §86 *intr* (SEIN) step forward; advance
Vor'schrift *f* order, direction; regulation; (med) prescription
vor'schriftsmäßig *adj* & *adv* according
to regulations
vor'schriftswidrig *adj* & *adv* against
regulations
Vor'schub *m* assistance; (mach) feed;
V. leisten (*dat*) encourage; (jur) aid
and abet
Vor'schule *f* prep school; (*Elementar-
schule*) elementary school
Vor'schuß *m* (*Geld-*) advance; (jur)
retainer
vor'schützen *tr* pretend, plead
Vor'schützung *f* (-;) pretense
vor'schweben *intr*—**mir schwebte etw
anderes vor** I had s.th. else in mind;
das schwebt mir dunkel vor I have a
dim recollection of it
vor'schwindeln *tr*—**j-m etw v.** fool s.o.
about s.th.
vor'sehen §138 *tr* schedule, plan; provide; (fin) earmark; **das Gesetz sieht
vor, daß** the law provides that || *ref*
be careful, take care; **sich mit etw
v.** provide oneself with s.th.; **sich v.
vor** (*dat*) be on one's guard against
Vor'sehung *f* (-;) Providence
vor'setzen *tr* put forward; (*Silbe*) prefix; **j-m etw v.** set s.th. before s.o.
(*to eat*); **j-m j-n v.** set s.o. over s.o.
Vor'sicht *f* caution, care; (*Umsicht*)
prudence; **V.!** watch out! (*auf
Kisten*) handle with care!; **V., Stufe!**
watch your step!
vor'sichtig *adj* cautious, careful
Vor'sichtigkeit *f* (-;) caution
vorsichtshalber ['fɔrzɪçtshalbər] *adv*
to be on the safe side, as a precaution
Vor'sichtsmaßnahme *f*, **Vor'sichts-
maßregel** *f* precaution
Vor'silbe *f* prefix
vor'singen §142 *tr*—**j-m etw v.** sing
s.th. to s.o. || *intr* lead the choir
Vor'sitz *m* chairmanship, chair; presidency; **den V. haben** (or **führen**) **bei**
preside over; **unter V. von** presided
over by
Vorsitzende ['fɔrzɪtsəndə] §5 *mf*
chairperson; president
Vor'sorge *f* provision; **V. tragen** (or
treffen) **für** make provision for, provide for
vor'sorgen *intr* (**für**) provide (for)
vorsorglich ['fɔrzɔrklɪç] *adv* as a precaution, just in case
Vor'spann *m* (cin) credits; (*Kurzfilm*)
(cin) short
Vor'speise *f* appetizer
vor'spiegeln *tr*—**j-m etw v.** delude s.o.
with s.th.; **j-m falsche Tatsachen v.**
misrepresent facts to s.o.
Vor'spiegelung *f* (-;) sham; pretense;
V. falscher Tatsachen misrepresenta-
tion of facts
Vor'spiel *n* prelude; (*beim Geschlechtsverkehr*) foreplay; (mus)
overture; (theat) curtain raiser; **das**

war nur das V.! (fig) that was only the beginning!
vor'spielen *tr*—**j**–**m etw v.** play s.th. for s.o.
vor'sprechen §64 *tr*—**j**–**m etw v.** pronounce s.th. for s.o.; teach s.o. how to pronounce s.th. ‖ *intr*—**bei j–m v.** drop in on s.o.; **j–m v.** audition before s.o.
vor'springen §142 *intr* (SEIN) leap forward; *(aus dem Versteck)* jump out; *(vorstehen)* stick out, protrude
Vor'sprung *m* projection; *(Sims)* ledge; *(Vorteil)* advantage; (sport) head start; (sport) lead
Vor'stadt *f* suburb
vor'städtisch *adj* suburban
Vor'stand *m* board of directors; executive committee, executive board; *(Person)* chairman of the board
vor'stehen §146 *intr* protrude; *(dat)* be at the head of, direct, manage
Vor'steher *m* (**-s;-**) head, director, manager; (educ) principal
Vor'steherdrüse *f* prostate gland
Vor'steherin *f* (**-;-nen**) head, director, manager; (educ) principal
vor'stellen *tr* place in front, put ahead; *(Uhr)* set ahead; *(einführen)* introduce, present; *(darstellen)* represent; *(bedeuten)* mean; *(hinweisen auf)* point out ‖ *ref*—**sich** [*dat*] **etw v.** imagine s.th., picture s.th.
Vor'stellung *f* (**-;-en**) introduction, presentation; *(Begriff)* idea; *(Einspruch)* remonstrance, protest; (cin) show; (theat) performance
Vor'stellungsvermögen *n* imagination
Vor'stoß *m* (fig & mil) thrust, drive
vor'stoßen §150 *tr* push forward ‖ *intr* (SEIN) push forward, advance
Vor'strafe *f* previous conviction
Vor'strafenregister *n* previous record
vor'strecken *tr* stretch out; *(Geld)* advance
Vor'stufe *f* preliminary stage
Vor'tag *m* previous day
vor'täuschen *tr* pretend, put on
Vor'teil *m* advantage; profit; (tennis) advantage
vor'teilhaft *adj* advantageous; profitable
Vortrag ['fortrɑk] *m* (**-[e]s;-̈e**) performance; *(Bericht)* report; *(e-s Gedichtes)* recitation; *(e-r Rede)* delivery; *(Vorlesung)* lecture; (acct) balance (carried over); (mus) recital; **e-n V. halten über** *(acc)* give a lecture on
vor'tragen §132 *tr* perform; present
Vortragende ['fortragəndə] §5 *mf* performer; speaker; lecturer
Vor'tragsfolge *f* program
vortrefflich ['fortreflɩç] *adj* excellent
vor'treten §152 *intr* (SEIN) step forward; (fig) stick out, protrude
Vor'tritt *m* (**-[e]s;-**) precedence
vorü'ber *adv* past, by, along; *(zeitlich)* over, gone by
vorü'bergehen §82 *intr* (SEIN) pass; (an *dat*) pass by; (fig) disregard
vorü'bergehend *adj* passing, transitory ‖ **Vorübergehende** §5 *mf* passer-by

vorü'berziehen §163 *intr* (SEIN) march by; *(Gewitter)* blow over
Vor'übung *f* warmup
Vor'untersuchung *f* preliminary investigation
Vor'urteil *n* prejudice
vor'urteilsfrei, vor'urteilslos *adj* unprejudiced
Vor'vergangenheit *f* (gram) past perfect
Vor'verkauf *m* advance sale; (theat) advance reservation
vor'verlegen *tr* advance, move up
Vor'wahl *f* (pol) primary
vor'wählen *intr* dial the area code
Vor'wählnummer *f* (telp) area code
Vor'wand *m* (**-[e]s;-̈e**) pretext; excuse
vorwärts ['forverts] *adv* forward, on, ahead ‖ *interj* go on!
vor'wärtsbringen §65 *tr* bring forward; (fig) advance
vor'wärtsgehen §82 *intr* (SEIN) progress
vor'wärtskommen §99 *intr* (SEIN) go ahead; progress, make headway
vorweg [for'vɛk] *adv* beforehand; out in front
Vorweg'nahme *f* anticipation
vorweg'nehmen §116 *tr* anticipate; presuppose, assume
vor'weisen §118 *tr* produce, show
Vor'welt *f* prehistoric world
vor'weltlich *adj* primeval
vor'werfen §160 *tr*—**j–m etw v.** throw s.th. to s.o.; (fig) throw s.th. up to s.o.
vorwiegend ['forvigənt] *adj* predominant ‖ *adv* predominantly, chiefly
Vor'wissen *n* foreknowledge
vor'witzig *adj* inquisitive; brash
Vor'wort *n* (**-[e]s;-e**) foreword
Vor'wurf *m* reproach, blame; *(e-s Dramas)* subject; **j–m Vorwürfe machen** blame s.o.
vor'wurfslos *adj* irreproachable
vor'wurfsvoll *adj* reproachful
vor'zählen *tr* enumerate
Vor'zeichen *n* omen; (math) sign; (mus) accidental; **negatives V.** minus sign
vor'zeichnen *tr*—**j–m etw v.** draw or sketch s.th. for s.o.
Vor'zeichnung *f* (**-;-en**) drawing; (mus) signature
vor'zeigen *tr* produce, show; *(Wechsel)* present
Vor'zeiger –in §6 *mf* bearer
Vor'zeigung *f* (**-;-en**) producing, showing; presentation
Vor'zeit *f* remote antiquity
vor'zeiten *adv* in days of old
vor'zeitig *adj* premature
vor'ziehen §163 *tr* draw forth; pull out; prefer; (mil) move up
Vor'zimmer *n* anteroom; entrance hall
Vor'zug *m* preference; *(Vorteil)* advantage; *(Überlegenheit)* superiority; *(Vorrang)* priority; *(Vorrecht)* privilege; *(Vorzüglichkeit)* excellence; **e-r Sache den V. geben** prefer s.th.
vorzüglich ['fortsyklɩç] *adj* excellent, first-rate ‖ *adv* especially
Vor'züglichkeit *f* (**-;**) excellence
Vor'zugsaktie *f* preferred stock

Vor'zugsbehandlung *f* preferential treatment
Vor'zugspreis *m* special price
Vor'zugsrecht *n* priority; privilege
vor'zugsweise *adv* preferably
votieren [vɔ'tirən] *intr* vote
Votiv– [vɔtif] *comb.fm.* votive
Vo·tum ['votʊm] *n* (-s;-ten [tən] & -ta [ta]) vote

vulgär [vʊl'ger] *adj* vulgar
Vulkan [vʊl'kɑn] *m* (-s;-e) volcano
Vulkan'ausbruch *m* eruption
vulkanisch [vʊl'kɑnɪʃ] *adj* volcanic
vulkanisieren [vʊlkɑnɪ'zirən] *tr* vulcanize
Vulkan'schlot *m* volcanic vent
VW *abbr* (**Volkswagen**) VW
V-Waffe *f* (**Vergeltungswaffe**) V-1, V-2

W

W, w [ve] *invar n* W, w
Waage ['vagə] *f* (-;-n) (pair of) scales; (astr) Libra; (gym) horizontal position; **die beiden Dinge halten sich** [dat] **die W.** the two things balance each other; **die W. halten** (*dat*) counterbalance; **j–m die W. halten** be a match for s.o.
waa'gerecht, waagrecht ['vakreçt] *adj* horizontal, level
Waagschale ['vakʃalə] *f* scale(s); **in die W. fallen** carry weight; **in die W. werfen** bring to bear
wabbelig ['vabəlɪç] *adj* (coll) flabby
Wabe ['vabə] *f* (-;-n) honeycomb
wach [vax] *adj* awake; (*lebhaft*) lively; (*Geist*) alert; **ganz w.** wide awake
Wach'ablösung *f* changing of the guard
Wach'dienst *m* guard duty
Wache ['vaxə] *f* (-;-n) guard, watch; (*Wachstube*) guardroom; (*Wachlokal*) guardhouse; (*Polizei–*) police station; (*Wachdienst*) guard duty; (*Posten*) guard, sentinel; **auf W.** on guard; **auf W. ziehen** mount guard; **W. schieben** (coll) pull guard duty
wachen ['vaxən] *intr* be awake; **bei j–m w.** sit up with s.o.; **w. über** (*acc*) watch over, guard
wach'habend *adj* on guard duty
wach'halten §90 *tr* keep awake; (fig) keep alive
Wach'hund *m* watchdog
Wach'lokal *n* guardroom; police station
Wach'mann *m* (-[e]s;-leute) (Aust) policeman
Wach'mannschaft *f* (mil) guard detail
Wacholder [va'xɔldər] *m* (-s;-) juniper
Wachol'derbranntwein *m* gin
Wach'posten *m* sentry
wach'rufen §122 *tr* wake up; (*Erinnerung*) bring back
Wachs [vaks] *n* (-es;-e) wax
wachsam ['vaxzam] *adj* vigilant
Wach'samkeit *f* (-;) vigilance
Wachs'bohne *f* wax bean
wachsen ['vaksən] *tr* wax || §155 *intr* (SEIN) grow; (*an dat*) increase (in)
wächsern ['vɛksərn] *adj* wax; (fig) waxy
Wachs'figurenkabinett *n* wax museum
Wachs'kerze *f*, **Wachs'licht** *n* wax candle
Wachs'leinwand *f* oilcloth

Wach'stube *f* guardroom
Wachs'tuch *n* oilcloth
Wachstum ['vaxstum] *n* (-s;) growth; increase
Wacht [vaxt] *f* (-;-en) guard, watch
Wächte ['veçtə] *f* (-;-n) snow cornice
Wachtel ['vaxtəl] *f* (-;-n) quail
Wach'telhund *m* spaniel
Wächter ['veçtər] *m* (-s;-) guard
Wacht'meister *m* police sergeant
Wach'traum *m* daydream
Wacht'turm *m* watchtower
wackelig ['vakəlɪç] *adj* wobbly; (*Zahn*) loose; (fig) shaky
Wackelkontakt ['vakəlkɔntakt] *m* (elec) loose connection, poor contact
wackeln ['vakəln] *intr* wobble; shake; (*locker sein*) be loose
wacker ['vakər] *adj* decent, honest; (*tapfer*) brave || *adv* heartily
wacklig ['vaklɪç] *adj* var of **wackelig**
Wade ['vadə] *f* (-;-n) (anat) calf
Wa'denbein *n* (anat) fibula
Wa'denkrampf *m* leg cramp
Wa'denstrumpf *m* calf-length stocking
Waffe ['vafə] *f* (-;-n) weapon; branch of service; **die Waffen strecken** surrender; (fig) give up; **zu den Waffen greifen** take up arms
Waffel ['vafəl] *f* (-;-n) waffle
Waf'fenbruder *m* comrade in arms
waf'fenfähig *adj* capable of bearing arms
Waf'fengang *m* armed conflict
Waf'fengattung *f* branch of service
Waf'fengewalt *f* force of arms
Waf'fenkammer *f* armory
Waf'fenlager *n* ordnance depot; **heimliches W.** cache of arms
waf'fenlos *adj* unarmed
Waf'fenruhe *f* truce
Waf'fenschein *m* gun permit
Waf'fenschmied *m* gunsmith
Waf'fenschmuggel *m* gunrunning
Waf'fen-SS *f* (-;) SS combat unit
Waf'fenstillstand *m* armistice
Wagehals ['vagəhals] *m* daredevil
Wagemut ['vagəmut] *m* daring
wagen ['vagən] *tr* dare; risk || *ref* venture, dare || **Wagen** *m* (-s;-) wagon; (*Fahrzeug; Teil e–r Schreibmaschine*) carriage; (aut, rr) car; **der Große Wagen** the Big Dipper; **j–m an den W. fahren** (fig) step on s.o.'s toes
wägen ['vegən] *tr* (& fig) weigh
Wa'genabteil *n* (rr) compartment

Wa'genburg *f* barricade of wagons
Wa'genheber *m* (aut) jack
Wa'genpark *m* fleet of cars
Wa'genpflege *f* (aut) maintenance
Wa'genschlag *m* car door, carriage door
Wa'genschmiere *f* (aut) grease
Wa'genspur *f* wheel track, rut
Wa'genwäsche *f* car wash
Wagestück ['vɑgə/tyk] *n* hazardous venture, daring deed
Waggon [va'gō] *m* (-s;-s) railroad car
waghalsig ['vɑkhalzɪç] *adj* foolhardy
Wagnis ['vɑknɪs] *n* (-ses;-se) risk
Wahl [val] *f* (-;-en) choice, option; (*Auswahl*) selection; (*Alternative*) alternative; (pol) election; **e-e W.** treffen make a choice; **vor der W.** stehen have the choice
wählbar ['velbɑr] *adj* eligible
Wähl'barkeit *f* (-;) eligibility
Wahl'beeinflussung *f* interference with the election process
wahl'berechtigt *adj* eligible to vote
Wahl'beteiligung *f* election turnout
Wahl'bezirk *m* ward
wählen ['velən] *tr* choose; select; (pol) elect; (telp) dial ‖ *intr* vote
Wäh'ler *m* (-s;-) voter
Wahl'ergebnis *n* election returns
Wäh'lerin *f* (-;-nen) voter
wählerisch ['verlərɪʃ] *adj* choosy, particular
Wäh'lerschaft *f* (-;-en) constituency
Wäh'lerscheibe *f* (telp) dial
Wahl'fach *n* (educ) elective
wahl'fähig *adj* eligible for election; having a vote
wahl'frei *adj* (educ) elective
Wahl'gang *m* ballot
Wahl'kampf *m* election campaign
Wahl'kreis *m* constituency; district
Wahl'leiter *m* campaign manager
Wahl'list *f* (pol) slate, ticket
Wahl'lokal *n* polling place
Wahl'lokomotive *f* (coll) vote getter
wahl'los *adj* indiscriminate
Wahl'parole *f* campaign slogan
Wahl'programm *n* (pol) platform
Wahl'recht *n* right to vote, suffrage
Wahl'rede *f* campaign speech
Wahl'spruch *m* motto; (com, pol) slogan
Wahl'urne *f* ballot box
Wahl'versammlung *f* campaign rally
wahl'verwandt *adj* congenial
Wahl'zelle *f* voting booth
Wahl'zettel *m* ballot
Wahn [van] *m* (-[e]s;) delusion; error; folly; madness
Wahn'bild *n* phantom, delusion
wähnen ['venən] *tr* fancy, imagine
Wahn'idee *f* delusion; (coll) crazy idea
Wahn'sinn *m* (& fig) madness
wahn'sinnig *adj* (vor *dat*) mad (with); (coll) terrible ‖ *adv* madly; (coll) awfully ‖ **Wahnsinnige** §5 *mf* lunatic
Wahn'vorstellung *f* hallucination
Wahn'witz *m* (& fig) madness
wahn'witzig *adj* mad; (*unverantwortlich*) irresponsible
wahr [var] *adj* true; (*wirklich*) real; (*echt*) genuine; **nicht w.?** right?

wahren ['varən] *tr* keep; (*Anschein*) keep up; (vor *dat*) protect (against)
währen ['verən] *intr* last
während ['verənt] *prep* (*genit*) during; (jur) pending ‖ *conj* while; whereas
wahr'haben §89 *tr* admit
wahr'haft, wahr'haftig *adj* true, truthful; (*wirklich*) real ‖ *adv* actually
Wahr'haftigkeit *f* (-;) truthfulness
Wahr'heit *f* (-;-en) truth; **j-m die W.** sagen give s.o. a piece of one's mind
wahr'heitsgemäß, wahr'heitsgetreu *adj* true, faithful; truthful
Wahr'heitsliebe *f* truthfulness
wahr'heitsliebend *adj* truthful
wahr'lich *adv* truly; (Bib) verily
wahrnehmbar ['varnembɑr] *adj* noticeable
wahr'nehmen §116 *tr* notice; (*benutzen*) make use of; (*Interesse*) protect; (*Recht*) assert
Wahr'nehmung *f* (-;) observation, perception; (*der Interessen*) safeguarding
wahr'sagen *ref*—**sich** [*dat*] **w. lassen** have one's fortune told ‖ *intr* prophesy; tell fortunes
Wahr'sagerin *f* (-;-nen) fortuneteller
wahrscheinlich [var'ʃainlɪç] *adj* probable, likely ‖ *adv* probably
Wahrschein'lichkeit *f* (-;) probability
Wahr'spruch *m* verdict
Wah'rung *f* (-;) safeguarding
Wäh'rung *f* (-;-en) currency; standard
Wäh'rungsabwertung *f* devaluation
Wäh'rungseinheit *f* monetary unit
Wahr'zeichen *n* landmark
Waise ['vaɪzə] *f* (-;-n) orphan
Wai'senhaus *n* orphanage
Wal [val] *m* (-[e]s;-e) whale
Wald [valt] *m* (-[e]s;ᵊer) forest, woods
Wald– *comb.fm.* forest; sylvan; wild
Wald'aufseher *m* forest ranger
Wald'brand *m* forest fire
waldig ['valdɪç] *adj* wooded
Waldung ['valduŋ] *f* (-;-en) forest
Wald'wirtschaft *f* forestry
Wal'fang *m* whaling
Wal'fänger *m* (-s;-) whaler
walken ['valkən] *tr* full
Wal'ker *m* (-s;-) fuller
Wall [val] *m* (-[e]s;ᵊe) mound; embankment; (mil) rampart
Wallach ['valax] *m* (-[e]s;-e) gelding
wallen ['valən] *intr* (*sieden*) boil; (*sprudeln*) bubble; (*Gewand, Haar*) flow, fall in waves ‖ *intr* (SEIN) go on a pilgrimage; travel, wander
wall'fahren *insep intr* (SEIN) go on a pilgrimage
Wall'fahrer –in §6 *mf* pilgrim
Wall'fahrt *f* pilgrimage
Wall'graben *m* moat
Wal'lung *f* (-;) simmering, boiling; bubbling; flow; flutter; (*Blutandrang*) congestion; **in W. bringen** enrage; **in W. geraten** fly into a rage; **Wallungen** hot flashes
Walnuß ['valnus] *f* walnut
Walroß ['valrɔs] *n* walrus
Wal'speck *m* blubber
walten ['valtən] *intr* rule; hold sway;

Gnade w. lassen show mercy; **seines Amtes w.** attend to one's duties
Wal′tran m whale oil
Walze ['valtsə] f (-;-n) cylinder, drum; roll, roller; (der Schreib-maschine) platen
walzen ['valtsən] tr roll
wälzen ['vɛltsən] tr roll; (Bücher) pore over; (Gedanken) turn over in one's mind; **die Schuld auf j–n w.** shift the blame to s.o. else || ref roll, toss; (im Kot) wallow; (im Blut) welter
Wal′zer m (-s;-) waltz
Wäl′zer m (-s;-) (coll) thick tome
Walz′werk n rolling mill
Wamme ['vamə] f (-;-n) dewlap; (coll) potbelly
Wampe ['vampə] f (-;-n) (coll) pot-belly
wand [vant] pret of **winden** || **Wand** f (-;⸚e) wall; partition; (Fels-) cliff; **spanische W.** folding screen
Wand′apparat m (telp) wall phone
Wand′bekleidung f wainscot
Wandel ['vandəl] m (-s;) change
wandelbar ['vandəlbar] adj changeable
Wan′delgang m, **Wan′delhalle** f lobby
wandeln ['vandəln] tr change || ref (in acc) change (into) || intr (SEIN) (poet) wander; (poet) walk
Wan′derer –in §6 mf wanderer; hiker
Wan′derlust f wanderlust, itch to travel
wandern ['vandərn] intr (SEIN) wander; hike; (Vögel) migrate
Wan′derniere f floating kidney
Wan′derpreis m challenge trophy
Wan′derschaft f (-;) travels, wanderings
Wan′derstab m walking stick
Wan′derung f (-;-en) hike; migration
Wan′dervogel m migratory bird; (coll) rover
Wand′gemälde n mural
Wand′karte f wall map
Wand′leuchter m sconce
Wand′lung f (-;-en) change, transformation; (eccl) consecration
Wand′malerei f wall painting
Wand′pfeiler m pilaster
Wand′schirm m folding screen
Wand′schrank m wall shelves
Wand′spiegel m wall mirror
Wand′steckdose f, **Wand′stecker** m (elec) wall outlet
Wand′tafel f blackboard
wandte ['vantə] pret of **wenden**
Wand′teppich m tapestry
Wange ['vaŋə] f (-;-n) cheek
-wangig [vaŋɪç] comb.fm. -cheeked
Wan′kelmut m fickleness
wan′kelmütig adj fickle
wanken ['vaŋkən] intr stagger; sway, rock; (fig) waver
wann [van] adv & conj when; **w. immer** anytime, whenever
Wanne ['vanə] f (-;-n) tub
Wanst [vanst] m (-es;⸚e) belly, paunch
-wanstig [vanstɪç] comb.fm. -bellied
Wanze ['vantsə] f (-;-n) bedbug
Wappen ['vapən] n (-s;-) coat of arms
Wap′penkunde f heraldry

Wap′penschild m escutcheon
wappnen ['vapnən] ref arm oneself; **sich mit Geduld w.** have patience
war [var] pret of **sein**
warb [varp] pret of **werben**
ward [vart] pret of **werden**
Ware ['varə] f (-;-n) ware; article; commodity; **Waren** goods, merchandise
-waren [varən] pl comb.fm. -ware
Wa′renaufzug m freight elevator
Wa′renausgabe f wrapping department
Wa′renbestand m stock
Wa′renbörse f commodity market
Wa′renhaus n department store
Wa′renlager n warehouse; stockroom
Wa′renmarkt m commodity market
Wa′renmuster n, **Wa′renprobe** f sample
Wa′renrechnung f invoice
Wa′renzeichen n trademark
warf [varf] pret of **werfen**
warm [varm] adj (wärmer ['vɛrmər]; wärmste ['vɛrmstə] §9) warm
Warmblüter ['varmblytər] m (-s;-) warm-blooded animal
warmblütig ['varmblytɪç] adj warm-blooded
Wärme ['vɛrmə] f (-;) warmth, heat
wär′mebeständig adj heatproof
Wär′meeinheit f thermal unit; calory
Wär′megrad m degree of heat, temperature
wärmen ['vɛrmən] tr warm, heat
Wär′meplatte f—**elektrische W.** hotplate
Wärm′flasche f hot-water bottle
warm′halten §90 tr keep warm
warm′herzig adj warm-hearted
warm′laufen §105 intr—**den Motor w. lassen** let the motor warm up
Warmluft′heizung f hot-air heating
Warmwas′serbehälter m hot-water tank
Warmwas′serheizung f hot-water heating
Warmwas′serspeicher m hot-water tank
Warn– [varn] comb.fm. warning
Warn′anlage f warning system
warnen ['varnən] tr (vor dat) warn (of), caution (against)
Warn′gebiet n danger zone
Warn′schuß m warning shot
Warn′signal n warning signal
War′nung f (-;-en) warning, caution; **zur W.** as a warning
War′nungsschild n, **Warn′zeichen** n danger sign
Warschau ['varʃau] n (-s;) Warsaw
Warte ['vartə] f (-;-n) watchtower, lookout
War′tefrau f attendant; nurse
War′tefrist f waiting period
warten ['vartən] tr tend, attend to; (pflegen) nurse || intr (auf acc) wait (for)
Wärter ['vɛrtər] m (-s;-) attendant; (Pfleger) male nurse; (Aufseher) caretaker; (Gefängnis-) guard; (rr) signalman
War′teraum m waiting room
Wärterin ['vɛrtərɪn] f (-;-nen) attendant; nurse

War'tesaal *m*, **War'tezimmer** *n* waiting room
War'tung *f* (-;) maintenance
warum [va'rum] *adv* why
Warze ['vartsə] *f* (-;-n) wart; (*Brust-*) nipple
was [vas] *indef pron* something; **na, so was!** well, I never! ‖ *interr pron* what; **ach was!** go on! **was für ein** what kind of, what sort of; **was haben wir gelacht!** how we laughed! ‖ *rel pron* what; which, that; **was auch immer** no matter what; **was immer** whatever
Wasch– [vaʃ] *comb.fm.* wash, washing
waschbar ['vaʃbɑr] *adj* washable
Wasch'bär *m* racoon
Wasch'becken *n* sink
Wasch'benzin *n* cleaning fluid
Wasch'blau *n* bluing
Wasch'bütte *f* washtub
Wäsche ['vɛʃə] *f* (-;-n) wash, laundry; linen; underwear
Wä'schebeutel *m* laundry bag
wasch'echt *adj* washable; (fig) genuine
Wä'scheklammer *f* clothespin
Wä'schekorb *m* clothesbasket
Wä'scheleine *f* clothesline
waschen ['vaʃən] §158 *tr* wash; launder; (*Gold*) pan; (*Haar*) shampoo; (*reinigen*) purify ‖ *ref* wash; **sich** [*dat*] **die Hände w.** wash one's hands ‖ *intr* wash
Wä'scher ['vɛʃər] *m* (-s;-) washer, laundryman
Wäscherei [vɛʃə'raɪ] *f* (-;-en) laundry
Wäscherin ['vɛʃərɪn] *f* (-;-nen) washerwoman, laundress
Wä'scherolle *f* mangle
Wä'scheschleuder *f* spin-drier
Wä'scheschrank *m* linen closet
Wä'schezeichen *n* laundry mark
Wasch'frau *f* laundress
Wasch'haus *n* laundry
Wasch'korb *m* clothesbasket
Wasch'küche *f* laundry
Wasch'lappen *m* washcloth; (fig) wishy-washy person
Wasch'maschine *f* washmachine, washer
Wasch'mittel *n* detergent
Wasch'raum *m* washroom, lavatory
Wasch'schüssel *f* wash basin
Wasch'tisch *m* washstand
Wasch'trog *m* washtub
Wa'schung *f* (-;-en) washing; ablution
Wasch'weib *n* (coll) gossip (*woman*)
Wasch'zettel *m* laundry list; (*am Schutzumschlag*) blurb
Wasser ['vasər] *n* (-s;-) water; **das W. läuft mir im Mund zusammen** my mouth is watering; **j-m das W. abgraben** pull the rug out from under s.o.; **mit allen Wassern gewaschen** sharp as a needle
was'serabstoßend *adj* water-repellent
was'serarm *adj* arid
Was'serball *m* water polo
Was'serbau *m* (-[e]s;) harbor and canal construction
Was'serbehälter *m* water tank; reservoir; cistern

Was'serblase *f* bubble; (*auf der Haut*) blister
Was'serbombe *f* depth charge
Was'serbüffel *m* water buffalo
Was'serdampf *m* steam
was'serdicht *adj* watertight, waterproof
Was'sereimer *m* bucket
Was'serfall *m* waterfall, cascade
Was'serfarbe *f* watercolor
Was'serflasche *f* water bottle
Was'serflugzeug *n* seaplane
Was'serfowl *n* waterfowl
Was'sergeflügel *n* waterfowl
Was'sergraben *m* drain; moat
Was'serhahn *m* faucet, spigot
Was'serhose *f* waterspout
wässerig ['vɛsərɪç] *adj* watery
Was'serjungfer *f* dragonfly
Was'serkessel *m* cauldron
Was'serklosett *n* toilet
Was'serkraftwerk *n* hydroelectric plant
Was'serkrug *m* water jug, water pitcher
Was'serkur *f* spa
Was'serland'flugzeug *n* amphibian plane
Was'serland'panzerwagen *m* amphibian tank
Was'serlauf *m* watercourse
Was'serleitung *f* water main; aqueduct
Was'sermangel *m* water shortage
Was'sermann *m* (-[e]s;) (astr) Aquarius
Was'sermelone *f* watermelon
wassern ['vasərn] *intr* land on water; (rok) splash down
wässern ['vɛsərn] *tr* water; irrigate; (phot) wash ‖ *intr* (*Augen, Mund*) water
Was'serratte *f* water rat; (fig) old salt
Was'serrinne *f* gutter
Was'serrohr *n* water pipe
Was'serscheide *f* watershed, divide
was'serscheu *adj* afraid of water
Was'serschi *m* water ski
Was'serschlauch *m* hose
Wasserspeier ['vasərʃpaɪ·ər] *m* (-s;-) gargoyle
Was'serspiegel *m* surface; water level
Was'sersport *m* aquatics
Was'serstand *m* water level
Was'serstiefel *m* rubber boots
Was'serstoff *m* hydrogen
was'serstoffblond *adj* peroxide-blond
Was'serstoffbombe *f* hydrogen bomb
Was'serstrahl *m* jet of water
Was'serstraße *f* waterway
Was'sersucht *f* dropsy
Was'serung *f* (-;-en) (aer) landing on water; (rok) splashdown
Wäs'serung *f* (-;) watering; irrigation
Was'serverdrängung *f* displacement
Was'serversorgung *f* water supply
Was'servogel *m* waterfowl
Was'serwaage *f* (carp) level
Was'serweg *m* waterway; **auf dem W.** by water
Was'serwerk *n* waterworks
Was'serzähler *m* water meter
Was'serzeichen *n* watermark
wässrig ['vɛsrɪç] *adj* watery
waten ['vatən] *intr* (SEIN) wade
Watsche ['vatʃə] *f* (-;-n) slap
watscheln ['vatʃəln] *intr* (SEIN) waddle
watschen ['vatʃən] *tr* slap

Watt [vat] *n* (-s;-) (elec) watt
Watte ['vatə] *f* (-;-en) absorbent cotton; wadding
Wat'tebausch *m* swab
Wat'tekugel *f* cotton ball
Wat'tenmeer *n* shallow coastal waters
Wat'testäbchen *n* Q-tip, cotton swab
wattieren [va'tirən] *tr* pad, wad
Wattie'rung *f* (-;-en) padding, wadding
wauwau ['vau'vau] *interj* bow-wow!
 ‖ **Wauwau** *m* (-s;-s) bow-wow, doggy
weben ['vebən] §109 & §94 *tr* & *intr* weave
We'ber *m* (-s;-) weaver
Weberei [vebə'raɪ] *f* (-;-en) weaving
We'berin *f* (-;-nen) weaver
We'berknecht *m* daddy-long-legs
Webstuhl ['vep/tul] *m* loom
Webwaren ['vepvɑrən] *pl* textiles
Wechsel ['vɛksəl] *m* (-s;-) change, shift; (*für Studenten*) allowance; (agr) rotation (*of crops*); (fin) bill of exchange; (hunt) run, beaten track; **gezogener W.** draft; **offener W.** letter of credit; **trockener** (or **eigener**) **W.** promissory note
Wech'selbeziehung *f* correlation
Wechselfälle ['vɛksəlfɛlə] *pl* ups and downs, vicissitudes
Wech'selfieber *n* intermittent fever; malaria
Wech'selfrist *f* period of grace (*before bill of exchange falls due*)
Wech'selgeld *n* change, small change
Wech'selgesang *m* antiphony
Wech'selgespräch *n* dialogue
wech'selhaft *adj* changeable
Wech'selkurs *m* rate of exchange
Wech'selmakler –in §6 *mf* bill-broker
wechseln ['vɛksəln] *tr* change; vary; (*austauschen*) exchange; **den Besitzer w.** change hands; **die Zähne w.** get one's second set of teeth; **seinen Wohnsitz w.** move ‖ *intr* change; vary
Wech'selnehmer *m* (fin) payee
Wech'selnotierung *f* foreign exchange rate
Wech'selrichter *m* (elec) vibrator (*producing a.c.*)
wech'selseitig *adj* mutual, reciprocal
Wech'selseitigkeit *f* (-;) reciprocity
Wech'selspiel *n* interplay
Wech'selsprechanlage *f* intercom
Wech'selstrom *m* alternating current
Wech'selstube *f* money-exchange office
Wech'seltierchen *n* amoeba
wech'selvoll *adj* (*Landschaft*) changing; (*Leben*) checkered; (*Wetter*) changeable
wech'selweise *adv* mutually; alternately
Wech'selwirkung *f* interaction
Wech'selwirtschaft *f* crop rotation
wecken ['vɛkən] *tr* wake, awaken, rouse
Wecker (**Wek'ker**) *m* (-s;-) alarm clock
Weck'ruf *m* (mil) reveille
Wedel ['vedəl] *m* (-s;-) brush, whisk; (*Schwanz*) tail; (eccl) sprinkler
wedeln ['vedəln] *tr* brush away ‖ *intr*

—mit dem Fächer w. fan oneself; mit dem Schwanz w. wag its tail
weder ['vedər] *conj*—**weder...noch** neither...nor
weg [vɛk] *adv* away, off; gone; lost ‖
Weg [vɛk] *m* (-[e]s;-e) way, path; road; route, course; (*Art und Weise*) way; (*Mittel*) means; **am Wege** by the roadside; **auf dem besten Wege sein** be well on the way; **auf gütlichem Wege** amicably; **auf halbem Wege** halfway; **aus dem Weg räumen** remove; (fig) bump off; **etw in die Wege leiten** prepare the way for s.th.; introduce s.th.; **j–m aus dem Wege gehen** make way for s.o.; steer clear of s.o.; **Weg und Steg kennen** know every turn in the road
weg/bekommen §99 *tr* (*Fleck*) get out; (*Krankheit*) catch; (*verstehen*) get the hang of; **e–e w.** (coll) get a crack
weg/bleiben §62 *intr* (SEIN) stay away; be omitted
weg/blicken *intr* glance away
weg/bringen §65 *tr* take away; (*Fleck*) get out
Wegebau ['vegəbau] *m* (-[e]s;) road building
Wegegeld ['vegəgɛlt] *n* mileage allowance; turnpike toll
wegen ['vegən] *prep* (genit) because of, on account of; for the sake of; (*mit Rücksicht auf*) in consideration of; (*infolge*) in consequence of; (jur) on (the charge of); **von Amts w.** officially; **von Rechts w.** by right
Wegerecht ['vegəreçt] *n* right of way
weg/essen §70 *tr* eat up
weg/fahren §71 *tr* remove ‖ *intr* (SEIN) drive away, leave
weg/fallen §72 *intr* (SEIN) fall away, fall off; (*ausgelassen werden*) be omitted; (*aufhören*) cease; (*abgeschafft werden*) be abolished
weg/fangen §73 *tr* snap away, snatch
weg/fliegen §57 *intr* (SEIN) fly away
weg/fressen §70 *tr* devour
weg/führen *tr* lead away
Weggang ['vɛkgan] *m* departure
weg/geben §80 *tr* give away
weg/gehen §82 *intr* (SEIN) go away; **w. über** (acc) pass over; **wie warme Semmeln w.** go like hotcakes
weg/haben §89 *tr* get rid of; (*Schläge, usw.*) have gotten one's share of; (*verstehen*) catch on to; **der hat eins weg** (sl) he has a screw loose; (sl) he's loaded
weg/jagen *tr* chase away
weg/kehren *tr* sweep away; (*Gesicht*) avert ‖ *ref* turn away
weg/kommen §99 *intr* (SEIN) come away; get away (*verlorengehen*) get lost; **nicht w. über** (acc) not get over
weg/können §100 *intr*—**nicht w.** not be able to get away
Wegkreuzung ['vɛkkrɔɪtsuŋ] *f* (-;-en) crossing, intersection
weg/kriegen *tr* get; (*Fleck*) get out
weg/lassen §104 *tr* leave out; let go; cross out; (gram) elide; (math) cancel
weg/legen *tr* put aside

weg'machen *tr* take away; *(Fleck)* take out
wegmüde ['vekmydə] *adj* travel-weary
weg'müssen §115 *intr* have to go
Wegnahme ['vɛknɑmə] *f* (-;-n) taking away; confiscation; (mil) capture
weg'nehmen §116 *tr* take away; *(Raum, Zeit)* take up; *(beschlagnahmen)* confiscate; (mil) capture
weg'packen *tr* pack away ‖ *ref* pack off
weg'raffen *tr* snatch away
Wegrand ['vekrant] *m* wayside
weg'räumen *tr* clear away
weg'reißen §53 *tr* tear off, tear away
weg'rücken *tr* move away
weg'schaffen *tr* remove; get rid of
weg'scheren §129 *tr* clip ‖ *ref* scram
weg'scheuchen *tr* scare away
weg'schicken *tr* send away
weg'schleichen §85 *ref & intr* (SEIN) sneak away, steal away
weg'schmeißen §53 *tr* (coll) throw away
weg'schneiden §106 *tr* cut away
weg'sehen §138 *intr* look away; **w. über** *(acc)* shut one's eyes to
weg'setzen *tr* put away ‖ *ref*—**sich w. über** *(acc)* not mind; feel superior to ‖ *intr* (SEIN)—**w. über** *(acc)* jump over
weg'spülen *tr* wash away; (geol) erode
weg'stehlen §147 *ref* slip away
weg'stellen *tr* put aside
weg'stoßen §150 *tr* shove aside
weg'streichen §85 *tr* cross out
weg'treten §152 *intr* (SEIN) step aside; (mil) break ranks; **weggetreten!** (mil) dismissed!; **w. lassen** (mil) dismiss
weg'tun §154 *tr* put away
Wegweiser ['vekvaɪzər] *m* (-s;-) road-sign; *(Buch, Reiseführer)* guide
weg'wenden §120 & §140 *tr & ref* turn away
weg'werfen §160 *tr* throw away ‖ *ref* degrade oneself
weg'werfend *adj* disparaging
weg'wischen *tr* wipe away
weg'zaubern *tr* spirit away
weg'ziehen §163 *tr* pull away ‖ *intr* (SEIN) move; (mil) pull out
weh [ve] *adj* painful, sore; **mir ist weh ums Herz** I am sick at heart ‖ *adv*—**sich** *[dat]* **weh tun** hurt oneself; **weh tun** ache ‖ *interj* woe! **weh mir!** woe is me! ‖ **Weh** *n* (-[e]s;-e) pain, ache
wehe ['ve·ə] *adj, adv, & interj* var of **weh** ‖ **Wehe** *f* (-;-n) drift
wehen ['ve·ən] *tr* blow; *(Schnee)* drift ‖ *intr (Wind)* blow; *(Fahne, Kerzenflamme)* flutter ‖ **Wehen** *pl* labor, labor pains; (fig) travail
Weh'geschrei *n* wails, wailing
Weh'klage *f* wail
weh'klagen *intr* (über *acc*) wail (over); **w. um** lament for
weh'leidig *adj* complaining, whining; **W. tun** whine
Weh'mut *f* (-;) melancholy; nostalgia
weh'mütig *adj* melancholy; nostalgic
Wehr [ver] *f* (-;-en) weapon; *(Abwehr)* defense, resistance; *(Brüstung)*

parapet; **sich zur W. setzen** offer resistance ‖ **Wehr** *n* (-[e]s;-e) dam
Wehr'dienst *m* military service
wehr'dienstpflichtig *adj* subject to military service
Wehr'dienstverweigerer *m* (-s;-) conscientious objector
wehren ['verən] *tr*—**j-m etw w.** keep s.o. (away) from s.th. ‖ *ref* defend oneself; resist, put up a fight; **sich seiner Haut w.** save one's skin ‖ *intr* (*dat*) resist; (*dat*) check
wehr'fähig *adj* fit for military service
wehr'haft *adj (Person)* full of fight; *(Burg)* strong
wehr'los *adj* defenseless
Wehr'macht *f* (hist) German armed forces
Wehr'meldeamt *n* draft board
Wehr'paß *m* service record
Wehr'pflicht *f* compulsory military service; **allgemeine W.** universal military training
wehr'pflichtig *adj* subject to military service
Weib [vaɪp] *n* (-[e]s;-er) woman; wife; **ein tolles W.** a luscious doll
Weibchen ['vaɪpçən] *n* (-s;-) *(Tier)* female; *(Ehefrau)* little woman
Weiberfeind ['vaɪbərfaɪnt] *m* woman-hater
Weiberheld ['vaɪbərhɛlt] *m* ladies' man
Weibervolk ['vaɪbərfɔlk] *n* womenfolk
weibisch ['vaɪbɪʃ] *adj* womanish, effeminate
weib'lich *adj* female; womanly; (& gram) feminine
Weib'lichkeit *f* (-;) womanhood; feminine nature; **die holde W.** (hum) the fair sex
Weibs'bild *n* female; (pej) wench
Weibs'stück *n* (sl) woman
weich [vaɪç] *adj* soft; *(Ei)* soft-boiled; *(zart)* tender; *(schwach)* weak; **w. machen** soften up; **w. werden** (& fig) soften; relent
Weich'bild *n* urban area, outskirts
Weiche ['vaɪçə] *f* (-;-n) (anat) side, flank; (rr) switch; **Weichen stellen** throw the switch
weichen ['vaɪçən] *tr & intr* soften; soak ‖ §85 *intr* (SEIN) yield; give ground; *(Boden)* give way; (*dat*) give in to; **j-m nicht von der Seite w.** not leave s.o.'s side; **nicht von der Stelle w.** not budge from the spot; **von j-m w.** leave s.o.
Weichensteller ['vaɪçənstelər] *m* (-s; -) (rr) switchman
Weich'heit *f* (-;) softness; tenderness
weich'herzig *adj* soft-hearted
Weich'käse *m* soft cheese
weich'lich *adj* soft; tender; flabby; insipid; *(weibisch)* effeminate; *(lässig)* indolent
Weichling ['vaɪçlɪŋ] *m* (-s;-e) weakling
Weich'tier *n* mollusk
Weide ['vaɪdə] *f* (-;-n) pasture; (bot) willow
Wei'deland *n* pasture land
weiden ['vaɪdən] *tr* graze; *(Augen)*

feast ‖ *ref*—**sich w. an** (*dat*) feast one's eyes on ‖ *intr* graze
Wei′denkorb *m* wicker basket
weidlich [′vaɪtlɪç] *adv* heartily
weidmännisch [′vaɪtmɛnɪʃ] *adj* (hunt) sportsmanlike
weigern [′vaɪgərn] *ref*—**sich w. zu** (*inf*) refuse to (*inf*)
Wei′gerung *f* (–;–en) refusal
Weihe [′vaɪ·ə] *f* (–;–n) consecration; (*e–s Priesters*) ordination
weihen [′vaɪ·ən] *tr* consecrate; (*zum Priester*) ordain; (*widmen*) dedicate; **dem Tode geweiht** doomed to death ‖ *ref* devote oneself
Wei′her *m* (–s;–) pond
wei′hevoll *adj* solemn
Weihnachten [′vaɪnaxtən] *n* (–s;) & *pl* Christmas; **zu W.** for or at Christmas
Weih′nachtsabend *m* Christmas Eve
Weih′nachtsbaum *m* Christmas tree; (coll) bombing markers
Weih′nachtsbescherung *f* exchange of Christmas presents
Weih′nachtsfeier *f* Christmas celebration; (*in Betrieben*) Christmas party
Weih′nachtsfest *n* feast of Christmas
Weih′nachtsgeschenk *n* Christmas present
Weih′nachtsgratifikation *f* Christmas bonus
Weih′nachtslied *n* Christmas carol
Weih′nachtsmann *m* (–[e]s;) Santa Claus
Weih′nachtsmarkt *m* Christmas fair (*at which Christmas decorations are sold*)
Weih′nachstag *m* Christmas day
Weih′rauch *m* incense
Weih′rauchfaß *n* censer
Weih′wasser *n* holy water
Weih′wedel *m* (eccl) sprinkler
weil [vaɪl] *conj* because, since
weiland [′vaɪlant] *adv* formerly
Weilchen [′vaɪlçən] *n* (–s;) little while
Weile [′vaɪlə] *f* (–;) while
weilen [′vaɪlən] *intr* stay, linger
Wein [vaɪn] *m* (–[e]s;–e) wine; (*Pflanze*) vine
Wein′bau *m* (–[e]s;) winegrowing
Wein′bauer –in §6 *mf* winegrower
Wein′beere *f* grape
Wein′berg *m* vineyard
Wein′blatt *n* vine leaf
Wein′brand *m* brandy
weinen [′vaɪnən] *tr* (*Tränen*) shed ‖ *intr* cry, weep; **vor Freude w.** weep for joy; **w. um** cry over
weinerlich [′vaɪnərlɪç] *adj* tearful; (*Stimme*)) whining
Wein′ernte *f* vintage
Wein′essig *m* wine vinegar
Wein′faß *n* wine barrel
Wein′händler *m* wine merchant
Wein′jahr *n* vintage year
Wein′karte *f* wine list
Wein′keller *m* wine cellar
Wein′kelter *f* wine press
Wein′kenner *m* connoisseur of wine
Wein′krampf *m* crying fit
Wein′laub *n* vine leaves
Wein′lese *f* grape picking
Wein′presse *f* wine press

Wein′ranke *f* vine tendril
Wein′rebe *f* grapevine
wein′selig *adj* tipsy, tight
Wein′stock *m* vine
Wein′traube *f* grape; bunch of grapes
weise [′vaɪzə] *adj* wise ‖ **Weise** §5 *m* wise man, sage ‖ *f* (–;–n) way; (*Melodie*) tune; **auf diese W. in** this way
-weise *comb.fm.* –wise; by, e.g., **dutzendweise** by the dozen; –ly, e.g., **glücklicherweise** luckily
weisen [′vaɪzən] §118 *tr* point out, show; (*aus dem Lande*) banish; (*aus der Schule*) expel; **j–n w. an** (*acc*) refer s.o. to; **j–n w. nach** direct s.o. to; **j–n w. von** order s.o. off (*premises, etc.*); **von der Hand w.** refuse; **weit von der Hand w.** have nothing to do with ‖ *ref*—**von sich w.** refuse ‖ *intr*—**w. auf** (*acc*) point to
Weis′heit *f* (–;–en) wisdom; wise saying; **Weisheiten** words of wisdom
Weis′heitszahn *m* wisdom tooth
weis′lich *adv* wisely, prudently
weismachen [′vaɪsmaxən] *tr*—**j–m etw w.** put s.th. over on s.o.; **mach das anderen weis!** tell it to the marines!
weiß [vaɪs] *adj* white
weissagen [′vaɪszɑgən] *tr* foretell
Weiß′blech *n* tin plate, tin
Weiß′blechdose *f* tincan
weiß′bluten *tr* bleed white
Weiß′brot *n* white bread
Weiß′dorn *m* (bot) hawthorn
Weiße [′vaɪsə] *f* (–;–n) whiteness; (Berlin) ale ‖ §5 *m* white man ‖ *f* white woman ‖ *n* (*im Auge, im Ei*) white
weißen [′vaɪsən] *tr* whiten; (*tünchen*) whitewash
weiß′glühend *adj* white-hot
Weiß′glut *f* white heat, incandescence
Weiß′kohl *m*, **Weiß′kraut** *n* cabbage
weiß′lich *adj* whitish
Weiß′metall *n* pewter; Babbitt metal
Weiß′waren *pl* linens
Weiß′wein *m* white wine
Wei′sung *f* (–;–en) directions, instructions; directive
weit [vaɪt] *adj* far, distant; (*ausgedehnt*) extensive; (*breit*) wide, broad; (*geräumig*) large; (*Gewissen*) elastic; (*Herz*) big; (*Kleid*) full, big; (*Meer*) broad; (*Reise, Weg*) long; (*Welt*) wide; **bei weitem besser** better by far; **von weitem** from afar ‖ *adv* far, way; widely; greatly; **w. besser** far better
weit′ab′ *adv* (**von**) far away (from)
weit′aus′ *adv* by far
Weit′blick *m* farsightedness
weit′blickend *adj* farsighted
Weite [′vaɪtə] *f* (–;–n) width, breadth; (*Ferne*) distance; (*Umfang*) size; (*Ausdehnung*) extent; (*Durchmesser*) diameter; (fig) range; **in die W. ziehen** go out into the world
weiten [′vaɪtən] *tr* widen; (*Loch*) enlarge; (*Schuh*) stretch ‖ *ref* widen
weiter [′vaɪtər] *adj* farther; further; wider; **bis auf weiteres** until further notice; **des weiteren** furthermore;

ohne weiteres without further ado ‖ *adv* farther; further; furthermore; (*voran*) on; **er kann nicht w.** he can't go on; **nur s. w.!** keep it up!; **und so w.** and so forth, and so on

weiter– *comb.fm.* on; keep on, continue to

wei'terbefördern *tr* forward

Wei'terbestand *m* continued existence

wei'terbestehen §146 *intr* survive

wei'terbilden *tr* develop ‖ *ref* continue one's studies

wei'tererzählen *tr* spread (*rumors*)

wei'terfahren §71 *intr* (SEIN) drive on

wei'tergeben §80 *tr* pass on, relay

wei'tergehen §82 *intr* (SEIN) go on

wei'terhin' *adv* furthermore; again

wei'terkommen §99 *intr* (SEIN) get ahead, make progress

wei'terkönnen §100 *intr* be able to go on; **ich kann nicht weiter** I'm stuck

wei'terleben *intr* live on, survive

wei'termachen *tr & intr* continue ‖ *interj* (mil) as you were!, carry on!

weit'gehend *adj* far-reaching

weit'gereist *adj* widely traveled

weit'greifend *adj* far-reaching

weit'her' *adv*—**von w.** from afar

weit'her'geholt *adj* far-fetched

weit'herzig *adj* broad-minded

weit'hin' *adv* far off

weitläufig ['vaɪtlɔɪfɪç] *adj* lengthy, detailed; complicated; (*Verwandte*) distant; (*geräumig*) roomy ‖ *adv* at length, in detail

weit'reichend *adj* far-reaching

weitschweifig ['vaɪtʃvaɪfɪç] *adj* detailed, lengthy; long-winded

weit'sichtig *adj* (& fig) far-sighted

Weit'sprung *m* (sport) long jump

Weit'streckenflug *m* long-distance flight

weit'tragend *adj* long-range; (fig) far-reaching

Weit'winkelobjektiv *n* wide-angle lens

Weizen ['vaɪtsən] *m* (-s;-) wheat

Wei'zenmehl *n* wheat flour

welch [vɛlç] *interr adj* which ‖ *interr pron* which one; (*in Ausrufen*) what ...!; **mit welcher** (or **mit welch einer**) **Begeisterung arbeitet er!** with what enthusiasm he works! ‖ *indef pron* any; some ‖ *rel pron* who, which, that

welcherlei ['vɛlçər'laɪ] *invar adj* what kind of; whatever

welk [vɛlk] *adj* withered; (*Haut, Lippen*) wrinkled; (fig) faded

welken ['vɛlkən] *intr* (SEIN) wither; (fig) fade

Wellblech ['vɛlblɛç] *n* corrugated iron

Well'blechhütte *f* Quonset hut

Welle ['vɛlə] *f* (-;-n) wave; (*Wellbaum*) shaft; (gym) circle (*around horizontal bar*); (mach) shaft

wellen ['vɛlən] *tr & ref* wave

Wel'lenbereich *m* wave band

Wel'lenberg *m* crest (*of wave*)

Wel'lenbewegung *f* undulation

Wel'lenbrecher *m* breakwater

wel'lenförmig *adj* wavy

Wel'lenlänge *f* wavelength

Wel'lenlinie *f* wavy line

wel'lenreiten §86 *intr* surf; waterski ‖

Wellenreiten *n* (-s;) surfing, surfboard riding; waterskiing

Wel'lenreiter –**in** §6 *mf* surfer; waterskier

Wel'lenreiterbrett *n* surfboard; water ski

Wel'lental *n* trough (*of wave*)

wellig ['vɛlɪç] *adj* wavy

Well'pappe *f* corrugated cardboard

Welt [vɛlt] *f* (-;-en) world

Welt'all *n* universe; outer space

Welt'anschauung *f* outlook on life; ideology

Welt'ausmaß *m*—**im W.** on a global scale

Welt'ausstellung *f* world's fair

welt'bekannt, welt'berühmt *adj* world-renowned

Wel'tenbummler *m* globetrotter

welt'erfahren *adj* sophisticated

Weltergewicht ['vɛltərgəvɪçt] *n* welterweight class

Weltergewichtler ['vɛltərgəvɪçtlər] *m* (-s;-) welterweight boxer

welt'erschütternd *adj* earth-shaking

welt'fremd *adj* secluded; innocent

Welt'friede *m* world peace

Welt'geistlicher *m* secular priest

welt'gewandt *adj* worldly-wise

Welt'karte *f* map of the world

welt'klug *adj* worldly-wise

Welt'körper *m* heavenly body

Welt'krieg *m* world war

Welt'kugel *f* globe

Welt'lage *f* international situation

welt'lich *adj* worldly; secular

Welt'macht *f* world power

Welt'mann *m* (-[e]s;-er) man of the world

welt'männisch *adj* sophisticated

Welt'meer *n* ocean

Welt'meinung *f* world opinion

Welt'meister –**in** §6 *mf* world champion

Welt'meisterschaft *f* world championship

Welt'ordnung *f* cosmic order

Welt'postverein *m* postal union

Welt'priester *m* secular priest

Welt'raum *m* (-[e]s;) outer space

Welt'raumfahrer *m* spaceman

Welt'raumfahrt *f* space travel

Welt'raumfahrzeug *n* spacecraft

Welt'raumforschung *f* exploration of outer space

Welt'raumgeschoß *n* space shot

Welt'raumkapsel *f* space capsule

Welt'raumstation *f* space station

Welt'raumstrahlen *pl* cosmic rays

Welt'reich *n* world empire

Welt'reise *f* trip around the world

Welt'rekord *m* world record

Welt'ruf *m* world-wide renown

Welt'ruhm *m* world-wide fame

Welt'schmerz *m* world-weariness

Welt'sicherheitsrat *m* U.N. Security Council

Welt'stadt *f* metropolis (*city with more than one million inhabitants*)

Welt'teil *m* continent

welt'umfassend *adj* world-wide

Welt'weisheit *f* philosophy

wem [vem] *interr & rel pron* to whom
Wem'fall *m* dative case
wen [ven] *interr & rel pron* whom
Wende ['vɛndə] *f* (−;−n) turn; turning point; (gym) face vault, front vault
Wen'dekreis *m* (geog) tropic
Wendeltreppe ['vɛndəltrɛpə] *f* spiral staircase
Wen'demarke *f* (aer) pylon; (sport) turn post
wenden ['vɛndən] §140 *tr* turn; turn around; turn over; (Geld, Mühe) spend ‖ *ref* turn; (Wind, Wetter) change ‖ *intr* turn, turn around
Wen'depunkt *m* turning point
wendig ['vɛndɪç] *adj* maneuverable; (Person) versatile, resourceful
Wen'dung *f* (−;−en) turn; change; (Redensart) idiomatic expression
Wen'fall *m* accusative case
wenig ['veːnɪç] *adj* little; **ein w.** a little, a bit of; **wenige** few, a few, some ‖ *adv* little; not very; seldom ‖ *indef pron* little; **wenige** few, a few
weniger ['veːnɪgər] *adj* fewer; less; (arith) minus
We'nigkeit *f* (−;) fewness; smallness; pittance; trifle; **meine W.** (coll) poor little me
wenigste ['veːnɪçstə] §9 *adj* least; very few, fewest; **am wenigsten** least of all
wenigstens ['veːnɪçstəns] *adv* at least
wenn [ven] *conj* if, in case; (zeitlich) when, whenever; **auch w.** even if; **außer** except when, except if, unless; **w. anders** provided that; **w. auch** although, even if; **w. schon, denn schon** go all the way ‖ **Wenn** *n* (−;−) if
wenngleich', wennschon' *conj* although
Wenzel ['vɛntsəl] *m* (−s;−) (cards) jack
wer [ver] *interr pron* who, which one; **wer auch immer** whoever; **wer da?** who goes there? ‖ *rel pron* he who, whoever ‖ *indef pron* somebody, anybody
Werbe− [vɛrbə] *comb.fm.* advertising; publicity; commercial
Wer'befernsehen *n* commercial television
Wer'befilm *m* commercial
Wer'befläche *f* advertising space
Wer'begraphik *f* commercial art
Wer'begraphiker −in §6 *mf* commercial artist
werben ['vɛrbən] §149 *tr* (neue Kunden) try to get; (mil) recruit ‖ *intr* advertise; **für e−n neuen Handelsartikel w.** advertise a new product; **um ein Mädchen w.** court a girl
Wer'beschrift *f* folder
Wer'bestelle *f* advertising agency
Wer'bung *f* (−;−en) advertising; publicity; courting; recruiting
Werdegang ['verdəgaŋ] *m* career, background; (Entwicklung) development; (Wachstum) growth; (Ablauf der Herstellung) process of production
werden ['verdən] §159 *intr* (SEIN) become, grow, get, turn; **w. zu** change into; **zu nichts w.** come to nought ‖

aux (SEIN) (to form the future) **er wird gehen** he will go; (to form the passive) **er wird geehrt** he is being honored ‖ **Werden** *n* (−s;) becoming, growing; (Entstehung) evolution; (Wachstum) growth; **im W. sein** be in the process of development; be in the making
wer'dend *adj* nascent; (Mutter) expectant; (Arzt) future
Werder ['verdər] *m* (−s;−) islet
Wer'fall *m* subjective case
werfen ['vɛrfən] §160 *tr* throw, cast; (Junge) produce; (Blasen) form, blow; **Falten w.** wrinkle ‖ *ref* (Holz) warp; **sich hin und her w.** toss; **sich in die Brust w.** throw out one's chest ‖ *intr* throw; (Tieren) produce young
Werft [verft] *f* (−;−e) shipyard
Werft'halle *f* (aer) repair hangar
Werg [verk] *n* (−[e]s;) oakum, tow
Werk [verk] *n* (−[e]s;−e) work; (Tat) deed; (Erzeugnis) production; (Leistung) performance; (Unternehmen) undertaking; (Fabrik) works, plant, mill; (horol) clockwork; **das ist dein W.** that's your doing; **gutes W.** good deed; **im Werke sein** be in the works; **zu Werke gehen** go to it
Werk'anlage *f* plant, works
Werk'bank *f* (−;−e) workbench
werk'fremd *adj* (Personen) unauthorized
Werk'meister *m* foreman
Werk'nummer *f* factory serial number
Werks'angehörige §5 *mf* employee
Werk'schutz *m* security force
Werks'kantine *f* factory cafeteria
Werk'statt *f*, **Werk'stätte** *f* workshop
Werk'stattwagen *m* maintenance truck
Werk'stoff *m* manufacturing material
Werk'stück *n* (indust) piece
Werk'tag *m* weekday; working day
werk'tägig *adj* workaday, ordinary
werk'tags *adv* (on) weekdays
werk'tätig *adj* working; practical
Werk'zeug *n* tool
Werk'zeugmaschine *f* machine tool
Wermut ['vermut] *m* (−[e]s;) vermouth; (bot) wormwood
wert [vert] *adj* worth; worthy; esteemed; **etw** [genit or acc] **w. sein** be worth s.th.; **nicht der Rede w. sein** not worth mentioning; **nichts w.** good for nothing; **Werter Herr X** Dear Mr. X ‖ **Wert** *m* (−[e]s;−e) worth, value; price, rate; (Wichtigkeit) importance; (chem) valence; **äußerer W.** face value; **im W. von** valued at; **innerer W.** intrinsic value; **Werte** (com) assets; (phys) data
Wert'angabe *f* valuation
wert'beständig *adj* of lasting value; (Währung) stable
Wert'bestimmung *f* appraisal
Wert'brief *m* insured letter
werten ['vertən] *tr* (bewerten) value; (nach Leistung) rate; (auswerten) evaluate
Wert'gegenstand *m* valuable article; **Wertgegenstände** valuables
−wertig [vertɪç] *comb.fm.* −value, −quality, e.g., **geringwertig** low-qual-

ity; (chem) –valent, e.g., **zweiwertig** bivalent

Wer'tigkeit *f* (–;–en) (chem) valence

wert'los *adj* worthless

Wert'papiere *pl* securities

Wert'sachen *pl* valuables

wert'voll *adj* valuable

Wert'zeichen *n* stamp; (*Briefmarke*) postage stamp; (*Banknote*) bill

Wesen ['vezən] *n* (–s;–) being, creature; entity; (*inneres Sein, Kern*) essence; (*Betragen*) conduct, way; (*Getue*) fuss; (*Natur*) nature, character; **einnehmendes W.** pleasing personality; **höchtes W.** Supreme Being

–wesen *n comb.fm.* system

we'senhaft *adj* real; characteristic

we'senlos *adj* unreal; incorporeal

wesentlich ['vezəntlıç] *adj* essential; (*beträchtlich*) substantial

Weser ['vezər] *f* (–;) Weser (River)

Wes'fall *m* genitive case

weshalb [vɛs'halp] *adv* why; wherefore

Wespe ['vɛspə] *f* (–;–n) wasp

wessen ['vɛsən] *interr pron* whose

West [vɛst] *m* (–s;) west; (poet) west wind

Weste ['vɛstə] *f* (–;–n) vest; **e–e reine W.** a clean slate

Westen ['vɛstən] *m* (–s;) west; **im W. von** west of; **nach W.** westward

Westfalen [vɛst'falən] *n* (–s;) Westphalia

westfälisch [vɛst'felıʃ] *adj* Westphalian

West'gote *m* (–n;–n) Visigoth

Westindien [vɛst'ındjən] *n* (–s;) the West Indies

west'lich *adj* west, western; westerly

Westmächte ['vɛstmɛçtə] *pl* Western Powers

westwärts ['vɛstvɛrts] *adv* westward

weswegen [vɛs'vegən] *adv* why; wherefore

wett [vɛt] *adj* even, quits

Wett– *comb.fm.* competitive

Wett'bewerb *m* (–s;–e) competition, contest; (*Treffen*) meet

Wett'bewerber –in §6 *mf* competitor

Wette ['vɛtə] *f* (–;–n) bet, wager; **e–e W. abschließen** (or **eingehen**) make a bet; **mit j–m um die W. laufen** race s.o.; **was gilt die W.?** what do you bet?

Wett'eifer *m* competitiveness, rivalry

wetteifern ['vɛtaıfərn] *insep intr* compete; **w. um** compete for

Wetter ['vɛtər] *n* (–s;) weather; (min) ventilation; **alle W.!** holy smokes!

wet'terbeständig, wet'terfest *adj* weatherproof

Wet'terglas *n* barometer

wet'terhart *adj* hardy

Wet'terkunde *f* meteorology

Wet'terlage *f* weather conditions

wet'terleuchten *insep impers*—es **wetterleuchtet** there is summer lightning ‖ **Wetterleuchten** *n* (–;) summer lightning, heat lightning

Wet'terverhältnisse *pl* weather conditions

Wet'tervorhersage *f* weather forecast

Wet'terwarte *f* meteorological station

Wet'terwechsel *m* change in the weather

wetterwendisch ['vɛtərvɛndıʃ] *adj* moody

Wett'fahrer –in §6 *mf* racer

Wett'fahrt *f* race

Wett'kampf *m* competition, contest

Wett'kämpfer –in §6 *mf* competitor, contestant

Wett'lauf *m* race, foot race

Wett'läufer –in §6 *mf* runner

wett'machen *tr* make up for

Wett'rennen *n* race

Wett'rudern *n* boat race

Wett'rüsten *n* armaments race

Wett'schwimmen *n* swimming meet

Wett'segeln *n* regatta

Wett'spiel *n* game, match

Wett'streit *m* contest, match, game

Wett'zettel *m* betting ticket

wetzen ['vɛtsən] *tr* whet, sharpen

Wetzstein ['vɛtsʃtaın] *m* whetstone

Whisky ['vɪski] *m* (–s;–s) whiskey

wich [vɪç] *pret* of **weichen**

Wichs [vɪks] *m* (es–;–e) gala; **in vollem W.** in full dress; **sich in W. werfen** dress up

Wichse ['vɪksə] *f* (–;–n) shoepolish ‖ *f* (–;) (coll) spanking

wichsen ['vɪksən] *tr* polish; (coll) spank, beat up

Wicht [vɪçt] *m* (–[e]s;–e) elf; dwarf

Wichtel ['vɪçtəl] *m* (–s;–) dwarf

wichtig ['vɪçtıç] *adj* important ‖ *adv* —**w. tun** act important

Wich'tigkeit *f* (–;) importance

Wichtigtuer ['vɪçtıçtu·ər] *m* (–s;–) busybody

wichtigtuerisch ['vɪçtıçtu·ərıʃ] *adj* officious

Wicke ['vɪkə] *f* (–;–n) (bot) vetch

Wickel ['vɪkəl] *m* (–s;–) wrapper; curler, roller; (*von Garn*) ball; (med) compress

wickeln ['vɪkəln] *tr* wrap; wind (*Haar*) curl; (*Kind*) diaper; (*Zigaretten*) roll

Widder ['vɪdər] *m* (–s;–) ram; (astr) Ram

wider ['vidər] *prep* (*acc*) against, contrary to

wider– *comb.fm.* re–, con–, un–, counter–, contra–, anti–, with–

wi'derborstig *adj* stubborn, contrary

widerfah'ren §71 *intr* (SEIN) (*dat*) befall, happen to

Wi'derhaken *m* barb

Wi'derhall *m* echo, reverberation; (fig) response, reaction

wi'derhallen *intr* echo, resound

Wi'derlager *n* abutment

widerle'gen *tr* refute

wi'derlich *adj* repulsive

wi'dernatürlich *adj* unnatural

widerra'ten §63 *tr*—j–m etw w. dissuade s.o. from s.th.

wi'derrechtlich *adj* illegal

Wi'derrede *f* contradiction

Wi'derruf *m* recall; cancellation; retraction; denial; **bis auf W.** until further notice

widerru'fen §122 *tr* revoke; (*Auftrag*)

cancel; (*Befehl*) countermand; (*Behauptung*) retract
Widersacher –in ['vidərzaxər(ın)] §6 *mf* adversary
Wi'derschein *m* reflection
widerset'zen *ref* (*dat*) oppose, resist
widersetz'lich *adj* insubordinate
wi'dersinning *adj* absurd, nonsensical
widerspenstig ['vidər∫pɛnstıç] *adj* refractory, contrary; (*Haar*) stubborn
wi'derspiegeln *tr* reflect ‖ *ref* (**in** *dat*) be reflected (in)
Wi'derspiel *n* contrary, reverse
widerspre'chen §64 *intr* (*dat*) contradict; (*dat*) oppose
widerspre'chend *adj* contradictory
Wi'derspruch *m* contradiction; opposition; **auf heftigen W. stoßen bei** meet with strong opposition from
widersprüchlich ['vidər/pryçlıç] *adj* contradictory
wi'derspruchsvoll *adj* full of contradictions
Wi'derstand *m* resistance; opposition; (elec) resistance; (elec) resistor
Wi'derstandsnest *n* pocket of resistance
widerste'hen §146 *intr* (*dat*) withstand, resist; (*dat*) be repugnant to
widerstre'ben *intr* (*dat*) oppose, resist; (*dat*) be repugnant to ‖ *impers*—**es widerstrebt mir zu** (*inf*) I hate to (*inf*)
widerstre'bend *adj* reluctant
Wi'derstreit *m* opposition, antagonism; (fig) conflict, clash
widerstrei'ten §86 *intr* (*dat*) clash with
widerwärtig ['vidərvɛrtıç] *adj* nasty
Wi'derwille *m* (**gegen**) dislike (of, for), aversion (to); (*Widerstreben*) reluctance; **mit W.** reluctantly
wi'derwillig *adj* reluctant, unwilling
widmen ['vıtmən] *tr* dedicate, devote ‖ *ref* (*dat*) devote oneself to
Wid'mung *f* (–;–en) dedication
widrig ['vidrıç] *adj* contrary; (*ungünstig*) unfavorable, adverse
wid'rigenfalls *adv* otherwise, or else
wie [vi] *adv* how; (*vergleichend*) as, such as, like; **so...wie as...as; und wie!** and how!; **wie, bitte?** what did you say?; **wie dem auch sei** be that as it may; **wie wäre es mit...?** how about...?
wieder ['vidər] *adv* again; anew; (*zurück*) back; (*als Vergeltung*) in return
wieder– *comb.fm.* re–
Wie'derabdruck *m* reprint
wiederan'knüpfen *tr* resume
Wiederauf'bau *m* (–[e]s;) rebuilding
wiederauf'bauen *tr* rebuild, reconstruct
wiederauf'erstehen §146 *intr* (SEIN) rise from the dead
Wiederauf'erstehung *f* resurrection
Wiederauf'führung *f* (theat) revival
wiederauf'kommen §99 *intr* (SEIN) (*Kranker*) recover; (*Mode*) come in again
Wiederauf'nahme *f* resumption; (jur) reopening
Wiederauf'nahmeverfahren *n* retrial
Wiederauf'rüstung *f* rearmament

Wie'derbeginn *m* reopening
wie'derbekommen §99 *tr* recover
wie'derbeleben *tr* revive, resuscitate
wie'derbeschaffen *tr* replace
wie'derbringen §65 *tr* bring back; restore, give back
wiederein'bringen §65 *tr* make up for
wiederein'setzen *tr* (**in** *acc*) reinstate (in); **in Rechte w.** restore to former rights
wiederein'stellen *tr* rehire; (mil) reenlist
Wie'dereintritt *m* (rok) reentry
wie'derergreifen §88 *tr* recapture
wie'dererhalten §90 *tr* get back
wie'dererkennen §97 *tr* recognize
wie'dererlangen *tr* recover, retrieve
wie'dererstatten *tr* restore; (*Geld*) refund
Wie'dergabe *f* return; reproduction; rendering
wie'dergeben §80 *tr* give back; (*Ton*) reproduce; (*spielen, übersetzen*) render; (*Ehre, Gesundheit*) restore
Wie'dergeburt *f* rebirth
wie'dergenesen §84 *intr* (SEIN) recover
wie'dergewinnen §52 *tr* regain
wiedergut'machen *tr* make good
Wiedergut'machung *f* (–;–en) reparation
wiederher'stellen *tr* restore
wie'derholen *tr* bring back; take back ‖ **wiederho'len** *tr* repeat
wiederholt [vidər'hɔlt] *adv* repeatedly
Wiederho'lung *f* (–;–en) repetition
Wiederho'lungszeichen *n* dittomarks; (mus) repeat
Wie'derhören *n*—**auf W.!** (telp) goodbye!
wie'derimpfen *tr* give (*s.o.*) a booster shot
wiederinstand'setzen *tr* repair
wiederkäuen ['vidərkɔɪ·ən] *tr* ruminate; (fig) repeat over and over ‖ *intr* chew the cud
Wiederkehr ['vidərker] *f* (–;) return; recurrence; anniversary
wie'derkehren *intr* (SEIN) return; recur
wie'derkommen §99 *intr* (SEIN) come back
Wiederkunft ['vidərkʊnft] *f* (–;) return
wie'dersehen §138 *tr* see again ‖ *recip* meet again ‖ **Wiedersehen** *n* (–s;–) meeting again; **auf W.!** see you!
Wie'dertäufer *m* Baptist
wie'dertun §154 *tr* do again, repeat
wie'derum *adv* again; on the other hand
wie'dervereinigen *tr* reunite; reunify
Wie'dervereinigung *f* reunion; (pol) reunification
wie'derverheiraten *tr* & *recip* remarry
Wie'derverkäufer –in §6 *mf* retailer
Wie'derwahl *f* reelection
wie'derwählen *tr* reelect
wiederzu'lassen §104 *tr* readmit
Wiege ['vigə] *f* (–;–n) cradle
wiegen ['vigən] *tr* (*schaukeln*) rock ‖ *ref*—**sich in den Hüften w.** sway one's hips; **sich w. in** (*acc*) lull oneself into ‖ §57 *tr* & *intr* weigh
Wie'gendruck *m* incunabulum
Wie'genlied *n* lullaby

wiehern ['vi·ərn] *intr* neigh; **wiehern-des Gelächter** horselaugh

Wien [vin] *n* (-s;) Vienna

Wiener –in ['vinər(ɪn)] §6 *mf* Viennese

wienerisch ['vinərɪʃ] *adj* Viennese

wies [vis] *pret* of **weisen**

Wiese ['vizə] *f* (-;-n) meadow

Wiesel ['vizəl] *n* (-s;-) weasel

Wie'senland *n* meadowland

wieso' *adv* why, how come

wieviel' *adj* how much; **w. Uhr ist es?** what time is it? || *adv & pron* how much || **vieviele** *adj & pron* how many

wievielte [vi'filtə] §9 *adj* which, what; **den wievielten haben wir?** (or **der w. ist heute?**) what day of the month is it?

wiewohl' *conj* although

wild [vɪlt] *adj* wild; savage; (*grausam*) ferocious; (*Flucht*) headlong; (**auf** *acc*) wild (about); **wilde Ehe** concubinage; **wilder Streik** wildcat strike || **Wild** *n* (-es;) game

Wild'bach *m* torrent

Wild'braten *m* roast venison

Wildbret ['vɪltbret] *n* (-s;) game; venison

Wild'dieb *m* poacher

Wilde ['vɪldə] §5 *mf* savage; **wie ein Wilder** like a madman

Wild'ente *f* wild duck

Wilderer ['vɪldərər] *m* (-s;-) poacher

wildern ['vɪldərn] *intr* poach

Wild'fleisch *n* game; venison

wild'fremd' *adj* completely strange

Wild'hüter *m* game warden

Wild'leder *n* doeskin, buckskin; chamois; suede

Wildnis ['vɪltnɪs] *f* (-;) wilderness

Wild'schwein *n* wild boar

Wild'wasser *n* rapids

Wildwest'film *m* western

wildwüchsig ['vɪltvyksɪç] *adj* wild

Wille ['vɪlə] *m* (-ns;-n), **Willen** ['vɪlən] *m* (-s;-) will; (*Absicht*) intention; **mit W.** on purpose; **um j–s willen** for s.o.'s sake; **wider Willen** unwillingly; unintentionally; **willens sein zu** (*inf*) be willing to (*inf*)

wil'lenlos *adj* irresolute; unstable

Wil'lensfreiheit *f* free will

Wil'lenskraft *f* will power

wil'lensschwach *adj* weak-willed

wil'lensstark *adj* strong-willed

willfah'ren *intr* (*dat*) comply with

willig ['vɪlɪç] *adj* willing, ready

Wil'ligkeit *f* (-;) willingness

willkom'men *adj* welcome; **j–n w. heißen** welcome s.o. || **Willkommen** *m & n* (-s;) welcome

Willkür ['vɪlkyr] *f* (-;) arbitrariness

will'kürlich *adj* arbitrary

wimmeln ['vɪməln] *intr* (**von**) team (with)

wimmern ['vɪmərn] *intr* whimper

Wimpel ['vɪmpəl] *m* (-s;-) streamer; pennant

Wimper ['vɪmpər] *f* (-;-n) eyelash; **ohne mit der W. zu zucken** without batting an eye

Wim'perntusche *f* mascara

Wind [vɪnt] *m* (-[e]s;-e) wind; flatulence; (hunt) scent

Wind'beutel *m* (fig) windbag; (aer) windsock; (culin) cream puff

Winde ['vɪndə] *f* (-;-n) winch, windlass; reel; (naut) capstan

Windel ['vɪndəl] *f* (-;-n) diaper

win'delweich *adj*—**w. schlagen** (coll) beat to a pulp

winden ['vɪndən] §59 *tr* wind; twist, coil; (*Kranz*) weave, make || *ref* wriggle; (*Fluß*) wind; (*vor Schmerzen*) writhe

Wind'fang *m* storm porch

Wind'hose *f* tornado

Wind'hund *m* greyhound; (coll) windbag

windig ['vɪndɪç] *adj* windy; (fig) flighty

Wind'kanal *m* wind tunnel

Wind'licht *n* hurricane lamp

Wind'mühle *f* windmill

Wind'pocken *pl* chicken pox

Wind'sack *m* windsock

Wind'schatten *m* lee

Wind'schutzscheibe *f* windshield

Wind'stärke *f* wind velocity

wind'still *adj* calm || **Windstille** *f* calm

Wind'stoß *m* gust

Wind'strömung *f* air current

Win'dung *f* (-;-en) winding, twisting; (*Kurve*) bend; (*e–r Schlange*) coil; (*e–r Schraube*) thread, worm; (*e–r Muschel*) whorl

Wind'zug *m* air current, draft

Wink [vɪŋk] *m* (-[e]s;-e) sign; (*Zwinkern*) wink; (*mit der Hand*) wave; (*mit dem Kopfe*) nod; (*Hinweis*) hint, tip; **W. mit dem Zaunpfahl** broad hint

Winkel ['vɪŋkəl] *m* (-s;-) corner; (carp) square; (geom) angle; (mil) chevron

winkelig ['vɪŋkəlɪç] *adj* angular; (*Straße*) crooked

Win'kellinie *f* diagonal

Win'kelmaß *n* (carp) square

Win'kelzug *m* subterfuge; evasion

winken ['vɪŋkən] *intr* signal; **mit der Hand** wave; (*mit dem Kopfe*) nod; (*mit dem Auge*) wink; **mit dem Taschentuch w.** wave the handkerchief

Win'ker *m* (-s;-) signalman; (aut) direction signal

winseln ['vɪnzəln] *intr* whimper, whine

Winter ['vɪntər] *m* (-s;-) winter

win'terfest *adj* winterized; (*Pflanzen*) hardy

win'terlich *adj* wintry

Win'terschlaf *m* hibernation; **W. halten** hibernate

Win'tersonnenwende *f* winter solstice

Winzer ['vɪntsər] *m* (-s;-) vinedresser; (*Traubenleser*) grape picker

winzig ['vɪntsɪç] *adj* tiny

Wipfel ['vɪpfəl] *m* (-s;-) treetop

Wippe ['vɪpə] *f* (-;-n) seesaw

wippen ['vɪpən] *intr* seesaw; rock; balance oneself

wir [vir] §11 *pers pron* we

Wirbel ['vɪrbəl] *m* (-s;-) whirl; eddy; whirlpool; (*Trommel*-) roll; (*Violin*-)

peg; (anat) vertebra; **e–n W. machen** (coll) raise Cain
wirbelig ['vɪrbəlɪç] *adj* whirling; giddy
Wir'belknochen *m* (anat) vertebra
wir'bellos *adj* spineless, invertebrate
wirbeln ['vɪrbəln] *tr* warble ‖ *intr* whirl; (*Wasser*) eddy; (*Trommel*) roll; (*Lerche*) warble; **mir wirbelt der Kopf** my head is spinning
Wir'belsäule *f* spinal column, spine
Wir'belsturm *m* hurricane, typhoon
Wir'beltier *n* vertebrate
Wir'belwind *m* whirlwind
wirken ['vɪrkən] *tr* work, bring about, effect; (*Teig*) knead; (*Teppich*) weave; (*Pullover*) knit; **Gutes w.** do good; **Wunder w.** work wonders ‖ *intr* work; be active; function; look, appear; (*Worte*) tell, hit home; **als Arzt w.** be a doctor; **an e–r Schule (als Lehrer) w.** teach school; **anregend w.** act as a stimulant; **berauschend w. auf** (*acc*) intoxicate; **beruhigend w. auf** (*acc*) have a soothing effect on; **gut w.** work well; **lächerlich w.** look ridiculous; **stark w. auf** (*acc*) touch deeply; **w. auf** (*acc*) affect, have an effect on; **w. bei** have an effect on; **w. für** work for; **w. gegen** work against, counteract ‖ **Wirken** *n* (–s;) action, performance; operation
wirk'lich *adj* real, actual; true ‖ *adv* really, actually; truly
Wirk'lichkeit *f* (–;–en) reality; actual fact
Wirk'lichkeitsform *f* indicative mood
wirksam ['vɪrkzɑm] *adj* active; effective; (*Hieb*) telling; **w. für** good for
Wirk'samkeit *f* (–;) effectiveness
Wirk'stoff *m* metabolic substance (*vitamin, hormone, or enzyme*)
Wir'kung *f* (–;–en) effect; result; operation, action; influence, impression
Wir'kungsbereich *m* scope; effective range; (mil) zone of fire
wir'kungsfähig *adj* active; effective; efficient
Wir'kungskreis *m* domain, province
wir'kungslos *adj* ineffective; inefficient
wir'kungsvoll *adj* effective; efficacious
Wirk'waren *pl* knitwear
wirr [vɪr] *adj* confused; (*verworren*) chaotic; (*Haar*) disheveled
Wirren ['vɪrən] *pl* disorders, troubles
Wirr'kopf *m* scatterbrain
Wirrwarr ['vɪrvar] *m* (–s;) mix-up, mess
Wirt [vɪrt] *m* (–[e]s;–e) host; innkeeper; landlord; (biol) host
Wirtin ['vɪrtɪn] *f* (–;–nen) hostess; innkeeper, innkeeper's wife; landlady
wirt'lich *adj* hospitable
Wirt'schaft *f* (–;–en) economy; business; industry and trade; (*Haushaltung*) housekeeping; (*Hauswesen*) household; (*Gasthaus*) inn; (*Treiben*) goings-on; (*Durcheinander*) mess; (*Umstände*) fuss, trouble; **die W. besorgen** (or **führen**) keep house; **gelenkte W.** planned economy
wirtschaften ['vɪrtʃaftən] *intr* keep

house; economize; (*herumhantieren*) bustle about; **gut w.** manage well
Wirt'schafter **–in** §6 *mf* manager ‖ *f* housekeeper
Wirt'schaftler **–in** §6 *mf* economist; economics teacher
wirt'schaftlich *adj* economical, thrifty; economic; industrial; (*vorteilhaft*) profitable
Wirt'schaftsgeld *n* housekeeping money
Wirt'schaftshilfe *f* economic aid
Wirt'schaftsjahr *n* fiscal year
Wirt'schaftslehre *f* economics
Wirt'schaftspolitik *f* economic policy
Wirt'schaftsprüfer **–in** §6 *mf* certified public accountant, CPA
Wirts'haus *n* inn, restaurant; bar
wischen ['vɪʃən] *tr* wipe
Wisch'lappen *m* dustcloth
Wisch'tuch *n* dishtowel
wispern ['vɪspərn] *tr* & *intr* whisper
Wißbegierde ['vɪsbəgɪrdə] *f* (–;) craving for knowledge; curiosity
wissen ['vɪsən] §161 *tr* & *intr* know ‖ **Wissen** *n* (–s;) knowledge; learning; know-how; **meines Wissens as far as** I know
Wis'senschaft *f* (–;–en) knowledge; science
Wis'senschaftler **–in** §6 *mf* scientist
wis'senschaftlich *adj* scientific; scholarly; learned
Wis'sensdrang *m,* **Wis'sensdurst** *m* thirst for knowledge
Wis'sensgebiet *n* field of knowledge
wis'senswert *adj* worth knowing
wis'sentlich *adj* conscious; willful ‖ *adv* knowingly; on purpose
wittern ['vɪtərn] *tr* scent, smell
Wit'terung *f* (–;–en) weather; (hunt) scent; **bei günstiger W.** weather permitting; **e–e feine W. haben** have a good nose
Wit'terungsverhältnisse *pl* weather conditions
Witwe ['vɪtvə] *f* (–;–n) widow
Witwer ['vɪtvər] *m* (–s;–) widower
Witz [vɪts] *m* (–es;–e) joke; wisecrack; wit; wittiness; **das ist der ganze W.** that's all; **Witze machen** (or **reißen**) crack jokes
Witz'blatt *n* comics
Witzbold ['vɪtsbɔlt] *m* (–[e]s;–e) joker
witzig ['vɪtsɪç] *adj* witty; funny
wo [vo] *adv* where; **wo auch** (or **wo immer**) wherever; **wo nicht** if not; **wo nur** wherever
woan'ders *adv* somewhere else
wob [vop] *pret* of **weben**
wobei' *adv* whereby; whereat; whereto; at which; in the course of which
Woche ['vɔxə] *f* (–;–n) week; **heute in e–r W.** a week from today; **in den Wochen sein** be in labor; **in die Wochen kommen** go into labor; **unter der W.** (coll) during the week
Wo'chenbeihilfe *f* maternity benefits
Wo'chenbett *n* post-natal period
Wo'chenblatt *n* weekly (newspaper)
Wo'chenende *n* weekend
Wo'chengeld *n* weekly allowance; (*für Mütter*) maternity benefits

wo'chenlang *adj* lasting many weeks ‖ *adv* for weeks

Wo'chenlohn *m* weekly wages

Wo'chenschau *f* (cin) newsreel

wöchentlich ['vœçəntlıç] *adj* weekly ‖ *adv* every week; **einmal w.** once a week

–wöchig [vœçıç] *comb.fm.* –week

Wöchnerin ['vœçnərın] *f* (–;–nen) recent mother

Wodka ['vɔtka] *m* (–s;) vodka

wodurch' *adv* whereby, by which; how

wofern' *conj* provided that; **w. nicht** unless

wofür' *adv* wherefore, for which; what for; **w. halten Sie mich?** what do you take me for?

wog [vok] *pret* of **wägen** & **wiegen**

Woge ['vogə] *f* (–;–n) billow; **Wogen der Erregung** waves of excitement

woge'gen *adv* against what; against which; in exchange for what

wogen ['vogən] *intr* billow, surge, heave; (*Getreide*) wave; **hin und her w.** fluctuate

woher' *adv* from where; **w. wissen Sie das?** how do you know this?

wohin' *adv* whereto, where

wohinge'gen *conj* whereas

wohl [vol] *adj* well ‖ *adv* well; (*freilich*) to be sure, all right; I guess; possibly, probably; perhaps; **es sich** [*dat*] **w. sein lassen** have a good time; **nun w.!** well!; **w. daran tun zu** (*inf*) do well to (*inf*); **w. dem, der** happy he who; **w. kaum** hardly; **w. oder übel** willy-nilly ‖ **Wohl** *n* (–[e]s;) good health, well-being; (*Wohlfahrt*) welfare; (*Gedeihen*) prosperity; **auf Ihr W.!** to your health! **gemeines W.** common good

wohlan' *interj* all right then!

wohlauf' *adj* in good health, well ‖ *interj* all right then!

wohlbedacht ['volbədaxt] *adj* well-thought-out

Wohl'befinden *n* (–;) well-being

Wohl'behagen *n* comfort, contentment

wohl'behalten *adj* safe and sound

wohl'bekannt *adj* well-known

wohl'beschaffen *adj* in good condition

Wohl'ergehen *n* well-being

wohl'erzogen *adj* well-bred

Wohl'fahrt *f* (–;) welfare

Wohl'fahrtsarbeit *f* social work

wohl'feil *adj* cheap

Wohl'gefallen *n* (–s;) pleasure, satisfaction

wohl'gefällig *adj* pleasant, agreeable

wohl'gemeint *adj* well-meant

wohlgemut ['volgəmut] *adj* cheerful

wohl'genährt *adj* well-fed

wohl'geneigt *adj* affectionate

Wohl'geruch *m* fragrance, perfume

wohl'gesinnt *adj* well-disposed

wohl'habend *adj* well-to-do

wohlig ['volıç] *adj* comfortable

Wohl'klang *m* melodious sound

wohl'klingend *adj* melodious

Wohl'leben *n* good living, luxury

wohl'riechend *adj* fragrant

wohl'schmeckend *adj* tasty

Wohl'sein *n* good health, well-being

Wohl'stand *m* prosperity, wealth

Wohl'tat *f* benefit; (*Gunst*) kindness, good deed; **e–e W. sein** hit the spot

Wohl'täter **–in** §6 *mf* benefactor

wohl'tätig *adj* charitable; beneficent

Wohl'tätigkeit *f* charity

wohltuend ['voltu·ənt] *adj* pleasant

wohl'tun §154 *intr* do good; (*dat*) be pleasant (to)

wohl'unterrichtet *adj* well-informed

wohl'verdient *adj* well-deserved

wohl'verstanden *interj* mark my words!

wohl'weislich *adv* very wisely

wohl'wollen §162 *intr* (*dat*) be well-disposed towards ‖ **Wollwollen** *n* (–s;) good will; (*Gunst*) favor

Wohn– [von] *comb.fm.* residential; dwelling, living

Wohn'anhänger *m* house trailer

Wohn'block *m* block of apartments

wohnen ['vonən] *intr* live, reside; (*als Mieter*) room

wohn'haft *adj* residing, living

Wohn'haus *n* dwelling; apartment house

Wohn'küche *f* efficiency apartment

Wohn'laube *f* garden house

wohn'lich *adj* livable; cozy

Wohn'möglichkeit *f* living accommodations

Wohn'ort *m* place of residence; (jur) domicile; **ständiger W.** permanent address

Wohn'raum *m* living space; room (*of a house*)

Wohn'sitz *m* place of residence

Woh'nung *f* (–;–en) dwelling, home; apartment; room; accommodations

Woh'nungsamt *n* housing authority

Woh'nungsbau *m* (–[e]s;) housing construction

Woh'nungsfrage *f* housing problem

Woh'nungsinhaber **–in** §6 *mf* occupant

Woh'nungsmangel *m*, **Woh'nungsnot** *f* housing shortage

Wohn'viertel *n* residential district

Wohn'wagen *m* mobile home

Wohn'wagenparkplatz *m* trailer camp

Wohn'zimmer *n* living room

wölben ['vœlbən] *tr* vault, arch ‖ *ref* (*über dat or acc*) arch (over)

Wöl'bung *f* (–;–en) curvature; vault

Wolf [vɔlf] *m* (–[e]s;⁼e) wolf; (*Fleisch–*) meat grinder; (astr) Lupus; (pathol) lupus

Wolfram ['vɔlfram] *n* (–s;) tungsten

Wolke ['vɔlkə] *f* (–;–n) cloud

Wol'kenbildung *f* cloud formation

Wol'kenbruch *m* cloudburst

Wol'kendecke *f* cloudcover

Wol'kenfetzen *m* wispy cloud

Wol'kenhöhe *f* (meteor) ceiling

Wol'kenkratzer *m* (–s;–) skyscraper

Wol'kenwand *f* cloud bank

wolkig ['vɔlkıç] *adj* cloudy, clouded

Wolldecke ['vɔldɛkə] *f* woolen blanket

Wolle ['vɔlə] *f* (–;–n) wool

wollen ['vɔlən] *adj* woolen, wool ‖ §162 *tr* want, wish; mean, intend; (*gern haben*) like ‖ *intr* wish, like; **dem sei, wie ihm wolle** be that as it may; **wie Sie w.** as you please ‖ *mod aux* want (to), wish (to), intend (to);

be going (to) ‖ **Wollen** *n* (-s;) will; volition
Wollfett ['vɔlfɛt] *n* lanolin
Wollgarn ['vɔlgarn] *n* worsted
wollig ['vɔlıç] *adj* woolly
Wolljacke ['vɔljakə] *f* cardigan
Wollsachen ['vɔlzaxən] *pl* woolens
Wollstoff ['vɔlʃtɔf] *m* woolen fabric
Wollust ['vɔllʊst] *f* (-;ᵉe) lust
wollüstig ['vɔllʏstıç] *adj* voluptuous; (*geil*) lewd, lecherous
Wollüstling ['vɔllʏstlıŋ] *m* (-s;-e) voluptuary
Wollwaren ['vɔlvarən] *pl* woolens
womit' *adv* with which; with what; wherewith; **w. kann ich dienen?** (com) can I help you?
womög'lich *adv* possibly, if possible
wonach' *adv* after which, whereupon; according to which
Wonne ['vɔnə] *f* (-;-n) delight; bliss
Won'negefühl *n* blissful feeling
Won'neschauer *m* thrill of delight
won'netrunken *adj* enraptured
won'nevoll, wonnig ['vɔnıç] *adj* blissful
woran' *adv* at which; at what; **ich weiß nicht, w. ich bin** I don't know where I stand
worauf' *adv* on which; on what; whereupon; **w. warten Sie?** what are you waiting for?
woraus' *adv* out of what, from what; out of which, from which; **w. ist das gemacht?** what is this made of?
worden ['vɔrdən] *pp* of **werden**
worin' *adv* in what; in which
Wort [vɔrt] *n* (-[e]s;ᵉer) word (*individual; literal*) ‖ *n* (-[e]s;-e) word (*expression; figurative*); (*Ausspruch*) saying; (*Ehrenwort*) word (*of honor*); **auf ein W.!** may I have a word with you!; **auf mein W.!** word of honor!; **aufs W.** implicitly, to the letter; **das W. ergreifen** begin to speak; (parl) take the floor; **das W. erhalten** (or **haben**) be allowed to speak; (parl) have the floor; **das W. führen** be the spokesman; **hast du Worte!** (coll) can you beat that!; **in Worten** in writing; **j-m das W. erteilen** allow s.o. to speak; **j-m ins W. fallen** cut s.o. short
Wort'art *f* (gram) part of speech
Wort'bedeutungslehre *f* semantics
Wort'beugung *f* declension
Wort'bildung *f* word formation
wort'brüchig *adj*—**w. werden** break one's word
Wörterbuch ['vœrtərbux] *n* dictionary
Wörterverzeichnis ['vœrtərfɛrtsaıçnıs] *n* word index; vocabulary; glossary
Wort'folge *f* word order
Wort'führer **-in** §6 *mf* spokesman
Wort'gefecht *n* dispute
wort'getreu *adj* literal; verbatim
wort'karg *adj* taciturn
Wortklauber **-in** ['vɔrtklaubər(ın)] §6 *mf* quibbler, hairsplitter
Wort'laut *m* wording; (fig) letter
wörtlich ['vœrtlıç] *adj* word-for-word; literal; (*Rede*) direct
wort'los *adv* without saying a word

Wort'register *n* word index
Wort'schatz *m* vocabulary
Wort'schwall *m* flood of words, verbiage
Wort'spiel *n* pun
Wort'stamm *m* stem
Wort'stellung *f* word order
Wort'streit *m*, **Wort'wechsel** *m* argument
worüber [vo'rybər] *adv* over what, over which
worum [vo'rʊm] *adv* about what, about which
worunter [vo'rʊntər] *adv* under what, under which; among which
wovon' *adv* from what, of what, from which, of which; **w. ist die Rede?** what are they talking about?
wovor' *adv* of what; before which
wozu' *adv* for what; why; to which
Wrack [vrak] *n* (-[e]s;-e & -s) (& fig) wreck
Wrack'gut *n* wreckage
wrang [vraŋ] *pret* of **wringen**
wringen ['vrıŋən] §142 *tr* wring
Wringmaschine ['vrıŋmaʃinə] *f* wringer
Wucher ['vuxər] *m* (-s;) profiteering; **das ist ja W.!** (coll) that's highway robbery!; **W. treiben** profiteer
Wu'cherer **-in** §6 *mf* profiteer; loan shark
Wu'chergewinn *m* excess profit
wu'cherhaft, wucherisch ['vuxərıʃ] *adj* profiteering, exorbitant
Wu'chermiete *f* excessive rent
wuchern ['vuxərn] *intr* grow luxuriantly; (*Wucher treiben*) profiteer
Wu'cherung *f* (-;-en) (bot) rank growth; (pathol) growth
Wu'cherzinsen *pl* excessive interest
wuchs [vuks] *pret* of **wachsen** ‖ **Wuchs** *m* (-es;) growth; **groß von W.** tall
-wüchsig [vyksıç] *comb.fm.* –growing, –grown
Wucht [vuxt] *f* (-;-en) weight, force
wuchten ['vuxtən] *tr* lift with effort
wuchtig ['vuxtıç] *adj* heavy; massive
Wühlarbeit ['vylarbaıt] *f* subversive activity
wühlen ['vylən] *intr* dig, burrow; (*Schwein*) root about; (*suchend*) rummage about; (pol) engage in subversive activities; **im Geld w.** be rolling in money; **in Schmutz w.** wallow in filth
Wüh'ler **-in** §6 *mf* subversive, agitator
Wulst [vulst] *m* (-es;ᵉe) & *f* (-;ᵉe) bulge; (aut) rim (*of tire*)
wulstig ['vulstıç] *adj* bulging; (*Lippen*) thick
wund [vunt] *adj* sore; (poet) wounded
Wunde ['vundə] *f* (-;-n) wound; sore
Wunder ['vundər] *n* (-s;-) wonder; miracle; **W. wirken** work wonders
wunderbar ['vundərbar] *adj* wonderful; (& fig) miraculous
Wun'derding *n* marvel
Wun'derdoktor *m* faith healer
Wun'derkind *n* child prodigy
Wun'derkraft *f* miraculous power
wun'derlich *adj* queer, odd
wundern ['vundərn] *tr* amaze ‖ *ref*

(über *acc*) be amazed (at) || *impers*
—es sollte mich w., wenn I'd be surprised if; es wundert mich, daß I am surprised that
wun'derschön' *adv* lovely, gorgeous
Wun'dertat *f* miracle
Wun'dertäter –in §6 *mf* wonder worker
wundertätig *adj* miraculous
wun'dervoll *adj* wonderful, marvelous
Wun'derwerk *n* (& fig) miracle
Wun'derzeichen *n* omen, prodigy
Wund'klammer *f* (surg) clamp
wund'liegen §108 *ref* get bedsores
Wund'mal *n* scar, sore; (relig) wound
wund'reiten §86 *ref* become saddlesore
Wunsch [vʊnʃ] *m* (–es;≃e) wish; (nach) desire (for); auf W. upon request; ein frommer W. wishful thinking; nach W. as desired
Wünschelrute ['vʏnʃəlrutə] *f* divining rod
Wün'schelrutengänger *m* dowser
wünschen ['vʏnʃən] *tr* wish; wish for, desire; was w. Sie? (com) may I help you? || *intr* wish, please
wün'schenswert *adj* desirable
Wunsch'form *f* (gram) optative
Wunsch'konzert *n* (rad) request program
wunsch'los *adj* contented || *adv*—w. glücklich perfectly happy
wuppdich ['vʊpdɪç] *interj* zip!, in a flash!; all of a sudden!
wurde ['vʊrdə] *pret* of werden
Würde ['vʏrdə] *f* (–;–n) honor; title; dignity; post, office; akademische W. academic degree; unter aller W. beneath contempt
wür'delos *adj* undignified
Wür'denträger –in §6 *mf* dignitary
wür'devoll *adj* dignified
würdig ['vʏrdɪç] *adj* dignified; (genit) worthy (of), deserving (of)
würdigen ['vʏrdɪgən] *tr* appreciate, value; (genit) deem worthy (of)
Wurf [vʊrf] *m* (–[e]s;≃e) throw, cast, pitch; (fig) hit, success; (zool) litter, brood
Wurf'anker *m* grapnel
Würfel ['vʏrfəl] *m* (–s;–) die; cube,

square; (geom) cube; W. spielen play dice
Wür'felbecher *m* dice box
würfelig ['vʏrfəlɪç] *adj* cube-shaped; (Muster) checkered
würfeln ['vʏrfəln] *intr* play dice
Wür'felzucker *m* cube sugar
Wurf'geschoß *n* projectile, missile
Wurf'pfeil *m* dart
würgen ['vʏrgən] *tr* choke; strangle || *intr* choke; am Essen w. gag on food
Wurm [vʊrm] *m* (–s;≃er) (& mach) worm
wurmen ['vʊrmən] *tr* (coll) bug
wurmig ['vʊrmɪç] *adj* wormy; wormeaten
wurmstichig ['vʊrmʃtɪçɪç] *adj* wormeaten
Wurst [vʊrst] *f* (–;≃e) sausage; es geht um die W. now or never; es ist mir W. I couldn't care less
Würstchen ['vʏrstçən] *n* (–s;–), Würstel ['vʏrstəl] *n* (–s;–n) hotdog
wursteln ['vʊrstəln] *intr* muddle along
Würze ['vʏrtsə] *f* (–;–n) spice, seasoning; (fig) zest
Wurzel ['vʊrtsəl] *f* (–;–n) root; W. fassen (or schlagen) take root
wurzeln ['vʊrtsəln] *intr* (HABEN & SEIN) take root; w. in (dat) be rooted in
würzen ['vʏrtsən] *tr* spice, season
würzig ['vʏrtsɪç] *adj* spicy; aromatic
Würz'stoff *m* seasoning
wusch [vʊʃ] *pret* of waschen
wußte ['vʊstə] *pret* of wissen
Wust [vʊst] *m* (–es;) jumble, mess
wüst [vʏst] *adj* desert, waste; (roh) coarse; (wirr) confused
Wüste ['vʏstə] *f* (–;–en) desert
Wüstling ['vʏstlɪŋ] *m* (–s;–e) debauchee
Wut [vut] *f* (–;) rage, fury; madness
Wut'anfall *m* fit of rage
wüten ['vytən] *intr* rage
wü'tend *adj* (auf acc) furious (at)
Wüterich ['vytərɪç] *m* (–s;–e) madman; bloodthirsty villain
wut'schäumend *adj* foaming with rage
wut'schnaubend *adj* in a towering rage
Wut'schrei *m* shout of anger

X

X, x [ɪks] *invar n* X, x
X'-Beine *pl* knock-knees
x'-beinig *adj* knock-kneed
x'-beliebig *adj* any, whatever || X-beliebige §5 *m*—jeder X. every Tom, Dick, and Harry
x'-fach *adj* (coll) hundredfold

x'-mal *adv* umpteen times
X'-Strahlen *pl* x-rays
X'-Tag *m* D-day
x-te ['ɪkstə] §9 *adj* umpteenth; die x-te Potenz (math) the nth power
Xylophon [ksʏlɔ'fon] *n* (–s;–e) xylophone

Y

Y, y [ypsilən] *invar n* Y, y
Yacht [jaxt] *f* (–;–en) yacht
Yamswurzel ['jamsvʊrtsəl] *f* (–;–n) (bot) yam

Yankee ['jeŋki] *m* (–s;–s) Yankee
Yoghurt ['jogurt] *m* & *n* (–s;) yogurt
Yo-Yo ['jo'jo] *n* (–s;–s) yo-yo
Ypsilon ['ypsilən] *n* (–[s];–s) y

Z

Z, z [tset] *invar n* Z, z
Zacke ['tsakə] *f* (–;–n) sharp point;
(*Zinke*) prong; (*Fels–*) crag; (*e–s
Kamms, e–r Säge*) tooth; (*am Kleid*)
scallop
zacken ['tsakən] *tr* notch; scallop ‖
Zacken *m* (–s;–) var of **Zacke**
zackig ['tsakıç] *adj* toothed; notched;
(*Felsen*) jagged; (*spitz*) pointed;
(*Kleid*) scalloped; (fig) sharp
zagen ['tsagən] *intr* be faint-hearted
zaghaft ['tsakhaft] *adj* timid
zäh [tse] *adj* tough; (*klebig*) viscous;
(*beharrlich*) persistent; (*Gedächtnis*)
tenacious; (*halsstarrig*) dogged
zäh'flüssig *adj* viscous
Zäh'flüssigkeit *f* (–;) viscosity
Zä'higkeit *f* (–;) toughness; tenacity;
viscosity; doggedness
Zahl [tsal] *f* (–;–en) number; (*Betrag,
Ziffer*) figure; **an Z. übertreffen** out-
number; **arabische Z.** Arabic numeral; **der Z. nach** in number; **ganze Z.**
integer; **gebrochene Z.** fraction; **gerade Z.** even number; **in roten Zahlen stecken** be in the red; **ungerade
Z.** odd number; **wenig an der Z.** few
in number
zahlbar ['tsalbar] *adj* payable; **z. bei
Lieferung** cash on delivery
zählebig ['tselebıç] *adj* hardy
zahlen ['tsalən] *tr* pay; (*Schuld*) pay
off ‖ *intr* pay
zählen ['tselən] *tr* count; number,
amount to ‖ *intr* count; be of importance, count; **nach Tausenden z.**
number in the thousands; **z. auf** (*dat*)
count on; **z. zu** be numbered among,
belong to
Zah'lenangaben *pl* figures
Zah'lenfolge *f* numerical order
zah'lenmäßig *adj* numerical
Zah'ler –in §6 *mf* payer
Zäh'ler (–s;–) counter; recorder; (*für
Gas, Elektrizität*) meter; (math) numerator; (parl) teller; (sport) score-
keeper
Zählerableser ['tseləraplezər] *m* (–s;–)
meter man
Zahl'karte *f* money-order form
zahl'los *adj* countless, innumerable
Zahl'meister *m* paymaster; (mil) pay
officer; (nav) purser
zahl'reich *adj* numerous
Zähl'rohr *n* Geiger counter
Zahl'stelle *f* cashier's window; (*e–r
Bank*) branch office
Zahl'tag *m* payday
Zah'lung *f* (–;–en) payment; (*e–r
Schuld*) settlement
Zäh'lung *f* (–;–en) counting; computa-
tion
Zah'lungsanweisung *f* draft; check;
postal money order
Zah'lungsausgleich *m* balance of pay-
ments
Zah'lungsbedingungen *pl* (fin) terms
Zah'lungsbestätigung *f* receipt

Zah'lungsbilanz *f* balance of payments;
aktive (or **passive**) **Z.** favorable (or
unfavorable) balance of payments
zah'lungsfähig *adj* solvent
Zah'lungsfähigkeit *f* (–;) solvency
Zah'lungsfrist *f* due date
Zah'lungsmittel *n* medium of exchange; **gesetzliches Z.** legal tender;
bargeldloses Z. instrument of credit
Zah'lungsschwierigkeiten *pl* financial
embarrassment
Zah'lungssperre *f* stoppage of payments
Zah'lungstermin *m* date of payment;
(fin) date of maturity
Zah'lungsverzug *m* (fin) default
Zähl'werk *n* meter
Zahl'wort *n* (–[e]s;–er) numeral
Zahl'zeichen *n* figure, cipher
zahm [tsam] *adj* tame; domesticated
zähmen ['tsemən] *tr* tame; domesti-
cate; (fig) control ‖ *ref* control one-
self
Zäh'mung *f* (–;) taming; domestica-
tion
Zahn [tsan] *m* (–[e]s;–e) tooth;
(mach) tooth, cog; **j–m auf den Z.
fühlen** sound s.o. out; **mit den Zäh-
nen knirschen** grind one's teeth
Zahn'arzt *m*, **Zahn'ärztin** *f* dentist
Zahn'bürste *f* toothbrush
Zahn'creme *f* toothpaste
zahnen ['tsanən] *intr* cut one's teeth
Zahn'ersatz *m* denture
Zahn'fäule *f* tooth decay, caries
Zahn'fleisch *n* gum
Zahn'füllung *f* (dent) filling
Zahn'heilkunde *f* dentistry
Zahn'klammer *f* (–;–n) (dent) brace
Zahn'krem *f* toothpaste
Zahn'krone *f* (dent) crown
Zahn'laut *m* (phonet) dental
Zahn'lücke *f* gap between the teeth
Zahn'paste *f* toothpaste
Zahn'pflege *f* dental hygiene
Zahn'pulver *n* tooth powder
Zahn'rad *n* cog wheel; (*Kettenrad*)
sprocket
Zahn'radbahn *f* cog railway
Zahn'schmerz *m* toothache
Zahn'spange *f* (–;–n) (dent) brace
Zahn'stein *m* (dent) tartar
Zahnstocher ['tsan/təxər] *m* (–s;–)
toothpick
Zahn'techniker –in §6 *mf* dental tech-
nician
Zahn'weh *n* toothache
Zange ['tsaŋə] *f* (–;–en) (pair of)
pliers; (pair of) tongs; (*Pinzette*)
(pair of) tweezers; (dent, surg, zool)
forceps; **j–n in die Z. nehmen** corner
s.o. (*with tough questioning*)
Zank ['tsaŋk] *m* (–[e]s;) quarrel, fight
Zank'apfel *m* apple of discord
zanken ['tsaŋkən] *tr* scold ‖ *recip &
intr* quarrel, fight
zank'haft, zänkisch ['tseŋkıʃ], **zank'-
süchtig** *adj* quarrelsome

Zäpfchen ['tsɛpfçən] *n* (**-s;-**) little peg; (anat) uvula; (med) suppository
zapfen ['tsapfən] *tr* (*Bier, Wein*) tap ‖ **Zapfen** *m* (**-s;-**) plug, bung; (*Stift*) stud; (*Drehpunkt*) pivot; (*Eis-*) icicle; (*Tannen-*) cone; (carp) tenon; (mach) pin; (mach) journal
Zap'fenstreich *m* (mil) taps
Zapfhahn ['tsapfhɑn] *m* tap, spigot
Zapfsäule ['tsapfzɔɪlə] *f* (**-;-n**) (aut) gasoline pump
Zapfstelle ['tsapfʃtɛlə] *f* (**-;-n**) (aut) service station, gas station
Zapfwart ['tsapfvart] *m* (**-[e]s;-e**) (aut) service station attendant
zappelig ['tsapəlɪç] *adj* fidgety
zappeln ['tsapəln] *intr* fidget; squirm; (*im Wasser*) founder
Zar [tsɑr] *m* (**-en;-en**) czar
Zarge ['tsargə] *f* (**-;-n**) border; frame
zart [tsɑrt] *adj* tender; (*Farbe, Haut*) soft; (*Gesundheit*) delicate
zart'fühlend *adj* tender; sensitive
Zart'gefühl *n* sensitivity; tact
Zart'heit *f* (**-;**) tenderness
zärtlich ['tsɛrtlɪç] *adj* tender, affectionate
Zärt'lichkeit *f* (**-;-en**) tenderness; (*Liebkosung*) caress
Zaster ['tsastər] *m* (**-s;**) (coll) dough
Zauber ['tsaʊbər] *m* (**-s;-**) spell; magic; (fig) charm, glamor
Zauber- *comb.fm.* magic
Zauberei [tsaʊbə'raɪ] *f* (**-;-en**) magic; witchcraft, sorcery
Zau'berer *m* (**-s;-**) magician; sorcerer
Zau'berformel *f* incantation, spell
zau'berhaft *adj* magic; enchanting
Zau'berin *f* (**-;-nen**) sorceress, witch; enchantress
zauberisch ['tsaʊbərɪʃ] *adj* magic
Zau'berkraft *f* magic power
Zau'berkunst *f* magic
Zau'berkünstler **-in** §6 *mf* magician
Zau'berkunststück *n* magic trick
Zau'berland *n* fairyland
zaubern ['tsaʊbərn] *tr* produce by magic ‖ *intr* practice magic; do magic tricks
Zau'berspruch *m* incantation, spell
Zau'berstab *m* magic wand
Zau'bertrank *m* magic potion
Zau'berwerk *n* witchcraft
Zau'berwort *n* (**-[e]s;-e**) magic word
zaudern ['tsaʊdərn] *intr* procrastinate; hesitate; linger
Zaum [tsaʊm] *m* (**-[e]s;ᵉe**) bridle; **im Z. halten** keep in check
zäumen ['tsɔɪmən] *tr* bridle
Zaun [tsaʊn] *m* (**-[e]s;ᵉe**) fence; **e-n Streit vom Z. brechen** pick a quarrel
Zaun'gast *m* non-paying spectator
Zaun'könig *m* (orn) wren
Zaun'pfahl *m* fence post
zausen ['tsaʊzən] *tr* tug at; tousle, ruffle ‖ *recip* tug at each other
Zebra ['tsebra] *n* (**-s;-s**) zebra
Ze'brastreifen *m* zebra stripe; (*auf der Fahrbahn*) passenger crossing
Zech- [tsɛç] *comb.fm.* drinking
Zech'bruder *m* boozehound
Zeche ['tsɛçə] *f* (**-;-n**) (*Wirtshausrechnung*) check; (min) mine **die Z.**

prellen (coll) sneak out without paying the bill
zechen ['tsɛçən] *intr* booze
Ze'cher **-in** §6 *mf* heavy drinker
Zech'gelage *n* drinking party
Zechpreller ['tsɛçprɛlər] *m* (**-s;-**) cheat, bilker
Zech'tour *f* binge; **e-e Z. machen** go on a binge
Zecke ['tsɛkə] *f* (**-;-n**) (ent) tick
Zeder ['tsedər] *f* (**-;-n**) cedar
Zehe ['tse.ə] *f* (**-;-n**) toe; (*Knoblauch-*) clove
Ze'hennagel *m* toenail
Ze'henspitze *f* tip of the toe; **auf den Zehenspitzen** (on) tiptoe
zehn [tsen] *invar adj & pron* ten ‖ **Zehn** *f* (**-;-en**) ten
Zehner ['tsenər] *m* (**-s;-**) ten; ten-mark bill
zehn'fach, zehn'fältig *adj* tenfold
Zehnfin'gersystem *n* touch-type system
Zehn'kampf *m* decathlon
zehn'mal *adv* ten times
zehnte ['tsentə] §9 *adj & pron* tenth ‖ **Zehnte** §5 *mfn* tenth
Zehntel ['tsentəl] *n* (**-s;-**) tenth (*part*)
zehren ['tserən] *intr* be debilitating; **an den Kräften z.** drain one's strength; **an der Gesundheit z.** undermine one's health; **z. an** (*dat*) (fig) gnaw at; **z. von** live on, live off
Zeh'rung *f* (**-;**) provisions; expenses
Zeichen ['tsaɪçən] *n* (**-s;-**) sign; signal; token; (*Merkmal*) distinguishing mark; (*Beweis*) proof; symbol; (astr) sign; (com) brand; (med) symptom; (rad) call sign; **er ist seines Zeichens Anwalt** he is a lawyer by profession; **zum Z., daß** as proof that
Zei'chenbrett *n* drawing board
Zei'chenbuch *n* sketchbook
Zei'chengerät *n* drafting equipment
Zei'chenheft *n* sketchbook
Zei'chenlehrer **-in** §6 *mf* art teacher
Zei'chenpapier *n* drawing paper
Zei'chensetzung *f* punctuation
Zei'chensprache *f* sign language
Zei'chentisch *m* drawing board
Zei'chentrickfilm *m* animated cartoon
Zei'chenunterricht *m* drawing lesson
zeichnen ['tsaɪçnən] *tr* draw; sketch; (*entwerfen*) design; (*brandmarken*) brand; (*Anleihe*) take out; (*Aktien*) buy; (*Geld*) pledge; (*Wäsche*) mark; (*Brief*) sign ‖ *intr* draw; sketch; (hunt) leave a trail of blood; **z. für** sign for
Zeich'ner **-in** §6 *mf* draftsman; (*Mode-*) designer; (*e-r Anleihe*) subscriber
zeichnerisch ['tsaɪçnərɪʃ] *adj* (*Begabung*) for drawing; (*Darstellung*) graphic
Zeich'nung *f* (**-;-en**) drawing; sketch; design; picture, illustration; diagram; signature; (*e-r Anleihe*) subscription; (*des Holzes*) grain
zeich'nungsberechtigt *adj* authorized to sign
Zeigefinger ['tsaɪgəfɪŋər] *m* index finger
zeigen ['tsaɪgən] *tr* show, indicate;

(*in e-r Rede*) point out; (*zur Schau stellen*) display; (*beweisen*) prove; (*dartun*) demonstrate ‖ *ref* appear, show up; prove to be ‖ *intr* point; **z. auf** (*acc*) point to; **z. nach** point toward ‖ *impers ref*—**es zeigt sich, daß** it turns out that; **es wird sich ja z., ob** we shall see whether
Zei'ger *m* (**-s;-**) pointer; indicator; (*e-r Uhr*) hand
Zeigestock ['tsaɪgəʃtɔk] *m* pointer
Zeile ['tsaɪlə] *f* (**-;-n**) line; (*Reihe*) row
Zeit [tsaɪt] *f* (**-;-en**) time; **auf Z.** (com) on credit, on time; **in der letzten Z.** lately; **in jüngster Z.** quite recently; **mit der Z.** in time, in the course of time; **vor Zeiten** in former times; **zu meiner Z.** in my time; **zu rechter Z.** in the nick of time; **on time; zur Z.** at present; **zur Z.** (*genit*) at the time of
Zeit'abschnitt *m* period, epoch
Zeit'abstand *m* interval of time
Zeit'alter *n* age
Zeit'angabe *f* time; date; exact date and hour; **ohne Z.** undated
Zeit'ansage *f* (rad) (giving of) time
Zeit'aufnahme *f* (phot) time exposure
Zeit'aufwand *m* loss of time; (**für**) time spent (on)
Zeit'dauer *f* term, period of time
Zeit'einteilung *f* timetable; timing
Zei'tenfolge *f* sequence of tenses
Zei'tenwende *f* beginning of the Christian era
Zeit'folge *f* chronological order
Zeit'form *f* tense
Zeit'geist *m* spirit of the times
zeit'gemäß *adj* timely; up-to-date
Zeit'genosse *m*, **Zeit'genossin** *f* contemporary
zeitgenössisch ['tsaɪtgənœsɪʃ] *adj* contemporary
Zeit'geschichte *f* contemporary history
zeitig ['tsaɪtɪç] *adj* early; (*reif*) mature, ripe
zeitigen ['tsaɪtɪgən] *tr* ripen
Zeit'karte *f* commuter ticket
Zeit'lage *f* state of affairs
Zeit'lang *f*—**e-e Z.** for some time
Zeit'lauf *m* course of time
zeit'lebens *adv* during my (his, your, etc.) life
zeit'lich *adj* temporal; chronological ‖ *adv* in time ‖ **Zeitliche §5** *n*—**das Z.** segnen depart this world
zeit'los *adj* timeless
Zeit'lupe *f* (cin) slow motion
Zeit'mangel *m* lack of time
Zeit'maß *n* (mus) tempo; (pros) quantity
Zeit'nehmer -in §6 *mf* timekeeper
Zeit'ordnung *f* chronological order
Zeit'punkt *m* point of time, moment
Zeitraffer ['tsaɪtrafər] *m* (**-s;**) time-lapse photography
zeit'raubend *adj* time-consuming
Zeit'raum *m* space of time, period
Zeit'rechnung *f* era
Zeit'schaltgerät *n* timer
Zeit'schrift *f* periodical, magazine
Zeit'spanne *f* span (of time)

Zeit'tafel *f* chronological table
Zei'tung *f* (**-;-en**) newspaper; journal
Zei'tungsarchiv *n* (journ) morgue
Zei'tungsartikel *m* newspaper article
Zei'tungsausschnitt *m* newspaper clipping
Zei'tungsbeilage *f* supplement
Zei'tungsdeutsch *n* journalese
Zei'tungsente *f* (journ) hoax, spoof
Zei'tungskiosk *m* newsstand
Zei'tungsmeldung *f*, **Zei'tungsnotiz** *f* newspaper item
Zei'tungspapier *n* newsprint
Zei'tungsverkäufer -in §6 *mf* newsvendor
Zei'tungswesen *n*—**das Z.** the press
Zeit'vergeudung *f* waste of time
zeit'verkürzend *adj* entertaining
Zeit'verlust *m* loss of time
Zeit'vermerk *m* date
Zeit'verschwendung *f* waste of time
Zeit'vertreib *m* pastime
zeitweilig ['tsaɪtvaɪlɪç] *adj* temporary; periodic ‖ *adv* temporarily; at times, from time to time
Zeit'wende *f* beginning of a new era
Zeit'wert *m* current value
Zeit'wort *n* (**-[e]s;⁈er**) verb
Zeit'zeichen *n* time signal
Zeit'zünder *m* time fuse
Zelle ['tsɛlə] *f* (**-;-n**) cell; (aer) fuselage; (telp) booth
Zel'lenlehre *f* cytology
Zellophan [tsɛlo'fan] *n* (**-s;**) cellophane
Zellstoff ['tsɛlʃtɔf] *m* cellulose
Zelluloid [tsɛlu'lɔɪt] *n* (**-s;**) celluloid
Zellulose [tsɛlu'lozə] *f* (**-;**) cellulose
Zelt ['tsɛlt] *n* (**-[e]s;-e**) tent
zelten ['tsɛltən] *intr* camp out
Zelt'leinwand *f* canvas
Zelt'pfahl *m* tent pole
Zelt'pflock *m* tent peg, tent stake
Zelt'stange *f*, **Zelt'stock** *m* tent pole
Zement [tsɛ'mɛnt] *m* (**-[e]s;**) cement
zementieren [tsɛmɛn'tirən] *tr* cement
Zenit [tsɛ'nit] *m* (**-[e]s;**) zenith
zensieren [tsɛn'zirən] *tr* censor; (educ) mark, grade
Zen·sor ['tsɛnzɔr] *m* (**-s;-soren** ['zorən]) censor
Zensur [tsɛn'zur] *f* (**-;-en**) censorship; (educ) grade, mark
Zentimeter [tsɛntɪ'metər] *m & n* centimeter
Zentner ['tsɛntnər] *m* (**-s;-**) hundredweight
Zent'nerlast *f* (fig) heavy load
zentral [tsɛn'tral] *adj* central
Zentral'behörde *f* central authority
Zentrale [tsɛn'tralə] *f* (**-;-n**) central office; telephone exchange, switchboard; (elec) power station
Zentral'heizung *f* central heating
Zen·trum ['tsɛntrum] *m* (**-s;-tren** [trən]) center
Zephir ['tsefir] *m* (**-s;-e**) zephyr
Zepter ['tsɛptər] *n* (**-s;-**) scepter
zer- [tsɛr] *pref* up, to pieces, apart
zerbei'ßen §53 *tr* bite to pieces
zerber'sten §55 *intr* (SEIN) split apart
zerbre'chen §64 *tr* break to pieces, shatter, smash ‖ *ref*—**sich** [*dat*] **den**

Kopf z. über (*acc*) rack one's brains over || *intr* (SEIN) shatter

zerbrech'lich *adj* fragile, brittle

zerbröckeln (**zerbrök'keln**) *tr* & *intr* (SEIN) crumble

zerdrücken (**zerdrük'ken**) *tr* crush; (*Kleid*) wrinkle; (*Kartoffeln*) mash

Zeremonie [tsɛrɛmɔˈni] *f* (–;–nien [ˈni·ən]) ceremony

zeremoniell [tsɛrɛmɔˈnjɛl] *adj* ceremonial || **Zeremoniell** *n* (–s;–e) ceremonial

Zeremo'nienmeister *m* master of ceremonies

zerfah'ren *adj* (*Weg*) rutted; (*zerstreut*) absent-minded; (*konfus*) scatterbrained

Zerfall' *m* (–s;) decay, ruin; disintegration; (*geistig*) decadence

zerfal'len *adj*—z. sein mit be at variance with || §72 *intr* (SEIN) fall into ruin; decay; disintegrate; **z. in** (*acc*) divide into; **z. mit** fall out with

zerfa'sern *tr* unravel || *intr* fray

zerfet'zen *tr* tear to shreds

zerflei'schen *tr* mangle; lacerate

zerflie'ßen §76 *intr* (SEIN) melt; (*Farben*) run

zerfres'sen §70 *tr* eat away, chew up; erode, eat a hole in; corrode

zerge'hen §82 *intr* (SEIN) melt

zerglie'dern *tr* dissect; analyze

zerhacken (**zerhak'ken**) *tr* chop up

zerkau'en *tr* chew well

zerkleinern [tsɛrˈklaɪnərn] *tr* cut into small pieces; chop up

zerklop'fen *tr* pound

zerklüftet [tsɛrˈklʏftət] *adj* jagged

zerknirscht [tsɛrˈknɪrʃt] *adj* contrite

Zerknir'schung *f* (–;) contrition

zerknit'tern *tr* (*Papier*) crumple; (*Kleider*) rumple

zerknül'len *tr* crumple up

zerko'chen *tr* overcook

zerkrat'zen *tr* scratch up

zerkrü'meln *tr* & *intr* (SEIN) crumble

zerlas'sen §104 *tr* melt, dissolve

zerlegbar [tsɛrˈlekbɑr] *adj* collapsible; (chem) decomposable; (math) divisible

zerle'gen *tr* take apart; (*zerstückeln*) cut up; (*Braten*) carve; (*Licht*) disperse; (anat) dissect; (chem) break down; (geom, mus) resolve; (gram & fig) analyze; (mach) tear down

zerle'sen *adj* well-thumbed

zerlö'chern *tr* riddle with holes

zerlumpt [tsɛrˈlʊmpt] *adj* tattered

zermah'len *tr* grind

zermal'men *tr* crush

zermür'ben *tr* wear down

Zermür'bung *f* (–;) attrition, wear

zerna'gen *tr* gnaw, chew up; (chem) corrode

zerplat'zen *intr* (SEIN) burst; explode

zerquet'schen *tr* crush; (culin) mash

Zerrbild [ˈtsɛrbɪlt] *n* distorted picture; caricature

zerrei'ben §62 *tr* grind, pulverize

zerrei'ßen §95 *tr* tear; tear up; (*zerfleischen*) mangle; (fig) split; (pathol) rupture; **j–m das Herz z.** break s.o.'s heart || *ref*—**sich z. für**

(fig) knock oneself out for || *intr* (SEIN) tear

zerren [ˈtsɛrən] *tr* drag; (*Sehne*) pull || *intr* (an *dat*) tug (at)

zerrin'nen §121 *intr* (SEIN) melt away

zerrissen [tsɛrˈrɪsən] *adj* torn

Zer'rung *f* (–;–en) strain, muscle pull

zerrütten [tsɛrˈrʏtən] *tr* disorganize; (*Geist*) unhinge; (*Gesundheit*) undermine; (*Nerven*) shatter; (*Ehe*) wreck

zersä'gen *tr* saw up

zerschel'len *intr* (SEIN) be wrecked; (*Schiff*) break up

zerschie'ßen §76 *tr* shoot up

zerschla'gen *adj* battered, broken; exhausted, beat || §132 *tr* beat up; break to pieces; smash; batter

zerschmel'zen *tr* & *intr* (SEIN) melt

zerschmet'tern *tr* smash, crush

zerschnei'den §106 *tr* cut up; mince

zerset'zen *tr* decompose; electrolyze; (fig) undermine || *ref* decompose, disintegrate

zerspal'ten *tr* split

zersplit'tern *tr* split up; splinter; (*Menge*) disperse; (*Kraft, Zeit*) fritter away || *ref* spread oneself thin

zerspren'gen *tr* blow up; (*Kette*) break; (mil) rout

zersprin'gen §142 *intr* (SEIN) break, burst; (*Glas*) crack; (*Saite*) snap; (*Kopf*) split; (*vor Wut*) explode; (*vor Freude*) burst

zerstamp'fen *tr* crush, pound; trample

zerstäu'ben *tr* pulverize, spray

Zerstäu'ber *m* (–s;–) sprayer; (*für Parfüm*) atomizer

zerste'chen §64 *tr* sting; bite

zerstie'ben *intr* §130 *intr* (SEIN) scatter

zerstö'ren *tr* destroy; (*Fernsprechleitung*) disrupt; (*Leben, Ehe, usw.*) ruin; (*Illusionen*) shatter

Zerstö'rer *m* (–s;–) (& nav) destroyer

Zerstö'rung *f* (–;–en) destruction; ruin; disruption

Zerstö'rungswerk *n* work of destruction

Zerstö'rungswut *f* vandalism

zersto'ßen §150 *tr* pound, crush

zerstreu'en *tr* scatter, disperse; (*Bedenken, Zweifel*) dispel; (*ablenken*) distract; (*Licht*) diffuse || *ref* scatter; amuse oneself

zerstreut' *adj* dispersed; (*Licht*) diffused; (fig) absent-minded

Zerstreut'heit *f* (–;) absent-mindedness

Zerstreu'ung *f* (–;) scattering; diffusion; diversion; absent-mindedness

zerstückeln [tsɛrˈʃtʏkəln] *tr* chop up; (*Körper*) dismember; (*Land*) parcel out

zertei'len *tr* divide; (*zerstreuen*) disperse; (*Braten, usw.*) cut up || *ref* divide, separate

Zertifikat [tsɛrtɪfiˈkɑt] *n* (–[e]s;–e) certificate

zertren'nen *tr* sever

zertre'ten §152 *tr* trample, squash; (*Feuer*) stamp out

zertrümmern [tsɛrˈtrʏmərn] *tr* smash, demolish; (*Atome*) split

zerwüh'len *tr* root up; (*Haar*) dishevel; (*Bett, Kissen*) rumple

Zerwürfnis [tsɛr'vʏrfnɪs] *n* (**-ses;-se**) disagreement, quarrel

zerzau'sen *tr* (*Haar*) muss; (*Federn*) ruffle

Zeter ['tsetər] *n* (**-s;**)—**Z. und Mordio schreien** (coll) cry bloody murder

zetern ['tsetərn] *intr* cry out, raise an outcry

Zettel ['tsɛtəl] *m* (**-s;-**) slip of paper; note; (*Anschlag*) poster; (*zum Ankleben*) sticker; (*zum Anhängen*) tag

Zet'telkartei *f*, **Zet'telkasten** *m*, **Zet'telkatalog** *m* card file

Zeug [tsɔɪk] *n* (**-[e]s;-e**) stuff, material; (*Stoff*) cloth, fabric; (*Sachen*) things; (*Waren*) goods; (*Geräte*) tools; (*Plunder*) junk; **dummes Z.** silly nonsense; **er hat das Z.** he has what it takes

-zeug *n comb.fm.* stuff; tools; equipment; tackle; instrument; things; **-wear**

Zeuge ['tsɔɪgə] *m* (**-n;-n**) witness; **als Z. aussagen** testify

zeugen ['tsɔɪgən] *tr* beget; (fig) produce, generate || *intr* produce offspring; testify; **z. für** testify in favor of; **z. von** bear witness to

Zeu'genaussage *f* deposition

Zeu'genbank *f* witness stand

Zeu'genbeeinflussung *f* suborning of witnesses

Zeu'genstand *m* witness stand

Zeugin ['tsɔɪgɪn] *f* (**-;-nen**) witness

Zeugnis ['tsɔɪknɪs] *n* (**-ses;-se**) evidence, testimony; proof; (*Schein*) certificate; (educ) report card; **j-m ein Z. ausstellen** (or **schreiben**) write s.o. a letter of recommendation; **Z. ablegen** testify; **zum Z. dessen** in witness whereof

Zeu'gung *f* (**-;**) procreation; breeding

Zeu'gungstrieb *m* sexual drive

zeu'gungsunfähig *adj* impotent

Zicke ['tsɪkə] *f* (**-;-n**) (pej) old nanny goat; **Zicken machen** (coll) play tricks

Zicklein ['tsɪklaɪn] *n* (**-s;-**) kid

Zickzack ['tsɪktsak] *m* (**-[e]s;-e**) zigzag; **im Z. laufen** run zigzag

Zick'zackkurs *m*—**im Z. fahren** zigzag

Ziege ['tsigə] *f* (**-;-n**) she-goat

Ziegel ['tsigəl] *m* (**-s;-**) brick; (*Dach-*) tile

Zie'gelbrenner *m* brickmaker; tilemaker

Zie'gelbrennerei *f* brickyard; tileworks

Zie'geldach *n* tiled roof

Zie'gelstein *m* brick

Zie'genbart *m* goatee

Zie'genbock *m* billy goat

Zie'genhirt *m* goatherd

Zie'genpeter *m* (pathol) mumps

Zieh- [tsi] *comb.fm.* draw; tow-; foster

Zieh'brunnen *m* well

ziehen ['tsi‧ən] *tr* pull; (*Folgerung, Kreis, Linie, Los, Schwert, Seitengewehr, Vorhang, Wechsel*) draw; (*Glocke*) ring; *aus der Tasche*) pull out; (*Zahn*) extract, pull; (*züchten*) grow, breed; (*Kinder*) raise; (*beim Schach*) move; (*den

Hut) tip; (*Graben*) dig; (*Mauer*) build; (*Schiff*) tow; (*Blasen*) raise; (*Vergleich*) make; (*Gewehrlauf*) rifle; (math) extract; **auf Fäden z.** string (*pearls*); **auf Flaschen z.** bottle; **auf seine Seite z.** win over to one's side; **den kürzeren z.** get the short end of it; **die Bilanz z.** balance accounts; **die Stirn kraus z.** knit the brows; **Grimassen z.** make faces; **ins Vertrauen z.** take into confidence; **j-n auf die Seite z.** take s.o. aside; **Nutzen z.** derive benefit; **Wasser z.** leak || *ref* (*Holz*) warp; (*Stoff*) stretch; (geog) extend, run; **an sich** (or **auf sich**) **z.** attract; **sich in die Länge z.** drag on || *intr* ache; (**an** *dat*) pull (on); (theat) (coll) pull them in; **an e-r Zigarette z.** puff on a cigarette || *intr* (SEIN) go; march; (*Vögel*) migrate; (*Wohnung wechseln*) move || *impers*—**es zieht** there is a draft; **es zieht mich nach I** feel drawn to || **Ziehen** *n* (**-s;**) drawing; cultivation; growing; raising; breeding; migration

Zieh'harmonika *f* accordion

Zieh'kind *n* foster child

Zie'hung *f* (**-;-en**) drawing (*of lots*)

Ziel [tsil] *n* (**-[e]s;-e**) aim; mark; goal; (*beim Rennsport*) finish line; (*e-r Reise*) destination; (*beim Schießen*) target; (*Grenze*) limit, boundary; (*Zweck*) end, object; (*des Spottes*) butt; (*Frist*) term; (mil) objective; **auf Z.** (com) on credit; **durchs Z. gehen** pass the finish line; **gegen zwei Jahre Z.** (or **mit zwei Jahren Z.**) with two years to pay; **j-m zwei Jahre Z. gewähren** give s.o. two years to pay; **seinem Ehrgeiz ein Z. setzen** set a limit to one's ambition

Ziel'anflug *m* (aer) bomb run

Ziel'band *n* (**-[e]s;-̈er**) (sport) tape

ziel'bewußt *adj* purposeful; single-minded

zielen ['tsilən] *intr* take aim; **z. auf** (*acc*) or **nach** aim at

Ziel'fernrohr *n* telescopic sight

Ziel'gerade *f* homestretch

Ziel'gerät *n* gunsight; (aer) bombsight

Ziel'landung *f* pinpoint landing

Ziel'linie *f* (sport) finish line

ziel'los *adj* aimless

Ziel'photographie *f* photo finish

Ziel'punkt *m* objective; bull's-eye

Ziel'scheibe *f* target; (fig) butt

Ziel'setzung *f* objective, target

ziel'sicher *adj* steady, unerring

Ziel'sprache *f* target language

zielstrebig ['tsil/trebɪç] *adj* single-minded, determined

Ziel'sucher *m* (rok) homing device

Ziel'vorrichtung *f* gunsight; bombsight

ziemen ['tsimən] *ref* be proper; **sich für j-n z.** become s.o. || *intr* (*dat*) be becoming to

ziemlich ['tsimlɪç] *adj* fit, suitable; (*leidlich*) middling; (*mäßig*) fair; (*beträchtlich*) considerable || *adv* pretty, rather, fairly; (*fast*) almost, practically

Zier [tsir] *f* (–;), **Zierat** ['tsirɑt] *m* (–s;) ornament, decoration
Zierde ['tsirdə] *f* (–;–n) ornament decoration; (fig) credit, honor
zieren ['tsirən] *tr* decorate, adorn ‖ *ref* be affected, be coy; (*beim Essen*) need to be coaxed; **zier dich doch nicht so!** don't be coy!
Zier'leiste *f* trim(ming)
zier'lich *adj* delicate; (*nett*) nice
Zier'pflanze *f* ornamental plant
Zier'puppe *f* glamour girl
Ziffer ['tsɪfər] *f* (–;–n) digit, figure
Zif'ferblatt *n* face (*of a clock*)
zig [tsɪç] *invar adj* (coll) umpteen
Zigarette [tsɪga'retə] *f* (–;–n) cigarette
Zigaret'tenautomat *m* cigarette machine
Zigaret'tenetui *n* cigarette case
Zigaret'tenspitze *f* cigarette holder
Zigaret'tenstummel *m* cigarette butt
Zigarre [tsɪ'garə] *f* (–;–n) cigar
Zigeuner –in [tsɪ'gɔɪnər(ɪn)] §6 *mf* gipsy
Zimbel ['tsɪmbəl] *f* (–;–n) cymbal
Zimmer ['tsɪmər] *n* (–s;–) room
Zim'merantenne *f* indoor antenna
Zim'merarbeit *f* carpentry
Zim'merdienst *m* room service
Zim'mereinrichtung *f* furniture
Zim'merer *m* (–s;–) carpenter
Zim'merflucht *f* suite
Zim'mermädchen *n* chambermaid
Zim'mer·mann *m* (–[e]s;–leute) carpenter
zimmern ['tsɪmərn] *tr* carpenter, build ‖ *intr* carpenter
Zim'mervermieter *m* landlord
–zimmrig [tsɪmrɪç] *comb.fm.* –room
zimperlich ['tsɪmpərlɪç] *adj* prudish; fastidious; (*gegen Kälte*) oversensitive
Zimt [tsɪmt] *m* (–[e]s;) cinnamon
Zink [tsɪŋk] *m & n* (–[e]s;) zinc
Zinke ['tsɪŋkə] *f* (–;–n) prong; (*e–s Kammes*) tooth; (carp) dovetail
zinken ['tsɪŋkən] *tr* dovetail; (*Karten*) mark ‖ **Zinken** *m* (–s;–) (sl) schnozzle
–zinkig [tsɪŋkɪç] *comb.fm.* –pronged
Zinn [tsɪn] *n* (–[e]s;) tin
Zinne ['tsɪnə] *f* (–;–n) pinnacle; battlement
zinnoberrot [tsɪ'nobərrot] *adj* vermilion
Zins [tsɪns] *m* (–es;–en) interest; (*Miete*) rent; **auf Zinsen anlegen** put out at interest; **j–m mit Zinsen (und Zinseszinsen) heimzahlen** (coll) pay s.o. back in full; **Zinsen berechnen** charge interest
zins'bringend *adj* interest-bearing
Zin'senbelastung *f* interest charge
Zinseszinsen ['tsɪnzəstsɪnzən] *pl* compound interest
zins'frei *adj* rent-free; interest-free
Zins'fuß *m*, **Zins'satz** *m* rate of interest
Zins'schein *m* (interest) coupon; dividend warrant
Zionismus [tsɪ·ɔ'nɪsmʊs] *m* (–;) Zionism
Zipfel ['tsɪpfəl] *m* (–s;–) tip, point;

edge; (*Ecke*) corner; (*e–r Wurst*) end piece
Zip'felmütze *f* nightcap, tasseled cap
zirka ['tsɪrka] *adv* approximately
Zirkel ['tsɪrkəl] *m* (–s;–) circle; (*Reißzeug*) compass; (fig) circle
Zir'kelschluß *m* vicious circle
Zirkon [tsɪr'kon] *m* (–s;–e) zircon
zirkulieren [tsɪrkʊ'lirən] *intr* (SEIN) circulate; **z. lassen** circulate
Zirkus ['tsɪrkʊs] *m* (–;–se) circus
zirpen ['tsɪrpən] *intr* chirp
zischeln ['tsɪʃəln] *tr & intr* whisper
zischen ['tsɪʃən] *intr* hiss; sizzle; (*schwirren*) whiz ‖ **Zischen** *n* (–s;) hissing; sizzle; whiz
Zisch'laut *m* hissing sound; (phonet) sibilant
ziselieren [tsize'lirən] *tr* chase
Zisterne [tsɪs'ternə] *f* (–;–n) cistern
Zitadelle [tsɪta'dɛlə] *f* (–;–n) citadel
Zitat [tsɪ'tat] *n* (–[e]s;–e) quotation
Zither ['tsɪtər] *f* (–;–n) zither
zitieren [tsɪ'tirən] *tr* quote; **j–n vor Gericht z.** issue a summons
Zitronat [tsɪtro'nat] *n* (–[e]s;–e) candied lemon peel
Zitrone [tsɪ'tronə] *f* (–;–n) lemon
Zitro'nenlimonade *f* lemonade; (*mit Sodawasser*) lemon soda
Zitro'nenpresse *f* lemon squeezer
Zitro'nensaft *m* lemon juice
Zitro'nensäure *f* citric acid
zitterig ['tsɪtərɪç] *adj* shaky
zittern ['tsɪtərn] *intr* quake, tremble; quiver; (*flimmern*) dance; (**vor** *dat*) shake (with), shiver (with); **beim dem Gedanken an etw** [*acc*] **z.** shudder at the thought of s.th.
Zit'terpappel ['tsɪtərpapəl] *f* aspen
Zitze ['tsɪtsə] *f* (–;–n) teat
zivil [tsɪ'vil] *adj* civil; civilian; (*Preise*) reasonable ‖ **Zivil** *n* (–s;) civilians; **in Z.** in plain clothes
Zivil'courage *f* courage of one's convictions, moral courage
Zivil'ehe *f* civil marriage
Zivilisation [tsɪvɪliza'tsjon] *f* (–;–en) civilization
zivilisieren [tsɪvɪli'zirən] *tr* civilize
Zivilist –in [tsɪvɪ'lɪst(ɪn)] §7 *mf* civilian
Zivil'klage *f* (jur) civil suit
Zivil'kleidung *f* civilian clothes
Zivil'person *f* civilian
Zobel ['tsobəl] *m* (–s;–) (zool) sable
Zofe ['tsofə] *f* (–;–n) lady-in-waiting
zog [tsok] *pret* of **ziehen**
zögern ['tsøgərn] *intr* hesitate; delay ‖ **Zögern** *n* (–s;) hesitation; delay
Zögling ['tsøklɪŋ] *m* (–s;–e) pupil
Zölibat [tsølɪ'bat] *m & n* (–[e]s;) celibacy
Zoll [tsɔl] *m* (–[e]s;¨e) duty, customs; (*Brückenzoll*) toll; (*Maß*) inch
Zoll'abfertigung *f* customs clearance
Zoll'amt *n* customs office
Zoll'beamte §5 *m* customs official
zollen ['tsɔlən] *tr* give, pay; **j–m Achtung z.** show s.o. respect; **j–m Beifall z.** applaud s.o.; **j–m Dank z.** thank s.o.; **j–m Lob z.** praise s.o.
Zoll'erklärung *f* customs declaration

zoll'frei adj duty-free
Zoll'grenze f customs frontier
–zöllig [tsœliç] comb.fm. –inch
Zoll'kontrolle f customs inspection
zoll'pflichtig adj dutiable
Zoll'schein m customs clearance
Zoll'schranke f customs barrier
Zoll'stab m, **Zoll'stock** m foot rule
Zoll'tarif m tariff
Zone ['tsonə] f (–;–n) zone; **blaue Z.**
 limited-parking area; **Z. der Wind-**
 stille doldrums
Zoo [tso] m (– & –s;–s) zoo
Zoologe [tsɔ·ɔ'logə] m (–n;–n) zool-
 ogist
Zoologie [tsɔ·ɔlɔ'gi] f (–;) zoology
Zoologin [tsɔ·ɔ'login] f (–;–nen) zoologist
zoologisch [tsɔ·ɔ'logiʃ] adj zoological
Zopf [tsɔpf] m (–[e]s;ˑ̈e) plait of hair;
 pigtail; twisted (bread) roll; **alter Z.**
 outdated custom
zopfig ['tsɔpfiç] adj pedantic; old-
 fashioned
Zorn [tsɔrn] m (–[e]s;) anger, rage
Zorn'anfall m fit of anger
Zorn'ausbruch m outburst of anger
zornig ['tsɔrniç] adj (**auf** acc) angry
 (at)
zorn'mütig adj hotheaded
Zote ['tsotə] f (–;–n) obscenity; dirty
 joke; **Zoten reißen** crack dirty jokes;
 talk dirty
zo'tenhaft, zotig ['tsotiç] adj obscene,
 dirty
Zotte ['tsɔtə] f (–;–n) tuft of hair;
 strand of hair
Zottel ['tsɔtəl] f (–;–n) strand of hair
Zot'telhaar n stringy hair
zottelig ['tsɔtəliç] adj stringy (hair)
zotteln ['tsɔtəln] intr (SEIN) (coll)
 saunter
zottig ['tsɔtiç] adj shaggy; matted
zu [tsu] adj closed, shut || adv too;
 immer zu! (or **nur zu!**) go on! || prep
 (dat) at, in, on; to; along with; in
 addition to; beside, near; **zu Anfang**
 at the beginning; **zu dritt** in threes;
 zu Wasser und zu Lande by land and
 by sea
zuallererst [tsu·alər'ɛrst] adv first of
 all
zuallerletzt [tsu·alər'lɛtst] adv last of
 all
zuballern ['tsubalərn] tr (coll) slam
zu'bauen tr wall up, wall in
Zubehör ['tsubəhør] m & n (–s;) accessories; fittings; trimmings; **Woh-**
 nung mit allem Z. apartment with
 all utilities
Zu'behörteil m accessory, attachment,
 component
zu'beißen §53 intr bite; snap at people
zu'bekommen §99 tr get in addition;
 (Tür, usw.) manage to close
zu'bereiten tr prepare; (Speise) cook;
 (Getränk) mix
Zu'bereitung f (–;–en) preparation
zu'billigen tr grant, allow, concede
zu'binden §59 tr tie up; **j–m die Augen**
 z. blindfold s.o.
zu'bleiben §62 intr (SEIN) remain
 closed

zu'blinzeln intr (dat) wink at
zu'bringen §65 tr (Zeit) spend; (coll)
 manage to shut; (tech) feed
Zu'bringer m (–s;–) (tech) feeder
Zu'bringerdienst m shuttle service
Zu'bringerstraße f access road
Zucht [tsuxt] f (–;) breeding; rearing;
 (Rasse) race, stock; (Pflanzen–)
 cultivation; (Schul–) education; discipline; training, drill; **Z. halten**
 maintain discipline
züchten ['tsYçtən] tr breed; rear, raise;
 (bot) grow, cultivate
Züch'ter –in §6 mf breeder; grower
Zucht'haus n penitentiary, hard labor;
 lebenslängliches Z. life imprisonment
Zuchthäusler –in ['tsuxthɔɪzlər(in)] §6
 mf convict, prisoner at hard labor
Zucht'hengst m studhorse
züchtig ['tsYçtiç] adj modest, chaste
züchtigen ['tsYçtigən] tr chastise
zucht'los adj undisciplined
Zucht'losigkeit f (–;) lack of discipline
Zucht'meister m disciplinarian
Zucht'perle f cultured pearl
Züch'tung f (–;) breeding; rearing;
 growing, cultivation
zucken ['tsukən] tr (Aschseln) shrug
 || intr twitch, jerk; (Blitz) flash; (vor
 Schmerzen) wince; **mit keiner Wim-**
 per z. not bat an eye; **ohne zu z.**
 without wincing || impers—**es zuckte**
 mir in den Fingern zu (inf) my fin-
 gers were itching to (inf) || **Zucken**
 n (–s;) twitch
zücken ['tsYkən] tr (Schwert) draw
Zucker ['tsukər] m (–s;) sugar
Zuckerdose (**Zuk'kerdose**) f sugar bowl
Zuckererbse (**Zuk'kererbse**) f sweet
 pea
Zuckerguß (**Zuk'kerguß**) m frosting
Zuckerharnruhr (**Zuk'kerharnruhr**) f
 diabetes
Zuckerhut (**Zuk'kerhut**) m sugar loaf
zuckerig ['tsukəriç] adj sugary
zuckerkrank (**zuk'kerkrank**) adj dia-
 betic || **Zuckerkranke** §5 mf diabetic
Zuckerkrankheit (**Zuk'kerkrankheit**) f
 diabetes
Zuckerlecken (**Zuk'kerlecken**) n (–s;)
 (fig) pushover, picnic
Zuckerrohr (**Zuk'kerrohr**) n sugar cane
Zuckerrübe (**Zuk'kerrübe**) f sugar beet
zuckersüß (**zuk'kersüß'**) adj sweet as
 sugar
Zuckerwerk (**Zuk'kerwerk**) n, **Zucker-**
 zeug (**Zuk'kerzeug**) n candy
Zuckung (**Zuk'kung**) f (–;–en) twitch,
 spasm, convulsion
Zu'decke f (coll) bed covering
zu'decken tr cover up
zudem [tsu'dem] adv moreover, besides
zu'denken §66 tr—**j–m etw z.** intend
 s.th. as a present for s.o.
Zu'drang m crowding, rush
zu'drehen tr turn off; **j–m den Rücken**
 z. turn one's back on s.o.
zu'dringlich adj obtrusive; **z. werden**
 make a pass
zu'drücken tr close, shut
zu'eignen tr dedicate
Zu'eignung f (–;–en) dedication

zu'erkennen §97 *tr* confer, award; (jur) adjudge, award
zuerst' *adv* first; at first
zu'erteilen *tr* award; confer, bestow
zu'fahren §71 *intr* (SEIN) drive on; z. auf (*acc*) drive in the direction of (*s.th.*); rush at (*s.o.*)
Zu'fahrt *f* access
Zu'fahrtsrampe *f* on-ramp
Zu'fahrtsstraße *f* access road
Zu'fall *m* chance; coincidence; accident; **durch Z.** by chance
zu'fallen §72 *intr* (SEIN) close, shut; **j–m z.** fall to s.o.'s share
zufällig ['tsufɛlɪç] *adj* chance, fortuitous; accidental; casual ǁ *adv* by chance; accidentally
zu'fälligerweise *adv* by chance
Zufalls– *comb.fm.* chance
zu'fassen *intr* set to work; lend a hand; (*e–e Gelegenheit wahrnehmen*) seize the opportunity
Zu'flucht *f* refuge; (fig) recourse; **seine Z. nehmen zu** take refuge in; have recourse to
Zu'fluß *m* influx; (*Nebenfluß*) tributary; (mach) feed
zu'flüstern *intr* (dat) whisper to
zufolge [tsu'fɔlgə] *prep* (*genit & dat*) in consequence of; according to
zufrieden [tsu'fridən] *adj* satisfied; **j–n z. lassen** leave s.o. alone
zufrie'dengeben §80 *ref* (mit) be satisfied (with), acquiesce (in)
Zufrie'denheit *f* (–;) satisfaction
zufrie'denstellen *tr* satisfy
zufrie'denstellend *adj* satisfactory
Zufrie'denstellung *f* satisfaction
zu'frieren §77 *intr* (SEIN) freeze up
zu'fügen *tr* add; (*Niederlage*) inflict; (*Kummer, Schaden, Schmerz*) cause
Zufuhr ['tsufur] *f* (–;) supply; importation; supplies; (mach) feed
zu'führen *tr* convey, bring; (*Waren*) supply; (mach) feed
Zu'führung *f* (–;–en) conveyance; supply; importation; (elec) lead; (mach) feed
Zug [tsuk] *m* (–[e]s;–̈e) train; pull, tug; drawing, pulling; (*Spannung*) tension; strain; (*beim Rauchen*) puff; (*beim Atmen*) breath, gasp; (*Schluck*) drink, gulp, swig; (*Luft–*) draft; (*Reihe*) row, line; (*Um–*) procession; parade; (*Kriegs–*) campaign; (*Geleit*) escort; (*von Vögeln*) flock; flight, migration; (*von Fischen*) school; (*Rudel*) pack; (*Trupp*) platoon; (*Gespann*) team, yoke; (*Gesichts–*) feature; (*Charakter–*) trait; characteristic; (*Neigung*) trend, tendency; (*im Gewehrlauf*) groove, rifling; (*Strich*) stroke; (*Schnörkel*) flourish; (*Umriß*) outline; (*beim Brettspiel*) move; **auf dem Zuge** on the march; **auf e–n Zug** in one gulp; at one stroke; at a stretch; **du bist am Zug** (& fig) it's your move; **e–n guten Zug haben** drink like a fish; **e–n Zug tun** take a puff; make a move; take a drink; **gut im Zuge sein** (or **im besten Zuge sein**) be going strong; **in e–m Zuge** in one

gulp; in one breath; at one stroke; at a stretch; **in großen Zügen** in broad outlines; **in vollen Zügen** thoroughly; **in Zug bringen start; nicht zum Zug kommen** not get a chance; **ohne rechten Zug** half-heartedly; **Zug um Zug** in rapid succession
Zu'gabe *f* addition; (theat) encore
Zu'gang *m* access; approach; entrance; (*Zunahme*) increase; (libr) accession
zugänglich ['tsugɛŋlɪç] *adj* accessible; (*Person*) affable; (*benutzbar*) available; (*dat, für*) open (to); **nicht z.** für proof against
Zug'artikel *m* (com) popular article
Zug'brücke *f* drawbridge
zu'geben §80 *tr* add; (*erlauben*) allow; (*anerkennen*) admit, concede; (*eingestehen*) confess; (com) throw into the bargain
zugegen [tsu'gegən] *adj* (**bei**) present (at)
zu'gehen §82 *intr* (SEIN) go on; walk faster; (*sich schließen*) shut; **auf j–n z.** go up to s.o.; **j–m etw z. lassen** send s.th. to s.o.
zu'gehören *intr* (dat) belong to
zu'gehörig *adj* (dat) belonging to
Zu'gehörigkeit *f* (–;) (**zu**) membership (in)
Zügel ['tsygəl] *m* (–s;–) rein; bridle; (fig) curb
zü'gellos *adj* (& fig) unbridled; (*ausschweifig*) dissolute
Zü'gellosigkeit *f* (–;) licentiousness
zügeln ['tsygəln] *tr* bridle; (fig) curb
Zu'geständnis *n* admission, concession
zu'gestehen §146 *tr* admit, concede
zu'getan *adj* (dat) fond of
Zug'feder *f* tension spring
Zug'führer *m* (mil) platoon leader; (rr) chief conductor
zu'gießen §76 *tr* add
zugig ['tsugɪç] *adj* drafty
zügig ['tsygɪç] *adj* speedy, fast
Zug'klappe *f* damper
Zug'kraft *f* tensile force; (fig) drawing power
zug'kräftig *adj* attractive, popular
zugleich' *adv* at the same time; **z. mit** together with
Zug'luft *f* draft
Zug'maschine *f* tractor
Zug'mittel *n* (fig) attraction, draw
zu'graben §87 *tr* cover up
zu'greifen §88 *intr* grab hold; lend a hand; (fig) go into action; **greifen Sie zu!** (*bei Tisch*) help yourself!; (*bei Reklamen*) don't miss this opportunity!
Zu'griff *m* grip; (fig) clutches
zugrunde [tsu'grundə] *adv*—**z. gehen** go to ruin; **z. legen** (dat) take as a basis (for); **z. liegen** (dat) underlie
Zug'tier *n* draft animal
zu'gucken *intr* (coll) look on
zugunsten [tsu'gunstən] *prep* (genit) in favor of; for the benefit of
zugute [tsu'gutə] *adv*—**j–m etw z. halten** make allowance to s.o. for s.th.; **j–m z. kommen** stand s.o. in good stead
Zug'verkehr *m* train service

Zug'vogel *m* migratory bird
zu'haben §89 *tr* (*Augen*) have closed; (*Mantel*) have buttoned up ‖ *intr* (*Geschäft*) be closed
zu'halten §90 *tr* keep closed; (*Ohren*) shut ‖ *intr*—**z. auf** (*acc*) head for
Zuhälter ['tsuheltər] *m* (-s;-) pimp
Zuhälterei [tsuhelte'raɪ] *f* (-;) pimping
zuhanden [tsu'handən] *prep* (*genit*) (*auf Briefumschlägen*) Attn:
Zuhause [tsu'hauzə] *n* (-s;) home
zu'heilen *intr* (SEIN) heal up
zu'hören *intr* (*dat*) listen (to)
Zu'hörer -in §6 *mf* hearer, listener; **die Z.** the audience
Zu'hörerschaft *f* (-;) audience
zu'jauchzen, zu'jubeln *intr* cheer
zu'klappen *tr* shut, slam shut
zu'kleben *tr* glue up, paste up
zu'knallen *tr* bang, slam shut
zu'kneifen §88 *tr*—**die Augen z.** blink; **ein Auge z.** wink
zu'knöpfen *tr* button up
zu'kommen §99 *intr* (SEIN) (*dat*) reach; (*dat*) be due to; **auf j-n z.** come up to s.o.; **das kommt dir nicht zu** you're not entitled to it; **j-m etw z. lassen** let s.o. have s.th.; send s.th. to s.o. ‖ *impers*—**mir kommt es nicht zu zu** (*inf*) it's not up to me to (*inf*)
zu'korken *tr* put the cork on
Zu'kost *f* vegetables; trimmings
Zukunft ['tsukʊnft] *f* (-;) future; (gram) future (tense)
zukünftig ['tsukʏnftɪç] *adj* future ‖ *adv* in the future ‖ **Zukünftige** §5 *m* (coll) fiancé ‖ *f* (coll) fiancée
Zu'kunftsmusik *f* wishful thinking
Zu'kunftsroman *m* science fiction
zu'lächeln *intr* (*dat*) smile at; (*dat*) smile on
Zu'lage *f* extra pay; pay raise
zulande [tsu'landə] *adv*—**bei uns z.** in my (or our) country
zu'langen *intr* suffice, do; (*bei Tisch*) help oneself
zu'länglich *adj* adequate, sufficient
zu'lassen §104 *tr* admit; (*erlauben*) allow; (*Tür*) leave shut; (*Fahrzeug*) license; (*Zweifel*) admit of
zulässig ['tsulesɪç] *adj* permissible; **zulässige Abweichung** allowance, tolerance
Zu'lassung *f* (-;-en) admission; permission; approval; license
Zu'lassungsprüfung *f* college entrance examination
Zu'lassungsschein *m* registration card
Zu'lauf *m* crowd, rush; **Z. haben** be popular; (theat) have a long run
zu'laufen §105 *intr* (SEIN) run on; run faster; (*dat*) flock to; **auf j-n z.** run up to s.o.; **spitz z.** end in a point
zu'legen *tr* add; **etw z.** up one's offer ‖ *ref*—**sich** [dat] **etw. z.** (coll) get oneself s.th.
zuleide [tsu'laɪdə] *adv*—**j-m etw z. tun** hurt s.o., do s.o. wrong
zu'leiten *tr* (*Wasser*) (*dat*) let in (to); (*dat*) direct (s.o.) (to); (*Schreiben*) (*dat*) pass on (to); *auf dem Amtsweg*) channel (to); (tech) feed

Zu'leitung *f* (-;-en) feed pipe; (elec) lead-in wire; (elec) conductor
zuletzt [tsu'letst] *adv* last; at last; finally; after all
zuliebe [tsu'libə] *prep* (*dat*) for (*s.o.'s*) sake
zum [tsum] *abbr* **zu dem; es ist zum** ...it's enough to make one...
zu'machen *tr* shut; (*Loch*) close up; (*zuknöpfen*) button up
zumal [tsu'mal] *adv* especially; **z. da** all the more because
zu'mauern *tr* wall up
zumindest [tsu'mɪndəst] *adv* at least
zumute [tsu'mutə] *adv*—**mir ist gut** (or **wohl**) **z.** I feel good; **mir ist nicht zum Lachen z.** I don't feel like laughing
zumuten ['tsumutən] *tr*—**j-m etw z.** expect s.th. of s.o. ‖ *ref*—**sich** [dat] **zuviel z.** attempt too much
Zu'mutung *f* (-;-en) imposition
zunächst [tsu'neçst] *adv* first, at first, first of all; (*erstens*) to begin with; (*vorläufig*) for the time being ‖ *prep* (*dat*) next to
zu'nageln *tr* nail up, nail shut
zu'nähen *tr* sew up
Zu'nahme *f* (-;-n) increase; growth; rise
Zu'name *m* last name, family name
Zünd- (tsʏnt) *comb.fm.* ignition
zünden ['tsʏndən] *tr* ignite; kindle; (*Sprengstoff*) detonate ‖ *intr* ignite, catch fire; (fig) catch on
Zün'der *m* (-s;-) fuse; detonator
Zünd'flamme *f* pilot light
Zünd'holz *n* match
Zünd'kerze *f* (aut) spark plug
Zünd'nadel *f* firing pin
Zünd'satz *m* primer
Zünd'schlüssel *m* ignition key
Zünd'schnur *f* fuse
Zünd'stein *m* flint
Zünd'stoff *m* fuel
Zün'dung *f* (-;-en) (aut) ignition
zu'nehmen §116 *intr* (**an** *dat*) increase (in); (*steigen*) rise; grow longer
zu'neigen *tr* (*dat*) tilt toward ‖ *ref &* *intr* (*dat*) incline toward(s); **sich dem Ende z.** draw to a close
Zu'neigung *f* (-;) (**für, zu**) liking (**for**)
Zunft [tsunft] *f* (-;-en) guild
Zunge ['tsuŋə] *f* (-;-n) tongue
züngeln ['tsʏŋəln] *intr* dart out the tongue; (*Flamme*) dart, leap up
Zun'genbrecher *m* tongue twister
zun'genfertig *adj* glib
Zun'genspitze *f* tip of the tongue
zunichte [tsu'nɪçtə] *adv*—**z. machen** destroy; (*Plan*) spoil; (*Theorie*) explode; **z. werden** come to nothing
zu'nicken *intr* (*dat*) nod to
zunutze [tsu'nutsə] *adv*—**sich etw z. machen** utilize s.th.
zuoberst [tsu'obərst] *adv* at the top
zupfen ['tsupfən] *tr* pull; pluck ‖ *intr* (**an** *dat*) tug (at)
zu'prosten *intr* (*dat*) toast
zur [tsur] *abbr* **zu der**
zu'rechnen *tr* add; (*dat*) number among, classify with; (*dat*) attribute to

zu'rechnungsfähig *adj* accountable; responsible; of sound mind
Zu'rechnungsfähigkeit *f* responsibility; sound mind
zurecht– [tsu'reçt] *comb.fm.* right, in order; at the right time
zurecht'biegen §57 *tr* straighten out
zurecht'bringen §65 *tr* set right
zurecht'finden §59 *ref* find one's way; (fig) see one's way
zurecht'kommen §99 *intr* (SEIN) come on time; get on, manage; turn out all right; **mit etw nicht z.** make a mess of s.th.; **mit j–m z.** get along with s.o.
zurecht'legen *tr* lay out in order ‖ *ref*—**sich** [*dat*] **z.** figure out
zurecht'machen *tr* & *ref* get ready
zurecht'schneiden §106 *tr* cut to size
zurecht'setzen *tr* set right, fix, adjust
zurecht'weisen §118 *tr* reprimand
zu'reden *intr* (*dat*) try to persuade; (*dat*) encourage
zu'reichen *tr* reach, pass ‖ *intr* do
zu'reichend *adj* sufficient
zu'reiten §86 *tr* break in
zu'richten *tr* prepare; cook
zu'riegeln *tr* bolt
zürnen ['tsʏrnən] *intr* (*dat*) be angry (with)
zurren ['tsurən] *tr* (naut) lash down
Zurschau'stellung *f* display
zurück [tsu'rʏk] *adv* back; backward; behind; **ein paar Jahre z.** a few years ago ‖ *interj* back up!
zurück– *comb.fm.* back; behind; re–
zurück'behalten §90 *tr* keep back
zurück'bekommen §99 *tr* get back
zurück'bleiben §62 *intr* (SEIN) stay behind; fall behind; (*Uhr*) lose time; (**hinter** *dat*) fall short (of)
Zurück'blenden *n* (cin) flashback
zurück'blicken *intr* look back
zurück'bringen §65 *tr* bring back; **z. auf** (*acc*) (math) reduce to
zurück'datieren *tr* antedate
zurück'drängen *tr* force back; repress
zurück'dürfen §69 *intr* be allowed to return
zurück'erobern *tr* reconquer, win back
zurück'erstatten *tr* return; (*Ausgaben*) refund; (*Kosten*) reimburse
zurück'fahren §71 *tr* drive back ‖ *intr* (SEIN) drive back, ride back; (*vor Schreck*) recoil, start
zurück'finden §59 *ref* find one's way back
zurück'fordern *tr* reclaim, demand back
zurück'führen *tr* lead back; trace back; **z. auf** (*acc*) refer to; attribute to
zurück'geben §80 *tr* give back, return
zurück'gehen §82 *intr* (SEIN) go back; (*Fieber, Preise*) drop; (*Geschwulst*) go down; (mil) fall back
zurück'gezogen *adj* secluded
zurück'greifen §88 *intr*—**z. auf** (*acc*) (fig) fall back on
zurück'halten §90 *tr* hold back; **j–n davon z. zu** (*inf*) keep s.o. from (*ger*) ‖ *intr* **mit etw z.** conceal s.th.
zurück'haltend *adj* reserved; shy
Zurück'haltung *f* (–;–en) reserve

zurück'kehren *intr* (SEIN) return
zurück'kommen §99 *intr* (SEIN) return; **z. auf** (*acc*) come back to, revert to; (*hinweisen*) refer to
zurück'können §100 *intr* be able to return
zurück'lassen §104 *tr* leave behind; outstrip, outrun
zurück'legen *tr* (*Kopf*) lean back; (*Geld*) put aside; (*Jahre*) complete; (*Strecke*) cover; (*Ware*) lay away ‖ *ref* lean back
zurück'lehnen *ref* lean back
zurück'liegen §108 *intr* belong to the past ‖ *impers*—**es liegt jetzt zehn Jahre zurück, daß** it's ten years now that
zurück'müssen §115 *intr* have to return
zurück'nehmen §116 *tr* take back; (*widerrufen*) revoke; (*Auftrag*) cancel; (*Vorwurf*) retract; (*Klage*) withdraw; (*Versprechen*) go back on; (*Truppen*) pull back; **das Gas z.** slow down
zurück'prallen *intr* (SEIN) rebound; (*vor Schreck*) start, be startled
zurück'rufen §122 *tr* call back, recall
zurück'schauen *intr* look back
zurück'schicken *tr* send back
zurück'schlagen §132 *tr* beat back, throw back ‖ *intr* strike back
zurück'schrecken *tr* frighten away; (**von**) deter (from) ‖ §109 & §134 *intr* (SEIN) (**von, vor** *dat*) shrink back (from)
zurück'sehnen *ref* yearn to return
zurück'sein §139 *intr* (SEIN) be back; (**in** *dat*) be behind (in)
zurück'setzen *tr* put back; (**im Preis**) reduce; (fig) snub ‖ *ref* sit back
zurück'stecken *tr* put back
zurück'stellen *tr* (*Uhr*) set back; (*Plan*) shelve; (mil) defer
zurück'stoßen §150 *tr* push back; repel
zurück'strahlen *tr* reflect
zurück'streifen *tr* (*Ärmel*) roll up
zurück'treten §152 *intr* (SEIN) step back; (*vom Amt*) resign; (*Wasser, Berge*) recede
zurück'tun §154 *tr* put back
zurück'verfolgen *tr* (*Schritte*) retrace; (fig) trace back
zurück'verweisen §118 *tr* (**an** *acc*) refer back (to); (parl) remand (to)
zurück'weichen §85 *intr* (SEIN) fall back, make way; (*Hochwasser*) recede; (*vor dem Feind*) give ground; **z. vor** (*dat*) shrink from
zurück'weisen §118 *tr* turn back; (*ablehnen*) turn down; (*Angriff*) repel ‖ *intr*—**z. auf** (*acc*) refer to
Zurück'weisung *f* (–;–en) rejection
zurück'wenden §140 *tr* & *ref* turn back
zurück'werfen §160 *tr* throw back; (*e–n Patienten*) set back; (*Strahlen*) reflect; (*Feind*) hurl back
zurück'wirken *intr* (**auf** *acc*) react (on); (*Gesetz*) be retroactive
zurück'zahlen *tr* pay back; (fin) refund
zurück'ziehen §163 *tr* draw back; (*Antrag*) withdraw; (*Geld*) call in; (*Truppen*) pull back; (sport) scratch ‖ *ref* withdraw; (*schlafengehen*) re-

tire; (mil) pull back ‖ *intr* (SEIN) move back; (mil) fall back, retreat
Zu'ruf *m* call; cheer; (parl) acclamation
zu'rufen §122 *tr—j-m etw z.* shout s.th. to s.o.
Zu'sage *f* (-;-n) assent; promise
zu'sagen *tr* promise ‖ *intr* accept an invitation; (*dat*) please; (*dat*) agree (with)
zusammen [tsʊ'zamən] *adv* together; in common; at the same time
Zusam'menarbeit *f* cooperation
zusam'menarbeiten *intr* cooperate
zusam'menballen *tr* (*Faust*) clench
zusam'menbeißen §53 *tr—die Zähne z.* grit one's teeth
zusam'menbinden §59 *tr* tie together
zusam'menbrauen *tr* concoct ‖ *ref* (*Sturm*) brew
zusam'menbrechen §64 *intr* (SEIN) break down; collapse
Zusam'menbruch *m* collapse; breakdown
zusam'mendrängen *tr* crowd together
zusam'mendrücken *tr* compress
zusam'menfahren §71 *intr* (SEIN) be startled; (mit) collide (with)
zusam'menfallen §72 *intr* (SEIN) fall in, collapse; (*Teig*) fall; (*Person*) lose weight; (mit) coincide (with)
Zusam'menfall *m* coincidence
zusam'menfalten *tr* fold
zusam'menfassen *tr* (*in sich fassen*) comprise; (*verbinden*) combine; (*Macht, Funktionen*) concentrate; (*Bericht*) summarize
zusam'menfassend *adj* comprehensive; summary
Zusam'menfassung *f* (-;-en) summary, résumé
zusam'menfinden §59 *ref* meet
zusam'menfügen *tr* join together; (*Scherben, Teile*) piece together
zusam'mengehen §82 *intr* (SEIN) go together; match; close; shrink
zusam'mengehören *intr* belong together
zusam'mengeraten §63 *intr* (SEIN) collide
zusammengewürfelt [tsʊ'zaməngevʏrfəlt] *adj* mixed, motely
Zusam'menhalt *m* cohesion; consistency
zusam'menhalten §90 *tr* hold together; compare ‖ *intr* stick together
Zusam'menhang *m* connection, relation; context; coherence
zusam'menhängend *adj* coherent; allied
zusam'menklappen *tr* fold up; **die Hacken z.** click one's heels ‖ *intr* (SEIN) collapse
zusam'menkommen §99 *intr* (SEIN) come together
Zusam'menkunft [tsʊ'zamənkʊnft] *f* (-;̈e) meeting
zusam'menlaufen §105 *intr* (SEIN) run together; come together; flock; (*Milch*) curdle; (*Farben*) run; (*einschrumpfen*) shrink up; (geom) converge
zusammenlegbar [tsʊ'zamənlekbɑr] *adj* collapsible
zusam'menlegen *tr* put together; (*fal-*

ten) fold; (*Geld*) pool; (*vereinigen*) combine, consolidate ‖ *intr* pool money
zusam'mennehmen §116 *tr* gather up; (*Gedanken*) collect; (*Kräfte, Mut*) muster; **alles zusammengenommen** considering everything ‖ *ref* pull oneself together
zusam'menpacken *tr* pack up
zusam'menpassen *tr & intr* match
zusam'menpferchen *tr* crowd together
Zusam'menprall *m* collision; (fig) (mit) impact (on)
zusam'menprallen *intr* collide
zusam'menraffen *tr* collect in haste; (*ein Vermögen*) amass; (*Kräfte*) summon up, marshal ‖ *ref* pull oneself together
zusam'menreißen §53 *ref* (coll) pull oneself together
zusam'menrollen *tr* roll up
zusam'menrotten *ref* band together, form a gang; (*Aufrührer*) riot
zusam'menrücken *tr* push together ‖ *intr* (SEIN) move closer together
zusam'menschießen *tr* (*Stadt*) shoot up; (*Menschen*) shoot down; (*Geld*) pool
zusam'menschlagen §132 *tr* smash up; (*Absätze*) click; (*Beine, Zeitung*) fold; (*Hände*) clap; (*zerschlagen*) beat up; **die Hände über den Kopf z.** (fig) throw up one's hands ‖ *intr* (SEIN)—**aneinander z.** clash
zusam'menschließen §76 *tr* join; link together ‖ *ref* join together, unite
Zusam'menschluß *m* union; alliance
zusam'menschmelzen *intr* (SEIN) fuse; melt away; (fig) dwindle
zusam'menschnüren *tr* tie up
zusam'menschrumpfen *intr* (SEIN) shrivel; (*Geld*) (coll) dwindle away
zusam'mensetzen *tr* put together; (mach) assemble ‖ *ref* sit down together; **sich z. aus** consist of
Zusam'mensetzung *f* (-;-en) composition; (*Bestandteile*) ingredients; (*Struktur*) structure; (chem, gram) compound
Zusam'menspiel *n* teamwork
zusam'menstauchen *tr* browbeat, chew out
zusam'menstellen *tr* put together; (*Liste*) compile; (*Farben*) match; organize
Zusam'menstoß *m* collision; (*der Meinungen*) clash; (*Treffen*) encounter; (mil) engagement
zusam'menstoßen §150 *tr* knock together; (*Gläser*) touch ‖ *intr* adjoin; **mit den Gläsern z.** clink glasses ‖ *intr* (SEIN) collide; (*Gegner*) clash
zusam'menstückeln *tr* piece together
zusam'menstürzen *intr* (SEIN) collapse
zusam'mentragen §132 *tr* collect
zusam'mentreffen §151 *intr* (SEIN) meet; coincide ‖ **Zusammentreffen** *n* (-s;) encounter; meeting; coincidence
zusam'mentreiben §62 *tr* round up; (*Geld*) scrape up
zusam'mentreten §152 *intr* (SEIN) meet
zusam'menwirken *intr* cooperate; col-

laborate; interact || **Zusammen-
wirken** n (-s;) cooperation; interaction
zusam'menzählen tr count up, add up
zusam'menziehen §163 tr draw together, contract; (*Lippen*) pucker;
(*Brauen*) knit; (*Summe*) add up;
(*kürzen*) shorten; (*Truppen*) concen-
trate || ref contract; (*Gewitter*) brew
|| intr (SEIN)—**mit j-m z.** move in
with s.o.
Zu'satz m addition; (*Ergänzung*) supplement; (*Anhang*) appendix; (*Nachschrift*) postscript; (*Beimischung*)
admixture; (*zu e-m Testament*) codicil; (parl) rider; **unter Z. von** with
the addition of
Zu'satzgerät n attachment
zusätzlich ['tsuzetslɪç] adj additional,
extra || adv in addition
zuschanden [tsu'ʃandən] adv—**z. machen** ruin; **z. werden** go to ruin
zu'schauen intr look on; (*dat*) watch
Zu'schauer –in §6 mf spectator
Zu'schauerraum m auditorium
zu'schicken tr (*dat*) send (to)
zu'schieben §130 tr close, shut; (*Riegel*) push forward; **j-m die Schuld z.**
push the blame on s.o.
Zu'schlag m extra charge; **den Z. erhalten** get the contract (*on a bid*)
zu'schlagen §132 tr (*Tür*) slam; (*Buch*)
shut; (*auf Auktionen*) knock down;
(*hinzurechnen*) add || intr hit hard
zu'schließen §76 tr shut, lock
zu'schnallen tr buckle (up)
zu'schnappen intr snap shut; **z. lassen**
snap shut
zu'schneiden §106 tr cut out; (*Anzug*)
cut to size
Zu'schnitt m cut; (fig) style
zu'schnüren tr lace up
zu'schrauben tr screw tight
zu'schreiben §62 tr ascribe; (*Bedeutung*) attach; (*Grundstück, usw.*)
transfer, sign over || ref—**er hat es
sich** [dat] **selbst zuzuschreiben** he
has himself to thank for it
Zu'schrift f letter, communication
zuschulden [tsu'ʃuldən] adv—**sich**
[dat] **etw. z. kommen lassen** take the
blame for s.th.
Zu'schuß m subsidy; grant; allowance
zu'schütten tr add; (*Graben*) fill up
zu'sehen §138 intr look on; (*dat*)
watch; **z., daß** see to it that
zusehends ['tsuze·ənts] adv visibly
zu'senden §120 & §140 tr (*dat*) send to
zu'setzen tr add; (*Geld*) lose || intr
(*dat*) pester; (*dat*) be hard on; (mil)
(*dat*) put pressure on
zu'sichern tr—**j-m etw z.** assure s.o.
of s.th.
Zu'sicherung f (-;-en) assurance
zu'siegeln tr seal up
Zu'speise f side dish
zu'sperren tr lock
zu'spielen tr—**j-m den Ball z.** pass the
ball to s.o.; **j-m etw z.** slip s.th. to
s.o.
zu'spitzen tr sharpen, make pointy ||
ref (*Lage*) come to a head
zu'sprechen §64 tr (& jur) award

Zu'spruch m consolation, encouragement; (com) customers, clientele
zu'springen §142 intr (SEIN) snap shut
Zu'stand m state, condition; **gegen-
wärtiger Z.** status quo; **in gutem Z.**
in good condition; **Zustände** state of
affairs
zustande [tsu'ʃtandə] adv—**z. bringen**
bring about; put across; get away
with; **z. kommen** come about, come
off; happen; be realized; (*Gesetz*)
pass; (*Vertrag*) be reached
zu'ständig adj competent; (*Behörde*)
proper; (*verantwortlich*) responsible
Zu'ständigkeit f (-;) jurisdiction
zustatten [tsu'ʃtatən] adv—**z. kommen**
come in handy
zu'stehen §146 intr (*dat*) be due to
zu'stellen tr deliver; (jur) serve
Zu'stellung f (-;-en) delivery; (jur)
serving
zu'steuern tr (*Geld*) contribute, kick
in || intr (*dat*, **auf** acc) head for
zu'stimmen intr (*dat*) agree to, approve
of (*s.th.*); (*dat*) agree with (*s.o.*)
Zu'stimmung f (-;) consent, approval
zu'stopfen tr plug up
zu'stoßen §150 tr slam || intr (SEIN)
lunge; (*dat*) happen to
zu'streben intr (*dat*) strive for
zutage [tsu'tagə] adv to light; **z. liegen**
be evident
Zutaten ['tsutatən] pl ingredients
zuteil [tsu'taɪl] adv—**j-m z. werden**
fall to s.o.'s share
zu'teilen tr allot; ration; award; (*gewähren*) grant; confer; (mil) assign
Zu'teilung f (-;-en) allotment, alloca-
tion; rationing; (mil) assignment
zu'tragen §132 tr carry; (*Neuigkeiten*)
report || ref happen
zuträglich ['tsutreklɪç] adj advantageous; (*Klima*) healthful; (*Nahrung*)
wholesome; **j-m z. sein** agree with
s.o.
zu'trauen tr—**j-m etw z.** give s.o.
credit for s.th.; imagine s.o. capable
of s.th. || **Zutrauen** n (-s;) (zu) con-
fidence (in)
zu'traulich adj trustful; (*zahm*) tame
zu'treffen §151 intr (SEIN) prove right;
come true; hold true, be conclusive;
z. auf (acc) apply to
zu'treffend adj correct; to the point;
(*anwendbar*) applicable
zu'trinken §143 intr (*dat*) drink to
Zu'tritt m access; admission, entrance;
kein Z.! no admittance!
zu'tun §154 tr close; (*hinzufügen*) add
zu'verlässig adj reliable; **von zuverläs-
siger Seite** on good authority
Zu'verlässigkeit f (-;) reliability
Zuversicht ['tsufɛrzɪçt] f (-;) confidence
zu'versichtlich adj confident
zuviel [tsu'fil] adv & indef pron too
much; **einer z.** one too many
zuvor [tsu'for] adv before, previously;
first (of all); **kurz z.** shortly before
zuvor- comb.fm. beforehand
zuvor'kommen §99 intr (SEIN) (*dat*)
anticipate; **j-m z.** get the jump on
s.o.

zuvor'kommend *adj* obliging; polite
zuvor'tun §154 *tr*—es **j-m z.** outdo s.o.
Zu'wachs *m* increase; growth; **auf Z.** (big enough) to allow for growth
zu'wachsen §155 *intr* (SEIN) grow together; (*Wunde*) heal up; (*dat*) accrue (to)
Zu'wachsrate *f* rate of increase
zuwege [tsʊ'vegə] *adv*—**z. bringen** bring about; achieve; finish; **gut z. sein** be fit as a fiddle
zuweilen [tsʊ'vaɪlən] *adv* sometimes
zu'weisen §118 *tr* assign, allot
zu'wenden §120 & §140 *tr* (*dat*) turn (*s.th.*) towards; (*dat*) give (*s.th.*) to, devote (*s.th.*) to || *ref* (*dat*) devote oneself to, concentrate on
Zu'wendung *f* (—;-en) gift, donation
zuwenig [tsʊ'venɪç] *adv* & *pron* too little
zu'werfen §160 *tr* (*Tür*) slam; (*Blick*) cast; (*Grube*) fill up; **j-m etw z.** throw s.o. s.th.
zuwider [tsʊ'vidər] *adj* (*dat*) distasteful (to) || *prep* (*dat*) contrary to
zuwi'derhandeln *intr* (*dat*) go against
Zuwi'derhandlung *f* (—;-en) violation
zu'winken *intr* (*dat*) wave to; beckon to
zu'zahlen *tr* pay extra
zu'zählen *tr* add
zuzeiten [tsʊ'tsaɪtən] *adv* at times
zu'ziehen §163 *tr* (*Vorhang*) draw; (*Knoten*) tighten; (*Arzt, Experten*) call in || *ref*—**sich** [*dat*] **etw z.** incur s.th.; contract s.th. || *intr* (SEIN) move in; move (*to a city*)
Zu'ziehung *f*—**unter Z.** (*genit* or **von**) in consultation with
zuzüglich ['tsutsyklɪç] *prep* (*genit*) plus; including
zwang [tsvaŋ] *pret of* **zwingen** || **Zwang** *m* (-[e]s;) coercion, force; restraint; obligation; (*Druck*) pressure; (jur) duress; **auf j-n Z. ausüben** put pressure on s.o. || *ref*—**sich** [*dat*] **keinen Z. antun** (or **auferlegen**) relax
zwängen ['tsvɛŋən] *tr* force, squeeze || *ref* (**durch**) squeeze (through)
zwang'los *adj* free and easy; informal
Zwang'losigkeit *f* (-;) ease; informality
Zwangs– [tsvaŋs] *comb.fm.* force, compulsory
Zwangs'arbeit *f* hard labor
Zwangs'arbeitslager *n* labor camp
Zwangs'jacke *f* strait jacket
Zwangs'lage *f* tight spot
zwangs'läufig *adj* inevitable
zwangs'mäßig *adj* forced; coercive
Zwangs'maßnahme *f*—**zu Zwangsmaßnahmen greifen** resort to force
Zwangs'verschleppte §5 *mf* displaced person
Zwangs'verwaltung *f* receivership
Zwangs'vorstellung *f* hallucination
zwangs'weise *adv* by force
Zwangs'wirtschaft *f* (econ) government control, controlled economy
zwanzig ['tsvantsɪç] *invar adj* & *pron* twenty || **Zwanzig** *f* (-;-en) twenty
zwanziger ['tsvantsɪgər] *invar adj* of the twenties; **die z. Jahre** the twenties

zwanzigste ['tsvantsɪçstə] §9 *adj* & *pron* twentieth
Zwanzigstel ['tsvantsɪçstəl] *n* (-s;-) twentieth (*part*)
zwar [tsvɑr] *adv* indeed, no doubt, it is true; **und z.** namely, that is
Zweck [tsvɛk] *m* (-[e]s;-e) purpose, aim, object, point; **es hat keinen Z.** there's no point to it
zweck'dienlich *adj* serviceable, useful
Zwecke ['tsvɛkə] *f* (-;-n) tack; thumbtack
zweck'entfremden *tr* misuse
zweck'entsprechend *adj* appropriate
zweck'los *adj* pointless
zweck'mäßig *adj* serving its purpose; (*Möbel*) functional
zwecks [tsvɛks] *prep* (*genit*) for the purpose of
zwei [tsvaɪ] *adj* & *pron* two; **alle z.** (coll) both; **zu zweien** in twos, two by two, in pairs; **zu zweien hintereinander** in double file || **Zwei** *f* (-;-en) two
zwei'beinig *adj* two-legged
Zwei'bettzimmer *n* double room
Zweidecker ['tsvaɪdɛkər] *m* (-s;-) biplane
zweideu'tig ['tsvaɪdɔɪtɪç] *adj* ambiguous; (*Witz*) off-color; (*schlüpfrig*) suggestive
zweierlei ['tsvaɪ·ər'laɪ] *invar adj* two kinds of; **das ist z.** (coll) that's different
zwei'fach, zwei'fältig *adj* twofold, double; **in zweifacher Ausfertigung** in duplicate
Zweifami'lienhaus *n* duplex
zwei'farbig *adj* two-tone
Zweifel ['tsvaɪfəl] *m* (-s;-) doubt; **in Z. stellen** (or **ziehen**) call into question; **über allen Zweifeln erhaben** beyond reproach
zwei'felhaft *adj* doubtful; questionable; (*Persönlichkeit*) suspicious
zwei'fellos *adj* doubtless
zweifeln ['tsvaɪfəln] *intr* be in doubt; waver, hesitate; **z. an** (*dat*) doubt
Zwei'felsfall *m*—**im Z.** in case of doubt
Zweif'ler –**in** §6 *mf* skeptic
Zweig [tsvaɪk] *m* (-[e]s;-e) branch
Zweig'anstalt *f*, **Zweig'geschäft** *n* (com) branch
Zweig'gesellschaft *f* (com) affiliate
Zweig'niederlassung *f*, **Zweig'stelle** *f* (com) branch
Zwei'kampf *m* duel, single combat
zwei'mal *adv* twice
zweimalig ['tsvaɪmalɪç] *adj* repeated
zweimotorig ['tsvaɪmotorɪç] *adj* two-engine, twin-engine
zweireihig ['tsvaɪraɪ·ɪç] *adj* (*Sakko*) double-breasted
zwei'schneidig *adj* double-edged
zwei'seitig *adj* bilateral; reversible
zweisprachig ['tsvaɪ∫praxɪç] *adj* bilingual
Zweistär'kenglas *n* bifocal lens; (*Brille*) bifocals
zwei'stimmig *adj* for two voices
zweistufig ['tsvaɪ∫tufɪç] *adj* (rok) two-stage
zwei'stündig *adj* two-hour

zwei'stündlich *adj & adv* every two hours

zweit [tsvaɪt] *adv—zu z.* by twos; wir sind zu z. there are two of us

Zwei'taktmotor *m* two-cycle engine

Zweit'ausfertigung *f* duplicate

zweit'beste §9 *adj* second-best

zweite ['tsvaɪtə] §9 *adj & pron* second; another; aus zweiter Hand second-hand; at second hand; zum zweiten secondly || Zweite §5 *mf* (sport) runner-up

zwei'teilig *adj* two-piece; two-part

zweitens ['tsvaɪtəns] *adv* secondly

zweit'klassig *adj* second-class

Zwerchfell ['tsvɛrçfɛl] *n* diaphragm

Zwerg [tsvɛrk] *m* (-[e]s;-e) dwarf

zwer'genhaft *adj* dwarfish

Zwetsche ['tsvɛtʃə] *f* (-;-n), Zwetsch-ge ['tsvɛtʃgə] *f* (-;-n) plum

Zwetsch'genwasser *n* plum brandy

zwicken ['tsvɪkən] *tr* pinch

Zwicker (Zwik'ker) *m* (-s;-) pince-nez

Zwickmühle ['tsvɪkmylə] *f* (fig) fix

zwie– [tsvi] *comb.fm.* dis-, two-, double

Zwieback ['tsvibak] *m* (-s;ˬe & -e) zwieback

Zwiebel ['tsvibəl] *f* (-;-n) onion; (*Blumen-*) bulb

Zwie'gespräch *n* dialogue

Zwie'licht *n* twilight

Zwiesel ['tsvizəl] *f* (-;-n) fork (*of tree*)

Zwie'spalt *m* dissension; schism; discrepancy; im Z. sein mit be at variance with

zwiespältig ['tsviʃpɛltɪç] *adj* disunited, divided; divergent

Zwie'tracht *f* (-;) discord

Zwilling ['tsvɪlɪŋ] *m* (-s;-e) twin; eineiige Zwillinge identical twins

Zwil'lingsbruder *m* twin brother

Zwil'lingsschwester *f* twin sister

Zwinge ['tsvɪŋə] *f* (-;-n) ferrule; clamp; (*Schraubstock*) vise

zwingen ['tsvɪŋən] §142 *tr* force, compel; (*schaffen*) accomplish, swing

zwin'gend *adj* forceful, cogent

Zwin'ger *m* (-s;-) dungeon; cage; dog kennel; bear pit; lists

zwinkern ['tsvɪŋkərn] *intr* blink

Zwirn [tsvɪrn] *m* (-[e]s;-e) thread

Zwirns'faden *m* thread

zwischen ['tsvɪʃən] *prep* (*dat & acc*) between, among

Zwi'schenbemerkung *f* interruption

Zwi'schendeck *n* steerage

Zwi'schending *n* cross, mixture

zwischendurch' *adv* in between; at times

Zwi'schenergebnis *n* incomplete result

Zwi'schenfall *m* (unexpected) incident

Zwi'schenhändler –in §6 *mf* middle-man

Zwi'schenlandung *f* stopover

Zwi'schenlauf *m* (sport) quarterfinal; (sport) semifinal

Zwi'schenpause *f* break, intermission

Zwi'schenraum *m* space, interval

Zwi'schenruf *m* boo; interruption

Zwi'schenrunde *f* (sport) quarterfinal; (sport) semifinal

Zwi'schenspiel *n* interlude

zwi'schenstaatlich *adj* international; interstate

Zwi'schenstation *f* (rr) way station

Zwi'schenstecker *m* (elec) adapter

Zwi'schenstellung *f* (-;-en) intermediate position

Zwi'schenstück *n* insert; (*Verbindung*) connection; (elec) adapter

Zwi'schenstufe *f* intermediate stage

Zwi'schenträger –in §6 *mf* gossip

Zwi'schenwand *f* partition wall

Zwi'schenzeit *f* interval, meanwhile

Zwist [tsvɪst] *m* (-es;-e) discord; quarrel; (*Feindschaft*) enmity

Zwi'stigkeit *f* (-;-en) hostility

zwitschern ['tsvɪtʃərn] *tr—e–n z.* (coll) have a shot of liquor || *intr* chirp

Zwitter ['tsvɪtər] *m* (-s;-) hermaphrodite

Zwit'terfahrzeug *n* (mil) half-track

zwo [tsvo] *adj & pron* (coll) two

zwölf ['tsvœlf] *invar adj & pron* twelve || Zwölf *f* (-;-en) twelve

Zwölffin'gerdarm *m* duodenum

zwölfte ['tsvœlftə] §9 *adj & pron* twelfth

Zwölftel ['tsvœftəl] *n* (-s;-) twelfth (*part*)

Zyklon [tsY'klon] *m* (-s;-e), Zyklone [tsY'klonə] *f* (-;-n) cyclone

Zyk·lus ['tsyklʊs] *m* (-;-len [lən]) cycle; (*Reihe*) series, course

Zylinder [tsY'lɪndər] *m* (-s;-) cylinder (*e–r Lampe*) chimney; (*Hut*) top hat

zylindrisch [tsY'lɪndrɪʃ] *adj* cylindrical

Zyniker ['tsynɪkər] *m* (-s;-) cynic; (philos) Cynic

zynisch ['tsynɪʃ] *adj* cynical

Zypern ['tsypərn] *n* (-s;) Cyprus

Zypresse [tsY'prɛsə] *f* (-;-n) cypress

Zyste ['tsYstə] *f* (-;-n) cyst

GRAMMATICAL EXPLANATIONS

German Pronunciation

All the German letters and their variant spellings are listed below (in column 1) with their IPA symbols (in column 2), a description of their sounds (in column 3), and German examples with phonetic transcription (in column 4).

VOWELS

SPELLING	SYMBOL	APPROXIMATE SOUND	EXAMPLES
a	[a]	Like *a* in English *swat*	**Apfel** ['apfəl], **lassen** ['lasən], **Stadt** [ʃtat]
a	[ɑ]	Like *a* in English *father*	**Vater** ['fɑtər], **laden** ['lɑdən]
aa	[ɑ]	" "	**Paar** [pɑr], **Staat** [ʃtɑt]
ah	[ɑ]	" "	**Hahn** [hɑn], **Zahl** [tsɑl]
ä	[ɛ]	Like *e* in English *met*	**Äpfel** ['ɛpfəl], **lässig** ['lɛsɪç], **Städte** ['ʃtɛtə]
ä	[e]	Like *e* in English *they* (without the following sound of *y*)	**mäßig** ['mesɪç], **Väter** ['fetər]
äh	[e]	" "	**ähnlich** ['enlɪç], **Zähne** ['tsenə]
e	[ə]	Like *e* in English *system*	**Bitte** ['bɪtə], **rufen** ['rufən]
e	[ɛ]	Like *e* in English *met*	**Kette** ['kɛtə], **messen** ['mɛsən]
e	[e]	Like *e* in English *they* (without the following sound of *y*)	**Feder** ['fedər], **regnen** ['regnən]
ee	[e]	" "	**Meer** [mer], **Seele** ['zelə]
eh	[e]	" "	**Ehre** ['erə], **zehn** [tsen]
i	[ɪ]	Like *i* in English *sin*	**bin** [bɪn], **Fisch** [fɪʃ]
i	[i]	Like *i* in English *machine*	**Maschine** [ma'ʃinə], **Lid** [lit]
ih	[i]	" "	**ihm** [im], **ihr** [ir]
ie	[i]	" "	**dieser** ['dizər], **tief** [tif]
o	[ɔ]	Like *o* in English *often*	**Gott** [gɔt], **offen** ['ɔfən]
o	[o]	Like *o* in English *note*, but without the diphthongal glide	**holen** ['holən], **Rose** ['rozə]
oo	[o]	" "	**Boot** [bot], **Moos** [mos]
oh	[o]	" "	**Bohne** ['bonə], **Kohle** ['kolə]
ö	[œ]	The lips are rounded for [ɔ] and held without moving while the sound [ɛ] is pronounced.	**Götter** ['gœtər], **öffnen** ['œfnən]

SPELLING	SYMBOL	APPROXIMATE SOUND	EXAMPLES
ö	[ø]	The lips are rounded for [o] and held without moving while the sound [e] is pronounced.	böse ['bøzə], Löwe ['løvə]
öh	[ø]	" "	Röhre ['rørə], Söhne ['zønə]
u	[ʊ]	Like *u* in English *bush*	Busch [buʃ], muß [mʊs], Hund [hʊnt]
u	[u]	Like *u* in English *rule*	Schule ['ʃulə], Gruß [grus]
uh	[u]	" "	Uhr [ur], Ruhm [rum]
ü	[ʏ]	The lips are rounded for [ʊ] and held without moving while the sound [ɪ] is pronounced.	Hütte ['hʏtə], müssen ['mʏsən]
ü	[y]	The lips are rounded for [u] and held without moving while the sound [i] is pronounced.	Schüler ['ʃylər], Grüße ['grysə]
üh	[y]	" "	Mühle ['mylə], kühn [kyn]
y	[ʏ]	Like **ü** [ʏ] above	Mystik ['mʏstɪk]
y	[y]	Like **ü** [y] above	Mythe ['mytə]

DIPHTHONGS

SPELLING	SYMBOL	APPROXIMATE SOUND	EXAMPLES
ai	[aɪ]	Like *i* in English *night*	Saite ['zaɪtə], Mais [maɪs]
au	[au]	Like *ou* in English *ouch*	kaufen ['kaufən], Haus [haus]
äu	[ɔɪ]	Like *oy* in English *toy*	träumen ['trɔɪmən], Gebäude [gə'bɔɪdə]
ei	[aɪ]	Like *i* in English *night*	Zeit [tsaɪt], nein [naɪn]
eu	[ɔɪ]	Like *oy* in English *toy*	heute ['hɔɪtə], Eule ['ɔɪlə]

CONSONANTS

SPELLING	SYMBOL	APPROXIMATE SOUND	EXAMPLES
b	[b]	Like *b* in English *boy*	Buch [bux], haben ['habən]
b	[p]	Like *p* in English *lap*	gelb [gɛlp], lieblich ['liplɪç]
c	[k]	Like *c* in English *car*	Clown [klaun], Café [ka'fe]
c	[ts]	Like *ts* in English *its*	Cäsar ['tsezar], Centrale [tsɛn'tralə]
ch	[x]	This sound is made by breathing through a space between the back of the tongue and the soft palate.	auch [aux], Buche ['buxə]
ch	[ç]	This sound is made by breathing through a space left when the front of the tongue is pressed close to the hard palate with the tip of the tongue behind the lower teeth.	ich [ɪç], Bücher ['byçər], Chemie [çɛ'mi], durch [durç]

SPELLING	SYMBOL	APPROXIMATE SOUND	EXAMPLES
ch	[k]	Like *k* in English *key*	**Charakter** [ka'raktər], **Chor** [kor]
ch	[ʃ]	Like *sh* in English *shall*	**Chef** [ʃɛf], **Chassis** [ʃa'si]
chs	[ks]	Like *x* in English *box*	**sechs** [zɛks], **Wachs** [vaks]
ck	[k]	Like *k* in English *key* When *ck* in a vocabulary entry in this Dictionary has to be divided by an accent mark, the word is first spelled with *ck* and is then repeated in parentheses with the *ck* changed to *kk* in accordance with the principle which requires this change when the division comes at the end of the line, e.g., **Deckenlicht (Dek'kenlicht)**.	**wecken** ['vɛkən], **Ruck** [rʊk]
d	[d]	Like *d* in English *door*	**laden** ['lɑdən], **deutsch** [dɔɪtʃ]
d	[t]	Like *t* in English *time*	**Freund** [frɔɪnt], **Hund** [hʊnt]
dt	[t]	" "	**verwandt** [fɛr'vant], **Stadt** [ʃtat]
f	[f]	Like *f* in English *five*	**Fall** [fal], **auf** [aʊf]
g	[g]	Like *g* in English *go*	**geben** ['gebən], **Regen** ['regən]
g	[k]	Like *k* in English *key*	**Krieg** [krik], **Weg** [vek]
g	[ç]	See **ch** [ç] above	**wenig** ['venɪç], **häufig** ['hɔɪfɪç]
h	[h]	Like *h* in English *hat*	**Haus** [haʊs], **Freiheit** ['fraɪhaɪt]
j	[j]	Like *y* in English *yet*	**Jahr** [jɑr], **jener** ['jenər]
k	[k]	Like *k* in English *key*	**Kaffee** [ka'fe], **kein** [kaɪn]
l	[l]	This sound is made with the tip of the tongue against the back of the upper teeth and the side edges of the tongue against the side teeth.	**laden** ['lɑdən], **fahl** [fɑl]
m	[m]	Like *m* in English *man*	**mehr** [mer], **Amt** [amt]
n	[n]	Like *n* in English *neck*	**Nase** ['nɑzə], **kaufen** ['kaʊfən]
n	[ŋ]	Like *n* in English *sink*	**sinken** ['zɪŋkən], **Funke** ['fʊŋkə]
ng	[ŋ]	" "	**Finger** ['fɪŋər], **Rang** [raŋ]
p	[p]	Like *p* in English *pond*	**Perle** ['pɛrlə], **Opfer** ['ɔpfər]
ph	[f]	Like *f* in English *five*	**Phase** ['fɑzə], **Graphik** ['grɑfɪk]
qu	[kv]	Does not occur in English.	**Quelle** ['kvɛlə], **bequem** [bə'kvem]
r	[r]	This sound is a trilled sound made by vibrating the tip of the tongue against the upper gums or by vibrating the uvula.	**rufen** ['rufən], **Rede** ['redə]

361

SPELLING	SYMBOL	APPROXIMATE SOUND	EXAMPLES
s	[s]	Like s in English *sock*	**Glas** [glɑs], **erst** [erst]
s	[z]	Like z in English *zest*	**sind** [zɪnt], **Eisen** ['aɪzən]
sch	[ʃ]	Like sh in English *shall*	**Schuh** [ʃu], **Schnee** [ʃne]
sp	[ʃp]	Does not occur in English in the initial position.	**sparen** ['ʃpɑrən], **Spott** [ʃpɔt]
ss	[s]	This spelling is used only in the intervocalic position and when the preceding vowel sound is one of the following: [a], [ɛ], [ɪ], [ə], [œ], [ʊ], [ʏ]	**Klasse** ['klasə], **essen** ['ɛsən], **wissen** ['vɪsən], **Gosse** ['gɔsə], **Rössel** ['rœsəl], **Russe** ['rʊsə], **müssen** ['mʏsən]
ß	[s]	This spelling is used instead of ss (a) when in the final position in a word or component, (b) when followed by a consonant, or (c) when intervocalic and preceded by a diphthong or one of the following vowel sounds: [ɑ], [e], [i], [o], [ø], [u], [y]	(a) **Fluß** [flʊs], **Flußufer** ['flʊsufər], (b) **läßt** [lɛst], (c) **dreißig** ['draɪsɪç], **Straße** ['ʃtrasə], **mäßig** ['mɛsɪç], **schießen** ['ʃisən], **stoßen** ['ʃtosən], **Stößel** ['ʃtøsəl], **Muße** ['musə], **müßig** ['mysɪç]
st	[ʃt]	Does not occur in English in the initial position.	**Staub** [ʃtaʊp], **stehen** ['ʃte·ən]
t	[t]	Like t in English *time*	**Teller** ['tɛlər], **Tau** [taʊ]
th	[t]	" "	**Theater** [tɛ'atər], **Thema** ['tema]
ti+ vowel	[tsj]	Does not occur in English.	**Station** [sta'tsjon], **Patient** [pa'tsjɛnt]
tz	[ts]	Like ts in English *its*	**schätzen** ['ʃɛtsən], **jetzt** [jɛtst]
v	[f]	Like f in English *five*	**Vater** ['fɑtər], **brav** [brɑf]
v	[v]	Like v in English *vat*	**November** [nɔ'vɛmbər], **Verb** [vɛrp]
w	[v]	" "	**Wasser** ['vasər], **wissen** ['vɪsən]
x	[ks]	Like x in English *box*	**Export** [ɛks'pɔrt], **Taxe** ['taksə]
z	[ts]	Like ts in English *its*	**Zahn** [tsɑn], **reizen** ['raɪtsən]

German Grammar References

§1. Declension of the Definite Article

	SINGULAR			PLURAL
	MASC	FEM	NEUT	MASC, FEM, NEUT
NOM	der	die	das	die
ACC	den	die	das	die
DAT	dem	der	dem	den
GENIT	des	der	des	der

§2. Declension of the Indefinite Article and the Numeral Adjective

1.	SINGULAR			PLURAL
	MASC	FEM	NEUT	MASC, FEM, NEUT
NOM	ein	eine	ein	
ACC	einen	eine	ein	
DAT	einem	einer	einem	
GENIT	eines	einer	eines	

2. Other words that are declined like **ein** are: **kein** *no, not any* and the possessive adjectives **mein** *my;* **dein** *thy, your;* **sein** *his; her; its;* **ihr** *her; their;* **Ihr** *your;* **unser** *our;* **euer** *your.* Unlike **ein**, they have plural forms, as shown in the following paradigm.

	SINGULAR			PLURAL
	MASC	FEM	NEUT	MASC, FEM, NEUT
NOM	kein	keine	kein	keine
ACC	keinen	keine	kein	keine
DAT	keinem	keiner	keinem	keinen
GENIT	keines	keiner	keines	keiner

3. The **e** of **er** of **unser** and **euer** is generally dropped when followed by an ending, as shown in the following paradigm. And instead of the **e** of **er** dropping, the **e** of final **em** and **en** in these words may drop.

	SINGULAR			PLURAL
	MASC	FEM	NEUT	MASC, FEM, NEUT
NOM	unser	uns(e)re	unser	uns(e)re
ACC	uns(e)ren or unsern	uns(e)re	unser	uns(e)re
DAT	uns(e)rem or unserm	uns(e)rer	uns(e)rem or unserm	uns(e)ren or unsern
GENIT	uns(e)res	uns(e)rer	uns(e)res	uns(e)rer

All adjectives that follow these words are declined in the mixed declension.

4. The pronouns **einer** and **keiner,** as well as all the possessive pronouns, are declined according to the strong declension of adjectives. The neuter forms **eines** and **keines** have the variants **eins** and **keins.**

5. When the possessive adjectives are used as possessive pronouns, they are declined according to the strong declension of adjectives. When preceded by the definite article, they are declined according to the weak declension of adjectives. There are also possessive pronouns with the infix **ig** which are always preceded by the definite article and capitalized and are declined according to the declension of adjectives, e.g., **der, die, das Meinige** *mine.*

§3. Declension of the Demonstrative Pronoun

| | SINGULAR | | | PLURAL |
	MASC	FEM	NEUT	MASC, FEM, NEUT
NOM	dieser	diese	dieses or dies	diese
ACC	diesen	diese	dieses or dies	diese
DAT	diesem	dieser	diesem	diesen
GENIT	dieses	dieser	dieses	dieser

Other words that are declined like **dieser** are **jeder** *each;* **jener** *that;* **mancher** *many a;* **welcher** *which.* All adjectives that come after these words are declined in the weak declension.

§4. Declension of Adjectives.
Adjectives have three declensions: 1) the strong declension, 2) the weak declension, and 3) the mixed declension. On both sides of this Dictionary, adjectives occurring in the expressions consisting solely of an adjective and a noun are entered in their weak forms.

1. ,The strong declension of adjectives, whose endings are shown in the following table, is used when the adjective is not preceded by **der** or by **dieser** or any of the other words listed in §3 or by **ein** or any of the other words listed in §2.

| | SINGULAR | | | PLURAL |
	MASC	FEM	NEUT	MASC, FEM, NEUT
NOM	−er	−e	−es	−e
ACC	−en	−e	−es	−e
DAT	−em	−er	−em	−en
GENIT	−en	−er	−en	−er

2. The weak declension of adjectives, whose endings are shown in the following table, is used when the adjective is preceded by **der** or **dieser** or any of the other words listed in §3.

| | SINGULAR | | | PLURAL |
	MASC	FEM	NEUT	MASC, FEM, NEUT
NOM	−e	−e	−e	−en
ACC	−en	−e	−e	−en
DAT	−en	−en	−en	−en
GENIT	−en	−en	−en	−en

3. The **der** component of **derselbe** and **derjenige** is the article **der** and is declined like it, while the **−selbe** and **−jenige** components are declined according to the weak declension of adjectives.

4. The mixed declension of adjectives, whose endings are shown in the following table, is used when the adjective is preceded by **ein** or **kein** or any of the other words listed in §2.

364

	SINGULAR			PLURAL
	MASC	FEM	NEUT	MASC, FEM, NEUT
NOM	–er	–e	–es	–en
ACC	–en	–e	–es	–en
DAT	–en	–en	–en	–en
GENIT	–en	–en	–en	–en

§5. Adjectives Used as Nouns. When an adjective is used as a masculine, feminine, or neuter noun, it is spelled with an initial capital letter and is declined as an adjective in accordance with the principles set forth in §4. We have, for example, **der** or **die Fremde** the foreigner; **der** or **die Angestellte** *the employee;* **ein Angestellter** *a (male) employee,* **eine Angestellte** *a (female) employee;* **das Deutsche** *German* (i.e., *language*). These nouns are entered on both sides of this Dictionary in the weak form of the adjective and their genitives and plurals are not shown.

§6. Many masculine nouns ending in **–er** and **–ier** have feminine forms made by adding **–in.** The masculine forms have genitives made by adding **s** and remain unchanged in the plural, while the feminine forms remain unchanged in the singular and have plurals made by adding **–nen.** For example:

	MASC	FEM
NOM SG	**Verkäufer** *salesperson (salesman)*	**Verkäuferin** *salesperson (saleslady)*
GENIT SG	**Verkäufers**	**Verkäuferin**
NOM PL	**Verkäufer**	**Verkäuferinnen**

§7. Many masculine nouns ending in **–at** (e.g., **Advokat**), or in **–ant** (e.g., **Musikant**), or in **–ist** (*e.g.,* **Artist**), or in **–ent** (e.g., **Student**), or in **–graph** (e.g., **Choreograph**), or in **–ot** (e.g., **Pilot**), or in **–et** (e.g.,**Analphabet**), or in **–it** (e.g., **Israelit**), or in **–ast** (e.g., **Phantast**), etc., have feminine forms made by adding **–in.** The masculine forms have genitives and plurals made by adding **–en,** while the femine forms remain unchanged in the singular and have plurals made by adding **–nen.** For example:

	MASC	FEM
NOM SG	**Advokat** *attorney*	**Advokatin** *attorney*
GENIT SG	**Advokaten**	**Advokatin**
NOM PL	**Advokaten**	**Advokatinnen**

§8. Many masculine nouns ending in **–ar** (e.g., **Antiquar**) or in **–är** (e.g., **Milliardär**) have feminine forms made by adding **–in.** The masculine forms have genitives made by adding **–(e)s** and plurals made by adding **–e,** while the feminine forms remain unchanged in the singular and have plurals made by adding **–nen.** For example:

	MASC	FEM
NOM SG	**Antiquar** *antique dealer*	**Antiquarin** *antique dealer*
GENIT SG	**Antiquar(e)s**	**Antiquarin**
NOM PL	**Antiquare**	**Antiquarinnen**

§9. Adjectives are generally given in their uninflected form, the form in which they appear in the predicate, e.g., **billig, reich, alt.** However, those adjectives which do not occur in an uninflected form are given with the weak ending **–e,** which in the nominative is the same for all genders, e.g., **andere, besondere, beste, hohe.**

§10. Adjectives which denote languages may be used as adverbs. When so used with **sprechen, schreiben, können,** and a few others, they are translated in English by the corresponding noun, and actual and immediate action is implied, e.g., **deutsch sprechen** *to speak German* (i.e., to be speaking German right now). Adjectives which denote languages may be capitalized and used as invariable nouns, and when so used with **sprechen, schreiben, können,** and a few other verbs, general action is implied, e.g., **Deutsch sprechen** *to speak German* (i.e., to know how to speak German, to be a speaker of German).

With other verbs, these adjectives used as adverbs are translated by the corresponding noun preceded by "auf" or "in", e.g., **sich auf** (or **in**) **deutsch unterhalten** *to converse in German.*

§11. Personal and Reflexive Pronouns

PERSONS	SUBJECT	PERSONAL DIRECT OBJECT	PERSONAL INDIRECT OBJECT	REFLEXIVE DIRECT OBJECT	REFLEXIVE INDIRECT OBJECT
SG					
1	**ich** *I*	**mich** *me*	**mir** *(to) me*	**mich** *myself*	**mir** *(to) myself*
2	**du** *you*	**dich** *you*	**dir** *(to) you*	**dich** *yourself*	**dir** *(to) yourself*
3 MASC	**er** *he; it*	**ihn** *him; it*	**ihm** *(to) him; (to) it*	**sich** *himself; itself*	**sich** *(to) himself; (to) itself*
3 FEM	**sie** *she; it*	**sie** *her; it*	**ihr** *(to) her; (to) it*	**sich** *herself; itself*	**sich** *(to) herself; (to) itself*
3 NEUT	**es** *it; she; he*	**es** *it; her; him*	**ihm** *(to) it; (to) her; (to) him*	**sich** *itself; herself; himself*	**sich** *(to) itself; (to) herself; (to) himself*
PL					
1	**wir** *we*	**uns** *us*	**uns** *(to) us*	**uns** *ourselves*	**uns** *(to) ourselves*
2	**ihr** *you*	**euch** *you*	**euch** *(to) you*	**euch** *yourselves*	**euch** *(to) yourselves*
3	**sie** *they*	**sie** *them*	**ihnen** *(to) them*	**sich** *themselves*	**sich** *(to) themselves*
2 FORMAL SG & PL	**Sie** *you*	**Sie** *you*	**Ihnen** *(to) you*	**sich** *yourself; yourselves*	**sich** *(to) yourself; (to) yourselves*

er means *it* when it stands for a masculine noun that is the name of an animal or a thing, as **Hund, Tisch.** **sie** means *it* when it stands for a feminine noun that is the name of an animal or a thing, as **Hündin, Feder.** **es** means *she* when it stands for a neuter noun that is the name of a female person, as **Fräulein, Mädchen, Weib;** it means *he* when it stands for a neuter noun that is the name of a male person, as **Söhnchen, Söhnlein.**

The dative means also *from me, from you,* etc., with certain verbs expressing separation such as **entnehmen.**

§12. Separable and Inseparable Prefixes. Many verbs can be compounded either with a prefix, which is always inseparable and unstressed, or with a combining form (conventionally called also a prefix), which can be separable and stressed or inseparable and unstressed. Exceptions are indicated by the abbreviations *sep* and *insep.*

1. The inseparable prefixes are **be–, emp–, ent–, er–, ge–, ver–,** and **zer–,** e.g., **beglei′ten, erler′nen, verste′hen.** They are never stressed.

2. The separable prefixes (i.e., combining forms) are prepositions, e.g., **auf–** as in **auf′tragen,** adverbs, e.g., **vorwärts–** as in **vor′wärtsbringen,** adjectives, e.g., **tot–** as in **tot′schlagen,** nouns, e.g., **maschine–** as in **maschi′neschreiben,** or other verbs, e.g., **stehen–** as in **ste′henbleiben.** They are always stressed except as provided for those listed in the following section.

3. The prefixes (combining forms) **durch, hinter, über, um, unter, wider,** and **wieder,** when their meaning is literal, are separable and stressed, e.g. **durch′schneiden** *cut through, cut in two,* and, when their meaning is figurative or derived, are inseparable and unstressed, e.g., **durchschnei′den** *cut across, traverse.*

4. A compound prefix is (a) inseparable if it consists of an inseparable prefix plus a separable prefix, e.g., **beauf′tragen,** (b) separable if it consists of a separable prefix plus an inseparable prefix, e.g.,**vor′bereiten—er bereitet etwas vor,** and (c) separable if it consists of two separable prefixes, e.g., **vorbei′laufen—sie lief vorbei.** Although verbs falling under (b) are separable, they do not take **–ge–** in the past participle, e.g., **vor′bereitet** (past participle of **vorbereiten**). But they do take the infix **–zu–** in the infinitive, e.g., **vor′-zubereiten.** Note that compound prefixes falling under (c) are stressed on the second of the two separable components.

§13. German verbs are regarded as reflexive regardless of whether the reflexive pronoun is the direct or indirect object of the verb.

§14. The declension of German nouns is shown by giving the genitive singular followed by the nominative plural, in parentheses after the abbreviation indicating gender. This is done by presenting the whole noun by a hyphen with which the ending and/or the umlaut may or may not be shown according to the inflection; e.g., **Stadt** [ʃtat] *f* (–;⸚e) means **der Stadt** and **die Städte.** If the noun has no plural, the closing parenthesis comes immediately after the semicolon following the genitive singular, e.g., **Kleidung** [ˈklaɪduŋ] *f* (–;). In loan words in which the ending changes in the plural, the centered period is used to mark off the portion of the word that has to be detached before the portion showing the plural form is added, e.g., **Da·tum** [ˈdɑtum] *n* (–s;–ten [tən]).

When a vowel is added to a word ending in **ß,** the **ß** remains if it is preceded by a diphthong or one of the following vowel sounds: [ɑ], [e], [i], [o], [ø], [y], e.g., **Stoß** [ʃtos], plural: **Stöße; Strauß,** plural: **Sträuße,** but changes to **ss** if it is preceded by one of the following vowel sounds: [a], [ɛ], [ɪ], [ɔ], [œ], [ʊ], [ʏ], e.g., **Roß** [rɔs], plural **Rosses.** In this Dictionary the inflection of words in which **ß** does not change is shown in the usual way, e.g., **Stoß** [ʃtos] *m* (–es;⸚e); **Strauß** [ʃtraʊs] *m* (–es;⸚e), while the inflection of words in which **ß** changes to **ss** is shown in monosyllables by repeating the full word in its inflected forms, e.g., **Roß** [rɔs] *n* (**Rosses; Rosse**) and in polysyllables by marking off with a centered dot the final syllable and then repeating it in its inflected forms, e.g., **Ver·laß** [fɛrˈlas] *m* (–lasses;).

§15. When a word ending in a double consonant is combined with a following word beginning with the same single consonant followed by a vowel, the resultant group of three identical consonants is shortened to two, e.g., **Schiff** combined with **Fahrt** makes **Schiffahrt** and **Schall** combined with **Lehre** makes

Schallehre.[1] However, when such a compound as a vocabulary entry has to be divided by an accent mark, the word is first spelled with two identical consonants and is then repeated in parentheses with three identical consonants, e.g., **Schiffahrt (Schiff'fahrt)**. Furthermore, when such a compound has to be divided because the first component comes at the end of a line and is followed by a hyphen and the second component begins the following line, the three consonants are used, e.g., **Schiff–fahrt** and **Schall–lehre.**

When the medial group **ck** in a vocabulary entry has to be divided by an accent mark, the word is first spelled with **ck** and is then repeated in parentheses with the **ck** changed to **kk** in accordance with the orthographic principle which requires this change when the division comes at the end of the line, e.g., **Deckenlicht (Dek'kenlicht).**

---

[1] If the intial consonant of the following word is followed by a consonant instead of a vowel, the group of three identical consonants remains, e.g., **Fetttropfen, Rohstofffrage.**

German Model Verbs

These verbs are models for all the verbs that appear as vocabulary entries in the German-English part of this Dictionary. If a section number referring to this table is not given with an entry, it is understood that the verb is a weak verb conjugated like **loben, reden, handeln,** or **warten.** If a section number is given, it is understood that the verb is a strong, mixed, or irregular verb and that it is identical in all forms with the model referred to in its radical vowel or diphthong and the consonants that follow the radical. Thus **schneiden** is numbered §106 to refer to the model **leiden.** Such words include the model itself, e.g., **denken,** numbered §66 to refer to the model **denken,** compounds of the model, e.g., **bekommen,** numbered §99 to refer to the model **kommen,** and verbs that have the same radical component, e.g., **empfehlen,** numbered §51 to refer to the model **befehlen.**

If a strong or mixed verb in a given function (transitive or intransitive) and/or meaning may be conjugated also as a weak verb, this is indicated by the insertion of the section number of the appropriate weak verb (**loben, handeln, reden,** or **warten**) after the section number of the model strong verb, e.g., **dingen** §142 & §109.

If a strong or mixed verb in a different function is conjugated as a weak verb, this is indicated by dividing the two functions by parallels and showing the conjugation of each by the insertion of the appropriate section numbers, e.g., **hängen** §92 *tr* . . . ‖ §109 *intr.*

If a strong or mixed verb in a different meaning is conjugated as a weak verb, this is indicated by dividing the two meanings by parallels and showing the conjugation of each by the insertion of the appropriate section numbers, e.g., **bewegen** *tr* move, set in motion . . . ‖ §56 *tr* move, induce.

It is understood that verbs with inseparable prefixes, verbs with compound separable prefixes of which the first component is separable and the second inseparable, and verbs ending in **–ieren** do not take **ge** in the past participle.

No account is taken here of the auxiliary used in forming compound tenses. The use of SEIN is indicated in the body of the Dictionary.

Alternate forms are listed in parentheses immediately below the corresponding principal part of the model verb.

370

	INFINITIVE	3D SG PRESENT INDICATIVE	IMPERFECT INDICATIVE	IMPERFECT SUBJUNCTIVE	PAST PARTICIPLE
§50	backen	bäckt	buk	büke	gebacken
§51	befehlen	befiehlt	befahl	beföhle	befohlen
§52	beginnen	beginnt	begann	begönne (begänne)	begonnen
§53	beißen	beißt	biß	bisse	gebissen
§54	bergen	birgt	barg	bärge (bürge)	geborgen
§55	bersten	birst (berstet)	barst	bärste (börste)	geborsten
§56	bewegen	bewegt	bewog	bewöge	bewogen
§57	biegen	biegt	bog	böge	gebogen
§58	bieten	bietet	bot	böte	geboten
§59	binden	bindet	band	bände	gebunden
§60	bitten	bittet	bat	bäte	gebeten
§61	blasen	bläst	blies	bliese	geblasen
§62	bleiben	bleibt	blieb	bliebe	geblieben
§63	braten	brät	briet	briete	gebraten
§64	brechen	bricht	brach	bräche	gebrochen
§65	bringen	bringt	brachte	brächte	gebracht
§66	denken	denkt	dachte	dächte	gedacht
§67	dreschen	drischt	drosch (drasch)	drösche (dräsche)	gedroschen
§68	dünken	dünkt (deucht)	dünkte (deuchte)	dünkte (deuchte)	gedünkt (gedeucht)

	INFINITIVE	3D SG PRESENT INDICATIVE	IMPERFECT INDICATIVE	IMPERFECT SUBJUNCTIVE	PAST PARTICIPLE
§69	dürfen	darf	durfte	dürfte	gedurft (dürfen)
§70	essen	ißt	aß	äße	gegessen
§71	fahren	fährt	fuhr	führe	gefahren
§72	fallen	fällt	fiel	fiele	gefallen
§73	fangen	fängt	fing	finge	gefangen
§74	fechten	ficht	focht	föchte	gefochten
§75	fliehen	flieht	floh	flöhe	geflohen
§76	fließen	fließt	floß	flösse	geflossen
§77	frieren	friert	fror	fröre	gefroren
§78	gären	gärt	gor	göre	gegoren
§79	gebären	gebiert	gebar	gebäre	geboren
§80	geben	gibt	gab	gäbe	gegeben
§81	gedeihen	gedeiht	gedieh	gediehe	gediehen
§82	gehen	geht	ging	ginge	gegangen
§83	gelten	gilt	galt	gälte (gölte)	gegolten
§84	genesen	genest	genas	genäse	genesen
§85	gleichen	gleicht	glich	gliche	geglichen
§86	gleiten	gleitet	glitt	glitte	geglitten
§87	graben	gräbt	grub	grübe	gegraben
§88	greifen	greift	griff	griffe	gegriffen
§89	haben	hat	hatte	hätte	gehabt
§90	halten	hält	hielt	hielte	gehalten

	INFINITIVE	3D SG PRESENT INDICATIVE	IMPERFECT INDICATIVE	IMPERFECT SUBJUNCTIVE	PAST PARTICIPLE
§91	handeln	handelt	handelte	handelte	gehandelt
§92	hängen	hängt	hing	hinge	gehangen
§93	hauen	haut	hieb	hiebe	gehauen
§94	heben	hebt	hob	höbe	gehoben
§95	heißen	heißt	hieß	hieße	geheißen
§96	helfen	hilft	half	hälfe (hülfe)	geholfen
§97	kennen	kennt	kannte	kennte	gekannt
§98	kiesen	kiest	kor	köre	gekoren
§99	kommen	kommt	kam	käme	gekommen
§100	können	kann	konnte	könnte	gekonnt (können)
§101	kreischen	kreischt	kreischte (krisch)	kreischte (krische)	gekreischt (gekrischen)
§102	kriechen	kriecht	kroch	kröche	gekrochen
§103	laden	lädt	lud	lüde	geladen
§104	lassen	läßt	ließ	ließe	gelassen
§105	laufen	läuft	lief	liefe	gelaufen
§106	leiden	leidet	litt	litte	gelitten
§107	lesen	liest	las	läse	gelesen
§108	liegen	liegt	lag	läge	gelegen
§109	loben	lobt	lobte	lobte	gelobt
§110	löschen	lischt	losch	lösche	geloschen
§111	lügen	lügt	log	löge	gelogen

	INFINITIVE	3D SG PRESENT INDICATIVE	IMPERFECT INDICATIVE	IMPERFECT SUBJUNCTIVE	PAST PARTICIPLE
§112	meiden	meidet	mied	miede	gemieden
§113	melken	melkt	molk	mölke	gemolken
§114	mögen	mag	mochte	möchte	gemocht
§115	müssen	muß	mußte	müßte	gemußt (mögen) (müssen)
§116	nehmen	nimmt	nahm	nähme	genommen
§117	pflegen	pflegt	pflog	pflöge	gepflogen
§118	preisen	preist	pries	priese	gepriesen
§119	quellen	quillt	quoll	quölle	gequollen
§120	reden	redet	redete	redete	geredet
§121	rinnen	rinnt	rann	ränne (rönne)	geronnen
§122	rufen	ruft	rief	riefe	gerufen
§123	salzen	salzt	salzte	salzte	gesalzen
§124	saufen	säuft	soff	söffe	gesoffen
§125	saugen	saugt	sog	söge	gesogen
§126	schaffen	schafft	schuf	schüfe	geschaffen
§127	schallen	schallt	scholl	schölle	geschollen
§128	scheinen	scheint	schien	schiene	geschienen
§129	scheren	schert (schiert)	schor	schöre	geschoren
§130	schieben	schiebt	schob	schöbe	geschoben
§131	schlafen	schläft	schlief	schliefe	geschlafen

	INFINITIVE	3D SG PRESENT INDICATIVE	IMPERFECT INDICATIVE	IMPERFECT SUBJUNCTIVE	PAST PARTICIPLE
§132	schlagen	schlägt	schlug	schlüge	geschlagen
§133	schmelzen	schmilzt	schmolz	schmölze	geschmolzen
§134	schrecken	schrickt	schrak	schräke	geschrocken
§135	schreien	schreit	schrie	schriee	geschrie(e)n
§136	schwimmen	schwimmt	schwamm	schwämme (schwömme)	geschwommen
§137	schwören	schwört	schwur (schwor)	schwüre	geschworen
§138	sehen	sieht	sah	sähe	gesehen
§139	sein	ist	war	wäre	gewesen
§140	senden	sendet	sandte	sendete	gesandt
§141	sieden	siedet	sott	sötte	gesotten
§142	singen	singt	sang	sänge	gesungen
§143	sinken	sinkt	sank	sänke	gesunken
§144	sitzen	sitzt	saß	säße	gesessen
§145	sollen	soll	sollte	sollte	gesollt (sollen)
§146	stehen	steht	stand	stände (stünde)	gestanden
§147	stehlen	stiehlt	stahl	stähle (stöhle)	gestohlen
§148	steigen	steigt	stieg	stiege	gestiegen
§149	sterben	stirbt	starb	stürbe	gestorben
§150	stoßen	stößt	stieß	stieße	gestoßen

	INFINITIVE	3D SG PRESENT INDICATIVE	IMPERFECT INDICATIVE	IMPERFECT SUBJUNCTIVE	PAST PARTICIPLE
§151	treffen	trifft	traf	träfe	getroffen
§152	treten	tritt	trat	träte	getreten
§153	triefen	trieft	troff	tröffe	getroffen
§154	tun	tut	tat	täte	getan
§155	wachsen	wächst	wuchs	wüchse	gewachsen
§156	wägen	wiegt	wog	wöge	gewogen
§157	warten	wartet	wartete	wartete	gewartet
§158	waschen	wäscht	wusch	wüsche	gewaschen
§159	werden	wird	wurde (ward)	würde	geworden (worden)
§160	werfen	wirft	warf	würfe	geworfen
§161	wissen	weiß	wußte	wüßte	gewußt
§162	wollen	will	wollte	wollte	gewollt (wollen)
§163	ziehen	zieht	zog	zöge	gezogen
§164	klimmen	klimmt	klomm	klömme	geklommen
§165	küren	kürt	kor	köre	gekoren
§166	schinden	schindet	schund	schünde	geschunden

Die Aussprache des Englischen

Die nachstehenden Lautzeichen bezeichnen fast alle Laute der englischen Sprache:

	VOKALE	
LAUTZEICHEN	**UNGEFÄHRER LAUT**	**BEISPIEL**
[æ]	Offener als *ä* in *hätte*	**hat** [hæt]
[ɑ]	Wie *a* in *Vater* Wie *a* in *Mann*	**father** [ˈfɑðər] **proper** [ˈprɑpər]
[ɛ]	Wie *e* in *Fett*	**met** [mɛt]
[e]	Offener als *eej* in *Seejungfrau*	**fate** [fet] **they** [ðe]
[ə]	Wie *e* in *finden*	**haven** [ˈhevən] **pardon** [ˈpardən]
[i]	Wie *ie* in *sie*	**she** [ʃi] **machine** [məˈʃin]
[ɪ]	Offener als *i* in *bitte*	**fit** [fɪt] **beer** [bɪr]
[o]	Offenes *o* mit anschließendem kurzem (halbvokalischem) *u*	**nose** [noz] **road** [rod] **row** [ro]
[ɔ]	Wie *o* in *oft*	**bought** [bɔt] **law** [lɔ]
[ʌ]	Wie *er* in *jeder* (umgangssprachlich)	**cup** [kʌp] **come** [kʌm] **mother** [ˈmʌðər]
[ʊ]	Wie *u* in *Fluß*	**pull** [pʊl] **book** [bʊk] **wolf** [wʊlf]
[u]	Wie *u* in *Fluß*	**move** [muv] **tomb** [tum]

	DIPHTHONGE	
LAUTZEICHEN	**UNGEFÄHRER LAUT**	**BEISPIEL**
[aɪ]	Wie *ei* in *nein*	**night** [naɪt] **eye** [aɪ]
[aʊ]	Wie *au* in *Haus*	**found** [faʊnd] **cow** [kaʊ]
[ɔɪ]	Wie *eu* in *heute*	**voice** [vɔɪs] **oil** [ɔɪl]

	KONSONANTEN	
LAUTZEICHEN	**UNGEFÄHRER LAUT**	**BEISPIEL**
[b]	Wie *b* in *bin*	**bed** [bɛd] **robber** [ˈrɑbər]

377

LAUTZEICHEN	UNGEFÄHRER LAUT	BEISPIEL
[d]	Wie *d* in *du*	dead [dɛd] add [æd]
[dʒ]	Wie *dsch* in *Dschungel*	gem [dʒɛm] jail [dʒel]
[ð]	*d* als Reibelaut ausgesprochen	this [ðɪs] Father ['faðər]
[f]	Wie *f* in *fett*	face [fes] phone [fon]
[g]	Wie *g* in *gehen*	go [go] get [gɛt]
[h]	Wie *h* in *Haus*	hot [hɑt] alcohol ['ælkə‚hɔl]
[j]	Wie *j* in *ja*	yes [jɛs] unit ['junɪt]
[k]	Wie *k* in *kann*	cat [kæt] chord [kɔrd] kill [kɪl]
[l]	Wie *l* in *lang*, aber mit angehobenem Zungenrücken	late [let] allow [ə'laʊ]
[m]	Wie *m* in *mehr*	more [mor] command [kə'mænd]
[n]	Wie *n* in *Nest*	nest [nɛst] manner ['mænər]
[ŋ]	Wie *ng* in *singen*	king [kɪŋ] conquer ['kɑŋkər]
[p]	Wie *p* in *Pech*	pen [pɛn] cap [kæp]
[r]	Im Gegensatz zum deutschen gerollten Zungenspitzen– oder Zäpfchen–r, ist das englische *r* mit retroflexer Zungenstel- lung und gerundeten Lippen zu artikulieren.	run [rʌn] far [fɑr] art [ɑrt] carry ['kæri]
[s]	Wie *s* in *es*	send [sɛnd] cellar ['sɛlər]
[ʃ]	Wie *sch* in *Schule*	shall [ʃæl] machine [mə'ʃin] nation ['neʃən]
[t]	Wie *t* in *Tee*	ten [tɛn] dropped [drɑpt]
[tʃ]	Wie *tsch* in *deutsch*	child [tʃaɪld] much [mʌtʃ] nature ['netʃər]
[θ]	Ist als stimmloser linguadentaler Lispellaut zu artikulieren	think [θɪŋk] truth [truθ]
[v]	Wie *w* in *was*	vest [vɛst] over ['ovər] of [ɑv]
[w]	Ist als Halbvokal zu artikulieren	work [wʌrk] tweed [twid] queen [kwin]
[z]	Ist stimmhaft zu artikulieren wie *s* in *so*	zeal [zil] busy ['bɪzi] his [hɪz] winds [wɪndz]
[ʒ]	Wie *j* in *Jalousie*	azure ['eʒər] measure ['mɛʒər]

Aussprache der zusammengesetzten Wörter

Im englisch-deutschen Teil dieses Wörterbuches ist die Aussprache aller einfachen englischen Wörter in einer Neufassung der Lautzeichen des Internationa-
len Phonetischen Alphabets in eckigen Klammern angegeben.

Außer den mit Präfixen, Suffixen und Wortbildungselementen gebildeten Zusammensetzungen gibt es im Englischen drei Arten von zusammengesetzten Wörtern: (1) zusammengeschriebene, z.B. **bookcase** Bücherregal, (2) mit Bindestrich geschriebene, z.B. **short-circuit** kurzschließen, und (3) getrennt geschriebene, z.B. **post card** Postkarte. Die Aussprache der englischen zusammengesetzten Wörter ist nicht angegeben, sofern die Aussprache der Bestandteile an der Stelle angegeben ist, wo sie als selbständige Stichwörter erscheinen; angegeben ist jedoch die Betonung durch Haupt- und Nebentonakzent und zwar jeweils am Ende der betonten Silben, z.B. **book′case′, short′-cir′cuit, post′ card′.**
In Hauptwörtern, in denen der Nebenton auf den Bestandteilen **–man** und **–men** liegt, wird der Vokal dieser Bestandteile wie in den Wörtern **man** und **men** ausgesprochen, z.B. **mailman** [′mel͵mæn] und **mailmen** [′mel͵mɛn]. In Hauptwörtern, in denen diese Bestandteile unbetont bleiben, wird der Vokal beider Bestandteile als schwa ausgesprochen, z.B. **policeman** [pə′lismən] und **policemen** [pə′lismən]. Es gibt Hauptwörter, in denen diese Bestandteile entweder mit dem Nebenton oder unbetont ausgesprochen werden, z.B. **doorman** [′dor͵mæn] oder [′dormən] und **doormen** [′dor͵men] oder [′dormən]. In diesem Wörterbuch ist die Lautschrift für diese Wörter nicht angegeben, sofern sie für den ersten Bestandteil dort angeführt ist, wo er als Stichwort erscheint; angegeben sind jedoch Haupt- und Nebenton:

> **mail′man** s (–men′)
> **police′man** s (–men)
> **door′man′** & **door′man** s (–men′ & –men)

Aussprache des Partizip Perfekt

Bei Wörtern, die auf **–ed** (oder **–d** nach stummem e) enden und nach den nachstehenden Regeln ausgesprochen werden, ist die Aussprache in diesem Wörterbuch nicht angegeben, sofern sie für die endungslose Form dort angegeben ist, wo diese als Stichwort erscheint. Die Doppelschreibung des Schlußkonsonanten nach einfachem betontem Vokal hat keinen Einfluß auf die Aussprache der Endung **–ed.**
Die Endung **–ed** (oder **–d** nach stummem e) der Vergangenheit, des Partizip Perfekt und gewisser Adjektive hat drei verschiedene Aussprachen je nach dem Klang des Konsonanten am Stammende.
1) Wenn der Stamm auf einen stimmhaften Konsonanten mit Ausnahme von [d] ausgeht, nämlich [b], [g], [l], [m], [n], [ŋ], [r], [v], [z], [ʒ], oder auf einen Vokal ausgeht, wird **–ed** als [d] ausgesprochen.

KLANG DES STAMMENDES	INFINITIV	VERGANGENHEIT UND PARTIZIP PERFEKT
[b]	ebb [ɛb] rob [rɑb] robe [rob]	ebbed [ɛbd] robbed [rɑbd] robed [robd]
[g]	egg [ɛg] sag [sæg]	egged [ɛgd] sagged [sægd]
[l]	mail [mel] scale [skel]	mailed [meld] scaled [skeld]
[m]	storm [stɔrm] bomb [bɑm] name [nem]	stormed [stɔrmd] bombed [bɑmd] named [nemd]
[n]	tan [tæn] sign [saɪn] mine [maɪn]	tanned [tænd] signed [saɪnd] mined [maɪnd]
[ŋ]	hang [hæŋ]	hanged [hæŋd]
[r]	fear [fɪr] care [kɛr]	feared [fɪrd] cared [kɛrd]
[v]	rev [rɛv] save [sev]	revved [rɛvd] saved [sevd]
[z]	buzz [bʌz]	buzzed [bʌzd]
[ð]	smooth [smuð] bathe [beð]	smoothed [smuðd] bathed [beðd]
[ʒ]	massage [mə′sɑʒ]	massaged [mə′sɑʒd]
[dʒ]	page [pedʒ]	paged [pedʒd]
Klang des Vokals	key [ki] sigh [saɪ] paw [pɔ]	keyed [kid] sighed [saɪd] pawed [pɔd]

2) Wenn der Stamm auf einen stimmlosen Konsonanten mit Ausnahme von [t] ausgeht, nämlich: [f], [k], [p], [s], [θ], [ʃ] oder [tʃ], wird –ed als [t] ausgesprochen.

KLANG DES STAMMENDES	INFINITIV	VERGANGENHEIT UND PARTIZIP PERFEKT
[f]	loaf [lof] knife [naɪf]	loafed [loft] knifed [naɪft]
[k]	back [bæk] bake [bek]	backed [bækt] baked [bekt]
[p]	cap [kæp] wipe [waɪp]	capped [kæpt] wiped [waɪpt]
[s]	hiss [hɪs] mix [mɪks]	hissed [hɪst] mixed [mɪkst]
[θ]	lath [læθ]	lathed [læθt]
[ʃ]	mash [mæʃ]	mashed [mæʃt]
[tʃ]	match [mætʃ]	matched [mætʃt]

3) Wenn der Stamm auf einen Dentallaut ausgeht, nämlich: [t] oder [d], wird –ed als [ɪd] oder [əd] ausgesprochen.

KLANG DES STAMMENDES	INFINITIV	VERGANGENHEIT UND PARTIZIP PERFEKT
[t]	wait [wet] mate [met]	waited ['wetɪd] mated ['metɪd]
[d]	mend [mɛnd] wade [wed]	mended ['mɛndɪd] waded ['wedɪd]

Es ist zu beachten, daß die Doppelschreibung des Schlußkonsonanten nach einem einfachen betonten Vokal die Aussprache der Endung –ed nicht beeinflußt: **batted** ['bætɪd], **dropped** [drɑpt], **robbed** [rɑbd].

Diese Regeln gelten auch für zusammengesetzte Adjektive, die auf –ed enden. Für diese Adjektive ist nur die Betonung angegeben, sofern die Aussprache der beiden Bestandteile ohne die Endung –ed dort angegeben ist, wo sie als Stichwörter erscheinen, z.B. **o'pen-mind'ed.**

Es ist jedoch zu beachten, daß bei manchen Adjektiven, deren Stamm auf einen anderen Konsonanten als [d] oder [t] ausgeht, das –ed als [ɪd] ausgesprochen wird; in diesem Fall ist die volle Aussprache in phonetischer Umschrift angegeben, z.B. **blessed** ['blɛsɪd], **crabbed** ['kræbɪd].

PART TWO

Englisch–Deutsch

A

A, a [e] s erster Buchstabe des englischen Alphabets; (mus) A n; A flat As n; A sharp Ais n

a [e], [ə] indef art ein ‖ prep pro; once a year einmal im Jahr

abandon [ə'bændən] s—with a. rückhaltlos ‖ tr (forsake) verlassen; (give up) aufgeben; (a child) aussetzen; (a position) (mil) überlassen; a. oneself to sich ergeben (dat)

abase [ə'bes] tr demütigen

abasement [ə'besmənt] s Demütigung f

abashed [ə'bæʃt] adj fassungslos

abate [ə'bet] tr mäßigen ‖ intr nachlassen

abbess ['æbɪs] s Äbtissin f

abbey ['æbi] s Abtei f

abbot ['æbət] s Abt m

abbreviate [ə'brivɪ ˌet] tr abkürzen

abbreviation [ə ˌbrivɪ'eʃən] s Abkürzung f

ABC's [ˌe ˌbi'siz] spl Abc n

abdicate ['æbdɪ ˌket] tr niederlegen; (a right, claim) verzichten auf (acc) ‖ intr abdanken

abdomen ['æbdəmən] s Unterleib m

abdominal [æb'dɑmɪnəl] adj Unterleibs-

abduct [æb'dʌkt] tr entführen

abet [ə'bet] v (pret & pp abetted; ger abetting) tr (a person) aufhetzen; (a crime) Vorschub leisten (dat)

abeyance [ə'be·əns] s—in a. in der Schwebe

ab·hor [æb'hər] v (pret & pp –horred; ger -horring) tr verabscheuen

abhorrent [æb'hərənt] adj verhaßt

abide [ə'baɪd] v (pret & pp abode [ə'bod] & abided) intr—a. by (an agreement) sich halten an (acc); (a promise) halten

ability [ə'bɪlɪti] s Fähigkeit f; to the best of one's a. nach bestem Vermögen

abject [æb'dʒekt] adj (servile) unterwürfig; (poverty) äußerst

ablative ['æblətɪv] s Ablativ m

ablaze [ə'blez] adj in Flammen; (with) glänzend (vor dat); (excited) (with) erregt (vor dat)

able ['ebəl] adj fähig, tüchtig; be a. to (inf) können (inf)

able-bodied ['ebəl'bɑdid] adj kräftig; (mil) wehrfähig; a. seaman Vollmatrose m

ably ['ebli] adv mit Geschick

abnormal [æb'nərməl] adj abnorm

abnormality [ˌæbnər'mælɪti] s Ungewöhnlichkeit f; (pathol) Mißbildung f

abnor'mal psychol'ogy s Psychopathologie f

aboard [ə'bord] adv an Bord; all a.! (a ship) alles an Bord! (a bus, plane, train) alles einsteigen! ‖ prep (a ship) an Bord (genit); (a bus, train) in (dat)

abode [ə'bod] s Wohnsitz m

abolish [ə'bɑlɪʃ] tr aufheben, abschaffen

abominable [ə'bɑmɪnəbəl] adj abscheulich

aborigines [ˌæbə'rɪdʒɪ ˌniz] spl Ureinwohner pl, Urvolk n

abort [ə'bɔrt] tr (rok) vorzeitig zur Explosion bringen ‖ intr fehlgebären; (fig) fehlschlagen

abortion [ə'bɔrʃən] s Abtreibung f

abortive [ə'bɔrtɪv] adj (fig) mißlungen; prove a. fehlschlagen

abound [ə'baʊnd] intr reichlich vorhanden sein; a. in reich sein an (dat)

about [ə'baʊt] adv umher, herum; (approximately) ungefähr, etwa; be a. to (inf) im Begriff sein zu (inf) ‖ prep (around) um (acc); (concerning) über (acc); (approximately at) gegen (acc)

about' face' interj kehrt!

about'-face' s—do an a. (fig) umschwenken; complete a. (fig) völliger Umschwung m

above [ə'bʌv] adj obig ‖ adv oben, droben ‖ prep (position) über (dat); (direction) über (acc); (physically) oberhalb (genit); a. all vor allem

above'board' adj & adv ehrlich, redlich

above'-men'tioned adj obenerwähnt, obig

abrasion [ə'breʒən] s Abschleifen n; (of the skin) Abschürfung f

abrasive [ə'bresɪv] adj abschleifend; (character) auf die Nerven gehend ‖ s Schleifmittel n

abreast [ə'brest] adj & adv nebeneinander; keep a. of Schritt halten mit

abridge [ə'brɪdʒ] tr verkürzen

abridgement [ə'brɪdʒmənt] s Verkürzung f

abroad [ə'brɔd] adv im Ausland; (direction) ins Ausland; (out of doors) draußen

abrogate ['æbrə ˌget] tr abschaffen

abrupt [ə'brʌpt] adj (sudden) jäh; (curt) schroff; (change) unvermittelt; (style) abgerissen

abscess ['æbsɛs] s Geschwür n, Abszeß m

abscond [æb'skɑnd] intr (with) durchgehen (mit)

absence ['æbsəns] s Abwesenheit f; (lack) Mangel m; in the a. of in Ermangelung von (or genit)

3

ab'sence without' leave' s unerlaubte Entfernung f von der Truppe
absent ['æbsənt] *adj* abwesend; **be a.** fehlen || [æb'sɛnt] *tr*—**a. oneself** (*stay away*) fernbleiben; (*go away*) sich entfernen
absentee [,æbsən'ti] s Abwesende *mf*
ab'sent-mind'ed *adj* geistesabwesend
absolute ['æbsə,lut] *adj* absolut
absolutely ['æbsə,lutli] *adv* absolut, völlig || [,æbsə'lutli] *adv* (*coll*) ganz bestimmt, jawohl; **a. not!** keine Rede!
absolve [æb'salv] *tr* (*from sin, an obligation*) lossprechen; (*sins*) vergeben
absorb [æb'sɔrb] *tr* aufsaugen; (*a shock*) dämpfen; (*engross*) ganz in Anspruch nehmen; **be absorbed in** vertieft sein in (*acc*)
absorbent [æb'sɔrbənt] *adj* aufsaugend
absor'bent cot'ton s Verbandswatte f
absorb'ing *adj* (fig) packend
abstain [æb'sten] *intr* (**from**) sich enthalten (*genit*); (parl) sich der Stimme enthalten
abstention [æb'stɛnʃən] s (**from**) Enthaltung f (von); (parl) Stimmenthaltung f
abstinence ['æbstɪnəns] s Enthaltsamkeit f; (**from**) Enthaltung f (von)
abstinent ['æbstɪnənt] *adj* enthaltsam
abstract ['æbstrækt] *adj* abstrakt || s (*summary*) Abriß m; **in the a.** an und für sich (betrachtet) || [æb-'strækt] *tr* (*the general from the specific*) abstrahieren; (*summarize*) kurz zusammenfassen; (*purloin*) entwenden
abstruse [æb'strus] *adj* dunkel
absurd [æb'sʌrd] *adj* unsinnig
absurdity [æb'sʌrdɪti] s Unsinn m
abundance [ə'bʌndəns] s (**of**) Fülle f (von), Überfluß m (an *dat*, von)
abundant [ə'bʌndənt] *adj* reichlich; **a. in** reich an (*dat*)
abuse [ə'bjus] s (*misuse*) Mißbrauch m; (*insult*) Beschimpfung f; (*physical ill-treatment*) Mißhandlung f || [ə'bjuz] *tr* mißbrauchen; (*insult*) beschimpfen; (*ill-treat*) mißhandeln; (*a girl*) schänden
abusive [ə'bjusɪv] *adj* mißbräuchlich; (*treatment*) beleidigend; **a. language** Schimpfworte pl; **become a.** ausfällig werden
abut [ə'bʌt] v (*pret & pp* **abutted; ger abutting**) *intr*—**a. on** grenzen an (*acc*)
abutment [ə'bʌtmənt] s (*of arch*) Strebepfeiler m; (*of bridge*) Widerlager n
abyss [ə'bɪs] s Abgrund m
academic [,ækə'dɛmɪk] *adj* akademisch
academ'ic gown' s Talar m
academy [ə'kædəmi] s Akademie f
accede [æk'sid] *intr* beistimmen; **a. to** (*s.o.'s wishes*) gewähren; (*an agreement*) beitreten (*dat*); **a. to the throne** den Thron besteigen
accelerate (æk'sɛlə,ret] *tr & intr* beschleunigen

accelerator [æk'sɛlə,retər] s Gashebel m
accent ['æksɛnt] s (*stress*) Betonung f; (*peculiar pronunciation*) Akzent m || [æk'sɛnt] *tr* betonen
ac'cent mark' s Tonzeichen n, Akzent m
accentuate [æk'sɛntʃu,et] *tr* betonen
accept [æk'sɛpt] *tr* annehmen; (*one's fate, blame*) auf sich [*acc*] nehmen; (*put up with*) hinnehmen; (*recognize*) anerkennen
acceptable [æk'sɛptəbəl] *adj* annehmbar; (*pleasing*) angenehm; (*welcome*) willkommen
acceptance [æk'sɛptəns] s Annahme f; (*recognition*) Anerkennung f
access ['ækses] s Zugang m; (*to a person*) Zutritt m; (data proc) Zugriff m
accessible [æk'sɛsɪbəl] *adj* (**to**) zugänglich (für)
accession [æk'sɛʃən] s (*to an office*) Antritt m; **a. to the throne** Thronbesteigung f
accessory [æk'sɛsəri] *adj* (*subordinate*) untergeordnet; (*additional*) zusätzlich || s Zubehörteil n; (*to a crime*) Teilnehmer –in *mf*; (*after the fact*) Begünstiger –in *mf*; (*before the fact*) Anstifter –in *mf*
ac'cess road' s Zufahrtsstraße f; (*on a turnpike*) Zubringerstraße f
accident ['æksɪdənt] s (*mishap*) Unfall m; (*chance*) Zufall m; **by a.** zufälligerweise; **have an a.** verunglücken
accidental [,æksɪ'dɛntəl] *adj* zufällig; **a. death** Unfalltod m || s (mus) Versetzungszeichen n
acclaim [ə'klem] s Beifall m || *tr* (*e.g., as king*) begrüßen, akklamieren
acclamation [,æklə'meʃən] s Beifall m
acclimate ['æklɪ,met] *tr* akklimatisieren || *intr* (**to**) sich gewöhnen (an *acc*)
accommodate [ə'kamə,det] *tr* (*oblige*) aushelfen (*dat*); (*have room for*) Platz haben für
accom'modating *adj* gefällig
accommodation [ə,kamə'deʃən] s (*convenience*) Annehmlichkeit f; (*adaptation, adjustment*) Anpassung f; (*willingness to please*) Gefälligkeit f; (*compromise*) Übereinkommen n; **accommodations** (*lodgings*) Unterkunft f
accompaniment [ə'kʌmpənɪmənt] s Begleitung f
accompanist [ə'kʌmpənɪst] s Begleiter –in *mf*
accompa·ny [ə'kʌmpəni] v (*pret & pp* **–nied**) *tr* begleiten
accomplice [ə'kamplɪs] m Mitschuldige *mf*
accomplish [ə'kamplɪʃ] *tr* (*a task*) vollenden; (*a goal*) erreichen
accom'plished *adj* (*skilled*) ausgezeichnet
accomplishment [ə'kamplɪʃmənt] s (*completion*) Vollendung f; (*achievement*) Leistung f
accord [ə'kɔrd] s Übereinstimmung f; **in a. with** übereinstimmend mit; **of**

one's own a. aus eigenem Antriebe || *tr* gewähren || *intr* übereinstimmen
accordingly [ə'kɔrdɪŋli] *adv* demgemäß
accord'ing to' *prep* gemäß *(dat)*, laut *(genit* or *dat)*, nach *(dat)*
accordion [ə'kɔrdɪ·ən] *s* Akkordeon *n*
accost [ə'kɔst] *tr* ansprechen
account [ə'kaunt] *s* Rechnung *f*; *(narrative)* Erzählung *f*; *(report)* Bericht *m*; *(importance)* Bedeutung *f*; *(com)* Konto *n*; **by all accounts** nach allem, was man hört; **call to a.** zur Rechenschaft ziehen; **on a.** of wegen; **on no a.** auf keinen Fall; **render an a.** of **s.th. to s.o.** j-m Rechenschaft von etw ablegen; **settle accounts with** (coll) abrechnen mit; **take into a.** in Betracht ziehen
accountable [ə'kauntəbəl] *adj (explicable)* erklärlich; *(responsible)* **(for)** verantwortlich (für)
accountant [ə'kauntənt] *s* Rechnungsführer –in *mf*, Buchhalter –in *mf*
account'ing *s* Rechnungswesen *n*
accouterments [ə'kutərmənts] *spl* Ausrüstung *f*
accredit [ə'kredɪt] *tr (e.g., an ambassador)* beglaubigen; *(a school)* bestätigen; *(a story)* als wahr anerkennen; *(give credit for)* gutschreiben
accrue [ə'kru] *intr* anwachsen; *(said of interest)* auflaufen || *intr* sich anhäufen
accumulation [ə,kjumjə'leʃən] *s* Anhäufung *f*
accuracy ['ækjərəsi] *s* Genauigkeit *f*
accurate ['ækjərɪt] *adj* genau
accursed [ə'kʌrsɪd], [ə'kʌrst] *adj* verwünscht
accusation [,ækjə'zeʃən] *s* Anschuldigung *f*; (jur) Anklage *f*
accusative [ə'kjuzətɪv] *s* Akkusativ *m*
accuse [ə'kjuz] *tr* (of) beschuldigen *(genit)*; (jur) **(of)** anklagen (wegen)
accustom [ə'kʌstəm] *tr* **(to)** gewöhnen (an *acc*); **become accustomed to** sich gewöhnen an *(acc)*
ace [es] *s* (aer, cards) As *n*
acetate ['æsɪ,tet] *s* Azetat *n*; (tex) Azetatseide *f*
ace'tic ac'id [ə'sitɪk] *s* Essigsäure *f*
acetone ['æsɪ,ton] *s* Azeton *n*
acet'ylene torch' [ə'setɪ,lin] *s* Schweißbrenner *m*
ache [ek] *s* Schmerz *m* || *intr* schmerzen; **a. for** (coll) sich sehnen nach
achieve [ə'tʃiv] *tr* erlangen; *(success)* erzielen; *(a goal)* erreichen
achievement [ə'tʃivmənt] *s (something accomplished)* Leistung *f*; *(great deed)* Großtat *f*; *(heroic deed)* Heldentat *f*; *(of one's object)* Erreichung *f*
achieve'ment test' *s* Leistungsprüfung *f*
Achil'les' ten'don [ə'kɪlis] *s* Achillessehne *f*
acid ['æsɪd] *adj* sauer || *s* Säure *f*
acidity [ə'sɪdɪti] *s* Säure *f*, Schärfe *f*; *(of the stomach)* Magensäure *f*
ac'id test' *s* (fig) Feuerprobe *f*
acidy ['æsɪdi] *adj* säuerlich, säurig
acknowledge [æk'nɑlɪdʒ] *tr* anerken-

nen; *(admit)* zugeben; *(receipt)* bestätigen
acknowledgment [æk'nɑlɪdʒmənt] *s* Anerkennung *f*; *(e.g., of a letter)* Bestätigung *f*
acme ['ækmi] *s* Höhepunkt *m*
acne ['ækni] *s* (pathol) Akne *f*
acolyte ['ækə,laɪt] *s* Ministrant *m*
acorn ['ekɔrn] *s* Eichel *f*
acoustic(al) [ə'kustɪk(əl)] *adj* akustisch, Gehör–, Hör–
acous'tical tile' *s* Dämmplatte *f*
acoustics [ə'kustɪks] *s* & *spl* Akustik *f*
acquaint [ə'kwent] *tr*—**a. s.o. with s.th.** j–n mit etw bekanntmachen; j–m etw mitteilen; **be acquainted with** kennen; **get acquainted with** kennenlernen
acquaintance [ə'kwentəns] *s* Bekanntschaft *f*; *(person)* Bekannte *mf*
acquiesce [,ækwɪ'ɛs] *intr* **(in)** einwilligen (in *acc*)
acquiescence [,ækwɪ'esəns] *s* **(in)** Einwilligung *f* (in *acc*)
acquire [ə'kwaɪr] *tr* erwerben, sich *[dat]* anschaffen; **a. a taste for** Geschmack gewinnen an *(dat)*
acquisition [,ækwɪ'zɪʃən] *s* Anschaffung *f*
acquisitive [ə'kwɪzɪtɪv] *adj* gewinnsüchtig
acquit [ə'kwɪt] *v (pret & pp* **acquitted;** *ger* **acquitting)** *tr* freisprechen
acquittal [ə'kwɪtəl] *s* Freispruch *m*
acre ['ekər] *s* Acre *m*
acreage ['ekərɪdʒ] *s* Fläche *f*
acrid ['ækrɪd] *adj* beißend, scharf
acrobat ['ækrə,bæt] *s* Akrobat –in *mf*
acrobatic [,ækrə'bætɪk] *adj* akrobatisch || **acrobatics** *spl* Akrobatik *f*; (aer) Kunstflug *m*
acronym ['ækrənɪm] *s* Akronym *n*
across [ə'krɔs] *adv* herüber, hinüber; **a. from** gegenüber *(dat)*; **ten feet a.** zehn Fuß im Durchmesser || *prep* (quer) über *(acc)*; *(on the other side of)* jenseits *(genit)*; **come a.** (a person) treffen; *(a thing)* stoßen auf *(acc)*; **come a. with it!** *(say it!)* heraus damit!; *(give it!)* her damit!
across'-the-board' *adj* allgemein
acrostic [ə'krɔstɪk] *s* Akrostichon *n*
act [ækt] *s* Tat *f*, Handlung *f*; (coll) Theater *n*; (jur) Gesetz *n*; (telv) Nummer *f*; (theat) Akt *m*, Aufzug *m*; **catch in the act** auf frischer Tat ertappen || *tr* spielen; || *intr (take action)* handeln; *(function)* wirken; *(behave)* (like) sich benehmen (wie); (theat & fig) Theater spielen; **act as** dienen als; **act as if** so tun, als ob; **act on** *(follow)* befolgen; *(affect)* (ein)wirken auf *(acc)*
act'ing *adj* stellvertretend; (theat) Bühnen– || *s (as an art)* Schauspielkunst *f*
action ['ækʃən] *s* Tätigkeit *f*, Tat *f*; *(effect)* Wirkung *f*; (jur) Klage *f*; (mil) Gefecht *n*; (tech) Wirkungsweise *f*; **go into a.** eingreifen; **put out of a.** (mil) außer Gefecht setzen; (tech) außer Betrieb setzen; **see a.** (mil) an der Front kämpfen

activate ['æktɪ‚vet] *tr* aktivieren; (mil) aufstellen

active ['æktɪv] *adj* tätig; (*member*) ordentlich; (gram, mil) aktiv

ac'tive voice' *s* Tätigkeitsform *f*

activist ['æktɪvɪst] *s* Aktivist –in *mf*

activity [æk'tɪvɪti] *s* Tätigkeit *f*

act' of God' *s* höhere Gewalt *f*

act' of war' *s* Angriffshandlung *f*

actor ['æktər] *s* Schauspieler *m*

actress ['æktrɪs] *s* Schauspielerin *f*

actual ['æktʃu‚əl] *adj* wirklich

actually ['æktʃu‚əli] *adv* (*really*) wirklich; (*as a matter of fact*) eigentlich

actuary ['æktʃu‚ɛri] *s* Aktuar –in *mf*

actuate ['æktʃu‚et] *tr* in Bewegung setzen; (*incite*) antreiben

acumen [ə'kjumən] *s* Scharfsinn *m*

acupuncture ['ækjə‚pʌŋkt/ər] *s* Akupunktur *f*

acute [ə'kjut] *adj* (*stage, appendicitis*) akut; (*pain*) scharf; (*need*) vordringlich; (*vision*) scharf; (*hearing*) fein; (*problem*) brennend; (*shortage*) bedenklich; (*angle*) spitz

A.D. *abbr* n. Chr. (*nach Christus*)

ad [æd] *s* (coll) Anzeige *f*; **put an ad in the papers** inserieren

adage ['ædɪdʒ] *s* Sprichwort *n*

adamant ['ædəmənt] *adj* unnachgiebig

Ad'am's ap'ple ['ædəmz] *s* Adamsapfel *m*

adapt [ə'dæpt] *tr* (to) anpassen (*dat* or an *acc*); **a. to the stage** für die Bühne bearbeiten; **a. to the screen** verfilmen || *intr* sich anpassen

adaptation [‚ædæp'teʃən] *s* (*adjustment*) (to) Anpassung *f* (an *acc*); (*reworking, rewriting*) (for) Bearbeitung *f* (für)

adapter [ə'dæptər] *s* Zwischenstück *n*; (elec) Zwischenstecker *m*

add [æd] *tr* hinzufügen; (math) addieren; **add** (*e.g., 10%*) **to the price** auf den Preis aufschlagen; **add up** zusammenrechnen || *intr* (math) addieren; **add to** (*in number*) vermehren; (*in size*) vergrößern; **add up** (coll) stimmen; **add up to** betragen

adder ['ædər] *s* Natter *f*, Otter *f*

addict ['ædɪkt] *s* Süchtige *mf* || [ə'dɪkt] *tr*—**a. oneself to** sich ergeben (*dat*)

addict'ed *adj* ergeben; **a. to drugs** rauschgiftsüchtig

addiction [ə'dɪkʃən] *s* (to) Sucht *f* (nach)

add'ing machine' *s* Addiermaschine *f*

addition [ə'dɪʃən] *s* Hinzufügung *f*, Zusatz *m*; (*to a family, possessions*) Zuwachs *m*; (*to a building*) Anbau *m*; (math) Addition *f*; **in a.** außerdem; **in a. to** außer

additional [ə'dɪʃənəl] *adj* zusätzlich

additive ['ædɪtɪv] *s* Zusatz *m*

address [ə'drɛs], ['ædrɛs] *s* Adresse *f*, Anschrift *f* || [ə'drɛs] *s* Rede *f*; **deliver an a.** e–e Rede halten || *tr* (*a letter*) (to) adressieren (an *acc*); (*words, a question*) (to) richten (an *acc*); (*an audience*) e–e Ansprache halten an (*acc*)

adduce [ə'd(j)us] *tr* anführen

adenoids ['ædə‚nɔɪdz] *spl* Polypen *pl*

adept [ə'dɛpt] *adj* (in) geschickt (in *dat*)

adequate ['ædɪkwɪt] *adj* angemessen; (to) ausreichend (für)

adhere [æd'hɪr] *intr* (to) haften (an *dat*); (fig) (to) festhalten (an *dat*)

adherence [æd'hɪrəns] *s* (to) Festhalten *n* (an *dat*); (fig) (to) Festhalten *n* (an *dat*), Beharren *n* (bei)

adherent [æd'hɪrənt] *s* Anhänger –in *mf*

adhesion [æd'hiʒən] *s* (*sticking*) Ankleben *n*; (*loyalty*) Anhänglichkeit *f*; (pathol, phys) Adhäsion *f*

adhesive [æd'hisɪv] *adj* anklebend || *s* Klebemittel *n*, Klebstoff *m*

adhe'sive tape' *s* Heftpflaster *m*

adieu [ə'd(j)u] *s* (**adieus** & **adieux**) Lebewohl *n* || *interj* lebe wohl!

adjacent [ə'dʒesənt] *adj* (to) angrenzend (an *acc*); (*angles*) Neben–

adjective ['ædʒɪktɪv] *s* Eigenschaftswort *n*, Adjektiv *n*

adjoin [ə'dʒɔɪn] *tr* angrenzen an (*acc*) || *intr* angrenzen, naheliegen

adjoin'ing *adj* angrenzend; **a. rooms** Nebenzimmer *pl*

adjourn [ə'dʒʌrn] *tr* vertagen || *intr* sich vertagen

adjournment [ə'dʒʌrnmənt] *s* Vertagung *f*

adjudge [ə'dʒʌdʒ] *tr* (*a prize*) zusprechen; **a. s.o. guilty** j–n für schuldig erklären

adjudicate [ə'dʒudɪ‚ket] *tr* gerichtlich entscheiden

adjunct ['ædʒʌŋkt] *s* (to) Zusatz *m* (zu)

adjust [ə'dʒʌst] *tr* (*to the right position*) einstellen; (*to an alternate position*) verstellen; (*fit*) (to) anpassen (*dat* or an *acc*); (*differences*) ausgleichen; (*an account*) bereinigen; (*ins*) berechnen || *intr* (to) sich anpassen (*dat* or an *acc*)

adjustable [ə'dʒʌstəbəl] *adj* verstellbar

adjuster [ə'dʒʌstər] *s* (ins) Schadenssachverständiger –in *mf*

adjustment [ə'dʒʌstmənt] *s* (to) Anpassung *f* (*dat* or an *acc*); (*of an account*) Bereinigung *f*; (ins) Berechnung *f*; (mach) Einstellung *f*

adjutant ['ædʒətənt] *s* Adjutant *m*

ad-lib [‚æd'lɪb] *v* (*pret & pp*) **–libbed**; *ger* **–libbing**) *tr & intr* improvisieren

ad-man ['ædmən] *s* (**–men**) Werbefachmann *m*; (*writer*) Werbetexter *m*

administer [æd'mɪnɪstər] *tr* verwalten; (*help*) leisten; (*medicine*) eingeben; (*an oath*) abnehmen; (*punishment*) verhängen; (*a sacrament*) spenden; **a. justice** Recht sprechen || *intr*— **a. to** dienen (*dat*)

administration [æd‚mɪnɪs'treʃən] *s* (*of an institution*) Verwaltung *f*; (*of an official*) Amtsführung *f*; (*government*) Regierung *f*; (*period of government*) Regierungszeit *f*; (*of a president*) Amtszeit *f*; (*of tests*) Durchführung *f*; (*of an oath*) Abnahme *f*; (*of a sacrament*) Spendung *f*; **a. of justice** Rechtspflege *f*

administrator [æd'mɪnɪs‚tretər] *s* Verwalter –in *mf*
admiral ['ædmɪrəl] *s* Admiral *m*
admiration [‚ædmɪ're/ən] *s* Bewunderung *f*
admire [æd'maɪr] *tr* (**for**) bewundern (wegen)
admirer [æd'maɪrər] *s* Bewunderer –in *mf;* (*of a woman*) Verehrer *m*
admissible [æd'mɪsɪbəl] *adj* (& jur) zulässig
admission [æd'mɪ/ən] *s* (*entry*) Eintritt *m;* (*permission to enter*) Eintrittserlaubnis *f;* (*entry fee*) Eintrittsgebühr *f;* (*of facts*) Anerkennung *f;* (*of guilt*) Eingeständis *n;* (*enrollment*) (**to, into**) Aufnahme *f* (in *acc*); (**to**) (*a profession*) Zulassung *f* (zu)
ad·mit [æd'mɪt] *v* (*pret & pp* **–mitted;** *ger* **–mitting**) *tr* (hin)einlassen; (**to**) (*a hospital, a society*) aufnehmen (in *acc*); (**to**) (*a profession*) zulassen (zu); (*accept*) anerkennen; (*concede*) zugeben; (*a crime, guilt*) eingestehen || *intr*—**a. of** zulassen
admittance [æd'mɪtəns] *s* Eintritt *m;* **no a.** Eintritt verboten
admittedly [æd'mɪtɪdli] *adv* anerkanntermaßen
admixture [æd'mɪkst/ər] *s* Beimischung *f*
admonish [æd'manɪ/] *tr* ermahnen
admonition [‚ædmə'nɪ/ən] *s* Ermahnung *f*
ado [ə'du] *s* Getue *n;* **much ado about nothing** viel Lärm um nichts; **without further ado** ohne weiteres
adobe [ə'dobi] *s* Lehmstein *m*
adolescence [‚ædə'lesəns] *s* Jugendalter *n*
adolescent [‚ædə'lesənt] *adj* jugendlich || *s* Jugendliche *mf*
adopt [ə'dapt] *tr* (*a child*) adoptieren; (*an idea*) annehmen
adopt′ed child′ *s* Adoptivkind *n*
adoption [ə'dap/ən] *s* (*of a child*) Adoption *f;* (*of an idea*) Annahme *f*
adorable [ə'dorəbəl] *adj* anbetungswürdig; (coll) entzückend
adore [ə'dor] *tr* anbeten; (coll) entzückend finden
adorn [ə'dɔrn] *tr* schmücken
adornment [ə'dɔrnmənt] *s* Schmuck *m*
adrenaline [ə'drenəlɪn] *s* Adrenalin *n*
adrift [ə'drɪft] *adj*—**be a.** treiben; (fig) weder aus noch ein wissen
adroit [ə'drɔɪt] *adj* geschickt, gewandt
adulation [‚ædjə'le/ən] *s* Schmeichelei *f*
adult [ə'dʌlt], ['ædʌlt] *adj* erwachsen || *s* Erwachsene *mf*
adult′ educa′tion *s* Erwachsenenbildung *f*
adulterate [ə'dʌltə‚ret] *tr* verfälschen; (*e.g., wine*) panschen
adulterer [ə'dʌltərər] *s* Ehebrecher *m*
adulteress [ə'dʌltərɪs] *s* Ehebrecherin *f*
adulterous [ə'dʌltərəs] *adj* ehebrecherisch
adultery [ə'dʌltəri] *s* Ehebruch *m*
advance [æd'væns] *s* Fortschritt *m;* (*money*) Vorschuß *m;* **in a.** im vor-

aus; **make advances to** (*e.g., a girl*) Annäherungsversuche machen bei || *tr* vorrücken; (*a clock*) vorstellen; (*money*) vorschießen; (*a date*) aufschieben; (*an opinion*) vorbringen; (*s.o.'s interests*) fördern; (*in rank*) befördern || *intr* vorrücken
advancement [æd'vænsmənt] *s* Fortschritt *m;* (*promotion*) Beförderung *f;* (*of a cause*) Förderung *f*
advance′ pay′ment *s* Voraus(be)zahlung *f*
advantage [æd'væntɪdʒ] *s* Vorteil *m;* **be of a.** nützlich sein; **take a. of** ausnutzen; **to a.** vorteilhaft
advantageous [‚ædvən'tedʒəs] *adj* vorteilhaft
advent ['ædvent] *s* Ankunft *f;* **Advent** Advent *m*, Adventszeit *f*
adventure [æd'vent/ər] *s* Abenteuer *n*
adventurer [æd'vent/ərər] *s* Abenteurer *m*
adventuress [æd'vent/ərɪs] *s* Abenteurerin *f*
adventurous [æd'vent/ərəs] *adj* (*person*) abenteuerlustig; (*undertaking*) abenteuerlich
adverb ['ædvʌrb] *s* Umstandswort *n*
adverbial [æd'vʌrbɪəl] *adj* adverbial
adversary ['ædvər‚seri] *s* Gegner –in *mf*
adverse [æd'vʌrs], ['ædvʌrs] *adj* ungünstig, nachteilig
adversity [æd'vʌrsɪti] *s* Unglück *n*, Not *f*
advertise ['ædvər‚taɪz] *tr* Reklame machen für || *intr* Reklame machen; **a. for** durch Inserat suchen
advertisement [‚ædvər'taɪzmənt], [æd'vʌrtɪsmənt] *s* Anzeige *f*, Reklame *f*
ad′vertising a′gency *s* Reklamebüro *n*
ad′vertising campaign′ *s* Werbfeldzug *m*
ad′vertising man′ *s* (*solicitor*) Anzeigenvermittler *m;* (*writer*) Werbetexter *m*
advice [æd'vaɪs] *s* Rat *m*, Ratschlag *m;* **a piece of a.** ein Rat *m;* **get a. from** sich [*dat*] Rat holen bei; **give a. to** raten (*dat*)
advisable [æd'vaɪzəbəl] *adj* ratsam
advise [æd'vaɪz] *tr* raten (*dat*); (**of**) benachrichtigen (*über acc*); (**on**) beraten (*über acc*); **a. s.o. against s.th.** j–m von etw abraten
advisement [æd'vaɪzmənt] *s*—**take under a.** in Betracht ziehen
adviser [æd'vaɪzər] *s* Berater –in *mf*
advisory [æd'vaɪzəri] *adj* Beratungs-
advi′sory board′ *s* Beirat *m*
advocate ['ædvə‚ket] *s* Fürsprecher –in *mf;* (jur) Advokat –in *mf* || *tr* befürworten
aeon ['i·ən], ['i·an] *s* Äon *m*
aerial ['erɪ·əl] *adj* Luft– || *s* Antenne *f*
aerodynamic [‚erodaɪ'næmɪk] *adj* aerodynamisch || **aerodynamics** *s* Aerodynamik *f*
aeronautic(al) [‚erə'nɔtɪk(əl)] *adj* aeronautisch || **aeronautics** *s* Aeronautik *f*, Luftfahrt *f*
aerosol ['erə‚sol] *s* Sprühdose *f*

aerospace ['erəspes] *adj* Raum–
aesthetic [ɛs'θetɪk] *adj* ästhetisch ‖
aesthetics *s* Ästhetik *f*
afar [ə'fɑr] *adv*—a. off weit weg; **from
a.** von weit her
affable ['æfəbəl] *adj* leutselig
affair [ə'fɛr] *s* Angelegenheit *f*; (*event,
performance*) Veranstaltung *f*; (*romantic involvement*) Verhältnis *n*
affect [ə'fɛkt] *tr* (*influence*) berühren;
(*injuriously*) angreifen; (*pretend*)
vortäuschen
affectation [,æfɛk'teʃən] *s* Geziertheit
f
affect'ed *adj* affektiert
affection [ə'fɛkʃən] *s* (**for**) Zuneigung
f (zu); (pathol) Erkrankung *f*
affectionate [ə'fɛkʃənɪt] *adj* liebevoll
affidavit [,æfɪ'devɪt] *s* (schriftliche)
eidesstattliche Erklärung *f*
affiliate [ə'fɪlɪ,et] *s* Zweiggesellschaft
f ‖ *tr* angliedern ‖ *intr* sich angliedern
affinity [ə'fɪnɪti] *s* Verwandschaft *f*
affirm [ə'fʌrm] *tr & intr* behaupten
affirmation [,æfər'meʃən] *s* Behauptung *f*
affirmative [ə'fʌrmətɪv] *adj* bejahend
‖ *s* Bejahung *f*; **in the a.** bejahend,
positiv
affix [ə'fɪks] *tr* (*a seal*) aufdrücken;
(**to**) befestigen (an *dat*), anheften (an
acc)
afflict [ə'flɪkt] *tr* plagen; **afflicted with**
erkrankt an (*dat*)
affliction [ə'flɪkʃən] *s* Elend *n*, Leiden
n; (*grief*) Betrübnis *f*
affluence ['æfluˑəns] *s* Wohlstand *m*
affluent ['æfluˑənt] *adj* wohlhabend
af'fluent socie'ty *s* Wohlstandsgesell-
schaft *f*
afford [ə'fɔrd] *tr* (*confer*) gewähren;
(*time*) erübrigen; (*be able to meet
the expense of*) sich [*dat*] leisten
affront [ə'frʌnt] *s* Beleidigung *f* ‖ *tr*
beleidigen
afire [ə'faɪr] *adj & adv* in Flammen
aflame [ə'flem] *adj & adv* in Flammen
afloat [ə'flot] *adj* flott, schwimmend;
(*awash*) überschwemmt; (*at sea*) auf
dem Meer; (*in circulation*) im Umlauf; **keep a.** (& fig) über Wasser
halten; **stay a.** (& fig) sich über
Wasser halten
afoot [ə'fut] *adj & adv* (*on foot*) zu
Fuß; (*in progress*) im Gange
aforesaid [ə'fɔr,sed] *adj* vorerwähnt
afoul [ə'faul] *adj* (*entangled*) verwickelt ‖ *adv*—**run a.** of the law mit
dem Gesetz in Konflikt geraten
afraid [ə'fred] *adj* ängstlich; **be a.** (**of**)
(*inf*) sich scheuen zu (*inf*)
afresh [ə'frɛʃ] *adv* aufs neue
Africa ['æfrɪkə] *s* Afrika *n*
African ['æfrɪkən] *adj* afrikanisch ‖
s Afrikaner –in *mf*
aft [æft] *adv* (nach) achtern
after ['æftər] *adj* später; (naut) achter
‖ *adv* nachher, darauf ‖ *prep* nach
(*dat*); **a. all** immerhin; **a. that** darauf; **be a. s.o.** hinter j–m her sein ‖
conj nachdem
af'ter-din'ner speech' *s* Tischrede *f*

af'tereffect' *s* Nachwirkung *f*; **have an
a.** nachwirken
af'terlife' *s* (*later life*) zukünftiges
Leben *n*; (*life after death*) Leben *n*
nach dem Tode
aftermath ['æftər,mæθ] *s* Nach-
wirkungen *pl*; (agr) Grummet *n*
af'ternoon' *s* Nachmittag *m*; **in the a.**
am Nachmittag, nachmittags; **this a.**
heute nachmittag
af'ter-shave' lo'tion *s* Rasierwasser *n*
af'tertaste' *s* Nachgeschmack *m*
af'terthought' *s* nachträglicher Einfall
m
afterward(s) ['æftərwərd(z)] *adv* später
af'terworld' *s* Jenseits *n*
again [ə'gɛn] *adv* wieder, noch einmal;
half as much a. anderthalbmal so
viel; **what's his name a.?** wie heißt
er doch schnell?
against [ə'gɛnst] *prep* gegen (*acc*); **a.
it** dagegen; **a. the rules** regelwidrig;
be up a. it (coll) in der Klemme sein
age [edʒ] *s* Alter *n*, Lebensalter *n*;
(*period of history*) Zeitalter *n*; **at the
age of** mit, im Alter von; **come of
age** mündig werden; **for ages** e-e
Ewigkeit; **of age** volljährig; **of the
same age** gleichaltrig; **twenty years
of age** zwanzig Jahre alt ‖ *tr* alt
machen; (*wine*) ablagern ‖ *intr*
altern; (*said of wine*) lagern
aged [edʒd] *adj* alt, e.g., **a. three** drei
Jahre alt ‖ ['edʒɪd] *adj* bejahrt
age' lim'it *s* Altersgrenze *f*
agency ['edʒənsi] *s* (*instrumentality*)
Vermittlung *f*; (*activity*) Tätigkeit
f; (adm) Behörde *f*; (com) Agentur *f*
agenda [ə'dʒɛndə] *s* Tagesordnung *f*
agent ['edʒənt] *s* Handelnde *mf*; (biol,
chem) Agens *n*; (com) Agent –in *mf*
agglomeration [ə,glɑmə'reʃən] *s* Anhäufung *f*
aggravate ['ægrə,vet] *tr* erschweren,
verschärfen; (coll) ärgern
aggravation [,ægrə've ʃən] *s* Erschwe-
rung *f*, Verschärfung *f*; (coll) Ärger
m
aggregate ['ægrɪ,get] *adj* gesamt ‖ *s*
Aggregat *n*; **in the a.** im ganzen ‖ *tr*
anhäufen
aggression [ə'grɛʃən] *s* Aggression *f*
aggressive [ə'grɛsɪv] *adj* aggressiv
aggressor [ə'grɛsər] *s* Aggressor *m*
aggrieved [ə'grivd] *adj* (*saddened*) betrübt; (jur) geschädigt
aghast [ə'gæst] *adj* entsetzt
agile ['ædʒɪl] *adj* flink; (*mind*) rege
agility [ə'dʒɪlɪti] *s* Flinkheit *f*; (*of the
mind*) Regsamkeit *f*
agitate ['ædʒɪ,tet] *tr* hin und her bewegen; (fig) beunruhigen ‖ *intr* agitieren
agitator ['ædʒɪ,tetər] *s* Unruhestifter
–in *mf*; (*in a washer*) Rührapparat *m*
aglow [ə'glo] *adj & adv* (er)glühend
agnostic [æg'nɑstɪk] *adj* agnostisch ‖
s Agnostiker –in *mf*
ago [ə'go] *adv* vor (*dat*), e.g., **a year
ago** vor e–m Jahr; **long ago** vor langer Zeit
agog [ə'gɑg] *adv* gespannt, erpicht
agonize ['ægə,naɪz] *intr* sich quälen

ag'onizing *adj* qualvoll
agony ['ægəni] *s* Qual *f;* (*death struggle*) Todeskampf *m*
agrarian [ə'grerɪ·ən] *adj* landwirtschaftlich, agrarisch
agree [ə'gri] *intr* übereinstimmen; **a. on** (or **upon**) sich einigen über (*acc*); **a. to** zustimmen (*dat*); **a. to** (*inf*) übereinkommen zu (*inf*); **a. with** (& gram) übereinstimmen mit; (*affect one's health*) bekommen (*dat*)
agreeable [ə'gri·əbəl] *adj* angenehm
agreed' *interj* abgemacht!, einverstanden!
agreement [ə'grimənt] *s* Abkommen *n*, Vereinbarung *f;* (*contract*) Vertrag *m;* (& gram) Übereinstimmung *f*
agriculture ['ægrɪ ‚kʌltʃər] *s* Landwirtschaft *f*, Ackerbau *m*
aground [ə'graund] *adv* gestrandet; **run a.** stranden, auf Grund laufen
ahead [ə'hɛd] *adj* & *adv* (*in the front*) vorn; (*to the front*) nach vorn; (*in advance*) voraus; (*forward*) vorwärts; **a. of** vor (*dat*); **get a.** vorwärtskommen; **go a.** vorangehen; **go a.!** los!; **go a. with** fortfahren mit; **look a.** an die Zukunft denken
ahoy [ə'hɔɪ] *interj* ahoi!
aid [ed] *s* Hilfe *f*, Beihilfe *f* ‖ *tr* helfen (*dat*); **aid and abet** Vorschub leisten (*dat*)
aide [ed] *s* Gehilfe *m*
aide-de-camp ['eddə'kæmp] *s* (**aides-de-camp**) Adjutant *m*
ail [el] *tr* schmerzen; **what ails you?** was fehlt Ihnen? ‖ *intr* (*have pain*) Schmerzen haben; (*be ill*) erkrankt sein
ail'ing *adj* leidend, kränklich
ailment ['elmənt] *s* Leiden *n*
aim [em] *s* Ziel *n;* (fig) Ziel *n*, Zweck *m;* **is your aim good?** zielen Sie gut?; **take aim** zielen ‖ *tr* (*a gun, words*) (**at**) richten auf (*acc*); **aim to** (*inf*) beabsichtigen zu (*inf*) ‖ *intr* zielen; **aim at** (& fig) zielen auf (*acc*); **aim for** streben nach
aimless ['emlɪs] *adj* ziellos, planlos
air [er] *s* Luft *f;* (mus) Melodie *f;* **be on the air** (*an announcer*) senden; (*a program*) gesendet werden; **be up in the air** (fig) in der Luft hängen; **by air** per Flugzeug; **go off the air** die Sendung beenden; **go on the air** die Sendung beginnen; **in the open air** im Freien; **put on airs** groß tun; **walk on air** sich wie im Himmel fühlen ‖ *tr* lüften
air'base' *s* Flugstützpunkt *m*
airborne ['ɛr ‚bɔrn] *adj* aufgestiegen; **a. troops** Luftlandetruppen *pl*
air'brake' *s* Druckluftbremse *f*
air'-condi'tion *tr* klimatisieren
air' condi'tioner *s* Klimaanlage *f*
air' cov'er *s* Luftsicherung *f*
air'craft' *s* (*pl* **aircraft**) Flugzeug *n*
air'craft car'rier *s* Flugzeugträger *m*
air' cur'rent *s* Luftströmung *f*
air' fare' *s* Flugpreis *m*
air'field' *s* Flugplatz *m*
air'force' *s* Luftstreitkräfte *pl*
air'ing *s* Lüftung *f*

air' lane' *s* Flugschneise *f*
air'lift' *s* Luftbrücke *f* ‖ *tr* auf dem Luftwege transportieren
air'line(s)' *s* Luftverkehrsgesellschaft *f*
air'line pi'lot *s* Flugkapitän *m*
air'lin'er *s* Verkehrsflugzeug *n*
air'mail' *s* Luftpost *f*
air'-mail let'ter *s* Luftpostbrief *m*
air'-mail stamp' *s* Luftpostbriefmarke *f*
air'plane' *s* Flugzeug *n*
air' pock'et *s* Luftloch *n*
air' pollu'tion *s* Luftverunreinigung *f*
air'port' *s* Flughafen *m*, Flugplatz *m*
air' raid' *s* Fliegerangriff *m*
air'-raid drill' *s* Luftschutzübung *f*
air'-raid shel'ter *s* Luftschutzraum *m*
air'-raid war'den *s* Luftschutzwart *m*
air'-raid warn'ing *s* Fliegeralarm *m*
air' recon'naissance *s* Luftaufklärung *f*
air'show' *s* Flugvorführung *f*
air'sick' *adj* luftkrank
air'sleeve', air'sock' *s* Windsack *m*
air'strip' *s* Start– und Landestreifen *m*
air' suprem'acy *s* Lufterrschaft *f*
air'tight' *adj* luftdicht
air' time' *s* (rad, telv) Sendezeit *f*
air'-traffic control' *s* Flugsicherung *f*
air'waves' *spl* Rundfunk *m;* **on the a.** im Rundfunk
air'way' *s* Luft(verkehrs)linie *f*
air'wor'thy *adj* lufttüchtig
airy ['ɛri] *adj* (*room*) luftig; (*lively*) lebhaft; (*flippant*) leichtsinnig
aisle [aɪl] *s* Gang *m;* (archit) Seitenschiff *n*
ajar [ə'dʒɑr] *adj* angelehnt
akimbo [ə'kɪmbo] *adj*—**with arms a.** die Arme in die Hüften gestemmt
akin [ə'kɪn] *adj* verwandt; **a. to** ähnlich (*dat*)
alabaster ['ælə ‚bæstər] *s* Alabaster *m*
alacrity [ə'lækrɪti] *s* Bereitwilligkeit *f*
alarm [ə'lɑrm] *s* Alarm *m;* (*sudden fear*) Bestürzung *f;* (*apprehension*) Unruhe *f* ‖ *tr* alarmieren
alarm' clock' *s* Wecker *m*
alas [ə'læs] *interj* o weh!
Albania [æl'benɪ·ə] *s* Albanien *n*
Albanian [æl'benɪ·ən] *adj* albanisch ‖ *s* Alban(i)er –in *mf*
albatross ['ælbə ‚trɔs] *s* Albatros *m*
album ['ælbəm] *s* Album *n*
albumen [æl'bjumən] *s* Eiweiß *n*
alchemy ['ælkɪmi] *s* Alchimie *f*
alcohol ['ælkə ‚hɔl] *s* Alkohol *m*
alcoholic [‚ælkə'hɔlɪk] *adj* alkoholisch ‖ *s* Alkoholiker –in *mf*
alcove ['ælkov] *s* Alkoven *m*
alder ['ɔldər] *s* (bot) Erle *f*
al'der·man *s* (**-men**) Stadtrat *m*
ale [el] *s* Ale *n*, englisches Bier *n*
alert [ə'lʌrt] *adj* wachsam ‖ *s* (*state of readiness*) Alarmbereitschaft *f;* **on the a.** alarmbereit; (fig) auf der Hut ‖ *tr* alarmieren
alfalfa [æl'fælfə] *s* Luzerne *f*
algae ['ældʒi] *spl* Algen *pl*
algebra ['ældʒɪbrə] *s* Algebra *f*
Algeria [æl'dʒɪrɪ·ə] *s* Algerien *n*
Algerian [æl'dʒɪrɪ·ən] *adj* algerisch ‖ *s* Algerier –in *mf*
Algiers [æl'dʒɪrz] *s* Algier *n*

alias ['eɪɪ·əs] *adv* alias, sonst...genannt ‖ *s* Deckname *m*
ali·bi ['ælɪ‚baɪ] *s* (**-bis**) Alibi *n*; (*excuse*) Ausrede *f*
alien ['eljən], ['elɪ·ən] *adj* fremd ‖ *s* Fremde *mf*, Ausländer –in *mf*
alienate ['eljə‚net], ['elɪ·ə‚net] *tr* entfremden; (jur) übertragen
alight [ə'laɪt] *v* (*pret & pp* **alighted &** **alit** [ə'lɪt]) *intr* aussteigen; (*said of a bird*) (**on**) sich niederlassen (auf *dat* or *acc*); (aer) landen
align [ə'laɪn] *tr* (**with**) ausrichten (nach); (aut) einstellen; **a. oneself** **with** sich anschließen an (*acc*) ‖ *intr* **—a. with** sich ausrichten nach
alignment [ə'laɪnmənt] *s* Ausrichten *n*; (pol) Ausrichtung *f*; **bring into a.** gleichschalten; **out of a.** schlecht ausgerichtet
alike [ə'laɪk] *adj* gleich, ähnlich; **look a.** sich [*dat*] ähnlich sehen; (*resemble completely*) gleich aussehen
alimony ['ælɪ‚moni] *s* Unterhaltskosten *pl*
alive [ə'laɪv] *adj* lebendig; (*vivacious*) lebhaft; **keep a.** am Leben bleiben; **keep s.o. a.** j–n am Leben erhalten
alka·li ['ælkə‚laɪ] *s* (**-lis &** **-lies**) Laugensalz *n*, Alkali *n*
alkaline ['ælkə‚laɪn] *adj* alkalisch
all [ɔl] *adj* all, ganz; **all day long** den ganzen Tag; **all kinds of** allerlei; **all the time** fortwährend; **for all that** trotzdem ‖ *adv* ganz, völlig; **all along** schon immer; **all at once** auf einmal; **all gone** alle; **all in** (coll) völlig erschöpft; **all over** (*everywhere*) überall; (*ended*) ganz vorbei; **all right** gut, schön; **all the better** um so besser; **all the same** dennoch; **not be all there** (coll) nicht ganz richtig im Kopf sein ‖ *s*—**after all** schließlich; **all in all** im großen und ganzen; **and all** gesamt, e.g., **he went, family and all** er ging mit gesamter Familie; **in all** insgesamt; **not at all** überhaupt nicht, gar nicht ‖ *indef pron* alle; (*everything*) alles
all′-around′ *adj* vielseitig
allay [ə'le] *tr* beschwichtigen; (*hunger, thirst*) stillen
all′-clear′ *s* Entwarnung *f*
allege [ə'lɛdʒ] *tr* behaupten; (*advance as an excuse*) vorgeben
alleged′ *adj* angeblich, mutmaßlich
allegiance [ə'lidʒəns] *s* Treue *f*
allegoric(al) [‚ælɪ'gɔrɪk(əl)] *adj* allegorisch
allegory ['ælɪ‚gori] *s* Allegorie *f*
allergic [ə'lʌrdʒɪk] *adj* allergisch
allergy ['ælərdʒi] *s* Allergie *f*
alleviate [ə'livɪ‚et] *tr* lindern
alley ['æli] *s* Gasse *f*; (*for bowling*) Kegelbahn *f*
alliance [ə'laɪ·əns] *s* Bündnis *n*
allied′ *adj* (*field*) benachbart; (*science*) verwandt; (mil, pol) alliiert
alligator ['ælɪ‚getər] *s* Alligator *m*
all′-inclu′sive *adj* Pauschal–
alliteration [ə‚lɪtə'reʃən] *s* Stabreim *m*, Alliteration *f*
all′-know′ing *adj* allwissend

allocate ['ælə‚ket] *tr* zuteilen
al·lot [ə'lɑt] (*pret & pp* **–lotted;** *ger* **–lotting**) *tr* zuteilen, austeilen
all′-out′ *adj* vollkommen, total
allow [ə'lau] *tr* erlauben, gestatten; (*admit*) zugeben; (e.g., *a discount*) gewähren; **be allowed to** (*inf*) dürfen (*inf*) ‖ *intr*—**a. for** bedenken
allowable [ə'lau·əbəl] *adj* zulässig
allowance [ə'lau·əns] *s* (*tolerance*) Duldung *f*; (*permission*) Erlaubnis *f*; (*ration*) Zuteilung *f*, Ration *f*; (*pocket money*) Taschengeld *n*; (*discount*) Abzug *m*; (*salary for a particular expense*) Zuschuß *m*, Zulage *f*; (*for groceries*) Wirtschaftsgeld *n*; (mach) Toleranz *f*; **make a. for** berücksichtigen
alloy ['ælɔɪ] *s* Legierung *f* ‖ [ə'lɔɪ] *tr* legieren
all′-pow′erful *adj* allmächtig
all′ right′ *adj*—**be a.** in Ordnung sein ‖ *interj* schon gut!
All′ Saints′′ Day′ *s* Allerheiligen *n*
All′ Souls′′ Day′ *s* Allerseelen *n*
all′spice′ *s* Nelkenpfeffer *m*
all′-star′ *adj* (*sport*) aus den besten Spielern bestehend
allude [ə'lud] *intr*—**a. to** anspielen auf (*acc*)
allure [ə'lur] *s* Charme *m* ‖ *tr* anlocken
allurement [ə'lurmənt] *s* Verlockung *f*
allur′ing *adj* verlockend
allusion [ə'luʒən] *s* (**to**) Anspielung *f* (auf *acc*)
al·ly ['ælaɪ], [ə'laɪ] *s* Alliierte *mf*, Verbündete *mf* ‖ [ə'laɪ] *v* (*pret & pp* **–lied**) *tr*—**a. oneself with** sich verbünden mit
almanac ['ɔlmə‚næk] *s* Almanach *m*
almighty [ɔl'maɪti] *adj* allmächtig
almond ['ɑmənd] *s* Mandel *f*
almost ['ɔlmost], [ɔl'most] *adv* fast
alms [ɑmz] *s & spl* Almosen *n*
aloft [ə'lɔft] *adv* (*position*) oben; (*direction*) nach oben; **raise a.** emporheben
alone [ə'lon] *adj* allein; **let a.** (*not to mention*) geschweige denn; (*not bother*) in Ruhe lassen ‖ *adv* allein
along [ə'lɔŋ] *adv* vorwärts, weiter; **all a.** schon immer; **a. with** zusammen mit; **get a. with** sich gut vertragen mit; **go a. with** mitgehen mit; (*agree with*) sich einverstanden erklären mit ‖ *prep* (*direction*) entlang (*acc*); (*position*) an (*dat*), längs (*genit*)
along′side′ *adv* (naut) längsseits; **a. of** im Vergleich zu ‖ *prep* neben (*dat*); (naut) längsseits (*genit*)
aloof [ə'luf] *adj* zurückhaltend ‖ *adv*—**keep a.** (**from**) sich fernhalten (von); **stand a.** für sich bleiben
aloud [ə'laud] *adv* laut
alphabet ['ælfə‚bet] *s* Alphabet *n*
alphabetic(al) [‚ælfə'betɪk(əl)] *adj* alphabetisch
alpine ['ælpaɪn] *adj* alpin, Alpen–
Alps [ælps] *spl* Alpen *pl*
already [ɔl'redi] *adv* schon, bereits
Alsace [æl'ses], ['ælsæs] *s* Elsaß *n*
Alsatian [æl'seʃən] *adj* elsässisch ‖ *s*

Elsässer –in *mf;* (*dog*) deutscher Schäferhund *m*

also ['ɔlso] *adv* auch

altar ['ɔltər] *s* Altar *m*

al'tar boy' *s* Ministrant *m*

alter ['ɔltər] *tr* ändern; (*castrate*) kastrieren || *intr* sich ändern

alteration [‚ɔltə'reʃən] *s* Änderung *f;* **alterations** (*in construction*) Umbau *m*

alternate ['ɔltərnɪt] *adj* abwechselnd || *s* Ersatzmann *m* || ['ɔltər‚net] *tr* (ab)wechseln; (*e.g., hot and cold compresses*) zwischen (*dat*) und (*dat*) abwechseln || *intr* miteinander abwechseln

al'ternating cur'rent *s* Wechselstrom *m*

alternative [ɔl'tʌrnətɪv] *adj* Ausweich-, Alternativ– || *s* Alternative *f*

although [ɔl'ðo] *conj* obgleich, obwohl

altimeter [æl'tɪmɪtər] *s* Höhenmesser *m*

altitude ['æltɪ‚t(j)ud] *s* Höhe *f*

al·to ['ælto] *s* (**-tos**) Alt *m,* Altstimme *f;* (*singer*) Altist *m*

altogether [‚ɔltə'geðər] *adv* durchaus; (*in all*) insgesamt

altruist ['æltrʊ·ɪst] *s* Altruist –in *mf*

alum ['æləm] *s* Alaun *m*

aluminum [ə'lumɪnəm] *s* Aluminium *n*

alu'minum foil' *s* Aluminiumfolie *f*

alum·na [ə'lʌmnə] *s* (**-nae** [ni]) ehemalige Studentin *f*

alum·nus [ə'lʌmnəs] *s* (**-ni** [naɪ]) ehemaliger Student *m*

always ['ɔlwɪz], ['ɔlwez] *adv* immer

A.M. *abbr* (**ante meridiem**) vormittags; (**amplitude modulation**) Amplitudenmodulation *f*

amalgam [ə'mælgəm] *s* Amalgam *n;* (fig) Mischung *f,* Gemenge *n*

amalgamate [ə'mælgə‚met] *tr* amalgamieren || *intr* sich amalgamieren

amass [ə'mæs] *tr* aufhäufen, ansammeln

amateur ['æmətʃər] *adj* Amateur– || *s* Amateur *m,* Liebhaber *m*

amaze [ə'mez] *tr* erstaunen

amaz'ing *adj* erstaunlich

Amazon ['æmə‚zɑn] *s* (*river*) Amazonas *m;* (fig) Mannweib *n;* (myth) Amazone *f*

ambassador [æm'bæsədər] *s* Botschafter –in §6 *mf;* (fig) Bote *m*

ambassadorial [æm‚bæsə'dorɪ·əl] *adj* Botschafts–

amber ['æmbər] *adj* Bernstein–; (*in color*) bernsteinfarben || *s* Bernstein *m*

ambiguity [‚æmbɪ'gju·ɪti] *s* Doppelsinn *m,* Zweideutigkeit *f*

ambiguous [æm'bɪgjʊ·əs] *adj* doppelsinnig, zweideutig

ambit ['æmbɪt] *s* Bereich *m*

ambition [æm'bɪʃən] *s* Ehrgeiz *m;* (*aim, object*) Ambition *f*

ambitious [æm'bɪʃəs] *adj* ehrgeizig

ambivalent [æm'bɪvələnt] *adj* (chem) ambivalent; (psychol) zwiespältig

amble ['æmbəl] *s* (*of a person*) gemächlicher Gang *m;* (*of a horse*) Paßgang *m* || *intr* schlendern; (*said of a horse*) im Paßgang gehen

ambulance ['æmbjələns] *s* Krankenwagen *m*

ambulatory ['æmbjələ‚tori] *adj* gehfähig

ambuscade [‚æmbəs'ked] *s* Hinterhalt *m*

ambush ['æmbuʃ] *s* Hinterhalt *m* || *tr* aus dem Hinterhalt überfallen

ameliorate [ə'miljə‚ret] *tr* verbessern || *intr* besser werden

amen ['e'mɛn], ['ɑ'mɛn] *s* Amen *n* || *interj* amen!

amenable [ə'mɛnəbəl] *adj* (*docile*) fügsam; **a. to** (*e.g., flattery*) zugänglich (*dat*); (*e.g., laws*) unterworfen (*dat*)

amend [ə'mɛnd] *tr* (*a law*) (ver)bessern; (*one's ways*) (ab)ändern || *intr* sich bessern

amendment [ə'mɛndmənt] *s* Änderungsantrag *m;* (by addition) Zusatzantrag *m;* (*to the constitution*) Zusatzartikel *m*

amends [ə'mɛndz] *s & spl* Genugtuung *f;* **make a. for** wiedergutmachen

amenity [ə'mɛnɪti] *s* (*pleasantness*) Annehmlichkeit *f;* **amenities** (*of life*) Annehmlichkeiten *pl*

America [ə'mɛrɪkə] *s* Amerika *n*

American [ə'mɛrɪkən] *adj* amerikanisch || *s* Amerikaner –in *mf*

Americanize [ə'mɛrɪkə‚naɪz] *tr* amerikanisieren

amethyst ['æmɪθɪst] *s* Amethyst *m*

amiable ['emɪ·əbəl] *adj* liebenswürdig

amicable ['æmɪkəbəl] *adj* freundschaftlich, gütlich

amid [ə'mɪd] *prep* inmitten (*genit*)

amidships [ə'mɪd/ɪps] *adv* mittschiffs

amiss [ə'mɪs] *adj* (*improper*) unpassend; (*wrong*) verkehrt; **there is s.th. a.** etwas stimmt nicht || *adv* verkehrt; **go a.** danebengehen; **take a.** übelnehmen

amity ['æmɪti] *s* Freundschaft *f*

ammo ['æmo] *s* (sl) Muni *m*

ammonia [ə'monɪ·ə] *s* (*gas*) Ammoniak *n;* (*solution*) Salmiakgeist *m*

ammunition [‚æmjə'nɪʃən] *s* Munition *f*

amnesia [æm'niʒɪ·ə] *s* Amnesie *f*

amnes·ty ['æmnɪsti] *s* Amnestie *f* || *v* (*pret & pp.* **–tied**) *tr* begnadigen

amoeba [ə'mibə] *s* Amöbe *f*

among [ə'mʌŋ] *prep* (*position*) unter (*dat*); (*direction*) unter (*acc*); **a. other things** unter anderem

amorous ['æmərəs] *adj* amourös

amortize ['æmər‚taɪz] *tr* tilgen

amount [ə'maunt] *s* (*sum*) Betrag *m;* (*quantity*) Menge *f* || *intr*—**a. to** betragen

ampere ['æmpɪr] *s* Ampere *n*

amphibian [æm'fɪbɪ·ən] *s* Amphibie *f*

amphibious [æm'fɪbɪ·əs] *adj* amphibisch

amphitheater ['æmfɪ‚θɪ·ətər] *s* Amphitheater *n*

ample ['æmpəl] *adj* (*sufficient*) genügend; (*spacious*) geräumig

amplifier ['æmplɪ‚faɪ·ər] *s* Verstärker *m*

ampli·fy ['æmplɪ‚faɪ] *v* (*pret & pp* **–fied**) *tr* (*a statement*) erweitern; (electron, rad, phys) verstärken

amplitude ['æmplɪ,t(j)ud] s Weite f; (electron, rad, phys) Amplitude f
am'plitude modula'tion s Amplitudenmodulation f
amputate ['æmpjə,tet] tr amputieren
amputee [,æmpje'ti] s Amputierte mf
amuck [ə'mʌk] adv—run a. Amok laufen
amulet ['æmjəlɪt] s Amulett n
amuse [ə'mjuz] tr amüsieren, belustigen
amusement [ə'mjuzmənt] s Vergnügen n
amuse'ment park' s Vergnügungspark m
amus'ing adj amüsant
an [æn], [ən] indef art ein
anachronism [ə'nækrə,nɪzəm] s Anachronismus m
analogous [ə'næləgəs] adj (to) analog (dat), ähnlich (dat)
analogy [ə'nælədʒi] s Analogie f
analy·sis [ə'nælɪsɪs] s (-ses [,siz]) Analyse f; (of a literary work) Zergliederung f
analyst ['ænəlɪst] s Analytiker –in mf
analytic(al) [,ænə'lɪtɪk(əl)] adj analytisch
analyze ['ænə,laɪz] tr analysieren
anarchist ['ænərkɪst] s Anarchist –in mf
anarchy ['ænərki] s Anarchie f
anatomic(al) [,ænə'tɑmɪk(əl)] adj anatomisch
anatomy [ə'nætəmi] s Anatomie f
ancestor ['ænsɛstər] s Vorfahr m, Ahne m
ancestral [æn'sɛstrəl] adj angestammt, Ahnen–; (inherited) Erb–, ererbt
ancestry ['ænsɛstri] s Abstammung f
anchor ['æŋkər] s Anker m; cast a. vor Anker gehen; weigh a. den Anker lichten || tr verankern || intr ankern
anchorage ['æŋkərɪdʒ] s Ankerplatz m
anchovy ['æntʃovi] s Anschovis f
ancient ['entʃənt] adj (very old) uralt; (civilization) antik || the ancients spl die alten Griechen und Römer
an'cient his'tory s alte Geschichte f
and [ænd], [ənd] conj und; and how! und ob! and so forth und so weiter
andiron ['ænd,aɪ·ərn] s Kaminbock m
anecdote ['ænɪk,dot] s Anekdote f
anemia [ə'nimɪ·ə] s Anämie f
anemic [ə'nimɪk] adj anämisch, blutarm
anesthesia [,ænɪs'θiʒə] s Anästhesie f; general a. Vollnarkose f; local a. Lokalanästhesie f
anesthetic [,ænɪs'θɛtɪk] adj betäubend || s Betäubungsmittel n; local a. örtliches Betäubungsmittel n
anesthetize [æ'nɛsθɪ,taɪz] tr betäuben
anew [ə'n(j)u] adv von neuem, aufs neue
angel ['endʒəl] s Engel m; (financial backer) Hintermann m
angelic(al) [æn'dʒɛlɪk(əl)] adj engelgleich, engelhaft
anger ['æŋgər] s Zorn m || tr erzürnen
angina pectoris [æn'dʒaɪnə'pɛktərɪs] s Brustbeklemmung f, Herzbräune f

angle ['æŋgəl] s Winkel m; (point of view) Gesichtswinkel m; (ulterior motive) Hintergedanken m; (side) Seite f
angler ['æŋglər] s Angler –in mf
angry ['æŋgri] adj zornig, böse; (wound) entzündet; a. at (s.th.) zornig über (acc); a. with (s.o.) zornig auf (acc)
anguish ['æŋgwɪʃ] s Qual f, Pein f
angular ['æŋgjələr] adj kantig
animal ['ænɪməl] adj tierisch, Tier— || s Tier n
animate ['ænɪmɪt] adj belebt; (lively) lebhaft || ['ænɪ,met] tr beleben, beseelen; (make lively) aufmuntern
an'imated cartoon' s Zeichentrickfilm m
animation [,ænɪ'meʃən] s Lebhaftigkeit f; (cin) Herstellung f von Zeichentrickfilm
animosity [,ænɪ'mɑsɪti] s Feindseligkeit f
anion ['æn,aɪ·ən] s Anion n
anise ['ænɪs] s Anis m
anisette [,ænɪ'sɛt] s Anisett m
ankle ['æŋkəl] s Fußknöchel m
an'kle support' s Knöchelstütze f
anklet ['æŋklɪt] s (ornament) Fußring m; (sock) Söckchen n
annals ['ænəlz] spl Annalen pl
anneal [ə'nil] tr ausglühen; (the mind) stählen
annex ['ænɛks] s (building) Anbau m, Nebengebäude n; (supplement) Zusatz m || [ə'nɛks] tr annektieren
annexation [,ænɛks'eʃən] s Einverleibung f; (pol) Annexion f
annihilate [ə'naɪ·ɪ,let] tr vernichten; (fig) zunichte machen
annihilation [ə,naɪ·ɪ'leʃən] s Vernichtung f
anniversary [,ænɪ'vʌrsəri] s Jahrestag m
annotate ['ænə,tet] tr mit Anmerkungen versehen
annotation [,ænə'teʃən] s Anmerkung f
announce [ə'naʊns] tr ankündigen, anmelden; (rad) ansagen, melden
announcement [ə'naʊnsmənt] s Ankündigung f; (rad) Durchsage f
announcer [ə'naʊnsər] s Ansager –in mf
annoy [ə'nɔɪ] tr ärgern; be annoyed at sich ärgern über (acc)
annoyance [ə'nɔɪ·əns] s Ärger m
annoy'ing adj ärgerlich
annual ['ænju·əl] adj jährlich, Jahres–; (plant) einjährig || s (book) Jahrbuch n; (bot) einjährige Pflanze f
annuity [ə'n(j)u·ɪti] s Jahresrente f
an·nul [ə'nʌl] v (pret & pp –nulled; ger –nulling) tr annullieren
annulment [ə'nʌlmənt] s Annullierung f; (of marriage) Nichtigkeitserklärung f
anode ['ænod] s Anode f
anoint [ə'nɔɪnt] tr salben
anomaly [ə'nɑməli] s Anomalie f
anonymous [ə'nɑnɪməs] adj anonym
another [ə'nʌðər] adj (a different) ein anderer; (an additional) noch ein; a. Caesar ein zweiter Cäsar || pron

(*a different one*) ein anderer; (*an additional one*) noch einer

answer ['ænsər] *s* Antwort *f;* (*to a problem*) Lösung *f* || *tr* (*a person*) antworten (*dat*); (*a question, letter*) beantworten; (*need, description*) entsprechen (*dat*); (*enemy fire*) antworten auf (*acc*); **a. an ad** sich auf e–e Anzeige melden; **a. the door** die Tür öffnen; **a. the telephone** ans Telefon gehen || *intr* antworten; (telp) sich melden; **a. back** e–n losen Mund haben; **a. for** verantworten; **a. to** (*a description*) entsprechen (*dat*)

an'swering serv'ice *s* Fernsprechauftragsdienst *m*

ant [ænt] *s* Ameise *f*

antagonism [æn'tægə,nɪzəm] *s* Feindseligkeit *f*

antagonize [æn'tægə,naɪz] *tr* sich [*dat*] zum Gegner machen

antarctic [ænt'arktɪk] *adj* antarktisch || **the Antarctic** *s* die Antarktis

Antarc'tic Cir'cle *s* südlicher Polarkreis *m*

Antarc'tic O'cean *s* südliches Eismeer *n*

ante ['ænti] *s* (cards) Einsatz *m;* (com) Scherflein *n* || *tr* (cards) einsetzen || *intr* (*in a joint venture*) sein Scherflein beitragen; (*pay up*) (coll) blechen; (cards) einsetzen

antecedent [,ænti'sidənt] *adj* vorhergehend || *s* (gram) Beziehungswort *n;* **antecedents** Antezedenzien *pl*

antechamber ['ænti,tʃembər] *s* Vorzimmer *n*

antelope ['ænti,lop] *s* Antilope *f*

anten·na [æn'tenə] *s* (-nae [ni]) (ent) Fühler *m* || *s* (-nas) (rad) Antenne *f*

antepenult [,ænti'pinʌlt] *s* drittletzte Silbe *f*

anthem ['ænθəm] *s* Hymne *f*

ant'hill' *s* Ameisenhaufen *m*

anthology [æn'θalədʒi] *s* Anthologie *f*

anthropology [,ænθrə'palədʒi] *s* Anthropologie *f*, Lehre *f* vom Menschen

antiaircraft [,ænti'ɛr,kræft] *adj* Flak-, Flugabwehr- || *s* Flak *f*

antiair'craft gun' *s* Flak *f*

antibiotic [,æntibaɪ'atɪk] *s* Antibiotikum *n*

antibody ['ænti,badi] *s* Antikörper *m*

anticipate [æn'tɪsɪ,pet] *tr* (*expect*) erwarten; (*remarks, criticism, etc.*) vorwegnehmen; (*trouble*) voraussahnen; (*pleasure*) vorausempfinden; (*s o.'s wish or desire*) zuvorkommen (*dat*)

anticipation [æn,tɪsɪ'peʃən] *s* Erwartung *f*, Vorfreude *f*

antics ['æntɪks] *spl* Possen *pl*

antidote ['ænti,dot] *s* Gegengift *n*

antifreeze ['ænti,friz] *s* Gefrierschutzmittel *n*

antiknock [,ænti'nak] *adj* klopffest || *s* Antiklopfmittel *n*

antipathy [æn'tɪpəθi] *s* Abneigung *f*, Antipathie *f*

antiquarian [,ænti'kwɛri·ən] *adj* altertümlich || *s* Altertumsforscher –in *mf*

antiquated ['ænti,kwetɪd] *adj* veraltet

antique [æn'tik] *adj* (ur)alt, antik || *s* Antiquität *f*

antique' deal'er *s* Antiquitätenhändler –in *mf*

antique' shop' *s* Antiquitätenladen *m*

antiquity [æn'tɪkwɪti] *s* Altertum *n,* Vorzeit *f;* **antiquities** Antiquitäten *pl*, Altertümer *pl*

antirust [,ænti'rʌst] *adj* Rostschutz–

anti-Semitic [,æntisɪ'mɪtɪk] *adj* antisemitisch, judenfeindlich

antiseptic [,ænti'septɪk] *adj* antiseptisch || *s* Antiseptikum *n*

antitank [,ænti'tæŋk] *adj* Panzer–: (*unit*) Panzerjäger–

antitank' mine' *s* Tellermine *f*

antithe·sis [æn'tɪθɪsɪs] *s* (-ses [,siz]) Gegensatz *m*, Antithese *f*

antitoxin [,ænti'taksɪn] *s* Gegengift *n*

antitrust [,ænti'trʌst] *adj* Antitrust–

antiwar [,ænti'wɔr] *adj* antimilitaristisch

antler ['æntlər] *s* Geweihsprosse *f;* (*pair of*) **antlers** Geweih *n*

antonym ['æntənɪm] *s* Antonym *n*

anus ['enəs] *s* After *m*

anvil ['ænvɪl] *s* Amboß *m*

anxiety [æŋ'zaɪ·əti] *s* (**over**) Besorgnis *f* (um); (psychol) Beklemmung *f*

anxious ['æŋkʃəs] *adj* (**about**) besorgt (um or wegen); (**for**) gespannt (auf *acc*), begierig (auf *acc*); **I am a. to** (*inf*) es liegt mir daran zu (*inf*)

any ['eni] *indef adj* irgendein, irgendwelch; (*a little*) etwas; **any** (**possible**) etwaig; **any** (**you wish**) jeder beliebige; **do you have any money on you?** haben Sie Geld bei sich?; **I do not have any money** ich habe kein Geld || *adv*—**any more** (*e.g., coffee*) noch etwas; (*e.g., apples*) noch ein paar; **not any better** keinwegs besser; **not ...any longer** nicht mehr; **not ...any more** nicht mehr

an'ybod'y *indef pron* var of **anyone**

an'yhow' *adv* sowieso, trotzdem; (*in any event*) jedenfalls

an'yone' *indef pron* (irgend)jemand, irgendeiner; **a. but you** jeder andere als du; **a. else** sonstnochwer; **ask a.** frag wen du willst; **I don't see a.** ich sehe niemand

an'yplace' *adv* (coll) var of **anywhere**

an'ything' *indef pron* (irgend)etwas, (irgend)was; **a. but** alles andere als; **a. else?** noch etwas?, sonst etwas?; **a. vou want** was du willst; **not ...a.** nichts; **not for a. in the world** um keinen Preis

an'ytime' *adv* zu jeder (beliebigen) Zeit; (*at some unspecified time*) irgendwann

an'yway' *adv* sowieso, trotzdem

an'ywhere' *adv* (*position*) irgendwo; (*everywhere*) an jedem beliebigen Ort; (*direction*) irgendwohin; (*everywhere*) an jeden beliebigen Ort; (*to any extent*) einigermaßen, e.g., **a. near correct** einigermaßen richtig; **get a.** (*achieve success*) es zu etwas bringen

apace [ə'pes] *adv* schnell, rasch

apart [ə'part] *adv* (*to pieces*) auseinander; (*separately*) einzeln, für sich; a. from abgesehen von

apartment [ə'pɑrtmənt] *s* Wohnung *f*

apart'ment house' *s* Apartmenthaus *n*

apathetic [ˌæpə'θetɪk] *adj* apathisch, teilnahmslos

apathy ['æpəθi] *s* Apathie *f*

ape [ep] *s* Affe *m* || *tr* nachäffen

aperture ['æpərtʃər] *s* Öffnung *f*; (phot) Blende *f*

apex ['epɛks] *s* (**apexes & apices** ['æpɪˌsiz]) Spitze *f*; (fig) Gipfel *m*

aphid ['æfɪd] *s* Blattlaus *f*

aphorism ['æfəˌrɪzəm] *s* Aphorismus *m*

apiary ['epɪˌeri] *s* Bienenhaus *n*

apiece [ə'pis] *adv* pro Stück; (*per person*) pro Person

aplomb [ə'plɔm] *s* sicheres Auftreten *n*

apogee ['æpəˌdʒi] *s* Erdferne *f*

apologetic [əˌpɑlə'dʒetɪk] *adj* (*remark*) entschuldigend; (*letter, speech*) Entschuldigungs–; **be a.** (**about**) Entschuldigungen vorbringen (für)

apologize [ə'pɑləˌdʒaɪz] *intr* sich entschuldigen; **a. to s.o. for s.th.** sich bei j–m wegen etw entschuldigen

apology [ə'pɑlədʒi] *s* (*excuse*) Entschuldigung *f*; (*apologia*) Verteidigung *f*

apoplec'tic stroke' [ˌæpə'plektɪk] *s* Schlaganfall *m*

apoplexy ['æpəˌplɛksi] *s* Schlaganfall *m*

apostle [ə'pɑsəl] *s* Apostel *m*

apostolic [ˌæpəs'tɑlɪk] *adj* apostolisch

apostrophe [ə'pɑstrəfi] *s* (gram) Apostroph *m*; (rhet) Anrede *f*

apothecary [ə'pɑθɪˌkeri] *s* (*druggist*) Apotheker *m*; (*drugstore*) Apotheke *f*

appall [ə'pɔl] *tr* entsetzen

appall'ing *adj* entsetzlich

appara·tus [ˌæpə'retəs], [ˌæpə'rætəs] *s* (**–tus & –tuses**) Apparat *m*

apparel [ə'pærəl] *s* Kleidung *f*, Tracht *f*

apparent [ə'pærənt] *adj* (*visible*) sichtbar; (*obvious*) offenbar; (*seeming*) scheinbar

apparition [ˌæpə'rɪʃən] *s* Erscheinung *f*; (*ghost*) Gespenst *n*

appeal [ə'pil] *s* (*request*) Appell *m*, dringende Bitte *f*; (*to reason, etc.*) Appell *m*; (*charm*) Anziehungskraft *f*; (jur) (**to**) Berufung *f* (an *acc*) || *tr*—**a. a case** Berufung einlegen in e-r Rechtssache || *intr*—**a. to** (*entreat*) dringend bitten; (*be attractive to*) reizen; (jur) appellieren an (*acc*)

appear [ə'pir] *intr* erscheinen; (*seem*) scheinen; (*come before the public*) sich zeigen; (jur) sich stellen; (theat) auftreten; **a. as a guest** (telv) gastieren

appearance [ə'pɪrəns] *s* Erscheinen *n*; (*outward look*) Aussehen *n*; (*semblance*) Anschein *m*; (*on the stage*) Auftreten *n*; (jur) Erscheinen *f*; **for the sake of appearances** anstandshalber; **to all appearances** allem Anschein nach

appease [ə'piz] *tr* beruhigen; (*hunger*)

stillen; (*pain*) mildern; (dipl) be schwichtigen

appeasement [ə'pizmənt] *s* Beruhigung *f*; (*of hunger*) Stillung *f*; (dipl) Be schwichtigung *f*

appel'late court' [ə'pɛlɪt] *s* Berufungs gericht *n*

append [ə'pend] *tr* anhängen; (*a sig nature*) hinzufügen

appendage [ə'pendɪdʒ] *s* Anhang *m*

appendectomy [ˌæpən'dɛktəmi] Blinddarmoperation *f*

appendicitis [əˌpendɪ'saɪtɪs] *s* Blind darmentzündung *f*, Appendizitis *f*

appen·dix [ə'pendɪks] *s* (**–dixes &** **–dices** [dɪˌsiz]) Anhang *m*; (anat. Appendix *m*

appertain [ˌæpər'ten] *intr* (**to**) gehöre (zu), gebühren (*dat*)

appetite ['æpɪˌtaɪt] *s* (**for**) Appetit *n* (auf *acc*)

appetizer ['æpɪˌtaɪzər] *s* Vorspeise

ap'petizing *adj* appetitlich

applaud [ə'plɔd] *tr* Beifall klatcher (*dat*); (*praise*) billigen || *intr* Beifal klatschen

applause [ə'plɔz] *s* Beifall *m*, Applau *m*

apple ['æpəl] *s* Apfel *m*

ap'plecart' *s*—**upset the a.** die Plän über den Haufen werfen

ap'ple of one's eye' *s* Augapfel *m*

ap'ple pie' *s* gedeckte Apfeltorte *f*

ap'ple-pol'isher *s* (coll) Speichellecker *m*

ap'plesauce' *s* Apfelmus *n*

ap'ple tree' *s* Apfelbaum *m*

appliance [ə'plaɪ·əns] *s* Gerät *n*, Vor richtung *f*

applicable ['æplɪkəbəl] *adj* (**to**) an wendbar (auf *acc*); **not a.** nicht zu treffend

applicant ['æplɪkənt] *s* Bewerber –in *mf*

application [ˌæplɪ'keʃən] *s* (*use*) An wendung *f*; (*for a job*) Bewerbung *f*; (*for a grant*) Antrag *m*; (*zeal*) Fleiß *m*; (med) Anlegen *n*

applica'tion blank' *s* (*for a job*) Be werbungsformular *n*; (*for a grant*) Antragsformular *n*

applied' *adj* angewandt

apply [ə'plaɪ] *v* (*pret & pp* **–plied**) *tr* anwenden; (med) anlegen; **a. oneself to** sich befleißigen (*genit*); **a. the brakes** bremsen || *intr* gelten; **a. for** (*a job*) sich bewerben um; (*a grant*) beantragen

appoint [ə'pɔɪnt] *tr* (*a person*) ernen nen; (*a time, etc.*) festsetzen

appointment [ə'pɔɪntmənt] *s* Ernen nung *f*; (*post*) Stelle *f*; (*engagement*) Verabredung *f*; **by a.** only nur nach Vereinbarung; **have an a. with** (*e.g., a dentist*) bestellt sein zu

appoint'ment book' *s* Terminkalender *m*

apportion [ə'pɔrʃən] *tr* zumessen

appraisal [ə'prezəl] *s* Abschätzung *f*

appraise [ə'prez] *tr* (ab)schätzen

appraiser [ə'prezər] *s* Schätzer –in *mf*

appreciable [ə'priʃɪ·əbəl] *adj* (*notice–*

able) merklich; (*considerable*) erheblich

appreciate [ə'priʃɪ‚et] *tr* dankbar sein für; (*danger*) erkennen; (*regard highly*) hochschätzen || *intr* (im Werte) steigen

appreciation [ə‚priʃɪ'eʃən] *s* (*gratitude*) Dank *m*. Anerkennung *f*; (*for art*) Verständnis *n*; (*high regard*) Schätzung *f*; (*increase in value*) Wertzuwachs *m*

appreciative [ə'priʃɪ‚ətɪv] *adj* (**of**) dankbar (für)

apprehend [‚æprɪ'hɛnd] *tr* verhaften, ergreifen; (*understand*) begreifen

apprehension [‚æprɪ'hɛnʃən] *s* (*arrest*) Verhaftung *f*; (*fear*) Befürchtung *f*; (*comprehending*) Begreifen *n*

apprehensive [‚æprɪ'hɛnsɪv] *adj* (**of**) besorgt (um)

apprentice [ə'prɛntɪs] *s* Lehrling *m*

appren′ticeship′ *s* Lehre *f*; **serve an a.** in der Lehre sein

apprise, apprize [ə'praɪz] *tr* (**of**) benachrichtigen (von)

approach [ə'protʃ] *s* Annäherung *f*; (*e.g., a road*) Zugang *m*, Zufahrt *f*; *e.g., to a problem*) Behandlung *f*; (*tentative sexual approach*) Annäherungsversuch *m; (*aer) anfliegen || *intr* sich nähern (*dat*); (*e.g., a problem*) behandeln; (*perfection*) nahekommen (*dat*); (aer) anfliegen || *intr* sich nähern

approachable [ə'protʃəbəl] *adj* zugänglich

approbation [‚æprə'beʃən] *s* (*approval*) Beifall *m;* (*sanction*) Billigung *f*

appropriate [ə'proprɪ‚ɪt] *adj* (**to**) angemessen (*dat*) || [ə'proprɪ‚et] *tr* (*take possession of*) sich [*dat*] aneignen; (*authorize*) bewilligen

approval [ə'pruvəl] *s* (*approbation*) Beifall *m;* (*sanction*) Billigung *f*; **meet with s.o.'s a.** j-s Beifall finden; **on a.** auf Probe

approve [ə'pruv] *tr* (*sanction*) genehmigen; (*judge favorably*) billigen; (*a bill*) (parl) annehmen || *intr*—**a. of** billigen

approvingly [ə'pruvɪŋli] *adv* beifällig

approximate [ə'proksɪmɪt] *adj* annähernd || [ə'proksɪ‚met] *tr* (*come close to*) nahekommen (*dat*); (*estimate*) schätzen; (*simulate closely*) täuschend nachahmen

approximately [ə'proksɪmɪtli] *adv* ungefähr, etwa

apricot ['eprɪ‚kɑt] *s* Aprikose *f*

ap′ricot tree′ *s* Aprikosenbaum *m*

April ['eprɪl] *s* April *m*

A′pril fool′ *interj* April, April!

A′pril Fools′′ Day′ *s* der erste April *m*

apron ['eprən] *s* Schürze *f*; (aer) Vorfeld *n;* (theat) Vorbühne *f*

apropos [‚æprə'po] *adj* passend || *adv* —**a. of** in Bezug auf (*acc*)

apse [æps] *s* Apsis *f*

apt [æpt] *adj* (*suited to the occasion*) passend; (*suited to the purpose*) geeignet; (*metaphor*) zutreffend; **be apt to** (*inf*) (*be prone to*) dazu neigen zu

(*inf*); **he is apt to believe it** er wird es wahrscheinlich glauben

aptitude ['æptɪ‚t(j)ud] *s* Eignung *f*

ap′titude test′ *s* Eignungsprüfung *f*

aqualung ['ækwə‚lʌŋ] *s* Tauchergerät *n*

aquamarine [‚ækwəmə'rin] *adj* blaugrün || *s* Aquamarin *m*

aquari·um [ə'kwɛrɪ·əm] *s* (**-ums & -a** [ə]) Aquarium *n*

aquatic [ə'kwætɪk] *adj* Wasser– || **aquatics** *spl* Wassersport *m*

aqueduct ['ækwə‚dʌkt] *s* Aquädukt *n*

aq′uiline nose′ ['ækwɪ‚laɪn] *s* Adlernase *f*

Arab ['ærəb] *adj* arabisch || *s* Araber –in *mf*

Arabia [ə'rebɪ·ə] *s* Arabien *n*

Arabic ['ærəbɪk] *adj* arabisch || *s* Arabisch *n*

arable ['ærəbəl] *adj* urbar, Acker–

arbiter ['ɑrbɪtər] *s* Schiedsrichter *m*

arbitrary ['ɑrbɪ‚treri] *adj* (*act*) willkürlich; (*number*) beliebig; (*person, government*) tyrannisch

arbitrate ['ɑrbɪ‚tret] *tr* schlichten || *intr* als Schiedsrichter fungieren

arbitration [‚ɑrbɪ'treʃən] *s* Schlichtung *f*

arbitrator ['ɑrbɪ‚tretər] *s* Schiedsrichter *m*

arbor ['ɑrbər] *s* Laube *f;* (mach) Achse *f*

arbore·tum [‚ɑrbə'ritəm] *s* (**-tums & -ta** [ə]) Baumgarten *m*

arc [ɑrk] *s* (astr, geom, mach) Bogen *m; (elec*) Lichtbogen *m*

arcade [ɑr'ked] *s* Bogengang *m*, Arkade *f*

arcane [ɑr'ken] *adj* geheimnisvoll

arch [ɑrtʃ] *adj* (*liar, etc.*) abgefeimt || *s* Bogen *m* || *tr* wölben; (*span*) überwölben || *intr* sich wölben

archaeologist [‚ɑrkɪ'alədʒɪst] *s* Archäolog(e) *m*, Archäologin *f*

archaeology [‚ɑrkɪ'alədʒi] *s* Archäologie *f*

archaic [ɑr'ke·ɪk] *adj* (*word*) veraltet; (*manner, notion*) antiquiert

archangel ['ɑrk‚endʒəl] *s* Erzengel *m*

archbishop ['ɑrtʃ'bɪʃəp] *s* Erzbischof *m*

archduke ['ɑrtʃ'd(j)uk] *s* Erzherzog *m*

archenemy ['ɑrtʃ‚ɛnɪmi] *s* Erzfeind *m*

archer ['ɑrtʃər] *s* Bogenschütze *m*

archery ['ɑrtʃəri] *s* Bogenschießen *n*

archipela·go [‚ɑrkɪ'pɛləgo] *s* (**-gos & -goes**) Inselmeer *n;* (*group of islands*) Inselgruppe *f*, Archipel *m*

architect ['ɑrkɪ‚tɛkt] *s* Architekt –in *mf*

architecture ['ɑrkɪ‚tɛktʃər] *s* Architektur *f*, Baukunst *f*

archives ['ɑrkaɪvz] *spl* Archiv *n*

arch′way′ *s* Bogengang *m*, Torbogen *m*

arctic ['ɑrktɪk] *adj* arktisch, nördlich || **the Arctic** *s* die Arktis

Arc′tic Cir′cle *s* nördlicher Polarkreis *m*

arc′ weld′ing *s* Lichtbogenschweißung *f*

ardent ['ɑrdənt] *adj* feurig, eifrig

ardor ['ɑrdər] *s* Eifer *m*, Inbrust *f*

arduous ['ardʒʊ·əs] *adj* mühsam
area ['erɪ·ə] *s* (*surface*) Fläche *f*; (*district*) Gegend *f*; (*field of enterprise*) Bereich *m*, Gebiet *n*; (*of danger*) Zone *f*
arena [ə'rinə] *s* Arena *f*, Kampfbahn *f*
Argentina [,ardʒən'tinə] *s* Argentinien *n*
argue ['argju] *tr* erörtern; (*maintain*) behaupten; **a. into** (*ger*) dazu überreden zu (*inf*) ‖ *intr* (**with**) streiten (mit); **a. for** (or **against**) *s.th.* für (or gegen) etw eintreten; **don't a.!** keine Widerrede!
argument ['argjəmənt] *s* (*discussion*) Erörterung *f*; (*point*) Beweisgrund *m*; (*disagreement*) Auseinandersetzung *f*; (*theme*) Thema *n*
argumentative [,argjə'mentətɪv] *adj* streitsüchtig
aria ['arɪ·ə], ['erɪ·ə] *s* Arie *f*
arid ['ærɪd] *adj* trocken, dürr
aridity [ə'rɪdɪti] *s* Trockenheit *f*
arise [ə'raɪz] *v* (*pret* **arose** [ə'roz]; *pp* **arisen** [ə'rɪzən]) *intr* (*come into being*) (**from**) entstehen (aus); (*get out of bed*) aufstehen; (*from a seat*) sich erheben; (*occur*) aufkommen, auftauchen; (*said of an opportunity*) sich bieten; (*stem*) (**from**) stammen (von)
aristocracy [,ærɪs'takrəsi] *s* Aristokratie *f*
aristocrat [ə'rɪstə,kræt] *s* Aristokrat –in *mf*
aristocratic [ə,rɪstə'krætɪk] *adj* aristokratisch
arithmetic [ə'rɪθmətɪk] *s* Arithmetik *f*
arithmetical [,ærɪθ'metɪkəl] *adj* arithmetisch, rechnerisch
ark [ark] *s* Arche *f*
ark' of the cov'enant *s* Bundeslade *f*
arm [arm] *s* Arm *m*; (*of a chair*) Seitenlehne *f*; (*weapon*) Waffe *f*; **keep s.o. at arm's length** sich j–m vom Leibe halten; **take up arms** zu den Waffen greifen; **up in arms** in Aufruhr ‖ *tr* bewaffnen; ‖ *intr* sich bewaffnen
armament ['arməmənt] *s* Kriegsausrüstung *f*, Bewaffnung *f*
ar'maments race' *s* Rüstungswettlauf *m*
armature ['armə,tʃər] *s* (*of doorbell or magnet*) Anker *m*; (*of a motor or dynamo*) Läufer *m*; (biol) Panzer *m*
arm'chair' *s* Lehnsessel *m*; (*unpadded*) Lehnstuhl *m*
armed' for'ces *spl* Streitkräfte *pl*
armed' rob'bery *s* bewaffneter Raubüberfall *m*
Armenia [ar'minɪ·ə] *s* Armenien *n*
armful ['arm,fʊl] *s* Armvoll *m*
armistice ['armɪstɪs] *s* Waffenstillstand *m*
armor ['armər] *s* Panzer *m* ‖ *tr* panzern
ar'mored car' *s* Panzerwagen *m*
armor-piercing ['armər,pɪrsɪŋ] *adj* panzerbrechend
ar'mor plat'ing ['pletɪŋ] *s* Panzerung *f*
armory ['arməri] *s* (*large arms storage*) Arsenal *n*; (*arms repair and storage room of a unit*) Waffenkam-

mer *f*; (*arms factory*) Waffenfabrik *f*; (*drill hall*) Exerzierhalle *f*
arm'pit' *s* Achselhöhle *f*
arm'rest' *s* Armlehne *f*
army ['armi] *adj* Armes–, Heeres– ‖ *s* Armee *f*, Heer *n*; **join the a.** zum Militär gehen
aroma [ə'romə] *s* Aroma *n*, Duft *m*
aromatic [,ærə'mætɪk] *adj* aromatisch
around [ə'raʊnd] *adv* ringsherum; **be a.** in der Nähe sein; **get a.** viel herumkommen; **get a. to** (*inf*) dazukommen zu (*inf*) ‖ *prep* um (*acc*) herum; (*approximately*) etwa; (*near*) bei (*dat*); **a. town** in der Stadt
arouse [ə'raʊz] *tr* aufwecken; (fig) erwecken
arraign [ə'ren] *tr* (*accuse*) anklagen; (jur) vor Gericht stellen
arrange [ə'rendʒ] *tr* arrangieren; (*in a certain order*) (an)ordnen; (*a time*) festsetzen; (mus) bearbeiten ‖ *intr*— **a. for** Vorkehrungen treffen für
arrangement [ə'rendʒmənt] *s* Anordnung *f*; (*agreement*) Vereinbarung *f*; (mus) Bearbeitung *f*; **make arrangements to** (*inf*) Vorbereitungen treffen, um zu (*inf*)
array [ə're] *s* (*of troops, facts*) Ordnung *f*; (*large number or quantity*) Menge *f*; (*apparel*) Staat *m* ‖ *tr* ordnen; (*dress up*) putzen
arrears [ə'rɪrz] *spl* Rückstand *m*; **in a.** rückständig
arrest [ə'rest] *s* Verhaftung *f*; **make an a.** e–e Verhaftung vornehmen; **place under a.** in Haft nehmen; **under a.** verhaftet ‖ *tr* verhaften; (*attention*) fesseln; (*a disease, progress*) hemmen
arrival [ə'raɪvəl] *s* Ankunft *f*; (*of merchandise*) Eingang *m*; (*a person*) Ankömmling *m*
arrive [ə'raɪv] *intr* ankommen; (*said of time, an event*) kommen; **a. at** (*a conclusion, decision*) erlangen
arrogance ['ærəgəns] *s* Anmaßung *f*
arrogant ['ærəgənt] *adj* anmaßend
arrogate ['ærə,get] *tr* sich (*dat*) anmaßen
arrow ['æro] *s* Pfeil *m*
ar'rowhead' *s* Pfeilspitze *f*
arsenal ['arsənəl] *s* Arsenal *n*
arsenic ['arsɪnɪk] *s* Arsen *n*
arson ['arsən] *s* Brandstiftung *f*
arsonist ['arsənɪst] *s* Brandstifter –in *mf*
art [art] *s* Kunst *f*
artery ['artəri] *s* Pulsader *f*; (*highway*) Verkehrsader *f*
artful ['artfəl] *adj* (*cunning*) schlau, listig; (*skillful*) kunstvoll
arthritic [ar'θrɪtɪk] *adj* arthritisch, gichtisch ‖ *s* Arthritiker –in *mf*
arthritis [ar'θraɪtɪs] *s* Arthritis *f*
artichoke ['artɪ,tʃok] *s* Artischocke *f*
article ['artɪkəl] *s* (*object*) Gegenstand *m*; (com, gram, journ, jur) Artikel *m*
articulate [ar'tɪkjəlɪt] *adj* deutlich ‖ [ar'tɪkjə,let] *tr* & *intr* deutlich aussprechen
artifact ['artɪ,fækt] *s* Artefakt *n*
artifice ['artɪfɪs] *s* Kunstgriff *m*
artificial [,artɪ'fɪʃəl] *adj* Kunst–,

künstlich; (*emotion, smile*) gekünstelt
artillery [ar'tıları] *s* Artillerie *f*
artil/lery·man *s* (**-men**) Artillerist *m*
artisan ['artızən] *s* Handwerker –in *mf*
artist ['artıst] *s* Künstler –in *mf*
artistic [ar'tıstık] *adj* künstlerisch
artistry ['artıstri] *s* Kunstfertigkeit *f*
artless ['artlıs] *adj* (*lacking art*) unkünstlerisch; (*made without skill*) stümperhaft; (*ingenuous*) unbefangen
arts' and crafts' *spl* Kunstgewerbe *n*
arts' and sci'ences *spl* Geistes- und Naturwissenschaften *pl*
arty ['arti] *adj* (coll) gekünstelt
Aryan ['erɪ-ən], ['arjən] *adj* arisch || *s* Arier –in *mf*; (*language*) Arisch *n*
as [æz], [əz] *adv* wie; **as…as** (eben)so …wie; **as far as Berlin** bis nach Berlin; **as far as I know** soviel ich weiß; **as far back as 1900** schon im Jahre 1900; **as for me** was mich betrifft; **as if** als ob; **as long as** solange; (*with the proviso that*) vorausgesetzt, daß; **as soon as** sobald wie; **as though** als ob; **as well** ebensogut, auch; **as yet** bis jetzt || *rel pron* wie, was || *prep* als; **as a rule** in der Regel || *conj* wie; (*while*) als, während; (*because*) da, weil, indem; **as it were** sozusagen
asbestos [æs'bestəs] *adj* Asbest– || *s* Asbest *m*
ascend [ə'send] *tr* (*stairs*) hinaufsteigen; (*a throne, mountain*) besteigen || *intr* emporsteigen; (*said of a balloon, plane*) aufsteigen
ascendancy [ə'sendənsi] *s* Überlegenheit *f*
ascension [ə'senʃən] *s* Aufsteigen *n*
Ascen/sion Day' *s* Himmelfahrtstag *m*
ascent [ə'sent] *s* (*on foot*) Besteigung *f*; (*by vehicle*) Auffahrt *f*; (*upward slope*) Steigung *f*; (*& fig*) Aufstieg *m*
ascertain [,æsər'ten] *tr* feststellen
ascetic [ə'setık] *adj* asketisch || *s* Asket –in *mf*
ascribe [ə'skraıb] *tr—a. to* zuschreiben (*dat*)
aseptic [ə'septık] *adj* aseptisch
ash [æʃ] *s* Asche *f*; (*tree*) Esche *f*; **ashes** Asche *f*; (*mortal remains*) sterbliche Überreste *pl*
ashamed [ə'ʃemd] *adj—be* (or *feel*) *a.* (**of**) sich schämen (*genit*)
ash/can' *s* Ascheneimer *m*
ashen ['æʃən] *adj* aschgrau
ashore [ə'ʃor] *adv* (*position*) am Land; (*direction*) ans Land
ash/tray' *s* Aschenbecher *m*
Ash' Wednes/day *s* Aschermittwoch *m*
Asia ['eʒə], ['eʃə] *s* Asien *n*
A'sia Mi'nor *s* Kleinasien *n*
aside [ə'saıd] *adv* zur Seite; **a. from** außer || *s* (theat) Seitenbemerkung *f*
asinine ['æsɪ,naın] *adj* eselhaft
ask [æsk] *tr* (*request*) bitten; (*demand*) auffordern; (*a high price*) fordern; (*inquire of*) fragen; **ask a question (of s.o.)** (j–m) e–e Frage stellen; **ask in** hereinbitten; **that is asking too much** das ist zuviel verlangt || *intr*

fragen; **ask for** bitten um; **ask for trouble** sich [*dat*] selbst Schwierigkeiten machen
askance [əs'kæns] *adv—look a. at** schief ansehen
askew [ə'skju] *adv* schräg
ask/ing *s—for the a.** umsonst
asleep [ə'slip] *adj* schlafend; (*numb*) eingeschlafen; **be a.** schlafen; **fall a.** einschlafen
asp [æsp] *s* Natter *f*
asparagus [ə'spærəgəs] *s* Spargel *m*
aspect ['æspɛkt] *s* Gesichtspunkt *m*
aspen ['æspən] *s* Espe *f*
aspersion [ə'spʌrʒən] *s* (eccl) Besprengung *f*; **cast aspersions on** verleumden
asphalt ['æsfɔlt], ['æsfælt] *s* Asphalt *m* || *tr* asphaltieren
asphyxiate [æs'fıksı,et] *tr* & *intr* ersticken
aspirant [ə'spaırənt] *s* Bewerber –in *mf*
aspirate ['æspırıt] *s* Hauchlaut *m* || ['æspı,ret] *tr* behauchen
aspire [ə'spaır] *intr* (**after, to**) streben (nach); **a. to** (*inf*) danach streben zu (*inf*)
aspirin ['æspırın] *s* Aspirin *n*
ass [æs] *s* Esel *m*; (vulg) Arsch *m*; **make an ass of oneself** (sl) sich lächerlich machen
assail [ə'sel] *tr* angreifen, anfallen; (*with questions*) bestürmen
assassin [ə'sæsın] *s* Meuchelmörder –in *mf*
assassinate [ə'sæsı,net] *tr* ermorden
assassination [ə,sæsı'neʃən] *s* Meuchelmord *m*, Ermordung *f*
assault [ə'sɔlt] *s* Überfall *m*; (*rape*) Vergewaltigung *f*; (*physical violence*) (jur) tätlicher Angriff *m*; (*threat of violence*) (jur) unmittelbare Bedrohung *f*; (mil) Sturm *m* || *tr* (er)stürmen, anfallen; (jur) tätlich beleidigen
assault' and bat'tery *s* schwere tätliche Beleidigung *f*
assay [ə'se], ['æse] *s* Prüfung *f* || [ə'se] *tr* prüfen
assemble [ə'sembəl] *tr* versammeln; (mach) montieren || *intr* sich versammeln
assembly [ə'sembli] *s* Versammlung *f*; (mach) Montage *f*; (pol) Unterhaus *n*
assem/bly line' *s* Fließband *n*
assent [ə'sent] *s* Zustimmung *f* || *intr* (**to**) zustimmen (*dat*)
assert [ə'sʌrt] *tr* behaupten; **a. oneself** sich behaupten
assertion [ə'sʌrʃən] *s* Behauptung *f*; (*of rights*) Geltendmachung *f*
assess [ə'ses] *tr* (*damage*) festsetzen; (*property*) (**at**) (ab)schätzen (auf *acc*); **assessed value** Schätzungswert *m*
assessment [ə'sesmənt] *s* (*of damage*) Festsetzung *f*; (*valuation*) Einschätzung *f*; (*of real estate*) Veranlagung *f*
assessor [ə'sesər] *s* Steuereinschätzer *m*

asset ['æset] s Vorzug m; (com) Aktivposten m; assets Vermögenswerte pl; assets and liabilities Aktiva und Passiva pl

assiduous [ə'sɪdʒʊ·əs] adj emsig

assign [ə'saɪn] tr zuweisen; (homework) aufgeben; (transfer) (jur) abtreten; (mil) zuteilen

assignment [ə'saɪnmənt] s Zuweisung f; (homework) Aufgabe f; (task) Auftrag m, Aufgabe f; (transference) (jur) Abtretung f; (to a unit) (mil) Zuteilung f

assimilate [ə'sɪmɪ,let] tr angleichen || intr sich angleichen

assimilation [ə,sɪmɪ'leʃən] s Assimilierung f, Angleichung f

assist [ə'sɪst] s (sport) Zuspiel n || tr beistehen (dat) || intr—a. in beistehen bei, behilflich sein bei

assistance [ə'sɪstəns] s Hilfe f

assistant [ə'sɪstənt] adj Hilfs-, Unter– || s (helper) Gehilfe m, Gehilfin f

associate [ə'soʃɪ·ɪt] adj Mit-, beigeordnet; (member) außerordentlich || s (companion) Gefährte m, Gefährtin f; (colleague) Kollege m, Kollegin f; (com) Partner –in mf [ə'soʃɪ,et] tr verbinden || intr (with) verkehren (mit)

asso'ciate profes'sor s außerordentlicher Professor m

association [ə,soʃɪ'eʃən] s (connection) Verbindung f; (social intercourse) Verkehr m; (society) Verband m; (suggested ideas, feelings) Assoziation f

assonance ['æsənəns] s Assonanz f

assorted [ə'sɔrtɪd] adj verschieden

assortment [ə'sɔrtmənt] s Sortiment n

assuage [ə'swedʒ] tr (pain) lindern; (hunger) befriedigen; (thirst) stillen

assume [ə's(j)um] tr (a fact as true; a certain shape, property, habit) annehmen; (a duty) auf sich nehmen; (office) antreten; (power) ergreifen; assuming that vorausgesetzt, daß

assumed' adj (feigned) erheuchelt; a. name Deckname m

assumption [ə'sʌmpʃən] s (supposition) Annahme f; (e.g., of power) Übernahme f

assurance [ə'ʃurəns] s Versicherung f

assure [ə'ʃur] tr versichern

aster ['æstər] s Aster f

asterisk ['æstə,rɪsk] s Sternchen n

astern [ə'stʌrn] adv achtern, achteraus

asthma ['æzmə] s Asthma n

astonish [ə'stanɪʃ] tr in Erstaunen setzen; be astonished at staunen über (acc), sich wundern über (acc)

aston'ishing adj erstaunlich

astonishment [ə'stanɪʃmənt] s Erstaunen n, Verwunderung f

astound [ə'staʊnd] tr überraschen

astound'ing adj erstaunlich

astray [ə'stre] adv—go a. irregehen; lead a. irreführen

astride [ə'straɪd] adv rittlings || prep (a road) an beiden Seiten (genit); (a horse) rittlings auf (dat)

astringent [əs'trɪndʒənt] adj stopfend || s Stopfmittel n

astrology [ə'straladʒi] s Astrologie f

astronaut ['æstrə,nɔt] s Astronaut m

astronautics [,æstrə'nɔtɪks] s Raumfahrtwissenschaft f, Astronautik f

astronomer [ə'stranəmər] s Astronom –in mf

astronomic(al) [,æstrə'namɪk(əl)] adj astronomisch

astronomy [ə'stranəmi] s Astronomie f

astute [ə'st(j)ut] adj scharfsinnig; (cunning) schlau

asunder [ə'sʌndər] adv auseinander

asylum [ə'saɪləm] s (refuge) Asyl n; (for the insane) Irrenhaus n

at [æt], [ət] prep (position) an (dat), auf (dat), in (dat), bei (dat), zu (dat); (direction) auf (acc), gegen (acc), nach (dat), zu (dat); (manner, circumstance) auf (acc), in (dat), unter (dat), bei (dat), zu (dat); (time) um (acc), bei (dat), auf (dat) zu (dat); at all (in questions) überhaupt; at high prices zu hohen Preisen; even at that sogar so

atheism ['eθi,ɪzəm] s Atheismus m

atheist ['eθi·ɪst] s Atheist –in mf

Athens ['æθɪns] s Athen n

athlete ['æθlit] s Sportler –in mf

ath'lete's foot' s Fußflechte f

athletic [æθ'lɛtɪk] adj athletisch, Sport-, Turn– || athletics s Athletik f

Atlantic [æt'læntɪk] adj atlantisch || s Atlantik m

atlas ['ætləs] s Atlas m

atmosphere ['ætməs,fɪr] s (& fig) Atmosphäre f

atmospheric [,ætməs'fɛrɪk] adj atmosphärisch

atom ['ætəm] s Atom n

atomic [ə'tamɪk] adj atomisch, atomar, Atom–

atom'ic age' s Atomzeitalter n

atom'ic bomb' s Atombombe f

atom'ic pow'er s Atomkraft f; atomic powers (pol) Atommächte pl

atomizer ['ætə,maɪzər] s Zerstäuber m

atone [ə'ton] intr—a. for büßen

atonement [ə'tonmənt] s Buße f

atrocious [ə'troʃəs] adj gräßlich

atrocity [ə'trasɪti] s Greueltat f

atro·phy ['ætrəfi] s Verkümmerung f, Atrophie f || v (pret & pp –phied) tr auszehren || intr verkümmern

attach [ə'tætʃ] tr (with glue, stitches, tacks) (to) anheften (an acc); (connect) (to) befestigen (an acc); (importance) (to) beimessen (dat); (a person) (jur) verhaften; (a thing) (jur) beschlagnahmen; (mil) (to) zuteilen (dat); a. oneself to sich anschließen an (acc); be attached to festhalten an (dat); (fig) verwachsen sein mit

attaché [,ætə'ʃe] s Attaché m

attaché' case' s Aktenköfferchen n

attachment [ə'tætʃmənt] s Befestigung f; (regard) (to) Zuneigung f (zu); (device) Zusatzgerät n; (of a person) (jur) Verhaftung f; (of a thing) (jur) Beschlagnahme f

attack [ə'tæk] s Angriff m; (pathol)

Anfall *m* ‖ *tr & intr* angreifen; (pathol) überfallen

attain [ə'ten] *tr* erreichen, erzielen ‖ *intr*—**a. to** erreichen

attainment [ə'tenmənt] *s* Erreichen *n;* **attainments** Fertigkeiten *pl*

attempt [ə'tɛmpt] *s* Versuch *m; (assault)* Attentat *n* ‖ *tr* versuchen

attend [ə'tɛnd] *tr* beiwohnen *(dat); (school, church)* besuchen; *(accompany)* begleiten; *(a patient)* behandeln ‖ *intr*—**a. to** nachgehen *(dat)*, erledigen

attendance [ə'tɛndəns] *s* Besuch *m; (number in attendance)* Besucherzahl *f;* (med) Behandlung *f*

attendant [ə'tɛndənt] *s (servant, waiter)* Diener –in *mf; (keeper)* Wärter –in *mf; (at a gas station)* Tankwart *m; (escort)* Begleiter –in *mf*

attention [ə'tɛnʃən] *s* Aufmerksamkeit *f;* Acht *f;* **a. Mr. X.** zu Händen von Herrn X; **call a. to** hinweisen auf *(acc);* **call s.o.'s a. to** j–n aufmerksam machen auf *(acc);* **pay a.** achtgeben; **pay a. to** achten auf *(acc);* **stand at a.** stillstehen ‖ *interj* (mil) Achtung!

attentive [ə'tɛntɪv] *adj* aufmerksam

attenuate [ə'tɛnjuˌet] *tr (dilute, thin)* verdünnen; *(weaken)* abschwächen

attest [ə'tɛst] *tr* bezeugen ‖ *intr*—**a. to** bezeugen

attic ['ætɪk] *s* Dachboden *m; (as living quarters)* Mansarde *f*

attire [ə'taɪr] *s* Putz *m* ‖ *tr* kleiden

attitude ['ætɪˌt(j)ud] *s* Haltung *f;* (aer, rok) Lage *f*

attorney [ə'tʌrni] *s* Rechtsanwalt *m*

attor'ney gen'eral *s* **(attorneys general)** Justizminister *m*

attract [ə'trækt] *tr* anziehen, reizen; *(attention)* erregen

attraction [ə'trækʃən] *s* Anziehungskraft *f; (that which attracts)* Anziehungspunkt *m; (in a circus, variety show)* Attraktion *f;* (theat) Zugstück *m*

attractive [ə'træktɪv] *adj* reizvoll; *(price, offer)* günstig

attribute ['ætrɪˌbjut] *s* Attribut *n* ‖ [ə'trɪbjut] *tr* (to) zuschreiben *(dat)*

attrition [ə'trɪʃən] *s* Abnutzung *f*, Verschleiß *m*

attune [ə't(j)un] *tr* **(to)** abstimmen (auf *acc)*

auburn ['ɔbərn] *adj* kastanienbraun

auction ['ɔkʃən] *s* Auktion *f* ‖ *tr*—**a. off** versteigern; **be auctioned off** unter den Hammer kommen

auctioneer [ˌɔkʃən'ɪr] *s* Versteigerer –in *mf*

audacious [ɔ'deʃəs] *adj (daring)* kühn; *(brazen)* keck

audacity [ɔ'dæsɪti] *s (daring)* Kühnheit *f; (insolence)* Unverschämtheit *f*

audience ['ɔdɪ·əns] *s (spectators)* Publikum *n; (formal hearing)* Audienz *f;* (rad) Zuhörerschaft *f;* (telv) Fernsehpublikum *n*

au'dio fre'quency ['ɔdɪˌo] *s* Tonfrequenz *f*, Hörfrequenz *f*

au'dio-vis'ual *adj* audiovisuell; **a. aids** Lehrmittel *pl*

audit ['ɔdɪt] *s* Rechnungsprüfung *f* ‖ *tr* prüfen, revidieren; *(a lecture)* als Gasthörer belegen

audition [ɔ'dɪʃən] *s* Hörprobe *f* ‖ *tr* vorspielen (or vorsingen) lassen ‖ *intr* vorspielen, vorsingen

auditor ['ɔdɪtər] *s* (com) Rechnungsprüfer –in *mf;* (educ) Gasthörer –in *mf*

auditorium [ˌɔdɪ'torɪ·əm] *s* Hörsaal *m*

auger ['ɔgər] *s* Bohrer *m*

augment [ɔg'mɛnt] *tr (in size)* vergrößern; *(in number)* vermehren ‖ *intr* sich vergrößern; sich vermehren

augur ['ɔgər] *s* Augur *m* ‖ *intr* weissagen; **a. well for** Gutes versprechen für

augury ['ɔgəri] *s* Weissagung *f*

august [ɔ'gʌst] *adj* erhaben ‖ **August** ['ɔgəst] *s* August *m*

aunt [ænt], [ɑnt] *s* Tante *f*

auricle ['ɔrɪkəl] *s* äußeres Ohr *n; (of the heart)* Herzohr *n*

auspices ['ɔspɪsɪz] *spl* Auspizien *pl*

auspicious [ɔs'pɪʃəs] *adj* glückverheißend

austere [ɔs'tɪr] *adj (stern)* streng; *(simple)* einfach; *(frugal)* genügsam; *(style)* schmucklos

Australia [ɔ'streljə] *s* Australien *n*

Australian [ɔ'streljən] *adj* australisch ‖ *s* Australier –in *mf*

Austria ['ɔstrɪ·ə] *s* Österreich *n*

Austrian ['ɔstrɪ·ən] *adj* österreichisch ‖ *s* Österreicher –in *mf; (dialect)* Österreichisch *n*

authentic [ɔ'θɛntɪk] *adj* authentisch

authenticate [ɔ'θɛntɪˌket] *tr (establish as genuine)* als echt erweisen; *(a document)* beglaubigen

author ['ɔθər] *s (of a book)* Autor –in *mf; (creator)* Urheber –in *mf*

authoritative [ɔ'θɔrɪˌtetɪv] *adj* maßgebend

authority [ɔ'θɔrɪti] *s (power; expert)* Autorität *f; (right)* Recht *n; (approval)* Genehmigung *f; (source)* Quelle *f; (commanding influence)* Ansehen *n; (authoritative body)* Behörde *f;* **on one's own a.** auf eigene Verantwortung; **the authorities** die Behörden

authorize ['ɔθəˌraɪz] *tr* autorisieren

au'thorship' *s* Autorschaft *f*

au·to ['ɔto] *s* **(-tos)** Auto *n*

autobiography [ˌɔtobaɪ'ɑgrəfi] *s* Selbstbiographie *f*

autocratic [ˌɔtə'krætɪk] *adj* autokratisch

autograph ['ɔtəˌgræf] *s* Autogramm *n* ‖ *tr* autographieren

automat ['ɔtəˌmæt] *s* Automatenrestaurant *n*

automatic [ˌɔtə'mætɪk] *adj* automatisch ‖ *s* Selbstladepistole *f*

automat'ic transmis'sion *s* Automatik *f*

automation [ˌɔtə'meʃən] *s* Automation *f*

automa·ton [ɔ'tɑməˌtɑn] *s* **(-tons & -ta** [tə]**)** Automat *m*

automobile [,ɔtəmo'bil] *s* Automobil *n*

automotive [,ɔtə'motɪv] *adj* Auto–

autonomous [ɔ'tʌnəməs] *adj* autonom

autonomy [ɔ'tɑnəmi] *s* Autonomie *f*

autopsy ['ɔtɑpsi] *s* Obduktion *f*

autumn ['ɔtəm] *adj* Herbst– ‖ *s* Herbst *m*

autumnal [ɔ'tʌmnəl] *adj* herbstlich

auxiliary [ɔg'zɪljəri] *adj* Hilfs– ‖ *s* (*helper*) Helfer –in *mf;* (gram) Hilfszeitwort *n;* **auxiliaries** (mil) Hilfstruppen *pl*

avail [ə'vel] *s*—**to no a.** nutzlos; **without a.** vergeblich ‖ *tr* nützen (*dat*); **a. oneself of** sich bedienen (*genit*) ‖ *intr* nützen

available [ə'veləbəl] *adj* vorhanden; (*articles, products*) erhältlich; (*e.g., documents*) zugänglich; **be a.** (*for consultation, etc.*) zu sprechen sein; **make a.** (**to**) zur Verfügung stellen (*dat*)

avalanche ['ævə,læntʃ] *s* Lawine *f*

avarice ['ævərɪs] *s* Habsucht *f*, Geiz *m*

avaricious [,ævə'rɪʃəs] *adj* geizig

avenge [ə'vendʒ] *tr* (*a person*) rächen; (*a crime*) ahnden; **a. oneself on** sich rächen an (*dat*)

avenger [ə'vendʒər] *s* Rächer –in *mf*

avenue ['ævə,n(j)u] *s* (*wide street*) Straße *f;* (fig) Weg *m*

average ['ævərɪdʒ] *adj* Durchschnitts– ‖ *s* Durchschnitt *m;* (naut) Havarie *f;* **on the a.** im Durchschnitt ‖ *tr* (*amount to, as a mean quantity*) durchschnittlich betragen; (*find the average of*) den Durchschnitt berechnen von; (*earn on the average*) durchschnittlich verdienen; (*travel on the average*) durchschnittlich zurücklegen

averse [ə'vʌrs] *adj* (**to**) abgeneigt (*dat*)

aversion [ə'vʌrʒən] *s* (**to**) Abneigung *f* (gegen)

avert [ə'vʌrt] *tr* abwenden

aviary ['evɪ,ɛri] *s* Vogelhaus *n*

aviation [,evɪ'eʃən] *s* Flugwesen *n*

aviator ['evɪ,etər] *s* Flieger –in *mf*

avid ['ævɪd] *adj* gierig

avocation [,ævə'keʃən] *s* Nebenbeschäftigung *f*

avoid [ə'vɔɪd] *tr* (*a person*) meiden; (*a thing*) vermeiden

avoidable [ə'vɔɪdəbəl] *adj* vermeidbar

avoidance [ə'vɔɪdəns] *s* (*of a person*) Meidung *f;* (*of a thing*) Vermeidung *f*

avow [ə'vau] *tr* bekennen, gestehen

avowal [ə'vau·əl] *s* Bekenntnis *n*

avowed' *adj* (*declared*) erklärt; (*acknowledged*) offen anerkannt

await [ə'wet] *tr* erwarten

awake [ə'wek] *adj* wach, munter ‖ *v* (*pret & pp* **awoke** [ə'wok] & **awaked**) *tr* wecken; (fig) erwecken ‖ *intr* erwachen

awaken [ə'weken] *tr* wecken; (fig) erwecken ‖ *intr* erwachen

awak'ening *s* Erwachen *n;* **a rude a.** ein unsanftes Erwachen

award [ə'wɔrd] *s* Preis *m*, Prämie *f* ‖ *tr* (**to**) zuerkennen (*dat*)

aware [ə'wer] *adj*—**be a. of** sich [*dat*] bewußt sein (*genit*)

awareness [ə'wernɪs] *s* Bewußtsein *n*

awash [ə'waʃ] *adj* überschwemmt

away [ə'we] *adj* abwesend; (*on a trip*) verreist; (sport) Auswärts– ‖ *adv* fort, (hin)weg; **do a. with** abschaffen; **make a. with** (*kill*) umbringen

awe [ɔ] *s* (**of**) Ehrfurcht *f* (vor *dat*); **stand in awe of s.o.** vor j–m Ehrfurcht haben

awesome ['ɔsəm] *adj* ehrfurchtgebietend

awful ['ɔfəl] *adj* ehrfurchtgebietend; (coll) furchtbar

awfully ['ɔfəli] *adv* (coll) furchtbar

awhile [ə'hwaɪl] *adv* eine Zeitlang

awkward ['ɔkwərd] *adj* ungeschickt; (*situation*) peinlich

awl [ɔl] *s* Ahle *f*, Pfriem *m*

awning ['ɔnɪŋ] *s* Markise *f*

awry [ə'raɪ] *adv*—**go a.** schiefgehen

ax [æks] *s* Axt *f*, Beil *n*

axiom ['æksɪ·əm] *s* Axiom *n*

axiomatic [,æksɪ·ə'mætɪk] *adj* axiomatisch

axis ['æksɪs] *s* (**axes** ['æksiz]) Achse *f*

axle ['æksəl] *s* Achse *f*

ay(e) [aɪ] *adv* (*yes*) ja; **aye, aye, sir!** zu Befehl, Herr (*Leutnant, etc.*) ‖ *s* Ja *n*, Jastimme *f;* **the ayes have it** die Mehrheit ist dafür

azalea [ə'zeljə] *s* Azalee *f*

azure ['æʒər] *adj* azurblau ‖ *s* Azur *m*

B

B, b [bi] zweiter Buchstabe des englischen Alphabets; (mus) H *n;* **B flat** B *n;* **B sharp** His *n*

babble ['bæbəl] *s* Geschwätz *n;* (*of brook*) Geplätscher *n* ‖ *tr* schwätzen ‖ *intr* schwätzen; (*said of a brook*) plätschern

babe [beb] *s* Kind *n;* (*naive person*) Kindskopf *m;* (*pretty girl*) Puppe *f*

baboon [bæ'bun] *s* (zool) Pavian *m*

ba·by ['bebi] *s* Baby *n;* (*youngest child*) Nesthäkchen *n* ‖ *v* (*pret & pp* –**bied**) *tr* verzärteln

ba'by bot'tle *s* Saugflasche *f*

ba'by car'riage *s* Kinderwagen *m*

ba'by grand' *s* Stutzflügel *m*

ba'by pow'der *s* Kinderpuder *m*

ba'by-sit' *v* (*pret & pp* –**sat;** *ger* –**sitting**) *intr* Kinder hüten

ba'by-sit'ter *s* Babysitter *m*

ba'by talk' s Babysprache f
ba'by teeth' spl Milchzähne pl
baccalaureate [ˌbækəˈlɔrɪ·ɪt] s (bachelor's degree) Bakkalaureat n; (service) Gottesdienst m bei der akademischen Promotion
bacchanal [ˈbækənəl] s (devotee) Bacchantin f; (orgy) Bacchanal n
bachelor [ˈbætʃələr] s Junggeselle m
bach'elorhood' s Junggesellenstand m
Bach'elor of Arts' s Bakkalaureus m der Geisteswissenschaften
Bach'elor of Sci'ence s Bakkalaureus m der Naturwissenschaften
bacil·lus [bəˈsɪləs] s (–li [laɪ]) Bazillus m, Stäbchenbakterie f
back [bæk] adj Hinter-, Rück– ‖ s (of a man, animal) Rücken m, Kreuz n; (of a hand, book, knife, mountain) Rücken m; (of a head, house, door, picture, sheet) Rückseite f; (of a fabric) linke Seite f; (of a seat) Rückenlehne f; (of a coin) Kehrseite f; (of clothing) Rückenteil m; (sport) Verteidiger m; at the b. of (e.g., a room) hinten in (dat); b. to b. (coll) nacheinander; behind s.o.'s b. hinter j–s Rücken; have one's b. to the wall an die Wand gedrückt sein; turn one's b. on s.o. (& fig) j–m den Rücken kehren ‖ adv zurück; b. and forth hin und her; b. home bei uns (zulande); ‖ tr (a person) den Rücken decken (dat); (a candidate, product) befürworten; (a horse) setzen auf (acc); b. up (a car) rückwärts laufen lassen; b. water rückwärts rudern; das Schiff rückwärts fahren lassen; (fig) sich zurückziehen ‖ intr —b. down klein beigeben; b. down from abstehen von; b. out of zurücktreten von; b. up zurückfahren; zurückgehen; (said of a sewer) zurückfließen
back'ache' s Rückenschmerzen pl
back'bit'ing s Anschwärzerei f
back'bone' s Rückgrat n; (fig) Willenskraft f
back'break'ing adj mühsam
back' door' s Hintertür f
back'drop' s (fig & theat) Hintergrund m
backer [ˈbækər] s Förderer m, Unterstützer m; (com) Hintermann m
back'fire' s Fehlzündung f ‖ intr fehlzünden; (fig) nach hinten losgehen
back'ground' adj Hintergrund– ‖ s (& fig) Hintergrund m; (e.g., of an applicant) Vorbildung f, Erfahrung f
back'hand' s (tennis) Ruckhandschlag m
back'hand'ed adj Rückhand–; (compliment) zweideutig
back'ing s Unterstützung f; (material) versteifende Ausfütterung f
back'lash' s (& fig) Rückschlag m; (mach) toter Gang m
back'log' s Rückstand m
back' or'der s rückständiger Auftrag m
back' pay' s rückständiger Lohn m
back' seat' s Rücksitz m
back'side' s Rückseite f; (coll) Gesäß n

back'space' intr den Wagen zurückschieben
back'space key' s Rücktaste f
back'spin' s Rückeffet n
back'stage' adv hinten auf der Bühne
back' stairs' spl Hintertreppe f
back'stop' s (baseball) Ballfang m
back' stretch' s Gegengerade f
back'stroke' s Rückenschwimmen n
back'swept' adj pfeilförmig
back' talk' s freche Antworten pl
back'track' intr denselben Weg zurückgehen; (fig) e–n Rückzieher machen
back'up' s (stand-by) Beistand m; (in traffic) Verkehrsstauung f
back'up light' s (aut) Rückfahrscheinwerfer m
backward [ˈbækwərd] adj rückwärts gerichtet, Rück–; (country) rückständig; (in development) zurückgeblieben; (shy) zurückhaltend ‖ adv rückwärts, zurück; (fig) verkehrt; b. and forward vor und zurück
backwardness [ˈbækwərdnɪs] s Rückständigkeit f; (shyness) Zurückhaltung f
back'wash' s zurücklaufende Strömung f
back'wa'ter s Rückstau m; (fig) Öde f
back'woods' spl Hinterwälder pl
back'yard' s Hinterhof m
bacon [ˈbekən] s Speck m; bring home the b. (sl) es schaffen
bacteria [bækˈtɪrɪ·ə] spl Bakterien pl
bacteriological [bækˌtɪrɪ·əˈladʒɪkəl] adj bakteriologisch
bacteriology [bækˌtɪrɪˈalədʒi] s Bakteriologie f, Bakterienkunde f
bacteri·um [bækˈtɪrɪ·əm] s (–a [ə]) Bakterie f
bad [bæd] adj schlecht, schlimm; (unfavorable) ungünstig; (risk) zweifelhaft; (debt) uneinbringlich; (check) ungedeckt; (blood) böse; (breath) übelriechend; (language) anstößig; (pain) stark; bad for schädlich (dat); from bad to worse immer schlimmer; I feel bad about it es tut mir leid; too bad! schade!
bad' egg' s (sl) übler Kunde m
badge [bædʒ] s Abzeichen n
badger [ˈbædʒər] s Dachs m ‖ tr quälen
bad' luck' s Unglück n, Pech n
badly [ˈbædli] adv schlecht, übel; (coll) dringend; b. wounded schwerverwundet; be b. off übel dran sein
badminton [ˈbædmɪntən] s Federballspiel n
bad'-tem'pered adj schlecht gelaunt
baffle [ˈbæfəl] s Sperre f; (on loudspeaker) Schallwand f ‖ tr verwirren; (gas) drosseln
baf'fling adj verwirrend
bag [bæg] s Sack m; (for small items) Tüte f; (for travel) Reisetasche f; (sl) Frauenzimmer n; (hunt) Strecke f; bag and baggage mit Sack und Pack; it's in the bag das haben wir in der Tasche ‖ v (pret & pp bagged; ger bagging) tr einsacken; (hunt) zur Strecke bringen ‖ intr sich bauschen
baggage [ˈbægɪdʒ] s Gepäck n

bag'gage car' s Gepäckwagen m
bag'gage check' s Gepäckschein m
bag'gage count'er s Gepäckabfertigung f
bag'gage room' s Gepäckaufbewahrung f
baggy ['bægi] adj bauschig
bag'pipe' s Dudelsack m; **play the b.** dudeln
bail [bel] s Kaution f; **be out on b.** gegen Kaution auf freiem Fuß sein; **put up b. for** bürgen für || tr—**b. out** (water) aussschöpfen; (fig) retten; (jur) durch Kaution aus der Haft befreien || intr Wasser schöpfen; **b. out** (aer) abspringen
bailiff ['belɪf] s (agr) Gutsverwalter m; (jur) Gerichtsvollzieher m
bailiwick ['belɪwɪk] s (fig) Spezialgebiet n; (jur) Amtsbezirk m
bait [bet] s (& fig) Köder m || tr (traps) mit Köder versehen; (lure) ködern; (harass) quälen
bake [bek] tr (bread) backen; (meat) braten; (in a kiln) brennen || intr backen; (meat) braten
baked' goods' spl Gebäck n, Backwaren pl
baked' pota'to s gebackene Pellkartoffel f
baker ['bekər] s Bäcker –in mf
bak'er's doz'en s dreizehn Stück pl
bakery ['bekəri] s Bäckerei f
bak'ing pow'der s Backpulver n
bak'ing so'da s Backpulver n
balance ['bæləns] s (equilibrium) Gleichgewicht n; (remainder) Rest m; (scales) Waage f; (in a bank account) Bankguthaben n; (fig) Fassung f; (com) Bilanz f; || tr balancieren; (offset) abgleichen; (make come out even) ausgleichen || intr balancieren
bal'ance of pay'ments s Devisenbilanz f
bal'ance of pow'er s Gleichgewicht n der Kräfte
bal'ance sheet' s Bilanz f
bal'ance wheel' s (horol) Unruh f
balcony ['bælkəni] s Balkon m; (theat) Rang m
bald [bɔld] adj kahl; (eagle) weißköpfig; (fig) unverblümt
bald'head'ed adj kahlköpfig
baldness ['bɔldnɪs] s Kahlheit f
bald' spot' s Kahlstelle f
bale [bel] s Ballen m || tr in Ballen verpacken
baleful ['belfəl] adj unheilvoll
balk [bɔk] intr (at) scheuen (vor dat)
Balkan ['bɔlkən] adj Balkan– || s—**the Balkans** der Balkan
balky ['bɔki] adj störrisch
ball [bɔl] s Ball m; (dance) Ball m; (of yarn) Knäuel m & n; (of the foot) Ballen m; **be on the b.** (coll) bei der Sache sein; **have a lot on the b.** (coll) viel auf dem Kasten haben
ballad ['bæləd] s Ballade f
ball'-and-sock'et joint' s Kugelgelenk n
ballast ['bæləst] s (aer, naut) Ballast m; (rr) Schotter m || tr (aer, naut) mit Ballast beladen; (rr) beschottern

ball' bear'ing s Kugellager n
ballerina [,bælə'rinə] s Ballerina f
ballet [bæ'le] s Ballett n
ball' han'dling s (sport) Balltechnik f
ballistic [bə'lɪstɪk] adj ballistisch || **ballistics** s Ballistik f
balloon [bə'lun] s Ballon m
ballot ['bælət] s Stimmzettel m || intr abstimmen
bal'lot box' s Wahlurne f
ball'-point pen' s Kugelschreiber m
ball'room' s Ballsaal m, Tanzsaal m
ballyhoo ['bælɪ,hu] s Tamtam n || tr Tamtam machen um
balm [bam] s (& fig) Balsam m
balmy ['bami] adj mild, lind; **be b.** (coll) e–n Tick haben
baloney [bə'loni] s (sausage) (coll) Bolognawurst f; (sl) Quatsch m
balsam ['bɔlsəm] s Balsam m
Baltic ['bɔltɪk] adj baltisch || s Ostsee f
baluster ['bæləstər] s Geländersäule f
balustrade ['bæləs,tred] s Brüstung f
bamboo [bæm'bu] s Bambus m, Bambusrohr n
bamboozle [bæm'buzəl] tr (cheat) anschmieren; (mislead) irreführen; (perplex) verwirren
ban [bæn] s Verbot n; (eccl) Bann m; || v (pret & pp banned; ger banning) tr verbieten
banal ['benəl] adj banal
banana [bə'nænə] s Banane f; (tree) Bananenbaum m
band [bænd] s (e.g., of a hat) Band n; (stripe) Steifen m; (gang) Bande f; (mus) Musikkapelle f; (rad) Band n || intr—**b. together** sich zusammenrotten
bandage ['bændɪdʒ] s Verband m || tr verbinden
Band'-Aid' s (trademark) Schnellverband m
bandit ['bændɪt] s Bandit m
band'lead'er s Kapellmeister m
band' saw' s Bandsäge f
band'stand' s Musikpavillon m
band'wag'on s—**climb the b.** mitlaufen
bane [ben] s Ruin m
baneful ['benfəl] adj verderblich
bang [bæŋ] s Knall m; **bangs** Ponyfrisur f; **with a b.** mit Krach || tr knallen lassen; (a door) zuschlagen; || intr knallen; (said of a door) zuschlagen; || interj bums! paff!
bang'-up' adj (sl) tipptopp, prima
banish ['bænɪʃ] tr verbannen
banishment ['bænɪʃmənt] s Verbannung f
banister ['bænɪstər] s Geländer n
bank [bæŋk] s Bank f; (of a river) Ufer n; (in a road) Überhöhung f; (aer) Schräglage f; (rr) Böschung f; || tr (money) in e–r Bank deponieren; (a road) überhöhen; (aer) in Schräglage bringen || intr (at) ein Bankkonto haben (bei); (aer) in die Kurve gehen; **b. on** bauen auf (acc)
bank' account' s Bankkonto n
bank' bal'ance s Bankguthaben n
bank'book' s Sparbuch n, Bankbuch n
banker ['bæŋkər] s Bankier –in mf

bank'ing s Bankwesen n
bank' note' s Geldschein m
bank'roll' s Rolle f von Geldscheinen || tr (sl) finanzieren
bankrupt ['bæŋkrʌpt] adj bankrott; **go b.** Pleite machen || tr bankrott machen
bankruptcy ['bæŋkrʌptsi] s Bankrott m
bank' state'ment s Bankausweis m
bank' tell'er s Kassierer –in mf
banner ['bænər] s Fahne f, Banner n
banquet ['baŋkwɪt] s Bankett n || intr tafeln
banter ['bæntər] s Neckerei f || intr necken
baptism ['bæptɪzəm] s Taufe f
baptismal [bæp'tɪzməl] adj Tauf–
baptis'mal certi'ficate s Taufschein m
bap'tism of fire' s Feuertaufe f
Baptist ['bæptɪst] s Baptist –in mf, Wiedertäufer m
baptistery ['bæptɪstəri] s Taufkapelle f
baptize [bæp'taɪz] tr taufen
bar [bɑr] s Stange f; (of a door, window) Riegel m; (of gold, etc.) Barren m; (of chocolate, soap) Riegel m; (barroom) Bar f; (counter) Schanktisch m; (obstacle) (to) Schranke f (gegen); (jur) Gerichtshof m, Anwaltschaft f; (bar line) (mus) Taktstrich m; (measure) Takt m; (naut) Barre f; **be admitted to the bar** zur Advokatur zugelassen werden; **behind bars** hinter Gittern; || prep— **bar none** ohne Ausnahme || v (pret & pp barred; ger barring) tr (a door) verriegeln; (a window) vergittern; (the way) versperren; **bar s.o. from** j–n hindern an (dat)
barb [bɑrb] s Widerhaken m; (fig) Stachelrede f; (bot) Bart m
barbarian [bɑr'berɪ-ən] s Barbar m
barbaric [bɑr'bærɪk] adj barbarisch
barbarism ['bɑrbə‚rɪzəm] s Barbarei f; (gram) Barbarismus m
barbarity [bɑr'berɪti] s Barbarei f
barbarous ['bɑrbərəs] adj barbarisch
barbecue ['bɑrbɪ‚kju] s am Spieß (or am Rost) gebratenes Fleisch n; (grill) Bratrost m; (outdoor meal) Gartengrillfest n || tr am Spieß (or am Rost) braten
barbed' wire' s Stacheldraht m
barbed'-wire entan'glement s Drahtverhau m
barber ['bɑrbər] s Friseur m
bar'ber chair' s Friseursessel m
bar'bershop' s Friseurladen m
bard [bɑrd] s Barde m
bare [ber] adj nackt, bloß; (tree, wall) kahl; (facts) nackt; (majority) knapp || tr entblößen; (heart, thoughts) offenbaren; (teeth) fletschen
bare'back' adj & adv sattellos
bare'faced' adj unverschämt
bare'foot' adj & adv barfuß
bare'head'ed adj & adv barhäuptig
barely ['berli] adv kaum, bloß
bar'fly' s Kneipenhocker m
bargain ['bɑrgɪn] s (deal) Geschäft n; (cheap purchase) Sonderangebot n; **into the b.** obendrein; **it's a b.!** abge-

macht! || tr—**b. away** mit Verlust verkaufen || intr handeln; **b. for** verhandeln über (acc)
bar'gain price' s Preisschlager m
bar'gain sale' s Sonderverkauf m
barge [bɑrdʒ] s Lastkahn m; || intr— **b. in** hereinstürzen; **b. into** stürzen in (acc)
baritone ['bærɪ‚ton] s Bariton m
barium ['berɪ-əm] s Barium n
bark [bɑrk] s (of a tree) Rinde f; (of a dog) Bellen n, Gebell n; (boat) Barke f; || tr—**b. out** bellend hervorstoßen || intr bellen; **b. at** anbellen
barker ['bɑrkər] s Anreißer m
barley ['bɑrli] s Gerste f; **grain of b.** Graupe f
bar'maid' s Schankmädchen n, Bardame f
barn [bɑrn] s Scheune f; (for animals) Stall m
barnacle ['bɑrnəkəl] s Entenmuschel f
barn'storm' intr auf dem Lande Theateraufführungen versanstalten; (pol) auf dem Lande Wahlreden halten
barn'yard' s Scheunenhof m
barometer [bə'rɑmɪtər] s Barometer n
barometric [‚bærə'metrɪk] adj barometrisch
baron ['bærən] s Baron m
baroness ['bærənɪs] s Baronin f
baroque [bə'rok] adj barock || s (style, period) Barock m & n
barracks ['bærəks] s (temporary wooden structure) Baracke f; (mil) Kaserne f
barrage [bə'rɑʒ] s Sperrfeuer n; **moving b.** Sperrfeuerwalze f
barrel ['bærəl] s Faß n, Tonne f; (of a gun) Lauf m; (of money, fun) große Menge f; **have over the b.** (sl) in der Gewalt haben || intr (coll) rasen, sausen
barren ['bærən] adj dürr, unfruchtbar; (landscape) kahl
barricade ['bærɪ‚ked] s Barrikade f || tr verbarrikadieren
barrier ['bærɪ-ər] s Schranke f, Schlagbaum m; (e.g., on a street) Sperre f
bar'room' s Schenkstube f, Bar f
bartend ['bɑr‚tend] intr Getränke ausschenken
bar'tend'er s Schankwirt m, Barmixer m
barter ['bɑrtər] s Tauschhandel m || tr tauschen || intr Tauschhandel treiben
basalt [bə'sɔlt], ['bæsɔlt] s Basalt m
base [bes] adj gemein, niedrig; (metal) unedel || s (cosmetic) Schminkunterlage f; (fig) Grundlage f; (archit) Basis f, Fundament n; (baseball) Mal n; (chem) Base f; (geom) Grundlinie f, Grundfläche f; (math) Basis f; (mil) Stützpunkt m || tr (mil) stationieren; **b. on** stützen auf (acc), gründen auf (acc)
base'ball' s Baseball m
base'board' s Wandleiste f
basement ['besmənt] s Kellergeschoß n
bash [bæʃ] s heftiger Schlag m
bashful ['bæʃfəl] adj schüchtern

basic ['besɪk] *adj* grundsätzlich; (*e.g.*, *salary*) Grund–; (chem) basisch
basically ['besɪkəli] *adv* grundsätzlich
ba'sic train'ing *s* Grundausbildung *f*
basilica [bə'sɪlɪkə] *s* Basilika *f*
basin ['besɪn] *s* Becken *n*; (geol) Mulde *f*; (naut) Bassin *n*
ba·sis ['besɪs] *s* (*-ses* [siz]) Basis *f*, Grundlage *f*; **b. of comparison** Vergleichsgrundlage *f*; **put on a firm b.** (fin) sanieren
bask [bæsk] *intr* (& fig) sich sonnen
basket ['bæskɪt] *s* (& sport) Korb *m*
bas'ketball' *s* Basketball *m*, Korbball *m*
bas-relief [ˌbɑrɪ'lif] *s* Flachrelief *n*
bass [bes] *s* (mus) Baß *m* ‖ [bæs] *s* (ichth) Flußbarsch *m*, Seebarsch *m*
bass' clef' *s* Baßschlüssel *m*
bass' drum' *s* große Trommel *f*
bass' fid'dle *s* Baßgeige *f*
bassoon [bə'sun] *s* Fagott *n*
bass viol ['bes'vaɪ·əl] *s* Gambe *f*
bastard ['bæstərd] *adj* Bastard–; (*illegitimate in birth*) unehelich ‖ *s* Bastard *m*; (vulg) Schweinehund *m*
baste [best] *tr* (*thrash*) verprügeln; (*scold*) schelten; (culin) begießen; (*sew*) lose (an)heften
bastion ['bæstʃən] *s* Bastion *f*
bat [bæt] *s* (sport) Schläger *m*; (zool) Fledermaus *f*; **go to bat for s.o.** (fig) für j–n eintreten ‖ *v* (*pret & pp* **bat'ted;** *ger* **bat'ting**) *tr* schlagen; **without batting an eye** ohne mit der Wimper zu zucken
batch [bætʃ] *s* Satz *m*, Haufen *m*; (*of bread*) Schub *m*; (*of letters*) Stoß *m*
bated ['betɪd] *adj*—**with b. breath** mit verhaltenem Atem
bath [bæθ] *s* Bad *n*; **take a b.** ein Bad nehmen
bathe [beʒ] *tr & intr* baden
bather ['beðər] *s* Badende *mf*
bath'house' *s* Umkleideräume *pl*
bath'ing *s* Baden *n*, Bad *n*
bath'ing cap' *s* Badehaube *f*
bath'ing suit' *s* Badeanzug *m*
bath'ing trunks' *spl* Badehose *f*
bath'robe' *s* Bademantel *m*
bath'room' *s* Badezimmer *n*
bath'room fix'tures *spl* Armaturen *pl*
bath'room scales *spl* Personenwaage *f*
bath' tow'el *s* Badetuch *n*
bath'tub' *s* Badewanne *f*
baton [bæ'tɑn] *s* (mil) Kommandostab *m*; (mus) Taktstock *m*
battalion [bə'tæljən] *s* Bataillon *n*
batter ['bætər] *s* Teig *m*; (baseball) Schläger –in *mf* ‖ *tr* zerschlagen; (aer) bombardieren; **b. down** niederschlagen; **b. in** einschlagen
bat'tering ram' *s* Sturmbock *m*
battery ['bætəri] *s* Batterie *f*; (*secondary cell*) Akkumulator *m*; (arti) Batterie *f*; (nav) Geschützgruppe *f*
battle ['bætəl] *s* Schlacht *f*; (& fig) Kampf *m*; **do b.** kämpfen; **in b.** im Felde ‖ *tr* bekämpfen ‖ *intr* kämpfen
bat'tle array' *s* Schlachtordnung *f*
bat'tleax' *s* Streitaxt *f*; (fig) Drachen *m*
bat'tle cruis'er *s* Schlachtkreuzer *m*

bat'tle cry' *s* Schlachtruf *m*; (fig) Schlagwort *m*
bat'tle fatigue' *s* Kriegsneurose *f*
bat'tlefield' *s* Schlachtfeld *n*
bat'tlefront' *s* Front *f*, Hauptkampflinie *f*
bat'tleground' *s* Kampfplatz *m*
battlement ['bætəlmənt] *s* Zinne *f*
bat'tle scar' *s* Kampfmal *n*
bat'tleship' *s* Schlachtschiff *n*
bat'tle wag'on *s* (coll) Schlachtschiff *n*
batty ['bæti] *adj* (sl) doof
bauble ['bɔbəl] *s* Tand *m*; (*jester's staff*) Narrenstab *m*
Bavaria [bə'verɪ·ə] *s* Bayern *n*
Bavarian [bə'verɪ·ən] *adj* bayerisch ‖ *s* Bayer –in *mf*
bawd [bɔd] *s* Dirne *f*
bawdy ['bɔdi] *adj* unzüchtig
bawl [bɔl] *s* Geplärr *n* ‖ *tr*—**b. out** (*names, etc.*) ausschreien; (*scold*) anschnauzen ‖ *intr* (coll) plärren
bay [be] *adj* kastanienbraun ‖ *s* Bucht *f*; (*horse*) Rotfuchs *m*; (bot) Lorbeer *m*; **keep at bay** in Schach halten ‖ *intr* laut bellen; **bay at** anbellen
bayo·net ['be·ənɪt] *s* Bajonett *n*, Seitengewehr *n*; **with fixed bayonets** mit aufgepflanztem Bajonett ‖ *v* (*pret & pp* **–net(t)ed;** *ger* **–net(t)ing**) *tr* mit dem Bajonett erstechen
bay' win'dow *s* Erkerfenster *n*
bazaar [bə'zɑr] *s* Basar *m*, Markt *m*
bazooka [bə'zukə] *s* Panzerfaust *f*
be [bi] *v* (*pres am* [æm], *is* [ɪz], *are* [ɑr]; *pret was* [wɑz], [wʌz], *were* [wʌr]; *pp* **been** [bɪn]) *intr* sein; **be about to** in der Nähe sein; **be about to** (*inf*) im Begriff sein zu (*inf*); **be after s.o.** hinter j–m her sein; **be along** hier sein; **be behind in** Rückstand sein mit; **be behind s.o.** j–m den Rücken decken; **be from** (*a country*) stammen aus, sein aus; **be in** zu Hause sein; **be in for** zu erwarten haben; **be in for it** in der Patsche sitzen; **be in on** dabei sein bei; **be off** weggehen; **be on to s.o.** j–m auf die Schliche kommen; **be out** nicht zu Hause sein, aus sein; **be out for s.th.** auf der Suche nach etw sein; **be up** auf sein; **be up to s.th.** etw im Sinn haben; **how are you?** wie geht es Ihnen?, wie befinden Sie sich?; **how much is that?** wieviel kostet das?; **there are, there is** es gibt (*acc*) ‖ *aux*—**he is studying** er studiert; **he is to go** er soll gehen; **he was hit** er ist getroffen worden ‖ *impers*—**how is it that...?** wie kommt es, daß...?; **it is cold** es ist kalt; **it is to be seen that** es ist darauf zu sehen, daß
beach [bitʃ] *s* Strand *m*; **on the b.** am Strand, an der See ‖ *tr* auf den Strand ziehen; **be beached** stranden
beach'comb'er *s* Strandgutjäger *m*; (*wave*) Strandwelle *f*
beach'head' *s* Landekopf *m*
beach' tow'el *s* Badetuch *n*
beach' umbrel'la *s* Strandschirm *m*
beacon ['bikən] *s* Leuchtfeuer *n*, Bake *f*; (*lighthouse*) Leuchtturm *m*; (aer)

Scheinwerfer *m* ‖ *tr* lenken ‖ *intr* leuchten

bead [bid] (*of glass, wood, sweat*) Perle *f*; (*of a gun*) Korn *n*; **beads** (eccl) Rosenkranz *m*; **draw a b. on** zielen auf (*acc*)

beagle ['bigəl] *s* Spürhund *m*

beak [bik] *s* Schnabel *m*; (*nose*) (sl) Rübe *f*

beam [bim] *s* (*of wood*) Balken *m*; (*of light, heat, etc.*) Strahl *m*; (*fig*) Glanz *m*; (aer) Leitstrahl *m*; (*width of a vessel*) (naut) größte Schiffsbreite *f*; (*horizontal structural member*) (naut) Deckbalken *m*; **b. of light** Lichtkegel *m*; **off the b.** (sl) auf dem Holzweg; **on the b.** (sl) auf Draht ‖ *intr* strahlen; **b. at** anstrahlen

bean [bin] *s* Bohne *f*; (*head*) (sl) Birne *f*; **spill the beans** (sl) alles ausquatschen

bean'pole' *s* (& coll) Bohnenstange *f*

bear [ber] *adj* (*market*) flau, Baisse– ‖ *s* Bär *m*; (st. exch.) Baissier *m* ‖ *v* (*pret* **bore** [bor]; *pp* **borne** [born]) *tr* (*carry*) tragen; (*endure*) dulden, ertragen; (*children*) gebären; (*date*) tragen; (*a name, sword*) führen; (*a grudge, love*) hegen; (*a message*) überbringen; (*the consequences*) auf sich [*acc*] nehmen; **bear in mind** bedenken, beachten; **bear fruit** Früchte tragen; (fig) Frucht tragen; **bear out** bestätigen ‖ *intr*—**bear down on** losgehen auf (*acc*); (naut) zufahren auf (*acc*); **bear left** sich links halten; **bear on** sich beziehen auf (*acc*); **bear up** (**well**) **against** gut ertragen; **bear with** Geduld haben mit

bearable ['berəbəl] *adj* erträglich

beard [bird] *s* Bart *m*

beard'ed *adj* bärtig

beardless ['birdlɪs] *adj* bartlos

bearer ['berər] *s* Träger –in *mf*; (*of a message*) Überbringer –in *mf*; (com) Inhaber –in *mf*

bear' hug' *s* (coll) Knutsch *m*

bear'ing *s* Körperhaltung *f*; (mach) Lager *n*; (**on**) Beziehung *f* (auf *acc*); **bearings** (aer, naut) Lage *f*, Richtung *f*, Peilung *f*; **lose one's bearings** die Richtung verlieren

bear'skin' *s* Bärenfell *n*

beast [bist] *s* Tier *n*; (fig) Bestie *f*

beastly ['bistli] *adj* bestialisch; **b. weather** Hundewetter *n*

beast' of bur'den *s* Lasttier *n*

beat [bit] *adj* (sl) erschöpft ‖ *s* (*of the heart*) Schlag *m*; (*of a policeman*) Runde *f*, Revier *n*; (mus) Takt *m* ‖ *v* (*pret* **beat**; *pp* **beat** & **beaten**) *tr* (*eggs, a child, record, team, etc.*) schlagen; (*a carpet*) ausklopfen; (*metal*) hämmern; (*a path*) treten; **b. it!** hau ab!; **b. one's brains out** sich [*dat*] den Kopf zerbrechen; **b. s.o. to it** j–m zuvorkommen; **b. up** verprügeln ‖ *intr* schlagen, klopfen; **b. against** peitschen gegen; **b. down** niederprallen

beati•fy [bɪˈætɪ ˌfaɪ] *v* (*pret* & *pp* **–fied**) *tr* seligsprechen

beat'ing *s* Prügel *pl*

beatitude [bɪˈætɪ ˌt(j)ud] *s* Seligpreisung *f*

beau [bo] *s* (**beaus** & **beaux** [boz]) Liebhaber *m*

beautician [bjuˈtɪʃən] *s* Kosmetiker –in *mf*; (*hairdresser*) Friseuse *f*

beautiful ['bjutɪfəl] *adj* schön

beauti•fy ['bjutɪ ˌfaɪ] *v* (*pret* & *pp* **–fied**) *tr* verschönern

beauty ['bjuti] *s* (*quality; woman*) Schönheit *f*; (coll) Prachtexemplar *n*

beau'ty queen' *s* Schönheitskönigin *f*

beau'ty shop' *s* Frisiersalon *m*

beau'ty sleep' *s* Schönheitsschlaf *m*

beau'ty spot' *s* Schönheitsmal *n*

beaver ['bivər] *s* Biber *m*

because [bɪˈkɔz] *conj* weil, da ‖ *interj* darum!

because' of' *prep* wegen (*genit*)

beck [bɛk] *s* Wink *m*; **be at s.o.'s b. and call** j–m ganz zu Diensten sein

beckon ['bɛkən] *tr* zuwinken (*dat*); (*summon*) heranwinken ‖ *intr* winken; **b. to s.o.** j–m zuwinken

become [bɪˈkʌm] *v* (*pret* **–came**; *pp* **–come**) *tr* (*said of clothes*) gut anstehen (*dat*); (*said of conduct*) sich schicken für ‖ *intr* werden; **what has b. of him?** was ist aus ihm geworden?

becom'ing *adj* (*said of clothes*) kleidsam; (*said of conduct*) schicklich

bed [bɛd] *s* (*for sleeping; of a river*) Bett *n*; (*of flowers*) Beet *n*; (*of straw*) Lager *n*; (geol) Lager *n*; (rr) Unterbau *m*; **put to bed** zu Bett bringen

bed'bug' *s* Wanze *f*

bed'clothes' *spl* Bettwäsche *f*

bed'ding *s* Bettzeug *n*; (*for animals*) Streu *f*

bed'fel'low *s*—**strange bedfellows** ein seltsames Paar *n*

bedlam ['bɛdləm] *s* (fig) Tollhaus *n*; **there was b.** es ging zu wie im Tollhaus

bed' lin'en *s* Bettwäsche *f*

bed'pan' *s* Bettschüssel *f*

bed'post' *s* Bettpfosten *m*

bedraggled [bɪˈdrægəld] *adj* beschmutzt

bedridden ['bɛd ˌrɪdən] *adj* bettlägerig

bed'rock' *s* Grundgestein *n*; (fig) Grundlage *f*

bed'room' *s* Schlafzimmer *n*

bed'side' *s*—**at s.o.'s b.** an j–s Bett

bed'sore' *s* wundgelegene Stelle *f*; **get bedsores** sich wundliegen

bed'spread' *s* Bettdecke *f*, Tagesdecke *f*

bed'spring' *s* (*one coil*) Sprungfeder *f*; (*framework of springs*) Sprungfedermatratze *f*

bed'stead' *s* Bettgestell *n*

bed'time' *s* Schlafenszeit *f*; **it's past b.** es ist höchste Zeit, zu Bett zu gehen

bee [bi] *s* Biene *f*

beech [bitʃ] *s* Buche *f*

beech'nut' *s* Buchecker *f*

beef [bif] *s* Rindfleisch *n*; (*brawn*) (coll) Muskelkraft *f*; (*human flesh*) (coll) Fleisch *n*; (*complaint*) (sl) Gemecker *n* ‖ *tr*—**b. up** (coll) ver-

stärken ‖ *intr (complain)* (sl) meckern
beef' broth' *s* Kraftbrühe *f*
beef'steak' *s* Beefsteak *n*
beefy ['bifi] *adj* muskulös
bee'hive' *s* Bienenstock *m*, Bienenkorb *m*
bee'line' *s*—**make a b. for** schnurstracks losgehen auf *(acc)*
beer [bɪr] *s* Bier *n*
bee' sting' *s* Bienenstich *m*
beeswax ['biz‚wæks] *s* Bienenwachs *n*
beet [bit] *s* Rübe *f*
beetle ['bitəl] *s* Käfer *m*
be·fall [bɪ'fɔl] *v (pret –fell* ['fɛl]; *pp –fallen* ['fɔlən] *tr* betreffen, zustoßen ‖ *intr* sich ereignen
befit'ting *adj* passend
before [bɪ'fɔr] *adv* vorher, früher ‖ *prep (position or time)* vor *(dat)*; *(direction)* vor *(acc)*; **b. long** binnen kurzem; **b. now** schon früher ‖ *conj* bevor, ehe
before'hand' *adv* zuvor, vorher
befriend [bɪ'frɛnd] *tr* sich *[dat]* *(j–n)* zum Freund machen, sich anfreunden mit
befuddle [bɪ'fʌdəl] *tr* verwirren
beg [bɛg] *v (pret & pp* begged; *ger* begging) *tr* bitten um; *(a meal)* betteln um; **beg s.o. to** *(inf)* j–n bitten zu *(inf)*; **I beg your pardon** (ich bitte um) Verzeihung! ‖ *intr* betteln; *(said of a dog)* Männchen machen; **beg for** bitten um, flehen um; **beg off** absagen
be·get [bɪ'gɛt] *v (pret –got* ['gɑt]; *pp –gotten & –got; ger –getting) tr* erzeugen
beggar ['bɛgər] *s* Bettler –in *mf*
be·gin [bɪ'gɪn] *v (pret –gan* ['gæn]; *pp –gun* ['gʌn]; *ger –ginning* ['gɪnɪŋ]) *tr* beginnen, anfangen ‖ *intr* beginnen, anfangen; **to b. with** zunächst
beginner [bɪ'gɪnər] *s* Anfänger –in *mf*
beginning *s* Beginn *m*, Anfang *m*
begrudge [bɪ'grʌdʒ] *tr*—**b. s.o. s.th.** j–m etw mißgönnen
beguile [bɪ'gaɪl] *tr (mislead)* verleiten; *(charm)* betören
behalf [bɪ'hæf] *s*—**on b. of** zugunsten *(genit)*, für; *(as a representative of)* im Namen *(genit)*, im Auftrag von
behave [bɪ'hev] *intr* sich benehmen
behavior [bɪ'hevjər] *s* Benehmen *n*
behead [bɪ'hɛd] *tr* enthaupten
behind [bɪ'haɪnd] *adj (in arrears)* (in) im Rückstand (mit); **the clock is ten minutes b.** die Uhr geht zehn Minuten nach ‖ *adv (in the rear)* hinten, hinterher; *(to the rear)* nach hinten, zurück; **from b.** von hinten ‖ *s* (sl) Hintern *m*, Popo *m* ‖ *prep (position)* hinter *(dat)*; *(direction)* hinter *(acc)*; **be b. schedule** sich verspäten; **b. time** zu spät; **b. the times** hinter dem Mond
be·hold [bɪ'hold] *v (pret & pp –held* ['hɛld]) *tr* betrachten ‖ *interj* schau!
behoove [bɪ'huv] *impers*—**it behooves me** es geziemt mir
beige [beʒ] *adj* beige *n*
be'ing *adj*—**for the time b.** einstweilen

‖ *s* Dasein *n*; *(creature)* Wesen *n*; **come into b.** entstehen
belabor [bɪ'lebər] *tr* herumreiten auf *(dat)*
belated [bɪ'letɪd] *adj* verspätet
belch [bɛltʃ] *s* Rülpser *m* ‖ *tr (fire)* ausspeien ‖ *intr* rülpsen
beleaguer [bɪ'ligər] *tr* belagern
belfry ['bɛlfri] *s* Glockenturm *m*
Belgian ['bɛlʒən] *adj* belgisch ‖ *s* Belgier –in *mf*
Belgium ['bɛldʒəm] *s* Belgien *n*
belief [bɪ'lif] *s* (in) Glaube(n) *m* (an *acc)*
believable [bɪ'livəbəl] *adj* glaublich
believe [bɪ'liv] *tr (a thing)* glauben; *(a person)* glauben *(dat)* ‖ *intr* glauben; **b. in** glauben an *(acc)*; **I don't b. in war** ich halte nicht viel vom Kriege
believer [bɪ'livər] *s* Gläubige *mf*
belittle [bɪ'lɪtəl] *tr* herabsetzen
bell [bɛl] *s* Glocke *f*; *(small bell)* Klingel *f*; *(of a wind instrument)* Schalltrichter *m*; *(box)* Gong *m*
bell'boy' *s* Hotelboy *m*
bell'hop' *s* (sl) Hotelpage *m*
belligerent [bə'lɪdʒərənt] *adj* streitlustig ‖ *s* kriegführender Staat *m*
bell' jar' *s* Glasglocke *f*
bellow ['bɛlo] *s* Gebrüll *n*; **bellows** Blasebalg *m*; *(phot)* Balgen *m* ‖ *tr & intr* brüllen
bell' tow'er *s* Glockenturm *m*
bel·ly ['bɛli] *s* Bauch *m*; *(of a sail)* Bausch *m* ‖ *v (pret & pp –lied) intr* bauschen
bel'lyache' *s* (coll) Bauchweh *n* ‖ *intr* (sl) jammern
bel'ly but'ton *s* Nabel *m*
bel'ly danc'er *s* Bauchtänzerin *f*
bel'ly flop' *s* Bauchklatscher *m*
bellyful ['bɛli‚ful] *s*—**have a b. of** die Nase voll haben von
bel'ly-land'ing *s* Bauchlandung *f*
belong [bɪ'lɔŋ] *intr* **b. to** *(designating ownership)* gehören *(dat)*; *(designating membership)* gehören zu; **where does this table b.?** wohin gehört dieser Tisch?
belongings [bɪ'lɔŋɪŋz] *spl* Sachen *pl*
beloved [bɪ'lʌvɪd], [bɪ'lʌvd] *adj* geliebt ‖ *s* Geliebte *mf*
below [bɪ'lo] *adv (position)* unten; *(direction)* nach unten, hinunter ‖ *prep (position)* unter *(dat)*, unterhalb *(genit)*; *(direction)* unter *(acc)*
belt [bɛlt] *s* Riemen *m*, Gurt *m*, Gürtel *m*; *(geol)* Gebiet *n*; *(mach)* Treibriemen *m*; **tighten one's b.** den Riemen enger schnallen ‖ *tr* (sl) e–n heftigen Schlag versetzen *(dat)*
belt' buck'le *s* Gürtelschnalle *f*
belt'way' *s* Verkehrsgürtel *m*
bemoan [bɪ'mon] *tr* betrauern, beklagen
bench [bɛntʃ] *s* Bank *f*; *(jur)* Gerichtshof *m*; *(sport)* Reservebank *f*, Bank *f*
bend [bɛnd] *s* Biegung *f*; *(in a road)* Kurve *f*; **bends** (pathol) Tauchkrankheit *f* ‖ *v (pret & pp* bent [bɛnt]) *tr* biegen, beugen; *(a bow)* spannen ‖

intr sich biegen, sich beugen; **b. down** sich bücken; **b. over backwards** (fig) sich [*dat*] übergroße Mühe geben

beneath [bɪ'niθ] *adv* unten || *prep* (*position*) unter (*dat*), unterhalb (*genit*); (*direction*) unter (*acc*); **b. me** unter meiner Würde

benediction [ˌbenɪ'dɪkʃən] *s* Segen *m*

benefactor ['benɪˌfæktər] *s* Wohltäter –in *mf*

beneficence [bɪ'nefɪsəns] *s* Wohltätigkeit *f*

beneficent [bɪ'nefɪsənt] *adj* wohltätig

beneficial [ˌbenɪ'fɪʃəl] *adj* heilbringend, gesund; (**to**) nützlich (*dat*)

beneficiary [ˌbenɪ'fɪʃɪˌeri] *s* Begünstigte *mf*; (ins) Bezugsberechtigte *mf*

benefit ['benɪfɪt] *s* Nutzen *m*; (*fundraising performance*) Benefiz *n*; (ins) Versicherungsleistung *f*

benevolence [bɪ'nevələns] *s* Wohlwollen *n*

benevolent [bɪ'nevələnt] *adj* wohlwollend

benign [bɪ'naɪn] *adj* gütig; (pathol) gutartig

bent [bent] *adj* krumm, verbogen; **b. on** versessen auf (*acc*) || *s* Hang *m*

benzene [ben'zin] *s* Benzol *n*

bequeath [bɪ'kwið] *tr* vermachen

bequest [bɪ'kwest] *s* Vermächtnis *n*

berate [bɪ'ret] *tr* ausschelten, rügen

be·reave [bɪ'riv] *v* (*pret & pp* –**reaved** & –**reft** ['reft]) *tr* (**of**) berauben (*genit*)

bereavement [bɪ'rivmənt] *s* Trauerfall *m*

beret [bə're] *s* Baskenmütze *f*

Berlin [bər'lɪn] *adj* Berliner, berlinerisch || *s* Berlin *n*

Berliner [bər'lɪnər] *s* Berliner –in *mf*

berry ['beri] *s* Beere *f*

berserk [bər'sʌrk] *adj* wütend || *adv*— **go b.** wütend werden

berth [bʌrθ] *s* Schlafkoje *f*; (naut) Liegeplatz *m*; (rr) Bett *n*; **give s.o. wide b.** um j–n e–n weiten Bogen machen || *tr* am Kai festmachen

be·seech [bɪ'sitʃ] *v* (*pret & pp* –**sought** ['sɔt] & –**seeched**) *tr* anflehen

be·set [bɪ'set] *v* (*pret & pp* –**set; ger** –**setting**) *tr* bedrängen, umringen

beside [bɪ'saɪd] *prep* (*position*) neben (*dat*), bei (*dat*); (*direction*) neben (*acc*); **be b. oneself with** außer sich [*dat*] sein vor (*dat*)

besides [bɪ'saɪdz] *adv* überdies, außerdem || *prep* außer (*dat*)

besiege [bɪ'sidʒ] *tr* belagern

besmirch [bɪ'smʌrtʃ] *tr* beschmutzen

be·speak [bɪ'spik] *v* (*pret* –**spoke** ['spok]; *pp* –**spoken** ['spokən]) *tr* bezeigen

best [best] *adj* beste; **b. of all, very b.** allerbeste || *adv* am besten; **had b.** es wäre am besten, wenn || *s*—**at b.** bestenfalls; **be at one's b.** in bester Form sein; **for the b.** zum Besten; **make the b. of** sich abfinden mit; **to the b. of one's ability** nach bestem Vermögen

bestial ['bestʃəl] *adj* bestialisch

best' man' *s* Brautführer *m*

bestow [bɪ'sto] *tr* verleihen

bestowal [bɪ'sto·əl] *s* Verleihung *f*

best' sel'ler *s* (*book*) Bestseller *m*

bet [bet] *s* Wette *f*; **make a bet** e–e Wette abschließen (or eingehen) || *v* (*pret & pp* **bet & betted; ger betting**) *tr* (**on**) wetten (auf *acc*) || *intr* wetten; **you bet!** aber sicher!

betray [bɪ'tre] *tr* verraten; (*a secret*) preisgeben; (*ignorance*) offenbaren; (*a trust*) mißbrauchen

betrayal [bɪ'tre·əl] *s* Verrat *m*

betrayer [bɪ'tre·ər] *s* Verräter –in *mf*

better ['betər] *adj* besser; **the b. part of** der größere Teil (*genit*) || *s*— **change for the b.** sich zum Besseren wenden; **get the b. of** übervorteilen; **one's betters** die Höherstehenden *pl*; || *adv* besser; **all the b.** um so besser; **b. off** besser daran; (*financially*) wohlhabender; **so much the b.** desto besser; **you had b. do it at once** am besten tust du es sofort; **you had b. not** das will ich dir nicht geraten haben || *tr* verbessern; **b. oneself** sich verbessern

bet' ter half' *s* (coll) bessere Hälfte *f*

betterment ['betərmənt] *s* Besserung *f*

bettor ['betər] *s* Wettende *mf*

between [bɪ'twin] *adv*—**in b.** dazwischen || *prep* (*position*) zwischen (*dat*); (*direction*) zwischen (*acc*); **just b. you and me** ganz unter uns gesagt

bev·el ['bevəl] *adj* schräg || *s* schräge Kante *f* || *v* (*pret & pp* –**el(l)ed; ger** –**el(l)ing**) *tr* abschrägen

beverage ['bevərɪdʒ] *s* Getränk *n*

bevy ['bevi] *s* Schar *f*

bewail [bɪ'wel] *tr* beklagen

beware [bɪ'wer] *intr* sich hüten; **b.!** gib acht!; **b. of** sich hüten vor (*dat*); **b. of imitations** vor Nachahmungen wird gewarnt

bewilder [bɪ'wɪldər] *tr* verblüffen

bewilderment [bɪ'wɪldərmənt] *s* Verblüffung *f*

bewitch [bɪ'wɪtʃ] *tr* (fig) bezaubern

beyond [bɪ'jand] *adv* jenseits || *s*— **the b.** das Jenseits || *prep* jenseits (*genit*), über (*acc*) hinaus; (fig) über (*acc*), außer (*dat*); **he is b. help** ihm ist nicht mehr zu helfen; **that's b. me** das geht über meinen Verstand

B'-girl' *s* (coll) Animiermädchen *n*

bias ['baɪ·əs] *s* Voreingenommenheit *f* || *tr* (**against**) einnehmen (gegen)

bi'ased *adj* voreingenommen

bib [bɪb] *s* Latz *m*, Lätzchen *n*

Bible ['baɪbəl] *s* Bibel *f*

Biblical ['bɪblɪkəl] *adj* biblisch

bibliographer [ˌbɪbli'agrəfər] *s* Bibliograph –in *mf*

bibliography [ˌbɪbli'agrəfi] *s* Bücherverzeichnis *n*; (*science*) Bücherkunde *f*

bi·ceps ['baɪseps] *s* (–**cepses** [sepsɪz] & –**ceps**) Bizeps *m*

bicker ['bɪkər] *intr* (sich) zanken

bick'ering *s* Gezänk *n*

bicuspid [baɪ'kʌspɪd] *s* kleiner Backenzahn *m*

bicycle ['baısıkəl] s Fahrrad n
bid [bɪd] s Angebot n; (cards) Meldung f; (com) Kostenvoranschlag m
|| v (pret **bade** [bæd] & **bid**; pp **bidden** ['bɪdən]) tr (ask) heißen; (at auction) bieten; (cards) melden, reizen || intr (cards) reizen; (com) ein Preisangebot machen; **bid for** sich bewerben um
bidder ['bɪdər] s (at an auction) Bieter –in mf; **highest b.** Meistbietende mf
bid'ding s (at an auction) Bieten n; (request) Geheiß n; (cards) Reizen n
bide [baɪd] tr—**b. one's time** seine Gelegenheit abwarten
biennial [baı'enı·əl] adj zweijährig
bier [bɪr] s Totenbahre f
bifocals [baı'fokəlz] spl Zweistärkenbrille f
big [bɪg] adj (**bigger; biggest**) groß
bigamist ['bɪgəmɪst] s Bigamist m
bigamous ['bɪgəməs] adj bigamisch
bigamy ['bɪgəmi] s Bigamie f
big'-boned' adj starkknochig
big' busi'ness s das große Geschäft; (collectively) Großunternehmertum n
Big' Dip'per s Großer Bär m
big' game' s Hochwild n
big'-heart'ed adj großherzig
big'mouth' s (sl) Großmaul n
bigot ['bɪgət] s Fanatiker –in mf
bigoted ['bɪgətɪd] adj bigott, fanatisch
bigotry ['bɪgətri] s Bigotterie f
big' shot' s (coll) hohes Tier n, Bonze m
big'-time' adj groß, erstklassig; **b. operator** Großschieber –in mf
big' toe' s große Zehe f
big' top' s (coll) großes Zirkuszelt n
big' wheel' s (coll) hohes Tier n
big'wig' s (coll) Bonze m
bike [baɪk] s (coll) Rad n
bikini [bɪ'kini] s Bikini m
bilateral [baı'lætərəl] adj beiderseitig verbindlich
bile [baɪl] s Galle f
bilge [bɪldʒ] s Bilge f, Kielraum m
bilge' wat'er s Bilgenwasser n
bilingual [baı'lɪŋgwəl] adj zweisprachig
bilk [bɪlk] tr (**out of**) prellen (um)
bill [bɪl] s Rechnung f; (paper money) Geldschein m, Schein m; (of a bird) Schnabel m; (parl) Gesetzesvorlage f; **pass a b.** ein Gesetz verabschieden || tr in Rechnung stellen
bill'board' s Anschlagtafel f
bill' collec'tor s Einkassierer –in mf
billet ['bɪlət] s (mil) Quartier n || tr (mil) einquartieren, unterbringen
bill'fold' s Brieftasche f
bil'liard ball' s Billardkugel f
billiards ['bɪljərdz] s Billard n
bil'liard ta'ble s Billardtisch m
billion ['bɪljən] s Milliarde f; (Brit) Billion f (million million)
bill' of exchange' s Tratte f, Wechsel m
bill' of fare' s Speisekarte f
bill' of health' s Gesundheitszeugnis n; **he gave me a clean b.** (fig) er hat mich für einwandfrei befunden
bill' of lad'ing ['ledɪŋ] s Frachtbrief m

bill' of rights' s erste zehn Zusatzartikel pl zur Verfassung (der U.S.A.)
bill' of sale' s Kaufurkunde f
billow ['bɪlo] s Woge f || intr wogen
bil'ly club' ['bɪli] s Polizeiknüppel m
bil'ly goat' s (coll) Ziegenbock m
bind [baɪnd] s—**in a b.** in der Klemme || v (pret & pp **bound** [baʊnd]) tr binden; (obligate) verpflichten; (bb) einbinden
binder ['baɪndər] s Binder –in mf; (e.g., cement) Bindemittel n; (for loose papers) Aktendeckel m; (mach) Garbenbinder m
bindery ['baɪndəri] s Buchbinderei f
bind'ing adj (on) verbindlich (für) || s Binden n; (for skis) Bindung f; (bb) Einband n
binge [bɪndʒ] s (sl) Zechtour f; **go on a b.** (sl) e-e Zechtour machen
binoculars [baı'nɑkjələrz] spl Fernglas n
biochemistry [,baı·ə'kemıstri] s Biochemie f
biographer [baı'ɑgrəfər] s Biograph –in mf
biographic(al) [,baı·ə'græfɪk(əl)] adj biographisch
biography [baı'ɑgrəfi] s Biographie f
biologic(al) [,baı·ə'lɑdʒɪk(əl)] adj biologisch
biologist [baı'ɑlədʒɪst] s Biologe m, Biologin f
biology [baı'ɑlədʒi] s Biologie f
biophysics [,baı·ə'fɪzɪks] s Biophysik f
biopsy ['baı·ɑpsi] s Biopsie f
bipartisan [baı'pɑrtızən] adj Zweiparteien–
biped ['baɪped] s Zweifüßer m
bird [bɪrd] s Vogel m; **for the birds** für die Katz; **kill two birds with one stone** zwei Fliegen mit e-r Klappe schlagen
bird'cage' s Bauer n, Vogelkäfig m
bird' call' s Vogelruf m, Lockpfeife f
bird' dog' s Hühnerhund m
bird' of prey' s Raubvogel m
bird'seed' s Vogelfutter n
bird's'-eye view' s Vogelperspektive f
birth [bʌrθ] s Geburt f; (origin) Herkunft f; **give b. to** gebären
birth' certi'ficate s Geburtsurkunde f
birth' control' s Geburtenbeschränkung f
birth'day' s Geburtstag m
birth'day cake' s Geburtstagskuchen m
birth'day par'ty s Geburtstagsfeier f
birth'day pres'ent s Geburtstagsgeschenk n
birth'day suit' s (hum) Adamskostüm n
birth'mark' s Muttermal n
birth'place' s Geburtsort m
birth' rate' s Geburtenziffer f
birth'right' s Geburtsrecht n
biscuit ['bɪskɪt] s Keks m
bisect [baı'sɛkt] tr halbieren || intr sich teilen
bishop ['bɪ/əp] s Bischof m; (chess) Läufer m
bison ['baɪsən] s Bison m
bit [bɪt] s Bißchen n; (of food) Stück-

chen *n;* (*of time*) Augenblick *m;* (*part of a bridle*) Gebiß *n;* (*drill*) Bohrer *m;* **a bit** (*somewhat*) ein wenig; **a little bit** ein klein wenig; **bit by bit** brockenweise; **bits and pieces** Brocken *pl;* **every bit as** ganz genauso

bitch [bɪtʃ] *s* Hündin *f;* (vulg) Weibsbild *n*

bite [baɪt] *s* Biß *m;* (*wound*) Bißwunde *f;* (*of an insect*) Stich *m;* (*of a snake*) Biß *m;* (*snack*) Imbiß *m;* (fig) Bissigkeit *f;* **I have a b.** (*in fishing*) es beißt e-r an ‖ *v* (*pret* **bit** [bɪt]; *pp* **bit** & **bitten** ['bɪtən]) *tr* beißen; (*said of insects*) stechen; (*said of snakes*) beißen; **b. one's nails** an den Nägeln kauen ‖ *intr* beißen; (*said of fish*) anbeißen; (*said of the wind*) schneiden; **b. into** anbeißen

bit'ing *adj* (*remark*) bissig; (*cold, wind*) schneidend

bit' part' *s* kleine Rolle *f*

bitter ['bɪtər] *adj* (& fig) bitter; (*Person, Blick*) bitterböse

bitterly ['bɪtərli] *adv* bitterlich

bitterness ['bɪtərnɪs] *s* Bitterkeit *f*

bitters ['bɪtərz] *spl* Magenbitter *m*

bitu'minous coal' [bɪ't(j)umɪnəs] *s* Fettkohle *f*

bivouac ['bɪvwæk] *s* Biwak *n* ‖ *intr* biwakieren

bizarre [bɪ'zɑr] *adj* bizarr

blab [blæb] *v* (*pret* & *pp* **blabbed;** *ger* **blabbing**) *tr* ausplaudern ‖ *intr* plaudern

blabber ['blæbər] *intr* schwatzen

blab'bermouth' *s* Schwatzmaul *n*

black [blæk] *adj* schwarz ‖ *s* Schwarz *n;* (*black person*) Neger –in *mf,* Schwarze *mf* ‖ *tr* schwärzen; **b. out** (mil) verdunkeln ‖ *intr*—**b. out** die Besinnung verlieren

black'-and-blue' *adj* blau unterlaufen; **beat s.o. b.** j–n grün und blau schlagen

black' and white' *s*—**in b.** schwarz auf weiß, schriftlich

black'-and-white' *adj* schwarzweiß

black'ball' *tr* (*ostracize*) ausschließen; (*vote against*) stimmen gegen

black'ber'ry *s* Brombeere *f*

black'berry bush' *s* Brombeerstrauch *m*

black'bird' *s* Amsel *f*

black'board' *s* Tafel *f,* Wandtafel *f*

blacken ['blækən] *tr* schwärzen; (*a name*) anschwärzen

black' eye' *s* blaues Auge *n;* **give s.o. a b.** (fig) j–m Schaden zufügen

black'head' *s* Mitesser *m*

blackish ['blækɪʃ] *adj* schwärzlich

black'jack' *s* (*club*) Totschläger *m;* (cards) Siebzehnundvier *n* ‖ *tr* niederknüppeln

black'list' *s* schwarze Liste *f* ‖ *tr* auf die schwarze Liste setzen

black' mag'ic *s* schwarze Kunst *f*

black'mail' *s* Erpressung *f* ‖ *tr* erpressen

blackmailer ['blæk,melər] *s* Erpresser –in *mf*

black' mar'ket *s* Schwarzmarkt *m*

black' marketeer' *s* Schwarzhändle –in *mf*

black'out' *s* (*fainting*) Bewußtlosigkei *f;* (*of memory*) kurze Gedächtnis störung *f;* (*of news*) Nachrichten sperre *f;* (mil) Verdunkelung *f;* (telv Sperre *f;* (theat) Auslöschen *n* alle Rampenlichter

black' sheep' *s* (fig) schwarzes Schaf *1*

black'smith' *s* Grobschmied *m;* (*persol who shoes horses*) Hufschmied *m*

bladder ['blædər] *s* Blase *f*

blade [bled] *s* (*of a sword, knife*) Klin ge *f;* (*of grass*) Halm *m;* (*of a saw ax, shovel, oar*) Blatt *n;* (*of a pro peller*) Flügel *m*

blame [blem] *s* Schuld *f* ‖ *tr* di Schuld geben (*dat*); **b. s.o. for** j–n Vorwürfe machen wegen; **I don't b you for laughing** ich nehme es Ihnei nicht übel, daß Sie lachen

blameless ['blemlɪs] *adj* schuldlos

blame'wor'thy *adj* tadelnswert, schul dig

blanch [blæntʃ] *tr* erbleichen lassen (*celery*) bleichen; (*almonds*) blan chieren ‖ *intr* erbleichen

bland [blænd] *adj* sanft, mild

blandish ['blændɪʃ] *tr* schmeichelr (*dat*)

blank [blæŋk] *adj* (*cartridge*) blind (*piece of paper, space, expression`* leer; (*form*) unausgefüllt; (*tape*) un bespielt; (*nonplussed*) verblüfft; **m} mind went b.** ich konnte mich ar nichts erinnern ‖ *s* (*cartridge*) Platz patrone *f;* (*unwritten space*) leere Stelle *f;* (*form*) Formular *n;* (*un finished piece of metal*) Rohling *m* ‖ *tr* (sport) auf Null halten

blank' check' *s* Blankoscheck *m*

blanket ['blæŋkɪt] *adj* generell, um fassend ‖ *s* Decke *f*

blank' verse' *s* Blankvers *m*

blare [blɛr] *s* Lärm *m;* (*of trumpets*) Geschmetter *n* ‖ *intr* schmettern; (aut) laut hupen

blasé [blɑ'ze] *adj* blasiert; **b. attitude** Blasiertheit *f*

blaspheme [blæs'fim] *tr* & *intr* lästern

blasphemous ['blæsfɪməs] *adj* lästerlich

blasphemy ['blæsfɪmi] *s* Lästerung *f*

blast [blæst] *s* (*of an explosion*) Luftdruck *m;* (*of a horn, trumpet, air*) Stoß *m;* (*of air*) Luftzug *m;* **at full b.** (fig) auf höchsten Touren ‖ *tr* (*e.g., a tunnel*) sprengen; (*ruin*) (fig) verderben; (*criticize*) wettern gegen; (*blight*) versengen; **b. it!** verdammt! ‖ *intr*—**b. off** (rok) starten

blast' fur'nace *s* Hochofen *m*

blast'-off' *s* (rok) Start *m*

blatant ['bletənt] *adj* (*lie, infraction*) eklatant; (*nonsense*) schreiend

blaze [blez] *s* Brand *m;* **b. of color** Farbenpracht *f;* **b. of glory** Ruhmesglanz *m;* **b. of light** Lichterglanz *m;* **go to blazes!** (sl) geh zum Teufel!; **like blazes** wie verrückt ‖ *tr*—**b. a trail** e–n Weg markiern; (fig) e–n Weg bahnen ‖ *intr* lodern; **b. away at** drauflosschießen auf (*acc*)

blazer ['blezər] s Sportjacke f
blaz'ing adj (sun) prall
bleach [blitʃ] s Bleichmittel n || tr bleichen; (hair) blondieren || intr bleichen
bleachers ['blitʃərs] spl Zuschauersitze pl im Freien
bleak [blik] adj öde, trostlos
bleary-eyed ['blɪri ˌaɪd] adj triefäugig
bleat [blit] s Blöken n || intr blöken; (said of a goat) meckern
bleed [blid] v (pret & pp bled [blɛd]) tr (brakes) entlüften; (med) zur Ader lassen; **b. white** (fig) zum Weißbluten bringen || intr bluten; **b. to death** verbluten
blemish ['blɛmɪʃ] s Fleck m, Makel m; (fig) Schandfleck m
blend [blɛnd] s Mischung f; (liquor) Verschnitt m || v (pret & pp blended & blent [blɛnt]) tr mischen; (wine, liquor) verschneiden || intr sich vermischen; (said of colors) zueinander passen, zusammenpassen
bless [blɛs] tr segnen; **God b. you!** (after a sneeze) Gesundheit!
blessed ['blɛsɪd] adj selig
bless'ing s Segen m, Gnade f; **b. in disguise** Glück n im Unglück
blight [blaɪt] s (fig) Gifthauch m; (agr) Brand m, Mehltau m || tr (fig) verderben; (agr) schädigen
blight'ed adj brandig
blimp [blɪmp] s unstarres Luftschiff n
blind [blaɪnd] adj blind; (curve) unübersichtlich; **go b.** erblinden || s Jalousie f; (hunt) Attrappe f || tr blenden; (fig) verblenden
blind' al'ley s (& fig) Sackgasse f
blind' date' s Verabredung f mit e-r (or e-m) Unbekannten
blinder ['blaɪndər] s Scheuklappe f
blind' fly'ing s Blindflug m
blind'fold' adj mit verbundenen Augen || adv blindlings || tr die Augen verbinden (dat)
blind' man' s Blinder m
blind'man's' bluff' s Blindekuhspiel n
blindness ['blaɪndnɪs] s Blindheit f
blink [blɪŋk] s Blinken n; (with the eyes) Blinzeln n; **on the b.** (sl) kaputt || tr—**b. one's eyes** mit den Augen zwinkern || intr (said of a light) blinken; (said of the eyes) blinzeln
blinker ['blɪŋkər] s (for horses) Scheuklappe f; (aut) Blinker m
blip [blɪp] s (radar) Leuchtfleck m
bliss [blɪs] s Wonne f
blissful ['blɪsfəl] adj glückselig
blister ['blɪstər] s Blase f; (from a burn) Brandblase f || intr (said of the skin) Blasen ziehen; (said of paint) Blasen werfen
blithe [blaɪð] adj fröhlich
blitzkrieg ['blɪts ˌkrig] s Blitzkrieg m
blizzard ['blɪzərd] s Blizzard m
bloat [blot] tr aufblähen || intr anschwellen
bloc [blɑk] s (parl) Stimmblock m; (pol) Block m
block [blɑk] s (of wood) Klotz m; (toy) Bauklotz m; (for chopping) Hackklotz m; (of houses) Häuser-

block m; (of seats) Reihe f; (mach) Rolle f; (sport) Block m; **five blocks from here** fünf Straßen weiter || tr versperren; (traffic, a street, a player) blockieren; (a ball) abfangen; (a hat) aufdämpfen; **be blocked** sich stauen; **b. off** (a street) absperren; **b. up** verstopfen, versperren
blockade [blɑ'ked] s Blockade f, Sperre f || tr blockieren, sperren
blockade' run'ner s Blockadebrecher m
blockage ['blɑkɪdʒ] s Stockung f
block' and tac'kle s Flaschenzug m
block'head' s Klotz m, Dummkopf m
blond [blɑnd] adj blond || s Blonde m
blonde [blɑnd] s Blondine f
blood [blʌd] s Blut n; (lineage) Geblüt n; **in cold b.** kaltblütig
blood' circula'tion s Blutkreislauf m
blood' clot' s Blutgerinnsel n
bloodcurdling ['blʌd ˌkʌrdlɪŋ] adj haarsträubend
blood' do'nor s Blutspender –in mf
blood'hound' s (& fig) Bluthund m
bloodless ['blʌdlɪs] adj blutlos; (revolution) unblutig
blood' poi'soning s Blutvergiftung f
blood' pres'sure s Blutdruck m
blood' rela'tion s Blutsverwandte mf
blood'shed' s Blutvergießen n
blood'shot' adj blutunterlaufen
blood'stain' s Blutfleck m, Blutspur f
blood'stained' adj blutbefleckt
blood'stream' s Blutstrom m
blood'suck'er s (& fig) Blutsauger m
blood' test' s Blutprobe f
blood'thirst'y adj blutdürstig
blood' transfu'sion s Blutübertragung f
blood' type' s Blutgruppe f
blood' ves'sel s Blutgefäß n
blood·y ['blʌdi] adj blutig; (bloodstained) blutbefleckt || v (pret & pp –ied) tr mit Blut beflecken
bloom [blum] s Blüte f || intr blühen
blossom ['blɑsəm] s Blüte f || intr blühen
blot [blɑt] s Fleck m; (fig) Schandfleck m || v (pret & pp blotted; ger blotting) tr (smear) beschmieren; (with a blotter) (ab)löschen; **b. out** ausstreichen; (fig) auslöschen || intr (said of ink) klecksen
blotch [blɑtʃ] s Klecks m; (on the skin) Ausschlag m
blotter ['blɑtər] s Löscher m
blot'ting pa'per s Löschpapier n
blouse [blaus] s Bluse f
blow [blo] s Schlag m, Hieb m; (fig) Schlag m; **come to blows** handgemein werden || v (pret blew [blu]; pp blown) tr blasen; (money) (sl) verschwenden; (a fuse) durchbrennen; **b. a whistle** pfeifen; **b. off steam** sich austoben; **b. one's top** (coll) hochgehen; **b. out** (a candle) ausblasen; **b. up** (inflate) aufblasen; (with explosives) sprengen; (phot) vergrößern || intr blasen; **b. out** (said of a candle) auslöschen; (said of a tire) platzen; **blow over** vorüberziehen; **b. up** (& fig) in die Luft gehen
blower ['blo·ər] s Gebläse n, Bläser m

blow'out' *s* (sl) Gelage *n;* (aut) Reifenpanne *f*
blow'pipe' *s* Blasrohr *n*
blow'torch' *s* Lötlampe *f*
blubber ['blʌbər] *s* Tran *m* || *intr* (*cry
noisily*) jaulen
bludgeon ['blʌdʒən] *s* Knüppel *m* || *tr*
mit dem Knüppel bearbeiten
blue [blu] *adj* blau; (fig) bedrückt || *s*
Blau *n;* **blues** (mus) Blues *m;* **have
the blues** trüb gestimmt sein; **out of
the b.** aus heiterem Himmel
blue'ber'ry *s* Heidelbeere *f*
blue'bird' *s* Blaukehlchen *n*
blue' chip' *s* (cards) blaue Spielmarke
f; (fin) sicheres Wertpapier *n*
blue'-col'lar work'er *s* Arbeiter *m*
blue' jeans' *spl* Jeans *pl*
blue' moon' *s*—**once in a b.** alle Jubel-
jahre einmal
blue'print' *s* Blaupause *f*
blue' streak' *s*—**talk a b.** (coll) in e-r
Tour reden
bluff [blʌf] *adj* schroff; (*person*) derb
|| *s* (coll) Bluff *m;* (geol) Steilküste
f; **call s.o.'s b.** j-m beim Wort neh-
men || *tr & intr* bluffen
bluffer ['blʌfər] *s* Bluffer *m*
blu'ing *s* Waschblau *n*
bluish ['blu·ɪʃ] *adj* bläulich
blunder ['blʌndər] *s* Schnitzer *m;* ||
intr e-n Schnitzer machen; **b. into**
stolpern in (*acc*); **b. upon** zufällig
geraten auf (*acc*)
blunt [blʌnt] *adj* stumpf; (fig) plump,
unverblümt || *tr* abstumpfen
bluntly ['blʌntli] *adv* unverblümt
blur [blʌr] *s* Verschwommenheit *f* || *v*
(*pret & pp* **blurred;** *ger* **blurring**) *tr*
verwischen || *intr* verschwommen
werden
blurb [blʌrb] *s* Reklametext *m*
blurred *adj* verschwommen; (*vision*)
unscharf
blurt [blʌrt] *tr*—**b. out** herausplatzen
blush [blʌʃ] *s* Röte *f,* Schamröte *f* ||
intr (at) erröten (über *acc*)
bluster ['blʌstər] *s* Prahlerei *f* || *intr*
(*said of a person*) prahlen, poltern;
(*said of wind*) toben
blustery ['blʌstəri] *adj* stürmisch
boa constrictor ['bo·ə kən'strɪktər] *s*
Abgottschlange *f,* Königsschlange *f*
boar [bor] *s* Eber *m;* (*wild boar*) Wildschwein *n*
board [bord] *s* Brett *n;* (*of administra-
tors*) Ausschuß *m,* Behörde *f,* Rat *m;*
(*meals*) Kost *f;* (*educ*) Schultafel *f;*
above b. offen; **on b.** an Bord || *tr*
(*a ship*) besteigen; (*a plane, train*)
einsteigen in (*acc*); (*paying guests*)
beköstigen; **b. up** mit Brettern ver-
nageln || *intr* (**with**) in Kost sein
(bei)
boarder ['bordər] *s* Kostgänger –in *mf*
board'inghouse' *s* Pension *f*
board'ing pass' *s* Bordkarte *f*
board'ing school' *s* Internat *n*
board'ing stu'dent *s* Interne *mf*
board' of direc'tors *s* Verwaltungsrat
m, Aufsichtsrat *m*
board' of educa'tion *s* Unterrichtsmi-
nisterium *n*

board' of health' *s* Gesundheitsbehörde
f
board' of trade' *s* Handelskammer *f*
board' of trustees' *s* Verwaltungsrat *m*
board'walk' *s* Strandpromenade *f*
boast [bost] *s* Prahlerei *f;* (*cause of
pride*) Stolz *m* || *tr* sich rühmen
(*genit*) || *intr* (**about**) prahlen (mit)
boastful ['bostfəl] *adj* prahlerisch
boat [bot] *s* Boot *n;* **in the same b.**
(fig) in der gleichen Lage
boat'house' *s* Bootshaus *n*
boat'ing *s* Bootsfahrt *f;* **go b. e–e** Boot-
fahrt machen
boat'race' *s* Bootrennen *n*
boat' ride' *s* Bootsfahrt *f*
boatswain ['bosən] *s* Hochbootsmann
m
bob [bab] *s* (*jerky motion*) Ruck *m;*
(*hairdo*) Bubikopf *m;* (*of a fishing
line*) Schwimmer *m;* (*of a plumb
line*) Senkblei *n* || *v* (*pret & pp*
bobbed; *ger* **bobbing**) *tr* (*hair*) kurz
schneiden || *intr* sich hin und her be-
wegen; **bob up and down** sich auf
und ab bewegen
bobbin ['babɪn] *s* Klöppel *m*
bobble ['babəl] *tr* (coll) ungeschickt
handhaben
bob'by pin' ['babi] *s* Haarklammer *f*
bob'sled' *s* Bob *m,* Rennschlitten *m*
bode [bod] *tr* bedeuten
bodily ['badɪli] *adj* leiblich; **b. injury**
Körperverletzung *f* || *adv* leibhaftig
body ['badi] *s* Körper *m;* (*of a person
or animal*) Körper *m;* (*corpse*) Leiche
f; (*collective group*) Körperschaft *f;*
(*of a plane, ship*) Rumpf *m;* (*of a
vehicle*) Karosserie *f;* (*of beer, wine*)
Schwere *f;* (*of a letter*) Text *m;* **b. of
water** Gewässer *n;* **in a b.** geschlossen
bod'yguard' *s* Leibgarde *f*
bod'y o'dor *s* Körpergeruch *m*
bog [bag] *s* Sumpf *m* || *v* (*pret & pp*
bogged; *ger* **bogging**) *intr*—**bog down**
steckenbleiben
bogey·man ['bogi‚mæn] *s* (**–men**) Kin-
derschreck *m*
bogus ['bogəs] *adj* schwindelhaft
Bohemia [bo'himɪ·ə] *s* Böhmen *n*
Bohemian [bo'himɪ·ən] *adj* böhmisch
|| *s* (*person*) Böhme *m,* Böhmin *f;*
(fig) Bohemien *m;* (*language*) Böhmisch *n*
boil [bɔɪl] *s* (pathol) Geschwür *n;*
bring to a b. zum Sieden bringen ||
tr kochen, sieden || *intr* kochen, sie-
den; **b. away** verkochen; **b. over**
überkochen
boiled' ham' *s* gekochter Schinken *m*
boiled' pota'toes *spl* Salzkartoffeln *pl*
boiler ['bɔɪlər] *s* (*electrical water
tank*) Boiler *m;* (*kettle*) Kessel *m*
boil'ermak'er *s* Kesselschmied *m*
boil'er room' *s* Heizraum *m*
boil'ing *adj* siedend || *adv*—**be b. mad**
vor Zorn kochen; **b. hot** siedeheiß
boil'ing point' *s* Siedepunkt *m*
boisterous ['bɔɪstərəs] *adj* ausgelassen
bold [bold] *adj* kühn, gewagt; (*outlines*) deutlich
bold'face' *s* Fettdruck *m*

boldness ['boldnɪs] *s* Kühnheit *f*
Bolshevik ['bolʃəvɪk] *adj* bolschewistisch || *s* Bolschewik –in *mf*
bolster ['bolstər] *s* Nackenrolle *f* || *tr* unterstützen
bolt [bolt] *s* Bolzen *m; (door lock)* Riegel *m; (of cloth)* Stoffballen *m; (of lightning)* Blitzstrahl *m;* **b. out of the blue** Blitz *m* aus heiterem Himmel || *tr (a door)* verriegeln; *(a political party)* im Stich lassen; *(food)* hinunterschlingen || *intr* davonstürzen; *(said of a horse)* durchgehen
bomb [bam] *s (dropped from the air)* Bombe *f; (planted)* Sprengladung *f; (fiasco)* (sl) Versager *m* || *tr (from the air)* bombardieren; *(blow up)* sprengen || *intr* (sl) versagen
bombard [bam'bard] *tr* bombardieren, beschießen; (fig) bombardieren
bombardier [,bambər'dɪr] *s* Bombenschütze *m*
bombardment [bam'bardmənt] *s* Bombardement *n,* Beschießung *f*
bombast ['bambæst] *s* Schwulst *m*
bombastic [bam'bæstɪk] *adj* schwülstig
bomb′ bay′ *s* Bombenschacht *m*
bomb′ cra′ter *s* Bombentrichter *m*
bomber ['bamər] *s* Bomber *m*
bomb′ing *s* Bombenabwurf *m*
bomb′ing run′ *s* Bomben(ziel)anflug *m*
bomb′proof′ *adj* bombenfest, bombensicher
bomb′shell′ *s* (& fig) Bombe *f*
bomb′ shel′ter *s* Bombenkeller *m*
bomb′sight′ *s* Bombenzielgerät *n*
bomb′ squad′ *s* Entschärfungskommando *n*
bona fide ['bonə ,faɪd] *adj* ehrlich, echt; *(offer)* solide
bonanza [bo'nænzə] *s* Goldgrube *f*
bond [band] *s* Fessel *f; (fin)* Obligation *f*
bondage ['bandɪdʒ] *s* Knechtschaft *f*
bond′hold′er *s* Inhaber –in *mf* e–r Obligation
bonds·man ['bandzmən] *s* (–men) Bürge *m*
bone [bon] *s* Knochen *m,* Bein *n; (of fish)* Gräte *f;* **bones** Gebein *n; (mortal remains)* Gebeine *pl;* **have a b. to pick with** ein Hühnchen zu rupfen haben mit; **make no bones about it** nicht viel Federlesens machen mit; **to the b.** bis ins Mark || *tr (meat)* ausbeinen; *(fish)* ausgräten || *intr—* **b. up for** (sl) büffeln für
bone′-dry′ *adj* knochentrocken
bone′head′ *s* Dummkopf *m*
boneless ['bonlɪs] *adj* ohne Knochen; *(fish)* ohne Gräten
boner ['bonər] *s* (coll) Schnitzer *m;* **pull a b.** (coll) e–n Schnitzer machen
bonfire ['ban ,faɪr] *s* Freudenfeuer *n*
bonnet ['banɪt] *s* Haube *f*
bonus ['bonəs] *s* Gratifikation *f*
bony ['boni] *adj* knochig; *(fish)* grätig
boo [bu] *s* Pfuiruf *m* || *tr* niederbrüllen || *intr* pfui rufen || *interj (to jeer)* pfui!; *(to scare someone)* huh!
boob [bub] *s* (sl) Blödkopf *m*
booby ['bubi] *s* Blödkopf *m*
boo′by hatch′ *s* (sl) Affenkasten *m*

boo′by prize′ *s* Trostpreis *m*
boo′by trap′ *s* Minenfalle *f*
boogey·man ['bugi ,mæn], ['bogi- ,mæn] *s* (–men′) Schreckgespenst *n*
book [buk] *s* Buch *n; (of stamps, tickets, matches)* Heftchen *n;* **keep books** Bücher führen || *tr* buchen; *(e.g., seats)* vorbestellen
book′bind′er *s* Buchbinder –in *mf*
book′bind′ery *s* Buchbinderei *f*
book′bind′ing *s* Buchbinderei *f*
book′case′ *s* Bücherschrank *m*
book′ end′ *s* Bücherstütze *f*
bookie ['buki] *s* (coll) Buchmacher –in *mf*
book′ing *s* Buchung *f*
bookish ['bukɪʃ] *adj* lesefreudig
book′keep′er *s* Buchhalter –in *mf*
book′keep′ing *s* Buchhaltung *f*
book′ learn′ing *s* Schulweisheit *f*
booklet ['buklɪt] *s* Büchlein *n*
book′mak′er *s* Buchmacher –in *mf*
book′mark′ *s* Lesezeichen *n*
book′rack′ *s* Büchergestell *n*
book′ review′ *s* Buchbesprechung *f*
book′sel′ler *s* Buchhändler –in *mf*
book′shelf′ *s* (–shelves) Bücherregal *n*
book′stand′ *s* Bücher(verkaufs)stand *m*
book′store′ *s* Buchhandlung *f*
book′worm′ *s* (& fig) Bücherwurm *m*
boom [bum] *s (noise)* dumpfes Dröhnen *n; (of a crane)* Ausleger *m;* (cin, telv) Galgen *m;* (econ) Boom *m,* Hochkonjunktur *f;* (naut) Baum *m,* Spiere *f;* (st.exch.) Hausse *f* || *intr* dröhnen; *(said of an organ)* brummen
boomerang ['bumə ,ræŋ] *s* Bumerang *m*
boon [bun] *s* Wohltat *f,* Segen *m*
boon′ compan′ion *s* Zechkumpan *m*
boor [bur] *s* Rüpel *m,* Flegel *m*
boorish ['burɪʃ] *adj* flegelhaft
boost [bust] *s (push)* Auftrieb *m; (in pay)* Gehaltserhöhung *f* || *tr* fördern; *(prices)* in die Höhe treiben; (elec) verstärken; **b. business** die Wirtschaft ankurbeln
booster ['bustər] *s (backer)* Förderer *m,* Förderin *f*
boost′er rock′et *s* Hilfsrakete *f*
boost′er shot′ *s* (med) Nachimpfung *f*
boot [but] *s* Stiefel *m; (kick)* Fußtritt *m;* **to b.** noch dazu; **you can bet your boots on that** (sl) darauf kannst du Gift nehmen || *tr* (sl) stoßen; (fb) kicken; **b. out** (sl) 'rausschmeißen
booth [buθ] *s (at a fair)* Marktbude *f; (for telephone, voting)* Zelle *f*
boot′leg′ *adj* geschmuggelt || *v (pret & pp –legged; ger –legging) tr (make illegally)* illegal brennen; *(smuggle)* schmuggeln
bootlegger ['but ,lɛgər] *s* Alkoholschmuggler *m,* Bootlegger *m*
bootlicker ['but ,lɪkər] *s* (sl) Kriecher *m*
booty ['buti] *s* Beute *f*
booze [buz] *s* (coll) Schnaps *m* || *intr* (coll) saufen
booze′ hound′ *s* Saufbold *m,* Saufaus *m*
border ['bordər] *s* Rand *m; (of a country)* Grenze *f; (of a dress, etc.)* Saum

m, Borte *f* ‖ *tr* umranden, begrenzen; **be bordered by** grenzen an (*acc*) ‖ *intr*—**b. on** (& fig) grenzen an (*acc*)
bor'derline' *s* Grenzlinie *f*
bor'derline case' *s* Grenzfall *m*
bore [bor] *s* (*drill hole*) Bohrloch *n*; (*of a gun*) Bohrung *f*; (*of a cylinder*) innerer Zylinderdurchmesser *m*; (fig) langweiliger Mensch *m* ‖ *tr* bohren; (fig) langweilen
boredom ['bordəm] *s* Langeweile *f*
bor'ing *adj* langweilig ‖ *s* Bohren *n*
born [bɔrn] *adj* geboren; **he was b.** (*said of a living person*) er ist geboren; (*said of a deceased person*) er war geboren
borough ['bʌro] *s* Städtchen *n*
borrow ['bɔro] *tr* leihen
borrower ['bɔro·ər] *s* Entleiher –in *mf*; (fin) Kreditnehmer –in *mf*
bor'rowing *s* Borgen *n*; (fin) Kreditaufnahme *f*; (ling) Lehnwort *n*
bosom ['buzəm] *s* Busen *m*; (fig) Schoß *m*
bos'om friend' *s* Busenfreund *m*
boss [bɔs] *s* (coll) Chef *m*, Boß *m*; (*of a shield*) Buckel *m*; (pol) Bonze *m* ‖ *tr* (**around**) herumkommandieren
bossy ['bɔsi] *adj* herrschsüchtig
botanical [bə'tænɪkəl] *adj* botanisch
botanist ['batənɪst] *s* Botaniker –in *mf*
botany ['batəni] *s* Botanik *f*
botch [batʃ] *tr* (coll) verpfuschen
both [boθ] *adj* & *pron* beide ‖ *conj*—**both…and** sowohl… als auch
bother ['baðər] *s* Belästigung *f*, Mühe *f* ‖ *tr* (*annoy*) belästigen, stören; (*worry*) bedrücken; (*said of a conscience*) quälen ‖ *intr* sich bemühen; **b. about** sich bekümmern um; **b. with** (*a thing*) sich befassen mit; (*a person*) verkehren mit
bothersome ['baðərsəm] *adj* lästig
bottle ['batəl] *s* Flasche *f* ‖ *tr* in Flaschen abfüllen; **bottled up** aufgestaut
bot'tleneck' *s* Flaschenhals *m*; (fig) Engpaß *m*, Stauung *f*
bot'tle o'pener *s* Flaschenöffner *m*
bottom ['batəm] *adj* niedrigste, unterste ‖ *s* Boden *m*; (*of a well, shaft, river, valley*) Sohle *f*; (*of a mountain*) Fuß *m*; (*of an affair*) Grund *m*; (*buttocks*) Hintern *m*; **at the b. of the page** unten auf der Seite; **bottoms up!** prosit. ex!; **get to the b. of a problem** e-r Frage auf den Grund gehen; **reach b.** (fig) den Nullpunkt erreichen
bottomless ['batəmlɪs] *adj* bodenlos
bough [bau] *s* Ast *m*
bouillon ['buljan] *s* Kraftbrühe *f*
bouil'lon cube' *s* Bouillonwürfel *m*
boulder ['boldər] *s* Felsblock *m*
bounce [bauns] *s* Aufprall *m*; (fig) Schwung *m* ‖ *tr* (*a ball*) aufprallen lassen; (*throw out*) (sl) 'rausschmeißen ‖ *intr* aufprallen, aufspringen; (*said of a check*) (coll) platzen
bouncer ['baunsər] *s* (sl) Rausschmeißer *m*
bounc'ing *adj* (*baby*) stramm
bound [baund] *adj* gebunden, gefes-

selt; (*book*) gebunden; (*in duty*) verpflichtet; **be b. for** unterwegs sein nach; **be b. up with** eng verbunden sein mit; **I am b. to** (*inf*) ich muß (*inf*) ‖ *s* Sprung *m*, Satz *m*; **bounds** Grenzen *pl*, Schranken *pl*; **in bounds** (sport) in; **keep within bounds** in Schranken halten; **know no bounds** weder Maß noch Ziel kennen; **out of bounds** (sport) aus; **within the bounds of** im Bereich (*genit*) ‖ *tr* begrenzen ‖ *intr* aufprallen, aufspringen
boundary ['baundəri] *s* Grenze *f*; (fig) Umgrenzung *f*
boun'dary line' *s* Grenzlinie *f*
boun'dary stone' *s* Grenzstein *m*
boundless ['baundlɪs] *adj* grenzenlos
bountiful ['bauntɪfəl] *adj* (*generous*) freigebig; (*ample*) reichlich
bounty ['baunti] *s* (*generosity*) Freigebigkeit *f*; (*gift*) Geschenk *n*; (*reward*) Prämie *f*
bouquet [bu'ke] *s* Strauß *m*; (*aroma*) Blume *f*
bout [baut] *s* (box) Kampf *m*; (fencing) Gang *m*; (pathol) Anfall *m*
bow [bau] *s* Verbeugung *f*; (naut) Bug *m* ‖ *intr* sich verbeugen; **bow and scrape before** sich schmiegen und biegen vor (*dat*); **bow down** sich bücken; **bow out** sich geschickt zurückziehen; **bow to** sich (ver)neigen vor (*dat*) ‖ [bo] *s* (*weapon*) Bogen *m*; (*of a violin*) Geigenbogen *m*; (*bowknot*) Schleife *f*; **bow and arrow** Pfeil *m* und Bogen *m* ‖ *intr* (mus) geigen
bowel ['bau·əl] *s* Darm *m*; **bowels** Eingeweide *pl*; **bowels of the earth** Erdinnere *n*
bow'el move'ment *s* Stuhlgang *m*
bowl [bol] *s* Napf *m*, Schüssel *f*; (*of a pipe*) Kopf *m*; (*washbowl, toilet bowl*) Becken *n*; (*of a spoon*) Höhlung *f*; (sport) Stadion *n* ‖ *tr* umhauen; (fig) umwerfen ‖ *intr* kegeln
bowlegged ['bo,leg(ɪ)d] *adj* O-beinig
bowler ['bolər] *s* Kegler –in *mf*
bowl'ing *s* Kegeln *n*
bowl'ing al'ley *s* Kegelbahn *f*
bowl'ing ball' *s* Kegelkugel *f*
bowl'ing pin' *s* Kegel *m*
bowstring ['bo,strɪŋ] *s* Bogensehne *f*
bow' tie' [bo] *s* Schleife *f*, Fliege *f*
bow' win'dow [bo] *s* Bogenfenster *n*
bowwow ['bau'wau] *interj* wauwau!
box [baks] *s* (*small and generally of cardboard*) Schachtel *f*; (*larger and generally of cardboard*) Karton *m*; (*generally of wood*) Kasten *m*; (*larger and generally of wood*) Kiste *f*; (*of strips of wood*) Spanschachtel *f*; (theat) Loge *f*; (typ) Kasten *m*; **box of candy** Bonbonniere *f*; **box on the ear** Ohrfeige *f* ‖ *tr* (sport) boxen; **box in** einschließen; **box s.o.'s ears** j-n ohrfeigen ‖ *intr* (sport) boxen
box'car' *s* geschlossener Güterwagen *m*
boxer ['baksər] *s* (sport, zool) Boxer *m*
box'ing *s* Boxen *n*, Boxsport *m*
box'ing glove' *s* Boxhandschuh *m*

box'ing match' *s* Boxkampf *m*
box' kite' *s* Kastendrachen *m*
box' of'fice *s* (cin, theat) Kasse *f*
box' seat' *s* Logenplatz *m*
box'wood' *s* Buchsbaum *m*
boy [bɔɪ] *s* Junge *m; (servant)* Boy *m*
boycott ['bɔɪkɑt] *s* Boykott *m* || *tr* boykottieren
boy'friend' *s* Freund *m*
boy'hood' *s* Knabenalter *n*
boyish ['bɔɪ·ɪʃ] *adj* jungenhaft
boy' scout' *s* Pfadfinder *m*
bra [brɑ] *s* (coll) BH *m*
brace [bres] *s* (carp) Strebe *f*, Stütze *f;* (dent) Zahnklammer *f,* Zahnspange *f;* (hunt) Paar *n;* (med) Schiene *f;* (typ) geschweifte Klammer *f* || *tr* verstreben; (fig) stärken; **b. oneself** sich zusammenreißen; **b. oneself against** sich stemmen gegen; **b. oneself for** seinen Mut zusammennehmen für; **b. up** (fig) aufpulvern
brace' and bit' *s* Bohrwinde *f*
bracelet ['breslɪt] *s* Armband *n*
brac'ing *adj (invigorating)* erfrischend
bracket ['brækɪt] *s* Winkelstütze *f,* Konsole *f; (wall bracket)* Wandarm *m; (mounting clip)* Befestigungsschelle *f;* (typ) eckige Klammer *f* || *tr* einklammern; (arti) eingabeln
brackish ['brækɪʃ] *adj* brackig
brag [bræg] *v (pret & pp* bragged; *ger* bragging) *intr* (about) prahlen (mit)
braggart ['brægərt] *s* Prahler –in *mf*
brag'ging *adj* prahlerisch || *s* Prahlerei *f*
braid [bred] *s (of hair)* Flechte *f; (flat trimming)* Tresse *f,* Litze *f; (round trimming)* Kordel *f* || *tr (hair, rope)* flechten; *(trim with braid)* mit Tresse (or Borten) besetzen
braille [brel] *s* Blindenschrift *f*
brain [bren] *s* Hirn *n;* brains Hirn *n;* (fig) Grütze *f* || *tr* (coll) den Schädel einschlagen *(dat)*
brain'child' *s* Geistesfrucht *f*
brainless ['brenlɪs] *adj* hirnlos
brain'storm' *s* (coll) Geistesblitz *m*
brain'wash' *tr* Gehirnwäsche vornehmen bei
brain'wash'ing *s* Gehirnwäsche *f*
brain' wave' *s* Hirnwelle *f;* (fig) Geistesblitz *m*
brain'work' *s* Gehirnarbeit *f*
brainy ['breni] *adj* geistreich
braise [brez] *tr* schmoren, dünsten
brake [brek] *s* Bremse *f;* **put on the brakes** bremsen || *intr* bremsen
brake' drum' *s* Bremstrommel *f*
brake' light' *s* Bremslicht *n*
brake' lin'ing *s* Bremsbelag *m*
brake'man *s* (–men) Bremser *m*
brake'ped'al *s* Bremspedal *n*
brake' shoe' *s* (aut) Bremsbacke *f*
bramble ['bræmbəl] *s* Dornbusch *m*
bran [bræn] *s* Kleie *f*
branch [bræntʃ] *s (of a tree)* Ast *m; (smaller branch; of lineage)* Zweig *m; (of river)* Arm *m; (of a road, railroad)* Abzweigung *f; (of science, work, a shop)* Branche *f,* Unterabteilung *f;* (com) Filiale *f,* Nebenstelle

f || *intr*—**b. off** abzweigen; **b. ou** sich verzweigen
branch' line' *s* Seitenlinie *f*
branch' of'fice *s* Zweigstelle *f*
branch' of serv'ice *s* Truppengattun *f*
brand [brænd] *s (kind)* Marke *f (trademark)* Handelsmarke *f; (o cattle)* Brandmal *n; (branding iron* Brandeisen *n; (dishonor)* Schand fleck *m* || *tr (& fig)* brandmarken
brand'ing i'ron *s* Brandeisen *n*
brandish ['brændɪʃ] *tr* schwingen *(threateningly)* schwenken
brand'-new' *adj* nagelneu
brandy ['brændi] *s* Branntwein *m*
brash [bræʃ] *adj* schnodd(e)rig, frecl
brass [bræs] *adj* Messing– || *s* Messin *n;* (mil) hohe Offiziere *pl;* (mus Blechinstrumente *pl*
brass' band' *s* Blechblaskapelle *f*
brassiere [brə'zɪr] *s* Büstenhalter *m*
brass' knuck'les *spl* Schlagring *m*
brass' tacks' *spl*—**get down to b.** (coll zur Sache kommen
brat [bræt] *s* (coll) Balg *m*
bravado [brə'vɑdo] *s* Bravour *f,* An gabe *f*
brave [brev] *adj* tapfer, mutig || *s* indi anischer Krieger *m* || *tr* trotzen *(dat)*
bravery ['brevəri] *s* Tapferkeit *f*
bra·vo ['brɑvo] *s* (–vos) Bravo *n* || *interj* bravo!
brawl [brɔl] *s* Rauferei *f* || *intr* raufen
brawler ['brɔlər] *s* Raufbold *m*
brawn [brɔn] *s* Muskelkraft *f*
brawny ['brɔni] *adj* muskulös, kräftig
bray [bre] *s* Eselsschrei *m* || *intr* schreien, iahen
braze [brez] *tr (brassplate)* mit Messing überziehen; *(solder)* hartlöten
brazen ['brezən] *adj* Messing–, ehern; (fig) unverschämt || *tr*—**b. it out** unverschämt durchsetzen
Brazil [brə'zɪl] *s* Brasilien *n*
Brazilian [brə'zɪljən] *adj* brasilianisch, brasilisch || *s* Brasilier –in *mf*
Brazil' nut' *s* Paranuß *f*
breach [britʃ] *s* Bruch *m;* (mil) Bresche *f* || *tr* (mil) durchbrechen
breach' of con'tract *s* Vertragsbruch *m*
breach' of prom'ise *s* Verlöbnisbruch *m*
breach' of the peace' *s* Friedensbruch *m*
breach' of trust' *s* Vertrauensbruch *m*
bread [bred] *s* Brot *n; (money)* (sl) Pinke *f* || *tr* (culin) panieren
bread' and but'ter *s* Butterbrot *n; (livelihood)* Lebensunterhalt *m*
bread' box' *s* Brotkasten *m*
bread' crumb' *s* Brotkrume *f*
bread'ed *adj* paniert
bread'ed veal' cut'let *s* Wiener Schnitzel *n*
bread' knife' *s* Brotmesser *m*
breadth [bredθ] *s* Breite *f*
bread'win'ner *s* Brotverdiener –in *mf*
break [brek] *s* Bruch *m;* (split, tear) Riß *m; (crack)* Sprung *m; (in relations)* Bruch *m; (in a forest)* Lichtung *f; (in the clouds)* Lücke *f; (recess)* Pause *f; (rest from work)*

Arbeitspause *f;* (*luck*) Glück *n;* (*chance*) Chance *f;* (box) Lösen *n;* **bad b.** Pech *n;* **b. in the weather** Wetterumschlag *m;* **give s.o. a b.** j–m e–e Chance geben; **make a b. for** losstürzen auf (*acc*); **take a b.** e–e Pause machen; **tough b.** Pech *n;* **without a b.** ohne Unterbrechung ‖ *v* (*pret* **broke** [brok]; *pp* **broken** ['brokən]) *tr* (& fig) brechen; (*snap*) zerreißen; (*a string*) durchreißen; (*a dish*) zerbrechen; (*an appointment* nicht einhalten; (*contact*) unterbrechen; (*an engagement*) auflösen; (*a law, limb*) verletzen; (*monotony*) auflockern; (*a record*) brechen; (*a seal*) erbrechen; (*a window*) einschlagen; (*one's word, promise*) nicht halten; **b. down** (*into constituents*) zerlegen; (*s.o.'s resistance*) überwinden; (mach) abmontieren; **b. in** (*a horse*) zureiten; (*a car*) einfahren; (*a person*) anlernen; **b. loose** losreißen; **b. off** abbrechen, losbrechen; (*an engagement*) auflösen; **b. open** aufbrechen; **b. s.o. from s.th.** j–m etw abgewöhnen; **b. the news (to)** die Nachricht eröffnen (*dat*), die Nachricht beibringen (*dat*); **b. to pieces** zerbrechen; (*a meeting*) auflösen; (*forcibly*) sprengen; **break wind** e–n Darmwind abgehen lassen ‖ *intr* brechen; (*snap*) reißen; (*said of the voice*) mutieren; (*said of waves*) sich brechen; (*said of large waves*) sich überschlagen; (*said of the weather*) umschlagen; **b. down** zusammenbrechen; (mach) versagen; **b. even** gerade die Unkosten decken; **b. loose** losbrechen, sich losreißen; **b. out** (*said of fire, an epidemic, prisoner*) ausbrechen; **b. up** (*said of a meeting*) sich auflösen
breakable ['brekəbəl] *adj* zerbrechlich
breakage ['brekɪdʒ] *s* Bruch *m;* (*cost of broken articles*) Bruchschaden *m*
break'down' *s* (*of health, discipline, morals*) Zusammenbruch *m;* (*disintegration*) Zersetzung *f;* (*of costs, etc.*) Aufgliederung *f;* (aut) Panne *f;* (chem) Analyse *f;* (elec) Durchschlag *m;* (*of a piece of equipment*) (mach) Versagen *n;* (*e.g., of power supply, factory equipment*) Betriebsstörung *f*
breaker ['brekər] *s* Sturzwelle *f;* **breakers** Brandung *f*
breakfast ['brɛkfəst] *s* Frühstück *n* ‖ *intr* frühstücken
break'neck' *adj* halsbrecherisch
break' of day' *s* Tagesanbruch *m*
break'through' *s* Durchbruch *m*
break'up' *s* Aufbrechen *n;* (*of a meeting*) Auflösung *f*
break'wa'ter *s* Wellenbrecher *m*
breast [brɛst] *s* Brust *f;* (*of a woman*) Brust *f,* Busen *m;* **beat one's b.** sich an die Brust schlagen; **make a clean b. of** sich [*dat*] vom Herzen reden
breast'bone' *s* Brustbein *n*
breast' feed'ing *s* Stillen *n*
breast'plate' *s* Brustharnisch *m*
breast'stroke' *s* Brustschwimmen *n*

breath [brɛθ] *s* Atem *m;* (*single inhalation*) Atemzug *m;* (fig) Hauch *m;* **b. of air** Lüftchen *n;* **gasp for b.** nach Luft schnappen; **have bad b.** aus dem Mund riechen; **in the same b.** im gleichen Atemzug; **save one's b.** sich [*dat*] seine Worte ersparen; **take a deep b.** tief Luft holen; **take one's b. away** j–m den Atem verschlagen; **waste one's b.** in den Wind reden
breathe [brið] *tr* atmen, schöpfen; **b. a sigh of relief** aufatmen; **b. life into** beseelen; **b. one's last** die Seele aushauchen; **b. out** ausatmen; **not b. a word about it** kein Wort davon verlauten lassen ‖ *intr* atmen, hauchen; **b. again** aufatmen; **b. on** anhauchen
breath'ing space' *s* Atempause *f*
breathless ['brɛθlɪs] *adj* atemlos
breath'-tak'ing *adj* atemberaubend
breech [britʃ] *s* Verschlußstück *n*
breed [brid] *s* Zucht *f,* Stamm *m;* (*sort, group*) Schlag *m;* (*of animals*) Rasse *f* ‖ *v* (*pret & pp* **bred** [brɛd]) *tr* (*beget*) erzeugen; (*raise*) züchten; (fig) hervorrufen ‖ *intr* sich vermehren
breeder ['bridər] *s* Züchter –in *mf*
breed'ing *s* (*of animals*) Züchtung *f,* Aufzucht *f;* (fig) Erziehung *f*
breeze [briz] *s* Lüftchen *n,* Brise *f* ‖ *intr*—**b. by** vorbeiflitzen; **b. in** frisch und vergnügt hereinkommen
breezy ['brizi] *adj* luftig; (fig) keß
brevity ['brɛvɪti] *s* Kürze *f*
brew [bru] *s* Brühe *f;* (*of beer*) Bräu *m* ‖ *tr* (*tea, coffee*) aufbrühen; (*beer*) brauen ‖ *intr* ziehen; (*said of a storm*) sich zusammenbrauen; **something is brewing** etwas ist im Anzuge
brewer ['bru·ər] *s* Brauer –in *mf*
brewery ['bru·əri] *s* Brauerei *f*
bribe [braɪb] *s* Bestechungsgeld *n* ‖ *tr* bestechen
bribery ['braɪbəri] *s* Bestechung *f*
brick [brɪk] *s* Ziegelstein *m*
bricklayer ['brɪk ‚le·ər] *s* Maurer *m*
brick'work' *s* Mauerwerk *n*
brick'yard' *s* Ziegelei *f*
bridal ['braɪdəl] *adj* Braut–, Hochzeits–
brid'al gown' *s* Brautkleid *n*
brid'al veil' *s* Brautschleier *m*
bride [braɪd] *s* Braut *f*
bride'groom' *s* Bräutigam *m*
brides'maid' *s* Brautjungfer *f*
bridge [brɪdʒ] *s* (*over a river*) Brücke *f;* (*of eyeglasses*) Steg *m;* (*of a nose*) Nasenrücken *m;* (cards) Bridge *n;* (dent) Zahnbrücke *f;* (naut) Kommandobrücke *f* ‖ *tr* (& fig) überbrücken
bridge'head' *s* Brückenkopf *m*
bridge'work' *s* (dent) Brückenarbeit *f*
bridle ['braɪdəl] *s* Zaum *m,* Zügel *m* ‖ *tr* aufzäumen, zügeln
bri'dle path' *s* Reitweg *m*
brief [brif] *adj* kurz; **be b.** sich kurz fassen ‖ *s* (jur) Schriftsatz *m* ‖ *tr* einweisen, orientieren
brief' case' *s* Aktentasche *f*

brief'ing s Einsatzbesprechung f
brier ['braɪ·ər] s Dornbusch m
brig [brɪg] s (naut) Brigg f; (nav) Knast m
brigade [brɪ'ged] s Brigade f
brigadier' gen'eral [ˌbrɪgə'dɪr] s Brigadegeneral m
brigand ['brɪgənd] s Brigant m
bright [braɪt] adj hell; (color) lebhaft; (face) strahlend; (weather) heiter; (smart) gescheit, aufgeweckt || adv —b. and early in aller Frühe
brighten ['braɪtən] tr aufhellen || intr sich aufhellen
bright'-eyed' adj helläugig
brightness ['braɪtnɪs] s Helle f
bright' side' s (fig) Lichtseite f
bright' spot' s (fig) Lichtblick m
brilliance ['brɪljəns], **brilliancy** ['brɪljənsi] s Glanz m
brilliant ['brɪljənt] adj (& fig) glänzend
brim [brɪm] s Rand m; (of a hat) Krempe f; **to the b.** bis zum Rande || v (pret & pp **brimmed**; ger **brimming**) intr—**b. over (with)** (fig) überschäumen (vor dat)
brimful ['brɪm ˌful] adj übervoll
brim'stone' s Schwefel m
brine [braɪn] s Salzwasser n, Sole f; (for pickling) Salzlake f
bring [brɪŋ] v (pret & pp **brought** [brɔt]) tr bringen; **b. about** zustande bringen; **b. back** zurückbringen; (memories) zurückrufen; **b. down** herunterbringen; (shoot down) abschießen; **b. down the house** (fig) Lachstürme entfesseln; **b. forth** (e.g., complaints) hervorbringen; **b. forward** vorbringen; **b. it about that** es durchsetzen, daß; **b. on** herbeiführen; **b. oneself to** (inf) sich überwinden zu (inf); **b. to** wieder zu sich bringen; **b. together** zusammenbringen; **b. up** (children) erziehen; (a topic) zur Sprache bringen
bring'ing-up' s Erziehung f
brink [brɪŋk] s (& fig) Rand m
brisk [brɪsk] adj (pace, business) flott; (air) frisch, scharf
bristle ['brɪsəl] s Borste f || intr sich sträuben
bristly ['brɪsli] adj borstig
Britain ['brɪtən] s Britannien n
British ['brɪtɪʃ] adj britisch || **the B.** spl die Briten pl
Britisher ['brɪtɪʃər] s Brite m, Britin f
Briton ['brɪtən] s Brite m, Britin f
Brittany ['brɪtəni] s die Bretagne f
brittle ['brɪtəl] adj brüchig, spröde
broach [brotʃ] tr zur Sprache bringen
broad [brɔd] adj breit; (daylight) hellicht; (outline) grob; (sense) weit; (view) allgemein, umfassend
broad'cast' s Sendung f, Übertragung f || v (pret & pp —**cast**) tr (rumors, etc.) ausposaunen || (pret & pp —**cast** & —**casted**) tr & intr senden, übertragen
broadcaster ['brɔd ˌkæstər] s Rundfunksprecher –in mf
broad'casting sta'tion s Sender m
broad'casting stu'dio s Senderaum m

broad'cloth' s feiner Wäschestoff m
broaden ['brɔdən] tr verbreitern || intr sich verbreitern
broad'-gauge' adj (rr) breitspurig
broad'-mind'ed adj großzügig
broad'-shoul'dered adj breitschultrig
broad'side' s (guns on one side of ship) Breitseite f; (fig) Schimpfkanonade f
brocade [bro'ked] s Brokat m
broccoli ['brɑkəli] s Spargelkohl m
brochure [bro'ʃur] s Broschüre f
broil [brɔɪl] tr am Rost braten, grillen
broiler ['brɔɪlər] s Bratrost m
broke [brok] adj (coll) abgebrannt, pleite; **go b.** (coll) pleite gehen
broken ['brokən] adj zerbrochen; (limb, spirit, English) gebrochen; (home) zerrüttet; (line) gestrichelt
bro'ken-down' adj erschöpft; (horse) abgearbeitet
bro'ken-heart'ed adj mit gebrochenem Herzen
broker ['brokər] s Makler –in mf
brokerage ['brokərɪdʒ] s Maklergeschäft n; (fee) Maklergebühr f
bromide ['bromaɪd] s Bromid n; (coll) Binsenweisheit f
bromine ['bromin] s Brom n
bronchial ['brɑŋkɪ·əl] adj bronchial
bron'chial tube' s Luftröhre f, Bronchie f
bronchitis [brɑŋ'kaɪtɪs] s Bronchitis f
bron·co ['brɑŋko] s (—cos) kleines halbwildes Pferd n
bronze [brɑnz] adj Bronze– || s Bronze f || tr bronzieren || intr sich bräunen
brooch [brotʃ], [brutʃ] s Brosche f
brood [brud] s Brut f, Junge pl || tr ausbrüten || intr brüten; (coll) sinnieren; **b. over** grübeln über (acc)
brook [bruk] s Bach m || tr dulden
broom [brum] s Besen m
broom'stick' s Besenstiel m
broth [brɔθ] s Brühe f
brothel ['brɑθəl] s Bordell n
brother ['brʌðər] s Bruder m; **brother(s) and sister(s)** Geschwister pl
broth'erhood' s (& relig) Brüderschaft f
broth'er-in-law' s (brothers-in-law) Schwager m
brotherly ['brʌðərli] adj brüderlich
brow [brau] s Stirn f
brow'beat' v (pret —**beat**; pp —**beaten**) tr einschüchtern
brown [braun] adj braun || s Bräune f || tr & intr bräunen
brownish ['braunɪʃ] adj bräunlich
brown'-nose' tr (sl) kriechen (dat)
brown' sug'ar s brauner Zucker m
browse [brauz] intr grasen, weiden; (through books) schmökern, stöbern; (through a store) herumsuchen
bruise [bruz] s Quetschung f || tr quetschen
brunette [bru'nɛt] adj brünett || s Brünette f
brunt [brʌnt] s Anprall m; **bear the b.** die Hauptlast tragen
brush [brʌʃ] s Bürste f; (of an artist; for shaving) Pinsel m; (brief encoun-

ter) kurzer Zusammenstoß *m; (light touch)* leichte Berührung *f; (bot)* Gebüsch *n;* (elec) Bürste *f;* || *tr* bürsten; **b. aside** beiseite schieben; **b. off** abbürsten; *(devour)* verschlingen; *(make light of)* abwimmeln || *intr*—**b. against** streifen; **b. up on** auffrischen

brush'-off' *s* (coll) Laufpaß *m*
brush'wood' *s* Unterholz *n,* Niederwald *m*
brusque [brʌsk] *adj* brüsk
Brussels ['brʌsəlz] *s* Brüssel *n*
Brus'sels sprouts' *spl* Rosenkohl *m*
brutal ['brutəl] *adj* brutal
brutality [bru'tælɪti] *s* Brutalität *f*
brute [brut] *adj* viehisch; *(strength)* roh || *s* Tier *n;* (fig) Unmensch *m*
brutish ['brutɪʃ] *adj* tierisch, roh
bubble ['bʌbəl] *s* Blase *f,* Bläschen *n* || *intr* sprudeln; **b. over (with)** übersprudeln (vor *dat*)
bub'ble bath' *s* Schaumbad *n*
bub'ble gum' *s* Knallkaugummi *m*
bubbly ['bʌbli] *adj* sprudelnd; *(Person)* lebhaft
buck [bʌk] *s* Bock *m;* (sl) Dollar *m;* **pass the b.** (coll) die Verantwortung abschieben || *tr* (fig) kämpfen gegen; **b. off** abwerfen || *intr* bocken; **b. for** *(a promotion)* sich bemühen um
bucket ['bʌkɪt] *s* Eimer *m*
buck'et seat' *s* Schalensitz *m*
buckle ['bʌkəl] *s* Schnalle *f; (bend)* Ausbuchtung *f* || *tr* zuschnallen || *intr (from heat, etc.)* zusammensacken; **b. down** sich auf die Hosen setzen
buck' pri'vate *s* gemeiner Soldat *m*
buckram ['bʌkrəm] *s* Buckram *n*
buck'shot' *s* Rehposten *m*
buck'tooth' *s* (**-teeth**) vorstehender Zahn *m*
buck'wheat' *s* Buchweizen *m*
bud [bʌd] *s* Knospe *f,* Keim *m;* **nip in the bud** (fig) im Keime ersticken || *v (pret & pp* **budded; ger budding)** *intr* knospen, keimen, ausschlagen
buddy ['bʌdi] *s* (coll) Kumpel *m*
budge [bʌdʒ] *tr* (von der Stelle) bewegen || *intr* sich (von der Stelle) bewegen
budget ['bʌdʒɪt] *s* Budget *n,* Haushaltsplan *m; (of a state)* Staatshaushalt *m* || *tr* einteilen, vorausplanen
budgetary ['bʌdʒɪˌteri] *adj* Budget–
buff [bʌf] *adj* lederfarben || *s* Lederfarbe *f;* (coll) Schwärmer –in *mf* || *tr* polieren
buffa·lo ['bʌfəˌlo] *s* (**-loes** & **-los**) Büffel *m*
buffer ['bʌfər] *s* Puffer *m; (polisher)* Polierer *m;* (rr) Prellbock *m*
buff'er state' *s* Pufferstaat *m*
buffet [bu'fe] *s (meal)* Büfett *n; (furniture)* Kredenz *f* || ['bʌfɪt] *tr* herumstoßen
buffoon [bə'fun] *s* Hanswurst *m*
bug [bʌg] *s* Insekt *n,* Käfer *m; (defect)* (coll) Defekt *m;* (electron) Abhörgerät *n,* Wanze *f;* **bugs** Ungeziefer *n* || *v (pret & pp* **bugged; ger bugging)** *tr (annoy)* (sl) ärgern;

(electron) (sl) Abhörgeräte einbauen in *(dat)*
bug'-eyed' *adj* (sl) mit großen Augen
buggy ['bʌgi] *adj* verwanzt; *(crazy)* (sl) verrückt || *s* Wagen *m*
bugle ['bjugəl] *s* Signalhorn *n*
bu'gle call' *s* Signal *n*
bugler ['bjuglər] *s* Hornist –in *mf*
build [bɪld] *s* Bauart *f,* Gestalt *f; (of a person)* Körperbau *m* || *v (pret & pp* **built** [bɪlt]) *tr* bauen; *(with stone or brick)* mauern; *(a fire)* anmachen; **b. up** aufbauen; *(an area)* ausbauen; *(hopes)* erwecken
builder ['bɪldər] *s* Baumeister *m*
build'ing *s* Gebäude *n*
build'ing and loan' associa'tion *s* Bausparkasse *f*
build'ing block' *s* Zementblock *m; (for children)* Bauklötzchen *n*
build'ing con'tractor *s* Bauunternehmer *m*
build'ing in'dustry *s* Bauindustrie *f*
build'ing lot' *s* Bauplatz *m,* Grundstück *n*
build'ing mate'rial *s* Baustoff *m*
build'-up' *s* (coll) Propaganda *f*
built'-in' *adj* Einbau–
built'-up' *adj* bebaut
bulb [bʌlb] *s* (bot) Knolle *f,* Zwiebel *f;* (elec) Glühbirne *f;* (phot) Blitzlampe *f*
Bulgaria [bʌl'gɑrɪ·ə] *s* Bulgarien *n*
Bulgarian [bʌl'gɑrɪ·ən] *adj* bulgarisch || *s* Bulgare *m,* Bulgarin *f; (language)* Bulgarisch *n*
bulge [bʌldʒ] *s* Ausbauchung *f,* Beule *f; (of a sail)* Bausch *m;* (mil) Frontvorsprung *m* || *intr* sich bauschen; *(said of eyes)* hervortreten
bulg'ing *adj (belly, muscles)* hervorspringend; *(eyes)* hervorquellend; *(sails)* gebläht; **b. with** bis zum Platzen gefüllt mit
bulk [bʌlk] *adj* Massen–, unverpackt || *s* Masse *f; (main part)* Hauptteil *m;* **in b.** unverpackt || *intr*—**b. large** e–e große Rolle spielen
bulk'head' *s* (aer) Spant *m;* (naut) Schott *n*
bulky ['bʌlki] *adj* sperrig
bull [bʊl] *s* Bulle *m,* Stier *m;* (sl) Quatsch *m;* (eccl) Bulle *f;* (st. exch.) Haussier *m;* **like a b. in a china shop** wie ein Elefant im Porzellanladen; **shoot the b.** (sl) quatschen; **take the b. by the horns** den Stier an den Hörnern packen; **throw the b.** (sl) aufschneiden
bull'dog' *s* Bulldogge *f*
bull'doze' *tr* planieren; (fig) überfahren
bulldozer ['bʌlˌdozər] *s* Planierraupe *f*
bullet ['bʊlɪt] *s* Kugel *f*
bul'let hole' *s* Schußöffnung *f*
bulletin ['bʊlətɪn] *s (report)* Bulletin *n; (flyer)* Flugschrift *f*
bul'letin board' *s* Anschlagbrett *n*
bul'letproof' *adj* kugelsicher
bull'fight' *s* Stierkampf *m*
bull'fight'er *s* Stierkämpfer –in *mf*
bull'frog' *s* Ochsenfrosch *m*

bull'-head'ed *adj* dickköpfig
bull' horn' *s* Richtungslautsprecher *m*
bullion ['buljən] *s* Barren *m;* (mil, nav) Kordel *f*
bull' mar'ket *s* Spekulationsmarkt *m*
bullock ['buIək] *s* Ochse *m*
bull'pen' *s* Stierpferch *m;* (baseball) Übungsplatz *m* für Reservewerfer
bull'ring' *s* Stierkampfarena *f*
bull' ses'sion *s* (sl) zwanglose Diskussion *f*
bull's'-eye' *s* (*of a target*) Schwarze *n;* (*round window*) Bullauge *n;* **hit the b.** ins Schwarze treffen
bul·ly ['buli] *adj*—**b. for you!** großartig! ‖ *s* Raufbold *m* ‖ *v* (*pret & pp* –**lied**) *tr* tyrannisieren
bulrush ['bul‚rʌʃ] *s* Binse *f*
bulwark ['bulwərk] *s* Bollwerk *n*
bum [bʌm] (sl) Strolch *m;* **give s.o. the bum's rush** j–n auf den Schub bringen ‖ *v* (*pret & pp* **bummed;** *ger* **bumming**) *tr* (sl) schinden, schnorren ‖ *intr*—**bum around** bummeln
bumblebee ['bʌmbəl‚bi] *s* Hummel *f*
bump [bʌmp] *s* Stoß *m,* Bums *m;* (*swelling*) Beule *f;* (*in the road*) holp(e)rige Stelle *f* ‖ *tr* (an)stoßen; **b. off** (sl) abknallen; **b. one's head against s.th.** mit dem Kopf gegen etw stoßen ‖ *intr* zusammenstoßen; **b. against** stoßen an (*acc*); **b. into** stoßen gegen; (*meet unexpectedly*) in die Arme laufen (*dat*)
bumper ['bʌmpər] *s* Stoßstange *f*
bumpkin ['bʌmpkɪn] *s* Tölpel *m*
bumpy ['bʌmpi] *adj* holperig; (aer) böig
bum' steer' *s*—**give s.o. a b.** (coll) nasführen
bun [bʌn] *s* Kuchenbrötchen *n;* (*of hair*) Haarknoten *m*
bunch [bʌntʃ] *s* Bündel *n;* (*of grapes*) Traube *f;* (*group*) Schar *f,* Bande *f;* **b. of flowers** Blumenstrauß *m;* **b. of grapes** Weintraube *f* ‖ *tr*—**b. together** zusammenfassen ‖ *intr*—**b. together** sich zusammendrängen
bundle ['bʌndəl] *s* Bündel *n;* (*heap*) Stoß *m;* (*of straw*) Schütte *f;* **b. of nerves** Nervenbündel *n* ‖ *tr* bündeln; **b. off** (coll) verfrachten; **b. up** sich warm anziehen
bung [bʌŋ] *s* Spund *m* ‖ *tr* verspunden
bungalow ['bʌŋgə‚lo] *s* Bungalow *m*
bung'hole' *s* Spundloch *n*
bungle ['bʌŋgəl] *s* Pfuscherei *f* ‖ *tr* verpfuschen ‖ *intr* pfuschen
bungler ['bʌŋglər] *s* Pfuscher –in *mf*
bun'gling *adj* stümperhaft ‖ *s* Stümperei *f*
bunk [bʌŋk] *s* Schlafkoje *f;* (sl) Unsinn *m* ‖ *intr* (**with**) schlafen (mit)
bunk' bed' *s* Etagenbett *n*
bunker ['bʌŋkər] *s* Bunker *m*
bunny ['bʌni] *s* Kaninchen *n*
bunt'ing *s* (*cloth*) Fahnentuch *n;* (*decoration*) Fahnenschmuck *m;* (orn) Ammer *f*
buoy [bɔɪ], ['bu·i] *s* Boje *f* ‖ *tr*—**b. up** flott erhalten; (fig) Auftrieb geben (*dat*)

buoyancy ['bɔɪ·ənsi] *s* Auftrieb *m;* (fig) Spannkraft *f*
buoyant ['bɔɪ·ənt] *adj* schwimmend; (fig) lebhaft
burden ['bʌrdən] *s* Bürde *f,* Last *f;* (fig) Belastung *f* ‖ *tr* belasten
bur'den of proof' *s* Beweislast *f*
burdensome ['bʌrdənsəm] *adj* lästig
bureau ['bjuro] *s* Kommode *f;* (*office*) Büro *n;* (*department*) Amt *n*
bureaucracy [bju'rɑkrəsi] *s* Bürokratie *f,* Beamtenschaft *f*
bureaucrat ['bjurə‚kræt] *s* Bürokrat *m*
bureaucratic [‚bjurə'krætɪk] *adj* bürokratisch
burglar ['bʌrglər] *s* Einbrecher –in *mf*
bur'glar alarm' *s* Einbruchssicherung *f* –in *mf*
burglarize ['bʌrglə‚raɪz] *tr* einbrechen in (*acc*)
bur'glarproof' *adj* einbruchssicher
burglary ['bʌrgləri] *s* Einbruchdiebstahl *m*
Burgundy ['bʌrgəndi] *s* Burgund *n;* (*wine*) Burgunder *m*
burial ['berɪ·əl] *s* Beerdigung *f*
bur'ial ground' *s* Begräbnisplatz *m*
burlap ['bʌrlæp] *s* Sackleinwand *f*
burlesque [bər'lesk] *adj* burlesk ‖ *s* Burleske *f* ‖ *tr* burlesk behandeln
burlesque' show' *s* Varièté *s*
burly ['bʌrli] *adj* stämmig, beleibt
Burma ['bʌrmə] *s* Birma *n*
Bur·mese [bər'miz] *adj* birmanisch ‖ *s* (–**mese**) (*person*) Birmane *m,* Birmanin *f;* (*language*) Birmanisch *n*
burn [bʌrn] *s* Brandwunde *f;* ‖ *v* (*pret & pp* **burned** & **burnt** [bʌrnt]) *tr* (ver)brennen; **be burned up** (coll) fauchen; **b. down** niederbrennen; **b. up** (coll) wütend machen ‖ *intr* (ver)brennen; (*said of food*) anbrennen; **b. out** ausbrennen; (elec) durchbrennen; **b. up** ganz verbrennen; (*during reentry*) verglühen
burner ['bʌrnər] *s* Brenner *m*
burn'ing *adj* (& fig) brennend
burnish ['bʌrnɪʃ] *tr* polieren
burn'out' *s* (rok) Brennschluß *m*
burnt *adj* verbrannt; (*smell*) brenzlig
burp [bʌrp] *s* Rülpser *m* ‖ *tr* rülpsen lassen ‖ *intr* rülpsen
burr [bʌr] *s* (*growth on a tree*) Auswuchs *m;* (*in metal*) Grat *m;* (bot) Klette *f*
burrow ['bʌro] *s* Bau *m* ‖ *tr* graben ‖ *intr* sich eingraben, wühlen
bursar ['bʌrsər] *s* Schatzmeister *m*
burst [bʌrst] *s* Bersten *n;* (*split*) Riß *m;* Bruch *m;* **b. of gunfire** Feuerstoß *m* ‖ *v* (*pret & pp* **burst**) *tr* (auf-)sprengen, zum Platzen bringen ‖ *intr* bersten, platzen; (*split*) reißen; (*said of a boil*) aufgehen; **b. into** (*e.g., a room*) hereinstürzen in (*acc*); **b. into tears** in Tränen ausbrechen; **b. open** aufplatzen; **b. out laughing** loslachen
bur·y ['beri] *v* (*pret & pp* –**ied**) *tr* beerdigen, begraben; **be buried in thought** in Gedanken versunken sein; **b. alive** verschütten
bus [bʌs] *s* (**busses** & **buses**) Autobus *m,* Bus *m* ‖ *v* (*pret & pp*) **bussed** &

bused; *ger* bussing & busing) *tr* & *intr* mit dem Bus fahren
bus' boy' *s* Pikkolo *m*
bus' driv'er *s* Autobusfahrer –in *mf*
bush [buʃ] *s* Busch *m;* beat around the b. um die Sache herumreden
bushed *adj* (coll) abgeklappert
bushel ['buʃəl] *s* Scheffel *m;* by the b. scheffelweise
bush'ing *s* Buchse *f*
bushy ['buʃi] *adj* strauchbewachsen; (*brows*) buschig
business ['bɪznɪs] *adj* Geschäfts– ‖ *s* Geschäft *n;* (*company*) Firma *f,* Betrieb *m;* (*employment*) Beruf *m,* Gewerbe *n;* (*duty*) Pflicht *f;* (*right*) Recht *n;* (coll) Sache *f;* be in b. geschäftlich tätig sein; do b. with Geschäfte machen mit; get down to b. (coll) zur Sache kommen; go about one's b. seiner Arbeit nachgehen; he means b. (coll) er meint es ernst; know one's b. seine Sache verstehen; make s.th. one's b. sich [*dat*] etw angelegen sein lassen; mind your own b. kümmere dich um deine eigenen Sachen; that's none of your b. das geht dich gar nichts an; the whole b. die ganze Geschichte; you have no b. here du hast hier nichts zu suchen
busi'ness call' *s* Dienstgespräch *n*
busi'ness card' *s* Geschäftskarte *f*
busi'ness cen'ter *s* Geschäftszentrum *n*
busi'ness col'lege *s* Handelsschule *f*
busi'ness dis'trict *s* Geschäftsviertel *n*
busi'ness expens'es *spl* Geschäftsspesen *pl*
busi'ness hours' *s* Geschäftszeit *f*
busi'ness let'ter *s* Geschäftsbrief *m*
busi'nesslike' *adj* sachlich; (pej) geschäftsmäßig
busi'ness·man' *s* (–men') Geschäftsmann *m*
busi'ness reply' card' *s* Rückantwortkarte *f*
busi'ness suit' *s* Straßenanzug *m*
busi'ness·wom'an *s* (–wom'en) Geschäftsfrau *f*
bus' line' *s* Autobuslinie *f*
bus' stop' *s* Autobushaltestelle *f*
bust [bʌst] *s* (*chest*) Busen *m;* (*measurement*) Oberweite *f;* (*statue*) Brustbild *n;* (*blow*) (sl) Faustschlag *m;* (*failure*) (sl) Platzen *n;* (*binge*) (sl) Sauftour *f* ‖ *tr* (sl) kaputtmachen; (mil) degradieren ‖ *intr* (*break*) (sl) kaputtgehen
bustle ['bʌsəl] *s* (*activity*) Hochbetrieb *m,* Trubel *m* ‖ *intr* umherhasten; b. about herumsausen
bus'tling *adj* geschäftig
bus·y ['bɪzi] *adj* tätig, beschäftigt; (*day, life*) arbeitsreich; (*street*) lebhaft, verkehrsstark; (telp) belegt, besetzt; be b. (*be occupied*) zu tun haben; (*be unavailable*) nicht zu sprechen sein ‖ *v* (*pret & pp* –ied) *tr* beschäftigen
bus'ybod'y *s* Wichtigtuer –in *mf*
bus'y sig'nal *s* (telp) Besetztzeichen *n*
but [bʌt] *adv* nur, lediglich, bloß; (*just, only*) erst; all but beinahe ‖

prep außer (*dat*); (*after negatives*) als; all but one alle bis auf einen ‖ *conj* aber; (*after negatives*) sondern
butcher ['butʃər] *s* Fleischer –in *mf* Metzger –in *mf;* (fig) Schlächter –in *mf* ‖ *tr* schlachten; (fig) abschlachten
butch'er knife' *s* Fleischermesser *n*
butch'er shop' *s* Metzgerei *f*
butchery ['butʃəri] *s* (*slaughterhouse*) Schlachthaus *n;* (fig) Gemetzel *n*
butler ['bʌtlər] *s* Haushofmeister *m*
butt [bʌt] *s* (*of a gun*) Kolben *m;* (*of a cigarette*) Stummel *m;* (*with the horns, head*) Stoß *m;* (*of ridicule*) Zielscheibe *f* ‖ *tr* stoßen ‖ *intr* stoßen; b. in (sl) sich einmischen, dazwischenfahren
butter ['bʌtər] *s* Butter *f* ‖ *tr* mit Butter bestreichen; (*bread*) schmieren; b. s.o. up (coll) j–m Honig um den Mund schmieren
but'terball' *s* Butterkugel *f;* (*chubby child*) Pummelchen *n*
but'tercup' *s* Butterblume *f,* Hahnenfuß *m*
but'ter dish' *s* Butterdose *f*
but'terfly' *s* Schmetterling *m;* (sport) Schmetterlingsstil *m*
but'ter knife' *s* Buttermesser *n*
but'termilk' *s* Buttermilch *f*
buttocks ['bʌtəks] *spl* Hinterbacken *pl*
button ['bʌtən] *s* Knopf *m* ‖ *tr* knöpfen; button up zuknöpfen
but'tonhole' *s* Knopfloch *n* ‖ *tr* im Gespräch festhalten
buttress ['bʌtrɪs] *s* Strebepfeiler *m;* (fig) Stütze *f* ‖ *tr* (durch Strebepfeiler) stützen; (fig) (unter)stützen
butt'-weld' *tr* stumpfschweißen
buxom ['bʌksəm] *adj* beleibt
buy [baɪ] *s* Kauf *m* ‖ *v* (*pret & pp* bought [bɔt]) *tr* kaufen; (*bus ticket, train ticket*) lösen; (*accept, believe*) glauben; buy off (*bribe*) bestechen; buy out auskaufen; buy up aufkaufen
buyer ['baɪ·ər] *s* Käufer –in *mf*
buzz [bʌz] *s* Summen *m,* Surren *n;* (telp) (coll) Anruf *m* ‖ *tr* (coll) (aer) dicht vorbeisausen an (*dat*); (telp) (coll) anrufen ‖ *intr* summen, surren; b. around herumsausen
buzzard ['bʌzərd] *s* Bussard *m*
buzz' bomb' *s* Roboterbombe *f,* V-Waffe *f*
buzzer ['bʌzər] *s* Summer *m;* did the b. sound? ist der Sommer ertönt
buzz' saw' *s* Kreissäge *f,* Rundsäge *f*
by [baɪ] *adv* vorüber, vorbei; by and by nach und nach; by and large im großen und ganzen ‖ *prep* (*agency*) von (*dat*), durch (*acc*); (*position*) bei (*dat*), an (*dat*), neben (*dat*); (*no later than*) bis spätestens; (*in division*) durch (*acc*); (*indicating mode of transportation*) mit (*dat*); (*indicating authorship*) von (*dat*); (*according to*) nach (*dat*); (*past*) an (*dat*) vorbei; (*by means of*) mit (*dat*); by (*acc*) indem (*ind*); by an inch um e–n Zoll; by day bei Tag, by far bei weitem; by heart auswendig; by itself (*automatically*) von selbst; by land zu Lande; by mail

per Post; **by myself** ganz allein; **by nature** von Natur aus; **by now** schon; **by the pound** per Pfund; **two by four** zwei mal vier
bye [baɪ] *s* (sport) Freilos *n*
bye'bye' *interj* Wiedersehen!
bygone ['baɪ‚gɔn] *adj* vergangen ‖ *s—* **let bygones be bygones** laß(t) das Vergangene ruhen
by'law' *s* Satzung *f;* **bylaws** (*of an organization*) Statuten *pl,* Satzungen *pl*
by'-line' *s* (journ) Verfasserangabe *f*

by'pass' *s* Umgehungsstraße *f,* Umleitung *f;* (elec) Nebenschluß *m* ‖ *tr* umgehen
by'prod'uct *s* Nebenprodukt *n*
bystander ['baɪ‚stændər] *s* Umstehende *mf*
by'way' *s* Seitenweg *m*
by'word' *s* Sprichwort *n*
Byzantine ['bɪzən‚tin], [bɪ'zæntin] *adj* byzantinisch ‖ *s* Byzantiner –in *mf*
Byzantium [bɪ'zænʃɪ‚əm], [bɪ'zæntɪ‚əm] *s* Byzanz *n*

C

C, c [si] *s* dritter Buchstabe des englischen Alphabets; (mus) C *n;* **C flat** Ces *n;* **C sharp** Cis *n*
cab [kæb] *s* Taxi *n;* (*of a truck*) Fahrerkabine *f*
cabaret [‚kæbə're] *s* Kabarett *n*
cabbage ['kæbɪdʒ] *s* Kohl *m,* Kraut *n*
cab'driv'er *s* Taxifahrer –in *mf*
cabin ['kæbɪn] *s* Hütte *f;* (aer) Kabine *f;* (naut) Kajüte *f,* Kabine *f*
cab'in boy' *s* Schiffsjunge *m*
cabinet ['kæbɪnɪt] *adj* Kabinetts– ‖ *s* (*in a kitchen*) Küchenschrank *m;* (*for a radio*) Gehäuse *n;* (pol) Kabinett *n,* Ministerrat *m*
cab'inetmak'er *s* Tischler *m*
cable ['kebəl] *s* Kabel *n,* Seil *n;* (naut) Tau *m;* (telg) Kabelnachricht *f* ‖ *tr & intr* kabeln
ca'ble car' *s* Seilbahn *f,* Schwebebahn *f*
ca'blegram' *s* Kabelnachricht *f*
caboose [kə'bus] *s* (rr) Dienstwagen *m*
cab'stand' *s* Taxistand *m*
cache [kæʃ] *s* Geheimlager *n,* Versteck *n;* **c. of arms** Waffenlager *n*
cachet [kæ'ʃe] *s* Siegel *n;* (fig) Stempel *m;* (pharm) Kapsel *f*
cackle ['kækəl] *s* (*of chickens*) Gegacker *n;* (*of geese*) Geschnatter *n* ‖ *intr* gackern, gackeln; schnattern
cac·tus ['kæktəs] *s* (**–tuses & –ti** [taɪ]) Kaktus *m*
cad [kæd] *s* (sl) Saukerl *m,* Schuft *m*
cadaver [kə'dævər] *s* Kadaver *m,* Leiche *f*
caddie ['kædi] *s* Golfjunge *m* ‖ *intr* die Schläger tragen
cadence ['kedəns] *s* (*rhythm*) Rhythmus *m;* (*flow of language*) Sprechrhythmus *m;* (mus) Kadenz *f*
cadet [kə'dɛt] *s* Offizier(s)anwärter –in *mf*
cadre ['kædri] *s* Kader *m*
Caesar'ean opera'tion [sɪ'zɛrɪ‚ən] *s* Kaiserschnitt *m*
café [kæ'fe] *s* Cafe *n*
cafeteria [‚kæfə'tɪrɪ‚ə] *s* Selbstbedienungsrestaurant *n*
caffeine [kæ'fin] *s* Koffein *n*
cage [kedʒ] *s* Käfig *m* ‖ *tr* in e-n Käfig sperren
cagey ['kedʒi] *adj* (coll) schlau

cahoots [kə'huts] *s—***be in c.** (sl) unter e–r Decke stecken
Cain [ken] *s—***raise C.** Krach schlagen
caisson ['kesən] *s* Senkkasten *m*
cajole [kə'dʒol] *tr* beschwatzen
cake [kek] *s* Kuchen *m;* (*round cake*) Torte *f;* (*of soap*) Riegel *m;* **he takes the c.** (coll) er schießt den Vogel ab; **that takes the c.** (coll) das ist die Höhe ‖ *intr* zusammenbacken; **c. on** anbacken
calamitous [kə'læmɪtəs] *adj* unheilvoll
calamity [kə'læmɪti] *s* Unheil *n*
calci-fy ['kælsɪ‚faɪ] *v* (*pret & pp* **–fied**) *tr & intr* verkalken
calcium ['kælsɪ‚əm] *s* Kalzium *n*
calculate ['kælkjə‚let] *tr* berechnen ‖ *intr* rechnen
cal'culated risk' *s—***take a c.** ein bewußtes Risiko eingehen
cal'culating *adj* berechnend
calculation [‚kælkjə'leʃən] *s* Berechnung *f;* **rough c.** Überschlagsrechnung *f*
calculator ['kælkjə‚letər] *s* Rechenmaschine *f;* (data proc) Rechner *m*
calcu·lus ['kælkjələs] *s* (**–luses & –li** [‚laɪ]) (math) Differenzial– und Integralrechnung *f;* (pathol) Stein *m*
caldron ['kɔldrən] *s* Kessel *m*
calendar ['kæləndər] *s* Kalender *m*
calf [kæf] *s* (**calves** [kævz]) (*of a cow*) Kalb *n;* (*of certain other mammals*) Junge *n;* (anat) Wade *f*
calf'skin' *s* Kalbleder *n*
caliber ['kælɪbər] *s* (& fig) Kaliber *n*
calibrate ['kælɪ‚bret] *tr* kalibrieren
cali·co ['kælɪ‚ko] *s* (**–coes & –cos**) Kaliko *m*
calisthenics [‚kælɪs'θɛnɪks] *spl* Leibesübungen *pl*
calk [kɔk] *tr* abdichten, kalfatern
calk'ing *s* Kalfaterung *f*
call [kɔl] *s* Ruf *m;* (*visit*) Besuch *m;* (*reason*) Grund *m;* (com) (**for**) Nachfrage *f* (nach); (naut) Anlaufen *n;* (telp) Anruf *m;* **on c.** auf Abruf ‖ *tr* rufen; (*name*) nennen; (*wake*) wecken; (*a meeting*) einberufen; (*a game*) absagen; (*a strike*) ausrufen; (*by phone*) anrufen; (*a witness*) vorladen; (*a doctor; taxi*) kommen las-

sen; **be called** heißen; **c. down** (coll) herunterputzen; **c. in** (*a doctor, specialist*) hinzuziehen; (*for advice*) zu Rate ziehen; (*currency*) einziehen; (*capital*) kündigen; **c. it a day** (coll) Schluß machen; **c. off** absagen; **c. out** ausrufen; (*the police*) einsetzen; **c. s.o. names** j–n beschimpfen; **c. up** (mil) einberufen; (telp) anrufen || *intr* rufen; (cards) ansagen; **c. for** (*require*) erfordern; (*fetch*) abholen; (*help*) rufen um; (*a person*) rufen nach; **c. on** (*a pupil*) aufrufen; (*visit*) e–n Besuch machen bei; **c. to s.o.** j–m zurufen; **c. upon** auffordern

call' bell' *s* Rufglocke *f*
call' boy' *s* Hotelpage *m;* (theat) Inspezientengehilfe *m*
caller ['kɔlər] *s* Besucher –in *mf*
call' girl' *s* Callgirl *n*
call'ing *s* Beruf *m;* (relig) Berufung *f*
call'ing card' *s* Visitenkarte *f*
call'ing-down' *s* (coll) Standpauke *f*
call' num'ber *s* (libr) Standortnummer *f*
callous ['kæləs] *adj* schwielig; (fig) gefühllos, abgestumpft
call'up' *s* (mil) Einberufung *f*
callus ['kæləs] *s* Schwiele *f*
calm [kɑm] *adj* ruhig || *s* Ruhe *f;* (naut) Flaute *f* || *tr* beruhigen; **c. down** beruhigen || *intr*—**c. down** sich beruhigen
calorie ['kæləri] *s* Kalorie *f*
calumny ['kæləmni] *s* Verleumdung *f*
Calvary ['kælvəri] *s* Golgatha *n*
calve [kæv] *intr* kalben
cam [kæm] *s* Nocken *m*
camel ['kæməl] *s* Kamel *n*
camellia [kə'miljə] *s* Kamelie *f*
came•o ['kæmɪ‚o] *s* (–os) Kamee *f*
camera ['kæmərə] *s* Kamera *f*
cam'era•man' *s* (–men') Kameramann *m*
camouflage ['kæmə‚flɑʒ] *s* Tarnung *f* || *tr* tarnen
camp [kæmp] *s* (& fig) Lager *n* || *intr* kampieren, lagern, campen
campaign [kæm'pen] *s* (& fig) Feldzug *m;* (pol) Wahlfeldzug *m* || *intr* an e–m Feldzug teilnehmen; **c. for** (pol) Wahlpropaganda machen für
campaigner [kæm'penər] *s* (for a specific cause) Befürworter –in *mf;* (pol) Wahlredner –in *mf*
campaign' slo'gan *s* Wahlparole *f*
campaign' speech' *s* Wahlrede *f*
camper ['kæmpər] *s* Camper *m*
camp'fire' *s* Lagerfeuer *n*
camp'ground *s* Campingplatz *m*
camphor ['kæmfər] *s* Kampfer *m*
camp'ing *s* Camping *n*
campus ['kæmpəs] *s* Universitätsgelände *n*
cam'shaft' *s* Nockenwelle *f*
can [kæn] *s* Dose *f*, Büchse *f;* (for gasoline, water) Kanister *m* || *v* (pret & pp canned; ger canning) *tr* einmachen; (sl) 'rausschmeißen || *v* (pret & cond) (could) *aux*—**I can come** ich kann kommen; **I cannot come** ich kann nicht kommen
Canada ['kænədə] *s* Kanada *n*

Canadian [kə'nedɪ‚ən] *adj* kanadisch || *s* Kanadier –in *mf*
canal [kə'næl] *s* Kanal *m;* (anat) Gang *m*
canary [kə'nɛri] *s* Kanarienvogel *m* || **the Canaries** *spl* die Kanarischen Inseln *pl*
can•cel ['kænsəl] *v* (pret & pp –el(l)ed; ger –el(l)ing) *tr* (an event) absagen; (an order) rückgängig machen; (something written) (aus)streichen, annulieren; (stamps) entwerten; (a debt) tilgen; (a newspaper) abbestellen; (math) streichen; **c. out** ausgleichen
cancellation [‚kænsə'leʃən] *s* (of an event) Absage *f;* (of an order) Annullierung *f;* (of something written) Streichung *f;* (of a debt) Tilgung *f;* (of a stamp) Entwertung *f;* (of a newspaper) Abbestellung *f*
cancer ['kænsər] *s* Krebs *m*
cancerous ['kænsərəs] *adj* krebsartig
candela•brum [‚kændə'lɑbrəm] *s* (–bra [brə] & –brums) Armleuchter *m*
candid ['kændɪd] *adj* offen
candidacy ['kændɪdəsi] *s* Kandidatur *f*
candidate ['kændɪ‚det] *s* (for) Kandidat –in *mf* (für)
candied ['kændid] *adj* kandiert
candle ['kændəl] *s* Kerze *f*
can'dlelight' *s* Kerzenlicht *n*
can'dlepow'er *s* Kerzenstärke *f*
can'dlestick' *s* Kerzenhalter *m*
candor ['kændər] *s* Offenheit *f*
can•dy ['kændi] *s* Süßwaren *pl;* **piece of c.** Bonbon *m & n* || *v* (pret & pp –died) *tr* glacieren, kandieren
can'dy store' *s* Süßwarengeschäft *n*
cane [ken] *s* (plant; stem) Rohr *n;* (walking stick) Stock *m* || *tr* mit e–m Stock züchtigen
cane' sug'ar *s* Rohrzucker *m*
canine ['kenaɪn] *adj* Hunde– || *s* (tooth) Eckzahn *m*, Reißzahn *m*
canister ['kænɪstər] *s* Dose *f*
canker ['kæŋkər] *s* (bot) Brand *m;* (pathol) Mundgeschwür *n*
canned' goods' *spl* Dosenkonserven *pl*
canned' mu'sic *s* Konservenmusik *f*
canned' veg'etables *spl* Gemüsekonserven *pl*
cannery ['kænəri] *s* Konservenfabrik *f*
cannibal ['kænɪbəl] *s* Kannibale *m*
can'ning *adj* Konserven– || *s* Konservenfabrikation *f*
cannon ['kænən] *s* Kanone *f*
cannonade [‚kænə'ned] *s* Kanonade *f*, Beschießung *f* || *tr* beschießen
can'nonball' *s* Kanonenkugel *f*
can'non fod'der *s* Kanonenfutter *n*
canny ['kæni] *adj* (shrewd) schlau; (sagacious) klug
canoe [kə'nu] *s* Kanu *n*
canoe'ing *s* Kanufahren *n*
canoeist [kə'nu·ɪst] *s* Kanufahrer *m*
canon ['kænən] *s* Kanon *m;* (of a cathedral) Domherr *m*
canonical [kə'nɑnɪkəl] *adj* kanonisch || **canonicals** *spl* kirchliche Amtstracht *f*

canonize ['kænə‚naız] *tr* heiligsprechen

can'on law' *s* kanonisches Recht *n*

can' o'pener *s* Dosenöffner *m*

canopy ['kænəpi] *s* Baldachin *m;* (*above a king or pope*) Thronhimmel *m;* (*of a bed*) Betthimmel *m*

cant [kænt] *s* (*insincere statements*) unaufrichtiges Gerede *n;* (*jargon of thieves*) Gaunersprache *f;* (*technical phraseology*) Jargon *m*

cantaloupe ['kæntə‚lop] *s* Kantalupe *f*

cantankerous [kæn'tæŋkərəs] *adj* mürrisch, zänkisch

cantata [kən'tatə] *s* Kantate *f*

canteen [kæn'tin] *s* (*service club, service store*) Kantine *f;* (*flask*) Feldflasche *f*

canter ['kæntər] *s* kurzer Galopp *m* ‖ *intr* im kurzen Galopp reiten

canticle ['kæntɪkəl] *s* Lobgesang *m*

canton ['kæntən] *s* Kanton *m*

canvas ['kænvəs] *s* Leinwand *f;* (naut) Segeltuch *n;* (*a painting*) Gemälde *n*

canvass ['kænvəs] *s* (econ) Werbefeldzug *m;* (pol) Wahlfeldzug *m* ‖ *tr* (*a district*) (pol) bearbeiten; (*votes*) (pol) werben

canyon ['kænjən] *s* Schlucht *f*

cap [kæp] *s* Kappe *f*, Mütze *f;* (*of a jar*) Deckel *m;* (*twist-off type*) Kapsel *f;* (*for a toy pistol*) Knallblättchen *n;* (typ) großer Buchstabe *m;* **use caps** (typ) großschreiben ‖ *v* (*pret & pp* **capped**; *ger* **capping**) *tr* (*a bottle*) mit e-r Kapsel versehen; (*e.g., with snow*) bedecken; (*outdo*) übertreffen; (*success*) krönen

capability [‚kepə'bɪlɪti] *s* Fähigkeit *f*

capable ['kepəbəl] *adj* tüchtig; **c. of** fähig (*genit*); (*ger*) fähig zu (*inf*)

capacious [kə'peʃəs] *adj* geräumig

capacity [kə'pæsɪti] *adj* maximal, Kapazitäts– ‖ *s* (*ability*) Fähigkeit *f;* (*content*) Fassungsvermögen *n;* (*of a truck, bridge*) Tragfähigkeit *f;* (tech) Kapazität *f;* **in my c. as** in meiner Eigenschaft als

cap' and gown' *s* Barett *n* und Talar *m*

cape [kep] *s* Umhang *m;* (geog) Kap *n*

Cape' of Good' Hope' *s* Kap *n* der Guten Hoffnung

caper ['kepər] *s* Luftsprung *m;* (*prank*) Schabernack *m;* (culin) Kaper *f* ‖ *intr* hüpfen

capita ['kæpɪtə] *spl*—**per c.** pro Kopf, pro Person

capital ['kæpɪtəl] *adj* (*importance*) äußerste, höchste; (*city*) Haupt–; (*crime*) Kapital– ‖ *s* (*city*) Hauptstadt *f;* (archit) Kapitell *n;* (fin) Kapital *n;* (typ) Großbuchstabe *m*

cap'ital gains' *spl* Kapitalzuwachs *m*

capitalism ['kæpɪtə‚lɪzəm] *s* Kapitalismus *m*

capitalist ['kæpɪtəlɪst] *s* Kapitalist –in *mf*

capitalistic [‚kæpɪtə'lɪstɪk] *adj* kapitalistisch

capitalize ['kæpɪtə‚laɪz] *tr* (fin) kapitalisieren; (typ) groß schreiben (or drucken) ‖ *intr*—**c. on** Nutzen ziehen aus

cap'ital let'ter *s* Großbuchstabe *m*

cap'ital pun'ishment *s* Todesstrafe *f*

capitol ['kæpɪtəl] *s* Kapitol *n*

capitulate [kə'pɪtʃə‚let] *intr* kapitulieren

capon ['kepɑn] *s* Kapaun *m*

caprice [kə'pris] *s* Grille *f*, Kaprice *f*

capricious [kə'prɪʃəs] *adj* kapriziös

capsize ['kæpsaɪz] *tr* zum Kentern bringen ‖ *intr* kentern

capsule ['kæpsəl] *s* Kapsel *f*

captain ['kæptən] *s* (*of police, of firemen, in the army*) Hauptmann *m;* (naut, sport) Kapitän *m;* (nav) Kapitän *m* zur See; (sport) Mannschaftsführer *m*

caption ['kæpʃən] *s* (*heading of an article*) Überschrift *f;* (*wording under a picture*) Bildunterschrift *f;* (cin) Untertitel *m*

captivate ['kæptɪ‚vet] *tr* fesseln

captive ['kæptɪv] *adj* gefangen ‖ *s* Gefangene *mf*

cap'tive au'dience *s* unfreiwillige Zuhörerschaft *f*

captivity [kæp'tɪvɪti] *s* Gefangenschaft *f*

captor ['kæptər] *s* Fänger –in *mf*

capture ['kæptʃər] *s* Fangen *n,* Gefangennahme *f;* (naut) Kaperung *f* ‖ *tr* (*animals*) fangen; (*soldiers*) gefangennehmen; (*a ship*) kapern; (*a town*) erobern; (*a prize*) gewinnen

car [kɑr] *s* (aut, rr) Wagen *m*

carafe [kə'ræf] *s* Karaffe *f*

caramel ['kærəməl] *s* Karamelle *f*

carat ['kærət] *s* Karat *n*

caravan ['kærə‚væn] *s* Karawane *f*

car'away seed' ['kærə‚we] *s* Kümmelkorn *n*

carbide ['kɑrbaɪd] *s* Karbid *n*

carbine ['kɑrbaɪn] *s* Karabiner *m*

carbohydrate [‚kɑrbo'haɪdret] *s* Kohlenhydrat *n*

carbol'ic ac'id [kɑr'bɑlɪk] *s* Karbolsäure *f*

carbon ['kɑrbən] *s* (chem) Kohlenstoff *m;* (elec) Kohlenstift *m*

carbonated ['kɑrbə‚netɪd] *adj* kohlensäurehaltig, Brause–

car'bon cop'y *s* Durchschlag *m;* **make a c. of** durchschlagen

car'bon diox'ide *s* Kohlendioxyd *n*

car'bon monox'ide *s* Kohlenoxyd *n*

car'bon pa'per *s* Kohlepapier *n*

carbuncle ['kɑrbʌŋkəl] *s* (*stone*) Karfunkel *m;* (pathol) Karbunkel *m*

carburetor ['kɑrb(j)ə‚retər] *s* Vergaser *m*

carcass ['kɑrkəs] *s* Kadaver *m,* Aas *n;* (*without offal*) Rumpf *m*

car' coat' *s* Stutzer *m*

card [kɑrd] *s* Karte *f;* (*person*) (coll) Kerl *m;* (text) Krempel *f* ‖ *tr* (text) kardätschen

card'board' *s* Kartonpapier *n;* (*thick pasteboard*) Pappe *f;* **piece of c.** Papp(en)deckel *m*

card'board box' *s* Pappkarton *m,* Pappschachtel *f*

card' cat'alogue *s* Kartothek *f*

card' file' s Kartei f
cardiac ['kɑrdɪ‚æk] adj Herz– ‖ s (remedy) Herzmittel n; (patient) Herzkranke mf
cardinal ['kɑrdɪnəl] adj Kardinal– ‖ s (eccl, orn) Kardinal m
card' in'dex s Karthotek f, Kartei f
card'sharp' s Falschspieler –in mf
card' trick' s Kartenkunststück n
care [ker] s (accuracy) Sorgfalt f; (worry) Sorge f, Kummer m; (prudence) Vorsicht f; (upkeep) Pflege f; **be under a doctor's c.** unter der Aufsicht e–s Arztes stehen; **c. of** (on letters) bei; **take c.** aufpassen; **take c. not to** (inf) sich hüten zu (inf); **take c. of s.o.** (provide for s.o.) für j–n sorgen; (attend to) sich um j–n kümmern; **take c. of s.th.** etw besorgen; (e.g., one's clothes) schonen ‖ intr—**c. about** sich kümmern um; **c. for** (like) mögen, gern haben; (have concern for) sorgen für; (attend to) pflegen; **c. to** (inf) Lust haben zu (inf); **for all I c.** von mir aus
careen [kə'rin] tr auf die Seite legen ‖ intr (aut) sich in die Kurve neigen
career [kə'rɪr] adj Berufs– ‖ s Karriere f
career' wo'man s berufstätige Frau f
care'free' adj unbelastet, sorgenfrei
careful ['kerfəl] adj (cautious) vorsichtig; (accurate) sorgfältig; **b. c.!** gib acht!
careless ['kerlɪs] adj (incautious) unvorsichtig; (remark) unbedacht; (inaccurate) nachlässig
carelessness ['kerlɪsnɪs] s Unvorsichtigkeit f; Nachlässigkeit f
caress [kə'res] s Liebkosung f ‖ tr liebkosen
caret ['kærət] s Auslassungszeichen n
caretaker ['ker‚tekər] s Verwalter m
care'worn' adj abgehärmt, vergrämt
car'fare' s Fahrgeld n
car·go ['kɑrgo] s (–goes & –gos) Fracht f
car'go compart'ment s Frachtraum m
car'go plane' s Frachtflugzeug n
Caribbean [‚kærɪ'bi·ən], [kə'rɪbɪ·ən] adj karibisch ‖ s Karibisches Meer n
caricature ['kærɪkətʃər] s Karikatur f ‖ tr karikieren
caries ['keriz] s (dent) Karies f
carillon ['kærɪ‚lɑn] s Glockenspiel n
car' lift' s (aut) Hebebühne f
car'load' s Wagenladung f
carnage ['kɑrnɪdʒ] s Blutbad n
carnal ['kɑrnəl] adj fleischlich
car'nal know'ledge s Geschlechtsverkehr m
carnation [kɑr'neʃən] s Nelke f
carnival ['kɑrnɪvəl] s Karneval m
carnivorous [kɑr'nɪvərəs] adj fleischfressend
car·ol ['kærəl] s Weihnachtslied n ‖ v (pret & pp –ol(l)ed; ger –l(l)ing) intr Weihnachtslieder singen
carom ['kærəm] s (billiards) Karambolage f ‖ intr (fig) zusammenstoßen; (billiards) karambolieren
carouse [kə'rauz] intr zechen

carp [kɑrp] s Karpfen m ‖ intr nörgeln
carpenter ['kɑrpəntər] s Zimmermann m
carpentry ['kɑrpəntri] s Zimmerei f
carpet ['kɑrpɪt] s Teppich m ‖ tr mit Teppichen belegen
car'pet sweep'er s Teppichkehrmaschine f
car'port' s Autoschuppen m
car'-ren'tal serv'ice s Autovermietung f
carriage ['kærɪdʒ] s Kutsche f; (of a typewriter) Wagen m; (bearing) Körperhaltung f; (econ) Transportkosten pl
car' ride' s Autofahrt f
carrier ['kærɪ‚ər] s Träger m; (company) Transportunternehmen n
car'rier pig'eon s Brieftaube f
carrion ['kærɪ‚ən] s Aas n
carrot ['kærət] s Karotte f, Mohrrübe f
carrousel [‚kærə'zɛl] s Karussell n
car·ry ['kæri] v (pret & pp –ried) tr tragen; (wares) führen; (a message) überbringen; (a tune) halten; (said of transportation) befördern; (insurance) haben; (math) übertragen; (parl) durchbringen; **be carried** (said of a motion, bill) angenommen werden; **be carried away by** (& fig) mitgerissen werden von; **c. away** (an audience) mitreißen; **c. off** (a prize) davontragen; **c. on** weiterführen; (a business) betreiben, führen; **c. out** hinaustragen; (a duty) erfüllen; (measures) durchführen; (a sentence) vollstrecken; (an order) ausführen; **c. over** (acct) übertragen; **c. s.th. too far** etw übertreiben; **c. through** durchsetzen; ‖ intr (said of sounds) tragen; (parl) durchgehen; **c. on** (continue) weitermachen; (act up) (coll) toben; **c. on with** ein Verhältnis haben mit
car'rying char'ges spl Kreditgebühren pl
car'ry-o'ver s Überbleibsel n; (acct) Übertrag m
cart [kɑrt] s Karren m ‖ tr mit dem Handwagen befördern; **c. away** (or **c. off**) abfahren
cartel [kɑr'tel] s Kartell n
cartilage ['kɑrtɪlɪdʒ] s Knorpel m
carton ['kɑrtən] s Karton m; **a c. of cigarettes** e–e Stange Zigaretten
cartoon [kɑr'tun] s Karikatur f; (comic strip) Karikaturenreihe f; (cin) Zeichentrickfilm m; (paint) Entwurf m natürlicher Größe ‖ tr karikieren
cartoonist [kɑr'tunɪst] s Karikaturenzeichner –in mf
cartridge ['kɑrtrɪdʒ] s Patrone f; (phot) Filmpatrone f
car'tridge belt' s Patronengurt m
cart'wheel' s Wagenrad n; **turn a c.** ein Rad schlagen
carve [kɑrv] tr (wood) schnitzen; (meat) tranchieren, vorschneiden; (stone) meißeln; **c. out** (e.g., a career) aufbauen

carver [ˈkɑrvər] *s* (*at table*) Vorschneider –in *mf*
carv'ing knife' *s* Tranchiermesser *n*
car' wash' *s* Wagenwäsche *f*
cascade [kæsˈked] *s* Kaskade *f* ‖ *intr* kaskadenartig herabstürzen
case [kes] *s* (*instance*) Fall *m*; (*situation*) Sache *f*; (*box*) Kiste *f*; (*for a knife, etc.*) Hülle *f*; (*for cigarettes*) Etui *n*; (*for eyeglasses*) Futteral *n*; (*for shipping*) Schutzkarton *m*; (*of a watch*) Gehäuse *n*; (*of sickness*) Krankheitsfall *m*; (*sick person*) Patient –in *mf*; (*gram*) Fall *m*; (*jur*) Fall *m*, Sache *f*, Prozeß *m*; (*typ*) Setzkasten *m*; **as the c. may be** je nachdem; **have a strong c.** schlüssige Beweise haben; **if that's the c.** wenn es sich so verhält; **in any c.** auf jeden Fall, jedenfalls; **in c. falls; in c. of** im Falle (*genit*); **in c. of emergency** im Notfall; **in no c.** keinesfalls ‖ *tr* (sl) genau ansehen; **the c. at issue** der vorliegende Fall
case' his'tory *s* Vorgeschichte *f*; (med) Krankengeschichte *f*
casement [ˈkesmənt] *s* Fensterflügel *m*
case'ment win'dow *s* Flügelfenster *n*
cash [kæʃ] *adj* Bar– ‖ *s* Bargeld *n*; (*cash payment*) Barzahlung *f*; **c. and carry** nur gegen Barzahlung und eigenen Transport; **in c.** per Kasse; **out of c.** nicht bei Kasse; **pay c. for** bar bezahlen ‖ *tr* einlösen ‖ *intr*— **c. in on** (coll) Nutzen ziehen aus
cash'box' *s* Schatulle *f*, Kasse *f*
cash' dis'count *s* Kassaskonto *n*
cashew' nut' [kəˈʃ/u], [ˈkæ/u] *s* Kaschunuß *f*
cashier [kæˈʃɪr] *s* Kassierer –in *mf*
cashmere [ˈkæʃmɪr] *s* Kaschmir *m*
cash' on deliv'ery *adv* per Nachnahme
cash' reg'ister *m* Registerkasse *f*
cas'ing *s* (*wrapping*) Verpackung *f*; (*housing*) Gehäuse *n*; (*of a window or door*) Futter *n*; (*of a tire*) Mantel *m*; (*of a sausage*) Wurstdarm *m*
casi·no [kəˈsino] *s* (**–nos**) Kasino *n*
cask [kæsk] *s* Faß *n*, Tonne *f*
casket [ˈkæskɪt] *s* Sarg *m*
casserole [ˈkæsəˌrol] *s* Kasserolle *f*
cassette [kæˈsɛt] *s* Kassette *f*
cassock [ˈkæsək] *s* (eccl) Soutane *f*
cast [kæst] *s* (*throw*) Wurf *m*; (*act of molding*) Guß *m*; (*mold*) Gußform *f*; (*object molded*) Abguß *m*; (*hue*) Abtönung *f*; (surg) Gipsverband *m*; (theat) Rollenbesetzung *f* ‖ *v* (*pret & pp cast*) *tr* werfen; (*a net, anchor*) auswerfen; (*a ballot*) abgeben; (*lots*) ziehen; (*skin, horns*) abwerfen; (*a shadow, glance*) werfen; (*metal*) gießen; (*a play or motion picture*) die Rollen besetzen in (*dat*); **be c. down** niedergeschlagen sein; **c. aside** (*reject*) verwerfen; ‖ *intr* (angl) die Angel auswerfen; **c. off** (naut) loswerfen
castanet [ˌkæstəˈnet] *s* Kastagnette *f*
cast'away' *adj* verworfen; (naut) schiffbrüchig ‖ *s* (naut) Schiffbrüchige *mf*
caste [kæst] *s* Kaste *f*

caster [ˈkæstər] *s* (*under furniture*) Rolle *f*; (*shaker*) Streuer *m*
castigate [ˈkæstɪˌget] *tr* züchtigen (fig) geißeln
cast'ing *s* Wurf *m*; (*act of casting* (metal) Guß *m*; (*the object cast* (metal) Gußstück *n*; (theat) Rollenverteilung *f*
cast'ing rod' *s* Wurfangel *f*
cast' i'ron *s* Gußeisen *n*
cast'-i'ron *adj* gußeisern; (fig) eisern
castle [ˈkæsəl] *s* Schloß *n*, Burg, *f* (chess) Turm *m* ‖ *intr* (chess) rochieren
cast'off' *adj* abgelegt ‖ *s* (*e.g., dress* abgelegtes Kleidungsstück *n*; (*per son*) Verstoßene *mf*
cas'tor oil' [ˈkæstər] *s* Rizinusöl *n*
castrate [ˈkæstret] *tr* kastrieren
casual [ˈkæʒʊ·əl] *adj* (*cursory*) bei läufig; (*occasional*) gelegentlich; (*in cidental*) zufällig; (*informal*) zwang los; (*unconcerned*) gleichgültig
casualty [ˈkæʒʊ·əlti] *s* (*victim*) Opfe *n*; (*accident*) Unfall *m*; (*person in jured*) Verunglückte *mf*; (*perso killed*) (mil) Gefallene *mf*; (*perso wounded*) (mil) Verwundete *mf*
casualties (*in an accident*) Verun glückte *pl*; (*in war*) Verluste *pl*
cas'ualty list' *s* Verlustliste *f*
cat [kæt] *s* Katze *f*; (*guy*) (sl) Typ *m* (*malicious woman*) (sl) falsche Katz *f*
catacomb [ˈkætəˌkom] *s* Katakombe
catalog(ue) [ˈkætəˌlɔg] *s* Katalog *m* (*list*) Verzeichnis *n*; (*of a university* Vorlesungsverzeichnis *n* ‖ *tr* kata logisieren
catalyst [ˈkætəlɪst] *s* Katalysator *m*
catapult [ˈkætəˌpʌlt] *s* Katapult *m & n* ‖ *tr* katapultieren, abschleudern
cataract [ˈkætəˌrækt] *s* Katarakt *m* (pathol) grauer Star *m*; **remov s.o.'s c.** j–m den Star stechen
catastrophe [kəˈtæstrəfi] *s* Katastrophe *f*
cat'call' *s* Auspfeifen *n* ‖ *tr* auspfeifer
catch [kætʃ] *s* Fang *m*; (*of fish*) Fischfang *m*; (*device*) Haken *m*, Klinke *f*; (*desirable partner*) Partie *f*; (fig) Haken *m*; ‖ *v* (*pret & pp caught* [kɔt]) *tr* fangen; (*s.o. or s.th. falling*) auffangen; (*by pursuing*) abfangen; (*s.o. or s.th. that has escaped*) einfangen; (*by surprise*) ertappen, erwischen; (*in midair*) aufschnappen; (*take hold of*) fassen; (*said of a storm*) überraschen; (*e.g., a train*) erreichen; **c. a cold** sich erkälten; **c. fire** in Brand geraten; **c. hold of** ergreifen; **c. it** (coll) sein Fett kriegen; **c. one's breath** wieder Atem schöpfen; **c. one's eye** j–m ins Auge fallen; **get caught on** hängenbleiben an (*dat*) ‖ *intr* (*said of a bolt, etc.*) einschnappen; **c. on** (*said of an idea*) Anklang finden; **c. on to** (fig) kapieren; **catch up** aufholen; **c. up on** nachholen; **c. up with** einholen
catch'ing *adj* (*disease*) ansteckend; (*attractive*) anziehend

catch'word' s (*slogan*) Schlagwort n; (*actor's cue*) Stichwort n; (pol) Parteiparole f
catchy ['kætʃi] adj einschmeichelnd
catechism ['kætɪˌkɪzəm] s Katechismus m
category ['kætɪˌgori] s Kategorie f
cater ['ketər] tr Lebensmittel liefern für ‖ intr—**c. to** schmeicheln (*dat*); (*deliver food to*) Lebensmittel liefern für
cater-corner ['kætər ˌkɔrnər] adj & adv diagonal
caterer ['ketərər] s Lebensmittellieferant –in mf
caterpillar ['kætərˌpɪlər] s (ent, mach) Raupe f
cat'fish' s Katzenwels m, Katzenfisch m
cat'gut' s (mus) Darmseite f; (surg) Katgut n
cathedral [kə'θidrəl] s Dom m
catheter ['kæθɪtər] s Katheter n
cathode ['kæθod] s Kathode f
catholic ['kæθəlɪk] adj universal; **Catholic** katholisch ‖ **Catholic** s Katholik –in mf
cat'nap' s Nickerchen n
catnip ['kætnɪp] s Baldrian m
catsup ['kætsəp], ['ketʃəp] s Ketchup m
cattle ['kætəl] spl Vieh n
cat'tle car' s (rr) Viehwagen m
cat'tle·man s (–men) Viehzüchter m
cat'tle ranch' s Viehfarm f
catty ['kæti] adj boshaft
cat'walk' s Steg m, Laufplanke f
Caucasian [kɔ'keʒən] adj kaukasisch ‖ s Kaukasier –in mf
caucus ['kɔkəs] s Parteiführerversammlung f
cauliflower ['kɔlɪˌflaʊ·ər] s Blumenkohl m
cause [kɔz] s (*origin*) Ursache f; (*reason*) Grund m; (*person*) Urheber –in mf; (*occasion*) Anlaß m; **for a good c.** für e–e gute Sache ‖ tr verursachen; **c. s.o. to** (*inf*) j–n veranlassen zu (*inf*)
cause'way' s Dammweg m
caustic ['kɔstɪk] adj (& fig) ätzend
cauterize ['kɔtəˌraɪz] tr verätzen
caution ['kɔʃən] s (*carefulness*) Vorsicht f; (*warning*) Warnung f ‖ tr (*against*) warnen (vor *dat*)
cautious ['kɔʃəs] adj vorsichtig
cavalcade ['kævəlˌked] s Kavalkade f
cavalier [ˌkævə'lɪr] adj hochmütig ‖ s Kavalier m
cavalry ['kævəlri] s Kavallerie f
cav'alry·man s (–men) Kavallerist m
cave [kev] s Höhle f ‖ intr—**c. in** (*collapse*) einstürzen
cave'-in' s Einsturz m
cave' man' s Höhlenmensch m
cavern ['kævərn] s (große) Höhle f
caviar ['kævɪˌar] s Kaviar m
cav·il ['kævɪl] v (*pret & pp* –l(l)ed; *ger* –l(l)ing) intr (at, about) herumnörgeln (an *dat*)
cavity ['kævɪti] s Hohlraum m; (anat) Höhle f; (dent) Loch n
cavort [kə'vɔrt] intr (coll) herumtollen

caw [kɔ] s Krächzen n ‖ intr krächzen
cease [sis] s—**without c.** unaufhörlich ‖ tr einstellen; (*ger*) aufhören (zu *inf*); **c. fire** das Feuer einstellen ‖ intr aufhören
cease'fire' s Feuereinstellung f
ceaseless ['sislɪs] adj unaufhörlich
cedar ['sidər] s Zeder f
cede [sid] tr abtreten, überlassen
cedilla [sɪ'dɪlə] s Cedille f
ceiling ['silɪŋ] s Decke f; (fin) oberste Grenze f; **hit the c.** (coll) platzen
ceil'ing light' s Deckenlicht n
ceil'ing price' s Höchstpreis m
celebrant ['sɛlɪbrənt] s Zelebrant m
celebrate ['sɛlɪˌbret] tr (*a feast*) feiern; (*mass*) zelebrieren ‖ intr feiern; (eccl) zelebrieren
cel'ebrat'ed adj (for) berühmt (wegen)
celebration [ˌsɛlɪ'breʃən] s Feier f; (eccl) Zelebrieren n; **in c. of** zur Feier (*genit*)
celebrity [sɪ'lɛbrɪti] s Berühmtheit f; (*person*) Prominente mf
celery ['sɛləri] s Selleriestengel m
celestial [sɪ'lɛstʃəl] adj himmlisch; (astr) Himmels–
celibacy ['sɛlɪbəsi] s Zölibat m & n
celibate ['sɛlɪbɪt] adj ehelos
cell [sɛl] s Zelle f
cellar ['sɛlər] s Keller m
cellist ['tʃɛlɪst] s Cellist –in mf
cel·lo ['tʃɛlo] s (–los) Cello n
cellophane ['sɛləˌfɛn] s Zellophan n
celluloid ['sɛljəˌlɔɪd] s Zelluloid n
Celt [sɛlt], [kɛlt] s Kelte m, Keltin f
Celtic ['sɛltɪk], ['kɛltɪk] adj keltisch
cement [sɪ'mɛnt] s (*glue*) Bindemittel n; (*used in building*) Zement m ‖ tr zementieren; (*glue*) kitten; (fig) (be)festigen
cement' mix'er s Betonmischmaschine f
cemetery ['sɛmɪˌteri] s Friedhof m
censer ['sɛnsər] s Räucherfaß n
censor ['sɛnsər] s (*of printed matter, films*) Zensor m; (*of morals*) Sittenrichter m ‖ tr zensieren
cen'sorship' s Zensur f
censure ['sɛnʃər] s Tadel m ‖ tr tadeln
census ['sɛnsəs] s Volkszählung f
cent [sɛnt] s Cent m
centaur ['sɛntɔr] s Zentaur m
centennial [sɛn'tɛnɪ·əl] adj hundertjährig ‖ s Hundertjahrfeier f
center ['sɛntər] s Zentrum n, Mittelpunkt m; (pol) Mitte f ‖ tr in den Mittelpunkt stellen; (tech) zentrieren ‖ intr—**c.** on sich konzentrieren auf (*acc*)
cen'ter aisle' s Mittelgang m
cen'ter cit'y s Stadtmitte f
cen'terpiece' s Tischaufsatz m
centigrade ['sɛntɪˌgred] s Celsius, e.g., **one degree c.** ein Grad Celsius
centimeter ['sɛntɪˌmitər] s Zentimeter m
centipede ['sɛntɪˌpid] s Hundertfüßler m
central ['sɛntrəl] adj zentral
Cen'tral Amer'ica s Mittelamerika n
centralize ['sɛntrəˌlaɪz] tr zentralisieren

centri'fugal force' [sɛn'trɪfjəgəl] s Fliehkraft f
centrifuge ['sɛntrɪ‚fjudʒ] s Zentrifuge f
century ['sɛntʃəri] s Jahrhundert n
ceramic [sɪ'ræmɪk] adj keramisch || ceramics s (art) Keramik f; spl Töpferwaren pl
cereal ['sɪrɪ·əl] adj Getreide– || s (grain) Getreide n; (dish) Getreideflockengericht n
cerebral ['sɛrɪbrəl] adj Gehirn–
ceremonial [‚sɛrɪ'monɪ·əl] adj zeremoniell, feierlich
ceremonious [‚sɛrɪ'monɪ·əs] adj zeremoniös, umständlich
ceremony ['sɛrɪ‚moni] s Zeremonie f
certain ['sʌrtən] adj (sure) sicher, bestimmt; (particular but unnamed) gewiß; be c. feststehen; for c. gewiß; make c. of sich vergewissern (genit); make c. that sich vergewissern, daß
certainly ['sʌrtənlɪ] adv sicher(lich); (as a strong affirmative) allerdings
certainty ['sʌrtəntɪ] s Sicherheit f
certificate [sər'tɪfɪkɪt] s Schein m; (educ) Abgangszeugnis n
certification [‚sʌrtɪfɪ'keʃən] s Bescheinigung f, Beglaubigung f
cer'tified adj beglaubigt
cer'tified check' s durch Bank bestätigter Scheck m
cer'tified pub'lic account'ant s amtlich zugelassener Wirtschaftsprüfer m
certi·fy ['sʌrtɪ‚faɪ] v (pret & pp –fied) bescheinigen, beglaubigen
cervix ['sʌrvɪks] s (cervices [sər'vaɪsiz]) Genick n
cessation [sɛ'seʃən] s (of territory) Abtretung f; (of activities) Einstellung f
cesspool ['sɛs‚pul] s Senkgrube f
chafe [tʃef] tr (the skin) wundscheuern || intr (rub) scheuern; (become sore) sich wundreiben; (be irritated) (at) sich ärgern über (acc)
chaff [tʃæf] s Spreu f
chaf'ing dish' s Speisenwärmer m
chagrin [ʃə'grɪn] s Verdruß m || tr verdrießen
chain [tʃen] s Kette f || tr (to) anketten (an acc)
chain' gang' s Kettensträflinge pl
chain' reac'tion s Kettenreaktion f
chain' smok'er s Kettenraucher –in mf
chain' store' s Kettenladen m
chair [tʃer] s Stuhl m; (upholstered) Sessel m; (of the presiding officer) Vorsitz m; (presiding officer) Vorsitzende mf; (educ) Lehrstuhl m || tr den Vorsitz führen von
chair'la·dy s Vorsitzende f
chair' lift' s Sessellift m
chair'man s (–men) Vorsitzende m
chair'manship' s Vorsitz m
chalice ['tʃælɪs] s Kelch m
chalk [tʃɔk] s Kreide f || tr—c. up ankreiden; (coll) verbuchen
challenge ['tʃælɪndʒ] s Aufforderung f; (to a duel) Herausforderung f; (jur) Ablehnung f; (mil) Anruf m || tr auffordern; (to a duel) herausfor-

dern; (a statement, right) bestreiten; (jur) ablehnen; (mil) anrufen
chamber ['tʃembər] s Kammer f; (parl) Sitzungssaal m
chamberlain ['tʃembərlɪn] s Kammerherr m
cham'bermaid' s Stubenmädchen n
cham'ber of com'merce s Handelskammer f
chameleon [kə'milɪ·ən] s Chamäleon n
chamfer ['tʃæmfər] s Schrägkante f || tr abschrägen; (furrow) auskehlen
cham·ois ['ʃæmi] s (–ois) Sämischleder n; (zool) Gemse f
champ [tʃæmp] s (coll) Meister m || tr kauen; champ the bit am Gebiß kauen
champagne [ʃæm'pen] s Champagner m, Sekt m
champion ['tʃæmpɪ·ən] s (of a cause) Verfechter –in mf; (sport) Meister –in mf || tr eintreten für
cham'pionship' s Meisterschaft f
chance [tʃæns] adj zufällig || s (accident) Zufall m; (opportunity) Chance f, Gelegenheit f; (risk) Risiko n; (possibility) Möglichkeit f; (lottery ticket) Los n; by c. zufällig; c. of a lifetime einmalige Gelegenheit f; chances are (that) aller Wahrscheinlichkeit nach; on the c. that für den Fall, daß; take a c. ein Risiko eingehen; take no chances nichts riskieren; || tr riskieren || intr geschehen; c. upon stoßen auf (acc)
chancel ['tʃænsəl] s Altarraum m
chancellery ['tʃænsələri] s Kanzlei f
chancellor ['tʃænsələr] s Kanzler m; (hist) Reichskanzler m
chandelier [‚ʃændə'lɪr] s Kronleuchter m
change [tʃendʒ] s Veränderung f; (in times, styles, etc.) Wechsel m; (in attitude, relations, etc.) Wandel m; (small coins) Kleingeld n; (of weather) Umschlag m; c. for the better Verbesserung f; c. for the worse Verschlechterung f; for a c. zur Abwechslung; give c. for a dollar auf e–n Dollar herausgeben; need a c. Luftveränderung brauchen || tr verändern; (plans) ändern; (money, subject, oil) wechseln; (a baby) trockenlegen; (stations, channels) umschalten; c. around umändern; c. hands den Besitzer wechseln; c. one's mind sich anders besinnen; c. trains or buses, streetcars) umsteigen || intr sich verändern; (said of a mood, wind, weather) umschlagen; (said of a voice) mutieren; (change clothes) sich umziehen change into sich wandeln in (acc)
changeable ['tʃendʒəbəl] adj veränderlich
changeless ['tʃendʒlɪs] adj unveränderlich
change' of heart' s Sinnesänderung f
change' of life' s Wechseljahre pl
change' of scen'ery s Ortsveränderung f
change'-o'ver s Umstellung f

chan·nel ['t∫ænəl] s (strait) Kanal m; (of a river) Fahrrinne f; (groove) Rinne f; (furrow) Furche f; (fig) Weg m; (telv) Kanal m; **through official channels** auf dem Amtswege || v (pret & pp **-nel(l)ed;** ger **-nel(l)ing)** tr lenken; (furrow) kanalisieren

chant [t∫ænt] s Gesang m; (singsong) Singsang m; (eccl) Kirchengesang m || tr singen

chanter ['t∫æntər] s Kantor m

chaos ['ke·as] s Chaos n

chaotic [ke'atık] adj chaotisch

chap [t∫æp] s (in the skin) Riß m; (coll) Kerl m || v (pret & pp **chapped;** ger **chapping)** tr (the skin) rissig machen || intr rissig werden, aufspringen

chapel ['t∫æpəl] s Kapelle f

chaperon ['∫æpə,ron] s Begleiter –in mf; (of a young couple) Anstandsdame f || tr als Anstandsdame begleiten

chaplain ['t∫æplɪn] s Kaplan m

chapter ['t∫æptər] s Kapitel n; (of an organization) Ortsgruppe f

char [t∫ar] v (pret & pp **charred;** ger **charring)** tr verkohlen

character ['kærıktər] s Charakter m; (letter) Schriftzeichen n; (typewriter space) Anschlag m; (coll) Kauz m; (theat) handelnde Person f; **be out of c.** nicht passen

characteristic [,kærıktə'rıstık] adj (of) charakteristisch (für) || s Charakterzug m, Kennzeichen n

characterize ['kærıktə,raız] tr charakterisieren, kennzeichnen

charade [∫ə'red] s Scharade f

charcoal ['t∫ar,kol] s Holzkohle f; (for sketching) Zeichenkohle f

charge [t∫ardʒ] s (accusation) Anklage f; (fee) Gebühr f; (custody) Obhut f; (responsibility) Pflicht f; (ward) Pflegebefohlene mf; (of an explosive or electricity) Ladung f; (assault) Ansturm m; (of a judge to the jury) Rechtsbelehrung f; **be in c. of** verantwortlich sein für; **charges** Spesen pl; **take c. of** die Verantwortung übernehmen für; **there is no c.** es kostet nichts; **under s.o.'s c.** unter j–s Aufsicht || tr (a battery) (auf)-laden; (with) anklagen (wegen); (a jury) belehren; (mil) stürmen; **c. s.o. ten marks for** j–m zehn Mark berechnen für; **c. s.o.'s account** auf j–s Rechnung setzen || intr (mil) anrechnen für; **c. to s.o.'s account** auf j–s Rechnung setzen || intr (mil) anstürmen

charge′ account′ s laufendes Konto n

charger ['t∫ardʒər] s (elec) Ladevorrichtung f; (hist) Schlachtroß n

chariot ['t∫arı·ət] s Kampfwagen m

charitable ['t∫ærıtəbəl] adj (generous) freigebig; (lenient) nachsichtig; **c. institution** wohltätige Stiftung f

charity ['t∫ærıti] s (giving of alms) Wohltätigkeit f; (alms) Almosen n; (institution) Wohlfahrtsinstitut n; (love of neighbor) Nächstenliebe f

charlatan ['∫arlətən] s Scharlatan m

Charles [t∫arlz] s Karl m

char′ley horse′ ['t∫arli] s (coll) Muskelkater m

charm [t∫arm] s Charme m; (trinket) Amulett n || tr verzaubern; (fig) entzücken

charm′ing adj scharmant, reizend

chart [t∫art] s Karte f; (table) Tabelle f; (naut) Seekarte f || tr entwerfen, auf e–r Karte graphisch darstellen

charter ['t∫artər] adj (plane, etc.) Charter– || s Freibrief m, Charter m; (of an organization) Gründungsurkunde f und Satzungen pl || tr chartern

char′ter mem′ber s gründendes Mitglied n

char·woman ['t∫ar,wumən] s (–women [,wımın] Putzfrau f

chase [t∫es] s (pursuit) Verfolgung f; (hunt) Jagd f || tr jagen; (girls) nachsteigen (dat); **c. away** verjagen; **c. out** vertreiben || intr—**c. after** nachlaufen (dat)

chasm ['kæzəm] s (& fig) Abgrund m

chas·sis ['t∫æsi] s (–sis [siz]) Chassis n; (aut) Fahrgestell n

chaste [t∫est] adj keusch

chasten ['t∫esən] tr züchtigen

chastise [t∫æs'taız] tr züchtigen

chastity ['t∫æstıtı] s Keuschheit f

chat [t∫æt] s Plauderei f || v (pret & pp **chatted;** ger **chatting)** intr plaudern

chattel ['t∫ætəl] s Sklave m; **chattels** Hab und Gut n

chatter ['t∫ætər] s (talk) Geplapper n; (of teeth) Klappern n || intr (talk) plappern; (said of teeth) klappern

chat′terbox′ s (coll) Plappermaul n

chauffeur ['∫ofər], [∫o'fʌr] s Chauffeur m || tr fahren

cheap [t∫ip] adj (inexpensive) billig; (shoddy) minderwertig; (base) gemein; (stingy) geizig; **feel c.** sich verlegen fühlen || adv billig; **get off c.** mit e–m blauen Auge davonkommen

cheapen ['t∫ipən] tr herabsetzen

cheat [t∫it] s Betrüger –in mf || tr (out of) betrügen (um) || intr schwindeln; (at cards) mogeln; **c. on** (e.g., a wife) betrügen

cheat′ing s Betrügerei f; (at cards) Mogelei f

check [t∫ɛk] s (of a bank) Scheck m; (for luggage) Schein m; (in a restaurant) Rechnung f; (inspection) Kontrolle f; (test) Nachprüfung f; (repulse) Rückschlag m; (restraint) (on) Hemmnis n (für); (square) Karo n; (chess) Schach n; **hold in c.** in Schach halten || tr (restrain) hindern; (inspect) kontrollieren; (test) nachprüfen, überprüfen; (a hat, coat, luggage) abgeben, aufgeben; (figures) nachrechnen; (chess) Schach bieten (dat); **c. off** abhaken || intr (agree) übereinstimmen; **c. out** (of a hotel) sich abmelden; **c. up on** überprüfen; (a person) sich erkundigen über (acc); **c. with** (correspond to) übereinstimmen mit; (consult) sich besprechen mit ‖ interj Schach!

check'book' s Scheckbuch n, Scheckheft n

checker ['tʃɛkər] s Kontrolleur m; (in checkers) Damestein m; **checkers** Damespiel n

check'erboard' s Damebrett n

check'ered adj kariert; (life, career) wechselvoll

check'ing account' s Scheckkonto n

check' list' s Kontrolliste f

check'mate' s Schachmatt n; (fig) Niederlage f ‖ tr (& fig) matt setzen ‖ interj schachmatt!

check'-out count'er s Kasse f

check'point' s Kontrollstelle f

check'room' s Garderobe f

check'up' s Überprüfung f; (med) ärztliche Untersuchung f

cheek [tʃik] s Backe f, Wange f; (coll) Frechheit f

cheek'bone' s Backenknochen m

cheek' by jowl' adv Seite an Seite

cheeky ['tʃiki] adj (coll) frech

cheer [tʃɪr] s (applause) Beifallsruf m; (encouragement) Ermunterung f; (sport) Ermunterungsruf m; **three cheers for** ein dreifaches Hoch auf (acc) ‖ tr zujubeln (dat); **c. on** anfeuern; **c. up** aufmuntern; **c. up!** nur Mut!

cheerful ['tʃɪrfəl] adj heiter; (room, surroundings) freundlich

cheer'lead'er s Anführer –in mf beim Beifallsrufen

cheerless ['tʃɪrlɪs] adj freudlos

cheese [tʃiz] s Käse m

cheeseburger ['tʃiz͵bʌrgər] s belegtes Brot n mit Frikadelle und überbackenem Käse

cheese' cake' s Käsekuchen m

cheese' cloth' s grobe Baumwollgaze f

cheesy ['tʃizi] adj (sl) minderwertig

chef [ʃɛf] s Küchenchef m

chemical ['kɛmɪkəl] adj chemisch; (fertilizer) Kunst– ‖ s Chemikalie f

chemist ['kɛmɪst] s Chemiker –in mf

chemistry ['kɛmɪstri] s Chemie f

cherish ['tʃɛrɪʃ] tr (hold dear) schätzen; (hopes, thoughts) hegen

cherry ['tʃɛri] s Kirsche f

cher'ry tree' s Kirschbaum m

cher·ub ['tʃɛrəb] s (–ubim [əbɪm]) Cherub m ‖ s (–ubs) Engelskopf m

chess [tʃɛs] s Schach n

chess'board' s Schachbrett n

chess'man' s (–men') Schachfigur f

chest [tʃɛst] s Truhe f; (anat) Brust f

chestnut ['tʃɛsnət] adj kastanienbraun ‖ s Kastanie f; (tree) Kastanienbaum m; (horse) Rotfuchs m

chest' of drawers' s Kommode f

chevron ['ʃɛvrən] s (mil) Winkel m

chew [tʃu] s Kauen n; (stick of tobacco) Priem m ‖ tr kauen; **c. the cud** wiederkauen; **c. the rag** (sl) schwatzen

chew'ing gum' s Kaugummi m

chew'ing tobac'co s Kautabak m

chic [ʃik] adj schick ‖ s Schick m

chicanery [ʃɪ'kenəri] s Schikane f

chick [tʃɪk] s Küken n; (girl) (sl) kesse Biene f

chicken ['tʃɪkən] adj Hühner–; (sl) feig(e) ‖ s Huhn n, Hühnchen n

chick'en coop' s Hühnerstall m

chick'en-heart'ed adj feig(e)

chick'en pox' s Windpocken pl

chick'en wire' s Maschendraht m

chick'pea' s Kichererbse f

chicory ['tʃɪkəri] s Zichorie f

chide [tʃaɪd] v (pret & pp **chided** & **chid** [tʃɪd]; pp **chided**) tr tadeln

chief [tʃif] adj Haupt–, Ober–, oberste; (leading) leitend ‖ s Chef m, Oberhaupt n; (of an Indian tribe) Häuptling m

chief' exec'utive s Regierungsoberhaupt n

chief' jus'tice s Vorsitzender m des obersten Gerichtshofes

chiefly ['tʃifli] adv vorwiegend

chief' of police' s Polizeipräsident m

chief' of staff' s Generalstabschef m

chief' of state' s Staatschef m

chieftain ['tʃiftən] s Häuptling m

chiffon [ʃɪ'fɑn] s Chiffon m

child [tʃaɪld] s (children ['tʃɪldrən]) Kind n; **with c.** schwanger

child' abuse' s Kindermißhandlung f

child'birth' s Niederkunft f

child'hood' s Kindheit f

childish ['tʃaɪldɪʃ] adj kindisch

childless ['tʃaɪldlɪs] adj kinderlos

child'like' adj kindlich

child' prod'igy s Wunderkind n

child's' play' s (fig) Kinderspiel n

child' support' s Alimente pl

child' wel'fare s Jugendfürsorge f

Chile ['tʃɪli] s Chile n

chili ['tʃɪli] s Cayennepfeffer m

chil'i sauce' s Chillisoße f

chill [tʃɪl] s (coldness) Kälte f; (sensation of cold or fear) Schau(d)er m; **chills** Fieberschau(d)er m ‖ tr kühlen; (hopes, etc.) dämpfen; (metals) abschrecken; **be chilled to the bone** durchfrieren ‖ intr abkühlen

chilly ['tʃɪli] adj (& fig) frostig; **feel chilly** frösteln

chime [tʃaɪm] s Geläut n; **chimes** Glockenspiel n ‖ intr (said of bells) läuten; (said of a doorbell) ertönen; (said of a clock) schlagen; **c. in** (coll) beipflichten

chimera [kaɪ'mɪrə] s Hirngespinst n

chimney ['tʃɪmni] s Schornstein m; (of a lamp) Zylinder m

chimpanzee [tʃɪm'pænzi] s Schimpanse m

chin [tʃɪn] s Kinn n; **keep one's c. up** die Ohren steifhalten; **up to the c.** bis über die Ohren

china ['tʃaɪnə] s Porzellan n ‖ **China** s China n

chi'na clos'et s Porzellanschrank m

chi'na·man s (–men) (pej) Chinese m

chin'aware' s Porzellanwaren pl

Chi·nese [tʃaɪ'niz] adj chinesisch ‖ s (–nese) Chinese m, Chinesin f; (language) Chinesisch n

Chi'nese lan'tern s Lampion m

chink [tʃɪŋk] s Ritze f; (of coins or

glasses) Klang *m* ‖ *tr* (*glasses*) anstoßen
chin'-up' *s* Klimmzug *m*
chip [tʃɪp] *s* Span *m*, Splitter *m*; (*in china*) angestoßene Stelle *f*; (*in poker*) Spielmarke *f*; **a c. off the old block** (coll) ganz der Vater; **have a c. on one's shoulder** (coll) vor Zorn geladen sein ‖ *v* (*pret & pp* **chipped**; *ger* **chipping**) *tr* (*e.g., a cup*) anschlagen; **c. in** (coll) beitragen; **c. off** abbrechen ‖ *intr* (leicht) abbrechen; **c. in** (**with**) einspringen (mit); **c. off** (*said of paint*) abblättern
chipmunk ['tʃɪp‚mʌŋk] *s* Streifenhörnchen *n*
chipper ['tʃɪpər] *adj* (coll) munter
chiropodist [kaɪ'rɑpədɪst], [kɪ'rɑpədɪst] *s* Fußpfleger –in *mf*
chiropractor ['kaɪrə‚præktər] *s* Chiropraktiker –in *mf*
chirp [tʃʌrp] *s* Gezwitscher *n* ‖ *intr* zwitschern
chis·el ['tʃɪzəl] *s* Meißel *m* ‖ *v* (*pret & pp* **-el[l]ed**; *ger* **-il[l]ing**) *tr* meißeln; (sl) bemogeln ‖ meißeln; (sl) mogeln
chiseler ['tʃɪzələr] *s* (sl) Mogler *m*
chitchat ['tʃɪt‚tʃæt] *s* Schnickschnack *m*
chivalrous ['ʃɪvəlrəs] *adj* ritterlich
chivalry ['ʃɪvəlri] *s* Rittertum *n*; (*politeness*) Ritterlichkeit *f*
chive [tʃaɪv] *s* Schnittlauch *m*
chloride ['klɔraɪd] *s* Chlorid *n*
chlorine ['klorin] *s* Chlor *n*
chloroform ['klɔrə‚fɔrm] *s* Chloroform *n* ‖ *tr* chloroformieren
chlorophyll ['klorəfɪl] *s* Chlorophyll *n*
chock-full ['tsɑk'fʊl] *adj* zum Bersten voll
chocolate ['tʃɔkəlɪt] *adj* Schokoladen–; (*in color*) schokoladenfarben ‖ *s* Schokolade *f*; (*chocolate-covered candy*) Praline *f*
choc'olate bar' *s* Schokoladentafel *f*
choice [tʃɔɪs] *adj* (aus)erlesen ‖ *s* Wahl *f*; (*selection*) Auswahl *f*
choir [kwaɪr] *s* Chor *m*; (archit) Chor *m*
choir'boy' *s* Chorknabe *m*
choir' loft' *s* Chorgalerie *f*
choir'mas'ter *s* Chordirigent *m*
choke [tʃok] *s* (aut) Starterklappe *f* ‖ *tr* erwürgen, ersticken; **c. back** (*tears*) herunterschlucken; **c. down** herunterwürgen; **c. up** verstopfen ‖ *intr* ersticken; **c. on** ersticken an (*dat*)
choker ['tʃokər] *s* enges Halsband *n*
cholera ['kɑlərə] *s* Cholera *f*
cholesterol [kə'lestə‚rol] *s* Blutfett *n*
choose [tʃuz] *v* (*pret* **chose** [tʃoz]; *pp* **chosen** ['tʃozən]) *tr & intr* wählen
choosy ['tʃuzi] *adj* (coll) wählerisch
chop [tʃɑp] *s* Hieb *m*; (culin) Kotelett *n*, Schnitzel *n*; **chops** (sl) Maul *n* ‖ *v* (*pret & pp* **chopped**; *ger* **chopping**) *tr* hacken; **c. down** niederhauen; **c. off** abhacken; **c. up** zerhacken
chopper ['tʃɑpər] *s* (ax) Hackbeil *n*; (coll) Hubschrauber *m*

chop'ping block' *s* Hackklotz *m*
choppy ['tʃɑpi] *adj* (sea) bewegt
chop'stick' *s* Eßstäbchen *n*
choral ['korəl] *adj* Chor–, Sänger–
chorale [ko'ral] *s* Choral *m*
chord [kɔrd] *s* (anat) Band *n*; (geom) Sehne *f*; (*combination of notes*) (mus) Akkord *m*; (mus & fig) Saite *f*
chore [tʃor] *s* Hausarbeit *f*
choreography [‚kɔrɪ'ɑgrəfi] *s* Choreographie *f*
chorus ['korəs] *s* Chor *m*; (*refrain*) Kehrreim *m*
cho'rus girl' *s* Revuetänzerin *f*
chowder ['tʃaʊdər] *s* Fischsuppe *f*
Christ [kraɪst] *s* Christus *m*
Christ' child' *s* Christkind *n*
christen ['krɪsən] *tr* taufen
Christendom ['krɪsəndəm] *s* Christenheit *f*
chris'tening *s* Taufe *f*; **c. of a ship** Schiffstaufe *f*
Christian ['krɪstʃən] *adj* christlich ‖ Christ –in *mf*
Chris'tian E'ra *s* christliche Zeitrechnung *f*
Christianity [‚krɪstɪ'æniti] *s* (*faith*) Christentum *n*; (*all Christians*) Christenheit *f*
Chris'tian name' *s* Taufname *m*
Christmas ['krɪsməs] *adj* Weihnachts– ‖ *s* Weihnachten *pl*, Weihnachtsfest *n*
Christ'mas card' *s* Weihnachtskarte *f*
Christ'mas car'ol *s* Weihnachtslied *n*
Christ'mas Eve' *s* Heiliger Abend *m*
Christ'mas gift' *s* Weihnachtsgeschenk *n*
Christ'mas tree' *s* Christbaum *m*
Christ'mas tree' lights' *spl* Weihnachtskerzen *pl*
Christopher ['krɪstəfər] *s* Christoph *m*
chromatic [kro'mætɪk] *adj* chromatisch
chrome [krom] *adj* Chrom– ‖ *s* Chrom *n* ‖ *tr* verchromen
chrome'plate' *tr* verchromen
chromium ['kromɪ·əm] *s* Chrom *n*
chromosome ['kromə‚som] *s* Chromosom *n*
chronic ['krɑnɪk] *adj* chronisch
chronicle ['krɑnɪkəl] *s* Chronik *f* ‖ *tr* aufzeichnen
chronicler ['krɑnɪklər] *s* Chronist –in *mf*
chronological [‚krɑnə'lɑdʒɪkəl] *adj* chronologisch
chronology [krə'nɑlədʒi] *s* Chronologie *f*
chronometer [krə'nɑmɪtər] *s* Chronometer *n*
chrysanthemum [krɪ'sænθɪməm] *s* Chrysantheme *f*
chubby ['tʃʌbi] *adj* pummelig
chuck [tʃʌk] *s* (culin) Schulterstück *n*; (mach) Klemmfutter *n* ‖ *tr* schmeißen
chuckle ['tʃʌkəl] *s* Glucksen *n* ‖ *intr* glucksen
chug [tʃʌg] *s* Tuckern *n* ‖ *v* (*pret & pp* **chugged**; *ger* **chugging**) *intr* tuckern; **c. along** tuckernd fahren

chum [tʃʌm] *s* (coll) Kumpel *m* ‖ *v* (*pret* & *pp* **chummed;** *ger* **chumming**) *intr*—**c. around with** sich eng anschließen an (*acc*)

chummy ['tʃʌmi] *adj* eng befreundet

chump [tʃʌmp] *s* (coll) Trottel *m*

chunk [tʃʌŋk] *s* Klotz *m*, Stück *n*

church [tʃʌrtʃ] *adj* Kirchen–, kirchlich ‖ *s* Kirche *f*

churchgoer ['tʃʌrtʃ͵go·ər] *s* Kirchgänger –in *mf*

church' pic'nic *s* Kirchweih *f*

church'yard' *s* Kirchhof *m*

churl [tʃʌrl] *s* Flegel *m*

churlish ['tʃʌrlɪʃ] *adj* flegelhaft

churn [tʃʌrn] *s* Butterfaß *n* ‖ *tr* (*cream*) buttern; **c. up** aufwühlen ‖ *intr* sich heftig bewegen

chute [ʃut] *s* (*for coal, etc.*) Rutsche *f*; (*for laundry, etc.*) Abwurfschacht *m*; (*sliding board*) Rutschbahn *f*; (*in a river*) Stromschnelle *f*; (aer) Fallschirm *m*

cider ['saɪdər] *s* Apfelwein *m*

cigar [sɪ'gɑr] *s* Zigarre *f*

cigarette [͵sɪgə'rɛt] *s* Zigarette *f*

cigarette' cough' *s* Raucherhusten *m*

cigarette' light'er *s* Feuerzeug *n*

cigar' store' *s* Rauchwarenladen *m*

cinch [sɪntʃ] *s* Sattelgurt *m*; (*sure thing*) totsichere Sache *f*; (*snap*) (sl) Kinderspiel *n*; (*likely candidate*) totsicherer Kandidat *m* ‖ *tr* (sl) sich [*dat*] sichern

cinder ['sɪndər] *s* (*ember*) glühende Kohle *f*; (*slag*) Schlacke *f*; **cinders** Asche *f*

Cinderella [͵sɪndə'rɛlə] *s* Aschenbrödel *n*

cin'der track' *s* (sport) Aschenbahn *f*

cinema ['sɪnəmə] *s* Kino *n*

cinematography [͵sɪnəmə'tɑgrəfi] *s* Kinematographie *f*

cinnamon ['sɪnəmən] *s* Zimt *m*

cipher ['saɪfər] *s* Ziffer *f*; (*zero*) Null *f*; (*code*) Chiffre *f* ‖ *tr* chiffrieren

circle ['sʌrkəl] *s* Kreis *m*; **circles under the eyes** Ränder *pl* unter den Augen ‖ *tr* einkreisen; (*go around*) umkreisen ‖ *intr* kreisen

circuit ['sʌrkɪt] *s* (*course*) Kreislauf *m*; (elec) Stromkreis *m*; (jur) Bezirk *m*

cir'cuit break'er *s* Ausschalter *m*

cir'cuit court' *s* Bezirksgericht *n*

circuitous [sər'kju·ɪtəs] *adj* weitschweifig

circular ['sʌrkjələr] *adj* kreisförmig; (*saw*) Kreis– ‖ *s* Rundschreiben *n*

circulate ['sʌrkjə͵let] *tr* in Umlauf setzen; (*a rumor*) verbreiten; (fin) girieren ‖ *intr* umlaufen; (*said of blood*) kreisen; (*said of a rumor*) umgehen

circulation [͵sʌrkjə'leʃən] *s* (*of blood*) Kreislauf *m*; (*of a newspaper*) Auflage *f*; (*of money*) Umlauf *m*

circumcize ['sʌrkəm͵saɪz] *tr* beschneiden

circumference [sər'kʌmfərəns] *s* Umfang *m*

circumflex ['sʌrkəm͵flɛks] *s* Zirkumflex *m*

circumlocution [͵sʌrkəmlo'kjuʃən] *s* Umschreibung *f*

circumscribe ['sʌrkəm͵skraɪb] *tr* (geom) umschreiben; (fig) umgrenzen

circumspect ['sʌrkəm͵spɛkt] *adj* umsichtig

circumstance ['sʌrkəm͵stæns] *s* Umstand *m*; **circumstances** (*financial situation*) Verhältnisse *pl*

cir'cumstan'tial ev'idence [͵sʌrkəm'stænʃəl] *s* Indizienbeweis *m*

circumvent [͵sʌrkəm'vɛnt] *tr* umgehen

circus ['sʌrkəs] *s* Zirkus *m*

cistern ['sɪstərn] *s* Zisterne *f*

citadel ['sɪtədəl] *s* Burg *f*

citation [saɪ'teʃən] *s* Zitat *n*; (jur) Vorladung *f*; (mil) Belobung *f*

cite [saɪt] *tr* (*quote*) anführen; (jur) vorladen; (mil) belobigen

citizen ['sɪtɪzən] *s* Bürger –in *mf*

cit'izenship' *s* Staatsangehörigkeit *f*

cit'rus fruit' ['sɪtrəs] *s* Zitrusfrucht *f*

city ['sɪti] *s* Stadt *f*

cit'y coun'cil *s* Stadtrat *m*

cit'y fa'ther *s* Stadtrat *m*

cit'y hall' *s* Rathaus *n*

cit'y plan'ning *s* Stadtplanung *f*

civic ['sɪvɪk] *adj* bürgerlich, Bürger– ‖ **civics** *s* Staatsbürgerkunde *f*

civil ['sɪvɪl] *adj* (*life, duty*) bürgerlich; (*service*) öffentlich; (*polite*) höflich; (jur) privatrechtlich

civ'il cer'emony *s* standesamtliche Trauung *f*

civ'il defense' *s* zivile Verteidigung *f*

civ'il engineer'ing *s* Hoch– und Tiefbau *m*

civilian [sɪ'vɪljən] *adj* bürgerlich, Zivil– ‖ *s* Zivilist –in *mf*

civilization [͵sɪvɪlɪ'zeʃən] *s* Zivilisation *f*, Kultur *f*

civilize ['sɪvɪ͵laɪz] *tr* zivilisieren

civ'il rights' *spl* Bürgerrechte *pl*

civ'il serv'ant *s* Staatsbeamte *m*, Staatsbeamtin *f*

civ'il serv'ice *s* Staatsdienst *m*

civ'il war' *s* Bürgerkrieg *m*

claim [klem] *s* Anspruch *m*; (*assertion*) Behauptung *f*; (*for public land*) beanspruchtes Land *n* ‖ *tr* beanspruchen; (*assert*) behaupten; (*attention*) erfordern; **c. to be** sich ausgeben für

claim' check' *s* Aufgabeschein *m*

clairvoyance [klɛr'vɔɪ·əns] *s* Hellsehen *n*

clairvoyant [klɛr'vɔɪ·ənt] *adj* hellseherisch; **be c.** hellsehen ‖ *s* Hellseher –in *mf*

clam [klæm] *s* eßbare Meermuschel *f*

clamber ['klæmər] *intr* klettern

clammy ['klæmi] *adj* feuchtkalt

clamor ['klæmər] *s* Geschrei *n* ‖ *intr* (for) schreien (nach)

clamorous ['klæmərəs] *adj* schreiend

clamp [klæmp] *s* Klammer *f*; (surg) Klemme *f* ‖ *tr* (ver)klammern ‖ *intr* —**c. down on** einschreiten gegen

clan [klæn] *s* Stamm *m*; (pej) Sippschaft *f*

clandestine [klæn'dɛstɪn] *adj* heimlich

clang [klæŋ] *s* Geklirr *n* ‖ *intr* klirren

clank [klæŋk] s Geklirr n, Gerassel n || intr klirren, rasseln
clannish ['klænɪʃ] adj stammesbewußt
clap [klæp] s (of the hands) Klatschen n; (of thunder) Schlag m || v (pret & pp clapped; ger clapping) tr (a tax, fine, duty) (on) auferlegen (dat); clap hands in die Hände klatschen || intr Beifall klatschen
clapper ['klæpər] s Klöppel m
clap'trap' s Phrasendrescherei f
claque [klæk] s Claque f
clari·fy ['klærɪ,faɪ] v (pret & pp -fied) tr erklären
clarinet [,klærɪ'nɛt] s Klarinette f
clarity ['klærɪti] s Klarheit f
clash [klæʃ] s (sound) Geklirr n; (of interests, etc.) Widerstreit m || intr (conflict) kollidieren; (said of persons) aufeinanderstoßen; (said of ideas) im Widerspruch stehen; (said of colors) nicht zusammenpassen
clasp [klæsp] s (fastener) Schließe f, Spange f; (on a necktie) Klammer f; (embrace) Umarmung f; (of hands) Händedruck m || tr umklammern; c. s.o.'s hand j–m die Hand drücken
class [klæs] s (group) Klasse f; (period of instruction) Stunde f; (year) Jahrgang m; have c. (sl) Niveau haben || tr einstufen
classic ['klæsɪk] adj klassisch || s Klassiker m
classical ['klæsɪkəl] adj klassisch; c. antiquity Klassik f; c. author Klassiker m
classicist ['klæsɪsɪst] s Kenner –in mf der Klassik
classification [,klæsɪfɪ'keʃən] s Klassifikation f, Anordnung f
clas'sified adj geheimzuhaltend
clas'sified ad' s kleine Anzeige f
classi·fy ['klæsɪ,faɪ] v (pret & pp -fied) tr klassifizieren
class'mate' s Klassenkamerad m
class' reun'ion s Klassentreffen n
class'room' s Klassenzimmer n
classy ['klæsi] adj (sl) pfundig
clatter ['klætər] s Geklapper n || intr klappern
clause [klɔz] s Satzteil m; (jur) Klausel f
clavicle ['klævɪkəl] s Schlüsselbein n
claw [klɔ] s Klaue f, Kralle f; (of a crab) Schere f || tr zerkratzen; (a hole) scharren || intr kratzen
clay [kle] adj tönern || s Ton m, Lehm m
clay' pig'eon s Tontaube f
clean [klin] adj sauber, rein; (cut) glatt; (features) klar || adv (coll) völlig || tr reinigen, putzen; c. out (clear out by force) räumen; (empty) ausleeren; (sl) ausbeuten; c. up (a room) aufräumen || intr putzen; c. up sich zurechtmachen; (in gambling (sl) schwer einheimsen
clean'-cut' adj (person) ordentlich; (clearly outlined) klar umrissen
cleaner ['klinər] s (person, device) Reiniger m; cleaners (establishment) Reinigungsanstalt f

clean'ing flu'id s flüssiges Reinigungsmittel n
clean'ing wo'man s Reinemachefrau f
cleanliness ['klɛnlɪnɪs] s Sauberkeit f
cleanse [klɛnz] tr reinigen
cleanser ['klɛnzər] s Reinigungsmittel n
clean'-shav'en adj glattrasiert
clean'up' s Reinemachen n; (e.g., of vice, graft) Säuberungsaktion f
clear [klɪr] adj klar; (sky, weather) heiter; (light) hell; (profit) netto; (conscience) rein; (proof) offenkundig || adv (coll) völlig; (fin) netto || tr klären; (streets) freimachen; (the table) abräumen; (a room) räumen; (a forest) roden; (the air) reinigen; (an obstacle without touching it) setzen über (acc); (a path) bahnen; (as profit) rein gewinnen; (at customs) zollamtlich abfertigen; (one's name) reinwaschen; c. away wegräumen; (doubts) beseitigen; c. up klarlegen || intr sich klären; c. out (coll) sich davonmachen; c. up sich aufklären
clearance ['klɪrəns] s (approval) Genehmigung f; (at customs) Zollabfertigung f; (of a bridge) lichte Höhe f; (aer) Starterlaubnis f; (mach) Spielraum m
clear'ance sale' s Räumungsverkauf m
clear'-cut' adj klar, eindeutig
clear'-head'ed adj verständig
clear'ing s (in a woods) Lichtung f
clear'ing house' s Abstimmungszentrale f; (fin) Verrechnungsstelle f
clear'-sight'ed adj scharfsichtig
cleat [klit] s Stollen m
cleavage ['klivɪdʒ] s Spaltung f
cleave [kliv] v (pret & pp cleft [klɛft] & cleaved) tr zerspalten || intr (split) sich spalten; (to) kleben (an dat)
cleaver ['klivər] s Hackbeil n
clef [klɛf] s Notenschlüssel m
cleft [klɛft] s Riß m, Spalt m
clemency ['klɛmənsi] s Milde f; (jur) Begnadigung f
clement ['klɛmənt] adj mild
clench [klɛntʃ] tr (a fist) ballen; (the teeth) zusammenbeißen
clerestory ['klɪr,stori] s Lichtgaden m
clergy ['klɛrdʒi] s Geistlichkeit f
cler'gy·man s (-men) Geistliche m
cleric ['klɛrɪk] s Kleriker m
clerical ['klɛrɪkəl] adj Schreib–, Büro–; (eccl) geistlich
cler'ical er'ror s Schreibfehler m
cler'ical staff' s Schreibkräfte pl
cler'ical work' s Büroarbeit f
clerk [klʌrk] s (in a store) Verkäufer –in mf; (in an office) Büroangestellte mf; (in a post office) Schalterbeamte m; (jur) Gerichtsschreiber –in mf
clever ['klɛvər] adj (intelligent) klug; (adroit) geschickt; (witty) geistreich; (ingenious) findig
cleverness ['klɛvərnɪs] s (intelligence) Klugheit f; (adroitness) Geschicklichkeit f; (ingeniousness) Findigkeit f

cliché [kli'ʃe] s Klischee n

click [klɪk] s Klicken n; (of the tongue) Schnalzen n; (of a lock) Einschnappen n || tr klicken lassen; **c. one's heels** die Hacken zusammenschlagen || intr klicken; (said of heels) knallen; (said of a lock) einschnappen || impers—**it clicks** (coll) es klappt

client ['klaɪ·ənt] s (customer) Kunde m, Kundin f; (of a company) Auftraggeber –in mf; (jur) Klient –in mf

clientele [ˌklaɪ·ən'tel] s Kundschaft f; (com, jur) Klientel f

cliff [klɪf] s Felsen m

climate ['klaɪmɪt] s Klima n

climax ['klaɪmæks] s Höhepunkt m

climb [klaɪm] s Aufsteig m, Besteigung f; (aer) Steigungsflug m || tr ersteigen, besteigen; (stairs) hinaufsteigen; **climb a tree** auf e–n Baum klettern; || intr steigen, klettern; (said of a street) ansteigen

climber ['klaɪmər] s Kletterer –in mf; (of a mountain) Bergsteiger –in mf; (bot) Kletterpflanze f

clinch [klɪntʃ] s (box) Clinch m || tr (settle) entscheiden || intr clinchen

clincher ['klɪntʃər] s (coll) Trumpf m

cling [klɪŋ] v (pret & pp clung [klʌŋ]) intr haften; **c. to** sich anklammern an (acc); (said of a dress) sich anschmiegen an (acc); (fig) festhalten an (dat)

clinic ['klɪnɪk] s Klinik f

clinical ['klɪnɪkəl] adj klinisch

clink [klɪŋk] s Klirren n; (prison) (sl) Kittchen n || tr—**c. glasses** mit den Gläsern anstoßen || intr klirren

clip [klɪp] s Klammer f; **go at a good c.** ein scharfes Tempo gehen || v (pret & pp clipped; ger clipping) tr (a hedge) beschneiden; (hair) schneiden; (wings) stutzen; (sheep) scheren; (from newspapers, etc.) ausschneiden; (syllables) verschlucken; (sl) schröpfen; **c. together** zusammenklammern

clip'board' s Manuskripthalter m

clip' joint' s (sl) Nepplokal n

clipper ['klɪpər] s (aer) Klipperflugzeug n; (naut) Klipper m; **clippers** Haarschneidemaschine f

clip'ping s (act) Stutzen n; (from newspapers) Ausschnitt m; **clippings** (of paper) Schnitzel pl; (scraps) Abfälle pl

clique [klik] s Sippschaft f

cliquish ['klikɪʃ] adj cliquenhaft

cloak [klok] s Umhang m; (fig) Deckmantel m; **under the c. of darkness** im Schutz der Dunkelheit || tr (fig) bemänteln

cloak'-and-dag'ger adj Spionage–

cloak'room' s Garderobe f

clobber ['klabər] tr (coll) verwichsen

clock [klak] s Uhr f || tr (a runner) abstoppen

clock'mak'er s Uhrmacher –in mf

clock' tow'er s Uhrturm m

clock'wise' adv im Uhrzeigersinn

clock'work' s Uhrwerk n; **like c.** wie am Schnürchen

clod [klad] s Klumpen m, Scholle f

clodhopper ['klad,hapər] s Bauerntölpel m

clog [klag] s Verstopfung f; (shoe) Holzschuh m || v (pret & pp clogged; ger clogging) tr verstopfen || intr sich verstopfen

cloister ['klɔɪstər] s Kloster n; (covered walk) Kreuzgang m

close [klos] adj (near) nahe; (tight) knapp; (air) schwül; (ties; friend) eng; (attention) gespannt; (game) beinahe gleich; (observer) scharf; (surveillance) streng; (supervision) genau; (inspection) eingehend; (resemblance; competition) stark; (shave) glatt; (translation) wortgetreu; (stingy) geizig; (order) (mil) geschlossen; **c. to** (position) nahe an (dat), neben (dat); (direction) nahe an (acc), neben (acc) || adv dicht, eng; **from c. up** in der Nähe || [kloz] s Schluß m, Ende n; **bring to a c.** zu Ende bringen; **draw to a c.** zu Ende gehen || tr schließen; (an account, deal) abschließen; **c. down** stillegen; **c. off** abschließen; (a road) sperren; **c. out** (com) ausverkaufen; **c. up** zumachen || intr sich schließen; **c. in** immer näher kommen; **c. in on** umschließen

close-by ['klos'baɪ] adj nebenan

close-cropped ['klos'krapt] adj kurz geschoren

closed [klozd] adj geschlossen; **c. today** (public sign) heute Betriebsruhe

closed' shop' s Unternehmen n mit Gewerkschaftszwang

closefisted ['klos'fɪstəd] adj geizig

close-fitting ['klos'fɪtɪŋ] adj eng anliegend

close-mouthed ['klos'mauðd] adj verschwiegen

close' or'der drill' [klos] s (mil) geschlosssenes Exerzieren n

closeout ['kloz,aut] s Räumungsausverkauf m

close' shave' [klos] s glatte Rasure f; (fig) knappes Entkommen n; **have a c.** mit knapper Not davonkommen

closet ['klazɪt] s Schrank m

close-up ['klos,ʌp] s Nahaufnahme f

clos'ing adj Schluß–; (day) scheidend || s Schließung f; (of an account) Abschluß m; (of a factory) Stillegung f; (of a road) Sperrung f

clos'ing price' s Schlußkurs m

clos'ing time' s (of a shop) Geschäftsschluß m; (of bars) Polizeistunde f

clot [klat] s Klumpen m; (of blood) Gerinnsel n || v (pret & pp clotted; ger clotting) intr gerinnen

cloth [klɔθ] s Stoff m, Tuch n; (for cleaning, etc.) Lappen m; **the c.** die Geistlichkeit

clothe [kloð] v (pret & pp clothed & clad [klæd]) tr ankleiden, (be)kleiden; (fig) (in) einhüllen (in acc)

clothes [kloz], [kloðz] spl Kleider pl; **change one's clothes** sich umziehen; **put on one's clothes** sich anziehen

clothes'bas'ket s Wäschekorb m

clothes'brush' s Kleiderbürste f

clothes' clos'et s Kleiderschrank m

clothes′ dri′er s Wäschetrockner m
clothes′ hang′er s Kleiderbügel m
clothes′line′ s Wäscheleine f
clothes′pin′ s Wäscheklammer f
clothier [′kloðjər] s Kleiderhändler m; (cloth maker) Tuchmacher m; (cloth dealer) Tuchhändler m
clothing [′kloðɪŋ] s Kleidung f
cloud [klaʊd] s Wolke f; **be up in the clouds** (fig) in höheren Regionen schweben || tr bewölken; (a liquid) trüben; (fig) verdunkeln || intr— **c. over** (or **up**) sich bewölken
cloud′burst′ s Wolkenbruch m
cloud′-capped′ adj von Wolken bedeckt
cloudiness [′klaʊdɪnɪs] s Bewölktheit f
cloudless [′klaʊdlɪs] adj unbewölkt
cloudy [′klaʊdi] adj bewölkt; (liquid) trüb(e)
clout [klaʊt] s (blow) (coll) Hieb m; (influence) (coll) Einfluß m || tr— **c. s.o.** (coll) j-m eins herunterhauen
clove [klov] s Gewürznelke f; **c. of garlic** Knoblauchzehe f
clo′ven hoof′ [′klovən] s (as a sign of the devil) Pferdefuß m
clover [′klovər] s Klee m
clo′ver·leaf′ s (–leaves) Kleeblatt n
clown [klaʊn] s Clown m, Hanswurst m
clownish [′klaʊnɪʃ] adj närrisch
cloy [klɔɪ] tr übersättigen
club [klʌb] s (weapon) Keule f; (organization) Klub m; (cards) Kreuz n; (golf) Schläger m || (pret & pp **clubbed;** ger **clubbing**) tr verprügeln
club′ car′ s (rr) Salonwagen m
club′house′ s Klubhaus n
cluck [klʌk] s Glucken n || intr glucken
clue [klu] s Schlüssel m, Anhaltspunkt m
clump [klʌmp] s (of earth) Klumpen m; (of hair, grass) Büschel n; (of trees) Gruppe f; (heavy tramping sound) schwerer Tritt m; **c. of bushes** Gebüsch n || intr—**c. along** trapsen
clumsy [′klʌmzi] adj ungeschickt, plump; **c. ox** Tölpel m
cluster [′klʌstər] s (bunch growing together) Büschel n; (of grapes) Traube f; (group) Gruppe f || intr— **c. around** sich zusammendrängen um
clutch [klʌtʃ] s Griff m; (aut) Kupplung f; **fall into s.o.'s clutches** j-m in die Klauen geraten; **let out the c.** einkuppeln; **step on the c.** auskuppeln || tr packen
clutter [′klʌtər] s Durcheinander n || tr—**c. up** vollstopfen
Co. abbr (Company) Gesellschaft f
c/o abbr (care of) per Adresse, bei
coach [kotʃ] s Kutsche f; (rr) Personenwagen m; (sport) Trainer m || tr Nachhilfeunterricht geben (dat); (sport) trainieren || intr (sport) trainieren
coach′ing s Nachhilfeunterricht m; (sport) Training n
coach′man s (–men) Kutscher m

coagulate [ko′ægjə‚let] tr gerinnen lassen || intr gerinnen
coal [kol] s Kohle f
coal′bin′ s Kohlenkasten m
coal′-black′ adj kohlrabenschwarz
coal′ car′ s (rr) Kohlenwagen m
coal′deal′er s Kohlenhändler m
coalesce [‚ko·ə′lɛs] intr zusammenwachsen, sich vereinigen
coalition [‚ko·ə′lɪʃən] s Koalition f
coal′ mine′ s Kohlenbergwerk n
coal′ min′ing s Kohlenbergbau m
coal′ oil′ s Petroleum n
coal′yard′ s Kohlenlager n
coarse [kors] adj (& fig) grob
coast [kost] s Küste f; **the c. is clear** (coll) die Luft ist rein || intr im Leerlauf fahren; **c. along** (fig) sich mühelos fortbewegen
coastal [′kostəl] adj küstennah, Küsten–
coaster [′kostər] s (for a glass) Untersatz m; (naut) Küstenfahrer m
coast′guard′ s Küstenwachdienst m
coast′line′ s Küstenlinie f
coat [kot] s (of a suit) Jacke f, Rock m; (topcoat) Mantel m; (of fur) Fell n; (of enamel, etc.) Belag m; (of paint) Anstrich m || tr (e.g., with teflon) beschichten; (e.g., with chocolate) überziehen; (e.g., with oil) beschmieren
coat′ed adj überzogen; (tongue) belegt
coat′ hang′er s Kleiderbügel m
coat′ing s Belag m, Überzug m
coat′ of arms′ s Wappen n
coat′rack′ s Kleiderständer m
coat′room′ s Garderobe f
coat′tail′ s Rockschoß m; (of formal wear) Frackschoß m
coauthor [′ko‚ɔθər] s Mitautor m
coax [koks] tr schmeicheln (dat); **c. s.o. to** (inf) j-n überreden zu (inf)
cob [kab] s Kolben m
cobalt [′kobɔlt] s Kobalt m
cobbler [′kablər] s Flickschuster m
cobblestone [′kabəl‚ston] s Pflasterstein m, Kopfstein m
cobra [′kobrə] s Kobra f
cob′web′ s Spinn(en)gewebe n
cocaine [ko′ken] s Kokain n
cock [kak] s Hahn m; (faucet) Wasserhahn m; (of a gun) Gewehrhahn m || tr (one's ears) spitzen; (one's hat) schief aufsetzen; (the firing mᵉchanism) spannen
cock-a-doodle-doo [′kakə‚dudəl′du] s Kikeriki n
cock′-and-bull′ sto′ry s Lügengeschichte f
cockeyed [′kak‚aɪd] adj (cross-eyed) nach innen schielend; (slanted to one side) (sl) schief; (drunk) (sl) blau; (absurd) (sl) verrückt
cock′fight′ s Hahnenkampf m
cock′pit′ s Hahnenkampfplatz m; (aer) Kabine f, Kanzel f
cock′roach′ s Schabe f
cock′sure′ adj todsicher
cock′tail′ s Cocktail m
cock′tail dress′ s Cocktailkleid n
cock′tail par′ty s Cocktailparty f

cock'tail shak'er *s* Cocktailmischgefäß *n*

cocky ['kɑki] *adj* (coll) frech

cocoa ['koko] *s* Kakao *m*

coconut ['kokə‚nʌt] *s* Kokosnuß *f*

co'conut palm', co'conut tree' *s* Kokospalme *f*

cacoon [kə'kun] *s* Kokon *m*

C.O.D., c.o.d. *abbr* (cash on delivery) per Nachnahme

cod [kɑd] *s* Kabeljau *m*

coddle ['kɑdəl] *tr* hätscheln

code [kod] *s* Geheimschrift *f;* (jur) Kodex *m* || *tr* verschlüsseln, chiffrieren

codefendant [‚kodɪ'fɛndənt] *s* Mitangeklagte *mf*

code' name' *s* Deckname *m*

code' of hon'or *s* Ehrenkodex *m*

code' of laws' *s* Gesetzsammlung *f*

code' word' *s* Kennwort *n*

codex ['kodɛks] *s* (**codices** ['kodɪ‚siz]) Kodex *m*

cod'fish' *s* Kabeljau *m*

codicil ['kɑdɪsɪl] *s* Kodizill *n*

codi·fy ['kodɪ‚faɪ] *v* (*pret* & *pp* –**fied**) *tr* kodifizieren

cod'-liver oil' *s* Lebertran *m*

coed, co-ed ['ko‚ɛd] *s* Studentin *f*

coeducation [‚ko‚ɛdʒə'keʃən] *s* Koedukation *f*

coeducational [‚ko‚ɛdʒə'keʃənəl] *adj* Koedukations–

coefficient [‚ko·ɪ'fɪʃənt] *s* Koeffizient *m*

coerce [ko'ʌrs] *tr* zwingen

coercion [ko'ʌrʃən] *s* Zwang *m*

coexist [‚ko·ɪg'zɪst] *intr* koexistieren

coexistence [‚ko·ɪg'zɪstəns] *s* Koexistenz *f*

coffee ['kɔfi] *s* Kaffee *m*

cof'fee bean' *s* Kaffeebohne *f*

cof'fee break' *s* Kaffeepause *f*

cof'fee fiend' *s* Kaffeetante *f*

cof'fee grounds' *spl* Kaffeesatz *m*

cof'fee pot' *s* Kaffeekanne *f*

cof'fee shop' *s* Kaffeestube *f*

coffer ['kɔfər] *s* Truhe *f;* (archit) Deckenfeld *n;* **coffers** Schatzkammer *f*

cof'ferdam' *s* (*caisson*) Kastendamm *m;* (naut) Kofferdamm *m*

coffin ['kɔfɪn] *s* Sarg *m*

cog [kɑg] *s* Zahn *m;* (*cogwheel*) Zahnrad *n*

cogency ['kodʒənsi] *s* Beweiskraft *f*

cogent ['kodʒənt] *adj* triftig

cognac ['konjæk], ['kɑnjæk] *s* Kognak *m*

cognizance ['kɑgnɪzəns] *s* Kenntnis *f;* **take c. of s.th.** etw zur Kenntnis nehmen

cognizant ['kɑgnɪzənt] *adj*—**be c. of** Kenntnis haben von

cog'wheel' *s* Zahnrad *n*

cohabit [ko'hæbɪt] *intr* in wilder Ehe leben

coheir [ko'ɛr] *s* Miterbe *m*, Miterbin *f*

cohere [ko'hɪr] *intr* zusammenhängen

cohesion [ko'hiʒən] *s* Kohäsion *f*

coiffeur [kwa'fʌr] *s* Friseur *m*

coiffure [kwa'fjur] *s* Frisur *f*

coil [kɔɪl] *s* (*something wound in a spiral*) Spirale *f*, Rolle *f;* (*of tubing*) Schlange *f;* (*single wind*) Windung *f* (elec) Spule *f* || *tr* aufrollen; (naut) aufschießen || *intr*—**c. up** sich zusammenrollen

coil' spring' *s* Spiralfeder *f*

coin [kɔɪn] *s* Münze *f*, Geldstück *n* *tr* münzen, (& fig) prägen

coinage ['kɔɪnɪdʒ] *s* (*minting*) Prägei *n;* (*coins collectively*) Münzen *pl* (fig) Prägung *f*

coincide [‚ko·ɪn'saɪd] *intr* (**with**) zu sammentreffen (mit); (*in time*) (with) gleichzeitig geschehen (mit)

coincidence [ko'ɪnsɪdəns] *s* Zufall *m* **by mere c.** rein zufällig

coin' machine' *s* Münzautomat *m*

coin' slot' *s* Münzeinwurf *m*

coition [ko'ɪʃən], **coitus** ['ko·ɪtəs] Koitus *m*, Beischlaf *m*

coke [kok] *s* Koks *m;* (coll) Coca Cola *n*

colander ['kʌləndər] *s* Sieb *n*

cold [kold] *adj* kalt || *s* Kälte *f;* (*in disposition*) Erkältung *f*

cold' blood' *s*—**in c.** kaltblütig

cold'-blood'ed *adj* kaltblütig

cold' chis'el *s* Kaltmeißel *m*

cold' com'fort *s* (fig) geringer Trost *n*

cold' cream' *s* Cold Cream *n*

cold' cuts' *spl* kalter Aufschnitt *m*

cold' feet' *spl*—**have c.** (fig) Angs haben

cold' front' *s* Kaltfront *f*

cold'-heart'ed *adj* kaltherzig

coldness ['koldnɪs] *s* Kälte *f*

cold' should'er *s*—**give s.o. the c.** j–n die kalte Schulter zeigen

cold' snap' *s* plötzlicher Kälteeinbrucl

cold' stor'age *s* Lagerung *f* im Kühl raum

cold' war' *s* kalter Krieg *m*

cold' wave' *s* (meteor) Kältewelle *f*

coleslaw ['kol‚slɔ] *s* Krautsalat *m*

colic ['kɑlɪk] *s* Kolik *f*

coliseum [‚kɑlɪ'si·əm] *s* Kolosseum *»*

collaborate [kə'læbə‚ret] *intr* mit arbeiten; (pol) kollaborieren

collaboration [kə‚læbə're ʃən] *s* Mit arbeit *f;* (pol) Kollaboration *f*

collaborator [kə'læbə‚retər] *s* Mit arbeiter –in *mf;* (pol) Kollaborateui *m*

collapse [kə'læps] *s* (*of a bridge, etc.*) Einsturz *m;* (com) Krach *m;* (pathol Zusammenbruch *m*, Kollaps *m* || *inti* einstürzen; (fig) zusammenbrechen

collapsible [kə'læpsɪbəl] *adj* zusam menklappbar

collaps'ible boat' *s* Faltboot *n*

collar ['kɑlər] *s* Kragen *m;* (*of a dog*, Halsband *n;* (*of a horse*) Kummei *n;* (mach) Ring *m*, Kragen *m*

col'larbone' *s* Schlüsselbein *n*

collate [kə'let] *tr* kollationieren

collateral [kə'lætərəl] *adj* kollateral Seiten– || *s* (fin) Deckung *f*

collation [kə'leʃən] *s* Kollation *f*

colleague ['kɑlig] *s* Kollege *m*, Kolle· gin *f*

collect ['kɑlɛkt] *s* (eccl) Kollekte *f* || [kə'lɛkt] *adj*—**make a c. call** ein R·

Gespräch führen || *adv*—**call c.** ein
R-Gespräch führen; **send c.** gegen
Nachnahme schicken || *tr (money)*
(ein)kassieren; *(stamps, coins)* sammeln; *(e.g., examination papers)* ein-
sammeln; *(taxes)* abheben; *(one's
thoughts)* zusammennehmen; **c. one-
self** sich fassen || *intr* sich (ver)-
sammeln; *(pile up)* sich anhäufen
collect'ed *adj (works)* gesammelt;
(self-possessed) gefaßt
collection [kə'lɛkʃən] *s (of stamps,
etc.)* Sammlung *f*; *(accumulation)*
Ansammlung *f*; *(of money)* Einzie-
hung *f*; *(in a church)* Kollekte *f*; *(of
mail)* Leerung *f* des Briefkastens;
(com) Kollektion *f*
collec'tion a'gency *s* Inkassobüro *n*
collec'tion bas'ket *s* Klingelbeutel *m*
collective [kə'lɛktɪv] *adj* kollektiv,
Sammel-, Gesamt- || *s* (pol) Kollek-
tiv *n*
collec'tive bar'gaining *s* Tarifverhand-
lungen *pl*
collec'tive farm' *s* Kolchose *f*
collector [kə'lɛktər] *s (e.g., of stamps)*
Sammler –in *mf*; *(bill collector)* Einkassierer –in *mf*; *(of taxes)* Einneh-
mer –in *mf*; *(of tickets)* Fahrkarten-
abnehmer –in *mf*
college ['kɑlɪdʒ] *s* College *n*; *(e.g., of
cardinals)* Kollegium *n*
collide [kə'laɪd] *intr* zusammenstoßen
collie ['kɑli] *s* Collie *m*
collision [kə'lɪʒən] *s* Zusammenstoß *m*
colloquial [kə'lokwɪ·əl] *adj* umgangssprachlich, Umgangs-
colloquialism [kə'lokwɪ·ə ,lɪzəm] *s*
Ausdruck *m* der Umgangssprache
colloquy ['kɑləkwi] *s* Gespräch *n*
collusion [kə'luʒən] *s* Kollusion *f*; **be
in c.** kolludieren
colon ['kolən] *s* (anat) Dickdarm *m*;
(gram) Doppelpunkt *m*
colonel ['kʌrnəl] *s* Oberst *m*
colonial [kə'lonɪ·əl] *adj* Kolonial- || *s*
Einwohner –in *mf* e-r Kolonie
colonialism [kə'lonɪ·ə ,lɪzəm] *s* Kolo-
nialismus *m*
colonize ['kɑlə ,naɪz] *tr* besiedeln
colonnade [,kɑlə'ned] *s* Säulengang *m*
colony ['kɑləni] *s* Kolonie *f*
color ['kʌlər] *adj (film, photo, pho-
tography, slide, television)* Farb- ||
s Farbe *f*; **lend c. to** beleben; **show
one's colors** sein wahres Gesicht zeigen; **the colors** die Flagge; **with fly-
ing colors** glänzend || *tr* färben;
(fig) (schön)färben || *intr* sich ver-
färben; *(become red)* erröten
col'or-blind' *adj* farbenblind
col'ored *adj* farbig
col'or-fast' *adj* farbecht
colorful ['kʌlərfəl] *adj* bunt, farben-
reich; (fig) farbig
col'oring *s* Kolorit *n*, Färbung *f*
col'oring book' *s* Malbuch *n*
colorless ['kʌlərlɪs] *adj* farblos
col'or ser'geant *s* Fahnenträger *m*
colossal [kə'lɑsəl] *adj* kolossal
colossus [kə'lɑsəs] *s* Koloß *m*
colt [kolt] *s* Füllen *n*
Columbus [kə'lʌmbəs] *s* Kolumbus *m*

column ['kɑləm] *s* Säule *f*; *(syndi-
cated article)* Kolumne *f*; (mil) Kolonne *f*; (typ) Spalte *f*, Rubrik *f*; **c.
of smoke** Rauchsäule *f*
columnist ['kɑləmɪst] *s* Kolumnist –in
mf
coma ['komə] *s* Koma *n*
comb [kom] *s* Kamm *m*; *(honeycomb)*
Wabe *f*; *(of a rooster)* Kamm *m* ||
tr kämmen; *(an area)* absuchen
com·bat ['kɑmbæt] *(e.g., pilot,
strength, unit, zone)* Kampf- || *s*
Kampf *m*, Streit *m* || ['kɑmbæt],
[kəm'bæt] *v (pret & pp –bat[t]ed;
ger –bat[t]ing)* *tr* bekämpfen || *intr*
kämpfen
combatant ['kɑmbətənt] *s* Kämpfer
–in *mf*
com'bat fatigue' *s* Kriegsneurose *f*
combative ['kɑmbətɪv] *adj* streitsüchtig
comber ['komər] *s* Sturzwelle *f*
combination [,kɑmbɪ'neʃən] *s* Verbindung *f*; (com) Konzern *m*
combine ['kɑmbaɪn] *s* (agr) Mähdrescher *m*; (com) Interessengemein-
schaft *f* || [kəm'baɪn] *tr* kombinie-
ren, verbinden
combustible [kəm'bʌstɪbəl] *adj* (ver)-
brennbar || *s* Brennstoff *m*
combustion [kəm'bʌstʃən] *s* Verbrennung *f*
combus'tion cham'ber *s* Brennkammer
f
combus'tion en'gine *s* Verbrennungs-
maschine *f*
come [kʌm] *v (pret* **came** [kem]; *pp*
come) *intr* kommen; **c. about** geschehen, sich ereignen; **c. across**
(discover) stoßen auf *(acc)*; *(said of
a speech, etc.)* ankommen; **c. across
with** (coll) blechen; **c. after** folgen
(dat); *(fetch)* holen kommen; **c.
along** mitkommen; (coll) vorwärtskommen; **c. apart** auseinanderfallen;
c. around herumkommen; *(said of a
special day)* wiederkehren; *(improve)* wieder zu sich kommen;
(change one's view) von e-r Ansicht
abgehen; **c. back** zurückkehren; *(recur to the mind)* wieder einfallen;
c. between treten zwischen *(acc)*; **c.
by** vorbeikommen; *(acquire)* geraten
an *(acc)*; **c. clean** (sl) mit der Wahrheit herausrücken; **c. down** *(said of
prices)* sinken; (& fig) herunterkom-
men; **c. down with** erkranken an
(dat); **c. first** *(have priority)* zuerst
an die Reihe kommen; **c. for** abholen; **c. forward** vortreten; **c. from**
herkommen; *(e.g., a rich family)*
stammen aus; *(e.g., school)* kommen
aus; **c. in** hereinkommen; **c. in for**
(coll) erhalten; **c. in second** den
zweiten Platz belegen; **c. off** *(said
of a button)* abgehen; *(come loose)*
losgehen; *(said of an event)* verlaufen; **c. on!** los!; **c. out** herauskommen; *(said of a spot)* herausgehen;
(said of a publication) erscheinen;
c. out against (or **for)** sich erklären
gegen (or für); **c. over** *(said of fear,
etc.)* überlaufen; **c. to** *(amount to)*

betragen; (after fainting) wieder zu
sich kommen; c. together zusammenkommen; c. true in Erfüllung gehen;
c. up (occur) vorkommen; (said of
a number) herauskommen; (said of
plants) aufgehen; (in conversation)
zur Sprache kommen; (said of a
storm) heranziehen; c. upon kommen auf (acc); c. up to entsprechen
(dat); for years to c. auf Jahre hinaus; how c.? (coll) wieso?; it comes
easy to me es fällt mir leicht
come'back' s Comeback n
comedian [kə'midɪ·ən] s Komiker m;
(pej) Komödiant –in mf
comedienne [kə,midɪ'en] s Komikerin
f
come'down' s (coll) Abstieg m
comedy ['kamədi] s Komödie f
comely ['kʌmli] adj anmutig
come'-on' s (sl) Lockmittel n
comet ['kamɪt] s Komet m
comfort ['kʌmfərt] s (solace) Trost m;
(of a room, etc.) Behaglichkeit f;
(person or thing that comforts) Trö-
ster m; (bed cover) Steppdecke f ||
tr trösten
comfortable ['kʌmfərtəbəl] adj behaglich, bequem; (income) ausreichend;
be (or feel) c. sich wohl fühlen
comforter ['kʌmfərtər] s Tröster m;
(bed cover) Steppdecke f
com'forting adj tröstlich
com'fort sta'tion s Bedürfnisanstalt f
comic ['kamɪk] adj komisch || s Ko-
miker m; comics Comics pl, Witzblatt n
comical ['kamɪkəl] adj komisch
com'ic op'era s Operette f
com'ic strip' s Bildstreifen m
com'ing adj künftig, kommend; c.
soon (notice at theater) demnächst
|| s Kommen n, Ankunft f; c. of age
Mündigwerden n
comma ['kamə] s Komma n, Beistrich
m
command [kə'mænd] s (order) Befehl
m; (of language) Beherrschung f;
(mil) Kommando n; (jurisdiction)
(mil) Kommandobereich m; at s.o.'s
c. auf j–s Befehl; be in c. of (mil)
das Kommando führen über (acc);
have a good c. of gut beherrschen;
take c. of (mil) das Kommando
übernehmen über (acc) || tr (a per-
son) befehlen (dat); (respect, silence) gebieten; (troops) führen; (a
high price) erzielen || intr (mil) kom-
mandieren
commandant [,kamən'dænt] s Kommandant m
commandeer [,kamən'dɪr] tr (coll)
organisieren; (mil) requirieren
commander [kə'mændər] s Truppen-
führer m; (of a company) Chef m;
(of a military unit from battalion to
corps) Kommandeur m; (of an
army) Befehlshaber m; (nav) Fre-
gattenkapitän m
comman'der in chief' s Oberbefehls-
haber m
command'ing adj (appearance) eindrucksvoll; (view) weit; (position)

beherrschend; (general) kommandie-
rend
command'ing of'ficer s Einheitsführer
m
commandment [kə'mændmənt] s Gebot n
command' post' s Befehlsstand m
commemorate [kə'mɛmə,ret] tr gedenken (genit), feiern
commemoration [kə,mɛmə're∫ən] s
Gedenkfeier f; in c. of zum Gedächtnis von
commence [kə'mɛns] tr & intr anfangen
commencement [kə'mɛnsmənt] s Anfang m; (educ) Schulentlassungsfeier
f
commend [kə'mɛnd] tr (praise) (&
mil) belob(ig)en; (entrust) empfehlen
commendable [kə'mɛndəbəl] adj lobenswert
commendation [,kamən'de∫ən] s Be-
lobigung f
comment ['kamənt] s Bemerkung f,
Stellungnahme f; no c.! kein Kom-
mentar! || intr Bemerkungen ma-
chen; c. on kommentieren
commentary ['kamən,tɛri] s Kommentar m
commentator ['kamən,tetər] s Kom-
mentator –in mf; (of a text) Erklärer
–in mf
commerce ['kamərs] s Handel m
commercial [kə'mʌr∫əl] adj Handels-,
Geschäfts-, kommerziell || s (rad,
telv) Werbesendung f
commer'cial art' s Gebrauchsgraphik f
commercialism [kə'mʌr∫ə,lɪzəm] s
Handelsgeist m
commercialize [kə'mʌr∫ə,laɪz] tr
kommerzialisieren
commiserate [kə'mɪzə,ret] intr—c.
with bemitleiden
commissar ['kamɪ,sar] s (pol) Kommissar m
commissary ['kamɪ,sɛri] s (deputy)
Kommissar m; (store) Militärversor-
gungsstelle f
commission [kə'mɪ∫ən] s (order) Auftrag m; (of a crime) Begehung f;
(committee) Kommission f; (percentage) Provision f; (mil) Offizierspatent n; out of c. außer Betrieb;
|| tr beauftragen; (a work) bestellen;
(a ship) in Dienst stellen; (mil) ein
Offizierspatent verleihen (dat)
commis'sioned of'ficer s Offizier –in
mf
commissioner [kə'mɪ∫ənər] s Kommissar –in mf
com·mit [kə'mɪt] v (pret & pp
–mitted; ger –mitting) tr (a crime)
begehen; (entrust) anvertrauen; (give
over) übergeben; (to an institution)
einweisen; c. oneself to sich festlegen auf (acc); c. to memory auswendig lernen; c. to writing zu Papier bringen
commitment [kə'mɪtmənt] s (to) Festlegung f (auf acc); (to an asylum)
Anstaltsüberweisung f
committee [kə'mɪti] s Ausschuß m
commode [kə'mod] s Kommode f

commodious [kə'modɪ·əs] *adj* geräumig
commodity [kə'madɪtɪ] *s* Ware *f*
common ['kamən] *adj* (*language*, *property*, *interest*) gemeinsam; (*general*) allgemein; (*people*) einfach; (*soldier*) gemein; (*coarse*, *vulgar*) gemein; (*frequent*) häufig ‖ *s*—**in c.** gemeinsam
com'mon denom'inator *s* gemeinsamer Nenner *m;* **reduce to a c.** auf e–n gemeinsamen Nenner bringen
commoner ['kamənər] *s* Bürger –in *mf*
com'mon-law mar'riage *s* wilde Ehe *f*
Com'mon Mar'ket *s* Gemeinsamer Markt *m*
com'mon noun' *s* Gattungsname *m*
com'monplace' *adj* alltäglich ‖ *s* Gemeinplatz *m*
com'mon sense' *s* gesunder Menschenverstand *m*
com'mon stock' *s* Stammaktien *pl*
commonweal ['kamən‚wil] *s* Gemeinwohl *n*
com'monwealth' *s* (*republic*) Republik *f;* (*state in U.S.A.*) Bundesstaat *m*
commotion [kə'moʃən] *s* Aufruhr *m*
commune ['kamjun] *s* Kommune *f* ‖ [kə'mjun] *intr* sich vertraulich besprechen
communicable [kə'mjunɪkəbəl] *adj* übertragbar
communicant [kə'mjunɪkənt] *s* Kommunikant –in *mf*
communicate [kə'mjunɪ‚ket] *tr* mitteilen; (*a disease*) (**to**) übertragen (auf *acc*) ‖ *intr* sich besprechen
communication [kə‚mjunɪ'keʃən] *s* Mitteilung *f;* (*message*) Nachricht *f;* **communications** Nachrichtenwesen *n;* (mil) Fernmeldewesen *n*
communicative [kə'mjunɪ‚ketɪv] *adj* mitteilsam
communion [kə'mjunjən] *s* Gemeinschaft *f;* (Prot) Abendmahl *n;* (R. C.) Kommunion *f*
commun'ion rail' *s* Altargitter *n*
communiqué [kə‚mjunɪ'ke] *s* Kommuniqué *n*
communism ['kamjə‚nɪzəm] *s* Kommunismus *m*
communist ['kamjənɪst] *s* kommunistisch ‖ *s* Kommunist –in *mf*
community [kə'mjunɪtɪ] *s* Gemeinschaft *f;* (*people living together*) Gemeinde *f*
communize ['kamjə‚naɪz] *tr* kommunistisch machen
commutation [‚kamjə'teʃən] *s* (jur) Umwandlung *f*
commuta'tion tick'et *s* Zeitkarte *f*
commutator ['kamjə‚tetər] *s* (elec) Kommutator *m*, Kollektor *m*
commute [kə'mjut] *tr* (jur) umwandeln ‖ *intr* pendeln
commuter [kə'mjutər] *s* Pendler –in *mf*
commut'er train' *s* Pendelzug *m*
compact [kəm'pækt] *adj* kompakt, dicht ‖ ['kampækt] *s* (*for cosmetics*) Kompaktdose *f;* (*agreement*) Vertrag *m;* (aut) Kompaktwagen *m*

companion [kəm'pænjən] *s* Kumpan –in *mf;* (*one who accompanies*) Begleiter –in *mf*
companionable [kəm'pænjənəbəl] *adj* gesellig
compan'ionship' *s* Gesellschaft *f*
compan'ionway' *s* Kajütstreppe *f*
company ['kʌmpəni] *s* (*companions*) Umgang *m;* (& com) Gesellschaft *f;* (mil) Kompanie *f;* (theat) Truppe *f;* **keep c. with** verkehren mit; **keep s.o. c.** j–m Gesellschaft leisten
com'pany command'er *s* Kompaniechef *m*
comparable ['kampərəbəl] *adj* vergleichbar
comparative [kəm'pærətɪv] *adv* vergleichend; (gram) komparativ ‖ *s* (gram) Komparativ *m*
comparatively [kəm'pærətɪvli] *adv* verhältnismäßig
compare [kəm'pɛr] *s*—**beyond c.** unvergleichlich ‖ *tr* (**with, to**) vergleichen (mit); (gram) steigern; **as compared with** im Vergleich zu
comparison [kəm'pærɪsən] *s* Vergleich *m;* (gram) Steigerung *f*
compartment [kəm'partmənt] *s* Fach *n;* (rr) Abteil *n*
compass ['kʌmpəs] *s* Kompaß *m;* (geom) Zirkel *m;* **within the c. of** innerhalb (*genit*)
com'pass card' *s* Kompaßrose *f*
compassion [kəm'pæʃən] *s* Mitleid *n*
compassionate [kəm'pæʃənɪt] *adj* mitleidig
compatible [kəm'pætɪbəl] *adj* vereinbar
com·pel [kəm'pɛl] *v* (*pret & pp* **–pelled;** *ger* **–pelling**) *tr* zwingen, nötigen
compendious [kəm'pɛndɪ·əs] *adj* gedrängt
compendi·um [kəm'pɛndɪ·əm] *s* (**–ums** & **–a** [ə]) Abriß *m*, Kompendium *n*
compensate ['kampən‚set] *tr* entschädigen ‖ *intr*—**c. for** Ersatz leisten (or bieten) für
compensation [‚kampən'seʃən] *s* (*for damages*) Entschädigung *f;* (*remuneration*) Entgeld *n*
compete [kəm'pit] *intr* (**with**) konkurrieren (mit); (**for**) sich mitbewerben (um); (sport) am Wettkampf teilnehmen
competence ['kampɪtəns] *s* (*mental state*) Zurechnungsfähigkeit *f;* (*ability*) (**in**) Fähigkeit *f* (zu)
competent ['kampɪtənt] *adj* (*able*) fähig, tüchtig; (*witness*) zulässig
competition [‚kampɪ'trɪʃən] *s* Wettbewerb *m;* (com) Konkurrenz *f;* (sport) Wettkampf *m*
competitive [kəm'petɪtɪv] *adj* (*bidding*) Konkurrenz–; (*prices*) konkurrenzfähig; (*person*) ehrgeizig; (*exam*) Auslese–
competitor [kəm'petɪtər] *s* Mitbewerber –in *mf;* (com) Konkurrent –in *mf;* (sport) Wettkämpfer –in *mf*
compilation [‚kampɪ'leʃən] *s* Zusammenstellung *f;* (*book*) Sammelwerk *n*

compile [kəm'paɪl] *tr* zusammenstellen, kompilieren; (*Material*) zusammentragen

complacence [kəm'plesəns], **complacency** [kəm'plesənsi] *s* Selbstgefälligkeit *f*

complacent [kəm'plesənt] *adj* selbstgefällig

complain [kəm'plen] *intr* klagen; **c. to s.o. about** sich bei j—m beklagen über (*acc*)

complaint [kəm'plent] *s* Klage *f*; (*ailment*) Beschwerde *f*

complement ['kamplɪmənt] *s* (& gram) Ergänzung *f*; (geom) Komplement *n*; (nav) Bemannung *f* ‖ ['kamplɪ‚ment] *tr* ergänzen

complete [kəm'plit] *adj* ganz, vollkommen, vollständig; (*works*) sämtlich ‖ *tr* (*make whole*) vervollständigen; (*make perfect*) vollenden; (*finish*) beenden; (*a job*) erledigen

completely [kəm'plitli] *adv* völlig

completion [kəm'pliʃən] *s* Vollendung *f*

complex [kəm'plɛks], ['kamplɛks] *adj* verwickelt ‖ ['kamplɛks] *s* Komplex *m*

complexion [kəm'plɛkʃən] *s* Gesichtsfarbe *f*; (*appearance*) Aussehen *n*

complexity [kəm'plɛksɪti] *s* Kompliziertheit *f*

compliance [kəm'plaɪ-əns] *s* Einwilligung *f*; **in c. with your wishes** Ihren Wünschen gemäß

complicate ['kamplɪ‚ket] *tr* komplizieren

com'plicat'ed *adj* kompliziert

complication [‚kamplɪ'keʃən] *s* Verwicklung *f*; (& pathol) Komplikation *f*

complicity [kəm'plɪsɪti] *s* (**in**) Mitschuld *f* (an *dat*)

compliment ['kamplɪmənt] *s* Kompliment *n*; (*praise*) Lob *n*; **compliments** Empfehlungen *pl*; **pay s.o. a** (**high**) **c.** j—m ein (großes) Lob spenden ‖ *tr* (**on**) beglückwünschen (zu)

complimentary [‚kamplɪ'mɛntəri] *adj* (*remark*) schmeichelhaft; (*free*) Frei—

com·ply [kəm'plaɪ] *v* (*pret* & *pp* —**plied**) *intr* sich fügen; **c. with** einwilligen in (*acc*); **c. with the rules** sich an die Vorschriften halten

component [kəm'ponənt] *adj* Teil— ‖ *s* Bestandteil *m*; (math, phys) Komponente *f*

compose [kəm'poz] *tr* (*writings*) verfassen; (*a sentence*) bilden; (mus) komponieren; (typ) setzen; **be composed of** bestehen aus; **c. oneself** sich fassen

composed' *adj* ruhig, gefaßt

composer [kəm'pozər] *s* Verfasser —in *mf*; (mus) Komponist —in *mf*

composite [kəm'pazɪt] *adj* zusammengesetzt ‖ *s* Zusammensetzung *f*

composition [‚kampə'zɪʃən] *s* (chem) Zusammensetzung *f*; (*educ*) Aufsatz *m*; (mus, paint) Komposition *f*; (typ) Schriftsatz *m*

composi'tion book' *s* Übungsheft *n*

compositor [kəm'pazɪtər] *s* Setzer —in *mf*

composure [kəm'poʒər] *s* Fassung *f*

compote ['kampot] *s* (*stewed fruit*) Kompott *n*; (*dish*) Kompottschale *f*

compound ['kampaund] *adj* zusammengesetzt; (*fracture*) kompliziert ‖ *s* Zusammensetzung *f*; (*enclosure*) umzäumtes Gelände *n*; (chem) Verbindung *f*; (gram) Kompositum *n*; (mil) Truppenlager *n* ‖ [kam'paund] *tr* zusammensetzen

com'pound in'terest *s* Zinseszinsen *pl*

comprehend [‚kamprɪ'hend] *tr* auffassen

comprehensible [‚kamprɪ'hensɪbəl] *adj* faßlich, begreiflich

comprehension [‚kamprɪ'hɛnʃən] *s* Auffassung *f*; (*ability to understand*) Fassungskraft *f*

comprehensive [‚kamprɪ'hɛnsɪv] *adj* umfassend

compress ['kampres] *s* (med) Kompresse *f* ‖ [kəm'pres] *tr* komprimieren

compressed' *adj* komprimiert; (*air*) Druck—; (fig) gedrängt

compression [kəm'prɛʃən] *s* Kompression *f*, Druck *m*

comprise [kəm'praɪz] *tr* umfassen; **be comprised of** bestehen aus

compromise ['kamprə‚maɪz] *s* Kompromiß *m* ‖ *tr* kompromittieren; (*principles*) preisgeben ‖ *intr* (**on**) e—n Kompromiß schließen (über *acc*)

comptroller [kəm'trolər] *s* Rechnungsprüfer *m*

compulsion [kəm'pʌlʃən] *s* Zwang *m*

compulsive [kəm'pʌlsɪv] *adj* triebhaft

compulsory [kəm'pʌlsəri] *adj* obligatorisch, Zwangs—; **c. military service** allgemeine Wehrpflicht *f*

compute [kəm'pjut] *tr* berechnen ‖ *intr* rechnen

computer [kəm'pjutər] *s* Computer *m*

comput'er lan'guage *s* Maschinensprache *f*

comrade ['kamræd] *s* Kamerad *m*

con [kan] *v* (*pret* & *pp* **conned;** *ger* **conning**) *tr* beschwindeln

concave [kan'kev] *adj* konkav

conceal [kan'sil] *tr* verheimlichen

concealment [kən'silmənt] *s* Verheimlichung *f*; (*place*) Versteck *n*

concede [kən'sid] *tr* zugestehen, zubilligen; **c. victory** (pol) den Wahlsieg überlassen ‖ *intr* nachgeben

conceit [kən'sit] *s* (*vanity*) Einbildung *f*, Dünkel *m*; (*witty expression*) Witz *m*

conceit'ed *adj* eingebildet

conceivable [kən'sivəbəl] *adj* denkbar

conceive [kən'siv] *tr* begreifen; (*a desire*) hegen; (*a child*) empfangen

concentrate ['kansən‚tret] *tr* konzentrieren; (*troops*) zusammenziehen ‖ *intr* (**on**) sich konzentrieren (auf *acc*); (*gather*) sich sammeln

concentration [‚kansən'treʃən] *s* Konzentration *f*

concentric [kən'sɛntrɪk] *adj* konzentrisch

concept ['kansɛpt] *s* Begriff *m*

conception [kən'sɛpʃən] s (idea) Vorstellung f; (design) Entwurf m; (biol) Empfängnis f
concern [kən'sʌrn] s (worry) Besorgnis f; (matter) Angelegenheit f; (com) Firma f; **that is no c. of mine** das geht mich nichts an || tr betreffen, angehen; **as far as I am concerned** von mir aus; **c. oneself about** sich bekümmern um; **c. oneself with** sich befassen mit; **to whom it may c.** Bescheinigung
concern'ing prep betreffend (acc), betreffs (genit), über (acc)
concert ['kɑnsərt] s (mus) Konzert n; **in c.** (with) im Einvernehmen (mit) || [kən'sʌrt] tr zusammenfassen
concession [kən'sɛʃən] s Konzession f
conciliate [kən'sɪlɪ‚et] tr versöhnen
conciliatory [kən'sɪlɪ·ə‚tori] adj versöhnlich
concise [kən'saɪs] adj kurz, bündig
conclude [kən'klud] tr schließen; **c. from s.th. that** aus etw schließen, daß; **to be concluded** Schluß folgt || intr (with) schließen (mit)
conclusion [kən'kluʒən] s Schluß m; **draw conclusions from** Schlüsse ziehen aus; **in c.** zum Schluß; **jump at conclusions** voreilige Schlüsse ziehen
conclusive [kən'klusɪv] adj (decisive) entscheidend; (proof) schlagkräftig
concoct [kən'kɑkt] tr (brew) zusammenbrauen; (plans) schmieden
concoction [kən'kɑkʃən] s Gebräu n
concomitant [kən'kɑmɪtənt] adj begleitend || s Begleitumstand m
concord ['kɑŋkərd] s Eintracht f
concordance [kən'kərdəns] s Übereinstimmung f; (book) Konkordanz f
concourse ['kɑŋkors] s (of people) Zusammenlaufen n, Anlauf m; (of rivers) Zusammenfluß m; (rr) Bahnhofshalle f
concrete ['kɑnkrit], [kɑn'krit] adj (not abstract) konkret; (solid) fest; (evidence) schlüssig; (of concrete) Beton–; (math) benannt || s Beton m || tr betonieren
con'crete block' s Betonblock m
con'crete noun' s Konkretum n
concubine ['kɑŋkjə‚baɪn] s Nebenfrau f; (mistress) Konkubine f
con·cur [kən'kʌr] v (pret & pp) –curred; ger –curring) intr (agree) übereinstimmen; (coincide) (with) zusammenfallen (mit); **c. in** (an opinion) beistimmen (dat)
concurrence [kən'kʌrəns] s (agreement) Einverständis n; (coincidence) Zusammentreffen n; (geom) Schnittpunkt m
condemn [kən'dɛm] tr verdammen; (& jur) verurteilen; (a building) für unbewohnlich erklären
condemnation [‚kɑndɛm'neʃən] s Verurteilung f; (of a building, ship, plane) Untauglichkeitserklärung f
condense [kən'dɛns] tr (make thicker) verdichten; (writing) zusammendrängen; || intr kondensieren
condenser [kən'dɛnsər] s Kondensator m

condescend [‚kɑndɪ'sɛnd] intr sic[ ] herablassen
condescend'ing adj herablassend
condescension [‚kɑndɪ'sɛnʃən] s Hei ablassung f
condiment ['kɑndɪmənt] s Würze f
condition [kən'dɪʃən] s (state) Zustan(m; (state of health) Verfassung f (stipulation) Bedingung f; **condition** (e.g. for working; of the weather Verhältnisse pl; **on c. that** unter de Bedingung, daß || tr (impose stipu lations on) bedingen; (accustom (to) gewöhnen (an acc); (sport) ii Form bringen
conditional [kən'dɪʃənəl] adj bedingt
condi'tional clause' s Bedingungssat m
conditionally [kən'dɪʃənəli] adv be dingungsweise
condole [kən'dol] intr (with) kondo lieren (dat)
condolence [kən'doləns] s Beileid n
condom ['kɑndəm] s Präservativ n
condominium [‚kɑndə'mɪnɪ·əm] Eigentumswohnung f
condone [kən'don] tr verzeihen
conducive [kən'd(j)usɪv] adj—**c. t(** förderlich (dat)
conduct ['kɑndʌkt] s (behavior) Be tragen n; (guidance) Führung f | [kən'dʌkt] tr (business, a campaign a tour) führen; (elec, phys) leiten (mus) dirigieren; **c. oneself** sich be tragen || intr (mus) dirigieren
conductor [kən'dʌktər] s (elec, phys‚ Leiter m; (mus) Dirigent m; (rr) Schaffner m
conduit ['kɑnd(ʊ)ɪt] s Röhre f; (elec) Isolierrohr n
cone [kon] s (ice cream cone; papei cone) Tüte f; (bot) Zapfen m; (geom) Kegel m, Konus m
confection [kən'fɛkʃən] s Konfekt n
confectioner [kən'fɛkʃənər] s Zucker bäcker –in mf
confec'tioner's sug'ar s Puderzucker m
confectionery [kən'fɛkʃə‚neri] s (shop) Konditorei f; (sweets) Zukkerwerk n
confederacy [kən'fɛdərəsi] s Bündnis n; (conspiracy) Verschwörung f
confederate [kən'fɛdərɪt] adj verbündet || s Bundesgenosse m, Bundesgenossin f; (accomplice) Helfershelfer –in mf || [kən'fɛdə‚ret] tr verbünden || intr sich verbünden
confederation [kən‚fɛdə'reʃən] s Bund m
con·fer [kən'fʌr] v (pret & pp –ferred; ger –ferring) tr (on, upon) verleihen (dat) || intr sich besprechen, konferieren
conference ['kɑnfərəns] s Konferenz f; (sport) Verband m
con'ference call' s Sammelverbindung f
confess [kən'fɛs] tr (ein)gestehen, bekennen; (sins) beichten || intr gestehen
confession [kən'fɛʃən] s Geständnis n, Bekenntnis n; (of sins) Beichte f; **go to c.** beichten

confessional [kən'feʃənəl] *s* Beicht-stuhl *m*
confes'sion of faith' *s* Glaubensbe-kenntnis *n*
confessor [kən'fesər] *s* Beichtvater *m*
confidant [,kɑnfı'dænt] *s* Vertraute *mf*
confide [kən'faıd] *tr* (to) anvertrauen (*dat*) ‖ *intr*—**c. in** vertrauen (*dat*)
confidence ['kɑnfıdəns] *s* (*trust*) (in) Vertrauen *n* (auf *acc,* zu); (*assurance*) Zuversicht *f;* **in c.** im Vertrauen
con'fidence man' *s* Bauernfänger *m*
confident ['kɑnfıdənt] *adj* zuversichtlich; **be c. of** sich [*dat*] sicher sein (*genit*)
confidential [,kɑnfı'dɛnʃəl] *adj* vertraulich
confine ['kɑnfaın] *s*—**the confines** die Grenzen *pl* ‖ *tr* [kən'faın] *tr* (*limit*) (to) beschränken (auf *acc*); (*shut in*) einsperren; **be confined** (*in pregnancy*) niederkommen; **be confined to bed** bettlägerig sein
confinement [kən'faınmənt] *s* Beschränkung *f;* (*arrest*) Haft *f;* (*childbirth*) Niederkunft *f*
confirm [kən'fʌrm] *tr* bestätigen; (Prot) konfirmieren; (R.C.) firmen; **confirm in writing** verbriefen
confirmation [,kɑnfər'meʃən] *s* Bestätigung *f;* (Prot) Konfirmation *f;* (R.C.) Firmung *f*
confirmed' *adj* (*e.g., report*) bestätigt; (*inveterate*) unverbesserlich; **c. bachelor** Hagestolz *m*
confiscate ['kɑnfıs,ket] *tr* beschlagnahmen, konfiszieren
confiscation [,kɑnfıs'keʃən] *s* Beschlagnahme *f*
conflagration [,kɑnflə'greʃən] *s* Brand *m,* Feuerbrunst *f*
conflict ['kɑnflıkt] *s* (*of interests, of evidence*) Konflikt *m;* (*fight*) Zusammenstoß *m* ‖ [kən'flıkt] *intr* (**with**) im Widerspruch stehen (zu)
conflict'ing *adj* einander widersprechend
con'flict of in'terest *s* Interessenkonflikt *m,* Interessenkollision *f*
confluence ['kɑnflu·əns] *s* Zusammenfluß *m*
conform [kən'fɔrm] *tr* anpassen ‖ *intr* übereinstimmen; (to) sich anpassen (*dat*)
conformity [kən'fɔrmıti] *s* (*adaptation*) (to) Anpassung *f* (an *acc*); (*agreement*) (with) Übereinstimmung *f* (mit)
confound [kɑn'faund] *tr* (*perplex*) verblüffen; (*throw into confusion*) verwirren; (*erroneously identify*) (with) verwechseln (mit) ‖ ['kɑn'faund] *tr*—**c. it!** zum Donnerwetter!
confound'ed *adj* (coll) verwünscht
confrere ['kɑnfrer] *s* Kollege *m*
confront [kən'frʌnt] *tr* (*face*) gegenüberstehen (*dat*); (*a problem, an enemy*) entgegentreten (*dat*); **be confronted with** gegenüberstehen (*dat*); **c. s.o. with** j-n konfrontieren mit

confrontation [,kɑnfrən'teʃən] *s* Konfrontation *f;* (*of witnesses*) Gegenüberstellung *f*
confuse [kən'fjuz] *tr* (*e.g., names*) verwechseln; (*persons*) verwirren
confused' *adj* konfus, verwirrt, wirr
confusion [kən'fjuʒən] *s* Verwechslung *f;* (*disorder, chaos*) Verwirrung *f*
confute [kən'fjut] *tr* widerlegen
congeal [kən'dʒil] *tr* erstarren lassen ‖ *intr* erstarren
congenial [kən'dʒinjəl] *adj* (*person*) sympathisch; (*surroundings*) angenehm
congenital [kən'dʒɛnıtəl] *adj* angeboren
congen'ital de'fect *s* Geburtsfehler *m*
congest [kən'dʒɛst] *tr* überfüllen
congest'ed *adj* überfüllt; (*area*) übervölkert; (*with traffic*) verkehrsreich
congestion [kən'dʒɛstʃən] *s* Überfüllung *f;* (*of traffic*) Verkehrsstockung *f;* (*of population*) Übervölkerung *f;* (*pathol*) Blutandrang *m*
congratulate [kən'grætʃə,let] *tr* gratulieren (*dat*); **c. s.o. on** j-m gratulieren zu
congratulations [kən,grætʃə'leʃənz] *spl* Glückwunsch *m; c.!* ich gratuliere!
congregate ['kɑŋgrı,get] *intr* sich (ver)sammeln, zusammenkommen
congregation [,kɑŋgrı'geʃən] *s* Versammlung *f;* (eccl) Gemeinde *f*
congress ['kɑŋgres] *s* Kongreß *m*
congressional [kən'greʃənəl] *adj* Kongreß-
congress·man ['kɑŋgrısmən] *s* (**–men**) Abgeordnete *m*
con'gress·wom'an *s* (**–wom'en**) Abgeordnete *f*
congruent ['kɑŋgru·ənt] *adj* kongruent
conical ['kɑnıkəl] *adj* kegelförmig
conjecture [kən'dʒɛk/ər] *s* Vermutung *f,* Mutmaßung *f* ‖ *tr & intr* vermuten
conjugal ['kɑndʒəgəl] *adj* ehelich
conjugate ['kɑndʒə,get] *tr* abwandeln
conjugation [,kɑndʒə'geʃən] *s* Abwandlung *f*
conjunction [kən'dʒʌŋkʃən] *s* Bindewort *n;* **in c. with** in Verbindung mit
conjure [kən'dʒur] *tr* (*appeal solemnly to*) beschwören ‖ ['kʌndʒər] *tr*—**c. away** wegzaubern; **c. up** heraufbeschwören
conk [kɑŋk] *tr* (sl) hauen ‖ *intr*—**c. out** (sl) versagen
connect [kə'nɛkt] *tr* verbinden; (& fig) verknüpfen; (elec) (to) anschließen (an *acc*); (telp) (with) verbinden (mit) ‖ *intr* verbunden sein; (*said of trains, etc.*) (with) Anschluß haben (an *acc*); (box) treffen
connect'ing *adj* Verbindungs-, Binde-; (*trains, buses*) Anschluß-; (*rooms*) mit Zwischentür
connect'ing rod' *s* Schubstange *f*
connection [kə'nɛkʃən] *s* (*e.g., of a pipe*) Verbindung *f;* (*of ideas*) Verknüpfung *f;* (*context*) Zusammenhang *m;* (*part that connects*) Verbindungsteil *m;* (elec) Schaltung *f;*

(mach, rr, telp) Verbindung *f;* **connections** Beziehungen *pl;* **in c. with** in Zusammenhang mit
con'ning tow'er ['kɑnɪŋ] *s* Kommandoturm *m*
connive [kə'naɪv] *intr—***c. at** ein Auge zudrücken bei; **c. with** im geheimen Einverständnis stehen mit
connotation [‚kɑno'teʃən] *s* Nebenbedeutung *f*
connote [kə'not] *tr* mitbezeichnen
conquer ['kɑŋkər] *tr (win in war)* erobern; *(overcome)* überwinden
conquerer ['kɑŋkərər] *s* Eroberer *m*
conquest ['kɑŋkwest] *s* Eroberung *f*
conscience ['kɑnʃəns] *s* Gewissen *n*
conscientious [‚kɑnʃɪ'enʃəs] *adj* gewissenhaft, pflichtbewußt
conscien'tious objec'tor [əb'dʒektər] *s* Wehrdienstverweigerer *m*
conscious ['kɑnʃəs] *adj* bei Bewußtsein; **c. of** bewußt *(genit)*
consciousness ['kɑnʃəsnɪs] *s* Bewußtsein *n; (awareness)* **(of)** Kenntnis *f (genit* or von); **regain c.** wieder zu sich kommen
conscript ['kɑnskrɪpt] *s* Dienstpflichtige *m;* (mil) Wehrdienstpflichtige *m* ‖ [kən'skrɪpt] *tr* ausheben
conscription [kən'skrɪpt/ən] *s* Dienstpflicht *f; (draft)* Aushebung *f*
consecrate ['kɑnsɪ ‚kret] *tr* weihen
consecration [‚kɑnsɪ'kreʃən] *s* Einweihung *f; (at Mass)* Wandlung *f*
consecutive [kən'sekjətɪv] *adj* aufeinanderfolgend
consensus [kən'sensəs] *s* allgemeine Übereinstimmung *f;* **the c. of opinion** die übereinstimmende Meinung
consent [kən'sent] *s* Zustimmung *f;* **by common c.** mit allgemeiner Zustimmung ‖ *intr* zustimmen; **c. to** *(inf)* sich bereit erklären zu *(inf)*
consequence ['kɑnsɪ ‚kwens] *s* Folge *f; (influence)* Einfluß *m;* **in c. of** infolge *(genit);* **it is of no c.** es hat nichts auf sich; **suffer the consequences** die Folgen tragen
consequently ['kɑnsɪ ‚kwentlɪ] *adv* folglich, infolgedessen, mithin
conservation [‚kɑnsər've/ən] *s* Bewahrung *f; (of energy, etc.)* Erhaltung *f; (supervision of natural resources)* Naturschutz *m; (ecology)* Umweltschutz *m*
conservatism [kən'sɑrvə ‚tɪzəm] *s* Konservatismus *m*
conservative [kən'sɑrvətɪv] *adj* konservativ; *(estimate)* vorsichtig ‖ *s* Konservative *mf*
conservatory [kən'sɑrvə ‚torɪ] *s* Treibhaus *n;* (mus) Konservatorium *n*
conserve [kən'sɑrv] *tr* sparsam umgehen mit
consider [kən'sɪdər] *tr (take into account)* berücksichtigen; *(show consideration for)* Rücksicht nehmen auf *(acc); (reflect on)* sich *[dat]* überlegen; *(regard as)* halten für, betrachten als; **all things considered** alles in allem
considerable [kən'sɪdərəbəl] *adj* beträchtlich, erheblich

considerate [kən'sɪdərɪt] *adj* **(towards)** rücksichtsvoll (gegen)
consideration [kən ‚sɪdə're/ən] *s (taking into account)* Berücksichtigung *f; (regard)* **(for)** Rücksicht *f (auf acc);* **be an important c.** e–e wichtige Rolle spielen; **be under c.** in Betracht gezogen werden; **for a c.** entgeltlich; **in c. of** in Anbetracht *(genit);* **take into c.** in Betracht ziehen; **with c.** rücksichtsvoll
consid'ering *adv* (coll) den Umständen nach ‖ *prep* in Anbetracht *(genit)*
consign [kən'saɪn] *tr (ship)* versenden; *(address)* adressieren
consignee [‚kɑnsaɪ'ni] *s* Adressat –in *mf*
consignment [kən'saɪnmənt] *s (act of sending)* Versand *m; (merchandise sent)* Sendung *f;* **on c.** in Kommission
consist [kən'sɪst] *intr—***c. in** bestehen in *(dat);* **c. of** bestehen aus
consistency [kən'sɪstənsɪ] *s* Konsequenz *f; (firmness)* Festigkeit *f; (viscosity)* Dickflüssigkeit *f; (agreement)* Übereinstimmung *f; (steadfastness)* **(in)** Beständigkeit *f* (in *dat)*
consistent [kən'sɪstənt] *adj (performer)* stetig; *(performance)* gleichmäßig; *(free from contradiction)* konsequent; **c. with** in Übereinstimmung mit
consistory [kən'sɪstərɪ] *s* Konsistorium *n*
consolation [‚kɑnsə'le/ən] *s* Trost *m*
console ['kɑnsol] *s (for radio or record player)* Musiktruhe *f; (of an organ)* Spieltisch *m; (television)* Fernsehtruhe *f* ‖ [kən'sol] *tr* trösten
consolidate [kən'sɑlɪ ‚det] *tr (a position)* festigen; *(debts)* konsolidieren; *(combine)* zusammenlegen
consonant ['kɑnsənənt] *adj* **(with)** im Einklang (mit) ‖ *s* Mitlaut *m*
consort ['kɑnsɔrt] *s (male)* Gemahl *m; (female)* Gemahlin *f* ‖ [kən'sɔrt] *intr* **(with)** Umgang haben (mit)
consorti•um [kən'sɔrtɪ•əm] *s (–a* [ə]) Konsortium *n*
conspicuous [kən'spɪkju•əs] *adj* auffallend, auffällig; **c. for** bemerkenswert wegen
conspiracy [kən'spɪrəsɪ] *s* Verschwörung *f*
conspirator [kən'spɪrətər] *s* Verschwörer –in *mf*
conspire [kən'spaɪr] *intr* sich verschwören
constable ['kɑnstəbəl] *s* Gendarm *m*
constancy ['kɑnstənsɪ] *s* Beständigkeit *f*
constant ['kɑnstənt] *adj (continuous)* dauernd, ständig; *(faithful)* treu; *(resolute)* standhaft; *(element, time element)* fest; (fig & tech) konstant ‖ *s* (math, phys) Konstante *f*
constantly ['kɑnstəntlɪ] *adv* immerfort
constellation [‚kɑnstə'le/ən] *s* Sternbild *n*
consternation [‚kɑnstər'ne/ən] *s* Bestürzung *f*

constipate ['kɑnstɪ ˌpet] *tr* verstopfen
constipation [ˌkɑnstɪ'peʃən] *s* Verstopfung *f*
constituency [kən'stɪtʃʊ·ənsi] *s* Wählerschaft *f*
constituent [kən'stɪtʃʊ·ənt] *adj* wesentlich; **c. part** Bestandteil *m* ‖ *s* Komponente *f;* (pol) Wähler –in *mf*
constitute ['kɑnstɪ ˌt(j)ut] *tr* (*make up*) ausmachen, bilden; (*found*) gründen
constitution [ˌkɑnstɪ't(j)uʃən] *s* (*of a country or organization*) Verfassung *f;* (*bodily condition*) Konstitution *f;* (*composition*) Zusammensetzung *f*
constitutional [ˌkɑnstɪ't(j)uʃənəl] *adj* (*according to a constitution*) konstitutionell; (*crisis, amendment, etc.*) Verfassungs–
constrain [kən'stren] *tr* zwingen
constraint [kən'strent] *s* Zwang *m;* (jur) Nötigung *f*
constrict [kən'strɪkt] *tr* zusammenziehen
construct [kən'strʌkt] *tr* errichten; (eng, geom, gram) konstruieren
construction [kən'strʌkʃən] *s* (*act of building*) Errichtung *f;* (*manner of building*) Bauweise *f;* (*interpretation*) Auslegung *f;* (eng, geom, gram) Konstruktion *f;* **under c.** im Bau
constructive [kən'strʌktɪv] *adj* konstruktiv
construe [kən'stru] *tr* (*interpret*) auslegen; (gram) konstruieren
consul ['kɑnsəl] *s* Konsul *m*
consular ['kɑns(j)ələr] *adj* konsularisch
consulate ['kɑns(j)əlɪt] *s* Konsulat *n*
con'sul gen'eral *s* Generalkonsul *m*
consult [kən'sʌlt] *tr* konsultieren, um Rat fragen; (*a book*) nachschlagen ‖ *intr*—**c. with** sich beraten mit
consultant [kən'sʌltənt] *s* Berater –in *mf*
consultation [ˌkɑnsəl'teʃən] *s* Beratung *f;* (& med) Konsultation *f*
consume [kən's(j)um] *tr* verzehren; (*use up*) verbrauchen; (*time*) beanspruchen
consumer [kən's(j)umər] *s* Konsument –in *mf*, Verbraucher –in *mf*
consum'er goods' *spl* Konsumgüter *pl*
consummate [kən'sʌmɪt] *adj* vollendet; (pej) abgefeimt ‖ ['kɑnsə ˌmet] *tr* vollziehen
consumption [kən'sʌmpʃən] *s* (*of food*) Verzehr *m;* (econ) (*of*) Verbrauch *m* (an *dat*); (pathol) Schwindsucht *f*
consumptive [kə'sʌmptɪv] *adj* schwindsüchtig ‖ *s* Schwindsüchtige *mf*
contact ['kɑntækt] *s* Kontakt *m*, Berührung *f;* (fig) (**with**) Verbindung *f* (mit); (elec) Kontakt *m* ‖ *tr* (coll) sich in Verbindung setzen mit
con'tact lens' *s* Haftschale *f*
contagion [kən'tedʒən] *s* Ansteckung *f*
contagious [kən'tedʒəs] *adj* ansteckend
contain [kən'ten] *tr* enthalten; (an

enemy) aufhalten; (*one's feelings* verhalten; **c. oneself** sich beherrschen
container [kən'tenər] *s* Behälter *m*
containment [kən'tenmənt] *s* (mil pol) Eindämmung *f*
contaminate [kən'tæmɪ ˌnet] *tr* verunreinigen; (fig) vergiften
contamination [kən ˌtæmɪ'neʃən] *s* Verunreinigung *f;* (fig) Vergiftung *f*
contemplate ['kɑntəm ˌplet] *tr* betrachten; (*intend*) beabsichtigen ‖ *intr* nachdenken
contemplation [ˌkɑntəm'pleʃən] *s* Betrachtung *f;* (*consideration*) Erwägung *f*
contemporaneous [kən ˌtempə'renɪ·əs] *adj* (**with**) gleichzeitig (mit)
contemporary [kən'tempə ˌreri] *adj* zeitgenössisch; (*modern*) modern ‖ *s* Zeitgenosse *m*, Zeitgenossin *f*
contempt [kən'tempt] *s* Verachtung *f;* **beneath c.** unter aller Kritik
contemptible [kən'temptɪbəl] *adj* verachtungswürdig
contempt' of court' *s* Mißachtung *f* des Gerichtes
contemptuous [kən'temptʃʊ·əs] *adj* verachtungsvoll, verächtlich
contend [kən'tend] *tr* behaupten ‖ *intr* (**for**) sich bewerben (um); (**with**) kämfen (mit)
contender [kən'tendər] *s* (**for**) Bewerber –in *mf* (um)
content [kən'tent] *adj* (**with**) zufrieden (mit); **c. to** (*inf*) bereit zu (*inf*) ‖ *s* Zufriedenheit *f;* **to one's heart's c.** nach Herzenslust ‖ ['kɑntənt] *s* Inhalt *m;* (chem) Gehalt *m;* contents Inhalt *m* ‖ [kən'tent] *tr* zufriedenstellen; **c. oneself with** sich begnügen mit
content'ed *adj* zufrieden
contention [kən'tenʃən] *s* (*strife*) Streit *m;* (*assertion*) Behauptung *f*
contest ['kɑntest] *s* (**for**) Wettkampf *m* (um); (*written competition*) Preisausschreiben *n* ‖ [kən'test] *tr* (*argue against*) bestreiten; (*a will*) anfechten; (mil) kämpfen um; **contested** umstritten
contestant [kən'tɛstənt] *s* Bewerber –in *mf;* (sport) Wettkämpfer –in *mf*
context ['kɑntekst] *s* Zusammenhang *m*
contiguous [kən'tɪgjʊ·əs] *adj* einander berührend; (**to**) angrenzend (an *acc*)
continence ['kɑntɪnəns] *s* Enthaltsamkeit *f*
continent ['kɑntɪnənt] *adj* enthaltsam ‖ *s* Kontinent *m*
continental [ˌkɑntɪ'nentəl] *adj* kontinental, Kontinental–
contingency [kən'tɪndʒənsi] *s* Zufall *m*
contingent [kən'tɪndʒənt] *adj* (**upon**) abhängig (von) ‖ *s* (mil) Kontingent *n*
continual [kən'tɪnju·əl] *adj* immer wiederkehrend
continuation [kən ˌtɪnju'eʃən] *s* Fortsetzung *f;* (*continued existence*) Fortdauer *f*
continue [kən'tɪnju] *tr* fortsetzen; **c.**

to (*inf*) fortfahren zu (*inf*); weiter-, e.g., **c. to read** weiterlesen; **to be continued** Fortsetzung folgt ‖ *intr* fortfahren; (*said of things*) anhalten

continuity [,kɑntɪ'n(j)u·ɪtɪ] *s* Stetigkeit *f*

continuous [kən'tɪnjʊ·əs] *adj* ununterbrochen, anhaltend

contortion [kən'tɔrʃən] *s* Verzerrung *f*

contour ['kɑntʊr] *s* Kontur *f*

con'tour line' *s* Schichtlinie *f*

con'tour map' *s* Landkarte *f* mit Schichtlinien

contraband ['kɑntrə,bænd] *adj* Schmuggel– ‖ *s* Konterbande *f*, Schmuggelware *f*

contraceptive [,kɑntrə'sɛptɪv] *adj* empfängnisverhütend ‖ *s* Empfängnisverhütungsmittel *n*

contract ['kɑntrækt] *s* Vertrag *m*, Kontrakt *m*; (*order*) Auftrag *m* ‖ [kən'trækt] *tr* (*marriage*) (ab)schließen; (*a disease*) sich [*dat*] zuziehen; (*e g., a muscle*) zusammenziehen; (*debts*) geraten in (*acc*); (ling) kontrahieren ‖ *intr* (*shrink*) sich zusammenziehen; **c. to** (*inf*) sich vertraglich verpflichten zu (*inf*)

contract'ing *adj* vertragsschließend

contraction [kən'trækʃən] *s* (& ling) Zusammenziehung *f*, Kontraktion *f*; (*contracted word*) Verkürzung *f*

contractor ['kɑntræktər] *s* (*supplier*) Lieferant *m*; (*builder*) Bauunternehmer *m*

contradict [,kɑntrə'dɪkt] *tr* widersprechen (*dat*)

contradiction [,kɑntrə'dɪkʃən] *s* Widerspruch *m*

contradictory [,kɑntrə'dɪktəri] *adj* widerspruchsvoll

contrail ['kɑn,trel] *s* Kondensstreifen *m*

contral·to [kən'trælto] *s* (–tos) (*person*) Altistin *f*; (*voice*) Alt *m*

contraption [kən'træpʃən] *s* (coll) Vorrichtung *f*; (*car*) (coll) Kiste *f*

contrary ['kɑntreri] *adj* konträr, gegensätzlich; (*person*) querköpfig; **c. to** entgegen (*dat*); **c. to nature** naturwidrig ‖ *s* Gegenteil *n*; **on the c.** im Gegenteil

contrast ['kɑntræst] *s* Gegensatz *m* ‖ [kən'træst] *tr* (**with**) gegenüberstellen (*dat*) ‖ *intr* (**with**) im Gegensatz stehen (zu)

contravene [,kɑntrə'vin] *tr* zuwiderhandeln (*dat*)

contribute [kən'trɪbjut] *tr* beitragen, spenden ‖ *intr*—**c. to** beitragen zu; (*with help*) mitwirken an (*dat*)

contribution [,kɑntrɪ'bjuʃən] *s* Beitrag *m*; (*of money*) Spende *f*

contributor [kən'trɪbjutər] *s* Spender –in *mf*; (*to a periodical*) Mitarbeiter –in *mf*

contrite [kən'traɪt] *adj* reuig

contrition [kən'trɪʃən] *s* Reue *f*

contrivance [kən'traɪvəns] *s* (*device*) Vorrichtung *f*; (*expedient*) Kunstgriff *m*; (*act of contriving*) Aushecken *n*

contrive [kən'traɪv] *tr* (*invent*) erfin-

den; (*devise*) ersinnen; **c. to** (*inf*) es fertig bringen zu (*inf*) ‖ *intr* Anschläge aushecken

con·trol [kən'trol] *s* Kontrolle *f*, Gewalt *f*; (mach) Steuerung *f*; (mach) (*devise*) Regler *m*; **be out of c.** nicht zu halten sein; **be under c.** in bester Ordnung sein; **controls** (aer) Steuerwerk *n*; **gain c. over** die Herrschaft gewinnen über (*acc*); **have c. over s.o.** über j–n Gewalt haben; **keep under c.** im Zaume halten ‖ *v* (*pret & pp* –**trolled**; *ger* –**trolling**) *tr* (*dominate*) beherrschen; (*verify*) kontrollieren; (*contain*) eindämmen; (*steer*) steuern; (*regulate*) regeln; **c. oneself** sich beherrschen

control' pan'el *s* Schaltbrett *n*

control' room' *s* Kommandoraum *m*; (rad) Regieraum *m*

control' stick' *s* (aer) Steuerknüppel *m*

control' tow'er *s* (*at an airport*) Kontrollturm *m*; (*on an aircraft carrier*) Kommandoturm *m*

controversial [,kɑntrə'vʌrʃəl] *adj* umstritten, strittig; **c. subject** Streitfrage *f*

controversy ['kɑntrə,vʌrsi] *s* Kontroverse *f*, Auseinandersetzung *f*

controvert [,kɑntrə'vʌrt] *tr* (*argue against*) bestreiten; (*argue about*) streiten über (*acc*)

contusion [kən't(j)uʒən] *s* Quetschung *f*

convalesce [,kɑnvə'lɛs] *intr* genesen

convalescence [,kɑnvə'lɛsəns] *s* Genesung *f*

convalescent [,kɑnvə'lɛsənt] *s* Genesende *mf*

convales'cent home' *s* Genesungsheim *n*

convene [kən'vin] *tr* versammeln ‖ *intr* sich versammeln

convenience [kən'vinjəns] *s* Bequemlichkeit *f*; **at one's c.** nach Belieben; **at your earliest c.** möglichst bald; **modern conveniences** moderner Komfort *m*

convenient [kən'vinjənt] *adj* gelegen

convent ['kɑnvɛnt] *s* Nonnenkloster *n*

convention [kən'vɛnʃən] *s* (*professional meeting*) Tagung *f*; (*political meeting*) Konvent *m*; (*accepted usage*) Konvention *f*

conventional [kən'vɛnʃənəl] *adj* konventionell, herkömmlich

converge [kən'vʌrdʒ] *intr* zusammenlaufen; **c. on** sich stürzen auf (*acc*)

conversation [,kɑnvər'seʃən] *s* Gespräch *n*

conversational [,kɑnvər'seʃənəl] *adj* Gesprächs–

converse ['kɑnvʌrs] *adj* gegenteilig ‖ *s* (**of**) Gegenteil *n* (von) ‖ [kən'vʌrs] *intr* sich unterhalten

conversion [kən'vʌrʒən] *s* (**into**) Umwandlung *f* (in *acc*); (*of a factory*) (**to**) Umstellung *f* (auf *acc*); (*of a building*) (**into**) Umbau *m* (zu); (*of currency*) (**into**) Umwechslung *f* (in *acc*); (elec) (**to**) Umformung *f* (in *acc*); (math) Umrechnung *f*; (phys) Umsetzung *f*; (relig) Bekehrung *f*

convert ['kɑnvʌrt] *s* **(to)** Bekehrte *mf* (zu) ‖ [kən'vʌrt] *tr* **(into)** umwandeln (in *acc*); (*a factory*) **(to)** umstellen (auf *acc*); (*a building*) **(into)** umbauen (zu); (*currency*) **(into)** umwechseln (in *acc*); (biochem) **(into)** umsetzen (in *acc*); (chem) **(into)** umwandeln (in *acc*), verwandeln (in *acc*); (elec) **(to)** umformen (in *acc*); (math) **(to)** umrechnen (in *acc*); (phys) **(to)** umsetzen (in *acc*); (relig) **(to)** bekehren (zu) ‖ *intr* **(to)** sich bekehren (zu)

converter [kən'vʌrtər] *s* (elec) Umformer *m*, Stromrichter *m*

convertible [kən'vʌrtɪbəl] *adj* umwandelbar; (fin) konvertierbar ‖ *s* (aut) Kabriolett *n*

convex ['kɑnvɛks], [kɑn'vɛks] *adj* konvex

convey [kən've] *tr* (*transport*) befördern; (*greetings, message*) übermitteln; (*sound*) fortpflanzen; (*meaning*) ausdrücken; (*a property*) abtreten

conveyance [kən've·əns] *s* (*act*) Beförderung *f*; (*means*) Transportmittel *n*; (jur) Abtretung *f*

conveyor [kən've·ər] *s* Beförderer –in *mf*

convey'or belt' *s* Förderband *n*

convict ['kɑnvɪkt] *s* Sträfling *m* ‖ [kən'vɪkt] *tr* (**of**) überführen (*genit*)

conviction [kən'vɪkʃən] *s* (*of a crime*) Verurteilung *f*; (*certainty*) Überzeugung *f*; **convictions** Gesinnung *f*

convince [kən'vɪns] *tr* (**of**) überzeugen (von)

convivial [kən'vɪvɪ·əl] *adj* gesellig

convocation [ˌkɑnvə'keʃən] *s* Zusammenberufung *f*; (educ) Eröffnungsfeier *f*

convoke [kən'vok] *tr* zusammenberufen

convoy ['kɑnvɔɪ] *s* (*of vehicles*) Kolonne *f*, Konvoi *m*; (nav) Geleitzug *m*

convulse [kən'vʌls] *tr* erschüttern

convulsion [kən'vʌlʃən] *s* Krampf *m*; **go into convulsions** Krämpfe bekommen

coo [ku] *intr* girren

cook [kʊk] *s* Koch *m*, Köchin *f* ‖ *tr* braten, backen; (*boil*) kochen; **c. up** (fig) zusammenbrauen ‖ *intr* braten, backen; (*boil*) kochen

cook'book' *s* Kochbuch *n*

cookie ['kʊki] *s* Plätzchen *n*, Keks *m* & *n*; **cookies** *pl* Gebäck *n*

cook'ing *s* Kochen *n*; **do one's own c.** sich selbst beköstigen

cool [kul] *adj* (& fig) kühl; **keep c.!** ruhig Blut!; **keep one's c.** (coll) ruhig Blut bewahren ‖ *s* Kühle *f* ‖ *tr* kühlen; **c. down** (fig) beruhigen; **c. off** abkühlen ‖ *intr* (& fig) sich abkühlen

cooler ['kulər] *s* Kühler *m*; (sl) Kittchen *n*

cool'-head'ed *adj* besonnen

coolie ['kuli] *s* Kuli *m*

coolness ['kulnɪs] *s* (& fig) Kühle *f*

coon [kun] *s* (zool) Waschbär *m*

coop [kup] *s* (*building*) Hühnerstall *m* (*enclosure*) Hühnerhof *m*; (*jail*) (sl Kittchen *n*; **fly the c.** (sl) auskneifer ‖ *tr*—**c. up** einsperren

co-op ['ko·ɑp] *s* Konsumverein *m*

cooper ['kupər] *s* Küfer *m*, Böttcher *n*

cooperate [ko'ɑpə‚ret] *intr* **(in)** mit wirken (an *dat*, bei); **(with)** mit arbeiten (mit)

cooperation [ko‚ɑpə're ʃən] *s* Mit wirkung *f*, Mitarbeit *f*

cooperative [ko'ɑpə‚retɪv] *adj* hilfs bereit

coordinate [ko'ɔrdɪnɪt] *adj* gleichrangig; (gram) beigeordnet ‖ *s* (math) Koordinate *f* ‖ [ko'ɔrdɪ‚net] *tr* koordinieren

coordination [ko‚ɔrdɪ'ne ʃən] *s* Koordination *f*; (gram) Beiordnung *f*

cootie ['kuti] *s* (sl) Laus *f*

co-owner ['ko‚onər] *s* Miteigentümer –in *mf*

cop [kɑp] *s* (sl) Bulle *m* ‖ *v* (*pret & pp* **copped**; *ger* **copped**) *tr* (*catch*) (sl) erwischen; (*steal*) (sl) klauen ‖ *intr*—**cop out** (coll) auskneifen

copartner [ko'pɑrtnər] *s* Mitinhaber –in *mf*

cope [kop] *intr*—**c. with** sich messen mit, aufkommen gegen

cope'stone' *s* Schlußstein *m*

copier ['kɑpɪ·ər] *s* Kopiermaschine *f*

copilot ['ko‚paɪlət] *s* Kopilot *m*

coping ['kopɪŋ] *s* Mauerkappe *f*

copious ['kopɪ·əs] *adj* reichlich

cop'-out' *s* (*act*) Kneifen *n*; (*person*) Drückeberger *m*

copper ['kɑpər] *adj* kupfern, Kupfer–; (*color*) kupferrot ‖ *s* Kupfer *n*; (*coin*) Kupfermünze *f*; (sl) Schupo *m*

cop'persmith' *s* Kupferschmied *m*

copter ['kɑptər] *s* (coll) Hubschrauber *m*

copulate ['kɑpjə‚let] *intr* sich paaren

cop·y ['kɑpi] *s* Kopie *f*; (*of a book*) Exemplar *n*; (typ) druckfertiges Manuskript *n* ‖ *v* (*pret & pp* **–ied**) *tr* kopieren; (*in school*) abschreiben

cop'ybook' *s* Schreibheft *n*, Heft *n*

cop'ycat' *s* (*imitator*) Nachäffer –in *mf*

cop'yright' *s* Urheberrecht *n*, Verlagsrecht *n* ‖ *tr* urheberrechtlich schützen, verlagsrechtlich schützen

cop'ywrit'er *s* Texter –in *mf*

coquette [ko'ket] *s* Kokette *f*

coquettish [ko'ketɪʃ] *adj* kokett

coral ['kɔrəl] *adj* Korallen– ‖ *s* Koralle *f*

cor'al reef' *s* Korallenriff *n*

cord [kɔrd] *s* Schnur *f*, Strick *m*; (*of wood*) Klafter *n*; (elec) Leitungsschnur *f*

cordial ['kɔrdʒəl] *adj* herzlich ‖ *s* Likör *m*; (med) Herzstärkung *f*

cordiality [kɔr'dʒælɪti] *s* Herzlichkeit *f*

cordon ['kɔrdən] *s* Kordon *m*, Absperrkette *f* ‖ *tr*—**c. off** absperren

corduroy ['kɔrdə‚rɔɪ] *s* Kordsamt *m*; **corduroys** Kordsamthose *f*

core [kor] *s* (*of fruit*) Kern *m*; (*of a*

cable) Seele *f;* (fig) Kern *m,* Mark *n;* (elec) Spulenkern *m*
cork [kɔrk] *s* Kork *m;* (*stopper*) Pfropfen *m,* Korken *m* || *tr* verkorken
corker ['kɔrkər] *s* (sl) Schlager *m*
cork'ing *adj* (sl) fabelhaft
cork'oak', cork' tree' *s* Korkeiche *f*
cork'screw' *s* Korkenzieher *m*
corn [kɔrn] *s* (*Indian corn*) Mais *m;* (*on a foot*) Hühnerauge *n;* (*joke*) (sl) Kalauer *m*
corn'bread' *s* Maisbrot *n*
corn'cob' *s* Maiskolben *m*
corn'cob pipe' *s* Maiskolbenpfeife *f*
corn'crib' *s* Maisspeicher *m*
cornea ['kɔrnɪ·ə] *s* Hornhaut *f*
corned' beef' ['kɔrnd] *s* Pökelfleisch *n*
corner ['kɔrnər] *adj* Eck– || *s* Ecke *f;* (*secluded spot*) Winkel *m;* (*curve*) Kurve *f;* **c. of the eye** Augenwinkel *m;* **from all corners of the world** von allen Ecken und Enden; **turn the c.** um die Ecke biegen || *tr* (*a person*) in die Zange nehmen; (*the market*) aufkaufen
cor'nerstone' *s* Eckstein *m;* (*of a new building*) Grundstein *m*
cornet [kɔr'nɛt] *s* (mus) Kornett *n*
corn' exchange' *s* Getreidebörse *f*
corn'field' *s* Maisfeld *n;* (*grain field*) (Brit) Kornfeld *n*
corn'flakes' *spl* Maisflocken *pl*
corn' flour' *s* Maismehl *n*
corn'flow'er *s* Kornblume *f*
corn' frit'ter *s* Maispfannkuchen *m*
corn'husk' *s* Maishülse *f*
cornice ['kɔrnɪs] *s* Gesims *n*
corn' liq'uor *s* Maisschnaps *m*
corn' meal' *s* Maismehl *n*
corn' on the cob' *s* Mais *m* am Kolben
corn' silk' *s* Maisfasern *pl*
corn'stalk' *s* Maisstengel *m*
corn'starch' *s* Maisstärke *f*
cornucopia [,kɔrnə'kopɪ·ə] *s* Füllhorn *n*
corny ['kɔrni] *adj* (*sentimental*) rührselig; (*joke*) blöd
corollary ['kɔrə,lɛri] *s* (**to**) Folge *f* (*von*)
coron·a [kə'ronə] *s* (**–nas** & **–nae** [ni]) (astr) Hof *m,* Korona *f;* (archit) Kranzleiste *f*
coronary ['kɔrə,nɛri] *adj* koronar
coronation [,kɔrə'neʃən] *s* Krönung *f*
coroner ['kɔrənər] *s* Gerichtsmediziner *m*
cor'oner's in'quest *s* Totenschau *f*
coronet ['kɔrə,nɛt] *s* Krönchen *n;* (*worn by the nobility*) Adelskrone *f;* (*worn by women*) Diadem *n*
corporal ['kɔrpərəl] *adj* körperlich || *s* (mil) Obergefreite *m*
corporate ['kɔrpərɪt] *adj* korporativ
corporation [,kɔrpə'reʃən] *s* (fin) Aktiengesellschaft *f;* (jur) Körperschaft *f*
corpora'tion law'yer *s* Syndikus *m*
corporeal [kɔr'porɪ·əl] *adj* körperlich
corps [kor] *s* (**corps** [korz]) Korps *n*
corpse [kɔrps] *s* Leiche *f,* Leichnam *m*
corps'man *s* (**–men**) Sanitäter *m*
corpulent ['kɔrpjələnt] *adj* beleibt

corpuscle ['kɔrpəsəl] *s* Blutkörperchen *n*
cor·ral [ke'ræl] *s* Pferch *m* || *v* (*pret* & *pp* **–ralled;** *ger* **–ralling**) *tr* zusammenpferchen
correct [kə'rɛkt] *adj* richtig; (*manners*) korrekt; (*time*) genau; **be c.** (*said of a thing*) stimmen; (*said of a person*) recht haben || *tr* korrigieren; (*examination papers*) verbessern; (*beat*) züchtigen; (*scold*) zurechtweisen; (*an unjust situation*) ausgleichen
correction [kə'rɛkʃən] *s* Berichtigung *f;* (*of examination papers*) Verbesserung *f,* Korrektur *f;* (*punishment*) Bestrafung *f*
corrective [kə'rɛktɪv] *adj* (*measures*) Gegen–; (*lenses, shoes*) Ausgleichs–
correctness [kə'rɛktnɪs] *s* Richtigkeit *f;* (*in manners*) Korrektheit *f*
correlate ['kɔrə,let] *tr* in Wechselbeziehung bringen || *intr* in Wechselbeziehung stehen
correlation [,kɔrə'leʃən] *s* Wechselbeziehung *f,* Korrelation *f*
correlative [kə'rɛlətɪv] *adj* korrelativ || *s* Korrelat *n*
correspond [,kɔrɪ'spand] *intr* einander übereinstimmen; (**to, with**) entsprechen (*dat*); (*exchange letters*) (**with**) im Briefwechsel stehen (mit)
correspondence [,kɔrɪ'spandəns] *s* (*act of corresponding*) Übereinstimmung *f;* (*instance of correspondence*) Entsprechung *f;* (*exchange of letters; letters*) Korrespondenz *f*
correspon'dence course' *s* Fernkursus *m*
correspondent [,kɔrɪ'spandənt] *s* Briefpartner **–in** *mf;* (journ) Korrespondent **–in** *mf*
correspond'ing *adj* entsprechend
corridor ['kɔrɪdər] *s* Korridor *m*
corroborate [kə'rabə,ret] *tr* bestätigen
corrode [kə'rod] *tr* & *intr* korrodieren
corrosion [kə'roʒən] *s* Korrosion *f*
corrosive [kə'rosɪv] *adj* ätzend; (*influence*) schädigend || *s* Ätzmittel *n*
cor'rugated card'board ['kɔrə,getɪd] *s* Wellpappe *f*
cor'rugated i'ron *s* Wellblech *n*
corrupt [kə'rʌpt] *adj* (*text*) verderbt; (*morally*) verdorben; (*open to bribes*) bestechlich || *tr* verderben; (*bribe*) bestechen
corruption [kə'rʌpʃən] *s* Verderbtheit *f;* (*bribery*) Korruption *f*
corsage [kɔr'saʒ] *s* Blumensträußchen *n* zum Anstecken
corsair ['kɔrsɛr] *s* Korsar *m*
corset ['kɔrsɪt] *s* Korsett *n*
Corsica ['kɔrsɪkə] *s* Korsika *n*
Corsican ['kɔrsɪkən] *adj* korsisch
cortege [kɔr'teʒ] *s* Gefolge *n;* (*at a funeral*) Leichenzug *m*
cor·tex ['kɔr,tɛks] *s* (**–tices** [tɪ,siz]) Rinde *f,* Kortex *m*
cortisone ['kɔrtɪ,son] *s* Cortison *n*
corvette [kɔr'vɛt] *s* (naut) Korvette *f*
cosmetic [kaz'mɛtɪk] *adj* kosmetisch || *s* Kosmetikum *n;* **cosmetics** Kosmetikartikel *pl*

cosmic ['kazmɪk] adj kosmisch
cosmonaut ['kazmə,nɔt] s Kosmonaut –in mf
cosmopolitan [,kazə'palɪtən] adj kosmopolitisch || s Kosmopolit –in mf
cosmos ['kazməs] s Kosmos m
cost [kɔst] s Preis m; **at all costs** (fig) um jeden Preis; **at c.** zum Selbstkostenpreis; **at the c. of** auf Kosten (genit); **costs** Kosten pl; (jur) Gerichtskosten pl || v (pret & pp cost) intr kosten
cost' account'ing s Kostenrechnung f
costly ['kɔstlɪ] adj kostspielig; (of great value) kostbar
cost' of liv'ing s Lebenshaltungskosten pl
costume ['kast(j)um] s Kostüm n; (national dress) Tracht f
cos'tume ball' s Kostümball m
cos'tume jew'elry s Modeschmuck m
cot [kat] s Feldbett n
coterie ['kotəri] s Klüngel m, Koterie f
cottage ['katɪdʒ] s Hütte f; (country house) Landhaus n
cot'tage cheese' s Quark m, Quarkkäse m
cot'ter pin' ['katər] s Schließbolzen m
cotton ['katən] s (fiber, yarn) Baumwolle f; (unspun cotton) Watte f; (sterilized cotton) Verbandswatte f
cot'ton field' s Baumwollfeld n
cot'ton gin' s Entkörnungsmaschine f
cot'ton mill' s Baumwollspinnerei f
cot'ton pick'er ['pɪkər] s Baumwollpflücker –in mf; (machine) Baumwollpflückmaschine f
cot'tonseed oil' s Baumwollsamenöl n
cot'ton waste' s Putzwolle f
couch [kautʃ] s Couch f, Liege f || tr (words) fassen; (thoughts) ausdrücken
cougar ['kugər] s Puma m
cough [kɔf] s Husten m || tr—c. up aushusten; (money) (sl) blechen || intr husten; (in order to attract attention) sich räuspern
cough' drop' s Hustenbonbon m & n
cough' syr'up s Hustentropfen pl
could [kud] aux—he c. (was able) er konnte; if he c. (were able) wenn er könnte
council ['kaunsəl] s Rat m; (eccl) Konzil n
coun'cil·man s (–men) Stadtratsmitglied n
councilor ['kaunsələr] s Rat m
coun·sel ['kaunsəl] s Rat m; (for the defense) Verteidiger –in mf; (for the prosecution) Anklagevertreter –in mf || v (pret & pp –sel[l]ed; ger –sel[l]ing) tr raten (dat) || intr Rat geben
counselor ['kaunsələr] s Berater –in mf
count [kaunt] s Zahl f; (nobleman) Graf m; (jur) Anklagepunkt m; lose c. sich verzählen || tr zählen; (the costs) berechnen; c. in einschließen; c. off abzählen; c. out (money, a boxer) auszählen || intr zählen; c. for little (or much) wenig (or viel)

gelten; **c. off** (mil) abzählen; **c. on** zählen auf (acc)
count'down' s Countdown m & n
countenance ['kauntɪnəns] s Antlitz n || tr (tolerate) zulassen; (approve) billigen
counter ['kauntər] adj Gegen– || adv —c. to wider; run c. to zuwiderlaufen (dat) || s Zähler m; (in games) Spielmarke f; (in a store) Ladentisch m, Theke f; (in a restaurant) Büffet n; (in a bank) Schalter m; under the c. (fig) heimlich || tr widerstreben (dat); (in speech) widersprechen (dat) || intr Gegenmaßnahmen treffen; (box) kontern, nachschlagen
coun'teract' tr entgegenwirken (dat)
coun'terattack' s Gegenangriff m || coun'terattack' tr e–n Gegenangriff machen auf (acc) || intr e–n Gegenangriff machen
coun'terbal'ance s Gegengewicht n || coun'terbal'ance tr das Gegengewicht halten (dat)
coun'terclock'wise adj linksläufig || adv entgegen der Uhrzeigerrichtung
coun'teres'pionage s Gegenspionage f
counterfeit ['kauntərfɪt] adj gefälscht || s Fälschung f; (money) Falschgeld n || tr fälschen
counterfeiter ['kauntər,fɪtər] s Falschmünzer –in mf
coun'terfeit mon'ey s Falschgeld n
coun'terintel'ligence s Spionageabwehr f
countermand ['kauntər,mænd] s Gegenbefehl m || tr widerrufen
coun'termeas'ure s Gegenmaßnahme f
coun'teroffen'sive s Gegenoffensive f
coun'terpart' s Gegenstück n; (person) Ebenbild n
coun'terpoint' s (mus) Kontrapunkt m
coun'terrevolu'tion s Konterrevolution f
coun'tersign' s Gegenzeichen n || tr & intr mitunterzeichnen
coun'tersink' v (pret & pp –sunk) tr (a screw) versenken; (a hole) ausfräsen
coun'terspy' s Gegenspion –in mf
coun'terstroke' s Gegenstoß m
coun'terweight' s Gegengewicht n
countess ['kauntɪs] s Gräfin f
countless ['kauntlɪs] adj zahllos
countrified ['kʌntri,faɪd] adj ländlich; (boorish) bäu(e)risch
country ['kʌntri] adj (air, house, life, road) Land– || s (state; rural area) Land n; (land of birth) Heimatland n; in the c. auf dem Lande; to the c. aufs Land
coun'try club' s exklusiver Klub m auf dem Lande
coun'tryfolk' spl Landvolk n
coun'try gen'tleman s Landedelmann m
coun'try·man s (–men) Landsmann m
coun'tryside' s Landschaft f, Land n
coun'try-wide' adj über das ganze Land verbreitet (or ausgedehnt)
county ['kaunti] s Kreis m
coun'ty seat' s Kreisstadt f

coup [ku] *s* Coup *m*
coup d'état [ku de 'ta] *s* Staatsstreich *m*
coupe [ku'pe], [kup] *s* Coupé *n*
couple ['kʌpəl] *s* Paar *n; (of lovers)* Liebespaar *n; (man and wife)* Ehepaar *n;* (phys) Kräftepaar *n;* **a c. of** ein paar, e.g., **a c. of days ago** vor ein paar Tagen || *tr* koppeln || *intr* sich paaren
couplet ['kʌplɪt] *s* Verspaar *n*
coupling ['kʌplɪŋ] *s* Verbindungsstück *n;* (rad) Kopplung *f;* (rr) Kupplung *f*
coupon ['k(j)upɑn] *s* Gutschein *m*
courage ['kʌrɪdʒ] *s* Mut *m,* Courage *f;* **get up the c. to** *(inf)* sich *[dat]* ein Herz fassen zu *(inf)*
courageous [kə'redʒəs] *adj* mutig
courier ['kʌrɪ·ər] *s* Eilbote *m; (tour guide)* Reiseleiter –in *mf*
course [kors] *s (direction)* Richtung *f,* Kurs *m; (of a river, of time)* Lauf *m; (method of procedure)* Weg *m,* Weise *f,* Kurs *m,* (in racing) Bahn *f;* (archit) Schicht *f;* (culin) Gang *m;* (educ) Kurs *m;* **c. of action** Handlungsweise *f;* **go off c.** (aer) sich verfliegen; **in due c.** zur rechten Zeit; **in the c. of** im Verlaufe von (or *genit*); **(with expressions of time)** im Laufe (*genit*); **of c.** natürlich; **run its c.** seinen Verlauf nehmen
court [kort] *s (of a king)* Hof *m; (of justice)* Gericht *n;* (yard) Hof *m;* (tennis) Platz *m;* **in c.** (or **into c.** or **to c.**) vor Gericht; **out of c.** außergerichtlich || *tr (a girl)* werben um; *(danger)* suchen; *(disaster)* heraufbeschwören
courteous ['kʌrtɪ·əs] *adj* höflich
courtesan ['kortɪʒən] *s* Kurtisane *f*
courtesy ['kʌrtɪsi] *s* Höflichkeit *f;* **by c. of** freundlicherweise zur Verfügung gestellt von
court'house' *s* Gerichtsgebäude *n*
courtier ['kortɪ·ər] *s* Höfling *m*
court' jest'er *s* Hofnarr *m*
courtly ['kortli] *adj* höfisch
court'-mar'tial *s* (courts-martial) Kriegsgericht *n* || *v (pret & pp* –tial[l]ed; *ger* –tial[l]ing) *tr* vor ein Kriegsgericht stellen
court'room' *s* Gerichtssaal *m*
court'ship' *s* Werbung *f*
court'yard' *s* Hof *m*
cousin ['kʌzɪn] *s* Vetter *m; (female)* Kusine *f*
cove [kov] *s* Bucht *f*
covenant ['kʌvənənt] *s* Vertrag *m;* (Bib) Bund *m*
cover ['kʌvər] *s* Decke *f; (lid)* Deckel *m; (wrapping)* Hülle *f; (e.g., of a bed)* Bezug *m; (of a book)* Einband *m; (protection)* Schutz *m;* (mil) Deckung *f;* **from c. to c.** von vorn bis hinten; **take c.** sich unterstellen; **under c.** im Geheimen; **under c. of night** im Schutz der Dunkelheit || *tr* bedecken, decken; *(conceal)* verdecken; *(distances)* zurücklegen; *(a sales territory)* bearbeiten; *(a bet)* die gleiche Summe setzen gegen; *(ex-*

penses, losses) decken; *(upholstered furniture)* beziehen; *(deal with)* behandeln; *(include)* umfassen; *(material in class)* durchnehmen; *(said of a reporter)* berichten über *(acc);* **(said of plants)** bewachsen; *(with insurance)* versichern, decken; *(protect with a gun)* sichern; *(threaten with a gun)* in Schach halten; *(have within range)* beherrschen; **c. up** zudecken; *(conceal)* verheimlichen || *intr*—**c. for** einspringen für
coverage ['kʌvərɪdʒ] *s (area covered)* Verbreitungsgebiet *n; (of news)* Berichterstattung *f;* (ins) Versicherungsschutz *m;* (rad, telv) Sendebereich *m*
coveralls ['kʌvər‚ɔlz] *spl* Monteuranzug *m*
cov'ered wag'on *s* Planwagen *m*
cov'er girl' *s* Covergirl *n*
cov'ering *s* Decke *f,* Bedeckung *f*
covert ['kovərt] *adj* verborgen
cov'erup' *s* Beschönigung *f,* Bemäntelung *f*
covet ['kʌvɪt] *tr* begehren
covetous ['kʌvɪtəs] *adj* begehrlich
covetousness ['kʌvɪtəsnɪs] *s* Begehrlichkeit *f*
covey ['kʌvɪ] *s (brood)* Brut *f; (small flock)* Schwarm *m; (bevy)* Schar *f*
cow [kau] *s* Kuh *f* || *tr* einschüchtern
coward ['kau·ərd] *s* Feigling *m,* Memme *f*
cowardice ['kau·ərdɪs] *s* Feigheit *f*
cowardly ['kau·ərdli] *adj* feig(e)
cow'bell' *s* Kuhglocke *f*
cow'boy' *s* Cowboy *m*
cower ['kau·ər] *intr* kauern
cow'herd' *s* Kuhhirt *m*
cow'hide' *s* Rindsleder *n*
cowl [kaul] *s (on a chimney)* Schornsteinkappe *f;* (aer) Motorhaube *f;* (eccl) Kapuze *f*
cowling ['kaulɪŋ] *s* (aer) Motorhaube *f*
co-worker ['ko ‚wʌrkər] *s* Mitarbeiter –in *mf*
cowpox ['kau ‚pɑks] *s* Kuhpocken *pl*
coxswain ['kɑksən] *s* Steuermann *m*
coy [kɔɪ] *adj* spröde
coyote [kaɪ'oti], ['kaɪ·ot] *s* Kojote *m,* Präriewolf *m,* Steppenwolf *m*
cozy ['kozi] *adj* gemütlich
C.P.A. ['si'pi'e] *s* (certified public accountant) amtlich zugelassener Wirtschaftsprüfer *m*
crab [kræb] *s* Krabbe *f; (grouch)* Sauertopf *m*
crab' ap'ple *s* Holzapfel *m*
crabbed ['kræbɪd] *adj* mürrisch; *(handwriting)* unleserlich; *(style)* schwer verständlich, verworren
crabby ['kræbi] *adj* mürrisch, grämlich
crack [kræk] *adj* erstklassig; *(troops)* Elite– || *s* Riß *m,* Sprung *m; (of a whip or rifle)* Knall *m; (blow)* (sl) Klaps *m; (opportunity)* (sl) Gelegenheit *f; (try)* (sl) Versuch *m; (cutting remark)* (sl) Seitenhieb *m;* **at the c. of dawn** bei Tagesanbruch; **take a c. at** (sl) versuchen || *tr* spalten; *(a nut, safe)* knacken; *(an egg)* aufschlagen;

(*a code*) entziffern; (*hit*) (sl) e–n Klaps geben (*dat*); (chem) spalten; **c. a joke** e–n Witz reißen; **c. a smile** lächeln ‖ *intr* (*make a cracking sound*) knacken, krachen; (*develop a crack*) rissig werden; (*said of a whip or rifle*) knallen; (*said of a voice*) umschlagen; (*said of ice*) (zer) springen; **c. down on** scharf vorgehen gegen; **c. up** (coll) überschnappen; (aut) aufknallen
cracked *adj* (*split*) rissig; (*crazy*) (sl) übergeschnappt
cracker ['krækər] *s* Keks *m* & *n*
crack'erjack' *adj* (coll) erstklassig ‖ *s* (coll) Kanone *f*
crackle ['krækəl] *s* Krakelierung *f* ‖ *tr* krakelieren ‖ *intr* prasseln
crack'pot' *adj* (sl) verrückt ‖ *s* (sl) Verrückte *mf*
crack' shot' *s* Meisterschütze *m*
crack'-up' *s* (aut) Zusammenstoß *m*
cradle ['kredəl] *s* Wiege *f;* (telp) Gabel *f* ‖ *tr* in den Armen wiegen
craft [kræft] *s* Handwerk *n*, Gewerbe *n;* (naut) Fahrzeug *n;* **by c.** durch List ‖ *spl* Fahrzeuge *pl*, Schiffe *pl;* **small c.** kleine Schiffe *pl*
craftiness ['kræftɪnɪs] *s* List *f*
crafts·man ['kræftsmən] *s* (**–men**) Handwerker *m*
crafts'manship' *s* Kunstfertigkeit *f*
crafty ['kræfti] *adj* arglistig
crag [kræg] *s* Felszacke *f*
cram [kræm] *v* (*pret & pp* **crammed;** *ger* **cramming**) *tr* vollstopfen; **c. into** hineinstopfen in (*acc*) ‖ *intr* (educ) büffeln, ochsen; **c. into** sich hineinzwängen in (*acc*)
cram' course' *s* Presse *f*
cramp [kræmp] *s* Krampf *m;* (*clamp*) Klammer *f* ‖ *tr* einschränken, beengen
cramped *adj* eng
cranberry ['kræn ‚bɛri] *s* Preiselbeere *f*
crane [kren] *s* (mach) Kran *m;* (orn) Kranich *m* ‖—**c. one's neck** den Hals recken
crani·um ['kreni·əm] *s* (**–a** [ə]) *s* Hirnschale *f*, Schädel *m*
crank [kræŋk] *s* Kurbel *f;* (*grouch*) (coll) Griesgram *m;* (*eccentric*) (coll) Sonderling *m* ‖ *tr* kurbeln; **c. up** ankurbeln
crank'case' *s* Kurbelgehäuse *n*
crank'shaft' *s* Kurbelwelle *f*
cranky ['kræŋki] *adj* launisch
cranny ['kræni] *s* Ritze *f*
crap [kræp] *s* (*nonsense*) (sl) Unsinn *m;* **craps** Würfel *pl;* **shoot craps** Würfel spielen
crash [kræʃ] *s* Krach *m;* (aer) Absturz *m;* (aut) Zusammenstoß *m;* (econ) Zusammenbruch *m* ‖ *tr* zerschmettern; (*a party*) hineinplatzen in (*acc*); (aer) zum Absturz bringen ‖ *intr* (*produce a crashing sound*) krachen; (*shatter*) zerbrechen; (*collapse*) zusammenstürzen; (aer) abstürzen; (aut) zusammenstoßen; **c. into** fahren gegen
crash' dive' *s* Schnelltauchen *n*

crash'-dive' *intr* schnelltauchen
crash' hel'met *s* Sturzhelm *m*
crash' land'ing *s* Bruchlandung *f*
crash' pro'gram *s* Gewaltkur *f*
crass [kræs] *adj* kraß
crate [kret] *s* Lattenkiste *f;* (*old car, old plane*) (coll) Kiste *f* ‖ *tr* in e–r Lattenkiste verpacken
crater ['kretər] *s* Krater *m;* (*of a bomb*) Trichter *m*
crave [krev] *tr* ersehnen ‖ *intr*—**c. for** verlangen nach
craven ['krevən] *adj* feige ‖ *s* Feigling *m*
crav'ing *s* (for) Verlangen *n* (nach)
craw [krɔ] *s* Kropf *m*
crawl [krɔl] *s* Kriechen *n* ‖ *intr* kriechen; (*said of the skin*) kribbeln; (*said of a swimmer*) kraulen; (*said of cars*) schleichen; **c. along** im Schneckentempo gehen (or fahren); **c. into a hole** (& fig) sich verkriechen; **c. with** wimmeln von
crayon ['kre·ən] *s* (*wax crayon*) Wachsmalkreide *f;* (*colored pencil*) Farbstift *m;* (*artist's crayon*) Zeichenkreide *f*
craze [krez] *s* Mode *f*, Verrücktheit *f* ‖ *tr* verrückt machen
crazy ['krezi] *adj* verrückt; (*senseless*) sinnlos; **c. about** verrückt nach; **c. idea** Wahnidee *f;* **drive c.** verrückt machen
cra'zy bone' *s* Musikantenknochen *m*
creak [krik] *s* (*high-pitched sound*) Quietschen *n;* (*low-pitched sound*) Knarren *n* ‖ *intr* quietschen; knarren
creaky ['kriki] *adj* quietschend; knarrend
cream [krim] *adj* Sahne-, Rahm-; (*color*) creme, cremefarben ‖ *s* Sahne *f*, Rahm *m;* (*cosmetic*) Creme *f;* (*color*) Cremefarbe *f;* (fig) Creme *f* ‖ *tr* (*milk*) abrahmen; (*trounce*) (sl) schlagen
cream' cheese' *s* Rahmkäse *m*, Sahnekäse *m*
creamery ['kriməri] *s* Molkerei *f*
cream' pit'cher *s* Sahnekännchen *n*
cream' puff' *s* Windbeutel *m*
cream' sep'arator *s* Milchschleuder *f*, Milchzentrifuge *f*
creamy ['krimi] *adj* sahnig
crease [kris] *s* Falte *f;* (*in trousers*) Bügelfalte *f* ‖ *tr* falten; (*trousers*) bügeln ‖ *intr* knittern
create [kri'et] *tr* (er)schaffen; (*excitement, an impression*) hervorrufen; (*noise*) verursachen; (*appoint*) ernennen, machen zu; (*a role, fashions*) kreieren
creation [kri'eʃən] *s* Schaffung *f;* (*of the world*) Schöpfung *f;* (*in fashions*) Modeschöpfung *f*
creative [kri'etɪv] *adj* schöpferisch
creator [kri'etər] *s* Schöpfer *m*
creature ['kritʃər] *s* Kreatur *f*, Geschöpf *n;* **every living c.** jedes Lebewesen *n*
credence ['kridəns] *s* Glaube *m*
credentials [krɪ'dɛn/əlz] *spl* Beglaubigungsschreiben *n*, Akkreditiv *n*
credenza [krɪ'dɛnzə] *s* Kredenz *f*

credibility [ˌkrɛdɪ'bɪlɪti] s Glaubwürdigkeit f
credibil'ity gap' s Vertrauenslücke f
credible ['krɛdɪbəl] adj glaubwürdig
credit ['krɛdɪt] s (credence) Glaube m; (honor) Ehre f; (recognition) Anerkennung f; (educ) Anrechnungspunkt m; (fin) Kredit m; (credit balance) (fin) Guthaben n; **be a c.** **to** Ehre machen (dat); **credits** (cin) Vorspann m; **give s.o. c. for s.th.** j-m etw hoch anrechnen; **on c.** auf Kredit; **on thirty days' c.** auf dreißig Tage Ziel; **take c. for** sich [dat] als Verdienst anrechnen; **to s.o.'s c.** zu j-s Ehre ‖ tr (believe) glauben (dat); (an account) gutschreiben (dat); **c. s.o. with s.th.** j-m etw hoch anrechnen
creditable ['krɛdɪtəbəl] adj ehrenwert
cre'dit card' s Kreditkarte f
cre'dit hour' s (educ) Anrechnungspunkt m
creditor ['krɛdɪtər] s Gläubiger –in mf
cre'dit rat'ing s Bonität f
credulous ['krɛdʒələs] adj leichtgläubig
creed [krid] s (& fig) Glaubensbekenntnis n
creek [krik] s Bach m
creep [krip] s Kriechen n; (sl) Spinner m; **it gives me the creeps** mir gruselt ‖ v (pret & pp **crept** [krɛpt]) intr kriechen, schleichen; (said of plants) kriechen; **c. along** dahinschleichen; **c. up on** heranschleichen an (acc); **it makes my flesh c.** es macht mich schaudern
creeper ['kripər] s Kletterpflanze f
creepy ['kripi] adj schaudererregend; (sensation) gruselig; **have a c. feeling** gruseln
cremate ['krimet] tr einäschern
cremation [krɪ'meʃən] s Einäscherung f
crematory ['krimə,tori] s Krematorium n
crepe [krep] s Krepp m; (mourning band) Trauerflor m
crepe' pa'per s Kreppapier n
crescent ['krɛsənt] s Mondsichel f
cres'cent roll' s Hörnchen n
cress [krɛs] s (bot) Kresse f
crest [krɛst] s (of a hill, wave, or rooster) Kamm m; (of a helmet) Helmbusch m; (of a bird) Federbüschel n
crestfallen ['krɛst,fɔlən] adj niedergeschlagen
Crete [krit] s Kreta n
crevice ['krɛvɪs] s Riß m
crew [kru] s Gruppe f; (aer, nav) Besatzung f; (of a boat) (sport) Mannschaft f; (rowing) (sport) Rudersport m
crew' cut' s Bürstenschnitt m
crib [krɪb] s (manger) Krippe f; (for children) Kinderbettstelle f; (bin) Speicher m; (student's pony) Eselsbrücke f ‖ v (pret & pp **cribbed;** ger **cribbing**) tr & intr abbohren
cricket ['krɪkɪt] s (ent) Grille f;

(sport) Kricketspiel n; **not c.** (coll) nicht fair
crime [kraɪm] s Verbrechen n
criminal ['krɪmɪnəl] adj verbrecherisch; (act, case, code, court, law) Straf–; (investigation, trial, police) Kriminal– ‖ s Verbrecher –in mf
crim'inal charge' s Strafanzeige f
crim'inal neg'ligence s grobe Fahrlässigkeit f
crim'inal offense' s strafbare Handlung f
crim'inal rec'ord s Strafregister n
crimp [krɪmp] s Welle f; **put a c. in** (coll) e-n Dämpfer aufsetzen (dat) ‖ tr wellen, riffeln
crimson ['krɪmzən] adj karmesinrot ‖ s Karmesin n
cringe [krɪndʒ] intr sich krümmen; (fawn) kriechen
crinkle ['krɪŋkəl] s Runzel f ‖ tr runzeln; (one's nose) rümpfen
cripple ['krɪpəl] s Krüppel m ‖ tr verkrüppeln; (fig) lähmen, lahmlegen
cri·sis ['kraɪsɪs] s (–ses [siz]) Krise f
crisp [krɪsp] adj (brittle) knusprig; (firm and fresh) mürb; (air, clothes) frisch; (manner) forsch
crisscross ['krɪs,krɔs] adj & adv kreuz und quer ‖ tr kreuz und quer markieren ‖ intr sich kreuzen
criteri·on [kraɪ'tɪrɪ·ən] s (–a [ə] & –ons) Kennzeichen n, Kriterium n
critic ['krɪtɪk] s Kritiker –in mf
critical ['krɪtɪkəl] adj kritisch
criticism ['krɪtɪ,sɪzəm] s Kritik f
criticize ['krɪtɪ,saɪz] tr kritisieren
critique [krɪ'tik] s (review) Rezension f; (critical discussion) Kritik f
croak [krok] s (of a frog) Quaken n; (of a raven) Krächzen n ‖ intr quaken; krächzen; (die) (sl) verrecken
cro·chet [kro'ʃə] s Häkelarbeit f ‖ v (pret & pp –cheted ['ʃed]; ger –cheting ['ʃe·ɪŋ]) tr & intr häkeln
crochet' nee'dle s Häkelnadel f
crock [krak] s irdener Topf m, Krug m
crockery ['krakəri] s irdenes Geschirr n
crocodile ['krakə,daɪl] s Krokodil n
croc'odile tears' spl Krokodilstränen pl
crocus ['krokəs] s (bot) Krokus m
crone [kron] s altes Weib n
crony ['kroni] s alter Kamerad m
crook [krʊk] s (of a shepherd) Hirtenstab m; (sl) Gauner m ‖ tr krümmen
crooked ['krʊkɪd] adj krumm; (dishonest) unehrlich
croon [krun] tr & intr schmalzig singen
crooner ['krunər] s Schnulzensänger m
crop [krap] s Ernte f; (whip) Peitsche f; (of a bird) Kropf m; (large number) Menge f; **the crops** die ganze Ernte ‖ v (pret & pp **cropped;** ger **cropping**) tr stutzen; (said of an animal) abfressen ‖ intr—**c. up** auftauchen
crop' fail'ure s Mißerte f
croquet [kro'ke] s Krocket n

croquette [kro'kɛt] *s* (culin) Krokette *f*

crosier ['kroʒər] *s* Bischofsstab *m*

cross [krɔs] *adj* Quer-, Kreuz-; (biol) Kreuzungs-; (*angry*) (**with**) ärgerlich (auf *acc*, über *acc*) || *s* (& fig) Kreuz *n*; (biol) Kreuzung *f* || *tr* (*arms, legs, streets, plans, breeds*) kreuzen; (*a mountain*) übersteigen; (*oppose*) in die Quere kommen (*dat*); **c. my heart!** Hand aufs Herz!; **c. oneself** sich bekreuzigen; **c. s.o.'s mind** j–m durch den Kopf gehen; **c. out** ausstreichen || *intr* sich kreuzen; **c. over to** hinübergehen zu

cross'bones' *spl* gekreuzte Skelettknochen *pl*

cross'bow' *s* (hist) Armbrust *f*

cross'breed' *v* (*pret & pp* –**bred**) *tr* kreuzen

cross'-coun'try *adj* (*vehicle*) geländegängig || **cross'-coun'try** *s* (sport) Langlauf *m*

cross'cur'rent *s* Gegenströmung *f*

cross'-exam'ine *tr* ins Kreuzverhör nehmen

cross'-examina'tion *s* Kreuzverhör *n*

cross'-eyed' *adj* schieläugig

cross'fire' *s* Kreuzfeuer *n*

cross'ing *s* (*of streets*) Kreuzung *f*; (*of the ocean*) Überfahrt *f*, Überquerung *f*; (rr) Übergang *m*

cross'piece' *s* Querstück *n*

cross'-pur'pose *s*—**be at cross-purposes** einander entgegenarbeiten

cross' ref'erence *s* Querverweis *m*

cross'road' *s* Querweg *m*; **crossroads** Straßenkreuzung *f*; (fig) Scheideweg *m*

cross' sec'tion *s* Querschnitt *m*

cross'wind' *s* Seitenwind *m*

cross'wise' *adj & adv* quer, in die Quere

cross'word puz'zle *s* Kreuzworträtsel *n*

crotch [krɑtʃ] *s* (*of a tree*) Gabelung *f*; (*of a body or trousers*) Schritt *m*

crotchety ['krɑtʃɪti] *adj* verschroben

crouch [krautʃ] *s* Hocke *f* || *intr* hocken

croup [krup] *s* (*of a horse*) Kruppe *f*; (pathol) Halsbräune *f*

croupier ['krupɪ·ər] *s* Croupier –in *mf*

crouton ['krutɑn] *s* gerösteter Brotwürfel *m*

crow [kro] *s* (*cry*) Krähen *n*; (bird) Krähe *f*; **as the c. flies** schnurgrade; **eat c.** klein beigeben || *intr* krähen

crow'bar' *s* Stemmeisen *n*

crowd [kraud] *s* Menge *f*; (*mob*) Masse *f*; (*set*) Gesellschaft *f* || *tr* vollstopfen; (*push*) stoßen; **c. out** verdrängen || *intr* (*around*) sich drängen (um); **c. into** sich hineindrängen in (*acc*)

crowd'ed *adj* überfüllt; (*street*) belebt

crown [kraun] *s* Krone *f*; (dent) Zahnkrone *f* || *tr* krönen, bekränzen; (checkers) zur Dame machen; (sl) eins aufs Dach geben (*dat*); (dent) überkronen

crown' jew'els *spl* Kronjuwelen *pl*

crown' prince' *s* Kronprinz *m*

crown' prin'cess *s* Kronprinzessin *f*

crow's'-feet' *spl* (*wrinkles*) Krähenfüße *pl*

crow's'-nest' *s* (naut) Krähennest *n*

crucial ['kruʃəl] *adj* entscheidend; (*point*) springend; **c. question** Gretchenfrage *f*; **c. test** Feuerprobe *f*

crucible ['krusɪbəl] *s* Schmelztiegel *m*

crucifix ['krusɪfɪks] *s* Kruzifix *n*

crucifixion [‚krusɪ'fɪkʃən] *s* Kreuzigung *f*

cruci·fy ['krusɪ‚faɪ] *v* (*pret & pp* –**fied**) *tr* kreuzigen

crude [krud] *adj* (*raw, unrefined*) roh; (*person*) grob, ungeschliffen; **c. joke** plumper Scherz *m*

crudity ['krudɪti] *s* Roheit *f*

cruel ['kru·əl] *adj* (**to**) grausam (gegen)

cruelty ['kru·əlti] *s* Grausamkeit *f*; **c. to animals** Tierquälerei *f*

cruet ['kru·ɪt] *s* Fläschchen *n*; (relig) Meßkännchen *n*

cruise [kruz] *s* Kreuzfahrt *f* || *intr* (aer) mit Reisegeschwindigkeit fliegen; (aut) herumfahren; (naut) kreuzen

cruiser ['kruzər] *s* (nav) Kreuzer *m*

cruise' ship' *s* Vergnügungsdampfer *m*

cruller ['krʌlər] *s* Krapfen *m*

crumb [krʌm] *s* Krümel *m*; (& fig) Bröckchen *n*; (sl) Schweinehund *m*

crumble ['krʌmbəl] *tr & intr* zerbröckeln

crumbly ['krʌmbli] *adj* bröcklig

crummy ['krʌmi] *adj* (sl) schäbig

crumple ['krʌmpəl] *tr* zerknittern || *intr* (*said of clothes*) faltig werden; (*collapse*) zusammenbrechen

crunch [krʌntʃ] *s* Knacken *n*; (*of snow*) Knirschen *n*; (*tight situation*) Druck *m* || *tr* knirschend kauen || *intr* (*said of snow*) knirschen; **c. on** knirschend kauen

crusade [kru'sed] *s* Kreuzzug *m*

crusader [kru'sedər] *s* Kreuzfahrer *m*

crush [krʌʃ] *s* Gedränge *n*; **have a c. on s.o.** (coll) in j–n vernarrt sein || *tr* (zer)quetschen, zerdrücken; (*grain*) schroten; (*stone*) zerkleinern; (*suppress*) unterdrücken; (*oppress*) bedrücken; (*hopes*) knicken; (*overwhelm*) zerschmettern; (min) pochen; **c. out** (*a cigarette*) ausdrücken || *intr* zerdrückt werden

crush'ing *adj* (*victory*) entscheidend; (*defeat*) vernichtend; (*experience*) überwältigend

crust [krʌst] *s* Kruste *f*; (sl) Frechheit *f*

crustacean [krʌs'teʃən] *s* Krebstier *n*

crustaceous [krʌs'teʃəs] *adj* Krebs-

crusty ['krʌsti] *adj* krustig, rösch; (*surly*) mürrisch

crutch [krʌtʃ] *s* (& fig) Krücke *f*

crux [krʌks] *s* Kern *m*, Kernpunkt *m*

cry [kraɪ] *s* (**cries**) (*shout*) Schrei *m*, Ruf *m*; (*weeping*) Weinen *n*; **a far cry from** etw ganz anderes als; **cry for help** Hilferuf *m*; **have a good cry** sich ordentlich ausweinen || *v* (*pret & pp* **cried**) *tr* schreien, rufen; **cry one's eyes out** sich [*dat*] die Augen aus dem Kopf weinen || *intr* (*weep*) weinen; (*shout*) schreien; **cry for help** um Hilfe rufen; **cry on s.o.'s shoulder** j–m seine Not klagen; **cry out against** scharf verurteilen; **cry out in** (*pain*) schreien vor (*dat*); **cry over** nachweinen (*dat*)

cry'ba'by *s* (**-bies**) Schreihals *m*

cry'ing *adj*—**c. jag** Schreikrampf *m;* **c. shame** schreiende Ungerechtigkeit *f* ‖ *s* Weinen *n;* **for c. out loud!** um Himmels willen!

crypt [krɪpt] *s* Totengruft *f*, Krypta *f*

cryptic(al) ['krɪptɪk(əl)] *adj* (*secret*) geheim; (*puzzling*) rätselhaft; (*coded*) verschlüsselt

crystal ['krɪstəl] *adj* Kristall– ‖ *s* Kristall *m;* (*cut glass*) Kristallglas *n;* (*of a watch*) Uhrglas *n*

crys'tal ball' *s* Kristall *m*

crystalline ['krɪstəlɪn], ['krɪstə,laɪn] *adj* kristallinisch, kristallen

crystallize ['krɪstə,laɪz] *tr* kristallisieren ‖ *intr* kristallisieren; (fig) feste Form annehmen

cub [kʌb] *s* Junge *n*

Cuba ['kjubə] *s* Kuba *n*

Cuban ['kjubən] *adj* kubanisch ‖ *s* Kubaner –in *mf*

cubbyhole ['kʌbɪ,hol] *s* gemütliches Zimmerchen *n*

cube [kjub] *s* Würfel *m;* (math) dritte Potenz *f* ‖ *tr* in Würfel schneiden; (math) kubieren

cubic ['kjubɪk] *adj* Raum–; (math) kubisch; **c. foot** Kubikfuß *m*

cub' report'er *s* unerfahrener Reporter *m*

cub' scout' *s* Wölfling *m*

cuckold ['kʌkəld] *s* Hahnrei *m* ‖ *tr* zum Hahnrei machen

cuckoo ['kuku] *adj* (sl) verrückt ‖ *s* Kuckuck *m*

cuck'oo clock' *s* Kuckucksuhr *f*

cucumber ['kjukʌmbər] *s* Gurke *f*

cud [kʌd] *s*—**chew the cud** wiederkäuen

cuddle ['kʌdəl] *tr* herzen ‖ *intr* sich kuscheln; **c. up** sich behaglich zusammenkuscheln

cudg·el ['kʌdʒəl] *s* Prügel *m* ‖ *v* (*pret & pp* **-el[l]ed;** *ger* **-el[l]ing**) *tr* verprügeln

cue [kju] *s* Hinweis *m;* (billiards) Billardstock *m;* (theat) Stichwort *n;* **take the cue from s.o.** sich nach j–m richten ‖ *tr* das Stichwort geben (*dat*)

cuff [kʌf] *s* (*of a shirt*) Manschette *f;* (*of trousers*) Aufschlag *m;* (*blow*) Ohrfeige *f;* **off the c.** aus dem Handgelenk

cuff' link' *s* Manschettenknopf *m*

cuisine [kwɪ'zin] *s* Küche *f*

culinary ['kjulɪ,nɛri] *adj* kulinarisch, Koch–; **c. art** Kochkunst *f*

cull [kʌl] *tr* (*choose*) auslesen; (*pluck*) pflücken

culminate ['kʌlmɪ,net] *intr* (**in**) kulminieren (in *dat*), gipfeln (in *dat*)

culmination [,kʌlmɪ'neʃən] *s* Gipfel *m*

culpable ['kʌlpəbəl] *adj* schuldhaft

culprit ['kʌlprɪt] *s* Schuldige *mf*

cult [kʌlt] *s* Kult *m*, Kultus *m*

cultivate ['kʌltɪ,vet] *tr* (*soil*) bearbeiten; (*plants*) ziehen; (*activities*) betreiben; (*an art*) pflegen; (*friendship*) hegen

cul'tivat'ed *adj* kultiviert

cultivation [,kʌltɪ'veʃən] *s* (*of the soil*) Bearbeitung *f;* (*of the arts*) Pflege *f;* (*of friendship*) Hegen *n;* **under c.** bebaut

cultivator ['kʌltɪ,vetər] *s* (mach) Kultivator *m*

cultural ['kʌltʃərəl] *adj* kulturell, Kultur–

culture ['kʌltʃər] *s* Kultur *f*

cul'tured *adj* kultiviert

cul'ture me'dium *s* Nährboden *m*

culvert ['kʌlvərt] *s* Rinnstein *m*

cumbersome ['kʌmbərsəm] *adj* (*unwieldy*) unhandlich; (*slow-moving*) schwerfällig; (*burdensome*) lästig

cunning ['kʌnɪŋ] *adj* (arg)listig ‖ *s* List *f*, Arglist *f*, Schlauheit *f*

cup [kʌp] *s* Tasse *f;* (*of a bra*) Körbchen *n;* (fig, bot, relig) Kelch *m;* (sport) Pokal *m* ‖ *v* (*pret & pp* **cupped;** *ger* **cupping**) *tr* (*the hands*) wölben; (med) schröpfen

cupboard ['kʌbərd] *s* Schrank *m*

cupidity [kju'pɪdɪti] *s* Habgier *f*

cupola ['kjupələ] *s* Kuppel *f*

cur [kʌr] *s* Köter *m;* (pej) Halunke *m*

curable ['kjurəbəl] *adj* heilbar

curate ['kjurɪt] *s* Kaplan *m*

curative ['kjurətɪv] *adj* heilend, Heil–

curator ['kju,retər] *s* Kustos *m*

curb [kʌrb] *s* (*of a street*) Randstein *m;* (*of a horse*) Kandare *f* ‖ *tr* (& fig) zügeln; (*a person*) an die Kandare nehmen

curb'stone' *s* Bordstein *m*

curd [kʌrd] *s* Quark *m;* **curds** Quark *m*

curdle ['kʌrdəl] *tr* gerinnen lassen; (fig) erstarren lassen ‖ *intr* gerinnen, stocken; (fig) erstarren

cure [kjur] *s* (*restoration to health*) Heilung *f;* (*remedy*) Heilmittel *n;* (*treatment*) Kur *f* ‖ *tr* (*a disease, evil*) heilen; (*by smoking*) räuchern; (*by drying*) trocknen; (*by salting*) einsalzen ‖ *intr* heilen

cure'-all' *s* Allheilmittel *n*

curfew ['kʌrfju] *s* Ausgehverbot *n;* (*enforced closing time*) Polizeistunde *f*

curi·o ['kjurɪ,o] *s* (**-os**) Kuriosität *f*

curiosity [,kjurɪ'ɑsɪti] *s* Neugier *f;* (*strange article*) Kuriosität *f*

curious ['kjurɪ·əs] *adj* neugierig; (*odd*) kurios, merkwürdig

curl [kʌrl] *s* (*of hair*) Locke *f;* (*of smoke*) Rauchkringel *m* ‖ *tr* locken; (*lips*) verächtlich schürzen ‖ *intr* sich kräuseln; **c. up** sich zusammenrollen; (*said of an edge*) sich umbiegen

curler ['kʌrlər] *s* Haarwickler *m*

curlicue ['kʌrlɪ,kju] *s* Schnörkel *m*

curly ['kʌrli] *adj* lockig; (*leaves, etc.*) gekräuselt

currant ['kʌrənt] *s* (*raisin*) Korinthe *f;* (genus *Ribes*) Johannisbeere *f*

currency ['kʌrənsi] *s* (*money*) Währung *f;* (*circulation*) Umlauf *m;* **foreign c.** Devisen *pl;* **gain c.** in Gebrauch kommen

current ['kʌrənt] *adj* (*year, prices, account*) laufend; (*events*) aktuell, Tages-; **be c.** Gültigkeit haben; (*said of money*) gelten ‖ *s* (& elec) Strom *m*

currently ['kʌrəntli] *adv* gegenwärtig

curricu·lum [kə'rıkjələm] *s* (-**lums** & -**la** [lə]) Lehrplan *m*

cur·ry ['kʌri] *s* Curry *m* ‖ *v* (*pret & pp* -**ried**) *tr* (*a horse*) striegeln; **c. favor with s.o.** sich bei j–m einzuschmeicheln suchen

cur'rycomb' *s* Striegel *m*

cur'ry pow'der *s* Currypulver *n*

curse [kʌrs] *s* Fluch *m;* **put a c. on** verwünschen ‖ *tr* verfluchen ‖ *intr* (**at**) fluchen (auf *acc*)

cursed ['kʌrsıd], [kʌrst] *adj* verflucht

curse' word' *s* Fluchwort *n*, Schimpfwort *n*

cursive ['kʌrsıv] *adj* Kurrent–

cursory ['kʌrsəri] *adj* flüchtig

curt [kʌrt] *adj* barsch, schroff

curtail [kər'tel] *tr* einschränken

curtain ['kʌrtın] *s* Gardine *f;* (*drape*) Vorhang *m;* (theat) Vorhang *m* ‖ *tr*—**c. off** mit Vorhängen abteilen

cur'tain call' *s* Vorhang *m*, Hervorruf *m*

cur'tain rod' *s* Gardinenstange *f*

curt·sy ['kʌrtsi] *s* Knicks *m* ‖ *v* (*pret & pp* -**sied**) *intr* (**to**) knicksen (vor *dat*)

curvaceous [kʌr'veʃəs] *adj* kurvenreich

curvature ['kʌrvətʃər] *s* (*of the spine*) Verkrümmung *f;* (*of the earth*) Krümmung *f*

curved *adj* krumm

cushion ['kuʃən] *s* Kissen *n*, Polster *m* & *n;* (billiards) Bande *f* ‖ *tr* polstern; (*a shock*) abfedern

cuss [kʌs] *s* (sl) Kerl *m;* (*curse*) (sl) Fluch *m* ‖ *tr* (sl) verfluchen ‖ *intr* (sl) fluchen

cussed ['kʌsıd] *adj* (sl) verflucht

cussedness ['kʌsıdnıs] *s* (sl) Bosheit *f*

custard ['kʌstərd] *s* Eierkrem *f*

custodian [kəs'todı·ən] *s* (*e.g., of records*) Verwalter *m;* (*of inmates*) Wärter *m;* (*caretaker*) Hausmeister *m*

custody ['kʌstədi] *s* Verwahrung *f*, Obhut *f;* (jur) Gewahrsam *m;* **c. of** (*children*) Sorgerecht für; **in the c. of** in der Obhut (*genit*); **take into c.** in Gewahrsam nehmen

custom ['kʌstəm] *s* Brauch *m*, Sitte *f;* (*habit*) Gewohnheit *f;* **customs** Zollkontrolle *f;* **pay customs on s.th.** für etw Zoll bezahlen

customary ['kʌstə,meri] *adj* gebräuchlich

cus'tom-built' *adj* nach Wunsch gebaut

customer ['kʌstəmər] *s* Kunde *m*, Kundin *f;* (*in a restaurant*) Gast *m;* (telp) Teilnehmer –in *mf*

cus'tom-made' *adj* nach Maß angefertigt

cus'toms clear'ance *s* Zollabertigung *f*

cus'toms declara'tion *s* Zollerklärung *f;* (*form*) Abfertigungsschein *m*

cus'toms inspec'tion *s* Zollkontrolle *f*

cus'toms of'fice *s* Zollamt *n*

customs of'ficer *s* Zollbeamte *m*, Zollbeamtin *f*

cus'tom tai'lor *s* Maßschneider *m*

cut [kʌt] *adj* (*glass*) geschliffen; **cut flowers** Schnittblumen *pl;* **cut out for** wie geschaffen für (or zu) ‖ *s* Schnitt *m;* (*piece cut off*) Abschnitt *m;* (*slice*) Schnitte *f;* (*wound*) Schnittwunde *f;* (*of a garment*) Schnitt *m*, Fasson *f;* (*of the profits*) Anteil *m;* (*in prices, pay*) Kürzung *f*, Senkung *f;* (*absence from school*) Schwänzen *n;* (*of meat*) Stück *n;* (cards) Abheben *n;* (tennis) Drehschlag *m;* **a cut above** e–e Stufe besser als ‖ *v* (*pret & pp* **cut;** *ger* **cutting**) *tr* schneiden; (*glass, precious stones*) schleifen; (*grass*) mähen; (*hedges*) stutzen; (*hay*) machen; (*a slice*) Schnitte *f;* (*a tunnel*) bohren; (*a motor*) abstellen; (*production*) drosseln; (*pay*) kürzen, vermindern; (*class*) (coll) schwänzen; (*prices*) herabsetzen, kürzen; (*whiskey*) (coll) panschen; (*cards*) abheben; (tennis) schneiden; **cut back** (*plants*) stutzen; (fig) abbauen; **cut down** fällen; **cut it out!** Schluß damit!; **cut off** abschneiden; (*a tail*) kupieren; (*gas, telephone, electricity*) absperren; (*troops*) absprengen; **cut one's finger** sich in den Finger schneiden; **cut out the nonsense!** laß den Quatsch!; **cut short** (*e.g., a vacation*) abkürzen; (*a person*) das Wort abschneiden (*dat*); **cut up** zerstückeln ‖ *intr* schneiden; **cut down on** einschränken, verringern; **cut in** sich einmischen; (*at a dance*) ablösen; **cut in ahead of s.o.** vor j–m einbiegen; **cut up** (sl) wild darauf losschießen

cut-and-dried ['kʌtən'draıd] *adj* fix und fertig

cut'away' *s* Cut *m*

cut'back' *s* Einschränkung *f*

cute [kjut] *adj* (*pretty*) niedlich; (*shrewd*) (coll) klug

cut' glass' *s* geschliffenes Glas *n*

cuticle ['kjutıkəl] *s* Nagelhaut *f*

cutie ['kjuti] *s* (sl) flotte Biene *f*

cut'lass ['kʌtləs] *s* Entermesser *n*

cutlery ['kʌtləri] *s* Schneidwerkzeuge *pl*

cutlet ['kʌtlıt] *s* Schnitzel *n*

cut'-off' *s* (*turn-off*) Abzweigung *f;* (*cut-off point*) (acct) gemeinsamer Endpunkt *m;* (elec) Ausschaltvorrichtung *f;* (mach) Absperrvorrichtung *f*

cut'-off date' *s* Abschlußtag *m*

cut'-out' *s* Ausschnitt *m;* (*design to be cut out*) Ausschneidemuster *n;* (aut) Auspuffklappe *f*

cut'-rate' *adj* (*price*) Schleuder–

cutter ['kʌtər] *s* (naut) Kutter *m*

cut'throat' *adj* halsabschneiderisch ‖ *s* Halsabschneider –in *mf*

cut'ting *adj* schneidend; (*tools*)

Schneide–; (remark) scharf ‖ s Abschnitt m; (of prices) Herabsetzung f; (hort) Steckling m; cuttings Abfälle pl
cut'ting board' s Schneidebrett n
cut'ting edge' s Schnittkante f
cut'ting room' s (cin) Schneideraum m
cuttlefish ['kʌtəl‚fɪʃ] s Tintenfisch m
cyanamide [saɪ'ænə‚maɪd] s (chem) Zyanamid n; (com) Kalkstickstoff m
cycle ['saɪkəl] s Kreis m; (of an internal combustion engine) Takt m; (phys) Periode f ‖ intr radeln
cyclic(al) ['sɪklɪk(əl)] adj zyklisch, kreisförmig
cyclist ['saɪklɪst] s Radfahrer –in mf
cyclone ['saɪklon] s Zyklon m
cyclotron ['saɪklə‚trɑn] s Zyklotron n, Beschleuniger m
cylinder ['sɪlɪndər] s Zylinder m
cyl'inder block' s Zylinderblock m
cyl'inder bore' s Zylinderbohrung f

cyl'inder head' s Zylinderkopf m
cylindric(al) [sɪ'lɪndrɪk(əl)] adj zylindrisch
cymbal ['sɪmbəl] s Becken n
cynic ['sɪnɪk] adj (philos) zynisch ‖ s Menschenverächter –in mf; (philos) Zyniker m
cynical ['sɪnɪkəl] adj zynisch
cynicism ['sɪnɪ‚sɪzəm] s Zynismus m; (cynical remark) zynische Bemerkung f
cypress ['saɪprəs] s Zypresse f
Cyprus ['saɪprəs] s Zypern n
Cyrillic [sɪ'rɪlɪk] adj kyrillisch
cyst [sɪst] s Zyste f
czar [zɑr] s Zar m
czarina [zɑ'rinə] s Zarin f
Czech [tʃɛk] adj tschechisch ‖ s Tscheche m, Tschechin f; (language) Tschechisch n
Czechoslovakia [‚tʃɛkəslo'vækɪ·ə] s die Tschechoslowakei f

D

D, d [di] s vierter Buchstabe des englischen Alphabets; (mus) D; D flat Des n; D sharp Dis n
D.A. abb (District Attorney) Staatsanwalt m
dab [dæb] s (of color) Klecks m; (e.g., of butter) Stückchen n ‖ v (pret & pp dabbed; ger dabbing) tr betupfen ‖ intr—dab at betupfen
dabble ['dæbəl] tr bespritzen ‖ intr (splash about) plantschen; d. in herumstümpern in (dat)
dachshund ['dɑks‚hʊnd] s Dachshund m
dad [dæd] s (coll) Vati m
daddy ['dædi] s (coll) Vati m
dad'dy-long'legs' s (-legs) Weberknecht m
daffodil ['dæfədɪl] s gelbe Narzisse f
daffy ['dæfi] adj (coll) doof
dagger ['dægər] s Dolch m; (typ) Kreuzzeichen n; look daggers at s.o. j–n mit Blicken durchbohren
dahlia ['dæljə] s Georgine f, Dahlie f
daily ['deli] adj täglich, Tages– ‖ adv täglich ‖ s Tageszeitung f
dainty ['denti] adj zart; (food) lecker; (finiky) wählerisch
dairy ['dɛri] s Molkerei f
dair'y farm' s Meierei f
dair'y farm'er s Meier –in mf
dais ['de·ɪs] s Tribüne f
daisy ['dezi] s Gänseblümchen n
dal·ly ['dæli] v (pret & pp –lied) intr (delay) herumtrödeln; (play amorously) liebäugeln
dam [dæm] s Damm m; (female quadruped) Muttertier n ‖ v (pret & pp dammed; ger damming) tr eindämmen; dam up anstauen
damage ['dæmɪdʒ] s Schaden m; damages (jur) Schadenersatz m; do d. Schaden anrichten; sue for damages

auf Schadenersatz klagen ‖ tr beschädigen; (a reputation) beeinträchtigen
dam'aging adj (influence) schädlich; (evidence) belastend
dame [dem] s Dame f; (sl) Weibsbild n
damn [dæm] adj (sl) verflucht ‖ s— I don't give a d. about it (sl) ich mache mir e–n Dreck daraus; not be worth a d. (sl) keinen Pfifferling wert sein ‖ tr verdammen; (curse) verfluchen; d. it! (sl) verflucht!
damnation [dæm'neʃən] s Verdammnis f
damned adj verdammt; (sl) verflucht ‖ adv (sl) verdammt ‖ the d. spl die Verdammten pl
damp [dæmp] adj feucht ‖ s Feuchtigkeit f ‖ tr (be)feuchten; (a fire; enthusiasm) dämpfen; (elec, mus, phys) dämpfen
dampen ['dæmpən] tr befeuchten; (fig) dämpfen
damper ['dæmpər] s (of a fireplace) Schieber m; (of a stove) Ofenklappe f; (mus) Dämpfer m; put a d. on e–n Dämpfer aufsetzen (dat)
dampness ['dæmpnɪs] s Feuchtigkeit f
damsel ['dæmzəl] s Jungfrau f
dance [dæns] s Tanz m ‖ tr & intr tanzen
dance' band' s Tanzkapelle f
dance' floor' s Tanzfläche f
dance' hall' s Tanzsaal m, Tanzlokal n
dancer ['dænsər] s Tänzer –in mf
dance' step' s Tanzschritt m
danc'ing part'ner s Tanzpartner –in mf
dandelion ['dændɪ‚laɪ·ən] s Löwenzahn m
dandruff ['dændrəf] s Schuppen pl

dandy ['dændi] *adj* (coll) pfundig, nett ‖ *s* Stutzer *m*
Dane [den] *s* Däne *m*, Dänin *f*
danger ['dendʒər] *s* (to) Gefahr *f* (für)
dan'ger list' *s*—**be on the d.** in Lebensgefahr sein
dangerous ['dendʒərəs] *adj* gefährlich
dangle ['dæŋgəl] *tr* schlenkern, baumeln lassen ‖ *intr* baumeln
Danish ['denɪʃ] *adj* dänisch ‖ *s* (*language*) Dänisch *n*
Dan'ish pas'try *s* feines Hefegebäck *n*
dank [dæŋk] *adj* feucht
Danube ['dænjub] *s* Donau *f*
dapper ['dæpər] *adj* schmuck
dappled ['dæpəld] *adj* scheckig, bunt
dare [dɛr] *s* Herausforderung *f* ‖ *tr* wagen; (*a person*) herausfordern; **d. to** (*inf*) es wagen zu (*inf*); **don't you d.** go unterstehen Sie sich, wegzugehen!; **I d. say** ich darf wohl behaupten ‖ *intr*—**don't you d.!** unterstehen Sie sich!
dare'dev'il *s* Waghals *m*, Draufgänger *m*
dar'ing *adj* (*deed*) verwegen; (*person*) wagemutig ‖ *s* Wagemut *m*
dark [dɑrk] *adj* finster; (*color, beer, complexion*) dunkel; (fig) düster ‖ *s* Finsternis *n*, Dunkel *n;* **be in the d.** about im unklaren sein über (*acc*)
Dark' A'ges *spl* frühes Mittelalter *n*
dark-complexioned ['dɑrkkəm'plɛkʃənd] *adj* dunkelhäutig
darken ['dɑrkən] *tr* (*a room*) verfinstern ‖ *intr* sich verfinstern; (fig) sich verdüstern
dark'-eyed' *adj* schwarzäugig
dark' horse' *s* Außenseiter *m*
darkly ['dɑrkli] *adv* geheimnisvoll
darkness ['dɑrknɪs] *s* Finsternis *f*
dark'room' *s* (phot) Dunkelkammer *f*
darling ['dɑrlɪŋ] *adj* lieb ‖ *s* Liebchen *n*
darn [dɑrn] *adj* (coll) verwünscht ‖ *adv* (coll) verdammt ‖ *s*—**I don't give a d. about** it ich pfeif drauf! ‖ *tr* (*stockings*) stopfen; **d. it!** (coll) verflixt!; **I'll be darned if** der Kukkuck soll mich holen, wenn
darn'ing nee'dle *s* Stopfnadel *f*
dart [dɑrt] *s* Wurfspieß *m*, Pfeil *m;* (sew) Abnäher *m;* **darts** (*game*) Pfeilwerfen *n;* **play darts** Pfeile werfen ‖ *intr* huschen; **d. ahead** vorschießen; **d. off** davonstürzen
dash [dæʃ] *s* (*rush*) Ansturm *m;* (*smartness*) Schneidigkeit *f;* (*spirit*) Schwung *m;* (*of solids*) Prise *f;* (*of liquids*) Schuß *m;* (sport) Kurzstreckenlauf *m;* (typ) Gedankenstrich *m;* **make a d. for** losstürzen auf (*acc*) ‖ *tr* (*throw*) schleudern; (*hopes*) niederschlagen, knicken; **d. off** (*a letter*) hinwerfen ‖ *intr* stürmen, stürzen
dash'board' *s* (aut) Armaturenbrett *n*
dash'ing *adj* schneidig, forsch
dastardly ['dæstərdli] *adj* feige
data ['detə] *s* or *spl* Daten *pl*, Angaben *pl*
da'ta proc'essing *s* Datenverarbeitung *f*

date [det] *s* Datum *n; (fixed time)* Termin *m;* (*period*) Zeitraum *m;* (*appointment*) (coll) Verabredung *f;* (*person on a date*) Freund –in *mf;* (bot) Dattel *f;* (jur) Termin *m;* **have a d. with** verabredet sein mit; **make a d. with** sich verabreden mit; **out of d.** veraltet; **to d.** bis heute; **what is the d. today?** der wievielte ist heute? ‖ *tr* datieren; (coll) ausgehen mit ‖ *intr*—**d. back to** zurückgehen auf (*acc*); **d. from** stammen aus
dat'ed *adj* (*provided with a date*) datiert; (*out-of-date*) zeitgebunden
date' line' *s* Datumsgrenze *f*
date'line' *s* (journ) Datumszeile *f*
date' palm' *s* Dattelpalme *f*
dative ['detɪv] *s* Dativ *m*, Wemfall *m*
daub [dɔb] *s* Bewurf *m* ‖ *tr* (*a canvas*) beschmieren; (*a wall*) bewerfen; (*e.g. mud, plaster*) (on) schmieren (auf *acc*) ‖ *intr* (paint) klecksen
daughter ['dɔtər] *s* Tochter *f*
daugh'ter-in-law' *s* **(daughters-in-law)** Schwiegertocher *f*
daunt [dɔnt] *tr* einschüchtern
dauntless ['dɔntlɪs] *adj* furchtlos
davenport ['dævən‚port] *s* Diwan *m*
davit ['dævɪt] *s* (naut) Bootskran *m*
daw [dɔ] *s* (orn) Dohle *f*
dawdle ['dɔdəl] *intr* trödeln, bummeln
dawn [dɔn] *s* Morgendämmerung *f;* (fig) Anbeginn *m* ‖ *intr* dämmern; **d. on s.o.** j–m zum Bewußtsein kommen
day [de] *adj* Tage-, Tages– ‖ *s* Tag *m;* (*specific date*) Termin *m;* **all day long** den ganzen Tag; **by day** am Tage, bei Tage; **by the day** tageweise; **call it a day** (coll) Feierabend machen; **day after day** Tag für Tag; **day by day** Tag für Tag; **day in, day out** tagaus, tagein; **day off** Urlaubstag *m*, Ruhetag *m;* **every other day** jeden zweiten Tag; **in days of old** in alten Zeiten; **in his day** zu seiner Zeit; **in those days** damals; **one day** e–s Tages; **one of these days** demnächst; **the day after** am folgenden Tag; **the day after tomorrow** übermorgen; **the day before** am Vortag; **the day before yesterday** vorgestern; **the other day** neulich, unlängst; **these days** heutzutage; **to this very day** bis auf den heutigen Tag; **what day of the week is it?** welchen Wochentag haben wir?
day' bed' *s* Ruhebett *n*, Liege *f*
day'break' *s* Tagesanbruch *m*
day'-by-day' *adj* tagtäglich, Tag für Tag
day'-care cen'ter *s* Kindertagesstätte *f*, Kindergarten *m*
day' coach' *s* (rr) Personenwagen *m*
day'dream' *s* Träumerei *f*, Wachtraum *m;* (*wild ideas*) Phantasterei *f* ‖ *intr* mit offenen Augen träumen
day'dream'er *s* Träumer –in *mf*
day' la'borer *s* Tagelöhner –in *mf*
day'light' *adj* Tageslicht– ‖ *s* Tageslicht *n;* **in broad d.** am hellichten Tag; **knock the daylights out of** (sl) zur Sau machen

day'light-sav'ing time' s Sommerzeit f
day' nurs'ery s Kleinkinderbewahranstalt f
day' of reck'oning s Jüngster Tag m
day' shift' s Tagsschicht f
day'time' s Tageszeit f; **in the d.** bei Tage, am Tage
daze [dez] s Benommenheit f; **be in a d.** benommen sein || tr betäuben
dazzle ['dæzəl] s Blenden n || tr (& fig) blenden
dazz'ling adj blendend
D-day ['di͵de] s X-Tag m; (hist) Invasionstag m
deacon ['dikən] s Diakon m
deaconess ['dikənɪs] s Diakonisse f
dead [dɛd] adj tot; (plant) abgestorben, dürr; (faint, sleep) tief; (numb) gefühllos; (volcano, fire) erloschen; (elec) stromlos; (sport) tot, nicht im Spiel; **d. as a doornail** mausetot; **d. shot** unfehlbarer Schütze m; **d. stop** völliger Stillstand m; **d. silence** Totenstille f || adv völlig, tod– || s— **in the d. of night** mitten in der Nacht; **in the d. of winter** im tiefsten Winter
dead' beat' s (sl) Nichtstuer –in mf
dead' bolt' s Absteller m
dead' calm' s Windstille f
dead' cen'ter s genaue Mitte f; (dead point) (mach) toter Punkt m
deaden ['dɛdən] tr (pain) betäuben; (a nerve) abtöten; (sound) dämpfen
dead' end' s (& fig) Sackgasse f
dead'head' s Dummkopf m
dead' heat' s totes Rennen n
dead'-let'ter of'fice s Abteilung f für unbestellbare Briefe
dead'line' s (letzter) Termin m; (journ) Redaktionsschluß m; **meet the d.** den Termin einhalten; **set a d. for** terminieren
dead'lock' s Stillstand m; **break the d.** den toten Punkt überwinden; **reach a d.** steckenbleiben || tr zum völligen Stillstand bringen; **become deadlocked** stocken
deadly ['dɛdli] adj (fatal) tödlich; **d. enemy** Todfeind –in mf; **d. fear** Todesangst f || adv—**d. dull** sterbenlangweilig; **d. pale** leichenblaß
dead'ly sins' spl Todsünden pl
dead'pan' adj (look) ausdruckslos; (person) schafsgesichtig
dead' pan' s (coll) Schafsgesicht n
dead' reck'oning s (naut) Koppelkurs m
dead' ring'er ['rɪŋər] s (coll) Doppelgänger m
dead'wood' s (& fig) totes Holz n
deaf [dɛf] adj taub; **d. and dumb** taubstumm; **d. to** (fig) taub gegen; **turn a d. ear to** taube Ohren haben für
deafen ['dɛfən] tr betäuben
deaf'ening adj ohrenbetäubend
deaf'-mute' adj taubstumm || s Taubstumme mf
deafness ['dɛfnɪs] s Taubheit f
deal [dil] s (business transaction) Geschäft n; (underhanded agreement) Schiebung f; (cards) Austeilen n, Geben n; **a good d. of** (coll) ziemlich

viel; **a good d. worse** (coll) viel (or weit) schlechter; **a great d. of** (coll) sehr viel; **give s.o. a good d.** (be fair to s.o.) j–n fair behandeln; (make s.o. a good offer) j–m ein gutes Angebot machen; **give s.o. a raw d.** j–m übel mitspielen; **it is my d.** (cards) ich muß geben; **it's a d.!** abgemacht!; **make a d.** (coll) ein Abkommen treffen || v (pret & pp **dealt** [dɛlt]) tr (a blow) versetzen; (cards) austeilen, geben || intr (cards) geben; **d. at** (a store) kaufen bei; **d. in** handeln mit; **d. with** (settle) erledigen; (occupy oneself or itself with) sich befassen mit; (treat, e.g., fairly) behandeln; (patronize) kaufen bei; (do business with) in Geschäftsbeziehungen stehen mit; **I'll d. with you later** mit Ihnen werde ich später abrechnen!
dealer ['dilər] s Geber –in mf; (com) Händler –in mf
deal'ings spl (business dealings) Handel m; (relations) Umgang m; **I'll have no d. with** ich will nichts zu tun haben mit
dean [din] s (eccl, educ) Dekan m
dean'ship' s (eccl, educ) Dekanat n
dear [dɪr] adj lieb, traut; (expensive) teuer; **Dear Madam** Sehr verehrte gnädige Frau!; **Dear Mrs. X** Sehr geehrte Frau X; **Dear Mr. X** Sehr geehrter Herr X!; **Dear Sir** Sehr geehrter Herr! || s Liebling m, Schatz m || interj—**oh d.!** ach herrje!
dearie ['dɪri] s (coll) Liebchen n
dearth [dʌrθ] s (of) Mangel m (an dat)
death [dɛθ] s Tod m; (in the family) Todesfall m; **at death's door** sterbenskrank; **catch a d. of a cold** sich [dat] den Tod holen; **he'll be the d. of me yet** er bringt mich noch ins Grab; **put to d.** hinrichten; **to the d.** bis aufs Messer; **work to d.** totarbeiten
death'bed' s Totenbett n, Sterbebett n
death'blow' s Gnadenstoß m; (fig) Todesstoß m
death' certif'icate s Totenschein m
death' house' s Todeshaus n
death' knell' s Grabgeläute n
deathless ['dɛθlɪs] adj unsterblich
deathly ['dɛθli] adj tödlich, Todes–, Toten– || adv toten–
death' mask' s Totenmaske f
death' pen'alty s Todesstrafe f
death' rate' s Sterblichkeitsziffer f
death' rat'tle s Todesröcheln n
death' sen'tence s Todesurteil n
death' strug'gle s Todeskampf m
death' trap' s (fig) Mausefalle f
death' war'rant s Hinrichtungsbefehl m
debacle [de'bɑkəl] s Zusammenbruch m
de·bar [dɪ'bɑr] v (pret & pp **–barred;** ger **–barring**) tr (from) ausschließen (aus)
debark [dɪ'bɑrk] tr ausschiffen || intr sich ausschiffen, an Land gehen
debarkation [͵dibɑr'keʃən] s Ausschiffung f

debase [dɪ'bes] *tr* entwürdigen; (*currency*) entwerten
debatable [dɪ'betəbəl] *adj* strittig
debate [dɪ'bet] *s* Debatte *f* ‖ *tr* & *intr* debattieren
debauch [dɪ'bɔtʃ] *s* Schwelgerei *f* ‖ *tr* verderben; (*seduce*) verführen; **d. oneself** verkommen
debauched *adj* ausschweifend
debauchee [‚debə'tʃi] *s* Wüstling *m*
debauchery [dɪ'bɔtʃəri] *s* Schwelgerei *f*
debenture [dɪ'bentʃər] *s* (*bond*) Obligation *f*; (*voucher*) Schuldschein *m*
debilitate [dɪ'bɪlɪ‚tet] *tr* entkräften
debility [dɪ'bɪlɪti] *s* Schwäche *f*
debit ['debɪt] *s* Debet *n*, Soll *n*; (*as entry*) Belastung *f*
de'bit bal'ance *s* Sollsaldo *n*
de'bit side' *s* Soll *n*, Sollseite *f*
debonair [‚debə'ner] *adj* (*courteous*) höflich; (*carefree*) heiter und sorglos
debris [de'bri] *s* Trümmer *pl*
debt [det] *s* Schuld *f*; **be in s.o.'s d.** j-m verpflichtet sein; **run into d.** in Schulden geraten
debtor ['detər] *s* Schuldner –in *mf*
de-bug [dɪ'bʌg] *v pret* & *pp* **–bugged**; *ger* **–bugging**) *tr* (*remove defects from*) bereinigen; (*electron*) Abhörgeräte entfernen aus
debut [de'bju], ['debju] *s* Debüt *n*; **make one's d.** debütieren
debutante ['debju‚tɑnt] *s* Debütantin *f*
decade ['deked] *s* Jahrzehnt *n*, Dekade *f*
decadence ['dekədəns] *s* Dekadenz *f*
decadent ['dekədənt] *adj* dekadent; (*art*) entartet
decal ['dikæl] *s* Abziehbild *n*
decanter [dɪ'kæntər] *s* Karaffe *f*
decapitate [dɪ'kæpɪ‚tet] *tr* enthaupten
decathlon [dɪ'kæθlɑn] *s* Zehnkampf *m*
decay [dɪ'ke] *s* (*rotting*) Verwesung *f*; (fig) Verfall *m*; (dent) Karies *f*; **fall into d.** (& fig) in Verfall geraten ‖ *intr* verfaulen; (fig) verfallen
decease [dɪ'sis] *s* Ableben *n*
deceased' *adj* verstorben ‖ *s* Verstorbene *mf*
deceit [dɪ'sit] *s* Betrügerei *f*
deceitful [dɪ'sitfəl] *adj* betrügerisch
deceive [dɪ'siv] *tr* betrügen ‖ *intr* trügen
decelerate [dɪ'selə‚ret] *tr* verlangsamen ‖ *intr* seine Geschwindigkeit verringern
December [dɪ'sembər] *s* Dezember *m*
decency ['disənsi] *s* Anstand *m*; **decencies** Anstandsformen *pl*
decent ['disənt] *adj* anständig
decentralize [dɪ'sentrə‚laɪz] *tr* dezentralisieren
deception [dɪ'sepʃən] *s* (*act of deceiving*) Betrug *m*; (*state of being deceived*) Täuschung *f*
deceptive [dɪ'septɪv] *adj* trügerisch; (*misleading*) irreführend; (*similarity*) täuschend
decide [dɪ'saɪd] *tr* entscheiden ‖ *intr* (**on**) sich entscheiden, sich entschließen (über *acc*, für)

deciduous [dɪ'sɪdʒu·əs] *adj* blattabwerfend; **d. tree** Laubbaum *m*
decimal ['desɪməl] *adj* dezimal ‖ *s* Dezimalzahl *f*
dec'imal place' *s* Dezimalstelle *f*
dec'imal point' *s* (*in German the comma is used to separate the decimal fraction from the integer*) Komma *n*
decimate ['desɪ‚met] *tr* dezimieren
decipher [dɪ'saɪfər] *tr* entziffern
decision [dɪ'sɪʒən] *s* Entscheidung *f*, Entschluß *m*; (jur) Urteil *n*
decisive [dɪ'saɪsɪv] *adj* entscheidend
deck [dek] *s* (*of cards*) Spiel *n*; (data proc) Kartensatz *m*; (naut) Deck *n*, Verdeck *n* ‖ *tr* (coll) zu Boden schlagen; **d. out** ausschmücken
deck' chair' *s* Liegestuhl *m*
deck' hand' *s* gemeiner Matrose *m*
deck' land'ing *s* (aer) Trägerlandung *f*
declaim [dɪ'klem] *tr* & *intr* deklamieren
declaration [‚deklə'reʃən] *s* Erklärung *f*; (*at customs*) Zollerklärung *f*
declarative [dɪ'klærətɪv] *adj*—**d. sentence** Aussagesatz *m*
declare [dɪ'kler] *tr* erklären; (*tourist's belongings*) verzollen; (*commercial products*) deklarieren; **d. oneself against** sich aussprechen gegen
declension [dɪ'klenʃən] *s* Deklination *f*
declinable [dɪ'klaɪnəbəl] *adj* deklinierbar
decline [dɪ'klaɪn] *s* (*decrease*) Abnahme *f*; (*in prices*) Rückgang *m*; (*deterioration*) Verschlechterung *f*; (*slope*) Abhang *m*; (fig) Niedergang *m*; **be on the d.** in Abnahme begriffen sein ‖ *tr* (*refuse*) ablehnen; (gram) deklinieren ‖ *intr* (*refuse*) ablehnen; (*descend*) sich senken; (*sink*) sinken; (*draw to a close*) zu Ende gehen
declivity [dɪ'klɪvɪti] *s* Abhang *m*
decode [di'kod] *tr* entschlüsseln
decompose [‚dikəm'poz] *tr* zerlegen ‖ *intr* sich zersetzen, verwesen
decomposition [‚dikɑmpə'zɪʃən] *s* Zersetzung *f*, Verwesung *f*
decompression [‚dikəm'preʃən] *s* Dekompression *f*
decontaminaiton [‚dikən‚tæmɪ'neʃən] *s* Entseuchung *f*
décor [de'kɔr] *s* Dekor *m*
decorate ['dekə‚ret] *tr* dekorieren, (aus)schmücken; (*a new room*) einrichten; (*e.g., with a badge*) auszeichnen
decoration [‚dekə'reʃən] *s* Schmuck *m*; (*medal*) Orden *m*, Ehrenzeichen *n*, Dekoration *f*
decorative ['dekərətɪv] *adj* dekorativ
decorator ['dekə‚retər] *s* Dekorateur –in *mf*
decorous ['dekərəs] *adj* schicklich
decorum [dɪ'korəm] *s* Schicklichkeit *f*
decoy ['dikɔɪ] *s* (*bird or person*) Lockvogel *m*; (*anything used as a lure*) Lockmittel *n* ‖ [dɪ'kɔɪ] *tr* locken
decrease ['dikris] *s* Abnahme *f* ‖

[dɪ'kris] *tr* verringern ‖ *intr* abnehmen

decree [dɪ'kri] *s* Dekret *n*, Verordnung *f* ‖ *tr* dekretieren, verordnen

decrepit [dɪ'krepɪt] *adj* (*age-worn*) altersschwach; (*frail*) gebrechlich

de·cry [dɪ'kraɪ] *v* (*pret* & *pp* **–cried**) *tr* (*disparage*) herabsetzen; (*censure openly*) kritisieren

dedicate ['dɛdɪ,ket] *tr* (*a book, one's life*) (**to**) widmen (*dat*); (*a building*) einweihen

dedication [,dɛdɪ'keʃən] *s* Widmung *f*; (*of a building, etc.*) Einweihung *f*; (**to**) Hingabe *f* (*an acc*)

deduce [dɪ'd(j)us] *tr* (**from**) schließen (*aus*)

deduct [dɪ'dʌkt] *tr* abziehen, abrechnen

deduction [dɪ'dʌkʃən] *s* Abzug *m*; (*conclusion*) Schluß *m*, Folgerung *f*

deed [did] *s* (*act*) Tat *f*; (*jur*) Besitzurkunde *f*

deem [dim] *tr* halten für; **d. s.o. worthy of my confidence** j–n meines Vertrauens für würdig halten

deep [dip] *adj* tief; (*recondite*) dunkel; (*impression*) tiefgehend; (*color, sound*) tief, dunkel; **be d. in debt** tief in Schulden stecken; **four (ranks) d. in** Viererreihen; **in d. water** (fig) in Schwierigkeiten; **that's too d. for me** das ist mir zu hoch ‖ *adv* tief; **d. down in** tief innen in (*dat*) ‖ *s* Tiefe *f*, Meer *n*

deepen ['dipən] *tr* (& fig) vertiefen ‖ *intr* sich vertiefen

deep'-freeze' *v* (*pret* **–freezed** & **–froze**; *pp* **–freezed** & **–frozen**) *tr* tiefkühlen

deep'-fry' *v* (*pret* & *pp* **–fried**) *tr* fritieren

deep'-laid' *adj* schlau angelegt

deep' mourn'ing *s* tiefe Trauer *f*

deep'-root'ed *adj* tiefsitzend

deep'-set' *adj* (*eyes*) tiefliegend

deer [dɪr] *s* Hirsch *m*, Reh *n*, Rotwild *n*

deer'skin' *s* Hirschleder *n*, Wildleder *n*

deface [dɪ'fes] *tr* (*disfigure*) verunstalten; (*make illegible*) unleserlich machen

defacement [dɪ'fesmənt] *s* Verunstaltung *f*

de facto [di'fækto] *adj* & *adv* tatsächlich, de facto

defamation [,dɛfə'meʃən] *s* Verleumdung *f*

defame [dɪ'fem] *tr* verleumden

default [dɪ'fɔlt] *s* (*in duties*) Unterlassung *f*; (fin) Verzug *m*; **by d.** (jur) durch Nichterscheinen; (sport) durch Nichtantreten; **in d. of** in Ermangelung (*genit*) ‖ *tr* nicht erfüllen; (fin) nicht zahlen ‖ *intr* seinen Verpflichtungen nicht nachkommen; (fin) in Verzug sein

defeat [dɪ'fit] *s* Niederlage *f*; (parl) Niederstimmen *n*; **admit d.** sich geschlagen geben ‖ *tr* besiegen, schlagen; (*frustrate*) hilflos machen; (*plans*) zunichte machen; (*a bill*) niederstimmen; **d. the purpose** den Zweck verfehlen

defeatism [dɪ'fitɪzəm] *s* Defätismus *m*

defeatist [dɪ'fitɪst] *s* Defätist –in *mf*

defecate ['dɛfɪ,ket] *intr* Stuhl haben

defect ['difɛkt] *s* Defekt *m*; (*physical or mental defect*) Gebrechen *n*; (*imperfection*) Mangel *m*; (*in manufacture*) Fabrikationsfehler *m* ‖ [dɪ'fɛkt] *intr* (**from**) (*a religion*) abfallen (von); (*a party*) abtrünnig werden (von); (**to**) überlaufen (zu)

defection [dɪ'fɛkʃən] *s* Abfall *m*; (**to**) Übertritt *m* (zu)

defective [dɪ'fɛktɪv] *adj* fehlerhaft; (gram) unvollständig; (tech) defekt

defector [dɪ'fɛktər] *s* (pol) Abtrünnige *mf*, Überläufer –in *mf*

defend [dɪ'fɛnd] *tr* verteidigen

defendant [dɪ'fɛndənt] *s* (*in civil suit*) Beklagte *mf*; (*in criminal suit*) Angeklagte *mf*

defender [dɪ'fɛndər] *s* Verteidiger –in *mf*; (sport) Titelverteidiger –in *mf*

defense [dɪ'fɛns] *s* (& jur, sport) Verteidigung *f*; (*tactical*) (mil) Abwehr *f*; **d. against** (*e.g., disease*) Schutz *m* vor (*dat*)

defenseless [dɪ'fɛnslɪs] *adj* schutzlos

defensible [dɪ'fɛnsɪbəl] *adj* verteidigungsfähig; (*argument, claim*) verfechtbar

defensive [dɪ'fɛnsɪv] *adj* defensiv; (mil) Verteidigungs–, Abwehr– ‖ *s* Defensive *f*; (*tactical*) Abwehr *f*; **be on the d.**—sich in der Defensive befinden

de·fer [dɪ'fʌr] *v* (*pret* & *pp* **–ferred**; *ger* **–ferring**) *tr* verschieben; (mil) zurückschieben ‖ *intr*—**d. to** nachgeben (*dat*)

deference ['dɛfərəns] *s* (*courteous regard*) Ehrerbietung *f*; (*yielding*) Nachgiebigkeit *f*; **in d. to** aus Rücksicht gegen; **with all due d. to** bei aller Achtung vor (*dat*)

deferential [,dɛfə'rɛnʃəl] *adj* ehrerbietig, rücksichtsvoll

deferment [dɪ'fʌrmənt] *s* Aufschub *m*; (mil) Zurückstellung *f*

defiance [dɪ'faɪəns] *s* Trotz *m*; **in d. of s.o.** i–m zum Trotz

defiant [dɪ'faɪənt] *adj* trotzig

deficiency [dɪ'fɪʃənsi] *s* (**of**) Mangel *m* (*an dat*); (*shortcoming*) Defekt *m*; (*deficit*) Defizit *n*

deficient [dɪ'fɪʃənt] *adj* mangelhaft; **be d. in** Mangel haben an (*dat*); **mentally d.** schwachsinnig

deficit ['dɛfɪsɪt] *s* Defizit *n*

defilade [,dɛfɪ'led] *s* Deckung *f* ‖ *tr* gegen Feuer sichern

defile [dɪ'faɪl], ['difaɪl] *s* Hohlweg *m* ‖ [dɪ'faɪl] *tr* beflecken

defilement [dɪ'faɪlmənt] *s* Befleckung *f*

define [dɪ'faɪn] *tr* definieren, bestimmen; (*e.g., boundaries*) festlegen

definite ['dɛfɪnɪt] *adj* bestimmt

definition [,dɛfɪ'nɪʃən] *s* Definition *f*, Bestimmung *f*; (opt) Bildschärfe *f*

definitive [dɪ'fɪnɪtɪv] *adj* endgültig

deflate [dɪ'flet] *tr* Luft ablassen aus; (*prices*) herabsetzen; (*s.o.'s ego, hopes*) e–n Stoß versetzen (*dat*)

deflation [dɪ'fleʃən] s (fin) Deflation f

deflect [dɪ'flɛkt] tr ablenken ‖ intr (from) abweichen (von)

deflection [dɪ'flɛkʃən] s Ablenkung f; Abweichung f; (of an indicator) Ausschlag m; (of light rays) Beugung f; (radar, telv) Ablenkung f

deflower [dɪ'flaʊ·ər] tr entjungfern

defoliate [di'folɪ,et] tr entblättern

deforest [di'fɔrɛst] tr abholzen

deform [dɪ'fɔrm] tr entstellen

deformed' adj verwachsen, mißförmig

deformity [dɪ'fɔrmɪti] s (state of being deformed) Mißgestalt f; (deformed part) Verwachsung f; (ugliness) Häßlichkeit f

defraud [dɪ'frɔd] tr (of) betrügen (um)

defray [dɪ'fre] tr tragen, bestreiten

defrock [di'frɑk] tr das Priesteramt entziehen (dat)

defrost [dɪ'frɔst] tr entfrosten

defroster [dɪ'frɔstər] s Entfroster m

deft [dɛft] adj flink, fingerfertig

defunct [dɪ'fʌŋkt] adj (person) verstorben; (no longer in operation) stillgelegt; (no longer in effect) außer Kraft (befindlich); (newspaper) eingegangen

de·fy [dɪ'faɪ] v (pret & pp –fied) tr trotzen (dat); (challenge) herausfordern; **d. description** sich nicht beschreiben lassen

degeneracy [dɪ'dʒɛnərəsi] s Entartung f

degenerate [dɪ'dʒɛnərɪt] adj entartet, verkommen ‖ [dɪ'dʒɛnə,ret] intr entarten; **(into)** ausarten (in acc)

degrade [dɪ'gred] tr degradieren; (bring into low esteem) entwürdigen

degrad'ing adj entwürdigend

degree [dɪ'gri] s Grad m; (gram) Steigerungsstufe f; **by degrees** gradweise; **d. of latitude** Breitengrad m; **d. of longitude** Längengrad m; **take one's d.** promovieren; **to a d.** einigermaßen; **to a high d.** in hohem Maße

dehumanize [dɪ'hjumə,naɪz] tr entmenschlichen

dehumidifier [,dihju'mɪdɪ,faɪ·ər] s Luftentfeuchter m

dehumidi·fy [,dihju'mɪdɪ,faɪ] v (pret & pp –fied) entfeuchten

dehydrate [di'haɪdret] tr (vegetables) dörren, das Wasser entziehen (dat); (chem) dehydrieren ‖ intr das Wasser verlieren

dehy'drated adj (vegetables) Trocken–; (body) dehydriert

deice [di'aɪs] tr enteisen

dei·fy ['di·ɪ,faɪ] v (pret & pp –fied) tr (a man) zum Gott erheben; (a woman) zur Göttin erheben

deject'ed adj niedergeschlagen

dejection [dɪ'dʒɛkʃən] s Niedergeschlagenheit f, Mutlosigkeit f

delay [dɪ'le] s Aufschub m, Verzögerung f; **without d.** unverzüglich ‖ tr (postpone) aufschieben; (detain) aufhalten ‖ intr zögern

delectable [dɪ'lɛktəbəl] adj ergötzlich

delegate ['dɛlɪ,get], ['dɛlɪgɪt] s De-legierte mf ‖ ['dɛlɪ,get] tr delegieren; (authority) übertragen

delegation [,dɛlɪ'geʃən] s (persons delegated) Delegation f; (e.g., of authority) Übertragung f

delete [dɪ'lit] tr tilgen

deletion [dɪ'liʃən] s Tilgung f

deliberate [dɪ'lɪbərɪt] adj (intentional) vorsätzlich, bewußt; (slow) gemessen, bedächtig ‖ [dɪ'lɪbə,ret] intr überlegen; (said of several persons) beratschlagen; **d. on** sich beraten über (acc)

deliberately [dɪ'lɪbərɪtli] adv mit Absicht

deliberation [dɪ,lɪbə'reʃən] s Überlegung f; (by several persons) Beratung f; (slowness) Bedächtigkeit f

delicacy ['dɛlɪkəsi] s Zartheit f; (fine food) Delikatesse f

delicate ['dɛlɪkɪt] adj fein, delikat; (situation) heikel; (health) zart

delicatessen [,dɛlɪkə'tɛsən] s (food) Delikatessen pl; (store) Delikatessengeschäft n

delicious [dɪ'lɪʃəs] adj köstlich

delight [dɪ'laɪt] s Freude f; (high degree of pleasure) Entzücken n; **take d. in** Freude finden an (dat) ‖ tr entzücken, erfreuen; **be delighted by** sich freuen an (dat); **I'll be delighted to come** ich komme mit dem größten Vergnügen ‖ intr—**d. in** sich ergötzen an (dat)

delightful [dɪ'laɪtfəl] adj entzückend

delimit [dɪ'lɪmɪt] tr abgrenzen

delineate [dɪ'lɪnɪ,et] tr zeichnen

delinquency [dɪ'lɪŋkwənsi] s Pflichtvergessenheit f; (misdeed) Vergehen n

delinquent [dɪ'lɪŋkwənt] adj pflichtvergessen; (guilty) straffällig; (overdue) rückständig; (in default) säumig ‖ s Straffällige mf

delirious [dɪ'lɪrɪ·əs] adj irre; **(with)** rasend (vor dat)

delirium [dɪ'lɪrɪ·əm] s Fieberwahn m

deliver [dɪ'lɪvər] tr liefern; (a message) überreichen; (free) befreien; (mail) zustellen; (a speech) halten; (a blow) versetzen; (a verdict) aussprechen; (a child) zur Welt bringen; (votes) bringen; (a ball) werfen; (relig) erlösen

deliverance [dɪ'lɪvərəns] s Erlösung f

delivery [dɪ'lɪvəri] s Lieferung f; (freeing) Befreiung f; (of mail) Zustellung f; (of a speaker, actor, singer) Vortragsweise f; (of a pitcher) Wurf m; (childbirth) Entbindung f

deliv'ery·man' s (–men') Austräger m

deliv'ery room' s Kreißsaal m

deliv'ery truck' s Lieferwagen m

dell [dɛl] s enges Tal n

delouse [di'laus] tr entlausen

delta ['dɛltə] s Delta n

delude [dɪ'lud] tr täuschen

deluge ['dɛljudʒ] s Überschwemmung f; (fig) Hochflut f; **Deluge** (Bib) Sintflut f ‖ tr überschwemmen; (with letters, etc.) überschütten

delusion [dɪ'luʒən] s (state of being deluded) Täuschung f; (misconcep-

tion) Wahnvorstellung *f;* (*psychiatry*) Wahn *m;* **delusions of grandeur** Größenwahn *m*

deluxe [dɪ'lʊks], [dɪ'lʌks] *adj* Luxus-

delve [dɛlv] *intr—***d. into** sich vertiefen in (*acc*)

demagogue ['dɛmə‚gag] *s* Volksverführer –in *mf*

demand [dɪ'mænd] *s* Verlangen *n;* (*com*) (**for**) Nachfrage *f* (nach); **in** (**great**) **d.** (sehr) gefragt; **make demands on** Ansprüche erheben auf (*acc*); **on d.** auf Verlangen || *tr* (**from** or **of**) verlangen (von), fordern (von)

demand'ing *adj* anspruchsvoll; (*strict*) streng

demarca'tion line' [‚dimɑr'keʃən] *s* Demarkationslinie *f*

demean [dɪ'min] *tr* erniedrigen

demeanor [dɪ'minər] *s* Benehmen *n*

demented [dɪ'mɛntɪd] *adj* wahnsinnig

demerit [di'mɛrɪt] *s* (*fault*) Fehler *m;* (*deficiency mark*) Minuspunkt *m*

demigod ['dɛmɪ‚gɑd] *s* Halbgott *m*

demijohn ['dɛmɪ‚dʒɑn] *s* Korbflasche *f*

demilitarize [di'mɪlɪtə‚raɪz] *tr* entmilitarisieren

demise [dɪ'maɪz] *s* Ableben *n*

demitasse ['dɛmɪ‚tæs], ['dɛmɪ‚tɑs] *s* Mokkatasse *f*

demobilize [di'mobɪ‚laɪz] *tr & intr* demobilisieren

democracy [dɪ'mɑkrəsi] *s* Demokratie *f*

democrat ['dɛmə‚kræt] *s* Demokrat –in *mf*

democratic [‚dɛmə'krætɪk] *adj* demokratisch

demolish [dɪ'mɑlɪʃ] *tr* (*raze*) niederreißen; (*destroy*) zertrümmern; (*an argument*) vernichten; (*devour*) (coll) verschlingen

demolition [‚dɛmə'lɪʃən], [‚dimə'lɪʃən] *s* (*act of razing*) Abbruch *m;* (*by explosives*) Sprengung *f;* **demolitions** Sprengstoff *m*

demoli'tion squad' *s* Sprengkommando *n*

demoli'tion work' *s* Sprengarbeiten *pl*

demon ['dimən] *s* Dämon *m,* böser Geist *m*

demonstrable [dɪ'mɑnstrəbəl] *adj* beweisbar

demonstrate ['dɛmən‚stret] *tr* (*prove*) beweisen; (*explain*) dartun; (*display*) zeigen; (*a product, process*) vorführen || *intr* (pol) demonstrieren

demonstration [‚dɛmən'streʃən] *s* (*com*) Vorführung *f;* (*pol*) Demonstration *f*

demonstrative [dɪ'mɑnstrətɪv] *adj* (*showing emotions*) gefühlvoll; (*illustrative*) anschaulich; (*gram*) hinweisend

demonstrator ['dɛmən‚stretər] *s* (*of products*) Vorführer –in *mf;* (*model used in demonstration*) Vorführmodell *n;* (*pol*) Demonstrant –in *mf*

demoralize [dɪ'mɔrə‚laɪz] *tr* demoralisieren

demote [dɪ'mot] *tr* (*an employee*) her-

abstufen; (*a student*) zurückversetzen; (mil) degradieren

demotion [dɪ'moʃən] *s* (*of an employee*) Herabstufung *f;* (*of a student*) Zurückversetzung *f;* (mil) Degradierung *f*

de·mur [dɪ'mʌr] *v* (*pret & pp* **-murred;** *ger* **-murring**) *intr* Einwände erheben

demure [dɪ'mjʊr] *adj* zimperlich

den [dɛn] *s* (*of animals; of thieves*) Höhle *f;* (*comfortable room*) Freizeitraum *m*

denaturalize [di'nætjərə‚laɪz] *tr* ausbürgern

denial [dɪ'naɪ·əl] *s* (*of an assertion*) Leugnung *f;* (*of guilt*) Leugnen *n;* (*of a request*) Ablehnung *f;* (*of faith*) Ableugnung *f;* (*of rights*) Verweigerung *f;* (*of a report*) Dementi *n*

denigrate ['dɛnɪ‚gret] *tr* anschwärzen

denim ['dɛnɪm] *s* Drillich *m*

denizen ['dɛnɪzən] *s* Bewohner –in *mf*

Denmark ['dɛnmɑrk] *s* Dänemark *n*

denomination [dɪ‚nɑmɪ'neʃən] *s* Bezeichnung *f;* (*class, kind*) Klasse *f,* (*of money*) Nennwert *m;* (*of shares*) Stückelung *f;* (relig) Konfession *f,* Bekenntnis *n;* **in denominations of five and ten dollars** in Fünf– und Zehndollarnoten

denotation [‚dino'teʃən] *s* Bedeutung *f*

denote [dɪ'not] *tr* (*mean*) bedeuten; (*indicate*) anzeigen

dénouement [‚denu'mɑ̃] *s* Auflösung *f*

denounce [dɪ'naʊns] *tr* (*inform against*) denunzieren; (*condemn openly*) brandmarken, anprangern; (*a treaty*) kündigen

dense [dɛns] *adj* dicht; (coll) beschränkt

density ['dɛnsɪti] *s* Dichte *f*

dent [dɛnt] *s* Beule *f* || *tr* einbeulen

dental ['dɛntəl] *adj* Zahn–; (ling) dental || *s* (ling) Zahnlaut *m*

den'tal hygiene' *s* Zahnpflege *f*

den'tal sur'geon *s* Zahnarzt *m,* Zahnärztin *f*

dentifrice ['dɛntɪfrɪs] *s* Zahnputzmittel *n*

dentist ['dɛntɪst] *s* Zahnarzt *m,* Zahnärztin *f*

dentistry ['dɛntɪstri] *s* Zahnheilkunde *f*

denture ['dɛntʃər] *s* künstliches Gebiß *n*

denunciation [dɪ‚nʌnsɪ'eʃən] *s* (*informing against*) Denunzierung *f;* (*public condemnation*) Brandmarkung *f*

de·ny [dɪ'naɪ] *v* (*pret & pp* **-nied**) *tr* (*a statement*) leugnen; (*officially*) dementieren; (*a request*) ablehnen; (*one's faith*) ableugnen; (*rights*) verweigern; **d. oneself s.th.** sich [*dat*] etw versagen; **d. s.o. s.th.** j-m etw aberkennen

deodorant [di'odərənt] *s* Deodorant *n*

deodorize [di'odə‚raɪz] *tr* desodorieren

deoxidize [di'ɑksɪ‚daɪz] *tr* desoxydieren

depart [dɪ'pɑrt] *intr* (*on foot*) fortgehen; (*in a vehicle or boat*) abfahren; (*by plane*) abfliegen; (*on horseback*) abreiten; (*on a trip*) abreisen; (*deviate*) abweichen

department [dɪ'pɑrtmənt] *s* (*subdivision*) Abteilung *f;* (*field*) Fach *n;* (*principal branch of government*) Ministerium *n;* (*government office*) Amt *n;* (educ) Abteilung *f*

depart'ment head' *s* Abteilungsleiter –in *mf*

depart'ment store' *s* Kaufhaus *n,* Warenhaus *n*

departure [dɪ'pɑrtʃər] *s* (*on foot*) Weggehen *n;* (*by car, boat, train*) Abfahrt *f,* Abreise *f;* (*by plane*) Abflug *m;* (*deviation*) Abweichung *f*

depend [dɪ'pɛnd] *intr* (on) abhängen (von); (*rely on*) sich verlassen (auf *acc*); **depending on** je nach; **depending on how** je nachdem; **it all depends** (coll) es kommt darauf an

dependable [dɪ'pɛndəbəl] *adj* zuverlässig

dependence [dɪ'pɛndəns] *s* Abhängigkeit *f*

dependency [dɪ'pɛndənsi] *s* Schutzgebiet *n*

dependent [dɪ'pɛndənt] *adj* (on) abhängig (von) ‖ *s* Abhängige *mf;* (*for tax purposes*) Unterhaltsberechtigte *mf*

depict [dɪ'pɪkt] *tr* schildern

deplete [dɪ'plit] *tr* entleeren; (fig) erschöpfen

deplorable [dɪ'plorəbəl] *adj* (*situation*) beklagenswert; (*regrettable*) bedauerlich; (*bad*) schlecht

deplore [dɪ'plor] *tr* bedauern

deploy [dɪ'plɔɪ] *tr* entfalten ‖ *intr* sich entfalten

deployment [dɪ'plɔɪmənt] *s* Entfaltung *f*

depolarize [di'polə,raɪz] *tr* depolarisieren

deponent [dɪ'ponənt] *s* (gram) Deponens *n;* (jur) Deponent –in *mf*

depopulate [di'pɑpjə,let] *tr* entvölkern

deport [dɪ'port] *tr* deportieren; **d. oneself** sich benehmen

deportation [,dipor'teʃən] *s* Deportation *f*

deportment [dɪ'portmənt] *s* Benehmen *n*

depose [dɪ'poz] *tr* (*from office*) absetzen; (jur) bezeugen ‖ *intr* (jur) unter Eid aussagen; (*in writing*) (jur) eidesstattlich versichern

deposit [dɪ'pɑzɪt] *s* (*partial payment*) Anzahlung *f;* (*at a bank*) Einlage *f;* (*for safekeeping*) Hinterlegung *f;* (geol) Ablagerung *f;* (min) Vorkommen *n;* **for d. only** nur zur Verrechnung ‖ *tr* (*set down*) niederlegen; (*money at a bank*) einlegen; (*a check*) verrechnen; (*as part payment*) anzahlen; (*for safekeeping*) deponieren; (geol) ablagern; (*a coin*) (telp) einwerfen

depositor [dɪ'pɑzɪtər] *s* Einzahler –in *mf;* (*of valuables*) Hinterleger –in *mf*

depos'it slip' *s* Einzahlungsbeleg *m*

depot ['dipo], ['dɛpo] *s* (*bus station; storage place*) Depot *n;* (*train station*) Bahnhof *m*

depraved [dɪ'prevd] *adj* verworfen

depravity [dɪ'præviti] *s* Verworfenheit *f*

deprecate ['dɛprɪ,ket] *tr* mißbilligen

depreciate [dɪ'priʃɪ,et] *tr* (*money, stocks*) abwerten; (*for tax purposes*) abschreiben; (*value or price*) herabsetzen; (*disparage*) geringschätzen ‖ *intr* im Wert sinken

depreciation [dɪ,priʃɪ'eʃən] *s* (*decrease in value*) Wertminderung *f;* (*of currency or stocks*) Abwertung *f;* (*for tax purposes*) Abschreibung *f*

depress [dɪ'prɛs] *tr* niederdrücken; (*sadden*) deprimieren; (*cause to sink*) herunterdrücken

depressed' *adj* (*saddened*) niedergeschlagen; (*market*) flau

depressed' ar'ea *s* Notstandsgebiet *n*

depress'ing *adj* deprimierend

depression [dɪ'prɛʃən] *s* (*mental state; economic crisis*) Depression *f;* (geol) Vertiefung *f*

deprive [dɪ'praɪv] *tr*—**d. s.o. of s.th.** j-m etw entziehen; (*withhold*) j-m etw vorenthalten

depth [dɛpθ] *s* Tiefe *f;* **go beyond one's d.** den Boden unter den Füßen verlieren; **in d.** gründlich

depth' charge' *s* Wasserbombe *f*

depth' of field' *s* (phot) Tiefenschärfe *f*

deputation [,dɛpjə'teʃən] *s* Abordnung *f*

deputize ['dɛpjə,taɪz] *tr* abordnen

deputy ['dɛpjəti] *s* Vertreter –in *mf;* (pol) Abgeordnete *mf*

derail [dɪ'rel] *tr* zum Entgleisen bringen ‖ *intr* entgleisen

derailment [dɪ'relmənt] *s* Entgleisung *f*

deranged [dɪ'rendʒd] *adj* geistesgestört

derangement [dɪ'rendʒmənt] *s* Geistesgestörtheit *f*

derby ['dʌrbi] *s* (*hat*) Melone *f;* (*race*) Derbyrennen *n*

derelict ['dɛrɪlɪkt] *adj* (*negligent*) (in) nachlässig (in *dat*); (*abandoned*) herrenlos ‖ *s* (*ship; bum*) Wrack *n*

dereliction [,dɛrɪ'lɪkʃən] *s* (*neglect*) Vernachlässigung *f*

deride [dɪ'raɪd] *tr* verspotten

derision [dɪ'rɪʒən] *s* Spott *m*

derivation [,dɛrɪ'veʃən] *s* (gram, math) Ableitung *f*

derivative [dɪ'rɪvətɪv] *adj* abgeleitet ‖ *s* (*chem*) Derivat *n;* (gram, math) Ableitung *f*

derive [dɪ'raɪv] *tr* (*obtain*) gewinnen; (gram, math) ableiten; **d. pleasure from s.th.** Freude an etw finden ‖ *intr* (from) herstammen (von)

dermatologist [,dʌrmə'tɑlədʒɪst] *s* Hautarzt *m,* Hautärztin *f*

derogatory [dɪ'rɑgə,tori] *adj* abfällig

derrick ['dɛrɪk] *s* (*over an oil well*) Bohrturm *m;* (naut) Ladebaum *m*

dervish ['dʌrvɪʃ] *s* Derwisch *m*

desalinization [di,sɛlɪnɪ'zeʃən] *s* Entsalzung *f*

desalt [di'sɔlt] *tr* entsalzen
descend [dɪ'sɛnd] *tr* hinuntergehen ||
intr (*dismount, alight*) absteigen;
(*said of a plane*) niedergehen; (*from
a tree, from heaven*) herabsteigen;
(*said of a road*) sich senken; (*pass
by inheritance*) (**to**) übergehen (auf
acc); **be descended from** abstammen
von; **d. upon** hereinbrechen über
(*acc*)
descendant [dɪ'sɛndənt] *s* Abkömmling *m*, Nachkomme *m*; **descendants**
Nachkommenschaft *f*
descendent [dɪ'sɛndənt] *adj* absteigend
descent [dɪ'sɛnt] *s* Abstieg *m*; (*lineage*) Herkunft *f*; (*of a plane or parachute*) Niedergehen *n*; (*slope*) Abhang *m*; (*hostile raid*) (**on**) Überfall
m (auf *acc*)
describe [dɪ'skraɪb] *tr* beschreiben
description [dɪ'skrɪpʃən] *s* Beschreibung *f*; (*type*) Art *f*; **beyond d.** unbeschreiblich
descriptive [dɪ'skrɪptɪv] *adj* beschrei-
bend
de·scry [dɪ'skraɪ] *v* (*pret & pp
–scried*) *tr* erspähen, erblicken
desecrate ['dɛsɪ‚kret] *tr* entweihen
desecration [‚dɛsɪ'kreʃən] *s* Entweihung *f*
desegregate [di'sɛgrɪ‚get] *tr* die Rassentrennung aufheben in (*dat*)
desegregation [di‚sɛgrɪ'geʃən] *s* Aufhebung *f* der Rassentrennung
desert ['dɛzərt] *adj* öde, wüst; (*sand,
warfare, etc.*) Wüsten– || *s* Wüste *f*;
(fig) Öde *f* || [dɪ'zʌrt] *s* Verdienst
m; **get one's just deserts** seinen wohl-
verdienten Lohn empfangen || *tr* ver-
lassen || *intr* (mil) desertieren; (**to**)
überlaufen (zu)
deserter [dɪ'zʌrtər] *s* Deserteur *m*
desertion [dɪ'zʌrʃən] *s* Verlassen *n*;
(*of a party*) Abfall *m*; (mil) Fahnen-
flucht *f*
deserve [dɪ'zʌrv] *tr* verdienen
deservedly [dɪ'zʌrvɪdli] *adv* mit Recht
deserv'ing *adj* (**of**) würdig (*genit*)
design [dɪ'zaɪn] *s* (*outline*) Entwurf
m; (*pattern*) Muster *n*; (*plan*) Plan
m; (*plot*) Anschlag *m*; (*of a building, etc.*) Bauart *f*; (*aim*) Absicht *f*;
designs on böse Absichten auf (*acc*)
|| *tr* (*make a preliminary sketch of*)
entwerfen; (*draw up detailed plans
for*) konstruieren; **designed for** gedacht für
designate ['dɛzɪg‚net] *tr* (**as**) bezeichnen (als); (**to**) ernennen (zu)
designation [‚dɛzɪg'neʃən] *s* (*act of
designating*) Kennzeichnung *f*; (*title*)
Bezeichnung *f*; (*appointment*) Ernennung *f*
designer [dɪ'zaɪnər] *s* (*of patterns*)
Musterzeichner –in *mf*; (*of fashions*)
Modeschöpfer –in *mf*; (theat) Dekorateur –in *mf*
design'ing *adj* intrigant; (*calculating*)
berechnend
desirable [dɪ'zaɪrəbəl] *adj* wünschenswert, begehrenswert
desire [dɪ'zaɪr] *s* (*wish*) Wunsch *m*;
(*interest*) Lust *f*; (*craving*) Begierde

f; (*thing desired*) Gewünschte *n* || *tr*
wünschen
desirous [dɪ'zaɪrəs] *adj* (**of**) begierig
(nach)
desist [dɪ'zɪst] *intr* (**from**) ablassen
(von)
desk [dɛsk] *s* Schreibtisch *m*; (*of a
teacher*) Pult *m*; (*of a pupil*) Schul-
bank *f*; (*in a hotel*) Kasse *f*
desk' cop'y *s* Freiexemplar *n*
desk' lamp' *s* Tischlampe *f*
desk' pad' *s* Schreibunterlage *f*
desolate ['dɛsəlɪt] *adj* (*barren*) öde;
(*joyless*) trostlos; (*deserted*) ver-
lassen; (*delapidated*) verfallen ||
['dɛsə‚let] *tr* verwüsten
desolation [‚dɛsə'leʃən] *s* (*devastation*) Verwüstung *f*; (*dreariness*)
Trostlosigkeit *f*
despair [dɪs'pɛr] *s* Verzweiflung *f* ||
intr (**of**) verzweifeln (an *dat*)
despair'ing *adj* verweifelt
despera·do [‚dɛspə'rado], [‚dɛspə-
'redo] *s* (*–does & –dos*) Desperado *m*
desperate ['dɛspərɪt] *adj* verzweifelt
desperation [‚dɛspə'reʃən] *s* Verzweiflung *f*
despicable ['dɛspɪkəbəl] *adj* verächtlich, verachtungswürdig
despise [dɪ'spaɪz] *tr* verachten
despite [dɪ'spaɪt] *prep* trotz (*genit*)
despondency [dɪ'spandənsi] *s* Klein-
mut *m*
despondent [dɪ'spandənt] *adj* kleinmütig
despot ['dɛspat] *s* Despot –in *mf*
despotic [dɛs'patɪk] *adj* despotisch
despotism ['dɛspə‚tɪzəm] *s* Despotie
f; (*as a system*) Despotismus *m*
dessert [dɪ'zʌrt] *s* Nachtisch *m*
destination [‚dɛstɪ'neʃən] *s* (*of a trip*)
Bestimmungsort *m*, Reiseziel *n*; (*purpose*) Bestimmung *f*
destine ['dɛstɪn] *tr* (**for**) bestimmen
(zu or für)
destiny ['dɛstɪni] *s* Schicksal *n*;
(*doom*) Verhängnis *n*
destitute ['dɛstɪ‚t(j)ut] *adj* mittellos;
d. of ohne
destitution [‚dɛstɪ't(j)uʃən] *s* äußerste
Armut *f*
destroy [dɪ'strɔɪ] *tr* vernichten, zerstören; (*animals, bacteria*) töten
destroyer [dɪ'strɔɪ·ər] *s* (nav) Zer-
störer *m*
destroy'er es'cort *s* Zerstörergeleit-
schutz *m*
destruction [dɪ'strʌkʃən] *s* Zerstörung
f; (*of species*) Ausrottung *f*
destructive [dɪ'strʌktɪv] *adj* zerstö-
rend; (*criticism*) vernichtend; (*tendency*) destruktiv
desultory ['dɛsəl‚tori] *adj* (*without
plan*) planlos; (*fitful*) sprunghaft;
(*remark*) deplaciert
detach [dɪ'tætʃ] *tr* ablösen; (*along a
perforation*) abtrennen; (mil) abkom-
mandieren
detachable [dɪ'tætʃəbəl] *tr* abnehmbar,
ablösbar
detached' *adj* (*building*) alleinstehend;
(*objective*) objektiv; (*aloof*) distan-
ziert

detachment [dɪ'tætʃmənt] s Objektivität f; (aloofness) Abstand m; (mil) Trupp m, Kommando n
detail [dɪ'tel], ['ditel] s Enzelheit f, Detail n; (mil) Kommando n, Trupp m; **details** (pej) Kleinkram m; **in d.** ausführlich || [dɪ'tel] (relate in detail) ausführlich berichten; (list) einzeln aufzählen; (mil) abkommandieren
de'tail draw'ing s Detailzeichnung f
detailed' adj ausführlich; **d. work** Kleinarbeit f
detain [dɪ'ten] tr zurückhalten; (jur) in Haft behalten
detect [dɪ'tɛkt] tr (discover) entdecken; (catch) ertappen
detection [dɪ'tɛkʃən] s Entdeckung f
detective [dɪ'tɛktɪv] s Detektiv m
detec'tive sto'ry s Kriminalroman m
detector [dɪ'tɛktər] s (e.g., of smoke) Spürgerät n; (of objects) Suchgerät n; (rad) Detektor m
détente [de'tant] s Entspannung f, Détente f
detention [dɪ'tɛnʃən] s (jur) Haft f
deten'tion camp' s Internierungslager n
deten'tion home' s Haftanstalt f
de·ter [dɪ'tʌr] v (pret & pp –terred; ger–terring) tr (from) abschrecken (von), abhalten (von)
detergent [dɪ'tʌrdʒənt] s Reinigungsmittel n; (in a washer) Waschmittel n
deteriorate [dɪ'tɪrɪ·ə‚ret] tr verschlechtern || intr sich verschlechtern
deterioration [dɪ‚tɪrɪ·ə're ʃən] s Verschlechterung f, Verfall m
determination [dɪ‚tʌrmɪ'neʃən] s Bestimmung f; (resoluteness) Entschlossenheit f; (of boundaries) Festlegung f
determine [dɪ'tʌrmɪn] tr (fix conclusively) bestimmen; (boundaries) festlegen; (decide) entscheiden
deter'mined adj entschlossen
deterrent [dɪ'tʌrənt] adj abschreckend || s Abschreckungsmittel n
detest [dɪ'tɛst] tr verabscheuen
detestable [dɪ'tɛstəbəl] adj abscheulich
dethrone [dɪ'θron] tr entthronen
detonate ['dɛtə‚net] tr explodieren lassen || intr explodieren
detour ['ditur] s (for cars) Umleitung f; (for pedestrians) Umweg m || tr umleiten || intr e-n Umweg machen
detract [dɪ'trækt] tr ablenken || intr— **d. from** beeinträchtigen
detraction [dɪ'trækʃən] s Beeinträchtigung f
detractor [dɪ'træktər] s Verleumder –in mf
detrain [dɪ'tren] tr ausladen || intr aussteigen
detriment ['dɛtrɪmənt] s Nachteil m
detrimental [‚dɛtrɪ'mɛntəl] adj (to) nachteilig (für), schädlich (für)
deuce [d(j)us] s (in cards or dice) Zwei f; (in tennis) Einstand m; **what the d.?** was zum Teufel?
devaluate [di'vælju‚et] tr abwerten

devaluation [di‚vælju'eʃən] s Abwertung f
devastate ['dɛvəs‚tet] tr verheeren
develop [dɪ'vɛləp] tr entwickeln; (one's mind) (aus)bilden; (a habit) annehmen; (a disease) sich [dat] zuziehen; (cracks) bekommen; (land) nutzbar machen; (a mine) ausbauen; (phot) entwickeln || intr sich entwickeln; (said of habits) sich herausbilden; **d. into** sich entwicklen zu
developer [dɪ'vɛləpər] s (of land) Spekulant –in mf; (phot) Entwickler m
development [dɪ'vɛləpmənt] s Entwicklung f; (of relations, of a mine) Ausbau m; (of land) Nutzbarmachung f; (of housing) Siedlung f; (an event) Ereignis n; (educ) Ausbildung f; (phot) Entwicklung f
deviate ['divɪ‚et] intr abweichen
deviation [‚divɪ'eʃən] s Abweichung f
device [dɪ'vaɪs] s Vorrichtung f, Gerät n; (means) Mittel n; (crafty scheme) Kniff m; (literary device) Kunstgriff m; (heral) Sinnbild n; **leave s.o. to his own devices** j–n sich [dat] selbst überlassen
dev·il ['dɛvəl] s Teufel m; **a d. of a** (coll) verteufelt; **between the d. and the deep blue sea** zwischen zwei Feuern; **poor d.** armer Teufel; **the d. with you!** (coll) scher dich zum Teufel!; **what** (who, etc.) **the d.?** was (wer, etc.) zum Teufel? || v (pret & pp –il[l]ed; ger –il[l]ing) tr (culin) mit viel Gewürz zubereiten
devilish ['dɛv(ə)lɪʃ] adj teuflisch
dev'il-may-care' adj (informal) wurstig; (reckless) verwegen
devilment ['dɛvɪlmənt] s Unfug m
deviltry ['dɛvɪltri] s Unfug m
devious ['divɪ·əs] adj abweichend; (tricky) unredlich; (reasoning) abwegig
devise [dɪ'vaɪz] tr ersinnen; (jur) vermachen
devoid [dɪ'vɔɪd] adj—**d. of** ohne
devolve [dɪ'valv] intr—**d. on** zufallen (dat)
devote [dɪ'vot] tr widmen
devot'ed adj (dedicated) ergeben; (affectionate) liebevoll
devotee [‚dɛvə'ti] s Anhänger –in mf
devotion [dɪ'voʃən] s Ergebenheit f; (devoutness) Frömmigkeit f; (special prayer) (to) Gebet n (zu); **devotions** Andacht f
devour [dɪ'vaur] tr verschlingen; (said of fire) verzehren
devout [dɪ'vaut] adj fromm; (e.g., hope) innig
dew [d(j)u] s Tau m; **dew is falling** es taut
dew'drop' s Tautropfen m
dew'lap' s Wamme f
dewy ['d(j)u·i] adj tauig
dexterity [dɛks'tɛrɪti] s Geschicklichkeit f, Handfertigkeit f
dexterous ['dɛkstərəs] adj handfertig
dextrose ['dɛkstroz] s Traubenzucker m
diabetes [‚daɪ·ə'bitɪs] s Zuckerkrankheit f

diabetic [‚daɪ·ə'bɛtɪk] *adj* zuckerkrank *mf*
diabolic(al) [‚daɪ·ə'bɑlɪk(ə)l] *adj* teuflisch
diacritical [‚daɪ·ə'krɪtɪkəl] *adj* diakritisch
diadem ['daɪ·ə‚dɛm] *s* Diadem *n*
diaere·sis [daɪ'ɛrɪsɪs] *s* (**-ses** [‚siz] Diäresis *f*; (*mark*) Trema *n*
diagnose [‚daɪ·əg'nos], [‚daɪ·əg'noz] *tr* diagnostizieren
diagno·sis [‚daɪ·əg'nosɪs] *s* (**-ses** [siz]) Diagnose *f*
diagonal [daɪ'ægənəl] *adj* diagonal ‖ *s* Diagonale *f*
diagonally [daɪ'ægənəli] *adv*—**d. across from** schräg gegenüber von
diagram ['daɪ·ə‚græm] *s* Diagramm *n*
di·al ['daɪ·əl] *s* Zifferblatt *n;* (tech) Skalenscheibe *f;* (telp) Wählscheibe *f* ‖ *v* (*pret* & *pp* **-al[l]ed;** *ger* **-al[l]ing**) *tr* & *intr* (telp) wählen
di'aling *s* (telp) Wählen *n* der Nummer
dialogue ['daɪ·ə‚lɔg] *s* Dialog *m*
di'al tel'ephone *s* Selbstanschlußtelefon *n*
di'al tone' *s* Summton *m*, Amtszeichen *n*
diameter [daɪ'æmɪtər] *s* Durchmesser *m*
diamond ['daɪmənd] *adj* diamanten; (*in shape*) rautenförmig ‖ *s* Diamant *m;* (*cut diamond*) Brillant *m;* (*rhombus*) Raute *f;* (baseball) Spielfeld *n;* (cards) Karo *n*
dia'mond ring' *s* Brillantring *m*
diaper ['daɪpər] *s* Windel *f;* **change the diapers of** trockenlegen, wickeln
diaphanous [daɪ'æfənəs] *adj* durchsichtig, durchscheinend
diaphragm ['daɪ·ə‚fræm] *s* (*for birth control*) Gebärmutterkappe *f;* (anat) Zwerchfell *n;* (phot) Blende *f;* (tech, telp) Membran *f*
diarrhea [‚daɪ·ə'ri·ə] *s* Durchfall *m*
diary ['daɪ·əri] *s* Tagebuch *n*
diastole [daɪ'æstəli] *s* Diastole *f*
diatribe ['daɪ·ə‚traɪb] *s* Schmährede *f*
dice [daɪs] *spl* Würfel *pl* ‖ *tr* in Würfel schneiden
dice'box' *s* Würfelbecher *m*
dichotomy [daɪ'kɑtəmi] *s* Zweiteilung *f;* (bot) Gabelung *f*
dicker ['dɪkər] *intr* (**about**) feilschen (um)
dickey ['dɪki] *s* Hemdbrust *f*
dictaphone ['dɪktə‚fon] *s* Diktaphon *n*
dictate ['dɪktet] *s* Diktat *n;* **the dictates of conscience** das Gebot des Gewissens ‖ *tr* & *intr* diktieren
dictation [dɪk'teʃən] *s* Diktat *n*
dictator ['dɪktetər] *s* Diktator *m*
dictatorial [‚dɪktə'tori·əl] *adj* diktatorisch; (*power*) unumschränkt
dic'tatorship' *s* Diktatur *f*
diction ['dɪkʃən] *s* Ausdrucksweise *f*
dictionary ['dɪkʃə‚neri] *s* Wörterbuch *n*
dic·tum ['dɪktəm] *s* (**-ta** [tə]) (*saying*) Spruch *m;* (*pronouncement*) Ausspruch *m*
didactic [daɪ'dæktɪk] *adj* lehrhaft

die [daɪ] *s* (**dice** [daɪs]) Würfel *m;* **the die is cast** die Würfel sind gefallen ‖ *s* (**dies**) (*coining die*) Prägestempel *m;* (*casting die*) Form *f;* (*forging die*) Gesenk *n;* (*threader*) Schneidkopf *m* ‖ *v* (*pret* & *pp* **died;** *ger* **dying**) *tr*—**die a natural death** e-s natürlichen Todes sterben ‖ *intr* sterben; (*said of plants and animals*) eingehen; **be dying for** (coll) sich sehnen nach; **die down** (*said of the wind*) sich legen; (*said of noise*) ersterben; **die from** sterben an (*dat*); **die laughing** sich totlachen; **die of hunger** verhungern; **die of thirst** verdursten; **die out** aussterben; (*said of fire*) erlöschen; **I am dying to** (*inf*) (coll) ich würde schrecklich gern (*inf*)
die'-hard' *s* Unentwegte *mf*
die'sel en'gine ['dizəl] *s* Dieselmotor *m*
die'sel oil' *s* Dieselöl *n*
die'stock' *s* Gewindeschneidkluppe *f*
diet ['daɪ·ət] *s* Kost *f;* (*special menu*) Diät *f;* (parl) Reichstag *m;* **be on a d.** diät leben; **put on a d.** auf Diät setzen ‖ *intr* diät leben
dietary ['daɪ·ə‚teri] *adj* Diät–; **d. laws** rituelle Diätvorschriften *pl*
dietetic [‚daɪ·ə'tɛtɪk] *adj* diätetisch ‖ **dietetics** *spl* Diätetik *f*
dietitian [‚daɪ·ə'tɪʃən] *s* Diätspezialist *-in mf*
differ ['dɪfər] *intr* sich unterscheiden; (*said of opinions*) auseinandergehen; **d. from** abweichen von; **d. in** verschieden sein in (*dat*); **d. with** anderer Meinung sein als
difference ['dɪfərəns] *s* Unterschied *m;* (*argument*) Streit *m;* (math) Differenz *f;* **d. of opinion** Meinungsverschiedenheit *f;* **it makes no d. to me** es ist mir gleich; **split the d.** den Rest teilen
different ['dɪfərənt] *adj* verschieden; **a d. kind of** e–e andere Art von; **d. from** anders als, verschieden von; **d. kinds of** verschiedene
differential [‚dɪfə'rɛnʃəl] *adj* (econ, elec, mach, math, phys) Differential– ‖ *s* (*difference*) Unterschied *m;* (mach) Differentialgetriebe *n;* (math) Differential *n*
dif'feren'tial cal'culus *s* Differentialrechnung *f*
differentiate [‚dɪfə'rɛnʃɪ‚et] *tr* unterscheiden; (math) differenzieren ‖ *intr* —**d. between** unterscheiden zwischen (*dat*)
difficult ['dɪfɪ‚kʌlt] *adj* schwierig, schwer
difficulty ['dɪfɪ‚kʌlti] *s* Schwierigkeit *f;* **I have d. in** (*ger*) es fällt mir schwer zu (*inf*); **with d.** mit Mühe
diffuse [dɪ'fjus] *adj* (weit) zerstreut; (*style*) diffus ‖ [dɪ'fjuz] *tr* (*spread*) verbreiten; (*pour out*) ausgießen; (phys) diffundieren ‖ *intr* sich zerstreuen
diffusion [dɪ'fjuʃən] *s* (*spread*) Verbreitung *f;* (phys) Diffusion *f*
dig [dɪg] *s* (*jab*) Stoß *m;* (*sarcasm*)

Seitenhieb *m;* (archeol) Ausgrabung *f* ‖ *v* (*pret & pp* dug [dʌg] & **digged;** *ger* **digging**) *tr* graben; (*a ditch*) auswerfen; (*potatoes*) ausgraben; (*understand*) (sl) kapieren; (*look at*) (sl) anschauen; (*appreciate*) (sl) schwärmen für; **dig up** ausgraben; (*find*) auftreiben; (*information*) ausfindig machen; (*money*) aufbringen; ‖ *intr* graben, wühlen; **dig in** (*with the hands*) hineinfassen; (*work hard*) (coll) schuften; (mil) sich eingraben; **dig for** (*e.g., gold*) schürfen nach

digest ['daɪdʒɛst] *s* Zusammenfassung *f;* (jur) Gesetzessammlung *f* ‖ [daɪ'dʒɛst] *tr* verdauen; (*in the mind*) verarbeiten ‖ *intr* verdauen

digestible [daɪ'dʒɛstɪbəl] *adj* verdaulich, verträglich

digestion [daɪ'dʒɛstʃən] *s* Verdauung *f*

digestive [daɪ'dʒɛstɪv] *adj* Verdauungs–; **d. tract** Verdauungsapparat *m*

digit ['dɪdʒɪt] *s* (math) Ziffer *f* (unter zehn); (math) Stelle *f*

digital ['dɪdʒɪtəl] *adj* digital, Digital– **dig'ital comput'er** *s* digitale Rechenanlage *f*

digitalis [dɪdʒɪ'tælɪs] *s* Digitalis *n*

dignified ['dɪgnɪ,faɪd] *adj* würdig

digni•fy ['dɪgnɪ,faɪ] *v* (*pret & pp* –fied*)* *tr* ehren

digni:ary ['dɪgnɪ,tɛri] *s* Würdenträger –in *mf*

dignity ['dɪgnɪti] *s* Würde *f;* **d. of man** Menschenwürde *f;* **stand on one's d.** sich [*dat*] nichts vergeben

digress [daɪ'grɛs] *intr* (**from**) abschweifen (von)

digression [daɪ'grɛʃən] *s* Abschweifung *f*

dike [daɪk] *s* Deich *m*

dilapidated [dɪ'læpɪ,detɪd] *adj* baufällig

dilate [daɪ'let] *tr* ausdehnen ‖ *intr* sich ausdehnen

dilation [daɪ'leʃən] *s* Ausdehnung *f*

dilatory ['dɪlə,tori] *adj* saumselig; (*tending to cause delay*) hinhaltend

dilemma [dɪ'lɛmə] *s* Dilemma *n*

dilettan•te [,dɪlə'tænti], ['dɪlə,tɑnt] *s* (**-tes & –ti** [ti]) Dilettant –in *mf*

diligence ['dɪlɪdʒəns] *s* Fleiß *m*

diligent ['dɪlɪdʒənt] *adj* fleißig

dill [dɪl] *s* Dill *m*

dillydal•ly ['dɪlɪ,dæli] *v* (*pret & pp* –lied*)* *intr* herumtrödeln

dilute [dɪ'lut], [daɪ'lut] *adj* verdünnt ‖ [dɪ'lut] *tr* verdünnen; (*with water*) verwässern ‖ *intr* sich verdünnen

dilution [dɪ'luʃən] *s* Verdünnung *f;* (*with water*) Verwässerung *f*

dim [dɪm] *adj* (**dimmer; dimmest**) *adj* (*light, eyesight*) schwach; (*poorly lighted*) schwach beleuchtet; (*dull*) matt; (*chances, outlook*) schlecht; (*indistinct*) undeutlich; **take a dim view of** (*disapprove of*) mißbilligen; (*be pessimistic about*) sich [*dat*] etw schwarz ausmalen ‖ *v* (*pret & pp* **dimmed;** *ger* **dimming**) *tr* trüben; (*lights*) abblenden ‖ *intr* sich verdunkeln; (*said of lights, hopes*) verblassen

dime [daɪm] *s* Zehncentstück *n*

dime' nov'el *s* Groschenroman *m*

dimension [dɪ'mɛnʃən] *s* Maß *n,* Ausdehnung *f;* **dimensions** Ausmaß *n*

diminish [dɪ'mɪnɪʃ] *tr* (ver)mindern, verringern ‖ *intr* sich vermindern

diminutive [dɪ'mɪnjətɪv] *adj* winzig; (gram) Verkleinerungs– ‖ *s* Verkleinerungsform *f*

dimmer ['dɪmər] *s* (aut) Abblendvorrichtung *f*

dimple ['dɪmpəl] *s* Grübchen *n*

dim'wit' *s* Schwachsinnige *mf*

din [dɪn] *s* Getöse *n* ‖ *v* (*pret & pp* **dinned;** *ger* **dinning**) *tr* betäuben; **din s.th. into s.o.** j–m etw einhämmern

dine [daɪn] *intr* speisen; **d. out** auswärts speisen

diner ['daɪnər] *s* Tischgast *m;* (*small restaurant*) speisewagenähnliches Speiselokal *n;* (rr) Speisewagen *m*

dinette [daɪ'nɛt] *s* Speisenische *f*

dingbat ['dɪŋ,bæt] *s* (sl) (*person*) Dingsda *m;* (*thing*) Dingsda *n*

ding-dong ['dɪŋ,dɔŋ] *interj* bimbam!, klingklang!

dinghy ['dɪŋgi] *s* Beiboot *n;* **rubber d.** Schlauchboot *n*

dingy ['dɪndʒi] *adj* (*gloomy*) düster; (*shabby*) schäbig

din'ing car' *s* (rr) Speisewagen *m*

din'ing hall' *s* Speisesaal *m*

din'ing room' *s* Eßzimmer *n*

dinner ['dɪnər] *s* (*supper*) Abendessen *n;* (*main meal*) Hauptmahlzeit *f;* (*formal meal*) Diner *n;* **after d.** nach Tisch; **at d.** bei Tisch; **before d.** vor Tisch

din'ner guest' *s* Tischgast *m*

din'ner jac'ket *s* Smoking *m*

din'ner mu'sic *s* Tafelmusik *f*

din'ner par'ty *s* Tischgesellschaft *f*

din'ner time' *s* Tischzeit *f*

dinosaur ['daɪnə,sɔr] *s* Dinosaurier *m*

dint [dɪnt] *s*—**by d. of** kraft (*genit*)

diocesan [daɪ'ɑsɪsən] *adj* Diözesan–

diocese ['daɪ-ə,sis] *s* Diözese *f*

diode ['daɪ-od] *s* (*electron*) Diode *f*

dioxide [daɪ'ɑksaɪd] *s* Dioxyd *n*

dip [dɪp] *s* (*in the road*) Neigung *f;* (*short swim*) kurzes Bad *n;* (*dunk*) Eintauchen *n;* (*sauce*) Tunke *f;* (*of ice cream*) Portion *f* ‖ *v* (*pret & pp* **dipped;** *ger* **dipping**) *tr* eintauchen; (*e.g., doughnuts*) eintunken; (*a flag*) senken ‖ *intr* sich senken; **dip into** (*e.g., reserves*) angreifen; **dip into one's pockets** (fig) in die Tasche greifen

diphtheria [dɪf'θɪrɪ-ə] *s* Diphtherie *f*

diphthong ['dɪfθɔŋ] *s* Doppelvokal *m*

diploma [dɪ'plomə] *s* Diplom *n*

diplomacy [dɪ'ploməsi] *s* Diplomatie *f*

diplomat ['dɪplə,mæt] *s* Diplomat –in *mf*

diplomatic [,dɪplə'mætɪk] *adj* (& *fig*) diplomatisch

dipper ['dɪpər] *s* Schöpflöffel *m*

dipsomania [,dɪpsə'menɪ-ə] *s* Trunksucht *f*

dip' stick' s (aut) Ölstandmesser m
dire [daɪr] adj (terrible) gräßlich;
(need) äußerste
direct [dɪ'rɛkt] adj direkt, unmittelbar; (frank) unverblümt; (quotation) wörtlich ‖ tr (order) beauftragen; (a company) leiten; (traffic) regeln; (a movie, play) Regie führen bei; (an orchestra) dirigieren; (attention, glance) (to) richten (auf acc); (a person) (to) verweisen (an acc); (words, letter) (to) richten (an acc)
direct' call' s Selbstwählverbindung f
direct' cur'rent s Gleichstrom m
direct' dis'course s direkte Rede f
direct' hit' s Volltreffer m
direction [dɪ'rɛkʃən] s Richtung f; (order) Anweisung f; (leadership) Leitung f, Führung f; (cin, theat) Regie f; (mus) Stabführung f; **directions** Weisungen pl; (for use) Gebrauchsanweisung f; **in all directions** nach allen Richtungen
directional [dɪ'rɛkʃənəl] adj Richt–
direc'tion find'er s Peilgerät n
direc'tion sig'nal s (aut) Richtungsanzeiger m
directive [dɪ'rɛktɪv] s Anweisung f
direct' ob'ject s direktes Objekt n
direct' op'posite s genaues Gegenteil n
director [dɪ'rɛktər] s Leiter –in mf, Direktor –in mf; (cin, theat) Regisseur –in mf; (mus) Dirigent –in mf; (rad, telv) Sendeleiter –in mf
direc'torship' s Direktorat n
directory [dɪ'rɛktəri] s Verzeichnis n
dirge [dʌrdʒ] s Trauergesang m
dirigible ['dɪrɪdʒɪbəl] s lenkbares Luftschiff n
dirt [dʌrt] s Schmutz m, Dreck m; (moral filth) Schmutz m; (soil) Erde f
dirt'-cheap' adj spottbillig
dirt' farm'er s kleiner Farmer m
dirt' road' s unbefestigte Straße f
dirt·y ['dʌrti] adj schmutzig, dreckig; (morally) schmutzig; **d. business** Schweinerei f; **d. dog** Sauhund m; **d. joke** Zote f; **d. lie** gemeine Lüge f; **d. linen** schmutzige Wäsche f; **d. look** böser Blick m; **d. trick** übler Streich m; **that's a d. shame** das ist e-e Gemeinheit! ‖ v (pret & pp –ied) tr beschmutzen
disability [,dɪsə'bɪlɪti] s Invalidität f
disable [dɪs'ebəl] tr (e.g., a worker) arbeitsunfähig machen; (make unsuited for combat) kampfunfähig machen; (jur) rechtsunfähig machen
disa'bled adj invalide; (mil) kampfunfähig; **d. veteran** Kriegsversehrte mf; **d. person** Invalide mf
disabuse [,dɪsə'bjuz] tr—**d. of** befreien von
disadvantage [,dɪsəd'væntɪdʒ] s Nachteil m; **place at a d.** benachteiligen
disadvantageous [dɪs,ædvən'tedʒəs] adj nachteilig
disagree [,dɪsə'gri] intr nicht übereinstimmen; (be contradictory) einander widersprechen; (quarrel) (sich) streiten; **d. with** (said of food) nicht bekommen (dat); **d. with s.o. on**

anderer Meinung über (acc) als j-d sein
disagreeable [,dɪsə'grɪ·əbəl] adj unangenehm
disagreement [,dɪsə'grimənt] s (unlikeness) Verschiedenheit f; (dissention) Uneinigkeit f; (quarrel) Meinungsverschiedenheit f
disappear [,dɪsə'pɪr] intr verschwinden
disappearance [,dɪsə'pɪrəns] s Verschwinden n
disappoint [,dɪsə'pɔɪnt] tr enttäuschen; **be disappointed at (or with)** enttäuscht sein über (acc)
disappointment [,dɪsə'pɔɪntmənt] s Enttäuschung f
disapproval [,dɪsə'pruvəl] s Mißbilligung f
disapprove [,dɪsə'pruv] tr mißbilligen; (e.g., an application) nicht genehmigen ‖ intr—**d. of** mißbilligen
disarm [dɪs'ɑrm] tr (& fig) entwaffnen; (a bomb) entschärfen ‖ intr abrüsten
disarmament [dɪs'ɑrməmənt] s Abrüstung f
disarm'ing adj (fig) entwaffnend
disarray [,dɪsə're] s Unordnung f ‖ tr in Unordnung bringen, verwirren
disassemble [,dɪsə'sɛmbəl] tr zerlegen
disaster [dɪ'zæstər] s Unheil n
disas'ter ar'ea s Katastrophengebiet n
disastrous [dɪ'zæstrəs] adj unheilvoll
disavow [,dɪsə'vau] tr ableugnen
disavowal [,dɪsə'vau·əl] s Ableugnung f
disband [dɪs'bænd] tr auflösen ‖ intr sich auflösen
dis·bar [dɪs'bɑr] v (pret & pp –barred; ger –barring) tr aus dem Anwaltsstand ausschließen
disbelief [,dɪsbɪ'lif] s Unglaube m
disbelieve [,dɪsbɪ'liv] tr & intr nicht glauben
disburse [dɪs'bʌrs] tr auszahlen
disbursement [dɪs'bʌrsmənt] s Auszahlung f
disc [dɪsk] s var of **disk**
discard [dɪs'kɑrd] s Ablegen n ‖ tr (clothes, cards, habits) ablegen; (a plan) verwerfen
discern [dɪ'sʌrn] tr (perceive) wahrnehmen; **be able to d. right from wrong** zwischen Gut und Böse unterscheiden können
discern'ing adj scharfsinnig
discernment [dɪ'sʌrnmənt] s Scharfsinn m
discharge [dɪs'tʃɑrdʒ] s (of a gun) Abfeuern n; (of a battery) Entladung f; (of water) Abfluß m; (of smoke) Ausströmen n; (of duties) Erfüllung f; (of debts) Tilgung f; (of employees, patients, soldiers) Entlassung f; (of a prisoner) Freilassung f; (pathol) Ausfluß m ‖ tr (a gun) abfeuern; (e.g., water) ergießen; (smoke) ausstoßen; (debts) tilgen; (duties) erfüllen; (an office) verwalten; (an employee, patient, soldier) entlassen ‖ intr (said of a gun) losgehen; (said of a battery)

sich entladen; (pour out) abfließen; (pathol) eitern

disciple [dɪˈsaɪpəl] s Jünger m

disciplinarian [ˌdɪsɪplɪˈnɛrɪ·ən] s Zuchtmeister m

disciplinary [ˈdɪsɪplɪˌnɛri] adj Disziplinar–

discipline [ˈdɪsɪplɪn] s Disziplin f; (punishment) Züchtigung f || tr disziplinieren; (punish) züchtigen

disclaim [dɪsˈklem] tr leugnen; (jur) verzichten auf (acc)

disclose [dɪsˈkloz] tr enthüllen

disclosure [dɪsˈkloʒər] s Enthüllung f

discolor [dɪsˈkʌlər] tr verfärben || intr sich verfärben

discoloration [dɪsˌkʌləˈreʃən] s Verfärbung f

discomfiture [dɪsˈkʌmfɪtʃər] s (defeat) Niederlage f; (frustration) Enttäuschung f; (confusion) Verwirrung f

discomfort [dɪsˈkʌmfərt] s Unbehagen n || tr Unbehagen verursachen (dat)

disconcert [ˌdɪskənˈsʌrt] tr aus der Fassung bringen

dis′concert′ed adj fassungslos

disconnect [ˌdɪskəˈnɛkt] tr trennen; (elec) ausschalten; (mach) auskuppeln; (telp) unterbrechen

disconsolate [dɪsˈkɑnsəlɪt] adj trostlos

discontent [ˌdɪskənˈtɛnt] s Unzufriedenheit f || tr unzufrieden machen

dis′content′ed adj (with) mißvergnügt (über acc)

discontinue [ˌdɪskənˈtɪnju] tr (permanently) einstellen; (temporarily) aussetzen; (a newspaper) abbestellen; **d.** (ger) aufhören zu (inf)

discord [ˈdɪskɔrd] s Mißklang m; (dissention) Zwietracht f

discordance [dɪsˈkɔrdəns] s Uneinigkeit f

discotheque [ˌdɪskoˈtɛk] s Diskothek f

discount [ˈdɪskaunt] s (in price) Rabatt m; (cash discount) Kassaskonto n; (deduction from nominal value) Diskont m; **at a d.** mit Rabatt; (st. exch.) unter pari || tr (disregard) außer acht lassen; (minimize) geringen Wert beimessen (dat); (for cash payment) e-n Abzug gewähren auf (acc); (e.g., a promissory note) diskontieren

dis′count store′ s Rabattladen m

discourage [dɪsˈkʌrɪdʒ] tr (dishearten) entmutigen; **d. s.o. from** (ger) (deter) j-n davon abschrecken zu (inf); (dissuade) j-m davon abraten zu (inf)

discour′aged adj mutlos

discouragement [dɪsˈkʌrɪdʒmənt] s (act) Entmutigung f; (state) Mutlosigkeit f; (deterrent) Abschreckung f

discourse [ˈdɪskors] s (conversation) Gespräch n; (formal treatment) Abhandlung f; (lecture) Vortrag m || [dɪsˈkors] intr (on) sich unterhalten (über acc)

discourteous [dɪsˈkʌrtɪ·əs] adj unhöflich

discourtesy [dɪsˈkʌrtəsi] s Unhöflichkeit f

discover [dɪsˈkʌvər] tr entdecken

discovery [dɪsˈkʌvəri] s Entdeckung f

discredit [dɪsˈkrɛdɪt] s (disrepute) Mißkredit m; (disbelief) Zweifel m || tr (destroy confidence in) in Mißkredit bringen; (disbelieve) anzweifeln; (disgrace) in Verruf bringen

discreditable [dɪsˈkrɛdɪtəbəl] adj schändlich

discreet [dɪsˈkrit] adj diskret

discrepancy [dɪsˈkrɛpənsi] s Unstimmigkeit f

discretion [dɪsˈkrɛʃən] s Diskretion f, Besonnenheit f; **at one's d.** nach Belieben; **leave to s.o.'s d.** in j-s Belieben stellen

discriminate [dɪsˈkrɪmɪˌnet] tr voneinander unterscheiden || intr—**d. against** diskriminieren

discrimination [dɪsˌkrɪmɪˈneʃən] s (distinction) Unterscheidung f; (prejudicial treatment) Diskriminierung f

discriminatory [dɪsˈkrɪmɪnəˌtori] adj diskriminierend

discus [ˈdɪskʌs] s Diskus m

discuss [dɪsˈkʌs] tr besprechen, diskutieren; (formally) erörtern

discussion [dɪsˈkʌʃən] s Diskussion f; (formal consideration) Erörterung f

disdain [dɪsˈden] s Geringschätzung f || tr geringschätzen

disdainful [dɪsˈdenfəl] adj geringschätzig; **be d. of** geringschätzen

disease [dɪˈziz] s Krankheit f

diseased′ adj krank, erkrankt

disembark [ˌdɪsɛmˈbark] tr ausschiffen, landen || intr an Land gehen, landen

disembarkation [dɪsˌɛmbarˈkeʃən] s Ausschiffung f

disembow·el [ˌdɪsɛmˈbau·əl] v (pret & pp -el[l]ed; ger -el[l]ing) tr ausweiden

disenchant [ˌdɪsɛnˈtʃænt] tr ernüchtern

disenchantment [ˌdɪsɛnˈtʃæntmənt] s Ernüchterung f

disengage [ˌdɪsɛnˈgedʒ] tr (a clutch) ausrücken; (the enemy) sich absetzen von; (troops) entflechten; **d. the clutch** auskuppeln || intr loskommen; (mil) sich absetzen

disengagement [ˌdɪsɛnˈgedʒmənt] s Lösung f; (mil) Truppenentflechtung f

disentangle [ˌdɪsɛnˈtæŋgəl] tr entwirren

disentanglement [ˌdɪsɛnˈtæŋgəlmənt] s Entwirrung f

disfavor [dɪsˈfevər] s Ungunst f

disfigure [dɪsˈfɪgjər] tr entstellen

disfigurement [dɪsˈfɪgjərmənt] s Entstellung f

disfranchise [dɪsˈfræntʃaɪz] tr die Bürgerrechte entziehen (dat)

disgorge [dɪsˈgɔrdʒ] tr ausspeien || intr sich ergießen

disgrace [dɪsˈgres] s Schande f; (of a family) Schandfleck m || tr in Schande bringen; (a girl) schänden; **be disgraced** in Schande kommen

disgraceful [dɪs'gresfəl] *adj* schändlich, schimpflich
disgruntled [dɪs'grʌntəld] *adj* mürrisch
disguise [dɪs'gaɪz] *s (clothing)* Verkleidung *f; (insincere manner)* Verstellung *f* ‖ *tr (by dress)* verkleiden; *(e.g., the voice)* verstellen
disgust [dɪs'gʌst] *s* (at) Ekel *m* (vor *dat)* ‖ *tr* anekeln
disgust'ing *adj* ekelhaft
dish [dɪʃ] *s* Schüssel *f*, Platte *f; (food)* Gericht *n; do the dishes* das Geschirr spülen ‖ *tr*—**d. out** (coll) austeilen
dish'cloth' *s* Geschirrlappen *m*
dishearten [dɪs'hɑrtən] *tr* entmutigen
disheveled [dɪ'ʃevəld] *adj* unordentlich
dishonest [dɪs'ɑnɪst] *adj* unehrlich
dishonesty [dɪs'ɑnɪsti] *s* Unehrlichkeit *f*
dishonor [dɪs'ɑnər] *s* Unehre *f* ‖ *tr* verunehren
dishonorable [dɪs'ɑnərəbəl] *adj (person)* ehrlos; *(action)* unehrenhaft
dishon'orable dis'charge *s* Entlassung *f* wegen Wehrunwürdigkeit
dish'pan' *s* Aufwaschschüssel *f*
dish'rack' *s* Abtropfkörbchen *n*
dish'rag' *s* Spüllappen *m*
dish'tow'el *s* Geschirrtuch *n*
dish'wash'er *s (person)* Aufwäscher –in *mf; (appliance)* Geschirrspülmaschine *f*
dish'wa'ter *s* Spülwasser *n*
disillusion [,dɪsɪ'luʒən] *s* Ernüchterung *f* ‖ *tr* ernüchtern
disillusionment [,dɪsɪ'luʒənmənt] *s* Ernüchterung *f*
disinclination [dɪs,ɪnklɪ'neʃən] *s* Abneigung *f*, Abgeneigtheit *f*
disinclined [,dɪsɪn'klaɪnd] *adj* abgeneight
disinfect [,dɪsɪn'fɛkt] *tr* desinfizieren
disinfectant [,dɪsɪn'fɛktənt] *adj* desinfizierend ‖ *s* Desinfektionsmittel *n*
disinherit [,dɪsɪn'hɛrɪt] *tr* enterben
disintegrate [dɪs'ɪntɪ,gret] *tr* (& fig) zersetzen ‖ *intr* zerfallen
disintegration [dɪs,ɪntɪ'greʃən] *s* (& fig) Zerfall *m*
disin·ter [,dɪsɪn'tʌr] *v (pret & pp –terred; ger –terring) tr* ausgraben
disinterested [dɪs'ɪntə,rɛstɪd] *adj (unbiased)* unparteiisch; *(uninterested)* desinteressiert
disjunctive [dɪs'dʒʌŋktɪv] *adj* disjunktiv
disk [dɪsk] *s* Scheibe *f*
disk' brake' *s* Scheibenbremse *f*
disk' jock'ey *s* Schallplattenjockei *m*
dislike [dɪs'laɪk] *s* (of) Abneigung *f* (gegen) ‖ *tr* nicht mögen
dislocate ['dɪslo,ket] *tr* verschieben; *(a shoulder)* verrenken; (fig) stören
dislocation [,dɪslo'keʃən] *s* Verschiebung *f; (of a shoulder)* Verrenkung *f;* (fig) Störung *f*
dislodge [dɪs'lɑdʒ] *tr* losreißen; (mil) aus der Stellung werfen
disloyal [dɪs'lɔɪ·əl] *adj* untreu
disloyalty [dɪs'lɔɪ·əlti] *s* Untreue *f*
dismal ['dɪzməl] *adj* trübselig, düster
dismantle [dɪs'mæntəl] *tr* demontieren

dismay [dɪs'me] *s* Bestürzung *f* ‖ *tr* bestürzen
dismember [dɪs'mɛmbər] *tr* zerstückeln
dismiss [dɪs'mɪs] *tr* verabschieden; *(an employee)* **(from)** entlassen (aus); *(a case)* (jur) abweisen; (mil) wegtreten lassen; **d. as** abtun als; **dismissed!** (mil) wegtreten!
dismissal [dɪs'mɪsəl] *s* Entlassung *f;* (jur) Abweisung *f*
dismount [dɪs'maunt] *tr (throw down)* abwerfen; (mach) abmontieren ‖ *intr (from a carriage)* herabsteigen; *(from a horse)* absitzen
disobedience [,dɪsə'bidɪ·əns] *s* Ungehorsam *m*, Unfolgsamkeit *f*
disobedient [,dɪsə'bidɪ·ənt] *adj* ungehorsam, unfolgsam
disobey [,dɪsə'be] *tr* nicht gehorchen *(dat)* ‖ *intr* nicht gehorchen
disorder [dɪs'ɔrdər] *s* Unordnung *f; (public disturbance)* Unruhe *f;* (pathol) Erkrankung *f;* **throw into d.** in Unordnung bringen
disorderly [dɪs'ɔrdərli] *adj* unordentlich, liederlich
disor'derly con'duct *s* ungebührliches Benehmen *n*
disor'derly house' *s* Bordell *n; (gambling house)* Spielhölle *f*
disorganize [dɪs'ɔrgə,naɪz] *tr* zerrütten, desorganisieren
disown [dɪs'on] *tr* verleugnen
disparage [dɪ'spærɪdʒ] *tr* herabsetzen, geringschätzen
disparate ['dɪspərɪt] *adj* ungleichartig
disparity [dɪ'spærɪti] *s (inequality)* Ungleichheit *f; (difference)* Unterschied *m*
dispassionate [dɪs'pæʃənɪt] *adj* leidenschaftslos
dispatch [dɪ'spætʃ] *s* Abfertigung *f; (message)* Depesche *f;* **with d.** in Eile ‖ *tr (send off)* absenden; *(e.g., a truck)* abfertigen; *(e.g., a task)* schnell erledigen; *(kill)* töten; *(eat fast)* (coll) verputzen
dispatcher [dɪ'spætʃər] *s (of vehicles)* Fahrbereitschaftsleiter –in *mf*
dis·pel [dɪ'spɛl] *v (pret & pp –pelled; ger –pelling) tr* vertreiben; *(thoughts, doubts)* zerstreuen
dispensary [dɪ'spɛnsəri] *s* Arzneiausgabestelle *f;* (mil) Krankenrevier *n*
dispensation [,dɪspɛn'seʃən] *s* (eccl) **(from)** Dispens *m* (von); **by divine d.** durch göttliche Fügung
dispense [dɪ'spɛns] *tr (exempt)* **(from)** entbinden (von); (pharm) zubereiten und ausgeben; **d. justice** Recht sprechen ‖ *intr*—**d. with** verzichten auf *(acc)*
dispersal [dɪ'spʌrsəl] *s* Auflockerung *f*
disperse [dɪ'spʌrs] *tr* zerstreuen; *(a crowd)* zersprengen; *(one's troops)* auflockern; *(the enemy)* auseinandersprengen ‖ *intr (said of clouds, etc.)* sich verziehen; *(said of crowds)* auseinandergehen
dispirited [dɪ'spɪrɪtɪd] *adj* niedergeschlagen

displace [dɪs'ples] *tr* (*people in war*) verschleppen; (phys) verdrängen
displacement [dɪs'plesmənt] *s* Vertreibung *f;* (phys) Verdrängung *f*
display [dɪ'sple] *s* (*of energy, wealth*) Entfaltung *f;* (*of goods*) Ausstellung *f;* (*pomp*) Aufwand *m;* **on d.** zur Schau || *tr* (*wares*) ausstellen; (*reveal*) entfalten; (*flaunt*) protzen mit
display' case' *s* Vitrine *f*
display' room' *s* Ausstellungsraum *m*
display' win'dow *s* Schaufenster *n*
displease [dɪs'pliz] *tr* mißfallen (*dat*); **be displeased with** Mißfallen finden an (*dat*) || *intr* mißfallen
displeas'ing *adj* mißfällig
displeasure [dɪs'pleʒər] *s* Mißfallen *n*
disposable [dɪ'spozəbəl] *adj* Einweg–
disposal [dɪ'spozəl] *s* (*riddance*) Beseitigung *f;* (*of a matter*) Erledigung *f;* (*distribution*) Anordnung *f;* **be at s.o.'s d.** j–m zur Verfügung stehen; **have at one's d.** verfügen über (*acc*); **put at s.o.'s d.** j–m zur Verfügung stellen
dispose [dɪ'spoz] *tr* (*incline*) (**to**) geneigt machen (zu); (*arrange*) anordnen || *intr*—**d. of** (*a matter*) erledigen; (*get rid of*) loswerden
disposed' *adj* gesinnt; **d. to** (*ger*) geneigt zu (*inf*)
disposition [,dɪspə'zɪʃən] *s* (*settlement*) Erledigung *f;* (*nature*) Gemütsart *f;* (*inclination*) Neigung *f*
dispossess [,dɪspə'zes] *tr*—**d. s.o. of s.th.** j–m etw enteignen
disproof [dɪs'pruf] *s* Widerlegung *f*
disproportionate [,dɪsprə'porʃənɪt] *adj* unverhältnismäßig; **be d. to** im Mißverhältnis stehen zu
disprove [dɪs'pruv] *tr* widerlegen
dispute [dɪs'pjut] *s* (*quarrel*) Streit *m;* (*debate*) Wortgefecht *n;* **beyond d.** unstreitig; **in d.** umstritten || *tr* bestreiten || *intr* disputieren
disqualification [dɪs,kwɑlɪfɪ'keʃən] *s* Disqualifizierung *f*
disquali•fy [dɪs'kwɑlɪ,faɪ] *v* (*pret & pp* **–fied**) *tr* (*make unfit*) (**for**) untauglich machen (für); (*declare ineligible*) disqualifizieren
disquiet [dɪs'kwaɪ•ət] *tr* beunruhigen
disqui'eting *adj* beunruhigend
disregard [,dɪsrɪ'gɑrd] *s* (*lack of attention*) Nichtbeachtung *f;* (*disrespect*) Mißachtung *f* || *tr* (*not pay attention to*) nicht beachten; (*treat without due respect*) mißachten
disrepair [,dɪsrɪ'per] *s* Verfall *m;* **fall into d.** verfallen
disreputable [dɪs'repjətəbəl] *adj* verrufen
disrepute [,dɪsrɪ'pjut] *s* Verruf *m*
disrespect [,dɪsrɪ'spekt] *s* Nichtachtung *f,* Mißachtung *f* || *tr* nicht achten
disrespectful [,dɪsrɪ'spektfəl] *adj* respektlos, unehrerbietig
disrobe [dɪs'rob] *tr* entkleiden || *intr* sich entkleiden
disrupt [dɪs'rʌpt] *tr* (*throw into confusion*) in Verwirrung bringen; (*interrupt*) unterbrechen; (*cause to*

break down) zum Zusammenbruch bringen
dissatisfaction [,dɪssætɪs'fækʃən] *s* Unzufriedenheit *f*
dissat'isfied' *adj* unzufrieden
dissatis•fy [dɪs'sætɪs,faɪ] *v* (*pret & pp* **–fied**) *tr* nicht befriedigen
dissect [dɪ'sekt] *tr* (fig) zergliedern; (anat) sezieren
dissection [dɪ'sekʃən] *s* (fig) Zergliederung *f;* (anat) Sektion *f*
dissemble [dɪ'sembəl] *tr* verbergen || *intr* heucheln
disseminate [dɪ'semɪ,net] *tr* verbreiten
dissension [dɪ'senʃən] *s* Uneinigkeit *f*
dissent [dɪ'sent] *s* abweichende Meinung *f* || *intr* (**from**) anderer Meinung sein (als)
dissenter [dɪ'sentər] *s* Andersdenkende *mf;* (relig) Dissident –in *mf*
dissertation [,dɪsər'teʃən] *s* Dissertation *f*
disservice [dɪ'sʌrvɪs] *s* schlechter Dienst *m;* **do s.o. a d.** j–m e–n schlechten Dienst erweisen
dissidence ['dɪsɪdəns] *s* Meinungsverschiedenheit *f*
dissident ['dɪsɪdənt] *adj* andersdenkend || *s* Dissident –in *mf*
dissimilar [dɪ'sɪmɪlər] *adj* unähnlich
dissimilate [dɪ'sɪmɪ,let] *tr* (phonet) dissimilieren
dissimulate [dɪ'sɪmjə,let] *tr* verheimlichen || *intr* heucheln
dissipate ['dɪsɪ,pet] *tr* (*squander*) vergeuden; (*scatter*) zerstreuen; (*dissolve*) auflösen || *intr* (*scatter*) sich zerstreuen; (*dissolve*) sich auflösen
dis'sipat'ed *adj* ausschweifend
dissipation [,dɪsɪ'peʃən] *s* (*squandering*) Vergeudung *f;* (*dissolute mode of life*) Ausschweifung *f;* (phys) Dissipation *f*
dissociate [dɪ'soʃɪ,et] *tr* trennen; **d. oneself from** abrücken von
dissolute ['dɪsə,lut] *adj* ausschweifend
dissolution [,dɪsə'luʃən] *s* Auflösung *f*
dissolve [dɪ'zɑlv] *s* (cin) Überblendung *f* || *tr* auflösen; (cin) überblenden || *intr* sich auflösen; (cin) überblenden
dissonance ['dɪsənəns] *s* Mißklang *m*
dissuade [dɪ'swed] *tr* (**from**) abbringen (von); **d. s.o. from** (*ger*) j–n davon abbringen zu (*inf*)
dissyllabic [,dɪsɪ'læbɪk] *adj* zweisilbig
distaff ['dɪstæf] *s* Spinnrocken *m;* (fig) Frauen *pl*
dis'taff side' *s* weibliche Linie *f*
distance ['dɪstəns] *s* Entfernung *f;* (*between two points*) Abstand *m;* (*stretch*) Strecke *f;* (*of a race*) Rennstrecke *f;* **from a d.** aus einiger Entfernung; **go the d.** bis zum Ende aushalten; **in the d.** in der Ferne; **keep one's d.** zurückhaltend sein; **keep your d.** bleib mir vom Leib!; **within easy d. of** nicht weit weg von; **within walking d. of** zu Fuß erreichbar von
distant ['dɪstənt] *adj* entfernt; (*reserved*) zurückhaltend

distaste [dɪs'test] s (for) Abneigung f (gegen), Ekel m (vor dat)
distasteful [dɪs'testfəl] adj (unpleasant) (to) unangenehm (dat); (offensive) (to) ekelhaft (dat)
distemper [dɪs'tempər] s (of dogs) Staupe f; (paint) Temperafarbe f
distend [dɪs'tend] tr (swell) aufblähen; (extend) ausdehnen || intr (swell) anschwellen; (extend) (aus)-dehnen
distension [dɪs'tenʃən] s Aufblähung f; Ausdehnung f
distill [dɪ'stɪl] tr destillieren; (e.g., whiskey) brennen
distillation [ˌdɪstɪ'leʃən] s Destillation f; (of whiskey) Brennen n
distiller [dɪs'tɪlər] s Brenner m
distillery [dɪs'tɪləri] s Brennerei f
distinct [dɪ'stɪŋkt] adj (clear) deutlich; (different) verschieden; **as d. from** zum Unterschied von; **keep d.** auseinanderhalten
distinction [dɪs'tɪŋkʃən] s (difference) Unterschied m; (differentiation) Unterscheidung f; (honor) Auszeichnung f; (eminence) Vornehmheit f; **have the d. of** (ger) den Vorzug haben zu (inf)
distinctive [dɪs'tɪŋktɪv] adj (distinguishing) unterscheidend; (characteristic) kennzeichnend
distinguish [dɪs'tɪŋgwɪʃ] tr (differentiate) unterscheiden; (classify) einteilen; (honor) auszeichnen; (characterize) kennzeichnen; (discern) erkennen || intr (between) unterscheiden (zwischen dat)
distin'guished adj (eminent) prominent; (for) berühmt (wegen)
distort [dɪs'tɔrt] tr verzerren; (the truth) entstellen; **distorted picture** Zerrbild n
distortion [dɪs'tɔrʃən] s Verzerrung f; (of the truth) Entstellung f
distract [dɪ'strækt] tr ablenken
distraction [dɪ'strækʃən] s (diversion of attention) Ablenkung f; (entertainment) Zerstreuung f; **drive s.o. to d.** j–n zum Wahnsinn treiben
distraught [dɪ'strɔt] adj (bewildered) verwirrt; (deeply agitated) (with) aufgewühlt (von); (crazed) (with) rasend (vor dat)
distress [dɪ'stres] s (anxiety) Kummer m; (mental pain) Betrübnis f; (danger) Notstand m, Bedrängnis f; (naut) Seenot f || tr betrüben
distress'ing adj betrüblich
distress' sig'nal s Notzeichen n
distribute [dɪ'strɪbjut] tr verteilen; (divide) einteilen; (apportion) (jur) aufteilen
distribution [ˌdɪstrɪ'bjuʃən] s Verteilung f; (geographic range) Verbreitung f; (of films) Verleih m; (marketing) Vertrieb m; (of dividends) Ausschüttung f; (jur) Aufteilung f
distributor [dɪ'strɪbjətər] s Verteiler –in mf; (of films) Verleiher –in mf; (dealer) Lieferant –in mf; (aut) Verteiler m
distri'butorship' s Vertrieb m

district ['dɪstrɪkt] s Bezirk m
dis'trict attor'ney s Staatsanwalt m
distrust [dɪs'trʌst] s Mißtrauen n || tr mißtrauen (dat)
distrustful [dɪs'trʌstfəl] adj (of) mißtrauisch (gegen)
disturb [dɪs'tʌrb] tr stören; (disquiet) beunruhigen; **d. the peace** die öffentliche Ruhe stören
disturbance [dɪs'tʌrbəns] s (interruption) Störung f; (breach of peace) Unruhe f
disunited [ˌdɪsju'naɪtɪd] adj uneinig
disunity [dɪs'junɪti] s Uneinigkeit f
disuse [dɪs'jus] s Nichtverwendung f; **fall into d.** außer Gebrauch kommen
ditch [dɪtʃ] s Graben m || tr (discard) (sl) wegschmeißen; (aer) (coll) auf dem Wasser notlanden mit || intr (aer) (coll) notwassern
dither ['dɪðər] s—**be in a d.** verdattert sein
dit·to ['dɪto] adj (coll) dito || s (–tos) Kopie f || tr vervielfältigen
dit'to mark' s Wiederholungszeichen n
ditty ['dɪti] s Liedchen n
diva ['dɪvɑ] s (mus) Diva f
divan ['daɪvæn], [dɪ'væn] s Diwan m
dive [daɪv] s Kopfsprung m; (coll) Spelunke f; (aer) Sturzflug m; (nav) Tauchen n; (sport) Kunstsprung m; **make a d. for** (fig) sich stürzen auf (acc) || v (pret & pp dived & dove [dov]) intr (submerge) tauchen; (plunge head first) e–n Kopfsprung machen; (aer) e–n Sturzflug machen; (nav) (unter)tauchen; (sport) e–n Kunstsprung machen
dive'-bomb' tr & intr im Sturzflug mit Bomben angreifen
dive' bomb'er s Sturzkampfbomber m
diver ['daɪvər] s Taucher –in mf; (orn) Taucher m; (sport) Kunstspringer –in mf
diverge [daɪ'vʌrdʒ] intr (said of roads, views) sich teilen; (from the norm) abweichen; (geom, phys) divergieren
diverse [daɪ'vʌrs] adj (different) verschieden; (of various kinds) vielförmig
diversi·fy [daɪ'vʌrsɪˌfaɪ] v (pret & pp –fied) tr abwechslungsreich gestalten
diversion [daɪ'vʌrʒən] s Ablenkung f; (recreation) Zeitvertreib m; (mil) Ablenkungsmanöver n
diversity [daɪ'vʌrsɪti] s Mannigfaltigkeit f
divert [daɪ'vʌrt] tr (attention) ablenken; (traffic) umleiten; (a river) ableiten; (money) abzweigen; (entertain) zerstreuen
divest [daɪ'vest] tr—**d. oneself of** sich entäußern (genit); **d. s.o. of** (e.g., office, power) j–n entkleiden (genit); (e.g., rights, property) j–m (seine Rechte, etc.) entziehen
divide [dɪ'vaɪd] s (geol) Wasserscheide f || tr teilen; (cause to disagree) entzweien; (math) (by) teilen (durch); **d. into** einteilen in (acc); **d. off** (a room) abteilen; **d. up** (among) aufteilen (unter acc) || intr

(*said of a road*) sich teilen; **d. into** sich teilen in (*acc*)
dividend ['dɪvɪ‚dend] s Dividende f; (math) Dividend m; **pay dividends** Dividenden ausschütten; (fig) sich lohnen
divid'ing line' s Trennungsstrich m
divination [‚dɪvɪ'neʃən] s Weissagung f
divine [dɪ'vaɪn] adj göttlich || s Geistlicher m || tr (er)ahnen
divine' prov'idence s göttliche Vorsehung f
divine' right' of kings' s Königtum n von Gottes Gnaden
div'ing s Tauchen n (sport) Kunstspringen n
div'ing bell' s Taucherglocke f
div'ing board' s Sprungbrett n
div'ing suit' s Taucheranzug m
divin'ing rod' s Wünschelrute f
divinity [dɪ'vɪnɪti] s (*divine nature*) Göttlichkeit f; (*deity*) Gottheit f
divisible [dɪ'vɪzɪbəl] adj teilbar
division [dɪ'vɪʒən] s Teilung f; (*dissention*) Uneinigkeit f; (adm) Abteilung f; (math, mil) Division f; (sport) Sportklasse f
divisor [dɪ'vaɪzər] s (math) Teiler m; Divisor m
divorce [dɪ'vors] s Scheidung f; **apply for a d.** die Scheidungsklage einreichen; **get a d.** sich scheiden lassen || tr (*said of a spouse*) sich scheiden lassen von; (*said of a judge*) scheiden; (*separate*) trennen
divorcee [dɪvor'si] s Geschiedene f
divulge [dɪ'vʌldʒ] tr ausplaudern
dizziness ['dɪzɪnɪs] s Schwindel m
dizzy ['dɪzi] adj schwindlig; (*causing dizziness*) schwindelerregend; (*mentally confused*) benommen; (*foolish*) damisch; (*feeling, spell*) Schwindel-
do [du] v (*3d pers does* [dʌz]; *pret* did [dɪd]; *pp* done [dʌn]; *ger doing* ['du·ɪŋ] tr tun, machen; (*damage*) anrichten; (*one's hair*) frisieren; (*an injustice*) antun; (*a favor, disservice*) erweisen; (*time in jail*) absitzen; (*miles per hour*) fahren; (*tour*) (coll) besichtigen; (*Shakespeare, etc., in class*) durchnehmen; **do duty as** dienen als; **do in** (sl) umbringen; **do over** (*with paint*) neu anstreichen; (*with covering*) neu überziehen; **what can I do for you?** womit kann ich dienen? || intr tun, machen; (*suffice*) genügen; **do away with** abschaffen; (*persons*) aus dem Wege räumen; **do away with oneself** sich |dat| das Leben nehmen; **do without** auskommen ohne; **I am doing well** es geht mir gut; (*financially*) ich verdiene gut; (*e.g., in history*) ich komme gut voran; **I'll make it do** ich werde schon damit auskommen; **nothing doing!** ausgeschlossen! **that will do!** genug davon!; **that won't do!** das geht nicht! || aux used in English but not specifically expressed in German: 1) in questions, e.g., **do you speak German?** sprechen Sie deutsch?; 2) in negative sentences,

e.g., **I do not live here** ich wohne hier nicht; 3) for emphasis, e.g., **I do feel better** ich fühle mich wirklich besser; 4) in imperative entreaties, e.g., **do come again** besuchen Sie mich doch wieder!; 5) in elliptical sentences, e.g., **I like Berlin. So do I** Mir gefällt Berlin. Mir auch.; **he drinks, doesn't he?** er trinkt, nicht wahr?; 6) in inversions after adverbs such as hardly, rarely, scarcely, little, e.g., **little did she realize that…**sie hatte keine Ahnung, daß… || impers—**it doesn't do to** (*inf*) es ist unklug zu (*inf*); **it won't do you any good to stay here** es wird Ihnen nicht viel nützen, hier zu bleiben
docile ['dɑsɪl] adj gelehrig; (*easy to handle*) fügsam, lenksam
dock [dɑk] s Anlegeplatz m; (jur) Anklagebank f; **docks** Hafenanlagen pl; **in the d.** (jur) auf der Anklagebank || tr (*a ship, space vehicle*) docken; (*a tail*) stutzen; (*pay*) kürzen; **d. an employee (for)** e-m Arbeitnehmer den Lohn kürzen (um) || intr (naut) (*am Kai*) anlegen; (rok) docken, koppeln
docket ['dɑkɪt] s (*agenda*) Tagesordnung f; (jur) Prozeßliste f
dock' hand' s Hafenarbeiter m
dock'ing s (naut) Anlegen n; (rok) Andocken n
dock' work'er s Dockarbeiter m
dock'yard' s Werft f
doctor ['dɑktər] s Doktor m; (*physician*) Arzt m, Ärztin f || tr (*records*) frisieren; (*adapt, e.g., a play*) zurechtmachen || intr (*coll*) in ärztlicher Behandlung stehen
doctorate ['dɑktərɪt] s Doktorwürde f
doctrine ['dɑktrɪn] s Doktrin f, Lehre f
document ['dɑkjəmənt] s Urkunde f || ['dɑkjə‚ment] tr dokumentieren
documentary [‚dɑkjə'mentəri] adj dokumentarisch || s Dokumentarfilm m
documentation [‚dɑkjəmən'teʃən] s Dokumentation f
doddering ['dɑdərɪŋ] adj zittrig
dodge [dɑdʒ] s Winkelzug m || tr (*e.g., a blow*) ausweichen (*dat*); (*e.g., a responsibility*) sich drücken vor (*dat*) || intr ausweichen
do·do ['dodo] s (*–does & –dos*) (coll) Depp m
doe [do] s Rehgeiß f, Damhirschkuh f
doer ['du·ər] s Täter –in mf
doe'skin' s Rehleder n
doff [dɔf] tr (*a hat*) abnehmen; (*clothes*) ausziehen; (*habits*) ablegen
dog [dɔg] s Hund m; **dog eats dog** jeder für sich; **go to the dogs** (coll) vor die Hunde gehen; **lucky dog!** (coll) Glückspitz!; **put on the dog** (coll) großtun || v (*pret & pp* **dogged;** *ger* **dogging**) tr nachspüren (*dat*)
dog' bis'cuit s Hundekuchen m
dog' days' spl Hundstage pl
dog'-eared' adj mit Eselsohren
dog'face' s (mil) Landser m

dog'fight' *s* (aer) Kurbelei *f*
dogged ['dɔgɪd] *adj* verbissen
doggerel ['dɔgərəl] *s* Knittelvers *m*
doggone ['dɔg'gɔn] *adj* (sl) verflixt
dog'house' *s* Hundehütte *f;* **in the d.** (fig) in Ungnade
dog' ken'nel *s* Hundezwinger *m*
dogma ['dɔgmə] *s* Dogma *n*
dogmatic [dɔg'mætɪk] *adj* dogmatisch
do-gooder ['du'gudər] *s* Humanitätsapostel *m*
dog' show' *s* Hundeschau *f*
dog's' life' *s* Hundeleben *n*
Dog' Star' *s* Hundestern *m*
dog' tag' *s* Hundemarke *f;* (mil) Erkennungsmarke *f*
dog'-tired' *adj* hundemüde
dog'wood' *s* Hartriegel *m*
doily ['dɔɪli] *s* Zierdeckchen *n*
do'ing *s* Werk *n;* **doings** Tun und Treiben *n;* (*events*) Ereignisse *pl*
doldrums ['dɔldrəmz] *spl* Kalmengürtel *m;* **in the d.** (fig) deprimiert
dole [dol] *s* Spende *f;* **be on the d.** stempeln gehen || *tr*—**d. out** verteilen
doleful ['dolfəl] *adj* trübselig
doll [dal] *s* Puppe *f* || *tr*—**d. up** (coll) aufdonnern || *intr* (coll) sich aufdonnern
dollar ['dalər] *s* Dollar *m*
doll' car'riage *s* Puppenwagen *m*
dolly ['dali] *s* Püppchen *n;* (*cart*) Schiebkarren *m*
dolphin ['dalfɪn] *s* Delphin *m*
dolt [dolt] *s* Tölpel *m*
domain [do'men] *s* (& fig) Domäne *f*
dome [dom] *s* Kuppel *f*
dome' light' *s* (aut) Deckenlicht *n*
domestic [də'mɛstɪk] *adj* (*of the home*) Haus-, häuslich, Haushalts-; (*produced at home*) einheimisch, inländisch, Landes-; (*tame*) Haus-; (*e.g., policy*) Innen-, innere || *s* Hausangestellte *mf*
domesticate [də'mɛstɪ ˌket] *tr* zähmen
domicile ['damɪ ˌsaɪl] *s* Wohnsitz *m*
dominance ['damɪnəns] *s* Vorherrschaft *f*
dominant ['damɪnənt] *adj* vorherrschend; (*factor*) entscheidend
dominate ['damɪ ˌnet] *tr* beherrschen || *intr* (**over**) herrschen (über *acc*)
domination [ˌdamɪ'neʃən] *s* Beherrschung *f*, Herrschaft *f*
domineer [ˌdamɪ'nɪr] *tr* & *intr* tyrannisieren
domineer'ing *adj* tyrannisch
dominion [də'mɪnjən] *s* (*sovereignty*) (**over**) Gewalt *f* (über *acc*); (*domain*) Domäne *f;* (*of British Empire*) Dominion *n*
domi·no ['damɪ ˌno] *s* (**-noes** & **nos**) Dominostein *m;* **dominoes** *ssg* Dominospiel *n*
don [dan] *s* Universitätsprofessor *m* || *v* (*pret* & *pp* **donned;** *ger* **donning**) *tr* anlegen; (*a hat*) sich [*dat*] aufsetzen
donate ['donet] *tr* schenken, spenden
donation [do'neʃən] *s* Schenkung *f;* (*small contribution*) Spende *f*
done [dʌn] *adj* erledigt; (culin) gar, fertig; **d. for** kaputt; **d. with** (com-

pleted) fertig; **get** (*s.th.*) **d.** fertigbekommen; **well d.** (culin) durchgebraten
donkey ['dʌŋki] *s* Esel *m*
donor ['donər] *s* Spender –in *mf*
doodad ['dudæd] *s* (*gadget*) Dings *n;* (*decoration*) Tand *m*
doodle ['dudəl] *s* Gekritzel *n* || *tr* bekritzeln || *intr* kritzeln
doom [dum] *s* Verhängnis *n* || *tr* verdammen, verurteilen
doomed *adj* todgeweiht
doomsday ['dumz ˌde] *s* der Jüngste Tag
door [dor] *s* Tür *f;* **from d. to d.** von Haus zu Haus; **out of doors** draußen, im Freien; **show s.o. the d.** j-m die Tür weisen; **two doors away** zwei Häuser weiter
door'bell' *s* Türklingel *f;* **the d. is ringing** es klingelt
door'bell but'ton *s* Klingelknopf *m*
door'frame' *s* Türrahmen *m*
door'han'dle *s* Türgriff *m*, Türklinke *f*
door'jamb' *s* Türpfosten *m*
door'knob' *s* Türknopf *m*
door'man' *s* (**-men'**) Portier *m*
door'mat' *s* Abtreter *m*, Türmatte *f*
door'nail' *s*—**dead as a d.** mausetot
door'post' *s* Türpfosten *m*
door'sill' *s* Türschwelle *f*
door'step' *s* Türstufe *f*
door'stop' *s* Türanschlag *m*
door'-to-door' sales'man *s* Hausierer *m*
door'-to-door sel'ling *s* Hausieren *n*
door'way' *s* Türöffnung *f;* (fig) Weg *m*
dope [dop] *s* (*drug*) (sl) Rauschgift *n;* (*information*) (sl) vertraulicher Tip *m;* (*fool*) (sl) Trottel *m;* (aer) Lack *m* || *tr* (*a racehorse*) (sl) dopen; (*a person*) (sl) betäuben, verdrogen; (aer) lackieren; **d. out** (sl) herausfinden, ausarbeiten; **d. up** (sl) verdrogen
dope' ad'dict *s* (sl) Rauschgiftsüchtige *mf*
dope' push'er *s* (sl) Rauschgiftschieber –in *mf*
dope'sheet' *s* (sl) vertraulicher Bericht *m*
dope' traf'fic *s* (sl) Rauschgifthandel *m*
dopey ['dopi] *adj* (**dopier; dopiest**) (sl) dämlich; (*from sleep*) (coll) schlaftrunken
dormant ['dɔrmənt] *adj* ruhend, untätig; (bot) in der Winterruhe
dormer ['dɔrmər] *s* Bodenfenster *n;* (*the whole structure*) Mansarde *f*
dor'mer win'dow *s* Bodenfenster *n*
dormitory ['dɔrmɪ ˌtori] *s* (*building*) Studentenheim *n;* (*room*) Schlafsaal *m*
dormouse ['dɔr ˌmaus] *s* (**mice** [ˌmaɪs]) Haselmaus *f*
dor'sal fin' ['dɔrsəl] *s* Rückenflosse *f*
dosage ['dosɪdʒ] *s* Dosierung *f*
dose [dos] *s* (& fig) Dosis *f*
dossier ['dasɪ ˌe] *s* Dossier *m*
dot [dat] *s* Punkt *m*, Tupfen *m;* **on the dot** auf die Sekunde; **three o'clock on the dot** Punkt drei Uhr || *v* (*pret*

& *pp* **dotted; ger dotting**) *tr* punktieren; tüpfeln; **dot one's i's** den Punkt aufs i setzen; (fig) übergenau sein

dotage ['dotɪdʒ] *s*—**be in one's d.** senil sein

dotard ['dotərd] *s* kindischer Greis *m*

dote [dot] *intr*—**d. on** vernarrt sein in (*acc*)

dot'ing *adj* (**on**) vernarrt (in *acc*)

dots' and dash'es *spl* (telg) Punkte und Striche *pl*

dot'ted *adj* (*pattern*) getüpfelt; (*with flowers, etc.*) übersät; (*line*) punktiert

double ['dʌbəl] *adj* doppelt ‖ *s* Doppelte *n*; (*person*) Doppelgänger *m* (cin, theat) Double *n*; **doubles** (tennis) Doppel *n*; **on the d.** im Geschwindschritt ‖ *tr* (ver)doppeln; (*the fist*) ballen; (*cards*) doppeln; (naut) umsegeln ‖ *intr* sich verdoppeln; (cards) doppeln; **d. back** umkehren; **d. up with** sich biegen vor (*dat*)

dou'ble-bar'reled *adj* (*gun*) doppelläufig; (fig) mit zweifacher Wirkung

dou'ble bass' [bes] *s* Kontrabaß *m*

dou'ble bed' *s* Doppelbett *n*

dou'ble-breast'ed *adj* doppelreihig

dou'ble' chin' *s* Doppelkinn *n*

dou'ble cross' *s* Schwindel *m*

dou'ble-cross' *tr* beschwindeln

dou'ble-cross'er *s* Schwindler –in *mf*

dou'ble date' *s* Doppelrendezvous *n*

dou'ble-deal'er *s* Betrüger –in *mf*

dou'ble-deal'ing *s* Doppelzüngigkeit *f*

dou'ble-deck'er *s* (*ship, bus*) Doppeldecker *m*; (*sandwich*) Doppelsandwich *n*; (*bed*) Etagenbett *n*

dou'ble-edged' *adj* (& fig) zweischneidig

double entendre ['dʌbəlanˈtandrə] *s* (*ambiguity*) Doppelsinn *m*; (*ambiguous term*) doppelsinniger Ausdruck *m*

dou'ble en'try *s* (com) doppelte Buchführung *f*

dou'ble expo'sure *s* Doppelbelichtung *f*

dou'ble fea'ture *s* Doppelprogramm *n*

dou'blehead'er *s* Doppelspiel *n*

dou'ble-joint'ed *adj* mit Gummigelenken

dou'blepark' *tr* & *intr* falsch parken

dou'ble-spaced' *adj* mit doppeltem Zeilenabstand

dou'ble stand'ard *s* zweierlei Maß *n*

doublet ['dʌblɪt] *s* (*duplicate; counterfeit stone*) Dublette *f*; (hist) Wams *m*; (ling) Doppelform *f*

dou'ble take' *s* (fig) Spätzündung *f*

dou'ble-talk' *s* zweideutige Rede *f*

dou'ble time' *s* (*wage rate*) doppelter Lohn *m*; (mil) Eilschritt *m*

dou'ble track' *s* (rr) doppelgleisige Bahnlinie *f*

doubly ['dʌbli] *adv* doppelt

doubt [daut] *s* Zweifel *m*; **be still in d.** (*said of things*) noch zweifelhaft sein; **beyond d.** ohne (jeden) Zweifel; **in case of d.** im Zweifelsfalle; **no d.** zweifellos; **raise doubts** Bedenken

erregen; **there is no d. that** es unterliegt keinem Zweifel, daß ‖ *tr* bezweifeln ‖ *intr* zweifeln

doubter ['dautər] *s* Zweifler –in *mf*

doubtful ['dautfəl] *adj* zweifelhaft

doubtless ['dautlɪs] *adj* & *adv* zweifellos

douche [duʃ] *s* (*device*) Irrigator *m*; (*act of cleansing*) Spülung *f* ‖ *tr* & *intr* spülen

dough [do] *s* Teig *m*; (sl) Pinke *f*

dough'boy' *s* (sl) Landser *m*

dough'nut' *s* Krapfen *m*

doughty ['dauti] *adj* wacker

doughy ['do·i] *adj* teigig

dour [daur], [dur] *adj* mürrisch

douse [daus] *tr* eintauchen; (**with**) übergießen (mit); (*a fire*) auslöschen

dove [dʌv] *s* (& pol) Taube *f*

dovecote ['dʌv‚kot] *s* Taubenschlag *m*

dove'tail' *s* (carp) Schwalbenschwanz *m* ‖ *tr* verzinken; (fig) ineinanderfügen ‖ *intr* sich verdoppeln

dowager ['dau·ədʒər] *s* Witwe *f* (von Stand); (coll) Matrone *f*

dowdy ['daudi] *adj* schlampig

dow·el ['dau·əl] *s* Dübel *m* ‖ *v* (*pret* & *pp* –el[l]ed; *ger* –el[l]ing) *tr* (ein)dübeln

down [daun] *adj* (*prices*) gesunken; (*sun*) untergegangen; **be d. for** vorgemerkt sein für; **be d. on s.o.** auf j–m herumtrampeln; **be d. three points** (sport) drei Punkte zurück sein; **be d. with a cold** mit e–r Erkältung im Bett liegen; **d. and out** völlig erledigt; **d. in the mouth** niedergedrückt ‖ *adv* herunter, hinunter; **d. from** von... herab; **d. there** da unten; **d. to** bis hinunter zu; **d. to the last man** bis zum letzten Mann; **d. with...!** nieder mit...! ‖ *s* (*of fowl*) Daune *f*; (*fine hair*) Flaum *m*; **downs** grasbedecktes Hügelland *n* ‖ *prep* (postpositive) (*acc*) herunter, hinunter; **a little way d. the road** etwas weiter auf der Straße; **d. the river** flußabwärts ‖ *tr* niederschlagen; (*a glass of beer*) (coll) hinunterstürzen; (aer) abschießen

down'cast' *adj* niedergeschlagen

down'draft' *s* Abwind *m*, Fallwind *m*

down'fall' *s* Untergang *m*

down'grade' *s* Gefälle *n*; **on the d.** (fig) im Niedergang ‖ *tr* herabsetzen; niedriger einstufen

down'heart'ed *adj* niedergeschlagen

down'hill' *adj* bergabgehend; (*in skiing*) Abfahrts– ‖ *adv* bergab; **he's going d.** (coll) mit ihm geht es abwärts

down' pay'ment *s* Anzahlung *f*

down'pour' *s* Regenguß *m*, Sturzregen *m*

down'right' *adj* ausgesprochen; (*lie*) glatt; (*contradiction*) schroff ‖ *adv* ausgesprochen

down'spout' *s* Fallrohr *n*

down'stairs' *adj* unten befindlich ‖ *adv* (*position*) unten; (*direction*) nach unten

down'stream' *adv* stromabwärts

down'stroke' s (*in writing*) Grundstrich m; (*of a piston*) Abwärtshub m
down'-the-line' adj vorbehaltlos
down-to-earth' adj nüchtern
down'town' adj im Geschäftsviertel gelegen ‖ adv (*position*) im Geschäftsviertel; (*direction*) ins Geschäftsviertel, in die Stadt ‖ s Geschäftsviertel n
down'trend' s Baissestimmung f
downtrodden ['daʊn‚trɑdən] adj unterdrückt
downward ['daʊnwərd] adj Abwärts– ‖ adv abwärts
downwards ['daʊnwərdz] adv abwärts
downy ['daʊni] adj flaumig; (*soft*) weich wie Flaum
dowry ['daʊri] s Mitgift f
dowser ['daʊzər] s (*rod*) Wünschelrute f; (*person*) Wünschelrutengänger m
doze [doz] s Schläfchen n ‖ intr dösen
dozen ['dʌzən] s Dutzend n; **a d. times** dutzendmal
Dr. abbr (**Doctor**) Dr.; (*in addresses:* **Drive**) Str.
drab [dræb] adj (**drabber; drabbest**) graubraun; (fig) trüb
drach·ma ['drækmə] s (**–mas** & **–mae** [mi]) Drachme f
draft [dræft] s (*of air; drink*) Zug m; (*sketch*) Entwurf m; (fin) Tratte f; (mil) Einberufung f; **on d.** vom Faß ‖ tr (*sketch*) entwerfen, abfassen; (mil) einberufen
draft' age' s wehrpflichtiges Alter n
draft' beer' s Schankbier n
draft' board' s Wehrmeldeamt n
draft' dodg'er ['dɑdʒər] s Drückeberger m
draftee [‚dræf'ti] s Dienstpflichtige mf
draft'ing s (*of a document*) Abfassung f; (*mechanical drawing*) Zeichnen n; (mil) Aushebung f
draft'ing board' s Zeichenbrett n
draft'ing room' s Zeichenbüro n
drafts·man ['dræftsmən] s (**–men**) Zeichner m
drafty ['dræfti] adj zugig
drag [dræg] s (*sledge*) Lastschlitten m; (*in smoking*) (coll) Zug m; (*boring person*) langweiliger Mensch m; (s.th. *tedious*) etwas langweiliges; (*encumbrance*) (on) Hemmschuh m (für); (aer) Luftwiderstand m; (*for recovering objects*) (naut) Schleppnetz n; (*for retarding motion*) (naut) Schleppanker m ‖ v (pret & pp **dragged; ger dragging**) tr schleppen, schleifen; **d. one's feet** schlurfen; (fig) sich [*dat*] Zeit lassen; **d. out** dahinschleppen; (*protract*) verschleppen; **d. through the mud** (fig) in den Schmutz zerren; **d. up** (fig) aufwärmen ‖ intr (*said of a long dress, etc.*) schleifen; (*said of time*) dahinschleichen; **d. on** (*be prolonged*) sich hinziehen
drag'net' s Schleppnetz n
dragon ['drægən] s Drache m
drag'onfly' s Libelle f

dragoon [drə'gun] s Dragoner m ‖ tr (*coerce*) zwingen
drag' race' s Straßenrennen n; (sport) Kurzstreckenrennen n
drain [dren] s (*sewer*) Kanal m; (*under a sink*) Abfluß m; (fig) (on) Belastung f (*genit*); (surg) Drain m; **down the d.** (fig) zum Fenster hinaus ‖ tr (*land*) entwässern; (*water*) ableiten; (*a cup, glass*) austrinken; (fig) verzehren ‖ intr ablaufen; (culin) abtropfen
drainage ['drenɪdʒ] s Ableitung f; (e.g., *of land*) Entwässerung f; (surg) Drainage f
drain'age ditch' s Abflußgraben m
drain' cock' s Entleerungshahn m
drain' pipe' s Abflußrohr n
drain' plug' s Abflußstöpsel m
drake [drek] s Enterich m
dram [dræm] s Dram n
drama ['drɑmə] s Drama n; (*art and genre*) Dramatik f
dra'ma crit'ic s Theaterkritiker –in mf
dramatic [drə'mætɪk] adj dramatisch ‖ **dramatics** s Dramatik f; spl (pej) Schauspielerei f
dramatist ['dræmətɪst] s Dramatiker –in mf
dramatize ['dræmə‚taɪz] tr dramatisieren
drape [drep] s Vorhang m; (*hang of a drape or skirt*) Faltenwurf m ‖ tr drapieren
drapery ['drepəri] s Vorhänge pl
dra'pery mate'rial s Vorhangstoff m
drastic ['dræstɪk] adj drastisch
draught [dræft] s & tr var of **draft**
draw [drɔ] s (*in a lottery*) Ziehen n; (*that which attracts*) Schlager m; (*power of attraction*) Anziehungskraft f; **end in a d.** unentschieden ausgehen ‖ v (pret **drew** [dru]; pp **drawn** [drɔn]) tr (*pictures*) zeichnen; (*a line, comparison, parallel, conclusion, lots, winner, sword, wagon*) ziehen; (*a crowd*) anlocken; (*a distinction*) machen; (*blood*) vergießen; (*curtains*) zuziehen; (*a check*) ausstellen; (*water*) schöpfen; (*cards*) nehmen; (*rations*) (mil) in Empfang nehmen; **d. a blank** (coll) e–e Niete ziehen; **d. aside** beiseiteziehen; **d. attention to** die Aufmerksamkeit lenken auf (*acc*); **d. into** (e.g., *an argument*) hineinziehen in (*acc*); **d. lots for** losen um; **d. out** (*protract*) in die Länge ziehen; (*money from a bank*) abheben; **d. s.o. out** j–n ausholen; **d. the line** (fig) e–e Grenze ziehen; **d. up** (*a document*) verfassen; (*plans*) entwerfen ‖ intr zeichnen; **d. away** sich entfernen; **d. back** sich zurückziehen; **d. near** herannahen; **d. on** zurückgreifen auf (*acc*); **d. to a close** sich dem Ende zuneigen
draw'back' s Nachteil m
draw'bridge' s Zugbrücke f
drawee [‚drɔ'i] s Trassat –in mf
drawer ['drɔ·ər] s Zeichner –in mf; (com) Trassant –in mf ‖ [drɔr] s Schublade f; **drawers** Unterhose f
draw'ing s (*of pictures*) Zeichnen n;

(*picture*) Zeichnung *f*; (*in a lottery*) Ziehung *f*, Verlosung *f*
draw'ing board' *s* Reißbrett *n*
draw'ing card' *s* Zugnummer *f*
draw'ing room' *s* Empfangszimmer *n*
drawl [drɔl] *s* gedehntes Sprechen *n* || *intr* gedehnt sprechen
drawn [drɔn] *adj* (*face*) (**with**) verzerrt (*vor dat*); (*sword*) blank
dray [dre] *s* niedriger Rollwagen *m*; (*sledge*) Schleife *f*
dread ⌊dred⌋ *adj* furchtbar || *s* Furcht *f* || *tr* fürchten
dreadful ['dredfəl] *adj* furchtbar
dream [drim] *s* Traum *m*; (*aspiration, ambition*) Wunschtraum *m*; (*ideal*) (*coll*) Gedicht *n* || *v* (*pret & pp* **dreamed** & **dreamt** [dremt] *tr* träumen; **d. away** verträumen; **d. up** zusammenträumen || *intr* träumen; **d. of** (*long for*) sich [*dat*] enträumen; **I dreamt of her** mir träumte von ihr
dreamer ['drimər] *s* Träumer –in *mf*
dream'land' *s* Traumland *n*
dream'-like' *adj* traumhaft
dream'world' *s* Traumwelt *f*
dreamy ['drimi] *adj* (*place*) verträumt; (*eyes*) träumerisch
dreary ['driri] *adj* trüb, trist
dredge [dredʒ] *s* Bagger *m* || *tr* (aus)baggern || *intr* baggern
dredger ['dredʒər] *s* Bagger *m*
dredg'ing *s* Baggern *n*
dregs [dregz] *spl* Bodensatz *m*; (*of society*) Abschaum *m*, Auswurf *m*
drench [drentʃ] *tr* durchnässen
Dres'den chi'na ['drezdən] *s* Meißner Porzellan *n*
dress [dres] *s* Kleidung *f*; (*woman's dress*) Kleid *n* || *tr* anziehen; (*a store window*) dekorieren; (*skins*) gerben; (*a salad, goose, chicken*) zubereiten; (*vines*) beschneiden; (*stones*) behauen; (*ore*) aufbereiten; (*wounds*) verbinden; (*hair*) frisieren; (*tex*) appretieren; **d. down** (*coll*) ausschimpfen; **d. ranks** die Glieder ausrichten; **get dressed** sich anziehen || *intr* sich anziehen; **d. up** sich fein machen
dress' affair' *s* Galaveranstaltung *f*
dresser ['dresər] *s* Frisierkommode *f*; **be a good d.** sich gut kleiden
dress'ing *s* (*stuffing for fowl*) Füllung *f*; (*for salad*) Soße *f*; (surg) Verband *m*
dress'ing down' *s* Gardinenpredigt *f*
dress'ing room' *s* Umkleideraum *m*; (theat) Garderobe *f*
dress'ing sta'tion *s* Verbandsplatz *m*
dress'ing ta'ble *s* Frisierkommode *f*
dress'mak'er *s* Schneiderin *f*
dress'mak'ing *s* Modenschneiderei *f*
dress' rehear'sal *s* Kostümprobe *f*
dress' shirt' *s* Frackhemd *n*
dress' shop' *s* Modenhaus *n*, Modengeschäft *n*
dress' suit' *s* Frackanzug *m*, Frack *m*
dress' un'iform *s* Paradeuniform *f*
dressy ['dresi] *adj* (*showy*) geschniegelt; (*stylish*) modisch; (*for formal affairs*) elegant
dribble ['dribəl] *s* (*trickle*) Getröpfel

n; (sport) Dribbeln *n* || *tr & intr* tröpfeln; (sport) dribbeln
driblet ['driblit] *s* Bißchen *n*
dried [draid] *adj* Trocken–, Dörr–
dried' beef' *s* Dörrfleisch *n*
dried' fruit' *s* Dörrobst *n*
dried'-up' *adj* ausgetrocknet, verdorrt
drier ['drai·ər] *s* Trockner *m*; (*for the hair*) Haartrockenhaube *f*; (*hand model*) Fön *m*
drift [drift] *s* (*of sand, snow*) Wehe *f*; (*tendency*) Richtung *f*, Neigung *f*; (*intent*) Absicht *f*; (*meaning*) Sinn *m*; (aer, naut, rad) Abtrift *f*; (*flow of the ocean current*) (naut) Drift *f* || *intr* (*said of sand, snow*) sich anhäufen; (*said of a boat*) treiben; **d. away** (*said of sounds*) verwehen; (*said of a crowd*) sich verlaufen; **d. shut** verweht werden
drifter ['driftər] *s* zielloser Mensch *m*
drift' ice' *s* Treibeis *n*
drift'wood' *s* Treibholz *n*
drill [dril] *s* (*tool*) Bohrer *m*; (*exercise*) Drill *m*; (tex) Drillich *m* || *tr* bohren; (*exercise*) drillen; **d. s.th. into s.o.** j-m etw einpauken || *intr* bohren; (*exercise*) drillen
drill'mas'ter *s* (mil) Ausbilder *m*
drill' press' *s* Bohrpresse *f*
drink [driŋk] *s* Trunk *m* || *v* (*pret* **drank** [dræŋk]; *pp* **drunk** [drʌŋk] *tr* trinken; (*said of animals*) saufen; (pej) saufen; **d. away** (*money*) versaufen; **d. down** hinunterkippen; **d. in** (*air*) einschlürfen; (*s.o.'s words*) verschlingen || *intr* trinken; (*excessively*) saufen; **d. to** trinken auf (*acc*); **d. up** austrinken
drinkable ['driŋkəbəl] *adj* trinkbar
drinker ['driŋkər] *s* Trinker –in *mf*; **heavy drinker** Zecher –in *mf*
drink'ing foun'tain *s* Trinkbrunnen *m*
drink'ing par'ty *s* Zechgelage *n*
drink'ing song' *s* Trinklied *n*
drink'ing straw' *s* Strohhalm *m*
drink'ing trough' *s* Viehtränke *f*
drink'ing wa'ter *s* Trinkwasser *n*
drip [drip] *s* Tröpfeln *n* || *v* (*pret & pp* **dripped**; *ger* **dripping**) *tr & intr* tröpfeln
drip' cof'fee *s* Filterkaffee *m*
drip'-dry' *adj* bügelfrei
drip' pan' *s* Bratpfanne *f*
drip'pings *spl* Bratenfett *n*
drive [draiv] *s* (*in a car*) Fahrt *f*; (*road*) Fahrweg *m*; (*energy*) Schwungkraft *f*; (*inner urge*) Antrieb *m*; (*campaign*) Aktion *f*; (*for raising money*) Spendeaktion *f*; (golf) Treibschlag *m*; (mach) Antrieb *m*; (mil) Vorstoß *m*; (tennis) Treibschlag *m*; **go for a d.** spazierenfahren || *v* (*pret* **drove** [drov]; *pp* **driven** ['drivən]) *tr* (*a car, etc.*) fahren; (*e.g., cattle*) treiben; (*a tunnel*) vortreiben; **d. a hard bargain** zäh um den Preis feilschen; **d. away** abtreiben; **d.** (*oneself, a horse*) hard abjagen; **d. home** nahebringen; **d. in** (*a nail*) einschlagen; **d. off course** (naut) verschlagen; **d. on** antreiben; **d. out** austreiben; **d. s.o. to** (*inf*) j-n

dazu bringen zu (*inf*); **d. to despair** zur Verzweiflung treiben ‖ *intr* fahren; **d. along** mitfahren; **d. at** abzielen auf (*acc*); **d. away** wegfahren; **d. by** vorbeifahren an (*dat*); **d. in** einfahren; **d. on** weiterfahren; **d. out** herausfahren; **d. up** anfahren

drive′ belt′ *s* Treibriemen *m*

drive′-in′ *s* Autorestaurant *n*; (cin) Autokino *n*

driv•el ['drɪvəl] *s* (*slobber*) Geifer *m*; (*nonsense*) Faselei *f* ‖ *v* (*pret & pp* –el[l]ed; *ger* –el[l]ing) *intr* sabbern; (fig) faseln

driver ['draɪvər] *s* (*of a car*) Fahrer –in *mf*; (*of a locomotive, streetcar*) Führer *m*; (golf) Treibschläger *m*; (mach) Treibhammer *m*

driv′er's li′cense *s* Führerschein *m*

drive′ shaft′ *s* Antriebswelle *f*

drive′way′ *s* Einfahrt *f*

drive′-yourself′ serv′ice *s* Autovermietung *f* an Selbstfahrer

driv′ing *adj* (*rain*) stürmisch ‖ *s* (aut) Steuerung *f*

driv′ing instruc′tor *s* Fahrlehrer –in *mf*

driv′ing les′son *s* Fahrstunde *f*

driv′ing school′ *s* Autofahrschule *f*

drizzle ['drɪzəl] *s* Nieselregen *m* ‖ *impers*—**it is drizzling** es nieselt

droll [drol] *adj* drollig

dromedary ['drɑmə͵dɛri] *s* Dromedar *n*

drone [dron] *s* (*bee; loafer*) Drohne *f*; (*buzz*) Gesumme *n*; (*monotonous speech*) Geleier *n* ‖ *tr* (*e.g., prayers*) leiern ‖ *intr* summen; (fig) leiern

drool [drul] *intr* sabbern

droop [drup] *s* Herabhängen *n*; (*stoop*) gebeugte Haltung *f* ‖ *intr* herabhängen; (*said of flowers*) zu welken beginnen; (fig) den Kopf hängen lassen

droopy ['drupi] *adj* (*saggy*) schlaff herabhängend; (*dejected*) mutlos; (*shoulders*) abfallend; (*flowers*) welkend

drop [drɑp] *s* (*of liquid*) Tropfen *m*; (*candy*) Fruchtbonbon *m & n*; (*fall*) Fall *m*; (*height differential*) Gefälle *n*; (*reduction*) Abnahme *f*; (*in prices*) Rückgang *m*; (*in temperature*) Sturz *m*; (*of bombs or supplies*) Abwurf *m*; (*of paratroopers*) Absprung *m*; **a fifty-meter d.** ein Fall *m* aus e–r Höhe von fünfzig Metern; **d. by d.** tropfenweise; **d. in the bucket** Tropfen *m* auf e–n heißen Stein ‖ *v* (*pret & pp* dropped; *ger* dropping) *tr* (*let fall*) fallenlassen; (*bombs, supplies*) abwerfen; (*a subject, remarks, hints*) fallenlassen; (*the eyes, voice*) senken; (*anchor; young of animals*) werfen; (*money in gambling*) (sl) verlieren; (*terminate*) einstellen; (*from membership roll*) ausschließen; (*paratroopers*) absetzen; **d. it!** laß das!; **d. s.o. a line** j–m ein Zeilen schreiben ‖ *intr* fallen; (*drip*) tropfen; (*said of prices, temperature*) sinken, fallen; (*keel over*) umfallen; (*said of a curtain*) niedergehen; **d. behind** zurück-

fallen; **d. dead!** (sl) laß dich begraben!; **d. in on s.o.** auf e–n Sprung bei j–m vorbeikommen; **d. off to sleep** einschlafen; **d. out** sich zurückziehen; (sport) ausscheiden; **d. out of school** von der Schule abgehen

drop′ ar′ea *s* (aer) Abwurfraum *m*

drop′ cur′tain *s* (bemalter) Vorhang *m*

drop′ ham′mer *s* Fallhammer *m*

drop′-leaf ta′ble *s* Tisch *m* mit herunterklappbaren Flügeln

drop′light′ *s* Hängelampe *f*

drop′out′ *s* Gescheiterte *mf*; (educ) Abgänger –in *mf*

dropper ['drɑpər] *s* (med) Tropfer *m*

drop′ping *adj* (*prices*) rückgängig ‖ *s* (*of bombs, supplies*) Abwurf *m*; **droppings** tierischer Kot *m*

dropsy ['drɑpsi] *s* Wassersucht *f*

drop′ ta′ble *s* Klapptisch *m*

dross [drɔs] *s* (*slag*) Schlacke *f*; (*waste*) Abfall *m*

drought [draut] *s* Dürre *f*

drove [drov] *s* Herde *f*

drown [draun] *tr* (& fig) ertränken; **d. out** übertönen ‖ *intr* ertrinken

drowse [drauz] *intr* dösen

drowsiness ['drauzɪnɪs] *s* Schläfrigkeit *f*

drowsy ['drauzi] *adj* schläfrig, dösig

drub [drʌb] *v* (*pret & pp* drubbed; *ger* drubbing) *tr* (*flog*) verprügeln; (sport) entscheidend schlagen

drudge [drʌdʒ] *s* Packesel *m* ‖ *intr* sich placken, schuften

drudgery ['drʌdʒəri] *s* Plackerei *f*

drug [drʌg] *s* Droge *f*, Arznei *f*; (*narcotic*) Betäubungsmittel *n*; (*addictive narcotic*) Rauschgift *n* ‖ *v* (*pret & pp* drugged; *ger* drugging) *tr* betäuben

drug′ ad′dict *s* Rauschgiftsüchtige *mf*

drug′ addic′tion *s* Rauschgiftsucht *f*

druggist ['drʌgɪst] *s* Apotheker –in *mf*

drug′store′ *s* Apotheke *f*, Drogerie *f*

drug′ traf′fic *s* Rauschgifthandel *m*

druid ['dru-ɪd] *s* Druide *m*

drum [drʌm] *s* (*musical instrument; container*) Trommel *f* ‖ *v* (*pret & pp* drummed; *ger* drumming) *tr* trommeln; **d. s.th. into s.o.** j–m etw einpauken; **d. the table** auf den Tisch trommeln; **d. up** zusammentrommeln ‖ *intr* trommeln

drum′ and bu′gle corps′ *s* Musikzug *m*

drum′beat′ *s* Trommelschlag *m*

drum′fire′ *s* (mil) Trommelfeuer *n*

drum′head′ *s* Trommelfell *n*

drum′ ma′jor *s* Tambourmajor *m*

drum′ majorette′ *s* Tambourmajorin *f*

drummer ['drʌmər] *s* Trommler –in *mf*

drum′stick′ *s* Trommelschlegel *m*; (culin) Unterschenkel *m*

drunk [drʌŋk] *adj* betrunken ‖ *s* Säufer –in *mf*

drunkard ['drʌŋkərd] *s* Trunkenbold *m*

drunken ['drʌŋkən] *adj* betrunken

dry [draɪ] *adj* trocken; (*boring*) trocken; (*wine*) herb; (*thirsty*) durstig; (*rainless*) regenarm; (*wood*) dürr ‖ *v* (*pret & pp* –dried) *tr* (ab)trocknen;

(*e.g.*, *fruit*) dörren; **dry off** abtrocknen; **dry out** austrocknen; **dry up** austrocknen; (fig) erschöpfen ‖ *intr* trocknen; **dry out** austrocknen; **dry up** vertrocknen; (*said of grass, flowers*) verdorren; (fig) versiegen; (*keep quiet*) (sl) die Klappe halten
dry′ bat′tery *s* Trockenbatterie *f*
dry′ cell′ *s* Tockenelement *n*
dry′-clean′ *tr* (*chemically*) reinigen
dry′ clean′er's *s* Reinigungsanstalt *f*
dry′ clean′ing *s* chemische Reinigung *f*
dry′ dock′ *s* Trockendock *n*
dry′-eyed′ *adj* ungerührt
dry′ goods′ *spl* Schnittwaren *pl*
dry′ ice′ *s* Trockeneis *n*
dry′ land′ *s* fester Boden *m*
dry′ meas′ure *s* Trockenmaß *n*
dryness ['draɪnɪs] *s* Trockenheit *f*, Dürre *f*; (fig) Nüchternheit *f*
dry′ nurse′ *s* Säuglingsschwester *f*
dry′ rot′ *s* Trockenfäule *f*
dry′ run′ *s* Vorübung *f*; (*test run*) Probelauf *m*; (*with blank ammunition*) Zielübung *f*
dry′ sea′son *s* Trockenzeit *f*
dual ['d(j)u‑əl] *adj* Zwei‑, doppelt; (tech) Doppel‑
dualism ['d(j)u‑ə‚lɪzəm] *s* Dualismus *m*
du′al‑pur′pose *adj* e‑m doppelten Zweck dienend
dub [dʌb] *v* (*pret & pp* **dubbed;** *ger* **dubbing**) *tr* (*nickname*) betiteln; (cin) synchronisieren; (golf) schlecht treffen; (hist) zum Ritter schlagen
dub′bing *s* (cin) Synchronisierung *f*
dubious ['d(j)ubɪ‑əs] *adj* zweifelhaft
ducal ['d(j)ukəl] *adj* herzoglich
duchess ['dʌt∫ɪs] *s* Herzogin *f*
duchy ['dʌt∫i] *s* Herzogtum *n*
duck [dʌk] *s* Ente *f* ‖ *tr* (*the head*) ducken; (*in water*) (unter)tauchen; (*evade*) sich drücken vor (*dat*) ‖ *intr* ducken; (*go under the surface*) untertauchen
duck′ing *s*—**give s.o. a d.** j‑n untertauchen
duck′ pond′ *s* Ententeich *m*
duck′ soup′ *s* (sl) Kinderspiel *n*
ducky ['dʌki] *adj* (coll) nett, lieb
duct [dʌkt] *s* Rohr *n*, Kanal *m*, Leitung *f*; (anat, elec) Kanal *m*
duct′less gland′ ['dʌktlɪs] *s* endokrine Drüse *f*
duct′work′ *s* Rohrleitungen *pl*
dud [dʌd] *s* (sl & mil) Versager *m*, Blindgänger *m*; **duds** (coll) Klamotten *pl*
dude [d(j)ud] *s* (*dandy*) Geck *m*
dude′ ranch′ *s* Vergnügungsfarm *f*
due [d(j)u] *adj* (*payment; bus, train*) fällig; (*proper*) gehörig; (*consideration*) reiflich; **be due to** (*as a cause*) beruhen auf (*dat*); (*said of an honor*) gebühren (*dat*); (*said of money*) zustehen (*dat*); **be due to** (*inf*) sollen, müssen; **in due course** im gegebenen Moment; **in due time** zur rechten Zeit ‖ *adv* (naut) genau ‖ *s*—**dues** Beitrag *m*; **get one's due** nach Verdienst behandelt werden; **give every-**

one his due jedem geben, was ihm gebührt
due′ date′ *s* (*of a payment*) Termin *m*
duel ['d(j)u‑əl] *s* Duell *n*; **fight a d.** sich duellieren ‖ *v* (*pret & pp* **duel[l]ed;** *ger* **duel[l]ing**) *intr* sich duellieren
dues‑paying ['d(j)uz‚pe‑ɪŋ] *adj* beitragzahlend
duet [d(j)u'ɛt] *s* Duett *n*
due′ to′ *prep* wegen (*genit*)
duf′fle bag′ ['dʌfəl] *s* (mil) Kleidersack *m*
dug′out′ *s* (*boat*) Einbaum *m*; (baseball, mil) Unterstand *m*
duke [d(j)uk] *s* Herzog *m*
dukedom ['d(j)ukdəm] *s* Herzogtum *n*
dull [dʌl] *adj* (*not sharp*) stumpf; (*pain*) dumpf; (*not shining*) glanzlos, matt; (*uninteresting*) nüchtern, geistlos; (*stupid*) stumpfsinnig; (com) flau ‖ *tr* stumpf machen; (fig) abstumpfen ‖ *intr* stumpf werden; (fig) abstumpfen
dullard ['dʌlərd] *s* Dummkopf *m*
dullness ['dʌlnɪs] *s* (*of a blade*) Stumpfheit *f*; (*of color*) Mattheit *f*; (*of a speech, etc.*) Stumpfsinn *m*
duly ['d(j)uli] *adv* ordnungsgemäß
dumb [dʌmb] *adj* stumm; (*stupid*) dumm ‖ *adv*—**play d.** sich unwissend stellen
dumb′bell′ *s* Hantel *f*; (sl) Dummkopf *m*
dumbstruck ['dʌm‚strʌk] *adj* wie auf den Mund geschlagen
dumb′ wait′er *s* (*elevator*) Speiseaufzug *m*; (*serving table*) Serviertisch *m*
dumdum ['dʌm‚dʌm] *s* Dumdumgeschoß *n*
dumfound ['dʌm‚faʊnd] *tr* verblüffen
dummy ['dʌmi] *adj* (*not real*) Schein‑; (mil) blind, Übungs‑ ‖ *s* (*representation for display*) Attrappe *f*; (*clothes form*) Schneiderpuppe *f*; (*dolt*) Ölgötze *m*; (cards) Strohmann *m*; (mil) Übungspatrone *f*; (typ) Blindband *m*
dump [dʌmp] *s* (*trash heap*) Schuttabladeplatz *m*; (sl) Bude *f*; (mil) Lager *n*; **be down in the dumps** (coll) Trübsal blasen ‖ *tr* (aus)kippen; (*fling down*) hinplumpsen; (*garbage*) abladen; (com) verschleudern; **be dumped** (*be fired*) entlassen werden; **no dumping** (public sign) Schuttabladen verboten
dumpling ['dʌmplɪŋ] *s* Kloß *m*, Knödel *m*
dump′ truck′ *s* Kipper *m*
dumpy ['dʌmpi] *adj* rundlich
dun [dʌn] *adj* schwarzbraun ‖ *v* (*pret & pp* **dunned;** *ger* **dunning**) *tr* drängen
dunce [dʌns] *s* Schwachkopf *m*
dunce′ cap′ *s* Narrenkappe *f*
dune [d(j)un] *s* Düne *f*
dung [dʌŋ] *s* Dung *m*, Mist *m* ‖ *tr* düngen
dungarees [‚dʌŋgə'riz] *spl* Drillichhose *f*, Drillichanzug *m*
dungeon ['dʌndʒən] *s* Verlies *n*; (hist) Bergfried *m*

dung'hill' s Düngerhaufen m
dunk [dʌŋk] tr eintunken
duo ['d(j)u·o] s (duet) Duett n; (a pair) Duo n
duode·num [‚d(j)u·ə'dinəm] s (-na [nə]) Zwölffingerdarm m
dupe [d(j)up] s Düpierte mf || tr düpieren, übertölpeln
duplex ['d(j)uplɛks] s Doppelhaus n
duplicate ['d(j)uplɪkɪt] adj Duplikat-; (parts) Ersatz-; **d. key** Nachschlüssel m || s Duplikat n, Abschrift f; **in d.** abschriftlich || ['d(j)uplɪ‚ket] tr (make a copy of) kopieren; (make many copies of) vervielfältigen; (reproduce by writing) abschreiben; (repeat) wiederholen; (perform again) nachmachen
duplication [‚d(j)uplɪ'keʃən] s Vervielfältigung f
duplicator ['d(j)uplɪ‚ketər] s Vervielfältigungsapparat m
duplicity [d(j)u'plɪsɪti] s Duplizität f
durable ['d(j)urəbəl] adj dauerhaft
duration [d(j)u're/ən] s Dauer f
duress ['d(j)ures] s (jur) Nötigung f
during ['d(j)urɪŋ] prep während (genit), bei (dat); **d. the meal** bei Tisch; **d. the day** tagsüber
dusk [dʌsk] s Abenddämmerung f
dust [dʌst] s Staub m; **cover with d.** bestauben; **make d.** stauben || tr (free of dust) abstauben; (sprinkle, spray with insecticides) bestäuben
dust' bowl' s Staubsturmgebiet n
dust' cloth' s Staubtuch n
dust' collec'tor s Staubfänger m
duster ['dʌstər] s (feather duster) Staubwedel m; (for insecticides) Zerstäuber m
dust'ing pow'der s Streupulver n
dust' jac'ket s Schutzumschlag m
dust' mop' s Mop m
dust'pan' s Kehrichtschaufel f
dust'proof' adj staubdicht
dust' rag' s Staublappen m
dusty ['dʌsti] adj staubig
Dutch [dʌtʃ] adj niederländisch; **go D.** (coll) getrennt bezahlen || s (language) Niederländisch n; **in D.** (coll)

in der Patsche; **the D.** die Niederländer
Dutch'man s (-men) Niederländer m
Dutch' treat' s (coll) Beisammensein n bei getrennter Kasse
dutiable ['d(j)utɪ·əbəl] adj steuerpflichtig
dutiful ['d(j)utɪfəl] adj pflichtgetreu
duty ['d(j)uti] s (to) Pflicht f (gegenüber dat); (service) Dienst m; (task) Aufgabe f; (tax) Zoll m, Abgabe f; **be in d. bound to** (inf) pflichtgemäß müssen (inf); **do d. as** (said of a thing) dienen als; (said of a person) Dienst tun als; **off d.** außer Dienst, dienstfrei; **on. d.** im Dienst; **pay d. on** verzollen
du'ty-free' adj zollfrei
du'ty ros'ter s (mil) Diensteinteilung f
dwarf [dwɔrf] adj zwergenhaft, Zwerg- || s Zwerg m || tr (stunt) in der Entwicklung behindern; (fig) in den Schatten stellen
dwell [dwɛl] v (pret & pp dwelled & dwelt [dwɛlt]) intr wohnen; **d. on** verweilen bei
dwell'ing s Wohnung f
dwell'ing house' s Wohnhaus n
dwindle ['dwɪndəl] intr schwinden, abnehmen; **d. away** dahinschwinden
dye [daɪ] s Farbe f || v (pret & pp dyed; ger dyeing) tr färben
dyed'-in-the-wool' adj (fig) in der Wolle gefärbt
dye'ing s Färben n
dyer ['daɪ·ər] s Färber -in mf
dy'ing adj (person) sterbend; (words) letzte || s Sterben n
dynamic [daɪ'næmɪk] adj dynamisch || **dynamics** s Dynamik f; **dynamics** spl (fig) Triebkraft f
dynamite ['daɪnə‚maɪt] s Dynamit n || tr sprengen
dyna·mo ['daɪnə‚mo] s (-mos) Dynamo m
dynastic [daɪ'næstɪk] adj dynastisch
dynasty ['daɪnəsti] s Dynastie f
dysentery ['dɪsən‚teri] s Ruhr f
dyspepsia [dɪs'pɛpsɪ·ə] s Verdauungsstörung f

E

E, e [i] s fünfter Buchstabe des englischen Alphabets; (mus) E n; **E flat** Es n; **E sharp** Eis n
each [itʃ] indef adj jeder; **e. and every** jeder einzelne || adv je, pro Person, pro Stück || indef pron jeder; **e. other** einander, sich
eager ['igər] adj eifrig; **e. for** begierig nach; **e. to** (inf) begierig zu (inf)
ea'ger bea'ver s (coll) Streber -in mf
eagerness ['igərnɪs] s Eifer m
eagle ['igəl] s Adler m
ea'gle-eyed' adj adleräugig
ear [ɪr] s Ohr n; (of corn, wheat) Ähre f; (fig) Gehör n; **be all ears**

ganz Ohr sein; **bend s.o.'s ears** (sl) j-m die Ohren vollreden; **be up to one's ears** in bis über die Ohren stecken in (dat); **by ear** nach Gehör; **ear for music** musikalisches Gehör n; **fall on deaf ears** kein Gehör finden; **in one ear and out the other** zu e-m Ohr hinein und zum anderen hinaus; **turn a deaf ear to** taub sein gegen
ear'ache' s Ohrenschmerzen pl
ear'drops' spl (med) Ohrentropfen pl
ear'drum' s Trommelfell n
earl [ʌrl] s Graf m
ear'lobe' s Ohrläppchen n

early ['ʌrli] *adj* früh; (*reply*) baldig; (*far back in time*) Früh–; **at the earliest possible moment** baldigst; **at your earliest convenience** bei erster Gelegenheit; **be too e.** sich verfrühen || *adv* früh, frühzeitig; (*too soon*) zu früh; **as e.** as schon
ear'ly bird' s Frühaufsteher –in *mf*
ear'ly ris'er s Frühaufsteher –in *mf*
ear'ly warn'ing sys'tem s Vorwarnungssystem *n*
ear'mark' s (fig) Kennzeichen *n* || *tr* (*mark out*) kennzeichnen; (*e.g., funds*) (**for**) bestimmen (für)
ear'muffs' *spl* Ohrenschützer *m*
earn [ʌrn] *tr* (*money*) verdienen; (*a reputation*) sich [*dat*] erwerben; (*interest*) einbringen
earnest ['ʌrnɪst] *adj* ernst, ernsthaft || *s*—**are you in e.?** ist das Ihr Ernst?; **be in e. about** es ernst meinen mit; **in e.** im Ernst
ear'phone' s Kopfhörer *m*
ear'piece' s (*earphone*) Hörer *m;* (*of eyeglasses*) Bügel *m*
ear'ring' s Ohrring *m*
ear'shot' *s*—**within e.** in Hörweite
ear'split'ting *adj* ohrenbetäubend
earth [ʌrθ] s Erde *f;* **come down to e.** auf den Boden der Wirklichkeit zurückkehren; **on e.** (coll) in aller Welt
earthen ['ʌrθən] *adj* irden
earth'enware' s Tonwaren *pl*
earthly ['ʌrθli] *adj* irdisch; **be of no e. use** völlig unnütz sein; **e. possessions** Glücksgüter *pl*
earth'quake' s Erdbeben *n*
earth'shak'ing *adj* welterschütternd
earth'work' s Schanze *f*
earth' worm' s Regenwurm *m*
earthy ['ʌrθi] *adj* erdig; (fig) deftig
ear'wax' s Ohrenschmalz *n*
ease [iz] s (*facility*) Leichtigkeit *f;* (*comfort*) Bequemlichkeit *f;* (*informality*) Zwanglosigkeit *f;* **at e.!** (mil) rührt euch!; **feel at e. with s.o.** sich in j–s Gegenwart wohl fühlen; **put at e.** beruhigen; **with e.** mühelos || *tr* (*work*) erleichtern; (*pain*) lindern; (*move carefully*) lavieren; **e. out** (*of a job*) hinausmanövrieren || *intr*— **e. up** nachlassen; **e. up on** (*work*) es sich [*dat*] leichter machen mit
easel ['izəl] s Staffelei *f*
easement ['izmənt] s (jur) Dienstbarkeit *f*
easily ['izəli] *adv* leicht, mühelos; **e. satisfied** genügsam
easiness ['izɪnɪs] s Leichtigkeit *f*
east [ist] *adj* Ost–, östlich || *adv* ostwärts, nach Osten; **e. of** östlich von || *s* Osten *m;* **the East** der Osten
east'bound' *adj* nach Osten fahrend
Easter ['istər] *adj* Oster– || *s* Ostern *n & pl*
easterly ['istərli] *adj* österlich
eastern ['istərn] *adj* Ost–
East'ertide' s Osterzeit *f*
East'-Ger'man mark' s Ostmark *f*
eastward ['istwərd] *adv* ostwärts
easy ['izi] *adj* leicht; (*terms*) günstig; (*virtue*) locker; (*pace*) gemächlich; **e. on the eye** knusprig; **e. to digest**

leichtverdaulich; **have an e. time of it** leichtes Spiel haben; **it's e. for you to talk** du hast gut reden!; **make e.** erleichtern || *adv*—**e. come, e. go** wie gewonnen, so zerronnen; **get off e.** gnädig davonkommen; **take it e.** (*relax*) es sich [*dat*] leicht machen; **take on'e time**) sich [*dat*] Zeit lassen; (*in parting*) mach's gut! (*remain calm*) reg dich nicht auf!; **take it e. on** (*a person*) schonend umgehen mit; (*a thing*) sparsam umgehen mit
eas'y chair' s Lehnsessel *m*
eas'ygo'ing *adj* ungeniert, ungezwungen
eas'y mark' s (coll) leichte Beute *f*
eat [it] *s*—**eats** *pl* (coll) Essen *n* || *v* (*pret* **ate** [et]; *pp* **eaten** ['itən]) *tr* essen; (*said of animals*) fressen; **eat away** zerfressen; **eat one's fill** sich satt essen; **eat one's heart out** sich in Kummer verzehren; **eat one's words** das Gesagte zurücknehmen; **eat up** aufessen; **what's eating him?** was hat er denn? || *intr* essen; **eat out** auswärts essen
eatable ['itəbəl] *adj* eßbar
eaves [ivz] *spl* Dachrinne *f*, Traufe *f*
eaves'drop' *v* (*pret & pp* **–dropped;** *ger* **–dropping**) *intr* horchen; **e. on** belauschen
eaves'drop'per s Horcher –in *mf*
ebb [ɛb] s Ebbe *f;* **at a low ebb** sehr heruntergekommen || *intr* ebben; (fig) nachlassen
ebb' and flow' s Ebbe und Flut *f*
ebb' tide' s Ebbe *f*
ebony ['ɛbəni] s Ebenholz *n*
ebullient [ɪ'bʌljənt] *adj* überschwenglich, hochbegeistert
eccentric [ɛk'sɛntrɪk] *adj* (& fig) exzentrisch || *s* Sonderling *m*, Kauz *m;* (mach) Exzenter *m*
eccentricity [,ɛksen'trɪsɪti] *s* Verschrobenheit *f*, Tick *m*
ecclesiastic [ɪ,klizɪ'æstɪk] *adj* kirchlich; (*law*) Kirchen– || *s* Geistlicher *m*
echelon ['ɛʃə,lɑn] s (*level*) Befehlsebene *f;* (*group occupying a particular level*) Stabsführung *f;* (*flight formation*) Staffel *f;* **in echelons** staffelförmig || *tr* staffeln
ech·o ['ɛko] s (**–oes**) Echo *n* || *tr* (*sounds*) zurückwerfen; (fig) nachsprechen || *intr* widerhallen, echoen
éclair [e'klɛr] s Eclair *n*
eclectic [ɛk'lɛktɪk] *adj* eklektisch || *s* Eklektiker –in *mf*
eclipse [ɪ'klɪps] s Verfinsterung *f;* **go into e.** sich verfinstern; **in e.** im Schwinden || *tr* verfinstern; (fig) in den Schatten stellen
eclogue ['ɛklɔg] s Ekloge *f*
ecological [,ɛkə'lɑdʒɪkəl] *adj* ökologisch
ecology [ɪ'kɑlədʒi] s Ökologie *f*
economic [,ikə'nɑmɪk], [,ɛkə'nɑmɪk] *adj* wirtschaftlich, Wirtschafts–
economical [,ikə'nɑmɪkəl], [,ɛkə-'nɑmɪkəl] *adj* sparsam
economics [,ikə'nɑmɪks], [,ɛkə'nɑmɪks] s Wirtschaftswissenschaften *pl*

economist [ɪ'kɑnəmɪst] *s* Volkswirtschaftler –in *mf*
economize [ɪ'kɑnə͵maɪz] *intr* sparen
economy [ɪ'kɑnəmi] *s* Wirtschaft *f; (thriftiness)* Sparsamkeit *f; (a saving)* Ersparnis *f*
ecstasy ['ɛkstəsi] *s* Verzückung *f;* **go into e.** in Verzückung geraten
ecstatic [ɛk'stætɪk] *adj* verzückt
ecumenic(al) [͵ɛkjə'mɛnɪk(əl)] *adj* ökumenisch
eczema [ɛg'zimə] *s* Ausschlag *m*
ed·dy ['ɛdi] *s* Strudel *m* ‖ *v (pret & pp* –**died**) *intr* strudeln
edelweiss ['edəl͵vaɪs] *s* Edelweiß *n*
edge [ɛdʒ] *s (of a knife)* Schneide *f; (of a forest, town, water, road)* Rand *m; (e.g., of a table)* Kante *f; (keenness)* Schärfe *f;* (bb) Schnitt *m;* **have an e. on s.o.** den Vorteil gegenüber j–m haben; **on e.** *(said of a person or teeth)* kribbelig; *(said of nerves)* aufs äußerste gespannt; **take the e. off** abstumpfen; (fig) die Schärfe nehmen *(dat)* ‖ *tr (a lawn)* beschneiden; *(put a border on)* einfassen; **e. out** (sport) knapp schlagen ‖ *intr* —**e. forward** langsam vorrücken
edge'wise' *adv*—**not get a word in e.** nicht zu Worte kommen können
edg'ing *s* Umrandung *f,* Besatz *m*
edgy ['ɛdʒi] *adj* kribbelig
edible ['ɛdɪbəl] *adj* eßbar, genießbar
edict ['idɪkt] *s* Edikt *n,* Erlaß *m*
edification [͵ɛdɪfɪ'keʃən] *s* Erbauung *f*
edifice ['ɛdɪfɪs] *s* Bauwerk *n,* Gebäude *n*
edi·fy ['ɛdɪ͵faɪ] *v (pret & pp* –**fied**) *tr* erbauen; **be edified by** sich erbauen an *(dat)*
ed'ifying *adj* erbaulich
edit ['ɛdɪt] *tr (a book)* herausgeben; *(a newspaper)* redigieren; (cin) schneiden
edition [ɛ'dɪʃən] *s* Ausgabe *f*
editor ['ɛdɪtər] *s (of a newspaper or magazine)* Redakteur –in *mf; (of a book)* Herausgeber –in *mf; (of editorials)* Leitartikler –in *mf;* (cin) Schnittmeister –in *mf*
editorial [͵ɛdɪ'torɪəl] *adj* redaktionell, Redaktions– ‖ *s* Leitartikel *m*
editorialize [͵ɛdɪ'torɪ·ə͵laɪz] *intr* **(on)** seine Meinung zum Ausdruck bringen (über *acc*); *(report with a slant)* tendenziös berichten
edito'rial of'fice *s* Redaktion *f*
edito'rial staff' *s* Redaktion *f*
ed'itor in chief' *s* Chefredakteur –in *mf*
educate ['ɛdʒʊ͵ket] *tr* bilden, erziehen
education [͵ɛdʒʊ'keʃən] *s* Bildung *f,* Erziehung *f;* (educ) Pädagogik *f*
educational [͵ɛdʒʊ'keʃənəl] *adj* Bildungs–; **e. background** Vorbildung *f;* **e. film** Lehrfilm *m;* **e. institution** Lehranstalt *f*
educator ['ɛdʒʊ͵ketər] *s* Erzieher –in *mf*
educe [ɪ'd(j)us] *tr* hervorholen
eel [il] *s* Aal *m*
eerie, eery ['ɪri] *adj* unheimlich

efface [ɪ'fes] *tr* austilgen; **e. oneself** sich zurückhalten
effect [ɪ'fɛkt] *s* **(on)** Wirkung *f* (auf *acc*); *(consequence)* **(on)** Auswirkung *f* (auf *acc*); *(impression)* Eindruck *m;* **effects** *(movable property)* Habe *f;* **for e.** zum Effekt; **go into e.** in Kraft treten; **have an e. on** wirken auf *(acc);* **in e.** praktisch; **put into e.** in Kraft setzen; **take e.** zur Geltung kommen; **to the e. that** des Inhalts, daß ‖ *tr* bewirken
effective [ɪ'fɛktɪv] *adj* wirkungsvoll; *(actual)* effektiv; **e. against** wirksam gegen; **e. date** Tag *m* des Inkrafttretens; **e. from** mit Wirkung von; **e. immediately** mit sofortiger Wirkung; **e. strength** (mil) Iststärke *f*
effectual [ɪ'fɛkt/ʊ·əl] *adj* wirksam
effectuate [ɪ'fɛkt/ʊ͵et] *tr* bewirken
effeminacy [ɪ'fɛmɪnəsi] *s* Verweichlichung *f*
effeminate [ɪ'fɛmɪnɪt] *adj* verweichlicht
effervesce [͵ɛfər'vɛs] *intr* aufbrausen
effervescence [͵ɛfər'vɛsəns] *s* Aufbrausen *n,* Moussieren *n*
effervescent [͵ɛfər'vɛsənt] *adj (liquid; personality)* aufbrausend
effete [ɪ'fit] *adj* entkräftet
efficacious [͵ɛfɪ'keʃəs] *adj* wirksam
efficacy ['ɛfɪkəsi] *s* Wirksamkeit *f,* Wirkungskraft *f*
efficiency [ɪ'fɪʃənsi] *s* Tüchtigkeit *f;* (phys) Nutzeffekt *m;* (tech) Leistungsfähigkeit *f*
efficient [ɪ'fɪʃənt] *adj* tüchtig; (tech) leistungsfähig
effigy ['ɛfɪdʒi] *s* Abbild *n;* **hang in e.** symbolisch hängen
effort ['ɛfɔrt] *s (exertion)* Mühe *f; (attempt)* Bestreben *n;* **efforts** Bemühungen *pl;* **make an honest e. to** *(inf)* sich redlich bemühen zu *(inf)*
effortless ['ɛfərtlɪs] *adj* mühelos
effrontery [ɪ'frʌntəri] *s* Frechheit *f,* Unverschämtheit *f*
effusion [ɪ'fjuʒən] *s* Erguß *m*
effusive [ɪ'fjusɪv] *adj* überschwenglich
egg [ɛg] *s* Ei *n;* **bad egg** (sl) übler Geselle *m;* **good egg** (sl) feiner Kerl *m;* **lay an egg** ein Ei legen; (fig) e–e völlige Niete sein ‖ *tr*—**egg on** anstacheln
egg'beat'er *s* Schneeschläger *m*
egg'cup' *s* Eierbecher *m*
egg'head' *s* (coll) Intelligenzler –in *mf*
eggnog ['ɛg͵nɑg] *s* Eierlikör *m,* Egg-Nog *m*
egg'plant' *s* Eierfrucht *f*
egg'shell' *s* Eierschale *f*
egg' white' *s* Eiweiß *n*
egg' yolk' *s* Eigelb *n,* Eidotter *m*
ego ['igo] *s* Ego *n,* Ich *n;* (coll) Ichsucht *f*
egocentric [͵igo'sɛntrɪk] *adj* egozentrisch
egoism ['igo͵ɪzəm] *s* Selbstsucht *f*
egoist ['igo·ɪst] *s* Egoist *m*
egotism ['igo͵tɪzəm] *s* Ichsucht *f*
egotistic(al) [͵igo'tɪstɪk(əl)] *adj* egotistisch, geltungsbedürtig

egregious [ɪ'gridʒəs] *adj* unerhört
egress ['igrɛs] *s* Ausgang *m*
Egypt ['idʒɪpt] *s* Ägypten *n*
Egyptian [ɪ'dʒɪp/ən] *adj* ägyptisch ||
s Ägypter –in *mf;* (*language*) Ägyptisch *n*
eiderdown ['aɪdər,daʊn] *s* Eiderdaunen *pl;* (*cover*) Daunenbett *n*
eight [et] *adj & pron* acht || *s* Acht *f*
eight'ball' *s*—**be behind the e.** (sl) in der Klemme sitzen
eighteen ['et'tin] *adj & pron* achtzehn
|| *s* Achtzehn *f*
eighteenth ['et'tinθ] *adj* achtzehnte ||
s (*fraction*) Achtzehntel *n;* **the e.**
(*in dates or in a series*) der Achzehnte
eighth [etθ] *adj* achte || *s* (*fraction*)
Achtel *n;* **the e.** (*in dates or in a series*) der Achte
eighth' note' *s* (mus) Achtelnote *f*
eightieth ['etɪ·ɪθ] *adj* achtzigste || *s*
(*fraction*) Achtzigstel *n;* **the e.** der Achtzigste
eighty ['eti] *adj & pron* achtzig || *s*
Achtzig *f;* **the eighties** die achtziger Jahre *pl*
eigh'ty-one' *adj & pron* einundachtzig
either ['iðər], ['aɪðər] *adj*—**e. one is
correct** beides ist richtig; **e. way** auf die e–e oder andere Art; **in e. case**
in jedem der beiden Fälle; **on e. side**
auf beiden Seiten || *adv*—**not...e.**
auch nicht || *pron* einer von beiden;
e. of you einer von euch beiden; **I
didn't see e.** ich habe beide nicht gesehen || *conj*—**e....or** entweder...
oder
ejaculate [ɪ'dʒækjə,let] *tr* ausstoßen;
(physiol) ejakulieren
eject [ɪ'dʒɛkt] *tr* ausstoßen; (*from a
property*) (**from**) hinauswerfen (aus)
ejection [ɪ'dʒɛk/ən] *s* Ausstoßung *f*
ejec'tion seat' *s* Schleudersitz *m*
eke [ik] *tr*—**eke out a living** das Leben fristen
el [ɛl] *s* (coll) Hochbahn *f*
elaborate [ɪ'læbərɪt] *adj* (*detailed*)
weitläufig; (*ornate*) kunstvoll; (*idea*)
compliziert || [ɪ'læbə,ret] *tr* ausarbeiten || *intr*—**e. on** sich verbreiten über (*acc*)
elaboration [ɪ,læbə're/ən] *s* Ausarbeitung *f*
elapse [ɪ'læps] *intr* verrinnen
elastic [ɪ'læstɪk] *adj* elastisch; (*conscience*) weit || *s* Gummiband *n*
elasticity [,ilæs'tɪsɪti] *s* Elastizität *f*
elated [ɪ'letɪd] *adj* freudig erregt
elation [ɪ'le/ən] *s* Hochgefühl *n*
elbow ['elbo] *s* Ellbogen *m;* (*of a pipe*)
Rohrknie *n;* **at one's e.** bei der Hand;
rub elbows with s.o. mit j–m in nähere Berührung kommen || *tr*—**e.
one's way** sich [*dat*] seinen Weg bahnen
el'bow grease' *s* (coll) Knochenschmalz *n*
el'bowroom' *s* Spielraum *m*
elder ['eldər] *adj* älter || *s* Ältere *mf;*
(bot) Holunder *m;* (eccl) Kirchenälteste *mf*
el'derber'ry *s* Holunderbeere *f*

elderly ['eldərli] *adj* ältlich
el'der states'man *s* profilierter Staatsmann *m*
eldest ['eldɪst] *adj* älteste
elect [ɪ'lɛkt] *adj* erlesen; (*elected but
not yet installed*) zukünftig; (relig)
auserwählt || **the e.** *spl* die Auserwählten *pl* || *tr* wählen; **e. s.o. president** j–n zum Präsidenten wählen
election [ɪ'lɛk/ən] *adj* Wahl– || *s*
Wahl *f*
elec'tion campaign' *s* Wahlkampf *m*
elec'tion day' *s* Wahltag *m*
electioneer [ɪ,lɛk/ə'nɪr] *intr* Stimmen werben
elective [ɪ'lɛktɪv] *adj* (educ) wahlfrei;
(pol) Wahl– || *s* (educ) Wahlfach *n*
electoral [ɪ'lɛktərəl] *adj* Wahl–
elec'toral col'lege *s* Wahlmänner *pl*
electorate [ɪ'lɛktərɪt] *s* Wählerschaft *f*
electric(al) [ɪ'lɛktrɪk(əl)] *adj* elektrisch, Elektro–
elec'trical appli'ance *s* Elektrogerät *n*
elec'trical engineer' *s* Elektroingenieur *m*
elec'trical engineer'ing *s* Elektrotechnik *f*
elec'tric blan'ket *s* Heizdecke *f*
elec'tric bulb' *s* Glühbirne *f*
elec'tric chair' *s* elektrischer Stuhl *m;*
(*penalty*) Hinrichtung *f* auf dem elektrischen Stuhl
elec'tric cir'cuit *s* Stromkreis *m*
elec'tric eel' *s* Zitteraal *m*
elec'tric eye' *s* Photozelle *f*
elec'tric fan' *s* Ventilator *m*
elec'tric fence' *s* elektrisch geladener Drahtzaun *m*
electrician [ɪ,lɛk'trɪ/ən] *s* Elektriker
–in *mf*
electricity [,ɪlɛk'trɪsɪti] *s* Elektrizität
f; (*current*) Strom *m*
elec'tric light' *s* elektrisches Licht *n*
elec'tric me'ter *s* Stromzähler *m*
elec'tric saw' *s* Motorsäge *f*
elec'tric shav'er *s* elektrischer Rasierapparat *m*
elec'tric storm' *s* Gewittersturm *m*
elec'tric stove' *s* Elektroherd *m*
electri·fy [ɪ'lɛktrɪ,faɪ] *v* (*pret & pp*
–**fied**) *tr* (& fig) elektrisieren; (*a
streetcar, railroad*) elektrifizieren
electrocute [ɪ'lɛktrə,kjut] *tr* durch elektrischen Strom töten; (jur) auf dem elektrischen Stuhl hinrichten
electrode [ɪ'lɛktrod] *s* Elektrode *f*
electrolysis [ɪ,lɛk'trɑlɪsɪs] *s* Elektrolyse *f*
electrolyte [ɪ'lɛktrə,laɪt] *s* Elektrolyt *m*
electromagnet [ɪ,lɛktrə'mægnət] *s*
Elektromagnet *m*
electromagnetic [ɪ,lɛktrəmæg'nɛtɪk]
adj elektromagnetisch
electron [ɪ'lɛktrɑn] *s* Elektron *n*
electronic [ɪ,lɛk'trɑnɪk] *adj* elektronisch, Elektronen– || **electronics** *s*
Elektronik *f*
electron'ic flash' *s* Röhrenblitz *m;*
(*device*) Blitzgerät *n*
electronic [ɪ,lɛk'trɑnɪk] *adj* elektroplattieren, galvanisieren

electrostatic [ɪˌlɛktrə'stætɪk] *adj* elektrostatisch
electrotype [ɪ'lɛktrəˌtaɪp] *s* Galvano *n* ‖ *tr* galvanoplastisch vervielfältigen
elegance ['ɛlɪgəns] *s* Eleganz *f*
elegant ['ɛləˌgənt] *adj* elegant
elegiac [ˌɛlɪ'dʒaɪ·æk] *adj* elegisch
elegy ['ɛlɪdʒɪ] *s* Elegie *f*
element ['ɛlɪmənt] *s* (& fig) Element *n; (e.g., of truth)* Körnchen *n*
elementary [ˌɛlɪ'mɛntərɪ] *adj* elementar, grundlegend
elemen'tary school' *s* Grundschule *f*
elephant ['ɛlɪfənt] *s* Elefant *m*
elevate ['ɛlɪˌvet] *tr* erheben, erhöhen
el'evated *adj (eyes)* erhoben; *(style)* erhaben ‖ *s* (coll) Hochbahn *f*
elevation [ˌɛlɪ've/ən] *s (height)* Höhe *f; (hill)* Anhöhe *f; (above sealevel)* Seehöhe *f; (to the throne)* Erhebung *f;* (archit) Aufriß *m;* (arti) Richthöhe *f;* (astr, relig) Elevation *f*
elevator ['ɛlɪˌvetər] *s* Aufzug *m,* Fahrstuhl *m;* (aer) Höhenruder *n;* (agr) Getreidespeicher *m*
el'evator op'erator *s* Fahrstuhlführer –in *mf*
el'evator shaft' *s* Fahrstuhlschacht *m*
eleven [ɪ'lɛvən] *adj & pron* elf ‖ *s* Elf *f*
eleventh [ɪ'lɛvənθ] *adj* elfte ‖ *s (fraction)* Elftel *n;* **the e.** *(in dates and in a series)* der Elfte
elev'enth hour' *s*—**at the e.** (fig) kurz vor Torschluß
elf [ɛlf] *s* (**elves** [ɛlvz]) Elf *m,* Elfe *f*
elicit [ɪ'lɪsɪt] *tr* hervorlocken; *(an answer)* entlocken
elide [ɪ'laɪd] *tr* elidieren
eligible ['ɛlɪdʒɪbəl] *adj* qualifiziert; *(entitled)* berechtigt; *(for office)* wählbar; *(for marriage)* heiratsfähig
el'igible bach'elor *s* Heiratskandidat *m*
eliminate [ɪ'lɪmɪˌnet] *tr* ausscheiden; (alg) eliminieren
elimination [ɪˌlɪmɪ'ne/ən] *s* Ausscheidung *f*
elimina'tion bout' *s* Ausscheidungskampf *m*
elision [ɪ'lɪʒən] *s* Auslassung *f*
elite [e'lit] *adj* Elite– ‖ *s* Elite *f*
elixir [ɪ'lɪksər] *s* Elixier *n*
elk [ɛlk] *s* Elch *m*
ellipse [ɪ'lɪps] *s* (geom) Ellipse *f*
ellip·sis [ɪ'lɪpsɪs] *s* (**–ses** [siz]) (gram) Ellipse *f*
elliptic(al) [ɪ'lɪptɪk(əl)] *adj* elliptisch
elm [ɛlm] *s* Ulme *f*
elocution [ˌɛlə'kju/ən] *s (art)* Vortragskunst *f; (style)* Vortragsweise *f*
elope [ɪ'lop] *intr* ausreißen
elopement [ɪ'lopmənt] *s* Ausreißen *n*
eloquence ['ɛləkwəns] *s* Beredsamkeit *f*
eloquent ['ɛləkwənt] *adj* beredt
else [ɛls] *adj* sonst; **someone else's house** das Haus e–s anderen; **what e.?** was sonst?; *(in addition)* was noch? ‖ *adv* sonst, anders; **nowhere e.** sonst nirgends; **or e.** sonst, andernfalls; **where e.?** wo sonst?
else'where' *adv (position)* woanders;

(direction) sonstwohin; **from e.** anderswoher
elucidate [ɪ'lusɪˌdet] *tr* erläutern
elucidation [ɪˌlusɪ'de/ən] *s* Erläuterung *f*
elude [ɪ'lud] *tr* entgehen *(dat)*
elusive [ɪ'lusɪv] *adj* schwer zu fassen; *(memory)* unzuverlässig
emaciated [ɪ'me/ɪˌetɪd] *adj* abgezehrt
emanate ['ɛməˌnet] *intr*—**e. from** *(said of gases)* ausströmen aus; *(said of rays)* ausstrahlen aus; (fig) ausgehen von
emancipate [ɪ'mænsɪˌpet] *tr* emanzipieren
emasculate [ɪ'mæskjəˌlet] *tr* (& fig) entmannen
embalm [ɛm'bam] *tr* einbalsamieren
embankment [ɛm'bæŋkmənt] *s* Damm *m*
embar·go [ɛm'bargo] *s* (**–goes**) Sperre *f,* Embargo *n* ‖ *tr* sperren
embark [ɛm'bark] *intr* (**for**) sich einschiffen (nach); **e. upon** sich einlassen auf *(acc)*
embarkation [ˌɛmbar'ke/ən] *s* Einschiffung *f*
embarrass [ɛm'bærəs] *tr* in Verlegenheit bringen
embar'rassed *adj* verlegen; **feel e.** sich genieren
embar'rassing *adj* peinlich
embarrassment [ɛm'bærəsmənt] *s* Verlegenheit *f*
embassy ['ɛmbəsɪ] *s* Botschaft *f*
em·bed [ɛm'bed] *v (pret & pp –bedded; ger –bedding) tr* einbetten; **e. in concrete** einbetonieren
embellish [ɛm'bɛlɪ/] *tr* verschönern
embellishment [ɛm'bɛlɪ/mənt] *s* Verschönerung *f*
ember ['ɛmbər] *s* glühende Kohle *f;* **embers** Glut *f*
Em'ber day' *s* Quatember *m*
embezzle [ɛm'bɛzəl] *tr* unterschlagen
embezzlement [ɛm'bɛzəlmənt] *s* Unterschlagung *f,* Veruntreuung *f*
embezzler [ɛm'bɛzlər] *s* Veruntreuer –in *mf*
embitter [ɛm'bɪtər] *tr* verbittern
emblazon [ɛm'blezən] *tr (decorate)* verzieren; *(extol)* verherrlichen; (heral) heraldisch darstellen
emblem ['ɛmbləm] *s* Sinnbild *n*
emblematic(al) [ˌɛmblə'mætɪk(əl)] *adj* sinnbildlich
embodiment [ɛm'badɪmənt] *s* Verkörperung *f*
embod·y [ɛm'badɪ] *v (pret & pp –ied) tr* verkörpern
embolden [ɛm'boldən] *tr* ermutigen
embolism ['ɛmbəˌlɪzəm] *s* Embolie *f*
emboss [ɛm'bas] *tr* bossieren
embossed' *adj* getrieben
embrace [ɛm'bres] *s* Umarmung *f* ‖ *tr* umarmen; *(include)* umfassen; *(a religion, idea)* annehmen ‖ *intr* sich umarmen
embrasure [ɛm'breʒər] *s* Schießscharte *f*
embroider [ɛm'brɔɪdər] *tr* sticken
embroidery [ɛm'brɔɪdərɪ] *s* Stickerei *f*
embroi'dery nee'dle *s* Sticknadel *f*

embroil [ɛm'brɔil] *tr* verwickeln
embroilment [ɛm'brɔilmənt] *s* Verwicklung *f*
embry·o ['ɛmbrɪ‚o] *s* (**-os**) Embryo *m*
embryology [‚ɛmbrɪ'ɑlədʒi] *s* Embryologie *f*
embryonic [‚ɛmbrɪ'ɑnɪk] *adj* embryonal
emend [ɪ'mɛnd] *tr* berichtigen
emendation [‚imɛn'deʃən] *s* Berichtigung *f*
emerald ['ɛmərəld] *adj* smaragdgrün ‖ *s* Smaragd *m*
emerge [ɪ'mʌrdʒ] *intr* (*come forth*) hervortreten; (*surface*) auftauchen; (*result*) (**from**) herauskommen (bei)
emergence [ɪ'mʌrdʒəns] *s* Hervortreten *n*; (*surfacing*) Auftauchen *n*
emergency [ɪ'mʌrdʒənsi] *adj* Not- ‖ *s* Notlage *f*; **in case of e.** im Notfall
emeritus [ɪ'mɛrɪtəs] *adj* emeritiert
emersion [ɪ'mʌrʒən] *s* Auftauchen *n*
emery ['ɛməri] *s* Schmirgel *m*
em'ery cloth' *s* Schmirgelleinwand *f*
em'ery wheel' *s* Schmirgelrad *n*
emetic [ɪ'mɛtɪk] *adj* Brech- ‖ *s* Brechmittel *n*
emigrant ['ɛmɪɡrənt] *s* Auswanderer -in *mf*
emigrate ['ɛmɪ‚ɡret] *intr* auswandern
emigration [‚ɛmɪ'ɡreʃən] *s* Auswanderung *f*
eminence ['ɛmɪnəns] *s* (*height*) Anhöhe *f*; (*fame*) Berühmtheit *f*; **Eminence** (*title of a cardinal*) Eminenz *f*; **rise to e.** zu Ruhm und Würde gelangen
eminent ['ɛmɪnənt] *adj* hervorragend
emissary ['ɛmɪ‚sɛri] *s* Abgesandte *mf*
emission [ɪ'mɪʃən] *s* (biol) Erguß *m*; (phys) Austrahlung *f*, Ausströmung *f*
emis'sion control' *s* Abgasentgiftung *f*
emit [ɪ'mɪt] *v* (*pret & pp* **emitted;** *ger* **emitting**) *tr* von sich geben; (*rays*) ausstrahlen; (*gases*) ausströmen; (*sparks*) sprühen
emolument [ɛ'mʌljəmənt] *s* Vergütung *f*
emotion [ɪ'moʃən] *s* Gemütsbewegung *f*
emotional [ɪ'moʃənəl] *adj* (*e.g., disorder*) Gemüts-; (*person*) gefühlvoll; (*e.g., sermon*) ergreifend; (*mawkish*) rührselig
emperor ['ɛmpərər] *s* Kaiser *m*
empha·sis ['ɛmfəsɪs] *s* (**-ses** [‚siz])
Betonung *f*
emphasize ['ɛmfə‚saɪz] *tr* betonen
emphatic [ɛm'fætɪk] *adj* nachdrücklich
emphysema [‚ɛmfɪ'simə] *s* Emphysem *n*
empire ['ɛmpaɪr] *s* Reich *n*; (*Roman period*) Kaiserzeit *f*
Em'pire fur'niture *s* Empiremöbel *n*
empiric(al) [ɛm'pɪrɪk(əl)] *adj* erfahrungsmäßig, empirisch
empiricist [ɛm'pɪrɪsɪst] *s* Empiriker -in *mf*
emplacement [ɛm'plesmənt] *s* Stellung *f*
employ [ɛm'plɔi] *s* Dienst *m* ‖ *tr* (*hire*) anstellen; (*keep in employ-*

ment) beschäftigen; (*use*) verwenden; (*troops, police*) einsetzen
employee [ɛm'plɔɪ·i], [‚ɛmplɔɪ'i] *s* Arbeitnehmer -in *mf*
employer [ɛm'plɔɪ·ər] *s* Arbeitgeber -in *mf*
employment [ɛm'plɔɪmənt] *s* (*work*) Beschäftigung *f*, Arbeit *f*; (*use*) Verwendung *f*; (*e.g., of troops*) Einsatz *m*; **out of e.** arbeitslos
employ'ment a'gency *s* Arbeitsvermittlung *f*
empower [ɛm'pau·ər] *tr* ermächtigen
empress ['ɛmprɪs] *s* Kaiserin *f*
emptiness ['ɛmptɪnɪs] *s* Leere *f*; (fig) Nichtigkeit *f*
emp·ty ['ɛmpti] *adj* leer; **e. talk** leere Worte *pl*; **on an e. stomach** auf nüchternen Magen ‖ **empties** *spl* Leergut *n* ‖ *v* (*pret & pp* **-tied**) *tr* (aus)leeren ‖ *intr*—**e. into** münden in (*acc*)
emp'ty-hand'ed *adj* mit leeren Händen
emp'ty-head'ed *adj* hohlköpfig
emulate ['ɛmjə‚let] *s* nacheifern (*dat*)
emulation [‚ɛmjə'leʃən] *s* Nacheiferung *f*
emulator [‚ɛmjə'letər] *s* Nacheiferer -in *mf*
emulsi·fy [ɪ'mʌlsɪ‚faɪ] *v* (*pret & pp* **-fied**) *tr* emulgieren
emulsion [ɪ'mʌlʃən] *s* Emulsion *f*; (phot) Schicht *f*
enable [ɛn'ebəl] *tr* befähigen
enact [ɛn'ækt] *tr* erlassen
enactment [ɛn'æktmənt] *s* Erlassen *n*
enam·el [ɪ'næməl] *s* Email *n*; (dent) Zahnscnmelz *m* ‖ *v* (*pret & pp* **-el[l]ed;** *ger* **-el[l]ing**) *tr* emaillieren
enam'el paint' *s* Emaillack *m*
enam'elware' *s* Emailwaren *pl*
enamored [ɛ'næmərd] *adj*—**be e. of** verliebt sein in (*acc*)
encamp [ɛn'kæmp] *tr* in e-m Lager unterbringen ‖ *intr* lagern, sich lagern
encampment [ɛn'kæmpmənt] *s* (*camping*) Lagern *n*; (*campsite*) Lager *n*
encase [ɛn'kes] *tr* einschließen
enchant [ɛn't/ænt] *tr* verzaubern; (fig) bezaubern
enchanter [ɛn't/æntər] *s* Zauberer -in *mf*
enchant'ing *adj* bezaubernd
enchantment [ɛn't/æntmənt] *s* (*state*) Verzauberung *f*; (*cause of enchantment*) Zauber *m*
enchantress [ɛn't/æntrɪs] *s* Zauberin *f*
encircle [ɛn'sʌrkəl] *tr* umgeben; (mil) einschließen
encirclement [ɛn'sʌrkəlmənt] *s* (mil) Einschließung *f*
enclave ['ɛnklev] *s* Enklave *f*
enclitic [ɛn'klɪtɪk] *adj* enklitisch ‖ *s* Enklitikon *n*
enclose [ɛn'kloz] *tr* einschließen; (*land*) umzäunen; (*in a letter*) beilegen; **e. in parentheses** einklammern; **please find enclosed** in der Anlage erhalten Sie
enclosure [ɛn'kloʒər] *s* Umzäunung *f*; (*in a letter*) Anlage *f*

encomi·um [εn'kɔmɪ·əm] s (–ums & –a [ə]) Lobpreisung f, Enkomion n

encompass [εn'kʌmpəs] tr umfassen

encore ['ankɔr] s (performance) Zugabe f; (recall) Dakaporuf m ‖ interj da capo!; noch einmal!

encounter [εn'kauntər] s Begegnung f; (hostile meeting) Zusammenstoß m; (mil) Gefecht n ‖ tr begegnen (dat)

encourage [εn'kʌrɪdʒ] tr ermutigen

encouragement [εn'kʌrɪdʒmənt] s Ermutigung f

encroach [εn'krotʃ] intr—e. on übergreifen auf (acc); (rights) beeinträchtigen

encroachment [εn'krotʃmənt] s Übergriff m

encrust [εn'krʌst] tr überkrusten

encumber [εn'kʌmbər] tr belasten; (with debts) verschulden

encumbrance [εn'krʌmbrəns] s Belastung f

encyclical [εn'sɪklɪkəl] s Enzyklika f

encyclopedia [εn,saɪklə'pidɪ·ə] s Enzyklopädie f

encyclopedic [εn,saɪklə'pidɪk] adj enzyklopädisch

end [εnd] s Ende n; (purpose) Zweck m; (goal) Ziel n; (closing) Schluß m; (outcome) Ausgang m, Ergebnis n; **at the end of one's strength** am Rande seiner Kraft; **come to a bad end** ein schlimmes Ende finden; **come to an end** zu Ende gehen; **end in itself** Selbstzweck m; **gain one's ends** seinen Vorsatz ausführen; **go off the deep end** sich unnötig aufregen; **in the end** schließlich; **make both ends meet** gerade auskommen; **no end of** unendlich viel(e); **on end** hochkant; (without letup) ununterbrochen; **put an end to** ein Ende machen (dat); **that will be the end of me** das überlebe ich nicht; **to no end** vergebens ‖ tr beenden ‖ intr enden; (gram) auslauten; **end in a point** spitz zulaufen; **end up (in)** (coll) landen (in dat); **end up with** beenden mit

end'-all' s Schluß m vom Ganzen

endanger [εn'dendʒər] tr gefährden

endear [εn'dɪr] tr—e. s.o. to j-n einschmeicheln bei

endear'ing adj gewinnend

endearment [εn'dɪrmənt] s Beliebtheit f

endeavor [εn'dεvər] s Bestreben n ‖ intr—e. to (inf) sich bestreben zu (inf), versuchen zu (inf)

endemic [εn'demɪk] adj endemisch ‖ s Endemie f, endemische Krankheit f

end'ing s Beendigung f, Abschluß m; (gram) Endung f

endive ['εndaɪv] s Endivie f

endless ['εndlɪs] adj endlos; **an e. number of** unendlich viele

end'most' adj entfernteste

endocrine ['εndo,kraɪn] adj endokrin

endorse [εn'dɔrs] tr (confirm) bestätigen; (a check) indossieren

endorsee [,εndɔr'si] s Indossat –in mf

endorsement [εn'dɔrsmənt] s Indossament n; (approval) Bestätigung f

endorser [εn'dɔrsər] s Indossant –in mf; (backer) Hintermann m

endow [εn'dau] tr (provide with income) dotieren; (with talent) begaben

endowment [εn'daumənt] s Dotierung f; (talent) Begabung f

endow'ment fund' s Stiftungsvermögen n

endurance [εn'd(j)urəns] s Dauer f; (ability to hold out) Ausdauer f

endur'ance test' s Dauerprobe f

endure [εn'd(j)ur] tr aushalten ‖ intr fortdauern

endur'ing adj dauerhaft

enema ['εnəmə] s Einlauf m

enemy ['εnəmi] adj feindlich, Feind– ‖ s Feind m; **become enemies** sich verfeinden

energetic [,εnər'dʒεtɪk] adj energisch

energy ['εnərdʒi] s Energie f

enervate ['εnər,vet] tr entkräften

enfeeble [εn'fibəl] tr entkräften

enfilade ['εnfɪ,led] s (mil) Flankenfeuer n ‖ tr mit Flankenfeuer bestreichen

enfold [εn'fold] tr einhüllen

enforce [εn'fɔrs] tr durchsetzen; (obedience) erzwingen

enforcement [εn'fɔrsmənt] s Durchsetzung f

enfranchise [εn'fræntʃaɪz] tr (admit to citizenship) einbürgern; (give the right to vote to) das Wahlrecht verleihen (dat)

engage [εn'gedʒ] tr (hire) anstellen; (reserve) vorbestellen; (attention) fesseln; (gears) einrücken; (one's own troops) einsetzen; (the enemy) angreifen; **be engaged in** beschäftigt sein mit; **e. in** verwickeln in (acc) ‖ intr (mach) (ein)greifen; **e. in** sich einlassen in (acc)

engaged' adj verlobt; **get e. (to)** sich verloben (mit)

engaged' cou'ple s Brautleute pl

engagement [εn'gedʒmənt] s (betrothal) Verlobung f; (appointment) Verabredung f; (obligation) Verpflichtung f; (mil) Gefecht n; **have a previous e.** verabredet sein

engage'ment ring' s Verlobungsring m

engag'ing adj gewinnend

engender [εn'dʒεndər] tr hervorbringen

engine ['εndʒɪn] s Maschine f; (aer, aut) Motor m; (rr) Lokomotive f

engineer [,εndʒə'nɪr] s Ingenieur m, Techniker m; (mil) Pionier m; (rr) Lokomotivführer m; **engineers** (mil) Pioniertruppe f ‖ tr errichten; (fig) bewerkstelligen

engineer'ing s Ingenieurwesen n

engineer'ing school' s Technikum n

en'gine house' s Spritzenhaus n

en'gine room' s Maschinenraum m

England ['ɪŋglənd] s England n

English ['ɪŋglɪʃ] adj englisch ‖ s (spin) Effet n; (language) Englisch n; **in plain E.** unverblümt; **the E.** die Engländer

Eng'lish Chan'nel s Ärmelkanal m
Eng'lish horn' s Englischhorn n
Eng'lish•man s (-men) Engländer m
Eng'lish-speak'ing adj englischsprechend
Eng'lish•wom'an s (-wom'en) Engländerin f
engraft [ɛn'græft] tr aufpropfen; (fig) einprägen
engrave [ɛn'grev] tr gravieren
engraver [ɛn'grevər] s Graveur m
engrav'ing s Kupferstich m
engross [ɛn'gros] tr in Anspruch nehmen; (a document) mit großen Buchstaben schreiben; **become engrossed in** sich versenken in (acc)
engross'ing adj fesselnd
engulf [ɛn'gʌlf] tr (fig) verschlingen
enhance [ɛn'hæns] tr erhöhen; **be enhanced** sich erhöhen
enhancement [ɛn'hænsmənt] s Erhöhung f
enigma [ɪ'nɪgmə] s Rätsel n
enigmatic(al) [,ɪnɪg'mætɪk(əl)] adj rätselhaft
enjoin [ɛn'dʒɔɪn] tr (forbid) (from ger) verbieten (dat) (zu inf); **e. s.o. to** (inf) j-m auferlegen zu (inf)
enjoy [ɛn'dʒɔɪ] tr (take pleasure in) Gefallen finden an (dat); (have the advantage of) genießen, sich erfreuen (genit); **e. doing s.th.** gern etw tun; **e. oneself** sich gut unterhalten; **e. to the full** auskosten; **I e. the wine** mir schmeckt der Wein
enjoyable [ɛn'dʒɔɪ•əbəl] adj erfreulich; **thoroughly e.** genußreich
enjoyment [ɛn'dʒɔɪmənt] s Genuß m
enkindle [ɛn'kɪndəl] tr entzünden
enlarge [ɛn'lardʒ] tr vergrößern || intr sich vergrößern; **e. upon** näher eingehen auf (acc)
enlargement [ɛn'lardʒmənt] s Vergrößerung f
enlarger [ɛn'lardʒər] s (phot) Vergrößerungsapparat m
enlighten [ɛn'laɪtən] tr aufklären
enlightenment [ɛn'laɪtənmənt] s (act) Aufklärung f; (state) Aufgeklärtheit f
enlist [ɛn'lɪst] tr (services) in Anspruch nehmen; (mil) anwerben; **e. s.o. in a cause** j-n für e-e Sache gewinnen || intr (in) sich freiwillig melden (zu)
enlist'ed man' s Soldat m; **enlisted men** Mannschaften pl
enlistment [ɛn'lɪstmənt] s Anwerbung f; (period of service) Militärdienstzeit f
enliven [ɛn'laɪvən] tr beleben
enmesh [ɛn'mɛʃ] tr verstricken
enmity ['ɛnmɪti] s Feindschaft f
ennoble [ɛn'nobəl] tr veredeln, adeln
ennui ['anwi] s Langeweile f
enormity [ɪ'nɔrmɪti] s Ungeheuerlichkeit f
enormous [ɪ'nɔrməs] adj enorm, ungeheuer
enough [ɪ'nʌf] adj & adv genug, genügend; **be e.** genügen; **I have e. of it** ich bin es satt; **it's e. to drive one crazy** es ist zum Verrücktwerden

enounce [ɪ'naʊns] tr (declare) verkünden; (pronounce) aussprechen
enrage [ɛn'redʒ] tr wütend machen
enraged' adj (at) wütend (über acc)
enrapture [ɛn'ræptʃər] tr hinreißen
enrich [ɛn'rɪtʃ] tr (a person with money; the mind, a program) bereichern; (soil) fruchtbarer machen; (food, metals, gases) anreichern
enrichment [ɛn'rɪtʃmənt] s Bereicherung f; (of food, metals, gases) Anreicherung f
enroll [ɛn'rol] tr als Mitglied aufnehmen || intr (educ) sich immatrikulieren lassen
enrollment [ɛn'rolmənt] s (in a course or school) Schülerzahl f; (of a society) Mitgliederzahl f
en route [an 'rut] adv unterwegs
ensconce [ɛn'skans] tr verbergen
ensemble [an'sambəl] s Ensemble n
ensign ['ɛnsɪn] s (flag) (mil) Fahne f; (flag) (nav) Flagge f; (emblem) Abzeichen n; (nav) Leutnant m zur See
enslave [ɛn'slev] tr versklaven
enslavement [ɛn'slevmənt] s Versklavung f
ensnare [ɛn'snɛr] tr (fig) umgarnen
ensue [ɛn's(j)u] intr (from) (er)folgen (aus)
ensu'ing adj darauffolgend
ensure [ɛn'ʃur] tr gewährleisten
entail [ɛn'tel] tr mit sich bringen
entangle [ɛn'tæŋgəl] tr verwickeln; **get entangled** sich verwickeln
entanglement [ɛn'tæŋgəlmənt] s Verwicklung f; (mil) Drahtverhau m
enter ['ɛntər] tr (a room) betreten, treten in (acc); (political office) antreten; (a university) beziehen; (a protest) erheben; (a career) einschlagen; (in the records) eintragen; **e. the army** Soldat werden || intr eintreten, hereinkommen; (by car) einfahren; (sport) melden; (theat) auftreten; **e. into** (an agreement) treffen; (a contract) abschließen; **e. upon** anfangen; (a career) einschlagen; (an office, inheritance) antreten; (year of life) eintreten in (acc)
enterprise ['ɛntər,praɪz] s Unternehmen n; (spirit) Unternehmungsgeist m
en'terprising adj unternehmungslustig
entertain [,ɛntər'ten] tr unterhalten; (guests) bewirten; (doubts, hopes, suspicions) hegen || intr Gäste haben
entertainer [,ɛntər'tenər] s Unterhaltungskünstler –in mf
entertain'ing adj unterhaltsam || s—**do a lot of e.** ein großes Haus führen
entertainment [,ɛntər'tenmənt] s Unterhaltung f
entertain'ment tax' s Vergnügungssteuer f
enthrall [ɛn'θrɔl] tr bezaubern, fesseln
enthrone [ɛn'θron] tr auf den Thron setzen; **be enthroned** thronen
enthuse [ɛn'θ(j)uz] tr (coll) begeistern
enthusiasm [ɛn'θ(j)uzɪ,æzəm] s Begeisterung f, Schwärmerei f

enthusiast [ɛn'θ(j)uzɪ‚æst] *s* Schwärmer –in *mf*
enthusiastic [ɛn‚θ(j)uzɪ'æstɪk] *adj* (about) begeistert (über *acc* or von)
entice [ɛn'taɪs] *tr* (ver)locken
enticement [ɛn'taɪsmənt] *s* Verlockung *f*
entic'ing *adj* verlockend
entire [ɛn'taɪr] *adj* ganz, gesamt; (trust) voll
entirely [ɛn'taɪrli] *adv* ganz, gänzlich
entirety [ɛn'taɪrti] *s*—**in its e.** in seiner Gesamtheit
entitle [ɛn'taɪtəl] *tr* (call) betiteln; (to) berechtigen (zu); **be entitled to** Anspruch haben auf (acc); **be entitled to** (inf) berechtigt sein zu (inf)
entity ['ɛntɪti] *s* Wesen *n*
entomb [ɛn'tum] *tr* bestatten
entombment [ɛn'tummənt] *s* Bestattung *f*
entomology [‚ɛntə'mɑlədʒi] *s* Entomologie *f*
entourage [‚ɑntu'rɑʒ] *s* Begleitung *f*
entrails ['ɛntrelz] *spl* Eingeweide *pl*
entrain [ɛn'tren] *tr* verladen ‖ *intr* einsteigen
entrance ['ɛntrəns] *s* Eingang *m;* (drive) Einfahrt *f;* (of a home) Flur *m;* (upon office) Antritt *m;* (theat) Auftritt *m;* **make one's e.** eintreten ‖ [ɛn'træns] *tr* mitreißen
en'trance examina'tion *s* Aufnahmeprüfung *f*
en'trance fee' *s* Eintrittspreis *m*
entrant ['ɛntrənt] *s* (in) Teilnehmer –in *mf* (an dat)
en·trap [ɛn'træp] *v* (pret & pp -trapped; ger -trapping) *tr* verleiten
entreat [ɛn'trit] *tr* anflehen
entreaty [ɛn'triti] *s* dringende Bitte *f;* **at his e.** auf seine Bitte
entrée ['ɑntre] *s* (access) Zutritt *m;* (before main course) Vorspeise *f;* (between courses) Zwischengericht *n;* (main course) Hauptgericht *n*
entrench [ɛn'trɛnt∫] *tr* verschanzen; **be entrenched in** (fig) eingewurzelt sein in (dat)
entrenchment [ɛn'trɛnt∫mənt] *s* (activity) Schanzbau *m;* (the result) Verschanzung *f*
entrepreneur [ɑntrəprə'nʌr] *s* Unternehmer –in *mf*
entrust [ɛn'trʌst] *tr* (to) anvertrauen (dat)
entry ['ɛntri] *s* Eintritt *m;* (by car) Einfahrt *f;* (door) Eingang *m,* Eingangstür *f;* (into a country) Einreise *f;* (into office) Antritt *m;* (in a dictionary) Stichwort *n;* (into a race) Nennung *f;* (contestant) Bewerber –in *mf* (com) Buchung *f;* (theat) Auftritt *m;* **unlawful e.** Hausfriedensbruch *m*
entwine [ɛn'twaɪn] *tr* umwinden
enumerate [ɪ'n(j)umə‚ret] *tr* aufzählen
enunciate [ɪ'nʌnsɪ‚et] *tr* aussprechen ‖ *intr* deutlich aussprechen
envelop [ɛn'vɛləp] *tr* (said of crowds, waves) verschlingen; (said of mist, clouds, darkness) umhüllen; (mil) umfassen

envelope ['ɛnvə‚lop] *s* Umschlag *m*
envelopment [ɛn'vɛləpmənt] *s* Umhüllung *f;* (mil) Umfassung *f*
envenom [ɛn'vɛnəm] *tr* vergiften
enviable ['ɛnvɪ‚əbəl] *adj* beneidenswert
envious ['ɛnvɪ‚əs] *adj* (of) neidisch (auf acc)
environment [ɛn'vaɪrənmənt] *s* (ecological condition) Umwelt *f;* (surroundings) Umgebung *f*
environmental [ɛn‚vaɪrən'mɛntəl] *adj* Umwelt–; umgebend, Umgebungs–
environmentalist [ɛn‚vaɪrən'mɛntəlɪst] Umweltschützer –in *mf*
environs [ɛn'vaɪrənz] *spl* Umgebung *f*
envisage [ɛn'vɪzɪdʒ] *tr* ins Auge fassen
envoy ['ɛnvɔɪ] *s* Gesandte *mf*
en·vy ['ɛnvi] *s* Neid *m* ‖ *v* (pret & pp -vied) *tr* (for) beneiden (um)
enzyme ['ɛnzaɪm] *s* Enzym *n*
epaulet, epaulette ['ɛpə‚lɛt] *s* Epaulette *f*, Schulterstück *n*
ephemeral [ɪ'fɛmərəl] *adj* flüchtig
epic ['ɛpɪk] *adj* episch; **e. poetry** Epik *f* ‖ *s* Epos *n,* Heldengedicht *n*
epicure ['ɛpɪ‚kjur] *s* Feinschmecker –in *mf*
epicurean [‚ɛpɪkju'ri‚ən] *adj* genußsüchtig; (philos) epikureisch ‖ *s* Genußmensch *m;* (philos) Epikureer *m*
epidemic [‚ɛpɪ'dɛmɪk] *adj* epidemisch ‖ *s* Epidemie *f,* Seuche *f*
epidermis [‚ɛpɪ'dʌrmɪs] *s* Oberhaut *f*
epigram ['ɛpɪ‚græm] *s* Epigramm *n*
epigraph ['ɛpɪ‚græf] *s* Inschrift *f*
epigraphy [ɛ'pɪgrəfi] *s* Inschriftenkunde *f*
epilepsy ['ɛpɪ‚lɛpsi] *s* Epilepsie *f*
epileptic [‚ɛpɪ'lɛptɪk] *adj* epileptisch ‖ *s* Epileptiker –in *mf*
epilogue ['ɛpɪ‚lɔg] *s* Nachwort *n*
Epiphany [ɪ'pɪfəni] *s* Dreikönigsfest *n*
episcopal [ɪ'pɪskəpəl] *adj* bischöflich
Episcopalian [ɪ‚pɪskə'peli‚ən] *adj* Episkopal– ‖ *s* Episkopale *m,* Episkopalin *f*
epis'copal see' *s* Bischofssitz *m*
episcopate [ɪ'pɪskə‚pet] *s* Bischofsamt *n*
episode ['ɛpɪ‚sod] *s* Episode *f*
epistemology [ɪ‚pɪstə'mɑlədʒi] *s* Epistemologie *f,* Erkenntnistheorie *f*
epistle [ɪ'pɪsəl] *s* Epistel *f*
epitaph ['ɛpɪtæf] *s* Grabinschrift *f*
epithet ['ɛpɪ‚θɛt] *s* Beiwort *n*
epitome [ɪ'pɪtəmi] *s* Auszug *m;* (fig) Verkörperung *f*
epitomize [ɪ'pɪtə‚maɪz] *tr*—e-n Auszug machen von or aus; (fig) verkörpern
epoch ['ɛpək], ['ipɑk] *s* Epoche *f*
epochal ['ɛpəkəl] *adj* epochal
e'poch-mak'ing *adj* bahnbrechend
Ep'som salts' ['ɛpsəm] *spl* Bittersalz *n*
equable ['ɛkwəbəl] *adj* gleichmäßig; (disposition) gleichmütig
equal ['ikwəl] *adj* gleich; (in birth or status) ebenbürtig; (in worth) gleichwertig; (in kind) gleichartig; **be e. to** (e.g., a task) gewachsen sein (dat); **be on e. terms** (be on the same level) auf gleichem Fuß stehen; **other**

things being e. bei sonst gleichen Verhältnissen ‖ *s* Gleiche *mfn;* **her or their e.(s)** ihresgleichen; **my (your,** *etc.***) e.(s)** meines– (deines–, *etc.*) gleichen ‖ *v* (*pret & pp* **equal[l]ed;** *ger* **equal[l]ing** *tr* gleichkommen (*dat*); (*a record*) erreichen; (math) ergeben
equality [ɪ'kwɑlɪti] *s* Gleichheit *f;* (*in standing*) Gleichberechtigung *f*
equalize ['ikwə‚laɪz] *tr* gleichmachen
equally ['ikwəli] *adv* gleich, ebenso
equanimity [‚ikwə'nɪmɪti] *s* Gleichmut *m*
equate [i'kwet] *tr* (**to** or **with**) gleichsetzen (*dat* or mit)
equation [i'kweʒən] *s* Gleichung *f*
equator [i'kwetər] *s* Äquator *m*
equatorial [‚ikwə'tɔrɪ·əl] *adj* äquatorial
equestrian [ɪ'kwɛstrɪ·ən] *adj* Reiter–; **e. statue** Reiterstandbild *n* ‖ *s* Kunstreiter –in *mf*
equilateral [‚ikwɪ'lætərəl] *adj* gleichseitig
equilibrium [‚ikwɪ'lɪbrɪ·əm] *s* Gleichgewicht *n;* (fig) Gleichmaß *n*
equinox ['ikwɪ‚nɑks] *s* Tagundnachtgleiche *f*
equip [ɪ'kwɪp] *v* (*pret & pp* **equipped;** *ger* **equipping**) *tr* ausrüsten, ausstatten
equipment [ɪ'kwɪpmənt] *s* Ausrüstung *f,* Ausstattung *f*
equipoise ['ikwɪ‚pɔɪz] *s* Gleichgewicht *n*
equitable ['ɛkwɪtəbəl] *adj* gerecht
equity ['ɛkwɪti] *s* (*fairness*) Unparteilichkeit *f;* (fin) Nettowert *m*
equivalent [ɪ'kwɪvələnt] *adj* gleichwertig; (**to**) gleichbedeutend (mit) ‖ *s* Gegenwert *m;* (**of**) Äquivalent *n* (für)
equivocal [ɪ'kwɪvəkəl] *adj* zweideutig
equivocate [ɪ'kwɪvə‚ket] *intr* zweideutig reden
equivocation [ɪ'kwɪvə‚keʃən] *s* Zweideutigkeit *f*
era ['ɪrə], ['irə] *s* Zeitalter *n*
eradicate [ɪ'rædɪ‚ket] *tr* ausrotten
erase [ɪ'res] *tr* ausradieren; (*a tape recording*) löschen; (*a blackboard*) abwischen; (fig) auslöschen
eraser [ɪ'resər] *s* Radiergummi *m;* (*for a blackboard*) Tafelwischer *m*
erasure [ɪ're/ər], [ɪ'reʒər] *s* (*action*) Ausradieren *n;* (*erased spot*) Rasur *f*
ere [ɛr] *prep* (poet) vor (*dat*) ‖ *conj* (poet) ehe, bevor
erect [ɪ'rɛkt] *adj* aufrecht, straff; (*hair*) gesträubt; **with head e.** erhobenen Hauptes ‖ *tr* errichten
erection [ɪ'rɛkʃən] *s* Errichtung *f;* (*of sexual organs*) Erektion *f*
erg [ʌrg] *s* Erg *n*
ermine ['ʌrmɪn] *s* Hermelinpelz *m*
erode [ɪ'rod] *tr* (*corrode*) zerfressen; (fig) unterhöhlen; (geol) erodieren ‖ *intr* zerfressen werden
erosion [ɪ'roʒən] *s* (*corrosion*) Zerfressen *n;* (fig) Unterhöhlung *f;* (geol) Erosion *f*
erotic [ɪ'rɑtɪk] *adj* erotisch

err [ʌr] *intr* irren, sich irren
errand ['ɛrənd] *s* Bersorgung *f;* **run an e.** e–e Besorgung machen
er'rand boy' *s* Laufbursche *m*
erratic [ɪ'rætɪk] *adj* regellos, ziellos; (geol) erratisch
erroneous [ɪ'ronɪ·əs] *adj* irrtümlich
erroneously [ɪ'ronɪ·əsli] *adv* irrtümlicherweise, versehentlich
error ['ɛrər] *s* Fehler *m,* Irrtum *m*
erudite ['ɛr(j)ʊ‚daɪt] *adj* gelehrt
erudition [‚ɛr(j)ʊ'dɪʃən] *s* Gelehrsamkeit *f*
erupt [ɪ'rʌpt] *intr* ausbrechen
eruption [ɪ'rʌpʃən] *s* Ausbruch *m;* (pathol) Ausschlag *m*
escalate ['ɛskə‚let] *tr & intr* eskalieren
escalation [‚ɛskə'leʃən] *s* Eskalierung *f*
escalator ['ɛskə‚letər] *s* Rolltreppe *f*
es'calator clause' *s* Indexklausel *f*
escapade ['ɛskə‚ped] *s* Eskapade *f*
escape [ɛs'kep] *s* Flucht *f;* (*of gas or liquid*) Ausströmen *n;* **have a narrow e.** mit knapper Not davonkommen ‖ *intr* (*said of gas or liquid*) ausströmen; (**from**) flüchten (aus)
escape' clause' *s* Ausweichklausel *f*
escapee [‚ɛskə'pi] *s* Flüchtling *m*
escape' hatch' *s* Notausstieg *m*
escapement [ɛs'kepmənt] *s* (horol) Hemmung *f*
escape' wheel' *s* (horol) Hemmungsrad *n*
escapism [ɛs'kepɪzəm] *s* Wirklichkeitsflucht *f*
escarpment [ɛs'kɑrpmənt] *s* (geol) Steilabhang *m;* (mil) Abdachung *f*
eschew [ɛs't/u] *tr* (ver)meiden
escort [ɛs'kɔrt] *s* Geleit *n,* Schutzgeleit *n;* (*person*) Begleiter *m;* (mil) Begleitmannschaft *f,* Bedeckung *f;* (nav) Geleitschutz *m* ‖ [ɛs'kɔrt] *tr* begleiten; (mil, nav) geleiten
es'cort ves'sel *s* Geleitschiff *n*
escutcheon [ɛs'kʌtʃən] *s* Wappenschild *m;* (*doorplate*) Schlüssellochschild *n*
Eskimo ['ɛskɪ‚mo] *adj* Eskimo– ‖ *s* (–**mos** & **–mo**) Eskimo *m*
esopha·gus [i'sɑfəgəs] *s* (**–gi** [‚dʒaɪ]) Speiseröhre *f*
esoteric [‚ɛso'tɛrɪk] *adj* esoterisch
especial [ɛs'pɛ/əl] *adj* besondere
especially [ɛs'pɛ/əli] *adv* besonders
espionage [‚ɛspɪ·ə'nɑʒ] *s* Spionage *f*
espousal [ɛs'pauzəl] *s* (**of**) Annahme *f* (von)
espouse [ɛs'pauz] *tr* annehmen
esprit de corps [ɛs'pri də 'kɔr] *s* Korpsgeist *m,* Gemeinschaftsgeist *m*
espy [ɛs'paɪ] *v* (*pret & pp* **espied**) *tr* erspähen
essay ['ɛse] *s* Aufsatz *m,* Essay *n* ‖ [ɛ'se] *tr* probieren
essayist ['ɛse·ɪst] *s* Essayist –in *mf*
essence ['ɛsəns] *s* Wesenheit *f;* (*scent*) Duft *m;* (*extract*) Essenz *f;* (philos) inneres Wesen *n;* **in e.** im wesentlichen
essential [ɛ'sɛnʃəl] *adj* (**to**) wesentlich (für) ‖ *s* Hauptsache *f;* **the essentials** die Grundzüge *pl*

establish [εs'tæblɪʃ] *tr* (*found*) gründen; (*a business, an account*) eröffnen; (*relations, connections*) herstellen; (*order*) schaffen; (*a record*) aufstellen; (*a fact*) feststellen

establishment [εs'tæblɪʃmənt] *s* (*act*) Gründung *f;* (*institution*) Anstalt *f;* (*business*) Unternehmen *n;* **the Establishment** das Establishment

estate [εs'tet] *s* (*landed property*) Landgut *n;* (*possessions*) Vermögen *n;* (*property of deceased person*) Nachlaß *m;* (*social station*) Stand *m*

esteem [εs'tim] *s* Hochachtung *f;* **hold in e.** achten || *tr* achten

esthete ['εsθit] *s* Ästhetiker –in *mf*

esthetic [εs'θεtɪk] *adj* ästhetisch || **esthetics** *s* Ästhetik *f*

estimable ['εstɪməbəl] *adj* schätzenswert

estimate ['εstɪ‚met], ['εstɪmɪt] *s* Kostenanschlag *m;* (*judgment of value*) Schätzung *f;* **rough e.** Überschlag *m* || ['εstɪ‚met] *tr* (*costs*) veranschlagen; (*the value*) abschätzen; (*homes, damages*) schätzen; (*at*) beziffern (auf *acc*); **e. roughly** überschlagen

estimation [‚εstɪ'meʃən] *s* Schätzung *f;* **in my e.** nach meiner Schätzung

Estonia [εs'tonɪ‚ə] *s* Estland *n*

estrangement [εs'trendʒmənt] *s* Entfremdung *f*

estuary ['εstʃu‚εri] *s* (*of a river*) Mündung *f;* (*inlet*) Meeresarm *m*

etch [εtʃ] *tr* radieren, ätzen

etcher ['εtʃər] *s* Radierer –in *mf*

etch'ing *s* Radierung *f;* (*as an art*) Radierkunst *f*

eternal [ɪ'tʌrnəl] *adj* ewig

eternity [ɪ'tʌrnɪti] *s* Ewigkeit *f*

ether ['iθər] *s* Äther *m*

ethereal [ɪ'θɪrɪ‚əl] *adj* ätherisch

ethical ['εθɪkəl] *adj* ethisch, sittlich

ethics ['εθɪks] *s* Ethik *f,* Sittenlehre *f*

Ethiopia [‚iθɪ'opɪ‚ə] *s* Äthiopien *n*

Ethiopian [‚iθɪ'opɪ‚ən] *adj* äthiopisch || *s* Äthiopier –in *mf;* (*language*) Äthiopisch *n*

ethnic(al) ['εθnɪk(əl)] *adj* völkisch; **e. group** Volksgruppe *f*

ethnography [εθ'nɑgrəfi] *s* Ethnographie *f*

ethnology [εθ'nɑlədʒi] *s* Völkerkunde *f*

ethyl ['εθɪl] *s* Äthyl *m*

ethylene ['εθɪ‚lin] *s* Äthylen *n*

etiquette ['εtɪ‚kεt] *s* Etikette *f*

etymology [‚εtɪ'mɑlədʒi] *s* Etymologie *f*

ety·mon ['εtɪ‚mɑn] *s* (**–mons** & **–ma** [mə]) Etymon *n*

eucalyp·tus [‚jukə'lɪptəs] *s* (**–tuses** & **–ti** [taɪ]) Eukalyptus *m*

Eucharist ['jukərɪst] *s*—**the E.** das heilige Abendmal, die Eucharistie *f*

eugenics [ju'dʒεnɪks] *s* Rassenhygiene *f*

eulogize ['julə‚dʒaɪz] *tr* lobpreisen

eulogy ['julədʒi] *s* Lobrede *f*

eunuch ['junək] *s* Eunuch *m*

euphemism ['jufɪ‚mɪzəm] *s* Euphemismus *m*

euphemistic [‚jufə'mɪstɪk] *adj* euphemistisch, verblümt

euphonic [ju'fɑnɪk] *adj* wohlklingend

euphony ['jufəni] *s* Wohlklang *m*

euphoria [ju'forɪ‚ə] *s* Euphorie *f*

euphoric [ju'forɪk] *adj* euphorisch

euphuism ['jufju‚ɪzəm] *s* gezierte Ausdrucksweise *f*

Europe ['jurəp] *s* Europa *n*

European [‚jurə'pi‚ən] *adj* europäisch || *s* Europäer –in *mf*

Europe'an plan' *s* Hotelpreis *m* ohne Mahlzeiten

euthanasia [‚juθə'neʒə] *s* Euthanasie *f*

evacuate [ɪ'vækju‚et] *tr* evakuieren; (*med*) entleeren; (*an area*) räumen || *intr* sich zurückziehen

evacuation [ɪ‚vækju'eʃən] *s* Evakuierung *f;* (*med*) Entleerung *f*

evade [ɪ'ved] *tr* ausweichen (*dat*); (*duties*) vernachlässigen; (*laws*) umgehen; (*prosecution, responsibility*) sich entziehen (*dat*); (*taxes*) hinterziehen

evaluate [ɪ'vælju‚et] *tr* (*e.g., jewels*) (ab)schätzen; (*e.g., a performance*) beurteilen

evaluation [ɪ‚vælju'eʃən] *s* Abschätzung *f;* (*judgment*) Beurteilung *f*

evangelic(al) [‚ivæn'dʒεlɪk(əl)], [‚εvən'dʒεlɪk(əl)] *adj* evangelisch

Evangelist [ɪ'vændʒəlɪst] *s* Evangelist *m*

evaporate [ɪ'væpə‚ret] *tr* eindampfen || *intr* (*above boiling point*) verdampfen; (*below boiling point*) verdunsten; (fig) sich verflüchtigen

eva'porated milk' *s* Kondensmilch *f*

evasion [ɪ've3ən] *s* (*dodge*) Ausweichen *n;* (*of the law*) Umgehung *f;* (*of responsibility*) Vernachlässigung *f;* (*in speech*) Ausflucht *f*

evasive [ɪ'vesɪv] *adj* ausweichend

eve [iv] *s* Vorabend *m*

even ['ivən] *adj* (*smooth*) eben, gerade; (*number*) gerade; (*uniform*) gleichmäßig; (*chance*) gleich; (*temperament*) ruhig, ausgeglichen; **an e. break** gleiche Aussichten *pl;* **an e. dozen** genau ein Dutzend; **be e.** (coll) quitt sein; **e. with** auf gleicher Höhe mit; **get e. with** mit j–m abrechnen || *adv* selbst, sogar; (*before comparatives*) noch; (*as intensifier before nouns and pronouns*) selbst; **break e.** gerade auf seine Kosten kommen; **e. if** selbst wenn, wenn auch; **e. so** trotzdem; **e. though** obgleich; **e. today** noch heute; **e. when** selbst wenn || *tr* ebnen; **e. up** ausgleichen

e'ven-hand'ed *adj* unparteiisch

evening ['ivnɪŋ] *adj* Abend– || *s* Abend *m;* **in the e.** am Abend; **this e.** heute abend

eve'ning gown' *s* Abendkleid *n*

eve'ning pa'per *s* Abendblatt *n*

eve'ning school' *s* Abendschule *f*

evenly ['ivənli] *adv* gleichmäßig; **e. matched** (sport) gleichwertig

ev'en-mind'ed *adj* gleichmütig

evenness ['ivənnɪs] *s* (*smoothness*)

Ebenheit *f;* (*uniformity*) Gleichmäßigkeit *f*

event [ı'vɛnt] *s* Ereignis *n;* (sport) Veranstaltung *f;* at all events, in any e. auf jeden Fall; in the e. of im Falle (*genit*)

eventful [ı'vɛntfəl] *adj* ereignisvoll

eventual [ı'vɛntʃʊ-əl] *adj* schließlich

eventuality [ı,vɛntʃʊ'ælıti] *s* Möglichkeit *f*

eventually [ı'vɛntʃʊ,əli] *adj* schließlich

ever ['ɛvər] *adv* je, jemals; (*before comparatives*) immer; did you e.! hat man schon sowas gehört!; e. after die ganze Zeit danach; e. so noch so; e. so much (coll) sehr; hardly e. fast nie

ev'ergreen' *adj* immergrün || *s* Immergrün *n*

ev'erlast'ing *adj* ewig; (*continual*) fortwährend; (iron) ewig

ev'ermore' *adv* immer; for e. in Ewigkeit

every ['ɛvri] *adj* jeder; (*confidence*) voll; e. bit (coll) völlig; e. now and then ab und zu; e. once in a while dann und wann; e. other day alle zwei Tage; e. time (that) jedesmal (wenn)

ev'erybod'y *indef pron* jeder, jedermann

ev'eryday' *adj* alltäglich, Alltags–

ev'eryone', ev'ery one' *indef pron* (of) jeder (von); e. else alle anderen

ev'erything' *indef pron* alles

ev'erywhere' *adv* (*position*) überall; (*direction*) überallhin

evict [ı'vıkt] *tr* delogieren

eviction [ı'vıkʃən] *s* Delogierung *f*

evidence ['ɛvıdəns] *s* Beweismaterial *n*, Beweise *pl;* (*piece of evidence*) Beweis *m;* as e. of zum Beweis (*genit*); for lack of e. wegen Mangels an Beweisen; give e. aussagen; in e. sichtbar

evident ['ɛvıdənt] *adj* (*obvious*) offensichtlich; (*visible*) ersichtlich; be e. zutage liegen

evidently ['ɛvıdəntli] *adv* offenbar

evil ['ivəl] *adj* übel, böse || *s* Übel *n*

e'vildo'er *s* Übeltäter –in *mf*

e'vildo'ing *s* Missetat *f*

e'vil eye' *s* böser Blick *m*

e'vil-mind'ed *adj* übelgesinnt

E'vil One' *s* Böse *m*

evince [ı'vıns] *tr* bekunden

evoke [ı'vok] *tr* hervorrufen

evolution [,ɛvə'luʃən] *s* Evolution *f*

evolve [ı'vɑlv] *tr* entwickeln, entfalten || *intr* sich entwickeln, sich entfalten

ewe [ju] *s* Mutterschaf *n*

ewer ['ju-ər] *s* Wasserkanne *f*

exact [ɛg'zækt] *adj* genau || *tr* (*e.g., money*) beitreiben; (*obedience*) erzwingen

exact'ing *adj* (*strict*) streng; (*task*) aufreibend; (*picky*) anspruchsvoll

exactly [ɛg'zæktli] *adv* genau

exactness [ɛg'zæktnıs] *s* Genauigkeit *f*

exact' sci'ences *spl* Realien *pl*

exaggerate [ɛg'zædʒə,ret] *tr* übertreiben

exaggeration [ɛg,zædʒə're ʃən] *s* Übertreibung *f*

exalt [ɛg'zɔlt] *tr* erheben

exam [ɛg'zæm] *s* (coll) Prüfung *f*

examination [ɛg,zæmı'neʃən] *s* Prüfung *f*, Examen *n;* (jur) Verhör *n*, Vernehmung *f;* (med) Untersuchung *f;* direct e. (jur) direkte Befragung *f;* fail an e. bei e-r Prüfung durchfallen; on closer e. bei näherer Prüfung; pass an e. e-e Prüfung bestehen; take an e. e-e Prüfung ablegen

examine [ɛg'zæmın] *tr* prüfen; (jur) verhören, vernehmen; (med) untersuchen

examinee [ɛg,zæmı'ni] *s* Prüfling *m*

examiner [ɛg'zæmınər] *s* (educ) Prüfer –in *mf;* (med) Untersucher –in *mf*

example [ɛg'zæmpəl] *s* Beispiel *n;* for e. zum Beispiel; make an e. of ein Exempel statuieren an (*dat*); set a good e. mit gutem Beispiel vorangehen

exasperate [ɛg'zæspə,ret] *tr* reizen

excavate ['ɛkskə,vet] *tr* ausgraben

excavation [,ɛkskə've ʃən] *s* Ausgrabung *f*

excavator ['ɛkskə,vetər] *s* (archeol) Ausgräber –in *mf;* (mach) Trockenbagger *m*

exceed [ɛk'sid] *tr* überschreiten

exceedingly [ɛk'sidıŋli] *adv* außerordentlich

ex•cel [ɛk'sɛl] *v* (*pret & pp* –celled; *ger* –celling) *tr* übertreffen || *intr* (in) sich auszeichnen (in *dat*)

excellence ['ɛksələns] *s* Vorzüglichkeit *f*

excellency ['ɛksələnsi] *s* Vorzüglichkeit *f;* Your Excellency Eure Exzellenz

excellent ['ɛksələnt] *adj* ausgezeichnet

excelsior [ɛk'sɛlsı-ər] *s* Holzwolle *f*

except [ɛk'sɛpt] *adv*—e. for abgesehen von; e. if außer wenn; e. that außer daß; e. when außer wenn || *prep* außer (*dat*), ausgenommen (*acc*) || *tr* ausnehmen, ausschließen

exception [ɛk'sɛpʃən] *s* Ausnahme *f;* by way of e. ausnahmsweise; take e. to Anstoß nehmen an (*dat*); without e. ausnahmslos; with the e. of mit Ausnahme von

exceptional [ɛk'sɛpʃənəl] *adj* außergewöhnlich. Sonder–

excerpt ['ɛksʌrpt] *s* Auszug *m* || [ɛk-'sʌrpt] *tr* exzerpieren

excess ['ɛksɛs], [ɛk'sɛs] *adj* überschüssig || [ɛk'sɛs] *s* (*surplus*) Überschuß *m;* (*immoderate amount*) (of) Übermaß *n* (von or an *dat*); carry to e. übertreiben; excesses Ausschreitungen *pl;* in e. of mehr als; to e. übermäßig

ex'cess bag'gage *s* Überfracht *f*

excessive [ɛk'sɛsıv] *adj* übermäßig

ex'cess-prof'its tax' *s* Mehrgewinnsteuer *f*

exchange [ɛks'tʃendʒ] *s* Austausch *m;* (*e.g., of purchases*) Umtausch *m;* (*of words*) Wechselgespräch *n;* (*of*

money) Geldwechsel *m;* (fin) Börse *f;* (mil) Kantine *f;* (telp) Vermittlung *f;* **e. of letters** Briefwechsel *m;* **in e.** dafür; **in e. for** für ‖ *tr (trade)* tauschen; *(replace)* auswechseln; **e. for** umtauschen gegen; **e. places with s.o.** mit j–m tauscnen
exchequer [ɛks'tʃɛkər] *s* Staatskasse *f; (department)* Schatzamt *n*
ex'cise tax' ['ɛksaɪz] *s* Verbrauchssteuer *f*
excitable [ɛk'saɪtəbəl] *adj* erregbar
excite [ɛk'saɪt] *tr* erregen, aufregen
excitement [ɛk'saɪtmənt] *s* Erregung *f,* Aufregung *f*
excit'ing *adj* erregend, aufregend
exclaim [ɛks'klem] *tr & intr* ausrufen
exclamation [,ɛksklə'meʃən] *s* Ausruf *m*
exclama'tion point' *s* Ausrufungszeichen *n*
exclude [ɛks'klud] *tr* ausschließen
exclusion [ɛks'kluʒən] *s* Ausschließung *f,* Ausschluß *m;* **to the e. of** unter Ausschluß *(genit)*
exclusive [ɛks'klusɪv] *adj (rights, etc.)* alleinig, ausschließlich; *(club)* exklusiv; *(shop)* teuer; **e. of** ausschließlich *(genit)*
excommunicate [,ɛkskə'mjunɪ,ket] *tr* exkommunizieren
excommunication [,ɛkskə,mjunɪ'keʃən] *s* Exkommunikation *f,* Kirchenbann *m*
excoriate [ɛks'korɪ,et] *tr* (fig) heruntermachen
excrement ['ɛkskrəmənt] *s* Exkremente *pl*
excrescence [ɛks'krɛsəns] *s* Auswuchs *m*
excruciating [ɛks'kruʃɪ,etɪŋ] *adj* qualvoll
exculpate ['ɛkskʌl,pet] *tr* entschuldigen
excursion [ɛks'kʌrʒən] *s (side trip)* Abstecher *m; (short trip)* Ausflug *m*
excusable [ɛks'kjuzəbəl] *adj* entschuldbar, verzeihlich
excuse [ɛks'kjus] *s* Ausrede *f;* **give as an e.** vorgeben; **make excuses** sich ausreden ‖ [ɛks'kjuz] *tr* entschuldigen; **e. me!** entschuldigen Sie!; **you may be excused now** Sie können jetzt gehen
execute ['ɛksɪ,kjut] *tr (a condemned man)* hinrichten; *(by firing squad)* erschießen; *(perform)* durchführen, vollziehen; *(a will, a sentence)* vollstrecken; (mus) vortragen
execution [,ɛksɪ'kjuʃən] *s* Hinrichtung *f; (by firing squad)* Erschießung *f; (performance)* Durchführung *f,* Vollziehung *f;* (mus) Vortrag *m*
executioner [,ɛksɪ'kjuʃənər] *s* Scharfrichter *m*
executive [ɛg'zɛkjətɪv] *adj* vollziehend, exekutiv ‖ *s* (com) Manager *m,* leitender Angestellte *mf;* **the Executive** *(pol)* die Exekutive *f*
exec'utive commit'tee *s* Vollzugsausschuß *m,* Vorstand *m*
exec'utive or'der *s* Durchführungsverordnung *f*

executor [ɛg'zɛkjətər] *s* Vollstrecker *m*
executrix [ɛg'zɛkjətrɪks] *s* Vollstreckerin *f*
exemplary [ɛg'zɛmpləri] *adj* vorbildlich, mustergültig
exempli·fy [ɛg'zɛmplɪ,faɪ] *v (pret & pp –fied) tr (demonstrate)* an Beispielen erläutern; *(embody)* als Beispiel dienen für
exempt [ɛg'zɛmpt] *adj* **(from)** befreit (von) ‖ *tr* befreien; (mil) freistellen
exemption [ɛg'zɛmpʃən] *s* Befreiung *f;* (mil) Freistellung *f*
exercise ['ɛksər,saɪz] *s* Übung *f; (of the body)* Bewegung *f; (of power)* Ausübung *f;* (mil) Exerzieren *n;* **take e.** sich *[dat]* Bewegung machen ‖ *tr* üben; *(the body, a horse)* bewegen; *(power, influence)* ausüben; (mil) exerzieren ‖ *intr* üben; (mil) exerzieren
exert [ɛg'zʌrt] *tr* ausüben; **e. every effort** alle Kräfte rühren; **e. oneself** sich anstrengen
exertion [ɛg'zʌrʃən] *s* Anstrengung *f; (e.g., of power)* Ausübung *f*
exhalation [,ɛks·hə'leʃən] *s* Ausatmung *f; (of gases)* Gasabgabe *f*
exhale [ɛks'hel] *tr & intr* ausatmen
exhaust [ɛg'zɔst] *s* (aut) Auspuff *m* ‖ *tr* erschöpfen
exhaust'ed *adj* erschöpft
exhaust' fan' *s* Absaugventilator *m*
exhaust' gas' *s* Abgas *n*
exhaust'ing *adj* anstrengend, mühselig
exhaustion [ɛg'zɔstʃən] *s* Erschöpfung *f*
exhaustive [ɛg'zɔstɪv] *adj* erschöpfend
exhaust' pipe' *s* Auspuffrohr *n*
exhaust' valve' *s* Auspuffventil *n*
exhibit [ɛg'zɪbɪt] *s (exhibition)* Ausstellung *f; (object exhibited)* Ausstellungsstück *n;* (jur) Beleg *m* ‖ *tr* zur Schau stellen; *(wares)* ausstellen; *(e.g., courage)* zeigen
exhibition [,ɛksɪ'bɪʃən] *s* Ausstellung *f*
exhilarating [ɛg'zɪlə,retɪŋ] *adj* erheiternd
exhort [ɛg'zɔrt] *tr* ermahnen
exhume [ɛks'hjum] *tr* exhumieren
exigency ['ɛksɪdʒənsi] *s (demand, need)* Erfordnis *n; (state of urgency)* Dringlichkeit *f*
exigent ['ɛksɪdʒənt] *adj* dringlich
exile ['ɛgzaɪl] *s* Exil *n; (person)* Verbannte *mf* ‖ *tr* verbannen
exist [ɛg'zɪst] *intr* existieren; *(continue to be)* bestehen; **e. from day to day** dahinleben
existence [ɛg'zɪstəns] *s* Existenz *f,* Dasein *n;* **be in e.** bestehen; **come into e.** entstehen
existential [,ɛgzɪs'tɛnʃəl] *adj* existentiell
existentialism [,ɛgzɪs'tɛnʃə,lɪzəm] *s* Existentialismus *m*
exit ['ɛgzɪt] *s* Ausgang *m; (by car)* Ausfahrt *f;* (theat) Abgang *m* ‖ *intr* (theat) abtreten
exodus ['ɛksədəs] *s* Abwanderung *f*
exonerate [ɛg'zɑnə,ret] *tr* entlasten

exorbitant [ɛg'zɔrbɪtənt] *adj* schwindelhaft; **e. price** Wucherpreis *m*
exorcise ['ɛksɔr,saɪz] *tr* exorzieren
exotic [ɛg'zɑtɪk] *adj* exotisch
expand [ɛks'pænd] *tr* (aus)dehnen; (*enlarge*) erweitern; (*math*) entwikkeln || *intr* sich ausdehnen
expanse [ɛks'pæns] *s* Weite *f*, Fläche *f*
expansion [ɛks'pænʃən] *s* Ausdehnung *f*; (*expanded part*) Erweiterung *f*
expansive [ɛks'pænsɪv] *adj* expansiv; (fig) mitteilsam
expatiate [ɛks'peʃɪ,et] *intr* (**on**) sich verbreiten (über *acc*)
expatriate [ɛks'petrɪ·ɪt] *adj* ausgebürgert || *s* Ausgebürgerte *mf* || [ɛks-'petrɪ,et] *tr* ausbürgern
expect [ɛks'pɛkt] *tr* erwarten || *intr*—**she's expecting** (coll) sie ist in anderen Umständen
expectancy [ɛks'pɛktənsi] *s* Ewartung *f*
expectant [ɛks'pɛktənt] *adj* erwartungsvoll; (*mother*) werdende
expectation [,ɛkspɛk'teʃən] *s* Erwartung *f*
expectorate [ɛks'pɛktə,ret] *tr* & *intr* spucken
expediency [ɛks'pidɪ·ənsi] *s* Zweckmäßigkeit *f*
expedient [ɛks'pidɪ·ənt] *adj* zweckmäßig || *s* Mittel *n*, Hilfsmittel *f*
expedite ['ɛkspɪ,daɪt] *tr* beschleunigen; (*a document*) ausstellen
expedition [,ɛkspɪ'dɪʃən] *s* Expedition *f*
expedi'tionary force' [,ɛkspɪ'dɪʃə,-nɛri] *s* (mil) Expeditionsstreitkräfte *pl*
expeditious [,ɛkspɪ'dɪʃəs] *adj* schleunig
ex·pel [ɛks'pɛl] *v* (*pret* & *pp* **–pelled**; *ger* **–pelling**) *tr* (aus)treiben; (*a student*) (**from**) verweisen (von)
expend [ɛks'pɛnd] *tr* (*time, effort, etc.*) aufwenden; (*money*) ausgeben
expendable [ɛks'pɛndəbəl] *adj* entbehrlich
expenditure [ɛks'pɛndɪtʃər] *s* Aufwand *m*; (*of money*) Ausgabe *f*
expense [ɛks'pɛns] *s* Ausgabe *f*; **at s.o.'s e.** (& fig) auf j-s Kosten; **expenses** Unkosten *pl*; **go to great e.** sich in Unkosten stürzen
expense' account' *s* Spesenkonto *n*
expensive [ɛks'pɛnsɪv] *adj* kostspielig
experience [ɛks'pɪrɪ·əns] *s* Erfahrung *f*; (*an event*) Erlebnis *n*; **no previous e. necessary** Vorkenntnisse nicht erforderlich || *tr* erfahren; (*pain*) erdulden; (*loss*) erleiden
expe'rienced *adj* erfahren
experiment [ɛks'pɛrɪmənt] *s* Experiment *n*, Versuch *m* || [ɛks'pɛrɪ,mɛnt] *intr* experimentieren, Versuche anstellen
experimental [ɛks,pɛrɪ'mɛntəl] *adj* experimentell, Versuchs–
expert ['ɛkspərt] *adj* fachmännisch, erfahren; **e. advice** Gutachten *n* || *s* Fachmann *m*; (jur) Sachverständige *mf*

expertise [,ɛkspər'tiz] *s* (*opinion*) Gutachten *n*; (*skill*) Sachkenntnis *f*
expiate ['ɛkspɪ,et] *tr* sühnen, büßen
expiation [,ɛkspɪ'eʃən] *s* Sühnung *f*
expiration [,ɛkspɪ'reʃən] *s* Verfall *m*
expira'tion date' *s* Verfalltag *m*
expire [ɛks'paɪr] *tr* ausatmen || *intr* verfallen; (*die*) verscheiden
explain [ɛks'plen] *tr* erklären, erläutern; (*justify*) rechtfertigen
explanation [,ɛksplə'neʃən] *s* Erklärung *f*, Erläuterung *f*
explanatory [ɛks'plænə,tori] *adj* erklärend, erläuternd
expletive ['ɛksplɪtɪv] *s* Füllwort *n*
explicit [ɛks'plɪsɪt] *adj* ausdrücklich
explode [ɛks'plod] *tr* explodieren lassen; (*a theory*) verwerfen || *intr* explodieren; (*said of a grenade*) krepieren; (**with**) platzen (vor *dat*)
exploit ['ɛksplɔɪt] *s* Heldentat *f*, Großtat *f* || [ɛks'plɔɪt] *tr* ausnutzen; (pej) ausbeuten; (min) abbauen
exploitation [,ɛksplɔɪ'teʃən] *s* Ausnutzung *f*; (pej) Ausbeutung *f*; (min) Abbau *m*
exploration [,ɛksplə'reʃən] *s* Erforschung *f*
explore [ɛks'plor] *tr* erforschen
explorer [ɛks'plorər] *s* Forscher –in *mf*
explosion [ɛks'ploʒən] *s* Explosion *f*
explosive [ɛks'plosɪv] *adj* explosiv, Spreng– || *s* (*explosive substance*) Sprengstoff *m*; (*device*) Sprengkörper *m*
explo'sive charge' *s* Sprengladung *f*
exponent [ɛks'ponənt] *s* Exponent *m*
export ['ɛksport] *adj* Ausfuhr– || *s* Ausfuhr *m*, Export *m*; **exports** Ausfuhrgüter *pl* || [ɛks'port] *tr* ausführen
exportation [,ɛkspor'teʃən] *s* Ausfuhr *m*
exporter ['ɛksportər], [ɛks'portər] *s* Ausfuhrhändler –in *mf*, Exporteur –in *mf*
expose [ɛks'poz] *tr* (*to danger, ridicule, sun*) aussetzen; (*bare*) entblößen; (*a person*) (**as**) bloßstellen (als), entlarven (als); (phot) belichten
exposé [,ɛkspo'ze] *s* Enthüllung *f*
exposition [,ɛkspə'zɪʃən] *s* Ausstellung *f*; (rhet) Exposition *f*
expostulate [ɛks'pastʃə,let] *intr* protestieren; **e. with s.o. about** j–m ernste Vorhaltungen machen über (*acc*)
exposure [ɛks'poʒər] *s* (*of a child*) Aussetzung *f*; (*laying bare*) Entblößung *f*; (*unmasking*) Entlarvung *f*; (*of a building*) Lage *f*; (phot) Belichtung *f*
expo'sure me'ter *s* Belichtungsmesser *m*
expound [ɛks'paund] *tr* erklären
express [ɛks'prɛs] *adj* ausdrücklich || *s* (rr) Expreß *m*; **by e.** als Eilgut || *tr* ausdrücken; (*feelings*) zeigen; **e. oneself** sich äußern
express' com'pany *s* Paketpostgesellschaft *f*
expression [ɛks'prɛʃən] *s* Ausdruck *m*

expressive [ɛks'prɛsɪv] *adj* ausdrucksvoll
express' train' *s* Expreßzug *m*
express'way' *s* Schnellverkehrsstraße *f*
expropriate [ɛks'proprɪ,et] *tr* enteignen
expulsion [ɛks'pʌlʃən] *s* Austreibung *f*; (*from school or a game*) Verweisung *f*
expunge [ɛks'pʌndʒ] *tr* ausstreichen
expurgate ['ɛkspər,get] *tr* säubern
exquisite ['ɛkskwɪzɪt], [ɛks'kwɪzɪt] *adj* exquisit, vorzüglich
ex-service-man [,ɛks'sʌrvɪs,mæn] *s* (**-men'**) ehemaliger Soldat *m*
extant ['ɛkstənt] *adj* noch bestehend
extemporaneous [ɛks,tɛmpə'renɪ-əs] *adj* aus dem Stegreif, unvorbereitet
extempore [ɛks'tɛmpəri] *adj* unvorbereitet || *adv* aus dem Stegreif
extemporize [ɛks'tɛmpə,raɪz] *tr & intr* extemporieren
extend [ɛks'tɛnd] *tr* (*expand*) ausdehnen; (*a line*) fortführen; (*time*) verlängern; (*congratulations, invitation*) aussprechen; (*one's hand*) ausstrecken; (*a building*) ausbauen || *intr* (**to**) sich erstrecken (bis); **e. beyond** hinausgehen über (*acc*)
extension [ɛks'tɛnʃən] *s* Ausdehnung *f*; (*of time, credit*) Verlängerung *f*; (archit) Anbau *m*; (telp) Nebenanschluß *m*
exten'sion cord' *s* Verlängerungsschnur *f*
exten'sion lad'der *s* Ausziehleiter *f*
exten'sion ta'ble *s* Ausziehtisch *m*
extensive [ɛks'tɛnsɪv] *adj* umfassend
extent [ɛks'tɛnt] *s* Umfang *m*, Ausmaß *n*; **to some e.** eingermaßen; **to the full e.** in vollem Umfang; **to what e.** inwiefern
extenuating [ɛks'tɛnju,etɪŋ] *adj* mildernd
exterior [ɛks'tɪrɪ-ər] *adj* Außen-, äußere || *s* Äußere *n*
exterminate [ɛks'tʌrmɪ,net] *tr* vertilgen, ausrotten
extermination [ɛks,tʌrmɪ'neʃən] *s* Vertilgung *f*; (*of vermin*) Raumentwesung *f*
exterminator [ɛks'tʌrmɪ,netər] *s* Raumentweser *m*
external [ɛks'tʌrnəl] *adj* Außen-, äußerlich || **externals** *spl* Äußerlichkeiten *pl*
extinct [ɛks'tɪŋkt] *adj* (*volcano*) erloschen; (*animal*) ausgestorben; **become e.** aussterben
extinguish [ɛks'tɪŋgwɪʃ] *tr* auslöschen; **be extinguished** erlöschen
extinguisher [ɛks'tɪŋgwɪʃər] *s* Löschgerät *n*
extirpate ['ɛkstər,pet] *tr* ausrotten
ex-tol [ɛks'tol] *v* (*pret & pp* **-tolled;** *ger* **-tolling**) *tr* erheben, lobpreisen
extort [ɛks'tort] *tr* erpressen
extortion [ɛks'torʃən] *s* Erpressung *f*
extortionate [ɛks'torʃənɪt] *adj* überhöht
extra ['ɛkstrə] *adj* übrig; (*special*) Sonder-, Extra-; **meals are e.** Mahlzeiten werden zusätzlich berechnet

|| *adv* extra, besonders || *s* (cin) Statist –in *mf*; (journ) Sonderausgabe *f*; (theat) Komparse *m*; **extras** (*expenses*) Nebenausgaben *pl*; (*accessories*) Zubehör *n*
extract ['ɛkstrækt] *s* Extrakt *m*, Auszug *m*; (*excerpt*) Ausschnitt *m* || [ɛks'trækt] *tr* extrahieren, ausziehen; (dent, math) ziehen
extraction [ɛks'trækʃən] *s* (*lineage*) Abstammung *f*; (dent) Zahnziehen *n*; (min) Gewinnung *f*
extracurricular [,ɛkstrəkə'rɪkjələr] *adj* außerplanmäßig
extradite ['ɛkstrə,daɪt] *tr* ausliefern
extradition [,ɛkstrə'dɪʃən] *s* Auslieferung *f*
ex'tra in'come *s* Nebeneinkünfte *pl*
ex'tra-mar'ital *adj* außerehelich
extramural [,ɛkstrə'mjurəl] *adj* außerhalb der Schule stattfindend
extraneous [ɛks'trenɪ-əs] *adj* unwesentlich
extraordinary [,ɛks'trordɪ,nɛri] *adj* außerordentlich
ex'tra pay' *s* Zulage *f*
extrapolate [ɛks'træpə,let] *tr & intr* extrapolieren
extrasensory [,ɛkstrə'sɛnsəri] *adj* übersinnlich
extravagance [ɛks'trævəgəns] *s* Verschwendung *f*
extravagant [ɛks'trævəgənt] *adj* verschwenderisch, extravagant; (*idea, plan*) überspannt
extreme [ɛks'trim] *adj* äußerst; (*radical*) extrem; (*old age*) höchst; (*necessity*) dringend || *s* Äußerste *n;* **at the other e.** am entgegengesetzten Ende; **carry to extremes** auf die Spitze treiben; **in the e.** äußerst
extremely [ɛks'trimli] *adj* äußerst
extreme' unc'tion *s* die Letzte Ölung
extremist [ɛks'trimɪst] *s* Extremist –in *mf*
extremity [ɛks'trɛmɪti] *s* Äußerste *n*, äußerstes Ende *n;* **be reduced to extremities** aus dem letzten Loch pfeifen; **extremities** (*hands and feet*) Extremitäten *pl*
extricate ['ɛkstrɪ,ket] *tr* befreien
extrinsic [ɛks'trɪnsɪk] *adj* äußerlich
extrovert ['ɛkstrə,vʌrt] *s* Extravertierte *mf*
extrude [ɛks'trud] *tr* ausstoßen
exuberant [ɛg'z(j)ubərənt] *adj* (*luxuriant*) üppig; (*lavish*) überschwenglich
exude [ɛg'zud] *tr* ausschwitzen; (fig) ausstrahlen
exult [ɛg'zʌlt] *intr* jauchzen
exultant [ɛg'zʌltənt] *adj* jauchzend
eye [aɪ] *s* Auge *n;* (*of a needle*) Öhr *n;* **an eye for an eye** Auge um Auge; **be all eyes** große Augen machen; **by eye** nach dem Augenmaß; **close one's eyes to** die Augen schließen vor (*dat*); **have an eye for** Sinn haben für; **have good eyes** gut sehen; **in my eyes** nach meiner Ansicht; **in the eyes of the law** vom Standpunkt des Gesetzes aus; **keep a close eye on** s.o. j–m auf die Finger sehen; **keep an eye on s.th.** ein wachsames Auge

auf etw [*acc*] haben; **keep one's eyes peeled** scharf aufpassen; **lay eyes on** zu Gesicht bekommen; **makes eyes at** verliebte Blicke zuwerfen (*dat*); **see eye to eye with** völlig übereinstimmen mit; **with an eye to** mit Rücksicht auf (*acc*) ‖ *v* (*pret* & *pp* **eyed;** *ger* **eying** & **eyeing**) *tr* mustern, schielen nach

eye'ball' *s* Augapfel *m*

eye'brow' *s* Augenbraue *f*

eye'brow pen'cil *s* Augenbrauenstift *m*

eye' cat'cher *s* Blickfang *m*

eye'cup' *s* Augenspülglas *n*

eye' drops' *spl* Augentropfen *pl*

eyeful ['aɪful] *s*—**get an e.** etw Hübsches sehen

eye'glass' *s* Augenglas *n;* **eyeglasses** Brille *f*

eye'lash' *s* Wimper *f*

eyelet ['aɪlɪt] *s* Öse *f*

eye'lid' *s* Lid *n,* Augenlid *n*

eye'o'pener *s* (*surprise*) Überraschung *f;* (*liquor*) Schnäpschen *n*

eye'piece' *s* Okular *n*

eye'shade' *s* Augenschirm *m*

eye' shad'ow *s* Lidschatten *m*

eye'shot' *s*—**within e.** in Sehweite

eye'sight' *s* Augenlicht *n,* Sehkraft *f;* (*range*) Sehweite *f;* **have bad (or good) e.** schlechte (or gute) Augen haben

eye' sock'et *s* Augenhöhle *f*

eye'sore' *s* (fig) Dorn *m* im Auge

eye'strain' *s* Überanstrengung *f* der Augen

eye'tooth' *s* (–**teeth**) Augenzahn *m;* **cut one's eyeteeth** (fig) erfahrener werden

eye'wash' *s* Augenwasser *n;* (sl) Schwindel *m*

eye'wit'ness *s* Augenzeuge *m,* Augenzeugin *f*

F

F, f [ɛf] *s* sechster Buchstabe des englischen Alphabets; (mus) F *n;* **F flat** Fes *n;* **F sharp** Fis *n*

fable ['febəl] *s* Fabel *f,* Märchen *n*

fabric ['fæbrɪk] *s* Gewebe *n;* (*cloth*) Stoff *m;* (fig) Gefüge *n*

fabricate ['fæbrɪ,ket] *tr* herstellen; (*lies*) erfinden

fabrication [,fæbrɪ'keʃən] *s* Herstellung *f;* (fig) Erfindung *f*

fabulous ['fæbjələs] *adj* fabelhaft

façade [fə'sɑd] *s* Fassade *f*

face [fes] *s* Gesicht *n;* (*dial*) Zifferblatt *n;* (tex) rechte Seite *f;* (typ) Satzspiegel *m;* **f. to f.** with Auge in Auge mit; **in the f. of** angesichts (*genit*); **lose f.** sich blamieren; **make faces at s.o.** j–m Gesichter schneiden; **on the f. of it** augenscheinlich; **save f.** das Gesicht wahren; **show one's f.** sich blicken lassen ‖ *tr* (& fig) ins Auge sehen (*dat*); (*said of a building*) liegen nach; (*e.g., with brick*) verkleiden; **be faced with** stehen vor (*dat*); **facing** gegenüber (*dat*); **have to f. the music** die Suppe löffeln müssen ‖ *intr* (*in some direction*) liegen; **about f.!** (mil) kehrt!; **he faced up to it like a man** er stellte seinen Mann

face' card' *s* Bildkarte *f,* Figur *f*

face' cream' *s* Gesichtskrem *f*

face' lift'ing *s* Gesichtsstraffung *f;* (*of a building*) Schönheitsreparatur *f*

face' pow'der *s* Gesichtspuder *m*

facet ['fæsɪt] *s* Facette *f;* (fig) Aspekt *m*

facetious [fə'siʃəs] *adj* scherzhaft

face' val'ue *s* Nennwert *m;* **take at f.** (fig) für bare Münze nehmen

facial ['feʃəl] *adj* Gesichts–; **f. expression** Miene *f* ‖ *s* Gesichtspflege *f*

facilitate [fə'sɪlɪ,tet] *tr* erleichtern

facility [fə'sɪlɪti] *s* (*ease*) Leichtigkeit *f;* (*skill*) Geschicklichkeit *f;* **facilities** Einrichtungen *pl*

fac'ing *s* (archit) Verkleidung *f;* (sew) Besatz *m*

facsimile [fæk'sɪmɪli] *s* Faksimile *n*

fact [fækt] *s* Tatsache *f;* **apart from the f. that** abgesehen davon, daß; **facts of the case** Tatbestand *m;* **in f.** tatsächlich; **it is a f. that** es steht fest, daß

fact'-find'ing *adj* Untersuchungs–

faction ['fækʃən] *s* Clique *f*

factional ['fækʃənəl] *adj* klüngelhaft

factor ['fæktər] *s* (& math) Faktor *m*

factory ['fæktəri] *s* Fabrik *f*

factual ['fæktʃʊ·əl] *adj* sachlich

faculty ['fækəlti] *s* Vermögen *n;* (educ) Lehrkörper *m*

fad [fæd] *s* Mode *f;* **latest fad** letzter Schrei *m*

fade [fed] *tr* verblassen lassen; **f. in** einblenden; **f. out** ausblenden ‖ *intr* (*said of colors, memories*) verblassen; (*said of cloth, wallpaper, etc.*) verschießen; (*said of flowers*) verwelken; **f. away** (*said of sounds*) abklingen; **f. in** (cin, rad, telv) einblenden; **f. out** (cin, rad, telv) ausblenden

fade'-in' *s* (cin, rad, telv) Einblenden *n*

fade'-out' *s* (cin, rad, telv) Ausblenden *n*

fag [fæg] *s* (*cigarette*) (sl) Glimmstengel *m;* (*homosexual*) (sl) Schwuler *m* ‖ *v* (*pret* & *pp* **fagged;** *ger* **fagging**) *tr*—**fag out** (sl) auspumpen

fagged *adj* (sl) erschöpft

fagot ['fægət] *s* Reisigbündel *n*

fail [fel] *s*—**without f.** ganz bestimmt ‖ *tr* (*an examination*) durchfallen bei; (*a student*) durchfallen lassen; (*friends*) im Stich lassen; (*a father*) enttäuschen; **failing this** widrigenfalls; **I f. to see** ich kann nicht einsehen; **words f. me** mir fehlen die

Worte ‖ *intr* (*said of a person or device*) versagen; (*said of a project, attempt*) fehlschlagen; (*said of crops*) schlecht ausfallen; (*said of strength*) abnehmen; (*said of health*) sich verschlechtern; (*com*) in Konkurs geraten
failure ['feljər] *s* Versagen *n;* (*person*) Versager –in *mf;* (*lack of success, unsuccessful venture*) Mißerfolg *m;* (*omission*) Versäumnis *n;* (*deterioration*) Schwäche *f;* (*educ*) ungenügende Zensur *f;* (*com*) Konkurs *m*
faint [fent] *adj* schwach; (*slight*) leise; **feel f.** sich schwach fühlen ‖ *s* Ohnmacht *f* ‖ *intr* ohnmächtig werden
faint'-heart'ed *adj* kleinmütig
faint'ing spell' *s* Ohnmachtsanfall *m*
fair [fɛr] *adj* (*just*) gerecht, fair; (*blond*) blond; (*complexion*) hell; (*weather*) heiter; (*chance, knowledge*) mittelmäßig; (*warning*) rechtzeitig; **f. to middling** gut bis mäßig ‖ *s* Jahrmarkt *m,* Messe *f*
fair' game' *s* (& fig) Freiwild *n*
fair'ground' *s* Jahrmarktplatz *m*
fairly ['fɛrli] *adv* ziemlich
fair'-mind'ed *adj* unparteiisch
fairness ['fɛrnɪs] *s* Gerechtigkeit *f;* **in f. to s.o.** um j–m Gerechtigkeit widerfahren zu lassen
fair' play' *s* fair Play *n*
fair' sex', the *s* das schöne Geschlecht
fair'way' *s* (golf) Spielbahn *f;* (naut) Fahrwasser *n*
fair'-weath'er *adj* (*friend*) unzuverlässig
fairy ['fɛri] *adj* Feen– ‖ *s* Fee *f;* (sl) Schwule *mf*
fair'y god'mother *s* gute Fee *f*
fair'yland' *s* Märchenland *n*
fair'ytale' *s* (& fig) Märchen *n*
faith [feθ] *s* Glaube(n) *m;* (*in*) Vertrauen *n* (auf *acc* or zu); **on the f. of** im Vertrauen auf (*acc*); **put one's f. in** Glauben schenken (*dat*)
faithful ['feθfəl] *adj* (to) (ge)treu (*dat*); (*exact*) genau, wahrheitsgemäß ‖ **the f.** *spl* die Gläubigen
faith' heal'er *s* Gesundbeter –in *mf*
faithless ['feθlɪs] *adj* treulos
fake [fek] *adj* verfälscht ‖ *s* Fälschung *f;* (*person*) Simulant –in *mf* ‖ *tr* vortäuschen, simulieren; (*forge*) fälschen
faker ['fekər] *s* Simulant –in *mf*
falcon ['fɔ(l)kən] *s* Falke *m*
falconer ['fɔ(l)kənər] *s* Falkner *m*
fall [fɔl] *adj* Herbst– ‖ *s* Fall *m;* (*of prices, of a government*) Sturz *m;* (*moral*) Verfall *m;* (*of water*) Fall *m;* (*autumn*) Herbst *m;* (Bib) Sündenfall *m;* ‖ *v* (*pret* **fell** [fɛl]; *pp* **fallen** ['fɔlən] *intr* (*said of a person, object, rain, snow, holiday, prices, temperature*) fallen; (*said of a town*) gestürzt werden; **f. apart** auseinanderfallen; **f. away** wegfallen; **f. back** zurückfallen; (mil) sich zurückziehen; **f. back on** zurückgreifen auf (*acc*); **f. behind** (in) zurückbleiben (mit); **f. below** unterschreiten; **f. down** umfallen; (*said only of persons*) hinfallen; **f. down on the job** versagen; **f. due** fällig werden; **f. flat** (coll) flachfallen; **f. for** reinfallen auf (*acc*); **f. from** abfallen von; **f.. from grace** in Ungnade fallen; **f. in** (*said of a roof*) einstürzen; (mil) antreten; **f. in love with** sich verlieben in (*acc*); **f. in step** Tritt fassen; **f. into** (*e.g., a hole*) hereinfallen in (*acc*); (*e.g., trouble*) geraten in (*acc*); **f. into ruin** zerfallen; **f. in with s.o.** j–n zufällig treffen; **f. off** abfallen; (com) zurückgehen; **f. out** (*said of hair*) ausfallen; **f. out with** sich verfeinden mit; **f. over** umfallen; **f. short** knapp werden; (arti) kurz gehen; **f. short of** zurückbleiben hinter (*dat*); **f. through** durchfallen; **f. to s.o.'s share** j–m zufallen; **f. under s.o.'s influence** unter j–s Einfluß geraten; **f. upon** herfallen über (*acc*)
fallacious [fə'lefəs] *adj* trügerisch
fallacy ['fæləsi] *s* Trugschluß *m,* Fehlschluß *m*
fall' guy' *s* (sl) Sündenbock *m*
fallible ['fælɪbəl] *adj* fehlbar
fall'ing off' *s* Rückschritt *m*
fall'ing rocks' *spl* (public sign) Steinschlag *m*
fall'ing star' *s* Sternschnuppe *f*
fall'out' *s* radioaktiver Niederschlag *m*
fallow ['fælo] *adj* (agr) brach; **lie f.** (& fig) brachliegen
false [fɔls] *adj* falsch, Miß–; (*start, step*) Fehl–; (*bottom*) doppelt; (*ceiling*) Zwischen–
false' alarm' *s* blinder Alarm *m;* (fig) Schreckschuß *m*
false' face' *s* Maske *f*
false' front' *s* (fig) (coll) Mache *f*
false'-heart'ed *adj* treulos
false'hood' *s* Unwahrheit *f*
false' pretens'es *spl* Hochstapelei *f*
false' teeth' *spl* (künstliches) Gebiß *n*
falset·to [fɔl'seto] *s* (–tos) Falset *n*
falsi·fy ['fɔlsɪ,faɪ] *v* (*pret & pp* –fied) *tr* (ver)fälschen
falsity ['fɔlsɪti] *s* Falschheit *f*
falter ['fɔltər] *intr* schwanken; (*in speech*) stocken
fame [fem] *s* Ruf, *m,* Ruhm *m*
famed *adj* (for) berühmt (wegen, durch)
familiar [fə'mɪljər] *adj* bekannt; (*expression*) geläufig; (*e.g., sight*) gewohnt; (*close*) vertraut; **become f. with** sich bekannt machen mit
familiarity [fə,mɪli'ærɪti] *s* Vertrautheit *f;* (*closeness*) Vertraulichkeit *f*
familiarize [fə'mɪljə,raɪz] *tr* bekannt machen
family ['fæm(ɪ)li] *adj* Familien–; **in a f. way** in anderen Umständen ‖ *s* Familie *f*
fam'ily doc'tor *s* Hausarzt *m*
fam'ily man' *s* häuslicher Mann *m*
fam'ily name' *s* Familienname *m*
fam'ily tree' *s* Stammbaum *m*
famine ['fæmɪn] *s* Hungersnot *f*
famish ['fæmɪʃ] *tr* (ver)hungern lassen ‖ *intr* verhungern
fam'ished *adj* ausgehungert

famous ['feməs] *adj* **(for)** berühmt (wegen, durch)

fan [fæn] *s* Fächer *m*, Wedel *m; (electric)* Ventilator *m;* (sl) Fan *m* ‖ *v (pret & pp* **fanned;** *ger* **fanning)** *tr* fächeln; *(a fire)* anfachen; *(passions)* entfachen ‖ *intr*—**fan out** *(said of roads)* fächerförmig auseinandergehen; (mil) ausschwärmen

fanatic [fə'nætɪk] *adj* fanatisch ‖ *s* Fanatiker –in *mf*

fanatical [fə'nætɪkəl] *adj* fanatisch

fanaticism [fə'nætɪ‚sɪzəm] *s* Fanatismus *m*

fan′ belt′ *s* (aut) Keilriemen *m*

fan′cied *adj* eingebildet

fancier ['fænsɪ‚ər] *s* Liebhaber –in *mf*

fanciful ['fænsɪfəl] *adj* phantastisch

fan·cy ['fænsi] *adj* (extra)fein; *(e.g., dress)* Luxus–; (sport) Kunst–; **f. price** Phantasiepreis *m* ‖ *s* Phantasie *f;* **passing f.** vorübergehender Spleen *m;* **take a f. to** Gefallen finden an *(dat)* ‖ *v (pret & pp* **–cied)** *tr* sich *[dat]* vorstellen

fan′cy foods′ *spl* Feinkost *f*

fan′cy-free′ *adj* ungebunden

fan′fare′ *s* Fanfare *f; (fuss)* Tamtam *n*

fang [fæŋ] *s* Fangzahn *m; (of a snake)* Giftzahn *m*

fan′ mail′ *s* Verehrerbriefe *pl*

fantastic(al) [fæn'tæstɪk(əl)] *adj* phantastisch, toll

fantasy ['fæntəsi] *s* Phantasie *f*

far [far] *adj (& fig)* weit; **at the far end** am anderen Ende; **far cry from** etw ganz anderes als; **far side** andere Seite *f;* **in the far future** in der fernen Zukunft ‖ *adv* weit; **as far as** soweit; *(up to)* bis zu, bis an *(acc);* **as far as I am concerned** was mich anbelangt; **as far as I know** soviel ich weiß; **as far as that goes** was das betrifft; **by far** weitaus, bei weitem; **far and away** weitaus; **far away** weit entfernt; **far below** tief unten; **far better** weit besser; **far from it!** weit gefehlt!; **far from ready** noch lange nicht fertig; **far into the night** tief in die Nacht hinein; **far out** (sl) ausgefallen; **from far** von weitem; *(from a distant place)* von weit her; **go far** es weit bringen; **go far towards** *(ger)* viel beitragen zu *(inf);* **go too far** das Maß überschreiten; **not far from** unweit von; **so far** soweit, bisher

far′away′ *adj* weit entfernt; (fig) träumerisch

farce [fars] *s* Possenspiel *n*, Farce *f;* (fig) Posse *f*, Schwank *m*

farcical ['farsɪkəl] *adj* possenhaft

fare [fer] *s (travel price)* Fahrpreis *m; (money for travel)* Fahrgeld *n; (passenger)* Fahrgast *m; (food)* Kost *f* ‖ *intr* (er)gehen; **how did you f., well or ill?** wie ist es Ihnen ergangen, gut oder schlecht?

Far′ East′, the *s* der Ferne Osten

Far′ East′ern *adj* fernöstlich

fare′well′ *s* Valet *n*, Lebewohl *n;* **bid s.o. f.** j–m Lebewohl sagen ‖ *interj* lebe wohl!; lebt wohl!

farewell′ din′ner *s* Abschiedsschmaus *m*

farewell′ par′ty *s* Abschiedsfeier *f*

far-fetched ['far'fet/t] *adj* gesucht

far-flung ['far'flʌŋ] *adj* weit ausgedehnt

farina [fə'rinə] *s* Grießmehl *n*

farm [farm] *adj* landwirtschaftlich ‖ *s* Farm *f*, Bauernhof *m* ‖ *tr* bebauen, bewirtschaften ‖ *intr* Landwirtschaft betreiben, Bauer sein

farm′ hand′ *s* Landarbeiter *m*

farm′house′ *s* Bauernhaus *n*

farm′ing *adj* landwirtschaftlich ‖ *s* Landwirtschaft *f*

farm′land′ *s* Ackerland *n*

farm′ machin′ery *s* Landmaschinen *pl*

farm′yard′ *s* Bauernhof *m*

far′-off′ *adj* fernliegend

far′-reach′ing *adj* weitreichend; *(decision)* folgenschwer

far′-sight′ed *adj* weitsichtig; (fig) weitblickend

farther ['farðər] *adj & adv* weiter

farthest ['farðɪst] *adj* weiteste ‖ *adv* am weitesten

farthing ['farðɪŋ] *s*—**not worth a f.** keinen Pfifferling wert

fascinate ['fæsɪ‚net] *tr* faszinieren

fas′cinating *adj* faszinierend

fascination [‚fæsɪ'ne/ən] *s* Faszination *f*

fascism ['fæ/ɪzəm] *s* Faschismus *m*

fascist ['fæ/ɪst] *s* Faschist –in *mf*

fashion ['fæ/ən] *s* Mode *f; (manner)* Art *f*, Weise *f;* **after a f.** in gewisser Weise; **in f.** in Mode; **out of f.** aus der Mode ‖ *tr* gestalten, bilden

fashionable ['fæ/ənəbəl] *adj (modern)* modisch; *(elegant)* elegant

fash′ion magazine′ *s* Modenzeitschrift *f*

fash′ion plate′ *s* Modedame *f*

fash′ion show′ *s* Mode(n)schau *f*

fast [fæst] *adj* schnell; *(dye)* dauerhaft; *(company)* flott; *(life)* locker; (phot) lichtstark; **be f.** *(said of a clock)* vorgehen; **f. train** Schnellzug *m;* **pull a f. one on s.o.** (coll) j–m ein Schnippchen schlagen ‖ *adv* schnell; *(firmly)* fest; **as f. as possible** schnellstens; **be f. asleep** im tiefen Schlaf liegen; **hold f.** festhalten; **not so f.!** nicht so stürmisch! ‖ *s* Fasten *n* ‖ *intr* fasten

fast′ day′ *s* Fasttag *m*

fasten ['fæsən] *tr* festmachen, sichern; *(a buckle)* schnallen; **(to)** befestigen (an *dat);* **f. one's seat belt** sich anschnallen; **f. the blame on** die Schuld zuschieben *(dat)* ‖ *intr*—**f. upon** sich heften an *(acc)*

fastener ['fæsənər] *s* Verschluß *m*

fastidious [fæs'tɪdɪ‚əs] *adj* wählerisch

fast′ing *s* Fasten *n*

fat [fæt] *adj* **(fatter; fattest)** fett; *(plump)* dick, fett; *(profits)* reich ‖ *s* Fett *n;* **chew the fat** (sl) schwatzen

fatal ['fetəl] *adj* tödlich; *(mistake)* verhängnisvoll; **f. to** verhängnisvoll für

fatalism ['fetə‚lɪzəm] *s* Fatalismus *m*

fatalist ['fetəlɪst] *s* Fatalist –in *mf*

fatality [fə'tælɪti] *s* Todesfall *m;* (*accident victim*) Todesopfer *n;* (*disaster*) Unglück *n*

fat′ cat′ *s* (sl) Geldgeber –in *mf*

fate [fet] *s* Schicksal *n,* Verhängnis *n;* **the Fates** die Parzen *pl*

fated ['fetɪd] *adj* vom Schicksal bestimmt

fateful ['fetfəl] *adj* verhängnisvoll

fat′head′ *s* (coll) dummes Luder *n*

father ['faðər] *s* Vater *m;* (eccl) Pater *m* || *tr* (*beget*) erzeugen; (*originate*) hervorbringen

fa′therhood′ *s* Vaterschaft *f*

fa′ther-in-law′ *s* (**fathers-in-law**) Schwiegervater *m*

fa′therland′ *s* Vaterland *n*

fatherless ['faðərlɪs] *adj* vaterlos

fatherly ['faðərli] *adj* väterlich

Fa′ther's Day′ *s* Vatertag *m*

fathom ['fæðəm] *s* Klafter *f* || *tr* sondieren; (fig) ergründen

fathomless ['fæðəmlɪs] *adj* unergründlich

fatigue [fə'tig] *s* Ermattung *f;* (mil) Arbeitsdienst *m;* **fatigues** (mil) Arbeitsanzug *m* || *tr* abmatten

fat·so ['fætso] *s* (**-sos** & **-soes**) (coll) Fettkloß *m*

fatten ['fætən] *tr* mästen || *intr*—**f. up** (coll) sich mästen

fatty ['fæti] *adj* fettig, fett; **f. tissue** Fettgewebe *n* || *s* (coll) Dicke *mf*

fatuous ['fætʃʊ·əs] *adj* albern

faucet ['fɔsɪt] *s* Wasserhahn *m*

fault [fɔlt] *s* (*blame*) Schuld *f;* (*misdeed*) Vergehen *n,* Fehler *m;* (*defect*) Defekt *m;* (geol) Verwerfung *f;* (tennis) Fehlball *m;* **at f. schuld;** **find f. with** etw zu tadeln finden an (*dat*); **to a f.** allzusehr || *intr* (geol) sich verwerfen

fault′find′er *s* Krittler –in *mf*

fault′find′ing *adj* tadelsüchtig || *s* Krittelei *f*

faultless ['fɔltlɪs] *adj* fehlerfrei

faulty ['fɔlti] *adj* fehlerhaft

faun [fɔn] *s* (myth) Faun *m*

fauna ['fɔnə] *s* Fauna *f*

favor ['fevər] *s* (*kind act*) Gefallen *m;* (*good will*) Gunst *f;* **in f. of** zugunsten (*genit*), für; **in s.o.'s f.** zu j–s Gunsten; **lose f. with s.o.** sich [*dat*] j–s Gunst verwirken; **speak in f. of s.th.** für etw aussprechen || *tr* begünstigen; (*prefer*) bevorzugen; (*a sore limb*) schonen

favorable ['fevərəbəl] *adj* günstig; (*criticism*) positiv; (*report*) beifällig

favorite ['fevərɪt] *adj* Lieblings- || *s* Liebling *m;* (sport) Favorit –in *mf*

favoritism ['fevərɪ,tɪzəm] *s* Günstlingswirtschaft *f*

fawn [fɔn] *s* Rehkalb *n* || *intr*—**f. on** schmeicheln (*dat*)

fawn′ing *adj* schmeichlerisch

faze [fez] *tr* (coll) auf die Palme bringen

FBI [,ɛf,bi'aɪ] *s* (**Federal Bureau of Investigation**) Bundessicherheitspolizei *f*

fear [fɪr] *s* (*of*) Furcht *f* (vor *dat*), Angst *f* (vor *dat*); **for f. of** aus Angst

vor (*dat*); **for f. of** (*ger*) um nicht zu (*inf*); **stand in f. of** sich fürchten vor (*dat*) || *tr* fürchten, sich fürchten vor (*dat*); **f. the worst** das Schlimmste befürchten || *intr* sich fürchten; **f. for** besorgt sein um

fearful ['fɪrfəl] *adj* (*afraid*) furchtsam; (*terrible*) furchtbar

fearless ['fɪrlɪs] *adj* furchtlos

feasible ['fizɪbəl] *adj* durchführbar

feast [fist] *s* Fest *n;* (*sumptuous meal*) Schmaus *m* || *tr*—**f. one's eyes on** seine Augen weiden an (*dat*) || *intr* schwelgen; **f. on** sich gütlich tun an (*dat*)

feast′day′ *s* Festtag *m*

feast′ing *s* Schmauserei *f*

feat [fit] *s* Kunststück *n;* **f. of arms** Waffentat *f*

feather ['fɛðər] *s* Feder *f;* **a f. in his cap** ein Triumph für ihn || *tr* mit Federn versehen; (aer) auf Segelstellung fahren; (crew) flach drehen; **f. one's nest** sich warm betten

feath′er bed′ *s* Federbett *n*

feath′erbed′ding *s* Anstellung *f* unnötiger Arbeitskräfte

feath′erbrain′ *s* Schwachkopf *m*

feath′er dust′er *s* Staubwedel *m*

feath′eredge′ *s* feine Kante *f*

feath′erweight′ *adj* Federgewichts- || *s* (*boxer*) Federgewichtler *m*

feathery ['fɛðəri] *adj* federartig; (*light as feathers*) federleicht

feature ['fitʃər] *s* (*of the face*) Gesichtszug *m;* (*characteristic*) Merkmal *n;* **f. film** Spielfilm *m;* **main f.** Grundzug *m;* (cin) Hauptfilm *m* || *tr* als Hauptschlager herausbringen; (cin) in der Hauptrolle zeigen

fea′ture writ′er *s* Sonderberichterstatter –in *mf*

February ['fɛbru,ɛri] *s* Februar *m*

feces ['fisiz] *spl* Kot *m,* Stuhl *m*

feckless ['fɛklɪs] *adj* (*incompetent*) unfähig; (*ineffective*) unwirksam; (*without spirit*) geistlos

fecund ['fikənd] *adj* fruchtbar

federal ['fɛdərəl] *adj* Bundes-, bundesstaatlich; **f. government** Bundesregierung *f*

federate ['fɛdə,ret] *adj* verbündet || *tr* zu e–m Bund vereinigen || *intr* sich verbünden

federation [,fɛdə'reʃən] *s* Staatenbund *m*

fed′ up′ [fɛd] *adj*—**be f.** die Nase voll haben; **be f. with s.th.** etw satt haben

fee [fi] *s* Gebühr *f;* (*of a doctor*) Honorar *n*

feeble ['fibəl] *adj* schwächlich

fee′ble-mind′ed *adj* schwachsinnig

feed [fid] *s* Futter *n;* (mach) Zuführung *f* || *v* (*pret* & *pp* **fed** [fɛd]) *tr* (*animals*) füttern; (*persons*) zu Essen geben; (*in a restaurant*) verpflegen; (*e.g., a nation*) nähren; (*a fire*) unterhalten; (mach) zuführen || *intr* fressen; **f. on** sich ernähren von

feed′back′ *s* Rückwirkung *f;* (electron) Rückkoppelung *f*

feed′ bag′ *s* Futtersack *m;* **put on the f.** (sl) futtern

feeder ['fidər] s (elec) Speiseleitung f; (mach) Zubringer m
feed'er line' s (aer, rr) Zubringerlinie f
feed'ing s (of animals) Fütterung f; (& mach) Speisung f
feed' trough' s Futtertrog m
feed' wire' s (elec) Zuleitungsdraht m
feel [fil] s Gefühl n; **get the f. of** sich gewöhnen an (acc) || v (pret & pp **felt** [fɛlt]) tr fühlen; (a pain) spüren; **f. one's way** sich vortasten; (fig) sondieren; **f. s.o. out** bei j—m vorfühlen || intr (sick, tired, well) sich fühlen; **f. about for** herumtasten nach; **f. for s.o.** mit j—m fühlen; **f. like** (ger) Lust haben zu (inf); **f. up to** sich gewachsen fühlen (dat); **his head feels hot** sein Kopf fühlt sich heiß an; **how do you f. about it?** was halten Sie davon?; **I don't quite f. myself** ich fühle mich nicht ganz wohl; **I f. as if** es ist mir, als wenn; **make itself felt** sich fühlbar machen
feeler ['filər] s (ent) Fühler m; **put out feelers to** vorfühlen bei
feel'ing s Gefühl n; **bad f.** Verstimmung f; **good f.** Wohlwollen n; **have a f. for** Sinn haben für; **have a f. that** das Gefühl haben, daß; **with f.** gefühlsvoll
feign [fen] tr vortäuschen; **f. death** sich totstellen
feint [fent] s Finte f, Scheinangriff m
feldspar ['fɛld,spɑr] s Feldspat m
feline ['filaɪn] adj katzenartig
fell [fɛl] adj grausam || tr fällen
fellow ['fɛlo] s (coll) Kerl m; (of a society) Mitglied n
fel'low be'ing s Mitmensch m
fel'low citizen s Mitbürger –in mf
fel'low coun'tryman s Landsmann m
fel'low crea'ture s Mitgeschöpf n
fel'lowman' s (-men') Mitmensch m
fel'low mem'ber s Mitglied n
fel'lowship' s Kameradschaft f; (educ) Stipendium n
fel'low stu'dent s Kommilitone m
fel'low trav'eler s Mitreisende mf; (pol) Mitläufer –in mf
felon ['fɛlən] s Schwerverbrecher –in mf
felony ['fɛləni] s Schwerverbrechen n
felt [fɛlt] adj Filz– || s Filz m
felt' pen' s Filzschreiber m, Faserstift m
female ['fimel] adj weiblich || s (of animals) Weibchen n; (pej) Weibsbild n
feminine ['fɛmɪnɪn] adj weiblich
feminism ['fɛmɪ,nɪzəm] s Feminismus m
fen [fɛn] s Bruch m & n
fence [fɛns] s Zaun m; (of stolen goods) Hehler m; **on the f.** (fig) unentschlossen || tr—**f. in** einzäunen; **f. off** abzäunen || intr (sport) fechten
fence' post' s Zaunpfahl m
fenc'ing s Fechten n
fend [fɛnd] tr—**f. off** abwehren || intr —**f. for oneself** für sich selbst sorgen
fender ['fɛndər] s (aut) Kotflügel m
fennel ['fɛnəl] s Fenchel m
ferment ['fɑrmɛnt] s Gärmittel n; (fig) Unruhe f || [fər'mɛnt] tr in Gärung bringen || intr gären
fermentation [,fɑrmən'teʃən] s Gärung f
fern [fɑrn] s Farn m
ferocious [fə'roʃəs] adj wild
ferocity [fə'rɑsɪti] s Wildheit f
ferret ['fɛrɪt] s Frettchen n || tr—**f. out** aufspüren
Fer'ris wheel' ['fɛrɪs] s Riesenrad n
ferrule ['fɛrul], ['fɛrəl] s Stockzwinge f, Zwinge f
fer·ry ['fɛri] s Fähre f || v (pret & pp –ried) tr übersetzen
fer'ryboat' s Fährboot n
fer'ry·man' s (-men') Fährmann m
fertile ['fɑrtɪl] adj fruchtbar
fertility [fər'tɪlɪti] s Fruchtbarkeit f
fertilization [,fɑrtɪlɪ'zeʃən] s Befruchtung f; (of soil) Dünung f
fertilize ['fɑrtɪ,laɪz] tr (a field) düngen; (an egg) befruchten
fertilizer ['fɑrtɪ,laɪzər] s Kunstdünger m
fervent ['fɑrvənt] adj inbrünstig
fervid ['fɑrvɪd] adj brennend
fervor ['fɑrvər] s Inbrunst f
fester ['fɛstər] intr schwären, eitern; (fig) nagen
festival ['fɛstɪvəl] adj festlich, Fest– || s Fest n; (mus, theat) Festspiele pl
festive ['fɛstɪv] adj festlich
festivity [fɛs'tɪvɪti] s Feierlichkeit f
festoon [fɛs'tun] s Girlande f || tr mit Girlanden schmücken
fetch [fɛtʃ] tr holen, abholen
fetch'ing adj entzückend
fete [fet] s Fest n
fetid ['fɛtɪd], ['fitɪd] adj stinkend
fetish ['fɛtɪʃ], ['fitɪʃ] s Fetisch m
fetlock ['fɛtlɑk] s Köte f; (tuft of hair) Kötenzopf m
fetter ['fɛtər] s Fessel f || tr fesseln
fettle ['fɛtəl] s—**in fine f.** in Form
fetus ['fitəs] s Leibesfrucht f
feud [fjud] s Fehde f
feudal ['fjudəl] adj feudal
feudalism ['fjudə,lɪzəm] s Feudalismus m
fever ['fivər] s Fieber n
feverish ['fivərɪʃ] adj fieberig; **be f.** fiebern
few [fju] adj & pron wenige; **a few** ein paar
fiancé [,fi·ɑn'se] s Verlobte m
fiancée [,fi·ɑn'se] s Verlobte f
fias·co [fi'æsko] s (-cos & -coes) Fiasko n
fib [fɪb] s Flunkerei f || v (pret & pp **fibbed;** ger **fibbing**) intr flunkern
fibber ['fɪbər] s Flunkerer –in mf
fiber ['faɪbər] s Faser f
fibrous ['faɪbrəs] adj faserig
fickle ['fɪkəl] adj wankelmütig
fickleness ['fɪkəlnɪs] s Wankelmut m
fiction ['fɪkʃən] s Dichtung f, Romanliteratur f
fictional ['fɪkʃənəl] adj romanhaft
fic'tion writ'er s Romanschriftsteller –in mf
fictitious [fɪk'tɪʃəs] adj fingiert
fiddle ['fɪdəl] s Fiedel f, Geige f || tr fiedeln; **f. away** (time) vergeuden ||

intr fiedeln; **f. with** herumfingern an (*dat*)

fiddler ['fɪdlər] *s* Fiedler –in *mf*

fid'dlestick' *s* Fiedelbogen *m* ‖ **fiddlesticks** *interj* Quatsch!

fidelity [fɪ'dɛlɪti] *s* Treue *f*

fidget ['fɪdʒɪt] *intr* zappeln; **f. with** nervös spielen mit

fidgety ['fɪdʒɪti] *adj* zappelig

fiduciary [fɪ'd(j)uʃɪ‚ɛri] *adj* treuhänderisch; (*note*) ungedeckt ‖ *s* Treuhänder –in *mf*

fief [fif] *s* (hist) Lehen *n*

field [fild] *adj* (*artillery, jacket, hospital, kitchen*) Feld– ‖ *s* Feld *n;* (*under cultivation*) Acker *m;* (*contestants collectively*) Wettbewerbsteilnehmer *pl;* (*specialty*) Gebiet *n;* (aer) Flugplatz *m;* (elec) Feld *n;* (*of a motor*) (elec) Magnetfeld *n;* (sport) Spielfeld *n*

field' am'bulance *s* Sanitätskraftwagen *m*

field' day' *s* (fig) großer Tag *m*

fielder ['fildər] *s* Feldspieler *m*

field' ex'ercise *s* Truppenübung *f*

field' glass'es *spl* Feldstecher *m*

field' hock'ey *s* Rasenhockey *n*

field'mar'shal *s* Feldmarschall *m*

field' mouse' *s* Feldmaus *f*

field' of vi'sion *s* Blickfeld *n*

field' pack' *s* (mil) Tornister *m*

field' piece' *s* Feldgeschütz *n*

field' trip' *s* Studienfahrt *f*

field' work' *s* praktische Arbeit *f*

fiend [find] *s* (*devil*) Teufel *m;* (*wicked person*) Unhold *m;* (*addict*) Süchtige *mf*

fiendish ['findɪʃ] *adj* teuflisch

fierce [fɪrs] *adj* wild, wütend; (*vehement*) heftig; (*menacing*) drohend; (*heat*) glühend

fiery ['faɪri], ['faɪ‚əri] *adj* feurig

fife [faɪf] *s* Querpfeife *f*

fifteen ['fɪf'tin] *adj & pron* fünfzehn ‖ *s* Fünfzehn *f*

fifteenth ['fɪf'tinθ] *adj & pron* fünfzehnte ‖ *s* (*fraction*) Fünfzehntel *n;* **the f.** (*in dates or a series*) der Fünfzehnte

fifth [fɪfθ] *adj & pron* fünfte ‖ *s* (*fraction*) Fünftel *n;* **the f.** (*in dates or a series*) der Fünfte *f*

fiftieth ['fɪftɪ‚ɪθ] *adj & pron* fünfzigste ‖ *s* (*fraction*) Fünfzigstel *n*

fifty ['fɪfti] *adj & pron* fünfzig ‖ *s* Fünfzig *f;* **the fifties** die fünfziger Jahre

fif'ty-fif'ty *adv* halbpart; **go f. with s.o.** mit j–m halbpart machen

fig [fɪg] *s* Feige *f;* (fig) Pfifferling *m*

fight [faɪt] *s* Kampf *m,* Gefecht *n;* (*quarrel*) Streit *m;* (*brawl*) Rauferei *f;* (box) Boxkampf *m;* **pick a f.** Zank suchen ‖ *tr* bekämpfen; (*a case*) durchkämpfen; **f. back** (*tears*) niederkämpfen; **f. it out** ausfechten; **f. one's way out** sich durchkämpfen ‖ *intr* kämpfen; (*quarrel*) streiten; (*brawl*) raufen

fighter ['faɪtər] *adj* (aer) Jagd– ‖ *s*

Kämpfer –in *mf;* (aer) Jäger *m;* (box) Boxkämpfer *m*

fight'er pi'lot *s* Jagdflieger *m*

fight'ing *s* Schlägerei *f;* (*quarreling*) Streiten *n;* (mil) Kampfhandlungen *pl*

fig' leaf' *s* Feigenblatt *n*

figment ['fɪgmənt] *s*—**f. of the imagination** Hirngespinst *n*

fig' tree' *s* Feigenbaum *m*

figurative ['fɪgjərətɪv] *adj* bildlich; (*meaning*) übertragen

figure ['fɪgjər] *s* Figur *f;* (*personage*) Persönlichkeit *f;* (*number*) Zahl *f;* **be good at figures** ein guter Rechner sein; **cut a fine** (or **poor**) **f.** e–e gute (or schlechte) Figur abgeben; **run into three figures** in die Hunderte gehen ‖ *tr* (coll) glauben, meinen; **f. out** ausknobeln ‖ *intr*—**f. large** e–e große Rolle spielen; **f. on** rechnen mit

fig'urehead' *s* Strohmann *m;* (naut) Bugfigur *f;* **a mere f.** e–e bloße Nummer

fig'ure of speech' *s* Redewendung *f*

fig'ure skat'ing *s* Kunstlauf *m*

figurine [‚fɪgjə'rin] *s* Figurine *f*

filament ['fɪləmənt] *s* Faser *f,* Faden *m;* (elec) Glühfaden *m*

filbert ['fɪlbərt] *s* Haselnuß *f*

filch [fɪltʃ] *tr* mausen

file [faɪl] *s* (*tool*) Feile *f;* (*record*) Akte *f;* (*cards*) Kartei *f;* (*row*) Reihe *f;* **put on f.** zu den Akten legen ‖ *tr* (*with a tool*) feilen; (*letters, etc.*) ablegen, abheften; (*a complaint*) erheben; (*a report*) erstatten; (*a claim*) anmelden; (*a petition*) einreichen; **f. suit** e–n Prozeß anstrengen ‖ *intr* —**f. for** sich bewerben um; **f. out** im Gänsemarsch herausmarschieren; **f. past** vorbeidefilieren (an *dat*)

file' cab'inet *s* Aktenschrank *m*

file' card' *s* Karteikarte *f*

filial ['fɪlɪ‚əl] *adj* kindlich

filibuster ['fɪlɪ‚bʌstər] *s* Obstruktion *f* ‖ *intr* Obstruktion treiben

filigree ['fɪlɪ‚gri] *s* Filigran *n*

fil'ing *s* Feilen *n;* (*of records*) Ablegen *n* von Akten; (*of a claim*) Anmeldung *f;* (*of a complaint*) Erhebung *f;* (*of a petition*) Einreichung *f;* **filings** Feilspäne *pl*

Filipi·no [‚fɪlɪ'pino] *adj* filipinisch ‖ *s* (**–nos**) Filipino *m*

fill [fɪl] *s* (*fullness*) Fülle *f;* (*land fill*) Aufschüttung *f;* **eat one's f.** sich satt essen; **I have had my f. of it** ich habe es satt ‖ *tr* füllen; (*an order*) ausführen; (*a pipe*) stopfen; (*a position*) besetzen; (dent) plombieren, füllen; **f. full** vollfüllen; **f. in** (*empty space*) ausfüllen; (*one's name*) einsetzen; (*a hole, grave*) zuwerfen; **f. it up** (aut) volltanken; **f. up** auffüllen; (*a tank*) nachfüllen; (*a bag*) anfüllen; (*a glass*) vollschenken; **f. with smoke** verräuchern ‖ *intr* sich füllen; (*said of sails*) sich blähen; **f. in for** einspringen für; **f. out** rund werden; **f. up** sich füllen

filler ['fɪlər] *s* Füller *m;* (*of a cigar*)

Einlage *f;* (journ) Lückenbüßer *m;* (paint) Grundierfirnis *m*
fillet [ˈfɪlət] *s* (*headband*) Kopfbinde *f;* (archit) Leiste *f* || [fɪˈle] *s* (culin) Filet *n* || *tr* filetieren
fillet' of beef' *s* Rinderfilet *n*
fillet' of sole' *s* Seezungenfilet *n*
fill'ing *s* (culin, dent) Füllung *f*
fill'ing sta'tion *s* Tankstelle *f*
fillip [ˈfɪlɪp] *s* Schnippchen *n;* (*on the nose*) Nasenstüber *m*
filly [ˈfɪli] *s* Stutenfüllen *n*
film [fɪlm] *s* (*thin layer*) Schicht *f;* (cin, phot) Film *m;* **f. of grease** Fettschicht *f*
film' fes'tival *s* Filmfestspiele *pl*
film' li'brary *s* Filmarchiv *n*
film' speed' *s* Filmempfindlichkeit *f*
film' star' *s* Filmstar *m*
film'strip' *s* Bildstreifen *m*
filmy [ˈfɪlmi] *adj* trüb
filter [ˈfɪltər] *s* Filter *m;* (rad) Sieb *n* || *tr* filtern; (rad) sieben
fil'tering *s* Filtrierung *f*
fil'ter pa'per *s* Filterpapier *n*
fil'ter tip' *s* Filtermundstück *n;* (coll) Filterzigarette *f*
filth [fɪlθ] *s* Schmutz *m;* (fig) Unflätigkeit *f*, Zote *f*
filthy [ˈfɪlθi] *adj* schmutzig (*talk*) unflätig; (*lucre*) schnöd(e) || *adv*—**f. rich** (sl) klotzig reich
filtrate [ˈfɪltret] *s* Filtrat *n* || *tr & intr* filtrieren
filtration [fɪlˈtreʃən] *s* Filtrierung *f*
fin [fɪn] *s* Flosse *f;* (*of a shark or whale*) Finne *f;* (*of a bomb*) Steuerschwanz *m;* (aer) Flosse *f*
final [ˈfaɪnəl] *adj* End–, Schluß–; (*definitive*) endgültig || *s* (educ) Abschlußprüfung *f;* **finals** (sport) Endrunde *f*, Endspiel *n*
finale [fɪˈnɑli] *s* Finale *n*
finalist [ˈfaɪnəlɪst] *s* Finalist –in *mf*
finality [faɪˈnælɪti] *s* Endgültigkeit *f*
finally [ˈfaɪnəli] *adv* schließlich
finance [ˈfaɪnæns], [fɪˈnæns] *s* Finanz *f;* **finances** Finanzwesen *n* || *tr* finanzieren
financial [fɪˈnænʃəl], [faɪˈnænʃəl] *adj* (*e.g., policy, situation, crisis, aid*) Finanz–; (*e.g. affairs, resources, embarrassment*) Geld–
financier [ˌfɪnənˈsɪr], [ˌfaɪnənˈsɪr] *s* Finanzmann *m*
financ'ing, fi'nancing *s* Finanzierung *f*
finch [fɪntʃ] *s* Fink *m*
find [faɪnd] *s* Fund *m;* (archeol) Bodenfund *m* || *v* (*pret & pp* found [faʊnd]) *tr* finden; (math) bestimmen; **f. one's way** sich zurechtfinden; **f. one's way back** zurückfinden; **f. out** herausfinden; **f. s.o. guilty** j–n für schuldig erklären || *intr*—**f. out about s.th.** hinter etw [*acc*] kommen
finder [ˈfaɪndər] *s* Finder –in *mf*
find'ing *s* Finden *n;* **findings** Tatbestand *m*
fine [faɪn] *adj* fein; (*excellent*) hervorragend; (*weather*) schön; **f.!** gut! || *s* Geldstrafe *f* || *tr* mit e–r Geldstrafe belegen
fine' arts' *spl* schöne Künste *pl*

fineness [ˈfaɪnnɪs] *s* Feinheit *f;* (*of a coin or metal*) Feingehalt *m*
fine' point' *s* Feinheit *f*
fine' print' *s* Kleindruck *m*
finery [ˈfaɪnəri] *s* Putz *m*, Staat *m*
fine-spun [ˈfaɪnˌspʌn] *adj* feingesponnen
finesse [fɪˈnɛs] *s* Finesse *f;* (cards) Impaß *m* || *tr & intr* impassieren
fine-toothed [ˈfaɪnˌtuθt] *adj* feingezahnt; **go over with a f. comb** unter die Lupe nehmen
fine' touch' *s* Feinheit *f*
fine' tun'ing *s* Feineinstellung *f*
finger [ˈfɪŋgər] *s* Finger *m;* **have a f. in the pie** die Hand im Spiel haben; **keep your fingers crossed** halten Sie mir den Daumen; **not lift a f.** keinen Finger rühren; **put the f. on s.o.** (sl) j–n verpetzen; **snap one's fingers** mit den Fingern schnellen; **twist around one's little f.** um den kleinen Finger wickeln || *tr* befingern
fin'ger bowl' *s* Fingerschale *f*
fin'gering *s* (mus) Fingersatz *m*
fin'gernail' *s* Fingernagel *m*
fin'gernail pol'ish *s* Nagellack *m*
fin'gerprint' *s* Fingerabdruck *m* || *tr*—**f. s.o.** j–m die Fingerabdrücke abnehmen
fin'gertip' *s* Fingerspitze *f;* **have at one's fingertips** parat haben
finicky [ˈfɪnɪki] *adj* wählerisch
finish [ˈfɪnɪʃ] *s* Ende *n*, Abschluß *m;* (*polish*) Lack *m*, Politur *f;* **put a f. on** fertig bearbeiten || *tr* beenden; (*complete*) vollenden; (*put a finish on*) fertig bearbeiten; (*smooth*) glätten; (*polish*) polieren; (*ruin*) kaputt machen; **f. drinking** austrinken; **f. eating** aufessen; **f. off** (*supplies*) aufbrauchen; (*food*) aufessen; (*a drink*) austrinken; (*kill*) (sl) erledigen; **f. reading** (*a book*) auslesen
fin'ished *adj* beendet, fertig; **be all f.** fix und fertig sein
fin'ished pro'duct *s* Fertigprodukt *n*
fin'ishing coat' *s* Deckanstrich *m*
fin'ishing mill' *s* Nachwalzwerk *n*
fin'ishing school' *s* Mädchenpensionat *n*
fin'ishing touch'es *spl*—**put the f. to** die letzte Hand legen an (*acc*)
fin'ish line' *s* Ziel *n*, Ziellinie *f*
finite [ˈfaɪnaɪt] *adj* endlich
fi'nite verb' *s* Verbum *n* finitum
fink [fɪŋk] *s* (*informer*) (sl) Verräter –in *mf;* (*strikebreaker*) (sl) Streikbrecher –in *mf*
Finland [ˈfɪnlənd] *s* Finnland *n*
Finn [fɪn] *s* Finne *m*, Finnin *f*
Finnish [ˈfɪnɪʃ] *adj* finnisch || *s* (*language*) Finnisch *n*
fir [fʌr] *s* Tanne *f*
fir' cone' *s* Tannenzapfen *m*
fire [faɪr] *s* Feuer *n;* (*conflagration*) Brand *m;* (mil) Feuer *n;* **come under f.** unter Beschuß geraten; **on f.** in Brand; **open f.** Feuer eröffnen; **set on f.** in Brand stecken || *tr* (*a gun, pistol, shot*) abfeuern; (*bricks, ceramics*) brennen; (*an oven*) befeuern; (*an employee*) entlassen; (*throw*

hard) feuern; **f. questions at s.o.** j-n mit Fragen bombardieren; **f. up** (& fig) anfeuern ‖ *intr* feuern, schießen; **f. away!** schieß los!; **f. on** (mil) beschießen
fire′ alarm′ *s* Feuermeldung *f;* (*box*) Feuermelder *m*
fire′arm′ *s* Schußwaffe *f*
fire′ball′ *s* Feuerball *m;* (*hustler*) Draufgänger *m*
fire′bomb′ *s* Brandbombe *f* ‖ *tr* mit Brandbomben belegen
fire′brand′ *s* (fig) Aufwiegler –in *mf*
fire′break′ *s* Feuerschneise *f*
fire′ brigade′ *s* Feuerwehr *f*
fire′bug′ *m* (coll) Brandstifter –in *mf*
fire′ chief′ *s* Branddirektor *m*
fire′ com′pany *s* Feuerwehr *f*
fire′crack′er *s* Knallfrosch *m*
fire′damp′ *s* Schlagwetter *pl*
fire′ depart′ment *s* Feuerwehr *f*
fire′ drill′ *s* Feueralarmübung *f;* (*by a fire company*) Feuerwehrübung *f*
fire′ en′gine *s* Spritze *f*
fire′ escape′ *s* Feuerleiter *f*
fire′ extin′guisher *s* Feuerlöscher *m*
fire′fly′ *s* Glühwurm *m*
fire′ hose′ *s* Spritzenschlauch *m*
fire′house′ *s* Feuerwache *f*
fire′ hy′drant *s* Hydrant *m*
fire′ insur′ance *s* Brandversicherung *f*
fire′ i′rons *spl* Kamingeräte *pl*
fire′lane′ *s* Feuer(schutz)schneise *f*
fire′man *s* (**–men**) Feuerwehrmann *m;* (*stoker*) Heizer *m*
fire′place′ *s* Kamin *m*, Herd *m*
fire′plug′ *s* Hydrant *m*
fire′ pow′er *s* (mil) Feuerkraft *f*
fire′proof′ *adj* feuerfest ‖ *tr* feuerfest machen
fire′ sale′ *s* Ausverkauf *m* von feuerbeschädigten Waren
fire′ screen′ *s* Feuervorhang *m*
fire′side′ *s* Kamin *m*, Herd *m*
fire′trap′ *s* feuergefährdetes Gebäude *n*
fire′ wall′ *s* Brandmauer *f*
fire′wa′ter *s* (coll) Feuerwasser *n*
fire′wood′ *s* Brennholz *n*
fire′works′ *spl* Feuerwerk *n*
fir′ing *s* (*of a weapon*) Abfeuern *n;* (*of an employee*) Entlassung *f*
fir′ing line′ *s* Feuerlinie *f*
fir′ing range′ *s* Schießstand *m*
fir′ing squad′ *s* Erschießungskommando *n;* (*for ceremonies*) Ehrensalutkommando *n;* **put to the f.** an die Wand stellen
firm [fʌrm] *adj* fest ‖ *s* (com) Firma *f*
firmament [′fʌrməmənt] *s* Firmament *n*
firmness [′fʌrmnɪs] *s* Festigkeit *f*
first [fʌrst] *adj* erste; **very f.** allererste ‖ *adv* erst, erstens; **f. of all** zunächst ‖ *s* (aut) erster Gang *m;* **at f.** zuerst; **f. come, f. served** wer zuerst kommt, mahlt zuerst; **from the f.** von vornherein; **the f.** (*in dates or in a series*) der Erste
first′ aid′ *s* Erste Hilfe *f*
first′-aid′ kit′ *s* Verbandpäckchen *n*
first′-aid′ sta′tion *s* Unfallstation *f;* (mil) Verbandsplatz *m*

first′-born′ *adj* erstgeboren
first′-class′ *adj* erstklassig ‖ *adv* erster Klasse
first′-class′ mail′ *s* Briefpost *f*
first′-class′ tic′ket *s* Fahrkarte *f* (or Flugkarte *f*) erster Klasse
first′ cous′in *s* leiblicher Vetter *m*, leibliche Cousine *f*
first′-degree′ *adj* ersten Grades
first′ draft′ *s* Konzept *n*
first′ fin′ger *s* Zeigefinger *m*
first′ floor′ *s* Parterre *n*, Erdgeschoß *n*
first′ fruits′ *spl* Erstlinge *pl*
first′ lieuten′ant *s* Oberleutnant *m*
firstly [′fɪrstli] *adv* erstens
first′ mate′ *s* Obersteuermann *m*
first′ name′ *s* Vorname *m*
first′ night′ *s* (theat) Erstaufführung *f*
first-nighter [′fɪrst′naɪtər] *s* (theat) Premierenbesucher –in *mf*
first′ offend′er *s* noch nicht Vorbestrafte *mf*
first′ of′ficer *s* erster Offizier *m*
first′ prize′ *s* Hauptgewinn *m*, Haupttreffer *m*
first′-rate′ *adj* erstklassig
first′ ser′geant *s* Hauptfeldwebel *m*
fir′ tree′ *s* Tannenbaum *m*
fiscal [′fɪskəl] *adj* (*period, year*) Rechnungs–; (*policy*) Finanz–
fish [fɪʃ] *s* Fisch *m;* **drink like a f.** wie ein Bürstenbinder saufen; **like a f. out of water** nicht in seinem Element ‖ *tr* fischen ‖ *intr* fischen; **f. for** angeln nach
fish′bone′ *s* Gräte *f*, Fischgräte *f*
fish′ bowl′ *s* Fischglas *n*
fisher [′fɪʃər] *s* Fischer –in *mf*
fish′er·man *s* (**–men**) Angler *m*
fishery [′fɪʃəri] *s* Fischerei *f*
fish′hook′ *s* Angelhaken *m*
fish′ing *adj* Fisch–, Angel– ‖ *s* Fischen *n*
fish′ing line′ *s* Angelschnur *f*
fish′ing reel′ *s* Angelschnurrolle *f*
fish′ing rod′ *s* Angelrute *f*
fish′ing tack′le *s* Fischgerät *n*
fish′ mar′ket *s* Fischmarkt *m*
fishmonger [′fɪʃˌmʌŋgər] *s* Fischhändler –in *mf*
fish′pond′ *s* Fischteich *m*
fish′ sto′ry *s* Jägerlatein *n*
fish′tail′ *s* (aer) Abbremsen *n* ‖ *intr* (aer) abbremsen
fishy [′fɪʃi] *adj* fischig; (*eyes, look*) ausdruckslos; (*suspicious*) anrüchig; **there's s.th. f. about it** das geht nicht mit rechten Dingen zu
fission [′fɪʃən] *s* (phys) Spaltung *f*
fissionable [′fɪʃənəbəl] *adj* spaltbar
fissure [′fɪʃər] *s* Riß *m*, Spalt *m*
fist [fɪst] *s* Faust *f;* **make a f.** die Faust ballen; **shake one's f. at s.o.** j-m mit der Faust drohen
fist′ fight′ *s* Handgemenge *n*
fisticuffs [′fɪstɪˌkʌfs] *spl* Faustschläge *pl*
fit [fɪt] *adj* (**fitter; fittest**) gesund; (**for**) tauglich (für, zu); (sport) gut in Form; **be fit as a fiddle** kerngesund sein; **be fit to be tied** Gift und Galle spucken; **feel fit** auf der Höhe sein; **fit for military service**

diensttauglich; **fit to eat** genießbar; **fit to drink** trinkbar; **keep fit** in Form bleiben; **see fit to** (*inf*) es für richtig halten zu (*inf*) || *s* (*of clothes*) Sitz *m;* **by fits and starts** ruckweise; **fit of anger** Wutanfall *m;* **fit of laughter** Lachkrampf *m;* **give s.o.** **fits** j–n auf die Palme bringen; **it is a good** (or **a bad**) **fit** es sitzt gut (or schlecht); **throw a fit** e–n Wutanfall kriegen || *v* (*pret & pp* **fitted;** *ger* **fitting**) *tr* passen (*dat*); **fit in** (*for an appointment*) einschieben; **fit out** ausrüsten, ausstatten || *intr* passen; **fit into** sich einfügen in (*acc*); **fit in with** passen zu; **fit together** zusammenpassen

fitful ['fɪtfəl] *adj* unregelmäßig

fitness ['fɪtnɪs] *s* Tauglichkeit *f;* **physical f.** gute körperliche Verfassung *f*

fit'ting *adj* passend, angemessen || *s* (*of a garment*) Anprobe *f;* (*mach*) Montage *f;* **fittings** Armaturen *pl*

five [faɪv] *adj & pron* fünf || *s* Fünf *f*

five'-year plan' *s* Fünfjahresplan *m*

fix [fɪks] *s* (*determination of a position*) Standortbestimmung *f;* (*position*) Standort *m;* (*injection of heroin*) (sl) Schuß *m;* **be in a fix** (coll) in der Klemme sein || *tr* befestigen; (*a price, time*) festsetzen; (*repair*) reparieren, wieder in Ordnung bringen; (*get even with*) (sl) erledigen, das Handwerk legen (*dat*); (*one's glance*) (**on**) heften (auf *acc*); (*the blame*) (**on**) zuschreiben (*dat*); (*a game* sl) auf unehrliche Weise beeinflussen; (*bayonets*) aufpflanzen; (phot) fixieren

fixed *adj* (*unmovable*) unbeweglich; (*stare*) starr; (*income*) fest; (*idea, cost*) fix; **f. date** Termin *m*

fixer ['fɪksər] *s* (phot) Fixiermittel *n*

fix'ing *s* (*making fast*) Befestigung *f;* (*of a date, etc.*) Festsetzung *f;* **fixings** (culin) Zutaten *pl*

fix'ing bath' *s* (phot) Fixierbad *n*

fixture ['fɪkst∫ər] *s* Installationsteil *m;* **he is a permanent f.** er gehört zum Inventar

fizz [fɪz] *s* Zischen *n* || *intr* zischen

fizzle ['fɪzəl] *s* (coll) Pleite *f* || *intr* aufzischen; **f. out** verpuffen

flabbergast ['flæbər‚gæst] *tr* verblüffen

flabby ['flæbi] *adj* schlaff, schlapp

flag [flæg] *s* Fahne *f,* Flagge *f* || *v* (*pret & pp* **flagged;** *ger* **flagging**) *tr* signalisieren || *intr* nachlassen

flag'pole' *s* Fahnenmast *m*

flagrant ['flegrənt] *adj* schreiend

flag'ship' *s* Flaggschiff *n*

flag'staff' *s* Flaggenmast *m*

flag'stone' *s* Steinfliese *f*

flag' stop' *s* (rr) Bedarfshaltestelle *f*

flail [flel] *s* Dreschflegel *m* || *tr* dreschen || *intr*—**f. about** um sich schlagen

flair [fler] *s* Spürsinn *m,* feine Nase *f*

flak [flæk] *s* Flak *f,* Flakfeuer *n*

flake [flek] *s* (*thin piece*) Schuppe *f;* (*of snow, soap*) Flocke *f* || *intr* Schuppen bilden; **f. off** abblättern

flaky ['fleki] *adj* (*skin*) schuppig; (*pastry*) blätterig; (sl) überspannt

flamboyant [flæm'bɔɪ‚ənt] *adj* (*person*) angeberisch; (*style*) überladen

flame [flem] *s* Flamme *f;* **be in flames** in Flammen stehen; **burst into flames** in Flammen aufgehen || *intr* flammen

flamethrower ['flem‚θro·ər] *s* Flammenwerfer *m*

flam'ing *adj* flammend

flamin·go [flə'mɪŋgo] *s* (**-gos &** **-goes**) (orn) Flamingo *m*

flammable ['flæməbəl] *adj* brennbar

Flanders ['flændərz] *s* Flandern *n*

flange [flændʒ] *s* (*of a pipe*) Flansch *m;* (*of a wheel*) (rr) Spurkranz *m*

flank [flæŋk] *s* (anat, mil, zool) Flanke *f* || *tr* flankieren

flank'ing move'ment *s* (mil) Umgehung *f*

flannel ['flænəl] *adj* flanellen || *s* Flanell *m*

flap [flæp] *s* Klappe *f;* **f. of the wing** Flügelschlag *m* || *v* (*pret & pp* **flapped;** *ger* **flapping**) *tr*—**f. the wings** mit den Flügeln schlagen || *intr* flattern

flare [fler] *s* Leuchtsignal *n;* (*of anger, excitement*) Aufbrausen *n;* (*of a skirt*) Glocke *f;* (mil) Leuchtrakete *f,* Leuchtbombe *f* || *intr* flackern; (*said of a skirt*) glockenförmig abstehen; **f. up** auflodern; (fig) aufbrausen

flare'-up' *s* Auflodern *n;* (*of anger*) Aufbrausen *n*

flash [flæ∫] *s* Blitz *m;* (*of a gun*) Mündungsfeuer *n;* (phot) Blitzlicht *n;* **f. of genious** Geistesblitz *m;* **f. of light** Lichtstrahl *m;* **f. of lightning** Blitzstrahl *m;* **in a f.** im Nu || *tr* (*a glance*) zuwerfen; (*a message*) funkeln; **f. a light in s.o.'s face** j–m ins Gesicht leuchten || *intr* blitzen; (*said of eyes*) funkeln; **f. by** vorbeisausen; **f. on** aufleuchten; **f. through one's mind** j–m durch den Kopf schießen

flash'back' *s* (cin) Rückblende *f*

flash' bulb' *s* Blitzlichtbirne *f*

flash' cube' *s* Blitzlichtwürfel *m*

flash' flood' *s* plötzliche Überschwemmung *f*

flash' gun' *s* Blitzlichtgerät *n*

flash'light' *s* Taschenlampe *f*

flash' pic'ture, flash' shot' *s* Blitzlichtaufnahme *f*

flashy ['flæʃi] *adj* auffällig; (*clothes*) protzig; (*colors*) grell

flask [flæsk] *s* Taschenflasche *f;* (*for laboratory use*) Glaskolben *m*

flat [flæt] *adj* (**flatter; flattest**) platt, flach; (*food*) fad(e); (*rate*) Pauschal–; (*tire*) platt; (*color*) matt; (*beer, soda*) schal; (*lie*) glatt; (*denial*) entschieden; (mus) erniedrigt; **be f.** (mus) zu tief singen || *adv* (*e.g., in exactly ten minutes*) genau; **fall f.** (fig) flachfallen; **go f.** schal werden; **lie f.** flach liegen || *s* (*apartment*) Wohnung *f;* (*tire*) Reifenpanne *f*

flat'boat' *s* Flachboot *n*

flat-broke ['flæt'brok] *adj* (coll) völlig
pleite
flat'car' *s* Plattformwagen *m*
flat' feet' *spl* Plattfüße *pl*
flat'-foot'ed *adj* plattfüßig; **catch f.**
auf frischer Tat ertappen
flat'i'ron *s* Bügeleisen *n*
flatly ['flætli] *adv* rundweg, reinweg
flatten ['flætən] *tr* (paper, cloth) glatt-
streichen; (raze) einebnen; **f. out**
abplatten; (aer) abfangen || *intr* sich
verflachen; (aer) ausschweben
flatter ['flætər] *tr* schmeicheln (dat);
be flattered sich geschmeichelt fühlen; **f. oneself** sich [dat] einbilden
flatterer ['flætərər] *s* Schmeichler –in
mf
flat'tering *adj* schmeichelhaft
flattery ['flætəri] *s* Schmeichelei *f*
flat' tire' *s* Reifenpanne *f*
flat'top' *s* (coll) Flugzeugträger *m*
flat' trajec'tory *s* Rasanz *f*
flatulence ['flætʃələns] *s* Blähung *f*
flat'ware' *s* (silverware) Eßbestecke *pl*
flaunt [flɔnt] *tr* prunken mit
flavor ['flevər] *s* Aroma *n* || *tr* würzen
fla'voring *s* Würze *f*
flavorless ['flevərlɪs] *adj* fad(e)
flaw [flɔ] *s* Fehler *m*; (crack) Riß *m*;
(in glass, precious stone) Blase *f*
flawless ['flɔlɪs] *adj* tadellos
flax [flæks] *s* Flachs *m*, Lein *m*
flaxen ['flæksən] *adj* flachsen
flax'seed' *s* Leinsamen *m*
flay [fle] *tr* ausbalgen
flea [fli] *s* Floh *m*
flea'bag' *s* (sleeping bag) (coll) Floh-
kiste *f*; (hotel) (coll) Penne *f*
flea'bite' *s* Flohbiß *m*
flea'mar'ket *s*, Flohmarkt *m*
fleck [flɛk] *s* Fleck *m*
fledgling ['flɛdʒlɪŋ] *s* eben flügge ge-
wordener Vogel *m*; (fig) Grün-
schnabel *m*
flee [fli] *v* (pret & pp fled [flɛd]) *intr*
fliehen
fleece [flis] *s* Vlies *n* || *tr* (coll) rupfen
fleecy ['flisi] *adj* wollig; **f. clouds**
Schäfchenwolken *pl*
fleet [flit] *adj* flink || *s* Flotte *f*; (aer)
Geschwader *n*; (nav) Kriegsflotte *f*;
f. of cars Wagenpark *m*
fleet'ing *adj* flüchtig
Flemish ['flɛmɪʃ] *adj* flämisch || *s*
Flämisch *n*
flesh [flɛʃ] *s* Fleisch *n*; **in the f.** leib-
haftig
flesh'-col'ored *adj* fleischfarben
fleshiness ['flɛʃɪnɪs] *s* Fleischigkeit *f*
flesh' wound' *s* Fleischwunde *f*
fleshy ['flɛʃi] *adj* fleischig
flex [flɛks] *tr* biegen; (muscles) anspannen
flexible ['flɛksɪbəl] *adj* biegsam
flex(i)time ['flɛks(ɪ) ,taɪm] *s* Gleitzeit
f
flick [flɪk] *s* Schnippen *n* || *tr* (away)
wegschnippen
flicker ['flɪkər] *s* (of a flame) Flak-
kern *n*; (of eyelids) Zucken *n* || *intr*
flackern
flier ['flaɪ·ər] *s* Flieger –in *mf*; (handbill) Flugblatt *n*

flight [flaɪt] *s* Flug *m*; (fleeing) Flucht
f; (of birds, geese) Schar *f*; (of
stairs) Treppe *f*; **f. of stairs** Trep-
penflucht *f*; **f. of the imagination**
Geistesschwung *m*; **live two flights up**
zwei Treppen hoch wohnen; **put to f.**
in die Flucht schlagen; **take to f.**
sich davonmachen
flight' bag' *s* (aer) Reisetasche *f*
flight' deck' *s* (nav) Landedeck *n*
flight' engineer' *s* Bordmechaniker *m*
flight' instruc'tor *s* Fluglehrer –in *mf*
flight' path' *s* Flugstrecke *f*
flighty ['flaɪti] *adj* leichtsinnig
flim·flam ['flɪm ,flæm] *s* (nonsense)
Unsinn *m*; (deception) Betrügerei *f*
|| *v* (pret & pp –flammed) ger
–flamming) *tr* (coll) betrügen
flimsy ['flɪmzi] *adj* (material) hauch-
dünn; (excuse, construction) schwach
flinch [flɪntʃ] *intr* (at) zurückweichen
(vor dat), zusammenfahren (vor dat)
flinch'ing *s*—**without f.** ohne mit der
Wimper zu zucken
fling [flɪŋ] *s* Wurf *m*; **go on** (or **have**)
a f. sich austoben; **have a f. at** ver-
suchen || *v* (pret & pp flung [flʌŋ])
tr schleudern; **f. off** abschleudern;
f. open aufreißen
flint [flɪnt] *s* Feuerstein *m*
flinty ['flɪnti] *adj* steinhart; (fig) hart
flip [flɪp] *adj* leichtfertig || *s* (of a
coin) Hochwerfen *n*; (somersault)
Purzelbaum *m* || *v* (pret & pp
flipped; ger flipping) *tr* schnellen;
(a coin) hochwerfen; **f. one's lid** (sl)
rasend werden; **f. over** umdrehen
flippancy ['flɪpənsi] *s* Leichtfertigkeit
f
flippant ['flɪpənt] *adj* leichtfertig
flipper ['flɪpər] *s* Flosse *f*
flirt [flʌrt] *s* Flirt *m* || *intr* koket-
tieren, flirten; (with an idea) liebäugeln
flirtation [flʌr'teʃən] *s* Liebelei *f*
flit [flɪt] *v* (pret & pp flitted; ger
flitting) *intr* flitzen; **f. by** vorbeiflitzen; (said of time) verfliegen
float [flot] *s* Schwimmkörper *m*; (of a
fishing line) Schwimmer *m*; (raft)
Floß *n*; (in parades) Festwagen *m* ||
tr (logs) flößen; (a loan) auflegen
|| *intr* schwimmen; (in the air) schwe-
ben; **f. about** herumtreiben
float'ing kid'ney *s* Wanderniere *f*
float'ing mine' *s* Treibmine *f*
flock [flɑk] *s* (of sheep) Herde *f*; (of
birds) Schar *f*, Schwarm *m*; (of peo-
ple) Menge *f* || *intr* herbeiströmen;
come flocking herbeigeströmt kommen; **f. around** sich scharen um; **f.
into** strömen in (acc); **f. to** zulaufen
(dat); **f. together** sich zusammen-
scharen
floe [flo] *s* Eisscholle *f*
flog [flɑg] *v* (pret & pp flogged; ger
flogging) *tr* prügeln
flood [flʌd] *s* Flut *f*; (caused by heavy
rains) Überschwemmung *f*; (sudden
rise of a river) Hochwasser *n*; (fig)
Schwall *m*; (Bib) Sintflut *f* || *tr* (&
fig) überschwemmen; (e.g., with
mail) überschütten

flood'gate' s (& fig) Schleusentor n
flood'light' s Flutlicht n ‖ tr anstrahlen
flood' tide' s Flut f; **at f.** zur Zeit der Flut
flood' wa'ters spl Flutwasser n
floor [flor] s Fußboden m; (story) Stock m; (parl) Sitzungssaal m; **have the f.** das Wort haben; **may I have the f.?** ich bitte ums Wort; **on the third f.** im zweiten Stock ‖ tr zu Boden strecken; (coll) verblüffen
floor'board' s Diele f
floor'ing s Fußbodenbelag m
floor' lamp' s Stehlampe f
floor' plan' s Grundriß m
floor' pol'ish s Bohnermasse f
floor' sam'ple s Vorführungsmuster n
floor' show' s Kabarett n
floor' tile' s Bodenfliese f
floor'walk'er s Abteilungsaufseher –in mf
floor' wax' s Bohnerwachs n
flop [flap] s (coll) Mißerfolg m; (person) Niete f; (fall) (coll) Plumps m; **take a f.** (coll) plumpsen ‖ v (pret & pp flopped; ger flopping) intr (fall) (coll) plumpsen; (fail) (coll) versagen; (theat) (coll) durchfallen; **f. down in** (coll) sich plumpsen lassen in (acc)
flora ['florə] s Pflanzenwelt f
floral ['florəl] adj Blumen-
Florence ['florəns] s Florenz n
florescence [flo'resəns] s Blüte f
florid ['florɪd] adj (ornate) überladen; (complexion) blühend
florist ['florɪst] s Blumenhändler –in mf
floss [flɔs] s Rohseide f; (of corn) Narbenfäden pl
floss' silk' s Florettseide f
flossy ['flɔsi] adj seidenweich
flotilla [flo'tɪlə] s Flotille f
flotsam ['flatsəm] s Wrackgut n
flot'sam and jet'sam s Treibgut n; (trifles) Kleinigkeiten pl
flounce [flauns] s Volant m ‖ tr mit Volants besetzen ‖ intr erregt stürmen
flounder ['flaundər] s Flunder f ‖ intr taumeln; (fig) ins Schwimmen kommen
flour [flaur] s Mehl n
flourish ['flʌrɪʃ] s (in writing) Schnörkel m; (in a speech) Floskel f; (gesture) große Geste f; (mus) Tusch m; **f. of trumpets** Trompetengeschmetter n ‖ tr (banners) schwenken; (swords) schwingen ‖ intr blühen, gedeihen
flour'ishing adj blühend; (business) schwunghaft
flour' mill' s Mühle f
floury ['flauri] adj mehlig
flout [flaut] tr verspotten ‖ intr—**f. at** spotten über (acc)
flow [flo] s Fluß m ‖ intr fließen, rinnen; (said of hair, clothes) wallen; **f. by** vorbeifließen; **f. into** zuströmen (dat)
flower ['flau·ər] s Blume f; **cut flowers** Schnittblumen pl ‖ intr blühen

flow'er bed' s Blumenbeet n
flow'er gar'den s Blumengarten m
flow'er girl' s Blumenmädchen n
flow'erpot' s Blumentopf m
flow'er shop' s Blumenladen m
flow'er show' s Blumenausstellung f
flow'er stand' s Blumenstand m
flowery ['flau·əri] adj blumig; (fig) geziert; **f. phrase** Floskel f
flu [flu] s (coll) Grippe f
flub [flʌb] v (pret & pp flubbed; ger flubbing) tr (coll) verkorksen
fluctuate ['flʌktʃu ˌet] intr schwanken
fluctuation [ˌflʌktʃu'eʃən] s Schwankung f
flue [flu] s Rauchrohr n
fluency ['flu·ənsi] s Geläufigkeit f
fluent ['flu·ənt] adj (speaker) redegewandt; (speech) fließend
fluently ['flu·əntli] adv fließend
fluff [flʌf] s Staubflocke f; (blunder) Schnitzer m ‖ tr verpfuschen; **f. up** (a pillow) schütteln; (a rug) aufrauhen
fluffy ['flʌfi] adj flaumig
fluid ['flu·ɪd] adj flüssig ‖ s Flüssigkeit f
fluke [fluk] s Ankerflügel m; (coll) Dusel m
flunk [flʌŋk] s Durchfallen n ‖ tr (a test) (coll) durchfallen in (dat); (a student) (coll) durchfallen lassen ‖ intr (coll) durchfallen
flunky ['flʌŋki] s Schranze mf
fluorescent [flo'resənt] adj fluoreszierend
fluores'cent light' s Leuchtstofflampe f
fluores'cent tube' s Leuchtröhre f
fluoridate ['florɪ ˌdet] tr mit e–m Fluorid versetzen
fluoride ['florard] s Fluorid n
fluorine ['florin] s Fluor n
fluorite ['florart] s Fluorkalzium n
fluoroscope ['florə ˌskop] s Fluoroskop n
flurry ['flʌri] s (of snow) Schneegestöber m; (st. exch.) kurzes Auffüllkern n; **f. of activity** fieberhafte Tätigkeit f
flush [flʌʃ] adj (even) eben, glatt; (well-supplied) gut bei Kasse; (full to overflowing) übervoll ‖ adv übervoll ‖ s (on the cheeks) Erröten n; (of youth) Blüte f; (of a toilet) Spülung f; (cards) Flöte f; **f. of victory** Siegesrausch m ‖ tr (a toilet) spülen; (hunt) auftreiben; **f. down** hinunterspülen; **f. out** (animals) auftreiben ‖ intr erröten
flush' switch' s Unterputzschalter m
flush' tank' s Spülkasten m
flush' toi'let s Spülklosett n
fluster ['flʌstər] s Verwirrung f ‖ tr verwirren
flute [flut] s (archit) Kannelüre f; (mus) Flöte f ‖ tr riffeln
flut'ing s (archit) Kannelierung f
flutist ['flutɪst] s Flötist –in mf
flutter ['flʌtər] s Flattern n; (excitement) Aufregung f ‖ tr—**f. one's eyelashes** mit den Wimpern klimpern ‖ intr flattern

flux [flʌks] *s* (*flow*) Fließen *n*, Fluß *m*; (*for fusing metals*) Schmelzmittel *n*; **in f.** im Fluß
fly [flai] *s* Fliege *f*; (*of trousers*) Schlitz *m*; (angl) künstliche Fliege *f*; **flies** (theat) Soffitten *pl*; **fly in the ointment** Haar *n* in der Suppe ‖ *v* (*pret* **flew** [flu]; *pp* **flown** [flon]) *tr* fliegen ‖ *intr* fliegen; (*rush*) stürzen; (*said of rumors*) schwirren; (*said of time*) verfliegen; **fly around** umherfliegen; (*e.g., the globe*) umfliegen; **fly at s.o.** auf j-n losgehen; **fly away** abfliegen; **fly in all directions** nach allen Seiten zerstieben; **fly low** tief fliegen; **fly off the handle** (fig) aus der Haut fahren; **fly open** aufspringen; **fly over** überfliegen; **fly past** vorbeifliegen (an *dat*); **let fly** (*e.g., an arrow*) schnellen
fly′ ball′ *s* (baseball) Flugball *m*
fly′-by-night′ *adj* unverläßlich ‖ *s* (coll) Schwindelunternehmen *n*
fly′ cast′ing *s* Fischen *n* mit der Wurfangel
flyer [′flaɪ·ər] *s* var of **flier**
fly′-fish′ *intr* mit künstlichen Fliegen angeln
fly′ing *adj* fliegend; (*boat, field, time*) Flug–; (*suit, club, school*) Flieger– ‖ *s* Fliegen *n*
fly′ing but′tress *s* Strebebogen *m*
fly′ing col′ors *spl*—**come through with f.** e–n glänzenden Sieg erringen
fly′ing sau′cer *s* fliegende Untertasse *f*
fly′leaf′ *s* (**-leaves′**) Vorsatzblatt *n*
fly′pa′per *s* Fliegenfänger *m*
fly′ rod′ *s* Angelrute *f*
fly′speck′ *s* Fliegendreck *m*
fly′ swat′ter [‚swɑtər] *s* Fliegenklappe *f*
fly′trap′ *s* Fliegenfalle *f*
fly′wheel′ *s* Schwungrad *n*
foal [fol] *s* Fohlen *n* ‖ *intr* fohlen
foam [fom] *s* Schaum *m*; (*of waves*) Gischt *m*; (*from the mouth*) Geifer *m* ‖ *intr* schäumen; (*said of waves*) branden
foam′ rub′ber *s* Schaumgummi *m*
foamy [′fomi] *adj* (*full of foam*) schaumig; (*beer*) schäumend; (*foam-like*) schaumartig
F.O.B., f.o.b. [‚ef ‚o ′bi] *adv* (**free on board**) frei an Bord
focal [′fokəl] *adj* fokal; **be the f. point** im Brennpunkt stehen; **f. point** (fig & opt) Brennpunkt *m*
fo·cus [′fokəs] *s* (**-cuses** & **-ci** [sai]) (math, opt) Brennpunkt *m*; (pathol) Herd *m*; **bring into f.** richtig (or scharf) einstellen; **in f.** scharf eingestellt; **out of f.** unscharf ‖ *v* (*pret* & *pp* **-cus[s]ed**; *ger* **-cus[s]ing**) *tr* (*a camera*) einstellen; (*attention, etc.*) (**on**) richten (auf *acc*) ‖ *intr* sich scharf einstellen
fo′cusing *s* Scharfeinstellung *f*
fodder [′fɑdər] *s* Futter *n*
foe [fo] *s* Feind –*in mf*
fog [fɔg] *s* Nebel *m*; (fig) Verwirrung *f*; (phot) Grauschleier *m* ‖ *v* (*pret* & *pp* **fogged**; *ger* **fogging**) *tr* vernebeln; (fig) umnebeln ‖ *intr* (phot) verschleiern; **fog up** beschlagen
fog′ bank′ *s* Nebelbank *f*
fog′ bell′ *s* Nebelglocke *f*
fog′-bound′ *adj* durch Nebel festgehalten
fogey [′fogi] *s* Kauz *m*
foggy [′fɔgi] *adj* neblig, nebelhaft; (phot) verschleiert; **he hasn't the foggiest idea** er hat nicht die leiseste Ahnung
fog′horn′ *s* Nebelhorn *n*
fog′ light′ *s* (aut) Nebelscheinwerfer *m*
foible [′fɔɪbəl] *s* Schwäche *f*
foil [fɔɪl] *s* (*of metal*) Folie *f*; (*of a mirror*) Spiegelbelag *m*; (fig) (**to**) Hintergrund *m* (für); (fencing) Florett *n* ‖ *tr* (*a plan*) durchkreuzen; (*an attempt*) vereiteln
foist [fɔɪst] *tr*—**f. s.th. on s.o.** j-m etw anhängen
fold [fold] *s* Falte *f*; (*in stiff material*) Falz *m*; (*for sheep*) Pferch *m*; (*flock of sheep*) Schafherde *f*; (relig) Herde *f* ‖ *tr* falten; (*stiff material*) (*e.g., a chair*) zusammenklappen; (*the arms*) kreuzen; (*the wash*) zusammenlegen ‖ *intr* sich (zusammen) falten; (com) zusammenbrechen
folder [′folder] *s* (*loose-leaf binder*) Schnellhefter *m*; (*manila folder*) Mappe *f*; (*brochure*) Prospekt *m*
fold′ing *adj* (*bed, chair, camera, wing*) Klapp–
fold′ing door′ *s* Falttür *f*
fold′ing screen′ *s* spanische Wand *f*
foliage [′folɪ·ɪdʒ] *s* Laubwerk *n*, Laub *n*
foli·o [′folɪ ‚o] *adj* Folio–, in Folio ‖ *s* (**-os**) (*page*) Folioblatt *n*; (*book*) Foliant *m* ‖ *tr* paginieren
folk [fok] *adj* Volks– ‖ **folks** *spl* (*people*) Leute *pl*; (*family*) Angehörige *pl*
folk′ dance′ *s* Volkstanz *m*
folk′lore′ *s* Volkskunde *f*
folk′ mu′sic *s* Volksmusik *f*
folk′ song′ *s* Volkslied *n*
folksy [′foksi] *adj* (*person*) leutselig; (*speech, expression*) volkstümlich
folk′ tale′ *s* Volkssage *f*
folk′ways′ *spl* volkstümliche Lebensweise *f*
follicle [′fɑlɪkəl] *s* Follikel *n*
follow [′fɑlo] *tr* folgen (*dat*); (*instructions*) befolgen; (*a goal, events, news*) verfolgen; (*in office*) folgen auf (*acc*); (*a profession*) ausüben; (*understand*) folgen können (*dat*); **f. one another** aufeinanderfolgen; (*said of events*) sich überstürzen; **f. up** nachgehen (*dat*); **f. your nose!** immer der Nase nach! ‖ *intr* (nach)-folgen; **as follows** folgendermaßen; **f. after** nachfolgen (*dat*); **f. through** (sport) ganz durchziehen; **f. upon** folgen auf (*acc*); **it follows that** daraus folgt, daß
follower [′fɑlo·ər] *s* Anhänger –*in mf*
fol′lowing *adj* nachstehend, folgend ‖ *s* Gefolgschaft *f*
fol′low-up′ *adj* Nach– ‖ *s* weitere Verfolgung *f*

folly ['fɑli] s Torheit f; **follies** (theat) Revue f
foment [fo'mɛnt] tr schüren, anstiften
fond [fɑnd] adj (hope, wish) sehnlich; **become f.** of lieb gewinnen; **be f.** of gern haben; **be f.** of reading gern lesen
fondle ['fɑndəl] tr liebkosen
fondness ['fɑndnıs] s Verliebtheit f; (for) Hang m (zu), Vorliebe f (für)
font [fɑnt] s (for holy water) Weihwasserbecken n; (for baptism) Taufbecken n; (typ) Schriftart f
food [fud] adj Nähr-, Speise- ‖ s (on the table) Essen n; (in a store) Lebensmittel pl; (requirement for life) Nahrung f; (for animals) Futter n; (for plants) Nährstoff m; **f. and drink** Speis' und Trank; **f. for thought** Stoff m zum Nachdenken
food' poi'soning s Nahrungsmittelvergiftung f
food'stuffs' spl Nahrungsmittel pl
food' val'ue s Nährwert m
fool [ful] s Narr m; **born f.** Mondkalb n; **make a f. of oneself** sich blamieren ‖ tr täuschen, anführen ‖ intr— **f. around** herumtrödeln; **f. around with** herumspielen mit; (romantically) sich herumtreiben mit
fool'har'dy adj tollkühn
fool'ing s Späße pl; **f. around** Firlefanz m; **no f.!** na, so was!
foolish ['fulıʃ] adj töricht, albern
foolishness ['fulıʃnıs] s Torheit f
fool'-proof' adj narrensicher
fools'cap' s Narrenkappe f; (paper size) Kanzleipapier n
foot [fut] s (feet [fit]) Fuß m; **be (back) on one's feet** (wieder) auf den Beinen sein; **f. of the bed** Fußende n des Bettes; **on f.** zu Fuß; **put one's best f. forward** sich ins rechte Licht setzen; **put one's f. down** (fig) ein Machtwort sprechen; **put one's f. in it** (coll) ins Fettnäpfchen treten; **stand on one's own two feet** auf eigenen Füßen stehen ‖ tr—**f. the bill** blechen
footage ['futıdʒ] s Ausmaß n in Fuß
foot'-and-mouth' disease' s Maul- und Klauenseuche f
foot'ball' s Fußball m
foot'board' s (in a car) Trittbrett n; (of a bed) Fußbrett n
foot'bridge' s Steg m
foot'fall' s Schritt m
foot'hills' spl Vorgebirge n
foot'hold' s (& fig) Halt m; **gain a f.** festen Fuß fassen
foot'ing s Halt m; **lose one's f.** ausgleiten; **on an equal f. with** auf gleichem Fuße mit
foot'lights' spl Rampenlicht n
foot'man s (-men) Lakai m
foot'note' s Fußnote f
foot'path' s Fußpfad m, Fußsteig m
foot'print' s Fußstapfe f
foot' race' s Wettlauf m
foot'rest' s Fußraste f
foot' rule' s Zollstock m
foot' sol'dier s Infanterist m
foot'sore' adj fußkrank

foot'step' s Tritt m; **follow in s.o.'s footsteps** in j–s Fußstapfen treten
foot'stool' s Schemel m
foot'wear' s Schuhwerk n
foot'work' s (sl) Lauferei f; (sport) Beinarbeit f
foot'worn' adj abgetreten
fop [fɑp] s Geck m
for [fɔr] prep für; (a destination) nach (dat); (with an English present perfect tense) schon (acc), e.g., **I have been living here for a month** ich wohne hier schone e–n Monat (or seit e–m Monat; (with an English future tense) für or auf (acc); **for good** für immer; **for joy** vor Freude; **for years** jahrelang ‖ conj denn
forage ['fɔrıdʒ] s Furage f ‖ intr furagieren
foray ['fɔre] s (raid) Raubzug m; (e.g., into politics) Streifzug m ‖ intr plündern
for·bear [fɔr'bɛr] v (pret –bore ['bor]; pp –borne ['born]) tr unterlassen ‖ intr ablassen
forbearance [fɔr'bɛrəns] s (patience) Geduld f; (leniency) Nachsicht f
for·bid [fɔr'bıd] v (pret –bade ['bæd] & –bad ['bæd]; pp –bidden ['bıdən]) tr verbieten
forbid'ding adj abschreckend; (dangerous) gefährlich
force [fɔrs] s (strength) Kraft f; (compulsion) Gewalt f; (phys) Kraft f; **be in f.** in Kraft sein; **by f.** gewaltsam; **come into f.** in Kraft treten; **forces** (mil) Streitkräfte pl; **have the f. of** gelten als; **resort to f.** zu Zwangsmaßnahmen greifen; **with full f.** mit voller Wucht ‖ tr zwingen; (plants) treiben; (a door) aufsprengen; (e.g., an issue) forcieren; (into) zwängen (in acc); **f. down** hinunterdrücken; (aer) zur Landung zwingen; **f. one's way** sich drängen; **f. s.th. on s.o.** j–m etw aufdrängen
forced' land'ing s Notlandung f
forced' march' s Gewaltmarsch m
forceful ['fɔrsfəl] adj eindrucksvoll
for·ceps ['fɔrsɛps] s (–ceps & –cipes [sı ,pız]) (dent, surg, zool) Zange f
forcible ['fɔrsıbəl] adj (strong) kräftig; (violent) gewaltsam
ford [fɔrd] s Furt f ‖ tr durchwaten
fore [fɔr] adj Vorder- ‖ adv (naut) vorn ‖ s—**come to the f.** hervortreten ‖ interj (golf) Achtung!
fore' and aft' adv längsschiffs
fore'arm' s Vorderarm m, Unterarm m
fore'bears' spl Vorfahren pl
forebode [for'bod] tr vorbedeuten
forebod'ing s (omen) Vorzeichen n; (presentiment) Vorahnung f
fore'cast' s Voraussage f ‖ v (pret & pp –cast & –casted) tr voraussagen
forecastle ['foksəl] s Back f
foreclose' tr (a mortgage) für verfallen erklären; (shut out) ausschließen
foredoom' tr im voraus verurteilen
fore'fa'thers spl Vorfahren pl
fore'fin'ger s Zeigefinger m
fore'front' s Spitze f
fore'go'ing adj vorhergehend

fore'gone' conclu'sion *s* ausgemachte Sache *f*
fore'ground' *s* Vordergrund *m*
forehead ['fɔrɪd] *s* Stirn(e) *f*
foreign ['fɔrɪn] *adj* (*e.g.*, *aid*, *product*) Auslands–; (*e.g.*, *body*, *language*, *word*, *worker*) Fremd–; (*e.g.*, *minister*, *office*, *policy*, *trade*) Außen–; (*e.g.*, *affairs*, *service*) auswärtig
foreigner ['fɔrɪnər] *s* Ausländer –in *mf*
for'eign exchange' *s* Devisen *pl*
fore'leg' *s* Vorderbein *n*
fore'lock' *s* Stirnlocke *f*
fore'man *s* (**-men**) Vorarbeiter *m*; (jur) Obmann *m*; (min) Steiger *m*
foremast ['fɔr‚mæst] *s* Fockmast *m*
fore'most' *adj* vorderste || *adv* zuerst
fore'noon' *s* Vormittag *m*
fore'part' *s* vorderster Teil *m*
fore'paw' *s* Vorderpfote *f*
fore'quart'er *s* Vorderviertel *n*
fore'run'ner *s* Vorbote *m*
fore'sail' *s* Focksegel *n*
fore·see' *v* (*pret* **-saw'**; *pp* **-seen'**) *tr* voraussehen
foreseeable [for'si·əbəl] *adj* absehbar
foreshad'ow *tr* ahnen lassen
foreshort'en *tr* verkürzen
fore'sight' *s* Voraussicht *f*
fore'sight'ed *adj* umsichtig
fore'skin' *s* Vorhaut *f*
forest ['fɔrɪst] *s* Wald *m*, Forst *m*
forestall' *tr* zuvorkommen (*dat*)
for'est fire' *s* Waldbrand *m*
for'est rang'er *s* Forstbeamte *m*
forestry ['fɔrɪstri] *s* Forstwirtschaft *f*
fore'taste' *s* Vorgeschmack *m*
fore·tell' *v* (*pret & pp* **-told'**) *tr* vorhersagen, weissagen
fore'thought' *s* Vorsorge *f*, Vorbedacht *m*
forev'er *adv* ewig, für immer; **f. and ever** auf immer und ewig
forewarn' *tr* (of) vorher warnen (vor *dat*)
fore'word' *s* Vorwort *n*
forfeit ['fɔrfɪt] *s* Einbuße *f* || *tr* einbüßen, verwirken
forfeiture ['fɔrfɪtʃər] *s* Verwirkung *f*
forgather [fɔr'gæðər] *intr* sich treffen
forge [fɔrdʒ] *s* Schmiede *f* || *tr* schmieden; (*documents*) fälschen || *intr*— **forge ahead** vordringen
forger ['fɔrdʒər] *s* Fälscher –in *mf*
forgery ['fɔrdʒəri] *s* Fälschung *f*; (*coin*) Falschgeld *n*
for·get [fɔr'gɛt] *v* (*pret* **-got**; *pp* **-got & -gotten**; *ger* **-getting**) *tr* vergessen; **f. it!** spielt keine Rolle!; **f. oneself** sich vergessen
forgetful fɔr'gɛtfəl] *adj* vergeßlich
forgetfulness [fɔr'gɛtfəlnɪs] *s* Vergeßlichkeit *f*
forget'-me-not' *s* Vergißmeinnicht *n*
forgivable [fɔr'gɪvəbəl] *adj* verzeihlich
for·give [fɔr'gɪv] *v* (*pret* **-gave**; *pp* **-given**) *tr* (*a person*) vergeben (*dat*); (*a thing*) vergeben
forgiveness [fɔr'gɪvnɪs] *s* Vergebung *f*
forgiv'ing *adj* versöhnlich
for·go [fɔr'go] *v* (*pret* **-went**; *pp* **-gone**) *tr* verzichten auf (*acc*)

fork [fɔrk] *s* Gabel *f*; (*in the road*) Gabelung *f*; (*of a tree*) Astgabelung *f* || *tr* gabeln; **f. over** (coll) übergeben
forked *adj* gabelförmig; (*tongue*) gespalten
fork'lift truck' *s* Gabelstapler *m*
forlorn [fɔr'lɔrn] *adj* (*forsaken*) verlassen; (*wretched*) elend; (*attempt*) verzweifelt
forlorn' hope' *s* aussichtsloses Unternehmen *n*
form [fɔrm] *s* Form *f*, Gestalt *f*; (*paper to be filled out*) Formular *n* || *tr* formen, bilden; (*a plan*) fassen; (*a circle*, *alliance*) schließen; (*suspicions*) schöpfen; (*a habit*) annehmen; (*blisters*) werfen || *intr* sich bilden
formal ['fɔrməl] *adj* formell, förmlich
for'mal call' *s* Höflichkeitsbesuch *m*
for'mal educa'tion *s* Schulbildung *f*
formality [fɔr'mælɪti] *s* Formalität *f*; **without f.** ohne Umstände
format ['fɔrmæt] *s* Format *n*
formation [fɔr'meʃən] *s* Bildung *f*; (aer) Verband *m*; (geol, mil) Formation *f*
former ['fɔrmər] *adj* ehemalig, früher; **the f.** jener
formerly ['fɔrmərli] *adv* ehemals, früher
form'-fit'ting *adj*—**be f.** e–e gute Paßform haben
formidable ['fɔrmɪdəbəl] *adj* (*huge*) gewaltig; (*dreadful*) schrecklich
formless ['fɔrmlɪs] *adj* formlos
form' let'ter *s* Rundbrief *m*
formu·la ['fɔrmjələ] *s* (**-las & -lae** [‚li]) Formel *f*; (*baby food*) Kindermilch *f*
formulate ['fɔrmjə‚let] *tr* formulieren
formulation [‚fɔrmjə'leʃən] *s* Formulierung *f*
fornicate ['fɔrnɪ‚ket] *intr* Unzucht treiben
fornication [‚fɔrnɪ'keʃən] *s* Unzucht *f*
for·sake [fɔr'sek] *v* (*pret* **-sook** ['suk]; *pp* **-saken** ['sekən]) *tr* verlassen
fort [fɔrt] *s* Burg *f*; (mil) Fort *n*
forte [fɔrt] *s* Stärke *f*
forth [forθ] *adv* hervor; **and so f.** und so fort; **from that day f.** von dem Tag an
forth'com'ing *adj* bevorstehend
forth'right' *adj* ehrlich, offen
forth'with' *adv* sofort
fortieth ['fɔrtɪ·ɪθ] *adj & pron* vierzigste || *s* (*fraction*) Vierzigstel *n*; (*in a series*) Vierzigste *mfn*
fortification [‚fɔrtɪfɪ'keʃən] *s* Befestigung *f*
forti·fy ['fɔrtɪ‚faɪ] *v* (*pret & pp* **-fied**) *tr* (*a place*) befestigen; (*e.g.*, *with liquor*) kräftigen; (*encourage*) ermutigen
fortitude ['fɔrtɪ‚t(j)ud] *s* Seelenstärke *f*
fortnight ['fɔrtnaɪt] *s* vierzehn Tage *pl*
fortress ['fɔrtrɪs] *s* Festung *f*
fortuitous [fɔr't(j)u·ɪtəs] *adj* zufällig
fortunate ['fɔrtʃənɪt] *adj* glücklich
fortunately ['fɔrtʃənɪtli] *adv* glücklicherweise

fortune ['fortʃən] *s* Glück *n;* (*money*) Vermögen *n;* **make a f.** sich [*dat*] ein Vermögen erwerben; **have one's f.** told sich [*dat*] wahrsagen lassen; **tell fortunes** wahrsagen
for'tune hunt'er *s* Mitgiftjäger –in *mf*
for'tunetell'er *s* Wahrsagerin *f*
forty ['forti] *adj & pron* vierzig ‖ *s* Vierzig *f;* **the forties** die vierziger Jahre
fo·rum ['forəm] *s* (–rums & –ra [rə]) (& fig) Forum *n*
forward ['forwərd] *adj* vordere, Vorwärts–; (*person*) keck; (mil) vorgeschoben ‖ *adv* vorwärts, nach vorn; **bring f.** (*an idea*) vorschlagen; (*a proposal*) vorbringen; **come f.** sich melden; **look f. to** sich freuen auf (*acc*); **put f.** vorlegen ‖ *s* (fb) Stürmer *m* ‖ *tr* befördern; **please f.** bitte nachsenden ‖ *interj*—**f., march!** im Gleichschritt, marsch!
fossil ['fasıl] *adj* versteinert ‖ *s* Fossil *n*
foster ['fostər] *adj* (*child, father, mother, home*) Pflege–; (*brother, sister*) Milch– ‖ *tr* pflegen
foul [faul] *adj* übel; (*in smell*) übelriechend; (*air, weather*) schlecht; (*language*) unflätig; (*means*) unfair ‖ *s* (sport) Foul *n* ‖ *tr* (*make dirty*) besudeln; (*the lines*) verwickeln; (sport) foulen; **f. up** durcheinanderbringen ‖ *intr* (sport) foulen
foul' line' *s* (*baseball*) Grenzlinie *f;* (basketball) Freiwurflinie *f*
foul-mouthed ['faul,mauðd], ['faul,mauθt] *adj* zotige Reden führend
foul' play' *s* unfaires Spiel *n;* (*crime*) Verbrechen *n*, Mord *m*
found [faund] *tr* gründen; (*cast*) gießen
foundation [faun'deʃən] *s* (*act*) Gründung *f;* (*of a structure*) Fundament *n;* (*fund*) Stiftung *f;* (fig) Grundlage *f;* **lay the foundation of** (& fig) den Grund legen zu
founda'tion gar'ments *spl* Miederwaren *pl*
founda'tion wall' *s* Grundmauer *f*
founder ['faundər] *s* Gründer –in *mf;* (metal) Gießer –in *mf* ‖ *intr* (*said of a ship*) sinken; (*fail*) scheitern
foundling ['faundlıŋ] *s* Findling *m*
foundry ['faundri] *s* Gießerei *f*
found'ry·man *s* (–men) Gießer *m*
fount [faunt] *s* Quelle *f*
fountain ['fauntən] *s* Springbrunnen *m*
foun'tainhead' *s* Urquell *m*
foun'tain pen' *s* Füller *m*
four [for] *adj & pron* vier ‖ *s* Vier *f;* **on all fours** auf allen vieren
four'-cy'cle *adj* (mach) Viertakt–
four'-en'gine *adj* viermotorig
fourflusher ['for,flʌʃər] *s* Angeber *m*
four'foot'ed *adj* vierfüßig
four' hun'dred *adj & pron* vierhundert ‖ *spl*—**the Four Hundred** die oberen Zehntausend
four'lane' *adj* Vierbahn–
four'-leaf' *adj* vierblätterig
four'-leg'ged *adj* vierbeinig
four'-letter word' *s* unanständiges Wort *n*

foursome ['forsəm] *s* Viererspiel *n;* (*group of four*) Quartet *n*
fourteenth [for'tinθ] *adj & pron* vierzehnte ‖ *s* (*fraction*) Vierzehntel *n;* **the f.** (*in dates and in a series*) der Vierzehnte
fourth [forθ] *adj & pron* vierte ‖ *s* (*fraction*) Viertel *n;* **the f.** (*in dates and in a series*) der Vierte
fourth' estate' *s* Presse *f*
fowl [faul] *s* Huhn *n*, Geflügel *n*
fox [faks] *s* (& fig) Fuchs *m*
fox'glove' *s* (bot) Fingerhut *m*
fox'hole' *s* (mil) Schützenloch *n*
fox' hound' *s* Hetzhund *m*
fox' hunt' *s* Fuchsjagd *f*
fox' ter'rier *s* Foxterrier *m*
fox' trot' *s* Foxtrott *m*
foyer ['foi·ər] *s* (*of a theater*) Foyer *n;* (*of a house*) Diele *f*
fracas ['frekəs] *s* Aufruhr *m*
fraction ['frækʃən] *s* Bruchteil *m;* **fractions** Bruchrechnung *f*
fractional ['frækʃənəl] *adj* Bruch–
fracture ['fræktʃər] *s* Bruch *m* ‖ *tr* sich [*dat*] brechen
fragile ['frædʒıl] *adj* zerbrechlich
fragment ['frægmənt] *s* Bruchstück *n;* (*of writing*) Fragment *n*
fragmentary ['frægmən,teri] *adj* bruchstückhaft; (*writing*) fragmentarisch
fragmenta'tion bomb' [,frægmən'teʃən] *s* Splitterbombe *f*
fragrance ['fregrəns] *s* Duft *m*
fragrant ['fregrənt] *adj* duftend; **be f.** duften
frail [frel] *adj* schwach, hinfällig; (*fragile*) zerbrechlich
frailty ['frelti] *s* Schwachheit *f*
frame [frem] *s* (*e.g., of a picture, door*) Rahmen *m;* (*of glasses*) Fassung *f;* (*of a house*) Balkenwerk *n;* (*structure*) Gestell *n;* (anat) Körperbau *m;* (cin, telv) Bild *n;* (naut) Spant *n* ‖ *tr* (*a picture*) einrahmen; (*a plan*) ersinnen; (sl) reinhängen
frame' house' *s* Holzhaus *n*
frame' of mind' *s* Gemütsverfassung *f*
frame' of ref'erence *s* Bezugspunkte *pl*
frame'-up' *s* abgekartete Sache *f*
frame'work' *s* Gebälk *n*, Fachwerk *n;* (fig) Rahmen *m;* (aer) Aufbau *m*
franc [fræŋk] *s* Franc *m;* (*Swiss*) Franken *m*
France [fræns] *s* Frankreich *n*
Frances ['frænsıs] *s* Franziska *f*
franchise ['fræntʃaız] *s* Konzession *f;* (*right to vote*) Wahlrecht *n*
Francis ['frænsıs] *s* Franz *m*
Franciscan [fræn'sıskən] *adj* Franziskaner– ‖ *s* Franziskaner *m*
frank [fræŋk] *adj* offen ‖ *s* Freivermerk *m;* **Frank** (*masculine name*) Franz *m;* (*medieval German person*) Franke *m*, Frankin *f* ‖ *tr* franieren
frankfurter ['fræŋkfərtər] *s* Würstel *n*
frankincense ['fræŋkın,sens] *s* Weihrauch *m*
Frankish ['fræŋkıʃ] *adj* fränkisch
frankness ['fræŋknıs] *s* Offenheit *f;* (*bluntness*) Freimut *m*
frantic ['fræntık] *adj* (**with**) außer sich (vor *dat*); (*efforts*) krampfhaft

fraternal [frə'tʌrnəl] *adj* brüderlich; (*twins*) zweieiig
fraternity [frə'tʌrnɪti] *s* Bruderschaft *f;* (*educ*) Studentenverbindung *f*
fraternize ['frætər‚naɪz] *intr* (**with**) sich anfreunden (mit)
fraud [frɔd] *s* Betrug *m;* (*person*) (coll) Betrüger –in *mf*
fraudulent ['frɔdjələnt] *adj* betrügerisch
fraught [frɔt] *adj*—**f. with** voll mit; **f. with danger** gefahrvoll
fray [fre] *s* Schlägerei *f;* (*battle*) Kampf *m* ‖ *tr* ausfranzen; (*the nerves*) aufreiben ‖ *intr* (*said of edges*) sich ausfranzen; (*become threadbare*) sich durchscheuern
freak [frik] *s* Mißbildung *f;* (*whimsy*) Laune *f;* (*enthusiast*) Enthusiast –in *mf;* (*abnormal person*) verrückter Kerl *m;* **f. of nature** Monstrum *n*
freakish ['frikɪʃ] *adj* grotesk; (*capricious*) launisch
freckle ['frɛkəl] *s* Sommersprosse *f*
freckled ['frɛkəld], **freckly** ['frɛkli] *adj* sommersprossig
Frederick ['frɛdərɪk] *s* Friedrich *m*
free [fri] *adj* (**freer** ['fri‧ər]; **freest** ['fri‧ɪst]) frei; (*off duty*) dienstfrei; **for f.** (coll) gratis; **f. with** (*e.g., money, praise*) freigebig mit; **go f.** frei ausgehen; **he is f. to** (*inf*) es steht ihm frei zu (*inf*); **set f.** freilassen ‖ *adv* umsonst, kostenlos ‖ *v* (*pret* & *pp* **freed** [frid]; *ger* **freeing** ['fri‧ɪŋ] *tr* (*liberate*) befreien; (*untie*) losmachen
free′ and ea′sy *adj* zwanglos
freebooter ['fri‚butər] *s* Freibeuter *m*
free′born′ *adj* freigeboren
freedom ['fridəm] *s* Freiheit *f*
free′dom of assem′bly *s* Versammlungsfreiheit *f*
free′dom of speech′ *s* Redefreiheit *f*
free′dom of the press′ *s* Pressefreiheit *f*
free′dom of wor′ship *s* Glaubensfreiheit *f*
free′ en′terprise *s* freie Wirtschaft *f*
free′-for-all′ *s* allgemeine Prügelei *f*
free′ hand′ *s* freie Hand *f*
free′-hand draw′ing *s* (*activity*) Freihandzeichnen *n;* (*product*) Freihandzeichnung *f*
free′hand′ed *adj* freigebig
free′hold′ *s* (jur) Freigut *n*
free′ kick′ *s* (fb) Freistoß *m*
free′-lance′ *adj* freiberuflich ‖ *intr* freiberuflich tätig sein
free-lancer ['fri‚lænsər] *s* Freiberufliche *mf*
free′ li′brary *s* Volksbibliothek *f*
free′man *s* (**–men**) Ehrenbürger *m*
Free′ma′son *s* Freimaurer *m*
Free′ma′sonry *s* Freimaurerei *f*
free′ of charge′ *adj* & *adv* kostenlos
free′ on board′ *adv* frei an Bord
free′ play′ *s* (fig & mach) Spielraum *m*
free′ port′ *s* Freihafen *m*
free′ sam′ple *s* (*of food*) Gratiskostprobe *f;* (*of products*) Gratismuster *n*

free′ speech′ *s* Redefreiheit *f*
free′-spo′ken *adj* freimütig
free′stone′ *adj* mit leicht auslösbarem Kern
free′think′er *s* Freigeist *m*
free′ thought′ *s* Freigeisterei *f*
free′ trade′ *s* Freihandel *m*
free′way′ *s* Autobahn *f*
free′ will′ *s* Willensfreiheit *f;* **of one's own f.** aus freien Stücken
freeze [friz] *s* Frieren *n* ‖ *v* (*pret* **froze** [froz]; *pp* **frozen** ['frozən]) *tr* frieren; (*assets*) einfrieren; (*prices*) stoppen; (*food*) tiefkühlen; (surg) vereisen ‖ *intr* (ge)frieren; (*e.g., with fear*) erstarren; **f. over** zufrieren; **f. to death** erfrieren; **f. up** vereisen
freeze′-dry′ *v* (*pret* & *pp* **–dried**) *tr* gefriertrocknen
freezer ['frizər] *s* (*chest*) Tiefkühltruhe *f;* (*cabinet*) Tiefkühlschrank *m*
freez′er compart′ment *s* Gefrierfach *n*
freez′ing *s* Einfrieren *n;* **below f.** unter dem Gefrierpunkt
freight [fret] *s* (*load*) Fracht *f;* (*cargo*) Frachtgut *n;* (*fee*) Frachtgebühr *f;* **by f.** als Frachtgut ‖ *tr* beladen
freight′ car′ *s* Güterwagen *m*
freight′ el′vator *s* Warenaufzug *m*
freighter ['fretər] *s* Frachter *m*
freight′ of′fice *s* Güterabfertigung *f*
freight′ train′ *s* Güterzug *m*
freight′ yard′ *s* Güterbahnhof *m*
French [frɛntʃ] *adj* französisch ‖ *s* (*language*) Französisch *n;* **the F.** die Franzosen
French′ doors′ *spl* Glastüre *pl*
French′ fries′ *spl* Pommes frites *pl*
French′ horn′ *s* (mus) Waldhorn *n*
French′ leave′ *s*—**take F.** sich französisch empfehlen
French′man *s* (**–men**) Franzose *m*
French′ roll′ *s* Schrippe *f*
French′ toast′ *s* arme Ritter *pl*
French′ win′dow *s* Flügelfenster *n*
French′ wom′an *s* (**–wom′en**) Französin *f*
frenzied ['frenzid] *adj* rasend
frenzy ['frenzi] *s* Raserei *f*
frequency ['frikwənsi] *s* Häufigkeit *f;* (phys) Frequenz *f*
fre′quency modula′tion *s* Frequenzmodulation *f*
frequent ['frikwənt] *adj* häufig ‖ [fri-'kwɛnt] *tr* besuchen, frequentieren
frequently ['frikwəntli] *adv* häufig
fres·co ['frɛsko] *s* (**–coes** & **–cos**) Fresko *n,* Freskogemälde *n*
fresh [frɛʃ] *adj* frisch; (coll) frech ‖ *adv* neu, kürzlich
fresh′-baked′ *adj* neugebacken
freshen ['frɛʃən] *tr* erfrischen; **f. up** auffrischen ‖ *intr*—**f. up** sich auffrischen
freshet ['frɛʃɪt] *s* Hochwasser *n;* (*fresh-water stream*) Fluß *m*
fresh′man *s* (**–men**) Fuchs *m*
freshness ['frɛʃnɪs] *s* Frische *f;* (coll) Naseweisheit *f*
fresh′ wa′ter *s* Süßwasser *n*
fresh′-wa′ter *adj* Süßwasser–
fret [frɛt] *s* Verdruß *m;* (carp) Laubsägewerk *n;* (mus) Bund *n* ‖ *v* (*pret*

& pp **fretted;** ger **fretting)** tr gitterförmig verzieren ‖ intr sich ärgern
fretful ['fretfəl] adj verdrießlich
fret'work' s Laubsägewerk n
Freudian ['frɔɪdɪ·ən] adj Freudsch ‖ s Freudianer –in mf
friar ['fraɪ·ər] s Klosterbruder m
fricassee [‚frɪkə'si] s Frikassee n
friction ['frɪkʃən] s Reibung f; (fig) Reiberei f, Mißhelligkeit f
fric'tion tape' s Isolierband n
Friday ['fraɪdɪ] s Freitag m
fried [fraɪd] adj gebraten, Brat–, Back–
fried' chick'en s Backhuhn n
fried' egg' s Spiegelei n
fried' pota'toes spl Bratkartoffeln pl
friend [frend] s Freund –in mf; be (close) friends (eng) befreundet sein; make friends (with) sich anfreunden (mit)
friendliness ['frendlɪnɪs] s Freundlichkeit f
friendly ['frendli] adj freundlich; on f. terms with in freundschaftlichem Verhältnis mit
friend'ship' s Freundschaft f
frieze [friz] s Fries m
frigate ['frɪgɪt] s Fregatte f
fright [fraɪt] s Schrecken m
frighten ['fraɪtən] tr schrecken; be frightened erschrecken; f. away verscheuchen, vertreiben
frightful ['fraɪtfəl] adj schrecklich
frigid ['frɪdʒɪd] adj eiskalt; (pathol) Frigid
frigidity [frɪ'dʒɪdɪti] s Kälte f; (pathol) Frigidität f
Frig'id Zone' s kalte Zone f
frill [frɪl] s (ruffle) Volant m, Krause f; (frippery) Schnörkel m; put on frills sich aufgeblasen benehmen; with all the frills mit allen Schikanen
fringe [frɪndʒ] s Franse f ‖ tr mit Fransen besetzen; (fig) einsäumen
fringe' ar'ea s Randgebiet n
fringe' ben'efit s zusätzliche Sozialleistung f
frippery ['frɪpəri] s (cheap finery, trifles) Flitterkram m
frisk [frɪsk] tr (sl) durchsuchen ‖ intr —f. about herumtollen
frisky ['frɪski] adj ausgelassen
fritter ['frɪtər] s Beignet m ‖ tr—f. away vertrödeln, verzetteln
fritz [frɪts] s—on the f. kaputt
frivolous ['frɪvələs] adj leichtfertig; (object) geringfügig
friz [frɪz] s (frizzes) Kraushaar n ‖ v (pret & pp frizzed; ger frizzing) tr kräuseln ‖ intr sich kräuseln
frizzle ['frɪzəl] s Kraushaar n ‖ tr (hair) kräuseln; (food) knusprig braten ‖ intr sich kräuseln; (sizzle) zischen
frizzy ['frɪzi] adj kraus
fro [fro] adv—to and fro hin und her
frock [frɑk] s Kleid n; (eccl) Mönchskutte f
frog [frɔg] s (animal; slight hoarseness) Frosch m
frog'man' s (-men') Froschmann m
frol·ic ['frɑlɪk] s Spaß m ‖ v (pret &

pp –icked; ger –icking) intr Spaß machen; (frisk about) herumtollen
frolicsome ['frɑlɪksəm] adj ausgelassen
from [frʌm] prep von (dat), aus (dat), von (dat) aus; f. afar von weitem; f. now on künftig; f. ... on von ... an
front [frʌnt] adj Vorder–, vordere ‖ s (façade) Vorderseite f; (of a shirt, dress) Einsatz m; (cover-up) Aushängeschild n; (meteor, mil) Front f; from the f. von vorn; in f. vorn; in f. of vor (dat or acc); in the f. of the book vorn im Buch; put on a bold f. Mut zeigen; they put on a big f. alles Fassade! ‖ tr gegenüberliegen (dat) ‖ intr—f. for s.o. j–m als Strohmann dienen; f. on mit der Front liegen nach
frontage ['frʌntɪdʒ] s Straßenfront f
frontal ['frʌntəl] adj Frontal–; (anat) Stirn–
fron'tal view' s Vorderansicht f
front' door' s Haustür f
front' foot' s Vorderfuß m
frontier [frʌn'tɪr] s (border) Grenze f; (area) Grenzland n; (fig) Grenzbereich m
frontiers'man s (–men) Pionier m
frontispiece ['frʌntɪs‚pis] s Titelbild n
front' line' s Front f, Frontlinie f
front'-line' adj Front–, Gefechts–
front' page' s Titelseite f
front' porch' s Veranda f
front' rank' s (mil) vorderes Glied n; be in the f. (fig) im Vordergrund stehen
front' row' s erste Reihe f
front' run'ner s (pol) Spitzenkandidat –in mf
front' seat' s Vordersitz m
front' steps' spl Vordertreppe f
front' yard' s Vorgarten m, Vorplatz m
frost [frɔst] s (freezing) Frost m; (frozen dew) Reif m ‖ tr mit Reif überziehen; (culin) glasieren
frost'bite' s Erfrierung f
frost'bit'ten adj erfroren
frost'ed glass' s Mattglas n
frost'ing s Glasur f
frost' line' s Frostgrenze f
frosty ['frɔsti] adj (& fig) frostig
froth [frɔθ] s (foam) Schaum m; (slaver) Geifer m ‖ intr schäumen, geifern
frothy ['frɔθi] adj schäumend
froward ['frowərd] adj eigensinnig
frown [fraun] s Stirnrunzeln n ‖ intr die Stirn runzeln; f. at böse anschauen; f. on mißbilligen
frowsy, frowzy ['frauzi] adj (slovenly) schlampig; (ill-smelling) muffig
froz'en as'sets ['frozən] spl eingefrorene Guthaben pl
froz'en foods' spl tiefgekühlte Lebensmittel pl
frugal ['frugəl] adj frugal
fruit [frut] adj (tree) Obst–, Südfrucht– ‖ s Frucht f, Obst n, Südfrüchte pl; (fig) Frucht f
fruit' cake' s Stolle f, Stollen m

fruit' cup' *s* gemischte Früchte *pl*
fruit' fly' *s* Obstfliege *f*
fruitful ['frutfəl] *adj* fruchtbar
fruition [fru'ɪ/ən] *s* Reife *f;* **come to f.** zur Reife gelangen
fruit' jar' *s* Konservenglas *n*
fruit' juice' *s* Fruchtsaft *m,* Obstsaft *m*
fruitless ['frutlɪs] *adj* (& *fig*) fruchtlos
fruit' sal'ad *s* Obstsalat *m*
fruit' stand' *s* Obststand *m*
frump [frʌmp] *s* Scharteke *f*
frumpish ['frʌmpɪ/] *adj* schlampig
frustrate ['frʌstret] *tr* (*discourage*) frustrieren; (*an endeavor*) vereiteln
frustration [frʌs'tre/ən] *s* Frustration *f;* (*of an endeavor*) Vereitelung *f*
fry [fraɪ] *s* Gebratenes *n* ‖ *v* (*pret* & *pp* **fried**) *tr* & *intr* braten
fry'ing pan' *s* Bratpfanne *f;* **jump out of the f. into the fire** vom Regen unter die Traufe kommen
fuchsia ['fju/ə] *s* (bot) Fuchsie *f*
fudge [fʌdʒ] *s* weiches, milchhaltiges, mit Kakao versetztes Zuckerwerk *n*
fuel ['fju·əl] *s* Brennstoff *m;* (*for engines*) Treibstoff *m;* (fig) Nahrung *f;* **add f. to the flames** Öl ins Feuer gießen ‖ *v* (*pret* & *pp* **fuel[l]ed**) *ger* **fuel[l]ing**) *tr* mit Brennstoff versorgen ‖ *intr* tanken
fu'el dump' *s* Treibstofflager *n*
fu'el gauge' *s* Benzinuhr *f*
fu'el tank' *s* Treibstoffbehälter *m*
fugitive ['fjudʒɪtɪv] *adj* flüchtig ‖ *s* Flüchtling *m*
fugue [fjug] *s* (mus) Fuge *f*
ful·crum ['fʌlkrəm] *s* (**-crums** & **-cra** [krə]) Stützpunkt *m,* Drehpunkt *m*
fulfill [ful'fɪl] *tr* erfüllen
fulfillment [ful'fɪlmənt] *s* Erfüllung *f*
full [ful] *adj* voll; (*with food*) satt; (*clothes*) weit; (*hour*) ganz; (*life*) inhaltsreich; (*voice*) wohlklingend; (*professor*) ordentlich; **f. of** voller, voll von; **too f.** übervoll; **work f. time** ganztägig arbeiten ‖ *adv*—**f. well** sehr gut ‖ *s*—**in f.** voll, ganz ‖ *tr* (tex) walken
full'back' *s* (fb) Außenverteidiger *m*
full'-blood'ed *adj* vollblütig
full-blown ['ful'blon] *adj* (*flower*) voll aufgeblüht; (fig) voll erblüht
full'-bod'ied *adj* (*wine*) stark, schwer
full' dress' *s* Gesellschaftsanzug *m;* (mil) Paradeanzug *m*
full'-dress' *adj* Gala–, formell
full'-faced' *adj* pausbackig; (*portrait*) mit voll zugewandtem Gesicht
full-fledged ['ful'fledʒd] *adj* richtiggehend
full-grown ['ful'gron] *adj* voll ausgewachsen
full' house' *s* (cards) Full house *n;* (theat) volles Haus *n*
full'-length' *adj* (*dress*) in voller Größe; (*portrait*) lebensgroß; (*movie*) abendfüllend
full' moon' *s* Vollmond *m*
full'-page' *adj* ganzseitig
full' pay' *s* volles Gehalt *n*
full' profes'sor *s* Ordinarius *m*
full'-scale' *adj* in voller Größe
full'-sized' *adj* in natürlicher Größe

full' speed' *adv* auf höchsten Touren
full' stop' *s* (gram) Punkt *m;* **come to a f.** völlig stillstehen
full' swing' *s*—**in f.** in vollem Gange
full' throt'tle *s* Vollgas *n*
full' tilt' *adv* auf höchsten Touren
full'-time' *adj* ganztägig
full' view' *s*—**in f.** direkt vor den Augen
fully ['ful(l)i] *adj* völlig; **be f. booked** ausverkauft sein
fulsome ['fulsəm] *adj* (*excessive*) übermäßig; (*offensive*) widerlich
fumble ['fʌmbəl] *tr* (*a ball*) fallen lassen ‖ *intr* fummeln; **f. for** umherfühlen nach
fume [fjum] *s* Gas *n,* Dampf *m* ‖ *intr* dampfen; (*smoke*) rauchen; **f. with rage** vor Wut schnauben
fumigate ['fjumɪ‚get] *tr* ausräuchern
fun [fʌn] *s* Spaß *m;* **be (great) fun** (viel) Spaß machen; **for fun** zum Spaß; **for the fun of it** spaßeshalber; **have fun!** viel Spaß!; **make fun of** sich lustig machen über (*acc*); **poke fun at** witzeln über (*acc*)
function ['fʌŋk/ən] *s* Funktion *f;* (*office*) Amt *n;* (*formal occasion*) Feier *f* ‖ *intr* funktionieren; (*officiate*) fungieren
functional ['fʌŋk/ənəl] *adj* (*practical*) Zweck–, zweckmäßig; (*disorder*) funktionell, Funktions–
functionary ['fʌŋk/ə‚neri] *s* Funktionär –in *mf*
fund [fʌnd] *s* Fonds *m;* (fig) Vorrat *m* **funds** Geldmittel *pl* ‖ *tr* fundieren
fundamental [‚fʌndə'mentəl] *adj* grundlegend, Grund– ‖ *s* Grundbegriff *m*
fundamentalist [‚fʌndə'mentəlɪst] *s* Fundamentalist –in *mf*
fundamentally [‚fʌndə'mentəli] *adv* im Grunde, prinzipiell
funeral ['fjunərəl] *adj* Leichen–, Trauer–, Begräbnis– ‖ *s* Begräbnis *n*
fu'neral direc'tor *s* Bestattungsunternehmer –in *mf*
fu'neral home' *s* Aufbahrungshalle *f*
fu'neral proces'sion *s* Trauergefolge *n*
fu'neral serv'ice *s* Trauergottesdienst *m*
fu'neral wreath' *s* Totenkranz *m*
funereal [fju'nɪrɪ·əl] *adj* düster
fungus ['fʌŋgəs] *s* (**funguses** & **fungi** ['fʌndʒaɪ]) Pilz *m,* Schwamm *m*
funicular [fju'nɪkjələr] *s* Drahtseilbahn *f*
funk [fʌŋk] *s* (*fear*) Mordsangst *f;* **be in a f.** niedergeschlagen sein
fun·nel ['fʌnəl] *s* Trichter *m;* (naut) Schornstein *m* ‖ *v* (*pret* & *pp* **-nel[l]ed**) *ger* **-nel[l]ing**) *tr* durch e-n Trichter gießen; (fig) (*into*) konzentrieren (auf *acc*)
funnies ['fʌniz] *spl* Witzseite *f*
funny ['fʌni] *adj* komisch; (*strange, suspicious*) sonderbar; **don't try anything f.** mach mir keine Dummheiten!
fun'ny bone' *s* Musikantenknochen *m*
fun'ny bus'iness *s* dunkle Geschäfte *pl*
fun'ny ide'as *spl* Flausen *pl*

fun'ny pa'per *s* Witzblatt *n*
fur [fʌr] *adj* (*coat, collar*) Pelz– ‖ *s* Pelz *m*; (*on the tongue*) Belag *m*
furbish ['fʌrbɪʃ] *tr* aufputzen
furious ['fjurɪ·əs] *adj* (**at**) wütend (*auf acc*); **be f.** wüten
furl [fʌrl] *tr* zusammenrollen
fur'-lined' *adj* pelzgefüttert
furlong ['fʌrlɔŋ] *s* Achtelmeile *f*
furlough ['fʌrlo] *s* (mil) Urlaub *m*; **go on f.** auf Urlaub kommen ‖ *tr* beurlauben
furnace ['fʌrnɪs] *s* Ofen *m*
furnish ['fʌrnɪʃ] *tr* (*a room*) möblieren; (*e.g., an office*) ausstatten; (*proof*) liefern; (*supply*) (**with**) versehen (mit)
fur'nished room' *s* möbliertes Zimmer *n*
furnishings ['fʌrnɪʃɪŋz] *spl* Ausstattung *f*
furniture ['fʌrnɪtʃər] *s* Möbel *pl*; **piece of f.** Möbelstück *n*
fur'niture store' *s* Möbelhandlung *f*
furor ['fjurɔr] *s* (*rage*) Wut *f*; (*uproar*) Furore *f*; (*vogue*) Mode *f*; **cause a f.** Furore machen
furrier ['fʌrɪ·ər] *s* Pelzhändler –in *mf*
furrow ['fʌro] *s* Furche *f* ‖ *tr* furchen
furry ['fʌri] *adj* pelzig
further ['fʌrðər] *adj* weiter; (*particulars*) näher ‖ *adv* weiter ‖ *tr* fördern
furtherance ['fʌrðərəns] *s* Förderung *f*
fur'thermore' *adv* überdies, außerdem
furthest ['fʌrðɪst] *adj* weiteste ‖ *adv* am weitesten
furtive ['fʌrtɪv] *adj* verstohlen

fury ['fjuri] *s* Wut *f*; **Fury** (myth) Furie *f*
fuse [fjuz] *s* (*of an explosive*) Zünder *m*; (elec) Sicherung *f*; **blown f.** durchgebrannte Sicherung *f* ‖ *tr* verschmelzen ‖ *intr* verschmelzen; (fig) sich vereinigen
fuse' box' *s* Sicherungskasten *m*
fuselage ['fjuzəlɪdʒ] *s* (aer) Rumpf *m*
fusible ['fjuzɪbəl] *adj* schmelzbar
fusillade ['fjusə‚led] *s* Feuersalve *f*; (fig) Hagel *m*
fusion ['fjuʒən] *s* Verschmelzung *f*; (pol, phys) Fusion *f*
fuss [fʌs] *s* Getue *n*; **make a f. over** viel Aufhebens machen von ‖ *intr* sich aufregen; **f. around** herumwirtschaften; **f. over** viel Aufhebens machen von; **f. with** herumspielen mit
fuss' bud'get, fuss'pot' *s* Umstandskrämer *m*
fussy ['fʌsi] *adj* (*given to detail*) umständlich; (*fastidious*) heikel; (*irritable*) reizbar; **be f.** Umstände machen
fustian ['fʌstʃən] *s* (*bombast*) Schwulst *m*; (tex) Barchent *m*
fusty ['fʌsti] *adj* (*musty*) muffig; (*old-fashioned*) veraltet
futile ['fjutəl] *adj* vergeblich, nutzlos
futility [fju'tɪlɪti] *s* Nutzlosigkeit *f*
future ['fjutʃər] *adj* (zu)künftig ‖ *s* Zukunft *f*; **futures** (econ) Termingeschäfte *pl*; **in the f.** künftig
fuzz [fʌz] *s* (*from cloth*) Fussel *f*; (*on peaches*) Flaum *m*
fuzzy ['fʌzi] *adj* flaumig; (*unclear*) unklar; (*hair*) kraus

G

G, g [dʒi] *s* siebenter Buchstabe des englischen Alphabets
gab [gæb] *s* (coll) Geschwätz *n* ‖ *v* (*pret & pp* **gabbed**; *ger* **gabbing**) *intr* schwatzen
gabardine ['gæbər‚din] *s* Gabardine *m*
gabble ['gæbəl] *s* Geschnatter *n* ‖ *intr* schnattern
gable ['gebəl] *s* Giebel *m*
ga'ble end' *s* Giebelwand *f*
ga'ble roof' *s* Giebeldach *m*
gad [gæd] *v* (*pret & pp* **gadded**; *ger* **gadding**) *intr*—**gad about** umherstreifen
gad'about' *s* Bummler –in *mf*
gad'fly' *s* Viehbremse *f*; (fig) Störenfried *m*
gadget ['gædʒɪt] *s* (coll) Gerät *n*
Gaelic ['gelɪk] *adj* gälisch ‖ *s* (*language*) Gälisch *n*
gaff [gæf] *s* Fischhaken *m*
gag [gæg] *s* (*something put into the mouth*) Knebel *m*; (*joke*) Witz *m*; (*hoax, trick*) amüsanter Trick *m* ‖ *v* (*pret & pp* **gagged**; *ger* **gagging**) *tr* knebeln; (*said of a tight collar*) würgen; (fig) mundtot machen ‖ *intr* (*on food*) würgen

gage [gedʒ] *s* (*challenge*) Fehdehandschuh *m*; (*pawn*) Pfand *m*
gaiety ['ge·ɪti] *s* Fröhlichkeit *f*
gaily ['geli] *adv* fröhlich
gain [gen] *s* Gewinn *m*; (*advantage*) Vorteil *m*; **g. in weight** Gewichtszunahme *f* ‖ *tr* gewinnen; (*pounds*) zunehmen; (*a living*) verdienen; (*a victory*) erringen; **g. a footing** festen Fuß fassen; **g. ground** (mil & fig) Terrain gewinnen; **g. speed** schneller werden; **g. weight** an Gewicht zunehmen ‖ *intr* (*said of a car*) aufholen; (*said of a clock*) vorgehen; **g. from** Gewinn haben von; **g. in** gewinnen an (*dat*); **g. on s.o.** j-m den Vorteil abgewinnen
gainful ['genfəl] *adj* einträglich
gainfully ['genfəli] *adv*—**g. employed** erwerbstätig
gain'say' *v* (*pret & pp* **–said** [‚sed], [‚sɛd]) *tr* (*a thing*) verneinen; (*a person*) widersprechen (*dat*)
gait [get] *s* Gang *m*, Gangart *f*
gala ['gælə], ['gelə] *adj* festlich ‖ *s* (*celebration*) Feier *f*; (*dress*) Gala *f*
galaxy ['gæləksi] *s* Galaxis *f*; (fig) glänzende Versammlung *f*

gale [gel] s Sturm *m*, Sturmwind *m;*
gales of laughter Lachensalven *pl*
gale' warn'ing s Sturmwarnung *f*
gall [gɔl] s Galle *f; (audacity)* Unver-
schämtheit *f* || *tr (rub)* wundreiben;
(vex) ärgern, belästigen
gallant ['gælənt] *adj (tapfer); (stately)*
stattlich || [gə'lænt] *adj* galant || *s*
Galan *m*
gallantry ['gæləntri] s *(bravery)* Tapferkeit *f; (courteous behavior)* Ritterlichkeit *f*
gall' blad'der s Gallenblase *f*
galleon ['gælɪ·ən] s Galeone *f*
gallery ['gæləri] s *(arcade)* Säulen-
halle *f;* (art, theat) Galerie *f;* (min)
Stollen *m;* play to the g. (coll) Effekthascherei treiben
galley ['gæli] s *(a ship)* Galeere *f; (a
kitchen)* Kombüse *f;* (typ) Setzschiff
n
gal'ley proof' s (typ) Fahne *f*
gal'ley slave' s Galeerensklave *m*
Gallic ['gælɪk] *adj* gallisch
gall'ing *adj* verdrießlich
gallivant ['gælɪ ˌvænt] *intr* bummeln
gallon ['gælən] s Gallone *f*
galloon [gə'lun] s Tresse *f*
gallop ['gæləp] s Galopp *m;* at full g.
in gestrecktem Galopp || *tr* in Ga-
lopp setzen || *intr* galoppieren
gal·lows ['gæloz] s (–lows & –lowses)
Galgen *m*
gal'lows bird' s (coll) Galgenvogel *m*
gall'stone' s Gallenstein *m*
galore [gə'lor] *adv* im Überfluß
galosh [gə'lɑʃ] s Galosche *f*
galvanize ['gælvə ˌnaɪz] *tr* galvanisieren
gambit ['gæmbɪt] s (fig) Schachzug
m; (chess) Gambit *n*
gamble ['gæmbəl] s Hasardspiel *n;*
(risk) Risiko *n;* (com) Spekulations-
geschäft *n* || *tr*—g. away verspielen
|| *intr* spielen, hasardieren
gambler ['gæmblər] s Spieler –in *mf;*
(fig) Hasardeur *m*, Hasardeuse *f*
gam'bling s Spielen *n*, Spiel *n*
gam'bling house' s Spielhölle *f*
gam'bling ta'ble s Spieltisch *m*
gam·bol ['gæmbəl] s Luftsprung *m* || *v*
(pret & pp –bol[l]ed; *ger* –bol[l]ing)
intr umhertollen
gambrel ['gæmbrəl] s *(hock)* Hachse
f; (in a butcher shop) Spriegel *m*
gam'brel roof' s Mansardendach *n*
game [gem] *adj* bereit; *(fight)* tapfer;
(leg) lahm; (hunt) Wild–, Jagd– || s
Spiel *n; (e.g., of chess)* Partie *f;* (fig)
Absicht *f;* (culin) Wildbret *n;* (hunt)
Wild *n*, Jagdwild *n;* have the g. in
the bag den Sieg in der Tasche haben; play a losing g. auf verlorenem
Posten kämpfen; the g. is up das
Spiel ist aus
game' bird' s Jagdvogel *m*
game' board' s Spielbrett *n*
game'cock' s Kampfhahn *m*
gameness ['gemnɪs] *f* Tapferkeit *f*
game' of chance' s Glücksspiel *n*
game' preserve' s Wildpark *m*
game' war'den s Jagdaufseher *m*
gamut ['gæmət] s Skala *f*

gamy ['gemi] *adj* nach Wild riechend;
g. flavor Wildgeschmack *m*
gander ['gændər] s Gänserich *m;* take
a g. at (coll) e–n Blick werfen auf
(acc)
gang [gæŋ] s *(group of friends)* Gesellschaft *f; (antisocial group)* Bande
f; (of workers) Kolonne *f* || *intr*—
g. up (on) sich zusammenrotten
(gegen)
gangling ['gæŋglɪŋ] *adj* schlaksig
gangli·on ['gæŋglɪ·ən] s (–ons & –a
[ə]) *(cystic tumor)* Überbein *n; (of
nerves)* Nervenknoten *m*
gangly ['gæŋgli] *adj* schlaksig
gang'plank' s Laufplanke *f*, Steg *m*
gangrene ['gæŋgrin] s Gangrän *n*,
Brand *m* || *intr* brandig werden
gangrenous ['gæŋgrɪnəs] *adj* brandig
gangster ['gæŋstər] s Gangster *m*
gang'way' s *(passageway)* Durchgang
m; (naut) Laufplanke *f* || *interj* aus
dem Weg!
gantlet ['gɔntlət] s (rr) Gleisverschlin-
gung *f*
gantry ['gæntri] s (rok) Portalkran *m;*
(rr) Signalbrücke *f*
gan'try crane' s Portalkran *m*
gap [gæp] s Lücke *f; (in the mountains)* Schlucht *f;* (mil) Bresche *f*
gape [gep] s Riß *m*, Sprung *m; (gap-
ing)* Gaffen *n* || *intr* gaffen; *(said of
wounds, etc.)* klaffen; g. at angaffen
garage [gə'raʒ] s Garage *f; (repair
shop)* Reparaturwerkstatt *f;* put into
the g. unterstellen
garb [gɑrb] s Tracht *f*
garbage ['gɑrbɪdʒ] s Müll *m; (nonsense)* Unsinn *m*
gar'bage can' s Mülltonne *f*
gar'bage dispos'al s Müllabfuhr *f*
gar'bage dump' s Müllplatz *m*
gar'bage man' s Müllfahrer *m*
gar'bage truck' s Müllabfuhrwagen *m*
garble ['gɑrbəl] *tr* verstümmeln
garden ['gɑrdən] s Garten *m;* gardens
Gartenanlage *f*
gardener ['gɑrdənər] s Gärtner –in *mf*
gar'den hose' s Gartenschlauch *m*
gardenia [gɑr'dinɪ·ə] s Gardenie *f*
gar'dening s Gartenarbeit *f*
gar'den par'ty s Gartengesellschaft *f*
gargle ['gɑrgəl] s Mundwasser *n* || *tr
& intr* gurgeln
gargoyle ['gɑrgɔɪl] s Wasserspeier *m*
garish ['gerɪʃ], ['gærɪʃ] *adj* grell
garland ['gɑrlənd] s Girlande *f*
garlic ['gɑrlɪk] s Knoblauch *m*
garment ['gɑrmənt] s Kleidungsstück *n*
garner ['gɑrnər] *tr (grain)* aufspeichern; *(gather)* ansammeln
garnet ['gɑrnɪt] s Granat *m*
garnish ['gɑrnɪʃ] s Verzierung *f;*
(culin) Garnierung *f* || *tr* verzieren;
(culin) garnieren
garret ['gærɪt] s Dachstube *f*
garrison ['gærɪsən] s *(troops)* Garnison *f*, Besatzung *f; (fort)* Festung *f*
|| *tr* mit e–r Garnison versehen;
(troops) in Garnison stationieren
gar'rison cap' s Schiffchen *n*
garrote [gə'rɑt], [gə'rot] s Garrotte *f*
|| *tr* garrottieren

garrulous ['gær(j)ələs] *adj* schwatzhaft
garter ['gɑrtər] *s* Strumpfband *n*
gar'ter belt' *s* Strumpfhaltergürtel *m*
gas [gæs] *adj* (e.g., *generator, light, main, meter*) Gas– ‖ *s* Gas *n;* (coll) Benzin *n,* Sprit *m;* (*empty talk*) (sl) leeres Geschwätz *n;* **get gas** (coll) tanken; **step on the gas** (coll) Gas geben ‖ *v* (*pret & pp* **gassed; ger gassing**) *tr* vergasen ‖ *intr* (sl) schwatzen; **gas up** (coll) volltanken
gas' attack' *s* Gasangriff *m*
gas' burn'er *s* Gasbrenner *m*
gas' en'gine *s* Gasmotor *m*
gaseous ['gæsɪ·əs], ['gæʃəs] *adj* gasförmig
gas' fit'ter *s* Gasinstallateur *m*
gash [gæʃ] *s* tiefe Schnittwunde *f* ‖ e–e tiefe Schnittwunde beibringen (*dat*)
gas' heat' *s* Gasheizung *f*
gas'hold'er *s* Gasbehälter *m*
gasi·fy ['gæsɪ‚faɪ] *v* (*pret & pp* **–fied**) *tr* in Gas verwandeln ‖ *intr* zu Gas werden
gas' jet' *s* Gasflamme *f*
gasket ['gæskɪt] *s* Dichtung *f*
gas' mask' *s* Gasmaske *f*
gasoline [‚gæsə'lin] *s* Benzin *n*
gasoline' pump' *s* Benzinzapfsäule *f*
gasp [gæsp] *s* Keuchen *n* ‖ *tr* (**out**) hervorstoßen ‖ *intr* keuchen; **g. for air** nach Luft schnappen; **g. for breath** nach Atem ringen
gas' range' *s* Gasherd *m*
gas' sta'tion *s* Tankstelle *f*
gas' sta'tion attend'ant *s* Tankwart *m*
gas' stove' *s* Gasherd *m*
gas' tank' *s* Benzinbehälter *m*
gastric ['gæstrɪk] *adj* gastrisch
gas'tric juice' *s* Magensaft *m*
gastronomy [gæs'trɑnəmi] *s* Gastronomie *f*
gas'works' *spl* Gasanstalt *f*
gate [get] *s* Tor *n,* Pforte *f;* (rr) Sperre *f;* (sport) eingenommenes Eintrittsgeld *n;* **crash the g.** ohne Eintrittskarte durchschlupfen
gate' crash'er [‚kræʃər] *s* unberechtigter Zuschauer *m*
gate'keep'er *s* Pförtner –in *mf*
gate'post' *s* Torpfosten *m*
gate'way' *s* Tor *n,* Torweg *m*
gather ['gæðər] *tr* (*things*) sammeln; (*people*) versammeln; (*flowers, fruit, peas*) pflücken; (*courage*) aufbringen; (*the impression*) gewinnen; (*information*) einziehen; (*strength, speed*) zunehmen an (*dat*); (*conclude*) (**from**) schließen (aus); **g. together** versammeln; **g. up** aufheben; (*curtains, dress*) raffen ‖ *intr* sich (*an*)sammeln; (*said of clouds*) sich zusammenziehen; **g. around** sich scharen um
gath'ered *adj* (*skirt*) gerafft
gath'ering *s* Versammlung *f;* (sew) Kräuselfalten *pl*
gaudy ['gɔdi] *adj* (*overdone*) überladen; (*color*) grell
gauge [gedʒ] *s* (*instrument*) Messer *m,* Anzeiger *m;* (*measurement*) Eichmaß *n;* (*of wire*) Stärke *f;* (*of a shot-gun*) Kaliber *n;* (fig) Maß *n;* (mach) Lehre *f;* (rr) Spurweite *f* ‖ *tr* messen; (*check for accuracy*) eichen; (fig) abschätzen
Gaul [gɔl] *s* Gallien *n;* (*native*) Gallier –in *mf*
Gaulish ['gɔlɪʃ] *adj* gallisch
gaunt [gɔnt] *adj* hager
gauntlet ['gɔntlɪt] *s* Panzerhandschuh *m;* (fig) Fehdehandschuh *m;* **run the g.** Spießruten laufen
gauze [gɔz] *s* Gaze *f*
gavel ['gævəl] *s* Hammer *m*
gawk [gɔk] *s* (coll) Depp *m* ‖ *intr*—**g. at** (coll) blöde anstarren
gawky ['gɔki] *adj* schlaksig
gay [ge] *adj* lustig; (*homosexual*) schwul
gay' blade' *s* lebenslustiger Kerl *m*
gaze [gez] *intr* starren; **g. at** anstarren; (*in astonishment*) anstaunen
gazelle [gə'zel] *s* Gazelle *f*
gazetteer [‚gæzə'tɪr] *s* Ortslexikon *n*
gear [gɪr] *s* (*equipment*) Ausrüstung *f;* (aut) Schaltgetriebe *n,* Gang *m;* (mach) Zahnrad *n;* **gears** Räderwerk *n;* **in g.** eingeschaltet; **in high g.** im höchsten Gang; (fig) auf Touren; **shift gears** umschalten; **throw into g.** einschalten; **throw out of g.** (fig) aus dem Gleichgewicht bringen ‖ *tr*—**g. to** anpassen (*dat*)
gear'box' *s* Schaltgetriebe *n*
gear'shift' *s* Gangschaltung *f;* (*lever*) Schalthebel *m*
gear'wheel' *s* Zahnrad *n*
gee [dʒi] *interj* nanu!
Geiger counter ['gaɪgər‚kauntər] *s* Geigerzähler *m*
gel [dʒel] *s* Gel *n* ‖ *v* (*pret & pp* **gelled; ger gelling**) *intr* gelieren; (coll) klappen
gelatin ['dʒelətɪn] *s* Gelatine *f*
geld [geld] *v* (*pret & pp* **gelded & gelt** [gelt]) *tr* kastrieren
geld'ing *s* Wallach *m*
gem [dʒem] *s* Edelstein *m;* (fig) Perle *f*
Gemini ['dʒemɪ‚naɪ] *s* (astr) Zwillinge *pl*
gender ['dʒendər] *s* Geschlecht *n*
gene [dʒin] *s* Gen *n,* Erbanlage *f*
genealogical [‚dʒini·ə'lɑdʒɪkəl] *adj* genealogisch, Stamm–
genealog'ical ta'ble *s* Stammtafel *f*
genealog'ical tree' *s* Stammbaum *m*
genealogy [‚dʒini'ælədʒi] *s* Genealogie *f*
general ['dʒenərəl] *adj* allgemein, Gesamt– ‖ *s* General *m;* **in g.** im allgemeinen
Gen'eral Assem'bly *s* Vollversammlung *f*
gen'eral deliv'ery *adv* postlagernd
gen'eral head'quarters *spl* Oberkommando *n*
generalissi·mo [‚dʒenərə'lɪsɪmo] *s* (**–mos**) Generalissimus *m*
generality [‚dʒenə'rælɪti] *s* Allgemeingültigkeit *f;* **generalities** Gemeinplätze *pl*
generalization [‚dʒenərəlɪ'zeʃən] *s* Verallgemeinerung *f*

generalize ['dʒɛnərə‚laɪz] *tr & intr* verallgemeinern
generally ['dʒɛnərəli] *adv* im allgemeinen; *(usually)* gewöhnlich; *(mostly)* meistens
gen'eral man'ager *s* Generaldirektor –in *mf*
gen'eral plan' *s* Übersichtsplan *m*
gen'eral post' of'fice *s* Oberpostamt *n*
gen'eral practi'tioner *s* praktischer Arzt *m*
gen'eralship' *s* Führereingenschaften *pl*
gen'eral staff' *s* Generalstab *m*
gen'eral store' *s* Gemischtwarenhandlung *f*
gen'eral strike' *s* Generalstreik *m*
generate ['dʒɛnə‚ret] *tr (procreate)* zeugen; *(fig)* verursachen; *(elec)* erzeugen; *(geom)* bilden
gen'erating sta'tion *s* Kraftwerk *n*
generation [‚dʒɛnə'reʃən] *s* Generation *f;* **present g.** Mitwelt *f;* **younger g.** junge Generation *f*
genera'tion gap' *s* Generationsproblem *n*
generator ['dʒɛnə‚retər] *s* Erzeuger *m;* (chem, elec) Generator *m;* (elec) Stromerzeuger *m*
generic [dʒɪ'nɛrɪk] *adj* generisch, Gattungs–; **g. name** Gattungsname *m*
generosity [‚dʒɛnə'rɑsɪti] *s* Freigebigkeit *f*
generous ['dʒɛnərəs] *adj* freigebig
gene•sis ['dʒɛnɪsɪs] *s* (**–ses** [‚siz]) Genese *f,* Entstehung *f;* **Genesis** (Bib) Genesis *f*
genetic [dʒɪ'nɛtɪk] *adj* genetisch
genet'ic engineer' *s* Gen-Ingineur *m*
genet'ic engineer'ing *s* Gen-Manipulation *f*
genetics [dʒɪ'nɛtɪks] *s* Genetik *f,* Vererbungslehre *f*
Geneva [dʒɪ'nivə] *adj* Genfer || *s* Genf *n*
Genevieve ['dʒɛnə‚viv] *s* Genoveva *f*
genial ['dʒinɪ‚əl] *adj* freundlich
genie ['dʒini] *s* Kobold *m*
genital ['dʒɛnɪtəl] *adj* Genital– || **genitals** *spl* Genitalien *pl*
genitive ['dʒɛnɪtɪv] *s* Genitiv *m,* Wesfall *m*
genius ['dʒinɪ‚əs] *s* (**geniuses**) Genie *n* || *s* (**genii** ['dʒini‚aɪ]) Genius *m*
Genoa ['dʒɛno‚ə] *s* Genua *n*
genocidal [‚dʒɛnə'saɪdəl] *adj* rassenmörderisch
genocide ['dʒɛnə‚saɪd] *s* Rassenmord *m*
genre ['ʒɑnrə] *s* Genre *n*
genteel [dʒɛn'til] *adj* vornehm
gentile ['dʒɛntaɪl] *adj* nichtjüdisch; *(pagan)* heidnisch || *s* Nichtjude *m,* Nichtjüdin *f;* *(pagan)* Heide *m,* Heidin *f*
gentility [dʒɛn'tɪlɪti] *s* Vornehmheit *f*
gentle ['dʒɛntəl] *adj* sanft, mild; *(tame)* zahm
gen'tle•man *s* (**–men**) Herr *m,* Gentleman *m*
gentlemanly ['dʒɛntəlmənli] *adj* weltmännisch
gen'tleman's agree'ment *s* Kavaliersab-

kommen *n,* Gentleman's Agreement *n*
gentleness ['dʒɛntəlnɪs] *s* Sanftmut *f*
gen'tle sex' *s* zartes Geschlecht *n*
gentry ['dʒɛntri] *s* feine Leute *pl*
genuflection [‚dʒɛnju'flɛkʃən] *s* Kniebeugung *f*
genuine ['dʒɛnju•ɪn] *adj* echt
genus ['dʒinəs] *s* (**genera** ['dʒɛnərə] & **genuses**) (biol, log) Gattung *f*
geographer [dʒɪ'ɑgrəfər] *s* Geograph –in *mf*
geographic(al) [‚dʒɪ•ə'græfɪk(əl)] *adj* geographisch
geography [dʒɪ'ɑgrəfi] *s* Geographie *f*
geologic(al) [‚dʒɪ•ə'lɑdʒɪk(əl)] *adj* geologisch
geolog'ical e'ra *s* Erdalter *n*
geologist [dʒɪ'ɑlədʒɪst] *s* Geologe *m,* Geologin *f*
geology [dʒɪ'ɑlədʒi] *s* Geologie *f*
geometric(al) [‚dʒi•ə'mɛtrɪk(əl)] *adj* geometrisch
geometrician [dʒɪ‚ɑmɪ'trɪʃən] *s* Geometer –in *mf*
geometry [dʒɪ'ɑmɪtri] *s* Geometrie *f*
geophysics [‚dʒi•ə'fɪzɪks] *s* Geophysik *f*
geopolitics [‚dʒi•ə'pɑlɪtɪks] *s* Geopolitik *f*
George [dʒɔrdʒ] *s* Georg *m*
geranium [dʒɪ'renɪ•əm] *s* Geranie *f*
geriatrics [‚dʒɛrɪ'ætrɪks] *s* Geriatrie *f*
germ [dʒʌrm] *s* Keim *m*
German ['dʒʌrmən] *adj & adv* deutsch || *s* Deutsche *mf;* *(language)* Deutsch *n;* **in G.** auf deutsch
germane [dʒɛr'men] *adj* (**to**) passend (zu)
Germanize ['dʒʌrmə‚naɪz] *tr* eindeutschen
Ger'man mea'sles *s & spl* Röteln *pl*
Ger'man shep'herd *s* deutscher Schäferhund *m*
Ger'man sil'ver *s* Alpaka *n,* Neusilber *n*
Germany ['dʒʌrməni] *s* Deutschland *n*
germ' cell' *s* Keimzelle *f*
germicidal [‚dʒʌrmɪ'saɪdəl] *adj* keimtötend
germicide ['dʒʌrmɪ‚saɪd] *s* Keimtöter *m*
germinate ['dʒʌrmɪ‚net] *intr* keimen
germ' war'fare *s* bakteriologische Kriegsführung *f*
gerontology [‚dʒɛrən'tɑlədʒi] *s* Gerontologie *f*
gerund ['dʒɛrənd] *s* Gerundium *n*
gerundive [dʒɪ'rʌndɪv] *s* Gerundiv *n*
gestation [dʒɛs'teʃən] *s* Schwangerschaft *f;* *(in animals)* Trächtigkeit *f*
gesticulate [dʒɛs'tɪkjə‚let] *intr* gestikulieren, sich gebärden
gesticulation [dʒɛs‚tɪkjə'leʃən] *s* Gebärdenspiel *n,* Gestikulation *f*
gesture ['dʒɛstʃər] *s* Geste *f* || *intr* Gesten machen
get [gɛt] *v (pret* **got** [gɑt]*; pp* **got** & **gotten** ['gɑtən]*; ger* **getting**) *tr (acquire)* bekommen; *(receive)* erhalten; *(procure)* beschaffen, besorgen; *(fetch)* holen; *(understand)* (coll) kapieren; *(s.o. to do s.th.)* dazu

bringen; (*reach by telephone*) erreichen; (*make, e.g., dirty*) machen; (*convey, e.g., a message*) übermitteln; **get across** klarmachen; **get back** zurückbekommen; **get down** (*depress*) verdrießen; (*swallow*) hinunterwürgen; **get going** in Gang setzen; **get hold of** (*a person*) erwischen; (*a thing*) erlangen; (*grip*) ergreifen; **get off** (*e.g., a lid*) abbekommen; **get out** (*e.g., a spot*) herausbekommen; **get s.o.** used to j–n gewöhnen an (*acc*); **get s.th.** into one's head sich [*dat*] etw in den Kopf setzen; **get the hang of** (coll) wegbekommen; **get the jump on s.o.** j–m zuvorkommen; **get the worst of it** am schlechtesten dabei wegkommen; get (*s.th.*) **wrong** falsch verstehen; **you're going to get it!** (coll) du wirst es kriegen! ‖ *intr* (*become*) werden; **get about** sich fortbewegen; **get ahead in the world** in der Welt fortkommen; **get along** auskommen; **get along with** zurechtkommen mit; **get around** herumkommen; **get around to it** dazu kommen; **get at** herankommen an (*acc*); (*e.g., the real reason*) herausfinden; **get away** (*run away*) entlaufen; (*escape*) entkommen; **get away from me!** geh weg von mir!; **get away with** davonkommen mit; **get back at s.o.** es j–m heimzahlen; **get by** (*e.g., the guards*) vorbeikommen an (*dat*); (*on little money*) durchkommen; **get down** (*step down*) absteigen; **get down to brass tacks** (*or* **business**) zur Sache kommen; **get going** sich auf den Weg machen; **get going!** mach, daß du weiter kommst!; **get into** (*a vehicle*) einsteigen in (*acc*); (*trouble, etc.*) geraten in (*acc*); **get loose** sich losmachen; **get lost** verloren gehen, abhanden kommen; (*lose one's way*) sich verirren; **get lost!** (sl) hau ab!; **get off** aussteigen; **get off with** (*a light sentence*) davonkommen mit; **get on** (*e.g., a train*) einsteigen (in *acc*); **get on one's feet again** sich hochrappeln; **get on with** (*s.o.*) zurechtkommen mit; **get out** aussteigen; **get out of a tight spot** sich aus der Schlinge ziehen; **get over** (*a hurdle*) nehmen; (*a misfortune*) überwinden; (*a sickness*) überstehen; **get ready** sich fertig machen; **get through** durchkommen; **get through to s.o.** sich verständlich machen (*dat*); (telp) erreichen; **get to be** werden; **get together** (*meet*) sich treffen; (*agree*) (on) sich einig werden (über *acc*); **get to the bottom of** ergründen; **get up** aufstehen; **get used to** sich gewöhnen an (*acc*); **get well** gesund werden; **get with it!** (coll) zur Sache!

get′away′ *s* Entkommen *n*; (sport) Start *m;* **make one's g.** entkommen
get′away car′ *s* Fluchtwagen *m*
get′-togeth′er *s* zwangloses Treffen *n*
get′up′ *s* (coll) Aufzug *m*

get′ up′ and go′ *s* Unternehmungsgeist *m*
gewgaw [′g(j)ugɔ] *s* Plunder *m*
geyser [′gaɪzər] *s* Geiser *m*
ghastly [′gæstli] *adj* (*ghostly*) gespenstisch; (*e.g., crime*) grausig; (*intensely unpleasant*) schrecklich
gherkin [′gʌrkɪn] *s* Essiggurke *f*
ghet·to [′geto] *s* (**-tos**) Getto *n*
ghost [gost] *s* Gespenst *n*, Geist *m;* (telv) Doppelbild *n;* **give up the g.** den Geist aufgeben; **not a g. of a chance** nicht die geringsten Aussichten
ghostly [′gostli] *adj* gespenstisch
ghost′ sto′ry *s* Spukgeschichte *f*
ghost′ town′ *s* Geisterstadt *f*
ghost′ writ′er *s* Ghostwriter *m*
ghoul [gul] *s* (& fig) Unhold *m*
ghoulish [′gulɪʃ] *adj* teuflisch
GHQ [′dʒi′et′′kju] *s* (**General Headquarters**) Oberkommando *n*
GI [′dʒi′aɪ] *s* (**GI's**) (coll) Landser *m*
giant [′dʒaɪ·ənt] *adj* riesig, Riesen– ‖ *s* Riese *m*, Riesin *f*
giantess [′dʒaɪ·əntɪs] *s* Riesin *f*
gibberish [′dʒɪbərɪʃ], [′gɪbərɪʃ] *s* Klauderwelsch *n*
gibbet [′dʒɪbɪt] *s* Galgen *m* ‖ *tr* hängen
gibe [dʒaɪb] *s* Spott *m* ‖ *intr* spotten; **g. at** verspotten
giblets [′dʒɪblɪts] *spl* Gänseklein *n*
giddiness [′gɪdɪnɪs] *s* Schwindelgefühl *n;* (*frivolity*) Leichtsinn *m*
giddy [′gɪdi] *adj* (*dizzy*) schwindlig; (*height*) schwindelerregend; (*frivolous*) leichtsinnig
gift [gɪft] *s* Geschenk *n;* (*natural ability*) Begabung *f*
gift′ed *adj* begabt
gift′horse′ *s*—**never look a g. in the mouth** e–m geschenkten Gaul schaut man nicht ins Maul
gift′ of gab′ *s* (coll) gutes Mundwerk *n*
gift′ shop′ *s* Geschenkartikelladen *m*
gift′-wrap′ *v* (*pret* & *pp* **–wrapped;** *ger* **–wrapping**) *tr* als Geschenk verpacken
gift′wrap′ping *s* Geschenkverpackung *f*
gigantic [dʒaɪ′gæntɪk] *adj* riesig
giggle [′gɪgəl] *s* Gekicher *n* ‖ *intr* kichern
gigly [′gɪgli] *adj* allezeit kichernd
gigo·lo [′dʒɪgə‚lo] *s* (**-los**) Gigolo *m*
gild [gɪld] *v* (*pret* & *pp* **gilded** & **gilt** [gɪlt]) *tr* vergolden
gild′ing *s* Vergoldung *f*
gill [gɪl] *s* (*of a fish*) Kieme *f;* (*of a cock*) Kehllappen *m*
gilt [gɪlt] *adj* vergoldet ‖ *s* Vergoldung *f*
gilt′ edge′ *s* Goldschnitt *m*
gilt′-edged′ *adj* mit Goldschnitt versehen; (*first-class*) (coll) erstklassig
gimlet [′gɪmlɪt] *s* Handbohrer *m*
gimmick [′gɪmɪk] *s* (sl) Trick *m*
gin [dʒɪn] *s* Wacholderbranntwein *m*, Gin *m;* (*snare*) Schlinge *f* ‖ *v* (*pret* & *pp* **ginned;** *ger* **ginning**) *tr* entkörnen
ginger [′dʒɪndʒər] *s* Ingwer *m*

gin'ger ale' *s* Ingwerlimonade *f*
gin'gerbread' *s* Pfefferkuchen *m*
gingerly ['dʒɪndʒərli] *adv* sacht(e)
gin'gersnap' *s* Ingwerplätzchen *n*
gingnam ['gɪŋəm] *s* Gingham *m*
giraffe [dʒɪ'ræf] *s* Giraffe *f*
gird [gʌrd] *v* (*pret & pp* girt [gʌrt] & girded) *tr* gürten; **g. oneself with a sword** sich ⌊*dat*⌋ ein Schwert umgürten
girder ['gʌrdər] *s* Tragbalken *m*
girdle ['gʌrdəl] *s* Gürtel *m*
girl [gʌrl] *s* Mädchen *n*, Mädel *n*
girl' friend' *s* Freundin *f*, Geliebte *f*
girl'hood' *s* Mädchenzeit *f*
girlish ['gʌrlɪʃ] *adj* mädchenhaft
girl' scout' *s* Pfadfinderin *f*
girth [gʌrθ] *s* Umfang *m*; (*for a horse*) Sattelgurt *m*
gist [dʒɪst] *s* Kernpunkt *m*; **g. of the matter** des Pudels Kern
give [gɪv] *s* Elastizität *f*; (*yielding*) Nachgeben *n* ‖ *v* (*pret* gave [gev]; *pp* given ['gɪvən]) *tr* geben; (*a gift, credence*) schenken; (*free of charge*) verschenken; (*contribute*) spenden; (*hand over*) übergeben; (*a report*) erstatten; (*a reason, the time*) angeben; (*attention, recognition*) zollen; (*a lecture*) halten; (*an award*) zusprechen; (*homework*) aufgeben; (*a headache, etc.*) verursachen; (*joy*) machen; (*a reception*) veranstalten; (*a blow*) versetzen; **g. away** weggeben; (*divulge*) verraten; **g. away the bride** Brautvater sein; **g. back** zurückgeben; **g. it to 'em!** (coll) hau zu!; **g. off** von sich geben; (*steam*) ausströmen lassen; **g. oneself away** sich verplappern; **g. oneself up** sich stellen; **g. or take** mehr oder weniger; **g. out** ausgeben; **g. rise to** Anlaß geben zu; **g. up** aufgeben; (*a business*) schließen; **g. up for lost** verlorengeben; **g. way** weichen; **g. way to** sich überlassen (*dat*) ‖ *intr* (*yield*) nachgeben; (*collapse*) einstürzen; **g. in to** nachgeben (*dat*), weichen (*dat*); **g. out** (*said of the voice, legs*) versagen; (*said of strength*) nachlassen; **g. up** aufgeben; (mil) die Waffen strecken; **g. up on** verzagen an (*dat*)
give'-and-take' *s* Kompromiß *m & n*; (*exchange of opinion*) Meinungsaustausch *m*
give'away' *s* (*betrayal of a secret*) unbeabsichtigte Preisgabe *f*; (*promotional article*) Gratisprobe *f*
give'away show' *s* Preisrätselsendung *f*
given ['gɪvən] *adj* gegeben; (*time*) festgesetzt; (math, philos) gegeben); **g. to drinking** dem Trunk ergeben
giv'en name' *s* Vorname *m*
giver ['gɪvər] *s* Geber –in *mf*; (*of a contribution*) Spender –in *mf*
gizzard ['gɪzərd] *s* Geflügelmagen *m*
gla'cial per'iod ['gleʃəl] *s* Eiszeit *f*
glacier ['gleʃər] *s* Gletscher *m*
glad [glæd] *adj* (gladder; gladdest) froh; **be g. (about)** sich freuen (über *acc*); **g. to** (*inf*) erfreut zu (*inf*); **g. to meet you** sehr erfreut!, sehr ange-

nehm!; **I'll be g. to do it for you** ich werde das gern für Sie tun
gladden ['glædən] *tr* erfreuen
glade [gled] *s* Waldwiese *f*, Waldlichtung *f*
gladiator ['glædɪ̩etər] *s* Gladiator *m*
gladiola [̩glædɪ'olə] *s* Gladiole *f*
gladly ['glædli] *adv* gern(e)
gladness ['glædnɪs] *s* Freude *f*
glad' rags' *spl* (sl) Sonntagsstaat *m*
glad' tid'ings *spl* Freundenbotschaft *f*
glamorous ['glæmərəs] *adj* bezaubernd
glamour ['glæmər] *s* (*of a girl*) Zauber *m*; (*of an event*) Glanz *m*
glam'our girl' *s* gefeierte Schönheit *f*; (pej) Zierpuppe *f*
glance [glæns] *s* Blick *m*; **at a g.**, **at first g.** auf den ersten Blick; ‖ *intr* (at) blicken (auf *acc* or nach); **g. around** umherblicken; **g. off** abgleiten an (*dat*); **g. through** (or over) flüchtig durchsehen; **g. up** aufblicken
gland [glænd] *s* Drüse *f*
glanders ['glændərz] *spl* Rotskrankheit *f*
glare [gler] *s* grelles Licht *n*; (*look*) böser Blick *m* ‖ *intr* blenden; (*look*) böse starren; **g. at** böse anstarren
glar'ing *adj* (*light*) grell; (fig) schreiend, aufdringlich
glass [glæs] *adj* gläsern, Glas– ‖ *s* Glas *n*; **glasses** Brille *f*
glass' bead' *s* Glasperle *f*
glass' blow'er ['blo-ər] *s* Glasbläser –in *mf*
glass' blow'ing *s* Glasbläserei *f*
glass' case' *s* Schaukasten *m*
glass' cut'ter *s* Glasschleifer –in *mf*; (*tool*) Glasschneider *m*
glassful ['glæsful] *s* Glas *n*
glass'ware' *s* Glaswaren *pl*
glass' wool' *s* Glaswolle *f*
glass'works' *s* Glasfabrik *f*, Glashütte *f*
glassy ['glæsi] *adj* (*surface*) spiegelglatt; (*eyes*) glasig
glaucoma [glau'komə] *s* Glaukom *n*, grüner Star *m*
glaze [glez] *s* (*on ceramics*) Glasur *f*; (*on paintings*) Lasur *f*; (*of ice*) Glatteis *n* ‖ *tr* (ceramics, baked goods) glasieren; (*a window*) verglasen; (*a painting*) lasieren
glazed *adj* (ceramics, baked goods) glasiert; (*eyes*) glasig; **g. tile** Kachel *f*
glazier ['gleʒər] *s* Glaser –in *mf*
gleam [glim] *s* Lichtstrahl *m*; **g. of hope** Hoffnungsschimmer *m* ‖ *intr* strahlen
glean [glin] *tr & intr* auflesen; (fig) zusammentragen
gleanings ['glinɪŋz] *spl* Nachlese *f*
glee [gli] *s* Frohsinn *m*
glee' club' *s* Gesangverein *m*
glen [glen] *s* Bergschlucht *f*
glib [glɪb] *adj* (glibber; glibbest) (*tongue*) beweglich; (*person*) zungenfertig
glide [glaɪd] *s* Gleiten *n*; (aer) Gleitflug *m*; (*with a glider*) (aer) Segelflug *m*; (ling) Gleitlaut *m*; (mus) Glissando *n* ‖ *intr* gleiten

glider ['glaɪdər] *s* (*porch swing*) Schaukelbett *n;* (aer) Segelflugzeug *n*

glid'er pi'lot *s* Segelflieger –in *mf*

glid'ing *s* Segelfliegen *n*

glimmer ['glɪmər] *s* Schimmer *m;* **g. of hope** Hoffnungsschimmer *m* || *intr* schimmern

glim'mering *adj* flimmernd || *s* Flimmern *n*

glimpse [glɪmps] *s* flüchtiger Blick *m;* **catch a g. of** flüchtig zu sehen bekommen || *tr* flüchtig erblicken || *intr*—**g. at** e–n flüchtigen Blick werfen auf (*acc*)

glint [glɪnt] *s* Lichtschimmer *m* || *intr* schimmern

glisten ['glɪsən] *s* Glanz *m* || *intr* glänzen

glitter ['glɪtər] *s* Glitzern *n,* Glanz *m* || *intr* glitzern, glänzen

gloat [glot] *intr* schadenfroh sein; **g. over** sich weiden an (*dat*)

gloat'ing *s* Schadenfreude *f*

global ['globəl] *adj* global, Welt-

globe [glob] *s* Erdkugel *f,* Globus *m*

globe'-trot'ter *s* Weltenbummler –in *mf*

globule ['glɑbjul] *s* Kügelchen *n*

glockenspiel ['glɑkən ˌspil] *s* Glockenspiel *n*

gloom [glum] *s* Düsternis *f;* (fig) Trübsinn *m*

gloominess ['glumɪnɪs] *s* Düsterkeit *f;* (fig) Trübsinn *m*

gloomy ['glumi] *adj* düster; (*depressing*) bedrückend; (*depressed*) trübsinning

glorification ['glorɪfɪ ˌkeʃən] *s* Verherrlichung *f*

glori·fy ['glorɪ ˌfaɪ] *v* (*pret & pp* –fied) *tr* verherrlichen

glorious ['glorɪ·əs] *adj* (*full of glory*) glorreich; (*magnificent*) herrlich

glo·ry ['glori] *s* Ruhm *m;* (*magnificence*) Herrlichkeit *f;* **be in one's g.** im siebenten Himmel sein || *v* (*pret & pp* –ried) *intr*—**g. in** frohlocken über (*acc*)

gloss [glɔs] *s* (*shine*) Glanz *m;* (*notation*) Glosse *f* || *tr* glossieren; **g. over** verschleiern

glossary ['glɔsəri] *s* Glossar *n*

glossy ['glɔsi] *adj* glänzend

glottis ['glɑtɪs] *s* Stimmritze *f*

glove [glʌv] *s* Handschuh *m;* **fit like a g.** wie angegossen passen

glove' compart'ment *s* Handschuhfach *n*

glow [glo] *s* Glühen *n* || *intr* glühen; **g. with** (fig) (er)glühen vor (*dat*)

glower ['glau·ər] *s* finsterer Blick *m* || *intr* finster blicken; **g. at** finster anblicken

glow'ing *adj* glühend; (*account*) begeistert

glow'worm' *s* Glühwurm *m*

glucose ['glukos] *s* Glukose *f*

glue [glu] *s* Leim *m,* Klebemittel *n* || *tr* (*wood*) leimen; (*paper*) kleben

gluey ['glu·i] *adj* leimig

glum [glʌm] *adj* (**glummer; glummest**) verdrießlich

glut [glʌt] *s* Übersättigung *f;* **a g. on the market** e-e Überschwemmung des Marktes || *v* (*pret & pp* **glutted;** *ger* **glutting**) *tr* übersättigen; (com) überschwemmen

glutton ['glʌtən] *s* Vielfraß *m*

gluttonous ['glʌtənəs] *adj* gefräßig

gluttony ['glʌtəni] *s* Gefräßigkeit *f*

glycerine ['glɪsərɪn] *s* Glyzerin *n*

gnarled [nɑrld] *adj* knorrig

gnash [næʃ] *tr*—**g. one's teeth** mit den Zähnen knirschen

gnat [næt] *s* Mücke *f*

gnaw [nɔ] *tr* zernagen; **g. off** abnagen || *intr* (**on**) nagen (an *dat*)

gnome [nom] *s* Gnom *m,* Berggeist *m*

go [go] *s*—**be on the go** auf den Beinen sein; **have a lot of go** viel Mumm in den Knochen haben; **it's no go** es geht nicht; **let's have a go at it** probieren wir's mal; **make a go of it** es zu e–m Erfolg machen || *v* (*pret* **went** [wɛnt]; *pp* **gone** [gɔn]) *tr*—**go it alone** es ganz allein(e) machen || *intr* gehen; (*depart*) weggehen; (*travel*) fahren, reisen; (*operate*) arbeiten; (*belong*) gehören; (*turn out*) verlaufen; (*collapse*) zusammenbrechen; (*fail, go out of order*) kaputtgehen; (*said of words*) lauten; (*said of bells*) läuten; (*said of a buzzer*) ertönen; (*said of awards*) zugeteilt werden; (*said of a road*) führen; **be going to,** e.g., **I am going to study** ich werde studieren; **go about** umhergehen; (*a task*) in Angriff nehmen; **go about it** darangehen; **go after** (*run after*) nachlaufen; (*strive for*) streben nach; **go against the grain** gegen den Strich gehen; **go ahead** vorausgehen; **go ahead!** voran!; **go along with** (*accompany*) mitgehen mit; (*agree with*) zustimmen mit; **go and see for yourself** überzeugen Sie sich selbst davon!; **go around** herumgehen; (*suffice*) (aus)reichen; (*an obstacle*) umgehen; **go at** (*a person*) losgehen auf (*acc*); (*a thing*) herangehen an (*acc*); **go away** weggehen; **go bad** schlecht werden; **go back** zurückkehren; (*ride back*) zurückfahren; **go back on** (*one's word*) brechen; **go beyond** überschreiten; **go by** (*pass by*) vorbeigehen (an *dat*); (*said of time*) vergehen; (*act according to*) sich richten nach; **go down** niedergehen; (*said of the sun or a ship*) untergehen; (*said of a swelling*) zurückgehen; (*said of a fever or a price*) sinken; **go down in history** in die Geschichte eingehen; **go for** (*fetch*) holen; (*apply to*) gelten für; (*be enthusiastic about*) schwärmen für; (*have a crush on*) verknallt sein in (*acc*); (*be sold for*) verkauft werden für; (*attack*) losgehen auf (*acc*); **go in hineingehen;** (*said of the sun*) verschwinden; **go in for** schwärmen für; (sport) treiben; **go into** eintreten in (*acc*); (arith) enthalten sein in (*dat*); **go**

into detail ins Detail gehen; **go in with s.o. on** sich beteiligen mit j-m an (dat); **go off** (depart) weggehen; (said of a gun) losgehen; (said of a bomb) explodieren; **go on** (happen) vorgehen; (continue) weitergehen; (with) fortfahren (mit); (theat) auftreten; **go on!** (expressing encouragement) nur zu!; (expressing disbelief) ach was!; **go on reading** weiterlesen; **go on to** (another theme) übergehen auf (acc); **go over** (check) überprüfen; (review) noch einmal durchgehen; (figures) nachrechnen; (be a success) einschlagen; **go over to** hinübergehen zu; (the enemy) übergehen zu; **go out** (e.g., of the house) hinausgehen; (on an errand or socially; said of a light) ausgehen; **go out of one's way** sich besonders anstrengen; **go out to dinner** auswärts essen; **go through** (penetrate) durchdringen; (a traffic signal) überfahren; (endure) durchmachen; **go through with** zu Ende führen; **go to** (said of a prize) zugeteilt werden (dat); **go together** zueinanderpassen; **go to it!** los!; **go to show** ein Beweis sein für; **go with** (fit, match) passen zu; (associate with) verkehren mit; **go without** entbehren; **go under an assumed name** e-n angenommenen Namen führen; **go up to s.o.** auf j-n zugehen
goad [god] s Stachel m ‖ tr antreiben; **g. on** (fig) anstacheln
go'-ahead sig'nal n freie Bahn f
goal [gol] s Ziel n; (sport) Tor n; **make a goal** (sport) ein Tor schießen
goalie ['goli] s Torwart m
goal'keep'er s Torwart m
goal' line' s Torlinie f
goal' post' s Torpfosten m
goat [got] s Ziege f, Geiß f; (male goat) Ziegenbock m; **get s.o.'s g.** (sl) j-n auf die Palme bringen
goatee [go'ti] s Ziegenbart m, Spitzbart m
goat' herd' s Ziegenhirt m
goat'skin' s Ziegenfell n
gob [gab] s (coll) Klumpen m; (sailor) (coll) Blaujacke f; **gobs of money** (coll) ein Haufen m Geld
gobble ['gabəl] s Kollern n ‖ tr verschlingen; **g. up** (food) herunterschlingen; (e.g., land) zusammenraffen ‖ intr (said of a turkey) kollern
gobbledegook ['gabəldɪ‚guk] s (coll) Amtssprache f
gobbler ['gablər] s (coll) Fresser –in mf; (orn) (coll) Puter m, Truthahn m
go'-between' s Vermittler –in mf, Unterhändler –in mf
goblet ['gablɪt] s Kelchglas n
goblin ['gablɪn] s Kobold m
go'cart' s (walker) Laufstuhl m; (stroller) Sportwagen m; (small racer) Go-Kart m; (handcart) Handwagen m
god [gad] s Gott m; **God forbid!** Gott bewahre!; **God knows** weiß Gott; **my God!** du lieber Gott!; **so help**

me **God!** so wahr mir Gott helfe!; ye **gods!** heiliger Strohsack!
god'child' s (–chil'dren) Patenkind n
goddess ['gadɪs] s Göttin f
god'fa'ther s Pate m; **be a g.** Pate stehen
God'-fear'ing adj gottesfürchtig
god'forsak'en adj gottverlassen
god'head' s Göttlichkeit f; **Godhead** Gott m
godless ['gadlɪs] adj gottlos
god'like' adj göttlich
godly ['gadli] adj gottselig
god'moth'er s Patin f; **be a g.** Patin stehen
god'send' s Segen m
God'speed' s—**wish s.o. G.** j-m Lebewohl sagen
go-getter ['go‚gɛtər] s Draufgänger m
goggle ['gagəl] intr glotzen
gog'gle-eyed' adj glotzäugig
goggles ['gagəlz] spl Schutzbrille f
go'ing adj (rate) gültig, üblich; **g. on** (e.g., six o'clock) gegen; **I'm g. to do it** ich werde es tun
go'ing concern' s schwunghaftes Geschäft n
go'ing-o'ver s Überprüfung f; (beating) Prügel pl
go'ings on' spl Treiben n, Wirtschaft f
goiter ['gɔɪtər] s Kropf m
gold [gold] adj Gold– ‖ s Gold n
gold' bar' s Goldbarren m
gold'brick' s (mil) Drückeberger m
gold'-brick' intr faulenzen
gold'-brick'ing s (mil) Drückebergerei f
gold'crest' s Goldhähnchen n
gold' dig'ger ['dɪgər] s Goldgräber m, (sl) Vamp m
golden ['goldən] adj golden; (opportunity) günstig
gold'en age' s Glanzzeit f, Goldenes Zeitalter n
gold'en calf', **the** s das Goldene Kalb
gold'en ea'gle s Goldadler m
Gold'en Fleece', **the** (myth) das Goldene Vlies
gold'en mean' s goldene Mitte f
gold'en rule' s goldene Regel f
gold'en wed'ding s goldene Hochzeit f
gold'-filled' adj vergoldet
gold' fill'ing s (dent) Goldplombe f
gold'finch' s Goldfink m, Stieglitz m
gold'fish' s Goldfisch m
goldilocks ['goldɪ‚laks] s (bot) Hahnenfuß m
gold' leaf' s Blattgold n
gold'mine' s Goldbergwerk n
gold' nug'get s Goldklumpen m
gold' plate' s Goldgeschirr n
gold'-plate' tr vergolden
gold'smith' s Goldschmied –in mf
gold' stand'ard s Goldwährung f
golf [galf] s Golf n ‖ intr Golf spielen
golf' bag' s Köcher m
golf' club' s Golfschläger m; (organization) Golfklub m
golf' course' s Golfplatz m
golfer ['galfər] s Golfspieler –in mf
golf' links' spl Golfplatz m
gondola ['gandələ] s Gondel f

gon'dola car' s offener Güterwagen m
gondolier [,gʌndə'lɪr] s Gondelführer m
gone [gɔn] adj hin, weg; (ruined) futsch; **all g.** ganz weg; (sold out) ausverkauft; **he is g.** er ist fort
goner ['gɔnər] s (coll) verlorener Mensch m
gong [gɔŋ] s Gong m, Tamtam n
gonorrhea [,ganə'ri·ə] s Tripper m
goo [gu] s (sl) klebrige Masse f
good [gʊd] adj (better; best) gut; (well behaved) brav, artig; (in health) gesund; (valid) gültig; **as g. as** so gut wie; **be g. enough to** (inf) so gut sein und; **g. and** recht, e.g., **g. and cheap** recht billig; **g. at** gut in (dat); **g. for** (suited to) geeignet zu; (effective against) wirksam für; (valid for) gültig für; **g. for you!** (serves you right!) das geschieht dir recht!; (expressing congratulations) ich gratuliere!, bravo!; **make g.** wiedergutmachen; (losses) vergüten; (a promise) erfüllen; || s Gut n; (welfare) Wohl n; (advantage) Nutzen m; (philos) Gut n, das Gute; **be up to no g.** nichts Gutes im Schilde führen; **catch with the goods** auf frischer Tat ertappen; **do g.** wohltun; **for g.** für immer; **goods** Waren pl; **to the g.** als Nettogewinn; **what g. is it?, what's the g. of it?** was nutzt es?
good'-by', **good'-bye'** s Lebewohl n; **say g. (to)** sich verabschieden (von) || interj auf Wiedersehen!; (on the telephone) auf Wiederhören!
good' day' interj guten Tag!
good' deed' s Wohltat f
good' egg' s (sl) feiner Kerl m
good' eve'ning interj guten Abend!
good' fel'low s netter Kerl m
good'-fel'lowship s gute Kameradschaft f
good'-for-noth'ing adj nichtsnutzig || s Taugenichts m, Nichtsnutz m
Good' Fri'day s Karfreitag m
good' grac'es spl—**be in s.o.'s g.** in j-s Gunst stehen
good'-heart'ed adj gutherzig
good'-hu'mored adj gutgelaunt, gutmütig
good'-look'ing adj gutaussehend, hübsch
goodly ['gʊdli] adj beträchtlich; **a g. number of** viele
good' morn'ing interj guten Morgen!
good'-na'tured adj gutmütig
goodness ['gʊdnɪs] s Güte f; **for g. sake!** um Himmels willen!; **g. knows** weiß Gott; **thank g.** Gott sei Dank!
good' night' interj gute Nacht!
good' sense' s Sinn m; (common sense) gesunder Menschenverstand m; **make g.** Sinn haben
good'-sized' adj ziemlich groß
good'-tem'pered adj ausgeglichen
good' time' s—**have a g.** sich gut unterhalten; **keep g.** taktfest sein
good' turn' s Gefallen m; **one g. deserves another** e–e Hand wäscht die andere

good' will' s Wohlwollen n; (com) Geschäftswert m
goody ['gʊdi] s Näscherei f || interj pfundig!
gooey ['gu·i] adj klebrig
goof [guf] s (person) (sl) Depp m; (mistake) (sl) Schnitzer m || tr (sl) verpfuschen || intr (sl) e–n Schnitzer machen; **g. off** (sl) fau!enzen
goof'ball' s (pill) (sl) Beruhigungspille f; (eccentric person) (sl) Sonderling m
goofy ['gufi] adj (sl) dämlich; **g. about** (sl) vernarrt in (acc)
goon [gun] s (sl) Dummkopf m; (in strikes) bestellter Schläger m
goose [gus] s (geese [gis]) Gans f; (culin) Gänsebraten m; **cook s.o.'s g.** j–n erledigen
goose'ber'ry s Stachelbeere f
goose' egg' s Gänseei n; (sl) Null f
goose' flesh' s Gänsehaut f
goose'neck' s Schwanenhals m
goose' pim'ples spl Gänsehaut f
goose' step' s Stechschritt m
goose'-step' v (pret & pp –stepped; ger –stepping) intr im Stechschritt marschieren
gopher ['gofər] s Taschenratte f
gore [gor] s geronnenes Blut n || tr aufspießen
gorge [gɔrdʒ] s Schlucht f || tr vollstopfen || intr schlingen
gorgeous ['gɔrdʒəs] adj prachtvoll
gorilla [gə'rɪlə] s Gorilla m
gorse [gɔrs] s Stechginster m
gory ['gori] adj blutig
gosh [gaʃ] interj herrjeh!
Gospel ['gaspəl] s Evangelium n
gos'pel truth' s reine Wahrheit f
gossamer ['gasəmər] s Sommerfäden pl
gossip ['gasɪp] s Klatsch m; (woman) Klatschweib n; (man) Schwätzer m || intr klatschen, tratschen
gos'sip col'umn s Klatschspalte f
gossipmonger ['gasɪp ,mʌŋgər] s Klatschbase f
gossipy ['gasɪpi] adj tratschsüchtig
Goth [gaθ] s Gote m, Gotin f
Gothic ['gaθɪk] adj gotisch || s (language) Gotisch n
Goth'ic arch' s Spitzbogen m
gouge [gaʊdʒ] s (tool) Hohlmeißel m; (hole made by a gouge) ausgemeißelte Vertiefung f || tr aushöhlen; (overcharge) übervorteilen; **g. out** (eyes) herausdrücken
gouger ['gaʊdʒər] s Wucherer –in mf
goulash ['gulaʃ] s Gulasch n
gourd [gord], [gʊrd] s Kürbis m
gourmand ['gurmənd] s (glutton) Schlemmer –in mf; (gourmet) Feinschmecker m
gourmet ['gurme] s Feinschmecker m
gout [gaʊt] s Gicht f
govern ['gʌvərn] tr regieren; (fig) beherrschen; (gram) regieren || intr regieren
governess ['gʌvərnɪs] s Gouvernante f
government ['gʌvərnmənt] adj Regierungs–, Staats– || s Regierung f

gov'ernment con'tract s Staatsauftrag m
gov'ernment control' s Zwangsbewirtschaftung f
gov'ernment employ'ee s Staatsbeamte m, Staatsbeamtin f
gov'ernment grant' s Staatszuschuß m
gov'ernment-in-ex'ile s Exilregierung f
governor ['gʌvərnər] s Statthalter m, Gouverneur m; (mach) Regler m
gov'ernorship' s Statthalterschaft f
gown [gaʊn] s Damenkleid n; (of a judge, professor) Robe f, Talar m
grab [græb] s—**make a g. for** grapschen nach ‖ v (pret & pp grabbed; ger grabbing) tr schnappen; **g. hold of** anpacken ‖ intr—**g. for** greifen nach
grab' bag' s Glückstopf m
grace [gres] s (mercy, divine favor) Gnade f; (charm) Grazie f; (table prayer) Tischgebet n; (charm) Grazie f; **Graces** (myth) Grazien pl
graceful ['gresfəl] adj graziös, anmutig
gracious ['greʃəs] adj gnädig; (living) angenehm ‖ interj lieber Himmel!
gradation [gre'deʃən] s Stufenfolge f
grade [gred] s (level) Stufe f, Grad m; (quality) Qualität f; (class year) Schulklasse f; (mark in a course, test) Zensur f; (slope) Steigung f; (mil) Dienstgrad m ‖ tr (sort) einstufen; (evaluate) bewerten; (make level) planieren; (educ) zensieren
grade' cross'ing s (rr) Schienenübergang m
grade' school' s Grundschule f
gradient ['gredɪ·ənt] s Neigung f
gradual ['grædʒu·əl] adj allmählich
graduate ['grædʒu·ɪt] adj (student) graduiert; (course) Graduierten– ‖ s Promovierte mf; (from a junior college) Abiturient –in mf; (from a university) Absolvent –in mf ‖ ['grædʒu,et] tr & intr graduieren, promovieren; **g. from** absolvieren
grad'uated adj (tax) abgestuft; (marked by divisions of measurement) graduiert; **g. scale** Gradmesser m
graduation [,grædʒu'eʃən] s Graduierung f, Promotion f; (marking on a vessel or instrument) Gradeinteilung f
gradua'tion ex'ercises spl Schlußfeier f
graft [græft] s (illegal gain) Schiebung f; (money involved in graft) Schmiergeld n; (twig) (hort) Pfropfreis n; (place where scion is inserted) (hort) Propfstelle f; (organ transplanted) (surg) verpflanztes Gewebe n; (transplanting) (surg) Gewebeverpflanzung f ‖ tr (hort) pfropfen; (surg) verpflanzen
gra'ham bread' ['gre·əm] s Grahambrot n
gra'ham crack'er s Grahamplätzchen n
gra'ham flour' s Grahammehl n
grain [gren] s Korn n; (of leather) Narbe f; (in wood, marble) Maserung f; (unit of weight) Gran n;

(cereals) Getreide n; (phot) Korn n **against the g.** (& fig) gegen der Strich; **g. of truth** Körnchen n Wahrheit
grain' el'evator s Getreidesilo m
grain'field' s Saatfeld n, Kornfeld n
gram [græm] s Gramm n
grammar ['græmər] s Grammatik f
gram'mar school' s Grundschule f
grammatical [grə'mætɪkəl] adj grammatisch, grammatikalisch
gramophone ['græmə,fon] s Grammophon n
granary ['grenəri] s Getreidespeicher m
grand [grænd] adj großartig; (large and striking) grandios; (lofty) erhaben; (wonderful) (coll) herrlich
grand'aunt' s Großtante f
grand'child' s (-chil'dren) Enkelkind n
grand'daugh'ter s Enkelin f
grand' duch'ess s Großfürstin f, Großherzogin f
grand' duch'y s Großfürstentum n, Großherzogtum n
grand' duke' s Großfürst m, Großherzog m
grandee [græn'di] s Grande m
grandeur ['grændʒər], ['grændʒʊr] s Großartigkeit f, Erhabenheit f
grand'fath'er s Großvater m
grand'father's clock' s Standuhr f
grandiose ['grændɪ,os] adj grandios
grand' ju'ry s Anklagekammer f
grand' lar'ceny s schwerer Diebstahl m
grand' lodge' s Großloge f
grandma ['græn(d),mɑ], ['græm,mɑ] s (coll) Oma f
grand'moth'er s Großmutter f
grand'neph'ew s Großneffe m
grand'niece' s Großnichte f
grandpa ['græn(d),pɑ], ['græm,pɑ] s (coll) Opa m
grand'par'ents spl Großeltern pl
grand' pian'o s Konzertflügel m
grand' slam' s Schlemm m
grand'son' s Enkel m
grand'stand' s Tribüne f
grand' to'tal s Gesamtsumme f
grand'un'cle s Großonkel m
grand' vizier' s Großwesir m
grange [grendʒ] s Farm f; (organization) Farmervereinigung f
granite ['grænɪt] adj Granit– ‖ s Granit m
granny ['græni] s (coll) Oma f
grant [grænt] s (of money) Beihilfe f; (of a pardon) Gewährung f; (of an award) Verleihung f ‖ tr (permission) geben; (credit) bewilligen; (a favor) gewähren; (a request) erfüllen; (a privilege, award) verleihen; (admit) zugeben; **granted that** angenommen, daß; **take for granted** als selbstverständlich hinnehmen
grantee [græn'ti] s Empfänger –in mf
grant'-in-aid' s (grants-in-aid) (by the government) Subvention f; (educ) Stipendium n
grantor ['græntər] s Verleiher –in mf
granular ['grænjələr] adj körnig
granulate ['grænjə,let] tr körnen

gran'ulated sug'ar s Streuzucker m
granule ['grænjul] s Körnchen n
grape [grep] s Weintraube f
grape' ar'bor s Weinlaube f
grape'fruit' s Pampelmuse f
grape' juice' s Most m, Traubensaft m
grape' pick'er s Weinleser –in mf
grape'vine' s Weinstock m; **through the g.** gerüchtweise
graph [græf] s Diagramm n
graphic(al) ['græfɪk(əl)] adj graphisch; (description) anschaulich, bildhaft
graph'ic arts' spl Graphik f
graphite ['græfaɪt] s Graphit m
graph' pa'per s Millimeterpapier n
grapnel ['græpnəl] s Wurfanker m
grapple ['græpəl] s Enterhaken m; (fight) Handgemenge n || tr packen || intr (use a grapple) (naut) e–n Enterhaken gebrauchen; **g. with** (& fig) ringen mit
grap'pling hook', **grap'pling i'ron** s Wurfanker m; (naut) Enterhaken m
grasp [græsp] s Griff m; (control) Gewalt f; (comprehension) Verständnis n; (reach) Reichweite f; **have a good g. of** gut beherrschen || tr (& fig) fassen || intr—**g. at** schnappen nach
grasp'ing adj habgierig, geldgierig
grass [græs] s Gras n; (lawn) Rasen m; (pasture land) Weide f
grass' court' s Rasenspielplatz m
grass'hop'per s Grashüpfer m
grass' land' s Weideland n, Grasland n
grass'-roots' adj (coll) volkstümlich
grass' seed' s Grassamen m
grass' wid'ow s Strohwitwe f
grassy ['græsi] adj grasig
grate [gret] s (on a window) Gitter n; (of a furnace) Rost m || tr (e.g., cheese) reiben; **g. the teeth** mit den Zähnen knirschen || intr knirschen; **g. on one's nerves** an den Nerven reißen
grateful ['gretfəl] adj dankbar
grater ['gretər] s (culin) Reibeisen n
grati·fy ['græti ,faɪ] v (pret & pp –fied) tr befriedigen; **be gratified by** sich freuen über (acc)
grat'ifying adj erfreulich
grat'ing adj knirschend || s Gitter n
gratis ['grætɪs], ['gretɪs] adj & adv unentgeltlich
gratitude ['græti ,t(j)ud] s Dankbarkeit f
gratuitous [grə't(j)u·ɪtəs] adj unentgeltlich; (undeserving) unverdient
gratuity [grə't(j)u·ɪti] s Trinkgeld n
grave [grev] adj (face) ernst; (condition) besorgniserregend; (mistake) folgenschwer; (sound) tief || s Grab n; (accent) Gravis m
gravedigger ['grev ,dɪgər] s Totengräber m
gravel ['grævəl] s (rounded stones) Kies m; (crushed stones) Schotter m; (pathol) Harngrieß m || tr mit Kies (or Schotter) bestreuen
gravelly ['grævəli] adj heiser
grav'el pit' s Kiesgrube f
grav'el road' s Schotterstraße f

grave'stone' s Grabstein m
grave'yard' s Friedhof m
gravitate ['grævɪ ,tet] intr gravitieren; **g. towards** (fig) neigen zu
gravitation [,grævɪ'teʃən] s Gravitation f, Massenanziehung f
gravitational [,grævɪ'teʃənəl] adj Gravitations-, Schwer-
gravita'tional force' s Schwerkraft f
gravita'tional pull' s Anziehungskraft f
gravity ['grævɪti] s (seriousness) Ernst m; (of a situation) Schwere f; (phys) Schwerkraft f
gravy ['grevi] s Soße f; (coll) leichter Gewinn m
gra'vy boat' s Soßenschüssel f
gra'vy train' s (sl) Futterkrippe f
gray [gre] adj grau || s Grau n || intr ergrauen
gray'beard' s Graubart m
gray'-haired' adj grauhaarig
grayish ['gre·ɪʃ] adj gräulich
gray' mat'ter s graue Substanz f
graze [grez] tr (said of a bullet) streifen; (cattle) weiden lassen || intr weiden
graz'ing land' s Weide f
grease [gris] s Fett n, Schmiere f || [gris], [griz] tr (aut) schmieren
grease' gun' [gris] s Schmierpresse f
grease' paint' s Schminke f
grease' pit' s (aut) Schmiergrube f
grease' spot' s Fettfleck m
greasy ['grisi], ['grizi] adj fett(ig)
great [gret] adj groß; (wonderful) (coll) großartig; **a g. many** (of) e–e große Anzahl von; **g. fun** Heidenspaß m; **g. guy** Prachtkerl m
great'-aunt' s Großtante f
Great' Bear' s Großer Bär m
Great' Brit'ain s Großbritannien n
Great' Dane' s deutsche Dogge f
great'-grand'child' s (–chil'dren) Urenkel m
great'-grand'daugh'ter s Urenkelin f
great'-grand'fa'ther s Urgroßvater m
great'-grand'moth'er s Urgroßmutter f
great'-grand'par'ents spl Urgroßeltern pl
great'-grand'son' s Urenkel m
greatly ['gretli] adv sehr, stark
great'-neph'ew s Großneffe m
greatness ['gretnɪs] s Größe f
great'-niece' s Großnichte f
great'-un'cle s Großonkel m
Grecian ['griʃən] adj griechisch
Greece [gris] s Griechenland n
greed [grid] s Habgier f, Gier f
greediness ['gridɪnɪs] s Gierigkeit f
greedy ['gridi] adj (for) gierig (nach)
Greek [grik] adj griechisch || s (person) Grieche m, Griechin f; (language) Griechisch n; **that's G. to me** das kommt mir spanisch vor
green [grin] adj grün; (unripe) unreif; (inexperienced) unerfahren, neu; **become g.** grünen; **turn g. with envy** grün vor Neid werden || s (& golf) Grün n; **greens** Blattgemüse n
green'back' s (coll) Geldschein m
greenery ['grinəri] s Grün n

green'-eyed' *adj* grünäugig; (fig) neidisch
green'gro'cer *s* Obst- und Gemüsehändler –in *mf*
green'horn' *s* Ausländer –in *mf*
green'house' *s* Gewächshaus *n*
greenish ['grinɪʃ] *adj* grünlich
Green'land *s* Grönland *n*
green' light' *s* (fig) freie Fahrt *f*
greenness ['grinnɪs] *s* Grün *n;* (*inexperience*) Unerfahrenheit *f*
green' pep'per *s* Paprikaschote *f*
green'room' *s* (theat) Aufenthaltsraum *m*
greensward ['grin ‚swɔrd] *s* Rasen *m*
green' thumb' *s*—**have a g.** gärtnerisches Geschick besitzen
greet [grit] *tr* grüßen; (*welcome*) begrüßen
greet'ing *s* Gruß *m;* (*welcoming*) Begrüßung *f;* **greetings** Grüße *pl*
greet'ing card' *s* Glückwunschkarte *f*
gregarious [grɪ'gɛrɪ·əs] *adj* gesellig
Gregor'ian cal'endar [grɪ'gorɪ·ən] *s* Gregorianischer Kalender *m*
Gregor'ian chant' *s* Gregorianischer Gesang *m*
grenade [grɪ'ned] *s* Granate *f*
grenade' launch'er *s* Gewehrgranatgerät *n*
grey [gre] *adj, s, & intr* var of **gray**
grey'hound' *s* Windhund *m*
grid [grɪd] *s* (*on a map*) Gitternetz *n;* (culin) Bratrost *m;* (electron) Gitter *n*
griddle ['grɪdəl] *s* Bratpfanne *f;* (*cookie sheet*) Backblech *n*
grid'dlecake' *s* Pfannkuchen *m*
grid'i'ron *s* Bratrost *m;* (sport) Spielfeld *n;* (theat) Schnürboden *m*
grid' leak' *s* (electron) Gitterwiderstand *m*
grief [grif] *s* Kummer *m;* **come to g.** zu Fall (or Schaden) kommen, scheitern
grief'-strick'en *adj* gramgebeugt
grievance ['grivəns] *s* Beschwerde *f*
grieve [griv] *tr* bekümmern || *intr* (**over**) sich grämen (über *acc*)
grievous ['grivəs] *adj* (*causing grief*) schmerzlich; (*serious*) schwerwiegend
griffin ['grɪfɪn] *s* Greif *m*
grill [grɪl] *s* Grill *m* || *tr* grillen; (*an accused person*) scharf verhören
grille [grɪl] *s* Gitter *n*
grim [grɪm] *adj* (**grimmer; grimmest**) grimmig; **g. humor** Galgenhumor *m*
grimace ['grɪməs], [grɪ'mes] *s* Grimasse *f* || *intr* Grimassen schneiden
grime [graɪm] *s* Schmutz *m*, Ruß *m*
grimness ['grɪmnɪs] *s* Grimmigkeit *f*
grimy ['graɪmɪ] *adj* schmutzig, rußig
grin [grɪn] *s* Grinsen *n*, Schmunzeln *n* || *v* (*pret & pp* **grinned;** *ger* **grinning**) *intr* grinsen, schmunzeln; **I had to g. and bear it** ich mußte gute Miene zum bösen Spiel machen
grind [graɪnd] *s* (*of coffee, grain*) Mahlen *n;* (*hard work*) Schinderei *f;* (*a student*) (coll) Streber –in *mf;* **the daily g.** der graue Alltag || *v* (*pret & pp* **ground** [graʊnd]) *tr* (*coffee,*

grain) mahlen; (*glass, tools*) schleifen; (*meat*) zermahlen; (*in a mortar*) stampfen; **g. down** zerreiben; **g. one's teeth** mit den Zähnen knirschen; **g. out** (*e.g., articles*) ausstoßen; (*tunes*) leiern
grinder ['graɪndər] *s* (*molar*) (dent) Backenzahn *m;* (*mach*) Schleifmaschine *f*
grind'stone' *s* Schleifstein *m*
grip [grɪp] *s* Griff *m;* (*handle*) Handgriff *m;* (*handbag*) Reisetasche *f;* (*power*) Gewalt *f;* **come to grips with** in Angriff nehmen; **have a good g. on** (fig) sicher beherrschen; **lose one's g.** (fig) den Halt verlieren || *v* (*pret & pp* **gripped;** *ger* **gripping**) *tr* (& fig) packen
gripe [graɪp] *s* Meckerei *f* || *intr* (**about**) meckern (über *acc*)
grippe [grɪp] *s* (pathol) Grippe *f*
grip'ping *adj* fesselnd, packend
grisly ['grɪzlɪ] *adj* gräßlich
grist [grɪst] *s* Mahlkorn *n;* **that's g. for his mill** das ist Wasser auf seine Mühle
gristle ['grɪsəl] *s* Knorpel *m*
gristly ['grɪslɪ] *adj* knorpelig
grist'mill' *s* Getreidemühle *f*
grit [grɪt] *s* (*abrasive particles*) Grieß *m;* (*pluck*) (coll) Mumm *m;* **grits** Schrotmehl *m* || *v* (*pret & pp* **gritted;** *ger* **gritting**) *tr* (*one's teeth*) zusammenbeißen
gritty ['grɪtɪ] *adj* grießig
grizzly ['grɪzlɪ] *adj* gräulich
griz'zly bear' *s* Graubär *m*
groan [gron] *s* Stöhnen *n;* **groans** Geächze *n* || *intr* stöhnen; (*grumble*) (coll) brumen
grocer ['grosər] *s* Lebensmittelhändler –in *mf*
grocery ['grosərɪ] *s* (*store*) Lebensmittelgeschäft *n;* **groceries** Lebensmittel *pl*
gro'cery store' *s* Lebensmittelgeschäft *n*
grog [grɑg] *s* Grog *m*
groggy ['grɑgɪ] *adj* benommen
groin [grɔɪn] *s* (anat) Leiste *f*, Leistengegend *f;* (archit) Rippe *f*
groom [grum] *s* Bräutigam *m;* (*stableboy*) Reitknecht *m* || *tr* (*a person, animal*) pflegen; (*for a position*) heranziehen
groove [gruv] *s* Kerbe *f;* (*for letting off water*) Rinne *f;* (*of a record*) Rille *f;* (*in a barrel*) Zug *m;* **in the g.** (fig) im richtigen Fahrwasser
grope [grop] *tr*—**g. one's way** sich vorwärtstasten || *intr* tappen; **g. about** herumtappen; **g. for** tappen nach, tasten nach
gropingly ['gropɪŋlɪ] *adv* tastend
gross [gros] *adj* (*coarse, vulgar*) roh, derb; (*mistake*) grob; (*crass, extreme*) kraß; (*without deductions*) Brutto– || *s* Gros *n* || *tr* e–n Bruttogewinn haben von
grossly ['groslɪ] *adv* sehr, stark
gross' na'tional prod'uct *s* Bruttosozialprodukt *n*

gross′ receipts′ *spl* Bruttoeinnahmen *pl*

grotesque [gro'tɛsk] *adj* grotesk

grot•to ['grɑto] *s* (**–toes** & **–tos**) Grotte *f*, Höhle *f*

grouch [graʊtʃ] *s* (coll) Brummbär *m*, Griesgram *m* ‖ *intr* brummen

grouchy ['graʊtʃi] *adj* (coll) brummig

ground [graʊnd] *s* Grund *m*, Boden *m*; (*reason*) Grund *m*; (elec) Erde f; **every inch of g.** jeder Fußbreit Boden; **grounds** (*e.g., of an estate*) Anlagen *pl*; (*reasons*) Gründe *pl*; (*of coffee*) Satz *m*; **break g.** mit dem Bau beginnen; **gain g.** (an) Boden gewinnen; **hold one's g.** seinen Standpunkt behaupten; **level to the g.** dem Erdboden gleichmachen; **lose g.** (an) Boden verlieren; **low g.** Niederung *f*; **new g.** (fig) Neuland *n*; **on the grounds that** mit der Begründung, daß; **run into the g.** (fig) bis zum Überdruß wiederholen; **stand one's g.** standhalten; **yield g.** (fig) nachgeben ‖ *tr* (*a pilot*) Startverbot erteilen (*dat*); (*a ship*) auflaufen lassen; (elec) erden; **be grounded by bad weather** wegen schlechten Wetters am Starten gehindert werden

ground′ connec′tion *s* (elec) Erdung *f*

ground′ crew′ *s* (aer) Bodenmannschaft *f*

ground′ floor′ *s* Parterre *n*, Erdgeschoß *n*

ground′ glass′ *s* Mattglas *n*

ground′ hog′ *s* Murmeltier *n*

groundless ['graʊndlɪs] *adj* grundlos

ground′ meat′ *s* Hackfleisch *n*

ground′ plan′ *s* Grundriß *m*; (fig) Entwurf *m*

ground′ speed′ *s* Geschwindigkeit *f* über Grund

ground′ swell′ *s* Dünung *f*; (fig) wogende Erregung *f*

ground′-to-air′ *adj* Boden-Bord-

ground′ wa′ter *s* Grundwasser *n*

ground′ wire′ *s* (elec) Erdleitung *f*

ground′work′ *s* Grundlage *f*

group [grup] *adj* Gruppen– ‖ *s* Gruppe *f*; (*consisting of 18 aircraft*) Geschwader *n* ‖ *tr* gruppieren ‖ *intr* sich gruppieren

group′ing *s* Gruppierung *f*

group′ insur′ance *s* Gruppenversicherung *f*

group′ ther′apy *s* Gruppentherapie *f*

grouse [graʊs] *s* Waldhuhn *n* ‖ *intr* (sl) meckern

grout [graʊt] *s* dünner Mörtel *m* ‖ *tr* verstreichen

grove [grov] *s* Gehölz *n*, Hain *m*

grov•el ['grʌvəl], ['grɑvəl] *v* (*pret* & *pp* **–eled; el[l]ed**; *ger* **–el[l]ing**) *intr* (& fig) kriechen; **g. in filth** in Schmutz wühlen

grow [gro] *v* (*pret* **grew** [gru]; *pp* **grown** [gron]) *tr* (*plants*) planzen, züchten; (*grain*) anbauen; (*a beard*) sich [*dat*] wachsen lassen; **the ram grows horns** dem Widder wachsen Hörner ‖ *intr* wachsen; (*become*) werden; (*become bigger*) größer wer-

den; **g. fond of** liebgewinnen; **g. luxuriantly** wuchern; **g. older an** Jahren zunehmen; **g. on s.o.** j–m ans Herz wachsen; **g. out of** (*clothes*) herauswachsen aus; (fig) entstehen aus; **g. pale** erblassen; **g. together** zusammenwachsen; (*close*) zuwachsen; **g. up** aufwachsen; **g. wild** (*luxuriantly*) wuchern; (*in the wild*) wild wachsen

grower ['gro-ər] *s* Züchter –in *mf*

growl [graʊl] *s* (*of a dog, stomach*) Knurren *n*; (*of a bear*) Brummen *n* ‖ *tr* (*words*) brummen ‖ *intr* knurren; (*said of a bear*) brummen; **g. at** anknurren

grown [gron] *adj* erwachsen

grown′-up′ *adj* erwachsen ‖ *s* (**grown-ups**) Erwachsene *mf*

growth [groθ] *s* Wachstum *n*; (*increase*) Zuwachs *m*; (pathol) Gewächs *n*; **full g.** volle Größe *f*

grub [grʌb] *s* Larve *f*, Made *f*; (sl) Fraß *m* ‖ *v* (*pret* & *pp* **grubbed**; *ger* **grubbing**) *tr* ausjäten ‖ *intr* wühlen; **g. for** graben nach

grubby ['grʌbi] *adj* (*dirty*) schmutzig

grudge [grʌdʒ] *s* Mißgunst *f*, Groll *m*; **bear** (or **have**) **a g. against s.o.** j–m grollen ‖ *tr* mißgönnen

grudg′ing *adj* mißgünstig

grudg′ingly *adv* (nur) ungern

gruel ['gru-əl] *s* Haferschleim *m*

gruel′ing *adj* strapaziös

gruesome ['grusəm] *adj* grausig

gruff [grʌf] *adj* barsch

grumble ['grʌmbəl] *s* Murren *n* ‖ *intr* (*over*) murren (über *acc*)

grumbler ['grʌmblər] *s* Brummbär *m*

grumpy ['grʌmpi] *adj* übellaunig

grunt [grʌnt] *s* Grunzen *n* ‖ *tr* & *intr* grunzen

G′-string′ *s* (*of a dancer*) letzte Hülle *f*; (*of a native*) Lendenschurz *m*

guarantee [ˌgærən'ti] *s* Garantie *f* ‖ *tr* garantieren für

guarantor ['gærənˌtɔr] *s* Garant –in *mf*

guaranty ['gærənti] *s* Garantie *f* ‖ *v* (*pret* & *pp* **–tied**) *tr* garantieren

guard [gɑrd] *s* (*watch; watchman*) Wache *f*; (*person*) Wächter –in *mf*; (fb) Verteidiger *m*; (mach) Schutzvorrichtung *f*; (*soldier*) (mil) Posten *m*; (*soldiers*) (mil) Wachmannschaft *f*, Wache *f*; **be on g. against** sich hüten vor (*dat*); **be on one's g. auf** der Hut sein; **keep under close g.** scharf bewachen; **mount g.** Wache beziehen; **relieve the g.** die Wache ablösen; **stand g.** Posten (or Wache) stehen; (*during a robbery*) Schmiere stehen ‖ *tr* bewachen; (fig) hüten; **g. one's tongue** seine Zunge im Zaum halten ‖ *intr*—**g. against** sich vorsehen gegen (*acc*); **g. over** wachen über (*acc*)

guard′ de′tail *s* Wachmannschaft *f*

guard′ du′ty *s* Wachdienst *m*; **pull g.** Wache schieben

guard′house′ *s* (*building used by guards*) Wache *f*; (*military jail*) Arrestlokal *n*

guardian ['gardɪ·ən] *s* (*custodian*) Wächter –in *mf*; (jur) Vormund *m*
guard'ian an'gel *s* Schutzengel *m*
guard'ianship' *s* Obhut *f*; (jur) Vormundschaft *f*
guard'rail' *s* Geländer *n*
guard'room' *s* Wachstube *f*, Wachlokal *n*
guerrilla [gə'rɪlə] *s* Guerillakämpfer –in *mf*
gueril'la war'fare *s* Guerillakrieg *m*
guess [gɛs] *s* Vermutung *f*; **anybody's g.** reine Vermutung *f*; **take a good g.** gut raten || *tr* vermuten; **you guessed it!** geraten! || *intr* raten; **g. at** schätzen
guesser ['gɛsər] *s* Rater –in *mf*
guess'work' *s* Raten *n*, Mutmaßung *f*
guest [gɛst] *adj* Gast–, Gäste– || *s* Gast *m*; **be a g. of** zu Gaste sein bei
guest' book' *s* Gästebuch *n*
guest' perform'ance *s* Gastspiel *n*; **give a g.** (theat) gastieren
guest' perform'er *s* Gast *m*
guest' room' *s* Gästezimmer *n*
guest' speak'er *s* Gastredner –in *mf*
guffaw [gə'fɔ] *s* Gewieher *n* || *intr* wiehern
guidance ['gaɪdəns] *s* Leitung *f*, Führung *f*; (educ) Studienberatung *f*; **for your g.** zu Ihrer Orientierung
guid'ance coun'selor *s* Studienberater –in *mf*
guide [gaɪd] *s* Führer –in *mf*; (*book*) Reiseführer *m*; (*tourist escort*) Reiseführer –in *mf*; (*for gardening, etc.*) Leitfaden *m* || *tr* führen; (rok) lenken
guide'book' *s* Reiseführer *m*, Führer *m*
guid'ed mis'sile *s* Fernlenkkörper *m*
guid'ed tour' *s* Führung *f*
guide'line' *s* Richtlinie *f*
guide'post' *s* Wegweiser *m*
guide' word' *s* Stichwort *n*
guild [gɪld] *s* Zunft *f*, Gilde *f*
guile [gaɪl] *s* Arglist *f*
guileful ['gaɪfəl] *adj* arglistig
guileless ['gaɪllɪs] *adj* arglos
guillotine ['gɪlə‚tin] *s* Fallbeil *n*, Guillotine *f* || *tr* mit dem Fallbeil (or mit der Guillotine) hinrichten
guilt [gɪlt] *s* Schuld *f*
guilt'-rid'den *adj* schuldbeladen
guilty ['gɪlti] *adj* (of) schuldig (*genit*); (*conscience*) schlecht; **plead g.** sich schuldig bekennen; **plead not g.** sich für nicht schuldig erklären
guil'ty par'ty *s* Schuldige *mf*
guil'ty ver'dict *s* Schuldspruch *m*
guin'ea fowl' ['gɪni], **guin'ea hen'** *s* Perlhuhn *n*
guin'ea pig' *s* Meerschweinchen *n*; (fig) Versuchskaninchen *n*
guise [gaɪz] *s* Verkleidung *f*; **under the g. of** unter dem Schein (*genit*)
guitar [gɪ'tar] *s* Gitarre *f*
guitarist [gɪ'tarɪst] *s* Gitarrenspieler –in *mf*
gulch [gʌltʃ] *s* Bergschlucht *f*
gulf [gʌlf] *s* Golf *m*; (fig) Kluft *f*
Gulf' Stream' *s* Golfstrom *m*
gull [gʌl] *s* Möwe *f*; (coll) Tölpel *m* || *tr* übertölpeln

gullet ['gʌlɪt] *s* Gurgel *f*, Schlund *m*
gullible ['gʌlɪbəl] *adj* leichtgläubig
gully ['gʌli] *s* Wasserrinne *f*
gulp [gʌlp] *s* Schluck *m*, Zug *m*; **at one g.** in e–m Zuge || *tr* schlucken; **g. down** schlingen || *intr* schlucken
gum [gʌm] *s* Gummi *m & n*; (*chewing gum*) Kaugummi *m & n*; (anat) Zahnfleisch *n* || *v* (*pret & pp* **gummed;** *ger* **gumming**) *tr* (*e.g., labels*) gummieren; **gum up the works** (coll) die Arbeit (or das Spiel) vermasseln
gum' ar'abic *s* Gummiarabikum *n*
gum'boil' *s* (pathol) Zahngeschwür *n*
gum'drop' *s* Gummibonbon *m & n*
gummy ['gʌmi] *adj* klebrig
gumption ['gʌmpʃən] *s* Unternehmungsgeist *m*, Mumm *m*
gun [gʌn] *s* Gewehr *n*; (*handgun*) Handfeuerwaffe *f*; (arti) Geschütz *n*; **stick to one's guns** bei der Stange bleiben || *v* (*pret & pp* **gunned;** *ger* **gunning**) *tr*—**gun down** niederschießen; **gun the engine** Gas geben || *intr* auf die Jagd gehen; **be out gunning for** auf dem Korn haben; **gun for game** auf die Jagd gehen
gun' bar'rel *s* Gewehrlauf *m*; (arti) Geschützrohr *n*
gun' bat'tle *s* Feuerkampf *m*
gun' belt' *s* Wehrgehänge *n*
gun'boat' *s* Kanonenboot *n*
gun' car'riage *s* Lafette *f*
gun'cot'ton *s* Schießbaumwolle *f*
gun' crew' *s* Bedienungsmannschaft *f*
gun' emplace'ment *s* Geschützstand *m*
gun' fight' *s* Schießerei *f*
gun'fire' *s* Geschützfeuer *n*
gun'man *s* (–**men**) bewaffneter Bandit *m*
gun' met'al *s* Geschützlegierung *f*
gun' mount' *s* Lafette *f*; (*of swivel type*) Schwenklafette *f*
gunner ['gʌnər] *s* Kanonier *m*; (aer) Bordschütze *m*
gunnery ['gʌnəri] *s* Geschützwesen *n*
gun'nery prac'tice *s* Übungsschießen *n*
gunnysack ['gʌni‚sæk] *s* Jutesack *m*
gun' per'mit *s* Waffenschein *m*
gun'point' *s*—**at g.** mit vorgehaltenem Gewehr
gun'pow'der *s* Schießpulver *n*
gun'run'ning *s* Waffenschmuggel *m*
gun'shot' *s* Schuß *m*; (*range*) Schußweite *f*
gun'shot wound' *s* Schußwunde *f*
gun'-shy' *adj* schußscheu
gun'sight' *s* Visier *n*
gun'smith' *s* Büchsenmacher *m*
gun'stock' *s* Gewehrschaft *m*
gun' tur'ret *s* Geschützturm *m*; (aer) Schwalbennest *n*
gunwale ['gʌnəl] *s* Schandeckel *m*
guppy ['gʌpi] *s* Millionenfisch *m*
gurgle ['gʌrgəl] *s* Glucksen *n*, Gurgeln *n* || *intr* glucksen, gurgeln
gush [gʌʃ] *s* Guß *m*; (fig) Erguß *m* || *intr* sich ergießen; **g. out** hervorströmen; **g. over** (fig) viel Aufhebens machen von
gusher ['gʌʃər] *s* Schwärmer –in *mf*; (*oil well*) sprudelnde Ölquelle *f*

gush'ing *adj* (fig) überschwenglich
gushy ['gʌʃi] *adj* schwärmerisch
gusset ['gʌsɪt] *s* Zwickel *m*
gust [gʌst] *s* Stoß *m;* (*of wind*) Windstoß *m*, Bö *f*
gusto ['gʌsto] *s* Gusto *m*
gusty ['gʌsti] *adj* böig
gut [gʌt] *s* Darm *m;* **guts** Eingeweide *pl;* (coll) Schneid *m* || *v* (*pret & pp* **gutted;** *ger* **gutting**) *tr* ausbrennen; **be gutted** ausbrennen
gutter ['gʌtər] *s* Gosse *f;* (*of a roof*) Dachrinne *f*
gut'tersnipe' *s* (coll) Straßenjunge *m*
guttural ['gʌtərəl] *adj* kehlig; (ling) Kehl– || *s* (ling) Kehllaut *m*
guy [gaɪ] *s* Halteseil *n;* (*of a tent*) Spannschnur *f;* (coll) Kerl *m;* **dirty guy** (coll) Sauigel *m;* **great guy** Prachtkerl *m* || *tr* verspannen
guy' wire' *s* Spanndraht *m*
guzzle ['gʌzəl] *tr & intr* saufen
guzzler ['gʌzlər] *s* Säufer –in *mf*
gym [dʒɪm] *adj* (coll) Turn– || *s* (coll) Turnhalle *f*
gym' class' *s* (coll) Turnstunde *f*

gymnasi·um [dʒɪm'nezɪ·əm] *s* (**–ums** & **–a** [ə]) Turnhalle *f*
gymnast ['dʒɪmnæst] *s* Turner –in *m*
gymnastic [dʒɪm'næstɪk] *adj* Turn–gymnastisch; **g. exercise** Turnübung *f* || **gymnastics** *spl* Gymnastik *f*, Turnen *n*
gynecologist [ˌgaɪnə'kɑlədʒɪst] *s* Gynäkologe *m*, Gynäkologin *f*
gynecology [ˌgaɪnə'kɑlədʒi] *s* Gynäkologie *f*
gyp [dʒɪp] *s* (sl) Nepp *m;* (*person*) Nepper *m;* **that's a gyp** das ist Nepp! || *v* (*pret & pp* **gypped;** *ger* **gypping**) *tr* neppen
gyp' joint' *s* Nepplokal *n*
gypper ['dʒɪpər] *s* Nepper *m*
gypsy ['dʒɪpsi] *adj* Zigeuner– || *s* Zigeuner –in *mf*
gyp'sy moth' *s* Großer Schwammspinner *m*
gyrate ['dʒaɪret] *intr* sich drehen; kreiseln
gyration [dʒaɪ're/ən] *s* Kreiselbewegung *f*
gyroscope ['dʒaɪrə,skop] *s* Kreisel *m*

H

H, h [etʃ] *s* achter Buchstabe des englischen Alphabets
haberdasher ['hæbər,dæʃər] *s* Inhaber –in *mf* e-s Herrenmodengeschäfts
haberdashery ['hæbər,dæʃəri] *s* Herrenmodengeschäft *n*
habit ['hæbɪt] *s* Gewohnheit *f;* (eccl) Ordenskleid *n;* **be in the h. of** (*ger*) pflegen zu (*inf*); **break s.o. of that h. of smoking** j–m das Rauchen abgewöhnen; **from h.** aus Gewohnheit; **get into the h. of smoking** sich [*dat*] das Rauchen angewöhnen; **make a h. of it** es zur Gewohnheit werden lassen
habitat ['hæbɪ,tæt] *s* Wohngebiet *n*
habitation [ˌhæbɪ'te/ən] *s* Wohnort *m*
habitual [hə'bɪt/ʊ·əl] *adj* gewohnheitsmäßig, Gewohnheits–
hack [hæk] *s* (*blow*) Hieb *m;* (*notch*) Kerbe *f;* (*rasping cough*) trockener Husten *m;* (*worn-out horse*) Schindmähre *f;* (*hackney*) Droschke *f;* (*taxi*) (coll) Taxi *n;* (*writer*) (coll) Schreiberling *m* || *tr* hacken, hauen; (basketball) auf den Arm schlagen || *intr* Taxi fahren
hackney ['hækni] *s* (*carriage*) Droschke *f;* (*horse*) gewöhnliches Gebrauchspferd *n*
hackneyed ['hæknid] *adj* abgedroschen
hack'saw' *s* Metallsäge *f*, Bügelsäge *f*
haddock ['hædək] *s* Schellfisch *m*
haft [hæft] *s* Griff *m*
hag [hæg] *s* Vettel *f;* (*witch*) Hexe *f*
haggard ['hægərd] *adj* hager
haggle ['hægəl] *intr* (**over**) feilschen (um)

hag'gling *s* Feilschen *n*
Hague, the [heg] *s* den Haag *m*
hail [hel] *s* Hagel *m;* **h. of bullets** Kugelhagel *m* || *tr* (*a taxi, ship*) anrufen; (*acclaim*) preisen; (**as**) begrüßen (als) || *intr* hageln; **h. from** stammen aus (or von) || *interj* Heil!
Hail' Mar'y *s* Ave Maria *n*
hail'stone' *s* Hagelkorn *n*, Schloße *f*
hail'storm' *s* Hagelschauer *m*
hair [her] *s* (*single hair*) Haar *n;* (*collectively*) Haare *pl;* **by a h.** um ein Haar; **do s.o.'s h.** j–n frisieren; **get in s.o.'s h.** j–m auf die Nerven gehen lassen; **split hairs** Haarspalterei treiben
hair'breadth' *s*—**by a h.** um Haaresbreite
hair'brush' *s* Haarbürste *f*
hair' clip' *s* Spange *f*, Klammer *f*
hair'cloth' *s* Haartuch *n*
hair'curl'er *s* Lockenwickler *m*
hair'cut' *s* Haarschnitt *m;* **get a h.** sich [*dat*] die Haare schneiden lassen
hair'do' *s* (**–dos**) Frisur *f*
hair'dress'er *s* Friseur *m*, Friseuse *f*
hair'dri'er *s* Haartrockner *m*
hair' dye' *s* Haarfärbemittel *n*
hariness ['herɪnɪs] *s* Behaartheit *f*
hairless ['herlɪs] *adj* haarlos
hair'line' *s* Haaransatz *m*
hair' net' *s* Haarnetz *n*
hair' oil' *s* Haaröl *n*
hair'piece' *s* Haarteil *n*
hair'pin' *s* Haarnadel *f*
hair'-pin curve' *s* Haarnadelkurve *f*
hair'-rais'ing *adj* haarsträubend
hair' rinse' *s* Spülmittel *n*

hair'roll'er s Haarwickler m
hair' set' s Wasserwelle f
hair' shirt' s Büßerhemd n
hair'split'ting s Haarspalterei f
hair' spray' s Haarspray m
hair'spring' s Haarfeder f, Spirale f
hair'style' s Frisur f
hair' ton'ic s Haarwasser n
hairy ['heri] adj haarig, behaart
Haiti ['heti] s Haiti n
halberd ['hælbərd] s Hellebarde f
hal'cyon days' ['hælsɪ·ən] spl (fig)
  glückliche Zeit f
hale [hel] adj gesund; **h. and hearty**
  gesund und munter
half [hæf] adj halb; **at h. price** zum
  halben Preis; **have h. a mind to** (inf)
  halb und halb entschlossen sein zu
  (inf); **one and a h.** eineinhalb || adv
  halb; **h. as much as** nur halb so wie;
  h. as much again um die Hälfte mehr;
  h. past three halb vier; **not h.** durch-
  aus nicht || s **(halves** [hævz]) Hälfte
  f; **cut in h.** in die Hälfte schneiden;
  go halves with halbpart machen mit
half'-and-half' adj & adv halb und
  halb || s Halb-und-halb-Mischung f
half'back' s (fb) Läufer m
half'-baked' adj halb gebacken; (plans,
  etc.) halbfertig; (person) unerfahren
half'-blood' s Halbblut n
half'-breed' s Halbblut n, Mischling m
half' broth'er s Halbbruder m
half'-cocked' adv (coll) nicht ganz
  vorbereitet
half'-day' adv halbtags
half'-full' adj halbvoll
half'-heart'ed adj zaghaft
half'-hour' adj halbstündig || s halbe
  Stunde f; **every h.** halbstündlich
half' leath'er s (bb) Halbleder n
half'-length' adj halblang; (portrait) in
  Halbfigur
half'-length por'trait s Brustbild n
half'-light' s Halbdunkel n
half'-mast' s—**at h.** auf halbmast
half'-meas'ure s Halbheit f
half'-moon' s Halbmond m
half' note' s (mus) halbe Note f
half' pay' s Wartegeld n; **be on h.**
  Wartegeld beziehen
half' pint' s (sl) Zwerg m
half' sis'ter s Halbschwester f
half' sleeves' spl halblange Ärmel pl
half' sole' s Halbsohle f
half'-staff' s—**at h.** auf halbmast
half'-tim'bered adj Fachwerk–
half' time' s (sport) Halbzeit f
half'-time' adj Halbzeit–
half' ti'tle s Schmutztitel m
half'tone' s (mus, paint, typ) Halbton
  m
half'-track' s Halbkettenfahrzeug n
half'-truth' s halbe Wahrheit f
half'way' adj auf halbem Wege liegend
  || adv halbwegs, auf halbem Wege;
  meet s.o. h. j–m auf dem halbem
  Wege entgegenkommen
half'way meas'ure s Halbheit f
half'-wit' s Schwachkopf m
half'-wit'ted adj blöd
halibut ['hælɪbət] s Heilbutt m

halitosis [ˌhælɪ'tosɪs] s Mundgeruch m
hall [hɔl] s (entranceway) Diele f, Flur
  m; (passageway) Gang m; (large
  meeting room) Saal m; (building)
  Gebäude n
hall'mark' s Kennzeichen n
hal·lo [hə'lo] s (–los) Hallo n || interj
  hallo!
hall' of fame' s Ruhmeshalle f
hallow ['hælo] tr heiligen
hallucination [həˌlusɪ'neʃən] s Sinnes-
  täuschung f, Halluzination f
hall'way' s Flur m, Diele f; (passageway) Gang m
ha·lo ['helo] s (–los) Glorienschein m;
  (astr) Ring m, Hof m
halogen ['hælədʒən] s Halogen n
halt [hɔlt] s Halt m, Stillstand m; (rest)
  Rast f; **bring to a h.** zum Stillstand
  bringen; **call a h. to** halten lassen;
  come to a h. stehenbleiben || tr an-
  halten || intr halten; (rest) rasten ||
  interj halt!
halter ['hɔltər] s (for a horse) Halfter
  m; (noose) Strick m
halt'ing adj (gait) hinkend; (voice)
  stockend
halve [hæv] tr halbieren
halyard ['hæljərd] s Fall n
ham [hæm] s (pork) Schinken m; (back
  of the knee) Kniekehle f; (actor)
  (sl) Schmierenschauspieler –in mf;
  (rad) (sl) Funkamateur m
hamburger ['hæmˌbʌrgər] s Hackfleisch n, deutsches Beefsteak n
hamlet ['hæmlɪt] s Dörfchen n
hammer ['hæmər] s Hammer m; (of a
  bell) Klöppel m; (sport) Wurfham-
  mer m || tr hämmern; **h. in** (a nail)
  einschlagen; (e.g., rules) einhäm-
  mern; **h. out** aushämmern || intr
  hämmern; **h. away at** (fig) herum-
  arbeiten an (dat)
hammock ['hæmək] s Hängematte f
hamper ['hæmpər] s Wäschebehälter
  m || tr behindern
hamster ['hæmstər] s Hamster m
ham'string' s Kniesehne f || v (pret &
  pp –strung) tr (fig) lähmen
hand [hænd] s Hand f; (applause) Beifall m; (handwriting) Handschrift f;
  (of a clock) Zeiger m; (help) Hilfe
  f; **all hands on deck!** (naut) alle
  Mann an Deck!; **at first h.** aus erster
  Hand; **at h.** vorhanden, zur Hand;
  at the hands of von seiten (genit);
  be on h. zur Stelle sein; **by h.** mit
  der Hand; **change hands** in andere
  Hände übergehen; **fall into s.o.'s
  hands** in j–s Hände fallen; **from h.
  to mouth** von der Hand in den Mund;
  get one's hands on in die Hände
  bekommen; **get the upper h.** die
  Oberhand gewinnen; **give s.o. a free
  h.** j–m freies Spiel lassen; **give s.o. a
  h.** (help s.o.) j–m helfen; (applaud
  s.o.) j–m Beifall spenden; **go h. in h.
  with** (fig) Hand in Hand gehen mit;
  h. and foot eifrig; **h. in h.** Hand in
  Hand; **hands off!** Hände weg!; **hands
  up!** Hände hoch!; **have a good h.**
  (cards) gute Karten haben; **have a h.**

in die Hand im Spiel haben bei; **have one's hands full** alle Hände voll zu tun haben; **have well in h.** gut in der Hand haben; **hold hands** sich bei den Händen halten; **in one's own h.** eigenhändig; **I wash my hands of it** ich wasche meine Hände in Unschuld; **join hands** (fig) sich zusammenschließen; **new h.** Neuling *m*; **on all hands** auf allen Seiten; **on h.** (com) vorrätig; **on one h.** ... **on the other** einerseits ... anderseits; **out of h.** außer Rand und Band; **play into s.o.'s hands** j–m in die Hände spielen; **put one's h. on** (fig) finden; **show one's h.** (fig) seine Karten aufdecken; **take a h.** in mitarbeiten an (*dat*); **throw up one's hands** verzweifelt die Hände hochwerfen; **try one's h. at** versuchen; **win hands down** spielend gewinnen; **with a heavy h.** streng || *tr* (zu)reichen; **h. down** (*to s.o. below*) herunterreichen; (*e.g., traditions*) überliefern; **h. in** (*e.g., homework*) abgeben; (*an application*) einreichen; **h. out** austeilen; **h. over** übergeben; (*relinquish*) aushändigen, hergeben; **I have to h. it to you** (coll) ich muß dir recht geben
hand'bag' *s* Handtasche *f*, Tasche *f*
hand'ball' *s* Handball *m*
hand'bill' *s* Handzettel *m*
hand'book' *s* Handbuch *n*
hand' brake' *s* (aut) Handbremse *f*
hand'breadth' *s* Handbreit *f*
hand' cart' *s* Handkarren *m*
hand'clasp' *s* Händedruck *m*
hand'cuff' *s* Handschelle *f* || *tr* Handschellen anlegen (*dat*)
–handed [ˌhændɪd] *suf* –händig
handful [ˈhændˌfʊl] *s* Handvoll *f*; (*a few*) ein paar; (fig) Nervensäge *f*
hand'glass' *s* Leselupe *f*
hand' grenade' *s* Handgranate *f*
handi·cap [ˈhændɪˌkæp] *s* Handikap *n*, Benachteiligung *f* || *v* (*pret & pp* –capped; *ger* –capping) *tr* handikapen, benachteiligen
hand'icap race' *s* Vorgaberennen *n*
handicraft [ˈhændɪˌkræft] *s* Handwerk *n*
handily [ˈhændɪli] *adv* (*dexterously*) geschickt; (*easily*) mit Leichtigkeit
handiwork [ˈhændɪˌwʌrk] *s* Handarbeit *f*; (fig) Werk *n*, Schöpfung *f*
handkerchief [ˈhæŋkərtʃɪf] *s* Taschentuch *n*
handle [ˈhændəl] *s* Griff *m*; (*of a pot*) Henkel *m*; (*of a frying pan, broom, etc.*) Stiel *m*; (*of a crank*) Handkurbel *f*; (*of a pump*) Schwengel *m*; (*of a door*) Drücker *m*; (*name*) (coll) Name *m*; (*title*) (coll) Titelkram *m*; **fly off the h.** vor Wut platzen || *tr* (*touch*) berühren; (*tools, etc.*) handhaben; (*operate*) bedienen; (fig) erledigen; (com) handeln mit; **h. with care!** Vorsicht!; **know how to h. customers** es verstehen, mit Kunden umzugehen || *intr*—**h. well** sich leicht lenken lassen

han'dlebars' *spl* Lenkstange *f*, (*mustache*) (coll) Schnauzbart *m*
handler [ˈhændlər] *s* (sport) Trainer *m*
han'dling *s* (*e.g., of a car*) Lenkbarkeit *f*; (*of merchandise, theme, ball*) Behandlung *f*; (*of a tool*) Handhabung *f*
han'dling charg'es *spl* Umschlagspesen *pl*
hand' lug'gage *s* Handgepäck *n*
hand'made' *adj* handgemacht
hand'-me-downs' *spl* getragene Kleider *pl*
hand' mir'ror *s* Handspiegel *m*
hand'-op'erated *adj* mit Handbetrieb
hand' or'gan *s* Drehorgel *f*
hand'out' *s* milde Gabe *f*; (*sheet*) Handzettel *m*
hand'-picked' *adj* handgepflückt; (fig) ausgesucht
hand'rail' *s* Geländer *n*
hand'saw' *s* Handsäge *f*
hand'shake' *s* Handschlag *m*, Händedruck *m*
handsome [ˈhænsəm] *adj* schön
hand'-to-hand' fight'ing *s* Nahkampf *m*
hand'-to-mouth' *adj* von der Hand in den Mund
hand'work' *s* Handarbeit *f*
hand'writ'ing *s* Handschrift *f*
handwritten [ˈhændˌrɪtən] *adj* handschriftlich; **h. letter** Handschreiben *n*
handy [ˈhændi] *adj* handlich; (*practical*) praktisch; (*person*) geschickt; **come in h.** gelegen kommen; **have h.** zur Hand haben
hand'y·man' *s* (–men') Handlanger *m*
hang [hæŋ] *s* (*of curtains, clothes*) Fall *m*; **get the h. of** (coll) sich einarbeiten in (*acc*); **I don't give a h. about it** (coll) es ist mir Wurst || *v* (*pret & pp* hung [hʌŋ]) *tr* hängen; (*a door*) einhängen; (*wallpaper*) ankleben; **h. one's head** den Kopf hängen lassen; **h. out** heraushängen; **h. up** aufhängen; (*the receiver*) (telp) auflegen; **I'll be hanged if** ich will mich hängen lassen, wenn || *intr* hängen; (*float*) schweben; **h. around** herumlungern; **h. around the bar** sich in der Bar herumtreiben; **h. around with** umgehen mit; **h. back** sich zurückhalten; **h. by** (*a thread, rope*) hängen an (*dat*); **h. down** niederhängen; **h. in the balance** in der Schwebe sein; **h. on** durchhalten; **h. on s.o.'s words** an j–s Worten hängen; **h. on to** festhalten; (*retain*) behalten; **h. together** zusammenhalten; **h. up** (telp) einhängen || *v* (*pret & pp* hanged & hung) *tr* hängen
hangar [ˈhæŋər] *s* Hangar *m*
hang'-dog look' *s* Armesündergesicht *n*
hanger [ˈhæŋər] *s* Kleiderbügel *m*
hang'er-on' *s* (hangers-on) Mitläufer *m* –in *mf*
hang'ing *adj* (herab)hängend || *s* Hängen *n*
hang'man *s* (–men) Henker *m*
hang'nail' *s* Niednagel *m*

hang'out' *s* Treffpunkt *m*
hang'o'ver *s* (coll) Kater *m*
hank [hæŋk] *s* Strähne *f*
hanker ['hæŋkər] *intr* (for) sich sehnen (nach)
hanky-panky ['hæŋki'pæŋki] *s* (coll) Schwindel *m*
haphazard [,hæp'hæzərd] *adj* wahllos
haphazardly [,hæp'hæzərdli] *adv* aufs Geratewohl
hapless ['hæplis] *adj* unglücklich
happen ['hæpən] *intr* geschehen; **h. to see** zufällig sehen; **h. upon** zufällig stoßen auf (*acc*); **what happens now?** was soll nun werden?
hap'pening *s* Ereignis *n*
happily ['hæpili] *adv* glücklich
happiness ['hæpinis] *s* Glück *n*
happy ['hæpi] *adj* glücklich; **be h. about s.th.** über etw erfreut sein; **be h. to** (*inf*) sich freuen zu (*inf*); **h. as a lark** quietschvergnügt
Hap'py Birth'day *interj* Herzlichen Glückwunsch zum Geburtstag!
hap'py-go-luck'y *adj* unbekümmert
hap'py me'dium *s*—**strike a h.** e-n glücklichen Ausgleich treffen
Hap'py New' Year' *interj* Glückliches Neujahr!
harangue [hə'ræŋ] *s* leidenschaftliche Rede *f* || *tr* e–e leidenschaftliche Rede halten an (*acc*)
harass [hə'ræs], ['hærəs] *tr* schikanieren; (mil) stören
harass'ing fire' *s* (mil) Störungsfeuer *n*
harassment [hə'ræsmənt], ['hærəsmənt] *s* Schikane *f*; (mil) Störung *f*
harbinger ['harbindʒər] *s* Vorbote *m* || *tr* anmelden
harbor ['harbər] *adj* Hafen– || *s* Hafen *m* || *tr* (*give refuge to*) beherbergen; (*hide*) verbergen; (*thoughts*) hegen
har'bor mas'ter *s* Hafenmeister *m*
hard [hard] *adj* (*substance, water, words*) hart; (*problem*) schwierig; (*worker*) fleißig; (*blow, times, work*) schwer; (*life*) mühsam; (*fact*) nackt; (*rain*) heftig; (*winter*) streng; (*drinks*) alkoholisch; **be h. on s.o.** j–m schwer zusetzen; **have a h. time** Schwierigkeiten haben; **h. to believe** kaum zu glauben; **h. to please** anspruchsvoll; **h. to understand** schwer zu verstehen || *adv* hart; (*energetically*) fleißig; **he was h. put to** (*inf*) es fiel ihm schwer zu (*inf*); **rain h.** stark regnen; **take h.** schwer nehmen; **try h.** mit aller Kraft versuchen
hard'-and-fast' *adj* fest
hard-bitten ['hard,bitən] *adj* verbissen
hard'-boiled' *adj* (*egg*) hartgekocht; (coll) hartgesotten
hard' can'dy *s* Bonbons *pl*
hard' cash' *s* bare Münze *f*
hard' ci'der *s* Apfelwein *m*
hard' coal' *s* Steinkohle *f*
hard'-earned' *adj* schwer verdient
harden ['hardən] *tr & intr* (er)härten
hard'ened *adj* (*criminal*) hartgesotten
hard'ening *s* Verhärtung *f*
hard'-head'ed *adj* nüchtern
hard'-heart'ed *adj* hartherzig

hardihood ['hardi,hud] *s* Kühnheit *f*; (*insolence*) Frechheit *f*
hardiness ['hardinis] *s* Ausdauer *f*, Widerstandsfähigkeit *f*
hard' la'bor *s* Zwangsarbeit *f*
hard' luck' *s* Pech *n*
hardly ['hardli] *adv* kaum, schwerlich; **h. ever** fast gar nicht
hardness ['hardnis] *s* Härte *f*
hard'-of-hear'ing *adj* schwerhörig
hard'-pressed' *adj* schwer bedrängt
hard'-shell' *adj* hartschalig; (coll) unnachgiebig
hard'ship' *s* Mühsal *f*
hard'top' *s* (aut) Hardtop *n*
hard' up' *adj* (*for money*) schlecht bei Kasse; **h. for** in Verlegenheit um
hard'ware' *s* Eisenwaren *pl*; (*e.g., on doors, windows*) Beschläge *pl*; **military h.** militärische Ausrüstung *f*
hard'ware store' *s* Eisenwarenhandlung *f*
hard'wood' *s* Hartholz *n*
hard'wood floor' *s* Hartholzboden *m*
hard'-work'ing *adj* fleißig
hardy ['hardi] *adj* (*plants*) winterfest; (*person*) widerstandsfähig
hare [her] *s* Hase *m*
hare'brained' *adj* unbesonnen
hare'lip' *s* Hasenscharte *f*
harem ['herəm] *s* Harem *m*
hark [hark] *intr* horchen; **h. back to** zurückgehen auf (*acc*)
harlequin ['harləkwin] *s* Harlekin *m*
harlot ['harlət] *s* Hure *f*
harm [harm] *s* Schaden *m*; **do h.** Schaden anrichten; **I meant no h. by it** ich meinte es nicht böse; **out of harm's way** in Sicherheit; **there's no h. in trying** ein Versuch kann nicht schaden || *tr* beschädigen; (*e.g., a reputation, chances*) schaden (*dat*); **h. s.o.** (*physically*) j–m etw zuleide tun; (fig) schaden (*dat*)
harmful ['harmfəl] *adj* schädlich
harmless ['harmlis] *adj* unschädlich
harmonic [har'manik] *adj* harmonisch || *s* (mus) Oberton *m*
harmonica [har'manikə] *s* Harmonika *f*
harmonious [har'moni·əs] *adj* harmonisch
harmonize ['harmə,naiz] *intr* harmonieren
harmony ['harməni] *s* Harmonie *f*; **be in h. with** im Einklang stehen mit
harness ['harnis] *s* Geschirr *n*; **die in the h.** in den Sielen sterben || *tr* anschirren; (*e.g., a river, power*) nutzbar machen
har'ness mak'er *s* Sattler *m*
har'ness rac'ing *s* Trabrennen *n*
harp [harp] *s* Harfe *f* || *intr*—**h. on** herumreiten auf (*dat*)
harpist ['harpist] *s* Harfner –in *mf*
harpoon [har'pun] *s* Harpune *f* || *tr* harpunieren
harpsichord ['harpsi,kɔrd] *s* Cembalo *n*
harpy ['harpi] *s* (myth) Harpyie *f*
harrow ['hæro] *s* Egge *f* || *tr* eggen
har'rowing *adj* schrecklich

har·ry ['hæri] v (*pret* & *pp* **–ried**) *tr* martern

Harry ['hæri] s Heinz *m*

harsh [harʃ] *adj* (*conditions*) hart; (*tone*) schroff; (*light*) grell; (*treatment*) rauh

harshness ['harʃnɪs] s Härte *f;* Schroffheit *f;* Grelle *f;* Rauheit *f*

hart [hart] s Hirsch *m*

harum-scarum ['hɛrəm'skɛrəm] *adj* wild || *adv* wie ein Wilder

harvest ['harvɪst] s Ernte *f;* **bad h.** Mißernte *f* || *tr* & *intr* ernten

harvester ['harvɪstər] s Schnitter –in *mf;* (mach) Mähmaschine *f*

har'vest moon' s Erntemond *m*

has-been ['hæz‚bɪn] s (coll) Gestrige *mf*

hash [hæʃ] s Gehacktes *n;* **make h. of** (coll) verwursteln || *tr* zerhacken

hashish ['hæʃiʃ] s Haschisch *n*

hasp [hæsp] s Haspe *f*

hassle ['hæsəl] s (coll) Streit *m*

hassock ['hæsək] s Hocker *m*

haste [hest] s Hast *f,* Eile *f;* **in (all) h. in** (aller) Eile; **make h.** sich beeilen

hasten ['hesən] *tr* beschleunigen || *intr* hasten, eilen

hasty ['hesti] *adj* eilig; (*rash*) hastig

hat [hæt] s Hut *m;* **keep under one's h.** für sich behalten

hat'band' s Hutband *n*

hat'block' s Hutform *f*

hat'box' s Hutschachtel *f*

hatch [hætʃ] s (*opening*) (aer, naut) Luke *f;* (*cover*) (naut) Lukendeckel *m* || *tr* (*eggs*) ausbrüten; (*a scheme*) aushecken; (*mark with strokes*) schraffieren || *intr* Junge ausbrüten; (*said of chicks*) aus dem Ei kriechen

hat'check girl' s Garderobe(n)fräulein *n*

hatchet ['hætʃɪt] s Beil *n;* **bury the h.** die Streitaxt begraben

hatch'ing s Schraffierung *f*

hatch'way' s (naut) Luke *f*

hate [het] s Haß *m* || *tr* hassen; **I h. to** (*inf*) es widerstrebt mir zu (*inf*)

hateful ['hetfəl] *adj* verhaßt

hatless ['hætlɪs] *adj* hutlos

hat'pin' s Hutnadel *f*

hat'rack' s Hutständer *m*

hatred ['hetrɪd] s Haß *m*

haughtiness ['hɔtɪnɪs] s Hochmut *m*

haughty ['hɔti] *adj* hochmütig

haul [hɔl] s Schleppen *n;* (*hauling distance*) Transportstrecke *f;* (*amount caught*) Fang *m;* **make a big h.** (fig) reiche Beute machen; **over the long h.** auf die Dauer || *tr* (*tug*) schleppen; (*transport*) transportieren; **h. ashore** ans Land ziehen; **h. down** (*a flag*) einholen; **h. into court** vor Gericht schleppen; **h. out of bed** aus dem Bett herausholen || *intr*—**h. off** (naut) abdrehen; **h. off and hit** ausholen um zu schlagen

haulage ['hɔlɪdʒ] s Transport *m;* (*costs*) Transportkosten *pl*

haunch [hɔntʃ] s (*hip*) Hüfte *f;* (*hind quarter of an animal*) Keule *f*

haunt [hɔnt] s Aufenthaltsort *m* || *tr*

verfolgen; **h. a place** an e–m Ort umgehen; **this place is haunted** es spukt hier

haunt'ed house' s Haus *n* in dem es spukt

have [hæv] s—**the haves and the havenots** die Besitzenden und die Besitzlosen || *v* (*pret* & *pp* **had** [hæd]) *tr* haben; (*a baby*) bekommen; (*a drink*) trinken; (*food*) essen; **h. back** (coll) zurückhaben; **h. in mind** vorhaben; **h. it in for s.o.** j–n auf dem Strich haben; **h. it out with s.o.** sich mit j–m aussprechen; **h. it your way** meinetwegen machen Sie es, wie Sie wollen; **h. left** übrig haben; **h. on** (*clothes*) anhaben; (*a hat*) aufhaben; (*e.g., a program*) vorhaben; **h. on one's person** bei sich tragen; **h. to do with s.o.** mit j–m zu tun haben; **h. what it takes** das Zeug dazu haben; **I've had it!** jetzt langt's mir aber!; **I will not h. it!** ich werde es nicht dulden!; **you had better** es wäre besser, wenn Sie; **what would you h. me do?** was soll ich machen? || *intr*—**h. done with it** fertig sein damit; **h. off** frei haben || *aux* (to form compound past tenses) haben, e.g., **he has paid the bill** er hat die Rechnung bezahlt; (to form compound past tenses of certain intransitive verbs of motion and change of condition, of the transitive verb **bleiben,** and of the transitive verb **eingehen**) sein, e.g., **she has gone to the theater** sie ist ins Theater gegangen; **they h. become rich** sie sind reich geworden; **you h. stayed too long** Sie sind zu lange geblieben; **I h. assumed an obligation** ich bin e–e Verpflichtung eingegangen, e.g., **I am having a new suit made** ich lasse mir e–n neuen Anzug machen; (to express necessity) müssen, e.g., **I h. to study now** jetzt muß ich studieren; **that will h. to do** das wird genügen müssen

haven ['hevən] s Hafen *m*

haversack ['hævər‚sæk] s Brotbeutel *m*

havoc ['hævək] s Verwüstung *f;* **wreak h. on** verwüsten

haw [hɔ] s (bot) Mehlbeere *f;* (*in speech*) Äh *n* || *tr* nach links lenken || *intr* nach links gehen || *interj* (*to a horse*) hü!

Hawaii [hə'waɪ·i] s Hawaii *n*

Hawaiian [hə'waɪjən] *adj* hawaiisch

Hawai'ian Is'lands *spl* Hawaii-Inseln *pl*

hawk [hɔk] s Habicht *m* || *tr* (*wares*) verhökern; **h. up** aushusten || *intr* sich räuspern

hawker ['hɔkər] s Straßenhändler –in *mf*

hawse [hɔz] s (*hole*) (naut) Klüse *f;* (*prow*) (naut) Klüsenwand *f*

hawse'hole' s (naut) Klüse *f*

hawser ['hɔzər] s (naut) Trosse *f,* Tau *n*

hawthorn ['hɔθɔrn] s Weißdorn *m*

hay [he] s Heu *n;* **hit the hay** (sl) sich

in die Falle hauen; **make hay** Heu machen
hay′ fe′ver s Heufieber n
hay′field′ s Kleefeld n
hay′fork′ s Heugabel f
hay′loft′ s Heuboden m
hay′mak′er s (box) Schwinger m
hay′rack′ s Heuraufe f
hayrick [′he ˌrɪk] s Heuschober m
hay′ride′ s Ausflug m in e–m teilweise mit Heu gefüllten Wagen
hay′seed′ s (coll) Bauerntölpel m
hay′stack′ s Heuschober m
hay′wire′ adj (sl) übergeschnappt; **go h.** (go wrong) schiefgehen; (go insane) überschnappen
hazard [′hæzərd] s (danger) Gefahr f; (risk) Risiko n ‖ tr riskieren
hazardous [′hæzərdəs] adj gefährlich
haze [hez] s Dunst m; (fig) Unklarheit f ‖ tr (students) piesacken
hazel [′hezəl] adj (eyes) nußbraun ‖ s (bush) Hasel f
ha′zelnut′ s Haselnuß f
haziness [′hezɪnɪs] s Dunstigkeit f; (fig) Verschwommenheit f
haz′ing s (of students) Piesacken n
hazy [′hezi] adj dunstig; (recollection) verschwommen
H-bomb [′etʃ ˌbɑm] s Wasserstoffbombe f
he [hi] pers pron er; **he who** wer ‖ s Männchen n
head [hed] adj Kopf–; (chief) Haupt–, Ober–, Chef– ‖ s (of a body, cabbage, nail, lettuce, pin) Kopf m; (of a gang, family) Haupt m; (of a firm) Chef m; (of a school) Direktor –in mf; (of a department) Leiter –in mf; (of a bed) Kopfende n; (of a coin) Bildseite f; (of a glass of beer) Blume f; (of cattle) Stück n; (of stairs) oberer Absatz m; (of a river) Quelle f; (of a parade, army) Spitze f; (toilet) Klo n; **a h.** pro Person, pro Kopf; **at the h.** of an der Spitze (genit); **be at the h.** of vorstehen (dat); **be h. and shoulders above s.o.** haushoch über j–m stehen; (be far superior to s.o.) j–m haushoch überlegen sein; **be over one's h.** über j–s Verstand gehen; **bring to a h.** zur Entscheidung bringen; **by a h.** um e–e Kopflänge; **from h. to foot** von Kopf bis Fuß; **go over s.o.'s h.** über j–s Verstand gehen; (adm) über j–s Kopf hinweg handeln; **go to s.o.'s h.** j–m zu Kopfe steigen; **have a good h. for** begabt sein für; **h. over heels** kopfüber; (in love) bis über die Ohren; (in debt) bis über den Hals; **heads or tails?** Kopf oder Wappen?; **heads up!** aufpassen!; **keep one's h.** kaltes Blut behalten; **keep one's h. above water** sich über Wasser halten; **lose one's h.** den Kopf verlieren; **my h. is spinning** es schwindelt mir; **not be able to make h. or tail of** nicht klug werden aus; **out of one's h.** nicht ganz richtig im Kopf; **per h.** pro Kopf; **put heads together** die Köpfe zusammenstecken; **talk over**

s.o.'s h. über j–s Kopf hinwegreden
talk s.o.'s h. off j–n dumm und däm lich reden; **take it into one's h.** e: sich [dat] in den Kopf setzen ‖ tr (be in charge of) leiten; (a parade army, expedition) anführen; (steer guide) lenken; **h. a list** als erster auf e–r Liste stehen; **h. off** abwehren: **h. up** (a committee) vorsitzen (dat) ‖ intr—**h. back** zurückkehren; **h. for** auf dem Wege sein nach; (aer) anfliegen; (naut) ansteuern; **h. home** sich heimbegeben; **where are you heading?** wo wollen Sie hin?
head′ache′ s Kopfweh n, Kopfschmerzen pl
head′band′ s Kopfband n
head′board′ s Kopfbrett n
head′cold′ s Schnupfen m
head′ doc′tor s Chefarzt m, Chefärztin f
head′dress′ s Kopfputz m
–headed [ˌhedɪd] suf –köpfig
head first adv kopfüber; (fig) Hals über Kopf
head′gear′ s Kopfbedeckung f
head′hunt′er s Kopfjäger m
head′ing s Überschrift f; (aer) Steuerkurs m
headland [′hedlənd] s Landspitze f
headless [′hedlɪs] adj kopflos; (without a leader) führerlos
head′light′ s (aut) Scheinwerfer m
head′line′ s (in a newspaper) Schlagzeile f; (at the top of a page) Überschrift f; **hit the headlines** (coll) Schlagzeilen liefern
head′lin′er s Hauptdarsteller –in mf
head′long′ adj stürmisch ‖ adv kopfüber
head′man s (–men) Häuptling m, Chef m
head′mas′ter s Direktor m
head′mis′tress s Direktorin f
head′ nurse′ s Oberschwester f
head′ of′fice s Hauptgeschäftsstelle f
head′ of gov′ernment s Regierungschef m
head′ of hair′ s—**beautiful h.** schönes volles Haar n
head′ of the fam′ily s Familienoberhaupt n
head′-on′ adj Frontal– ‖ adv frontal
head′phones′ spl Kopfhörer pl
head′piece′ s Kopfbedeckung f; (brains) (coll) Kopf m; (typ) Zierleiste f
head′quar′ters s Hauptquartier n; (of police) Polizeidirektion f; (mil) Hauptquartier n, Stabsquartier n
head′quarters com′pany s Stabskompanie f
head′rest′ s Kopflehne f; (aut) Kopfstütze f
head′ restrain′er s (aut) Kopfstütze f
head′set′ s Kopfhörer m
head′ shrink′er s (coll) Psychiater –in mf
head′stand′ s Kopfstand m
head′ start′ s Vorsprung m
head′stone′ s Grabstein m
head′strong′ adj starrköpfig

head′ wait′er s Oberkellner m
head′wa′ters spl Quellflüsse pl
head′way′ s Vorwärtsbewegung f; (fig) Fortschritte pl
head′wear′ s Kopfbedeckung f
head′wind′ s Gegenwind m
head′work′ s Kopfarbeit f
heady [′hɛdi] adj (wine) berauschend; (news) spannend; (impetuous) unbesonnen
heal [hil] tr & intr heilen; **h. up** zuheilen
healer [′hilər] s Heilkundige mf
heal′ing s Heilung f
health [hɛlθ] s Gesundheit f; **drink to s.o.'s h.** auf j–s Wohl trinken; **in good h.** gesund; **in poor h.** kränklich; **to your h.!** auf Ihr Wohl!
health′ certi′ficate s Gesundheitspaß m
healthful [′hɛlθfəl] adj heilsam; (climate) bekömmlich
health′ insur′ance s Krankenversicherung f
health′ resort′ s Kurort m
healthy [′hɛlθi] adj gesund; (respect) gehörig; **keep h.** sich gesund halten
heap [hip] s Haufen m; **in heaps** haufenweise ‖ tr beladen; **h.** (e.g., praise) **on s.o.** j–n überhäufen mit; **h. up** anhäufen
hear [hɪr] v (pret & pp heard [hʌrd]) tr hören; (find out) erfahren; (get word) Bescheid bekommen; **h. s.o.'s lessons** j–n überhören; **h. s.o. out** j–n ganz ausreden lassen ‖ intr hören; **h. about** hören über (acc) or von; **h. from** Nachricht bekommen von; **h. of** hören von; **h. wrong** sich verhören; **he wouldn't h. of it** er wollte nichts davon hören
hearer [′hɪrər] s Hörer –in mf; **hearers** Zuhörer pl
hear′ing s Hören n, Gehör n; (jur) Verhör n; **within h.** in Hörweite
hear′ing aid′ s Hörgerät n, Hörapparat m
hear′say′ s Hörensagen n; **know s.th. by h.** etw nur vom Hörensagen kennen; **that's mere h.** das ist bloßes Gerede
hearse [hʌrs] s Leichenwagen m
heart [hɑrt] s Herz n; **after my own h.** nach meinem Herzen; **at h.** im Grunde genommen; **be the h. and soul of** die Seele sein (genit); **by h.** auswendig; **cross my h.!** Hand aufs Herz!; **cry one's h. out** sich ausweinen; **eat one's h. out** sich vor Kummer verzehren; **get to the h. of** auf den Grund kommen (dat); **have a h.** (coll) ein Herz haben; **have one's h. in s.th.** mit dem Herzen bei etw sein; **have the h. to** (inf) es übers Herz bringen zu (inf); **h. and soul** mit Leib und Seele; **hearts** (cards) Herz n; **lose h.** den Mut verlieren; **lose one's h. to** sein Herz verlieren an (acc); **set one's h. on** sein Herz hängen an (acc); **take h.** Mut fassen; **take to h.** beherzigen; **to one's heart's content** nach Herzenslust; **wear one's h. on one's sleeve** das Herz auf der

Zunge tragen; **with all one's h.** mit ganzem Herzen
heart′ache′ s Herzweh n
heart′ attack′ s Herzanfall m
heart′beat′ s Herzschlag m
heart′break′ s Herzeleid n
heart′break′er s Herzensbrecher –in mf
heartbroken [′hɑrt‚brokən] adj trostlos
heart′burn′ s Sodbrennen n
heart′ disease′ s Herzleiden n
–hearted [‚hɑrtɪd] suf –herzig
hearten [′hɑrtən] tr ermutigen
heart′ fail′ure s Herzschlag m
heartfelt [′hɑrt‚fɛlt] adj herzinnig, tiefempfunden; (wishes) herzlich
hearth [hɑrθ] s Herd m
hearth′stone′ s Kaminplatte f
heartily [′hɑrtɪli] adv (with zest) herzhaft; (sincerely) von Herzen
heartless [′hɑrtlɪs] adj herzlos
heart′ mur′mur s Herzgeräusch n
heart′-rend′ing adj herzzerreißend
heart′sick′ adj tief betrübt
heart′ strings′ spl—**pull at s.o.'s h.** j–m ans Herz greifen
heart′ throb′ s Schwarm m
heart′ trans′plant s Herzverpflanzung f
heart′ trou′ble s Herzbeschwerden pl
heart′wood′ s Kernholz n
hearty [′hɑrti] adj herzhaft; (meal) reichlich; (eater) stark; (appetite) gut
heat [hit] s Hitze f, Wärme f; (heating) Heizung f; (sexual) Brunst f; (in the case of dogs) Läufigkeit f; (of battle) Eifer m; (sport) Rennen n, Einzelrennen n; **be in h.** brunsten; (said of dogs) läufig sein; **final h.** Schlußrennen n; **put the h. on** (sl) unter Druck setzen; **qualifying h.** Vorlauf m ‖ tr (e.g., food) wärmen; (fluids) erhitzen; (a house) heizen; **h. up** aufwärmen ‖ intr—**h. (up)** warm (or heiß) werden
heat′ed adj erhitzt; (fig) erregt
heater [′hitər] s Heizkörper m; (oven) Heizofen m
heath [hiθ] s Heide f
hea·then [′hiðən] adj heidnisch ‖ s (–then & –thens) Heide m, Heidin f
heathendom [′hiðəndəm] s Heidentum n
heather [′hɛðər] s Heiderkraut n
heat′ing s Heizung f
heat′ing pad′ s Heizkissen n
heat′ing sys′tem s Heizanlage f
heat′ light′ning s Wetterleuchten n
heat′ prostra′tion s Hitzekollaps m
heat′-resis′tant adj hitzebeständig
heat′ shield′ s (rok) Hitzeschild m
heat′stroke′ s Hitzschlag m
heat′ treat′ment s Wärmebehandlung f
heat′ wave′ s Hitzewelle f
heave [hiv] s Hub m; (throw) Wurf m; **heaves** (vet) schweres Atmen n ‖ v (pret & pp heaved & hove [hov]) tr heben; (throw) werfen; (a sigh) ausstoßen; (the anchor) lichten ‖ intr (said of the breast or sea) wogen; (retch) sich übergeben; **h. in sight** auftauchen; **h. to** (naut) stoppen

heaven ['hevən] *s* Himmel *m;* **for heaven's sake** um Himmels willen; **good heavens!** ach du lieber Himmel!; **the heavens** der Himmel
heavenly ['hevənli] *adj* himmlisch
hea'venly bod'y *s* Himmelskörper *m*
heavenwards ['hevənwərdz] *adv* himmelwärts
heavily ['hevɪli] *adv* schwer; **h. in debt** überschuldet
heavy ['hevi] *adj* schwer; (*food*) schwer verdaulich; (*fine, price*) hoch; (*walk*) schwerfällig; (*heart*) bedrückt, schwer; (*traffic, frost, rain*) stark; (*fog*) dicht; (*role*) (theat) ernst, düster; **h. drinker** Gewohnheitstrinker –in *mf;* **h. seas** Sturzsee *f;* **h. with sleep** schlaftrunken
heavy'-armed' *adj* schwerbewaffnet
heav'y-du'ty *adj* Hochleistungs-, Schwerlast–
heav'y-du'ty truck' *s* Schwerlastwagen *m*
heav'y-heart'ed *adj* bedrückt
heav'y in'dustry *s* Schwerindustrie *f*
heav'yset' *adj* untersetzt
heav'y weight' *adj* Schwergewicht– ‖ *s* Schwergewichtler *m*
Hebrew ['hibru] *adj* hebräisch ‖ *s* Hebräer –in *mf;* (*language*) Hebräisch *n*
hecatomb ['hekə‚tom] *s* Hekatombe *f*
heck [hek] *s*—**give s.o. h.** (sl) j-m tüchtig einheizen; **what the h. are you doing?** (sl) was zum Teufel tust du? ‖ *interj* (sl) verflixt!
heckle ['hekəl] *tr* durch Zwischenrufe belästigen
heckler ['heklər] *s* Zwischenrufer –in *mf*
hectic ['hektɪk] *adj* hektisch
hectograph ['hektə‚græf] *s* Hektograph *m* ‖ *tr* hektographieren
hedge [hedʒ] *s* Hecke *f* ‖ *tr*—**h. in** (or **h. off**) einhegen ‖ *intr* sich den Rücken decken
hedge'hog' *s* Igel *m*
hedge'hop' *v* (*pret & pp* –**hopped;** *ger* **hopping**) *intr* (aer) heckenspringen
hedge'hop'ping *s* (aer) Heckenhüpfen *n*
hedge'row' *s* Hecke *f*
hedonism ['hidə‚nɪzəm] *s* Hedonismus *m*
hedonist ['hidənɪst] *s* Hedonist –in *mf*
heed [hid] *s* Acht *f;* **pay h. to** achtgeben auf (*acc*); **take h.** achtgeben ‖ *tr* beachten ‖ *intr* achtgeben
heedful ['hidfəl] *adj* (of) achtsam (auf *acc*)
heedless ['hidlɪs] *adj* achtlos; **h. of** ungeachtet (*genit*)
heehaw ['hi‚hɔ] *s* Iah *n* ‖ *interj* iah!
heel [hil] *s* (*of the foot*) Ferse *f;* (*of a shoe*) Absatz *m;* (*of bread*) Brotende *n;* (sl) Schurke *m;* **down at the h.** abgerissen; **cool one's heels** sich [*dat*] die Beine in den Bauch stehen; **take to one's heels** Fersengeld geben ‖ *intr* (*said of a dog*) auf den Fersen folgen
hefty ['hefti] *adj* (*heavy*) schwer; (*muscular*) stämmig; (*blow*) zünftig

heifer ['hefər] *s* Färse *f*
height [haɪt] *s* Höhe *f;* (*e.g., of power*) Gipfel *m;* **h. of the season** Hochsaison *f*
heighten ['haɪtən] *tr* erhöhen; (fig) verschärfen
heinous ['henəs] *adj* abscheulich
heir [er] *s* Erbe; *m;* **become h. to** erben; **become s.o.'s h.** j-n beerben
heir' appar'ent *s* (**heirs apparent**) Thronerbe *m*
heiress ['erɪs] *s* Erbin *f*
heir'loom' *s* Erbstück *n*
heir' presump'tive *s* (**heirs presumptive**) mutmaßlicher Erbe *m*
Helen ['helən] *s* Helene *f*
helicopter ['helɪ‚kaptər] *s* Hubschrauber *m*
heliport ['helɪ‚pɔrt] *s* Hubschrauberlandeplatz *m*
helium ['hilɪ‚əm] *s* Helium *n*
helix ['hilɪks] *s* (**helixes & helices** ['helɪ‚siz]) Spirale *f;* (archit) Schnecke *f*
hell [hel] *s* Hölle *f*
hell'bent' *adj*—**h. on** (sl) erpicht auf (*acc*)
hell'cat' *s* (*shrew*) Hexe *f*
Hellene ['helin] *s* Hellene *m*, Hellenin *f*
Hellenic [he'lenɪk] *adj* hellenisch
hell'fire' *s* Höllenfeuer *n*
hellish ['helɪʃ] *adj* höllisch
hel·lo ['he'lo] *s* (–**los**) Hallo *n* ‖ *interj* guten Tag!; (in southern Germany and Austria) Grüß Gott!; (to get s.o.'s attention and in answering the telephone) hallo!
helm [helm] *s* (& fig) Steuerruder *n*
helmet ['helmɪt] *s* Helm *m*
helms'man *s* (–**men**) Steuermann *m*
help [help] *s* Hilfe *f;* (*domestic*) Hilfe *f*, Hilfskraft *f;* (*temporary*) Aushilfe *f;* **h. wanted** (in *newspapers*) Stellenangebot *n;* **there's no h. for it** da ist nicht zu helfen; **with the h. of** mit Hilfe (*genit*) ‖ *tr* helfen (*dat*); **can I h. you?** womit kann ich (Ihnen) dienen?; **h. along** nachhelfen (*dat*); **h. down from** herunterhelfen (*dat*) von (*dat*); **h. oneself** sich bedienen; (*at table*) zugreifen; **h. oneself to** sich [*dat*] nehmen; **h. out** aushelfen (*dat*); **h. s.o. on** (or **off**) **with the coat** j-m in den (or aus dem) Mantel helfen; **I cannot h.** (*ger*), **I cannot h. but** (*inf*) ich kann nicht umhin zu (*inf*); **sorry, that can't be helped** es tut mir leid, aber es geht nicht anders ‖ *intr* ‖ *interj* Hilfe!
helper ['helpər] *s* Gehilfe *m*, Gehilfin *f*
helpful ['helpfəl] *adj* (*person*) hilfsbereit; (*e.g., suggestion*) nützlich
help'ing *s* Portion *f*
help'ing hand' *s* hilfreiche Hand *f*
helpless ['helplɪs] *adj* hilflos, ratlos
helter-skelter ['heltər'skeltər] *adj* wirr ‖ *adv* holterdipolter
hem [hem] *s* Saum *m* ‖ *v* (*pret & pp* **hemmed;** *ger* **hemming**) *tr* säumen; **hem in** umringen ‖ *intr* stocken; **hem**

and haw nicht mit der Sprache herauswollen || *interj* hm!
hemisphere ['hemɪ͵sfɪr] *s* Halbkugel *f*
hemistich ['hemɪ͵stɪk] *s* Halbvers *m*
hem·line' *s* Rocklänge *f*
hem'lock' *s* (*conium*) Schierling *m;* (*poison*) Schierlingsgift *n;* (*Tsuga canadensis*) Kanadische Hemmlocktanne *f*
hemoglobin [͵hɪmə'globɪn] *s* Blutfarbstoff *m*, Hämoglobin *n*
hemophilia [͵hɪmə'fɪlɪ·ə] *s* Bluterkrankheit *f*, Hämophilie *f*
hemorrhage ['hemərɪdʒ] *s* Blutung *f*
hemorrhoids ['hemə͵rɔɪdz] *spl* Hämorrhoiden *pl*
hemostat ['hɪmə͵stæt] *s* Unterbindungssklemme *f*
hemp [hemp] *s* Hanf *m*
hem'stitch' *s* Hohlsaum *m* || *tr* mit e–m Hohlsaum versehen
hen [hen] *s* Henne *f*, Huhn *n*
hence [hens] *adv* von hier; (*therefore*) daher, daraus; **a year h.** in e–m Jahr
hence'forth' *adv* hinfort, von nun an
hench·man ['hentʃmən] *s* (**–men**) Anhänger *m;* (*gang member*) Helfershelfer *m*
hen'house' *s* Hühnerstall *m*
henna ['henə] *s* Henna *f*
hen' par'ty *s* (coll) Damengesellschaft *f*
hen'peck' *tr* unter dem Pantoffel haben; **be henpecked** unter dem Pantoffel stehen; **henpecked husband** Pantoffelheld *m*
Henry ['henri] *s* Heinrich *m*
hep [hep] *adj* (**to**) eingeweiht (in *acc*)
her [hʌr] *poss adj* ihr; (if the antecedent is neuter, e.g., Fräulein) sein || *pers pron* sie; (if the antecedent is neuter) es; (indirect object) ihr; (if the antecedent is neuter) ihm
herald ['herəld] *s* Herold *m;* (fig) Vorbote *m* || *tr* ankündigen; **h. in** einführen
heraldic [he'rældɪk] *adj* heraldisch; **h. figure** Wappenbild *n;* **h. motto** Wappenspruch *m*
heraldry ['herəldri] *s* Wappenkunde *f*
herb [(h)ʌrb] *s* Kraut *n*, Gewürz *n;* (pharm) Arzneikraut *n*
herculean [hʌrkju'li·ən] *adj* herkulisch
herd [hʌrd] *s* Herde *f;* (of game) Rudel *n;* **the common h.** der Pöbel || *tr* hüten; **h. together** zusammenpferchen || *intr* in e–r Herde gehen (or leben)
herds'man *s* (**–men**) Hirt *m*
here [hɪr] *adv* (*position*) hier; (*direction*) hierher, her; **h. and there** hie(r) und da; **h. below** in diesem Leben; **h. goes!** jetzt gilt's!; **here's to you!** auf Ihr Wohl!; **neither h. nor there** belanglos || *interj* hier!
hereabouts ['hɪrə͵bauts] *adv* hier in der Nähe
hereaf'ter *adv* hiernach || *s* Jenseits *n*
hereby' *adv* hierdurch
hereditary [hɪ'redɪ͵teri] *adj* erblich, Erb–; **be h.** sich vererben
heredity [hɪ'redɪti] *s* Vererbung *f*

herein' *adv* hierin
hereof' *adv* hiervon
hereon' *adv* hierauf
heresy ['herəsi] *s* Ketzerei *f*
heretic ['herətɪk] *s* Ketzer –in *mf*
heretical [hɪ'retɪkəl] *adj* ketzerisch
heretofore [͵hɪrtu'for] *adv* zuvor
here'upon' *adv* daraufhin
herewith' *adv* hiermit; (*in a letter*) anbei, in der Anlage
heritage ['herɪtɪdʒ] *s* Erbe *n*
hermet'ically sealed' [hʌr'metɪkəli] *adj* hermetisch verschlossen
hermit ['hʌrmɪt] *s* Einsiedler –in *mf;* (eccl) Eremit *m*
hermitage ['hʌrmɪtɪdʒ] *s* Eremitage *f*
herni·a ['hʌrnɪ·ə] *s* (**–as & –ae** [͵i]) Bruch *m*
he·ro ['hɪro] *s* (**–roes**) Held *n*
heroic [hɪ'ro·ɪk] *adj* heldenhaft, Helden–; (pros) heroisch || **heroics** *spl* Heldentaten *pl*
hero'ic age' *s* Helden(zeit)alter *n*
hero'ic coup'let *s* heroisches Reimpaar *n*
hero'ic verse' *s* heroisches Vermaß *n*
heroin ['hɪro·ɪn] *s* Heroin *n*
heroine ['hɪro·ɪn] *s* Heldin *f*
heroism ['hɪro͵ɪzəm] *s* Heldenmut *m*
heron ['herən] *s* (orn) Fischreiher *m*
he'ro wor'ship *s* Heldenverehrung *f*
herring ['herɪŋ] *s* Hering *m*
her'ringbone' *s* (*pattern*) Grätenmuster *n;* (*parquetry*) Riemenparkett *n*
hers [hʌrz] *poss pron* der ihre (or ihrige), ihrer
herself' *reflex pron* sich; **she's not h. today** sie ist heute gar nicht wie sonst || *intens pron* selbst, selber
hesitancy ['herzɪtənsi] *s* Zaudern *n*
hesitant ['hezɪtənt] *adj* zögernd
hesitate ['hezɪ͵tet] *intr* zögern
hesitation [͵hezɪ'te/ən] *s* Zögern *n*
heterodox ['hetərə͵daks] *adj* andersgläubig, heterodox
heterodyne ['hetərə͵daɪn] *adj* Überlagerungs– || *tr & intr* überlagern
heterogeneous [͵hetərə'dʒinɪ·əs] *adj* heterogen
hew [hju] *v* (*pret* **hewed** & **hewn**) *tr* (*stone*) hauen; (*trees*) fällen; **hew down** umhauen
hex [heks] *s* (*spell*) Zauber *m;* (*witch*) Hexe *f;* **put a hex on** (coll) behexen || *tr* (coll) behexen
hexagon ['heksəgɑn] *s* Hexagon *n*
hey [he] *interj* hei!; **hey there!** heda!
hey'day' *s* Hochblüte *f*, Glanzzeit *f*
H'-hour' *s* (mil) X-Zeit *f*
hi [haɪ] *interj* hei!; **hi there!** heda!
hia·tus [haɪ'etəs] *s* (**–tuses & –tus**) Lücke *f;* (ling) Hiatus *m*
hibernate ['haɪbər͵net] *intr* (& fig) Winterschlaf halten
hibernation [͵haɪbər'ne/ən] *s* Winterschlaf *m*
hibiscus [haɪ'bɪskəs] *s* Hibiskus *m*
hiccough, hiccup ['hɪkəp] *s* Schluckauf *m*
hick [hɪk] *s* Tölpel *m*
hickory ['hɪkəri] *s* Hickorybaum *m*
hick' town' *s* Kuhdorf *n*

hidden ['hɪdən] *adj* verborgen, versteckt; (*secret*) geheim
hide [haɪd] *s* Haut *f*, Fell *n* || *v* (*pret* **hid** [hɪd]; *pp* **hid** & **hidden** ['hɪdən] *tr* verstecken; (*a view*) verdecken; (fig) verbergen; **h. from** verheimlichen vor (*dat*) || *intr* (**out**) sich verstecken
hide'-and-seek' *s* Versteckspiel *n;* **play h.** Versteck spielen
hide'away' *s* Schlupfwinkel *m*
hide'bound' *adj* engherzig
hideous ['hɪdɪ·əs] *adj* gräßlich
hide'out' *s* (coll) Versteck *n*
hid'ing *s* Verstecken *n;* **be in h.** sich versteckt halten; **get a h.** (coll) Prügel bekommen
hid'ing place' *s* Versteck *n*
hierarchy ['haɪ·ə‚rɑrki] *s* Hierarchie *f*
hieroglyphic [‚haɪ·ərə'glɪfɪk] *adj* Hieroglphen– || *s* Hieroglyphe *f*
hi-fi ['haɪ'faɪ] *adj* Hif-fi– || *s* Hi-Fi *n*
high [haɪ] *adj* hoch; (*wind*) stark; (*hopes*) hochgespannt; (*fever*) heftig (*spirits*) gehoben; **h. and dry** auf dem Trockenen; **h. and mighty** hochfahrend; **it is h. time** es ist höchste Zeit || *adv* hoch; **h. and low** weit und breit || *s* (e.g., *in prices*) Hochstand *m;* (aut) höchster Gang *m;* (meteor) Hoch *n;* **on h.** oben; **shift into h.** den höchsten Gang einschalten
high' al'tar *s* Hochaltar *m*
high'ball' *s* Highball *m*
high'born' *adj* hochgeboren
high'boy' *s* hochbeinige Kommode *f*
high'brow' *adj* intellektuell || *s* Intellektuelle *mf*
high' chair' *s* Kinderstuhl *m*
High' Church' *s* Hochkirche *f*
high'-class' *adj* vornehm, herrschaftlich
high' command' *s* Oberkommando *n*
high' cost' of liv'ing *s* hohe Lebenshaltungskosten *pl*
high' div'ing *s* Turmspringen *n*
high'er educa'tion *s* Hochschulbildung *f*
high'er-up' *s* (coll) hohes Tier *n*
high'est bid' ['haɪ·ɪst] *s* Meistgebot *n*
high'est bid'der *s* Meistbietende *mf*
high' explo'sive *s* hochexplosiver Sprengstoff *m*
highfalutin [‚haɪfə'lutən] *adj* hochtönend
high' fidel'ity *s* äußerst getreue Tonwiedergabe *f*, High Fidelity *f*
high'-fidel'ity *adj* klanggetreu
high' fre'quency *s* Hochfrequenz *f*
high'-fre'quency *adj* hochfrequent
high' gear' *s* höchster Gang *m;* **shift into h.** den höchsten Gang einschalten; (fig) auf Hochtouren gehen
High' Ger'man *s* Hochdeutsch *n*
high'-grade' *adj* hochfein, Qualitäts–
high'-grade steel' *s* Edelstahl *m*
high'-hand'ed *adj* anmaßend
high' heel' *s* Stöckel *m*
high'-heeled shoe' *s* Stöckelschuh *m*
high' horse' *s*—**come off one's h.** klein beigeben; **get up on one's h.** sich aufs hohe Roß setzen

high' jinks' [‚dʒɪŋks] *spl* Ausgelassenheit *f*
high' jump' *s* (sport) Hochsprung *m*
highland ['haɪlənd] *s* Hochland *n;* **highlands** Hochland *n*
highlander ['haɪləndər] *s* Hochländer –in *mf*
high' life' *s* Prasserei *f*, Highlife *n*
high'light' *s* (*big moment*) Höhepunkt *m;* (*in a picture*) Glanzlicht *n* || *tr* hervorheben; (*in a picture*) Glanzlichter aufsetzen (*dat*)
highly ['haɪli] *adv* hoch, hoch–, höchst; **h. sensitive** hochempfindlich; **speak h. of** in den höchsten Tönen sprechen von; **think h. of** große Stücke halten auf (*acc*)
High' Mass' *s* Hochamt *n*
high'-mind'ed *adj* hochgesinnt
high'-necked' *adj* hochgeschlossen
highness ['haɪnɪs] *s* Höhe *f;* **Highness** (*title*) Hoheit *f*
high' noon' *s*—**at h.** am hellen Mittag
high'-oc'tane *adj* mit hoher Oktanzahl
high'-pitched' *adj* (*voice*) hoch; (*roof*) steil
high'-pow'ered *adj* starkmotorig; **h. engine** Hochleistungsmotor *m*
high' pres'sure *s* Hochdruck *m*
high'-pres'sure *adj* Hochdruck–; **h. area** Hochdruckgebiet *n* || *tr* (com) bearbeiten
high'-priced' *adj* kostspielig
high' priest' *s* Hohe(r)priester *m*
high'-qual'ity *adj* Qualitäts–, hochwertig
high'-rank'ing *adj* hochgestellt
high' rise' *s* Hochbau *m*, Hochhaus *n*
high'road' *s* (fig) sicherer Weg *m*
high' school' *s* Oberschule *f*
high' sea' *s*—**on the high seas** auf offenem Meer
high' soci'ety *s* vornehme Welt *f*, High Society *f*
high'-sound'ing *adj* hochtönend
high'-speed' *adj* Schnell–; (phot) lichtstark
high'-speed steel' *s* Schnelldrehstahl *m*
high'-spir'ited *adj* hochgemut; (*horse*) feurig
high' spir'its *spl* gehobene Stimmung *f*
high-strung ['haɪ'strʌŋ] *adj* überempfindlich
high' ten'sion *s* Hochspannung *f*
high'-ten'sion *adj* Hochspannungs–
high'-test' gas'oline *s* Superbenzin *n*
high' tide' *s* Flut *f*
high' time' *s* höchste Zeit *f;* (sl) Heidenspaß *m*
high' trea'son *s* Hochverrat *m*
high' volt'age *s* Hochspannung *f*
high'-volt'age *adj* Hochspannungs–
high'-wa'ter mark' *s* Hochwassermarke *f;* (fig) Höhepunkt *m*
high'way' *s* Landstraße *f*, Chaussee *f*
high'way'man *s* (–men) Straßenräuber *m*
high'way patrol' *s* Straßenstreife *f*
high'way rob'bery *s* Straßenraub *m*
hijack ['haɪ‚dʒæk] *tr* (*a truck*) überfallen und rauben; (*a plane*) entführen

hijacker ['haɪ‚dʒækər] s (of a truck) Straßenräuber –in mf; (of a plane) Entführer –in mf
hi'jack'ing s Entführung f
hike [haɪk] s Wanderung f; (in prices) Erhöhung f ‖ tr (prices) erhöhen ‖ intr wandern
hiker ['haɪkər] s Wanderer –in mf
hik'ing s Wandern n
hilarious [hɪ'lɛrɪ·əs] adj heiter
hill [hɪl] s Hügel m; **go over the h.** (mil) ausbüxen; **over the h.** (coll) auf dem absteigenden Ast ‖ tr häufeln
hill'bil'ly adj hinterwäldlerisch ‖ s Hinterwäldler –in mf
hill' coun'try s Hügelland n
hillock ['hɪlək] s Hügelchen n
hill'side' s Hang m
hilly ['hɪli] adj hügelig
hilt [hɪlt] s Griff m; **armed to the h.** bis an die Zähne bewaffnet; **to the h.** (fig) gründlich
him [hɪm] pers pron (dative) ihm; (accusative) ihn
himself' reflex pron sich; **he is not h. today** er ist heute gar nicht wie sonst ‖ intens pron selbst, selber
hind [haɪnd] adj Hinter– ‖ s Hirschkuh f
hinder ['hɪndər] tr (ver)hindern
hind'most' adj hinterste
hind'quar'ter s Hinterviertel n; (of a horse) Hinterhand f; (of venison) Ziemer m
hindrance ['hɪndrəns] s (to) Hindernis n (für)
hind'sight' s späte Einsicht f
Hindu ['hɪndu] adj Hindu– ‖ s Hindu m
hinge [hɪndʒ] s Scharnier n; (of a door) Angel f ‖ intr—**h. on** abhängen von
hint [hɪnt] s Wink m, Andeutung f; **give a broad h.** e-n Wink mit dem Zaunpfahl geben; **take the h.** den Wink verstehen ‖ intr—**h. at** andeuten
hinterland ['hɪntər‚lænd] s Hinterland n
hip [hɪp] adj (sl) im Bild ‖ s Hüfte f; (of a roof) Walm m
hip'bone' s Hüftbein n
hip'joint' s Hüftgelenk n
hipped adj—**h. on** (coll) erpicht auf (acc)
hippopota·mus [‚hɪpə'patəməs] s (–muses & –mi [‚maɪ]) Nilpferd n
hip' roof' s Walmdach n
hire [haɪr] s Miete f; (salary) Lohn m; **for h.** zu vermieten ‖ tr (workers) anstellen; (rent) mieten; **h. oneself out** to sich verdingen bei; **h. out** vermieten
hired' hand' s Lohnarbeiter –in mf
hireling ['haɪrlɪŋ] s Mietling m
his [hɪz] poss adj sein ‖ poss pron seiner, der seine (or seinige)
Hispanic [hɪs'pænɪk] adj hispanisch
hiss [hɪs] s Zischen n ‖ tr auszischen ‖ intr zischen
hiss'ing s Zischen n, Gezisch n

hiss'ing sound' s Zischlaut m
hist [hɪst] interj st!
historian [hɪs'torɪ·ən] s Historiker –in mf
historic [hɪs'tɔrɪk] adj historisch bedeutsam
historical [hɪs'tɔrɪkəl] adj historisch, geschichtlich
history ['hɪstəri] s Geschichte f
historionic [‚hɪstrɪ'anɪk] adj schauspielerisch; (fig) übertrieben ‖ **histrionics** spl theatralisches Benehmen n
hit [hɪt] s Schlag m, Stoß m; (a success) Schlager m; (sport) Treffer m; (theat) Zugstück n ‖ v (pret & pp hit; ger hitting) tr (e.g., with the fist) schlagen; (a note, target) treffen; **hit bottom** (fig) auf dem Nullpunkt angekommen sein; **hit it off** gut miteinander auskommen; **hit one's head against** mit dem Kopf stoßen gegen; **hit s.o. hard** (said of misfortunes, etc.) schwer treffen; **hit the road** sich auf den Weg machen; **hit the sack** sich hinhauen ‖ intr schlagen; **hit on** (or **upon**) kommen auf (acc)
hit'-and-run' adj (driver) flüchtig; **h. accident** Unfall m mit Fahrerflucht; **h. attack** Zerstörangriff m
hitch [hɪtʃ] s (difficulty) Haken m; (knot) Stich m; (term of service) Dienstzeit f; **that's the h.** das ist ja gerade der Haken; **without a h.** reibungslos ‖ tr spannen; **h. a ride** (to) per Anhalter fahren (nach); **h. to the wagon** vor (or an) den Wagen spannen; **h. up** (horses) anspannen; (trousers) hochziehen
hitch'hike' intr per Anhalter fahren
hitch'ing post' s Pfosten m (zum Anbinden von Pferden)
hither ['hɪðər] adv her, hierher; **h. and thither** hierhin und dorthin
hitherto' adv bisher
hit' or miss' adv aufs Geratewohl
hit'-or-miss' adj planlos
hitter ['hɪtər] s Schläger m
hive [haɪv] s Bienenstock m; **hives** (pathol) Nesselausschlag m
hoard [hord] s Hort m ‖ tr & intr horten; (food) hamstern
hoarder ['hordər] s Hamsterer –in mf
hoard'ing s Horten n; (of food) Hamstern n
hoarfrost ['hor‚frɔst] s Rauhreif m
hoarse [hors] adj heiser
hoarseness ['horsnɪs] s Heiserkeit f
hoary ['hori] adj ergraut; (fig) altersgrau
hoax [hoks] s Schnabernack m ‖ tr anführen
hob [hab] s Kamineinsatz m
hobble ['habəl] s Humpeln n ‖ intr humpeln
hobby ['habi] s Hobby n
hob'byhorse' s (stick with horse's head) Steckenpferd n; (rocking horse) Schaukelpferd n
hob'gob'lin s Kobold m; (bogy) Schreckgespenst n
hob'nail' s grober Schuhnagel m

hob·nob ['hɑb ‚nɑb] v (*pret & pp* –**nobbed;** *ger* –**nobbing**) *intr*—**h. with** freundschaftlich verkehren mit
ho·bo ['hobo] s (**-bos & -boes**) Landstreicher m
hock [hɑk] s (*of a horse*) Sprunggelenk n; **in h.** verpfändet ‖ *tr* (*hamstring*) lähmen; (*pawn*) (coll) verpfänden
hockey ['hɑki] s Hockey n
hoc'key stick' s Hockeystock m
hock'shop' s (coll) Leihhaus n
hocus-pocus ['hokəs'pokəs] s Hokuspokus m
hod [hɑd] s Mörteltrog m
hodgepodge ['hɑdʒ ‚pɑdʒ] s Mischmasch m
hoe [ho] s Hacke f, Haue f ‖ *tr* hacken
hog [hɔg] s Schwein n ‖ v (*pret & pp* **hogged;** *ger* **hogging**) *tr* (sl) gierig an sich reißen; **hog the road** rücksichtslos fahren
hog'back' s scharfer Gebirgskamm m
hog' bris'tle s Schweinsborste f
hoggish ['hɔgɪʃ] adj schweinisch, gefräßig
hog'wash' s (*nonsense*) Quatsch m
hoist [hɔɪst] s (*apparatus for lifting*) Hebezeug n; (*act of lifting*) Hochwinden n ‖ *tr* hochwinden; (*a flag, sail*) hissen
hokum ['hokəm] s (*nonsense*) (coll) Quatsch m; (*flimflam*) (coll) Effekthascherei f
hold [hold] s Halt m, Griff m; (naut) Raum m; (sport) Griff m; **get h. of** (*catch*) erwischen; (*acquire*) erwerben; **get h. of oneself** sich fassen; **take h. of** anfassen ‖ v (*pret & pp* **held** [hɛld] *tr* halten; (*contain*) enthalten; (*regard as*) halten für; (*one's breath*) anhalten; (*an audience*) fesseln; (*a meeting, election, court*) abhalten; (*an office, position*) bekleiden, innehaben; (*talks*) führen; (*a viewpoint*) vertreten; (*a meet*) (sport) veranstalten; **able to h. one's liquor** trinkfest; **h. back** zurückhalten; (*news*) geheimhalten; **h. dear** werthalten; **h. down** niederhalten; **h. in contempt** verachten; **h. it!** halt!; **h. off** abhalten; **h. office** amtieren; **h. one's ground** die Stellung halten; **h. one's own** seinen Mann stehen; **h. one's own against** sich behaupten gegen; **h. one's tongue** den Mund halten; **h. open** (*a door*) aufhalten; **h. out** (*a hand*) hinhalten; (*proffer*) vorhalten; **h. over** (*e.g., a play*) verlängern; **h. s.th. against s.o.** j-m etw nachtragen; **h. sway** walten; **h. under** niederhalten; **h. up** (*raise*) hochhalten; (*detain*) aufhalten; (*traffic*) behindern; (*rob*) (räuberisch) überfallen; **h. up to ridicule** dem Spott preisgeben; **h. the line** (telp) am Apparat bleiben; **h. the road well** e-e gute Straßenlage haben; **h. together** zusammenhalten; **h. water** (fig) stichhaltig sein ‖ *intr* (*said of a knot*) halten; **h. back** sich zurückhalten; **h. forth** (coll) dozieren; **h. on** warten; **h. on to** festhalten, sich

festhalten an (*dat*); **h. out** aushalten; **h. out for** abwarten; **h. true** gelten; **h. true for** zutreffen auf (*acc*); **h. up** (*wear well*) halten
holder ['holdər] s (*device*) Halter m; (*e.g., of a title*) Inhaber –in mf
hold'ing s (*of a meeting*) Abhaltung f; (*of an office*) Bekleidung f; **holdings** Besitz m, Bestand m
hold'ing com'pany s Holdinggesellschaft f
hold'ing pat'tern s (aer) Platzrunde f
hold'-o'ver s Überbleibsel n
hold'up' s (*delay*) Aufenhalt m; (*robbery*) Raubüberfall m; (*in traffic*) Verkehrsstauung f
hold'up man' s Räuber m
hole [hol] s Loch n; (*of animals*) Bau m; **h. in the wall** Loch n; **in a h.** in der Patsche; **in the h.** hängengeblieben, e.g., **I am ten dollars in the h.** ich bin mit zehn Dollar hängengeblieben; **pick holes in** (fig) herumkritisieren an (*dat*); **wear holes in** völlig abtragen ‖ *intr*—**h. out** (golf) ins Loch spielen; **h. up** sich vergraben; (fig) sich verstecken
holiday ['hɑlı ‚de] s Feiertag m; (*vacation*) Ferien pl; **take a h.** e-n freien Tag machen, Urlaub nehmen
hol'iday mood' s Ferienstimmung f
holiness ['holinis] s Heiligkeit f; **His Holiness** Seine Heiligkeit
Holland ['hɑlənd] s Holland n
Hollander ['hɑləndər] s Holländer –in mf
hollow ['hɑlo] adj hohl ‖ s Höhle f, Höhlung f; (geol) Talmulde f ‖ *tr*— **h. out** aushöhlen
hol'low-cheeked' adj hohlwangig
hol'low-eyed' adj hohläugig
holly ['hɑli] s Stechpalme f
holm' oak' [hom] s Steineiche f
holocaust ['hɑlə ‚kɔst] s Brandopfer n; (*disaster*) Brandkatastrophe f
holster ['holstər] s Pistolentasche f
holy ['holi] adj heilig; **h. smokes!** (coll) heiliger Strohsack!
Ho'ly Commun'ion s Kommunion f, das Heilige Abendmahl
ho'ly day' s Feiertag m
Ho'ly Ghost' s Heiliger Geist m
Ho'ly of Ho'lies s Allerheiligste n
ho'ly or'ders spl Priesterweihe f
Ho'ly Scrip'ture s die Heilige Schrift
Ho'ly See' s Heiliger Stuhl m
Ho'ly Sep'ulcher s Heiliges Grab n
Ho'ly Spir'it s Heiliger Geist m
ho'ly wa'ter s Weihwasser n
Ho'ly Week' s Karwoche f
Ho'ly Writ' s die Heilige Schrift
homage ['(h)ɑmɪdʒ] s Huldigung f; **pay h. to** huldigen (*dat*)
home [hom] adj inländisch, Innen– ‖ adv nach Hause, heim; **bring h. to s.o.** j-m beibringen ‖ s Heim n; (*house*) Haus n, Wohnung f; (*place of residence*) Wohnort m; (*institution*) Heim n; **at h.** zu Hause, daheim; **at h. and abroad** im In– und Ausland; **feel at h.** sich zu Hause fühlen; **for the h.** für den Hausbe-

darf; **from h.** von zu Hause; **h. for the aged** Altersheim *n;* **h. for the blind** Blindenheim *n;* **h. of one's own** Zuhause *n*
home′ address′ *s* Privatadresse *f*
home′-baked′ *adj* hausbacken
home′ base′ *s* (aer) Heimatflughafen *m*
home′bod′y *s* Stubenhocker –in *mf*
homebred ['hom,brɛd] *adj* einheimisch
home′-brew′ *s* selbstgebrautes Getränk *n*
home′-brewed′ *adj* selbstgebraut
home′com′ing *s* Heimkehr *f*
home′ comput′er *s* Heimcomputer *m*
home′ coun′try *s* Heimatstaat *m*
home′ econom′ics *s* Hauswirtschaftslehre *f*
home′-fried pota′toes *spl,* **home′ fries′** [,fraɪz] *spl* Bratkartoffeln *pl*
home′ front′ *s* Heimatfront *f*
home′-grown′ *adj* selbstgezogen
home′ guard′ *s* Landsturm *m*
home′land′ *s* Heimatland *n*
homeless ['homlɪs] *adj* obdachlos ‖ *s* Obdachlose *mf*
home′like′ *adj* anheimelnd
homely ['homli] *adj* unschön
home′made′ *adj* selbstgemacht; (culin) selbstgebacken
home′mak′er *s* Hausfrau *f*
home′ of′fice *s* Hauptbüro *n*
home′ own′er *s* Hausbesitzer –in *mf*
home′ plate′ *s* Schlagmal *n*
home′ rem′edy *s* Hausmittel *n*
home′ rule′ *s* Selbstverwaltung *f*
home′ run′ *s* (baseball) Vier-Mal-Lauf *m*
home′sick′ *adj*—**be h.** Heimweh haben
home′sick′ness *s* Heimweh *n*
homespun ['hom,spʌn] *adj* selbstgemacht; (fig) einfach
home′stead′ *s* Siedlerstelle *f*
home′stretch′ *s* Zielgerade *f*
home′ team′ *s* Ortsmannschaft *f*
home′town′ *adj* Heimat– ‖ *s* Heimatstadt *f*
homeward ['homwərd] *adv* heimwärts
home′ward jour′ney *s* Heimreise *f*
home′work′ *s* Hausaufgabe *f*
homey ['homi] *adj* anheimelnd
homicidal [,hɑmɪ'saɪdəl] *adj* mörderisch
homicide ['hɑmɪ,saɪd] *s* (*act*) Totschlag *m;* (*person*) Totschläger –in *mf*
hom′icide squad′ *s* Mordkommission *f*
homily ['hɑmɪli] *s* Homilie *f*
hom′ing device′ ['homɪŋ] *s* Zielsucher *m*
hom′ing pi′geon *s* Brieftaube *f*
homogeneous [,homə'dʒɪnɪ·əs] *adj* homogen
homogenize [hɑ'mɑdʒə,naɪz] *tr* homogenisieren
homonym ['hɑmənɪm] *s* Homonym *n*
homosexual [,homə'sɛkʃʊ·əl] *adj* homosexuell ‖ *s* Homosexuelle *mf*
hone [hon] *s* Wetzstein *m* ‖ *tr* honen
honest ['ɑnɪst] *adj* ehrlich, aufrecht
honestly ['ɑnɪstli] *adv* erhlich; **to tell you h.** offengestanden ‖ *interj* auf mein Wort!

honesty ['ɑnɪsti] *s* Ehrlichkeit *f*
hon·ey ['hʌni] *s* Honig *m;* (*as a term of endearment*) Schatz *m,* Liebling *m* ‖ *v* (*pret* & *pp* –eyed & –ied) *tr* versüßen; (*speak sweetly to*) schmeicheln (*dat*)
hon′eybee′ *s* Honigbiene *f*
hon′eycomb′ *s* Honigwabe *f* ‖ *tr* (*e.g., a hill*) wabenartig durchlöchern
hon′eyed *adj* mit Honig gesüßt; (fig) honigsüß
hon′ey lo′cust *s* Honigdorn *m*
hon′eymoon′ *s* Fiitterwochen *pl* ‖ *intr* die Flitterwochen verbringen
hon′eysuck′le *s* Geißblatt *n*
honk [hɑŋk] *s* (aut) Hupensignal *n* ‖ *tr*—**h. the horn** hupen ‖ *intr* hupen
honkytonk ['hɑŋkɪ,tɑŋk] *s* (sl) Tingeltangel *m* & *n*
honor ['ɑnər] *s* Ehre *f;* (*award*) Auszeichnung *f;* (*chastity*) Ehre *f;* **be held in h.** in Ehren gehalten werden; **consider it an h.** es sich [*dat*] zur Ehre anrechnen; **do the honors** die Honneurs machen; **have the h. of** (*ger*) sich beehren zu (*inf*); **in s.o.'s h.** j–m zu Ehren; **your Honor** Euer Gnaden ‖ *tr* ehren; (*favor*) beehren; (*a check*) honorieren; **feel honored** sich geehrt fühlen
honorable ['ɑnərəbəl] *adj* (*person*) ehrbar; (*intentions*) ehrlich; (*peace treaty*) ehrenvoll
honorari·um [,ɑnə'rɛrɪ·əm] *s* (–ums & –a [ə]) Honorar *n;* **give an h. to** honorieren
hon′orary degree′ *s* Ehrendoktorat *n*
honorific [,ɑnə'rɪfɪk] *adj* ehrend, Ehren– ‖ *s* Ehrentitel *m*
hooch [hutʃ] *s* (sl) Fusel *m,* Schnaps *m*
hood [hʊd] *s* Haube *f;* (*of a monk*) Kapuze *f;* (*of a baby carriage*) Verdeck *n;* (sl) Gangster *m;* (aut) Motorhaube *f;* (culin) Rauchabzug *m;* (educ) Talarüberwurf *m* ‖ *tr* mit e–r Haube versehen; (fig) verhüllen
hoodlum ['hudləm] *s* Ganove *m*
hoodoo ['hudu] *s* Unglücksbringer *m* ‖ *tr* Unglück bringen (*dat*)
hood′wink′ *tr* täuschen
hooey ['hu·i] *s* (sl) Quatsch *m*
hoof [huf], [hʊf] *s* Huf *m* ‖ *tr*—**h. it** auf Schusters Rappen reiten
hoof′beat′ *s* Hufschlag *m*
hook [hʊk] *s* Haken *m;* (angl) Angelhaken *m;* (baseball) Kurvball *m;* (box) Haken *m;* (golf) Hook *m;* **by h. or by crook** so oder so; **h., line, and sinker** mit allem Drum und Dran; **off the h.** (coll) aus der Schlinge; **on one's own h.** (coll) auf eigene Faust ‖ *tr* festhaken, einhaken; (*e.g., a boyfriend*) angeln; (*steal*) schnappen; (box) e–n Haken versetzen (*dat*); (golf) nach links verziehen; **h. up** zuhaken; (elec) anschließen ‖ *intr* sich krümmen; **h. up with s.o.** sich j–m anschließen
hook′ and eye′ *s* Haken *m* und Öse *f*
hook′-and-lad′der truck′ *s* Feuerwehrfahrzeug *n* mit Drehleiter

hooked adj hakenförmig; **h. on drugs** rauschgiftsüchtig

hooker ['hʊkər] s (sl) Nutte f

hook'nose' s Hakennase f

hook'up' s (elec, electron) Schaltung f; (electron) Schaltbild n; (rad, telv) Gemeinschaftsschaltung f

hook'worm' s Hakenwurm m

hooky ['hʊki] s—**play h.** schwänzen

hooligan ['hulɪgən] s Straßenlümmel m

hoop [hup] s Reifen m || tr binden

hoop' skirt' s Reifrock m

hoot [hut] s Geschrei n; **not give a h. about** keinen Pfifferling geben für || intr schreien; **h. at** anschreien

hoot' owl' s Waldkauz m

hop [hap] s Hopser m; (dance) Tanz m; **hops** (bot) Hopfen m || v (pret & pp **hopped**; ger **hopping**) tr (e.g., a train) aufspringen auf (acc); **hop a ride** (coll) mitfahren || intr hüpfen; **hop around** herumhüpfen

hope [hop] s (of) Hoffnung f (auf acc); **beyond h.** hoffnungslos; **not get up one's hopes** sich [dat] keine Hoffnungen machen || tr hoffen || intr hoffen; **h. for** hoffen auf (acc); **h. for the best** das Beste hoffen; **I h.** (parenthetical) hoffentlich

hope' chest' s Aussteuertruhe f

hopeful ['hopfəl] adj hoffnungsvoll || s (pol) Kandidat –in mf

hopefully ['hopfəli] adv hoffentlich

hopeless ['hoplɪs] adj hoffnungslos

hopper ['hapər] s Fülltrichter m; (in a toilet) Spülkasten m; (storage container) Vorratsbehälter m; (data proc) Kartenmagazin n

hop'per car' s (rr) Selbstentladewagen m

hop'ping mad' adj fuchsteufelswild

hop'scotch' s Himmel und Hölle

horde [hord] s Horde f

horehound ['hor‚haʊnd] s (lozenge) Hustenbonbon m; (bot) Andorn m

horizon [hə'raɪzən] s Horizont m

horizontal [‚harɪ'zɑntəl] adj horizontal, waagrecht || s Horizontale f

horizon'tal bar' s (gym) Reck m

horizon'tal controls' spl (aer) Seitenleitwerk n

horizon'tal sta'bilizer s (aer) Höhenflosse f

hormone ['hormon] s Hormon n

horn [horn] s (of an animal; wind instrument) Horn n; (aut) Hupe f; **blow one's own h.** (coll) ins eigene Horn stoßen; **blow the h.** (aut) hupen; **horns** (of an animal) Geweih n || intr—**h. in (on)** (coll) sich eindrängen (in acc)

hornet ['hornɪt] s Hornisse f

hor'net's nest' s—**stir up a h.** in ein Wespennest stechen

horn' of plen'ty s Füllhorn n

horn'-rimmed glass'es spl Hornbrille f

horny ['horni] adj (callous) schwielig; (having horn-like projections) verhornt; (sl) geil

horoscope ['horə‚skop] s Horoskop n; **cast s.o.'s h.** j-m das Horoskop stellen

horrible ['horɪbəl] adj (& coll) schrecklich

horrid ['horɪd] adj abscheulich

horri•fy ['horɪ‚faɪ] v (pret & pp **–fied**) tr erschrecken, entsetzen

horror ['horər] s Schrecken m, Entsetzen n

hor'ror sto'ry s Schaudergeschichte f

hors d'oeuvre [ɔr'dʌrv] s (hors d'oeuvres** [ɔr'dʌrvz]) Vorspeise f

horse [hors] s Pferd n; (carp) Sägebock m; **back the wrong h.** (fig) auf's falsche Pferd setzen; **bet on a h.** auf ein Pferd setzen; **hold your horses** immer mit der Ruhe!; **h. of another color** e-e andere Sache; **mount a h.** zu Pferd steigen; **straight from the horse's mouth** direkt von der Quelle || intr—**h. around** (sl) herumalbern; **stop horsing around** laß den Unsinn!

horse'back' s—**on h.** zu Pferd || adv—**ride h.** reiten

horse'back rid'ing s Reiten n

horse' blan'ket s Pferdedecke f

horse' chest'nut s Roßkastanie f

horse' col'lar s Kummet n

horse' doc'tor s (coll) Roßarzt m

horse'fly' s Pferdebremse f

horse'hair' s Roßhaar n, Pferdehaar n

horse'laugh' s wieherndes Gelächter n

horse'man s (–men) Reiter m

horse'manship' s Reitkunst f

horse' meat' s Pferdefleisch n

horse' op'era s (coll) Wildwestfilm m

horse'play' s grober Unfug m

horse'pow'er s Pferdestärke f

horse' race' s Pferderennen n

horse'rad'ish s Meerrettich m, Kren m

horse' sense' s gesunder Menschenverstand m

horse' shoe' s Hufeisen n || tr beschlagen

horse'shoe mag'net s Hufeisenmagnet m

horse' show' s Pferdeschau f

horse' tail' s Pferdeschwanz m

horse' trad'er s Pferdehändler m; (fig) Kuhhändler m

horse' trad'ing s Pferdehandel m; (fig) Kuhhandel m

horse'whip' s Reitpeitsche f || v (pret & pp **–whipped**; ger **–whipping**) tr mit der Reitpeitsche schlagen

horse'wom'an s (–wom'en) Reiterin f

horsy ['horsi] adj pferdeartig; (horse-loving) pferdeliebend

horticultural [‚hortɪ'kʌltʃərəl] adj Gartenbau-

horticulture ['hortɪ‚kʌltʃər] s Gartenbau m, Gärtnerei f

hose [hoz] s Schlauch m || s (hose) Strumpf m; (collectively) Strümpfe pl

hosiery ['hoʒəri] s Strumpfwaren pl; (mill) Strumpffabrik f

hospice ['haspɪs] s Hospiz n

hospitable ['haspɪtəbəl], [has'pɪtəbəl] adj gastlich, gastfreundlich

hospital ['haspɪtəl] s Hospital n, Krankenhaus n; (mil) Lazarett n

hospitality [‚haspɪ'tælɪti] s Gast-

freundschaft *f;* **show s.o. h.** j–m Gastfreundschaft gewähren
hospitalize ['hɑspɪtə,laɪz] *tr* ins Krankenhaus einweisen
hos'pital ship' *s* Lazarettschiff *f*
hos'pital train' *s* Sanitätszug *m*
hos'pital ward' *s* Kranken(haus)station *f*
host [host] *s* Gastgeber *m;* (*at an inn*) Wirt *m;* (*in a television show*) Leiter *m;* (*multitude*) Heerschar *f;* (*army*) Heer *n;* **Host** (relig) Hostie *f*
hostage ['hɑstɪdʒ] *s* Geisel *mf*
hostel ['hɑstəl] *s* Herberge *f*
hostelry ['hɑstəlri] *s* Gasthaus *n*
hostess ['hostɪs] *s* Gastgeberin *f;* (*at an inn*) Wirtin *f;* (*on an airplane*) Stewardeß *f;* (*in a restaurant*) Empfangsdame *f;* (*on a television show*) Leiterin *f*
hostile ['hɑstɪl] *adj* feindlich; (**to**) feindselig (gegen)
hostility [hɑs'tɪlɪti] *s* Feindseligkeit *f;* **hostilities** Feindseligkeiten *pl*
hot [hɑt] *adj* heiß; (*spicy*) scharf; (*meal*) warm; (*stolen, sought by the police, radioactive; jazz, tip*) heiß; (*trail, scent*) frisch; (*in heat*) geil; **be hot** (*said of the sun*) stechen; **get into hot water** in die Patsche geraten; **hot and bothered** aufgeregt; **hot from the press** frisch von der Presse; **hot on s.o.'s trail** j–m dicht auf der Spur; **hot stuff** (sl) toller Kerl *m;* **I am hot** mir ist heiß; **I don't feel so hot** (coll) ich fühle mich nicht besonders; **she's not so hot** (coll) sie is nicht so toll
hot' air' *s* Heißluft *f;* (sl) blauer Dunst *m*
hot'-air heat' *s* Heißluftheizung *f*
hot'bed' *s* Frühbeet *n;* (fig) Brutstätte *f*
hot'-blood'ed *adj* heißblütig
hot' cake' *s* Pfannkuchen *m;* **sell like hot cakes** wie warme Semmeln weggehen
hotchpotch ['hɑtʃ,pɑtʃ] *s* (coll) Mischmasch *m*
hot' dog' *s* warmes Würstel *n*
hotel [ho'tɛl] *adj* Hotel– ‖ *s* Hotel *n;* (*small hotel*) Gasthof *m*
hotel' busi'ness *s* Hotelgewerbe *n*
hotel'man *s* (–men) Hotelbesitzer *m*
hot'foot' *adv* in aller Eile ‖ *tr*—**h. it** schleunigst eilen; **h. it after s.o.** j–m nacheilen
hot'head' *s* Hitzkopf *m*
hot'-head'ed *adj* hitzköpfig
hot'house' *s* Treibhaus *n,* Gewächshaus *n*
hot' line' *s* (telp) heißer Draht *m*
hot' mon'ey *s* (sl) Fluchtkapital *n*
hot' pep'per *s* scharfe Paprikaschote *f*
hot' plate' *s* Heizplatte *f*
hot' pota'to *s* (coll) schwieriges Problem *n*
hot' rod' *s* (sl) frisiertes altes Auto *n*
hot' rod'der [,rɑdər] *s* (sl) Fahrer *m* e–s frisierten Autos
hot' seat' *s* (sl) elektrischer Stuhl *m*
hot' springs' *spl* Thermalquellen *pl*
hot' tem'per *s* hitziges Temperament *n*

hot'-tem'pered *adj* hitzig, hitzköpfig
hot' war' *s* Schießkrieg *m*
hot' wa'ter *s* Heißwasser *n;* **be in h.** (fig) in der Tinte sitzen; **get into h.** (fig) in die Patsche geraten
hot'-wa'ter bot'tle *s* Gummiwärmflasche *f*
hot'-wa'ter heat'er *s* Heißwasserbereiter *m*
hot'-wa'ter heat'ing *s* Heißwasserheizung *f*
hot'-wa'ter tank' *s* Heißwasserspeicher *m*
hound [haund] *s* Jagdhund *m* ‖ *tr* hetzen
hour [aur] *s* Stunde *f;* **after hours** nach Arbeitsschluß; **at any h.** zu jeder Tageszeit; **by the h.** stundenweise; **every h.** stündlich; **for an h.** e–e Stunde lang; **for a solid h.** e–e geschlagene Stunde lang; **for hours** stundenlang; **h. of death** Todesstunde *f;* **h. overtime** Überstunde *f;* **in the small hours** in den frühen Morgenstunden; **keep late hours** spät zu Bett gehen; **keep regular hours** zur Zeit aufstehen und schlafengehen; **on the h.** zur vollen Stunde
–hour *suf* –stündig
hour'glass' *s* Stundenglas *n*
hour' hand' *s* Stundenzeiger *m*
hourly ['aurli] *adj* stündlich; **h. rate** Stundensatz *m;* **h. wages** Stundenlohn *m* ‖ *adv* stündlich
house [haus] *adj* (*boat, dress*) Haus– ‖ *s* (**houses** ['hauzɪz]) Haus *n;* **h. and home** Haus und Hof; **is h. for rent** Haus *n* zu vermieten; **keep h. (for s.o.)** (j–m) den Haushalt führen; **on the h.** auf Kosten des Wirts; **put one's h. in order** (fig) seine Angelegenheiten in Ordnung bringen ‖ [hauz] *tr* unterbringen
house' arrest' *s* Hausarrest *m*
house'boat' *s* Hausboot *n*
house'break'ing *s* Einbruchsdiebstahl *m*
housebroken ['haus,brokən] *adj* stubenrein
house' clean'ing *s* Hausputz *m;* (fig) Säuberungsaktion *f*
house'fly' *s* Stubenfliege *f*
houseful ['haus,ful] *s* Hausvoll *n*
house'guest' *s* Logierbesuch *m*
house'hold' *adj* Haushalts– ‖ *s* Haushalt *m*
house'hold'er *s* Haushaltsvorstand *m*
house'hold fur'nishings *spl* Hausrat *m*
house'hold needs' *spl* Hausbedarf *m*
house'hold word' *s* Alltagswort *n*
house' hunt'ing *s* Wohungssuche *f*
house'keep'er *s* Haushälterin *f*
house'keep'ing *s* Hauswirtschaft *f*
house'maid' *s* Dienstmädchen *n*
house'moth'er *s* Hausmutter *f*
house' of cards' *s* Kartenhaus *n*
House' of Com'mons *s* Unterhaus *n*
house' of corec'tion *s* Zuchthaus *n,* Besserungsanstalt *f*
house' of ill' repute' *s* öffentliches Haus *n*
House' of Lords' *s* Oberhaus *n*

house' physi'cian *s* Krankenhausarzt *m*; (*in a hotel*) Hausarzt *m*
house'-to-house' *adv* von Haus zu Haus; **sell h.** hausieren
house'warm'ing *s* Einzugsfest *n*
house'wife' *s* (**wives'**) Hausfrau *f*
house'work' *s* Hausarbeit *f*
hous'ing *s* Unterbringung *f*, Wohnung *f*; (mach) Gehäuse *n*
hous'ing devel'opment *s* Siedlung *f*
hous'ing pro'ject *s* Sozialsiedlung *f*
hous'ing short'age *s* Wohnungsnot *f*
hous'ing un'it *s* Wohneinheit *f*
hovel [ˈhʌvəl], [ˈhɑvəl] *s* Hütte *f*
hover [ˈhʌvər] *intr* schweben; (fig) pendeln; **h. about** sich herumtreiben in der Nähe von
Hov'ercraft' *s* (trademark) Schwebefahrzeug *n*
how [haʊ] *adv* wie; **and how!** und wie!; **how about ...?** (*would you care for ...?*) wie wäre es mit ...?; (*what's the progress of ...?*) wie steht es mit ...?; (*what do you think of ...?*) was halten Sie von ...?; **how are you?** wie befinden Sie sich?; **how beautiful!** wie schön!; **how come?** wieso?, wie kommt es?; **how do you do?** (*as a greeting*) guten Tag!; (*at an introduction*) freut mich sehr!; **how many** wie viele; **how much** wieviel; **how on earth** wie in aller Welt; **how the devil** wie zum Teufel || *s* Wie *n*
how-do-you-do [ˈhaʊdəjəˈdu] *s*—**that's a fine h.!** (coll) das ist e-e schöne Geschichte!
howev'er *adv* jedoch, aber; (with adjectives and adverbs) wie ... auch immer; **h. it may be** wie es auch sein mag
howitzer [ˈhaʊ·ɪtsər] *s* Haubitze *f*
howl [haʊl] *s* Geheul *n*, Gebrüll *n* || *tr* heulen, brüllen; **h. down** (*a speaker*) niederschreien; **h. out** hinausbrüllen || *intr* (*said of a dog, wolf, wind, etc.*) heulen; (*in pain, anger*) brüllen; **h. with laughter** vor Lachen brüllen
howler [ˈhaʊlər] *s* (coll) Schnitzer *m*
hub [hʌb] *s* Nabe, *f*, Radnabe *f*
hubbub [ˈhʌbʌb] *s* Rummel *m*
hubby [ˈhʌbi] *s* (coll) Mann *m*
hub'cap' *s* Radkappe *f*
huckleberry [ˈhʌkəlˌberi] *s* Heidelbeere *f*
huckster [ˈhʌkstər] *s* (*hawker*) Straßenhändler *m*; (*peddler*) Hausierer *m*; (*adman*) Reklamefachmann *m* || *tr* verhökern
huddle [ˈhʌdəl] *s* (fb) Zusammendrängen *n*; **go into a h.** die Köpfe zusammenstecken || *intr* sich zusammendrängen; (fb) sich um den Mannschaftsführer drängen
hue [hju] *s* Farbton *m*
hue' and cry' *s* Zetergeschrei *n*
huff [hʌf] *s* Aufbrausen *n*; **in a h.** beleidigt
huffy [ˈhʌfi] *adj* übelnehmerisch
hug [hʌg] *s* Umarmung *f*; **give s.o. a hug** j–n an sich drücken || *v* (*pret & pp* **hugged**; *ger* **hugging**) *tr* umar-

men; **hug the road** gut auf der Straße liegen; **hug the shore** sich dicht an der Küste halten || *intr* einander herzen
huge [hjudʒ] *adj* riesig, ungeheuer; **h. success** (theat) Bombenerfolg *m*
hulk [hʌlk] *s* (*body of an old ship*) Schiffsrumpf *m*; (*old ship used as a warehouse, etc.*) Hulk *m* & *f*; **h. of a man** Koloß *m*
hulk'ing *adj* ungeschlacht
hull [hʌl] *s* (*of seed*) Schale *f*; (naut) Schiffsrumpf *m* || *tr* schälen
hullabaloo [ˌhʌləbəˈlu] *s* Heidenlärm *m*
hum [hʌm] *s* Summen *n* || *v* (*pret & pp* **hummed**; *ger* **humming**) *tr* summen; **hum** (*e.g., a tune*) **to oneself** vor sich hin summen || *intr* summen; (fig) in lebhafter Bewegung sein
human [ˈhjumən] *adj* menschlich, Menschen–
hu'man be'ing *s* Mensch *m*, menschliches Wesen *n*
humane [hju'men] *adj* human
humaneness [hju'mennɪs] *s* Humanität *f*
humanistic [hjumə'nɪstɪk] *adj* humanistisch
humanitarian [hjuˌmænɪ'terɪ·ən] *adj* menschenfreundlich || *s* Menschenfreund –in *mf*
humanity [hju'mænɪti] *s* (*mankind*) Menschheit *f*; (*humaneness*) Humanität *f*, Menschlichkeit *f*; **humanities** Geisteswissenschaften *pl*; (*Greek and Latin studies*) klassische Philologie *f*
humanize [ˈhjuməˌnaɪz] *tr* zivilisieren
hu'mankind' *s* Menschengeschlecht *n*
humanly [ˈhjumənli] *adv* menschlich; **h. possible** menschenmöglich; **h. speaking** nach menschlichen Begriffen
hu'man na'ture *s* menschliche Natur *f*
hu'man race' *s* Menschengeschlecht *n*
humble [ˈ(h)ʌmbəl] *adj* demütig; (*origens*) niedrig; **in my h. opinion** nach meiner unmaßgeblichen Meinung || *tr* demütigen
hum'ble pie' *s*—**eat h.** sich demütigen
hum'bug' *s* Humbug *m*
hum'drum' *adj* eintönig
humer·us [ˈhjumərəs] *s* (**-i** [ˌaɪ]) Oberarmknochen *m*
humid [ˈhjumɪd] *adj* feucht
humidifier [hju'mɪdɪˌfaɪ·ər] *s* Verdunster *m*
humidity [hju'mɪdɪti *s* Feuchtigkeit *f*
humiliate [hju'mɪlɪˌet] *tr* erniedrigen
humil'iating *adj* schmachvoll
humiliation [hjuˌmɪlɪ'eʃən] *s* Erniedrigung *f*
hum'mingbird' *s* Kolibri *m*
humor [ˈ(h)jumər] *s* (*comic quality*) Komik *f*; (*frame of mind*) Laune *f*; **in bad** (or **good**) **h.** bei schlechter (or guter) Laune || *tr* bei guter Laune halten
humorist [ˈ(h)jumərɪst] *s* Humorist –in *mf*
humorous [ˈ(h)jumərəs] *adj* humorvoll
hump [hʌmp] *s* Buckel *m*; (*of a camel*)

Höcker *m;* (*slight elevation*) kleiner Hügel *m;* **over the h.** (fig) über den Berg ‖ *tr*—**h.** its **back** (*said of an animal*) e–n Buckel machen
hump′back′ *s* Buckel *m;* (*person*) Bucklige *mf*
Hun [hʌn] *s* (hist) Hunne *m,* Hunnin *f*
hunch [hʌntʃ] *s* (*hump*) Buckel *m;* (coll) Ahnung *f* ‖ *intr*—**h. over** sich bücken über (*acc*)
hunch′back′ *s* Bucklige *mf*
hunch′backed′ *adj* bucklig
hunched *adj*—**h. up** zusammengekauert
hundred [′hʌndrəd] *adj & pron* hundert ‖ *s* Hundert *n;* **by the h.**(**s**) hundertweise; **hundreds (and hundreds) of** Hunderte (und aber Hunderte) von
hun′dredfold′ *adj & adv* hundertfach
hundredth [′hʌndrədθ] *adj & pron* hundertste; **for the h. time** (fig) zum X-ten Male; **h. anniversary** Hundertjahrfeier *f* ‖ *s* (*fraction*) Hundertstel *n*
hun′dredweight′ *s* Zentner *n*
Hungarian [hʌŋ′gɛrɪ·ən] *adj* ungarisch ‖ *s* (*person*) Ungar –in *mf;* (*language*) Ungarisch *n*
Hungary [′hʌŋgəri] *s* Ungarn *n*
hunger [′hʌŋgər] *s* Hunger *m* ‖ *intr* hungern; **h. for** hungern nach
hun′ger strike′ *s* Hungerstreik *m*
hungry [′hʌŋgri] *adj* hungrig; **be h.** Hunger haben; **be h. for** (fig) begierig sein nach; **go h.** am Hungertuch nagen; **I feel h.** es hungert mich
hunk [hʌŋk] *s* großes Stück *n*
hunt [hʌnt] *s* Jagd *f;* (*search*) (**for**) Suche *f* (nach); **on the h. for** auf der Suche nach ‖ *tr* jagen; (*a horse*) jagen mit; (*look for*) suchen; **h. down** erjagen ‖ *intr* jagen; **h. for** suchen; (*game*) jagen; (*a criminal*) fahnden nach; **go hunting** auf die Jagd gehen
hunter [′hʌntər] *s* Jäger –in *mf;* (*horse*) Jagdpferd *n*
hunt′ing *adj* (*e.g., dog, knife, season*) Jagd– ‖ *s* Jägerei *f;* (*on horseback*) Parforcejagd *f*
hunt′ing ground′ *s* Jagdrevier *n*
hunt′ing li′cense *s* Jagdschein *m*
hunt′ing lodge′ *s* Jagdhütte *f*
huntress [′hʌntrɪs] *s* Jägerin *f*
hunts′man *s* (**–men**) Weidmann *m*
hurdle [′hʌrdəl] *s* Hürde *f;* (fig) Hindernis *n;* **hurdles** (sport) Hürdenlauf *m* ‖ *tr* überspringen; (fig) überwinden
hurdygurdy [′hʌrdi′gʌrdi] *s* Drehorgel *f*
hurl [hʌrl] *s* Wurf *m* ‖ *tr* scheudern; **h. abuse at s.o.** j–m Beleidigungen ins Gesicht schleudern; **h. down** zu Boden werfen
hurrah [hə′rɑ], **hurray** [hə′re] *s* Hurra *n* ‖ *interj* hurra!
hurricane [′hʌrɪ‚ken] *s* Orkan *m*
hur′ricane lamp′ *s* Sturmlaterne *f*
hurried [′hʌrid] *adj* eilig, flüchtig
hurriedly [′hʌrɪdli] *adv* eilig, eilends
hur·ry [′hʌri] *s* Eile *f;* **be in too much of a h.** sich übereilen; **in a h.** in Eile; **there's no h.** es hat keine Eile ‖ *v*

(*pret & pp* **–ried**) *tr* (*prod*) antreiben; (*expedite*) beschleunigen; (*an activity*) zu schnell tun; (*to overhasty action*) drängen ‖ *intr* eilen; **h. away** wegeilen; **h. over s.th.** etw flüchtig erledigen; **h. up** sich beeilen
hurt [hʌrt] *adj* (*injured, offended*) verletzt; **feel h.** (**about**) sich verletzt (or gekränkt) fühlen (durch) ‖ *s* Verletzung *f* ‖ *v* (*pret & pp* **hurt**) *tr* (*a person, animal, feelings*) verletzen; (*e.g., a business*) schaden (*dat*); **it hurts him to think of it** es schmerzt ihn, daran zu denken ‖ *intr* (*& fig*) weh tun, schmerzen; **my arm hurts** mir tut der Arm weh; **that won't h.** das schadet nichts; **will it h. if I'm late?** macht es etw aus, wenn ich zu spät komme?
hurtle [′hʌrtəl] *tr* schleudern ‖ *intr* stürzen
husband [′hʌzbənd] *s* Ehemann *m;* **my h.** mein Mann *m* ‖ *tr* haushalten mit
hus′bandman *s* (**–men**) Landwirt *m*
husbandry [′hʌzbəndri] *s* Landwirtschaft *f*
hush [hʌʃ] *s* Stille *f* ‖ *tr* zur Ruhe bringen; **h. up** (*suppress*) vertuschen ‖ *intr* schweigen ‖ *interj* still!
hush′-hush′ *adj* streng vertraulich und geheim
hush′ mon′ey *s* Schweigegeld *n*
husk [hʌsk] *s* Hülse *f;* (*of corn*) Maishülse *f* ‖ *tr* enthülsen
husky [′hʌski] *adj* stämmig; (*voice*) belegt ‖ *s* Eskimohund *m*
hussy [′hʌsi] *s* (*prostitute*) Dirne *f;* (*saucy girl*) Fratz *m*
hustle [′hʌsəl] *s* (coll) Betriebsamkeit *f;* **h. and bustle** Getriebe *n* ‖ *tr* (*jostle, rush*) drängen; (*wares, girls*) an den Mann bringen; (*customers*) bearbeiten; (*money*) betteln ‖ *intr* rührig sein; (*shove*) sich drängen; (*hasten*) hasten; (*make money by fraud*) Betrügereien verüben; (*engage in prostitution*) Prostitution betreiben
hustler [′hʌslər] *s* rühriger Mensch *m*
hut [hʌt] *s* Hütte *f;* (mil) Baracke *f*
hutch [hʌtʃ] *s* Stall *m*
hyacinth [′haɪ·əsɪnθ] *s* Hyazinthe *f*
hybrid [′haɪbrɪd] *adj* hybrid ‖ *s* Kreuzung *f*
hydrant [′haɪdrənt] *s* Hydrant *m*
hydrate [′haɪdret] *s* Hydrat *n* ‖ *tr* hydratisieren, hydrieren
hydraulic [haɪ′drɔlɪk] *adj* hydraulisch ‖ **hydraulics** *s* Hydraulik *f*
hydrau′lic brakes′ *spl* Öldruckbremsen *pl*
hydrocarbon [‚haɪdrə′kɑrbən] *s* Kohlenwasserstoff *m*
hydrochlor′ic ac′id [‚haɪdrə′klorɪk] *s* Salzsäure *f*
hydroelectric [‚haɪdro·ɪ′lɛktrɪk] *adj* hydroelektrisch
hydroelec′tric plant′ *s* Wasserkraftwerk *n*
hydrofluo′ric ac′id [‚haɪdrəflu′ɔrɪk] *s* Flußsäure *f*
hydrofoil [′haɪdrə‚fɔɪl] *s* Tragflügelboot *n*

hydrogen ['haɪdrədʒən] s Wasserstoff m
hy'drogen bomb' s Wasserstoffbombe f
hy'drogen perox'ide s Wasserstoffsuperoxyd n
hydrometer [haɪ'drɑmɪtər] s Hydrometer m
hydrophobia [‚haɪdrə'fobɪ-ə] s Wasserscheu f; (rabies) Tollwut f
hydrophone ['haɪdrə‚fon] s Unterwasserhorchgerät n, Hydrophon n
hydroplane ['haɪdrə‚plen] s (aer) Wasserflugzeug n; (aer) Gleitfläche f; (naut) Gleitboot n; (in a submarine) (nav) Tiefenruder n
hydroxide [haɪ'drɑksaɪd] s Hydroxyd n
hyena [haɪ'inə] s Hyäne f
hygiene ['haɪdʒin] s Hygiene f; (educ) Gesundheitslehre f
hygienic [haɪ'dʒinɪk] adj hygienisch
hymn [hɪm] s Hymne f; (eccl) Kirchenlied n
hymnal ['hɪmnəl] s Gesangbuch n
hymn'book' s Gesangbuch n
hyperacidity [‚haɪpərə'sɪdɪti] s Übersäuerung f
hyperbola [haɪ'pʌrbələ] s Hyperbel f
hyperbole [haɪ'pʌrbəli] s Hyperbel f
hypersensitive [‚haɪpər'sensɪtɪv] adj (to) überempfindlich (gegen)
hypertension [‚haɪpər'tenʃən] s Hypertonie f
hyphen ['haɪfən] s Bindestrich m

hyphenate ['haɪfə‚net] tr mit Bindestrich schreiben
hypnosis [hɪp'nosɪs] s Hypnose f
hypnotic [hɪp'nɑtɪk] adj hypnotisch
hypnotism ['hɪpnə‚tɪzəm] s Hypnotismus m
hypnotist ['hɪpnətɪst] s Hypnotiseur m
hypnotize ['hɪpnə‚taɪz] tr hypnotisieren
hypochondriac [‚haɪpə'kɑndrɪ‚æk] s Hypochonder m
hypocrisy [hɪ'pɑkrəsi] s Heuchelei f
hypocrite ['hɪpəkrɪt] s Heuchler –in mf; be a h. heucheln
hypocritical [‚hɪpə'krɪtɪkəl] adj heuchlerisch
hypodermic [‚haɪpə'dʌrmɪk] adj subkutan ‖ s (injection) subkutane Spritze f
hypoderm'ic nee'dle s Injektionsnadel f
hypotenuse [haɪ'pɑtɪ‚n(j)us] s Hypotenuse f
hypothe·sis [haɪ'pɑθɪsɪs] s (–ses [‚siz]) Hypothese f
hypothetic(al) [‚haɪpə'θetɪk(əl)] adj hypothetisch
hysterectomy [‚hɪstə'rektəmi] s Hysterektomie f
hysteria [hɪs'tɪrɪ-ə] s Hysterie f
hysteric [hɪs'terɪk] adj hysterisch ‖ **hysterics** spl Hysterie f; go into hysterics e–n hysterischen Anfall bekommen
hysterical [hɪs'terɪkəl] adj hysterisch

I

I, i [ai] s elfter Buchstabe des englischen Alphabets
I pers pron ich
iambic [aɪ'æmbɪk] adj jambisch
Iberian [aɪ'bɪrɪ-ən] adj iberisch
ibex ['aɪbɛks] s (ibexes & ibices ['ɪbɪ‚siz]) Steinbock m
ice [aɪs] s Eis n; break the ice (coll) das Eis brechen; cut no ice (coll) nicht ziehen ‖ tr (a cake) glasieren ‖ intr—ice up vereisen
ice' age' s Eiszeit f
iceberg ['aɪs‚bʌrg] s Eisberg m
ice'boat' s (sport) Segelschlitten m
ice'bound' adj (boat) eingefroren; (port, river) zugefroren
ice'box' s Eisschrank m; (refrigerator) Kühlschrank m
ice'break'er s Eisbrecher m
ice' buck'et s Sektkübel m
ice'cap' s Eiskappe f
ice' cream' s Eis n, Eiskrem f
ice'-cream cone' s Tüte f Eis
ice' cube' s Eiswürfel m
ice'-cube tray' s Eiswürfelschale f
iced' tea' s Eistee m
ice' floe' s Eisscholle f
ice' hock'ey s Eishockey n
Iceland ['aɪslənd] s Island n

Icelander ['aɪs‚lændər] s Isländer –in mf
Icelandic [aɪs'lændɪk] adj isländisch ‖ s (language) Isländisch n
ice'man' s (–men') Eismann m
ice' pack' s (geol) Packeis n; (med) Eisbeutel m
ice' pick' s Eispfriem m; (mount) Eispickel m
ice' skate' s Schlittschuh m
ice'-skate' intr eislaufen
ichthyology [‚ɪkθɪ'ɑlədʒi] s Ichthyologie f, Fischkunde f
icicle ['aɪsɪkəl] s Eiszapfen m
icing ['aɪsɪŋ] s Glasur f, Zuckerguß m; (aer) Vereisung f
icon ['aɪkɑn] s Ikone f
iconoclast [aɪ'kɑnə‚klæst] s Bilderstürmer –in mf
icy ['aɪsi] adj (& fig) eisig
id [ɪd] s (psychol) Es n
I.D. card [aɪ'di'kard] s Ausweis m
idea [aɪ'di-ə] s Idee f, Vorstellung f; (intimation) Ahnung f; crazy i. Schnapsidee f; have big ideas große Rosinen im Kopf haben; that's the i.! so ist's richtig!; the i.! na so was!; what's the i.? wie kommen Sie darauf?

ideal [aɪ'di·əl] *adj* ideal || *s* Ideal *n*
idealism [aɪ'di·ə‚lɪzəm] *s* Idealismus *m*
idealist [aɪ'di·əlɪst] *s* Idealist –in *mf*
idealistic [aɪ‚di·əl'ɪstɪk] *adj* idealistisch
idealize [aɪ'di·ə‚laɪz] *tr* idealisieren
identical [aɪ'dɛntɪkəl] *adj* identisch
identification [aɪ'dɛntɪfɪ'keʃən] *s* Identifizierung *f*
identifica'tion tag' *s* Erkennungsmarke *f*
identi·fy [aɪ'dɛntɪ‚faɪ] *v* (*pret & pp* –fied) *tr* identifizieren; **i. oneself** sich ausweisen || *intr*—**i. with** sich einfühlen in (*acc*)
identity [aɪ'dɛntɪti] *s* Identität *f;* **prove one's i.** sich ausweisen
iden'tity card' *s* Ausweis *m*
ideological [‚aɪdɪ·ə'lɑdʒɪkəl] *adj* ideologisch
ideology [‚aɪdɪ'ɑlədʒi] *s* Ideologie *f*
idiocy ['ɪdɪ·əsi] *s* Idiotie *f*
idiom ['ɪdɪ·əm] *s* (*phrase*) Redewendung *f;* (*language*, *style*) Idiom *n*
idiomatic [‚ɪdɪ·ə'mætɪk] *adj* idiomatisch; **i. expression** (idiomatische) Redewendung *f*
idiosyncrasy [‚ɪdɪ·ə'sɪnkrəsi] *s* Idiosynkrasie *f*
idiot ['ɪdɪ·ət] *s* Idiot *m*, Trottel *m*
idiotic [‚ɪdɪ'ɑtɪk] *adj* idiotisch
idle ['aɪdəl] *adj* (*person*, *question*, *hours*) müßig; (*machine*, *factory*) stillstehend; (*capital*) tot; (*fears*) grundlos; (*talk*, *threats*) leer; **lie i.** stilliegen; **stand i.** stillstehen || *s* (aut) Leerlauf *m* || *tr* arbeitslos machen; **i. away** vertrödeln || *intr* (aut) leerlaufen
idleness ['aɪdəlnɪs] *s* Müßiggang *m*
idler ['aɪdlər] *s* Müßiggänger *m*
i'dling *s* (aut) Leerlauf *m*
idol ['aɪdəl] *s* Abgott *m;* (fig) Idol *n*
idolatry [aɪ'dɑlətri] *s* Abgötterei *f*
idolize ['aɪdə‚laɪz] *tr* verhimmeln
idyll ['aɪdəl] *s* Idyll *n*, Idylle *f*
idyllic [aɪ'dɪlɪk] *adj* idyllisch
if [ɪf] *s* Wenn *n* || *conj* wenn; (*whether*) ob
igloo ['ɪglu] *s* Schneehütte *f*, Iglu *m & n*
ignite [ɪg'naɪt] *tr & intr* zünden
ignition [ɪg'nɪʃən] *adj* Zünd– || *s* Entzünden *n;* (aut) Zündung *f*
igni'tion key' *s* Zündschlüssel *m*
igni'tion switch' *s* Zündschloß *n*
ignoble [ɪg'nobəl] *adj* unedel
ignominious [‚ɪgnə'mɪnɪ·əs] *adj* schmachvoll, schändlich
ignoramus [‚ɪgnə'reməs] *s* Ignorant –in *mf*
ignorance ['ɪgnərəns] *s* Unwissenheit *f;* (of) Unkenntnis *f* (*genit*)
ignorant ['ɪgnərənt] *adj* unwissend; **be i. of** nicht wissen
ignore [ɪg'nor] *tr* ignorieren; (*words*) überhören; (*rules*) nicht beachten
ilk [ɪlk] *s*—**of that ilk** derselben Art
ill [ɪl] *adj* (**worse** [wʌrs]); **worst** [wʌrst]) krank; (*repute*) schlecht; (*feelings*) feindselig; **fall** (*or* **take**)

ill krank werden || *adv* schlecht; **he can ill afford to** (*inf*) er kann es sich [*dat*] kaum leisten zu (*inf*); **take s.th. ill** etw übelnehmen
ill'-advised' *adj* (*person*) schlecht beraten; (*action*) unbesonnen
ill'-at-ease' *adj* unbehaglich
ill'-bred' *adj* ungezogen
ill'-consid'ered *adj* unbesonnen
ill'-disposed' *adj*—**be i. towards** übelgesinnt sein (*dat*)
illegal [ɪ'ligəl] *adj* illegal
illegible [ɪ'lɛdʒɪbəl] *adj* unlesbar
illegitimate [‚ɪlɪ'dʒɪtɪmɪt] *adj* unrechtmäßig; (*child*) illegitim
ill'-fat'ed *adj* unglücklich
illgotten ['ɪl‚gɑtən] *adj* unrechtmäßig erworben
ill' health' *s* Kränklichkeit *f*
ill'-hu'mored *adj* übelgelaunt
illicit [ɪ'lɪsɪt] *adj* unerlaubt
illiteracy [ɪ'lɪtərəsi] *s* Analphabetentum *n*
illiterate [ɪ'lɪtərɪt] *adj* analphabetisch || *s* Analphabet –in *mf*
ill'-man'nered *adj* ungehobelt
ill'-na'tured *adj* bösartig
illness ['ɪlnɪs] *s* (& fig) Krankheit *f*
illogical [ɪ'lɑdʒɪkəl] *adj* unlogisch
ill'-spent' *adj* verschwendet
ill'-starred' *adj* unglücklich
ill'-suit'ed *adj* (to) unpassend (*dat*)
ill'-tem'pered *adj* schlechtgelaunt
ill'-timed' *adj* unpassend
ill'-treat' *tr* mißhandeln
illuminate [ɪ'lumɪ‚net] *tr* beleuchten; (*public buildings*, *manuscripts*) illuminieren; (*enlighten*) erleuchten; (*explain*) erklären
illumination [ɪ‚lumɪ'neʃən] *s* Beleuchten *n;* Erleuchtung *f;* Illuminierung *f*
illusion [ɪ'luʒən] *s* Illusion *f*
illusive [ɪ'lusɪv] *adj* trügerisch
illusory [ɪ'lusəri] *adj* illusorisch
illustrate ['ɪləs‚tret] *tr* (*exemplify*) erläutern; (*a book*) illustrieren; **illustrated lecture** Lichtbildervortrag *m;* **richly illustrated** bilderreich
illustration [‚ɪləs'treʃən] *s* Erläuterung *f;* (*in a book*) Abbildung *f*
illustrative [ɪ'lʌstrətɪv] *adj* erläuternd; **i. material** Anschauungsmaterial *n*
illustrator ['ɪləs‚tretər] *s* Illustrator *m*
illustrious [ɪ'lʌstrɪ·əs] *adj* berühmt
ill' will' *s* Feindschaft *f*
image ['ɪmɪdʒ] *s* Bild *n;* (*reflection*) Spiegelbild *n;* (*statue*) Standbild *n;* (*before the public*) Image *n;* (opt, phot, telv) Bild *n;* **the spitting i. of his father** ganz der Vater
imagery ['ɪmɪdʒ(ə)ri] *s* Bildersprache *f*
imaginable [ɪ'mædʒɪnəbəl] *adj* erdenklich
imaginary [ɪ'mædʒɪ‚neri] *adj* imaginär
imagination [ɪ‚mædʒɪ'neʃən] *s* Phantasie *f*, Einbildungskraft *f;* **that's pure i.** das ist pure Einbildung
imaginative [ɪ'mædʒɪnətɪv] *adj* phantasievoll
imagine [ɪ'mædʒɪn] *tr* sich [*dat*] vorstellen, sich [*dat*] denken; **i. oneself**

in sich hineindenken in (acc); **you're only imagining things** das bilden Sie sich [*dat*] nur ein || *intr*—**I can i.** das läßt sich denken; **I i.** so ich glaube schon; **just i.** denken Sie nur mal!

imbecile ['ɪmbɪsɪl] *adj* geistesschwach || *s* Geistesschwache *mf*

imbecility [,ɪmbɪ'sɪlɪti] *s* Geistesschwäche *f*, Blödheit *f*

imbibe [ɪm'baɪb] *tr* aufsaugen; (coll) trinken; (fig) (geistig) aufnehmen

imbue [ɪm'bju] *tr* durchfeuchten; (fig) (**with**) durchdringen (mit)

imitate ['ɪmɪ,tet] *tr* nachahmen, nachmachen; **i. s.o. in everything** j–m alles nachmachen

imitation [,ɪmɪ'teʃən] *adj* unecht, nachgemacht || *s* Nachahmung *f*; **in i. of** nach dem Muster (*genit*)

imita'tion leath'er *s* Kunstleder *n*

imitator ['ɪmɪ,tetər] *s* Nachahmer –in *mf*

immaculate [ɪ'mækjəlɪt] *adj* makellos; (*sinless*) unbefleckt

immaterial [,ɪmə'tɪrɪ·əl] *adj* immateriell, unkörperlich; (*unimportant*) unwesentlich; **it's i. to me** es ist mir gleichgültig

immature [,ɪmə'tjʊr] *adj* unreif

immaturity [,ɪmə'tjʊrɪti] *s* Unreife *f*

immeasurable [ɪ'mɛʒərəbəl] *adj* unermeßlich

immediacy [ɪ'midɪ·əsi] *s* Unmittelbarkeit *f*

immediate [ɪ'midɪ·ɪt] *adj* sofortig; (*direct*) unmittelbar

immediately [ɪ'midɪ·ɪtli] *adv* sofort; **i. afterwards** gleich darauf

immemorial [,ɪmɪ'morɪ·əl] *adj* uralt; **since time i.** seit Menschengedenken

immense [ɪ'mɛns] *adj* unermeßlich

immensity [ɪ'mɛnsɪti] *s* Unermeßlichkeit *f*

immerse [ɪ'mʌrs] *tr* (unter)tauchen; **immersed in** (*books, thought, work*) vertieft in (*acc*); **i. oneself in** sich vertiefen in (*acc*)

immersion [ɪ'mʌrʒən] *s* Untertauchen *n*; (fig) Versunkenheit *f*

immigrant ['ɪmɪgrənt] *adj* einwandernd || *s* Einwanderer –in *mf*

immigrate ['ɪmɪ,gret] *intr* einwandern

immigration [,ɪmɪ'greʃən] *s* Einwanderung *f*

imminent ['ɪmɪnənt] *adj* drohend

immobile [ɪ'mobɪl] *adj* unbeweglich

immobilize [ɪ'mobɪ,laɪz] *tr* unbeweglich machen; (*tanks*) bewegungsunfähig machen; (*troops*) fesseln; (med) ruhigstellen

immoderate [ɪ'madərɪt] *adj* unmäßig

immodest [ɪ'madɪst] *adj* unbescheiden

immolate ['ɪmə,let] *tr* opfern

immoral [ɪ'mɔrəl] *adj* unsittlich

immorality [,ɪmə'rælɪti] *s* Unsittlichkeit *f*

immortal [ɪ'mɔrtəl] *adj* unsterblich

immortality [,ɪmɔr'tælɪti] *s* Unsterblichkeit *f*

immortalize [ɪ'mɔrtə,laɪz] *tr* unsterblich machen

immovable [ɪ'muvəbəl] *adj* unbeweglich

immune [ɪ'mjun] *adj* (*free, exempt*) (**from**) immun (gegen); (*not responsive*) (**to**) gefeit (gegen); (med) (**to**) immun (gegen)

immunity [ɪ'mjunɪti] *s* Immunität *f*

immunization [,ɪmjunɪ'zeʃən] *s* Schutzimpfung *f*, Immunisierung *f*

immunize ['ɪmjə,naɪz] *tr* (**against**) immunisieren (gegen)

immutable [ɪ'mjutəbəl] *adj* unwandelbar

imp [ɪmp] *s* Schlingel *m*

impact ['ɪmpækt] *s* Anprall *m;* (*of a shell*) Aufschlag *m;* (fig) Einwirkung *f*

impair [ɪm'pɛr] *tr* beeinträchtigen

impale [ɪm'pel] *tr* pfählen

impan·el [ɪm'pænəl] *v* (*pret & pp* **-el[l]ed;** *ger* **-el[l]ing**) *tr* in die Geschworenenliste eintragen

impart [ɪm'part] *tr* mitteilen

impartial [ɪm'parʃəl] *adj* unparteiisch

impassable [ɪm'pæsɪbəl] *adj* (*on foot*) ungangbar; (*by car*) unbefahrbar

impasse ['ɪmpæs] *s* Sackgasse *f;* **reach an i.** in e-e Sackgasse geraten

impassible [ɪm'pæsɪbəl] *adj* (**to**) unempfindlich (für)

impassioned [ɪm'pæʃənd] *adj* leidenschaftlich

impassive [ɪm'pæsɪv] *adj* (*person*) teilnahmslos; (*expression*) ausdruckslos

impatience [ɪm'peʃəns] *s* Ungeduld *f*

impatient [ɪm'peʃənt] *adj* ungeduldig

impeach [ɪm'pitʃ] *tr* (*an official*) wegen Amtsmißbrauchs unter Anklage stellen; (*a witness, motives*) in Zweifel ziehen

impeachment [ɪm'pitʃmənt] *s* (*of an official*) öffentliche Anklage *f;* (*of a witness, motives*) Anzweiflung *f*

impeccable [ɪm'pɛkəbəl] *adj* makellos

impecunious [,ɪmpɪ'kjunɪ·əs] *adj* mittellos

impede [ɪm'pid] *tr* behindern, erschweren

impediment [ɪm'pɛdɪmənt] *s* Behinderung *f;* (*of speech*) Sprachfehler *m*

im·pel [ɪm'pel] *v* (*pret & pp* **-pelled;** *ger* **-pelling**) *tr* antreiben

impending [ɪm'pɛndɪŋ] *adj* nahe bevorstehen; (*threatening*) drohend

impenetrable [ɪm'pɛnətrəbəl] *adj* undurchdringlich; (fig) unergründlich

impenitent [ɪm'pɛnɪtənt] *adj* unbußfertig

imperative [ɪm'pɛrətɪv] *adj* dringend nötig || *s* Imperativ *m*

imper'ative mood' *s* Befehlsform *f*

imperceptible [,ɪmpər'sɛptɪbəl] *adj* nicht wahrnehmbar, unmerklich

imperfect [ɪm'pɑrfɪkt] *adj* unvollkommen || *s* (gram) Imperfekt(um) *n*

imperfection [,ɪmpər'fɛkʃən] *s* Unvollkommenheit *f;* (*flaw*) Fehler *m*

imperial [ɪm'pɪrɪ·əl] *adj* kaiserlich

imperialism [ɪm'pɪrɪ·ə,lɪzəm] *s* Imperialismus *m*

imperialist [ɪm'pɪrɪ·əlɪst] *adj* imperialistisch || *s* Imperialist –in *mf*

imper·il [ɪm'perɪl] v (pret & pp
-il[l]ed; ger -il[l]ing) tr gefährden
imperious [ɪm'perɪ·əs] adj herrisch, anmaßend
imperishable [ɪm'perɪʃəbəl] adj unver-
gänglich
impersonal [ɪm'pʌrsənəl] adj unpersönlich
impersonate [ɪm'pʌrsə‚net] tr (imitate) nachahmen; (e.g., an officer)
sich ausgeben als; (theat) darstellen
impersonator [ɪm'pʌrsə‚netər] s Imitator -in mf
impertinence [ɪm'pʌrtɪnəns] s Ungezogenheit f
impertinent [ɪm'pʌrtɪnənt] adj ungezogen
imperturbable [‚ɪmpʌr'tʌrbəbəl] adj
unerschütterlich
impetuous [ɪm'petʃu·əs] adj ungestüm
impetus ['ɪmpɪtəs] s (& fig) Antrieb
m
impiety [ɪm'paɪ·əti] s Gottlosigkeit f
impinge [ɪm'pɪndʒ] intr—i. on (an)
stoßen an (acc); (said of rays) fallen
auf (acc); (fig) eingreifen in (acc)
impious ['ɪmpɪ·əs] adj gottlos
impish ['ɪmpɪʃ] adj spitzbübisch
implant [ɪm'plænt] tr einpflanzen
implement ['ɪmplɪmənt] s Werkzeug
n, Gerät n || ['ɪmplɪ‚ment] tr durch-
führen
implicate ['ɪmplɪ‚ket] tr (in) verwickeln (in acc)
implication [‚ɪmplɪ'keʃən] s (involvement) Verwicklung f; (implying) Andeutung f; **implications** Folgerungen
pl
implicit [ɪm'plɪsɪt] adj (approval) stillschweigend; (trust) unbedingt
implied [ɪm'plaɪd] adj stillschweigend
implore [ɪm'plor] tr anflehen
im·ply [ɪm'plaɪ] v (pret & pp -plied)
tr (express indirectly) andeuten; (involve) in sich schließen; (said of
words) besagen
impolite [‚ɪmpə'laɪt] adj unhöflich
import ['ɪmport] s Import m, Einfuhr
f; (meaning) Bedeutung f; **imports**
Einfuhrwaren pl || [ɪm'port], ['ɪm-
port] tr importieren, einführen
importance [ɪm'portəns] s Wichtigkeit
f; **a man of i.** ein Mann m von Bedeutung; **of no i.** unwichtig
important [ɪm'portənt] adj wichtig
im'port du'ty s Einfuhrzoll m
importer [ɪm'portər] s Importeur m
importune [‚ɪmpər't(j)un] adj auf-
dringlich || tr bestürmen
impose [ɪm'poz] tr (on, upon) auf-
erlegen (dat) || intr—i. on über Ge-
bühr beanspruchen
impos'ing adj imposant
imposition [‚ɪmpə'zɪʃən] s (of hands,
of an obligation) Auferlegung f; (taking unfair advantage) Zumutung f
impossible [ɪm'pasɪbəl] adj unmöglich
impostor [ɪm'pastər] s Hochstapler m
imposture [ɪm'pastʃər] s Hochstapelei
f
impotence ['ɪmpətəns] s Machtlosig-
keit f; (pathol) Impotenz f

impotent ['ɪmpətənt] adj machtlos;
(pathol) impotent
impound [ɪm'paund] tr beschlagnahmen
impoverish [ɪm'pavərɪʃ] tr arm machen; **become impoverished** verarmen
impracticable [ɪm'præktɪkəbəl] adj unausführbar
impractical [ɪm'præktɪkəl] adj un-
praktisch
impregnable [ɪm'prɛgnəbəl] adj unein-
nehmbar
impregnate [ɪm'prɛgnet] tr (saturate)
imprägnieren; (& fig) schwängern
impresari·o [‚ɪmprɪ'sarɪ‚o] s (-os)
Impresario m
impress [ɪm'pres] tr (affect) imponieren (dat), beeindrucken; (imprint,
emphasize) einprägen; **i. s.th. on s.o.**
j-m etw einprägen
impression [ɪm'preʃən] s Eindruck m;
(stamp) Gepräge n; **try to make an i.**
Eindruck schinden
impressive [ɪm'presɪv] adj eindrucksvoll
imprint ['ɪmprɪnt] s Aufdruck m; (fig)
Eindruck m || [ɪm'prɪnt] tr (on) auf-
drucken (auf acc); **i. on s.o.'s memory** j-m ins Gedächtnis einprägen
imprison [ɪm'prɪzən] tr einsperren
imprisonment [ɪm'prɪzənmənt] s Haft
f; (penalty) Freiheitsstrafe f; (captivity) Gefangenschaft f
improbable [ɪm'prabəbəl] adj unwahrscheinlich
impromptu [ɪm'prampt(j)u] adj & adv
aus dem Stegreif || s Stegreifstück n
improper [ɪm'prapər] adj ungehörig,
unschicklich; (use) unzulässig
improve [ɪm'pruv] tr verbessern; (relations) ausbauen; (land) kultivieren;
(a salary) aufbessern; **i. oneself** sich
bessern; (financially) sich verbessern
|| intr bessern; (com) sich erholen;
i. on Verbesserungen vornehmen an
(dat)
improvement [ɪm'pruvmənt] s Verbesserung f; (reworking) Umarbeitung
f; (of money value) Erholung f; (of
a salary) Aufbesserung f; (in health)
Besserung f; **be an i. on** ein Fortschritt sein gegenüber
improvident [ɪm'pravɪdənt] adj unbedacht
improvise ['ɪmprə‚vaɪz] tr improvisie-
ren || intr improvisieren; (mus) phan-
tasieren
imprudence [ɪm'prudəns] s Unklugheit
f
imprudent [ɪm'prudənt] adj unklug
impudence ['ɪmpjədəns] s Unverschämtheit f
impudent ['ɪmpjədənt] adj unverschämt
impugn [ɪm'pjun] tr bestreiten
impulse ['ɪmpʌls] s Impuls m; **act on i.**
impulsiv handeln
impulsive [ɪm'pʌlsɪv] adj impulsiv
impunity [ɪm'pjunɪti] s Straffreiheit
f; **with i.** ungestraft
impure [ɪm'pjur] adj (& fig) unrein

impurity [ɪmˈpjʊrɪtɪ] *s* (& fig) Unreinheit *f*
impute [ɪmˈpjut] *tr* (**to**) unterstellen (*dat*)
in [ɪn] *adv* (*position*) drin, drinnen; (*direction away from the speaker*) hinein; (*direction toward the speaker*) herein; **be all in** ganz erschöpft sein; **be in** da sein; (*said of a political party*) an der Macht sein; (*be in style*) in Mode sein; **be in for** zu erwarten haben; **have it in for** auf dem Strich haben ‖ *s*—**the ins and outs of** die Einzelheiten (*genit*) ‖ *prep* (*position*) in (*dat*); (*direction*) in (*acc*); (e.g., *the morning, afternoon, evening*) am; (*a field, the country; one eye*) auf (*dat*); (*one's opinion; all probability*) nach (*dat*); (*circumstances; a reign*) unter (*dat*); (*ink; one stroke*) mit (*dat*); (*because of pain, joy, etc.*) vor (*dat*); **he doesn't have it in him to** (*inf*) er hat nicht das Zeug dazu zu (*inf*); **in German** auf deutsch
inability [ˌɪnəˈbɪlɪtɪ] *s* Unfähigkeit *f*; **i. to pay** Zahlungsunfähigkeit *f*
inaccessible [ˌɪnækˈsɛsɪbəl] *adj* unzugänglich
inaccuracy [ɪnˈækjərəsɪ] *s* Ungenauigkeit *f*
inaccurate [ɪnˈækjərɪt] *adj* ungenau
inaction [ɪnˈækʃən] *s* Untätigkeit *f*
inactive [ɪnˈæktɪv] *adj* untätig; (chem) unwirksam; (st. exch.) lustlos
inactivity [ˌɪnækˈtɪvɪtɪ] *s* Untätigkeit *f*
inadequate [ɪnˈædɪkwɪt] *adj* unangemessen
inadmissible [ˌɪnədˈmɪsɪbəl] *adj* unstatthaft, unzulässig
inadvertent [ˌɪnədˈvʌrtənt] *adj* versehentlich
inadvisable [ˌɪnədˈvaɪzəbəl] *adj* nicht ratsam
inalienable [ɪnˈeljənəbəl] *adj* unveräußerlich
inane [ɪnˈen] *adj* leer, unsinnig
inanimate [ɪnˈænɪmɪt] *adj* unbeseelt
inappropriate [ˌɪnəˈproprɪ-ɪt] *adj* unangemessen
inarticulate [ˌɪnɑrˈtɪkjəlɪt] *adj* unartikuliert, undeutlich
inartistic [ˌɪnɑrˈtɪstɪk] *adj* unkünstlerisch, kunstlos
inasmuch as [ˌɪnəzˈmʌtʃ ˌæz] *conj* da
inattentive [ˌɪnəˈtɛntɪv] *adv* (**to**) unaufmerksam (or unachtsam) (gegenüber)
inaudible [ɪnˈɔdɪbəl] *adj* unhörbar
inaugural [ɪnˈɔg(j)ərəl] *adj* Antritts–
inaugurate [ɪnˈɔg(j)ə ˌret] *tr* feierlich eröffnen; (*a new policy*) einleiten
inauguration [ɪn ˌɔg(j)əˈreʃən] *s* Eröffnung *f*; (*of an official*) Amtsantritt *m*
inauspicious [ˌɪnɔˈspɪʃəs] *adj* ungünstig
inborn [ˈɪn ˌbɔrn] *adj* angeboren
inbred [ˈɪn ˌbred] *adj* angeboren, ererbt
in'breed'ing *s* Inzucht *f*

incalculable [ɪnˈkælkjələbəl] *adj* unberechenbar
incandescent [ˌɪnkənˈdɛsənt] *adj* Glüh–
incantation [ˌɪnkænˈteʃən] *s* Beschwörung *f*
incapable [ɪnˈkepəbəl] *adj* untüchtig; **i. of** (*ger*) nicht fähig zu (*inf*)
incapacitate [ˌɪnkəˈpæsɪ ˌtet] *tr* unfähig machen; (jur) für geschäftsunfähig erklären
incarcerate [ɪnˈkɑrsə ˌret] *tr* einkerkern
incarnate [ɪnˈkɑrnet] *adj*—**God i.** Gottmensch *m*; **the devil i.** der Teufel in Menschengestalt
incarnation [ˌɪnkɑrˈneʃən] *s* (fig) Verkörperung *f*; (eccl) Fleischwerdung *f*
incendiary [ɪnˈsɛndɪ ˌerɪ] *adj* Brand–; (fig) aufhetzend ‖ *s* Brandstifter –in *mf*
incense [ˈɪnsəns] *s* Weihrauch *m* ‖ *tr* (eccl) beräuchern ‖ [ɪnˈsɛns] *tr* erzürnen
in'cense burn'er *s* Räuchergefäß *n*
incentive [ɪnˈsɛntɪv] *s* Anreiz *m*
inception [ɪnˈsɛpʃən] *s* Anfang *m*
incessant [ɪnˈsɛsənt] *adj* unaufhörlich
incest [ˈɪnsɛst] *s* Blutschande *f*
incestuous [ɪnˈsɛstʃʊ-əs] *adj* blutschänderisch
inch [ɪntʃ] *s* Zoll *m*; **beat within an i. of one's life** fast zu Tode prügeln; **by inches** nach und nach; **not yield an i.** keinen Fußbreit nachgeben ‖ *intr*—**i. along** dahinschleichen; **i. forward** langsam vorrücken
incidence [ˈɪnsɪdəns] *s* Vorkommen *n*
incident [ˈɪnsɪdənt] *s* Vorfall *m*; (*adverse event*) Zwischenfall *m*
incidental [ˌɪnsɪˈdɛntəl] *adj* zufällig; **i. to** gehörig zu ‖ **incidentals** *spl* Nebenausgaben *pl*
incidentally [ˌɪnsɪˈdɛntəlɪ] *adv* übrigens
incinerate [ɪnˈsɪnə ˌret] *tr* einäschern
incinerator [ɪnˈsɪnə ˌretər] *s* Verbrennungsofen *m*
incipient [ɪnˈsɪpɪ-ənt] *adv* beginnend
incision [ɪnˈsɪʒən] *s* Schnitt *m*
incisive [ɪnˈsaɪsɪv] *adj* (*biting*) beißend; (*penetrating*) durchdringend; (*sharp*) scharf
incisor [ɪnˈsaɪzər] *s* Schneidezahn *m*
incite [ɪnˈsaɪt] *tr* aufreizen, aufhetzen
inclement [ɪnˈklɛmənt] *adj* ungünstig
inclination [ˌɪnklɪˈneʃən] *s* (& fig) Neigung *f*
incline [ˈɪnklaɪn] *s* Abhang *m* ‖ [ɪnˈklaɪn] *tr* neigen ‖ *intr* (**towards**) sich neigen (nach or zu); (fig) (**towards**) neigen (zu); **the roof inclines sharply** das Dach fällt steil ab
include [ɪnˈklud] *tr* einschließen; **i. among** rechnen unter (*acc*); **i. in** einrechnen in (*acc*)
includ'ed *adj* (mit) inbegriffen
includ'ing *prep* einschließlich (*genit*)
inclusive [ɪnˈklusɪv] *adj* umfassend, gesamt; **all i.** alles inbegriffen; **from ... to ... i.** von ... zu ... einschließlich (or inklusive); **i. of** einschließlich (*genit*)

incognito [ɪn'kagnɪ‚to] *adv* inkognito
incoherent [‚ɪnko'hɪrənt] *adj* unzusammenhängend; **be i.** (*said of a person*) nicht ganz bei sich sein
incombustible [‚ɪnkəm'bʌstɪbəl] *adj* unverbrennbar
income ['ɪnkʌm] *s* (**from**) Einkommen *n* (aus)
in'come tax' *s* Einkommensteuer *f*
in'come-tax return' *s* Einkommensteuererklärung *f*
in'com'ing *adj* (*e.g., tide*) hereinkommend; (*bus, train*) ankommend; (*official*) neu eintretend; **i. goods, i. mail** Eingänge *pl*
incomparable [ɪn'kampərəbəl] *adj* unvergleichlich
incompatible [‚ɪnkəm'pætɪbəl] *adj* (**with**) unvereinbar (mit); (*persons*) unverträglich
incompetent [ɪn'kampɪtənt] *adj* untauglich; (*not legally qualified*) nicht zuständig; (*not legally capable*) geschäftsunfähig; (*inadmissible*) unzulässig || *s* Nichtkönner –in *mf*
incomplete [‚ɪnkəm'plit] *adj* unvollständig
incomprehensible [‚ɪnkamprɪ'hɛnsɪbəl] *adj* unbegreiflich
inconceivable [‚ɪnkən'sivəbəl] *adj* undenkbar
inconclusive [‚ɪnkən'klusɪv] *adj* (*not convincing*) nicht überzeugend; (*leading to no result*) ergebnislos
incongruous [ɪn'kaŋgru‚əs] *adj* nicht übereinstimmend
inconsequential [ɪn‚kansɪ'kwɛnʃəl] *adj* belanglos
inconsiderate [‚ɪnkən'sɪdərɪt] *adj* unüberlegt; (**towards**) rücksichtslos (gegen)
inconsistency [‚ɪnkən'sɪstənsi] *s* (*lack of logical connection*) Inkonsequenz *f*; (*contradiction*) Unstimmigkeit *f*; (*instability*) Unbeständigkeit *f*
inconsistent [‚ɪnkən'sɪstənt] *adj* inkonsequent; (*uneven*) unbeständig
inconspicuous [‚ɪnkən'spɪkju‚əs] *adj* unauffällig
inconstant [ɪn'kanstənt] *adj* unbeständig
incontinent [ɪn'kantɪnənt] *adj* zügellos
incontrovertible [‚ɪnkantrə'vʌrtɪbəl] *adj* unwiderlegbar
inconvenience [‚ɪnkən'vini‚əns] *s* Ungelegenheit *f* || *tr* bemühen, belästigen
inconvenient [‚ɪnkən'vini‚ənt] *adj* ungelegen
incorporate [ɪn'kɔrpə‚ret] *tr* einverleiben; (*an organization*) zu e–r Körperschaft machen || *intr* e–e Körperschaft werden
incorporation [ɪn‚kɔrpə'reʃən] *s* Einverleibung *f*; (*jur*) Körperschaftsbildung *f*
incorrect [‚ɪnkə'rɛkt] *adj* unrichtig, falsch; (*conduct*) unschicklich
incorrigible [ɪn'kɔrɪdʒɪbəl] *adj* unverbesserlich
increase ['ɪnkris] *s* Zunahme *f*; **be on the i.** steigen; **i. in costs** Kostensteigerung *f*; **i. in pay** Gehaltser-

höhung *f*; (mil) Solderhöhung *f*; **i. in population** Bevölkerungszunahme *f*; **i. in prices** Preiserhöhung *f*; **i. in rent** Mieterhöhung *f*; **i. in taxes** Steuererhöhung *f*; **i. in value** Wertsteigerung *f*; **i. in weight** Gewichtszunahme *f* || ['ɪn'kris] *tr* (*in size*) vergrößern; (*in height*) erhöhen; (*in quantity*) vermehren; (*in intensity*) verstärken; (*prices*) heraufsetzen || *intr* zunehmen, sich vergrößern; (*rise*) sich erhöhen; (*in quantity*) sich vermehren; (*in intensity*) sich verstärken; **i. in** zunehmen an (*dat*)
increasingly [ɪn'krisɪŋli] *adv* immer mehr; **i. more difficult** immer schwieriger
incredible [ɪn'krɛdɪbəl] *adj* unglaublich
incredulous [ɪn'krɛdʒələs] *adj* ungläubig
increment ['ɪnkrɪmənt] *s* Zunahme *f*, Zuwachs *m*; (*in pay*) Gehaltszulage *f*
incriminate [ɪn'krɪmɪ‚net] *tr* belasten
incrust [ɪn'krʌst] *tr* überkrusten
incubate ['ɪnkjə‚bet] *tr & intr* brüten
incubator ['ɪnkjə‚betər] *s* Brutapparat *m*
inculcate [ɪn'kʌlket], ['ɪnkʌl‚ket] *tr* (**in**) einprägen (*dat*)
incumbency [ɪn'kʌmbənsi] *s* (*obligation*) Obliegenheit *f*; (*term of office*) Amtszeit *f*
incumbent [ɪn'kʌmbənt] *adj*—**be i. on** obliegen (*dat*) || *s* Amtsinhaber –in *mf*
incunabula [‚ɪnkju'næbjələ] *spl* (typ) Wiegendrucke *pl*
in·cur [ɪn'kʌr] *v* (*pret & pp* **-curred;** *ger* **-curring**) *tr* sich (*dat*) zuziehen; (*debts*) machen; (*a loss*) erleiden; (*a risk*) eingehen
incurable [ɪn'kjurəbəl] *adj* unheilbar || *s* unheilbarer Kranke *m*
incursion [ɪn'kʌrʒən] *s* Einfall *m*
indebted [ɪn'dɛtɪd] *adj* (**to**) verschuldet (bei); **be i. to s.o. for s.th.** j–m etw zu verdanken haben
indecency [ɪn'disənsi] *s* Unsittlichkeit *f*
indecent [ɪn'disənt] *adj* unsittlich; **i. assault** Sittlichkeitsvergehen *n*
indecision [‚ɪndɪ'sɪʒən] *s* Unentschlossenheit *f*
indecisive [‚ɪndɪ'saɪsɪv] *adj* (*person*) unentschlossen; (*battle*) nicht entscheidend
indeclinable [‚ɪndɪ'klaɪnəbəl] *adj* undeklinierbar
indeed [ɪn'did] *adv* ja, zwar || *interj* jawohl!
indefatigable [‚ɪndɪ'fætɪgəbəl] *adj* unermüdlich
indefensible [‚ɪndɪ'fɛnsɪbəl] *adj* nicht zu verteidigen(d); (*argument*) unhaltbar; (*behavior*) unentschuldbar
indefinable [‚ɪndɪ'faɪnəbəl] *adj* undefinierbar
indefinite [ɪn'dɛfɪnɪt] *adj* (*unlimited*) unbegrenzt; (*not exact*) unbestimmt; (*answer*) ausweichend; (*vague*) undeutlich; (gram) unbestimmt

indelible [ɪn'delɪbəl] *adj* (*ink, pencil*) wasserfest; (fig) unauslöschlich
indelicate [ɪn'delɪkɪt] *adj* unzart
indemnification [ɪn,demnɪfɪ'keʃən] *s* Schadenersatzleistung *f*
indemni·fy [ɪn'demnɪ,faɪ] *v* (*pret & pp* –**fied**) *tr* entschädigen
indemnity [ɪn'demnɪti] *s* Schadenersatz *m*
indent [ɪn'dent] *tr* (*notch*) einkerben; (*the coast*) tiefe Einschnitte bilden in (*dat*); (typ) einrücken || *intr* (typ) einrücken
indentation [,ɪnden'teʃən] *s* Kerbe *f*; (typ) Absatz *m*
indenture [ɪn'dentʃər] *s* (*service contract*) Arbeitsvertrag *m*; (*apprentice contract*) Lehrvertrag *m* || *tr* vertraglich binden
independence [,ɪndɪ'pendəns] *s* Unabhängigkeit *f*
independent [,ɪndɪ'pendənt] *adj* (**of**) unabhängig (**von**) || *s* Unabhängige *mf*
indescribable [,ɪndɪ'skraɪbəbəl] *adj* unbeschreiblich
indestructible [,ɪndɪ'strʌktɪbəl] *adj* unzerstörbar
index ['ɪndeks] *s* (**indexes & indices** ['ɪndɪ,siz]) (*in a book*) Register *n*; (fig) (**to**) Hisweis *m* (auf *acc*); **Index** Index *m* || *tr* registrieren; (*a book*) mit e–m Register versehen
in'dex card' *s* Karteikarte *f*
in'dex fin'ger *s* Zeigefinger *m*
India ['ɪndɪ·ə] *s* Indien *n*
In'dia ink' *s* chinesische Tusche *f*
Indian ['ɪndɪ·ən] *adj* indisch; (*e.g., chief, tribe*) Indianer– || *s* (*of India*) Inder –in *mf*; (*of North America*) Indianer –in *mf*; (*of Central or South America*) Indio *m*
In'dian corn' *s* Mais *m*
In'dian file' *adv* in Gänsemarsch
In'dian O'cean *s* Indischer Ozean *m*
In'dian sum'mer *s* Altweibersommer *m*
indicate ['ɪndɪ,ket] *tr* angeben, anzeigen
indication [,ɪndɪ'keʃən] *s* Angabe *f*; (*of s.th. imminent*) (**of**) Anzeichen *n* (**für**); **give i. of** anzeigen
indicative [ɪn'dɪkətɪv] *adj* (gram) indikativ; **be i. of** hindeuten auf (*acc*) || *s* (gram) Wirklichkeitsform *f*, Indikativ *m*
indicator ['ɪndɪ,ketər] *s* Zeiger *m*
indict [ɪn'daɪt] *tr* (**for**) anklagen (wegen)
indictment [ɪn'daɪtmənt] *s* Anklage *f*
indifference [ɪn'dɪfərəns] *s* (**to**) Gleichgültigkeit *f* (**gegen** *or* **gegenüber**)
indifferent [ɪn'dɪfərənt] *adj* (*mediocre*) mittelmäßig; (**to**) gleichgültig (**gegen**)
indigenous [ɪn'dɪdʒɪnəs] *adj* (**to**) einheimisch (in *dat*)
indigent ['ɪndɪdʒənt] *adj* bedürftig
indigestible [,ɪndɪ'dʒestɪbəl] *adj* unverdaulich
indigestion [,ɪndɪ'dʒestʃən] *s* Verdauungsstörung *f*, Magenverstimmung *f*
indignant [ɪn'dɪgnənt] *adj* (**at**) empört (**über** *acc*)

indignation [,ɪndɪg'neʃən] *s* (**at**) Empörung *f* (über *acc*)
indignity [ɪn'dɪgnɪti] *s* Beleidigung *f*
indigo ['ɪndɪ,go] *adj* Indigo– || *s* Indigo *m & n*
indirect [,ɪndɪ'rekt] *adj* indirekt
in'direct dis'course *s* indirekte Rede *f*
in'direct ques'tion *s* indirekter Fragesatz *m*
indiscreet [,ɪndɪs'krit] *adj* indiskret
indiscretion [,ɪndɪs'kreʃən] *s* Indiskretion *f*
indiscriminate [,ɪndɪs'krɪmɪnɪt] *adj* unterschiedslos
indispensable [,ɪndɪs'pensəbəl] *adj* unentbehrlich
indisposed *adj* (*ill*) unpäßlich; **i. to** abgeneigt (*dat*)
indissoluble [,ɪndɪ'saljəbəl] *adj* unauflösbar
indistinct [,ɪndɪ'stɪŋkt] *adj* undeutlich
individual [,ɪndɪ'vɪdʒʊ·əl] *adj* individuell, Einzel–, einzeln || *s* Individuum *n*
individuality [,ɪndɪ,vɪdʒʊ'ælɪti] *s* Individualität *f*
individually [,ɪndɪ'vɪdʒʊ·əli] *adv* einzeln
indivisible [,ɪndɪ'vɪzɪbəl] *adj* unteilbar
Indochina ['ɪndo't'faɪnə] *s* Indochina *n*
indoctrinate [ɪn'daktrɪ,net] *tr* (**in**) schulen (in *dat*), unterweisen (in *dat*)
indoctrination [,ɪndaktrɪ'neʃən] *s* Schulung *f*, Unterweisung *f*
Indo-European ['ɪndo,jʊrə'pi·ən] *adj* indogermanisch || *s* (*language*) Indogermanisch *n*
indolence ['ɪndələns] *s* Trägheit *f*
indolent ['ɪndələnt] *adj* träge
Indonesia [,ɪndo'niʒə] *s* Indonesien *n*
Indonesian [,ɪndo'niʒən] *adj* indonesisch || *s* Indonesier –in *mf*
indoor ['ɪn,dor] *adj* Haus–, Zimmer, Innen–; (sport) Hallen–
indoors [ɪn'dorz] *adv* innen, drin(nen)
in'door shot' *s* (phot) Innenaufnahme *f*
induce [ɪn'd(j)us] *tr* veranlassen, bewegen; (*bring about*) verursachen; (elec, phys) induzieren
inducement [ɪn'd(j)usmənt] *s* Anreiz *m*
induct [ɪn'dʌkt] *tr* (**into**) einführen (in *acc*); (mil) (**into**) einberufen (zu)
inductee [,ɪn'dʌkti] *s* Einberufene *mf*
induction [ɪn'dʌkʃən] *s* Einführung *f*; (elec, log) Induktion *f*; (mil) Einberufung *f*
induc'tion coil' *s* Induktionsspule *f*
indulge [ɪn'dʌldʒ] *tr* (*a desire*) frönen (*dat*); (*a person*) befriedigen; (*children*) verwöhnen; **i. oneself in** schwelgen in (*dat*) || *intr* (coll) trinken; **i. in s.th.** sich (*dat*) etw gestatten
indulgence [ɪn'dʌldʒəns] *s* (*of a desire*) Frönen *n*; (*tolerance*) Duldung *f*; (relig) Ablaß *m*; **ask s.o.'s i.** j–n um Nachsicht bitten
indulgent [ɪn'dʌldʒənt] *adj* schonend; (**toward**) nachsichtig (**gegen**)
industrial [ɪn'dʌstrɪ·əl] *adj* (*e.g., bank,*

center, alcohol, product, worker) Industrie–; *(e.g., accident, medicine)* Betriebs–; *(e.g., revolution)* industriell; *(e.g., school, engineering)* Gewerbe–
industrialist [ɪn'dʌstrɪ·əlɪst] *s* Industrielle *mf*
industrialize [ɪn'dʌstrɪ·ə‚laɪz] *tr* industrialisieren
indus'trial man'agement *s* Betriebswirtschaft *f*
industrious [ɪn'dʌstrɪ·əs] *adj* fleißig
industry ['ɪndəstrɪ] *s* Industrie *f; (energy)* Fleiß *m*
inebriated [ɪn'ibrɪ‚etɪd] *adj* betrunken
inedible [ɪn'ɛdɪbəl] *adj* ungenießbar
ineffable [ɪn'ɛfəbəl] *adj* unaussprechlich
ineffective [‚ɪnɪ'fɛktɪv] *adj* unwirksam; *(person)* untüchtig
ineffectual [‚ɪnɪ'fɛktʃu·əl] *adj* unwirksam
inefficient [‚ɪnɪ'fɪʃənt] *adj* untüchtig; *(process, procedure)* unrationell; *(mach)* nicht leistungsfähig
ineligible [ɪn'ɛlɪdʒɪbəl] *adj* nicht wählbar; *(not suitable)* ungeeignet
inept [ɪn'ɛpt] *adj* ungeschickt
inequality [‚ɪnɪ'kwɑlɪtɪ] *s* Ungleichheit *f*
inequity [ɪn'ɛkwɪtɪ] *s* Ungerechtigkeit *f*
inertia [ɪn'ʌrʃə] *s* Trägheit *f*
inescapable [‚ɪnɛs'kepəbəl] *adj* unentrinnbar, unabwendbar
inevitable [ɪn'ɛvɪtəbəl] *adj* unvermeidlich, unausweichlich
inexact [‚ɪnɛg'zækt] *adj* ungenau
inexcusable [‚ɪnɛks'kjuzəbəl] *adj* unentschuldbar
inexhaustible [‚ɪnɛg'zɔstɪbəl] *adj* unerschöpflich
inexorable [ɪn'ɛksərəbəl] *adj* unerbittlich
inexpensive [‚ɪnɛk'spɛnsɪv] *adj* billig
inexperience [‚ɪnɛk'spɪrɪ·əns] *s* Unerfahrenheit *f*
inexpe'rienced *adj* unerfahren
inexplicable [ɪn'ɛksplɪkəbəl] *adj* unerklärlich
inexpressible [‚ɪnɛk'sprɛsɪbəl] *adj* unaussprechlich
infallibility [‚ɪnfælɪ'bɪlɪtɪ] *s* Unfehlbarkeit *f*
infallible [ɪn'fælɪbəl] *adj* unfehlbar
infamous ['ɪnfəməs] *adj* schändlich
infamy ['ɪnfəmɪ] *s* Schändlichkeit *f*
infancy ['ɪnfənsɪ] *s* Kindheit *f;* **be still in its i.** (fig) noch in den Kinderschuhen stecken
infant ['ɪnfənt] *adj* Säuglings– || *s* Kleinkind *n,* Säugling *m*
infantile ['ɪnfən‚taɪl] *adj* infantil
in'fantile paral'ysis *s* Kinderlähmung *f*
infantry ['ɪnfəntrɪ] *s* Infanterie *f*
in'fantry·man *s* (–men) Infanterist *m*
infatuated [ɪn'fætʃu‚etɪd] *adj* betört
infatuation [ɪn‚fætʃu'eʃən] *s* Betörung *f*
infect [ɪn'fɛkt] *tr* anstecken, infizieren; **become infected** sich anstecken
infection [ɪn'fɛkʃən] *s* Ansteckung *f*

infectious [ɪn'fɛkʃəs] *adj* (& *fig*) ansteckend
in·fer [ɪn'fʌr] *v* (*pret* & *pp* –ferred; *ger* –ferring) *tr* folgern
inference ['ɪnfərəns] *s* Folgerung *f*
inferior [ɪn'fɪrɪ·ər] *adj* (*in rank*) niedriger; (*in worth*) minderwertig; (**to**) unterlegen (*dat*)
inferiority [ɪn‚fɪrɪ'ɑrɪtɪ] *s* Unterlegenheit *f;* (*in worth*) Minderwertigkeit *f*
inferior'ity com'plex *s* Minderwertigkeitskomplex *m*
infernal [ɪn'fʌrnəl] *adj* höllisch
infest [ɪn'fɛst] *tr* in Schwärmen überfallen; **be infested with** wimmeln von
infidel ['ɪnfɪdəl] *adj* ungläubig || *s* Ungläubige *mf*
infidelity [‚ɪnfɪ'dɛlɪtɪ] *s* Untreue *f*
in'field' *s* (baseball) Innenfeld *n*
infiltrate [ɪn'fɪltret], ['ɪnfɪl‚tret] *tr* (*filter through*) infiltrieren; (mil) durchsickern durch; (pol) unterwandern || *intr* infiltrieren
infinite ['ɪnfɪnɪt] *adj* unendlich
infinitive [ɪn'fɪnɪtɪv] *s* (gram) Nennform *f,* Infinitiv *m*
infinity [ɪn'fɪnɪtɪ] *s* Unendlichkeit *f;* **to i.** endlos
infirm [ɪn'fʌrm] *adj* schwach; (*from age*) altersschwach
infirmary [ɪn'fʌrmərɪ] *s* Krankenstube *f;* (mil) Revier *n*
infirmity [ɪn'fʌrmɪtɪ] *s* Schwachheit *f*
inflame [ɪn'flem] *tr* (fig & pathol) entzünden; **become inflamed** sich entzünden
inflammable [ɪn'flæməbəl] *adj* entzündbar, feuergefährlich
inflammation [‚ɪnflə'meʃən] *s* Entzündung *f*
inflammatory [ɪn'flæmə‚torɪ] *adj* aufrührerisch; (pathol) Entzündungs–
inflate [ɪn'flet] *tr* aufblasen; (tires) aufpumpen
inflation [ɪn'fleʃən] *s* (econ) Inflation *f*
inflationary [ɪn'fleʃə‚nɛri] *adj* inflationistisch
inflect [ɪn'flɛkt] *tr* (*the voice*) modulieren; (gram) flektieren
inflection [ɪn'flɛkʃən] *s* (*of the voice*) Tonfall *m;* (gram) Flexion *f*
inflexible [ɪn'flɛksɪbəl] *adj* unbiegsam; (*person*) unbeugsam; (*law*) unabänderlich
inflict [ɪn'flɪkt] *tr* (*punishment*) (on) auferlegen (*dat*); (*a defeat*) (on) zufügen (*dat*); (*a wound*) (on) beibringen (*dat*)
influence ['ɪnflu·əns] *s* (on) Einfluß *m* (auf *acc*) || *tr* beeinflussen
influential [ɪnflu'ɛnʃəl] *adj* einflußreich, maßgebend
influenza [‚ɪnflu'ɛnzə] *s* Grippe *f*
influx ['ɪnflʌks] *s* Zufluß *m*
inform [ɪn'fɔrm] *tr* (of) benachrichtigen (von) || *intr*—**i. against** anzeigen
informal [ɪn'fɔrməl] *adj* zwanglos
informant [ɪn'fɔrmənt] *s* Gewährsmann *m*
information [‚ɪnfər'meʃən] *s* Nachricht *f,* Auskunft *f; (items of information)*

Informationen *pl;* **a piece of i.** e–e Auskunft *f;* **for your i.** zu Ihrer Information
informa'tion desk' *s* Auskunftsstelle *f*
informative [ɪn'fɔrmətɪv] *adj* belehrend
informed' *adj* unterrichtet
informer [ɪn'fɔrmər] *s* Denunziant –in *mf*
infraction [ɪn'fræk/ən] *s* (of) Verstoß *m* (gegen)
infrared [ˌɪnfrə'rɛd] *adj* infrarot
infrequent [ɪn'frikwənt] *adj* selten
infringe [ɪn'frɪndʒ] *tr* verletzen || *intr* **—i. on** eingreifen in (*acc*)
infringement [ɪn'frɪndʒmənt] *s* (*of a law*) Verletzung *f;* (*of a right*) Eingriff *m* (in *acc*)
infuriate [ɪn'fjʊrɪˌet] *tr* wütend machen
infuse [ɪn'fjuz] *tr* (& fig) (into) einflößen (*dat*)
infusion [ɪn'fjuʒən] *s* (& fig) Einflößung *f;* (med) Infusion *f*
ingenious [ɪn'dʒinɪ·əs] *adj* erfinderisch
ingenuity [ˌɪndʒɪ'n(j)u·ɪti] *s* Erfindungsgabe *f,* Scharfsinn *m*
ingenuous [ɪn'dʒɛnju·əs] *adj* aufrichtig; (*naive*) naiv
ingest [ɪn'dʒɛst] *tr* zu sich nehmen
inglorious [ɪn'glɔrɪ·əs] *adj* (*shameful*) unrühmlich; (*without honor*) ruhmlos
ingot ['ɪŋgət] *s* Block *m;* (*of gold or silver*) Barren *m*
ingrained', **in'grained** *adj* eingewurzelt
ingrate ['ɪŋgret] *s* Undankbare *mf*
ingratiate [ɪn'gre/ɪˌet] *tr—i.* **oneself with** sich einschmeicheln bei
ingra'tiating *adj* einschmeichelnd
ingratitude [ɪn'grætɪˌt(j)ud] *s* Undankbarkeit *f,* Undank *m*
ingredient [ɪn'gridɪ·ənt] *s* Bestandteil *m;* (culin) Zutat *f*
in'grown' *adj* eingewachsen
inhabit [ɪn'hæbɪt] *tr* bewohnen
inhabitant [ɪn'hæbɪtənt] *s* Bewohner –in *mf,* Einwohner –in *mf*
inhale [ɪn'hel] *tr & intr* einatmen; inhalieren
inherent [ɪn'hɪrənt] *adj* innewohnend; (*right*) angeboren
inherit [ɪn'hɛrɪt] *tr* (biol, jur) erben
inheritance [ɪn'hɛrɪtəns] *s* Erbschaft *f*
inher'itance tax' *s* Erbschaftssteuer *f*
inheritor [ɪn'hɛrɪtər] *s* Erbe *m,* Erbin *f*
inhibit [ɪn'hɪbɪt] *tr* hemmen, inhibieren
inhibition [ˌɪnɪ'bɪ/ən] *s* Hemmung *f*
inhospitable [ɪn'hɑspɪtəbəl] *adj* ungastlich; (*place*) unwirtlich
inhuman [ɪn'hjumən] *adj* unmenschlich
inhumane [ˌɪnju'men] *adj* inhuman
inhumanity [ˌɪnhju'mænɪti] *s* Unmenschlichkeit *f*
inimical [ɪ'nɪmɪkəl] *adj* (to) abträglich (*dat*)
iniquity [ɪ'nɪkwɪti] *s* Niederträchtigkeit *f,* Ungerechtigkeit *f*
ini·tial [ɪn'ɪ/əl] *adj* anfänglich || *s* Anfangsbuchstabe *m,* Initiale *f* || *v*

(*pret & pp* –tial[l]ed; *ger* –tial[l]ing) *tr* mit den Initialen unterzeichnen
initially [ɪ'nɪ/əli] *adv* anfangs
initiate [ɪ'nɪ/ɪˌet] *tr* einführen; (*reforms*) einleiten; (**into**) aufnehmen in (*acc*)
initiation [ɪˌnɪ/ɪ'e/ən] *s* Einführung *f;* (**into**) Aufnahme *f* (in *acc*)
initiative [ɪ'nɪ/(ɪ)ətɪv] *s* Unternehmungsgeist *m;* **take the i.** die Initiative ergreifen
inject [ɪn'dʒɛkt] *tr* (*a needle*) einführen; (*a word*) dazwischenwerfen; (*e.g., bigotry into a campaign*) einfließen lassen; (*a liquid*) (med) injizieren
injection [ɪn'dʒɛk/ən] *s* (mach) Einspritzung *f;* (med) Injektion *f*
injudicious [ˌɪndʒu'dɪ/əs] *adj* unverständig
injunction [ɪn'dʒʌŋk/ən] *s* Gebot *n,* (jur) gerichtliche Verfügung *f*
injure ['ɪndʒər] *tr* verletzen; (fig) schädigen
injurious [ɪn'dʒʊrɪ·əs] *adj* schädlich
injury ['ɪndʒəri] *s* Verletzung *f;* (**to**) Schädigung *f* (*genit*)
injustice [ɪn'dʒʌstɪs] *s* Ungerechtigkeit *f*
ink [ɪŋk] *s* Tinte *f* || *tr* schwärzen
inkling ['ɪŋklɪŋ] *s* leise Ahnung *f*
ink' pad' *s* Stempelkissen *n*
ink' spot' *s* Tintenklecks *m*
inky ['ɪŋki] *adj* tiefschwarz
inlaid ['ɪnˌled] *adj* eingelegt
in'laid floor' *s* Parkettfußboden *m*
inland ['ɪnlənd] *adj* Binnen– || *adv* landeinwärts || *s* Binnenland *n*
in'-laws' *spl* angeheiratete Verwandte *pl*
inlay ['ɪnˌle] *s* Einlegearbeit *f;* (dent) gegossene Plombe *f*
in'let *s* Meeresarm *m;* (*opening*) Öffnung *f*
in'mate *s* Insasse *m,* Insassin *f*
inn [ɪn] *s* Gasthaus *n,* Wirtshaus *n*
innards ['ɪnərdʒ] *spl* (coll) Innere *n*
innate [ɪ'net] *adj* angeboren
inner ['ɪnər] *adj* innere, inwendig, Innen–
in'nermost' *adj* innerste
in'nerspring mat'tress *s* Federkernmatratze *f*
in'ner tube' *s* Schlauch *m*
inning ['ɪnɪŋ] *s* Runde *f*
inn'keep'er *s* Wirt *m,* Wirtin *f*
innocence ['ɪnəsəns] *s* Unschuld *f;* (*of a crime*) Schuldlosigkeit *f*
innocent ['ɪnəsənt] *adj* (of) unschuldig (an *dat*); (*harmless*) harmlos; (*guileless*) arglos || *s* Unschuldige *mf*
innocuous [ɪ'nɑkju·əs] *adj* harmlos
innovation [ˌɪnə've/ən] *s* Neuerung *f*
innovative ['ɪnəˌvetɪv] *adj* (*person*) neuerungssüchtig; (*thing*) Neuerungs–
innuen·do [ˌɪnju'ɛndo] *s* (**-does**) Unterstellung *f*
innumerable [ɪ'n(j)umərəbəl] *adj* unzählbar, unzählig
inoculate [ɪn'ɑkjəˌlet] *tr* impfen
inoculation [ɪnˌɑkjə'le/ən] *s* Impfung *f*

inoffensive [ˌɪnə'fɛnsɪv] *adj* unschädlich

inopportune [ɪn ˌapər't(j)un] *adj* ungelegen

inordinate [ɪn'ɔrdɪnɪt] *adj* übermäßig

inorganic [ˌɪnɔr'gænɪk] *adj* unorganisch; (chem) anorganisch

in'put' *adj* (data proc) Eingabe– || *s* (*in production*) Aufwand *m;* (data proc) Eingabe *f,* Eingangsinformation *f;* (elec) Stromzufuhr *f*

inquest ['ɪnkwɛst] *s* Untersuchung *f*

inquire [ɪn'kwaɪr] *intr* anfragen; **i. about** sich erkundigen nach; **i. into** untersuchen; **i. of** sich erkundigen bei

inquiry [ɪn'kwaɪri], ['ɪnkwɪri] *s* Anfrage *f;* (*investigation*) Untersuchung *f;* **make inquiries** (**about**) Erkundigungen einziehen (über *acc*)

inquisition [ˌɪnkwɪ'zɪʃən] *s* Inquisition *f*

inquisitive [ɪn'kwɪzɪtɪv] *adj* wißbegierig

in'road *s* (*raid*) Einfall *m;* (fig) Eingriff *m*

ins' and outs' *spl* alle Kniffe *pl*

insane [ɪn'sen] *adj* wahnsinnig; (*absurd*) unsinnig

insane' asy'lum *s* Irrenanstalt *f*

insanity [ɪn'sænɪti] *s* Wahnsinn *m*

insatiable [ɪn'seʃəbəl] *adj* unersättlich

inscribe [ɪn'skraɪb] *tr* (*a name*) einschreiben; (*a book*) widmen; (*a monument*) mit e-r Inschrift versehen

inscription [ɪn'skrɪpʃən] *s* Inschrift *f;* (*of a book*) Widmung *f*

inscrutable [ɪn'skrutəbəl] *adj* unerforschlich

insect ['ɪnsɛkt] *s* Insekt *n,* Kerbtier *n*

insecticide [ɪn'sɛktɪ ˌsaɪd] *s* Insektenvertilgungsmittel *n,* Insektizid *n*

insecure [ˌɪnsɪ'kjur] *adj* unsicher

insecurity [ˌɪnsɪ'kjurɪti] *s* Unsicherheit *f*

insensitive [ɪn'sɛnsɪtɪv] *adj* (**to**) unempfindlich (gegen)

inseparable [ɪn'sɛpərəbəl] *adj* untrennbar; (*friends*) unzertrennlich

insert ['ɪnsʌrt] *s* Einsatzstück *n* || [ɪn'sʌrt] *tr* einfügen; (*a coin*) einwerfen

insertion [ɪn'sʌrʃən] *s* Einfügung *f;* (*of a coin*) Einwurf *m*

in'set' (*of a map*) Nebenkarte *f;* (*inserted piece*) Einsatz *m*

in'shore' *adj* Küsten– || *adv* auf die Küste zu

in'side' *adj* innere, Innen–; (*information*) vertraulich || *adv* innen, drinnen; **come i.** hereinkommen; **i. of** innerhalb von; **i. out** verkehrt; **know i. out** in– und auswendig kennen; **turn i. out** umdrehen || *s* Innenseite *f,* Innere *n;* **on the i.** innen || *prep* innerhalb (*genit*)

insider [ɪn'saɪdər] *s* Eingeweihte *mf*

in'side track' *s* (sport) Innenbahn *f;* **have the i.** (fig) im Vorteil sein

insidious [ɪn'sɪdɪ·əs] *adj* hinterlistig

in'sight' *s* Einsicht *f*

insigni·a [ɪn'sɪgnɪ·ə] *s* (**-a & -as**) Abzeichen *n;* **i. of office** Amtsabzeichen *pl;* **i. of rank** Rangabzeichen *pl*

insignificant [ˌɪnsɪg'nɪfɪkənt] *adj* bedeutungslos, geringfügig

insincere [ˌɪnsɪn'sɪr] *adj* unaufrichtig

insincerity [ˌɪnsɪn'sɛrɪti] *s* Unaufrichtigkeit *f*

insinuate [ɪn'sɪnju ˌet] *tr* andeuten

insipid [ɪn'sɪpɪd] *adj* (& fig) fad(e)

insist [ɪn'sɪst] *intr*—**i. on** bestehen auf (*dat*); **i. on** (*ger*) darauf bestehen zu (*inf*)

insistent [ɪn'sɪstənt] *adj* beharrlich

insofar as [ˌɪnso'far ˌæz] *conj* insoweit als

insolence ['ɪnsələns] *s* Unverschämtheit *f*

insolent ['ɪnsələnt] *adj* unverschämt

insoluble [ɪn'saljəbəl] *adj* unlösbar

insolvency [ɪn'salvənsi] *s* Zahlungsunfähigkeit *f,* Insolvenz *f*

insolvent [ɪn'salvənt] *adj* zahlungsunfähig

insomnia [ɪn'samnɪ·ə] *s* Schlaflosigkeit *f*

insomuch as [ˌɪnso'mʌtʃəz] *conj* insofern als

inspect [ɪn'spɛkt] *tr* (*view closely*) besichtigen; (*check*) kontrollieren; (aut) untersuchen; (mil) besichtigen

inspection [ɪn'spɛkʃən] *s* Besichtigung *f;* Kontrolle *f;* (aut) Untersuchung *f;* (mil) Truppenbesichtigung *f*

inspector [ɪn'spɛktər] *s* Kontrolleur *m;* (*of police*) Inspektor *m*

inspiration [ˌɪnspɪ'reʃən] *s* Begeisterung *f*

inspire [ɪn'spaɪr] *tr* begeistern; (*feelings*) erwecken

inspir'ing *adj* begeisternd

instability [ˌɪnstə'bɪlɪti] *s* Unbeständigkeit *f*

install [ɪn'stɔl] *tr* (*appliances*) installieren; (*in office*) einführen

installation [ˌɪnstə'leʃən] *s* (*of appliances*) Installation *f;* (mil) Anlage *f*

installment [ɪn'stɔlmənt] *s* Installation *f;* (*in a serialized story*) Fortsetzung *f;* (*partial payment*) Rate *f;* **in installments** ratenweise

install'ment plan' *s* Teilzahlungsplan *m*

instance ['ɪnstəns] *s* (*case*) Fall *m;* (*example*) Beispiel *n;* (jur) Instanz *f;* **for i.** zum Beispiel

instant ['ɪnstənt] *adj* augenblicklich; (*foods*) gebrauchsfertig || *s* Augenblick *m;* **this i.** sofort

instantaneous [ˌɪnstən'tenɪ·əs] *adj* augenblicklich, sofortig

instead [ɪn'stɛd] *adv* statt dessen

instead' of *prep* (an)statt (*genit*); (*ger*) anstatt zu (*inf*)

in'step' *s* Rist *m*

instigate ['ɪnstɪ ˌget] *tr* anstiften

instigation [ˌɪnstɪ'geʃən] *s* Anstiftung *f*

instigator ['ɪnstɪ ˌgetər] *s* Anstifter –in *mf*

instill [ɪn'stɪl] *tr* einflößen

instinct ['ɪnstɪŋkt] *s* Trieb *m,* Instinkt *m;* **by i.** instinktiv

instinctive [ɪn'stɪŋktɪv] *adj* instinktiv

institute ['ɪnstɪ,t(j)ut] s Institut n ‖
tr einleiten
institution [,ɪnstɪ't(j)uʃən] s Anstalt f
instruct [ɪn'strʌkt] tr anweisen, beauftragen; (teach) unterrichten
instruction [ɪn'strʌkʃən] s (teaching)
Unterricht m; **instructions** Anweisun-
gen pl; **instructions for use** Gebrauchsanweisung f
instructive [ɪn'strʌktɪv] adj lehrreich
instructor [ɪn'strʌktər] s Lehrer –in
mf; (at a university) Dozent –in mf
instrument ['ɪnstrəmənt] s Instrument
n; (tool) Werkzeug n; (jur) Dokument n
instrumental [,ɪnstrə'mentəl] adj (mus)
instrumental; **he was i. in my getting
an award** er war mir behilflich, e–n
Preis zu erlangen
instrumentality [,ɪnstrəmən'tælɪti] s
Vermittlung f
in'strument land'ing s Instrumenten-
landung f
in'strument pan'el s Armaturenbrett n
insubordinate [,ɪnsə'bɔrdɪnɪt] adj wi-
dersetzlich
insubordination [,ɪnsəbɔrdɪ'neʃən] s
Widersetzlichkeit f
insufferable [ɪn'sʌfərəbəl] adj unausstehlich
insufficient [,ɪnsə'fɪʃənt] adj unge-
nügend, unzureichend
insular ['ɪns(j)ələr] adj insular
insulate ['ɪnsə,let] tr isolieren
insulation [,ɪnsə'leʃən] s Isolierung f;
(insulating material) Isolierstoff m
insulator ['ɪnsə,letər] s Isolator m
insulin ['ɪnsəlɪn] s Insulin n
insult ['ɪnsʌlt] s Beleidigung f ‖ [ɪn-
'sʌlt] tr beleidigen, beschimpfen
insurance [ɪn'ʃʊrəns] adj Versiche-
rungs– ‖ s Versicherung f
insure [ɪn'ʃʊr] tr versichern
insured' adj (letter, package) Wert– ‖
s Versicherungsnehmer –in mf
insurer [ɪn'ʃʊrər] s Versicherer –in mf
insurgent [ɪn'sʌrdʒənt] adj aufständisch ‖ s Aufständische mf
insurmountable [,ɪnsər'maʊntəbəl] adj
unübersteigbar; (fig) unüberwindlich
insurrection [,ɪnsə'rekʃən] s Aufstand
m
intact [ɪn'tækt] adj unversehrt
in'take' s (aut) Einlaß m; **i. of food**
Nahrungsaufnahme f
in'take valve' s Einlaßventil n
intangible [ɪn'tændʒɪbəl] adj immateriell
integer ['ɪntɪdʒər] s ganze Zahl f
integral ['ɪntɪgrəl] adj wesentlich;
(math) Integral– ‖ s Integral n
integrate ['ɪntɪ,gret] tr eingliedern;
(a school) die Rassentrennung aufheben in (dat); (& math) integrieren
integration [,ɪntɪ'greʃən] s Integration f; (of schools) Aufhebung f der
Rassentrennung
integrity [ɪn'tegrɪti] s Redlichkeit f
intellect ['ɪntə,lekt] s Intellekt m
intellectual [,ɪntə'lektʃu-əl] adj intel-
lektuell; (freedom, history) Geistes–
‖ s Intellektuelle mf

intelligence [ɪn'telɪdʒəns] s Intelligenz
f, Klugheit f; (information) Nachricht f; (department) Nachrichten-
dienst m; **gather i.** Nachrichten einziehen
intel'ligence quo'tient s Intelligenz-
Quotient m
intel'ligence test' s Begabungsprüfung
f
intelligent [ɪn'telɪdʒənt] adj intelligent,
klug
intelligentsia [ɪn,telɪ'dʒentsɪ-ə] s Intelligenz f, geistige Oberschicht f
intelligible [ɪn'telɪdʒɪbəl] adj (to) verständlich (dat)
intemperate [ɪn'tempərɪt] adj unmäßig;
(in drink) trunksüchtig
intend [ɪn'tend] tr beabsichtigen; **be
intended for** bestimmt sein für, ge-
münzt sein auf (acc) **i. by** bezwecken
mit; **i. for s.o.** j–m zudenken
intend'ed s (coll) Verlobte mf
intense [ɪn'tens] adj intensiv, stark
intensi•fy [ɪn'tensɪ,faɪ] v (pret & pp
–fied) tr steigern, verstärken ‖ intr
sich steigern, stärker werden
intensity [ɪn'tensɪti] s Stärke f
intensive [ɪn'tensɪv] adj intensiv;
(gram) verstärkend
inten'sive care' s Intensivstation f
intent [ɪn'tent] adj (on) erpicht (auf
acc) ‖ s Absicht f; **to all intents and
purposes** praktisch genommen
intention [ɪn'tenʃən] s Absicht f; **good
i.** guter Wille m; **have honorable intentions** es ehrlich meinen; **with the
i. of** (ger) in der Absicht zu (inf)
intentional [ɪn'tenʃənəl] adj absichtlich
intently [ɪn'tentli] adv gespannt
in•ter [ɪn'tʌr] v (pret & pp –terred;
ger –terring) tr beerdigen
interact [,ɪntər'ækt] intr zusammen-
wirken, aufeinander wirken
interaction [,ɪntər'ækʃən] s Wechsel-
wirkung f
inter•breed [,ɪntər'brid] v (pret & pp
–bred) tr kreuzen ‖ intr sich kreuzen
intercede [,ɪntər'sid] intr Fürsprache
einlegen; **i. for s.o. with** Fürsprache
einlegen für j–n bei
intercept [,ɪntər'sept] tr (a letter, aircraft) abfangen; (a radio message)
abhören; (cut off, check) den Weg
abschneiden (dat)
interceptor [,ɪntər'septər] s (aer) Ab-
fangjäger m
intercession [,ɪntər'seʃən] s Fürsprache f; (relig) Fürbitte f
interchange ['ɪntər,tʃendʒ] s Wechsel
m; (on a highway) Anschlußstelle f
‖ [,ɪntər'tʃendʒ] tr auswechseln ‖
intr (with) abwechseln (mit)
interchangeable [,ɪntər'tʃendʒəbəl] adj
auswechselbar, austauschbar
intercom ['ɪntər,kɑm] s Wechsel-
sprachanlage f
intercourse ['ɪntər,kors] s Verkehr m;
(sexual) Geschlechtsverkehr m
interdependent [,ɪntərdɪ'pendənt] adj
voneinander abhängig
interdict ['ɪntər,dɪkt] s Verbot n;
(eccl) Interdikt n ‖ [,ɪntər'dɪkt] tr

verbieten; **i. s.o.** from (*ger*) j–m verbieten zu (*inf*)
interest ['int(ə)rist] *s* (**in**) Interesse *n* (an *dat*, für); (fin) Zinsen *pl*; **at i.** gegen Zinsen; **be in s.o.'s i.** in j–s Interesse liegen; **have an i.** in beteiligt sein an (*dat*) or bei; **interests** Belange *pl*; **pay i.** (*bring in interest*) Zinsen abwerfen; (*pay out interest*) Zinsen zahlen; **take an i.** in sich interessieren für; **with i.** (& fig) mit Zinsen ‖ *tr* (**in**) interessieren (für)
in'terested *adj*—**i.** in interessiert an (*dat*); **the i.** parties die Beteiligten *pl*
in'teresting *adj* interessant
in'terest rate' *s* Zinsfuß *m*, Zinssatz *m*
interfere [,intər'fir] *intr* (*said of a thing*) dazwischenkommen; (*said of a person*) eingreifen; (**in** or **with**) sich (ein)mengen (in *acc*); **i. with** (rad, telv) stören; **i. with s.o.'s work** j–n bei seiner Arbeit stören
interference [,intər'firəns] *s* Einmischung *f*; (phys) Interferenz *f*; (rad, telv) Störung *f*
interim ['intərim] *adj* Zwischen– ‖ *s* Zwischenzeit *f*
interior [in'tiri·ər] *adj* innere, Innen– ‖ *s* Innere *n*; (*of a building*) Innenraum *m*; (*of a country*) Inland *n*
inte'rior dec'orator *s* Innenarchitekt –in *mf*
interject [,intər'dʒɛkt] *tr* dazwischenwerfen
interjection [,intər'dʒɛkʃən] *s* Zwischenwurf *m*; (gram) Interjektion *f*
interlard [,intər'lard] *tr* (& fig) spicken
interlinear [,intər'lini·ər] *adj* Interlinear–
interlock [,intər'lak] *tr* miteinander verbinden ‖ *intr* sich ineinanderschließen
interloper [,intər'lopər] *s* Eindringling *m*
interlude ['intər,lud] *s* (*interval*) Pause *f*; (fig, mus, theat) Zwischenspiel *n*
intermediary [,intər'midi,ɛri] *adj* vermittelnd ‖ *s* Vermittler –in *mf*
intermediate [,intər'midi·it] *adj* zwischenliegend, Zwischen–
interment [in'tʌrmənt] *s* Beerdigung *f*
intermez·zo [,intər'mɛtso] *s* (**-zos &** zi [tsi]) Intermezzo *n*
intermingle [,intər'miŋgəl] *tr* vermischen ‖ *intr* sich vermischen
intermission [,intər'miʃən] *s* Unterbrechung *f*; (theat) Pause *f*
intermittent [,intər'mitənt] *adj* intermittierend
intermix [,intər'miks] *tr* vermischen ‖ *intr* sich vermischen
intern ['intʌrn] *s* Assistenzarzt *m*, Assistenzärztin *f*
internal [in'tʌrnəl] *adj* innere, intern; (*domestic*) einheimisch; (*trade, rhyme*) Binnen–
inter'nal-combus'tion en'gine *s* Verbrennungsmotor *m*
inter'nal med'icine *s* innere Medizin *f*
inter'nal rev'enue *s* Steueraufkommen *n*

international [,intər'næʃənəl] *adj* international
interna'tional date' line' *s* internationale Datumsgrenze *f*
interna'tional law' *s* Völkerrecht *n*
interne'cine war' [,intər'nisin] *s* gegenseitiger Vernichtungskrieg *m*
internee [,intər'ni] *s* Internierte *mf*
internment [in'tʌrnmənt] *s* Internierung *f*
in'ternship' *s* Pflichtzeit *f* als Assistenzarzt (or Assistenzärztin)
interoffice [,intər'afis] *adj* Haus–
interplanetary [,intər'plæni,tɛri] *adj* interplanetarisch
interplay ['intər,ple] *s* Wechselspiel *n*
interpolate [in'tʌrpə,let] *tr* interpolieren
interpose [,intər'poz] *tr* (*an obstacle*) dazwischensetzen; (*a remark*) einwerfen
interpret [in'tʌrprit] *tr* (& mus) interpretieren; (*translate*) verdolmetschen ‖ *intr* dolmetschen
interpretation [in,tʌrpri'teʃən] *s* (& mus) Interpretation *f*
interpreter [in'tʌrpritər] *s* Dolmetscher –in *mf*; **act as i.** dolmetschen
interrogate [in'tɛrə,get] *tr* ausfragen; (jur) verhören, vernehmen
interrogation [in,tɛrə'geʃən] *s* Verhör *n*
interrogative [,intər'ragətiv] *adj* Frage–
interrupt [,intə'rʌpt] *tr* unterbrechen
interruption [,intə'rʌpʃən] *s* Unterbrechung *f*; (*in industry*) Betriebsstörung *f*
intersect [,intər'sɛkt] *tr* durchschneiden ‖ *ref* sich kreuzen
intersection [,intər'sɛkʃən] *s* Straßenkreuzung *f*; (math) Schnittpunkt *m*
intersperse [,intər'spʌrs] *tr* durchsetzen
interstate ['intər,stet] *adj* zwischenstaatlich
interstellar [,intər'stɛlər] *adj* interstellar
interstice [in'tʌrstis] *s* Zwischenraum *m*
intertwine [,intər'twain] *tr* verflechten ‖ *intr* sich verflechten
interval ['intərvəl] *s* Abstand *m*; (mus) Stufe *f*, Intervall *n*
intervene [,intər'vin] *intr* dazwischenkommen; (*interfere*) eingreifen; (*intercede*) intervenieren
intervention [,intər'vɛnʃən] *s* Dazwischenkommen *n*; Eingreifen *n*; Intervention *f*
interview ['intər,vju] *s* Interview *n* ‖ *tr* interviewen
inter·weave [,intər'wiv] *v* (*pret* **–wove** **& –weaved;** *pp* **–wove, –woven & –weaved**) *tr* durchweben, durchflechten
intestate [in'testet] *adj* ohne Testament
intestine [in'testin] *s* Darm *m*; **intestines** Gedärme *pl*
intimacy ['intiməsi] *s* Vertraulichkeit *f*; **intimacies** Intimitäten *pl*
intimate ['intimit] *adj* intim, vertraut

|| s Vertraute *mf* || ['ıntı͵met] *tr* andeuten

intimation [͵ıntı'meʃən] s Andeutung *f*

intimidate [ın'tımı͵det] *tr* einschüchtern

intimidation [͵ıntımı'deʃən] s Einschüchterung *f*

into ['ıntu], ['ıntʊ] *prep* in (*acc*)

intolerable [ın'talərəbəl] *adj* unerträglich

intolerance [ın'talərəns] s (**of**) Intoleranz *f* (gegen)

intolerant [ın'talərənt] *adj* (**of**) intolerant (gegen)

intonation [͵ınto'neʃən] s Tonfall *m*

intone [ın'ton] *tr* intonieren

intoxicate [ın'taksı͵ket] *tr* berauschen; (*poison*) vergiften

intoxication [ın͵taksı'keʃən] s (& fig) Rausch *m*; (*poisoning*) Vergiftung *f*

intractable [ın'træktəbəl] *adj* (*person*) störrisch; (*thing*) schwer zu bearbeiten(d)

intransigent [ın'trænsıdʒənt] *adj* unversöhnlich

intransitive [ın'trænsıtıv] *adj* intransitiv

intravenous [͵ıntrə'vinəs] *adj* intravenös

intrepid [ın'trepıd] *adj* unerschrocken

intricate ['ıntrıkıt] *adj* verwickelt

intrigue [ın'trig], ['ıntrig] s Intrige *f* || [ın'trig] *tr* fesseln || *intr* intrigieren

intrigu/ing *adj* fesselnd

intrinsic(al) [ın'trınsık(əl)] *adj* innere, innerlich; (*value*) wirklich

introduce [͵ıntrə'd(j)us] *tr* einführen; (*strangers*) vorstellen

introduction [͵ıntrə'dʌkʃən] s Einführung *f*; (*of strangers*) Vorstellung *f*; (*in a book*) Einleitung *f*

introductory [͵ıntrə'dʌktəri] *adj* (*offer, price*) Einführungs-; (*remarks*) einleitend

introspection [͵ıntrə'spɛkʃən] s Selbstbeobachtung *f*

introspective [͵ıntrə'spɛktıv] *adj* introspektiv

introvert ['ıntrə͵vʌrt] s Introvertierte *mf*

intrude [ın'trud] *intr* (**on**) sich aufdrängen (dat); **am I intruding?** störe ich?

intruder [ın'trudər] s Eindringling *m*

intrusion [ın'truʒən] s Eindrängen *n*, Stören *n*

intrusive [ın'trusıv] *adj* störend, lästig

intuition [͵ınt(j)u'ıʃən] s Intuition *f*

inundate ['ınən͵det] *tr* überschwemmen

inundation [͵ınən'deʃən] s Überschwemmung *f*

inure [ın'jur] *tr* (**to**) abhärten (gegen)

invade [ın'ved] *tr* (*a country*) eindringen in (*acc*); (*rights*) verletzen; (*privacy*) stören

invader [ın'veder] s Eindringling *m*; (mil) Angreifer *m*

invalid [ın'vælıd] *adj* ungültig || ['ınvəlıd] *adj* kränklich || s Invalide *m*

invalidate [ın'vælı͵det] *tr* ungültig machen; (*a law*) außer Kraft setzen

invalidity [͵ınvə'lıdıtı] s Ungültigkeit *f*

invaluable [ın'vælju·əbəl] *adj* unschätzbar

invariable [ın'verı·əbəl]*ˊ adj* unveränderlich

invasion [ın'veʃən] s Invasion *f*

invective [ın'vɛktıv] s Schmähung *f*

inveigh [ın've] *intr*—**i. against** schimpfen über (*acc*) or auf (*acc*)

inveigle [ın'vigel] *tr* verleiten; **i. s.o. into** (*ger*) j–n verleiten zu (*inf*)

invent [ın'vent] *tr* erfinden; (*a story*) sich [*dat*] ausdenken

invention [ın'venʃən] s Erfindung *f*

inventive [ın'ventıv] *adj* erfinderisch

inventiveness [ın'ventıvnıs] s Erfindungsgabe *f*

inventor [ın'ventər] s Erfinder –in *mf*

invento·ry ['ınvən͵tɔri] s (*stock*) Inventar *n*; (*act*) Inventur *f*; (*list*) Bestandsverzeichnis *n*; **take i.** Inventur machen || *v* (*pret & pp* –**ried**) *tr* inventarisieren

inverse [ın'vʌrs] *adj* umgekehrt

inversion [ın'vʌrʒən] s Umkehrung *f*; (gram) Umstellung *f*

invert [ın'vʌrt] *tr* umkehren; (gram) umstellen

invertebrate [ın'vʌrtı͵bret] *adj* wirbellos || s wirbelloses Tier *n*

invest [ın'vest] *tr* (**in**) investieren (in *acc*); (mil) belagern; **i. with** ausstatten mit

investigate [ın'vestı͵get] *tr* untersuchen

investigation [ın͵vestı'geʃən] s Untersuchung *f*

investigator [ın'vestı͵getər] s Untersucher –in *mf*

investment [ın'vestmənt] s Anlage *f*, Investition *f*; (*with an office*) Amtseinführung *f*; (mil) Belagerung *f*

investor [ın'vestər] s Investor –in *mf*

inveterate [ın'vetərıt] *adj* (*habitual*) eingefleischt; (*firmly established*) eingewurzelt

invidious [ın'vıdı·əs] *adj* haßerregend

invigorate [ın'vıgə͵ret] *tr* beleben

invig/orating *adj* belebend

invincible [ın'vınsıbəl] *adj* unbesiegbar

invisible [ın'vızıbəl] *adj* unsichtbar

invis/ible ink/ s Geheimtinte *f*

invitation [͵ınvı'teʃən] s Einladung *f*

invite [ın'vaıt] *tr* einladen; **i. in** hereinbitten

invit/ing *adj* lockend

invocation [͵ınvə'keʃən] s Anrufung *f*; (relig) Bittgebet *n*

invoice ['ınvɔıs] s Faktura *f*, Warenrechnung *f*; **as per i.** laut Rechnung || *tr* fakturieren

invoke [ın'vok] *tr* anrufen; (*cite*) zitieren

involuntary [ın'valən͵teri] *adj* (*against one's will*) unfreiwillig; (*without one's will*) unwillkürlich

invol/untary man/slaughter s unbeabsichtigte Tötung *f*

involve [ɪn'vɑlv] *tr* verwickeln; (*include*) einschließen; (*affect*) betreffen; (*entail*) zur Folge haben
involved' *adj* verwickelt, kompliziert; **be i. in** (*e.g., construction*) beschäftigt sein bei; (*e.g., a crime*) verwickelt sein in (*acc*); **be i. with** (*e.g., a married person*) e-e Affäre haben mit
involvement [ɪn'vɑlʌmənt] *s* Verwicklung *f*
invulnerable [ɪn'vʌlnərəbəl] *adj* unverwundbar
inward ['ɪnwərd] *adj* inner(lich) ‖ *adv* nach innen
inwardly ['ɪnwərdli] *adv* innerlich
iodine ['aɪ·ə‚din] *s* (chem) Jod *n* ‖ ['aɪ·ə‚daɪn] *s* (pharm) Jodtinktur *f*
ion ['aɪ·ən], ['aɪ·ɑn] *s* Ion *n*
ionize ['aɪ·ə‚naɪz] *tr* ionisieren
IOU ['aɪ‚o'ju] *s* (**I owe you**) Schuldschein *m*
I.Q. ['aɪ'kju] *s* (**intelligence quotient**) Intelligenz-Quotient *m*
Iran [ɪ'rɑn], [aɪ'ræn] *s* Iran *m*
Iranian [aɪ'renɪ·ən] *adj* iranisch ‖ *s* Iran(i)er –in *mf*
Iraq [ɪ'rɑk] *s* Irak *m*
Ira·qi [ɪ'rɑki] *adj* irakisch ‖ *s* (**–qis**) Iraker –in *mf*
irascible [ɪ'ræsɪbəl] *adj* jähzornig
irate ['aɪret], [aɪ'ret] *adj* zornig
ire [aɪr] *s* Zorn *m*
Ireland ['aɪrlənd] *s* Irland *n*
iris ['aɪrɪs] *s* (anat, bot) Iris *f*
Irish ['aɪrɪʃ] *adj* irisch ‖ *s* (*language*) Irisch *n;* **the I.** die Iren *pl*
I'rish·man *s* (**–men**) Ire *m*
I'rishwom'an *s* (**–wom'en**) Irin *f*
irk [ʌrk] *tr* ärgern
irksome ['ʌrksəm] *adj* ärgerlich
iron ['aɪ·ərn] *adj* (& fig) eisern ‖ *s* Eisen *n;* (*for pressing clothes*) Bügeleisen *n* ‖ *tr* bügeln; **i. out** ausbügeln; (fig) ins Reine bringen
ironclad ['aɪ·ərn‚klæd] *adj* (fig) umstößlich
i'ron cur'tain *s* eiserner Vorhang *m*
ironic(al) [aɪ'rɑnɪk(əl)] *adj* ironisch
i'roning *s* (*act*) Bügeln *n;* (*clothes*) Bügelwäsche *f*
i'roning board' *s* Bügelbrett *n*
i'ron lung' *s* eiserne Lunge *f*
i'ron ore' *s* Eisenerz *n*
irony ['aɪrəni] *s* Ironie *f*
irradiate [ɪ'redɪ‚et] *tr* bestrahlen; (*light*) ausstrahlen; (*a face*) aufheitern
irrational [ɪ'ræʃənəl] *adj* irrational
irreconcilable [‚ɪrekən'saɪləbəl] *adj* unversöhnlich
irredeemable [‚ɪrɪ'diməbəl] *adj* (*loan, bond*) nicht einlösbar; (*hopeless*) hoffnungslos
irrefutable [‚ɪrɪ'fjutəbəl] *adj* unwiderlegbar
irregular [ɪ'regjələr] *adj* unregelmäßig
irregularity [ɪ‚regjə'lærɪti] *s* Unregelmäßigkeit *f*
irrelevant [ɪ'reləvənt] *adj* (**to**) nicht anwendbar (auf *acc*)
irreligious [‚ɪrɪ'lɪdʒəs] *adj* irreligiös

irreparable [ɪ'repərəbəl] *adj* unersetzlich
irreplaceable [‚ɪrɪ'plesɪbəl] *adj* unersetzlich
irrepressible [‚ɪrɪ'presɪbəl] *adj* unbezähmbar
irreproachable [‚ɪrɪ'protʃəbəl] *adj* untadelig
irresistible [‚ɪrɪ'zɪstɪbəl] *adj* unwiderstehlich
irresolute [ɪ'rezəlut] *adj* unentschlossen, unschlüßig
irrespective [‚ɪrɪ'spektɪv] *adj*—**i. of** ohne Rücksicht auf (*acc*)
irresponsible [‚ɪrɪ'spɑnsɪbəl] *adj* unverantwortlich
irretrievable [‚ɪrɪ'trivəbəl] *adj* unwiederbringlich, unrettbar
irreverent [ɪ'revərənt] *adj* unehrerbietig
irrevocable [ɪ'revəkəbəl] *adj* unwiderruflich
irrigate ['ɪrɪ‚get] *tr* verwässern; (med) irrigieren
irrigation [‚ɪrɪ'geʃən] *s* Bewässerung *f*
irritable ['ɪrɪtəbəl] *adj* reizbar
irritant ['ɪrɪtənt] *s* Reizstoff *m*
irritate ['ɪrɪ‚tet] *tr* reizen, irritieren
ir'ritating *adj* ärgerlich
irritation [‚ɪrɪ'teʃən] *s* Reizung *f*
irruption ['ɪrʌpʃən] *s* Einbruch *m*
isinglass ['aɪzɪŋ‚glæs] *s* Fischleim *m;* (*mica*) Glimmer *m*
Islam ['ɪsləm] *s* Islam *m*
island ['aɪlənd] *s* Insel *f*
islander ['aɪləndər] *s* Insulaner –in *mf*
isle [aɪl] *s* kleine Insel *f*
isolate ['aɪsə‚let] *tr* isolieren
isolation [‚aɪsə'leʃən] *s* Isolierung *f*
isolationist [‚aɪsə'leʃənɪst] *s* Isolationist –in *mf*
isola'tion ward' *s* Isolierstation *f*
isometric [‚aɪsə'metrɪk] *adj* isometrisch
isosceles [aɪ'sɑsə‚liz] *adj* gleichschenklig
isotope ['aɪsə‚top] *s* Isotop *n*
Israel ['ɪzrɪ·əl] *s* Israel *n*
Israe·li [ɪz'reli] *adj* israelisch ‖ *s* (**–li**) Israeli *m*
Israelite ['ɪzrɪ·ə‚laɪt] *adj* israelitisch ‖ *s* Israelit –in *mf*
issuance ['ɪʃu·əns] *s* Ausgabe *f*
issue ['ɪʃu] *s* (*of a magazine*) Nummer *f;* (*result*) Ausgang *m;* (*e.g., of securities*) Ausgabe *f,* Emission *f;* (*under discussion*) Streitpunkt *m;* (*offspring*) Nachkommenschaft *f;* **avoid the i.** der Frage ausweichen; **be at i.** zur Debatte stehen; **make an i. of it** e-e Streitfrage daraus machen; **take i. with** anderer Meinung sein als ‖ *tr* (*orders, supplies, stamps, stocks*) ausgeben; (*a pass*) ausstellen ‖ *intr* (**from**) herauskommen (aus)
isthmus ['ɪsməs] *s* Landenge *f*
it [ɪt] *pron* es; **about it** darüber, davon; **it is I** ich bin es
Italian [ɪ'tæljən] *adj* italienisch ‖ *s* (*person*) Italiener –in *mf;* (*language*) Italienisch *n*
italicize [ɪ'tælɪ‚saɪz] *tr* kursiv drucken

italics [ɪ'tælɪks] *spl* Kursivschrift *f*
Italy ['ɪtəli] *s* Italien *n*
itch [ɪtʃ] *s* Jucken *n;* (pathol) Krätze
f ‖ *intr* jucken; **I am itching to** (*inf*)
es reizt mich zu (*inf*); **my nose itches
me** es juckt mich in der Nase
itchy ['ɪtʃi] *adj* juckend; (pathol) krät-
zig
item ['aɪtəm] *s* Artikel *m;* (*in a list*)
Punkt *m;* (com) Posten *m;* (journ)
Nachricht *f;* **hot i.** (coll) Schlager *m*
itemize ['aɪtə,maɪz] *tr* einzeln aufführen

itinerant [aɪ'tɪnərənt], [ɪ'tɪnərənt] *adj*
Wander-, reisend ‖ *s* Reisende *mf*
itinerary [aɪ'tɪnə,rɛri] *s* Reiseplan *m*
its [ɪts] *poss adj* sein
itself *reflex pron* sich; **in i.** an und für
sich ‖ *intens pron* selbst, selber
ivied ['aɪvɪd] *adj* efeubewachsen
ivory ['aɪvəri] *adj* elfenbeinern, Elfenbein–; (*color*) kremfarben ‖ *s* Elfenbein *n;* **tickle the ivories** in die Tasten
greifen
i'vory tow'er *s* (fig) Elfenbeinturm *m*
ivy ['aɪvi] *s* Efeu *m*

J

J, j [dʒe] *s* zehnter Buchstabe des englischen Alphabets
jab [dʒæb] *s* Stoß *m;* (box) Gerade *f* ‖
v (*pret & pp* **jabbed;** *ger* **jabbing**) *tr*
stoßen; (box) mit der Gerade stoßen
jabber ['dʒæbər] *tr & intr* plappern
jack [dʒæk] *s* (*money*) (sl) Pinke *f;*
(aut) Wagenheber *m;* (cards) Bube
m; (telp) Klinke *f;* **Jack** Hans *m* ‖
tr—**j. up** (aut) heben; (*prices*) hin-
aufschrauben
jackal ['dʒækəl] *s* Schakal *m*
jack'ass' *s* Esel *m*
jacket ['dʒækɪt] *s* Jacke *f;* (*of a book*)
Umschlag *m;* (*of a potato*) Schale *f*
Jack' Frost' *s* Herr Winter *m*
jack'ham'mer *s* Preßlufthammer *m*
jack'-in-the-box' *s* Kastenteufel *m*
jack'knife' *s* (–knives) Klappmesser *n;*
(*dive*) Hechtbeuge *f* ‖ *intr* zusammenklappen
jack'-of-all'-trades' *s* Hansdampf *m* in
allen Gassen
jack'pot' *s* Jackpot *m;* **hit the j.** das
Große Los gewinnen
jack' rab'bit *s* Hase *m*
Jacob ['dʒekəb] *s* Jakob *m*
jade [dʒed] *adj* jadegrün ‖ *s* (*stone*)
Jade *m;* (*color*) Jadegrün *n;* (*horse*)
Schindmähre *f*
jad'ed *adj* ermattet
jag [dʒæg] *s* Zacke *f;* **have a jag on**
(sl) e–n Schwips haben
jagged ['dʒægɪd] *adj* zackig, schartig
jaguar ['dʒægwar] *s* Jaguar *m*
jail [dʒel] *s* Gefängnis *n*, Untersuch-
ungsgefängnis *n;* **be in j.** sitzen ‖ *tr*
einsperren
jail'bird' *s* Knastbruder *m*
jailer ['dʒelər] *s* Gefängniswärter *m*
jalopy [dʒə'lɑpi] *s* Rumpelkasten *m*
jal'ousie win'dow ['dʒæləsi] *s* Glas-
jalousie *f*
jam [dʒæm] *s* Marmelade *f;* **be in a
jam** (coll) in der Patsche sitzen ‖ *v*
(*pret & pp* **jammed;** *ger* **jamming**)
tr (*a room*) überfüllen; (*a street*)
verstopfen; (*a finger*) quetschen;
(rad) stören; **be jammed** in einge-
zwängt sein; **jam on the brakes** auf
die Bremsen drücken; **jam s.th. into**

etw stopfen in (*acc*) ‖ *intr* (*said of
a window*) klemmen; (*said of gears*)
sich verklemmen; (*said of a gun*)
Ladehemmung haben; **jam into** sich
hineinquetschen in (*acc*)
jamb [dʒæm] *s* Pfosten *m*
jamboree [,dʒæmbə'ri] *s* Trubel *m;*
(*of scouts*) Pfadfindertreffen *n*
James [dʒemz] *s* Jakob *m*
jam'ming *s* (rad) Störung *f*
Jane [dʒen] *s* Johanna *f*
Janet ['dʒænɪt] *s* Hanna *f*
jangle ['dʒæŋgəl] *s* Rasseln *n* ‖ *tr* rasseln lassen; **j. s.o.'s nerves** j–m auf
die Nerven gehen ‖ *intr* rasseln
janitor ['dʒænɪtər] *s* Hausmeister *m*
January ['dʒænju,ɛri] *s* Januar *m*
Japan [dʒə'pæn] *s* Japan *n*
Japanese [,dʒæpə'niz] *adj* japanisch
‖ *s* Japaner –in *mf;* (*language*) Japanisch *n*
Jap'anese bee'tle *s* Japankäfer *m*
jar [dʒar] *s* Krug *m;* (*e.g., of jam*)
Glas *n;* (*jolt*) Stoß *m* ‖ *v* (*pret & pp*
jarred; *ger* **jarring**) *tr* (*jolt*) anstoßen;
(fig) erschüttern ‖ *intr* nicht harmonieren; **jar on the nerves** auf die
Nerven gehen
jargon ['dʒargən] *s* Jargon *m*
jasmine ['dʒæzmɪn] *s* Jasmin *m*
jaundice ['dʒɔndɪs] *s* Gelbsucht *f*
jaun'diced *adj* gelbsüchtig
jaunt [dʒɔnt] *s* Ausflug *m*
jaunty ['dʒɔnti] *adj* (*sprightly*) lebhaft;
(*clothes*) fesch
javelin ['dʒævəlɪn] *s* Speer *m*
jaw [dʒɔ] *s* Kiefer *m;* **the jaws of death**
die Klauen des Todes
jaw'bone' *s* Kiefer *m* ‖ *intr* (sl) sich
stark machen
jay [dʒe] *s* (orn) Häher *m*
jay'walk' *intr* verkehrswidrig die Straße
überqueren
jazz [dʒæz] *s* Jazz *m* ‖ *tr*—**j. up** (coll)
aufmöbeln
jazz' band' *s* Jazzband *f*
jazzy ['dʒæzi] *adj* bunt, grell
jealous ['dʒeləs] *adj* (*of*) eifersüchtig
(auf *acc*)
jealousy ['dʒeləsi] *s* Eifersucht *f*
jeans [dʒinz] *spl* Jeans *pl*

jeep [dʒip] s Jeep m
jeer [dʒɪr] s Hohn m || tr verhöhnen || intr höhnen; **j. at** verhöhnen
Jeffrey ['dʒɛfri] s Gottfried m
Jehovah [dʒɪ'hovə] s Jehova m
jell [dʒɛl] s Gelee n || intr gelieren; (fig) zum Klappen kommen
jellied ['dʒɛlid] adj geliert
jelly ['dʒɛli] s Gallerte f
jel'lyfish' s Qualle f; (pej) Waschlappen m
jeopardize ['dʒɛpər,daɪz] tr gefährden
jeopardy ['dʒɛpərdi] s Gefahr f
jerk [dʒʌrk] s Ruck m; (sl) Knülch m || tr ruckweise ziehen || intr zucken
jerky ['dʒʌrki] adj ruckartig
jersey ['dʒʌrzi] s (material) Jersey m; (shirt) Jersey n; (sport) Trikot n
jest [dʒɛst] s Scherz m; **in j.** scherzweise || intr scherzen
jester ['dʒɛstər] s Hofnarr m; (joker) Spaßvogel m
Jesuit ['dʒɛʒʊ·ɪt] adj Jesuiten– || s Jesuit m
Jesus ['dʒizəs] s Jesus m
jet [dʒɛt] adj Düsen– || s (stream) Strahl m; (nozzle) Düse f; (plane) Jet m, Düsenflugzeug n || v (pret & pp jetted; ger jetting) herausströmen; (aer) jetten
jet'-black' adj rabenschwarz
jet' propul'sion s Düsenantrieb m
jetsam ['dʒɛtsəm] s Seewurfgut n
jet' stream' s Strahlströmung f
jettison ['dʒɛtɪsən] s Seewurf m || tr (aer) abwerfen; (naut) über Bord werfen
jetty ['dʒɛti] s (warf) Landungsbrücke f; (breakwater) Hafendamm m
Jew [dʒu] s Jude m, Jüdin f
jewel ['dʒu·əl] s (& fig) Juwel n; (in a watch) Stein m
jew'el box' s Schmuckkästchen n
jewel(l)er ['dʒu·ələr] s Juwelier –in mf
jewelry ['dʒu·əlri] s Jewelen pl; **piece of j.** Schmuckstück n
jew'elry store' s Juweliergeschäft n
Jewish ['dʒu·ɪʃ] adj jüdisch
Jew's' harp' s Maultrommel f
jib [dʒɪb] s Ausleger m; (naut) Klüver m
jibe [dʒaɪb] intr (coll) übereinstimmen
jiffy ['dʒɪfi] s—**in a j.** im Nu
jig [dʒɪg] s (dance) Gigue f; (tool) Spannvorrichtung f; **the jig is up** (sl) das Spiel ist aus
jigger ['dʒɪgər] s Schnapsglas n; (gadget) Dingsbums n; (naut) Besan m
jiggle ['dʒɪgəl] tr & intr rütteln
jig'saw' s Laubsäge f
jig'saw puz'zle s Puzzlespiel n
jilt [dʒɪlt] tr (a girl) sitzenlassen; (a boy) den Laufpaß geben (dat)
jim·my ['dʒɪmi] s Brecheisen n || v (pret & pp –mied) tr mit dem Brecheisen aufbrechen
jingle ['dʒɪŋgəl] s (of coins) Klimpern n; (bell) Schelle f; (verse) Verseklingel n || tr klimpern mit || intr klimpern; (said of verses) klingeln
jin·go ['dʒɪŋgo] s (–goes) Chauvinist –in mf; **by j.!** alle Wetter!

jinx [dʒɪŋks] s Unglücksrabe m || tr Pech bringen (dat); **be jinxed** vom Pech verfolgt sein
jitters ['dʒɪtərz] spl—**have the j.** wahnsinnig nervös sein; **give s.o. the j.** j-n wahnsinnig nervös machen
jittery ['dʒɪtəri] adj durchgedreht
Joan [dʒon] s Johanna f
job [dʒab] s (employment) Job m; (task, responsibility) Aufgabe f; **bad job** Machwerk n; **do a good job** gute Arbeit leisten; **fall down on the job** seine Pflicht nicht erfüllen; **know one's job** seine Sache verstehen; **on the job** bei der Arbeit; (fig) auf Draht; **out of a job** arbeitslos
jobber ['dʒabər] s (middleman) Zwischenhändler –in mf; (pieceworker) Akkordarbeiter –in mf
job'hold'er s Stelleninhaber –in mf
jobless ['dʒablɪs] adj stellungslos
jockey ['dʒaki] s Jockei m || tr manövrieren
jog [dʒag] s Dauerlauf m; (of a horse) Trott m || v (pret & pp jogged; ger jogging) tr (shake) rütteln; (the memory) auffrischen || intr trotten; (for exercise) langsam rennen, Dauerlauf machen
John [dʒan] s Johann m; **john** (sl) Klo n
Johnny ['dʒani] s Hans m
John'ny-come'-late'ly s Neuling m, Nachzügler m
join [dʒɔɪn] tr verbinden; (a club) beitreten (dat); (a person) sich anschließen (dat); (two parts) zusammenfügen; **j. the army** zum Militär gehen || intr sich verbinden; **j. in** sich beteiligen an (dat); **j. up** (mil) einrücken
joiner ['dʒɔɪnər] s (coll) Vereinsmeier m; (carp) Tischler m
joint [dʒɔɪnt] adj (account, venture) gemeinschaftlich; (return) gemeinsam; (committee) gemischt; (heir, owner) Mit– || s Verbindungspunkt m; (in plumbing) Naht f; (sl) Bumslokal n; (anat, bot, mach) Gelenk n; (carp) Fuge f; (culin) Bratenstück n; **throw out of j.** auskugeln
jointly ['dʒɔɪntli] adv gemeinsam
joint'-stock' com'pany s Aktiengesellschaft f
joist [dʒɔɪst] s Tragbalken m
joke [dʒok] s Witz m; **he can't take a j.** er versteht keinen Spaß; **make a j. of** ins Lächerliche ziehen; **play a j. on** e-n Streich spielen (dat) || intr Spaß machen; **j. about** witzeln über (acc); **j. around** schäkern; **joking aside** Spaß beiseite
joker ['dʒokər] s Spaßvogel m; (pej) Knülch m; (cards) Joker m
jolly ['dʒali] adj lustig
jolt [dʒolt] s Stoß m || tr stoßen || intr holpern; **j. along** dahinholpern
Jordan ['dʒɔrdən] s (country) Jordanien n; (river) Jordan m
josh [dʒaʃ] tr & intr hänseln
jostle ['dʒasəl] tr & intr drängeln
jot [dʒat] s—**not a jot** kein Jota || v

(*pret & pp* **jotted**; *ger* **jotting**) *tr—*
jot down notieren
journal ['dʒʌrnəl] *s (daily record)* Tagebuch *n; (magazine)* Zeitschrift *f*
journalism ['dʒʌrnə‚lɪzəm] *s* Journalismus *m*, Zeitungswesen *n*
journalist ['dʒʌrnəlɪst] *s* Journalist –in *mf*
journey ['dʒʌrni] *s* Reise *f;* **go on a j.** verreisen || *intr* reisen
jour'ney·man *adj* tüchtig || *s* (**-men**) Geselle *m*
joust [dʒaust] *s* Tjost *f* || *intr* turnieren
jovial ['dʒovɪ·əl] *adj* jovial
jowls [dʒaulz] *spl* Hängebacken *pl*
joy [dʒɔɪ] *s* Freude *f*
joyful ['dʒɔɪfəl] *adj* froh, freudig
joyless ['dʒɔɪlɪs] *adj* freudlos
joy' ride' *s* (coll) Schwarzfahrt *f*
joy' stick' *s* (aer) Steuerknüppel *m*
Jr. *abbr* (**Junior**) jr., jun.
jubilant ['dʒubɪlənt] *adj* frohlockend
jubilation [‚dʒubɪ'leʃən] *s* Jubel *m*
jubilee ['dʒubɪ‚li] *s* Jubiläum *n*
Judaea [dʒu'di·ə] *s* Judäa *n*
Judaic [dʒu'de·ɪk] *adj* jüdisch
Judaism ['dʒudə‚ɪzəm] *s* Judaismus *m*
judge [dʒʌdʒ] *s (in a competition)* Preisrichter –in *mf;* (box) Punktrichter *m;* (jur) Richter –in *mf* || *tr* (**by**) beurteilen (nach); *(distances)* abschätzen; (jur) richten || *intr* urteilen; (jur) richten; **judging by his words** seinen Worten nach zu urteilen
judge' ad'vocate *s* Kriegsgerichtsrat *m*
judgment ['dʒʌdʒmənt] *s (& jur)* Urteil *n;* **in my j.** meines Erachtens; **show good j.** ein gutes Urteilsvermögen haben; **sit in j. over** zu Gericht sitzen über *(acc)*
Judg'ment Day' *s* Tag *m* des Gerichts
judicial [dʒu'dɪʃəl] *adj* Rechts–
judiciary [dʒu'dɪʃɪ‚ɛri] *adj* richterlich || *s (branch)* richterliche Gewalt *f; (judges)* Richterstand *m*
judicious [dʒu'dɪʃəs] *adj* klug
judo ['dʒudo] *s* Judo *n*
jug [dʒʌg] *s* Krug *m; (jail)* Kittchen *n*
juggle ['dʒʌgəl] *tr* jonglieren; *(accounts)* frisieren || *intr* jonglieren
juggler ['dʒʌglər] *s* Gaukler –in *mf*
Jugoslav ['jugo‚slav] *adj* jugoslawisch || *s* Jugoslawe *m*, Jugoslawin *f*
Jugoslavia [‚jugo'slavɪ·ə] *s* Jugoslawien *n*
jug'ular vein' ['dʒʌgjələr] *s* Halsader *f*
juice [dʒus] *s* Saft *m*
juicy ['dʒusi] *adj* saftig
jukebox ['dʒuk‚baks] *s* Musikautomat *m*
July [dʒu'laɪ] *s* Juli *m*
jumble ['dʒʌmbəl] *s* Wust *m* || *tr* durcheinanderwerfen
jumbo ['dʒʌmbo] *adj* Riesen–
jump [dʒʌmp] *s* Sprung *m;* (aer) Absprung *m;* **get the j. on** zuvorkommen *(dat)* || *tr* überspringen; *(attack)* überfallen; *(a hurdle)* nehmen; *(in*

checkers) schlagen; **j. bail** die Kaution verfallen lassen; **j. channels** den amtlichen Weg nicht einhalten; **j. rope** seilspringen; **j. ship** vom Schiff weglaufen; **j. the gun** übereilt handeln; (sport) zu früh starten; **j. the track** entgleisen || *intr* springen; *(be startled)* auffahren; **j. at** *(a chance)* stürzen auf *(acc);* **j. down s.o.'s throat** j–n anfahren
jump' ball' *s* (basketball) Sprungball *m*
jumper ['dʒʌmpər] *s (dress)* Jumper *m;* (elec) Kurzschlußbrücke *f*
jump'-off' *s* Beginn *m;* (sport) Start *m*
jump' rope' *s* Springseil *n*
jumpy ['dʒʌmpi] *adj* unruhig, nervös
junction ['dʒʌŋkʃən] *s* Verbindung *f; (of roads, rail lines)* Knotenpunkt *m*
juncture ['dʒʌŋktʃər] *s* Verbindungsstelle *f;* **at this j.** in diesem Augenblick
June [dʒun] *s* Juni *m*
June' bug' *s* Maikäfer *m*
jungle ['dʒʌŋgəl] *s* Dschungel *m, n & f*
junior ['dʒunjər] *adj* jünger || *s* Student –in *mf* im dritten Studienjahr
juniper ['dʒunɪpər] *s* Wacholder *m*
junk [dʒʌŋk] *s* Altwaren *pl; (scrap iron)* Schrott *m; (useless stuff)* Plunder *m;* (naut) Dschunke *f*
junket ['dʒʌŋkɪt] *s* Vergnügungsreise *f* auf öffentliche Kosten
junk' mail' *s* Wurfsendung *f*
junk'yard' *s* Schrottplatz *m*
junta ['hʌntə], ['dʒʌntə] *s* Junta *f*
jurisdiction [‚dʒurɪs'dɪkʃən] *s* Zuständigkeit *f;* **have j. over** zuständig sein für
jurisprudence [‚dʒurɪs'prudəns] *s* Rechtswissenschaft *f*
jurist ['dʒurɪst] *s* Jurist –in *mf*
juror ['dʒurər] *s* Geschworene *mf*
jury ['dʒuri] *s* Geschworene *pl*
ju'ry box' *s* Geschworenenbank *f*
ju'ry tri'al *s* Schwurgerichtsverfahren *n*
just [dʒʌst] *adj* gerecht || *adv* gerade; *(only)* nur; *(simply)* einfach
justice ['dʒʌstɪs] *s* Gerechtigkeit *f; (of a claim)* Berechtigung *f; (judge)* Richter *m;* **bring to j.** vor Gericht bringen; **do j. to** *(a meal)* wacker zusprechen *(dat); (said of a picture)* gerecht werden *(dat)*
jus'tice of the peace' *s* Friedensrichter *m*
justification [‚dʒʌstɪfɪ'keʃən] *s* Rechtfertigung *f*
justi·fy ['dʒʌstɪ‚faɪ] *v (pret & pp* **-fied**) *tr* rechtfertigen
justly ['dʒʌstli] *adv* mit Recht
jut [dʒʌt] *v (pret & pp* **jutted**; *ger* **jutting**) *intr—***jut out** hervorragen
juvenile ['dʒuvə‚naɪl] *adj (books, court)* Jugend–; *(childish)* unreif
ju'venile delin'quency *s* Jugendkriminalität *f*
ju'venile delin'quent *s* jugendlicher Verbrecher *m*
juxtapose [‚dʒʌkstə'poz] *tr* nebeneinanderstellen

K

K, k [ke] *s* elfter Buchstabe des englischen Alphabets
kale [kel] *s* Grünkohl *m*
kaleidoscopic [kə͵laɪdə'skɑpɪk] *adj* (& fig) kaleidoskopisch
kangaroo [͵kæŋgə'ru] *s* Känguruh *n*
kangaroo court' *s* Scheingericht *n*
kashmir ['kaeʃmɪr] *s* (tex) Kaschmir *m*
kayo ['ke'o] *s* K.o. *m* ‖ *tr* k.o. schlagen
keel [kil] *s* Kiel *m;* **on an even k.** (fig) gleichmäßig ‖ *intr*—**k. over** umkippen; (naut) kentern
keen [kin] *adj* (*sharp*) scharf; (*interest*) lebhaft; **k. on** scharf auf (*acc*)
keenness ['kinnɪs] *s* Schärfe *f*
keep [kip] *s* Unterhalt *m;* (*of a castle*) Bergfried *m;* **for keeps** (*forever*) für immer; (*seriously*) im Ernst ‖ *v* (*pret & pp* **kept** [kɛpt]) *tr* (*retain*) behalten; (*detain*) aufhalten; (*save for s.o.*) aufbewahren; (*a secret*) bewahren; (*a promise*) (ein)halten; (*animals*) halten; (*books*) (acct) führen; **be kept in school** nachsitzen müssen; **k. at arm's length** vom Leibe halten; **k. at bay** sich erwehren (*genit*); **k. away** fernhalten; **k. back** zurückhalten; (*retain*) zurückbehalten; **k.** (*s.o.*) **company** Gesellschaft leisten (*dat*); **k. down** (*one's head*) niederhalten; (*one's voice*) verhalten; (*prices*) niedrig halten; **k. from** abhalten von; **k. from** (*ger*) daran hindern zu (*inf*); **k. going** im Gange halten; **k. good time** gut gehen; **k. guard** Wache halten; **k. house** den Haushalt führen; **k. in good condition** instand halten; **k. in mind** sich [*dat*] merken; **k. it up!** nur so weiter; **k. on** (*a garment*) anbehalten; (*a hat*) aufbehalten; **k. oneself from** (*ger*) es fertigbringen nicht zu (*inf*); **k. one's temper** sich beherrschen; **k. out** ausschließen; (*light*) nicht durchlassen; (*rain*) abhalten; **k. posted** auf dem laufenden halten; **k. score** die Punktliste führen; **k. secret** geheimhalten; **k. step** Tritt halten; **k. s.th. from s.o.** j-m etw verschweigen; **k. track of** sich [*dat*] merken; **k. under wraps** (coll) totschweigen; **k. up** instand halten; (*appearances*) wahren; (*correspondence*) unterhalten; **k. up the good work!** arbeiten Sie weiter so gut!; **k. waiting** warten lassen; **k. warm** warm halten; **k. your shirt on!** (coll) daß du die Nase im Gesicht behältst! ‖ *intr* (*said of food*) sich halten; **k. at** beharren bei; **k. at it!** bleib dabei!; **k. away** sich fernhalten; **k. cool** (fig) die Nerven behalten; **k. cool!** ruhig Blut!; **k. from** sich enthalten (*genit*); **k. from** (*ger*) es unterlassen zu (*inf*); **k. from laughing** sich das Lachen verkneifen;

k. going weitermachen; **k. moving** weitergehen; **k. on** (*ger*) weiter (*inf*), e.g., **k. on driving** weiterfahren; **k. out!** Eintritt verboten! **k. out of sich** fernhalten von; **k. quiet** sich ruhig verhalten; **k. quiet!** sei still!; **k. to the right** sich rechts halten; **k. up with** (*work*) nachkommen mit; **k. up with the Joneses** mit den Nachbarn Schritt halten; **k. within** bleiben innerhalb (*genit*)
keeper ['kipər] *s* (*of animals*) Halter –in *mf;* (*at a zoo*) Tierwärter –in *mf;* (*watchman*) Wächter *m*
keep'ing *s* Verwahrung *f;* **in k. with** in Einklang mit
keep'sake' *s* Andenken *n*
keg [kɛg] *s* Faß *n*
ken [kɛn] *s* Gesichtskreis *m*
kennel ['kɛnəl] *s* Hundezwinger *m*
kep·i ['kepi], ['kɛpi] *s* (–is) Kappi *n*
kerchief ['kʌrtʃɪf] *s* (*for the head*) Kopftuch *n;* (*for the neck*) Halstuch *n*
kernel ['kʌrnəl] *s* (*of fruit*) Kern *m;* (*of grain*) Korn *n;* (fig) Kern *m*
kerosene [͵kɛrə'sin] *s* Petroleum *n*
kerplunk [kər'plʌŋk] *interj* bums!
ketchup ['kɛtʃəp] *s* Ketchup *m & n*
kettle ['kɛtəl] *s* Kessel *m*
ket'tledrum' *s* Kesselpauke *f*
key [ki] *s* (*ring, hole, industry, position*) Schlüssel– ‖ *s* (& fig) Schlüssel *m;* (*of a map*) Zeichenerklärung *f;* (*of a typewriter, piano, organ*) Taste *f;* (*of windinstrument*) Klappe *f;* (*reef*) Riff *n;* (*low island*) Insel *f;* (mus) Tonart *f;* **key of C major** C-dur; **off key** falsch ‖ *tr* (mach) festkeilen
key'board' *s* Tastatur *f*
keyed *adj*—**k. to** gestimmt auf (*acc*); **k. up** in Hochspannung
key' man' *s* Schlüsselfigur *f*
key'note *s* Grundgedanke *m;* (mus) Tonika *f*
key'note address' *s* programmatische Rede *f*
keynoter ['ki ͵notər] *s* Programmatiker –in *mf*
keypuncher ['ki ͵pʌntʃər] *s* Locher –in *mf*
key'stone' *s* Schlußstein *m;* (fig) Grundlage *f*
key' word' *s* Stichwort *n*
kha·ki ['kæki] *adj* Khaki– ‖ *s* (–kis) Khaki *m;* **khakis** Khakiuniform *f*
kibitz ['kɪbɪts] *intr* (coll) kiebitzen
kibitzer ['kɪbɪtsər] *s* (coll) Kiebitz *m*
kick [kɪk] *s* Fußtritt *m;* (*of a rifle*) Rückstoß *m;* (*of a horse*) Schlag *m;* (*final spurt*) (sport) Endspurt *m;* **give s.o. a k.** j-m e-n Fußtritt versetzen; **I get a (great) k. out of him** er macht mir (riesigen) Spaß ‖ *tr* treten, stoßen; (fb) kicken; **be kicked upstairs** (coll) die Treppe hinauffallen;

I could k. myself ich könnte mich ohrfeigen; **k. a goal** (fb) ein Tor schießen; **k.** (*s.o.*) **around** schlecht behandeln; (*e.g., an idea*) beschwatzen; **k. in** (*money*) beisteuern; **k. open** (*a door*) aufstoßen; **k. out** (coll) rausschmeißen; **k. s.o. in the shins** j–n gegen das Schienbein treten; **k. the bucket** (sl) krepieren; **k. up a storm** Krach schlagen || *intr* (*said of a gun*) stoßen; (*said of a horse*) ausschlagen; (*complain*) (*about*) meckern (über *acc*); **k. around Europe** in Europa herumbummeln; **k. off** (fb) anspielen

kick'back' *s* Schmiergeld *n*
kick'off' *s* (*commencement*) Beginn *m;* (fb) Anstoß *m*
kid [kɪd] *s* Zicklein *n;* (coll) Kind *n* || *v* (*pret & pp* **kidded;** *ger* **kidding**) *tr* necken || *intr* scherzen; **no kidding!** mach keine Witze!
kid' gloves' *spl* Glacéhandschuhe *pl;* **handle with k.** (fig) mit Glacéhandschuhen anfassen
kid'nap' *v* (*pret & pp* **–nap(p)ed;** *ger* **–nap(p)ing**) *tr* kidnappen, entführen
kidnap(p)er ['kɪd,næpər] *s* Kidnapper *m*
kid'nap(p)ing *s* Kidnapping *s*
kidney ['kɪdni] *s* Niere *f*
kid'ney bean' *s* rote Bohne *f*
kid'ney-shaped' *adj* nierenförmig
kid'ney stone' *s* Nierenstein *m*
kid'ney trans'plant *s* Nierenverpflanzung *f;* (*transplanted kidney*) verpflanzte Niere *f*
kid'ney trou'ble *s* Nierenleiden *n*
kid' stuff' *s* (coll) Kinderei *f*
kill [kɪl] *s* (aer) Abschuß *m;* (hunt) Jagdbeute *f;* (nav) Versenkung *f* || *tr* töten; (*murder*) ermorden, killen; (*plants*) zum Absterben bringen; (*time*) totschlagen; (*a proposal, plans, competition*) zu Fall bringen; (*the motor*) abwürgen; (*the ball*) stark schlagen; (*a bottle*) austrinken; **be killed in action** (im Felde) fallen; **it won't k. you** (coll) es wird dich nicht umbringen; **k. off** abschlachten; **k. oneself** sich umbringen; **k. two birds with one stone** zwei Fliegen mit e–r Klappe schlagen; **she is dressed to k.** sie ist totschick angezogen
killer ['kɪlər] *s* Totschläger –in *mf,* Killer *m*
kill'er whale' *s* Schwertwal *m*
kill'ing *s* Tötung *f;* **make a k.** e–n unerhofften Gewinn erzielen
kill'joy' *s* Spaßverderber *m*
kiln ['kɪl(n)] *s* Brennofen *m*
kil·o ['kɪlo], ['kilo] *s* (**–os**) Kilo *n*
kilocycle ['kɪlə,saɪkəl] *s* Kilohertz *n*
kilogram ['kɪlə,græm] *s* Kilogramm *n*
kilohertz ['kɪlə,hɑrts] *s* Kilohertz *n*
kilometer [kɪ'lɑmɪtər] *s* Kilometer *m;* **kilometers per hour** Stundenkilometer *pl*
kilowatt ['kɪlə,wɑt] *s* Kilowatt *n*
kil'owatt'-hour' *s* Kilowattstunde *f*
kilt [kɪlt] *s* Kilt *m*

kilter ['kɪltər] *s*—**out of k.** nicht in Ordnung
kimo·no [kɪ'mono] *s* (**–nos**) Kimono *m*
kin [kɪn] *s* Sippe *f;* **the next of kin** die nächsten Angehörigen
kind [kaɪnd] *adj* liebenswürdig; **(to)** gütig (zu), freundlich (zu); **would you be so k. as to** (*inf*)? würden Sie so gefällig sein zu (*inf*)?; **with k. regards** mit freundlichen Grüßen || *s* Art *f,* Sorte *f;* **all kinds of** allerlei; **another k. of** ein anderer; **any k. of** irgendwelcher; **every k. of** jede Art von; **in. k.** (fig) auf gleiche Weise; **k. of** (coll) etwas; **nothing of the k.** nichts dergleichen; **that k. of** derartig; **two (three) kinds of** zweierlei (dreierlei); **what k. of** was für ein
kindergarten ['kɪndər,gɑrtən] *s* Vorschule *f,* Vorschuljahr *n*
kind'-heart'ed *adj* gutmütig
kindle ['kɪndəl] *tr* anzünden; (fig) erwecken || *intr* sich entzünden
kindling ['kɪndlɪŋ] *s* Entzündung *f;* (*wood*) Kleinholz *n*
kindly ['kaɪndli] *adj* gütig, freundlich || *adv* freundlich; (*please*) bitte
kindness ['kaɪndnɪs] *s* Freundlichkeit *f;* (*deed*) Gefälligkeit *f*
kindred ['kɪndrɪd] *adj* verwandtschaftlich; (fig) verwandt || *s* Verwandtschaft *f*
kinescope ['kɪnɪ,skop] *s* (trademark) Fernsehempfangsröhre *f*
kinetic [kɪ'nɛtɪk] *adj* kinetisch || **kinetics** *s* Kinetik *f*
king [kɪŋ] *s* König *m;* (cards, chess) König *m;* (checkers) Dame *f*
kingdom ['kɪŋdəm] *s* Königreich *n;* (*of animals, etc.*) Reich *n;* **k. of heaven** Himmelreich *n*
king'fish'er *s* Königsfischer *m*
kingly ['kɪŋli] *adj* königlich
king'pin' *s* (coll) Boß *m;* (bowling) König *m*
king'ship' *s* Königtum *n*
king'-size' *adj* übergroß
kink [kɪŋk] *s* (*in a wire*) Knick *m;* (*in the hair*) Kräuselung *f;* (*in a muscle*) Muskelkrampf *m;* (*flaw*) Fehler *m*
kinky ['kɪŋki] *adj* gekräuselt
kin'ship' *s* Verwandtschaft *f*
kins'man *s* (**–men**) Blutsverwandte *m*
kins'wom'an *s* (**–wom'en**) Blutsverwandte *f*
kipper ['kɪpər] *s* Räucherhering *m* || *tr* einsalzen und räuchern
kiss [kɪs] *s* Kuß *m* || *tr & intr* küssen
kisser ['kɪsər] *s* (sl) Fresse *f*
kit [kɪt] *s* (*equipment*) Ausrüstung *f;* (*tool kit*) Werkzeugkasten *m;* (*for models*) Modellsatz *m;* (*e.g., for a convention*) Mappe *f;* **the whole kit and caboodle** (*things*) der ganze Kram; (*persons*) die ganze Sippschaft
kitchen ['kɪtʃən] *s* Küche *f*
kitchenette [,kɪtʃə'nɛt] *s* Kochnische *f*
kit'chen knife' *s* Küchenmesser *n*
kit'chen police' *s* (mil) Küchendienst *m*
kit'chen range' *s* Herd *m,* Kochherd *m*

kit'chen sink' s Ausguß m
kit'chenware' s Küchengeschirr n
kite [kaɪt] s Drachen m; (orn) Weih m; **fly a k.** e–n Drachen steigen lassen; **go fly a k.!** (coll) scher dich zum Kuckuck!
kith' and kin' [kɪθ] spl Freunde and Verwandte pl
kitten ['kɪtən] s Kätzchen n
kitty ['kɪti] s Kätzchen n; (cards) gemeinsame Kasse f; **Kitty** Käthchen n
kleptomaniac [ˌkleptə'menɪˌæk] s Kleptomane m, Kleptomanin f
knack [næk] s—**have a k. for** Talent haben für; **have the k. of it** den Griff heraus haben
knapsack ['næpˌsæk] s Rucksack m
knave [nev] s Schelm m; (cards) Bube m
knavery ['nevəri] s Schelmenstreich m
knead [nid] tr kneten
knead'ing trough' s Teigmulde f
knee [ni] s Knie n; **bring s.o. to his knees** j–n auf die Knie zwingen; **go down on one's knees** niederknien; **on bended knees** kniefällig
knee' bend' s Kniebeuge f
knee' breech'es spl Kniehose f
knee'cap' s Kniescheibe f
knee'-deep' adj knietief
knee'-high' adj kniehoch
knee' jerk' s Patellarreflex m
kneel [nil] v (pret & pp **knelt** [nɛlt] & **kneeled**) intr knien
knee'-length' adj kniefreit
knee'pad' s (sport) Knieschützer m
knee'pan' s Kniescheibe f
knee' swell' s (of organ) Knieschweller m
knell [nɛl] s Totengeläute n
knickers ['nɪkərz] spl Knickerbockerhosen pl
knicknack ['nɪkˌnæk] s Nippsache f
knife [naɪf] s (knives [naɪvz]) Messer n || tr erstechen
knife' sharp'ener s Messerschleifer m
knife' switch' s (elec) Messerschalter m
knight [naɪt] s Ritter m; (chess) Springer m || tr zum Ritter schlagen
knight'hood' s Ritterschaft f
knightly ['naɪtli] adj ritterlich
knit [nɪt] v (pret & pp **knitted** & **knit;** ger **knitting**) tr stricken; **k. one's brows** die Brauen runzeln || intr stricken; (said of bones) zusammenheilen
knit' goods' spl Trikotwaren pl
knit'ted dress' s Strickkleid n
knit'ting s (act) Strickerei f; (materials) Strickzeug n
knit'ting machine' s Strickmaschine f
knit'ting nee'dle s Stricknadel f
knit'ting yarn' s Strickgarn n
knit'wear' s Strickwaren pl
knob [nab] s (of a door) Drücker m; (lump) Auswuchs m; (in wood) Knorren m; (of a radio) Knopf m
knock [nak] s (& aut) Klopfen n || tr (criticize) tadeln; **k. a hole through** durchbrechen; **k. around** herumstoßen; (mistreat) unsanft behandeln;

k. down niederschlagen; (with a car) umfahren; (trees) umbrechen; (at auctions) zuschlagen; **k. it off!** (sl) hör mal auf!; **k. oneself out over** sich [dat] die Zähne ausbeißen an (dat); **k. one's head against the wall** mit dem Kopf gegen die Wand rennen; **k. out** ausschlagen; (coll) strapazieren; (a tank) abschießen; (box) k.o. schlagen; **k. over** umwerfen; **k. together** (build hurriedly) schnell zusammenhauen; **k. to the ground** zu Boden schlagen; **k. up a girl** (sl) e–m Mädchen ein Kind anhängen || intr (an)klopfen; (aut) klopfen; **k. about** herumbummeln; **k. against** stoßen an (acc); **k. off** (from) (coll) aufhören (mit)
knock'down' s (box) Niederschlag m
knocker ['nakər] s Türklopfer m; **knockers** (sl) Brüste pl
knock-kneed ['nakˌnid] adj x-beinig
knock'-knees' spl X-beine pl
knock'out' s (woman) (coll) Blitzmädel n; (box) Knockout m
knock'out drops' spl Betäubungsmittel n
knock'-out punch' s K.o.-Schlag m
knoll [nol] s Hügel m
knot [nat] s Knoten m; (in wood) Knorren m; (of people) Gruppe f; (naut) Knoten m; **tie a k.** e–n Knoten machen; **tie the k.** (coll) sich verheiraten || tr e–n Knoten machen in (acc); (two ends) zusammenknoten
knot'hole' s Astloch n
knotty ['nati] adj knorrig; (problem) knifflig
know [no] s—**be in the k.** Bescheid wissen || v (pret **knew** [n(j)u]; pp **known**) tr (facts) wissen; (be familiar with) kennen; (a language) können; **come to k.** erfahren; **get to k.** kennenlernen; **known** bekannt; **k. one's way around** sich auskennen; **k. the ropes** (coll) Bescheid wissen; **k. what's what** (coll) den Rummel kennen || intr wissen; **he ought to k. better** er sollte mehr Verstand haben; **k. about** wissen über (acc); **k. of** wissen von; **not that I k. of** (coll) nicht, daß ich wüßte; **you k.** (coll) wissen Sie
knowable ['no·əbəl] adj kenntlich
know'-how' s Sachkenntnis f
know'ing adj (glance) vielsagend
knowingly ['no·ɪŋli] adv wissentlich; (intentionally) absichtlich
know'-it-all' s Naseweis m
knowledge ['nalɪdʒ] s Wissen n, Kenntnisse pl; (information) (of) Kenntnis f (von); **basic k. of** Grundkenntnisse pl in (dat); **come to s.o.'s k.** j–m zur Kenntnis kommen; **to my k.** soweit (or soviel) ich weiß; **to the best of my k.** nach bestem Wissen; **without my k.** ohne mein Mitwissen; **working k. of** praktisch verwertbare Kenntnisse pl (genit)
knowledgeable ['nalɪdʒəbəl] adj kenntnisreich
known [non] adj bekannt; **become k.**

kundwerden; **k. all over town** stadtbekannt; **make k.** bekanntgeben
know'-noth'ing s Nichtswisser *m*
knuckle ['nʌkəl] s Knöchel *m*, Fingerknöchel *m;* (mach) Gelenkstück *n;* **k. of ham** Eisbein *n* || *intr*—**k. down to work** sich ernsthaft an die Arbeit machen; **k. under** klein beigeben
k.o. ['ke'o] s K.o. *m* || *tr* k.o.-schlagen
Koran [ko'ræn] s Koran *m*
Korea [ko'ri·ə] s Korea *n*

Korean [ko'ri·ən] *adj* koreanisch || *s* Koreaner –in *mf;* (*language*) Koreanisch *n*
kosher ['koʃər] *adj* (& coll) koscher
kowtow ['kau'tau] *intr* e–n Kotau machen; **k. to** kriechen vor (*dat*)
K.P. ['ke'pi] s (**kitchen police**) (mil) Küchendienst *m*
Kremlin ['kremlɪn] s Kreml *m*
kudos ['k(i)udas] s (coll) Ruhm *m*, Renommee *n*

L

L, l [ɛl] s zwölfter Buchstabe des englischen Alphabets
lab [læb] s (coll) Labor *n*
la·bel ['lɛbəl] s Etikett *n;* (*brand*) Marke *f;* (fig) Bezeichnung *f* || *v* (*pret & pp* –bel[l]ed; *ger* —bel[l]ing) *tr* etikettieren; (fig) bezeichnen
labial ['lebɪ·əl] *adj* Lippen– || *s* Lippenlaut *m*, Labial *m*
labor ['lebər] *adj* Arbeits–, Arbeiter– || *s* Arbeit *f;* (*toil*) Mühe *f;* **be in l.** in den Wehen liegen || *tr* (*a point*) ausführlich eingehen auf (*acc*) || *intr* sich abmühen; (**at**) arbeiten (an *dat*); (*exert oneself*) sich anstrengen; (*said of a ship*) stampfen; **l. under** zu leiden haben unter (*dat*)
la'bor and man'agement *spl* Arbeitnehmer und Arbeitgeber *pl*
laboratory ['læbərə,tori] s Laboratorium *n*
lab'oratory techni'cian s Laborant –in *mf*
la'bor camp' s Zwangsarbeitslager *n*
la'bor con'tract s Tarifvertrag *m*
la'bor dis'pute s Arbeitsstreitigkeit *f*
la'bored *adj* (e.g., *breathing*) mühsam; (*style*) gezwungen
laborer ['lebərər] s Arbeiter –in *mf;* (*unskilled*) Hilfsarbeiter –in *mf*
la'bor force' s Arbeitskräfte *pl*
laborious [lə'borɪ·əs] *adj* mühsam, schwierig
la'bor law' s Arbeitsrecht *n*
la'bor lead'er s Arbeiterführer –in *mf*
la'bor mar'ket s Arbeitsmarkt *m*
la'bor move'ment s Arbeiterbewegung *f*
la'bor pains' *spl* Geburtswehen *pl*
la'bor-sav'ing *adj* arbeitssparend; **l. device** Hilfsgerät *n*
la'bor short'age s Mangel *m* an Arbeitskräften
la'bor supply' s Arbeitsangebot *n*
la'bor un'ion s Gewerkschaft *f*
laburnum [lə'bʌrnəm] s Goldregen *m*
labyrinth ['læbɪrɪnθ] s Labyrinth *n*
lace [les] *adj* (*collar*, *dress*) Spitzen– || *s* Spitze *f;* (*shoestring*) Schnürsenkel *m* || *tr* (e.g., *shoes*) schnüren; (*braid*) flechten; (*drinks*) (coll) mit e–m Schuß Branntwein versetzen; (*beat*) (coll) prügeln; **l. up** zuschnüren

lacerate ['læsə,ret] *tr* zerfleischen
laceration [,læsə'reʃən] s Fleischwunde *f*
lace' **trim'ming** s Spitzenbesatz *m*
lace'work' s Spitzenarbeit *f*
lachrymose ['lækrɪ,mos] *adj* tränenreich
lac'ing s Schnürung *f;* (coll) Prügel *pl*
lack [læk] s (**of**) Mangel *m* (an *dat*); **for l. of** aus Mangel an (*dat*); **l. of space** Raummangel *m;* **l. of time** Zeitmangel *m* || *tr*—**I l. es** mangelt mir an (*dat*) || *intr*—**be lacking** fehlen; **he is lacking in courage** ihm fehlt der Mut
lackadaisical [,lækə'dezɪkəl] *adj* teilnahmslos, gleichgültig
lackey ['læki] s Lakai *m*
lack'ing *prep* mangels (*genit*)
lack'lus'ter *adj* glanzlos
laconic [lə'kanɪk] *adj* lakonisch
lacquer ['lækər] s Lack *m* || *tr* lackieren
lac'quer ware' s Lackwaren *pl*
lacrosse [lə'krɔs] s Lacrosse *n*
lacu·na [lə'kjunə] s (**–nas** & **–nae** [ni]) Lücke *f*, Lakune *f*
lacy ['lesi] *adj* spitzenartig
lad [læd] s Bube *m*
la'dies' man' s Weiberheld *m*, Salonlöwe *m*
la'dies' room' s Damentoilette *f*
ladle ['ledəl] s Schöpflöffel *m* || *tr* ausschöpfen
lady ['ledi] s Dame *f;* **ladies and gentlemen** meine Damen und Herren!
la'dybird', la'dybug' s Marienkäfer *m*
la'dy compan'ion s Gesellschaftsdame *f*
la'dyfin'ger s Löffelbiskuit *m & n*
la'dy-in-wait'ing s (**ladies-in-waiting**) Hofdame *f*
la'dy-kil'ler s Schwerenöter *m*
la'dylike' *adj* damenhaft
la'dylove' s Geliebte *f*
la'dy of the house' s Hausherrin *f*
la'dy's maid' s Zofe *f*
la'dy's man' s var of **ladies' man**
lag [læg] s Zurückbleiben *n;* (aer) Rücktrift *f;* (phys) Verzögerung *f* || *v* (*pret & pp* lagged; *ger* lagging) *intr* (**behind**) zurückbleiben (hinter *dat*)
la'ger beer' ['lagər] s Lagerbier *n*
laggard ['lægərd] s Nachzügler *m*

lagoon [lə'guːn] s Lagune f
laid' up' adj (with) bettlägerig (infolge von); **be l. in bed** auf der Nase liegen
lair [lɛr] s Höhle f, Lager n
laity ['leˑɪti] s Laien pl
lake [lek] s See m
Lake' Con'stance ['kɑnstəns] s der Bodensee
lamb [læm] s Lamm n; (culin) Lammfleisch n
lambaste [læm'best] tr (berate) (coll) herunterputzen; (beat) (coll) verdreschen
lamb' chop' s Hammelrippchen n
lambkin ['læmkɪn] s Lammfell n
lame [lem] adj (person, leg; excuse) lahm; **be l. in one leg** auf e-m Bein lahm sein || tr lähmen
lament [lə'mɛnt] s Jammer m; (dirge) Klagelied n || tr beklagen || intr wehklagen
lamentable ['læməntəbəl] adj beklagenswert; (pej) jämmerlich
lamentation [ˌlæmə'teʃən] s Wehklage f
laminate ['læmɪˌnet] tr schichten
lamp [læmp] s Lampe f
lamp' chim'ney s Lampenzylinder m
lamp'light' s Lampenlicht n
lamp'light'er s Laternenanzünder m
lampoon [læm'pun] s Schmähschrift f || tr mit e-r Schmähschrift verspotten
lamp'post' s Laternenpfahl m
lamp'shade' s Lampenschirm m
lance [læns] s Lanze f; (surg) Lanzette f || tr (surg) aufstechen
lance' cor'poral s (Brit) Hauptgefreite m
lancet ['lænsɪt] s Lanzette f
land [lænd] s (dry land; country) Land n; (ground) Boden m; **by l.** zu Lande || tr (a plane, troops, punch) landen; (a ship, fish) an Land bringen; (a job) (coll) kriegen; **l. s.o. in trouble** j-n in Schwierigkeiten bringen || intr (aer, naut, & fig) landen; (said of a blow) treffen; **l. on s.o.'s head** j-m auf den Kopf fallen; **l. on water** auf dem Wasser aufsetzen
land' breeze' s Landwind m
land'ed prop'erty s Landbesitz m
land'fall' s (sighting of land) Sichten n von Land; **make l.** landen
land' forc'es spl Landstreitkräfte pl
land'ing s Landung f; (of a staircase) Absatz m; **l. on the moon** Mondlandung f
land'ing craft' s Landungsboot n
land'ing field' s Landeplatz m
land'ing force' s Landekorps n
land'ing gear' s Fahrgestell n
land'ing par'ty s Landeabteilung f
land'ing stage' s Landungssteg m
land'ing strip' s Start– und Landestreifen m
land'la'dy s (of an apartment) Hauswirtin f; (of an inn) Gastwirtin f
land'locked' adj landumschlossen
land'lord' s (of an apartment) Hauswirt m; (of an inn) Gastwirt m
landlubber ['lænd,lʌbər] s Landratte f

land'mark' s Landmarke f; (cardinal event) Markstein m
land' of'fice s Grundbuchamt n
land'-office bus'iness s (fig) Bombengeschäft n
land'own'er s Grundbesitzer –in mf
landscape ['lænd,skep] s Landschaft f; (paint) Landschaftsbild n || tr landschaftlich gestalten
land'scape ar'chitect s Landschaftsarchitekt –in mf
land'scape paint'er s Landschaftsmaler –in mf
land'slide' s Bergrutsch m; (pol) Stimmenrutsch m
landward ['lændwərd] adv landwärts
land' wind' [wɪnd] s Landwind m
lane [len] s Bahn f; (country road) Feldweg m; (aer) Flugschneise f; (aut) Fahrbahn f; (naut) Fahrtroute f; (sport) Laufbahn f; (sport) Schwimmbahn f
language ['læŋgwɪdʒ] s Sprache f
lan'guage instruc'tion s Sprachunterricht m
lan'guage teach'er s Sprachlehrer –in mf
languid ['læŋgwɪd] adj schlaff
languish ['læŋgwɪʃ] intr schmachten
languor ['læŋgər] s Mattigkeit f
languorous ['læŋgərəs] adj matt
lank [læŋk] adj schlank; (hair) glatt
lanky ['læŋki] adj schlaksig
lanolin ['lænəlɪn] s Lanolin n
lantern ['læntərn] s Laterne f
lan'tern slide' s Diapositiv n
lanyard ['lænjərd] s (around the neck) Halsschnur f; (naut) Taljereep n
Laos ['leˑɑs] s Laos n
Laotian [le'oʃən] adj laotisch || s Laote m, Laotin f; (language) Laotisch n
lap [læp] s (of the body or clothing) Schoß m; (of the waves) Plätschern n; (sport) Runde f || v (pret & pp lapped; ger lapping) tr schlappen; (sport) überrunden; **lap up** auf(sch)lecken || intr—**lap against** (e.g., a boat, shore) plätschern gegen; **lap over** hinausragen über (acc)
lap' dog' s Schoßhund m
lapel [lə'pɛl] s Aufschlag m
Lap'land' s Lappland n
Laplander ['læp,lændər] s Lappländer –in mf
Lapp [læp] s Lappe m, Lappin f; (language) Lappisch n
lapse [læps] s (error) Versehen n; (of time) Ablauf m; **after a l. of** nach Ablauf von; **l. of duty** Pflichtversäumnis f; **l. of memory** Gedächtnislücke f || intr (said of a right, an insurance policy) verfallen; (said of time) ablaufen; **l. into** verfallen in (acc); **l. into unconsciousness** das Bewußtsein verlieren
lap'wing' s Kiebitz m
larceny ['lɑrsəni] s Diebstahl m
larch [lɑrtʃ] s (bot) Lärche f
lard [lɑrd] s Schmalz n || tr spicken
larder ['lɑrdər] s Speisekammer f
large [lɑrdʒ] adj groß; **at l.** (as a whole) gesamt; (at liberty) auf freiem

Fuß; (said of an official) zur besonderen Verfügung; become larger sich vergrößern; on a l. scale in großem Umfang
large' intes'tine s Dickdarm m
largely ['lɑrdʒli] adv größtenteils
largeness ['lɑrdʒnɪs] s Größe f
large'-scale' adj Groß–; (map) in großem Maßstab; (production) Serien–
largesse ['lɑrdʒɛs] s (generosity) Freigebigkeit f; (handout) Geldverteilung f
lariat ['lærɪ·ət] s Lasso m & n; (for grazing animals) Halteseil n
lark [lɑrk] s (orn) Lerche f; for a l. zum Spaß
lark'spur' s (bot) Rittersporn m
lar·va ['lɑrvə] s (-vae [vi]) Larve f
laryngitis [,lærɪn'dʒaɪtɪs] s Kehlkopfentzündung f, Laryngitis f
larynx ['lærɪŋks] s (larynxes & larynges [lə'rɪndʒɪz]) Kehlkopf m
lascivious [lə'sɪvɪ·əs] adj wollüstig
lasciviousness [lə'sɪvɪ·əsnɪs] s Wollüstigkeit f
laser ['lezər] s Laser m
lash [læʃ] s Peitsche f; (as a punishment) Peitschenhieb m; (of the eye) Wimper f || tr (whip) peitschen; (bind) (to) anbinden (an acc); (said of rain, storms) peitschen || intr—l. out (at) ausschlagen (nach)
lass [læs] s Mädel n
lassitude ['læsɪ,t(j)ud] s Mattigkeit f
last [læst] adj letzte; very l. allerletzte || adv zuletzt; l. of all zuallerletzt || s Letzte mfn; (of a cobbler) Schuhleisten m; at l. schließlich; at long l. zu guter Letzt; look one's l. on zum letzten Mal blicken auf (acc); see the l. of s.o. j–n nicht mehr wiedersehen; to the l. bis zum Letzten || intr (remain unchanged) anhalten; (for a specific time) dauern; (said of money, supplies) reichen; (said of a person) aushalten
last'ing adj dauerhaft, andauernd; l. effect Dauerwirkung f; l. for months monatelang
Last' Judg'ment s Jüngstes Gericht n
lastly ['læstli] adv zuletzt
last'-min'ute adj in letzter Minute
last'-minute news' s neueste Nachrichten pl
last' night' adv gestern abend
last' quar'ter s (astr) abnehmendes Mondviertel n; (com) letztes Quartal n
last' resort' s letztes Mittel n
last' sleep' s Todesschlaf m
last' straw' s—that's the l. das schlägt dem Faß den Boden aus
Last' Sup'per, the s das Letzte Abendmahl
last' week' adv vorige Woche
last' will' and test'ament s letztwillige Verfügung f
last' word' s letztes Wort n; the l. (fig) der letzte Schrei
latch [lætʃ] s Klinke f || tr zuklinken || intr einschnappen; l. on to (coll) spitzkriegen

latch'key' s Hausschlüssel m
late [let] adj (after the usual time) spät; (at a late hour) zu später Stunde; (deceased) verstorben; be l. sich verspäten; (said of a train) Verspätung haben; keep l. hours spät aufbleiben || adv spät; come l. zu spät kommen; of l. kürzlich; see you later! bis später!
latecomer ['let,kʌmər] s Nachzügler m
lateen' sail' [læ'tin] s Lateinsegel n
lateen' yard' s Lateinrah f
lately ['letli] adv neulich, unlängst
lateness ['letnɪs] s Verspätung f
latent ['letənt] adj latent, verborgen
later ['letər] adj später || adv später, nachher; l. on späterhin
lateral ['lætərəl] adj seitlich, Seiten–
lath [læθ] s Latte f || tr belatten
lathe [leð] s Drehbank f; turn on a l. drechseln
lather ['læðər] s Seifenschaum m; (of a horse) schäumender Schweiß m || tr einseifen || intr schäumen
lathing ['læðɪŋ] s Lattenwerk n
Latin ['lætɪn] adj lateinisch || s (Romance-speaking person) Romane m, Romanin f; (language) Lateinisch n
La'tin Amer'ica s Lateinamerika n
La'tin-Amer'ican adj lateinamerikanisch || s Lateinamerikaner –in mf
latitude ['lætɪ,t(j)ud] s Breite f; (fig) Spielraum m
latrine [lə'trin] s Latrine f
latter ['lætər] adj (later) später; (final) End–; (recent) letzte; in the l. part of (e.g., the year) in der zweiten Hälfte (genit); the l. dieser
lat'ter-day' adj (later) später; (recent) letzte
Lat'ter-day Saint' s Heilige mf der Jüngsten Tage
lattice ['lætɪs] s Gitter n || tr vergittern
lat'ticework' s Gitterwerk n
Latvia ['lætvɪ·ə] s Lettland n
Latvian ['lætvɪ·ən] adj lettisch || s Lette m, Lettin f; (language) Lettisch n
laud [lɔd] tr loben, preisen
laudable ['lɔdəbəl] adj löblich
laudanum ['lɔd(ə)nəm] s Opiumtinktur f
laudatory ['lɔdə,tɔri] adj Lob–
laugh [læf] s Lachen n, Gelächter n; for laughs zum Spaß; have a good l. sich auslachen || tr—l. off sich lachend hinwegsetzen über (acc) || intr lachen; it's easy for you to l. Sie haben leicht lachen!; l. about lachen über (acc); l. at (deride) auslachen; (find amusement in) lachen über (acc)
laughable ['læfəbəl] adj lächerlich
laugh'ing adj lachend; it's no l. matter es ist nichts zum Lachen
laugh'ing gas' s Lachgas n
laugh'ingstock' s Gespött n
laughter ['læftər] s Gelächter n, Lachen n; roar with l. vor Lachen brüllen
launch [lɔntʃ] s (open boat) Barkasse

f || *tr* (*a boat*) aussetzen; (*a ship*) vom Stapel laufen lassen; (*a plane*) katapultieren; (*a rocket*) starten; (*a torpedo*) abschießen; (*an offensive*) beginnen; **be launched** (naut) vom Stapel laufen; (rok) starten || *intr*—
l. into sich stürzen in (*acc*)
launch'ing *s* (*of a ship*) Stapellauf *m*; (*of a torpedo*) Ausstoß *m*; (*of a rocket*) Abschuß *m*, Start *m*
launch' pad' *s* (rok) Startrampe *f*
launder ['lɔndər] *tr* waschen
laundress ['lɔndrɪs] *s* Wäscherin *f*
laundry ['lɔndrɪ] *s* (*clothes*) Wäsche *f*; (*room*) Waschküche *f*; (*business*) Wäscherei *f*
laun'drybag' *s* Wäschebeutel *m*
laun'drybas'ket *s* Wäschekorb *m*
laun'dry list' *s* Waschzettel *m*
laun'dry•man' *s* (**-men'**) Wäscher *m*
laun'dry•wom'an *s* (**-wom'en**) Wäscherin *f*
laurel ['lɔrəl] *s* Lorbeer *m*
lau'rel tree' *s* Lorbeerbaum *m*
lava ['lavə] *s* Lava *f*
lavatory ['lævə‚tori] *s* Waschraum *m*; (*toilet*) Toilette *f*
lavender ['lævəndər] *adj* lavendelfarben || *s* (bot) Lavendel *m*
lavish ['lævɪʃ] *adj* (*person*) verschwenderisch; (*dinner*) üppig || *tr*—**l. care on** hegen und pflegen; **l. s.th. on s.o.** j-n mit etw überhäufen
lavishness ['lævɪʃnɪs] *s* Üppigkeit *f*
law [lɔ] *s* Gesetz *n*; (*system*) Recht *n*; (*as a science*) Rechtswissenschaft *f*; (relig) Gebot *n*; **according to law** dem Recht entsprechend; **act within the law** sich ans Gesetz halten; **against the law** gesetzwidrig; **become law** Gesetzkraft erlangen; **by law** gesetzlich; **go against the law** gegen das Gesetz handeln; **lay down the law** gebieterisch auftreten; **practice law** den Anwaltsberuf ausüben; **study law** Jura studieren; **take the law into one's own hands** sich [*dat*] selbst sein Recht verschaffen; **under the law** nach dem Gesetz
law'-abid'ing *adj* friedlich
law' and or'der *s* Ruhe und Ordnung *pl*
law'-and-or'der *adj* für Ruhe und Ordnung
law'break'er *s* Rechtsbrecher –in *mf*
law'break'ing *s* Rechtsbruch *m*
law'court' *s* Gerichtshof *m*, Gericht *n*
lawful ['lɔfəl] *adj* gesetzmäßig
lawless ['lɔlɪs] *adj* gesetzlos
lawlessness ['lɔlɪsnɪs] *s* Gesetzlosigkeit *f*
law'mak'er *s* Gesetzgeber *m*
lawn [lɔn] *s* Rasen *m*; (tex) Batist *m*
lawn' mow'er *s* Rasenmäher *m*
lawn' par'ty *s* Gartenfest *n*
lawn' sprin'kler *s* Rasensprenger *m*
law' of dimin'ishing returns' *s* Gesetz *n* der abnehmenden Erträge
law' of'fice *s* Anwaltsbüro *n*
law' of na'tions *s* Völkerrecht *n*
law' of na'ture *s* Naturgesetz *n*
law' of probabil'ity *s* Wahrscheinlichkeitsgesetz *n*

law' of supply' and demand' *s* Gesetz *n* von Angebot und Nachfrage
law' of the land' *s* Landesgesetz *n*
law' school' *s* juristiche Fakultät *f*
law' stu'dent *s* Student –in *mf* der Rechtswissenschaft
law'suit' *s* Klage *f*, Prozeß *m*
lawyer ['lɔjər] *s* Advokat –in *m*, Anwalt –in *mf*
lax [læks] *adj* lax, nachlässig
laxative ['læksətɪv] *s* Abführmittel *n*
laxity ['læksɪtɪ] *s* Laxheit *f*
lay [le] *adj* (*not of the clergy*) Laien–, weltlich; (*non-expert*) laienhaft || *s* (*poem*) Lied *n* || *v* (*pret & pp* **laid** [led]) *tr* legen; (*eggs; foundation, bricks, lineoleum*) legen; (*cables, pipes, tracks*) verlegen; (vulg) umlegen; **be laid up with** das Bett hüten müssen wegen (*genit*); **I'll lay you two to one** ich wette mit dir zwei zu eins; **lay aside** beiseite legen; (*save*) sparen; **lay bare** bloßlegen; **lay down** niederlegen; (*principles*) aufstellen; **lay claim to** Anspruch erheben auf (*acc*); **lay it on thick** dick auftragen; **lay low** (*said of an illness*) bettlägerig machen; **lay off** (*workers*) vorübergehend entlassen; **lay open** freilegen; **lay out** auslegen; (*a garden*) anlegen; (*money*) aufwenden; (*a corpse*) aufbahren; (surv) abstecken; **lay siege to** belagern; **lay waste** verwüsten || *intr* (*said of hens*) legen; **lay for** auflauern (*dat*); **lay into** (*beat*) (coll) verdreschen; (*scold*) (coll) heruntermachen; **lay off** (*abstain from*) sich enthalten (*genit*); (*let alone*) in Ruhe lassen; **lay over** (*on a trip*) sich aufhalten; **lay to** (naut) stilliegen
lay' broth'er *s* Laienbruder *m*
layer ['le·ər] *s* Schicht *f*; (bot) Ableger *m*; **in layers** schichtenweise; **l. of fat** Fettschicht *f*; **thin l.** Hauch *m*
lay'er cake' *s* Schichttorte *f*
layette [le'ɛt] *s* Babyausstattung *f*
lay' fig'ure *s* Gliederpuppe *f*
lay'man *s* (**-men**) Laie *m*; **layman's** laienhaft
lay'off' *s* vorübergehende Entlassung *f*
lay' of the land' *s* Gestaltung *f* des Terrains; (fig) Gesichtspunkt *m* der Angelegenheit
lay'out' *s* Anlage *f*, Anordnung *f*; (typ) Layout *n*; **l. of rooms** Raumverteilung *f*
laziness ['lezɪnɪs] *s* Faulheit *f*
lazy ['lezɪ] *adj* faul
la'zybones' *s* (coll) Faulpelz *m*
la'zy Su'san *s* drehbares Tablett *n*
lea [li] *s* (poet) Aue *f*
lead [led] *adj* Blei– || *s* Blei *n*; (*in a pencil*) Mine *f*; (*plumb line*) Bleilot *n* || *v* (*pret & pp* **leaded**; *ger* **leading**) *tr* verbleien; (typ) durchschießen || [lid] *s* Führung *f*; (cards) Vorhand *f*; (elec) Zuführung *f*; (sport) Vorsprung *m*; (theat) Hauptrolle *f*; **be in the l.** an der Spitze stehen; **have the l.** die Führung haben; **take the l.** die Führung übernehmen || *v* (*pret & pp*

led [lɛd]) *tr* führen, leiten; (*to error, drinking, etc.*) verleiten; (*a parade*) anführen; (*a life*) führen; **l. astray** verführen; **l. away** wegführen; (*e.g., a criminal*) abführen; **l. back** zurückführen; **l. by the nose** an der Nase herumführen; **l. on** weiterführen; (*deceive*) täuschen; **l. the way** vorangehen || *intr* führen; (*cards*) anspielen; **l. nowhere** zu nichts führen; **l. off** den Anfang machen; **l. to** hinausgehen auf (*acc*); **l. up to** hinauswollen auf (*acc*) **where will all this l. to?** wo soll das alles hinführen?

leaden ['lɛdən] *adj* bleiern; (*in color*) bleifarbig; (*sluggish*) schwerfällig; **l. sky** bleierner Himmel *m*

leader ['lidər] *s* Führer –in *mf*; (*of a band*) Dirigent –in *mf*; (*of a film*) Vorspann *m*; (*lead article*) Leitartikel *m*

lead'ership' *s* Führung *f*

leading ['lidɪŋ] *adj* (*person, position, power*) führend

lead'ing ide'a *s* Leitgedanke *m*

lead'ing la'dy *s* Hauptdarstellerin *f*

lead'ing man' *s* Hauptdarsteller *m*

leading' ques'tion *s* Suggestivfrage *f*

lead'ing role' *s* Hauptrolle *f*

lead'-in wire' *s* Zuleitungsdraht *m*

lead' pen'cil [lɛd] *s* Bleistift *m*

lead' pipe' [lɛd] *s* Bleirohr *n*

lead' poi'soning [lɛd] *s* Bleivergiftung *f*

leaf [lif] *s* (**leaves** [livz]) Blatt *n*; (*of a folding door*) Flügel *m*; (*of a folding table*) Tischklappe *f*; (*insertable table board*) Einlegebrett *n*; **turn over a new l.** ein neues Leben anfangen || *intr*—**l. through** durchblättern

leafage ['lifɪdʒ] *s* Laubwerk *n*

leafless ['liflɪs] *adj* blattlos

leaflet ['liflɪt] *s* Werbeprospekt *m*, Flugblatt *n*; (bot) Blättchen *n*

leafy ['lifi] *adj* (*abounding in leaves*) belaubt; (*e.g., vegetables*) Blatt–

league [lig] *s* Bund *m*; (*unit of distance*) Meile *f*; (sport) Liga *f*; **in l. with** verbündet mit || *tr* verbünden || *intr* sich verbünden

League' of Na'tions *s* Völkerbund *m*

leak [lik] *s* Leck *n*; **spring a l.** ein Leck bekommen; **take a l.** (vulg) schiffen || *tr* (*e.g., a story to the press*) durchsickern lassen || *intr* (*said of a container*) leck sein; (*said of a boat*) lecken; (*said of a fluid*) auslaufen; (*said of a spigot*) tropfen; **l. out** (& fig) durchsickern

leakage ['likɪdʒ] *s* Lecken *n*; (& fig) Durchsickern *n*; (com) Schwund *m*; (elec) Streuung *f*

leaky ['liki] *adj* leck

lean [lin] *adj* mager || *v* (*pret & pp* **leaned** & **leant** [lɛnt]) *tr* (*against*) lehnen (an *acc* or gegen) || *intr* lehnen; **l. against** sich anlehnen an (*acc*); **l. back** sich zurücklehnen; **l. forward** sich vorbeugen; **l. on** sich stützen auf (*acc*); **l. over** (*e.g., a railing*) sich neigen über (*acc*); **l. toward** (fig) neigen zu

lean'ing *adj* sich neigend; (*tower*) schief || *s* (*toward*) Neigung *f* (zu)

leanness ['linnɪs] *s* Magerkeit *f*

lean'-to' *s* (–tos) Anbau *m* mit Pultdach

lean' years' *spl* magere Jahre *pl*

leap [lip] *s* Sprung *m*, Satz *m*; **by leaps and bounds** sprungweise; **l. in the dark** (fig) Sprung *m* ins Ungewisse || *v* (*pret & pp* **leaped** & **leapt** [lɛpt]) *tr* überspringen || *intr* springen; **l. at** anspringen; **l. at an opportunity** e-e Gelegenheit beim Schopf ergreifen; **l. forward** vorspringen; **l. up** emporschnellen

leap'frog' *s* Bocksprung *m*; **play l.** Bocksprünge machen

leap' year' *s* Schaltjahr *n*

learn [lʌrn] *v* (*pret & pp* **learned** & **learnt** [lʌrnt]) *tr* lernen; (*find out*) erfahren; **l. s.th. from s.o.**

learned ['lʌrnɪd] *adj* (*person, word*) gelehrt; (*for or of scholars*) Gelehrten–

learn'ed jour'nal *s* Gelehrtenzeitschrift *f*

learn'ed soci'ety *s* Gelehrtenvereinigung *f*

learn'ed world' *s* Gelehrtenwelt *f*

learn'ing *s* (*act*) Lernen *n*; (*erudition*) Gelehrsamkeit *f*

lease [lis] *s* Mietvertrag *m*; (*of land*) Pachtvertrag *m* || *tr* (*in the role of landlord*) vermieten; (*land*) verpachten; (*in the role of tenant*) mieten; (*land*) pachten

lease'hold' *adj* Pacht– || *s* Pachtbesitz *m*

leash [liʃ] *s* Leine *f*, Hundeleine *f*; **keep on the l.** an der Leine führen; **strain at the l.** (fig) an der Leine zerren || *tr* an die Leine nehmen

leas'ing *s* Miete *f*; (*of land*) Pachtung *f*; **l. out** Vermietung *f*; (*of land*) Verpachtung *f*

least [list] *adj* mindeste, wenigste || *adv* am wenigsten; **l. of all** am wenigsten von allen || *s* Geringste *mfn*; **at l.** mindestens, wenigstens; **at the very l.** zum mindesten; **not in the l.** nicht im mindeste

leather ['lɛðər] *adj* ledern || *s* Leder *n*

leath'er bind'ing *s* Ledereinband *m*

leath'erbound' *adj* ledergebunden

leath'erneck' *s* (sl) Marineinfanterist *m*

leathery ['lɛðəri] *adj* (*e.g., steak*) (coll) lederartig

leave [liv] *s* (*permission*) Erlaubnis *f*; (mil) Urlaub *m*; **on l.** auf Urlaub; **take l.** (**from**) Abschied nehmen (von); **take l. of one's senses** (coll) den Verstand verlieren || *v* (*pret & pp* **left** [lɛft]) *tr* (*go away from*) verlassen; (*undone, open, etc.*) lassen; (*a message, bequest*) hinterlassen; (*a job*) aufgeben; (*a scar*) zurücklassen; (*forget*) liegenlassen, stehenlassen; (*e.g., some food for s.o.*) übriglassen; **be left** übrig sein; **l. alone** (*a thing*) bleibenlassen; (*a person*) in Frieden lassen; **l. behind** (*said of a deceased person*) hinterlassen; (*forget*) liegenlassen; **l. home von zu Hause** fortgehen; **l. it at that!** überlaß es mir!; **l. lying about her-** umliegen lassen; **l. nothing to chance** nichts dem Zufall überlassen; **l. nothing undone** nichts unversucht lassen; **l. open** offen lassen; **l. out** auslassen; **l. standing** stehenlassen; **l.** (*e.g., work*) **undone** liegenlassen || *intr* fortgehen; (*on travels*) abreisen; (*said of vehicles*) abfahren; (aer) abfliegen; **l. off** (*e.g., from reading*) aufhören

leaven ['lɛvən] *s* Treibmittel *n* || *tr* säuern

leav'ening *s* Treibstoff *m*

leave' of ab'sence *s* Urlaub *m*

leave'-tak'ing *s* Abschiednehmen *n*

leavings ['liːvɪŋz] *spl* Überbleibsel *pl*

Leba·nese [ˌlɛbə'niz] *adj* libanesisch || *s* (-nese) Libanese *m*, Libanesin *f*

Lebanon ['lɛbənən] *s* Libanon *n*

lecher ['lɛtʃər] *s* Lüstling *m*

lecherous ['lɛtʃərəs] *adj* wollüstig

lechery ['lɛtʃəri] *s* Wollust *f*

lectern ['lɛktərn] *s* Lesepult *n*

lector ['lɛktər] *s* (eccl) Lektor *m*

lecture ['lɛktʃər] *s* Vorlesung *f*, Vortrag *m*; (coll) Standpauke *f*; **give a l. on** e-n Vortrag halten über (*acc*); **give s.o. a l.** j-m den Text lesen || *tr* (coll) abkanzeln || *intr* lesen

lecturer ['lɛktʃərər] *s* Vortragende *mf*; (*at a university*) Dozent –in *mf*

lec'ture room' *s* Hörsaal *m*

ledge [lɛdʒ] *s* Sims *m* & *n*; (*of a cliff*) Felsenriff *n*

ledger ['lɛdʒər] *s* (acct) Hauptbuch *n*

lee [li] *s* Lee *f*

leech [liːtʃ] *s* Blutegel *m*; (fig) Blutsauger –in *mf*

leek [lik] *s* (bot) Porree *m*, Lauch *m*

leer [lɪr] *s* lüsterner Seitenblick *m* || *intr* (at) lüstern schielen (nach)

leery ['lɪri] *adj* mißtrauisch; **be l. of** mißtrauen (*dat*)

lees [liz] *spl* Hefe *f*

lee' side' *s* Leeseite *f*

leeward ['liːwərd] *adv* leewärts || *s* Leeseite *f*

Lee'ward Is'lands *spl* Inseln *pl* unter dem Winde

lee'way' *s* (coll) Spielraum *m*; (aer, naut) Abtrift *f*

left [lɛft] *adj* linke; (*left over*) übrig || *adv* links; **l. face!** (mil) links um! || *s* (*left hand*) Linke *f*; **on our l.** zu unserer Linken; **the l.** (pol) die Linke; **the third street to the l.** die dritte Querstraße links; **to the l.** nach links; **to the l. of** links von

left' field' *s* (baseball) linkes Außenfeld *n*

left' field'er ['fildər] *s* Spieler *m* im linken Außenfeld

left'-hand drive' *s* Linkssteuerung *f*

left'-hand'ed *adj* linkshändig; (*compliment*) fragwürdig; (*counterclockwise*) linksgängig; (*clumsy*) linkisch

left-hander ['lɛft'hændər] *s* Linkshänder –in *mf*

leftish ['lɛftɪʃ] *adj* linksgerichtet

leftist ['lɛftɪst] *s* Linksradikaler *m*; (pol) Linkspolitiker –in *mf*

left'o'ver *adj* übriggeblieben || **leftovers** *spl* Überbleibsel *pl*

left'-wing' *adj* Links–

left' wing' *s* (pol) linker Flügel *m*; (sport) Linksaußen *m*

left-winger ['lɛft'wɪŋər] *s* (coll) Linkspolitiker –in *mf*

lefty ['lɛfti] *adj* (coll) linkshändig || *s* (coll) Linkshänder –in *mf*

leg [lɛg] *s* (*of a body, of furniture, of trousers*) Bein *n*; (*stretch*) Etappe *f*; (*of a compass*) Schenkel *m*; (*of a boot*) Schaft *m*; **be on one's last legs** auf dem letzten Loche pfeifen; **pull s.o.'s leg** (coll) j–n auf die Schippe nehmen; **run one's legs off** sich abrennen; **you don't have a leg to stand on** Sie haben keinerlei Beweise

legacy ['lɛgəsi] *s* Vermächtnis *n*

legal ['ligəl] *adj* (*according to the law*) gesetzlich, legal; (*pertaining to or approved by law*) Rechts–, juristisch; **take l. action** den Rechtweg beschreiten; **take l. steps against s.o.** gerichtlich gegen j–n vorgehen

le'gal advice' *s* Rechtsberatung *f*

le'gal advis'er *s* Rechtsberater –in *mf*

le'gal age' *s* Volljährigkeit *f*; **of l.** großjährig

le'gal aid' *s* Rechtshilfe *f*

le'gal ba'sis *s* Rechtsgrundlage *f*

le'gal case' *s* Rechtsfall *m*

le'gal claim' *s* Rechtsanspruch *m*

le'gal en'tity *s* juristische Person *f*

le'gal force' *s* Rechtskraft *f*

le'gal grounds' *spl* Rechtsgrund *m*

le'gal hol'iday *s* gesetzlicher Feiertag *m*

legality [lɪ'gælɪti] *s* Gesetzlichkeit *f*, Rechtlichkeit *f*

legalize ['ligə,laɪz] *tr* legalisieren

le'gal jar'gon *s* Kanzleisprache *f*

le'gal profes'sion *s* Rechtsanwaltsberuf *m*

le'gal rem'edy *s* Rechtsmittel *n*

le'gal ten'der *s* gesetzliches Zahlungsmittel *n*; **be l.** gelten

le'gal ti'tle *s* Rechtsanspruch *m*

legate ['lɛgɪt] *s* Legat –in *mf*

legatee [ˌlɛgə'ti] *s* Legatar –in *mf*

legation [lɪ'geʃən] *s* Gesandtschaft *f*

legend ['lɛdʒənd] *s* Legende *f*

legendary ['lɛdʒən,dɛri] *adj* legendär

legerdemain [ˌlɛdʒərdɪ'men] *s* Taschenspielerei *f*

leggings ['lɛgɪŋz] *spl* hohe Gamaschen *pl*

leggy ['lɛgi] *adj* langbeinig

Leg'horn' *s* (chicken) Leghorn *n*; (*town in Italy*) Livorno *n*

legibility [ˌlɛdʒɪ'bɪlɪti] *s* Lesbarkeit *f*

legible ['lɛdʒɪbəl] *adj* lesbar

legion ['lidʒən] *s* Legion *f*; (fig) Heerschar *f*

legionnaire [ˌlidʒə'nɛr] *s* Legionär *m*

legislate ['lɛdʒɪs,let] *tr* durch Gesetzgebung bewirken || *intr* Gesetze geben

legislation [ˌlɛdʒɪs'leʃən] *s* Gesetzgebung *f*

legislative ['lɛdʒɪs‚letɪv] *adj* gesetzgebend
legislator ['lɛdʒɪs‚letər] *s* Gesetzgeber –in *mf*
legislature ['lɛdʒɪs‚letʃər] *s* Legislatur *f*
legitimacy [lɪ'dʒɪtɪməsi] *s* Rechtmäßigkeit *f*
legitimate [lɪ'dʒɪtɪmɪt] *adj* gesetzmäßig, legitim; (*child*) ehelich || [lɪ'dʒɪtɪ‚met] *tr* legitimieren
legit'imate the'ater *s* literarisch wertvolles Theater *n*
legitimize [lɪ'dʒɪtɪ‚maɪz] *tr* legitimieren
leg' of lamb' *s* Lammkeule *f*
leg' of mut'ton *s* Hammelkeule *f*
leg' room' *s* Beinfreiheit *f*
leg'work' *s* Vorarbeiten *pl*
leisure ['liʒər] *s* Muße *f*; at l. mit Muße; at s.o.'s l. wenn es j–m paßt
lei'sure class' *s* wohlhabende Klasse *f*
lei'sure hours' *spl* Mußestunden *pl*
leisurely ['liʒərli] *adj & adv* gemächlich
lei'sure time' *s* Freizeit *f*
lemon ['lɛmən] *adj* Zitronen– || *s* Zitrone *f*; (sl) Niete *f*
lemonade [‚lɛmɪ'ned] *s* Zitronenlimonade *f*
lem'on squeez'er *s* Zitronenpresse *f*
lend [lɛnd] *v* (*pret & pp* lent [lɛnt]) *tr* leihen, borgen; l. at five percent interest zu fünf Prozent Zinsen anlegen; l. itself to sich eignen zu or für; l. oneself to sich hergeben zu; l. out ausleihen, verborgen; l. s.o. a hand j–m zur Hand gehen
lender ['lɛndər] *s* Verleiher –in *mf*
lend'ing li'brary *s* Leihbücherei *f*
length [lɛŋθ] *s* Länge *f*; (*of time*) Dauer *f*; (*in horse racing*) Pferdelänge *f*; at great l. sehr ausführlich; at l. ausführlich; (*finally*) schließlich; at some l. ziemlich ausführlich; go to any l. alles Erdenkliche tun; go to great lengths sich sehr bemühen; keep s.o. at arm's l. zu j–m Abstand wahren; stretch out full l. sich der Länge nach ausstrecken
lengthen ['lɛŋθən] *tr* verlängern; (*a vowel*) dehnen
length'ening *s* Verlängerung *f*; (ling) Dehnung *f*
length'wise' *adj & adv* der Länge nach
lengthy ['lɛŋθi] *adj* langwierig
leniency ['linɪ‧ənsi] *s* Milde *f*
lens [lɛnz] *s* Linse *f*; (*combination of lenses*) Objektiv *n*
Lent [lɛnt] *s* Fastenzeit *f*
Lenten ['lɛntən] *adj* Fasten–
lentil ['lɛntɪl] *s* (bot) Linse *f*
leopard ['lɛpərd] *s* Leopard *m*
leper ['lɛpər] *s* Aussätzige *mf*
leprosy ['lɛprəsi] *s* Aussatz *m*, Lepra *f*
lesbian ['lɛzbɪ‧ən] *adj* lesbisch || *s* Lesbierin *f*
lesbianism ['lɛzbɪ‧ə‚nɪzəm] *s* lesbische Liebe *f*
lesion ['liʒən] *s* Wunde *f*
less [lɛs] *comp adj* weniger, geringer;

l. and l. immer weniger || *adv* weniger, minder; l. than weniger als || s—do with l. mit weniger auskommen; for l. billiger; in l. than no time in Null Komma nichts || *prep* abzüglich (*genit* or *acc*); (arith) weniger (*acc*), minus (*acc*)
lessee [lɛ'si] *s* Mieter –in *mf*; (*of land*) Pächter –in *mf*
lessen ['lɛsən] *tr* vermindern || *intr* sich vermindern, abnehmen
lesser ['lɛsər] *comp adj* minder, geringer
lesson ['lɛsən] *s* Unterrichtsstunde *f*, Stunde *f*; (*in a textbook*) Lektion *f*; (*warning*) Lehre *f*; learn a l. from e–e Lehre ziehen aus; let that be l. to you! lassen Sie sich das e–e Lehre sein
lessor ['lɛsər] *s* Vermieter –in *mf*; (*of land*) Verpächter –in *mf*
lest [lɛst] *conj* damit nicht; (after expressions of fear) daß
let [lɛt] *v* (*pret & pp* let; *ger* letting) *tr* lassen; I really let him have it! (coll) ich hab's ihm ordentlich gegeben!; let alone in Ruhe lassen; (*not to mention*) geschweige denn; let down herunterlassen; (*disappoint*) enttäuschen; let drop fallen lassen; let fly fliegen lassen; (coll) loslassen; let go fortlassen, loslassen; let go ahead vorlassen; let in hereinlassen; (*water*) zuleiten; let in on (*e.g., a secret*) einweihen in (*acc*); let it go, e.g., I'll let it go this time diesmal werde ich es noch hingehen lassen; let lie liegenlassen; let know wissen lassen, Bescheid geben (*dat*); let off (*e.g., at the next corner*) absetzen; let off easy noch so davonkommen lassen; let off scot-free straflos laufen lassen; let one's hair down (fig) sich gehenlassen; let out (*seams, air, water*) auslassen; (*e.g., a yell*) von sich geben; let pass durchlassen; let s.o. have s.th. j–m etw zukommen lassen; let stand (fig) gelten lassen; let through durchlassen; let things slide die Dinge laufen lassen; let things take their course den Dingen ihren Lauf lassen; let's go! los!; let us (or let's) (*inf*), e.g., let's (or let us) sing singen wir || *intr* (*be rented out*) (for) vermietet werden (für); let fly with (coll) loslegen mit; let go of loslassen; let on that sich [*dat*] anmerken lassen, daß; let up nachlassen; let up on (coll) ablassen von
let'down' *s* Hereinfall *m*
lethal ['liθəl] *adj* tödlich
lethargic [lɪ'θardʒɪk] *adj* lethargisch
lethargy ['lɛθərdʒi] *s* Lethargie *f*
letter ['lɛtər] *s* Brief *m*, Schreiben *n*; (*of the alphabet*) Buchstabe *m*; by l. brieflich, schriftlich; to the l. aufs Wort || *tr* beschriften
let'ter box' *s* Briefkasten *m*
let'ter car'rier *s* Briefträger –in *mf*
let'ter drop' *s* Briefeinwurf *m*
let'tered *adj* gelehrt
let'ter file' *s* Briefordner *m*

let'terhead' s Briefkopf m
let'tering s (act) Beschriften n; (inscription) Beschriftung f
let'ter of condol'ence s Beileidsbrief m
let'ter of cred'it s Kreditbrief m
let'ter of recommenda'tion s Empfehlungsbrief m
letter o'pener s Brieföffner m
let'terper'fect adj buchstabengetreu
let'terpress' s (typ) Hochdruck m
let'ter scales' spl Briefwaage f
let'ter to the ed'itor s Leserbrief m
lettuce ['letɪs] s Salat m
let'up' s Nachlassen n; **without l.** ohne Unterlaß
leukemia [lu'kimɪ·ə] s Leukämie f
Levant [lɪ'vænt] s Levante f
Levantine [lɪ'væntin] adj levantinisch || s Levantiner –in mf
levee ['levi] s Uferdamm m
lev·el ['levəl] adj eben, gerade; (flat) flach; (spoonful) gestrichen; **be l. with** so hoch sein wie; **do one's l. best** sein Möglichstes tun; **have a l. head** ausgeglichen sein; **keep a l. head** e–n klaren Kopf behalten || s (& fig) Niveau n; (tool) Wasserwaage f; **at higher levels** höheren Ortes; **be up to the usual l.** (fig) auf der gewöhnlichen Höhe sein; **on a l. with** (& fig) auf gleicher Höhe mit; **on the l.** (fig) ehrlich || v (pret & pp –el[l]ed; ger –el[l]ing tr (a street, ground) planieren; **l.** (e.g., a rifle) **at** richten auf (acc); (e.g., complaints) richten gegen; **l. off** nivellieren; (aer) abfangen; **l. to the ground** dem Erdboden gleichmachen || intr— **l. off** sich verflachen; (said of prices) sich stabilisieren; (aer) in Horizontalflug übergehen; **l. with s.o.** mit j–m offen sein
lev'elhead'ed adj besonnen, vernünftig
lever ['livər] s Hebel m, Brechstange f || tr mit e–r Brechstange fortbewegen
leverage ['livərɪdʒ] s Hebelkraft f; (fig) Einfluß m
leviathan [lɪ'vaɪ·əθən] s Leviathan m
levitate ['levɪˌtet] tr schweben lassen || intr frei schweben
levitation [ˌlevɪ'teʃən] s Schweben n
levity ['levɪti] s Leichtsinn m
lev·y ['levi] s Truppenaushebung f; (of taxes) Erhebung f; (tax) Steuer f || v (pret & pp –vied) tr (troops) ausheben; (taxes) erheben; **l. war on** Krieg führen gegen
lewd [lud] adj unzüchtig
lewdness ['ludnɪs] s Unzucht f
lexical ['leksɪkəl] adj lexikalisch
lexicographer [ˌleksɪ'kɑgrəfər] s Lexikograph –in mf
lexicographic(al) [ˌleksɪkə'græfɪk(əl)] adj lexikographisch
lexicography [ˌleksɪ'kɑgrəfi] s Lexikographie f
lexicology [ˌleksɪ'kɑlədʒi] s Wortforschung f, Lexikologie f
lexicon ['leksɪkən] s Wörterbuch n
liability [ˌlaɪ·ə'bɪlɪti] s (ins) Haftpflicht f; (jur) Haftung f; **liabilities** Schulden pl; (acct) Passiva pl

liabil'ity insur'ance s Haftpflichtversicherung f
liable ['laɪ·əbəl] adj (jur) (for) haftbar (für); **be l. to** (inf) (coll) leicht können (inf); **l. for damages** schadenersatzpflichtig
liaison [li'ezən] s Verbindung f; (illicit affair) Liaison f; (ling) Bindung f
liai'son of'ficer s Verbindungsoffizier m
liar ['laɪ·ər] s Lügner –in mf
libation [laɪ'beʃən] s Opfertrank m
li·bel ['laɪbəl] s Verleumdung f; (in writing) Schmähschrift f || v (pret & pp –bel[l]ed; ger –bel[l]ing) tr verleumden
libelous ['laɪbələs] adj verleumderisch
li'bel suit' s Verleumdungsklage f
liberal ['lɪbərəl] adj (views) liberal, freisinnig; (with money) freigebig; (gift) großzügig; (interpretation) weitherzig; (education) allgemeinbildend; (pol) liberal || s Liberale mf
lib'eral arts' spl Geisteswissenschaften pl
liberalism ['lɪbərəˌlɪzəm] s Liberalismus m
liberality [ˌlɪbə'rælɪti] s Freigebigkeit f, Großzügigkeit f
liberate ['lɪbəˌret] tr befreien; (chem) freimachen
liberation [ˌlɪbə'reʃən] s Befreiung f; (chem) Freimachen n
liberator ['lɪbəˌretər] s Befreier –in mf
libertine ['lɪbərˌtin] s Wüstling m
liberty ['lɪbərti] s Freiheit f; **take liberties** sich [dat] Freiheiten herausnehmen; **you are at l. to** (inf) es steht Ihnen frei zu (inf)
libidinous [lɪ'bɪdɪnəs] adj wollüstig
libido [lɪ'bido] s Libido f
librarian [laɪ'brerɪ·ən] s Bibliothekar –in mf
library ['laɪˌbreri] s Bibliothek f
li'brary card' s Benutzerkarte f
libret·to [lɪ'breto] s (–tos) Operntext m, Libretto n
Libya ['lɪbɪ·ə] s Libyen n
Libyan ['lɪbɪ·ən] adj libysch || s Libyer –in mf
license ['laɪsəns] s Lizenz f, Genehmigung f; (document) Zulassungsschein m; (for a business, restaurant) Konzession f; (to drive) Führerschein m; (excessive liberty) Zügellosigkeit f || tr konzessionieren; (aut) zulassen
li'cense num'ber s (aut) Kennzeichen n
li'cense plate' or **tag'** s Nummernschild n
licentious [laɪ'senʃəs] adj unzüchtig
lichen ['laɪkən] s (bot) Flechte f
lick [lɪk] s Lecken n || tr lecken; (thrash) (coll) wichsen; (defeat) (coll) schlagen; (said of a flame) züngeln an (dat); **l. clean** auslecken; **l. into shape** auf Hochglanz bringen; **l. off** ablecken; **l. one's chops** sich [dat] die Lippen lecken; **l. s.o.'s boots** vor j–m kriechen; **l. up** auflecken
lick'ing s Prügel pl; **give s.o. a good l.** j–n versohlen

licorice [ˈlɪkərɪs] s Lakritze f
lid [lɪd] s Deckel m
lie [laɪ] s Lüge f; **give the lie to s.o.**
(or **s.th.**) j-n (or etw) Lügen strafen;
tell a lie lügen ‖ v (pret & pp **lied**;
ger **lying**) tr—**lie one's way out of**
sich herauslügen aus ‖ intr lügen;
lie like mad das Blaue vom Himmel
herunter lügen; **lie to** belügen ‖ v
(pret **lay** [le]; pp **lain** [len]; ger
lying) intr liegen; **lie down** sich hin-
legen; **lie down!** (to a dog) leg dich!;
lie in wait auf der Lauer liegen; **lie
in wait for** auflauern (dat); **lie low**
sich versteckt halten; (bide one's
time) abwarten; **take s.th. lying down**
etw widerspruchslos hinnehmen
lie′ detec′tor s Lügendetektor m
lien [lin] s Pfandrecht n
lieu [lu] s—**in l. of** statt (genit)
lieutenant [luˈtɛnənt] s Leutnant m;
(nav) Kapitänleutnant m
lieuten′ant colo′nel s Oberstleutnant m
lieuten′ant comman′der s Korvetten-
kapitän m
lieuten′ant gen′eral s Generalleutnant
m
lieuten′ant gov′ernor s Vizegouverneur
m
lieuten′ant jun′ior grade′ s (nav) Oberleutnant m zur See
lieuten′ant sen′ior grade′ s (nav) Kapitänleutnant m
life [laɪf] adj (imprisonment) lebenslänglich ‖ s (lives [laɪvz]) Leben n;
(e.g., of a car) Lebensdauer f; **all
my l.** mein ganzes Leben lang; **as big
as l.** in voller Lebensgröße; **bring
back to l.** wieder zum Bewußtsein
bringen; **bring to l.** ins Leben bringen; **for dear l.** ums liebe Leben;
for l. auf Lebenszeit; **full of l.** voller
Leben; **I can't for the l. of me** ich
kann beim besten Willen nicht; **lives
lost** Menschenleben pl; **not on your
l.** auf keinen Fall; **put l. into** beleben; **such is l.!** so ist nun mal das
Leben; **take one's l.** sich [dat] das
Leben nehmen; **upon my l!** so wahr
ich lebe!; **you can bet your l. on
that!** darauf kannst du Gift nehmen!
life′-and-death′ adj auf Leben und Tod
life′ annu′ity s Lebensrente f
life′ belt′ s Schwimmgürtel m
life′blood′ s Lebensblut n
life′boat′ s Rettungsboot n
life′ buoy′ s Rettungsboje f
life′ expect′ancy s Lebenserwartung f
life′ guard′ s (at a pool) Bademeister
–in mf; (at the shore) Strandwärter
–in mf
life′ impris′onment s lebenslängliche
Haft f
life′ insur′ance s Lebensversicherung f
life′ jack′et s Schwimmweste f
lifeless [ˈlaɪflɪs] adj leblos; (fig)
schwunglos
life′-like′ adj naturgetreu, lebensecht
life′ line′ s Rettungsleine f; (for a
diver) Signalleine f; (supply line)
Lebensader f
life′long′ adj lebenslänglich

life′ mem′ber s Mitglied n auf Lebenszeit
life′ of lei′sure s Wohlleben n
life′ of plea′sure s Wohlleben n
life′ of Ri′ley [ˈraɪli] s Herrenleben n
life′ of the par′ty s—**be the l.** die ganze
Gesellschaft unterhalten
life′ preserv′er [prɪ ˌzʌrvər] s Rettungs-
ring m
lifer [ˈlaɪfər] s (sl) Lebenslängliche mf
life′ raft′ s Rettungsfloß n
lifesaver [ˈlaɪfˌsevər] s Rettungs-
schwimmer –in mf; (fig) rettender
Engel m
life′ sen′tence s Verurteilung f zu le-
benslänglicher Haft
life′-size(d)′ adj lebensgroß
life′ span′ s Lebensdauer f
life′ style′ s Lebensweise f
life′time′ adj lebenslänglich ‖ s Leben
n; **for a l.** auf Lebenszeit; **once in a
l.** einmal im Leben
life′ vest′ s Schwimmweste f
life′work′ s Lebenswerk n
lift [lɪft] s (elevator) Aufzug m; (aer
& fig) Auftrieb m; **give s.o. a l.** j-n
im Wagen mitnehmen ‖ tr heben;
(gently) lüpfen; (with effort) wuchten; (weights) stemmen; (the receiver) abnehmen; (an embargo) aufheben; (steal) (sl) klauen; **l. up** aufheben; (the eyes) erheben; **not l. a
finger** keinen Finger rühren ‖ intr
(said of a mist) steigen; **l. off** (rok)
starten
lift′-off′ s (rok) Start m
lift′ truck′ s Lastkraftwagen m mit
Hebevorrichtung
ligament [ˈlɪgəmənt] s Band n
ligature [ˈlɪgətʃər] s (mus) Bindung f;
(act) (surg) Abbinden n; (filament)
(surg) Abbindungsschnur f; (typ)
Ligatur f
light [laɪt] adj (clothing, meal, music,
heart, wine, sleep, punishment,
weight) leicht; (day, beer, color,
complexion, hair) hell; **as l. as day**
tageshell; **l. as a feather** federleicht;
make l. of auf die leichte Schulter
nehmen; (belittle) als bedeutungslos
hinstellen ‖ s Licht n; **according to
his lights** nach dem Maß seiner Einsicht; **bring to l.** ans Licht bringen;
come to l. ans Licht kommen; **do
you have a l.?** haben Sie Feuer?;
in the l. of im Lichte (genit), angesichts (genit); **put in a false l.** in ein
falsches Licht stellen; **see the l. of
day** (be born) das Licht der Welt
erblicken; **shed l. on** Licht werfen
auf (acc); **throw quite a different l.
on** ein ganz anderes Licht werfen
auf (acc) ‖ v (pret & pp **lighted &
lit** [lɪt]) tr (a fire, cigarette) anzünden; (an oven) anheizen; (a
street) beleuchten; (a hall) erleuchten; (a face) aufleuchten lassen ‖
intr sich entzünden; **l. up** (said of a
face) aufleuchten; (light a cigarette)
sich [dat] e-e Zigarette anstecken
light′-blue′ adj lichtblau, hellblau
light′ bulb′ s Glühbirne f

light-complexioned ['laɪtkəm'plɛkʃənd] *adj* von heller Hautfarbe

lighten ['laɪtən] *tr* (*in weight*) leichter machen; (*brighten*) erhellen; (fig) erleichtern ‖ *intr* (*become brighter*) sich aufhellen; (*during a storm*) blitzen

lighter ['laɪtər] *s* Feuerzeug *n*; (naut) Leichter *m*

ligh'ter flu'id *s* Feuerzeugbenzin *n*

light'-fin'gered *adj* geschickt; (*thievish*) langfingerig

light'-foot'ed *adj* leichtfüßig

light'-head'ed *adj* leichtsinnig; (*dizzy*) schwindlig

light'-heart'ed *adj* leichtherzig

light'-heavy'weight' *adj* (box) Halbschwergewichts– ‖ *s* Halbschwergewichtler *m*

light'house' *s* Leuchtturm *m*

light'ing *s* Beleuchtung *f*

light'ing effects' *spl* Lichteffekte *pl*

light'ing fix'ture *s* Beleuchtungskörper *m*

lightly ['laɪtli] *adv* leicht; (*without due consideration*) leichthin; (*disparagingly*) geringschätzig

light' me'ter *s* Lichtmesser *m*

lightness ['laɪtnɪs] *s* (*in weight*) Leichtigkeit *f*; (*in shade*) Helligkeit *f*

lightning ['laɪtnɪŋ] *s* Blitz *m* ‖ *impers* —it is l. es blitzt

light'ning arrest'er [ə‚rɛstər] *s* Blitzableiter *m*

light'ning bug' *s* Leuchtkäfer *m*

light'ning rod' *s* Blitzableiter *m*

light'ning speed' *s* Windeseile *f*

light' op'era *s* Operette *f*

light' read'ing *s* Unterhaltungslektüre *f*

light'ship' *s* Leuchtschiff *n*

light' sleep' *s* Dämmerschlaf *m*

light' switch' *s* Lichtschalter *m*

light' wave' *s* Lichtwelle *f*

light'weight' *adj* (box) Leichtgewichts– ‖ *s* (coll) geistig Minderbemittelter *m*; (box) Leichtgewichtler *m*

light'-year' *s* Lichtjahr *n*

likable ['laɪkəbəl] *adj* sympathisch, lieb

like [laɪk] *adj* gleich, ähnlich; **be l.** gleichen (*dat*) ‖ *adv*—**l. crazy** (coll) wie verrückt ‖ *s*—**and the l.** und dergleichen; **likes and dislikes** Neigungen und Abneigungen *pl* ‖ *tr* gern haben, mögen; **I l. him** er ist mir sympathisch; **I l. the picture** das Bild gefällt mir; **I l. the food** das Essen schmeckt mir; **l. to** (*inf*), e.g., **I l. to read** ich lese gern ‖ *intr*—**as you l.** wie Sie wollen; **if you l.** wenn Sie wollen ‖ *prep* wie; **feel l.** (*ger*) Lust haben zu (*inf*); **feel l. hell** (sl) sich elend fühlen; **it looks l. es** sieht nach … aus; **l. greased lightning** wie geschmiert; **that's just l. him** das sieht ihm ähnlich; **there's nothing l. traveling** es geht nichts übers Reisen

likelihood ['laɪklɪ‚hʊd] *s* Wahrscheinlichkeit *f*

likely ['laɪkli] *adj* wahrscheinlich; **a l. story!** (iron) e–e glaubhafte Ge-

schichte!; **it's l. to rain** es wird wahrscheinlich regen

like'-mind'ed *adj* gleichgesinnt

liken ['laɪkən] *tr* (to) vergleichen (mit)

likeness ['laɪknɪs] *s* Ähnlichkeit *f*; **a good l.** of ein gutes Portrait (*genit*)

like'wise' *adv* gleichfalls, ebenso

lik'ing *s* (for) Zuneigung *f* (*zu*); **not to my l.** nicht nach meinem Geschmack; **take a l. to** Zuneigung fassen zu

lilac ['laɪlək] *adj* lila ‖ *s* Flieder *m*

lilt [lɪlt] *s* rhythmischer Schwung *m*; (*lilting song*) lustiges Lied *n*

lily ['lɪli] *s* Lilie *f*

lil'y of the val'ley *s* Maiglöckchen *n*

lil'y pad' *s* schwimmendes Seerosenblatt *n*

lil'y-white' *adj* lilienweiß

li'ma bean' ['laɪmə] *s* Limabohne *f*

limb [lɪm] *s* Glied *n*; (*of a tree*) Ast *m*; **go out on a l.** (fig) sich exponieren; **limbs** Gliedmaßen *pl*

limber ['lɪmbər] *adj* geschmeidig ‖ *tr* —**l. up** geschmeidig machen ‖ *intr*— sich geschmeidig machen

lim·bo ['lɪmbo] *s* (–bos) Vorhölle *f*; (fig) Vergessenheit *f*

lime [laɪm] *s* Kalk *m*; (bot) Limonelle *f*

lime'kiln' *s* Kalkofen *m*

lime'light' *s* (& fig) Rampenlicht *n*

limerick ['lɪmərɪk] *s* Limerick *m*

lime'stone' *adj* Kalkstein– ‖ *s* Kalkstein *m*

limit ['lɪmɪt] *s* Grenze *f*; **go the l.** zum Äußersten gehen; **off limits** Zutritt verboten; **set a l. to** e–e Grenze ziehen (*dat*); **that's the l.!** das ist denn doch die Höhe!; **there's a l. to everything** alles hat seine Grenzen; **within limits** in Grenzen; **without l.** schrankenlos ‖ *tr* begrenzen; (to) beschränken (auf *acc*)

limitation [‚lɪmɪ'teʃən] *s* Begrenzung *f*, Beschränkung *f*

lim'ited *adj* (to) beschränkt (*auf* acc)

lim'ited-ac'cess high'way *s* Autobahn *f*

lim'ited mon'archy *s* konstitutionelle Monarchie *f*

limitless ['lɪmɪtlɪs] *adj* grenzenlos

limousine ['lɪmə‚zin], [‚lɪmə'zin] *s* Limousine *f*

limp [lɪmp] *adj* (& fig) schlaff ‖ *s* Hinken *n*; **walk with a l.** hinken ‖ *intr* (& fig) hinken

limpid ['lɪmpɪd] *adj* durchsichtig

linchpin ['lɪntʃ‚pɪn] *s* Achsnagel *m*

linden ['lɪndən] *s* Linde *f*, Lindenbaum *m*

line [laɪn] *s* Linie *f*, Strich *m*; (*boundary*) Grenze *f*; (*of a page*) Zeile *f*; (*of verse*) Verszeile *f*; (*of a family*) Zweig *m*; (*sphere of activity*) Fach *n*; (e.g., *of a streetcar*) Linie *f*, Strecke *f*; (*wrinkle*) Furche *f*; (*of articles for sale*) Sortiment *n*; (*for wash*) Leine *f*; (*queue*) Schlange *f*; (sl) zungenfertiges Gerede *n*; (angl) Schnur *f*; (mil) Linie *f*, Front *f*; (telp) Leitung *f*; **all along the l.** (fig) auf der ganzen Linie; **along the lines**

of nach dem Muster von; **draw the l. (at)** (fig) e-e Grenze ziehen (bei); **fall into l.** sich einfügen; **forget one's lines** (theat) steckenbleiben; **form a l.** sich in e-r Reihe aufstellen; **get a l. on** (coll) herausklamüsern; **give s.o. a l.** (sl) j-m schöne Worte machen; **hold the l.** die Stellung halten; (telp) am Apparat bleiben; **in l. of duty** im Dienst; **in l. with** in Übereinstimmung mit; **keep in l.** in der Reihe bleiben; **keep s.o. in l.** j-n im Zaum halten; **stand in l.** Schlange stehen; **the l. is busy** (telp) Leitung besetzt! || tr linieren; (e.g., a coat) füttern; (a face) furchen; (a drawer) ausschlagen; (a wall) verkleiden; **l. one's purse** sich [dat] den Beutel spicken; **l. the streets** in den Straßen Spalier bilden; **l. up** ausrichten; (mil) aufstellen || intr—**l. up** Schlange stehen; (mil) antreten; **l. up for** sich anstellen nach
lineage ['lɪnɪ·ɪdʒ] s Abkunft f, Abstammung f
lineal ['lɪnɪ·əl] adj (descent) direkt; (linear) geradlinig
lineaments ['lɪnɪ·əmənts] spl Gesichtszüge pl
linear ['lɪnɪ·ər] adj (arranged in a line) geradlinig; (involving a single dimension) Längen–; (using lines) Linien–; (math) linear
lined' pa'per s Linienpapier n
line'man s (–men) (rr) Streckenwärter m; (telp) Telephonarbeiter m
linen ['lɪnən] adj Leinen– || s Leinen n; (in the household) Wäsche f; (of the bed) Bettwäsche f; **linens** Weißzeug n; **put fresh l. on the bed** das Bett überziehen
lin'en clos'et s Wäscheschrank m
lin'en cloth' s Leinwand f
lin'en goods' spl Weißwaren pl
line' of approach' s (aer) Anflugschneise f
line' of bus'iness s Geschäftszweig m
line' of communica'tion s Verbindungslinie f
line' of fire' s Schußlinie f
line' of sight' s (of a gun) Visierlinie f; (astr) Sichtlinie f
liner ['laɪnər] s Einsatz m; (naut) Linienschiff n
lines'man s (–men) (sport) Linienrichter m
line'up' s (at a police station) Gegenüberstellung f; (sport) Aufstellung f
linger ['lɪŋgər] intr (tarry) verweilen; (said of memories) nachwirken; (said of a melody) nachtönen; **l. over** verweilen bei
lingerie [,lænʒə'ri] s Damenunterwäsche f
lin'gering adj (disease) schleichend; (tune) nachklingend; (memory, taste, feeling) nachwirkend
lingo ['lɪŋgo] s Kauderwelsch n
linguist ['lɪŋgwɪst] s Sprachwissenschaftler –in mf
linguistic [lɪŋ'gwɪstɪk] adj (e.g., skill) sprachlich; (of linguistics) sprach-

wissenschaftlich || **linguistics** s Sprachwissenschaft f
liniment ['lɪnɪmənt] s Einreibemittel n
lin'ing s (of a coat) Futter n; (of a brake) Bremsbelag m; (e.g., of a wall) Verkleidung f
link [lɪŋk] s Glied n; (fig) Bindeglied n || tr verbinden; (fig) verketten; **l. to** verbinden mit; (fig) in Verbindung bringen mit || intr—**l. up** (rok) dokken; **l. up with** sich anschließen an (acc)
linnet ['lɪnɪt] s (orn) Hänfling m
linoleum [lɪ'nolɪ·əm] s Linoleum n
linotype ['laɪnə,taɪp] s (trademark) Linotype f
lin'seed oil' ['lɪn,sid] s Leinöl n
lint [lɪnt] s Fussel f
lintel ['lɪntəl] s Sturz m
lion ['laɪ·ən] s Löwe m
li'on cage' s Löwenzwinger m
lioness ['laɪ·ənɪs] s Löwin f
lionize ['laɪ·ə,naɪz] tr zum Helden des Tages machen
li'ons' den' s Löwengrube f
li'on's share' s Löwenanteil m
li'on tam'er s Löwenbändiger –in mf
lip [lɪp] s Lippe f; (edge) Rand m; **bite one's lips** sich auf die Lippen beißen; **smack one's lips** sich [dat] die Lippen lecken
lip' read'ing s Lippenlesen n
lip' serv'ice s Lippenbekenntnis n; **pay l. to** ein Lippenbekenntnis ablegen zu
lip'stick' s Lippenstift m
lique·fy ['lɪkwɪ,faɪ] v (pret & pp –fied) tr verflüssigen || intr sich verflüssigen
liqueur [lɪ'kʌr] s Likör m
liquid ['lɪkwɪd] adj flüssig; (clear) klar || s Flüssigkeit f
liq'uid as'sets spl flüssige Mittel pl
liquidate ['lɪkwɪ,det] tr (a debt) tilgen; (an account) abrechnen; (a company) liquidieren
liquidation [,lɪkwɪ'deʃən] s (of a debt) Tilgung f; (of an account) Abrechnung f; (of a company) Liquidation f
liquidity [lɪ'kwɪdɪti] s flüssiger Zustand m; (fin) Liquidität f
liq'uid meas'ure s Hohlmaß m
liquor ['lɪkər] s Spirituosen pl, Schnaps m; **have a shot of l.** einen zwitschern
liquorice ['lɪkərɪs] s Lakritze f
li'quor li'cense s Schankerlaubnis f
Lisbon ['lɪzbən] s Lissabon n
lisp [lɪsp] s Lispeln n || tr & intr lispeln
lissome ['lɪsəm] adj biegsam, gelenkig
list [lɪst] s Liste f, Verzeichnis n; (naut) Schlagseite f; **enter the lists** (& fig) in die Schranken treten; **make a l. of** verzeichnen || tr verzeichnen || intr (naut) Schlagseite haben
listen ['lɪsən] intr horchen, zuhören; **l. closely** die Ohren aufsperren; **l. for** achten auf (acc); **l. in** mithören; **l. to** zuhören (dat); (a thing) horchen auf (acc); (obey) gehorchen (dat); (take advice from) hören auf (acc); **l. to reason** auf e-n Rat hören; **l. to the radio** Radio hören

listener ['lısənər] s Zuhörer –in mf;
(rad) Rundfunkhörer –in mf
lis'tening adj Abhör-, Horch-
lis'tening post' s Horchposten m
listless ['lıstlıs] adj lustlos
list' price' s Listenpreis m
litany ['lıtəni] s (& fig) Litanei f
liter ['litər] s Liter m & n
literacy ['lıtərəsi] s Kenntnis f des
Lesens und Schreibens
literal ['lıtərəl] adj buchstäblich; (person) pedantisch; **l. sense** wörtlicher
Sinn m
literally ['lıtərəli] adv buchstäblich
literary ['lıtə‚rɛri] adj literarisch; **l.
language** Literatursprache f; **l. reference** Schrifttumsangabe f
literate ['lıtərıt] adj des Lesens und
des Schreibens kundig; (educated)
gebildet || s Gebildete mf
literati [‚lıtə'rɑti] spl Literaten pl
literature ['lıtərət/ər] s Literatur f;
(com) Drucksachen pl
lithe [laıð] adj gelenkig
lithia ['lıθı‚ə] s (chem) Lithiumoxyd n
lithium ['lıθı‚əm] s Lithium n
lithograph ['lıθə‚græf] s Steindruck m
|| tr lithographieren
lithographer [lı'θɑgrəfər] s Lithograph
–in mf
lithography [lı'θɑgrəfi] s Steindruck
m, Lithographie f
Lithuania [‚lıθu'enı‚ə] s Litauen n
Lithuanian [‚lıθu'enı‚ən] adj litauisch || s Litauer –in mf; (language)
Litauisch n
litigant ['lıtıgənt] adj prozessierend;
the l. parties die streitenden Parteien
|| s Prozeßführer –in mf
litigate ['lıtı‚get] tr prozessieren gegen
|| intr prozessieren
litigation [‚lıtı'ge/ən] s Rechsstreit m
lit'mus pa'per ['lıtməs] s Lackmuspapier n
litter ['lıtər] s (stretcher) Tragbahre
f; (bedding for animals) Streu f; (of
pigs, dogs) Wurf m; (trash) herumliegender Abfall m; (hist) Sänfte f ||
tr verunreinigen || intr (bear young)
werfen; (strew litter) Abfälle wegwerfen; **no littering!** das Wegwerfen
von Abfällen ist verboten!
lit'terbug' s—**don't be a l.** wirf keine
Abfälle weg
little ['lıtəl] adj (in size) klein; (in
amount) wenig || adv wenig; **l. by l.**
nach und nach || s—**after a l.** nach
kurzer Zeit; **a l.** ein wenig, ein
bißchen; **make l. of** wenig halten von
Lit'tle Bear' s Kleiner Bär m
Lit'tle Dip'per s Kleiner Wagen m,
Kleiner Bär m
lit'tle fin'ger s kleiner Finger m
lit'tle peo'ple s kleine Leute pl; (myth)
Heinzelmännchen pl
Lit'tle Red Rid'inghood' s Rotkäppchen n
lit'tle slam' s (cards) Klein-Schlemm
m
liturgic(al) [lı'tʌrdʒık(əl)] adj liturgisch
liturgy ['lıtərdʒi] s Liturgie f

livable ['lıvəbəl] adj (place) wohnlich;
(life) erträglich
live [laıv] adj lebendig; (coals) glühend; (ammunition) scharf; (elec)
stromführend; (rad, telv) live; **l. program** Originalsendung f || adv (rad,
telv) live || [lıv] tr leben; (a life)
führen; **l. down** durch einwandfreien
Lebenswandel vergessen machen; **l.
it up** (coll) das Leben genießen; **l.
out** (survive) überleben || intr leben;
(reside) wohnen; (reside temporarily)
sich aufhalten; **l. and learn!** man
lernt nie aus!; **l. for the moment** in
den Tag hineinleben; **l. high off the
hog** in Saus und Braus leben; **l. off
s.o.** j–m auf der Tasche liegen; **l. on**
(subsist on) sich nähren von; (continue to live) fortleben; **l. through**
durchmachen; **l. to see** erleben; **l.
up to** gerecht werden (dat)
livelihood ['laıvlı‚hud] s Lebensunterhalt m
liveliness ['laıvlınıs] s Lebhaftigkeit f
livelong ['lıv‚lɔŋ] adj—**all the l. day**
den lieben langen Tag
lively ['laıvli] adj lebhaft; (street) belebt
liven ['laıvən] tr aufmuntern || intr
munter werden
liver ['lıvər] s (anat) Leber f
liverwurst ['lıvər‚wurst] s Leberwurst f
livery ['lıvəri] s Livree f
liv'ery sta'ble s Mietstallung f
live' show' [laıv] s Originalsendung f,
Livesendung f
livestock ['laıv‚stɑk] s Viehstand m
live' wire' [laıv] s geladener Draht m;
(coll) energiegeladener Mensch m
livid ['lıvıd] adj bleifarben; (enraged)
wütend
liv'ing adj (alive) lebend, lebendig; (for
living) Wohn-; **not a l. soul** keine
Mutterseele f || s Unterhalt n; **good
l.** Wohlleben n; **make a l. (as)** sein
Auskommen haben (als); **what do
you do for a l.?** wie verdienen Sie
Ihren Lebensunterhalt?
liv'ing accommoda'tions spl Unterkunft f
liv'ing be'ing s Lebewesen n
liv'ing condi'tions spl Lebensbedingungen pl
liv'ing expens'es spl Unterhaltskosten
pl
liv'ing quar'ters spl Unterkunft f
liv'ing room' s Wohnzimmer n
liv'ing-room set' (or **suite**) s Polstergarnitur f
liv'ing space' s Lebensraum m
liv'ing wage' s Existenzminimum n
lizard ['lızərd] s Eidechse f
load [lod] s Last f, Belastung f; (in a
truck) Fuhre f; **get a l. of that!** schau
dir das mal an!; **have a l. on** (sl)
einen sitzen haben; **loads of** (coll)
Mengen von; **that's a l. off my mind**
mir ist dabei ein Stein vom Herzen
gefallen || tr (a truck, gun) laden;
(cargo on a ship) einladen; (with
work) überladen; (with worries) belasten; **l. down** belasten; **l. the cam-**

era den Film einlegen; **l. up** aufladen || *intr* das Gewehr laden

load'ed *adj* (*rifle*) scharf geladen; (*dice*) falsch; (*question*) verfänglich; (*very rich*) (sl) steinreich; (*drunk*) (sl) sternhagelvoll; **fully l.** (aut) mit allen Schikanen

loader ['lodər] *s* (*worker*) Ladearbeiter –in *mf;* (*device*) Verladevorrichtung *f*

load'ing *s* Ladung *f*, Verladung *f*

load'ing plat'form *s* Ladebühne *f*

load'ing ramp' *s* Laderampe *f*

load' lim'it *s* Tragfähigkeit *f;* (elec) Belastungsgrenze *f*

load'stone' *s* Magneteisenstein *m*

loaf [lof] *s* (**loaves** [lovz]) Laib *m* || *intr* faulenzen; **l. around** herumlungern

loafer ['lofər] *s* Faulenzer *m*

loaf'ing *s* Faulenzen *n*

loam [lom] *s* Lehm *m*

loamy ['lomi] *adj* lehmig

loan [lon] *s* Anleihe *f*, Darlehe(n) *n* || *tr* (ver)leihen, borgen; **l. out** leihen

loan' com'pany *s* Leihanstalt *f*

loan' shark' *s* (coll) Wucherer *m*

loan' word' *s* Lehnwort *n*

loath [loθ] *adj*—**be l. to** (*inf*) abgeneigt sein zu (*inf*)

loathe [loð] *tr* verabscheuen

loathing ['loðıŋ] *s* (for) Abscheu *m* (vor *dat*)

loathsome ['loðsəm] *adj* abscheulich

lob [lɑb] *s* (tennis) Lobball *m* || *v* (*pret & pp* **lobbed; ger lobbing**) *tr* lobben, hochschlagen

lob·by ['lɑbi] *s* (*of a hotel or theater*) Vorhalle *f*, Foyer *n;* (pol) Interessengruppe *f* || *v* (*pret & pp* –**bied**) *intr* antichambrieren

lob'bying *s* Beeinflussung *f* von Abgeordneten, Lobbying *n*

lobbyist ['lɑbɪ·ɪst] *s* Lobbyist –in *mf*

lobe [lob] *s* (anat) Lappen *m*

lobster ['lɑbstər] *s* Hummer *m;* **red as a l.** (fig) krebsrot

local ['lokəl] *adj* örtlich, Orts–; (*produce*) heimisch || *s* (*group*) Ortsgruppe *f;* (rr) Personenzug *m*

lo'cal anesthe'sia *s* Lokalanästhese *f*

lo'cal call' *s* (telp) Ortsgespräch *n*

lo'cal col'or *s* Lokalkolorit *n*

lo'cal deliv'ery *s* Ortszustellung *f*

locale [lo 'kæl] *s* Ort *m*

lo'cal gov'ernment *s* Gemeindeverwaltung *f*

locality [lo 'kælɪti] *s* Örtlichkeit *f*

localize ['lokə ̦laɪz] *tr* lokalisieren

lo'cal news' *s* Lokalnachrichten *pl*

lo'cal pol'itics *s* Kommunalpolitik *f*

lo'cal show'er *s* Strichregen *m*

lo'cal tax' *s* Gemeindesteuer *f*

lo'cal time' *s* Ortszeit *f*

lo'cal traf'fic *s* Nahverkehr *m*, Ortsverkehr *m*

locate [lo 'ket], ['loket] *tr* (*find*) ausfindig machen; (*a ship, aircraft*) orten; (*the trouble*) finden, feststellen; (*set up, e.g., an office*) errichten; **be located** liegen, gelegen sein || *intr* sich niederlassen

location [lo 'keʃən] *s* Lage *f;* **on l.** (cin) auf Außenaufnahme

lock [lɑk] *s* Schloß *n;* (*of hair*) Locke *f;* (*of a canal*) Schleuse *f;* **l., stock, and barrel** mit allem Drum und Dran; **under l. and key** unter Verschluß || *tr* zusperren; (*arms*) verschränken; **l. in** einsperren; **l. out** aussperren; **l. up** (*a house*) zusperren; (*imprison*) einsperren || *intr* (*said of a lock*) zuschnappen; (*said of brakes*) sperren; **l. together** (*said of bumpers*) sich ineinander verhaken

locker ['lɑkər] *s* (*as in a gym or barracks*) Spind *m & n;* (*for luggage*) Schließfach *n*

lock'er room' *s* Umkleideraum *m*

locket ['lɑkɪt] *s* Medaillon *n*

lock'jaw' *s* Maulsperre *f*

lock' nut' *s* Gegenmutter *f*

lock'out' *s* Aussperrung *f*

lock'smith' *s* Schlosser –in *mf*

lock'smith shop' *s* Schlosserei *f*

lock' step' *s* Marschieren *n* in dicht geschlossenen Gliedern

lock' stitch' *s* Kettenstich *m*

lock'up' *s* (coll) Gefängnis *n*

lock' wash'er *s* Sicherungsring *m*

locomotion [̦lokə 'moʃən] *s* (act) Fortbewegung *f;* (*power*) Fortbewegungsfähigkeit *f*

locomotive [̦lokə 'motɪv] *s* Lokomotive *f*

lo·cus ['lokəs] *s* (–**ci** [saɪ]) Ort *m;* (geom) geometrischer Ort *m*

locust ['lokəst] *s* (*black locust*) (bot) Robinie *f;* (*carob*) (bot) Johannisbrotbaum *m;* (Cicada) (ent) Zikade *f*

lode [lod] *s* (min) Gang *m*

lode'star' *s* Leitstern *m*

lodge [lɑdʒ] *s* (*of Masons*) Loge *f;* (*for hunting*) Jagdhütte *f;* (*for weekending*) Wochenendhäuschen *n;* (*summer house*) Sommerhäuschen *n* || *tr* unterbringen; **l. a complaint** e–e Beschwerde einreichen || *intr* wohnen; (*said of an arrow, etc.*) steckenbleiben

lodger ['lɑdʒər] *s* Untermieter –in *mf*

lodg'ing *s* Unterkunft *f;* **lodgings** Logis *n*

loft [lɔft] *s* Speicher *m;* (*for hay*) Heuboden *m;* (*of a church*) Chor *m;* (*of a golf club*) Hochschlaghaltung *f* || *tr* (*a golf club*) in Hochschlaghaltung bringen; (*a golf ball*) hochschlagen

loftiness ['lɔftɪnɪs] *s* Erhabenheit *f*

lofty ['lɔfti] *adj* (*style*) erhaben; (*high*) hochragend; (*elevated in rank*) gehoben; (*haughty*) anmaßend

log [lɔg] *s* (*trunk*) Baumstamm *m;* (*for the fireplace*) Holzklotz *m;* (*record book*) Tagebuch *n;* (aer, naut) Log *n;* **sleep like a log** wie ein Klotz schlafen || *v* (*pret & pp* **logged; ger logging**) *tr* (*trees*) fällen und abästen; (*cut into logs*) in Klötze schneiden; (*an area*) abholzen; (*enter into a logbook*) in das Logbuch eintragen; (*traverse*) zurücklegen

logarithm ['lɔgə ̦rɪðəm] *s* Logarithmus *m*

log'book' s (aer, naut) Logbuch n
log' cab'in s Blockhaus n, Blockhütte f
logger ['lɔgər] s Holzfäller m
log'gerhead' s—at loggerheads auf Kriegsfuß
log'ging s Holzarbeit f
logic ['lɑdʒɪk] s Logik f
logical ['lɑdʒɪkəl] adj logisch
logician [lo'dʒɪʃən] s Logiker –in mf
logistic(al) [lo'dʒɪstɪk(əl)] adj logistisch
logistics [lo'dʒɪstɪks] s Logistik f
log'jam' s aufgestaute Baumstämme pl; (fig) völlige Stockung f
log'wood' s Kampescheholz n
loin [lɔɪn] s (of beef) Lendenstück n; (anat) Lende f; gird up one's loins (fig) sich rüsten
loin'cloth' s Lendentuch n
loin' end' s (of pork) Rippenstück n
loiter ['lɔɪtər] tr—l. away vertrödeln || intr trödeln; (hang around) herumlungern
loiterer ['lɔɪtərər] s Bummler –in mf
loi'tering s Trödelei f; no l. Herumlungern verboten!
loll [lɑl] intr sich bequem ausstrecken
lollipop ['lɑlɪ ˌpɑp] s Lutschbonbon m & n
Lombardy ['lɑmbərdi] s die Lombardei
London ['lʌndən] adj Londoner || s London n
Londoner ['lʌndənər] s Londoner –in mf
lone [lon] adj (sole) alleinig; (solitary) einzelstehend
loneliness ['lonlɪnɪs] s Einsamkeit f
lonely ['lonli] adj einsam; become l. vereinsamen
loner ['lonər] s Einzelgänger m
lonesome ['lonsəm] adj einsam; be l. for sich sehnen nach
lone' wolf' s (fig) Einzelgänger m
long [lɔŋ] adj (longer ['lɔŋgər]; longest ['lɔŋgɪst]) lang; (way, trip) weit; (detour) groß; a l. time lange; a l. time since schon lange her, daß; in the l. run auf die Dauer || adv lange; as l. as so lange wie; but not for l. aber nicht lange; l. after lange nach; l. ago vor langer Zeit; l. live ...! es lebe ...!; l. since längst; so l.! bis dann! || intr—l. for sich sehnen nach; l. to (inf) sich danach sehnen zu (inf)
long'boat' s Pinasse f
long' dis'tance s (telp) Ferngespräch n; call l. ein Ferngespräch anmelden
long'-dis'tance adj (sport) Langstrecken-
long'-dis'tance call' s Ferngespräch n
long'-dis'tance flight' s Langstreckenflug m
long'-drawn'-out' adj ausgedehnt; (story) langatmig
longevity [lɑn'dʒɛvɪti] s Langlebigkeit f
long' face' s langes Gesicht n
long'hair' adj (fig) intellektuell || s (fig) Intellektueller m; (mus) (coll) konservativer Musiker m
long'hand' s Langschrift f; in l. mit der Hand geschrieben

long'ing adj sehnsüchtig || s (for) Sehnsucht f (nach)
longitude ['lɑndʒɪ ˌt(j)ud] s Länge f
longitudinal [ˌlɑndʒɪ't(j)udɪnəl] adj Longitudinal–
long' jump' s Weitsprung m
long-lived ['lɔŋ'laɪvd] adj langlebig
long'-play'ing rec'ord s Langspielplatte f
long'-range' adj (plan) auf lange Sicht; (aer) Langstrecken–
long'shore'man s (–men) Hafenarbeiter m
long' shot' s (coll) riskante Wette f; by a l. bei weitem
long'stand'ing adj althergebracht, alt
long'-suf'fering adj langmütig
long' suit' s (fig) Stärke f; (cards) lange Farbe f
long'-term' adj langfristig
long-winded ['lɔŋ 'wɪndɪd] adj langatmig
look [lʊk] s (glance) Blick m; (appearance) Aussehen n; (expression) Ausdruck m; from the looks of things wie die Sache aussieht; give a second l. sich [dat] genauer ansehen; have a l. around Umschau halten; have a l. at s.th. sich [dat] etw ansehen; I don't like the looks of it die Sache gefällt mir nicht; looks Ansehen n; new l. verändertes Aussehen n; (latest style) neueste Mode f; take a l. at s.th. sich [dat] etw ansehen || tr—he looks his age man sieht ihm sein Alter an; l. one's best sich in bester Verfassung zeigen; l. one's last at zum letzten Mal ansehen; l. s.o. in the eye j–m in die Augen sehen; l. s.o. over j–n mustern; l. s.th. over etw (über)prüfen (or durchsehen); l. up (e.g., a word) nachschlagen; (e.g., a friend) aufsuchen; l. up and down von oben bis unten mustern || intr schauen; (appear, seem) aussehen; l. after (e.g., children) betreuen; (a household, business) besorgen; (a departing person) nachblicken (dat); l. ahead vorausschauen; l. around (for) sich [dat] umsehen (nach); l. at anschauen; l. back (on) zurücksehen (auf acc); l. down herabsehen; (cast the eyes down) die Augen niederschlagen; l. down on herabsehen auf (acc); (in contempt) über die Achseln ansehen; l. for suchen; (e.g., a criminal) fahnden nach; l. forward to sich freuen auf (acc); l. hard at scharf ansehen; l. into (a mirror, the future) blicken in (acc); (a matter) nachgehen (dat); l. like gleichen (dat); (e.g., rain) aussehen nach; l. on zuschauen; l. on s.o. as j–n betrachten als; l. out aufpassen; l. out for aussehen nach; l. out on (a view) hinausgehen auf (acc); l. sharp! jetzt aber hoppla!; l. through (e.g., a window) blicken durch; (s.o. or s.o.'s motives) durchschauen; l. up (raise one's gaze) aufschauen; l. up to s.o. zu j–m hinaufsehen; things

are beginning to l. up es wird langsam besser; **things don't l. so good for** est steht übel mit; **what does he l. like?** wie sieht er aus?

look'ing glass' s Spiegel m

look'out' s (*watchman*) Wachposten m; (*observation point*) Ausguck m; (*matter of concern*) Sache f; **be a l.** Schmiere stehen; **be on the l. (for)** Auschau halten (nach)

look'out man' s—**be the l.** Schmiere stehen

look'out tow'er s Aussichtsturm m

loom [lum] s Webstuhl m ‖ intr undeutlich und groß auftauchen; **l. large** von großer Bedeutung scheinen

loon [lun] s (orn) Taucher m

loony ['luni] adj verrückt; **be l.** spinnen

loop [lup] s Schleife f, Schlinge f; (e.g., *on a dress for a hook*) Öse f; (aer) Looping m; **do a l.** (aer) e-n Looping drehen ‖ tr schlingen ‖ intr Schlingen (or Schleifen) bilden

loop'hole' s Guckloch n; (in a *fortification*) Schießscharte f; (in a *law*) Lücke f

loose [lus] adj locker, los; (*wobbly*) wackelig; (*morally*) locker, unsolid; (*unpacked*) unverpackt; (*translation*) frei; (*interpretation*) dehnbar; (*dress, tongue*) lose; (*skin*) schlaff; **l. connection** (elec) Wackelkontakt m ‖ adv—**break l.** (*from an enclosure*) ausbrechen; (e.g., *from a hitching*) sich losmachen; (*said of a storm, hell*) losbrechen; **come l.** losgehen; **cut l.** (*act up*) (coll) außer Rand und Band geraten; **turn l.** befreien; **work l.** sich lockern; (*said of a button*) abgehen; (*said of a brick, stone, shoestring*) sich lösen ‖ s—**on the l.** ungehemmt, frei ‖ tr (a *boat*) losmachen; (a *knot*) lösen

loose' change' s Kleingeld n

loose' end' s (fig) unerledigte Kleinigkeit f; **at loose ends** im ungewissen

loose'-leaf note'book s Loseblattbuch n

loosen ['lusən] tr lockern, locker machen ‖ intr locker werden

looseness ['lusnɪs] s Lockerheit f

loot [lut] s Beute f ‖ tr erbeuten; (*plunder*) plündern; (e.g., *art treasures*) verschleppen

lop [lɑp] v (*pret & pp* lopped; *ger* lopping) tr—**lop off** abhacken

lope [lop] s Trab m ‖ intr—**l. along** in großen Schritten laufen

lop'sid'ed adj schief; (*score*) einseitig

loquacious [lo'kweʃəs] adj geschwätzig

lord [lɔrd] s Herr m; (Brit) Lord m; **Lord** Herrgott m ‖ tr—**l. it over** sich als Herr aufspielen über (acc)

lordly ['lɔrdli] adj würdig; (*haughty*) hochmütig

Lord's' Day' s Tag m des Herrn

lord'ship' s Herrschaft f

Lord's' Prayer' s Vaterunser n

Lord's' Sup'per s heiliges Abendmahl n

lore [lor] s Kunde f; (*traditional wisdom*) überlieferte Kunde f

lorry ['lɔri] s (Brit) Lastkraftwagen m

lose [luz] v (*pret & pp* lost [lɔst]) tr verlieren; (*several minutes, as a clock does*) zurückbleiben; (in *betting*) verwetten; (in *gambling*) verspielen; (*the page in a book*) verblättern; **l. one's way** sich verirren; (on *foot*) sich verlaufen; (by *car*) sich verfahren ‖ intr verlieren; (sport) geschlagen werden; **l. to** (sport) unterliegen (dat)

loser ['luzər] s Unterlegene mf; **be the l.** mit langer Nase abziehen

los'ing adj verlierend; (com) verlustbringend ‖ **losings** spl Verluste pl

los'ing game' s aussichtsloses Spiel n

loss [lɔs] s (in) Verlust m (an dat); **at a l.** in Verlegenheit; (com) mit Verlust; **be at a l. for words** nach Worten suchen; **inflict l. on s.o.** j-m Schaden zufügen; **l. of appetite** Appetitlosigkeit f; **l. of blood** Blutverlust m; **l. of face** Blamage f; **l. of life** Verluste pl an Menschenleben; **l. of memory** Gedächtnisverlust m; **l. of sight** Erblindung f; **l. of time** Zeitverlust m; **straight l.** Barverlust m

lost [lɔst] adj verloren; **be l.** (*said of a thing*) verlorengehen; (*not know one's way*) sich verirrt haben; **be l. on s.o.** auf j-n keinen Eindruck machen; **get l.** in Verlust geraten; **get l.!** hau ab!; **l. in thought** in Gedanken versunken

lost'-and-found' depart'ment s Fundbüro n

lost' cause' s aussichtslose Sache f

lot [lɑt] s (*fate*) Los n, Schicksal n; (in a *drawing*) Los n; (*portion of land*) Grundstück n; (cin) Filmgelände n; (com) Posten m, Partie f; **a lot** viel, sehr; **a lot of** (or **lots of**) viel(e); **the lot** das Ganze

lotion ['loʃən] s Wasser n

lottery ['lɑtəri] s Lotterie f

lot'tery tick'et s Lotterielos n

lotto ['lɑto] s Lotto n

lotus ['lotəs] s Lotos m

loud [laud] adj laut; (*colors*) schreiend

loud-mouthed ['laud ˌmauðd] adj laut

loud'speak'er s Lautsprecher m

lounge [laundʒ] s Aufenthaltsraum m ‖ intr sich recken; **l. around** herumlungern

lounge' chair' s Klubsessel m

lounge' liz'ard s (sl) Salonlöwe m

louse [laus] s (*lice* [laɪs]) Laus f; (sl) Sauhund m ‖ tr—**l. up** (sl) versauen

lousy ['lauzi] adj verlaust; (sl) lausig; **l. with** (*people*) wimmelnd von; **l. with money** stinkreich

lout [laut] s Lümmel m

louver ['luvər] s Jalousie f

lovable ['lʌvəbəl] adj liebenswürdig

love [lʌv] adj Liebes– ‖ s (for, of) Liebe f (zu); **be in l. with** verliebt sein in (acc); **for the l. of God** um Gottes willen; **fall (madly) in l. with** sich (heftig) verlieben in (acc); **Love** (at the end of a letter) herzliche Grüße; **l. at first sight** Liebe f auf den ersten Blick; **make l. to** herzen;

(sl) geschlechtlich verkehren mit; **not for l. or money** nicht für Gold und gute Worte; **there's no l. lost between them** sie schätzen sich nicht || *tr* lieben; (*like*) gern haben; **l. to dance** sehr gern tanzen

love′ affair′ *s* Liebeshandel *m*, Liebesverhältnis *n*

love′birds′ *spl* (coll) Unzertrennlichen *pl*

love′ child′ *s* Kind *n* der Liebe

love′ feast′ *s* (eccl) Liebesmahl *n*

love′ game′ *s* (tennis) Nullpartie *f*

love′ knot′ *s* Liebesschleife *f*

loveless [ˈlʌvlɪs] *adj* lieblos

love′ let′ter *s* Liebesbrief *m*

lovelorn [ˈlʌvˌlɔrn] *adj* vor Liebe vergehend

lovely [ˈlʌvli] *adj* lieblich

love′-mak′ing *s* Geschlechtsverkehr *m*

love′ match′ *s* Liebesheirat *f*

love′ po′em *s* Liebesgedicht *n*

love′ po′tion *s* Liebestrank *m*

lover [ˈlʌvər] *s* Liebhaber *m*; **lovers** Liebespaar *n*

love′ scene′ *s* Liebesszene *f*

love′ seat′ *s* Sofasessel *n*

love′sick′ *adj* liebeskrank

love′ song′ *s* Liebeslied *n*

love′ to′ken *s* Liebespfand *n*

lov′ing *adj* liebevoll; **Your l. . . .** Dich liebender . . .

lov′ing-kind′ness *s* Herzensgüte *f*

low [lo] *adj* (*building, mountain, forehead, birth, wages, estimate, prices, rent*) niedrig; (*number*) nieder; (*altitude, speed*) gering; (*not loud*) leise; (*vulgar*) gemein; (*grades, company*) schlecht; (*fever*) leicht; (*pulse, pressure*) schwach; (*ground*) tiefgelegen; (*bow, voice*) tief; (*almost empty*) fast leer; (*supplies, funds*) knapp; **be low** (*said of the sun, water*) niedrigstehen; **be low in funds** knapp bei Kasse sein; **feel low** niedergeschlagen sein; **have a low opinion of** e-e geringe Meinung haben von || *adv* niedrig; **lay low** über den Haufen werfen; **lie low** sich versteckt halten; (*bide one's time*) abwarten; **run low** knapp werden; **sing low** tief singen; **sink low** tief sinken || *s* (*low point*) (fig) Tiefstand *m*; (meteor) Tief *n* || *intr* muhen, brüllen

low′ blow′ *s* (box) Tiefschlag *m*

low′born′ *adj* von niederer Herkunft

low′brow′ *s* Spießbürger *m*

low′-cost hous′ing *s* sozial geförderter Wohnungsbau *m*

Low′ Coun′tries, the *spl* die Niederlande

low′-cut′ *adj* tiefausgeschnitten

low′-down′ *adj* schurkisch || *s* (*unadorned facts*) unverblümte Wahrheit *f*; (*inside information*) Geheimnachrichten *pl*

lower [ˈloər] *comp adj* untere; (*e.g., deck, house, jaw, lip*) Unter– || *tr* herunterlassen; (*the eyes, voice, water level, temperature*) senken; (*prices*) herabsetzen; (*a flag, sail*) streichen; (*lifeboats*) aussetzen; **l.**

oneself sich herablassen || [ˈlauər] *intr* finster blicken; **l. at** finster anblicken

low′er ab′domen [ˈlo·ər] *s* Unterbauch *m*

low′er berth′ [ˈlo·ər] *s* untere Koje *f*

low′er case′ [ˈlo·ər] *s* Kleinbuchstaben *pl*

lower-case [ˈlo·ərˈkes] *adj* klein

low′er course′ [ˈlo·ər] *s* (*of a river*) Unterlauf *m*

low′er mid′dle class′ [ˈlo·ər] *s* Kleinbürgertum *n*

lowermost [ˈlo·ərˌmost] *adj* niedrigste

low′er world′ [ˈlo·ər] *s* Unterwelt *f*

low′-fly′ing *adj* tiefffliegend

low′ fre′quency *s* Niederfrequenz *f*

low′-fre′quency *adj* Niederfrequenz–

low′ gear′ *s* erster Gang *m*

low′-grade′ *adj* minderwertig

low′ing *s* Gebrüll *n*

lowland [ˈloland] *s* Flachland *n*; **Lowlands** (*in Scotland*) Unterland *n*

low′ lev′el *s* Tiefstand *m*

low′-lev′el attack′ *s* Tiefangriff *m*

low′-lev′el flight′ *s* Tiefflug *m*

lowly [ˈloli] *adj* bescheiden; (*humble in spirit*) niederträchtig

low′-ly′ing *adj* tiefliegend

Low′ Mass′ *s* stille Messe *f*

low′-mind′ed *adj* niedrig gesinnt

low′ neck′ *s* (*of a dress*) Ausschnitt *m*

low′-necked′ *adj* tief ausgeschnitten

low′-pitched′ *adj* (*sound*) tief; (*roof*) mit geringer Neigung

low′-pres′sure *adj* Tiefdruck–, Unterdruck–

low′-priced′ *adj* billig

low′ shoe′ *s* Halbschuh *m*

low′-speed′ *adj* mit geringer Geschwindigkeit; (*film*) unempfindlich

low′-spir′ited *adj* niedergeschlagen

low′ spir′its *spl* Niedergeschlagenheit *f*; **be in l.** niedergeschlagen sein

low′ tide′ *s* Ebbe *f*; (fig) Tiefstand *m*

low′ wa′ter *s* Niedrigwasser *n*

low′-wa′ter mark′ *s* (fig) Tiefpunkt *m*

loyal [ˈlɔɪ·əl] *adj* treu, loyal

loyalist [ˈlɔɪ·əlɪst] *s* Regierungstreue *mf*

loyalty [ˈlɔɪ·əlti] *s* Treue *f*

lozenge [ˈlazɪndʒ] *s* Pastille *f*

LP [ˈelˈpi] *s* (trademark) (**long-playing record**) Langspielplatte *f*

Ltd. *abbr* (Brit) (**Limited**) Gesellschaft *f* mit beschränkter Haftung

lubricant [ˈlubrɪkənt] *s* Schmiermittel *n*

lubricate [ˈlubrɪˌket] *tr* (ab)schmieren

lubrication [ˌlubrɪˈkeʃən] *s* Schmierung *f*

lucerne [luˈsʌrn] *s* (bot) Luzerne *f*; Lucerne Luzern *n*

lucid [ˈlusɪd] *adj* (*clear*) klar, deutlich; (*bright*) hell

luck [lʌk] *s* Glück *n*; (*chance*) Zufall *m*; **as l. would have it** wie es der Zufall wollte; **be down on one's l.** an seinem Glück verzagen; **be in l.** Glück haben; **be out of l.** Unglück haben; **dumb l.** (coll) Sauglück *n*; **have tough l.** (coll) Pech haben;

rotten l. (coll) Saupech n; try one's l. sein Glück versuchen; with l. you should win wenn Sie Glück haben, werden Sie gewinnen

luckily ['lʌkɪli] adv zum Glück

luckless ['lʌklɪs] adj glücklos

lucky ['lʌki] adj glücklich; be l. Glück haben; l. dog (coll) Glückspilz m; l. penny Glückspfennig m

luck'y shot' s Glückstreffer m

lucrative ['lukrətɪv] adj gewinnbringend

ludicrous ['ludɪkrəs] adj lächerlich

lug [lʌg] s (pull, tug) Ruck m; (lout) (sl) Lümmel m; (elec) Öse f ‖ v (pret & pp lugged; ger lugging) tr schleppen

luggage ['lʌgɪdʒ] s Gepäck n; excess l. Mehrgepäck n; piece of l. Gepäckstück n

lug'gage car'rier s Gepäckträger m

lug'gage compart'ment s (aer) Frachtraum m

lug'gage rack' s Gepäckablage f; (on the roof of a car) Dachgepäckträger m

lug'gage receipt' s Aufgabeschein m

lugubrious [lʊ'g(j)ubrɪ·əs] adj tieftraurig

lukewarm ['luk,wɔrm] adj lau, lauwarm

lull [lʌl] s Windstille f; (com) Flaute f ‖ tr einlullen; (e.g., fears) beschwichtigen; l. to sleep einschläfern ‖ intr nachlassen

lullaby ['lʌlə,baɪ] s Wiegenlied n

lumbago [lʌm'bego] s Hexenschluß m

lumber ['lʌmbər] s Bauholz n ‖ intr sich schwerfällig fortbewegen

lum'berjack' s Holzfäller m

lum'ber·man' s (-men') (dealer) Holzhändler m; (lumberjack) Holzfäller m

lum'beryard' s Holzplatz m

luminary ['lumɪ,neri] s Leuchtkörper m; (fig) Leuchte f

luminescent [,lumɪ'nesənt] adj lumineszierend

luminous ['lumɪnəs] adj leuchtend, Leucht–

lu'minous di'al s Leuchtzifferblatt n

lu'minous paint' s Leuchtfarbe f

lummox ['lʌməks] s Lümmel m

lump [lʌmp] s (e.g., of clay) Klumpen m; (on the body) Beule f; have a l. in one's throat e–n Kloß (or Knödel) im Hals haben; l. of sugar Würfel m Zucker ‖ tr—l. together (fig) zusammenwerfen

lumpish ['lʌmpɪʃ] adj klumpig

lump' sug'ar s Würfelzucker m

lump' sum' s Pauschalbetrag m

lumpy ['lʌmpi] adj klumpig; (sea) bewegt

lunacy ['lunəsi] s Irrsinn m

lu'nar eclipse' ['lunər] s Mondfinsternis f

lu'nar land'ing s Mondlandung f

lu'nar mod'ule s (rok) Mondfähre f

lu'nar year' s Mondjahr n

lunatic ['lunətɪk] s Irre mf

lu'natic asy'lum s Irrenhaus n

lu'natic fringe' s Extremisten pl

lunch [lʌntʃ] s (at noon) Mittagessen n, Lunch m; (light meal) Zwischenmahlzeit f; eat l. zu Mittag essen; have (s.th.) for l. zum Mittagessen haben ‖ intr zu Mittag essen, lunchen

lunch' coun'ter s Theke f

luncheon ['lʌntʃən] s gemeinsames Mittagessen n

luncheonette [,lʌntʃə'net] s Imbißstube f

lunch' hour' s Mittagsstunde f

lunch'room' s Imbißhalle f

lunch'time' s Mittagszeit f

lung [lʌŋ] s Lunge f; at the top of one's lungs aus voller Kehle

lunge ['lʌndʒ] s Sprung m vorwärts; (fencing) Ausfall m ‖ tr (a horse) an der Longe laufen lassen ‖ intr— e–n Sprung vorwärts machen; (with a sword) (at) e–n Ausfall machen (gegen); l. at losstürzen auf (acc)

lurch [lʌrtʃ] s Torkeln n, Taumeln n; leave in a l. im Stich lassen ‖ intr torkeln; (said of a ship) zur Seite rollen

lure [lur] s Köder m ‖ tr ködern; (fig) verlocken; l. away weglocken

lurid ['lurɪd] adj (light) gespenstisch; (sunset) düsterrot; (gruesome) grausig; (pallid) fahl

lurk [lʌrk] intr lauern

luscious ['lʌʃəs] adj köstlich; a l. doll (coll) ein tolles Weib

lush [lʌʃ] adj üppig

lust [lʌst] s Wollust f; (for) Begierde f (nach) ‖ intr (after, for) gieren (nach)

luster ['lʌstər] s Glanz m; (e.g., chandelier) Lüster m

lusterless ['lʌstərlɪs] adj matt

lus'terware' s Tongeschirr n mit Lüster

lustful ['lʌstfəl] adj lüstern, geil

lustrous ['lʌstrəs] adj glänzend

lusty ['lʌsti] adj kräftig

lute [lut] s Laute f

Lutheran ['luθərən] adj lutherisch ‖ s Lutheraner –in mf

luxuriance [lʌg'ʒurɪ·əns] s Üppigkeit f

luxuriant [lʌg'ʒurɪ·ənt] adj üppig

luxuriate [lʌg'ʒurɪ,et] intr (thrive) gedeihen; (delight) (in) schwelgen (in dat)

luxurious [lʌg'ʒurɪ·əs] adj luxuriös; l. living Prasserei f

luxury ['lʌgʒəri] s Extravaganz f, Luxus m; (object of luxury) Luxusartikel m; live a life of l. im vollen leben

lye [laɪ] s Lauge f

ly'ing adj lügenhaft ‖ s Lügen n

ly'ing-in' hos'pital s Entbindungsanstalt f

lymph [lɪmf] s Lymphe f

lymphatic [lɪm'fætɪk] adj lymphatisch

lynch [lɪntʃ] tr lynchen

lynch'ing s Lynchen n

lynch' law' s Lynchjustiz f

lynx [lɪŋks] s Luchs m

lynx'-eyed' adj luchsäugig

lyre [laɪr] s (mus) Leier f
lyric ['lɪrɪk] adj lyrisch; **l. poetry**
Lyrik f ‖ s lyrisches Gedicht n; (of
a song) Text m

lyrical ['lɪrɪkəl] adj lyrisch
lyricism ['lɪrɪ,sɪzəm] s Lyrik f
lyricist ['lɪrɪsɪst] s (of a song) Texter
–in mf; (poet) lyrischer Dichter m

M

M, m [ɛm] s dreizehnter Buchstabe des
englischen Alphabets
ma [mɑ] s (coll) Mama f
ma'am [mæm] s (coll) gnädige Frau f
macadam [məˈkædəm] s Makadam-
decke f
macadamize [məˈkædə,maɪz] tr ma-
kadamisieren
maca'dam road' s Straße f mit Maka-
damdecke
macaroni [,mækəˈroni] spl Makkaroni
pl
macaroon [,mækəˈrun] s Makrone f
macaw [məˈkɔ] s (orn) Ara m
mace [mes] s Stab m, Amtsstab m
mace'bear'er s Träger m des Amts-
stabes
machination [,mækɪˈneʃən] s Intrige
f; **machinations** Machenschaften pl
machine [məˈʃin] s Maschine f; (pol)
Apparat m; **by m.** maschinell ‖ tr
spannabhebend formen
machine'-driv'en adj mit Maschinenan-
trieb
machine' gun' s Maschinengewehr n
machine'-gun' v (pret & pp –gunned;
ger –gunning) tr unter Maschinenge-
wehrfeuer nehmen
machine' gun'ner s Maschinengewehr-
schütze m
machine'-made' adj maschinell herge-
stellt
machinery [məˈʃinəri] s (& fig) Maschinerie f
machine' screw' s Maschinenschraube
f
machine' shop' s Maschinenhalle f
machine' tool' s Werkzeugmaschine f
machinist [məˈʃinɪst] s (maker and
repairer of machines) Maschinen-
bauer m; (machine operator) Ma-
schinenschlosser –in mf
mackerel ['mækərəl] s Makrele f
mad [mæd] adj (madder; maddest) verrückt; (angry) böse; **be mad about**
vernarrt sein in (acc); **be mad at**
böse sein auf (acc); **drive mad** verrückt machen; **go mad** verrückt
werden
madam ['mædəm] s gnädige Frau f;
(of a brothel) (sl) Bordellmutter f
mad'cap' adj ausgelassen ‖ s Wildfang
m
madden ['mædən] tr verrückt machen;
(make angry) zornig machen
made'-to-or'der adj nach Maß angefertigt
made'-up' adj (story) erfunden; (artificial) künstlich; (with cosmetics) ge-
schminkt

mad'house' s Irrenhaus n, Narrenhaus
n
madly ['mædli] adv (coll) wahnsinnig
mad'man' s (–men') Verrückter m
madness ['mædnɪs] s Wahnsinn m
Madonna [məˈdɑnə] s Madonna f
maelstrom ['melstrəm] s (& fig) Strudel m
magazine [,mægəˈzin] s (periodical)
Zeitschrift f; (illustrated) Illustrierte
f; (warehouse for munitions; cartridge container) Magazin n; (for a
camera) Kassette f
magazine' rack' s Zeitschriftenständer
m
Maggie ['mægi] s Gretchen n
maggot ['mægət] s Made f
Magi ['medʒaɪ] spl—**the three M.**
(Bib) die drei Weisen pl aus dem
Morgenland
magic ['mædʒɪk] adj (enchanting) zau-
berhaft; (trick, word, wand) Zauber–
‖ s Zauberkunst f
magician [məˈdʒɪʃən] s Zauberer –in
mf
ma'gic lan'tern s Laterna magica f
magisterial [,mædʒɪsˈtɪrɪ-əl] adj (of
a magistrate) obrigkeitlich; (authoritative) autoritativ; (pompous) anmaßend
magistrate ['mædʒɪs,tret] s Polizei-
richter m
magnanimous [mægˈnænɪməs] adj groß-
mütig
magnate ['mægnet] s Magnat m
magnesium [mægˈnizɪ-əm] s Magnesium n
magnet ['mægnɪt] s Magnet m
magnetic [mægˈnetɪk] adj magnetisch;
(personality) fesselnd
magnetism ['mægnɪ,tɪzəm] s Magnetismus m; (fig) Anziehungskraft f
magnetize ['mægnɪ,taɪz] tr magnetisieren
magnificence [mægˈnɪfɪsəns] s Pracht
f
magnificent [mægˈnɪfɪsənt] adj prächtig
magnifier ['mægnɪ,faɪ-ər] s (electron)
Verstärker m
magni-fy ['mægnɪ,faɪ] v (pret & pp
–fied) tr vergrößern; (fig) übertreiben
mag'nifying glass' s Lupe f
magnitude ['mægnɪ,t(j)ud] s (& astr)
Größe f
magno'lia tree' [mægˈnolɪ-ə] s Magno-
lia f
magpie ['mæg,paɪ] s (& fig) Elster f
mahlstick ['mɑl,stɪk] s Malerstock m

mahogany [mə'hagəni] s Mahagoni n
mahout [mə'haut] s Elefantentreiber m
maid [med] s Dienstmädchen n
maiden ['medən] s Jungfer f; (poet) Maid f
maid'enhair' s (bot) Jungfernhaar n
maid'enhead' s Jungfernhäutchen n
maid'enhood' s Jungfräulichkeit f
maidenly ['medənli] adj jungfräulich
maid'en name' s Mädchenname m
maid'en voy'age s Jungfernfahrt f
maid'-in-wait'ing s (maids-in-waiting) Hofdame f
maid' of hon'or s erste Brautjungfer f
maid'serv'ant s Dienstmädchen n
mail [mel] adj Post– || s Post f; (armor) Kettenpanzer m; by m. brieflich; by return m. postwendend || tr (put into the mail) aufgeben; (send) abschicken; m. to zuschicken (dat)
mail'bag' s Postsack m
mail'boat' s Postschiff n
mail'box' s Briefkasten m
mail' car'rier s Briefträger –in mf
mail' deliv'ery s Postzustellung f
mail' drop' s Briefeinwurf m
mailer ['melər] s (phot) Versandbeutel m
mail'ing s Absendung f
mail'ing list' s Postversandliste f
mail'ing per'mit s Zulassung f zum portofreien Versand
mail'man' s (–men') Briefträger m
mail' or'der s Bestellung f durch die Post
mail'-order house' s Versandhaus n
mail' plane' s Postflugzeug n
mail' train' s Postzug m
mail' truck' s Postauto n
maim [mem] tr verstümmeln
main [men] adj Haupt– || s Hauptleitung f; in the main hauptsächlich
main' clause' s (gram) Hauptsatz m
main' course' s Hauptgericht n
main' deck' s Hauptdeck n
main' floor' s Erdgeschoß n
mainland ['men,lænd] s Festland n
main' line' s (rr) Hauptstrecke f
mainly ['menli] adv größtenteils
mainmast ['men,mæst] s Großmast m
main' of'fice s Hauptbüro n, Zentrale f
main' point' s springender Punkt m
mainsail ['men,sel] s Großsegel m
main'spring' s (horol & fig) Triebfeder f
main'stay' s (fig) Hauptstütze f; (naut) Großstag n
main' street' s Hauptstraße f
maintain [men'ten] tr aufrechterhalten; (e.g., a family) unterhalten; (assert) behaupten; (one's reputation) wahren; (e.g., in good condition) bewahren; (order, silence) halten; (a road) instand halten
maintenance ['mentɪnəns] s (upkeep) Instandhaltung f; (support) Unterhalt m; (e.g., of an automobile) Wardirektor m
maître d'hôtel [,metərdo'tɛl] s (head waiter) Oberkellner m; (owner)

Hotelbesitzer m; (manager) Hoteltung f
majestic [mə'dʒestɪk] adj majestätisch
majesty ['mædʒɪsti] s Majestät f
major ['medʒər] adj Haupt–; (mus) –Dur || s (educ) Hauptfach n; (mil) Major m || intr—m. in als Hauptfach studieren
majordomo ['medʒər'domo] s Haushofmeister m
ma'jor gen'eral s Generalmajor m
majority [mə'dʒərɪti] adj Mehrheits– || s Mehrheit f; (full age) Mündigkeit f; (mil) Majorsrang m; (parl) Stimmenmehrheit f; be in the m. in der Mehrheit sein; in the m. of cases in der Mehrzahl der Fälle; the m. of people die meisten Menschen
major'ity vote' s Mehrheitsbeschluß m
ma'jor league' s Oberliga f
make [mek] s Fabrikat n, Marke f || tr machen; (in a factory) herstellen; (cause) lassen; (force) zwingen; (clothes) anfertigen; (money) verdienen; (a reputation, name) erwerben; (a choice) treffen; (a confession) ablegen; (a report) erstatten; (plans) schmieden; (changes) vornehmen; (a movie) drehen; (contact) herstellen; (a meal) (zu)bereiten; (conditions) stellen; (rules, assertions) aufstellen; (a bet, compromise, peace) schließen; (excuses, requests, objections) vorbringen; (a protest) erheben; (a goal) schießen (or erzielen); (a comparison) ziehen; (a speech) halten; (e.g., a good father) abgeben; (be able to fit through, e.g., a window) gehen durch; (e.g., a train, bus, destination) erreichen; (e.g., ten miles) zurücklegen; (a girl) (sl) verführen; (arith) machen; m. (s.o.) believe weismachen (dat); m. into verarbeiten zu; m. of halten von; m. out (e.g., writing) entziffern; (e.g., a person at a distance) erkennen; (understand) kapieren; (a blank or form) ausfüllen; (a check, receipt) ausstellen; m. over to (jur) überschreiben auf (acc); m. s.o. out to be a liar j-n als Lügner hinstellen; m. s.th. of oneself es weit bringen; m. the most of ausnutzen; m. time Zeit gewinnen; m. time with (a woman) (coll) flirten mit; m. up (e.g., a list) zusammenstellen; (a bill) ausstellen; (a sentence) bilden; (a story) sich [dat] ausdenken; m. up one's mind (about) sich [dat] schlüssig werden (über acc); m. way! Platz da!; m. way for ausweichen vor (dat) || intr—m. believe schauspielern; m. believe that nur so tun, als ob; m. do with sich behelfen mit; m. for lossteuern auf (acc); m. off with durchbrennen mit; m. out well gut auskommen; m. sure of sich vergewissern (genit); m. sure that vergewissern, daß; m. up (after a quarrel) sich versöhnen; m. up for (past mistakes) wieder gutmachen; (lost time) wieder einbringen

make'-believe' adj Schein-, vorgetäuscht ‖ s Schein m, Mache f
maker ['mekər] s Hersteller –in mf;
Maker Schöpfer m
make'shift' adj behelfsmäßig, Behelfs-
‖ s Notbehelf m
make'-up' s Aufmachung f; (cosmetic)
Make-up n, Schminke f; (of a team)
Aufstellung f; (theat) Maske f; (typ)
Umbruch m; **apply m.** sich schminken
make'weight' s Gewichtszugabe f
mak'ing s Herstellung f; **be in the m.**
im Werden sein; **have the makings
of** das Zeug haben zu; **this is of his
own m.** dies ist sein eigenes Werk
maladjusted [,mælə'dʒʌstɪd] adj unausgeglichen
maladroit [,mælə'drɔɪt] adj unge-
scnickt
malady ['mælədi] s (& fig) Krankheit
f
malaise [mæ'lez] s (physical) Unwohl-
sein n; (mental) Unbehagen n
malaria [mə'lɛrɪ·ə] s Malaria f
Malaya [mə'le·ə] s Malaya n
Malaysia [mə'leʒɪ·ə] s Malaysia n
malcontent ['mælkən,tɛnt] adj unzufrieden ‖ s Unzufriedene mf
male [mel] adj männlich ‖ s Mann m;
(bot) männliche Pflanze f; (zool)
Männchen n
malediction [,mælɪ'dɪkʃən] s Ver-
wünschung f
malefactor ['mælɪ,fæktər] s Übeltäter
–in mf
male' nurse' s Pfleger m
malevolence [mæ'lɛvələns] s Böswillig-
keit f
malevolent [mə'lɛvələnt] adj böswillig
malfeasance [,mæl'fizəns] s strafbare
Handlung f; **m. in office** Amtsvergehen n
malice ['mælɪs] s Bosheit f
malicious [mə'lɪʃəs] adj boshaft
malign [mə'laɪn] adj böswillig ‖ tr
verleumden
malignancy [mə'lɪgnənsi] s (pathol)
Bösartigkeit f
malignant [mə'lɪgnənt] adj böswillig;
(pathol) bösartig
malinger [mə'lɪŋgər] intr simulieren
malingerer [mə'lɪŋgərər] s Simulant
–in mf
mall [mɔl] s (promenade) Lauben-
promenade f; (shopping center) über-
dachtes Einkaufszentrum n, Mall f
mallard ['mælərd] s Stockente f
malleable ['mælɪ·əbəl] adj schmiedbar
mallet ['mælɪt] s Schlegel m
mallow ['mælo] s Malve f
malnutrition [,mæln(j)u'trɪʃən] s Unterernährung f
malodorous [mæl'odərəs] adj übelriechend
malpractice [mæl'præktɪs] s ärztlicher
Kunstfehler m
malt [mɔlt] s Malz n
maltreat [mæl'trit] tr mißhandeln
mamma ['mɑmə] s Mama f, Mutti f

mammal ['mæməl] s Säugetier n
mammalian [mæ'melɪ·ən] adj Säu-
getier- ‖ s Säugetier n
mam'mary gland' ['mæməri] s Milch-
drüse f
mam'ma's boy' s Muttersöhnchen n
mammoth ['mæmə θ] adj ungeheuer
(groß) ‖ s (zool) Mammut n
man [mæn] s (men [mɛn]) (adult male)
Mann m; (human being) Mensch m;
(servant) Diener m; (worker) Arbeiter m; (mankind) die Menschheit
f; (checkers) Stein m; **man alive!**
Menschenskind! ‖ v (pret & pp
manned; ger manning) tr besetzen;
(nav, rok) bemannen
man' about town' s weltgewandter
Mann m
manacle ['mænəkəl] s Handschelle f ‖
tr fesseln
manage ['mænɪdʒ] tr (a business,
household) leiten; (an estate) verwalten; (tools, weapons) handhaben;
(e.g., a boat, car) völlig in der Gewalt haben; (children) fertig werden
mit; **I'll m.** it ich werde es schon
schaffen; **m. the situation** die Sache
deichseln ‖ intr zurechtkommen;
(with, on) auskommen (mit); **m. to**
(inf) es fertigbringen zu (inf)
manageable ['mænɪdʒəbəl] adj handlich; (hair) fügsam
management ['mænɪdʒmənt] s Unter-
nehmensführung f; (group which
manages) Direktion f; (as opposed
to labor) Management n
man'agement consult'ant s Unterneh-
mungsberater –in mf
manager ['mænədʒər] s Manager m,
Geschäftsführer –in mf; (of a bank
or hotel) Direktor –in mf; (of an
estate) Verwalter –in mf; (of a department) Abteilungsleiter –in mf;
(of a star, theater, athlete) Manager
m
managerial [,mænə'dʒɪrɪ·əl] adj Lei-
tungs-, Führungs–
man'aging adj geschäftsführend
man'aging direc'tor s Geschäftsführer
–in mf
Manchuria [mæn'tʃʊrɪ·ə] s Mandschurei f
man'darin or'ange ['mændərɪn] s
Mandarine f
mandate ['mændet] s Mandat n ‖ tr
(to) zuweisen (dat)
mandatory ['mændə,tori] adj verbindlich
mandolin ['mændəlɪn] s Mandoline f
mandrake ['mændrek] s (bot) Alraune
f
mane [men] s Mähne f
maneuver [mə'nuvər] s Manöver n; **go
on maneuvers** (mil) ins Manöver ziehen ‖ tr manövrieren; **m. s.o. into**
(ger) j-n dazubringen zu (inf)
maneuverability [mə,nuvərə'bɪlɪti] s
Manövrierbarkeit f
maneuverable [mə'nuvərəbəl] adj ma-
növrierfähig
manful ['mænfəl] adj mannhaft
manganese ['mæŋgə,niz] s Mangan n

mange ['mendʒ] s Räude f
manger ['mendʒər] s Krippe f
mangle ['mæŋgəl] s Mangel f || tr
(tear apart) zerfleischen; (wash)
mangeln
mangy ['mendʒi] adj räudig; (fig)
schäbig
man'han'dle tr grob behandeln
man'hole' s Kanalschacht m, Mann-
loch n
man'hole cov'er s Schachtdeckel m
man'hood' s (virility) Männlichkeit f;
(age) Mannesalter n
man'-hour' s Arbeitsstunde f pro Mann
man'hunt' s Fahndung f
mania ['menɪ·ə] s Manie f
maniac ['menɪ‚æk] s Geisteskranke
mf
maniacal [mə'naɪ·əkəl] adj manisch
manicure ['mænɪ‚kjʊr] s Maniküre f,
Handpflege f || tr maniküren
manicurist ['mænɪ‚kjʊrɪst] s Maniküre f
manifest ['mænɪ‚fɛst] adj offenkundig,
offenbar || s (aer, naut) Manifest n
|| tr bekunden, bezeigen
manifestation [‚mænɪfɛs'teʃən] s
(manifesting) Offenbarung f; (indication) Anzeichen n
manifes•to [‚mænɪ'fɛsto] s (-toes)
Manifest n
manifold ['mænɪ‚fold] adj mannigfal-
tig || s (aut) Rohrverzweigung f
manikin ['mænɪkɪn] s Männchen n;
(for teaching anatomy) anatomisches
Modell n; (mannequin) Mannequin n
man' in the moon' s Mann m im Mond
man' in the streets' s Durchschnitts-
mensch m
manipulate [mə'nɪpjə‚let] tr manipulieren
man'kind' s Menschheit f
manliness ['mænlɪnɪs] s Männlichkeit
f
manly ['mænli] adj mannhaft, männlich
man'-made' adj künstlich
manna ['mænə] s Manna n, Himmels-
brot n
manned' space'craft s bemanntes
Raumfahrzeug n
mannequin ['mænɪkɪn] s (clothes
model) Mannequin n; (in a display
window) Schaufensterpuppe f
manner ['mænər] s Art f, Weise f;
(custom) Sitte f; after the m. of
nach der Art von; by all m. of means
auf jeden Fall; by no m. of means
auf keinen Fall; in a m. gewissermaßen; in a m. of speaking sozusagen; in like m. gleicherweise; in
the following m. folgendermaßen; in
this m. auf diese Weise; it's bad
manners to (inf) es schickt sich nicht
zu (inf); m. of death Todesart f;
manners Manieren pl
mannerism ['mænə‚rɪzəm] s Manie-
riertheit f
mannerly ['mænərli] adj manierlich
mannish ['mænɪʃ] adj männisch;
(woman) unweiblich
man' of let'ters s Literat m

man' of the world' s Weltmann m
man' of war' s Kriegsschiff n
manor ['mænər] s Herrengut n
man'or house' s Herrenhaus n
man'pow'er s Arbeitskräfte pl; (mil)
Kriegsstärke f
man'serv'ant s (menservants) Diener m
mansion ['mænʃən] s Herrenhaus n
man'slaugh'ter s Totschlag m
mantel ['mæntəl] s Kaminsims m & n
man'telpiece' s Kaminsims m & n
mantilla [mæn'tɪlə] s Mantille f
mantle ['mæntəl] s (& fig) Mantel m;
(of a gaslight) Glühstrumpf m; (geol)
Mantel m || tr verhüllen
manual ['mænjʊ·əl] adj manuell, Hand-
|| s (book) Handbuch n, Leitfaden
m; (mus) Manual n
man'ual control' s Handbedienung f
man'ual dexter'ity s Handfertigkeit f
man'ual la'bor s Handarbeit f
man'ual of arms' s (mil) Dienstvor-
schrift f
man'ual train'ing s Werkunterricht m
manufacture [‚mænjə'fæktʃər] s Herstellung f; (production) Erzeugnis n
|| tr herstellen; (clothes) konfektio-
nieren
manufac'tured goods' spl Fertigwaren
pl
manufacturer [‚mænjə'fæktʃərər] s
Hersteller –in mf
manure [mə'n(j)ʊr] s Mist m || tr
misten
manuscript ['mænjə‚skrɪpt] adj hand-
schriftlich || s Manuskript n
many ['meni] adj viele; a good (or
great) m. sehr viele; how m. wieviele; in so m. words ausdrücklich;
m. a mancher, manch ein; m. a person manch einer; m. a time manchmal; twice as m. noch einmal so
viele || pron viele; as m. as ten nicht
weniger als zehn; how m. wieviele
man'y-sid'ed adj vielseitig
map [mæp] s Karte f, Landkarte f; (of
a city) Plan m; (of a local area)
Spezialkarte f; map of the world
Weltkarte f; put on the map (coll)
ausposaunen || v (pret & pp mapped;
ger mapping) tr kartographisch aufnehmen; map out planen
maple ['mepəl] s Ahorn m
ma'ple sug'ar s Ahornzucker m
ma'ple syr'up s Ahornsirup m
mar [mar] v (pret & pp marred; ger
marring) tr (detract from the beauty
of) verunzieren; (e.g., a reputation)
beeinträchtigen
marathon ['mærə‚θɑn] s Dauerwett-
bewerb m
mar'athon race' s Marathonlauf m
maraud [mə'rɔd] tr & intr plündern
marauder [mə'rɔdər] s Plünderer m
marble ['marbəl] adj marmorn || s
Marmor m; (little glass ball) Murmel
f; marbles (game) Murmelspiel n ||
tr marmorieren
mar'ble quar'ry s Marmorbruch m
march [martʃ] s Marsch m; (festive
parade) Umzug m; **March** März m;
on the m. auf dem Marsch; steal a

m. on s.o. j–m den Rang ablaufen; the m. of time der Lauf der Zeit || *tr* marschieren || *intr* marschieren; m. by vorbeimarschieren (an *dat*); m. off abmarschieren || *interj* marsch!

marchioness ['marʃənɪs] *s* Marquise *f*

mare ⌊mer⌋ *s* Stute *f*

Margaret ['margərɪt] *s* Margarete *f*

margarine ['mardʒərɪn] *s* Margarine *f*

margin ['mardʒɪn] *s* (*of a page*) Rand *m*; (*leeway*) Spielraum *m*; (fin) Spanne *f*; **by a narrow m.** mit knappem Abstand; **leave a m.** am Rande Raum lassen; **m. of profit** Gewinnspanne *f*; **m. of safety** Sicherheitsfaktor *m*; **win by a ten-second m.** mit zehn Sekunden Abstand gewinnen; **write in the m.** an dem Rand schreiben

marginal ['mardʒɪnəl] *adj* (*costs, profits, case*) Grenz–; (*in the margin*) Rand–

mar'ginal note' *s* Randbemerkung *f*

mar'gin release' *s* Randauslöser *m*

mar'gin set'ter *s* Randsteller *m*

marigold ['mærɪ‚gold] *s* Ringelblume *f*

marijuana [‚marɪ'hwanə] *s* Marihuana *n*

marinate ['mærɪ‚net] *tr* marinieren

marine [mə'rin] *adj* See–, Meer(es)– || *s* (*fleet*) Marine *f*; (*fighter*) Marineinfanterist *m*; **marines** Marinetruppen *pl*

Marine' Corps' *s* Marineinfanteriekorps *n*

mariner ['mærɪnər] *s* Seemann *m*

marionette [‚mærɪ‑ə'net] *s* Marionette *f*

marital ['mærɪtəl] *adj* ehelich, Gatten–

mar'ital sta'tus *s* Familienstand *m*

maritime ['mærɪ‚taɪm] *adj* See–

marjoram ['mardʒərəm] *s* Majoran *m*

mark [mark] *s* (& fig) Zeichen *n*; (*stain, bruise*) Fleck *m*, Mal *n*; (*German unit of currency*) Mark *f*; (*educ*) Zensur *f*; **be an easy m.** (coll) leicht reinzulegen sein; **hit the m.** ins Schwarze treffen; **make one's m.** sich durchsetzen; **m. of confidence** Vertrauensbeweis *m*; **m. of favor** Gunstbezeichnung *f*; **m. of respect** Zeichen *n* der Hochachtung; **on your marks!** auf die Plätze!; **wide of the m.** am Ziel vorbei || *tr* (aus)zeichnen, bezeichnen; (*student papers*) zensieren; (*cards*) zinken; (*labels*) beschriften; (*laundry*) zeichnen; (*the score*) anschreiben; **m. down** aufschreiben, niederschreiben; (com) im Preis herabsetzen; **m. my words!** merken Sie sich, was ich sage!; **m. off** abgrenzen; (surv) abstecken; **m. time** (mil & fig) auf der Stelle treten; (mus) den Takt schlagen; **m. up** (*e.g., a wall*) beschmieren; (com) im Preis heraufsetzen

mark'down' *s* Preisnachlaß *m*

marked *adj* (*difference*) merklich; **a m. man** ein Gezeichneter *m*

marker ['markər] *s* (*of scores*) Anschreiber –in *mf*; (*commemorative*

marker) Gedenktafel *f*; (*on a firing range*) Anzeiger *m*; (*bombing marker*) Leuchtbombe *f*; (*felt pen*) Filzschreiber *m*

market ['markɪt] *s* Markt *m*; (*grocery store*) Lebensmittelgeschäft *n*; (*stock exchange*) Börse *f*; (*ready sale*) Absatz *m*; **be in the m. for** Bedarf haben an (*dat*); **be on the m.** zum Verkauf stehen; **put on the m.** auf den Markt bringen || *tr* verkaufen

marketable ['markɪtəbəl] *adj* marktfähig

mar'ket anal'ysis *s* Marktanalyse *f*

mar'keting *s* (econ) Marketing *n*; **do the m.** Einkäufe machen

mar'keting research' *s* Absatzforschung *f*

mar'ketplace' *s* Marktplatz *m*

mar'ket price' *s* Marktpreis *m*

mar'ket town' *s* Marktflecken *m*

mar'ket val'ue *s* Marktwert *m*; (st. exch.) Kurswert *m*

mark'ing *s* Kennzeichen *n*

marks•man ['marksmən] *s* (–men) Schütze *m*

marks'manship' *s* Schießkunst *f*

mark'up' *s* (com) Gewinnaufschlag *m*

marl [marl] *s* Mergel *m* || *tr* mergeln

marmalade ['marmə‚led] *s* Marmelade *f*

maroon [mə'run] *adj* rotbraun, kastanienbraun || *s* Kastanienbraun *n* || *tr* aussetzen; **be marooned** von der Außenwelt abgeschnitten sein

marquee [mar'ki] *s* Schutzdach *n*

marquess ['markwɪs] *s* Marquis *m*

marquis ['markwɪs] *s* Marquis *m*

marquise [mar'kiz] *s* Marquise *f*

marriage ['mærɪdʒ] *s* Heirat *f*; (*state*) Ehe *f*, Ehestand *m*; **by m.** angeheiratet, schwägerlich; **give in m.** verheiraten

marriageable ['mærɪdʒəbəl] *adj* heiratsfähig; **m. age** (*of a girl*) Mannbarkeit *f*

mar'riage brok'er *s* Heiratsvermittler –in *mf*

mar'riage cer'emony *s* Trauung *f*

mar'riage li'cense *s* Heiratsurkunde *f*

mar'riage of conven'ience *s* Vernunftehe *f*

mar'riage por'tion *s* Mitgift *f*

mar'riage propos'al *s* Heiratsantrag *m*

mar'riage vow' *s* Ehegelöbnis *n*

mar'ried cou'ple *s* Ehepaar *n*

mar'ried state' *s* Ehestand *m*

marrow ['mæro] *s* Knochenmark *n*; (fig) Mark *n*

mar•ry ['mæri] *v* (*pret & pp* –ried) *tr* heiraten; (*said of a priest or minister*) trauen; **m. off (to)** verheiraten (mit) || *intr* heiraten; **m. rich** e–e gute Partie machen

Mars [marz] *s* Mars *m*

marsh [marʃ] *s* Sumpf *m*

mar•shal ['marʃəl] *s* Zeremonienmeister *m*; (*police officer*) Bezirkspolizeichef *m*; (mil) Marschall *m* || *v* (*pret & pp* –shal[l]ed) *ger* –shal[l]ing) *tr* (*troops*) ordnungsgemäß aufstellen; (*strength*) zusammenraffen

marsh'land' *s* Sumpfland *n*
marsh' mal'low *s* (bot) Eibisch *m*
marsh'mal'low *s* (*candy*) Konfekt *n* aus Stärkesirup, Zucker, Stärke, Gelatine, und geschlagenem Eiweiß
marshy ['marʃi] *adj* sumpfig
mart [mart] *s* Markt *m*
marten ['martən] *s* (zool) Marder *m*
Martha ['marθə] *s* Martha *f*
martial ['marʃəl] *adj* Kriegs–
mar'tial law' *s* Standrecht *n;* declare m. das Standrecht verhängen; under m. standrechtlich
martin ['martɪn] *s* Mauerschwalbe *f;* Martin Martin *m*
martinet [,martɪ'nɛt] *s* Pauker –in *mf;* (mil) Schleifer *m*
martyr ['martər] *s* Märtyrer –in *mf* || *tr* martern
martyrdom ['martərdəm] *s* Märtyrertum *n*
mar·vel ['marvəl] *s* Wunder *n* || *v* (*pret* & *pp* –vel[l]ed; *ger* –vel[l]ing) *intr* (at) sich wundern (über *acc*)
marvelous ['marvələs] *adj* wundervoll; (coll) pfundig
Marxist ['marksɪst] *adj* marxistisch || Marxist –in *mf*
marzipan ['marzɪ,pæn] *s* Marzipan *n*
mascara [mæs'kærə] *s* Lidtusche *f*
mascot ['mæskat] *s* Maskotte *f*
masculine ['mæskjəlɪn] *adj* männlich
mash [mæʃ] *s* Brei *m;* (*in brewing*) Maische *f* || *tr* zerquetschen; (*potatoes*) zerdrücken
mashed' pota'toes *spl* Kartoffelbrei *m*
mask [mæsk] *s* Maske *f* || *tr* maskieren
masked' ball' *s* Maskenball *m*
mason ['mesən] *s* Maurer *m;* Mason Freimaurer *m*
Masonic [mə'sanɪk] *adj* Freimaurer–
masonite ['mesə,naɪt] *s* Holzfaserplatte *f*
masonry ['mesənri] *s* Mauerwerk *n;* Masonry Freimaurerei *f*
masquerade [,mæskə'red] *s* (& fig) Maskerade *f* || *intr* (& fig) sich maskieren; m. as sich ausgeben als
mass [mæs] *adj* Massen– || *s* Masse *f;* (eccl) Messe; the masses die breite Masse *f* || *tr* massieren || *intr* sich ansammeln
massacre ['mæsəkər] *s* Massaker *n* || *tr* massakrieren, niedermetzeln
massage [mə'saʒ] *s* Massage *f* || *tr* massieren
masseur [mə'sʌr] *s* Masseur *m*
masseuse [mə'suz] *s* Masseuse *f*
massif ['mæsɪf] *s* Gebirgsstock *m*
massive ['mæsɪv] *adj* massiv
mass' me'dia ['midɪ-ə] *spl* Massenmedien *pl*
mass' meet'ing *s* Massenversammlung *f*
mass' mur'der *s* Massenmord *m*
mass'-produce' *tr* serienmäßig herstellen
mass' produc'tion *s* Serienherstellung *f*
mast [mæst] *s* Mast *m;* (*food for swine*) Mast *f*
master ['mæstər] *adj* (*bedroom, key, switch, cylinder*) Haupt– || *s* Herr *m,*

Meister *m;* (*male head of a household*) Hausherr *m;* (*of a ship*) Kapitän *m* || *tr* beherrschen
mas'ter build'er *s* Baumeister *m*
mas'ter car'penter *s* Zimmermeister *m*
mas'ter cop'y *s* Originalkopie *f*
masterful ['mæstərfəl] *adj* herrisch; (*masterly*) meisterhaft
masterly ['mæstərli] *adj* meisterhaft
mas'ter mechan'ic *s* Schlossermeister *m*
mas'termind' *s* führender Geist *m* || *tr* planen und überwachen
Mas'ter of Arts' *s* Magister *m* der freien Künste
mas'ter of cer'emonies *s* Zeremonienmeister *m*
mas'ter of the house' *s* Hausherr *m*
mas'terpiece' *s* Meisterstück *n*
mas'ter ser'geant *s* Oberfeldwebel *m*
mas'ter stroke' *s* Meisterstreich *m*
mas'terwork' *s* Meisterwerk *n*
mastery ['mæstəri] *s* (of) Beherrschung *f* (*genit*); gain m. over die Oberhand gewinnen über (*acc*)
mast'head' *s* (naut) Topp *m;* (typ) Impressum *n*
masticate ['mæstɪ,ket] *tr* zerkauen || *intr* kauen
mastiff ['mæstɪf] *s* Mastiff *m*
masturbate ['mæstər,bet] *intr* onanieren
masturbation [,mæstər'beʃən] *s* Onanie *f*
mat [mæt] *s* (*for a floor*) Matte *f;* (*before the door*) Türvorleger *m;* (*under cups, vases, etc.*) Zierdeckchen *n* || *v* (*pret* & *pp* matted; *ger* matting) *tr* (*cover with matting*) mit Matten belegen; (*the hair*) verfilzen || *intr* sich verfilzen
match [mætʃ] *s* Streichholz *n;* (*for marriage*) Partie *f;* (sport) Match *n;* be a good m. zueinanderpassen; be a m. for gewachsen sein (*dat*); be no m. for sich nicht messen können mit; meet one's m. seinen Mann finden || *tr* (*fit together*) zusammenstellen; (*harmonize with*) passen zu; (*equal*) (in) gleichkommen (in *dat*); (*funds*) in gleicher Höhe aufbringen; (*adapt*) in Übereinstimmung bringen mit; be well matched auf gleicher Höhe sein; m. up zusammenpassen; m. wits with sich geistig messen mit || *intr* zueinanderpassen
match'book' *s* Streichholzbrief *m*
match' box' *s* Streichholzschachtel *f*
match'ing *adj* (*clothes*) passend; (*funds*) in gleicher Höhe || *s* Paarung *f*
match'mak'er *s* Heiratsvermittler –in *mf;* (sport) Veranstalter *m*
mate [met] *s* Genosse *m,* Kamerad *m;* (*in marriage*) Ehepartner *m;* (*one of a pair, e.g., of gloves*) Gegenstück *n;* (*especially of birds*) Männchen *n,* Weibchen *n;* (naut) Maat *m* || *tr* paaren || *intr* sich paaren
material [mə'tɪrɪ,əl] *adj* materiell; (*important*) wesentlich || *s* Material *n,* Stoff *m;* (tex) Stoff *m*

materialist [mə'tırı·əlıst] s Materialist
-in mf
materialistic [mə,tırı·ə'lıstık] adj materialistisch
materialize [mə'tırı·ə,laız] intr sich verwirklichen
materiel [mə,tırı'el] s Material n; (mil) Kriegsmaterial n
maternal [mə'tʌrnəl] adj mütterlich; (relatives) mütterlicherseits
maternity [mə'tʌrnıti] s Mutterschaft f
mater'nity dress' s Umstandskleid n
mater'nity hos'pital s Wöchnerinnenheim n
mater'nity ward' s Wöchnerinnenstation f
math [mæθ] s (coll) Mathe f
mathematical [,mæθı'mætıkəl] adj mathematisch
mathematician [,mæθımə'tıʃən] s Mathematiker -in mf
mathematics [,mæθı'mætıks] s Mathematik f
matinée [,mætı'ne] s Nachmittagsvorstellung f
mat'ing sea'son s Paarungszeit f
matins ['mætınz] spl Frühmette f
matriarch ['metrı,ɑrk] s Stammesmutter f
matriarchal [,metrı'ɑrkəl] adj matriarchalisch
matriarchy ['metrı,ɑrki] s Matriarchat n
matricide ['mætrı,saıd] s (act) Muttermord m; (person) Muttermörder -in mf
matriculate [mə'trıkjə,let] tr immatrikulieren || intr sich immatrikulieren
matriculation [mə,trıkjə'leʃən] s Immatrikulation f
matrimonial [,mætrı'monı·əl] adj Ehe–
matrimony ['mætrı,moni] s Ehestand m
ma·trix ['metrıks] s (-trices [trı,siz] & -trixes) (mold) Gießform f; (math) Matrix f; (typ) Matrize f
matron ['metrən] s Matrone f
matronly ['metrənli] adj matronenhaft, gesetzt
matt [mæt] adj (phot) matt
matter ['mætər] s Stoff m; (affair) Sache f, Angelegenheit f; (pus) Eiter m; (phys) Materie f; as a m. of course routinemäßig; as matters now stand wie die Sache jetzt liegt; for that m. was das betrifft; it's a m. of es handelt sich um; it's a m. of life and death es geht um Leben und Tod; m. of opinion Ansichtssache f; m. of taste Geschmackssache f; something is the m. with his heart er hat was am Herz; no laughing m. nichts zum Lachen; no m. ganz gleich; what's the m. (with)? was ist los (mit)? || intr von Bedeutung sein; it doesn't m. es macht nichts (aus); it doesn't m. to me es liegt mir nichts daran; it matters a great deal to me es liegt mir sehr viel daran

mat'ter of fact' s Tatsache f; as a m. tatsächlich
mat'ter-of-fact' adj sachlich, nüchtern
Matthew ['mæθju] s Matthäus m
mattock ['mætək] s Breithacke f
mattress ['mætrıs] s Matratze f
mature [mə'tʃur] adj (& fig) reif || tr reifen lassen || intr reifen; (fin) fällig werden
maturity [mə'tʃurıti] s Reife f; (fin) Verfall m
maudlin ['mɔdlın] adj rührselig
maul [mɔl] tr schlimm zurichten
maulstick ['mɔl,stık] s Mahlstock m
mausole·um [,mɔsə'li·əm] s (-ums & -a [ə]) Mausoleum n
maw [mɔ] s (mouth of an animal) Rachen m; (stomach of an animal) Tiermagen m; (of birds) Kropf m
mawkish ['mɔkıʃ] adj rührselig
maxim ['mæksım] s Maxime f, Lehrspruch m
maximum ['mæksıməm] adj Höchst–; **m. load** Höchstbelastung f || s Maximum n
May [me] s Mai m || **may** v (pret **might** [maıt] aux (expressing possibility) mögen, können; (expressing permission) dürfen; (expressing a wish) mögen; **be that as it may** wie dem auch sei; **come what may** komme, was da wolle; **it may be too late** es ist vielleicht zu spät; **that may be** das kann (or mag) sein
maybe ['mebi] adv vielleicht
May' Day' s der erste Mai
mayhem ['mehəm] s Körperverletzung f
mayonnaise [,me·ə'nez] s Mayonnaise f
mayor [mer] s Bürgermeister m; (of a large city) Oberbürgermeister m
May'pole' s Maibaum m
May' queen' s Maikönigin f
maze [mez] s Irrgarten m; (fig) Gewirr n
me [mi] pers pron (direct object) mich; (indirect object) mir; **this one is on me** das geht auf meine Rechnung
mead [mid] s (hist) Met m; (poet) Aue f
meadow ['medo] s Wiese f
mead'owland' s Wiesenland n
meager ['migər] adj karg, kärglich
meal [mil] s Mahl n, Mahlzeit f; (grain) grobes Mehl n
meal' tick'et s Gutschein m für e-e Mahlzeit
meal'time' s Essenszeit f
mealy ['mili] adj mehlig
mealy-mouthed ['mili,mauðd] adj zurückhaltend
mean [min] adj (nasty) bösartig; (lowly) gemein, niedrig; (shabby) schäbig; (in statistics) mittlere; no m. kein schlecter || s (log) Mittelbegriff m; (math) Mittel n; **by all means** unbedingt; **by every means** mit allen Mitteln; **by fair means or foul** ganz gleich wie; **by lawful means** auf dem Rechtswege; **by means of**

mittels (*genit*); **by no means** keineswegs; **live beyond one's means** über seine Verhältnisse leben; **live within one's means** seinen Verhältnissen entsprechend leben; **means** (*way*) Mittel *n*; (*resources*) Mittel *pl*, Vermögen *n*; **means of transportation** Verkehrsmittel *n*; **means to an end** Mittel *pl* zum Zweck; **of means** bemittelt ‖ *v* (*pret & pp* **meant** [ment]) *tr* (*intend, intend to say*) meinen; (*signify*) bedeuten; **be meant for** (*said, e.g., of a remark*) gelten (*dat*); (*said, e.g., of a gift*) bestimmt sein für; **it means a lot to me to** (*inf*) mir liegt viel daran zu (*inf*); **m. business** es ernst meinen; **m. little** (or much) wenig (or viel) gelten; **m. no harm** es nicht böse meinen; **m. s.o. no harm** j–n nicht verletzen wollen; **m. the world to s.o.** j–m alles bedeuten; **what is meant by ...?** was versteht man unter ...? ‖ *intr*—**m. well** recht gut meinen
meander [mɪˈændər] *intr* sich winden
mean'ing *s* Bedeutung *f*; **take on m.** e–n Sinn bekommen; **what's the m. of this?** was soll das heißen?
meaningful [ˈminɪŋfəl] *adj* sinnvoll
meaningless [ˈminɪŋlɪs] *adj* sinnlos
mean'-look'ing *adj* bösartig aussehend
meanness [ˈminnɪs] *s* Gemeinheit *f*; (*nastiness*) Bösartigkeit *f*
mean'time', **mean'while'** *adv* mittlerweile ‖ *s*—**in the m.** mittlerweile, in der Zwischenzeit
measles [ˈmizəlz] *s* Masern *pl*; (*German measles*) Röteln *pl*
measly [ˈmizli] *adj* kümmerlich, lumpig
measurable [ˈmeʒərəbəl] *adj* meßbar
measure [ˈmeʒər] *s* Maß *n*; (*step*) Maßnahme *f*; (*law*) Gesetz *n*; (*mus*) Takt *m*; **beyond m.** übermäßig; **for good m.** obendrein; **in a great m.** in großem Maß; **to some m.** gewissermaßen; **take drastic measures** durchgreifen; **take measures to** (*inf*) Maßnahmen ergreifen um zu (*inf*); **take s.o.'s m.** (fig) j–n einschätzen ‖ *tr* messen; **m. off** abmessen; **m. out** ausmessen ‖ *intr* messen; **m. up to** gewachsen sein (*dat*)
measurement [ˈmeʒərmənt] *s* (*measured dimension*) Maß *n*; (*measuring*) Messung *f*; **measurements** Maße *pl*; **take s.o.'s measurements for** j–m Maß nehmen zu
meas'uring cup' *s* Meßbecher *m*
meas'uring tape' *s* Meßband *n*
meat [mit] *s* Fleisch *n*; (*of a nut, of the matter*) Kern *m*
meat'ball' *m* Fleischklößchen *n*
meat' grind'er *s* Fleischwolf *m*
meat'hook' *s* Fleischhaken *m*
meat'mar'ket *s* Fleischmarkt *m*
meat' pie' *s* Fleischpastete *f*
meaty [ˈmiti] *adj* fleischig; (fig) kernig
Mecca [ˈmekə] *s* Mekka *n*
mechanic [məˈkænɪk] *s* Mechaniker *m*, Schlosser *m*; (aut) Autoschlosser *m*; **mechanics** Mechanik *f*

mechanical [məˈkænɪkəl] *adj* mechanisch
mechan'ical engineer' *s* Maschinenbauingenieur *m*
mechan'ical engineer'ing *s* Maschinenbau *m*
mechanism [ˈmekəˌnɪzəm] *s* Mechanismus *m*
mechanize [ˈmekəˌnaɪz] *tr* mechanisieren
medal [ˈmedəl] *s* Medaille *f*, Orden *m*
medallion [mɪˈdæljən] *s* Medaillon *n*
meddle [ˈmedəl] *intr* sich einmischen; **m. with** sich abgeben mit
meddler [ˈmedlər] *s* zudringliche Person *f*
meddlesome [ˈmedəlsəm] *adj* zudringlich
media [ˈmidɪ-ə] *spl* Medien *pl*
median [ˈmidɪ-ən] *adj* mittlere, Mittel- ‖ *s* (arith) Mittelwert *m*; (geom) Mittellinie *f*
me'dian strip' *s* Mittelstreifen *m*
mediate [ˈmidɪˌet] *tr & intr* vermitteln
mediation [ˌmidɪˈeʃən] *s* Vermittlung *f*
mediator [ˈmidɪˌetər] *s* Vermittler –in *mf*
medic [ˈmedɪk] *s* (mil) Sanitäter *m*
medical [ˈmedɪkəl] *adj* (*of a doctor*) ärztlich; (*of medicine*) medizinisch; (*of the sick*) Kranken—
med'ical bul'letin *s* Krankheitsbericht *m*
med'ical corps' *s* Sanitätstruppe *f*
med'ical profes'sion *s* Arztberuf *m*
med'ical school' *s* medizinische Fakultät *f*
med'ical sci'ence *s* Heilkunde *f*
med'ical stu'dent *s* Medizinstudent –in *mf*
medication [ˌmedɪˈkeʃən] *s* Medikament *n*
medicinal [məˈdɪsɪnəl] *adj* medizinisch
medicine [ˈmedɪsən] *s* Medizin *f*, Arznei *f*; (*profession*) Medizin *f*; **practice m.** den Arztberuf ausüben
med'icine cab'inet *s* Hausapotheke *f*
med'icine kit' *s* Reiseapotheke *f*
med'icine man' *s* Medizinmann *m*
medic·o [ˈmedɪˌko] *s* (–cos) (coll) Mediziner –in *mf*
medieval [ˌmidɪˈivəl], [ˌmedɪˈivəl] *adv* mittelalterlich
mediocre [ˌmidɪˈokər] *adj* mittelmäßig
mediocrity [ˌmidɪˈɑkrɪti] *s* Mittelmäßigkeit *f*
meditate [ˈmedɪˌtet] *tr* vorhaben ‖ *intr* (on) meditieren (über *acc*)
meditation [ˌmedɪˈteʃən] *s* Meditation *f*
Mediterranean [ˌmedɪtəˈrenɪ-ən] *adj* Mittelmeer– ‖ *s* Mittelmeer *n*
medi·um [ˈmidɪ-əm] *adj* Mittel-, mittlere ‖ *s* (–ums & –a [ə]) Mittel *n*; (*culture*) Nährboden *m*; (*in spiritualism, communications*) Medium *n*; **through the m. of** vermittels (*genit*)
me'dium of exchange' *s* Tauschmittel *n*
me'dium-rare' *adj* halb durchgebraten
me'dium size' *s* Mittelgröße *f*

med'ium-sized' *adj* mittelgroß
medley ['medli] *s* Mischmasch *m*; (mus) Potpourri *n*
medul·la [mɪ'dʌlə] *s* (–las & –lae [li]) Knochenmark *n*, Mark *n*
meek [mik] *adj* sanftmütig; **m. as a lamb** lammfromm
meekness ['miknɪs] *s* Sanftmut *m*
meerschaum ['mɪrʃəm] *s* Meerschaum *m*
meet [mit] *adj* passend ‖ *s* (sport) Treffen *n*, Veranstaltung *f* ‖ *v* (*pret* & *pp* **met** [mɛt]) *tr* begegnen (*dat*), treffen; (*make the acquaintance of*) kennenlernen; (*demands*) befriedigen; (*obligations*) nachkommen (*dat*); (*wishes*) erfüllen; (*a deadline*) einhalten; **m. s.o. at the train** j–n von der Bahn abholen; **m. s.o. halfway** j–m auf halbem Wege entgegenkommen; **m. the train** zum Zug gehen; **pleased to m. you** freut mich sehr, sehr angenehm ‖ *intr* (*said of persons, of two ends*) zusammenkommen; (*said of persons*) sich treffen; (*in conference*) tagen; (*said of roads, rivers*) sich vereinigen; **make both ends m.** gerade mit dem Geld auskommen; **m. again** sich wiedersehen; **m. up with s.o.** j–n einholen; **m. with** zusammentreffen mit; **m. with an accident** verunglücken; **m. with a refusal** e–e Fehlbitte tun; **m. with approval** Beifall finden; **m. with success** Erfolg haben
meet'ing *s* (*of an organization*) Versammlung *f*; (*e.g., of a committee*) Sitzung *f*; (*of individuals*) Zusammenkunft *f*
meet'ing place' *s* Treffpunkt *m*
megacycle ['mɛgə͵saɪkəl], **megahertz** ['mɛgə͵hʌrts] *s* (elec) Megahertz *n*
megalomania [͵mɛgəlo'menɪə] *s* Größenwahn *m*
megaphone ['mɛgə͵fon] *s* Sprachrohr *n*
megohm ['mɛg͵om] *s* Megohm *n*
melancholy ['mɛlən͵kɑli] *adj* schwermütig ‖ *s* Schwermut *f*
melee ['mele], ['mɛle] *s* Gemenge *n*
mellow ['mɛlo] *adj* (*very ripe*) mürb(e); (*wine*) abgelagert; (*voice*) schmelzend; (*person*) gereift ‖ *tr* zur Reife bringen; (fig) mildern ‖ *intr* mürb(e) werden; (fig) mild werden
melodic [mɪ'lɑdɪk] *adj* melodisch
melodious [mɪ'lodɪ·əs] *adj* melodisch
melodrama ['mɛlo͵drɑmə] *s* (& fig) Melodrama *n*
melody ['mɛlədi] *s* Melodie *f*
melon ['mɛlən] *s* Melone *f*
melt [mɛlt] *tr* & *intr* schmelzen
melt'ing point' *s* Schmelzpunkt *m*
melt'ing pot' *s* (& fig) Schmelztiegel *m*
member ['mɛmbər] *s* Glied *n*; (*person*) Mitglied *n*, Angehörige *mf*; **m. of the family** Familienangehörige *mf*
mem'bership' *s* Mitgliedschaft *f*; (*collectively*) Mitglieder *pl*; (*number of members*) Mitgliederzahl *f*
mem'bership card' *s* Mitgliedskarte *f*

membrane ['mɛmbren] *s* Häutchen *n*, Membran(e) *f*
memen·to [mɪ'mɛnto] *s* (–tos & –toes) Erinnerung *f*, Memento *n*
mem·o' ['mɛmo] *s* (–os) (coll) Notiz *f*
mem'o book' *s* Notizbuch *n*, Agenda *f*
memoirs ['mɛmwɑrz] *spl* Memoiren *pl*
mem'o pad' *s* Notizblock *m*, Agenda *f*
memorable ['mɛmərəbəl] *adj* denkwürdig
memoran·dum [͵mɛmə'rændəm] *s* (–dums & –da [də]) Notiz *f*, Vermerk *m*; (dipl) Memorandum *n*
memorial [mɪ'morɪ·əl] *adj* Gedächtnis–. Erinnerungs– ‖ *s* Denkmal *n*
Memor'ial Day' *s* Gefallenengedenktag *m*
memorialize [mɪ'morɪ·ə͵laɪz] *tr* gedenken (*genit*)
memorize ['mɛmə͵raɪz] *tr* auswendig lernen
memory ['mɛməri] *s* (*faculty*) Gedächtnis *n*; (of) Gedenken *n* (an *acc*), Erinnerung *f* (an *acc*); **commit to m.** auswendig lernen; **escape one's m.** seinem Gedächtnis entfallen; **from m.** aus dem Gedächtnis; **in m. of** zur Erinnerung an (*acc*); **of blessed m.** seligen Angedenkens; **within the m. of men** seit Menschengedenken
menace ['mɛnɪs] *s* (to) Drohung *f* (*genit*) ‖ *tr* bedrohen
menagerie [mə'nædʒəri] *s* Menagerie *f*
mend [mɛnd] *s* Besserung *f*; **on the m.** auf dem Wege der Besserung ‖ *tr* (*clothes*) ausbessern; (*socks*) stopfen; (*repair*) reparieren
mendacious [mɛn'deʃəs] *adj* lügnerisch
mendicant ['mɛndɪkənt] *adj* Bettel– ‖ *s* Bettelmönch *m*
menfolk ['mɛn͵fok] *spl* Mannsleute *pl*
menial ['minɪ·əl] *adj* niedrig ‖ *s* Diener –in *mf*
menopause ['mɛnə͵pɔz] *s* Wechseljahre *pl*
menses ['mɛnsiz] *spl* Monatsfluß *m*
men's' room' *s* Herrentoilette *f*
men's' size' *s* Herrengröße *f*
men's' store' *s* Herrenbekleidungsgeschäft *n*
menstruate ['mɛnstru͵et] *intr* menstruieren
menstruation [͵mɛnstru'eʃən] *s* Menstruation *f*
men's' wear' *s* Herrenbekleidung *f*
mental ['mɛntəl] *adj* geistig, Geistes–
men'tal an'guish *s* Seelenpein *f*
men'tal arith'metic *s* Kopfrechnen *n*
men'tal capac'ity *s* Fassungskraft *f*
men'tal disor'der *s* Geistesstörung *f*
men'tal institu'tion *s* Nervenheilanstalt *f*
mentality [mɛn'tælɪti] *s* Mentalität *f*
mentally ['mɛntəli] *adv* geistig, Geistes–; **m. alert** geistesgegenwärtig; **m. disturbed** geistesgestört; **m. lazy** denkfaul
men'tal reserva'tion *s* geistiger Vorbehalt *m*
men'tal telep'athy *s* Gedankenübertragung *f*
mention ['mɛnʃən] *s* Erwähnung *f*;

make m. of erwähnen ‖ *tr* erwähnen, nennen; **be mentioned** zur Sprache kommen; **don't m. it!** keine Ursache!; **not worth mentioning** nicht der Rede wert

menu ['menju] *s* Speisekarte *f*

meow [mi'au] *s* Miauen *n* ‖ *intr* miauen

mercantile ['mʌrkən‚til], ['mʌrkən‚tail] *adj* Handels-, kaufmännisch

mercenary ['mʌrsə‚neri] *adj* gewinnsüchtig ‖ *s* Söldner *m*

merchandise ['mʌrtʃən‚daiz] *s* Ware *f* ‖ *tr* handeln

mer'chandising *s* Verkaufspolitik *f*

merchant ['mʌrtʃənt] *s* Händler, Kaufmann *m*

mer'chant·man *s* (–men) Handelsschiff *n*

mer'chant marine' *s* Handelsmarine *f*

mer'chant ves'sel *s* Handelsschiff *n*

merciful ['mʌrsifəl] *adj* barmherzig

merciless ['mʌrsilis] *adj* erbarmungslos

mercurial [mer'kjuri·əl] *adj* quecksilbrig

mercury ['mʌrkjəri] *s* Quecksilber *n*

mercy ['mʌrsi] *s* Barmherzigkeit *f*; **be at s.o.'s m.** in j–s Gewalt sein; **be at the m. of** (*e.g., the wind, waves*) preisgegeben sein (*dat*); **beg for m.** um Gnade flehen; **show no m.** keine Gnade walten lassen; **show s.o. m.** sich j–s erbarmen; **throw oneself on the m. of** sich auf Gnade und Ungnade ergeben (*dat*); **without m.** ohne Gnade

mere [mir] *adj* bloß, rein

merely ['mirli] *adv* nur, lediglich

meretricious [‚meri'triʃəs] *adj* (*tawdry*) flitterhaft; (*characteristic of a prostitute*) dirnenhaft

merge [mʌrdʒ] *tr* verschmelzen ‖ *intr* sich verschmelzen

merger ['mʌrdʒər] *s* (com) Fusion *f*; (jur) Verschmelzung *f*

meridian [mə'ridi·ən] *s* (astr) Meridian *m*; (geog) Meridian *m*, Längenkreis *m*

meringue [mə'ræŋ] *s* (*topping*) Eierschnee *m*; (*pastry*) Schaumgebäck *n*

merit ['merit] *s* Verdienst *n*; **of great m.** hochverdient ‖ *tr* verdienen

meritorious [‚meri'tori·əs] *adj* verdienstvoll

merlin ['mʌrlin] *s* (orn) Merlinfalke *m*

mermaid ['mʌr‚med] *s* Seejungfer *f*

merriment ['merimənt] *s* Fröhlichkeit *f*

merry ['meri] *adj* fröhlich, heiter

Mer'ry Christ'mas *s* fröhliche Weihnachten *pl*

mer'ry-go-round' *s* Karussell *n*

mer'rymak'er *s* Zecher –in *mf*

mesh [meʃ] *s* Masche *f*; (*network*) Netzwerk *n*; (mach) Ineinandergreifen *n*; **meshes** (fig) Schlingen *pl* ‖ *intr* ineinandergreifen

mesmerize ['mesmə‚raiz] *tr* hypnotisieren

mess [mes] *s* (*disorder*) Durcheinander *n*; (*dirty condition*) Schweinerei *f*; (*for officers*) Messe *f*; **a nice m.!** e–e schöne Wirtschaft!; **get into a m.** in die Klemme geraten; **make a m.** Schmutz machen; **make a m. of** verpfuschen; **what a m.!** nette Zustände! ‖ *tr*—**m. up** (*dirty*) beschmutzen; (*put into disarray*) in Unordnung bringen ‖ *intr*—**m. around** herumtrödeln; **m. around with** herummurksen an (*dat*)

message ['mesidʒ] *s* Botschaft *f*

messenger ['mesəndʒər] *s* Bote *m*, Botin *f*

mess' hall' *s* Messe *f*

Messiah [mə'sai·ə] *s* Messias *m*

mess' kit' *s* Eßgeschirr *n*

messy ['mesi] *adj* (*disorderly*) unordentlich; (*dirty*) dreckig

metabolism [mə'tæbə‚lizəm] *s* Stoffwechsel *m*

metal ['metəl] *s* Metall *n*

metallic [mi'tælik] *adj* metallisch

metallurgy ['metə‚lʌrdʒi] *s* Hüttenwesen *n*, Metallurgie *f*

met'alwork' *s* Metallarbeit *f*

metamorpho·sis [‚metə'mɔrfəsis] *s* (–ses [‚siz]) Verwandlung *f*

metaphor ['metə‚fɔr] *s* Metapher *f*

metaphorical [‚metə'fɔrikəl] *adj* bildlich

metaphysical [‚metə'fizikəl] *adj* metaphysisch

metaphysics [‚metə'fiziks] *s* Metaphysik *f*

metathe·sis [mi'tæθisis] *s* (–ses [‚siz]) Metathese *f*, Lautversetzung *f*

mete [mit] *tr*—**m. out** austeilen

meteor ['miti·ər] *s* Meteor *m*

meteoric [‚miti'ɔrik] *adj* meteorisch; (fig) kometenhaft

meteorite ['miti·ə‚rait] *s* Meteorit *m*

meteorologist [‚miti·ə'ralədʒist] *s* Meteorologe *m*, Meteorologin *f*

meteorology [‚miti·ə'ralədʒi] *s* Meteorologie *f*, Wetterkunde *f*

meter ['mitər] *s* Meter *m* & *n*; (*instrument*) Messer *m*, Zähler *m*; (pros) Versmaß *n*

me'ter read'er *s* Zählerableser –in *mf*

methane ['meθen] *s* Methan *n*, Sumpfgas *n*

method ['meθəd] *s* Methode *f*

methodic(al) [mi'θadik(əl)] *adj* methodisch

Methodist ['meθədist] *s* Methodist –in *mf*

methodology [‚meθə'dalədʒi] *s* Methodenlehre *f*

Methuselah [mi'θuzələ] *s* Methusalem *m*

meticulous [mi'tikjələs] *adj* übergenau

metric(al) ['metrik(əl)] *adj* metrisch

metrics ['metriks] *s* Metrik *f*

metronome ['metrə‚nom] *s* Metronom *n*

metropolis [mi'trapəlis] *s* Metropole *f*

metropolitan [‚metrə'palitən] *adj* großstädtisch ‖ *s* (eccl) Metropolit *m*

mettle ['metəl] *s* (*temperament*) Veranlagung *f*; (*courage*) Mut *m*

mettlesome ['metəlsəm] *adj* mutig

mew [mju] s Miau n ‖ intr miauen
Mexican ['mɛksɪkən] adj mexikanisch
‖ s Mexikaner –in mf
Mexico ['mɛksɪˌko] s Mexiko n
mezzanine ['mɛzəˌnin] s Zwischenge-
schoß n
mica ['maɪkə] s Glimmer m, Marienglas n
Michael ['maɪkəl] s Michel m
microbe ['maɪkrob] s Mikrobe f
microbiology [ˌmaɪkrəbaɪ'alədʒi] s
Mikrobiologie f
microcosm ['maɪkrəˌkazəm] s Mikro-
kosmos m
microfilm ['maɪkrəˌfɪlm] s Mikrofilm
m ‖ tr mikrofilmen
microgroove ['maɪkrəˌgruv] s Mikro-
rille f
mic'rogroove rec'ord s Schallplatte f
mit Mikrorillen
microphone ['maɪkrəˌfon] s Mikrophon n
microscope ['maɪkrəˌskop] s Mikroskop n
microscopic [ˌmaɪkrə'skapɪk] adj mikroskopisch
microwave ['maɪkrəˌwev] s Mikro-
welle f
mid [mɪd] adj mittlere
midair' s—in m. mitten in der Luft
mid'day' adj mittäglich, Mittags– ‖ s
Mittag m
middle ['mɪdəl] adj mittlere ‖ s Mitte
f, Mittel n; in the m. of inmitten
(genit), mitten in (dat)
mid'dle age' s mittleres Lebensalter n;
Middle Ages Mittelalter n
middle-aged ['mɪdəlˌedʒd] adj mittleren Alters
mid'dle class' s Mittelstand m
mid'dle-class' adj bürgerlich
mid'dle dis'tance s Mittelgrund m
mid'dle ear' s Mittelohr n
Mid'dle East', the s der Mittlere Osten
mid'dle fin'ger s Mittelfinger m
Mid'dle High' Ger'man s Mittelhochdeutsch n
Mid'dle Low' Ger'man s Mittelnieder-
deutsch n
mid'dle-man' s (–men') Mittelsmann
m, Zwischenhändler m
mid'dleweight box'er s Mittelgewichtler
m
mid'dleweight divi'sion s Mittelgewicht
n
middling ['mɪdlɪŋ] adj mittelmäßig ‖
adv leidlich, ziemlich
middy ['mɪdi] s (nav) Fähnrich m zur
See
midget ['mɪdʒɪt] s Zwerg m
mid'get rail'road s Liliputbahn f
mid'get submarine' s Kleinst-U-Boot n
midland ['mɪdlənd] adj binnenländisch
mid'night' adj mitternächtlich; **burn the
m.** oil bis in die tiefe Nacht arbeiten
‖ s Mitternacht f; **at m.** um Mitternacht
midriff ['mɪdrɪf] s (of a dress) Mittel-
teil m; (diaphragm) Zwerchfell n;
(middle part of the body) Magengrube f; **have a bare m.** die Taille
frei lassen

mid'shipman' s (–men') Fähnrich m zur
See
midst [mɪdst] s Mitte f; **from our m.**
aus unserer Mitte; **in the m. of** mitten in (dat)
mid'stream' s—in m. in der Mitte des
Stromes
mid'sum'mer s Mittsommer m
mid'-term' adj mitten im Semester ‖
midterms spl Prüfungen pl mitten im
Semester
mid'way' adj in der Mitte befindlich ‖
adv auf halbem Weg ‖ s Mitte f des
Weges; (at a fair) Mittelstraße f
mid'week' s Wochenmitte f
mid'wife' s (–wives') Hebamme f
mid'win'ter s Mittwinter m
mid'year' adj in der Mitte des Studienjahres ‖ midyears spl Prüfungen pl
in der Mitte des Studienjahres
mien [min] s Miene f
miff [mɪf] s kleine Auseinandersetzung
f ‖ tr ärgern
might [maɪt] s Macht f, Kraft f; **with
m. and main** mit aller Kraft ‖ aux
used to form the potential mood,
e.g., she m. lose her way sie könnte
sich verirren; **we m. as well go** es ist
wohl besser, wenn wir gehen
mightily ['maɪtəli] adv gewaltig; (coll)
enorm
mighty ['maɪti] adj mächtig ‖ adv
(coll) furchtbar
migraine ['maɪgren] s Migräne f
mi'grant work'er ['maɪgrənt] s Wan-
derarbeiter –in mf
migrate ['maɪgret] intr wandern, ziehen
migration [maɪ'greʃən] s Wanderung
f; (e.g., of birds) Zug m
migratory ['maɪgrəˌtori] adj Wander–
mi'gratory bird' s Zugvogel m
Milan [mɪ'læn] s Mailand n
mild [maɪld] adj mild, lind
mildew ['mɪlˌd(j)u] s Mehltau m
mildly ['maɪldli] adv leicht, schwach;
to put it m. gelinde gesagt
mildness ['maɪldnɪs] s Milde f
mile [maɪl] s Meile f; **for miles** meilenweit; **miles apart** meilenweit auseinander; **miles per hour** Stundenge-
schwindigkeit
mileage ['maɪlɪdʒ] s Meilenzahl f;
(charge) Meilengeld n
mile'post' s Wegweiser m mit Entfer-
nungsangabe
mile'stone' s (& fig) Meilenstein m
militancy ['mɪlɪtənsi] s Kampfgeist m
militant ['mɪlɪtənt] adj militant ‖ s
Kämpfer –in mf
militarism ['mɪlɪtəˌrɪzəm] s Militarismus m
militarize ['mɪlɪtəˌraɪz] tr auf den
Krieg vorbereiten
military ['mɪləˌteri] adj militärisch;
(academy, band, government) Militär– ‖ s Militär n
mil'itary campaign' s Feldzug m
mil'itary cem'etery s Soldatenfriedhof
m
mil'itary obliga'tions spl Wehrpflicht f
mil'itary police' s Militärpolizei f

mil'itary police'man *s* (**-men**) Militärpolizist *m*

mil'itary sci'ence *s* Kriegswissenschaft *f*

militate ['mɪlɪ‚tet] *intr* (**against**) entgegenwirken (*dat*)

militia [mɪ'lɪʃə] *s* Miliz *f*

mili'tia·man *s* (**-men**) Milizsoldat *m*

milk [mɪlk] *s* Milch *f* || *tr* (& *fig*) melken

milk' bar' *s* Milchbar *f*

milk' car'ton *s* Milchtüte *f*

milk'maid' *s* Milchmädchen *n*

milk'man' *s* (**-men'**) Milchmann *m*

milk' pail' *s* Melkeimer *m*

milk'shake' *s* Milchmischgetränk *n*

milk'sop' *s* Milchbart *m*

milk' tooth' *s* Milchzahn *m*

milk'weed' *s* Wolfsmilch *f*, Seidenpflanze *f*

milky ['mɪlki] *adj* milchig

Milk'y Way' *s* Milchstraße *f*

mill [mɪl] *s* Mühle *f*; (*factory*) Fabrik *f*, Werk *n*; **put through the m.** (coll) durch e-e harte Schule schicken || *tr* (*grain*) mahlen; (*coins*) rändeln; (*with a milling machine*) fräsern; (*chocolate*) quirlen || *intr*—**m. around** durcheinanderlaufen

millenial [mɪ'lɛnɪ·əl] *adj* tausendjährig

millenni·um [mɪ'lɛnɪ·əm] *s* (**-ums &** **-a** [ə]) Jahrtausend *n*

miller ['mɪlər] *s* Müller *m*

millet ['mɪlɪt] *s* Hirse *f*

milligram ['mɪlɪ‚græm] *s* Milligramm *n*

millimeter ['mɪlɪ‚mitər] *s* Millimeter *n*

milliner ['mɪlɪnər] *s* Putzmacher *-in* *mf*

mil'linery shop' ['mɪlɪ‚nɛri] *s* Damenhutgeschäft *n*

mill'ing *s* (*of grain*) Mahlen *n*; (*of wood or metal*) Fräsen *n*

mill'ing machine' *s* Fräsmaschine *f*

million ['mɪljən] *adj*—**one m.** people e-e Million Menschen; **two m.** people zwei Millionen Menschen || *s* Million *f*

millionaire [‚mɪljən'ɛr] *s* Millionär *-in* *mf*

millionth ['mɪljənθ] *adj* & *pron* millionste || *s* (*fraction*) Millionstel *n*

mill'pond' *s* Mühlteich *m*

mill'stone' *s* Mühlstein *m*

mill' wheel' *s* Mühlrad *n*

mime [maɪm] *s* Mime *m*, Mimin *f* || *tr* mimen

mimeograph ['mɪmɪ·ə‚græf] *s* Vervielfältigungsapparat *m* || *tr* vervielfältigen

mim·ic ['mɪmɪk] *s* Mimiker *-in* *mf* || *v* (*pret & pp* **-icked**; *ger* **-icking**) *tr* nachäffen

mimicry ['mɪmɪkri] *s* Nachäffen *n*; (zool) Mimikry *f*

mimosa [mɪ'mosə] *s* Mimose *f*

minaret [‚mɪnə'rɛt] *s* Minarett *n*

mince [mɪns] *tr* (*meat*) zerhacken; **not m. words** kein Blatt vor den Mund nehmen

mince'meat' *s* Pastetenfüllung *f*;

(*chopped meat*) Hackfleisch *n*; **make m. of** (fig) in die Pfanne hauen

mind [maɪnd] *s* Geist *m*; **bear in m.** denken an (*acc*); **be of one m.** eir Herz und e-e Seele sein; **be of two minds** geteilter Meinung sein; **be oul of one's m.** nicht bei Trost sein; **call to m.** erinnern; (*remember*) sich erinnern; **change one's m.** sich anders besinnen; **give s.o. a piece ol one's m.** j-m gründlich die Meinung sagen; **have a good m. to** (*inf*) große Lust haben zu (*inf*); **have in m.** im Sinn haben zu (*inf*); **have one's m. on s.th.** ständig an etw denken müssen; **I can't get her out of my m.** sie will mir nicht aus dem Sinn; **know one's own m.** wissen, was man will; **of sound m.** zurechnungsfähig; **put s.th. out of one's m.** sich [*dat*] etw aus dem Sinn schlagen; **set one's m. on** sein Sinnen und Trachten richten auf (*acc*); **slip s.o.'s m.** j-m entfallen; **to my m.** meines Erachtens || *tr* (*watch over*) aufpassen auf (*acc*); (*obey*) gehorchen (*dat*); (*be troubled by; take care of*) sich kümmern um; **do you m. if I smoke?** macht es Ihnen etw aus, wenn ich rauche?; **do you m. the smoke?** macht Ihnen der Rauch etw aus?; **I don't m. your smoking** ich habe nichts dagegen, daß (or wenn) Sie rauchen; **m. your own business!** kümmere dich um deine Angelegenheit!; **m. you!** wohlgemerkt! || *intr*—**I don't m.** es macht mir nichts aus; **I don't m. if I do** (coll) ja, recht gern; **never m.!** schon gut!

-minded [‚maɪndɪd] *suf* –mütig. -gesinnt, -sinnig

mindful ['maɪndfəl] *adj* (**of**) eingedenk (*genit*); **be m. of** achten auf (*acc*)

mind' read'er *s* Gedankenleser *-in* *mf*

mind' read'ing *s* Gedankenlesen *n*

mine [maɪn] *s* Bergwerk *n*, Mine *f*; (fig) Fundgrube *f*; (mil) Mine *f* || *poss pron* meiner || *tr* (*e.g., coal*) abbauen; (mil) verminen || *intr*—**m. for** graben nach

mine' detec'tor *s* Minensuchgerät *n*

mine'field' *s* Minenfeld *n*

minelayer ['maɪn‚le·ər] *s* Minenleger *m*

miner ['maɪnər] *s* Bergarbeiter *m*

mineral ['mɪnərəl] *adj* mineralisch, Mineral– || *s* Mineral *n*

mineralogy [‚mɪnə'ralədʒi] *s* Mineralogie *f*

min'eral resourc'es *spl* Bodenschätze *pl*

min'eral wa'ter *s* Mineralwasser *n*

mine'sweep'er *s* Minenräumboot *n*

mingle ['mɪŋgəl] *tr* vermengen || *intr* (**with**) sich mischen (unter *acc*)

miniature ['mɪni·ət∫ər], ['mɪnɪt∫ər] *adj* Miniatur–, Klein– || *s* Miniatur *f*

minimal ['mɪnɪməl] *adj* minimal, Mindest–

minimize ['mɪnə‚maɪz] *tr* auf das Minimum herabsetzen; (fig) bagatellisieren

minimum ['mɪnɪməm] *adj* minimal, Mindest– ‖ *s* Minimum *n; (lowest price)* untere Preisgrenze *f*
min'imum wage' *s* Mindestlohn *m*
min'ing *adj* Bergbau– ‖ *s* Bergbau *m*, Bergwesen *n;* (mil) Minenlegen *n*
minion ['mɪnjən] *s* Günstling *m*
miniskirt ['mɪnɪ,skʌrt] *s* Minirock *m*
minister ['mɪnɪstər] *s* (eccl) Geistlicher *m;* (pol) Minister *m* ‖ *intr*—m. to dienen *(dat); (aid)* Hilfe leisten *(dat)*
ministerial [,mɪnɪs'tɪrɪ·əl] *adj* (eccl) geistlich; (pol) ministeriell
ministry ['mɪnɪstri] *s (office)* (eccl) geistliches Amt *n; (the clergy)* (eccl) geistlicher Stand *m;* (pol) Ministerium *n*
mink [mɪŋk] *s* (zool) Nerz *m; (fur)* Nerzfell *n*
mink' coat' *s* Nerzmantel *m*
minnow ['mɪno] *s* Pfrille *f*, Elritze *f*
minor ['maɪnər] *adj* minder, geringer, Neben– ‖ *s (person)* Minderjährige *mf;* (educ) Nebenfach *n;* (log) Untersatz *m;* (mus) Moll *n* ‖ *intr*—m. in als Nebenfach studieren
minority [mɪ'nɔrɪti] *adj* Minderheits– ‖ *s* Minderheit *f; (of votes)* Stimmenminderheit *f; (ethnic group)* Minorität *f*
mi'nor key' *s* Molltonart *f;* **in a m.** in Moll
minstrel ['mɪnstrəl] *s* (hist) Spielmann *m*
mint [mɪnt] *s* Münzanstalt *f;* (bot) Minze *f* ‖ *tr* münzen
mintage ['mɪntɪdʒ] *s* Prägung *f*
minuet [,mɪnju'et] *s* Menuett *n*
minus ['maɪnəs] *adj* negativ ‖ *prep* minus, weniger; *(without)* (coll) ohne *(acc)*
mi'nus sign' *s* Minuszeichen *n*
minute [maɪ'n(j)ut] *adj* winzig ‖ ['mɪnɪt] *s* Minute *f;* **minutes** Protokoll *n;* **take the minutes** das Protokoll führen
–minute [mɪnɪt] *suf* –minutig
min'ute hand' *s* Minutenzeiger *m*
minutiae [mɪ'n(j)uʃɪ·i] *spl* Einzelheiten *pl*
minx [mɪŋks] *s* Range *f*
miracle ['mɪrəkəl] *s* Wunder *n*
mir'acle play' *s* Mirakelspiel *n*
miraculous [mɪ'rækjələs] *adj* wunderbar; *(e.g., power)* Wunder–
mirage [mɪ'rɑʒ] *s* Luftspiegelung *f;* (fig) Luftbild *n*, Täuschung *f*
mire [maɪr] *s* Morast *m*, Schlamm *m*
mirror ['mɪrər] *s* Spiegel *m* ‖ *tr* spiegeln
mirth [mʌrθ] *s* Fröhlichkeit *f*
miry ['maɪri] *adj* sumpfig, schlammig
misadventure [,mɪsəd'ventʃər] *s* Mißgeschick *n*
misanthrope ['mɪsən,θrop] *s* Menschenfeind *m*
misapprehension [,mɪsæprɪ'henʃən] *s* Mißverständnis *n*
misappropriate [,mɪsə'propri,et] *tr* sich *[dat]* widerrechtlich aneignen
misbehave [,mɪsbɪ'hev] *intr* sich schlecht benehmen

misbehavior [,mɪsbɪ'hevɪ·ər] *s* schlechtes Benehmen *n*
miscalculate [mɪs'kælkjə,let] *tr* falsch berechnen ‖ *intr* sich verrechnen
miscalculation [,mɪskælkjə'leʃən] *s* Rechenfehler *m*
miscarriage [mɪs'kærɪdʒ] *s* Fehlgeburt *f;* (fig) Fehlschlag *m*
miscar'riage of jus'tice *s* Justizirrtum *m*
miscar·ry [mɪs'kæri] *v (pret & pp –ried) intr* e–e Fehlgeburt haben; *(said of a plan)* scheitern, fehlschlagen
miscellaneous [,mɪsə'lenɪ·əs] *adj* vermischt
miscellany ['mɪsə,leni] *s* Gemisch *n; (of literary works)* Sammelband *m*
mischief ['mɪstʃɪf] *s* Unfug *m;* **be up to m.** e–n Unfug im Kopf haben; **cause m.** Unfug treiben; **get into m.** etw anstellen
mis'chief-mak'er *s* Störenfried *m*
mischievous ['mɪstʃɪvəs] *adj* mutwillig
misconception [,mɪskən'sepʃən] *s* falsche Auffassung *f*
misconduct [mɪs'kɑndʌkt] *s* schlechtes Benehmen *n;* **m. in office** Amtsvergehen *n* ‖ [,mɪskən'dʌkt] *tr* schlecht verwalten; **m. oneself** sich schlecht benehmen
misconstrue [,mɪskən'stru] *tr* falsch auffassen
miscount [mɪs'kaʊnt] *s* Rechenfehler *m* ‖ *tr* falsch zählen ‖ *intr* sich verzählen
miscreant ['mɪskrɪ·ənt] *s* Schurke *m*
miscue [mɪs'kju] *s* (fig) Fehler *m;* (billiards) Kicks *m* ‖ *intr* (billiards) kicksen; (theat) den Auftritt verpassen
mis·deal ['mɪs,dɪl] *s* falsches Geben *n* ‖ [mɪs'dɪl] *v (pret & pp –dealt* [delt]*) tr* falsch geben ‖ *intr* sich vergeben
misdeed [mɪs'did] *s* Missetat *f*
misdemeanor [,mɪsdɪ'minər] *s* Vergehen *n*
misdirect [,mɪsdɪ'rekt], [,mɪsdaɪ'rekt] *tr* (& fig) fehlleiten
misdoing [mɪs'du·ɪŋ] *s* Missetat *f*
miser ['maɪzər] *s* Geizhals *m*
miserable ['mɪzərəbəl] *adj* elend; **feel m.** sich elend fühlen; **make life m. for s.o.** j–m das Leben sauer machen
miserly ['maɪzərli] *adj* geizig
misery ['mɪzəri] *s* Elend *n*
misfeasance [mɪs'fizəns] *s* (jur) Amtsmißbrauch *m*
misfire [mɪs'faɪr] *s* Versagen *n* ‖ *intr* versagen
misfit ['mɪsfɪt] *s (clothing)* schlecht sitzendes Kleidungsstück *n; (person)* Gammler *m*
misfortune [mɪs'fɔrtʃən] *s* Unglück *n*
misgiving [mɪs'gɪvɪŋ] *s* böse Ahnung *f;* **full of misgivings** ahnungsvoll
misgovern [mɪs'gʌvərn] *tr* schlecht verwalten
misguidance [mɪs'gaɪdəns] *s* Irreführung *f*
misguide [mɪs'gaɪd] *tr* irreleiten
misguid'ed *adj* irregeleitet

mishap ['mɪshæp] *s* Unfall *m*
mishmash ['mɪʃ͵mæʃ] *s* Mischmasch
m
misinform [͵mɪsɪn'fɔrm] *tr* falsch informieren, falsch unterrichten
misinterpret [͵mɪsɪn'tʌrprɪt] *tr* miß-
deuten, falsch auffassen
misjudge [mɪs'dʒʌdʒ] *tr* (e.g., a person, situation) falsch beurteilen; (distance) falsch schätzen
mis·lay [mɪs'le] *v* (pret & pp –laid)
tr verlegen, verkramen
mis·lead [mɪs'lid] *v* (pret & pp –led)
tr irreführen
mislead'ing *adj* irreführend
mismanage [mɪs'mænɪdʒ] *tr* schlecht
verwalten; (funds) verwirtschaften
mismanagement [mɪs'mænɪdʒmənt] *s*
Mißwirtschaft *f*, schlechte Verwaltung *f*
mismarriage [mɪs'mærɪdʒ] *s* Mißheirat
f
misnomer [mɪs'nomər] *s* Felhbezeich-
nung *f*
misplace [mɪs'ples] *tr* verlegen
misprint ['mɪs͵prɪnt] *s* Druckfehler *m*
‖ [mɪs'prɪnt] *tr* verdrucken
mispronounce [͵mɪsprə'naʊns] *tr*
falsch aussprechen
mispronunciation [͵mɪsprənʌnsɪ'eʃən]
s falsche Aussprache *f*
misquote [mɪs'kwot] *tr* falsch zitieren
misread [mɪs'rid] *v* (pret & pp –read
['red]) *tr* falsch lesen ‖ *intr* sich
verlesen
misrepresent [͵mɪsreprɪ'zent] *tr* falsch
darstellen; m. the facts to s.o. j-m
falsche Tatsachen vorspiegeln
miss [mɪs] *s* Fehlschlag *m*, Versager *m;*
Miss Fräulein *n;* Miss America die
Schönheitskönigin von Amerika ‖ *tr*
(a target; one's calling; a person,
e.g., at the station; a town along the
road; one's way) verfehlen; (feel the
lack of) verpassen; (school, a train,
an opportunity) versäumen; m. one's
step fehltreten; m. the mark vorbeischießen; (fig) sein Ziel verfehlen;
m. the point die Pointe nicht verstanden haben ‖ *intr* fehlen; (in
shooting) vorbeischießen
missal ['mɪsəl] *s* Meßbuch *n*
misshapen [mɪs'ʃepən] *adj* mißgestaltet
missile ['mɪsɪl] *s* Geschoß *n;* (rok)
Rakete *f*
missing ['mɪsɪŋ] *adj*—be m. fehlen;
(said, e.g., of a child) vermißt werden; m. in action vermißt
miss'ing per'son *s* Vermißte *mf*
miss'ing-per'sons bu'reau *s* Suchdienst
m
mission ['mɪʃən] *s* Mission *f;* m. in life
Lebensaufgabe *f*
missionary ['mɪʃən͵erɪ] *adj* Missions–
‖ *s* Missionar –in *mf*
missis ['mɪsɪz] *s*—the m. (the wife)
die Frau; (of the house) (coll) die
Frau des Hauses
missive ['mɪsɪv] *s* Sendschreiben *n*
mis·spell [mɪs'spel] *v* (pret & pp
–spelled & –spelt) *tr* & *intr* falsch
schreiben

misspell'ing *s* Schreibfehler *m*
misspent [mɪs'spent] *adj* vergeudet
misstate [mɪs'stet] *tr* falsch angeben
misstatement [mɪs'stetmənt] *s* falsche
Angabe *f*
misstep [mɪs'step] *s* (& fig)Fehltritt *m*
mist [mɪst] *s* feiner Nebel *m* ‖ *tr* umnebeln ‖ *intr* (said of the eyes) sich
trüben; mist over nebeln
mis·take [mɪs'tek] *s* Fehler *m;* by m.
aus Versehen ‖ *v* (pret –took ['tʊk];
pp –taken) *tr* verkennen; m. s.o. for
s.o. else j–n mit e–m anderen verwechseln
mistaken [mɪs'tekən] *adj* falsch, irrig;
be m. (about) sich irren (in dat);
unless I'm m. wenn ich mich nicht
irre
mistak'en iden'tity *s* Personenverwechs-
lung *f*
mistakenly [mɪs'tekənlɪ] *adv* versehentlich
mister ['mɪstər] *s* Herr *m* ‖ *interj*
(pej) Herr!
mistletoe ['mɪsəl͵to] *s* Mistel *f*
mistreat [mɪs'trit] *tr* mißhandeln
mistreatment [mɪs'tritmənt] *s* Miß-
handlung *f*
mistress ['mɪstrɪs] *s* Herrin *f;* (lover)
Mätresse *f*, Geliebte *f*
mistrial [mɪs'traɪ·əl] *s* fehlerhaft ge-
führter Prozeß *m*
mistrust [mɪs'trʌst] *s* Mißtrauen *n* ‖
tr mißtrauen (dat)
misty ['mɪsti] *adj* neblig; (eyes) um-
flort; (fig) unklar
misunder·stand [͵mɪsʌndər'stænd] *v*
(pret & pp –stood) *tr* & *intr* mißver-
stehen
misunderstanding [͵mɪsʌndər'stændɪŋ]
s Mißverständnis *n*
misuse [mɪs'jus] *s* Mißbrauch *m* ‖
[mɪs'juz] *tr* mißbrauchen; (mistreat)
mißhandeln
misword [mɪs'wʌrd] *tr* in falsche
Worte fassen
mite [maɪt] *s* (ent) Milbe *f*
miter ['maɪtər] *s* Bischofsmütze *f* ‖ *tr*
auf Gehrung verbinden
mi'ter box' *s* Gehrlade *f*
mitigate ['mɪtɪ͵get] *tr* lindern
mitigation [͵mɪtɪ'geʃən] *s* Linderung
f
mitt [mɪt] *s* Fausthandschuh *m;* (sl)
Flosse *f;* (baseball) Fängerhandschuh
m
mitten ['mɪtən] *s* Fausthandschuh *m*
mix [mɪks] *s* Mischung *f*, Gemisch *n* ‖
tr (ver)mischen; (a drink) mixen; (a
cake) anrühren; mix in beimischen;
mix up vermischen; (confuse) verwirren ‖ *intr* sich (ver)mischen; mix
with vekehren mit
mixed *adj* vermischt; (feelings, company, doubles) gemischt
mixed' drink' *s* Mixgetränk *n*
mixed' mar'riage *s* Mischehe *f*
mixer ['mɪksər] *s* Mischer –in *mf;* (of
cocktails) Mixer –in *mf;* (mach)
Mischmaschine *f;* a good m. ein
guter Gesellschafter
mixture ['mɪkstʃər] *s* (e.g., of gases)

Gemisch *n; (e.g., of tobacco, coffee)* Mischung *f;* (pharm) Mixtur *f*
mix'-up' *s* Wirrwar *m,* Verwechslung *f*
mizzen ['mɪzən] *s* Besan *m*
mnemonic [nə'manık] *s* Gedächtnishilfe *f*
moan [mon] *s* Stöhnen *n* ‖ *intr* stöhnen; **m.** about jammern über *(acc)* or um
moat [mot] *s* Schloßgraben *m*
mob [mab] *s (populace)* Pöbel *m;* *(crush of people)* Andrang *m;* *(gang of criminals)* Verbrecherbande *f* ‖ *v* *(pret & pp* mobbed; *ger* mobbing) *tr (crowd into)* lärmend eindringen in *(acc); (e.g., a consulate)* angreifen; *(a celebrity)* umringen
mobile ['mobɪl] *adj* fahrbar; (mil) motorisiert
mo'bile home' *s* Wohnwagen *m*
mobility [mo'bɪlɪti] *s* (& mil) Beweglichkeit *f*
mobilization [ˌmobɪlɪ'zeʃən] *s* Mobilisierung *f*
mobilize ['mobɪˌlaɪz] *tr* mobilisieren; *(strength)* aufbieten
mob' rule' *s* Pöbelherrschaft *f*
mobster ['mabstər] *s* Gangster *m*
moccasin ['makəsın] *s* Mokassin *m;* *(snake)* Mokassinschlange *f*
Mo'cha cof'fee ['mokə] *s* Mokka *m*
mock [mak] *adj* Schein- ‖ *tr* verspotten; *(imitate)* nachäffen ‖ *intr* spotten; **m.** at sich lustig machen über *(acc);* **m.** up improvisieren
mocker ['makər] *s* Spötter –in *mf*
mockery ['makəri] *s* Spott *m,* Spöttelei *f;* **make a m.** of hohnsprechen *(dat)*
mock'ing *adj* spöttisch
mock'ingbird' *s* Spottdrossel *f*
mock' tri'al *s* Schauprozeß *m*
mock' tur'tle soup' *s* falsche Schildkrötensuppe *f*
mock'-up' *s* Schaumodell *n*
modal ['modəl] *adj* modal, Modal–
mode [mod] *s* Modus *m;* (mus) Tonart *f*
mod·el ['madəl] *adj* vorbildlich; *(student, husband)* Muster– ‖ *s (e.g., of a building)* Modell *n; (at a fashion show)* Vorführdame *f; (for art or photography)* Modell *n; (example for imitation)* Vorbild *n,* Muster *n; (make)* Typ *m,* Bauart *f* ‖ *v (pret & pp* –el[l]ed; *ger* –el[l]ing) *tr (clothes)* vorführen; **m. oneself on** sich *[dat]* ein Muster nehmen an *(dat);* **m. s.th. on** etw formen nach; (fig) etw gestalten nach ‖ *intr* (for) Modell stehen (zu *dat)*
mod'el air'plane *s* Flugzeugmodell *n*
mod'el num'ber *s* (aut) Typennummer *f*
moderate ['madərɪt] *adj (climate)* gemäßigt; *(demand)* maßvoll; *(price)* angemessen; *(e.g., in drinking)* mäßig; **of m. means** minderbemittelt ‖ ['madəˌret] *tr* mäßigen; *(a meeting)* den Vorsitz führen über *(acc)* or bei; *(a television show)* moderieren ‖ *intr* sich mäßigen
moderation [ˌmadə'reʃən] *s* Mäßigung

f, Maß *n;* **in m.** mit Maß; **observe m.** Maß halten
moderator ['madəˌretər] *s* Moderator *m*
modern ['madərn] *adj* modern, zeitgemäß
mod'ern Eng'lish *s* Neuenglisch *n*
mod'ern his'tory *s* Neuere Geschichte *f*
modernize ['madərˌnaɪz] *tr* modernisieren
mod'ern lan'guages *spl* neuere Sprachen *pl*
mod'ern times' *spl* die Neuzeit *f*
modest ['madɪst] *adj* bescheiden
modesty ['madɪsti] *s* Bescheidenheit *f*
modicum ['madɪkəm] *s* bißchen; **a m.** of truth ein Körnchen Wahrheit
modification [ˌmadɪfɪ'keʃən] *s* Abänderung *f*
modifier ['madɪˌfaɪ·ər] *s* (gram) nähere Bestimmung *f*
modi·fy ['madɪˌfaɪ] *v (pret & pp* –fied) *tr* abändern; (gram) näher bestimmen
modish ['modɪʃ] *adj* modisch
modulate ['madjəˌlet] *tr & intr* modulieren
modulation [ˌmadjə'leʃən] *s* Modulation *f*
mohair ['mo ˌhɛr] *s* Mohair *m*
Mohammedan [mo'hæmɪdən] *adj* mohammedanisch ‖ *s* Mohammedaner –in *mf*
Mohammedanism [mo'hæmɪdəˌnɪzəm] *s* Mohammedanismus *m*
moist [mɔɪst] *adj* feucht; *(eyes)* tränenfeucht
moisten ['mɔɪsən] *tr* anfeuchten; *(lips)* befeuchten ‖ *intr* feucht werden
moisture ['mɔɪstʃər] *s* Feuchtigkeit *f*
molar ['molər] *s* Backenzahn *m*
molasses [mə'læsɪz] *s* Melasse *f*
mold [mold] *s* Form *f; (mildew)* Schimmel *m;* (typ) Matrize *f* ‖ *tr* formen ‖ *intr* (ver)schimmeln
molder ['moldər] *s* Former –in *mf;* (fig) Bildner –in *mf* ‖ *intr* modern
mold'ing *s* Formen *n;* (carp) Gesims *n*
moldy ['moldi] *adj* mod(e)rig, schimmlig
mole [mol] *s (breakwater)* Hafendamm *m; (blemish)* Muttermal *n;* (zool) Maulwurf *m*
molecular [mə'lɛkjələr] *adj* molekular
molecule ['malɪˌkjul] *s* Molekül *n*
mole'skin' *s (fur)* Maulwurfsfell *n;* (tex) Englischleder *n*
molest [mə'lɛst] *tr* belästigen
molli·fy ['malɪˌfaɪ] *v (pret & pp* –fied) *tr* besänftigen
mollusk ['maləsk] *s* Weichtier *n*
mollycoddle ['malɪˌkadəl] *s* Weichling *m* ‖ *tr* verweichlichen
Mol'otov cock'tail ['malətəf] *s* Flaschengranate *f*
molt [molt] *s intr* sich mausern
molten ['moltən] *adj* schmelzflüssig
molybdenum [mə'lɪbdɪnəm] *s* Molybdän *n*
mom [mam] *s* (coll) Mama *f,* Mutti *f*
moment ['momənt] *s* Moment *m,* Au-

genblick *m;* **a m. ago** nur eben; **at a moment's notice** jeden Augenblick; **at any m.** jederzeit; **at the m.** im Augenblick, zur Zeit; **of great m.** von großer Tragweite; **the very m. I spotted her** sobald ich sie erblickte
momentarily ['moumən,terɪli] *adv* momentan; (*in a moment*) gleich
momentary ['moumən,teri] *adj* vorübergehend
momentous [mo'mentəs] *adj* folgenschwer
momen·tum [mo'mentəm] *s* (**-tums & -ta** [tə]) (phys) Moment *n;* (fig) Schwung *m;* **gather m.** Schwung bekommen
monarch ['mɑnərk] *s* Monarch *m*
monarchical [mə'nɑrkɪkəl] *adj* monarchisch
monarchy ['mɑnərki] *s* Monarchie *f*
monastery ['mɑnes,teri] *s* Kloster *n*
monastic [mə'næstɪk] *adj* Kloster-, Mönchs–
monasticism [mə'næstɪ,sɪzəm] *s* Mönchswesen *n*
Monday ['mʌndi], ['mʌnde] *s* Montag *m;* **on M.** am Montag
monetary ['mɑnɪ,teri] *adj* (*e.g., crisis, unit*) Währungs–; (*e.g., system, value*) Geld–
mon'etary stand'ard *s* Münzfuß *m*
money ['mʌni] *adj* Geld– ‖ *s* Geld *n;* **big m.** schweres Geld; **get one's money's worth** reell bedient werden; **make m. (on)** Geld verdienen (an *dat*); **put m. on** Geld setzen auf (*acc*)
mon'eybag' *s* Geldbeutel *m;* **money-bags** (coll) Geldsack *m*
mon'ey belt' *s* Geldgürtel *m*
moneychanger ['mʌni,tʃendʒər] *s* Wechsler –in *mf*
moneyed ['mʌnid] *adj* vermögend
mon'ey exchange' *s* Geldwechsel *m*
mon'eylend'er *s* Geldverleiher –in *mf*
mon'eymak'er *s* (fig) Goldgrube *f*
mon'ey or'der *s* Postanweisung *f*
Mongol ['mɑŋgəl] *adj* mongolid ‖ *s* Mongole *m,* Mongolin *f*
Mongolian [mɑŋ'golɪ·ən] *adj* mongolisch ‖ *s* (*language*) Mongolisch *n*
mon·goose ['mɑŋgus] *s* (**-gooses**) Mungo *m*
mongrel ['mʌŋgrəl] *s* Bastard *m*
monitor ['mɑnɪtər] *s* (*at school*) Klassenordner *m;* (rad, telv) Überwachungsgerät *n,* Monitor *m* ‖ *tr* überwachen
monk [mʌŋk] *s* Mönch *m*
monkey ['mʌŋki] *s* Affe *m;* (*female*) Äffin *f;* **make a m. of** zum Narren halten ‖ *intr*—**m. around** (*trifle idly*) herumalbern; **m. around with s.o.** es mit j–m treiben; **m. around with s.th.** an etw [*dat*] herummurksen
mon'keybusi'ness *s* (*underhanded conduct*) Gaunerei *f;* (*frivolous behavior*) (sl) Unfug *m*
mon'keyshine' *s* (sl) Possen *m*
mon'key wrench' *s* Engländer *m*
monocle ['mɑnəkəl] *s* Monokel *n*
monogamous [mə'nɑgəməs] *adj* monogam

monogamy [mə'nɑgəmi] *s* Einehe *f*
monogram ['mɑnə,græm] *s* Monogramm *n*
monograph ['mɑnə,græf] *s* Monographie *f*
monolithic [,mɑnə'lɪθɪk] *adj* (& fig) monolithisch
monologue ['mɑnə,lɔg] *s* Monolog *m*
monomania [,mɑnə'menɪ·ə] *s* Monomanie *f*
monoplane ['mɑnə,plen] *s* Eindecker *m*
monopolize [mə'nɑpə,laɪz] *tr* monopolisieren
monorail ['mɑnə,rel] *s* Einschienenbahn *f*
monosyllable ['mɑnə,sɪləbəl] *s* einsilbiges Wort *n*
monotheism [,mɑnə'θi·ɪzəm] *s* Monotheismus *m*
monotonous [mə'nɑtənəs] *adj* eintönig
monotony [mə'nɑtəni] *s* Eintönigkeit *f*
monotype ['mɑnə,taɪp] *s* Monotype *f*
monoxide [mə'nɑksaɪd] *s* Monoxyd *n*
monsignor [mɑn'sinjər] *s* (**monsignors & monsignori** [,mɑnsi'njori]) (eccl) Monsignore *m*
monsoon [mɑn'sun] *s* Monsun *m*
monster ['mɑnstər] *s* (& fig) Ungeheuer *n*
monstrance ['mɑnstrəns] *s* Monstranz *f*
monstrosity [mɑns'trɑsɪti] *s* Monstrosität *f,* Ungeheuerlichkeit *f*
monstrous ['mɑnstrəs] *adj* ungeheuer(lich)
month [mʌnθ] *s* Monat *m*
monthly ['mʌnθli] *adj & adv* monatlich ‖ *s* Monatszeitschrift *f*
monument ['mɑnjəmənt] *s* Denkmal *n*
monumental [,mɑnjə'mentəl] *adj* monumental
moo [mu] *s* Muhen *n* ‖ *intr* muhen
mood [mud] *s* Laune *f,* Stimmung *f;* (gram) Aussageweise *f,* Modus *m;* **be in a bad m.** schlechtgelaunt sein; **be in the m. for s.th.** zu etw gelaunt sein
moody ['mudi] *adj* launisch
moon [mun] *s* Mond *m* ‖ *intr*—**m. about** herumlungern
moon'beam' *s* Mondstrahl *m*
moon'light' *s* Mondschein *m* ‖ *intr* schwarzarbeiten
moon'light'er *s* Doppelverdiener –in *mf*
moon'light'ing *s* Schwarzarbeit *f*
moon'lit' *adj* mondhell
moon'shine' *s* Mondschein *m;* (sl) schwarz gebrannter Whisky *m*
moonshiner ['mun,ʃaɪnər] *s* Schwarzbrenner –in *mf*
moon'shot' *s* Mondgeschoß *n*
moor [mur] *s* Moor *n,* Heidemoor *n;* **Moor** Mohr *m* ‖ *tr* (naut) vertäuen ‖ *intr* (naut) festmachen
moor'ing *s* (act) Festmachen *n;* **moorings** (*cables*) Vertäuung *f;* (*place*) Liegeplatz *m*
Moorish ['murɪʃ] *adj* maurisch
moose [mus] *s* (**moose**) amerikanischer Elch *m*
moot [mut] *adj* umstritten

mop [map] *s* Mop *m;* (*of hair*) Wust *m* ‖ *v* (*pret & pp* **mopped;** *ger* **mopping**) *tr* mit dem Mop wischen; **mop up** mit dem Mop aufwischen; (mil) säubern

mope [mop] *intr* Trübsal blasen

moped ['mopəd] *s* Moped *n*

mop'ping-up' opera'tion *s* (mil) Säuberungsaktion *f*

moral ['mɔrəl] *adj* moralisch ‖ *s* Moral *f;* **morals** Sitten *pl*

morale [mə'ræl] *s* Moral *f*

morality [mə'rælɪti] *s* Sittlichkeit *f*

moralize ['mɔrə,laɪz] *intr* moralisieren

morass [mə'ræs] *s* Morast *m*

moratori·um [,mɔrə'tɔrɪ·əm] *s* (-ums & a- [ə]) Moratorium *n*

Moravia [mə'revɪ·ə] *s* Mähren *n*

morbid ['mɔrbɪd] *adj* krankhaft, morbid

mordacious [mɔr'deʃəs] *adj* bissig

mordant ['mɔrdənt] *adj* beißend

more [mor] *comp adj* mehr; **one m.** minute noch e–e Minute ‖ *comp adv* mehr; **all the m.** erst recht; **all the m.** because zumal, da; **m. and m.** immer mehr; **m. and m. expensive** immer teurer; **m. or less** gewissermaßen; **m. than anything** über alles; **no m.** nicht mehr; **not any m.** nicht mehr; **once m.** noch einmal; **the more … the** (expressing quantity) je mehr … desto; (expressing frequency) je öfter … desto ‖ *s* mehr; **see m. of s.o.** j–n noch öfter sehen; **what's m.** außerdem ‖ *pron* mehr

more'o'ver *adv* außerdem, übrigens

morgue [mɔrg] *s* Leichenschauhaus *n;* (journ) Archiv *n,* Zeitungsarchiv *n*

morning ['mɔrnɪŋ] *adj* Morgen– ‖ *s* Morgen *m;* **from m. till night** von früh bis spät; **in the early m.** in früher Morgenstunde; **in the m.** am Morgen; **this m.** heute morgen; **to-morrow m.** morgen früh

morn'ing-af'ter pill' *s* Pille *f* danach

morn'ing-glo'ry *s* Trichterwinde *f*

morn'ing sick'ness *s* morgendliches Erbrechen *n*

morn'ing star' *s* Morgenstern *m*

Moroccan [mə'rakən] *adj* marokkanisch ‖ *s* Marokkaner –in *mf*

morocco [mə'rako] *s* (*leather*) Saffian *m;* **Morocco** Marokko *n*

moron ['mɔran] *s* Schwachsinnige *mf*

morose [mə'ros] *adj* mürrisch

morphine ['mɔrfin] *s* Morphium *n*

morphology [mɔr'falədʒi] *s* Morphologie *f*

morrow ['mɔro] *s*—**on the m.** am folgenden Tag

Morse' code' [mɔrs] *s* Morsealphabet *n*

morsel ['mɔrsəl] *s* Bröckchen *n*

mortal ['mɔrtəl] *adj* sterblich ‖ *s* Sterbliche *mf*

mor'tal dan'ger *s* Lebensgefahr *f*

mor'tal en'emy *s* Todfeind *m*

mor'tal fear' *s* Heidenangst *f*

mortality [mɔr'tælɪti] *s* Sterblichkeit *f*

mortally ['mɔrtəli] *adv* tödlich

mor'tal remains' *spl* irdische Überreste *pl*

mor'tal sin' *s* Todsünde *f*

mor'tal wound' *s* Todeswunde *f*

mortar ['mɔrtər] *s* (*vessel*) Mörser *m;* (archit) Mörtel *m;* (mil) Granatwerfer *m*

mor'tarboard' *s* Mörtelbrett *n*

mor'tar fire' *s* Granatwerferfeuer *n*

mor'tar shell' *s* Granate *f*

mortgage ['mɔrgɪdʒ] *s* Hypothek *f* ‖ *tr* mit e–r Hypothek belasten

mortgagee [,mɔrgɪ'dʒi] *s* Hypothengläubiger –in *mf*

mortgagor ['mɔrgɪdʒər] *s* Hypothekenschuldner –in *mf*

mortician [mɔr'tɪʃən] *s* Leichenbestatter –in *mf*

morti·fy ['mɔrtɪ,faɪ] *v* (*pret & pp* **-fied**) *tr* (*the flesh*) abtöten; (*humiliate*) demütigen; **m. oneself** sich kasteien

mortise ['mɔrtɪs] *s* (carp) Zapfenloch *n* ‖ *tr* (carp) verzapfen

mortuary ['mɔrtʃʊ,ɛri] *s* Leichenhalle *f*

mosaic [mo'ze·ɪk] *adj* mosaisch ‖ *s* Mosaik *n*

Moscow ['masko], ['maskau] *s* Moskau *n*

Moses ['mozɪz], ['mozɪs] *s* Moses *m*

mosey ['mozi] *intr* (coll) dahinschlürfen

Mos·lem ['mazləm] *adj* muselmanisch ‖ *s* (-lems & -lem) Moslem –in *mf*

mosque [mask] *s* Moschee *f*

mosqui·to [məs'kito] *s* (-toes & -tos) Moskito *m,* Mücke *f*

mosqui'to net' *s* Moskitonetz *n*

moss [mɔs] *s* Moos *n*

mossy ['mɔsi] *adj* bemoost

most [most] *super adj* meist ‖ *super adv* am meisten; (*very*) höchst; **m. of all** am allermeisten ‖ *s*—**at (the) m.** höchstens; **make the m. of** möglichst gut ausnützen; **m. of die** meisten; **m. of the day** der größte Teil des Tages; **the m.** das meiste, das Höchste ‖ *pron* die meisten

mostly ['mostli] *adv* meistens

motel [mo'tɛl] *s* Motel *n*

moth [mɔθ] *s* Nachtfalter *m;* (*clothes moth*) Motte *f*

moth'ball' *s* Mottenkugel *f;* **put into mothballs** (nav) stillegen, einmotten ‖ *tr* (& fig) einmotten

moth-eaten ['mɔθ,itən] *adj* mottenzerfressen

mother ['mʌðər] *s* Mutter *f* ‖ *tr* (*produce*) gebären; (*take care of as a mother*) bemuttern

moth'er coun'try *s* Mutterland *n*

moth'erhood' *s* Mutterschaft *f*

moth'er-in-law' *s* (mothers-in-law) Schwiegermutter *f*

motherless ['mʌðərlɪs] *adj* mutterlos

motherly ['mʌðərli] *adj* mütterlich

mother-of-pearl ['mʌðərəv'pʌrl] *adj* perlmuttern ‖ *s* Perlmutter *f*

Moth'er's Day' *s* Muttertag *m*

moth'er's help'er *s* Stütze *f* der Hausfrau

moth'er supe'rior s (Schwester) Oberin f

moth'er tongue' s Muttersprache f
moth' hole' s Mottenfraß m
mothy ['mɔθi] adj mottenzerfressen
motif [mo'tif] s (mus, paint) Motiv n
motion ['moʃən] s Bewegung f; (parl) Antrag m; **make a m.** e–n Antrag stellen; **set in m.** in Bewegung setzen || tr zuwinken (dat); **m. s.o.** to (inf) j–n durch e–n Wink auffordern zu (inf)
motionless ['moʃənlɪs] adj bewegungslos
mo'tion pic'ture s Film m; **be in motion pictures** beim Film sein
mo'tion-pic'ture adj Film–
mo'tion-pic'ture the'ater s Kino n
motivate ['motɪ‚vet] tr begründen, motivieren
motive ['motɪv] s Anlaß m, Beweggrund m
mo'tive pow'er s Triebkraft f
motley ['mɑtli] adj bunt zusammengewürfelt
motor ['motər] adj Motor– || s Motor m
motorcade ['motər‚ked] s Wagenkolonne f
mo'torcy'cle s Motorrad n
mo'torcyc'list s Motorradfahrer –in mf
mo'toring s Autofahren n
motorist ['motərɪst] s Autofahrer –in mf
motorize ['motə‚raɪz] tr motorisieren
mo'tor launch' s Motorbarkasse f
mo'tor·man s (–men) Straßenbahnführer m
mo'tor pool' s Fahrbereitschaft f
mo'tor scoot'er s Motorroller m
mo'tor ve'hicle s Kraftfahrzeug n
mottle ['mɑtəl] tr sprenkeln
mot·to ['mɑto] s (–toes & –tos) Motto n
mound [maʊnd] s Wall m, Erdhügel m
mount [maʊnt] s (mountain) Berg m; (riding horse) Reittier n || tr (a horse, mountain) besteigen; (stairs) hinaufgehen; (e.g., a machinegun) in Position bringen; (a precious stone) fassen; (photographs in an album) einkleben; (photographs on a backing) aufkleben; **m.** (e.g., a gun) **on** montieren auf (acc)
mountain ['maʊntən] s Berg m; **down the m.** bergab; **up the m.** bergauf
moun'tain clim'ber s Bergsteiger –in mf
moun'tain climb'ing s Bergsteigen n
mountaineer [‚maʊmtə'nɪr] s Bergbewohner –in mf
mountainous ['maʊntənəs] adj gebirgig
moun'tain pass' s Gebirgspaß m, Paß m
moun'tain rail'road s Bergbahn f
moun'tain range' s Gebirge n
moun'tain scen'ery s Berglandschaft f
mountebank ['maʊntə‚bæŋk] s Quacksalber m; (charlatan) Scharlatan m
mount'ing s Montage f; (of a precious stone) Fassung f
mourn [morn] tr betrauren || intr

trauern; **mourn for** betrauern, trauern um
mourner ['mornər] s Leidtragende mf
mournful ['mornfəl] adj traurig
mourn'ing s Trauer f; **be in m.** Trauer tragen
mourn'ing band' s Trauerflor m
mourn'ing clothes' spl Trauerkleidung f; **wear m.** Trauer tragen
mouse [maʊs] s (mice [maɪs]) Maus f
mouse'hole' s Mauseloch n
mouse'trap' s Mausefalle f
moustache [məs'tæʃ] s Schnurbart m
mouth [maʊθ] s (mouths [maʊðz]) Mund m; (of an animal) Maul n; (of a gun, bottle, river) Mündung f; (sl) Maul n; **keep one's m.** shut den Mund halten; **make s.o.'s m.** water j–m das Wasser im Munde zusammenlaufen lassen
mouthful ['maʊθ‚ful] s Mundvoll m; (sl) großes Wort n
mouth' or'gan s Mundharmonika f
mouth'piece' s (of an instrument) Ansatz m; (box) Mundstück n; (fig) Sprachrohr n
mouth'wash' s Mundwasser n
movable ['muvəbəl] adj beweglich, mobil || **movables** spl Mobilien pl
move [muv] s (movement) Bewegung f; (step, measure) Maßnahme f; (resettlement) Umzug m; (checkers) Zug m; (parl) Vorschlag m; **be on the m.** unterwegs sein; **don't make a m.!** keinen Schritt!; **get a m. on** (coll) sich rühren; **it's your m.** (& fig) du bist am Zug; **she won't make a m. without him** sie macht keinen Schritt ohne ihn || tr bewegen; (emotionally) rühren; (shove) rücken; (checkers) e–n Zug machen mit; (parl) beantragen; **m. the bowels** abführen; **m. up** (mil) vorschieben || intr (stir) sich bewegen; (change residence) umziehen; (in society) verkehren; (checkers) ziehen; (com) Absatz haben; **m. away** wegziehen; **m. back** zurückziehen; **m. for** (e.g., a new trial) beantragen; **m. in** zuziehen; **m. into** (a home) beziehen; **m. on** fortziehen; **m. out** (of) ausziehen (aus); **m. over** (make room) zur Seite rücken; **m. up** (to a higher position) vorrücken; (into a vacated position) nachrücken; (said of a team) aufsteigen
movement ['muvmənt] s (& fig) Bewegung f; (mus) Satz m
mover ['muvər] s Möbeltransporteur m; (parl) Antragsteller –in mf
movie ['muvi] adj (actor, actress, camera, projector) Film– || s (coll) Film m; **movies** Kino n; **go to the movies** ins Kino gehen
mov'ie cam'era s Filmkamera f
moviegoer ['muvi‚go·ər] s Kinobesucher –in mf
mov'ie house' s Kino n
mov'ie screen' s Filmleinwand f
mov'ie set' s Filmkulisse f
mov'ie the'ater s Kino n
mov'ing adj beweglich; (force) trei-

bend; (fig) herzergreifend ‖ s
(*change of residence*) Umzug m
mov'ing pic'ture s Lichtspiel n, Film m
mov'ing spir'it s führender Kopf m
mow [mo] v (pret **mowed;** pp **mowed**
& **mown**) tr mähen; **mow down** (*enemies*) niedermähen
mower ['mo·ər] s Mäher m
m.p.h. ['em'pi'et∫] spl (**miles per hour**)
Stundenmeilen; **drive sixty m.p.h.**
mit sechzig Stundenmeilen fahren
Mr. [mɪstər] s Herr m
Mrs. ['mɪsɪz] s Frau f
Ms. [mɪz] s Fräulein n
much [mʌt∫] adj, adv & pron viel; **as
m. again** noch einmal soviel; **how m.**
wieviel; **m. less** (*not to mention*) geschweige denn; **not so m. as** nicht
einmal; **so m.** so sehr; **so m. the
better** um so besser; **very m.** sehr
mucilage ['mjusɪlɪdʒ] s Klebstoff m
muck [mʌk] s (& fig) Schmutz m
muck'rake' intr (coll) Korruptionsfälle
enthüllen
muckraker ['mʌk,rekər] s (coll) Korruptionsschnüffler –in mf
mucky ['mʌki] adj schmutzig
mucous ['mjukəs] adj schleimig
muc'ous mem'brane s Schleimhaut f
mucus ['mjukəs] s Schleim m
mud [mʌd] s Schlamm m; **drag through
the mud** (fig) in den Schmutz ziehen
mud' bath' s Schlammbad n, Moorbad
n
muddle ['mʌdəl] s Durcheinander n ‖
tr durcheinanderbringen ‖ intr—**m.
through** sich durchwursteln
mud'dlehead' s Wirrkopf m
mud·dy ['mʌdi] adj schlammig; (fig)
trüb ‖ v (pret & pp –died) trüben
mud'hole' s Schlammloch n
mudslinging ['mʌd,slɪŋɪŋ] s (fig) Verleumdung f
muff [mʌf] s Muff m ‖ tr (coll) verpfuschen
muffin ['mʌfɪn] s Teekuchen m aus
Backpulverteig
muffle ['mʌfəl] tr (*sounds*) dämpfen;
m. up (*wrap up*) einhüllen
muf'fled adj dumpf
muffler ['mʌflər] s (*scarf*) Halstuch n;
(aut) Auspufftopf m
mufti ['mʌfti] s Zivil n
mug [mʌg] s Krug m; (*for beer*) Seidel
n; (*thug*) (sl) Rocker m; (*face*) (sl)
Fratze f ‖ v (pret & pp **mugged**; ger
mugging) tr (sl) photographieren;
(*assault*) (sl) überfallen ‖ intr (sl)
Gesichter schneiden
muggy ['mʌgi] adj schwül
mug' shot' s (sl) Polizeiphoto n
mulat·to [mə'læto] s (**–toes**) Mulatte
m, Mulattin f
mulberry ['mʌl,beri] s Maulbeere f
mul'berry tree' s Maulbeerbaum m
mulch [mʌlt∫] s Streu n
mulct [mʌlkt] tr (**of**) betrügen (um)
mule [mjul] s Maulesel m, Maultier n
mulish ['mjulɪ∫] adj störrisch
mull [mʌl] intr—**m. over** nachgrübeln
über (*acc*)
mullion ['mʌljən] s Mittelpfosten m

multicolored ['mʌltɪ,kələrd] adj bunt
multigraph ['mʌltɪ,græf] s (trademark) Vervielfältigungsmaschine f ‖
tr vervielfältigen
multilateral [,mʌltɪ'lætərəl] adj mehrseitig
multimillionaire ['mʌltɪ,mɪljə'ner] s
vielfacher Millionär m
multiple ['mʌltɪpəl] adj mehrfach,
Vielfach– ‖ s (math) Vielfaches n
multiplication [,mʌltɪplɪ'ke∫ən] s Vermehrung f; (arith) Multiplikation f
multiplica'tion ta'ble s Einmaleins n
multiplicity [,mʌltɪ'plɪsɪti] s Vielfältigkeit f
multi·ply ['mʌltɪ,plaɪ] v (pret & pp
–plied) tr vervielfältigen; (biol) vermehren; (math) multiplizieren ‖ intr
sich vervielfachen; (biol) sich vermehren
multistage ['mʌltɪ,stedʒ] adj mehrstufig
multistory ['mʌltɪ,stori] adj mehrstöckig
multitude ['mʌltɪ,t(j)ud] s (*large number*) Vielheit f; (*of people*) Masse f
mum [mʌm] adj still; **keep mum about**
Stillschweigen beobachten über (*acc*);
mum's the word! Mund halten!
mumble ['mʌmbəl] tr & intr murmeln
mummery ['mʌməri] s Hokuspokus m
mummy ['mʌmi] s Mumie f
mumps [mʌmps] s Ziegenpeter m,
Mumps m
munch [mʌnt∫] tr & intr geräuschvoll
kauen
mundane [mʌn'den] adj irdisch
municipal [mju'nɪsɪpəl] adj städtisch
muni'cipal bond' s Kommunalobligation f
municipality [mju,nɪsɪ'pælɪti] s Stadt
f, Gemeinde f; (*governing body*)
Stadtverwaltung f
munificent [mju'nɪfɪsənt] adj freigebig
munificence [mju'nɪfɪsəns] s Freigebigkeit f
munitions [mju'nɪ∫əns] s Kriegsmaterial n, Munition f
muni'tions dump' s Munitionsdepot n
muni'tions fac'tory s Rüstungsfabrik f
mural ['mjurəl] s Wandgemälde n
murder ['mʌrdər] s Mord m ‖ tr
(er)morden; (*a language*) radebrechen
murderer ['mʌrdərər] s Mörder m
murderess ['mʌrdərɪs] s Mörderin f
mur'der mys'tery s Krimi m
murderous ['mʌrdərəs] adj mörderisch
mur'der plot' s Mordanschlag m
murky ['mʌrki] adj düster
murmur ['mʌrmər] s Gemurmel n ‖
tr & intr murmeln
muscle ['mʌsəl] s Muskel m; **muscles**
Muskulatur f
muscular ['mʌskjələr] adj muskulös
Muse [mjuz] s Muse f ‖ **muse** intr
(**over**) nachsinnen (über acc)
museum [mju'zi·əm] s Museum n
mush [mʌ∫] s (*corn meal*) Maismehlbrei m; (*soft mass*) Matsch m; (*sentimental talk*) Süßholzraspeln n
mush'room' s Pilz m, Champignon m

|| *intr* wie Pilze aus dem Boden schießen
mushy ['mʌʃi] *adj* matschig; (*sentimental*) rührselig
music ['mjusɪk] *s* Musik *f;* (*score*) Noten *pl;* **face the m.** die Sache ausbaden; **set to m.** vertonen
musical ['mjuzɪkəl] *adj* musikalisch **||** *s* (cin) Singspielfilm *m;* (theat) Musical *n,* Singspiel *n*
mu'sical in'strument *s* Musikinstrument *n*
musicale [,mjusɪ'kæl] *s* Musikabend *m*
mu'sic box' *s* Spieldose *f*
musician [mju'zɪʃən] *s* Musikant –in *mf;* (*accomplished artist*) Musiker –in *mf*
musicology [,mjuzɪ'kɑlədʒi] *s* Musikwissenschaft *f*
mu'sic stand' *s* Notenständer *m*
mus'ing *s* Grübelei *f*
musk [mʌsk] *s* Moschus *m*
musket ['mʌskɪt] *s* Muskete *f*
musk'rat' *s* Bisamratte *f*
muslin ['mʌzlɪn] *s* Musselin *m*
muss [mʌs] *tr* (*hair*) zerzausen; (*dirty*) schmutzig machen; (*rumple*) zerknittern
mussel ['mʌsəl] *s* Muschel *f*
mussy ['mʌsi] *adj* (*hair*) zerzaust; (*clothes*) zerknittert
must [mʌst] *s* (*a necessity*) Muß *n;* (*new wine*) Most *m;* (*mold*) Moder *m* **||** *mod*—**I m.** (*inf*) ich muß (*inf*)
mustache [məs'tæʃ] *s* Schnurrbart *m*
mustard ['mʌstərd] *s* Senf *m*
mus'tard plas'ter *s* Senfpflaster *n*
muster ['mʌstər] *s* Appell *m;* **pass m.** die Prüfung bestehen **||** *tr* (*troops*) antreten lassen; (*courage, strength*) aufbringen; **m. out** ausmustern
musty ['mʌsti] *adj* mod(e)rig
mutation [mju'teʃən] *s* (biol) Mutation *f*
mute [mjut] *adj* (& ling) stumm **||** *s* (ling) stummer Buchstabe *m;* (mus) Dämpfer **||** *tr* (mus) dämpfen
mutilate ['mjutɪ,let] *tr* verstümmeln

mutineer [,mjutɪ'nɪr] *s* Meuterer *m*
mutinous ['mjutɪnəs] *adj* meuterisch
muti·ny ['mjutɪni] *s* Meuterei *f* **||** *v* (*pret & pp* –nied) *intr* meutern
mutt [mʌt] *s* (coll) Köter *m*
mutter ['mʌtər] *s* Gemurmel *n* **||** *tr* & *intr* murmeln
mutton ['mʌtən] *s* (culin) Hammel *m*
mut'ton-head' *s* (sl) Hammel *m*
mutual ['mjutʃu·əl] *adj* gegenseitig; (*friends*) gemeinsam
mu'tual fund' *s* Investmentfond *m*
mu'tual insur'ance com'pany *s* Versicherungsgesellschaft *f* auf Gegenseitigkeit
mutually ['mjutʃu·əli] *adv* gegenseitig
muzzle ['mʌzəl] *s* Maulkorb *m;* (*of a gun*) Rohrmündung *f;* (*snout*) Schnauze *f* **||** *tr* (*an animal*) e–n Maulkorb anlegen (*dat*); (e.g., *the press*) mundtot machen
muz'zle flash' *s* Mündungsfeuer *n*
my [maɪ] *poss adj* mein
myopic [maɪ'ɑpɪk] *adj* kurzsichtig
myriad ['mɪrɪ·əd] *adj* Myriade *f*
myrrh [mʌr] *s* Myrrhe *f*
myrtle ['mʌrtəl] *s* Myrte *f*
myself ['maɪ'self] *reflex pron* mich; (*indirect object*) mir **||** *intens pron* selbst, selber
mysterious [mɪs'tɪrɪ·əs] *adj* mysteriös
mystery ['mɪstəri] *s* Geheimnis *n;* (fi) Rätsel *n;* (relig) Mysterium *n*
mys'tery nov'el *s* Kriminalroman *m*
mys'tery play' *s* Mysterienspiel *n*
mystic ['mɪstɪk] *adj* mystisch **||** *s* Mystiker –in *mf*
mystical ['mɪstɪkəl] *adj* mystisch
mysticism ['mɪstɪ,sɪzəm] *s* Mystik *f*
mystification [,mɪstɪfɪ'keʃən] *s* Verwirrung *f*
mysti·fy ['mɪstɪ,faɪ] *v* (*pret & pp* –fied) *tr* verwirren
myth [mɪθ] *s* Mythe *f,* Mythos *m;* (*ill-founded belief*) Märchen *n*
mythical ['mɪθɪkəl] *adj* mythisch
mythological [,mɪθə'lɑdʒɪkəl] *adj* mythologisch
mythology [mɪ'θɑlədʒi] *s* Mythologie *f*

N

N, n [ɛn] *s* vierzehnter Buchstabe des englischen Alphabets
nab [næb] *v* (*pret & pp* nabbed; *ger* –nabbing) *tr* (coll) schnappen
nadir ['nedɪr] *s* (fig) Tiefpunkt *m;* (astr) Nadir *m*
nag [næg] *s* Gaul *m;* **old nag** Schindmähre *f* **||** *v* (*pret & pp* nagged; *ger* nagging) *tr* zusetzen (*dat*) **||** *intr* nörgeln; **nag at** herumnörgeln an (*dat*)
nag'ging *adj* nörgelnd **||** *s* Nörgelei *f*
naiad ['naɪ·æd] *s* Najade *f*
nail [nel] *s* Nagel *m;* **hit the n. on the head** den Nagel auf den Kopf treffen **||** *tr* (**to**) annageln (an *acc*); (*catch*)

(coll) erwischen; (box) (coll) treffen; **n. down** (fig) festnageln; **n. shut** zunageln
nail' clip'pers *spl* Nagelzange *f*
nail' file' *s* Nagelfeile *f*
nail' pol'ish *s* Nagellack *m*
nail' scis'sors *s* & *spl* Nagelschere *f*
naïve [nɑ'iv] *adj* naiv
naked ['nekɪd] *adj* nackt; (*eye*) bloß
nakedness ['nekɪdnɪs] *s* Nacktheit *f*
name [nem] *s* Name *m;* (*reputation*) Name *m,* Ruf *m;* **by n.** dem Namen nach; **by the n. of** namens; **in n. only** nur dem Namen nach; **of the same n.** gleichnamig; **spell one's n.** sich

schreiben; **what is your n.?** wie heißen Sie? ‖ *tr* nennen; (*nominate*) ernennen; **be named after** heißen nach; **n. after** nennen nach; **named** namens
name'-call'ng s Beschimpfung *f*
name' day' s Namenstag *m*
nameless ['nemlɪs] *adj* namenlos
namely ['nemli] *adv* nämlich, und zwar
name'plate' s Namensschild *n*
name'sake' s Namensvetter *m*
nanny ['næni] s Kindermädchen *n*
nan'ny goat' s (coll) Ziege *f*
nap [næp] s Schläfchen *n;* (tex) Noppe *f;* **take a nap** ein Schläfchen machen ‖ *v* (*pret & pp* **napped;** *ger* **napping**) *intr* schlummern; **catch s.o. napping** (fig) j–n überrumpeln
napalm ['nepɑm] s Napalm *n*
nape [nep] s—**n. of the neck** Nacken *m*
naphtha ['næfθə] s Naphtha *f & n*
napkin ['næpkɪn] s Serviette *f*
nap'kin ring' s Serviettenring *m*
narcissism ['nɑrsɪ ˌsɪzəm] s Narzißmus *m*
narcissus [nɑr'sɪsəs] s (bot) Narzisse *f*
narcotic [nɑr'kɑtɪk] *adj* narkotisch ‖ s (med) Betäubungsmittel *n,* Narkotikum *n;* (*addictive drug*) Rauschgift *n;* (*addict*) Rauschgiftsüchtige *mf*
narrate [næ'ret] *tr* erzählen
narration [næ'reʃən] s Erzählung *f*
narrative ['nærətɪv] *adj* erzählend ‖ s Erzählung *f*
narrator [næ'retər] s Erzähler *m;* (telv) Moderator *m*
narrow ['næro] *adj* eng, schmal; (*e.g., margin*) knapp ‖ **narrows** *spl* Meerenge *f* ‖ *tr* verengen ‖ *intr* sich verengen
nar'row escape' s—**have a n.** mit knapper Not entkommen
nar'row-gauge rail'road s Schmalspurbahn *f*
narrowly ['næroli] *adv* mit knapper Not
nar'row-mind'ed *adj* engstirnig
nasal ['nezəl] *adj* (*of the nose*) Nasen–; (*sound*) näselnd ‖ s (phonet) Nasenlaut *m*
nasalize ['nezə ˌlaɪz] *tr* nasalieren ‖ *intr* näseln
na'sal twang' s Näseln *n*
nascent ['nesənt] *adj* werdend
nastiness ['næstɪnɪs] s Ekligkeit *f*
nasturtium [nə'stʌrʃəm] s Kapuzinerkresse *f*
nasty ['næsti] *adj* (*person, smell, taste*) ekelhaft; (*weather*) scheußlich; (*dog, accident, tongue*) böse; **n. to** garstig zu or gegen
nation ['neʃən] s Nation *f,* Volk *n*
national ['næʃənəl] *adj* national, Landes– ‖ s Staatsangehörige *mf*
na'tional an'them s Nationalhymne *f*
na'tional defense' s Landesverteidigung *f*
nationalism ['næʃənə ˌlɪzəm] s Nationalismus *m*
nationality [ˌnæʃə'nælɪti] s (*citizen-*

ship) Staatsangehörigkeit *f;* (*ethnic identity*) Nationalität *f*
nationalization [ˌnæʃənəlɪ'zeʃən] s Verstaatlichung *f*
nationalize ['næʃənə ˌlaɪz] *tr* verstaatlichen
na'tional park' s Naturschutzpark *m*
na'tional so'cialism s Nationalsozialismus *m*
na'tionwide' *adj* im ganzen Land
native ['netɪv] *adj* eingeboren; (*products*) heimisch, Landes– ‖ s Eingeborene *mf;* **be a n. of** beheimatet sein in (*dat*)
na'tive coun'try s Vaterland *n*
na'tive land' s Heimatland *n*
na'tive tongue' s Muttersprache *f*
nativity [nə'tɪvɪti] s Geburt *f;* (astrol) Nativität *f;* **the Nativity** die Geburt Christi
NATO ['neto] s (**North Atlantic Treaty Organization**) NATO *f*
natty ['næti] *adj* elegant
natural ['nætʃərəl] *adj* natürlich; (*behavior*) ungezwungen ‖ s (mus) weiße Taste *f;* (*symbol*) (mus) Auflösungszeichen *n;* **a n.** (*person*) (coll) ein Naturtalent *n;* (*thing*) (coll) e–e totsichere Sache *f*
na'tural his'tory s Naturgeschichte *f*
naturalism ['nætʃərə ˌlɪzəm] s Naturalismus *m*
naturalist ['nætʃərəlɪst] s (*student of natural history*) Naturforscher –in *mf;* (paint, philos) Naturalist –in *mf*
naturalization [ˌnætʃərəlɪ'zeʃən] s Einbürgerung *f*
naturalize ['nætʃərə ˌlaɪz] *tr* einbürgern
na'tural law' s Naturgesetz *n*
na'tural phenom'enon s (*occurring in nature*) Naturereignis *n;* (*not supernatural*) natürliche Erscheinung *f*
na'tural re'sources *spl* Bodenschätze *pl*
na'tural sci'ence s Naturwissenschaft *f*
na'tural state' s Naturzustand *m*
nature ['netʃər] s die Natur; (*qualities*) Natur *f,* Beschaffenheit *f;* **by n.** von Natur aus
naught [nɔt] s Null *f;* **all for n.** ganz umsonst; **bring to n.** zuschanden machen; **come to n.** zunichte werden
naughty ['nɔti] *adj* unartig, ungezogen
nausea ['nɔʃi·ə], ['nɔsɪ·ə] s Übelkeit *f*
nauseate ['nɔʃi ˌet], ['nɔsɪ ˌet] *tr* Übelkeit erregen (*dat*)
naus'eating *adj* Übelkeit erregend
nauseous ['nɔʃi·əs], ['nɔsɪ·əs] *adj* (*causing nausea*) Übelkeit erregend; **I feel n.** mir ist übel
nautical ['nɔtɪkəl] *adj* See–, nautisch
nau'tical mile' ['nɔtɪkəl] s Seemeile *f*
nau'tical term' s Ausdruck *m* der Seemannssprache *f*
naval ['nevəl] *adj* (*e.g., battle, blockade, cadet, victory*) See–; (*unit*) Flotten–; (*academy, officer*) Marine–
na'val base' s Flottenstützpunkt *m*
na'val cap'tain s Kapitän *m* zur See
na'val engage'ment s Seegefecht *n*
na'val forc'es s Seestreitkräfte *pl*
na'val suprem'acy s Seeherrschaft *f*

nave [nev] *s (of a church)* Schiff *n;* *(of a wheel)* Nabe *f*
navel ['nevəl] *s* Nabel *m*
na'vel or'ange *s* Navelorange *f*
navigable ['nævɪgəbəl] *adj* schiffbar
navigate ['nævɪ,get] *tr (traverse)* befahren; *(steer)* steuern || *intr* (aer, naut) navigieren
navigation [,nævɪ'geʃən] *s (plotting courses)* Navigation *f;* *(sailing)* Schiffahrt *f*
naviga'tion chart' *s* Navigationskarte *f*
naviga'tion light' *s* (aer, naut) Positionslicht *n*
navigator ['nævɪ,getər] *s* Seefahrer *m;* (aer) Navigator *m*
navy ['nevi] *adj* Marine– || *s* Kriegsmarine *f*
na'vy bean' *s* Weiße Bohne *f*
na'vy blue' *adj* marineblau || *s* Marineblau *n*
na'vy yard' *s* Marinewerft *f*
nay [ne] *adv* nein || *s* Nein *n;* (parl) Neinstimme *f;* **the nays have it** die Mehrheit stimmt dagegen
Nazarene [,næzə'rin] *adj* aus Nazareth || *s* Nazarener *m*
Nazi ['natsi] *adj* Nazi– || *s* Nazi *m*
Nazism ['natsɪzəm] *s* Nazismus *m*
N.C.O. ['ɛn'si'o] *s* **(noncommissioned officer)** Unteroffizier *m*
neap' tide' [nip] *s* Nippflut *f*
near [nɪr] *adj* nahe(liegend); *(escape)* knapp; **n. at hand** zur Hand || *adv* nahe; **draw n. (to)** sich nähern *(dat);* **live n.** *(e.g., a church)* in der Nähe wohnen *(genit)* || *prep* nahe *(dat),* nahe an *(dat),* bei *(dat);* **n. here** hier in der Nähe
near'by' *adj* nahe(gelegen) || *adv* in der Nähe
Near' East', **the** *s* der Nahe Osten
nearly ['nɪrli] *adv* beinahe, fast
nearness ['nɪrnɪs] *s* Nähe *f*
near'-sight'ed *adj* kurzsichtig
near'-sight'edness *s* Kurzsichtigkeit *f*
neat [nit] *adj* sauber, ordentlich; *(simple but tasteful)* nett; *(cute)* niedlich; *(tremendous)* (coll) prima
neatness ['nitnɪs] *s* Sauberkeit *f*
nebu·la ['nɛbjələ] *s (–lae* [,li] & **–las)** (astr) Nebelfleck *m*
nebulous ['nɛbjələs] *adj* nebelhaft; (astr) Nebel–
necessarily [,nɛsɪ'sɛrɪli] *adv* notwendigerweise, unbedingt
necessary ['nɛsɪ,sɛri] *adj* notwendig, nötig; *(consequence)* zwangsläufig; **if n.** notfalls
necessitate [nɪ'sɛsɪ,tet] *tr* notwendig machen, enfordern
necessity [nɪ'sɛsɪti] *s (state of being necessary)* Notwendigkeit *f;* *(something necessary)* Bedürfnis *n;* *(poverty)* Not *f;* **in case of n.** im Notfall; **necessities of life** Lebensbedürfnisse *pl;* **of n.** notwendigerweise
neck [nɛk] *s* Hals *m;* *(of a dress)* Halsausschnitt *m;* **break one's n.** (& fig) sich *[dat]* den Hals brechen; **get it in the n.** (sl) eins aufs Dach kriegen; **get s.o. off one's n.** sich *[dat]* j–n

vom Halse schaffen; **n. and n.** Seite an Seite || *intr* (coll) sich knutschen
–necked [,nɛkt] *suf* –halsig, –nackig
neckerchief ['nɛkərtʃɪf] *s* Halstuch *n*
neck'ing *s* Abknutscherei *f*
necklace ['nɛklɪs] *s* Halsband *n;* *(metal chain)* Halskette *f*
neck'line' *s* Halsausschnitt *m;* **with a low n.** tief ausgeschnitten
neck'tie' *s* Krawatte *f,* Schlips *m*
necrology [nɛ'kralədʒi] *s (list of the dead)* Totenliste *f;* *(obituary)* Nekrolog *m*
necromancer ['nɛkrə,mænsər] *s* Geistesbeschwörer –in *mf*
necromancy ['nɛkrə,mænsi] *s* Geistesbeschwörung *f*
necropolis [nɛ'krapəlɪs] *s* Nekropolis *f*
nectar ['nɛktər] *s* (bot, myth) Nektar *m*
nectarine [,nɛktə'rin] *s* Nektarine *f*
nee [ne] *adj* geborene, e.g., **Mrs. Mary Schmidt, nee Müller** Frau Maria Schmidt, geborene Müller
need [nid] *s* Bedarf *m,* Bedürfnis *n;* **be in n.** in Not sein; **be in n. of repair** reparaturbedürftig sein; **be in n. of s.th.** etw nötig haben; **if n. be** erforderlichenfalls; **meet s.o.'s needs** j–s Bedarf decken; **needs** Bedarfsartikel *pl* || *tr* benötigen, brauchen; **as needed** nach Bedarf
needful ['nidfəl] *adj* nötig
needle ['nidəl] *s* Nadel *f* || *tr (prod)* anstacheln; **n. s.o. about** gegen j–n sticheln wegen
nee'dlepoint', **nee'dlepoint lace'** *s* Nadelspitze *f*
needless ['nidlɪs] *adj* unnötig; **n. to say** es erübrigt sich zu sagen
nee'dlework' *s* Näharbeit *f*
needy ['nidi] *adj* bedürftig
ne'er [nɛr] *adv* nie
ne'er'-do-well' *s* Tunichtgut *m*
nefarious [nɪ'feri·əs] *adj* ruchlos
negate [nɪ'get] *tr* verneinen
negation [nɪ'geʃən] *s* Verneinung *f*
negative ['nɛgətɪv] *adj* negativ || *s* Verneinung *f;* (elec) negativer Pol *m;* (gram) Verneinungswort *n;* (phot) Negativ *n*
neglect [nɪ'glɛkt] *s* Vernachlässigung *f* || *tr* vernachlässigen; **n. to** *(inf)* unterlassen zu *(inf)*
négligée, negligee [,nɛglɪ'ʒe] *s* Negligé *n*
negligence ['nɛglɪdʒəns] *s* Fahrlässigkeit *f*
negligent ['nɛglɪdʒənt] *adj* fahrlässig
negligible ['nɛglɪdʒɪbəl] *adj* geringfügig
negotiable [nɪ'goʃɪ·əbəl] *adj* diskutierbar; (fin) übertragbar, bankfähig
negotiate [nɪ'goʃɪ,et] *tr (a contract)* abschließen; *(a curve)* nehmen || *intr* verhandeln
negotiation [nɪ,goʃɪ'eʃən] *s* Verhandlung *f;* **carry on negotiations with;** **enter negotiations with** in Verhandlungen treten mit

negotiator [nɪ'goʃɪ,etər] *s* Unterhändler –in *mf*

Ne·gro ['nigro] *s* (**-groes**) Neger –in *mf*

neigh [ne] *s* Wiehern *n* ‖ *intr* wiehern

neighbor ['nebər] *s* Nachbar –in *mf*; (*fellow man*) Nächste *m* ‖ *tr* angrenzen an (*acc*) ‖ *intr*—**n. on** angrenzen an (*acc*)

neigh'borhood' *s* Nachbarschaft *f*; (*vicinity*) Umgebung *f*; **in the n. of** (coll) etwa

neigh'boring *adj* benachbart, Nachbar–, angrenzend

neighborliness ['nebərlɪnɪs] *s* gutnachbarliche Beziehungen *pl*

neighborly ['nebərli] *adj* (gut)nachbarlich

neither [niðər] *indef adj* keiner ‖ *indef pron* (**of**) keiner (von); **n. of them** keiner von beiden ‖ *conj* noch, ebensowenig; auch nicht, e.g., **n. do I** ich auch nicht; **neither ... nor** weder ... noch; **that's n.** here nor there das hat nichts zu sagen

neme·sis ['nɛməsɪs] *s* (**-ses** [,siz]) Nemesis *f*

Neolith'ic Age' [,ni·ə'lɪθɪk] *s* Neusteinzeit *f*

neologism [ni'alə,dʒɪzəm] *s* Neubildung *f*, Neologismus *m*

neon ['ni·an] *s* Neon *n*

ne'on light' *s* Neonröhre *f*

ne'on sign' *s* Neonreklame *f*

neophyte ['ni·ə,faɪt] *s* Neuling *m*; (relig) Neubekehrte *mf*

nephew ['nɛfju] *s* Neffe *m*

nepotism ['nɛpə,tɪzəm] *s* Nepotismus *m*

Neptune ['nɛpt(j)un] *s* Neptun *m*

neptunium [nɛp't(j)unɪ·əm] *s* Neptunium *n*

nerve [nʌrv] *adj* Nerven– ‖ *s* Nerv *m*; (*courage*) Wagemut *m*; (*gall*) (coll) Unverfrorenheit *f*; **get on s.o.'s nerves** j–m auf die Nerven gehen; **lose one's n.** die Nerven verlieren; **nerves of steel** Nerven *pl* wie Drahtseile

nerve' cen'ter *s* Nervenzentrum *n*

nerve'-rack'ing *adj* nervenaufreibend

nervous ['nʌrvəs] *adj* nervös; (*system*) Nerven–; (*horse*) kopfscheu; **be a n. wreck** mit den Nerven herunter sein

ner'vous break'down *s* Nervenzusammenbruch *m*

nervousness ['nʌrvəsnɪs] *s* Nervosität *f*

nervy ['nʌrvi] *adj* (*brash*) unverschämt; (*courageous*) mutig

nest [nɛst] *s* Nest *n* ‖ *intr* nisten

nest' egg' *s* (fig) Sparpfennig *m*

nestle ['nɛsəl] *intr* (**up to**) sich anschmiegen (an *acc*)

net [nɛt] *adj* Rein– ‖ *s* Netz *n*; (*for fire victims*) Sprungtuch *n* ‖ *v* (*pret & pp* **netted;** *ger* **netting**) *tr* (e.g., *fish, butterflies*) mit dem Netz fangen; (*said of an enterprise*) netto einbringen; (*said of a person*) rein verdienen

net'ball' *s* (*tennis*) Netzball *m*

Netherlander ['nɛðər,lændər] *s* Niederländer –in *mf*

Netherlands, the ['nɛðərləndz] *s & spl* die Niederlande

net'ting *s* Netzwerk *n*

nettle ['nɛtəl] *s* Nessel *f* ‖ *tr* reizen

net'work' *s* Netzwerk *n*; (rad, telv) Sendergruppe *f*

neuralgia [n(j)ʊ'rældʒə] *s* Neurologie *f*

neuritis [n(j)ʊ'raɪtɪs] *s* Nervenentzündung *f*

neurologist [n(j)ʊ'ralədʒɪst] *s* Nervenarzt *m*, Nervenärztin *f*

neurology [n(j)ʊ'ralədʒi] *s* Nervenheilkunde *f*, Neurologie *f*

neuron ['n(j)ʊran] *s* Neuron *n*

neuro·sis [n(j)ʊ'rosɪs] *s* (**-ses** [siz]) Neurose *f*

neurotic [n(j)ʊ'ratɪk] *adj* neurotisch ‖ *s* Neurotiker –in *mf*

neuter ['n(j)utər] *adj* (gram) sächlich ‖ *s* (gram) Neutrum *n*

neutral ['n(j)utrəl] *adj* neutral ‖ *s* Neutrale *mf*; (aut) Leerlauf *m*

neutrality [n(j)u'trælɪti] *s* Neutralität *f*

neutralize ['n(j)utrə,laɪz] *tr* (*a bomb*) entschärfen; (& chem) neutralisieren; (*troops*) lahmlegen; (*an attack*) unterbinden

neutron ['n(j)utran] *s* Neutron *n*

never ['nɛvər] *adv* nie(mals); **n. again** nie wieder; **n. before** noch nie; **n. mind!** spielt keine Rolle!

ne'vermore' *adv* nimmermehr

ne'vertheless' *adv* nichtsdestoweniger

new [n(j)u] *adj* neu; (*wine*) jung; (*inexperienced*) unerfahren; **what's new?** was gibt's Neues?

new' arriv'al *s* Neuankömmling *m*

new'born' *adj* neugeboren

New'cas'tle *s*—**carry coals to N.** Eulen nach Athen tragen

newcomer ['n(j)u,kʌmər] *s* Neuankömmling *m*

newel ['n(j)u·əl] *s* Treppenspindel *f*

new'el post' *s* Geländerpfosten *m*

newfangled ['n(j)u,fæŋgəld] *adj* neumodisch

Newfoundland ['n(j)ufənd,lænd] Neufundland *n* ‖ [n(j)u'faʊndlənd] *s* (*dog*) Neufundländer *m*

newly ['n(j)uli] *adv* neu, Neu–

new'lyweds' *spl* Neuvermählten *pl*

new' moon' *s* Neumond *m*

new-mown ['n(j)u ,mon] *adj* frischgemäht

newness ['n(j)unɪs] *s* Neuheit *f*

news [n(j)uz] *s* Nachricht *f*; (rad, telv) Nachrichten *pl*; **that's not n. to me** das ist mir nicht neu; **piece of n.** Neuigkeit *f*

news' a'gency *s* Nachrichtenagentur *f*

news'boy' *s* Zeitungsjunge *m*

news' bul'letin *s* Kurznachricht *f*

news'cast' *s* Nachrichtensendung *f*

news'cast'er *s* Nachrichtensprecher –in *mf*

news'deal'er *s* Zeitungshändler –in *mf*

news' ed'itor *s* Nachrichtenredakteur –in *mf*

news'let'ter s Rundschreiben n
news'man' s (–men') Journalist m; (dealer) Zeitungshändler m
news'pa'per adj Zeitungs– || s Zeitung f
news'paper clip'ping s Zeitungsausschnitt m
news'paper·man' s (–men') Journalist m; (dealer) Zeitungshändler m
news'paper se'rial s Zeitungsroman m
news'print' s Zeitungspapier n
news'reel' s Wochenschau f
news' report' s Nachrichtensendung f
news' report'er s Zeitungsreporter –in mf
news' room' s Nachrichtenbüro n
news'stand' s Zeitungskiosk m
news'wor'thy adj berichtenswert
New' Tes'tament s Neues Testament n
New' World' s Neue Welt f
New' Year' s Neujahr n; **happy N.!** glückliches Neues Jahr!
New' Year's' Eve' s Silvesterabend m
New' Zea'land ['ziland] s Neuseeland n
next [nɛkst] adj nächste; **be n.** an der Reihe sein; **come n.** folgen; **in the n. place** darauf; **n. best** nächstbeste; **n. time** das nächste Mal; **n. to** (locally) gleich neben (dat); (almost) sogut wie; **the n. day** am nächsten Tag || adv dann, danach; **what should I do n.?** was soll ich als Nächstes tun?
next'-door' adj—n. neighbor unmittelbarer Nachbar m || **next'-door'** adv nebenan; **n. to** direkt neben (dat)
next' of kin' s (pl: next of kin) nächster Angehöriger m
niacin ['naɪ·əsɪn] s Niacin n
Niag'ara Falls' [naɪ'ægrə] s Niagarafall m
nib [nɪb] s Spitze f; (of a pen) Federspitze f
nibble ['nɪbəl] tr knabbern || intr (on) knabbern (an dat)
Nibelung ['nibəluŋ] s (myth) Nibelung m
nice [naɪs] adj nett; (pretty) hübsch; (food) lecker; (well-behaved) artig; (distinction) fein; **have a n. time** sich gut unterhalten; **n. and warm** schön warm
nicely ['naɪsli] adv nett; **he's doing n.** es geht ihm recht gut; **that will do n.** das paßt gut
nicety ['naɪsəti] s Feinheit f; **niceties of life** Annehmlichkeiten pl des Lebens
niche [nɪtʃ] s Nische f; (fig) rechter Platz m
nick [nɪk] s Kerbe f, Scharte f; **in the n. of time** gerade im rechten Augenblick || tr kerben
nickel ['nɪkəl] s Nickel n; (coin) Fünfcentstück n || tr vernickeln
nick'el-plate' tr vernickeln
nick'name' s Spitzname m || tr e–n Spitznamen geben (dat)
nicotine ['nɪkə·tin] s Nikotin n; **low in n.** nikotinarm
niece [nis] s Nichte f
nifty ['nɪfti] adj (coll) fesch, prima

niggard ['nɪgərd] s Knauser –in mf
niggardly ['nɪgərdli] adj knauserig
night [naɪt] adj (light, shift, train, watch) Nacht– || s Nacht f; **all n.** (long) die ganze Nacht (über); **at n.** nachts; **last n.** gestern abend; **n. after n.** Nacht für Nacht; **n. before last** vorgestern abend
night' cap' s Nachtmütze f; (drink) Schlummertrunk m
night' club' s Nachtklub m
night'fall' s Anbruch m der Nacht; **at n.** bei Anbruch der Nacht
night'gown' s Damennachthemd n
nightingale ['naɪtən‚gel] s Nachtigall f
night'light' s Nachtlicht n
night'long' adj & adv die ganze Nacht dauernd
nightly ['naɪtli] adj & adv allnächtlich
night'mare' s Alptraum m
nightmarish ['naɪt‚merɪʃ] adj alpartig
night' owl' s (coll) Nachteule f
night' school' s Abendschule f
night'time' s Nachtzeit f; **at n.** zur Nachtzeit
night' watch'man s Nachtwächter m
nihilism ['naɪ·ɪ‚lɪzəm] s Nihilismus m
nil [nɪl] s Nichts m, Null f
Nile [naɪl] s Nil m
nimble ['nɪmbəl] adj flink
nincompoop ['nɪnkəm‚pup] s Trottel m
nine [naɪn] adj & pron neun || s Neun f
nineteen ['naɪn'tin] adj & pron neunzehn || s Neunzehn f
nineteenth ['naɪn'tinθ] adj & pron neunzehnte || s (fraction) Neunzehntel n; **the nineteenth** (in dates or in a series) der Neunzehnte
ninetieth ['naɪnti·ɪθ] adj & pron neunzigste || s (fraction) Neunzigstel n
ninety ['naɪnti] adj & pron neunzig || s Neunzig f; **the nineties** die neunziger Jahre
nine'ty-first' adj & pron einundneunzigste
nine'ty-one' adj & pron einundneunzig
ninny ['nɪni] s (coll) Trottel m
ninth [naɪnθ] adj & pron neunte || s (fraction) Neuntel n; **the n.** (in dates or in a series) der Neunte
nip [nɪp] s (pinch) Kneifen n; (of cold weather) Schneiden n; (of liquor) Schluck m || v (pret & pp nipped; ger nipping) tr (pinch) kneifen; (alcohol) nippen; **nip in the bud** im Keime ersticken
nippers ['nɪpərz] spl Zwickzange f
nipple ['nɪpəl] s (of a nursing bottle) Lutscher m; (anat) Brustwarze f; (mach) Schmiernippel m
nippy ['nɪpi] adj schneidend
nirvana [nɪr'vanə] s Nirwana n
nit [nɪt] s (ent) Nisse f
niter ['naɪtər] s Salpeter m
nit'pick'er s (coll) Pedant –in mf
nitrate ['naɪtret] s Nitrat n || tr nitrieren
ni'tric ac'id ['naɪtrɪk] s Salpetersäure f

nitride ['naɪtraɪd] s Nitrid n
nitrogen ['naɪtrədʒən] s Stickstoff m
nitroglycerin [ˌnaɪtrə'glɪsərɪn] s Nitroglyzerin n
ni'trous ac'id ['naɪtrəs] s salpetrige Säure f
ni'trous ox'ide s Stickstoffoxydul n
nit'wit' s Trottel m
no [no] adj kein; **no admittance** Zutritt verboten; **no ... of any kind** keinerlei; **no offense!** nichts für ungut!; **no parking** Parkverbot; **no smoking** Rauchen verboten; **no thoroughfare** Durchgang verboten; **no ... whatever** überhaupt kein ‖ adv nein; **no?** nicht wahr?; **no longer** (or **no more**) nicht mehr ‖ s Nein n; **give no for an answer** mit (e–m) Nein antworten
No'ah's Ark' ['no·əz] s Arche f Noah(s)
nobility [no'bɪlɪti] s (nobleness; aristocracy) Adel m; (noble rank) Adelsstand m; **n. of mind** Seelenadel m
noble ['nobəl] adj (rank) ad(e)lig; (character, person) edel ‖ s Adliger m; **nobles** Edelleute pl
no'ble·man s (–men) Edelmann m
no'blemind'ed adj edelgesinnt
nobleness ['nobəlnɪs] s Vornehmheit f
no'ble·wom'an s (–wom'en) Edelfrau f
nobody ['no ˌbadi] s indef pron niemand, keiner; **n. else** sonst keiner ‖ s (coll) Null f
nocturnal [nak'tʌrnəl] adj nächtlich
nod [nad] s Kopfnicken n ‖ v (pret & pp **nodded;** ger **nodding**) tr—**nod one's head** mit dem Kopf nicken ‖ intr nicken; **nod to** zunicken (dat)
node [nod] s (anat, astr, math, phys) Knoten m
nodule ['nadʒul] s Knötchen n; (bot) Knollen m
noise [nɔɪz] s Geräusch n; (disturbingly loud) Lärm m ‖ tr—**n. abroad** ausposaunen
noiseless ['nɔɪzlɪs] adj geräuschlos
noisy ['nɔɪzi] adj lärmend, geräuschvoll
nomad ['nomæd] s Nomade m, Nomadin f
no' man's' land' s Niemandsland n
nomenclature ['nomən ˌkletʃər] s Nomenklatur f
nominal ['namɪnəl] adj nominell
nominate ['namɪ ˌnet] tr ernennen; **n. as candidate** als Kandidaten aufstellen
nomination [ˌnamɪ'neʃən] s Ernennung f; (of a candidate) Aufstellung f
nominative ['namɪnətɪv] s Nominativ m
nominee [ˌnamɪ'ni] s Designierte mf
non– [nan] pref Nicht-, nicht–
non'accept'ance s Nichtannahme f
non'belli'gerent adj nicht am Krieg teilnehmend
non'break'able adj unzerbrechlich
non'-Cath'olic nichtkatholisch ‖ s Nichtkatholik –in mf
nonchalant [ˌnanʃə'lant] adj zwanglos

noncom ['nan ˌkam] s (coll) Kapo m
non'com'batant s Nichtkämpfer m
non'commis'sioned of'ficer s Unteroffizier m
noncommittal [ˌnankə'mɪtəl] adj nichtssagend; (person) zurückhaltend
nondescript ['nandɪ ˌskrɪpt] adj unbestimmbar
none [nʌn] adv—**n. too** keineswegs zu ‖ indef pron keiner; **that's n. of your business** das geht dich nichts an
nonen'tity s Nichts n; (fig) Null f
non'exis'tent adj nichtexistent
nonfic'tion s Sachbücher pl
nonfulfill'ment s Nichterfüllung f
non'interven'tion s Nichteinmischung f
non'met'al s Nichtmetall n, Metalloid n
non'nego'tiable adj unübertragbar; (demands) unabdingbar
nonpar'tisan adj überparteilich
nonpay'ment s Nichtbezahlung f
non'polit'ical adj unpolitisch
non·plus [nan'plʌs] s Verlegenheit f ‖ v (pret & pp **–plus[s]ed;** ger **–plus[s]ing**) tr verblüffen
nonprof'it adj gemeinnützig
nonres'ident adj nich ansässig ‖ s Nichtansässige mf
non'return'able adj (bottles, etc.) Einweg–; (merchandise) nicht rücknehmbar
non'scienti'fic adj nichtwissenschaftlich
non'sectar'ian adj keiner Sekte angehörend
nonsense ['nansəns] s Unsinn m
nonsen'sical adj unsinnig, widersinnig
non'skid' adj rutschsicher
nonsmok'er s Nichtraucher –in mf
non'stop' adj & adv ohne Zwischenlandung
nonvi'olence s Gewaltlosigkeit f
nonvi'olent adj gewaltlos
noodle ['nudəl] s Nudel f; (head) (coll) Birne f
noo'dle soup' s Nudelsuppe f
nook [nʊk] s Ecke f; (fig) Winkel m
noon [nun] s Mittag m; **at n.** zu Mittag
no' one', no'-one' indef pron niemand, keiner; **n. else** kein anderer
noon' hour' s Mittagsstunde f
noon'time' adj mittäglich ‖ s Mittagszeit f
noose [nus] s Schlinge f
nor [nɔr] conj (after **neither**) noch; auch nicht, e.g., **nor do I** ich auch nicht
Nordic ['nɔrdɪk] adj nordisch
norm [nɔrm] s Norm f
normal ['nɔrməl] adj normal
normalcy ['nɔrməlsi] s Normalzustand m
normalize ['nɔrmə ˌlaɪz] tr normalisieren
Norman ['nɔrmən] adj normannisch ‖ s Normanne m, Normannin f
Normandy ['nɔrməndi] s die Normandie
Norse [nɔrs] adj altnordisch ‖ s (language) Altnordisch n; **the N.** die Skandinavier pl
Norse'man s (–men) Nordländer m

north [nɔrθ] *adj* nördlich, Nord– ‖ *adv* nach Norden ‖ *s* Norden *m;* **to the n.** of im Norden von
North′ Amer′ica *s* Nordamerika *n*
North′ Amer′ican *adj* nordamerikanisch ‖ *s* Nordamerikaner –in *mf*
north′east′ *adj & adv* nordöstlich ‖ *s* Nordosten *m*
north′east′er *s* Nordostwind *m*
northerly [′nɔrðərli] *adj* nördlich
northern [′nɔrðərn] *adj (direction)* nördlich; *(race)* nordisch
north′ern expo′sure *s* Nordseite *f*
North′ern Hem′isphere *s* nördliche Halbkugel *f*
north′ern lights′ *spl* Nordlicht *n*
nor′thernmost′ *adj* nördlichst
North′ Pole′ *s* Nordpol *m*
North′ Sea′ *s* Nordsee *f*
northward [′nɔrθwərd] *adv* nach Norden
north′west′ *adj & adv* nordwestlich ‖ *s* Nordwesten *m*
north′ wind′ *s* Nordwind *m*
Norway [′nɔrwe] *s* Norwegen *n*
Norwegian [nɔr′widʒən] *adj* norwegisch ‖ *s* Norweger –in *mf; (language)* Norwegisch *n*
nose [noz] *s* Nase *f;* (aer) Nase *f,* Bug *m;* **by a n.** (sport) um e–e Nasenlänge; **blow one's n.** sich schneuzen; **lead around by the n.** an der Nase herumführen; **pay through the n.** e–n zu hohen Preis bezahlen; **turn one's n. up** at die Nase rümpfen über *(acc)* ‖ *tr*—**n. out** (fig) mit knappem Vorsprung besiegen; (sport) um e–e Nasenlänge schlagen ‖ *intr*—**n. about** herumschnüffeln; **n. over** (aer) sich überschlagen
nose′bleed′ *s* Nasenbluten *n*
nose′ cone′ *s* (rok) Raketenspitze *f*
nose′ dive′ *s* (aer) Sturzflug *m*
nose′-dive′ *intr* e–n Sturzflug machen
nose′ drops′ *spl* Nasentropfen *pl*
nose′gay′ *s* Blumenstrauß *m*
nose′-heav′y *adj* (aer) vorderlastig
nostalgia [nɑ′stældʒə] *s* Heimweh *n*
nostalgic [nɑ′stældʒɪk] *adj* wehmütig
nostril [′nɑstrɪl] *s* (anat) Nasenloch *n;* (zool) Nüster *f*
nostrum [′nɑstrəm] *s* Allheilmittel *n*
nosy [′nozi] *adj* neugierig
not [nɑt] *adv* nicht; **not at all** überhaupt nicht; **not even** nicht einmal; **not one** keiner; **not only ... but also** nicht nur ... sondern auch
notable [′notəbəl] *adj* bemerkenswert ‖ *s* Standesperson *f*
notarial [no′tɛrɪ·əl] *adj* notariell
notarize [′notə‚raɪz] *tr* notariell beglaubigen
no′tary pub′lic [′notəri] *s* **(notaries public)** Notar *m,* Notarin *f*
notation [no′teʃən] *s (note)* Aufzeichnung *f; (system of symbols)* Bezeichnung *f; (method of noting)* Schreibweise *f*
notch [nɑtʃ] *s* Kerbe *f; (in a belt)* Loch *n; (degree, step)* Grad *m; (of a wheel)* Zahn *m* ‖ *tr* einkerben
note [not] *s* Notiz *f; (to a text)* An-

merkung *f; (slip)* Zettel *m; (e.g., of doubt)* Ton *m;* (mus) Note *f;* **jot down notes** sich [*dat*] Notizen machen; **make a n.** of sich [*dat*] notieren; **take n.** of zur Kenntnis nehmen; **take notes** sich [*dat*] Notizen machen ‖ *tr* beachten; **n. down** notieren; **n. in passing** am Rande bemerken
note′book′ *s* Heft *n,* Notizbuch *n*
note′ pad′ *s* Schreibblock *m*
note′wor′thy *adj* beachtenswert
nothing [′nʌθɪŋ] *indef pron* nichts; **be for n.** vergebens sein; **come to n.** platzen; **for n.** *(gratis)* umsonst; **have n. to go on** keine Unterlagen haben; **next to n.** soviel wie nichts; **n. at all** gar nichts; **n. but** lauter; **n. doing!** kommt nicht in Frage!; **n. else** sonst nichts; **n. new** nichts Neues; **there is n. like** es geht nichts über *(acc)*
nothingness [′nʌθɪŋnɪs] *s (nonexistence)* Nichts *n; (utter insignificance)* Nichtigkeit *f*
notice [′notɪs] *s (placard)* Anschlag *m; (in the newspaper)* Anzeige *f; (attention)* Beachtung *f; (announcement)* Ankündigung *f; (notice of termination)* Kündigung *f;* **at a moment's n.** jeden Moment; **escape s.o.'s n.** j–m entgehen; **give s.o. a week's n.** j–m acht Tage vorher kündigen; **take n.** of Notiz nehmen von; **until further n.** bis auf weiteres ‖ *tr* (be)merken, wahrnehmen; **be noticed by s.o.** j–m auffallen; **n. s.th. about s.o.** j–m etw anmerken
noticeable [′notɪsəbəl] *adj* wahrnehmbar
notification [‚notɪfɪ′keʃən] *s* Benachrichtigung *f*
noti·fy [′notɪ‚faɪ] *v (pret & pp –fied) tr (about)* benachrichtigen (von)
notion [′noʃən] *s (idea)* Vorstellung *f;* **I have a good n. to** *(inf)* ich habe gute Lust zu *(inf);* **notions** Kurzwaren *pl*
notoriety [‚notə′raɪ·ɪti] *s* Verruf *m*
notorious [no′tori·əs] *adj* (for) notorisch (wegen)
no′-trump′ *adj* ohne Trumpf ‖ *s* Ohne Trumpf-Ansage *f*
notwithstanding [‚nɑtwɪθ′stændɪŋ] *adv* trotzdem ‖ *prep* trotz (genit)
noun [naʊn] *s* Hauptwort *n*
nourish [′nʌrɪʃ] *tr* (er)nähren
nour′ishing *adj* nahrhaft, Nähr–
nourishment [′nʌrɪʃmənt] *s (feeding)* Ernährung *f; (food)* Nahrung *f*
Nova Scotia [′novə′skoʃə] *s* Neuschottland *n*
novel [′nɑvəl] *adj* neuartig ‖ *s* Roman *m*
novelist [′nɑvəlɪst] *s* Romanschriftsteller –in *mf*
novelty [′nɑvəlti] *s* Neuheit *f*
November [no′vɛmbər] *s* November *m*
novena [no′vinə] *s* Novene *f*
novice [′nɑvɪs] *s* Neuling *m;* (eccl) Novize *m,* Novizin *f*
novitiate [no′vɪʃɪ·ɪt] *s* Noviziat *n*
novocaine [′novə‚ken] *s* Novokain *n*
now [naʊ] *adv* jetzt; *(without tem-*

poral force) nun; **before now** schon
früher; **by now** nachgerade; **from
now on** von nun ab, fortan; **now and
then** dann und wann; **now ... now**
bald ... bald; **now or never** jetzt
oder nie
nowadays ['nau·ə‚dez] *adv* heutzutage
no'way', **no'ways'** *adv* keineswegs
no'where' *adv* nirgends
noxious ['nɑk/əs] *adj* schädlich
nozzle ['nɑzəl] *s* Düse *f;* (*on a can*)
Schnabel *m*
nth [ɛnθ] *adj*—**nth times** zig mal; **to
the nth degree** (fig) im höchsten
Maße
nuance ['n(j)u·ɑns] *s* Nuance *f*
nub [nʌb] *s* Knoten *m;* (*gist*) Kernpunkt *m*
nuclear ['n(j)uklɪ·ər] *adj* nuklear;
(*energy, fission, fusion, physics, reactor, weapon*) Kern-
nu'clear pow'er *s* Atomkraft *f*
nu'clear pow'er plant' *s* Atomkraft-
werk *n*
nucleolus [n(j)u'kli·ələs] *s* Nukleolus
m
nucleon ['n(j)ukli·ɑn] *s* Nukleon *n*
nucle·us ['n(j)ukli·əs] *s* (-**uses** & **i-**
[‚aɪ] *s* Kern *m*
nude [n(j)ud] *adj* nackt ‖ *s* (*nude figure*) Akt *m;* **in the n.** nackt
nudge [nʌdʒ] *s* Stups *m* ‖ *tr* stupsen
nudist ['n(j)udɪst] *s* Nudist –in *mf*
nudity ['n(j)udɪti] *s* Nacktheit *f*
nugget ['nʌgɪt] *s* Klumpen *m*
nuisance ['n(j)usəns] *s* Ärgernis *n;* **be
a n.** lästig sein
nui'sance raid' *s* Störungsangriff *m*
null' and void' [nʌl] *adj* null und
nichtig
nulli·fy ['nʌlɪ‚faɪ] *v* (*pret & pp* –**fied**)
tr (*e.g., a law*) für ungültig erklären;
(*e.g., the effects*) aufheben
numb [nʌm] *adj* taub; (**with**) starr (vor
dat); (fig) betäubt; **grow n.** erstarren
‖ *tr* (& fig) betäuben; (*said of cold*)
starr machen
number ['nʌmbər] *s* Nummer *f;* (*count*)
Zahl *f*, Anzahl *f;* (*article*) (com)
Artikel *m;* (gram) Zahl *f;* (mus)
Stück *n;* **in n.** der Zahl nach; **get
s.o.'s n.** (coll) j-m auf die Schliche
kommen ‖ *tr* (*e.g., pages*) numerieren; (*amount to*) zählen; **be numbered among** zählen zu; **n. among**
zählen zu
numberless ['nʌmbərlɪs] *adj* zahllos
num'bers game' *s* Zahlenlotto *n*
numbness ['nʌmnɪs] *s* Taubheit *f;*
(*from cold*) Starrheit *f*
numeral ['n(j)umərəl] *adj* Zahl– ‖ *s*
Zahl *f*, Ziffer *f;* (gram) Zahlwort *n*

numerator ['n(j)umə‚retər] *s* Zähler *m*
numerical [n(j)u'merɪkəl] *adj* numerisch; **n. order** Zahlenfolge *f;* **n. superiority** Überzahl *f;* **n. value** Zahlen-
wert *m*
numerous ['n(j)umərəs] *adj* zahlreich
numismatic [‚n(j)umɪz'mætɪk] *adj* nu-
mismatisch ‖ **numismatics** *s* Münz-
kunde *f*
numskull ['nʌm‚skʌl] *s* Dummkopf *m*
nun [nʌn] *s* Nonne *f*
nunci·o ['nʌn/ɪ·o] *s* (-**os**) Nuntius *m*
nuptial ['nʌp/əl] *adj* Braut-, Hochzeits– ‖ **nuptials** *spl* Trauung *f*
Nuremberg ['n(j)urəm‚bʌrg] *s* Nürnberg *n*
nurse [nʌrs] *s* Krankenschwester *f;*
(*male*) Krankenpfleger *m;* (*wet
nurse*) Amme *f* ‖ *tr* (*the sick*) pflegen; (*a child*) stillen; (*hopes*) hegen;
n. a cold e–e Erkältung kurieren
nurse'maid' *s* Kindermädchen *n*
nursery ['nʌrsəri] *s* Kinderstube *f;* (*for
day care*) Kindertagesstätte *f;* (hort)
Baumschule *f*, Pflanzschule *f*
nurs'ery·man *s* (-**men**) Kunstgärtner *m*
nurs'ery rhyme' *s* Kinderlied *n*
nurs'ery school' *s* Kindergarten *m*
nurse''s aide' *s* Schwesterhelferin *f*
nurs'ing *s* (*as a profession*) Kranken-
pflege *f;* (*of a person*) Pflege *f;* (*of
a baby*) Stillen *n*
nurs'ing home' *s* Pflegeheim *n*
nurture ['nʌrt/ər] *s* Nahrung *f* ‖ *tr*
(er)nähren
nut [nʌt] *s* Nuß *f;* (sl) verrückter Kerl
m; (mach) Mutter *f*, Schraubenmut-
ter *f;* **be nuts** (sl) verrückt sein; **be
nuts about** (sl) vernarrt sein in (*acc*)
go nuts (sl) e–n Klaps kriegen
nut'crack'er *s* Nußknacker *m*
nutmeg ['nʌt‚meg] *s* (*spice*) Muskat-
nuß *f;* (*tree*) Muskat *m*
nutrient ['nutrɪ·ənt] *s* Nährstoff *m*
nutriment ['n(j)utrɪmənt] *s* Nährstoff
m
nutrition [n(j)u'trɪ/ən] *s* Ernährung *f*
nutritious [n(j)u'trɪ/əs] *adj* nahrhaft
nutritive ['n(j)utrɪtɪv] *adj* nahrhaft,
Nähr–
nut'shell' *s* Nußschale *f;* **in a n.** mit
wenigen Worten
nutty ['nʌti] *adj* nußartig; (sl) spleenig,
verrückt
nuzzle ['nʌzəl] *tr* sich mit der Schnauze
(or Nase) reiben an (*dat*) ‖ *intr*
(*burrow*) mit der Schnauze wühlen;
n. up to sich anschmiegen an (*acc*)
nylon ['naɪlɑn] *s* Nylon *n*
nymph [nɪmf] *s* Nymphe *f*
nymphomaniac [‚nɪmfə'menɪ·æk] *s*
Nymphomanin *f*

O

O, o [o] fünfzehnter Buchstabe des
englischen Alphabets
oaf [of] *s* Tölpel *m*
oak [ok] *adj* eichen ‖ *s* Eiche *f*

oak' leaf' clus'ter *s* Eichenlaub *n*
oak' tree' *s* Eichbaum *m*
oakum ['okəm] *s* Werg *n*
oar [or], [ɔr] *s* Ruder *n*, Riemen *m*

oar'lock' s Ruderdolle f
oars'man' s (**-men'**) Ruderer m
oa·sis [o'esɪs] s (**-ses** [siz]) Oase f
oath [oθ] s (**oaths** [oðz]) Eid m; **o. of allegiance** Treueid m; **o. of office** Amtseid m; **under o.** eidlich
oat'meal' s Hafergrütze f, Hafermehl n
oats [ots] spl Hafer m; **he's feeling his o.** (coll) ihn sticht der Hafer; **sow one's wild o.** (coll) sich [dat] die Hörner ablaufen
obbligato [,ablɪ'gato] adj hauptstimmig || s Obligato m
obdurate ['abdjərɪt] adj verstockt
obedience [o'bidɪ·əns] s (**to**) Gehorsam m (gegenüber dat, gegen); **blind o.** Kadavergehorsam m
obedient [o'bidɪ·ənt] adj (**to**) gehorsam (dat)
obeisance [o'bisəns] s Ehrerbietung f
obelisk ['abəlɪsk] s Obelisk m
obese [o'bis] adj fettleibig
obesity [o'bisɪti] s Fettleibigkeit f
obey [o'be] tr gehorchen (dat); (a law, order) befolgen || intr gehorchen
obfuscate [ab'fʌsket] tr verdunkeln
obituary [o'bɪtʃʊ,ɛri] adj Todes– || s Todesanzeige f, Nachruf m
object ['abdʒɪkt] s Gegenstand m; (aim) Ziel n, Zweck m; (gram) Ergänzung f, Objekt n; **money is no o.** Geld spielt keine Rolle || [ab'dʒɛkt] intr (**to**) Einwände erheben (gegen)
objection [ab'dʒɛkʃən] s Einwand m; **I have no o. to his staying** ich habe nichts dagegen (einzuwenden), daß er bleibe
objectionable [ab'dʒɛkʃənəbəl] adj nicht einwandfrei
objective [ab'dʒɛktɪv] adj sachlich, objektiv || s Ziel n
objec'tive case' s Objektsfall m
ob'ject les'son s Lehre f
obligate ['ablɪ,get] tr verpflichten; **be obligated to s.o.** j–m zu Dank verbunden sein
obligation [,ablɪ'geʃən] s Verpflichtung f
obligatory ['abləgə,tori], [ə'blɪgə,tori] adj verpflichtend, obligatorisch
oblige [ə'blaɪdʒ] tr (bind) verpflichten; (do a favor to) gefällig sein (dat); **be obliged to** (inf) müssen (inf); **feel obliged to** (inf) sich bemüßigt fühlen zu (inf); **I'm much obliged to you** ich bin Ihnen sehr verbunden
oblig'ing adj gefällig
oblique [ə'blik] adj schief
obliterate [ə'blɪtə,ret] tr auslöschen; (traces) verwischen; (writing) unleserlich machen
oblivion [ə'blɪvɪ·ən] s Vergessenheit f
oblivious [ə'blɪvɪ·əs] adj—**be o. of** sich [dat] nicht bewußt sein (genit)
oblong ['ablɔŋ] adj länglich || s Rechteck n
obnoxious [ab'nakʃəs] adj widerlich
oboe ['obo] s Oboe f
oboist ['obo·ɪst] s Oboist –in mf
obscene [ab'sin] adj obszön

obscenity [ab'sɛnɪti] s Obszönität f
obscure [əb'skjʊr] adj dunkel, obskur || tr verdunkeln
obscurity [əb'skjʊrɪti] s Dunkelheit f
obsequies ['absɪkwiz] spl Totenfeier f
obsequious [əb'sikwɪ·əs] adj unterwürfig
observance [əb'zʌrvəns] s Beachtung f, Befolgung f; (celebration) Feier f
observant [əb'zʌrvənt] adj beobachtend
observation [,abzər'veʃən] s Beobachtung f; **keep under o.** beobachten
observa'tion tow'er s Aussichtsturm m
observatory [əb'zʌrvə,tori] s Sternwarte f, Observatorium n
observe [əb'zʌrv] tr (a person, rules) beobachten; (a holiday) feiern; **o. silence** Stillschweigen bewahren
obsess [əb'sɛs] tr verfolgen; **obsessed** (by) besessen (von)
obsession [əb'sɛʃən] s Besessenheit f
obsolescent [,absə'lɛsənt] adj veraltend
obsolete ['absə,lit] adj veraltet; **become o.** veralten
obstacle ['abstəkəl] s Hindernis n
ob'stacle course' s Hindernisbahn f
obstetrical [ab'stetrɪkəl] adj Geburtshilfe–, Entbindungs–
obstetrician [,abstə'trɪʃən] s Geburtshelfer –in mf
obstetrics [ab'stetrɪks] s Geburtshilfe f
obstinacy ['abstɪnəsi] s Starrheit f
obstinate ['abstɪnɪt] adj starr
obstreperous [əb'strɛpərəs] adj (clamorous) lärmend; (unruly) widerspenstig
obstruct [əb'strʌkt] tr (e.g., a pipe) verstopfen; (a view, way) versperren; (traffic) behindern; **o. justice** die Rechtspflege behindern
obstruction [əb'strʌkʃən] s (of a view, way) Versperrung f; (of traffic) Behinderung f; (obstacle) Hindernis n; (parl, pathol) Obstruktion f
obtain [əb'ten] tr erhalten, erlangen || intr bestehen
obtrusive [əb'trusɪv] adj aufdringlich
obtuse [əb't(j)us] adj (& fig) stumpf
obviate ['abvɪ,et] tr erübrigen
obvious ['abvɪ·əs] adj naheliegend; **it is o.** es liegt auf der Hand
occasion [ə'keʒən] s Gelegenheit f; (reason) Anlaß m; **on o.** gelegentlich; **on the o. of** anläßlich (genit) || tr veranlassen
occasional [ə'keʒənəl] adj gelegentlich
occasionally [ə'keʒənəli] adv gelegentlich, zuweilen
occident ['aksɪdənt] s Abendland n
occidental [,aksɪ'dɛntəl] adj abendländisch || s Abendländer –in mf
occlusion [ə'kluʒən] s Okklusion f
occult [ə'kʌlt] adj geheim, okkult
occupancy ['akjəpənsi] s Besitz m, Besitzergreifung f; (of a home) Einzug m
occupant ['akjəpənt] s Besitzer –in mf; (of a home) Inhaber –in mf; (of a car) Insasse m, Insassin f
occupation [,akjə'peʃən] s (employ-

ment) Beruf *m*, Beschäftigung *f*; (mil) Besetzung *f*, Besatzung *f*
occup'ational disease' [ˌɑkjə'peʃənəl] *s* Berufskrankheit *f*
occupa'tional ther'apy *s* Beschäftigungstherapie *f*
occupa'tion troops' *spl* Besatzungstruppen *pl*
occu·py ['ɑkjə ˌpaɪ] *v* (*pret & pp* **–pied**) *tr* in Besitz nehmen; (*a house*) bewohnen; (*time*) in Anspruch nehmen; (*keep busy*) beschäftigen; (mil) besetzen; **occupied** (*said of a seat or toilet*) besetzt; (*said of a person*) beschäftigt; **o. oneself with** sich befassen mit
oc·cur [ə'kʌr] *v* (*pret & pp* **–curred; ger –curring**) *intr* sich ereignen; (*come to mind*) (**to**) einfallen (*dat*)
occurrence [ə'kʌrəns] *s* Ereignis *n*; (*e.g., of a word*) Vorkommen *n*
ocean ['oʃən] *s* Ozean *m*
oceanic [ˌoʃɪ'ænɪk] *adj* Ozean–, ozeanisch
o'cean lin'er *s* Ozeandampfer *m*
oceanography [ˌoʃən'ɑgrəfi] *s* Ozeanographie *f*
ocher ['okər] *s* Ocker *m & n*
o'clock [ə'klɑk] *adv* Uhr; **at ... o'clock** um ... Uhr
octane ['ɑkten] *s* Oktan *n*
oc'tane num'ber *s* Oktanzahl *f*
octave ['ɑktɪv], ['ɑktev] *s* Oktave *f*
October [ɑk'tobər] *s* Oktober *m*
octogenarian [ˌɑktədʒɪ'nɛrɪ·ən] *s* Achtzige *mf*
octo·pus ['ɑktəpəs] *s* (**–puses & –pi** [ˌpaɪ]) Seepolyp *m*
ocular ['ɑkjələr] *adj* Augen–
oculist ['ɑkjəlɪst] *s* Augenarzt *m*, Augenärztin *f*
odd [ɑd] *adj* (*strange*) seltsam, eigenartig; (*number*) ungerade; (*e.g., glove*) einzeln; **two hundred odd pages** etwas über zweihundert Seiten || **odds** *spl* (*probability*) Wahrscheinlichkeit *f*; (*advantage*) Vorteil *m*; (*in gambling*) Vorgabe *f*; **at odds** uneinig; **lay** (*or* **give**) **odds** vorgeben; **the odds are two to one** die Chancen stehen zwei zu eins
odd' ball' *s* (sl) Sonderling *m*
oddity ['ɑdɪti] *s* Seltsamkeit *f*
odd' jobs' *spl* Gelegenheitsarbeit *f*; (*chores*) kleine Aufgaben *pl*
odds' and ends' *spl* Kleinkram *m*
ode [od] *s* Ode *f*
odious ['odɪ·əs] *adj* verhaßt
odor ['odər] *s* Duft *m*, Geruch *m*; **be in bad o.** in schlechtem Ruf stehen
odorless ['odərlɪs] *adj* geruchlos
odyssey ['ɑdɪsi] *s* Irrfahrt *f*; **Odyssey** Odyssee *f*
of [ɑv], [əv] *prep* von (*dat*); genit, e.g., **the name of the dog** der Name des Hundes
off [ɔf] *adj* (*free from work*) dienstfrei; (*poor, bad*) schlecht; (*electric current*) ausgeschaltet, abgeschaltet; **be badly off** in schlechten Verhältnissen sein; **be off** (*said of a clock*) nachgehen; (*said of a measurement*)

falsch sein; (*said of a person*) im Irrtum sein; (*be crazy*) nicht ganz richtig im Kopf sein; **be well off** in guten Verhältnissen sein; **the deal** (*or* **party**) **is off** es ist aus mit dem Geschäft (*or* mit der Party) || *adv* (*distant*) weg; **he was off in a flash** er war im Nu weg; **I must be off** ich muß fort || *prep* von (*dat*); **off duty** außer Dienst; **off limits** Zutritt verboten
offal ['ɔfəl] *s* (*refuse*) Abfall *m*; (*of butchered meat*) Innereien *pl*
off' and on' *adv* ab und zu
off'beat' *adj* (sl) ungewöhnlich
off' chance' *s* geringe Chance *f*
off'-col'or *adj* schlüpfrig
off'-du'ty *adj* außerdienstlich
offend [ə'fend] *tr* beleidigen || *intr*— **o. against** verstoßen gegen
offender [ə'fendər] *s* Missetäter –in *mf*; **first o.** nicht Vorbestrafte *mf*; **second o.** Vorbestrafte *mf*
offense [ə'fens] *s* (**against**) Vergehen *n* (gegen); **give o.** Anstoß geben; **no o.!** nichts für ungut!; **take o.** (**at**) Anstoß nehmen (an *dat*)
offensive [ə'fensɪv] *adj* anstößig; (*odor*) ekelhaft; (*action*) offensiv || *s* Offensive *f*; **take the o.** die Offensive ergreifen
offer ['ɔfər] *s* Angebot *n* || *tr* anbieten; (*a price*) bieten; (*help, resistance*) leisten; (*friendship*) schenken; **o. an excuse** e–e Entschuldigung vorbringen; **o. as an excuse** als Entschuldigung vorbringen; **o. for sale** feilbieten; **o. one's services** sich anbieten; **o. up** aufopfern || *intr*—**o. to** (*inf*) sich erbieten zu (*inf*)
of'fering *s* (*act*) Opferung *f*; (*gift*) Opfergabe *f*
offertory ['ɔfər ˌtori] *s* Offertorium *n*
off'hand' *adj* (*excuse*) unvorbereitet; (*manner*) lässig || *adv* kurzerhand
office ['ɔfɪs] *s* (*room*) Büro *n*, Amt *n*; (*position*) Amt *n*; (*of a doctor*) Sprechzimmer *n*; **be in o.** amtieren; **through the good offices of** durch die freundliche Vermittlung (*genit*); **run for o.** für ein Amt kandidieren
of'fice boy' *s* Bürojunge *m*
of'fice build'ing *s* Bürogebäude *n*
of'ficehold'er *s* Amtsträger –in *mf*
of'fice hours' *spl* Dienststunden *pl*; (*of a doctor, lawyer*) Sprechstunde *f*
officer ['ɔfɪsər] *s* (adm) Beamte *m*, Beamtin *f*; (com) Direktor –in *mf*; (mil) Offizier –in *mf*
of'ficer can'didate *s* Offiziersanwärter –in *mf*
of'ficers' mess' *s* Offizierskasino *n*; (nav) Offiziersmesse *f*
of'fice seek'er *s* Amtsbewerber –in *mf*
of'fice supplies' *spl* Bürobedarf *m*
of'fice work' *s* Büroarbeit *f*
official [ə'fɪʃəl] *adj* amtlich; (*in line of duty*) Dienst–; (*visit*) offiziell; (*document*) öffentlich; **on o. business** dienstlich || *s* Beamte *m*, Beamtin *f*; **top officials** Spitzenkräfte *pl*
offi'cial busi'ness *s* Dienstsache *f*

offi′cial call′ s (telp) Dienstgespräch n
officialdom [ə'fɪʃəldəm] s Beamtentum n
officialese [ə,fɪʃə'liz] s Amtssprache f
officially [ə'fɪʃəli] adv offiziell
offi′cial use′ s Dienstgebrauch m
officiate [ə'fɪʃɪ,et] intr amtieren; **o. at a marriage** e–n Traugottesdienst halten
officious [ə'fɪʃəs] adj dienstbeflissen
offing ['ɔfɪŋ] s—**in the o.** in Aussicht
off′-lim′its adj gesperrt
off′print′ s Abdruck m, Sonderdruck m
off′-seas′on adj—**o. prices** Preise pl während der Vor– und Nachsaison || s Vor– und Nachsaison f
off′set′ s (compensation) Ausgleich m; (typ) Offsetdruck m || **off′set′** v (pret –set; ger –setting) tr ausgleichen
off′set press′ s Offsetdruck m
off′shoot′ s Ableger m
off′shore′ adj küstennah
off′side′ adv (sport) abseits
off′spring′ s Sprößling m
off′stage′ adj hinter der Bühne befindlich || adv hinter der Bühne
off′-the-cuff′ adj aus dem Stegreif
off′-the-rec′ord adj im Vertrauen
often ['ɔfən] adv oft, häufig; **every so o.** von Zeit zu Zeit; **quite o.** öfters
of′tentimes′ adv oftmals
ogive ['odʒaɪv] s (diagonal vaulting rib) Gratrippe f; (pointed arch) Spitzbogen m
ogle ['ogəl] tr liebäugeln mit || intr liebäugeln
ogre ['ogər] s Scheusal n; (myth) Menschenfresser m
oh [o] interj oh!; **oh, dear!** o weh!
ohm [om] s Ohm n
oil [ɔɪl] s Öl n; **strike oil** auf Öl stoßen || tr ölen
oil′ burn′er s Ölbrenner m
oil′can′ s Ölkanne f
oil′cloth′ s Wachsleinwand f
oil′ col′or s Ölfarbe f
oil′ drum′ s Ölfaß n
oil′ field′ s Ölfeld n
oil′ gauge′ s Ölstandsanzeiger m
oil′ heat′ s Ölheizung f
oil′ lev′el s Ölstand m
oil′man′ s (–men′) Ölhändler m
oil′ paint′ing s Ölgemälde n
oil′ pres′sure s Öldruck m
oil′ rig′ s Ölbohrinsel f
oil′ shale′ s Ölschiefer m
oil′ slick′ s Öllache f
oil′ tank′ s Ölbehälter m
oil′ tank′er s Öltanker m
oil′ well′ s Ölquelle f
oily ['ɔɪli] adj ölig; (unctious) salbungsvoll
ointment ['ɔɪntmənt] s Salbe f
O.K. ['o'ke] adj in Ordnung, okay || s Billigung f || v (pret & pp O.K.'d; ger O.K.'ing) tr billigen || intr okay!
old [old] adj alt; **as old as the hills** uralt; (said of a person) steinalt
old′ age′ s Alter n, Greisenalter n
old′-age′ home′ s Altersheim n
old′ coun′try s Heimatland n
olden ['oldən] adj alt

old′-fash′ioned adj altmodisch
old′ fog′(e)y ['fogi] s alter Kauz m
Old′ Glo′ry s Sternenbanner n
old′ hand′ s alter Hase m
old′ hat′ adj bärtig
old′ la′dy s Greisin f; (wife) (pej) Alte f
old′ maid′ s alte Jungfer f
old′ man′ s Greis m; (mil) Alter m
old′ mas′ter s (paint) alter Meister m
old′ moon′ s letztes Viertel n
old′ salt′ s alter Seebär m
oldster ['oldstər] s alter Knabe m
Old′ Tes′tament s Altes Testament n
old′-time′ adj altväterisch
old′-tim′er s (coll) alter Hase m
old′ wives′′ tale′ s Altweibergeschichte f
Old′ World′ s alte Welt f
oleander [,olɪ'ændər] s Oleander m
olfactory [al'fæktəri] adj Geruchs–
oligarchy ['alɪ,garki] s Oligarchie f
olive ['alɪv] s Olive f
ol′ive branch′ s Ölzweig m
ol′ive grove′ s Olivenhain m
ol′ive oil′ s Olivenöl n
ol′ive tree′ s Ölbaum m, Olivenbaum m
olympiad [o'lɪmpɪ,æd] s Olympiade f
Olympian [o'lɪmpɪ-ən] adj olympisch
Olympic [o'lɪmpɪk] adj olympisch || **the Olympics** spl die Olympischen Spiele
omelet, omelette ['amə,let] s Eierkuchen m, Omelett n
omen ['oman] s Omen n, Vorzeichen n
ominous ['amɪnəs] adj ominös, unheilvoll
omission [o'mɪʃən] s Auslassung f; (of a deed) Unterlassung f
omit [o'mɪt] v (pret & pp omitted; ger omitting) tr (a word) auslassen; (a deed) unterlassen; **be omitted** ausfallen; **o.** (ger) es unterlassen zu (inf)
omnibus ['amnɪ,bʌs] adj Sammel–, Mantel– || s Omnibus m, Autobus m
omnipotent [am'nɪpətənt] adj allmächtig
omnipresent [,amnɪ'prezənt] adj allgegenwärtig
omniscient [am'nɪʃənt] adj allwissend
on [ɔn] adj (in progress) im Gange; (light, gas, water) an; (radio, television) angestellt; (switch) eingeschaltet; (brakes) angezogen; **be on to s.o.** j–n durchsehen; **be on to s.th.** über etw [acc] im Bilde sein || adv weiter; **on and off** dann und wann; **on and on** in e–m fort || prep auf (dat or acc), an (dat or acc); (concerning) über (acc)
once [wʌns] adv einmal; (formerly) einst; **at o.** auf einmal; (immediately) sofort; **not o.** nicht ein einziges Mal; **o. and for all** ein für allemal; **o. before** früher einmal; **o. in a while** ab und zu; **o. more** noch einmal; **o. upon a time there was** es war einmal || s—**this o.** dieses (eine) Mal || conj sobald
once′-o′ver s—**give** (s.o. or s.th.) **the o.** rasch mustern
one [wʌn] adj ein; (one certain, e.g.,

Mr. Smith) ein gewisser; **for one thing** zunächst; **her one care** ihre einzige Sorge; **it's all one to me** es ist mir ganz gleich; **one and a half hours** anderthalb Stunden; **one day** e–s Tages; **one more** noch ein; **one more thing** noch etwas; **one o'clock** ein Uhr, eins; **on the one hand ... on the other** einerseits ... andererseits ‖ *s* Eins *f* ‖ *pron* einer; **I for one** was mich betrifft, ich jedenfalls; **one after another** einer nach dem anderen; **one after the other** nacheinander; **one another** einander, sich; **one at a time, please!** einer nach dem anderen, bitte!; **one behind the other** hintereinander; **one by one** einer nach dem anderen; **one of these days** früher oder später; **one on top of the other** übereinander, aufeinander; **one to nothing** eins zu Null; **this one** dieser da, der da; **with one another** miteinander ‖ *indef pron* man; **one's** sein

one'-armed' *adj* einarmig

one'-eyed' *adj* einäugig

one'-horse town' *s* Kuhdorf *n*

one'-leg'ged *adj* einbeinig

onerous ['ɒnərəs] *adj* lästig

oneself' *reflex pron* sich; **be o.** sein, wie man immer ist; **by o.** allein; **to o.** vor sich [*acc*] hin

one'-sid'ed *adj* (& fig) einseitig

one'-track' *adj* eingleisig; (fig) einseitig

one'-way street' *s* Einbahnstraße *f*

one'-way tick'et *s* einfache Fahrkarte *f*

one'-week' *adj* achttägig

onion ['ʌnjən] *s* Zwiebel *f;* **know one's onions** (coll) Bescheid wissen

on'ionskin' *s* Durchschlagpapier *n*

on'look'er *s* Zuschauer –in *mf*

only ['onli] *adj* (*son, hope*) einzig ‖ *adv* nur; **not only ... but also** nicht nur ... sondern auch; **o. too** nur (all)zu; **o. too well** zur Genüge; **o. yesterday** erst gestern ‖ *conj* aber; **o. that** nur daß

on'ly-begot'ten *adj* eingeboren

onomatopoeia [ˌɑnəˌmætə'pi·ə] *s* Lautmalerei *f*

on'-ramp' *s* Zufahrtsrampe *f*

on'rush' *s* Ansturm *m*

on'set' *s* Anfang *m; (attack)* Angriff *m*

onslaught ['ɒnˌslɔt] *s* Angriff *m*

on'to *prep* auf (*acc*) hinauf; **be o. s.o.** hinter j–s Schliche kommen; **be o. s.th.** über etw [*acc*] im Bilde sein

onus ['onəs] *s* Last *f;* **o. of proof** Beweislast *f*

onward(s) ['ɒnwərd(z)] *adv* vorwärts

onyx ['ɑnɪks] *s* Onyx *m*

oodles ['udəlz] *spl* (coll) (of) Unmengen *pl* (von)

ooze [uz] *s* Sickern *n; (mud)* Schlamm *m* ‖ *tr* ausschwitzen ‖ *intr* sickern; **o. out** durchsickern

opal ['opəl] *s* Opal *m*

opaque [o'pek] *adj* undurchsichtig; (*stupid*) stumpf

open ['opən] *adj* (*window, position, sea, question, vowel*) offen; (*air, field, seat*) frei; (*business, office*)

geöffnet; (*seam*) geplatzt; (*account*) laufend; (*meeting*) öffentlich; **be o.** offenstehen; **get o.** aufbekommen; **have an o. mind about s.th.** sich noch nicht auf etw [*acc*] festgelegt haben; **keep o.** offenhalten; **lay oneself o. to** sich aussetzen (*dat*); **o. to** (*the public*) zugänglich (*dat*); (*criticism*) ausgesetzt (*dat*); (*doubt*) unterworfen (*dat*); **o. to bribery** bestechlich; **o. to question** strittig ‖ *s*—**come out into the o.** (fig) mit seinen Gedanken herauskommen; **in the o.** im Freien ‖ *tr* öffnen, aufmachen; (*a business, account, meeting, hostilities, fire*) eröffnen; (*a book*) aufschlagen; (*eyes in surprise*) aufreißen; (*a box, bottle*) anbrechen; (*an umbrella*) aufspannen; **o. the attack** losschlagen; **o. to traffic** dem Verkehr übergeben; **o. wide** weit aufreißen ‖ *intr* sich öffnen, aufgehen; (*said of a school, speech, play*) beginnen; **o. onto** hinausgehen auf (*acc*); **o. up** sich auftun; **o. with hearts** (cards) Herz ausspielen

o'pen-air' *adj* Freiluft–; (theat) Freilicht–; **o. concert** Konzert *n* im Freien

opener ['opənər] *s* Öffner *m*, **for openers** (coll) für den Anfang

o'pen-eyed' *adj* mit offenen Augen

o'pen-hand'ed *adj* freigebig

o'pen-heart'ed *adj* offenherzig

o'pen house' *s* allgemeiner Besuchstag *m*

o'pening *adj* (*scene*) erste; (*remarks*) Eröffnungs– ‖ *s* Öffnung *f;* (*of a speech, play*) Anfang *m;* (*of a store, etc.*) Eröffnung *f;* (*vacant job*) freie (or offene) Stelle *f;* (*in the woods*) Lichtung *f;* (*good opportunity*) günstige Gelegenheit *f;* (theat) Erstaufführung *f*

o'pening night' *s* Eröffnungsvorstellung *f*, Premiere *f*

o'pening num'ber *s* erstes Stück *n*

o'pen-mind'ed *adj* aufgeschlossen

openness ['opɴnɪs] *s* Offenheit *f*

o'pen sea'son *s* Jagdzeit *f*

o'pen se'cret *s* offenes Geheimnis *n*

o'pen shop' *s* offener Betrieb *m* (für den kein Gewerkschaftszwang besteht)

opera ['ɑpərə] *s* Oper *f*

op'era glass'es *spl* Opernglas *n*

op'era house' *s* Opernhaus *n*

operate ['ɑpəˌret] *tr* (*a machine, gun*) bedienen; (*a tool*) handhaben; (*a business*) betreiben; **be operated by electricity** elektrisch betrieben werden ‖ *intr* (*said of a device, machine*) funktionieren, laufen; (surg) operieren; **o. on** (surg) operieren

operatic [ˌɑpə'rætɪk] *adj* opernhaft

op'erating costs' *spl* Betriebskosten *pl*

op'erating instruc'tions *spl* Bedienungsanweisung *f*

op'erating room' *s* Operationssaal *m*

op'erating ta'ble *s* Operationstisch *m*

operation [ˌɑpə'reʃən] *s* (*process*) Verfahren *n;* (*of a machine*) Bedienung *f;* (*of a business*) Leitung *f;* (mil) Operation *f,* Aktion *f;* (surg) Operation *f;* **be in o.** (*said of a machine*) in Betrieb sein; (*said of a law*) in Kraft sein; **have** (or **undergo**) **an o.** sich e-r Operation unterziehen; **in a single o.** in e-m einzigen Arbeitsgang; **put into o.** in Betrieb setzen

operational [ˌapəˈreʃənəl] *adj* (*ready to be used*) betriebsbereit; (*pertaining to operations*) Betriebs– Arbeits–; (mil) Einsatz–, Operations–

opera'tions room' *s* (aer) Bereitschaftsraum *m*

operative [ˈapərətɪv] *adj* funktionsfähig, wirkend; **become o.** in Kraft treten || *s* Agent –in *mf*

operator [ˈapəˌretər] *s* (*of a machine*) Bedienende *mf;* (*of an automobile*) Fahrer –in *mf;* (sl) Schieber –in *mf;* (telp) Telephonist –in *mf;* **o.!** (telp) Zentrale!

op'erator's li'cense *s* Führerschein *m*

operetta [ˌapəˈretə] *s* Operette *f*

ophthalmologist [ˌafθəlˈmalədʒɪst] *s* Augenarzt *m*, Augenärztin *f*

ophthalmology [ˌafθəlˈmalədʒi] *s* Augenheilkunde *f*, Ophthalmologie *f*

opiate [ˈopɪˌet] *s* Opiat *n;* (fig) Betäubungsmittel *n*

opinion [əˈpɪnjən] *s* Meinung *f;* **be of the o.** der Meinung sein; **give an o. on** begutachten; **have a high o. of** große Stücke halten auf (*acc*); **in my o.** meiner Meinung nach, meines Erachtens

opinionated [əˈpɪnjəˌnetɪd] *adj* von sich eingenommen

opin'ion poll' *s* Meinungsumfrage *f*

opium [ˈopɪ·əm] *s* Opium *n*

o'pium den' *s* Opiumhöhle *f*

o'pium pop'py *s* Schlafmohn *m*

opossum [əˈpasəm] *s* Opossum *n*

opponent [əˈponənt] *s* Gegner –in *mf*

opportune [ˌapərˈt(j)un] *adj* gelegen

opportunist [ˌapərˈt(j)unɪst] *s* Opportunist –in *mf*

opportunity [ˌapərˈt(j)unɪti] *s* Gelegenheit *f*

oppose [əˈpoz] *tr* sich widersetzen (*dat*); (*for comparison*) gegenüberstellen; **be opposed to s.th.** gegen etw sein

oppos'ing *adj* (*team, forces*) gegnerisch; (*views*) entgegengesetzt

opposite [ˈapəsɪt] *adj* (*side, corner*) gegenüberliegend; (*meaning*) entgegengesetzt; (*view*) gegenteilig; **o. angle** (geom) Gegenwinkel *m;* **o. to** gegenüber (*dat*) || *s* Gegensatz *m,* Gegenteil *n* || *prep* gegenüber (*dat*)

op'posite num'ber *s* Gegenstück *n,* Gegenspieler –in *mf*

opposition [ˌapəˈzɪʃən] *s* Widerstand *m;* (pol) Opposition *f;* **meet with stiff o.** auf heftigen Widerstand stoßen; **offer o.** Widerstand leisten

oppress [əˈpres] *tr* unterdrücken

oppression [əˈpreʃən] *s* Unterdrückung *f*

oppressive [əˈpresɪv] *adj* bedrückend

oppressor [əˈpresər] *s* Unterdrücker –in *mf*

opprobrious [əˈprobrɪ·əs] *adj* schändlich

opprobrium [əˈprobrɪ·əm] *s* Schande *f*

opt [apt] *intr*—**opt for** optieren für

optic [ˈaptɪk] *adj* Augen– || **optics** *s* Optik *f*

optical [ˈaptɪkəl] *adj* optisch

op'tical illus'ion *s* optische Täuschung *f*

optician [apˈtɪʃən] *s* Optiker –in *mf*

op'tic nerve' *s* Augennerv *m*

optimism [ˈaptɪˌmɪzəm] *s* Optimismus *m*

optimist [ˈaptɪmɪst] *s* Optimist –in *mf*

optimistic [ˌaptɪˈmɪstɪk] *adj* optimistisch

option [ˈapʃən] *s* (*choice*) Wahl *f;* (*alternative*) Alternative *f;* (ins) Option *f*

optional [ˈapʃənəl] *adj* wahlfrei; **be o.** freistehen

optometrist [apˈtamɪtrɪst] *s* Augenoptiker –in *mf*

optometry [apˈtamɪtri] *s* Optometrie *f*

opulent [ˈapjələnt] *adj* (*wealthy*) reich; (*luxurious*) üppig

or [ɔr] *conj* oder

oracle [ˈɔrəkəl] *s* Orakel *n*

oracular [oˈrækjələr] *adj* orakelhaft

oral [ˈorəl] *adj* mündlich

o'ral hygiene' *s* Mundpflege *f*

orange [ˈorɪndʒ] *adj* orange || *s* Orange *f,* Apfelsine *f*

orangeade [ˌorɪndʒˈed] *s* Orangeade *f*

or'ange blos'som *s* Orangenblüte *f*

or'ange grove' *s* Orangenhain *m*

or'ange tree' *s* Orangenbaum *m*

orang-outang [oˈræŋuˌtæŋ] *s* Orang-Utan *m*

oration [oˈreʃən] *s* Rede *f*

orator [ˈɔrətər] *s* Redner –in *mf*

oratorical [ˌɔrəˈtɔrɪkəl] *adj* rednerisch

oratori·o [ɔrəˈtɔrɪˌo] *s* (**–os**) Oratorium *n*

oratory [ˈɔrəˌtori] *s* Redekunst *f*

orb [ɔrb] *s* Kugel *f;* (*of the moon or sun*) Scheibe *f*

orbit [ˈɔrbɪt] *s* Umlaufbahn *f;* **send into o.** in die Umlaufbahn schicken || *tr* umkreisen

orbital [ˈɔrbɪtəl] *adj* Kreisbahn–

orchard [ˈɔrtʃərd] *s* Obstgarten *m*

orchestra [ˈɔrkɪstrə] *s* Orchester *n*

or'chestra pit' *s* Orchesterraum *m*

orchestrate [ˈɔrkɪˌstret] *tr* orchestrieren

orchid [ˈɔrkɪd] *s* Orchidee *f*

ordain [ɔrˈden] *tr* verordnen; (eccl) ordinieren, zum Priester weihen

ordeal [ɔrˈdil] *s* Qual *f;* (hist) Gottesurteil *n;* **o. by fire** Feuerprobe *f*

order [ˈɔrdər] *s* (*command*) Befehl *m;* (*decree*) Verordnung *f;* (*order, arrangement*) Ordnung *f;* (*medal*) Orden *m;* (*sequence*) Reihenfolge *f;* (archit, bot, zool) Ordnung *f;* (com) (*for*) Auftrag *m* (auf *acc*), Bestellung *f* (auf *acc*); (eccl) Orden *m;* (jur) Beschluß *m;* **according to orders** befehlsgemäß; **be in good o.** in gutem

Zustand sein; **be the o. of the day** (coll) an der Tagesordnung sein; **be under orders to** (inf) Befehl haben zu (inf); **by o. of** auf Befehl von (or genit); **call to o.** (a meeting) für eröffnet erklären; (reestablish order) zur Ordnung rufen; **in o.** (functioning) in Ordnung; (proper, in place) angebracht; **in o. of** geordnet nach; **in o. that** damit; **in o. to** (inf) um ... zu (inf); **make to o.** nach Maß machen; **of a high o.** von ausgezeichneter Art; **on o.** (com) in Auftrag; **o.!, o.!** zur Ordnung! **out of o.** (defective) außer Betrieb; (not functioning at all) nicht in Ordnung; (disarranged) in Unordnung; (parl) im Widerspruch zur Geschäftsordnung, unzulässig; **put in o.** in Ordnung bringen; **restore to o.** die Ordnung wiederherstellen; **you are out of o.** Sie haben nicht das Wort || tr (command) befehlen, anordnen; (decree) verordnen; (com) bestellen; **as ordered** auftragsgemäß; **o. around** herumkommandieren; **o. in advance** vor(her)bestellen; **o. more of** nachbestellen; **o. s.o. off** (e.g., the premises) j-n weisen von
or'der blank' s Auftragsformular n
orderliness ['ɔrdərlɪnɪs] s (of a person) Ordnungsliebe f; (of a room, etc.) Ordnung f
orderly ['ɔrdərli] adj ordentlich || s (med) Krankenwärter m; (mil) Bursche m
or'derly room' s (mil) Schreibstube f
or'der slip' s Bestellzettel m
ordinal ['ɔrdɪnəl] adj Ordnungs– || s Ordnungszahl f
ordinance ['ɔrdɪnəns] s Verfügung f; (of a city) Verordnung f
ordinary ['ɔrdɪ,nɛri] adj gewöhnlich; (member) ordentlich; **o. person** Alltagsmensch m || s Gewöhnliche n; (eccl) Ordinarius m; **nothing out of the o.** nichts Ungewöhnliches; **out of the o.** außerordentlich
ordination [,ɔrdɪ'neʃən] s Priesterweihe f
ordnance ['ɔrdnəns] s Waffen und Munition pl; (arti) Geschützwesen n
ore [or] s Erz n
organ ['ɔrgən] s (means) Werkzeug n; (publication) Organ n; (adm, biol) Organ n; (mus) Orgel f
organdy ['ɔrgəndi] s Organdy m
or'gan grind'er s Drehorgelspieler m
organic [ɔr'gænɪk] adj organisch
organism ['ɔrgə,nɪzəm] s Organismus m
organist ['ɔrgənɪst] s Organist –in mf
organization [,ɔrgənɪ'zeʃən] s Organisation f
organizational [,ɔrgənɪ'zeʃənəl] adj organisatorisch
organize ['ɔrgə,naɪz] tr organisieren
organizer ['ɔrgə,naɪzər] s Organisator –in mf
or'gan loft' s Orgelbühne f
orgasm ['ɔrgæzəm] s Orgasmus m
orgy ['ɔrdʒi] s Orgie f

Orient ['orɪ·ənt] s Orient m || **orient** ['orɪ,ɛnt] tr orientieren
oriental [,orɪ'ɛntəl] adj orientalisch || **Oriental** s Orientale m, Orientalin f
orientation [,orɪ·ən'teʃən] s Orientierung f; (of new staff members) Einführung f
orifice ['orɪfɪs] s Öffnung f
origin ['orɪdʒɪn] s Ursprung m; (of a person or word) Herkunft f
original [ə'rɪdʒɪnəl] adj ursprünglich; (first) Ur–; (novel, play) originell; (person) erfinderisch || s Original n
originality [ə,rɪdʒɪ'nælɪti] s Originalität f
ori'ginal research' s Quellenstudium n
ori'ginal sin s Erbsünde f, Sündenfall m
originate [ə'rɪdʒɪ,net] tr hervorbringen || intr (from) entstehen (aus); **o. in** seinen Ursprung haben in (dat)
originator [ə'rɪdʒɪ,netər] s Urheber –in mf
oriole ['orɪ,ol] s Goldamsel f, Pirol m
ormolu ['ɔrmə,lu] s Malergold n
ornament ['ɔrnəmənt] s Verzierung f, Schmuck m || ['ɔrnə,mɛnt] tr verzieren
ornamental [,ɔrnə'mɛntəl] adj Zier–
ornamentation [,ɔrnəmən'teʃən] s Verzierung f
ornate [ɔr'net] adj überladen; (speech) bilderreich
ornery ['ɔrnəri] adj (cantankerous) mürrisch; (vile) gemein
ornithology [,ɔrnɪ'θɑlədʒi] s Vogelkunde f, Ornithologie f
orphan ['ɔrfən] s Waise f; **become an o.** verwaisen
orphanage ['ɔrfənɪdʒ] s Waisenhaus n
or'phaned adj verwaist; **be o.** verwaisen
or'phans' court' s Vormundschaftsgericht n
orthodox ['ɔrθə,dɑks] adj orthodox
orthography [ɔr'θɑgrəfi] s Orthographie f, Rechtschreibung f
orthopedist [,ɔrθə'pidɪst] s Orthopäde m, Orthopädin f
oscillate ['ɑsɪ,let] intr schwingen
oscillation [,ɑsɪ'leʃən] s Schwingung f
oscillator ['ɑsɪ,letər] s Oszillator m
osier ['oʒər] s Korbweide f
osmosis [ɑs'mosɪs] s Osmose f
osprey ['ɑspri] s Fischadler m
ossi·fy ['ɑsɪ,faɪ] v (pret & pp –fied) tr verknöchern lassen || intr verknöchern
ostensible [ɑs'tɛnsɪbəl] adj vorgeblich
ostentation [,ɑstən'teʃən] s Zurschaustellung f, Prahlerei f
ostentatious [,ɑstən'teʃəs] adj prahlerisch, prunksüchtig
osteopath [,ɑstɪ·ə,pæθ] s Osteopath –in mf
osteopathy [,ɑstɪ'apəθi] s Osteopathie f
ostracism ['ɑstrə,sɪzəm] s Ächtung f; (hist) Scherbengericht n
ostracize ['ɑstrə,saɪz] tr verfemen
ostrich ['ɑstrɪtʃ] s Strauß m
Ostrogoth ['ɑstrə,gɑθ] s Ostgote m

other [ˈʌðər] *adj* andere, sonstig; **among o. things** unter anderem; **every o. day** jeden zweiten Tag; **none o. than he** kein anderer als er; **on the o. hand** andererseits; **o. things being equal** unter gleichen Voraussetzungen; **someone or o.** irgend jemand; **some ... or o.** irgendein; **the o. day** unlängst ‖ *adv*—**o. than** anders als ‖ *indef pron* andere; **the others** die anderen

otherwise [ˈʌðər‚waɪz] *adj* sonstig ‖ *adv* sonst; **I can't do o.** ich kann nicht umhin; **o.** engaged anderweitig beschäftigt; **think o.** anders denken

otter [ˈɑtər] *s* Otter *m*; (*snake*) Otter *f*

Ottoman [ˈɑtəmən] *adj* osmanisch ‖ **ottoman** *s* (*couch*) Ottomane *m*; (*cushioned stool*) Polsterschemel *m*; **O.** Osmane *m*

ouch [aʊtʃ] *interj* au!

ought [ɔt] *aux* used to express obligation, e.g., **you o.** to tell her Sie sollten es ihr sagen; **they o. to have been here** sie hätten hier sein sollen

ounce [aʊns] *s* Unze *f*

our [aʊr] *poss adj* unser

ours [aʊrz] *poss pron* der uns(e)rige, der uns(e)re, uns(e)rer; **a friend of o.** ein Freund von uns; **this is o.** das gehört uns

ourselves [aʊrˈsɛlvz] *reflex pron* uns; **we are by o.** wir sind doch unter uns ‖ *intens pron* selbst, selber

oust [aʊst] *tr* (**from**) verdrängen (aus); **o. from office** seines Amtes entheben

ouster [ˈaʊstər] *s* Amtsenthebung *f*

out [aʊt] *adj*—**an evening out** ein Ausgehabend *m*; **be out** (*of the house*) ausgegangen sein; (*said of a light, fire*) aus sein; (*said of a new book*) erschienen sein; (*said of a secret*) enthüllt sein; (*said of flowers*) aufgeblüht sein; (*said of a dislocated limb*) verrenkt sein; (*be out of style*) aus der Mode sein; (*be at an end*) aus sein; (*be absent from work*) der Arbeit fernbleiben; (*be on strike*) streiken; **be out after s.o.** hinter j-m her sein; **be out for a good time** dem Vergnügen nachgehen; **be out on one's feet** (coll) erledigt sein; **be out ten marks** zehn Mark eingebüßt haben; **be out to** (*inf*) darauf ausgehen (or aus sein) zu (*inf*); **that's out** das kommt nicht in Frage; **the best thing out** das Beste, was es gibt ‖ *adv* (*gone forth; ended, terminated*) aus; **out of** (*curiosity, pity, etc.*) aus (*dat*); (*fear*) vor (*dat*); (*a certain number*) von (*dat*); (*deprived of*) beraubt (*genit*); **out of breath** außer Atem; **out of money** ohne Geld; **out of place** verlegt; (*not appropriate or proper*) unpassend; **out of the window** zum Fenster hinaus ‖ *s* (*pretext*) Ausweg *m*; **be on the outs with s.o.** mit j-m auf gespanntem Fuße sein ‖ *prep* aus (*dat*) ‖ *interj* (sport) aus!; **out with it!** heraus damit!

out′ and away′ *adv* bei weitem

out′-and-out′ *adj* abgefeimt

out′-ar′gue *tr* in Grund und Boden argumentieren

out′bid′ *v* (*pret* –**bid**; *pp* –**bid** & –**bidden**; *ger* –**bidding**) *tr* überbieten

out′board mo′tor *s* Außenbordmotor *m*

out′bound′ *adj* nach auswärts bestimmt; (*traffic*) aus der Stadt fließend

out′break′ *s* Ausbruch *m*

out′build′ing *s* Nebengebäude *n*

out′burst′ *s* Ausbruch *m*; **o. of anger** Zornausbruch *m*

out′cast′ *adj* ausgestoßen ‖ *s* Ausgestoßene *mf*

out′come′ *s* Ergebnis *n*

out′cry′ *s* Ausruf *m*; **raise an o.** ein Zetergeschrei erheben

out′-dat′ed *adj* zeitlich überholt

out′dis′tance *tr* hinter sich [*dat*] lassen

out′do′ *v* (*pret* –**did**; *pp* –**done**) *tr* überbieten, übertreffen; **not to be outdone by s.o. in zeal** j-m nichts an Eifer nachgeben; **o. oneself in** sich überbieten in (*dat*)

out′door′ *adj* Außen—

out′doors′ *adv* draußen, im Freien ‖ *s*—**in the outdoors** im Freien

out′door shot′ *s* (*phot*) Außenaufnahme *f*

out′door swim′ming pool′ *s* Freibad *n*

out′door the′ater *s* Naturtheater *n*

out′door toil′et *s* Abtritt *m*

outer [ˈaʊtər] *adj* äußere, Außen—

out′er ear′ *s* Ohrmuschel *f*

out′er gar′ment *s* Überkleid *n*

out′ermost′ *adj* äußerste

out′er space′ *s* Weltall *n*, Weltraum *m*

out′field′ *s* (baseball) Außenfeld *n*

out′fit′ *s* (*equipment*) Ausrüstung *f*; (*set of clothes*) Ausstattung *f*; (*uniform*) Kluft *f*; (*business firm*) Gesellschaft *f*; (mil) Einheit *f* ‖ *v* (*pret* –**fitted**; *ger* –**fitting**) *tr* (*with equipment*) ausrüsten; (*with clothes*) neu ausstaffieren

out′flank′ *tr* überflügeln, umfassen

out′flow′ *s* Ausfluß *m*

out′go′ing *adj* (*sociable*) gesellig; (*officer*) bisherig; (*tide*) zurückgehend; (*train, plane*) abgehend

out′grow′ *v* (*pret* –**grew**; *pp* –**grown**) *tr* herauswachsen aus; (fig) entwachsen (*dat*)

out′growth′ *s* Auswuchs *m*; (fig) Folge *f*

out′ing *s* Ausflug *m*

outlandish [aʊtˈlændɪʃ] *adj* fremdartig; (*prices*) überhöht

out′last′ *tr* überdauern

out′law′ *s* Geächtete *mf* ‖ *tr* ächten

out′lay′ *s* Auslage *f*, Kostenaufwand *m* ‖ **out′lay′** *v* (*pret* & *pp* –**laid**) *tr* auslegen

out′let′ *s* (*for water*) Abfluß *m*, Ausfluß *m*; (fig) (**for**) Ventil *n* (für); (com) Absatzmarkt *m*; (elec) Steckdose *f*; **find an o. for** (fig) Luft machen (*dat*); **no o.** Sackgasse *f*

out′line′ *s* (*profile*) Umriß *m*; (*sketch*) Umrißzeichnung *f*; (*summary*) Grundriß *m*; **rough o.** knapper Umriß *m* ‖ *tr* umreißen

out'live' *tr* überleben
out'look' *s* (*place giving a view*) Ausguck *m*; (*view from a place*) Ausblick *m*; (*point of view*) Anschauung *f*; (*prospects*) Aussichten *pl*
out'ly'ing *adj* Außen—
out'maneu'ver *tr* ausmanövrieren; (fig) überlisten
outmoded [ˌaʊt'moʊdɪd] *adj* unmodern
out'num'ber *tr* an Zahl übertreffen
out'-of-bounds' *adj* (fig) nicht in den Schranken; (sport) im Aus
out'-of-court' **set'tlement** *s* außergerichtlicher Vergleich *m*
out'-of-date' *adj* veraltet
out'-of-door' *adj* Außen—
out'-of-doors' *adj* Außen— ‖ *adv* im Freien, draußen ‖ *s*—**in the o.** im Freien
out'-of-pock'et *adj*—**o. expenses** Barauslagen *pl*
out' of print' *adj* vergriffen
out'-of-the-way' *adj* abgelegen
out' of tune' *adj* verstimmt
out' of work' *adj* arbeitslos, erwerbslos
out'pace' *tr* überholen
out'pa'tient *s* ambulant Behandelte *mf*
out'patient clin'ic *s* Ambulanz *f*
out'play' *tr* überspielen
out'point' *tr* (sport) nach Punkten schlagen
out'post' *s* (mil) Vorposten *m*
out'pour'ing *s* (& fig) Erguß *m*
out'put' *s* (*of a machine or factory*) Arbeitsleistung *f*; (*of a factory*) Produktion *f*; (mech) Nutzleistung *f*; (min) Förderung *f*
out'rage' *s* Unverschämtheit *f*; (**against**) Verletzung *f* (*genit*) ‖ *tr* gröblich beleidigen
outrageous [aʊt'redʒəs] *adj* unverschämt
out'rank' *tr* im Rang übertreffen
out'rid'er *s* Vorreiter *m*
outrigger ['aʊtˌrɪɡər] *s* Ausleger *m*; (*of a racing boat*) Outrigger *m*
out'right' *adj* (*lie, refusal*) glatt; (*loss*) total; (*frank*) offen ‖ *adv* (*completely*) völlig; (*without reserve*) ohne Vorbehalt; (*at once*) auf der Stelle; **buy o.** per Kasse kaufen; **refuse o.** glatt ablehnen
out'run' *v* (*pret* —**ran;** *pp* —**run;** *ger* —**running**) *tr* hinter sich [*dat*] lassen
out'sell' *v* (*pret & pp* —**sold**) *tr* e-n größeren Umsatz haben als
out'set' *s* Anfang *m*
out'shine' *v* (*pret & pp* —**shone**) *tr* überstrahlen
out'side' *adj* (*help, interference*) von außen; (*world, influence, impressions*) äußere; (*lane, work*) Außen— ‖ *adv* draußen ‖ *s* Außenseite *f*, Äußere *n*; **at the** (**very**) **o.** (aller-)höchstens; **from the o.** von außen ‖ *prep* außerhalb (*genit*)
outsider [ˌaʊt'saɪdər] *s* Außenstehende *mf*; (sport) Außenseiter *m*
out'size' *adj* übergroß ‖ *s* Übergröße *f*
out'skirts' *spl* Randgebiet *n*, Stadtrand *m*

out'smart' *tr* überlisten
out'spo'ken *adj* freimütig
out'spread' *adj* (*legs*) gespreizt; (*arms, wings*) ausgebreitet
out'stand'ing *adj* hervorragend, profiliert; (*money, debts*) ausstehend
out'strip' *v* (*pret & pp* —**stripped;** *ger* —**stripping**) *tr* (& fig) hinter sich [*dat*] lassen
out'vote' *tr* überstimmen
outward ['aʊtwərd] *adj* äußerlich, äußere ‖ *adv* auswärts, nach außen
outwardly ['aʊtwərdli] *adv* äußerlich
outwards ['aʊtwərdz] *adv* auswärts
out'weigh' *tr* an Gewicht übertreffen; (fig) überwiegen
out'wit' *v* (*pret & pp* —**witted;** *ger* —**witting**) *tr* überlisten
oval ['oʊvəl] *adj* oval ‖ *s* Oval *n*
ovary ['oʊvəri] *s* Eierstock *m*
ovation [oʊ'veʃən] *s* Huldigung *f*, Ovation *f*
oven ['ʌvən] *s* Ofen *m*; (*for baking*) Backofen *m*
over ['oʊvər] *adj* (*ended*) vorbei, aus; **it's all o. with him** es ist vorbei mit ihm; **o. and done with** total erledigt ‖ *adv*—**all o.** (*everywhere*) überall; (*on the body*) über und über; **children of twelve and o.** Kinder von zwölf Jahren und darüber; **come o.!** komm herüber!; **o.!** (*turn the page*) bitte wenden!; **o. again** noch einmal; **o. against** gegenüber (*dat*); **o. and above** obendrein; **o. and out!** (rad) Ende!; **o. and o. again** immer wieder; **o. in Europe** drüben in Europa; **o. there** dort, da drüben ‖ *prep* (*position*) über (*dat*); (*motion*) über (*acc*); (*because of*) wegen (*genit*); (*in the course of, e.g., a cup of tea*) bei (*dat*); (*during; more than*) über (*acc*); **all o. town** (*position*) in der ganzen Stadt; (*direction*) durch die ganze Stadt; **be o. s.o.** über j-m stehen; **b. o. s.o.'s head** j-m zu hoch sein; **from all o. Germany** aus ganz Deutschland; **o. and above** außer (*genit*); **o. the radio** im Radio
o'veract' *tr & intr* (theat) übertreiben
o'verac'tive *adj* übermäßig tätig
overage ['oʊvər'edʒ] *adj* über das vorgeschriebene Alter hinaus
o'verall' *adj* Gesamt— ‖ **o'veralls'** *spl* Monteuranzug *m*; (*trousers*) Überziehhose *f*
o'verambi'tious *adj* allzu ehrgeizig
o'veranx'ious *adj* überängstlich; (*overeager*) übereifrig
o'verawe' *tr* einschüchtern
o'verbear'ing *adj* überheblich
o'verboard' *adv* über Bord; **go o. about** sich übermäßig begeistern für
o'vercast' *adj* bewölkt, bedeckt; **become o.** sich bewölken ‖ *s* Bewölkung *f*
o'vercharge' *s* Überteuerung *f*; (elec) Überladung *f* ‖ **o'vercharge'** *tr* e-n Überpreis abverlangen (*dat*); (elec) überladen
o'vercoat' *s* Mantel *m*, Überrock *m*
o'ver•come' *v* (*pret* —**came;** *pp* —**come**)

tr überwältigen; **be o. with joy** vor Freude hingerissen sein

o'vercon'fidence *s* zu großes Selbstvertrauen *n*

o'vercon'fident *adj* zu vertrauensvoll

o'vercook' *tr* (*overboil*) zerkochen; (*overbake*) zu lange backen, zu lange braten

o'vercrowd' *tr* überfüllen; (*a room, hotel, hospital*) überbelegen

o'ver·do' *v* (*pret* –**did**; *pp* –**done**) *tr* übertreiben; **o. it** sich überanstrengen

o'verdone' *adj* (culin) übergar

o'verdose' *s* Überdosis *f*

o'verdraft' *s* Überziehung *f*

o'ver·draw' *v* (*pret* –**drew**; *pp* –**drawn**) *tr* überziehen

o'verdress' *intr* sich übertrieben kleiden

o'verdrive' *s* (aut) Schongang *m*

o'verdue' *adj* überfällig

o'ver·eat' *v* (*pret* –**ate**; *pp* –**eaten**) *intr* sich überessen

o'verem'phasis *s* Überbetonung *f*

o'verem'phasize *tr* überbetonen

o'veres'timate *tr* überschätzen

o'verexcite' *tr* überreizen

o'verexert' *tr* überanstrengen

o'verexer'tion *s* Überanstrengung *f*

o'verexpose' *tr* (phot) überbelichten

o'verexpo'sure *s* Überbelichtung *f*

o'verextend' *tr* übermäßig ausweiten

o'verflow' *s* (*inundation*) Überschwemmung *f*; (*surplus*) Überschuß *m*; (*outlet for surplus liquid*) Überlauf *m*; **filled to o.** bis zum Überfließen gefüllt ‖ **o'verflow'** *tr* überfluten; **o. the banks** über die Ufer treten ‖ *intr* überfließen

o'ver·fly' *v* (*pret* –**flew**; *pp* –**flown**) *tr* überfliegen

o'verfriend'ly *adj* katzenfreundlich

o'vergrown' *adj* überwachsen; (*child*) lang aufgeschossen; **become o.** (*said of a garden*) verwildern; **become o. with** überwuchert werden von

o'verhang' *s* Überhang *m* ‖ **o'ver·hang'** *v* (*pret & pp* –**hung**) *tr* hervorragen über (*acc*); (*threaten*) bedrohen ‖ *intr* überhängen

o'verhaul' *s* Überholung *f* ‖ **o'verhaul'** *tr* (*repair; overtake*) überholen

o'verhead' *adj* (*line*) oberirdisch; (*valve*) obengesteuert ‖ *adv* droben ‖ *s* (econ) Gemeinkosten *pl*, laufende Unkosten *pl*

o'verhead door' *s* Federhubtor *f*

o'verhead line' *s* (*of a trolley*) Oberleitung *f*

o'ver·hear' *v* (*pret & pp* –**heard**) *tr* mitanhören; **be o.** belauscht werden

o'verheat' *tr* überhitzen; (*a room*) überheizen ‖ *intr* heißlaufen

o'verindulge' *tr* verwöhnen ‖ *intr* (**in**) sich allzusehr ergehen (in *dat*)

o'verkill' *s* Overkill *m*

overjoyed [‚ovər'dʒɔɪd] *adj* überglücklich

overland ['ovər‚lænd] *adj* Überland–; **o. route** Landweg *m* ‖ *adv* über Land

o'verlap' *s* Überschneiden *n* ‖ **o'verlap'** *v* (*pret & pp* –**lapped**; *ger* –**lapping**) *tr* sich überschneiden mit ‖ *intr* (& fig) sich überschneiden

o'verlap'ping *s* (& fig) Überschneidung *f*

o'verlay' *s* Auflage *f*; (*for a map*) Planpause *f*; **o. of gold** Goldauflage *f*

o'verload' *s* Überbelastung *f*; (elec) Überlast *f* ‖ **o'verload'** *tr* überlasten; (*a truck*) überladen; (*in radio communications*) übersteuern; (elec) überlasten

o'verlook' *tr* (*by mistake*) übersehen; (*a mistake*) hinwegsehen über (*acc*); (*a view*) überblicken

overly ['ovərli] *adv* übermäßig

o'vernight' *adj*—**o. stop** Aufenthalt *m* von e–r Nacht; **o. things** Nachtzeug *n* ‖ *adv* über Nacht; **stay o.** übernachten

o'vernight' bag' *s* Nachtzeugtasche *f*

o'verpass' *s* Überführung *f*

o'ver·pay' *v* (*pret & pp* –**paid**) *tr & intr* überbezahlen

o'verpay'ment *s* Überbezahlung *f*

o'verpop'ulat'ed *adj* übervölkert

o'verpop'ula'tion *s* Übervölkerung *f*

o'verpow'er *tr* (& fig) überwältigen

o'verproduc'tion *s* Überproduktion *f*

o'verrate' *tr* zu hoch schätzen

o'verreach' *tr* (*extend beyond*) hinausragen über (*acc*); (*an arm*) zu weit ausstrecken; **o. oneself** sich übernehmen

o'verrefined' *adj* überspitzt

o'verripe' *adj* überreif

o'verrule' *tr* (*an objection*) zurückweisen; (*a proposal*) verwerfen; (*a person*) überstimmen

o'verrun' *s* Überproduktion *f* ‖ **o'ver·run'** *v* (*pret* –**ran**; *pp* –**run**; *ger* –**running**) *tr* überrennen; (*said of a flood*) überschwemmen; **o. with** (*weeds*) überwuchert von; (*tourists*) überlaufen von; (*vermin*) wimmeln von

o'versalt' *tr* versalzen

o'versea(s)' *adj* Übersee– ‖ *adv* nach Übersee

o'ver·see' *v* (*pret & pp* –**saw**; *pp* –**seen**) *tr* beaufsichtigen

o'verse'er *s* Aufseher –in *mf*

o'versen'sitive *adj* überempfindlich

o'vershad'ow *tr* überschatten; (fig) in den Schatten stellen

o'vershoe' *s* Überschuh *m*

o'ver·shoot' *v* (*pret & pp* –**shot**) *tr* (& fig) hinausschießen über (*acc*)

o'versight' *s* Versehen *n*; **through an o.** aus Versehen

o'versimplifica'tion *s* allzu große Vereinfachung *f*

o'versize' *adj* übergroß ‖ *s* Übergröße *f*

o'ver·sleep' *v* (*pret & pp* –**slept**) *tr & intr* verschlafen

o'verspe'cialized *adj* überspezialisiert

o'verstaffed' *adj* (mit Personal) übersetzt

o'verstay' *tr* überschreiten

o'ver·step' *v* (*pret & pp* –**stepped**; *ger* –**stepping**) *tr* überschreiten

o'verstock' *tr* überbevorraten
o'verstrain' *tr* überanstrengen
o'verstuffed' *adj* überfüllt; (*furniture*) überpolstert
o'versupply' *s* zu großer Vorrat *m;* (com) Überangebot *n* || o'versup•ply' *v* (*pret & pp* –plied) *tr* überreichlich versehen; (com) überreichlich anbieten
overt ['ovərt], [o'vʌrt] *adj* offenkundig
o'ver•take' *v* (*pret* –took; *pp* –taken) *tr* (*catch up to*) einholen; (*pass*) überholen; (*suddenly befall*) überfallen
o'vertax' *tr* überbesteuern; (fig) überfordern, übermäßig in Anspruch nehmen
o'ver-the-coun'ter *adj* (pharm) rezeptfrei; (st. exch.) freihändig
o'verthrow' *s* Sturz *m* || o'ver•throw' (*pret* –threw; *pp* –thrown) *tr* stürzen
o'vertime' *adj* Überstunden– || *adv*—work o. Überstunden arbeiten; work five hours o. fünf Überstunden machen || *s* Überstunden *pl;* (sport) Spielverlängerung *f*
o'vertired' *adj* übermüdet
o'vertone' *s* (fig) Nebenbedeutung *f;* (mus) Oberton *m*
o'vertrump' *tr* überstechen
overture ['ovərtʃər] *s* Antrag *m;* (mus) Ouvertüre *f*
o'verturn' *tr* umstürzen || *intr* umkippen; (aut) sich überschlagen
overweening [,ovər'winɪŋ] *adj* hochmütig
o'verweight' *adj* zu schwer || *s* Übergewicht *n;* (*of freight*) Überfracht *f*
overwhelm [,ovər'whelm] *tr* (*with some feeling*) überwältigen; (*e.g., with questions, gifts*) überschütten; (*with work*) überbürden
o'verwhelm'ing *adj* überwältigend
overwind [,ovər'waɪnd] *v* (*pret & pp* –wound) *tr* überdrehen
o'verwork' *s* Überarbeitung *f,* Überanstrengung *f* || o'verwork' *tr* überfordern || *intr* sich überarbeiten
o'verwrought' *adj* überreizt

o'verzeal'ous *adj* übereifrig
ow [aʊ] *interj* au!
owe [o] *tr* schulden (*dat*), schuldig sein (*dat*); he owes her everything er verdankt ihr alles
ow'ing *adj*—it is o. to you that es ist dein Verdienst, daß; o. to infolge (*genit*)
owl [aʊl] *s* Eule *f;* (*barn owl, screech owl*) Schleiereule *f*
own [on] *adj* eigen || *s*—be left on one's own sich (*dat*) selbst überlassen sein; be on one's own auf eigenen Füßen stehen; come into one's own zu seinem Recht kommen; hold one's own sich behaupten; of one's own für sich allein; on one's own (*initiative*) aus eigener Initiative; (*responsibility*) auf eigene Faust || *tr* besitzen; (*acknowledge*) anerkennen; who owns this house? wem gehört dieses Haus? || *intr*—own to sich bekennen zu; own up to zugeben (*dat*)
owner ['onər] *s* Eigentümer –in *mf*
own'ership' *s* Eigentum *n;* (*legal right of possession*) Eigentumsrecht *n;* under new o. unter neuer Leitung
ox [aks] *s* (oxen ['aksən]) Ochse *m*
ox'cart' *s* Ochsenkarren *m*
oxfords ['aksfərdz] *spl* Halbschuhe *pl*
oxide ['aksaɪd] *s* Oxyd *n*
oxidize ['aksɪ,daɪz] *tr & intr* oxydieren
oxydation [,aksɪ'deʃən] *s* Oxydation *f*
oxygen ['aksɪdʒən] *s* Sauerstoff *m*
oxygenate ['aksɪdʒə,net] *tr* mit Sauerstoff anreichern
ox'ygen mask' *s* Sauerstoffmaske *f*
ox'ygen tank' *s* Sauerstoffflasche *f*
ox'ygen tent' *s* Sauerstoffzelt *n*
oxytone ['aksɪ,ton] *adj* oxytoniert || *s* Oxytonon *n*
oyster ['ɔɪstər] *s* Auster *f*
oys'ter bed' *s* Austernbank *f*
oys'ter farm' *s* Austernpark *m*
oys'ter•man *s* (–men) Austernfischer *m*
oys'tershell' *s* Austernschale *f*
oys'ter stew' *s* Austernragout *n*
ozone ['ozon] *s* Ozon *n*
O'zone layer' *s* Ozonschicht *f*

P

P, p [pi] *s* sechzehnter Buchstabe des englischen Alphabets
pace [pes] *s* Schritt *m;* (*speed*) Tempo *n;* at a fast p. in schnellem Tempo; keep p. with Schritt halten mit; put s.o. through his paces j–n auf Herz und Nieren prüfen; set the p. das Tempo angeben; (sport) Schrittmacher sein || *tr* (*the room, floor*) abschreiten; p. off abschreiten || *intr*—p. up and down (in) auf und ab schreiten (in *dat*)
pace'mak'er *s* Schrittmacher *m*
pacific [pə'sɪfɪk] *adj* pazifisch; the

Pacific Ocean der Pazifische (or Stille) Ozean || *s*—the Pacific der Pazifik
pacifier ['pæsɪ,faɪ·ər] *s* Friedensvermittler –in *mf;* (*for a baby*) Schnuller *m*
pacifism ['pæsɪ,fɪzəm] *s* Pazifismus *m*
pacifist ['pæsɪfɪst] *s* Pazifist –in *mf*
paci•fy ['pæsɪ,faɪ] *v* (*pret & pp* –fied) *tr* (*a country*) befrieden; (*a person*) beruhigen
pack [pæk] *s* Pack *m,* Packen *m;* (*of a soldier*) Gepäck *n;* (*of wolves, submarines*) Rudel *n;* (*of hounds*) Meute

f; (of cigarettes) Päckchen *n,* Schachtel *f; (on pack animals)* Last *f; (med)* Packung *f;* **p. of cards** Spiel *n* Karten; **p. of lies** Lug und Trug ‖ *tr (a trunk)* packen; *(clothes)* einpacken; *(seal)* abdichten; **p. in** *(above normal capacity)* einpferchen; **p. up** zusammenpacken ‖ *intr* packen; **send s.o. packing** j–m Beine machen
package ['pækɪdʒ] *adj (price, tour, agreement)* Pauschal– ‖ *s* Paket *n* ‖ *tr* (ver)packen
pack'age deal' *s* Koppelgeschäft *n*
pack' an'imal *s* Packtier *n*
packet ['pækɪt] *s* Paket *n,* Päckchen *n;* (naut) Postschiff *n*
pack'ing *s (act)* Packen *n; (seal)* Dichtung *f; (wrapper)* Verpackung *f*
pack'ing case' *s* Packkiste *f*
pack'ing house' *s* Konservenfabrik *f*
pack'sad'dle *s* Packsattel *m*
pact [pækt] *s* Pakt *m;* **make a p.** paktieren
pad [pæd] *s (of writing paper)* Block *m; (ink pad)* Stempelkissen *n; (cushion)* Kissen *n; (of butter)* Stück *n; (under a rug)* Unterlage *f; (living quarters)* Bude *f;* (rok) Abschußrampe *f;* (sport) Schützer *m;* (surg) Bausch *m* ‖ *v (pret & pp* **padded;** *ger* **padding)** *tr (e.g., the shoulders)* wattieren; *(writing)* ausbauschen
pad'ded cell' *s* Gummizelle *f*
pad'ding *s* Wattierung *f;* (coll) Ballast *m*
paddle ['pædəl] *s (of a canoe)* Paddel *n; (for table tennis)* Schläger *m* ‖ *tr* paddeln; *(spank)* prügeln ‖ *intr* paddeln
pad'dle wheel' *s* Schaufelrad *n*
paddock ['pædək] *s* Pferdekoppel *f; (at the races)* Sattelplatz *m*
pad'dy wag'on ['pædi] *s* (sl) Grüne Minna *f*
pad'lock' *s* Vorhängeschloß *n* ‖ *tr* mit e–m Vorhängeschloß verschließen
paean ['pi·ən] *s* Siegeslied *n*
pagan ['pegən] *adj* heidnisch ‖ *s* Heide *m,* Heidin *f*
paganism ['pegə‚nɪzəm] *s* Heidentum *n*
page [pedʒ] *s* Seite *f; (in a hotel or club; at court)* Page *m* ‖ *tr (summon)* über den Lautsprecher (or durch Pagen) holen lassen ‖ *intr*— **p. through** durchblättern
pageant ['pædʒənt] *s* Festspiel *n; (procession)* Festzug *m*
pageantry ['pædʒəntri] *s* Schaugepränge *n*
page'boy' *s* Pagenfrisur *f*
page' proof' *s* Umbruchabzug *m*
pagoda [pə'godə] *s* Pagode *f*
paid' in full' [ped] *adj* voll bezahlt
paid'-up' *adj(debts)* abgezahlt; *(policy, capital)* voll eingezahlt
pail [pel] *s* Eimer *m*
pain [pen] *s* Schmerz *m;* **on p. of death** bei Todesstrafe; **take pains** sich bemühen ‖ *tr & intr* schmerzen ‖ *impers*—**it pains me to** *(inf)* es fällt mir schwer zu *(inf)*

painful ['penfəl] *adj* schmerzhaft; (fig) peinlich
pain' in the neck' *s* (coll) Nervensäge *f*
pain'kill'er *s* schmerzstillendes Mittel *n*
painless ['penlɪs] *adj* schmerzlos
pains'tak'ing *adj (work)* mühsam; *(person)* sorgfältig
paint [pent] *s* Farbe *f; (for a car)* Lack *m* ‖ *tr* (be)malen; *(e.g., a house)* (an) streichen; *(a car)* lackieren; *(with watercolors)* aquarellieren; (fig) schildern; **p. the town red** tüchtig auf die Pauke hauen ‖ *intr* malen; *(with house paint)* überstreichen
paint'box' *s* Malkasten *m*
paint'brush' *s* Pinsel *m*
paint' can' *s* Farbendose *f*
painter ['pentər] *s* Maler –in *mf; (of houses, etc.)* Anstreicher –in *mf*
paint'ing *s* Malerei *f; (picture)* Gemälde *n*
paint' remov'er *s* Farbenabbeizmittel *n*
paint' spray'er *s* Farbspritzpistole *f*
pair [per] *s* Paar *n;* **a p. of glasses** e–e Brille *f;* **a p. of gloves** ein Paar *n* Handschuhe; **a p. of pants** e–e Hose *f;* **a p. of scissors** e–e Schere *f;* **a p. of twins** ein Zwillingspaar *n;* **in pairs** paarweise ‖ *tr* paaren; **p. off** paarweise ordnen; (coll) verheiraten ‖ *intr*—**p. off** sich paarweise absondern
pajamas [pə'dʒɑməz] *s* Pyjama *m*
Pakistan ['pækɪ‚stæn] *s* Pakistan *n*
Pakista·ni [‚pækɪ'stæni] *adj* pakistanisch ‖ *s* (–nis) Pakistaner –in *mf*
pal [pæl] *s* Kamerad *m* ‖ *v (pret & pp* **palled;** *ger* **palling)** *intr*—**pal around with** dick befreundet sein mit
palace ['pælɪs] *s* Palast *m*
palatable ['pælətəbəl] *adj* (& fig) mundgerecht
palatal ['pælətəl] *adj* Gaumen– ‖ *s* (phonet) Gaumenlaut *m*
palate ['pælɪt] *s* Gaumen *m*
palatial [pə'le/əl] *adj* palastartig
Palatinate [pə'lætɪ‚net] *s* Rheinpfalz *f*
pale [pel] *adj (face, colors, recollection)* blaß; **turn pale** erblassen, erbleichen ‖ *s* Pfahl *m* ‖ *intr* erblassen; **pale beside** (fig) verblassen neben *(dat)*
pale'face' *s* Bleichgesicht *n*
Palestine ['pælɪs‚taɪn] *s* Palästina *n*
palette ['pælɪt] *s* Palette *f*
palisade [‚pælɪ'sed] *s* Palisade *f; (line of cliffs)* Flußklippen *pl*
pall [pɔl] *s* Bahrtuch *n; (of smoke, gloom)* Hülle *f* ‖ *intr* **(on)** zuviel werden *(dat)*
pall'bear'er *s* Sargträger *m*
pallet ['pælɪt] *s* Lager *n*
palliate ['pæli‚et] *tr* lindern; (fig) bemänteln
pallid ['pælɪd] *adj* blaß, bleich
pallor ['pælər] *s* Blässe *f*
palm [pɑm] *s (of the hand)* Handfläche *f; (tree)* Palme *f;* **grease s.o.'s palm** j–n schmieren; **palm of victory** Siegespalme *f* ‖ *tr (a card)* in der Hand verbergen; **palm s.th. off on s.o.** j–m etw andrehen

palmette [pæl'met] s Palmette f
palmet·to [pæl'meto] s (-tos & -toes) Fächerpalme f
palmist ['pɑmɪst] s Wahrsager –in mf
palmistry ['pɑmɪstri] s Handlesekunst f
palm' leaf' s Palmblatt n
Palm' Sun'day s Palmsonntag m
palm' tree' s Palme f
palpable ['pælpəbəl] adj greifbar
palpitate ['pælpɪ,tet] intr klopfen
palsied ['pɔlzid] adj lahm, gelähmt
palsy ['pɔlzi] s Lähmung f
paltry ['pɔltri] adj armselig
pamper ['pæmpər] tr verwöhnen
pamphlet ['pæmflɪt] s Flugschrift f
pan [pæn] s Pfanne f; (sl) Visage f || tr (gold) waschen; (a camera) schwenken; (criticize sharply) (coll) verreißen || intr (cin) panoramieren; **pan out** glücken, klappen
panacea [,pænə'si·ə] s Allheilmittel n
Panama ['pænəmɑ] s Panama n
Pan'ama Canal' s Panamakanal m
Pan-American [,pænə'merɪkən] adj panamerikanisch
pan'cake' s (flacher) Pfannkuchen m || intr (aer) absacken, bumslanden
pan'cake land'ing s Bumslandung f
panchromatic [,pænkro'mætɪk] adj panchromatisch
pancreas ['pænkrɪ·əs] s Bauchspeicheldrüse f
pandemic [pæn'dɛmɪk] adj pandemisch
pandemonium [,pændə'moni·əm] s Höllenlärm m
pander ['pændər] s Kuppler m || intr kuppeln; **p. to** Vorschub leisten (dat)
pane [pen] s Scheibe f
panegyric [,pænɪ'dʒɪrɪk] s Lobrede f
pan·el ['pænəl] s Tafel f, Feld n; (in a door) Füllung f; (for instruments) Schlattafel f; (of experts) Diskussionsgruppe f; (archit) Paneel n; (jur) Geschworenenliste f || v (pret & pp -el[l]ed; ger -el[l]ing) tr täfeln
pan'el discus'sion s Podiumsdiskussion f
pan'eling s Täfelung f
panelist ['pænəlɪst] s Diskussionsteilnehmer –in mf
pang [pæŋ] s stechender Schmerz m; (fig) Angst f; **pangs of conscience** Gewissensbisse pl; **pangs of hunger** nagender Hunger m
pan'han'dle s Pfannenstiel m; (geog) Landzunge f || intr (sl) betteln
pan'han'dler s (sl) Bettler –in mf
pan·ic ['pænɪk] s Panik f || v (pret & pp –icked; ger –icking) tr in Panik versetzen || intr von panischer Angst erfüllt werden
pan'ic-strick'en adj von panischem Schrecken erfaßt
panicky ['pænɪki] adj übernervös
panoply ['pænəpli] s Pracht f; (full suit of armor) vollständige Rüstung f
panorama [,pænə'ræmə] s Panorama n
pansy ['pænzi] s Stiefmütterchen n
pant [pænt] s Keuchen n; **pants** Hose f, Hosen pl || intr keuchen; **p. for or after** gieren nach

pantheism ['pænθɪ,ɪzəm] s Pantheismus m
pantheon ['pænθɪ,ɑn] s Pantheon n
panther ['pænθər] s Panther m
panties ['pæntiz] spl Schlüpfer m
pantomime ['pæntə,maɪm] s Pantomime f
pantry ['pæntri] s Speisekammer f
pap [pæp] s Brei m, Kleister m
papa ['pɑpə] s Papa m, Vati m
papacy ['pepəsi] s Papsttum n
papal ['pepəl] adj päpstlich
Pa'pal State' s Kirchenstaat m
paper ['pepər] adj (money, plate, towel) Papier– || s Papier n; (before a learned society) Referat n; (newspaper) Zeitung f; **papers** (documents) Papiere pl || tr tapezieren
pa'perback' s Taschenbuch n, Pappband m
pa'per bag' s Papiertüte f, Tüte f
pa'perboy' s Zeitungsjunge m
pa'per clip' s Büroklammer f
pa'per cone' s Tüte f
pa'per cup' s Papierbecher m
pa'per cut'ter s Papierschneidemaschine f
pa'perhang'er s Tapezierer –in mf
pa'perhang'ing s Tapezierarbeit f
pa'pering s Tapezieren n
pa'per mill' s Papierfabrik f
pa'per nap'kin s Papierserviette f
pa'perweight' s Briefbeschwerer m
pa'perwork' s Schreibarbeit f
papier-mâché [,pepərmə'ʃe] s Papiermaché n, Pappmaché n
paprika [pæ'prikə] s Paprika m
papy·rus [pə'paɪrəs] s (-ri [raɪ]) Papyrus m
par [pɑr] s (fin) Pari n; (golf) festgesetzte Schlagzahl f; **at par** pari, auf Pari; **on a par with** auf gleicher Stufe mit; **up to par** (coll) auf der Höhe
parable ['pærəbəl] s Gleichnis n
parabola [pə'ræbələ] s Parabel f
parachute ['pærə,ʃut] s Fallschirm m || tr mit dem Fallschirm abwerfen || intr abspringen
par'achute jump' s Fallschirmabsprung m
parachutist ['pærə,ʃutɪst] s Fallschirmspringer –in mf
parade [pə'red] s Parade f || tr zur Schau stellen || intr paradieren; (mil) aufmarschieren
paradigm ['pærədɪm], ['pærə,daɪm] s Musterbeispiel n, Paradigma n
paradise ['pærə,daɪs] s Paradies n
paradox ['pærə,dɑks] s Paradox n
paradoxical [,pærə'dɑksɪkəl] adj paradox
paraffin ['pærəfɪn] s Paraffin n
paragon ['pærə,gɑn] s Musterbild n
paragraph ['pærə,græf] s Absatz m, Paragraph m
parakeet ['pærə,kit] s Sittich m
paral·lel ['pærə,lel] adj parallel; **be (or run) p. to** parallel verlaufen zu || s Parallele f; (of latitude) Breiten-

kreis *m*; (fig) Gegenstück *n*; **without p.** ohnegleichen ‖ *v* (*pret & pp* –lel[l]ed; *ger* –lel[l]ing) *tr* parallel verlaufen zu; (*match*) gleichkommen (*dat*); (*correspond to*) entsprechen (*dat*)
par'allel bars' *spl* Barren *m*
paraly·sis [pə'rælɪsɪs] *s* (–ses [ˌsiz]) Lähmung *f*, Paralyse *f*
paralytic [ˌpærə'lɪtɪk] *adj* paralytisch ‖ *s* Paralytiker –in *mf*
paralyze ['pærəˌlaɪz] *tr* lähmen, paralysieren; (*traffic*) lahmlegen
parameter [pə'ræmɪtər] *s* Parameter *m*
paramilitary [ˌpærə'mɪlɪˌteri] *adj* halbmilitärisch
paramount ['pærəˌmaʊnt] *adj* oberste; **be p.** an erster Stelle stehen; **of p. importance** von äußerster Wichtigkeit
paranoia [ˌpærə'nɔɪ·ə] *s* Paranoia *f*
paranoiac [ˌpærə'nɔɪ·æk] *adj* paranoisch ‖ *s* Paranoiker –in *mf*
paranoid ['pærəˌnɔɪd] *adj* paranoid
parapet ['pærəˌpet] *s* (*of a wall*) Brustwehr *f*; (*of a balcony*) Geländer *n*
paraphernalia [ˌpærəfər'neli·ə] *s* Zubehör *n*, Ausrüstung *f*
paraphrase ['pærəˌfrez] *s* Umschreibung *f* ‖ *tr* umschreiben
parasite ['pærəˌsaɪt] *s* (& fig) Parasit *m*
parasitic(al) [ˌpærə'sɪtɪk(əl)] *adj* parasitisch
parasol ['pærəˌsɔl] *s* Sonnenschirm *m*
paratrooper ['pærəˌtrupər] *s* Fallschirmjäger *m*
par·cel ['pɑrsəl] *s* Paket *n*; (com) Posten *m* ‖ *v* (*pret & pp* –cel[l]ed; *ger* –cel[l]ing) *tr*—**p. out** aufteilen
par'cel post' *s* Paketpost *f*
parch [pɑrtʃ] *tr* ausdörren; **my throat is parched** mir klebt die Zunge am Gaumen
parchment ['pɑrtʃmənt] *s* Pergament *n*
pardon ['pɑrdən] *s* Verzeihung *f*; (jur) Begnadigung *f*; **I beg your p.** ich bitte um Entschuldigung; **p.?** wie, bitte? ‖ *tr* (*a person*) verzeihen (*dat*); (*an act*) verzeihen; (*officially*) begnadigen
pardonable ['pɑrdənəbəl] *adj* verzeihlich
pare [per] *tr* (*nails*) schneiden; (*e.g., potatoes*) (ab)schälen; (*costs*) beschneiden
parent ['perənt] *s* Elternteil *m*; **parents** Eltern *pl*
parentage ['perəntɪdʒ] *s* Abstammung *f*
parental [pə'rentəl] *adj* elterlich
parenthe·sis [pə'rɛnθɪsɪs] *s* (–ses [ˌsiz]) Klammer *f*; (*expression in parentheses*) Parenthese *f*
parenthetic(al) [ˌperən'θɛtɪk(əl)] *adj* parenthetisch
parenthood ['perəntˌhʊd] *s* Elternschaft *f*
pariah [pə'raɪ·ə] *s* Paria *m*
par'ing knife' *s* Schälmesser *n*
Paris ['pærɪs] *s* Paris *n*

parish ['pærɪʃ] *adv* Pfarr– ‖ *s* Pfarrgemeinde *f*
parishioner [pə'rɪʃənər] *s* Gemeindemitglied *n*, Pfarrkind *n*
Parisian [pə'rɪʒən] *adj* Pariser ‖ *s* Pariser –in *mf*
parity ['pærɪti] *s* Parität *f*
park [pɑrk] *s* Park *m* ‖ *tr* abstellen, parken ‖ *intr* parken
park'ing *s* Parken *n*; **no p.** (public sign) Parken verboten
park'ing light' *s* Parklicht *n*
park'ing lot' *s* Parkplatz *m*
park'ing lot' atten'dant' *s* Parkplatzwärter –in *mf*
park'ing me'ter *s* Parkuhr *f*
park'ing place', park'ing space *s* Parkplatz *m*, Parkstelle *f*
park'ing tick'et *s* gebührenpflichtige Verwarnung *f* (wegen falschen Parkens)
park'way' *s* Aussichtsautobahn *f*
parley ['pɑrli] *s* Unterhandlung *f* ‖ *intr* unterhandeln
parliament ['pɑrləmənt] *s* Parlament *n*
parliamentary [ˌpɑrlə'mentəri] *adj* parlamentarisch
parlor ['pɑrlər] *s* Salon *m*; (*living room*) Wohnzimmer *n*
par'lor game' *s* Gesellschaftsspiel *n*
parochial [pə'roki·əl] *adj* Pfarr–; (fig) beschränkt
paro'chial school' *s* Pfarrschule *f*
paro·dy ['pærədi] *s* Parodie *f* ‖ *v* (*pret & pp* –died) *tr* parodieren
parole [pə'rol] *s* bedingte Strafaussetzung *f*; **be out on p.** bedingt entlassen sein ‖ *tr* bedingt entlassen
par·quet [pɑr'ke], [pɑr'ket] *v* (*pret & pp* –queted ['ked]; *ger* –queting ['keˌɪŋ]) *tr* parkettieren
parquetry ['pɑrkɪtri] *s* Parkettfußboden *m*
parrot ['pærət] *s* Papagei *m* ‖ *tr* nachplappern
par·ry ['pæri] *s* Parade *f* ‖ *v* (*pret & –ried*) *tr* parieren
parse [pɑrs] *tr* zergliedern
parsimonious [ˌpɑrsɪ'moni·əs] *adj* sparsam
parsley ['pɑrsli] *s* Petersilie *f*
parsnip ['pɑrsnɪp] *s* Pastinak *m*
parson ['pɑrsən] *s* Pfarrer *m*
parsonage ['pɑrsənɪdʒ] *s* Pfarrhaus *n*
part [pɑrt] *adv*—**p. ... p.** zum Teil ... zum Teil ‖ *s* Teil *m & n*; (*section*) Abschnitt *m*; (*spare part*) Ersatzteil *m*; (*of a machine, etc.*) Bestandteil *m*; (*share*) Anteil *m*; (*of the hair*) Scheitel *m*; (mus) Partie *f*; (theat) Rolle *f*; **do one's p.** das Seinige tun; **for his p.** seinerseits; **for the most p.** größtenteils; **have a p. in** Anteil haben an (*dat*); **in p.** zum Teil, teilweise; **make a p.** (*in the hair*) e–n Scheitel ziehen; **on his p.** seinerseits; **part and parcel** ein wesentlicher Bestandteil *m*; **take p.** (in) teilnehmen (an *dat*); **take s.o.'s p.** j–s Partei ergreifen ‖ *tr* (ab)scheiden; (*the hair*) scheiteln; **p. company** von

einander scheiden ‖ *intr* sich trennen; **p. with** hergeben
par·take [pɑr'tek] *v* (*pret* –**took;** *pp* **taken**) *intr*—**p. in** teilnehmen an (*dat*); **p. of** zu sich nehmen
partial ['pɑrʃəl] *adj* Teil-, partiell; (*prejudiced*) parteiisch; **be p. to** bevorzugen
partiality [ˌpɑrʃɪ'ælɪti] *s* Parteilichkeit *f*, Befangenheit *f*
partially ['pɑrʃəli] *adv* teilweise
participant [pɑr'tɪsɪpənt] *s* Teilnehmer –in *mf*
participate [pɑr'tɪsɪˌpet] *intr* (**in**) teilnehmen (an *dat*)
participation [pɑrˌtɪsɪ'peʃən] *s* (**in**) Teilnahme *f* (*an* dat)
participle ['pɑrtɪˌsɪpəl] *s* Mittelwort *n*, Partizip *n*
particle ['pɑrtɪkəl] *s* Teilchen *n;* (gram, phys) Partikel *f*
particular [pɑr'tɪkjələr] *adj* (*specific*) bestimmt; (*individual*) einzeln; (*meticulous*) peinlich genau; (*especial*) peinlich genau; (*choosy*) heikel ‖ *s* Einzelheit *f;* **in p.** insbesondere
partisan ['pɑrtɪzən] *adj* parteiisch ‖ *s* (mil) Partisan –in *mf;* (pol) Parteigänger –in *mf*
partition [pɑr'tɪʃən] *s* Teilung *f;* (*wall*) Scheidewand *f* ‖ *tr* (auf)teilen; **p. off** abteilen
partly ['pɑrtli] *adv* teils, teilweise
partner ['pɑrtnər] *s* Partner –in *mf*
part'nership' *s* Partnerschaft *f*
part' of speech' *s* Wortart *f*
partridge ['pɑrtrɪdʒ] *s* Rebhuhn *n*
part'-time' *adj & adv* nicht vollzeitlich
part'-time work' *s* Teilzeitarbeit *f*
party ['pɑrti] *s* Gesellschaft *f*, Party *f;* (jur) Partei *f;* (mil) Kommando *n;* (pol) Partei *f;* (telp) Teilnehmer –in *mf;* **be a p. to** sich hergeben zu
par'ty affilia'tion *s* Parteizugehörigkeit *f*
par'ty line' *s* (pol) Parteilinie *f;* (telp) Gemeinschaftsanschluß *m*
par'ty mem'ber *s* Parteigenosse *m*, Parteigenossin *f*
par'ty pol'itics *s* Parteipolitik *f*
paschal ['pæskəl] *adj* Oster-
pass [pæs] *s* (*over a mountain; permit*) Paß *m;* (*erotic advance*) Annäherungsversuch *m;* (fencing) Stoß *m;* (fb) Paßball *m;* (mil) Urlaubsschein *m;* (theat) Freikarte *f;* **make a p. at** (*flirt with*) e–n Annäherungsversuch machen bei; (aer) vorbeifliegen an (*dat*) ‖ *tr* (*go by*) vorbeigehen an (*dat*), passieren; (*a test*) bestehen; (*a student in a test*) durchlassen; (*a bill*) verabschieden; (*hand over*) reichen; (*judgment*) abgeben; (*sentence*) sprechen; (*time*) verbringen; (*counterfeit money*) in Umlauf bringen; (*a car*) überholen; (*e.g., a kidney stone*) ausscheiden; (*a ball*) weitergeben; (*to*) zuspielen (*dat*); **p. around** herumgeben lassen; **p. away** (*time*) vertreiben; **p. in** einhändigen; **p. off as** ausgeben als; **p. on** weiterleiten; (*e.g., news*) weitersagen; **p.**

out ausgeben; **p. over in silence** unerwähnt lassen; **p. up** verzichten auf (*acc*) ‖ *intr* (by) vorbeikommen (an *dat*), vorbeigehen (an *dat*); (*in a car*) (by) vorbeifahren (an *dat*); (*in a test*) durchkommen; (*e.g., from father to son*) übergehen; (cards) passen; (parl) zustandekommen; **bring to p.** herbeiführen; **come to p.** geschehen; **p.!** (cards) passe!; **p. away** verscheiden; **p. for** gelten als; **p. on** abscheiden; **p. out** ohnmächtig werden; **p. over** (*disregard*) hinweggehen über (*acc*); **p. through** durchgehen (*durch*); (*said of an army*) durchziehen (*durch*); (*said of a train*) berühren
passable ['pæsəbəl] *adj* (*road*) gangbar; (*by car*) befahrbar; (*halfway good*) leidlich, passabel
passage ['pæsɪdʒ] *s* Korridor *m*, Gang *m;* (*crossing*) Überfahrt *f;* (*in a book*) Stelle *f;* (*of a law*) Annahme *f;* (*of time*) Ablauf *m;* **book p. for** e–e Schiffskarte bestellen nach
pas'sageway' *s* Durchgang *m*, Passage *f*
pass'book' *s* Sparbuch *n*
passenger ['pæsəndʒər] *s* Passagier –in *mf;* (*in public transportation*) Fahrgast *m;* (*in a car*) Insasse *m*, Insassin *f*
pas'senger car' *s* Personenkraftwagen *m*
pas'senger plane' *s* Passagierflugzeug *n*
pas'senger train' *s* Personenzug *m*
passer-by ['pæsər'baɪ] *s* (passers-by) Passant –in *mf*
pass'ing *adj* vorübergehend; **a p. grade** die Note „befriedigend" ‖ *s* (*act of passing*) Vorbeigehen *n;* (*of a law*) Verabschiedung *f;* (*of time*) Verstreichen *n;* (*dying*) Hinscheiden *n;* **in p.** im Vorbeigehen; (*as understatement*) beiläufig; **no p.** (public sign) Überholen verboten
passion ['pæʃən] *s* Leidenschaft *f;* (*of Christ*) Passion *f;* **fly into a p.** in Zorn geraten; **have a p. for** e–e Vorliebe haben für
passionate ['pæʃənɪt] *adj* leidenschaftlich
pas'sion play' *s* Passionsspiel *n*
passive ['pæsɪv] *adj* (& gram) passiv ‖ *s* Passiv(um) *n*
pass'key' *s* (*master key*) Hauptschlüssel *m;* (*skeleton key*) Nachschlüssel *m*
Pass'o'ver *s* Passah *n*
pass'port *s* Paß *m*, Reisepaß *m*
pass'port of'fice *s* Paßamt *n*
pass'word' *s* (mil) Kennwort *n*
past [pæst] *adj* (*e.g., week*) vergangen; (*e.g., president*) ehemalig, früher; (*gone*) vorbei; **for some time p.** seit einiger Zeit ‖ *s* Vergangenheit *f* ‖ *prep* (*e.g., one o'clock*) nach; (*beyond*) über (*acc*) hinaus; **get p.** (*an opponent*) (sport) umspielen; **go p.** vorbeigehen an (*dat*); **it's way p. bedtime** es ist schon längst Zeit zum Schlafengehen
paste [pest] *s* (*glue*) Kleister *m;* (culin) Brei *m*, Paste *f* ‖ *tr* (*e.g., a wall*) (with) bekleben (mit); **p. on** aufkle-

ben auf (*acc*); **p. together** zusammenkleben

paste'board' *s* Pappe *f*

pastel [pæs'tel] *adj* pastellfarben || *s* Pastell *n*

pastel' col'or *s* Pastellfarbe *f*

pasteurize ['pæstə‚raɪz] *tr* pasteurisieren

pastime ['pæs‚taɪm] *s* Zeitvertreib *m*

past' mas'ter *s* Experte *m*

pastor ['pæstər] *s* Pastor *m*

pastoral ['pæstərəl] *adj* Schäfer-, Hirten-; (eccl) Hirten-, pastoral || *s* Schäfergedicht *n*

pas'toral let'ter *s* Hirtenbrief *m*

pastorate ['pæstərɪt] *s* Pastorat *n*

pastry ['pestri] *s* Gebäck *n;* **pastries** Backwaren *pl*

pas'try shop' *s* Konditorei *f*

past' tense' *s* Vergangenheit *f*

pasture ['pæst/ər] *s* Weide *f* || *tr & intr* weiden

pas'ture land' *s* Weideland *n*

pasty ['pesti] *adj* (*sticky*) klebrig; (*complexion*) bläßlich

pat [pæt] *adj* (*answer*) treffend; **have s.th. down pat** etw in- und auswendig wissen || *adv*—**stand pat** bei der Stange bleiben || *s* Klaps *m;* (*of butter*) Klümpchen *n* || *tr* tätscheln; **pat s.o. on the back** j–m auf die Schulter klopfen; (fig) j–n beglückwünschen

patch [pæt/] *s* (*of clothing, land, color*) Fleck *m;* (*garden bed*) Beet *n;* (*for clothing, inner tube*) Flicken *m;* (*over the eye*) Binde *f;* (*for a wound*) Pflaster *n* || *tr* flicken; **p. together** (& fig) zusammenflicken; **p. up** (*a friendship*) kitten; (*differences*) beilegen

patch'work' *s* Flickwerk *n;* (fig) Stückwerk *n*

patch'work quilt' *s* Flickendecke *f*

pate [pet] *s* (coll) Schädel *m*

patent ['petənt] *adj* öffentlich || ['pætənt] *adj* Patent-, e.g., **p. lawyer** Patentanwalt *m* || *s* Patent *n;* **p. pending** Patent angemeldet || *tr* patentieren

pa'tent leath'er ['pætənt] *s* Lackleder *n*

pa'tent-leath'er shoe' *s* Lackschuh *m*

pat'ent med'icine ['pætənt] *s* rezeptfreies Medikament *n*

pat'ent rights' ['pætənt] *spl* Schutzrechte *pl*

paternal [pə'tʌrnəl] *adj* väterlich

paternity [pə'tʌrnɪti] *s* Vaterschaft *f*

path [pæθ] *s* Pfad *m;* (astr) Lauf *m;* **clear a p.** e–n Weg bahnen; **cross s.o.'s p.** j–s Weg kreuzen

pathetic [pə'θɛtɪk] *adj* (*moving*) rührend; (*evoking contemptuous pity*) kläglich

path'find'er *s* Pfadfinder *m;* (aer) Beleuchter *m*

pathologist [pə'θɑlədʒɪst] *s* Pathologe *m,* Pathologin *f*

pathology [pə'θɑlədʒi] *s* Pathologie *f*

pathos ['peθɑs] *s* Pathos *n*

path'way' *s* Weg *m,* Pfad *m*

patience ['pe/əns] *s* Geduld *f*

patient ['pe/ənt] *adj* geduldig || *s* Patient –in *mf*

pati‧o ['pætɪ‧o] *s* (**-os**) Terasse *f*

patriarch ['petri‚ɑrk] *s* Patriarch *m*

patrician [pə'trɪ/ən] *adj* patrizisch || *s* Patrizier –in *mf*

patricide ['pætri‚saɪd] *s* (*act*) Vatermord *m;* (*person*) Vatermörder –in *mf*

patrimony ['pætri‚moni] *s* väterliches Erbe *n*

patriot ['petri‧ət] *s* Patriot –in *mf*

patriotic [‚petri'ɑtɪk] *adj* patriotisch

patriotism ['petri‧ə‚tɪzəm] *s* Patriotismus *m*

pa‧trol [pə'trol] *s* Patrouille *f,* Streife *f* || *v* (*pret & pp* **-trolled;** *ger* **-trolling**) *tr & intr* patrouillieren

patrol' car' *s* Streifenwagen *m*

patrol'man *s* (**-men**) Polizeistreife *f*

patrol' wag'on *s* Gefangenenwagen *m*

patron ['petrən] *s* Schutzherr *m;* (com) Kunde *m,* Kundin *f;* (eccl) Schutzpatron *m*

patronage ['petrənɪdʒ] *s* Patronat *n*

patroness ['petrənɪs] *s* Schutzherrin *f;* (eccl) Schutzpatronin *f*

patronize ['petrə‚naɪz] *tr* beschützen, protegieren; (com) als Kunde besuchen; (theat) regelmäßig besuchen

pa'tronizing *adj* gönnerhaft

pa'tron saint' *s* Schutzheilige *mf*

patter ['pætər] *s* (*of rain*) Prasseln *n;* (*of feet*) Getrappel *n* || *intr* (*said of rain*) prasseln; (*said of feet*) trappeln

pattern ['pætərn] *s* Muster *n;* (sew) Schnittmuster *n*

patty ['pæti] *s* Pastetchen *n*

paucity ['pɔsɪti] *s* Knappheit *f*

paunch [pɔnt/] *s* Wanst *m*

paunchy ['pɔn/i] *adj* dickbäuchig

pauper ['pɔpər] *s* Arme *mf;* (*person on welfare*) Unterstützte *mf*

pause [pɔz] *s* Pause *f;* (mus) Fermate *f* || *intr* pausieren

pave [pev] *tr* pflastern; **p. the way for** (fig) anbahnen

pavement ['pevmənt] *s* Pflaster *n;* (*sidewalk*) Bürgersteig *m,* Trottoir *n*

pavilion [pə'vɪljən] *s* Pavillon *m*

pav'ing *s* Pflasterung *f*

pav'ing stone' *s* Pflasterstein *m*

paw [pɔ] *s* Pfote *f* || *tr* (*scratch*) kratzen; (coll) befummeln; **paw the ground** auf dem Boden scharren || *intr* (*said of a horse*) mit dem Huf scharren

pawl [pɔl] *s* Sperrklinke *f*

pawn [pɔn] *s* Pfand *n;* (fig) Schachfigur *f;* (chess) Bauer *m* || *tr* verpfänden

pawn'brok'er *s* Pfandleiher –in *mf*

pawn'shop' *s* Pfandhaus *n*

pawn' tick'et *s* Pfandschein *m*

pay [pe] *s* Lohn *m;* (mil) Sold *m* || *v* (*pret & pp* **paid** [ped]) *tr* bezahlen; (*a visit*) abstatten; (*a dividend*) ausschütten; (*a compliment*) machen; **pay back** zurückzahlen; **pay damages** Schadenersatz leisten; **pay down** anzahlen; **pay extra** nachzahlen; **pay in advance** vorausbezahlen; **pay in full**

begleichen; **pay interest on** verzinsen; **pay off** (*a debt*) abbezahlen; (*a person*) entlohnen; **pay one's way** ohne Verlust arbeiten; **pay out** auszahlen; **pay s.o. back for s.th.** j–m etw heimzahlen; **pay taxes on** versteuern; **pay up** (*a debt*) abbezahlen; (ins) voll einzahlen ‖ *intr* zahlen; (*be worthwhile*) sich lohnen; **pay extra** zuzahlen; **pay for** (*a purchase*) (be)zahlen für; (*suffer for*) büßen
payable ['pe·əbəl] *adj* fällig, zahlbar
pay' check' *s* Lohnscheck *m*
pay'day' *s* Zahltag *m*
pay' dirt' *s*—**hit p.** sein Glück machen
payee [pe'i] *s* (*of a draft*) Zahlungsempfänger –in *mf*; (*of a check*) Wechselnehmer –in *mf*
pay' en'velope *s* Lohntüte *f*
payer ['pe·ər] *s* Zahler –in *mf*
pay'load' *s* Nutzlast *f*; (*explosive energy*) Sprengladung *f*
pay'mas'ter *s* Zahlmeister *m*
payment ['pemənt] *s* Zahlung *f*; **in p. of** zur Bezahlung (*genit*)
pay' phone' *s* Münzfernsprecher *m*
pay' raise' *s* Gehaltserhöhung *f*
pay' rate' *s* Lohnsatz *m*
pay'roll' *s* Lohnliste *f*; (*money paid*) gesamte Lohnsumme *f*
pay' sta'tion *s* Telephonautomat *m*
pea [pi] *s* Erbse *f*
peace [pis] *s* Friede(n) *m*; (*quiet*) Ruhe *f*; **be at p. with** in Frieden leben mit; **keep the p.** die öffentliche Ruhe bewahren
peaceable ['pisəbəl] *adj* friedfertig
Peace' Corps' *s* Friedenskorps *n*
peace'-lov'ing *adj* friedliebend
peace'mak'er *s* Friedensstifter –in *mf*
peace' negotia'tions *spl* Friedensverhandlungen *pl*
peace' of mind' *s* Seelenruhe *f*
peace'pipe' *s* Friedenspfeife *f*
peace'time' *adj* Friedens– ‖ *s*—**in p.** in Friedenszeiten
peace' trea'ty *s* Friedensvertrag *m*
peach [pit/] *s* Pfirsich *m*
peach' tree' *s* Pfirsichbaum *m*
peachy ['pit/i] *adj* (coll) pfundig
pea'cock' *s* Pfau *m*
pea'hen' *s* Pfauenhenne *f*
pea' jack'et *s* (nav) Matrosenjacke *f*
peak [pik] *adj* Spitzen– ‖ *s* (& fig) Gipfel *m*; (*of a cap*) Mützenschirm *m*; (elec) Leistungsspitze *f*; (phys) Scheitelwert *m*
peak' hours' *spl* (*of traffic*) Hauptverkehrszeit *f*; (elec) Stoßzeit *f*
peak' load' *s* (elec) Spitzenlast *f*
peak' vol'tage *s* Spitzenspannung *f*
peal [pil] *s* Geläute *n* ‖ *intr* erschallen
peal' of laugh'ter *s* Lachsalve *f*
peal' of thun'der *s* Donnergetöse *n*
pea'nut' *s* Erdnuß *f*; **peanuts** (coll) kleine Fische *pl*
pea'nut but'ter *s* Erdnußbutter *f*
pear [per] *s* Birne *f*
pearl [pʌrl] *adj* Perlen– ‖ *s* Perle *f*
pearl' neck'lace *s* Perlenkette *f*
pearl' oys'ter *s* Perlenauster *f*
pear' tree' *s* Birnbaum *m*

peasant ['pεzənt] *adj* Bauern–, bäuerlich ‖ *s* Bauer *m*, Bäuerin *f*
peasantry ['pεzəntri] *s* Bauernstand *m*
pea'shoot'er *s* Blasrohr *n*
pea' soup' *s* Erbsensuppe *f*; (fig) Waschküche *f*
peat [pit] *s* Torf *m*
peat' moss' *s* Torfmull *m*
pebble ['pεbəl] *s* Kiesel *m*; **pebbles** Geröll *n*
peck [pεk] *s* (*measure*) Viertelscheffel *m*; (*e.g., of a bird*) Schnabelhieb *n*; (*kiss*) (coll) flüchtiger Kuß *m*; (*of trouble*) (coll) Menge *f* ‖ *tr* hacken; (*food*) aufpicken ‖ *intr* hacken, picken; (*eat food*) picken; **p. at** hacken nach; (*food*) (coll) herumstochern in (*dat*)
peculation [,pεkjə'le/ən] *s* Gelduntschlagung *f*
peculiar [pɪ'kjuljər] *adj* eigenartig, absonderlich; **p. to** eigen (*dat*)
peculiarity [,pɪkjulɪ'ærɪti] *s* Eigenheit *f*, Absonderlichkeit *f*
pedagogic(al) [,pεdə'gadʒɪk(əl)] *adj* pädagogisch, erzieherisch
pedagogue ['pεdə,gag] *s* Pädagoge *m*, Erzieher *m*
pedagogy ['pεdə,gadʒi] *s* Pädagogik *f*, Erziehungskunde *f*
ped·al ['pεdəl] *s* Pedal *n* ‖ *v* (*pret & pp* –al[l]ed; *ger* –al[l]ing) *tr* fahren ‖ *intr* die Pedale treten
pedant ['pεdənt] *s* Pedant –in *mf*
pedantic [pɪ'dæntɪk] *adj* pedantisch
pedantry ['pεdəntri] *s* Pedanterie *f*
peddle ['pεdəl] *tr* hausieren mit ‖ *intr* hausieren
peddler ['pεdlər] *s* Hausierer –in *mf*
pedestal ['pεdɪstəl] *s* Sockel *m*, Postament *n*; **put s.o. on a p.** (fig) j–n aufs Podest erheben
pedestrian [pɪ'dεstrɪ·ən] *adj* Fußgänger–; (fig) schwunglos ‖ *s* Fußgänger –in *mf*
pediatrician [,pidɪ·ə'trɪ/ən] *s* Kinderarzt *m*, Kinderärztin *f*
pediatrics [,pidɪ'ætrɪks] *s* Kinderheilkunde *f*
pediment ['pεdɪmənt] *s* Giebelfeld *n*
peek [pik] *s* schneller Blick *m* ‖ *intr* gucken; **p. at** angucken
peekaboo ['pikə,bu] *adj* durchsichtig ‖ *interj* guck, guck!
peel [pil] *s* Schale *f* ‖ *tr* schälen; **p. off** abschälen ‖ *intr* sich schälen; (*said of paint*) abbröckeln; **p. off** (aer) sich aus dem Verband lösen
peep [pip] *s* schneller Blick *m*; heimlicher Blick *m*; **not another p. out of you!** kein Laut mehr aus dir! ‖ *intr* gucken; (*look carefully*) lugen; **p. out** hervorlugen
peep'hole' *s* Guckloch *n*
peep' show' *s* Fleischbeschau *f*
peer [pɪr] *s* Gleichgestellte *mf* ‖ *intr* blicken; **p. at** mustern
peerless ['pɪrlɪs] *adj* unvergleichlich
peeve [piv] *s* (coll) Beschwerde *f* ‖ *tr* (coll) ärgern
peeved *adj* verärgert
peevish ['pivɪ/] *adj* sauertöpfisch

peg [pɛg] *s* Pflock *m*; *(for clothes)* Haken *m*; *(e.g., of a violin)* Wirbel *m*; **take down a peg or two** ducken ‖ *v* *(pret & pp* **pegged**; *ger* **pegging)** *tr* festpflocken; *(prices)* festlegen; *(throw)* (sl) schmeißen; *(identify)* (sl) erkennen

peg'board' *s* Klammerplatte *f*

Peggy ['pɛgi] *s* Gretchen *n*, Gretl *f* & *n*

peg' leg' *s* Stelzbein *n*

Pekin·ese [,pikɪ'niz] *s* (**-ese**) Pekinese *m*

pelf [pɛlf] *s* (pej) Mammon *m*

pelican ['pɛlɪkən] *s* Pelikan *m*

pellet ['pɛlɪt] *s* Kügelchen *n*; *(bullet)* Schrotkugel *f*, Schrotkorn *n*

pell-mell ['pɛl'mɛl] *adj* verworren ‖ *adv* durcheinander

pelt [pɛlt] *s* Fell *n*, Pelz *m*; *(whack)* Schlag *m* ‖ *tr* (**with**) bewerfen (mit); *(with questions)* bombardieren

pelvis ['pɛlvɪs] *s* Becken *n*

pen [pɛn] *s* Feder *f*; *(fountain pen)* Füllfederhalter *m*; *(enclosure)* Pferch *m*; *(prison)* (sl) Kittchen *n* ‖ *v* *(pret & pp* **penned**; *ger* **penning)** *tr* *(a letter)* verfassen ‖ *(pret & pp* **penned** & **pent**; *ger* **penning)** *tr*—**pen in** pferchen

penal ['pinəl] *adj* strafrechtlich, Straf—

pe'nal code' *s* Strafgesetzbuch *n*

penalize ['pinə,laɪz] *tr* bestrafen; (box) mit Strafpunkten belegen

penalty ['pɛnəlti] *s* Strafe *f*; *(point deducted)* (sport) Strafpunkt *m*; **under p. of death** bei Todesstrafe

pen'alty ar'ea *s* (sport) Strafraum *m*

pen'alty box' *s* Strafbank *f*

pen'alty kick' *s* Strafstoß *m*

penance ['pɛnəns] *s* Buße *f*

penchant ['pɛnʃənt] *s* (**for**) Hang *m* (zu)

pen·cil ['pɛnsəl] *s* Bleistift *m* ‖ *v* *(pret & pp* **-cil[l]ed**; *ger* **-cil[l]ing)** *tr* mit Bleistift anzeichnen

pen'cil push'er *s* (coll) Schreiberling *m*

pen'cil sharp'ener *s* Bleistiftspitzer *m*

pendant ['pɛndənt] *s* Anhänger *m*; *(electrical fixture)* Hängeleuchter *m*

pendent ['pɛndənt] *adj* (herab)hängend

pend'ing *adj* schwebend; **be p. in** (der) Schwebe sein ‖ *prep* *(during)* während *(genit)*; *(until)* bis zu *(dat)*

pendulum ['pɛndʒələm] *s* Pendel *n*

pen'dulum bob' *s* Pendelgewicht *n*

penetrate ['pɛnɪ,tret] *tr* eindringen in *(acc)* ‖ *intr* eindringen

penetration [,pɛnɪ'treʃən] *s* Durchdringen *n*; *(of, e.g., a country)* Eindringen *n* *(in acc)*; *(in ballistics)* Durchschlagskraft *f*

penguin ['pɛngwɪn] *s* Pinguin *m*

penicillin [,pɛnɪ'sɪlɪn] *s* Penizillin *n*

peninsula [pə'nɪnsələ] *s* Halbinsel *f*

pe·nis ['pinɪs] *s* (**-nes** [niz] & **-nises**) Penis *m*

penitence ['pɛnɪtəns] *s* Bußfertigkeit *f*

penitent ['pɛnɪtənt] *adj* bußfertig ‖ *s* Büßer –in *mf*; *(eccl)* Beichtkind *n*

penitentiary [,pɛnɪ'tɛnʃəri] *s* Zuchthaus *n*

pen'knife' *s* (**-knives'**) Federmesser *n*

penmanship ['pɛnmən,ʃɪp] *s* Schreibkunst *f*

pen' name' *s* Schriftstellername *m*

pennant ['pɛnənt] *s* Wimpel *m*; (nav) Stander *m*

penniless ['pɛnɪlɪs] *adj* mittellos

penny ['pɛni] *s* Pfennig *m*; *(U.S.A.)* Cent *m*

pen'ny pinch'er [,pɪntʃər] *s* Pfennigfuchser *m*

pen' pal' *s* Schreibfreund –in *mf*

pension ['pɛnʃən] *s* Pension *f*, Rente *f*; **put on p.** pensionieren ‖ *tr* pensionieren

pensioner ['pɛnʃənər] *s* Pensionär –in *mf*; (ins) Rentenempfänger –in *mf*

pen'sion fund' *s* Pensionskasse *f*

pensive ['pɛnsɪv] *adj* sinnend

pentagon ['pɛntə,gan] *s* Fünfeck *n*; **the Pentagon** das Pentagon

Pentecost ['pɛntɪ,kɔst] *s* Pfingsten *n*

penthouse ['pɛnt,haʊs] *s* Wetterdach *n*; *(exclusive apartment)* Penthouse *n*

pent-up ['pɛnt'ʌp] *adj* verhalten

penult ['pinʌlt] *s* vorletzte Silbe *f*

penurious [pɪ'nʊrɪ-əs] *adj* karg

penury ['pɛnjəri] *s* Kargheit *f*

peony ['pi-əni] *s* Pfingstrose *f*

people ['pipəl] *spl* Leute *pl*, Menschen *pl*; **his p. die Seinen**; **p. like him** seinesgleichen; **p.** say man sagt, die Leute sagen ‖ *s* (**peoples**) Volk *n* ‖ *tr* bevölkern

pep [pɛp] *s* (coll) Schwungkraft *f* ‖ *v* *(pret & pp* **pepped**; *ger* **pepping)** *tr*— **pep up** aufpulvern

pepper ['pɛpər] *s* *(spice)* Pfeffer *m*; *(plant)* Paprika *f*; *(vegetable)* Paprikaschote *f* ‖ *tr* pfeffern

pep'per mill' *s* Pfeffermühle *f*

pep'permint' *adj* Pfefferminz– ‖ *s* Pfefferminze *f*

pep'per shak'er *s* Pfefferstreuer *m*

peppery ['pɛpəri] *adj* pfefferig

per [pʌr] *prep* pro *(acc)*; **as per** laut *(genit & dat)*

perambulator [pər'æmbjə,letər] *s* Kinderwagen *m*

per capita [pər'kæpɪtə] pro Kopf

perceivable [pər'sivəbəl] *adj* wahrnehmbar

perceive [pər'siv] *tr* wahrnehmen

percent [pər'sɛnt] *s* Prozent *n*

percentage [pər'sɛntɪdʒ] *s* Prozentsatz *m*; **p. of** *(e.g., the profit)* Anteil *m* an *(dat)*; *(e.g., of a group)* Teil *m* *(genit)*

perceptible [pər'sɛptəbəl] *adj* wahrnehmbar

perception [pər'sɛpʃən] *s* Wahrnehmung *f*

perch [pʌrtʃ] *s* Stange *f*; (ichth) Barsch *m* ‖ *tr* setzen ‖ *intr* sitzen

percolate ['pʌrkə,let] *tr* durchseihen; *(coffee)* perkolieren ‖ *intr* durchsickern

percolator ['pʌrkə,letər] *s* Perkolator *m*

percussion [pər'kʌʃən] *s* Schlag *m*; (med) Perkussion *f*

percus'sion in'strument *s* Schlaginstrument *n*

per di'em allow'ance [pər'daɪ·əm] *s* Tagegeld *n*
perdition [pər'dɪʃən] *s* Verdammnis *f*
perennial [pə'renɪ·əl] *adj* immerwährend; (bot) ausdauernd ‖ *s* ausdauernde Pflanze *f*
perfect ['pʌrfɪkt] *adj* perfekt, vollkommen; **he is a p.** stranger to me er ist mir völlig fremd ‖ *s* (gram) Perfekt(um) *n* ‖ [pər'fɛkt] *tr* vervollkommen
perfection [pər'fɛkʃən] *s* Vollkommenheit *f;* **to p.** vollkommen
perfectionist [pər'fɛkʃənɪst] *s* Perfektionist –in *mf*
perfectly ['pʌrfɪktli] *adv* völlig, durchaus; **p.** well ganz genau
perfidious [pər'fɪdɪ·əs] *adj* treulos
perfidy ['pʌrfɪdi] *s* Treubruch *m*
perforate ['pʌrfə‚ret] *tr* durchlöchern
per'forated line' *s* durchlochte Linie *f*
perforation [‚pʌrfə're ʃən] *s* gelochte Linie *f*
perforce [pər'fɔrs] *adv* notgedrungen
perform [pər'fɔrm] *tr* ausführen; (an operation) vornehmen; (theat) aufführen ‖ *intr* (öffentlich) auftreten; (mach) funktionieren
performance [pər'fɔrməns] *s* Ausführung *f;* (mach) Leistung *f;* (theat) Aufführung *f*
performer [pər'fɔrmər] *s* Künstler –in *mf*
perform'ing arts' *spl* darstellende Künste *pl*
perfume [pər'fjum] *s* Parfüm *n* ‖ *tr* parfümieren
perfunctorily [pər'fʌŋktərɪli] *adv* oberflächlich
perfunctory [pər'fʌŋktəri] *adj* oberflächlich
perhaps [pər'hæps] *adv* vielleicht
per hour' pro Stunde, in der Stunde
peril ['perɪl] *s* Gefahr *f;* **at one's own p.** auf eigene Gefahr
perilous ['perɪləs] *adj* gefährlich
perimeter [pə'rɪmɪtər] *s* (math) Umfang *m;* (mil) Rand *m*
period ['pɪrɪ·əd] *s* Periode *f,* Zeitabschnitt *m;* (menstrual period) Periode *f;* (educ) Stunde *f;* (gram) Punkt *m;* (sport) Viertel *n;* **extra p.** (sport) Verlängerung *f;* **for a p. of** für die Dauer von; **p.!** und damit punktum!; **p. of grace** Frist *f;* **p. of life** Lebensalter *n;* **p. of time** Zeitdauer *pl*
pe'riod fur'niture *s* Stilmöbel *pl*
periodic [‚pɪrɪ'ɑdɪk] *adj* zeitweilig
periodical [‚pɪrɪ'ɑdɪkəl] *s* Zeitschrift *f*
peripheral [pə'rɪfərəl] *adj* peripher
periphery [pə'rɪfəri] *s* Peripherie *f*
periscope ['perɪ‚skop] *s* Periskop *n*
perish ['perɪʃ] *intr* umkommen; (said of wares) verderben
perishable ['perɪʃəbəl] *adj* vergänglich; (food) leicht verderblich
perjure ['pʌrdʒər] *tr—***p. oneself** Meineid begehen
perjury ['pʌrdʒəri] *s* Meineid *m;* **commit p.** e–n Meineid leisten
perk [pʌrk] *tr—***p. up** (the head) aufwerfen; (the ears) spitzen ‖ *intr*

(percolate) (coll) perkolieren; **p. up** lebhaft werden
permanence ['pʌrmənəns] *s* Dauer *f*
permanent ['pʌrmənənt] *adj* (for*t*)-dauernd, bleibend ‖ *s* Dauerwelle *f*
per'manent address' *s* ständiger Wohnort *m*
per'manent job' *s* Dauerstellung *f*
per'manent wave' *s* Dauerwelle *f*
permeable ['pʌrmɪ·əbəl] *adj* durchlässig
permeate ['pʌrmɪ‚et] *tr* durchdringen ‖ *intr* durchsickern
permissible [pər'mɪsɪbəl] *adj* zulässig
permission [pər'mɪʃən] *s* Erlaubnis *f;* **with your p.** mit Verlaub
permissive [pər'mɪsɪv] *adj* nachsichtig
per·mit ['pʌrmɪt] *s* Erlaubnis *f;* (document) Erlaubnisschein *m* ‖ [pər'mɪt] *v* (pret & pp –mitted; ger –mitting) *tr* erlauben, gestatten; **be permitted to** (inf) dürfen (inf)
permute [pər'mjut] *tr* umsetzen; (math) permutieren
pernicious [pər'nɪʃəs] *adj* **(to)** schädlich (für)
perox'ide blonde' [pə'rɑksaɪd] *s* Wasserstoffblondine *f*
perpendicular [‚pʌrpən'dɪkjələr] *adj* senkrecht ‖ *s* Senkrechte *f*
perpetrate ['pʌrpɪ‚tret] *tr* verüben
perpetual [pər'petʃu·əl] *adj* (everlasting) ewig; (continual) unaufhörlich
perpetuate [pər'petʃu‚et] *tr* verewigen
perplex [pər'pleks] *tr* verblüffen
perplexed' *adj* verblüfft
perplexity [pər'pleksɪti] *s* Verblüffung *f*
persecute ['pʌrsɪ‚kjut] *tr* verfolgen
persecution [‚pʌrsɪ'kjuʃən] *s* Verfolgung *f*
persecutor ['pʌrsɪ‚kjutər] *s* Verfolger –in *mf*
perseverance [‚pʌrsɪ'vɪrəns] *s* Ausdauer *f,* Beharrlichkeit *f*
persevere [‚pʌrsɪ'vɪr] *intr* ausdauern; **p. in** (cling to) beharren auf (acc); (e.g., efforts, studies) fortfahren mit
Persia ['pʌrʒə] *s* Persien *n*
Persian ['pʌrʒən] *adj* persisch ‖ *s* Perser –in *mf;* (language) Persisch *n*
Per'sian rug' *s* Perserteppich *m*
persimmon [pər'sɪmən] *s* Persimone *f*
persist [pər'sɪst] *intr* andauern; **p. in** verbleiben bei
persistent [pər'sɪstənt] *adj* andauernd
person ['pʌrsən] *s* Person *f;* **in p.** persönlich; **per p.** pro Person
personable ['pʌrsənəbəl] *adj* (attractive) ansehnlich; (good-natured) verträglich
personage ['pʌrsənɪdʒ] *s* Persönlichkeit *f*
personal ['pʌrsənəl] *adj* persönlich; (private) Privat–; **become p.** anzüglich werden
per'sonal da'ta *spl* Personalien *pl*
per'sonal hygiene' *s* Körperpflege *f*
per'sonal in'jury *s* Personenschaden *m*
personality [‚pʌrsə'nælɪti] *s* Persönlichkeit *f*
personally ['pʌrsənəli] *adv* persönlich

per'sonal pro'noun *s* Personalpronomen *n*

personi·fy [pər'sɑnɪ,faɪ] *v* (*pret & pp* –**fied**) *tr* personifizieren, verkörpern

personnel [,pʌrsə'nɛl] *s* Personal *n*

per'son-to-per'son call' *s* Gespräch *n* mit Voranmeldung

perspective [pər'spɛktɪv] *s* Perspektive *f*

perspicacious [,pʌrspɪ'keʃəs] *adj* scharfsinnig

perspiration [,pʌrspɪ'reʃən] *s* Schweiß *m;* (*perspiring*) Schwitzen *n*

perspire [pər'spaɪr] *intr* schwitzen

persuade [pər'swed] *tr* überreden

persuasion [pər'sweʒən] *s* Überredung *f*

persuasive [pər'swesɪv] *adj* redegewandt

pert [pʌrt] *adj* keck; (*sprightly*) lebhaft

pertain [pər'ten] *intr*—**p. to** betreffen, sich beziehen auf (*acc*)

pertinacious [,pʌrtɪ'neʃəs] *adj* beharrlich

pertinent ['pʌrtɪnənt] *adj* einschlägig; **be p. to** sich beziehen auf (*acc*)

perturb [pər'tʌrb] *tr* beunruhigen

peruse [pə'ruz] *tr* sorgfältig durchlesen

pervade [pər'ved] *tr* durchdringen

perverse [pər'vʌrs] *adj* (*abnormal*) pervers; (*obstinate*) verstockt

perversion [pər'vʌrʒən] *s* Perversion *f;* (*of truth*) Verdrehung *f*

perversity [pər'vʌrsɪti] *s* Perversität *f*

pervert ['pʌrvərt] *s* perverser Mensch *m* || [pər'vʌrt] *tr* (*corrupt*) verderben; (*twist*) verdrehen; (*misapply*) mißbrauchen

pesky ['pɛski] *adj* (coll) lästig

pessimism ['pɛsɪ,mɪzəm] *s* Pessimismus *m*

pessimist ['pɛsɪmɪst] *s* Pessimist –in *mf*

pessimistic [,pɛsɪ'mɪstɪk] *adj* pessimistisch

pest [pɛst] *s* (*insect*) Schädling *m;* (*annoying person*) Plagegeist *m;* (*pestilence*) Pest *f*

pest' control' *s* Schädlingsbekämpfung *f*

pester ['pɛstər] *tr* piesacken; (*with questions*) belästigen

pesticide ['pɛstɪ,saɪd] *s* Pestizid *n*

pestilence ['pɛstɪləns] *s* Pestilenz *f*

pestle ['pɛsəl] *s* Stößel *m*

pet [pɛt] *adj* Lieblings– || *s* (*animal*) Haustier *n;* (*person*) Liebling *m;* (*favorite child*) Schoßkind *n* || *v* (*pret & pp* **petted;** *ger* **petting**) *tr* streicheln || *intr* sich abknutschen

petal ['pɛtəl] *s* Blumenblatt *n*

Peter ['pitər] *s* Peter *m* || *intr*—**peter out** im Sande verlaufen

pet' ide'a *s* Lieblingsgedanke *m*

petition [pɪ'tɪʃən] *s* Eingabe *f;* (jur) Gesuch *n* || *tr* (*s.o.*) ersuchen

pet' name' *s* Kosename *m*

petri·fy ['pɛtrɪ,faɪ] *v* (*pret & pp* –**fied**) *tr* (& fig) versteinern; **be petrified** versteinern; (fig) zu Stein werden

petroleum [pə'trolɪ·əm] *s* Petroleum *n*

pet' shop' *s* Tierhandlung *f*

petticoat ['pɛtɪ,kot] *s* Unterrock *m*

pet'ting *s* Petting *n*

petty ['pɛti] *adj* klein, geringfügig; (*narrow*) engstirnig

pet'ty cash' *s* Handkasse *f*

pet'ty lar'ceny *s* geringer Diebstahl *m*

pet'ty of'ficer *s* (nav) Bootsmann *m*

petulant ['pɛtjələnt] *adj* verdrießlich

petunia [pə't(j)unɪ·ə] *s* Petunie *f*

pew [pju] *s* Bank *f*, Kirchenstuhl *m*

pewter ['pjutər] *s* Weißmetall *n*

Pfc. ['pi'ɛf'si] *s* (**private first class**) Gefreiter *m*

phalanx ['fælæŋks] *s* Phalanx *f*

phantasm ['fæntæzəm] *s* Trugbild *n*

phantom ['fæntəm] *s* Phantom *n*

Pharaoh ['fɛro] *s* Pharao *m*

Pharisee ['færɪ,si] *s* Pharisäer *m*

pharmaceutical [,fɑrmə'sutɪkəl] *adj* pharmazeutisch

pharmacist ['fɑrməsɪst] *s* Apotheker –in *mf*

pharmacy ['fɑrməsi] *s* Apotheke *f;* (*science*) Pharmazie *f*

pharynx ['færɪŋks] *s* Rachenhöhle *f*

phase [fez] *s* Phase *f* || *tr* in Phasen einteilen; **p. out** abwickeln

pheasant ['fɛzənt] *s* Fasan *m*

phenobarbital [,fino'bɑrbɪ,tæl] *s* Phenobarbital *n*

phenomenal [fɪ'nɑmɪnəl] *adj* phänomenal

phenome·non [fɪ'nɑmɪ,nɑn] *s* (–**na** [nə]) (& fig) Phänomen *n*, Erscheinung *f*

phial ['faɪ·əl] *s* Phiole *f*

philanderer [fɪ'lændərər] *s* Schürzenjäger *m*

philanthropist [fɪ'lænθrəpɪst] *s* Menschenfreund –in *mf*, Philanthrop –in *mf*

philanthropy [fɪ'lænθrəpi] *s* Menschenliebe *f*, Philanthropie *f*

philately [fɪ'lætəli] *s* Briefmarkenkunde *f*

Philippine ['fɪlɪ,pin] *adj* philippinisch || **the Philippines** *spl* die Philippinen

Philistine ['fɪlɪstin] *adj* (& fig) philisterhaft || *s* (& fig) Philister *m*

philologist [fɪ'lɑlədʒɪst] *s* Philologe *m*, Philologin *f*

philology [fɪ'lɑlədʒi] *s* Philologie *f*

philosopher [fɪ'lɑsəfər] *s* Philosoph *m*

philosophic(al) [,fɪlə'sɑfɪk(əl)] *adj* philosophisch

philosophy [fɪ'lɑsəfi] *s* Philosophie *f*

phlebitis [flɪ'baɪtɪs] *s* Venenentzündung *f*

phlegm [flɛm] *s* Schleim *m*

phlegmatic(al) [flɛg'mætɪk(əl)] *adj* phlegmatisch

phobia ['fobɪ·ə] *s* Phobie *f*

Phoenicia [fɪ'nɪ/ə] *s* Phönizien *f*

Phoenician [fɪ'nɪʃən] *adj* phönizisch || *s* Phönizier *m*

phoenix ['finɪks] *s* Phönix *m*

phone [fon] *s* (coll) Telephon *n;* **on the p.** am Apparat || *tr* (coll) anrufen || *intr* telephonieren

phone' call' *s* (coll) Anruf *m*

phonetic [fo'nɛtɪk] *adj* phonetisch, Laut– || **phonetics** *s* Lautlehre *f*, Phonetik *f*
phonograph ['fonə‚græf] *s* Grammophon *n*
pho'nograph rec'ord *s* Schallplatte *f*
phonology [fə'nalədʒi] *s* Lautlehre *f*
phony ['foni] *adj* falsch, Schein– || *s* Schwindler –in *mf*
phosphate ['fasfet] *s* Phosphat *n*
phosphorescent [‚fasfə'resənt] *adj* phosphoreszierend
phospho·rus ['fasfərəs] *s* (–ri [‚raɪ]) Phosphor *m*
pho·to ['foto] *s* (–tos) (coll) Photo *n*
pho'tocop'y *s* Photokopie *f* || *v* (*pret & pp* –ied) *tr* photokopieren
pho'toengrav'ing *s* Lichtdruckverfahren *n*
pho'to fin'ish *s* Zielphotographie *f*
photogenic [‚foto'dʒenɪk] *adj* photogen
photograph ['fotə‚græf] *s* Photographie *f* || *tr & intr* photographieren
photographer [fə'tagrəfər] *s* Photograph –in *mf*
photography [fə'tagrəfi] *s* Photographie *f*
photostat ['fotə‚stæt] *s* (trademark) Photokopie *f* || *tr* photokopieren
phrase [frez] *s* Sinngruppe *f* || *tr* formulieren; (mus) phrasieren
phrenology [frə'nalədʒi] *s* Schädellehre *f*
physic ['fɪzɪk] *s* Abführmittel *n;* **physics** *s* Physik *f*
physical ['fɪzɪkəl] *adj* körperlich, physisch || *s* (*examination*) ärztliche Untersuchung *f*
phys'ical condi'tion *s* Gesundheitszustand *m*
phys'ical de'fect *s* körperliches Gebrechen *n*
phys'ical educa'tion *s* Leibeserziehung *f*
phys'ical ex'ercise *s* Leibesübungen *pl;* (*calisthenics*) Bewegung *f*
phys'ical hand'icap *s* Körperbehinderung *f*
physician [fɪ'zɪʃən] *s* Arzt *m*, Ärztin *f*
physicist ['fɪzɪsɪst] *s* Physiker –in *mf*
physics ['fɪzɪks] *s* Physik *f*
physiognomy [‚fɪzɪ'agnəmi] *s* Gesichtsbildung *f*, Physiognomie *f*
physiological [‚fɪzɪ·ə'ladʒɪkəl] *adj* physiologisch
physiology [‚fɪzɪ'alədʒi] *s* Physiologie *f*
physique [fɪ'zik] *s* Körperbau *m*
pi [paɪ] *s* (math) Pi *n* || *tr* (typ) zusammenwerfen
pianist ['pi·ənɪst] *s* Pianist –in *mf*
pian·o [pɪ'æno] *s* (–os) Klavier *n*
pian'o stool' *s* Klavierschemel *m*
picayune [‚pɪkə'jun] *adj* (*paltry*) geringfügig; (*person*) kleinlich
picco·lo ['pɪkəlo] *s* (–los) Pikkoloflöte *f*
pick [pɪk] *s* (*tool*) Spitzhacke *f;* (*choice*) Auslese *f;* **the p. of the crop** das Beste von allem || *tr* (*choose*) sich [*dat*] aussuchen; (*e.g., fruit*)

pflücken; (*one's teeth*) stochern in (*dat*); (*one's nose*) bohren in (*dat*); (*a lock*) mit e–m Dietrich öffnen; (*a quarrel*) suchen; (*a bone*) abnagen; **p. off** abpflücken; (*shoot*) (coll) abknallen; **p. out** auswählen; **p. s.o.'s brains** j–s Ideen klauen; **p. s.o.'s pocket** j–m die Tasche ausräumen; **p. up** (*lift up*) aufheben; (*a girl*) (coll) aufgabeln; (*a suspect*) aufgreifen; (*with a car*) abholen; (*passengers; the scent*) aufnehmen; (*a language; news*) aufschnappen; (*a habit*) annehmen; (*a visual object*) erkennen; (*strength*) wieder erlangen; (*weight*) zunehmen an (*dat*); **p. up speed** in Fahrt kommen || *intr*—**p. and choose** wählerisch suchen; **p. at** herumstochern in (*dat*); **p. on** herumreiten auf (*dat*); **p. up** (*improve in health or business*) sich (wieder) erholen
pick'ax' *s* Picke *f*, Pickel *m*
picket ['pɪkɪt] *s* Holzpfahl *m; (of strikers*) Streikposten *m* || *tr* durch Streikposten absperren, Streikposten stehen vor (*dat*) || *intr* Streikposten stehen
pick'et fence' *s* Lattenzaun *m*
pick'et line' *s* Streikkette *f*
pickle ['pɪkəl] *s* Essiggurke *f;* **be in a p.** (coll) im Schlamassel sitzen || *tr* (ein)pökeln
pick'led *adj* (sl) blau
pick'led her'ring *s* Rollmops *m*
pick'pock'et *s* Taschendieb *m*
pick'up' *s* (*of a car*) Beschleunigungsvermögen *n;* (*girl*) Straßenbekanntschaft *f;* (*restorative*) Stärkungsmittel *n*, Erfrischung *f;* (*a stop to pick up*) Abholung *f;* (*of a phonograph*) Schalldose *f*
pick'up truck' *s* offener Lieferwagen *m*
picky ['pɪki] *adj* wählerisch
pic·nic ['pɪknɪk] *s* Picknick *n* || *v* (*pret & pp* –nicked; *ger* –nicking) *intr* picknicken
pictorial [pɪk'tori·əl] *adj* illustriert || *s* Illustrierte *f*
picture ['pɪktʃər] *s* Bild *n;* (fig) Vorstellung *f;* **look the p. of health** kerngesund aussehen || *tr* sich [*dat*] vorstellen
pic'ture gal'lery *s* Gemäldegalerie *f*
pic'ture post'card *s* Ansichtspostkarte *f*
picturesque [‚pɪktʃə'resk] *adj* malerisch, pittoresk; (*language*) bilderreich
pic'ture tube' *s* Bildröhre *f*
pic'ture win'dow *s* Panoramafenster *n*
piddling ['pɪdlɪŋ] *adj* lumpig
pie [paɪ] *s* Torte *f;* (*meat-filled*) Pastete *f;* **pie in the sky** Luftschloß *n*
piece [pis] *s* Stück *n;* (checkers) Stein *m;* (chess) Figur *f;* (mil) Geschütz *n;* (mus, theat) Stück *n;* **a p. of advice** ein Rat *m;* **a p. of bad luck** ein unglücklicher Zufall *m;* **a p. of furniture** ein Möbelstück *n;* **a p. of luggage** ein Gepäckstück *n;* **a p. of**

news e–e Neuigkeit *f;* **a p. of paper** ein Blatt Papier; **a p. of toast** e–e geröstete Brotscheibe *f;* **say one's p.** seine Meinung sagen
piece'meal' *adv* stückweise
piece'work' *s* Akkordarbeit *f;* **do p.** in Akkord arbeiten
piece'work'er *s* Akkordarbeiter –in *mf*
pier [pɪr] *s* Landungsbrücke *f,* Pier *m & f; (of a bridge)* Pfeiler *m*
pierce [pɪrs] *tr* durchstechen, durchbohren
pierc'ing *adj (look, pain)* scharf, stechend; *(cry)* gellend; *(cold)* schneidend
piety ['paɪ·əti] *s* Frömmigkeit *f*
pig [pɪg] *s* Schwein *n*
pigeon ['pɪdʒən] *s* Taube *f*
pi'geonhole' *s* Fach *n* ‖ *tr* auf die lange Bank schieben
pi'geon loft' *s* Taubenschlag *m*
pi'geon-toed' *adj & adv* mit einwärts gerichteten Zehen
piggish ['pɪgɪʃ] *adj* säuisch
piggyback ['pɪgi‚bæk] *adv* huckepack
pig'gy bank' *s* Sparschweinchen *n*
pig'head'ed *adj* dickköpfig
pig' i'ron *s* Roheisen *n*
pigment ['pɪgmənt] *s* Pigment *n*
pig'pen' *s* Schweinekoben *m*
pig'skin' *s* Schweinsleder *n;* (sport) (coll) Fußball *m*
pig'sty' *s* Schweinestall *m*
pig'tail' *s (hair style)* Rattenschwanz *m*
pike [paɪk] *s* Pike *f,* Spieß *m; (highway)* Landstraße *f;* (ichth) Hecht *m*
piker ['paɪkər] *s* (coll) Knicker *m*
pilaster [pɪ'læstər] *s* Wandpfeiler *m*
pile [paɪl] *s (heap)* Haufen *m; (e.g., of papers)* Stoß *m; (stake)* Pfahl *m; (fortune)* (coll) Menge *f;* (atom. phys) Meiler *m,* Reaktor *m;* (elec, phys) Säule *f;* (tex) Flor *m;* **piles** (pathol) Hämorrhoiden *pl;* **piles of money** (coll) Heidengeld *n* ‖ *tr* anhäufen, aufhäufen; **p. it on** (coll) dick auftragen ‖ *intr*—**p. into** sich drängen in *(acc);* **p. on** sich übereinander stürzen; **p. out of** sich hinausdrängen aus; **p. up** sich (an)häufen
pile' driv'er *s* Pfahlramme *f,* Rammbär *m*
pilfer ['pɪlfər] *tr* mausen, stibitzen
pilgrim ['pɪlgrɪm] *s* Pilger –in *mf*
pilgrimage ['pɪlgrɪmɪdʒ] *s* Pilgerfahrt *f;* **go on a p.** pilgern
pill [pɪl] *s (& fig)* Pille *f*
pillar ['pɪlər] *s* Pfeiler *m,* Säule *f*
pill'box' *s* Pillenschachtel *f;* (mil) Bunker *m*
pillo·ry ['pɪləri] *s* Pranger *m* ‖ *v (pret & pp –ried)* *tr* an den Pranger stellen; (fig) anprangern
pillow ['pɪlo] *s* Kopfkissen *n*
pil'lowcase' *s* Kopfkissenbezug *m*
pilot ['paɪlət] *adj (experimental)* Versuchs– ‖ *s* (aer) Pilot *m,* Flugzeugführer –in *mf;* (naut) Lotse *m* ‖ *tr* (aer) steuern, führen; (naut) steuern, lotsen
pi'lothouse' *s* (naut) Ruderhaus *m*
pi'lot light' *s* Sparflamme *f*

pi'lot's li'cense *s* Flugzeugführerschein *m*
pimp [pɪmp] *s* Zuhälter *m* ‖ *intr* kuppeln
pimp'ing *s* Zuhälterei *f*
pimple ['pɪmpəl] *s* Pickel *m*
pimply ['pɪmpli] *adj* pickelig
pin [pɪn] *s* Stecknadel *f; (ornament)* Anstecknadel *f;* (bowling) Kegel *m;* (mach) Pinne *f,* Zapfen *m;* **be on pins and needles** wie auf Nadeln sitzen ‖ *v (pret & pp* pinned*; ger* pinning*) tr (fasten with a pin)* mit e–r Nadel befestigen; *(e.g., a dress)* abstecken; *(e.g., under a car)* einklemmen; *(e.g., against the wall)* drücken; *(in wrestling)* auf die Schultern legen; **pin down** *(a person)* festlegen; *(troops)* niederhalten; **pin one's hopes on** seine Hofnungen setzen auf *(acc);* **pin s.th. on s.o.** (fig) j–m etw anhängen; **pin up** *(a sign)* anschlagen; *(the hair, a dress)* aufstecken
pinafore ['pɪnə‚for] *s* Latz *m*
pin'ball machine' *s* Spielautomat *m*
pin' boy' *s* Kegeljunge *m*
pincers ['pɪnsərz] *s & spl* Kneifzange *f*
pinch [pɪntʃ] *s* Kneifen *n; (of salt)* Prise *f;* **give s.o. a p.** j–n kneifen; **in a p.** zur Not, in der Not ‖ *tr* kneifen, zwicken; *(steal)* (sl) klauen; *(arrest)* (coll) schnappen; **I got my finger pinched in the door** ich habe mir den Finger in der Tür geklemmt; **p. and scrape every penny** sich *[dat]* jeden Groschen vom Munde absparen; **p. off** abzwicken ‖ *intr (said of shoe)* (& fig) drücken
pinchers ['pɪntʃərz] *s & spl* Kneifzange *f*
pinch'-hit' *v (pret & pp –hit; ger –hitting) intr* einspringen
pinch' hit'ter *s* Ersatzmann *m*
pin'cush'ion *s* Nadelkissen *n*
pine [paɪn] *adj* Kiefern– ‖ *s* Kiefer *f* ‖ *intr*—**p. away** sich abzehren; **p. for** sich sehnen nach
pine'ap'ple *s* Ananas *f*
pine' cone' *s* Kiefernzapfen *m*
pine' nee'dle *s* Kiefernnadel *f*
ping [pɪŋ] *s* Päng *n; (of a motor)* Klopfen *n* ‖ *intr* (aut) klopfen
ping-pong ['pɪŋ‚paŋ] *s* Ping-pong *n*
pin'head' *s* (& fig) Stechnadelkopf *m*
pink [pɪŋk] *adj* rosa ‖ *s* Rosa *n*
pin' mon'ey *s* Nadelgeld *n*
pinnacle ['pɪnəkəl] *s* Zinne *f*
pin'point' *adj* haarscharf; **p. landing** Ziellandung *f* ‖ *tr* markieren
pin'prick' *s* Nadelstich *m*
pint [paɪnt] *s* Schoppen *m,* Pinte *f*
pin'up girl' *s* Pin-up-Girl *n*
pin'wheel' *s (toy)* Windmühle *f; (fireworks)* Feuerrad *n*
pioneer [‚paɪ·ə'nɪr] *s* Bahnbrecher –in *mf;* (fig & mil) Pionier *m* ‖ *tr* (fig) den Weg freimachen für ‖ *intr* (fig) Pionierarbeit leisten
pious ['paɪ·əs] *adj* fromm
pip [pɪp] *s (in fruit)* Kern *m; (on dice)* Punkt *m; (on a radarscope)* Leuchtpunkt *m; (of chickens)* Pips *m*

pipe [paɪp] *s* Rohr *n*; (*for smoking; of an organ*) Pfeife *f* ‖ *tr* durch ein Rohr (weiter)leiten ‖ *intr* pfeifen; **p. down** (sl) das Maul halten; **p. up** (coll) anfangen zu sprechen, loslegen
pipe′ clean′er *s* Pfeifenreiniger *m*
pipe′ dream′ *s* Wunschtraum *m*
pipe′ joint′ *s* Rohranschluß *m*
pipe′ line′ *s* Rohrleitung *f*, Pipeline *f*; (*of information*) Informationsquelle *f*
pipe′ or′gan *s* Orgel *f*
piper [′paɪpər] *s* Pfeifer –in *mf*
pipe′ wrench′ *s* Rohrzange *f*
piping [′paɪpɪŋ] *adv*—**p. hot** siedend heiß ‖ *s* Rohrleitung *f*; (*on uniforms*) Biese *f*; (*sew*) Paspel *f*
piquancy [′pikənsi] *s* Pikanterie *f*
piquant [′pikənt] *adj* pikant
pique [pik] *s* Pik *m* ‖ *tr* verärgern; **be piqued at** pikiert sein über (*acc*)
piracy [′paɪrəsi] *s* Seeräuberei *f*
pirate [′paɪrɪt] *s* Seeräuber *m* ‖ *tr* (*a book*) (ungesetzlich) nachdrucken
pirouette [͵pɪru′ɛt] *s* Pirouette *f*
pista′chio nut′ [pɪs′tæʃɪ·o] *s* Pistaziennuß *f*
pistol [′pɪstəl] *s* Pistole *f*
pis′tol point′ *s*—**at p.** mit vorgehaltener Pistole
piston [′pɪstən] *s* Kolben *m*
pis′ton ring′ *s* Kolbenring *m*
pis′ton rod′ *s* Kolbenstange *f*
pis′ton stroke′ *s* Kolbenhub *m*
pit [pɪt] *s* Grube *f*; (*in fruit*) Kern *m*; (*trap*) Fallgrube *f*; (*in the skin*) Narbe *f*; (*from corrosion*) Rostgrübchen *n*; (*in auto racing*) Box *f*; (*for cockfights*) Kampfplatz *m*; (min) Schacht *m*; (theat) Parkett *n*; (mus) Orchester *n*; **pit of the stomach** Magengrube *f* ‖ *v* (*pret & pp* **pitted**; ger **pitting**) *tr* (*a face*) mit Narben bedecken; (*fruit*) entkernen; (*through corrosion*) anfressen; **pit A against B** A gegen B ausspielen; **pit one's strength against s.th.** seine Kraft mit etw messen
pitch [pɪtʃ] *s* Pech *n*; (*of a roof*) Dachschräge *f*; (*downward slope*) Gefälle *n*; (*of a ship*) Stampfen *n*; (*of a screw, thread*) Teilung *f*; (*of a propeller*) Steigung *f*; (*throw*) Wurf *m*; (*sales talk*) Verkaufsgespräch *n*; (mus) Tonhöhe *f* ‖ *tr* (*seal with pitch*) verpichen; (*a tent*) aufschlagen; (*a ball*) dem Schläger zuwerfen; (*hay*) mit der Heugabel werfen ‖ *intr* (naut) stampfen; **p. and toss** schlingern; **p. in** mithelfen
pitch′ ac′cent *s* musikalischer Tonakzent *m*
pitch′-black′ *adj* pechrabenschwarz
pitcher [′pɪtʃər] *s* (*jug*) Krug *m*
pitch′fork′ *s* Heugabel *f*
pitch′ing *s* (naut) Stampfen *n*
pit′fall′ *s* Fallgrube *f*; (fig) Falle *f*
pith [pɪθ] *s* (& fig) Mark *n*
pithy [′pɪθi] *adj* (& fig) markig
pitiable [′pɪtɪ·əbəl] *adj* erbarmenswert
pitiful [′pɪtɪfəl] *adj* erbärmlich
pitiless [′pɪtɪlɪs] *adj* erbarmungslos

pit′ted *adj* (*by corrosion*) angefressen; (*fruit*) entkernt
pit·y [′pɪti] *s* Erbarmen *n*, Mitleid *n*; **have p. on** Mitleid haben mit; **it's a p. that** (es ist) schade, daß; **move to p.** jammern; **what a p.!** wie schade! ‖ *v* (*pret & pp* –ied) *tr* sich erbarmen (*genit*), bemitleiden
pivot [′pɪvət] *s* Drehpunkt *m* ‖ *intr* (on) sich drehen (um); (mil) schwenken
placard [′plækɑrd] *s* Plakat *n*
placate [′pleket] *tr* begütigen
place [ples] *s* (*seat; room*) Platz *m*; (*area, town, etc.*) Ort *m*, Ortschaft *f*; (*in a book; in a room*) Stelle *f*; (*situation*) Lage *f*; (*spot to eat in, dance in, etc.*) Lokal *n*; **all over the p.** überall; **at your p.** (coll) bei Ihnen; **in my p.** an meiner Stelle; **in p. of** anstelle von (or *genit*); **in the first p.** erstens; **know one's p.** wissen, wohin man gehört; **out of p.** (& fig) nicht am Platz; **p. to stay** Unterkunft *f*; **put s.o. in his p.** j–n in seine Schranken verweisen; **take one's p.** antreten; **take p.** stattfinden; **take s.o.'s p.** an j–s Stelle treten ‖ *tr* setzen, stellen; (*an advertisement*) aufgeben; (*an order*) erteilen; (*find a job for*) unterbringen; **I can't p. him** ich weiß nicht, wo ich ihn hintun soll; **p. a call** (telp) ein Gespräch anmelden ‖ *intr* (*in horseracing*) sich als Zweiter placieren; (sport) sich placieren
place·bo [plə′sibo] *s* (**–bos** & **–boes**) Placebo *n*
place′ card′ *s* Tischkarte *f*
place′ mat′ *s* Tischmatte *f*
placement [′plesmənt] *s* Unterbringung *f*
place′-name′ *s* Ortsname *m*
place′ of birth′ *s* Geburtsort *m*
place′ of employ′ment *s* Arbeitsstätte *f*
place′ of res′idence *s* Wohnsitz *m*
placid [′plæsɪd] *adj* ruhig, sanftmütig
plagiarism [′pledʒə͵rɪzəm] *s* Plagiat *n*
plagiarist [′pledʒərɪst] *s* Plagiator –in *mf*
plagiarize [′pledʒə͵raɪz] *intr* ein Plagiat begehen
plague [pleg] *s* Seuche *f* ‖ *tr* heimsuchen
plaid [plæd] *adj* buntkariert ‖ *s* Schottenkaro *n*
plain [plen] *adj* (*simple*) einfach; (*clear*) klar; (*fabric*) einfarbig; (*homely*) unschön; (*truth*) rein; (*food*) bürgerlich; (*paper*) unlin(i)iert; (*speech*) unverblümt; (*alcohol*) unverdünnt ‖ *s* Ebene *f*
plain′ clothes′ *spl*—**in p.** in Zivil
plain′-clothes′ man′ *s* Geheimpolizist *m*
plaintiff [′plentɪf] *s* Kläger –in *mf*
plaintive [′plentɪv] *adj* Klage-, klagend
plait [plet], [plæt] *s* Flechte *f*; **p. of hair** Zopf *m* ‖ *tr* flechten
plan [plæn] *s* Plan *m*; (*intention*) Vorhaben *n*; **according to p.** planmäßig;

what are your plans for this evening?
was haben Sie für heute abend vor?
‖ _v (pret & pp_ **planned; ger planning)** _tr_ planen; _(one's time)_ einteilen; **p. to** _(inf)_ vorhaben zu _(inf)_ ‖
intr—**p. for** Pläne machen für; **p. on**
rechnen mit
plane [plen] _s (airplane)_ Flugzeug _n,_
Maschine _f; (airfoil)_ Tragfläche _f;_
(carp) Hobel _m;_ (geom) Ebene _f;_
on a high p. (fig) auf e–m hohen
Niveau ‖ _tr_ hobeln; **p. down** ab-
hobeln
plane′ connec′tion _s_ Fluganschluß _m_
plane′ geom′etry _s_ Planimetrie _f_
planet [′plænɪt] _s_ Planet _m_
planetari·um [ˌplænɪ′terɪ-əm] _s_ **(–a**
[ə] & **–ums)** Planetarium _n_
planetary [′plænəˌteri] _adj_ Planeten-
plane′ tick′et _s_ Flugkarte _f_
plane′ tree′ _s_ Platane _f_
plank [plæŋk] _s_ Brett _n,_ Planke _f;_
(pol) Programmpunkt _m_
planned′ par′enthood _s_ Familienpla-
nung _f_
plant [plænt] _s (factory)_ Anlage _f;_
(spy) Spion _–in mf;_ (bot) Pflanze _f_
‖ _tr_ (an)pflanzen; _(a field)_ bepflan-
zen; _(a colony)_ gründen; _(as a spy)_
als Falle aufstellen; _(a bomb)_ verstecken; **p. oneself** sich hinstellen
plantation [plæn′teʃən] _s_ Plantage _f_
planter [′plæntər] _s (person who
plants; plantation owner)_ Pflanzer
–in mf; (decorative container) Blu-
mentrog _m;_ (mach) Pflanzmaschine
_f_
plasma [′plæzmə] _s_ Plasma _n_
plaster [′plæstər] _s_ Verputz _m;_ (med)
Pflaster _n_ ‖ _tr_ verputzen; _(e.g., with
posters)_ bepflastern; **be plastered**
(sl) besoffen sein
plas′terboard′ _s_ Gipsdiele _f_
plas′ter cast′ _s_ (med) Gipsverband _m;_
(sculp) Gipsabguß _m_
plasterer [′plæstərər] _s_ Stukkateur _m_
plas′tering _s_ Verputz _m_
plas′ter of Par′is _s_ Gips _m_
plastic [′plæstɪk] _adj_ Plastik- ‖ _s_
Plastik _n_
plas′tic sur′gery _s_ Plastik _f_
plas′tic wood′ _s_ Holzpaste _f_
plate [plet] _s (dish)_ Teller _m; (of
metal)_ Platte _f; (in a book)_ Tafel _f;_
(elec, phot, typ) Platte _f;_ (electron)
Plattenelektrode _f_ ‖ _tr_ plattieren
plateau [plæ′to] _s_ Plateau _n_
plate′ glass′ _s_ Tafelglas _n_
platen [′plætən] _s_ Schreibmaschinen-
walze _f_
platform [′plætˌfɔrm] _s_ Plattform _f;_
(for a speaker) Bühne _f; (for loading)_ Rampe _f;_ (pol) Programm _n;_
(rr) Bahnsteig _m_
plat′form shoes′ _spl_ Plateauschuhe _pl_
plat′ing _s (e.g., of gold)_ Plattierung _f;_
(armor) Panzerung _f_
platinum [′plætɪnəm] _s_ Platin _n_
plat′inum blonde′ _s_ Platinblondine _f_
platitude [′plætɪˌt(j)ud] _s_ Gemeinplatz _m_
Plato [′pleto] _s_ Plato _m_

Platonic [plə′tɑnɪk] _adj_ platonisch
platoon [plə′tun] _s_ Zug _m_
platter [′plætər] _s_ Platte _f_
plausible [′plɔzɪbəl] _adj_ plausibel
play [ple] _s_ Spiel _n;_ (mach) Spielraum
_m;_ (sport) Spielzug _m;_ (theat) Stück
_n;_ **in p.** im Spiel; **out of p.** aus dem
Spiel ‖ _tr_ spielen; _(a card)_ ausspielen; _(an opponent)_ spielen gegen;
p. back _(a tape, record)_ abspielen;
p. down bagatellisieren; **p. the horses**
bei Pferderennen wetten ‖ _intr_ spielen; _(records, tapes)_ abspielen; **p.
about** _(the lips)_ umspielen; **p. along**
mitspielen; **p. around with** herumspielen mit; **p. for** _(stakes)_ spielen
um; _(a team)_ spielen für; **p. into**
s.o.'s hands j–m in die Hände spielen; **p. safe** auf Nummer Sicher gehen; **p. up to** schmeicheln _(dat)_
play′back′ _s (reproduction)_ Wiedergabe
f; (device) Abspielgerät _n_
play′boy′ _s_ Playboy _m_
player [′ple·ər] _s_ Spieler _–in mf;_
(sport) Sportler _–in mf;_ (theat)
Schauspieler _–in mf_
playful [′plefəl] _adj_ spielerisch
play′ground′ _s_ Spielplatz _m_
play′house′ _s_ Theater _n; (for children)_
Spielhaus _n_
play′ing card′ _s_ Spielkarte _f_
play′ing field′ _s_ Spielfeld _n_
play′mate′ _s_ Spielkamerad _–in mf_
play′-offs′ _spl_ Vorrunde _f_
play′ on words′ _s_ Wortspiel _n_
play′pen′ _s_ Laufgitter _n_
play′room′ _s_ Spielzimmer _n_
play′-school′ _s_ Kindergarten _m_
play′thing′ _s_ (& fig) Spielzeug _n_
playwright [′pleˌraɪt] _s_ Schauspiel-
dichter _–in mf_
plea [pli] _s_ Bitte _f;_ (jur) Plädoyer _n_
plead [plid] _v (pret & pp_ **pleaded &
pled** [pled]) _tr (ignorance)_ vorschüt-
zen ‖ _intr_ plädieren; **p. guilty** sich
schuldig bekennen; **p. not guilty** sich
als nichtschuldig erklären; **p. with**
s.o. j–n anflehen
pleasant [′plezənt] _adj_ angenehm
pleasantry [′plezəntri] _s_ Heiterkeit _f;_
(remark) Witz _m_
please [pliz] _tr_ gefallen _(dat);_ **be
pleased to** _(inf)_ sich freuen zu _(inf);_
be pleased with sich freuen über
(acc); **pleased to meet you!** sehr angenehm ‖ _intr_ gefallen; **as one
pleases** nach Gefallen; **do as you p.**
tun Sie, wie Sie wollen; **if you p.**
wenn ich bitten darf; (iron) gefälligst;
p.! bitte!
pleas′ing _adj_ angenehm, gefällig
pleasure [′pleʒər] _s_ Vergnügen _n_
pleas′ure trip′ _s_ Vergnügungsreise _f_
pleat [plit] _s_ Plissee _n_ ‖ _tr_ plissieren
pleat′ed skirt′ _s_ Plisseerock _m_
plebeian [plɪ′bi·ən] _adj_ plebejisch ‖ _s_
Plebejer _–in mf_
plect·rum [′plektrəm] _s_ **(–rums & –ra**
[rə]) Plektron _n; (for zither)_ Schlagring _m_
pledge [pledʒ] _s (solemn promise)_ Gelübde _n; (security for a payment)_

Pfand *n;* (fig) Unterpfand *n* ‖ *tr* geloben; (*money*) zeichnen
plenary ['pli:nəri] *adj* Plenar-, Vollple'nary indul'gence *s* vollkommener Ablaß *m*
ple'nary ses'sion *s* Plenum *n*
plenipotentiary [ˌplenɪpə'tenʃɪˌeri] *adj* bevollmächtigt ‖ *s* Bevollmächtigte *mf*
plentiful ['plentɪfəl] *adj* reichlich
plenty ['plenti] *s* Fülle *f;* **have p. of** Überfluß haben an (*dat*); **have p. to do** vollauf zu tun haben ‖ *adv* (coll) reichlich
pleurisy ['plʊrɪsi] *s* Brustfellentzündung *f*
plexiglass ['pleksɪˌglæs] *s* Plexiglas *n*
pliant ['plaɪ·ənt] *adj* biegsam; (fig) gefügig
pliers ['plaɪ·ərz] *s & spl* Zange *f*
plight [plaɪt] *s* Notlage *f*
plod [plɑd] *v* (*pret & pp* **plodded;** *ger* **plodding**) *intr* stapfen; **p. along** mühsam weitermachen
plop [plɑp] *v* (*pret & pp* **plopped;** *ger* **plopping**) *tr* plumpsen lassen ‖ *intr* plumpsen ‖ *interj* plumps!
plot [plɑt] *s* (*conspiracy*) Komplott *n;* (*of a story*) Handlung *f;* (*of ground*) Grundstück *n* ‖ *v* (*pret & pp* **plotted;** *ger* **plotting**) *tr* (*a course*) abstecken; (*intrigues*) schmieden; (*e.g., murder*) planen ‖ *intr* sich verschwören
plough [plaʊ] *s, tr & intr* var of **plow**
plow [plaʊ] *s* Pflug *m* ‖ *tr* pflügen; **p. up** umpflügen; **p. under** unterpflügen ‖ *intr* pflügen; **p. through the waves** durch die Wellen streichen
plow'man *s* (**-men**) Pflüger *m*
plow'share *s* Pflugschar *f*
pluck [plʌk] *s* (*tug*) Ruck *m;* (fig) Schneid *m* ‖ *tr* (*e.g., a chicken*) rupfen; (*flowers, fruit*) pflücken; (*eyebrows*) auszupfen; (mus) zupfen ‖ *intr*—**p. up** Mut fassen
plug [plʌg] *s* (*for a sink*) Pfropfen *m;* (*of tobacco*) Priem *m;* (*old horse*) alter Klepper *m;* (*advertising*) Befürwortung *f;* (aut) Zündkerze *f;* (elec) Stecker *m* ‖ *v* (*pret & pp* **plugged;** *ger* **plugging**) *tr* (*a hole*) zustopfen; **p. in** an die Steckdose anschließen ‖ *intr*—**p. away** (*work hard*) schuften; (*study hard*) pauken
plum [plʌm] *s* Pflaume *f*
plumage ['plumɪdʒ] *s* Gefieder *n*
plumb [plʌm] *adj* lotrecht ‖ *adv* (coll) völlig ‖ *s* Lot *n;* **out of p.** aus dem Lot ‖ *tr* loten, sondieren
plumb' bob' *s* Lot *n*
plumber ['plʌmər] *s* Installateur *m*
plumb'ing *s* (*plumbing work*) Installateurarbeit *f;* (*pipes*) Rohrleitung *f*
plumb' line' *s* Lotschnur *f*
plume [plum] *s* Feder *f;* (*on a helmet*) Helmbusch *m;* **p. of smoke** Rauchfahne *f* ‖ *tr* (*adorn with plumes*) mit Federn schmücken; **p. itself** sich putzen
plummet ['plʌmɪt] *s* Lot *n* ‖ *intr* stürzen

plump [plʌmp] *adj* rundlich ‖ *tr* plumpsen; **p. oneself down** sich schwerfällig hinwerfen
plum' tree' *s* Pflaumenbaum *m*
plunder ['plʌndər] *s* (*act*) Plünderung *f;* (*booty*) Beute *f* ‖ *tr & intr* plündern
plunderer ['plʌndərər] *s* Plünderer *m*
plunge [plʌndʒ] *s* Sturz *m* ‖ *tr* stürzen ‖ *intr* (*fall*) stürzen; (*throw oneself*) sich stürzen
plunger ['plʌndʒər] *s* Saugglocke *f*
plunk [plʌŋk] *adv* (*squarely*) (coll) genau ‖ *tr* (*e.g., a guitar*) zupfen; **p. down** klirrend auf den Tisch legen
pluperfect [ˌplu'pʌrfekt] *s* Vorvergangenheit *f,* Plusquamperfekt(um) *n*
plural ['plʊrəl] *adj* Plural- ‖ *s* Mehrzahl *f,* Plural *m*
plurality [plʊ'rælɪti] *s* Mehrheit *f;* (pol) Stimmenmehrheit *f*
plus [plʌs] *adj* Plus-; (elec) positiv ‖ *s* Plus *n* ‖ *prep* plus (*acc*)
plush [plʌʃ] *adj* (coll) luxuriös
plus' sign' *s* Pluszeichen *n*
plutonium [plu'toni·əm] *s* Plutonium *n*
ply [plaɪ] *s* (*of wood, etc.*) Schicht *f;* (*of yarn*) Strähne *f* ‖ *v* (*pret & pp* **plied**) *tr* (*e.g., a needle*) (eifrig) handhaben; (*a trade*) betreiben; (*with questions*) bestürmen; (*a waterway*) regelmäßig befahren ‖ *intr* (*between*) verkehren (zwischen *dat*)
ply'wood' *s* Sperrholz *n*
pneumatic [n(j)u'mætɪk] *adj* pneumatisch
pneumat'ic drill' *s* Preßluftbohrer *m*
pneumonia [n(j)u'moni·ə] *s* Lungenentzündung *f*
poach [potʃ] *tr* (*eggs*) pochieren ‖ *intr* wildern
poached' egg' *s* verlorenes Ei *n*
poacher ['potʃər] *s* Wilderer *m*
pock [pɑk] *s* Pocke *f,* Pustel *f*
pocket ['pɑkɪt] *adj* (*comb, flap, knife, money, watch*) Taschen- ‖ *s* Tasche *f;* (billiards) Loch *n;* (mil) Kessel *m* ‖ *tr* in die Tasche stecken; (billiards) ins Loch spielen
pock'etbook' *s* Handtasche *f;* (*book*) Taschenbuch *n*
pock'et cal'culator *s* Taschenrechner *m*
pock'mark' *s* Pockennarbe *f*
pock'marked' *adj* pockennarbig
pod [pɑd] *s* Hülse *f*
podi·um ['podi·əm] *s* (**-ums & -a** [ə]) Podium *n*
poem ['po·ɪm] *s* Gedicht *n*
poet ['po·ɪt] *s* Dichter *m,* Poet *m*
poetaster ['po·ɪtˌæstər] *s* Dichterling *m*
poetess ['po·ɪtɪs] *s* Dichterin *f*
poetic [po'etɪk] *adj* dichterisch, poetisch ‖ **poetics** *s* Poetik *f*
poetry ['po·ɪtri] *s* Dichtung *f;* **write p.** dichten, Gedichte schreiben
poignant ['pɔɪn(j)ənt] *adj* (*touching*) ergreifend; (*pungent*) scharf; (*cutting*) beißend
point [pɔɪnt] *s* (*dot, score*) Punkt *m;*

(*tip*) Spitze *f*; (*of a joke*) Pointe *f*; (*of a statement*) Hauptpunkt *m*; (*side of a character*) Seite *f*; (*purpose*) Sinn *m*; (*matter, subject*) Sache *f*; (*of a compass*) Kompaßstrich *m*; (*to show decimals*) Komma *n*; (aut) Zündkontakt *m*; (geog) Landspitze *f*; (typ) Punkt *m*; **at this p.** in diesem Augenblick; **be on the p. of** (*ger*) gerade im Begriff sein zu (*inf*); **come to the p.!** zur Sache!; **get the p.** verstehen; **in p. of fact** tatsächlich; **make a p. of** bestehen auf (*dat*); **make it a p. to** (*inf*) es sich [*dat*] zur Pflicht machen zu (*inf*); **not to the p.** nicht zur Sache gehörig; **off the p.** unzutreffend; **on points** (sport) nach Punkten; **p. at issue** strittiger Punkt *m*; **p. of order!** zur Tagesordnung!; **p. of time** Zeitpunkt *m*; **score a p.** (fig) e-n Punkt für sich buchen; **that's beside the p.** darum handelt es sich nicht; **there's no p. to it** es hat keinen Zweck; **to the p.** zutreffend; **up to a certain p.** bis zu e-m gewissen Grade ‖ *tr* (*e.g., a gun*) (**at**) richten (*auf acc*); **p. out** (auf)zeigen; **p. s.th. out to s.o.** j-n auf etw [*acc*] hinweisen; **p. the finger at** mit dem Finger zeigen auf (*acc*) ‖ *intr* mit dem Finger zeigen; **p. to** deuten auf (*acc*); (fig) hinweisen auf (*acc*)

point'-blank' *adj* (*refusal*) glatt; (*shot*) rasant, Kernschuß–; **at p. range** auf Kernschußweite ‖ *adv* (*at close range*) aus nächster Nähe; (fig) glatt; (arti) auf Kernschußweite

point'ed *adj* spitzig; (*remark*) anzüglich; (*gun*) gerichtet; (*arch, nose*) Spitz–

pointer ['pɔɪntər] *s* (*of a meter*) Zeiger *m*; (*stick*) Zeigestock *m*; (*advice*) Tip *m*; (*hunting dog*) Vorstehhund *m*

pointless ['pɔɪntlɪs] *adj* zwecklos

point' of hon'or *s* Ehrensache *f*

point' of law' *s* Rechtsfrage *f*

point' of view' *s* Gesichtspunkt *m*

poise [pɔɪz] *s* sicheres Auftreten *n* ‖ *tr* im Gleichgewicht halten ‖ *intr* schweben

poison ['pɔɪzən] *s* Gift *n* ‖ *tr* (& fig) vergiften

poi'son gas' *s* Giftgas *n*

poi'son i'vy *s* Giftsumach *m*

poisonous ['pɔɪzənəs] *adj* giftig

poke [pok] *s* Stoß *m*, Knuff *m* ‖ *tr* anstoßen, knuffen; (*the fire*) schüren; (*head, nose*) stecken; **p. fun at** sich lustig machen über (*acc*); **p. out** (*an eye*) ausstechen; **p. s.o. in the ribs** j-m e-n Rippenstoß geben ‖ *intr* bummeln; **p. around** herumstochern; (*be slow*) herumbummeln; (*in another's business*) herumstöbern

poker ['pokər] *s* Schürhaken *m*; (cards) Poker *n*

pok'er face' *s* Pokergesicht *n*

poky ['poki] *adj* bummelig

Poland ['polənd] *s* Polen *n*

polar ['polər] *adj* Polar–

po'lar bear' *s* Eisbär *m*

polarity [po'lærɪti] *s* Polarität *f*

polarize ['polə‚raɪz] *tr* polarisieren

pole [pol] *s* (*rod*) Stange *f*; (*for telephone lines, flags, etc.*) Mast *m*; (astr, geog, phys) Pol *m*; **Pole** Pole *m*, Polin *f* ‖ *tr* (*a raft, boat*) staken

pole'cat' *s* Iltis *m*

polemic(al) [pə'lɛmɪk(əl)] *adj* polemisch

polemics [pə'lɛmɪks] *s* Polemik *f*

pole'star' *s* Polarstern *m*

pole'-vault' *intr* stabhochspringen

pole' vault'ing *s* Stabhochsprung *m*

police [pə'lis] *adj* polizeilich ‖ *s* Polizei *f* ‖ *tr* polizeilich überwachen; (*clean up*) (mil) säubern

police' es'cort *s* Polozeibedeckung *f*

police'man *s* (**–men**) Polizist *m*

police' of'ficer *s* Polizeibeamte *m*, Polizeibeamtin *f*

police' pre'cinct *s* Polizeirevier *n*

police' state' *s* Polizeistaat *m*

police' sta'tion *s* Polizeiwache *f*

police'wom'an *s* (**–wom'en**) Polizistin *f*

policy ['palɪsi] *s* Politik *f*; (ins) Police *f*

polio ['polɪ‚o] *s* Polio *f*

polish ['palɪʃ] *s* (*material; shine*) Politur *f*; (*for shoes*) Schuhcreme *f*; (fig) Schliff *m* ‖ *tr* polieren; (*fingernails*) lackieren; (*shoes, silver, etc.*) putzen; (*floors*) bohnern; (fig) abschleifen; **p. off** (*eat*) (sl) verdrücken; (*an opponent*) (sl) erledigen; (*work*) (sl) hinhauen ‖ *intr*—**p. up on** aufpolieren ‖ **Polish** ['polɪʃ] *adj* polnisch ‖ *s* Polnisch *n*

polite [pə'laɪt] *adj* höflich

politeness [pə'laɪtnɪs] *s* Höflichkeit *f*

politic ['palɪtɪk] *adj* diplomatisch

political [pə'lɪtɪkəl] *adj* politisch

poli'tical econ'omy *s* Volkswirtschaft *f*

poli'tical sci'ence *s* Staatswissenschaften *pl*

politician [‚palɪ'tɪʃən] *s* Politiker –in *mf*

politics ['palɪtɪks] *s* Politik *f*; **be in p.** sich politisch betätigen; **talk p.** politisieren

polka ['po(l)kə] *s* Polka *f*

pol'ka-dot' *adj* getupft

poll [pol] *s* (*voting*) Abstimmung *f*; (*of public opinion*) Umfrage *f*; **be defeated at the polls** e-e Wahlniederlage erleiden; **go to the polls** zur Wahl gehen; **polls** (*voting place*) Wahllokal *n*; **take a p.** e-e Umfrage halten ‖ *tr* befragen

pollen ['palən] *s* Pollen *m*

poll'ing booth' *s* Wahlzelle *f*

pollster ['polstər] *s* Meinungsforscher –in *mf*

poll' tax' *s* Kopfsteuer *f*

pollute [pə'lut] *tr* verunreinigen

pollution [pə'luʃən] *s* Verunreinigung *f*

polo ['polo] *s* (sport) Polo *n*

po'lo shirt' *s* Polohemd *n*

polygamist [pə'lɪgəmɪst] *s* Polygamist *m*

polygamy [pə'lɪgəmi] *s* Polygamie *f*

polyglot ['palɪ‚glat] *s* Polyglott *m*

polygon ['palı ,gan] s Vieleck n
polyp ['palıp] s Polyp m
polytheism [,palı'θi ,ızəm] s Vielgötterei f, Polytheismus m
polytheistic [,palıθi'ıstık] adj polytheistisch
pomade [pə'med] s Pomade f
pomegranate ['pam ,grænıt] s Granatapfel m; (tree) Granatapfelbaum m
Pomerania [,pamə'renı·ə] s Pommern n
pom·mel ['pʌməl] s (of a sword) Degenkopf m; (of a saddle) Sattelknopf m || v (pret & pp –mel[l]ed; ger –el[l]ing) tr mit der Faust schlagen
pomp [pamp] s Pomp m, Prunk m
pompous ['pampəs] adj hochtrabend
pon·cho ['pant/o] s (–chos) Poncho m
pond [pand] s Teich m
ponder ['pandər] tr erwägen; (words) abwägen || intr (over) nachsinnen (über acc)
ponderous ['pandərəs] adj schwerfällig
pontiff ['pantıf] s (eccl) Papst m; (hist) Pontifex m
pontifical [pan'tıfıkəl] adj pontifikal
pontoon [pan'tun] s Ponton m; (aer) Schwimmer m
pony ['poni] s (small horse; hair style) Pony m; (crib) Eselsbrücke f
poodle ['pudəl] s Pudel m
pool [pul] s (small pond) Tümpel m; (of blood) Lache f; (swimming pool) Schwimmbecken n; (in betting) Pool m; (game) Billiard n; (fin) Pool m || tr zusammenlegen
pool'room' s Billardsalon m
pool' ta'ble s Billardtisch m
poop [pup] s Heck n || tr (sl) erschöpfen; **be pooped (out)** erschöpft sein
poor [pʊr] adj arm; (e.g., in spelling) schwach; (soil, harvest) schlecht; (miserable) armselig; **p. in** arm an (dat)
poor' box' s Opferstock m
poor'house' s Armenhaus n
poorly ['pʊrli] adv schlecht
pop [pap] adj (concert, singer, music) Pop– || s Puff m, Knall m; (dad) Vati m; (soda) Brauselimonade f; (mus) Popmusik f || v (pret & pp popped; ger popping) tr (corn) rösten; (cause to pop) knallen lassen; **pop the question** (coll) e-n Heiratsantrag machen || intr (make a popping noise) knallen; (said of popcorn) aufplatzen; **pop in** (visit unexpectedly) (coll) hereinplatzen; **pop off** (sl) das Maul aufreißen; **pop up** (appear) (coll) auftauchen; (jump up) hochfahren
pop'corn' s Puffmais m
pope [pop] s Papst m
pop'eyed' adj glotzäugig
pop'gun' s Knallbüchse f
poplar ['paplər] s Pappel f
poppy ['papi] s Mohnblume f, Mohn m
pop'pycock' s (coll) Quatsch m
pop'pyseed' s Mohn m
popsicle ['pap ,sıkəl] s Eis n am Stiel
populace ['papjəlıs] s Pöbel m

popular ['papjələr] adj populär; (e.g., music, expression) volkstümlich; **p. with** beliebt bei
popularity [,papjə'lærıti] s Popularität f, Beliebtheit f
popularize ['papjələ ,raız] tr popularisieren
populate ['papjə ,let] tr bevölkern
population [,papjə'le/ən] s Bevölkerung f
popula'tion explo'sion s Bevölkerungsexplosion f
populous ['papjələs] adj volkreich
porcelain ['pɔrs(ə)lın] s Porzellan n
porch [port/] s Vorbau m, Veranda f
porcupine ['pɔrkjə ,paın] s Stachelschwein n
pore [por] s Pore f || intr–**p. over** eifrig studieren
pork [pork] adj Schweine– || s Schweinefleisch n
pork'chop' s Schweinekotelett n
pornography [pɔr'nagrəfi] s Pornographie f
porous ['porəs] adj porös
porphyry ['pɔrfıri] s Porphyr m
porpoise ['pɔrpəs] s Tümmler m
porridge ['pɔrıdʒ] s Brei m
port [port] s Hafen m; (wine) Portwein m; (slit for shooting) Schießscharte f; (naut) Backbord m & n; **to p.** (naut) backbord
portable ['portəbəl] adj tragbar; (radio, television, typewriter) Koffer–
portal ['pɔrtəl] s Portal n
portend [pɔr'tend] tr vorbedeuten
portent ['pɔrtənt] s schlimmes Vorzeichen n, böses Omen n
portentous [pɔr'tentəs] adj unheildrohend
porter ['portər] s (in a hotel) Hausdiener m; (at a station) Gepäckträger m; (doorman) Portier m
portfoli·o [port'folı ,o] s (–os) Aktenmappe f; (fin) Portefeuille n; **without p.** ohne Geschäftsbereich
port'hole' s (for shooting) Schießscharte f; (naut) Bullauge n
porti·co ['portı ,ko] s (–coes & –cos) Säulenvorbau m, Portikus m
portion ['por/ən] s Anteil m; (serving) Portion f; (dowry) Heiratsgut n || tr —**p. out** austeilen, einteilen
portly ['portli] adj wohlbeleibt
port' of call' s Anlaufhafen m
port' of en'try s Einfuhrhafen m
portrait ['portret] s Porträt n
portray [por'tre] tr porträtieren; (fig) beschreiben; (theat) darstellen
portrayal [por'tre·əl] s Porträtieren n; (fig) Beschreibung f; (theat) Darstellung f
port'side' s Backbord m & n
Portugal ['port/əgəl] s Portugal n
Portuguese ['port/ə ,giz] adj portugiesisch || s Portugiese m, Portugiesin f; (language) Portugiesisch n
port' wine' s Portwein m
pose [poz] s Haltung f, Pose f || tr (a question, problem) stellen || intr posieren; **p. as** sich ausgeben als; **p. for an artist** e-m Künstler Modell ste-

hen; **p. for a picture** sich e-m Photographen stellen
posh [paʃ] *adj* (sl) großartig
position [pə'ziʃən] *s* Stellung *f;* (*situation, condition*) Lage *f;* (*job; place of defense*) Stellung *f;* (*point of view*) Standpunkt *m;* (aer, naut) Standort *m;* (astr, mil, naut) Position *f;* **be in a p. to** (*inf*) in der Lage sein zu (*inf*); **in p.** am rechten Platz; **p. wanted** (*as in an ad*) Stelle gesucht; **take a p. on** Stellung nehmen zu; **take one's p.** sich aufstellen
positive ['pazɪtɪv] *adj* (*reply, result, attitude*) positiv; (*answer*) zustimmend; (*sure*) sicher; (*offer*) fest; (elec, math, med, phot, phys) positiv ‖ *s* (gram) Positiv *m;* (phot) Positiv *n*
posse ['pasi] *s* Polizeiaufgebot *n*
possess [pə'zɛs] *tr* besitzen; **be possessed by the devil** von dem Teufel besessen sein
possession [pə'zɛʃən] *s* Besitz *m;* (*property*) Eigentum *n;* **be in p. of s.th.** etw besitzen; **take p. of s.th.** etw in Besitz nehmen
possessive [pə'zɛsɪv] *adj* eifersüchtig; (gram) besitzanzeigend, Besitz–
possibility [,pasɪ'bɪlɪti] *s* Möglichkeit *f*
possible ['pasɪbəl] *adj* möglich; **make p.** ermöglichen
possibly ['pasɪbli] *adv* möglicherweise
possum ['pasəm] *s* Opossum *n;* **play p.** sich verstellen; (*play dead*) sich tot stellen
post [post] *s* (*pole*) Pfahl *m;* (*job; of a sentry*) Posten *m;* (*military camp*) Standort *m* ‖ *tr* (*a notice*) anschlagen; (*a guard*) aufstellen; **p. bond** Kaution stellen; **p. no bills** Plakatankleben verboten
postage ['postɪdʒ] *s* Porto *n*
post'age due' *s* Nachporto *n*
post'age stamp' *s* Briefmarke *f*
postal ['postəl] *adj* Post–
post'al mon'ey or'der *s* Postanweisung *f*
post'card' *s* Ansichtskarte *f*
post'date' *tr* nachdatieren
post'ed *adj*—**keep s.o. p.** j–n auf dem laufenden halten
poster ['postər] *s* Plakat *n*
posterity [pas'terɪti] *s* Nachkommenschaft *f*, Nachwelt *f*
postern ['postərn] *s* Hintertür *f*
post' exchange' *s* Marketenderei *f*
post'haste' *adv* schnellstens
posthumous ['pastʃuməs] *adj* posthum
post'man *s* (–**men**) Briefträger *m*
post'mark' *s* Poststempel *m* ‖ *tr* abstempeln
post'mas'ter *s* Postmeister *m*
post'master gen'eral *s* Postminister *m*
post-mortem [,post'mortəm] *s* Obduktion *f*
post' of'fice *s* Post *f*, Postamt *n*
post'-office box' *s* Postschließfach *n*
post'paid' *adv* frankiert
postpone [post'pon] *tr* (**till, to**) aufschieben (auf *acc*)

postponement [post'ponmənt] *s* Aufschub *m*
post'script' *s* Nachschrift *f*
posture ['pastʃər] *s* Haltung *f*
post'war' *adj* Nachkriegs–
posy ['pozi] *s* Sträußchen *n*
pot [pat] *s* Topf *m;* (*for coffee, tea*) Kanne *f;* (*in gambling*) Einsatz *m;* **go to pot** (sl) hops gehen; **pots and pans** Kochgeschirr *n*
potash ['pat,æʃ] *s* Pottasche *f*, Kali *n*
potassium [pə'tæsɪ·əm] *s* Kalium *n*
pota·to [pə'teto] *s* (–**toes**) Kartoffel *f*
pota'to chips' *spl* Kartoffelchips *pl*
potbellied ['pat,bɛlid] *adj* dickbäuchig
pot'bel'ly *s* Spitzbauch *m*
potency ['potənsi] *s* Stärke *f;* (physiol) Potenz *f*
potent ['potənt] *adj* (*powerful*) mächtig; (*persuasive*) überzeugend; (*e.g., drugs*) wirksam; (physiol) potent
potentate ['potən,tet] *s* Potentat *m*
potential [pə'tɛnʃəl] *adj* möglich; (phys) potentiell ‖ *s* (& elec, math, phys) Potential *n*
pot'hold'er *s* Topflappen *m*
pot'hole' *s* Schlagloch *n*
potion ['poʃən] *s* Trank *m*
pot'luck' *s*—**take p.** mit dem vorliebnehmen, was es gerade gibt
pot' roast' *s* Schmorbraten *m*
pot'sherd' *s* Topfscherbe *f*
pot' shot' *s* müheloser Schuß *m;* **take a p. at** unfair bekritteln
pot'ted *adj* Topf–
potter ['patər] *s* Töpfer *m*
pot'ter's clay' *s* Töpferton *m*
pot'ter's wheel' *s* Töpferscheibe *f*
pottery ['patəri] *s* Tonwaren *pl*
potty ['pati] *s* (coll) Töpfchen *n*
pouch [pautʃ] *s* Beutel *m*
poultice ['poltɪs] *s* Breiumschlag *m*
poultry ['poltri] *s* Geflügel *n*
poul'try·man *s* (–**men**) Geflügelzüchter *m;* (*dealer*) Geflügelhändler *m*
pounce [pauns] *intr*—**p. on** sich stürzen auf (*acc*)
pound [paund] *s* Pfund *n;* (*for animals*) Pferch *m* ‖ *tr* (zer)stampfen; (*meat*) klopfen; **p. the sidewalks** Pflaster treten ‖ *intr* (*said of the heart*) klopfen; **p. on** (*e.g., a door*) hämmern an (*acc*)
–pound *suf* –pfündig
pound' ster'ling *s* Pfund *n* Sterling
pour [por] *tr* gießen; (*e.g., coffee*) einschenken; **p. away** wegschütten ‖ *intr* (meteor) gießen; **p. out of** (*e.g., a theater*) strömen aus ‖ *impers*—**it's pouring** es gießt
pout [paut] *s* Schmollen *n* ‖ *intr* schmollen
pout'ing *adj* (*lips*) aufgeworfen ‖ *s* Schmollen *n*
poverty ['pavərti] *s* Armut *f*
pov'erty-strick'en *adj* verarmt
POW ['pi'o'dʌb'l,ju] *s* (**prisoner of war**) Kriegsgefangener *m*
powder ['paudər] *s* Pulver *n;* (*cosmetic*) Puder *m* ‖ *tr* (*e.g., the face*) pudern; (*plants*) stäuben; (*a cake*) bestreuen ‖ *intr* zu Pulver werden

pow'der box' *s* Puderdose *f*
pow'dered milk' *s* Milchpulver *n*
pow'dered sug'ar *s* Staubzucker *m*
pow'der keg' *s* Pulverfaß *n*
pow'der puff' *s* Puderquaste *f*
pow'der room' *s* Damentoilette *f*
powdery ['paʊdəri] *adj* pulverig
power ['paʊ·ər] *s* Macht *f*; *(personal control)* Gewalt *f*; *(electricity)* Strom *m*; (math) Potenz *f*; (opt) Vergrößerungskraft *f*; (phys) Leistung *f*; (pol) Macht *f*; **be in p.** an der Macht sein; **be in s.o.'s p.** in j–s Gewalt sein; **be within s.o.'s p.** in j–s Macht liegen; **come to p.** an die Macht gelangen; **have the p. to** (*inf*) vermögen zu (*inf*); **more p. to you!** viel Erfolg!; **the powers that be** die Obrigkeit *f* ‖ *tr* antreiben
pow'er brake' *s* (aut) Servobremse *f*
pow'er dive' *s* (aer) Vollgassturzflug *m*
pow'er drill' *s* Elektrobohrer *m*
pow'er-driv'en *adj* mit Motorantrieb
pow'er fail'ure *s* Stromausfall *m*
powerful ['paʊ·ərfəl] *adj* mächtig; (opt) stark
pow'erhouse' *s* Kraftwerk *n*; (coll) Kraftprotz *m*
pow'erhun'gry *adj* herrschsüchtig
powerless ['paʊ·ərlɪs] *adj* machtlos
pow'er line' *s* Starkstromleitung *f*
pow'er mow'er *s* Motorrasenmäher *m*
pow'er of attorn'ey *s* Vollmacht *f*
pow'er plant' *s* *(powerhouse)* Kraftwerk *n*; (aer, aut) Triebwerk *n*
pow'er shov'el *s* Löffelbagger *m*
pow'er sta'tion *s* Kraftwerk *n*
pow'er steer'ing *s* Servolenkung *f*
pow'er supply' *s* Stromversorgung *f*
practicable ['præktɪkəbəl] *adj* praktikabel, durchführbar
practical ['præktɪkəl] *adj* praktisch
prac'tical joke' *s* Streich *m*
practically ['præktɪkəli] *adv* praktisch; *(almost)* fast, so gut wie
prac'tical nurse' *s* praktisch ausgebildete Krankenschwester *f*
practice ['præktɪs] *s* *(exercise)* Übung *f*; *(habit)* Gewohnheit *f*; *(of medicine, law)* Praxis *f*; **in p.** *(in training)* in der Übung; *(in reality)* in der Praxis; **make it a p. to** (*inf*) es sich *[dat]* zur Gewohnheit machen zu (*inf*); **out of p.** aus der Übung ‖ *tr* *(a profession)* tätig sein als; *(patience, reading, dancing, etc.)* sich üben in *(dat)*; *(music, gymnastics)* treiben; *(piano, etc.)* üben ‖ *intr* üben; *(said of a doctor)* praktizieren; **p. on** *(e.g., the violin, piano, parallel bars)* üben auf *(dat)*
prac'tice game' *s* Übungsspiel *n*
prac'tice teach'er *s* Studienreferendar –in *mf*
practitioner [præk'tɪʃənər] *s* Praktiker –in *mf*
pragmatic [præg'mætɪk] *adj* pragmatisch
pragmatism ['prægmə‚tɪzəm] *s* Sachlichkeit *f*; (philos) Pragmatismus *m*
Prague [prɑg] *s* Prag *n*
prairie ['prɛri] *s* Steppe *f*, Prärie *f*

praise [prez] *s* Lob *n* ‖ *tr* **(for)** loben *(wegen)*; **p. to the skies** verhimmeln
praise'wor'thy *adj* lobenswert
prance [præns] *intr* tänzeln
prank [præŋk] *s* Schelmenstreich *m*
prate [pret] *intr* schwätzen
prattle ['prætəl] *s* Geplapper *n* ‖ *intr* plappern, schwätzen
prawn [prɔn] *s* Garnele *f*
pray [pre] *tr & intr* beten
prayer [prer] *s* Gebet *n*; **say a p.** ein Gebet sprechen
prayer' book' *s* Gebetbuch *n*
preach [pritʃ] *tr & intr* predigen
preacher ['pritʃər] *s* Prediger *m*
preamble ['pri‚æmbəl] *s* Präambel *f*
precarious [prɪ'kɛrɪ·əs] *adj* prekär
precaution [prɪ'kɔʃən] *s* Vorsichtsmaßnahme *f*; **as a p.** vorsichtshalber; **take precautions** Vorkehrungen treffen
precede [prɪ'sid] *tr* vorausgehen *(dat)* ‖ *intr* vorangehen
precedence ['prɛsɪdəns] *s* Vorrang *m*; **take p. over** den Vorrang haben vor *(dat)*
precedent ['prɛsɪdənt] *s* Präzedenzfall *m*; **set a p.** e–n Präzedenzfall schaffen
preced'ing *adj* vorhergehend
precept ['prisept] *s* Vorschrift *f*
precinct ['prisɪŋkt] *s* Bezirk *m*
precious ['prɛʃəs] *adj* *(expensive)* kostbar; *(valuable)* wertvoll; *(excessively refined)* geziert; *(child)* lieb ‖ *adv* **p. few** (coll) herzlich wenige
pre'cious stone' *s* Edelstein *m*
precipice ['prɛsɪpɪs] *s* Abgrund *m*
precipitate [prɪ'sɪpɪ‚tet] *adj* steil abfallend ‖ *s* (chem) Niederschlag *m* ‖ *tr* *(hurl)* **(into)** stürzen (in *acc*); *(bring about)* heraufbeschwören; *(vapor)* (chem) niederschlagen; *(from a solution)* (chem) ausfällen ‖ *intr* (chem, meteor) sich niederschlagen
precipitation [prɪ‚sɪpɪ'teʃən] *s* (meteor) Niederschlag *m*
precipitous [prɪ'sɪpɪtəs] *adj* jäh
precise [prɪ'saɪs] *adj* präzis, genau
precision [prɪ'sɪʒən] *s* Präzision *f*
preclude [prɪ'klud] *tr* ausschließen
precocious [prɪ'koʃəs] *adj* frühreif
preconceived [‚prikən'sivd] *adj* vorgefaßt
predatory ['prɛdə‚tori] *adj* Raub–
predecessor ['prɛdɪ‚sɛsər] *s* Vorgänger –in *mf*
predestination [‚pridɛstɪ'neʃən] *s* Prädestination *f*
predicament [prɪ'dɪkəmənt] *s* Mißliche Lage *f*
predicate ['prɛdɪkɪt] *s* (gram) Aussage *f*, Prädikat *n* ‖ ['prɛdɪ‚ket] *tr* **(of)** aussagen (über *acc*); *(base)* **(on)** gründen (auf *acc*)
predict [prɪ'dɪkt] *tr* voraussagen
prediction [prɪ'dɪkʃən] *s* Voraussage *f*
predispose [‚pridɪs'poz] *tr* **(to)** im voraus geneigt machen (zu); (pathol) empfänglich machen (für)
predominant [prɪ'dɑmɪnənt] *adj* vorwiegend

preeminent [prɪ'emɪnənt] *adj* hervorragend

preempt [prɪ'empt] *tr* (*a program*) ersetzen; (*land*) durch Vorkaufsrecht erwerben

preen [prin] *tr* putzen

prefabricated [pri'fæbrɪ͵ketɪd] *adj* Fertig–

preface ['prefɪs] *s* Vorwort *n*, Vorrede *f* || *tr* einleiten

prefer [prɪ'fʌr] *v* (*pret & pp* –ferred; *ger* –ferring) *tr* bevorzugen; (*charges*) vorbringen; **I p. to wait** ich warte lieber

preferable ['prefərəbəl] *adj* (**to**) vorzuziehen(d) (*dat*)

preferably ['prefərəbli] *adv* vorzugsweise

preferred' stock' *s* Vorzugsaktie *f*

prefix ['prifɪks] *s* Vorsilbe *f*, Präfix *n* || *tr* vorsetzen

pregnancy ['pregnənsi] *s* Schwangerschaft *f*; (*of animals*) Trächtigkeit *f*

pregnant ['pregnənt] *adj* schwanger; (*animals*) trächtig; (*fig*) inhaltsschwer

prehistoric [͵prihɪs'tɔrɪk] *adj* vorgeschichtlich, prähistorisch

prejudice ['predʒədɪs] *s* Voreingenommenheit *f*; (*detriment*) Schaden *m* || *tr* beeinträchtigen; **p. s.o. against** j-n einnehmen gegen

pre'judiced *adj* voreingenommen

prejudicial [͵predʒə'dɪʃəl] *adj* (**to**) schädlich (für)

prelate ['prelɪt] *s* Prälat *m*

preliminary [prɪ'lɪmɪ͵neri] *adj* einleitend, Vor– || *s* Vorbereitung *f*

prelude ['prel(j)ud] *s* (fig, mus, theat) Vorspiel *n*

premarital [pri'mærɪtəl] *adj* vorehelich

premature [͵primə't(j)ʊr] *adj* verfrüht; **p. birth** Frühgeburt *f*

premeditated [pri'medɪ͵tetɪd] *adj* vorbedacht; (*murder*) vorsätzlich

premier [prɪ'mɪr] *s* Premier *m*

premiere [prɪ'mɪr] *s* Erstaufführung *f*

premise ['premɪs] *s* Voraussetzung *f*; **on the premises** an Ort und Stelle; **the premises** das Lokal

premium ['primɪ·əm] *s* Prämie *f*; **at a p.** (*in demand*) sehr gesucht; (*at a high price*) über pari

premonition [͵primə'nɪʃən] *s* Vorahnung *f*

preoccupation [pri͵ɑkjə'peʃən] *s* (**with**) Beschäftigtsein *n* (mit)

preoccupied [pri'ɑkjə͵paɪd] *adj* ausschließlich beschäftigt

preparation [͵prepə're ʃən] *s* Vorbereitung *f*; (med) Präparat *n*

preparatory [prɪ'pærə͵tori] *adj* vorbereitend; **p. to** vor (*dat*)

prepare [prɪ'per] *tr* vorbereiten; (*a meal*) zubereiten; (*a prescription*) anfertigen; (*a document*) abfassen

preparedness [prɪ'perɪdnɪs] *s* Bereitschaft *f*; (mil) Einsatzbereitschaft *f*

pre·pay [pri'pe] *v* (*pret & pp* –paid) *tr* im voraus bezahlen

preponderant [prɪ'pɑndərənt] *adj* überwiegend

preposition [͵prepə'zɪʃən] *s* Präposition *f*, Verhältniswort *n*

prepossessing [͵pripə'zesɪŋ] *adj* einnehmend

preposterous [prɪ'pɑstərəs] *adj* lächerlich

prep' school' [prep] *s* Vorbereitungsschule *f*

prerecorded [͵prirɪ'kɔrdɪd] *adj* vorher aufgenommen

prerequisite [pri'rekwɪzɪt] *s* Voraussetzung *f*, Vorbedingung *f*

prerogative [prɪ'rɑgətɪv] *s* Vorrecht *n*

presage ['presɪdʒ] *s* Vorzeichen *n* || [prɪ'sedʒ] *tr* ein Vorzeichen sein für

Presbyterian [͵prezbɪ'tɪrɪ·ən] *adj* presbyterianisch || *s* Presbyterianer –in *mf*

prescribe [prɪ'skraɪb] *tr* vorschreiben; (med) verordnen

prescription [prɪ'skrɪpʃən] *s* Vorschrift *f*; (med) Rezept *n*, Verordnung *f*

presence ['prezəns] *s* Anwesenheit *f*; **pres'ence of mind'** *s* Geistesgegenwart *f*

present ['prezənt] *adj* (*at this place*) anwesend; (*of the moment*) gegenwärtig || *s* (*gift*) Geschenk *n*; (*present time or tense*) Gegenwart *f*; **at p.** zur Zeit; **for the p.** vorläufig || [prɪ'zent] *tr* bieten; (*facts*) darstellen; (*introduce*) vorstellen; (theat) vorführen; **p. s.o. with s.th.** j-m etw verehren

presentable [prɪ'zentəbəl] *adj* presentabel

presentation [͵prezən'teʃən] *s* Vorstellung *f*; (theat) Aufführung *f*

pres'ent-day' *adj* heutig, aktuell

presentiment [prɪ'zentɪmənt] *s* Ahnung *f*

presently ['prezəntli] *adv* gegenwärtig; (*soon*) alsbald

preservation [͵prezər'veʃən] *s* Erhaltung *f*; (**from**) Bewahrung *f* (vor *dat*)

preservative [prɪ'zʌrvətɪv] *s* Konservierungsmittel *n*

preserve [prɪ'zʌrv] *s* Revier *n*; **preserves** Konserven *pl* || *tr* konservieren; **p. from** schützen vor (*dat*)

preside [prɪ'zaɪd] *intr* (**over**) den Vorsitz führen (über *acc* or bei)

presidency ['prezɪdənsi] *s* Präsidentschaft *f*

president ['prezɪdənt] *s* Präsident –in *mf*; (*of a university*) Rektor –in *mf*; (*of a board*) Vorsitzende *mf*

presidential [͵prezɪ'dentʃəl] *adj* Präsidenten–

press [pres] *adj* (*agency, agent, conference, gallery, report, secretary*) Presse– || *s* (*wine press; printing press; newspapers*) Presse *f*; **go to p.** in Druck gehen || *tr* drucken; (*a suit*) (auf)bügeln; (*a person*) bedrängen; (*fruit*) ausdrücken; **be pressed for** knapp sein an (*dat*); **p. s.o. to** (*inf*) j-n dringend bitten zu (*inf*); **p. the button** auf den Knopf drücken || *intr* (*said of time*) drängen; **p. for** drängen auf (*acc*); **p. forward** sich vorwärtsdrängen

press' box' *s* Pressekabine *f*
press' card' *s* Presseausweis *m*
press'ing *adj* dringend, dringlich
press' release' *s* Pressemitteilung *f*
pressure ['prɛʃər] *s* Druck *m*; (of
work) Andrang *m*; (aut) Reifendruck
m; put p. on unter Druck setzen || *tr*
drängen
pres'sure cook'er *s* Schnellkochtopf *m*
pres'sure group' *s* Interessengruppe *f*
pressurize ['prɛʃəˌraɪz] *tr* druckfest
machen
prestige [prɛs'tiʒ] *s* Prestige *n*
presumably [prɪ'z(j)uməbli] *adv* vermutlich
presume [prɪ'z(j)um] *tr* vermuten ||
intr vermuten; p. on pochen auf
(acc)
presumption [prɪ'zʌmpʃən] *s* Vermutung *f*; (presumptuousness) Anmaßung *f*
presumptuous [prɪ'zʌmptʃu·əs] *adj* anmaßend
presuppose [ˌprisə'poz] *tr* vorausset-
zen
pretend [prɪ'tɛnd] *tr* vorgeben; he
pretended that he was a captain er
gab sich für e-n Hauptmann aus ||
intr so tun, als ob
pretender [prɪ'tɛndər] *s* Quaksalber *m*;
p. to the throne Thronbewerber *m*
pretense [prɪ'tɛns], ['pritəns] *s* Schein
m; under false pretenses unter Vor-
spiegelung falscher Tatsachen; under
the p. of unter dem Vorwand (genit)
pretentious [prɪ'tɛnʃəs] *adj* (person)
anmaßend; (home) protzig
pretext ['pritɛkst] *s* Vorwand *m*
pretty ['prɪti] *adj* hübsch || *adv* (coll)
ziemlich
pretzel ['prɛtsəl] *s* Brezel *f*
prevail [prɪ'vel] *intr* (predominate)
(vor)herrschen; (triumph) (against)
sich behaupten (gegen); p. on überreden
prevail'ing *adj* (fashion, view) (vor)-
herrschend; (situation) obwaltend
prevalence ['prɛvələns] *s* Vorherrschen
n
prevalent ['prɛvələnt] *adj* vorherrschend; be p. herrschen
prevaricate [prɪ'værɪˌket] *intr* Ausflüchte machen
prevent [prɪ'vɛnt] *tr* verhindern; (war,
danger) abwenden; p. s.o. from j-n
hindern an (dat); p. s.o. from (ger)
j-n daran hindern zu (inf)
prevention [prɪ'vɛnʃən] *s* Verhütung *f*
preventive [prɪ'vɛntɪv] *adj* vorbeugend
|| *s* Schutzmittel *n*
preview ['priˌvju] *s* Vorschau *f*
previous ['privɪ·əs] *adj* vorhergehend,
vorig; Vor–, e.g., p. conviction Vor-
strafe *f*; p. day Vortag *m*; p. record
Vorstrafenregister *n*
previously ['privɪ·əsli] *adv* vorher
prewar ['priˌwɔr] *adj* Vorkriegs–
prey [pre] *s* Beute *f*, Raub *m*; (fig)
Opfer *n*; fall p. to (& fig) zum Opfer
fallen (dat) || *intr*—p. on erbeuten;
(exploit) ausbeuten; p. on s.o.'s mind
an j-s Gewissen nagen

price [praɪs] *s* Preis *m*; (st. exch.)
Kurs *m*; at any p. um jeden Preis
at the p. of im Wert von || *tr* mi
Preisen versehen; (inquire about the
price of) nach dem Preis frager
(genit)
price' control' *s* Preiskontrolle *f*
price' fix'ing *s* Preisbindung *f*
price' freeze' *s* Preisstopp *m*
priceless ['praɪslɪs] *adj* unbezahlbar
(coll) sehr komisch
price' range' *s* Preislage *f*
price' rig'ging *s* Preistreiberei *f*
price' tag' *s* Preiszettel *m*, Preisschilc
n
price'-wage' spi'ral *s* Preis-Lohn-Spi-
rale *f*
price' war' *s* Preiskrieg *m*
prick [prɪk] *s* (& fig) Stich *m* || *t*
stechen; p. up (ears) spitzen
prickly ['prɪkli] *adj* stachelig, Stech–
prick'ly heat' *s* Hitzepickel *pl*
pride [praɪd] *s* Stolz *m*; (pej) Hochmu
m; swallow one's p. seinen Stolz ir
die Tasche stecken; take p. in stoLz
sein auf (acc) || *tr*—p. oneself oi
sich viel einbilden auf (acc)
priest [prist] *s* Priester *m*
priestess ['prɪstɪs] *s* Priesterin *f*
priest'hood' *s* Priestertum *n*
priestly ['pristli] *adj* priesterlich
prig [prɪg] *s* Tugendbold *m*
prim [prɪm] *adj* (primmer; primmest
spröde
primacy ['praɪməsi] *s* Primat *m* & *n*
primarily [praɪ'mɛrɪli] *adv* vor allen
primary ['praɪˌmɛri] *adj* primär
Haupt–; (e.g., color, school) Grund-
|| *s* (pol) Vorwahl *f*
primate ['praɪmet] *s* (zool) Primat *n*
prime [praɪm] *adj* (chief) Haupt–
(best) erstklassig || *s* Blüte *f*; (math
Primzahl *f*; p. of life Lenz *m* de:
Lebens || *tr* (a pump) ansaugen las
sen; (ammunition) scharfmachen; (a
surface for painting) grundieren
(with information) vorher informie
ren
prime' min'ister *s* Ministerpräsident *m*
(in England) Premierminister *m*
primer ['praɪmər] *s* Fibel *f* || ['praɪmər
s (for painting) Grundierfarbe *f*; (o,
an explosive) Zündsatz *m*; (aut) Ein
spritzpumpe *f*
prime' time' *s* schönste Zeit *f*
primeval [praɪ'mivəl] *adj* urweltlich
Ur–; p. world Urwelt *f*
primitive ['prɪmɪtɪv] *adj* primitiv ||
Primitive *mf*, Urmensch *m*
primp [prɪmp] *tr* aufputzen || *intr* sicl
aufputzen, sich zieren
prim'rose' *s* Himmelschlüssel *m*
prince [prɪns] *s* Prinz *m*, Fürst *m*
Prince' Al'bert *s* Gehrock *m*
princely ['prɪnsli] *adj* prinzlich
princess ['prɪnsɪs] *s* Prinzessin *f*, Für
stin *f*
principal ['prɪnsɪpəl] *adj* Haupt– ||
(educ) Schuldirektor –in *mf*; (fin
Kapitalbetrag *m*, Kapital *n*
principality [ˌprɪnsɪ'pæliti] *s* Fürsten
tum *n*

principally ['prɪnsɪpəli] *adv* größtenteils
principle ['prɪnsɪpəl] *s* Grundsatz *m*, Prinzip *n;* **in p.** im Prinzip
print [prɪnt] *s* (*lettering; design on cloth*) Druck *m;* (*printed dress*) bedrucktes Kleid *n;* (phot) Abzug *m;* **in cold p.** schwarz auf weiß; **out of p.** vergriffen ‖ *tr* drucken; (*e.g., one's name*) in Druckschrift schreiben; (phot) kopieren; (tex) bedrucken
print'ed mat'ter *s* Drucksache *f*
printer ['prɪntər] *s* Drucker *m;* (phot) Kopiermaschine *f*
prin'ter's ink' *s* Druckerschwärze *f*
print'ing *s* Drucken *n;* (*of a book*) Buchdruck *m;* (*subsequent printing*) Abdruck *m;* (phot) Kopieren *n*, Abziehen *n*
print'ing press' *s* Druckerpresse *f*
print' shop' *s* Druckerei *f*
prior ['praɪ·ər] *adj* vorherig; **p. to** vor (*dat*) ‖ *s* (eccl) Prior *m*
priority [praɪ'ɔrɪti] *s* Priorität *f*
prism ['prɪzəm] *s* Prisma *n*
prison ['prɪzən] *s* Gefängnis *n*
pris'on camp' *s* Gefangenenlager *n*
prisoner ['prɪz(ə)nər] *s* Gefangene *mf;* (*in a concentration camp*) Häftling *m;* **be taken p.** in Gefangenschaft geraten; **take p.** gefangennehmen
pris'oner of war' *s* Kriegsgefangene *mf*
prissy ['prɪsi] *adj* zimperlich
privacy ['praɪvəsi] *s* Zurückgezogenheit *f;* **disturb s.o.'s p.** j–s Ruhe stören
private ['praɪvɪt] *adj* privat; (*personal*) persönlich; **keep p.** geheimhalten ‖ *s* (mil) Gemeine *mf;* **in p.** privat(im); **privates** Geschlechtsteile *pl*
pri'vate cit'izen *s* Privatperson *f*
pri'vate eye' *s* (coll) Privatdetektiv *m*
pri'vate first' class' *s* Gefreite *mf*
privately ['praɪvɪtli] *adv* privat(im)
privet ['prɪvɪt] *s* Liguster *m*
privilege ['prɪvɪlɪdʒ] *s* Privileg *n*
privy ['prɪvi] *adj*—**p. to** eingeweiht in (*acc*) ‖ *s* Abtritt *m*
prize [praɪz] *s* Preis *m*, Prämie *f;* (nav) Prise *f* ‖ *tr* schätzen
prize' fight' *s* Preisboxkampf *m*
prize' fight'er *s* Berufsboxer *m*
prize' ring' *s* Boxring *m*
pro [pro] *s* (**pros**) (coll) Profi *m;* **the pros and the cons** das Für und Wider ‖ *prep* für (*acc*)
probability [ˌprɑbə'bɪlɪti] *s* Wahrscheinlichkeit *f;* **in all p.** aller Wahrscheinlichkeit nach
probable ['prɑbəbəl] *adj* wahrscheinlich
probate ['probet] *s* Testamentsbestätigung *f* ‖ *tr* bestätigen
pro'bate court' *s* Nachlaßgericht *n*
probation [pro'beʃən] *s* Probe *f;* (jur) Bewährungsfrist *f;* **on p.** auf Probe; (jur) mit Bewährung
proba'tion of'ficer *s* Bewährungshelfer –in *mf*
probe [prob] *s* (jur) Untersuchung *f;*

(mil) Sondierungsangriff *m;* (rok) Versuchsrakete *f;* (surg) Sonde *f* ‖ *tr* (*with the hands*) abtasten; (fig & surg) sondieren
problem ['prɑbləm] *s* Problem *n;* (math) Aufgabe *f*
prob'lem child' *s* Sorgenkind *n*
procedure [pro'sidʒər] *s* Verfahren *n*
proceed [pro'sid] *intr* (*go on*) fortfahren; (*act*) verfahren; **p. against** (jur) vorgehen gegen; **p. from** kommen von; **p. to** (*inf*) darangehen zu (*inf*)
proceed'ing *s* Vorgehen *n;* **proceedings** (*of a society*) Sitzungsberichte *pl;* (jur) Verfahren *n*
proceeds ['prosidz] *spl* Erlös *n*
process ['prɑsɛs] *s* Verfahren *n*, Prozeß *m;* **be in p.** im Gang sein; **in the p.** dabei ‖ *tr* (*raw materials*) verarbeiten; (*applications*) bearbeiten; (*persons*) abfertigen; (phot) entwickeln und vervielfältigen
procession [pro'sɛʃən] *s* Prozession *f*
proclaim [pro'klem] *tr* ankündigen; (*a law*) bekanntmachen; **p. (as) a holiday** zum Feiertag erklären
proclamation [ˌprɑklə'meʃən] *s* Aufruf *m*, Proklamation *f*
procrastinate [pro'kræstɪˌnet] *intr* zaudern
proctor ['prɑktər] *s* Aufsichtsführende *mf* ‖ *tr* beaufsichtigen
procure [pro'kjʊr] *tr* besorgen, verschaffen; (*said of a pimp*) verkuppeln
procurement [pro'kjʊrmənt] *s* Besorgung *f*
procurer [pro'kjʊrər] *s* Kuppler *m*
prod [prɑd] *s* Stoß *m;* (*stick*) Stachelstock *m* ‖ *v* (*pret & pp* **prodded;** *ger* **prodding**) *tr* stoßen; **prod s.o. into** (*ger*) j–n dazu anstacheln zu (*inf*)
prodigal ['prɑdɪgəl] *adj* verschwenderisch
prod'igal son' *s* verlorener Sohn *m*
prodigious [pro'dɪdʒəs] *adj* großartig
prodigy ['prɑdɪdʒi] *s* Wunderzeichen *n;* (*talented child*) Wunderkind *n*
produce ['prɑd(j)us] *s* (*product*) Erzeugnis *n;* (*amount produced*) Ertrag *m;* (*fruits and vegetables*) Bodenprodukte *pl* ‖ [pro'd(j)us] *tr* produzieren; (*manufacture*) herstellen; (*said of plants, trees*) hervorbringen; (*interest, profit*) abwerfen; (*proof*) beibringen; (*papers*) vorlegen; (cin) produzieren; (theat) inszenieren ‖ *intr* (bot) tragen; (econ) Gewinne abwerfen
pro'duce depart'ment *s* Obst– und Gemüseabteilung *f*
producer [pro'd(j)usər] *s* Hersteller *m;* (cin, theat) Produzent –in *mf*
product ['prɑdʌkt] *s* Erzeugnis *n*, Produkt *n*
production [pro'dʌkʃən] *s* Erzeugung *f*, Produktion *f;* (fa, lit) Werk *n*
productive [pro'dʌktɪv] *adj* produktiv
profane [pro'fen] *adj* profan; **p. language** Fluchen *n* ‖ *tr* profanieren
profanity [pro'fænɪti] *s* Fluchen *n;* **profanities** Flüche *pl*

profess [pro'fɛs] *tr* gestehen
profession [pro'fɛʃən] *s* Beruf *m; (of faith)* Bekenntnis *n;* **by p.** von Beruf
professional [pro'fɛʃənəl] *adj* berufsmäßig, professionell ‖ *s (expert)* Fachmann *m;* (sport) Profi *m*
profes'sional jea'lousy *s* Brotneid *m*
professor [pro'fɛsər] *s* Professor –in *mf*
profes'sorship' *s* Professur *f*
proffer ['prɑfər] *s* Angebot *n* ‖ *tr* anbieten
proficient [pro'fɪʃənt] *adj* tüchtig
profile ['profaɪl] *s* Profil *n; (biographical sketch)* Kurzbiographie *f*
profit ['prɑfɪt] *s* Gewinn *m;* **show a p.** e–n Gewinn abwerfen ‖ *tr* nutzen ‖ *intr* (**by**) Nutzen ziehen aus
profitable ['prɑfɪtəbəl] *adj* einträglich
profiteer [,prɑfɪ'tɪr] *s* Wucherer *m,* Schieber *m* ‖ *intr* wuchern, schieben
prof'it shar'ing *s* Gewinnbeteiligung *f*
profligate ['prɑflɪgɪt] *adj* verkommen; *(extravagant)* verschwenderisch ‖ *s* verkommener Mensch *m; (spendthrift)* Verschwender –in *mf*
profound [pro'faʊnd] *adj (knowledge)* gründlich; *(change)* tiefgreifend
profuse [prə'fjus] *adj* überreichlich
progeny ['prɑdʒəni] *s* (& bot) Nachkommenschaft *f; (of animals)* Junge *pl*
progno·sis [prɑg'nosɪs] *s* (–**ses** [siz]) Prognose *f*
prognosticate [prɑg'nɑstɪ,ket] *tr* voraussagen
pro·gram ['progræm] *s* Programm *n; (radio or television show)* Sendung *f* ‖ *v (pret & pp* –**grammed; ger** –**gramming)** *tr* programmieren
progress ['prɑgrɛs] *s* Fortschritt *m;* **be in progress** im Gang sein ‖ [prə'grɛs] *intr (make progress)* fortschreiten; *(develop)* sich fortentwickeln
progressive [prə'grɛsɪv] *adj* fortschrittlich; *(party)* Fortschritts– ‖ *s* Fortschrittler –in *mf*
prog'ress report' *s* Tätigkeitsbericht *m*
prohibit [pro'hɪbɪt] *tr* verbieten
prohibition [,pro·ə'bɪʃən] *s* Verbot *n;* (hist) Prohibition *f*
prohibitive [pro'hɪbɪtɪv] *adj (costs)* unertragbar; *(prices)* unerschwinglich
project ['prɑdʒɛkt] *s* Project *n,* Vorhaben *n* ‖ [prə'dʒɛkt] *tr (light, film)* projizieren; *(plan)* vorhaben ‖ *intr* vorspringen, vorragen
projectile [prə'dʒɛktɪl] *s (fired from a gun)* Projektil *n; (thrown object)* Wurfgeschoß *n*
projection [prə'dʒɛkʃən] *s (jutting out)* Vorsprung *m,* Vorbau *m;* (cin) Projektion *f*
projector [prə'dʒɛktər] *s* Projektor *m*
proletarian [,prolɪ'tɛrɪ·ən] *adj* proletarisch ‖ *s* Proletarier –in *mf*
proletariat [,prolɪ'tɛrɪ·ət] *s* Proletariat *n*
proliferate [prə'lɪfə,ret] *intr* sich stark vermehren
prolific [prə'lɪfɪk] *adj* fruchtbar
prolix [pro'lɪks] *adj* weitschweifig

prologue ['prolɔg] *s* Prolog *m*
prolong [pro'lɔŋ] *tr* verlängern
promenade [,prɑmɪ'ned] *s* Promenade *f* ‖ *intr* promenieren
promenade' deck' *s* Promenadendeck *n*
prominent ['prɑmɪnənt] *adj* hervorragend, prominent; *(chin)* vorstehend
promiscuity [,prɑmɪs'kju·ɪti] *s* Promiskuität *f*
promiscuous [pro'mɪskju·əs] *adj* unterschiedslos; *(sexually)* locker
promise ['prɑmɪs] *s* Versprechen *n* ‖ *tr* versprechen
prom'ising *adj (thing)* aussichtsreich; *(person)* vielversprechend
prom'issory note' ['prɑmɪ,sori] *s* Eigenwechsel *m*
promontory ['prɑmən,tori] *s* Landspitze *f*
promote [prə'mot] *tr (in rank)* befördern; *(a cause)* fördern; *(a pupil)* versetzen; *(wares)* werben für
promoter [prə'motər] *s* Förderer –in *mf;* (sport) Veranstalter –in *mf*
promotion [prə'moʃən] *s (in rank)* Beförderung *f; (of a cause)* Förderung *f; (of a pupil)* Versetzung *f*
prompt [prɑmpt] *adj* prompt ‖ *tr* veranlassen; (theat) soufflieren *(dat)*
prompter ['prɑmptər] *s* Souffleur *m,* Souffleuse *f*
promp'ter's box' *s* Souffleurkasten *m*
promptness ['prɑmptnɪs] *s* Pünktlichkeit *f*
promulgate [pro'mʌlget] *tr* bekanntmachen
prone [pron] *adj*—**be p. to** neigen zu; **in the p. position** auf Anschlag liegend
prong [prɔŋ] *s (of a fork)* Zinke *f; (of a deer)* Sprosse *f*
pronoun ['pronaʊn] *s* Fürwort *n*
pronounce [prə'naʊns] *tr (enunciate)* aussprechen; **p. sentence** das Strafausmaß festsetzen; **p. s.o.** *(e.g., guilty, insane, man and wife)* erklären für
pronouncement [prə'naʊnsmənt] *s (announcement)* Erklärung *f; (of a sentence)* (jur) Verkündung *f*
pronunciation [prə,nʌnsɪ'eʃən] *s* Aussprache *f*
proof [pruf] *adj*—**p. against** (fig) gefeit gegen; **90 p.** 45 prozentig ‖ *s* Beweis *m;* (phot) Probebild *n;* (typ) Korrekturbogen *m*
proof'read'er *s* Korrektor –in *mf*
prop [prɑp] *s* Stütze *f;* **props** (coll) Beine *pl;* (theat) Requisiten *pl* ‖ *v (pret & pp* **propped; ger propping)** *tr* stützen; **p. oneself up** sich aufstemmen; **p. up** abstützen
propaganda [,prɑpə'gændə] *s* Propaganda *f*
propagate ['prɑpə,get] *tr* fortpflanzen; (fig) propagieren ‖ *intr* sich fortpflanzen
pro·pel [prə'pɛl] *v (pret & pp* –**pelled; ger** –**pelling)** *tr* antreiben
propeller [prə'pɛlər] *s* (aer) Propeller *m;* (naut) Schraube *f*
propensity [prə'pɛnsɪti] *s* Neigung *f*

proper ['prɑpər] *adj* passend; (*way, time*) richtig; (*authority*) zuständig; (*strictly so-called*) selbst, e.g., Germany p. Deutschland selbst
properly ['prɑpərli] *adj* gehörig
prop'er name' *s* Eigenname *m*
property ['prɑpərti] *s* Eigentum *n*; (*land*) Grundstück *n*; (*quality*) Eigenschaft *f*
prop'erty dam'age *s* Sachschaden *m*
prop'erty tax' *s* Grundsteuer *f*
prophecy ['prɑfɪsi] *s* Prophezeiung *f*
prophe·sy ['prɑfɪ͵saɪ] *v* (*pret & pp* –sied) *tr* prophezeien
prophet ['prɑfɪt] *s* Prophet *m*
prophetess ['prɑfɪtɪs] *s* Prophetin *f*
prophylactic [͵profɪ'læktɪk] *adj* prophylaktisch || *s* Prophylaktikum *n*; (*condom*) Präservativ *n*
propitiate [prə'pɪʃɪ͵et] *tr* versöhnen
propitious [prə'pɪʃəs] *adj* günstig
prop'jet' *s* Flugzeug *n* mit Turboprop
proportion [prə'porʃən] *s* Verhältnis *n*; in p. to im Verhältnis zu; out of p. to in keinem Verhältnis zu; proportions Proportionen *pl* || *tr* bemessen; well proportioned gut proportioniert
proposal [prə'pozəl] *s* Vorschlag *m*; (*of marriage*) Heiratsantrag *m*
propose [prə'poz] *tr* vorschlagen; (*intend*) beabsichtigen; p. a toast to e–n Toast ausbringen auf (*acc*) || *intr* (to) e–n Heiratsantrag machen (*dat*)
proposition [͵prɑpə'zɪʃən] *s* Vorschlag *m*; (*log, math*) Lehrsatz *m* || *tr* ansprechen
propound [prə'paund] *tr* vortragen
proprietor [prə'praɪ·ətər] *s* Inhaber *m*
proprietress [prə'praɪ·ətrɪs] *s* Inhaberin *f*
propriety [prə'praɪ·əti] *s* Anstand *m*; proprieties Anstandsformen *pl*
propulsion [prə'pʌlʃən] *s* Antrieb *m*
prorate [pro'ret] *tr* anteilmäßig verteilen
prosaic [pro'ze·ɪk] *adj* prosaisch
proscribe [pro'skraɪb] *tr* proskribieren
prose [proz] *adj* Prosa– || *s* Prosa *f*
prosecute ['prɑsɪ͵kjut] *tr* verfolgen
prosecutor ['prɑsɪ͵kjutər] *s* Ankläger –in *mf*
proselytize ['prɑsɪlə͵taɪz] *intr* Anhänger gewinnen
prose' writ'er *s* Prosaiker –in *mf*
prosody ['prɑsədi] *s* Silbenmessung *f*
prospect ['prɑspɛkt] *s* Aussicht *f*; (*person*) Interessent –in *mf*; hold out the p. of s.th. etw in Aussicht stellen || *intr* (for) schürfen (nach)
prospector ['prɑspɛktər] *s* Schürfer *m*
prospectus [prə'spɛktəs] *s* Prospekt *m*
prosper ['prɑspər] *intr* gedeihen
prosperity [prɑs'pɛrɪti] *s* Wohlstand *m*
prosperous ['prɑspərəs] *adj* wohlhabend
prostitute ['prɑstɪ͵t(j)ut] *s* Prostituierte *f* || *tr* prostituieren
prostrate ['prɑstret] *adj* hingestreckt; (*exhausted*) erschöpft || *tr* niederwerfen; (*fig*) niederzwingen

prostration [prɑs'treʃən] *s* Niederwerfen *n*; (*abasement*) Demütigung *f*
protagonist [pro'tægənɪst] *s* Protagonist *m*, Hauptfigur *f*
protect [prə'tɛkt] *tr* (be)schützen; (*interests*) wahrnehmen; p. from schützen vor (*dat*)
protection [prə'tɛkʃən] *s* (from) Schutz *m* (vor *dat*)
protector [prə'tɛktər] *s* Beschützer *m*
protein ['protin] *s* Protein *n*
protest ['protɛst] *s* Protest *m* || [pro'tɛst] *tr & intr* protestieren
Protestant ['prɑtɪstənt] *adj* protestantisch || *s* Protestant –in *mf*
protocol ['protə͵kal] *s* Protokoll *n*
proton ['protan] *s* Proton *n*
protoplasm ['protə͵plæzəm] *s* Protoplasma *n*
prototype ['protə͵taɪp] *s* Prototyp *m*
protozo·an [͵protə'zo·ən] *s* (–a [ə]) Einzeller *m*
protract [pro'trækt] *tr* hinziehen
protrude [pro'trud] *intr* hervorstehen
proud [praud] *adj* (of) stolz (auf *acc*)
prove [pruv] *v* (*pret* proved; *pp* proved & proven ['pruvən]) *tr* beweisen; p. a failure sich nicht bewähren; p. one's worth sich bewähren || *intr*— p. right zutreffen; p. to be sich erweisen als
proverb ['prɑvərb] *s* Sprichwort *n*
proverbial [prə'vʌrbɪ·əl] *adj* sprichwörtlich
provide [prə'vaɪd] *tr* (*s.th.*) besorgen; p. s.o. with s.th. j–n mit etw versorgen || *intr*—p. for (*e.g., a family*) sorgen für; (*e.g., a special case*) vorsehen; (*the future*) voraussehen
provid'ed *adj* (with) versehen (mit) || *conj* vorausgesetzt, daß
Providence ['prɑvɪdəns] *s* Vorsehung *f*
providential [͵prɑvɪ'dɛntʃəl] *adj* von der Vorsehung beschlossen
provid'ing *conj* vorausgesetzt, daß
province ['prɑvɪns] *s* (*district*) Provinz *f*; (*special field*) Ressort *n*
provision [prə'vɪʒən] *s* (*providing*) Versorgung *f*; (*stipulation*) Bestimmung *f*; make p. for Vorsorge treffen für; provisions Lebensmittelvorräte *pl* || *tr* (*mil*) verpflegen
provisional [prə'vɪʒənəl] *adj* vorläufig
provi·so [prə'vaɪzo] *s* (–sos & –soes) Vorbehalt *m*
provocation [͵prɑvə'keʃən] *s* Provokation *f*
provocative [prə'vɑkətɪv] *adj* aufreizend
provoke [prə'vok] *tr* (*a person*) provozieren; (*e.g., laughter*) erregen
provok'ing *adj* ärgerlich
prow [prau] *s* Bug *m*
prowess ['prau·ɪs] *s* Tapferkeit *f*
prowl [praul] *intr* herumschleichen
prowl' car' *s* Streifenwagen *m*
prowler ['praulər] *s* mutmaßlicher Einbrecher *m*
proximity [prak'sɪmɪti] *s* Nähe *f*
proxy ['prɑksi] *s* Stellvertreter –in *mf*; by p. in Vertretung

prude [prud] *s* prüde Person *f*
prudence ['prudəns] *s* Klugheit *f;* (*caution*) Vorsicht *f*
prudent ['prudənt] *adj* klug; (*cautious*) umsichtig
prudish ['prudɪʃ] *adj* prüde
prune [prun] *s* Zwetschge *f* || *tr* stuzen
Prussia ['prʌʃɪə] *s* Preußen *n*
Prussian ['prʌʃən] *adj* preußisch || *s* Preuße *m*, Preußin *f*
pry [praɪ] *v* (*pret & pp* **pried**) *tr*—**pry open** aufbrechen; **pry s.th. out of s.o.** etw aus j-m herauspressen || *intr* herumschnüffeln; **pry into** seine Nase stecken in (*acc*)
P.S. ['pi'es] *s* (**postscript**) NS
psalm [sɑm] *s* Psalm *m*
pseudo– ['sudo] *adj* Pseudo–, falsch
pseudonym ['sudənɪm] *s* Deckname *m*
psyche ['saɪki] *s* Psyche *f*
psychiatrist [saɪ'kaɪətrɪst] *s* Psychiater –in *mf*
psychiatry [saɪ'kaɪətri] *s* Psychiatrie *f*
psychic ['saɪkɪk] *adj* psychisch || *s* Medium *n*
psychoanalysis [ˌsaɪko·ə'nælɪsɪs] *s* Psychoanalyse *f*
psychoanalyze [ˌsaɪko'ænə ˌlaɪz] *tr* psychoanalytisch behandeln
psychologic(al) [ˌsaɪko'ludʒɪk(əl)] *adj* psychologisch
psychologist [saɪ'kɑlədʒɪst] *s* Psychologe *m*, Psychologin *f*
psychology [saɪ'kɑlədʒi] *s* Psychologie *f*
psychopath ['saɪkə ˌpæθ] *s* Psychopath –in *mf*
psycho·sis [saɪ'kosɪs] *s* (**–ses** [siz]) Psychose *f*
psychotic [saɪ'kɑtɪk] *adj* psychotisch || *s* Psychosekranke *mf*
pto'main poi'soning ['tomen] *s* Fleischvergiftung *f*
pub [pʌb] *s* Kneipe *f*
puberty ['pjubərti] *s* Pubertät *f*
public ['pʌblɪk] *adj* öffentlich || *s* Öffentlichkeit *f*, Publikum *n*
pub'lic address' sys'tem *s* Lautsprecheranlage *f*
publication [ˌpʌblɪ'keʃən] *s* Veröffentlichung *f*
pub'lic domain' *n*—**in the p. d.** gemeinfrei
publicity [pʌb'lɪsɪti] *s* Publizität *f*
publicize ['pʌblɪ ˌsaɪz] *tr* bekanntmachen
pub'lic opin'ion *s* öffentliche Meinung *f*
pub'lic-opin'ion poll' *s* öffentliche Meinungsumfrage *f*
pub'lic pros'ecutor *s* Staatsanwalt *m*
pub'lic rela'tions *spl* Kontaktpflege *f*
pub'lic serv'ant *s* Staatsangestellte *mf*
pub'lic util'ity *s* öffentlicher Versorgungsbetrieb *m*
publish ['pʌblɪʃ] *tr* veröffentlichen
publisher ['pʌblɪʃər] *s* Verleger –in *mf*
pub'lishing house' *s* Verlag *m*
puck [pʌk] *s* Puck *m*
pucker ['pʌkər] *tr* (*the lips*) spitzen || *intr*—**p. up** den Mund spitzen
pudding ['pudɪŋ] *s* Pudding *m*

puddle ['pʌdəl] *s* Pfütze *f*, Lache *f*
pudgy ['pʌdʒi] *adj* dicklich
puerile ['pju·ərɪl] *adj* knabenhaft
puff [pʌf] *s* (*on a cigarette*) Zug *m;* (*of smoke*) Rauchwölkchen *n;* (*on sleeves*) Puff *m* || *tr* (*e.g., a cigar*) paffen; **p. oneself up** sich aufblähen; **p. out** ausblasen || *intr* keuchen; **p. on** (*a pipe, cigar*) paffen an (*dat*)
pugilist ['pjudʒɪlɪst] *s* Faustkämpfer *m*
pugnacious [pʌg'neʃəs] *adj* kampflustig
pug-nosed ['pʌg ˌnozd] *adj* stupsnasig
puke [pjuk] *s* (sl) Kotze *f* || *intr* (sl) kotzen
pull [pul] *s* Ruck *m;* (*influence*) Beziehungen *pl;* (*of gravity*) Anziehungskraft *f* || *tr* ziehen; (*a muscle*) zerren; (*proof*) (typ) abziehen; **p. down** (*e.g., a shade*) herunterziehen; (*a building*) niederreißen; **p. off** (coll) zuwegebringen; **p. oneself together** sich zusammennehmen; **p. out** (*weeds*) herausreißen; **p. up** (*e.g., a chair*) heranrücken || *intr* (on) ziehen (an *dat*); **p. back** sich zurückziehen; **p. in** (*arrive*) ankommen; **p. out** (*depart*) abfahren; **p. over to the side** an den Straßenrand heranfahren; **p. through** durchkommen; **p. up** (*e.g., in a car*) vorfahren
pullet ['pulɪt] *s* Hühnchen *n*
pulley ['puli] *s* Rolle *f;* (*pulley block*) Flaschenzug *m*
pull'o'ver *s* Pullover *m*
pulmonary ['pʌlmə ˌneri] *adj* Lungen–
pulp [pʌlp] *s* Brei *m;* (*to make paper*) Papierbrei *m;* **beat to a p.** windelweich schlagen
pulpit ['pulpɪt] *s* Kanzel *f*
pulsate ['pʌlset] *intr* pulsieren
pulsation [pʌl'seʃən] *s* Pulsieren *n*
pulse [pʌls] *s* Puls *m;* **take s.o.'s p.** j–m den Puls fühlen
pulverize ['pʌlvə ˌraɪz] *tr* pulverisieren
pum'ice stone' ['pʌmɪs] *s* Bimsstein *m*
pum·mel ['pʌməl] *v* (*pret & pp* –**mel[l]**-ed; *ger* –**mel[l]ing**) *tr* mit der Faust schlagen
pump [pʌmp] *s* Pumpe *f;* (*shoe*) Pump *m* || *tr* pumpen; (*for information*) ausfragen; **p. up** (*a tire*) aufpumpen
pump'han'dle *s* Pumpenschwengel *m*
pumpkin ['pʌmpkɪn] *s* Kürbis *m*
pun [pʌn] *s* Wortspiel *n* || *v* (*pret & pp* **punned**; *ger* **punning**) *intr* ein Wortspiel machen
punch [pʌntʃ] *s* Faustschlag *m;* (*to make holes*) Locher *m;* (*drink*) Punsch *m* || *tr* mit der Faust schlagen; (*a card*) lochen; (*a punch clock*) stechen
punch' bowl' *s* Punschschüssel *f*
punch' card' *s* Lochkarte *f*
punch' clock' *s* Kontrolluhr *f*
punch'-drunk' *adj* von Faustschlägen betäubt
punch'ing bag' *s* Punchingball *m*
punch' line' *s* Pointe *f*
punctilious [pʌŋk'tɪlɪ·əs] *adj* förmlich
punctual ['pʌŋktʃu·əl] *adj* pünktlich
punctuate ['pʌŋktʃu ˌet] *tr* interpunktieren

punctuation [ˌpʌŋktʃʊ'eʃən] s Interpunktion f
punctua'tion mark' s Satzzeichen n
puncture ['pʌŋktʃər] s Loch n ‖ tr durchstechen; **p. a tire** e-e Reifenpanne haben
punc'ture-proof' adj pannensicher
pundit ['pʌndɪt] s Pandit m
pungent ['pʌndʒənt] adj beißend, scharf
punish ['pʌnɪʃ] tr (be)strafen
punishment ['pʌnɪʃmənt] s Strafe f, Bestrafung f; (educ) Strafarbeit f
punk [pʌŋk] adj (sl) mies; **I feel p.** mir ist mies ‖ s (sl) Rocker m
punster ['pʌnstər] s Wortspielmacher m
puny ['pjuni] adj kümmerlich, winzig
pup [pʌp] s junger Hund m
pupil ['pjupəl] s Schüler –in mf; (of the eye) Pupille f
puppet ['pʌpɪt] s Marionette f
pup'pet gov'ernment s Marionettenregierung f
pup'pet show' s Marionettentheater n
puppy ['pʌpi] s Hündchen n
pup'py love' s Jugendliebe f
purchase ['pʌrtʃəs] s Kauf m; (leverage) Hebelwirkung f ‖ tr kaufen
pur'chasing pow'er s Kaufkraft f
pure [pjʊr] adj (& fig) rein
purgative ['pʌrgətɪv] s Abfuhrmittel n
purgatory ['pʌrgə‚tori] s Fegefeuer n
purge [pʌrdʒ] s (pol) Säuberungsaktion f ‖ tr reinigen; (pol) säubern
puri·fy ['pjʊrɪ‚faɪ] v (pret & pp –fied) tr reinigen, läutern
puritan ['pjʊrɪtən] adj puritanisch ‖ **Puritan** s Puritaner –in mf
purity ['pjʊrɪti] s Reinheit f
purloin [pər'lɔɪn] tr entwenden
purple ['pʌrpəl] adj purpurn ‖ s Purpur m
purport ['pʌrport] s Sinn m ‖ [pər'port] tr vorgeben; (imply) besagen
purpose ['pʌrpəs] s Absicht f; (goal) Zweck m; **on p.** absichtlich; **to no p.** ohne Erfolg
purposely ['pʌrpəsli] adv absichtlich
purr [pʌr] s Schnurren n ‖ intr schnurren
purse [pʌrs] s Beutel m; (handbag) Handtasche f ‖ tr—**p. one's lips** den Mund spitzen
purse' strings' spl—**hold the p.** über das Geld verfügen
pursue [pər's(j)u] tr (a person; a plan, goal) verfolgen; (studies, profession) betreiben; (pleasures) suchen
pursuit [pər's(j)ut] s Verfolgung f; **in hot p.** hart auf den Fersen
pursuit' plane' s Jäger m
purvey [pər've] tr liefern, versorgen
pus [pʌs] s Eiter m
push [pʊʃ] s Schub m; (mil) Offensive f ‖ tr (e.g., a cart) schieben; (jostle) stoßen; (a button) drücken auf (acc); **p. around** (coll) schlecht behandeln; **p. aside** beiseite schieben; (curtains) zurückschlagen; **p. one's way through** sich durchdrängen; **p. through** durchsetzen ‖ intr drängen

push' but'ton s Druckknopf m
push' cart' s Verkaufskarren m
push'o'ver s (snap) (coll) Kinderspiel n; (sucker) Gimpel m; (easy opponent) leicht zu besiegender Gegner m
push'-up' s (gym) Liegestütz m
pushy ['pʊʃi] adj zudringlich
puss [pʊs] s (cat) Mieze f; (face) (sl) Fresse f
pussy ['pʌsi] adj eit(e)rig ‖ ['pʊsi] s Mieze f
puss'y wil'low s Salweide f
put [pʊt] v (pret & pp **put**; ger **putting**) tr (stand) stellen; (lay) legen; (set) setzen; **feel put out** ungehalten sein; **put across to** beibringen (dat); **put aside** beiseite legen; **put down** (a load) abstellen; (a rebellion) niederschlagen; (in writing) aufschreiben; **put in** (e.g., a windowpane) einsetzen; (e.g., a good word) einlegen; (time) (on) verwenden (auf acc); **put off** (a person) hinhalten; (postpone) aufschieben; **put on** (clothing) anziehen; (a hat) aufsetzen; (a ring) anstecken; (an apron) umbinden; (the brakes) betätigen; (to cook) ansetzen; (a play) aufführen; **put on an act** sich in Szene setzen; **put oneself into** sich hineindenken in (acc); **put oneself out** sich [dat] Umstände machen; **put on its feet again** (com) auf die Beine stellen; **put s.o. on to s.th.** j-n auf etw [acc] bringen; **put out** (a fire) löschen; (lights) auslöschen; (throw out) herauswerfen; (a new book) herausbringen; **put out of action** kampfunfähig machen; **put over on** s.o. j-n übers Ohr hauen; **put through** durchsetzen; (a call) (telp) herstellen; **put** (s.o.) **through to** (telp) j-n verbinden mit; **put to good use** gut verwenden; **put up** (erect) errichten; (bail) stellen; (for the night) unterbringen; **put up a fight** sich zur Wehr setzen; **put up to** anstiften zu; **to put it mildly** gelinde gesagt ‖ intr —**put on** sich verstellen; **put out to sea** (said of a ship) in See gehen; **put up with** sich abfinden mit
put'-on' adj vorgetäuscht ‖ s (affectation) Affektiertheit f; (parody) Jux m
put-put ['pʌt'pʌt] s Tacktack n ‖ intr —**p. along** knattern
putrid ['pjutrɪd] adj faul(ig)
putt [pʌt] tr & intr (golf) putten
putter ['pʌtər] s (golf) Putter m ‖ intr—**p. around** herumwursteln
put·ty ['pʌti] s Kitt m ‖ v (pret & pp –tied) tr (ver)kitten
put'ty knife' s Spachtel m & f
put'-up job' s abgekartete Sache f
puzzle ['pʌzəl] s Rätsel n; (game) Geduldspiel n ‖ tr verwirren; **be puzzled** verwirrt sein; **p. out** enträtseln ‖ intr—**p. over** tüfteln an (dat)
puzzler ['pʌzlər] s Rätsel n
puz'zling adj rätselhaft
PW ['pi'dʌbəl‚ju] s (prisoner of war) Kriegsgefangene mf

pygmy ['pɪgmi] s Pygmäe m, Pygmäin f
pylon ['paɪlɑn] s (entrance to Egyptian temple) Pylon m; (aer) Wendemarke f; (elec) Leitungsmast m
pyramid ['pɪrəmɪd] s Pyramide f

pyre [paɪr] s Scheiterhaufen m
Pyrenees ['pɪrɪ‚niz] spl Pyrenäen pl
pyrotechnics [‚paɪrə'tɛknɪks] spl Feuerwerkskunst f, Pyrotechnik f
python ['paɪθɑn] s Pythonschlange f
pyx [pɪks] s (eccl) Pyxis f

Q

Q, q [kju] s siebzehnter Buchstabe des englischen Alphabets
quack [kwæk] s Quacksalber m, Kurpfuscher m ‖ intr schnattern
quadrangle ['kwɑd‚ræŋgəl] s Viereck n; (inner yard) Innenhof m, Lichthof m
quadrant ['kwɑdrənt] s Quadrant m
quadratic [kwɑd'rætɪk] adj quadratisch
quadruped ['kwɑdrʊ‚pɛd] s Vierfüßer m
quadruple [kwɑd'rupəl] adj vierfach ‖ s Vierfache n ‖ tr vervierfachen ‖ intr sich vervierfachen
quadruplets [kwɑd'ruplɛts] spl Vierlinge pl
quaff [kwɑf] tr in langen Zügen trinken
quagmire ['kwæg‚maɪr] s Morast m
quail [kwel] s Wachtel f ‖ intr verzagen
quaint [kwent] adj seltsam
quake [kwek] s Zittern n; (geol) Beben n ‖ intr zittern; (geol) beben
Quaker ['kwekər] s Quäker –in mf
qualification [‚kwɑlɪfɪ'keʃən] s (for) Qualifikation f (für)
quali·fy ['kwɑlɪ‚faɪ] v (pret & pp –fied) tr qualifizieren; (modify) einschränken ‖ intr sich qualifizieren
quality ['kwɑlɪti] s (characteristic) Eigenschaft f; (grade) Qualität f
qualm [kwɑm] s Bedenken n
quandary ['kwɑndəri] s Dilemma n
quantity ['kwɑntɪti] s Menge f, Quantität f; (math) Größe f; (pros) Silbenmaß n; **buy in q.** auf Vorrat kaufen
quan'tum the'ory ['kwɑntəm] s Quantentheorie f
quarantine ['kwɔrən‚tin] s Quarantäne f ‖ tr unter Quarantäne stellen
quar·rel ['kwɔrəl] s Streit m; **pick a q.** Händel suchen ‖ v (pret & pp –rel[l]ed; ger –el[l]ing) intr (over) streiten (über acc or um)
quarrelsome ['kwɔrəlsəm] adj streitsüchtig, händelsüchtig
quar·ry ['kwɔri] s Steinbruch m; (hunt) Jagdbeute f ‖ v (pret & pp –ried) tr brechen
quart [kwɔrt] s Quart n
quarter ['kwɔrtər] s Viertel n; (of a city) Stadtviertel n; (of the moon) Mondviertel n; (of the sky) Himmelsrichtung f; (coin) Vierteldollar m; (econ) Quartal n; (sport) Viertelzeit f; **a q. after one** (ein) Viertel nach

eins; **a q. of an hour** e–e Viertelstunde f; **a q. to eight** dreiviertel acht, (ein) viertel vor acht; **at close quarters** im Nahkampf; **from all quarters** von überall; **give no q.** keinen Pardon geben; **quarters** (& mil) Unterkunft f, Quartier n ‖ tr (lodge) einquartieren; (divide into four, tear into quarters) vierteilen ‖ intr im Quartier liegen
quar'ter-deck' s Quarterdeck n
quar'terfi'nal s Zwischenrunde f
quar'ter-hour' s Viertelstunde f
quarterly ['kwɔrtərli] adj vierteljährig; (econ) Quartals– ‖ s Vierteljahresschrift f
quar'termas'ter s Quartiermeister m
Quar'termaster Corps' s Versorgungstruppen pl
quar'ter note' s (mus) Viertelnote f
quar'ter rest' s (mus) Viertelpause f
quartet [kwɔr'tɛt] s Quartett n
quartz [kwɔrts] s Quarz m
quash [kwɑʃ] tr niederschlagen
quatrain ['kwɑtren] s Vierzeiler m
quaver ['kwevər] s Zittern n; (mus) Triller m ‖ intr zittern; (mus) trillern, tremolieren
queasy ['kwizi] adj übel
queen [kwin] s Königin f; (cards) Dame f
queen' bee' s Bienenkönigin f
queen' dow'ager s Königinwitwe f
queenly ['kwinli] adj königlich
queen' moth'er s Königinmutter f
queer [kwɪr] adj sonderbar; (homosexual) schwul ‖ s (homosexual) Schwule mf
queer' duck' s (coll) Unikum n
quell [kwɛl] tr unterdrücken
quench [kwɛntʃ] tr (thirst) löschen; (a fire) (aus)löschen
que·ry ['kwɪri] s Frage f ‖ v (pret & pp –ried) tr befragen; (cast doubt on) bezweifeln
quest [kwɛst] s Suche f; **in q. of** auf der Suche nach
question ['kwɛstʃən] s Frage f; **ask (s.o.) a q.** (j–m) e–e Frage stellen; **be out of the q.** außer Frage stehen; **beyond q.** außer Frage; **call into q.** in Frage stellen; **call the q.** (parl) um Abstimmung bitten; **in q.** betreffend; **it is a q. of** (ger) es handelt sich darum zu (inf); **q. of time** Zeitfrage f; **that's an open q.** darüber läßt sich streiten; **there's no q. about it** darüber besteht kein Zweifel ‖ tr be-

fragen; (*said of the police*) verhören; (*cast doubt on*) bezweifeln
questionable ['kwestʃənəbəl] *adj* fraglich, fragwürdig; (*doubtful*) zweifelhaft; (*character*) bedenklich
ques'tioning *s* Verhör *n*, Vernehmung *f*
ques'tion mark' *s* Fragezeichen *n*
questionnaire [ˌkwestʃə'ner] *s* Frage-
bogen *m*
queue [kju] *s* Schlange *f* ‖ *intr*—**q. up**
sich anstellen
quibble ['kwɪbəl] *s* Deutelei *f* ‖ *intr*
(*about*) deuteln (an *dat*)
quibbler ['kwɪblər] *s* Wortklauber *m*
quick [kwɪk] *adj* schnell, fix ‖ *s*—**cut
to the q.** bis ins Mark treffen
quicken ['kwɪkən] *tr* beschleunigen ‖
intr sich beschleunigen
quick'lime' *s* gebrannter ungelöschter
Kalk *m*
quick' lunch' *s* Schnellimbiß *m*
quick'sand' *s* Treibsand *m*
quick'sil'ver *s* Quecksilber *n*
quick'-tem'pered *adj* jähzornig
quick'-wit'ted *adj* scharfsinnig
quiet ['kwaɪ-ət] *adj* ruhig; (*person*)
schweigsam; (*still*) still; (*street*) un-
belebt; **be q.!** sei still!; **keep q.**
schweigen ‖ *s* Stille *f* ‖ *tr* beruhigen
‖ *intr*—**q. down** sich beruhigen; (*said
of excitement, etc.*) sich legen
quill [kwɪl] *s* Feder *f*, Federkiel *m*;
(*of a porcupine*) Stachel *m*
quilt [kwɪlt] *s* Steppdecke *f* ‖ *tr* steppen
quince [kwɪns] *s* Quitte *f*
quince' tree' *s* Quittenbaum *m*
quinine ['kwaɪnaɪn] *s* Chinin *n*
quintessence [kwɪn'tesəns] *s* Inbegriff
m
quintet [kwɪn'tet] *s* Quintett *n*
quintuplets [kwɪn'tʌplets] *spl* Fünf-
linge *pl*
quip [kwɪp] *s* witziger Seitenhieb *m* ‖
v (*pret & pp* **quipped; ger quipping**)
tr witzig sagen ‖ *intr* witzeln

quire [kwaɪr] *s* (bb) Lage *f*
quirk [kwʌrk] *s* Eigenart *f*; (*subterfuge*) Ausflucht *f*; (*sudden change*)
plötzliche Wendung *f*
quit [kwɪt] *adj* quitt; **let's call it quits!**
(coll) Strich drunter! ‖ *v* (*pret & pp*
quit & quitted; ger quitting) *tr* aufgeben; (*e.g., a gang*) abspringen von;
q. it! hören Sie damit auf! ‖ *intr*
aufhören; (*at work*) seine Stellung
aufgeben
quite [kwaɪt] *adv* recht, ganz; **q. a disappointment** e–e ausgesprochene Enttäuschung *f*; **q. recently** in jüngster
Zeit; **q. the reverse** genau das Gegenteil
quitter ['kwɪtər] *s* Schlappmacher *m*
quiver ['kwɪvər] *s* Zittern *n*; (*to hold
arrows*) Köcher *m* ‖ *intr* zittern
quixotic [kwɪks'ɑtɪk] *adj* überspannt
quiz [kwɪz] *s* Prüfung *f*; (*game*) Quiz
n ‖ *v* (*pret & pp* **quizzed; ger quiz-
zing**) *tr* ausfragen; **q. s.o. on s.th.**
j–n etw abfragen
quiz'mas'ter *s* Quizonkel *m*
quiz' show' *s* Quizshow *f*
quizzical ['kwɪzɪkəl] *adj* (*puzzled*)
verwirrt; (*strange*) seltsam; (*mocking*) spöttisch
quoit [kwɔɪt] *s* Wurfring *m*
quondam ['kwɑndæm] *adj* ehemalig
Quon'set hut' ['kwɔnsət] *s* Nissen-
hütte *f*
quorum ['kworəm] *s* beschlußfähige
Anzahl *f*
quota ['kwotə] *s* Quote *f*, Anteil *m*;
(*work*) Arbeitsleistung *f*
quotation [kwo'teʃən] *s* Zitat *n*; (*price*)
Notierung *f*
quota'tion marks' *spl* Anführungszei-
chen *pl*
quote [kwot] *s* Zitat *n*; (*of prices*)
Notierung *f* ‖ *tr* zitieren; (*prices*)
notieren ‖ *interj*—**q. ... unquote** Beginn des Zitats! ... Ende des Zitats!
quotient ['kwoʃənt] *s* Quotient *m*

R

R, r [ɑr] *s* achtzehnter Buchstabe des
englischen Alphabets
rabbet ['ræbɪt] *s* Falz *m* ‖ *tr* falzen
rabbi ['ræbaɪ] *s* Rabbiner *m*
rabbit ['ræbɪt] *s* Kaninchen *n*
rabble ['ræbəl] *s* Pöbel *m*
rab'ble-rous'er *s* Volksaufwiegler –in
mf
rabid ['ræbɪd] *adj* rabiat; (*dog*) toll-
wütig
rabies ['rebiz] *s* Tollwut *f*
raccoon [ræ'kun] *s* Waschbär *m*
race [res] *s* Rasse *f*; (*contest*) Wettren-
nen *n*; (fig) Wettlauf *m* ‖ *tr* um die
Wette laufen mit; (*in a car*) um die
Wette fahren mit; (*a horse*) rennen
lassen; (*an engine*) hochjagen ‖ *intr*

rennen; (*on foot*) um die Wette laufen; (*in a car*) um die Wette fahren
race' driv'er *s* Rennfahrer –in *mf*
race' horse' *s* Rennpferd *n*
racer ['resər] *s* (*person*) Wettfahrer
–in *mf*; (*car*) Rennwagen *m*; (*in
speed skating*) Schnelläufer –in *mf*
race' ri'ot *s* Rassenaufruhr *m*
race' track' *s* Rennbahn *f*
racial ['reʃəl] *adj* rassisch, Rassen–
rac'ing *s* Rennsport *m*
racism ['resɪzəm] *s* Rassenhaß *m*
rack [ræk] *s* (*shelf*) Regal *n*, Ablage *f*;
(*for clothes, bicycles, hats*) Ständer
m; (*for luggage*) Gepäcknetz *n*; (*for
fodder*) Futterraufe *f*; (*for torture*)
Folter *f*; (*toothed bar*) Zahnstange *f*;

go to r. and ruin völlig zugrunde gehen; **put to the r.** auf die Folter spannen || *tr (with pain)* quälen; **r. one's brains (over)** sich *[dat]* den Kopf zerbrechen (über *acc*)
racket ['rækɪt] *s (noise)* Krach *m; (illegal business)* Schiebergeschäft *n; (tennis)* Rakett *n*
racketeer [,rækɪ'tɪr] *s* Schieber –in *mf*
racketeer'ing *s* Schiebertum *n*
rack' rail'way *s* Zahnradbahn *f*
racy ['resi] *adj (off-color)* schlüpfrig; *(vivacious, pungent)* rassig
radar ['redɑr] *s* Radar *n*
ra'darscope' *s* Radarschirm *m*
radial ['redɪ·əl] *adj* radial
radiance ['redɪ·əns] *s* Strahlung *f*
radiant ['redɪ·ənt] *adj (with)* strahlend (vor *dat*); *(phys)* Strahlungs–
radiate ['redɪ,et] *tr & intr* ausstrahlen
radiation [,redɪ'eʃən] *s* Strahlung *f*
radia'tion belt' *s* Strahlungsgürtel *m*
radia'tion treat'ment *s* Bestrahlung *f;* **give r. treatment to** bestrahlen
radiator ['redɪ,etər] *s* Heizkörper *m; (aut)* Kühler *m*
ra'diator cap' *s* Kühlerverschluß *m*
radical ['rædɪkəl] *adj* radikal || *s* Radikale *mf*
radically ['rædɪkəli] *adv* von Grund auf
radi·o ['redɪ,o] *s (–os)* Radio *n,* Rundfunk *m;* **go on the r.** im Rundfunk sprechen || *tr* funken
ra'dioac'tive *adj* radioaktiv
ra'dio announc'er *s* Rundfunkansager –in *mf*
ra'dio bea'con *s (aer)* Funkfeuer *n*
ra'dio beam' *s* Funkleitstrahl *m*
ra'dio broad'cast *s* Rundfunksendung *f*
radiocar'bon dat'ing *s* Radiokarbonmethode *f*
ra'diofre'quency *s* Hochfrequenz *f*
radiogram ['redɪ·o,græm] *s* Radiogramm *n*
radiologist [,redɪ'alədʒɪst] *s* Röntgenologe *m,* Röntgenologin *f*
radiology [redɪ'alədʒi] *s* Röntgenologie *f*
ra'dio net'work *s* Rundfunknetz *n*
ra'dio op'erator *s* Funker –in *mf*
radioscopy [,redɪ'askəpi] *s* Durchleuchtung *f*
ra'dio set' *s* Radioapparat *m*
ra'dio sta'tion *s* Rundfunkstation *f*
radish ['rædɪʃ] *s* Radieschen *n*
radium ['redɪ·əm] *s* Radium *n*
radi·us ['redɪ·əs] *s (–i [,aɪ] & –uses)* Halbmesser *m; (anat)* Speiche *f;* **within a r. of** in e-m Umkreis von
raffish ['ræfɪʃ] *adj* gemein, niedrig
raffle ['ræfəl] *s* Tombola *f* || *tr—***r. off** in e-r Tombola verlosen
raft [ræft] *s* Floß *n;* **a r. of** *(coll)* ein Haufen *m*
rafter ['ræftər] *s* Dachsparren *m;* **rafters** Sparrenwerk *n*
rag [ræg] *s* Lumpen *m;* **chew the rag** *(sl)* quasseln
ragamuffin ['rægə,mʌfɪn] *s* Lump *m*
rag' doll' *s* Stoffpuppe *f*
rage [redʒ] *s* Wut *f;* **all the r.** letzter

Schrei *m;* **be the r.** die große Mode sein; **fly into a r.** in Wut geraten || *intr* wüten, toben
ragged ['rægɪd] *adj* zerlumpt, lumpig
rag'man *s (–men)* Lumpenhändler *m*
ragout [ræ'gu] *s* Ragout *n*
rag'weed' *s* Ambrosiapflanze *f*
raid [red] *s* Beutezug *m; (by police)* Razzia *f; (mil)* Überfall *m* || *tr* überfallen; **e-e Razzia machen auf** *(acc)*
raider ['redər] *s (naut)* Kaperkreuzer *m;* **raiders** *(mil)* Kommandotruppe *f*
rail [rel] *s* Geländerstange *f; (naut)* Reling *f; (rr)* Schiene *f;* **by r.** per Bahn || —**r. at** beschimpfen
rail'head' *s* Schienenkopf *m*
rail'ing *s* Geländer *n; (naut)* Reling *f*
rail'road' *s* Eisenbahn *f* || *tr (a bill)* durchpeitschen
rail'road cross'ing *s* Bahnübergang *m*
rail'road embank'ment *s* Bahndamm *m*
rail'road sta'tion *s* Bahnhof *m*
rail'road tie' *s* Schwelle *f*
rail'way' *adj* Eisenbahn– || *s* Eisenbahn *f*
raiment ['remənt] *s* Kleidung *f*
rain [ren] *s* Regen *m;* **it looks like r.** es sieht nach Regen aus; **r. or shine** bei jedem Wetter || *tr*—**r. cats and dogs** Bindfäden regnen; **r. out** verregnen || *intr* regnen
rainbow ['ren,bo] *s* Regenbogen *m*
rain'coat' *s* Regenmantel *m*
rain'drop' *s* Regentropfen *m*
rain'fall' *s* Regenfall *m; (amount of rain)* Regenmenge *f*
rain' gut'ter *s* Dachrinne *f*
rain' pipe' *s* Fallrohr *n*
rain'proof' *adj* regenfest, regendicht
rainy ['reni] *adj* regnerisch; *(e.g., day, weather)* Regen–; **save money for a r. day** sich *[dat]* e-n Notpfennig aufsparen
rain'y sea'son *s* Regenzeit *f*
raise [rez] *s* Lohnerhöhung *f; (in poker)* Steigerung *f* || *tr (lift)* heben, erheben; *(increase)* erhöhen, steigern; *(erect)* aufstellen; *(children)* großziehen; *(a family)* ernähren; *(grain, vegetables)* anbauen; *(animals)* züchten; *(dust)* aufwirbeln; *(money, troops)* aufbringen; *(blisters)* ziehen; *(a question)* aufwerfen; *(hopes)* erwecken; *(a laugh, smile)* hervorrufen; *(the ante)* steigern; *(a siege)* aufheben; *(from the dead)* auferwecken; **r. Cain** (or **hell**) Krach schlagen; **r. the arm** *(before striking)* mit dem Arm ausholen; **r. the price of** verteuern; **r. to a higher power** potenzieren || *intr (in poker)* höher wetten
raisin ['rezən] *s* Rosine *f*
rake [rek] *s* Rechen *m; (person)* Wüstling *m* || *tr* rechen; *(with gunfire)* bestreichen; **r. in** *(money)* kassieren; **r. together** (or **up**) zusammenrechen
rake'-off' *s (coll)* Gewinnanteil *m*
rakish ['rekɪʃ] *adj (dissolute)* liederlich; *(jaunty)* schmissig
ral·ly ['ræli] *s (meeting)* Massenversammlung *f; (recovery)* Erholung *f;*

(mil) Umgruppierung *f* ‖ *v* (*pret &
pp* –**lied**) *tr* (wieder) sammeln ‖ *intr*
sich (wieder) sammeln; (*recover*) sich
erholen
ram [ræm] *s* Schafbock *m* ‖ *v* (*pret &
pp* **rammed**; *ger* **ramming**) *tr* rammen; **ram s.th. down s.o.'s throat**
j–m etw aufdrängen
ramble ['ræmbəl] *intr*—**r. about** her-
umwandern; **r. on** daherreden
ramification [͵ræmɪfɪ'keʃən] *s* Ver-
zweigung *f*
ramp [ræmp] *s* Rampe *f*
rampage ['ræmpedʒ] *s* Toben *n*, Wüten
n; **go on a r.** toben, wüten
rampant ['ræmpənt] *adj*—**be r.** grassieren
rampart ['ræmpɑrt] *s* Wall *m*, Ring-
wall *m*
ram'rod' *s* Ladestock *m*; (*cleaning rod*)
Reinigungsstock *m*
ram'shack'le *adj* baufällig
ranch [rænt∫] *s* Ranch *f*
rancid ['rænsɪd] *adj* ranzig
random ['rændəm] *adj* zufällig, Zufalls–; **at r.** aufs Geratewohl
range [rendʒ] *s* (row) Reihe *f*; (*mountains*) Bergkette *f*; (*stove*) Herd *m*;
(*for firing practice*) Schießplatz *m*;
(*of a gun*) Schießweite *f*; (*distance*)
Reichweite *f*; (mus) Umfang *m*; **at
a r. of** in e–r Entfernung von; **at
close r.** auf kurze Entfernung; **come
within s.o.'s r.** j–m vor den Schuß
kommen; **out of r.** außer Reichweite;
(*in shooting*) außer Schußweite;
within r. in Reichweite; (*in shooting*)
in Schußweite ‖ *tr* reihen ‖ *intr*—
r. from . . . to sich bewegen zwischen
(*dat*) . . . und
range' find'er *s* Entfernungsmesser *m*
ranger ['rendʒər] *s* Förster *m*; **rangers**
Stoßtruppen *pl*
rank [ræŋk] *adj* (*rancid*) ranzig;
(*smelly*) stinkend; (*absolute*) kraß;
(*excessive*) übermäßig; (*growth*)
üppig ‖ *s* Rang *m*; **according to r.**
standesgemäß; **person of r.** Standesperson *f* ‖ *tr* einreihen, rangieren;
be ranked as gelten als ‖ *intr* rangieren; **r. above** stehen über (*dat*);
r. among zählen zu; **r. below** stehen
unter (*dat*); **r. with** mitzählen zu
rank' and file' *s* die breite Masse
rank'ing of'ficer *s* Rangälteste *mf*
rankle ['ræŋkəl] *tr* nagen an (*dat*) ‖
intr nagen
ransack ['rænsæk] *tr* durchstöbern
ransom ['rænsəm] *s* Lösegeld *n* ‖ *tr*
auslösen
rant [rænt] *intr* schwadronieren
rap [ræp] *s* (*on the door*) Klopfen *n*;
(*blow*) Klaps *m*; **not give a rap for**
husten auf (*acc*); **take the rap** den
Kopf hinhalten; **there was a rap on
the door** es klopfte an der Tür ‖ *v*
(*pret & pp* **rapped**; *ger* **rapping**) *tr*
(*strike*) schlagen; (*criticize*) tadeln ‖
intr (*talk freely*) offen reden; (**on**)
klopfen (an *dat*)
rapacious [rə'peʃəs] *adj* raffgierig;
(*animal*) raubgierig

rape [rep] *s* Vergewaltigung *f* ‖ *tr*
vergewaltigen
rapid ['ræpɪd] *adj* rapid(e); (*river*)
reißend ‖ **rapids** *spl* Stromschnelle *f*
rap'id-fire' *adj* Schnell–; (mil) Schnell-
feuer–
rap'id trans'it *s* Nahschnellverkehr *m*
rapier ['repɪ-ər] *s* Rapier *n*
rapist ['repɪst] *s* sexueller Gewaltver-
brecher *m*
rap' ses'sion *s* zwanglose Diskussion *f*
rapt [ræpt] *adj* (*attention*) gespannt;
(*in thought*) vertieft
rapture ['ræptʃər] *s* Entzückung *f*; **go
into raptures** in Entzücken geraten
rare [rer] *adj* selten; (culin) halbgar
rare' bird' *s* (fig) weißer Rabe *m*
rare·fy ['rerɪ͵faɪ] *v* (*pret & pp* –**fied**)
tr verdünnen
rarely ['rerli] *adv* selten
rarity ['rerɪti] *s* Rarität *f*
rascal ['ræskəl] *s* Bengel *m*
rash [ræʃ] *adj* vorschnell, unbesonnen
‖ *s* Ausschlag *m*
rasp [ræsp] *s* (*sound*) Kratzlaut *m*;
(*tool*) Raspel *f* ‖ *tr* raspeln
raspberry ['ræz͵beri] *s* Himbeere *f*
rat [ræt] *s* Ratte *f*; (*deserter*) (sl)
Überläufer –in *mf*; (*informer*) (sl)
Spitzel *m*; (*scoundrel*) (sl) Gauner
m; **smell a rat** (coll) den Braten
riechen ‖ *intr*—**rat on** (sl) verpetzen
ratchet ['rætʃɪt] *s* (*wheel*) Sperrad *n*;
(*pawl*) Sperrklinke *f*
rate [ret] *s* Satz *m*; (*for mail, freight*)
Tarif *m*; **at any r.** auf jeden Fall;
at the r. of (*a certain speed*) mit der
Geschwindigkeit von; (*a certain
price*) zum Preis von; **at the r. of a
dozen per week** ein Dutzend pro
Woche; **at this** (or that) **r.** bei diesem
Tempo ‖ *tr* bewerten ‖ *intr* (coll)
hochgeschätzt sein
rate' of exchange' *s* Kurs *m*
rate' of in'terest *s* Zinssatz *m*
rather ['ræðər] *adv* ziemlich; **I would
r. wait** ich würde lieber warten; **r.
. . . than** lieber . . . als ‖ *interj* na ob!
rati·fy ['rætɪ͵faɪ] *v* (*pret & pp* –**fied**)
tr ratifizieren, bestätigen
rat'ing *s* Beurteilung *f*; (mach) Leistung *f*; (mil) Dienstgrad *m*; (sport)
Bewertung *f*
ra·tio ['reʃ(ɪ)͵o] *s* (–**tios**) Verhältnis
n
ration ['ræʃən], ['reʃən] *s* Ration *f*;
rations (mil) Verpflegung *f* ‖ *tr*
rationieren
ra'tion card' *s* Bezugsschein *m*
ra'tioning *s* Rationierung *f*
rational ['ræʃənəl] *adj* vernünftig
rationalize ['ræʃənə͵laɪz] *tr & intr*
rationalisieren
rat' poi'son *s* Rattengift *n*
rat' race' *s* (fig) Hetzjagd *f*
rattle ['rætəl] *s* Geklapper *n*; (*toy*)
Klapper *f*, Schnarre *f* ‖ *tr* (*confuse*)
verwirren; **get s.o. rattled** j–n aus
dem Konzept bringen; **r. off** herun-
terschnarren; **r. the dishes** mit dem
Geschirr klappern ‖ *intr* klappern;
(*said of a machine gun*) knattern;

(*said of windows*) klirren; **r. on** daherplappern
rat′tlebrain′ *s* Hohlkopf *m*
rat′tlesnake′ *s* Klapperschlange *f*
rat′tletrap′ *s* (coll) Kiste *f*, Karre *f*
rat′trap′ *s* Rattenfalle *f*
raucous ['rɔkəs] *adj* heiser
ravage ['rævɪdʒ] *s* Verwüstung *f*, Verheerung *f* || *tr* verwüsten, verheeren
rave [rev] *s* (coll) Modeschrei *m* || *intr* irrereden; **r. about** schwärmen von
raven ['revən] *adj* (black) rabenschwarz || *s* Kolkrabe *m*, Rabe *m*
ravenous ['rævənəs] *adj* rasend
ravine [rə'vin] *s* Bergschlucht *f*
rav′ing *adj* (coll) toll || *adv*—**r. mad** tobsüchtig
ravish ['rævɪʃ] *tr* vergewaltigen
rav′ishing *adv* entzückend
raw [rɔ] *adj* roh; (weather) naßkalt; (throat) rauh; (recruit) unausgebildet; (skin) wundgerieben; (leather) ungegerbt; (wool) ungesponnen
raw′-boned′ *adj* hager
raw′ deal′ *s* (sl) unfaire Behandlung *f*
raw′hide′ *s* Rohhaut *f*
raw′ mate′rial *s* Rohstoff *m*
ray [re] *s* Strahl *m;* (ichth) Rochen *m;* **ray of hope** Hoffnungsstrahl *m*
rayon ['re-ɑn] *adj* kunstseiden || *s* Kunstseide *f*, Rayon *n*
raze [rez] *tr* abtragen; **r. to the ground** dem Erdboden gleichmachen
razor ['rezər] *s* Rasiermesser *n;* (safety razor) Rasierapparat *m*
ra′zor blade′ *s* Rasierklinge *f*
razz [ræz] *tr* (sl) aufziehen
re [ri] *prep* betreffs (genit)
reach [ritʃ] *s* Reichweite *f;* **beyond the r. of s.o.** für j–n unerreichbar; **out of r.** unerreichbar; **within easy r.** leicht zu erreichen; **within r.** in Reichweite || *tr* (a goal, person, city, advanced age, an understanding) erreichen; (a certain amount) sich belaufen auf (acc); (a compromise) schließen; (an agreement) treffen; (e.g., the ceiling) heranreichen an (acc); **r. out** ausstrecken || *intr* (extend) reichen, sich erstrecken; **r. for** greifen nach; **r. into one's pocket** in die Tasche greifen
react [rɪ'ækt] *intr* (to) reagieren (auf acc); **r. upon** zurückwirken auf (acc)
reaction [rɪ'ækʃən] *s* Reaktion *f*
reactionary [rɪ'ækʃən‚eri] *adj* reaktionär || *s* Reaktionär –in *mf*
reac′tion time′ *s* Reaktionszeit *f*
reactor [rɪ'æktər] *s* Reaktor *m*
read [rid] *v* (pret & pp read [red]) *tr* lesen; **r. a paper on** referieren über (acc); **r. off** verlesen; **r. over** durchlesen; **r. to** vorlesen (dat) || *intr* lesen; (said of a passage) lauten; (said of a thermometer) zeigen; **r. up on** studieren
readable ['ridəbəl] *adj* lesbar
reader ['ridər] *s* (person) Leser –in *mf;* (book) Lesebuch *n*
readily ['redɪli] *adv* gern(e)
readiness ['redɪnɪs] *s* Bereitwilligkeit *f;* (preparedness) Bereitschaft *f*

read′ing *s* (act) Lesen *n;* (material) Lektüre *f;* (version) Lesart *f;* (eccl, parl) Lesung *f*
read′ing glass′es *spl* Lesebrille *f*
read′ing lamp′ *s* Leselampe *f*
read′ing room′ *s* Lesesaal *m*
readjustment [‚ri·ə'dʒʌstmənt] *s* Umstellung *f*
read‧y ['redi] *adj* (done) fertig; **be r.** (stand in readiness) in Bereitschaft stehen; **get r.** sich fertig (or bereit) machen; **get s.th. r.** etw fertigstellen; **r. for** bereit zu; **r. for take-off** startbereit; **r. for use** gebrauchsfertig; **r. to** (inf) bereit zu (inf) || *v* (pret & pp –ied) *tr* fertigmachen
read′y cash′ *s* flüssiges Geld *n*
read′y-made′ *adj* von der Stange
read′y-made′ clothes′ *spl* Konfektion *f*
reaffirm [‚ri·ə'fʌrm] *tr* nochmals beteuern
real ['ri·əl] *adj* wirklich; (genuine) echt; (friend) wahr
re′al estate′ *s* Immobilien *pl*
re′al-estate′ a′gent *s* Immobilienmakler –in *mf*
re′al-estate tax′ *s* Grundsteuer *f*
realist ['ri·əlɪst] *s* Realist –in *mf*
realistic [ri·ə'lɪstɪk] *adj* wirklichkeitsnah, realistisch
reality [ri'ælɪti] *s* Wirklichkeit *f;* **in r.** wirklich; **realities** (facts) Tatsachen *pl*
realize ['ri·ə‚laɪz] *tr* einsehen; (a profit) erzielen; (a goal) verwirklichen; (a good) realisieren
really ['ri·əli] *adv* wirklich; **not r.** eigentlich nicht
realm [relm] *s* Königreich *n;* (fig) Reich *n*, Gebiet *n;* **within the r. of possibility** im Rahmen des Möglichen
realtor ['ri·əltər] *s* Immobilienmakler –in *mf*
ream [rim] *s* Ries *n* || *tr* ausbohren
reamer ['rimər] *s* Reibahle *f*
reap [rip] *tr* (cut) mähen; (& fig) ernten
reaper ['ripər] *s* Mäher –in *mf;* (mach) Mähmaschine *f*
reappear [‚ri·ə'pɪr] *intr* wiederauftauchen, wiedererscheinen
rearmament [ri'ɑrməmənt] *s* Wiedererscheinen *n*
reappoint [‚ri·ə'pɔɪnt] *tr* wieder anstellen
rear [rɪr] *adj* hintere, rückwärtig || *s* Hinterseite *f;* (of an army) Nachhut *f;* (sl) Hintern *m;* **bring up the r.** den Schluß bilden; (mil) den Zug beschließen; **from the r.** von hinten; **to the r.** nach hinten; **to the r.,** **march!** kehrt, marsch! || *tr* (children) aufziehen; (animals) züchten; (a structure, one's head) aufrichten || *intr* sich bäumen
rear′ ad′miral *s* Konteradmiral *m*
rear′ ax′le *s* Hinterachse *f*
rear′ end′ *s* (sl) Hintern *m*
rear′ guard′ *s* (mil) Nachhut *f*
rear′ gun′ner *s* Heckschütze *m*

rearm [ri'arm] *tr* wieder aufrüsten
rearmament [ri'arməmənt] *s* Wiederaufrüstung *f*
rearrange [ˌri·ə'rendʒ] *tr* umstellen
rear' seat' *s* Hintersitz *m*
rear'-view mir'ror *s* Rückspiegel *m*
rear'-wheel drive' *s* Hinterradantrieb *m*
rear' win'dow *s* (aut) Heckfenster *n*
reason ['rizən] *s* Vernunft *f;* (*cause*) Grund *m;* by **r.** of auf Grund (*genit*); for this **r.** aus diesem Grund; listen to **r.** sich belehren lassen; not listen to **r.** sich [*dat*] nichts sagen lassen; not without good **r.** nicht umsonst || *tr*—**r.** out durchdenken || *intr*—**r.** with vernünftig reden mit
reasonable ['rizənəbəl] *adj* (*person*) vernünftig; (*price*) solid; (*wares*) preiswert
reassemble [ˌri·ə'sembəl] *tr* (*people*) wieder versammeln; (mach) wieder zusammenbauen || *intr* sich wieder sammeln
reassert [ˌri·ə'sɛrt] *tr* wieder behaupten
reassurance [ˌri·ə'ʃurəns] *s* Beruhigung *f*
reassure [ri·ə'ʃur] *tr* beruhigen
reawaken [ˌri·ə'wekən] *tr* wieder erwecken || *intr* wieder erwachen
rebate ['ribet] *s* Rabatt *m*
re·bel ['rɛbəl] *adj* Rebellen- || *s* Rebell –in *mf* || [rɪ'bɛl] *v* (*pret & pp* –belled; *ger* –belling) *intr* rebellieren
rebellion [rɪ'bɛljən] *s* Aufstand *m*, Rebellion *f*
rebellious [rɪ'bɛljəs] *adj* aufständisch
rebirth ['ribʌrθ] *s* Wiedergeburt *f*
rebore [ri'bor] *tr* nachbohren
rebound ['riˌbaund] *s* Rückprall *m* || [ri'baund] *intr* zurückprallen
rebroad·cast [ri'brɔdˌkæst] *s* Wiederholungssendung *f* || *v* (*pret & pp* –cast & –casted) *tr* nochmals übertragen
rebuff [rɪ'bʌf] *s* Zurückweisung *f* || *tr* schroff abweisen
re·build [ri'bɪld] *v* (*pret & pp* –built) *tr* wiederaufbauen; (mach) überholen; (*confidence*) wiederherstellen
rebuke [rɪ'bjuk] *s* Verweis *m* || *tr* verweisen
re·but [rɪ'bʌt] *v* (*pret & pp* –butted; *ger* –butting) *tr* widerlegen
rebuttal [rɪ'bʌtəl] *s* Widerlegung *f*
recall [rɪ'kɔl], ['rikɔl] *s* (*recollection*) Erinnerungsvermögen *n;* (com) Zurücknahme *f;* (dipl, pol) Abberufung *f;* beyond **r.** unwiderruflich || [rɪ'kɔl] *tr* (*remember*) sich erinnern an (*dat*); (*an ambassador*) abberufen; (*workers*) zurückrufen; (mil) wiedereinberufen
recant [rɪ'kænt] *tr & intr* (öffentlich) widerrufen
re·cap ['ri,kæp] *s* Zusammenfassung *f* || *v* (*pret & pp* –capped; *ger* –capping) *tr* zusammenfassen; (*a tire*) runderneuern
recapitulate [ˌrikə'pɪtʃə,let] *tr* zusammenfassen

recapitulation [ˌrikəˌpɪtʃə'leʃən] *s* Rekapitulation *f,* Zusammenfassung *f*
re·cast ['ri,kæst] *s* Umguß *m* || [ri'kæst] *v* (*pret & pp* –cast) *tr* umgießen; (*a sentence*) umarbeiten; (theat) neubesetzen
recede [rɪ'sid] *intr* zurückgehen; (*become more distant*) zurückweichen
reced'ing *adj* (*forehead, chin*) fliehend
receipt [rɪ'sit] *s* Quittung *f;* **acknowledge r.** of den Empfang bestätigen (*genit*); **receipts** Eingänge *pl* || *tr* quittieren
receive [rɪ'siv] *tr* bekommen, erhalten; (*a guest*) empfangen; (*pay*) beziehen; (rad) empfangen
receiver [rɪ'sivər] *s* Empfänger –in *mf;* (jur) Zwangsverwalter –in *mf;* (telp) Hörer *m*
receiv'ership' *s* Zwangsverwaltung *f*
recent ['risənt] *adj* neu, jung; **in r. years** in den letzten Jahren; **of r. date** neueren Datums
recently ['risəntli] *adv* kürzlich
receptacle [rɪ'sɛptəkəl] *s* Behälter *m;* (elec) Steckdose *f*
reception [rɪ'sɛpʃən] *s* (& rad) Empfang *m*
recep'tion desk' *s* Empfang *m*
receptionist [rɪ'sɛpənɪst] *s* Empfangsdame *f;* (med) Sprechstundenhilfe *f*
receptive [rɪ'sɛptɪv] *adj* (to) aufgeschlossen (für)
recess [rɪ'sɛs], ['rises] *s* (*alcove*) Nische *f;* (*cleft*) Einschnitt *m;* (at *school*) Pause *f;* (jur) Unterbrechung *f;* (parl) Ferien *pl* || [rɪ'ses] *tr* (*place in a recess*) versenken || *intr* (until) sich vertagen (auf *acc*)
recession [rɪ'sɛʃən] *s* Rezession *f,* Rückgang *m*
recharge [ri'tʃardʒ] *tr* wieder aufladen
recipe ['rɛsɪˌpi] *s* Rezept *n*
recipient [rɪ'sɪpɪ·ənt] *s* Empfänger –in *mf*
reciprocal [rɪ'sɪprəkəl] *adj* gegenseitig
reciprocate [rɪ'sɪprə,ket] *tr* sich erkenntlich zeigen für || *intr* sich erkenntlich zeigen
reciprocity [ˌrɛsɪ'prɑsɪti] *s* Gegenseitigkeit *f*
recital [rɪ'saɪtəl] *s* Vortrag *m*
recite [rɪ'saɪt] *tr* vortragen
reckless ['rɛklɪs] *adj* (*careless of consequences*) unbekümmert; (*lacking caution*) leichtsinnig; (*negligent*) fahrlässig
reck'less driv'ing *s* rücksichtsloses Fahren *n*
reckon ['rɛkən] *tr* (*count*) rechnen; (*compute*) (coll) schätzen || *intr* rechnen; (coll) schätzen; **r. on** rechnen auf (*acc*); **r. with** (*deal with*) abrechnen mit; (*take into consideration*) rechnen mit
reck'oning *s* (*accounting*) Abrechnung *f;* (*computation*) Berechnung *f;* (aer, naut) Besteck *n*
reclaim [rɪ'klem] *tr* (*demand back*) zurückfordern; (*from wastes*) rückgewinnen; (*land*) urbar machen

reclamation [,rɛklə'meʃən] s (of land) Urbarmachung f
recline [rɪ'klaɪn] intr ruhen; **r. against** sich lehnen an (acc); **r. in** (a chair) sich zurücklehnen in (dat)
recluse ['rɛklus] s Einsiedler –in mf
recognition [,rɛkəg'nɪʃən] s Wiedererkennung f; (acknowledgement) Anerkennung f; **gain r.** zur Geltung kommen
recognizable [,rɛkəg'naɪzəbəl] adj erkennbar
recognize ['rɛkəg,naɪz] tr (by) erkennen (an dat); **r. as** anerkennen als
recoil ['rikɔɪl] s (of a rifle) Rückstoß m; (arti) Rücklauf m ‖ [rɪ'kɔɪl] intr (in fear) zurückfahren; (from, e.g., a challenge) zurückschrecken vor (dat); (said of a rifle) zurückstoßen; (arti) zurücklaufen
recoilless [rɪ'kɔɪllɪs] adj rückstoßfrei
recollect [,rɛkə'lɛkt] tr sich erinnern an (acc)
recollection [,rɛkə'lɛkʃən] s Erinnerung f
recommend [,rɛkə'mɛnd] tr empfehlen
recommendation [,rɛkəmən'deʃən] s Empfehlung f
recompense ['rɛkəm,pɛns] s (for) Vergütung f (für) ‖ tr vergüten
reconcile ['rɛkən,saɪl] tr (with) versöhnen (mit); **become reconciled** sich versöhnen; **r. oneself to** sich abfinden mit
reconciliation [,rɛkən,sɪlɪ'eʃən] s Versöhnung f, Aussöhnung f
recondite ['rɛkən,daɪt] adj (deep) tiefgründig; (obscure) dunkel
recondition [,rikən'dɪʃən] tr wiederinstandsetzen
reconnaissance [rɪ'kɑnɪsəns] s Aufklärung f
reconnoiter [,rɛkə'nɔɪtər] tr erkunden ‖ intr aufklären
reconquer [ri'kɑŋkər] tr zurückerobern
reconquest [ri'kɑŋkwɛst] s Zurückeroberung f
reconsider [,rikən'sɪdər] tr noch einmal erwägen
reconstruct [,rikən'strʌkt] tr (rebuild) wiederaufbauen; (make over) umbauen; (e.g., events of a case) rekonstruieren
record ['rɛkərd] adj Rekord– ‖ s (highest achievement) Rekord m; (document) Akte f, Protokoll n; (documentary evidence) Aufzeichnung f; (mus) Schallplatte f; **have a criminal r.** vorbestraft sein; **keep a r. of** Buch führen über (acc); **make a r. of** zu Protokoll nehmen; **off the r.** inoffiziell; **on r.** bisher registriert; **set a r.** e–n Rekord aufstellen ‖ [rɪ'kɔrd] tr (in writing) aufzeichnen; (officially) protokollieren; (on tape or disk) aufnehmen ‖ intr Schallplatten aufnehmen
rec'ord chang'er s Plattenwechsler m
recorder [rɪ'kɔrdər] s Protokollführer –in mf; (device) Zähler m; (on tape

or disk) Aufnahmegerät; (mus) Blockflöte f
rec'ord hold'er s Rekordler –in mf
record'ing adj aufzeichnend; (on tape or disk) Aufnahme– ‖ s Aufzeichnung f; (on tape or disk) Tonaufnahme f
record'ing sec'retary s Protokollführer –in mf
rec'ord play'er s Plattenspieler m
recount ['ri,kaunt] s Nachzählung f ‖ [ri'kaunt] tr (count again) nachzählen ‖ [rɪ'kaunt] tr (relate) im einzelnen erzählen
recoup [rɪ'kup] tr (losses) wieder einbringen; (a fortune) wiedererlangen; (reimburse) entschädigen
recourse [rɪ'kors], ['rikors] s (to) Zuflucht f (zu); (jur) Regreß m; **have r. to** seine Zuflucht nehmen zu
recover [rɪ'kʌvər] tr (get back) wiedererlangen; (losses) wiedereinbringen; (e.g., a spent rocket) bergen; (one's balance) wiederfinden; (e.g., a chair) neu beziehen ‖ intr (from) sich erholen (von)
recovery [rɪ'kʌvəri] s Wiedererlangung f, Rückgewinnung f; (of health) Genesung f; (of a rocket) Bergung f
recreation [,rɛkrɪ'eʃən] s Erholung f
recrea'tion room' s Unterhaltungsraum m
recruit [rɪ'krut] s Rekrut m ‖ (& mil) rekrutieren; **be recruited from** sich rekrutieren aus
recruit'ing of'ficer s Werbeoffizier m
recruitment [rɪ'krutmənt] s Rekrutierung f; (mil) Rekrutenaushebung f
rectangle ['rɛk,tæŋgəl] s Rechteck n
rectangular [rɛk'tæŋgjələr] adj rechteckig
rectifier ['rɛktə,faɪ-ər] s Berichtiger m; (elec) Gleichrichter m
recti·fy ['rɛktɪ,faɪ] v (pret & pp –fied) tr berichtigen; (elec) gleichrichten
rector ['rɛktər] s Rektor m
rectory ['rɛktəri] s Pfarrhaus n
rec·tum ['rɛktəm] s (–ta [tə]) Mastdarm m
recumbent [rɪ'kʌmbənt] adj liegend
recuperate [rɪ'k(j)upə,ret] intr sich (wieder) erholen
re·cur [rɪ'kʌr] v (pret & pp –curred) ger –curring) intr wiederkehren
recurrence [rɪ'kʌrəns] s Wiederkehr f
red [rɛd] adj (redder; reddest) rot ‖ s Rot n, Röte f; **be in the red** in den Roten Zahlen stecken; **Red** (pol) Rote mf; **see red** wild werden
red' ant' s rote Waldameise f
red'bird' s Kardinal m
red'blood'ed adj lebensprühend
red'breast' s Rotkehlchen n
red' cab'bage s Rotkohl m
red' car'pet s (fig) roter Teppich m
red' cent' s—**not give a r. for** keinen roten Heller geben für
red'-cheeked adj rotbäckig
Red' Cross', the s das Rote Kreuz
redden ['rɛdən] tr röten, rot machen ‖ intr erröten, rot werden
reddish ['rɛdɪʃ] adj rötlich

redecorate [rɪ'dɛkə‚ret] *tr* neu dekorieren
redeem [rɪ'dim] *tr* zurückkaufen; (*a pawned article, promise*) einlösen; **r.** oneself seine Ehre wiederherstellen
redeemable [rɪ'diməbəl] *adj* (fin) ablösbar, kündbar
Redeemer [rɪ'dimər] *s* Erlöser *m*
redemption [rɪ'dɛmpʃən] *s* Rückkauf *m*, Wiedereinlösung *f*; (relig) Erlösung *f*
red'-haired' *adj* rothaarig
red'-hand'ed *adj*—catch s.o. **r.** j-n auf frischer Tat ertappen
red'head' *s* Rotkopf *m*
red' her'ring *s* Bückling *m*; (fig) Ablenkungsmanöver *n*
red'-hot' *adj* glühend heiß, rotglühend
redirect [‚ridɪ'rɛkt] *tr* umdirigieren
rediscover [‚ridɪs'kʌvər] *tr* wiederentdecken
red'-let'ter day' *s* Glückstag *m*
red' light' *s* rotes Licht *n*
red'-light' dis'trict *s* Bordellviertel *n*
red' man' *s* Rothaut *f*
redness ['rɛdnɪs] *s* Röte *f*
re•do ['ri'du] *v* (*pret* –did; *pp* –done) *tr* neu machen; (*redecorate*) renovieren
redolent ['rɛdələnt] *adj* (**with**) duftend (**nach**)
redoubt [rɪ'daʊt] *s* Redoute *f*
redound [rɪ'daʊnd] *intr*—**r.** to gereichen zu
red' pep'per *s* spanischer Pfeffer *m*
redress [rɪ'drɛs] *s* Wiedergutmachung *f* ‖ *tr* wiedergutmachen
Red' Rid'inghood' *s* Rotkäppchen *n*
red'skin' *s* Rothaut *f*
red' tape' *s* Amtsschimmel *m*
reduce [rɪ'd(j)us] *tr* reduzieren, verringern; (*prices*) herabsetzen; (math) (ab)kürzen
reduction [rɪ'dʌkʃən] *s* Verminderung *f*; (*gradual reduction*) Abbau *m*; (*in prices*) Absetzung *f*; (*in weight*) Abnahme *f*
redundant [rɪ'dʌndənt] *adj* überflüssig
red' wine' *s* Rotwein *m*
red'wing' *s* Rotdrossel *f*
red'wood' *s* Rotholz *n*
reecho [ri'ɛko] *tr* wiederhallen lassen ‖ *intr* wiederhallen
reed [rid] *s* Schilf *n*; (*in mouthpiece*) Rohrblatt *n*; (*of metal*) Zunge *f*; (*pastoral pipe*) Hirtenflöte *f*
reedit [ri'ɛdɪt] *tr* neu herausgeben
reeducate [ri'ɛdʒʊ‚ket] *tr* umerziehen
reef [rif] *s* Riff *n*; (naut) Reff *n* ‖ *tr* (naut) reffen
reek [rik] *intr* (**of**) riechen (**nach**)
reel [ril] *s* (*sway*) Taumeln *n*; (*for cables*) Trommel *f*; (angl, cin) Spule *f*; (min, naut) Haspel *f* ‖ *tr* (angl, cin) spulen; (min, naut) haspeln; **r. in** (*a fish*) einholen; **r. off** abhaspeln; (fig) herunterrasseln ‖ *intr* taumeln
reelect [‚ri·ɪ'lɛkt] *tr* wiederwählen
reelection [‚ri·ɪ'lɛkʃən] *s* Wiederwahl *f*
reenlist [‚ri·ɛn'lɪst] *tr* wieder anwerben ‖ *intr* sich weiterverpflichten

reenlistment [‚ri·ɛn'lɪstmənt] *s* Weiterverpflichtung *f*
reentry [ri'ɛntri] *s* Wiedereintritt *m*
reexamination [‚ri·ɛg‚zæmɪ'neʃən] *s* Nachprüfung *f*
re•fer [rɪ'fʌr] *v* (*pret & pp* –ferred; *ger* –ferring) *tr*—**r.** s.o. to j-n verweisen an (*acc*) ‖ *intr*—**r.** to hinweisen auf (*acc*); (*e.g., to an earlier correspondence*) sich beziehen auf (*acc*)
referee [‚rɛfə'ri] *s* (box) Ringrichter *m*; (sport) Schiedsrichter *m* ‖ *tr* als Schiedsrichter fungieren bei ‖ *intr* als Schiedsrichter fungieren
reference ['rɛfərəns] *s* (**to**) Hinweis *m* (auf *acc*); (*person or document*) Referenz *f*; **in r. to** in Bezug auf (*acc*); **make r. to** hinweisen auf (*acc*)
ref'erence lib'rary *s* Handbibliothek *f*
ref'erence work' *s* Nachschlagewerk *n*
referen•dum [‚rɛfə'rɛndəm] *s* (**–da** [də]) Volksentscheid *m*
referral [rɪ'fʌrəl] *s* (**to**) Zuweisung *f* (an *acc*, auf *acc*); **by r.** auf Empfehlung
refill ['rifɪl] *s* Nachfüllung *f*; (*for a pencil, ball-point pen*) Ersatzmine *f* ‖ [ri'fɪl] *tr* nachfüllen
refine [rɪ'faɪn] *tr* (*metal*) läutern; (*oil, sugar*) raffinieren; (fig) verfeinern
refinement [rɪ'faɪnmənt] *s* Läuterung *f*; (*of oil, sugar*) Raffination *f*; (fig) Verfeinerung *f*
refinery [rɪ'faɪnəri] *s* Raffinerie *f*
reflect [rɪ'flɛkt] *tr* (& fig) widerspiegeln ‖ *intr* (*throw back rays*) reflektieren; (**on**) nachdenken (über *acc*); **r. on** (*comment on*) sich äußern über (*acc*); (*bring reproach on*) ein schlechtes Licht werfen auf (*acc*)
reflection [rɪ'flɛkʃən] *s* (*e.g., of light*) Reflexion *f*; (*reflected image*) Spiegelbild *n*; (*thought*) Überlegung *f*; **that's no r. on you** das färbt nicht auf Sie ab
reflector [rɪ'flɛktər] *s* Reflektor *m*
reflex ['riflɛks] *s* Reflex *m*
reflexive [rɪ'flɛksɪv] *adj* (gram) reflexiv ‖ *s* Reflexivform *f*
reforestation [‚rifɔrɪs'teʃən] *s* Aufforstung *f*
reform [rɪ'fɔrm] *s* Reform *f* ‖ *tr* reformieren, verbessern ‖ *intr* sich bessern
reformation [‚rɛfər'meʃən] *s* Besserung *f*; **Reformation** Reformation *f*
reformatory [rɪ'fɔrmə‚tori] *s* Besserungsanstalt *f*
reformer [rɪ'fɔrmər] *s* Reformator –in *mf*
reform' school' *s* Besserungsanstalt *f*
refraction [rɪ'frækʃən] *s* Ablenkung *f*
refrain [rɪ'fren] *s* Kehrreim *m* ‖ *intr*—**r. from** sich enthalten (*genit*); **r. from** (*ger*) es unterlassen zu (*inf*)
refresh [rɪ'frɛʃ] *tr* erfrischen; (*the memory*) auffrischen
refresh'er course' [rɪ'frɛʃər] *s* Auffrischungskurs *m*
refresh'ing *adj* erfrischend

refreshment [rɪˈfreʃmənt] s Erfrischung *f*

refresh'ment stand' s Erfrischungsstand *m*

refrigerant [rɪˈfrɪdʒərənt] s Kühlmittel *n*

refrigerate [rɪˈfrɪdʒə͵ret] *tr* kühlen

refrigerator [rɪˈfrɪdʒə͵retər] s Kühlschrank *m;* (*walk-in type*) Kühlraum *m*

refrig'erator car' s (rr) Kühlwagen *m*

re·fuel [riˈfjul] *v* (*pret & pp* –fuel[l]ed; *ger* –fuel[l]ing) *tr* auftanken ‖ *intr* tanken

refuge [ˈrefjudʒ] s Zuflucht *f;* **take r. in** (sich) flüchten in (*acc*)

refugee [͵refjuˈdʒi] s Flüchtling *m*

refugee' camp' s Flüchtlingslager *n*

refund [ˈrifʌnd] s Zurückzahlung *f* ‖ [rɪˈfʌnd] *tr* (*pay back*) zurückzahlen ‖ [rɪˈfʌnd] *tr* (*fund again*) neu fundieren

refurnish [rɪˈfʌrnɪʃ] *tr* neu möblieren

refusal [rɪˈfjuzəl] s Ablehnung *f*

refuse [ˈrefjus] s Abfall *m* ‖ [rɪˈfjuz] *tr* ablehnen; **r. to** (*inf*) sich weigern zu (*inf*)

refutation [͵refjuˈteʃən] s Widerlegung *f*

refute [rɪˈfjut] *tr* widerlegen

regain [rɪˈgen] *tr* zurückgewinnen

regal [ˈrigəl] *adj* königlich

regale [rɪˈgel] *tr* (*delight*) ergötzen; (*entertain*) reichlich bewirten

regalia [rɪˈgelɪ·ə] *spl* Insignien *pl*

regard [rɪˈgɑrd] s (**for**) Rücksicht *f* (auf *acc*); **best regards to** herzlichster Gruß an (*acc*); **have little r. for** wenig achten; **in every r.** in jeder Hinsicht; **in** (or **with**) **r. to** in Hinsicht auf (*acc*); **in this r.** in dieser Hinsicht; **without r. for** ohne Rücksicht auf (*acc*) ‖ *tr* betrachten; **as regards** in Bezug auf (*acc*)

regard'ing *prep* hinsichtlich (*genit*)

regardless [rɪˈgɑrdlɪs] *adv* (coll) ungeniert; **r. of** ungeachtet (*genit*)

regatta [rɪˈgætə] s Regatta *f*

regency [ˈridʒənsi] s Regentschaft *f*

regenerate [rɪˈdʒɛnə͵ret] *tr* regenerieren

regent [ˈridʒənt] s Regent –in *mf*

regicide [ˈredʒɪ͵saɪd] s (*act*) Königsmord *m;* (*person*) Königsmörder –in *mf*

regime [reˈʒim] s Regime *n*

regiment [ˈredʒɪmənt] s (mil) Regiment *n* ‖ [ˈredʒɪ͵ment] *tr* reglementieren

regimental [͵redʒɪˈmɛntəl] *adj* Regiments-

region [ˈridʒən] s Gegend *f*, Region *f*

regional [ˈridʒənəl] *adj* regional

register [ˈredʒɪstər] s Register *n*, Verzeichnis *n* ‖ *tr* registrieren; (*students*) immatrikulieren; (*feelings*) erkennen lassen ‖ *intr* sich einschreiben lassen; (*at a hotel*) sich eintragen lassen

reg'istered let'ter s eingeschriebener Brief *m*

reg'istered nurse' s (staatlich) geprüfte Krankenschwester *f*

registrar [ˈredʒɪstrɑr] s Registrator –in *mf*

registration [͵redʒɪsˈtreʃən] s (*e.g., of firearms*) Registrierung *f;* (*for a course; at a hotel*) Anmeldung *f;* (*of a trademark*) Eintragung *f;* (aut) Zulassung *f;* (educ) Einschreibung *f*

registra'tion blank' s Meldeformular *n*

registra'tion fee' s Anmeldegebühr *f*

registra'tion num'ber s Registriernummer *f*

regression [rɪˈgreʃən] s Rückgang *m*

regret [rɪˈgret] s (**over**) Bedauern *n* (über *acc*) ‖ *v* (*pret & pp* –regretted; *ger* regretting) *tr* bedauern; **I r. to say** es tut mir leid, sagen zu müssen

regrettable [rɪˈgretəbəl] *adj* bedauerlich

regroup [rɪˈgrup] *tr* umgruppieren

regular [ˈregjələr] *adj* (*usual*) gewöhnlich; (*pulse, breathing, features, intervals*) regelmäßig; **r. army** stehendes Heer *n;* **r. guy** (coll) Pfundskerl *m;* **r. officer** Berufsoffizier –in *mf*

regularity [͵regjəˈlærɪti] s Regelmäßigkeit *f*

regulate [ˈregjə͵let] *tr* regeln

regulation [͵regjəˈleʃən] s Regelung *f;* (*rule*) Vorschrift *f*, Bestimmung *f;* **against regulations** vorschriftswidrig

regulator [ˈregjə͵letər] s Regler *m*

rehabilitate [͵rihəˈbɪlɪ͵tet] *tr* rehabilitieren

rehash [riˈhæʃ] *tr* (coll) aufwärmen

rehearsal [rɪˈhʌrsəl] s Probe *f*

rehearse [rɪˈhʌrs] *tr & intr* proben

rehire [rɪˈhaɪr] *tr* wiedereinstellen

reign [ren] s Regierung *f;* (*period of rule*) Regierungszeit *f* ‖ *intr* regieren; **r. over** herrschen über (*acc*)

reimburse [ri·ɪmˈbʌrs] *tr* (*costs*) rückerstatten; **r. s.o. for s.th.** j–m etw vergüten

rein [ren] s Zügel *m;* **give free r. to** die Zügel schießen lassen (*dat*) ‖ *tr* —**r. in** (*a horse*) parieren

reincarnation [͵ri·ɪnkɑrˈneʃən] s Reinkarnation *f*, Wiedergeburt *f*

rein'deer' s Rentier *n*

reinforce [͵ri·ɪnˈfors] *tr* verstärken

reinforced' concrete' s Stahlbeton *m*

reinforcement [͵ri·ɪnˈforsmənt] s Verstärkung *f;* **reinforcements** (mil) Verstärkungen *pl*

reinstate [͵ri·ɪnˈstet] *tr* (**in**) wiedereinsetzen (in *acc*)

reiterate [riˈɪtə͵ret] *tr* wiederholen

reject [ˈridʒekt] s Ausschußware *f* ‖ [rɪˈdʒekt] *tr* ablehnen, zurückweisen; (*a request, appeal*) abweisen

rejection [rɪˈdʒekʃən] s Ablehnung *f;* (*of a request, appeal*) Abweisung *f*

rejoice [rɪˈdʒɔɪs] *intr* frohlocken

rejoin [rɪˈdʒɔɪn] *tr* (*answer*) erwidern; (*a group*) sich wieder anschließen (*dat*)

rejoinder [rɪˈdʒɔɪndər] s Erwiderung *f;* (jur) Duplik *f*

rejuvenate [rɪˈdʒuvɪ͵net] *tr* verjüngen

rekindle [riˈkɪndəl] *tr* wieder anzünden; (fig) wieder entzünden

relapse [rɪˈlæps] s (& pathol) Rückfall

m ‖ *intr* (**into**) wieder verfallen (in *acc*)

relate [rɪ'let] *tr* (*a story*) erzählen; (*connect*) verknüpfen; **r. s.th. to s.th.** etw auf etw [*acc*] beziehen ‖ *intr*—**r. to** in Beziehung stehen mit

relat'ed *adj* (*by blood*) verwandt; (*by marriage*) verschwägert; (*subjects*) benachbart

relation [rɪ'leʃən] *s* Beziehung *f*, Verhältnis *n*; (*relative*) Verwandte *mf*; **in r. to** in Bezug auf (*acc*); **relations** (*sex*) Verkehr *m*

rela'tionship' *s* (*connection*) Beziehung *f*; (*kinship*) Verwandschaft *f*

relative ['relɪtɪv] *adj* relativ, verhältnismäßig; **r. to** bezüglich (*genit*) ‖ *s* Verwandte *mf*

rel'ative clause' *s* Relativsatz *m*

rel'ative pro'noun *s* Relativpronomen *n*

relativity [,relə'tɪvɪti] *s* Relativität *f*

relax [rɪ'læks] *tr* auflockern; (*muscles*) entspannen ‖ *intr* sich entspannen

relaxation [,rɪlæk'seʃən] *s* Entspannung *f*; **r. of tension** Entspannung *f*

relay ['rɪle] *s* Relais *n*; (sport) Staffel *f* ‖ [rɪ'le] *v* (*pret & pp* –**layed**) *tr* übermitteln; (*through relay stations*) übertragen

re'lay race' *s* Staffellauf *m*

re'lay team' *s* Staffel *f*

release [rɪ'lis] *s* (**from**) Entlassung *f* (aus); (*of bombs*) Abwurf *m*; (*of news*) Mitteilung *f* ‖ *tr* entlassen; (*a film, book*) freigeben; (*bombs*) abwerfen; (*energy*) freisetzen; (*brakes*) lösen; **r. the clutch** auskuppeln

relegate ['relɪ,get] *tr* (**to**) verweisen (an *acc*); **r. to second position** auf den zweiten Platz verweisen

relent [rɪ'lent] *intr* (*let up*) nachlassen; (*yield*) sich erweichen lassen

relentless [rɪ'lentlɪs] *adj* (*tireless*) unermüdlich; (*unappeasable*) unerbittlich; (*never-ending*) unaufhörlich

relevant ['relɪvənt] *adj* sachdienlich

reliable [rɪ'laɪ-əbəl] *adj* zuverlässig

reliance [rɪ'laɪ-əns] *s* Vertrauen *n*

relic ['relɪk] *s* Reliquie *f*; **r. of the past** Zeuge *m* der Vergangenheit

relief [rɪ'lif] *s* Erleichterung *f*; (*for the poor*) Armenunterstützung *f*; (*replacement*) Ablösung *f*; (*sculpture*) Relief *n*; **on r.** von Sozialhilfe lebend; **bring r.** Linderung schaffen; **go on r.** stempeln gehen

relief' map' *s* Reliefkarte *f*

relieve [rɪ'liv] *tr* erleichtern; (*from guard duty*) ablösen; **r. oneself** seine Notdurft verrichten

religion [rɪ'lɪdʒən] *s* Religion *f*

religious [rɪ'lɪdʒəs] *adj* religiös; (*order*) geistlich

relinquish [rɪ'lɪŋkwɪʃ] *tr* aufgeben; **r. the right to s.th. to s.o.** j-m das Recht auf etw [*acc*] überlassen

relish ['relɪʃ] *s* (**for**) Genuß *m* (an *acc*); (*condiment*) Würze *f* ‖ *tr* genießen

reluctance [rɪ'lʌktəns] *s* Widerstreben *n*

reluctant [rɪ'lʌktənt] *adj* widerstrebend; **be r. to do s.th.** etw ungern tun

reluctantly [rɪ'lʌktəntli] *adv* ungern

re·ly [rɪ'laɪ] *v* (*pret & pp* –**lied**) *intr*—**r. on** sich verlassen auf (*acc*)

remain [rɪ'men] *s*—**remains** Überreste *pl*; (*corpse*) sterbliche Reste *pl* ‖ *intr* bleiben; (*at end of letter*) verbleiben; **r. behind** zurückbleiben; **r. seated** sitzenbleiben; **r. steady** (*said of prices*) sich behaupten

remainder [rɪ'mendər] *s* Restbestand *m*, Rest *m* ‖ *tr* verramschen

remark [rɪ'mɑrk] *s* Bemerkung *f* ‖ *tr* bemerken

remarkable [rɪ'mɑrkəbəl] *adj* markant, bemerkenswert

remar·ry [rɪ'mæri] *v* (*pret & pp* –**ried**) *tr* sich wiederverheiraten mit ‖ *intr* sich wiederverheiraten

reme·dy ['remɪdi] *s* (**for**) Heilmittel *n* (für); (fig) (**for**) Gegenmittel *n* (gegen) ‖ *v* (*pret & pp* –**died**) *tr* abhelfen (*dat*); (*damage, shortage*) abheben

remember [rɪ'membər] *tr* sich erinnern an (*acc*); **r. me to** empfehlen Sie mich (*dat*) ‖ *intr* sich erinnern

remembrance [rɪ'membrəns] *s* Erinnerung *f*; **in r. of** zum Andenken an (*acc*)

remind [rɪ'maɪnd] *tr* (**of**) erinnern (an *acc*); **r. s.o. to** (*inf*) j-n mahnen zu (*inf*)

reminder [rɪ'maɪndər] *s* (*note*) Zettel *m*; (*from a creditor*) Mahnung *f*

reminisce [,remɪ'nɪs] *intr* in Erinnerungen schwelgen

remiss [rɪ'mɪs] *adj* nachlässig

remission [rɪ'mɪʃən] *s* Nachlaß *m*

re·mit [rɪ'mɪt] *v* (*pret & pp* –**mitted**; *ger* –**mitting**) *tr* (*in cash*) übersenden; (*by check*) überweisen; (*forgive*) vergeben

remittance [rɪ'mɪtəns] *s* (*in cash*) Übersendung *f*; (*by check*) Überweisung *f*

remnant ['remnənt] *s* Rest *m*; (*of cloth*) Stoffrest *m*

remod·el [rɪ'mɑdəl] *v* (*pret & pp* –**el[l]ed**; *ger* –**el[l]ing**) *tr* umgestalten; (*a house*) umbauen

remonstrate [rɪ'mɑnstret] *intr* protestieren; **r. with s.o.** j-m Vorwürfe machen

remorse [rɪ'mɔrs] *s* Gewissensbisse *pl*

remorseful [rɪ'mɔrsfəl] *adj* reumütig

remote [rɪ'mot] *adj* fern; (*possibility*) vage; (*idea*) blaß; (*resemblance*) entfernt; (*secluded*) abgelegen

remote' control' *s* Fernsteuerung *f*; (telv) Fernbedienung *f*; **guide by r.** fernlenken

removable [rɪ'muvəbəl] *adj* entfernbar

removal [rɪ'muvəl] *s* Entfernung *f*; (*by truck*) Abfuhr *f*; (*from office*) Absetzung *f*

remove [rɪ'muv] *tr* entfernen; (*clothes*) ablegen; (*one's hat*) abnehmen; (*e.g., dishes from the table*) abräumen; (*a stain*) entfernen; (*from office*) absetzen; (*furniture*) ausräumen

remuneration [rɪ͵mjunə'reʃən] *s* Vergütung *f*
renaissance [͵renə'sɑns] *s* Renaissance *f*
rend [rend] *v* (*pret* & *pp* rent [rent]) *tr* (& fig) zerreißen
render ['rendər] *tr* (*give*) geben; (*a service*) leisten; (*honor*) erweisen; (*thanks*) abstatten; (*a verdict*) fällen; (*translate; play, e.g., on the piano*) wiedergeben; **r.** harmless unschädlich machen
rendez·vous ['rɑndə͵vu] *s* (**–vous** [͵vuz]) Rendezvous *n*, Treffpunkt *m;* (mil) Sammelplatz *m* ‖ *v* (*pret* & *pp* **–voused** [͵vud]; *ger* **–vousing** [͵vu·ɪŋ]) *intr* sich treffen; (mil) sich versammeln
rendition [ren'dɪʃən] *s* Wiedergabe *f*
renegade ['renɪ͵ged] *s* Renegat –in *mf*
renege [rɪ'nɪg] *s* Renonce *f* ‖ *intr* (cards) nicht bedienen; **r.** on nicht einhalten
renew [rɪ'n(j)u] *tr* erneuern; (*e.g., a passport*) verlängern lassen
renewable [rɪ'n(j)u·əbəl] *adj* erneuerbar
renewal [rɪ'n(j)u·əl] *s* Erneuerung *f;* (*e.g., of a passport*) Verlängerung *f*
renounce [rɪ'nauns] *tr* verzichten auf (*acc*)
renovate ['renə͵vet] *tr* renovieren; (fig) erneuern
renovation [͵renə've ʃən] *s* Renovierung *f*
renown [rɪ'naun] *s* Ruhm *m*
renowned [rɪ'naund] *adj* (for) berühmt (wegen)
rent [rent] *adj* zerrissen ‖ *s* Miete *f;* (*tear*) Riß *m* ‖ *tr* mieten; **r.** out vermieten
rental ['rentəl] *s* Miete *f*
rent'al serv'ice *s* Verleih *m*
rent'ed car' *s* Mietwagen *m*, Mietauto *n*
renter ['rentər] *s* Mieter –in *mf*
renunciation [rɪ͵nʌnsɪ'eʃən] *s* (of) Verzicht *m* (auf *acc*)
reopen [ri'opən] *tr* wieder öffnen; (*a business*) wieder eröffnen; (*an argument; school year*) wieder beginnen ‖ *intr* (*said of a shop or business*) wieder geöffnet werden; (*said of a school year*) wieder beginnen
reopening [ri'opənɪŋ] *s* (*of a business*) Wiedereröffnung *f;* (*of school*) Wiederbeginn *m;* (jur) Wiederaufnahme *f*
reorder [ri'ɔrdər] *tr* nachbestellen
reorganization [͵ri·ɔrgənɪ'zeʃən] *s* Reorganisation *f*, Neuordnung *f*
reorganize [ri'ɔrgə͵naɪz] *tr* reorganisieren; (*an administration*) umbilden
repack [ri'pæk] *tr* umpacken
repair [rɪ'per] *s* Ausbesserung *f*, Reparatur *f;* in bad r. in schlechtem Zustand; keep in good r. im Stande halten ‖ *tr* ausbessern, reparieren ‖ *intr* (to) sich begeben (nach, zu)
repair' gang' *s* Störungstrupp *m*
repair' shop' *s* Reparaturwerkstatt *f*
repaper [ri'pepər] *tr* neu tapezieren

reparation [͵repə'reʃən] *s* Wiedergutmachung *f;* **reparations** Reparationen *pl*, Kriegsentschädigung *f*
repartee [͵repɑr'ti] *s* schlagfertige Antwort *f*
repast [rɪ'pæst] *s* Mahl *n*
repatriate [ri'petrɪ͵et] *tr* repatriieren
re·pay [rɪ'pe] *v* (*pret* & *pp* **–paid**) *tr* (*e.g., a loan*) zurückzahlen; (*a person*) entschädigen; **r.** a favor e–n Gefallen erwidern
repayment [rɪ'pemənt] *s* Rückzahlung *f;* (*reprisal*) Vergeltung *f*
repeal [rɪ'pil] *s* Aufhebung *f* ‖ *tr* aufheben, außer Kraft setzen
repeat [rɪ'pit] *tr* wiederholen; (*a story, gossip*) weitererzählen; **r.** s.th. after s.o. j–m etw nachsagen
repeat'ed *adj* abermalig, mehrmalig
repeatedly [rɪ'pitɪdli] *adv* wiederholt
re·pel [rɪ'pel] *v* (*pret* & *pp* **–pelled;** *ger* **–pelling**) *tr* (*an enemy, an attack*) zurückschlagen; (*e.g., water*) abstoßen
repellent [rɪ'pelənt] *s* Bekämpfungsmittel *n*
repent [rɪ'pent] *tr* bereuen ‖ *intr* Reue empfinden; **r.** of bereuen
repentance [rɪ'pentəns] *s* Reue *f*
repentant [rɪ'pentənt] *adj* reuig
repercussion [͵ripər'kʌʃən] *s* Rückwirkung *f*
repertory ['repər͵tori] *s* Repertoire *n*
repetition [͵repɪ'tɪʃən] *s* Wiederholung *f*
replace [rɪ'ples] *tr* (with) ersetzen (durch)
replaceable [rɪ'plesəbəl] *adj* ersetzbar
replacement [rɪ'plesmənt] *s* (*act*) Ersetzen *n;* (*substitute part*) Ersatz *m;* (*person*) Ersatzmann *m*
replay ['riple] *s* (sport) Wiederholungsspiel *n* ‖ [ri'ple] *tr* nochmals spielen
replenish [rɪ'plenɪʃ] *tr* wieder auffüllen
replete [rɪ'plit] *adj* angefüllt
replica ['replɪkə] *s* Replik *f*
re·ply [rɪ'plaɪ] *s* Erwiderung *f;* (*letter*) Antwortschreiben *n;* in r. to your letter in Beantwortung Ihres Schreibens ‖ *v* (*pret* & *pp* **–plied**) *tr* & *intr* erwidern
report [rɪ'port] *s* Bericht *m;* (*rumor*) Gerücht *n;* (*e.g., of a gun*) Knall *m* ‖ *tr* (*give an account of*) berichten; (*give notice of*) melden; **r.** s.o. to the police j–n bei der Polizei anzeigen ‖ *intr* (to) sich melden (bei); **r.** in sich anmelden
report' card' *s* Zeugnis *n*
reportedly [rɪ'portɪdli] *adv* angeblich
reporter [rɪ'portər] *s* Reporter –in *mf*
repose [rɪ'poz] *s* Ruhe *f* ‖ *intr* ruhen
repository [rɪ'pazɪ͵tori] *s* Verwahrungsort *m;* (*of information*) Fundgrube *f*
represent [͵reprɪ'zənt] *tr* vertreten; (*depict*) darstellen
representation [͵reprɪzen'teʃən] *s* Vertretung *f;* (*depiction*) Darstellung *f*
representative [͵reprɪ'zentətɪv] *adj* (*function*) stellvertretend; (*government*) parlamentarisch; (*typical*) (of)

typisch (für) ‖ *s* Vertreter –in *mf;* (pol) Abgeordnete *mf*
repress [rɪ'prɛs] *tr* unterdrücken; (psychoanal) verdrängen
repression [rɪ'prɛʃən] *s* Unterdrückung *f;* (psychoanal) Verdrängung *f*
reprieve [rɪ'priv] *s* Strafaufschub *m;* (fig) Gnadenfrist *f,* Atempause *f*
reprimand ['rɛprɪ‚mænd] *s* Verweis *m;* **give s.o. a r.** j–m e–n Verweis erteilen ‖ *tr* **(for)** zurechtweisen (wegen, für), rügen (wegen, für)
reprint ['riprɪnt] *s* Nachdruck *m* ‖ [ri'prɪnt] *tr* nachdrucken
reprisal [rɪ'praɪzəl] *s* Vergeltung *f;* **take reprisals against** or **on** Repressalien ergreifen gegen
reproach [rɪ'protʃ] *s* Vorwurf *m* ‖ *tr* **(for)** tadeln (wegen); **r. s.o. with s.th.** j–m etw vorwerfen
reproduce [‚riprə'd(j)us] *tr* reproduzieren; *(copies)* vervielfältigen; *(an experiment)* wiederholen; *(a play* neuaufführen; *(a sound)* wiedergeben; *(a lost limb)* regenerieren ‖ *intr* sich fortpflanzen
reproduction [‚riprə'dʌkʃən] *s* Reproduktion *f;* *(making copies)* Vervielfältigung *f;* *(of sound)* Wiedergabe *f;* (biol) Fortpflanzung *f*
reproductive [‚riprə'dʌktɪv] *adj* Fortpflanzungs–
reproof [rɪ'pruf] *s* Rüge *f*
reprove [rɪ'pruv] *tr* rügen
reptile ['rɛptaɪl] *s* Kriechtier *n*
republic [rɪ'pʌblɪk] *s* Republik *f*
republican [rɪ'pʌblɪkən] *adj* republikanisch ‖ *s* Republikaner –in *mf*
repudiate [rɪ'pjudɪ‚et] *tr* *(disown)* verleugnen; *(a charge)* zurückweisen; *(a debt)* nicht anerkennen; *(a treaty)* für unverbindlich erklären; *(a woman)* verstoßen
repugnant [rɪ'pʌgnənt] *adj* widerwärtig
repulse [rɪ'pʌls] *s* *(refusal)* Zurückweisung *f;* *(setback)* Rückschlag *m* ‖ *tr* zurückweisen; (mil) zurückschlagen
repulsive [rɪ'pʌlsɪv] *adj* abstoßend
reputable ['rɛpjətəbəl] *adj* anständig
reputation [‚rɛpjə'teʃən] *s* Ruf *m,* Ansehen *n;* **have the r. of being** im Rufe stehen zu sein
repute [rɪ'pjut] *s*—**be held in high r.** hohes Ansehen genießen; **bring into bad r.** in üble Nachrede bringen; **of r.** von Ruf ‖ *tr*—**she is reputed to be a beauty** sie soll e–e Schönheit sein
reputedly [rɪ'pjutɪdli] *adv* angeblich
request [rɪ'kwɛst] *s* Bitte *f,* Gesuch *n;* **at his r.** auf seine Bitte; **on r.** auf Wunsch ‖ *tr (a person)* bitten; *(a thing)* bitten um, ersuchen
Requiem ['rɛkwɪ‚ɛm] *s (Mass)* Seelenmesse *f;* *(chant, composition)* Requiem *n*
require [rɪ'kwaɪr] *tr* erfordern; **if required** erforderlichenfalls
requirement [rɪ'kwaɪrmənt] *s* Anforderung *f*
requisite ['rɛkwɪzɪt] *adj* erforderlich ‖

s Erfordernis *n;* *(required article)* Requisit *n*
requisition [‚rɛkwɪ'zɪʃən] *s* Anforderung *f;* (mil) Requisition *f* ‖ *tr* anfordern; (mil) beschlagnahmen
requital [rɪ'kwaɪtəl] *s (retaliation)* Vergeltung *f;* *(for a kindness)* Belohnung *f*
requite [rɪ'kwaɪt] *tr* vergelten; **r. s.o. for a favor** sich j–m für e–n Gefallen erkenntlich zeigen
re·read [ri'rid] *v (pret & pp –read* [rɛd]) *tr* nachlesen
rerun ['rirʌn] *s* (cin) Reprise *f*
resale ['ri‚sɛl] *s* Wiederverkauf *m*
rescind [rɪ'sɪnd] *tr (an order)* rückgängig machen; *(a law)* aufheben
rescue ['rɛskju] *s* Rettung *f,* Bergung *f* ‖ *tr* retten, bergen
rescuer ['rɛskju·ər] *s* Retter –in *mf*
research [rɪ'sʌrtʃ], ['risʌrtʃ] *s* Forschung *f;* **do r. on** Forschungen betreiben über (acc) ‖ *intr* forschen
researcher ['risʌrtʃər] *s* Forscher –in *mf*
re·sell [ri'sɛl] *v (pret & pp –sold) tr* wiederverkaufen, weiterverkaufen
resemblance [rɪ'zɛmbləns] *s* **(to)** Ähnlichkeit *f* (mit); **bear a close r. to s.o.** große Ähnlichkeit mit j–m haben
resemble [rɪ'zɛmbəl] *tr* ähneln *(dat)*
resent [rɪ'zɛnt] *tr*—**I r. your remark** Ihre Bemerkung paßt mir nicht
resentful [rɪ'zɛntfəl] *adj* grollend
resentment [rɪ'zɛntmənt] *s* Groll *m;* **feel r. toward** Groll hegen gegen
reservation [‚rɛzər've·ʃən] *s* Vorbestellung *f;* *(Indian land)* Reservation *f;* **do you have a r.?** haben Sie vorbestellt?; **make reservations** vorbestellen
reserve [rɪ'zʌrv] *s (discretion)* Zurückhaltung *f;* (econ, mil) Reserve *f;* **without r.** rückhaltlos ‖ *tr (e.g., seats)* reservieren, belegen; **r. judgment** mit seinem Urteil zurückhalten
reserved' *adj (place)* belegt; *(person)* zurückhaltend
reserve' of·ficer *s* Reserveoffizier *m*
reservist [rɪ'zʌrvɪst] *s* Reservist –in *mf*
reservoir ['rɛzər‚vwɑr] *s* Staubecken *m*
re·set [ri'sɛt] *v (pret & pp –set; ger –setting) tr (a gem)* neu fassen; (mach) nachstellen; (typ) neu setzen
resettle [ri'sɛtəl] *tr & intr* umsiedeln
reshape [rɪ'ʃep] *tr* umformen
reshuffle [rɪ'ʃʌfəl] *tr (cards)* neu mischen; (pol) umgruppieren
reside [rɪ'zaɪd] *intr* wohnen
residence ['rɛzɪdəns] *s* Wohnsitz *m;* *(for students)* Studentenheim *n*
resident ['rɛzɪdənt] *adj* wohnhaft ‖ *s* Einwohner –in *mf*
residential [‚rɛzɪ'dɛntʃəl] *adj* Wohn–
residue ['rɛzɪ‚d(j)u] *s* Rest *m;* (chem) Rückstand *m*
resign [rɪ'zaɪn] *tr (an office)* niederlegen; **r. oneself to** sich ergeben in *(acc)* ‖ *intr* zurücktreten
resignation [‚rɛzɪg'neʃən] *s (from an office)* Rücktritt *m;* *(submissive*

resilience 272 resuscitate

state) Ergebung *f;* **hand in one's r.**
sein Entlassungsgesuch einreichen
resilience [rɪ'zɪlɪ·əns] *s* Elastizität *f;*
(fig) Spannkraft *f*
resilient [rɪ'zɪlɪ·ənt] *adj* elastisch;
(fig) unverwüstlich
resin ['rɛzɪn] *s* Harz *m*
resist [rɪ'zɪst] *tr* widerstehen *(dat)* ‖
intr Widerstand leisten
resistance [rɪ'zɪstəns] *s* (& elec) Widerstand *m*
resole [ri'sol] *tr* neu besohlen
resolute ['rɛzə‚lut] *adj* entschlossen
resolution [rɛzə'luʃən] *s* (*resoluteness*)
Entschlossenheit *f;* (parl) Beschluß
m; **make good resolutions** gute Vor-
sätze fassen
resolve [rɪ'zɔlv] *s* Vorsatz *m* ‖ *tr* auflösen; (*a question, problem*) lösen;
r. to (*inf*) beschließen zu (*inf*) ‖ *intr*
—**r. into** sich auflösen in (*acc*); **r.
upon s.th.** sich [*dat*] etw vornehmen
resonance ['rɛzənəns] *s* Resonanz *f*
resort [rɪ'zɔrt] *s* (*refuge*) Zuflucht *f;*
(*for health*) Kurort *m;* (*for vacation*)
Ferienort *m,* Sommerfrische *f;* **as a
last r.** als letztes Mittel ‖ *intr*—**r. to**
greifen zu
resound [rɪ'zaund] *intr* widerhallen
resource ['risors] *s* Mittel *n;* **resources**
(fin) Geldmittel *pl*
resourceful [rɪ'sorsfəl] *adj* findig
respect [rɪ'spɛkt] *s* (*esteem*) Achtung
f, Respekt *m;* (*reference*) Hinsicht *f;*
in every r. in jeder Hinsicht; **pay
one's respects to s.o.** j-m seine Auf-
wartung machen; **with r. to** mit Bezug auf (*acc*) ‖ *tr* achten
respectable [rɪ'spɛktəbəl] *adj* achtbar;
(*e.g., firm*) angesehen
respect'ed *adj* angesehen
respectful [rɪ'spɛktfəl] *adj* ehrerbietig
respectfully [rɪ'spɛktfəli] *adv*—**r. yours**
hochachtungsvoll, Ihr ... or Ihre ...
respective [rɪ'spɛktɪv] *adj* jeweilig
respectively [rɪ'spɛktɪvli] *adv* beziehungsweise
respiration [‚rɛspɪ'reʃən] *s* Atmung *f*
respirator ['rɛspɪ‚retər] *s* Atemgerät *n*
respiratory ['rɛspɪrə‚tori] *adj* At-
mungs-
respite ['rɛspɪt] *s* (*pause*) Atempause
f; (*reprieve*) Aufschub *m;* **without r.**
ohne Unterlaß
resplendent [rɪ'splɛndənt] *adj* glänzend
respond [rɪ'spand] *tr* antworten ‖ *intr*
(*reply*) (**to**) antworten (auf *acc*); (*react*) (**to**) ansprechen (auf *acc*)
response [rɪ'spans] *s* Antwort *f;* (*reaction*) Reaktion *f;* (fig) Widerhall
m; **in r. to** als Antwort auf (*acc*)
responsibility [rɪ‚spansɪ'bɪlɪti] *s* Verantwortung *f*
responsible [rɪ'spansɪbəl] *adj* (*position*) verantwortlich; (*person*) verant-
wortungsbewußt; **be held r. for** verantwortlich gemacht werden für; **be
r. for** (*be answerable for*) verantwortlich sein für; (*be to blame for*) schuld
sein an (*dat*); (*be the cause of*) die
Ursache sein (*genit*); (*be liable for*)
haften für

responsive [rɪ'spansɪv] *adj*—**be r. to**
ansprechen auf (*acc*)
rest [rɛst] *s* (*repose*) Ruhe *f;* (*from
work*) Ruhepause *f;* (*e.g., from walking*) Rast *f;* (*remainder*) Rest *m;*
(*support*) Stütze *f;* (mus) Pause *f;*
all the r. (*in number*) alle andern;
(*in quantity*) alles übrige; **be at r.**
(*be calm*) beruhigt sein; (*be dead*)
ruhen; (*not be in motion*) sich in
Ruhelage befinden; **come to r.** stehenbleiben; **put one's mind to r.** sich
beruhigen; **take a r.** sich ausruhen;
the r. of the boys die übrigen (or
andern) Jungen ‖ *tr* ruhen lassen,
ausruhen; (*support, e.g., one's elbow*)
stützen ‖ *intr* sich ausruhen; **r. on**
lasten auf (*dat*); (*be based on*) beruhen auf (*dat*); **r. with** liegen bei
restaurant ['rɛstərənt] *s* Restaurant *n*
restful ['rɛstfəl] *adj* ruhig
rest' home' *s* Erholungsheim *n*
rest'ing place' *s* Ruheplatz *m;* **final r.**
letzte Ruhestätte *f*
restitution [‚rɛstɪ't(j)uʃən] *s* Wiedergutmachung *f;* **make r.** Genugtuung
leisten
restive ['rɛstɪv] *adj* (*restless*) unruhig;
(*balky*) störrisch
restless ['rɛstlɪs] *adj* ruhelos
restock [ri'stak] *tr* wieder auffüllen;
(*waters*) wieder mit Fischen besetzen
restoration [‚rɛstə'reʃən] *s* (*of a work
of art or building*) Restaurierung *f*
restore [rɪ'stor] *tr* (*order*) wiederherstellen; (*a painting, building*) restau-
rieren; (*stolen goods*) zurückerstat-
ten; **r. to health** wiederherstellen
restrain [rɪ'stren] *tr* zurückhalten;
(*feelings; a horse*) zügeln; (*e.g.,
trade*) einschränken; **r. s.o. from**
(*ger*) j-n davon abhalten zu (*inf*)
restrain'ing or'der *s* Unterlassungsur-
teil *n*
restraint [rɪ'strent] *s* Zurückhaltung *f;*
(*force*) Zwang *m*
restrict [rɪ'strɪkt] *tr* begrenzen; **r. to**
beschränken auf (*acc*)
restrict'ed ar'ea *s* Sperrgebiet *n*
rest' room' *s* Abort *m,* Toilette *f*
result [rɪ'zʌlt] *s* Ergebnis *n,* Resultat
n; (*consequence*) Folge *f;* **as a r. of**
als Folge (*genit*); **without r.** ergebnislos ‖ *intr*—**r. from** sich ergeben
aus; **r. in** führen zu
result' clause' *s* Folgesatz *m*
resume [rɪ'zum] *tr* wieder aufnehmen;
(*a journey*) fortsetzen
résumé ['rɛzu‚me] *s* Zusammenfassung *f*
resumption [rɪ'zʌmpʃən] *s* Wiederaufnahme *f*
resurface [ri'sʌrfɪs] *tr*—**r. the road
with** die Straßendecke erneuern von
‖ *intr* (naut & fig) wiederauftauchen
resurrect [‚rɛzə'rɛkt] *tr* (*the dead*)
wieder zum Leben erwecken; (fig)
wieder aufleben lassen
resurrection [‚rɛzə'rɛkʃən] *s* Auferste-
hung *f*
resuscitate [rɪ'sʌsɪ‚tet] *tr* wiederbe-
leben

retail ['ritel] *adj* Kleinhandels– || *adv* im Kleinhandel || *tr* im Kleinhandel verkaufen || *intr*—**r.** at two dollars im Kleinverkauf zwei Dollar kosten
re'tail busi'ness *s* Kleinhandel *m*
retailer ['ritelər] *s* Kleinhändler –in *mf*
retain [rɪ'ten] *tr* (zurück)behalten; (*a lawyer*) sich [*dat*] nehmen
retainer [rɪ'tenər] *s* (hist) Gefolgsmann *m;* (jur) Honorarvorschuß *m*
retain'ing wall' *s* Stützmauer *f*
retake ['ritek] *s* (cin) Neuaufnahme *f* || [ri'tek] *tr* (*a town*) zurückerobern; (cin) nochmals aufnehmen
retaliate [rɪ'tælɪˌet] *intr* (**against**) Vergeltung üben (an *dat*)
retaliation [rɪˌtælɪ'eʃən] *s* Vergeltung *f*
retaliatory [rɪ'tælɪ·əˌtori] *adj* Vergeltungs–
retard [rɪ'tɑrd] *tr* verzögern
retard'ed *adj* zurückgeblieben
retch [rɛtʃ] *intr* würgen
retch'ing *s* Würgen *n*
retell [ri'tɛl] *tr* wiedererzählen
retention [rɪ'tɛnʃən] *s* Beibehaltung *f*
re·think [ri'θɪŋk] *v* (*pret & pp* –thought*) *tr* umdenken
reticence ['rɛtɪsəns] *s* Verschwiegenheit *f*
reticent ['rɛtɪsənt] *adj* verschwiegen
retina ['rɛtɪnə] *s* Netzhaut *f*, Retina *f*
retinue ['rɛtɪˌn(j)u] *s* Gefolge *n*
retire [rɪ'taɪr] *tr* pensionieren || *intr* (*from employment*) in den Ruhestand treten; (*withdraw*) sich zurückziehen; (*go to bed*) sich zur Ruhe begeben
retired' *adj* pensioniert
retirement [rɪ'taɪrmənt] *s* Ruhestand *m;* **go into r.** in den Ruhestand treten, sich pensionieren lassen
retire'ment pay' *s* Pension *f*
retire'ment plan' *s* Pensionsplan *m*
retir'ing *adj* zurückhaltend
retort [rɪ'tort] *s* schlagfertige Erwiderung *f;* (chem) Retorte *f* || *tr & intr* erwidern
retouch [ri'tʌtʃ] *tr* retuschieren
retrace [ri'tres] *tr* zurückverfolgen
retract [rɪ'trækt] *tr* (*a statement*) widerrufen; (*claws; landing gear*) einziehen
retract'able land'ing gear' [rɪ'træktəbəl] *s* Verschwindfahrgestell *n*
retrain [ri'tren] *tr* umschulen
retread ['riˌtrɛd] *s* (*aut*) runderneuerter Reifen *m* || *tr* runderneuern
retreat [rɪ'trit] *s* (*quiet place*) Ruhesitz *m;* (mil) Rückzug *m;* (rel) Exerzitien *pl;* **beat a hasty r.** eilig den Rückzug antreten || *intr* sich zurückziehen
retrench [rɪ'trɛnʃ] *tr* einschränken || *intr* sich einschränken
retribution [ˌrɛtrɪ'bjuʃən] *s* Vergeltung *f*
retrieval [rɪ'trivəl] *s* Wiedererlangung *f*
retrieve [rɪ'triv] *tr* wiedererlangen; (*a loss*) wettmachen; (hunt) apportieren
retriever [rɪ'trivər] *s* Apportierhund *m*

retroactive [ˌrɛtro'æktɪv] *adj* (**from**) rückwirkend von … an
retrogressive [ˌrɛtrə'grɛsɪv] *adj* rückläufig
retrorocket ['rɛtroˌrɑkɪt] *s* Bremsrakete *f*
retrospect ['rɛtrəˌspɛkt] *s*—**in r.** rückblickend
re·try [ri'traɪ] *v* (*pret & pp* –tried*) *tr* (jur) nochmals verhandeln
return [rɪ'tʌrn] *s* Rückkehr *f;* (*giving back*) Rückgabe *f;* (*the way back*) Rückweg *m;* (*tax form*) Steuererklärung *f;* (*profit*) Umsatz *m;* (tennis) Rückschlag *m;* **in r.** dafür; **in r. for** als Entgelt für; **returns** (*profits*) Ertrag *m;* (*of an election*) Ergebnisse *pl* || *tr* zurückgeben; (*send back*) zurücksenden; (*put back*) zurückstellen; (*thanks*) abstatten; (*a verdict*) fällen; (*a favor, love, gun fire*) erwidern; (tennis) zurückschlagen || *intr* zurückkehren; **r. to** (e.g., *a topic*) zurückkommen auf (*acc*)
return' address' *s* Rückadresse *f*
return' flight' *s* Rückflug *m*
return' match' *s* Revanchepartie *f*
return' tick'et *s* Rückfahrkarte *f;* (aer) Rückflugkarte *f*
reunification [riˌjunɪfɪ'keʃən] *s* (pol) Wiedervereinigung *f*
reunion [ri'junjən] *s* Treffen *n*
rev [rɛv] *v* (*pret & pp* revved; *ger* revving) *tr* (up) auf Touren bringen || *intr* auf Touren kommen
revamp [ri'væmp] *tr* umgestalten
reveal [rɪ'vil] *tr* offenbaren
reveille ['rɛvəli] *s* Wecken *n*
rev·el ['rɛvəl] *s* Gelage *n* || *v* (*pret & pp* –el[l]ed; *ger* –el[l]ing) *intr* ein Gelage halten; **r. in** (fig) schwelgen in (*dat*)
revelation [ˌrɛvə'leʃən] *s* Offenbarung *f;* **Revelations** (Bib) Offenbarung *f*
reveler ['rɛvələr] *s* Zecher –in *mf*
revelry ['rɛvəlri] *s* Zechgelage *n*
revenge [rɪ'vɛndʒ] *s* Rache *f;* **take r. on s.o. for s.th.** sich an j–m für etw rächen || *tr* rächen
revengeful [rɪ'vɛndʒfəl] *adj* rachsüchtig
revenue ['rɛvəˌn(j)u] *s* (*yield*) Ertrag *m;* (*internal revenue*) Steueraufkommen *n*
rev'enue stamp' *s* Banderole *f*
reverberate [rɪ'vʌrbəˌret] *intr* widerhallen
revere [rɪ'vɪr] *tr* verehren
reverence ['rɛvərəns] *s* (*respect given or received*) Ehrerbietung *f;* (*respect felt*) Ehrfurcht *f*
reverend ['rɛvərənd] *adj* ehrwürdig; **the Reverend** … Hochwürden …
reverie ['rɛvəri] *s* Träumerei *f;* **be lost in r.** in Träumen versunken sein
reversal [rɪ'vʌrsəl] *s* Umkehrung *f;* (*of opinion*) Umschwung *m*
reverse [rɪ'vʌrs] *adj* umgekehrt; (*side*) linke || *s* (*back side*) Rückseite *f;* (*opposite*) Gegenteil *n;* (*setback*) Rückschlag *m;* (*of a coin*) Revers *m;*

(aut) Rückwärtsgang *m* ‖ *tr* umkehren, umdrehen; (*a decision*) umstoßen ‖ *intr* sich rückwärts bewegen
reverse' side' *s* Rückseite *f*, Kehrseite *f*
reversible [rɪ'vʌrsɪbəl] *adj* (*decision*) umstoßbar; (*material*) zweiseitig; (chem, phys) umkehrbar; (mach) umsteuerbar
revert [rɪ'vʌrt] *intr*—r. to zurückkommen auf (*acc*); (jur) zurückfallen an (*acc*)
review [rɪ'vju] *s* (of) Überblick *m* (über *acc*); (*of a lesson*) Wiederholung *f*; (*of a book*) Besprechung *f*; (*periodical*) Rundschau *m*; (mil) Besichtigung *f*; pass in r. mustern ‖ *tr* (*a lesson*) wiederholen; (*a book*) besprechen; (e.g., *the events of the day*) überblicken; (mil) besichtigen
reviewer [rɪ'vju·ər] *s* Besprecher –in *mf*
revile [rɪ'vaɪl] *tr* schmähen
revise [rɪ'vaɪz] *tr* (*a book*) umarbeiten; (*one's opinion*) revidieren
revised' edi'tion *s* verbesserte Auflage *f*
revision [rɪ'vɪʒən] *s* Neubearbeitung *f*
revival [rɪ'vaɪvəl] *s* Wiederbelebung *f*; (rel) Erweckung *f*; (theat) Reprise *f*
reviv'al meet'ing *s* Erweckungsversammlung *f*
revive [rɪ'vaɪv] *tr* wieder aufleben lassen; (*memories*) aufrühren; (*a victim*) wieder zu Bewußtsein bringen ‖ *intr* wieder aufleben
revoke [rɪ'vok] *tr* widerrufen
revolt [rɪ'volt] *s* Aufstand *m* ‖ *tr* abstoßen ‖ *intr* revoltieren
revolt'ing *adj* abstoßend
revolution [,revə'luʃən] *s* Revolution *f*; (*turn*) Umdrehung *f*; **revolutions per minute** Drehzahl *f*
revolutionary [,revə'luʃə,nɛri] *adj* revolutionär ‖ *s* Revolutionär –in *mf*
revolve [rɪ'valv] *intr* (around) sich drehen (um)
revolver [rɪ'valvər] *s* Revolver *m*
revolv'ing *adj* Dreh–
revue [rɪ'vju] *s* (theat) Revue *f*
revulsion [rɪ'vʌl/ən] *s* Abscheu *m*
reward [rɪ'wɔrd] *s* Belohnung *f* ‖ *tr* belohnen
reward'ing *adj* lohnend
re·wind [ri'waɪnd] *v* (*pret & pp* –wound*) *tr* (*a tape, film*) umspulen; (*a clock*) wieder aufziehen
rewire [ri'waɪr] *tr* Leitungen neu legen in (*dat*)
rework [ri'wʌrk] *tr* umarbeiten
re·write [ri'raɪt] *v* (*pret* –wrote; *pp* –written) *tr* umschreiben
rhapsody ['ræpsədi] *s* Rhapsodie *f*
rheostat ['ri·ə,stæt] *s* Rheostat *m*
rhetoric ['retərɪk] *s* Redekunst *f*
rhetorical [rɪ'tɔrɪkəl] *adj* rhetorisch
rheumatic [ru'mætɪk] *adj* rheumatisch
rheumatism ['rumə,tɪzəm] *s* Rheumatismus *m*
Rhine [raɪn] *s* Rhein *m*
Rhineland ['raɪn,lænd] *s* Rheinland *n*
rhine'stone' *s* Rheinkiesel *m*
rhinoceros [raɪ'nasərəs] *s* Nashorn *n*

rhubarb ['rubɑrb] *s* Rhabarber *m*; (sl) Krach *m*
rhyme [raɪm] *s* Reim *m* ‖ *tr & intr* reimen
rhythm ['rɪðəm] *s* Rhythmus *m*
rhythmic(al) ['rɪðmɪk(əl)] *adj* rhythmisch
rib [rɪb] *s* Rippe *f* ‖ *v* (*pret & pp* ribbed; *ger* ribbing) *tr* (coll) sich lustig machen über (*acc*)
ribald ['rɪbəld] *adj* zotig
ribbon ['rɪbən] *s* Band *n*; (*decoration*) Ordensband *n*; (*for a typewriter*) Farbband *n*
rice [raɪs] *s* Reis *m*
rich [rɪt/] *adj* reich; (*voice*) volltönend; (*soil*) fruchtbar; (*funny*) (coll) köstlich; r. in reich an (*dat*) ‖ **riches** *spl* Reichtum *n*
rickets ['rɪkɪts] *s* Rachitis *f*
rickety ['rɪkɪti] *adj* (*building*) baufällig; (*furniture*) wackelig
rid [rɪd] *v* (*pret & pp* rid; *ger* ridding) *tr* (of) befreien (von); **get rid of** loswerden
riddance ['rɪdəns] *s* Befreiung *f*; **good r.!** den (or die or das) wäre ich glücklich los!
riddle ['rɪdəl] *s* Rätsel *n*
ride [raɪd] *s* Fahrt *f*; **give s.o. a r.** j–n im Auto mitnehmen; **take for a r.** (*murder*) entführen und umbringen; (*dupe*) hochnehmen ‖ *v* (*pret* rode [rod]; *pp* ridden ['rɪdən]) *tr* (*a bicycle*) fahren; (*a horse*) reiten; (*a train, bus*) fahren mit; (*harass*) hetzen; **r. out** (*a storm*) gut überstehen ‖ *intr* (e.g., *in a car*) fahren; (*on a horse*) reiten; **let s.th. r.** sich mit etw abfinden
rider ['raɪdər] *s* (*on horseback*) Reiter –in *mf*; (*on a bicycle*) Radfahrer –in *mf*; (*in a vehicle*) Fahrer –in *mf*; (*to a document*) Zusatzklausel *f*
ridge [rɪdʒ] *s* (*of a hill; of the nose*) Rücken *m*; (*of a roof*) Dachfirst *m*
ridge'pole' *s* Firstbalken *m*
ridicule ['rɪdɪ,kjul] *s* Spott *m* ‖ *tr* verspotten
ridiculous [rɪ'dɪkjələs] *adj* lächerlich; **look r.** lächerlich wirken
rid'ing acad'emy *s* Reitschule *f*
rid'ing boot' *s* Reitstiefel *m*
rid'ing breech'es *spl* Reithose *f*
rid'ing hab'it *s* Reitkostüm *n*
rife [raɪf] *adj* häufig; **r. with** voll von
riffraff ['rɪf,ræf] *s* Gesindel *n*
rifle ['raɪfəl] *s* Gewehr *n* ‖ *tr* ausplündern
rift [rɪft] *s* (& fig) Riß *m*
rig [rɪg] *s* (*gear*) Ausrüstung *f*; (*horse and carriage*) Gespann *n*; (*truck*) Laster *m*; (*oil drill*) Bohrturm *m*; (*getup*) (coll) Aufmachung *f*; (naut) Takelung *f* ‖ *v* (*pret & pp* rigged; *ger* rigging) *tr* (auf)takeln; (*prices, elections, accounts*) manipulieren
rig'ging *s* Takelung *f*
right [raɪt] *adj* (*side, glove, angle*) recht; (*just*) gerecht; (*correct*) richtig; (*moment*) richtig; **do you have the r. time?** können Sie mir die ge-

naue Uhrzeit sagen?; **be in one's r. mind** bei klarem Verstand sein; **it is all r.** es ist schon gut; **r.?** nicht wahr?; **that's r.!** eben!; **the r. thing** das Richtige; **you are r.** Sie haben Leviten lesen recht || *adv* direkt; *(to the right)* rechts; **r. along** durchaus; **r. away** sofort, gleich; **r. behind the door** gleich hinter der Tür; **r. glad** (coll) recht froh; **r. here** gleich hier; **r. now** *(at the moment)* momentan; *(immediately)* sofort; **r. through** durch und durch || *s* Recht *n;* (box) Rechte *f;* **all rights reserved** alle Rechte vorbehalten; **by rights** von Rechts wegen; **in the r.** im Recht; **on the r.** rechts, zur Rechten || *tr* aufrichten; *(an error)* berichtigen; *(a wrong)* wiedergutmachen || *interj* stimmt!

righteous ['raɪtʃəs] *adj* gerecht, rechtschaffen; *(smug)* selbstgerecht
rightful ['raɪtfəl] *adj* *(owner)* rechtmäßig; *(claim, place)* berechtigt
right'-hand' *adj* zur Rechten; *(glove)* recht
right'-hand'ed *adj* rechtshändig
right-hander ['raɪt'hændər] *s* Rechtshänder –in *mf*
right'-hand man' *s* rechte Hand *f*
rightist ['raɪtɪst] *adj* rechtsstehend || *s* Rechtspolitiker –in *mf*
rightly ['raɪtli] *adv* richtig; *(rightfully)* rechtmäßig
right' of way' *s* *(in traffic)* Vorfahrtsrecht *n;* *(across another's land)* Grunddienstbarkeit *f*
right' wing' *s* rechter Flügel *m*
rigid ['rɪdʒɪd] *adj* steif, starr
rigmarole ['rɪgmə‚rol] *s* *(meaningless talk)* Geschwafel *n;* *(fuss)* Getue *n*
rigorous ['rɪgərəs] *adj* hart, streng
rile [raɪl] *tr* aufbringen
rill [rɪl] *s* Bächlein *n*
rim [rɪm] *s* Rand *m;* *(of eyeglasses)* Fassung *f;* *(of a wheel)* Felge *f*
rind [raɪnd] *s* Rinde *f*
ring [rɪŋ] *s* *(for the fingers; for boxing; of criminals or spies; of a circus; circle under the eyes)* Ring *m;* *(of a bell, voice, laughter)* Klang *m;* **give s.o. a r.** (telp) j–n anrufen; **run rings around s.o.** j–n in die Tasche stecken || *v* *(pret & pp* **ringed)** *tr* umringen; **r. in** einschließen || *v* *(pret* **rang** [ræŋ]; *pp* **rung** [rʌŋ]) *tr* läuten; **r. the bell** läuten, klingeln; **r. out** ausläuten; **r. up** anrufen || *intr* läuten, klingeln; **my ears are ringing** mir klingen die Ohren; **r. for s.o.** nach j–m klingeln; **r. out** laut schallen; **the bell is ringing** es läutet
ring'ing *adj* schallend || *s* Läuten *n;* *(in the ears)* Klingen *n*
ring'lead'er *s* Rädelsführer *m*
ring'mas'ter *s* Zirkusdirektor *m*
ring'side' *s* Ringplatz *m*
ring'worm' *s* Scherpilzflechte *f*
rink [rɪŋk] *s* Eisbahn *f;* *(for roller-skating)* Rollschuhbahn *f*
rinse [rɪns] *s* Spülen *n* || *tr* ausspülen
riot ['raɪ·ət] *s* Aufruhr *m;* **r. of colors**

Farbengemisch *n;* **run r.** sich austoben; *(said of plants)* wuchern || *intr* sich zusammenrotten
ri'ot act' *s*—read the r. to s.o. j–m die Leviten lesen
rioter ['raɪ·ətər] *s* Aufrührer –in *mf*
rip [rɪp] *s* Riß *m* || *v* *(pret & pp* **ripped;** *ger* **ripping)** *tr* (zer)reißen; **rip off** abreißen; *(the skin)* abziehen; *(cheat)* betrügen || *intr* reißen
rip' cord' *s* Reißlinie *f*
ripe [raɪp] *adj* reif
ripen ['raɪpən] *tr* (& fig) reifen lassen || *intr* (& fig) reifen
rip' off' *s* (sl) Wucher *m*
ripple ['rɪpəl] *s* leichte Welle *f* || *intr* leichte Wellen schlagen
rise [raɪz] *s* Aufsteigen *n;* *(in prices)* Steigerung *f;* *(of heavenly bodies)* Aufgang *m;* *(increase, e.g., in population)* Zunahme *f;* *(in the ground)* Erhebung *f;* **get a r. out of s.o.** j–n zu e–r Reaktion veranlassen; **give r. to** veranlassen || *v* *(pret* **rose** [roz]; *pp* **risen** ['rɪzən]) *intr* *(said of the sun, of a cake)* aufgehen; *(said of a river, prices, temperature, barometer)* steigen; *(said of a road)* ansteigen; *(get out of bed)* aufstehen; *(stand up)* sich erheben; *(from the dead)* auferstehen; *(said of anger)* hochsteigen; **r. to the occasion** sich der Lage gewachsen zeigen; **r. up from the ranks** von der Pike auf dienen
riser ['raɪzər] *s* *(of a staircase)* Futterbrett *n;* **early r.** Frühaufsteher –in *mf;* **late r.** Langschläfer –in *mf*
risk [rɪsk] *s* Risiko *n;* **run the r. of** *(ger)* Gefahr laufen zu *(inf)* || *tr* wagen, aufs Spiel setzen
risky ['rɪski] *adj* riskant, gewagt
risque [rɪs'ke] *adj* schlüpfrig
rite [raɪt] *s* Ritus *m;* **last rites** Sterbesakramente *pl*
ritual ['rɪtʃu·əl] *adj* rituell || *s* Ritual *n*
ri·val ['raɪvəl] *adj* rivalisierend || *s* Rivale *m,* Rivalin *f* || *v* *(pret & pp* **–val[l]ed;** *ger* **–val[l]ing)** *tr* rivalisieren, wetteifern mit
rivalry ['raɪvəlri] *s* Rivalität *f*
river ['rɪvər] *adj* Fluß– || *s* Fluß *m*
riv'er ba'sin *s* Flußgebiet *n*
riv'erfront' *s* Flußufer *n*
riv'erside' *adj* am Flußufer gelegen || *s* Flußufer *n*
rivet ['rɪvɪt] *s* Niet *m* || *tr* nieten
riv'et gun' *s* Nietmaschine *f*
riv'eting *s* (act) Vernieten *n;* *(connection)* Nietnaht *f*
rivulet ['rɪvjəlɪt] *s* Flüßchen *n*
R.N. ['ɑr'en] *s* (registered nurse) staatlich geprüfte Krankenschwester *f*
roach [rotʃ] *s* (ent) Schabe *f;* (ichth) Plötze *f*
road [rod] *s* (& fig) Weg *m;* **be (much) on the r.** (viel) auf Reisen sein; **go on the r.** auf Tour gehen; (theat) auf Tournee gehen
road'bed' *s* Bahnkörper *m*
road'block' *s* Straßensperre *f*

road' hog' s rücksichtsloser Autofahrer m

road' house' s Wirtshaus n, Rasthaus n

road' map' s Straßenkarte f, Autokarte f

road'side' adj Straßen– ‖ s Straßenrand m

road'side inn' s Rasthaus n

road'sign' s Wegweiser m

road'stead' s Reede f

road' test' s (aut) Probefahrt f

road'way' s Fahrweg m

roam [rom] tr durchstreifen ‖ intr herumstreifen

roar [ror] s Gebrüll n; (of a waterfall, sea, wind) Brausen n; (of an engine) Dröhnen n; (laughter) schallendes Gelächter n ‖ intr brüllen; (said of a waterfall, sea, wind) brausen; **r. at** anbrüllen; (e.g., a joke) schallend lachen über (acc); **r. by** vorbeibrausen; **r. with** brüllen vor (dat)

roast [rost] adj gebraten ‖ s Braten m ‖ tr (meat, fish) braten, rösten; (coffee, chestnuts) rösten; (a person) (coll) durch den Kakao ziehen ‖ intr braten

roast' beef' s Roastbeef n

roaster ['rostər] s (appliance) Röster m, Röstapparat m; (fowl) Brathuhn n

roast' pork' s Schweinsbraten m

rob [rɑb] v (pret & pp robbed; ger robbing) tr (a thing) rauben; (a person) (of) berauben (genit)

robber ['rɑbər] s Räuber –in mf

robbery ['rɑbəri] s Raubüberfall m

robe [rob] s Robe f; (house robe) Hausrock m ‖ tr feierlich ankleiden ‖ intr sich feierlich ankleiden

robin ['rɑbɪn] s Rotkehlchen n

robot ['robɑt] s Roboter m

robust [ro'bʌst] adj robust

rock [rɑk] adj (mus) Rock– ‖ s Fels m; (one that is thrown) Stein m; (mus) Rockmusik f; **on the rocks** mit Eiswürfeln; (ruined) kaputt ‖ tr schaukeln, wiegen; **r. the boat** (fig) die Sache ins Wanken bringen; **r. to sleep** in den Schlaf wiegen ‖ intr schwanken, wanken; (said of a boat) schaukeln

rock'-bot'tom adj äußerst niedrig ‖ s Tiefpunkt m

rock' can'dy s Kandiszucker m

rock' crys'tal s Bergkristall m

rocker ['rɑkər] s Schaukelstuhl m; **go off one's r.** (coll) den Verstand verlieren

rocket ['rɑkɪt] s Rakete f

rock'et launch'er s Raketenwerfer m

rocketry ['rɑkətri] s Raketentechnik f

rock'et ship' s Raketenflugkörper m

rock' gar'den s Steingarten m

rock'ing chair' s Schaukelstuhl m

rock'ing horse' s Schaukelpferd n

rock-'n'-roll ['rɑkən'rol] s Rock 'n Roll m

rock' salt' s Steinsalz n

rocky ['rɑki] adj felsig; (shaky) wacklig

rod [rɑd] s Stab m, Stange f; (whip)

Zuchtrute f; (of the retina; of a microorganism) Stäbchen n; (revolver) (sl) Schießeisen n; (angl) Angelrute f; (Bib) Reis n; (mach) Pleuelstange f; (surg) Absteckpfahl m

rodent ['rodənt] s Nagetier n

roe [ro] s (deer) Reh n; (ichth) Rogen m

rogue [rog] s Schuft m, Schurke m

rogues'' gal'lery s Verbrecheralbum n

roguish ['rogɪʃ] adj schurkisch

role, rôle [rol] s Rolle f

roll [rol] s Rolle f; (bread) Brötchen n; (of thunder, of a ship) Rollen n; (of drums) Wirbel m; (of fat) Wulst m; **call the r.** die Namen verlesen; (mil) Appell halten ‖ tr rollen; (cigarettes) drehen; (metals, roads) walzen; **r. over** überrollen; **r. up** zusammenrollen; (sleeves) zurückstreifen ‖ intr sich wälzen; **be rolling in money** im Geld wühlen

roll'back' s (com) Senkung f

roll'call' s Namensverlesung f; (mil) Appell m

roll'er bear'ing s Rollenlager n

roll'er coast'er s Berg-und-Tal-Bahn f

roll'er skate' s Rollschuh m

roll'er-skate' intr rollschuhlaufen

roll'er tow'el s Rollhandtuch n

roll'ing mill' s Walzwerk n

roll'ing pin' s Nudelholz n, Teigrolle f

roll'ing stock' s (rr) rollendes Material n

roly-poly ['roli'poli] adj dick und rund

roman ['romən] adj (typ) Antiqua–; **Roman** römisch ‖ s (typ) Antiqua f; **Roman** Römer –in mf

Ro'man can'dle s Leuchtkugel f

Ro'man Cath'olic adj römisch-katholisch ‖ s Katholik –in mf

romance [ro'mæns] adj (ling) romanisch ‖ s Romanze f

Romanesque [,romə'nesk] adj romanisch ‖ s das Romanische

Ro'man nose' s Römernase f

Ro'man nu'meral s römische Ziffer f

romantic [ro'mæntɪk] adj romantisch

romanticism [ro'mæntɪ,sɪzəm] s Romantik f

romp [rɑmp] intr umhertollen

rompers ['rɑmpərz] spl Spielanzug m

roof [ruf] s Dach n; (aut) Verdeck n; **raise the r.** (coll) Krach machen; **r. of the mouth** Gaumendach n

roofer ['rufər] s Dachdecker m

roof' gar'den s Dachgarten m

roof' tile' s Dachziegel m

rook [rʊk] s (chess) Turm m; (orn) Saatkrähe f ‖ tr (coll) (out of) beschwindeln (um)

rookie ['rʊki] s (coll) Neuling m

room [rum] s Zimmer n; (space) Raum m, Platz m; **make r.** Platz machen; **r. for complaint** Anlaß m zur Klage; **take up too much r.** zu viel Platz in Anspruch nehmen ‖ intr wohnen

room' and board' s Kost und Quartier

room' clerk' s Empfangschef m

roomer ['rumər] s Mieter –in mf

room'ing house' s Pension f
room'mate' s Zimmergenosse m
room' serv'ice s Bedienung f aufs Zimmer
roomy ['rumi] adj geräumig
roost [rust] s Hühnerstange f; **rule the r.** Hahn im Korb sein || intr auf der Stange sitzen
rooster ['rustər] s Hahn m
root [rut] s Wurzel f; **get to the r. of s.th.** etw [dat] auf den Grund gehen; **take r.** Wurzel schlagen; (fig) sich einbürgern || tr—**be rooted in** wurzeln in (dat); **rooted to the spot** festgewurzelt; **r. out** ausrotten || intr —**r. about** wühlen; **r. for** zujubeln (dat)
rope [rop] s Strick m, Seil n; **know the ropes** alle Kniffe kennen || tr mit e-m Seil festbinden; (a steer) mit e-m Lasso einfangen; **r. in** (coll) einwickeln; **r. off** absperren
rosary ['rozəri] s Rosenkranz m
rose [roz] adj rosenrot || s Rose f
rose'bud' s Rosenknospe f
rose'bush' s Rosenstock m
rose'-col'ored adj rosenfarbig; (fig) rosa(rot)
rosemary ['roz‚meri] s Rosmarin m
rosin ['razin] s Harz n; (for violin bow) Kolophonium n
roster ['rastər] s Namenliste f; (educ) Stundenplan m; (mil, naut) Dienstplan m
rostrum ['rastrəm] s Rednerbühne f
rosy ['rozi] adj (& fig) rosig
rot [rat] s Fäulnis f; (sl) Quatsch m || v (pret & pp **rotted**; ger **rotting**) tr faulen lassen || intr verfaulen
rotate ['rotet] tr rotieren lassen; (tires) auswechseln; (agr) wechseln || intr rotieren; (take turns) sich abwechseln
rotation [ro'teʃən] s Rotation f; **in r.** wechselweise; **r. of crops** Wechselwirtschaft f
rote [rot] s—**by r.** mechanisch
rotisserie [ro'tɪsəri] s Fleischbraterei f
rotten ['ratən] adj faul; (trick) niederträchtig; **feel r.** (sl) sich elend fühlen
rotund [ro'tʌnd] adj rundlich
rotunda [ro'tʌndə] s Rotunde f
rouge [ruʒ] s Rouge n || tr schminken
rough [rʌf] adj (hands, voice, person) rauh; (piece of wood) roh; (work, guess, treatment) grob; (water, weather) stürmisch; (road) uneben; **have it r.** viel durchmachen || tr—**r. in** roh entwerfen; (carp) grob bearbeiten; **r. it** primitiv leben; **r. up** grob behandeln
rough' draft' s Konzept n
roughen ['rʌfən] tr aufrauhen
rough'house' s Radau m || intr Radau machen
roughly ['rʌfli] adv grob; (about) etwa
rough'neck' s (coll) Rauhbein n
roulette [ru'lɛt] s Roulett n
round [raund] adj rund || s Runde f; (of applause) Salve f; (shot) Schuß m; (of drinks) Lage f; (of a sentinel,

policeman, inspector, mailman) Rundgang m; **daily r.** Alltag m || prep um (acc) herum || tr (make round) runden; (a corner) herumgehen (or herumfahren) um (acc); **r. off** abrunden; (finish) vollenden; **r. up** (animals) zusammentreiben; (persons) zusammenbringen; (criminals) ausheben
round'house' s (rr) Lokomotivschuppen m
round'-shoul'dered adj mit runden Schultern
round' steak' s Kugel f
round'-ta'ble adj am runden Tisch
round' trip' s Hin-und Rückfahrt f; (aer) Hin- und Rückflug m
round'-trip' tick'et s Rückfahrkarte f
round'up' s (of cattle) Zusammentreiben n; (of criminals) Aushebung f
rouse [rauz] tr (from) aufwecken (aus)
rout [raut] s völlige Niederlage f; (mil) wilde Flucht f; **put to r.** in die Flucht schlagen || tr (mil) zersprengen
route [rut], [raut] s Route f, Weg m || tr leiten
routine [ru'tin] adj routinemäßig || s Routine f; **be r.** die Regel sein
rove [rov] intr umherwandern
row [rau] s Krach m; **raise a row** (coll) Krach machen || [ro] Reihe f; **in a row** hintereinander || tr rudern
rowboat ['ro‚bot] s Ruderboot n
rowdy ['raudi] adj flegelhaft || s Flegel m
rower ['ro·ər] s Ruderer –in m/f
rowing ['ro·ɪŋ] s Rudersport m
royal ['rɔɪ·əl] adj königlich
royalist ['rɔɪ·əlɪst] adj königstreu || s Königstreue m/f
royalty ['rɔɪ·əlti] s (royal status) Königswürde f; (personage) fürstliche Persönlichkeit f; (collectively) fürstliche Persönlichkeiten pl; (author's compensation) Tantieme f; (inventor's compensation) Lizenzgebühr f
r.p.m. ['ar'pi'em] spl (revolutions per minute) Drehzahl f
R.S.V.P. abbr u.A.w.g. (um Antwort wird gebeten)
rub [rʌb] s Reiben n; **there's the rub** (coll) da sitzt der Haken || v (pret & pp **rubbed**; ger **rubbing**) tr reiben; **rub down** abreiben; **rub elbows with** verkehren mit; **rub in** einreiben; **rub it in** (sl) es (j-m) unter die Nase reiben; **rub out** ausradieren; (sl) umbringen; **rub s.o. the wrong way** j-m auf die Nerven gehen || intr reiben; **rub against** sich reiben an (dat); **rub off on** (fig) abfärben auf (acc)
rubber ['rʌbər] adj Gummi– || s Gummi m & n; (cards) Robber m; **rubbers** Gummischuhe pl
ru'ber band' s Gummiband n
rubberize ['rʌbə‚raɪz] tr gummieren
rub'ber plant' s Kautschukpflanze f
rub'ber stamp' s Gummistempel m
rub'ber-stamp' tr abstempeln; (coll) automatisch genehmigen
rubbery ['rʌbəri] adj gummiartig
rub'bing al'cohol s Franzbranntwein m

rubbish ['rʌbɪʃ] *s* (*trash*) Abfall *m*; (*nonsense*) dummes Zeug *n*
rubble ['rʌbəl] *s* Schutt *m*; (*used in masonry*) Bruchstein *m*
rub'down' *s* Abreibung *f*
rubric ['rubrɪk] *s* Rubrik *f*
ruby ['rubi] *adj* rubinrot ‖ *s* Rubin *m*
ruckus ['rʌkəs] *s* (coll) Krawall *m*
rudder ['rʌdər] *s* (aer) Seitenruder *n*; (naut) Steuerruder *n*
ruddy ['rʌdi] *adj* rosig
rude [rud] *adj* grob
rudeness ['rudnɪs] *s* Grobheit *f*
rudiments ['rudɪmənts] *spl* Grundlagen *pl*
rue [ru] *tr* bereuen
rueful ['rufəl] *adj* reuig; (*pitiable*) kläglich; (*mournful*) wehmütig
ruffian ['rʌfɪ·ən] *s* Raufbold *m*
ruffle ['rʌfəl] *s* Rüsche *f*; (*in water*) Kräuseln *n*; (*of a drum*) gedämpfter Trommelwirbel *m* ‖ *tr* kräuseln; (*feathers, hair*) sträuben
rug [rʌg] *s* Teppich *m*
rugged ['rʌgɪd] *adj* (*country*) wild; (*robust*) kräftig; (*life*) hart
ruin ['ru·ɪn] *s* Ruine *f*; (*undoing*) Ruin *m*; **go to r.** zugrunde gehen; **lie in ruins** in Trümmern liegen; **ruins** (*debris*) Trümmer *pl* ‖ *tr* ruinieren
rule [rul] *s* (*reign*) Herrschaft *f*; (*regulation*) Regel *f*; **as a r.** in der Regel; **become the r.** zur Regel werden ‖ *tr* beherrschen; (*paper*) linieren; **r. out** ausschließen ‖ *intr* (over) herrschen (über *acc*)
rule' of law' *s* Rechtsstaatlichkeit *f*
rule' of thumb' *s* Faustregel *f*; **by r.** über den Daumen gepeilt
ruler ['rulər] *s* Herrscher –in *mf*; (*for measuring*) Lineal *n*
rul'ing *adj* herrschend ‖ *s* Regelung *f*
rum [rʌm] *s* Rum *m*
Rumania [ru'menɪ·ə] *s* Rumänien *n*
Rumanian [ru'menɪ·ən] *adj* rumänisch ‖ *s* Rumäne *m*, Rumänin *f*; (*language*) Rumänisch *n*
rumble ['rʌmbəl] *s* (*of thunder*) Rollen *n*; (*of a truck*) Rumpeln *n* ‖ *intr* rollen; rumpeln
ruminate ['rumɪ‚net] *tr & intr* wiederkäuen
rummage ['rʌmɪdʒ] *intr*—**r. through** durchsuchen
rum'mage sale' *s* Ramschverkauf *m*
rumor ['rumər] *s* Gerücht *n* ‖ *tr*—**it is rumored that** es geht das Gerücht, daß
rump [rʌmp] *s* (*of an animal*) Hinterteil *m & n*; (*buttocks*) Gesäß *n*
rumple ['rʌmpəl] *tr* (*clothes*) zerknittern; (*hair*) zerzausen
rump' steak' *s* Rumpsteak *n*
rumpus ['rʌmpəs] *s* (coll) Krach *m*; **raise a r.** (coll) Krach machen
rum'pus room' *s* Spielzimmer *n*
run [rʌn] *s* Lauf *m*; (*in stockings*) Laufmasche *f*; (fin) Run *m*; (theat) Laufzeit *f*; **be on the run** auf der Flucht sein; **in the long run** auf die Dauer; **run of bad luck** Pechsträhne *f*; **run of good luck** Glücksträhne *f* ‖

v (*pret* **ran** [ræn]; *pp* **run**; *ger* **running**) *tr* (*a machine*) bedienen; (*a business, household*) führen; (*a distance*) laufen; (*a blockade*) brechen; (*a cable*) verlegen; **run a race** um die Wette laufen; **run down** (*with a car*) niederfahren; (*clues*) nachgehen (*dat*); (*a citation*) aufspüren; (*through gossip*) schlechtmachen; **run off** (typ) Abzüge machen von; **run over** (*with a vehicle*) überfahren; (*rehearse*) nochmal durchgehen; **run through** (*with a sword*) erstechen; **run up** (*bills*) auflaufen lassen; (*prices*) in die Höhe treiben; (*a flag*) hissen ‖ *intr* laufen, rennen; (*flow*) fließen; (*said of buses, etc.*) verkehren; (*said of the nose*) laufen, e.g., **ihm läuft die Nase** his nose is running; (*said of colors*) auslaufen; (*said of a meeting*) dauern; (*said of a lease*) (**for**) gelten (auf *acc*); **run across** zufällig treffen; **run after** nachlaufen (*dat*); **run around** herumlaufen; **run around with** sich herumtreiben mit; **run away** weglaufen; (*said of a spouse*) durchgehen; **run down** (*said of a clock*) ablaufen; **run dry** austrocknen; **run for** kandidieren für; **run high**, e.g., **feelings ran high** die Gemüter waren erhitzt; **run in the family** in der Familie liegen; **run into** (*e.g., a tree*) fahren gegen; (*e.g., trouble, debt*) geraten in (*acc*); (*e.g., a friend*) unerwartet treffen; **run into the thousands** in die Tausende gehen; **run low** knapp werden; **run out** (*said of liquids*) ausgehen; (*said of supplies, time*) zu Ende gehen; **run out of** ausgehen, e.g., **they ran out of supplies** die Vorräte gingen ihnen aus; **run over** (*said of a pot*) überlaufen; **run up against** stoßen auf (*acc*); **run up to s.o.** j–m entgegenlaufen; **run wild** verwildern
run'-around' *s*—**give s.o. the r.** j–n von Pontius zu Pilatus schicken
run'away' *adj* flüchtig; (*horse*) durchgegangen ‖ *s* Ausreißer *m*; (*horse*) Durchgänger *m*
run'down' *s* kurze Zusammenfassung *f*
run'-down' *adj* (*condition*) heruntergekommen; (*clock*) abgelaufen; (*battery*) entladen
rung [rʌŋ] *s* (*of a ladder*) Sprosse *f*; (*of a chair*) Querleiste *f*
run-in' *s* (coll) Zusammenstoß *m*
runner ['rʌnər] *s* Läufer –in *mf*; (*of a sled or skate*) Kufe *f*; (*of a sliding door*) Laufschiene *f*; (*rug*) Läufer *m*; (bot) Ausläufer *m*; (mil) Meldegänger *m*
run'ner-up' *s* (**runners-up**) Zweitbeste *mf*; (sport) Zweite *mf*
run'ning *adj* (*water*) fließend; (*debts, expenses, sore*) laufend ‖ *s* Laufen *n*, Lauf *m*; **be in the r.** gut im Rennen liegen; **be out of the r.** (*out of the race*) aus dem Rennen ausgeschieden sein; (*not among the front runners*) keine Aussichten haben

run'ning board' s Trittbrett n
run'ning start' s fliegender Start m
run'off' s (sport) Entscheidungslauf m
run'off elec'tion s entscheidende Vorwahl f
run'-of-the-mill' adj Durchschnitts–
runt [rʌnt] s Dreikäsehoch m
run'way' s Startbahn f
rupture ['rʌptʃər] s Bruch m ‖ tr (relations) abbrechen; be ruptured e–n Bruch (or Riß) bekommen; r. oneself sich [dat] e–n Bruch zuziehen ‖ intr platzen
rural ['rʊrəl] adj ländlich
ruse [ruz] s List f
rush [rʌʃ] adj dringend ‖ s Eile f; (for) Ansturm m (auf acc); (bot) Binse f; be in a r. es eilig haben; what's your r.? wozu die Eile? ‖ tr (a person) hetzen; (a defensive position) im Sturm nehmen; (work) schnell erledigen; (goods) schleunigst schicken; (e.g., to a hospital) schleunigst schaffen; be rushed for time sehr wenig Zeit haben; r. through (a bill) durchpeitschen; r. up (reinforcements) schnell herbeischaffen ‖ intr eilen, sich stürzen; r. at zustürzen auf

(acc); r. forward vorstürmen; r. into stürzen in (acc); r. up to zuschießen auf (acc); the blood rushed to his head ihm stieg das Blut in den Kopf
rush' hours' spl Hauptverkehrszeit f
rush' or'der s Eilauftrag m
russet ['rʌsɪt] adj rotbraun
Russia ['rʌʃə] s Russland n
Russian ['rʌʃən] adj russisch ‖ s Russe m, Russin f; (language) Russisch n
rust [rʌst] s Rost m ‖ tr rostig machen ‖ intr (ver)rosten
rustic ['rʌstɪk] adj (rural) ländlich; (countryish) bäuerlich ‖ s Bauer m
rustle ['rʌsəl] s Rauschen n; (of silk) Knistern n ‖ tr rascheln mit; (cattle) stehlen ‖ intr rauschen; (said of silk) knistern
rust'proof' adj rostfrei
rusty ['rʌsti] adj rostig; (fig) eingerostet
rut [rʌt] s Geleise n, Spur f; (fig) alter Trott m
ruthless ['ruθlɪs] adj erbarmungslos
rye [raɪ] s (grain) Roggen m; (whiskey) Roggenwhisky m
rye' bread' s Roggenbrot n
rye' grass' s Raigras n

S

S, s [ɛs] s neunzehnter Buchstabe des englischen Alphabets
Sabbath ['sæbəθ] s Sabbat m
sabbat'ical year' [sə'bætɪkəl] s einjähriger Urlaub m (e–s Professors)
saber ['sebər] s Säbel m
sable ['sebəl] adj schwarz ‖ s (fur) Zobelpelz m; (zool) Zobel m
sabotage ['sæbə‚tɑʒ] s Sabotage f ‖ tr sabotieren
saboteur [‚sæbə'tʌr] s Saboteur –in mf
saccharin ['sækərɪn] s Saccharin n
sachet [sæ'ʃe] s Duftkissen n
sack [sæk] s Sack m; (bed) (coll) Falle f; hit the s. (coll) in die Falle gehen ‖ tr einsacken; (dismiss) (coll) an die Luft setzen; (mil) ausplündern
sack'cloth' s Sacktuch n; in s. and ashes in Sack und Asche
sacrament ['sækrəmənt] s Sakrament n
sacramental [‚sækrə'mentəl] adj sakramental
sacred ['sekrəd] adj heilig; s. to geweiht (dat)
sacrifice ['sækrɪ‚faɪs] s Opfer n; at a s. mit Verlust ‖ tr opfern
sacrilege ['sækrɪlɪdʒ] s Sakrileg n
sacrilegious [‚sækrɪ'lɪdʒəs] adj frevelhaft, gotteslästerlich
sacristan ['sækrɪstən] s Sakristan m
sacristy ['sækrɪsti] s Sakristei f
sad [sæd] adj traurig; (plight) schlimm
sadden ['sædən] tr traurig machen
saddle ['sædəl] s Sattel m ‖ tr satteln; be saddled with auf dem Halse haben

sad'dlebag' s Satteltasche f
sadism ['sedɪzəm] s Sadismus m
sadistic [se'dɪstɪk] adj sadistisch
sadness ['sædnɪs] s Traurigkeit f
sad' sack' s (sl) Trauerkloß m
safe [sef] adj (from) sicher (vor dat); (arrival) glücklich; s. and sound heil und gesund; (said of a thing) unversehrt; to be on the s. side vorsichtshalber ‖ s Geldschrank m
safe'-con'duct s sicheres Geleit n
safe'-depos'it box' s Schließfach n
safe' dis'tance s Sicherheitsabstand m
safe'guard' s Schutz m ‖ tr schützen
safe'keep'ing s sicherer Gewahrsam m
safety ['sefti] adj Sicherheits– ‖ s Sicherheit f
safe'ty belt' s Sicherheitsgurt m
safe'ty pin' s Sicherheitsnadel f
safe'ty ra'zor s Rasierapparat m
safe'ty valve' s Sicherheitsventil n
saffron ['sæfrən] adj safrangelb ‖ s Safran m
sag [sæg] s Senkung f ‖ v (pret & pp sagged; ger sagging) intr sich senken; (said of a cable) durchhängen; (fig) sinken
sagacious [sə'geʃəs] adj scharfsinnig
sage [sedʒ] adj weise, klug ‖ s Weise m; (plant) Salbei f
sage'brush' s Beifuß m
sail [sel] s Segel n; set s. for in See stechen nach ‖ tr (a boat) fahren; (the sea) segeln über (acc) ‖ intr segeln; (depart) abfahren; s. across übersegeln; s. along the coast an der

Küste entlangsegeln; **s. into** (coll) herunterputzen
sail'boat' *s* Segelboot *n*
sail'cloth' *s* Segeltuch *n*
sail'ing *s* Segelfahrt *f;* (sport) Segelsport *m;* **it will be smooth s.** (fig) es wird alles glattgehen
sail'ing ves'sel *s* Segelschiff *n*
sailor ['selər] *s* Matrose *m*
Saint [sent] *s* Heilige *mf;* **S. George** der heilige Georg, Sankt Georg
Saint' Bernard' *s (dog)* Bernhardiner *m*
sake [sek] *s*—**for her s.** ihretwegen; **for his s.** seinetwegen; **for my s.** meinetwegen; **for our s.** unsertwegen; **for their s.** ihretwegen; **for the s. of** um *(genit)* willen; **for your s.** deinetwegen, Ihretwegen
salable ['seləbəl] *adj* verkäuflich
salacious [sə'le/əs] *adj (person)* geil; *(writing, pictures)* obszön
salad ['sæləd] *s* Salat *m*
sal'ad bowl' *s* Salatschüssel *f*
sal'ad dress'ing *s* Salatsoße *f*
sal'ad oil' *s* Salatöl *n*
salami [sə'lɑmi] *s* Salami *f*
salary ['sæləri] *s* Gehalt *n*
sale [sel] *s* Verkauf *m;* *(special sale)* Ausverkauf *m;* **be up for s.** zum Kauf stehen; **for s.** zu verkaufen; **sales** (com) Absatz *m,* Umsatz *m;* **put up for s.** zum Verkauf anbieten
sales'' clerk' *s* Verkäufer –in *mf*
sales'girl' *s* Ladenmädchen *n*
sales'la'dy *s* Verkäuferin *f*
sales'man *s* (–men) Verkäufer *m*
sales'manship' *s* Verkaufstüchtigkeit *f*
sales' promo'tion *s* Verkaufsförderung *f*
sales' slip' *s* Kassenzettel *m,* Bon *m*
sales' tax' *s* Umsatzsteuer *f*
saliva [sə'laɪvə] *s* Speichel *m*
sallow ['sælo] *adj* bläßlich
sal·ly ['sæli] *s (side trip)* Abstecher *m;* (mil) Ausfall *m* ‖ *v (pret & pp* –**lied)** *intr* (mil) ausfallen; **s. forth** sich aufmachen
salmon ['sæmən] *adj* lachsfarben ‖ *s* Lachs *m*
saloon [sə'lun] *s* Kneipe *f;* (naut) Salon *m*
salt [sɔlt] *s* Salz *n* ‖ *tr* salzen; **s. away** (coll) auf die hohe Kante legen
salt'cel'lar *s* Salzfaß *n*
salt'ed meat' *s* Salzfleisch *n*
salt' mine' *s* Salzbergwerk *n;* **back to the salt mines** zurück zur Tretmühle
salt'pe'ter *s* Salpeter *m*
salt' shak'er *s* Salzfaß *n*
salty ['sɔlti] *adj* salzig
salutary ['sæljə,teri] *adj* heilsam
salute [sə'lut] *s* Salut *m* ‖ *tr & intr* salutieren
salvage ['sælvɪdʒ] *s (saving by ship)* Bergung *n;* *(property saved by ship)* Bergungsgut *n;* *(discarded material)* Altmaterial *n* ‖ *tr* bergen; *(discarded material)* verwerten
salvation [sæl've/ən] *s* Heil *n*
Salva'tion Ar'my *s* Heilsarmee *f*
salve [sæv] *s* Salbe *f* ‖ *tr (one's conscience)* beschwichtigen

sal·vo ['sælvo] *s* (–vos & –voes) Salve *f*
Samaritan [sə'mærɪtən] *s* Samariter –in *mf;* **good S.** barmherziger Samariter *m*
same [sem] *adj*—**at the s. time** gleichzeitig; **it's all the s. to me** es ist mir ganz gleich; **just the s.** trotzdem; **thanks, s. to you!** danke, gleichfalls!; **the s.** derselbe
sameness ['semnɪs] *s* Eintönigkeit *f*
sample ['sæmpəl] *s* Muster *n,* Probe *f* ‖ *tr* (aus)probieren
sancti·fy ['sæŋktɪ,faɪ] *v (pret & pp* –**fied)** *tr* heiligen
sanctimonious [,sæŋktɪ'monɪ·əs] *adj* scheinheilig
sanction ['sæŋkʃən] *s* Sanktion *f* ‖ *tr* sanktionieren
sanctity ['sæŋktɪti] *s* Heiligkeit *f*
sanctuary ['sæŋktʃu,eri] *s (shrine)* Heiligtum *n;* *(of a church)* Altarraum *m;* *(asylum)* Asyl *n*
sand [sænd] *s* Sand *m* ‖ *tr* mit Sandpapier abschleifen; *(a road, sidewalk)* mit Sand bestreuen
sandal ['sændəl] *s* Sandale *f*
san'dalwood' *s* Sandelholz *n*
sand'bag' *s* Sandsack *m*
sand'bank' *s* Sandbank *f*
sand' bar' *s* Sandbank *f*
sand'blast' *tr* sandstrahlen
sand'box' *s* Sandkasten *m*
sand' cas'tle *s* Strandburg *f*
sand' dune' *s* Sanddüne *f*
sand'glass' *s* Sanduhr *f*
sand'man *s* (–men) (fig) Sandmann *m*
sand'pa'per *s* Sandpapier *n* ‖ *tr* mit Sandpapier abschleifen
sand'stone' *s* Sandstein *m*
sand'storm' *s* Sandsturm *m*
sandwich ['sændwɪtʃ] *s* belegtes Brot *n,* Sandwich *n* ‖ *tr* **(in between)** einzwängen (zwischen *dat)*
sandy ['sændi] *adj* sandig; *(color)* sandfarben
sane [sen] *adj* geistig gesund; *(e.g., advice)* vernünftig
sanguine ['sæŋgwɪn] *adj* **(about)** zuversichtlich (in Bezug auf *acc)*
sanitarium [,sænɪ'terɪ·əm] *s* Heilanstalt *f,* Sanatorium *n*
sanitary ['sænɪ,teri] *adj* sanitär
san'itary nap'kin *s* Damenbinde *f*
sanitation [,sænɪ'te/ən] *s* Gesundheitswesen *n;* *(in a building)* sanitäre Einrichtungen *pl*
sanity ['sænɪti] *s* geistige Gesundheit *f*
Santa Claus ['sæntə,klɔz] *s* der Weihnachtsmann *m,* der Nikolaus
sap [sæp] *s* Saft *m;* (coll) Schwachkopf *m* ‖ *v (pret & pp* **sapped)** *ger* **sapping)** *tr (strength)* erschöpfen
sapling ['sæplɪŋ] *s* junger Baum *m*
sapphire ['sæfaɪr] *s* Saphir *m*
Saracen ['særəsən] *adj* sarazenisch ‖ *s* Sarazene *m,* Sarazenin *f*
sarcasm ['sɑrkæzəm] *s* Sarkasmus *m*
sarcastic [sɑr'kæstɪk] *adj* sarkastisch
sarcophagus [sɑr'kɑfəgəs] *s* Sarkophag *m*
sardine [sɑr'din] *s* Sardine *f;* **packed**

in like **sardines** zusammengedrängt wie die Heringe

Sardinia [sɑr'dɪnɪ·ə] s Sardinien n

Sardinian [sɑr'dɪnɪ·ən] adj sardinisch ‖ s Sardinier –in mf; (language) Sardinisch n

sash [sæʃ] s Schärpe f; (of a window) Fensterrahmen m

sass [sæs] s (coll) Revolverschnauze f ‖ tr (coll) (off) patzig antworten (dat)

sassy ['sæsi] adj (coll) patzig

Satan ['setən] s Satan m

satanic(al) [sə'tænɪk(əl)] adj satanisch

satchel ['sætʃəl] s Handtasche f

sate [set] tr übersättigen

satellite ['sætə,laɪt] s Satellit m

sat'ellite coun'try s Satellitenstaat m

satiate ['seʃɪ,et] tr sättigen

satin ['sætɪn] s Seidenatlas m

satire ['sætaɪr] s Satire f

satiric(al) [sə'tɪrɪk(əl)] adj satirisch

satirize ['sætɪ,raɪz] tr verspotten

satisfaction [,sætɪs'fækʃən] s Befriedigung f, Genugtuung f

satisfactory [,sætɪs'fæktəri] adj friedenstellend, genügend

satis·fy ['sætɪs,faɪ] v (pret & pp –fied) tr (desires, needs) befriedigen; (requirements) genügen (dat); (a person) zufriedenstellen; **be satisfied with** zufrieden sein mit ‖ intr befriedigen

saturate ['sætʃə,ret] tr (& chem) sättigen, saturieren

satura'tion bomb'ing s Bombenteppich m

satura'tion point' s Sättigungspunkt m

Saturday ['sætər,de] s Samstag m; **on S.** am Samstag

sauce [sɔs] s Soße f; (coll) Frechheit f ‖ tr mit Soße zubereiten; (season) würzen

sauce'pan' s Stielkasserolle f

saucer ['sɔsər] s Untertasse f

saucy ['sɔsi] adj (impertinent) frech; (amusingly flippant) keß; (trim) flott

sauerkraut ['saʊr,kraʊt] s Sauerkraut n

saunter ['sɔntər] s Schlendern n ‖ intr schlendern

sausage ['sɔsɪdʒ] s Wurst f

saute [so'te] v (pret & pp sauteed) tr sautieren

savage ['sævɪdʒ] adj wild ‖ s Wilde mf

savant ['sævənt] s Gelehrte m

save [sev] tr (rescue) retten; (money, fuel) sparen; (keep, preserve) aufheben; (trouble) ersparen; (time) gewinnen; (stamps) sammeln; **s. face** das Gesicht wahren; **s. from** bewahren vor (dat) ‖ prep außer (dat)

sav'ing adj (grace) seligmachend; (quality) ausgleichend ‖ s (of souls) Rettung f; (in) Ersparnis f (an dat); savings Ersparnisse pl

sav'ings account' s Sparkonto n

sav'ings bank' s Sparkasse f

sav'ings certi'ficate s Sparbon m

sav'ings depos'it s Spareinlage f

savior ['sevjər] s Retter –in mf; **Saviour** Heiland m

savor ['sevər] s Wohlgeschmack m ‖ tr auskosten ‖ intr—**s. of** (smell of) riechen nach; (taste of) schmecken nach

savory ['sevəri] adj wohlschmeckend

saw [sɔ] s Säge f; (saying) Sprichwort n ‖ tr sägen; **saw up** zersägen

saw'dust' s Sägespäne pl

saw'horse' s Sägebock m

saw'mill' s Sägemühle f

Saxon ['sæksən] adj sächsisch ‖ s Sachse m, Sachsin f

Saxony ['sæksəni] s Sachsen n

saxophone ['sæksə,fon] s Saxophon n

say [se] s—**have a** (or no) **say in etw** (or nichts) zu sagen haben bei; **have one's say** (about) seine Meinung äußern (über acc) ‖ v (pret & pp said [sɛd]) tr sagen; (Mass) lesen; (a prayer) sprechen; (one's prayers) verrichten; (said of a newspaper article, etc.) besagen; **it says in the papers** in der Zeitung steht; (let's) say sagen wir; **no sooner said than done** gesagt, getan; **say!** (to draw attention) sag mal!; (to elicit agreement) gelt!; **say s.th. behind s.o.'s back** j–m etw nachsagen; **she is said to be clever** sie soll klug sein; **that is not to say** das will nicht sagen; **that is to say** das heißt; **they say** man sagt; **to say nothing of** ganz zu schweigen von; **you don't say so!** tatsächlich!

say'ing s Sprichwort n; **as the s. goes** wie man zu sagen pflegt; **it goes without s.** das versteht sich von selbst

say'-so' s (assertion) Behauptung f; (order) Anweisung f; (final authority) letztes Wort n

scab [skæb] s Schorf m; (sl) Streikbrecher –in mf

scabbard ['skæbərd] s Schwertscheide f

scabby ['skæbi] adj schorfig

scads [skædz] spl (sl) e–e Menge f

scaffold ['skæfəld] s Gerüst n; (for executions) Schafott n

scaf'folding s Baugerüst n

scald [skɔld] tr verbrühen; (milk) aufkochen

scale [skel] s (on fish, reptiles) Schuppe f; (pan of a balance) Waagschale f; (of a thermometer, wages) Skala f; (mus) Tonleiter f; **on a grand s.** im großen Stil; **on a large** (or small) **s.** in großem (or kleinem) Maßstab; **s. 1:1000** Maßstab 1:1000; **scales** Waage f; **to s.** maßstabgerecht ‖ tr erklettern; **s. down** maßstäblich verkleinern; (prices) herabsetzen

scallop ['skæləp] s Kammuschel f; (sew) Zacke f ‖ tr auszacken; (culin) überbacken

scalp [skælp] s Kopfhaut f; (Indian trophy) Skalp m ‖ tr skalpieren

scalpel ['skælpəl] s Skalpell n

scaly ['skeli] adj schuppig

scamp [skæmp] s Fratz m, Wildfang m

scamper ['skæmpər] intr herumtollen; **s. away** davonlaufen

scan [skæn] v (pret & pp scanned; ger

scanning) *tr* (*a page*) überfliegen; (*a verse*) skandieren; (*examine*) genau prüfen; (radar, telv) abtasten

scandal ['skændəl] *s* Skandal *m*

scandalize ['skændə,laɪz] *tr* schockieren

scandalmonger ['skændəl,mʌŋgər] *s* Lästermaul *n*

scandalous ['skændələs] *adj* skandalös

scan'dal sheet' *s* Sensationsblatt *n*

Scandinavia [,skændɪ'nevɪ·ə] *s* Skandinavien *n*

Scandinavian [,skændɪ'nevɪ·ən] *adj* skandinavisch || *s* Skandinavier –in *mf*; (*language*) Skandinavisch *n*

scansion ['skænʃən] *s* Skandieren *n*

scant [skænt] *adj* gering; **a s. two hours** knapp zwei Stunden

scantily ['skæntɪli] *adv*—**s. clad** leicht bekleidet

scanty ['skænti] *adj* kärglich, knapp

scapegoat ['skep,got] *s* Sündenbock *m*

scar [skɑr] *s* Narbe *f*; (fig) Makel *m* || *v* (*pret* & *pp* **scarred**; *ger* **scarring**) *tr* (*e.g.*, *a face*) entstellen; (*e.g.*, *a tabletop*) verschrammen; (fig) beinträchtigen

scarce [skɛrs] *adj* knapp, rar; **make oneself s.** (coll) das Weite suchen

scarcely ['skɛrsli] *adv* kaum; **be s. able to** (*inf*) Not haben zu (*inf*)

scarcity ['skɛrsɪti] *s* (of) Knappheit *f* (an *dat*), Mangel *m* (an *dat*)

scare [skɛr] *s* Schrecken *m*; **be scared** erschrecken; **be scared stiff** e–e Hundeangst haben; **give s.o. a s.** j–m e–n Schrecken einjagen || *tr* erschrecken; **s. away** verscheuchen; **s. up** (*money*) auftreiben || *intr* erschrecken

scare'crow' *s* Vogelscheuche *f*

scarf [skɑrf] *s* (**scarfs** & **scarves** [skɑrvz]) Schal *m*

scarlet ['skɑrlɪt] *adj* scharlachrot || *s* Scharlachrot *n*

scar'let fe'ver *s* Scharlach *m*

scarred *adj* narbig, schrammig

scary ['skɛri] *adj* schreckerregend

scat [skæt] *interj* weg!

scathing ['skeðɪŋ] *adj* vernichtend

scatter ['skætər] *tr* zerstreuen || *intr* sich zerstreuen

scat'terbrain' *s* Wirrkopf *m*

scat'tered show'ers *spl* einzelne Schauer *pl*

scenari·o [sɪ'nɛrɪ·o] *s* (–os) Drehbuch *n*

scene [sin] *s* Szene *f*; **be on the s.** zur Stelle sein; **behind the scenes** hinter den Kulissen; **make a s.** e–e Szene machen; **s. of the crime** Tatort *m*

scenery ['sinəri] *s* Landschaft *f*; (theat) Bühnenausstattung *f*

scenic ['sinɪk] *adj* landschaftlich; (theat) szenisch

scent [sɛnt] *s* Duft *m*; (*of a dog*) Witterung *f*; (hunt) Spur *f*; **have a s.** duften || *tr* wittern

scepter ['sɛptər] *s* Zepter *n*

sceptic ['skɛptɪk] *s* Skeptiker –in *mf*

scepticism ['skɛptɪ,sɪzəm] *s* (*doubt*) Skepsis *f*; (*doctrine*) Skeptizismus *m*

schedule ['skɛdjʊl] *s* Plan *m*; (*for work*) Arbeitsplan *m*; (*in travel*) Fahrplan *m*; (*at school*) Stundenplan *m*; (*appendix to a tax return*) Einkommensteuerformular *n*; (*table*) Einkommensteuertabelle *f*; **on s.** fahrplanmäßig || *tr* ansetzen; **the plane is scheduled to arrive at six** nach dem Flugplan soll die Maschine um sechs Uhr ankommen

scheme [skim] *s* (*schematic*) Schema *n*; (*plan, program*) Plan *m*; (*intrigue*) Intrige *f* || *tr* planen || *intr* Ränke schmieden

schemer ['skimər] *s* Ränkeschmied *m*

schilling ['ʃɪlɪŋ] *s* (Aust) Schilling *m*

schism ['sɪzəm] *s* (fig) Spaltung *f*; (eccl) Schisma *n*

schizophrenia [,skɪtso'frinɪ·ə] *s* Schizophrenie *f*, Bewußtseinsspaltung *f*

schizophrenic [,skɪtso'frɛnɪk] *adj* schizophren

schmaltzy ['ʃmɔltsi] *adj* schmalzig

scholar ['skɑlər] *s* Gelehrte *mf*

scholarly ['skɑlərli] *adj* gelehrt

schol'arship' *s* Gelehrsamkeit *f*; (*award*) Stipendium *n*

scholastic [skə'læstɪk] *adj* Schul–, Bildungs–; (hist) scholastisch

school [skul] *adj* (*book, house, master, room, teacher, yard, year*) Schul– || *s* Schule *f*; (*of a university*) Fakultät *f*; (*of fish*) Schwarm *m*; **s. is over** die Schule ist aus || *tr* schulen

school' age' *s* schulpflichtiges Alter *n*; **of s.** schulpflichtig

school'bag' *s* Schulranzen *m*

school' board' *s* Schulausschuß *m*

school'boy' *s* Schüler *m*

school'girl' *s* Schülerin *f*

school'ing *s* (*formal education*) Schulbildung *f*; (*training*) Schulung *f*

school'mate' *s* Mitschüler –in *mf*

schooner ['skunər] *s* Schoner *m*

sciatica [saɪ'ætɪkə] *s* Hüftschmerz *m*

science ['saɪ·əns] *s* Wissenschaft *f*; **the sciences** die Naturwissenschaften *pl*

sci'ence fic'tion *s* Science-fiction *f*

scientific [,saɪ·ən'tɪfɪk] *adj* wissenschaftlich

scientist ['saɪ·əntɪst] *s* Wissenschaftler –in *mf*

scimitar ['sɪmɪtər] *s* Türkensäbel *m*

scintillate ['sɪntɪ,let] *intr* funkeln

scion ['saɪ·ən] *s* Sprößling *m*; (bot) Pfropfreis *n*

scissors ['sɪzərz] *s* & *spl* Schere *f*; (*in wrestling*) Zangengriff *m*

scoff [skɔf] *s* Spott *m* || *intr* (at) spotten (über *acc*)

scold [skold] *tr* & *intr* schelten

scold'ing *s* Schelte *f*; **get a s.** Schelte bekommen

sconce [skɑns] *s* Wandleuchter *m*

scoop [skup] *s* (*ladle*) Schöpfkelle *f*; (*for sugar, flour*) Schaufel *f*; (*amount scooped*) Schlag *m*; (journ) Knüller *m* || *tr* schöpfen; **s. out** ausschaufeln; **s. up** scheffeln

scoot [skut] *intr* (coll) flitzen

scooter ['skutər] *s* Roller *m*

scope [skop] *s* (*extent*) Umfang *m*;

(range) Reichweite *f;* **give free s. to the imagination** der Phatasie freien Lauf lassen; **give s.o. free s.** j–m freie Hand geben; **within the s. of** im Rahmen *(genit)* or von
scorch [skɔrtʃ] *tr* versengen
scorched'-earth' pol'icy *s* Politik *f* der verbrannten Erde
scorch'ing *adj* & *adv* sengend
score [skor] *s (of a game)* Punktzahl *f;* *(final score)* Ergebnis *n;* *(notch)* Kerbe *f;* (mus) Partitur *f;* **a s. of** zwanzig; **have an old s. to settle with s.o.** mit j–m e–e alte Rechnung zu begleichen haben; **keep s.** die Punktzahl anschreiben; **know the s.** (coll) auf Draht sein; **on that s.** diesbezüglich; **what's the s.?** wie steht das Spiel? ‖ *tr (points)* erzielen; *(goals)* schießen; *(notch)* einkerben; (mus) in Partitur setzen ‖ *intr* e–n Punkt erzielen
score'board' *s* Anzeigetafel *f*
score'card' *s* Punktzettel *m*
score'keep'er *s* Anschreiber –in *mf*
score'sheet' *s* Spielberichtsbogen *m*
scorn [skɔrn] *s* Verachtung *f;* **laugh to s.** auslachen ‖ *tr* verachten
scornful ['skɔrnfəl] *adj* verächtlich
scorpion ['skɔrpɪ-ən] *s* Skorpion *m*
Scot [skɑt] *s* Schotte *m*, Schottin *f*
Scotch [skɑtʃ] *adj* schottisch; (sl) geizig ‖ *s* schottischer Whisky *m;* *(dialect)* Schottisch *n* ‖ *tr (a rumor)* ausrotten; *(with a chock)* blockieren; *(render harmless)* unschädlich machen
Scotch'man *s* (–men) Schotte *m*
Scotch' pine' *s* gemeine Kiefer *f*
Scotch' tape' *s* (trademark) durchsichtiger Klebstreifen *m*
scot'-free' *adj* ungestraft
Scotland ['skɑtlənd] *s* Schottland *n*
Scottish ['skɑtɪʃ] *adj* schottisch ‖ *s (dialect)* Schottisch *n;* **the S.** die Schotten *pl*
scoundrel ['skaundrəl] *s* Lump *m*
scour [skaʊr] *tr* scheuern; *(the city)* absuchen
scourge [skʌrdʒ] *s* Geißel *f* ‖ *tr* geißeln
scout [skaʊt] *s* Pfadfinder *m;* (mil, sport) Kundschafter *m* ‖ *tr* aufklären ‖ *intr* kundschaften
scout'mas'ter *s* Pfadfinderführer *m*
scowl [skaʊl] *s* finsterer Blick *m* ‖ *intr* finster blicken; **s. at** grollend ansehen
scram [skræm] *v (pret* & *pp* **scrammed;** *ger* **scramming)** *intr* (coll) abhauen
scramble ['skræmbəl] *s* **(for)** Balgerei *f* (um) ‖ *tr (mix up)* durcheinandermischen; *(a message)* unverständlich machen; **s. eggs** Rührei machen ‖ *intr (e.g., over rocks)* klettern; **s. for s.th.** sich um etw reißen; **s. to one's feet** sich aufrappeln
scram'bled eggs' *spl* Rührei *n*
scrap [skræp] *s (of metal)* Schrott *m;* *(of paper)* Fetzen *m;* *(of food)* Rest *m;* *(refuse)* Abfall *m;* *(quarrel)* (coll) Zank *m;* *(fight)* (coll) Rauferei *f* ‖ *v (pret* & *pp* **scrapped;** *ger*

scrapping) *tr* ausrangieren ‖ *intr (quarrel)* (coll) zanken; *(fight)* (coll) raufen
scrap'book' *s* Einklebebuch *n*
scrape [skrep] *s* Kratzer *m;* (coll) Patsche *f* ‖ *tr* schaben; *(the skin)* abscheuern; **s. off** abschaben; **s. together** (or **up)** zusammenkratzen
scrap' heap' *s* Schrotthaufen *m;* *(refuse heap)* Abfallhaufen *m*
scrap' i'ron *s* Schrott *m*, Alteisen *n*
scrapper ['skræpər] *s* Zänker –in *mf*
scrappy ['skræpi] *adj (made of scraps)* zusammengestoppelt; (coll) rauflustig
scratch [skrætʃ] *s* Kratzer *m*, Schramme *f;* **start from s.** wieder ganz von vorne anfangen ‖ *tr* kratzen; (sport) streichen; **s. open** aufkratzen; **s. out** *(a line)* ausstreichen; *(eyes)* aushacken; **s. the surface of** nur streifen ‖ *intr* kratzen; *(scratch oneself)* sich kratzen
scratch' pad' *s* Notizblock *m*
scratch' pa'per *s* Schmierpapier *n*
scrawl [skrɔl] *s* Gekritzel *n* ‖ *tr* & *intr* kritzeln
scrawny ['skrɔni] *adj* spindeldürr
scream [skrim] *s* Aufschrei *m;* **he's a s.!** er ist zum Schreien! ‖ *tr* & *intr* schreien
screech [skritʃ] *s* Kreischen *n* ‖ *intr (said of tires, brakes)* kreischen; *(said of an owl)* schreien
screech' owl' *s* Kauz *m*
screen [skrin] *s* Wandschirm *m;* *(for a window)* Fliegengitter *n;* *(camouflage)* Tarnung *f;* (aer) (of) Abschirmung *f* (durch); (cin) Leinwand *f;* (nav) Geleitschutz *m;* (radar, telv) Leinwand *f* ‖ *tr (sand, gravel, coal; applications)* durchsieben; *(applicants)* überprüfen; *(a porch, windows)* mit Fliegengittern versehen; (mil) verschleiern; **s. off** abschirmen
screen'play' *s* Filmdrama *n;* *(scenario)* Drehbuch *n*
screen' test' *s* Probeaufnahme *f*
screw [skru] *s* Schraube *f;* **he has a s. loose** (coll) bei ihm ist e–e Schraube locker ‖ *tr* schrauben; *(cheat)* (sl) hereinlegen; *(vulg)* vögeln; **s. tight** festschrauben; **s. up** *(courage)* aufbringen; *(bungle)* (coll) verpfuschen
screw'ball' *adj* (coll) verrückt ‖ *s* (coll) Wirrkopf *m*
screw'driv'er *s* Schraubenzieher *m*
screw'-on cap' *s* Schraubendeckel *m*
screwy ['skru-i] *adj* (sl) verrückt
scribble ['skrɪbəl] *s* Gekritzel *n* ‖ *tr* & *intr* kritzeln
scribe [skraɪb] *s* Schreiber *m;* (Bib) Schriftgelehrte *m*
scrimmage ['skrɪmɪdʒ] *s* (fb) Übungsspiel *n*
scrimp [skrɪmp] *tr* knausern mit ‖ *intr* (on) knausern (mit)
scrimpy ['skrɪmpi] *adj* knapp
script [skrɪpt] *s (handwriting)* Handschrift *f;* (cin) Drehbuch *n;* (rad) Textbuch *n;* (typ) Schreibschrift *f*
scriptural ['skrɪptʃərəl] *adj* biblisch; **s. passage** Bibelstelle *f*

Scripture ['skrɪptʃər] s die Heilige Schrift; (*Bible passage*) Bibelzitat n
script'writ'er s (cin) Drehbuchautor m
scrofula ['skrɑfjələ] s Skrofeln pl
scroll [skrol] s Schriftrolle f; (archit) Schnörkel m
scroll'work' s Schnörkelverzierung f
scro·tum ['skrotəm] s (-ta [tə] or -tums) Hodensack m
scrounge [skraʊndʒ] tr stibitzen ‖ intr —s. around for herumstöbern nach
scrub [skrʌb] s Schrubben n; (*shrubs*) Buschwerk n; (sport) Ersatzmann m ‖ v (*pret & pp* scrubbed; ger scrubbing) tr schrubben
scrub'bing brush' s Scheuerbürste f
scrub'wom'an s (-wom'en) Scheuerfrau f
scruff [skrʌf] s—s. of the neck Genick n
scruple ['skrupəl] s Skrupel m
scrupulous ['skrupjələs] adj skrupulös
scrutinize ['skrutɪ,naɪz] tr genau prüfen; (*a person*) mustern
scrutiny ['skrutɪni] s genaue Prüfung f
scud [skʌd] s Wolkenfetzen m
scuff [skʌf] tr (*a shoe, waxed floor*) abschürfen ‖ intr (*shuffle*) schlurfen
scuffle ['skʌfəl] s Rauferei f ‖ intr raufen
scuff' mark' s Schmutzfleck m
scull [skʌl] s (sport) Skull m ‖ intr (sport) skullen
scullery ['skʌləri] s Spülküche f
scul'lery maid' s Spülerin f
sculptor ['skʌlptər] s Bildhauer m
sculptress ['skʌlptrɪs] s Bildhauerin f
sculptural ['skʌlptʃərəl] adj bildhauerisch
sculpture ['skʌlptʃər] s (*art*) Bildhauerei f; (*work of art*) Skulptur f ‖ tr meißeln ‖ intr bildhauern
scum [skʌm] s (& fig) Abschaum m
scummy ['skʌmi] adj schaumig; (fig) niederträchtig
scurrilous ['skʌrɪləs] adj skurril
scur·ry ['skʌri] v (*pret & pp* -ried) intr huschen
scurvy ['skʌrvi] adj gemein ‖ s Skorbut m
scuttle ['skʌtəl] s (naut) Springluke f ‖ tr (*hopes, plans*) vernichten; (naut) selbst versenken
scut'tlebutt' s (coll) Latrinenparole f
scut'tling s Selbstversenkung f
scythe [saɪð] s Sense f
sea [si] s See f, Meer n; at sea auf See; go to sea zur See gehen; heavy seas hoher (or schwerer) Seegang m
sea'board' s Küstenstrich m
sea' breeze' s Seebrise f
sea'coast' s Seeküste f, Meeresküste f
seafarer ['si,ferər] s Seefahrer m
seafaring ['si,ferɪŋ] s Seefahrt f
sea'food' s Fischgerichte pl
sea'go'ing adj seetüchtig
sea' gull' s Seemöwe f, Möwe f
seal [sil] s Siegel n; (zool) Seehund m ‖ tr (*a document*) siegeln; (*a deal, s.o.'s fate*) besiegeln; (*against leakage*) verschließen, abdichten; s. off (mil) abriegeln; s. up abdichten

sea' legs' spl—get one's s. seefest werden
sea'lev'el s Meereshöhe f
seal'ing wax' s Siegellack m
seal'skin' s Seehundsfell n
seam [sim] s (*groove*) Fuge f; (geol) Lager n; (min) Flöz n; (sew) Naht f
sea'man s (-men) Seemann m; (nav) Matrose m
sea' mile' s Seemeile f
seamless ['simlɪs] adj nahtlos
sea' mon'ster s Meeresungeheuer n
seamstress ['simstrɪs] s Näherin f
seamy ['simi] adj verrufen; s. side (fig) Schattenseite f
séance ['se·ɑns] s Séance f
sea'plane' s Seeflugzeug n
sea'port' s Seehafen m
sea'port town' s Hafenstadt f
sea' pow'er s Seemacht f
sear [sɪr] tr versengen
search [sʌrtʃ] s Durchsuchung f; (*for a person*) (for) Fahndung f (nach); in s. of auf der Suche nach ‖ tr durchsuchen ‖ intr suchen; s. for suchen, fahnden nach
search'ing adj gründlich; (*glance*) forschend
search'light' s Scheinwerfer m
search' war'rant s Haussuchungsbefehl m
seascape ['si,skep] s Seegemälde n
sea' shell' s Muschel f
sea'shore' s Strand m
sea'shore resort' s Seebad n
sea'sick' adj seekrank
sea'sick'ness s Seekrankheit f
sea'side' adj Meeres-, See–
season ['sizən] s Jahreszeit f; (*appropriate period*) Saison f; closed s. (hunt) Schonzeit f; dry s. Trockenzeit f; in and out of s. jederzeit; in s. zur rechten Zeit; out of s. (*game*) außerhalb der Saison; (*fruits, vegetables*) nicht auf dem Markt; peak s. Hochsaison f ‖ tr (*food*) würzen; (*wine*) lagern; (*wood*) austrocknen lassen; (*tobacco*) reifen lassen; (*soldiers*) abhärten ‖ intr (e.g., *said of wine*) (ab)lagern
seasonal ['sizənəl] adj jahreszeitlich; (*caused by seasons*) saisonbedingt
sea'sonal work' s Saisonarbeit f
sea'soned adj erfahren; (*troops*) kampfgewohnt, fronterfahren
sea'soning s Würze f
sea'son's greet'ings spl Festgrüße pl
sea'son tick'et s Dauerkarte f
seat [sit] s Sitz m, Platz m; (*of trousers*) Gesäß n; have a s. Platz nehmen; keep one's s. sitzenbleiben ‖ tr (*a person*) e-n Platz anweisen (*dat*); (*said of a room*) Sitzplätze bieten für; be seated sich hinsetzen
seat' belt' s (aer, aut) Sicherheitsgurt m; fasten seat belts! bitte anschnallen!
seat' cov'er s (aut) Auto-Schonbezug m
seat'ing capac'ity s (for) Sitzgelegenheit f (für); have a s. of fassen
seat' of gov'ernment s Regierungssitz m
sea'wall' s Strandmauer f

sea'way' s Seeweg m; (heavy sea) schwerer Seegang m
sea'weed' s Alge f, Seetang m
sea'wor'thy adj seetüchtig
secede [sɪ'sid] intr sich trennen
secession [sɪ'sɛʃən] s Sezession f
seclude [sɪ'klud] tr abschließen
seclud'ed adj abgeschieden; (life) zurückgezogen; (place) abgelegen
seclusion [sɪ'kluʒən] s Zurückgezogenheit f, Abgeschiedenheit f
second ['sɛkənd] adj zweite; **be s. to none** niemandem nachstehen; **in the s. place** zweitens; **s. in command** stellvertretender Kommandeur m || s (unit of time) Sekunde f; (moment) Augenblick m; (in boxing or duelling) Sekundant m; **George the Second** Georg der Zweite; **the s.** (of the month) der zweite || pron zweite || tr unterstützen
secondary ['sɛkən‚dɛri] adj sekundär, Neben– || s (elec) Sekundärwicklung f; (fb) Spieler pl in der zweiten Reihe
sec'ondary school' s Oberschule f
sec'ondary-school teach'er s Oberlehrer –in mf
sec'ondary sourc'es spl Sekundärliteratur f
sec'ondary tar'get s Ausweichziel n
sec'ond best' s Zweitbeste mfn
sec'ond-best' adj zweitbeste; **come off s.** den kürzeren ziehen
sec'ond-class' adj zweitklassig; **s. ticket** Fahrkarte f zweiter Klasse
sec'ond cous'in s Cousin m (or Kusine f) zweiten Grades
sec'ond fid'dle s—**play s.** die zweite Geige spielen
sec'ond hand' s (horol) Sekundenzeiger m
sec'ondhand' adj (car) gebraucht (information) aus zweiter Hand; (books) antiquarisch
sec'ondhand book'store s Antiquariat n
sec'ondhand deal'er s Altwarenhändler –in mf
sec'ond lieuten'ant s Leutnant m
secondly ['sɛkəndli] adv zweitens
sec'ond mate' s (naut) zweiter Offizier m
sec'ond na'ture s zweite Natur f
sec'ond-rate' adj zweitklassig
sec'ond sight' s zweites Gesicht n
sec'ond thought' s—**have second thoughts** Bedenken hegen; **on s.** bei weiterem Nachdenken
sec'ond wind' s—**get one's s.** wieder zu Kräften kommen
secrecy ['sikrəsi] s Heimlichkeit f
secret ['sikrɪt] adj geheim || s Geheimnis n; **in s.** insgeheim; **keep no secrets from** keine Geheimnisse haben vor (dat); **keep s.** geheimhalten; **make no s. of** kein Hehl machen aus
secretary ['sɛkrə‚tɛri] s (man, desk, bird) Sekretär m; (female) Sekretärin f; (in government) Minister m
sec'retary-gen'eral s Generalsekretär m
sec'retary of com'merce s Handelsminister m

sec'retary of defense' s Verteidigungsminister m
sec'retary of la'bor s Arbeitsminister m
sec'retary of state' s Außenminister m
sec'retary of the inter'ior s Innenminister m
sec'retary of the treas'ury s Finanzminister n
se'cret bal'lot s geheime Abstimmung f
secrete [sɪ'krit] tr (hide) verstecken; (physiol) absondern, ausscheiden
secretive ['sikrɪtɪv] adj verschwiegen
se'cret police' s Geheimpolizei f
se'cret serv'ice s Geheimdienst m
sect [sɛkt] s Sekte f
sectarian [sɛk'tɛrɪ‚ən] adj sektiererisch; (school) Konfessions–
section ['sɛkʃən] s (segment, part) Teil m; (of a newspaper, chapter) Abschnitt m; (of a city) Viertel n; (group) Abteilung f; (cross section; thin slice, e.g., of tissue) Schnitt m; (jur) Paragraph m; (mil) Halbzug m; (rr) Strecke f; (surg) Sektion f || tr—**s. off** abteilen
sectional ['sɛkʃənəl] adj (view) Teil–; (pride) Lokal–
sec'tional fur'niture s Anbaumöbel n
sec'tion hand' s Schienenleger m
sector ['sɛktər] s Sektor m
secular ['sɛkjələr] adj weltlich || s Weltpriester m, Weltgeistlicher m
secularism ['sɛkjələ‚rɪzəm] s Weltlichkeit f, Säkularismus m
secure [sɪ'kjʊr] adj sicher || tr (make fast) sichern; (obtain) sich [dat] beschaffen
security [sɪ'kjʊrɪti] s (& jur) Sicherheit f; **securities** Wertpapiere pl
sedan [sɪ'dæn] s Limousine f
sedan' chair' s Sänfte f
sedate [sɪ'det] adj gesetzt
sedation [sɪ'deʃən] s Beruhigung f
sedative ['sɛdətɪv] s Beruhigungsmittel n
sedentary ['sɛdən‚tɛri] adj sitzend
sedge [sɛdʒ] s (bot) Segge f
sediment ['sɛdɪmənt] s Bodensatz m; (geol) Ablagerung f, Sediment n
sedition [sɪ'dɪʃən] s Aufruhr m
seditious [sɪ'dɪʃəs] adj aufrührerisch
seduce [sɪ'd(j)us] tr verführen
seducer [sɪ'd(j)usər] s Verführer –in mf
seduction [sɪ'dʌkʃən] s Verführung f
seductive [sɪ'dʌktɪv] adj verführerisch
sedulous ['sɛdʒələs] adj emsig
see [si] s (eccl) (erz)bischöflicher Stuhl m || v (pret **saw** [sɔ]; pp **seen** [sin]) tr sehen; (comprehend) verstehen; (realize) einsehen; (a doctor) gehen zu; **see red** rasend werden; **see s.o. off** j–n an den Zug (ans Flugzeug) bringen; **see s.o. to the door** j–n zur Tür geleiten; **see s.th. through** etw durchstehen; **that remains to be seen** das wird man erst sehen || intr sehen; **see through** (fig) durchschauen; **see to** sich kümmern um; **see to it that** sich darum kümmern,

daß; **you see** (*parenthetical*) wissen Sie
seed [sid] *s* Samen *m;* (*collective &* fig) Saat *f;* (*in fruit*) Kern *m;* (physiol) Samen *m;* **go to s.** in Samen schießen; **seeds** (fig) Keim *m* ‖ *tr* besäen
seed′bed′ *s* Samenbeet *n*
seed′ed rye′ bread′ *s* Kümmelbrot *n*
seedless [ˈsidlɪs] *adj* kernlos
seedling [ˈsidlɪŋ] *s* Sämling *m*
seedy [ˈsidi] *adj* (*person*) heruntergekommen; (*thing*) schäbig
see′ing *s* Sehen *n* ‖ *conj*—**s. that** in Anbetracht dessen, daß
See′ing Eye′ dog′ *s* Blindenhund *m*
seek [sik] *v* (*pret & pp* **sought** [sɔt]) *tr* suchen; **s. s.o.'s advice** j–s Rat erbitten; **s. to** (*inf*) versuchen zu (*inf*) ‖ *intr*—**s. after** suchen nach
seem [sim] *intr* scheinen ‖ *impers*—**it seems to me** es kommt mir vor
seemingly [ˈsimɪŋli] *adv* anscheinend
seemly [ˈsimli] *adj* schicklich
seep [sip] *intr* sickern
seepage [ˈsipɪdʒ] *s* Durchsickern *n*
seer [sɪr] *s* Seher *m*
seeress [ˈsɪrɪs] *s* Seherin *f*
see′saw′ *s* Schaukelbrett *n*, Wippe *f* ‖ *intr* wippen; (fig) schwanken
seethe [siδ] *intr* sieden; **s. with** (fig) sieden vor (*dat*)
segment [ˈsɛgmənt] *s* Abschnitt *m*
segregate [ˈsɛgrɪˌget] *tr* trennen, absondern
segregation [ˌsɛgrɪˈgeʃən] *s* Absonderung *f;* (*of races*) Rassentrennung *f*
seismograph [ˈsaɪzməˌgræf] *s* Erdbebenmesser *m*, Seismograph *m*
seismology [saɪzˈmɑlədʒi] *s* Erdbebenkunde *f*, Seismologie *f*
seize [siz] *tr* anfassen; (*a criminal*) festnehmen; (*a town, fortress*) einnehmen; (*an opportunity*) ergreifen; (*power*) an sich reißen; (*confiscate*) beschlagnahmen
seizure [ˈsiʒər] *s* Besitzergreifung *f;* (*confiscation*) Beschlagnahme *f;* (pathol) plötzlicher Anfall *m*
seldom [ˈsɛldəm] *adv* selten
select [sɪˈlɛkt] *adj* erlesen ‖ *tr* auslesen, auswählen
select′ed *adj* ausgesucht
selection [sɪˈlɛkʃən] *s* Auswahl *f*
selective [sɪˈlɛktɪv] *adj* Auswahl–; (rad) trennscharf
selec′tive serv′ice *s* allgemeine Wehrpflicht *f*
self [sɛlf] *s* (**selves** [sɛlvz]) Selbst *n*, Ich *n;* **be one's old s. again** wieder der alte sein; **his better s.** sein besseres Ich ‖ *pron*—**payable to s.** auf Selbst ausgestellt
self′-addressed en′velope *s* mit Anschrift versehener Freiumschlag *m*
self′-assur′ance *s* Selbstbewußtsein *n*
self′-cen′tered *adj* ichbezogen
self′-conceit′ed *adj* eingebildet
self′-con′fident *adj* selbstsicher
self′-con′scious *adj* befangen
self′-control′ *s* Selbstbeherrschung *f*
self′-decep′tion *s* Selbsttäuschung *f*

self′-defense′ *s* Selbstverteidigung *f;* **in s.** aus Notwehr
self′-deni′al *s* Selbstverleugnung *f*
self′-destruc′tion *s* Selbstvernichtung *f*
self′-determina′tion *s* Selbstbestimmung *f*
self′-dis′cipline *s* Selbstzucht *f*
self′-ed′ucated per′son *s* Autodidakt –in *mf*
self′-employed′ *adj* selbständig
self′-esteem′ *s* Selbsteinschätzung *f*
self′-ev′ident *adj* selbstverständlich
self′-explan′ator′y *adj* keiner Erklärung bedürftig
self′-gov′ernment *s* Selbstverwaltung *f*
self′-impor′tant *adj* eingebildet
self′-indul′gence *s* Genußsucht *f*
self′-in′terest *s* Eigennutz *m*
selfish [ˈsɛlfɪʃ] *adj* eigennützig
selfishness [ˈsɛlfɪʃnɪs] *s* Eigennutz *m*
selfless [ˈsɛlflɪs] *adj* selbstlos
self′-love′ *s* Selbstliebe *f*
self′-made man′ *s* Selfmademan *m*
self′-por′trait *s* Selbstbildnis *n*
self′-possessed′ *adj* selbstbeherrscht
self′-praise′ *s* Eigenlob *n*
self′-preserva′tion *s* Selbsterhaltung *f*
self′-reli′ant *adj* selbstsicher
self′-respect′ *s* Selbstachtung *f*
self′-right′eous *adj* selbstgerecht
self′-sac′rifice *s* Selbstaufopferung *f*
self′same′ *adj* ebenderselbe
self′-sat′isfied *adj* selbstzufrieden
self′-seek′ing *adj* selbstsüchtig
self′-serv′ice *adj* mit Selbstbedienung ‖ *s* Selbstbedienung *f*
self′-styled′ *adj* von eigenen Gnaden
self′-suffi′cient *adj* selbstgenügsam
self′-support′ing *adj* finanziell unabhängig
self′-taught′ *adj* autodidaktisch
self′-willed′ *adj* eigenwillig
self′-wind′ing *adj* automatisch
sell [sɛl] (*pret & pp* **sold** [sold]) *tr* verkaufen; (*at auction*) versteigern; (*wares*) führen; **be sold on** (coll) begeistert sein von; **s. dirt cheap** verramschen; **s. s.o. on s.th.** (coll) j–n zu etw überreden; **s. out** ausverkaufen; (*betray*) verraten; **s. short** (st. exch.) in blanko verkaufen ‖ *intr* sich verkaufen; **s. for** verkauft werden für; **s. short** fixen
seller [ˈsɛlər] *s* Verkäufer –in *mf;* **good s.** (com) Reißer *m*
Seltzer [ˈsɛltsər] *s* Selterswasser *n*
selvage [ˈsɛlvɪdʒ] *s* (*of fabric*) Salleiste *f;* (*of a lock*) Eckplatte *f*
semantic [sɪˈmæntɪk] *adj* semantisch ‖ **semantics** *s* Wortbedeutungslehre *f*
semaphore [ˈsɛməˌfor] *s* Winkzeichen *n;* (rr) Semaphor *m* ‖ *intr* winken
semblance [ˈsɛmbləns] *s* Anschein *m*
semen [ˈsimən] *s* Samen *m*
semicircle [ˈsɛmɪˌsʌrkəl] *s* Halbkreis *m*
semicolon [ˈsɛmɪˌkolən] *s* Strichpunkt *m*
semiconductor [ˌsɛmɪkənˈdʌktər] *s* Halbleiter *m*
semiconscious [ˌsɛmɪˈkɑnʃəs] *adj* halbbewußt

semifinal [ˌsɛmɪ'faɪnəl] *adj* Halbfinale– ‖ *s* Halbfinale *n*, Vorschlußrunde *f*
seminar ['sɛmɪ ˌnɑr] *s* Seminar *n*
seminarian [ˌsɛmɪ'nɛrɪ·ən] *s* Seminarist *m*
seminary ['sɛmɪ ˌnɛri] *s* Seminar *n*
semiprecious [ˌsɛmɪ'prɛʃəs] *adj* halbedel
Semite ['sɛmaɪt] *s* Semit –in *mf*
Semitic [sɪ'mɪtɪk] *adj* semitisch
semitrailer ['sɛmɪ ˌtrelər] *s* Schleppanhänger *m*
senate ['sɛnɪt] *s* Senat *m*
senator ['sɛnətər] *s* Senator *m*
senatorial [ˌsɛnə'torɪ·əl] *adj* (*of one senator*) senatorisch; (*of the senate*) Senats–
send [sɛnd] *v* (*pret & pp* **sent** [sɛnt]) *tr* schicken, senden; (rad, telv) senden; **s. back** zurückschicken; **s. back word** zurücksagen lassen; **s. down** (box) niederschlagen; **s. forth** (*leaves*) treiben; **s. off** absenden; **s. on** (*forward*) weiterbefördern; **s. word that** benachrichtigen, daß ‖ *intr*—**s. for** (*e.g., free samples*) bestellen; (*e.g., a doctor*) rufen lassen
sender ['sɛndər] *s* Absender –in *mf;* (telg) Geber –in *mf*
send'-off' *s* Abschiedsfeier *f*
senile ['sinaɪl] *adj* senil
senility [sɪ'nɪlɪti] *s* Senilität *f*
senior ['sinjər] *adj* (*in age*) älter; (*in rank*) ranghöher; (*class*) oberste; **Mr. John Smith Senior** Herr John Smith senior ‖ *s* Älteste *mf;* (*student*) Student –in *mf* im letzten Studienjahr
sen'ior cit'izen *s* bejahrter Mitbürger *m*
seniority [sin'jɑrɪti] *s* Dienstalter *n*
sen'ior of'ficer *s* Vorgesetzte *mf*
sen'ior part'ner *s* geschäftsführender Partner *m*
sen'ior year' *s* letztes Studienjahr *n*
sensation [sɛn'seʃən] *s* (*feeling*) Gefühl *n;* (*cause of interest*) Sensation *f*
sensational [sɛn'seʃənəl] *adj* sensationell
sensationalism [sɛn'seʃənə ˌlɪzəm] *s* Sensationsgier *f*
sense [sɛns] *s* (*e.g., of sight; meaning*) Sinn *m;* (*feeling*) Gefühl *n;* (*common sense*) Verstand *m;* **be out of one's senses** von Sinnen sein; **bring s.o. to his senses** j–n zur Vernunft bringen; **in a s.** in gewissem Sinne; **in the broadest s.** im weitesten Sinne; **make s.** Sinn haben; **there's no s. to it** da steckt kein Sinn drin ‖ *tr* spüren, fühlen
senseless ['sɛnslɪs] *adj* sinnlos; (*from a blow*) bewußtlos
sense' of direc'tion *s* Ortssinn *m*
sense' of du'ty *s* Pflichtgefühl *n*
sense' of guilt' *s* Schuldgefühl *n*
sense' of hear'ing *s* Gehör *n*
sense' of hon'or *s* Ehrgefühl *n*
sense' of hu'mor *s* Humor *m*
sense' of jus'tice *s* Gerechtigkeitsgefühl *n*

sense' of responsibil'ity *s* Verantwortungsbewußtsein *n*
sense' of sight' *s* Gesichtssinn *m*
sense' of smell' *s* Geruchssinn *m*
sense' of taste' *s* Geschmackssinn *m*
sense' of touch' *s* Tastsinn *m*
sense' or'gan *s* Sinnesorgan *n*
sensibility [ˌsɛnsɪ'bɪlɪti] *s* Empfindlichkeit *f*
sensible ['sɛnsɪbəl] *adj* vernünftig
sensitive ['sɛnsɪtɪv] *adj* (**to,** *e.g., cold*) empfindlich (gegen); (*touchy*) überempfindlich; **s. post** Vertrauensposten *m;* **very s.** überempfindlich
sensitize ['sɛnsɪ ˌtaɪz] *tr* (phot) lichtempfindlich machen
sensory ['sɛnsəri] *adj* Sinnes–
sen'sory depriva'tion *s* Reizentzug *m*
sensual ['sɛnʃu·əl] *adj* sinnlich
sensuality [ˌsɛnʃu'ælɪti] *s* Sinnlichkeit *f*, Sinnenlust *f*
sensuous ['sɛnʃu·əs] *adj* sinnlich
sentence ['sɛntəns] *s* (gram) Satz *m;* (jur) Urteil *n;* **pronounce s.** das Urteil verkünden ‖ *tr* verurteilen
sentiment ['sɛntɪmənt] *s* Empfindung *f*
sentimental [ˌsɛntɪ'mɛntəl] *adj* sentimental, rührselig
sentinel ['sɛntɪnəl] *s* Posten *m;* **stand s.** Wache stehen
sentry ['sɛntri] *s* Wachposten *m*
sen'try box' *s* Schilderhaus *n*
separable ['sɛpərəbəl] *adj* trennbar
separate ['sɛpərɪt] *adj* getrennt; **under s. cover** separat ‖ ['sɛpə ˌret] *tr* trennen; (*segregate*) absondern; (*scatter*) zerstreuen; (*discharge*) entlassen; **s. into** teilen in (*acc*) ‖ *intr* sich trennen, sich scheiden
sep'arated *adj* (*couple*) getrennt
separation [ˌsɛpə'reʃən] *s* Trennung *f*
September [sɛp'tɛmbər] *s* September *m*
sep'tic tank' ['sɛptɪk] *s* Kläranlage *f*
sepulcher ['sɛpəlkər] *s* Grabmal *n*
sequel ['sikwəl] *s* Fortsetzung *f;* (fig) Nachspiel *n*
sequence ['sikwəns] *s* Reihenfolge *f*
se'quence of tens'es *s* Zeitenfolge *f*
sequester [sɪ'kwɛstər] *tr* (*remove*) entfernen; (*separate*) absondern; (jur) sequestrieren
sequins ['sikwɪnz] *spl* Flitter *m*
ser·aph ['sɛrəf] *s* (**-aphs** & **–aphim** [əfɪm]) Seraph *m*
Serb [sɑrb] *adj* serbisch ‖ *s* Serbe *m*, Serbin *f*
Serbia ['sɑrbɪ·ə] *s* Serbien *n*
serenade [ˌsɛrə'ned] *s* Ständchen *n* ‖ *tr* ein Ständchen bringen (*dat*)
serene [sɪ'rin] *adj* heiter; (*sea*) ruhig
serenity [sɪ'rɛnɪti] *s* Heiterkeit *f*
serf [sɑrf] *s* Leibeigene *mf*
serfdom ['sɑrfdəm] *s* Leibeigenschaft *f*
serge [sɑrdʒ] *s* (tex) Serge *f*
sergeant ['sɑrdʒənt] *s* Feldwebel *m*
ser'geant-at-arms' *s* (**sergeants-at-arms**) Ordnungsbeamter *m*
ser'geant first' class' *s* Oberfeldwebel *m*

ser'geant ma'jor *s* (sergeant majors) Hauptfeldwebel *m*
serial ['sɪrɪ·əl] *s* Fortsetzungsroman *m*, Romanfolge *f*
serialize ['sɪrɪ·ə‚laɪz] *tr* in Fortsetzungen veröffentlichen
se'rial num'ber *s* laufende Nummer *f*; (*of a product*) Fabriknummer *f*
se·ries ['sɪriz] *s* (–ries) Serie *f*, Reihe *f*; **in s.** reihenweise; (elec) hintereinandergeschaltet
serious ['sɪrɪ·əs] *adj* ernst; (*mistake*) schwerwiegend; (*illness*) gefährlich
seriously ['sɪrɪ·əsli] *adv* ernstlich; **s. wounded** schwerverwundet; **take s. ernst** nehmen
seriousness ['sɪrɪ·əsnɪs] *s* Ernst *m*
sermon ['sʌrmən] *s* Predigt *f*
sermonize ['sʌrmə‚naɪz] *intr* e–e Moralpredigt halten
serpent ['sʌrpənt] *s* Schlange *f*
serrated ['sɛretɪd] *adj* sägeartig
se·rum ['sɪrəm] *s* (–rums & –ra [rə]) Serum *n*
servant ['sʌrvənt] *s* Diener –in *mf*; (*domestic*) Hausdiener –in *mf*
serv'ant girl' *s* Dienstmädchen *n*
serve [sʌrv] *s* (tennis) Aufschlag *m* ‖ *tr* (*a master, God*) dienen (*dat*); (*food*) servieren; (*a meal*) anrichten; (*guests*) bedienen; (*time in jail*) verbüßen; (*one's term in the service*) abdienen; (*the purpose*) erfüllen; (tennis) aufschlagen; **s. mass** (eccl) zur Messe dienen; **s. notice on s.o.** j–n vorladen; **s. up** (*food*) auftragen ‖ *intr* (& mil) dienen; (*at table*) servieren; **s. as** dienen als; **s. on a committe** e–m Ausschuß angehören
server ['sʌrvər] *s* (eccl) Ministrant *m*; (tennis) Aufschläger *m*
service ['sʌrvɪs] *s* (*diplomatic, secret, foreign, public, etc.*) Dienst *m*; (*in a restaurant*) Bedienung *f*; (*set of table utensils*) Besteck *n*; (*set of dishes*) Service *n*; (*assistance at a repair shop*) Service *m*; (*maintenance*) Wartung *f*; (*transportation*) Verkehr *m*; (relig) Gottesdienst *m*; (tennis) Aufschlag *m*; **at your s.** zu Ihren Diensten; **be in s.** (mach) in Betrieb sein; **be in the s.** (mil) beim Militär sein; **be of s.** behilflich sein; **do s.o. a s.** j–m e–n Dienst erweisen; **essential services** lebenswichtige Betriebe *pl*; **fit for active s.** kriegverwendungsfähig; **see s.** Kriegsdienst tun; **the services** die Waffengattungen *pl* ‖ *tr* (mach) warten
serviceable ['sʌrvɪsəbəl] *adj* (*usable*) verwendungsfähig; (*helpful*) nützlich; (*durable*) haltbar
serv'ice club' *s* (mil) Soldatenklub *m*
serv'ice en'trance *s* Dienstboteneingang *m*
serv'ice·man' *s* (–men') Monteur *m*; (*at a gas station*) Tankwart *m*; (mil) Soldat *m*
serv'ice rec'ord *s* Wehrpaß *m*
serv'ice sta'tion *s* Tankstelle *f*
serv'ice-station atten'dant *s* Tankwart *m*

serv'ice troops' *spl* Versorgungstruppen *pl*
servile ['sʌrvaɪl] *adj* kriecherisch
serv'ing *s* Portion *f*; (*e.g., of a subpoena*) Zustellung *f*
serv'ing cart' *s* Servierwagen *m*
servitude ['sʌrvɪ‚t(j)ud] *s* Knechtschaft *f*
ses'ame seed' ['sɛsəmi] *s* Sesamsamen *m*
session ['sɛʃən] *s* Sitzung *f*, Tagung *f*; (educ) Semester *n*; **be in session** tagen
set [sɛt] *adj* (*price, time*) festgesetzt; (*rule*) festgelegt; (*speech*) wohlüberlegt; **be all set** fix und fertig sein; **be set in one's ways** festgefahren sein ‖ *s* (*group of things belonging together*) Satz *m*, Garnitur *f*; (*of chess or checkers*) Spiel *n*; (*clique*) Sippschaft *f*; (rad, telv) Apparat *m*; (*tennis*) Satz *m*; (theat) Bühnenbild *n*; **younger set** Nachwuchs *m* ‖ *v* (*pret* & *pp* **set**; *ger* **setting**) *tr* (*put*) setzen; (*stand*) stellen; (*lay*) legen; (*a clock, a trap*) stellen; (*the hair*) legen; (*a record*) aufstellen; (*an example*) geben; (*a time, price*) festsetzen; (*the table*) decken; (*jewels*) (ein)fassen; (*a camera*) einstellen; (surg) einrenken; (typ) setzen; **set ahead** (*a clock*) vorstellen; **set back** (*a clock*) nachstellen; (*a patient*) zurückwerfen; **set down** niedersetzen; **set down in writing** schriftlich niederlegen; **set foot in** (or on) betreten; **set forth** (*explain*) erklären; **set free** freilassen; **set in order** in Ordnung bringen; **set limits to** Schranken setzen (*dat*); **set off** (*a bomb*) sprengen lassen; **set (s.o.) over** (j–n) überordnen (*dat*); **set right** wieder in Ordnung bringen; **set store by** Gewicht beimessen (*dat*); **set straight (on)** aufklären (über *acc*); **set the meeting for two** die Versammlung auf zwei Uhr ansetzen; **set up** (*at the bar*) (coll) zu e–m Gläschen einladen; (mach) montieren; (typ) (ab)setzen; **set up housekeeping** Wirtschaft führen; **set up in business** etablieren ‖ *intr* (*said of cement*) abbinden; (astr) untergehen; **set about** (*ger*) darangehen zu (*inf*); **set in** einsetzen; **set out** (*for*) sich auf den Weg machen (nach); **set out on** (*a trip*) antreten; **set to work** sich an die Arbeit machen
set'back' *s* Rückschlag *m*, Schlappe *f*
set'screw' *s* Stellschraube *f*
settee [sɛ'ti] *s* Polsterbank *f*
setter ['sɛtər] *s* Vorstehhund *m*
set'ting *s* (*of the sun*) Niedergang *m*; (*of a story*) Ort *m* der Handlung; (*of a gem*) Fassung *f*; (theat) Bühnenbild *n*
settle ['sɛtəl] *tr* (*conclude*) erledigen; (*decide*) entscheiden; (*an argument*) schlichten; (*a problem*) erledigen; (*an account*) begleichen; (*one's affairs*) in Ordnung bringen; (*a creditor's claim*) befriedigen; (*a lawsuit*) durch Vergleich beilegen; (*a region*)

besiedeln; (*people*) ansiedeln || *intr* (*in a region*) sich niederlassen; (*said of a building*) sich senken; (*said of a ship*) absacken; (*said of dust*) sich legen; (*said of a liquid*) sich klären; (*said of suspended particles*) sich setzen; (*said of a cold*) (**in**) sich festsetzen (in *dat*); **s. down** (*in a chair*) sich niederlassen; (*calm down*) sich beruhigen; **s. down to** (*e.g., work*) sich machen an (*acc*); **s. for** sich einigen auf (*acc*); **s. on** sich entscheiden für; **s. up** (fin) die Verbindlichkeit vergleichen
settlement ['sɛtəlmənt] *s* (*colony*) Siedlung *f*; (*agreement*) Abkommen *n*; (*of an argument*) Beilegung *f*; (*of accounts*) Abrechnung *f*; (*of a debt*) Begleichung *f*; **reach a s.** e–n Vergleich schließen
settler ['sɛtlər] *s* Ansiedler –in *mf*
set'up' *s* Aufbau *m*, Anlage *f*
seven ['sɛvən] *adj & pron* sieben || *s* Sieben *f*
seventeen ['sɛvən'tin] *adj & pron* siebzehn || *s* Siebzehn *f*
seventeenth ['sɛvən'tinθ] *adj & pron* siebzehnte || *s* (*fraction*) Siebzehntel *n;* **the s.** (*in dates or a series*) der Siebzehnte
seventh ['sɛvənθ] *adj & pron* sieb(en)te || *s* (*fraction*) Sieb(en)tel *n;* **the s.** (*in dates or a series*) der Sieb(en)te
seventieth ['sɛvəntɪ·ɪθ] *adj & pron* siebzigste || *s* (*fraction*) Siebzigstel *n*
seventy ['sɛvənti] *adj & pron* siebzig || *s* Siebzig *f;* **the seventies** die siebziger Jahre
sev'enty-first' *adj & pron* einundsiebzigste
sev'enty-one' *adj* einundsiebzig
sever ['sɛvər] *tr* (ab)trennen; (*relations*) abbrechen
several ['sɛvərəl] *adj & indef pron* mehrere; **s. times** mehrmals
severance ['sɛvərəns] *s* Trennung *f;* (*of relations*) Abbruch *m*
sev'erance pay' *s* (& mil) Abfindungsentschädigung *f*
severe [sɪ'vɪr] *adj* (*judge, winter, cold*) streng; (*blow, sentence, winter*) hart; (*illness, test*) schwer; (*criticism*) scharf
severity [sɪ'vɛrɪti] *s* Strenge *f;* Härte *f;* Schärfe *f*
sew [so] *v* (*pret* **sewed;** *pp* **sewed &** **sewn**) *tr & intr* nähen
sewage ['su·ɪdʒ] *s* Abwässer *pl*
sew'age-dispos'al plant' *s* Kläranlage *f*
sewer ['su·ər] *s* Kanal *m* || ['so·ər] *s* Näher –in *mf*
sewerage ['su·ərɪdʒ] *s* Kanalisation *f*
sew'er pipe' ['su·ər] *s* Abwasserleitung *f*
sew'ing *s* Näharbeit *f*
sew'ing bas'ket *s* Nähkasten *m*
sew'ing kit' *s* Nähzeug *n*
sew'ing machine' *s* Nähmaschine *f*
sex [sɛks] *adj* (*crime, education, harmone*) Sexual– || *s* Geschlecht *n;* (*intercourse*) Sex *m*

sex appeal' *s* Sex-Appeal *m*
sex' pot' *s* (coll) Sexbombe *f*
sextent ['sɛkstənt] *s* Sextant *m*
sexton ['sɛkstən] *s* Küster *m*
sexual ['sɛkʃu·əl] *adj* geschlechtlich, Geschlechts–, sexuell
sex'ual in'tercourse *s* Geschlechtsverkehr *m*
sexuality [sɛkʃu'ælɪti] *s* Sexualität *f*
sexy ['sɛksi] *adj* sexy
shabbily ['ʃæbɪli] *adv* schäbig; (*in treatment*) stiefmütterlich
shabby ['ʃæbi] *adj* schäbig
shack [ʃæk] *s* Bretterbude *f*
shackle ['ʃækəl] *s* (naut) Schäkel *m;* **shackles** Fesseln *pl* || *tr* fesseln
shad [ʃæd] *s* Shad *m*, Alse *f*
shade [ʃed] *s* Schatten *m;* (*for a window*) Rollo *n;* (*of a lamp*) Schirm *m;* (*hue*) Schattierung *f;* **throw into the s.** (fig) in den Schatten stellen || *tr* beschatten; (paint) schattieren
shad'ing *s* Schattierung *f*
shadow ['ʃædo] *s* Schatten *m* || *tr* (*a person*) beschatten
shad'ow box'ing *s* Schattenboxen *n*
shadowy ['ʃædo·i] *adj* (*like a shadow*) schattenhaft; (*indistinct*) verschwommen; (*shady*) schattig
shady ['ʃedi] *adj* schattig; (coll) dunkel; **s. character** Dunkelmann *m;* **s. deal** Lumperei *f;* **s. side** (& fig) Schattenseite *f*
shaft [ʃæft] *s* Schaft *m;* (*of an elevator*) Schacht *m;* (*handle*) Stiel *m;* (*of a wagon*) Deichsel *f;* (*of a column*) Säulenschaft *m;* (*of a transmission*) Welle *f*
shaggy ['ʃægi] *adj* zottig, struppig
shake [ʃek] *s* Schütteln *n;* **he's no great shakes** mit ihm ist nicht viel los || *v* (*pret* **shook** [ʃuk]; *pp* **shaken**) *tr* schütteln; **s. a leg!** (coll) rühr dich ein bißchen; **s. before using** vor Gebrauch schütteln; **s. down** (sl) erpressen; **s. hands** sich [*dat*] die Hand geben; **s. hands with s.o.** j–m die Hand drücken; **s. off** (& fig) abschütteln; **s. one's head** mit dem Kopf schütteln; **s. out** (*a rug*) ausschütteln; **s. up** aufschütteln; (fig) aufrütteln || *intr* (**with**) zittern (vor *dat*), beben (vor *dat*)
shake'down' *s* (sl) Erpressung *f*
shake'down cruise' *s* Probefahrt *f*
shaker ['ʃekər] *s* (*for salt*) Streuer *m;* (*for cocktails*) Shaker *m*
shake'-up' *s* Umgruppierung *f*
shaky ['ʃeki] *adj* (& fig) wacklig
shale [ʃel] *s* Schiefer *m*
shale' oil' *s* Schieferöl *n*
shall [ʃæl] *v* (*pret* **should** [ʃud]) *aux* (*to express future tense*) werden, e.g., **I s.** go ich werde gehen; (*to express obligation*) sollen, e.g., **s. I stay?** soll ich bleiben?
shallow ['ʃælo] *adj* (*river, person*) seicht; (*water, bowl*) flach || **shallows** *spl* Untiefe *f*
sham [ʃæm] *adj* Schein– || *s* Schein *m* || *v* (*pret & pp* **shammed;** *ger* **shamming**) *tr* vortäuschen

sham′ bat′tle s Scheingefecht n
shambles [′ʃæmbəlz] s Trümmerhaufen m
shame [ʃem] s Schande f; (feeling of shame) Scham f; **put s.o. to s.** (outdo s.o.) j-n in den Schatten stellen; **s. on you!** schäm dich!; **what a s.!** wie schade! ‖ tr beschämen
shame′faced′ adj verschämt
shameful [′ʃemfəl] adj schändlich
shameless [′ʃemlɪs] adj unverschämt
shampoo [ʃæm′pu] s Shampoo n ‖ tr shampoonieren
shamrock [′ʃæmrɑk] s Kleeblatt n
Shanghai [ʃæŋ′haɪ] s Schanghai n ‖ **shanghai** [′ʃæŋhaɪ] tr schanghaien
shank [ʃæŋk] s Unterschenkel m; (of an anchor, column, golf club) Schaft m; (cut of meat) Schenkel m
shanty [′ʃænti] s Bude f
shan′tytown′ s Bretterbudensiedlung f
shape [ʃep] s Form f, Gestalt f; **in bad s.** (coll) in schlechter Form; **in good s.** in gutem Zustand; **out of s.** aus der Form; **take s.** sich gestalten ‖ tr formen, gestalten ‖ intr—**s. up** (coll) sich zusammenfassen
shapeless [′ʃeplɪs] adj formlos
shapely [′ʃepli] adj wohlgestaltet
share [ʃɛr] s Anteil m; (st. exch.) Aktie f; **do one's s.** das Seine tun ‖ tr teilen ‖ intr—**s. in** teilhaben an (dat)
share′hold′er s Aktionär –in mf
shark [ʃɑrk] s Hai m, Haifisch m
sharp [ʃɑrp] adj scharf; (pointed) spitzig; (keen) pfiffig ‖ adv pünktlich ‖ s (mus) Kreuz n
sharpen [′ʃɑrpən] tr schärfen; (a pencil) spitzen
sharply [′ʃɑrpli] adv scharf
sharp′shoot′er s Scharfschütze m
shatter [′ʃætər] tr zersplittern; (the nerves) zerrütten; (dreams) zerstören ‖ intr zersplittern
shat′terproof′ adj splittersicher
shave [ʃev] s—**get a s.** sich rasieren lassen ‖ tr rasieren ‖ intr sich rasieren
shav′ing brush′ s Rasierpinsel m
shav′ing cream′ s Rasierkrem m
shav′ing mug′ s Rasiernapf m
shawl [ʃɔl] s Schal m
she [ʃi] s Weibchen n ‖ pers pron sie
sheaf [ʃif] s (sheaves [ʃivz]) Garbe f
shear [ʃɪr] s—**shears** Schere f ‖ v (pret **sheared**; pp **sheared** & **shorn** [ʃorn]) tr scheren; **s. off** abschneiden
sheath [ʃiθ] s Scheide f
sheathe [ʃið] tr in die Scheide stecken
shed [ʃɛd] s Schuppen m ‖ v (pret & pp **shed**; ger **shedding**) tr (leaves) abwerfen; (tears) vergießen; (hair, leaves) verlieren; (peace) verbreiten; **s. light on** (fig) Licht werfen auf (acc)
sheen [ʃin] s Glanz m
sheep [ʃip] s (sheep) Schaf n
sheep′dog′ s Schäferhund m
sheep′fold′ s Schafhürde f, Schafpferch m
sheepish [′ʃipɪʃ] adj (embarrassed) verlegen; (timid) schüchtern

sheep′skin′ s Schaffell n; (coll) Diplom n
sheep′skin coat′ s Schafpelz m
sheer [ʃɪr] adj rein; (tex) durchsichtig; **by s. force** durch bloße Gewalt ‖ intr—**s. off** (naut) abscheren
sheet [ʃit] s (for the bed) Leintuch n; (of paper) Blatt n, Bogen m; (of metal) Blech n; (naut) Segelleine f; **come down in sheets** (fig) in Strömen regnen; **s. of ice** Glatteis n; **s. of flame** Feuermeer n
sheet′ i′ron s Eisenblech n
sheet′ mu′sic s Notenblatt n
she′-goat′ s Ziege f
sheik [ʃik] s Scheich m
shelf [ʃɛlf] s (shelves [ʃɛlvz]) Regal n; **put on the s.** (fig) auf die lange Bank schieben
shell [ʃɛl] s Schale f; (conch) Muschel f; (of a snail) Gehäuse n; (of a tortoise) Panzer m; (explosive) Granate f; (bullet) Patrone f ‖ tr (eggs) schälen; (nuts) aufknacken; (mil) beschießen; **s. out money** (coll) mit dem Geld herausrücken ‖ intr—**s. out** (coll) blechen
shel·lac [ʃə′læk] s Schellack m ‖ v (pret & pp **–lacked**; ger **–lacking**) tr mit Schellack streichen; (sl) verdreschen
shell′fish′ s Schalentier n
shell′ hole′ s Granattrichter m
shell′ shock′ s Bombenneurose f
shelter [′ʃɛltər] s Obdach n; (fig) Schutz m ‖ tr schützen
shelve [ʃɛlv] tr auf ein Regal stellen; (fig) auf die lange Bank schieben
shenanigans [ʃɪ′nænɪgənz] spl Possen pl
shepherd [′ʃɛpərd] s Hirt m; (fig) Seelenhirt m ‖ tr hüten
shep′herd dog′ s Schäferhund m
shepherdess [′ʃɛpərdɪs] s Hirtin f
sherbet [′ʃɑrbət] s Speiseeis n
sheriff [′ʃɛrɪf] s Sheriff m
sherry [′ʃɛri] s Sherry m
shield [ʃild] s Schild m; (fig) Schutz m; (rad) Röhrenabschirmung f ‖ tr (from) schützen (vor dat); (elec, mach) abschirmen
shift [ʃɪft] adj (worker, work) Schicht– ‖ s Schicht f; (change) Verschiebung f; (loose-fitting dress) Kittelkleid n ‖ tr (a meeting) verschieben; (the blame) (on) (ab)schieben (auf acc); **s. gears** umschalten ‖ intr (said of the wind) umspringen; **s. for oneself** sich allein durchschlagen; **s. into second gear** in den zweiten Gang umschalten
shift′ key′ s Umschalttaste f
shiftless [′ʃɪftlɪs] adj träge
shifty [′ʃɪfti] adj schlau, gerissen
shimmer [′ʃɪmər] s Schimmer m ‖ intr schimmern, flimmern
shin [ʃɪn] s Schienbein n
shin′bone′ s Schienbein n
shine [ʃaɪn] s Schein m, Glanz m ‖ v (pret & pp **shined**) tr polieren; (shoes) wichsen ‖ v (pret & pp **shone** [ʃon]) intr scheinen; (said of the

eyes) leuchten; (*be outstanding*) (**in**) glänzen (in *dat*)
shiner ['ʃaɪnər] *s* (sl) blaues Auge *n*
shingle ['ʃɪŋgəl] *s* (*for a roof*) Schindel *f*; (e.g., *of a doctor*) Aushängeschild *n* ‖ *tr* mit Schindeln decken
shin'ing *adj* (*eyes*) leuchtend, strahlend; (*example*) glänzend
shiny ['ʃaɪni] *adj* blank, glänzend
ship [ʃɪp] *s* Schiff *n* ‖ *v* (*pret & pp* **shipped;** *ger* **shipping**) *tr* senden; **s. water** e–e Sturzsee bekommen ‖ *intr*—**s. out** absegeln
ship'board' *s* Bord *m;* **on s.** an Bord
ship'build'er *s* Schiffbauer *m*
ship'build'ing *s* Schiffbau *m*
shipment ['ʃɪpmənt] *s* Lieferung *f*
ship'ping *s* Absendung *f*, Verladung *f*; (*ships*) Schiffe *pl*
ship'ping clerk' *s* Expedient –in *mf*
ship'ping depart'ment *s* Versandabteilung *f*
ship'shape' *adj* ordentlich
ship'wreck' *s* Schiffbruch *m* ‖ *tr* scheitern lassen; **be s.** schiffbrüchig sein ‖ *intr* Schiffbruch erleiden
ship'yard' *s* Werft *f*
shirk [ʃɪrk] *tr* sich drücken vor (*dat*) ‖ *intr* (**from**) sich drücken (vor *dat*)
shirt [ʃʌrt] *s* Hemd *n;* **keep your s. on!** (sl) regen Sie sich nicht auf!
shirt' col'lar *s* Hemdkragen *m*
shirt'sleeve' *s* Hemdsärmel *m*
shirttail' *s* Hemdschoß *m*
shit [ʃɪt] *s* (vulg) Scheiße *f* ‖ *v* (*pret & pp* **shit**) *tr & intr* (vulg) scheißen
shiver ['ʃɪvər] *s* Schauder *m* ‖ *intr* (**at**) schaudern (vor *dat*); (**with**) zittern (vor *dat*)
shoal [ʃol] *s* Untiefe *f*
shock [ʃak] *s* Schock *m;* (*of hair*) Schopf *m;* (agr) Schober *m;* (elec) Schlag *m* ‖ *tr* schockieren; (elec) e–n Schlag versetzen (*dat*)
shock' absorb'er [æb‚sɔrbər] *s* Stoßdämpfer *m*
shock'ing *adj* schockierend
shock' troops' *spl* Stoßtruppen *pl*
shock' wave' *s* Stoßwelle *f*
shoddy ['ʃadi] *adj* schäbig
shoe [ʃu] *s* Schuh *m* ‖ *v* (*pret & pp* **shod** [ʃad]) *tr* beschlagen
shoe'horn' *s* Schuhlöffel *m*
shoe'lace' *s* Schuhband *n,* Schnürsenkel *m*
shoe'mak'er *s* Schuster *m*
shoe' pol'ish *s* Schuhwichse *f*
shoe'shine' *s* Schuhputzen *n*
shoe' store' *s* Schuhladen *m*
shoe' string' *s* Schuhband *m;* **on a s.** mit ein paar Groschen
shoe'tree' *s* Schuhspanner *m*
shoo [ʃu] *tr* (**away**) wegscheuchen ‖ *interj* sch!
shook-up ['ʃuk'ʌp] *adj* (coll) verdattert
shoot [ʃut] *s* Schößling *m* ‖ *v* (*pret & pp* **shot** [ʃat]) *tr* (an)schießen, (ab)schießen; (*kill*) erschießen; (*dice*) werfen; (cin) drehen; (phot) aufnehmen; **s. down** (aer) abschießen; **s. the breeze** zwanglos plaudern; **s. up** (e.g., *a town*) zusammenschie-

ßen ‖ *intr* schießen; **s. at** schießen auf (*acc*); **s. by** vorbeisausen an (*dat*); **s. up** (*in growth*) aufschießen; (*said of flames*) emporschlagen; (*said of prices*) emporschnellen
shoot'ing *s* Schießerei *f;* (*execution*) Erschießung *f;* (*of a film*) Drehen *n*
shoot'ing gal'lery *s* Schießbude *f*
shoot'ing match' *s* Preisschießen *n*
shoot'ing star' *s* Sternschnuppe *f*
shoot'ing war' *s* heißer Krieg *m*
shop [ʃap] *s* Laden *m,* Geschäft *n;* **talk s.** fachsimpeln ‖ *v* (*pret & pp* **shopped;** *ger* **shopping**) *intr* einkaufen; **go shopping** einkaufen gehen; **s. around for** sich in einigen Läden umsehen nach
shop'girl' *s* Ladenmädchen *n*
shop'keep'er *s* Ladeninhaber –in *mf*
shoplifter ['ʃap‚lɪftər] *s* Ladendieb –in *mf*
shop'lift'ing *s* Ladendiebstahl *m*
shopper ['ʃapər] *s* Einkäufer –in *mf*
shop'ping *s* Einkaufen *n;* (*purchases*) Einkäufe *pl*
shop'ping bag' *s* Einkaufstasche *f*
shop'ping cen'ter *s* Einkaufcenter *n*
shop'ping dis'trict *s* Geschäftsviertel *n*
shop'ping spree' *s* Einkaufsorgie *f*
shop'talk' *s* Fachsimpelei *f*
shop'win'dow *s* Schaufenster *n*
shop'worn' *adj* (fig) abgerissen
shore [ʃor] *s* Küste *f;* (*beach*) Strand *m;* (*of a river*) Ufer *n;* **go to the s.** ans Meer fahren ‖ *tr*—**s. up** abstützen
shore' leave' *s* Landurlaub *m*
shore'line' *s* Küstenlinie *f;* (*of a river*) Uferlinie *f*
shore' patrol' *s* Küstenstreife *f*
short [ʃɔrt] *adj* kurz; (*person*) klein; (*loan*) kurzfristig; **a s. time ago** vor kurzem; **be s. of,** e.g., **I am s. of bread** das Brot geht mir aus; **be s. with s.o.** j–n kurz abfertigen; **cut s.** abbrechen; **fall s. of** zurückbleiben hinter (*dat*); **get the s. end** das Nachsehen haben; **I am three marks s.** es fehlen mir drei Mark; **in s.** kurzum; **s. of breath** außer Atem; **s. of cash** knapp bei Kasse ‖ *s* (cin) Kurzfilm *m;* (elec) Kurzschluß *m* ‖ *tr* (elec) kurzschließen
shortage ['ʃɔrtɪdʒ] *s* (**of**) Mangel *m* (an *dat*); (com) Minderbetrag *m*
short'cake' *s* Mürbekuchen *m*
short'-change' *tr* zu wenig Wechselgeld herausgeben (*dat*); (fig) betrügen
short' cir'cuit *s* Kurzschluß *m*
short'-cir'cuit *tr* kurzschließen
short'com'ing *s* Fehler *m,* Mangel *m*
short'cut' *s* Abkürzung *f;* **take a s.** den Weg abkürzen
shorten ['ʃɔrtən] *tr* abkürzen
short'ening *s* Abkürzung *f;* (culin) Backfett *m*
short'hand' *adj* stenographisch ‖ *s* Stenographie *f;* **in s.** stenographisch; **take down in s.** stenographieren
short-lived ['ʃɔrt'laɪvd] *adj* kurzlebig
shortly ['ʃɔrtli] *adv* in kurzem; **s. after** kurz nach

short'-or'der cook' s Schnellimbißkoch
m, Schnellimbißköchin f
short'-range' adj Nah-, auf kurze Sicht
shorts [ʃɔrts] s (underwear) Unterhose
f; (walking shorts) kurze Hose f;
(sport) Sporthose f
short'-sight'ed adj kurzsichtig
short' sto'ry s Novelle f
short'-tem'pered adj leicht aufbrausend
short'-term' adj kurzfristig
short'wave' adj Kurzwellen– || s Kurz-
welle f
short'wind'ed adj kurzatmig
shot [ʃɑt] (sl) kaputt; (drunk) (sl)
besoffen; **my nerves are s.** ich bin
mit meinen Nerven ganz herunter ||
s Schuß m; (shooter) Schütze m;
(pellets) Schrot m; (injection) Spritze
f; (snapshot) Aufnahme f; (of liquor)
Gläschen n; **be a good s.** gut schießen; **s. in the arm** (fig) Belebungs-
spritze f; **s. in the dark** Sprung m
ins Ungewisse; **take a s. at** e–n Schuß
abgeben auf (acc); (fig) versuchen;
wild s. Schuß m ins Blaue
shot'gun' s Schrotflinte f
shot'gun wed'ding s Mußehe f
shot'-put' s (sport) Kugelstoßen n
should [ʃud] aux (to express softened
affirmation) **I s. like to know** ich
möchte wissen; **I s. think so** das will
ich meinen; (to express obligation)
how s. I know? wie sollte ich das
wissen?; **you shouldn't do that** Sie
sollten das nicht tun; (in conditional
clauses) **if it s. rain tomorrow** wenn
es morgen regnen sollte
shoulder [ʃoldər] s Schulter f, Achsel
f; (of a road) Bankett n; **have broad
shoulders** e–n breiten Rücken haben
|| tr (a rifle) schultern; (responsibil-
ity) auf sich nehmen
shoul'der bag' s Umhängetasche f
shoul'der blade' s Schulterblatt n
shoul'der strap' s (of underwear) Trä-
gerband n; (mil) Schulterriemen m
shout [ʃaut] s Schrei m, Ruf m || tr
schreien, rufen; **s. down** (coll) nieder-
schreien || intr schreien, rufen
shove [ʃʌv] s Stoß m; **give s.o. a s.**
j–m e–n Stoß versetzen || tr stoßen;
(e.g., furniture) rücken; **s. around**
(coll) herumschubsen; **s. forward**
vorschieben || intr drängeln; **s. off**
(coll) abschieben; (naut) vom Land
abstoßen
shov·el [ʃʌvəl] s Schaufel f || v (pret
& pp -el[l]ed; ger -el[l]ing) tr schaufeln
show [ʃo] s (exhibition) Ausstellung f;
(outer appearance) Schau f; (spectacle) Theater n; (cin, theat) Vorstellung f; **by s. of hands** durch
Handzeichen; **make a s. of s.th.** mit
etw Staat machen; **only for s.** nur zur
Schau || v (pret showed; pp shown
[ʃon] & showed) tr zeigen; (prove)
beweisen, nachweisen; (said of evidence, tests) ergeben; (tickets, passport, papers) vorweisen; **s. around**
(a person) herumführen; (a thing)
herumzeigen || intr zu sehen sein;

(said of a slip) vorgucken; **s. off**
(with) großtun (mit); **s. up** erscheinen
show' busi'ness s Unterhaltungsindu-
strie f
show'case' s Schaukasten m, Vitrine f
show'down' s entscheidender Wendepunkt m; (e.g., in a western) Kraft-
probe f; (cards) Aufdecken n der
Karten
shower [ʃau·ər] s (rain) Schauer m;
(bath) Dusche f; (shower room)
Duschraum m; (of stones, arrows)
Hagel m; (of bullets, sparks) Regen
m; (for a bride) Party f zur Über-
reichung der Brautgeschenke; **take a
s.** (sich) duschen || intr (with gifts)
überschütten || intr duschen; (me-
teor) schauern
show'er bath' s Dusche f, Brausebad n
show' girl' s Revuegirl n
show'ing s Zeigen n; (cin) Vorführung
f
show'ing off' s Großtuerei f
show'man s (-men) s Schauspieler m
show'-off' s Protz m
show'piece' s Schaustück n
show'room' s Ausstellungsraum m
show' win'dow s Schaufenster n
showy [ʃo·i] adj prunkhaft
shrapnel [ʃræpnəl] s Schrapnell n
shred [ʃred] s Fetzen m; (least bit)
Spur f; **tear to shreds** in Fetzen reißen; (an argument) gründlich wider-
legen || v (pret & pp **shredded &
shred;** ger **shredding**) tr zerfetzen;
(paper) in Streifen schneiden; (culin)
schnitzeln
shredder [ʃredər] s (of paper) Reiß-
wolf m; (culin) Schnitzelmaschine f
shrew [ʃru] s böse Sieben f
shrewd [ʃrud] adj schlau
shriek [ʃrik] s Gekreische n, gellender
Schrei m || intr kreischen
shrill [ʃrɪl] adj schrill
shrimp [ʃrɪmp] s Garnele f; (coll)
Knirps m
shrine [ʃraɪn] s Heiligtum n
shrink [ʃrɪŋk] s (pret **shrank** [ʃræŋk]
& **shrunk** [ʃrʌŋk]; pp **shrunk &
shrunken**) tr einlaufen lassen || intr
schrumpfen; **s. back from** zurückschrecken vor (dat); **s. from** sich
scheuen vor (dat); **s. up** einschrumpfen
shrinkage [ʃrɪŋkɪdʒ] s Schrumpfung f
shriv·el [ʃrɪvəl] s (pret & pp -el[l]ed;
ger -el[l]ing) intr schrumpfen; **s. up**
zusammenschrumpfen
shriv'eled adj schrumpelig
shroud [ʃraud] s Leichentuch n; (fig)
Hülle f; (naut) Want f || tr (in) ein-
hüllen (in acc)
shrub [ʃrʌb] s Strauch m
shrubbery [ʃrʌbəri] s Strauchwerk n
shrug [ʃrʌg] s Zucken n || v (pret &
pp **shrugged;** ger **shrugging**) tr zuk-
ken; **s. off** mit e–m Achselzucken
abtun; **s. one's shoulders** mit den
Achseln zucken || intr mit den Ach-
seln zucken
shuck [ʃʌk] tr enthülsen
shudder [ʃʌdər] s Schau(d)er m ||

intr (at) schau(d)ern (vor *dat*); **s. at the thought of s.th.** bei dem Gedanken an etw [*acc*] zittern
shuffle ['ʃʌfəl] *s* Schlurfen *n;* (cards) Mischen *n;* **get lost in the s.** (fig) unter den Tisch fallen ‖ *tr* (*cards*) mischen; (*the feet*) schleifen; ‖ *intr* die Karten mischen; (*walk*) schlurfen; **s. along** latschen
shun [ʃʌn] *v* (*pret & pp* **shunned; ger shunning**) *tr* (*a person*) meiden; (*a thing*) (ver)meiden
shunt [ʃʌnt] *s* (elec) Nebenschluß *m* ‖ *tr* (*shove aside*) beiseite schieben; (*across*) parallelschalten (zu); (rr) rangieren
shut [ʃʌt] *adj* zu ‖ (*pret & pp* **shut; ger shutting**) *tr* schließen, zumachen; **be s. down** stilliegen; **s. down** stillegen; **s. off** absperren; **s. one's eyes to** hinwegsehen über (*acc*); **s. out** ausperren; **s. s.o. up** j–m den Mund stopfen ‖ *intr* sich schließen; **s. up!** (coll) halt's Maul!
shut'down' *s* Stillegung *f*
shutter ['ʃʌtər] *s* Laden *m;* (phot) Verschluß *m*
shuttle ['ʃʌtəl] *s* Schiffchen *n* ‖ *intr* pendeln, hin– und herfahren
shut'tle bus' *s* Pendelbus *m*
shut'tlecock' *s* Federball *m*
shut'tle serv'ice *s* Pendelverkehr *m*
shut'tle train' *s* Pendelzug *m*
shy [ʃaɪ] *adj* (**shyer; shyest**) schüchtern; **be a dollar shy** e–n Dollar los sein ‖ *intr* (*said of a horse*) stutzen; **shy at** zurückscheuen vor (*dat*); **shy away from** sich scheuen vor (*dat*)
shyness ['ʃaɪnɪs] *s* Scheu *f*
shyster ['ʃaɪstər] *s* Winkeladvokat *m*
Siamese' twins' [ˌsaɪ·ə'miz] *spl* Siamesische Zwillinge *pl*
Siberia [saɪ'bɪrɪ·ə] *s* Sibirien *n*
Siberian [saɪ'bɪrɪ·ən] *adj* sibirisch ‖ *s* Sibirier –in *mf*
sibilant ['sɪbɪlənt] *s* Zischlaut *m*
siblings ['sɪblɪŋz] *spl* Geschwister *pl*
sibyl ['sɪbɪl] *s* Sibylle *f*
sic [sɪk] *adv* sic ‖ *v* (*pret & pp* **sicked;** *ger* **sicking**) *tr*—**sic 'em!** (coll) faß!; **sic the dog on s.o.** den Hund auf j–n hetzen
Sicilian [sɪ'sɪljən] *adj* sizilianisch ‖ *s* Sizilianer –in *mf*
Sicily ['sɪsɪli] *s* Sizilien *n*
sick [sɪk] *adj* krank; **be s. and tired of s.th.** etw gründlich satt haben; **be s. as a dog** sich hundeelend fühlen; **I am s. to my stomach** mir ist übel; **play s.** krankfeiern
sick' bay' *s* Schiffslazarett *n*
sick'bed' *s* Krankenbett *n*
sicken ['sɪkən] *tr* krank machen; (*disgust*) anekeln ‖ *intr* krank werden
sick'ening *adj* (fig) ekelhaft
sick' head'ache *s* Kopfschmerzen *pl* mit Übelkeit
sickle ['sɪkəl] *s* Sichel *f*
sick' leave' *s* Krankenurlaub *m*
sickly ['sɪkli] *adj* kränklich; (*smile*) erzwungen

sickness ['sɪknɪs] *s* Krankheit *f*
sick' room' *s* Krankenzimmer *n*
side [saɪd] *adj* Neben–, Seiten– ‖ *s* Seite *f;* (*of a team, government*) Partei *f;* (*edge*) Rand *m;* **at my s.** mir zur Seite; **dark s.** Schattenseite *f;* **off sides** (sport) abseits; **on the father's s.** väterlicherseits; **on the s.** (coll) nebenbei; **this s. up** Vorsicht, nicht stürzen; **to be on the safe s.** um ganz sicher zu gehen ‖ *intr*—**s. with s.o.** j–s Partei ergreifen
side' aisle' *s* Seitengang *m;* (*of a church*) Seitenschiff *n*
side' al'tar *s* Nebenaltar *m*
side'arm' *s* Seitengewehr *n*
side'board' *s* Anrichte *f*, Büffet *n*
side'burns' *spl* Koteletten *pl*
side' dish' *s* Nebengericht *n*
side' door' *s* Seitentür *f*
side' effect' *s* Nebenwirkung *f*
side' en'trance *s* Seiteneingang *m*
side' glance' *s* Seitenblick *m*
side' is'sue *s* Nebenfrage *f*
side' job' *s* Nebenverdienst *m*
side'kick' *s* (coll) Kumpel *m*
side'line' *s* (*occupation*) Nebenbeschäftigung *f;* (fb) Seitenlinie *f* ‖ *tr* (coll) an der aktiven Teilnahme hindern
side' of ba'con *s* Speckseite *f*
side' road' *s* Seitenweg *m*
side'sad'dle *adv*—**ride s.** im Damensattel reiten
side' show' *s* Nebenvorstellung *f;* (fig) Episode *f*
side'split'ting *adj* zwerchfellerschütternd
side'-step' *v* (*pret & pp* **–stepped;** *ger* **–stepping**) *tr* ausweichen (*dat*)
side' street' *s* Seitenstraße *f*
side'stroke' *s* Seitenschwimmen *n*
side'track' *s* Seitengeleise *n* ‖ *tr* (& fig) auf ein Seitengeleise schieben
side' trip' *s* Abstecher *m*
side' view' *s* Seitenansicht *f*
side'walk' *s* Bürgersteig *m*, Gehsteig *m*
sideward ['saɪdwərd] *adj* nach der Seite gerichtet ‖ *adv* seitwärts
side'ways' *adv* seitlich, seitwärts
sid'ing *s* (*of a house*) Verkleidung *f;* (rr) Nebengeleise *n*
sidle ['saɪdəl] *intr*—**s. up to s.o.** sich heimlich an j–n heranmachen
siege [sidʒ] *s* Belagerung *f;* **lay s. to** belagern
siesta [si'ɛstə] *s* Mittagsruhe *f*
sieve [sɪv] *s* Sieb *n* ‖ *tr* durchsieben
sift [sɪft] *tr* (fig) durch(sieben); (fig) sichten; **s. out** aussieben
sigh [saɪ] *s* Seufzer *m;* **with a s.** seufzend ‖ *intr* seufzen
sight [saɪt] *s* Anblick *m;* (*faculty*) Sehvermögen *n;* (*on a weapon*) Visier *n;* **at first s.** auf den ersten Blick; **at s.** sofort; **be a s.** (coll) unmöglich aussehen; **by s.** vom Sehen; **catch s. of** erblicken; **in s.** in Sicht; **lose s. of** aus den Augen verlieren; **out of s.** außer Sicht; **s. for sore eyes** Augentrost *m;* **sights** Sehenswürdigkeiten *pl;* **s. unseen** unbesehen; **within s.** in Sehweite ‖ *tr* sichten

sight'see'ing s Besichtigung *f;* **go s.** sich [*dat*] die Sehenswürdigkeiten ansehen
sight'seeing tour' s Rundfahrt *f*
sightseer [ˈsaɪtˌsi·ər] s Tourist –in *mf*
sign [saɪn] s (*signboard*) Schild *n;* (*symbol, omen, signal*) Zeichen *n;* (*symptom, indication*) Kennzeichen *n;* (*trace*) Spur *f;* (math, mus) Vorzeichen *n;* **s. of life** Lebenszeichen *n* || *tr* unterschreiben; **s. away** aufgeben; **s. over (to)** überschreiben (auf *acc*) || *intr* unterschreiben; **s. for** zeichnen für; **s. in** sich eintragen; **s. off** (rad) die Sendung beenden; **s. out** sich austragen; **s. up** (mil) sich anwerben lassen; **s. up for** (*e.g., courses, work*) sich anmelden für
sig·nal [ˈsɪgnəl] *adj* auffallend || s (*by gesture*) Zeichen *n,* Wink *m;* (aut, rad, rr, telv) Signal *n* || *v* (*pret & pp* –nal[l]ed; *ger* –nal[l]ing) *tr* signalisieren; (*a person*) ein Zeichen geben (*dat*)
sig'nal corps' s Fernmeldetruppen *pl*
sig'nal·man s (–men) (nav) Signalgast *m;* (rr) Bahnwärter *m*
signatory [ˈsɪgnəˌtori] s Unterzeichner –in *mf*
signature [ˈsɪgnətʃər] s Unterschrift *f*
sign'board' s Aushängeschild *n*
signer [ˈsaɪnər] s Unterzeichner –in *mf*
sig'net ring' [ˈsɪgnɪt] s Siegelring *m*
significance [sɪgˈnɪfɪkəns] s Bedeutung *f*
significant [sɪgˈnɪfɪkənt] *adj* bedeutsam
signi·fy [ˈsɪgnɪˌfaɪ] *v* (*pret & pp* –fied) bedeuten, bezeichnen
sign' lan'guage s Zeichensprache *f*
sign' of the cross' s Kreuzzeichen *n;* **make the s.** sich bekreuzigen
sign'post' s Wegweiser *m*
silence [ˈsaɪləns] s Ruhe *f,* Stille *f;* (*reticence*) Schweigen *n;* **in s.** schweigend || *tr* zum Schweigen bringen; (*a conscience*) beschwichtigen
silent [ˈsaɪlənt] *adj* (*night, partner*) still; (*movies*) stumm; (*person*) schweigend; **be s.** stillschweigen; **keep s.** schweigen
silhouette [ˌsɪluˈet] s Schattenbild *n,* Silhouette *f* || *tr* silhouettieren
silicon [ˈsɪlɪkən] s Silizium *n*
silicone [ˈsɪlɪkon] s Silikon *n*
silk [sɪlk] *adj* seiden || s Seide *f*
silken [ˈsɪlkən] *adj* seiden
silk' hat' s Zylinder *m*
silk' mill' s Seidenfabrik *f*
silk' worm' s Seidenraupe *f*
silky [ˈsɪlki] *adj* seiden, seidenartig
sill [sɪl] s (*of a window*) Sims *m & n;* (*of a door*) Schwelle *f*
silliness [ˈsɪlɪnɪs] s Albernheit *f*
silly [ˈsɪli] *adj* albern, blöd(e)
si·lo [ˈsaɪlo] s (–los) Getreidesilo *m;* (rok) Raketenbunker *m,* Silo *m*
silt [sɪlt] s Schlick *m* || *intr*—**s. up** verschlammen
silver [ˈsɪlvər] *adj* silbern || s Silber *n;* (*for the table*) Silberzeug *n;* (*money*) Silbergeld *n*

sil'verfish' s Silberfischchen *n*
sil'ver foil' s Silberfolie *f*
sil'ver lin'ing s (fig) Silberstreifen *m*
sil'ver plate' s Silbergeschirr *n*
sil'ver-plat'ed *adj* versilbert
sil'versmith' s Silberschmied *m*
sil'ver spoon' s—**be born with a s. in one's mouth** ein Sonntagskind sein
sil'verware' s Silbergeschirr *n*
silvery [ˈsɪlvəri] *adj* silbern
similar [ˈsɪmɪlər] *adj* (**to**) ähnlich (*dat*)
similarity [ˌsɪmɪˈlærɪti] s Ähnlichkeit *f*
simile [ˈsɪmɪli] s Gleichnis *n*
simmer [ˈsɪmər] *tr* leicht kochen lassen || *intr* brodeln; **s. down** (coll) sich abreagieren
simper [ˈsɪmpər] s selbstgefälliges Lächeln *n* || *intr* selbstgefällig lächeln
simple [ˈsɪmpəl] *adj* einfach; (*truth*) rein; (*fact*) bloß
sim'ple-mind'ed *adj* einfältig
simpleton [ˈsɪmpəltən] s Einfaltspinsel *m*
simpli·fy [ˈsɪmplɪˌfaɪ] *v* (*pret & pp* –fied) *tr* vereinfachen
simply [ˈsɪmpli] *adv* einfach
simulate [ˈsɪmjəˌlet] *tr* (*illness*) simulieren; (*e.g., a rocket flight*) am Modell vorführen
sim'ulated *adj* unecht
simultaneous [ˌsaɪməlˈtenɪ·əs] *adj* gleichzeitig, simultan
sin [sɪn] s Sünde *f* || *v* (*pret & pp* sinned; *ger* sinning) *intr* sündigen; **sin against** sich versündigen an (*dat*)
since [sɪns] *adv* seitdem, seither || *prep* seit (*dat*); **s. then** seither; **s. when** seit wann || *conj* (*temporal*) seit(dem); (*causal*) da
sincere [sɪnˈsɪr] *adj* aufrichtig
sincerely [sɪnˈsɪrli] *adv* aufrichtig, ehrlich; **Sincerely yours** Ihr ergebener, Ihre ergebene
sincerity [sɪnˈserɪti] s Aufrichtigkeit *f*
sinecure [ˈsaɪnɪˌkjur] s Sinekure *f*
sinew [ˈsɪnju] s Sehne *f,* Flechse *f;* (fig) Muskelkraft *f*
sinewy [ˈsɪnju·i] *adj* sehnig; (fig) kräftig, nervig
sinful [ˈsɪnfəl] *adj* sündhaft
sing [sɪŋ] *v* (*pret* sang [sæŋ] & sung [sʌŋ]; *pp* sung) *tr & intr* singen
singe [sɪndʒ] *v* (**singeing**) *tr* sengen; (*the hair*) versengen
singer [ˈsɪŋər] s Sänger –in *mf*
single [ˈsɪŋgəl] *adj* einzeln; (*unmarried*) ledig; **not a s. word** kein einziges Wort || *tr*—**s. out** herausgreifen
sin'gle bed' s Einzelbett *n*
sin'glebreast'ed *adj* einreihig
sin'gle file' s Gänsemarsch *m*
sin'gle-hand'ed *adj* einhändig
sin'gle-lane' *adj* einbahnig
sin'gle life' s Ledigenstand *m*
sin'gle-mind'ed *adj* zielstrebig
sin'gle room' s Einzelzimmer *n*
sin'gle-track' *adj* (& fig) eingleisig
sing'song' *adj* eintönig || s Singsang *m*
singular [ˈsɪŋgjələr] *adj* (*outstanding*) ausgezeichnet; (*unique*) einzig; (*odd*) seltsam || s (gram) Einzahl *f*

sinister ['sɪnɪstər] *adj* unheimlich
sink [sɪŋk] *s* (*in the kitchen*) Ausguß *m*; (*in the bathroom*) Waschbecken *n* ‖ *v* (*pret* sank [sæŋk] & sunk [sʌŋk]; *pp* sunk) *tr* (*a ship; a post*) versenken; (*money*) investieren; (*min*) abteufen; **s. a well** e–n Brunnen bohren ‖ *intr* sinken; (*said of a building*) sich senken; **he is sinking fast** seine Kräfte nehmen rapide ab; **s. in** (coll) einleuchten; **s. into** (*an easychair*) sich fallen lassen in (*acc*); (*poverty*) geraten in (*acc*); (*unconsciousness*) fallen in (*acc*)
sink'ing feel'ing *s* Beklommenheit *f*
sink'ing fund' *s* Schuldentilgungsfonds *m*
sinless ['sɪnlɪs] *adj* sünd(en)los
sinner ['sɪnər] *s* Sünder –in *mf*
sinuous ['sɪnju·əs] *adj* gewunden
sinus ['saɪnəs] *s* Stirnhöhle *f*
sip [sɪp] *s* Schluck *m* ‖ *v* (*pret* & *pp* sipped; *ger* sipping) *tr* schlürfen
siphon ['saɪfən] *s* Siphon *m*, Saugheber *m* ‖ *tr* entleeren; **s. off** absaugen; (*profits*) abschöpfen
sir [sɪr] *s* Herr *m*; **yes sir!** jawohl!; **Dear Sir** Sehr geehrter Herr
sire [saɪr] *s* (& zool) Vater *m* ‖ *tr* zeugen
siren ['saɪrən] *s* (& myth) Sirene *f*
sirloin ['sʌrlɔɪn] *s* Lendenbraten *m*
sissy ['sɪsi] *s* Schlappschwanz *m*
sister ['sɪstər] *s* Schwester *f*
sis'ter-in-law' *s* (sisters-in-law) Schwägerin *f*
sisterly ['sɪstərli] *adj* schwesterlich
sit [sɪt] *v* (*pret* & *pp* sat [sæt]; *ger* sitting) *intr* sitzen; **sit down** sich (hin)setzen; **sit for a painter** e–m Maler Modell stehen; **sit in on** (*a meeting*) dabeisein bei; **sit up and beg** Männchen machen
sit'down strike' *s* Sitzstreik *m*
site [saɪt] *s* (*position, location*) Lage *f*; (*piece of ground*) Gelände *n*
sit'ting *s*—**at one s.** auf e–n Sitz
sit'ting duck' *s* wehrloses Ziel *n*
sit'ting room' *s* Gemeinschaftsraum *m*
situated ['sɪtʃu,etɪd] *adj* gelegen; **be s.** liegen
situation [,sɪtʃu'eʃən] *s* Lage *f*; **s. wanted** Stelle gesucht
six [sɪks] *adj* & *pron* sechs ‖ *s* Sechs *f*
sixteen ['sɪks'tin] *adj* & *pron* sechzehn ‖ *s* Sechzehn *f*
sixteenth ['sɪks'tinθ] *adj* & *pron* sechzehnte ‖ *s* (*fraction*) Sechzehntel *n*; **the s.** (*in dates or in series*) der Sechzehnte
sixth [sɪksθ] *adj* & *pron* sechste ‖ *s* (*fraction*) Sechstel *n*; **the s.** (*in dates or in series*) der Sechste
sixtieth ['sɪkstɪ·ɪθ] *adj* & *pron* sechzig ‖ *s* (*fraction*) Sechzigstel *n*
sixty ['sɪksti] *adj* & *pron* sechzig ‖ *s* Sechzig *f*; **the sixties** die sechziger Jahre
six'ty-four dol'lar ques'tion *s* Preisfrage *f*
sizable ['saɪzəbəl] *adj* beträchtlich
size [saɪz] *s* Größe *f*; (*of a book,*

paper) Format *n* ‖ *tr* grundieren; **s. up** einschätzen
sizzle ['sɪzəl] *s* Zischen *n* ‖ *intr* zischen
skate [sket] *s* Schlittschuh *m* ‖ *intr* Schlittschuh laufen
skat'ing rink' *s* Eisbahn *f*
skein [sken] *s* Strähne *f*
skeleton ['skelɪtən] *s* Gerippe *n*
skel'eton crew' *s* Minimalbelegschaft *f*
skel'eton key' *s* Dietrich *m*
skeptic ['skeptɪk] *s* Zweifler –in *mf*
skeptical ['skeptɪkəl] *adj* skeptisch
skepticism ['skeptɪ,sɪzəm] *s* (*doubt*) Skepsis *f*; (philos) Skeptizismus *m*
sketch [sketʃ] *s* Skizze *f*; (theat) Sketch *m* ‖ *tr* & *intr* skizzieren
sketch'book' *s* Skizzenbuch *n*
sketchy ['sketʃi] *adj* skizzenhaft
skewer ['skju·ər] *s* Fleischspieß *m*
ski [ski] *s* Schi *m* ‖ *intr* schilaufen
ski' boot' *s* Schistiefel *m*
skid [skɪd] *s* Rutschen *n*, Schleudern *n*; **go into a s.** ins Schleudern geraten ‖ *v* (*pret* & *pp* skidded; *ger* skidding) *intr* rutschen, schleudern
skid' mark' *s* Bremsspur *f*
skid'proof' *adj* bremssicher
skid' row' [ro] *s* Elendsviertel *n*
skiff [skɪf] *s* Skiff *n*
ski'ing *s* Schilaufen *n*
ski' jack'et *s* Anorak *m*
ski' jump' *s* Schisprung *m*; (*chute*) Sprungschanze *f*
ski' jump'ing *s* Schispringen *n*
ski' lift' *s* Schilift *m*
skill [skɪl] *s* Fertigkeit *f*
skilled *adj* gelernt
skillet ['skɪlɪt] *s* Bratpfanne *f*
skillful ['skɪfəl] *adj* geschickt
skim [skɪm] *v* (*pret* & *pp* skimmed; *ger* skimming) *tr* (*milk*) abrahmen; (*a book*) überfliegen; **s. off** abschöpfen ‖ *intr*—**s. over the water** über das Wasser streichen; **s. through** (*a book*) flüchtig durchblättern
skim' milk' *s* entrahmte Milch *f*
skimp [skɪmp] *intr* (**on**) knausern (mit)
skimpy ['skɪmpi] *adj* (*person*) knauserig; (*thing*) knapp, dürftig
skin [skɪn] *s* Haut *f*; (*fur*) Fell *n*; (*of fruit*) Schale *f*; **by the s. of one's teeth** mit knapper Not; **get under s.o.'s s.** j–m auf die Nerven gehen ‖ *v* (*pret* & *pp* skinned; *ger* skinning) *tr* (*an animal*) enthäuten; (*a knee*) aufschürfen; (*fleece*) das Fell über die Ohren ziehen (*dat*); (*defeat*) schlagen; **s. alive** zur Sau machen
skin'-deep' *adj* oberflächlich
skin' div'er *s* Schwimmtaucher –in *mf*
skin'flint' *s* Geizhals *m*
skin' graft' *s* Hautverpflanzung *f*
skinny ['skɪni] *adj* spindeldürr, mager
skin'tight' *adj* hauteng
skip [skɪp] *s* Sprung *m* ‖ *v* (*pret* & *pp* skipped; *ger* skipping) *tr* (*omit*) auslassen; (*a page*) überblättern; **s. it!** Schwamm drüber!; **s. rope** Seil springen; **s. school** Schule schwänzen ‖ *intr* springen; **s. out** abhauen
ski' pole' *s* Schistock *m*

skipper ['skɪpər] s Kapitän m
skirmish ['skʌrmɪʃ] s Scharmützel n ‖ intr scharmützeln
skir'mish line' s (mil) Schützenlinie f
skirt [skʌrt] s Rock m ‖ tr (border) umsäumen; (pass along) sich entlangziehen (an dat)
ski' run' s Schipiste f
skit [skɪt] s Sket(s)ch m
skittish ['skɪtɪʃ] adj (lively) lebhaft; (horse) scheu
skull [skʌl] s Schädel m
skull' and cross'bones s Totenkopf m
skull'cap' s Käppchen n
skunk [skʌŋk] s Stinktier n; (sl) Saukerl m
sky [skaɪ] s Himmel m; out of the clear blue sky wie aus heiterem Himmel; praise to the skies über den grünen Klee loben
sky'-blue' adj himmelblau
sky'div'er s Fallschirmspringer –in mf
sky'div'ing s Fallschirmspringen n
sky'lark' s Feldlerche f
sky'light' s Dachluke f
sky'line' s Horizontlinie f; (of a city) Stadtsilhouette f
sky'rock'et s Rakete f ‖ intr in die Höhe schießen
sky'scrap'er s Wolkenkratzer m
sky'writ'ing s Himmelsschrift f
slab [slæb] s Platte f, Tafel f
slack [slæk] adj schlaff; (period) flau ‖ s Spielraum m; slacks Herrenhose f, Damenhose f ‖ intr—s. off nachlassen
slacken ['slækən] tr (slow down) verlangsamen; (loosen) lockern ‖ intr nachlassen
slack' per'iod s Flaute f
slack' sea'son s Sauregurkenzeit f
slag [slæg] s Schlacke f
slag' pile' s Schlackenhalde f
slake [slek] tr (thirst, lime) löschen
slalom ['slɑləm] s Slalom m
slam [slæm] s Knall m; (cards) Schlemm m ‖ v (pret & pp slammed; ger slamming) tr zuknallen; s. down hinknallen ‖ intr knallen
slander ['slændər] s Verleumdung f ‖ tr verleumden
slanderous ['slændərəs] adj verleumderisch
slang [slæŋ] s Slang m
slant [slænt] s Schräge f; (view) Einstellung f; (personal point of view) Tendenz f ‖ tr abschrägen; (fig) färben
slap [slæp] s Klaps m; s. in the face Ohrfeige f ‖ v (pret & pp slapped; ger slapping) tr schlagen; (s.o.'s face) ohrfeigen; s. together zusammenhauen
slap'stick' adj Radau– ‖ s Radaukomödie f
slash [slæʃ] s Schnittwunde f ‖ tr aufschlitzen; (prices) drastisch herabsetzen
slat [slæt] s Stab m
slate [slet] s Schiefer m; (to write on) Schiefertafel f; (of candidates) Vorschlagsliste f ‖ tr (a roof) mit Schiefer decken; (schedule) planen; he is slated to speak er soll sprechen
slate' roof' s Schieferdach n
slattern ['slætərn] s (slovenly woman) Schlampe f; (slut) Dirne f
slaughter ['slɔtər] s Schlachten n; (massacre) Metzelei f ‖ tr schlachten; (massacre) niedermetzeln
slaugh'terhouse' s Schlachthaus n
Slav [slɑv], (slæv) adj slawisch ‖ s (person) Slawe m, Slawin f
slave [slev] s Sklave m, Sklavin f ‖ intr (coll) schuften; s. at a job sich mit e–r Arbeit abquälen
slave' driv'er s (fig) Leuteschinder m
slaver ['slævər] s Geifer m
slavery ['slevəri] s Sklaverei f
slave' trade' s Sklavenhandel m
Slavic ['slɑvɪk], ['slævɪk] adj slawisch
slavish ['slevɪʃ] adj sklavisch
slay [sle] v (pret slew [slu]; pp slain [slen]) tr erschlagen
slayer ['sle·ər] s Totschläger –in mf
sled [slɛd] s Schlitten m ‖ v (pret & pp sledded; ger sledding) intr Schlitten fahren
sledge [slɛdʒ] s Schlitten m
sledge' ham'mer s Vorschlaghammer m
sleek [slik] adj (hair) glatt; (cattle) fett ‖ tr glätten
sleep [slip] s Schlaf m; get enough s. sich ausschlafen ‖ v (pret & pp slept [slɛpt]) tr (accommodate) Schlafgelegenheiten bieten für; s. off a hangover seinen Kater ausschlafen ‖ intr schlafen; I didn't s. a wink ich habe kein Auge zugetan; s. like a log wie ein Murmeltier schlafen; s. with (a woman) schlafen mit
sleeper ['slipər] s Schläfer –in mf; (sleeping car) Schlafwagen m; (fig) überraschender Erfolg m
sleepiness ['slipɪnɪs] s Schläfrigkeit f
sleep'ing bag' s Schlafsack m
Sleep'ing Beau'ty s Dornröschen n
sleep'ing car' s Schlafwagen m
sleep'ing compart'ment s Schlafabteil n
sleep'ing pill' s Schlaftablette f
sleep'ing sick'ness s Schlafkrankheit f
sleepless ['sliplɪs] adj schlaflos
sleep'walk'er s Nachtwandler –in mf
sleepy ['slipi] adj schläfrig
sleep'yhead' s Schlafmütze f
sleet [slit] s Schneeregen m; (on the ground) Glatteis n ‖ impers—it is sleeting es gibt Schneeregen, es graupelt
sleeve [sliv] s Ärmel m; (mach) Muffe f; have s.th. up one's s. etw im Schilde führen; roll up one's sleeves die Ärmel hochkrempeln
sleeveless ['slivlɪs] adj ärmellos
sleigh [sle] s Schlitten m
sleigh' bell' s Schlittenschelle f
sleigh' ride' s Schlittenfahrt f; go for a
sleight' of hand' [slaɪt] s Taschenspielertrick m
slender ['slɛndər] adj schlank; (means) gering
sleuth [sluθ] s Detektiv m
slice [slaɪs] s Scheibe f, Schnitte f;

(tennis) Schnittball *m* ‖ *tr* aufschneiden

slicer ['slaɪsər] *s* Schneidemaschine *f*

slick [slɪk] *adj* glatt; (*talker*) raffiniert

slicker ['slɪkər] *s* Regenmantel *m*

slide [slaɪd] *s* (*slip*) Rutsch *m*; (*chute*) Rutschbahn *f*; (*of a microscope*) Objektträger *m*; (phot) Diapositiv *n* ‖ *v* (*pret & pp* **slid** [slɪd]) *tr* schieben ‖ *intr* rutschen; **let things s.** die Dinge laufen lassen

slide' rule' *s* Rechenschieber *m*

slide' valve' *s* Schieberventil *n*

slide' view'er *s* Bildbetrachter *m*

slid'ing door' *s* Schiebetür *f*

slid'ing scale' *s* gleitende Skala *f*

slight [slaɪt] *adj* gering(fügig); (*illness*) leicht; (*petite*) zart ‖ *tr* mißachten

slim [slɪm] *adj* schlank; (*chance*) gering ‖ *intr*—**s. down** abnehmen

slime [slaɪm] *s* Schlamm *m*; (*e.g., of fish, snakes*) Schleim *m*

slimy ['slaɪmi] *adj* schleimig; (*muddy*) schlammig

sling [slɪŋ] *s* (*to hurl stones*) Schleuder *f*; (*for a broken arm*) Schlinge *f* ‖ *v* (*pret & pp* **slung** [slʌŋ]) *tr* schleudern; **s. over the shoulders** umhängen

sling'shot' *s* Schleuder *f*

slink [slɪŋk] *v* (*pret & pp* **slunk** [slʌŋk]) *intr* schleichen; **s. away** wegschleichen

slip [slɪp] *s* (*slide*) Ausrutschen *n*; (*cutting*) Ableger *m*; (*underwear*) Unterrock *m*; (*paper*) Zettel *m*; (*pillowcase*) Kissenbezug *m*; (*error*) Flüchtigkeitsfehler *m*; (*for ships*) Schlipp *m*; **give s.o. the s.** j—m entwischen; **s. of the pen** Schreibfehler *m*; **s. of the tongue** Sprechfehler *m* ‖ *v* (*pret & pp* **slipped**; *ger* **slipping**) *tr*—**s. in** (*a remark*) einfließen lassen; (*poison*) heimlich schütten; **s. on** (*a glove*) überstreifen; (*a coat*) überziehen; (*a ring*) auf den Finger streifen; **s. s.o. money** j—m etw Geld zustecken; **s. s.o.'s mind** j—m entfallen ‖ *intr* rutschen; (*e.g., out of or into a room*) schlüpfen; (*lose one's balance*) ausgleiten; **let s.** sich [*dat*] entgehen lassen; **s. by** verstreichen; **s. in** (*said of errors*) unterlaufen; **s. through one's fingers** durch die Finger gleiten; **s. out on s.o.** j—m entschlüpfen; **s. up** (on) danebenhauen (bei); **you are slipping** (coll) Sie lassen in der Leistung nach

slip'cov'er *s* Schonbezug *m*

slip'knot' *s* Schleife *f*

slipper ['slɪpər] *s* Pantoffel *m*

slippery ['slɪpəri] *adj* glatt

slipshod ['slɪp‚ʃɑd] *adj* schlampig; **do s. work** schludern

slip'stream *s* Luftschraubenstrahl *m*

slip'-up' *s* (coll) Flüchtigkeitsfehler *m*

slit [slɪt] *s* Schlitz *m* ‖ *v* (*pret & pp* **slit**; *ger* **slitting**) *tr* schlitzen; **s. open** aufschlitzen

slit'-eyed' *adj* schlitzäugig

slither ['slɪðər] *intr* gleiten

slit' trench' *s* (mil) Splittergraben *m*

sliver ['slɪvər] *s* Splitter *m*, Span *m*

slob [slɑb] *s* (sl) Schmutzfink *m*

slobber ['slɑbər] *s* Geifer *m* ‖ *intr* geifern

sloe [slo] *s* (bot) Schlehe *f*

sloe'-eyed' *adj* schlitzäugig

slog [slɑg] *v* (*pret & pp* **slogged**; *ger* **slogging**) *intr* stapfen

slogan ['slogən] *s* Schlagwort *n*

sloop [slup] *s* Schaluppe *f*

slop [slɑp] *s* Spülicht *n*; (*bad food*) (sl) Fraß *m* ‖ *v* (*pret & pp* **slopped**; *ger* **slopping**) *tr* (*hogs*) füttern; (*spill*) verschütten

slope [slop] *s* Abhang *m*; (*of a road*) Gefälle *n*; (*of a roof*) Neigung *f* ‖ *tr* abschrägen ‖ *intr* sich neigen; (*said of a road*) abfallen

sloppy ['slɑpi] *adj* schlampig; (*weather*) matschig

slosh [slɑʃ] *intr* schwappen

slot [slɑt] *s* Schlitz *m*

sloth [sloθ] *s* Faulheit *f*, Trägheit *f*; (zool) Faultier *n*

slothful ['sloθfəl] *adj* faul, träge

slot' machine' *s* Spielautomat *m*

slouch [slautʃ] *s* nachlässige Haltung *f*; (*person*) Schlappschwanz *m* ‖ *intr* in schlechter Haltung sitzen; **s. along** latschen

slouch' hat' *s* Schlapphut *m*

slough [slau] *s* Sumpf *m* ‖ [slʌf] *s* (*of a snake*) abgestreifte Haut *f*; (pathol) Schorf *m* ‖ *tr* (& fig) abstreifen ‖ *intr* (*said of a snake*) sich häuten

Slovak ['slovɑk], ['slovæk] *adj* slowakisch ‖ *s* (*person*) Sklowake *m*, Slowakin *f*; (*language*) Slowakisch *n*

slovenly ['slʌvənli] *adj* schlampig

slow [slo] *adj* langsam; (*dawdling*) bummelig; (*mentally*) schwer von Begriff; (com) flau; **be s.** (horol) nachgehen ‖ *adv* langsam ‖ *tr*—**s. down** verlangsamen ‖ *intr*—**s. down** (in *driving*) langsamer fahren; (in *working*) nachlassen; **s. down** (public sign) Schritt fahren

slow'down' *s* Bummelstreik *m*

slow' mo'tion *s* (cin) Zeitlupe *f*; **in s.** (cin) im Zeitlupentempo

slow'-mo'tion *adj* Zeitlupen–

slow'poke' *s* (coll) langsamer Mensch *m*

slow'-wit'ted *adj* schwer von Begriff

slug [slʌg] *s* Rohling *m*; (*drink*) Zug *m* (zool) Wegschnecke *f* ‖ *v* (*pret & pp* **slugged**; *ger* **slugging**) *tr* (coll) hart mit der Faust treffen

sluggard ['slʌgərd] *s* Faulpelz *m*

sluggish ['slʌgɪʃ] *adj* träge

sluice [slus] *s* Schleuse *f*

sluice' gate' *s* Schleusentor *n*

slum [slʌm] *s* Elendsviertel *n*

slumber ['slʌmbər] *s* Schlummer *m* ‖ *intr* schlummern

slum' dwell'ing *s* Elendsquartier *n*

slump [slʌmp] *s* (st. exch.) Baisse *f*; **s. in sales** Absatzstockung *f* ‖ *intr* zusammensacken; (*said of prices*) stürzen

slur [slʌr] *s* (*insult*) Verleumdung *f*; (mus) Bindezeichen *n* ‖ *v* (*pret & pp* **slurred**; *ger* **slurring**) *tr* (*words*)

verschleifen; (mus) binden; **s. over** hinweggehen über (acc)
slurp [slʌrp] s Schlürfen n || tr & intr schlürfen
slush [slʌʃ] s Matsch m, Schneematsch m
slush' fund' s Schmiergeld n
slushy ['slʌʃi] adj matschig
slut [slʌt] s Nutte f
sly [slaɪ] adj (**slyer** & **slier**; **slyest** & **sliest**) schlau || s—**on the sly** im Verborgenen
sly' fox' s Pfiffikus m
smack [smæk] s (blow) Klaps m; (sound) Klatsch m; (kiss) Schmatz m; **s. in the face** Backpfeife f || tr klapsen; **s. one's lips** schmatzen || intr—**s. of** riechen nach
small [smɔl] adj klein; (difference) gering; (comfort) schlecht; (petty) kleinlich
small' arms' spl Handwaffen pl
small' busi'ness s Kleinbetrieb m
small' cap'ital s (typ) Kapitälchen n
small' change' s Kleingeld n
small' fry' s kleine Fische pl
small' intes'tine s Dünndarm m
small'-mind'ed adj engstirnig
small' of the back' s Kreuz n
smallpox ['smɔl ,pɑks] s Pocken pl
small' print' s Kleindruck m
small' talk' s Geplauder n
small'-time' adj klein
small'-town' adj kleinstädtisch
smart [smɑrt] adj (bright) klug; (neat, trim) schick; (car) schneidig; (pej) überklug || s Schmerz m || intr weh tun; (burn) brennen
smart' al'eck s [,ælɪk] s Neunmalkluge mf
smart'-look'ing adj schnittig
smart' set' s elegante Welt f
smash [smæʃ] s (hit) (coll) Bombe f; (tennis) Schmetterschlag m || tr zerschmettern; (e.g., a window) einschlagen; (sport) schmettern; **s. up** zerknallen || intr zerbrechen; **s. into** krachen gegen
smash' hit' s (theat) Bombenerfolg m
smash'-up' s (aut) Zusammenstoß m
smattering ['smætərɪŋ] s (of) oberflächliche Kenntnis f (genit)
smear [smɪr] s Schmiere f; (smudge) Schmutzfleck m; (vilification) Verunglimpfung f; (med) Abstrich m || tr (spread) schmieren; (make dirty) beschmieren; (vilify) verunglimpfen; (trounce) vollständig fertigmachen
smear' campaign' s Verleumdungsfeldzug m
smell [smɛl] s Geruch m; (aroma) Duft m; (sense) Geruchssinn m || v (pret & pp smelled & smelt [smɛlt]) tr riechen; (danger, trouble) wittern || intr (of) riechen (nach)
smell'ing salts' pl Riechsalz n
smelly ['smɛli] adj übelriechend
smelt [smɛlt] s (fish) Stint m || tr schmelzen, verhütten
smile [smaɪl] s Lächeln n || intr lächeln; **s. at** anlächeln; (clandestinely) zulächeln (dat); **s. on** lächeln (dat)

smirk [smɪrk] s Grinsen n || intr grinsen
smite [smaɪt] v (pret **smote** [smot]; pp **smitten** ['smɪtən] & **smit** [smɪt]) tr schlagen; (said of a plague) befallen; **smitten with** hingerissen von
smith [smɪθ] s Schmied m
smithy ['smɪθi] s Schmiede f
smock [smɑk] s Kittel m, Bluse f
smog [smɑg] s Smog m
smoke [smok] s Rauch m; (heavy smoke) Qualm m; **go up in s.** (fig) in Dunst und Rauch aufgehen || tr rauchen; (meat) räuchern || intr rauchen; (said of a chimney) qualmen
smoke' bomb' s Rauchbombe f
smoked' ham' s Räucherschinken m
smoker ['smokər] s Raucher –in mf; (sl) obszöner Film m
smoke' screen' s Rauchvorhang m
smoke'stack' s Schornstein m
smok'ing s Rauchen n; **no s.** (public sign) Rauchen verboten
smok'ing car' s Raucherwagen m
smok'ing jack'et s Hausjacke f
smoky ['smoki] adj rauchig
smolder ['smoldər] intr (& fig) schwelen
smooch [smutʃ] intr sich abknutschen
smooth [smuð] adj (surface; talker; landing, operation) glatt; (wine) mild || tr glätten; **s. away** glätten; **s. out** glätten; **s. over** beschönigen
smooth'-faced' adj glattwangig
smooth-shaven ['smuð'ʃevən] adj glattrasiert
smooth'-talk'ing adj schönrednerisch
smoothy ['smuði] s Schönredner –in mf
smother ['smʌðər] tr ersticken; **s. with kisses** abküssen
smudge [smʌdʒ] s Schmutzfleck m || tr beschmutzen || intr schmutzig werden
smug [smʌg] adj (smugger; smuggest) selbstgefällig
smuggle ['smʌgəl] tr & intr schmuggeln
smuggler ['smʌglər] s Schmuggler –in mf
smug'gling s Schmuggel m
smut [smʌt] s Schmutz m
smutty ['smʌti] adj schmutzig, obszön
snack [snæk] s Imbiß m
snack' bar' s Imbißstube f, Snack Bar f
snaffle ['snæfəl] s Trense f
snag [snæg] s—**hit a s.** auf Schwierigkeiten stoßen || v (pret & pp snagged; ger snagging) tr hängenbleiben mit
snail [snel] s Schnecke f; **at a snail's pace** im Schneckentempo
snake [snek] s Schlange f || intr sich schlängeln
snake'bite' s Schlangenbiß m
snake' in the grass' s heimtückischer Mensch m
snap [snæp] s (sound) Knacks m; (on clothes) Druckknopf m; (of a dog) Biß m; (liveliness) Schwung m; (easy work) Kinderspiel n || v (pret & pp snapped; ger snapping) tr (break) zerreißen, entzweibrechen; (a picture) knipsen; **s. a whip** mit der

Peitsche knallen; **s. back** (*words*) hervorstoßen; (*the head*) zurückwerfen; **s. off** abbrechen; **s. one's fingers** mit den Fingern schnalzen; **s. s.o.'s head off** j-n zusammenstauchen; **s. up** gierig an sich reißen; (*buy up*) aufkaufen ‖ *intr* (*tear*) zerreißen; (*break*) entzweibrechen; **s. at** schnappen nach; (*fig*) anfahren; **s. out of it!** komm zu dir!; **s. shut** zuschnappen; **s. to it!** mach zu!

snap'drag'on *s* (bot) Löwenmaul *n*

snap' fas'tener *s* Druckknopf *m*

snap' judg'ment *s* vorschnelles Urteil *n*

snap'per soup' ['snæpər] *s* Schildkrötensuppe *f*

snappish ['snæpıʃ] *adj* bissig

snappy ['snæpi] *adj* (*caustic*) bissig; (*lively*) energisch; **make it s.!** mach schnell!

snap'shot' *s* Schnappschuß *m*

snare [sner] *s* Schlinge *f* ‖ *tr* mit e-r Schlinge fangen; (fig) fangen

snare' drum' *s* Schnarrtrommel *f*

snarl [snɑrl] *s* (*tangle*) Verwicklung *f*; (*sound*) Knurren *n* ‖ *tr* verwickeln; **s. traffic** e-e Verkehrsstockung verursachen ‖ *intr* knurren

snatch [snætʃ] *s*—**in snatches** ruckweise; **snatches** (*of conversation*) Bruchstücke *pl* ‖ *tr* schnappen; **s. away from** entreißen (*dat*); **s. up** schnappen

snazzy ['snæzi] *adj* (sl) schmissig

sneak [snik] *s* Schleicher –in *mf* ‖ *tr* (*e.g., a drink*) heimlich trinken; **s. in** einschmuggeln ‖ *intr* schleichen; **s. away** sich davonschleichen; **s. in** sich einschleichen; **s. out** sich herausschleichen; **s. up on s.o.** an j-n heranschleichen

sneaker ['snikər] *s* Tennisschuh *m*

sneaky ['sniki] *adj* heimtückisch

sneer [snır] *s* Hohnlächeln *n* ‖ *intr* höhnisch grinsen; **s. at** spötteln über (*acc*)

sneeze [sniz] *s* Niesen *n* ‖ *tr*—**not to be sneezed at** nicht zu verachten ‖ *intr* niesen

snicker ['snıkər] *s* Kichern *n* ‖ *intr* kichern

snide' remark' [snaɪd] *s* Anzüglichkeit *f*

sniff [snıf] *s* Schnüffeln *n* ‖ *tr* (be)riechen; **s. out** ausschnüffeln ‖ *intr* (at) schnüffeln (an *dat*)

sniffle ['snıfəl] *s* Geschnüffel *n*; **sniffles** Schnupfen *m* ‖ *intr* schniefen

snip [snıp] *s* (*cut*) Einschnitt *m*; (*small piece snipped off*) Schnippel *m* ‖ *v* (*pret & pp* **snipped**; *ger* **snipping**) *tr & intr* schnippeln

snipe [snaɪp] *intr*—**s. at** aus dem Hinterhalt schießen auf (*acc*)

sniper ['snaɪpər] *s* Heckenschütze *m*

snippet ['snıpıt] *s* Schnippelchen *n*; (*small person*) Knirps *m*

snippy ['snıpi] *adj* schroff, barsch

snitch [snıtʃ] *tr* (coll) klauen ‖ *intr* (coll) petzen; **s. on** (coll) verpfeifen

sniv·el ['snıvəl] *s* (*whining*) Gewimmer *n*; (*mucus*) Nasenschleim *m* ‖ *v*

(*pret & pp* –el[l]ed; *ger* –el[l]ing) *intr* (*whine*) wimmern; (*cry with sniffling*) schluchzen; (*have a runny nose*) e-e tropfende Nase haben

snob [snɑb] *s* Snob *m*

snob' appeal' *s* Snobappeal *m*

snobbery ['snɑbəri] *s* Snobismus *m*

snobbish ['snɑbıʃ] *adj* snobistisch

snoop [snup] *s* (coll) Schnüffler –in *mf* ‖ *intr* (coll) schnüffeln

snoopy ['snupi] *adj* schnüffelnd

snoot [snut] *s* (sl) Rüssel *m*; **make a s.** e-e Schnute ziehen

snooty ['snuti] *adj* hochnäsig

snooze [snuz] *s* (coll) Nickerchen *n* ‖ *intr* (coll) ein Nickerchen machen

snore [snor] *s* Schnarchen *n* ‖ *intr* schnarchen

snort [snɔrt] *s* Schnauben *n* ‖ *tr* wütend schnauben ‖ *intr* prusten; (*said of a horse*) schnauben; (*with laughter*) vor Lachen prusten

snot [snɑt] *s* (sl) Rotz *m*

snotty ['snɑti] *adj* (sl & fig) rotzig

snout [snaut] *s* Schnauze *f*, Rüssel *m*

snow [sno] *s* Schnee *m* ‖ *tr* (sl) einwickeln; **s. in** einschneien; **s. under** mit Schnee bedecken ‖ *impers*—**it is snowing** es schneit

snow'ball' *s* Schneeball *m* ‖ *intr* (fig) lawinenartig anwachsen

snow'bank' *s* Schneeverwehung *f*

snow'bird' *s* Schneefink *m*

snow' blind'ness *s* Schneeblindheit *f*

snow' blow'er *s* Schneefräse *f*

snow'bound' *adj* eingeschneit

snow'-capped' *adj* schneebedeckt

snow' chain' *s* (aut) Schneekette *f*

snow'-clad' *adj* verschneit

snow'drift' *s* Schneeverwehung *f*

snow'fall' *s* Schneefall *m*

snow'flake' *s* Schneeflocke *f*

snow' flur'ry *s* Schneegestöber *n*

snow' job' *s*—**give s.o. a s.** (sl) j-n hereinlegen

snow'man *s* (–men) Schneemann *m*

snow'mobile' *s* Motorschlitten *m*

snow'plow' *s* Schneepflug *m*

snow'shoe' *s* Schneeteller *m*

snow' shov'el *s* Schneeschaufel *f*

snow'storm' *s* Schneesturm *m*

snow' tire' *s* Winterreifen *m*

Snow' White' *s* Schneewittchen *n*

snow'-white' *adj* schneeweiß

snowy ['sno·i] *adj* schneeig

snub [snʌb] *s* verächtliche Behandlung *f* ‖ *v* (*pret & pp* **snubbed**; *ger* **snubbing**) *tr* (*ignore*) schneiden; (*treat contemptuously*) verächtlich behandeln

snubby ['snʌbi] *adj* (*nose*) etwas abgestumpft; (*person*) abweisend

snub'-nosed' *adj* stupsnasig

snuff [snʌf] *s* Schnupftabak *m*; (*of a candle*) Schnuppe *f*; **up to s.** (sl) auf Draht ‖ *tr*—**s. out** (*a candle*) auslöschen; (*suppress*) unterdrücken

snuff'box' *s* Schnupftabakdose *f*

snug [snʌg] *adj* (**snugger**; **snuggest**) behaglich; (*fit*) eng angeschmiegt; **s. as a bug in a rug** wie die Made im Speck

snuggle ['snʌgəl] *intr—s.* **up (to)** sich schmiegen (an *acc*)

so [so] *adv* (with adjectives or adverbs) so; (*thus*) so; (*for this reason*) daher; (*then*) also; **and so forth** und so weiter; **or so** etwa, e.g., **ten miles or so** etwa zehn Meilen; **so as to** (*inf*) um zu (*inf*); **so far** bisher; **so far as** soviel; **so far, so good** soweit ganz gut; **so I see!** das seh' ich!; **so long!** (coll) bis bald!; **so much** soviel; **so much the better** um so besser; **so that** damit; **so what?** na, und?

soak [sok] *s* Einweichen *n* ‖ *tr* einweichen; (*soak through and through*) durchnässen; (*overcharge*) (sl) schröpfen; **soaked to the skin** bis auf die Haut durchnäßt ‖ *intr* weichen

so'-and-so' *s* (–sos) Soundso *mf*

soap [sop] *s* Seife *f* ‖ *tr* einseifen

soap'box der'by *s* Seifenkistenrennen *n*

soap'box or'ator *s* Straßenredner –in *mf*

soap' bub'ble *s* Seifenblase *f*

soap' dish' *s* Seifenschale *f*

soap' flakes' *spl* Seifenflocken *pl*

soap' op'era *s* (rad) rührselige Hörspielreihe *f*; (telv) rührselige Fernsehspielreihe *f*

soap' pow'der *s* Seifenpulver *n*

soap'stone' *s* Seifenstein *m*

soap'suds' *spl* Seifenlauge *f*

soapy ['sopi] *adj* seifig; (*like soap*) seifenartig

soar [sor] *intr* schweben, (auf)steigen; (*prices*) steigen

sob [sab] *s* Schluchzen *n* ‖ *v* (*pret & pp* **sobbed;** *ger* **sobbing**) *intr* schluchzen

sober ['sobər] *adj* nüchtern ‖ *tr* (**up**) ernüchtern ‖ *intr—s.* **up** wieder nüchtern werden

sobriety [so'braɪ·əti] *s* Nüchternheit *f*

sob' sto'ry *s* Schmachtfetzen *m*

so'-called' *adj* sogenannt

soccer ['sakər] *s* Fußball *m*

soc'cer play'er *s* Fußballer *m*

sociable ['soʃəbəl] *adj* gesellig

social ['soʃəl] *adj* gesellschaftlich ‖ *s* geselliges Beisammensein *n*

so'cial climb'er *s* Streber –in *mf*

socialism ['soʃə‚lɪzəm] *s* Sozialismus *m*

socialist ['soʃəlɪst] *s* Sozialist –in *mf*

socialistic [‚soʃə'lɪstɪk] *adj* sozialistisch

socialite ['soʃə‚laɪt] *s* Prominente *mf*

socialize ['soʃə‚laɪz] *intr* (**with**) verkehren (mit)

so'cialized med'icine *s* staatliche Gesundheitspflege *f*

so'cial reg'ister *s* Register *n* der prominenten Mitglieder der oberen Gesellschaftsklasse

so'cial sci'ence *s* Sozialwissenschaft *f*

so'cial secu'rity *s* Sozialversicherung *f*

so'cial wel'fare *s* Sozialfürsorge *f*

so'cial work'er *s* Sozialfürsorger –in *mf*

society [sə'saɪ·əti] *s* Gesellschaft *f*; (*an organization*) Verein *m*

soci'ety col'umn *s* Gesellschaftsspalte *f*

soci'ety for the preven'tion of cru'elty to an'imals *s* Tierschutzverein *m*

sociological [‚sosɪ·ə'lɑdʒɪkəl] *adj* sozialwissenschaftlich, soziologisch

sociologist [‚sosɪ'alədʒɪst] *s* Soziologe *m*, Soziologin *f*

sociology [‚sosɪ'alədʒi] *s* Soziologie *f*

sock [sak] *s* Socke *f*; (sl) Faustschlag *m* ‖ *tr—s.* **it to him!** gib's ihm!; **s. s.o.** j–m eine 'runterhauen

socket ['sakɪt] *s* (anat) Höhle *f*; (elec) Steckdose *f*; (mach) Muffe *f*

sock'et joint' *s* (anat) Kugelgelenk *n*

sock'et wrench' *s* Steckschlüssel *m*

sod [sad] *s* Rasenstück *n* ‖ *v* (*pret & pp* **sodded;** *ger* **sodding**) *tr* mit Rasen bedecken

soda ['sodə] *s* (*refreshment*) Limonade *f*; (*in mixed drinks*) Selterswasser *n;* (chem) Soda *f & n*

so'da crack'er *s* Keks *m*

so'da wa'ter *s* Sodawasser *n*

sodium ['sodɪ·əm] *s* Natrium *n*

sofa ['sofə] *s* Sofa *n*

soft [saft] *adj* (*not hard or tough*) weich; (*not loud*) leise; (*light, music*) sanft; (*sleep, breeze*) leicht; (*effeminate*) verweichlicht; (*muscles*) schlaff; **be s. on** weich sein gegenüber (*dat*)

soft'-boiled egg' *s* weichgekochtes Ei *n*

soft' coal' *s* Braunkohle *f*

soft' drink' *s* alkoholfreies Getränk *n*

soften ['safən] *tr* aufweichen; (*palliate*) lindern; (*water*) enthärten; **s. up** (mil) zermürben ‖ *intr* (& fig) weich werden

soft'-heart'ed *adj* weichherzig

soft' job' *s* Druckposten *m*

soft' land'ing *s* (rok) weiche Landung *f*

soft' pal'ate *s* Hintergaumen *m*

soft'-ped'al *v* (*pret & pp* **–al[l]ed;** *ger* **–al[l]ing**) *tr* zurückhaltender vorbringen

soft'-soap' *tr* (coll) schmeicheln (*dat*)

soggy ['sagi] *adj* (*soaked*) durchnäßt; (*ground*) sumpfig

soil [sɔɪl] *s* Boden *m* ‖ *tr* beschmutzen ‖ *intr* schmutzen

soil' pipe' *s* Abflußrohr *n*

sojourn ['sodʒʌrn] *s* Aufenthalt *m* ‖ *intr* sich vorübergehend aufhalten

solace ['salɪs] *s* Trost *m* ‖ *tr* trösten

solar ['solər] *adj* Sonnen-

so'lar plex'us ['plɛksəs] *s* (anat) Sonnengeflecht *n*

solder ['sadər] *s* Lötmetall *n* ‖ *tr* löten

sol'dering i'ron *s* Lötkolben *m*

soldier ['soldʒər] *s* Soldat *m*

sole [sol] *adj* einzig, alleinig ‖ *s* (*of a shoe, foot*) Sohle *f*; (*fish*) Scholle *f* ‖ *tr* (be)sohlen

solely ['soli] *adv* einzig und allein

solemn ['saləm] *adj* feierlich; (*expression*) ernst

solemnity [sə'lɛmnɪti] *s* Feierlichkeit *f*

solicit [sə'lɪsɪt] *tr* (*beg for*) dringend bitten um; (*accost*) ansprechen; (*new members, customers*) werben

solicitor [sə'lɪsɪtər] *s* (com) Agent –in *mf*; (jur) Rechtsanwalt *m*

solicitous [sə'lısıtəs] *adj* fürsorglich
solid ['salıd] *adj* (*hard, firm, e.g., ice, ground*) fest; (*sturdy, e.g., person, furniture; firm, e.g., foundation; learning; financially sound*) solid(e); (*compact*) kompakt, massiv; (*durable*) dauerhaft; (*gold*) gediegen; (*meal, blow*) kräftig; (*hour*) ganz, geschlagen; (*of one color*) einfarbig; (*color*) getönt; (*of one mind*) einmütig; (*grounds, argument*) stichhaltig; (*row of houses*) geschlossen; (*clouds, fog*) dicht; (geom) Raum– || *s* (geom, phys) Körper *m*
solidarity [,salı'dærıtı] *s* Solidarität *f*, Verbundenheit *f*
sol'id food' *s* feste Nahrung *f*
sol'id geo'metry *s* Stereometrie *f*
solidi-fy [sə'lıdı,faı] *v* (*pret* & *pp* –fied) *tr* fest werden lassen; (fig) konsolidieren || *intr* fest werden
solidity [sə'lıdıtı] *s* (*state*) Festigkeit *f*; (*soundness*) Solidität *f*
solidly ['salıdli] *adv*—**be s. behind s.o.** sich mit j–m solidarisch erklären
sol'id-state' *adj* Transistor–
soliloquy [sə'lıləkwi] *s* Selbstgespräch *n*
solitaire ['salı,ter] *s* Solitär *m*
solitary ['salı,teri] *adj* allein; (*life*) zurückgezogen; (*exception*) einzig; (*lonely*) einsam
sol'itary confine'ment *s* Einzelhaft *f*
solitude ['salı,t(j)ud] *s* Einsamkeit *f*; (*lonely spot*) abgelegener Ort *m*
so·lo ['solo] *adj* & *adv* solo || *s* (–los) Solo *n*
so'lo flight' *s* Soloflug *m*
soloist ['solo·ıst] *s* Solist –in *mf*
so'lo part' *s* (mus) Solostimme *f*
solstice ['salstıs] *s* Sonnenwende *f*
soluble ['saljəbəl] *adj* (fig) (auf)lösbar; (chem) löslich
solution [sə'luʃən] *s* Lösung *f*
solvable ['salvəbəl] *adj* (auf)lösbar
solve [salv] *tr* (auf)lösen
solvency ['salvənsi] *s* Zahlungsfähigkeit *f*
solvent ['salvənt] *adj* zahlungsfähig; (chem) (auf)lösend || *s* Lösungsmittel *n*
somber ['sambər] *adj* düster, trüb(e)
some [sʌm] *indef adj* (with singular nouns) etwas; (with plural nouns) manche; (sometimes not translated) e.g., **I am buying s. stockings** ich kaufe Strümpfe; (coll) toll, e.g., **s. girl!** tolles Mädchen!; **at s. time or other** irgendeinmal, irgendwann; **s. ... or other** irgendein; **s. other way** sonstwie || *adv* (*with numerals*) etwa, ungefähr || *indef pron* manche; (*part of*) ein Teil *m*; **s. of these people** einige Leute; **s. of us** manche von uns
some'bod'y *indef pron* jemand, irgendwer; **s. else** jemand anderer || *s*—**be a s.** etwas Besonderes sein
some'day' *adv* e–s Tages
some'how' *adv* irgendwie; (*for some reason or other*) aus irgendeinem Grunde

some'one' *indef pron* jemand, irgendwer; **s. else** jemand anderer; **s. else's** fremd, e.g., **s. else's property** fremdes Eigentum
some'place' *adv* irgendwo; (*direction*) irgendwohin
somersault ['sʌmər,sɔlt] *s* Purzelbaum *m*; (gym) Überschlag *m*; **do a s.** e–n Purzelbaum schlagen || *intr* sich überschlagen
some'thing' *indef pron* etwas; **he is s. of an expert** er ist e–e Art Experte; **s. else** etwas anderes; **s. or other** irgend etwas
some'time' *adv* einmal; **s. today** irgendwann heute
some'times' *adv* manchmal; **sometimes ... sometimes ...** mal ... mal ...
some'way', **some'ways'** *adv* irgendwie
some'what' *adv* etwas
some'where' *adv* irgendwo; (*direction*) irgendwohin; **from s. else** sonstwoher; **s. else** sonstwo
somnambulist [sam'næmbjəlıst] *s* Nachtwandler –in *mf*
somnolent ['samnələnt] *adj* schläfrig
son [sʌn] *s* Sohn *m*
sonar ['sonar] *s* Sonar *n*
sonata [sə'natə] *s* Sonate *f*
song [sɔŋ] *s* Lied *n*; (*of birds*) Gesang *m*; **for a s.** (coll) um ein Spottgeld
Song' of Songs' *s* (Bib) Hohelied *n*
sonic ['sanık] *adj* Schall–
son'ic boom' *s* Kopfwellenknall *m*
son'-in-law' *s* (sons-in-law) Schwiegersohn *m*
sonnet ['sanıt] *s* Sonett *n*
sonny ['sʌni] *s* Söhnchen *n*, Kleiner *m*
Son' of Man', **the** *s* (Bib) der Menschensohn
sonorous [sə'norəs] *adj* sonor
soon [sun] *adv* bald; **as s. as** sobald; **as s. as possible** sobald wie möglich; **just as s.** (*expressing preference*) genauso gern(e); **no sooner said than done** gesagt, getan; **sooner** (*expressing time*) früher, eher; (*expressing preference*) lieber, eher; **sooner or later** über kurz oder lang; **the sooner the better** je eher, je besser; **too s.** zu früh
soot [sʊt] *s* Ruß *m*
soothe [suð] *tr* beschwichtigen, beruhigen; **have a soothing effect on** beruhigend wirken auf (*acc*)
soothsayer ['suθ,se·ər] *s* Wahrsager *m*
sooty ['suti] *adj* rußig
sop [sap] *s* eingetunktes Stück *n* Brot; (*something given to pacify*) Beschwichtigungsmittel *n*; (*bribe*) Schmiergeld *n*; (*spineless person*) Waschlappen *m* || *v* (*pret* & *pp* sopped; *ger* sopping) *tr* (*dip*) eintunken; **sop up** aufsaugen
sophist ['safıst] *s* Sophist –in *mf*
sophisticated [sə'fıstı,ketıd] *adj* (*person*) weltklug; (*way of life*) verfeinert; (*highly developed*) hochentwickelt
sophistication [sə,fıstı'keʃən] *s* Weltklugheit *f*
sophistry ['safıstri] *s* Sophisterei *f*

sophomore ['sɑfə‚mor] *s* Student –in *mf* im zweiten Studienjahr

sop'ping *adj* klatschnaß ‖ *adv*—s. **wet** klatschnaß

sopran·o [sə'præno] *adj* Sopran– ‖ *s* (–os) (*uppermost voice*) Sopran *m*; (*soprano part*) Sopranpartie *f*; (*singer*) Sopranist –in *mf*

sorcerer ['sɔrsərər] *s* Zauberer *m*

sorceress ['sɔrsərɪs] *s* Zauberin *f*

sorcery ['sɔrsəri] *s* Zauberei *f*

sordid ['sɔrdɪd] *adj* schmutzig; (*improper*) unlauter

sore [sor] *adj* wund; (*sensitive*) empfindlich; (coll) (at) bös (auf *acc*); be **s.** weh tun; **s.** spot (& fig) wunder Punkt *m* ‖ *s* Wunde *f*

sore'head' *s* (coll) Verbitterte *mf*

sorely ['sorli] *adv* sehr

soreness ['sornɪs] *s* Empfindlichkeit *f*

sore' throat' *s* Halsweh *n*

sorority [sə'rɔrɪti] *s* Studentinnenvereinigung *f*

sorrel ['sɔrəl] *adj* fuchsrot ‖ *s* Fuchs *m*; (bot) Sauerampfer *m*

sorrow ['sɔro] *s* Kummer *m* ‖ *intr* (for or over) Kummer haben (um)

sorrowful ['sɔrəfəl] *adj* betrübt

sorry ['sɔri] *adj* traurig, betrübt; (*appearance*) armselig; **I am s.** es tut mir leid; **I am** (or **feel**) **s. for him** er tut mir leid

sort [sɔrt] *s* Art *f*, Sorte *f*; **all sorts of** alle möglichen; **nothing of the s.** nichts dergleichen; **out of sorts** unpäßlich; **s. of** (coll) (with adjectives) etwas; (with verbs) irgendwie; (with nouns) so 'n, e.g., **I had a s. of feeling that** ich hatte so 'ne Ahnung, daß; **these sorts of** derartige; **what s. of** was für ein ‖ *tr* sortieren; **s. out** aussortieren; (fig) sichten

sortie ['sɔrti] *s* (*from a fortress*) Ausfall *m*; (aer) Einzeleinsatz *m* ‖ *intr* e–n Ausfall machen

so'-so' *adj* & *adv* soso, leidlich

sot [sɑt] *s* Trunkenbold *m*

soul [sol] *s* (*spiritual being; inhabitant*) Seele *f*; **not a s.** (coll) keine Seele *f*; **upon my s.**! meiner Seele!

sound [saund] *adj* Schall-, Ton–; (*healthy*) gesund; (*valid*) einwandfrei; (*basis*) tragfähig; (*sleep*) fest; (*beating*) (coll) tüchtig; (*business*) solid; (*judgment*) treffsicher ‖ *s* Laut *m*, Ton *m*; (*noise*) Geräusch *n*; (*of one's voice*) Klang *m*; (*narrow body of water*) Sund *m*; (phys) Schall *m*; (surg) Sonde *f* ‖ *adv*—be **s. asleep** fest schlafen ‖ *tr* ertönen lassen; (med) sondieren; (naut) loten; **s. s.o. out** (coll) j–m auf den Zahn fühlen; **s. the alarm** Alarm schlagen; **s. the all-clear** entwarnen ‖ *intr* (er)klingen, (er)tönen; (*seem*) klingen; (naut) loten; **it sounds good to me** es kommt mir gut vor; **s. off** (coll) sich laut beschweren

sound' bar'rier *s* Schallgrenze *f*, Schallmauer *f*

sound' effects' *spl* Klangeffekte *pl*

sound' film' *s* Tonfilm *m*

sound'ing *s* Lotung *f*; **take soundings** loten

sound'ing board' *s* (*on an instrument*) Resonanzboden *m*; (*over an orchestra or speaker*) Schallmuschel *f*; (*board for damping sounds*) Schalldämpfungsbrett *n*

soundly ['saundli] *adv* tüchtig

sound'proof' *adj* schalldicht ‖ *tr* schalldicht machen

sound' stu'dio *s* (cin) Tonatelier *n*

sound' techni'cian *s* Tontechniker *m*

sound' track' *s* (cin) Tonstreifen *m*

sound' truck' *s* Lautsprecherwagen *m*

sound' wave' *s* Schallwelle *f*

soup [sup] *s* Suppe *f*; (*thick fog*) (coll) Waschküche *f*; **in the s.** (coll) in der Patsche ‖ *tr*—s. **up** (aut) frisieren

soup' kitch'en *s* Volksküche *f*

soup'meat' *s* Suppenfleisch *n*

soup' plate' *s* Suppenteller *m*

soup'spoon' *s* Suppenlöffel *m*

sour [saur] *adj* (& fig) sauer ‖ *tr* säuern; (fig) verbittern ‖ *intr* säuern; (fig) versauern

source [sors] *s* Quelle *f*

source' lan'guage *s* Ausgangssprache *f*

source' mate'rial *s* Quellenmaterial *n*

sour' cher'ry *s* Weichsel *f*

sour' grapes' *spl* (fig) saure Trauben *pl*

sour' note' *s* (& fig) Mißklang *m*

sour'puss' *s* (sl) Sauertopf *m*

souse [saus] *s* (sl) Säufer –in *mf*

soused *adj* (sl) besoffen

south [sauθ] *adj* Süd-, südlich ‖ *adv* (*direction*) nach Süden; **s. of** südlich von ‖ *s* Süd(en) *m*

South' Amer'ica *s* Südamerika *n*

south'east' *adj* Südost– ‖ *adv* (*direction*) südöstlich; **s. of** südöstlich von ‖ *s* Südost(en) *m*

south'east'ern *adj* südöstlich

southerly ['sʌðərli] *adj* südlich

southern ['sʌðərn] *adj* südlich

southerner ['sʌðərnər] *s* Südländer –in *mf*; (*in the U.S.A.*) Südstaatler –in *mf*

south'paw' *adj* (coll) linkshändig ‖ *s* (coll) Linkshänder –in *mf*

South' Pole' *s* Südpol *m*

South' Seas' *spl* Südsee *f*

southward ['sauθwərd] *adv* südwärts

south'west' *adj* Südwest– ‖ *adv* südwestlich; **s. of** südwestlich von ‖ *s* Südwest(en) *m*

south'west'ern *adj* südwestlich

souvenir [‚suvə'nɪr] *s* Andenken *n*

sovereign ['savrɪn] *adj* souverän ‖ *s* Souverän *m*, Landesfürst *m*

sov'ereign rights' *spl* Hoheitsrechte *pl*

sovereignty ['savrɪnti] *s* Souveränität *f*

soviet ['sovɪ‚ɛt] *adj* sowjetisch ‖ *s* Sowjet *m*; **the Soviets** die Sowjets *pl*

So'viet Rus'sia *s* Sowjetrußland *n*

So'viet Un'ion *s* Sowjetunion *f*

sow [sau] *s* Sau *f* ‖ [so] *v* (*pret* **sowed**; *pp* **sowed** & **sown**) *tr* & *intr* säen

soybean ['sɔɪ‚bin] *s* Sojabohne *f*

spa [spɑ] *s* Bad *n*, Badekurort *m*

space [spes] *s* Raum *m*; (*between ob-*

jects) Zwischenraum *m;* (typ) Spatium *n;* **take up s.** Platz einnehmen ‖ *tr* in Abständen anordnen; (typ) spationieren
space' age' *s* Weltraumzeitalter *n*
space' bar' *s* (typ) Leertaste *f*
space' cap'sule *s* (rok) Raumkapsel *f*
space'craft' *s* Weltraumfahrzeug *n*
space' flight' *s* Raumflug *m*
space'man' *s* (**-men'**) Raumfahrer *m*
space' probe' *s* Sonde *f*
space'ship' *s* Raumschiff *n*
space' shot' *s* Weltraumabschuß *m*
space' shut'tle *s* Raumfähre *f*
space' suit' *s* Raumanzug *m*
space' trav'el *s* Raumfahrt *f*
spacious [ˈspeʃəs] *adj* geräumig
spade [sped] *s* Spaten *m;* (cards) Pik *n;* **call a s. a s.** das Kind beim richtigen Namen nennen
spade'work' *s* (fig) Pionierarbeit *f*
spaghetti [spəˈgeti] *s* Spahetti *pl*
Spain [spen] *s* Spanien *n*
span [spæn] *s* (& fig) Spanne *f;* (*of a bridge*) Joch *n;* **s. of time** Zeitspanne *f* ‖ *v* (*pret & pp* **spanned;** *ger* **spanning**) *tr* (e.g., *the waist*) umspannen; (*a river*) überbrücken; (*said of a bridge*) überspannen
spangle [ˈspæŋgəl] *s* Flitter *m* ‖ *tr* mit Flitter besetzen
Spaniard [ˈspænjərd] *s* Spanier –in *mf*
spaniel [ˈspænjəl] *s* Wachtelhund *m*
Spanish [ˈspænɪʃ] *adj* spanisch ‖ *s* Spanisch *n;* **the S.** die Spanier
Span'ish-Amer'ican *adj* spanischamerikanisch ‖ *s* Amerikaner –in *mf* mit spanischer Muttersprache
Span'ish moss' *s* Moosbärte *pl*
spank [spæŋk] *tr* (ver)hauen
spank'ing *adj* (*quick*) flink; (*breeze*) frisch ‖ *adv*—**s. new** funkelnagelneu ‖ *s* Schläge *pl*
spar [spɑr] *s* (aer) Holm *m;* (mineral) Spat *m;* (naut) Spiere *f* ‖ *v* (*pret & pp* **sparred;** *ger* **sparring**) *intr* sparren
spare [sper] *adj* Ersatz–; (*thin*) mager; (*time*) frei; (*leftover*) übrig ‖ *s* (aut) Ersatzreifen *m* ‖ *tr* (*a person*) schonen; (*time, money*) erübrigen; (*expense*) scheuen; (*do without*) entbehren; **have to s.** übrig haben; **s. s.o. s.th.** j–m etw ersparen
spare' bed' *s* Gastbett *n*
spare' part' *s* Ersatzteil *n*
spare'rib' *s* Rippenspeer *n*
spare' time' *s* Freizeit *f*
spare'-time' *adj* nebenberuflich
spare' tire' *s* Ersatzreifen *m*
spar'ing *adj* sparsam; **be s. with** sparsam umgehen mit
spark [spɑrk] *s* Funke(n) *m* ‖ *tr* (*set off*) auslösen; (*stimulate*) anregen ‖ *intr* Funken sprühen
spark' gap' *s* Funkenstrecke *f*
sparkle [ˈspɑrkəl] *s* Funkeln *n* ‖ *intr* funkeln; (*said of wine*) moussieren
spark' plug' *s* Zündkerze *f*
spar'ring part'ner *s* Übungspartner *m*
sparrow [ˈspæro] *s* Spatz *m*, Sperling *m*

spar'row hawk' *s* Sperber *m*
sparse [spɑrs] *adj* spärlich
Spartan [ˈspɑrtən] *adj* spartanisch ‖ *s* Spartaner –in *mf*
spasm [ˈspæzəm] *s* Krampf *m*, Zuckung *f*
spasmodic [spæzˈmɑdɪk] *adj* sprunghaft; (pathol) krampfartig
spastic [ˈspæstɪk] *adj* spastisch
spat [spæt] *s* (coll) Wortwechsel *m*
spatial [ˈspeʃəl] *adj* räumlich
spatter [ˈspætər] *s* Spritzen *n;* (*stain*) Spritzfleck *m* ‖ *tr* verspritzen
spatula [ˈspætʃələ] *s* Spachtel *m & f*
spawn [spɔn] *s* Fischlaich *m* ‖ *tr* hervorbringen ‖ *intr* (*said of fish*) laichen
spay [spe] *tr* die Eierstöcke entfernen aus
speak [spik] *v* (*pret* **spoke** [spok]; *pp* **spoken**) *tr* sprechen; **s. one's mind** sich aussprechen ‖ *intr* (**about**) sprechen (über *acc*, von); **generally speaking** im allgemeinen; **so to s.** sozusagen; **speaking!** (telp) am Apparat!; **s. to** sprechen mit; (*give a speech to*) sprechen zu; **s. up** lauter sprechen; (*say something*) den Mund aufmachen; **s. up!** heraus mit der Sprache!; **s. up for** eintreten für
speak'-eas'y *s* Flüsterkneipe *f*
speaker [ˈspikər] *s* Sprecher –in *mf;* (*before an audience*) Redner –in *mf;* (parl) Sprecher –in *mf;* (rad) Lautsprecher *m*
spear [spɪr] *s* Speer *m* ‖ *tr* durchbohren; (*a piece of meat*) aufspießen; (*fish*) mit dem Speer fangen
spear'head' *s* Speerspitze *f;* (mil) Stoßkeil *m* ‖ *tr* an der Spitze stehen von
spear'mint' *s* Krauseminze *f*
special [ˈspeʃəl] *adj* besonder, Sonder– ‖ *s* (rr) Sonderzug *m;* **today's s.** Stammgericht *n*
spe'cial deliv'ery *s* Eilzustellung *f;* (*tab on envelope*) Eilsendung *f*
spec'ial-deliv'ery let'ter *s* Eilbrief *m*
specialist [ˈspeʃəlɪst] *s* Spezialist –in *mf*
specialization [ˌspeʃəlɪˈzeʃən] *s* Spezialisierung *f*
specialize [ˈspeʃəˌlaɪz] *intr* sich spezialisieren; **specialized knowledge** Fachkenntnisse *pl*
spe'cial of'fer *s* (com) Sonderangebot *n*
specialty [ˈspeʃəlti] *s* Spezialität *f;* (*special field*) Spezialfach *n*
spe'cialty shop' *s* Spezialgeschäft *n*
specie [ˈspisi] *s*—**in s.** der Art nach
spe•cies [ˈspisiz] *s* (**-cies**) Gattung *f*
specific [spɪˈsɪfɪk] *adj* spezifisch
specification [ˌspɛsɪfɪˈkeʃən] *s* Spezifizierung *f;* **specifications** (tech) technische Beschreibung *f*
specif'ic grav'ity *s* spezifisches Gewicht *n*
speci•fy [ˈspɛsɪˌfaɪ] *v* (*pret & pp* **-fied**) *tr* spezifizieren; (*stipulate*) bestimmen
specimen [ˈspɛsɪmən] *s* (*example*) Exemplar *n;* (*test sample*) Probe *f*
specious [ˈspiʃəs] *adj* Schein–

speck [spɛk] *s* Fleck *m; (in the distance)* Pünktchen *n;* s. of dust Stäubchen *n;* s. of grease Fettauge *n*
speckle ['spɛkəl] *s* Sprenkel *m* || *tr* sprenkeln
spectacle ['spɛktəkəl] *s* Schauspiel *n,* Anblick *m;* spectacles Brille *f*
spec'tacle case' *s* Brillenfutteral *n*
spectacular [spɛk'tækjələr] *adj* sensationell || *s* (cin) Monsterfilm *m*
spectator ['spɛktetər] *s* Zuschauer –in *mf*
specter ['spɛtər] *s* Gespenst *n*
spec·trum ['spɛktrəm] *s* (–tra [trə]) Spektrum *n*
speculate ['spɛkjə,let] *intr* spekulieren; s. in spekulieren in *(dat);* s. on Überlegungen anstellen über *(acc)*
speculation [,spɛkjə'leʃən] *s* Spekulation *f*
speculative ['spɛkjələtɪv] *adj* (com) Spekulations–; (philos) spekulativ
speculator ['spɛkjə,letər] *s* Spekulant –in *mf*
speech [spitʃ] *s* Sprache *f; (address)* Rede *f;* give a s. e–e Rede halten
speech' defect' *s* Sprachfehler *m*
speech' imped'iment *s* Sprachstörung *f*
speechless ['spitʃlɪs] *adj* sprachlos
speed [spid] *s* Geschwindigkeit *f; (gear)* Gang *m;* at top s. mit Höchstgeschwindigkeit; pick up s. auf Touren kommen || *v (pret & pp* speeded & sped [spɛd]) *tr* beschleunigen; s. up forcieren; s. it up (coll) ein scharfes Tempo vorlegen || *intr* (aut) rasen; *(above the speed limit)* (aut) zu schnell fahren
speed'boat' *s* Schnellboot *n*
speed'ing *s* (aut) Schnellfahren *n;* be arrested for s. wegen Überschreitung der Höchstgeschwindigkeit verhaftet werden; no s. *(public sign)* Schnellfahren verboten
speed' lim'it *s* Geschwindigkeitsgrenze *f*
speed' of light' *s* Lichtgeschwindigkeit *f*
speed' of sound' *s* Schallgeschwindigkeit *f*
speedometer [spi'dɑmɪtər] *s* Tachometer *n; (mileage indicator)* Meilenzähler *m,* Kilometerzähler *m*
speed' rec'ord *s* Geschwindigkeitsrekord *m*
speed' trap' *s* Autofalle *f*
speed'way' *s* (aut) Rennstrecke *f*
speedy ['spidi] *adj* schnell, schleunig; *(reply)* baldig
speed' zone' *s* Geschwindigkeitsbeschränkung *f*
spell [spɛl] *s (short period)* Zeitlang *f; (attack)* Anfall *m; (magical influence)* Bann *m;* be under s.o.'s s. in j–s Bann stehen; cast a s. bannen || *v (pret & pp* spelled & spelt [spɛlt]) *tr* buchstabieren; *(in writing)* schreiben; s. out Buchstaben für Buchstaben lesen; (fig) auseinanderklamüsern; s. trouble Schwie-

rigkeiten bedeuten || *intr* buchstabieren
spell'bind'er *s* faszinierender Redne *m*
spell'ing *s* Schreibweise *f; (orthogra phy)* Rechtschreibung *f*
spell'ing bee' *s* orthographischer Wett bewerb *m*
spelt [spɛlt] *s* Spelz *m*
spelunker [spɪ'lʌŋkər] *s* Höhlenfor scher –in *mf*
spend [spend] *v (pret & pp* spen [spɛnt]) *tr (money)* ausgeben; *(time* verbringen; s. the night übernachten s. time and effort on Zeit und Müh verwenden auf *(acc)*
spend'thrift' *s* Verschwender –in *mf*
spent [spɛnt] *adj (exhausted)* erschöpft *(cartridge)* leergeschossen
sperm [spʌrm] *s* Sperma *n*
sperm' whale' *s* Pottwal *m*
spew [spju] *tr* erbrechen; (fig) aus speien || *intr* sich erbrechen; (fig) herausströmen
sphere [sfɪr] *s* Kugel *f,* Sphäre *f;* (fig) Bereich *m;* s. of influence Einfluß sphäre *f*
spherical ['sfɛrɪkəl] *adj* sphärisch, ku gelförmig
sphinx [sfɪŋks] *s* (sphinxes & sphinge: ['sfɪndʒiz]) Sphinx *f*
spice [spaɪs] *s* Gewürz *n,* Würze *f,* (fig) Würze *f* || *tr* würzen
spick-and-span ['spɪkənd'spæn] *ad, blitzblank
spicy ['spaɪsi] *adj* würzig; (fig) pikan
spider ['spaɪdər] *s* Spinne *f*
spi'derweb' *s* Spinnengewebe *n*
spiffy ['spɪfi] *adj* (sl) fesch
spigot ['spɪgət] *s* Wasserhahn *m*
spike [spaɪk] *s (nail)* langer Nagel *m; (in volleyball)* Schmetterball *m;* (bot) Ähre *f;* (rr) Schwellenschraube *f;* (sport) Dorn *m* || *tr (a drink)* e–n Schuß Alkohol tun in *(acc);* (in volleyball) schmettern
spill [spɪl] *s (spilling)* Vergießen *n; (stain)* Fleck *m,* Klecks *m; (fall)* Sturz *m;* take a s. stürzen || *v (pret & pp* spilled & spilt [spɪlt]) *tr* verschütten; *(a rider)* abwerfen; s. out ausschütten; s. the beans (sl) alles ausplaudern || *intr* überlaufen; s. over into (fig) übergreifen auf *(acc)*
spill'way' *s* Überlauf *m*
spin [spɪn] *s (rotation)* Umdrehung *f; (short ride)* kurze Fahrt *f;* (aer) Trudeln *n;* go for a s. e–e Spritztour machen; go into a s. (aer) ins Trudeln kommen || *v (pret & pp* spun [spʌn]) *ger* spinning] *tr (rotate)* drehen; (tex) spinnen; s. out *(a story)* ausspinnen; s. s.o. around j–n im Kreise herumwirbeln || *intr* kreiseln, sich drehen; (tex) spinnen; my head is spinning mir dreht sich alles im Kopf
spinach ['spɪnɪtʃ] *s* Spinat *m*
spi'nal col'umn ['spaɪnəl] *s* Wirbelsäule *f*
spi'nal cord' *s* Rückenmark *n*

spi′nal flu′id *s* Rückenmarksflüssigkeit *f*
spindle ['spɪndəl] *s* Spindel *f*
spin′-dry′ *v* (*pret & pp* **–dried**) *tr* schleudern
spin′-dry′er *s* Trockenschleuder *m*
spine [spaɪn] *s* Rückgrat *n*, Wirbelsäule *f;* (bb) Buchrücken *m*
spineless ['spaɪnlɪs] *adj* (& fig) rückgratlos
spinet ['spɪnɪt] *s* Spinett *n*
spinner ['spɪnər] *s* Spinner –in *mf;* (mach) Spinnmaschine *f*
spin′ning *adj* (*rotating*) sich drehend; (tex) Spinn– ‖ *s* (tex) Spinnen *n*
spin′ning wheel′ *s* Spinnrad *n*
spinster ['spɪnstər] *s* alte Jungfer *f*
spi·ral ['spaɪrəl] *adj* spiralig ‖ *s* Spirale *f; s.* **of rising prices and wages** Lohn-Preis-Spirale *f* ‖ *v* (*pret & pp* **–ral[l]ed;** *ger* **–ral[l]ing**) *intr* sich in die Höhe schrauben
spi′ral stair′case *s* Wendeltreppe *f*
spire [spaɪr] *s* Spitze *f*
spirit ['spɪrɪt] *s* Geist *m;* (*enthusiasm*) Schwung *m;* (*ghost*) Geist *m;* **in high spirits** in gehobener Stimmung; **low spirits** in gedrückter Stimmung; **spirits** Spirituosen *pl;* **that's the right s.!** das ist die richtige Einstellung! ‖ *tr—s.* **away** wegzaubern
spir′ited *adj* lebhaft; (*horse*) feurig
spiritless ['spɪrɪtlɪs] *adj* schwunglos
spiritual ['spɪrɪtʃu·əl] *adj* (*incorporeal*) geistig; (*of the soul*) seelisch; (*religious*) geistlich ‖ *s* geistliches Negerlied *n*
spiritualism ['spɪrɪtʃuə‚lɪzəm] *s* Spiritismus *m*
spiritualist ['spɪrɪtʃu·əlɪst] *s* Spiritist –in *mf*
spir′itual life′ *s* Seelenleben *n*
spit [spɪt] *s* Spucke *f;* (culin) Spieß *m* ‖ *v* (*pret & pp* **spat** [spæt] & **spit;** *ger* **spitting**) *tr & intr* spucken
spite [spaɪt] *s* Trotz *m;* **for s.** aus Trotz; **in s. of** trotz (*genit*) ‖ *tr* kränken; **he did it to s. me** er hat es mir zum Trotz getan
spiteful ['spaɪtfəl] *adj* gehässig
spit′fire′ *s* (coll) Sprühteufel *m*
spit′ting im′age *s* (coll) Ebenbild *n*
spittoon [spɪ'tun] *s* Spucknapf *m*
splash [splæʃ] *s* Platschen *n;* (*noise of falling into water*) Klatschen *n;* **make a s.** (coll) Aufsehen erregen ‖ *tr* (*a person, etc.*) bespritzen; (*e.g., water*) spritzen ‖ *intr* klatschen, patschen; **s. about** planschen; **s. down** (rok) wassern ‖ *interj* schwaps!, platsch!
splash′down′ *s* (rok) Wasserung *f*
splatter ['splætər] *tr & intr* kleckern
spleen [splin] *s* Milz *f;* (fig) schlechte Laune *f;* **vent one's s.** on seiner schlechten Laune Luft machen gegenüber (*dat*)
splendid ['splendɪd] *adj* prächtig, herrlich; (coll) großartig
splendor ['splendər] *s* Herrlichkeit *f*
splice [splaɪs] *s* Spleiß *m* ‖ *tr* (*a rope*) spleißen; (*film*) zusammenkleben

splint [splɪnt] *s* Schiene *f;* **put in splints** schienen
splinter ['splɪntər] *s* Splitter *m* ‖ *tr* (zer)splittern
splin′ter group′ *s* Splittergruppe *f*
split [splɪt] *adj* rissig ‖ *s* Riß *m*, Spalt *m;* (fig) Spaltung *f;* (gym) Spagat *m* ‖ *v* (*pret & pp* **split;** *ger* **splitting**) *tr* spalten; (*pants*) platzen; (*profits, the difference*) sich teilen in (*acc*); **s. hairs** Haarspalterei treiben; **s. one's sides laughing** vor Lachen platzen; **s. open** aufbrechen ‖ *intr* (into) sich spalten (in *acc*); **splitting headache** rasende Kopfschmerzen *pl;* **s. up** (*said of a couple*) sich trennen
split′ infin′itive *s* gespaltener Infinitiv *m*
split′-lev′el *adj* mit Zwischenstockwerk versehen
split′ personal′ity *s* gespaltene Persönlichkeit *f*
split′ sec′ond *s* Sekundenbruchteil *m*
splotch [splatʃ] *s* Klecks *m* ‖ *tr* kleckern
splotchy ['splatʃi] *adj* fleckig
splurge [splʌrdʒ] *s—***go on a s.** verschwenderischen Aufwand treiben ‖ *tr* verschwenden ‖ *intr* (**on**) verschwenderische Ausgaben machen (für)
splutter ['splʌtər] *s* Geplapper *n* ‖ *tr* (*words*) heraussprudeln; (*besplatter*) bespritzen ‖ *intr* plappern; (*said, e.g., of grease*) spritzen
spoil [spɔɪl] *s—***spoils** Beute *f* ‖ *v* (*pret & pp* **spoiled & spoilt** [spɔɪlt]) *tr* (*perishable goods; fun*) verderben; (*a child*) verziehen, verwöhnen ‖ *intr* verderben, schlecht werden; **spoiling for a fight** zanksüchtig
spoilage ['spɔɪlɪdʒ] *s* Verderb *m*
spoil′ sport′ *s* Spielverderber –in *mf*
spoils′ sys′tem *s* Futterkrippensystem *n*
spoke [spok] *s* Speiche *f*
spokes′man *s* (**–men**) Wortführer –in *mf*
sponge [spʌndʒ] *s* Schwamm *m* ‖ *tr* schnorren ‖ *intr* schnorren; **s. on** (coll) schmarotzen bei
sponge′ cake′ *s* Sandtorte *f*
sponger ['spʌndʒər] *s* Schmarotzer –in *mf*
sponge′ rub′ber *s* Schaumgummi *m* & *n*
spongy ['spʌndʒi] *adj* schwammig
sponsor ['spansər] *s* Förderer –in *mf; (of a program*) Sponsor *m; (of an immigrant*) Bürge *m*, Bürgin *f; (at baptism or confirmation*) Pate *m*, Patin *f* ‖ *tr* fördern; (*a program*) finanziell fördern
spontaneity [spantə'ni·ɪti] *s* Spontaneität *f*
spontaneous [span'tenɪ·əs] *adj* spontan
sponta′neous combus′tion *s* Selbstverbrennung *f*
spontaneously [span'tenɪ·əsli] *adv* von selbst, unaufgefordert

spoof [spuf] *s* (*hoax*) Jux *m;* (*parody*) (**on**) Parodie *f* (auf *acc*) || *intr* albern
spook [spuk] *s* (coll) Spuk *m*
spooky ['spuki] *adj* spukhaft
spool [spul] *s* Spule *f,* Rolle *f*
spoon [spun] *s* Löffel *m;* **wooden s.** Kochlöffel *m* || *tr* (**out**) löffeln
spoonerism ['spunə͵rɪzəm] *s* Schüttelreim *m*
spoon′-feed′ *v* (*pret* & *pp* –**fed**) *tr* (fig) es leicht machen (*dat*)
spoonful ['spunful] *s* Löffel *m*
sporadic [spə'rædɪk] *adj* vereinzelt
spore [spor] *s* Spore *f*
sport [sport] *adj* Sport– || *s* Sport *m;* (biol) Spielart *f;* **a good s.** ein Pfundskerl *m;* **go in for sports** sporteln; **in s.** im Spaß; **make s. of** sich lustig machen über (*acc*); **play sports** Sport treiben; **poor s.** Spielverderber –in *mf;* **sports** Sport *m;* (*sportscast*) Sportbericht *m* || *intr* sich belustigen
sport′ing event′ *s* Sportveranstaltung *f*
sport′ing goods′ *spl* Sportwaren *pl*
sport′ jac′ket *s* Sportjacke *f*
sports′ car′ *s* Sportwagen *m*
sports′cast′ *s* Sportbericht *m*
sports′cast′er *s* Sportberichterstatter *m*
sports′ fan′ *s* Sportfreund –in *mf*
sport′ shirt′ *s* Sporthemd *n*
sports′man *s* (–**men**) Sportsmann *m*
sports′manlike *adj* sportlich
sports′manship′ *s* sportliches Verhalten *n*
sports′ news′ *s* Sportnachrichten *pl*
sports′wear′ *s* Sportkleidung *f*
sports′ world′ *s* Sportwelt *f*
sports′ writ′er *s* Sportjournalist –in *mf*
sporty ['sporti] *adj* auffallend
spot [spɑt] *s* (*stain*) Fleck(en) *m;* (*place*) Platz *m,* Ort *m;* (*as on a leopard*) Tüpfel *m* & *n;* **be on the s.** (*be present*) zur Stelle sein; (*be in difficulty*) in der Klemme sein; **hit the s.** gerade das Richtige sein; **on the s.** auf der Stelle; **put on the s.** in Verlegenheit bringen || *v* (*pret* & *pp* **spotted**; *ger* **spotting**) *tr* (*stain*) beflecken; (*espy*) erblicken; (*points in betting*) vorgeben
spot′ announce′ment *s* Durchsage *f*
spot′ cash′ *s* ungebundene Barmittel *pl*
spot′ check′ *s* Stichprobe *f*
spot′-check′ *tr* stichprobenweise prüfen
spotless ['spɑtlɪs] *adj* makellos
spot′light′ *s* Scheinwerfer *m;* **in the s.** (fig) im Rampenlicht der Öffentlichkeit || *tr* (fig) in den Vordergrund stellen
spot′ remov′er [rɪ͵muvər] *s* Fleckputzmittel *n*
spotty ['spɑti] *adj* fleckig; (*uneven*) ungleichmäßig
spot′ weld′ing *s* Punktschweißung *f*
spouse [spaus] *s* Gatte *m,* Gattin *f*
spout [spaut] *s* (*of a pot*) Tülle *f;* (*jet of water*) Strahl *m* || *tr* (& fig) hervorsprudeln || *intr* spritzen; (coll) große Reden schwingen

sprain [spren] *s* Verstauchung *f* || *tr* verstauchen; **s. one's ankle** sich [*dat*] den Fuß vertreten
sprat [spræt] *s* (ichth) Sprotte *f*
sprawl [sprɔl] *intr* (**out**) alle viere von sich ausstrecken; (*said of a city*) sich weit ausbreiten
spray [spre] *s* (*of ocean*) Gischt *m;* (*from a can*) Spray *n;* (*from a fountain*) Sprühwasser *n;* **s. of flowers** Blütenzweig *m* || *tr* spritzen; (*liquids*) zerstäuben; (*plants*) besprühen
sprayer ['spre·ər] *s* Zerstäuber *m;* (*for a garden*) Gartenspritze *f*
spray′ gun′ *s* Spritzpistole *f*
spray′ paint′ *s* Spritzfarbe *f*
spread [spred] *s* (*act of spreading*) Ausbreitung *f;* (*extent*) Verbreitung *f;* (e.g., *of a tree*) Umfang *m;* (*on bread*) Aufstrich *m;* (*bedspread*) Bettdecke *f;* (*large piece of land*) weite Fläche *f;* (*of a shot*) Streubereich *m* & *n;* (*sumptuous meal*) Gelage *n* || *v* (*pret* & *pp* **spread**) *tr* (*warmth, light, news, rumors*) verbreiten; (*mortar, glue*) auftragen; (e.g., *butter*) aufstreichen; (*the legs*) spreizen; (*manure*) streuen; **s. oneself too thin** sich verzetteln; **s. out over a year** über ein Jahr verteilen || *intr* sich verbreiten; (*said of margarine*) sich aufstreichen lassen
spree [spri] *s* Bummel *m;* (*carousal*) Zechgelage *n;* **go on a buying s.** sich in e–e Kauforgie stürzen
sprig [sprɪg] *s* Zweiglein *n*
sprightly ['spraɪtli] *adj* lebhaft; (*gait*) federnd
spring [sprɪŋ] *adj* Frühlings– || *s* (*of water*) Quelle *f;* (*season*) Frühling *m;* (*resilience*) Sprungkraft *f;* (*of metal*) Feder *f;* (*jump*) Sprung *m;* **springs** (aut) Federung *f* || *v* (*pret* **sprang** [spræŋ] & **sprung** [sprʌŋ]; *pp* **sprung** [sprʌŋ]) *tr* (*a trap*) zuschnappen lassen; (*a leak*) bekommen; (*a question*) (**on**) plötzlich stellen (*dat*); (*a surprise*) (**on**) bereiten (*dat*); **s. the news on s.o.** j–n mit der Nachricht überraschen || *intr* springen; **s. back** zurückschnellen; **s. from** entspringen (*dat*); **s. up** aufspringen; (*said of industry, towns*) aus dem Boden schießen
spring′board′ *s* (& fig) Sprungbrett *n*
spring′ chic′ken *s* Hähnchen *n;* **she's no s.** (sl) sie ist nicht die Jüngste
spring′ fe′ver *s* Frühlingsmüdigkeit *f*
spring′time′ *s* Frühlingszeit *f*
spring′ wa′ter *s* Quellwasser *n*
springy ['sprɪŋi] *adj* federnd
sprinkle ['sprɪŋkəl] *s* Spritzen *n;* (*light rain*) Sprühregen *m* || *tr* (*water, streets, lawns, laundry*) sprengen; (e.g., *sugar*) streuen || *intr* sprühen
sprinkler ['sprɪŋklər] *s* (*truck*) Sprengwagen *m;* (*for the lawn*) Rasensprenger *m;* (eccl) Sprengwedel *m*
sprin′kling *s* Sprengung *f;* **a s. of** (e.g., *sugar*) ein bißchen; (e.g., *of people*) ein paar

sprin'kling can' *s* Gießkanne *f*
sprin'kling sys'tem *s* Feuerlöschanlage *f*
sprint [sprɪnt] *s* Sprint *m* ‖ *intr* sprinten
sprinter ['sprɪntər] *s* Sprinter –in *mf*
sprite [spraɪt] *s* Kobold *m*, Elfe *f*
sprocket ['sprɑkɪt] *s* Zahnrad *n*
sprout [spraut] *s* Sproß *m* ‖ *intr* sprießen
spruce [sprus] *adj* schmuck ‖ *s* (bot) Fichte *f* ‖ *intr*—**s. up** sich schmücken
spry [spraɪ] *adj* (**spryer & sprier; spryest & spriest**) flink
spud [spʌd] *s* (*for weeding*) Jäthacke *f*; (*potatoe*) (coll) Kartoffel *f*
spume [spjum] *s* Schaum *m*
spun' glass' *s* Glasfaser *f*
spunk [spʌŋk] *s* (coll) Mumm *m*
spunky ['spʌŋki] *adj* (coll) feurig
spur [spʌr] *s* (*on riding boot; on a rooster*) Sporn *m*; (*of a mountain*) Ausläufer *m*; (fig) Ansporn *m*; (archit) Strebe *f*; (bot) Stachel *m*; (rr) Seitengleis *n*; **on the s. of the moment** der Eingebung des Augenblicks folgend ‖ *v* (*pret & pp* **spurred; ger spurring**) *tr* die Sporen geben (*dat*); **s. on** anspornen
spurious ['spjʊrɪ-əs] *adj* unecht
spurn [spʌrn] *tr* verschmähen
spurt [spʌrt] *s* Ruck *m*; (sport) Spurt *m*; **in spurts** ruckweise ‖ *tr* speien ‖ *intr* herausspritzen; (sport) spurten
sputnik ['spʌtnɪk] *s* Sputnik *m*
sputter ['spʌtər] *s* Stottern *n* ‖ *tr* umherspritzen; (*words*) hervorsprudeln ‖ *intr* (*said of a person, engine*) stottern; (*said of a candle, fire*) flackern
sputum ['spjutəm] *s* Sputum *n*
spy [spaɪ] *s* Spion –in *mf* ‖ *v* (*pret & pp* **spied**) *tr*—**spy out** ausspionieren ‖ *intr* spionieren
spy'glass' *s* Fernglas *n*
spy'ing *s* Spionage *f*
spy' ring' *s* Spionageorganization *f*
squabble ['skwɑbəl] *s* Zank *m* ‖ *intr* zanken
squad [skwɑd] *s* (gym) Riege *f*; (mil) Gruppe *f*; (sport) Mannschaft *f*
squad' car' *s* Funkstreifenwagen *m*
squad' lead'er *s* (mil) Gruppenführer *m*
squadron ['skwɑdrən] *s* (aer) Staffel *f*; (nav) Geschwader *n*
squalid ['skwɑlɪd] *adj* verkommen
squall [skwɔl] *s* Bö *f*
squander ['skwɑndər] *tr* verschwenden
square [skwɛr] *adj* quadratisch; (*mile, meter, foot*) Quadrat–; (*fellow; meal*) anständig; (*even*) quitt; **ten meters s.** zehn Meter im Quadrat; **ten s. meters** zehn Quadratmeter ‖ *s* Quadrat *n*; (*city block*) Häuserblock *m*; (*open area*) Platz *m*; (*of a checkerboard or chessboard*) Feld *n*; (carp) Winkel *m*; (math) zweite Potenz *f* ‖ *tr* quadrieren; (*a number*) ins Quadrat erheben; (*accounts*) abrechnen ‖ *intr*—**s. off** in Kampfstellung gehen; **s. with** (*agree with*)

übereinstimmen mit; (*be frank with*) aufrichtig sein zu
square' dance' *s* Reigen *m*
square' deal' *s* reelles Geschäft *n*
square' root' *s* Quadratwurzel *f*
squash [skwɑʃ] *s* (bot) Kürbis *m* ‖ *tr* (*a hat*) zerdrücken; (*a finger, grape*) quetschen; (fig) unterdrücken ‖ *intr* zerdrückt (or zerquetscht) werden
squashy ['skwɑʃi] *adj* weich, matschig
squat [skwɑt] *adj* gedrungen, untersetzt ‖ *s* Hocken *n* ‖ *v* (*pret & pp* **squatted; ger squatting**) *intr* hocken; **s. down** sich (hin)hocken
squatter ['skwɑtər] *s* Ansiedler –in *mf* ohne Rechtstitel
squaw [skwɔ] *s* Indianerin *f*
squawk [skwɔk] *s* Geschrei *n*; (sl) Schimpferei *f* ‖ *intr* schreien; (sl) schimpfen
squeak [skwik] *s* (*of a door*) Quietschen *n*; (*of a mouse*) Pfeifen *n* ‖ *intr* quietschen; (*said of a mouse*) pfeifen
squeal [skwil] *s* Quieken *n* ‖ *intr* (*said of a pig*) quieken; (*said of a mouse*) pfeifen; (sl) petzen; **s. for joy** vor Vergnügen quietschen; **s. on** (sl) (*a pupil*) verpetzen; (*to the police*) verpfeifen
squealer ['skwilər] *s* (sl) Petze *f*
squeamish ['skwimɪʃ] *adj* zimperlich
squeeze [skwiz] *s* Druck *m*; **s. of the hand** Händedruck *m* ‖ *tr* drücken; (*oranges*) auspressen; **s. into** (e.g., *a trunk*) hineinquetschen; **s. out** auspressen; **s. together** zusammenpressen; (e.g., *people*) zusammenpferchen ‖ *intr*—**s. in** sich eindrängen; **s. through** sich durchzwängen (durch)
squelch [skwɛltʃ] *s* schlagfertige Antwort *f* ‖ *tr* niederschmettern
squid [skwɪd] *s* Tintenfisch *m*
squill [skwɪl] *s* (bot) Meerzwiebel *f*; (zool) Heuschreckenkrebs *m*
squint [skwɪnt] *s* Schielen *n* ‖ *intr* (*look with eyes partly closed*) blinzeln; (*be cross-eyed*) schielen; (*look askance*) (at) argwöhnisch blicken (auf *acc*)
squint'-eyed' *adj* schielend
squire [skwaɪr] *s* (hist) Knappe *m*; (jur) Friedensrichter *m*
squirm [skwʌrm] *intr* (**through**) sich winden (durch); (*be restless*) zappeln; **s. out of** sich herauswinden aus
squirrel ['skwʌrəl] *s* Eichhörnchen *n*
squirt [skwʌrt] *s* Spritzer *m*; (*boy*) (coll) Stöpsel *m* ‖ *tr* (ver)spritzen ‖ *intr* spritzen; **s. out** herausspritzen
S'S' troops' ['ɛs'ɛs] *spl* Schutzstaffel *f*
stab [stæb] *s* Stich *m*; (*wound*) Stichwunde *f*; **make a s. at** (coll) probieren ‖ *v* (*pret & pp* **stabbed; ger stabbing**) *tr* stechen; (*kill*) erstechen; (*a pig*) abstechen; **s. s.o. in the back** j–m in den Rücken fallen
stability [stə'bɪlɪti] *s* Stabilität *f*
stabilization [ˌstɛbɪlɪ'zeʃən] *s* (e.g., *of prices*) Stabilisierung *f*; (aer) Dämpfung *f*

stabilize ['stebɪˌlaɪz] *tr* stabilisieren
stabilizer ['stebɪˌlaɪzər] *s* (aer) Flosse *f*
stab' in the back' *s* Stoß *m* aus dem Hinterhalt
stable ['stebəl] *adj* stabil || *s* Stall *m* || *tr* unterbringen
sta'ble boy' *s* Stalljunge *m*
stack [stæk] *s* (*of papers, books*) Stapel *m;* (*of wheat*) Schober *m;* (*of a ship*) Schornstein *m;* (*of rifles*) Pyramide *f;* **stacks** (libr) Bücherregale *pl* || *tr* (*wood, wheat*) aufstapeln; (*rifles*) zusammensetzen; (cards) packen
stadi·um ['stedɪ·əm] *s* (**–ums** & **–a** [ə]) Stadion *n*
staff [stæf] *s* (*rod*) Stab *m;* (*personnel*) Personal *n;* (*of a newspaper*) Redaktion *f;* (mil) Stab *m;* (mus) Notensystem *n* || *tr* mit Personal besetzen
staff' of'ficer *s* Stabsoffizier *m*
staff' ser'geant *s* Feldwebel *m*
stag [stæg] *adj* Herren– || *adv*—**go s.** ohne Damenbegleitung sein || *s* Hirsch *m*
stage [stedʒ] *s* (*of a theater*) Bühne *f;* (*phase*) Stadium *n;* (*stretch*) Strecke *f;* (*of life*) Etappe *f;* (*of a rocket*) Stufe *f;* (*scene*) Szene *f;* **at this s.** in diesem Stadium; **by easy stages** etappenweise; **final stages** Endstadien *pl* || *tr* (*a play*) inszenieren; (*a comeback*) veranstalten
stage'coach' *s* Postkutsche *f*
stage'craft' *s* Bühnenkunst *f*
stage' direc'tion *s* Bühnenanweisung *f*
stage' door' *s* Bühneneingang *m*
stage' effect' *s* Bühnenwirkung *f*
stage' fright' *s* Lampenfieber *n*
stage' hand' *s* Bühnenarbeiter –in *mf*
stage' light'ing *s* Bühnenbeleuchtung *f*
stage' man'ager *s* Bühnenleiter –in *mf*
stage' play' *s* Bühnenstück *n*
stage' prop'erties *spl* Theaterrequisiten *pl*
stagestruck ['stedʒˌstrʌk] *adj* theaterbegeistert
stagger ['stægər] *s* Taumeln *n* || *tr* (*e.g., lunch hours*) staffeln; (& fig) erschüttern || *intr* taumeln
stag'gering *adj* taumelnd; (*blow, loss*) vernichtend; (*news*) erschütternd
stagnant ['stægnənt] *adj* (*water*) stillstehend; (*air*) schlecht; (fig) träge
stagnate ['stægnet] *intr* stagnieren
stag' par'ty *s* Herrenabend *m*
staid [sted] *adj* gesetzt
stain [sten] *s* Fleck *m;* (*paint*) Beize *f* || *tr* beflecken; (*wood*) beizen
stained'-glass win'dow *s* buntes Glasfenster *n*
stainless ['stenlɪs] *adj* rostfrei
stair [ster] *s* Stufe *f;* **stairs** Treppe *f*
stair'case' *s* Treppenhaus *n*
stair'way' *s* Treppenaufgang *m*
stair'well' *s* Treppenschacht *m*
stake [stek] *s* Pfahl *m;* (*bet*) Einsatz *m;* **be at s.** auf dem Spiel stehen; **die at the s.** auf dem Scheiterhaufen sterben; **play for high stakes** viel riskieren; **pull up stakes** (coll) ab-

hauen || *tr* (*plants*) mit e-m Pfahl stützen; **s. off** abstecken; **s. out a claim** (fig) e-e Forderung umreißen
stake'-out' *s* polizeiliche Überwachung *f*
stalactite [stə'læktaɪt] *s* Stalaktit *m*
stalagmite [stə'lægmaɪt] *s* Stalagmit *m*
stale [stel] *adj* (*baked goods*) altbacken; (*e.g., beer*) schal; (*air*) verbraucht; (*joke*) abgedroschen; **get s.** abstehen
stale'mate' *s* (fig) Sackgasse *f;* (chess) Patt *n* || *tr* (fig) in e–e Sackgasse treiben; (chess) patt setzen
stalk [stɔk] *s* (*of grain*) Halm *m;* (*of a plant*) Stiel *m* || *tr* beschleichen; **s. game** pirschen
stall [stɔl] *s* (*for animals*) Stall *m;* (*booth*) Bude *f;* (sl) Vorwand *m* || *tr* (*a motor*) abwürgen; (*a person*) aufhalten || *intr* ausweichen; (aut) absterben; **s. for time** Zeit zu gewinnen suchen
stallion ['stæljən] *s* Hengst *m*
stalwart ['stɔlwərt] *adj* stämmig; (*supporter*) treu
stamen ['stemən] *s* Staubfaden *m*
stamina ['stæmɪnə] *s* Ausdauer *f*
stammer ['stæmər] *s* Stammeln *n* || *tr* & *intr* stammeln
stammerer ['stæmərər] *s* Stammler –in *mf*
stamp [stæmp] *s* (*mark*) Gepräge *n;* (*device for stamping*) Stempel *m;* (*for postage*) Briefmarke *f* || *tr* (*e.g., a document*) stempeln; (*a letter*) freimachen; (*the earth*) stampfen; **s. one's foot** mit dem Fuß aufstampfen; **s. out** (*a fire*) austreten; (*a rebellion*) niederschlagen
stampede [stæm'pid] *s* panische Flucht *f* || *tr* in die Flucht jagen || *intr* in wilder Flucht davonrennen
stamped' en'velope *s* Freiumschlag *m*
stamp'ing grounds' *spl* Lieblingsplatz *m*
stamp' machine' *s* Briefmarkenautomat *m*
stamp' pad' *s* Stempelkissen *n*
stance [stæns] *s* Haltung *f*, Stellung *f*
stanch [stɑntʃ] *tr* stillen
stand [stænd] *s* (*booth*) Stand *m;* (*platform*) Tribüne *f;* (*e.g., for bicycles*) Ständer *m;* (*view, position*) Standpunkt *m;* (*piece of furniture*) Ständer *m;* **take a s. (on)** Stellung nehmen (zu); **take one's s.** (*e.g., near the door*) sich stellen; **s. of timber** Waldbestand *m;* **stands** (sport) Tribüne *f;* **take the s.** (jur) als Zeuge auftreten || *v* (*pret* & *pp* **stood** [stʊd]) *tr* (*put*) stellen; (*the cold, hardships*) aushalten; (*a person*) leiden; **s. a chance** e–e Chance haben; **s. guard** Posten stehen; **s. one's ground** sich behaupten; **s. s.o. up** j–n aufsitzen lassen; **s. the test** sich bewähren || *intr* stehen; (*have validity*) gelten; **she wants to know where she stands** sie will wissen, wie sie daran ist; **s. aside** auf die Seite treten; **s. at attention** stillstehen; **s.**

back zurückstehen; **s. behind** s.o. (fig) hinter j–m stehen; **s. by** (in *readiness*) in Bereitschaft stehen; (a *decision*) bleiben bei; (e.g., *for the latest news*) am Apparat bleiben; **s. by** s.o. j–m beistehen; **s. firm** fest bleiben; **s. for** (*champion*) eintreten für; (*tolerate*) sich [*dat*] gefallen lassen; (*mean*) bedeuten; **s. good for** gutstehen für; **s. idle** stillstehen; **s. on end** sich sträuben, e.g., **my hair stood on end** mir sträubten sich die Haare; **s. on one's head** kopfstehen; **s. out** (*project*) abstehen; (*be conspicuous*) hervorstechen; **s. out against** sich abzeichnen gegen; **s.o. in good stead** j–m zugute kommen; **s. up** aufstehen; **s. up against** aufkommen gegen; **s. up for** (a *thing*) verfechten; (a *person*) die Stange halten (*dat*); **s. up to** s.o. j–m die Stirn bieten; **s. up under** aushalten

standard ['stændərd] *adj* Standard–, Normal– ‖ *s* Standard *m*; (*banner*) Banner *n*

stand'ard-bear'er *s* Bannerträger *m*
stand'ard-gauge track' *s* Normalspur *f*
standardize ['stændər‚daɪz] *tr* normen
stand'ard of liv'ing *s* Lebensstandard *m*
stand'ard time' *s* Normalzeit *f*
stand'-by' *adj* Reserve– ‖ *s*—**on s. in** Bereitschaft
standee [stæn'di] *s* Stehplatzinhaber –in *mf*
stand'in' *s* (coll) Ersatzmann *m*; (cin, theat) Double *m*
stand'ing *adj* (*army, water, rule*) stehend; (*committee*) ständig; (*jump*) aus dem Stand ‖ *s* Stehen *n*; (*social*) Stellung *f*; (*of a team*) Stand *m*; **in good s.** treu; **of long s.** langjährig
stand'ing or'der *s* (com) Dauerauftrag *m*
stand'ing room' *s* Stehplatz *m*; **s. only** nur noch Stehplätze
stand'-off' *s* Unentschieden *n*
stand-offish ['stænd'ɔfɪʃ] *adj* zurückhaltend
stand'out' *s* Blickfang *m*
stand'point' *s* Standpunkt *m*
stand'still' *s* Stillstand *m*; **come to a s.** zum Stillstand kommen
stanza ['stænzə] *s* Strophe *f*
staple ['stepəl] *adj* Haupt–, Stapel– ‖ *s* (*food*) Hauptnahrungsmittel *n*; (*product*) Hauptprodukt *n*; (*clip*) Heftklammer *f* ‖ *tr* mit Draht heften
stapler ['steplər] *s* Heftmaschine *f*
star [star] *adj* Spitzen–; (astr) Stern– ‖ *s* Stern *m*; (cin, rad, telv, theat) Star *m*; **I saw stars** (fig) Sterne tanzten mir vor den Augen ‖ *v* (*pret & pp* **starred;** *ger* **starring**) *tr* (cin, rad, sport, telv, theat) als Star herausstellen; (typ) mit Sternchen kennzeichnen ‖ *intr* Star sein
starboard ['starbərd] *adj* Steuerbord– ‖ *s* Steuerbord *n*
starch [startʃ] *s* Stärke *f* ‖ *tr* stärken
starchy ['startʃi] *adj* stärkenhaltig
stare [ster] *s* starrer Blick *m* ‖ *tr*—

s. down durch Anstarren aus der Fassung bringen ‖ *intr* starren; **s. at** anstarren; **s. into space** ins Leere blicken, ins Blaue starren
star'fish' *s* Seestern *m*
stargazer ['star‚gezər] *s* Sterngucker –in *mf*
stark [stark] *adj* (*landscape*) kahl; (*sheer*) völlig ‖ *adv* völlig
stark'-na'ked *adj* splitter(faser)nackt
starlet ['starlət] *s* Sternchen *n*
star'light' *s* Sternenlicht *n*
starling ['starlɪŋ] *s* (orn) Star *m*
star'lit' *adj* sternhell
Star' of Da'vid *s* David(s)stern *m*
starry ['stari] *adj* gestirnt; (*night*) sternklar; (*sky*) Stern–
star'ry-eyed' *adj* verträumt
Stars' and Stripes' *spl* Sternenbanner *n*
Star'-Spangled Ban'ner *s* Sternenbanner *n*
start [start] *s* Anfang *m*; (*sudden springing movement*) plötzliches Hochfahren *n*; (*lead, advantage*) Vorgabe *f*, Vorsprung *m*; (*of a race*) Start *m*; **give s.o. a s.** j–m auf die Beine helfen ‖ *tr* anfangen; (a *motor*) anlassen; (a *rumor*) in die Welt setzen; (a *conversation*) anknüpfen; **s. a fire** ein Feuer anmachen; (*said of an arsonist*) e–n Brand legen ‖ *intr* anfangen; **s. in to** (*inf*) anfangen zu (*inf*); **s. out** (*begin*) anfangen; (*start walking*) losgehen; **s. out on** (a *trip*) antreten; **to s. with** zunächst
start'ing gate' *s* Startmaschine *f*
start'ing gun' *s* Startpistole *f*; **at the s.** beim Startschuß
start'ing point' *s* Ausgangspunkt *m*
startle ['startəl] *tr* erschrecken; **be startled** zusammenfahren
starvation [star've ʃən] *s* Hunger *m*; **die of s.** verhungern
starva'tion di'et *s* Hungerkur *f*
starva'tion wag'es *spl* Hungerlohn *m*
starve [starv] *tr* verhungern lassen; **s. out** aushungern ‖ *intr* hungern; (coll) furchtbaren Hunger haben; **s. to death** verhungern
state [stet] *adj* staatlich, Staats–; (*as opposed to federal*) bundesstaatlich ‖ *s* (*condition*) Zustand *m*; (*government*) Staat *m*; (*of the U.S.A.*) Bundesstaat *m* ‖ *tr* angeben; (a *rule, problem*) aufstellen; **as stated above** wie oben angegeben
State' Depart'ment *s* Außenministerium *n*
stateless ['stetlɪs] *adj* staatenlos
stately ['stetli] *adj* stattlich
statement ['stetmənt] *s* Angabe *f*; (*from a bank*) Abrechnung *f*; (jur) Aussage *f*
state' of affairs' *s* Lage *f*
state' of emer'gency *s* Notstand *m*
state' of health' *s* Gesundheitszustand *m*
state' of mind' *s* Geisteszustand *m*
state' of war' *s* Kriegszustand *m*
state'-owned' *adj* staatseigen; (*in communistic countries*) volkseigen
state' police' *s* Staatspolizei *f*

state'room' s (*in a palace*) Prunkzimmer n; (*on a ship*) Passagierkabine f
states'man s (**-men**) Staatsmann m
states'manlike' adj staatsmännisch
states'manship' s Staatskunst f
static ['stætɪk] adj statisch ‖ s (rad) Nebengeräusche pl
station ['steʃən] s (*social*) Stellung f; (*of a bus, rail line*) Bahnhof m; (mil) Standort m ‖ tr aufstellen; (mil) stationieren
stationary ['steʃə,nɛri] adj stationär
sta'tion break' s Werbepause f
stationer ['steʃənər] s Schreibwarenhändler –in mf
stationery ['steʃə,nɛri] s Briefpapier n
sta'tionery store' s Schreibwarenhandlung f
sta'tion house' s Polizeiwache f
sta'tion identifica'tion s (rad) Pausenzeichen n
sta'tionmas'ter s Bahnhofsvorsteher m
sta'tions of the cross' spl Kreuzweg m
sta'tion wag'on s Kombiwagen m
statistic [stə'tɪstɪk] s Angabe f; **statistics** (*science*) Statistik f ‖ spl (*data*) Statistik f
statistical [stə'tɪstɪkəl] adj statistisçh
statistician [,stætɪs'tɪʃən] s Statistiker –in mf
statue ['stætʃʊ] s Statue f
statuesque [,stætʃʊ'ɛsk] adj statuenhaft
stature ['stætʃər] s Gestalt f; (fig) Format n
status ['stetəs] s (*in society*) Stellung f; (*e.g., mental*) Stand m
sta'tus quo' [kwo] s Status m quo
sta'tus sym'bol s Statussymbol n
statute ['stætʃut] s Satzung f, Statut n
statutory ['stætʃʊ,tori] adj statutenmäßig
staunch [stɔntʃ] adj unentwegt
stave [stev] s (*of a barrel*) Daube f; (*of a chair*) Steg m; (*of a ladder*) Sprosse f; (mus) Notensystem n ‖ tr—**s. off** abwenden
stay [ste] s (*visit*) Aufenthalt m; (prop) Stütze f; (*of execution*) Aufschub m ‖ intr bleiben; **have to s. in** (*after school*) nachsitzen müssen; **s. away** wegbleiben; **s. behind** zurückbleiben; (*in school*) sitzenbleiben
stay'-at-home' s Stubenhocker –in mf
stead [stɛd] s Statt f; **in s.o.'s s. an** j–s Statt
stead'fast' adj standhaft
stead·y ['stedi] adj fest, beständig; (*hands*) sicher; (*ladder*) fest; (*pace*) gleichmäßig; (*progress*) ständig; (*nerves*) stark; (*prices*) stabil; (*work*) regelmäßig; **s. customer** Stammkunde m, Stammkundin f; **s. now!** immer langsam! ‖ v (pret & pp **–ied**) tr festigen
steak [stek] s Beefsteak n
steal [stil] s—**it's a s.** (coll) das ist geschenkt ‖ v (pret **stole** [stol]; pp **stolen**) tr stehlen; (*a kiss*) rauben; **s. s.o.'s thunder** j–m den Wind aus den Segeln nehmen; **s. the show** den Vogel abschießen ‖ intr stehlen; **s.**

away wegstehlen; **s. up on s.o.** sich an j–n heranschleichen
stealth [stɛlθ] s—**by s.** heimlich
stealthy ['stɛlθi] adj verstohlen
steam [stim] s Dampf m; (*vapor*) Dunst m; (fig) Kraft f; **full s. ahead!** Volldampf voraus!; **let off s.** Dampf ablassen; (fig) sich [*dat*] Luft machen; **put on s.** (fig) Dampf dahinter machen ‖ tr dämpfen; (culin) dünsten; **s. up** beschlagen ‖ intr dampfen; (culin) dünsten; **s. up** sich beschlagen
steam' bath' s Dampfbad n
steam'boat' s Dampfer m
steam' en'gine s Dampfmaschine f
steamer ['stimər] s Dampfer m
steam' heat' s Dampfheizung f
steam' i'ron s Dampfbügeleisen n
steam' roll'er s (& fig) Dampfwalze f ‖ tr glattwalzen; (fig) niederwalzen
steam'ship' s Dampfschiff n
steam'ship line' s Dampfschiffahrtslinie f
steam' shov'el s Dampflöffelbagger m
steamy ['stimi] adj dampfig, dunstig
steed [stid] s Streitroß n
steel [stil] adj stählern, Stahl– ‖ s Stahl m ‖ tr stählen; **s. oneself against s.th.** sich gegen etw wappnen
steel' wool' s Stahlwolle f
steel'works' spl Stahlwerk n
steely ['stili] adj (fig) stählern
steelyard ['stiljərd] s Schnellwaage f
steep [stip] adj steil; (*prices*) happig ‖ tr (*immerse*) eintauchen; (*soak*) einweichen; **be steeped in** (*e.g., prejudice*) durchdrungen sein von; (*be expert in*) ein Kenner sein (*genit*); **s. oneself in** sich versenken in (*acc*)
steeple ['stipəl] s Kirchturm m
stee'plechase' s Hindernisrennen n
steer [stɪr] s Stier m ‖ tr lenken, steuern; **s. a middle course** e–n Mittelweg einschlagen ‖ intr lenken, steuern; **s. clear of** vermeiden
steerage ['stɪrɪdʒ] s Zwischendeck n
steer'ing wheel' s Steuerrad n
stellar ['stɛlər] adj (*role*) Star–; (*attraction*) Haupt–; (astr) Stern(en)–
stem [stem] s (*of a plant*) Halm m; (*of a word; of a tree*) Stamm m; (*of a leaf, fruit; of a glass; of a smoke pipe*) Stiel m; (*of a watch*) Aufziehwelle f; (naut) Steven m; **from s. to stern** von vorn bis achtern ‖ v (pret & pp **stemmed**; ger **stemming**) tr (*check*) hemmen; (*fruit*) entstielen; (*the flow*) (an)stauen; (*the blood*) stillen; (*in skiing*) stemmen ‖ intr—**s. from** (ab)stammen von
stench [stɛntʃ] s Gestank m
sten·cil ['stɛnsɪl] s (*for printing*) Schablone f; (*for typing*) Matrize f ‖ v (pret & pp **–cil**[l]**ed**; ger **–cil**[l]**ing**) tr mittels Schablone aufmalen
stenographer [stə'nɑgrəfər] s Stenograph –in mf
stenography [stə'nɑgrəfi] s Stenographie f
step [stɛp] s Schritt m; (*of a staircase*) Stufe f; (*footprint*) Fußtritt m;

(*measure*) Maßnahme *f;* **be out of s.** nicht Schritt halten; **in. s.** im Takt; **keep in s. with the times** mit der Zeit Schritt halten; **s. by s.** schrittweise; **watch your s.!** Vorsicht! ‖ *v* (*pret & pp* stepped; *ger* stepping) *tr*—**s. down** (elec) heruntertransformieren; **s. off** abschreiten ‖ *intr* schreiten, treten; **s. aside** beiseitetreten; **s. back** zurücktreten; **s. forward** vortreten; **s. on betreten; s. on it** (coll) sich beeilen; **s. on s.o.'s toes** (fig) j–m auf die Zehen treten; **s. out** hinausgehen; **s. out on** (*a marriage partner*) betrügen
step'broth'er *s* Stiefbruder *m*
step'child' *s* (–chil'dren) Stiefkind *n*
step'daugh'ter *s* Stieftochter *f*
step'fa'ther *s* Stiefvater *m*
step'lad'der *s* Stehleiter *f*
step'moth'er *s* Stiefmutter *f*
steppe [stɛp] *s* Steppe *f*
step'ping stone' *s* Trittstein *m;* (fig) Sprungbrett *n*
step'sis'ter *s* Stiefschwester *f*
step'son' *s* Stiefsohn *m*
stere•o ['stɛrɪˌo] *adj* Stereo– ‖ *s* (–os) (*sound*) Stereoton *m,* Raumton *m;* (*reproduction*) Raumtonwiedergabe *f;* (*set*) Stereoapparat *m*
stereotyped ['stɛrɪˌ-əˌtaɪpt] *adj* (& fig) stereotyp
sterile ['stɛrɪl] *adj* keimfrei
sterility [steˈrɪlɪti] *s* Sterilität *f*
sterilize ['stɛrɪˌlaɪz] *tr* sterilisieren
sterling ['stʌrlɪŋ] *adj* (fig) gediegen ‖ *s* (*currency*) Sterling *m;* (*sterling silver*) Sterlingsilber *n;* (*articles of sterling silver*) Sterlingsilberwaren *pl*
stern [stʌrn] *adj* streng; (*look*) finster ‖ *s* (naut) Heck *n*
stethoscope ['stɛθəˌskop] *s* Stethoskop *n*
stevedore ['stivəˌdor] *s* Stauer *m*
stew [st(j)u] *s* Ragout *n,* Stew *n* ‖ *tr & intr* dünsten; (& fig) schmoren
steward ['st(j)u•ərd] *s* (aer, naut) Steward *m;* (*of an estate*) Gutsverwalter *m;* (*of a club*) Tafelmeister *m*
stewardess ['st(j)u•ərdɪs] *s* (aer, naut) Stewardeß *f*
stewed' fruit' *s* Kompott *n*
stick [stɪk] *s* Stecken *m,* Stock *m;* (*for punishment*) Prügel *pl;* (*of candy or gum*) Stange *f;* **the sticks** (coll) die Provinz *f* ‖ *tr* (*with a sharp point; into one's pocket*) stecken; (*paste*) (**on**) ankleben (an *acc*); **s. it out** durchhalten; **s. one's finger** sich in den Finger stechen; **s. out** herausstrecken; **s. up** (sl) überfallen und berauben ‖ *intr* (*adhere*) kleben; (*be stuck, be tight*) klemmen; **nothing sticks in his mind** (coll) bei ihm bleibt nichts haften; **s. around** (coll) in der Nähe bleiben; **s. by** (coll) bleiben bei; **s. close to** sich heften an (*acc*); **s. out** (*said of ears*) abstehen; (*be visible*) heraushängen; **s. to** (fig) beharren auf (*dat*); **s. together** zusammenkleben; (fig) zusammenhalten; **s. up for** sich einsetzen für

sticker ['stɪkər] *s* Klebezettel *m*
stick'-in-the-mud' *s* (coll) Schlafmütze *f*
stickler ['stɪklər] *s* (**for**) Pedant *m* (in *dat*)
stick'pin' *s* Krawattennadel *f*
stick'-up' *s* (sl) Raubüberfall *m*
sticky ['stɪki] *adj* klebrig; (*air*) schwül; (*ticklish*) heikel
stiff [stɪf] *adj* steif; (*difficult*) schwer; (*drink*) stark; (*opposition*) hartnäckig; (*sentence*) streng; (*bearing*) steif; (*price*) hoch; **s. as a board** stocksteif ‖ *s* (*corpse*) (sl) Leiche *f;* **big s.** (sl) blöder Kerl *m*
stiffen ['stɪfən] *tr* versteifen ‖ *intr* sich versteifen
stiffly ['stɪfli] *adv* gezwungen
stiff'-necked' *adj* mit steifem Hals; (fig) eigensinnig
stifle ['staɪfəl] *tr* (*a yawn*) unterdrücken; (*a person*) ersticken
stig•ma ['stɪgmə] *s* (–mas & mata [mətə]) Brandmal *n;* **stigmata** Wundmale *pl* Christi
stigmatize ['stɪgməˌtaɪz] *tr* brandmarken
stile [staɪl] *s* Stiege *f*
stilet•to [stɪˈlɛto] *s* (–os) Stilett *n*
still [stɪl] *adj* still, ruhig ‖ *adv* (up to this time, as yet, even) noch; (yet, nevertheless) dennoch; **keep s.** stillbleiben ‖ *s* (*stillness*) Stille *f;* (*for whiskey*) Brennapparat *m;* (cin) Einzelphotographie *f;* (phot) Standphoto *n* ‖ *tr* stillen
still'born' *adj* totgeboren
still' life' *s* (**still lifes & still lives**) Stilleben *n*
stilt [stɪlt] *s* Stelze *f*
stilt'ed *adj* (*style*) geschraubt; (archit) auf Pfeilern ruhend
stimulant ['stɪmjələnt] *s* Reizmittel *n;* **act as a s.** anregend wirken
stimulate ['stɪmjəˌlet] *tr* anregen
stimulation [ˌstɪmjəˈleʃən] *s* Anregung *f*
stimu•lus ['stɪmjələs] *s* (–li [ˌlaɪ]) (& fig) Reizmittel *n;* (fig) Ansporn *m*
sting [stɪŋ] *s* Biß *m,* Stich *m;* (*sting-ing organ*) Stachel *m* ‖ *v* (*pret & pp* stung [stʌŋ]) *tr & intr* stechen
stingy ['stɪndʒi] *adj* geizig
stink [stɪŋk] *s* Gestank *m;* (sl) Krach *m* ‖ *v* (*pret* stank [stæŋk]; **stunk** [stʌŋk]) *tr*—**s. up** verstänkern ‖ *intr* stinken
stinker ['stɪŋkər] *s* (sl) Stinker *m*
stinky ['stɪŋki] *adj* stinkend, stinkig
stint [stɪnt] *s* bestimmte Arbeit *f;* **without s.** freigebig ‖ *tr* einschränken ‖ *intr* (**on**) knausern (mit)
stipend ['staɪpənd] *s* (*salary*) Gehalt *n;* (*of a scholarship*) Zuwendung *f*
stipple ['stɪpəl] *tr* punktieren
stipulate ['stɪpjəˌlet] *tr* bedingen; **as stipulated** wie vertraglich festgelegt
stipulation [ˌstɪpjəˈleʃən] *s* Bedingung *f*
stir [stʌr] *s* (*movement*) Bewegung *f;* (*unrest*) Unruhe *f;* (*commotion, ex-*

citement) Aufsehen *n;* **create quite a s.** großes Aufsehen erregen ‖ *v* (*pret & pp* **stirred; ger stirring**) *tr e.g., with a spoon*) (um)rühren; (*said of a breeze*) bewegen; (*the fire*) schüren; **s. up** (*hatred*) entfachen; (*trouble*) stiften; (*people*) aufhetzen ‖ *intr* sich rühren

stir'ring *adj* erregend; (*times*) bewegt; (*speech*) mitreißend; (*song*) schwungvoll

stirrup ['stʌrəp] *s* Steigbügel *m*

stitch [stɪtʃ] *s* Stich *m;* (*in knitting*) Masche *f;* **stitches** (surg) Naht *f;* **s. in the side** Seitenstechen *n* ‖ *tr* heften; (surg) nähen

stock [stɑk] *s* (*supplies*) Lager *n;* (*of a gun*) Schaft *m;* (*lineage*) Zucht *f;* (*of paper*) Papierstoff *m;* (culin) Fond *m;* (st. exch.) Aktie *f;* **in s.** vorrätig, auf Lager; **not put much s. in** nicht viel Wert legen auf (*acc*); **out of s.** nicht (mehr) vorrätig; (*books*) vergriffen; **stocks** (hist) Stock *m;* **take s.** den Bestand aufnehmen; **take s. of** (fig) in Betracht ziehen ‖ *tr* auf Lager halten; (*a stream*) (mit Fischen) besetzen; (*a farm*) ausstatten ‖ *intr*—**s. up (on)** sich eindrecken (mit)

stockade [stɑ'ked] *s* Palisade *f;* (mil) Gefängnis *n*

stock'breed'er *s* Viehzüchter –in *mf*

stock'brok'er *s* Börsenmakler –in *mf*

stock' car' *s* (aut) Serienwagen *m;* (sport) als Rennwagen hergerichteter Personenkraftwagen *m*

stock' com'pany *s* (com) Aktiengesellschaft *f;* (theat) Repertoiregruppe *f*

stock' div'idend *s* Aktiendividende *f*

stock' exchange' *s* Börse *f*

stock'hold'er *s* Aktionär –in *mf*

stock'ing *s* Strumpf *m*

stock' in trade' *s* Warenbestand *m;* (fig) Rüstzeug *n*

stock'pile' *s* Vorrat *m* ‖ *tr* aufstapeln

stock'room' *s* Lagerraum *m*

stocky ['stɑki] *adj* untersetzt

stock'yard' *s* Viehhof *m*

stodgy ['stɑdʒi] *adj* gezwungen

stogy ['stogi] *s* (coll) Glimmstengel *m*

stoic ['sto·ɪk] *adj* stoisch ‖ *s* Stoiker *m*

stoke [stok] *tr* (*a fire*) schüren; (*a furnace*) heizen

stoker ['stokər] *s* Heizer *m*

stole [stol] *s* (*woman's fur piece*) Pelzstola *f;* (eccl) Stola *f*

stolid ['stɑlɪd] *adj* unempfindlich

stomach ['stʌmək] *s* Magen *m;* (fig) (**for**) Lust *f* (zu) ‖ *tr* (*food*) verdauen; (fig) vertragen

stom'ach ache' *s* Magenschmerzen *pl*

stone [ston] *adj* steinern ‖ *s* Stein *m;* (*of fruit*) Kern *m;* (pathol) Stein *m* ‖ *tr* steinigen; (*fruit*) entsteinen

stone' age' *s* Steinzeit *f*

stone'-broke' *adj* (coll) völlig abgebrannt

stone'-deaf' *adj* stocktaub

stone' ma'son *s* Steinmetz *m*

stone' quar'ry *s* Steinbruch *m*

stone's' throw' *s* Katzensprung *m*

stony ['stoni] *adj* steinig

stooge [studʒ] *s* Lakai *m*

stool [stul] *s* Schemel *m;* (*e.g., at a bar*) Hocker *m;* (*bowel movement*) Stuhl *m*

stool' pi'geon *s* Polizeispitzel *m*

stoop [stup] *s* Beugung *f;* (*condition of the body*) gebeugte Körperhaltung *f;* (*porch*) kleine Verande *f* ‖ *intr* sich bücken; (*demean oneself*) sich erniedrigen

stoop'-shoul'dered *adj* gebeugt

stop [stɑp] *s* (*for a bus or streetcar*) Haltestelle *f;* (*layover*) Aufenthalt *m;* (*station*) Station *f;* (*of an organ*) Register *m;* (ling) Verschlußlaut *m;* **bring to a s.** zum Halten bringen; **come to a s.** anhalten; **put a s. to** ein Ende machen (*dat*) ‖ *v* (*pret & pp* **stopped; ger stopping**) *tr* (*an activity*) aufhören mit; (*ger*) aufhören (zu *inf*); (*e.g., a thief, car*) anhalten; (*bring to a stop with difficulty*) zum Halten bringen; (*delay, detain*) aufhalten; (*a leak*) stopfen; (*a check*) sperren; (*payment*) einstellen; (*the blood*) stillen; (*traffic*) lahmlegen; **s. down** (phot) abblenden; **s. s.o. from** (*ger*) j–n davonhalten zu (*inf*) ‖ *intr* (*cease*) aufhören; (*come to a stop; break down*) stehenbleiben; (*said of a person stopping for a short time or of a vehicle at an unscheduled stop*) anhalten; (*said of a vehicle at a scheduled stop*) halten; **s. at nothing** vor nichts zurückschrecken; **s. dead** plötzlich stehenbleiben; **s. in** vorbeikommen; **s. off** at e–n kurzen Halt machen bei

stop'gap' *adj* Not–, Behelfs– ‖ *s* Notbehelf *m*

stop'light' *s* (*on a car*) Bremslicht *n;* (*traffic light*) Verkehrsampel *f*

stop'o'ver *s* Fahrtunterbrechung *f;* (aer) Zwischenlandung *f*

stoppage ['stɑpɪdʒ] *s* (*of a pipe*) Verstopfung *f;* (*of payment, of work*) Einstellung *f;* (pathol) Verstopfung *f*

stopper ['stɑpər] *s* Stöpsel *m;* (*made of cork*) Korken *m*

stop' sign' *s* Haltezeichen *n*

stop'watch' *s* Stoppuhr *f*

storage ['storɪdʒ] *s* Lagerung *f*

stor'age bat'tery *s* Akkumulator *m*

stor'age charge' *s* Lagergebühr *f*

stor'age room' *s* Rumpelkammer *f;* (com) Lagerraum *m*

stor'age tank' *s* Sammelbehälter *m*

store [stor] *s* (*small shop*) Laden *m;* (*large shop*) Geschäft *n;* (*supply*) Vorrat *m;* **be in s. for** bevorstehen (*dat*); **have in s. for** bereithalten für; **set great s. by** viel Wert legen auf (*acc*); **s. of knowledge** Wissenschatz *m* ‖ *tr* einlagern; (*in the attic*) auf den Speicher stellen; **s. up** aufspeichern

store'house' *s* Lagerhaus *n;* (fig) Schatz *m,* Fundgrube *f*

store'keep'er *s* Ladeninhaber –in *mf*

store'room' s Lagerraum m, Vorratsraum m
stork [stɔrk] s Storch m
storm [stɔrm] s Sturm m; (thunderstorm) Gewitter n; (fig) Sturm m; **take by s.** (& fig) im Sturm nehmen || tr (er)stürmen || intr stürmen
storm' cloud' s Gewitterwolke f
storm' door' s Doppeltür f
storm' warn'ing s Sturmwarnung f
storm' win'dow s Doppelfenster n
stormy ['stɔrmi] adj stürmisch
story ['stori] s Geschichte f; (floor) Stock m, Stockwerk n; **that's another s.** das ist e-e Sache für sich
sto'rybook' s Geschichtenbuch n
sto'rytell'er s Erzähler –in mf
stout [staut] adj beleibt; (heart) tapfer || s Starkbier n
stout'-heart'ed adj beherzt
stove [stov] s Ofen m, Küchenherd m
stove'pipe' s Ofenrohr n; (coll) Angströhre f
stow [sto] tr stauen; **s. away** verstauen || intr—s. away als blinder Passagier mitreisen
stowage ['sto·idʒ] s Stauen n; (costs) Staugebühr f
stow'away' s blinder Passagier m
straddle ['strædəl] tr mit gespreizten Beinen sitzen auf (dat)
strafe [stref] tr im Tiefflug mit Bordwaffen angreifen
straggle ['strægəl] intr abschweifen
straggler ['stræglər] s Nachzügler –in mf; (mil) Versprengte m
straight [stret] adj gerade; (honest) aufrecht; (candid) offen; (hair) glatt; (story) wahr; (uninterrupted) unterbrochen; (whiskey) unverdünnt || adv (directly) direkt; (without interruption) ununterbrochen; **give it to s.o. s.** j–m die ungeschminkte Wahrheit sagen; **go s.** (fig) seinen geraden Weg gehen; **is my hat on s.?** sitzt mein Hut richtig?; **make s. for** zuhalten auf (acc); **set the record s.** den Sachverhalt klarstellen; **s. ahead** (immer) geradeaus; **s. as an arrow** pfeilgerade; **s. from the horse's mouth** (coll) aus erster Hand; **s. home** schnurstracks nach Hause; **s. off** ohne weiteres || s (cards) Buch n
straight'away' adv geradewegs, sofort || s (sport) Gerade f
straighten ['stretən] tr gerade machen; (e.g., a tablecloth) glattziehen; **s. out** (fig) wieder in Ordnung bringen; **s. s.o.'s tie** j–m die Krawatte zurechtrücken; **s. up** (a room) aufräumen || intr gerade werden; **s. up** sich aufrichten
straight' face' s—**keep a s.** keine Miene verziehen
straight'for'ward adj aufrichtig
straight' left' s (box) linke Gerade f
straight' man' s Stichwortgeber m
straight' ra'zor s Rasiermesser n
straight' right' s (box) rechte Gerade f
straight'way' adv auf der Stelle
strain [stren] s Belastung f; (of a muscle or tendon) Zerrung f; (task re-

quiring effort) (coll) Strapaze f; (stock, family) Linie f; (trait) Erbeigenschaft f; (bot) Art f; **without s.** mühelos || tr (filter) durchseihen; (the eyes, nerves) überanstrengen; **s. oneself** (make a great effort) sich überanstrengen; (in lifting) sich überheben; **s. the truth** übertreiben || intr sich anstrengen; **s. after** sich abmühen um; **s. at** ziehen an (dat), zerren an (dat)
strained adj (smile) gezwungen; (relations) gespannt
strainer ['strenər] s Seiher m, Filter m
strait [stret] s Straße f; **financial straits** finanzielle Schwierigkeiten pl; **straits** Meerenge f
strait' jack'et s Zwangsjacke f
strait'-laced' adj sittenstreng
strand [strænd] s Strähne f; (beach) Strand m; **s. of pearls** Perlenschnur f || tr auf den Strand setzen; (fig) stranden lassen; **be stranded** (fig) in der Patsche sitzen; **get stranded** auflaufen; **leave s.o. stranded** j–n im Stich lassen
strange [strendʒ] adj (quaint) sonderbar; (foreign) fremd; **s. character** Sonderling m || adv—**s. to say** merkwürdigerweise
stranger ['strendʒər] s Fremde mf
strangle ['stræŋgəl] tr erwürgen || intr ersticken
stran'glehold' s Würgegriff m
strap [stræp] s Riemen m, Gurt m; (of metal) Band n || v (pret & pp strapped; ger strapping) tr (to) anschnallen (an acc); (a razor) abziehen
strap'ping adj stramm
stratagem ['strætədʒəm] s Kriegslist f
strategic(al) [strə'tidʒɪk(əl)] adj strategisch
strategist ['strætɪdʒɪst] s Stratege m
strategy ['strætɪdʒi] s Strategie f
stratification [,strætɪfɪ'keʃən] s Schichtung f
strati·fy ['strætɪ,faɪ] v (pret & pp -fied) tr schichten || intr Schichten bilden
stratosphere ['strætə,sfɪr] s Stratosphäre f
stra·tum ['stretəm], ['strætəm] s (-ta [tə] & -tums) Schicht f
straw [strɔ] adj (e.g., hat, man, mat) Stroh– || s Stroh n; (single stalk; for drinking) Strohhalm m; **that's the last s.!** das schlägt dem Faß den Boden aus!
straw'ber'ry s Erdbeere f
straw'berry blond' adj rotblond
straw' mat'tress s Strohsack m
straw' vote' s Probeabstimmung f
stray [stre] adj (e.g., bullet) verirrt; (cat, dog) streunend; **s. shell** (mil) Ausreißer m || s verirrtes Tier n || intr herumirren; (fig) abschweifen
streak [strik] s Streifen m; **like a s.** wie der Blitz; **s. of bad luck** Pechsträhne f; **s. of luck** Glückssträhne f; **s. of light** Lichtstreifen m || tr streifen || intr streifig werden; **s. along** vorbeisausen

streaky ['striki] *adj* gestreift; *(uneven)* (coll) ungleich(mäßig)

stream [strim] *s* Fluß *m; (of people, cars, air, blood, lava)* Strom *m; (of words)* Schwall *m; (of tears)* Flut *f; (of a liquid)* Strahl *m* ‖ *intr* (aus)-strömen

streamer ['strimər] *s (pennant)* Wimpel *m; (ribbon)* herabhängendes Band *n; (rolled crepe paper)* Papierschlange *f*

stream'line' *tr* in Stromlinienform bringen; (fig) reorganizieren

stream'lined' *adj* stromlinienförmig

street [strit] *s* Straße *f*

street'car' *s* Straßenbahn *f*

street' clean'er *s* Straßenkehrer –in *mf; (truck)* Straßenkehrmaschine *f*

street' fight' *s* Straßenschlacht *f*

street'light' *s* Straßenlaterne *f*

street' sign' *s* Straßenschild *n*

street' ven'dor *s* Straßenhändler –in *mf*

street'walk'er *s* Straßendirne *f*

strength [strɛŋθ] *s* Kraft *f; (strong point; potency of alcohol; moral or mental power)* Stärke *f;* (mil) Kopfstärke *f;* **bodily s.** Körperkraft *f;* **on the s.** of auf Grund *(genit)*

strengthen ['strɛŋθən] *tr* stärken; (fig) bestärken ‖ *intr* stärker werden

strenuous ['strɛnjuˌəs] *adj* anstrengend; **s. effort** Kraftanstrengung *f*

stress [strɛs] *s (emphasis, weight)* Nachdruck *m; (mental)* Belastung *f;* (mus, pros) Ton *m,* Betonung *f;* (phys) Beanspruchung *f,* Spannung *f* ‖ *tr* (& mus, pros) betonen

stress' ac'cent *s* Betonungsakzent *m*

stress' mark' *s* Betonungszeichen *n*

stretch [strɛtʃ] *s (of road)* Strecke *f; (of the limbs)* Strecken *n; (of water)* Fläche *f; (of a racetrack)* Gerade *f; (of years)* Zeitspanne *f;* **do a s.** (sl) brummen; **in one s.** in e–m Zug ‖ *tr (a rope)* spannen; *(one's neck)* rekken; *(shoes, gloves)* ausdehnen; *(wire)* ziehen; *(strings of an instrument)* straffziehen; **s. a point** es nicht allzu genau nehmen; **s. oneself** sich strecken; **s. one's legs** sich [*dat*] die Beine vertreten; **s. out** *(e.g., hands)* ausstrecken ‖ *intr* sich (aus)-dehnen; *(said of a person)* sich strecken; **s. out on** sich ausstrecken auf *(dat)*

stretcher ['strɛtʃər] *s* Tragbahre *f*

stretch'erbear'er *s* Krankenträger *m*

strew [stru] *v (pret* **strewed;** *pp* **strewed & strewn)** *tr* (aus)streuen; **s. with** bestreuen mit

stricken ['strɪkən] *adj* **(with** *e.g., misfortune)* heimgesucht (von); **(with** *e.g., fear, grief)* ergriffen (von); **(with** *a disease)* befallen (von)

strict [strɪkt] *adj* streng; **in s. con-fidence** streng vertraulich

strictly ['strɪktli] *adv* streng; **s. speaking** genau genommen

stricture ['strɪktʃər] *s* **(on)** kritische Bemerkung *f* (über *acc*)

stride [straɪd] *s* Schritt *m;* **hit one's s.** auf Touren kommen; **make great**

strides große Fortschritte machen; **take in s.** ruhig hinnehmen ‖ *v (pret* **strode** [strod]; *pp* **stridden** ['strɪdən]) *intr* schreiten; **s. along** tüchig ausschreiten

strident ['straɪdənt] *adj* schrill

strife [straɪf] *s* Streit *m,* Hader *m*

strike [straɪk] *s (work stoppage)* Streik *m; (blow)* Schlag *m; (discovery, e.g., of oil)* Fund *m;* (baseball) Fehlschlag *m;* **go on s.** in Streik treten ‖ *v (pret & pp* **struck** [strʌk]) *tr (a person, the hours, coins, strings of an instrument)* schlagen; *(a match)* anstreichen; *(a bargain)* schließen; *(a note)* greifen; **(go on strike against)** bestreiken; *(a tent)* abbrechen; *(oil)* stoßen auf *(acc); (run into)* auffahren auf *(acc); (s.o. blind, dumb)* machen; *(s.o. with fear)* erfüllen; *(a blow)* versetzen; *(a pose)* einnehmen; *(seem to s.o.)* erscheinen *(dat);* **s. it rich** auf e–e Goldader stoßen; **s. fear into s.o.** j–m e–n Schrecken einjagen; **s. up** *(a conversation, an acquaintance)* anknüpfen; *(a song)* anstimmen ‖ *intr (said of a person or clock)* schlagen; *(said of workers)* streiken; *(said of lightning)* einschlagen; **s. home** Eindruck machen; **s. out** (& fig) fehlschlagen

strike'break'er *s* Streikbrecher –in *mf*

striker ['straɪkər] *s* Streikende *mf*

strik'ing *adj* auffallend; *(example)* treffend; *(workers)* streikend

strik'ing pow'er *s* Schlagkraft *f*

string [strɪŋ] *s* Bindfaden *m; (row, series)* Reihe *f; (of a bow)* Sehne *f; (of a musical instrument)* Saite *f;* **pull strings** (fig) der Drahtzieher sein; **s. of pearls** Perlenkette *f;* **strings** (mus) Streicher *pl;* **with no strings attached** ohne einschränkende Bedingungen ‖ *v (pret & pp* **strung** [strʌŋ]) *tr (pearls)* auf e–e Schnur (auf)reihen; *(a bow)* spannen; **s. along** hinhalten; **s. up** (coll) aufknüpfen

string' band' *s* Streichorchester *n*

string' bean' *s* grüne Bohne *f; (tall, thin person)* Bohnenstange *f*

stringed' in'strument *s* Saiteninstrument *n*

stringent ['strɪndʒənt] *adj* streng

string' quartet' *s* Streichquartett *n*

stringy ['strɪŋi] *adj (vegetables)* holzig; *(meat)* sehnig; *(hair)* zottelig

strip [strɪp] *s* Streifen *m* ‖ *v (pret & pp* **stripped;** *ger* **stripping)** *tr* (off) abziehen; *(clothes)* (off) abstreifen; *(a thread)* überdrehen; *(gears)* beschädigen; **s. down** abmontieren; **s. s.o. of office** j–n seines Amtes entkleiden ‖ *intr* sich ausziehen

stripe [straɪp] *s* Streifen *m; (elongated welt)* Striemen *m;* (mil) Tresse *f* ‖ *tr* streifen

strip' mine' *s* Tagebau *m*

stripper ['strɪpər] *s* Stripperin *f*

strip'tease' *s* Entkleidungsnummer *f*

stripteaser ['strɪpˌtizər] *s* Stripperin *f*

strive [straɪv] *v (pret* **strove** [strov];

pp **striven** ['strɪvən]) *intr* (**for**) streben (nach); **s. to** (*inf*) sich bemühen zu (*inf*)

stroke [strok] *s* Schlag *m;* (*caress with the hand*) Streicheln *n;* (*of a piston*) Hub *m;* (*of a pen, brush*) Strich *m;* (*of a sword*) Hieb *m;* (*in swimming*) Schwimmstoß *m;* (*of the leg*) Beinstoß *m;* (*of an oar*) Schlag *m;* (*pathol*) Schlaganfall *m;* **at a single s.** mit e–m Schlag; **at the s. of twelve** Schlag zwölf Uhr; **not do a s. of work** keinen Strich tun; **she'll have a s.** (coll) dann trifft sie der Schlag; **s. of genius** Genieblitz *m;* **s. of luck** Glücksfall *m;* **with a s. of the pen** mit e–m Federstrich ‖ *tr* streicheln

stroll [strol] *s* Spaziergang *m* ‖ *intr* spazieren

stroller ['strolər] *s* Spaziergänger –in *mf;* (*for a baby*) Kindersportwagen *m*

strong [strɔŋ] *adj* kräftig; (*firm*) fest; (*drink, smell, light, wind, feeling*) stark; (*glasses*) scharf; (*wine*) schwer; (*suspicion*) dringend; (*memory*) gut; (*candidate*) aussichtsreich; (*argument*) triftig

strong'-arm' *adj* (*e.g., methods*) Zwangs–

strong'box' *s* Geldschrank *m*

strong'hold' *s* Feste *f;* (fig) Hochburg *f*

strong' lan'guage *s* Kraftausdrücke *pl*

strongly ['strɔŋli] *adv* nachdrücklich; **feel s. about** sich sehr einsetzen für

strong'-mind'ed *adj* willensstark

strontium ['stranʃɪ·əm] *s* Strontium *n*

strop [strɑp] *s* Streichriemen *m* ‖ *v* (*pret & pp* **stropped;** *ger* **stropping**) *tr* abziehen

strophe ['strofi] *s* Strophe *f*

structural ['strʌktʃərəl] *adj* strukturell, Bau–

structure ['strʌktʃər] *s* Struktur *f;* (*building*) Bau *m*

struggle ['strʌgəl] *s* Kampf *m* ‖ *intr* (**for**) kämpfen (um); **s. against** ankämpfen gegen; **s. to one's feet** sich mit Mühe erheben

strum [strʌm] *v* (*pret & pp* **strummed;** *ger* **strumming**) *tr* klimpern auf (*dat*)

strumpet ['strʌmpɪt] *s* Dirne *f*

strut [strʌt] *s* (*brace*) Strebebalken *m;* (*haughty walk*) stolzer Gang *m* ‖ *v* (*pret & pp* **strutted;** *ger* **strutting**) *intr* stolzieren

strychnine ['strɪknaɪn] *s* Strychnin *n*

stub [stʌb] *s* (*of a checkbook*) Abschnitt *m;* (*of a ticket*) Kontrollabschnitt *m;* (*of a candle, pencil, cigarette*) Stummel *m* ‖ *v* (*pret & pp* **stubbed;** *ger* **stubbing**) *tr*—**s. one's toe** sich an der Zehe stoßen

stubble ['stʌbəl] *s* Stoppel *f;* (*facial hair*) Bartstoppeln *pl*

stubbly ['stʌbli] *adj* stopp(e)lig

stubborn ['stʌbərn] *adj* eigensinnig; (*e.g., resistance*) hartnäckig; (*hair*) widerspenstig

stubby ['stʌbi] *adj* kurz und dick; (*person*) untersetzt

stuc·co ['stʌko] *s* (**–coes & –cos**) Verputz *m* ‖ *tr* verputzen

stuc'co work' *s* Verputzarbeit *f*

stuck [stʌk] *adj*—**be s.** feststecken; (*said, e.g., of a lock*) klemmen; **be s. on** vernarrt sein in (*acc*); **get s.** steckenbleiben

stuck'-up' *adj* (coll) hochnäsig

stud [stʌd] *s* (*ornament*) Ziernagel *m;* (*horse*) Zuchthengst *m;* (*archit*) Wandpfosten *m* ‖ *v* (*pret & pp* **studded;** *ger* **studding**) *tr* mit Ziernägeln verzieren

stud' bolt' *s* Schraubenbolzen *m*

student ['st(j)udənt] *adj* Studenten– ‖ *s* (*in college*) Student –in *mf;* (*in grammar or high school*) Schüler –in *mf;* (*scholar*) Gelehrte *mf*

stu'dent bod'y *s* Studentenschaft *f*

stu'dent nurse' *s* Krankenpflegerin *f* in Ausbildung

stud' farm' *s* Gestüt *n*

stud'horse' *s* Zuchthengst *m*

stud'ied *adj* gesucht

studi·o ['st(j)udɪ‚o] *s* (**–os**) (fa, phot) Atelier *n;* (cin, fa, phot, telv) Studio *n*

studious ['st(j)udɪ·əs] *adj* fleißig

stud·y ['stʌdi] *s* Studium *n;* (*room*) Studierzimmer *n;* (paint) Studie *f* ‖ *v* (*pret & pp* **–ied**) *tr & intr* studieren

stuff [stʌf] *s* Stoff *m;* (coll) Kram *m;* **do your s.!** (coll) schieß los!; **know one's s.** (coll) sich auskennen ‖ *tr* (*animals*) ausstopfen; (*a cushion*) polstern; (*e.g., cotton in the ears*) sich [*dat*] stopfen; (culin) füllen; **s. oneself** sich vollstopfen

stuffed' shirt' *s* steifer, eingebildeter Mensch *m*

stuff'ing *s* Polstermaterial *n;* (culin) Fülle *f*

stuffy ['stʌfi] *adj* (*room*) stickig; (*nose*) verstopft; (*person*) steif

stumble ['stʌmbəl] *intr* stolpern; (*in reading*) holpern; **s. across** stoßen auf (*acc*)

stum'bling block' *s* Stein *m* des Anstoßes

stump [stʌmp] *s* (*of an arm, tree, cigarette, pencil*) Stummel *m* ‖ *tr* (*a cigarette*) ausdrücken; (*nonplus*) verblüffen; (*a district, state*) als Wahlredner bereisen

stump' speak'er *s* Wahlredner –in *mf*

stun [stʌn] *v* (*pret & pp* **stunned;** *ger* **stunning**) *tr* betäuben

stun'ning *adj* (coll) phantastisch

stunt [stʌnt] *s* Kunststück *n;* **do stunts** Kunststücke vorführen ‖ *tr* hemmen

stunt'ed *adj* verkümmert

stunt' fly'ing *s* Kunstflug *m*

stunt' man' *s* (**men'**) Sensationsdarsteller *m*

stupe·fy ['st(j)upɪ‚faɪ] *v* (*pret & pp* **–fied**) *tr* verblüffen

stupendous [st(j)u'pɛndəs] *adj* erstaunlich

stupid ['st(j)upɪd] *adj* dumm, blöd

stupidity [st(j)u'pɪdɪti] *s* Dummheit *f*

stupor ['st(j)upər] *s* Stumpfsinn *m*

sturdy ['stʌrdi] *adj* (*person*) kräftig;

(*thing*) stabil; (*resolute*) standhaft; (*plant*) widerstandsfähig
sturgeon ['stʌrdʒən] *s* Stör *m*
stutter ['stʌtər] *s* Stottern *n* || *tr* & *intr* stottern
sty [staɪ] *s* Schweinestall *m*; (pathol) Gerstenkorn *n*
style [staɪl] *s* Stil *m*; (*manner*) Art *f*; (*fashion*) Mode *f*; (*cut of suit*) Schnitt *m*; **be in s.** in Mode sein; **go out of s.** veralten; **live in s.** auf großem Fuße leben || *tr* (*title*) betiteln; (*e.g., clothes*) gestalten; (*hair*) nach der Mode frisieren
stylish ['staɪlɪʃ] *adj* modisch; (*person*) modisch gekleidet
stylistic [staɪ'lɪstɪk] *adj* stilistisch
stymie ['staɪmi] *tr* vereiteln
styp'tic pen'cil ['stɪptɪk] *s* Alaunstift *m*
suave [swɑv] *adj* verbindlich
sub [sʌb] *s* (naut) U-boot *n*; (sport) Ersatzspieler –in *mf*
sub'chas'er *s* U-bootjäger *m*
sub'commit'tee *s* Unterausschuß *m*
subconscious [sʌb'kɑnʃəs] *adj* unterbewußt || *s* Unterbewußtsein *n*
sub'con'tinent *s* Subkontinent *m*
sub'con'tract *s* Nebenvertrag *m* || *tr* e–n Nebenvertrag abschließen über (*acc*)
sub'con'tractor *s* Unterlieferant –in *mf*
sub'divide', **sub'divide'** *tr* unterteilen || *intr* sich unterteilen
sub'divi'sion *s* (*act*) Unterteilung *f*; (*unit*) Unterabteilung *f*
subdue [sʌb'd(j)u] *tr* (*an enemy*) unterwerfen; (*one who is struggling*) überwältigen; (*light, sound*) dämpfen; (*feelings, impulses*) bändigen
sub'floor' *s* Blindboden *m*
sub'head' *s* Untertitel *m*
subject ['sʌbdʒɪkt] *adj* (**to**) untertan (*dat*); **be s. to** (*e.g., approval, another country*) abhängig sein von; (*e.g., colds*) neigen zu; (*e.g., laws of nature, change*) unterworfen sein (*dat*); **s. to change without notice** Änderungen vorbehalten || *s* Thema *n*; (*of a kingdom*) Untertan –in *mf*; (educ) Fach *n*; (fa) Vorwurf *m*; (gram) Satzgegenstand *m*, Subjekt *n*; (libr) Stichwort *n*; **change the s.** das Thema wechseln; **get off the s.** vom Thema abkommen || [sʌb'dʒɛkt] *tr* (& fig) unterwerfen (*dat*)
subjection [sʌb'dʒɛkʃən] *s* Unterwerfung *f*
subjective [sʌb'dʒɛktɪv] *adj* subjektiv; **s. case** Werfall *m*
sub'ject mat'ter *s* Inhalt *m*
subjugate ['sʌbdʒə‚get] *tr* unterjochen
subjunctive [sʌb'dʒʌŋktɪv] *adj* konjunktiv(isch) || *s* Konjunktiv *m*
sub'lease' *s* Untermiete *f* || **sub'lease'** *tr* & *intr* (*to s.o.*) untervermieten; (*from s.o.*) untermieten
sublet [sʌb'lɛt] *v* (*pret* & *pp* –**let**; *ger* –**letting**) *tr* & *intr* (*to s.o.*) untervermieten; (*from s.o.*) untermieten
sublimate ['sʌblɪmət] *s* (chem) Sublimat *n* || ['sʌblɪ‚met] *tr* sublimieren

sublime [sə'blaɪm] *adj* erhaben || *s* Erhabene *n*
submachine' gun' *s* Maschinenpistole *f*
sub'marine' *adj* U-boot– || *s* U-boot *n*
sub'marine' base' *s* U-bootstützpunkt *m*
submerge [səb'mʌrdʒ] *tr* & *intr* untertauchen; **ready to s.** tauchklar
submersion [səb'mʌrʒən] *s* Untertauchen *n*
submission [səb'mɪʃən] *s* (**to**) Unterwerfung *f* (unter *acc*); (*of a document*) Vorlage *f*; (*of a question*) Unterbreitung *f*
submissive [səb'mɪsɪv] *adj* unterwürfig
sub·mit [səb'mɪt] *v* (*pret* & *pp* –**mitted**; *ger* –**mitting**) *tr* (*a question*) unterbreiten; (*a document*) vorlegen; (*suggest*) der Ansicht sein || *intr* (**to**) sich unterwerfen (*dat*)
subordinate [səb'ɔrdɪnɪt] *adj* (*lower in rank*) untergeordnet; (*secondary*) Neben– || *s* Untergebene *mf* || [səb'ɔrdɪ‚net] *tr* (**to**) unterordnen (*dat*)
subor'dinate clause' *s* Nebensatz *m*
suborn [sə'bɔrn] *tr* verleiten; (*bribe*) bestechen
sub'plot' *s* Nebenhandlung *f*
subpoena [sʌb'pina] *s* Vorladung *f* || *tr* (unter Strafandrohung) vorladen
subscribe [səb'skraɪb] *tr* unterschreiben; (*money*) zeichnen || *intr*—**s. to** (*a newspaper*) abonnieren; (*to a series of volumes*) subskribieren; (*an idea*) billigen
subscriber [səb'skraɪbər] *s* Abonnent –in *mf*
subscription [səb'skrɪpʃən] *s* (**to**) Abonnement *n* (auf *acc*); (*to a series of volumes*) Subskription *f* (auf *acc*); **take out a s. to** sich abonnieren auf (*acc*)
sub'sec'tion *s* Unterabteilung *f*
subsequent ['sʌbsɪkwənt] *adj* (nach)folgend; **s. to** anschließend an (*acc*)
subsequently ['sʌbsɪkwəntli] *adv* anschließend
subservient [səb'sʌrvɪ·ənt] *adj* (**to**) unterwürfig (gegenüber *dat*)
subside [səb'saɪd] *intr* nachlassen; (geol) sich senken
subsidiary [səb'sɪdɪ‚ɛri] *adj* Tochter– || *s* Tochtergesellschaft *f*
subsidize ['sʌbsɪ‚daɪz] *tr* subventionieren
subsidy ['sʌbsɪdi] *s* Subvention *f*
subsist [səb'sɪst] *intr* (*exist*) existieren; **s. on** leben von
subsistence [səb'sɪstəns] *s* (*existence*) Dasein *n*; (*livelihood*) Lebensunterhalt *m*; (philos) Subsistenz *f*
subsist'ence allow'ance *s* Unterhaltszuschuß *m*
sub'soil' *s* Untergrund *m*
subsonic [səb'sɑnɪk] *adj* Unterschall–
sub'spe'cies *s* Unterart *f*
substance ['sʌbstəns] *s* Substanz *f*, Stoff *m*; **in s.** im wesentlichen
substand'ard *adj* unter dem Niveau
substantial [səb'stænʃəl] *adj* (*sum, amount*) beträchtlich; (*difference*)

wesentlich; (*meal*) kräftig; **be in s. agreement** im wesentlichen übereinstimmen

substantiate [səb'stænʃɪ‚et] *tr* begründen, nachweisen

substantive ['sʌbstəntɪv] *adj* wesentlich ‖ *s* (gram) Substantiv *m*

sub'sta'tion *s* Nebenstelle *f*; (*post-office*) Zweigpostamt *n*; (elec) Umspannwerk *n*

substitute ['sʌbstɪ‚t(j)ut] *s* (*person*) Stellvertreter –in *mf*; (*material*) Austauschstoff *m*; (pej) Ersatz *m*; (sport) Ersatzspieler –in *mf*; **act as a s. for** vertreten; **beware of substitutes** vor Nachamung wird gewarnt ‖ *tr*—**s. A for B** B durch A ersetzen ‖ *intr*—**s. for** einspringen für

sub'stitute teach'er *s* Aushilfslehrer –in *mf*

substitution [‚sʌbstɪ't(j)uʃən] *s* Einsetzung *f*; (chem, math, ling) Substitution *f*; (sport) Auswechseln *n*

sub'stra'tum *s* (–ta [tə] & –tums) Unterlage *f*; (biol) Nährboden *m*

sub'struc'ture *s* Unterbau *m*

subsume [sʌb'sjum] *tr* unterordnen

subterfuge ['sʌbtər‚fjudʒ] *s* Winkelzug *m*

subterranean [‚sʌbtə'renɪ‚ən] *adj* unterirdisch

sub'ti'tle *s* Untertitel *m*

subtle ['sʌtəl] *adj* fein; (*poison*) schleichend; (*cunning*) raffiniert

subtlety ['sʌtəlti] *s* Feinheit *f*

subtract [səb'trækt] *tr* subtrahieren

subtraction [səb'trækʃən] *s* Subtraktion *f*

suburb ['sʌbʌrb] *s* Vorstadt *f*, Vorort *m*; **the suburbs** der Stadtrand

suburban [sə'bʌrbən] *adj* Vorstadt–

suburbanite [sə'bʌrbə‚naɪt] *s* Vorstadtbewohner –in *mf*

subvention [səb'vɛnʃən] *s* Subvention *f*

subversion [səb'vʌrʒən] *s* Umsturz *m*

subversive [səb'vʌrsɪv] *adj* umstürzlerisch ‖ *s* Umstürzler –in *mf*

subver'sive activ'ity *s* Wühlarbeit *f*

subvert [səb'vʌrt] *tr* (*a government*) stürzen; (*the law*) umstoßen; (*corrupt*) (sittlich) verderben

sub'way' *s* U-Bahn *f*, Untergrundbahn *f*

succeed [sək'sid] *tr* folgen (*dat*) ‖ *intr* (*said of persons*) (**in**) Erfolg haben (mit); (*said of things*) gelingen; **I succeeded in** (*ger*) es gelang mir zu (*inf*); **not s.** mißglücken; **s. to the throne** die Thronfolge antreten

success [sək'sɛs] *s* Erfolg *m*; (*play, song, piece of merchandise*) Knüller *m*; **be a s.** Erfolg haben; **without s.** erfolglos

successful [sək'sɛsfəl] *adj* erfolgreich

succession [sək'sɛʃən] *s* Reihenfolge *f*; (*as heir*) Erbfolge *f*; **in s.** nacheinander; **s. to** (*e.g., an office, estate*) Übernahme *f* (*genit*)

successive [sək'sɛsɪv] *adj* aufeinanderfolgend

successor [sək'sɛsər] *s* Nachfolger –in

mf; **s. to the throne** Thronfolger –in *mf*

succor ['sʌkər] *s* Beistand *m* ‖ *tr* beistehen (*dat*)

succotash ['sʌkə‚tæʃ] *s* Gericht *n* aus Süßmais und grünen Bohnen

succulent ['sʌkjələnt] *adj* saftig

succumb [sə'kʌm] *intr* (**to**) erliegen (*dat*)

such [sʌtʃ] *adj* solch; **as s.** als solcher; **no s. thing** nichts dergleichen; **some s. thing** irgend so (et)was; **s. and s.** der und der; **s. as** wie (etwa); **s. a long time** so lange; **s. as it is wie es** nun einmal ist

suck [sʌk] *s* Saugen *n*; (*licking*) Lutschen *n* ‖ *tr* saugen; **s. in** einsaugen; (sl) reinlegen ‖ *intr* saugen; **s. on** (*e.g., candy*) lutschen

sucker ['sʌkər] *s* (coll) Gimpel *m*; (*carp*) Karpfenfisch *m*; (bot) Wurzelschößling *m*; (zool) Saugröhre *f*

suckle ['sʌkəl] *tr* stillen; (*animals*) säugen

suck'ling *s* Säugling *m*

suck'ling pig' *s* Spanferkel *n*

suction ['sʌkʃən] *s* Saugen *n*, Sog *m*

suc'tion cup' *s* Saugnapf *m*

suc'tion pump' *s* Saugpumpe *f*

sudden ['sʌdən] *adj* plötzlich, jäh; **all of a s.** (ganz) plötzlich

suddenly ['sʌdənli] *adv* plötzlich

suds [sʌdz] *spl* Seifenschaum *m*

sudsy ['sʌdzi] *adj* schaumig

sue [s(j)u] *tr* (**for**) verklagen (auf *acc*) ‖ *intr* (**for**) klagen (auf *acc*)

suede [swed] *adj* Wildleder– ‖ *s* Wildleder *n*

suet ['s(j)u‚ɪt] *s* Talg *m*

suffer ['sʌfər] *tr* erleiden; (*damage*) nehmen; (*put up with*) ertragen ‖ *intr* (**from**) leiden (an *dat*)

sufferance ['sʌfərəns] *s* stillschweigende Einwilligung *f*

suf'fering *s* Leiden *n*

suffice [sə'faɪs] *intr* ausreichen

sufficient [sə'fɪʃənt] *adj* (**for**) ausreichend (für)

suffix ['sʌfɪks] *s* Nachsilbe *f*

suffocate ['sʌfə‚ket] *tr* & *intr* ersticken

suffrage ['sʌfrɪdʒ] *s* Stimmrecht *n*

suffuse [sə'fjuz] *tr* übergießen

sugar ['ʃugər] *s* Zucker *m* ‖ *tr* zuckern

sug'ar beet' *s* Zuckerrübe *f*

sug'ar bowl' *s* Zuckerdose *f*

sug'ar cane' *s* Zuckerrohr *n*

sug'ar-coat' *tr* (& fig) überzuckern

sug'ar dad'dy *s* Geldonkel *m*

sug'ar ma'ple *s* Zuckerahorn *m*

sug'ar tongs' *spl* Zuckerzange *f*

sugary ['ʃugəri] *adj* zuckerig

suggest [səg'dʒɛst] *tr* vorschlagen; (*hint*) andeuten

suggestion [səg'dʒɛstʃən] *s* Vorschlag *m*

suggestive [səg'dʒɛstɪv] *adj* (*remark*) zweideutig; (*thought-provoking*) anregend; (*e.g., dress*) hauteng; **be s. of** erinnern an (*acc*)

suicidal [‚su·ɪ'saɪdəl] *adj* selbstmörderisch

suicide ['su·ɪ‚saɪd] *s* Selbstmord *m*;

(*person*) Selbstmörder –in *mf;* **commit s.** Selbstmord begehen

suit [sut] *s* (*men's*) Anzug *m;* (*women's*) Kostüm *n;* (cards) Farbe *f;* (jur) Prozeß *m;* **bring s.** (against) e–e Klage einbringen (gegen); **follow s.** Farbe bekennen; (fig) sich nach den anderen richten ‖ *tr* (*please*) passen (*dat*); (*correspond to*) entsprechen (*dat*); (*said, e.g., of colors, style*) gut passen (*dat*); **be suited for** sich eignen für; **s. s.th.** to etw anpassen (*dat*); **s. yourself!** wie Sie wollen!

suitable ['sutəbəl] *adj* (**to**) geeignet (für)

suit'case' *s* Handkoffer *m*

suit' coat' *s* Sakko *m & n*

suite [swit] *s* (*series of rooms*) Zimmerflucht *f;* (*set of furniture*) Zimmergarnitur *f;* (mus) Suite *f*

suitor ['sutər] *s* Freier *m*

sul'fa drug' *s* Sulfonamid *n*

sulfate ['sʌlfet] *s* Sulfat *n*

sulfide ['sʌlfaɪd] *s* Sulfid *n*

sulfur ['sʌlfər] *adj* Schwefel– ‖ *s* Schwefel *m* ‖ *tr* einschwefeln

sulfur'ic ac'id [sʌl'f(j)ʊrɪk] *s* Schwefelsäure *f*

sul'fur mine' *s* Schwefelgrube *f*

sulk [sʌlk] *intr* trotzen

sulky ['sʌlki] *adj* trotzend, mürrisch ‖ *s* (sport) Traberwagen *m*

sulk'y race' *s* Trabrennen *n*

sullen ['sʌlən] *adj* mißmutig

sul·ly ['sʌli] *v* (*pret & pp* –**lied**) *tr* besudeln

sulphur ['sʌlfər] var of **sulfur**

sultan ['sʌltən] *s* Sultan *m*

sultry ['sʌltri] *adj* schwül

sum [sʌm] *s* Summe *f,* Betrag *m;* **in sum** kurz gesagt ‖ *v* (*pret & pp* **summed;** *ger* **summing**)—**sum up** summieren; (*summarize*) zusammenfassen; (*make a quick estimate of*) kurz abschätzen

sumac, sumach ['ʃumæk] *s* Sumach *m*

summarize ['sʌmə,raɪz] *tr* zusammenfassen

summary ['sʌməri] *adj* summarisch ‖ *s* Zusammenfassung *f*

sum'mary court'martial *s* summarisches Militärgericht *n*

summer ['sʌmər] *s* Sommer *m*

sum'mer cot'tage *s* Sommerwohnung *f*

sum'mer resort' *s* Sommerfrische *f*

sum'mer school' *s* Sommerkurs *m*

sum'mertime' *s* Sommerzeit *f*

summery ['sʌməri] *adi* sommerlich

summit ['sʌmɪt] *s* (& fig) Gipfel *m*

sum'mit con'ference *s* Gipfelkonferenz *f*

sum'mit talks' *spl* Gipfelgespräche *pl*

summon ['sʌmən] *tr* (*e.g., a doctor*) kommen lassen; (*a conference*) einberufen; (jur) vorladen; **s. up** (*courage, strength*) aufbieten

summons ['sʌmənz] *s* (jur) Vorladung *f*

sumptuous ['sʌmptʃu·əs] *adj* üppig

sun [sʌn] *s* Sonne *f* ‖ *v* (*pret & pp* **sunned;** *ger* **sunning**) *tr* sonnen; **sun oneself** sich sonnen

sun' bath' *s* Sonnenbad *n*

sun'beam' *s* Sonnenstrahl *m*

sun'burn' *s* Sonnenbrand *m*

sun'burned' *adj* sonnverbrannt

sundae ['sʌnde] *s* Eisbecher *m* mit Sirup, Nüssen, Früchten und Schlagsahne

Sunday ['sʌnde] *adj* sonntäglich; **dressed in one's S.** best sonntäglich gekleidet ‖ *s* Sonntag *m;* **on S.** am Sonntag

Sun'day driv'er *s* Sonntagsfahrer –in *mf*

Sun'day school' *s* Sonntagsschule *f*

sunder ['sʌndər] *tr* trennen

sun'di'al *s* Sonnenuhr *f*

sun'down' *s* Sonnenuntergang *m*

sun'-drenched' *adj* sonnenüberflutet

sundries ['sʌndriz] *pl* Diverses *n*

sundry ['sʌndri] *adj* verschiedene

sun'fish' *s* Sonnenfisch *m*

sun'flow'er *s* Sonnenblume *f*

sun'glass'es *pl* Sonnenbrille *f*

sun' hel'met *s* Tropenhelm *m*

sunken ['sʌŋkən] *adj* (*ship*) gesunken; (*eyes; garden*) tiefliegend; (*treasure*) versunken; (*cheeks*) eingefallen; **s. rocks** blinde Klippe *f*

sun' lamp' *s* Höhensonne *f*

sun'light' *s* Sonnenlicht *n*

sunny ['sʌni] *adj* sonnig

sun'ny side' *s* Sonnenseite *f*

sun' par'lor *s* Glasveranda *f*

sun'rise' *s* Sonnenaufgang *m*

sun' roof' *s* (aut) Schiebedach *n*

sun'set' *s* Sonnenuntergang *m*

sun'shade' *s* Sonnenschirm *m;* (*awning*) Sonnendach *n;* (phot) Gegenlichtblende *f*

sun'shine' *s* Sonnenschein *m*

sun'spot' *s* Sonnenfleck *m*

sun'stroke' *s* Sonnenstich *m*

sun'tan' *s* Sonnenbräune *f*

sun'tanned' *adj* sonnengebräunt

sun' vis'or *s* (aut) Sonnenblende *f*

sup [sʌp] *v* (*pret & pp* **supped;** *ger* **supping**) *intr* zu Abend essen

super ['supər] *adj* (*oversized*) Super–; (sl) prima ‖ *s* (theat) Komparse *m*

su'perabun'dance *s* (of) Überfülle *f* (an *dat*)

su'perabun'dant *adj* überreichlich

superannuated [,supər'ænju,etɪd] *adj* (*person*) pensioniert; (*thing*) veraltet

superb [su'pɜrb] *adj* prachtvoll, herrlich

su'perbomb' *s* Superbombe *f*

su'perbomb'er *s* Riesenbomber *m*

supercilious [,supər'sɪlɪ·əs] *adj* hochnäsig

superficial [,supər'fɪʃəl] *adj* oberflächlich

superfluous [su'pʌrfluːəs] *adj* überflüssig

su'perhigh'way' *s* Autobahn *f*

su'perhu'man *adj* übermenschlich

su'perimpose' *tr* darüberlegen; (elec, phys) überlagern

su'perintend' *tr* die Aufsicht führen über (*acc*), beaufsichtigen

superintendent [,supərɪn'tendənt] *s* Oberaufseher –in *mf;* (*in industry*)

Betriebsleiter –in *mf;* (*of a factory*) Werksleiter –in *mf;* (*of a building*) Hausverwalter –in *mf;* (*educ*) Schulinspektor –in *mf*
superior [sə'pɪrɪ·ər] *adj* (*physically*) höher; (*in rank*) übergeordnet; (*quality*) hervorragend; **s. in** überlegen an (*dat*); **s. to** überlegen (*dat*) || *s* Vorgesetzte *mf*
supe'rior court' *s* Obergericht *n*
superiority [sə‚pɪrɪ'ɑrɪti] *s* (**in**) Überlegenheit *f* (in *dat,* an *dat*); (mil) Übermacht *f*
superlative [su'pʌrlətɪv] *adj* hervorragend; (gram) superlativisch, Superlativ– || *s* (gram) Superlativ *m*
su'perman' *s* (**–men'**) Übermensch *m*
su'permar'ket *s* Supermarkt *m*
su'pernat'ural *adj* übernatürlich || *s* Übernatürliche *n*
supersede [‚supər'sid] *tr* ersetzen
su'persen'sitive *adj* überempfindlich
su'person'ic *adj* Überschall–
superstition [‚supər'stɪʃən] *s* Aberglaube *m;* (*superstitious idea*) abergläubische Vorstellung *f*
superstitious [‚supər'stɪʃəs] *adj* abergläubisch
su'perstruc'ture *s* Überbau *m;* (*of a bridge*) Oberbau *m;* (*of a building or ship*) Aufbauten *pl*
supervise ['supər‚vaɪz] *tr* beaufsichtigen
supervision [‚supər'vɪʒən] *s* Beaufsichtigung *f*
supervisor ['supər‚vaɪzər] *s* Vorgesetzte *mf*
su'pine posi'tion ['supaɪn] *s* Rückenlage *f*
supper ['sʌpər] *s* Abendessen *n; eat s.* zu Abend essen
sup'pertime' *s* Abendbrotzeit *f*
supplant [sə'plænt] *tr* ersetzen
supple ['sʌpəl] *adj* geschmeidig; (*mind*) beweglich
supplement ['sʌplɪmənt] *s* (*e.g., to a diet*) (**to**) Ergänzung *f* (*genit*); (*to a writing*) Anhang *m;* (*to a newspaper*) Beilage *f* || ['sʌplɪ‚mɛnt] *tr* ergänzen
supplementary [‚sʌplɪ'mɛntəri] *adj* ergänzend
suppliant ['sʌplɪ·ənt] *adj* flehend || *s* Bittsteller –in *mf*
supplicant ['sʌplɪkənt] *s* Bittsteller –in *mf*
supplicate ['sʌplɪ‚ket] *tr* flehen
supplication [‚sʌplɪ'keʃən] *s* Flehen *n*
supplier [sə'plaɪ·ər] *s* Lieferant –in *mf*
sup•ply [sə'plaɪ] *s* (*supplying*) Versorgung *f;* (*stock*) (**of**) Vorrat *m* (an *dat*); (com) Angebot *n;* **supplies** Vorräte *pl;* (*e.g., office supplies, dental supplies*) Bedarfsartikel *pl;* (mil) Nachschub *m* || *v* (*pret & pp* **–plied**) *tr* (**with**) versorgen (mit); (*deliver*) liefern; (*procure*) beschaffen; (*with a truck*) zuführen; (*equip*) (**with**) versehen (mit); (*a demand*) befriedigen; (*a loss*) ausgleichen; (*missing words*) ergänzen; (mil) mit Nachschub versorgen

supply' and demand' *spl* Angebot *n* und Nachfrage *f*
supply' base' *s* Nachschubstützpunkt *m*
supply' line' *s* Versorgungsweg *m;* (mil) Nachschubweg *m*
support [sə'port] *adj* Hilfs– || *s* (*prop, brace, stay; person*) Stütze *f;* (*of a family*) Unterhalt *m;* **in s. of** zur Unterstützung (*genit*); **without s.** (*unsubstantiated*) haltlos; (*unprovided*) unversorgt; **with the s. of** mit dem Beistand von || *tr* stützen, tragen; (*back*) unterstützen; (*a family*) erhalten; (*a charge*) erhärten; (*a claim*) begründen
supporter [sə'portər] *s* (*of a family*) Ernährer –in *mf;* (*backer*) Förderer –in *mf;* (*jockstrap*) Suspensorium *n*
support'ing role' *s* Nebenrolle *f*
suppose [sə'poz] *tr* annehmen; **be supposed to** sollen; **I s. so** ich glaube schon; **s. it rains** gesetzt den Fall (or angenommen), es regnet; **s. we take a walk** wie wäre es, wenn wir e–n Spaziergang machten?; **what is that supposed to mean?** was soll das bedeuten? || *intr* vermuten
supposed' *adj* mutmaßlich
supposedly [sə'pozɪdli] *adv* angeblich
supposition [‚sʌpə'zɪʃən] *s* Annahme *f*
suppository [sə'pɑzɪ‚tori] *s* Zäpfchen *n*
suppress [sə'prɛs] *tr* unterdrücken; (*news, scandal*) verheimlichen
suppression [sə'prɛʃən] *s* Unterdrükkung *f;* (*of news, truth, scandal*) Verheimlichung *f*
suppurate ['sʌpjə‚ret] *intr* eitern
supremacy [sə'prɛməsi] *s* Oberherrschaft *f*
supreme [sə'prim] *adj* Ober–, höchste
supreme' author'ity *s* Obergewalt *f*
Supreme' Be'ing *s* höchstes Wesen *n*
supreme' command' *s* Oberkommando *n;* **have s.** den Oberbefehl führen
supreme' command'er *s* oberster Befehlshaber *m*
Supreme' Court' *s* Oberster Gerichtshof *m*
surcharge ['sʌr‚tʃɑrdʒ] *s* (**on**) Zuschlag *m* (zu)
sure [ʃur] *adj* sicher, gewiß; (*shot, cure*) unfehlbar; (*shot, footing, ground, way, proof*) sicher; **are you s. you won't come?** kommen Sie wirklich nicht?; **be s. of** sicher sein (*genit*); **be s. to** (*inf*) vergiß nicht zu (*inf*); **feel s. of oneself** s–r selbst sicher sein; **for s.** sicherlich; **she is s. to come** sie wird sicher(lich) kommen; **s. enough** wirklich; **to be s.** (*parenthetically*) zwar
sure'-foot'ed *adj* trittsicher
surely ['ʃurli] *adv* sicher(lich), gewiß
surety ['ʃur(ɪ)ti] *s* Bürgschaft *f;* **stand s.** (**for**) bürgen (für)
surf [sʌrf] *s* Brandung *f* || *intr* wellenreiten
surface ['sʌrfɪs] *adj* (*superficial*) oberflächlich; (*apparent rather than real*)

Schein– ‖ *s* Oberfläche *f; (of a road)* Belag *m;* (aer) Tragfläche *f;* **on the s.** oberflächlich (betrachtet) ‖ *tr (a road)* mit e–m Belag versehen ‖ *intr* auftauchen
sur'face mail' *s* gewöhnliche Post *f*
sur'face-to-air' **mis'sile** *s* Boden-Luft-Rakete *f*
sur'face-to-sur'face **mis'sile** *s* Boden-Boden-Rakete *f*
surf'board' *s* Wellenreiterbrett *n*
surf'board'ing *s* Wellenreiten *n*
surfeit ['sʌrfɪt] *s* Übersättigung *f* ‖ *tr* übersättigen
surfer ['sʌrfər] *s* Wellenreiter –in *mf*
surf'ing *s* Wellenreiten *n*
surge [sʌrdʒ] *s (forward rush of a wave or crowd)* Wogen *n; (swelling wave)* Woge *f; (swelling sea)* Wogen *n;* (elec) Stromstoß *m* ‖ *intr (said of waves or a crowd)* wogen; *(said of emotions, blood)* (**up**) (auf)wallen
surgeon ['sʌrdʒən] *s* Chirurg –in *mf*
surgery ['sʌrdʒəri] *s* Chirurgie *f; (room)* Operationssaal *m;* **undergo s.** sich e–r Operation unterziehen
surgical ['sʌrdʒɪkəl] *adj* chirurgisch; *(resulting from surgery)* Operations–
surly ['sʌrli] *adj* bärbeißig
surmise [sər'maɪz] *s* Vermutung *f* ‖ *tr & intr* vermuten
surmount [sər'maʊnt] *tr* überwinden
surname ['sʌr‚nem] *s (family name)* Zuname *m; (epithet)* Beiname *m* ‖ *tr* e–n Zunamen (or Beinamen) geben *(dat)*
surpass [sər'pæs] *tr* (**in**) übertreffen (an *dat)*
surplice ['sʌrplɪs] *s* Chorhemd *n*
surplus ['sʌrplʌs] *adj* überschüssig, Über– ‖ *s* (**of**) Überschuß *m* (an *dat)*
surprise [sər'praɪz] *adj* Überraschungs– ‖ *s* Überraschung *f;* **take by s.** überraschen; **to my (great) s.** zu meiner (großen) Überraschung ‖ *tr* überraschen; **be surprised at** sich wundern über *(acc);* **be surprised to see how** staunen, wie; **I am surprised that** es wundert mich, daß
surpris'ing *adj* überraschend
surrealism [sə'riˌə‚lɪzəm] *s* Surrealismus *m*
surrender [sə'rɛndər] *s (e.g., of a fortress)* Übergabe *f; (of an army or unit)* Kapitulation *f; (of rights)* Aufgabe *f; (of a prisoner)* Auslieferung *f* ‖ *tr* übergeben; *(rights)* aufgeben; *(a prisoner)* ausliefern ‖ *intr* sich ergeben
surren'der val'ue *s* (ins) Rückkaufswert *m*
surreptitious [‚sʌrep'tɪʃəs] *adj* heimlich; *(glance)* verstohlen
surround [sə'raʊnd] *tr* umgeben; *(said of a crowd, police)* umringen; (mil) einschließen
surround'ing *adj* umliegend ‖ **surroundings** *spl* Umgebung *f*
surtax ['sʌr‚tæks] *s* Steuerzuschlag *m*
surveillance [sər'vel(j)əns] *s* Überwachung *f;* **keep under s.** unter Polizeiaufsicht halten

survey ['sʌrve] *s* (**of**) Überblick *m* (über *acc);* *(of opinions)* Umfrage *f; (of land)* Vermessung *f; (plan or description of the survey)* Lageplan *m* ‖ [sʌr've] *tr* überblicken; *(a person)* mustern; *(land)* vermessen; *(people for their opinion)* befragen
sur'vey course' *s* Einführungskurs *m*
survey'ing *s* Landvermessung *f*
surveyor [sər've‐ər] *s* Landmesser *m*
survival [sər'vaɪvəl] *s* Überleben *n; (after death)* Weiterleben *n*
surviv'al of the fit'test *s* Überleben *n* des Tüchtigsten
survive [sər'vaɪv] *tr (a person)* überleben; *(a thing)* überstehen; **be survived by** hinterlassen ‖ *intr* am Leben bleiben
surviv'ing *adj* überlebend
survivor [sər'vaɪvər] *s* Überlebende *mf*
susceptible [sə'sɛptɪbəl] *adj (impressionable)* eindrucksfähig; **be s. of** zulassen; **be s. to** *(disease, infection)* anfällig sein für; *(flattery)* empfänglich sein für
suspect ['sʌspɛkt] *adj* verdächtig ‖ *s* Verdächtige *mf* ‖ [səs'pɛkt] *tr* in Verdacht haben; *(surmise)* vermuten; *(have a hint of)* ahnen; **s. s.o. of** j-n verdächtigen *(genit)*
suspend [səs'pɛnd] *tr (from a job, office)* suspendieren; *(payment, hostilities, proceedings, a game)* einstellen; *(a rule)* zeitweilig aufheben; *(a sentence)* aussetzen; *(a player)* sperren; *(from a club)* zeitweilig ausschließen; *(from)* hängen (an *dat)*
suspenders [səs'pɛndərz] *spl* Hosenträger *pl*
suspense [səs'pɛns] *s* Spannung *f;* **hang in s.** in der Schwebe sein; **keep in s.** im ungewissen lassen
suspension [səs'pɛnʃən] *s* Aufhängung *f; (of a sentence)* Aussetzung *f; (of work)* Einstellung *f; (e.g., of telephone service)* Sperrung *f;* (aut) Federung *f;* (chem) Suspension *f;* **s. of driver's license** Führerscheinentzug *m*
suspen'sion bridge' *s* Hängebrücke *f*
suspen'sion points' *spl (indicating unfinished thoughts)* Gedankenpunkte *pl; (indicating omission)* Auslassungspunkte *pl*
suspicion [səs'pɪʃən] *s* Verdacht *m;* **above s.** über jeden Verdacht erhaben; **be under s.** unter Verdacht stehen; **on s. of murder** unter Mordverdacht
suspicious [səs'pɪʃəs] *adj (person)* verdächtig; *(e.g., glance)* argwöhnisch; *(character)* zweifelhaft
sustain [səs'ten] *tr* aufrechterhalten; *(a loss, defeat, injury)* erleiden; *(a family)* ernähren; *(an army)* verpflegen; *(a motion, an objection)* stattgeben *(dat);* *(a theory, position)* erhärten; *(a note)* dehnen
sustenance ['sʌstɪnəns] *s (nourishment)* Nahrung *f; (means of livelihood)* Unterhalt *m*
swab [swɑb] *s* (med, surg) Tupfer *m;*

(*matter collected on a swab*) Abstrich *m;* (naut) Schwabber *m* ‖ *v* (*pret & pp* **swabbed;** *ger* **swabbing**) *tr* (med, surg) abtupfen; (naut) schrubben
Swabia ['swebɪ·ə] *s* Schwaben *n*
Swabian ['swebɪ·ən] *adj* schwäbisch ‖ *s* Schwabe *m,* Schwäbin *f;* (*dialect*) Schwäbisch *n*
swad'dling clothes' ['swɑdlɪŋ] *spl* Windeln *pl*
swagger ['swægər] *s* (*strut*) Stolzieren *n;* (*swaggering manner*) Prahlerei *f* ‖ *intr* stolzieren; (*show off*) prahlen
swain [swen] *s* (*lover*) Liebhaber *m;* (*country lad*) Bauernbursche *m*
swallow ['swɑlo] *s* Schluck *m;* (orn) Schwalbe *f* ‖ *tr* schlucken; (fig) hinunterschlucken ‖ *intr* schlucken; **s. the wrong way** sich verschlucken
swamp [swɑmp] *s* Sumpf *m,* Moor *n* ‖ *tr* überfluten; (*with work*) überhäufen
swamp'land' *s* Moorland *n*
swampy ['swɑmpi] *adj* sumpfig
swan [swɑn] *s* Schwan *m*
swan' dive' *s* Schwalbensprung *m*
swank [swæŋk], **swanky** ['swæŋki] *adj* (*luxurious*) schick; (*ostentatious*) protzig
swan's'-down' *s* Schwanendaunen *pl*
swan' song' *s* Schwanengesang *n*
swap [swɑp] *s* (coll) Tauschgeschäft *n* ‖ *v* (*pret & pp* **swapped;** *ger* **swapping**) *tr & intr* (coll) tauschen
swarm [swɑrm] *s* Schwarm *m;* (*of children*) Schar *f* ‖ *intr* schwärmen; **s. around** umschwärmen; **s. into** sich drängen in (*acc*); **s. with** (fig) wimmeln von
swarthy ['swɔrði] *adj* dunkelhäutig
swashbuckler ['swɑʃ͵bʌklər] *s* Eisenfresser *m*
swastika ['swɑstɪkə] *s* Hakenkreuz *n*
swat [swɑt] *s* Schlag *m* ‖ (*pret & pp* **swatted;** *ger* **swatting**) *tr* schlagen
swath [swɑθ] *s* Schwaden *m*
swathe [sweð] *tr* umwickeln, einwikkeln
sway [swe] *s* Schwanken *n,* Schwingen *n;* (*domination*) Herrschaft *f* ‖ *tr* (e.g., *tree*) hin- und herbewegen; (*influence*) beeinflussen; (*cause to vacillate*) ins Wanken bringen ‖ *intr* schwanken
sway'-back' *s* Senkrücken *m*
swear [swɛr] *v* (*pret* **swore** [swor]; *pp* **sworn** [sworn]) *tr* schwören; **s. in** vereidigen; **s. s.o. to secrecy** j–n auf Geheimhaltung vereidigen ‖ *intr* schwören; (coll) fluchen; **s. at** schimpfen über (*acc*) or auf (*acc*); **s. by** schwören bei; **s. off** abschwören (*dat*); **s. on a stack of Bibles** Stein und Bein schwören; **s. to** (*a statement*) beschwören; **s. to it** darauf schwören
swear'ing-in' *s* Vereidigung *f*
swear'word' *s* Fluchwort *n*
sweat [swɛt] *s* Schweiß *m;* **break out in s.** in Schweiß geraten ‖ *v* (*pret & pp* **sweat & sweated**) *tr* (*blood*)

schwitzen; (*metal*) seigern; (*a horse*) in Schweiß bringen; **s. off** abschwitzen; **s. out** (sl) geduldig abwarten; **s. up** durchschwitzen ‖ *intr* schwitzen
sweater ['swɛtər] *s* Sweater *m,* Pullover *m*
sweat'er girl' *s* vollbusiges Mädchen *n*
sweat' shirt' *s* Trainingsbluse *f*
sweat' shop' *s* (sl) Knochenmühle *f*
sweaty ['swɛti] *adj* verschwitzt; (*hand*) schweißig
Swede [swid] *s* Schwede *m,* Schwedin *f*
Swedish ['swidɪʃ] *adj* schwedisch ‖ *s* Schwedisch *n*
sweep [swip] *s* (*sweeper*) Kehrer –in *mf;* (*of the arm, scythe, weapon*) Schwung *m;* (*of an oar*) Schlag *m;* (*range*) Reichweite *f;* (*continuous stretch*) ausgedehnte Strecke *f;* **in one clean s.** mit e–m Schlag; **make a clean s. of it** reinen Tisch machen ‖ *v* (*pret & pp* **swept** [swɛpt]) *tr* kehren, fegen; (*mines*) räumen; (*with machine-gun fire*) bestreichen; (*with a searchlight*) absuchen; **he swept her off her feet** er hat sie im Sturm erobert; **s. clean** reinemachen ‖ *intr* kehren, fegen
sweeper ['swipər] *s* Kehrer –in *mf;* (*carpet sweeper*) Teppichkehrer *m*
sweep'ing *adj* weitreichend ‖ **sweepings** *spl* Kehricht *m & n*
sweep'-sec'ond *s* Zentralsekundenzeiger *m*
sweep'stakes' *s & spl* Lotterie *f;* (sport) Toto *m & n*
sweet [swit] *adj* süß; (*person*) lieb; (*butter*) ungesalzen; **be s. on** scharf sein auf (*acc*) ‖ **sweets** *spl* Süßigkeiten *pl*
sweet'bread' *s* Bries *n*
sweet'bri'er *s* Heckenrose *f*
sweet' corn' *s* Zuckermais *m*
sweeten ['switən] *tr* süßen; (fig) versüßen ‖ *intr* süß(er) werden
sweet'heart' *s* Liebste *mf,* Schatz *m*
sweetish ['switɪʃ] *adj* süßlich
sweet' mar'joram *s* Gartenmajoran *m*
sweet'meats' *spl* Zuckerwerk *n*
sweetness ['switnɪs] *s* Süßigkeit *f*
sweet' pea' *s* Gartenwicke *f*
sweet' pep'per *s* grüner Paprika *m*
sweet' pota'to *s* Süßkartoffel *f*
sweet'-scent'ed *adj* wohlriechend
sweet' tooth' *s*—**have a s.** gern naschen
sweet' wil'liam *s* Fleischnelke *f*
swell [swɛl] *adj* (coll) prima ‖ *s* (*of the sea*) Wellengang *m;* (*of an organ*) Schweller *m* ‖ *v* (*pret* **swelled;** *pp* **swelled & swollen** ['swolən]) *tr* zum Schwellen bringen; (*the number*) vermehren; (*a musical tone*) anschwellen lassen ‖ *intr* schwellen
swell'ing *s* Schwellung *f*
swelter ['swɛltər] *intr* unter der Hitze leiden
swept'-back' *adj* (aer) keilförmig
swerve [swʌrv] *s* Abweichung *f* ‖ *tr* ablenken ‖ *intr* scharf abbiegen
swift [swɪft] *adj* geschwind, rasch
swig [swɪg] *s* (coll) kräftiger Schluck

m || *v* (*pret & pp* **swigged;** *ger* **swig- ging**) *tr* in langen Zügen trinken

swill [swɪl] *s* Spülicht *n;* (*for swine*) Schweinefutter *n;* (*deep drink*) tüchtiger Schluck *m* || *tr & intr* gierig trinken

swim [swɪm] *s* Schwimmen *n;* **take a s.** schwimmen || *v* (*pret* **swam** [swæm]; *pp* **swum** [swʌm]; *ger* **swimming**) *tr* (*e.g., a lake*) durchschwimmen; (*cause to swim*) schwimmen lassen; (*challenge in swimming*) um die Wette schwimmen mit || *intr* schwimmen; **my head is swimming** mir schwindelt der Kopf

swimmer ['swɪmər] *s* Schwimmer –in *mf*

swim′ming *adj* Schwimm– || *s* Schwimmen *n;* (sport) Schwimmsport *m*

swim′ming pool′ *s* Schwimmbecken *n*

swim′ming suit′ *s* Badeanzug *m*

swim′ming trunks′ *spl* Badehose *f*

swindle ['swɪndəl] *s* Schwindel *m* || *tr* gaunern; **s. s.th. out of** etw er- schwindeln von

swindler ['swɪndlər] *s* Schwindler –in *mf*

swind′ling *s* Schwindelei *f*

swine [swaɪn] *s* Schwein *n*

swine′herd′ *s* Schweinehirt *m*

swing [swɪŋ] *s* (*for children*) Schaukel *f;* (*swinging movement*) Hin– und Herschwingen *n;* (box) Schwinger *m;* (mus) Swing *m;* **in full s.** in vollem Gang; **take a s. at s.o.** nach j–m schlagen || *v* (*pret & pp* **swung** [swʌŋ]) *tr* schwingen; (*children on a swing*) schaukeln; (*an election*) entscheidend beeinflussen; **s.** (*e.g., a car*) **around** herumdrehen; **we'll s. it somhow** (coll) wir werden es schon schaffen || *intr* pendeln; (*on a swing*) schaukeln; **s. around** sich um- drehen; **things are swinging around here** (coll) hier geht es lustig zu

swing′ing door′ *s* Pendeltür *f*

swinish ['swaɪnɪʃ] *adj* schweinisch

swipe [swaɪp] *s* (coll) Hieb *m;* **take a s. at** (coll) schlagen nach || *tr* (*hit with full force*) (coll) kräftig schla- gen; (*steal*) (sl) mausen

swirl [swʌrl] *s* Wirbel *m* || *tr* (**about**) herumwirbeln || *intr* wirbeln; (*said of water*) Strudel bilden

swish [swɪʃ] *s* (*e.g., of a whip*) Sausen *n;* (*of a dress*) Rauschen *n* || *tr* (*a whip*) sausen lassen; **s. its tail** mit dem Schwanz wedeln || *intr* (*said of a whip*) sausen; (*said of a dress*) rauschen

Swiss [swɪs] *adj* schweizerisch || *s* Schweizer –in *mf*

Swiss′ cheese′ *s* Schweizer Käse *m*

Swiss′ franc′ *s* Schweizerfranken *m*

Swiss′ Guard′ *s* Schweizergarde *f*

switch [swɪtʃ] *s* (*exchange*) Wechsel *m,* Umschwung *m;* (*stick*) Rute *f;* (elec) Schalter *m;* (rr) Weiche *f* || *tr* wechseln; (*e.g., coats by mistake*) verwechseln; (rr) rangieren; **s. off** (elec, rad, telv) ausschalten; **s. on**

(elec, rad, telv) einschalten || *intr* Plätze wechseln

switch′-blade knife′ *s* feststellbares Messer *n*

switch′board′ *s* Schaltbrett *n,* Zentrale *f*

switch′board op′erator *s* Telephonist –in *mf*

switch′ box′ *s* Schaltkasten *m*

switch′man *s* (–men) (rr) Weichenstel- ler *m*

switch′ tow′er *s* (rr) Blockstation *f*

switch′yard′ *s* Rangierbahnhof *m*

Switzerland ['swɪtsərlənd] *s* die Schweiz

swiv·el ['swɪvəl] *s* Drehlager *n* || *v* (*pret & pp* –el[l]ed; *ger* –el[l]ing) *tr* herumdrehen || *intr* sich drehen

swiv′el chair′ *s* Drehstuhl *m*

swiz′zle stick′ ['swɪzəl] *s* Rührstäb- chen *n*

swollen ['swolən] *adj* (an)geschwollen; (*eyes*) verquollen

swoon [swun] *s* Ohnmacht *f* || *intr* ohnmächtig werden

swoop [swup] *s* Herabstoßen *n;* **in one fell s.** mit e–m Schlag || *intr*—**s. down** (**on**) herabstoßen (auf *acc*)

sword [sord] *s* Schwert *n;* **put to the s.** mit dem Schwert hinrichten

sword′ belt′ *s* Schwertgehenk *n*

sword′fish′ *s* Schwertfisch *m*

swords′man *s* (–men) Fechter *m*

sworn [sworn] *adj* (*statement*) eidlich; **s. enemy** Todfeind *m*

sycamore ['sɪkəmor] *s* Platane *f*

sycophant ['sɪkəfənt] *s* Sykophant *m*

syllabary ['sɪlə,beri] *s* Silbenschrift *f*

syllabification [sɪ,læbɪfɪ'keʃən] *s* Sil- bentrennung *f*

syllable ['sɪləbəl] *s* Silbe *f*

sylla·bus ['sɪləbəs] *s* (**–bai** [,baɪ] & **–buses**) Lehrplan *m*

syllogism ['sɪlə,dʒɪzəm] *s* Syllogismus *m*

sylvan ['sɪlvən] *adj* Wald–

symbol ['sɪmbəl] *s* Sinnbild *n,* Symbol *n*

symbolic(al) [sɪm'bɑlɪk(əl)] *adj* sinn- bildlich, symbolisch

symbolism ['sɪmbə,lɪzəm] *s* Symbolik *f*

symbolize ['sɪmbə,laɪz] *tr* symbolisie- ren

symmetric(al) [sɪ'metrɪk(əl)] *adj* sym- metrisch

symmetry ['sɪmɪtri] *s* Symmetrie *f*

sympathetic [,sɪmpə'θetɪk] *adj* mit- fühlend; (physiol) sympathisch

sympathize ['sɪmpə,θaɪz] *intr*—**s. with** mitfühlen mit; (*be in accord with*) sympathisieren mit

sympathizer ['sɪmpə,θaɪzər] *s* Sym- pathisant –in *mf*

sympathy ['sɪmpəθi] *s* Mitleid *n;* **be in s. with** im Einverständnis sein mit; **offer one's sympathies to s.o.** j–m sein Beileid bezeigen

sym′pathy card′ *s* Beileidskarte *f*

sym′pathy strike′ *s* Sympathiestreik *m*

symphonic [sɪm'fɑnɪk] *adj* sinfonisch

symphony ['sɪmfəni] *s* Sinfonie *f*

symposi·um [sɪm'poʊzɪ·əm] *s* (**-a** [ə] &
-ums) Symposion *n*
symptom ['sɪmptəm] *s* (**of**) Symptom
n (für)
symptomatic [ˌsɪmtə'mætɪk] *adj* (**of**)
symptomatisch (für)
synagogue ['sɪnəˌgɔg] *s* Synagoge *f*
synchronize ['sɪŋkrəˌnaɪz] *tr* synchronisieren
synchronous ['sɪŋkrənəs] *adj* synchron;
(elec) Synchron–
syncopate ['sɪŋkəˌpet] *tr* synkopieren
syncopation [ˌsɪŋkə'peʃən] *s* Synkope
f
syncope ['sɪŋkəˌpi] *s* Synkope *f*
syndicate ['sɪndɪkɪt] *s* Interessenge-
meinschaft *f*, Syndikat *n* ‖ ['sɪndɪ-
ˌket] *tr* zu e–m Syndikat zusammen-
schließen; (*a column*) in mehreren
Zeitungen zugleich veröffentlichen ‖
intr ein Syndikat bilden
synod ['sɪnəd] *s* Synode *f*
synonym ['sɪnənɪm] *s* Synonym *n*
synonymous [sɪ'nɑnəməs] *adj* sinnver-
wandt; **s. with** gleichbedeutend mit

synop·sis [sɪ'nɑpsɪs] *s* (**-ses** [siz])
Zusammenfassung *f*
synoptic [sɪ'nɑptɪk] *adj* synoptisch
syntax ['sɪntæks] *s* Satzlehre *f*, Syntax
f
synthe·sis ['sɪnθɪsɪs] *s* (**-ses** [ˌsiz])
Synthese *f*
synthesize ['sɪnθɪˌsaɪz] *tr* (& chem)
zusammenfügen
synthetic [sɪn'θetɪk] *adj* künstlich,
Kunst– ‖ *s* Kunststoff *m*
syphilis ['sɪfɪlɪs] *s* Syphilis *f*
Syria ['sɪrɪ·ə] *s* Syrien *n*
Syrian ['sɪrɪ·ən] *adj* syrisch ‖ *s* Syrer
–in *mf*; (*language*) Syrisch *n*
syringe [sɪ'rɪndʒ] *s* Spritze *f* ‖ *tr* (*inject*) einspritzen; (*wash*) ausspritzen
syrup ['sɪrəp] *s* Sirup *m*
system ['sɪstəm] *s* System *n*; (*bodily
system*) Organismus *m*
systematic(al) [ˌsɪstə'mætɪk(əl)] *adj*
systematisch, planmäßig
systematize ['sɪstəməˌtaɪz] *tr* syste-
matisieren, systematisch ordnen
systole ['sɪstəli] *s* Systole *f*

T

T, t [ti] *s* zwanzigster Buchstabe des
englischen Alphabets
tab [tæb] *s* (*label*) Etikett *n;* (*on file
cards*) Karteireiter *m;* **keep tabs on**
(coll) genau kontrollieren; **pick up
the tab** (coll) die Zeche bezahlen ‖
v (*pret & pp* **tabbed;** *ger* **tabbing**) *tr*
(*designate*) ernennen
tabby ['tæbi] *s* getigerte Katze *f*
tabernacle ['tæbərˌnækəl] *s* Tabernakel *n*
table ['tebəl] *s* Tisch *m;* (*list, chart*)
Tafel *f*, Tabelle *f;* (geol) Tafel *f;* **at
t.** bei Tisch; **the tables have turned**
das Blatt hat sich gewendet ‖ *tr*
(parl) verschieben
tab·leau ['tæblo] *s* (**-leaus** & **leaux**
[loz]) Tableau *n*
ta'blecloth' *s* Tischtuch *n*
ta'bleland' *s* Tafelland *n*
ta'ble man'ners *spl* Tischmanieren *pl*
ta'ble of con'tents *s* Inhaltsverzeichnis
n
ta'ble salt' *s* Tafelsalz *n*
ta'ble set'ting *s* Gedeck *n*
ta'blespoon' *s* Eßlöffel *m*
tablespoonful ['tebəlˌspun ˌful] *s* Eßlöffel *m*
tablet ['tæblɪt] *s* (*writing pad*) Schreibblock *m;* (med) Tablette *f*
ta'ble talk' *s* Tischgespräch *n*
ta'ble ten'nis *s* Tischtennis *n*
ta'bletop' *s* Tischplatte *f*
ta'bleware' *s* Tafelgeschirr *n*
ta'ble wine' *s* Tafelwein *m*
tabloid ['tæblɔɪd] *adj* konzentriert ‖ *s*
Bildzeitung *f;* (pej) Sensationsblatt *n*
taboo [tə'bu] *adj* tabu ‖ *s* Tabu *n* ‖
tr für Tabu erklären

tabular ['tæbjələr] *adj* tabellarisch
tabulate ['tæbjəˌlet] *tr* tabellarisieren
tabulator ['tæbjəˌletər] *s* Tabellier-
maschine *f*
tacit ['tæsɪt] *adj* stillschweigend
taciturn ['tæsɪtərn] *adj* schweigsam
tack [tæk] *s* (*nail*) Zwecke *f*, Stift *m;*
(*stitch*) Heftstich *m;* (*stickiness*)
Klebrigkeit *f;* (*course of action*)
Kurs *m;* (*gear for a riding horse*)
Reitgeschirr *n;* (*course run obliquely
to the wind*) Schlag *m;* **be on the
wrong t.** (fig) auf dem Holzweg sein
‖ *tr* (**down**) mit Zwecken befestigen;
(sew) heften; **t. on** (**to**) anfügen (an
acc) ‖ *intr* (fig & naut) lavieren
tackle ['tækəl] *s* (*gear*) Ausrüstung *f;*
(*for lifting*) Flaschenzug *m;* (fb)
Halbstürmer *m;* (naut) Takelwerk *n*
‖ *tr* (*a problem*) anpacken; (fb)
packen
tacky ['tæki] *adj* klebrig; (*gaudy*) geschmacklos
tact [tækt] *s* Takt *m*, Feingefühl *n*
tactful ['tæktfəl] *adj* taktvoll
tactical ['tæktɪkəl] *adj* taktisch
tac'tical u'nit *s* Kampfeinheit *f*
tactician [tæk'tɪʃən] *s* Taktiker *m*
tactics ['tæktɪks] *spl* (& fig) Taktik *f*
tactless ['tæktlɪs] *adj* taktlos
tadpole ['tædˌpol] *s* Kaulquappe *f*
taffeta ['tæfɪtə] *s* Taft *m*
taffy ['tæfi] *s* Sahnebonbon *n*
tag [tæg] *s* (*label*) Etikett *n;* (*loose
end*) loses Ende *n;* (*on a shoestring*)
Stift *m;* (*loop for hanging up a coat*)
Aufhänger *m;* (*on a fish hook*) Glit-
zerschmuck *m;* (*game*) Haschen *n;*
play tag sich haschen; **tags** (aut)

Nummernschild *n* ‖ *v* (*pret & pp* **tagged;** *ger* **tagging**) *tr* (*mark with a tag*) mit e–m Etikett versehen; (*touch*) haschen; (*hit solidly*) heftig schlagen; (*give a traffic ticket to*) e–n Strafzettel geben (*dat*) ‖ *intr—* **tag after** *s.o.* sich an j–s Sohlen heften

tag′ line′ *s* (*e.g., of a play*) Schlußworte *pl;* (*favorite phrase*) stehende Redensart *f*

tail [tel] *s* Schwanz *m;* (*of a horse, comet*) Schweif *m;* (*of a shirt*) Schoß *m;* (*aer*) Heck *n;* **tails** ein Frack *m;* (*of a coin*) Rückseite *f;* **turn t.** ausreißen; **wag its t.** mit dem Schwanz wedeln ‖ *tr* (coll) beschatten ‖ *intr* **—t. after** nachlaufen (*dat*); **t. off** abflauen

tail′ end′ *s* (*e.g., of a conversation*) Schlußteil *n;* **come in at the t. end** als letzter durchs Ziel gehen

tail′gate′ *s* (*of a station wagon*) Hecktür *f;* (*of a truck*) Ladeklappe *f* ‖ *intr* dicht hinter e–m anderen fahren

tail′ gun′ner *s* (aer) Heckschütze *m*

tail′-heav′y *adj* schwanzlastig

tail′light′ *s* (aer) Hecklicht *n;* (aut) Rücklicht *n*

tailor [′telər] *s* Schneider *m* ‖ *tr & intr* schneidern

tai′loring *s* Schneiderarbeit *f*

tai′lor-made suit′ *s* Maßanzug *m*

tai′lor shop′ *s* Schneiderei *f*

tail′piece′ *s* (*appendage*) Anhang *m;* (*of a stringed instrument*) Saitenhalter *m;* (typ) Zierleiste *f*

tail′ pipe′ *s* (aut) Auspuffrohr *n*

tail′skid′ *s* (aer) Sporn *m*

tail′spin′ *s*—**go into a t.** abtrudeln

tail′ wheel′ *s* (aer) Spornrad *n*

tail′wind′ *s* Rückenwind *m*

taint [tent] *s* Fleck *m;* (fig) Schandfleck *m* ‖ *tr* beflecken; (*food*) verderben

take [tek] *s* (*income*) (sl) Einnahmen *pl;* (*loot*) (sl) Beute *f;* (angl) Fang *m;* (cin) Szenenaufnahme *f;* **be on the t.** (sl) sich bestechen lassen ‖ *v* (*pret* **took** [tʊk]; *pp* **taken**) *tr* nehmen; (*in a car*) mitnehmen; (*bring, carry*) bringen; (*subtract*) abziehen; (*require*) erfordern; (*insults, criticism*) hinnehmen; (*bear, stand*) ertragen; (*with a camera*) aufnehmen; (*food, pills*) einnehmen; (*s.o.'s temperature*) messen; (*courage*) schöpfen; (*a deep breath*) holen; (*precautions*) treffen; (*responsibility*) übernehmen; (*an oath, test*) ablegen; (*inventory*) aufnehmen; (*a walk, trip, examination, turn, notes*) machen; (*the consequences*) tragen; (*measures*) ergreifen; (*a certain amount of time to travel*) in Anspruch nehmen; (*a step*) tun; (*advice*) befolgen; (*a game*) gewinnen; (*e.g., third place*) belegen; (*a trick*) (cards) stechen; (gram) regieren; **be able to t. a lot** e–n breiten Rücken haben; **be taken in by s.o.** j–m auf den Leim gehen; **I'm not going to t. that**

das lasse ich nicht auf mir sitzen; **t. along** mitnehmen; **t. aside** beiseitenehmen; **t. at one's word** beim Wort nehmen; **t. away** wegschaffen; **t. away from** wegnehmen (*dat*); **t. back** zurücknehmen; **t.** (*e.g., s.o.'s hat*) **by mistake** verwechseln; **t. down** herunternehmen; (*in writing*) aufschreiben; (*dictation*) aufnehmen; (*minutes*) zu Protokoll nehmen; **t. in** (*money*) einnehmen; (*washing*) ins Haus nehmen; (*as guest*) beherbergen; (*deceive*) täuschen; (*encompass*) umfassen; (*observe*) beobachten; (*sightsee*) besichtigen; (*sew*) enger machen; **t. it out on s.o.** seinen Zorn an j–m auslassen; **t. it that** annehmen, daß; **taken** (*occupied*) besetzt; **t. off** (*subtract*) abziehen; (*clothes*) ausziehen; (*a coat*) ablegen; (*gloves*) abstreifen; (*a hat*) abnehmen; (*a tire, wheel*) abmontieren; (*e.g., a day from work*) sich [*dat*] freinehmen; **t.** (*e.g., wares*) **off s.o.'s hands** j–m abnehmen; **t. on** (*hire*) anstellen; (*passengers*) aufnehmen; **t. out** (*from a container*) herausnehmen; (*a spot*) entfernen; (*a girl*) ausführen; (*a mortgage, loan*) aufnehmen; (ins) abschließen; (libr) sich [*dat*] ausleihen; **t. over** übernehmen; **t. s.o. for** j–n halten für; **t. up** aufnehmen; (*absorb*) aufsaugen; (*a profession*) ergreifen; (*room, time*) wegnehmen; (*a collection*) veranstalten; (*a skirt*) kürzer machen; **t. upon oneself** auf sich nehmen; **t. up** (*a matter*) **with** besprechen mit ‖ *intr* (*said of an injection*) anschlagen; (*said of seedlings, skin transplants*) anwachsen; **how long does it t.?** wie lange dauert es?; **how long does it t. to** (*inf*)? wie lange braucht man, um zu (*inf*)?; **t. after** nachgeraten (*dat*); **t. off** (*depart*) (coll) abhauen; (*from work*) wegbleiben; (aer, rok) starten; (aut) abfahren; **t. over for s.o.** für j–n einspringen; **t. to** (*a person*) warm werden mit; (*an idea*) aufgreifen; **t. up with** sich abgeben mit

take′-home pay′ *s* Nettolohn *m*

take′-off′ *s* Karikatur *f;* (aer) Start *m*

take′-off ramp′ *s* (*in skiing*) Schanzentisch *m*

take′o′ver *s* Übernahme *f*

tal′cum pow′der [′tælkəm] *s* Federweiß *n*

tale [tel] *s* Geschichte *f;* **tell tales out of school** aus der Schule plaudern

tale′bear′er *s* Zuträger –in *mf*

talent [′tælənt] *s* Talent *n*

tal′ented *adj* talentiert, begabt

talisman [′tælısmən] *s* Talisman *m*

talk [tɔk] *s* Gespräch *n;* (*gossip*) Geschwätz *n;* (*lecture*) Vortrag *m;* (*speech*) Rede *f;* **cause t.** von sich reden machen; **give a t. on** e–n Vortrag halten über (*acc*); **t. of the town** Stadtgespräch *n* ‖ *tr* reden; (*business, politics, etc.*) sprechen über (*acc*); **t. down** zum Schweigen bringen; (aer) heruntersprechen; **t. one-**

self hoarse sich heiser reden; **t. one's way out of** sich herausreden aus; **t. over** besprechen; **t. sense** vernünftig reden; **t. s.o. into** (*ger*) j–n überreden zu (*inf*); **t. up** Reklame machen für || *intr* reden; (*chat*) schwätzen; **t. back** scharf erwidern; **t. big** große Töne reden; **t. dirty** Zoten reißen; **t. down to** herablassend reden zu; **talking of food** à propos Essen; **t. on** (*a topic*) e–n Vortrag halten über (*acc*); **t. to the walls** in den Wind reden
talkative ['tɔkətɪv] *adj* redselig
talker ['tɔkər] *s* Plauderer –in *mf;* **big t.** Schaumschläger *m*
talkie ['tɔki] *s* (cin) Sprechfilm *m*
talk'ing-to' *s* Denkzettel *m*
tall [tɔl] *adj* hoch; (*person*) hochgewachsen; **t. story** Mordsgeschichte *f*
tallow ['tælo] *s* Talg *m*
tal·ly ['tæli] *s* (*reckoning*) Rechnung *f;* (*game score*) Punktzahl *f* || *v* (*pret & pp* –lied) *tr* (**up**) berechnen || *intr* (**with**) übereinstimmen (**mit**)
tallyho [ˌtælɪ'ho] *interj* hallo!
tal'ly sheet' *s* Zählbogen *m*
talon ['tælən] *s* Klaue *f*
tambourine [ˌtæmbə'rin] *s* Tamburin *n*
tame [tem] *adj* zahm; (*docile*) gefügig; (*dull*) langweilig || *tr* zähmen; (e.g., *lions*) bändigen || *intr*—**t. down** (*said of a person*) gesetzter werden
tamp [tæmp] *tr* (*a tobacco pipe*) stopfen; (*earth, cement*) stampfen; (*a drill hole*) zustopfen
tamper ['tæmpər] *s* Stampfer *m* || *intr* —**t. with** sich einmischen in (*acc*); (*machinery*) herumbasteln an (*dat*); (*documents*) frisieren
tampon ['tæmpɑn] *s* Damenbinde *f;* (surg) Tampon *m* || *tr* (surg) tamponieren
tan [tæn] *adj* gelbbraun || *s* Sonnenbräunung *f* || *v* (*pret & pp* **tanned;** *ger* **tanning**) *tr* (*the skin*) bräunen; (*leather*) gerben || *intr* sich bräunen
tandem ['tændəm] *adj & adv* hintereinander (geordnet) || *s* Tandem *n;* **in t.** hintereinander
tang [tæŋ] *s* Herbheit *f;* (*sound*) Geklingel *n*
tangent ['tændʒənt] *adj*—**be t. to** tangieren || *s* Tangente *f;* **fly off on a t.** plötzlich vom Thema abschweifen
tangerine [ˌtændʒə'rin] *s* Mandarine *f*
tangible ['tændʒɪbəl] *adj* (& fig) greifbar
tangle ['tæŋɡəl] *s* Verwicklung *f;* (*twisted strands; confused jumble*) Gewirr *n;* (*conflict*) Auseinandersetzung *f* || *tr* verwirren; **get tangled** sich verfilzen || *intr* sich verwirren; **t. with** sich in e–n Kampf einlassen mit
tango ['tæŋgo] *s* Tango *m* || *intr* Tango tanzen
tangy ['tæŋi] *adj* herb
tank [tæŋk] *s* Behälter *m;* (*of a toilet*) Spülkasten *m;* (mil) Panzer *m*
tank' attack' *s* Panzerangriff *m*

tank' car' *s* (rr) Kesselwagen *m*, Tankwagen *m*
tanker ['tæŋkər] *s* (*truck*) Tankwagen *m;* (*ship*) Tanker *m;* (*plane*) Tankflugzeug *n*
tank' trap' *s* Panzersperre *f*
tank' truck' *s* Tankwagen *m*
tanned *adj* gebräunt
tanner ['tænər] *s* Gerber –in *mf*
tannery ['tænəri] *s* Gerberei *f*
tantalize ['tæntəˌlaɪz] *tr* quälen
tantamount ['tæntəˌmaʊnt] *adj*—**be t. to** gleichkommen (*dat*)
tantrum ['tæntrəm] *s* Koller *m;* **throw a t.** e–n Koller kriegen
tap [tæp] *s* (*light blow*) Klaps *m;* (*on a window or door*) Klopfen *n;* (*faucet*) Wasserhahn *m;* (*in a cask*) Faßhahn *m;* (elec) Anzapfung *f;* (mach) Gewindebohrer *m;* (surg) Punktion *f;* **on tap** vom Faß; **play taps** (mil) den Zapfenstreich blasen || *v* (*pret & pp* **tapped;** *ger* **tapping**) *tr* (*a cask, powerline, telephone*) anzapfen; (*fluids*) abzapfen; (*a person on the shoulder*) antippen; (*a hole*) mit e–m Gewinde versehen; **tap one's foot** (*to mark time*) Takt treten; **tap s.o. for** (*money*) (coll) j–n anpumpen um; **tap s.o.'s spine** j–n punktieren; **tap the window** am Fenster klopfen || *intr* tippen
tap' dance' *s* Steptanz *m*
tap'-dance' *intr* steppen
tap' dan'cer *s* Stepper –in *mf*
tape [tep] *s* Band *n;* (electron) Tonband *n;* (*friction tape*) Isolierband *n;* (*of paper*) Papierstreifen *m;* (med) Klebestreifen *m;* (sport) Zielband *n* || *tr* (mit Band) umwickeln; (electron) auf Tonband aufnehmen
tape' meas'ure *s* Meßband *n*
taper ['tepər] *s* Wachsfaden *m* || *tr* zuspitzen || *intr* spitz zulaufen; **t. off** langsam abnehmen
tape' record'er *s* Tonbandgerät *n*
ta'pered *adj* kegelförmig, Keil–
tapestry ['tæpɪstri] *s* Wandteppich *m*
tape'worm' *s* Bandwurm *m*
tapioca [ˌtæpɪ'okə] *s* Tapioka *f*
tappet ['tæpɪt] *s* (mach) Stößel *m*
tap'room' *s* Ausschank *m*
tap'root' *s* Pfahlwurzel *f*
tap' wa'ter *s* Leitungswasser *n*
tap' wrench' *s* Gewindeschneidkluppe *f*
tar [tɑr] *s* Teer *m* || *v* (*pret & pp* **tarred;** *ger* **tarring**) *tr* teeren
tardy ['tɑrdi] *adj* säumig
target ['tɑrgɪt] *s* Ziel *n;* (*on a firing range; of ridicule*) Zielscheibe *f*
tar'get ar'ea *s* Zielraum *m*
tar'get date' *s* Zieltag *m*
tar'get lan'guage *s* Zielsprache *f*
tar'get prac'tice *s* Scheibenschießen *n*
tariff ['tærɪf] *s* Tarif *m*
tarnish ['tɑrnɪʃ] *tr* matt (or blind) machen; (fig) beflecken || *intr* matt (or blind) werden
tar' pa'per *s* Teerpappe *f*
tarpaulin ['tɑrpəlɪn] *s* Plane *f*
tar·ry ['tɑri] *adj* teerig || ['tæri] *v*

(*pret* & *pp* **–ried**) *intr* verweilen; (*stay*) bleiben
tart [tɑrt] *adj* sauer; (*reply*) scharf || *s* Tortelett *n*
tartar ['tɑrtər] *s* (dent) Zahnstein *m*
tar'tar sauce' *s* pikante Soße *f*
task [tæsk] *s* Aufgabe *f;* **take to t.** zur Rede stellen
task' force' *s* Sonderverband *m*
task'mas'ter *s* Zuchtmeister *m*
tassel ['tæsəl] *s* Quaste *f;* (*on corn*) Narbenfäden *pl*
taste [test] *s* (& fig) Geschmack *m;* **develop a t.** for Geschmack gewinnen an (*dat*); **have a bad t.** schlecht || *intr*—**t.** like (or of) schmecken schmecken; **have bad t.** e–n schlechten Geschmack haben; **in bad t.** geschmacklos; **in good t.** geschmackvoll; **to t.** (culin) nach Gutdünken || *tr* schmecken; (*try out*) kosten; (*e.g., the pepper in soup*) herausschmecken; **t. blood** (fig) Blut lecken nach
taste' bud' *s* Geschmacksknospe *f*
tasteful ['testfəl] *adj* geschmackvoll
tasteless ['testlɪs] *adj* (& fig) geschmacklos
tasty ['testi] *adj* schmackhaft
tatter ['tætər] *s* Lumpen *m* || *tr* zerfetzen
tat'tered *adj* zerlumpt
tattle ['tætəl] *intr* petzen
tattler ['tætlər] *s* Petze *f*
tat'tletale' *s* Petze *f*
tattoo [tæ'tu] *s* Tätowierung *f* || *tr* tätowieren
taunt [tɔnt] *s* Stichelei *f* || *tr* sticheln gegen
taut [tɔt] *adj* straff, prall
tavern ['tævərn] *s* Schenke *f*
tawdry ['tɔdri] *adj* aufgedonnert
tawny ['tɔni] *adj* gelbbraun
tax [tæks] *s* Steuer *f* || *tr* besteuern; (fig) beanspruchen; **tax s.o. with** j–n rügen wegen
taxable ['tæksəbəl] *adj* steuerpflichtig
tax' assess'ment *s* Steuereinschätzung *f*
taxation [tæk'seʃən] *s* Besteuerung *f*
tax' brac'ket *s* Steuerklasse *f*
tax' collec'tor *s* Steuereinnehmer –in *mf*
tax' cut' *s* Steuersenkung *f*
tax' evas'ion *s* Steuerhinterziehung *f*
tax' exemp'tion *s* steuerfreier Betrag *m*
tax·i ['tæksi] *s* Taxi *n;* **go by t.** mit e–m Taxi fahren || *v* (*pret* & *pp* **–ied**; *ger* **–iing** & **–ying**) *tr* (aer) rollen lassen || *intr* mit e–m Taxi fahren; (aer) rollen
tax'icab' *s* Taxi *n*
tax'i danc'er *s* Taxigirl *n*
taxidermist ['tæksɪ ˌdɑrmɪst] *s* Tierpräparator –in *mf*
tax'i driv'er *s* Taxifahrer –in *mf*
tax'ime'ter *s* Taxameter *m*
tax'i stand' *s* Taxistand *m*
tax'pay'er *s* Steuerzahler –in *mf*
tax' rate' *s* Steuersatz *m*
tax' return' *s* Steuererklärung *f*
tea [ti] *s* Tee *m*
tea' bag' *s* Teebeutel *m*

tea' cart' *s* Teewagen *m*
teach [titʃ] *v* (*pret* & *pp* **taught** [tɔt]) *tr* lehren; (*instruct*) unterrichten; **t. school** an e–r Schule unterrichten; **t. s.o. manners** j–m Manieren beibringen; **t. s.o. music** j–n in Musik unterrichten; **t. s.o. (to play) tennis** j–m das Tennisspielen beibringen || *intr* lehren, unterrichten
teacher ['titʃər] *s* Lehrer –in *mf*
teach'er's pet' *s* Liebling *m* des Lehrers (or der Lehrerin)
teach'ing *s* Lehren *n;* (*profession*) Lehrberuf *m*
teach'ing aid' *s* Lehrmittel *n*
teach'ing staff' *s* Lehrkörper *m*
tea'cup' *s* Teetasse *f*
teak [tik] *s* Teakholz *n*
tea'ket'tle *s* Teekessel *m*
tea' leaves' *spl* Teesatz *m*
team [tim] *s* Team *n;* (*of draught animals*) Gespann *n;* (sport) Mannschaft *f* || *tr* (*draft animals*) zusammenspannen || *intr*—**t.** up with sich vereinigen mit
team' cap'tain *s* Spielführer –in *mf*
team'mate' *s* Mannschaftskamerad –in *mf*
teamster ['timstər] *s* Fuhrmann *m;* (*trucker*) Lastwagenfahrer *m*
team'work' *s* Gemeinschaftsarbeit *f;* (sport) Zusammenspiel *n*
tea'pot' *s* Teekanne *f*
tear [tɪr] *s* Träne *f;* **bring tears to the eyes** Tränen in die Augen treiben; **burst into tears** in Tränen ausbrechen || [tɛr] *s* Riß *m* || *v* (*pret* **tore** [tor]; *pp* **torn** [tɔrn]) *tr* (zer)reißen; **t. apart** (*meat*) zerreißen; (*a speech*) zerpflücken; **t. away** wegreißen; **t. down** (*a building*) abreißen; (mach) zerlegen; (*a person*) sich [*dat*] das Maul zerreißen über (*acc*); **t. off** abreißen; **t. open** aufreißen; **t. oneself away** sich losreißen; **t. out** ausreißen; **t. up** (*a street*) aufreißen; (*e.g., letter*) zerreißen || *intr* (zer)reißen; **t. along** (*at high speed*) dahinsausen
teardrop ['tɪr ˌdrɑp] *s* Träne *f*
tear' gas' [tɪr] *s* Tränengas *n*
tear-jerker ['tɪr ˌdʒʌrkər] *s* (sl) Schnulze *f*
tea'room' *s* Teestube *f*
tease [tiz] *tr* necken; (*e.g., a dog*) quälen; (*hair*) auflockern
teas'ing *s* Neckerei *f*
tea'spoon' *s* Teelöffel *m*
teaspoonful ['ti ˌspun ˌfʊl] *s* Teelöffel *m*
teat [tit] *s* Zitze *f*
technical ['tɛknɪkəl] *adj* technisch, Fach-
tech'nical in'stitute *s* technische Hochschule *f*
technicality [ˌtɛknɪ 'kælɪti] *s* technische Einzelheit *f*
tech'nical school' *s* Technikum *n*
tech'nical term' *s* Fachausdruck *m*
technician [tɛk'nɪʃən] *s* Techniker –in *mf*
technique [tɛk'nik] *s* Technik *f*

technocrat ['tɛknə‚kræt] s Technokrat m

technological [‚tɛknə'lɑdʒɪkəl] adj technologisch

technology [tɛk'nɑlɪdʒi] s Technologie f

ted'dy bear' ['tɛdi] s Teddybär m

tedious ['tidɪ‧əs] adj langweilig

tee [ti] s (mound) Abschlagplatz m; (wooden or plastic peg) Aufsatz m; **to a tee** aufs Haar || tr—**tee off** (sl) aufregen; **tee up** (golf) auf den Aufsatz stellen || intr—**tee off** (golf) abschlagen

teem [tim] intr (**with**) wimmeln (von)

teem'ing adj wimmelnd; (rain) strömend

teen-age ['tin‚edʒ] adj halbwüchsig

teen-ager ['tin‚edʒər] s Teenager m

teens [tinz] spl Jugendalter n (vom dreizehnten bis neunzehnten Lebensjahr); **in one's t.** in den Jugendjahren

teeny ['tini] adj (coll) winzig

tee' shot' s (golf) Abschlag m

teeter ['titər] s Schaukeln n || intr schaukeln

teethe [tið] intr zahnen

teeth'ing ring' s Beißring m

teetotaler [ti'totələr] s Abstinenzler –in mf

tele-cast ['tɛlɪ‚kæst] s Fernsehsendung f || v (pret & pp –cast & –casted) tr im Fernsehen übertragen

telecommunications [‚tɛlɪkə‚mjunɪ'keʃəns] spl Fernmeldewesen n

telegram ['tɛlɪ‚græm] s Telegramm n

telegraph ['tɛlɪ‚græf] s Telegraph m || tr & intr telegraphieren

telegrapher [tɪ'lɛgrəfər] s Telegraphist –in mf

tel'egraph pole' s Telegraphenstange f

telemeter [tɪ'lɛmɪtər] s Telemeter n

telepathy [tɪ'lɛpəθi] s Telepathie f

telephone ['tɛlɪ‚fon] s Telephon n, Fernsprecher m; **be on the t.** am Apparat sein; **by t.** telephonisch; **speak on the t. with** telephonieren mit || tr & intr anrufen

tel'ephone booth' s Telephonzelle f

tel'ephone call' s Telephonanruf m

tel'ephone direc'tory s Teilnehmerverzeichnis n

tel'ephone exchange' s Telephonzentrale f

tel'ephone num'ber s Telephonnummer f

tel'ephone op'erator s Telephonist –in mf

tel'ephone receiv'er s Telephonhörer m

tel'ephoto lens' ['tɛlɪ‚foto] s Teleobjektiv n

telescope ['tɛlɪ‚skop] s Fernrohr n, Perspektiv n || tr ineinanderschieben; (fig) verkürzen || intr sich ineinanderschieben

telescopic [‚tɛlɪ'skɑpɪk] adj teleskopisch

telescop'ic sight' s Zielfernrohr n

Teletype ['tɛlɪ‚taɪp] s (trademark) Fernschreiber m || **teletype** tr durch Fernschreiber übermitteln || intr fernschreiben

tel'etype'writ'er s Fernschreiber m

televiewer ['tɛlɪ‚vju‧ər] s Fernsehteilnehmer –in mf

televise ['tɛlɪ‚vaɪz] tr im Fernsehen übertragen (or senden)

television ['tɛlɪ‚vɪʒən] adj Fernseh– || s Fernsehen n; **watch t.** fernsehen

tel'evision net'work s Fernsehnetz n

tel'evision screen' s Bildschirm m

tel'evision set' s Fernsehapparat m; **color t.** Farbfernsehapparat m

tel'evision show' s Fernschau f

telex ['tɛlɛks] s Fernschreiber m; (message) Telex n || tr fernschreiben

tell [tɛl] v (pret & pp **told** [told]) tr (the truth, a lie) sagen; (relate) erzählen; (a secret) anvertrauen; (let know) Bescheid sagen (dat); (inform) bestellen; (express) ausdrücken; (the reason) angeben; (distinguish) auseinanderhalten; **be able to t.** time die Uhr lesen können; **t. apart** auseinanderhalten; **t. me another!** (sl) das machst du mir nicht weis!; **t. s.o. off** j–n abkanzeln; **t. s.o. that** (assure s.o. that) j–m versichern, daß; **t. s.o. to** (inf) j–m sagen, daß er (inf) soll; **t. s.o. where to get off** (sl) j–m e–e Zigarre verpassen; **to t. the truth** ehrlich gesagt; **you can t. by looking at her** that man sieht es ihr an, daß || intr—**don't t. me!** na, so was!; **t. on** (betray) verraten; (produce a marked effect on) sehr mitnehmen; **you're telling me!** wem sagst du das!

teller ['tɛlər] s (of a bank) Kassierer –in mf; (of votes) Zähler –in mf

tell'ing adj (blow) wirksam

tell'-tale' adj verräterisch

temper ['tɛmpər] s (anger) Zorn m; (of steel) Härtegrad m; **bad t.** großer Zorn m; **even t.** Gleichmut m; **lose one's t.** in Wut geraten || tr (with) mildern (durch); (steel) härten; (mus) temperieren

temperament ['tɛmpərəmənt] s Temperament n

temperamental [‚tɛmpərə'mɛntəl] adj launisch, temperamentvoll

temperance ['tɛmpərəns] s Mäßigkeit f

temperate ['tɛmpərɪt] adj mäßig; (climate) gemäßigt

Tem'perate Zone' s gemäßigte Zone f

temperature ['tɛmərətʃər] s Temperatur f

tempest ['tɛmpɪst] s Sturm m; **a t. in a teapot** ein Sturm im Wasserglas

tempestuous [tɛm'pɛstʃu‧əs] adj stürmisch

temple ['tɛmpəl] s Tempel m; (of glasses) Bügel m; (anat) Schläfe f

tem·po ['tɛmpo] s (–pos & –pi [pi]) Tempo n

temporal ['tɛmpərəl] adj zeitlich

temporary ['tɛmpə‚rɛri] adj zeitweilig; (credit, solution) Zwischen–

temporize ['tɛmpə‚raɪz] intr Zeit zu gewinnen suchen

tempt [tɛmpt] tr versuchen; (said of things) reizen, locken

temptation [temp'teʃən] s Versuchung f

tempter ['temptər] s Versucher m

tempt'ing adj verlockend

temptress ['temptrɪs] s Versucherin f

ten [ten] adj & pron zehn ‖ s Zehn f

tenable ['tenəbəl] adj haltbar

tenacious [tɪ'neʃəs] adj (obstinate) nartnäckig; (memory) verläßlich

tenacity [tɪ'næsɪtɪ] s Hartnäckigkeit f

tenant ['tenənt] s Mieter –in mf

ten'ant farm'er s Pächter –in mf

tend [tend] tr (flocks) hüten; (the sick) pflegen; (a machine) bedienen ‖ intr—t. to (attend to) sich kümmern um; (inf) dazu neigen zu (inf); t. toward(s) neigen zu

tendency ['tendənsi] s Tendenz f

tender ['tendər] adj zart ‖ s Angebot n; (nav, rr) Tender m ‖ tr anbieten

ten'derfoot' s Neuankömmling m; (boyscout) neu aufgenommener Pfadfinder m

ten'derheart'ed adj zartfühlend

ten'derloin' s Rindslendenstück n

tenderness ['tendərnɪs] s Zartheit f

tendon ['tendən] s Sehne f

tendril ['tendrɪl] s Ranke f

tenement ['tenɪmənt] s (dwelling) Wohnung f; (rented dwelling) Mietwohnung f

ten'ement house' s Mietskaserne f

tenet ['tenɪt] s Grundsatz m, Lehrsatz m

ten'fold' adj & adv zehnfach

tennis ['tenɪs] s Tennis n

ten'nis court' s Tennisplatz m

ten'nis rack'et s Tennisschläger m

tenor ['tenər] s (drift, meaning; singer; voice range) Tenor m

ten'pin' s Kegel m

tense [tens] adj gespannt, straff; **make t.** spannen ‖ s (gram) Tempus n, Zweitform f

tension ['tenʃən] s (& elec) Spannung f; (phys) Spannkraft f

tent [tent] s Zelt n

tentacle ['tentəkəl] s Fühler m; (bot) Tentakel m

tentative ['tentətɪv] adj vorläufig

tenth [tenθ] adj & pron zehnte ‖ s (fraction) Zehntel n; **the t.** (in dates and in series) der Zehnte

tent' pole' s Zeltstange f

tenuous ['tenju-əs] adj (thin) dünn; (rarefied) verdünnt; (insignificant) unbedeutend; (weak) schwach

tenure ['tenjər] s (possession) Besitz m; (educ) Anstellung f auf Lebenszeit; **t. of office** Amtsdauer f

tepid ['tepɪd] adj lauwarm

term [tʌrm] s (expression) Ausdruck m; (time period) Frist f; (of office) Amtszeit f; (jur) Sitzungsperiode f; (math) Glied n; (log) Begriff m; **be on good terms with** in guten Beziehungen stehen mit; **come to terms with** handelseinig werden mit; **in plain terms** unverblümt; **in terms of** im Sinne von; **in terms of praise** mit lobenden Worten; **on easy terms** zu günstigen Bedingungen; **on equal**

terms auf gleichem Fuß; **on t.** (com) auf Zeit; **not be on speaking terms with** nicht sprechen mit; **tell s.o. in no uncertain terms** j–m gründlich die Meinung sagen; **terms** (of a contract, treaty, payment) Bedingungen pl ‖ tr bezeichnen

termagant ['tʌrməgənt] s Xanthippe f

terminal ['tʌrmɪnəl] adj End–; (disease) unheilbar ‖ s (aer) Flughafenempfangsgebäude n; (pole) (elec) Pol m; (rr) Kopfbahnhof m

terminate ['tʌrmɪ‚net] tr (end) beenden; (limit) begrenzen ‖ intr enden, endigen; (gram) (in) auslauten (auf acc)

termination [‚tʌrmɪ'neʃən] s Beendigung f; (gram) Endung f

terminology [‚tʌrmɪ'nɑlɪdʒi] s Terminologie f

term' insur'ance s Versicherung f auf Zeit

terminus ['tʌrmɪnəs] s (end) Endpunkt m; (boundary) Grenze f; (rr) Endstation f

termite ['tʌrmaɪt] s Termite f

term' pa'per s Referat n

terrace ['terəs] s Terrasse f ‖ tr abstufen, terrassieren

terra cotta ['terə'kɑtə] s Terrakotta f

ter'ra-cot'ta adj Terrakotta–

terrain [te'ren] s Gelände n, Terrain n

terrestrial [tə'restrɪ-əl] adj irdisch

terrible ['terɪbəl] adj furchtbar

terribly ['terɪbli] adv (coll) furchtbar

terrier ['terɪ-ər] s Terrier m

terrific [tə'rɪfɪk] adj (frightful) fürchterlich; (intense) (coll) gewaltig; (splendid) (coll) prima

terri•fy ['terɪ‚faɪ] v (pret & pp –fied) tr Entsetzen einjagen (dat)

ter'rifying adj schrecklich

territorial [‚terɪ'torɪ-əl] adj territorial; **t. waters** Hoheitsgewässer pl

territory ['terɪ‚tori] s Gebiet n, Territorium n; (of a salesman) Absatzgebiet n; (pol) Hoheitsgebiet n; (sport) Spielhälfte f

terror ['terər] s Schrecken m; **in t. vor** Schrecken

terrorism ['terə‚rɪzəm] s Terrorismus m

terrorist ['terərɪst] s Terrorist –in mf

terrorize ['terə‚raɪz] tr terrorisieren

ter'ror-strick'en adj schreckerfüllt

ter'ry cloth' ['teri] s Frottee m & n

terse [tʌrs] adj knapp

tertiary ['tʌrʃɪ‚eri] adj Tertiär–

test [test] s Probe f, Prüfung f; (criterion) Prüfstein m; (med) Probe f; **put to the t.** auf die Probe stellen ‖ tr (for) prüfen (auf acc); (chem) (for) analysieren (auf acc); **t. out** (coll) ausprobieren

testament ['testəmənt] s Testament n

testator [tes'tetər] s Erblasser –in mf

test' ban' s Atomstopp m

test' case' s Probefall m; (jur) Präzedenzfall m

test' flight' s Probeflug m

testicle ['testɪkəl] s Hoden m

testi•fy ['testɪ‚faɪ] v (pret & pp –fied)

intr (**against**) zeugen (gegen), aussagen (gegen); **t. to** bezeugen

testimonial [ˌtestɪ'monɪ·əl] *adj* (*dinner*) Ehren– ‖ *s* Anerkennungsschreiben *n*

testimony ['testɪˌmoni] *s* Zeugnis *n*

test′ pa′per *s* Prüfungsarbeit *f*

test′ pi′lot *s* Versuchsflieger –in *mf*

test′ tube′ *s* Reagenzglas *n*

testy ['testi] *adj* reizbar

tetanus ['tetənəs] *s* Starrkrampf *m*

tether ['teðər] *s* Haltestrick *m;* **be at the end of one's t.** nicht mehr weiter wissen ‖ *tr* anbinden

Teuton ['t(j)utən] *s* Teutone *m*, Teutonin *f*

Teutonic [t(j)u'tɑnɪk] *adj* teutonisch

text [tekst] *s* Text *m*

text′book′ *s* Lehrbuch *n*

textile ['tekstaɪl] *adj* Textil– ‖ *s* Webstoff *m;* **textiles** Textilien *pl*

textual ['tekstʃʊ·əl] *adj* textlich

texture ['tekstʃər] *s* (*structure*) Gefüge *n;* (*of a fabric*) Gewebe *n;* (*of a play*) Aufbau *m*

Thai [taɪ] *adj* Thai– ‖ *s* (*person*) Thai –in *mf;* (*language*) Thai *n*

Thailand ['taɪlənd] *s* Thailand *n*

Thames [temz] *s* Themse *f*

than [ðæn] *conj* als; **t. ever** denn je

thank [θæŋk] *adj* (*offering*) Dank– ‖ **thanks** *spl* Dank *m;* **give thanks to** danken (*dat*); **many thanks!** vielen Dank!; **return thanks** danksagen; **thanks a lot!** danke vielmals!; **thanks to her, I** ich verdanke es ihr, daß ich ‖ *tr* danken (*dat*); **t. God!** Gott sei Dank!; **t. goodness!** gottlob!; **t. you!** danke schön!; **t. you ever so much!** verbindlichsten Dank!; **you have only yourself to t. for that** das hast du dir nur selbst zu verdanken

thankful ['θæŋkfəl] *adj* dankbar

thankless ['θæŋklɪs] *adj* undankbar

Thanksgiv′ing Day′ *s* Danksagungstag *m*

that [ðæt] *adj* jener, der; **t. one** der da, jener ‖ *adv* (coll) so, derart ‖ *rel pron* der, welcher; (after indefinite pronouns) was ‖ *dem pron* das; **about t.** darüber; **after t.** danach; **and that's t.** und damit punktum!; **at t.** so, dabei; **by t.** dadurch; **for all t.** trotz alledem; **for t.** dafür; **from t.** daraus; **in t.** darin, daran; **on t.** darauf, drauf; **t. is** das heißt; **that's out** das kommt nicht in Frage!; **t. will do!** das reicht! ‖ *conj* daß

thatch [θætʃ] *s* Dachstroh *n*

thatched′ roof′ *s* Strohdach *n*

thaw [θɔ] *s* Tauwetter *n* ‖ *tr & intr* (auf)tauen

the [ðə], [ði] *def art* der, die, das ‖ *adv*—**so much the better** um so besser; **the ... the** je ... desto, je ... um so

theater ['θi·ətər] *s* Theater *n*

the′atergo′er *s* Theaterbesucher –in *mf*

the′ater of war′ *s* Kriegsschauplatz *m*

theatrical [θɪ'ætrɪkəl] *adj* (& fig) theatralisch

thee [ði] *pers pron* dich; **to t.** dir

theft [θeft] *s* Diebstahl *m*

their [ðer] *poss adj* ihr

theirs [ðerz] *poss pron* ihrer

them [ðem] *pron* sie; **to t.** ihnen

theme [θim] *s* Thema *n;* (*essay*) Aufsatz *m;* (mus) Thema *n*

theme′ song′ *s* Kennmelodie *f*

themselves′ *intens pron* selbst, selber ‖ *reflex pron* sich

then [ðen] *adv* (*next; in that case*) dann; (*at that time*) damals; **by t.** bis dahin; **from t. on** von da an; **t. and there** auf der Stelle; **till t.** bis dahin; **what t.?** was dann?

thence [ðens] *adv* von da, von dort; (*from that fact*) daraus

thence′forth′ *adv* von da an

theologian [ˌθi·ə'lodʒən] *s* Theologe *m*, Theologin *f*

theological [ˌθi·ə'lɑdʒɪkəl] *adj* theologisch

theology [θi'ɑlədʒi] *s* Theologie *f*

theorem ['θi·ərəm] *s* Lehrsatz *m*

theoretical [ˌθi·ə'retɪkəl] *adj* theoretisch

theorist ['θi·ərɪst] *s* Theoretiker –in *mf*

theorize ['θi·əˌraɪz] *intr* theoretisieren

theory ['θi·əri] *s* Theorie *f*, Lehre *f*

the′ory of relativ′ity *s* Relativitätstheorie *f*

therapeutic [ˌθerə'pjutɪk] *adj* therapeutisch ‖ **therapeutics** *s* Therapeutik *f*

therapy ['θerəpi] *s* Therapie *f*

there [ðer] *adv* (*position*) da; (*direction*) dahin; **down t.** da unten; **not be all t.** (coll) nicht ganz richtig sein; **over t.** da drüben; **t. are** es gibt, es sind; **t. is** es gibt, es ist; **t.!** sachte, sachte!; **up t.** da (or dort) oben

there′abouts′ *adv* daherum; **ten people or t.** so ungefähr zehn Leute

there′af′ter *adv* danach

there′by′ *adv* dadurch, damit

therefore ['ðerˌfor] *adv* deshalb, darum

there′in′ *adv* darin

there′of′ *adv* davon

there′to′ *adv* dazu

there′upon′ *adv* daraufhin, danach

there′with′ *adv* damit

thermal ['θʌrməl] *adj* Thermal–, Wärme–

thermodynamic [ˌθʌrmodaɪ'næmɪk] *adj* thermodynamisch ‖ **thermodynamics** *s* Thermodynamik *f*, Wärmelehre *f*

thermometer [θer'mɑmɪtər] *s* Thermometer *n*

thermonuclear [ˌθermo'n(j)uklɪ·ər] *adj* thermonuklear

ther′mos bot′tle ['θʌrməs] *s* Thermosflasche *f*

thermostat ['θʌrməˌstæt] *s* Thermostat *m*

thesau·rus [θɪ'sɔrəs] *s* (**–ri** [raɪ]) Thesaurus *m*

these [ðiz] *dem adj & pron* diese

the·sis ['θisɪs] *s* (**–ses** [siz]) These *f*

they [ðe] *pers pron* sie; **t. say** man sagt

thick [θɪk] *adj* dick; (*dense*) dicht;

(*stupid*) stumpfsinnig; (*lips*) wulstig; (*intimate*) (coll) dick; t. with dust dick bedeckt mit Staub || *adv*—be in t. with (coll dicke Beziehungen haben mit; come t. and fast Schlag auf Schlag gehen; lay it on t. (coll) dick auftragen || *s*—in the t. of mitten in (*dat*); through t. and thin durch dick und dünn

thicken ['θɪkən] *tr* verdicken; (*make denser*) verdichten; (*a sauce*) eindicken || *intr* sich verdicken; (*become denser*) sich verdichten; (*said of liquids*) sich verfestigen; (*said of a sauce*) eindicken; the plot thickens der Knoten schürzt sich

thicket ['θɪkɪt] *s* Dickicht *n*
thick'head' *s* (coll) Dickkopf *m*
thick'-head'ed *adj* (coll) dickköpfig
thickness ['θɪknɪs] *s* Dicke *f*
thick'-set' *adj* stämmig
thick'skinned' *adj* (coll) dickfellig
thief [θif] *s* (thieves [θivz] Dieb –in *mf*
thieve [θiv] *intr* stehlen
thievery ['θivəri] *s* Dieberei *f*
thievish ['θivɪʃ] *adj* diebisch
thigh [θaɪ] *s* Schenkel *m*, Oberschenkel *m*
thighbone' *s* Oberschenkelknochen *m*
thimble ['θɪmbəl] *s* Fingerhut *m*
thin [θɪn] *adj* (thinner; thinnest) dünn; (*hair*) schütter; (*lean*) mager; (*excuse*) schwach; (*soup*) wäßrig || *v* (*pret & pp* thinned; *ger* thinning) *tr* (*a liquid*) verdünnen; (*a forest*) lichten; t. out (*plants*) vereinzeln || *intr* (*said of hair*) sich lichten; t. out (*said of a crowd*) sich verlaufen
thing [θɪŋ] *s* Ding *n*, Sache *f*; among other things unter anderem; first t. zu allerest; how are things? wie geht's?; I'll do no such t.! ich werde mich schön hüten; of all things! na sowas!; the real t. das Richtige; things (*the situation*) die Lage *f*; (*belongings*) Sachen *pl*
think [θɪŋk] *v* (*pret & pp* thought [θɔt]) *tr* denken; (*regard*) halten; (*believe*) glauben, denken; he thinks he's clever er hält sich für klug; that's what you t.! ja, denkste!; t. better of it sich e–s Besseren besinnen; t. it best to (*inf*) es für das Beste halten zu (*inf*); t. little of nicht viel halten von; t. nothing of it! es ist nicht der Rede wert!; t. over sich [*dat*] überlegen; t. up sich [*dat*] ausdenken; what do you t. you're doing? was soll das? || *intr* denken; be thinking of (*ger*) beabsichtigen zu (*inf*); do you t. so? meinen Sie?; t. about (*call to consciousness*) denken an (*acc*); (*reflect on*) nachdenken über (*acc*); (*be concerned about*) bedacht sein auf (*acc*); t. twice before es sich [*dat*] zweimal überlegen, bevor
thinker ['θɪŋkər] *s* Denker –in *mf*
thin'-lipped' *adj* dünnlippig
thinner ['θɪnər] *s* Verdünnungsmittel *n*
third [θɪrd] *adj & pron* dritte || *s* (*frac-*

tion) Drittel *n*; (mus) Terz *f*; the third (*in dates and in series*) der Dritte
third'-class' *adj & adv* dritter Klasse
third' degree' *s*—give s.o. the t. j–n e–m Folterverhör unterwerfen
third' par'ty *s* Dritter *m*, dritte Seite *f*
third'-rate' *adj* drittrangig
thirst [θʌrst] *s* (for) Durst *m* (nach); t. for knowledge Wissensdurst *m*; t. for power Herrschsucht *f* || *intr* (for) dürsten (nach)
thirsty ['θʌrsti] *adj* durstig; be t. Durst haben
thirteen ['θʌr'tin] *adj & pron* dreizehn || *s* Dreizehn *f*
thirteenth ['θʌr'tinθ] *adj & pron* dreizehnte || *s* (*fraction*) Dreizehntel *n*; the t. (*in dates and in series*) der Dreizehnte
thirtieth ['θʌrtɪ·ɪθ] *adj & pron* dreißigste || *s* (*fraction*) Dreißigstel *n*; the t. (*in dates and in series*) der Dreißigste
thirty ['θʌrti] *adj & pron* dreißig || *s* Dreißig *f*; the thirties die dreißiger Jahre
thir'ty-one' *adj & pron* einundreißig
this [ðɪs] *dem adj* dieser; t. afternoon heute nachmittag; t. evening heute abend; t. minute augenblicklich; t. one dieser || *adv* (coll) so || *dem pron* dieser, der; about t. hierüber; (*concerning this*) davon; t. and that dies und jenes
thistle ['θɪsəl] *s* Distel *f*
thither ['θɪðər] *adv* dorthin, hinzu
thong [θɔŋ] *s* Riemen *m*; (*sandal*) Sandale *f*
tho·rax ['θoræks] *s* (–raxes & –races [rə̩siz]) Brustkorb *m*
thorn [θɔrn] *s* Dorn *m*; t. in the side Dorn *m* im Fleisch
thorny ['θɔrni] *adj* dornig; (fig) heikel
thorough ['θʌro] *adj* gründlich; (coll) tüchtig
thor'oughbred' *adj* reinrassig || *s* Vollblut *n*; (*horse*) Vollblutpferd *n*, Rassepferd *n*
thor'oughfare' *s* Durchgang *m*; no t. (public sign) Durchgang verboten
thor'oughgo'ing *adj* gründlich
thoroughly ['θʌroli] *adv* gründlich
those [ðoz] *dem adj & pron* jene, die da
thou [ðaʊ] *pers pron* du
though [ðo] *adv* immerhin || *conj* obwohl
thought [θɔt] *s* Gedanke(n) *m*; be lost in t. in Gedanken versunken sein; give some t. to sich [*dat*] Gedanken machen über (*acc*); have second thoughts sich [*dat*] eines Besseren besinnen; on second t. nach reiflicher Überlegung; the mere t. schon der Gedanke
thoughtful ['θɔtfəl] *adj* (*reflective*) nachdenklich; (*e.g., essay*) gedankenvoll; (*considerate*) aufmerksam; (*gift*) sinnig; t. of bedacht auf (*acc*)
thoughtless ['θɔtlɪs] *adj* gedankenlos
thought'-provok'ing *adj* anregend

thousand ['θauzənd] *adj & pron* tausend; **a t. times** tausendmal ‖ *s* Tausend *f;* **by the t.** zu Tausenden
thousandth ['θauzəndθ] *adj & pron* tausendste ‖ *s (fraction)* Tausendstel *n*
thrash [θræʃ] *tr (& fig)* dreschen; **t. out** *(debate)* gründlich erörten ‖ *intr* dreschen; **t. about** sich hin- und herwerfen
thrash'ing *s* Dreschen *n; (beating)* Dresche *f*
thread [θrɛd] *s* Faden *m; (of a screw)* Gewinde *n; (of a story)* Faden *m;* **hang by a t.** an e-m Faden hängen ‖ *tr (a needle)* einfädeln; *(pearls)* aufreihen; *(mach)* Gewinde schneiden in *(acc)*
thread'bare' *adj* fadenscheinig
threat [θrɛt] *s* Drohung *f*
threaten ['θrɛtən] *tr* drohen *(dat)*, bedrohen; **t. so. with s.th.** j-m etw androhen ‖ *intr* drohen
three [θri] *adj & pron* drei ‖ *s* Drei *f;* **in threes** zu dritt
three' cheers' *spl* ein dreimaliges Hoch *n*
three'-dimen'sional *adj* dreidimensional
three'-en'gine *adj* dreimotorig
three'-piece' *adj (suit)* dreiteilig
three'-ply' *adj* dreischichtig
three'-point land'ing *s* Dreipunktlandung *f*
threnody ['θrɛnədi] *s* Klagelied *n*
thresh [θrɛʃ] *tr* dreschen; **t. out** *(debate)* gründlich erörten ‖ *intr* dreschen
thresh'ing floor' *s* Dreschtenne *f*
thresh'ing machine' *s* Dreschmaschine *f*
threshold ['θrɛʃold] *s* Türschwelle *f;* (psychol) Schwelle *f*
thrice [θraɪs] *adv* dreimal
thrift [θrɪft] *s* Sparsamkeit *f*
thrifty ['θrɪfti] *adj* sparsam
thrill [θrɪl] *s* Nervenkitzel *m* ‖ *tr* erregen, packen
thriller ['θrɪlər] *s* Thriller *m*
thrill'ing *adj* packend, spannend
thrive [θraɪv] *v (pret* **thrived** & **throve** [θrov]; *pp* **thrived** & **thriven** ['θrɪvən]) *intr* gedeihen
throat [θrot] *s* Kehle *f;* **clear one's t.** sich räuspern; **cut one another's t.** (fig) sich gegenseitig kaputt machen; **cut one's own t.** (fig) sich *[dat]* sein eigenes Grab schaufeln; **jump down s.o.'s t.** j-m an die Gurgel fahren; **sore t.** Halsweh *n*
throb [θrɑb] *s* Schlagen *n; (of a motor)* Dröhnen *n* ‖ *v (pret & pp* **throbbed;** *ger* **throbbing)** *intr* schlagen; *(said of a motor or head)* dröhnen
throes [θroz] *spl* Schmerzen *pl;* **be in the t. of death** im Todeskampf liegen
thrombosis [θrʌm'bosɪs] *s* Thrombose *f*
throne [θron] *s* Thron *m*
throng [θrɔŋ] *s* Menschenmenge *f* ‖ *tr* umdrängen; *(the streets)* sich drängen in *(acc)* ‖ *intr (around)* sich drängen (um)
throttle ['θrɑtəl] *s* Drossel(klappe) *f*

‖ *tr* drosseln; *(a person)* erwürgen ‖ *intr*—**t. back** *(aut)* das Gas zurücknehmen
through [θru] *adj (traffic, train)* Durchgangs-; *(street)* durchgehend; *(finished)* fertig; *(coll)* quitt ‖ *adv*— **t. and t.** durch und durch ‖ *prep* durch *(acc)*
throughout' *adv* durch und durch ‖ *prep* hindurch *(acc)* (postpositive), e.g., **t. the summer** den ganzen Sommer hindurch; **t. the world** in der ganzen Welt
throw [θro] *s* Wurf *m; (scarf)* Überwurf *m* ‖ *v (pret* **threw** [θru]; *pp* **thrown** [θron]) *tr* werfen; *(a rider)* abwerfen; *(sparks)* sprühen; *(a party, banquet)* geben; *(a game)* absichtlich verlieren; *(into confusion)* bringen; **t. away** wegwerfen; **t. down** niederwerfen; *(overturn)* umwerfen; **t. in** *(e.g., a few extras)* als Zugabe geben; **t. off** *(fig)* aus dem Gleichgewicht bringen; **t. out** hinauswerfen; *(a person)* vor die Tür setzen; *(the chest)* herausdrücken; **t. out of the game** vom Platz verweisen; **t. the book at s.o.** (fig) j-n zur Höchststrafe verurteilen; **t. up to s.o.** j-m vorwerfen ‖ *intr* werfen; **t. up** sich erbrechen
throw'away' *adj* Einweg-
throw'back' *s* (to) Rückkehr *f* (zu)
throw' rug' *s* Vorleger *m*
thrum [θrʌm] *v (pret & pp* **thrummed;** *ger* **thrumming)** *intr* (on) mit den Fingern trommeln (auf *acc)*
thrush [θrʌʃ] *s* (orn) Drossel *f*
thrust [θrʌst] *s (shove)* Stoß *m; (stab)* Hieb *m;* (aer, archit, geol, rok) Schub *m;* (mil) Vorstoß *m* ‖ *v (pret & pp* **thrust)** *tr* stoßen
thud [θʌd] *s* Bums *m* ‖ *v (pret & pp* **thudded;** *ger* **thudding)** *tr & intr* bumsen ‖ *interj* bums!
thug [θʌg] *s* Rocker *m*
thumb [θʌm] *s* Daumen *m;* **be all thumbs** zwei linke Hände haben; **be under s.o.'s t.** unter j-s Fuchtel stehen; **thumbs down!** pfui!; **thumbs up!** Kopf hoch! ‖ *tr (a book)* abgreifen; **t. a ride** per Anhalter fahren; **t. one's nose at s.o.** j-m e-e lange Nase machen ‖ *intr*—**t. through** durchblättern
thumb' in'dex *s* Daumenindex *m*
thumb'print' *s* Daumenabdruck *m*
thumb'screw' *s* Flügelschraube *f*
thumb'tack' *s* Reißnagel *m*
thump [θʌmp] *s* Bums *m* ‖ *tr & intr* bumsen ‖ *interj* bums!
thump'ing *adj* (coll) enorm
thunder ['θʌndər] *s* Donner *m* ‖ *tr & intr* donnern
thun'derbolt' *s* Donnerkeil *m*
thun'derclap' *s* Donnerschlag *m*
thunderous ['θʌndərəs] *adj* donnernd
thun'dershow'er *s* Gewitterregen *m*
thun'derstorm' *s* Gewitter *n*
thunderstruck ['θʌndər‚strʌk] *adj* (fig) wie vom Schlag getroffen
Thursday ['θʌrzde] *s* Donnerstag *m;* **on T.** am Donnerstag

thus [ðʌs] *adv* so; (*consequently*) also; **t. far** soweit

thwack [θwæk] *s* heftiger Schlag *m* ‖ *tr* klatschen

thwart [θwɔrt] *adj* Quer– ‖ *s* (naut) Ruderbank *f* ‖ *tr* (*plans*) durchkreuzen; (*a person*) in die Quere kommen (*dat*)

thy [ðaɪ] *poss adj* dein

thyme [taɪm] *s* Thymian *m*

thy'roid gland' ['θaɪrɔɪd] *s* Schilddrüse *f*

thyself [ðaɪ'sɛlf] *intens pron* selbst, selber ‖ *reflex pron* dich

tiara [taɪ'ɛrə] *s* Tiara *f*; (*lady's headdress*) Diadem *n*

tibia ['tɪbɪ·ə] *s* Schienbein *n*

tic [tɪk] *s* (pathol) Tick *m*

tick [tɪk] *s* (*of a clock*) Ticken *n*; (*mattress case*) Überzug *m*; (ent) Zecke *f*; **on t.** (coll) auf Pump ‖ *tr*— **be ticked off** (at) (sl) verärgert sein (über *acc*); **t. off** (*names, items*) abhaken; (*the minutes*) ticken ‖ *intr* ticken; **t. by** vergehen

ticker ['tɪkər] *s* (*watch*) (sl) Uhr *f*, Armbanduhr *f*; (*heart*) (sl) Herz *n*; (st. exch.) Börsentelegraph *m*

tick'er tape' *s* Papierstreifen *m* (des Börsentelegraphen)

tick'er-tape parade' *s* Konfettiregenparade *f*

ticket ['tɪkɪt] *s* Karte *f*; (*for travel*) Fahrkarte *f*; (*by air*) Flugkarte *f*; (*for admission*) Eintrittskarte *f*; (*in a lottery*) Los *n*; (*for a traffic violation*) Strafzettel *m*; (pol) Wahlliste *f* ‖ *tr* etikettieren; (*aut*) mit e-m Strafzettel versehen

tick'et a'gency *s* Vorverkaufsstelle *f*

tick'et a'gent *s* Fahrkartenverkäufer –in *mf*

tick'et of'fice *s* Kartenverkaufsstelle *f*

tick'et win'dow *s* Schalter *m*

tick'ing *s* Ticken *n*

tickle ['tɪkəl] *s* Kitzel *m* ‖ *tr* kitzeln ‖ *intr* jucken

ticklish ['tɪklɪʃ] *adj* kitzlig; (*touchy*) heikel

ticktock ['tɪk‚tɑk] *adv*—**go t.** ticktack machen ‖ *s* Ticken *n*

tid'al wave' ['taɪdəl] *s* Flutwelle *f*

tidbit ['tɪd‚bɪt] *s* Leckerbissen *m*

tiddlywinks ['tɪdlɪ‚wɪŋks] *s* Flohhüpfspiel *n*

tide [taɪd] *s* Gezeiten *pl*; **against the t.** (fig) gegen den Strom; **the t. is coming in** die Flut steigt; **the t. is going out** die Flut fällt ‖ *tr*—**t. s.o. over** j–n über Wasser halten

tide'land' *s* Watt *n*

tide'wa'ter *s* Flutwasser *n*

tidings ['taɪdɪŋz] *spl* Botschaft *f*

ti·dy ['taɪdi] *adj* ordentlich; (*sum*) hübsch ‖ *v* (*pret & pp* –died) *tr* in Ordnung bringen; **t. up** aufräumen ‖ *intr*—**t. up** aufräumen

tie [taɪ] *adj* (sport) unentschieden ‖ *s* (*cord*) Schnur *f*; (*ribbon*) Band *n*; (*necktie*) Krawatte *f*; (*knot*) Schleife *f*; (mus) Ligatur *f*; (parl) Stimmengleichheit *f*; (rr) Schwelle *f*; (sport) Unentschieden *n*; **end in a tie** punktgleich enden; **ties** (*e.g., of friendship*) Bande *pl* ‖ *v* (*pret & pp* **tied**; *ger* **tying**) *tr* binden; **be tied up** (*said of a person or telephone*) besetzt sein; **get tied up** (*in traffic*) steckenbleiben; **my hands are tied** mir sind die Hände gebunden; **tie in with** verknüpfen mit; **tie oneself down** sich festlegen; **tie to** festbinden an (*dat*); **tie up** (*a wound*) verbinden; (*traffic*) lahmlegen; (*money*) fest anlegen; (*production*) stillegen; (*the telephone*) blockieren; (*a boat*) festmachen

tie'back' *s* Gardinenhalter *m*

tie'clasp' *s* Krawattenhalter *m*

tie'pin' *s* Krawattennadel *f*

tier [tɪr] *s* Reihe *f*; (theat) Rang *m*

tie'rod' *s* (aut) Zugstange *f*

tie'-up' *s* (*of traffic*) Stockung *f*

tiger ['taɪgər] *s* Tiger *m*

ti'ger shark' *s* Tigerhai *m*

tight [taɪt] *adj* (*firm*) fest; (*clothes*) eng; (*taut*) straff; (*scarce*) knapp; (*container*) dicht; (*drunk*) beschwipst; (*with money*) knaus(e)rig; **feel t. in the chest** sich beengt fühlen ‖ *adv* fest; **hold t.** festhalten; **sit t.** sich nicht rühren; **pull t.** strammziehen ‖ **tights** *spl* Trikot *m & n*

tighten ['taɪtən] *tr* (*a rope*) straff spannen; (*a belt*) enger schnallen; (*a jar lid*) festziehen; (*a screw*) anziehen; (*a spring*) spannen; (*a knot*) zuziehen

tight'-fist'ed *adj* knaus(e)rig

tight'-fit'ting *adj* eng anliegend

tight'-lipped' *adj* verschlossen

tight'rope' *s* Drahtseil *n*; **walk a t.** auf e–m festgespannten Drahtseil gehen

tight' spot' *s* (coll) Klemme *f*

tight' squeeze' *s* (coll) Zwickmühle *f*

tight'wad' *s* Geizkragen *m*

tigress ['taɪgrɪs] *s* Tigerin *f*

tile [taɪl] *s* (*for the floor or wall*) Fliese *f*; (*for the roof*) Dachziegel *m*; (*glazed tile*) Kachel *f* ‖ *tr* (*a roof*) mit Ziegeln decken; (*a floor*) mit Fliesen auslegen; (*a bathroom*) kacheln

tile' roof' *s* Ziegeldach *n*

till [tɪl] *s* Kasse *f* ‖ *tr* ackern ‖ *prep* bis (*acc*); **t. now** bisher ‖ *conj* bis

tiller ['tɪlər] *s* (naut) Pinne *f*

tilt [tɪlt] *s* Kippen *n*; **full t.** mit voller Wucht ‖ *tr* kippen; (*a bottle, the head*) neigen; **t. back** (*e.g., a chair*) zurücklehnen; **t. over** umkippen ‖ *intr* kippen; **t. over** umkippen

timber ['tɪmbər] *s* Holz *n*; (*for structural use*) Bauholz *n*; (*rafter*) Balken *m*

tim'berland' *s* Waldland *n*

tim'ber line' *s* Baumgrenze *f*

timbre ['tɪmbər] *s* Klangfarbe *f*

time [taɪm] *s* Zeit *f*; (*limited period*) Frist *f*; (*instance*) Mal *n*; (mus) Takt *m*; **all the t.** ständig; **all this t.** die ganze Zeit; **any number of times** x–mal; **at no t.** nie; **at one t.** einst; **at some t.** irgendwann; **at that t.**

damals; **at the present t.** derzeit; **at times** manchmal; **at what t.?** um wieviel Uhr?; **by this t.** nunmehr; **do t.** (sl) sitzen; **do you have the t.?** können Sie mir sagen, wie spät es ist?; **for a t.** e–e Zeitlang; **for the last t.** zum letzten Mal; **for the t.** being vorläufig; **give s.o. a hard t.** j–m das Leben schwer machen; **have a good t.** sich gut unterhalten; **have a hard t.** (ger) es schwer haben zu (inf); **in no t.** im Nu; **in t.** zur rechten Zeit; (in the course of time) mit der Zeit; **make good t.** Fortschritte machen; **on one's own t.** in der Freizeit; **on t.** pünktlich; (on schedule) fahrplanmäßig; (com) auf Raten; **several times** mehrmals; **take one's t.** sich [dat] Zeit lassen; **there's t. for that** das hat Zeit; **this t. tomorrow** morgen um diese Zeit; **t.!** (sport) Zeit!; **t. is up!** die Zeit ist um!; **t. of life** Lebensalter n; **times** Zeiten pl; (math) mal, e.g., **two times** two zwei mal zwei; **t. will tell** die Zeit wird es lehren; **what t. is it?** wieviel Uhr ist es? ‖ tr (mit der Uhr) messen; **t. s.th. right** die richtige Zeit wählen für

time′ bomb′ s Zeitbombe f
time′card′ s Stechkarte f
time′ clock′ s Stechuhr f
time′-consum′ing adj zeitraubend
time′ expo′sure s (phot) Zeitaufnahme f
time′ fuse′ s Zeitzünder m
time′-hon′ored adj altehrwürdig
time′keep′er s Zeitnehmer –in mf
time′-lag′ s Verzögerung f
timeless ['taɪmlɪs] adj zeitlos
time′ lim′it s Frist f; **set a t. on** befristen
timely ['taɪmli] adj zeitgerecht; (topic) aktuell
time′ pay′ment s Ratenzahlung f
time′piece′ s Uhr f
timer ['taɪmər] s (person) Zeitnehmer –in mf; (device) Schaltuhr f; (aut) Zündunterbrecher m; (phot) Zeitauslöser m
time′ sig′nal s Zeitzeichen n
time′ stud′y s Zeitstudien pl
time′ta′ble s Zeittabelle f; (aer) Flugplan m; (rr) Fahrplan m
time′work′ s Zeitlohnarbeit f
time′worn′ adj abgenutzt
time′ zone′ s Zeitzone f
timid ['tɪmɪd] adj ängstlich
tim′ing s genaue zeitliche Berechnung f; (aut) Zündeinstellung f
timorous ['tɪmərəs] adj furchtsam
tin [tɪn] adj Zinn– ‖ s (element) Zinn n; (tin plate) Weißblech n
tin′ can′ s Blechdose f
tincture ['tɪŋktʃər] s Tinktur f
tinder ['tɪndər] s Zunder m
tin′derbox′ s (fig) Pulverfaß n
tin′ foil′ s Zinnfolie f
ting-a-ling ['tɪŋəˌlɪŋ] s Klingeling m
tinge [tɪndʒ] s (of color) Stich m; (fig) Spur f ‖ v (pret tingeing & tinging) tr leicht färben

tingle ['tɪŋgəl] s Kribbeln n, Prickeln n ‖ intr kribbeln, prickeln
tinker ['tɪŋkər] s (bungler) Pfuscher m ‖ intr basteln
tinkle ['tɪŋkəl] s Klingeln n ‖ intr klingeln
tin′ mine′ s Zinnbergwerk n
tinsel ['tɪnsəl] s Lametta f; (fig) Flitterkram m
tin′smith′ s Klempner m
tin′ sol′dier s Zinnsoldat m
tint [tɪnt] s Farbton m ‖ tr tönen, leicht färben
tint′ed glass′ s (aut) blendungsfreies Glas n
tiny ['taɪni] adj winzig
tip [tɪp] s Spitze f; (gratuity) Trinkgeld n; (hint) Tip m; **it's on the tip of my tongue** es schwebt mir auf der Zunge ‖ v (pret & pp tipped; ger tipping) tr schief halten; (a waiter) ein Trinkgeld geben (dat); **tip off** e–n Tip geben (dat); **tip one's hat** auf den Hut tippen ‖ intr—**tip over** umtippen
tip′-off′ s Tip m, rechtzeitiger Wink m
tipple ['tɪpəl] tr & intr süffeln
tippler ['tɪplər] s Säufer –in mf
tipster ['tɪpstər] s Wettberater m
tipsy ['tɪpsi] adj beschwipst
tip′toe′ s—**on t.** auf den Zehenspitzen ‖ v (pret & pp –toed; ger –toeing) intr auf den Zehenspitzen gehen
tip′top′ adj tipptopp
tirade ['taɪred] s Tirade f
tire [taɪr] s Reifen m ‖ tr ermüden; **t. out** strapazieren ‖ intr ermüden
tired adj müde; **be t. of** (ger) es satt haben zu (inf); **be t. of coffee** den Kaffee satt haben; **t. out** abgespannt
tire′ gauge′ s Reifendruckmesser m
tireless ['taɪrlɪs] adj unermüdlich
tire′ pres′sure s Reifendruck m
tiresome ['taɪrsəm] adj (tiring) ermüdend; (boring) langweilig
tissue ['tɪʃju] s Gewebe n; (thin paper) Papiertaschentuch n; **t. of lies** Lügengewebe n
tis′sue pa′per s Seidenpapier n
tit [tɪt] s (sl) Brust f; **tit for tat** wie du mir, so ich dir
Titan ['taɪtən] s Titan(e) m
titanic [taɪ'tænɪk] adj titanisch
titanium [taɪ'tenɪˌəm] s Titan n
tithe [taɪð] s Kirchenzehnt m ‖ tr (pay one tenth of) den Zehnten bezahlen von; (exact a tenth from) den Zehnten erheben von
Titian ['tɪʃən] adj tizianrot
titillate ['tɪtɪˌlet] tr & intr kitzeln, (angenehm) reizen
title ['taɪtəl] s Titel m; (to a property) Eigentumsrecht n; (claim) Rechtstitel m; (of a chapter) Überschrift f; (honor) Würde f; (aut) Kraftfahrzeugbrief m ‖ tr titulieren
ti′tle bout′ s (box) Titelkampf m
ti′tle deed′ s Eigentumsurkunde f
ti′tle hold′er s Titelverteidiger –in mf
ti′tle page′ s Titelblatt n
ti′tle role′ s Titelrolle f

titter ['tɪtər] s Gekicher n ‖ intr kichern

titular ['tɪtələr] adj Titular–

to [tu], [tʊ] adv—to and fro hin und her ‖ prep zu (dat); (a city, country, island) nach (dat); (as far as) bis (acc); (in order to) um ... zu (inf); (against, e.g., a wall) an (dat or acc); a quarter to eight viertel vor acht; how far is it to the town? wie weit ist es bis zur Stadt?; to a T haargenau

toad [tod] s Kröte f

toad'stool' s Giftpilz m

toad•y ['todi] s Schranze m & f ‖ v (pret & pp –ied) intr (to) scharwenzeln (um)

to-and-fro ['tu•ənd'fro] adj Hin– und Her– ‖ adv hin und her

toast [tost] s (bread; salutation) Toast m; drink a t. to e–n Toast ausbringen auf (acc) ‖ tr (bread) rösten

toaster ['tostər] s Toaster m

toast'mas'ter s Toastmeister m

tobac•co [tə'bæko] s (–cos) Tabak m

tobac'co pouch' s Tabaksbeutel m

toboggan [tə'bagən] s Rodel m & f ‖ intr rodeln

tocsin ['taksɪn] s Alarmglocke f

today [tu'de] adv heute ‖ s—from t. on von heute an; today's heutig

toddle ['tadəl] s Watscheln n ‖ intr watscheln

toddler ['tadlər] s Kleinkind n

toddy ['tadi] s Toddy m

to-do [tə'du] s Getue n

toe [to] s Zehe f; be on one's toes auf Draht sein; step on s.o.'s toes j–m auf die Zehen treten ‖ v (pret & pp toed; ger toeing) tr—toe the line nicht aus der Reihe tanzen

toe' dance' s Spitzentanz m

toe'-in' s (aut) Spur f

toe'nail' s Zehennagel m

together [tu'gɛðər] adv zusammen; t. with mitsamt (dat), samt (dat)

togetherness [tu'gɛðərnɪs] s Zusammengehörigkeit f

tog'gle switch' ['tagəl] s (elec) Kippschalter m

togs [tagz] spl Klamotten pl

toil [tɔɪl] s Mühe f; toils Schlingen pl ‖ intr sich mühen

toilet ['tɔɪlɪt] s (room) Toilette f; (bathroom fixture) Klosett n

toi'let ar'ticle s Toilettenartikel m

toi'let bowl' s Klosettschüssel f

toi'let pa'per s Klosettpapier n

toi'let seat' s Toilettenring m

token ['tokən] adj (payment) symbolisch; (strike) Warn– ‖ Zeichen n; (proof) Beweis m; by the same t. aus dem gleichen Grund; as (or in) t. of zum Beweis (genit)

tolerable ['talərəbəl] adj erträglich

tolerably ['talərəbli] adv leidlich

tolerance ['talərəns] s Duldsamkeit f; (mach) Toleranz f

tolerant ['talərənt] adj (of) duldsam (gegen), tolerant (gegen)

tolerate ['talə‚ret] tr dulden

toleration [‚talə'reʃən] s Duldung f

toll [tol] adj (road) gebührenpflichtig s Wegezoll m; (at a bridge) Brücker zoll m; (of bells) Läuten n; (numbe of victims) Zahl f der Opfer; (fig Tribut m; (telp) Gebühr f für ei Ferngespräch; take a heavy t. o life viele Menschenleben kosten ‖ t & intr läuten

toll' booth' s Zahlkasse f

toll' bridge' s Zollbrücke f

toll' call' s Ferngespräch n

toll' collec'tor s Zolleinnehmer –in m

toma•to [tə'meto] s (–toes) Tomate

toma'to juice' s Tomatensaft f

tomb [tum] s Grab n, Grabmal n

tomboy ['tam‚bɔɪ] s Wildfang m

tomb'stone' s Grabstein m

tomcat ['tam‚kæt] s Kater m

tome [tom] s Band m

tomfoolery [tam'fuləri] s Albernhei f

Tom'my gun' ['tami] s Maschinen pistole f

tom'myrot' s Blödsinn m

tomorrow [tu'mɔro] adv morgen; t evening morgen abend; t. mornin₁ morgen früh; t. night morgen abend t. noon morgen mittag ‖ s morgen tomorrow's morgig

tom-tom ['tam‚tam] s Hindutromme f

ton [tʌn] s Tonne f

tone [ton] s Ton m; (of color) Farbton m; (phot) Tönung f ‖ tr tönen; (phot) tönen; t. down dämpfen ‖ intr milde₁ werden

tone'-control knob' s (rad) Klangregler m

tongs [taŋz] spl Zange f

tongue [tʌŋ] s Zunge f; (language) Sprache f; (of a shoe) Zunge f; (of a buckle) Dorn m; (of a bell) Klöppel m; (of a wagon) Deichsel f; (carp) Feder f; hold one's t. den Mund halten

tongue'-tied' adj zungenlahm; (fig) sprachlos

tongue' twist'er s Zungenbrecher m

tonic ['tanɪk] adj tonisch ‖ s (med) Tonikum n; (mus) Tonika f

tonight [tu'naɪt] adv heute nacht; (this evening) heute abend

tonnage ['tʌnɪdʒ] s Tonnage f

tonsil ['tansɪl] s Mandel f

tonsilitis [‚tansɪ'laɪtɪs] s Mandelentzündung f

tonsure ['tanʃər] s Tonsur f

too [tu] adv (also) auch; (excessively) zu; too bad! Schade!

tool [tul] s (& fig) Werkzeug n ‖ tr (with tools) bearbeiten

tool'box' s Werkzeugkasten m

tool'mak'er s Werkzeugmacher m

tool' shed' s Geräteschuppen m

toot [tut] s (aut) Hupen n ‖ tr (a trumpet) blasen; t. the horn (aut) hupen ‖ intr (aut) hupen

tooth [tuθ] s (teeth [tiθ]) Zahn m; (of a rake) Zinke f; t. and nail mit aller Gewalt

tooth'ache' s Zahnschmerz m, Zahnweh n

tooth'brush' *s* Zahnbürste *f*
tooth' decay' *s* Zahnfäule *f*
toothless ['tuθlɪs] *adj* zahnlos
tooth'paste' *s* Zahnpaste *f*
tooth'pick' *s* Zahnstocher *m*
tooth' pow'der *s* Zahnpulver *n*
top [tɑp] *adj* oberste; (*speed, price, form*) Höchst–; (*team*) Spitzen–; (*first-class*) erstklassig || *s* Spitze *f*; (*of a mountain*) Gipfel *m*; (*of a tree*) Wipfel *m*; (*of a car*) Verdeck *n*; (*of a box*) Deckel *m*; (*of a garment*) Oberteil *m & n*; (*of a bottle*) Verschluß *m*; (*of an object*) obere Seite *f*; (*of the water*) Oberfläche *f*; (*of a turnip*) Kraut *n*; (*toy*) Kreisel *m*; **at the top of one's voice** aus voller Kehle; **at the top of the page** oben auf der Seite; **be tops with s.o.** (coll) bei j–m ganz groß angeschrieben sein; **from top to bottom** von oben bis unten; **on top** (& fig) obenauf; **on top of** (*position*) auf (*dat*); (*direction*) auf (*acc*); **on top of that** obendrein || *v* (*pret & pp* **topped;** *ger* **topping**) *tr* (*a tree*) kappen; (*surpass*) übertreffen; **that tops everything** das übersteigt alles; **top off** (*a meal, an evening*) abschließen; **to top it off** zu guter Letzt
topaz ['topæz] *s* Topas *m*
top' brass' *s* (mil) hohe Tiere *pl*
top'coat' *s* Überzieher *m*
top' dog' *s* (coll) Erste *mf*
top' ech'elon *s* Führungsspitze *f*
top' hat' *s* Zylinder *m*
top'-heav'y *adj* oberlastig
topic ['tɑpɪk] *s* Gegenstand *m*, Thema *n*
topical ['tɑpɪkəl] *adj* aktuell
top' kick' *s* (mil) Spieß *m*
topless ['tɑplɪs] *adj* Oben-ohne–
topmast ['tɑp ˌmest] *s* Toppmast *m*
top'most' *adj* oberste
top'notch' *adj* erstklassig
top' of the head' *s* Scheitel *m*
topography [tə'pɑgrəfi] *s* Topographie *f*
topple ['tɑpəl] *tr & intr* stürzen
topsail ['tɑpsəl] *s* Toppsegel *n*
top'-se'cret *adj* streng geheim
top' ser'geant *s* Hauptfeldwebel *m*
top'side' *adv* auf Deck || *s* Oberseite *f*
top'soil' *s* Mutterboden *m*
topsy-turvy ['tɑpsi'tʌrvi] *adj* drunter und drüber || *adv*–**turn t.** durcheinanderbringen
torch [tɔrtʃ] *s* Fackel *f*; (Brit) Taschenlampe *f*; **carry the t. for** (coll) verknallt sein in (*acc*)
torch'bear'er *s* (& fig) Fackelträger *m*
torch'light' *s* Fackelschein *m*
torch'light parade' *s* Fackelzug *m*
torment ['tɔrment] *s* Qual *f* || [tɔr'ment] *tr* quälen
tormentor [tɔr'mentər] *s* Quäler –in *mf*
torn [tɔrn] *adj* zerrissen, rissig
torna·do [tɔr'nedo] *s* (**–does & –dos**) Tornado *m*, Windhose *f*
torpe·do [tɔr'pido] *s* (**–does**) Torpedo *m* || *tr* torpedieren

torpe'do boat' *s* Torpedoboot *n*
torpe'do tube' *s* Ausstoßrohr *n*
torpid ['tɔrpɪd] *adj* träge
torque [tɔrk] *s* Drehmoment *n*
torrent ['tɔrənt] *s* Sturzbach *m*; (*of words*) Schwall *m*; **in torrents** stromweise
torrential [tə'rentʃəl] *adj*–**t. rain** Wolkenbruch *m*
torrid ['tɔrɪd] *adj* brennend
Tor'rid Zone' *s* heiße Zone *f*
tor·so ['tɔrso] *s* (**–sos**) (*of a statue*) Torso *m*; (*of a human body*) Rumpf *m*
tortoise ['tɔrtəs] *s* Schildkröte *f*
tor'toise shell' *s* Schildpatt *n*
torture ['tɔrtʃər] *s* Folter *f*, Qual *f* || *tr* foltern, quälen
toss [tɔs] *s* Wurf *m*; (*of the head*) Zurückwerfen *n*; (*of a ship*) Schlingern *n*; (*of a coin*) Loswurf *m* || *tr* (*throw*) werfen; (*the head*) zurückwerfen; (*a ship*) hin– und herwerfen; (*a coin*) hochwerfen; **t. off** (*work*) hinhauen; **t. s.o. for** mit j–m losen um || *intr* (naut) schlingern; **t. for** e–e Münze hochwerfen um; **t. in bed** sich im Bett hin –und herwerfen
toss'up' *s* Loswurf *m*; **it's a t. whether** es hängt ganz vom Zufall ab, ob
tot [tɑt] *s* Knirps *m*
to·tal ['totəl] *adj* Gesamt–, total || *s* Gesamtsumme *f* || *v* (*pret & pp* **–tal[l]ed;** *ger* **–tal[l]ling**) *tr* (*add up*) zusammenrechnen; (*amount to*) sich belaufen auf (*acc*); (sl) (*Wagen*) ganz kaputt machen
totalitarian [to ˌtælɪ'terɪ·ən] *adj* totalitär
tote [tot] *tr* schleppen
totem ['totəm] *s* Totem *n*
totter ['tɑtər] *intr* schwanken
touch [tʌtʃ] *s* Berührung *f*; (*sense of touch*) Tastsinn *m*; (*e.g., of a fever*) Anflug *m*; (*trace, small bit*) Spur *f*; (*of a pianist*) Anschlag *m*; **get in t. with** in Verbindung treten mit; **keep in t. with** in Verbindung bleiben mit; **put in t. with** in Verbindung setzen mit; **with sure t.** mit sicherer Hand || *tr* berühren; (fig) rühren; **he's a little touched** (coll) er hat e–n kleinen Klaps; **t. bottom** anstoßen; **t. glasses** mit den Gläsern anstoßen; **t. off** auslösen; **t. s.o. for** (coll) j–n anpumpen um; **t. up** (*with cosmetics*) auffrischen; (paint, phot) retuschieren || *intr* sich berühren; **t. down** (aer) aufsetzen; **t. on** (*a topic*) berühren; (*e.g., arrogance*) grenzen an (*acc*)
touch' and go' *s*—**be t.** auf der Kippe stehen
touch'ing *adj* rührend, herzergreifend
touch'stone' *s* (fig) Prüfstein *m*
touch'-type' *intr* blindschreiben
touchy ['tʌtʃi] *adj* (*spot, person*) empfindlich; (*situation*) heikel
tough [tʌf] *adj* (*strong*) derb; (*meat*) zäh; (*life*) mühselig; (*difficult*) schwierig || *s* Gassenjunge *m*
toughen ['tʌfən] *tr* zäher machen; **t.**

up (*through training*) ertüchtigen ||
intr (**up**) zäher werden
tough′ luck′ *s* Pech *n*
tour [tʊr] *s* (*of a country*) Tour *f;* (*of
a city*) Rundfahrt *f;* (*of a museum*)
Führung *f;* (mus, theat) Tournee *f;*
go on t. auf Tournee gehen || *tr* be-
sichtigen; (*a country*) bereisen || *intr*
auf der Reise sein; (theat) auf Tournee sein
tour′ guide′ *s* Reiseführer –in *mf*
tourism ['tʊrɪzəm] *s* Touristik *f*
tournament ['tʊrnəmənt] *s* Turnier *n*
tourney ['tʊrni] *s* Turnier *n*
tourniquet ['tʊrnɪ͵kɛt] *s* Aderpresse *f*
tousle ['taʊzəl] *tr* (zer)zausen
tow [to] *s*—**have in tow** im Schlepptau
haben; **take in tow** ins Schlepptau
nehmen || *tr* schleppen; **tow away**
abschleppen
toward(s) [tord(z)] *prep* (*with respect
to*) gegenüber (*dat*); (*a goal, direction*) auf (*acc*), zu; (*shortly before*)
gegen (*acc*); (*for*) für (*acc*); (*facing*)
zugewandt (*dat*)
tow′boat′ *s* Schleppschiff *n*
tow•el ['taʊ·əl] *s* Handtuch *n* || *v* (*pret
& pp* **-el[l]ed**; *ger* **-el[l]ing**) *tr* mit
e–m Handtuch abtrocknen
tow′el rack′ *s* Handtuchhalter *m*
tower ['taʊ·ər] *s* Turm *m;* **t. of strength**
starker Hort *m* || *intr* ragen; **t. over**
überragen
tow′ering *adj* hochragend; (*rage*) rasend
tow′ing serv′ice *s* Schleppdienst *m*
tow′line′ *s* Schlepptau *n*
town [taʊn] *adj* städtisch, Stadt– || *s*
Stadt *f;* **in t.** in der Stadt; **out of t.**
verreist; **go to t. on** Feuer und
Flamme sein für
town′ coun′cil *s* Stadtrat *m*
town′ hall′ *s* Rathaus *n*
town′ house′ *s* Stadthaus *n*
town′ship *s* Gemeinde *f*
tow′rope′ *s* Schlepptau *n;* (*for a
glider*) Startseil *n*
tow′ truck′ *s* Abschleppwagen *m*
toxic ['taksɪk] *adj* Gift–, toxisch || *s*
Giftstoff *m*
toy [tɔɪ] *adj* Spielzeug– || *s* Spielzeug
n; **toys** Spielsachen *pl;* (com) Spiel-
waren *pl* || *intr* spielen; **toy with**
(fig) herumspielen mit
toy′ dog′ *s* Schoßhund *m*
toy′ shop′ *s* Spielwarengeschäft *n*
toy′ sol′dier *s* Spielzeugsoldat *m*
trace [tres] *s* Spur *f;* (*of a harness*)
Strang *m;* **without a t.** spurlos || *tr*
(*a drawing*) durchpausen; (*lines*)
nachziehen; (*track*) ausfindig machen; **t. (back) to** zurückführen auf
(*acc*)
tracer ['tresər] *s* Suchzettel *m*
trac′er bul′let *s* Leuchtspurgeschoß *n*
trac′ing pa′per *s* Pauspapier *n*
track [træk] *s* Spur *f;* (*of a foot*) Fuß-
spur *f;* (*of a wheel*) Radspur *f;*
(*chain of a tank*) Raupenkette *f;*
(*parallel rails*) Geleise *n;* (*single rail*)
Gleis *n,* Schiene *f;* (*station platform*)
Bahnsteig *m;* (*path*) Pfad *m;* (*course

for running) Laufbahn *f;* (*course for
motor and horse racing*) Rennbahn *f;*
(*running as a sport*) Laufen *n;* **be off
the t.** (fig) auf dem Holzweg sein;
go off the t. (derail) entgleisen; **in
one's tracks** mitten auf dem Weg;
jump the t. aus den Schienen sprin-
gen || *tr* verfolgen; **t. down** (*game,
a criminal*) zur Strecke bringen; (*a
rumor, reference*) nachgehen (*dat*);
t. up (*a rug*) schmutzig treten
track′-and-field′ *adj* Leichtathletik–
trackless ['træklɪs] *adj* pfadlos; (*vehicle*) schienenlos
track′ meet′ *s* Leichtathletikwettkampf
m
tract [trækt] *s* Strich *m;* (*treatise*)
Traktat *n;* **t. of land** Grundstück *n*
traction ['trækʃən] *s* (med) Ziehen *n;*
(*of the road*) Griffigkeit *f*
tractor ['træktər] *s* Traktor *m;* (*of
a tractor-trailer*) Zugmaschine *f*
trac′tor-trail′er *s* Sattelschlepper *m* mit
e–m Anhänger
trade [tred] *s* Handel *m;* (*calling, job*)
Gewerbe *n;* (*exchange*) Tausch *m;*
by t. von Beruf || *tr* (aus)tauschen;
t. in (*e.g., a used car*) in Zahlung
geben || *intr* Handel treiben
trade′ agree′ment *s* Handelsabkommen
n
trade′ bar′riers *spl* Handelsschranken
pl
trade′-in val′ue *s* Handelswert *m*
trade′mark′ *s* Warenzeichen *n*
trade′ name′ *s* (*of products*) Handels-
bezeichnung *f;* (*of a firm*) Firmen-
name *m*
trader ['tredər] *s* Händler –in *mf*
trade′ school′ *s* Gewerbeschule *f*
trade′ se′cret *s* Geschäftsgeheimnis *n*
trades′man *s* (**-men**) Handelsmann *n*
trade′ un′ion *s* Gewerkschaft *f*
trade′wind′ *s* Passatwind *m*
trad′ing post′ *s* Handelsniederlassung *f*
trad′ing stamp′ *s* Rabattmarke *f*
tradition [trə'dɪʃən] *s* Tradition *f*
traditional [trə'dɪʃənəl] *adj* herkömmlich, traditionell
traf•fic ['træfɪk] *s* Verkehr *m;* (*trade*)
(in) Handel *m* (in *dat*) || *v* (*pret &
pp* **-ficked**; *ger* **-ficking**) *intr*—**t. in**
handeln in (*dat*)
traf′fic ac′cident *s* Verkehrsunfall *m*
traf′fic cir′cle *s* Kreisverkehr *m*
traf′fic is′land *s* Verkehrsinsel *f*
traf′fic jam′ *s* Verkehrsstockung *f*
traf′fic lane′ *s* Fahrbahn *f*
traf′fic light′ *s* Verkehrsampel *f;* **go
through a t.** bei Rot durchfahren
traf′fic sign′ *s* Verkehrszeichen *n*
traf′fic tick′et *s* Strafzettel *m*
traf′fic viola′tion *s* Verkehrsdelikt *n*
tragedian [trə'dʒɪdɪ·ən] *s* Tragiker *m*
tragedy ['trædʒɪdi] *s* (& *fig*) Tragödie *f*
tragic ['trædʒɪk] *adj* tragisch
trail [trel] *s* (*path*) Fährte *f;* **be on
s.o.'s t.** j–m auf der Spur sein; **t. of
smoke** Rauchfahne *f* || *tr* (*on foot*)
nachgehen (*dat*); (*in a vehicle*) nach-
fahren (*dat*); (*in a race*) nachhinken
(*dat*) || *intr* (*said of a robe*) schleifen

trailer ['treilər] s Anhänger m; (mobile home) Wohnwagen m
trail'er camp' s Wohnwagenparkplatz m
train [tren] s (of railway cars) Zug m; (of a dress) Schleppe f; (following) Gefolge n; (of events) Folge f; **go by t.** mit dem Zug fahren; **t. of thought** Gedankengang m || tr ausbilden; (for a particular job) anlernen; (the memory) üben; (plants) am Spalier aufziehen; (an animal) dressieren; (a gun) (on) zielen (auf acc); (sport) trainieren || intr üben; (sport) trainieren
trained adj geschult, ausgebildet
trainee [tre'ni] s Anlernling m
trainer ['trenər] s (of domestic animals) Dresseur m, Dresseuse f; (of wild animals) Dompteur m, Dompteuse f; (aer) Schulflugzeug n; (sport) Sportwart –in mf
train'ing s Ausbildung f; (of animals) Dressur f; (sport) Training n
train'ing school' s (vocational school) Berufsschule f; (reformatory) Erziehungsanstalt f
trait [tret] s Charakterzug m
traitor ['tretər] s Verräter –in mf; (of a country) Hochverräter –in mf
trajectory [trə'dʒɛktəri] s Flugbahn f
tramp [træmp] s Landstreicher –in mf; (loose woman) Frauenzimmer n || tr trampeln; (traverse on foot) durchstreifen || intr vagabundieren; **t. on** herumtrampeln auf (dat)
trample ['træmpəl] s Getrampel n || tr trampeln; **t. to death** tottreten; **t. under foot** (fig) mit Füßen treten || intr—**t. on** herumtrampeln auf (dat); (fig) mit Füßen treten
trampoline ['træmpə,lin] s Trampolin n
trance [træns] s Trance f
tranquil ['træŋkwɪl] adj ruhig
tranquilize ['træŋkwɪ,laɪz] tr beruhigen
tranquilizer ['træŋkwɪ,laɪzər] s Beruhigungsmittel n
tranquillity [træn'kwɪlɪti] s Ruhe f
transact [træn'zækt] tr abwickeln
transaction [træn'zækʃən] s Abwicklung f; **transactions** (of a society) Sitzungsbericht m
transatlantic [,trænsət'læntɪk] adj transatlantisch
transcend [træn'sɛnd] tr übersteigen
transcendental [,trænsən'dɛntəl] adj übersinnlich; (philos) transzendental
transcribe [træn'skraɪb] tr (copy) umschreiben; (dictated or recorded material) übertragen; (mus) transkribieren; (phonet) in Lautschrift wiedergeben; (rad) auf Band aufnehmen
transcript ['trænskrɪpt] s Transkript n
transcription [træn'skrɪpʃən] s Umschrift f; (mus) Transkription f
transept ['trænsɛpt] s Querschiff n
trans·fer ['trænsfər] s (of property) Übertragung f (of money) Überweisung f; (of an employee) Versetzung f; (of a passenger) Umsteigen n; (ticket) Umsteigefahrschein

m || [træns'fʌr], ['trænsfər] v (pret & pp –ferred; ger –ferring) tr (property) übertragen; (money) überweisen; (to another account) umbuchen; (an employee) versetzen || intr (to) versetzt werden (nach, zu); (said of a passenger) umsteigen
transfix [træns'fɪks] tr durchbohren
transform [træns'fɔrm] tr (a person) verwandeln; (into) umwandeln (in acc); (elec) umspannen
transformer [træns'fɔrmər] s (elec) Stromwandler m, Transformator m
transfusion [træns'fjuʒən] s (med) Übertragung f, Transfusion f
transgress [træns'grɛs] tr überschreiten
transgression [træs'grɛʃən] s Vergehen n
transient ['trænʃənt] adj vorübergehend; (fleeting) flüchtig || s Durchreisende mf
transistor [træn'sɪstər] adj Transistor– || s Transistor m
transistorize [træn'sɪstə,raɪz] tr transistorisieren
transit ['trænzɪt] s (astr) Durchgang m; (com) Transit m; **in t.** unterwegs
transition [træn'zɪʃən] s Übergang m
transitional [træn'zɪʃənəl] adj Übergangs–
transitive ['trænsɪtɪv] adj transitiv
transitory ['trænsɪ,tori] adj vergänglich
translate [træns'let] tr übersetzen; **t. into action** in die Tat umsetzen
translation [træns'leʃən] s Übersetzung f
translator [træns'letər] s Übersetzer –in mf
transliterate [træns'lɪtə,ret] tr transkribieren
translucent [træns'lusənt] adj durchscheinend, lichtdurchlässig
transmigration [,trænsmaɪ'greʃən] s— **t. of the soul** Seelenwanderung f
transmission [træns'mɪʃən] s (of a text) Textüberlieferung f; (of news, information) Übermittlung f; (aut) Getriebe n; (rad, telv) Sendung f
trans·mit [træns'mɪt] v (pret & pp –mitted; ger –mitting) tr (send forward) übersenden; (disease, power, light, heat) übertragen; (e.g., customs) überliefern; (by inheritance) vererben; (rad, telp, telv) senden
transmitter [træns'mɪtər] s (rad, telg, telv) Sender m
transmutation [,trænsmu'teʃən] s Umwandlung f; (biol) Transmutation f; (chem, phys) Umwandlung f
transmute [træns'mjut] tr umwandeln
transoceanic [,trænzoʃɪ'ænɪk] adj überseeisch, Übersee–
transom ['trænsəm] s (crosspiece) Querbalken m; (window over a door) Oberlicht n mit Kreuzsprosse; (of a boat) Spiegel m
transparency [træns'perənsi] s Durchsichtigkeit f, Transparenz f; (phot) Diapositiv n
transparent [træns'perənt] adj durchsichtig, transparent

transpire ['træns'paɪr] *intr* (*happen*) sich ereignen; (*leak out*) (fig) durchsickern

transplant ['træns,plænt] *s* (bot, surg) Verpflanzung *f* || [træns'plænt] *tr* (bot, surg) verpflanzen

transport ['trænsport] *s* Beförderung *f*, Transport *m;* (nav) Truppentransporter *m* || [træns'port] *tr* befördern

transportation [,trænspor'teʃən] *s* Beförderung *f;* (*public transportation*) Verkehrsmittel *n;* **do you need t.?** brauchen Sie e-e Fahrgelegenheit?

trans'port plane' *s* Transportflugzeug *n*

transpose [træns'poz] *tr* umstellen; (math, mus) transponieren

trans·ship [træns'ʃɪp] *v* (*pret & pp* –shipped; *ger* –shipping) *tr* (com, naut) umladen

trap [træp] *s* (& fig) Falle *f;* (*snare*) Schlinge *f;* (*pit*) Fallgrube *f;* (*under a sink*) Geruchsverschluß *m;* (*mouth*) (sl) Klappe *f;* (chem) Abscheider *m;* (golf) Sandbunker *m;* **fall** (or **walk**) **into a t.** in die Falle gehen; **set a trap** e–e Falle stellen || *v* (*pret & pp* **trapped;** *ger* **trapping**) *tr* mit e–r Falle fangen; (fig) erwischen; (mil) einfangen

trap' door' *s* Falltür *f*, Klapptür *f;* (theat) Versenkung *f*

trapeze [trə'piz] *s* Trapez *n;* (gym) Schwebereck *n*

trapezoid ['træpɪ,zɔɪd] *s* Trapez *n*

trapper ['træpər] *s* Fallensteller *m*

trappings ['træpɪŋz] *spl* Staat *m;* (*caparison*) Staatsgeschirr *n*

trap'shoot'ing *s* Tontaubenschießen *n*

trash [træʃ] *s* Abfälle *pl;* (*junk*) Schund *m;* (*artistically inferior material*) Kitsch *m;* (*worthless people*) Gesindel *n*

trash' can' *s* Mülleimer *m*, Abfalleimer *m*

trashy ['træʃi] *adj* kitschig; (*literature*) Schund-

travail [trə'vel] *s* Plackerei *f;* (*labor of childbirth*) Wehen *pl*

trav·el ['trævəl] *s* Reisen *n;* (*trip*) Reise *f;* (*e.g., of a bullet, rocket*) Bewegung *f;* (*of moving parts*) Lauf *m;* **travels** Reiseerlebnisse *pl* || *v* (*pret & pp* –el[l]ed; *ger* –el[l]ing) *tr* bereisen || *intr* reisen; (*said of a vehicle or passenger*) fahren; (astr, aut, mach, phys) sich bewegen

trav'el a'gency *s* Reisebüro *n*

traveler ['trævələr] *s* Reisende *mf*

trav'eler's check' *s* Reisescheck *m*

trav'el fold'er *s* Reiseprospekt *m*

trav'eling bag' *s* Reisetasche *f*

trav'eling sales'man *s* (–men) Geschäftsreisende *m*

travelogue ['trævə,lɔg] *s* Reisebericht *m;* (cin) Reisefilm *m*

traverse [trə'vʌrs] *tr* durchqueren || *intr* (*said of a gun*) sich drehen

traves·ty ['trævɪsti] *s* Travestie *f* || *v* (*pret & pp* –tied) *tr* travestieren

trawl [trɔl] *s* Schleppnetz *n* || *tr* mit dem Schleppnetz fangen || *intr* mit dem Schleppnetz fischen

trawler ['trɔlər] *s* Schleppnetzboot *n*

tray [tre] *s* Tablett *n;* (phot) Schale *f*

treacherous ['trɛtʃərəs] *adj* verräterisch; (*e.g., ice*) trügerisch

treachery ['trɛtʃəri] *s* Verrat *m*

tread [trɛd] *s* (*step*) Tritt *m;* (*imprint*) Spur *f;* (*on a tire*) Profil *n* || *v* (*pret* **trod** [trɑd]; *pp* **trodden** ['trɑdən] & **trod**) *tr* betreten || *intr* (**on**) treten (auf *acc*)

treadle ['trɛdəl] *s* Trittbrett *n*

tread'mill' *s* (& fig) Tretmühle *f*

treason ['trizən] *s* Verrat *m*

treasonable ['trizənəbəl] *adj* verräterisch

treasure ['trɛʒər] *s* Schatz *m* || *tr* sehr schätzen

treasurer ['trɛʒərər] *s* Schatzmeister –in *mf*

treasury ['trɛʒəri] *s* Schatzkammer *f;* (*chest*) Tresor *m;* (*public treasury*) Staatsschatz *m;* **Treasury** Finanzministerium *n*

treat [trit] *s* Hochgenuß *m* || *tr* behandeln; (*regard*) (as) betrachten (als); **t. oneself to s.th.** sich [*dat*] etw genehmigen; **t. s.o. to s.th** j–n bewirten mit

treatise ['tritɪs] *s* Abhandlung *f*

treatment ['tritmənt] *s* Behandlung *f*

treaty ['triti] *s* Vertrag *m*

treble ['trɛbəl] *adj* (*threefold*) dreifach; (mus) Diskant– || *s* Diskant *m;* (*voice*) Diskantstimme *f* || *tr* verdreifachen || *intr* sich verdreifachen

tre'ble clef' *s* Violinschlüssel *m*

tree [tri] *s* Baum *m*

treeless ['trilɪs] *adj* baumlos

tree'top' *s* Baumwipfel *m*

tree' trunk' *s* Baumstamm *m*

trellis ['trɛlɪs] *s* Spalier *n;* (*gazebo*) Gartenhäuschen *n*

tremble ['trɛmbəl] *s* Zittern *n* || *intr* zittern; (geol) beben; **t. all over** am ganzen Körper zittern

tremendous [trɪ'mɛndəs] *adj* ungeheuer

tremor ['trɛmər] *s* Zittern *n;* (geol) Beben *n*

trench [trɛntʃ] *s* Graben *m;* (mil) Schützengraben *m*

trenchant ['trɛntʃənt] *adj* schneidend; (*policy*) durchschlagend

trench' war'fare *s* Stellungskrieg *m*

trend [trɛnd] *s* Richtung *f*, Trend *m*

trespass ['trɛspəs] *s* unbefugtes Betreten *n;* (*sin*) Sünde *f* || *intr* unbefugt fremdes Eigentum betreten; **no trespassing** (public sign) Betreten verboten; **t. on** unbefugt betreten

trespasser ['trɛspəsər] *s* Unbefugte *mf*

tress [trɛs] *s* Flechte *f*

trestle ['trɛsəl] *s* Gestell *n;* (*of a bridge*) Brückenbock *m*

trial ['traɪ·əl] *s* (*attempt*) Versuch *m;* (*hardship*) Beschwernis *f;* (jur) Prozeß *m;* **a week's t.** e–e Woche Probezeit; **be on t. for** vor Gericht stehen wegen; **be brought up** (or **come up**) **for t.** zur Verhandlung kommen; **new t.** Wiederaufnahmeverfahren *n;* **on t.** (com) auf Probe; **put on t.** vor Gericht bringen

tri'al and er'ror s—by t. durch Ausprobieren

tri'al balloon' s Versuchsballon m

tri'al by ju'ry s Verhandlung f vor dem Schwurgericht

tri'al or'der s Probeauftrag m

tri'al run' s Probelauf m

triangle ['traɪ,æŋgəl] s Dreieck n

triangular [traɪ'æŋgjələr] adj dreieckig

tribe [traɪb] s Stamm m; (pej) Sippschaft f

tribunal [traɪ'bjunəl] s Tribunal n

tributary ['trɪbjə,teri] adj zinspflichtig || s Nebenfluß m

tribute ['trɪbjut] s Tribut m, Zins m; **pay t.** to Anerkennung zollen (dat)

trice [traɪs] s—**in a t.** im Nu

trick [trɪk] s Trick m; (prank) Streich m; (technique) Kniff m; (artifice) Schlich m; (cards) Stich m; **be on to s.o.'s tricks** j–s Schliche kennen; **be up to one's old tricks** sein Unwesen treiben; **do the t.** die Sache schaffen; **play a dirty t. on s.o.** j–m e–n gemeinen Streich spielen || tr reinlegen; **t. s.o. into** (ger) j–n durch Kniffe dazu bringen zu (inf)

trickery ['trɪkəri] s Gaunerei f

trickle ['trɪkəl] s Tröpfeln n || intr tröpfeln, rieseln

trickster ['trɪkstər] s Gauner m

tricky ['trɪki] adj (wily) listig; (touchy) heikel; (difficult) verzwickt

trident ['traɪdənt] s Dreizack m

tried [traɪd] adj bewährt, probat

trifle ['traɪfəl] s Kleinigkeit f; **a t.** (e.g., too big) ein bißchen || tr—**t. away** vertändeln || intr tändeln

trif'ling adj geringfügig || s Tändelei f

trigger ['trɪgər] s Abzug m; **pull the t.** abdrücken || tr auslösen

trig'ger-hap'py adj schießwütig

trigonometry [,trɪgə'namətri] s Trigonometrie f

trill [trɪl] s Triller m || tr & intr trillern

trillion ['trɪljən] s Billion f; (Brit) Trillion f

trilogy ['trɪlədʒi] s Trilogie f

trim [trɪm] adj (trimmer; trimmest) (figure) schick; (well-kept) gepflegt || s (e.g., of a hat) Zierleiste f; (naut) Trimm m; **be in t.** in Form sein || v (pret & pp trimmed; ger trimming) tr (clip) stutzen; (decorate) dekorieren; (a Christmas tree) schmücken; (beat) (coll) schlagen; (naut) trimmen

trim'ming s (e.g., of a dress) Besatz m; (of hedges) Stutzen n; **take a t.** (coll) e–e Niederlage erleiden; **trimmings** (decorations) Verzierungen pl; (food) Zutaten pl; (scraps) Abfälle pl; **with all the trimmings** (fig) mit allen Schikanen

trinity ['trɪnɪti] s Dreiheit f; **Trinity** Dreifaltigkeit f

trinket ['trɪŋkɪt] s Schmuckgegenstand m

tri·o ['tri·o] s (-os) (& mus) Trio n

trip [trɪp] s Reise f; (on drugs) Trip m; **go on** (or **take**) **a t.** e–e Reise machen || v (pret & pp **tripped**; ger **tripping**) tr ein Bein stellen (dat); **t. up** (fig) zu Fall bringen || intr stolpern

tripartite [traɪ'partaɪt] adj Dreiparteien–; (of three powers) Dreimächte–

tripe [traɪp] s Kutteln pl; (sl) Schund m

trip'ham'mer s Schmiedehammer m

triple ['trɪpəl] adj dreifach || s Dreifache n || tr verdreifachen

triplet ['trɪplɪt] s (offspring) Drilling m; (mus) Triole f

triplicate ['trɪplɪkɪt] adj dreifach || s—**in t.** in dreifacher Ausfertigung

tripod ['traɪpad] s Dreifuß m; (phot) Stativ n

triptych ['trɪptɪk] s Triptychon n

trite [traɪt] adj abgedroschen

triumph ['traɪ·əmf] s Triumph m || intr (over) triumphieren (über acc)

triumphal [traɪ'ʌmfəl] adj Sieges–

triumphant [traɪ'ʌmfənt] adj triumphierend

trivia ['trɪvɪ·ə] spl Nichtigkeiten pl

trivial ['trɪvɪ·əl] adj trivial, alltäglich; (person) oberflächlich

triviality [,trɪvɪ'ælɪti] s Trivialität f, Nebensächlichkeit f

Trojan ['trodʒən] adj trojanisch || s Trojaner –in mf

troll [trol] s (myth) Troll m || tr & intr mit der Schleppangel fischen

trolley ['trali] s Straßenbahn f

trollop ['traləp] s (slovenly woman) Schlampe f; (prostitute) Dirne f

trombone ['trambon] s Posaune f

troop [trup] s Trupp m; (mil) Truppe f

trooper ['truper] s Kavallerist m; **swear like a t.** fluchen wie ein Kutscher

troop'ship' s Truppentransporter m

trophy ['trofi] s Trophäe f; (sport) Pokal m

tropical ['trapɪkəl] adj Tropen–

tropics ['trapɪks] spl Tropen pl

trot [trat] s Trab m || v (pret & pp trotted; ger trotting) tr—**t. out** (coll) zur Schau stellen || intr traben

troubadour ['trubə,dor] s Minnesänger m

trouble ['trʌbəl] s (inconvenience, bother) Mühe f; (difficulty) Schwierigkeit f; (physical distress) Leiden n; (civil disorder) Unruhe f; **ask for t.** das Schicksal herausfordern; **be in t.** in Schwierigkeiten sein; (be pregnant) schwanger sein; **cause s.o. a lot of t.** j–m viel zu schaffen machen; **get into t.** in Schwierigkeiten geraten; **go to a lot of t.** sich (dat) viel Mühe machen; **it was no t. at all!** gern geschehen!; **make t.** Geschichten machen; **take the t. to** (inf) sich der Mühe unterziehen zu (inf); **that's the t.** da liegt die Schwierigkeit; **what's the t.?** was ist los? || tr (worry) beunruhigen; (bother) belästigen; (disturb) stören; (said of ills) plagen

trou'blemak'er s Unruhestifter –in mf

troubleshooter ['trʌbəl,ʃutər] s Stö-

rungssucher –in *mf;* (*in disputes*) Friedensstifter –in *mf*
troublesome ['trʌbəlsəm] *adj* lästig
trough [trɔf] *s* Trog *m;* (*of a wave*) Wellental *n*
troupe [trup] *s* Truppe *f*
trousers ['trauzərz] *spl* Hose *f*
trous·seau [tru'so] *s* (–seaux & –seaus) Brautausstattung *f*
trout [traut] *s* Forelle *f*
trowel ['trau·əl] *s* Kelle *f*
truant ['tru·ənt] *adj* schwänzend ‖ *s—* **play t.** die Schule schwänzen
truce [trus] *s* Waffenruhe *f*
truck [trʌk] *s* Last(kraft)wagen *m;* (*for luggage*) Gepäckwagen *m* ‖ *tr* mit Lastkraftwagen befördern
truck'driv'er *s* Lastwagenfahrer *m*
trucker ['trʌkər] *s* (*driver*) Lastwagenfahrer *m;* (*owner of a trucking firm*) Fuhrunternehmer –in *mf*
truck' farm'ing *s* Gemüsebau *m*
truculent ['trʌkjələnt] *adj* gehässig
trudge [trʌdʒ] *intr* stapfen
true [tru] *adj* wahr; (*loyal*) (ge)treu; (*genuine*) echt; (*sign*) sicher; **come t.** sich verwirklichen; **prove t.** sich als wahr erweisen; **that's t.** das stimmt
truffle ['trʌfəl] *s* Trüffel *f*
truism ['tru·izəm] *s* Binsenwahrheit *f*
truly ['truli] *adv* wirklich; **Yours t.** Hochachtungsvoll
trump [trʌmp] *s* Trumpf *m* ‖ *tr* trumpfen; **t. up** erdichten ‖ *intr* trumpfen
trumpet ['trʌmpɪt] *s* Trompete *f* ‖ *intr* (*said of an elephant*) trompeten
truncheon ['trʌntʃən] *s* Gummiknüppel *m*
trunk [trʌŋk] *s* (*chest*) Koffer *m;* (*of a tree*) Stamm *m;* (*of a living body*) Rumpf *m;* (*of an elephant*) Rüssel *m;* (*aut*) Kofferraum *m;* **trunks** (sport) Sporthose *f*
trunk' line' *s* Fernverkehrsweg *m*
truss [trʌs] *s* (ɛrchit) Tragwerk *n;* (med) Bruchband *n* ‖ *tr* (archit) stützen; (*bind*) festbinden
trust [trʌst] *s* (**in**) Vertrauen *n* (auf *acc*); (com) Trust *m;* (jur) Treuhand *f* ‖ *tr* trauen (*dat*); (*hope*) hoffen ‖ *intr*—**t. in** vertrauen auf (*acc*)
trust' com'pany *s* Treuhandgesellschaft *f*
trustee [trʌs'ti] *s* Aufsichtsrat *m;* (jur) Treuhänder –in *mf*
trustee'ship *s* Treuhandverwaltung *f*
trustful ['trʌstfəl] *adj* zutraulich
trust' fund' *s* Treuhandfonds *m*
trust'wor'thy *adj* vertrauenswürdig
trusty ['trʌsti] *adj* treu ‖ *s* Kalfaktor *m*
truth [truθ] *s* Wahrheit *f;* **in t.** wahrlich
truthful ['truθfəl] *adj* (*person*) ehrlich; (*e.g., account*) wahrheitsgemäß
try [traɪ] *s* Versuch *m* ‖ *v* (*pret & pp* **tried**) *tr* versuchen; (*one's patience*) auf e–e harte Probe stellen; (*a cause*) verhandeln; **be tried for** vor Gericht kommen wegen; **try on** anprobieren; (*a hat*) aufprobieren; **try out** erproben; (*new food*) kosten; **try s.o. for**

gegen j–n verhandeln wegen ‖ *intr* versuchen
try'ing *adj* anstrengend
try'out' *s* (sport) Ausscheidungskampf *m*
T'-shirt' *s* T-Shirt *n*
tub [tʌb] *s* Wanne *f;* (*boat*) Kasten *m*
tubby ['tʌbi] *adj* (coll) kugelrund
tube [t(j)ub] *s* (*pipe*) Rohr *n,* Röhre *f;* (*e.g., of toothpaste*) Tube *f;* (*of rubber*) Schlauch *m;* (rad) Röhre *f*
tuber ['t(j)ubər] *s* (bot) Knolle *f*
tubercle ['t(j)ubərkəl] *s* Tuberkel *m*
tuberculosis [t(j)u ˌbʌrkjə'losɪs] *s* Lungenschwindsucht *f*
tuck [tʌk] *s* (sew) Abnäher *m* ‖ *tr* (*into one's pocket, under a mattress*) stecken; (*under one's arm*) klemmen; (*into bed*) packen; **t. in** reinstecken; **t. up** (*trousers*) hochkrempeln; (*a skirt, dress*) hochschürzen
Tuesday ['t(j)uzde] *s* Dienstag *m;* **on T.** am Dienstag
tuft [tʌft] *s* Büschel *m & n* ‖ *tr* (*e.g., a mattress*) durchheften
tug [tʌg] *s* (*pull*) Zug *m;* (*boat*) Schlepper *m* ‖ *v* (*pret & pp* **tugged;** *ger* **tugging**) *tr* schleppen ‖ *intr* (**at**) zerren (an *dat*)
tug'boat' *s* Schleppdampfer *m*
tug' of war' *s* Tauziehen *n*
tuition [t(j)u'ɪʃən] *s* Schulgeld *n*
tulip ['t(j)ulɪp] *s* Tulpe *f*
tumble ['tʌmbəl] *s* (*fall*) Sturz *m;* (gym) Purzelbaum *m* ‖ *intr* (*fall*) stürzen; (gym) Saltos machen; **t. down the stairs** die Treppe herunterpurzeln
tum'ble-down' *adj* baufällig
tumbler ['tʌmblər] *s* (*glass*) Trinkglas *n;* (*of a lock*) Zuhaltung *f;* (*acrobat*) Akrobat –in *mf*
tumor ['t(j)umər] *s* Geschwulst *f*
tumult ['t(j)umʌlt] *s* Getümmel *n*
tuna ['tunə] *s* Thunfisch *m*
tune [t(j)un] *s* Melodie *f;* **be in t.** richtig gestimmt sein; **be out of t.** falsch singen; (*said of a piano*) verstimmt sein; **change one's t.** e–n anderen Ton anschlagen ‖ *tr* stimmen; **t. up** (aut) neu einstellen ‖ *intr*— **t. in on** (rad) einstellen; **t. up** (*said of an orchestra*) stimmen
tungsten ['tʌŋstən] *s* Wolfram *n*
tunic ['t(j)unɪk] *s* Tunika *f*
tun'ing fork' *s* Stimmgabel *f*
tun·nel ['tʌnəl] *s* Tunnel *m;* (min) Stollen *m* ‖ *v* (*pret & pp* **–nel[l]ed;** *ger* **–nel[l]ing**) *intr* e–n Tunnel bohren
turban ['tʌrbən] *s* Turban *m*
turbid ['tʌrbɪd] *adj* trüb(e)
turbine ['tʌrbɪn] *s* Turbine *f*
turboprop ['tʌrbo ˌprɑp] *s* Turboprop *m*
turbulence ['tʌrbjələns] *s* Turbulenz *f*
tureen [t(j)u'rin] *s* Terrine *f*
turf [tʌrf] *s* Rasendecke *f;* (*of a gang*) (sl) Gebiet *n;* **the t.** der Turf
Turk [tʌrk] *s* Türke *m,* Türkin *f*
turkey ['tʌrki] *s* Truthahn *m;* (*female*) Truthenne *f;* **Turkey** die Türkei

Turkish ['tʌrkɪʃ] *adj* türkisch ‖ *s* Türkische *n*

Tur'kish tow'el *s* Frottiertuch *n*

turmoil ['tʌrmɔɪl] *s* Getümmel *n*

turn [tʌrn] *s* (*rotation*) Drehung *f;* (*change of direction or condition*) Wendung *f;* (*curve*) Kurve *f;* (*by a driver*) Abbiegen *n;* (*of a century*) Wende *f;* (*of a spool*) Windung *f;* at every **t.** bei jeder Gelegenheit; good **t.** Gunst *f;* **it's his t.** er ist dran; out of **t.** außer der Reihe; take turns sich abwechseln ‖ *tr* drehen; (*the page*) umblättern; (*one's head*) wenden; **t.** down (*refuse*) ablehnen; (*a radio*) leiser stellen; (*a bed*) aufdecken; (*a collar*) umschlagen; (*an appeal*) (jur) verwerfen; **t.** in (*an application, resignation*) einreichen; (*lost articles*) abgeben; (*a person*) anzeigen; **t.** into verwandeln in (*acc*); **t.** loose frei lassen; **t.** off (*light, gas*) abdrehen; (rad, telv) abstellen; **t.** on (*gas, light*) andrehen; (*excite*) (coll) in Erregung versetzen; (rad, telv) anstellen; **t.** out produzieren; (*pockets*) umkehren; (*eject*) vor die Tür setzen; **t.** over (*property*) abtreten; (*a business*) übertragen; (*e.g., weapons*) abliefern; **t.** up (*a card, sleeve*) aufschlagen ‖ *intr* (*rotate*) sich drehen; (*in some direction*) sich wenden; **it turned out that** es stellte sich heraus, daß; **t.** against (fig) sich wenden gegen; **t.** around sich herumdrehen; **t.** back umdrehen; **t.** down (*a street*) einbiegen in (*acc*); **t.** in (*go to bed*) zu Bett gehen; **t.** into werden zu; **t.** out ausfallen; **t.** out for sich einfinden zu; **t.** out for the best sich zum Guten wenden; **t.** out in force vollzählig erscheinen; **t.** out to be sich erweisen als; **t.** over (*tip over*) umkippen; (aut) anspringen; **t.** to s.o. for help sich an j-n um Hilfe wenden; **t.** towards sich wenden gegen; **t.** up auftauchen

turn'coat' *s* Überläufer –in *mf*

turn'ing point' *s* Wendepunkt *m*

turnip ['tʌrnɪp] *s* Steckrübe *f*

turn'out' *s* Beteiligung *f*

turn'o'ver *s* Umsatz *m*

turn'pike' *s* Autobahn *f*

turnstile ['tʌrn ˌstaɪl] *s* Drehkreuz *n*

turn'ta'ble *s* Plattenteller *m;* (rr) Drehscheibe *f*

turpentine ['tʌrpən ˌtaɪn] *s* Terpentin *n*

turpitude ['tʌrpɪ ˌt(j)ud] *s* Verworfenheit *f*

turquoise ['tʌrk(w)ɔɪz] *adj* türkisfarben ‖ *s* Türkis *m*

turret ['tʌrɪt] *s* Turm *m*

turtle ['tʌrtəl] *s* Schildkröte *f*

tur'tledove' *s* Turteltaube *f*

tur'tleneck' *s* Rollkragen *m*

tusk [tʌsk] *s* (*of an elephant*) Stoßzahn *m;* (*of a boar*) Hauer *m*

tussle ['tʌsəl] *s* Rauferei *f* ‖ *intr* raufen

tutor ['t(j)utər] *s* Hauslehrer –in *mf*

tuxe·do [tʌk'sido] *s* (**–dos**) Smoking *m*

twang [twæŋ] *s* (*of a musical instrument*) Schwirren *n;* (*of the voice*) Näseln *n* ‖ *intr* schwirren; näseln

tweed [twid] *adj* aus Tweed ‖ *s* Tweed *m*

tweet [twit] *s* Gezwitscher *n* ‖ *intr* zwitschern

tweezers ['twizərz] *spl* Pinzette *f*

twelfth [twɛlfθ] *adj* & *pron* zwölfte ‖ *s* (*fraction*) Zwölftel *n;* **the t.** (*in dates or in series*) der Zwölfte

twelve [twɛlv] *adj* & *pron* zwölf ‖ *s* Zwölf *f*

twentieth ['twɛntɪ·ɪθ] *adj* & *pron* zwanzigste ‖ *s* (*fraction*) Zwanzigstel *n;* **the t.** (*in dates or in series*) der Zwanzigste

twenty ['twɛnti] *adj* & *pron* zwanzig ‖ *s* Zwanzig *f;* **the twenties** die zwanziger Jahre

twen'ty-one' *adj* & *pron* einundzwanzig

twice [twaɪs] *adv* zweimal

twiddle ['twɪdəl] *tr* müßig herumdrehen; **t.** one's thumbs Daumen drehen

twig [twɪg] *s* Zweig *m*

twilight ['twaɪ ˌlaɪt] *adj* dämmerig ‖ *s* Abenddämmerung *f*

twin [twɪn] *adj* (*brother, sister*) Zwillings–; (*double*) Doppel– ‖ *s* Zwilling *m*

twine [twaɪn] *s* (*for a package*) Bindfaden *m;* (sew) Zwirn *m* ‖ *tr*—**t.** around winden um

twin'-en'gine *adj* zweimotorig

twinge [twɪndz] *s* stechender Schmerz *m*

twinkle ['twɪŋkəl] *s* Funkeln *n;* **in a t.** im Nu ‖ *intr* funkeln

twirl [twʌrl] *s* Wirbel *m* ‖ *tr* herumwirbeln ‖ *intr* wirbeln

twist [twɪst] *s* (*turn*) Drehung *f;* (*distortion*) Verdrehung *f;* (*strand*) Flechte *f;* (*bread roll*) Zopf *m;* (*dance*) Twist *m* ‖ *tr* (*revolve*) drehen; (*wind*) winden; (*an arm, words*) verdrehen; **t.** one's ankle sich [*dat*] den Knöchel vertreten ‖ *intr* sich drehen; (*wind*) winden

twister ['twɪstər] *s* (coll) Windhose *f*

twit [twɪt] *s* (sl) Depp *m* ‖ *v* (*pret* & *pp* **twitted;** *ger* **twitting**) *tr* verspotten; (*upbraid*) rügen

twitch [twɪtʃ] *s* Zucken *n* ‖ *intr* zucken

twitter ['twɪtər] *s* Zwitschern *n* ‖ *intr* zwitschern

two [tu] *adj* & *pron* zwei ‖ *s* Zwei *f;* **by twos** zu zweit; **in two** entzwei; **put two and two together** Schlußfolgerungen ziehen

two'-edged' *adj* zweischneidig

two'-faced' *adj* doppelzüngig

two' hun'dred *adj* & *pron* zweihundert

two'-piece' *adj* (*suit*) zweiteilig

twosome ['tusəm] *s* (*of lovers*) Liebespaar *n;* (golf) Einzelspiel *n*

two'-time' *tr* untreu sein (*dat*)

two'-tone' *adj* zweifarbig

two'-way traf'fic *s* Gegenverkehr *m*

tycoon [taɪ'kun] *s* Industriekapitän *m*

type [taɪp] *s* (*kind*) Art *f;* (*of person; of manufacture*) Typ *m;* (typ) Drucktype *f*, Letter *f* ‖ *tr* & *intr* tippen

type'face' *s* Schriftbild *n*
type'script' *s* Maschinenschrift *f*
type'set'ter *s* Schriftsetzer –in *mf*
type'write' *v* (*pret* –wrote; *pp* –written) *tr* & *intr* mit der Maschine schreiben
type'writ'er *s* Schreibmaschine *f*
type'writer rib'bon *s* Farbband *n*
ty'phoid fe'ver ['taɪfɔɪd] *s* Typhus *m*
typhoon [taɪ'fun] *s* Taifun *m*
typical ['tɪpɪkəl] *adj* (of) typisch (für)
typi·fy ['tɪpɪ‚faɪ] *v* (*pret* & *pp* –fied) *tr* (*characterize*) typisch sein für; (*exemplify*) ein typisches Beispiel sein für
typ'ing er'ror *s* Tippfehler *m*

typist ['taɪpɪst] *s* Maschinenschreiber –in *mf*
typographic(al) [‚taɪpə'græfɪk(əl)] *adj* typographisch; (*error*) Druck–
typography [taɪ'pɑgrəfi] *s* (*the skill*) Buchdruckerkunst *f*; (*the work*) Buchdruck *m*
tyrannical [tɪ'rænɪkəl] *adj* tyrannisch
tyrannize ['tɪrə‚naɪz] *tr* tyrannisieren
tyranny ['tɪrəni] *s* Tyrannei *f*
tyrant ['taɪrənt] *s* Tyrann *m*
ty·ro ['taɪro] *s* (–ros) Neuling *m*
Tyrol [tɪ'rol] *s* Tirol *n*
Tyrolean [tɪ'roli·ən] *adj* tirolerisch || *s* Tiroler –in *mf*

U

U, u [ju] *s* einundzwanzigster Buchstabe des englischen Alphabets
ubiquitous [ju'bɪkwɪtəs] *adj* allgegenwärtig
udder ['ʌdər] *s* Euter *n*
ugliness ['ʌglɪnɪs] *s* Häßlichkeit *f*
ugly ['ʌgli] *adj* häßlich
Ukraine [ju'kren] *s* Ukraine *f*
Ukrainian [ju'krenɪ·ən] *adj* ukrainisch || *s* (*person*) Ukrainer –in *mf*; (*language*) Ukrainisch *n*
ulcer ['ʌlsər] *s* Geschwür *n*
ulcerate ['ʌlsə‚ret] *intr* eitern
ulte'rior mo'tive [ʌl'tɪrɪ·ər] *s* Hintergedanke *m*
ultimate ['ʌltɪmɪt] *adj* äußerste; (*goal*) höchst; (*result*) End– || *s* Letzte *n*
ultima·tum [‚ʌltɪ'metəm] *s* (–tums & –ta [tə]) Ultimatum *n*
ul'trahigh fre'quency ['ʌltrə‚haɪ] *s* Ultrahochfrequenz *f*
ultramodern [‚ʌltrə'mɑdərn] *adj* ultramodern
ultraviolet [‚ʌltrə'vaɪ·əlɪt] *adj* ultraviolett || *s* Ultraviolett *n*
ultravi'olet lamp' *s* Höhensonne *f*
umbil'ical cord' [ʌm'bɪlɪkəl] *s* Nabelschnur *f*
umbrage ['ʌmbrɪdʒ] *s*—take u. at Anstoß nehmen an (*dat*)
umbrella [ʌm'brelə] *s* Regenschirm *m*; (*aer*) Abschirmung *f*
umlaut ['umlaut] *s* Umlaut *m* || *tr* umlauten
umpire ['ʌmpaɪr] *s* Schiedsrichter –in *mf* || *tr* als Schiedsrichter leiten || *intr* Schiedsrichter sein
umpteen [ʌmp'tin] *adj* zig; **u. times** zigmal
UN ['ju'en] *s* (**United Nations**) UNO *f*
unable [ʌn'ebəl] *adj* unfähig
unabridged [ʌnə'brɪdʒd] *adj* ungekürzt
unaccented [‚ʌnæk'sentɪd] *adj* unbetont
unacceptable [‚ʌnæk'septɪbəl] *adj* unannehmbar
unaccountable [‚ʌnə'kauntəbəl] *adj*

nicht verantwortlich; (*strange*) seltsam
unaccounted-for [‚ʌnə'kauntɪd‚fɔr] *adj* unerklärt; (*acct*) nicht belegt
unaccustomed [‚ʌnə'kʌstəmd] *adj* (**to**) nicht gewöhnt (an *acc*)
unaffected [‚ʌnə'fektɪd] *adj* nicht affektiert; **u. by** unbeeinflusst von
unafraid [‚ʌnə'fred] *adj*—**be u.** (of) sich nicht fürchten (vor *dat*)
unalterable [ʌn'ɔltərəbəl] *adj* unabänderlich
unanimity [‚junə'nɪmɪti] *s* Stimmeneinheit *f*
unanimous [ju'nænɪməs] *adj* (*persons*) einmütig; (*vote*) einstimmig
unannounced [‚ʌnə'naunst] *adj* unangemeldet
unanswered [ʌn'ænsərd] *adj* (*question*) unbeantwortet; (*claim, statement*) unwiderlegt; (*request*) nicht erhört
unappreciative [‚ʌnə'priʃɪ·ətɪv] *adj* (of) unempfänglich (für)
unapproachable [‚ʌnə'protʃəbəl] *adj* unzugänglich
unarmed [ʌn'ɑrmd] *adj* unbewaffnet
unasked [ʌn'æskt] *adj* (*advice*) unerbeten; (*uninvited*) ungeladen
unassailable [‚ʌnə'seləbəl] *adj* unangreifbar
unassuming [‚ʌnə's(j)umɪŋ] *adj* nicht anmaßend
unattached [‚ʌnə'tætʃt] *adj* (**to**) nicht befestigt (an *dat*); (*person*) ungebunden; (*mil*) zur Verfügung stehend
unattainable [‚ʌnə'tenəbəl] *adj* unerreichbar
unattended [‚ʌnə'tendɪd] *adj* unbeaufsichtigt
unattractive [‚ʌnə'træktɪv] *adj* reizlos
unauthorized [ʌn'ɔθəraɪzd] *adj* unberechtigt
unavailable [‚ʌnə'veləbəl] *adj* (*person*) unabkömmlich; (*thing*) nicht verfügbar
unavenged [‚ʌnə'vendʒd] *adj* ungerächt
unavoidable [‚ʌnə'vɔɪdəbəl] *adj* unvermeidlich

unaware [ˌʌnə'wer] adj (of) nicht bewußt (genit)

unawares [ˌʌnə'werz] adv (unexpectedly) unversehens; (unintentionally) versehentlich; catch u. überraschen

unbalanced [ʌn'bælənst] adj nicht im Gleichgewicht; (fig) unausgeglichen

un·bar [ʌn'bɑr] v (pret & pp –barred; ger –barring) tr aufriegeln

unbearable [ʌn'berəbəl] adj unerträglich

unbeaten [ʌn'bitən] adj (& fig) ungeschlagen

unbecoming [ˌʌnbɪ'kʌmɪŋ] adj (improper) ungeziemend; (clothing) unkleidsam

unbelievable [ˌʌnbɪ'livəbəl] adj unglaublich

unbeliever [ˌʌnbɪ'livər] s Ungläubige mf

unbending [ʌn'bendɪŋ] adj unbeugsam

unbiased [ʌn'baɪ·əst] adj unvoreingenommen

unbidden [ʌn'bɪdən] adj ungebeten

un·bind [ʌn'baɪnd] v (pret & pp –bound) tr losbinden

unbleached [ʌn'blit/t] adj ungebleicht

unbolt [ʌn'bolt] tr aufriegeln

unborn ['ʌnbɔrn] adj ungeboren

unbosom [ʌn'buzəm] tr—u. oneself to sich offenbaren (dat)

unbowed [ʌn'baud] adj ungebeugt

unbreakable [ʌn'brekəbəl] adj unzerbrechlich

unbridled [ʌn'braɪdəld] adj ungezügelt

unbroken [ʌn'brokən] adj (intact) ungebrochen; (line, series) ununterbrochen; (horse) nicht zugeritten

unbuckle [ʌn'bʌkəl] tr aufschnallen

unburden [ʌn'bʌrdən] tr entlasten; u. oneself sein Herz ausschütten

unburied [ʌn'berid] adj unbeerdigt

unbutton [ʌn'bʌtən] adj aufknöpfen

uncalled-for [ʌn'kɔld ˌfɔr] adj unangebracht

uncanny [ʌn'kæni] adj unheimlich

uncared-for [ʌn'kerd ˌfɔr] adj verwahrlost

unceasing [ʌn'sisɪŋ] adj unaufhörlich

unceremonious [ˌʌnserɪ'moni·əs] adj (informal) ungezwungen; (rude) unsanft

uncertain [ʌn'sʌrtən] adj unsicher

uncertainty [ʌn'sʌrtənti] s Unsicherheit f

unchain [ʌn't/en] tr losketten; (fig) entfesseln

unchangeable [ʌn't/endʒəbəl] adj unveränderlich

uncharacteristic [ˌʌnkærɪktə'rɪstɪk] adj wesensfremd

uncharted [ʌn't/ɑrtɪd] adj auf keiner Karte verzeichnet

unchaste [ʌn't/est] adj unkeusch

unchecked [ʌn't/ekt] adj ungehemmt

unchristian [ʌn'krɪst/ən] adj unchristlich

uncivilized [ʌn'sɪvɪ ˌlaɪzd] adj unzivilisiert

unclad [ʌn'klæd] adj unbekleidet

unclaimed [ʌn'klemd] adj nicht abgeholt

unclasp [ʌn'klæsp] tr loshaken; (the arms, hands) öffnen

unclassified [ʌn'klæsɪ ˌfaɪd] adj nicht klassifiziert; (not secret) nicht geheim

uncle ['ʌnkəl] s Onkel m

unclean [ʌn'klin] adj unsauber; (relig) unrein

unclear [ʌn'klɪr] adj unklar

un·clog [ʌn'klɑg] v (pret & pp –clogged; ger –clogging) tr von e-m Hindernis befreien

uncombed [ʌn'komd] adj ungekämmt

uncomfortable [ʌn'kʌmfərtəbəl] adj unbequem; feel u. sich nicht recht wohl fühlen

uncommitted [ˌʌnkə'mɪtɪd] adj (troops) nicht eingesetzt; (delegates, nations) unentschieden

uncommon [ʌn'kɑmən] adj ungewöhnlich; (outstanding) außergewöhnlich

uncomplaining [ˌʌnkʌm'plenɪŋ] adj klaglos

uncompromising [ʌn'kɑmprə ˌmaɪzɪŋ] adj unbeugsam

unconcealed [ˌʌnkən'sild] adj unverholen

unconcerned [ˌʌnkən'sʌrnd] adj (about) unbesorgt (um)

unconditional [ˌʌnkən'dɪ/ənəl] adj bedingungslos

unconfirmed [ˌʌnkən'fɪrmd] adj unbestätigt, unverbürgt

unconquerable [ʌn'kɑŋkərəbəl] adj unüberwindlich

unconquered [ʌn'kɑŋkərd] adj unbezwungen

unconscious [ʌn'kɑn/əs] adj bewußtlos; (of) nicht bewußt (genit) || s— the u. das Unbewußte

unconstitutional [ˌʌnkɑnstɪ't(j)u/ənəl] adj verfassungswidrig

uncontested [ˌʌnkən'testɪd] adj unbestritten

uncontrollable [ˌʌnkən'troləbəl] adj unkontrollierbar; (fig) unbändig

unconventional [ˌʌnkən'vent/ənəl] adj unkonventionell

uncork [ʌn'kɔrk] tr entkorken

uncouple [ʌn'kʌpəl] tr abkoppeln

uncouth [ʌn'kuθ] adj ungehobelt; (appearance) ungeschlacht

uncover [ʌn'kʌvər] tr aufdecken

unctuous ['ʌŋkt/u·əs] adj salbungsvoll

uncultivated [ʌn'kʌltɪ ˌvetɪd] adj unbebaut

uncultured [ʌn'kʌlt/ərd] adj (fig) unkultiviert

uncut [ʌn'kʌt] adj nicht abgeschnitten; (gem) ungeschliffen; (grain) ungemäht

undamaged [ʌn'dæmɪdʒd] adj unbeschädigt, unversehrt

undaunted [ʌn'dɔntɪd] adj unverzagt

undecided [ˌʌndɪ'saɪdɪd] adj (person) unschlüssig; (thing) unentschieden

undefeated [ˌʌndɪ'fitɪd] adj unbesiegt

undefended [ˌʌndɪ'fendɪd] adj unverteidigt

undefiled [ˌʌndɪ'faɪld] adj unbefleckt

undefined [ˌʌndɪ'faɪnd] adj unklar

undeliverable [ˌʌndɪ'lɪvərəbəl] adj unbestellbar

undeniable [ˌʌndɪ'naɪ·əbəl] *adj* un-leugbar

under ['ʌndər] *adj* Unter– || *adv* unter–, e.g., **go u.** untergehen || *prep* unter (*position*) (*dat*); (*direction*) unter (*acc*)

un'derage' *adj* unmündig

un'der·bid' *v* (*pret & pp* –bid; *ger* –bidding) *tr* unterbieten

un'derbrush' *s* Unterholz *n*

un'dercar'riage *s* Fahrgestell *n*

un'derclothes' *spl* Unterwäsche *f*

un'dercov'er *adj* Geheim–; **u. agent** Spitzel *m*

un'dercur'rent *s* (*& fig*) Unterströmmung *f*

un'dercut' *v* (*pret & pp* –cut; *ger* –cutting) *tr* unterbieten

un'derdevel'oped *adj* unterentwickelt

un'derdog' *s* (coll) Unterlegene *mf*

un'derdone' *adj* nicht durchgebraten

un'deres'timate *tr* unterschätzen

un'derexpose' *tr* (phot) unterbelichten

un'dergar'ment *s* Unterkleidung *f*

un'der·go' *v* (*pret* –went; *pp* –gone) durchmachen; (*an operation*) sich unterziehen (*dat*)

un'dergrad'uate *s* Collegestudent –in *mf*

un'derground' *adj* unterirdisch; (fig) Untergrund–; (*water*) Grund–; (min) unter Tage || **un'derground'** *s* (*secret movement*) Untergrundbewegung *f*; **go u.** untertauchen

un'dergrowth' *s* Buschholz *n*, Unterholz *n*

un'derhand' *adj* (*throw*) unter Schulterhöhe (ausgeführt)

un'derhand'ed *adj* hinterhältig

un'derline', **un'derline'** *tr* unterstreichen

underling ['ʌndərlɪŋ] *s* Handlanger *m*

un'dermine' *tr* (*& fig*) untergraben

underneath [ˌʌndər'niθ] *adj* Unter– || *adv* unten || *s* Unterseite *f* || *prep* (*position*) unter (*dat*), unterhalb (*genit*); (*direction*) unter (*acc*)

un'dernour'ished *adj* unterernährt

un'dernour'ishment *s* Unterernährung *f*

un'derpad' *s* (*of a rug*) Unterlage *f*

un'derpaid' *adj* unterbezahlt

un'derpass' *s* Straßenunterführung *f*

un'der·pin' *v* (*pret & pp* –pinned; *ger* –pinning) *tr* untermauern

un'derplay' *tr* unterspielen

un'derpriv'ileged *adj* benachteiligt

un'derrate' *tr* unterschätzen

un'derscore' *tr* (*& fig*) unterstreichen

un'dersea' *adj* Unterwasser–

un'dersec'retar'y *s* Untersekretär –in *mf*

un'der·sell' *v* (*pret & pp* –sold; *ger* –selling) *tr* (*a person*) unterbieten; (*goods*) verschleudern

un'dershirt' *s* Unterhemd *n*

un'derside' *s* Unterseite *f*

un'dersigned' *adj* unterschrieben || **un'dersigned'** *s* Unterzeichnete *mf*

un'der·stand' *v* (*pret & pp* –stood) *tr* verstehen; **it's understood that** es ist selbstverständlich, daß; **make oneself understood** sich verständlich machen

understandable [ˌʌndər'stændəbəl] *adj* verständlich

understandably [ˌʌndər'stændəbli] *adv* begreiflicherweise

un'derstand'ing *adj* verständnisvoll || *s* (of) Verständnis *n* (für); (*between persons*) Einvernehmen *n*; (*agreement*) Übereinkommen *n*; **come to an u. with s.o.** sich mit j–m verständigen; **it is my u. that** wie ich verstehe

un'derstud'y *s* Ersatzmann *m*; (cin, theat) Ersatzschauspieler –in *mf*

un'der·take' *v* (*pret* –took; *pp* –taken) *tr* unternehmen

undertaker ['ʌndər‚tekər] *s* Leichenbestatter –in *mf*

un'dertak'ing *s* Unternehmen *n*

un'dertone' *s* leise Stimme *f*; (fig) Unterton *m*

un'dertow' *s* Sog *m*

un'derwa'ter *adj* Unterwasser–

un'derwear' *s* Unterwäsche *f*

un'derweight' *adj* untergewichtig

un'derworld' *s* (*of criminals*) Unterwelt *f*; (myth) Totenreich *n*

un'der·write', **un'der·write'** *v* (*pret* –wrote; *pp* –written) *tr* unterschreiben; (ins) versichern

un'derwrit'er *s* Unterzeichner –in *mf*; (ins) Versicherer –in *mf*; (st. exch.) Wertpapiermakler –in *mf*; **underwriters** Emissionsfirma *f*

undeserved [ˌʌndɪ'zʌrvd] *adj* unverdient

undeservedly [ˌʌndɪ'zʌrvɪdli] *adv* unverdientermaßen

undesirable [ˌʌndɪ'zaɪrəbəl] *adj* unerwünscht || *s* Unerwünschte *mf*

undeveloped [ˌʌndɪ'vɛləpt] *adj* unentwickelt; (*land*) unerschlossen

undies ['ʌndiz] *spl* (coll) Unterwäsche *f*

undigested [ˌʌndɪ'dʒɛstɪd] *adj* (*& fig*) unverdaut

undignified [ʌn'dɪgnɪ‚faɪd] *adj* würdelos

undiluted [ˌʌndɪ'lutɪd] *adj* unverdünnt

undiminished [ˌʌndɪ'mɪnɪʃt] *adj* unvermindert

undisciplined [ʌn'dɪsəplɪnd] *adj* undiszipliniert, zuchtlos

undisputed [ˌʌndɪs'pjutɪd] *adj* unbestritten, unangefochten

undisturbed [ˌʌndɪs't ʌrbd] *adj* ungestört

undivided [ˌʌndɪ'vaɪdɪd] *adj* ungeteilt

un·do [ʌn'du] *v* (*pret* –did; *pp* –done) *tr* (*a knot*) aufschnüren; (*a deed*) ungeschehen machen

undo'ing *s* Ruin *m*

undone [ʌn'dʌn] *adj* (*not done*) ungetan; (*ruined*) ruiniert; **come u.** sich lösen; **leave nothing u.** nichts unversucht lassen

undoubtedly [ʌn'dautɪdli] *adv* zweifellos

undramatic [ˌʌndrə'mætɪk] *adj* undramatisch

undress [ʌn'drɛs] *s*—**in a state of u.** (*nude*) in unbekleidetem Zustand; (*in a negligee*) im Negligé || *tr* ausziehen || *intr* sich ausziehen

undrinkable [ʌn'drɪŋkəbəl] *adj* nicht trinkbar
undue [ʌn'd(j)u] *adj* (*inappropriate*) unangemessen; (*excessive*) übermäßig
undulate ['ʌndjə,let] *intr* wogen
undulating ['ʌndjə,letɪŋ] *adj* wellenförmig
unduly [ʌn'd(j)uli] *adv* übermäßig
undying [ʌn'daɪ·ɪŋ] *adj* unsterblich
un'earned in'come ['ʌnʌrnd] *s* Kapitalrente *f*
unearth [ʌn'ʌrθ] *tr* ausgraben; (fig) aufstöbern
unearthly [ʌn'ʌrθli] *adj* unirdisch; (*cry*) schauerlich; **at an u. hour** (*early*) in aller Herrgottsfrühe
uneasy [ʌn'izi] *adj* (*worried*) ängstlich; (*ill at ease*) unbehaglich
uneatable [ʌn'itəbəl] *adj* ungenießbar
uneconomic(al) [,ʌnɛkə'nɑmɪk(əl)] *adj* unwirtschaftlich
uneducated [ʌn'ɛdjə,ketɪd] *adj* ungebildet
unemployed [,ʌnɛm'plɔɪd] *adj* arbeitslos ‖ *s* Arbeitslose *mf*
unemployment [,ʌnɛm'plɔɪmənt] *s* Arbeitslosigkeit *f*
unemploy'ment compensa'tion *s* Arbeitslosenunterstützung *f;* **collect u.** (sl) Stempeln gehen
unencumbered [,ʌnən'kʌmbərd] *adj* unbelastet
unending [ʌn'ɛndɪŋ] *adj* endlos
unequal [ʌn'ikwəl] *adj* ungleich; **u. to** nicht gewachsen (*dat*)
unequaled [ʌn'ikwəld] *adj* ohnegleichen
unequivocal [,ʌnə'kwɪvəkəl] *adj* eindeutig
unerring [ʌn'ɛrɪŋ] *adj* unfehlbar
UNESCO [ju'nɛsko] *s* (**United Nations Educational, Scientific, and Cultural Organization**) UNESCO *f*
unessential [,ʌnɛ'sɛnʃəl] *adj* unwesentlich
uneven [ʌn'ivən] *adj* (*not smooth*) uneben; (*unbalanced*) ungleich; (*not uniform*) ungleichmäßig; (*number*) ungerade
uneventful [,ʌnɪ'vɛntfəl] *adj* ereignislos
unexceptional [,ʌnɛk'sɛpʃənəl] *adj* nicht außergewöhnlich
unexpected [,ʌnɛk'spɛktɪd] *adj* unerwartet
unexplained [,ʌnɛk'splend] *adj* unerklärt
unexplored [,ʌnɛk'splord] *adj* unerforscht
unexposed [,ʌnɛk'spozd] *adj* (phot) unbelichtet
unfading [ʌn'fedɪŋ] *adj* unverwelklich
unfailing [ʌn'felɪŋ] *adj* unfehlbar
unfair [ʌn'fɛr] *adj* unfair; (*competition*) unlauter
unfaithful [ʌn'feθfəl] *adj* treulos
unfamiliar [,ʌnfə'mɪljər] *adj* unbekannt
unfasten [ʌn'fæsən] *tr* losbinden; (*e.g., a seat belt*) aufschnallen
unfathomable [ʌn'fæðəməbəl] *adj* unergründlich

unfavorable [ʌn'fevərəbəl] *adj* ungünstig
unfeasible [ʌn'fizəbəl] *adj* unausführbar
unfeeling [ʌn'filɪŋ] *adj* unempfindlich
unfilled [ʌn'fɪld] *adj* ungefüllt; (*post*) unbesetzt
unfinished [ʌn'fɪnɪʃt] *adj* unfertig; (*business*) unerledigt
unfit [ʌn'fɪt] *adj* (**for**) ungeeignet (für); (*not qualified*) (**for**) untauglich (für); **u. for military service** wehrdienstuntauglich
unfold [ʌn'fold] *tr* (*a chair*) aufklappen; (*cloth, paper*) entfalten; (*ideas, plans*) offenbaren
unforeseeable [,ʌnfor'si·əbəl] *adj* un absehbar
unforeseen [,ʌnfor'sin] *adj* unvorhergesehen
unforgettable [,ʌnfor'gɛtəbəl] *adj* unvergeßlich
unfortunate [ʌn'fortʃənɪt] *adj* unglücklich
unfortunately [ʌn'fortʃənɪtli] *adv* leider
unfounded [ʌn'faundɪd] *adj* unbegründet
un·freeze [ʌn'friz] *v* (*pret* **–froze;** *pp* **–frozen**) *tr* auftauen; (*prices*) freigeben
unfriendly [ʌn'frɛndli] *adj* unfreundlich
unfruitful [ʌn'frutfəl] *adj* unfruchtbar
unfulfilled [,ʌnfəl'fɪld] *adj* unerfüllt
unfurl [ʌn'fʌrl] *tr* (*a flag*) entrollen; (*sails*) losmachen
unfurnished [ʌn'fʌrnɪʃt] *adj* unmöbliert
ungainly [ʌn'genli] *adj* plump
ungentlemanly [ʌn'dʒɛntəlmənli] *adj* unfein, unedel
ungodly [ʌn'gɑdli] *adj* (*hour*) ungehörig
ungracious [ʌn'greʃəs] *adj* ungnädig
ungrammatical [,ʌngrə'mætɪkəl] *adj* ungrammatisch
ungrateful [ʌn'gretfəl] *adj* undankbar
ungrudgingly [ʌn'grʌdʒɪŋli] *adv* gern
unguarded [ʌn'gɑrdɪd] *adj* unbewacht; (*moment*) unbedacht
unguent ['ʌŋgwɛnt] *s* Salbe *f*
unhandy [ʌn'hændi] *adj* unhandlich; (*person*) unbeholfen
unhappy [ʌn'hæpi] *adj* unglücklich
unharmed [ʌn'hɑrmd] *adj* unversehrt
unharness [ʌn'hɑrnɪs] *tr* abschirren
unhealthful [ʌn'hɛlθfəl] *adj* ungesund
unhealthy [ʌn'hɛlθi] *adj* ungesund
unheard-of [ʌn'hʌrd,ɑv] *adj* unerhört
unheated [ʌn'hitɪd] *adj* ungeheizt
unhesitating [ʌn'hɛzɪ,tetɪŋ] *adj* (*immediate*) unverzüglich; (*unswerving*) unbeirrbar; (*support*) bereitwillig
unhinge [ʌn'hɪndʒ] *tr* (fig) aus den Angeln heben
unhitch [ʌn'hɪtʃ] *tr* (*horses*) ausspannen; (*undo*) losmachen
unholy [ʌn'holi] *adj* unheilig
unhook [ʌn'huk] *tr* losmachen; (*a dress*) aufhaken; (*the receiver*) abnehmen

unhoped-for [ʌn'hopt ,fɔr] *adj* unverhofft

unhurt [ʌn'hʌrt] *adj* unbeschädigt; (*person*) unversehrt

unicorn ['junɪ ,kɔrn] *s* Einhorn *n*

unification [,junɪfɪ'keʃən] *s* Vereinigung *f*

uniform ['junɪ ,fɔrm] *adj* gleichförmig || *s* Uniform *f*

uniformity [,junɪ'fɔrmɪtɪ] *s* Gleichförmigkeit *f*

uni·fy ['junɪ ,faɪ] *v* (*pret & pp* –fied) *tr* vereinigen

unilateral [,junɪ'lætərəl] *adj* einseitig

unimpaired [,ʌnɪm'pɛrd] *adj* ungeschwächt

unimpeachable [,ʌnɪm'pitʃəbəl] *adj* unantastbar

unimportant [,ʌnɪm'pɔrtənt] *adj* unwichtig

uninflected [,ʌnɪn'flɛktɪd] *adj* (gram) unflektiert

uninhabited [,ʌnɪn'hæbɪtɪd] *adj* unbewohnt

uninspired [,ʌnɪn'spaɪrd] *adj* schwunglos

unintelligible [,ʌnɪn'tɛlɪdʒəbəl] *adj* unverständlich

unintentional [,ʌnɪn'tɛnʃənəl] *adj* unabsichtlich

uninterested [ʌn'ɪntə ,rɛstɪd] *adj* (in) uninteressiert (an *dat*)

uninteresting [ʌn'ɪntə ,rɛstɪŋ] *adj* uninteressant

uninterrupted [,ʌnɪntə'rʌptɪd] *adj* ununterbrochen

uninvited [,ʌnɪn'vaɪtɪd] *adj* ungeladen

union ['junjən] *adj* Gewerkschafts– || *s* Vereinigung *f;* (*harmony*) Eintracht *f;* (*of workers*) Gewerkschaft *f;* (pol) Union *f*

unionize ['junjə ,naɪz] *tr* gewerkschaftlich organisieren || *intr* sich gewerkschaftlich organisieren

un'ion shop' *s* Betrieb *m*, der nur Gewerkschaftsmitglieder beschäftigt

unique [ju'nik] *adj* einzigartig

unison ['junɪsən] *s* Einklang *m*

unit ['junɪt] *s* (& mil) Einheit *f*

unite [ju'naɪt] *tr* vereinigen; (chem) verbinden || *intr* sich vereinigen; (chem) sich verbinden

Unit'ed King'dom *s* Vereinigtes Königreich *n*

Unit'ed Na'tions *spl* Vereinte Nationen *pl*

Unit'ed States' *s* Vereinigte Staaten *pl*

unity ['junɪtɪ] *s* (*harmony*) Einigkeit *f;* (*e.g., of a nation*) Einheit *f;* (fa) Einheitlichkeit *f*

universal [,junɪ'vʌrsəl] *adj* universal, allgemein || *s* Allgemeine *n;* (philos) Allgemeinbegriff *m*

u'niver'sal joint' *s* Kardangelenk *n*

u'niver'sal mil'itary train'ing *s* allgemeine Wehrpflicht *f*

universe ['junɪ ,vʌrs] *s* Universum *n*

university [,junɪ'vɛrsɪtɪ] *adj* Universitäts– || *s* Universität *f*

unjust [ʌn'dʒʌst] *adj* ungerecht

unjustified [ʌn'dʒʌstɪ ,faɪd] *adj* ungerechtfertigt

unjustly [ʌn'dʒʌstlɪ] *adv* zu Unrecht

unkempt [ʌn'kɛmpt] *adj* ungekämmt; (fig) verwahrlost

unkind [ʌn'kaɪnd] *adj* unfreundlich

unknown [ʌn'non] *adj* unbekannt

un'known quan'tity *s* Unbekannte *f*

Un'known Sol'dier *s* Unbekannter Soldat *m*

unlatch [ʌn'lætʃ] *tr* aufklinken

unlawful [ʌn'lɔfəl] *adj* gesetzwidrig

unleash [ʌn'liʃ] *tr* losbinden; (fig) entfesseln

unleavened [ʌn'lɛvənd] *adj* ungesäuert

unless [ʌn'lɛs] *conj* wenn ... nicht

unlettered [ʌn'lɛtərd] *adj* ungebildet

unlicensed [ʌn'laɪsənst] *adj* unerlaubt

unlike [ʌn'laɪk] *adj* (*unequal*) ungleich; (*dissimilar*) unähnlich || *prep* im Gegensatz zu (*dat*); **be u. s.o.** anders als jemand sein

unlikely [ʌn'laɪklɪ] *adj* unwahrscheinlich

unlimited [ʌn'lɪmɪtɪd] *adj* unbeschränkt

unlined [ʌn'laɪnd] *adj* (*clothes*) ungefüttert; (*paper*) unliniert; (*face*) faltenlos

unload [ʌn'lod] *tr & intr* ausladen

unload'ing *s* Ausladen *n;* (naut) Löschen *n*

unlock [ʌn'lɑk] *tr* aufsperren

unloose [ʌn'lus] *tr* lösen

unloved [ʌn'lʌvd] *adj* ungeliebt

unlucky [ʌn'lʌkɪ] *adj* unglücklich

un·make [ʌn'mek] *v* (*pret & pp* –made) *tr* rückgängig machen; (*a bed*) abdecken

unmanageable [ʌn'mænɪdʒəbəl] *adj* (*person, animal*) widerspenstig; (*thing*) unhandlich

unmanly [ʌn'mænlɪ] *adj* unmännlich

unmanned [ʌn'mænd] *adj* (rok) unbemannt

unmannerly [ʌn'mænərlɪ] *adj* unmännlich

unmarketable [ʌn'mɑrkɪtəbəl] *adj* nicht marktgängig

unmarriageable [ʌn'mærɪdʒəbəl] *adj* nicht heiratsfähig

unmarried [ʌn'mærɪd] *adj* unverheiratet

unmask [ʌn'mæsk] *tr* (& fig) demaskieren || *intr* sich demaskieren

unmatched [ʌn'mætʃt] *adj* (*not matched*) ungleichartig; (*unmatchable*) unvergleichlich

unmerciful [ʌn'mʌrsɪfəl] *adj* unbarmherzig

unmesh [ʌn'mɛʃ] *tr* (mach) ausrücken

unmindful [ʌn'maɪndfəl] *adj* uneingedenk

unmistakable [,ʌnmɪs'tekəbəl] *adj* unmißverständlich

unmitigated [ʌn'mɪtɪ ,getɪd] *adj* ungemildert; (*liar*) Erz–

unmixed [ʌn'mɪkst] *adj* ungemischt

unmoor [ʌn'mur] *tr* losmachen || *intr* sich losmachen

unmoved [ʌn'muvd] *adj* (fig) ungerührt

unmuzzle [ʌn'mʌzəl] *tr* den Maulkorb abnehmen (*dat*)

unnatural [ʌn'nætʃərəl] *adj* unnatürlich; *(forced)* gezwungen
unnecessary [ʌn'nesəˌseri] *adj* unnötig
unneeded [ʌn'nidɪd] *adj* nutzlos
unnerve [ʌn'nʌrv] *tr* entnerven
unnoticeable [ʌn'notɪsəbəl] *adj* unbemerkbar
unnoticed [ʌn'notɪst] *adj* unbemerkt
unobserved [ˌʌnəb'zʌrvd] *adj* unbeobachtet
unobtainable [ˌʌnəb'tenəbəl] *adj* nicht erhältlich
unobtrusive [ˌʌnəb'trusɪv] *adj* unaufdringlich
unoccupied [ʌn'akjəˌpaɪd] *adj (room, house)* leerstehend; *(seat)* unbesetzt; *(person)* unbeschäftigt
unofficial [ˌʌnə'fɪʃəl] *adj* inoffiziell
unopened [ʌn'opənd] *adj* ungeöffnet
unopposed [ˌʌnə'pozd] *adj (without opposition)* widerspruchslos; *(unresisted)* unbehindert
unorthodox [ʌn'ɔrθəˌdaks] *adj* unorthodox; *(relig)* nicht orthodox
unpack [ʌn'pæk] *tr* auspacken
unpalatable [ʌn'pælətəbəl] *adj* unschmackhaft; *(fig)* widerlich
unparalleled [ʌn'pærəˌleld] *adj* unvergleichlich
unpardonable [ʌn'pardənəbəl] *adj* unverzeihlich
unpatriotic [ˌʌnpetrɪ'atɪk] *adj* unpatriotisch
unpaved [ʌn'pevd] *adj* ungepflastert
unperceived [ˌʌnpər'sivd] *adj* unbemerkt
unpleasant [ʌn'plezənt] *adj* unangenehm; *(person)* unsympathisch
unpopular [ʌn'papjələr] *adj* unbeliebt
unpopularity [ʌnˌpapjə'læriti] *s* Unbeliebtheit *f*
unprecedented [ʌn'presɪˌdentɪd] *adj* unerhört; *(jur)* ohne Präzedenzfall
unpredictable [ˌʌnprɪ'dɪktəbəl] *adj* unberechenbar; *(weather)* wechselhaft
unprejudiced [ʌn'predʒədɪst] *adj* unvoreingenommen
unprepared [ˌʌnprɪ'perd] *adj* unvorbereitet
unpresentable [ˌʌnprɪ'zentəbəl] *adj* nicht präsentabel
unpretentious [ˌʌnprɪ'tenʃəs] *adj* anspruchslos
unprincipled [ʌn'prɪnsɪpəld] *adj* haltlos
unproductive [ˌʌnprə'dʌktɪv] *adj* unproduktiv; *(of)* unergiebig (an *dat*)
unprofessional [ˌʌnprə'feʃənəl] *adj (work)* unfachmännisch; *(conduct)* berufswidrig
unprofitable [ʌn'prafɪtəbəl] *adj (useless)* nutzlos; *(fin)* unrentabel
unpronounceable [ˌʌnprə'naunsəbəl] *adj* unaussprechlich
unprotected [ˌʌnprə'tektɪd] *adj (place)* ungeschützt; *(person)* unbeschützt
unpropitious [ˌʌnprə'pɪʃəs] *adj* ungünstig
unpublished [ʌn'pʌblɪʃt] *adj* unveröffentlich
unpunished [ʌn'pʌnɪʃt] *adj* ungestraft
unqualified [ʌn'kwaləˌfaɪd] *adj* un-

qualifiziert; *(full, complete)* unbedingt
unquenchable [ʌn'kwentʃəbəl] *adj* unstillbar
unquestionably [ʌn'kwestʃənəbli] *adv* fraglos, unbezweifelbar
unquestioning [ʌn'kwestʃənɪŋ] *adj (obedience)* bedingungslos
unquiet [ʌn'kwaɪ-ət] *adj* unruhig
unravel [ʌn'rævəl] *v (pret & pp –el[l]ed; ger –el[l]ling) tr (a knitted fabric)* auftrennen; *(fig)* entwirren ‖ *intr* sich fasern; *(fig)* sich entwirren
unreachable [ʌn'ritʃəbəl] *adj* unerreichbar
unreal [ʌn'ri-əl] *adj* unwirklich
unreality [ˌʌnrɪ'æliti] *s* Unwirklichkeit *f*
unreasonable [ʌn'rizənəbəl] *adj* unvernünftig
unrecognizable [ʌn'rekəgˌnaɪzəbəl] *adj* unerkennbar
unreel [ʌn'ril] *tr* abspulen
unrefined [ˌʌnrɪ'faɪnd] *adj* roh
unrelated [ˌʌnrɪ'letɪd] *adj (to)* ohne Beziehung (zu)
unrelenting [ˌʌnrɪ'lentɪŋ] *adj* unerbittlich
unreliable [ˌʌnrɪ'laɪ-əbəl] *adj* unzuverlässig; *(fin)* unsolid(e)
unremitting [ˌʌnrɪ'mitɪŋ] *adj* unablässig
unrepentant [ˌʌnrɪ'pentənt] *adj* unbußfertig
unrequited [ˌʌnrɪ'kwaitɪd] *adj* unerwidert
unreserved [ˌʌnrɪ'zʌrvd] *adj* vorbehaltlos
unresponsive [ˌʌnrɪ'spansɪv] *adj (to)* unempfänglich (für)
unrest [ʌn'rest] *s* Unruhe *f*
unrestricted [ˌʌnrɪ'strɪktɪd] *adj* uneingeschränkt
unrewarded [ˌʌnrɪ'wɔrdɪd] *adj* unbelohnt
unrhymed [ʌn'raɪmd] *adj* ungereimt
un·rig [ʌn'rɪg] *v (pret & pp –rigged; ger –rigging) tr* abtakeln
unripe [ʌn'raɪp] *adj* unreif
unrivaled [ʌn'raɪvəld] *adj* unübertrefflich
unroll [ʌn'rol] *tr* aufrollen; *(e.g., a cable)* abrollen ‖ *intr* sich aufrollen; sich abrollen
unromantic [ˌʌnro'mæntɪk] *adj* unromantisch
unruffled [ʌn'rʌfəld] *adj* unerschüttert
unruly [ʌn'ruli] *adj* ungebärdig
unsaddle [ʌn'sædəl] *tr (a horse)* absatteln; *(a rider)* aus dem Sattel werfen
unsafe [ʌn'sef] *adj* unsicher
unsaid [ʌn'sed] *adj* ungesagt
unsalable [ʌn'seləbəl] *adj* unverkäuflich
unsanitary [ʌn'sænɪˌteri] *adj* unhygienisch
unsalted [ʌn'sɔltɪd] *adj* ungesalzen
unsatisfactory [ʌnˌsætɪs'fæktəri] *adj* unbefriedigend
unsatisfied [ʌn'sætɪsˌfaɪd] *adj* unbefriedigt

unsavory [ʌn'sevəri] *adj* unschmackhaft; (fig) widerlich
unscathed [ʌn'skeðd] *adj* unversehrt
unscientific [ˌʌnsaɪ·ən'tɪfɪk] *adj* unwissenschaftlich
unscramble [ʌn'skræmbəl] *tr* (a message) entziffern; (fig) entflechten
unscrew [ʌn'skru] *tr* aufschrauben
unscrupulous [ʌn'skrupjələs] *adj* skrupellos
unseal [ʌn'sil] *tr* entsiegeln; (eyes, lips) öffnen
unseasonable [ʌn'sizənəbəl] *adj* unzeitig; (weather) nicht der Jahreszeit entsprechend
unseasoned [ʌn'sizənd] *adj* ungewürzt
unseat [ʌn'sit] *tr* (a rider) aus dem Sattel heben; (an official) aus dem Posten verdrängen
unseemly [ʌn'simli] *adj* ungehörig
unseen [ʌn'sin] *adj* ungesehen
unselfish [ʌn'sɛlfɪʃ] *adj* selbstlos
unsettle [ʌn'sɛtəl] *tr* beunruhigen
unsettled [ʌn'sɛtəld] *adj* (matter, bill) unerledigt; (without a residence) ohne festen Wohnsitz; (restless) unruhig; (life) unstet
unshackle [ʌn'ʃækəl] *tr* die Fesseln abnehmen (dat)
unshakable [ʌn'ʃekəbəl] *adj* unerschütterlich
unshapely [ʌn'ʃepli] *adj* mißgestaltet
unshaven [ʌn'ʃevən] *adj* unrasiert
unsheathe [ʌn'ʃið] *tr* aus der Scheide ziehen
unshod [ʌn'ʃad] *adj* unbeschuht
unsightly [ʌn'saɪtli] *adj* unansehnlich
unsinkable [ʌn'sɪŋkəbəl] *adj* nicht versenkbar
unskilled [ʌn'skɪld] *adj* ungelernt; **u. laborer** Hilfsarbeiter –in *mf*
unskillful [ʌn'skɪlfəl] *adj* ungewandt
unsnarl [ʌn'snarl] *tr* entwirren
unsociable [ʌn'soʃəbəl] *adj* ungesellig
unsolicited [ˌʌnso'lɪsɪtɪd] *adj* unverlangt
unsold [ʌn'sold] *adj* unverkauft
unsophisticated [ˌʌnsə'fɪstɪˌketɪd] *adj* unverfälscht; (naive) arglos
unsound [ʌn'saund] *adj* ungesund; (sleep) unruhig; **of u. mind** geisteskrank
unspeakable [ʌn'spikəbəl] *adj* unsagbar
unspoiled [ʌn'spɔɪld] *adj* unverdorben
unsportsmanlike [ʌn'sportsmən ˌlaɪk] *adj* unsportlich
unstable [ʌn'stebəl] *adj* unbeständig; (e.g., ladder) wacklig; (hand) zittrig; (market, walk) schwankend; (inconstant) unbeständig; (chem) unbeständig
unstinted [ʌn'stɪntɪd] *adj* uneingeschränkt
unstinting [ʌn'stɪntɪŋ] *adj* freigebig
unstitch [ʌn'stɪtʃ] *tr* auftrennen
unstressed [ʌn'strɛst] *adj* unbetont
unsuccessful [ˌʌnsək'sɛsfəl] *adj* erfolglos
unsuitable [ʌn'sutəbəl] *adj* ungeeignet; (inappropriate) unangemessen
unsullied [ʌn'sʌlɪd] *adj* unbefleckt

unsung [ʌn'sʌŋ] *adj* unbesungen
unsuspected [ˌʌnsəs'pɛktɪd] *adj* unverdächtig; (not known to exist) ungeahnt
unsuspecting [ˌʌnsəs'pɛktɪŋ] *adj* arglos
unswerving [ʌn'swʌrvɪŋ] *adj* unentwegt
unsympathetic [ˌʌnsɪmpə'θɛtɪk] *adj* teilnahmslos
unsystematic(al) [ˌʌnsɪstə'mætɪk(əl)] *adj* unsystematisch
untactful [ʌn'tæktfəl] *adj* taktlos
untalented [ʌn'tæləntɪd] *adj* unbegabt
untamed [ʌn'temd] *adj* ungezähmt
untangle [ʌn'tæŋgəl] *tr* (& fig) entwirren
untenable [ʌn'tenəbəl] *adj* unhaltbar
untested [ʌn'tɛstɪd] *adj* ungeprüft
unthankful [ʌn'θæŋkfəl] *adj* undankbar
unthinking [ʌn'θɪŋkɪŋ] *adj* gedankenlos
untidy [ʌn'taɪdi] *adj* unordentlich
un·tie [ʌn'taɪ] *v* (pret & pp –tied; ger –tying) *tr* aufbinden; (a knot) lösen; **my shoe is untied** mein Schuh ist aufgegangen
until [ʌn'tɪl] *prep* bis (acc); **u. further notice** bis auf weiteres || *conj* bis
untimely [ʌn'taɪmli] *adj* frühzeitig; (at the wrong time) unzeitgemäß
untiring [ʌn'taɪrɪŋ] *adj* unermüdlich
untold [ʌn'told] *adj* (suffering) unsäglich; (countless) zahllos
untouched [ʌn'tʌtʃt] *adj* unangetastet; (fig) ungerührt
untoward [ʌn'tord] *adj* (unfavorable) ungünstig; (unruly) widerspenstig
untrained [ʌn'trend] *adj* unausgebildet; (eye) ungeschult; (sport) untrainiert
untried [ʌn'traɪd] *adj* (unattempted) unversucht; (untested) unerprobt; (case) (jur) nicht verhandelt
untroubled [ʌn'trʌbəld] *adj* (mind, times) ruhig; (peace) ungestört
untrue [ʌn'tru] *adj* unwahr; (unfaithful) un(ge)treu; (not exact) ungenau
untrustworthy [ʌn'trʌst ˌwʌrði] *adj* unglaubwürdig
untruth [ʌn'truθ] *s* Unwahrheit *f*
untruthful [ʌn'truθfəl] *adj* (statement) unwahr; (person) unaufrichtig
untwist [ʌn'twɪst] *tr* aufflechten || *intr* aufgehen
unusable [ʌn'juzəbəl] *adj* nicht verwendbar; (unconsumable) unbenutzbar
unusual [ʌn'juʒʊ·əl] *adj* ungewöhnlich
unutterable [ʌn'ʌtərəbəl] *adj* unaussprechlich
unvarnished [ʌn'varnɪʃt] *adj* nicht gefirnißt; (truth) ungeschminkt
unveil [ʌn'vel] *tr* (a monument) enthüllen; (a face) entschleiern
unventilated [ʌn'vɛntɪ ˌletɪd] *adj* ungelüftet
unvoiced [ʌn'vɔɪst] *adj* (ling) stimmlos
unwanted [ʌn'wantɪd] *adj* unerwünscht
unwarranted [ʌn'warəntɪd] *adj* ungerechtfertigt
unwary [ʌn'weri] *adj* unvorsichtig

unwavering [ʌnˈwevərɪŋ] *adj* standhaft
unwelcome [ʌnˈwɛlkəm] *adj* unwillkommen
unwell [ʌnˈwɛl] *adj* unwohl
unwept [ʌnˈwept] *adj* unbeweint
unwholesome [ʌnˈholsəm] *adj* schädlich; (& fig) unbekömmlich
unwieldy [ʌnˈwildi] *adj* (*person*) schwerfällig; (*thing*) unhandlich
unwilling [ʌnˈwilɪŋ] *adj* (*involuntary*) unfreiwillig; (*reluctant*) widerwillig; (*obstinate*) eigensinnig; be u. to (*inf*) nicht (*inf*) wollen
unwillingly [ʌnˈwilɪŋli] *adv* ungern
un·wind [ʌnˈwaɪnd] *v* (*pret & pp* –wound*) *tr* abwickeln || *intr* sich abwickeln; (fig) sich entspannen
unwise [ʌnˈwaɪz] *adj* unklug
unwished-for [ʌnˈwɪʃtˌfɔr] *adj* unerwünscht
unwitting [ʌnˈwitɪŋ] *adj* unwissentlich
unworkable [ʌnˈwʌrkəbəl] *adj* (*plan*) unausführbar; (*material*) nicht zu bearbeiten(d)
unworldly [ʌnˈwʌrldli] *adj* nicht weltlich; (*naive*) weltfremd
unworthy [ʌnˈwʌrði] *adj* unwürdig
un·wrap [ʌnˈræp] *v* (*pret & pp* –wrapped*; *ger* –wrapping) *tr* auspacken || *intr* aufgehen
unwrinkled [ʌnˈrɪŋkəld] *adj* faltenlos
unwritten [ʌnˈrɪtən] *adj* ungeschrieben; (*agreement*) mündlich
unyielding [ʌnˈjildɪŋ] *adj* unnachgiebig
up [ʌp] *adj & adv* (*at a height*) oben; (*to a height*) hinauf; be up (*be out of bed; said of a shade*) aufsein; (baseball) am Schlag sein; be up and around again wieder auf dem Damm sein; be up to (*be ready for*) gewachsen sein (*dat*); (*e.g., mischief*) vorhaben; from ten dollars and up von zehn Dollar aufwärts; it's up to you es hängt von Ihnen ab; prices are up die Preise sind gestiegen; up and down (*back and forth*) auf und ab; (*from head to toe*) von oben bis unten; up there da oben; up to (*e.g., one hour*) bis zu; up to the ears in debt bis über die Ohren in Schulden || *v* (*pret & pp* upped) *ger* upping) *tr* erhöhen || *prep* (*acc*) hinauf (postpositive)
up-and-coming [ˈʌpənˈkʌmɪŋ] *adj* (coll) unternehmungslustig
up-and-up [ˈʌpənˈʌp] *s*—be on the u. aufrichtig sein
upbraid' *tr* Vorwürfe machen (*dat*)
upbringing [ˈʌpˌbrɪŋɪŋ] *s* Erziehung *f*
update' *tr* aufs laufende bringen
up'draft' *s* Aufwind *m*
upend' *tr* hochkant stellen
up'grade' *s* Steigung *f;* on the u. (fig) im Aufsteigen || up'grade' *tr* (*reclassify*) höher einstufen; (*improve*) verbessern
upheaval [ʌpˈhivəl] *s* Umbruch *m*
up'hill' *adj* ansteigend; (fig) mühsam; u. struggle harter Kampf *m* || *adv* bergauf
uphold' *v* (*pret & pp* –held) *tr* (*the law*) unterstützen; (*a verdict*) bestätigen

upholster [ʌpˈholstər] *tr* (auf)polstern
upholsterer [ʌpˈholstərər] *s* Polstere –in *mf*
upholstery [ʌpˈholstəri] *s* Polsterung
up'keep' *s* Instandhaltung *f;* (*maintenance costs*) Instandhaltungskostei *pl*
upland [ˈʌplənd] *adj* Hochlands- Berg– || the uplands *spl* das Hochland
up'lift' *s* (fig) Aufschwung *m;* moral u moralischer Auftrieb *m* || up'lift' *t.* (fig) geistig (or moralisch) erhebei
upon [əˈpɑn] *prep* (*position*) an (*dat*) auf (*dat*); (*direction*) an (*acc*), au (*acc*); u. my word! auf mein Wort
upper [ˈʌpər] *adj* obere, Ober– || up pers *spl* Oberleder *n*
up'per-case' *adj* in Großbuchstaber gedruckt (or geschrieben)
up'per class'es *spl* Oberschicht *f*
up'percut' *s* (box) Aufwärtshaken *n*
up'per deck' *s* Oberdeck *n*
up'per hand' *s* Oberhand *f*
up'per lip' *s* Oberlippe *f*
up'permost' *adj* oberste
uppish [ˈʌpɪʃ] *adj* (coll) hochnäsig
uppity [ˈʌpɪti] *adj* (coll) eingebildet
upraise' *tr* erheben
up'right' *adj* aufrecht; (fig) redlich || ˌ (fb) Torpfosten *m*
up'ris'ing *s* Aufstand *m*
up'roar' *s* Aufruhr *m*
uproarious [ʌpˈrɔri-əs] *adj* (*noisy*) lärmend; (*laughter*) schallend; (applause) tosend; (*very funny*) zwerchfellerschütternd
uproot' *tr* entwurzeln
ups' and downs' *spl* Auf und Ab *n*
upset' *adj* (*over*) verstimmt (über *acc*) || up'set' *s* unerwartete Niederlage *j* || up'set' *v* (*pret & pp* –set; *ger* –setting) *tr* (*throw over*) umwerfen; (*tip over*) umkippen; (*plans*) umstoßen; (*a person*) aufregen; (*the stomach*) verderben
up'shot' *s* Ergebnis *n*
up'side down' *adv* verkehrt; turn u. auf den Kopf stellen
up'stage' *adv* in den (or im) Hintergrund der Bühne || *tr* (coll) ausstechen
up'stairs' *adj* im oberen Stockwerk || *adv* (*position*) oben; (*direction*) nach oben || *s* oberes Stockwerk *n*
upstand'ing *adj* aufrecht; (*sincere*) aufrichtig
up'start' *s* Emporkömmling *m*
up'stream' *adj* weiter stromaufwärts gelegen || *adv* stromaufwärts
up'stroke' *s* Aufstrich *m;* (mach) Hub *m*
up'surge' *s* Aufwallung *f*
up'sweep' *s* Hochfrisur *f*
up'swing' *s* (fig) Aufschwung *m*
upsy-daisy [ˈʌpsiˈdezi] *interj* hopsasa!
up-to-date [ˈʌptəˈdet] *adj* (*modern*) zeitgemäß; (*with latest information*) auf dem neuesten Stand
up'-to-the-min'ute news' [ˈʌptəðəˈmɪnɪt] *s* Zeitfunk *m*
up'trend' *s* steigende Tendenz *f*

up'turn' s Aufschwung m
upturned' adj nach oben gebogen; **u. nose** Stupsnase f
upward ['ʌpwərd] adj nach oben gerichtet; (tendency) steigend ‖ adv aufwärts
U'ral Moun'tains ['jurəl] spl Ural m
uranium [ju'renɪ·əm] adj Uran- ‖ s Uran n
urban ['ʌrbən] adj städtisch, Stadt-
urbane [ʌr'ben] adj weltgewandt
urbanite ['ʌrbə‚naɪt] s Städter –in mf
urbanize ['ʌrbə‚naɪz] tr verstädtern
ur'ban renew'al s Altstadtsanierung f
urchin ['ʌrtʃɪn] s Bengel m
ure·thra [ju'riθrə] s (–thras & –thrae [θri]) Harnröhre f
urge [ʌrdʒ] s Drang m, Trieb m ‖ tr drängen; **u. on** antreiben
urgency ['ʌrdʒənsi] s Dringlichkeit f
urgent ['ʌrdʒənt] adj dringend
urinal ['jurɪnəl] s (in a toilet) Urinbecken n; (in a sick bed) Urinflasche f
urinary ['jurɪ‚neri] adj Harn-, Urin-
urinate ['jurɪ‚net] intr harnen
urine ['jurɪn] s Harn m, Urin m
urn [ʌrn] s Urne f; (for coffee) Kaffeemaschine f
urology [jɪ'ralədʒi] s Urologie f
us [ʌs] per pron uns
U.S.A. ['ju'es'e] s (United States of America) USA pl
usable ['juzəbəl] adj (consumable items) verwendbar; (non-consumable items) benutzbar
usage ['jusɪdʒ] s (using) Gebrauch m; (treatment) Behandlung f; (ling) Sprachgebrauch m; **rough u.** starke Beanspruchung f
use [jus] s (of consumable items) Verwendung f, Gebrauch m; (of non-consumable items) Benutzung f; (application) Anwendung f; (advantage) Nutzen m; (purpose) Zweck m; (consumption) Verbrauch m; **I have no use for him** ich habe nichts für ihn übrig; **in use** in Gebrauch; **it's no use** es nützt nichts; **make use of** ausnutzen; **of use** von Nutzen; **there's no use in** (ger) es hat keinen Zweck zu (inf) ‖ [juz] tr (ge)brauchen, verwenden; (non-consumable items) benutzen; (apply) anwenden; (e.g.,

troops) einsetzen; **use up** verbrauchen ‖ intr—**he used to live here** er wohnte früher hier
used [juzd] adj gebraucht; (car) Gebraucht–; **be u. to** gewöhnt sein an (acc); **be u. to** (ger) gewöhnt sein zu (inf); **get s.o. u. to** j–n gewöhnen an (acc); **get u. to** sich gewöhnen an (acc)
useful ['jusfəl] adj nützlich
usefulness ['jusfəlnɪs] s Nützlichkeit f; (usability) Brauchbarkeit f
useless ['juslɪs] adj nutzlos; (not usable) unbrauchbar
user ['juzər] s (of gas, electric) Verbraucher –in mf; (e.g., of a book) Benutzer –in mf
usher ['ʌʃər] s Platzanweiser –in mf ‖ tr—**u. in** hereinführen; (a new era) einleiten
U.S.S.R. ['ju'es'es'ar] s (Union of Soviet Socialist Republics) UdSSR f
usual ['juʒu·əl] adj gewöhnlich; **as u.** wie gewöhnlich
usually ['juʒu·əli] adv gewöhnlich
usurp [ju'zʌrp] tr usurpieren
usurper [ju'zʌrpər] s Usurpator –in mf
usury ['juʒəri] s Wucher m
utensil [ju'tensɪl] s Gerät n; **utensils** Utensilien pl
uter·us ['jutərəs] s (–i [‚aɪ]) Gebärmutter f
utilitarian [‚jutɪlɪ'terɪ·ən] adj utilitaristisch, Nützlichkeits–
utility [ju'tɪlɪti] s (usefulness) Nützlichkeit f; (company) öffentlicher Versorgungsbetrieb m; **apartment with all utilities** Wohnung f mit allem Zubehör; **utilities** Gas, Wasser, Strom pl
utilize ['jutɪ‚laɪz] tr verwerten
utmost ['ʌt‚most] adj äußerste, höchste ‖ s—**do one's u.** sein Äußerstes tun; **to the u.** auf äußerste; **to the u. of one's power** nach besten Kräften
utopia [ju'topɪ·ə] s Utopie f
utopian [ju'topɪ·ən] adj utopisch
utter ['ʌtər] adj völlig, Erz– ‖ tr (a sigh) ausstoßen; (a sound) hervorbringen; (feelings) ausdrücken; (words) äußern
utterance ['ʌtərəns] s Äußerung f
utterly ['ʌtərli] adv ganz und gar, völlig

V

V, v [vi] s zweiundzwanzigster Buchstabe des englischen Alphabets
vacancy ['vekənsi] s (emptiness) Leere f; (unfilled job) freie Stelle f; **no v.** (public sign) kein freies Zimmer
vacant ['vekənt] adj frei; (stare) geistesabwesend; (lot) unbebaut
vacate [ve'ket] tr (a home) räumen; (a seat) freimachen ‖ intr ausziehen
vacation [ve'keʃən] s Urlaub m; (educ)

Ferien pl; **on v.** auf Urlaub ‖ intr Urlaub machen
vacationer [ve'keʃənər] s Urlauber –in mf
vaccinate ['væksɪ‚net] tr impfen
vaccination [‚væksɪ'neʃən] s Impfung f
vaccina'tion certi'ficate s Impfschein m
vaccine [væk'sin] s Impfstoff m

vacillate ['væsɪ ˌlet] *intr* schwanken
vacuous ['vækju·əs] *adj* nichtssagend
vacu·um ['vækju·əm] *s* (**-ums** & **-a** [ə]) Vakuum *n* ‖ *tr* & *intr* staubsaugen
vac'uum clean'er *s* Staubsauger *m*
vac'uum pump' *s* Absaugepumpe *f*
vac'uum tube' *s* Vakuumröhre *f*
vagabond ['vægə ˌband] *s* Landstreicher –in *mf*
vagary ['vegəri] *s* Laune *f*
vagina [və'dʒaɪnə] *s* Scheide *f*
vagrancy ['vegrənsi] *s* Landstreicherei *f*
vagrant ['vegrənt] *adj* vagabundierend ‖ *s* Landstreicher –in *mf*
vague [veg] *adj* unbestimmt, vage
vain [ven] *adj* (*proud*) eitel; (*pointless*) vergeblich; **in v.** vergebens
vainglo'rious *adj* prahlerisch
valance ['væləns] *s* Quervolant *m*
vale [vel] *s* Tal *n*
valedictory [ˌvælɪ'dɪktəri] *s* Abschiedsrede *f*
valence ['veləns] *s* Wertigkeit *f*
valentine ['vælən ˌtaɪn] *s* Valentinsgruß *m*
vale' of tears' *s* Jammertal *n*
valet ['vælɪt] *s* Kammerdiener *m*
valiant ['væljənt] *adj* tapfer
valid ['vælɪd] *adj* (*law, ticket*) gültig; (*argument, objection*) wohlbegründet; (*e.g., contract*) rechtsgültig; **be v.** gelten
validate ['vælɪ ˌdet] *tr* bestätigen
validation [ˌvælɪ'deʃən] *s* Bestätigung *f*
validity [və'lɪdɪti] *s* Gültigkeit *f*
valise [və'lis] *s* Reisetasche *f*
valley ['væli] *s* Tal *n*
valor ['vælər] *s* Tapferkeit *f*
valorous ['vælərəs] *adj* tapfer
valuable ['vælju·əbəl] *adj* wertvoll ‖ **valuables** *spl* Wertsachen *pl*
value ['vælju] *s* Wert *m* ‖ *tr* (at) schätzen (auf *acc*)
val'ue judg'ment *s* Werturteil *n*
valueless ['væljulɪs] *adj* wertlos
valve [vælv] *s* (anat, mach, zool) Klappe *f*; (mach, mus) Ventil *n*
vamp [væmp] *s* (coll) Vamp *m*
vampire ['væmpaɪr] *s* Vampir *m*
van [væn] *s* Möbelwagen *m*; (*panel truck*) Kastenwagen *m*; (fig) Avantgarde *f*; (mil) Vorhut *f*
vandal ['vændəl] *s* Vandale *m*; **Vandal** Vandale *m*
vandalism ['vændə ˌlɪzəm] *s* Vandalismus *m*
vane [ven] *s* (*of a windmill, fan, propeller*) Flügel *m*; (*in a turbine*) Schaufel *f*
vanguard ['væn ˌgard] *s* (fig) Spitze *f*; (mil) Vorhut *f*
vanilla [və'nɪlə] *s* Vanille *f*
vanish ['vænɪʃ] *intr* (ver)schwinden; **v. into thin air** sich in blauen Dunst auflösen
van'ishing cream' *s* Tagescreme *f*
vanity ['vænɪti] *s* (*arrogance*) Anmaßung *f*; (*emptiness*) Nichtigkeit *f*; (*furniture*) Frisiertisch *m*

van'ity case' *s* Kosmetikköfferchen *n*
vanquish ['væŋkwɪʃ] *tr* besiegen
van'tage point' ['væntɪdʒ] *s* (*advantage*) günstiger Ausgangspunkt *m*; (*view*) Aussichtspunkt *m*
vapid ['væpɪd] *adj* schal, fad(e)
vapor ['vepər] *s* Dampf *m*, Dunst *m*
vaporize ['vepə ˌraɪz] *tr* & *intr* verdampfen
vaporizer ['vepə ˌraɪzər] *s* Inhalationsapparat *m*
va'por trail' *s* Kondensstreifen *m*
variable ['verɪ·əbəl] *adj* veränderlich; (*wind*) aus wechselnden Richtungen ‖ *s* (math) Veränderliche *f*
variance ['verɪ·əns] *s* Veränderung *f*; (*difference*) Abweichung *f*; (*argument*) Streit *m*; **be at v. with** (*a person*) in Zwiespalt sein mit; (*a thing*) in Widerspruch stehen zu
variant ['verɪ·ənt] *adj* abweichend ‖ *s* Variante *f*
variation [ˌverɪ'eʃən] *s* Veränderung *f*; (alg, biol, mus) Variation *f*
var'icose vein' ['verɪ ˌkos] *s* Krampfader *f*
varied ['verid] *adj* abwechslungsreich; (*diverse*) verschieden
variegated ['verɪ·ə ˌgetɪd] *adj* (*diverse*) verschieden; (*in color*) bunt
variety [və'raɪ·əti] *s* (*choice*) Auswahl *f*; (*difference*) Verschiedenheit *f*; (*sort*) Art *f*; (biol) Spielart *f*; **for a v. of reasons** aus verschiedenen Gründen
vari'ety show' *s* Varietévorstellung *f*
various ['verɪ·əs] *adj* verschieden; (*several*) mehrere
varnish ['varnɪʃ] *s* Firnis *m*, Lack *m* ‖ *tr* firnissen
varsity ['varsɪti] *adj* Auswahl– ‖ *s* Auswahlmannschaft *f*
var·y ['veri] *v* (*pret* & *pp* **–ied**) *tr* & *intr* abwechseln, variieren
vase [ves], [vez] *s* Vase *f*
vaseline ['væsə ˌlin] *s* (trademark) Vaseline *f*
vassal ['væsəl] *s* Lehensmann *m*
vast [væst] *adj* riesig; (*majority*) überwiegend; **v. amount** Unmasse *f*
vastness ['væstnɪs] *s* Unermeßlichkeit *f*
vat [væt] *s* Bottich *m*
Vatican ['vætɪkən] *adj* vatikanisch; (*city*) Vatikan– ‖ *s* Vatikan *m*
Vat'ican Coun'cil *s* Vatikanisches Konzil *n*
vaudeville ['vɔdvɪl] *s* Varieté *n*
vaude'ville show' *s* Varietévorstellung *f*
vault [vɔlt] *s* (*underground chamber*) Gruft *f*; (*of a bank*) Tresor *m*; (archit) Gewölbe *n*; **v. of heaven** Himmelsgewölbe *n* ‖ *tr* überspringen
vaunt [vɔnt] *s* Prahlerei *f* ‖ *tr* sich rühmen (genit) ‖ *intr* sich rühmen
veal [vil] *s* Kalbfleisch *n*
veal' cut'let *s* Kalbskotelett *n*
veer [vɪr] *intr* drehen, wenden
vegetable ['vedʒɪtəbəl] *adj* pflanzlich; (*garden, soup*) Gemüse–; (*kingdom, life, oil, dye*) Pflanzen– ‖ *s* Gemüse *n*; **vegetables** Gemüse *n*

vegetarian [,vedʒɪ'terɪ·ən] *adj* vegetarisch ‖ *s* Vegetarier –in *mf*
vegetate ['vedʒɪ,tet] *intr* vegetieren
vegetation [,vedʒɪ'teʃən] *s* Vegetation *f*
vehemence ['vi·ɪməns] *s* Heftigkeit *f*
vehement ['vi·ɪmənt] *adj* heftig
vehicle ['vi·ɪkəl] *s* Fahrzeug *n*
veil [vel] *s* Schleier *m* ‖ *tr* (& fig) verschleiern
veiled *adj* verschleiert; (*threat*) verhüllt
vein [ven] *s* Vene *f;* (geol, min) Ader *f*
vellum ['veləm] *s* Velin *n*
velocity [vɪ'lɑsɪti] *s* Geschwindigkeit *f*
velvet ['velvɪt] *adj* Samt– ‖ *s* Samt *m*
velveteen [,velvɪ'tin] *s* Baumwollsamt *m*
velvety ['velvɪti] *adj* samtartig
vend [vend] *tr* verkaufen
vend'ing machine' *s* Automat *m*
vendor ['vendər] *s* Verkäufer –in *mf*
veneer [və'nɪr] *s* Furnier *n;* (fig) Tünche *f* ‖ *tr* furnieren
venerable ['venərəbəl] *adj* ehrwürdig
venerate ['venə,ret] *tr* verehren
veneration [,venə'reʃən] *s* Verehrung *f*
Venetian [vɪ'niʃən] *adj* venezianisch ‖ *s* Venezianer –in *mf*
Vene'tian blind' *s* Fensterjalousie *f*
vengeance ['vendʒəns] *s* Rache *f;* **take v. on** sich rächen an (*dat*); **with a v.** mit Gewalt
vengeful ['vendʒfəl] *adj* rachsüchtig
venial ['vinɪ·əl] *adj* (*sin*) läßlich
Venice ['venɪs] *s* Venedig *n*
venison ['venɪsən] *s* Wildbret *n*
venom ['venəm] *s* Gift *n;* (fig) Geiger *m*
venomous ['venəməs] *adj* giftig
vent [vent] *s* Öffnung *f;* **give v. to** Luft machen (*dat*) ‖ *tr* auslassen
ventilate ['ventɪ,let] *tr* ventilieren
ventilation [,ventɪ'leʃən] *s* Ventilation *f*
ventilator ['ventɪ,letər] *s* Ventilator *m*
ventricle ['ventrɪkəl] *s* Ventrikel *m*
ventriloquist [ven'trɪləkwɪst] *s* Bauchredner –in *mf*
venture ['ventʃər] *s* Unternehmen *n* ‖ *tr* wagen ‖ *intr* (**on**) sich wagen (an *acc*); **v. out** sich hinauswagen; **v. to** (*inf*) sich vermessen zu (*inf*)
venturesome ['ventʃərsəm] *adj* (*person*) wagemutig; (*deed*) gewagt
venue ['venju] *s* zuständiger Gerichtsort *m;* **change of v.** Änderung *f* des Gerichtsstandes
Venus ['vinəs] *s* Venus *f*
veracity [vɪ'ræsɪti] *s* Wahrhaftigkeit *f*
veranda [və'rændə] *s* Veranda *f*
verb [vɜrb] *s* Verb *n*, Zeitwort *n*
verbal ['vɜrbəl] *adj* (*oral*) mündlich; (gram) verbal
verbatim [vər'betɪm] *adj* wortgetreu
verbiage ['vɜrbɪ·ɪdʒ] *s* Wortschwall *m*
verbose [vər'bos] *adj* weitschweifig
verdant ['vɜrdənt] *adj* grün
verdict ['vɜrdɪkt] *s* Urteilsspruch *m* (der Geschworenen); **give a v.** e–n Spruch fällen

verdigris ['vɜrdɪ,gris] *s* Grünspan *m*
verge [vɜrdʒ] *s* (fig) Rand *m;* **on the v. of** (*ger*) nahe daran zu (*inf*) ‖ *intr*—**v. on** grenzen an (*acc*)
verifiable [,verɪ'faɪ·əbəl] *adj* nachprüfbar
verification [,verɪfɪ'keʃən] *s* Nachprüfung *f*
veri·fy ['verɪ,faɪ] *v* (*pret & pp* –fied) *tr* nachprüfen
verily ['verɪli] *adv* (Bib) wahrlich
veritable ['verɪtəbəl] *adj* echt
vermilion [vər'mɪljən] *adj* zinnoberrot
vermin ['vʌrmɪn] *s* (*objectionable person*) Halunke *m;* **v.** *spl* Schädlinge *pl;* (*objectionable persons*) Gesindel *n*
vermouth [vər'muθ] *s* Wermut *m*
vernacular [vər'nækjələr] *adj* volkssprachlich ‖ *s* Volkssprache *f*
ver'nal e'quinox ['vʌrnəl] *s* Frühlingstagundnachtgleiche *f*
versatile ['vʌrsətɪl] *adj* beweglich
verse [vʌrs] *s* (& Bib) Vers *m;* (*stanza*) Strophe *f*
versed [vʌrst] *adj* (**in**) bewandert in (*dat*)
versification [,vʌrsɪfɪ'keʃən] *s* (*metrical structure*) Versbau *m;* (*versifying*) Verskunst *f;* (*metrical version*) Versfassung *f*
versifier ['vʌrsɪ,faɪ·ər] *s* Verseschmied *m*
version ['vʌrʒən] *s* Version *f*
ver·so ['vʌrso] *s* (–sos) (*of a coin*) Revers *m;* (typ) Verso *n*
versus ['vʌrsəs] *prep* gegen (*acc*)
verte·bra ['vʌrtɪbrə] *s* (–brae [,bri] & –bras) Rückenwirbel *m*, Wirbel *m*
vertebrate ['vʌrtɪ,bret] *s* Wirbeltier *n*
ver·tex ['vʌrteks] *s* (–texes & –tices [tɪ,siz]) Scheitelpunkt *m*
vertical ['vʌrtɪkəl] *adj* senkrecht ‖ *s* Vertikale *f*
ver'tical hold' *s* (telv) Vertikaleinstellung *f*
ver'tical take'off *s* Senkrechtstart *m*
vertigo ['vʌrtɪ,go] *s* Schwindel *m*, Schwindelgefühl *n*
very ['veri] *adj*—**that v. day** an demselben Tag; **the v. thought** der bloße Gedanke; **the v. truth** die reine Wahrheit; **the v. man** genau der Mann ‖ *adv* sehr; **the v. best** der allerbeste; **the v. same** ebenderselbe
vesicle ['vesɪkəl] *s* Bläschen *n*
vespers ['vespərz] *spl* Vesper *f*
vessel ['vesəl] *s* (*ship*) Schiff *n;* (*container*) Gefäß *n*
vest [vest] *s* Weste *f;* (*for women*) Leibchen *n* ‖ *tr* (**with**) bekleiden (mit); **be vested in** zustehen (*dat*)
vest'ed in'terest *s* (*for personal benefits*) persönliches Interesse *n;* (jur) rechtmäßiges Interesse *n*
vestibule ['vestɪ,bjul] *s* Vestibül *n*
vestige ['vestɪdʒ] *s* Spur *f*
vestment ['vestmənt] *s* Gewand *n*
vest'-pock'et *adj* Westentaschen–
vestry ['vestri] *s* Sakristei *f;* (*committee*) Gemeindevertretung *f*
vetch [vetʃ] *s* Wicke *f*

veteran ['vetərən] *s* Veteran *m;* (sport) Senior *m*
veterinarian [ˌvetərɪ'nerɪ·ən] *s* Tierarzt *m*, Tierärztin *f*
veterinary ['vetərɪˌneri] *adj (college)* tierärztlich; **v. medicine** Tierheilkunde *f*
ve·to ['vito] *s* (–toes) Veto *n* ǁ *tr* ein Veto einlegen gegen
vex [veks] *tr* ärgern
vexation [vek'seʃən] *s* Ärger *m*
V'-forma'tion *s* (aer) Staffelkeil *m*
via ['vi·ə] *prep* über *(acc)*
viable ['vaɪ·əbəl] *adj* lebensfähig
viaduct ['vaɪ·əˌdʌkt] *s* Viadukt *m*
vial ['vaɪ·əl] *s* Phiole *f*
viands ['vaɪ·əndz] *spl* Lebensmittel *pl*
vibrate ['vaɪbret] *intr* vibrieren; **cause to v.** in Schwingung versetzen
vibration [vaɪ'breʃən] *s* Schwingung *f*
vicar ['vɪkər] *s* Vikar *m*
vicarage ['vɪkərɪdʒ] *s* Pfarrhaus *n*
vicarious [vaɪ'kerɪ·əs] *adj (pleasure)* nachempfunden; *(taking the place of another)* stellvertretend; **v. experience** Ersatzbefriedigung *f*
vice [vaɪs] *s* Laster *n*
vice'-ad'miral *s* Vizeadmiral *m*
vice'-con'sul *s* Vizekonsul *m*
vice'-pres'ident *s* Vizepräsident –in *mf*
viceroy ['vaɪsrɔɪ] *s* Vizekönig *m*
vice' squad' *s* Sittenpolizei *f*
vice versa ['vaɪsə'vʌrsə] *adv* umgekehrt
vicinity [vɪ'sɪnɪti] *s* Umgebung *f;* **in the v. of** in der Nähe *(genit)*
vicious ['vɪʃəs] *adj (temper)* bösartig; *(dog)* bissig; *(person, gossip)* heimtückisch
vi'cious cir'cle *s* Zirkelschluß *m*
vicissitudes [vɪ'sɪsɪˌtjudz] *spl* Wechselfälle *pl*
victim ['vɪktɪm] *s* Opfer *n;* *(animal)* Opfertier *n;* **fall v. to** zum Opfer fallen *(dat)*
victimize ['vɪktɪˌmaɪz] *tr (make a victim of)* benachteiligen; *(dupe)* hereinlegen
victor ['vɪktər] *s* Sieger –in *mf*
victorious [vɪk'torɪ·əs] *adj* siegreich
victory ['vɪktəri] *adj* Sieges– ǁ *s* Sieg *m;* (myth) Siegesgöttin *f;* **flushed with v.** siegestrunken
victuals ['vɪtəlz] *spl* Viktualien *pl*
vid'eo sig'nal ['vɪdɪ·ˌo] *s* Bildsignal *n*
vid'eo tape' *s* Bildband *n*
vid'eo tape' record'er *s* Bildbandgerät *n*
vid'eo tape' record'ing *s* Bildbandaufnahme *f*
vie [vaɪ] *v (pret & pp* **vied;** *ger* **vying)** *intr* **(with)** wetteifern (mit)
Vienna [vɪ'enə] *s* Wien *n*
Vien·nese [ˌvi·ə'niz] *adj* wienerisch ǁ *s* (–nese) Wiener –in *mf*
Vietnam [ˌvɪ·ɛt'nɑm] *s* Vietnam *n*
Vietnam·ese [vɪˌɛtnɑ'miz] *adj* vietnamesisch ǁ *s* (–se) Vietnamese *m*, Vietnamesin *f*
view [vju] *s* Aussicht *f;* *(opinion)* Ansicht *f;* **come into v.** in Sicht kommen; **in my v.** meiner Ansicht nach;

in v. of angesichts *(genit);* **with a v. to** *(ger)* in der Absicht zu (inf) ǁ *tr* betrachten; *(sights)* besichtigen
viewer ['vju·ər] *s* Zuschauer –in *mf*
view'find'er *s* Bildsucher *m*
view'point' *s* Standpunkt *m*
vigil ['vɪdʒɪl] *s* Nachtwache *f;* **keep v.** wachen
vigilance ['vɪdʒɪləns] *s* Wachsamkeit *f*
vigilant ['vɪdʒɪlənt] *adj* wachsam
vignette [vɪn'jet] *s* Vignette *f*
vigor ['vɪgər] *s* *(physical)* Kraft *f;* *(mental)* Energie *f;* *(intensity)* Wucht *f*
vigorous ['vɪgərəs] *adj (strong)* kräftig; *(act)* energisch
vile [vaɪl] *adj* gemein; (coll) scheußlich
vileness ['vaɪlnɪs] *s* Gemeinheit *f*
vili·fy ['vɪlɪˌfaɪ] *v (pret & pp* **–fied)** *tr* verleumden
villa ['vɪlə] *s* Villa *f*
village ['vɪlɪdʒ] *s* Dorf *n*, Ort *m*
villager ['vɪlɪdʒər] *s* Dorfbewohner –in *mf*
villain ['vɪlən] *s* Bösewicht *m*, Schurke *m*
villainous ['vɪlənəs] *adj* schurkisch
villainy ['vɪləni] *s* Schurkerei *f*
vim [vɪm] *s* Mumm *m*
vindicate ['vɪndɪˌket] *tr* rechtfertigen
vindictive [vɪn'dɪktɪv] *adj* rachsüchtig
vine [vaɪn] *s* Rebe *f;* *(creeper)* Ranke *f*
vinegar ['vɪnɪgər] *s* Essig *m*
vine' grow'er [ˌgro·ər] *s* Winzer *m*
vineyard ['vɪnjərd] *s* Weinberg *m*
vintage ['vɪntɪdʒ] *adj* Qualitäts– ǁ *s* Weinernte *f*
vin'tage year' *s* Weinjahr *n*
vintner ['vɪntnər] *s* Weinbauer –in *mf*
vinyl ['vaɪnɪl] *adj* Vinyl–
viola [vaɪ'olə] *s* Bratsche *f*, Viola *f*
violate ['vaɪ·əˌlet] *tr (a law)* verletzen; *(a promise)* brechen; *(the peace)* stören; *(a custom, shrine)* entweihen; *(a girl)* vergewaltigen
violation [ˌvaɪ·ə'leʃən] *s* *(of the law)* Verletzung *f;* *(of a shrine)* Entweihung *f;* *(of a girl)* Vergewaltigung *f*
violence ['vaɪ·ələns] *s* Gewalt *f*
violent ['vaɪ·ələnt] *adj (person)* gewalttätig; *(deed)* gewaltsam; *(anger, argument)* heftig
violet ['vaɪ·əlɪt] *adj* violett ǁ *s* Veilchen *n*
violin [ˌvaɪ·ə'lɪn] *s* Geige *f*
violinist [ˌvaɪ·ə'lɪnɪst] *s* Geiger –in *mf*
violoncel·lo [ˌvaɪ·ələn't͡ʃɛlo] *s* (–los) Violoncello *n*
viper ['vaɪpər] *s* Natter *f*, Viper *f*
virgin ['vʌrdʒɪn] *adj* Jungfern–; *(land)* unberührt ǁ *s* Jungfrau *f*
virginity [vər'dʒɪnɪti] *s* Jungfräulichkeit *f*
virility [vɪ'rɪlɪti] *s* Zeugungskraft *f*
virology [vaɪ'ralədʒi] *s* Virusforschung *f*
virtual ['vʌrt͡ʃu·əl] *adj* faktisch; (opt, tech) virtuell
virtue ['vʌrt͡ʃu] *s* Tugend *f;* **by v. of** kraft *(genit)*, vermöge *(genit)*

virtuosity [‚vʌrtʃu'asɪti] *s* Virtuosität *f*

virtuo·so [‚vʌrtʃu'oso] *s* (**–sos** & **–si** [si]) Virtuose *m*, Virtuosin *f*

virtuous ['vʌrtʃu·əs] *adj* tugendhaft

virulence ['vɪrjələns] *s* Virulenz *f*

virulent ['vɪrjələnt] *adj* virulent

virus ['vaɪrəs] *s* Virus *n*

visa ['vizə] *s* Visum *n*

visage ['vɪzɪdʒ] *s* Antlitz *n*

viscera ['vɪsərə] *s* Eingeweide *pl*

viscosity [vɪs'kasɪti] *s* Viskosität *f*

viscount ['vaɪkaunt] *s* Vicomte *m*

viscountess ['vaɪkauntɪs] *s* Vicomtesse *f*

viscous ['vɪskəs] *adj* zähflüssig

vise [vaɪs] *s* Schraubstock *m*

visibility [‚vɪzɪ'bɪlɪti] *s* Sichtbarkeit *f*; (meteor) Sicht *f*

visible ['vɪzɪbəl] *adj* sichtbar

visibly ['vɪzɪbli] *adv* zusehends

vision ['vɪʒən] *s* (*faculty*) Sehvermögen *n*; (*appearance*) Vision *f*; **of great v.** von großem Weitblick

visionary ['vɪʒə‚neri] *adj* visionär ‖ *s* Visionär –in *mf*

visit ['vɪzɪt] *s* Besuch *m*; (*official*) Visite *f* ‖ *tr* besuchen; (*a museum, town*) besichtigen

visitation [‚vɪzɪ'teʃən] *s* Visitation *f*; **Visitation of our Lady** Heimsuchung *f* Mariä

vis'iting hours' *spl* Besuchszeit *f*

vis'iting nurse' *s* Fürsorgerin *f*

visitor ['vɪzɪtər] *s* Besucher –in *mf*; **have visitors** Besuch haben

visor ['vaɪzər] *s* Schirm *m*; (*on a helmet*) Visier *n*

vista ['vɪstə] *s* (& fig) Ausblick *m*

Vistula ['vɪstʃulə] *s* Weichsel *f*

visual ['vɪʒu·əl] *adj* visuell

vis'ual aids' *spl* Anschauungsmaterial *n*

visualize ['vɪʒu·ə‚laɪz] *tr* sich [*dat*] vorstellen

vital ['vaɪtəl] *adj* (lebens)wichtig; (*signs, functions*) Lebens– ‖ **vitals** *spl* edle Teile *pl*

vitality [vaɪ'tælɪti] *s* Lebenskraft *f*

vitalize ['vaɪtə‚laɪz] *tr* beleben

vitamin ['vaɪtəmɪn] *s* Vitamin *n*

vi'tamin defi'ciency *s* Vitaminmangel *m*

vitiate ['vɪʃɪ‚et] *tr* verderben

vitreous ['vɪtrɪ·əs] *adj* glasartig

vitriolic [‚vɪtrɪ'alɪk] *adj* (fig) beißend; (chem) Vitriol–

vituperate [vaɪ't(j)upə‚ret] *tr* schelten

vivacious [vɪ'veʃəs] *adj* lebhaft

vivid ['vɪvɪd] *adj* lebhaft

vivi·fy ['vɪvɪ‚faɪ] *v* (*pret* & *pp* **–fied**) *tr* beleben

vivisection [‚vɪvɪ'sɛkʃən] *s* Vivisektion *f*

vixen ['vɪksən] *s* Füchsin *f*

viz. *abbr* nämlich

vizier [vɪ'zɪr] *s* Vezier *m*, Wesir *m*

vocabulary [vo'kæbjə‚leri] *s* (*word range*) Wortschatz *m*; (*list*) Wörterverzeichnis *n*

vocal ['vokəl] *adj* stimmlich, Stimm–; (*outspoken*) redselig

voc'al cord' *s* Stimmband *n*

vocalist ['vokəlɪst] *s* Sänger –in *mf*

vocalize ['vokə‚laɪz] *tr* (phonet) vokalisieren ‖ *intr* singen; (phonet) in e–n Vokal verwandelt werden

vocation [vo'keʃən] *s* Beruf *m*; (relig) Berufung *f*

voca'tional guid'ance [vo'keʃənəl] *s* Berufsberatung *f*

voca'tional school' *s* Berufsschule *f*

voca'tional train'ing *s* Berufsausbildung *f*

vocative ['vakətɪv] *s* Vokativ *m*

vociferous [vo'sɪfərəs] *adj* laut

vodka ['vadkə] *s* Wodka *m*

vogue [vog] *s* (herrschende) Mode *f*; **be in v.** Mode sein

voice [vɔɪs] *s* Stimme *f*; **in a low v.** mit leiser Stimme ‖ *tr* äußern; (phonet) stimmhaft aussprechen

voiced *adj* (phonet) stimmhaft

voiceless ['vɔɪslɪs] *adj* stimmlos

void [vɔɪd] *adj* leer; (*invalid*) ungültig ‖ *s* Leere *f* ‖ *tr* für ungültig erklären; (*the bowels*) entleeren

volatile ['valətɪl] *adj* (*explosive*) jähzornig; (*changeable*) unbeständig; (chem) flüchtig

volcanic [val'kænɪk] *adj* vulkanisch

volca·no [val'keno] *s* (**–noes** & **–nos**) Vulkan *m*

volition [və'lɪʃən] *s* Wollen *n*; **of one's own v.** aus eigenem Antrieb

volley ['vali] *s* (*of gunfire*) Salve *f*; (*of stones*) Hagel *m*; (sport) Flugschlag *m*

vol'leyball' *s* Volleyball *m*

volt [volt] *s* Volt *n*

voltage ['voltɪdʒ] *s* Spannung *f*

voluble ['valjəbəl] *adj* redegewandt

volume ['valjəm] *s* (*book*) Band *m*; (*of a magazine series*) Jahrgang *m*; (*of sound*) Lautstärke *f*; (*amount*) Ausmaß *n*; (*of a container*) Rauminhalt *m*; **speak volumes** Bände sprechen; **v. of sales** Umsatz *m*

vol'ume control' *s* Lautstärkeregler *m*

voluminous [və'luminəs] *adj* (*writer*) produktiv; (*of great extent or size*) umfangreich

voluntary ['valən‚teri] *adj* freiwillig

volunteer [‚valən'tɪr] *adj* Freiwilligen– ‖ *s* Freiwillige *mf* ‖ *tr* freiwillig anbieten ‖ *intr* (**for**) sich freiwillig erbieten (für, zu)

voluptuary [və'lʌptʃu‚eri] *s* Wollüstling *m*

voluptuous [və'lʌptʃu·əs] *adj* wollüstig

vomit ['vamɪt] *s* Erbrechen *n* ‖ *tr* (er)brechen; (*smoke*) ausstoßen; (*fire*) speien; (*lava*) auswerfen ‖ *intr* sich erbrechen

voodoo ['vudu] *adj* Wudu– ‖ *s* Wudu *m*

voracious [və'reʃəs] *adj* gefräßig

voracity [və'ræsɪti] *s* Gefräßigkeit *f*

vor·tex ['vɔrtɛks] *s* (**–texes** & **–tices** [tɪ‚siz]) (& fig) Wirbel *m*

votary ['votəri] *s* Verehrer –in *mf*

vote [vot] *s* Stimme *f*; (*act of voting*) Abstimmung *f*; (*right to vote*) Stimmrecht *n*; **put to a v.** zur Abstimmung

bringen ‖ *tr* (*approve of, e.g., money*) (*for*) bewilligen (für); **v. down** niederstimmen ‖ *intr* stimmen; **v. by acclamation** durch Zuruf stimmen; **v. for** wählen; **v. on** abstimmen über (*acc*)
vote′ get′ter [ˌgetər] *s* Wahllokomotive *f*
vote′ of con′fidence *s* Vertrauensvotum *n*
vote′ of no′ con′fidence *s* Mißvertrauensvotum *n*
voter [ˈvotər] *s* Wähler –in *mf*
vot′ing booth′ *s* Wahlzelle *f*
vot′ing machine′ *s* Stimmenzählapparat *m*
votive [ˈvotɪv] *adj* Votiv–, Weih–
vo′tive of′fering *s* Weihgabe *f*
vouch [vaʊtʃ] *tr* bezeugen ‖ *intr*—**v. for** bürgen für
voucher [ˈvaʊtʃər] *s* Beleg *m*
vouchsafe′ *tr* gewähren

vow [vaʊ] *s* Gelübde *n;* **take a vow of** geloben ‖ *tr* geloben; (*revenge*) schwören; **vow to** (*inf*) sich [*dat*] geloben zu (*inf*)
vowel [ˈvaʊ‐əl] *s* Selbstlaut *m*, Vokal *m*
voyage [ˈvɔɪ‐ɪdʒ] *s* Reise *f;* (*by sea*) Seereise *f* ‖ *intr* reisen
voyager [ˈvɔɪ‐ɪdʒər] *s* Reisende *mf;* (*by sea*) Seereisende *mf*
V′-sign′ *s* Siegeszeichen *n*
vulcanize [ˈvʌlkəˌnaɪz] *tr* vulkanisieren
vulgar [ˈvʌlgər] *adj* vulgär
vulgarity [vʌlˈgærɪti] *s* Gemeinheit *f*
Vul′gar Lat′in *s* Vulgärlatein *n*
Vulgate [ˈvʌlget] *s* Vulgata *f*
vulnerable [ˈvʌlnərəbəl] *adj* verwundbar; (*position*) ungeschützt; (fig) angreifbar; **v. to** anfällig für
vulture [ˈvʌltʃər] *s* Geier *m*

W

W, w [ˈdʌbəl ˌju] *s* dreiunzwanzigster Buchstabe des englischen Alphabets
wad [wɑd] *s* (*of cotton*) Bausch *m;* (*of money*) Bündel *n;* (*of papers*) Stoß *m;* (*of tobacco*) Priem *m*
waddle [ˈwɑdəl] *s* Watscheln *n* ‖ *intr* watscheln
wade [wed] *intr* waten; **w. into** (fig) anpacken; **w. through** (fig) sich mühsam durcharbeiten durch
wafer [ˈwefər] *s* Oblate *f*
waffle [ˈwɑfəl] *s* Waffel *f*
waf′fle i′ron *s* Waffeleisen *n*
waft [wæft], [wɑft] *tr & intr* wehen
wag [wæg] *s* (*nod*) Nicken *n;* (*shake*) Schütteln *n;* (*of the tail*) Wedeln *n;* (*mischievous person*) Schalk *m* ‖ *v* (*pret & pp* **wagged;** *ger* **wagging**) *tr* (*the tail*) wedeln mit; (*nod*) nicken mit; (*shake*) schütteln ‖ *intr* (*said of a tail*) wedeln; (*said of tongues*) nicht still sein
wage [wedʒ] *adj* Lohn– ‖ *s* Lohn *m;* **wages** Lohn *m* ‖ *tr* (*war*) führen
wage′ cut′ *s* Lohnabbau *m*
wage′ freeze′ *s* Lohnstopp *m*
wager [ˈwedʒər] *s* Wette *f;* **lay a w.** e–e Wette eingehen ‖ *tr & intr* wetten
waggish [ˈwægɪʃ] *adj* schalkhaft
wagon [ˈwægən] *s* Wagen *m*
wag′on load′ *s* Wagenladung *f*
waif [wef] *s* (*child*) verwahrlostes Kind *n;* (*animal*) verwahrlostes Tier *n*
wail [wel] *s* Wehklage *f* ‖ *intr* (**over**) wehklagen (über *acc*)
wain·scot [ˈwenskət] *s* Täfelung *f* ‖ *v* (*pret & pp* –**scot**[t]**ed;** *ger* –**scot**[t]**ing**) *tr* täfeln
waist [west] *s* Taille *f;* **strip to the w.** den Oberkörper freimachen
waist′-deep′ *adj* bis an die Hüften (reichend)

waist′line′ *s* Taille *f;* **watch one's w.** auf die schlanke Linie achten
wait [wet] *s* Warten *n;* **an hour's w.** e–e Stunde Wartezeit ‖ *intr* warten; **that can w.** das hat Zeit; **w. for** (*a person*) warten auf (*acc*); (*e.g., an answer*) abwarten; **w. on** bedienen; **w. up for** aufbleiben und warten auf (*acc*)
wait′-and-see′ pol′icy *s* Politik *f* des Abwartens
waiter [ˈwetər] *s* Kellner *m;* **w.!** Herr Ober!
wait′ing line′ *s* Schlange *f*
wait′ing list′ *s* Warteliste *f*
wait′ing room′ *s* Warteraum *m;* (*e.g., in a railroad station*) Wartesaal *m*
waitress [ˈwetrɪs] *s* Kellnerin *f*
waive [wev] *tr* verzichten auf (*acc*)
waiver [ˈwevər] *s* Verzicht *m*
wake [wek] *s* (*at a funeral*) Totenwache *f;* (naut) Kielwasser *n;* **in the w. of** im Gefolge (*genit*) ‖ *v* (*pret* **waked &** **woke** [wok]; *pp* **waked**) *tr* wecken; **w. up** aufwecken ‖ *intr* erwachen; **w. up** aufwachen; **w. up to** (fig) bewußt werden (*genit*)
wakeful [ˈwekfəl] *adj* wachsam
waken [ˈwekən] *tr* (auf)wecken ‖ *intr* erwachen
walk [wɔk] *s* Spaziergang *m;* (*gait*) Gang *m;* (*path*) Spazierweg *m;* **a five-minute w.** to fünf Minuten zu Fuß zu; **from all walks of life** aus allen Ständen; **go for a w.** spazierengehen; **take for a w.** spazierenführen ‖ *tr* (*a dog*) spazierenführen; (*a person*) begleiten; (*a horse*) führen; (*the streets*) ablaufen ‖ *intr* (zu Fuß) gehen, laufen; **w. off with** klauen; **w. out on** sitzenlassen; **w. up to** zugehen auf (*acc*)
walk′-away′ *s* (coll) leichter Sieg *m*

walker ['wɔkər] s Fußgänger –in mf
walkie-talkie ['wɔki'tɔki] s Sprechfunkgerät n
walk'-in' adj (closet) begehbar
walk'ing pa'pers spl Laufpaß m
walk'ing shoes' spl Straßenschuhe pl
walk'ing stick' s Spazierstock m
walk'-on' s (theat) Statist –in mf
walk'out' s Ausstand m
walk'-o'ver s (sport) leichter Sieg m
walk'-up' s Mietwohnung f ohne Fahrstuhl
wall [wɔl] s Mauer f; (between rooms) Wand f || tr—**w.** up vermauern
wall' brack'et s Konsole f
wall' clock' s Wanduhr f
wallet ['wɑlɪt] s Brieftasche f
wall'flow'er s (coll) Wandblümchen n
wall' map' s Wandkarte f
wallop ['wɑləp] s Puff m; **have a w.** Schlagkraft haben || tr verprügeln; (defeat) schlagen
wal'loping adj (sl) mordsgroß
wallow ['wɑlo] intr sich wälzen; **w. in** (fig) schwelgen in (dat)
wall'pa'per s Tapete f || tr tapezieren
walnut ['wɔlnət] s Walnuß f; (wood) Walnußholz n; (tree) Walnußbaum m
walrus ['wɔlrəs] s Walroß n
waltz [wɔlts] s Walzer m || intr Walzer tanzen
wan [wɑn] adj (**wanner; wannest**) bleich; (smile) schwach, matt
wand [wɑnd] s Stab m; (in magic) Zauberstab m
wander ['wɑndər] intr wandern; (from a subject) abschweifen
wanderer ['wɑndərər] s Wanderer –in mf
wan'derlust' s Wanderlust f
wane [wen] s—**be on the w.** abnehmen || intr abnehmen
wangle ['wæŋgəl] tr sich [dat] erschwindeln
want [wɔnt] s Bedürfnis n; **for w. of** mangels (genit) || tr wollen; **wanted** (sought, desired) gesucht
want' ad' s Kleinanzeige f
want'ing adj—**be w. in** ermangeln (genit)
war [wɔr] s Krieg m; **at war** im Kriege; **go to war with** e-n Krieg beginnen gegen; **make war on** Krieg führen gegen || v (pret & pp **warred; ger warring**) intr kämpfen
warble ['wɑrbəl] s Trillern n || intr trillern
war' bond' s Kriegsanleihe f
war' cry' s Schlachtruf m
ward [wɔrd] s (in a hospital) Station f; (of a city) Bezirk m; (person under protection) Schützling m; (person under guardianship) Mündel n; (guardianship) Vormundschaft f || tr—**w. off** abwehren
warden ['wɔrdən] s Gefängnisdirektor m
ward'robe' s Garderobe f
ward'room' s (nav) Offiziersmesse f
ware [wer] s Ware f
ware'house' s Lagerhaus n, Warenlager n

ware'house'man s (–men) Lagerist m
war'fare' s Kriegsführung f, Krieg m
war' foot'ing s Kriegsbereitschaft f
war'head' s Gefechtskopf m
war'-horse' s (coll) alter Kämpe m
war'like' adj kriegerisch
war' lord' s Kriegsherr m
warm [wɔrm] adj warm; (friends) intim || tr wärmen; **w. up** aufwärmen || intr—**w.** up warm werden; (sport) in Form kommen
warm'-blood'ed adj warmblütig
warm'front' s Warmfront f
warm'-heart'ed adj warmherzig
warmonger ['wɔr,mʌŋgər] s Kriegshetzer –in mf
warmth [wɔrmθ] s Wärme f
warm'-up' s (sport) Lockerungsübungen pl
warn [wɔrn] tr (against) warnen (vor dat)
warn'ing s Warnung f; **let this be a w. to you** lassen Sie sich das zur Warnung dienen
warn'ing shot' s Warnschuß m
war' of attri'tion s Zermürbungskrieg m
warp [wɔrp] s (of a board) Verziehen n || tr (wood) verziehen; **w. s.o.'s mind** j–n verschroben machen || intr sich verziehen
war'path' s Kriegspfad m
warped adj (wood) verzogen; (mind, opinion) verschroben
war'plane' s Kampfflugzeug n
warrant ['wɔrənt] s (justification) Rechtfertigung f; (authorization) Berechtigung f; **w. for arrest** Haftbefehl m || tr (justify) rechtfertigen; (guarantee) garantieren
war'rant of'ficer s (mil) Stabsfeldwebel m; (nav) Deckoffizier m
warranty ['wɔrənti] s Gewährleistung f
war'ranty serv'ice s Kundendienst m
warren ['wɔrən] s Kaninchengehege n
war'ring adj kriegsführend
warrior ['wɔrɪər] s Krieger m
Warsaw ['wɔrsɔ] s Warschau n
war'ship' s Kriegsschiff n
wart [wɔrt] s Warze f
war'time' adj Kriegs– || s Kriegszeit f
war'-torn' adj vom Krieg verwüstet
wary ['weri] adj vorsichtig
war' zone' s Kriegsgebiet n
wash [wɔʃ] adj Wasch– || s Wäsche f; (aer) Luftstrudel m; (paint) dünner Farbüberzug m; **do the w.** die Wäsche waschen || tr waschen; (metal) schlämmen; (paint) tuschen; (phot) wässern; **w. ashore** anschwemmen; **w. away** wegspülen; **w. off** abwaschen; **w. out** auswaschen; (a bridge) wegreißen; **w. up** aufwaschen || intr waschen; **w. ashore** ans Land spülen
washable ['wɔʃəbəl] adj waschbar
wash'-and-wear' adj bügelfrei
wash'ba'sin s Waschbecken n
wash'bas'ket s Wäschekorb m
wash'board' s Waschbrett n
wash'bowl' s Waschbecken n
wash'cloth' s Waschlappen m

wash'day' s Waschtag m
washed'-out' adj verwaschen; (tired) schlapp
washer ['wɔʃər] s Waschmaschine f; (of rubber) Dichtungsring m; (of metal) Unterlegscheibe f
washed'-up' adj (coll) erledigt
wash'er·wom'an s (-wom'en) Waschfrau f
wash'ing s Waschen n; (clothes) Wäsche f
wash'ing machine' s Waschmaschine f
wash'out' s Auswaschung f; (failure) Pleite f; (person who fails) Versager –in mf
wash'rag' s Waschlappen m
wash'room' s Waschraum m
wash'stand' s Waschtisch m
wash'tub' s Waschtrog m
wasp [wɑsp] s Wespe f
wasp' waist' s Wespentaille f
waste [west] adj (superfluous) überflüssig; (land) öde || s (of material goods, time, energy) Verschwendung f; (waste material) Müll m; (wilderness) Wildnis f; **go to w.** vergeudet werden || tr verschwenden, vergeuden || intr—**w. away** verfallen
waste'bas'ket s Papierkorb m
wasteful ['westfəl] adj verschwenderisch
waste'land' s Ödland n
waste'pa'per s Makulatur f
waste'pipe' s Abflußrohr n
waste'pro'duct s Abfallprodukt n
wastrel ['westrəl] s Verschwender –in mf
watch [wɑtʃ] s Uhr f; (lookout) Wache f; **be on the w. for** acht haben auf (acc) || tr (observe) beobachten; (guard) bewachen; (oversee) aufpassen auf (acc); **w. how I do it** passen Sie auf, wie ich es mache; **w. your step!** Vorsicht, Stufe! || intr (keep guard) wachen; (observe) zuschauen; **w. for** abwarten; **w. over** überwachen; **w. out!** Vorsicht!; **w. out for** ausschauen nach; (some danger) sich hüten vor (dat); **w. out for oneself** sich vorsehen
watch'band' s Uhrarmband n
watch'case' s Uhrgehäuse n
watch' crys'tal s Uhrglas n
watch'dog' s Wachhund m
watch'dog commit'tee s Überwachungsausschuß m
watchful ['wɑtʃfəl] adj wachsam
watchfulness ['wɑtʃfəlnɪs] s Wachsamkeit f
watch'mak'er s Uhrmacher –in mf
watch'man s (-men) Wächter m
watch' pock'et s Uhrtasche f
watch' strap' s Uhrarmband n
watch'tow'er s Wachturm m
watch'word' s Kennwort n, Parole f
water ['wɔtər] s Wasser n; (body of water) Gewässer n; **pass w.** Wasser lassen || tr (e.g., flowers) begießen; (fields) bewässern; (animals) tränken; (the garden, streets) sprengen; **w. down** (& fig) verwässern || intr (said of the eyes) tränen; **my mouth**

waters das Wasser läuft mir im Mund zusammen
wa'ter boy' s Wasserträger m
wa'ter clos'et s Wasserklosett n
wa'tercol'or s (paint) Aquarellfarbe f; (painting) Aquarell n
wa'tercourse' s Wasserlauf m
wa'tercress' s Brunnenkresse f
wa'terfall' s Wasserfall m
wa'terfront' s Hafenviertel n
wa'ter heat'er s Warmwasserbereiter m
wa'tering can' s Wasserkanne f
wa'tering place' s (for cattle) Tränke f; (for tourists) Badeort m
wa'ter lev'el s Wasserstand m
wa'terlogged' adj vollgesogen
wa'ter main' s Wasserleitung f
wa'termark' s Wasserzeichen n
wa'ter mat'tress s Wasserbett n
wa'termel'on s Wassermelone f
wa'ter me'ter s Wasserzähler m
wa'ter pipe' s Wasserrohr n
wa'ter po'lo s Wasserball m
wa'ter pow'er s Wasserkraft f
wa'terproof' adj wasserdicht || tr imprägnieren
wa'ter-repel'lent adj wasserabstoßend
wa'tershed' s Wasserscheide f
wa'ter-ski' intr wasserschifahren
wa'terspout' s (orifice) Wasserspeier m; (pipe) Ablaufrohr n
wa'ter supply' s Wasserversorgung f
wa'ter ta'ble s Grundwasserspiegel m
wa'ter tank' s Wasserbehälter m
wa'tertight' adj wasserdicht; (fig) eindeutig
wa'ter wag'on s—**be on the w.** Abstinenzler sein
wa'terway' s Wasserstraße f
wa'ter wheel' s (for raising water) Schöpfwerk n; (water-driven) Wasserrad n
wa'ter wings' spl Schwimmkissen n
wa'terworks' s Wasserwerk n
watery ['wɔtəri] adj wäss(e)rig
watt [wɑt] s Watt n
wattage ['wɑtɪdʒ] s Wattleistung f
wattles ['wɑtəlz] spl Flechtwerk s
watt'me'ter s Wattmeter m
wave [wev] s (fig, meteor, mil, phys, rad) Welle f; **w. of the hand** Wink m mit der Hand || tr (a hat, flag) schwenken; (a hand, handkerchief) winken mit; (hair) wellen; **w. one's hands about** mit den Händen herumfuchteln; **w. s.o. away** j–n abwinken || intr (said of a flag) wehen; (said of grain) wogen; (with the hand) winken; **w. to** zuwinken (dat)
wave'length' s Wellenlänge f
waver ['wevər] intr schweben, wanken
wavy ['wevi] adj wellenförmig; **w. line** Wellenlinie f
wax [wæks] adj Wachs– || s Wachs n || tr (the floor) bohnern; (skis) wachsen || intr werden; (said of the moon) zunehmen; **wax and wane** zu– und abnehmen
wax' muse'um s Wachsfigurenkabinett n
wax' pa'per s Wachspapier n
way [we] adv weit; **way ahead** weit

voraus ‖ s Weg m; (manner) Art f; (means) Mittel n; (condition) Verfassung f; (direction) Richtung f; **across the way** gegenüber; **a long way from** weit weg von; **a long way off** weit weg; **by the way** übrigens; **by way of** über (acc); **by way of comparison** vergleichsweise; **get s.th. out of the way** etw aus dem Wege schaffen; **get under way** in Gang kommen; **go all the way** aufs Ganze gehen; **go one's own way** aus der Reihe tanzen; **have a way with s.o.** mit j-m umzugehen verstehen; **have in the way of** (merchandise) haben an (dat); **have it both ways** es sich [dat] aussuchen können; **have one's own way** seinen Willen durchsetzen; **I'm on my way!** ich komme schon!; **in a way** gewissermaßen; **in no way** keineswegs; **in the way** im Weg; **in this way** auf diese Weise; **in what way** in welcher Hinsicht; **make one's way through the crowd** sich [dat] e-n Weg durch die Menge bahnen; **one way or another** irgendwie: **on the way** unterwegs; **on the way out** (fig) im Begriff unmodern zu werden; **see one's way clear** bereit sein; **that way** auf diese Weise; (in that direction) in jener Richtung; **the way it looks** voraussichtlich; **way back** Rückweg m; **way here** Herweg m; **way out** Ausgang m; (fig) Ausweg m; **way there** Hinweg m
wayfarer ['we͵ferər] s Wanderer m
way'lay' v (pret & pp –laid) tr auflauern (dat)
way' of life' s Lebensweise f
way' of think'ing s Denkweise f
ways' and means' spl Mittel und Wege pl
way'side' adj an der Straße gelegen ‖ s Wegrand m; **fall by the w.** dem Untergang anheimfallen
wayward ['wewərd] adj ungeraten
we [wi] pers pron wir
weak [wik] adj schwach
weaken ['wikən] tr (ab)schwächen ‖ intr schwach werden
weakling ['wiklɪŋ] s Schwächling m
weak'-mind'ed adj willenlos
weakness ['wiknɪs] s (& fig) Schwäche f
weak' spot' s schwache Stelle f
weal [wil] s Strieme f, Striemen m
wealth [wɛlθ] s (of) Reichtum m (an dat)
wealthy ['wɛlθi] adj wohlhabend
wean [win] tr (from) entwöhnen (genit)
weapon ['wepən] s Waffe f
weaponry ['wepənri] s Bewaffnung f
wear [wer] s (use) Gebrauch m; (durability) Haltbarkeit f; (clothing) Kleidung f; (wearing down) Verschleiß m ‖ v (pret wore [wor]; pp worn [worn])tr tragen; **w. down** (a heel) abtreten; (a person) zermürben; **w. out** abnützen; (tires) abfahren; (a person) erschöpfen; **w. the pants in the family** die Hosen anhaben ‖ intr sich tragen; **w. off** sich abtragen; **w.**

out sich abnützen; **w. thin** (said of clothes) fadenscheinig werden; (said of patience) zu Ende gehen
wearable ['werəbəl] adj tragbar
wear' and tear' [ter] s Verschleiß m; **takes a lot of w.** strapazierfähig sein
weariness ['wirɪnɪs] s Müdigkeit f
wearisome ['wirɪsəm] adj mühsam
wea·ry ['wiri] adj müde ‖ v (pret & pp –ried) tr ermüden ‖ intr (of) müde werden (genit)
weasel ['wizəl] s Wiesel n ‖ intr—**w. out** of sich herauswinden aus
weather ['weðər] s Wetter n; **be under the w.** unpäßlich sein; **w. permitting** bei günstiger Witterung ‖ tr dem Wetter aussetzen; (the storm) (fig) überstehen ‖intr verwittern
weath'erbeat'en adj verwittert
weath'er bu'reau s Wetterdienst m
weath'er condi'tions spl Wetterverhältnisse pl
weath'er fore'cast s Wettervoraussage f
weath'erman' s (–men') Wetteransager m
weath'er report' s Wetterbericht m
weath'erstrip'ping s Dichtungsstreifen pl
weath'er vane' s (& fig) Wetterfahne f
weave [wiv] s Webart f ‖ v (pret wove [wov] & weaved; pp woven ['wovən]) tr weben; (a rug) wirken; (a basket) flechten; (a wreath) winden; **w. one's way through traffic** sich durch den Verkehr schlängeln ‖ intr weben
weaver ['wivər] s Weber –in mf
web [wɛb] s (of a spider) Spinngewebe n; (of ducks) Schwimmhaut f; **web of lies** Lügengewebe n
web'-foot'ed adj schwimmfüßig
wed [wɛd] v (pret & pp wed & wedded; ger wedding) tr & intr heiraten
wed'ding adj (cake, present, day, reception) Hochzeits–; (ring) Trau– ‖ s Hochzeit f; (ceremony) Trauung f
wedge [wɛdʒ] s Keil m ‖ tr—**w. in** einkeilen
wed'lock' s Ehestand m; **out of w.** unehelich
Wednesday ['wɛnzde] s Mittwoch m; **on W.** am Mittwoch
wee [wi] adj winzig; **a wee bit** ein klein wenig
weed [wid] s Unkraut n; (marijuana) (sl) Marihuana n; (cigarette) (sl) Zigarette f; **pull weeds** jäten ‖ tr jäten; **w. out** (fig) aussondern
weed' kill'er s Unkrautvertilgungsmittel n
week [wik] s Woche f; **a w. from today** heute in e-r Woche; **a w. ago today** heute vor acht Tagen; **for weeks** wochenlang
week'day' s Wochentag m
week'end' s Wochenende n
weekender ['wik͵endər] s Wochenendausflügler –in mf
weekly ['wikli] adj wöchentlich; (wages) Wochen– ‖ s Wochenblatt n
weep [wip] v (pret & pp wept [wɛpt]) tr & intr weinen

weep′ing wil′low *s* Trauerweide *f*
weevil [′wivəl] *s* Rüsselkäfer *m*
weft [wɛft] *s* (tex) Schußfaden *m*
weigh [we] *tr* wiegen; (*ponder*) wägen;
(*anchor*) lichten ‖ *intr* wiegen; **w.
heavily on** schwer lasten auf (*dat*)
weight [wet] *s* Gewicht *n*; (*burden*)
Last *f*; (*influence*) Einfluß *m*; (*importance*) Bedeutung *f*; **carry great
w.** sehr ins Gewicht fallen; **lift
weights** Gewichte heben; **pull one's
w.** das Seine tun; **throw one's w.
about** sich breitmachen
weightless [′wetlɪs] *adj* schwerelos
weightlessness [′wetlɪsnɪs] *s* Schwere-
losigkeit *f*
weighty [′weti] *adj* (& fig) gewichtig
weird [wɪrd] *adj* unheimlich
weir·do [′wɪrdo] *s* (–dos) (sl) Kauz *m*
welcome [′wɛlkəm] *adj* willkommen;
(*news*) erfreulich; **you're w.!** bitte
sehr!; **you're w. to** (*inf*) es steht
Ihnen frei zu (*inf*) ‖ *s* Empfang *m*,
Willkomm *m* ‖ *tr* empfangen; (*an
opportunity*) mit Freude begrüßen ‖
interj (to) willkommen! (**in** *dat*)
weld [wɛld] *s* Schweißnaht *n* ‖ *tr* &
intr schweißen
welder [′wɛldər] *s* Schweißer –in *mf*
weld′ing *s* Schweißung *f*, Schweißarbeit
f
welfare [′wɛl ˌfɛr] *s* Wohlfahrt *f*
wel′fare work′er *s* Wohlfahrtspfleger
–in *mf*
well [wɛl] *adj* gesund; **all is w.** alles
ist in Ordnung; **feel w.** sich wohl
fühlen ‖ *adv* gut, wohl; **as w.** ebenso;
as w. as so gut wie; (*in addition to*)
sowohl … als auch; **he is doing w.**
es geht ihm gut; **his company is
doing w.** seine Firma geht gut; **leave
w. enough alone** es gut sein lassen;
w. on in years schon bejahrt; **w. on
the way** mitten auf dem Wege; (fig)
auf dem besten Wege; **w. over** weit
über ‖ *s* Brunnen *m*; (*hole*) Bohrloch *n*; (*source*) Quelle *f* ‖ *intr*—
w. up hervorquellen ‖ *interj* na!; (*in
surprise*) nanu!
well′-behaved′ *adj* artig
well′-be′ing *s* Wohlergehen *n*
well′born′ *adj* aus guter Familie
wellbred [′wɛl′brɛd] *adj* wohlerzogen
well′-deserved′ *adj* wohlverdient
well′-disposed′ *adj* (**toward**) wohlge-
sinnt (*dat*)
well-done [′wɛl′dʌn] *adj* (culin) durchgebraten ‖ *interj* gut gemacht!
well′-dressed′ *adj* gut angezogen
well′-found′ed *adj* wohlbegründet
well′-groomed′ *adj* gut gepflegt
well′-heeled′ *adj* (coll) steinreich
well′-informed′ *adj* wohlunterrichtet
well′-inten′tioned *adj* wohlmeinend
well-kept [′wɛl′kɛpt] *adj* gut gepflegt;
(*secret*) gut gehütet
well′-known′ *adj* wohlbekannt
well′-mean′ing *adj* wohlmeinend
well′-nigh′ *adv* fast
well′-off′ *adj* wohlhabend, vermögend
well′-preserved′ *adj* gut erhalten
well-read [′wɛl′rɛd] *adj* belesen

well′-spent′ *adj* (*money*) gut verwen-
det; (*time*) gut verbracht
well′spring′ *s* Brunnquell *m*
well′-thought′-of′ *adj* angesehen
well′-timed′ *adj* wohl berechnet
well-to-do [′wɛltə′du] *adj* wohlhabend
well-wisher [′wɛl′wɪʃər] *s* Gratulant
–in *mf*
well′-worn′ *adj* (*clothes*) abgetragen;
(*phrase, subject*) abgedroschen
Welsh [wɛlʃ] *adj* walisisch ‖ *s* Walisisch *n*; **the W.** die Waliser *pl* ‖
welsh *intr*—**welsh on** (*a promise*)
brechen
Welsh′ rab′bit or **rare′bit** [′rɛrbɪt] *s*
geröstete Käseschnitte *f*
welt [wɛlt] *s* Striemen *m*
welter [′wɛltər] *s* Durcheinander *n* ‖
intr sich wälzen
wel′terweight′ *s* Weltergewichtler *m*
we′lterweight divi′sion *s* Weltergewicht
n
wench [wɛntʃ] *s* Dirne *f*, Weibsbild *n*
wend [wɛnd] *tr*—**w. one's way** seinen
Weg nehmen
werewolf [′wer ˌwʌlf] *s* Werwolf *m*
west [wɛst] *adj* westlich ‖ *adv* nach
Westen ‖ *s* Westen *m*
western [′wɛstərn] *adj* westlich ‖ *s*
(cin) Wildwestfilm *m*
West′ Ger′many *s* Westdeutschland *n*
West′ In′dies, the [′ɪndiz] *spl* Westindien *n*
Westphalia [ˌwɛst′fɛlɪ·ə] *s* Westfalen
n
westward [′wɛstwərd] *adv* westwärts
wet [wɛt] *adj* (**wetter; wettest**) naß;
all wet (coll) auf dem Holzwege ‖ *v*
(*pret & pp* **wet** & **wetted; ger wetting**)
tr naß machen
wet′ blan′ket *s* (fig) Miesepeter *m*
wet′ nurse′ *s* Amme *f*
whack [wæk] *s* (coll) Klaps *m* ‖ *tr*
(coll) klapsen
whale [wel] *s* Wal(fisch) *m*; **have a w.
of a time** sich großartig unterhalten
whaler [′welər] *s* Walfänger *m*
wharf [wɔrf] *s* (**wharves** [wɔrvz]) Kai-
anlage *f*
what [wɑt] *interr adj* welcher, was für
ein ‖ *interr pron* was; **so w.?** na
und?; **w. about me?** und was geschieht mit mir?; **w. if** was geschieht,
wenn; **w. is more** außerdem; **w. next?**
was noch?; **w. of it?** was ist da schon
dabei?; **what's new?** was gibt es
Neues? **what's that to you?** was geht
Sie das an? ‖ *interj* was für ein
whatev′er *adj* welch … auch immer;
no … w. überhaupt kein ‖ *pron*
was auch immer; **w. I have** alles,
was ich habe; **w. you please** was Sie
wollen
what′not′ *s*—**and w.** und was weiß ich
noch (alles)
what's-his-name′ *s* (coll) Dingsda *m*
wheal [wil] *s* Pustel *f*; (*welt*) Striemen
m
wheat [wit] *s* Weizen *m*
wheedle [′hwidəl] *tr*—**w. s.o. into** (*ger*)
j-n beschwatzen zu (*inf*); **w. s.th.
out of s.o.** j-m etw abschwatzen

wheel [wil] s Rad n; **at the w.** (aut) am Steuer ‖ tr fahren ‖ intr sich drehen; **w. around** sich umdrehen

wheelbarrow ['wil‚bæro] s Schubkarre f

wheel'chair' s Krankenfahrstuhl m

wheeler-dealer ['wilər'dilər] s Drahtzieher –in mf

wheeze [wiz] s Schnaufen n ‖ intr schnaufen

whelp [wɛlp] s Welpe m ‖ tr werfen

when [wɛn] adv wann ‖ conj (once in the past) als; (whenever; at a future time) wenn

whence [wɛns] adv & conj woher

whenev'er conj wenn, wann immer

where [wɛr] adv & conj wo; (whereto) wohin; **from w.** woher

whereabouts ['wɛrə‚bauts] adv wo ungefähr ‖ s & spl Verbleib m

whereas' conj während, wohingegen

whereby' conj wodurch

where'fore' adv & conj weshalb

wherefrom' adv woher

wherein' adv & conj worin

whereof' adv & conj wovon

whereto' adv wohin

where'upon' adv worauf, wonach

wherever [wɛr'ɛvər] conj wo auch

wherewith' adv womit

wherewithal ['wɛrwɪð‚ɔl] s Geldmittel pl

whet [wɛt] v (pret & pp **whetted;** ger **whetting)** tr wetzen, schleifen; (the appetite) anregen

whether ['wɛðər] conj ob

whet'stone' s Wetzstein m, Schleifstein m

whew [hwju] interj hui!; ui!

which [wɪtʃ] interr adj welcher ‖ interr pron welcher ‖ rel pron der, welcher

whichev'er rel adj & rel pron welcher

whiff [wɪf] s Geruch m, Nasevoll f

while [waɪl] s Weile f ‖ conj während ‖ tr—**w. away** sich [dat] vertreiben

whim [wɪm] s Laune f, Grille f

whimper ['wɪmpər] s Wimmern n ‖ tr & intr wimmern

whimsical ['wɪmzɪkəl] adj schrullig

whine [waɪn] s Wimmern n; (of a siren, engine, storm) Heulen n ‖ intr wimmern; heulen

whin·ny ['wɪni] s Wiehern n ‖ v (pret & pp –nied) intr wiehern

whip [wɪp] s Peitsche f ‖ v (pret & pp **whipped;** ger **whipping)** tr peitschen; (egg whites) zu Schaum schlagen; (defeat) schlagen; **w. out** blitzschnell ziehen; **w. up** (a meal) hervorzaubern; (enthusiasm) erregen

whip'lash' s Peitschenhieb m; (fig) Peitschenhiebeffekt n

whipped' cream' s Schlagsahne f

whipper-snapper ['wɪpər‚snæpər] s Frechdachs m

whip'ping s Prügel pl

whip'ping boy' s Prügelknabe m

whip'ping post' s Schandpfahl m

whir [wʌr] s Schnurren n ‖ v (pret & pp **whirred;** ger **whirring)** intr schnurren

whirl [wʌrl] s Wirbel m; **give s.th. a w.** (coll) etw ausprobieren ‖ tr wirbeln ‖ intr wirbeln; **my head is whirling** mir ist schwindlig

whirl'pool' s Strudel m, Wirbel m

whirl'wind' s Wirbelwind m

whirlybird ['wʌrli‚bʌrd] s (coll) Hubschrauber m

whisk [wɪsk] s Wedel m; (culin) Schneebesen m ‖ tr wischen; **w. away** (fig) eilends mitnehmen; **w. off** wegfegen

whisk' broom' s Kleiderbesen m

whiskers ['wɪskərz] spl Bart m; (on the cheeks) Backenbart m; (of a cat) Barthaare pl

whiskey ['wɪski] s Whisky m

whisper ['wɪspər] s Flüsterton m ‖ tr & intr flüstern

whistle ['wɪsəl] s (sound) Pfiff m; (device) Trillerpfeife f; **wet one's w.** sich [dat] die Nase begießen ‖ tr pfeifen ‖ intr pfeifen; (said of the wind, bullet) sausen; **w. for** (coll) vergeblich warten auf (acc)

whit [wɪt] s—**not care a w. about** sich keinen Deut kümmern um

white [waɪt] adj weiß; **w. as a sheet** kreidebleich ‖ s Weiß n; (of the eye) Weiße f

white'caps' spl Schaumkronen pl

white'-col'lar work'er s Angestellte mf

white'fish' s Weißfisch m

white'-haired' adj weißhaarig

white'-hot' adj weißglühend

white' lie' s Notlüge f

white' meat' s weißes Fleisch n

whiten ['waɪtən] tr weiß machen ‖ intr weiß werden

whiteness ['waɪtnɪs] s Weiße f

white' slav'ery s Mädchenhandel m

white' tie' s Frackschleife f; (formal) Frack m

white'wash' s Tünche f; (fig) Beschönigung f ‖ tr tünchen; (fig) beschönigen

whither ['wɪðər] adv wohin

whitish ['waɪtɪʃ] adj weißlich

whittle ['wɪtəl] tr schnitzeln; **w. away** (or **down**) verringern ‖ intr—**w. away at** herumschnitzeln an (dat); (fig) verringern

whiz(z) [wɪz] s Zischen n; (fig) Kanone f ‖ v (pret & pp **whizzed;** ger **whizzing)** intr zischen; **w. by** flitzen

who [hu] interr pron wer; **who the devil** wer zum Teufel ‖ rel pron der; **he who** wer

whoa [wo] interj halt!

whoev'er rel pron wer, wer auch immer

whole [hol] adj ganz ‖ s Ganze n; **as a w.** im großen und ganzen

whole'-heart'ed adj ernsthaft

whole' note' s (mus) ganze Note f

whole' rest' s (mus) ganze Pause f

whole'sale' adj Massen–; (com) Großhandels– ‖ adv en gros ‖ s Großhandel m ‖ tr en gros verkaufen ‖ intr im großen handeln

wholesaler ['hol‚selər] s Großhändler –in mf

wholesome ['holsəm] *adj* gesund; (*food*) zuträglich
whole'-wheat' bread' *s* Vollkornbrot *n*
wholly ['holi] *adv* ganz, völlig
whom [hum] *interr pron* wen; **to w.** wem ‖ *rel pron* den, welchen; **to w.** dem, welchem
whomev'er *rel pron* wen auch immer; **to w.** wem auch immer
whoop [hup], [hwup] *s* Ausruf *m* ‖ *tr—w.* **it up** Radau machen
whoop'ing cough' *s* Keuchhusten *m*
whopper ['wapər] *s* Mordsding *n;* (*lie*) (coll) faustdicke Lüge *f*
whop'ping *adj* (coll) enorm, Riesen—
whore [hor] *s* Hure *f* ‖ *intr—w.* **around** huren
whose [huz] *interr pron* wessen ‖ *rel pron* dessen
why [waɪ] *adv* warum; **that's why** deswegen; **why, there you are!** da sind Sie ja!; **why, yes!** aber ja! ‖ *s* Warum *n;* **the whys and the wherefores** das Warum und Weshalb
wick [wɪk] *s* Docht *m*
wicked ['wɪkɪd] *adj* (*evil*) böse; (*roguish*) boshaft; (*vicious*) bösartig; (*unpleasant*) ekelhaft; (*cold, pain, storm, wound*) (coll) schlimm; (*fantastic*) (coll) großartig
wicker ['wɪkər] *adj* (*basket, chair*) Weiden— ‖ *s* (*wickerwork*) Flechtwerk *n*
wide [waɪd] *adj* breit; (*selection*) reich ‖ *adv* weit
wide'-an'gle lens' *s* Weitwinkelobjektiv *n*
wide'-awake' *adj* hellwach
wide'-eyed' *adj* mit weit aufgerissenen Augen; (*innocence*) naiv
widely ['waɪdli] *adv* weit
widen ['waɪdən] *tr* ausweiten, verbreiten ‖ *intr* sich ausweiten
wide'-o'pen *adj* weit geöffnet
wide' screen' *s* (cin) Breitleinwand *f*
wide'spread' *adj* weitverbreitet; (*damage*) weitgehend
widow ['wɪdo] *s* Witwe *f*
widower ['wɪdo·ər] *s* Witwer *m*
wid'owhood' *s* Witwenstand *m*
width [wɪdθ] *s* Breite *f;* **in w.** breit
wield [wild] *tr* (*a weapon*) führen; (*power, influence*) ausüben
wife [waɪf] *s* (**wives** [waɪvz]) Frau *f*
wig [wɪg] *s* Perücke *f*
wiggle ['wɪgəl] *s* Wackeln *n* ‖ *tr* wackeln mit
wigwag ['wɪg,wæg] *s* Winksignal *n*
wigwam ['wɪgwam] *s* Wigwam *m & n*
wild [waɪld] *adj* wild; **w. about** scharf auf (*acc*); **go w.** verwildern; **grow w.** (*become neglected*) verwildern; **make s.o. w.** (coll) j–n rasend machen ‖ *adv*—**grow w.** (*grow in the wild*) wild wachsen; **run w.** verwildern
wild' boar' *s* Wildschwein *n*
wild' card' *s* wilde Karte *f*
wild'cat' *s* Wildkatze *f*
wild'cat strike' *s* wilder Streik *m*
wilderness ['wɪldərnɪs] *s* Wildnis *f*
wild'fire' *s*—**like w.** wie Lauffeuer
wild' flow'er *s* Feldblume *f*

wild'-goose' chase' *s*—**go on a w.** sich [*dat*] vergeblich Mühe machen
wild'life' *s* Wild *n*
wild' oats' *spl*—**sow one's w.** sich [*dat*] die Hörner abstoßen
wile [waɪl] *s* List *f* ‖ *tr—w.* **away** sich [*dat*] vertreiben
will [wɪl] *s* Wille(n) *m;* (jur) Testament *n;* **at w.** nach Belieben ‖ *tr* (*bequeath*) vermachen ‖ *v* (*pret & cond* **would** [wʊd]) *aux* werden
willful ['wɪlfəl] *adj* absichtlich; (*stubborn*) eigensinnig
William ['wɪljəm] *s* Wilhelm *m*
will'ing *adj* bereitwillig; **be w. to** (*inf*) bereit sein zu (*inf*)
willingly ['wɪlɪŋli] *adv* gern
willingness ['wɪlɪŋnɪs] *s* Bereitwilligkeit *f*
will-o'-the-wisp ['wɪləðə'wɪsp] *s* (& fig) Irrlicht *n*
willow ['wɪlo] *s* Weide *f*
willowy ['wɪlo·i] *adj* biegsam
will' pow'er *s* Willenskraft *f*
willy-nilly ['wɪli'nɪli] *adv* wohl oder übel
wilt [wɪlt] *tr* verwelken lassen ‖ *intr* verwelken
wilt'ed *adj* welk
wily ['waɪli] *adj* schlau, listig
wimple ['wɪmpəl] *s* Kinntuch *n*
win [wɪn] *s* Gewinn *m;* (sport) Sieg *m* ‖ *v* (*pret & pp* **won** [wʌn]; *ger* **winning**) *tr* gewinnen; **win over to one's side** auf seine Seite ziehen ‖ *intr* gewinnen, siegen
wince [wɪns] *s* Zucken *n* ‖ *intr* zucken
winch [wɪntʃ] *s* (*windlass*) Winde *f;* (*handle*) Kurbel *f;* (min, naut) Haspel *f & m*
wind [wɪnd] *s* Wind *m;* **break w.** e–n Darmwind lassen; **get w. of** Wind bekommen von; **take the w. out of s.o.'s sails** j–m den Wind aus den Segeln nehmen; **there is s.th. in the w.** es liegt etw in der Luft ‖ [waɪnd] *v* (*pret & pp* **wound** [waʊnd]) *tr* wickeln, winden; (*a timepiece*) aufziehen; **w. up** aufwickeln; (*affairs*) abwickeln; (*a speech*) abschließen ‖ *intr* (*said of a river, road*) sich winden; **w. around** (*said of a plant*) sich ranken um
windbag ['wɪnd,bæg] *s* (coll) Schaumschläger –in *mf*
windbreak ['wɪnd,brek] *s* Windschutz *m*
windbreaker ['wɪnd,brekər] *s* Windjacke *f*
winded ['wɪndɪd] *adj* außer Atem, atemlos
windfall ['wɪnd,fɔl] *s* (*fallen fruit*) Fallobst *n;* (fig) Glücksfall *m*
wind'ing road' ['waɪndɪŋ] *s* Serpentinenstraße *f;* (public sign) kurvenreiche Straße *f*
wind'ing sheet' ['waɪndɪŋ] *s* Leichentuch *n*
wind' in'strument [wɪnd] *s* Blasinstrument *n*
windlass ['wɪndləs] *s* Winde *f*
windmill ['wɪnd,mɪl] *s* Windmühle *f*

window ['wɪndo] *s* Fenster *n; (of a ticket office)* Schalter *m; (for display)* Schaufenster *n*
win'dow display' *s* Schaufensterauslage *f*
win'dow dress'er *s* Schaufensterdekorateur –in *mf*
win'dow dress'ing *s* Schaufensterdekoration *f*
win'dow en'velope *s* Fensterumschlag *m*
win'dow frame' *s* Fensterrahmen *m*
win'dowpane' *s* Fensterscheibe *f*
win'dow screen' *s* Fliegengitter *n*
win'dow shade' *s* Rollvorhang *m*, Rollo *n*
win'dow-shop' *v (pret & pp –shopped; ger –shopping) intr* e–n Schaufensterbummel machen
win'dow shut'ter *s* Fensterladen *m*
win'dow sill' *s* Fensterbrett *n*
windpipe ['wɪnd‚paɪp] *s* Luftröhre *f*
windshield ['wɪnd‚ʃild] *s* Windschutzscheibe *f*
wind'shield wash'er *s* Scheibenwäscher *m*
wind'shield wip'er *s* Scheibenwischer *m*
windsock ['wɪnd‚sɑk] *s* Windsack *m*
windstorm ['wɪnd‚stɔrm] *s* Sturm *m*
wind' tun'nel [wɪnd] *s* Windkanal *m*
wind-up ['waɪnd‚ʌp] *s (of affairs)* Abwicklung *f; (of a speech)* Schluß *m*
windward ['wɪndwərd] *adj (side)* Wind– || *adv* windwärts || *s* Windseite *f;* **turn to w.** anluven
windy ['wɪndi] *adj* windig; *(speech)* weitschweifig; *(person)* redselig
wine [waɪn] *s* Wein *m* || *tr* mit Wein bewirten
wine' cel'lar *s* Weinkeller *m*
wine'glass' *s* Weinglas *n*
winegrower ['waɪn‚gro·ər] *s* Weinbauer –in *mf*
wine'grow'ing *s* Weinbau *m*
wine' list' *s* Weinkarte *f*
wine' press' *s* Weinpresse *f*
winery ['waɪnəri] *s* Weinkellerei *f*
wine'skin' *s* Weinschlauch *m*
wing [wɪŋ] *s (of a bird, building, party)* Flügel *m; (unit of three squadrons)* Geschwader *n; (theat)* Kulisse *f* || *tr (shoot)* in den Flügel treffen; **w. one' way** dahinfliegen
wing' chair' *s* Ohrensessel *m*
wing' nut' *s* Flügelmutter *f*
wing'spread' *s* Spannweite *f*
wink [wɪŋk] *s* Augenwink *m; **quick as a w.** im Nu || *intr* blinzeln; **w. at** zublinzeln *(dat); (overlook)* ein Auge zudrücken bei *(dat)*
winner ['wɪnər] *s* Gewinner –in *mf*, Sieger –in *mf; (e.g., winning ticket)* Treffer *m*
win'ning *adj (e.g., smile)* gewinnend; *(sport)* siegreich || **winnings** *spl* Gewinn *m*
winsome ['wɪnsəm] *adj* reizend
winter ['wɪntər] *s* Winter *m* || *intr* überwintern
winterize ['wɪntə‚raɪz] *tr* winterfest machen

wintry ['wɪntri] *adj* winterlich; *(fig)* frostig
wipe [waɪp] *tr* wischen; **w. clean** abwischen; **w. out** auswischen; *(e.g., a debt)* tilgen; *(destroy)* vernichten; *(fin)* ruinieren; **w. up** aufwischen
wire [waɪr] *s* Draht *m; (telg)* Telegramm *n;* **get in under the w.** es gerade noch schaffen || *tr* mit Draht versehen; *(a house)* (elec) elektrische Leitungen legen in *(dat); (a message)* drahten; *(a person)* telegraphieren *(dat)*
wire' cut'ter *s* Drahtschere *f*
wire'draw' *v (pret –drew; pp –drawn) tr* drahtziehen
wire' entan'glement *s* Drahtverhau *m*
wire' gauge' *s* Drahtlehre *f*
wire'-haired' *adj* drahthaarig
wireless ['waɪrlɪs] *adj* drahtlos
wire' nail' *s* Drahtnagel *m*
Wire'pho'to *s* (–tos) (trademark) Bildtelegramm *n*
wire' record'er *s* Drahttonaufnahmegerät *n*
wire'tap' *s* Abhören *n* || *v (pret & pp –tapped; ger –tapping) tr* abhören
wir'ing *s* Leitungen *pl;* **do the w.** die elektrischen Leitungen legen
wiry ['waɪri] *adj* drahtig
wisdom ['wɪzdəm] *s* Weisheit *f*
wis'dom tooth' *s* Weisheitszahn *m*
wise [waɪz] *adj (person, decision)* klug; *(impertinent)* naseweis; **be w. to** sich *[dat]* klar werden über *(acc);* **put s.o. w. to** j–n einweihen in *(acc)* || *s—***in no w.** keineswegs || *intr—* **w. up** endlich mal vernünftig werden
wise'a'cre *s* Neunmalkluge *mf*
wise'crack' *s* schnippische Bemerkung *f*
wise' guy' *s* (sl) Naseweis *m*
wisely ['waɪzli] *adv* wohlweislich
wish [wɪʃ] *s* Wunsch *m* || *tr* wünschen || *intr—***w. for** sich *[dat]* wünschen
wish'bone' *s* Gabelbein *n*
wish'ful think'ing ['wɪʃfəl] *s* ein frommer Wunsch *m*
wishy-washy ['wɪʃi‚wɑʃi] *adj* charakterlos; **be w.** ein Waschlappen sein
wisp [wɪsp] *s (of hair)* Strähne *f*
wistful ['wɪstfəl] *adj* versonnen
wit [wɪt] *s* Geist *m; (person)* geistreicher Mensch *m;* **be at one's wit's end** sich *[dat]* keinen Rat mehr wissen; **keep one's wits about one** e–n klaren Kopf behalten; **live by one's wits** sich durchschlagen
witch [wɪtʃ] *s* Hexe *f*
witch'craft' *s* Hexerei *f*
witch' doc'tor *s* Medizinmann *m*
witch' ha'zel *s* Zaubernuß *f; (ointment)* Präperat *n* aus Zaubernuß
witch' hunt' *s* Hexenjagd *f*
with [wɪð], [wɪθ] *prep* mit *(dat); (at the house of)* bei *(dat); (because of)* vor *(dat),* e.g., **green w. envy** grün vor Neid; *(despite)* trotz *(genit);* **not be w. it** nicht bei der Sache sein
with'draw' *v (pret –drew; pp –drawn) tr* zurückziehen; *(money)* abheben || *intr* sich zurückziehen

withdrawal [wɪð'drɔ·əl] s Zurückziehung f; (retraction) Zurücknahme f; (from a bank) Abhebung f; (mil) Rückzug m
withdraw'al slip' s Abhebungsformular n
wither ['wɪðər] intr verwelken
with·hold' v (pret & pp –held) tr (pay) einbehalten; (information) (from) vorenthalten (dat)
withhold'ing tax' s einbehaltene Steuer f
within' adv drin(nen); from w. von innen || prep (time) binnen (dat), innerhalb von (dat); (place) innerhalb (genit); w. walking distance in Gehweite
without' adv draußen || prep ohne (acc); w. (ger) ohne zu (inf), ohne daß; w. reason ohne allen Anlaß
with·stand' v (pret & pp –stood) tr widerstehen (dat)
witness ['wɪtnɪs] s Zeuge m, Zeugin f; (evidence) Zeugnis n; bear w. to Zeugnis ablegen von; in w. whereof zum Zeugnis dessen; w. for the defense Entlastungszeuge m; w. for the prosecution Belastungszeuge m || tr (an event) anwesend sein bei; (an accident, crime) Augenzeuge sein (genit); (e.g., a contract, will) als Zeuge unterschreiben
wit'ness stand' s Zeugenstand m
witticism ['wɪtɪ‚sɪzəm] s Witzelei f
wittingly ['wɪtɪŋli] adv wissentlich
witty ['wɪti] adj geistreich, witzig
wizard ['wɪzərd] s Hexenmeister m
wizardry ['wɪzərdri] s (& fig) Hexerei f
wizend ['wɪzənd] adj runzelig
wobble ['wɑbəl] intr wackeln
wobbly ['wɑbli] adj wackelig
woe [wo] s Weh n || interj—woe is me! weh mir!
woebegone ['wobɪ‚gɔn] adj jammervoll
woeful ['wofəl] adj jammervoll
wolf [wʊlf] s (wolves [wʊlvz]) Wolf m; (coll) Schürzenjäger m; cry w. blinden Alarm schlagen; keep the w. from the door sich über Wasser halten || tr—w. down verschlingen
wolf'pack' s Wolfsrudel n; (nav) U-bootrudel n
wolfram ['wʊlfrəm] s (chem) Wolfram n; (mineral) Wolframit n
woman ['wʊmən] s (women ['wɪmən]) Frau f
wom'an doc'tor s Ärztin f
wom'anhood' s Frauen pl; reach w. e–e Frau werden
womanish ['wʊmənɪʃ] adj weibisch
wom'ankind' s Frauen pl
womanly ['wʊmənli] adj fraulich
womb [wʊm] s Mutterleib m
wom'enfolk' spl Weibsvolk n
wom'en's dou'bles spl (tennis) Damendoppelspiel n
wom'en's sin'gles spl (tennis) Dameneinzelspiel n
wonder ['wʌndər] s Wunder n || intr (be surprised) sich wundern; (ask

oneself) sich fragen; (reflect) überlegen; wonder at sich verwundern über (acc)
wonderful ['wʌndərfəl] adj wunderbar
won'derland' s Wunderland n
won'der work'er s Wundertäter –in mf
wont [wʌnt], [wɔnt] adj—be w. to (inf) pflegen zu (inf) || s Gepflogenheit f
wont'ed adj gewöhnlich, üblich
woo [wu] tr den Hof machen (dat)
wood [wʊd] s Holz n; out of the woods (fig) über den Berg; woods Wald m
wood' al'cohol s Methylalkohol m
woodbine ['wʊd‚baɪn] s Geißblatt n; (Virginia creeper) wilder Wein m
wood' carv'ing s Holzschnitzerei f
wood'chuck' s Murmeltier n
wood'cock' s Holzschnepfe f
wood'cut' s (block) Holzplatte f; (print) Holzschnitt m
wood'cut'ter s Holzfäller m
wood'ed adj bewaldet
wooden ['wʊdən] adj (& fig) hölzern
wood' engrav'ing s Holzschnitt m
wood'en leg' s Stelzbein n
wood'en shoe' s Holzschuh m
woodland ['wʊdlənd] adj Wald– || s Waldland n
wood'man s (–men) Holzhauer m
woodpecker ['wʊd‚pɛkər] s Specht m
wood' pi'geon s Ringeltaube f
wood'pile' s Holzhaufen m
wood'pulp' s Holzfaserstoff m
wood' screw' s Holzschraube f
wood'shed' s Holzschuppen m
woods'man s (–men) Förster m; (lumberman) Holzhauer m
wood'winds' spl Holzblasinstrumente pl
wood'work' s Holzarbeit f; (structure in wood) Gebälk n
wood'work'er s Holzarbeiter –in mf
wood'worm' s (ent) Holzwurm m
woody ['wʊdi] adj waldig; (woodlike) holzig
wooer ['wu·ər] s Verehrer m
woof [wuf] s (of a dog) unterdrücktes Bellen n; (tex) Gewebe n
woofer ['wufər] s (rad) Tieftöner m
wool [wʊl] adj wollen || s Wolle f
woolen ['wʊlən] adj wollen, Woll– || woolens spl Wollwaren pl
woolly ['wʊli] adj wollig; (e.g., thinking) verschwommen
woozy ['wuzi] adj benebelt
word [wʌrd] s Wort n; be as good as one's w. zu seinem Wort stehen; by w. of mouth mündlich; get w. from Nachricht haben von; give one's w. sein Wort geben; have a w. with ein ernstes Wort sprechen mit; have words e–n Wortwechsel haben; in a w. mit e–m Wort; in other words mit anderen Worten; in so many words ausdrücklich; leave w. Bescheid hinterlassen; not another w.! kein Wort mehr!; not a w. of truth in it kein wahres Wort daran; put in a good w. for s.o. ein gutes Wort für j–n einlegen; put into words in

Worte kleiden; **put words in s.o.'s mouth** j-m Worte in den Mund legen; **send w. to s.o.** j-n benachrichtigen; **take s.o.'s w. for it** j-n beim Wort nehmen; **w. for w.** Wort für Wort || *tr* formulieren
word'-for-word' *adj* wörtlich
word'ing *s* Formulierung *f*
word' of hon'or *s* Ehrenwort *n;* **w.!** auf mein Wort!
word' or'der *s* Wortfolge *f*
wordy ['wʌrdi] *adj* wortreich
work [wʌrk] *s* Arbeit *f; (production, book)* Werk *n;* **be in the works** (coll) im Gang sein; **get to w.** sich an die Arbeit machen; *(travel to work)* zum Arbeitsplatz kommen; **give s.o. the works** (coll) j-n fertigmachen; **have one's w. cut out** zu tun haben; **it took a lot of w. to** *(inf)* es hat viel Arbeit gekostet zu *(inf);* **make short w. of** kurzen Prozeß machen mit; **out of w.** arbeitslos; **works** (horol) Uhrwerk *n* || *tr (a machine)* bedienen; *(a pedal)* treten; *(a mine)* abbauen; *(the soil)* bearbeiten; *(metal)* treiben; *(dough)* kneten; *(wonders)* wirken; **w. in** einarbeiten; **w. off** *(a debt)* abarbeiten; **w. oneself to death** sich totarbeiten; **w. one's way up** sich hocharbeiten; **w. out** *(a solution)* ausarbeiten; *(a problem)* lösen; **w. to death** abhetzen; **w. up an appetite** sich *[dat]* Appetit machen || *intr* arbeiten; *(function)* funktionieren; *(succeed)* klappen; **w. against** wirken gegen; **w. away** at losarbeiten auf *(acc);* **w. at** *(a trade)* ausüben; **w. both ways** für beide Fälle gelten; **w. loose** sich lockern; **w. on** *(a person)* bearbeiten; *(a patient, car)* arbeiten an *(dat);* **w. out** (sport) trainieren; **w. out well** gut ausgehen
workable ['wʌrkəbəl] *adj* brauchbar; *(plan)* durchführbar
work'bench' *s* Werkbank *f*
work'book' *s* Übungsheft *n*
work' camp' *s* Arbeitslager *n*
work'day' *s* Arbeitstag *m*
work' detail' *s* (mil) Arbeitskommando *n*
worked'-up' *adj* erregt; **get s.o. w.** j-n erregen; **get w.** sich erregen
worker ['wʌrkər] *s* Arbeiter –in *mf*
work' force' *s* Belegschaft *f*
work'horse' *s* Arbeitspferd *n*
work'ing day' *s* Arbeitstag *m*
work'ing girl' *s* Arbeiterin *f*
work'ing hours' *spl* Arbeitsstunden *pl*
work'ingman' *s* (-men') Arbeiter *m*
work'ing or'der *s*—**in w.** betriebsfähig
work'ingwom'an *s* (-wom'en) Arbeiterin *f; (professionally)* berufstätige Frau *f*
work'man *s* (-men) Arbeiter *m*
work'manship' *s* Ausführung *f*
work'men's compensa'tion insur'ance *s* Arbeiterunfallversicherung *f*
work' of art' *s* Kunstwerk *n*
work'out' *s* Training *n*
work' per'mit *s* Arbeitsgenehmigung *f*
work'room' *s* Arbeitszimmer *n*

work' sche'dule *s* Dienstplan *m*
work'shop' *s* Werkstatt *f*
work' stop'page *s* Arbeitseinstellung *f*
world [wʌrld] *adj* Welt– || *s* Welt *f;* **a w. of** groß; **from all over the w.** aus aller Herren Ländern; **not for all the w.** nicht um die Welt; **see the w.** in der Welt herumkommen; **they are worlds apart** es liegen Welten zwischen den beiden; **think the w. of** große Stücke halten auf *(acc);* **who (where) in the w.** wer (wo) in aller Welt
world' affairs' *spl* internationale Angelegenheiten *pl*
world'-fa'mous *adj* weltberühmt
worldly ['wʌrldli] *adj (goods, pleasures)* irdisch; *(person)* weltlich; *(wisdom)* Welt–
world'ly-wise' *adj* weltklug
world's' fair' *s* Weltausstellung *f*
world'-shak'ing *adj* weltbewegend
world'-wide' *adj* weltweit
worm [wʌrm] *s* Wurm *m* || *tr*—**w. one's way** sich schlängeln; **w. secrets out of s.o.** j-m die Würmer aus der Nase ziehen
worm-eaten ['wʌrm‚itən] *adj (& fig)* wurmstichig
wormy ['wʌrmi] *adj* wurmig
worn [wɔrn] *adj (clothes)* getragen; *(tires)* abgenutzt; *(wearied)* müde
worn'-out' *adj (clothes)* abgetragen; *(tires)* abgenutzt; *(exhausted)* erschöpft
worrisome ['wʌrɪsəm] *adj (causing worry)* beunruhigend; *(inclined to worry)* sorgenvoll
wor·ry ['wʌri] *s* Sorge *f; (source of worry)* Ärger *m* || *v (pret & pp* –**ried)** *tr* beunruhigen; **be worried** besorgt sein || *intr (about)* sich *[dat]* Sorgen machen (um); **don't w.!** keine Sorge!
worse [wʌrs] *comp adj* schlechter, schlimmer; **be w. off** schlimmer daran sein; **he's none the w. for it** es hat ihm nichts geschadet; **what's w.** was noch schlimmer ist
worsen ['wʌrsən] *tr* verschlimmern || *intr* sich verschlimmern
wor·ship ['wʌrʃɪp] *s* Anbetung *f; (services)* Gottesdienst *m* || *v (pret & pp* –**ship[p]ed)** *ger* –**ship[p]ing)** *tr (& fig)* anbeten || *intr* seine Andacht verrichten
worship(p)er ['wʌrʃɪpər] *s* Anbeter –in *mf; (in church)* Andächtige *mf*
worst [wʌrst] *super adj* schlimmste || *super adv* am schlimmsten || *s* Schlimmste *n;* **at the w.** schlimmstenfalls; **get the w. of** den kürzeren ziehen bei; **if w. comes to w.** wenn alle Stricke reißen; **the w. is yet to come** das dicke Ende kommt noch || *tr* schlagen
worsted ['wʊstɪd] *adj* Kammgarn–
worth [wʌrθ] *adj* wert; **it is w.** (ger) es lohnt sich zu *(inf);* **it is w. the trouble** es ist der Mühe wert; **ten dollars' w. of meat** für zehn Dollar Fleisch; **w. seeing** sehenswert || *s* Wert *m*

worthless ['wʌrθlɪs] *adj* wertlos; (*person*) nichtsnutzig
worth'while' *adj* lohnend
worthy ['wʌrði] *adj* (of) würdig (*genit*)
would [wʊd] *aux* used to express 1) indirect statements, e.g., **he said he w.** come er sagte, er würde kommen; 2) the present conditional, e.g., **he w. do it if he could** er würde es tun, wenn er könnte; 3) past conditional, e.g., **he w. have paid, if he had had the money** er würde gezahlt haben, wenn er das Geld gehabt hätte; 4) habitual action in the past, e.g., **he w. always buy the morning paper** er kaufte immer das Morgenblatt; 5) polite requests, e.g., **w. you please pass me the butter?** würden Sie mir bitte die Butter reichen; 6) a wish, e.g., **w. that I had never seen it** wenn ich es nur nie gesehen hätte!; **w. rather** möchte lieber, e.g., **I w. rather go on foot** ich möchte lieber zu Fuß gehen
would'-be' *adj* angeblich, Möchtegern—
wound [wund] *s* Wunde *f* ‖ *tr* verwunden
wound'ed *adj* verwundet ‖ **the w.** *spl* die Verwundeten *pl*
wow [waʊ] *s* (coll) Bombenerfolg *m* ‖ *tr* (coll) erstaunen ‖ *interj* nanu!
wrack [ræk] *s*—**go to w. and ruin** untergehen, in Brüche gehen
wraith [reθ] *s* (*apparition*) Erscheinung *f*; (*spirit*) Geist *m*
wrangle ['ræŋgəl] *s* Streit *m* ‖ *intr* streiten
wrap [ræp] *s* Überwurf *m* ‖ *v* (*pret & pp* **wrapped;** *ger* **wrapping**) *tr* wikkeln; (*a package*) einpacken; **be wrapped up in** (*e.g., thoughts*) versunken sein in (*dat*); **wrapped in darkness** in Dunkelheit gehüllt; **w. up** (*a deal*) abwickeln
wrapper ['ræpər] *s* Verpackung *f*; (*for mailing newspapers*) Streifband *n*
wrap'ping *s* Verpackung *f*
wrap'ping pa'per *s* Packpapier *n*
wrath [ræθ] *s* Zorn *m*, Wut *f*
wrathful ['ræθfəl] *adj* zornig, wütend
wreak [rik] *tr* (*vengeance*) üben; **w. havoc** schlimm hausen
wreath [riθ] *s* (**wreaths** [riðz]) Kranz *m*; **w. of smoke** Rauchfahne *f*
wreathe [rið] *tr* bekränzen, umwinden
wreck [rɛk] *s* (*of a car or train*) Unglück *n*; (*wrecked ship, car, person*) Wrack *n* ‖ *tr* (*e.g., a car*) zertrümmern; (*a building*) in Trümmer legen; (*a marriage*) zerrütten; (fig) zum Scheitern bringen; **be wrecked** (fig & naut) scheitern
wreckage ['rɛkɪdʒ] *s* Wrackgut *n*; (*of an accident*) Trümmer *pl*
wrecker ['rɛkər] *s* Abschleppwagen *m*
wren [rɛn] *s* (orn) Zaunkönig *m*
wrench [rɛntʃ] *s* (*tool*) Schraubenschlüssel *m*; (*of a muscle*) Verrenkung *f* ‖ *tr* verrenken
wrest [rɛst] *tr* (*from*) entreißen (*dat*)
wrestle ['rɛsəl] *tr* ringen mit ‖ *intr* ringen

wrestler ['rɛslər] *s* Ringer *m*; (*professional wrestler*) Catcher *m*
wrestling ['rɛslɪŋ] *s* Ringen *n*; (*professional wrestling*) Catchen *n*
wres'tling match' *s* Ringkampf *m*
wretch [rɛtʃ] *s* armer Kerl *m*; (*vile person*) Schuft *m*
wretched ['rɛtʃɪd] *adj* elend; (*terrible*) scheußlich
wriggle ['rɪgəl] *s* Krümmung *f*; (*of a worm*) schlängelnde Bewegung *f* ‖ *tr* hin- und herbewegen; **w. one's way** sich dahinschlängeln ‖ *intr* sich winden
wring [rɪŋ] *v* (*pret & pp* **wrung** [rʌŋ]) *tr* (*the hands*) ringen; **w. out** (*the wash*) auswinden; **w. s.o.'s neck** j–m den Hals umdrehen
wringer ['rɪŋər] *s* Wringmaschine *f*
wrinkle ['rɪŋkəl] *s* Falte *f*; **new w.** (fig) neuer Kniff *m*; **take out the wrinkles** (fig) den letzten Schliff geben ‖ *tr* falten, runzeln; (*paper, clothes*) zerknittern ‖ *intr* Falten werfen
wrin'kle-proof' *adj* knitterfrei
wrinkly ['rɪŋkli] *adj* faltig, runzelig
wrist [rɪst] *s* Handgelenk *n*
wrist'band' *s* Armband *n*
wrist' watch' *s* Armbanduhr *f*
writ [rɪt] *s* gerichtlicher schriftlicher Befehl *m*
write [raɪt] *v* (*pret* **wrote** [rot]; *pp* **written** ['rɪtən]) *tr* schreiben; (*compose*) verfassen; **it is written** (*in the Bible*) es steht geschrieben; **it is written all over his face** es steht ihm im Gesicht geschrieben; **w. down** aufschreiben; **w. off** abschreiben; **w. out** ausschreiben; (*a check*) ausstellen ‖ *intr* schreiben; **w. for information** Informationen anfordern
write'-off' *s* Abschreibung *f*
writer ['raɪtər] *s* Schreiber –in *mf*; (*author*) Schriftsteller –in *mf*
writ'er's cramp' *s* Schreibkrampf *m*
write'-up' *s* Pressebericht *m*
writhe [raɪð] *intr* (**in**) sich krümmen (*vor dat*)
writ'ing *s* Schreiben *n*; (*handwriting*) Schrift *f*; **in w.** schriftlich; **put in w.** niederschreiben
writ'ing desk' *s* Schreibtisch *m*
writ'ing pad' *s* Schreibblock *m*
writ'ing pa'per *s* Schreibpapier *n*; (*stationery*) Briefpapier *n*
written ['rɪtən] *adj* schriftlich; (*law*) geschrieben; (*language*) Schrift-
wrong [rɔŋ] *adj* (*incorrect*) falsch; (*unjust*) unrecht; **be w.** (*be incorrect*) nicht stimmen; (*be in error*) Unrecht haben; (*said of a situation*) nicht in Ordnung sein; **be. w. with** fehlen (*dat*); **sorry, w. number!** (telp) falsch verbunden! ‖ *s* Unrecht *n*; **be in the w.** im Unrecht sein; **do w.** ein Unrecht begehen; **do w. to s.o.** j–m ein Unrecht zufügen; **get in w. with s.o.** es sich (*dat*) mit j–m verderben ‖ *adv* falsch, unrecht; **go w.** (*morally*) auf Abwege geraten; (*in walking*) sich verirren; (*in reckoning*)

irregehen; (in driving) sich verfahren; (said of plans) schief gehen
wrongdoer ['rɔŋ͵du·ər] s Missetäter –in mf

wrong'do'ing s Missetat f
wrought' i'ron [rɔt] s Schmiedeeisen n
wrought'-up' adj aufgebracht
wry [raɪ] adj schief

X

X, x [ɛks] s vierundzwanzigster Buchstabe des englischen Alphabets
xenophobia [͵zɛnə'fobɪ·ə] s Fremdenhaß m
Xerox ['zɪrɑks] s (trademark) Xerographie f || **xerox** tr ablichten
Xer'ox-cop'y s Ablichtung f

Xmas ['krɪsməs] adj Weihnachts– || s Weihnachten pl
x'-ray' adj Röntgen– || s (picture) Röntgenbild n; **x-rays** Röntgenstrahlen pl || tr röntgen
x'-ray ther'apy s Röntgentherapie f
xylophone ['zaɪlə͵fon] s Xylophon n

Y

Y, y [waɪ] s fünfundzwanzigster Buchstabe des englischen Alphabets
yacht [jɑt] s Jacht f
yacht' club' s Jachtklub m
yam [jæm] s Yamwurzel f
yank [jæŋk] s Ruck m; **Yank** Ami m || tr—y. s.th. out of reißen aus || intr —y. on heftig ziehen an (dat)
Yankee ['jæŋki] s Yankee m
yap [jæp] s (talk) (sl) Geschwätz n; (mouth) (sl) Maul n; (bark) Gekläff n || v (pret & pp **yapped; ger yapping**) intr (bark) kläffen; (talk) (sl) schwätzen
yard [jɑrd] s (measure) Yard n; (ground adjoining a building) Hof m; (naut) Rahe f; (rr) Rangierbahnhof m
yard'arm' s (naut) Nock f & n
yard' mas'ter s (rr) Rangiermeister m
yard'stick' s Yardmaß n; (fig) Maßstab m
yarn [jɑrn] s (thread; story) Garn n; **spin yarns** (fig) Garne spinnen
yaw [jɔ] s (aer, rok) Schwanken n; (naut) Gieren n || intr (aer, rok) schwanken; (naut) gieren
yawl [jɔl] s (naut) Jolle f
yawn [jɔn] s Gähnen n || intr gähnen; (said, e.g., of a gorge) klaffen
ye [ji] pers pron ihr
yea [je] s Jastimme f || adv ja
yeah [jɛ] adv ja
year [jɪr] s Jahr n; **all y. round** das ganze Jahr hindurch; **a y. from to-day** heute übers Jahr; **for years** seit Jahren; jahrelang; **in years** seit Jahren; **y. in y. out** jahraus jahrein
year'book' s Jahrbuch n
yearling ['jɪrlɪŋ] s Jährling m
yearly ['jɪrli] adj & adv jährlich
yearn [jʌrn] intr—y. **for** sich sehnen nach; **y. to** (inf) sich danach sehnen zu (inf)
yearn'ing s Sehnsucht f

yeast [jist] s Hefe f
yell [jɛl] s Ruf m, Aufschrei m; (sport) Kampfruf m || tr (gellend) schreien; **y. one's lungs out** sich tot schreien || intr schreien; **y. at** anschreien
yellow ['jɛlo] adj gelb; (sl) feige || s Gelb n || tr gelb machen || intr vergilben
yellowish ['jɛlo·ɪʃ] adj gelblich
yel'lowjack'et s Wespe f
yel'low jour'nalism s Sensationspresse f
yel'low streak' s Zug m von Feigheit
yelp [jɛlp] s Gekläff n || intr kläffen
yen [jɛn] s (Japanese money) Yen m; (for) brennendes Verlangen n (nach)
yeo·man ['jomən] s (–men) (nav) Verwaltungsunteroffizier m
yeo'man's serv'ice s großer Dienst m
yes [jɛs] adv ja; **yes, Sir** jawohl || s Ja n; **say yes to** bejahen
yes' man' s Jasager m
yesterday ['jɛstər͵de] adv gestern; **y. morning** gestern früh || s Gestern n; **yesterday's** gestrig
yet [jɛt] adv (still) noch; (however) doch; (already) schon; **and yet** trotzdem, dennoch; **as yet** schon; **not yet** noch nicht || conj aber
yew [ju] s Eibe f
Yiddish ['jɪdɪʃ] adj jiddisch || s Jiddisch n
yield [jild] s Ertrag m || tr (profit) einbringen; (interest) tragen; (crops) hervorbringen; (give up) überlassen || intr (to) nachgeben (dat)
yo·del ['jodəl] s Jodler m || v (pret & pp **–del[l]ed; ger –del[l]ing**) intr jodeln
yodeler ['jodələr] s Jodler –in mf
yogurt ['jogurt] s Yoghurt m & n
yoke [jok] s (part of harness; burden) Joch n; **pass under the y.** sich in ein Joch fügen; **y. of oxen** Ochsengespann n || tr ins Joch spannen

yokel ['jokəl] s Bauerntölpel m
yolk [jok] s Dotter m & n
yonder ['jɑndər] adv dort drüben
yore [jor] s—**of y.** vormals
you [ju] pers pron du; (plural form) ihr; (polite form) Sie; **to you** dir; (plural form) euch; (polite form) Ihnen; **you of all people!** ausgerechnet Sie! || indef pron man
young [jʌŋ] adj (younger ['jʌŋgər]; youngest ['jʌŋgɪst]) jung; **y. for one's age** jugendlich für sein Alter || spl (of animals) Jungen pl; **the y.** die Jungen, die Jugend; **with y.** (pregnant) trächtig
young′ la′dy s Fräulein n
young′ man′ s junger Mann m; (boyfriend) Freund m
youngster ['jʌŋstər] s Jugendliche mf
your [jʊr] poss adj dein; (plural form) euer; (polite form) Ihr
yours [jʊrz] poss pron deiner; (plural form) euerer; (polite form) Ihrer; **y. truly** hochachtungsvoll
your·self [jʊr'sɛlf] intens pron (–selves ['sɛlvz]) selbst, selber || reflex pron dich; (plural form) euch; (polite form) Sich; **to y.** dir; (polite form) Sich; **to yourselves** euch; (polite form) Sich
youth [juθ] s (youths [juθs], [juðz]) (age) Jugend f; (person) Jugendliche mf
youthful ['juθfəl] adj jugendlich
youth′ hos′tel s Jugendherberge f
yowl [jaʊl] s Gejaule n || tr & intr jaulen
Yugoslav ['jugo'slɑv] adj jugoslawisch || s Jugoslawe m, Jugoslawin f
Yugoslavia ['jugo'slɑvɪ·ə] s Jugoslavien n
yule′ log′ [jul] s Weihnachtsscheit n
yule′tide′ s Weihnachtszeit f

Z

Z, z [zi] s sechsundzwanzigster Buchstabe des englischen Alphabets
zany ['zeni] adj närrisch || s Hanswurst m
zeal [zil] s Eifer m
zealot ['zɛlət] s Zelot –in mf
zealous ['zɛləs] adj eifrig
zebra ['zibrə] s Zebra n
zenith ['zinɪθ] s Scheitelpunkt m, Zenit m
zephyr ['zɛfər] s Zephir m
zeppelin ['zɛpəlɪn] s Zeppelin m
ze·ro ['ziro] s (–ros & –roes) Null f || tr—**z. in a rifle** Visier e–s Gewehrs justieren || intr—**z. in on** zielen auf (acc)
ze′ro hour′ s Stunde f Null
zest [zɛst] s Würze f
Zeus [zus] s Zeus m
zig·zag ['zɪg‚zæg] adj Zickzack– || adv im Zickzack || s Zickzack m || (pret & pp –zagged; ger –zagging) intr im Zickzack fahren
zinc [zɪŋk] s Zink n
Zionism ['zaɪ·ə‚nɪzəm] s Zionismus m
zip [zɪp] s (coll) Schmiß m || v (pret & pp zipped; ger zipping) tr (convey with speed) mit Schwung befördern; (fasten with a zipper) mit e–m Reißverschluß schließen || intr sausen; **zip by** vorbeisausen || interj wuppdich!
zip′ code′ s Postleitzahl f
zipper ['zɪpər] s Reißverschluß m
zircon ['zʌrkɑn] s Zirkon m
zither ['zɪθər] s Zither f
zodiac ['zodɪ‚æk] s Tierkreis m
zombie ['zɔmbi] s (sl) Depp m
zone [zon] s (& geol) Zone f; (postal zone) Postbezirk m; (mil) Bereich m
zoo [zu] s Zoo m, Tiergarten m
zoologic(al) [‚zo·ə'lɑdʒɪk(əl)] adj zoologisch
zoologist [zo'ɑlədʒɪst] s Zoologe m, Zoologin f
zoology [zo'ɑlədʒi] s Zoologie f
zoom [zum] s lautes Summen n; (aer) Hochreißen n || intr laut summen; **z. up** (aer) hochreißen
zoom′ lens′ s Gummilinse f

METRIC CONVERSIONS

Multiply:	By:	To Obtain:
acres	43,560	sq. ft.
	0.4047	hectares
	0.0015625	sq. mi.
ampere-hours	3600	coulombs
atmospheres	76.0	cm. of mercury
	33.90	ft. of water
	14.70	lbs./sq. in.
British thermal units	1054	joules
	777.5	ft.-lbs.
	252.0	gram calories
	0.0003927	horsepower-hrs.
	0.0002928	kilowatt-hrs.
B.T.U./hr.	0.2928	watts
B.T.U./min.	12.96	ft.-lbs./sec.
	0.02356	horsepower
bushels	3523.8	hectoliters
	2150.42	cu. ins.
	35.238	liters
°C + 17.78	1.8	°F
centimeters	0.3937	inches
cm-grams	980.1	cm.-dynes
chains	66	ft.
circumference	6.2832	radians
cubic centimeters	0.0610	cu. ins.
cu. feet	1728	cu. ins.
	62.43	lbs. of water
	7.481	gals. (liq.)
	0.0283	cu. m.
cu. ft./min.	62.43	lbs. water/min.
cu. ft./sec.	448.831	gals./min.
cu. inches	16.387	cu. cm.
	0.0005787	cu. ft.
cu. meters	264.2	gals. (liq.)
	35.3147	cu. ft.
	1.3079	cu. yds.
cu. yards	27	cu. ft.
	0.765	cu. m.
days	86,400	seconds
degrees/sec.	0.1667	revolutions/min.
°F − 32	0.5556	°C
faradays/sec.	96,500	amperes
feet	30.48	cm.
	0.3048	meters
	0.0001894	mi. (stat.)
	0.0001645	mi. (Brit. naut.)
ft. of water	62.43	lbs./sq. ft.
	0.4335	lbs./sq. in.
ft./min.	0.5080	cm./sec.
ft./sec.	0.6818	mi./hr.
	0.5921	knots

Multiply:	By:	To Obtain:
fluid ounces	29.573	milliliters
furlongs	660	feet
	0.125	mi.
gallons	231	cu. ins.
	8.345	lbs. of water
	8	pts.
	4	qts.
	3.785	liters
	0.003785	cu. m.
gals./min.	8.0208	cu. ft./hr.
grains	0.0648	grams
grams	980.1	dynes
	15.43	grains
	0.0353	oz. (avdp.)
	0.0022	lbs. (avdp.)
hectares	107,600	sq. ft.
	2.47	acres
hectoliters	2.838	bushels
horsepower	33,000	ft.-lbs./min.
	2545	B.T.U./hr.
	745.7	watts
	42.44	B.T.U./min.
	0.7457	kilowatts
inches	25.40	mm.
	2.540	cm.
	0.00001578	mi.
ins. of water	0.03613	lbs./sq. in.
kilograms	980,100	dynes
	2.2046	lbs. (avdp.)
kg. calories	3086	ft.-lbs.
	3.968	B.T.U.
kg. cal./min.	51.43	ft.-lbs./sec.
	0.06972	kilowatts
kilometers	3280.8	ft.
	0.621	mi.
km./hr.	0.621	mi./hr.
	0.5396	knots
kilowatts	737.6	ft.-lbs./sec.
	56.92	B.T.U./min.
	1.341	horsepower
kilowatt-hrs.	2,655,000	ft.-lbs.
	3415	B.T.U.
	1.341	horsepower-hrs.
knots	6080	ft./hr.
	1.151	stat. mi./hr.
	1	(Brit.) naut. mi./hr.
liters	61.02	cu. ins.
	2.113	pts. (liq.)
	1.057	qts. (liq.)
	0.264	gals. (liq.)
	1.816	pts. (dry)
	0.908	qts. (dry)
	0.1135	pecks
	0.0284	bushels
meters	39.37	inches
	3.2808	ft.
	1.0936	yds.
	0.0006215	mi. (stat.)
	0.0005396	mi. (Brit. naut.)
miles		
statute	5280	ft.
	1.609	km.
	0.8624	mi. (Brit. naut.)
nautical (Brit.)	6080	ft.
	1.151	mi. (stat.)
mi./hr.	1.467	ft./sec.
milligrams/liter	1	parts/million
milliliters	0.0338	fluid oz.
millimeters	0.03937	inches

Multiply:	By:	To Obtain:
ounces		
avoirdupois	28.349	grams
	0.9115	oz. (troy)
	0.0625	lbs. (avdp.)
troy	31.103	grams
	1.0971	oz. (avdp.)
pecks	8.8096	liters
pints		
liquid	473.2	cu. cm.
	28.875	cu. ins.
	0.473	liters
dry	0.550	liters
pounds		
avoirdupois	444,600	dynes
	453.6	grams
	32.17	poundals
	14.58	oz. (troy)
	1.21	lbs. (troy)
	0.4536	kg.
troy	0.373	kg.
lbs. (avdp.)/sq. in.	70.22	g./sq. cm.
	2.307	ft. of water
quarts		
liquid	57.75	cu. ins.
	32	fluid oz.
	2	pts.
	0.946	liters
dry	67.20	cu. ins.
	1.101	liters
quires	25	sheets
radians	3437.7	minutes
	57.296	degrees
reams	500	sheets
revolutions/min.	6	degrees/sec.
rods	16.5	ft.
	5.5	yds.
	5.029	meters
slugs	32.17	lbs. (mass)
square centimeters	0.155	sq. ins.
sq. feet	0.093	sq. m.
sq. inches	6.451	sq. cm.
sq. kilometers	247.1	acres
	0.3861	sq. mi.
sq. meters	10.76	sq. ft.
	1.1960	sq. yds.
sq. miles	27,878,400	sq. ft.
	640	acres
	2.5889	sq. km.
sq. yards	0.8361	sq. m.
tons		
long	2240	lbs. (avdp.)
	1.12	short tons
	1.0160	metric tons
metric	2204.6	lbs. (avdp.)
	1000	kg.
	1.1023	short tons
	0.9842	long tons
short	2000	lbs. (avdp.)
	0.9072	metric tons
	0.8929	long tons
watts	3.415	B.T.U./hr.
	0.001341	horsepower
yards	36	inches
	3	ft.
	0.9144	meters
	0.0005682	mi. (stat.)
	0.0004934	mi. (Brit. naut.)

LABELS AND ABBREVIATIONS

BEZEICHNUNGEN DER SACHGEBIETE UND ABKÜRZUNGEN

abbr abbreviation—Abkürzung
acc accusative—Akkusativ
(acct) accounting—Rechnungswesen
adj adjective—Adjektiv
(adm) administration—Verwaltung
adv adverb—Adverb
(aer) aeronautics—Luftfahrt
(agr) agriculture—Landwirtschaft
(alg) algebra—Algebra
(Am) American—amerikanisch
(anat) anatomy—Anatomie
(angl) angling—Angeln
(archeol) archeology—Archäologie
(archit) architecture—Architektur
(arith) arithmetic—Rechnen
art article—Artikel
(arti) artillery—Artillerie
(astr) astronomy—Astronomie
(atom. phys.) Atomic physics—
  Atomphysik
(Aust) Austrian—österreichisch
(aut) automobile—Automobile
aux auxiliary verb—Hilfsverb
(bact) bacteriology—Bakteriologie
(baseball) Baseball
(basketball) Korbball
(bb) bookbinding—Buchbinderei
(Bib) Biblical—biblisch
(billiards) Billard
(biochem) biochemistry—Biochemie
(biol) biology—Biologie
(bot) botany—Botanik
(bowling) Kegeln
(box) boxing—Boxen
(Brit) British—britisch
(cards) Kartenspiel
(carp) carpentry—Zimmerhandwerk
(checkers) Damespiel
(chem) chemistry—Chemie
(chess) Schachspiel
(cin) cinematography—
  Kinematographie
(coll) colloquial—
  umgangssprachlich
(com) commercial—Handels-
comb.fm. combining form—
  Wortbildungselement
comp comparative—Komparativ
conj conjunction—Konjunktion
(crew) Rudersport
(culin) culinary—kulinarisch

(data proc.) data processing—
  Datenverarbeitung
dem demonstrative—hinweisend
(dent) dentistry—Zahnheilkunde
(dial) dialectical—dialektisch
(dipl) diplomacy—Diplomatie
(eccl) ecclesiastical—kirchlich
(econ) economics—Wirtschaft
(educ) education—Schulwesen
e–e a(n)—eine
e.g. for example—zum Beispiel
(elec) electricity—Elektrizität
(electron) electronics—Elektronik
e–m to a(n)—einem
e–n a(n)—einen
(eng) engineering—Technik
(ent) entomology—Entomologie
e–r of a(n), to a(n)—einer
e–s of a(n)—eines
etw something—etwas
f feminine noun—Femininum
(fa) fine arts—schöne Künste
fem feminine—weiblich
(fencing) Fechtkunst
(fig) figurative—bildlich
(& fig) literal and figurative—
  buchstäblich und bildlich
(fin) finance—Finanzwesen
(fb) football, soccer—Fußball
fut future—Zukunft
genit genitive—Genitiv
(geog) geography, Geographie
(geol) geology—Geologie
(geom) geometry—Geometrie
ger gerund—Gerundium
(golf) Golf
(gram) grammar—Grammatik
(gym) gymnastics—Gymnastik
(heral) heraldry—Wappenkunde
(hist) history—Geschichte
(horol) horology—Zeitmessung
(hort) horticulture—Gartenbau
(hum) humorous—scherzhaft
(hunt) hunting—Jagdwesen
(ichth) ichthyology—Ichthyologie
imperf imperfect—Imperfekt
impers impersonal—unpersönlich
ind indicative—Indikativ
indecl indeclinable—undeklinierbar
indef indefinite—unbestimmt
(indust) industry—Industrie

373

inf infinitive—Infinitiv
(ins) insurance—
   Versicherungswesen
insep inseparable—untrennbar
intens intensive—verstärkend
interj interjection—Interjektion
interr interrogative—Frage-
intr intransitive—intransitiv
invar invariable—unveränderlich
(iron) ironical—ironisch
j-m to someone—jemandem
j-n someone—jemanden
(journ) journalism—Zeitungswesen
j-s someone's—jemand(e)s
(jur) jurisprudence—
   Rechtswissenschaft
(libr) library science—
   Bibliothekswissenschaft
(ling) linguistics—Linguistik
(lit) literary—literarisch
(log) logic—Logik
m masculine noun—Maskulinum
(mach) machinery—Maschinen
(mech) mechanics—Mechanik
(med) medicine—Medizin
(metal) metallurgy—Metallurgie
(meteor) meteorology—
   Meteorologie
mf masculine or feminine noun
   according to sex—Maskulinum
   oder Femininum je nach
   Geschlecht
(mil) military—Militär-
(min) mining—Bergwerkswesen
(mineral) mineralogy—Mineralogie
mod aux modal auxiliary—
   Modalverb
(mount) mountain climbing—
   Bergsteigerei
(mus) music—Musik
(myth) mythology—Mythologie
m & f masculine and feminine noun
   without regard to sex—
   Maskulinum oder Femininum
   ohne Rücksicht auf Geschlecht
(naut) nautical—nautisch
(nav) navy—Kriegsmarine
neut neuter—sächlich
(obs) obsolete—veraltet
(obstet) obstetrics—Geburtshilfe
(opt) optics—Optik
(orn) ornithology—Ornithologie
(paint) painting—Malerei
(parl) parliamentary—
   parlamentarisch
(pathol) pathology—Pathologie
(pej) pejorative—pejorativ
pers personal—Personal-
(pharm) pharmacy—Pharmazie
(philos) philosophy—Philosophie
(phonet) phonetics—Phonetik

(phot) photography—Photographie
(phys) physics—Physik
(physiol) physiology—Physiologie
pl plural—Plural
(poet) poetical—dichterisch
(pol) politics—Politik
poss possessive—besitzanzeigend
pp past participal—Partizip Perfekt
pref prefix—Präfix
prep preposition—Präposition
pres present—Gegenwart
pret preterit—Präteritum
pron pronoun—Pronomen
pros prosody—Prosodie
(Prot) Protestant—protestantisch
(psychol) psychology—Psychologie
(public sign) Hinweisschild
(rad) radio—Radio
(radar) Radar
recip reciprocal—wechselseitig
ref reflexive verb—Reflexivverb
reflex reflexive—reflexiv
rel relative—relativ
(relig) religion—Religion
(rhet) rhetoric—Rhetorik
(rok) rocketry—Raketen
(rr) railroad—Eisenbahn
s substantive—Substantiv
(sculp) sculpture—Bildhauerkunst
sep separable—trennbar
(sewing) Näherei
sg singular—Einzahl
(sl) slang—Slang
s.o. someone—jemand
s.o.'s someone's—jemand(e)s
spl substantive plural—pluralisches
   Substantiv
(sport) sports—Sports
(st. exch.) stock exchange—Börse
subj subjunctive—Konjunktiv
suf suffix—Suffix
super superlative—Superlativ
(surg) surgery—Chirurgie
(surv) surveying—Vermessungswesen
(tech) technical—Fachsprache
(telg) telegraphy—Telegraphie
(telp) telephone—Fernsprechwesen
(telv) television—Fernsehen
(tennis) Tennis
(tex) textiles—Textilien
(theat) theater—Theater
(theol) theology—Theologie
tr transitive—transitiv
(typ) typography—Typographie
usw. and so forth—und so weiter
v verb—Verb
var variant—Variante
(vet) veterinary medicine—
   Veterinärmedizin
(vulg) vulgar—vulgär
(zool) zoology—Zoologie